PRESENTED

TO

_____

_____

_____

BY

_____

_____

ON

_____

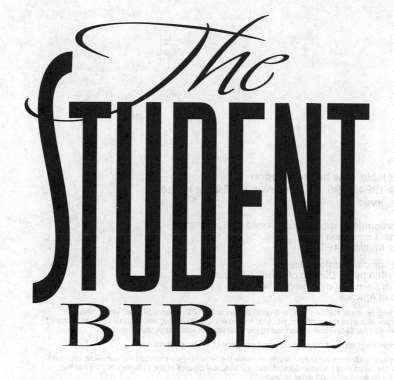

The STUDENT BIBLE

Notes by Philip Yancey and Tim Stafford

New Revised Standard Version

Zondervan Publishing House
Grand Rapids, Michigan 49530, USA

Contents

The Books of the Old Testament

The Books of the New Testament

Alphabetical Order
OF THE BOOKS OF THE BIBLE

The books of the New Testament are indicated by *italics*.

Acts 1121	James 1276	Nehemiah 490
Amos. 924	Jeremiah 766	Numbers 153
1 Chronicles 417	Job 514	Obadiah 934
2 Chronicles 444	Joel 918	*1 Peter*. 1282
Colossians 1230	*John*. 1090	*2 Peter*. 1289
1 Corinthians 1182	*1 John* 1293	*Philemon* 1260
2 Corinthians 1198	*2 John* 1299	*Philippians*. 1224
Daniel 888	*3 John* 1301	Proverbs 648
Deuteronomy 193	Jonah 937	Psalms 552
Ecclesiastes 681	Joshua 231	*Revelation* 1306
Ephesians 1217	*Jude* 1303	*Romans* 1163
Esther 505	Judges 257	Ruth 283
Exodus. 79	1 Kings. 353	1 Samuel. 288
Ezekiel 838	2 Kings. 385	2 Samuel. 323
Ezra 478	Lamentations 829	Song of Solomon 691
Galatians. 1210	Leviticus 122	*1 Thessalonians* 1235
Genesis 23	*Luke* 1051	*2 Thessalonians* 1240
Habakkuk 954	Malachi 978	*1 Timothy* 1244
Haggai 964	*Mark* 1025	*2 Timothy* 1251
Hebrews. 1262	*Matthew* 987	*Titus*. 1256
Hosea 906	Micah 941	Zechariah 967
Isaiah 698	Nahum. 950	Zephaniah 959

Why the Student Bible?

THE BIBLE IS THE MOST important book ever written—a gift to us from God himself. Styles and tastes change, but people all through history have recognized the Bible's uniqueness. They have treated it with special reverence, yet, strangely, even people who value the Bible often fail to read it. Most Americans believe the Bible to be from God. But Gallop polls reveal that only a small percentage of them can name basic Biblical facts, such as four of the Ten Commandments. Their Bibles sit somewhere on a shelf or coffee table, impressive to look at, but unread.

Christians we meet mention repeatedly their guilt about not reading the Bible consistently. They believe in the Bible. They expect to find help there. But they do not read the Bible nearly as often as they think they should.

Troubled by this reality, we began work on *The Student Bible*. Our aim: to produce an edition of the New International Version of the Bible that ordinary people could—and would—read on a regular, sustained basis. We used modern research techniques to try to find an answer to the question, "What keeps you from reading the Bible?" We discovered three main reasons. In developing this edition of the Bible, we worked hard to address those three reasons.

"I Get Discouraged"

Simple discouragement was the most common reason we heard for not reading the Bible. Many people we surveyed had tried to read the Bible regularly, but such experiments usually ended in failure.

The Bible is a big book—about 1,000 pages long. People who plan to read through the whole Bible starting with Genesis often get bogged down somewhere around Numbers or Deuteronomy. Fatigue sets in.

Other people never even start a reading plan. With busy schedules and limited confidence, they feel sure they'll fall such a project. Instead, they occasionally turn to familiar passages from the Gospel of John or the Psalms. They wouldn't know where to start venturing out into unfamiliar books.

We spent much time and research trying to find an answer to the discouragement problem. The result: the **3-Track Reading Plan**, which recognizes that people approach the Bible at different levels. All three "tracks" suggest reading one chapter a day—just 5 or 10 minutes, for most readers.

Track 1 requires a commitment of two weeks at a time, reading one chapter a day. By following it, a reader can encounter some of the most fundamental parts of the Bible. Pages 7-8 present two-week selections on Jesus and Paul, and a two-week sampling of the Old Testament. Pages 15-16 list a variety of further options depending on your personal interests. Just a few hours of investment can yield a solid introduction into the best of books.

Track 2 represents the next level of commitment. It takes six months, reading about one chapter a day. In Track 2 you will read at least one chapter from every book in the Bible. When you finish, you will have read the best-known, most-quoted, easiest-to-understand portions of the Bible. (The Zondervan book *Discovering God* offers a more detailed overview of the Bible based on Track 2.)

Track 3 includes every word of the Bible. Reading about one chapter a day, you devote three years to reading the entire Bible.

We believe the 3-track plan offers a handy, realistic method for approaching the Bible. It builds in several levels of success to combat the discouragement that afflicts Bible readers. A complete description for the 3-track plan follows on the next pages. In addition, the How to Read section in the Introduction to each Bible book uses the icon above and describes how the 3-track plan fits into that book.

"I Can't Understand It"

Many readers grow up with very little exposure to the Bible. They may never have heard of Goliath or Abraham. Often they ask, "What is the point of reading about spears and chariots and village wells and leprosy?"

Because it was written several thousand years ago, the Bible presents a culture gap. It mentions hard-to-pronounce names and refers to many outdated customs. For most readers, the Bible is the most ancient book in their library.

Most of us need some coaching on how to jump the 2,000-year gap back to when the Bible was written. *The Student Bible* addresses this problem with hundreds of additional notes scattered throughout the book. Each of these features is marked with a distinctive design element or icon.

Introductions: Each of the 66 books of the Bible is preceded by an Introduction that gives crucial background on the book and tells why it was written. By reading these Introductions, you'll gain a sense of how one particular book is different from, and yet fits together with, every other book in the Bible. In addition, you'll get clues to each book's contemporary relevance.

Insights: Throughout *The Student Bible,* you'll find short articles marked with this "Insight" icon. Written in the style of a modern magazine article, Insights include important background information right in the Bible, near the passage they shed light on. They condense the material that, in our judgment, will most help you understand and find meaning in the Bible. At the end of each Insight, **Life Questions** help relate the passage to practical life situations.

Profiles: We have selected "100 People You Should Know" in the Bible. Profiles marked with this icon give background material to help introduce these people. In a few cases these Profiles are combined with Insights or are found in a book's Introduction; these, too, are marked with the Profiles icon. Each of these Profiles also features a **Life Question**.

1:7 Paul's Partners
Strong-minded though he was, Paul never worked alone. The warmth in this book comes partly from his confidence that the Philippian Christians were his partners (verse 5), sharing in God's grace. He counted on their prayers (verse 19). At the end of this letter, Paul returns to this theme of partnership, rejoicing in the Philippians' love and thoughtfulness (4:10–19).

Highlights: Much shorter notes, marked off from the text in this manner, appear frequently in *The Student Bible*. These explain confusing verses, point out interesting facts, and, in effect, highlight something in the passage that might get easily overlooked. They're designed to catch your attention and draw you to read the Bible more closely.

"I Can't Find It"

"I spend a lot of time just flipping through the Bible, looking for something," we were told again and again. Many Bible readers are searching for help on specific issues—but they don't know where to find it.

Everybody has heard of something in the Bible—the Ten Commandments, the Golden Rule, the story of Daniel in the lions' den. But how do you know where to look for them? The Bible is too large just to flip through on a random search.

To aid in such a search, this edition of *The Student Bible* has greatly expanded a section called **"Where to Find It."** It appears at the back of this book, just before the maps section. You'll notice that the side of the book is marked with a colored tab that indicates this section's location. We hope this becomes the first place you turn when you want to find something in the Bible. The "Where to Find It" section includes the following features: a glossary of the proper names mentioned in the Bible notes; a list of miracles, parables, and other important Bible events and teachings; a guide to familiar psalms; a capsule history of the Old Testament kings and prophets. This is also where you'll find an index of the "100 People You Should Know" Profiles.

In addition to all these features, "Where to Find It" includes a Subject Guide. The Guide concentrates on major passages, not single verses. Whether you are looking for information about a familiar passage or are searching for help with a crucial life question, the Subject Guide should eliminate the "I can't find it" problem.

We hope these notes and features will help you learn some of the basic facts about the background and message of each book in the Bible. *The Student Bible* does not, of course, take the place of a Bible commentary or concordance. It is primarily a *reading* Bible. We believe that the habit of regular Bible reading is the best way for ordinary Christians to become familiar with the full breadth of God's Word.

In publishing *The Student Bible,* we are not trying to add to the Bible or to enliven it. The Bible speaks for itself. It is the most powerful book ever written, and it needs no help. We, its readers, are the ones who need help, and *The Student Bible* merely offers practical aids for the average reader. A good measure of our success will be whether this book helps you to read the Bible for yourself. That, after all, is our ultimate goal.

—Philip Yancey and Tim Stafford

3-Track Plan for Reading the Bible

Of all the reasons people mention for not reading the Bible, simple discouragement ranks highest. The Bible's length alone, about 1,000 pages, is imposing. More like a self-contained library than a book, it includes 66 different books, by several dozen authors. Little wonder people get confused and discouraged.

The following 3-Track Reading Plan helps break the Bible into more manageable portions. If you're new to the Bible, begin with Track 1, then proceed to Track 2, and finally—if you're ambitious—tackle Track 3. Your understanding and appreciation for the Bible should gradually increase.

All three tracks share one thing in common: They each assign usually one chapter a day. Reading an average Bible chapter should take only 5-10 minutes.

Note that the 3-track plan for each book is included within the Introduction to the book (see, for example, "How to Read Genesis," page 24). You can record your progress by checking off the boxes here or within each individual book.

TRACK 1: Introduction to the Bible

Track 1 is a place to begin reading the Bible. Three two-week reading courses take you quickly into passages of the Bible every Christian should know. These were selected with two concerns in mind: first, they are frequently quoted or referred to. Second, they are relatively easy to read and understand. Track 1 is a sampler, designed to whet your appetite for more.

If you like Track 1, but feel unready to tackle Track 2, you can find more Track 1 courses on pages 15-16.

TIME COMMITMENT:
Two Weeks

GOAL:
To survey basic biblical foundations

1. Two Weeks on the Life and Teachings of Jesus

☐ Day 1. LUKE 1: Preparing for Jesus' arrival

☐ Day 2. LUKE 2: The story of Jesus' birth

☐ Day 3. MARK 1: The beginning of Jesus' ministry

☐ Day 4. MARK 9: A day in the life of Jesus

☐ Day 5. MATTHEW 5: The Sermon on the Mount

☐ Day 6. MATTHEW 6: The Sermon on the Mount

☐ Day 7. LUKE 15: Parables of Jesus

☐ Day 8. JOHN 3: A conversation with Jesus

☐ Day 9. JOHN 14: Jesus' final instructions

☐ Day 10. JOHN 17: Jesus' prayer for his disciples

☐ Day 11. MATTHEW 26: Betrayal and arrest

☐ Day 12. MATTHEW 27: Jesus' execution on a cross

☐ Day 13. JOHN 20: Resurrection

☐ Day 14. LUKE 24: Jesus' appearance after resurrection

2. Two Weeks on the Life and Teachings of Paul

☐ Day 1. ACTS 9: The conversion of Saul
☐ Day 2. ACTS 16: Paul's Macedonian call and a jailbreak
☐ Day 3. ACTS 17: Scenes from Paul's missionary journey
☐ Day 4. ACTS 26: Paul tells his life story to a king
☐ Day 5. ACTS 27: Shipwreck on the way to Rome
☐ Day 6. ACTS 28: Paul's arrival in Rome
☐ Day 7. ROMANS 3: Paul's theology in a nutshell
☐ Day 8. ROMANS 7: Struggle with sin
☐ Day 9. ROMANS 8: Life in the Spirit
☐ Day 10. 1 CORINTHIANS 13: Paul's description of love
☐ Day 11. 1 CORINTHIANS 15: Thoughts on the afterlife
☐ Day 12. GALATIANS 5: Freedom in Christ
☐ Day 13. EPHESIANS 3: Paul's summary of his mission
☐ Day 14. PHILIPPIANS 2: Imitating Christ

3. Two Weeks on the Old Testament

☐ Day 1. GENESIS 1: The story of creation
☐ Day 2. GENESIS 3: The origin of sin
☐ Day 3. GENESIS 22: Abraham and Isaac
☐ Day 4. EXODUS 3: Moses' encounter with God
☐ Day 5. EXODUS 20: The gift of the Ten Commandments
☐ Day 6. 1 SAMUEL 17: David and Goliath
☐ Day 7. 2 SAMUEL 11: David and Bathsheba
☐ Day 8. 2 SAMUEL 12: Nathan's rebuke of the king
☐ Day 9. 1 KINGS 18: Elijah and the prophets of Baal
☐ Day 10. JOB 38: God's answer to Job
☐ Day 11. PSALM 51: A classic confession
☐ Day 12. ISAIAH 40: Words of comfort from God
☐ Day 13. DANIEL 6: Daniel and the lions
☐ Day 14. AMOS 4: A prophet's stern warning

TIME COMMITMENT:
Six Months

GOAL:
To gain an overview of the entire Bible

Track 2 includes 186 of the 1,189 chapters in the Bible. Many well-known parts of the Bible are not represented, and from some books (Leviticus, for example), you will read only a single chapter. These 186 chapters have been selected because they are understandable to the average reader without commentary. Taken together, they provide a good foundation of Bible understanding.

If you miss a few days, don't worry. Just resume reading when you can, about a chapter a day. In 180 total days, you will get an overview that includes something from every book in the Bible.

Track 2 recommends reading the Introduction to each book. You may also find it helpful to read the Insights that appear next to the assigned chapters.

GENESIS	□1	□2	□3	□4
	□7	□8	□15	□19
	□22	□27	□28	□37
	□41	□45		
EXODUS	□3	□10-11	□14	□20
	□32			
LEVITICUS	□26			
NUMBERS	□11	□14		
DEUTERONOMY	□4	□8	□28	
JOSHUA	□2	□6	□7	□24
JUDGES	□6	□7	□16	
RUTH	□1			
1 SAMUEL	□3	□16	□17	□20
2 SAMUEL	□6	□11	□12	
1 KINGS	□3	□8	□17	□18
2 KINGS	□5	□17	□22	
1 CHRONICLES	□17			
2 CHRONICLES	□20	□30	□32	
EZRA	□3			
NEHEMIAH	□2	□8		
ESTHER	□4			
JOB	□1-2	□38	□42	
PSALMS	□19	□23	□27	□51
	□84	□103	□139	
PROVERBS	□4	□10	□The proverbs listed in "Verbal Dynamite" (page 664)	
ECCLESIASTES	□3			
SONG OF SOLOMON	□2			
ISAIAH	□6	□25	□40	□52
	□53	□55		
JEREMIAH	□2	□15	□31	□38
LAMENTATIONS	□3			
EZEKIEL	□1	□2-3	□4	□37
DANIEL	□1	□3	□5	□6
HOSEA	□2-3	□11		
JOEL	□2			
AMOS	□4			
OBADIAH	□Obadiah			
JONAH	□3-4			
MICAH	□6			

NAHUM	□1			
HABAKKUK	□1			
ZEPHANIAH	□3			
HAGGAI	□1			
ZECHARIAH	□8			
MALACHI	□3			
MATTHEW	□5	□6	□13	□19
	□26	□27	□28	
MARK	□1	□2	□3	□4
	□5	□6	□7	□8
	□9	□10	□11	□12
	□13	□14	□15-16	
LUKE	□1	□2	□10	□12
	□15	□16	□18	□24
JOHN	□3	□6	□10	□14
	□15	□16	□17	□20
ACTS	□1	□2	□5	□9
	□16	□17	□26	□27
	□28			
ROMANS	□3	□7	□8	□12
1 CORINTHIANS	□13	□15		
2 CORINTHIANS	□4	□12		
GALATIANS	□3			
EPHESIANS	□2	□3		
PHILIPPIANS	□2			
COLOSSIANS	□1			
1 THESSALONIANS	□3-4			
2 THESSALONIANS	□2			
1 TIMOTHY	□1			
2 TIMOTHY	□2			
TITUS	□2			
PHILEMON	□Philemon			
HEBREWS	□2	□11	□12	
JAMES	□1			
1 PETER	□1			
2 PETER	□1			
1 JOHN	□3			
2 and 3 JOHN	□2, 3 John			
JUDE	□Jude			
REVELATION	□1	□12	□21	

TIME COMMITMENT:
Three Years

GOAL:
To read all the way through the Bible with understanding

Track 3 takes you completely through the Bible, reading every word. Other Bible-reading plans allot only a year for this project, requiring that at least 3 chapters be read each day. But many readers find such a pace to be unrealistic and discouraging. For this reason, Track 3 assigns usually only one chapter a day. (Some short chapters have been combined, so occasionally you will read two brief chapters in a day.) In all, the reading plan works out evenly to a three-year total.

The Track 3 plan alternates between the Old Testament and New Testament. This mixing provides variety and reduces the fatigue that may set in from reading long sections of the Old Testament.

GENESIS

□ 1	□ 2	□ 3	□ 4
□ 5	□ 6	□ 7	□ 8
□ 9	□ 10-11	□ 12	□ 13
□ 14	□ 15	□ 16	□ 17
□ 18	□ 19	□ 20	□ 21
□ 22	□ 23	□ 24	□ 25
□ 26	□ 27	□ 28	□ 29
□ 30	□ 31	□ 32	□ 33
□ 34	□ 35	□ 36	□ 37
□ 38	□ 39	□ 40	□ 41
□ 42	□ 43	□ 44	□ 45
□ 46	□ 47	□ 48	□ 49
□ 50			

MATTHEW 1-9

□ 1	□ 2	□ 3	□ 4
□ 5	□ 6	□ 7	□ 8
□ 9			

EXODUS

□ 1	□ 2	□ 3	□ 4
□ 5	□ 6	□ 7	□ 8
□ 9	□ 10-11	□ 12	□ 13
□ 14	□ 15	□ 16	□ 17
□ 18	□ 19	□ 20	□ 21
□ 22	□ 23	□ 24	□ 25
□ 26	□ 27	□ 28	□ 29
□ 30	□ 31	□ 32	□ 33
□ 34	□ 35	□ 36	□ 37
□ 38	□ 39	□ 40	

MATTHEW 10-20

□ 10	□ 11	□ 12	□ 13
□ 14	□ 15	□ 16	□ 17
□ 18	□ 19	□ 20	

LEVITICUS 1-14

□ 1	□ 2	□ 3	□ 4
□ 5	□ 6	□ 7	□ 8
□ 9	□ 10	□ 11-12	□ 13
□ 14			

MATTHEW 21-28

□ 21	□ 22	□ 23	□ 24
□ 25	□ 26	□ 27	□ 28

LEVITICUS 15-27

□ 15	□ 16	□ 17	□ 18
□ 19	□ 20	□ 21	□ 22
□ 23	□ 24	□ 25	□ 26
□ 27			

MARK 1-8

□ 1	□ 2	□ 3	□ 4
□ 5	□ 6	□ 7	□ 8

NUMBERS

□ 1-2	□ 3	□ 4	□ 5
□ 6	□ 7	□ 8	□ 9
□ 10	□ 11	□ 12	□ 13
□ 14	□ 15	□ 16	□ 17
□ 18	□ 19	□ 20	□ 21
□ 22	□ 23	□ 24	□ 25
□ 26	□ 27	□ 28	□ 29
□ 30	□ 31	□ 32	□ 33
□ 34	□ 35	□ 36	

MARK 9-16

□ 9	□ 10	□ 11	□ 12
□ 13	□ 14	□ 15-16	

DEUTERONOMY 1-17

□ 1	□ 2	□ 3	□ 4
□ 5	□ 6	□ 7	□ 8
□ 9	□ 10	□ 11	□ 12
□ 13	□ 14	□ 15	□ 16
□ 17			

LUKE 1-8

□ 1	□ 2	□ 3	□ 4
□ 5	□ 6	□ 7	□ 8

DEUTERONOMY 18-34

□ 18	□ 19	□ 20	□ 21
□ 22	□ 23	□ 24	□ 25

☐ 26 ☐ 27 ☐ 28 ☐ 29
☐ 30 ☐ 31 ☐ 32 ☐ 33
☐ 34

LUKE 9-16

☐ 9 ☐ 10 ☐ 11 ☐ 12
☐ 13 ☐ 14 ☐ 15 ☐ 16

JOSHUA

☐ 1 ☐ 2 ☐ 3 ☐ 4
☐ 5 ☐ 6 ☐ 7 ☐ 8
☐ 9 ☐ 10 ☐ 11 ☐ 12-13
☐ 14-15 ☐ 16-17 ☐ 18 ☐ 19
☐ 20 ☐ 21 ☐ 22 ☐ 23
☐ 24

LUKE 17-24

☐ 17 ☐ 18 ☐ 19 ☐ 20
☐ 21 ☐ 22 ☐ 23 ☐ 24

JUDGES

☐ 1 ☐ 2 ☐ 3 ☐ 4
☐ 5 ☐ 6 ☐ 7 ☐ 8
☐ 9 ☐ 10 ☐ 11 ☐ 12
☐ 13 ☐ 14 ☐ 15 ☐ 16
☐ 17 ☐ 18 ☐ 19 ☐ 20
☐ 21

JOHN 1-7

☐ 1 ☐ 2 ☐ 3 ☐ 4
☐ 5 ☐ 6 ☐ 7

RUTH

☐ 1 ☐ 2 ☐ 3 ☐ 4

1 SAMUEL 1-15

☐ 1 ☐ 2 ☐ 3 ☐ 4
☐ 5 ☐ 6 ☐ 7 ☐ 8
☐ 9 ☐ 10 ☐ 11 ☐ 12
☐ 13 ☐ 14 ☐ 15

JOHN 8-14

☐ 8 ☐ 9 ☐ 10 ☐ 11
☐ 12 ☐ 13 ☐ 14

1 SAMUEL 16-31

☐ 16 ☐ 17 ☐ 18 ☐ 19
☐ 20 ☐ 21 ☐ 22 ☐ 23
☐ 24 ☐ 25 ☐ 26 ☐ 27
☐ 28 ☐ 29 ☐ 30 ☐ 31

JOHN 15-21

☐ 15 ☐ 16 ☐ 17 ☐ 18
☐ 19 ☐ 20 ☐ 21

2 SAMUEL

☐ 1 ☐ 2 ☐ 3 ☐ 4
☐ 5 ☐ 6 ☐ 7 ☐ 8
☐ 9 ☐ 10 ☐ 11 ☐ 12
☐ 13 ☐ 14 ☐ 15 ☐ 16
☐ 17 ☐ 18 ☐ 19 ☐ 20
☐ 21 ☐ 22 ☐ 23 ☐ 24

ACTS 1-7

☐ 1 ☐ 2 ☐ 3 ☐ 4
☐ 5 ☐ 6 ☐ 7

1 KINGS 1-11

☐ 1 ☐ 2 ☐ 3 ☐ 4-5
☐ 6 ☐ 7 ☐ 8 ☐ 9
☐ 10 ☐ 11

ACTS 8-14

☐ 8 ☐ 9 ☐ 10 ☐ 11
☐ 12 ☐ 13 ☐ 14

1 KINGS 12-22

☐ 12 ☐ 13 ☐ 14 ☐ 15
☐ 16 ☐ 17 ☐ 18 ☐ 19
☐ 20 ☐ 21 ☐ 22

ACTS 15-21

☐ 15 ☐ 16 ☐ 17 ☐ 18
☐ 19 ☐ 20 ☐ 21

2 KINGS

☐ 1 ☐ 2 ☐ 3 ☐ 4
☐ 5 ☐ 6 ☐ 7 ☐ 8
☐ 9 ☐ 10 ☐ 11 ☐ 12
☐ 13 ☐ 14 ☐ 15 ☐ 16
☐ 17 ☐ 18 ☐ 19 ☐ 20
☐ 21 ☐ 22 ☐ 23 ☐ 24
☐ 25

ACTS 22-28

☐ 22 ☐ 23 ☐ 24 ☐ 25
☐ 26 ☐ 27 ☐ 28

1 CHRONICLES 1-14

☐ 1-9 ☐ 10 ☐ 11 ☐ 12
☐ 13 ☐ 14

ROMANS 1-8

☐ 1 ☐ 2 ☐ 3 ☐ 4
☐ 5 ☐ 6 ☐ 7 ☐ 8

1 CHRONICLES 15-29

☐ 15 ☐ 16 ☐ 17 ☐ 18
☐ 19 ☐ 20 ☐ 21 ☐ 22
☐ 23-27 ☐ 28 ☐ 29

ROMANS 9-16

☐ 9 ☐ 10 ☐ 11 ☐ 12-13
☐ 14 ☐ 15-16

2 CHRONICLES 1-18

☐ 1 ☐ 2 ☐ 3 ☐ 4
☐ 5 ☐ 6 ☐ 7 ☐ 8
☐ 9 ☐ 10 ☐ 11 ☐ 12
☐ 13 ☐ 14 ☐ 15 ☐ 16-17
☐ 18

1 CORINTHIANS 1-9

☐ 1 ☐ 2 ☐ 3 ☐ 4-5
☐ 6 ☐ 7 ☐ 8-9

2 CHRONICLES 19-36

☐ 19 ☐ 20 ☐ 21 ☐ 22
☐ 23 ☐ 24 ☐ 25 ☐ 26-27
☐ 28 ☐ 29 ☐ 30 ☐ 31
☐ 32 ☐ 33 ☐ 34 ☐ 35
☐ 36

1 CORINTHIANS 10-16

☐ 10 ☐ 11 ☐ 12 ☐ 13
☐ 14 ☐ 15 ☐ 16

EZRA

☐ 1-2 ☐ 3 ☐ 4 ☐ 5
☐ 6 ☐ 7 ☐ 8 ☐ 9
☐ 10

NEHEMIAH

☐ 1 ☐ 2-3 ☐ 4 ☐ 5
☐ 6 ☐ 7 ☐ 8 ☐ 9
☐ 10 ☐ 11 ☐ 12 ☐ 13

2 CORINTHIANS

☐ 1 ☐ 2-3 ☐ 4 ☐ 5
☐ 6 ☐ 7 ☐ 8-9 ☐ 10
☐ 11 ☐ 12-13

ESTHER

☐ 1 ☐ 2 ☐ 3 ☐ 4
☐ 5 ☐ 6-7 ☐ 8 ☐ 9-10

JOB 1-21

☐ 1 ☐ 2 ☐ 3 ☐ 4
☐ 5 ☐ 6 ☐ 7 ☐ 8
☐ 9 ☐ 10 ☐ 11 ☐ 12
☐ 13 ☐ 14 ☐ 15 ☐ 16
☐ 17 ☐ 18 ☐ 19 ☐ 20
☐ 21

GALATIANS

☐ 1 ☐ 2 ☐ 3 ☐ 4
☐ 5-6

JOB 22-42

☐ 22 ☐ 23 ☐ 24 ☐ 25-26
☐ 27 ☐ 28 ☐ 29 ☐ 30
☐ 31 ☐ 32 ☐ 33 ☐ 34
☐ 35 ☐ 36 ☐ 37 ☐ 38
☐ 39 ☐ 40 ☐ 41 ☐ 42

EPHESIANS

☐ 1 ☐ 2 ☐ 3 ☐ 4
☐ 5 ☐ 6

PSALMS 1-40

☐ 1-2 ☐ 3-4 ☐ 5 ☐ 6
☐ 7 ☐ 8 ☐ 9 ☐ 10
☐ 11-12 ☐ 13-14 ☐ 15-16 ☐ 17
☐ 18 ☐ 19 ☐ 20-21 ☐ 22
☐ 23-24 ☐ 25 ☐ 26 ☐ 27
☐ 28-29 ☐ 30 ☐ 31 ☐ 32
☐ 33 ☐ 34 ☐ 35 ☐ 36
☐ 37 ☐ 38 ☐ 39 ☐ 40

PHILIPPIANS

☐ 1 ☐ 2 ☐ 3 ☐ 4

PSALMS 41-80

☐ 41 ☐ 42-43 ☐ 44 ☐ 45
☐ 46-47 ☐ 48 ☐ 49 ☐ 50
☐ 51 ☐ 52 ☐ 53-54 ☐ 55
☐ 56 ☐ 57 ☐ 58 ☐ 59
☐ 60-61 ☐ 62 ☐ 63-64 ☐ 65
☐ 66 ☐ 67 ☐ 68 ☐ 69
☐ 70 ☐ 71 ☐ 72 ☐ 73
☐ 74 ☐ 75 ☐ 76 ☐ 77
☐ 78 ☐ 79 ☐ 80

COLOSSIANS

☐ 1 ☐ 2 ☐ 3 ☐ 4

PSALMS 81-121

☐ 81 ☐ 82 ☐ 83 ☐ 84
☐ 85 ☐ 86 ☐ 87 ☐ 88
☐ 89 ☐ 90 ☐ 91 ☐ 92-93
☐ 94 ☐ 95 ☐ 96 ☐ 97
☐ 98-99 ☐ 100-101 ☐ 102 ☐ 103
☐ 104 ☐ 105 ☐ 106 ☐ 107
☐ 108 ☐ 109 ☐ 110-111 ☐ 112
☐ 113 ☐ 114 ☐ 115 ☐ 116-117
☐ 118 ☐ 119.1-48 ☐ 119.49-96 ☐ 119.97-144
☐ 119.145-176 ☐ 120-121

1 THESSALONIANS

☐ 1-2 ☐ 3-4 ☐ 5

2 THESSALONIANS

☐ 1-2 ☐ 3

PSALMS 122-150

☐ 122-123 ☐ 124-125 ☐ 126-128 ☐ 129-130
☐ 131-132 ☐ 133-134 ☐ 135 ☐ 136
☐ 137-138 ☐ 139 ☐ 140 ☐ 141-142
☐ 143 ☐ 144 ☐ 145 ☐ 146
☐ 147 ☐ 148 ☐ 149-150

PROVERBS

☐ 1 ☐ 2 ☐ 3 ☐ 4
☐ 5 ☐ 6 ☐ 7 ☐ 8
☐ 9 ☐ 10 ☐ 11 ☐ 12
☐ 13 ☐ 14 ☐ 15 ☐ 16
☐ 17 ☐ 18 ☐ 19 ☐ 20
☐ 21 ☐ 22 ☐ 23 ☐ 24
☐ 25 ☐ 26 ☐ 27 ☐ 28
☐ 29 ☐ 30 ☐ 31

1 TIMOTHY

☐ 1-2 ☐ 3-4 ☐ 5 ☐ 6

ECCLESIASTES

☐ 1 ☐ 2 ☐ 3 ☐ 4
☐ 5 ☐ 6 ☐ 7 ☐ 8
☐ 9 ☐ 10 ☐ 11 ☐ 12

SONG OF SOLOMON

☐ 1 ☐ 2 ☐ 3 ☐ 4
☐ 5 ☐ 6 ☐ 7 ☐ 8

2 TIMOTHY

☐ 1 ☐ 2 ☐ 3 ☐ 4

ISAIAH 1-36

☐ 1 ☐ 2 ☐ 3 ☐ 4-5

☐ 6 ☐ 7 ☐ 8 ☐ 9
☐ 10 ☐ 11 ☐ 12 ☐ 13
☐ 14 ☐ 15 ☐ 16 ☐ 17
☐ 18 ☐ 19-20 ☐ 21 ☐ 22
☐ 23 ☐ 24 ☐ 25 ☐ 26
☐ 27 ☐ 28 ☐ 29 ☐ 30
☐ 31 ☐ 32 ☐ 33 ☐ 34
☐ 35 ☐ 36

TITUS

☐ 1 ☐ 2-3

ISAIAH 37-66

☐ 37 ☐ 38-39 ☐ 40 ☐ 41
☐ 42 ☐ 43 ☐ 44 ☐ 45
☐ 46 ☐ 47 ☐ 48 ☐ 49
☐ 50 ☐ 51 ☐ 52 ☐ 53
☐ 54 ☐ 55 ☐ 56 ☐ 57
☐ 58 ☐ 59 ☐ 60 ☐ 61
☐ 62 ☐ 63 ☐ 64 ☐ 65
☐ 66

PHILEMON

☐ Philemon

JEREMIAH 1-26

☐ 1 ☐ 2 ☐ 3 ☐ 4
☐ 5 ☐ 6 ☐ 7 ☐ 8
☐ 9 ☐ 10 ☐ 11 ☐ 12
☐ 13 ☐ 14 ☐ 15 ☐ 16
☐ 17 ☐ 18 ☐ 19 ☐ 20
☐ 21 ☐ 22 ☐ 23 ☐ 24
☐ 25 ☐ 26

HEBREWS 1-7

☐ 1 ☐ 2 ☐ 3-4 ☐ 5-6
☐ 7

JEREMIAH 27-52

☐ 27 ☐ 28 ☐ 29 ☐ 30
☐ 31 ☐ 32 ☐ 33 ☐ 34
☐ 35 ☐ 36 ☐ 37 ☐ 38
☐ 39 ☐ 40 ☐ 41 ☐ 42
☐ 43 ☐ 44-45 ☐ 46 ☐ 47
☐ 48 ☐ 49 ☐ 50 ☐ 51
☐ 52

HEBREWS 8-13

☐ 8 ☐ 9 ☐ 10 ☐ 11
☐ 12 ☐ 13

LAMENTATIONS

☐ 1   ☐ 2   ☐ 3   ☐ 4
☐ 5

EZEKIEL 1-24

☐ 1   ☐ 2-3   ☐ 4   ☐ 5
☐ 6   ☐ 7   ☐ 8   ☐ 9
☐ 10   ☐ 11   ☐ 12   ☐ 13
☐ 14   ☐ 15   ☐ 16   ☐ 17
☐ 18   ☐ 19   ☐ 20   ☐ 21
☐ 22   ☐ 23   ☐ 24

JAMES

☐ 1   ☐ 2   ☐ 3-4   ☐ 5

EZEKIEL 25-48

☐ 25   ☐ 26   ☐ 27   ☐ 28
☐ 29   ☐ 30   ☐ 31   ☐ 32
☐ 33   ☐ 34   ☐ 35   ☐ 36
☐ 37   ☐ 38   ☐ 39   ☐ 40
☐ 41   ☐ 42   ☐ 43   ☐ 44
☐ 45   ☐ 46   ☐ 47   ☐ 48

1 PETER

☐ 1   ☐ 2   ☐ 3   ☐ 4-5

DANIEL

☐ 1   ☐ 2   ☐ 3   ☐ 4
☐ 5   ☐ 6   ☐ 7   ☐ 8
☐ 9   ☐ 10   ☐ 11   ☐ 12

2 PETER

☐ 1   ☐ 2   ☐ 3

HOSEA

☐ 1   ☐ 2-3   ☐ 4   ☐ 5
☐ 6-7   ☐ 8   ☐ 9   ☐ 10
☐ 11-12 ☐ 13-14

1 JOHN

☐ 1-2   ☐ 3   ☐ 4   ☐ 5

JOEL

☐ 1   ☐ 2   ☐ 3

AMOS

☐ 1   ☐ 2   ☐ 3   ☐ 4

☐ 5   ☐ 6   ☐ 7   ☐ 8
☐ 9

OBADIAH

☐ Obadiah

JONAH

☐ 1-2   ☐ 3-4

2 and 3 JOHN

☐ 2 John, 3 John

MICAH

☐ 1   ☐ 2   ☐ 3   ☐ 4
☐ 5   ☐ 6   ☐ 7

NAHUM

☐ 1   ☐ 2   ☐ 3

JUDE

☐ Jude

HABAKKUK

☐ 1   ☐ 2   ☐ 3

ZEPHANIAH

☐ 1   ☐ 2   ☐ 3

REVELATION 1-7

☐ 1   ☐ 2   ☐ 3   ☐ 4-5
☐ 6   ☐ 7

HAGGAI

☐ 1   ☐ 2

REVELATION 8-14

☐ 8   ☐ 9   ☐ 10-11   ☐ 12
☐ 13   ☐ 14

ZECHARIAH

☐ 1   ☐ 2-3   ☐ 4-5   ☐ 6
☐ 7   ☐ 8   ☐ 9   ☐ 10
☐ 11   ☐ 12-13   ☐ 14

MALACHI

☐ 1   ☐ 2   ☐ 3-4

REVELATION 15-22

☐ 15-16   ☐ 17   ☐ 18   ☐ 19
☐ 20   ☐ 21   ☐ 22

TWO WEEKS ON BECOMING A CHRISTIAN

☐ Day 1. Genesis 3: The first sin creates a need.
☐ Day 2. Isaiah 52: Salvation prophesied.
☐ Day 3. Isaiah 53: The role of the suffering servant.
☐ Day 4. Luke 15: Three stories about God's love.
☐ Day 5. John 3: Jesus explains "born again."
☐ Day 6. John 10: The good shepherd.
☐ Day 7. Acts 8: Conversions spread outside the Jews.
☐ Day 8. Acts 26: Paul testifies of his conversion before a king.
☐ Day 9. Romans 3: God's provision for sin.
☐ Day 10. Romans 5: Peace with God.
☐ Day 11. Galatians 3: Salvation unavailable by obeying the law.
☐ Day 12. Ephesians 2: New life in Christ.
☐ Day 13. 1 Peter 1: Future rewards of salvation.
☐ Day 14. 2 Peter 1: Making your salvation sure.

TWO WEEKS ON PRAYERS OF THE BIBLE

☐ Day 1. Genesis 18: Abraham's plea for Sodom.
☐ Day 2. Exodus 15: Moses' song to the Lord.
☐ Day 3. Exodus 33: Moses meets with God.
☐ Day 4. 2 Samuel 7: David's response to God's promises.
☐ Day 5. 1 Kings 8: Solomon's dedication of the temple.
☐ Day 6. 2 Chronicles 20: Jehoshaphat prays for victory.
☐ Day 7. Ezra 9: Ezra's prayer for the people's sins.
☐ Day 8. Psalm 22: A cry to God for help.
☐ Day 9. Psalm 104: A prayer of praise.
☐ Day 10. Daniel 9: Daniel's prayer for the salvation of Jerusalem.
☐ Day 11. Habakkuk 3: A prophet's prayer of acceptance.
☐ Day 12. Matthew 6: The Lord's prayer.
☐ Day 13. John 17: Jesus' prayer for his disciples.
☐ Day 14. Colossians 1: Paul's prayer of thanksgiving.

TWO WEEKS ON THE HOLY SPIRIT

☐ Day 1. Judges 14: The Spirit gives Samson strength.
☐ Day 2. 1 Samuel 10: King Saul's experience.
☐ Day 3. Matthew 3:1–4:10: Role in Jesus' baptism and temptation.
☐ Day 4. John 14: Jesus promises the Spirit.
☐ Day 5. John 16: The work of the Spirit.
☐ Day 6. Acts 2: The Spirit comes at Pentecost.
☐ Day 7. Acts 10: The Spirit guides Peter to accept Gentiles.
☐ Day 8. Romans 8: Christians' victory in the Spirit.
☐ Day 9. 1 Corinthians 2: Wisdom from the Spirit.
☐ Day 10. 1 Corinthians 12: Gifts of the Spirit.
☐ Day 11. 1 Corinthians 14: Gifts of tongues and prophecy.
☐ Day 12. Galatians 5: Life in the Spirit.
☐ Day 13. Ephesians 4: Unity and gifts.
☐ Day 14. 1 John 4: Signs of the Spirit.

TWO WEEKS ON WOMEN OF THE BIBLE

☐ Day 1. Genesis 2: Eve, the first woman.
☐ Day 2. Genesis 18: Sarah laughs at God's promise.
☐ Day 3. Genesis 24: Rebekah's marriage to Isaac.
☐ Day 4. Genesis 27: Rebekah, the manipulative mother.
☐ Day 5. Judges 4: Deborah's leadership frees her people.
☐ Day 6. Ruth 1: Ruth and Naomi's deep friendship.
☐ Day 7. 1 Samuel 1: Hannah prays for a son.
☐ Day 8. 1 Kings 17: A poor widow and the prophet Elijah.
☐ Day 9. 1 Kings 21: Jezebel, an emblem of wickedness.
☐ Day 10. Esther 2: Esther is chosen as queen.
☐ Day 11. Esther 4: Esther's courage at the risk of death.

☐ Day 12. Luke 1: Mary and Elizabeth receive great news.
☐ Day 13. Luke 2: Mary gives birth to Jesus.
☐ Day 14. John 11: Mary and Martha and their brother's death.

TWO WEEKS ON MEN OF THE OLD TESTAMENT

☐ Day 1. Judges 6: God calls Gideon to rescue his people.
☐ Day 2. Judges 7: Gideon conquers his fears—and his enemies.
☐ Day 3. 1 Samuel 3: God calls young Samuel.
☐ Day 4. 1 Kings 3: Solomon is given wisdom.
☐ Day 5. 1 Kings 19: Elijah runs for his life.
☐ Day 6. 2 Kings 5: Elisha heals a powerful foreign general.
☐ Day 7. Isaiah 6: God calls the prophet Isaiah.
☐ Day 8. 2 Kings 18: King Hezekiah under military siege.
☐ Day 9. 2 Kings 19: Isaiah speaks God's word to King Hezekiah.
☐ Day 10. 2 Chronicles 34: Josiah sets his nation back on course.
☐ Day 11. Nehemiah 2: Nehemiah courageously begins rebuilding a wall.
☐ Day 12. Jeremiah 38: Jeremiah, in prison, refuses to change his message.
☐ Day 13. Daniel 1: Daniel risks his life in captivity.
☐ Day 14. Daniel 5: Daniel's word to a royal orgy.

TWO WEEKS ON SOCIAL JUSTICE

☐ Day 1. Exodus 3: God hears the cries of the slaves.
☐ Day 2. Leviticus 25: The year of jubilee, a time of economic revolution.
☐ Day 3. Ruth 2: A poor woman finds help.
☐ Day 4. 1 Kings 21: Elijah speaks to a land-grabbing, murderous king.
☐ Day 5. Nehemiah 5: Nehemiah demands justice for the poor.
☐ Day 6. Isaiah 5: Warning to fun-loving materialists.
☐ Day 7. Isaiah 58: Worship that God appreciates.
☐ Day 8. Jeremiah 34: Freedom for slaves.
☐ Day 9. Amos 2: Sins against God by his own people.
☐ Day 10. Amos 6: Warning to the complacent.
☐ Day 11. Micah 6: What the Lord requires.
☐ Day 12. Luke 3: John the Baptist tells how to prepare for Jesus.
☐ Day 13. Matthew 6: Jesus speaks on material things.
☐ Day 14. James 2: How to treat the rich and the poor.

TWO WEEKS ON GOD AND NATURE

☐ Day 1. Genesis 1: God creates the earth.
☐ Day 2. Genesis 2: God creates human beings.
☐ Day 3. Proverbs 8: Wisdom's view of creation.
☐ Day 4. Genesis 7: God preserves the species.
☐ Day 5. Job 38: The greatness of nature.
☐ Day 6. Job 39: The wildness of nature.
☐ Day 7. Job 40: God's mastery of nature.
☐ Day 8. Psalm 8: Praise for the Creator.
☐ Day 9. Psalm 98: Nature joins in the praise.
☐ Day 10. Psalm 104: God sustains the earth.
☐ Day 11. Isaiah 40: The ruler of all creation.
☐ Day 12. Romans 8: The "groanings" of our present state.
☐ Day 13. Isaiah 65: Preview of a restored earth.
☐ Day 14. Revelation 22: The end of history.

FURTHER TWO-WEEK COURSES FOR PERSONAL STUDY

Two weeks on Abraham, Isaac, and Jacob:
Genesis 12, 13, 15, 17, 18, 19, 22, 24, 27, 28, 29, 31, 32, 33.
Two weeks on Moses and the exodus:
Exodus 2, 3, 4, 7, 12, 14, 16, 19, 32; Numbers 14; Deuteronomy 1, 2, 4, 31.
Two weeks on David:
1 Samuel 16, 17, 18, 20, 21, 22, 24; 2 Samuel 6, 7, 11, 12, 13, 15, 18.

Overview:
THE OLD TESTAMENT

The Five Books

The first five books of the Bible tell the origins of the Jewish race and culture.

GENESIS: The book of beginnings describes creation, the first rebellions against God, and God's choosing of Abraham and his offspring.

EXODUS: God rescued the Israelites from slavery in Egypt and led them to the Desert of Sinai. There, he gave Moses the laws to govern the new nation.

LEVITICUS: God set up laws for the Israelites, mostly regarding holiness and worship.

NUMBERS: Because of their rebellion and disobedience, the Israelites had to wander in a wilderness for 40 years before entering the promised land.

DEUTERONOMY: Just before his death, Moses made three emotional farewell speeches, recapping history and warning the Israelites against further mistakes.

History Books

The next 12 books continue the history of the Israelites. They moved into the land of Canaan and established a kingdom that lasted almost 500 years.

JOSHUA: After Moses' death, Joshua commanded the armies that conquered much of the territory in the promised land.

JUDGES: The new nation fell into a series of dismal failures. God raised up leaders called "judges."

RUTH: This story of love and loyalty between two widows shines out brightly in an otherwise dark period.

1 SAMUEL: Samuel became a transition leader between the time of the judges and that of the kings. He appointed Israel's first king, Saul. After his own failure, Saul tried violently to prevent God's king-elect David from taking the throne.

2 SAMUEL: David, a man after God's own heart, brought the nation together. But after committing adultery and murder, he was haunted by family and national crises.

1 KINGS: Solomon succeeded David, with mixed success. At his death, a civil war tore apart the nation. Successive kings were mostly bad, and the prophet Elijah had dramatic confrontations with King Ahab.

2 KINGS: This book continues the record of the rulers of the divided kingdom. None of the northern kings followed God consistently, and so Israel was finally destroyed by an invader. The South, Judah, lasted much longer, but finally Babylon conquered Judah and deported its citizens.

1 CHRONICLES: The book opens with the most complete genealogical record in the Bible, then adds many incidents from the life of David (often the same as those in 2 Samuel).

2 CHRONICLES: Often paralleling the books of Kings, this book records the history of the rulers of Judah, emphasizing the good kings.

EZRA: After being held captive in Babylon for decades, the Jews were allowed to return to their homeland. Ezra, a priest, emerged from one of the first waves of refugees.

NEHEMIAH: Nehemiah returned from the Babylonian captivity after the temple had been rebuilt. He concentrated on restoring the protective wall around Jerusalem and joined Ezra in leading a religious revival.

ESTHER: This story is set among captive Jews in Persia. A courageous Jewish queen foiled a plan to exterminate her people.

Books of Poetry

Almost one-third of the Old Testament was originally written in poetry. These books concentrate on questions about pain, God, life, and love.

JOB: The best man of his day suffers the greatest personal tragedy. The entire book deals with the question, "Why?"

PSALMS: These prayers and hymns cover the full range of human emotion; together, they represent a personal journal of how to relate to God. Some were also used in public worship services.

PROVERBS: The proverbs offer advice on every imaginable area of life. The style of wise living described here leads to a fulfilled life.

ECCLESIASTES: A life without God, "under the sun," leads to meaninglessness and despair, says the Teacher in a strikingly modern book.

SONG OF SOLOMON: This beautiful poem celebrates romantic and physical love.

Books of the Prophets

During the years when kings ruled Israel and Judah, God spoke through prophets. Though some prophets did predict future events, their primary role was to call God's people back to him.

ISAIAH: The most eloquent of the prophets, Isaiah analyzed the failures of all the nations around him and pointed to a future Messiah who would bring peace.

JEREMIAH: Jeremiah led an emotionally tortured life, yet held to his stern message. He spoke to Judah in the last decades before Babylon destroyed the nation.

LAMENTATIONS: All Jeremiah's warnings about Jerusalem came true, and Lamentations records five poems of sorrow for the fallen city.

EZEKIEL: Ezekiel spoke to the Jews who were captive in Babylon. He often used dramatic stories and "enacted parables" to make his points.

DANIEL: A captive in Babylon, Daniel rose to the office of prime minister. Despite intense political pressure, he lived a model life of integrity and left highly symbolic prophecies about the future.

HOSEA: By marrying a loose-living wife, Hosea lived out his message: that Israel had committed spiritual adultery against God.

JOEL: Beginning with a recent catastrophe in Judah (a locust plague), Joel foretold God's judgment on Judah.

AMOS: A country boy, Amos preached to Israel at the height of its prosperity. His grim warnings focused on materialism.

OBADIAH: Obadiah warned Edom, a nation bordering Judah.

JONAH: Jonah reluctantly went to Nineveh and found Israel's enemies responsive to God's message.

MICAH: Micah exposed corruption in every level of society, but closed with a promise of forgiveness and restoration.

NAHUM: Long after Jonah had stirred Nineveh to repentance, Nahum foretold the mighty city's total destruction.

HABAKKUK: Habakkuk addressed his book to God, not people. In a frank dialogue with God, he discussed problems of suffering and justice.

ZEPHANIAH: Zephaniah focused on the coming day of the Lord, which would purge Judah, resulting in a remnant used to bless the entire world.

HAGGAI: After returning from the Babylonian captivity, the Jews began rebuilding the temple of God. But before long they set aside that task to work on their own homes. Haggai reminded them to put God first.

ZECHARIAH: Writing around the same time as Haggai, Zechariah also urged the Jews to work on the temple. He used a more uplifting approach, describing how the temple would point to the coming Messiah.

MALACHI: The last Old Testament prophet, Malachi faced a nation that had grown indifferent. He sought to stir them from apathy.

History Books

The word *gospel* means "good news." Almost half of the New Testament consists of four accounts of the life of Jesus and the good news he brought to earth. Each of these four books, or Gospels, has a different focus and a different audience; taken together, they give a complete picture of Jesus' life and teaching. About a third of their pages are devoted to the events of his last week on earth, including the crucifixion and resurrection.

Acts continues the history into the period after Jesus left earth.

MATTHEW: Written to a Jewish audience, this Gospel links the Old and New Testaments. It presents Jesus as the Messiah and King promised in the Old Testament. Matthew emphasizes Jesus' authority and power.

MARK: Mark probably had pragmatic Roman readers in mind. His Gospel stresses action and gives a straightforward, blow-by-blow account of Jesus' work on earth.

LUKE: A doctor, Luke was also a fine writer. His Gospel provides many details of human interest, especially in Jesus' treatment of the poor and needy. A joyful tone characterizes Luke's book.

JOHN: John has a different, more reflective style than the other Gospels. Its author selected seven signs that pointed to Jesus as the Son of God and wove together everything else to underscore that point.

ACTS: Acts tells what happened to Jesus' followers after he left them. Peter and Paul soon emerged as leaders of the rapidly spreading church.

The Letters

The young church was nourished spiritually by apostles who set down their beliefs and messages in a series of letters. The first 13 such letters (Romans through Philemon) were written by the apostle Paul, who led the advance of Christianity to non-Jewish people.

Paul's Letters:

ROMANS: Written for a sophisticated audience, Romans sets forth theology in a logical, organized form.

1 CORINTHIANS: A very practical book, 1 Corinthians takes up the problems of a tumultuous church in Corinth: marriage, factions, immorality, public worship, and lawsuits.

2 CORINTHIANS: Paul wrote this follow-up letter to defend himself against a rebellion led by certain false apostles.

GALATIANS: A short version of the message of Romans, this book addresses legalism. It shows how Christ came to bring freedom, not bondage to a set of laws.

EPHESIANS: Although written in jail, this letter is Paul's most optimistic and encouraging. It tells of the advantages a believer has in Christ.

PHILIPPIANS: The church at Philippi ranked among Paul's favorites. This friendly letter stresses that joy can be found in any situation.

COLOSSIANS: Written to oppose certain cults, Colossians tells how faith in Christ is complete. Nothing needs to be added to what Christ did.

1 THESSALONIANS: Composed early in Paul's ministry, this letter gives a capsule history of one church, as well as Paul's direct advice about specific problems.

2 THESSALONIANS: Stronger in tone than his first letter to the Thessalonians, the sequel goes over the same topics, especially the church's questions about Christ's second coming.

1 TIMOTHY: As Paul neared the end of his life, he chose young men such as Timothy to carry on his work. His two letters to Timothy form a leadership manual for a young pastor.

2 TIMOTHY: Written just before Paul's death, 2 Timothy offers Paul's final words to his young assistant.

TITUS: Titus was left in Crete, a notoriously difficult place to nurture a church. Paul's letter gave practical advice on how to go about it.

PHILEMON: Paul urged Philemon, owner of runaway slave Onesimus, to forgive his slave and accept him as a brother in Christ.

Other Letters:

HEBREWS: No one knows who wrote Hebrews, but it probably first went to Christians in danger of slipping back into Judaism. It interprets the Old Testament, explaining many Jewish practices as symbols that prepared the way for Christ.

JAMES: James, a man of action, emphasized the right kind of behavior for a believer. Someone who calls himself or herself a Christian ought to act like it, James believed, and his letter spells out the specifics.

1 PETER: Early Christians often met violent opposition, and Peter's letter comforted and encouraged Christians who were being persecuted for their faith.

2 PETER: In contrast to Peter's first letter, this one focused on problems that sprang up from the inside. It warns against false teachers.

1 JOHN: John could fill simple words—*light, love, life*—with deep meaning, and in this letter, he elegantly explains basic truths about the Christian life.

2 JOHN: Warning against false teachers, John counseled churches on how to respond to them.

3 JOHN: Balancing 2 John, this companion letter mentions the need to be hospitable to true teachers.

JUDE: Jude gave a brief but fiery exposé of heretics.

REVELATION: A book of visions and symbols, Revelation is the only New Testament book that concentrates on prophecy. It completes the story, begun in Genesis, of the cosmic battle between good and evil being waged on earth. It ends with a picture of a new heaven and new earth.

THE OLD TESTAMENT

GENESIS

God at Work
Everything—literally everything—begins here

THE BIBLE BEGINS WITH WORDS that have become famous, "In the beginning when God created." God, like an artist, fashioned a universe. How can we grasp the grandeur of this?

Michelangelo, perhaps the greatest artist in history, may help us to understand. He painted Rome's famous Sistine Chapel to retell Genesis' story of creation. His experience proves one thing: Creativity is work.

> So God blessed the seventh day and hallowed it, because on it God rested from all the work that he had done in creation. 2.3

An Exhausting Effort

Michelangelo had 6,000 square feet of ceiling to cover—the size of four average house roofs. Anyone who has painted a ceiling with a paint roller has caught a hint of the physical difficulty of such a task. But Michelangelo's plan called for 300 separate, detailed portraits of men and women. For more than three years the 5'4" artist devoted all his labors to the exhausting strain of painting the vast overhead space with his tiny brushes.

Sometimes he painted standing on a huge scaffold, a paintbrush high over his head. Sometimes he sat, his nose inches from the ceiling. Sometimes he painted while lying on his back. His back, shoulders, neck, and arms cramped painfully.

In the long days of summer, he had light to paint 17 hours a day, taking food and a chamber pot with him on the 60-foot scaffold. For 30 days at a stretch he slept in his clothes, not even taking off his boots. Paint dribbled into his eyes so he could barely see. Freezing in the winter, sweating in the summer, he painted until at last the ceiling looked like a ceiling no more. He had transformed it into the creation drama, with creatures so real they seemed to breathe. Never before or since have paint and plaster been so changed.

The Miracle of Life

But, as Michelangelo knew very well, his work was a poor, dim image of what God had created. Over the plaster vault of the Sistine Chapel rose the immense dome of God's sky, breathtaking in its simple beauty. Mountains, seas, the continents—all these, and much more, are the creative work of God, the Master Artist.

God's world, so much bigger and more beautiful than Michelangelo's masterpiece, is the product of incomparably greater energy. As author Eugene Peterson has written, "The Bible begins with the announcement, 'In the beginning God created,' not 'sat majestic in the heavens' and not 'was filled with beauty and love.' He created. He did something." In the beginning, God went to work. Genesis focuses attention on this creative, hardworking God. The word God appears 30 times in the 31 verses of chapter 1. He grabs our attention in action. Genesis is an account of his deeds, ringing splendidly with the magnificent effort of creation.

Mending Broken Pieces

Genesis also talks about the work of humankind—but the tone changes abruptly. God had barely finished creating the universe when human rebellion marred it, like a delinquent spraying graffiti on the Sistine Chapel. Chapters 3–11 of Genesis portray a series of disasters: Adam and Eve's rebellion, Cain's calculated murder of his brother, the worldwide wickedness leading to the great flood, and human arrogance at Babel.

God immediately began to mend the pieces his creatures had broken. He narrowed his scope from the whole universe to a single man—not a king or wealthy landowner, but a childless nomad, Abraham. Abraham, Sarah, Isaac, Rebekah, Jacob, Rachel, Joseph—the upward thrust from chapter 12 on came through God's work in these startlingly human individuals. They were far from perfect, yet God picked them up where they were and carried them forward. He promised them great things. He moved through them to restore his art. His creative activity did not stop on the seventh day.

Genesis and Revelation

Many people read the Old Testament as though it portrayed the "bad old days" before Jesus. But that's not an accurate picture. Actually, the first three chapters of Genesis link to the last book of the Bible, Revelation. They are like brackets of perfection around the sadness of life marred by sin, death, suffering, and hatred. In Genesis we learn that life didn't start out that way. In Revelation we find out it won't end that way either. But the Old and New Testaments take place between those brackets. Through Abraham, through Moses, ultimately in Jesus, God is hard at work to make things right.

How to Read Genesis

Genesis is one of the most enjoyable Old Testament books, full of memorable stories of people and events. It is a crucial book to know, for the rest of the Bible often refers back to it.

Genesis tells the story of many beginnings—the beginning of the universe, the beginning of sin, and perhaps most important, the beginning of God's work to restore a sinful humanity.

The book breaks into two major sections. The first 11 chapters take a big view. They give the origins of human society, including the familiar stories of Adam and Eve, Cain and Abel, Noah's ark, and the tower of Babel. Here, a few words carry great significance. You need to read slowly and reflectively, for what happens in a single line may echo off events for centuries to come. For instance, Adam and Eve's sin, because it was the first sin, became an emblem of disobedience against God.

Beginning at chapter 12, Genesis tells a different kind of story—that of a single family. The pace of the story slows to develop the personalities of Abraham, Isaac, Jacob, and Joseph. These fathers and sons are full of human faults and oddities. Do you recognize any of their traits in people you know?

Seeing their fully human personalities, try to understand what God's plans were for them as individuals—and through them, for the restoration of a whole world marred by sin.

PEOPLE YOU'LL MEET IN GENESIS

ADAM AND EVE *(p. 26)* **ISHMAEL** *(p. 39)* **LABAN** *(p. 56)*
CAIN AND ABEL *(p. 30)* **SARAH** *(p. 41)* **RACHEL** *(p. 58)*
NOAH *(p. 32)* **ISAAC** *(p. 44)* **ESAU** *(p. 61)*
ABRAHAM *(p. 35)* **REBEKAH** *(p. 48)* **JOSEPH** *(p. 75)*
LOT *(p. 37)* **JACOB** *(p. 52)*

3-TRACK READING PLAN

For an explanation and complete listing of the 3-track reading plan, turn to page 7.

TRACK 1: *Two-Week Courses on the Bible*
The Track 1 reading program on the Old Testament includes three chapters from Genesis. See page 7 for a complete listing of this course.

TRACK 2: *An Overview of Genesis in 14 Days*
☐ Day 1. Read the Introduction to Genesis and chapter 1, the story of creation.
☐ Day 2. Read chapter 2, the story of Adam and Eve.
☐ Day 3. Read chapter 3, where sin enters a perfect world.
☐ Day 4. Read chapter 4, the story of Cain and Abel.
☐ Day 5. Read chapter 7, the story of Noah and the great flood.
☐ Day 6. Read chapter 8, the end of the great flood.
☐ Day 7. Read chapter 15, God's covenant with Abraham.
☐ Day 8. Read chapter 19, the destruction of Sodom and Gomorrah.
☐ Day 9. Read chapter 22, God's testing of Abraham.
☐ Day 10. Read chapter 27, in which Jacob cheats his brother Esau.
☐ Day 11. Read chapter 28, when Jacob, fleeing Esau, dreams about God.
☐ Day 12. Read chapter 37, the story of Joseph sold into slavery.

☐ Day 13. Read chapter 41, in which Joseph is raised to the highest position in Egypt.

☐ Day 14. Read chapter 45, in which Joseph reveals his identity to his brothers.

Now turn to page 9 for your next Track 2 reading project.

TRACK 3: *All of Genesis in 49 Days*

After you have read through Genesis, turn to pages 10–14 for your next Track 3 reading project.

☐1	☐2	☐3	☐4	☐5	☐6	☐7	☐8
☐9	☐10–11	☐12	☐13	☐14	☐15	☐16	☐17
☐18	☐19	☐20	☐21	☐22	☐23	☐24	☐25
☐26	☐27	☐28	☐29	☐30	☐31	☐32	☐33
☐34	☐35	☐36	☐37	☐38	☐39	☐40	☐41
☐42	☐43	☐44	☐45	☐46	☐47	☐48	☐49
☐50							

Six Days of Creation and the Sabbath

1 In the beginning when God created*a* the heavens and the earth, ²the earth was a formless void and darkness covered the face of the deep, while a wind from God*b* swept over the face of the waters. ³Then God said, "Let there be light"; and there was light. ⁴And God saw that the light was good; and God separated the light from the darkness. ⁵God called the light Day, and the darkness he called Night. And there was evening and there was morning, the first day.

6 And God said, "Let there be a dome in the midst of the waters, and let it separate the waters from the waters." ⁷So God made the dome and separated the waters that were under the dome from the waters that were above the dome. And it was so. ⁸God called the dome Sky. And there was evening and there was morning, the second day.

9 And God said, "Let the waters under the sky be gathered together into one place, and let the dry land appear." And it was so. ¹⁰God called the dry land Earth, and the waters that were gathered together he called Seas. And God saw that it was good. ¹¹Then God said, "Let the earth put forth vegetation: plants yielding seed, and fruit trees of every kind on earth that bear fruit with the seed in it." And it was so. ¹²The earth brought forth vegetation: plants yielding seed of every kind, and trees of every kind bearing fruit with the seed in it. And God saw that it was good. ¹³And there was evening and there was morning, the third day.

14 And God said, "Let there be lights in the dome of the sky to separate the day from the night; and let them be for signs and for seasons and for days and years, ¹⁵and let them be lights in the dome of the sky to give light upon the earth." And it was so. ¹⁶God made the two great lights—the greater light to rule the day and the lesser light to rule the night—and the stars. ¹⁷God set them in the dome of the sky to give light upon the earth, ¹⁸to rule over the day and over the night, and to separate the light from the darkness. And God saw that it was good. ¹⁹And there was evening and there was morning, the fourth day.

20 And God said, "Let the waters bring forth swarms of living creatures, and let birds fly above the earth across the dome of the sky." ²¹So God created the great sea monsters and every living creature that moves, of every kind, with which the waters swarm, and every winged bird of every kind. And God saw that it was good. ²²God blessed them, saying, "Be fruitful and multiply and fill the waters in the seas, and let birds multiply on the earth." ²³And there was evening and there was morning, the fifth day.

24 And God said, "Let the earth bring forth living creatures of every kind: cattle and creeping things and wild animals of the earth of every kind." And it was so. ²⁵God made the wild animals of the earth of every kind, and the cattle of every kind, and everything that creeps upon the ground of every kind. And God saw that it was good.

26 Then God said, "Let us make humankind*c* in our image, according to our likeness; and let them have dominion over the fish of the sea, and over the birds of the air, and over the cattle, and over all the wild animals of the earth,*d* and over every creeping thing that creeps upon the earth."

27 So God created humankind*c* in his
    image,
  in the image of God he created them;*e*
    male and female he created them.

²⁸God blessed them, and God said to them, "Be fruitful and multiply, and fill the earth and subdue it; and have dominion over the fish of the sea and over the birds of the air and over every living

---

a Or *when God began to create* or *In the beginning God created*   *b* Or *while the spirit of God* or *while a mighty wind*
c Heb *adam*   *d* Syr: Heb *and over all the earth*   *e* Heb *him*

thing that moves upon the earth." 29God said, "See, I have given you every plant yielding seed that is upon the face of all the earth, and every tree with seed in its fruit; you shall have them for food. 30And to every beast of the earth, and to every bird of the air, and to everything that creeps on the earth, everything that has the breath of life, I have given every green plant for food." And it was so. 31God saw everything that he had made, and indeed, it was very good. And there was evening and there was morning, the sixth day.

1.31 God Takes Time

Why did God take "six days" to create? Why not make it all instantaneously—as he certainly could have? Genesis introduces God's normal way of working: through a process. Work that begins with a word may take time to complete. Similarly, Israel was freed from slavery overnight, but required forty years to reach the promised land. Christians are born anew in an instant, and, in a process that lasts a lifetime, God makes them new. The new heaven and new earth have been a long time coming, but God is in the process of making all things new.

2 Thus the heavens and the earth were finished, and all their multitude. 2And on the seventh day God finished the work that he had done, and he rested on the seventh day from all the work that he had done. 3So God blessed the seventh day

and hallowed it, because on it God rested from all the work that he had done in creation.

4 These are the generations of the heavens and the earth when they were created.

Another Account of the Creation

In the day that the LORD God made the earth and the heavens, 5when no plant of the field was yet in the earth and no herb of the field had yet sprung up—for the LORD God had not caused it to rain upon the earth, and there was no one to till the ground; 6but a stream would rise from the earth, and water the whole face of the ground— 7then the LORD God formed man from the dust of the ground,ƒ and breathed into his nostrils the breath of life; and the man became a living being. 8And the LORD God planted a garden in Eden, in the east; and there he put the man whom he had formed. 9Out of the ground the LORD God made to grow every tree that is pleasant to the sight and good for food, the tree of life also in the midst of the garden, and the tree of the knowledge of good and evil.

10 A river flows out of Eden to water the garden, and from there it divides and becomes four branches. 11The name of the first is Pishon; it is the one that flows around the whole land of Havilah, where there is gold; 12and the gold of that land is good; bdellium and onyx stone are there. 13The name of the second river is Gihon; it is the one that flows around the whole land of Cush. 14The name of the third river is Tigris, which

ƒ Or *formed a man* (Heb *adam*) *of dust from the ground* (Heb *adamah*)

ADAM AND EVE *First in Everything*

THEY WERE THE FIRST HUMAN beings on earth, part of God's original creation. As such, Adam and Eve set the standard for everything that followed. Their lives illustrate what God expects and loves from human beings—as well as what he loathes.

First ecologists. They were the first to name animals, the first to tend a garden, the first to be placed in charge of all the creatures. They took on the huge task of caring for earth and guiding its proper use.

First to form a relationship with God. Adam and Eve were made in God's image. He conversed with them and gave them responsibilities. When they failed God they felt ashamed and feared meeting him.

First married couple. God himself made the introductions and gave the first couple the delight of each other, body and soul. They also became the first parents, though their very first child (Cain) brought much pain as well as joy.

First to sin against God. They had only to follow directions, but they failed. In response they hid from God and blamed each other. "Think of all the squabbles Adam and Eve must have had in the course of their nine hundred years," wrote Martin Luther. "Eve would say, 'You ate the apple,' and Adam would retort, 'You gave it to me.'"

In the end, the first two human beings were banished from Eden and driven out into a world full of problems God had never intended for them to confront. In that, as in everything, these two led the way for all of us.

Life Questions: Are you ever in a position to set an example for others? What can you learn from Adam and Eve's experience?

flows east of Assyria. And the fourth river is the Euphrates.

15 The LORD God took the man and put him in the garden of Eden to till it and keep it. [16]And the LORD God commanded the man, "You may freely eat of every tree of the garden; [17]but of the tree of the knowledge of good and evil you shall not eat, for in the day that you eat of it you shall die."

18 Then the LORD God said, "It is not good that the man should be alone; I will make him a helper as his partner." [19]So out of the ground the LORD God formed every animal of the field and every bird of the air, and brought them to the man to see what he would call them; and whatever the man called every living creature, that was its name. [20]The man gave names to all cattle, and to the birds of the air, and to every animal of the field; but for the man[g] there was not found a helper as his partner. [21]So the LORD God caused a deep sleep to fall upon the man, and he slept; then he took one of his ribs and closed up its place with flesh. [22]And the rib that the LORD God had taken from the man he made into a woman and brought her to the man. [23]Then the man said,

"This at last is bone of my bones
    and flesh of my flesh;
this one shall be called Woman,[h]
    for out of Man[i] this one was taken."

2.23–25 The First Marriage

Adam joyfully recognized that he and Eve belonged together. As verse 24 suggests, this suitability is the basis for all marriages. This passage was quoted by Jesus (Matthew 19.5; Mark 10.7–8) and Paul (1 Corinthians 6.16; Ephesians 5.31) in their comments on sex and marriage.

[24]Therefore a man leaves his father and his mother and clings to his wife, and they become one flesh. [25]And the man and his wife were both naked, and were not ashamed.

The First Sin and Its Punishment

3 Now the serpent was more crafty than any other wild animal that the LORD God had made. He said to the woman, "Did God say, 'You shall not eat from any tree in the garden'?" [2]The woman said to the serpent, "We may eat of the fruit of the trees in the garden; [3]but God said, 'You shall not eat of the fruit of the tree that is in the middle of the garden, nor shall you touch it, or you shall die.'" [4]But the serpent said to the woman, "You will not die; [5]for God knows that

when you eat of it your eyes will be opened, and you will be like God,[j] knowing good and evil." [6]So when the woman saw that the tree was good for food, and that it was a delight to the eyes, and that the tree was to be desired to make one wise, she took of its fruit and ate; and she also gave some to her husband, who was with her, and he ate. [7]Then the eyes of both were opened, and they knew that they were naked; and they sewed fig leaves together and made loincloths for themselves.

3.7 Sin and Shame

When Adam and Eve disobeyed God, they immediately became ashamed of their bodies and wanted to hide. Ever since, sinful human beings have been "hiding" from each other and from God.

God asked Adam and Eve three questions, typical of the questions he puts to anyone "in hiding": 1) Where are you? (And why are you hiding from me?) 2) Who told you that you were naked? (And why did you believe somebody else, not me?) 3) What is this that you have done? (And are you ready to take responsibility for it?)

8 They heard the sound of the LORD God walking in the garden at the time of the evening breeze, and the man and his wife hid themselves from the presence of the LORD God among the trees of the garden. [9]But the LORD God called to the man, and said to him, "Where are you?" [10]He said, "I heard the sound of you in the garden, and I was afraid, because I was naked; and I hid myself." [11]He said, "Who told you that you were naked? Have you eaten from the tree of which I commanded you not to eat?" [12]The man said, "The woman whom you gave to be with me, she gave me fruit from the tree, and I ate." [13]Then the LORD God said to the woman, "What is this that you have done?" The woman said, "The serpent tricked me, and I ate." [14]The LORD God said to the serpent,

"Because you have done this,
    cursed are you among all animals
    and among all wild creatures;
upon your belly you shall go,
    and dust you shall eat
    all the days of your life.
15 I will put enmity between you and the
        woman,
    and between your offspring and hers;
he will strike your head,
    and you will strike his heel."

[16]To the woman he said,

---

g Or for Adam   h Heb ishshah   i Heb ish   j Or gods

"I will greatly increase your pangs in
      childbearing;
   in pain you shall bring forth children,
yet your desire shall be for your husband,
   and he shall rule over you."
17And to the man[k] he said,
"Because you have listened to the voice of
      your wife,
   and have eaten of the tree
about which I commanded you,
   'You shall not eat of it,'
cursed is the ground because of you;
   in toil you shall eat of it all the days of
      your life;
18   thorns and thistles it shall bring forth for
      you;
   and you shall eat the plants of the
      field.
19   By the sweat of your face

you shall eat bread
   until you return to the ground,
   for out of it you were taken;
you are dust,
   and to dust you shall return."
20 The man named his wife Eve,[l] because
she was the mother of all living. 21And the LORD
God made garments of skins for the man[m] and
for his wife, and clothed them.
22 Then the LORD God said, "See, the man
has become like one of us, knowing good and
evil; and now, he might reach out his hand and
take also from the tree of life, and eat, and live
forever"— 23therefore the LORD God sent him
forth from the garden of Eden, to till the ground
from which he was taken. 24He drove out the
man; and at the east of the garden of Eden he
placed the cherubim, and a sword flaming and
turning to guard the way to the tree of life.

k Or to Adam   l In Heb Eve resembles the word for living   m Or for Adam

Where We Came From
Above all else, Genesis says this: God did it

THE BIOLOGY TEACHER DISPLAYS A chart showing six animals. At one end is an ape standing upright, its hands swinging below its knees. At the other end, a rather hairy, stooped man in skins. "These are the stages of human evolution," the teacher declares, "over a period of several million years."

One agonized student shoots up his hand. "I believe in the Bible," he stammers, "that God made the earth and that the first man was Adam."

The teacher lets him finish, then dismisses his view. "Everybody is free to have his own religious beliefs. But science has proven that evolution is a fact."

Scenes like this have thrown confusion over the first three chapters of the Bible. It's impossible to read about Adam and Eve without wondering how they fit in with the bones scientists proclaim as "earliest man."

> The LORD God formed man from the dust of the ground, and breathed into his nostrils the breath of life; and the man became a living being. 2.7

The Main Point

These differences stir up controversy, even court cases. Certainly they are important issues. It's unfortunate, though, that the debate over process diverts attention from the main truth Genesis teaches.

Above everything else, it proclaims this: God did it. We are not here by accident, nor are we here merely to please ourselves. We owe our very existence to God. Every helium atom, every spiral galaxy, every living creature exists because God wants it to. Genesis 1–3 is the artist's signature on the painting, saying, "This is mine."

God Made Us Good

Genesis 1–3 pays humanity its highest compliment. After making all the glories of the world, God topped off his work with man and woman. He put them in charge. Unlike the animals, they were like him, "in his image." "Very good," he said to himself when he had finished. With humans he quit, satisfied.

Nobody, including God, has been satisfied with human beings since then. We were made good, but we disobeyed God right from the beginning. We've been suffering the consequences ever since. Genesis helps us understand why the universe is so flagrantly lovely, and yet so tragic. It is lovely because God made it. But it is tragic because he entrusted it to us—and we failed.

Life Questions: People say they can see God reflected in stars, forests, sunsets. What about people? How can you see God's artistry in them?

Cain Murders Abel

4 Now the man knew his wife Eve, and she conceived and bore Cain, saying, "I have produced[n] a man with the help of the LORD." [2]Next she bore his brother Abel. Now Abel was a keeper of sheep, and Cain a tiller of the ground. [3]In the course of time Cain brought to the LORD an offering of the fruit of the ground, [4]and Abel for his part brought of the firstlings of his flock, their fat portions. And the LORD had regard for

4.4 Improper Offerings

Why God preferred Abel's offering to Cain's is uncertain; later in the Old Testament both animal and agricultural offerings were accepted by God. Quite possibly, Cain's problem was his attitude. Cain certainly became instantly angry with God when things did not go his way.

Abel and his offering, [5]but for Cain and his offering he had no regard. So Cain was very angry, and his countenance fell. [6]The LORD said to Cain, "Why are you angry, and why has your countenance fallen? [7]If you do well, will you not be accepted? And if you do not do well, sin is lurking at the door; its desire is for you, but you must master it."

[8] Cain said to his brother Abel, "Let us go out to the field."[o] And when they were in the field, Cain rose up against his brother Abel, and killed him. [9]Then the LORD said to Cain, "Where is your brother Abel?" He said, "I do not know; am I my brother's keeper?" [10]And the LORD said, "What have you done? Listen; your brother's blood is crying out to me from the ground! [11]And now you are cursed from the ground, which has opened its mouth to receive your brother's blood from your hand. [12]When you till the ground, it will no longer yield to you its strength; you will be a fugitive and a wanderer on the earth." [13]Cain said to the LORD, "My punishment is greater than I can bear! [14]Today you have driven me away from the soil, and I shall be hidden from your face; I shall be a fugitive and a wanderer on the earth, and anyone who meets me may kill me." [15]Then the LORD said to him, "Not so![p] Whoever kills Cain will suffer a sevenfold vengeance." And the LORD put a mark on Cain, so that no one who came upon him would kill him. [16]Then Cain went away from the presence of the LORD, and settled in the land of Nod,[q] east of Eden.

Beginnings of Civilization

[17] Cain knew his wife, and she conceived and bore Enoch; and he built a city, and named it Enoch after his son Enoch. [18]To Enoch was born Irad; and Irad was the father of Mehujael, and Mehujael the father of Methushael, and Methushael the father of Lamech. [19]Lamech took two wives; the name of the one was Adah, and the name of the other Zillah. [20]Adah bore Jabal; he was the ancestor of those who live in tents and have livestock. [21]His brother's name was Jubal; he was the ancestor of all those who play the lyre and pipe. [22]Zillah bore Tubal-cain, who made all kinds of bronze and iron tools. The sister of Tubal-cain was Naamah.

[23] Lamech said to his wives:
"Adah and Zillah, hear my voice;
    you wives of Lamech, listen to what I
        say:
I have killed a man for wounding me,
    a young man for striking me.
[24] If Cain is avenged sevenfold,
    truly Lamech seventy-sevenfold."

[25] Adam knew his wife again, and she bore a son and named him Seth, for she said, "God has appointed[r] for me another child instead of Abel, because Cain killed him." [26]To Seth also a son was born, and he named him Enosh. At that time people began to invoke the name of the LORD.

Adam's Descendants to Noah and His Sons

5 This is the list of the descendants of Adam. When God created humankind,[s] he made them[t] in the likeness of God. [2]Male and female he created them, and he blessed them and named them "Humankind"[s] when they were created.

[3] When Adam had lived one hundred thirty years, he became the father of a son in his likeness, according to his image, and named him Seth. [4]The days of Adam after he became the father of Seth were eight hundred years; and he had other sons and daughters. [5]Thus all the days that Adam lived were nine hundred thirty years; and he died.

[6] When Seth had lived one hundred five years, he became the father of Enosh. [7]Seth lived after the birth of Enosh eight hundred seven years, and had other sons and daughters. [8]Thus all the days of Seth were nine hundred twelve years; and he died.

[9] When Enosh had lived ninety years, he became the father of Kenan. [10]Enosh lived after the birth of Kenan eight hundred fifteen years, and had other sons and daughters. [11]Thus all the days of Enosh were nine hundred five years; and he died.

[12] When Kenan had lived seventy years, he became the father of Mahalalel. [13]Kenan lived after the birth of Mahalalel eight hundred and forty

---

[n] The verb in Heb resembles the word for *Cain*   [o] Sam Gk Syr Compare Vg: MT lacks *Let us go out to the field*
[p] Gk Syr Vg: Heb *Therefore*   [q] That is *Wandering*   [r] The verb in Heb resembles the word for *Seth*   [s] Heb *adam*
[t] Heb *him*

years, and had other sons and daughters. 14Thus all the days of Kenan were nine hundred and ten years; and he died.

15 When Mahalalel had lived sixty-five years, he became the father of Jared. 16Mahalalel lived after the birth of Jared eight hundred thirty years, and had other sons and daughters. 17Thus all the days of Mahalalel were eight hundred ninety-five years; and he died.

18 When Jared had lived one hundred sixty-two years he became the father of Enoch. 19Jared lived after the birth of Enoch eight hundred years, and had other sons and daughters. 20Thus all the days of Jared were nine hundred sixty-two years; and he died.

21 When Enoch had lived sixty-five years, he became the father of Methuselah. 22Enoch walked with God after the birth of Methuselah three hundred years, and had other sons and daughters. 23Thus all the days of Enoch were three hundred sixty-five years. 24Enoch walked with God; then he was no more, because God took him.

5.24 The Man Who Did Not Die

All but one of the brief biographies in chapter 5 end with the words, "and he died." We know very little about the exception, Enoch, except that he walked with God. Enoch did not die; he "was no more, because God took him." Based on this evidence, Hebrews 11.5–6 commends Enoch as a man of faith, since "without faith it is impossible to please God."

25 When Methuselah had lived one hundred eighty-seven years, he became the father of Lamech. 26Methuselah lived after the birth of La-

u Meaning of Heb uncertain

mech seven hundred eighty-two years, and had other sons and daughters. 27Thus all the days of Methuselah were nine hundred sixty-nine years; and he died.

28 When Lamech had lived one hundred eighty-two years, he became the father of a son; 29he named him Noah, saying, "Out of the ground that the LORD has cursed this one shall bring us relief from our work and from the toil of our hands." 30Lamech lived after the birth of Noah five hundred ninety-five years, and had other sons and daughters. 31Thus all the days of Lamech were seven hundred seventy-seven years; and he died.

32 After Noah was five hundred years old, Noah became the father of Shem, Ham, and Japheth.

The Wickedness of Humankind

6 When people began to multiply on the face of the ground, and daughters were born to them, 2the sons of God saw that they were fair; and they took wives for themselves of all that they chose. 3Then the LORD said, "My spirit shall not abide*u* in mortals forever, for they are flesh; their days shall be one hundred twenty years." 4The Nephilim were on the earth in those days—and also afterward—when the sons of God went in to the daughters of humans, who bore children to them. These were the heroes that were of old, warriors of renown.

5 The LORD saw that the wickedness of humankind was great in the earth, and that every inclination of the thoughts of their hearts was only evil continually. 6And the LORD was sorry that he had made humankind on the earth, and it grieved him to his heart. 7So the LORD said, "I will

CAIN AND ABEL *Blood Brothers*

THEIR PARENTS HAD STARTED THE rebellion against God. Not much time passed before Cain took sin to its logical conclusion. The first child on earth became the first murderer.

Cain and Abel were the first of many feuding siblings. After them came Isaac and Ishmael, Jacob and Esau, Rachel and Leah, Joseph and his brothers. It's a theme song in Genesis (and in life): Blood kin have a hard time getting along. They can make bitter rivals.

The Bible tells us little about Abel and a good deal about Cain. That makes sad sense because as sinful humans we see more of ourselves in Cain than in Abel. Cain wears his emotions on his sleeve: first murderous anger, then defensiveness and finally shame and fear. In response to Cain's great crime, God both punishes and protects him. He must leave home to wander all his life, yet God also provides him with a measure of protection, "the mark of Cain" (4.15).

Cain's children set the pattern for humanity as it has lived ever since, a mixture of good and bad. On the one hand, as musicians, metalworkers and farmers, they helped civilize the earth. On the other hand, Cain's problems got passed down to future generations. Where Cain felt shame for his crime and punishment, his descendant Lamech would boast about his own murderous deed (Genesis 4.23–24).

Life Questions: Which of Cain's responses to God—anger, defensiveness, fear, shame—do you identify with most easily?

blot out from the earth the human beings I have created—people together with animals and creeping things and birds of the air, for I am sorry that I have made them." [8]But Noah found favor in the sight of the LORD.

6.2 The Sons of God

This mysterious description may refer to the "sons of Seth," the line of God's people from Adam to Noah, or it may refer to angels, often called "sons of God" in the Old Testament. However you interpret it, the point is that evil behavior increased in the world, a fact that led to punishment by a flood.

Noah Pleases God

9 These are the descendants of Noah. Noah was a righteous man, blameless in his generation; Noah walked with God. [10]And Noah had three sons, Shem, Ham, and Japheth.

11 Now the earth was corrupt in God's sight, and the earth was filled with violence. [12]And God saw that the earth was corrupt; for all flesh had corrupted its ways upon the earth. [13]And God said to Noah, "I have determined to make an end of all flesh, for the earth is filled with violence because of them; now I am going to destroy them along with the earth. [14]Make yourself an ark of cypress[u] wood; make rooms in the ark, and cover it inside and out with pitch. [15]This is how you are to make it: the length of the ark three hundred cubits, its width fifty cubits, and its height thirty cubits. [16]Make a roof[v] for the ark, and finish it to a cubit above; and put the door of the ark in its side; make it with lower, second, and third decks. [17]For my part, I am going to bring a flood of waters on the earth, to destroy from under heaven all flesh in which is the breath of life; everything that is on the earth shall die. [18]But I will establish my covenant with you; and you shall come into the ark, you, your sons, your wife, and your sons' wives with you. [19]And of every living thing, of all flesh, you shall bring two of every kind into the ark, to keep them alive with you; they shall be male and female. [20]Of the birds according to their kinds, and of the animals according to their kinds, of every creeping thing of the ground according to its kind, two of every kind shall come in to you, to keep them alive. [21]Also take with you every kind of food that is eaten, and store it up; and it shall serve as food for you and for them." [22]Noah did this; he did all that God commanded him.

The Great Flood

7 Then the LORD said to Noah, "Go into the ark, you and all your household, for I have seen that you alone are righteous before me in this generation. [2]Take with you seven pairs of all clean animals, the male and its mate; and a pair of the animals that are not clean, the male and its mate; [3]and seven pairs of the birds of the air also, male and female, to keep their kind alive on the face of all the earth. [4]For in seven days I will send rain on the earth for forty days and forty nights; and every living thing that I have made I will blot out from the face of the ground." [5]And Noah did all that the LORD had commanded him.

6 Noah was six hundred years old when the flood of waters came on the earth. [7]And Noah with his sons and his wife and his sons' wives went into the ark to escape the waters of the flood. [8]Of clean animals, and of animals that are not clean, and of birds, and of everything that creeps on the ground, [9]two and two, male and female, went into the ark with Noah, as God had commanded Noah. [10]And after seven days the waters of the flood came on the earth.

11 In the six hundredth year of Noah's life, in the second month, on the seventeenth day of the month, on that day all the fountains of the great deep burst forth, and the windows of the heavens were opened. [12]The rain fell on the earth forty days and forty nights. [13]On the very same day Noah with his sons, Shem and Ham and Japheth, and Noah's wife and the three wives of his sons entered the ark, [14]they and every wild animal of every kind, and all domestic animals of every kind, and every creeping thing that creeps on the earth, and every bird of every kind—every bird, every winged creature. [15]They went into the ark with Noah, two and two of all flesh in which was the breath of life. [16]And those that entered, male and female of all flesh, went in as God had commanded him; and the LORD shut him in.

17 The flood continued forty days on the earth; and the waters increased, and bore up the ark, and it rose high above the earth. [18]The waters swelled and increased greatly on the earth; and the ark floated on the face of the waters. [19]The waters swelled so mightily on the earth that all the high mountains under the whole heaven were covered; [20]the waters swelled above the mountains, covering them fifteen cubits deep. [21]And all flesh died that moved on the earth, birds, domestic animals, wild animals, all swarming creatures that swarm on the earth, and all human beings; [22]everything on dry land in whose nostrils was the breath of life died. [23]He blotted out every living thing that was on the face of the ground, human beings and animals and creeping things and birds of the air; they were blotted out from the earth. Only Noah was left, and those that were with him

[u] Meaning of Heb uncertain   [v] Or *window*

in the ark. 24And the waters swelled on the earth for one hundred fifty days.

The Flood Subsides

8 But God remembered Noah and all the wild animals and all the domestic animals that were with him in the ark. And God made a wind blow over the earth, and the waters subsided; 2the fountains of the deep and the windows of the heavens were closed, the rain from the heavens was restrained, 3and the waters gradually receded from the earth. At the end of one hundred fifty days the waters had abated; 4and in the seventh month, on the seventeenth day of the month, the ark came to rest on the mountains of Ararat. 5The waters continued to abate until the tenth month; in the tenth month, on the first day of the month, the tops of the mountains appeared.

6 At the end of forty days Noah opened the window of the ark that he had made 7and sent out the raven; and it went to and fro until the waters were dried up from the earth. 8Then he sent out the dove from him, to see if the waters had subsided from the face of the ground; 9but the dove found no place to set its foot, and it returned to him to the ark, for the waters were still on the face of the whole earth. So he put out his hand and took it and brought it into the ark with him. 10He waited another seven days, and again he sent out the dove from the ark; 11and the dove came back to him in the evening, and there in its beak was a freshly plucked olive leaf; so Noah knew that the waters had subsided from the earth. 12Then he waited another seven days, and sent out the dove; and it did not return to him any more.

13 In the six hundred first year, in the first month, on the first day of the month, the waters were dried up from the earth; and Noah removed the covering of the ark, and looked, and saw that the face of the ground was drying. 14In the second

month, on the twenty-seventh day of the month, the earth was dry. 15Then God said to Noah, 16"Go out of the ark, you and your wife, and your sons and your sons' wives with you. 17Bring out

8.11 Peace Symbol

The dove with an olive branch stands as a symbol for peace, and the origin of that symbol traces back to this account of restored peace between God and his creation. The olive leaf carried by the dove told Noah that lower elevations (where olives grow) were above water and had sprouted new life.

with you every living thing that is with you of all flesh—birds and animals and every creeping thing that creeps on the earth—so that they may abound on the earth, and be fruitful and multiply on the earth." 18So Noah went out with his sons and his wife and his sons' wives. 19And every animal, every creeping thing, and every bird, everything that moves on the earth, went out of the ark by families.

God's Promise to Noah

20 Then Noah built an altar to the LORD, and took of every clean animal and of every clean bird, and offered burnt offerings on the altar. 21And when the LORD smelled the pleasing odor, the LORD said in his heart, "I will never again curse the ground because of humankind, for the inclination of the human heart is evil from youth; nor will I ever again destroy every living creature as I have done.
22 As long as the earth endures,
    seedtime and harvest, cold and heat,
        summer and winter, day and night,
            shall not cease."

NOAH *Starting Over*

THE PROBLEM WITH THE PLANET God made was not its geology, biology or meteorology. The problem centered, rather, in a single species: *Homo sapiens*. Sin, spreading like a disease, had taken over human thought and action. As a result God chose to blot out much of his creation and start all over again, using Noah for this new beginning.

Characteristically, Noah obeyed right away when God announced his plans. Noah "walked with God," says Genesis (6.9). He worked hard, building a gigantic, seaworthy structure and storing up food for hundreds of animals. Repeatedly the Bible says that Noah "did all that God commanded him."

Noah and his family spent more than a year confined in the ark. When they emerged at last to step out on muddy ground, their first action was to worship God. Impressed, God made a new covenant with Noah, promising never again to destroy the earth. He urged Noah and his family to be fruitful and multiply, just as he had urged Adam and Eve in the beginning.

Did this new beginning work? The last we hear of Noah shows that sin had not been remedied. Noah got drunk, shamed himself in front of his sons, and cursed one of his grandsons (9.20–24). Not even a flood could solve the problem of sin, for it lived on inside the best of people, even Noah.

Life Questions: If you were given an assignment like Noah's, how would you respond?

The Covenant with Noah

9 God blessed Noah and his sons, and said to them, "Be fruitful and multiply, and fill the earth. ²The fear and dread of you shall rest on every animal of the earth, and on every bird of the air, on everything that creeps on the ground, and on all the fish of the sea; into your hand they are delivered. ³Every moving thing that lives shall be food for you; and just as I gave you the green plants, I give you everything. ⁴Only, you shall not

9.4 Reverence for Life

In the Garden of Eden God had provided plants for humanity's food. Here, for the first time, he gave permission to add meat to their diet. Still, an animal was not to be eaten "with its life, that is, its blood." Kosher dietary requirements kept by Orthodox Jews today derive partly from this statement. Leviticus 17.10–14 gives more detail.

The intent, many commentators believe, was to remind God's people to reverence life, including animal life. This passage makes clear, however, that human life has a special significance. Ironically, capital punishment derives its legitimacy from this. Murderers who destroy human life actually attack the image of God. Therefore God demands an accounting.

eat flesh with its life, that is, its blood. ⁵For your own lifeblood I will surely require a reckoning: from every animal I will require it and from human beings, each one for the blood of another, I will require a reckoning for human life.

⁶ Whoever sheds the blood of a human,
   by a human shall that person's blood
      be shed;
   for in his own image
      God made humankind.

⁷And you, be fruitful and multiply, abound on the earth and multiply in it."

8 Then God said to Noah and to his sons with him, ⁹"As for me, I am establishing my covenant with you and your descendants after you, ¹⁰and with every living creature that is with you, the birds, the domestic animals, and every animal of the earth with you, as many as came out of the ark.ʷ ¹¹I establish my covenant with you, that never again shall all flesh be cut off by the waters of a flood, and never again shall there be a flood to destroy the earth." ¹²God said, "This is the sign of the covenant that I make between me and you and every living creature that is with you, for all future generations: ¹³I have set my bow in the clouds, and it shall be a sign of the covenant between me and the earth. ¹⁴When I bring clouds over the earth and the bow is seen in the clouds,

¹⁵I will remember my covenant that is between me and you and every living creature of all flesh; and the waters shall never again become a flood to destroy all flesh. ¹⁶When the bow is in the

9.12 The Reason for Rainbows

Throughout the Bible, God makes covenant agreements with the people he loves. This first recorded covenant was marked by an appropriate symbol—the rainbow. While later covenants applied specifically to the Israelites, this one extended—and still extends—to every living creature.

clouds, I will see it and remember the everlasting covenant between God and every living creature of all flesh that is on the earth." ¹⁷God said to Noah, "This is the sign of the covenant that I have established between me and all flesh that is on the earth."

Noah and His Sons

18 The sons of Noah who went out of the ark were Shem, Ham, and Japheth. Ham was the father of Canaan. ¹⁹These three were the sons of Noah; and from these the whole earth was peopled.

20 Noah, a man of the soil, was the first to plant a vineyard. ²¹He drank some of the wine and became drunk, and he lay uncovered in his tent. ²²And Ham, the father of Canaan, saw the nakedness of his father, and told his two brothers outside. ²³Then Shem and Japheth took a garment, laid it on both their shoulders, and walked backward and covered the nakedness of their father; their faces were turned away, and they did not see their father's nakedness. ²⁴When Noah awoke from his wine and knew what his youngest son had done to him, ²⁵he said,

"Cursed be Canaan;
   lowest of slaves shall he be to his
      brothers."
²⁶He also said,
"Blessed by the LORD my God be Shem;
   and let Canaan be his slave.
²⁷ May God make space forˣ Japheth,
   and let him live in the tents of Shem;
   and let Canaan be his slave."

28 After the flood Noah lived three hundred fifty years. ²⁹All the days of Noah were nine hundred fifty years; and he died.

Nations Descended from Noah

10 These are the descendants of Noah's sons, Shem, Ham, and Japheth; children were born to them after the flood.

ʷ Gk: Heb adds *every animal of the earth*   ˣ Heb *yapht*, a play on *Japheth*

2 The descendants of Japheth: Gomer, Magog, Madai, Javan, Tubal, Meshech, and Tiras. [3]The descendants of Gomer: Ashkenaz, Riphath, and Togarmah. [4]The descendants of Javan: Elishah, Tarshish, Kittim, and Rodanim.[y] [5]From these the coastland peoples spread. These are the descendants of Japheth[z] in their lands, with their own language, by their families, in their nations.

6 The descendants of Ham: Cush, Egypt, Put, and Canaan. [7]The descendants of Cush: Seba, Havilah, Sabtah, Raamah, and Sabteca. The descendants of Raamah: Sheba and Dedan. [8]Cush became the father of Nimrod; he was the first on earth to become a mighty warrior. [9]He was a mighty hunter before the LORD; therefore it is said, "Like Nimrod a mighty hunter before the LORD." [10]The beginning of his kingdom was Babel, Erech, and Accad, all of them in the land of Shinar. [11]From that land he went into Assyria, and built Nineveh, Rehoboth-ir, Calah, and [12]Resen between Nineveh and Calah; that is the great city. [13]Egypt became the father of Ludim, Anamim, Lehabim, Naphtuhim, [14]Pathrusim, Casluhim, and Caphtorim, from which the Philistines come.[a]

15 Canaan became the father of Sidon his firstborn, and Heth, [16]and the Jebusites, the Amorites, the Girgashites, [17]the Hivites, the Arkites, the Sinites, [18]the Arvadites, the Zemarites, and the Hamathites. Afterward the families of the Canaanites spread abroad. [19]And the territory of the Canaanites extended from Sidon, in the direction of Gerar, as far as Gaza, and in the direction of Sodom, Gomorrah, Admah, and Zeboiim, as far as Lasha. [20]These are the descendants of Ham, by their families, their languages, their lands, and their nations.

21 To Shem also, the father of all the children of Eber, the elder brother of Japheth, children were born. [22]The descendants of Shem: Elam, Asshur, Arpachshad, Lud, and Aram. [23]The descendants of Aram: Uz, Hul, Gether, and Mash. [24]Arpachshad became the father of Shelah; and Shelah became the father of Eber. [25]To Eber were born two sons: the name of the one was Peleg,[b] for in his days the earth was divided, and his brother's name was Joktan. [26]Joktan became the father of Almodad, Sheleph, Hazarmaveth, Jerah, [27]Hadoram, Uzal, Diklah, [28]Obal, Abimael, Sheba, [29]Ophir, Havilah, and Jobab; all these were the descendants of Joktan. [30]The territory in which they lived extended from Mesha in the direction of Sephar, the hill country of the east. [31]These are the descendants of Shem, by their families, their languages, their lands, and their nations.

32 These are the families of Noah's sons, according to their genealogies, in their nations; and from these the nations spread abroad on the earth after the flood.

The Tower of Babel

11 Now the whole earth had one language and the same words. [2]And as they migrated from the east,[c] they came upon a plain in the land of Shinar and settled there. [3]And they said to one another, "Come, let us make bricks, and burn them thoroughly." And they had brick for stone, and bitumen for mortar. [4]Then they said, "Come, let us build ourselves a city, and a tower with its top in the heavens, and let us make a name for ourselves; otherwise we shall be scattered abroad upon the face of the whole earth." [5]The LORD came down to see the city and the tower, which mortals had built. [6]And the LORD said, "Look, they are one people, and they have all one language; and this is only the beginning of what they will do; nothing that they propose to do will now

11.6 Human Ambition

People are ambitious—they want to succeed. Genesis portrays humans as so ambitious that they try to compete with, rather than serve, God. This was Adam and Eve's sin (3.5,22), and at Babel people were at it again, in a citywide effort. God frustrated their plans by confusing their language.

be impossible for them. [7]Come, let us go down, and confuse their language there, so that they will not understand one another's speech." [8]So the LORD scattered them abroad from there over the face of all the earth, and they left off building the city. [9]Therefore it was called Babel, because there the LORD confused[d] the language of all the earth; and from there the LORD scattered them abroad over the face of all the earth.

Descendants of Shem

10 These are the descendants of Shem. When Shem was one hundred years old, he became the father of Arpachshad two years after the flood; [11]and Shem lived after the birth of Arpachshad five hundred years, and had other sons and daughters.

12 When Arpachshad had lived thirty-five years, he became the father of Shelah; [13]and Arpachshad lived after the birth of Shelah four hundred three years, and had other sons and daughters.

14 When Shelah had lived thirty years, he became the father of Eber; [15]and Shelah lived after

[y] Heb Mss Sam Gk See 1 Chr 1.7: MT *Dodanim*   [z] Compare verses 20, 31. Heb lacks *These are the descendants of Japheth*   [a] Cn: Heb *Casluhim, from which the Philistines come, and Caphtorim*   [b] That is *Division*   [c] Or *migrated eastward*   [d] Heb *balal*, meaning *to confuse*

the birth of Eber four hundred three years, and had other sons and daughters.

16 When Eber had lived thirty-four years, he became the father of Peleg; [17]and Eber lived after the birth of Peleg four hundred thirty years, and had other sons and daughters.

18 When Peleg had lived thirty years, he became the father of Reu; [19]and Peleg lived after the birth of Reu two hundred nine years, and had other sons and daughters.

20 When Reu had lived thirty-two years, he became the father of Serug; [21]and Reu lived after the birth of Serug two hundred seven years, and had other sons and daughters.

22 When Serug had lived thirty years, he became the father of Nahor; [23]and Serug lived after the birth of Nahor two hundred years, and had other sons and daughters.

24 When Nahor had lived twenty-nine years, he became the father of Terah; [25]and Nahor lived after the birth of Terah one hundred nineteen years, and had other sons and daughters.

26 When Terah had lived seventy years, he became the father of Abram, Nahor, and Haran.

Descendants of Terah

27 Now these are the descendants of Terah. Terah was the father of Abram, Nahor, and Haran; and Haran was the father of Lot. [28]Haran died before his father Terah in the land of his birth, in Ur of the Chaldeans. [29]Abram and Nahor took wives; the name of Abram's wife was Sarai,

Abraham
God begins to rebuild

AFTER SCANNING CENTURIES, GENESIS CHANGES dramatically at chapter 12. Leaving the big picture of world history, it settles on one lonely individual—not a great king or a wealthy landowner, but a childless nomad, Abraham.

At God's call, Abraham had uprooted himself from civilization and begun wandering in the wilderness. With a few changes (cattle substituted for sheep, Conestoga wagons for tents), you could make a cowboy movie out of his life. Moving his flocks from place to place, fighting skirmishes and pitched battles with hostile local people, Abraham had to be tough to survive. But this hardly made him unique; lots of tough nomads wandered the Middle East. What made this particular wanderer so important?

"I will make of you a great nation, and I will bless you . . . and in you all the families of the earth shall be blessed." 12.2–3

God's New Way of Working

Abraham was important, first of all, simply because God chose him. Shortly after the destruction caused by the great flood, God picked Abraham as the foundation of a new humanity. On several remarkable occasions God spoke directly to him, promising to make his family great in the land he roamed. The promises were hard to believe: Abraham's wife was barren, Abraham was getting too old to have children, he owned no land and had no prospect of any. Nonetheless, God asked Abraham to trust him.

The second reason why Abraham matters follows from the first: When God spoke to him, Abraham listened. He was far from perfect. Sometimes he strayed from the path God put him on, lying and trying to make the promises work out in his own way. Yet in the decisive moments of life, he listened to God and obeyed. He was willing to sacrifice anything for God—even his only son. God put his brand on Abraham, the mark of circumcision. His descendants were to be forever known as "God's people."

Uncensored Truth

The life of Abraham is a fascinating story, true to life, full of bad moments as well as good. He was hardly a theologian; a more comprehensive understanding of God would have to wait for Moses. But Abraham's faith is the root of Judaism and, thus, of Christianity. In his encounters with God we get raw, uncensored truth; not religion invented by a philosopher, but religion as it really happens when God meets man.

No wonder the New Testament cites Abraham more than 80 times, and Paul tells Christians they are the true descendants of Abraham (Galatians 3.6–9). Abraham's life began to unfold the story of God's long-range plans. Two thousand years later, Abraham's descendant Jesus came to fulfill the promises made to Abraham and his descendants.

Life Questions: God asked Abraham to leave his home and family and go to a far-off foreign country. If you were in his place, how would you have responded? Has God ever asked anything hard or risky of you?

and the name of Nahor's wife was Milcah. She was the daughter of Haran the father of Milcah and Iscah. ³⁰Now Sarai was barren; she had no child.

31 Terah took his son Abram and his grandson Lot son of Haran, and his daughter-in-law Sarai, his son Abram's wife, and they went out together from Ur of the Chaldeans to go into the land of Canaan; but when they came to Haran, they settled there. ³²The days of Terah were two hundred five years; and Terah died in Haran.

The Call of Abram

12 Now the LORD said to Abram, "Go from your country and your kindred and your father's house to the land that I will show you. ²I will make of you a great nation, and I will bless you, and make your name great, so that you will be a blessing. ³I will bless those who bless you, and the one who curses you I will curse; and in you all the families of the earth shall be blessed."ᵉ

4 So Abram went, as the LORD had told him; and Lot went with him. Abram was seventy-five years old when he departed from Haran. ⁵Abram took his wife Sarai and his brother's son Lot, and all the possessions that they had gathered, and the persons whom they had acquired in Haran; and they set forth to go to the land of Canaan. When they had come to the land of Canaan, ⁶Abram passed through the land to the place at Shechem, to the oakᶠ of Moreh. At that time the Canaanites were in the land. ⁷Then the LORD appeared to Abram, and said, "To your offspringᵍ I will give this land." So he built there an altar to the LORD, who had appeared to him. ⁸From there he moved on to the hill country on the east of Bethel, and pitched his tent, with Bethel on the west and Ai on the east; and there he built an altar to the LORD and invoked the name of the LORD. ⁹And Abram journeyed on by stages toward the Negeb.

Abram and Sarai in Egypt

10 Now there was a famine in the land. So Abram went down to Egypt to reside there as an alien, for the famine was severe in the land.

12.13 Abraham's Half-Truth

"A lie is an attempt to deceive," according to one definition, and by that standard Abraham was lying when he claimed Sarai was his sister. Yet he was telling half the truth, for she was his half sister (20.12). Abraham pulled this same trick years later and got caught again (chapter 20). On both occasions he had feared for his life, a situation in which half-truths are particularly appealing.

¹¹When he was about to enter Egypt, he said to his wife Sarai, "I know well that you are a woman beautiful in appearance; ¹²and when the Egyptians see you, they will say, 'This is his wife'; then they will kill me, but they will let you live. ¹³Say you are my sister, so that it may go well with me because of you, and that my life may be spared on your account." ¹⁴When Abram entered Egypt the Egyptians saw that the woman was very beautiful. ¹⁵When the officials of Pharaoh saw her, they praised her to Pharaoh. And the woman was taken into Pharaoh's house. ¹⁶And for her sake he dealt well with Abram; and he had sheep, oxen, male donkeys, male and female slaves, female donkeys, and camels.

17 But the LORD afflicted Pharaoh and his house with great plagues because of Sarai, Abram's wife. ¹⁸So Pharaoh called Abram, and said, "What is this you have done to me? Why did you not tell me that she was your wife? ¹⁹Why did you say, 'She is my sister,' so that I took her for my wife? Now then, here is your wife, take her, and be gone." ²⁰And Pharaoh gave his men orders concerning him; and they set him on the way, with his wife and all that he had.

Abram and Lot Separate

13 So Abram went up from Egypt, he and his wife, and all that he had, and Lot with him, into the Negeb.

2 Now Abram was very rich in livestock, in silver, and in gold. ³He journeyed on by stages from the Negeb as far as Bethel, to the place where his tent had been at the beginning, between

13.3 On the Road

The main trade route through Canaan passed north to south through Shechem, Bethel, Hebron, and Beersheba. As Abraham and his children traveled, they naturally stopped in those places. These place-names crop up again and again in the story of God's work.

Bethel and Ai, ⁴to the place where he had made an altar at the first; and there Abram called on the name of the LORD. ⁵Now Lot, who went with Abram, also had flocks and herds and tents, ⁶so that the land could not support both of them living together; for their possessions were so great that they could not live together, ⁷and there was strife between the herders of Abram's livestock and the herders of Lot's livestock. At that time the Canaanites and the Perizzites lived in the land.

8 Then Abram said to Lot, "Let there be no strife between you and me, and between your herders and my herders; for we are kindred. ⁹Is

ᵉ Or *by you all the families of the earth shall bless themselves*   ᶠ Or *terebinth*   ᵍ Heb *seed* not the whole land before you? Separate yourself from me. If you take the left hand, then I will go to the right; or if you take the right hand, then I will go to the left." ¹⁰Lot looked about him, and saw that the plain of the Jordan was well watered everywhere like the garden of the LORD, like the land of Egypt, in the direction of Zoar; this was before the LORD had destroyed Sodom and Gomorrah. ¹¹So Lot chose for himself all the plain of the Jordan, and Lot journeyed eastward; thus they separated from each other. ¹²Abram settled in the land of Canaan, while Lot settled among the cities of the Plain and moved his tent as far as Sodom. ¹³Now the people of Sodom were wicked, great sinners against the LORD.

14 The LORD said to Abram, after Lot had separated from him, "Raise your eyes now, and look from the place where you are, northward and southward and eastward and westward; ¹⁵for all the land that you see I will give to you and to your offspring^h forever. ¹⁶I will make your offspring like the dust of the earth; so that if one can count the dust of the earth, your offspring also can be counted. ¹⁷Rise up, walk through the length and the breadth of the land, for I will give it to you." ¹⁸So Abram moved his tent, and came and settled by the oaksⁱ of Mamre, which are at Hebron; and there he built an altar to the LORD.

Lot's Captivity and Rescue

14 In the days of King Amraphel of Shinar, King Arioch of Ellasar, King Chedorlaomer of Elam, and King Tidal of Goiim, ²these kings made war with King Bera of Sodom, King Birsha of Gomorrah, King Shinab of Admah, King Shemeber of Zeboiim, and the king of Bela (that is, Zoar). ³All these joined forces in the Valley of Siddim (that is, the Dead Sea).^j ⁴Twelve years they had served Chedorlaomer, but in the thirteenth year they rebelled. ⁵In the fourteenth year Chedorlaomer and the kings who were with him came and subdued the Rephaim in Ashteroth-karnaim, the Zuzim in Ham, the Emim in Shaveh-kiriathaim, ⁶and the Horites in the hill country of Seir as far as El-paran on the edge of the wilderness; ⁷then they turned back and came to En-mishpat (that is, Kadesh), and subdued all the country of the Amalekites, and also the Amorites who lived in Hazazon-tamar. ⁸Then the king of Sodom, the king of Gomorrah, the king of Admah, the king of Zeboiim, and the king of Bela (that is, Zoar) went out, and they joined battle in the Valley of Siddim ⁹with King Chedorlaomer of Elam, King Tidal of Goiim, King Amraphel of Shinar, and King Arioch of Ellasar, four kings against five. ¹⁰Now the Valley of Siddim was full of bitumen pits; and as the kings of Sodom and Gomorrah fled, some fell into them, and the rest fled to the hill country. ¹¹So the enemy took all the goods of Sodom and Gomorrah, and all their provisions, and went their way; ¹²they also took Lot, the son of Abram's brother, who lived in Sodom, and his goods, and departed.

13 Then one who had escaped came and told Abram the Hebrew, who was living by the oaksⁱ of Mamre the Amorite, brother of Eshcol and of Aner; these were allies of Abram. ¹⁴When Abram heard that his nephew had been taken captive, he led forth his trained men, born in his house, three hundred eighteen of them, and went in pursuit as

h Heb *seed*   *i* Or *terebinths*   *j* Heb *Salt Sea*

LOT *Different Pathways*

PEOPLE WHO GROW UP CLOSE together—neighbors, friends, cousins, even siblings—sometimes end up in very different places in life. Looking back, one wonders what made the difference.

Take Lot as an example. Abraham's nephew, he apparently latched on to his uncle after losing his own father. When God called Abraham to leave home and strike out for unknown territory, Lot packed up and joined Abraham on the long trip.

Abraham reciprocated with love. Even after the two men had separated to make better use of grazing lands, Abraham cared enough about his nephew to stage a daring raid to rescue Lot from kidnappers. Later, when God announced he would destroy Lot's adopted town of Sodom, Abraham pleaded with God to save it.

Though Lot started out close to Abraham, he ultimately chose a very different pathway. Abraham remained a nomad, following God all his days. Lot preferred the cushy surroundings of the city—despite Sodom's reputation as a center of immorality. Soon Lot grew attached.

Even when God sent angels warning him to escape the coming judgment, Lot had a hard time tearing himself away. He lost everything and ended up in a cave, engaged in drunken incest with his own daughters. In contrast, the more faithful Abraham became the father of God's chosen people and one of the great patriarchs of the Old Testament.

Life Questions: If someone offered you a comfortable, successful position in a morally questionable situation, would you accept? Why or why not?

far as Dan. [15]He divided his forces against them by night, he and his servants, and routed them and pursued them to Hobah, north of Damascus. [16]Then he brought back all the goods, and also brought back his nephew Lot with his goods, and the women and the people.

Abram Blessed by Melchizedek

17   After his return from the defeat of Chedorlaomer and the kings who were with him, the king of Sodom went out to meet him at the Valley of Shaveh (that is, the King's Valley). [18]And King Melchizedek of Salem brought out bread and wine; he was priest of God Most High.[k] [19]He blessed him and said,
    "Blessed be Abram by God Most High,[k]
        maker of heaven and earth;
[20]   and blessed be God Most High,[k]
        who has delivered your enemies into
            your hand!"
And Abram gave him one-tenth of everything.

14.20 Mystery Man

Melchizedek appeared to Abraham without warning, received tremendous honor, and then disappeared. Yet hundreds of years later he earned mention in Psalm 110, and hundreds of years after that in Hebrews 7.11–17. Melchizedek remains a mysterious figure, but he does set an important precedent for the Messiah: The same man can serve as both priest and king. (Jewish priests came from one tribe, and kings from another, different tribe.) Though Melchizedek did not have the proper family lineage, his spiritual power impressed Abraham, the father of Judaism.

[21]Then the king of Sodom said to Abram, "Give me the persons, but take the goods for yourself." [22]But Abram said to the king of Sodom, "I have sworn to the LORD, God Most High,[k] maker of heaven and earth, [23]that I would not take a thread or a sandal-thong or anything that is yours, so that you might not say, 'I have made Abram rich.' [24]I will take nothing but what the young men have eaten, and the share of the men who went with me—Aner, Eshcol, and Mamre. Let them take their share."

God's Covenant with Abram

15 After these things the word of the LORD came to Abram in a vision, "Do not be afraid, Abram, I am your shield; your reward shall be very great." [2]But Abram said, "O Lord GOD, what will you give me, for I continue childless, and the heir of my house is Eliezer of Damascus?"[l] [3]And Abram said, "You have given me no offspring, and so a slave born in my house is to be my heir." [4]But the word of the LORD came to him, "This man shall not be your heir; no one but your very own issue shall be your heir." [5]He brought him outside and said, "Look toward heaven and count the stars, if you are able to count them." Then he said to him, "So shall your descendants be." [6]And he believed the LORD; and the LORD [m] reckoned it to him as righteousness.

15.6 What God Looks For

God accepted Abraham not because he led a perfect life but because of his responsiveness to God's promises. This verse was quoted three times in the New Testament to demonstrate that salvation by faith was nothing new (Romans 4.3; Galatians 3.6; James 2.23). Even in the Old Testament, God looked for faith, not moral perfection.

7   Then he said to him, "I am the LORD who brought you from Ur of the Chaldeans, to give you this land to possess." [8]But he said, "O Lord GOD, how am I to know that I shall possess it?" [9]He said to him, "Bring me a heifer three years old, a female goat three years old, a ram three years old, a turtledove, and a young pigeon." [10]He brought him all these and cut them in two, laying each half over against the other; but he did not cut the birds in two. [11]And when birds of prey came down on the carcasses, Abram drove them away.

12   As the sun was going down, a deep sleep fell upon Abram, and a deep and terrifying darkness descended upon him. [13]Then the LORD [m] said to Abram, "Know this for certain, that your offspring shall be aliens in a land that is not theirs, and shall be slaves there, and they shall be oppressed for four hundred years; [14]but I will bring judgment on the nation that they serve, and afterward they shall come out with great possessions. [15]As for yourself, you shall go to your ancestors in peace; you shall be buried in a good old age. [16]And they shall come back here in the fourth generation; for the iniquity of the Amorites is not yet complete."

17   When the sun had gone down and it was dark, a smoking fire pot and a flaming torch passed between these pieces. [18]On that day the LORD made a covenant with Abram, saying, "To your descendants I give this land, from the river of Egypt to the great river, the river Euphrates, [19]the land of the Kenites, the Kenizzites, the Kadmonites, [20]the Hittites, the Perizzites, the Rephaim, [21]the Amorites, the Canaanites, the Girgashites, and the Jebusites."

---

[k] Heb *El Elyon*   [l] Meaning of Heb uncertain   [m] Heb *he*

The Birth of Ishmael

16 Now Sarai, Abram's wife, bore him no children. She had an Egyptian slave-girl whose
name was Hagar, [2]and Sarai said to Abram, "You
see that the LORD has prevented me from bearing
children; go in to my slave-girl; it may be that I
shall obtain children by her." And Abram listened
to the voice of Sarai. [3]So, after Abram had lived
ten years in the land of Canaan, Sarai, Abram's
wife, took Hagar the Egyptian, her slave-girl, and
gave her to her husband Abram as a wife. [4]He
went in to Hagar, and she conceived; and when
she saw that she had conceived, she looked with
contempt on her mistress. [5]Then Sarai said to
Abram, "May the wrong done to me be on you!
I gave my slave-girl to your embrace, and when
she saw that she had conceived, she looked on me
with contempt. May the LORD judge between you
and me!" [6]But Abram said to Sarai, "Your slave-
girl is in your power; do to her as you please."
Then Sarai dealt harshly with her, and she ran
away from her.

16.2 A Substitute Wife

According to custom, a man could sleep with a servant and include her children in his household. Abraham was trying to get the children he and his wife longed for and to "help God out" in fulfilling his promise of a son. Abraham's way was not God's way, however, and Abraham's attempt led to considerable jealousy and sorrow. The same practice also led to trouble for Jacob's family (chapter 30).

7 The angel of the LORD found her by a spring
of water in the wilderness, the spring on the way
to Shur. [8]And he said, "Hagar, slave-girl of Sarai,
where have you come from and where are you
going?" She said, "I am running away from my
mistress Sarai." [9]The angel of the LORD said to
her, "Return to your mistress, and submit to her."
[10]The angel of the LORD also said to her, "I will so
greatly multiply your offspring that they cannot
be counted for multitude." [11]And the angel of the
LORD said to her,

"Now you have conceived and shall bear
a son;
you shall call him Ishmael,[n]
for the LORD has given heed to your
affliction.

12 He shall be a wild ass of a man,
with his hand against everyone,
and everyone's hand against him;
and he shall live at odds with all his kin."

[13]So she named the LORD who spoke to her, "You
are El-roi";[o] for she said, "Have I really seen God
and remained alive after seeing him?"[p] [14]There-
fore the well was called Beer-lahai-roi;[q] it lies
between Kadesh and Bered.
15 Hagar bore Abram a son; and Abram
named his son, whom Hagar bore, Ishmael.
[16]Abram was eighty-six years old when Hagar
bore him[r] Ishmael.

The Sign of the Covenant

17 When Abram was ninety-nine years old,
the LORD appeared to Abram, and said to
him, "I am God Almighty;[s] walk before me, and
be blameless. [2]And I will make my covenant between me and you, and will make you exceedingly
numerous." [3]Then Abram fell on his face; and

[n] That is *God hears* [o] Perhaps *God of seeing* or *God who sees* [p] Meaning of Heb uncertain [q] That is *the Well of the Living One who sees me* [r] Heb *Abram* [s] Traditional rendering of Heb *El Shaddai*

ISHMAEL *Second Best*

YOU MIGHT CALL ISHMAEL A mistake. His birth came about when Sarah and Abraham doubted God's promise to provide them a child in their old age. The two conspired to "help God out" by using an Egyptian servant, Hagar, as a substitute wife for Abraham. Then, when God fulfilled his promise and Sarah bore a son of her own, she cruelly drove the servant and her son out into the desert. Ishmael, the innocent victim of this scheming, suffered the consequences.

Yet God also blessed Ishmael. He "heard the voice of the boy" when Ishmael was nearly dying of thirst in the desert (21.17). God promised that Ishmael's descendants would comprise a great nation. The Bible records that Ishmael had twelve sons, and that "the Ishmaelites" were Israel's neighbors for centuries. In fact, Arabs today traditionally trace their lineage to Ishmael.

Ishmael apparently kept in contact with his original family; he attended Abraham's funeral, and his daughter would marry Abraham's grandson Esau. Yet his place in Abraham's "covenant" with God was lost. In a similar way, Ishmael's son-in-law Esau would enjoy the earthly blessings of success, even though God's greatest blessing was reserved for his brother Jacob. In the Bible's accounting, God's "covenant blessing" always matters more than earthly success.

Life Questions: Have you ever tried to "help God out" when you thought he couldn't possibly help you in the way you wanted? What was the result?

God said to him, 4"As for me, this is my covenant with you: You shall be the ancestor of a multitude of nations. 5No longer shall your name be Abram,*t* but your name shall be Abraham;*u* for I have made you the ancestor of a multitude of nations. 6I will make you exceedingly fruitful; and I will make nations of you, and kings shall come from you. 7I will establish my covenant between me and you, and your offspring after you throughout their generations, for an everlasting covenant, to be God to you and to your offspring*v* after you. 8And I will give to you, and to your offspring after you, the land where you are now an alien, all the land of Canaan, for a perpetual holding; and I will be their God."

9 God said to Abraham, "As for you, you shall keep my covenant, you and your offspring after you throughout their generations. 10This is my covenant, which you shall keep, between me and you and your offspring after you: Every male among you shall be circumcised. 11You shall circumcise the flesh of your foreskins, and it shall be a sign of the covenant between me and you. 12Throughout your generations every male among you shall be circumcised when he is eight days old, including the slave born in your house and the one bought with your money from any foreigner who is not of your offspring. 13Both the slave born in your house and the one bought with your money must be circumcised. So shall my covenant be in your flesh an everlasting covenant. 14Any uncircumcised male who is not circumcised in the flesh of his foreskin shall be cut off from his people; he has broken my covenant."

15 God said to Abraham, "As for Sarai your wife, you shall not call her Sarai, but Sarah shall be her name. 16I will bless her, and moreover I will give you a son by her. I will bless her, and she shall give rise to nations; kings of peoples shall come from her." 17Then Abraham fell on his face and laughed, and said to himself, "Can a child be born to a man who is a hundred years old? Can Sarah, who is ninety years old, bear a child?" 18And Abraham said to God, "O that Ishmael might live in your sight!" 19God said, "No, but your wife Sarah shall bear you a son, and you shall name him Isaac.*w* I will establish my covenant with him as an everlasting covenant for his offspring after him. 20As for Ishmael, I have heard you; I will bless him and make him fruitful and exceedingly numerous; he shall be the father of twelve princes, and I will make him a great nation. 21But my covenant I will establish with Isaac, whom Sarah shall bear to you at this season next year." 22And when he had finished talking with him, God went up from Abraham.

23 Then Abraham took his son Ishmael and all the slaves born in his house or bought with his money, every male among the men of Abraham's house, and he circumcised the flesh of their foreskins that very day, as God had said to him. 24Abraham was ninety-nine years old when he was circumcised in the flesh of his foreskin. 25And his son Ishmael was thirteen years old when he was circumcised in the flesh of his foreskin. 26That very day Abraham and his son Ishmael were circumcised; 27and all the men of his house, slaves born in the house and those bought with money from a foreigner, were circumcised with him.

A Son Promised to Abraham and Sarah

18 The LORD appeared to Abraham*x* by the oaks*y* of Mamre, as he sat at the entrance of his tent in the heat of the day. 2He looked up and saw three men standing near him. When he saw them, he ran from the tent entrance to meet them, and bowed down to the ground. 3He said, "My lord, if I find favor with you, do not pass by your servant. 4Let a little water be brought, and wash your feet, and rest yourselves under the tree. 5Let me bring a little bread, that you may refresh yourselves, and after that you may pass on— since you have come to your servant." So they said, "Do as you have said." 6And Abraham hastened into the tent to Sarah, and said, "Make ready quickly three measures*z* of choice flour, knead it, and make cakes." 7Abraham ran to the herd, and took a calf, tender and good, and gave it to the servant, who hastened to prepare it. 8Then he took curds and milk and the calf that he had prepared, and set it before them; and he stood by them under the tree while they ate.

9 They said to him, "Where is your wife Sarah?" And he said, "There, in the tent." 10Then one said, "I will surely return to you in due season, and your wife Sarah shall have a son." And Sarah was listening at the tent entrance behind him. 11Now Abraham and Sarah were old, advanced in age; it had ceased to be with Sarah after the manner of women. 12So Sarah laughed to herself, saying, "After I have grown old, and my husband is old, shall I have pleasure?" 13The LORD said to

17.17 Laughing at God

Abraham was a man of faith, but his faith was less than 100 percent. Here, nearing the age of 100, he laughed heartily at God's promise that he would father a son, and he demonstrated his lack of belief by suggesting that God accept Ishmael as an adequate substitute. Some time later Sarah, his wife, shared in the "joke" (18.12).

---

t That is *exalted ancestor*　　*u* Here taken to mean *ancestor of a multitude*　　*v* Heb *seed*　　*w* That is *he laughs*
x Heb *him*　　*y* Or *terebinths*　　*z* Heb *seahs*

Abraham, "Why did Sarah laugh, and say, 'Shall I indeed bear a child, now that I am old?' ¹⁴Is anything too wonderful for the LORD? At the set time I will return to you, in due season, and Sarah shall have a son." ¹⁵But Sarah denied, saying, "I did not laugh"; for she was afraid. He said, "Oh yes, you did laugh."

Judgment Pronounced on Sodom

16 Then the men set out from there, and they looked toward Sodom; and Abraham went with them to set them on their way. ¹⁷The LORD said, "Shall I hide from Abraham what I am about to do, ¹⁸seeing that Abraham shall become a great and mighty nation, and all the nations of the earth

18.18 The Gospel to Abraham

God predicted here (and in several other places) that all nations on earth would be blessed through Abraham. About two thousand years later the apostle Paul, seeing in this a prediction of God reaching out through Jews to non-Jews with the message of Christianity, wrote that God had "declared the gospel beforehand to Abraham" (Galatians 3.8).

shall be blessed in him?[a] ¹⁹No, for I have chosen[b] him, that he may charge his children and his household after him to keep the way of the LORD by doing righteousness and justice; so that the LORD may bring about for Abraham what he has promised him." ²⁰Then the LORD said, "How great is the outcry against Sodom and Gomorrah

and how very grave their sin! ²¹I must go down and see whether they have done altogether according to the outcry that has come to me; and if not, I will know."

22 So the men turned from there, and went toward Sodom, while Abraham remained standing before the LORD.[c] ²³Then Abraham came near and said, "Will you indeed sweep away the righteous with the wicked? ²⁴Suppose there are fifty righteous within the city; will you then sweep away the place and not forgive it for the fifty righteous who are in it? ²⁵Far be it from you to do such a thing, to slay the righteous with the wicked, so that the righteous fare as the wicked! Far be that from you! Shall not the Judge of all the earth do what is just?" ²⁶And the LORD said, "If I find at Sodom fifty righteous in the city, I will forgive the whole place for their sake." ²⁷Abraham answered, "Let me take it upon myself to speak to the Lord, I who am but dust and ashes. ²⁸Suppose five of the fifty righteous are lacking? Will you destroy the whole city for lack of five?" And he said, "I will not destroy it if I find forty-five there." ²⁹Again he spoke to him, "Suppose forty are found there." He answered, "For the sake of forty I will not do it." ³⁰Then he said, "Oh do not let the Lord be angry if I speak. Suppose thirty are found there." He answered, "I will not do it, if I find thirty there." ³¹He said, "Let me take it upon myself to speak to the Lord. Suppose twenty are found there." He answered, "For the sake of twenty I will not destroy it." ³²Then he said, "Oh do not let the Lord be angry if I speak just once more. Suppose ten are found there." He answered, "For the sake of ten I will not destroy it." ³³And the LORD went his way, when he had fin-

[a] Or *and all the nations of the earth shall bless themselves by him while the LORD remained standing before Abraham*   [b] Heb *known*   [c] Another ancient tradition reads

SARAH *Who's Laughing?*

SHE WAS BEAUTIFUL. SHE HAD a wonderful, wealthy husband. Sarah should have been content. Instead her life revolved around the one thing she lacked—a child. Although God had promised that her husband Abraham would father a great nation, as the decades passed Sarah remained childless. The odds of giving birth gradually dwindled. More descendants than the stars in the sky? God's promise seemed laughable as Sarah celebrated her ninetieth birthday.

A resourceful woman, Sarah came up with an alternate plan. She would use her servant Hagar as a surrogate mother. Obviously Sarah felt deep inner conflict about this decision, for when Abraham got Hagar pregnant, Sarah mistreated her and sent her away. Hagar returned, but Sarah's inner conflict persisted. She would ultimately drive both mother and son into the desert.

Meanwhile, God kept repeating the amazing promise that Sarah would become the mother of a nation. Once, Abraham fell face down and laughed incredulously at the notion. Sarah cackled too. But the joke turned on them both when old Sarah finally got pregnant. After all her years of waiting, her longings were fulfilled.

"God has brought laughter for me," Sarah said when her son was born (21.6). It was a wonderful pun; in obedience to God (17.19), Abraham named his son Isaac, which means "he laughs" in Hebrew.

Life Questions: When a person has deep longings that seem impossible to fulfill, what should he or she do?

ished speaking to Abraham; and Abraham returned to his place.

The Depravity of Sodom

19 The two angels came to Sodom in the evening, and Lot was sitting in the gateway of Sodom. When Lot saw them, he rose to meet them, and bowed down with his face to the ground. ²He said, "Please, my lords, turn aside to your servant's house and spend the night, and wash your feet; then you can rise early and go on your way." They said, "No; we will spend the night in the square." ³But he urged them strongly; so they turned aside to him and entered his house; and he made them a feast, and baked unleavened bread, and they ate. ⁴But before they lay down, the men of the city, the men of Sodom, both young and old, all the people to the last man, surrounded the house; ⁵and they called to Lot, "Where are the men who came to you tonight? Bring them out to us, so that we may know

them." ⁶Lot went out of the door to the men, shut the door after him, ⁷and said, "I beg you, my brothers, do not act so wickedly. ⁸Look, I have two daughters who have not known a man; let me

19.1 A Man of Substance

The angels found Lot in the gateway to Sodom—a fact loaded with significance. Traditionally, city fathers gathered in the gateway to make important decisions. Lot's presence suggests that he had become "one of them" during his time in Sodom, which may explain why he struggled against leaving.

bring them out to you, and do to them as you please; only do nothing to these men, for they have come under the shelter of my roof." ⁹But they replied, "Stand back!" And they said, "This fellow came here as an alien, and he would play

A Catastrophe Sent from God
Sodom: a city that earned destruction

SHOULD A CATASTROPHE BE READ as a punishment from God? Do floods, famines, earthquakes come because God is angry? The Bible's answer is, "Sometimes, and sometimes not." In Genesis, several catastrophes seemed to "just happen"—they were not a punishment or a warning, though God used them to advance his plans. These included several famines such as the one that brought Joseph to power (chapter 41), a war (chapter 14), a rape (chapter 34).

But a few catastrophes God took full credit for—like the one at Sodom and Gomorrah. As usual, the Bible shows little or no interest in telling us the scientific facts about the destruction. Was it a volcanic eruption? The Bible doesn't say, and the area, now apparently at the bottom of the Dead Sea, cannot easily be investigated. The Bible stresses not how it happened, but why.

> *"Have you anyone else here? Sons-in-law, sons, daughters, or anyone you have in the city— bring them out of the place. For we are about to destroy this place."*
> *19.12–13*

Gang Rape

Sodom was a wretched place. The whole town saw the coming of strangers as a chance for homosexual gang rape. Sexual violence was not the town's only problem. Ezekiel 16.49 says that Sodom had "pride, excess of food, and prosperous ease, but did not aid the poor and needy." God would have let the city stand if Abraham could have located just ten righteous people. Apparently, ten such people did not exist. God's great patience finally ran out.

Years earlier, Abraham had refused to accept even a well-earned reward from the government of Sodom (14.21–24). He wanted nothing to do with such a society. But Lot had chosen the path of prosperity, the easy and successful life on the fertile plain near Sodom.

Lot had become a somebody there, a civic heavy who made important decisions in the city gateway. He was so entangled with life in Sodom he hesitated to leave until it was nearly too late. When Sodom went up in smoke, his hard-earned importance disappeared too. The shock was too great for him. Unable to start over, he ended up in a cave, too drunk to know that his two daughters were having sex with him. He is the perfect example of a man who, excessively tangled in a corrupt system, cannot bear to leave it behind.

Jesus did not let his followers think of Sodom simply as "those terrible people." He warned them that God would be even harder on those who saw Jesus' miracles, but ignored them (Matthew 11.24). God's patience has a limit.

Life Questions: Are any catastrophes of our time punishments from God? How would you know?

the judge! Now we will deal worse with you than with them." Then they pressed hard against the man Lot, and came near the door to break it down. [10]But the men inside reached out their hands and brought Lot into the house with them, and shut the door. [11]And they struck with blindness the men who were at the door of the house, both small and great, so that they were unable to find the door.

Sodom and Gomorrah Destroyed

12 Then the men said to Lot, "Have you anyone else here? Sons-in-law, sons, daughters, or anyone you have in the city—bring them out of the place. [13]For we are about to destroy this place, because the outcry against its people has become great before the LORD, and the LORD has sent us to destroy it." [14]So Lot went out and said to his sons-in-law, who were to marry his daughters, "Up, get out of this place; for the LORD is about to destroy the city." But he seemed to his sons-in-law to be jesting.

15 When morning dawned, the angels urged Lot, saying, "Get up, take your wife and your two daughters who are here, or else you will be consumed in the punishment of the city." [16]But he lingered; so the men seized him and his wife and his two daughters by the hand, the LORD being merciful to him, and they brought him out and left him outside the city. [17]When they had brought them outside, they[d] said, "Flee for your life; do not look back or stop anywhere in the Plain; flee to the hills, or else you will be consumed." [18]And Lot said to them, "Oh, no, my lords; [19]your servant has found favor with you, and you have shown me great kindness in saving my life; but I cannot flee to the hills, for fear the disaster will overtake me and I die. [20]Look, that city is near enough to flee to, and it is a little one. Let me escape there—is it not a little one?—and my life will be saved!" [21]He said to him, "Very well, I grant you this favor too, and will not overthrow the city of which you have spoken. [22]Hurry, escape there, for I can do nothing until you arrive there." Therefore the city was called Zoar.[e] [23]The sun had risen on the earth when Lot came to Zoar.

24 Then the LORD rained on Sodom and Gomorrah sulfur and fire from the LORD out of heaven; [25]and he overthrew those cities, and all the Plain, and all the inhabitants of the cities, and what grew on the ground. [26]But Lot's wife, behind him, looked back, and she became a pillar of salt.

27 Abraham went early in the morning to the place where he had stood before the LORD; [28]and he looked down toward Sodom and Gomorrah and toward all the land of the Plain and saw the smoke of the land going up like the smoke of a furnace.

29 So it was that, when God destroyed the cities of the Plain, God remembered Abraham, and sent Lot out of the midst of the overthrow, when he overthrew the cities in which Lot had settled.

19.26 Don't Look Back

Lot and his family found it hard to leave their adopted home of Sodom, despite its immorality. Angel messengers warned them to hurry, not even stopping to look back. When Lot's wife disobeyed, she turned into a pillar of salt—perhaps caught in volcanic explosions that engulfed Sodom. For this she became a symbol of indecision. Jesus urged his followers to remember her example when their time of trouble came (Luke 17.32).

The Shameful Origin of Moab and Ammon

30 Now Lot went up out of Zoar and settled in the hills with his two daughters, for he was afraid to stay in Zoar; so he lived in a cave with his two daughters. [31]And the firstborn said to the younger, "Our father is old, and there is not a man on earth to come in to us after the manner of all the world. [32]Come, let us make our father drink wine, and we will lie with him, so that we may preserve offspring through our father." [33]So they made their father drink wine that night; and the firstborn went in, and lay with her father; he did not know when she lay down or when she rose. [34]On the next day, the firstborn said to the younger, "Look, I lay last night with my father; let us make him drink wine tonight also; then you go in and lie with him, so that we may preserve offspring through our father." [35]So they made their father drink wine that night also; and the younger rose, and lay with him; and he did not know when she lay down or when she rose. [36]Thus both the daughters of Lot became pregnant by their father. [37]The firstborn bore a son, and named him Moab; he is the ancestor of the Moabites to this day. [38]The younger also bore a

19.37 Family Quarrels

Lot's determination to enjoy life in Sodom ended tragically here, in drunken incest. The resulting sons founded the family-nations of Moab and Ammon, which for centuries fought with their distant relatives in Israel and tempted them to sin.

---

d Gk Syr Vg: Heb *he*   *e* That is *Little*

son and named him Ben-ammi; he is the ancestor of the Ammonites to this day.

Abraham and Sarah at Gerar

20 From there Abraham journeyed toward the region of the Negeb, and settled between Kadesh and Shur. While residing in Gerar as an alien, ²Abraham said of his wife Sarah, "She is my sister." And King Abimelech of Gerar sent and took Sarah. ³But God came to Abimelech in a dream by night, and said to him, "You are about to die because of the woman whom you have taken; for she is a married woman." ⁴Now Abimelech had not approached her; so he said, "Lord, will you destroy an innocent people? ⁵Did he not himself say to me, 'She is my sister'? And she herself said, 'He is my brother.' I did this in the integrity of my heart and the innocence of my hands." ⁶Then God said to him in the dream, "Yes, I know that you did this in the integrity of your heart; furthermore it was I who kept you from sinning against me. Therefore I did not let you touch her. ⁷Now then, return the man's wife; for he is a prophet, and he will pray for you and you shall live. But if you do not restore her, know that you shall surely die, you and all that are yours."

8 So Abimelech rose early in the morning, and called all his servants and told them all these things; and the men were very much afraid. ⁹Then Abimelech called Abraham, and said to him, "What have you done to us? How have I sinned against you, that you have brought such great guilt on me and my kingdom? You have done things to me that ought not to be done." ¹⁰And Abimelech said to Abraham, "What were you thinking of, that you did this thing?" ¹¹Abraham said, "I did it because I thought, There is no fear of God at all in this place, and they will kill me because of my wife. ¹²Besides, she is indeed my sister, the daughter of my father but not the daughter of my mother; and she became my wife. ¹³And when God caused me to wander from my father's house, I said to her, 'This is the kindness you must do me: at every place to which we come, say of me, He is my brother.'" ¹⁴Then Abimelech took sheep and oxen, and male and female slaves, and gave them to Abraham, and restored his wife Sarah to him. ¹⁵Abimelech said, "My land is before you; settle where it pleases you." ¹⁶To Sarah he said, "Look, I have given your brother a thousand pieces of silver; it is your exoneration before all who are with you; you are completely vindicated." ¹⁷Then Abraham prayed to God; and God healed Abimelech, and also healed his wife and female slaves so that they bore children. ¹⁸For the LORD had closed fast all the wombs of the house of Abimelech because of Sarah, Abraham's wife.

The Birth of Isaac

21 The LORD dealt with Sarah as he had said, and the LORD did for Sarah as he had promised. ²Sarah conceived and bore Abraham a son in his old age, at the time of which God had spoken to him. ³Abraham gave the name Isaac to his son whom Sarah bore him. ⁴And Abraham circumcised his son Isaac when he was eight days old, as God had commanded him. ⁵Abraham was a hundred years old when his son Isaac was born to him. ⁶Now Sarah said, "God has brought

ISAAC *Ordinary People*

ISAAC SPENT HIS LIFE SURROUNDED by strong people. His father Abraham was a giant of faith who uprooted his family at God's call and moved to unknown territory. Isaac married a strong-willed woman, Rebekah, who dominated him and sometimes manipulated him to get her way. One of Isaac's sons, Jacob, grew up to become a major figure of the Old Testament, father of the twelve tribes of Israel.

For all that strength around him, Isaac was a rather ordinary, almost passive person. Maybe it was because his parents had dreamed of his birth for so long that they sheltered him, their only child. Maybe his personality formed in reaction to all those other, powerful figures. Regardless, the Bible portrays Isaac as a person who fit into other people's plans. Even when his father led him up a mountain to sacrifice him to God, Isaac did not protest or rebel (Genesis 22).

When famine drove Isaac to a foreign land, he lied about his relationship with Rebekah rather than risk a conflict with the local king. When his herdsmen bickered with other shepherds over water rights, Isaac simply moved on, avoiding a fight. In Isaac's old age, when his grown sons Jacob and Esau quarreled, Isaac seemed powerless to stop them. Instead of sorting out the details and resolving the feud, he sent Jacob away.

Despite his weaknesses, Isaac is counted among the three famous patriarchs of Old Testament faith: Abraham, Isaac and Jacob. In bringing blessings to the entire world, God uses all kinds—even quiet, ordinary people.

Life Questions: Think of an organization or cause you consider important. How many of those involved could be described as "ordinary people"? What do they contribute?

laughter for me; everyone who hears will laugh with me." ⁷And she said, "Who would ever have said to Abraham that Sarah would nurse children? Yet I have borne him a son in his old age."

Hagar and Ishmael Sent Away

8 The child grew, and was weaned; and Abraham made a great feast on the day that Isaac was weaned. ⁹But Sarah saw the son of Hagar the Egyptian, whom she had borne to Abraham, playing with her son Isaac.ᶠ ¹⁰So she said to Abraham, "Cast out this slave woman with her son; for the son of this slave woman shall not inherit along with my son Isaac." ¹¹The matter was very distressing to Abraham on account of his son. ¹²But God said to Abraham, "Do not be distressed because of the boy and because of your slave woman; whatever Sarah says to you, do as she tells you, for it is through Isaac that offspring shall be named for you. ¹³As for the son of the slave woman, I will make a nation of him also, because he is your offspring." ¹⁴So Abraham rose early in the morning, and took bread and a skin of water, and gave it to Hagar, putting it on her shoulder, along with the child, and sent her away. And she departed, and wandered about in the wilderness of Beer-sheba.

15 When the water in the skin was gone, she cast the child under one of the bushes. ¹⁶Then she went and sat down opposite him a good way off, about the distance of a bowshot; for she said, "Do not let me look on the death of the child." And as she sat opposite him, she lifted up her voice and wept. ¹⁷And God heard the voice of the boy; and the angel of God called to Hagar from heaven, and said to her, "What troubles you, Hagar? Do not be afraid; for God has heard the voice of the boy where he is. ¹⁸Come, lift up the boy and hold him fast with your hand, for I will make a great nation of him." ¹⁹Then God opened her eyes and she saw a well of water. She went, and filled the skin with water, and gave the boy a drink.

20 God was with the boy, and he grew up; he lived in the wilderness, and became an expert with the bow. ²¹He lived in the wilderness of Paran; and his mother got a wife for him from the land of Egypt.

Abraham and Abimelech Make a Covenant

22 At that time Abimelech, with Phicol the commander of his army, said to Abraham, "God is with you in all that you do; ²³now therefore swear to me here by God that you will not deal falsely with me or with my offspring or with my posterity, but as I have dealt loyally with you, you will deal with me and with the land where you have resided as an alien." ²⁴And Abraham said, "I swear it."

25 When Abraham complained to Abimelech about a well of water that Abimelech's servants had seized, ²⁶Abimelech said, "I do not know who has done this; you did not tell me, and I have not heard of it until today." ²⁷So Abraham took sheep and oxen and gave them to Abimelech, and the two men made a covenant. ²⁸Abraham set apart seven ewe lambs of the flock. ²⁹And Abimelech said to Abraham, "What is the meaning of these seven ewe lambs that you have set apart?" ³⁰He said, "These seven ewe lambs you shall accept from my hand, in order that you may be a witness for me that I dug this well." ³¹Therefore that place was called Beer-sheba;ᵍ because there both of them swore an oath. ³²When they had made a covenant at Beer-sheba, Abimelech, with Phicol the commander of his army, left and returned to the land of the Philistines. ³³Abrahamʰ planted a tamarisk tree in Beer-sheba, and called there on the name of the LORD, the Everlasting God.ⁱ ³⁴And Abraham resided as an alien many days in the land of the Philistines.

The Command to Sacrifice Isaac

22 After these things God tested Abraham. He said to him, "Abraham!" And he said, "Here I am." ²He said, "Take your son, your only son Isaac, whom you love, and go to the land of Moriah, and offer him there as a burnt offering on one of the mountains that I shall show you." ³So Abraham rose early in the morning, saddled his donkey, and took two of his young men with him, and his son Isaac; he cut the wood for the burnt offering, and set out and went to the place in the distance that God had shown him. ⁴On the third day Abraham looked up and saw the place far away. ⁵Then Abraham said to his young men, "Stay here with the donkey; the boy and I will go over there; we will worship, and then we will come back to you." ⁶Abraham took the wood of the burnt offering and laid it on his son Isaac, and he himself carried the fire and the knife. So the two of them walked on together. ⁷Isaac said to his father Abraham, "Father!" And he said, "Here I am, my son." He said, "The fire and the wood are here, but where is the lamb for a burnt offering?" ⁸Abraham said, "God himself will provide the lamb for a burnt offering, my son." So the two of them walked on together.

9 When they came to the place that God had shown him, Abraham built an altar there and laid the wood in order. He bound his son Isaac, and laid him on the altar, on top of the wood. ¹⁰Then Abraham reached out his hand and took the knife to killʲ his son. ¹¹But the angel of the LORD called to him from heaven, and said, "Abraham, Abra-

---

ᶠ Gk Vg: Heb lacks *with her son Isaac*   ᵍ That is *Well of seven* or *Well of the oath*   ʰ Heb *He*   ⁱ Or *the LORD, El Olam*   ʲ Or *to slaughter*

ham!" And he said, "Here I am." [12]He said, "Do not lay your hand on the boy or do anything to him; for now I know that you fear God, since you have not withheld your son, your only son, from me." [13]And Abraham looked up and saw a ram, caught in a thicket by its horns. Abraham went and took the ram and offered it up as a burnt offering instead of his son. [14]So Abraham called that place "The LORD will provide";[k] as it is said to this day, "On the mount of the LORD it shall be provided."[l]

15 The angel of the LORD called to Abraham a second time from heaven, [16]and said, "By myself I have sworn, says the LORD: Because you have done this, and have not withheld your son, your only son, [17]I will indeed bless you, and I will make your offspring as numerous as the stars of heaven and as the sand that is on the seashore. And your offspring shall possess the gate of their enemies, [18]and by your offspring shall all the nations of the earth gain blessing for themselves, because you have obeyed my voice." [19]So Abraham returned to his young men, and they arose and went to-gether to Beer-sheba; and Abraham lived at Beer-sheba.

The Children of Nahor

20 Now after these things it was told Abraham, "Milcah also has borne children, to your brother Nahor: [21]Uz the firstborn, Buz his brother, Kemuel the father of Aram, [22]Chesed, Hazo, Pildash, Jidlaph, and Bethuel." [23]Bethuel became the father of Rebekah. These eight Milcah bore to Nahor, Abraham's brother. [24]Moreover, his concubine, whose name was Reumah, bore Tebah, Gaham, Tahash, and Maacah.

Sarah's Death and Burial

23 Sarah lived one hundred twenty-seven years; this was the length of Sarah's life. [2]And Sarah died at Kiriath-arba (that is, Hebron) in the land of Canaan; and Abraham went in to mourn for Sarah and to weep for her. [3]Abraham rose up from beside his dead, and said to the Hittites, [4]"I am a stranger and an alien residing among you; give me property among you for a

---

[k] Or *will see*; Heb traditionally transliterated *Jehovah Jireh*   [l] Or *he shall be seen*

Promises, Promises
God promised to give Abraham all that he longed for . . . and more

> *"By your offspring shall all the nations of the earth gain blessing for themselves, because you have obeyed my voice." 22.18*

HUMAN BEINGS HAVEN'T CHANGED MUCH in 4,000 years. The longing for children and the desire for land still surge up with surprising emotional power.

Consider the estimated six million American couples—one in seven would-be parents—who are unable to have children. For most of them, this brings deep anguish. Or think about the people who work double shifts, sacrificing their free time in order to own a home rather than rent.

Abraham would have understood. When God wanted his attention, he promised him land and more sons than he could count. To a Babylonian emigrant, 75 years old and childless, owning nothing but his tents and animals, the promises sounded wonderful. In fact, they sounded impossible. Yet, because God himself was making the promise, Abraham "believed the LORD; and the LORD reckoned it to him as righteousness" (15.6).

For the God who had created the heavens and the earth, making good on the promises ought to have been a snap. But God did not make it easy for Abraham. Not until 25 years later, when Abraham was 100, did the promise of a son come true. Then, incredibly, God told Abraham to make a human sacrifice of his little boy. It was really asking too much.

Astonishingly, Abraham followed God's orders. And God gave him back his son.

Far from Fulfilled

When Abraham died, God's promises were far from fully realized. Abraham had only that one son to cling to. His only land was a burial plot. He still lived in a tent, and his only permanent structures were altars erected to worship the God who had made all those promises.

God, having promised him everything a man of that time could want, apparently wanted Abraham to think even bigger thoughts. He had slipped some words in along with the promises of offspring and land: "In you all the families of the earth shall be blessed" (12.3). God wanted to bless, not just Abraham, but the whole world. Thousands of years later, in the time of Jesus, the full meaning of those words became clear (see Galatians 3.6–9,16–18).

Life Questions: What kind of promises does God make today? What longings does he fulfill?

burying place, so that I may bury my dead out of my sight." [5]The Hittites answered Abraham, [6]"Hear us, my lord; you are a mighty prince among us. Bury your dead in the choicest of our burial places; none of us will withhold from you any burial ground for burying your dead." [7]Abraham rose and bowed to the Hittites, the people of the land. [8]He said to them, "If you are willing that I should bury my dead out of my sight, hear me, and entreat for me Ephron son of Zohar, [9]so that he may give me the cave of Machpelah, which he owns; it is at the end of his field. For the full price let him give it to me in your presence as a possession for a burying place." [10]Now Ephron was sitting among the Hittites; and Ephron the Hittite answered Abraham in the hearing of the Hittites, of all who went in at the gate of his city, [11]"No, my lord, hear me; I give you the field, and I give you the cave that is in it; in the presence of my people I give it to you; bury your dead." [12]Then Abraham bowed down before the people of the land. [13]He said to Ephron in the hearing of the people of the land, "If you only will listen to me! I will give the price of the field; accept it from me, so that I may bury my dead there." [14]Ephron answered Abraham, [15]"My lord, listen to me; a piece of land worth four hundred shekels of silver—what is that between you and me? Bury your

23.15 Let's Make a Deal

This may be the oldest recorded business deal. The elaborate politeness sounds very much like bargaining in the Middle East today. Underneath the smooth words, shrewd negotiating is going on. The Hittites were probably reluctant to allow Abraham, an alien, to own property of any kind lest he gain a legal foothold in their country. Abraham zeroed in on Ephron, who stood to gain financially from the sale.

dead." [16]Abraham agreed with Ephron; and Abraham weighed out for Ephron the silver that he had named in the hearing of the Hittites, four hundred shekels of silver, according to the weights current among the merchants.

17 So the field of Ephron in Machpelah, which was to the east of Mamre, the field with the cave that was in it and all the trees that were in the field, throughout its whole area, passed [18]to Abraham as a possession in the presence of the Hittites, in the presence of all who went in at the gate of his city. [19]After this, Abraham buried Sarah his wife in the cave of the field of Machpelah facing Mamre (that is, Hebron) in the land of Canaan. [20]The field and the cave that is in it passed from the Hittites into Abraham's possession as a burying place.

The Marriage of Isaac and Rebekah

24 Now Abraham was old, well advanced in years; and the LORD had blessed Abraham in all things. [2]Abraham said to his servant, the oldest of his house, who had charge of all that he had, "Put your hand under my thigh [3]and I will make you swear by the LORD, the God of heaven and earth, that you will not get a wife for my son from the daughters of the Canaanites, among

24.3 Marrying Foreigners

From this earliest period of Israelite history, there was an emphasis on not marrying foreigners. The reason had to do with religion, not race—in many cases foreigners were distant relatives. When foreigners were willing to worship Israel's God, they were welcomed (see the book of Ruth, for example).

whom I live, [4]but will go to my country and to my kindred and get a wife for my son Isaac." [5]The servant said to him, "Perhaps the woman may not be willing to follow me to this land; must I then take your son back to the land from which you came?" [6]Abraham said to him, "See to it that you do not take my son back there. [7]The LORD, the God of heaven, who took me from my father's house and from the land of my birth, and who spoke to me and swore to me, 'To your offspring I will give this land,' he will send his angel before you, and you shall take a wife for my son from there. [8]But if the woman is not willing to follow you, then you will be free from this oath of mine; only you must not take my son back there." [9]So the servant put his hand under the thigh of Abraham his master and swore to him concerning this matter.

10 Then the servant took ten of his master's camels and departed, taking all kinds of choice gifts from his master; and he set out and went to Aram-naharaim, to the city of Nahor. [11]He made the camels kneel down outside the city by the well of water; it was toward evening, the time when women go out to draw water. [12]And he said, "O LORD, God of my master Abraham, please grant me success today and show steadfast love to my master Abraham. [13]I am standing here by the spring of water, and the daughters of the townspeople are coming out to draw water. [14]Let the girl to whom I shall say, 'Please offer your jar that I may drink,' and who shall say, 'Drink, and I will water your camels'—let her be the one whom you have appointed for your servant Isaac. By this I shall know that you have shown steadfast love to my master."

15 Before he had finished speaking, there was Rebekah, who was born to Bethuel son of Milcah, the wife of Nahor, Abraham's brother, coming

out with her water jar on her shoulder. [16]The girl was very fair to look upon, a virgin, whom no man had known. She went down to the spring, filled her jar, and came up. [17]Then the servant ran to meet her and said, "Please let me sip a little water from your jar." [18]"Drink, my lord," she said, and quickly lowered her jar upon her hand and gave him a drink. [19]When she had finished giving him a drink, she said, "I will draw for your camels also, until they have finished drinking." [20]So she quickly emptied her jar into the trough and ran again to the well to draw, and she drew for all his camels. [21]The man gazed at her in silence to learn whether or not the LORD had made his journey successful.

22 When the camels had finished drinking, the man took a gold nose-ring weighing a half shekel, and two bracelets for her arms weighing ten gold shekels, [23]and said, "Tell me whose daughter you are. Is there room in your father's house for us to spend the night?" [24]She said to him, "I am the daughter of Bethuel son of Milcah, whom she bore to Nahor." [25]She added, "We have plenty of straw and fodder and a place to spend the night." [26]The man bowed his head and worshiped the LORD [27]and said, "Blessed be the LORD, the God of my master Abraham, who has not forsaken his steadfast love and his faithfulness toward my master. As for me, the LORD has led me on the way to the house of my master's kin."

28 Then the girl ran and told her mother's household about these things. [29]Rebekah had a brother whose name was Laban; and Laban ran out to the man, to the spring. [30]As soon as he had seen the nose-ring, and the bracelets on his sis-

ter's arms, and when he heard the words of his sister Rebekah, "Thus the man spoke to me," he went to the man; and there he was, standing by the camels at the spring. [31]He said, "Come in, O blessed of the LORD. Why do you stand outside when I have prepared the house and a place for the camels?" [32]So the man came into the house; and Laban unloaded the camels, and gave him straw and fodder for the camels, and water to wash his feet and the feet of the men who were with him. [33]Then food was set before him to eat; but he said, "I will not eat until I have told my errand." He said, "Speak on."

34 So he said, "I am Abraham's servant. [35]The LORD has greatly blessed my master, and he has become wealthy; he has given him flocks and herds, silver and gold, male and female slaves, camels and donkeys. [36]And Sarah my master's wife bore a son to my master when she was old; and he has given him all that he has. [37]My master made me swear, saying, 'You shall not take a wife for my son from the daughters of the Canaanites, in whose land I live; [38]but you shall go to my father's house, to my kindred, and get a wife for my son.' [39]I said to my master, 'Perhaps the woman will not follow me.' [40]But he said to me, 'The LORD, before whom I walk, will send his angel with you and make your way successful. You shall get a wife for my son from my kindred, from my father's house. [41]Then you will be free from my oath, when you come to my kindred; even if they will not give her to you, you will be free from my oath.'

42 "I came today to the spring, and said, 'O LORD, the God of my master Abraham, if now

---

REBEKAH *Forceful Woman*

"I'D RATHER BE A HAMMER than a nail," sang Paul Simon, meaning it's better to be an active force than to let others drive you. Rebekah followed that philosophy. When Abraham's servant asked for a drink of water, she took the initiative. "I'll draw for your camels also, until they have finished drinking," she said (24.19). And although camels require a lot of water, Rebekah didn't just walk to the well to draw it—she ran (v. 20).

When offered marriage to an unknown relative hundreds of miles' journey across dangerous wilderness, Rebekah grabbed the chance. Her family wanted time to adjust to the idea, but she got ready to leave the next day, never to see her home again.

Initiative is admirable, but an overdose can lead to trouble. Rebekah waited twenty years to have a child and then gave birth to twins. God told her that Jacob, the younger, would be God's chosen. In an attempt to manage Jacob's success, Rebekah pushed him into deceiving his father and stealing his brother's blessing. "Only obey my word," she told him (27.13). Rebekah thought she could control everything, regardless of whether her actions pleased God.

The ploy worked as she predicted, but Rebekah had not foreseen the fury of Esau, Jacob's outwitted brother. Fearing for Jacob's life, she arranged to send him back to her childhood home. "Stay with him a while, until . . . your brother's anger against you turns away . . . then I will send, and bring you back from there," she told Jacob (27.45). For Rebekah, that time never came—she died without seeing her favorite child again.

Life Questions: When can initiative like Rebekah's be helpful? Under what conditions can it lead to trouble?

you will only make successful the way I am going! [43]I am standing here by the spring of water; let the young woman who comes out to draw, to whom I shall say, "Please give me a little water from your jar to drink," [44]and who will say to me, "Drink, and I will draw for your camels also"—let her be the woman whom the LORD has appointed for my master's son.'

45 "Before I had finished speaking in my heart, there was Rebekah coming out with her water jar on her shoulder; and she went down to the spring, and drew. I said to her, 'Please let me drink.' [46]She quickly let down her jar from her shoulder, and said, 'Drink, and I will also water your camels.' So I drank, and she also watered the camels. [47]Then I asked her, 'Whose daughter are you?' She said, 'The daughter of Bethuel, Nahor's son, whom Milcah bore to him.' So I put the ring on her nose, and the bracelets on her arms. [48]Then I bowed my head and worshiped the LORD, and blessed the LORD, the God of my master Abraham, who had led me by the right way to obtain the daughter of my master's kinsman for his son. [49]Now then, if you will deal loyally and truly with my master, tell me; and if not, tell me, so that I may turn either to the right hand or to the left."

50 Then Laban and Bethuel answered, "The thing comes from the LORD; we cannot speak to you anything bad or good. [51]Look, Rebekah is before you, take her and go, and let her be the wife of your master's son, as the LORD has spoken."

52 When Abraham's servant heard their words, he bowed himself to the ground before the LORD. [53]And the servant brought out jewelry of silver and of gold, and garments, and gave them to Rebekah; he also gave to her brother and to her mother costly ornaments. [54]Then he and the men who were with him ate and drank, and they spent the night there. When they rose in the morning, he said, "Send me back to my master." [55]Her brother and her mother said, "Let the girl remain with us a while, at least ten days; after that she may go." [56]But he said to them, "Do not delay me, since the LORD has made my journey successful; let me go that I may go to my master." [57]They said, "We will call the girl, and ask her." [58]And they called Rebekah, and said to her, "Will you go with this man?" She said, "I will." [59]So they sent away their sister Rebekah and her nurse along with Abraham's servant and his men. [60]And they blessed Rebekah and said to her,

"May you, our sister, become
    thousands of myriads;
may your offspring gain possession
    of the gates of their foes."

[61]Then Rebekah and her maids rose up, mounted the camels, and followed the man; thus the servant took Rebekah, and went his way.

62 Now Isaac had come from[m] Beer-lahai-roi, and was settled in the Negeb. [63]Isaac went out in the evening to walk[n] in the field; and looking up, he saw camels coming. [64]And Rebekah looked up, and when she saw Isaac, she slipped quickly from the camel, [65]and said to the servant, "Who is the man over there, walking in the field to meet us?" The servant said, "It is my master." So she took her veil and covered herself. [66]And the servant told Isaac all the things that he had done. [67]Then Isaac brought her into his mother Sarah's tent. He took Rebekah, and she became his wife; and he loved her. So Isaac was comforted after his mother's death.

Abraham Marries Keturah

25 Abraham took another wife, whose name was Keturah. [2]She bore him Zimran, Jokshan, Medan, Midian, Ishbak, and Shuah. [3]Jokshan was the father of Sheba and Dedan. The sons of Dedan were Asshurim, Letushim, and Leummim. [4]The sons of Midian were Ephah, Epher, Hanoch, Abida, and Eldaah. All these were the children of Keturah. [5]Abraham gave all he had to Isaac. [6]But to the sons of his concubines Abraham gave gifts, while he was still living, and he sent them away from his son Isaac, eastward to the east country.

The Death of Abraham

7 This is the length of Abraham's life, one hundred seventy-five years. [8]Abraham breathed his last and died in a good old age, an old man and full of years, and was gathered to his people. [9]His sons Isaac and Ishmael buried him in the cave of Machpelah, in the field of Ephron son of Zohar the Hittite, east of Mamre, [10]the field that Abraham purchased from the Hittites. There Abraham was buried, with his wife Sarah. [11]After the death of Abraham God blessed his son Isaac. And Isaac settled at Beer-lahai-roi.

Ishmael's Descendants

12 These are the descendants of Ishmael, Abraham's son, whom Hagar the Egyptian, Sarah's slave-girl, bore to Abraham. [13]These are the names of the sons of Ishmael, named in the order of their birth: Nebaioth, the firstborn of Ishmael; and Kedar, Adbeel, Mibsam, [14]Mishma, Dumah, Massa, [15]Hadad, Tema, Jetur, Naphish, and Kedemah. [16]These are the sons of Ishmael and these are their names, by their villages and by their encampments, twelve princes according to their tribes. [17](This is the length of the life of Ishmael, one hundred thirty-seven years; he breathed his last and died, and was gathered to his people.) [18]They settled from Havilah to Shur, which is op-

---

[m] Syr Tg: Heb *from coming to*   [n] Meaning of Heb word is uncertain

posite Egypt in the direction of Assyria; he settled down[o] alongside of[p] all his people.

The Birth and Youth of Esau and Jacob

19 These are the descendants of Isaac, Abraham's son: Abraham was the father of Isaac, [20]and Isaac was forty years old when he married Rebekah, daughter of Bethuel the Aramean of Paddan-aram, sister of Laban the Aramean. [21]Isaac prayed to the LORD for his wife, because she was barren; and the LORD granted his prayer, and his wife Rebekah conceived. [22]The children struggled together within her; and she said, "If it is to be this way, why do I live?"[q] So she went to inquire of the LORD. [23]And the LORD said to her,

"Two nations are in your womb,
    and two peoples born of you shall be
        divided;
the one shall be stronger than the other,
    the elder shall serve the younger."

[24]When her time to give birth was at hand, there were twins in her womb. [25]The first came out red, all his body like a hairy mantle; so they named him Esau. [26]Afterward his brother came out, with his hand gripping Esau's heel; so he was named Jacob.[r] Isaac was sixty years old when she bore them.

27 When the boys grew up, Esau was a skillful hunter, a man of the field, while Jacob was a quiet man, living in tents. [28]Isaac loved Esau, because he was fond of game; but Rebekah loved Jacob.

Esau Sells His Birthright

29 Once when Jacob was cooking a stew, Esau came in from the field, and he was famished. [30]Esau said to Jacob, "Let me eat some of that red stuff, for I am famished!" (Therefore he was called Edom.[s]) [31]Jacob said, "First sell me your birthright." [32]Esau said, "I am about to die; of what use is a birthright to me?" [33]Jacob said, "Swear to me first."[t] So he swore to him, and sold his birthright to Jacob. [34]Then Jacob gave Esau bread and lentil stew, and he ate and drank, and rose and went his way. Thus Esau despised his birthright.

25.33 No Sympathy for Esau

Esau's birthright, which he sold for a meal, was his inheritance as the firstborn son. He stood to be head of a large extended family and its property. Though his brother Jacob took advantage of him, the Bible gives Esau little sympathy for his role as victim: he "despised his birthright" (verse 34) by letting his hunger overwhelm his concern for things of lasting value. Because of this, he was later labeled "godless" (Hebrews 12.16).

Isaac and Abimelech

26 Now there was a famine in the land, besides the former famine that had occurred in the days of Abraham. And Isaac went to Gerar, to King Abimelech of the Philistines. [2]The LORD appeared to Isaac[u] and said, "Do not go down to Egypt; settle in the land that I shall show you. [3]Reside in this land as an alien, and I will be with you, and will bless you; for to you and to your descendants I will give all these lands, and I will fulfill the oath that I swore to your father Abraham. [4]I will make your offspring as numerous as the stars of heaven, and will give to your offspring all these lands; and all the nations of the earth shall gain blessing for themselves through your offspring, [5]because Abraham obeyed my voice and kept my charge, my commandments, my statutes, and my laws."

6 So Isaac settled in Gerar. [7]When the men of the place asked him about his wife, he said, "She is my sister"; for he was afraid to say, "My wife," thinking, "or else the men of the place might kill me for the sake of Rebekah, because she is attractive in appearance." [8]When Isaac had been there a long time, King Abimelech of the Philistines looked out of a window and saw him fondling his wife Rebekah. [9]So Abimelech called for Isaac, and said, "So she is your wife! Why then did you say, 'She is my sister'?" Isaac said to him, "Because I thought I might die because of her." [10]Abimelech said, "What is this you have done to us? One of the people might easily have lain with your wife, and you would have brought guilt upon us." [11]So Abimelech warned all the people, saying, "Whoever touches this man or his wife shall be put to death."

12 Isaac sowed seed in that land, and in the same year reaped a hundredfold. The LORD blessed him, [13]and the man became rich; he prospered more and more until he became very wealthy. [14]He had possessions of flocks and herds, and a great household, so that the Philistines envied him. [15](Now the Philistines had stopped up and filled with earth all the wells that his father's servants had dug in the days of his father Abraham.) [16]And Abimelech said to Isaac, "Go away from us; you have become too powerful for us."

17 So Isaac departed from there and camped in the valley of Gerar and settled there. [18]Isaac dug again the wells of water that had been dug in the days of his father Abraham; for the Philistines had stopped them up after the death of Abraham; and he gave them the names that his father had given them. [19]But when Isaac's servants dug in the valley and found there a well of spring water, [20]the herders of Gerar quarreled with Isaac's herders,

---

o Heb *he fell / He supplants*   p Or *down in opposition to*   q Syr: Meaning of Heb uncertain   r That is *He takes by the heel* or
s That is *Red*   t Heb *today*   u Heb *him*

saying, "The water is ours." So he called the well Esek,ᵛ because they contended with him. ²¹Then they dug another well, and they quarreled over that one also; so he called it Sitnah.ʷ ²²He moved from there and dug another well, and they did not quarrel over it; so he called it Rehoboth,ˣ saying, "Now the LORD has made room for us, and we shall be fruitful in the land."

23 From there he went up to Beer-sheba. ²⁴And that very night the LORD appeared to him and said, "I am the God of your father Abraham; do not be afraid, for I am with you and will bless you and make your offspring numerous for my servant Abraham's sake." ²⁵So he built an altar there, called on the name of the LORD, and pitched his tent there. And there Isaac's servants dug a well.

26 Then Abimelech went to him from Gerar, with Ahuzzath his adviser and Phicol the commander of his army. ²⁷Isaac said to them, "Why have you come to me, seeing that you hate me and have sent me away from you?" ²⁸They said, "We see plainly that the LORD has been with you; so we say, let there be an oath between you and us, and let us make a covenant with you ²⁹so that you will do us no harm, just as we have not touched you and have done to you nothing but good and have sent you away in peace. You are now the blessed of the LORD." ³⁰So he made them a feast, and they ate and drank. ³¹In the morning they rose early and exchanged oaths; and Isaac set them on their way, and they departed from him in peace. ³²That same day Isaac's servants came and told him about the well that they had dug, and said to him, "We have found water!" ³³He called it Shibah;ʸ therefore the name of the city is Beer-shebaᶻ to this day.

Esau's Hittite Wives

34 When Esau was forty years old, he married Judith daughter of Beeri the Hittite, and Basemath daughter of Elon the Hittite; ³⁵and they made life bitter for Isaac and Rebekah.

Isaac Blesses Jacob

27 When Isaac was old and his eyes were dim so that he could not see, he called his elder son Esau and said to him, "My son"; and he answered, "Here I am." ²He said, "See, I am old; I do not know the day of my death. ³Now then, take your weapons, your quiver and your bow, and go out to the field, and hunt game for me. ⁴Then prepare for me savory food, such as I like, and bring it to me to eat, so that I may bless you before I die."

5 Now Rebekah was listening when Isaac spoke to his son Esau. So when Esau went to the field to hunt for game and bring it, ⁶Rebekah said to her son Jacob, "I heard your father say to your brother Esau, ⁷'Bring me game, and prepare for me savory food to eat, that I may bless you before the LORD before I die.' ⁸Now therefore, my son, obey my word as I command you. ⁹Go to the flock, and get me two choice kids, so that I may prepare from them savory food for your father, such as he likes; ¹⁰and you shall take it to your father to eat, so that he may bless you before he dies." ¹¹But Jacob said to his mother Rebekah, "Look, my brother Esau is a hairy man, and I am a man of smooth skin. ¹²Perhaps my father will feel me, and I shall seem to be mocking him, and bring a curse on myself and not a blessing." ¹³His mother said to him, "Let your curse be on me, my son; only obey my word, and go, get them for me." ¹⁴So he went and got them and brought them to his mother; and his mother prepared savory food, such as his father loved. ¹⁵Then Rebekah took the best garments of her elder son Esau, which were with her in the house, and put them on her younger son Jacob; ¹⁶and she put the skins of the kids on his hands and on the smooth part of his neck. ¹⁷Then she handed the savory food, and the bread that she had prepared, to her son Jacob.

18 So he went in to his father, and said, "My father"; and he said, "Here I am; who are you, my son?" ¹⁹Jacob said to his father, "I am Esau your firstborn. I have done as you told me; now sit up and eat of my game, so that you may bless me." ²⁰But Isaac said to his son, "How is it that you have found it so quickly, my son?" He answered, "Because the LORD your God granted me success." ²¹Then Isaac said to Jacob, "Come near, that I may feel you, my son, to know whether you are really my son Esau or not." ²²So Jacob went up to his father Isaac, who felt him and said, "The voice is Jacob's voice, but the hands are the hands of Esau." ²³He did not recognize him, because his hands were hairy like his brother Esau's hands; so he blessed him. ²⁴He said, "Are you really my son Esau?" He answered, "I am." ²⁵Then he said, "Bring it to me, that I may eat of my son's game and bless you." So he brought it to him, and he ate; and he brought him wine, and he drank. ²⁶Then his father Isaac said to him, "Come near and kiss me, my son." ²⁷So he came near and kissed him; and he smelled the smell of his garments, and blessed him, and said,

"Ah, the smell of my son
    is like the smell of a field that the LORD
        has blessed.
28 May God give you of the dew of heaven,
    and of the fatness of the earth,
    and plenty of grain and wine.
29 Let peoples serve you,
    and nations bow down to you.

ᵛ That is Contention   ʷ That is Enmity   ˣ That is Broad places or Room   ʸ A word resembling the word for oath   ᶻ That is Well of the oath or Well of seven

Con Man in God's Family?
The Bible doesn't cover up Jacob's scheming

ASK PEOPLE WHY THEY DON'T go to church, and you'll often hear this answer: "There are too many hypocrites." It may be an excuse, but there's a troubling reality behind it. How can a religion with such high standards include so many people with such low standards?

Jacob's life poses the same question. The Bible does not mince words in describing his grasping, con-man character. He took advantage of his twin brother's impulsiveness to switch places with him in the family will (25.29–34). Later, seeing that his father Isaac still favored Esau, Jacob (with his mother) tricked the old man into blessing him in place of his brother. (A father's blessing was not merely symbolic. It had a permanent significance, like a swearing-in ceremony.)

The Tricks Backfire

Dressed up in Esau's clothes and some fresh goatskins, Jacob flatly lied to his father and took the Lord's name in vain. Isaac, trusting his nose over his ears, fell for it (27.1–40). Yet the trick backfired. Jacob had to run for his life, and he spent 20 years in exile with his uncle. Uncle Laban gave Jacob a dose of his own medicine, planting an unwanted sister in his wedding bed and repeatedly changing his wages as head shepherd.

You might think Jacob would learn that tricks aren't nice. Yet Jacob didn't noticeably improve his ways. He made a poor husband, neglecting one of his wives and creating rivalry. He favored two sons, so that the neglected ones grew jealous to the point of murder. He certainly doesn't seem like choice material for a religious leader.

God Makes the Choice

But God chose Jacob. He was always making those kinds of choices, sometimes with no apparent reason at all. Often he went against the time-honored practice of letting the firstborn son be number one, as he did in choosing number-two sons Abel, Jacob, and Ephraim. In fact, an inspired prophecy marked Jacob as God's choice before he was even born—before he had done a single thing to merit the choice.

So God's choice did not necessarily depend on how a person behaved. God chose the one he wanted—it was as simple as that.

Is this fair? That's what the apostle Paul asked in Romans 9. He concluded that we have no right to find fault with God's choices, knowing as little as we do compared to his infinite understanding. And while we may never understand God's choices, we should note that all the "rejected" brothers of Genesis—Cain, Canaan, Ishmael, Reuben, Esau, and Manasseh—were treated more than fairly. Their offspring multiplied into nations under God's protection.

No One Excluded

For his chosen people, God had a much greater honor. Good or bad, they would be made a channel of blessing for the whole world. He told Abraham, right from the beginning, "In you all the families of the earth shall be blessed" (12.3). By selecting a few, God planned to extend his blessings to all. And that is how it worked out: Abraham's small, fault-ridden family grew into a sizable, fault-ridden nation that brought forth, in the fullness of time, a faultless Jesus.

No wonder Paul wrote that we have no business questioning the wisdom of God. We may not see why he chose people like Jacob. But unquestionably, those choices worked for good—and the whole world became eligible to join the "chosen people." As Paul wrote, "You are all children of God through faith . . . There is no longer Jew or Greek, there is no longer slave or free, there is no longer male and female; for all of you are one in Jesus Christ. And if you belong to Christ, then you are Abraham's offspring" (Galatians 3.26–29). God has a habit of choosing flawed people to achieve great good. Who can say what he is doing with the hypocrites of our day?

Life Questions: Why do you think God chooses imperfect people like Jacob? Why did he choose you?

Be lord over your brothers,
and may your mother's sons bow
down to you.
Cursed be everyone who curses you,
and blessed be everyone who blesses
you!"

27.27 Sense of Smell

An old man, Isaac had lost his eyesight and apparently much of his sense of touch. He could still smell though, and thought he recognized his son by the scent of his clothes. In an age before deodorants and frequent laundering, people had distinctive scents.

Esau's Lost Blessing

30 As soon as Isaac had finished blessing Jacob, when Jacob had scarcely gone out from the presence of his father Isaac, his brother Esau came in from his hunting. ³¹He also prepared savory food, and brought it to his father. And he said to his father, "Let my father sit up and eat of his son's game, so that you may bless me." ³²His father Isaac said to him, "Who are you?" He answered, "I am your firstborn son, Esau." ³³Then Isaac trembled violently, and said, "Who was it then that hunted game and brought it to me, and I ate it all[a] before you came, and I have blessed him?—yes, and blessed he shall be!" ³⁴When Esau heard his father's words, he cried out with an exceedingly great and bitter cry, and said to his father, "Bless me, me also, father!" ³⁵But he said, "Your brother came deceitfully, and he has taken away your blessing." ³⁶Esau said, "Is he not rightly named Jacob?[b] For he has supplanted me these two times. He took away my birthright; and look, now he has taken away my blessing." Then he said, "Have you not reserved a blessing for me?" ³⁷Isaac answered Esau, "I have already made him your lord, and I have given him all his brothers as servants, and with grain and wine I have sustained him. What then can I do for you, my son?" ³⁸Esau said to his father, "Have you only one blessing, father? Bless me, me also, father!" And Esau lifted up his voice and wept.

39 Then his father Isaac answered him:
"See, away from[c] the fatness of the earth
shall your home be,
and away from[d] the dew of heaven on
high.
40 By your sword you shall live,
and you shall serve your brother;
but when you break loose,[e]
you shall break his yoke from your
neck."

Jacob Escapes Esau's Fury

41 Now Esau hated Jacob because of the blessing with which his father had blessed him, and Esau said to himself, "The days of mourning for my father are approaching; then I will kill my brother Jacob." ⁴²But the words of her elder son Esau were told to Rebekah; so she sent and called her younger son Jacob and said to him, "Your brother Esau is consoling himself by planning to kill you. ⁴³Now therefore, my son, obey my voice; flee at once to my brother Laban in Haran, ⁴⁴and stay with him a while, until your brother's fury turns away— ⁴⁵until your brother's anger against you turns away, and he forgets what you have done to him; then I will send, and bring you back from there. Why should I lose both of you in one day?"

46 Then Rebekah said to Isaac, "I am weary of my life because of the Hittite women. If Jacob marries one of the Hittite women such as these, one of the women of the land, what good will my life be to me?"

28 Then Isaac called Jacob and blessed him, and charged him, "You shall not marry one of the Canaanite women. ²Go at once to Paddan-aram to the house of Bethuel, your mother's father; and take as wife from there one of the daughters of Laban, your mother's brother. ³May God Almighty[f] bless you and make you fruitful and numerous, that you may become a company of peoples. ⁴May he give to you the blessing of Abraham, to you and to your offspring with you, so that you may take possession of the land where you now live as an alien—land that God gave to Abraham." ⁵Thus Isaac sent Jacob away; and he went to Paddan-aram, to Laban son of Bethuel the Aramean, the brother of Rebekah, Jacob's and Esau's mother.

Esau Marries Ishmael's Daughter

6 Now Esau saw that Isaac had blessed Jacob and sent him away to Paddan-aram to take a wife from there, and that as he blessed him he charged him, "You shall not marry one of the Canaanite women," ⁷and that Jacob had obeyed his father and his mother and gone to Paddan-aram. ⁸So when Esau saw that the Canaanite women did not please his father Isaac, ⁹Esau went to Ishmael and took Mahalath daughter of Abraham's son Ishmael, and sister of Nebaioth, to be his wife in addition to the wives he had.

Jacob's Dream at Bethel

10 Jacob left Beer-sheba and went toward Haran. ¹¹He came to a certain place and stayed there for the night, because the sun had set. Taking one of the stones of the place, he put it under his head and lay down in that place. ¹²And he

---

[a] Cn: Heb *of all*   [b] That is *He supplants* or *He takes by the heel*   [c] Or *See, of*   [d] Or *and of*   [e] Meaning of Heb uncertain   [f] Traditional rendering of Heb *El Shaddai*

dreamed that there was a ladder^g set up on the earth, the top of it reaching to heaven; and the angels of God were ascending and descending on it. ^{13}And the LORD stood beside him^h and said, "I

28.12 A Stairway to Heaven

God's grace: this is what Jacob found while traveling alone in the desert. Through his own greedy scheming he had won the family birthright and then, ironically, had had to run away from the family. Yet God came to him full of promises, not the reproaches he deserved. Jacob had not looked for God, but God looked for him. Jacob's vision of a stairway to heaven looked forward to Jesus, who himself is the bridge between heaven and earth (John 1.51).

---

am the LORD, the God of Abraham your father and the God of Isaac; the land on which you lie I will give to you and to your offspring; ^{14}and your offspring shall be like the dust of the earth, and you shall spread abroad to the west and to the east and to the north and to the south; and all the families of the earth shall be blessed^i in you and in your offspring. ^{15}Know that I am with you and will keep you wherever you go, and will bring you back to this land; for I will not leave you until I have done what I have promised you." ^{16}Then Jacob woke from his sleep and said, "Surely the LORD is in this place—and I did not know it!" ^{17}And he was afraid, and said, "How awesome is this place! This is none other than the house of God, and this is the gate of heaven."

18 So Jacob rose early in the morning, and he took the stone that he had put under his head and set it up for a pillar and poured oil on the top of it. ^{19}He called that place Bethel;^{j} but the name of the city was Luz at the first. ^{20}Then Jacob made a vow, saying, "If God will be with me, and will keep me in this way that I go, and will give me bread to eat and clothing to wear, ^{21}so that I come again to my father's house in peace, then the LORD shall be my God, ^{22}and this stone, which I have set up for a pillar, shall be God's house; and of all that you give me I will surely give one-tenth to you."

Jacob Meets Rachel

29 Then Jacob went on his journey, and came to the land of the people of the east. ^{2}As he looked, he saw a well in the field and three flocks of sheep lying there beside it; for out of that well the flocks were watered. The stone on the well's mouth was large, ^{3}and when all the flocks were gathered there, the shepherds would roll the stone from the mouth of the well, and water the sheep,

and put the stone back in its place on the mouth of the well.

4 Jacob said to them, "My brothers, where do you come from?" They said, "We are from Haran." ^{5}He said to them, "Do you know Laban son of Nahor?" They said, "We do." ^{6}He said to them, "Is it well with him?" "Yes," they replied, "and here is his daughter Rachel, coming with the sheep." ^{7}He said, "Look, it is still broad daylight; it is not time for the animals to be gathered together. Water the sheep, and go, pasture them." ^{8}But they said, "We cannot until all the flocks are gathered together, and the stone is rolled from the mouth of the well; then we water the sheep."

9 While he was still speaking with them, Rachel came with her father's sheep; for she kept them. ^{10}Now when Jacob saw Rachel, the daughter of his mother's brother Laban, and the sheep of his mother's brother Laban, Jacob went up and rolled the stone from the well's mouth, and watered the flock of his mother's brother Laban. ^{11}Then Jacob kissed Rachel, and wept aloud. ^{12}And Jacob told Rachel that he was her father's kinsman, and that he was Rebekah's son; and she ran and told her father.

13 When Laban heard the news about his sister's son Jacob, he ran to meet him; he embraced him and kissed him, and brought him to his house. Jacob^k told Laban all these things, ^{14}and Laban said to him, "Surely you are my bone and my flesh!" And he stayed with him a month.

Jacob Marries Laban's Daughters

15 Then Laban said to Jacob, "Because you are my kinsman, should you therefore serve me for nothing? Tell me, what shall your wages be?" ^{16}Now Laban had two daughters; the name of the elder was Leah, and the name of the younger was Rachel. ^{17}Leah's eyes were lovely,^{l} and Rachel was graceful and beautiful. ^{18}Jacob loved Rachel; so he said, "I will serve you seven years for your younger daughter Rachel." ^{19}Laban said, "It is better that I give her to you than that I should give her to any other man; stay with me." ^{20}So Jacob served seven years for Rachel, and they seemed to him but a few days because of the love he had for her.

21 Then Jacob said to Laban, "Give me my wife that I may go in to her, for my time is completed." ^{22}So Laban gathered together all the people of the place, and made a feast. ^{23}But in the evening he took his daughter Leah and brought her to Jacob; and he went in to her. ^{24}(Laban gave his maid Zilpah to his daughter Leah to be her maid.) ^{25}When morning came, it was Leah! And Jacob said to Laban, "What is this you have done to me? Did I not serve with you for Rachel? Why then have you deceived me?" ^{26}Laban said, "This

---

^{g} Or *stairway* or *ramp* ^{h} Or *stood above it* ^{i} Or *shall bless themselves* ^{j} That is *House of God* ^{k} Heb *He*
^{l} Meaning of Heb uncertain

The Women of Genesis

Despite their low status, they were anyone's equal

PARTNER SOUGHT FOR VAST CREATIVE endeavor. Global plans. Unlimited compensation. Immediate responsibilities include maintenance of large property, care and authority over all kinds of creatures—flying, walking, creeping, crawling. Object: teamwork and companionship. Female only. Contact Adam.

> The man said, "This at last is bone of my bones and flesh of my flesh; this one shall be called Woman, for out of Man this one was taken." 2.23

No woman after Eve got such an opportunity. After sin came into the picture, the original idea of marriage got twisted. " 'To love and to cherish' became 'to desire and to dominate,' " as author Derek Kidner put it. Throughout the Old Testament you catch only glimpses of the original spontaneous joy with which man greeted woman and regarded her as a partner. Granted, the people of God had a higher view of women than did their pagan neighbors. Still, women had value chiefly as seconds to men, whose children they bore, whose desires they fulfilled.

Yet the women of Genesis were no pushovers. They had strong characters, minds of their own. They exerted all the influence they were allowed, and then some.

The Joke Was on Her

Sarah, Abraham's partner, was caught laughing at God's astonishing promise (18.12–15). She thought she knew better than to expect babies at the age of 90. She later had the grace to admit the joke was on her (21.6). Though the New Testament commends her as an ideal submissive wife (1 Peter 3.5–6), she certainly expressed her views strongly to Abraham. Twice she had her rival Hagar driven out of their home and into the desert.

Hagar, though only a servant girl, showed backbone too. After her first expulsion from Abraham and Sarah's home she met God himself, who comforted her and sent her back to Abraham with promises of a great future. Later she showed strength of character by bringing up her son alone in the desert.

A Scheme that Backfired

Rebekah shows up in Chapter 24 as a young girl drawing water for a stranger's camels. By the next day you know she has a mind of her own—and enough courage to set off with a stranger for marriage in unknown territory. Her husband Isaac loved her, and so did her son Jacob. From her, it seems, Jacob got his strong, scheming personality. She initiated the plan to install him in family leadership, against the custom of firstborn sons—and against his father's will. Sadly for Rebekah, her scheme partly backfired, and she never saw Jacob again.

Rachel and Leah, sisters, fought for years over Jacob. Rachel had the looks, as well as a corner on her husband's love. Jacob neglected Leah, whom he hadn't wanted to marry in the first place. But to make up for that slight, God gave Leah children—four sons in a row. Rachel took each one like a fist to the face, which is probably what Leah intended. After a while, Jacob seemed to be just a tool in the struggle for dominance between two sisters, especially when Leah cooly informed him that she had hired his services for the night (30.16).

Who won? It's hard to say. Rachel held the love of Jacob to the end, her two sons most favored by him though last in line. But Leah's sons gained prominence of their own, especially Judah who, became the ancestor of kings—and Jesus. Leah would have enjoyed knowing that she, not Rachel, was great-great-great-grandmother to the King of kings.

Hardly Delicate Violets

In short, the women in Genesis were not delicate violets, but tough, pioneer women. One cannot approve of everything they did, by a long shot. But their toughness and courage demolish any theory that women are, by nature, weak. They used every advantage they had, fairly or unfairly—and did it skillfully. For instance, Rachel displayed classic chutzpah in facing down her father as he searched for some idols she had stolen. She sweetly claimed she couldn't stand up because she was having her period. In truth, she was sitting on the goods, knowing perfectly well even Laban lacked the nerve to try moving a woman in that condition (31.25–35).

They were a match for their men: in courage, in character, in independence, in determination, in orneriness. In that culture they were second-class citizens. But in real life these women were, as God intended, the equal of anybody.

Life Questions: Creative people often find ways to transcend the limits put on them. What do you feel hemmed in by? How can you achieve God's will despite obstacles?

is not done in our country—giving the younger before the firstborn. 27Complete the week of this one, and we will give you the other also in return for serving me another seven years." 28Jacob did so, and completed her week; then Laban gave him his daughter Rachel as a wife. 29(Laban gave his maid Bilhah to his daughter Rachel to be her maid.) 30So Jacob went in to Rachel also, and he loved Rachel more than Leah. He served Laban*m* for another seven years.

29.30 Playing Favorites

Throughout his life, Jacob's favoritism would cause problems in his family. He must have learned the habit from his own parents (see 25.28). Here, he favors one wife over the other. Later, he spoiled his son Joseph with favors, making his other sons so jealous they wanted to kill Joseph (see 37.4,18).

31 When the LORD saw that Leah was unloved, he opened her womb; but Rachel was barren. 32Leah conceived and bore a son, and she named him Reuben;*n* for she said, "Because the LORD has looked on my affliction; surely now my husband will love me." 33She conceived again and bore a son, and said, "Because the LORD has heard*o* that I am hated, he has given me this son also"; and she named him Simeon. 34Again she conceived and bore a son, and said, "Now this time my husband will be joined*p* to me, because I have borne him three sons"; therefore he was named Levi. 35She conceived again and bore a son, and said, "This time I will praise*q* the LORD";

therefore she named him Judah; then she ceased bearing.

30 When Rachel saw that she bore Jacob no children, she envied her sister; and she said to Jacob, "Give me children, or I shall die!" 2Jacob became very angry with Rachel and said, "Am I in the place of God, who has withheld from you the fruit of the womb?" 3Then she said, "Here is my maid Bilhah; go in to her, that she may bear upon my knees and that I too may have children through her." 4So she gave him her maid Bilhah as a wife; and Jacob went in to her. 5And Bilhah conceived and bore Jacob a son. 6Then Rachel said, "God has judged me, and has also heard my voice and given me a son"; therefore she named him Dan.*r* 7Rachel's maid Bilhah conceived again and bore Jacob a second son. 8Then Rachel said, "With mighty wrestlings I have wrestled*s* with my sister, and have prevailed"; so she named him Naphtali.

9 When Leah saw that she had ceased bearing children, she took her maid Zilpah and gave her to Jacob as a wife. 10Then Leah's maid Zilpah bore Jacob a son. 11And Leah said, "Good fortune!" so she named him Gad.*t* 12Leah's maid Zilpah bore Jacob a second son. 13And Leah said, "Happy am I! For the women will call me happy"; so she named him Asher.*u*

14 In the days of wheat harvest Reuben went and found mandrakes in the field, and brought them to his mother Leah. Then Rachel said to Leah, "Please give me some of your son's mandrakes." 15But she said to her, "Is it a small matter that you have taken away my husband? Would you take away my son's mandrakes also?" Rachel said, "Then he may lie with you tonight for your son's mandrakes." 16When Jacob came from the

m Heb *him*   *n* That is *See, a son*   *o* Heb *shama*   *p* Heb *lawah*   *q* Heb *hodah*   *r* That is *He judged*
s Heb *niphtal*   *t* That is *Fortune*   *u* That is *Happy*

LABAN *Cheater*

HOW FITTING THAT JACOB, WHO had cheated his brother at least twice, fell into the hands of his uncle Laban, a notorious double-crosser. Deceit must have run in the family: Laban was brother to Rebekah, who had helped her son Jacob dupe his own father. Now Jacob learned how it felt to have the joke turned on him.

Laban won the first match by palming off his older daughter Leah on Jacob, who had just worked seven years to earn the beautiful Rachel. Throughout the rest of their working relationship, Jacob and Laban competed to outwit each other. Time and again Jacob accused Laban of changing his wages. Meanwhile Jacob schemed to get the biggest and best flock while tending Laban's animals.

Caught up in their wiles, neither man seemed to notice the obvious: Each trick damaged relationships. For example, deceit enabled Leah to share Rachel's husband, yet what did she really gain? For the rest of their lives the two quarreled miserably over Jacob's favor.

Jacob's flocks increased due to his cunning, but in the process Laban's sons grew hostile. Laban got cheap labor from Jacob, but Jacob resented it that one day he left without warning, taking Laban's daughters with him. Laban never learned that, though cheating may get you what you want, it usually involves a heavy cost.

Life Questions: What is the best way to respond when someone tries to cheat you?

field in the evening, Leah went out to meet him, and said, "You must come in to me; for I have hired you with my son's mandrakes." So he lay with her that night. [17]And God heeded Leah, and she conceived and bore Jacob a fifth son. [18]Leah said, "God has given me my hire[v] because I gave my maid to my husband"; so she named him Issachar. [19]And Leah conceived again, and she bore Jacob a sixth son. [20]Then Leah said, "God has endowed me with a good dowry; now my husband will honor[w] me, because I have borne him six sons"; so she named him Zebulun. [21]Afterwards she bore a daughter, and named her Dinah.

22 Then God remembered Rachel, and God heeded her and opened her womb. [23]She conceived and bore a son, and said, "God has taken away my reproach"; [24]and she named him Joseph,[x] saying, "May the LORD add to me another son!"

Jacob Prospers at Laban's Expense

25 When Rachel had borne Joseph, Jacob said to Laban, "Send me away, that I may go to my own home and country. [26]Give me my wives and my children for whom I have served you, and let me go; for you know very well the service I have given you." [27]But Laban said to him, "If you will allow me to say so, I have learned by divination that the LORD has blessed me because of you; [28]name your wages, and I will give it." [29]Jacob said to him, "You yourself know how I have served you, and how your cattle have fared with me. [30]For you had little before I came, and it has increased abundantly; and the LORD has blessed you wherever I turned. But now when shall I provide for my own household also?" [31]He said, "What shall I give you?" Jacob said, "You shall not give me anything; if you will do this for me, I will again feed your flock and keep it: [32]let me pass through all your flock today, removing from it every speckled and spotted sheep and every black lamb, and the spotted and speckled among the goats; and such shall be my wages. [33]So my honesty will answer for me later, when you come to look into my wages with you. Every one that is not speckled and spotted among the goats and black among the lambs, if found with me, shall be counted stolen." [34]Laban said, "Good! Let it be as you have said." [35]But that day Laban removed the male goats that were striped and spotted, and all the female goats that were speckled and spotted, every one that had white on it, and every lamb that was black, and put them in charge of his sons; [36]and he set a distance of three days' journey between himself and Jacob, while Jacob was pasturing the rest of Laban's flock.

37 Then Jacob took fresh rods of poplar and almond and plane, and peeled white streaks in them, exposing the white of the rods. [38]He set the rods that he had peeled in front of the flocks in the troughs, that is, the watering places, where the flocks came to drink. And since they bred when they came to drink, [39]the flocks bred in front of the rods, and so the flocks produced young that were striped, speckled, and spotted. [40]Jacob separated the lambs, and set the faces of the flocks toward the striped and the completely black animals in the flock of Laban; and he put his own droves apart, and did not put them with Laban's flock. [41]Whenever the stronger of the flock were breeding, Jacob laid the rods in the troughs before the eyes of the flock, that they might breed among the rods, [42]but for the feebler of the flock he did not lay them there; so the feebler were Laban's, and the stronger Jacob's. [43]Thus the man grew exceedingly rich, and had large flocks, and male and female slaves, and camels and donkeys.

30.33 Misplaced Faith

In this classic encounter between two schemers, each trying to take advantage of the other, Jacob placed considerable faith in an animal-breeding trick. Many people have believed in similar methods over the centuries. Modern genetics indicates that Jacob's results had nothing to do with such techniques. God's intervening power increased Jacob's flocks, as Jacob himself acknowledged (31.7–9).

Jacob Flees with Family and Flocks

31 Now Jacob heard that the sons of Laban were saying, "Jacob has taken all that was our father's; he has gained all this wealth from what belonged to our father." [2]And Jacob saw that Laban did not regard him as favorably as he did before. [3]Then the LORD said to Jacob, "Return to the land of your ancestors and to your kindred, and I will be with you." [4]So Jacob sent and called Rachel and Leah into the field where his flock was, [5]and said to them, "I see that your father does not regard me as favorably as he did before. But the God of my father has been with me. [6]You know that I have served your father with all my strength; [7]yet your father has cheated me and changed my wages ten times, but God did not permit him to harm me. [8]If he said, 'The speckled shall be your wages,' then all the flock bore speckled; and if he said, 'The striped shall be your wages,' then all the flock bore striped. [9]Thus God has taken away the livestock of your father, and given them to me.

10 During the mating of the flock I once had a dream in which I looked up and saw that the

male goats that leaped upon the flock were striped, speckled, and mottled. ¹¹Then the angel of God said to me in the dream, 'Jacob,' and I said, 'Here I am!' ¹²And he said, 'Look up and see that all the goats that leap on the flock are striped, speckled, and mottled; for I have seen all that Laban is doing to you. ¹³I am the God of Bethel,ʸ where you anointed a pillar and made a vow to me. Now leave this land at once and return to the land of your birth.'" ¹⁴Then Rachel and Leah answered him, "Is there any portion or inheritance left to us in our father's house? ¹⁵Are we not regarded by him as foreigners? For he has sold us, and he has been using up the money given for us. ¹⁶All the property that God has taken away from our father belongs to us and to our children; now then, do whatever God has said to you."

17 So Jacob arose, and set his children and his wives on camels; ¹⁸and he drove away all his livestock, all the property that he had gained, the livestock in his possession that he had acquired in Paddan-aram, to go to his father Isaac in the land of Canaan.

19 Now Laban had gone to shear his sheep, and Rachel stole her father's household gods. ²⁰And Jacob deceived Laban the Aramean, in that he did not tell him that he intended to flee. ²¹So he fled with all that he had; starting out he crossed

ʸ Cn: Meaning of Heb uncertain   ᶻ Heb the river

the Euphrates,ᶻ and set his face toward the hill country of Gilead.

Laban Overtakes Jacob

22 On the third day Laban was told that Jacob had fled. ²³So he took his kinsfolk with him and pursued him for seven days until he caught up with him in the hill country of Gilead. ²⁴But God came to Laban the Aramean in a dream by night, and said to him, "Take heed that you say not a word to Jacob, either good or bad."

25 Laban overtook Jacob. Now Jacob had pitched his tent in the hill country, and Laban with his kinsfolk camped in the hill country of Gilead. ²⁶Laban said to Jacob, "What have you done? You have deceived me, and carried away my daughters like captives of the sword. ²⁷Why did you flee secretly and deceive me and not tell me? I would have sent you away with mirth and songs, with tambourine and lyre. ²⁸And why did you not permit me to kiss my sons and my daughters farewell? What you have done is foolish. ²⁹It is in my power to do you harm; but the God of your father spoke to me last night, saying, 'Take heed that you speak to Jacob neither good nor bad.' ³⁰Even though you had to go because you longed greatly for your father's house, why did you steal my gods?" ³¹Jacob answered Laban,

RACHEL *Love and Grief*

JACOB ARRIVED PENNILESS AT HIS cousin Rachel's home, having traveled hundreds of miles on foot. To some he might appear a poor catch—a fugitive from his family, his character tainted with the grasping, scheming qualities that had created the problem. Rachel, however, could grasp and scheme quite well herself. In strength and cunning, Jacob had met his match.

In an age not known for romance, when young people often waited for their parents to arrange their marriages, Jacob fell profoundly in love with Rachel. He worked fourteen years to gain her (after being tricked into marrying her sister along the way). Clearly, to him, beautiful Rachel was worth the labor. He loved her from first sight to last breath.

Rachel knew what it was to be deeply loved, but she also knew piercing sorrow. More than anything she wanted children, and while her sister produced six sons for Jacob and two servants also bore him children, Rachel remained childless. Her rivalry with her sister Leah, told in Genesis 29 and 30, was profound and bitter. Finally Rachel gave birth to Joseph, her first son. Some years later she died in childbirth bearing Benjamin, her second. (Showing love even after her death, Jacob counted these two sons as his favorites.)

Rachel's fierce love for her children became an emblem for Israel. More than a thousand years after she lived, the prophet Jeremiah, mulling over the destruction of Israel, heard "lamentation and bitter weeping. Rachel is weeping for her children; she refuses to be comforted . . . because they are no more" (Jeremiah 31.15). The same haunting poetry is quoted in Matthew 2.18 regarding the slaughter of babies by King Herod. Even today the phrase "Rachel weeping" serves as shorthand for the sufferings of the Jewish people.

Rachel was a strong woman whose loyalty to her husband and desire for children outweighed everything else. She and her sister became part of a traditional Jewish wedding blessing: "May the LORD make the woman who is coming into your house like Rachel and Leah, who together built up the house of Israel" (Ruth 4.11).

Life Questions: Jacob longed for a wife. Rachel longed for children. What do you want more than anything else?

"Because I was afraid, for I thought that you would take your daughters from me by force. [32]But anyone with whom you find your gods shall not live. In the presence of our kinsfolk, point out what I have that is yours, and take it." Now Jacob did not know that Rachel had stolen the gods.[a]

33 So Laban went into Jacob's tent, and into Leah's tent, and into the tent of the two maids, but he did not find them. And he went out of Leah's tent, and entered Rachel's. [34]Now Rachel had taken the household gods and put them in the camel's saddle, and sat on them. Laban felt all about in the tent, but did not find them. [35]And she said to her father, "Let not my lord be angry that I cannot rise before you, for the way of women is upon me." So he searched, but did not find the household gods.

31.35 Household Gods

The "gods" Rachel had stolen from her father (verse 19) were small idols or "charms" supposed to protect the family from harm. They may also have served as something like a title deed for the family inheritance. Such idols continued to water down Israel's commitment to God for many generations to come.

36 Then Jacob became angry, and upbraided Laban. Jacob said to Laban, "What is my offense? What is my sin, that you have hotly pursued me? [37]Although you have felt about through all my goods, what have you found of all your household goods? Set it here before my kinsfolk and your kinsfolk, so that they may decide between us two. [38]These twenty years I have been with you; your ewes and your female goats have not miscarried, and I have not eaten the rams of your flocks. [39]That which was torn by wild beasts I did not bring to you; I bore the loss of it myself; of my hand you required it, whether stolen by day or stolen by night. [40]It was like this with me: by day the heat consumed me, and the cold by night, and my sleep fled from my eyes. [41]These twenty years I have been in your house; I served you fourteen years for your two daughters, and six years for your flock, and you have changed my wages ten times. [42]If the God of my father, the God of Abraham and the Fear[b] of Isaac, had not been on my side, surely now you would have sent me away empty-handed. God saw my affliction and the labor of my hands, and rebuked you last night."

Laban and Jacob Make a Covenant

43 Then Laban answered and said to Jacob, "The daughters are my daughters, the children are my children, the flocks are my flocks, and all that you see is mine. But what can I do today about these daughters of mine, or about their children whom they have borne? [44]Come now, let us make a covenant, you and I; and let it be a witness between you and me." [45]So Jacob took a stone, and set it up as a pillar. [46]And Jacob said to his kinsfolk, "Gather stones," and they took stones, and made a heap; and they ate there by the heap. [47]Laban called it Jegar-sahadutha:[c] but Jacob called it Galeed.[d] [48]Laban said, "This heap is a witness between you and me today." Therefore he called it Galeed, [49]and the pillar[e] Mizpah,[f] for he said, "The LORD watch between you and me, when we are absent one from the other. [50]If you ill-treat my daughters, or if you take wives in addition to my daughters, though no one else is with us, remember that God is witness between you and me."

51 Then Laban said to Jacob, "See this heap and see the pillar, which I have set between you and me. [52]This heap is a witness, and the pillar is a witness, that I will not pass beyond this heap to you, and you will not pass beyond this heap and this pillar to me, for harm. [53]May the God of Abraham and the God of Nahor"—the God of their father—"judge between us." So Jacob swore by the Fear[b] of his father Isaac, [54]and Jacob offered a sacrifice on the height and called his kinsfolk to eat bread; and they ate bread and tarried all night in the hill country.

[55g] Early in the morning Laban rose up, and kissed his grandchildren and his daughters and blessed them; then he departed and returned home.

32 Jacob went on his way and the angels of God met him; [2]and when Jacob saw them he said, "This is God's camp!" So he called that place Mahanaim.[h]

Jacob Sends Presents to Appease Esau

3 Jacob sent messengers before him to his brother Esau in the land of Seir, the country of Edom, [4]instructing them, "Thus you shall say to my lord Esau: Thus says your servant Jacob, 'I have lived with Laban as an alien, and stayed until now; [5]and I have oxen, donkeys, flocks, male and female slaves; and I have sent to tell my lord, in order that I may find favor in your sight.'"

6 The messengers returned to Jacob, saying, "We came to your brother Esau, and he is coming to meet you, and four hundred men are with him." [7]Then Jacob was greatly afraid and distressed; and he divided the people that were with him, and the flocks and herds and camels, into two companies, [8]thinking, "If Esau comes to the one company and destroys it, then the company that is left will escape."

9 And Jacob said, "O God of my father Abra-

---

[a] Heb *them* [b] Meaning of Heb uncertain [c] In Aramaic *The heap of witness* [d] In Hebrew *The heap of witness*
[e] Compare Sam: MT lacks *the pillar* [f] That is *Watchpost* [g] Ch 32.1 in Heb [h] Here taken to mean *Two camps*

ham and God of my father Isaac, O LORD who said to me, 'Return to your country and to your kindred, and I will do you good,' 10I am not worthy of the least of all the steadfast love and all the faithfulness that you have shown to your servant, for with only my staff I crossed this Jordan; and now I have become two companies. 11Deliver me, please, from the hand of my brother, from the hand of Esau, for I am afraid of him; he may come and kill us all, the mothers with the children. 12Yet you have said, 'I will surely do you good, and make your offspring as the sand of the sea, which cannot be counted because of their number.'"

13 So he spent that night there, and from what he had with him he took a present for his brother Esau, 14two hundred female goats and twenty male goats, two hundred ewes and twenty rams, 15thirty milch camels and their colts, forty cows and ten bulls, twenty female donkeys and ten male donkeys. 16These he delivered into the hand of his servants, every drove by itself, and said to his servants, "Pass on ahead of me, and put a space between drove and drove." 17He instructed the foremost, "When Esau my brother meets you, and asks you, 'To whom do you belong? Where are you going? And whose are these ahead of you?' 18then you shall say, 'They belong to your servant Jacob; they are a present sent to my lord Esau; and moreover he is behind us.'" 19He likewise instructed the second and the third and all who followed the droves, "You shall say the same thing to Esau when you meet him, 20and you shall say, 'Moreover your servant Jacob is behind us.'" For he thought, "I may appease him with the present that goes ahead of me, and afterwards I shall see his face; perhaps he will accept me." 21So the present passed on ahead of him; and he himself spent that night in the camp.

Jacob Wrestles at Peniel

22 The same night he got up and took his two wives, his two maids, and his eleven children, and crossed the ford of the Jabbok. 23He took them and sent them across the stream, and likewise everything that he had. 24Jacob was left alone; and a man wrestled with him until daybreak. 25When

32.24 Wrestling with God
This nighttime encounter, as strange as any in the Bible, sounds somewhat similar to Jacob's previous on-the-road encounter with God (28.12) in a dream. But this time God left Jacob evidence of his physical presence—a limp.

the man saw that he did not prevail against Jacob, he struck him on the hip socket; and Jacob's hip was put out of joint as he wrestled with him. 26Then he said, "Let me go, for the day is breaking." But Jacob said, "I will not let you go, unless you bless me." 27So he said to him, "What is your name?" And he said, "Jacob." 28Then the man*i* said, "You shall no longer be called Jacob, but Israel,*j* for you have striven with God and with humans,*k* and have prevailed." 29Then Jacob asked him, "Please tell me your name." But he said, "Why is it that you ask my name?" And there he blessed him. 30So Jacob called the place Peniel,*l* saying, "For I have seen God face to face, and yet my life is preserved." 31The sun rose upon him as he passed Penuel, limping because of his hip. 32Therefore to this day the Israelites do not eat the thigh muscle that is on the hip socket, because he struck Jacob on the hip socket at the thigh muscle.

Jacob and Esau Meet

33 Now Jacob looked up and saw Esau coming, and four hundred men with him. So he divided the children among Leah and Rachel and the two maids. 2He put the maids with their children in front, then Leah with her children, and Rachel and Joseph last of all. 3He himself went on ahead of them, bowing himself to the ground seven times, until he came near his brother.

4 But Esau ran to meet him, and embraced him, and fell on his neck and kissed him, and they wept. 5When Esau looked up and saw the women and children, he said, "Who are these with you?" Jacob said, "The children whom God has graciously given your servant." 6Then the maids drew near, they and their children, and bowed down; 7Leah likewise and her children drew near and bowed down; and finally Joseph and Rachel drew near, and they bowed down. 8Esau said, "What do you mean by all this company that I met?" Jacob answered, "To find favor with my lord." 9But Esau said, "I have enough, my brother; keep what you have for yourself." 10Jacob said, "No, please; if I find favor with you, then accept my present from my hand; for truly to see your face is like seeing the face of God—since you have received me with such favor. 11Please accept my gift that is brought to you, because God has dealt graciously with me, and because I have everything I want." So he urged him, and he took it.

12 Then Esau said, "Let us journey on our way, and I will go alongside you." 13But Jacob said to him, "My lord knows that the children are frail and that the flocks and herds, which are nursing, are a care to me; and if they are overdriven for one day, all the flocks will die. 14Let my lord pass

i Heb *he*   *j* That is *The one who strives with God* or *God strives*   *k* Or *with divine and human beings*   *l* That is *The face of God*

on ahead of his servant, and I will lead on slowly, according to the pace of the cattle that are before me and according to the pace of the children, until I come to my lord in Seir."

15 So Esau said, "Let me leave with you some of the people who are with me." But he said,

---

33.15 Surface Reconciliation

On the surface, Jacob and Esau had reconciled. Underneath the niceties, however, mistrust continued, at least on Jacob's part. He did not want Esau to accompany him on his way, nor did he wish Esau to leave some of his men for "protection." He let his brother think he was on his way to Seir (verse 14), but turned north to Succoth as soon as Esau was out of sight.

"Why should my lord be so kind to me?" [16]So Esau returned that day on his way to Seir. [17]But Jacob journeyed to Succoth,[m] and built himself a house, and made booths for his cattle; therefore the place is called Succoth.

Jacob Reaches Shechem

18 Jacob came safely to the city of Shechem, which is in the land of Canaan, on his way from Paddan-aram; and he camped before the city. [19]And from the sons of Hamor, Shechem's father,

he bought for one hundred pieces of money[n] the plot of land on which he had pitched his tent. [20]There he erected an altar and called it El-Elohe-Israel.[o]

The Rape of Dinah

34 Now Dinah the daughter of Leah, whom she had borne to Jacob, went out to visit the women of the region. [2]When Shechem son of Hamor the Hivite, prince of the region, saw her, he seized her and lay with her by force. [3]And his soul was drawn to Dinah daughter of Jacob; he loved the girl, and spoke tenderly to her. [4]So Shechem spoke to his father Hamor, saying, "Get me this girl to be my wife."

5 Now Jacob heard that Shechem[p] had defiled his daughter Dinah; but his sons were with his cattle in the field, so Jacob held his peace until they came. [6]And Hamor the father of Shechem went out to Jacob to speak with him, [7]just as the sons of Jacob came in from the field. When they heard of it, the men were indignant and very angry, because he had committed an outrage in Israel by lying with Jacob's daughter, for such a thing ought not to be done.

8 But Hamor spoke with them, saying, "The heart of my son Shechem longs for your daughter; please give her to him in marriage. [9]Make marriages with us; give your daughters to us, and take our daughters for yourselves. [10]You shall live with us; and the land shall be open to you; live

---

[m] That is *Booths*   [n] Heb *one hundred qesitah*   [o] That is *God, the God of Israel*   [p] Heb *he*

ESAU *Surprising Choice*

MANY PEOPLE FIND ESAU MORE attractive than his brother Jacob. Esau was an outdoorsman—rugged, impulsive, simple and unaffected. Jacob was the stay-at-home mama's boy who angled deceitfully for any personal advantage. He virtually stole his brother's inheritance from him.

Anyone can understand Esau's murderous feelings toward Jacob. As the oldest brother, Esau stood next in line to lead the family. Instead he became the lost brother, holding no significant place in God's plan.

Why God's surprising choice of the younger brother? The apostle Paul reflects on this question in Romans 9.10–18, pointing out that God's preference for Jacob began even before his birth. Again and again in history, God narrowed his focus to a single person in order to carry out his plan to save the world. God couldn't choose everyone—moreover, those individuals God did choose were not always the ones we admire. God makes his own judgments, Paul says, and God's people must bow before him even when they do not understand.

Yet in the stories recorded here, the reasons behind God's unexpected choice become clearer. Esau had major character flaws. At every crossroads he consistently followed his own desires, showing little spiritual sensitivity and no long-term vision. Jacob the grasper at least recognized that the family inheritance was precious; to Esau, momentary hunger mattered more (Genesis 27). And when it came to marriage, Esau chose the local women, even though they came from the wrong heritage and displeased his parents.

God seemed to hold no place in Esau's thinking. Jacob, however unattractively, set his sights higher. God channeled Jacob's passion and strong ambition toward divine purposes.

Life Questions: Do ordinary desires—for food, romance, peer approval, success—conflict with spiritual ambitions in your life? How can you deal with such conflicts?

and trade in it, and get property in it." [11]Shechem also said to her father and to her brothers, "Let me find favor with you, and whatever you say to me I will give. [12]Put the marriage present and gift as high as you like, and I will give whatever you ask me; only give me the girl to be my wife."

13 The sons of Jacob answered Shechem and his father Hamor deceitfully, because he had defiled their sister Dinah. [14]They said to them, "We cannot do this thing, to give our sister to one who is uncircumcised, for that would be a disgrace to us. [15]Only on this condition will we consent to you: that you will become as we are and every male among you be circumcised. [16]Then we will give our daughters to you, and we will take your daughters for ourselves, and we will live among you and become one people. [17]But if you will not listen to us and be circumcised, then we will take our daughter and be gone."

18 Their words pleased Hamor and Hamor's son Shechem. [19]And the young man did not delay to do the thing, because he was delighted with Jacob's daughter. Now he was the most honored of all his family. [20]So Hamor and his son Shechem came to the gate of their city and spoke to the men of their city, saying, [21]"These people are friendly with us; let them live in the land and trade in it, for the land is large enough for them; let us take their daughters in marriage, and let us give them our daughters. [22]Only on this condition will they agree to live among us, to become one people: that every male among us be circumcised as they are circumcised. [23]Will not their livestock, their property, and all their animals be ours? Only let us agree with them, and they will live among us." [24]And all who went out of the city gate heeded Hamor and his son Shechem; and every male was circumcised, all who went out of the gate of his city.

Dinah's Brothers Avenge Their Sister

25 On the third day, when they were still in pain, two of the sons of Jacob, Simeon and Levi, Dinah's brothers, took their swords and came against the city unawares, and killed all the males. [26]They killed Hamor and his son Shechem with the sword, and took Dinah out of Shechem's house, and went away. [27]And the other sons of Jacob came upon the slain, and plundered the city, because their sister had been defiled. [28]They took their flocks and their herds, their donkeys, and whatever was in the city and in the field. [29]All their wealth, all their little ones and their wives, all that was in the houses, they captured and made their prey. [30]Then Jacob said to Simeon and Levi, "You have brought trouble on me by making me odious to the inhabitants of the land, the Canaanites and the Perizzites; my numbers are few, and if they gather themselves against me and attack me, I shall be destroyed, both I and my household." [31]But they said, "Should our sister be treated like a whore?"

Jacob Returns to Bethel

35 God said to Jacob, "Arise, go up to Bethel, and settle there. Make an altar there to the God who appeared to you when you fled from your brother Esau." [2]So Jacob said to his household and to all who were with him, "Put away the foreign gods that are among you, and purify yourselves, and change your clothes; [3]then come, let us go up to Bethel, that I may make an altar there to the God who answered me in the day of my distress and has been with me wherever I have gone." [4]So they gave to Jacob all the foreign gods that they had, and the rings that were in their ears; and Jacob hid them under the oak that was near Shechem.

5 As they journeyed, a terror from God fell upon the cities all around them, so that no one pursued them. [6]Jacob came to Luz (that is, Bethel), which is in the land of Canaan, he and all the people who were with him, [7]and there he built an altar and called the place El-bethel,[q] because it was there that God had revealed himself to him when he fled from his brother. [8]And Deborah, Rebekah's nurse, died, and she was buried under an oak below Bethel. So it was called Allon-bacuth.[r]

9 God appeared to Jacob again when he came from Paddan-aram, and he blessed him. [10]God said to him, "Your name is Jacob; no longer shall you be called Jacob, but Israel shall be your name." So he was called Israel. [11]God said to him, "I am God Almighty:[s] be fruitful and multiply; a nation and a company of nations shall come from you, and kings shall spring from you. [12]The land that I gave to Abraham and Isaac I will give to you, and I will give the land to your offspring after you." [13]Then God went up from him at the place where he had spoken with him. [14]Jacob set up a pillar in the place where he had spoken with him, a pillar of stone; and he poured out a drink offering on it, and poured oil on it. [15]So Jacob called the place where God had spoken with him Bethel.

The Birth of Benjamin and the Death of Rachel

16 Then they journeyed from Bethel; and when they were still some distance from Ephrath, Rachel was in childbirth, and she had hard labor. [17]When she was in her hard labor, the midwife said to her, "Do not be afraid; for now you will have another son." [18]As her soul was departing (for she died), she named him Ben-oni;[t] but his

[q] That is *God of Bethel* [r] That is *Oak of weeping* [s] Traditional rendering of Heb *El Shaddai* [t] That is *Son of my sorrow*

father called him Benjamin.ᵘ ¹⁹So Rachel died, and she was buried on the way to Ephrath (that is, Bethlehem), ²⁰and Jacob set up a pillar at her grave; it is the pillar of Rachel's tomb, which is there to this day. ²¹Israel journeyed on, and pitched his tent beyond the tower of Eder.

22 While Israel lived in that land, Reuben went and lay with Bilhah his father's concubine; and Israel heard of it.

35.22 A Sin that Lies Sleeping

This passage offers no indication that what Reuben did was wrong, let alone subject to punishment. Yet his deed was not forgotten. Decades later, when Jacob called his sons in for a final blessing, he brought up this sin (49.4) and predicted that leadership would pass from Reuben, the firstborn.

Now the sons of Jacob were twelve. ²³The sons of Leah: Reuben (Jacob's firstborn), Simeon, Levi, Judah, Issachar, and Zebulun. ²⁴The sons of Rachel: Joseph and Benjamin. ²⁵The sons of Bilhah, Rachel's maid: Dan and Naphtali. ²⁶The sons of Zilpah, Leah's maid: Gad and Asher. These were the sons of Jacob who were born to him in Paddan-aram.

The Death of Isaac

27 Jacob came to his father Isaac at Mamre, or Kiriath-arba (that is, Hebron), where Abraham and Isaac had resided as aliens. ²⁸Now the days of Isaac were one hundred eighty years. ²⁹And Isaac breathed his last; he died and was gathered to his people, old and full of days; and his sons Esau and Jacob buried him.

Esau's Descendants

36 These are the descendants of Esau (that is, Edom). ²Esau took his wives from the Canaanites: Adah daughter of Elon the Hittite, Oholibamah daughter of Anah sonᵛ of Zibeon the Hivite, ³and Basemath, Ishmael's daughter, sister of Nebaioth. ⁴Adah bore Eliphaz to Esau; Basemath bore Reuel; ⁵and Oholibamah bore Jeush, Jalam, and Korah. These are the sons of Esau who were born to him in the land of Canaan.

6 Then Esau took his wives, his sons, his daughters, and all the members of his household, his cattle, all his livestock, and all the property he had acquired in the land of Canaan; and he moved to a land some distance from his brother Jacob. ⁷For their possessions were too great for them to live together; the land where they were

staying could not support them because of their livestock. ⁸So Esau settled in the hill country of Seir; Esau is Edom.

9 These are the descendants of Esau, ancestor of the Edomites, in the hill country of Seir. ¹⁰These are the names of Esau's sons: Eliphaz son of Adah the wife of Esau; Reuel, the son of Esau's wife Basemath. ¹¹The sons of Eliphaz were Teman, Omar, Zepho, Gatam, and Kenaz. ¹²(Timna was a concubine of Eliphaz, Esau's son; she bore Amalek to Eliphaz.) These were the sons of Adah, Esau's wife. ¹³These were the sons of Reuel: Nahath, Zerah, Shammah, and Mizzah. These were the sons of Esau's wife, Basemath. ¹⁴These were the sons of Esau's wife Oholibamah, daughter of Anah sonʷ of Zibeon: she bore to Esau Jeush, Jalam, and Korah.

Clans and Kings of Edom

15 These are the clansˣ of the sons of Esau. The sons of Eliphaz the firstborn of Esau: the clansˣ Teman, Omar, Zepho, Kenaz, ¹⁶Korah, Gatam, and Amalek; these are the clansˣ of Eliphaz in the land of Edom; they are the sons of Adah. ¹⁷These are the sons of Esau's son Reuel: the clansˣ Nahath, Zerah, Shammah, and Mizzah; these are the clansˣ of Reuel in the land of Edom; they are the sons of Esau's wife Basemath. ¹⁸These are the sons of Esau's wife Oholibamah: the clansˣ Jeush, Jalam, and Korah; these are the clansˣ born of Esau's wife Oholibamah, the daughter of Anah. ¹⁹These are the sons of Esau (that is, Edom), and these are their clans.ˣ

20 These are the sons of Seir the Horite, the inhabitants of the land: Lotan, Shobal, Zibeon, Anah, ²¹Dishon, Ezer, and Dishan; these are the clansˣ of the Horites, the sons of Seir in the land of Edom. ²²The sons of Lotan were Hori and Heman; and Lotan's sister was Timna. ²³These are the sons of Shobal: Alvan, Manahath, Ebal, Shepho, and Onam. ²⁴These are the sons of Zibeon: Aiah and Anah; he is the Anah who found the springsʸ in the wilderness, as he pastured the donkeys of his father Zibeon. ²⁵These are the children of Anah: Dishon and Oholibamah daughter of Anah. ²⁶These are the sons of Dishon: Hemdan, Eshban, Ithran, and Cheran. ²⁷These are the sons of Ezer: Bilhan, Zaavan, and Akan. ²⁸These are the sons of Dishan: Uz and Aran. ²⁹These are the clansˣ of the Horites: the clansˣ Lotan, Shobal, Zibeon, Anah, ³⁰Dishon, Ezer, and Dishan; these are the clansˣ of the Horites, clan by clanᶻ in the land of Seir.

31 These are the kings who reigned in the land of Edom, before any king reigned over the Israelites. ³²Bela son of Beor reigned in Edom, the name of his city being Dinhabah. ³³Bela died, and Jobab son of Zerah of Bozrah succeeded him as

ᵘ That is *Son of the right hand* or *Son of the South*   ᵛ Sam Gk Syr: Heb *daughter*   ʷ Gk Syr: Heb *daughter*
ˣ Or *chiefs*   ʸ Meaning of Heb uncertain   ᶻ Or *chief by chief*

king. [34]Jobab died, and Husham of the land of the Temanites succeeded him as king. [35]Husham died, and Hadad son of Bedad, who defeated Midian in the country of Moab, succeeded him as king, the name of his city being Avith. [36]Hadad died, and Samlah of Masrekah succeeded him as king. [37]Samlah died, and Shaul of Rehoboth on the Euphrates succeeded him as king. [38]Shaul died, and Baal-hanan son of Achbor succeeded him as king. [39]Baal-hanan son of Achbor died, and Hadar succeeded him as king, the name of his city being Pau; his wife's name was Mehetabel, the daughter of Matred, daughter of Me-zahab.

[40] These are the names of the clans[a] of Esau, according to their families and their localities by

their names: the clans[a] Timna, Alvah, Jetheth, [41]Oholibamah, Elah, Pinon, [42]Kenaz, Teman, Mibzar, [43]Magdiel, and Iram; these are the clans[a] of Edom (that is, Esau, the father of Edom), according to their settlements in the land that they held.

Joseph Dreams of Greatness

37 Jacob settled in the land where his father had lived as an alien, the land of Canaan. [2]This is the story of the family of Jacob.

Joseph, being seventeen years old, was shepherding the flock with his brothers; he was a helper to the sons of Bilhah and Zilpah, his father's wives; and Joseph brought a bad report of them

[a] Or chiefs

Family Battles
The closer they are, the harder they fight

JOSEPH AND HIS BROTHERS FOUGHT bitterly—almost to the death. Nobody, it seems, can fight like brothers and sisters. Their very closeness seems to rub salt in their wounds.

They said to one another, "Here comes this dreamer. Come now, let us kill him." 37.19–20

Take a contemporary example: Esther Pauline Friedman came into this world 17 minutes before her sister Pauline Esther Friedman. The identical twins dressed alike, took the same classes, even shared the same purse, with one set of keys, one comb, one lipstick. They slept in the same twin bed. The first time they were separated, in fact, was after their double wedding.

The middle-aged Esther Pauline hooked a job replacing the original Ann Landers at the *Chicago Sun Times*. Two months later Pauline Esther started her own column with the *San Francisco Chronicle*, calling herself Abigail Van Buren. Ann sniffed to *Time* that her sister Abby's column was "very imitative." The feud was on. For eight years the two women who had dispensed advice to thousands could not resolve a petty family squabble.

Finally, the two were partially reconciled. They told journalists they were "very close." Yet bitter feelings lived on. Seventeen years after making up, Abby said about Ann, "If she looked old, if she needed a face-lift, believe me, it's because she needed it. I'm quite opposed to chopping myself up, but it was her right. Why not? When you cry a lot, it's got to show."

A Father's Favorite

Joseph's story is the last of the brotherly battles of Genesis. Cain and Abel, Isaac and Ishmael, Jacob and Esau all quarreled. Joseph set his 11 brothers against him by telling his dream of their bowing down to him. He was his father's favorite and perhaps flaunted it. So when his brothers got a chance, they paid him back. They sold him as a slave to traveling merchants, who took him to Egypt. Never expecting to see him again, they cooked up a story that he had been killed by wild animals.

God had other plans. In Egypt, he gave Joseph the interpretation to several dreams. It was a ticket to prominence. Egyptians of that day were fascinated by dreams: Archaeologists have uncovered lengthy textbooks on dream interpretation. Joseph soon found himself at the top of Pharaoh's government.

But success was not enough. The Bible story goes on from there, for God wanted forgiveness within the family. A famine forced Joseph's brothers out of Palestine; they came to Egypt looking for food. Kneeling before Joseph—so Egyptian by now that they did not recognize him—they begged for the right to buy food.

A Strange Struggle

So began one of the strangest struggles of the Bible. Joseph could have made up with his brothers on the spot, welcoming them with open arms. Or he could have taken revenge, putting them to death. He did neither. He began a series of elaborate tests, demanding things from them, playing tricks on

to their father. ³Now Israel loved Joseph more than any other of his children, because he was the son of his old age; and he had made him a long robe with sleeves.[b] ⁴But when his brothers saw that their father loved him more than all his brothers, they hated him, and could not speak peaceably to him.

5 Once Joseph had a dream, and when he told it to his brothers, they hated him even more. ⁶He said to them, "Listen to this dream that I dreamed. ⁷There we were, binding sheaves in the field. Suddenly my sheaf rose and stood upright; then your sheaves gathered around it, and bowed down to my sheaf." ⁸His brothers said to him, "Are you indeed to reign over us? Are you indeed to have dominion over us?" So they hated him even more because of his dreams and his words.

9 He had another dream, and told it to his brothers, saying, "Look, I have had another dream: the sun, the moon, and eleven stars were bowing down to me." ¹⁰But when he told it to his father and to his brothers, his father rebuked him, and said to him, "What kind of dream is this that you have had? Shall we indeed come, I and

your mother and your brothers, and bow to the ground before you?" ¹¹So his brothers were jealous of him, but his father kept the matter in mind.

37.8 Big Mouth

God revealed Joseph's future by way of two dreams. Foolishly, Joseph told everything to his brothers, who hated him all the more. The spoiled, naive Joseph we meet here is a different character from the careful, prudent leader who would emerge from prison years later to lead Egypt.

Joseph Is Sold by His Brothers

12 Now his brothers went to pasture their father's flock near Shechem. ¹³And Israel said to Joseph, "Are not your brothers pasturing the flock at Shechem? Come, I will send you to them." He answered, "Here I am." ¹⁴So he said to him, "Go now, see if it is well with your brothers and with the flock; and bring word back to me." So he sent him from the valley of Hebron.

[b] Traditional rendering (compare Gk): *a coat of many colors*; Meaning of Heb uncertain

them, accusing them. For nearly two years he played these games. They brought confusion and fear to his brothers—and an admission of guilt.

Twenty years had not erased the brothers' memory of Joseph. The moment their troubles began, their guilt surfaced. 'They said to one another, 'Alas, we are paying the penalty for what we did to our brother; we saw his anguish when he pleaded with us, but we would not listen' " (42.21). For Joseph, the drama brought tremendous emotional strain. Five times Genesis records that he broke into tears, once weeping so loudly that people in the next room heard him.

Joseph felt the strain of forgiveness. He wanted to reconcile with his brothers, whom he loved, but it was not easy. And until they had been pushed to the point of admitting and accepting their guilt, reconciliation could not occur. Their sins had planted deep-rooted bitterness, and only an emotionally wrenching struggle could pull it out.

Seeds of Bitterness

In this sense Joseph's story is the story of God and his people—the struggle to root out the sin that began in Genesis 3. Victory over sin does not happen automatically or easily. Ultimately, it demanded the death of God's Son.

Joseph's story points toward Jesus—a man God sent to save his people, one who was hated and betrayed by them just as Joseph was. But God's will to save conquers all. As Joseph told his brothers, "Though you intended to do harm to me, God intended it for good, in order to preserve a numerous people" (50.20).

The Birth of a Nation

Joseph closes one chapter in the story of Israel. The children of Abraham were transformed from a chain of individuals to a nation. God did not choose Joseph over his brothers, as he did Abraham over Lot, Isaac over Ishmael, Jacob over Esau. The brothers' reconciliation opened the way for them to become one family of 12 tribes—a single nation.

But the story leads on. Prosperous and numerous though the 12 were to become, they still had no land. And so Genesis ends happily, but on a note of suspense: When will Joseph's bones go back to the land God promised? When will God's promises be fulfilled?

Life Questions: Have you ever fought hard with a person close to you, and then experienced reconciliation? What process did you go through?

He came to Shechem, [15]and a man found him wandering in the fields; the man asked him, "What are you seeking?" [16]"I am seeking my brothers," he said; "tell me, please, where they are pasturing the flock." [17]The man said, "They have gone away, for I heard them say, 'Let us go to Dothan.'" So Joseph went after his brothers, and found them at Dothan. [18]They saw him from a distance, and before he came near to them, they conspired to kill him. [19]They said to one another, "Here comes this dreamer. [20]Come now, let us kill him and throw him into one of the pits; then we shall say that a wild animal has devoured him, and we shall see what will become of his dreams." [21]But when Reuben heard it, he delivered him out of their hands, saying, "Let us not take his life." [22]Reuben said to them, "Shed no blood; throw him into this pit here in the wilderness, but lay no hand on him"—that he might rescue him out of their hand and restore him to his father. [23]So when Joseph came to his brothers, they stripped him of his robe, the long robe with sleeves[c] that he wore; [24]and they took him and threw him into a pit. The pit was empty; there was no water in it.

25 Then they sat down to eat; and looking up they saw a caravan of Ishmaelites coming from Gilead, with their camels carrying gum, balm, and resin, on their way to carry it down to Egypt. [26]Then Judah said to his brothers, "What profit is it if we kill our brother and conceal his blood? [27]Come, let us sell him to the Ishmaelites, and not lay our hands on him, for he is our brother, our own flesh." And his brothers agreed. [28]When some Midianite traders passed by, they drew Joseph up, lifting him out of the pit, and sold him to the Ishmaelites for twenty pieces of silver. And they took Joseph to Egypt.

29 When Reuben returned to the pit and saw that Joseph was not in the pit, he tore his clothes. [30]He returned to his brothers, and said, "The boy is gone; and I, where can I turn?" [31]Then they took Joseph's robe, slaughtered a goat, and dipped the robe in the blood. [32]They had the long robe with sleeves[c] taken to their father, and they said, "This we have found; see now whether it is your son's robe or not." [33]He recognized it, and said, "It is my son's robe! A wild animal has devoured him; Joseph is without doubt torn to pieces." [34]Then Jacob tore his garments, and put sackcloth on his loins, and mourned for his son many days. [35]All his sons and all his daughters sought to comfort him; but he refused to be comforted, and said, "No, I shall go down to Sheol to my son, mourning." Thus his father bewailed him. [36]Meanwhile the Midianites had sold him in Egypt to Potiphar, one of Pharaoh's officials, the captain of the guard.

Judah and Tamar

38 It happened at that time that Judah went down from his brothers and settled near a certain Adullamite whose name was Hirah. [2]There Judah saw the daughter of a certain Canaanite whose name was Shua; he married her and went in to her. [3]She conceived and bore a son; and he named him Er. [4]Again she conceived and bore a son whom she named Onan. [5]Yet again she bore a son, and she named him Shelah. She[d] was in Chezib when she bore him. [6]Judah took a wife for Er his firstborn; her name was Tamar. [7]But Er, Judah's firstborn, was wicked in the sight of the LORD, and the LORD put him to death. [8]Then Judah said to Onan, "Go in to your brother's wife and perform the duty of a brother-in-law to her; raise up offspring for your brother." [9]But since Onan knew that the offspring

38.8 A Brother's Duty

Having children was so important in Old Testament times that if a man died childless, his brother was required to sleep with his widow in order to produce a family for him. (The regulations are found in Deuteronomy 25.5–10.)

Onan's sin was a deliberate refusal to treat his brother's widow fairly by giving her children. Family quarrels had split Jacob and Esau and had sent Jacob's son Joseph into slavery; now the next generation was carrying on in the same way.

would not be his, he spilled his semen on the ground whenever he went in to his brother's wife, so that he would not give offspring to his brother. [10]What he did was displeasing in the sight of the LORD, and he put him to death also. [11]Then Judah said to his daughter-in-law Tamar, "Remain a widow in your father's house until my son Shelah grows up"—for he feared that he too would die, like his brothers. So Tamar went to live in her father's house.

12 In course of time the wife of Judah, Shua's daughter, died; when Judah's time of mourning was over,[e] he went up to Timnah to his sheepshearers, he and his friend Hirah the Adullamite. [13]When Tamar was told, "Your father-in-law is going up to Timnah to shear his sheep," [14]she put off her widow's garments, put on a veil, wrapped herself up, and sat down at the entrance to Enaim, which is on the road to Timnah. She saw that Shelah was grown up, yet she had not been given to him in marriage. [15]When Judah saw her, he thought her to be a prostitute, for she had covered her face. [16]He went over to her at the roadside,

c See note on 37.3   d Gk: Heb He   e Heb when Judah was comforted and said, "Come, let me come in to you," for he did not know that she was his daughter-in-law. She said, "What will you give me, that you may come in to me?" ¹⁷He answered, "I will send you a kid from the flock." And she said, "Only if you give me a pledge, until you send it." ¹⁸He said, "What pledge shall I give you?" She replied, "Your signet and your cord, and the staff that is in your hand." So he gave them to her, and went in to her, and she conceived by him. ¹⁹Then she got up and went away, and taking off her veil she put on the garments of her widowhood.

20 When Judah sent the kid by his friend the Adullamite, to recover the pledge from the woman, he could not find her. ²¹He asked the townspeople, "Where is the temple prostitute who was at Enaim by the wayside?" But they said, "No prostitute has been here." ²²So he returned to Judah, and said, "I have not found her; moreover the townspeople said, 'No prostitute has been here.'" ²³Judah replied, "Let her keep the things as her own, otherwise we will be laughed at; you see, I sent this kid, and you could not find her."

24 About three months later Judah was told, "Your daughter-in-law Tamar has played the whore; moreover she is pregnant as a result of whoredom." And Judah said, "Bring her out, and let her be burned." ²⁵As she was being brought out, she sent word to her father-in-law, "It was the owner of these who made me pregnant." And she said, "Take note, please, whose these are, the signet and the cord and the staff." ²⁶Then Judah acknowledged them and said, "She is more in the right than I, since I did not give her to my son Shelah." And he did not lie with her again.

27 When the time of her delivery came, there were twins in her womb. ²⁸While she was in labor, one put out a hand; and the midwife took and bound on his hand a crimson thread, saying, "This one came out first." ²⁹But just then he drew back his hand, and out came his brother; and she said, "What a breach you have made for yourself!" Therefore he was named Perez.ᶠ ³⁰Afterward his brother came out with the crimson thread on his hand; and he was named Zerah.ᵍ

Joseph and Potiphar's Wife

39 Now Joseph was taken down to Egypt, and Potiphar, an officer of Pharaoh, the captain of the guard, an Egyptian, bought him from the Ishmaelites who had brought him down there. ²The LORD was with Joseph, and he became a successful man; he was in the house of his Egyptian master. ³His master saw that the LORD was with him, and that the LORD caused all that he did to prosper in his hands. ⁴So Joseph found favor in his sight and attended him; he made him overseer of his house and put him in charge of all that he had. ⁵From the time that he made him overseer in his house and over all that he had, the LORD blessed the Egyptian's house for Joseph's sake; the blessing of the LORD was on all that he had, in house and field. ⁶So he left all that he had in Joseph's charge; and, with him there, he had no concern for anything but the food that he ate.

Now Joseph was handsome and good-looking. ⁷And after a time his master's wife cast her eyes on Joseph and said, "Lie with me." ⁸But he refused and said to his master's wife, "Look, with me here, my master has no concern about anything in the house, and he has put everything that he has in my hand. ⁹He is not greater in this house than I am, nor has he kept back anything from me except yourself, because you are his wife. How then could I do this great wickedness, and sin against God?" ¹⁰And although she spoke to Joseph day after day, he would not consent to lie beside her or to be with her. ¹¹One day, however, when he went into the house to do his work, and while no one else was in the house, ¹²she caught hold of his garment, saying, "Lie with me!" But he left his garment in her hand, and fled and ran outside. ¹³When she saw that he had left his garment in her hand and had fled outside, ¹⁴she called out to the members of her household and said to them, "See, my husbandʰ has brought among us a Hebrew to insult us! He came in to me to lie with me, and I cried out with a loud voice; ¹⁵and when he heard me raise my voice and cry out, he left his garment beside me, and fled outside." ¹⁶Then she kept his garment by her until his master came home, ¹⁷and she told him the same story, saying, "The Hebrew servant, whom you have brought among us, came in to me to insult me; ¹⁸but as soon as I raised my voice and cried out, he left his garment beside me, and fled outside."

19 When his master heard the words that his wife spoke to him, saying, "This is the way your servant treated me," he became enraged. ²⁰And Joseph's master took him and put him into the prison, the place where the king's prisoners were confined; he remained there in prison. ²¹But the LORD was with Joseph and showed him steadfast love; he gave him favor in the sight of the chief jailer. ²²The chief jailer committed to Joseph's care all the prisoners who were in the prison, and whatever was done there, he was the one who did it. ²³The chief jailer paid no heed to anything that was in Joseph's care, because the LORD was with him; and whatever he did, the LORD made it prosper.

The Dreams of Two Prisoners

40 Some time after this, the cupbearer of the king of Egypt and his baker offended their lord the king of Egypt. ²Pharaoh was angry with his two officers, the chief cupbearer and the chief

---

ᶠ That is A breach   ᵍ That is Brightness; perhaps alluding to the crimson thread   ʰ Heb he

baker, ³and he put them in custody in the house of the captain of the guard, in the prison where Joseph was confined. ⁴The captain of the guard charged Joseph with them, and he waited on

40.2 Important Officials

When Joseph was thrown into prison on a false charge, his future seemed to vanish. Yet in prison he came into contact with men who would eventually help raise him to the highest post in the nation. The "chief baker" and "chief cupbearer" were important officials in Pharaoh's court.

them; and they continued for some time in custody. ⁵One night they both dreamed—the cupbearer and the baker of the king of Egypt, who were confined in the prison—each his own dream, and each dream with its own meaning. ⁶When Joseph came to them in the morning, he saw that they were troubled. ⁷So he asked Pharaoh's officers, who were with him in custody in his master's house, "Why are your faces downcast today?" ⁸They said to him, "We have had dreams, and there is no one to interpret them." And Joseph said to them, "Do not interpretations belong to God? Please tell them to me."

9 So the chief cupbearer told his dream to Joseph, and said to him, "In my dream there was a vine before me, ¹⁰and on the vine there were three branches. As soon as it budded, its blossoms came out and the clusters ripened into grapes. ¹¹Pharaoh's cup was in my hand; and I took the grapes and pressed them into Pharaoh's cup, and placed the cup in Pharaoh's hand." ¹²Then Joseph said to him, "This is its interpretation: the three branches are three days; ¹³within three days Pharaoh will lift up your head and restore you to your office; and you shall place Pharaoh's cup in his hand, just as you used to do when you were his cupbearer. ¹⁴But remember me when it is well with you; please do me the kindness to make mention of me to Pharaoh, and so get me out of this place. ¹⁵For in fact I was stolen out of the land of the Hebrews; and here also I have done nothing that they should have put me into the dungeon."

16 When the chief baker saw that the interpretation was favorable, he said to Joseph, "I also had a dream: there were three cake baskets on my head, ¹⁷and in the uppermost basket there were all sorts of baked food for Pharaoh, but the birds were eating it out of the basket on my head." ¹⁸And Joseph answered, "This is its interpretation: the three baskets are three days; ¹⁹within three days Pharaoh will lift up your head—from you!—and hang you on a pole; and the birds will eat the flesh from you."

20 On the third day, which was Pharaoh's birthday, he made a feast for all his servants, and lifted up the head of the chief cupbearer and the head of the chief baker among his servants. ²¹He restored the chief cupbearer to his cupbearing, and he placed the cup in Pharaoh's hand; ²²but the chief baker he hanged, just as Joseph had interpreted to them. ²³Yet the chief cupbearer did not remember Joseph, but forgot him.

40.23 A Forgotten Man

Joseph had carefully prepared the way for his release from prison (verses 14–15). Everything worked according to plan except for one detail: the chief cupbearer forgot all about Joseph. Humanly speaking, Joseph was a forgotten man, stuck in prison with no hope of ever getting out. God alone remembered his existence.

Joseph Interprets Pharaoh's Dream

41 After two whole years, Pharaoh dreamed that he was standing by the Nile, ²and there came up out of the Nile seven sleek and fat cows, and they grazed in the reed grass. ³Then seven other cows, ugly and thin, came up out of the Nile after them, and stood by the other cows on the bank of the Nile. ⁴The ugly and thin cows ate up the seven sleek and fat cows. And Pharaoh awoke. ⁵Then he fell asleep and dreamed a second time; seven ears of grain, plump and good, were growing on one stalk. ⁶Then seven ears, thin and blighted by the east wind, sprouted after them. ⁷The thin ears swallowed up the seven plump and full ears. Pharaoh awoke, and it was a dream. ⁸In the morning his spirit was troubled; so he sent and called for all the magicians of Egypt and all its wise men. Pharaoh told them his dreams, but there was no one who could interpret them to Pharaoh.

9 Then the chief cupbearer said to Pharaoh, "I remember my faults today. ¹⁰Once Pharaoh was angry with his servants, and put me and the chief baker in custody in the house of the captain of the guard. ¹¹We dreamed on the same night, he and I, each having a dream with its own meaning. ¹²A young Hebrew was there with us, a servant of the captain of the guard. When we told him, he interpreted our dreams to us, giving an interpretation to each according to his dream. ¹³As he interpreted to us, so it turned out; I was restored to my office, and the baker was hanged."

14 Then Pharaoh sent for Joseph, and he was hurriedly brought out of the dungeon. When he had shaved himself and changed his clothes, he came in before Pharaoh. ¹⁵And Pharaoh said to Joseph, "I have had a dream, and there is no one who can interpret it. I have heard it said of you

that when you hear a dream you can interpret it." [16]Joseph answered Pharaoh, "It is not I; God will give Pharaoh a favorable answer." [17]Then Pharaoh said to Joseph, "In my dream I was standing on the banks of the Nile; [18]and seven cows, fat and sleek, came up out of the Nile and fed in the reed grass. [19]Then seven other cows came up after them, poor, very ugly, and thin. Never had I seen such ugly ones in all the land of Egypt. [20]The thin and ugly cows ate up the first seven fat cows, [21]but when they had eaten them no one would have known that they had done so, for they were still as ugly as before. Then I awoke. [22]I fell asleep a second time[i] and I saw in my dream seven ears of grain, full and good, growing on one stalk, [23]and seven ears, withered, thin, and blighted by the east wind, sprouting after them; [24]and the thin ears swallowed up the seven good ears. But when I told it to the magicians, there was no one who could explain it to me."

25 Then Joseph said to Pharaoh, "Pharaoh's dreams are one and the same; God has revealed to Pharaoh what he is about to do. [26]The seven good cows are seven years, and the seven good ears are seven years; the dreams are one. [27]The seven lean and ugly cows that came up after them are seven years, as are the seven empty ears blighted by the east wind. They are seven years of famine. [28]It is as I told Pharaoh; God has shown to Pharaoh what he is about to do. [29]There will come seven years of great plenty throughout all the land of Egypt. [30]After them there will arise seven years of famine, and all the plenty will be forgotten in the land of Egypt; the famine will consume the land. [31]The plenty will no longer be known in the land because of the famine that will follow, for it will be very grievous. [32]And the doubling of Pharaoh's dream means that the thing is fixed by God, and God will shortly bring it about. [33]Now therefore let Pharaoh select a man who is discerning and wise, and set him over the land of Egypt. [34]Let Pharaoh proceed to appoint overseers over the land, and take one-fifth of the produce of the land of Egypt during the seven plenteous years. [35]Let them gather all the food of these good years that are coming, and lay up grain under the authority of Pharaoh for food in the cities, and let them keep it. [36]That food shall be a reserve for the land against the seven years of famine that are to befall the land of Egypt, so that the land may not perish through the famine."

Joseph's Rise to Power

37 The proposal pleased Pharaoh and all his servants. [38]Pharaoh said to his servants, "Can we find anyone else like this—one in whom is the spirit of God?" [39]So Pharaoh said to Joseph,

"Since God has shown you all this, there is no one so discerning and wise as you. [40]You shall be over my house, and all my people shall order themselves as you command; only with regard to the throne will I be greater than you." [41]And Pharaoh said to Joseph, "See, I have set you over all the land of Egypt." [42]Removing his signet ring from his hand, Pharaoh put it on Joseph's hand; he arrayed him in garments of fine linen, and put a gold chain around his neck. [43]He had him ride in the chariot of his second-in-command; and they cried out in front of him, "Bow the knee!"[j] Thus he set him over all the land of Egypt. [44]Moreover Pharaoh said to Joseph, "I am Pharaoh, and without your consent no one shall lift up hand or foot in all the land of Egypt." [45]Pharaoh gave Joseph the name Zaphenath-paneah; and he gave him Asenath daughter of Potiphera, priest of On, as his wife. Thus Joseph gained authority over the land of Egypt.

41.45 Erasing Joseph's Past

Proud Egyptians did not care for Hebrews. In order that Joseph's ethnic past be erased as quickly as possible, Pharaoh gave Joseph an Egyptian name and married him into a prominent Egyptian family. Joseph gave his own sons Hebrew names, however, a practice that suggests he maintained his own identity.

46 Joseph was thirty years old when he entered the service of Pharaoh king of Egypt. And Joseph went out from the presence of Pharaoh, and went through all the land of Egypt. [47]During the seven plenteous years the earth produced abundantly. [48]He gathered up all the food of the seven years when there was plenty[k] in the land of Egypt, and stored up food in the cities; he stored up in every city the food from the fields around it. [49]So Joseph stored up grain in such abundance—like the sand of the sea—that he stopped measuring it; it was beyond measure.

50 Before the years of famine came, Joseph had two sons, whom Asenath daughter of Potiphera, priest of On, bore to him. [51]Joseph named the firstborn Manasseh,[l] "For," he said, "God has made me forget all my hardship and all my father's house." [52]The second he named Ephraim,[m] "For God has made me fruitful in the land of my misfortunes."

53 The seven years of plenty that prevailed in the land of Egypt came to an end; [54]and the seven years of famine began to come, just as Joseph had said. There was famine in every country, but throughout the land of Egypt there was bread.

---

[i] Gk Syr Vg: Heb lacks *I fell asleep a second time*   [j] *Abrek*, apparently an Egyptian word similar in sound to the Hebrew word meaning *to kneel*   [k] Sam Gk: MT *the seven years that were*   [l] That is *Making to forget*
[m] From a Hebrew word meaning *to be fruitful*

55When all the land of Egypt was famished, the people cried to Pharaoh for bread. Pharaoh said to all the Egyptians, "Go to Joseph; what he says to you, do." 56And since the famine had spread over all the land, Joseph opened all the storehouses,ⁿ and sold to the Egyptians, for the famine was severe in the land of Egypt. 57Moreover,

41.56 An Unusual Famine

Famine is common in the Middle East. There are records of two Egyptian famines so severe that starving people killed and ate each other. But it was rare for famine to affect both Egypt and Palestine at the same time, for they depended on totally different sources of water—Egypt on the Nile and Palestine on local rainfall.

all the world came to Joseph in Egypt to buy grain, because the famine became severe throughout the world.

Joseph's Brothers Go to Egypt

42 When Jacob learned that there was grain in Egypt, he said to his sons, "Why do you keep looking at one another? 2I have heard," he said, "that there is grain in Egypt; go down and buy grain for us there, that we may live and not die." 3So ten of Joseph's brothers went down to buy grain in Egypt. 4But Jacob did not send Joseph's brother Benjamin with his brothers, for he feared that harm might come to him. 5Thus the sons of Israel were among the other people who came to buy grain, for the famine had reached the land of Canaan.

6 Now Joseph was governor over the land; it was he who sold to all the people of the land. And Joseph's brothers came and bowed themselves before him with their faces to the ground. 7When Joseph saw his brothers, he recognized them, but he treated them like strangers and spoke harshly to them. "Where do you come from?" he said. They said, "From the land of Canaan, to buy food." 8Although Joseph had recognized his brothers, they did not recognize him. 9Joseph also remembered the dreams that he had dreamed about them. He said to them, "You are spies; you have come to see the nakedness of the land!" 10They said to him, "No, my lord; your servants have come to buy food. 11We are all sons of one man; we are honest men; your servants have never been spies." 12But he said to them, "No, you have come to see the nakedness of the land!" 13They said, "We, your servants, are twelve brothers, the sons of a certain man in the land of Canaan; the youngest, however, is now with our father, and one is no more." 14But Joseph said to

them, "It is just as I have said to you; you are spies! 15Here is how you shall be tested: as Pharaoh lives, you shall not leave this place unless your youngest brother comes here! 16Let one of you go and bring your brother, while the rest of you remain in prison, in order that your words may be tested, whether there is truth in you; or else, as Pharaoh lives, surely you are spies." 17And he put them all together in prison for three days.

18 On the third day Joseph said to them, "Do this and you will live, for I fear God: 19if you are honest men, let one of your brothers stay here where you are imprisoned. The rest of you shall go and carry grain for the famine of your households, 20and bring your youngest brother to me. Thus your words will be verified, and you shall not die." And they agreed to do so. 21They said to one another, "Alas, we are paying the penalty for what we did to our brother; we saw his anguish when he pleaded with us, but we would not listen. That is why this anguish has come upon us." 22Then Reuben answered them, "Did I not tell you not to wrong the boy? But you would not listen. So now there comes a reckoning for his blood." 23They did not know that Joseph understood them, since he spoke with them through an interpreter. 24He turned away from them and wept; then he returned and spoke to them. And he picked out Simeon and had him bound before

42.24 Joseph in Tears

Five times Genesis tells about Joseph weeping as he dealt with his brothers (43.30; 45.2,14–15; 50.17). They had sold him into slavery, and all those years had not erased his hurt and anger. Yet he loved his brothers, and wanted to be reconciled. He felt his conflicting emotions intensely: love versus anger, forgiveness versus bitterness.

their eyes. 25Joseph then gave orders to fill their bags with grain, to return every man's money to his sack, and to give them provisions for their journey. This was done for them.

Joseph's Brothers Return to Canaan

26 They loaded their donkeys with their grain, and departed. 27When one of them opened his sack to give his donkey fodder at the lodging place, he saw his money at the top of the sack. 28He said to his brothers, "My money has been put back; here it is in my sack!" At this they lost heart and turned trembling to one another, saying, "What is this that God has done to us?"

29 When they came to their father Jacob in the land of Canaan, they told him all that had happened to them, saying, 30"The man, the lord

---

ⁿ Gk Vg Compare Syr: Heb *opened all that was in* (or, *among*) *them* of the land, spoke harshly to us, and charged us with spying on the land. 31But we said to him, 'We are honest men, we are not spies. 32We are twelve brothers, sons of our father; one is no more, and the youngest is now with our father in the land of Canaan.' 33Then the man, the lord of the land, said to us, 'By this I shall know that you are honest men: leave one of your brothers with me, take grain for the famine of your households, and go your way. 34Bring your youngest brother to me, and I shall know that you are not spies but honest men. Then I will release your brother to you, and you may trade in the land.'"

35 As they were emptying their sacks, there in each one's sack was his bag of money. When they and their father saw their bundles of money, they were dismayed. 36And their father Jacob said to them, "I am the one you have bereaved of children: Joseph is no more, and Simeon is no more, and now you would take Benjamin. All this has happened to me!" 37Then Reuben said to his father, "You may kill my two sons if I do not bring him back to you. Put him in my hands, and I will bring him back to you." 38But he said, "My son shall not go down with you, for his brother is dead, and he alone is left. If harm should come to him on the journey that you are to make, you would bring down my gray hairs with sorrow to Sheol."

The Brothers Come Again, Bringing Benjamin

43 Now the famine was severe in the land. 2And when they had eaten up the grain that they had brought from Egypt, their father said to them, "Go again, buy us a little more food." 3But Judah said to him, "The man solemnly warned us, saying, 'You shall not see my face unless your brother is with you.' 4If you will send our brother with us, we will go down and buy you food; 5but if you will not send him, we will not go down, for the man said to us, 'You shall not see my face, unless your brother is with you.'" 6Israel said, "Why did you treat me so badly as to tell the man that you had another brother?" 7They replied, "The man questioned us carefully about ourselves and our kindred, saying, 'Is your father still alive? Have you another brother?' What we told him was in answer to these questions. Could we in any way know that he would say, 'Bring your brother down'?" 8Then Judah said to his father Israel, "Send the boy with me, and let us be on our way, so that we may live and not die—you and we and also our little ones. 9I myself will be surety for him; you can hold me accountable for him. If I do not bring him back to you and set him before you, then let me bear the blame forever. 10If we had not delayed, we would now have returned twice."

11 Then their father Israel said to them, "If it must be so, then do this: take some of the choice fruits of the land in your bags, and carry them down as a present to the man—a little balm and a little honey, gum, resin, pistachio nuts, and almonds. 12Take double the money with you. Carry

43.11 The Perfect Gift

What kind of gift can you send to a man who has everything? Egypt was among the richest and most sophisticated countries in the world, and Israel (Jacob), a desert nomad. He wisely chose simple gifts of local produce—things that might not be available in Egypt.

back with you the money that was returned in the top of your sacks; perhaps it was an oversight. 13Take your brother also, and be on your way again to the man; 14may God Almighty° grant you mercy before the man, so that he may send back your other brother and Benjamin. As for me, if I am bereaved of my children, I am bereaved." 15So the men took the present, and they took double the money with them, as well as Benjamin. Then they went on their way down to Egypt, and stood before Joseph.

16 When Joseph saw Benjamin with them, he said to the steward of his house, "Bring the men into the house, and slaughter an animal and make ready, for the men are to dine with me at noon." 17The man did as Joseph said, and brought the men to Joseph's house. 18Now the men were afraid because they were brought to Joseph's house, and they said, "It is because of the money, replaced in our sacks the first time, that we have been brought in, so that he may have an opportunity to fall upon us, to make slaves of us and take our donkeys." 19So they went up to the steward of Joseph's house and spoke with him at the entrance to the house. 20They said, "Oh, my lord, we came down the first time to buy food; 21and when we came to the lodging place we opened our sacks, and there was each one's money in the top of his sack, our money in full weight. So we have brought it back with us. 22Moreover we have brought down with us additional money to buy food. We do not know who put our money in our sacks." 23He replied, "Rest assured, do not be afraid; your God and the God of your father must have put treasure in your sacks for you; I received your money." Then he brought Simeon out to them. 24When the steward ᵖ had brought the men into Joseph's house, and given them water, and they had washed their feet, and when he had given their donkeys fodder, 25they made the present

---

° Traditional rendering of Heb *El Shaddai*   ᵖ Heb *the man*

ready for Joseph's coming at noon, for they had heard that they would dine there.

26 When Joseph came home, they brought him the present that they had carried into the house, and bowed to the ground before him. 27He inquired about their welfare, and said, "Is your father well, the old man of whom you spoke? Is he still alive?" 28They said, "Your servant our father is well; he is still alive." And they bowed their heads and did obeisance. 29Then he looked up and saw his brother Benjamin, his mother's son, and said, "Is this your youngest brother, of whom you spoke to me? God be gracious to you, my son!" 30With that, Joseph hurried out, because he was overcome with affection for his brother, and he was about to weep. So he went into a private room and wept there. 31Then he washed his face and came out; and controlling himself he said, "Serve the meal." 32They served him by himself, and them by themselves, and the Egyptians who ate with him by themselves, because the Egyptians could not eat with the Hebrews, for that is an

43.32 Prejudice

Despite his high rank, Joseph still fell victim to Egyptian prejudice: They would not eat at the same table with a Hebrew. Chapter 46 (verses 33–34) adds that Egyptians detested shepherds—and Hebrews herded sheep.

abomination to the Egyptians. 33When they were seated before him, the firstborn according to his birthright and the youngest according to his youth, the men looked at one another in amazement. 34Portions were taken to them from Joseph's table, but Benjamin's portion was five times as much as any of theirs. So they drank and were merry with him.

Joseph Detains Benjamin

44 Then he commanded the steward of his house, "Fill the men's sacks with food, as much as they can carry, and put each man's money in the top of his sack. 2Put my cup, the silver cup, in the top of the sack of the youngest, with his money for the grain." And he did as Joseph told him. 3As soon as the morning was light, the men were sent away with their donkeys. 4When they had gone only a short distance from the city, Joseph said to his steward, "Go, follow after the men; and when you overtake them, say to them, 'Why have you returned evil for good? Why have you stolen my silver cup?q 5Is it not from this that my lord drinks? Does he not indeed use it for divination? You have done wrong in doing this.'"

6 When he overtook them, he repeated these words to them. 7They said to him, "Why does my lord speak such words as these? Far be it from your servants that they should do such a thing! 8Look, the money that we found at the top of our sacks, we brought back to you from the land of Canaan; why then would we steal silver or gold from your lord's house? 9Should it be found with any one of your servants, let him die; moreover the rest of us will become my lord's slaves." 10He said, "Even so; in accordance with your words, let it be: he with whom it is found shall become my slave, but the rest of you shall go free." 11Then each one quickly lowered his sack to the ground, and each opened his sack. 12He searched, beginning with the eldest and ending with the youngest; and the cup was found in Benjamin's sack. 13At this they tore their clothes. Then each one loaded his donkey, and they returned to the city.

14 Judah and his brothers came to Joseph's house while he was still there; and they fell to the ground before him. 15Joseph said to them, "What deed is this that you have done? Do you not know that one such as I can practice divination?" 16And Judah said, "What can we say to my lord? What can we speak? How can we clear ourselves? God has found out the guilt of your servants; here we are then, my lord's slaves, both we and also the one in whose possession the cup has been found." 17But he said, "Far be it from me that I should do so! Only the one in whose possession the cup was found shall be my slave; but as for you, go up in peace to your father."

Judah Pleads for Benjamin's Release

18 Then Judah stepped up to him and said, "O my lord, let your servant please speak a word in my lord's ears, and do not be angry with your servant; for you are like Pharaoh himself. 19My lord asked his servants, saying, 'Have you a father or a brother?' 20And we said to my lord, 'We have a father, an old man, and a young brother, the child of his old age. His brother is dead; he alone is left of his mother's children, and his father loves him.' 21Then you said to your servants, 'Bring him down to me, so that I may set my eyes on him.' 22We said to my lord, 'The boy cannot leave his father, for if he should leave his father, his father would die.' 23Then you said to your servants, 'Unless your youngest brother comes down with you, you shall see my face no more.' 24When we went back to your servant my father we told him the words of my lord. 25And when our father said, 'Go again, buy us a little food,' 26we said, 'We cannot go down. Only if our youngest brother goes with us, will we go down; for we cannot see the man's face unless our youngest brother is with us.' 27Then your servant my father said to us, 'You know that my wife bore me two sons; 28one left me, and I said, Surely he has been torn to

pieces; and I have never seen him since. ²⁹If you take this one also from me, and harm comes to him, you will bring down my gray hairs in sorrow to Sheol.' ³⁰Now therefore, when I come to your servant my father and the boy is not with us, then, as his life is bound up in the boy's life, ³¹when he sees that the boy is not with us, he will die; and your servants will bring down the gray hairs of your servant our father with sorrow to Sheol. ³²For your servant became surety for the boy to my father, saying, 'If I do not bring him back to you, then I will bear the blame in the sight of my father all my life.' ³³Now therefore, please let your servant remain as a slave to my lord in place of the boy; and let the boy go back with his brothers. ³⁴For how can I go back to my father if the boy is not with me? I fear to see the suffering that would come upon my father."

Joseph Reveals Himself to His Brothers

45 Then Joseph could no longer control himself before all those who stood by him, and he cried out, "Send everyone away from me." So no one stayed with him when Joseph made himself known to his brothers. ²And he wept so loudly that the Egyptians heard it, and the household

45.2 Weeping and Terror

This is one of the Bible's most intensely emotional scenes: it shows Joseph weeping so loudly people heard it in the next room, and Joseph's brothers speechless with terror and guilt. Though the moment ended with embraces and kissing (verses 14–15), years later the brothers were still afraid of revenge (50.15).

of Pharaoh heard it. ³Joseph said to his brothers, "I am Joseph. Is my father still alive?" But his brothers could not answer him, so dismayed were they at his presence.

4 Then Joseph said to his brothers, "Come closer to me." And they came closer. He said, "I am your brother, Joseph, whom you sold into Egypt. ⁵And now do not be distressed, or angry with yourselves, because you sold me here; for God sent me before you to preserve life. ⁶For the famine has been in the land these two years; and there are five more years in which there will be neither plowing nor harvest. ⁷God sent me before you to preserve for you a remnant on earth, and to keep alive for you many survivors. ⁸So it was not you who sent me here, but God; he has made me a father to Pharaoh, and lord of all his house and ruler over all the land of Egypt. ⁹Hurry and go up to my father and say to him, 'Thus says your son Joseph, God has made me lord of all

Egypt; come down to me, do not delay. ¹⁰You shall settle in the land of Goshen, and you shall be near me, you and your children and your children's children, as well as your flocks, your herds, and all that you have. ¹¹I will provide for you there—since there are five more years of famine to come—so that you and your household, and all that you have, will not come to poverty.' ¹²And now your eyes and the eyes of my brother Benjamin see that it is my own mouth that speaks to you. ¹³You must tell my father how greatly I am honored in Egypt, and all that you have seen. Hurry and bring my father down here." ¹⁴Then he fell upon his brother Benjamin's neck and wept, while Benjamin wept upon his neck. ¹⁵And he kissed all his brothers and wept upon them; and after that his brothers talked with him.

16 When the report was heard in Pharaoh's house, "Joseph's brothers have come," Pharaoh and his servants were pleased. ¹⁷Pharaoh said to Joseph, "Say to your brothers, 'Do this: load your animals and go back to the land of Canaan. ¹⁸Take your father and your households and come to me, so that I may give you the best of the land of Egypt, and you may enjoy the fat of the land.' ¹⁹You are further charged to say, 'Do this: take wagons from the land of Egypt for your little ones and for your wives, and bring your father, and come. ²⁰Give no thought to your possessions, for the best of all the land of Egypt is yours.'"

21 The sons of Israel did so. Joseph gave them wagons according to the instruction of Pharaoh, and he gave them provisions for the journey. ²²To each one of them he gave a set of garments; but to Benjamin he gave three hundred pieces of silver and five sets of garments. ²³To his father he sent the following: ten donkeys loaded with the good things of Egypt, and ten female donkeys loaded with grain, bread, and provision for his father on the journey. ²⁴Then he sent his brothers on their way, and as they were leaving he said to them, "Do not quarrelʳ along the way."

25 So they went up out of Egypt and came to their father Jacob in the land of Canaan. ²⁶And they told him, "Joseph is still alive! He is even ruler over all the land of Egypt." He was stunned; he could not believe them. ²⁷But when they told him all the words of Joseph that he had said to them, and when he saw the wagons that Joseph had sent to carry him, the spirit of their father Jacob revived. ²⁸Israel said, "Enough! My son Joseph is still alive. I must go and see him before I die."

Jacob Brings His Whole Family to Egypt

46 When Israel set out on his journey with all that he had and came to Beer-sheba, he offered sacrifices to the God of his father Isaac. ²God spoke to Israel in visions of the night, and

ʳ Or be agitated

said, "Jacob, Jacob." And he said, "Here I am." [3]Then he said, "I am God,[s] the God of your father; do not be afraid to go down to Egypt, for I will make of you a great nation there. [4]I myself will go down with you to Egypt, and I will also bring you up again; and Joseph's own hand shall close your eyes."

5 Then Jacob set out from Beer-sheba; and the sons of Israel carried their father Jacob, their little ones, and their wives, in the wagons that Pharaoh had sent to carry him. [6]They also took their livestock and the goods that they had acquired in the land of Canaan, and they came into Egypt, Jacob and all his offspring with him, [7]his sons, and his sons' sons with him, his daughters, and his sons' daughters; all his offspring he brought with him into Egypt.

8 Now these are the names of the Israelites, Jacob and his offspring, who came to Egypt. Reuben, Jacob's firstborn, [9]and the children of Reuben: Hanoch, Pallu, Hezron, and Carmi. [10]The children of Simeon: Jemuel, Jamin, Ohad, Jachin, Zohar, and Shaul,[t] the son of a Canaanite woman. [11]The children of Levi: Gershon, Kohath, and Merari. [12]The children of Judah: Er, Onan, Shelah, Perez, and Zerah (but Er and Onan died in the land of Canaan); and the children of Perez were Hezron and Hamul. [13]The children of Issachar: Tola, Puvah, Jashub,[u] and Shimron. [14]The children of Zebulun: Sered, Elon, and Jahleel [15](these are the sons of Leah, whom she bore to Jacob in Paddan-aram, together with his daughter Dinah; in all his sons and his daughters numbered thirty-three). [16]The children of Gad: Ziphion, Haggi, Shuni, Ezbon, Eri, Arodi, and Areli. [17]The children of Asher: Imnah, Ishvah, Ishvi, Beriah, and their sister Serah. The children of Beriah: Heber and Malchiel [18](these are the children of Zilpah, whom Laban gave to his daughter Leah; and these she bore to Jacob—sixteen persons). [19]The children of Jacob's wife Rachel: Joseph and Benjamin. [20]To Joseph in the land of Egypt were born Manasseh and Ephraim, whom Asenath daughter of Potiphera, priest of On, bore to him. [21]The children of Benjamin: Bela, Becher, Ashbel, Gera, Naaman, Ehi, Rosh, Muppim, Huppim, and Ard [22](these are the children of Rachel, who were born to Jacob—fourteen persons in all). [23]The children of Dan: Hashum.[v] [24]The children of Naphtali: Jahzeel, Guni, Jezer, and Shillem [25](these are the children of Bilhah, whom Laban gave to his daughter Rachel, and these she bore to Jacob—seven persons in all). [26]All the persons belonging to Jacob who came into Egypt, who were his own offspring, not including the wives of his sons, were sixty-six persons in all. [27]The children of Joseph, who were born to him in Egypt, were two; all the persons of the house of Jacob who came into Egypt were seventy.

Jacob Settles in Goshen

28 Israel[w] sent Judah ahead to Joseph to lead the way before him into Goshen. When they came to the land of Goshen, [29]Joseph made ready his chariot and went up to meet his father Israel in Goshen. He presented himself to him, fell on his neck, and wept on his neck a good while. [30]Israel said to Joseph, "I can die now, having seen for myself that you are still alive." [31]Joseph said to his brothers and to his father's household, "I will go up and tell Pharaoh, and will say to him, 'My brothers and my father's household, who were in the land of Canaan, have come to me. [32]The men are shepherds, for they have been keepers of livestock; and they have brought their flocks, and their herds, and all that they have.' [33]When Pharaoh calls you, and says, 'What is your occupation?' [34]you shall say, 'Your servants have been keepers of livestock from our youth even until now, both we and our ancestors'—in order that you may settle in the land of Goshen, because all shepherds are abhorrent to the Egyptians."

47 So Joseph went and told Pharaoh, "My father and my brothers, with their flocks and herds and all that they possess, have come from the land of Canaan; they are now in the land of Goshen." [2]From among his brothers he took five men and presented them to Pharaoh. [3]Pharaoh said to his brothers, "What is your occupation?" And they said to Pharaoh, "Your servants are shepherds, as our ancestors were." [4]They said to Pharaoh, "We have come to reside as aliens in the land; for there is no pasture for your servants' flocks because the famine is severe in the land of Canaan. Now, we ask you, let your servants settle in the land of Goshen." [5]Then Pharaoh said to Joseph, "Your father and your brothers have come to you. [6]The land of Egypt is before you; settle your father and your brothers in the best part of the land; let them live in the land of Goshen; and if you know that there are capable men among them, put them in charge of my livestock."

7 Then Joseph brought in his father Jacob, and presented him before Pharaoh, and Jacob blessed Pharaoh. [8]Pharaoh said to Jacob, "How many are the years of your life?" [9]Jacob said to Pharaoh, "The years of my earthly sojourn are one hundred thirty; few and hard have been the years of my life. They do not compare with the years of the life of my ancestors during their long sojourn." [10]Then Jacob blessed Pharaoh, and went out from the presence of Pharaoh. [11]Joseph settled his father and his brothers, and granted them a holding in the land of Egypt, in the best

---

[s] Heb the God   [t] Or Saul   [u] Compare Sam Gk Num 26.24; 1 Chr 7.1: MT Iob   [v] Gk: Heb Hushim
[w] Heb He

part of the land, in the land of Rameses, as Pharaoh had instructed. [12]And Joseph provided his father, his brothers, and all his father's household with food, according to the number of their dependents.

The Famine in Egypt

13 Now there was no food in all the land, for the famine was very severe. The land of Egypt and the land of Canaan languished because of the famine. [14]Joseph collected all the money to be found in the land of Egypt and in the land of Canaan, in exchange for the grain that they bought; and Joseph brought the money into Pharaoh's house. [15]When the money from the land of Egypt and from the land of Canaan was spent, all the Egyptians came to Joseph, and said, "Give us food! Why should we die before your eyes? For our money is gone." [16]And Joseph answered, "Give me your livestock, and I will give you food in exchange for your livestock, if your money is gone." [17]So they brought their livestock to Joseph; and Joseph gave them food in exchange for the horses, the flocks, the herds, and the donkeys. That year he supplied them with food in exchange for all their livestock. [18]When that year was ended, they came to him the following year, and said to him, "We can not hide from my lord that our money is all spent; and the herds of cattle are my lord's. There is nothing left in the sight of my lord but our bodies and our lands. [19]Shall we die before your eyes, both we and our land? Buy us and our land in exchange for food. We with our land will become slaves to Pharaoh;

just give us seed, so that we may live and not die, and that the land may not become desolate."

20 So Joseph bought all the land of Egypt for Pharaoh. All the Egyptians sold their fields, because the famine was severe upon them; and the land became Pharaoh's. [21]As for the people, he made slaves of them[x] from one end of Egypt to the other. [22]Only the land of the priests he did not buy; for the priests had a fixed allowance from Pharaoh, and lived on the allowance that Pharaoh gave them; therefore they did not sell their land. [23]Then Joseph said to the people, "Now that I have this day bought you and your land for Pharaoh, here is seed for you; sow the land. [24]And at the harvests you shall give one-fifth to Pharaoh, and four-fifths shall be your own, as seed for the field and as food for yourselves and your households, and as food for your little ones." [25]They said, "You have saved our lives; may it please my lord, we will be slaves to Pharaoh." [26]So Joseph made it a statute concerning the land of Egypt, and it stands to this day, that Pharaoh should have the fifth. The land of the priests alone did not become Pharaoh's.

The Last Days of Jacob

27 Thus Israel settled in the land of Egypt, in the region of Goshen; and they gained possessions in it, and were fruitful and multiplied exceedingly. [28]Jacob lived in the land of Egypt seventeen years; so the days of Jacob, the years of his life, were one hundred forty-seven years.

29 When the time of Israel's death drew near, he called his son Joseph and said to him, "If I have found favor with you, put your hand under my

x Sam Gk Compare Vg: MT *He removed them to the cities*

JOSEPH *School of Hard Knocks*

JOSEPH WAS A SPOILED BRAT, favored by his father over ten older brothers. He got the fancy clothes and preferential treatment and apparently thought he deserved them. When he had a dream of his brothers bowing down to him, he had the gall to tell them all about it.

What could make such a boy grow up? In Joseph's case, maturity came only through calamity. His resentful brothers threatened to kill him, then sold him to slave-traders. As a slave he resisted sexual temptation, and for his troubles was accused of rape and thrown into prison. Basically, the bottom fell out of Joseph's life.

Yet the man emerged with a wholly different character than the boy. Summoned before Pharaoh on a whim, Joseph the prisoner behaved with confidence and tact. Pharaoh gave him a huge government program to administer, and he carried out his tasks with tremendous skill.

Most remarkably, Joseph resisted the chance to get even. When his brothers fell into his hands, he struggled to forgive them rather than paying them back for their actions. In a time of famine, he saved his brothers—and his entire extended family—by bringing them down to Egypt to live with him.

Joseph's story shows how struggles and disappointments can turn out for good. They resulted in good for Joseph's family, who was able to escape a terrible famine. And they resulted in good for Joseph, who gained a whole new perspective on life. Looking back, he could see God at work even in all the trials he had experienced.

Life Questions: What struggles have you gone through? Can you see some positive effects on your personality as a result of these struggles?

thigh and promise to deal loyally and truly with me. Do not bury me in Egypt. [30]When I lie down with my ancestors, carry me out of Egypt and bury me in their burial place." He answered, "I will do as you have said." [31]And he said, "Swear to me"; and he swore to him. Then Israel bowed himself on the head of his bed.

Jacob Blesses Joseph's Sons

48 After this Joseph was told, "Your father is ill." So he took with him his two sons, Manasseh and Ephraim. [2]When Jacob was told, "Your son Joseph has come to you," he[y] summoned his strength and sat up in bed. [3]And Jacob said to Joseph, "God Almighty[z] appeared to me at Luz in the land of Canaan, and he blessed me, [4]and said to me, 'I am going to make you fruitful and increase your numbers; I will make of you a company of peoples, and will give this land to your offspring after you for a perpetual holding.' [5]Therefore your two sons, who were born to you in the land of Egypt before I came to you in Egypt, are now mine; Ephraim and Manasseh shall be mine, just as Reuben and Simeon are. [6]As for the offspring born to you after them, they shall be yours. They shall be recorded under the names of their brothers with regard to their inheritance. [7]For when I came from Paddan, Rachel, alas, died in the land of Canaan on the way, while there was still some distance to go to Ephrath; and I buried her there on the way to Ephrath" (that is, Bethlehem).

8 When Israel saw Joseph's sons, he said, "Who are these?" [9]Joseph said to his father, "They are my sons, whom God has given me here." And he said, "Bring them to me, please, that I may bless them." [10]Now the eyes of Israel were dim with age, and he could not see well. So Joseph brought them near him; and he kissed them and embraced them. [11]Israel said to Joseph, "I did not expect to see your face; and here God has let me see your children also." [12]Then Joseph removed them from his father's knees,[a] and he bowed himself with his face to the earth. [13]Joseph took them both, Ephraim in his right hand toward Israel's left, and Manasseh in his left hand toward Israel's right, and brought them near him. [14]But Israel stretched out his right hand and laid it on the head of Ephraim, who was the younger, and his left hand on the head of Manasseh, crossing his hands, for Manasseh was the firstborn. [15]He blessed Joseph, and said,

"The God before whom my ancestors
　　Abraham and Isaac walked,
the God who has been my shepherd all
　　my life to this day,
[16]　the angel who has redeemed me from all
　　harm, bless the boys;

and in them let my name be perpetuated,
　　and the name of my ancestors
　　　Abraham and Isaac;
and let them grow into a multitude on
　　the earth."

48.14–20 The Younger Brother

Jacob gave his firstborn blessings to the younger of Joseph's boys, just as had been done for Isaac over Ishmael, for Jacob over Esau, and for Joseph over Reuben. In adopting both Manasseh and Ephraim as his own sons, Jacob was also giving Joseph's family a double share in the inheritance—these two grandsons would each receive a full share along with Jacob's other 11 sons. The "12 tribes" of Israel were the offspring of Jacob's sons; substituting Manasseh and Ephraim for Joseph made a total of 13.

17 When Joseph saw that his father laid his right hand on the head of Ephraim, it displeased him; so he took his father's hand, to remove it from Ephraim's head to Manasseh's head. [18]Joseph said to his father, "Not so, my father! Since this one is the firstborn, put your right hand on his head." [19]But his father refused, and said, "I know, my son, I know; he also shall become a people, and he also shall be great. Nevertheless his younger brother shall be greater than he, and his offspring shall become a multitude of nations." [20]So he blessed them that day, saying,

"By you[b] Israel will invoke blessings,
　　saying,
'God make you[b] like Ephraim and like
　　Manasseh.'"

So he put Ephraim ahead of Manasseh. [21]Then Israel said to Joseph, "I am about to die, but God will be with you and will bring you again to the land of your ancestors. [22]I now give to you one portion[c] more than to your brothers, the portion[c] that I took from the hand of the Amorites with my sword and with my bow."

Jacob's Last Words to His Sons

49 Then Jacob called his sons, and said: "Gather around, that I may tell you what will happen to you in days to come.
[2]　Assemble and hear, O sons of Jacob;
　　listen to Israel your father.

[3]　Reuben, you are my firstborn,
　　my might and the first fruits of my
　　　vigor,
　　excelling in rank and excelling in
　　　power.

---

[y] Heb *Israel*　　[z] Traditional rendering of Heb *El Shaddai*　　[a] Heb *from his knees*　　[b] *you* here is singular in Heb
[c] Or *mountain slope* (Heb *shekem*, a play on the name of the town and district of Shechem)

4 Unstable as water, you shall no longer
    excel
  because you went up onto your father's
    bed;
  then you defiled it—you[d] went up
    onto my couch!

5 Simeon and Levi are brothers;
    weapons of violence are their swords.
6 May I never come into their council;
  may I not be joined to their
    company—
  for in their anger they killed men,
    and at their whim they hamstrung
    oxen.
7 Cursed be their anger, for it is fierce,
    and their wrath, for it is cruel!
  I will divide them in Jacob,
    and scatter them in Israel.

8 Judah, your brothers shall praise you;
    your hand shall be on the neck of your
    enemies;
  your father's sons shall bow down
    before you.
9 Judah is a lion's whelp;
  from the prey, my son, you have gone
    up.
  He crouches down, he stretches out like a
    lion,
  like a lioness—who dares rouse him
    up?
10 The scepter shall not depart from Judah,
    nor the ruler's staff from between his
    feet,
  until tribute comes to him;[e]
    and the obedience of the peoples is his.
11 Binding his foal to the vine
    and his donkey's colt to the choice
    vine,
  he washes his garments in wine
    and his robe in the blood of grapes;
12 his eyes are darker than wine,
    and his teeth whiter than milk.

13 Zebulun shall settle at the shore of the
    sea;
  he shall be a haven for ships,
    and his border shall be at Sidon.

14 Issachar is a strong donkey,
    lying down between the sheepfolds;
15 he saw that a resting place was good,
    and that the land was pleasant;
  so he bowed his shoulder to the burden,
    and became a slave at forced labor.

16 Dan shall judge his people
    as one of the tribes of Israel.
17 Dan shall be a snake by the roadside,
    a viper along the path,
  that bites the horse's heels
    so that its rider falls backward.

18 I wait for your salvation, O LORD.

19 Gad shall be raided by raiders,
    but he shall raid at their heels.

20 Asher's[f] food shall be rich,
    and he shall provide royal delicacies.

21 Naphtali is a doe let loose
    that bears lovely fawns.[g]

22 Joseph is a fruitful bough,
    a fruitful bough by a spring;
  his branches run over the wall.[h]
23 The archers fiercely attacked him;
    they shot at him and pressed him hard.
24 Yet his bow remained taut,
    and his arms[i] were made agile
  by the hands of the Mighty One of Jacob,
    by the name of the Shepherd, the Rock
    of Israel,
25 by the God of your father, who will help
    you,
  by the Almighty[j] who will bless you
    with blessings of heaven above,
  blessings of the deep that lies beneath,
    blessings of the breasts and of the
    womb.
26 The blessings of your father
    are stronger than the blessings of the
    eternal mountains,
  the bounties[k] of the everlasting hills;
  may they be on the head of Joseph,
    on the brow of him who was set apart
    from his brothers.

27 Benjamin is a ravenous wolf,
    in the morning devouring the prey,
    and at evening dividing the spoil."

28 All these are the twelve tribes of Israel, and
this is what their father said to them when he
blessed them, blessing each one of them with a
suitable blessing.

Jacob's Death and Burial

29 Then he charged them, saying to them, "I
am about to be gathered to my people. Bury me
with my ancestors—in the cave in the field of

[d] Gk Syr Tg: Heb he   [e] Or until Shiloh comes or until he comes to Shiloh or (with Syr) until he comes to whom it
belongs   [f] Gk Vg Syr: Heb From Asher   [g] Or that gives beautiful words   [h] Meaning of Heb uncertain
[i] Heb the arms of his hands   [j] Traditional rendering of Heb Shaddai   [k] Cn Compare Gk: Heb of my progenitors to
the boundaries

Ephron the Hittite, [30]in the cave in the field at Machpelah, near Mamre, in the land of Canaan, in the field that Abraham bought from Ephron the Hittite as a burial site. [31]There Abraham and his wife Sarah were buried; there Isaac and his wife Rebekah were buried; and there I buried Leah— [32]the field and the cave that is in it were purchased from the Hittites." [33]When Jacob ended his charge to his sons, he drew up his feet into the bed, breathed his last, and was gathered to his people.

50 Then Joseph threw himself on his father's face and wept over him and kissed him. [2]Joseph commanded the physicians in his service to embalm his father. So the physicians embalmed Israel; [3]they spent forty days in doing this, for that is the time required for embalming. And the Egyptians wept for him seventy days.

50.3 An Egyptian Funeral

Joseph's political importance is underlined by this elaborate mummification procedure for his father. Jacob's mourning period was only two days shorter than that given for a pharaoh. All the court dignitaries went along for the funeral, a substantial journey (verse 7).

4 When the days of weeping for him were past, Joseph addressed the household of Pharaoh, "If now I have found favor with you, please speak to Pharaoh as follows: [5]My father made me swear an oath; he said, 'I am about to die. In the tomb that I hewed out for myself in the land of Canaan, there you shall bury me.' Now therefore let me go up, so that I may bury my father; then I will return." [6]Pharaoh answered, "Go up, and bury your father, as he made you swear to do."

7 So Joseph went up to bury his father. With him went up all the servants of Pharaoh, the elders of his household, and all the elders of the land of Egypt, [8]as well as all the household of Joseph, his brothers, and his father's household. Only their children, their flocks, and their herds were left in the land of Goshen. [9]Both chariots and charioteers went up with him. It was a very great company. [10]When they came to the threshing floor of Atad, which is beyond the Jordan, they held there a very great and sorrowful lamentation; and he observed a time of mourning for his father seven days. [11]When the Canaanite inhabitants of the land saw the mourning on the threshing floor of Atad, they said, "This is a grievous mourning on the part of the Egyptians." Therefore the place was named Abel-mizraim;[l] it is beyond the Jordan. [12]Thus his sons did for

him as he had instructed them. [13]They carried him to the land of Canaan and buried him in the cave of the field at Machpelah, the field near Mamre, which Abraham bought as a burial site from Ephron the Hittite. [14]After he had buried his father, Joseph returned to Egypt with his brothers and all who had gone up with him to bury his father.

Joseph Forgives His Brothers

15 Realizing that their father was dead, Joseph's brothers said, "What if Joseph still bears a grudge against us and pays us back in full for all the wrong that we did to him?" [16]So they approached[m] Joseph, saying, "Your father gave this instruction before he died, [17]'Say to Joseph: I beg you, forgive the crime of your brothers and the wrong they did in harming you.' Now therefore please forgive the crime of the servants of the God of your father." Joseph wept when they spoke to him. [18]Then his brothers also wept,[n] fell down before him, and said, "We are here as your slaves." [19]But Joseph said to them, "Do not be afraid! Am I in the place of God? [20]Even though you intended to do harm to me, God intended it for good, in order to preserve a numerous people, as he is doing today. [21]So have no fear; I myself will provide for you and your little ones." In this way he reassured them, speaking kindly to them.

50.20 You Intended Evil

Joseph's summation of his experience might apply to many human situations: You intended evil, but God intended good. Joseph's trust that God can bring good out of bad intentions enabled him finally to forgive his brothers, leaving judgment to God.

Joseph's Last Days and Death

22 So Joseph remained in Egypt, he and his father's household; and Joseph lived one hundred ten years. [23]Joseph saw Ephraim's children of the third generation; the children of Machir son of Manasseh were also born on Joseph's knees.

24 Then Joseph said to his brothers, "I am about to die; but God will surely come to you, and bring you up out of this land to the land that he swore to Abraham, to Isaac, and to Jacob." [25]So Joseph made the Israelites swear, saying, "When God comes to you, you shall carry up my bones from here." [26]And Joseph died, being one hundred ten years old; he was embalmed and placed in a coffin in Egypt.

---

[l] That is *mourning* (or *meadow*) *of Egypt*   [m] Gk Syr: Heb *they commanded*   [n] Cn: Heb *also came*

EXODUS

Free at Last
The slaves in Egypt get a liberator

NOTHING STIRS A NATION'S BLOOD like a liberator. The United States remembers two especially: Washington and Lincoln. George Washington led the original fight for independence. A century later Abraham Lincoln set three million people free when he signed the Emancipation Proclamation.

Other places, too, have liberators. India called a scrawny little man named Gandhi "Mahatma" (or "the great one") for leading his people to freedom. Poles honored Lech Walesa, the first freely elected head of state, for liberating Poland from Soviet communism. For the Israelites, one liberator named Moses accomplished what all these did—and more.

The Bible devotes one-eighth of its pages to the story of Moses' time (a bulk of material two-thirds the length of the entire New Testament). And when Jesus came as the great Liberator who set all humanity free, the New Testament reached back to Moses for a comparison (Hebrews 3.1–6).

> Then the LORD said, "I have observed the misery of my people who are in Egypt; I have heard their cry on account of their taskmasters. Indeed, I know their sufferings." 3.7

Bondage in Egypt

The time was ripe for a liberator. Genesis closed with Jacob's family of 70 moving to Egypt. But in the opening scene of Exodus, 350 years later, hundreds of thousands of their ancestors were toiling on Pharaoh's huge construction projects—not as guests but as slaves.

One particularly ruthless pharaoh ordered the murder of all male Israelite babies, unwittingly setting the stage for one of the great ironies of history. Moses' parents hid him in a watertight basket among the grasses of a swamp. There, the tiny baby caught the eye of the pharaoh's daughter. The very edict intended to destroy the Israelites led to their deliverance.

Adopted into the palace, Moses got the benefit of a superb classical education. His Egyptian upbringing was balanced by Israelite nurture: In another striking irony, the pharaoh's daughter paid Moses' own mother to nurse him. The son of slaves, yet brought up in the seat of power, Moses prepared for his eventual goal of forging a nation out of a ragtag band of captives.

His career had to wait, though, for a period of humbling in the desert. Moses fled Egypt as a brash, self-confident man who liked to take matters into his own hands. Forty years later he reluctantly returned, with little besides a stick and a donkey.

Free at Last

The Israelites had endured nearly four centuries of oppression—almost twice as long as the history of America as a nation—before liberation. So far as we know, during those years they received no direct communication from heaven. Surely God must have seemed silent.

Moses faced a formidable challenge. Somehow he had to earn the trust of the slaves and inspire hope in them so that they could indeed throw off their chains. He had to prove that God had not forgotten them. When the time was right, God unleashed a spectacle of might and power that brought a cruel pharaoh to his knees—and convinced the Israelites that God really did care for them.

God used Moses in remarkable ways. He was the first person recorded in the Bible to work miracles. He met God in intimate ways granted no other human. He had a hand in the authorship of a good portion of the Old Testament. But in Jewish history he earned a place primarily as a liberator. He led the march from slavery to freedom, from Egypt to the promised land.

How to Read Exodus

Exodus divides neatly into two parts. The first 20 chapters, on the Israelites' flight from Egypt, read like an exciting novel. Movies based on the action here have strained Hollywood special-effects crews. Everything else in the Old Testament flows out of the events of the exodus—these 20 chapters simply cannot be missed.

As you read Exodus, look for important lessons that apply to your life. For example, study the life of Moses, one of a handful of truly great leaders in history. Chapter 18 shows Moses learning an important leadership principle, and chapters 32–35 include encounters and conversations with God that have no equal in the Bible.

Exodus contains much material about the nature of God. Search for each place where God makes an appearance. Exodus shows a greater proportion of miracles—direct supernatural acts of God—than any part of the Bible except the Gospels. Why were these miracles done? Can you see a pattern? What should the Israelites have learned from them? Did they?

The last 20 chapters mainly consist of laws and regulations, given at Mount Sinai, to govern the life of the nation. Read them to note the concerns and priorities important to God as he designs an entire culture.

The instructions are usually clustered in groups, encompassing every area of life:

1. Moral rules, such as the Ten Commandments
2. Civil and social rules, much like a criminal code
3. Religious and ceremonial rules for the Israelites.

See "A National Law Library," page 143, for more information on these laws.

The religious rituals with their many sacrifices and feasts seem strange to modern Westerners, but they were not at all unusual then. Also, they prepared the way for a Redeemer who was greater than Moses: Jesus Christ. You will need study books and commentaries to find all the symbols that apply to Jesus' life, as shown, for example, in the Passover. Fortunately, the Bible includes a brief but powerful commentary in Hebrews (see especially Hebrews 7–10). This book should be read alongside Exodus and the three books that follow.

PEOPLE YOU'LL MEET IN EXODUS

MOSES *(p. 79)*
JETHRO *(p. 97)*

3-TRACK READING PLAN

For an explanation and complete listing of the 3-track reading plan, turn to page 7.

TRACK 1: *Two-Week Courses on the Bible*
The Track 1 reading program on the Old Testament includes two chapters from Exodus. See page 7 for a complete listing of this course.

TRACK 2: *An Overview of Exodus in 5 Days*
- ☐ Day 1. Read the Introduction to Exodus and then chapter 3, God's call of Moses.
- ☐ Day 2. Read chapter 10 and the very brief chapter 11; they record three of the ten plagues against Egypt.
- ☐ Day 3. Read chapter 14, which contains the exciting story of crossing the Red Sea.
- ☐ Day 4. Read the Ten Commandments as recorded in chapter 20. (If you have time, chapter 19 gives the dramatic setting for these laws.)
- ☐ Day 5. Read chapter 32. It records the most striking example of what was to become a characteristic of the Israelites: mass rebellion.

Now turn to page 9 for your next Track 2 reading project.

TRACK 3: *All of Exodus in 39 Days*
After you have read through Exodus, turn to pages 10–14 for your next Track 3 reading project.

☐1	☐2	☐3	☐4	☐5	☐6	☐7	☐8
☐9	☐10–11	☐12	☐13	☐14	☐15	☐16	☐17
☐18	☐19	☐20	☐21	☐22	☐23	☐24	☐25
☐26	☐27	☐28	☐29	☐30	☐31	☐32	☐33
☐34	☐35	☐36	☐37	☐38	☐39	☐40	

1 These are the names of the sons of Israel who came to Egypt with Jacob, each with his household: ²Reuben, Simeon, Levi, and Judah, ³Issachar, Zebulun, and Benjamin, ⁴Dan and Naphtali, Gad and Asher. ⁵The total number of people born to Jacob was seventy. Joseph was already in Egypt. ⁶Then Joseph died, and all his brothers, and that whole generation. ⁷But the Israelites were fruitful and prolific; they multiplied and grew exceedingly strong, so that the land was filled with them.

The Israelites Are Oppressed

8 Now a new king arose over Egypt, who did not know Joseph. ⁹He said to his people, "Look, the Israelite people are more numerous and more powerful than we. ¹⁰Come, let us deal shrewdly with them, or they will increase and, in the event of war, join our enemies and fight against us and escape from the land." ¹¹Therefore they set taskmasters over them to oppress them with forced labor. They built supply cities, Pithom and Rameses, for Pharaoh. ¹²But the more they were oppressed, the more they multiplied and spread, so that the Egyptians came to dread the Israelites. ¹³The Egyptians became ruthless in imposing tasks on the Israelites, ¹⁴and made their lives bitter with hard service in mortar and brick and in every kind of field labor. They were ruthless in all the tasks that they imposed on them.

15 The king of Egypt said to the Hebrew midwives, one of whom was named Shiphrah and the other Puah, ¹⁶"When you act as midwives to the Hebrew women, and see them on the birthstool, if it is a boy, kill him; but if it is a girl, she shall

1.16 New Tyrant in Town

Dictators often take out their wrath on a helpless minority: witness Hitler and the Jews or Saddam Hussein and the Kurds. At first pharaohs welcomed their Hebrew guests, and God used the peace and quiet of Egypt, far from the squabbling tribes of Canaan, to "grow" the people of Israel. But now the Israelites' very size and strength threatened the new pharaoh, who ruthlessly clamped down on them.

live." ¹⁷But the midwives feared God; they did not do as the king of Egypt commanded them, but they let the boys live. ¹⁸So the king of Egypt summoned the midwives and said to them, "Why have you done this, and allowed the boys to live?" ¹⁹The midwives said to Pharaoh, "Because the Hebrew women are not like the Egyptian women; for they are vigorous and give birth before the midwife comes to them." ²⁰So God dealt well with the midwives; and the people multiplied and be-

came very strong. ²¹And because the midwives feared God, he gave them families. ²²Then Pharaoh commanded all his people, "Every boy that is born to the Hebrews[a] you shall throw into the Nile, but you shall let every girl live."

Birth and Youth of Moses

2 Now a man from the house of Levi went and married a Levite woman. ²The woman conceived and bore a son; and when she saw that he was a fine baby, she hid him three months. ³When she could hide him no longer she got a papyrus basket for him, and plastered it with bitumen and pitch; she put the child in it and placed it among the reeds on the bank of the river. ⁴His sister stood at a distance, to see what would happen to him.

5 The daughter of Pharaoh came down to bathe at the river, while her attendants walked beside the river. She saw the basket among the reeds and sent her maid to bring it. ⁶When she opened it, she saw the child. He was crying, and she took pity on him. "This must be one of the Hebrews' children," she said. ⁷Then his sister said to Pharaoh's daughter, "Shall I go and get you a nurse from the Hebrew women to nurse the child for you?" ⁸Pharaoh's daughter said to her, "Yes." So the girl went and called the child's mother. ⁹Pharaoh's daughter said to her, "Take this child and nurse it for me, and I will give you your wages." So the woman took the child and nursed it. ¹⁰When the child grew up, she brought him to Pharaoh's daughter, and she took him as her son. She named him Moses,[b] "because," she said, "I drew him out[c] of the water."

Moses Flees to Midian

11 One day, after Moses had grown up, he went out to his people and saw their forced labor. He saw an Egyptian beating a Hebrew, one of his kinsfolk. ¹²He looked this way and that, and seeing no one he killed the Egyptian and hid him in the sand. ¹³When he went out the next day, he

2.10 Selective History

Exodus illustrates how selective the Bible's history is. The first chapter, for example, skips over the name of the Egyptian pharaoh (leaving a riddle for scholars to argue over ever since), and yet identifies by name two Hebrew midwives (1.15). After compressing three-and-a-half centuries into a few verses, Exodus devotes chapters 3–40 to the events of a single year. In contrast to Genesis's large cast of characters, Exodus focuses on one main character, Moses.

---

a Sam Gk Tg: Heb lacks *to the Hebrews*   *b* Heb *Mosheh*   *c* Heb *mashah*

saw two Hebrews fighting; and he said to the one who was in the wrong, "Why do you strike your fellow Hebrew?" [14]He answered, "Who made you a ruler and judge over us? Do you mean to kill me as you killed the Egyptian?" Then Moses was afraid and thought, "Surely the thing is known." [15]When Pharaoh heard of it, he sought to kill Moses.

But Moses fled from Pharaoh. He settled in the land of Midian, and sat down by a well. [16]The priest of Midian had seven daughters. They came to draw water, and filled the troughs to water their father's flock. [17]But some shepherds came and drove them away. Moses got up and came to their defense and watered their flock. [18]When they returned to their father Reuel, he said, "How is it that you have come back so soon today?" [19]They said, "An Egyptian helped us against the shepherds; he even drew water for us and watered the flock." [20]He said to his daughters, "Where is he? Why did you leave the man? Invite him to break bread." [21]Moses agreed to stay with the man, and he gave Moses his daughter Zipporah in marriage. [22]She bore a son, and he named him Gershom; for he said, "I have been an alien[d] residing in a foreign land."

23 After a long time the king of Egypt died. The Israelites groaned under their slavery, and cried out. Out of the slavery their cry for help rose up to God. [24]God heard their groaning, and God remembered his covenant with Abraham, Isaac, and Jacob. [25]God looked upon the Israelites, and God took notice of them.

Moses at the Burning Bush

3 Moses was keeping the flock of his father-in-law Jethro, the priest of Midian; he led his flock beyond the wilderness, and came to Horeb, the mountain of God. [2]There the angel of the LORD appeared to him in a flame of fire out of a bush; he looked, and the bush was blazing, yet it was not consumed. [3]Then Moses said, "I must turn aside and look at this great sight, and see why the bush is not burned up." [4]When the LORD saw that he had turned aside to see, God called to him out of the bush, "Moses, Moses!" And he said, "Here I am." [5]Then he said, "Come no closer! Remove the sandals from your feet, for the place on which you are standing is holy ground." [6]He said further, "I am the God of your father, the God of Abraham, the God of Isaac, and the God of Jacob." And Moses hid his face, for he was afraid to look at God.

7 Then the LORD said, "I have observed the misery of my people who are in Egypt; I have heard their cry on account of their taskmasters. Indeed, I know their sufferings, [8]and I have come down to deliver them from the Egyptians, and to bring them up out of that land to a good and broad land, a land flowing with milk and honey, to the country of the Canaanites, the Hittites, the Amorites, the Perizzites, the Hivites, and the Jebusites. [9]The cry of the Israelites has now come to me; I have also seen how the Egyptians oppress them. [10]So come, I will send you to Pharaoh to bring my people, the Israelites, out of Egypt." [11]But Moses said to God, "Who am I that I should go to Pharaoh, and bring the Israelites out of

3.11–13 Who, Me?

Moses had big doubts about his ability to lead. He resisted God, bringing up his unworthiness (here) and lack of authority (verse 13), his fear of the people's distrust (4.1), his speech difficulties (4.10), and his sheer cowardice (4.13). The remainder of Exodus should give people with similar self-doubts great hope, for it traces Moses' personal development from this fumbling start to his emergence as one of history's most decisive and powerful leaders.

Egypt?" [12]He said, "I will be with you; and this shall be the sign for you that it is I who sent you: when you have brought the people out of Egypt, you shall worship God on this mountain."

The Divine Name Revealed

13 But Moses said to God, "If I come to the Israelites and say to them, 'The God of your ancestors has sent me to you,' and they ask me, 'What is his name?' what shall I say to them?" [14]God said to Moses, "I AM WHO I AM."[e] He said further, "Thus you shall say to the Israelites, 'I AM has sent me to you.'" [15]God also said to Moses, "Thus you shall say to the Israelites, 'The LORD,[f] the God of your ancestors, the God of Abraham, the God of Isaac, and the God of Jacob, has sent me to you':

This is my name forever,
and this my title for all generations.

[16]Go and assemble the elders of Israel, and say to them, 'The LORD, the God of your ancestors, the God of Abraham, of Isaac, and of Jacob, has appeared to me, saying: I have given heed to you and to what has been done to you in Egypt. [17]I declare that I will bring you up out of the misery of Egypt, to the land of the Canaanites, the Hittites, the Amorites, the Perizzites, the Hivites, and the Jebusites, a land flowing with milk and honey.' [18]They will listen to your voice; and you and the elders of Israel shall go to the king of Egypt and say to him, 'The LORD, the God of the Hebrews, has met with us; let us now go a three days' journey into the wilderness, so that we may sacri-

---

[d] Heb *ger*   [e] Or *I AM WHAT I AM* or *I WILL BE WHAT I WILL BE*   [f] The word "LORD" when spelled with capital letters stands for the divine name, *YHWH*, which is here connected with the verb *hayah*, "to be"

fice to the LORD our God.' ¹⁹I know, however, that the king of Egypt will not let you go unless compelled by a mighty hand.⁸ ²⁰So I will stretch out my hand and strike Egypt with all my wonders that I will perform in it; after that he will let you go. ²¹I will bring this people into such favor with the Egyptians that, when you go, you will not go empty-handed; ²²each woman shall ask her neighbor and any woman living in the neighbor's house for jewelry of silver and of gold, and clothing, and you shall put them on your sons and on your daughters; and so you shall plunder the Egyptians."

Moses' Miraculous Power

4 Then Moses answered, "But suppose they do not believe me or listen to me, but say, 'The LORD did not appear to you.'" ²The LORD said to him, "What is that in your hand?" He said, "A staff." ³And he said, "Throw it on the ground." So he threw the staff on the ground, and it became a snake; and Moses drew back from it. ⁴Then the LORD said to Moses, "Reach out your hand, and seize it by the tail"—so he reached out his hand and grasped it, and it became a staff in his hand— ⁵"so that they may believe that the LORD, the God of their ancestors, the God of Abraham, the God of Isaac, and the God of Jacob, has appeared to you."

6 Again, the LORD said to him, "Put your hand inside your cloak." He put his hand into his cloak; and when he took it out, his hand was leprous,ʰ as white as snow. ⁷Then God said, "Put your hand back into your cloak"—so he put his hand back into his cloak, and when he took it out, it was restored like the rest of his body— ⁸"If they will not believe you or heed the first sign, they may believe the second sign. ⁹If they will not believe even these two signs or heed you, you shall take some water from the Nile and pour it on the dry ground; and the water that you shall take from the Nile will become blood on the dry ground."

10 But Moses said to the LORD, "O my Lord, I have never been eloquent, neither in the past nor even now that you have spoken to your servant; but I am slow of speech and slow of tongue." ¹¹Then the LORD said to him, "Who gives speech to mortals? Who makes them mute or deaf, seeing or blind? Is it not I, the LORD? ¹²Now go, and I will be with your mouth and teach you what you are to speak." ¹³But he said, "O my Lord, please send someone else." ¹⁴Then the anger of the LORD was kindled against Moses and he said, "What of your brother Aaron the Levite? I know that he can speak fluently; even now he is coming out to meet you, and when he sees you his heart will be glad. ¹⁵You shall speak to him and put the words in his mouth; and I will

be with your mouth and with his mouth, and will teach you what you shall do. ¹⁶He indeed shall speak for you to the people; he shall serve as a mouth for you, and you shall serve as God for him. ¹⁷Take in your hand this staff, with which you shall perform the signs."

Moses Returns to Egypt

18 Moses went back to his father-in-law Jethro and said to him, "Please let me go back to my kindred in Egypt and see whether they are still living." And Jethro said to Moses, "Go in peace." ¹⁹The LORD said to Moses in Midian, "Go back to Egypt; for all those who were seeking your life are dead." ²⁰So Moses took his wife and his sons, put them on a donkey, and went back to the land of Egypt; and Moses carried the staff of God in his hand.

21 And the LORD said to Moses, "When you go back to Egypt, see that you perform before Pharaoh all the wonders that I have put in your power; but I will harden his heart, so that he will not let the people go. ²²Then you shall say to Pharaoh, 'Thus says the LORD: Israel is my firstborn son. ²³I said to you, "Let my son go that he may worship me." But you refused to let him go; now I will kill your firstborn son.'"

24 On the way, at a place where they spent the night, the LORD met him and tried to kill him. ²⁵But Zipporah took a flint and cut off her son's foreskin, and touched Moses'ⁱ feet with it, and said, "Truly you are a bridegroom of blood to me!" ²⁶So he let him alone. It was then she said, "A bridegroom of blood by circumcision."

27 The LORD said to Aaron, "Go into the wilderness to meet Moses." So he went; and he met him at the mountain of God and kissed him. ²⁸Moses told Aaron all the words of the LORD with which he had sent him, and all the signs with which he had charged him. ²⁹Then Moses and Aaron went and assembled all the elders of the Israelites. ³⁰Aaron spoke all the words that the LORD had spoken to Moses, and performed the signs in the sight of the people. ³¹The people believed; and when they heard that the LORD had given heed to the Israelites and that he had seen their misery, they bowed down and worshiped.

Bricks without Straw

5 Afterward Moses and Aaron went to Pharaoh and said, "Thus says the LORD, the God of Israel, 'Let my people go, so that they may celebrate a festival to me in the wilderness.'" ²But Pharaoh said, "Who is the LORD, that I should heed him and let Israel go? I do not know the LORD, and I will not let Israel go." ³Then they said, "The God of the Hebrews has revealed himself to us; let us go a three days' journey into the wilderness to sacrifice to the LORD our God, or he will

g Gk Vg: Heb no, not by a mighty hand   *h A term for several skin diseases; precise meaning uncertain*   *i Heb his*

fall upon us with pestilence or sword." ⁴But the king of Egypt said to them, "Moses and Aaron, why are you taking the people away from their work? Get to your labors!" ⁵Pharaoh continued, "Now they are more numerous than the people of the land ʲ and yet you want them to stop working!" ⁶That same day Pharaoh commanded the taskmasters of the people, as well as their supervisors, ⁷"You shall no longer give the people straw to make bricks, as before; let them go and gather straw for themselves. ⁸But you shall require of them the same quantity of bricks as they have made previously; do not diminish it, for they are lazy; that is why they cry, 'Let us go and offer sacrifice to our God.' ⁹Let heavier work be laid on them; then they will labor at it and pay no attention to deceptive words."

10 So the taskmasters and the supervisors of the people went out and said to the people, "Thus

5.10 Three Kinds of Bricks

Archaeologists digging up settlements from ancient Egypt have unearthed three kinds of sun-dried bricks—some made of good straw, some containing mere roots and bits of straw, and some with no straw—confirming this account of slave labor.

says Pharaoh, 'I will not give you straw. ¹¹Go and get straw yourselves, wherever you can find it; but your work will not be lessened in the least.'" ¹²So the people scattered throughout the land of Egypt, to gather stubble for straw. ¹³The taskmasters were urgent, saying, "Complete your work, the same daily assignment as when you were given straw." ¹⁴And the supervisors of the Israelites, whom Pharaoh's taskmasters had set over them, were beaten, and were asked, "Why did you not finish the required quantity of bricks yesterday and today, as you did before?"

15 Then the Israelite supervisors came to Pharaoh and cried, "Why do you treat your servants like this? ¹⁶No straw is given to your servants, yet they say to us, 'Make bricks!' Look how your servants are beaten! You are unjust to your own people."ᵏ ¹⁷He said, "You are lazy, lazy; that is why you say, 'Let us go and sacrifice to the LORD.' ¹⁸Go now, and work; for no straw shall be given you, but you shall still deliver the same number of bricks." ¹⁹The Israelite supervisors saw that they were in trouble when they were told, "You shall not lessen your daily number of bricks." ²⁰As they left Pharaoh, they came upon Moses and Aaron who were waiting to meet them. ²¹They said to them, "The LORD look upon you and judge! You have brought us into bad

odor with Pharaoh and his officials, and have put a sword in their hand to kill us."

22 Then Moses turned again to the LORD and said, "O LORD, why have you mistreated this people? Why did you ever send me? ²³Since I first came to Pharaoh to speak in your name, he has mistreated this people, and you have done nothing at all to deliver your people."

Israel's Deliverance Assured

6 Then the LORD said to Moses, "Now you shall see what I will do to Pharaoh: Indeed, by a mighty hand he will let them go; by a mighty hand he will drive them out of his land."

2 God also spoke to Moses and said to him: "I am the LORD. ³I appeared to Abraham, Isaac, and Jacob as God Almighty,ˡ but by my name 'The LORD'ᵐ I did not make myself known to them. ⁴I also established my covenant with them, to give them the land of Canaan, the land in which they resided as aliens. ⁵I have also heard the groaning of the Israelites whom the Egyptians are holding as slaves, and I have remembered my covenant. ⁶Say therefore to the Israelites, 'I am the LORD, and I will free you from the burdens of the Egyptians and deliver you from slavery to them. I will redeem you with an outstretched arm and with mighty acts of judgment. ⁷I will take you as my people, and I will be your God. You shall know that I am the LORD your God, who has freed you from the burdens of the Egyptians. ⁸I will bring you into the land that I swore to give to Abraham, Isaac, and Jacob; I will give it to you for a possession. I am the LORD.'" ⁹Moses told this to the Israelites; but they would not listen to Moses, because of their broken spirit and their cruel slavery.

6.6–9 Oppressed by Egypt

With Egypt at the peak of its power, Pharaoh used slaves to build massive monuments, enforcing his rule with an army of renowned charioteers and bowmen. Egyptian hieroglyphics pictured the word for foreigner as a bound man with blood flowing from a wound in his head; the Israelites felt the full weight of such oppression. For a while, the increasing cruelty of Egyptian taskmasters turned the Israelites against Moses and his campaign to free them. But this oppression also made them anxious to leave.

10 Then the LORD spoke to Moses, ¹¹"Go and tell Pharaoh king of Egypt to let the Israelites go out of his land." ¹²But Moses spoke to the LORD, "The Israelites have not listened to me; how then shall Pharaoh listen to me, poor speaker that I

ʲ Sam: Heb *The people of the land are now many*   ᵏ Gk Compare Syr Vg: Heb *beaten, and the sin of your people*
ˡ Traditional rendering of Heb *El Shaddai*   ᵐ Heb *YHWH*; see note at 3.15

am?"[n] 13 Thus the LORD spoke to Moses and Aaron, and gave them orders regarding the Israelites and Pharaoh king of Egypt, charging them to free the Israelites from the land of Egypt.

The Genealogy of Moses and Aaron

14 The following are the heads of their ancestral houses: the sons of Reuben, the firstborn of Israel: Hanoch, Pallu, Hezron, and Carmi; these are the families of Reuben. 15 The sons of Simeon: Jemuel, Jamin, Ohad, Jachin, Zohar, and Shaul,[o] the son of a Canaanite woman; these are the families of Simeon. 16 The following are the names of the sons of Levi according to their genealogies: Gershon,[p] Kohath, and Merari, and the length of Levi's life was one hundred thirty-seven years. 17 The sons of Gershon:[p] Libni and Shimei, by their families. 18 The sons of Kohath: Amram, Izhar, Hebron, and Uzziel, and the length of Kohath's life was one hundred thirty-three years. 19 The sons of Merari: Mahli and Mushi. These are the families of the Levites according to their genealogies. 20 Amram married Jochebed his father's sister and she bore him Aaron and Moses, and the length of Amram's life was one hundred thirty-seven years. 21 The sons of Izhar: Korah, Nepheg, and Zichri. 22 The sons of Uzziel: Mishael, Elzaphan, and Sithri. 23 Aaron married Elisheba, daughter of Amminadab and sister of Nahshon, and she bore him Nadab, Abihu, Eleazar, and Ithamar. 24 The sons of Korah: Assir, Elkanah, and Abiasaph; these are the families of the Korahites. 25 Aaron's son Eleazar married one of the daughters of Putiel, and she bore him Phinehas. These are the heads of the ancestral houses of the Levites by their families.

26 It was this same Aaron and Moses to whom the LORD said, "Bring the Israelites out of the land of Egypt, company by company." 27 It was they who spoke to Pharaoh king of Egypt to bring the Israelites out of Egypt, the same Moses and Aaron.

Moses and Aaron Obey God's Commands

28 On the day when the LORD spoke to Moses in the land of Egypt, 29 he said to him, "I am the LORD; tell Pharaoh king of Egypt all that I am speaking to you." 30 But Moses said in the LORD's presence, "Since I am a poor speaker,[q] why would Pharaoh listen to me?"

7 The LORD said to Moses, "See, I have made you like God to Pharaoh, and your brother Aaron shall be your prophet. 2 You shall speak all that I command you, and your brother Aaron shall tell Pharaoh to let the Israelites go out of his land. 3 But I will harden Pharaoh's heart, and I will multiply my signs and wonders in the land of Egypt. 4 When Pharaoh does not listen to you, I will lay my hand upon Egypt and bring my people the Israelites, company by company, out of the land of Egypt by great acts of judgment. 5 The Egyptians shall know that I am the LORD, when I stretch out my hand against Egypt and bring the Israelites out from among them." 6 Moses and Aaron did so; they did just as the LORD commanded them. 7 Moses was eighty years old and Aaron eighty-three when they spoke to Pharaoh.

Aaron's Miraculous Rod

8 The LORD said to Moses and Aaron, 9 "When Pharaoh says to you, 'Perform a wonder,' then you shall say to Aaron, 'Take your staff and throw it down before Pharaoh, and it will become a snake.'" 10 So Moses and Aaron went to Pharaoh and did as the LORD had commanded; Aaron threw down his staff before Pharaoh and his officials, and it became a snake. 11 Then Pharaoh summoned the wise men and the sorcerers; and they also, the magicians of Egypt, did the same by their secret arts. 12 Each one threw down his staff, and they became snakes; but Aaron's staff swallowed up theirs. 13 Still Pharaoh's heart was hardened, and he would not listen to them, as the LORD had said.

The First Plague: Water Turned to Blood

14 Then the LORD said to Moses, "Pharaoh's heart is hardened; he refuses to let the people go. 15 Go to Pharaoh in the morning, as he is going out to the water; stand by at the river bank to meet him, and take in your hand the staff that was turned into a snake. 16 Say to him, 'The LORD, the God of the Hebrews, sent me to you to say, "Let my people go, so that they may worship me in the wilderness." But until now you have not listened. 17 Thus says the LORD, "By this you shall know that I am the LORD." See, with the staff that is in my hand I will strike the water that is in the Nile, and it shall be turned to blood. 18 The fish in the river shall die, the river itself shall stink, and the Egyptians shall be unable to drink water from the Nile.'" 19 The LORD said to Moses, "Say to Aaron, 'Take your staff and stretch out your hand over the waters of Egypt—over its rivers, its canals, and its ponds, and all its pools of water—so that they may become blood; and there shall be blood throughout the whole land of Egypt, even in vessels of wood and in vessels of stone.'"

20 Moses and Aaron did just as the LORD commanded. In the sight of Pharaoh and of his officials he lifted up the staff and struck the water in the river, and all the water in the river was turned into blood, 21 and the fish in the river died. The river stank so that the Egyptians could not drink its water, and there was blood throughout the whole land of Egypt. 22 But the magicians of

[n] Heb *me? I am uncircumcised of lips* [o] Or *Saul* [p] Also spelled *Gershom*; see 2.22 [q] Heb *am uncircumcised of lips*; see 6.12

Egypt did the same by their secret arts; so Pharaoh's heart remained hardened, and he would not listen to them, as the LORD had said. 23Pharaoh turned and went into his house, and he did not take even this to heart. 24And all the Egyptians had to dig along the Nile for water to drink, for they could not drink the water of the river.

25 Seven days passed after the LORD had struck the Nile.

The Second Plague: Frogs

8 r Then the LORD said to Moses, "Go to Pharaoh and say to him, 'Thus says the LORD: Let my people go, so that they may worship me. 2If you refuse to let them go, I will plague your whole country with frogs. 3The river shall swarm with frogs; they shall come up into your palace, into your bedchamber and your bed, and into the houses of your officials and of your people,s and into your ovens and your kneading bowls. 4The frogs shall come up on you and on your people and on all your officials.'" 5 t And the LORD said to Moses, "Say to Aaron, 'Stretch out your hand with your staff over the rivers, the canals, and the pools, and make frogs come up on the land of Egypt.'" 6So Aaron stretched out his hand over

r Ch 7.26 in Heb   s Gk: Heb upon your people   t Ch 8.1 in Heb

Day of the Locusts
The ten plagues proved a point for both Jews and Egyptians

LOCUSTS, OR GRASSHOPPERS, NORMALLY LIVE a solitary life, hopping from stalk to stalk and placidly munching on leaves and flowers. Then something happens—whether in response to climate, food supply, or crowded conditions—that triggers a change. The locusts grow restive, flush an ominous pink color, and begin to seek other locusts.

They become a plague. Great clattering hordes of them, millions strong, blacken the sky, shutting out sunlight. Groups of them fall to the ground like cluster bombs and disperse to destroy every sign of vegetation. Pesticide spraying may kill a few million, but the migratory swarm will barely notice such losses.

A single swarm crossing the Red Sea was once measured at 15 miles wide, three miles deep, and 100 miles long. Upon landing, the locusts consumed crops, leather, fences, and even tool handles, leaving behind total devastation over 2,000 square miles.

"The Egyptians shall know that I am the LORD, when I stretch out my hand against Egypt and bring the Israelites out from among them." 7.5

Why the Ten Plagues?

Exodus (7–12) depicts ten cataclysmic plagues on Egypt—including a locust swarm—in brief but graphic detail. The Bible does not concern itself with the question of how these natural phenomena occurred; it merely affirms that something supernatural took place. The miracles were an unprecedented display of God's power.

A nation was about to be born, and the Israelites' uprooting from Egypt called for such power. They had, after all, lived for centuries in Egypt. It would take a strong incentive indeed to motivate a massive, abrupt departure. And Egypt would not easily let thousands of valuable slaves walk away free.

Two Reputations at Stake

The ten plagues convincingly established Moses' authority. He had hesitated to accept a leadership role, doubting whether the other Israelites would trust him (4.1). But Moses' dramatic confrontations with Pharaoh dispelled all doubts. He and he alone could lead them to freedom.

Someone else's credibility was also at stake: that of God himself. In Egypt, religion centered around idolatry, with scores of gods—including even snakes and dung beetles—held up as objects of worship. Against that background, the plagues appear as God's open warfare against the false gods of Egypt. He said as much: "On all the gods of Egypt I will execute judgments" (12.12).

Exodus asserts more than a dozen times that the plagues were given so that Israel and Egypt would know the power of Israel's God. Evidently they worked. Egyptians became so convinced of God's power that they let thousands of slaves leave, with the wealth of Egypt showered upon them as farewell presents. The Israelites were so convinced that they left their home and history and marched out behind a single man toward a desert and a new life.

Life Questions: Do you know of any modern countries that treat minorities cruelly, like the Egyptians treated the Israelites? What would make such a government change its ways?

the waters of Egypt; and the frogs came up and covered the land of Egypt. 7But the magicians did the same by their secret arts, and brought frogs up on the land of Egypt.

8 Then Pharaoh called Moses and Aaron, and said, "Pray to the LORD to take away the frogs from me and my people, and I will let the people go to sacrifice to the LORD." 9Moses said to Pharaoh, "Kindly tell me when I am to pray for you and for your officials and for your people, that the frogs may be removed from you and your houses and be left only in the Nile." 10And he said, "Tomorrow." Moses said, "As you say! So that you may know that there is no one like the LORD our God, 11the frogs shall leave you and your houses and your officials and your people; they shall be left only in the Nile." 12Then Moses and Aaron went out from Pharaoh; and Moses cried out to the LORD concerning the frogs that he had brought upon Pharaoh.u 13And the LORD did as Moses requested: the frogs died in the houses, the courtyards, and the fields. 14And they gathered them together in heaps, and the land stank. 15But when Pharaoh saw that there was a respite, he hardened his heart, and would not listen to them, just as the LORD had said.

8.15 Pharaoh's Hard Heart

The Bible describes Pharaoh's stubbornness in three ways. Sometimes, as here, it says Pharaoh "hardened his heart," sometimes, God "hardened his heart" (10.1), and also, "Pharaoh's heart was hardened" (7.13). This is consistent with the Old Testament view: all of history was an act of God. Beyond that, the writers did not normally make clear distinctions on questions of who caused what.

The Third Plague: Gnats

16 Then the LORD said to Moses, "Say to Aaron, 'Stretch out your staff and strike the dust of the earth, so that it may become gnats throughout the whole land of Egypt.'" 17And they did so; Aaron stretched out his hand with his staff and struck the dust of the earth, and gnats came on humans and animals alike; all the dust of the earth turned into gnats throughout the whole land of Egypt. 18The magicians tried to produce gnats by their secret arts, but they could not. There were gnats on both humans and animals. 19And the magicians said to Pharaoh, "This is the finger of God!" But Pharaoh's heart was hardened, and he would not listen to them, just as the LORD had said.

The Fourth Plague: Flies

20 Then the LORD said to Moses, "Rise early in the morning and present yourself before Pharaoh, as he goes out to the water, and say to him, 'Thus says the LORD: Let my people go, so that they may worship me. 21For if you will not let my people go, I will send swarms of flies on you, your officials, and your people, and into your houses; and the houses of the Egyptians shall be filled with swarms of flies; so also the land where they live. 22But on that day I will set apart the land of Goshen, where my people live, so that no swarms of flies shall be there, that you may know that I the LORD am in this land. 23Thus I will make a distinctionv between my people and your people. This sign shall appear tomorrow.'" 24The LORD did so, and great swarms of flies came into the house of Pharaoh and into his officials' houses; in all of Egypt the land was ruined because of the flies.

25 Then Pharaoh summoned Moses and Aaron, and said, "Go, sacrifice to your God within the land." 26But Moses said, "It would not be right to do so; for the sacrifices that we offer to the LORD our God are offensive to the Egyptians. If we offer in the sight of the Egyptians sacrifices that are offensive to them, will they not stone us? 27We must go a three days' journey into the wilderness and sacrifice to the LORD our God as he

8.27 Oriental Bargaining

Those who have lived in the Middle East recognize in Moses' encounters with Pharaoh an example of high-level Oriental bargaining. As the pressure increased, Pharaoh kept raising his offers: from allowing sacrifices within Egypt (verse 25), to permitting sacrifices nearby in the desert (verse 28), to letting only the adult males go (10.11), to releasing all people but no flocks (10.24). Finally, with the tenth and final plague Pharaoh agreed to all Moses' demands (12.32).

commands us." 28So Pharaoh said, "I will let you go to sacrifice to the LORD your God in the wilderness, provided you do not go very far away. Pray for me." 29Then Moses said, "As soon as I leave you, I will pray to the LORD that the swarms of flies may depart tomorrow from Pharaoh, from his officials, and from his people; only do not let Pharaoh again deal falsely by not letting the people go to sacrifice to the LORD."

30 So Moses went out from Pharaoh and prayed to the LORD. 31And the LORD did as Moses asked: he removed the swarms of flies from Pharaoh, from his officials, and from his people; not

---

u Or *frogs, as he had agreed with Pharaoh*   v Gk Vg: Heb *will set redemption*

one remained. ³²But Pharaoh hardened his heart this time also, and would not let the people go.

The Fifth Plague: Livestock Diseased

9 Then the LORD said to Moses, "Go to Pharaoh, and say to him, 'Thus says the LORD, the God of the Hebrews: Let my people go, so that they may worship me. ²For if you refuse to let them go and still hold them, ³the hand of the LORD will strike with a deadly pestilence your livestock in the field: the horses, the donkeys, the camels, the herds, and the flocks. ⁴But the LORD will make a distinction between the livestock of Israel and the livestock of Egypt, so that nothing shall die of all that belongs to the Israelites.'" ⁵The LORD set a time, saying, "Tomorrow the LORD will do this thing in the land." ⁶And on the next day the LORD did so; all the livestock of the Egyptians died, but of the livestock of the Israelites not one died. ⁷Pharaoh inquired and found that not one of the livestock of the Israelites was dead. But the heart of Pharaoh was hardened, and he would not let the people go.

9.7 "Smart" Plagues

Like "smart bombs," targeted precisely, most of the plagues affected the Egyptians but not the Israelites—a miracle in itself. This fact should have convinced Pharaoh that he was contending against supernatural force, not just the caprice of nature. But it took ten plagues in all to persuade him to allow his main supply of cheap labor to walk away, and even then he had second thoughts and chased after them (14.5).

The Sixth Plague: Boils

8 Then the LORD said to Moses and Aaron, "Take handfuls of soot from the kiln, and let Moses throw it in the air in the sight of Pharaoh. ⁹It shall become fine dust all over the land of Egypt, and shall cause festering boils on humans and animals throughout the whole land of Egypt." ¹⁰So they took soot from the kiln, and stood before Pharaoh, and Moses threw it in the air, and it caused festering boils on humans and animals. ¹¹The magicians could not stand before Moses because of the boils, for the boils afflicted the magicians as well as all the Egyptians. ¹²But the LORD hardened the heart of Pharaoh, and he would not listen to them, just as the LORD had spoken to Moses.

The Seventh Plague: Thunder and Hail

13 Then the LORD said to Moses, "Rise up early in the morning and present yourself before Pharaoh, and say to him, 'Thus says the LORD, the God of the Hebrews: Let my people go, so that

they may worship me. ¹⁴For this time I will send all my plagues upon you yourself, and upon your officials, and upon your people, so that you may know that there is no one like me in all the earth. ¹⁵For by now I could have stretched out my hand and struck you and your people with pestilence, and you would have been cut off from the earth. ¹⁶But this is why I have let you live: to show you my power, and to make my name resound through all the earth. ¹⁷You are still exalting yourself against my people, and will not let them go. ¹⁸Tomorrow at this time I will cause the heaviest hail to fall that has ever fallen in Egypt from the day it was founded until now. ¹⁹Send, therefore, and have your livestock and everything that you have in the open field brought to a secure place; every human or animal that is in the open field and is not brought under shelter will die when the hail comes down upon them.'" ²⁰Those officials of Pharaoh who feared the word of the LORD hurried their slaves and livestock off to a secure place. ²¹Those who did not regard the word of the LORD left their slaves and livestock in the open field.

22 The LORD said to Moses, "Stretch out your hand toward heaven so that hail may fall on the whole land of Egypt, on humans and animals and all the plants of the field in the land of Egypt." ²³Then Moses stretched out his staff toward heaven, and the LORD sent thunder and hail, and fire came down on the earth. And the LORD rained hail on the land of Egypt; ²⁴there was hail with fire flashing continually in the midst of it, such heavy hail as had never fallen in all the land of Egypt since it became a nation. ²⁵The hail struck down everything that was in the open field throughout all the land of Egypt, both human and animal; the hail also struck down all the plants of the field, and shattered every tree in the field. ²⁶Only in the land of Goshen, where the Israelites were, there was no hail.

27 Then Pharaoh summoned Moses and Aaron, and said to them, "This time I have sinned; the LORD is in the right, and I and my people are in the wrong. ²⁸Pray to the LORD! Enough of God's thunder and hail! I will let you go; you need stay no longer." ²⁹Moses said to him, "As soon as I have gone out of the city, I will stretch out my hands to the LORD; the thunder will cease, and there will be no more hail, so that you may know that the earth is the LORD's. ³⁰But as for you and your officials, I know that you do not yet fear the LORD God." ³¹(Now the flax and the barley were ruined, for the barley was in the ear and the flax was in bud. ³²But the wheat and the spelt were not ruined, for they are late in coming up.) ³³So Moses left Pharaoh, went out of the city, and stretched out his hands to the LORD; then the thunder and the hail ceased, and the rain no longer poured down on the earth. ³⁴But when Pharaoh saw that the rain and the hail and the thunder had ceased, he sinned once more and hardened

his heart, he and his officials. [35]So the heart of Pharaoh was hardened, and he would not let the Israelites go, just as the LORD had spoken through Moses.

The Eighth Plague: Locusts

10 Then the LORD said to Moses, "Go to Pharaoh; for I have hardened his heart and the heart of his officials, in order that I may show these signs of mine among them, [2]and that you may tell your children and grandchildren how I have made fools of the Egyptians and what signs I have done among them—so that you may know that I am the LORD."

3 So Moses and Aaron went to Pharaoh, and said to him, "Thus says the LORD, the God of the Hebrews, 'How long will you refuse to humble yourself before me? Let my people go, so that they may worship me. [4]For if you refuse to let my people go, tomorrow I will bring locusts into your country. [5]They shall cover the surface of the land, so that no one will be able to see the land. They shall devour the last remnant left you after the hail, and they shall devour every tree of yours that grows in the field. [6]They shall fill your houses, and the houses of all your officials and of all the Egyptians—something that neither your parents nor your grandparents have seen, from the day they came on earth to this day.' " Then he turned and went out from Pharaoh.

7 Pharaoh's officials said to him, "How long shall this fellow be a snare to us? Let the people go, so that they may worship the LORD their God; do you not yet understand that Egypt is ruined?" [8]So Moses and Aaron were brought back to Pharaoh, and he said to them, "Go, worship the LORD your God! But which ones are to go?" [9]Moses said, "We will go with our young and our old; we will go with our sons and daughters and with our flocks and herds, because we have the LORD's festival to celebrate." [10]He said to them, "The LORD indeed will be with you, if ever I let your little ones go with you! Plainly, you have some evil purpose in mind. [11]No, never! Your men may go and worship the LORD, for that is what you are asking." And they were driven out from Pharaoh's presence.

12 Then the LORD said to Moses, "Stretch out your hand over the land of Egypt, so that the locusts may come upon it and eat every plant in the land, all that the hail has left." [13]So Moses stretched out his staff over the land of Egypt, and the LORD brought an east wind upon the land all that day and all that night; when morning came, the east wind had brought the locusts. [14]The locusts came upon all the land of Egypt and settled on the whole country of Egypt, such a dense swarm of locusts as had never been before, nor ever shall be again. [15]They covered the surface of the whole land, so that the land was black; and they ate all the plants in the land and all the fruit of the trees that the hail had left; nothing green was left, no tree, no plant in the field, in all the land of Egypt. [16]Pharaoh hurriedly summoned Moses and Aaron and said, "I have sinned against the LORD your God, and against you. [17]Do forgive my sin just this once, and pray to the LORD your God that at the least he remove this deadly thing from me." [18]So he went out from Pharaoh and prayed to the LORD. [19]The LORD changed the wind into a very strong west wind, which lifted the locusts and drove them into the Red Sea;[w] not a single locust was left in all the country of Egypt. [20]But the LORD hardened Pharaoh's heart, and he would not let the Israelites go.

The Ninth Plague: Darkness

21 Then the LORD said to Moses, "Stretch out your hand toward heaven so that there may be darkness over the land of Egypt, a darkness that

10.21 Attack on False Gods

God used ten plagues as a form of warfare against the gods of Egypt (12.12). Some scholars see in each individual punishment an attack against a specific Egyptian idol. Thus they believe the plague on the Nile River opposed the Egyptians' river god, the plague of flies flouted worship of the sacred fly, the plague of darkness attacked the sun-god Ra, and the plague on livestock countered the sacred bull.

can be felt." [22]So Moses stretched out his hand toward heaven, and there was dense darkness in all the land of Egypt for three days. [23]People could not see one another, and for three days they could not move from where they were; but all the Israelites had light where they lived. [24]Then Pharaoh summoned Moses, and said, "Go, worship the LORD. Only your flocks and your herds shall remain behind. Even your children may go with you." [25]But Moses said, "You must also let us have sacrifices and burnt offerings to sacrifice to the LORD our God. [26]Our livestock also must go with us; not a hoof shall be left behind, for we must choose some of them for the worship of the LORD our God, and we will not know what to use to worship the LORD until we arrive there." [27]But the LORD hardened Pharaoh's heart, and he was unwilling to let them go. [28]Then Pharaoh said to him, "Get away from me! Take care that you do not see my face again, for on the day you see my face you shall die." [29]Moses said, "Just as you say! I will never see your face again."

w Or Sea of Reeds

Warning of the Final Plague

11 The LORD said to Moses, "I will bring one more plague upon Pharaoh and upon Egypt; afterwards he will let you go from here; indeed, when he lets you go, he will drive you away. ²Tell the people that every man is to ask his neighbor and every woman is to ask her neighbor for objects of silver and gold." ³The LORD gave the people favor in the sight of the Egyptians. More-over, Moses himself was a man of great importance in the land of Egypt, in the sight of Pharaoh's officials and in the sight of the people.

4 Moses said, "Thus says the LORD: About midnight I will go out through Egypt. ⁵Every firstborn in the land of Egypt shall die, from the firstborn of Pharaoh who sits on his throne to the firstborn of the female slave who is behind the handmill, and all the firstborn of the livestock.

Independence Day
An unusual style of celebrating freedom

THE UNITED STATES CELEBRATES JULY 4 like no other day. The parades, the picnics, and the fireworks boisterously express national pride. We showed 'em, say the politicians in their speeches. With our own sweat and blood we created a nation. We're proud to be Americans.

> "There will be a loud cry throughout the whole land of Egypt, such as has never been or will ever be again."
> 11.6

A Different Mood for the Jews

Our style of celebration—noisy and flag-waving and proud—captures something of the original spirit that led a young nation to declare independence. A similar spirit surges up in France on Bastille Day and in many other nations on their birthdays. But these celebrations bear a striking *unlikeness* to the Jewish independence day, a day called passover.

The Jews trace their cultural birthday back to a dark, foreboding night—the Israelites' last in Egypt (Exodus 12). There are no blaring bands nor balloons nor fireworks to commemorate this event. Everything takes place inside a home, with a family or cluster of families gathered around a table. Participants taste morsels of food, pausing before each portion to hear Old Testament accounts of the history they are reliving. Their independence day resembles a worship service, not a party.

A Work of God Alone

More than anything else, the Jewish independence day expresses this one fact: God did it. No Israelite armies stood against the mighty Egyptians. Freedom came in the blackest night while Israelite families huddled around the passover table, their bags packed, waiting for deliverance.

When God's time came, the Egyptian captors not only released the Israelites, but begged them to go and showered them with gold and riches. The Jews remember that event with humility and praise; there is no room for pride. Later, when Pharaoh changed his mind and set his chariots loose upon the fleeing tribes, God came through again. Israelites stood trembling like cowards, already second-guessing their freedom. But God destroyed the great Egyptian army.

For the children of Israel, independence from Egypt meant dependence on God. In fact, God came back to this event throughout the Bible as a way of describing himself: "I am the LORD your God, who brought you out of the land of Egypt."

The pattern of dependence was to continue all through Exodus. When the wilderness wanderers ran out of water, God provided. When food supplies failed, God provided. When raiders attacked, God provided. Independence day merely set the tone for a national history that was an active movement of God.

Passover's New Meaning

Much later, passover night would take on an even broader significance. During one particular passover feast, as thousands of Jews were bringing their choice lambs to Jerusalem, one man was selected as the Passover Lamb for all humanity (1 Corinthians 5.7). The words "When I see the blood, I will pass over you" (12.13) came to convey a whole new meaning.

Today, though Jewish people still celebrate passover, most Christians do not. Rather, that ceremony has been incorporated into a new one called the Eucharist, or the Lord's Supper, with Christ representing the passover lamb. Although much of the ceremony's content has changed, one thing has not. The Lord's Supper, too, memorializes a time of pain and of bloodshed, a time of freedom and deliverance. It, too, was God's act alone. He gets the credit.

Life Questions: Does your church's celebration of the Eucharist, or Lord's Supper, resemble the Jewish passover described here? How are they similar or different?

⁶Then there will be a loud cry throughout the whole land of Egypt, such as has never been or will ever be again. ⁷But not a dog shall growl at any of the Israelites—not at people, not at animals—so that you may know that the LORD makes a distinction between Egypt and Israel. ⁸Then all these officials of yours shall come down to me, and bow low to me, saying, 'Leave us, you and all the people who follow you.' After that I will leave." And in hot anger he left Pharaoh.

9 The LORD said to Moses, "Pharaoh will not listen to you, in order that my wonders may be multiplied in the land of Egypt." ¹⁰Moses and Aaron performed all these wonders before Pharaoh; but the LORD hardened Pharaoh's heart, and he did not let the people of Israel go out of his land.

The First Passover Instituted

12 The LORD said to Moses and Aaron in the land of Egypt: ²This month shall mark for you the beginning of months; it shall be the first month of the year for you. ³Tell the whole congregation of Israel that on the tenth of this month they are to take a lamb for each family, a lamb for each household. ⁴If a household is too small for a whole lamb, it shall join its closest neighbor in obtaining one; the lamb shall be divided in proportion to the number of people who eat of it. ⁵Your lamb shall be without blemish, a year-old male; you may take it from the sheep or from the goats. ⁶You shall keep it until the fourteenth day of this month; then the whole assembled congregation of Israel shall slaughter it at twilight. ⁷They shall take some of the blood and put it on the two doorposts and the lintel of the houses in which they eat it. ⁸They shall eat the lamb that same night; they shall eat it roasted over the fire with

12.8–11 Fast Food

God's instructions for the passover stress the need for haste. Roasting over fire cooks meat faster than boiling, and (unlike frying or baking) requires no pan or oven. Likewise, bread without yeast doesn't need time to rise. The emphasis on speed indicated to the Israelites how terrible this plague would be, and how swiftly they had to flee from Egypt.

unleavened bread and bitter herbs. ⁹Do not eat any of it raw or boiled in water, but roasted over the fire, with its head, legs, and inner organs. ¹⁰You shall let none of it remain until the morning; anything that remains until the morning you shall burn. ¹¹This is how you shall eat it: your loins girded, your sandals on your feet, and your staff in your hand; and you shall eat it hurriedly. It is the passover of the LORD. ¹²For I will pass

through the land of Egypt that night, and I will strike down every firstborn in the land of Egypt, both human beings and animals; on all the gods of Egypt I will execute judgments: I am the LORD. ¹³The blood shall be a sign for you on the houses where you live: when I see the blood, I will pass over you, and no plague shall destroy you when I strike the land of Egypt.

14 This day shall be a day of remembrance for you. You shall celebrate it as a festival to the LORD; throughout your generations you shall observe it as a perpetual ordinance. ¹⁵Seven days you shall eat unleavened bread; on the first day you shall remove leaven from your houses, for whoever eats leavened bread from the first day until the seventh day shall be cut off from Israel. ¹⁶On the first day you shall hold a solemn assembly, and on the seventh day a solemn assembly; no work shall be done on those days; only what everyone must eat, that alone may be prepared by you. ¹⁷You shall observe the festival of unleavened bread, for on this very day I brought your companies out of the land of Egypt: you shall observe this day throughout your generations as a perpetual ordinance. ¹⁸In the first month, from the evening of the fourteenth day until the evening of the twenty-first day, you shall eat unleavened bread. ¹⁹For seven days no leaven shall be found in your houses; for whoever eats what is leavened shall be cut off from the congregation of Israel, whether an alien or a native of the land. ²⁰You shall eat nothing leavened; in all your settlements you shall eat unleavened bread.

21 Then Moses called all the elders of Israel and said to them, "Go, select lambs for your families, and slaughter the passover lamb. ²²Take a bunch of hyssop, dip it in the blood that is in the basin, and touch the lintel and the two doorposts with the blood in the basin. None of you shall go outside the door of your house until morning. ²³For the LORD will pass through to strike down the Egyptians; when he sees the blood on the lintel and on the two doorposts, the LORD will pass over that door and will not allow the destroyer to enter your houses to strike you down. ²⁴You shall observe this rite as a perpetual ordinance for you and your children. ²⁵When you come to the land that the LORD will give you, as he has promised, you shall keep this observance. ²⁶And when your children ask you, 'What do you mean by this observance?' ²⁷you shall say, 'It is the passover sacrifice to the LORD, for he passed over the houses of the Israelites in Egypt, when he struck down the Egyptians but spared our houses.'" And the people bowed down and worshiped.

28 The Israelites went and did just as the LORD had commanded Moses and Aaron.

The Tenth Plague: Death of the Firstborn

29 At midnight the LORD struck down all the firstborn in the land of Egypt, from the firstborn

of Pharaoh who sat on his throne to the firstborn of the prisoner who was in the dungeon, and all the firstborn of the livestock. ³⁰Pharaoh arose in the night, he and all his officials and all the Egyptians; and there was a loud cry in Egypt, for there was not a house without someone dead. ³¹Then he summoned Moses and Aaron in the night, and said, "Rise up, go away from my people, both you and the Israelites! Go, worship the LORD, as you said. ³²Take your flocks and your herds, as you said, and be gone. And bring a blessing on me too!"

The Exodus: From Rameses to Succoth

33 The Egyptians urged the people to hasten their departure from the land, for they said, "We shall all be dead." ³⁴So the people took their dough before it was leavened, with their kneading bowls wrapped up in their cloaks on their shoulders. ³⁵The Israelites had done as Moses told them; they had asked the Egyptians for jewelry of silver and gold, and for clothing, ³⁶and the LORD had given the people favor in the sight of the Egyptians, so that they let them have what they asked. And so they plundered the Egyptians.

37 The Israelites journeyed from Rameses to Succoth, about six hundred thousand men on foot, besides children. ³⁸A mixed crowd also went up with them, and livestock in great numbers, both flocks and herds. ³⁹They baked unleavened cakes of the dough that they had brought out of Egypt; it was not leavened, because they were driven out of Egypt and could not wait, nor had they prepared any provisions for themselves.

40 The time that the Israelites had lived in Egypt was four hundred thirty years. ⁴¹At the end of four hundred thirty years, on that very day, all the companies of the LORD went out from the land of Egypt. ⁴²That was for the LORD a night of vigil, to bring them out of the land of Egypt. That same night is a vigil to be kept for the LORD by all the Israelites throughout their generations.

Directions for the Passover

43 The LORD said to Moses and Aaron: This is the ordinance for the passover: no foreigner shall eat of it, ⁴⁴but any slave who has been purchased may eat of it after he has been circumcised; ⁴⁵no bound or hired servant may eat of it. ⁴⁶It shall be eaten in one house; you shall not take any of the animal outside the house, and you shall not break any of its bones. ⁴⁷The whole congregation of Israel shall celebrate it. ⁴⁸If an alien who resides with you wants to celebrate the passover to the LORD, all his males shall be circumcised; then he may draw near to celebrate it; he shall be regarded as a native of the land. But no uncircumcised person shall eat of it; ⁴⁹there shall be one law for the native and for the alien who resides among you.

50 All the Israelites did just as the LORD had commanded Moses and Aaron. ⁵¹That very day the LORD brought the Israelites out of the land of Egypt, company by company.

13 The LORD said to Moses: ²Consecrate to me all the firstborn; whatever is the first to

13.2 The Firstborn Principle

At the time of the passover and the exodus from Egypt, God introduced an important principle: every firstborn male, including animals, was to be dedicated to him. Later, the Levites were established as a symbolic firstborn for all the people, with very precise accounting (Numbers 3.40–51).

open the womb among the Israelites, of human beings and animals, is mine.

The Festival of Unleavened Bread

3 Moses said to the people, "Remember this day on which you came out of Egypt, out of the house of slavery, because the LORD brought you out from there by strength of hand; no leavened bread shall be eaten. ⁴Today, in the month of Abib, you are going out. ⁵When the LORD brings you into the land of the Canaanites, the Hittites, the Amorites, the Hivites, and the Jebusites, which he swore to your ancestors to give you, a land flowing with milk and honey, you shall keep this observance in this month. ⁶Seven days you shall eat unleavened bread, and on the seventh day there shall be a festival to the LORD. ⁷Unleavened bread shall be eaten for seven days; no leavened bread shall be seen in your possession, and no leaven shall be seen among you in all your territory. ⁸You shall tell your child on that day, 'It is because of what the LORD did for me when I came out of Egypt.' ⁹It shall serve for you as a sign on your hand and as a reminder on your forehead, so that the teaching of the LORD may be on your lips; for with a strong hand the LORD brought you out of Egypt. ¹⁰You shall keep this ordinance at its proper time from year to year.

The Consecration of the Firstborn

11 "When the LORD has brought you into the land of the Canaanites, as he swore to you and your ancestors, and has given it to you, ¹²you shall set apart to the LORD all that first opens the womb. All the firstborn of your livestock that are males shall be the LORD's. ¹³But every firstborn donkey you shall redeem with a sheep; if you do not redeem it, you must break its neck. Every firstborn male among your children you shall redeem. ¹⁴When in the future your child asks you, 'What does this mean?' you shall answer, 'By strength of hand the LORD brought us out of Egypt, from the house of slavery. ¹⁵When Phar-

aoh stubbornly refused to let us go, the LORD killed all the firstborn in the land of Egypt, from human firstborn to the firstborn of animals. Therefore I sacrifice to the LORD every male that first opens the womb, but every firstborn of my sons I redeem.' 16It shall serve as a sign on your hand and as an emblem˟ on your forehead that by strength of hand the LORD brought us out of Egypt."

The Pillars of Cloud and Fire

17 When Pharaoh let the people go, God did not lead them by way of the land of the Philistines, although that was nearer; for God thought, "If the people face war, they may change their minds and return to Egypt." 18So God led the people by the roundabout way of the wilderness toward the Red Sea.ʸ The Israelites went up out of the land of Egypt prepared for battle. 19And Moses took with him the bones of Joseph who had required a solemn oath of the Israelites, saying, "God will surely take notice of you, and then you must carry my bones with you from here." 20They set out from Succoth, and camped at Etham, on the edge of the wilderness. 21The LORD went in front of them in a pillar of cloud by day, to lead them along the way, and in a pillar of fire by night, to give them light, so that they might travel by day and by night. 22Neither the pillar of cloud by day nor the pillar of fire by night left its place in front of the people.

Crossing the Red Sea

14 Then the LORD said to Moses: 2Tell the Israelites to turn back and camp in front of Pi-hahiroth, between Migdol and the sea, in front of Baal-zephon; you shall camp opposite it, by the sea. 3Pharaoh will say of the Israelites, "They are wandering aimlessly in the land; the wilderness has closed in on them." 4I will harden Pharaoh's heart, and he will pursue them, so that I will gain glory for myself over Pharaoh and all his army; and the Egyptians shall know that I am the LORD. And they did so.

5 When the king of Egypt was told that the people had fled, the minds of Pharaoh and his officials were changed toward the people, and they said, "What have we done, letting Israel leave our service?" 6So he had his chariot made ready, and took his army with him; 7he took six hundred picked chariots and all the other chariots of Egypt with officers over all of them. 8The LORD hardened the heart of Pharaoh king of Egypt and he pursued the Israelites, who were going out boldly. 9The Egyptians pursued them, all Pharaoh's horses and chariots, his chariot drivers and his army; they overtook them camped by the sea, by Pi-hahiroth, in front of Baal-zephon.

10 As Pharaoh drew near, the Israelites looked back, and there were the Egyptians advancing on them. In great fear the Israelites cried out to the LORD. 11They said to Moses, "Was it because there were no graves in Egypt that you have taken us away to die in the wilderness? What have you done to us, bringing us out of Egypt? 12Is this not the very thing we told you in Egypt, 'Let us alone and let us serve the Egyptians'? For it would have been better for us to serve the Egyptians than to die in the wilderness." 13But Moses said to the people, "Do not be afraid, stand firm, and see the deliverance that the LORD will accomplish for you today; for the Egyptians whom you see today you shall never see again. 14The LORD will fight for you, and you have only to keep still."

15 Then the LORD said to Moses, "Why do you cry out to me? Tell the Israelites to go forward. 16But you lift up your staff, and stretch out your hand over the sea and divide it, that the Israelites may go into the sea on dry ground. 17Then I will harden the hearts of the Egyptians so that they will go in after them; and so I will gain glory for myself over Pharaoh and all his army, his chariots, and his chariot drivers. 18And the Egyptians shall know that I am the LORD, when I have gained glory for myself over Pharaoh, his chariots, and his chariot drivers."

19 The angel of God who was going before the Israelite army moved and went behind them; and the pillar of cloud moved from in front of them and took its place behind them. 20It came between the army of Egypt and the army of Israel. And so the cloud was there with the darkness, and it lit up the night; one did not come near the other all night.

21 Then Moses stretched out his hand over the sea. The LORD drove the sea back by a strong east wind all night, and turned the sea into dry

14.21 Final Escape

Hemmed in by mountains, the sea, and the Egyptian army, the Israelites seemed doomed until God opened a highway through the sea. This miracle closed an important chapter in the Israelites' history. Never again would the powerful Egyptian empire rule over them; most of their future enemies swept in from the north and east.

land; and the waters were divided. 22The Israelites went into the sea on dry ground, the waters forming a wall for them on their right and on their left. 23The Egyptians pursued, and went into the sea after them, all of Pharaoh's horses, chariots, and chariot drivers. 24At the morning watch the LORD in the pillar of fire and cloud looked down upon the Egyptian army, and threw the Egyptian army

---

˟ Or *as a frontlet*; Meaning of Heb uncertain   ʸ Or *Sea of Reeds*

into panic. [z]He clogged[z] their chariot wheels so that they turned with difficulty. The Egyptians said, "Let us flee from the Israelites, for the LORD is fighting for them against Egypt."

The Pursuers Drowned

26 Then the LORD said to Moses, "Stretch out your hand over the sea, so that the water may come back upon the Egyptians, upon their chariots and chariot drivers." [27]So Moses stretched out his hand over the sea, and at dawn the sea returned to its normal depth. As the Egyptians fled before it, the LORD tossed the Egyptians into the sea. [28]The waters returned and covered the chariots and the chariot drivers, the entire army of Pharaoh that had followed them into the sea; not one of them remained. [29]But the Israelites walked on dry ground through the sea, the waters forming a wall for them on their right and on their left.

30 Thus the LORD saved Israel that day from the Egyptians; and Israel saw the Egyptians dead on the seashore. [31]Israel saw the great work that the LORD did against the Egyptians. So the people feared the LORD and believed in the LORD and in his servant Moses.

The Song of Moses

15 Then Moses and the Israelites sang this song to the LORD:

"I will sing to the LORD, for he has
triumphed gloriously;
horse and rider he has thrown into the
sea.

15.1 A Story for All Time

Moses' song celebrates the event from which this book gets its name: "the exodus" from Egypt, when a band of slaves escaped from the most powerful civilization on earth. The psalmists never tired of celebrating that event in song (see, for example, Psalms 78 and 105), and the prophets later harked back to the days of the exodus to stir the conscience of their nation. The Israelites' liberation gave inspiration to the slaves of the American South, who often memorialized the exodus in their spirituals.

2 The LORD is my strength and my might,[a]
and he has become my salvation;
this is my God, and I will praise him,
my father's God, and I will exalt him.
3 The LORD is a warrior;
the LORD is his name.

4 "Pharaoh's chariots and his army he cast
into the sea;

his picked officers were sunk in the
Red Sea.[b]
5 The floods covered them;
they went down into the depths like a
stone.
6 Your right hand, O LORD, glorious in
power—
your right hand, O LORD, shattered the
enemy.
7 In the greatness of your majesty you
overthrew your adversaries;
you sent out your fury, it consumed
them like stubble.
8 At the blast of your nostrils the waters
piled up,
the floods stood up in a heap;
the deeps congealed in the heart of the
sea.
9 The enemy said, 'I will pursue, I will
overtake,
I will divide the spoil, my desire shall
have its fill of them.
I will draw my sword, my hand shall
destroy them.'
10 You blew with your wind, the sea covered
them;
they sank like lead in the mighty
waters.

11 "Who is like you, O LORD, among the
gods?
Who is like you, majestic in holiness,
awesome in splendor, doing wonders?
12 You stretched out your right hand,
the earth swallowed them.

13 "In your steadfast love you led the people
whom you redeemed;
you guided them by your strength to
your holy abode.
14 The peoples heard, they trembled;
pangs seized the inhabitants of
Philistia.
15 Then the chiefs of Edom were dismayed;
trembling seized the leaders of Moab;
all the inhabitants of Canaan melted
away.
16 Terror and dread fell upon them;
by the might of your arm, they became
still as a stone
until your people, O LORD, passed by,
until the people whom you acquired
passed by.
17 You brought them in and planted them
on the mountain of your own
possession,
the place, O LORD, that you made your
abode,

z Sam Gk Syr: MT *removed*   a Or *song*   b Or *Sea of Reeds*

the sanctuary, O LORD, that your hands
have established.

18 The LORD will reign forever and ever."

19 When the horses of Pharaoh with his chariots and his chariot drivers went into the sea, the
LORD brought back the waters of the sea upon
them; but the Israelites walked through the sea on
dry ground.

The Song of Miriam

20 Then the prophet Miriam, Aaron's sister,
took a tambourine in her hand; and all the wom-
en went out after her with tambourines and with
dancing. 21 And Miriam sang to them:
"Sing to the LORD, for he has triumphed
gloriously;
horse and rider he has thrown into the
sea."

Bitter Water Made Sweet

22 Then Moses ordered Israel to set out from
the Red Sea,c and they went into the wilderness
of Shur. They went three days in the wilderness
and found no water. 23 When they came to Marah,
they could not drink the water of Marah because
it was bitter. That is why it was called Marah.d
24 And the people complained against Moses, saying, "What shall we drink?" 25 He cried out to
the LORD; and the LORD showed him a piece of
wood;e he threw it into the water, and the water
became sweet.

There the LORD f made for them a statute and
an ordinance and there he put them to the test.
26 He said, "If you will listen carefully to the voice
of the LORD your God, and do what is right in his
sight, and give heed to his commandments and
keep all his statutes, I will not bring upon you any
of the diseases that I brought upon the Egyptians;
for I am the LORD who heals you."

27 Then they came to Elim, where there were
twelve springs of water and seventy palm trees;
and they camped there by the water.

Bread from Heaven

16 The whole congregation of the Israelites set
out from Elim; and Israel came to the wilderness of Sin, which is between Elim and Sinai,
on the fifteenth day of the second month after
they had departed from the land of Egypt. 2 The
whole congregation of the Israelites complained
against Moses and Aaron in the wilderness. 3 The
Israelites said to them, "If only we had died by the
hand of the LORD in the land of Egypt, when we
sat by the fleshpots and ate our fill of bread; for
you have brought us out into this wilderness to
kill this whole assembly with hunger."

4 Then the LORD said to Moses, "I am going
to rain bread from heaven for you, and each day
the people shall go out and gather enough for that

day. In that way I will test them, whether they will
follow my instruction or not. 5 On the sixth day,
when they prepare what they bring in, it will be
twice as much as they gather on other days." 6 So
Moses and Aaron said to all the Israelites, "In the
evening you shall know that it was the LORD who
brought you out of the land of Egypt, 7 and in the
morning you shall see the glory of the LORD, because he has heard your complaining against the
LORD. For what are we, that you complain against
us?" 8 And Moses said, "When the LORD gives you
meat to eat in the evening and your fill of bread
in the morning, because the LORD has heard the
complaining that you utter against him—what
are we? Your complaining is not against us but
against the LORD."

9 Then Moses said to Aaron, "Say to the
whole congregation of the Israelites, 'Draw near
to the LORD, for he has heard your complaining.'"
10 And as Aaron spoke to the whole congregation
of the Israelites, they looked toward the wilderness, and the glory of the LORD appeared in the
cloud. 11 The LORD spoke to Moses and said, 12 "I
have heard the complaining of the Israelites; say
to them, 'At twilight you shall eat meat, and in the
morning you shall have your fill of bread; then
you shall know that I am the LORD your God.'"

16.12–15 Food Supply

*The word manna means literally, "What is it?"
recalling the Israelites' first reaction to it (verse
15). Manna is a clear example of the Israelites'
enforced dependence on God; they had to rely
on him every day for 40 years, just to survive.
God's provision of manna made greed
impossible: it could not be hoarded and was
distributed with precise equity (verses 17–21).*

*Quail, referred to here and in Numbers 11,
still migrate across the Sinai peninsula, flying
in great flocks between Europe and Arabia.
Exhausted by their long flight, they roost on the
ground or in low bushes at night, making
capture easy.*

13 In the evening quails came up and covered
the camp; and in the morning there was a layer of
dew around the camp. 14 When the layer of dew
lifted, there on the surface of the wilderness was
a fine flaky substance, as fine as frost on the
ground. 15 When the Israelites saw it, they said to
one another, "What is it?"g For they did not
know what it was. Moses said to them, "It is the
bread that the LORD has given you to eat. 16 This
is what the LORD has commanded: 'Gather as
much of it as each of you needs, an omer to a
person according to the number of persons, all
providing for those in their own tents.'" 17 The

---

c Or *Sea of Reeds*   d That is *Bitterness*   e Or *a tree*   f Heb *he*   g Or "*It is manna*" (Heb *man hu*, see verse 31)

Israelites did so, some gathering more, some less. [18]But when they measured it with an omer, those who gathered much had nothing over, and those who gathered little had no shortage; they gathered as much as each of them needed. [19]And Moses said to them, "Let no one leave any of it over until morning." [20]But they did not listen to Moses; some left part of it until morning, and it bred worms and became foul. And Moses was angry with them. [21]Morning by morning they gathered it, as much as each needed; but when the sun grew hot, it melted.

22 On the sixth day they gathered twice as much food, two omers apiece. When all the leaders of the congregation came and told Moses, [23]he said to them, "This is what the LORD has commanded: 'Tomorrow is a day of solemn rest, a holy sabbath to the LORD; bake what you want to bake and boil what you want to boil, and all that is left over put aside to be kept until morning.'" [24]So they put it aside until morning, as Moses commanded them; and it did not become foul, and there were no worms in it. [25]Moses said, "Eat it today, for today is a sabbath to the LORD; today you will not find it in the field. [26]Six days you shall gather it; but on the seventh day, which is a sabbath, there will be none."

27 On the seventh day some of the people went out to gather, and they found none. [28]The LORD said to Moses, "How long will you refuse to keep my commandments and instructions? [29]See! The LORD has given you the sabbath, therefore on the sixth day he gives you food for two days; each of you stay where you are; do not leave your place on the seventh day." [30]So the people rested on the seventh day.

31 The house of Israel called it manna; it was like coriander seed, white, and the taste of it was like wafers made with honey. [32]Moses said, "This is what the LORD has commanded: 'Let an omer of it be kept throughout your generations, in order that they may see the food with which I fed you in the wilderness, when I brought you out of the land of Egypt.'" [33]And Moses said to Aaron, "Take a jar, and put an omer of manna in it, and place it before the LORD, to be kept throughout your generations." [34]As the LORD commanded Moses, so Aaron placed it before the covenant,[h] for safekeeping. [35]The Israelites ate manna forty years, until they came to a habitable land; they ate manna, until they came to the border of the land of Canaan. [36]An omer is a tenth of an ephah.

Water from the Rock

17 From the wilderness of Sin the whole congregation of the Israelites journeyed by stages, as the LORD commanded. They camped at Rephidim, but there was no water for the people to drink. [2]The people quarreled with Moses, and said, "Give us water to drink." Moses said to them, "Why do you quarrel with me? Why do you test the LORD?" [3]But the people thirsted there for water; and the people complained against Moses and said, "Why did you bring us out of Egypt,

17.1 Change of Scenery

Unlike the Sahara and Saudi Arabian deserts, the Sinai peninsula is no dry, sandy wasteland. A high plateau in the north gives way to a broad belt of sandstone and sand, and then a tumbled mass of mountains (some reaching 9,000 feet) in the south. Herbs and acacia trees grow, and widely scattered springs permit some farming, although the Sinai cannot support a large population. Moses' 40-year stint as a shepherd here would have taught him much about wilderness survival.

to kill us and our children and livestock with thirst?" [4]So Moses cried out to the LORD, "What shall I do with this people? They are almost ready to stone me." [5]The LORD said to Moses, "Go on ahead of the people, and take some of the elders of Israel with you; take in your hand the staff with which you struck the Nile, and go. [6]I will be standing there in front of you on the rock at Horeb. Strike the rock, and water will come out of it, so that the people may drink." Moses did so, in the sight of the elders of Israel. [7]He called the place Massah[i] and Meribah,[j] because the Israelites quarreled and tested the LORD, saying, "Is the LORD among us or not?"

Amalek Attacks Israel and Is Defeated

8 Then Amalek came and fought with Israel at Rephidim. [9]Moses said to Joshua, "Choose some men for us and go out, fight with Amalek. Tomorrow I will stand on the top of the hill with the staff of God in my hand." [10]So Joshua did as Moses told him, and fought with Amalek, while Moses, Aaron, and Hur went up to the top of the hill. [11]Whenever Moses held up his hand, Israel prevailed; and whenever he lowered his hand, Amalek prevailed. [12]But Moses' hands grew weary; so they took a stone and put it under him, and he sat on it. Aaron and Hur held up his hands, one on one side, and the other on the other side; so his hands were steady until the sun set. [13]And Joshua defeated Amalek and his people with the sword.

14 Then the LORD said to Moses, "Write this as a reminder in a book and recite it in the hearing of Joshua: I will utterly blot out the remembrance of Amalek from under heaven." [15]And Moses built an altar and called it, The LORD is my banner. [16]He said, "A hand upon the banner of

---

[h] Or *treaty* or *testimony*; Heb *eduth*   [i] That is *Test*   [j] That is *Quarrel*

the LORD[k] The LORD will have war with Amalek from generation to generation."

Jethro's Advice

18 Jethro, the priest of Midian, Moses' father-in-law, heard of all that God had done for Moses and for his people Israel, how the LORD had brought Israel out of Egypt. [2]After Moses had sent away his wife Zipporah, his father-in-law Jethro took her back, [3]along with her two sons. The name of the one was Gershom (for he said, "I have been an alien[l] in a foreign land"), [4]and the name of the other, Eliezer[m] (for he said, "The God of my father was my help, and delivered me from the sword of Pharaoh"). [5]Jethro, Moses' father-in-law, came into the wilderness where Moses was encamped at the mountain of God, bringing Moses' sons and wife to him. [6]He sent word to Moses, "I, your father-in-law Jethro, am coming to you, with your wife and her two sons." [7]Moses went out to meet his father-in-law; he bowed down and kissed him; each asked after the other's welfare, and they went into the tent. [8]Then Moses told his father-in-law all that the LORD had done to Pharaoh and to the Egyptians for Israel's sake, all the hardship that had beset them on the way, and how the LORD had delivered them. [9]Jethro rejoiced for all the good that the LORD had done to Israel, in delivering them from the Egyptians.

10 Jethro said, "Blessed be the LORD, who has delivered you from the Egyptians and from Pharaoh. [11]Now I know that the LORD is greater than all gods, because he delivered the people from the Egyptians,[n] when they dealt arrogantly with them." [12]And Jethro, Moses' father-in-law, brought a burnt offering and sacrifices to God; and Aaron came with all the elders of Israel to eat bread with Moses' father-in-law in the presence of God.

13 The next day Moses sat as judge for the people, while the people stood around him from morning until evening. [14]When Moses' father-in-law saw all that he was doing for the people, he said, "What is this that you are doing for the people? Why do you sit alone, while all the people stand around you from morning until evening?" [15]Moses said to his father-in-law, "Because the people come to me to inquire of God. [16]When they have a dispute, they come to me and I decide

17.14 First Writing

Civilization mastered the skill of writing at least as early as 3400 B.C., when a society near present-day Iraq introduced it, but this is the Bible's first mention of the practice. Moses' training in Egypt would have included writing on "paper" made from pulpy reeds of the papyrus plant. A basket fashioned out of such reeds had helped save Moses' life as an infant (2.3).

---

[k] Cn: Meaning of Heb uncertain   [l] Heb ger   [m] Heb Eli, my God; ezer, help   [n] The clause because . . . Egyptians has been transposed from verse 10

JETHRO *Advice from an In-Law*

A NEWLYWED HUSBAND CAN COUNT on one thing from his father-in-law: advice. He has, after all, married the woman his father-in-law has cared for from birth. And his father-in-law is older and more experienced than he. Under such conditions, advice is virtually inevitable.

After Moses led Israel out of Egypt, his father-in-law Jethro brought Moses' wife and children to join the rest of the Israelites. The old man stayed for a visit and observed Moses at work. Quickly he saw that the sheer volume of the work was overwhelming Moses. Jethro suggested that Moses appoint sub-officials to settle disputes, reserving only the most difficult cases for himself. Moses recognized this good advice, and acted on it.

Moses apparently liked and respected his father-in-law, and with good reason—Jethro took him in when he was running for his life after killing an Egyptian. And in addition to letting Moses marry his daughter, Jethro gave him a job. These men lived and worked together for forty years before God called Moses back to his people.

Jethro was, furthermore, a "priest of Midian." We don't know exactly how much of the true God Jethro knew before Moses came. Midianites, descended from Abraham, may have remembered "the God of Abraham, the God of Isaac and the God of Jacob." Surely Jethro and Moses talked often of their faith. After the Exodus, when Moses told Jethro how God had liberated the slaves from Pharaoh, Jethro acknowledged Moses' God as greater than all other gods.

Even so, Jethro did not accompany the Israelites on their journey to the promised land. He returned to his home, a believer in God remaining apart from God's chosen people.

Life Questions: Can you think of advice that proved especially helpful to you? What was it, and why was it beneficial?

between one person and another, and I make known to them the statutes and instructions of God." [17]Moses' father-in-law said to him, "What you are doing is not good. [18]You will surely wear yourself out, both you and these people with you. For the task is too heavy for you; you cannot do it alone. [19]Now listen to me. I will give you counsel, and God be with you! You should represent the people before God, and you should bring their cases before God; [20]teach them the statutes and instructions and make known to them the way they are to go and the things they are to do. [21]You should also look for able men among all the people, men who fear God, are trustworthy, and hate dishonest gain; set such men over them as officers over thousands, hundreds, fifties and tens. [22]Let them sit as judges for the people at all times; let them bring every important case to you, but decide every minor case themselves. So it will be easier for you, and they will bear the burden with you. [23]If you do this, and God so commands you, then you will be able to endure, and all these people will go to their home in peace."

24 So Moses listened to his father-in-law and did all that he had said. [25]Moses chose able men from all Israel and appointed them as heads over the people, as officers over thousands, hundreds, fifties, and tens. [26]And they judged the people at all times; hard cases they brought to Moses, but any minor case they decided themselves. [27]Then

The Covenant
What difference does a stone tablet make?

MANY SCHOLARS CALL THE NEXT few chapters the most pivotal section of the Old Testament. The Israelites, called before a trembling and smoking mountain by loud trumpet blasts, were about to receive something unique in all history: a stone document to be deposited in the most valuable piece of furniture in the nation, the ark of the covenant. What made a stone tablet so valuable? The "covenant" it summarized was sacred, signed by the finger of God himself.

"Now therefore, if you obey my voice and keep my covenant, you shall be my treasured possession out of all the peoples." 19.5

And yet someone who simply turned to Exodus and started reading the contents of the covenant might have trouble understanding all the fuss. The covenant begins with the familiar Ten Commandments. It proceeds from there to rules on cursing parents and knocking out teeth, oddly mixed in with rules on interest rates and cooking young goats in their mothers' milk. What is so special, after all, about the laws and instructions described here?

Since we don't normally communicate on stone tablets today, the question "What made a stone tablet so valuable?" might better be rephrased, "What makes a piece of paper valuable?" Seen in that light, our society, like the Israelites', stakes an awful lot on certain pieces of paper. Take just three examples: a constitution, a birth certificate, and a marriage certificate.

Constitution

Resting in a helium-filled bronze case in the Library of Congress, the United States Constitution is arguably the most valuable single piece of paper in the entire country. At a moment's notice it can be lowered into a fireproof, shockproof safe. But dollars alone barely hint at the Constitution's value; its real importance comes to light in a marble building down the street, where the Supreme Court hears hundreds of legal cases.

Each case has climbed up from lower courts through an arduous, expensive process, and now only one decision remains. Whatever the Supreme Court decides will rule as the law of the land. The Supreme Court bases its decision on one final authority: the Constitution. If the nine members judge a law "constitutional," the law will stand. If not, it will be overturned.

For Israel, the covenant became their Constitution. Details of the law came out in three main places: here at Sinai (Exodus and Leviticus), during the wilderness wanderings (Numbers), and on the plains of Moab (Deuteronomy). The complete legal code, far longer than the U.S. Constitution, extended from the grand sweep of national policy to petty disputes of living together. God was shaping an entire culture for a group of homeless pilgrims. In all, 613 separate commands ordered their political, social, and spiritual lives.

Other nations were haunted by the unpredictability of their gods. Who could tell what would anger or please them? But because of the covenant, Israelites knew exactly what God required and where they stood before him. They had a basis for trust and security as a nation.

Birth Certificate

This piece of paper, with its smudged baby footprint and fancy script, sits in a file drawer

Moses let his father-in-law depart, and he went off to his own country.

The Israelites Reach Mount Sinai

19 On the third new moon after the Israelites had gone out of the land of Egypt, on that very day, they came into the wilderness of Sinai. ²They had journeyed from Rephidim, entered the wilderness of Sinai, and camped in the wilderness; Israel camped there in front of the mountain. ³Then Moses went up to God; the LORD called to him from the mountain, saying, "Thus you shall say to the house of Jacob, and tell the Israelites: ⁴You have seen what I did to the Egyptians, and how I bore you on eagles' wings and brought you to myself. ⁵Now therefore, if you obey my voice and keep my covenant, you shall be my treasured possession out of all the peoples. Indeed, the whole earth is mine, ⁶but you shall be for me a priestly kingdom and a holy nation. These are the words that you shall speak to the Israelites."

7 So Moses came, summoned the elders of the people, and set before them all these words that the LORD had commanded him. ⁸The people all answered as one: "Everything that the LORD has spoken we will do." Moses reported the words of the people to the LORD. ⁹Then the LORD said to

Moses, "I am going to come to you in a dense cloud, in order that the people may hear when I speak with you and so trust you ever after."

The People Consecrated

When Moses had told the words of the people

19.5 Book of the Covenant

The word covenant appears throughout the next portion of Exodus. Chapter 19 gives the dramatic setting, and chapters 20–23 contain the actual covenant, a treaty between God and the Israelites. Chapter 24 shows the covenant being confirmed. Another word for covenant is testament, and, in fact, the rest of the Old Testament builds on what took place in these six chapters. Centuries later, Biblical writers would dust off the old word covenant and apply it to Jesus Christ (as in 1 Corinthians 11.25). He fulfilled and completed the reconciliation with God begun at Sinai.

---

to the LORD, ¹⁰the LORD said to Moses: "Go to the people and consecrate them today and tomorrow. Have them wash their clothes ¹¹and prepare for

---

99 percent of the time. But when you need it, you really need it. It can prove that a young-looking person deserves a driver's license or that an older person qualifies for Social Security payments. It establishes your rights as a United States citizen. A birth certificate is valuable indeed.

For Israel, the covenant established its birth as a nation. God said he had chosen the children of Israel as a treasured possession (19.5–6). He wanted a nation unlike any other, a model society centered around a commitment to him. He needed a pure people, kept separate.

The next few books of the Bible spell out the obligations, but also the rewards, of being God's chosen people, his "family." If they obeyed, the Israelites would live free from diseases, their crops would grow bountifully, their women would give birth to many children, their armies would prove victorious—in short, they would enjoy unprecedented national wealth and security (23.20–28). The covenant defined those benefits—all part of being born as the children of God.

Marriage Certificate

Marriage is far more than a piece of paper, surely. It involves love and trust, sexuality, the thousand details involved in two people sharing life together. But in the eyes of the law, marriage requires a piece of paper. The document makes formal and legal the most intimate, personal relationship human beings ever have.

Later, the prophets Hosea, Jeremiah, and Ezekiel would poignantly compare the covenant to marriage. They pointed out that Israel's treatment of God amounted to adultery, and they called the nation back to its original covenant. The laws listed in numbing detail are merely the formal expression of a love relationship between God and his people.

Pieces of paper define the boundaries of a relationship, but in no way can they express it adequately. You cannot get an adequate picture of life in the United States by reading the Constitution's dry prose, nor can you understand the mystery of marriage by studying a certificate in a county courthouse. In the same way, the laws and rules in the book of the covenant surely do not yield a complete picture of life in a nation bound to God. But the covenant, and the context in which it came, show much about what God desired from his followers.

Life Questions: Do you own any valuable papers that express a kind of "covenant"? If you drew up a covenant between yourself and God, what would it say?

the third day, because on the third day the LORD will come down upon Mount Sinai in the sight of all the people. [12]You shall set limits for the people all around, saying, 'Be careful not to go up the mountain or to touch the edge of it. Any who touch the mountain shall be put to death. [13]No hand shall touch them, but they shall be stoned or shot with arrows;[o] whether animal or human being, they shall not live.' When the trumpet sounds a long blast, they may go up on the mountain." [14]So Moses went down from the mountain to the people. He consecrated the people, and they washed their clothes. [15]And he said to the people, "Prepare for the third day; do not go near a woman."

16 On the morning of the third day there was thunder and lightning, as well as a thick cloud on the mountain, and a blast of a trumpet so loud that all the people who were in the camp trembled. [17]Moses brought the people out of the camp to meet God. They took their stand at the foot of the mountain. [18]Now Mount Sinai was wrapped in smoke, because the LORD had descended upon it in fire; the smoke went up like the smoke of a kiln, while the whole mountain shook violently. [19]As the blast of the trumpet grew louder and louder, Moses would speak and God would answer him in thunder. [20]When the LORD descended upon Mount Sinai, to the top of the mountain, the LORD summoned Moses to the top of the mountain, and Moses went up. [21]Then the LORD said to Moses, "Go down and warn the people not to break through to the LORD to look; otherwise many of them will perish. [22]Even the priests who approach the LORD must consecrate themselves or the LORD will break out against them." [23]Moses said to the LORD, "The people are not permitted to come up to Mount Sinai; for you yourself warned us, saying, 'Set limits around the mountain and keep it holy.'" [24]The LORD said to him, "Go down, and come up bringing Aaron with you; but do not let either the priests or the people break through to come up to the LORD; otherwise he will break out against them." [25]So Moses went down to the people and told them.

The Ten Commandments

20 Then God spoke all these words:
2 I am the LORD your God, who brought you out of the land of Egypt, out of the house of slavery; [3]you shall have no other gods before[p] me.

4 You shall not make for yourself an idol, whether in the form of anything that is in heaven above, or that is on the earth beneath, or that is in the water under the earth. [5]You shall not bow down to them or worship them; for I the LORD your God am a jealous God, punishing children for the iniquity of parents, to the third and the fourth generation of those who reject me, [6]but showing steadfast love to the thousandth generation[q] of those who love me and keep my commandments.

7 You shall not make wrongful use of the name of the LORD your God, for the LORD will not acquit anyone who misuses his name.

8 Remember the sabbath day, and keep it holy. [9]Six days you shall labor and do all your work. [10]But the seventh day is a sabbath to the LORD your God; you shall not do any work—you, your son or your daughter, your male or female slave, your livestock, or the alien resident in your towns. [11]For in six days the LORD made heaven and earth, the sea, and all that is in them, but rested the seventh day; therefore the LORD blessed the sabbath day and consecrated it.

12 Honor your father and your mother, so that your days may be long in the land that the LORD your God is giving you.

13 You shall not murder.[r]

14 You shall not commit adultery.

15 You shall not steal.

16 You shall not bear false witness against your neighbor.

17 You shall not covet your neighbor's house; you shall not covet your neighbor's wife, or male or female slave, or ox, or donkey, or anything that belongs to your neighbor.

20.1–17 Long-lasting Laws

The Ten Commandments given here and in Deuteronomy 5 form a central core of morality, a major advance from other legal codes of the day. The phrase "Judeo-Christian ethics," heard often in U.S. courtrooms and legislative chambers, refers to the broad moral principles derived from laws outlined here and in the next three books.

18 When all the people witnessed the thunder and lightning, the sound of the trumpet, and the mountain smoking, they were afraid[s] and trembled and stood at a distance, [19]and said to Moses, "You speak to us, and we will listen; but do not let God speak to us, or we will die." [20]Moses said to the people, "Do not be afraid; for God has come only to test you and to put the fear of him upon you so that you do not sin." [21]Then the people stood at a distance, while Moses drew near to the thick darkness where God was.

The Law concerning the Altar

22 The LORD said to Moses: Thus you shall say to the Israelites: "You have seen for yourselves that I spoke with you from heaven. [23]You shall not make gods of silver alongside me, nor shall

---

o Heb lacks *with arrows*   *p* Or *besides*   *q* Or *to thousands*   *r* Or *kill*   *s* Sam Gk Syr Vg: MT *they saw*

you make for yourselves gods of gold. [24]You need make for me only an altar of earth and sacrifice on it your burnt offerings and your offerings of well-being, your sheep and your oxen; in every place where I cause my name to be remembered I will come to you and bless you. [25]But if you make for me an altar of stone, do not build it of hewn stones; for if you use a chisel upon it you profane it. [26]You shall not go up by steps to my altar, so that your nakedness may not be exposed on it."

The Law concerning Slaves

21 These are the ordinances that you shall set before them:

2 When you buy a male Hebrew slave, he shall serve six years, but in the seventh he shall go

21.2 Slave Rights

Many of these laws set a new standard of morality: societies of that day oppressed aliens, mistreated slaves, exploited the poor, and awarded lost animals to their finder. The Israelites' rules governing slavery, for example, were enlightened for their time. Other ancient societies treated slaves as things rather than persons; Israelites were the first to honor them with formal rights. By beginning with laws protecting the lowest on the social scale, God was teaching the value of every human being.

out a free person, without debt. [3]If he comes in single, he shall go out single; if he comes in married, then his wife shall go out with him. [4]If his master gives him a wife and she bears him sons or daughters, the wife and her children shall be her master's and he shall go out alone. [5]But if the slave declares, "I love my master, my wife, and my children; I will not go out a free person," [6]then his master shall bring him before God.[t] He shall be brought to the door or the doorpost; and his master shall pierce his ear with an awl; and he shall serve him for life.

7 When a man sells his daughter as a slave, she shall not go out as the male slaves do. [8]If she does not please her master, who designated her for himself, then he shall let her be redeemed; he shall have no right to sell her to a foreign people, since he has dealt unfairly with her. [9]If he designates her for his son, he shall deal with her as with a daughter. [10]If he takes another wife to himself, he shall not diminish the food, clothing, or marital rights of the first wife.[u] [11]And if he does not do these three things for her, she shall go out without debt, without payment of money.

The Law concerning Violence

12 Whoever strikes a person mortally shall be put to death. [13]If it was not premeditated, but came about by an act of God, then I will appoint for you a place to which the killer may flee. [14]But if someone willfully attacks and kills another by treachery, you shall take the killer from my altar for execution.

15 Whoever strikes father or mother shall be put to death.

16 Whoever kidnaps a person, whether that person has been sold or is still held in possession, shall be put to death.

17 Whoever curses father or mother shall be put to death.

18 When individuals quarrel and one strikes the other with a stone or fist so that the injured party, though not dead, is confined to bed, [19]but recovers and walks around outside with the help of a staff, then the assailant shall be free of liability, except to pay for the loss of time, and to arrange for full recovery.

20 When a slaveowner strikes a male or female slave with a rod and the slave dies immediately, the owner shall be punished. [21]But if the slave survives a day or two, there is no punishment; for the slave is the owner's property.

22 When people who are fighting injure a pregnant woman so that there is a miscarriage, and yet no further harm follows, the one responsible shall be fined what the woman's husband demands, paying as much as the judges determine. [23]If any harm follows, then you shall give life for life, [24]eye for eye, tooth for tooth, hand for hand, foot for foot, [25]burn for burn, wound for wound, stripe for stripe.

26 When a slaveowner strikes the eye of a male or female slave, destroying it, the owner shall let the slave go, a free person, to compensate for the eye. [27]If the owner knocks out a tooth of a male or female slave, the slave shall be let go, a free person, to compensate for the tooth.

Laws concerning Property

28 When an ox gores a man or a woman to death, the ox shall be stoned, and its flesh shall not be eaten; but the owner of the ox shall not be liable. [29]If the ox has been accustomed to gore in the past, and its owner has been warned but has not restrained it, and it kills a man or a woman, the ox shall be stoned, and its owner also shall be put to death. [30]If a ransom is imposed on the owner, then the owner shall pay whatever is imposed for the redemption of the victim's life. [31]If it gores a boy or a girl, the owner shall be dealt with according to this same rule. [32]If the ox gores a male or female slave, the owner shall pay to the slaveowner thirty shekels of silver, and the ox shall be stoned.

[t] Or *to the judges*   [u] Heb *of her*

33 If someone leaves a pit open, or digs a pit and does not cover it, and an ox or a donkey falls into it, ³⁴the owner of the pit shall make restitution, giving money to its owner, but keeping the dead animal.

35 If someone's ox hurts the ox of another, so that it dies, then they shall sell the live ox and divide the price of it; and the dead animal they shall also divide. ³⁶But if it was known that the ox was accustomed to gore in the past, and its owner has not restrained it, the owner shall restore ox for ox, but keep the dead animal.

Laws of Restitution

22 ᵛ When someone steals an ox or a sheep, and slaughters it or sells it, the thief shall pay five oxen for an ox, and four sheep for a sheep.ʷ The thief shall make restitution, but if unable to do so, shall be sold for the theft. ⁴When the animal, whether ox or donkey or sheep, is found alive in the thief's possession, the thief shall pay double.

2ˣ If a thief is found breaking in, and is beaten to death, no bloodguilt is incurred; ³but if it happens after sunrise, bloodguilt is incurred.

5 When someone causes a field or vineyard to be grazed over, or lets livestock loose to graze in someone else's field, restitution shall be made from the best in the owner's field or vineyard.

6 When fire breaks out and catches in thorns so that the stacked grain or the standing grain or the field is consumed, the one who started the fire shall make full restitution.

7 When someone delivers to a neighbor money or goods for safekeeping, and they are stolen from the neighbor's house, then the thief, if caught, shall pay double. ⁸If the thief is not caught, the owner of the house shall be brought before God,ʸ to determine whether or not the owner had laid hands on the neighbor's goods.

9 In any case of disputed ownership involving ox, donkey, sheep, clothing, or any other loss, of which one party says, "This is mine," the case of both parties shall come before God;ʸ the one whom God condemnsᶻ shall pay double to the other.

10 When someone delivers to another a donkey, ox, sheep, or any other animal for safekeeping, and it dies or is injured or is carried off, without anyone seeing it, ¹¹an oath before the LORD shall decide between the two of them that the one has not laid hands on the property of the other; the owner shall accept the oath, and no restitution shall be made. ¹²But if it was stolen, restitution shall be made to its owner. ¹³If it was mangled by beasts, let it be brought as evidence; restitution shall not be made for the mangled remains.

14 When someone borrows an animal from another and it is injured or dies, the owner not being present, full restitution shall be made. ¹⁵If the owner was present, there shall be no restitution; if it was hired, only the hiring fee is due.

22.9 Punishment by Restitution

In contrast to the punishments of other contemporary codes (such as Sumer and Babylonia), the penalties for wrongdoing described in the next few chapters emphasize punishments fitted to the crime. They stress restitution rather than vengeance. Modern courtrooms are once again practicing restitution—making the criminal serve society or "make good" to the victim.

Social and Religious Laws

16 When a man seduces a virgin who is not engaged to be married, and lies with her, he shall give the bride-price for her and make her his wife. ¹⁷But if her father refuses to give her to him, he shall pay an amount equal to the bride-price for virgins.

18 You shall not permit a female sorcerer to live.

19 Whoever lies with an animal shall be put to death.

20 Whoever sacrifices to any god, other than the LORD alone, shall be devoted to destruction.

21 You shall not wrong or oppress a resident alien, for you were aliens in the land of Egypt. ²²You shall not abuse any widow or orphan. ²³If you do abuse them, when they cry out to me, I will surely heed their cry; ²⁴my wrath will burn, and I will kill you with the sword, and your wives shall become widows and your children orphans.

25 If you lend money to my people, to the poor among you, you shall not deal with them as a creditor; you shall not exact interest from them. ²⁶If you take your neighbor's cloak in pawn, you shall restore it before the sun goes down; ²⁷for it may be your neighbor's only clothing to use as cover; in what else shall that person sleep? And if your neighbor cries out to me, I will listen, for I am compassionate.

28 You shall not revile God, or curse a leader of your people.

29 You shall not delay to make offerings from the fullness of your harvest and from the outflow of your presses.ᵃ

The firstborn of your sons you shall give to me. ³⁰You shall do the same with your oxen and with your sheep: seven days it shall remain with its mother; on the eighth day you shall give it to me.

ᵛ Ch 21.37 in Heb   ʷ Verses 2, 3, and 4 rearranged thus: 3b, 4, 2, 3a   ˣ Ch 22.1 in Heb   ʸ Or *before the judges*
ᶻ Or *the judges condemn*   ᵃ Meaning of Heb uncertain

31 You shall be people consecrated to me; therefore you shall not eat any meat that is mangled by beasts in the field; you shall throw it to the dogs.

Justice for All

23 You shall not spread a false report. You shall not join hands with the wicked to act as a malicious witness. 2You shall not follow a majority in wrongdoing; when you bear witness in a lawsuit, you shall not side with the majority so as to pervert justice; 3nor shall you be partial to the poor in a lawsuit.

4 When you come upon your enemy's ox or donkey going astray, you shall bring it back.

5 When you see the donkey of one who hates you lying under its burden and you would hold back from setting it free, you must help to set it free.*b*

6 You shall not pervert the justice due to your poor in their lawsuits. 7Keep far from a false charge, and do not kill the innocent and those in the right, for I will not acquit the guilty. 8You shall take no bribe, for a bribe blinds the officials, and subverts the cause of those who are in the right.

9 You shall not oppress a resident alien; you know the heart of an alien, for you were aliens in the land of Egypt.

Sabbatical Year and Sabbath

10 For six years you shall sow your land and gather in its yield; 11but the seventh year you shall let it rest and lie fallow, so that the poor of your people may eat; and what they leave the wild animals may eat. You shall do the same with your vineyard, and with your olive orchard.

12 Six days you shall do your work, but on the seventh day you shall rest, so that your ox and your donkey may have relief, and your homeborn slave and the resident alien may be refreshed. 13Be attentive to all that I have said to you. Do not invoke the names of other gods; do not let them be heard on your lips.

The Annual Festivals

14 Three times in the year you shall hold a festival for me. 15You shall observe the festival of unleavened bread; as I commanded you, you shall eat unleavened bread for seven days at the appointed time in the month of Abib, for in it you came out of Egypt.

No one shall appear before me empty-handed.

16 You shall observe the festival of harvest, of the first fruits of your labor, of what you sow in the field. You shall observe the festival of ingathering at the end of the year, when you gather in from the field the fruit of your labor. 17Three times in the year all your males shall appear before the Lord GOD.

18 You shall not offer the blood of my sacrifice with anything leavened, or let the fat of my festival remain until the morning.

19 The choicest of the first fruits of your ground you shall bring into the house of the LORD your God.

You shall not boil a kid in its mother's milk.

The Conquest of Canaan Promised

20 I am going to send an angel in front of you, to guard you on the way and to bring you to the place that I have prepared. 21Be attentive to him and listen to his voice; do not rebel against him, for he will not pardon your transgression; for my name is in him.

22 But if you listen attentively to his voice and do all that I say, then I will be an enemy to your enemies and a foe to your foes.

23 When my angel goes in front of you, and brings you to the Amorites, the Hittites, the Perizzites, the Canaanites, the Hivites, and the Jebusites, and I blot them out, 24you shall not bow down to their gods, or worship them, or follow their practices, but you shall utterly demolish them and break their pillars in pieces. 25You shall worship the LORD your God, and I*c* will bless your bread and your water; and I will take sickness away from among you. 26No one shall miscarry or be barren in your land; I will fulfill the number of your days. 27I will send my terror in front of you, and will throw into confusion all the people against whom you shall come, and I will make all your enemies turn their backs to you. 28And I will send the pestilence*d* in front of you, which shall drive out the Hivites, the Canaanites, and the Hittites from before you. 29I will not drive them out from before you in one year, or the land would become desolate and the wild animals would multiply against you. 30Little by little I will drive them out from before you, until you have increased and possess the land. 31I will set your borders from the Red Sea*e* to the sea of the Philistines, and from the wilderness to the Euphrates; for I will hand over to you the inhabitants of the land, and you shall drive them out before you. 32You shall make no covenant with them and their gods. 33They shall not live in your land, or they will make you sin against me; for if you worship their gods, it will surely be a snare to you.

The Blood of the Covenant

24 Then he said to Moses, "Come up to the LORD, you and Aaron, Nadab, and Abihu, and seventy of the elders of Israel, and worship at a distance. 2Moses alone shall come near the LORD; but the others shall not come near, and the people shall not come up with him."

3 Moses came and told the people all the words of the LORD and all the ordinances; and all

---

b Meaning of Heb uncertain *c* Gk Vg: Heb *he* *d* Or *hornets*: Meaning of Heb uncertain *e* Or *Sea of Reeds*

the people answered with one voice, and said, "All the words that the LORD has spoken we will do." ⁴And Moses wrote down all the words of the LORD. He rose early in the morning, and built an altar at the foot of the mountain, and set up twelve pillars, corresponding to the twelve tribes of Israel. ⁵He sent young men of the people of Israel, who offered burnt offerings and sacrificed oxen as offerings of well-being to the LORD. ⁶Moses took half of the blood and put it in basins, and half of the blood he dashed against the altar. ⁷Then he took the book of the covenant, and read it in the hearing of the people; and they said, "All that the LORD has spoken we will do, and we will be obedient." ⁸Moses took the blood and dashed it on the people, and said, "See the blood of the covenant that the LORD has made with you in accordance with all these words."

On the Mountain with God

9 Then Moses and Aaron, Nadab, and Abihu, and seventy of the elders of Israel went up, ¹⁰and they saw the God of Israel. Under his feet there was something like a pavement of sapphire stone,

When God Was Obvious
Few atheists, but many rebels

WHY DOESN'T GOD INTERVENE MORE? Why doesn't he directly feed the hungry, heal all the sick, and stop all wars? If God really exists, at the least why doesn't he make himself more obvious?

People who ask such questions often assume that if God ever did spectacularly reveal himself, all doubts would vanish. Everyone would line up to believe in him.

The appearance of the glory of the LORD was like a devouring fire on the top of the mountain in the sight of the people of Israel. 24.17

Astonishing Reactions

Exodus tells of a time when God made himself perfectly obvious. The plagues on Egypt revealed his mighty power. An enormous miracle at the Red Sea provided sensational deliverance. A recurring miracle supplied food for the Israelites every morning. And, if questions about God's existence arose, doubters needed only to look to the ever-present glory cloud or pillar of fire. It must have been hard to be an atheist in those days.

Yet every instance of God's faithfulness seemed to summon up astonishing human *un*faithfulness. The same Israelites who had watched God crush a pharaoh quaked at the first sign of Egyptian chariots. Three days after a miraculous escape across the Red Sea they were grumbling to Moses and God about water supplies.

A month or so later, when hunger pangs began to gnaw at them, they bitterly complained, "If only we had died by the hand of the LORD in the land of Egypt, when we sat by the fleshpots and ate our fill of bread; for you have brought us out into this wilderness to kill this whole assembly with hunger" (16.3). God responded with a provision of manna (that would continue for 40 years) and quail, but the Israelites were soon grousing about the water supplies again.

The Great Rebellion

Exodus 32 shows the Israelites at their worst. People who had eaten manna for breakfast, who had just solemnly agreed to keep every word of the covenant, who were at that moment standing beside a mountain stormy with the Lord's presence—those very people proceeded to melt down their gold jewelry and flagrantly flout the first commandment.

"Stiff-necked," God called the Israelites as he burned in anger against them. Only Moses' eloquent appeal saved their lives.

The history of the Israelites should nail a coffin lid on the notion that impressive displays of God's power will guarantee faith. (Jesus would later say, "If they do not listen to Moses and the prophets, neither will they be convinced even if someone rises from the dead," Luke 16.31.) People who had everyday proof of God demonstrated only one thing: the monotonous consistency of human nature.

The offenders would pay for their acts by wandering 40 years in a desolate wilderness while a new, untainted generation grew up to replace them. But a pattern was beginning to emerge: If the Israelites failed God in the shadow of Mount Sinai, how would they possibly withstand the seduction of new cultures in the promised land? The next generation, too, would fail God, as would all their descendants. The old covenant, as Paul would so convincingly argue in the book of Galatians, succeeded mainly by proving undeniably the need for a new one.

Life Questions: Do you ever have doubts about God's existence? What would it take to completely convince you?

like the very heaven for clearness. [11]God[f] did not lay his hand on the chief men of the people of Israel; also they beheld God, and they ate and drank.

24.8 Covenant Blood

This chapter depicts one of the most important transactions in Israel's history. Since Aaron and his sons had not yet been named or consecrated, Moses served as priest for the dramatic personal encounter with God. A unique sacrifice formally set Israel apart as the people of God and laid the foundation for all the sacrifices to follow.

The New Testament applies the very phraseology from this solemn ceremony to the new covenant made possible by Christ's sacrifice. The phrase "blood of the covenant" appears six times in the New Testament, in each case referring to the death of Christ. Jesus himself used the phrase at the Last Supper (Matthew 26.28), and it became a part of the ceremony of the Lord's Supper.

12 The LORD said to Moses, "Come up to me on the mountain, and wait there; and I will give you the tablets of stone, with the law and the commandment, which I have written for their instruction." [13]So Moses set out with his assistant Joshua, and Moses went up into the mountain of God. [14]To the elders he had said, "Wait here for us, until we come to you again; for Aaron and Hur are with you; whoever has a dispute may go to them."

15 Then Moses went up on the mountain, and the cloud covered the mountain. [16]The glory of the LORD settled on Mount Sinai, and the cloud covered it for six days; on the seventh day he called to Moses out of the cloud. [17]Now the appearance of the glory of the LORD was like a devouring fire on the top of the mountain in the sight of the people of Israel. [18]Moses entered the cloud, and went up on the mountain. Moses was on the mountain for forty days and forty nights.

Offerings for the Tabernacle

25 The LORD said to Moses: [2]Tell the Israelites to take for me an offering; from all whose hearts prompt them to give you shall receive the offering for me. [3]This is the offering that you shall receive from them: gold, silver, and bronze, [4]blue, purple, and crimson yarns and fine linen, goats' hair, [5]tanned rams' skins, fine leather,[g] acacia wood, [6]oil for the lamps, spices for the anointing oil and for the fragrant incense, [7]onyx stones and gems to be set in the ephod and for the breastpiece. [8]And have them make me a sanctuary, so

that I may dwell among them. [9]In accordance with all that I show you concerning the pattern of the tabernacle and of all its furniture, so you shall make it.

The Ark of the Covenant

10 They shall make an ark of acacia wood; it shall be two and a half cubits long, a cubit and a half wide, and a cubit and a half high. [11]You shall overlay it with pure gold, inside and outside you shall overlay it, and you shall make a molding of gold upon it all around. [12]You shall cast four rings of gold for it and put them on its four feet, two rings on the one side of it, and two rings on the other side. [13]You shall make poles of acacia wood, and overlay them with gold. [14]And you shall put the poles into the rings on the sides of the ark, by which to carry the ark. [15]The poles shall remain in the rings of the ark; they shall not be taken from it. [16]You shall put into the ark the covenant[h] that I shall give you.

25.8 The Skills of Civilization

The children of Jacob, or Israel, had arrived in Egypt as a band of nomads. But 400 years in an advanced culture permitted them time to master the arts and trades of civilization. Crafting the sacred objects of the tabernacle put all these learned skills to use. In addition, God gave specific abilities to some key workmen (see 31.1–6).

17 Then you shall make a mercy seat[i] of pure gold; two cubits and a half shall be its length, and a cubit and a half its width. [18]You shall make two cherubim of gold; you shall make them of hammered work, at the two ends of the mercy seat.[j] [19]Make one cherub at the one end, and one cherub at the other; of one piece with the mercy seat[j] you shall make the cherubim at its two ends. [20]The cherubim shall spread out their wings above, overshadowing the mercy seat[j] with their wings. They shall face one to another; the faces of the cherubim shall be turned toward the mercy seat.[j] [21]You shall put the mercy seat[j] on the top of the ark; and in the ark you shall put the covenant[h] that I shall give you. [22]There I will meet with you, and from above the mercy seat,[j] from between the two cherubim that are on the ark of the covenant,[h] I will deliver to you all my commands for the Israelites.

The Table for the Bread of the Presence

23 You shall make a table of acacia wood, two cubits long, one cubit wide, and a cubit and a half high. [24]You shall overlay it with pure gold, and make a molding of gold around it. [25]You shall

---

[f] Heb *He*   [g] Meaning of Heb uncertain   [h] Or *treaty*, or *testimony*; Heb *eduth*   [i] Or *a cover*   [j] Or *the cover*

make around it a rim a handbreadth wide, and a molding of gold around the rim. ²⁶You shall make for it four rings of gold, and fasten the rings to the four corners at its four legs. ²⁷The rings that hold the poles used for carrying the table shall be close to the rim. ²⁸You shall make the poles of acacia wood, and overlay them with gold, and the table shall be carried with these. ²⁹You shall make its plates and dishes for incense, and its flagons and bowls with which to pour drink offerings; you shall make them of pure gold. ³⁰And you shall set the bread of the Presence on the table before me always.

The Lampstand

31 You shall make a lampstand of pure gold. The base and the shaft of the lampstand shall be made of hammered work; its cups, its calyxes, and its petals shall be of one piece with it; ³²and there shall be six branches going out of its sides, three branches of the lampstand out of one side of it and three branches of the lampstand out of the other side of it; ³³three cups shaped like almond blossoms, each with calyx and petals, on one branch, and three cups shaped like almond blossoms, each with calyx and petals, on the other branch—so for the six branches going out of the lampstand. ³⁴On the lampstand itself there shall be four cups shaped like almond blossoms, each with its calyxes and petals. ³⁵There shall be a calyx of one piece with it under the first pair of branches, a calyx of one piece with it under the next pair of branches, and a calyx of one piece with it under the last pair of branches—so for the six branches that go out of the lampstand. ³⁶Their calyxes and their branches shall be of one piece with it, the whole of it one hammered piece of pure gold. ³⁷You shall make the seven lamps for it; and the lamps shall be set up so as to give light on the space in front of it. ³⁸Its snuffers and trays shall be of pure gold. ³⁹It, and all these utensils, shall be made from a talent of pure gold. ⁴⁰And see that you make them according to the pattern for them, which is being shown you on the mountain.

The Tabernacle

26 Moreover you shall make the tabernacle with ten curtains of fine twisted linen, and blue, purple, and crimson yarns; you shall make them with cherubim skillfully worked into them. ²The length of each curtain shall be twenty-eight cubits, and the width of each curtain four cubits; all the curtains shall be of the same size. ³Five curtains shall be joined to one another; and the other five curtains shall be joined to one another. ⁴You shall make loops of blue on the edge of the outermost curtain in the first set; and likewise you shall make loops on the edge of the outermost curtain in the second set. ⁵You shall make fifty loops on the one curtain, and you shall make fifty loops on the edge of the curtain that is in the second set; the loops shall be opposite one another. ⁶You shall make fifty clasps of gold, and join the curtains to one another with the clasps, so that the tabernacle may be one whole.

7 You shall also make curtains of goats' hair for a tent over the tabernacle; you shall make eleven curtains. ⁸The length of each curtain shall be thirty cubits, and the width of each curtain four cubits; the eleven curtains shall be of the same size. ⁹You shall join five curtains by themselves, and six curtains by themselves, and the sixth curtain you shall double over at the front of the tent. ¹⁰You shall make fifty loops on the edge of the curtain that is outermost in one set, and fifty loops on the edge of the curtain that is outermost in the second set.

11 You shall make fifty clasps of bronze, and put the clasps into the loops, and join the tent together, so that it may be one whole. ¹²The part that remains of the curtains of the tent, the half curtain that remains, shall hang over the back of the tabernacle. ¹³The cubit on the one side, and the cubit on the other side, of what remains in the length of the curtains of the tent, shall hang over the sides of the tabernacle, on this side and that side, to cover it. ¹⁴You shall make for the tent a covering of tanned rams' skins and an outer covering of fine leather.^k

The Framework

15 You shall make upright frames of acacia wood for the tabernacle. ¹⁶Ten cubits shall be the length of a frame, and a cubit and a half the width of each frame. ¹⁷There shall be two pegs in each frame to fit the frames together; you shall make these for all the frames of the tabernacle. ¹⁸You shall make the frames for the tabernacle: twenty frames for the south side; ¹⁹and you shall make forty bases of silver under the twenty frames, two bases under the first frame for its two pegs, and two bases under the next frame for its two pegs; ²⁰and for the second side of the tabernacle, on the north side twenty frames, ²¹and their forty bases of silver, two bases under the first frame, and two bases under the next frame; ²²and for the rear of the tabernacle westward you shall make six frames. ²³You shall make two frames for corners of the tabernacle in the rear; ²⁴they shall be separate beneath, but joined at the top, at the first ring; it shall be the same with both of them; they shall form the two corners. ²⁵And so there shall be eight frames, with their bases of silver, sixteen bases; two bases under the first frame, and two bases under the next frame.

26 You shall make bars of acacia wood, five for the frames of the one side of the tabernacle,

²⁷and five bars for the frames of the other side of the tabernacle, and five bars for the frames of the side of the tabernacle at the rear westward. ²⁸The middle bar, halfway up the frames, shall pass through from end to end. ²⁹You shall overlay the frames with gold, and shall make their rings of gold to hold the bars; and you shall overlay the bars with gold. ³⁰Then you shall erect the tabernacle according to the plan for it that you were shown on the mountain.

The Curtain

31 You shall make a curtain of blue, purple, and crimson yarns, and of fine twisted linen; it shall be made with cherubim skillfully worked into it. ³²You shall hang it on four pillars of acacia overlaid with gold, which have hooks of gold and rest on four bases of silver. ³³You shall hang the curtain under the clasps, and bring the ark of the covenant¹ in there, within the curtain; and the curtain shall separate for you the holy place

26.33 A Torn Curtain

The thick curtain described here separated the holy place from the most holy place. Anyone who ventured beyond that curtain would die. The New Testament, however, records that at Jesus' crucifixion the curtain tore in two, from top to bottom. The tearing symbolized what Christ had accomplished: he broke down the separation between God and humanity (Matthew 27.51; Hebrews 10.20).

from the most holy. ³⁴You shall put the mercy seat^m on the ark of the covenant¹ in the most holy place. ³⁵You shall set the table outside the curtain, and the lampstand on the south side of the tabernacle opposite the table; and you shall put the table on the north side.

36 You shall make a screen for the entrance of the tent, of blue, purple, and crimson yarns, and of fine twisted linen, embroidered with needlework. ³⁷You shall make for the screen five pillars of acacia, and overlay them with gold; their hooks shall be of gold, and you shall cast five bases of bronze for them.

The Altar of Burnt Offering

27 You shall make the altar of acacia wood, five cubits long and five cubits wide; the altar shall be square, and it shall be three cubits high. ²You shall make horns for it on its four corners; its horns shall be of one piece with it, and you shall overlay it with bronze. ³You shall make pots for it to receive its ashes, and shovels and basins and forks and firepans; you shall make all its utensils of bronze. ⁴You shall also make for it

a grating, a network of bronze; and on the net you shall make four bronze rings at its four corners. ⁵You shall set it under the ledge of the altar so that the net shall extend halfway down the altar. ⁶You shall make poles for the altar, poles of acacia wood, and overlay them with bronze; ⁷the poles shall be put through the rings, so that the poles shall be on the two sides of the altar when it is carried. ⁸You shall make it hollow, with boards. They shall be made just as you were shown on the mountain.

The Court and Its Hangings

9 You shall make the court of the tabernacle. On the south side the court shall have hangings of fine twisted linen one hundred cubits long for that side; ¹⁰its twenty pillars and their twenty bases shall be of bronze, but the hooks of the pillars and their bands shall be of silver. ¹¹Likewise for its length on the north side there shall be hangings one hundred cubits long, their pillars twenty and their bases twenty, of bronze, but the hooks of the pillars and their bands shall be of silver. ¹²For the width of the court on the west side there shall be fifty cubits of hangings, with ten pillars and ten bases. ¹³The width of the court on the front to the east shall be fifty cubits. ¹⁴There shall be fifteen cubits of hangings on the one side, with three pillars and three bases. ¹⁵There shall be fifteen cubits of hangings on the other side, with three pillars and three bases. ¹⁶For the gate of the court there shall be a screen twenty cubits long, of blue, purple, and crimson yarns, and of fine twisted linen, embroidered with needlework; it shall have four pillars and with them four bases. ¹⁷All the pillars around the court shall be banded with silver; their hooks shall be of silver, and their bases of bronze. ¹⁸The length of the court shall be one hundred cubits, the width fifty, and the height five cubits, with hangings of fine twisted linen and bases of bronze. ¹⁹All the utensils of the tabernacle for every use, and all its pegs and all the pegs of the court, shall be of bronze.

The Oil for the Lamp

20 You shall further command the Israelites to bring you pure oil of beaten olives for the light, so that a lamp may be set up to burn regularly. ²¹In the tent of meeting, outside the curtain that is before the covenant,¹ Aaron and his sons shall tend it from evening to morning before the LORD. It shall be a perpetual ordinance to be observed throughout their generations by the Israelites.

Vestments for the Priesthood

28 Then bring near to you your brother Aaron, and his sons with him, from among the Israelites, to serve me as priests—Aaron and

---

¹ Or *treaty*, or *testimony*; Heb *eduth*   ^m Or *the cover*

Aaron's sons, Nadab and Abihu, Eleazar and Ithamar. [2]You shall make sacred vestments for the glorious adornment of your brother Aaron. [3]And you shall speak to all who have ability, whom I have endowed with skill, that they make Aaron's vestments to consecrate him for my priesthood. [4]These are the vestments that they shall make: a breastpiece, an ephod, a robe, a checkered tunic, a turban, and a sash. When they make these sacred vestments for your brother Aaron and his sons to serve me as priests, [5]they shall use gold, blue, purple, and crimson yarns, and fine linen.

The Ephod

6 They shall make the ephod of gold, of blue, purple, and crimson yarns, and of fine twisted linen, skillfully worked. [7]It shall have two shoulder-pieces attached to its two edges, so that it may be joined together. [8]The decorated band on it shall be of the same workmanship and materials, of gold, of blue, purple, and crimson yarns, and of fine twisted linen. [9]You shall take two onyx stones, and engrave on them the names of the sons of Israel, [10]six of their names on the one stone, and the names of the remaining six on the other stone, in the order of their birth. [11]As a gem-cutter engraves signets, so you shall engrave the two stones with the names of the sons of Israel; you shall mount them in settings of gold filigree. [12]You shall set the two stones on the shoulder-pieces of the ephod, as stones of remembrance for the sons of Israel; and Aaron shall bear their names before the LORD on his two shoulders for remembrance. [13]You shall make settings of gold filigree, [14]and two chains of pure gold, twisted like cords; and you shall attach the corded chains to the settings.

The Breastplate

15 You shall make a breastpiece of judgment, in skilled work; you shall make it in the style of the ephod; of gold, of blue and purple and crimson yarns, and of fine twisted linen you shall make it. [16]It shall be square and doubled, a span in length and a span in width. [17]You shall set in it four rows of stones. A row of carnelian,[n] chrysolite, and emerald shall be the first row; [18]and the second row a turquoise, a sapphire[o] and a moonstone; [19]and the third row a jacinth, an agate, and an amethyst; [20]and the fourth row a beryl, an onyx, and a jasper; they shall be set in gold filigree. [21]There shall be twelve stones with names corresponding to the names of the sons of Israel; they shall be like signets, each engraved with its name, for the twelve tribes. [22]You shall make for the breastpiece chains of pure gold, twisted like cords; [23]and you shall make for the breastpiece two rings of gold, and put the two rings on the two edges of the breastpiece. [24]You shall put the two cords of gold in the two rings at the edges of the breastpiece; [25]the two ends of the two cords you shall attach to the two settings, and so attach it in front to the shoulder-pieces of the ephod. [26]You shall make two rings of gold, and put them at the two ends of the breastpiece, on its inside edge next to the ephod. [27]You shall make two rings of gold, and attach them in front to the lower part of the two shoulder-pieces of the ephod, at its joining above the decorated band of the ephod. [28]The breastpiece shall be bound by its rings to the rings of the ephod with a blue cord, so that it may lie on the decorated band of the ephod, and so that the breastpiece shall not come loose from the ephod. [29]So Aaron shall bear the names of the sons of Israel in the breastpiece of judgment on his heart when he goes into the holy place, for a continual remembrance before the LORD. [30]In the breastpiece of judgment you shall put the Urim and the Thummim, and they shall be on Aaron's heart when he goes in before the LORD; thus Aaron shall bear the judgment of the Israelites on his heart before the LORD continually.

Other Priestly Vestments

31 You shall make the robe of the ephod all of blue. [32]It shall have an opening for the head in the middle of it, with a woven binding around the opening, like the opening in a coat of mail,[p] so that it may not be torn. [33]On its lower hem you shall make pomegranates of blue, purple, and crimson yarns, all around the lower hem, with bells of gold between them all around—[34]a golden bell and a pomegranate alternating all around the lower hem of the robe. [35]Aaron shall wear it when he ministers, and its sound shall be heard when he goes into the holy place before the LORD, and when he comes out, so that he may not die.

36 You shall make a rosette of pure gold, and engrave on it, like the engraving of a signet, "Holy to the LORD." [37]You shall fasten it on the turban with a blue cord; it shall be on the front of the turban. [38]It shall be on Aaron's forehead, and Aaron shall take on himself any guilt incurred in the holy offering that the Israelites consecrate as their sacred donations; it shall always be on his forehead, in order that they may find favor before the LORD.

39 You shall make the checkered tunic of fine linen, and you shall make a turban of fine linen, and you shall make a sash embroidered with needlework.

40 For Aaron's sons you shall make tunics and sashes and headdresses; you shall make them for their glorious adornment. [41]You shall put them on your brother Aaron, and on his sons with him, and shall anoint them and ordain them and consecrate them, so that they may serve me

---

n The identity of several of these stones is uncertain   o Or *lapis lazuli*   p Meaning of Heb uncertain

as priests. ⁴²You shall make for them linen under-garments to cover their naked flesh; they shall reach from the hips to the thighs; ⁴³Aaron and his sons shall wear them when they go into the tent of meeting, or when they come near the altar to minister in the holy place; or they will bring guilt on themselves and die. This shall be a perpetual ordinance for him and for his descendants after him.

The Ordination of the Priests

29 Now this is what you shall do to them to consecrate them, so that they may serve me as priests. Take one young bull and two rams without blemish, ²and unleavened bread, unleavened cakes mixed with oil, and unleavened wafers spread with oil. You shall make them of choice wheat flour. ³You shall put them in one basket and bring them in the basket, and bring the bull and the two rams. ⁴You shall bring Aaron and his sons to the entrance of the tent of meeting, and wash them with water. ⁵Then you shall take the vestments, and put on Aaron the tunic and the robe of the ephod, and the ephod, and the breast-piece, and gird him with the decorated band of the ephod; ⁶and you shall set the turban on his head, and put the holy diadem on the turban. ⁷You shall take the anointing oil, and pour it on his head and anoint him. ⁸Then you shall bring his sons, and put tunics on them, ⁹and you shall gird them with sashes*q* and tie headdresses on them; and the priesthood shall be theirs by a per-petual ordinance. You shall then ordain Aaron and his sons.

10 You shall bring the bull in front of the tent of meeting. Aaron and his sons shall lay their hands on the head of the bull, ¹¹and you shall slaughter the bull before the LORD, at the entrance of the tent of meeting, ¹²and shall take some of the blood of the bull and put it on the horns of the altar with your finger, and all the rest of the blood you shall pour out at the base of the altar. ¹³You shall take all the fat that covers the entrails, and the appendage of the liver, and the two kidneys with the fat that is on them, and turn them into smoke on the altar. ¹⁴But the flesh of the bull, and its skin, and its dung, you shall burn with fire outside the camp; it is a sin offering.

15 Then you shall take one of the rams, and Aaron and his sons shall lay their hands on the head of the ram, ¹⁶and you shall slaughter the ram, and shall take its blood and dash it against all sides of the altar. ¹⁷Then you shall cut the ram into its parts, and wash its entrails and its legs, and put them with its parts and its head, ¹⁸and turn the whole ram into smoke on the altar; it is a burnt offering to the LORD; it is a pleasing odor, an offering by fire to the LORD.

19 You shall take the other ram; and Aaron

and his sons shall lay their hands on the head of the ram, ²⁰and you shall slaughter the ram, and take some of its blood and put it on the lobe of Aaron's right ear and on the lobes of the right ears of his sons, and on the thumbs of their right hands, and on the big toes of their right feet, and dash the rest of the blood against all sides of the

29.20 The Whole Body

As part of their purification, the priests daubed blood on their ears (which hear God's laws), their hands (which do his will), and their toes (which were prepared to follow in his steps).

altar. ²¹Then you shall take some of the blood that is on the altar, and some of the anointing oil, and sprinkle it on Aaron and his vestments and on his sons and his sons' vestments with him; then he and his vestments shall be holy, as well as his sons and his sons' vestments.

22 You shall also take the fat of the ram, the fat tail, the fat that covers the entrails, the appen-dage of the liver, the two kidneys with the fat that is on them, and the right thigh (for it is a ram of ordination), ²³and one loaf of bread, one cake of bread made with oil, and one wafer, out of the basket of unleavened bread that is before the LORD; ²⁴and you shall place all these on the palms of Aaron and on the palms of his sons, and raise them as an elevation offering before the LORD. ²⁵Then you shall take them from their hands, and turn them into smoke on the altar on top of the burnt offering of pleasing odor before the LORD; it is an offering by fire to the LORD.

26 You shall take the breast of the ram of Aaron's ordination and raise it as an elevation offering before the LORD; and it shall be your portion. ²⁷You shall consecrate the breast that was raised as an elevation offering and the thigh that was raised as an elevation offering from the ram of ordination, from that which belonged to Aaron and his sons. ²⁸These things shall be a perpetual ordinance for Aaron and his sons from the Israel-ites, for this is an offering; and it shall be an offering by the Israelites from their sacrifice of offerings of well-being, their offering to the LORD.

29 The sacred vestments of Aaron shall be passed on to his sons after him; they shall be anointed in them and ordained in them. ³⁰The son who is priest in his place shall wear them seven days, when he comes into the tent of meet-ing to minister in the holy place.

31 You shall take the ram of ordination, and boil its flesh in a holy place; ³²and Aaron and his sons shall eat the flesh of the ram and the bread that is in the basket, at the entrance of the tent of

q Gk: Heb sashes, Aaron and his sons

meeting. [33]They themselves shall eat the food by which atonement is made, to ordain and consecrate them, but no one else shall eat of them, because they are holy. [34]If any of the flesh for the ordination, or of the bread, remains until the morning, then you shall burn the remainder with fire; it shall not be eaten, because it is holy.

35 Thus you shall do to Aaron and to his sons, just as I have commanded you; through seven days you shall ordain them. [36]Also every day you shall offer a bull as a sin offering for atonement. Also you shall offer a sin offering for the altar, when you make atonement for it, and shall anoint it, to consecrate it. [37]Seven days you shall make atonement for the altar, and consecrate it, and the altar shall be most holy; whatever touches the altar shall become holy.

The Daily Offerings

38 Now this is what you shall offer on the altar: two lambs a year old regularly each day. [39]One lamb you shall offer in the morning, and the other lamb you shall offer in the evening; [40]and with the first lamb one-tenth of a measure of choice flour mixed with one-fourth of a hin of beaten oil, and one-fourth of a hin of wine for a drink offering. [41]And the other lamb you shall offer in the evening, and shall offer with it a grain offering and its drink offering, as in the morning, for a pleasing odor, an offering by fire to the LORD. [42]It shall be a regular burnt offering throughout your generations at the entrance of the tent of meeting before the LORD, where I will meet with you, to speak to you there. [43]I will meet with the Israelites there, and it shall be sanctified by my glory; [44]I will consecrate the tent of meeting and the altar; Aaron also and his sons I will consecrate, to serve me as priests. [45]I will dwell among the Israelites, and I will be their God. [46]And they shall know that I am the LORD their God, who brought them out of the land of Egypt that I might dwell among them; I am the LORD their God.

The Altar of Incense

30 You shall make an altar on which to offer incense; you shall make it of acacia wood. [2]It shall be one cubit long, and one cubit wide; it shall be square, and shall be two cubits high; its horns shall be of one piece with it. [3]You shall overlay it with pure gold, its top, and its sides all around and its horns; and you shall make for it a molding of gold all around. [4]And you shall make two golden rings for it; under its molding on two opposite sides of it you shall make them, and they shall hold the poles with which to carry it. [5]You shall make the poles of acacia wood, and overlay them with gold. [6]You shall place it in front of the curtain that is above the ark of the covenant,[r] in front of the mercy seat[s] that is over the covenant,[r] where I will meet with you. [7]Aaron shall offer fragrant incense on it; every morning when he dresses the lamps he shall offer it, [8]and when Aaron sets up the lamps in the evening, he shall offer it, a regular incense offering before the LORD throughout your generations. [9]You shall not offer unholy incense on it, or a burnt offering, or a grain offering; and you shall not pour a drink offering on it. [10]Once a year Aaron shall perform the rite of atonement on its horns. Throughout your generations he shall perform the atonement for it once a year with the blood of the atoning sin offering. It is most holy to the LORD.

30.10 Jewish Holy Days

Orthodox Jews still faithfully honor the day of atonement described here, the holy day of Yom Kippur. But the New Testament book of Hebrews reinterprets this period of time as a copy, or shadow, of the real thing to come in Jesus Christ. What a high priest accomplished, through elaborate ceremony, once a year on the day of atonement, Christ did once for all (Hebrews 8–9). As a consequence, all of us—not just a purified priest—can confidently "enter the most holy place."

The Half Shekel for the Sanctuary

11 The LORD spoke to Moses: [12]When you take a census of the Israelites to register them, at registration all of them shall give a ransom for their lives to the LORD, so that no plague may come upon them for being registered. [13]This is what each one who is registered shall give: half a shekel according to the shekel of the sanctuary (the shekel is twenty gerahs), half a shekel as an offering to the LORD. [14]Each one who is registered, from twenty years old and upward, shall give the LORD's offering. [15]The rich shall not give more, and the poor shall not give less, than the half shekel, when you bring this offering to the LORD to make atonement for your lives. [16]You shall take the atonement money from the Israelites and shall designate it for the service of the tent of meeting; before the LORD it will be a reminder to the Israelites of the ransom given for your lives.

The Bronze Basin

17 The LORD spoke to Moses: [18]You shall make a bronze basin with a bronze stand for washing. You shall put it between the tent of meeting and the altar, and you shall put water in it; [19]with the water[t] Aaron and his sons shall wash their hands and their feet. [20]When they go into the tent of meeting, or when they come near

---

[r] Or *treaty*, or *testimony*; Heb *eduth*   [s] Or *the cover*   [t] Heb *it*

the altar to minister, to make an offering by fire to the LORD, they shall wash with water, so that they may not die. 21They shall wash their hands and their feet, so that they may not die: it shall be a perpetual ordinance for them, for him and for his descendants throughout their generations.

The Anointing Oil and Incense

22 The LORD spoke to Moses: 23Take the finest spices: of liquid myrrh five hundred shekels, and of sweet-smelling cinnamon half as much, that is, two hundred fifty, and two hundred fifty of aromatic cane, 24and five hundred of cassia—measured by the sanctuary shekel—and a hin of olive oil; 25and you shall make of these a sacred anointing oil blended as by the perfumer; it shall be a holy anointing oil. 26With it you shall anoint the tent of meeting and the ark of the covenant,u 27and the table and all its utensils, and the lampstand and its utensils, and the altar of incense, 28and the altar of burnt offering with all its utensils, and the basin with its stand; 29you shall consecrate them, so that they may be most holy; whatever touches them will become holy. 30You shall anoint Aaron and his sons, and consecrate them, in order that they may serve me as priests. 31You shall say to the Israelites, "This shall be my holy anointing oil throughout your generations. 32It shall not be used in any ordinary anointing of the body, and you shall make no other like it in composition; it is holy, and it shall be holy to you. 33Whoever compounds any like it or whoever puts any of it on an unqualified person shall be cut off from the people."

34 The LORD said to Moses: Take sweet spices, stacte, and onycha, and galbanum, sweet spices with pure frankincense (an equal part of each), 35and make an incense blended as by the perfumer, seasoned with salt, pure and holy; 36and you shall beat some of it into powder, and put part of it before the covenantu in the tent of meeting where I shall meet with you; it shall be for you most holy. 37When you make incense according to this composition, you shall not make it for yourselves; it shall be regarded by you as holy to the LORD. 38Whoever makes any like it to use as perfume shall be cut off from the people.

Bezalel and Oholiab

31 The LORD spoke to Moses: 2See, I have called by name Bezalel son of Uri son of Hur, of the tribe of Judah: 3and I have filled him with divine spirit,v with ability, intelligence, and knowledge in every kind of craft, 4to devise artistic designs, to work in gold, silver, and bronze, 5in cutting stones for setting, and in carving wood, in every kind of craft. 6Moreover, I have appointed with him Oholiab son of Ahisamach, of the tribe

of Dan; and I have given skill to all the skillful, so that they may make all that I have commanded you: 7the tent of meeting, and the ark of the covenant,u and the mercy seatw that is on it, and all the furnishings of the tent, 8the table and its utensils, and the pure lampstand with all its utensils, and the altar of incense, 9and the altar of burnt offering with all its utensils, and the basin with its stand, 10and the finely worked vestments, the holy vestments for the priest Aaron and the vestments of his sons, for their service as priests, 11and the anointing oil and the fragrant incense for the holy place. They shall do just as I have commanded you.

The Sabbath Law

12 The LORD said to Moses: 13You yourself are to speak to the Israelites: "You shall keep my sabbaths, for this is a sign between me and you throughout your generations, given in order that you may know that I, the LORD, sanctify you. 14You shall keep the sabbath, because it is holy for you; everyone who profanes it shall be put to death; whoever does any work on it shall be cut off from among the people. 15Six days shall work be done, but the seventh day is a sabbath of solemn rest, holy to the LORD; whoever does any work on the sabbath day shall be put to death. 16Therefore the Israelites shall keep the sabbath, observing the sabbath throughout their generations, as a perpetual covenant. 17It is a sign forever between me and the people of Israel that in six days the LORD made heaven and earth, and on the seventh day he rested, and was refreshed."

The Two Tablets of the Covenant

18 When Godx finished speaking with Moses on Mount Sinai, he gave him the two tablets of the covenant,u tablets of stone, written with the finger of God.

The Golden Calf

32 When the people saw that Moses delayed to come down from the mountain, the people gathered around Aaron, and said to him, "Come, make gods for us, who shall go before us; as for this Moses, the man who brought us up out of the land of Egypt, we do not know what has become of him." 2Aaron said to them, "Take off the gold rings that are on the ears of your wives, your sons, and your daughters, and bring them to me." 3So all the people took off the gold rings from their ears, and brought them to Aaron. 4He took the gold from them, formed it in a mold,y and cast an image of a calf; and they said, "These are your gods, O Israel, who brought you up out of the land of Egypt!" 5When Aaron saw this, he built an altar before it; and Aaron made procla-

---

u Or treaty, or testimony; Heb eduth   v Or with the spirit of God   w Or the cover   x Heb he   y Or fashioned it
with a graving tool; Meaning of Heb uncertain

mation and said, "Tomorrow shall be a festival to the LORD." 6They rose early the next day, and offered burnt offerings and brought sacrifices of well-being; and the people sat down to eat and drink, and rose up to revel.

32.4–8 Recent Discovery

Not until 1990 did archaeologists unearth the first golden calf in Palestine, and, to their surprise, it stood only a few inches tall. Contrary to popular depictions in movies and historical books, Aaron's solid gold calf too may have been very small, but elevated on a pedestal for visual emphasis. Undoubtedly the Israelites knew of the bull-god Apis, one of Egypt's important gods.

Moses stayed on Mount Sinai for nearly six weeks (24.18), which helps explain the Israelites' panicky behavior. Had Moses died or run away? Would he ever come back? Nevertheless, by flagrantly breaking the second commandment they failed their first test under the new covenant with God.

7 The LORD said to Moses, "Go down at once! Your people, whom you brought up out of the land of Egypt, have acted perversely; 8they have been quick to turn aside from the way that I commanded them; they have cast for themselves an image of a calf, and have worshiped it and sacrificed to it, and said, 'These are your gods, O Israel, who brought you up out of the land of Egypt!'" 9The LORD said to Moses, "I have seen this people, how stiff-necked they are. 10Now let me alone, so that my wrath may burn hot against them and I may consume them; and of you I will make a great nation."

11 But Moses implored the LORD his God, and said, "O LORD, why does your wrath burn hot against your people, whom you brought out of the land of Egypt with great power and with a mighty hand? 12Why should the Egyptians say, 'It was with evil intent that he brought them out to kill them in the mountains, and to consume them from the face of the earth'? Turn from your fierce wrath; change your mind and do not bring disaster on your people. 13Remember Abraham, Isaac, and Israel, your servants, how you swore to them by your own self, saying to them, 'I will multiply your descendants like the stars of heaven, and all this land that I have promised I will give to your descendants, and they shall inherit it forever.'" 14And the LORD changed his mind about the disaster that he planned to bring on his people.

15 Then Moses turned and went down from the mountain, carrying the two tablets of the covenant[z] in his hands, tablets that were written on both sides, written on the front and on the back. 16The tablets were the work of God, and the writing was the writing of God, engraved upon the tablets. 17When Joshua heard the noise of the people as they shouted, he said to Moses, "There is a noise of war in the camp." 18But he said,

"It is not the sound made by victors,
or the sound made by losers;
it is the sound of revelers that I hear."

19As soon as he came near the camp and saw the calf and the dancing, Moses' anger burned hot, and he threw the tablets from his hands and broke them at the foot of the mountain. 20He took the calf that they had made, burned it with fire, ground it to powder, scattered it on the water, and made the Israelites drink it.

21 Moses said to Aaron, "What did this people do to you that you have brought so great a sin upon them?" 22And Aaron said, "Do not let the anger of my lord burn hot; you know the people, that they are bent on evil. 23They said to me, 'Make us gods, who shall go before us; as for this Moses, the man who brought us up out of the land of Egypt, we do not know what has become of him.' 24So I said to them, 'Whoever has gold, take it off'; so they gave it to me, and I threw it into the fire, and out came this calf!"

25 When Moses saw that the people were running wild (for Aaron had let them run wild, to the derision of their enemies), 26then Moses stood in the gate of the camp, and said, "Who is on the LORD's side? Come to me!" And all the sons of Levi gathered around him. 27He said to them, "Thus says the LORD, the God of Israel, 'Put your sword on your side, each of you! Go back and forth from gate to gate throughout the camp, and each of you kill your brother, your friend, and your neighbor.'" 28The sons of Levi did as Moses commanded, and about three thousand of the people fell on that day. 29Moses said, "Today you have ordained yourselves[a] for the service of the LORD, each one at the cost of a son or a brother, and so have brought a blessing on yourselves this day."

30 On the next day Moses said to the people, "You have sinned a great sin. But now I will go up to the LORD; perhaps I can make atonement for your sin." 31So Moses returned to the LORD and said, "Alas, this people has sinned a great sin; they have made for themselves gods of gold. 32But now, if you will only forgive their sin—but if not, blot me out of the book that you have written." 33But the LORD said to Moses, "Whoever has sinned against me I will blot out of my book. 34But now go, lead the people to the place about which I have spoken to you; see, my angel shall go in front of you. Nevertheless, when the day comes for punishment, I will punish them for their sin."

35 Then the LORD sent a plague on the people,

---

[z] Or treaty, or testimony; Heb eduth   [a] Gk Vg Compare Tg: Heb Today ordain yourselves

because they made the calf—the one that Aaron made.

The Command to Leave Sinai

33 The LORD said to Moses, "Go, leave this place, you and the people whom you have brought up out of the land of Egypt, and go to the land of which I swore to Abraham, Isaac, and Jacob, saying, 'To your descendants I will give it.' [2]I will send an angel before you, and I will drive out the Canaanites, the Amorites, the Hittites, the Perizzites, the Hivites, and the Jebusites. [3]Go up to a land flowing with milk and honey; but I will not go up among you, or I would consume you on the way, for you are a stiff-necked people."

33.3 Why the Israelites?

This remarkable scene shows Moses pleading with God not to abandon the Israelites, his chosen people. Eventually, God did agree to lead them on (verse 17). Why were the children of Israel chosen? Why not some other race? When the Bible touches on the question at all, it gives no comprehensive answer. Usually, the reply boils down to something like this, "I will show mercy on whom I will show mercy" (verse 19). God reserves the right to choose whomever he wants. But Exodus makes one thing clear. Israelites were not chosen because of their bravery or impressiveness or even faithfulness. Their selection was an act of God's pure grace; no one else can take the credit.

[4] When the people heard these harsh words, they mourned, and no one put on ornaments. [5]For the LORD had said to Moses, "Say to the Israelites, 'You are a stiff-necked people; if for a single moment I should go up among you, I would consume you. So now take off your ornaments, and I will decide what to do to you.'" [6]Therefore the Israelites stripped themselves of their ornaments, from Mount Horeb onward.

The Tent outside the Camp

[7] Now Moses used to take the tent and pitch it outside the camp, far off from the camp; he called it the tent of meeting. And everyone who sought the LORD would go out to the tent of meeting, which was outside the camp. [8]Whenever Moses went out to the tent, all the people would rise and stand, each of them, at the entrance of their tents and watch Moses until he had gone into the tent. [9]When Moses entered the tent, the pillar of cloud would descend and stand at the entrance of the tent, and the LORD would speak with Moses. [10]When all the people saw the pillar of cloud standing at the entrance of the tent, all the people

would rise and bow down, all of them, at the entrance of their tent. [11]Thus the LORD used to speak to Moses face to face, as one speaks to a friend. Then he would return to the camp; but his young assistant, Joshua son of Nun, would not leave the tent.

Moses' Intercession

[12] Moses said to the LORD, "See, you have said to me, 'Bring up this people'; but you have not let me know whom you will send with me. Yet you have said, 'I know you by name, and you have also found favor in my sight.' [13]Now if I have found favor in your sight, show me your ways, so that I may know you and find favor in your sight. Consider too that this nation is your people." [14]He said, "My presence will go with you, and I will give you rest." [15]And he said to him, "If your presence will not go, do not carry us up from here. [16]For how shall it be known that I have found favor in your sight, I and your people, unless you go with us? In this way, we shall be distinct, I and your people, from every people on the face of the earth."

[17] The LORD said to Moses, "I will do the very thing that you have asked; for you have found favor in my sight, and I know you by name." [18]Moses said, "Show me your glory, I pray." [19]And he said, "I will make all my goodness pass before you, and will proclaim before you the name, 'The LORD';[b] and I will be gracious to whom I will be gracious, and will show mercy on whom I will show mercy. [20]But," he said, "you cannot see my face; for no one shall see me and live." [21]And the LORD continued, "See, there is a place by me where you shall stand on the rock; [22]and while my glory passes by I will put you in a cleft of the rock, and I will cover you with my hand until I have passed by; [23]then I will take away my hand, and you shall see my back; but my face shall not be seen."

Moses Makes New Tablets

34 The LORD said to Moses, "Cut two tablets of stone like the former ones, and I will write on the tablets the words that were on the former tablets, which you broke. [2]Be ready in the morning, and come up in the morning to Mount Sinai and present yourself there to me, on the top of the mountain. [3]No one shall come up with you, and do not let anyone be seen throughout all the mountain; and do not let flocks or herds graze in front of that mountain." [4]So Moses cut two tablets of stone like the former ones; and he rose early in the morning and went up on Mount Sinai, as the LORD had commanded him, and took in his hand the two tablets of stone. [5]The LORD descended in the cloud and stood with him there,

b Heb *YHWH*; see note at 3.15

and proclaimed the name, "The LORD."[c] [6]The LORD passed before him, and proclaimed,

"The LORD, the LORD,
a God merciful and gracious,
slow to anger,
and abounding in steadfast love and
    faithfulness,

34.6–7 Capsule Description

The self-description of God found in these two verses became for the Jews a profound summary of God's nature. The Old Testament quotes or alludes to this passage more than any other.

[7] keeping steadfast love for the thousandth
        generation,[d]
forgiving iniquity and transgression and
        sin,
yet by no means clearing the guilty,
but visiting the iniquity of the parents
        upon the children
and the children's children,
to the third and the fourth generation."

[8]And Moses quickly bowed his head toward the earth, and worshiped. [9]He said, "If now I have found favor in your sight, O Lord, I pray, let the Lord go with us. Although this is a stiff-necked people, pardon our iniquity and our sin, and take us for your inheritance."

The Covenant Renewed

10 He said: I hereby make a covenant. Before all your people I will perform marvels, such as have not been performed in all the earth or in any nation; and all the people among whom you live shall see the work of the LORD; for it is an awesome thing that I will do with you.

11 Observe what I command you today. See, I will drive out before you the Amorites, the Canaanites, the Hittites, the Perizzites, the Hivites, and the Jebusites. [12]Take care not to make a covenant with the inhabitants of the land to which you are going, or it will become a snare among you. [13]You shall tear down their altars, break their pillars, and cut down their sacred poles[e] [14](for you shall worship no other god, because the LORD, whose name is Jealous, is a jealous God). [15]You shall not make a covenant with the inhabitants of the land, for when they prostitute themselves to their gods and sacrifice to their gods, someone among them will invite you, and you will eat of the sacrifice. [16]And you will take wives from among their daughters for your sons, and their

daughters who prostitute themselves to their gods will make your sons also prostitute themselves to their gods.

17 You shall not make cast idols.

18 You shall keep the festival of unleavened bread. Seven days you shall eat unleavened bread, as I commanded you, at the time appointed in the month of Abib; for in the month of Abib you came out from Egypt.

19 All that first opens the womb is mine, all your male[f] livestock, the firstborn of cow and sheep. [20]The firstborn of a donkey you shall redeem with a lamb, or if you will not redeem it you shall break its neck. All the firstborn of your sons you shall redeem.

No one shall appear before me empty-handed.

21 Six days you shall work, but on the seventh day you shall rest; even in plowing time and in harvest time you shall rest. [22]You shall observe the festival of weeks, the first fruits of wheat harvest, and the festival of ingathering at the turn of the year. [23]Three times in the year all your males shall appear before the LORD God, the God of Israel. [24]For I will cast out nations before you, and enlarge your borders; no one shall covet your land when you go up to appear before the LORD your God three times in the year.

25 You shall not offer the blood of my sacrifice with leaven, and the sacrifice of the festival of the passover shall not be left until the morning.

26 The best of the first fruits of your ground you shall bring to the house of the LORD your God.

You shall not boil a kid in its mother's milk.

27 The LORD said to Moses: Write these words; in accordance with these words I have made a covenant with you and with Israel. [28]He was there with the LORD forty days and forty nights; he neither ate bread nor drank water. And he wrote on the tablets the words of the covenant, the ten commandments.[g]

The Shining Face of Moses

29 Moses came down from Mount Sinai. As he came down from the mountain with the two tablets of the covenant[h] in his hand, Moses did not know that the skin of his face shone because he had been talking with God. [30]When Aaron and all the Israelites saw Moses, the skin of his face was shining, and they were afraid to come near him. [31]But Moses called to them; and Aaron and all the leaders of the congregation returned to him, and Moses spoke with them. [32]Afterward all the Israelites came near, and he gave them in commandment all that the LORD had spoken with him on Mount Sinai. [33]When Moses had finished speaking with them, he put a veil on his face;

---

[c] Heb YHWH; see note at 3.15   [d] Or *for thousands*   [e] Heb *Asherim*   [f] Gk Theodotion Vg Tg: Meaning of Heb uncertain   [g] Heb *words*   [h] Or *treaty*, or *testimony*; Heb *eduth*

³⁴but whenever Moses went in before the LORD to speak with him, he would take the veil off, until he came out; and when he came out, and told the Israelites what he had been commanded, ³⁵the Israelites would see the face of Moses, that the skin of his face was shining; and Moses would put the veil on his face again, until he went in to speak with him.

Sabbath Regulations

35 Moses assembled all the congregation of the Israelites and said to them: These are the things that the LORD has commanded you to do:

2 Six days shall work be done, but on the seventh day you shall have a holy sabbath of solemn rest to the LORD; whoever does any work on

A Portable Cathedral
An unlikely sight in the desert

IN A.D. 1144 A GREAT building began to take shape in a village in northwest France. Enthusiasm for the project soon spread across the entire country, and volunteer workers streamed to the site. Working together, the people managed to construct one of the most beautiful buildings in the world, the magnificent cathedral at Chartres.

Fifty years later, after a terrible fire, the villagers of France rebuilt their cathedral from scratch. Today, tourists throng to marvel at what was splendidly fashioned to the glory of God so long ago.

> And they came, everyone whose heart was stirred, and everyone whose spirit was willing, and brought the LORD's offering to be used for the tent of meeting. 35.21

Inspired Builders

A work of art took shape in similar fashion thousands of years earlier than Chartres, and the last chapters of Exodus provide a wealth of details. In a hostile desert landscape, a tribe of just-liberated slaves built something of exquisite beauty: a portable cathedral, or tabernacle.

God directed the project personally, specially endowing the craftsmen with skill (31.1–6) and elaborating right down to the color choice of woven yarns, the precise length of curtains and wooden frames, and the design of gold filigree. The people of Israel joined together in a flurry of activity, carefully following God's pattern. A ton of gold went into the project, as well as nearly four tons of silver and stockpiles of precious gems and rare woods.

God Moves In

After describing the tabernacle construction in great detail, the Bible devotes just five verses, the last five in Exodus, to its culmination. In a matter-of-fact tone, those sentences record a remarkable event.

Throughout the book of Exodus God had been progressively revealing himself to Moses: once in a burning bush, once in a mysterious appearance beside a rock, once on a trembling mountain, and often in a cloud-covered tent of meeting. God's presence caused such fear and awe that the people of Israel begged that he not speak to them directly (20.19). When Moses had come down from Mount Sinai after meeting with God, he glowed as if radioactive, and everyone was too frightened to go near him (34.30).

Yet, on the day the tabernacle was completed, this same God moved in. His glory filled the new tabernacle. God took up residence with his people.

A Visible Reminder

From then on, whenever the Israelites marched or camped, their portable cathedral stayed in the exact center of the camp, with their tents and personal belongings radiating out from the most holy place and ark of the covenant. The tabernacle gave them a visible reminder of God's central place. Each day priests performed functions of sacrifice and worship there.

The story of the tabernacle, which takes up one-third of Exodus, reveals much about the character of God. He can never be taken lightly—the rituals here and in the next three books show that God must be approached with care and reverence. He cannot be experienced directly, in his fullness, by ordinary people; a holy God is simply too overwhelming. Even Moses, Exodus says, could not look on God's face and live (33.20).

And yet, amazingly, that same God who seemed so distant came near. Despite the huge gulf separating God and humanity—a gulf that all the rules on holiness and purification only hint at—God allowed personal access to himself. He made himself available.

Life Questions: Where does God "live" now?

it shall be put to death. ³You shall kindle no fire in all your dwellings on the sabbath day.

Preparations for Making the Tabernacle

4 Moses said to all the congregation of the Israelites: This is the thing that the LORD has commanded: ⁵Take from among you an offering to the LORD; let whoever is of a generous heart bring the LORD's offering: gold, silver, and bronze; ⁶blue, purple, and crimson yarns, and fine linen; goats' hair, ⁷tanned rams' skins, and fine leather;ⁱ acacia wood, ⁸oil for the light, spices for the anointing oil and for the fragrant incense, ⁹and onyx stones and gems to be set in the ephod and the breastpiece.

10 All who are skillful among you shall come and make all that the LORD has commanded: the tabernacle, ¹¹its tent and its covering, its clasps and its frames, its bars, its pillars, and its bases; ¹²the ark with its poles, the mercy seat,ʲ and the curtain for the screen; ¹³the table with its poles and all its utensils, and the bread of the Presence; ¹⁴the lampstand also for the light, with its utensils and its lamps, and the oil for the light; ¹⁵and the altar of incense, with its poles, and the anointing oil and the fragrant incense, and the screen for the entrance, the entrance of the tabernacle; ¹⁶the altar of burnt offering, with its grating of bronze, its poles, and all its utensils, the basin with its stand; ¹⁷the hangings of the court, its pillars and its bases, and the screen for the gate of the court; ¹⁸the pegs of the tabernacle and the pegs of the court, and their cords; ¹⁹the finely worked vestments for ministering in the holy place, the holy vestments for the priest Aaron, and the vestments of his sons, for their service as priests.

Offerings for the Tabernacle

20 Then all the congregation of the Israelites withdrew from the presence of Moses. ²¹And they came, everyone whose heart was stirred, and everyone whose spirit was willing, and brought the LORD's offering to be used for the tent of meeting, and for all its service, and for the sacred vestments. ²²So they came, both men and women; all who were of a willing heart brought brooches and earrings and signet rings and pendants, all sorts of gold objects, everyone bringing an offering of gold to the LORD. ²³And everyone who possessed blue or purple or crimson yarn or fine linen or goats' hair or tanned rams' skins or fine leather,ⁱ brought them. ²⁴Everyone who could make an offering of silver or bronze brought it as the LORD's offering; and everyone who possessed acacia wood of any use in the work, brought it. ²⁵All the skillful women spun with their hands, and brought what they had spun in blue and purple and crimson yarns and fine linen; ²⁶all the women whose hearts moved them to use their skill spun

the goats' hair. ²⁷And the leaders brought onyx stones and gems to be set in the ephod and the breastpiece, ²⁸and spices and oil for the light, and for the anointing oil, and for the fragrant incense. ²⁹All the Israelite men and women whose hearts made them willing to bring anything for the work that the LORD had commanded by Moses to be done, brought it as a freewill offering to the LORD.

Bezalel and Oholiab

30 Then Moses said to the Israelites: See, the LORD has called by name Bezalel son of Uri son of Hur, of the tribe of Judah; ³¹he has filled him with divine spirit,ᵏ with skill, intelligence, and knowledge in every kind of craft, ³²to devise artistic designs, to work in gold, silver, and bronze, ³³in cutting stones for setting, and in carving wood, in every kind of craft. ³⁴And he has inspired him to teach, both him and Oholiab son of Ahisamach, of the tribe of Dan. ³⁵He has filled them with skill to do every kind of work done by an artisan or by a designer or by an embroiderer in blue, purple, and crimson yarns, and in fine linen, or by a weaver—by any sort of artisan or skilled designer.

36 Bezalel and Oholiab and every skillful one to whom the LORD has given skill and understanding to know how to do any work in the construction of the sanctuary shall work in accordance with all that the LORD has commanded.

2 Moses then called Bezalel and Oholiab and every skillful one to whom the LORD had given skill, everyone whose heart was stirred to come to do the work; ³and they received from Moses all the freewill offerings that the Israelites had brought for doing the work on the sanctuary. They still kept bringing him freewill offerings every morning, ⁴so that all the artisans who were doing every sort of task on the sanctuary came, each from the task being performed, ⁵and said to Moses, "The people are bringing much more than enough for doing the work that the LORD has commanded us to do." ⁶So Moses gave command, and word was proclaimed throughout the camp: "No man or woman is to make anything else as an offering for the sanctuary." So the people were restrained from bringing; ⁷for what they had already brought was more than enough to do all the work.

Construction of the Tabernacle

8 All those with skill among the workers made the tabernacle with ten curtains; they were made of fine twisted linen, and blue, purple, and crimson yarns, with cherubim skillfully worked into them. ⁹The length of each curtain was twenty-eight cubits, and the width of each curtain four cubits; all the curtains were of the same size. 10 He joined five curtains to one another, and

---

ⁱ Meaning of Heb uncertain   ʲ Or the cover   ᵏ Or the spirit of God

the other five curtains he joined to one another. [11]He made loops of blue on the edge of the outermost curtain of the first set; likewise he made them on the edge of the outermost curtain of the

second set; [12]he made fifty loops on the one curtain, and he made fifty loops on the edge of the curtain that was in the second set; the loops were opposite one another. [13]And he made fifty clasps of gold, and joined the curtains one to the other with clasps; so the tabernacle was one whole.

14 He also made curtains of goats' hair for a tent over the tabernacle; he made eleven curtains. [15]The length of each curtain was thirty cubits, and the width of each curtain four cubits; the eleven curtains were of the same size. [16]He joined five curtains by themselves, and six curtains by themselves. [17]He made fifty loops on the edge of the outermost curtain of the one set, and fifty loops on the edge of the other connecting curtain. [18]He made fifty clasps of bronze to join the tent together so that it might be one whole. [19]And he made for the tent a covering of tanned rams' skins and an outer covering of fine leather.[l]

20 Then he made the upright frames for the tabernacle of acacia wood. [21]Ten cubits was the length of a frame, and a cubit and a half the width of each frame. [22]Each frame had two pegs for fitting together; he did this for all the frames of the tabernacle. [23]The frames for the tabernacle he made in this way: twenty frames for the south side; [24]and he made forty bases of silver under the twenty frames, two bases under the first frame for its two pegs, and two bases under the next frame for its two pegs. [25]For the second side of the tabernacle, on the north side, he made twenty frames [26]and their forty bases of silver, two bases under the first frame and two bases under the next frame. [27]For the rear of the tabernacle westward he made six frames. [28]He made two frames for corners of the tabernacle in the rear. [29]They were separate beneath, but joined at the top, at the first ring; he made two of them in this way, for the two corners. [30]There were eight frames with their bases of silver: sixteen bases, under every frame two bases.

31 He made bars of acacia wood, five for the frames of the one side of the tabernacle, [32]and five bars for the frames of the other side of the tabernacle, and five bars for the frames of the tabernacle at the rear westward. [33]He made the middle bar to pass through from end to end halfway up the frames. [34]And he overlaid the frames with gold, and made rings of gold for them to hold the bars, and overlaid the bars with gold.

35 He made the curtain of blue, purple, and crimson yarns, and fine twisted linen, with cherubim skillfully worked into it. [36]For it he made four pillars of acacia, and overlaid them with gold; their hooks were of gold, and he cast for them four bases of silver. [37]He also made a screen for the entrance to the tent, of blue, purple, and crimson yarns, and fine twisted linen, embroidered with needlework; [38]and its five pillars with their hooks. He overlaid their capitals and their bases with gold, but their five bases were of bronze.

Making the Ark of the Covenant

37 Bezalel made the ark of acacia wood; it was two and a half cubits long, a cubit and a

half wide, and a cubit and a half high. [2]He overlaid it with pure gold inside and outside, and made a molding of gold around it. [3]He cast for it four rings of gold for its four feet, two rings on its one side and two rings on its other side. [4]He made poles of acacia wood, and overlaid them with gold, [5]and put the poles into the rings on the sides of the ark, to carry the ark. [6]He made a mercy seat[m] of pure gold; two cubits and a half was its length, and a cubit and a half its width. [7]He made two cherubim of hammered gold; at the two ends of the mercy seat[n] he made them, [8]one cherub at the one end, and one cherub at the other end; of one piece with the mercy seat[n] he made the cherubim at its two ends. [9]The cherubim spread out their wings above, overshadowing the mercy seat[n] with their wings. They faced one another; the faces of the cherubim were turned toward the mercy seat.[n]

Making the Table for the Bread of the Presence

10 He also made the table of acacia wood, two

cubits long, one cubit wide, and a cubit and a half high. [11]He overlaid it with pure gold, and made a molding of gold around it. [12]He made around it a rim a handbreadth wide, and made a molding of gold around the rim. [13]He cast for it four rings of gold, and fastened the rings to the four corners at its four legs. [14]The rings that held the poles used for carrying the table were close to the rim. [15]He made the poles of acacia wood to carry the table, and overlaid them with gold. [16]And he made the vessels of pure gold that were to be on the table, its plates and dishes for incense, and its bowls and flagons with which to pour drink offerings.

Making the Lampstand

17 He also made the lampstand of pure gold. The base and the shaft of the lampstand were made of hammered work; its cups, its calyxes, and its petals were of one piece with it. [18]There were six branches going out of its sides, three branches of the lampstand out of one side of it and three branches of the lampstand out of the other side of it; [19]three cups shaped like almond blossoms, each with calyx and petals, on one branch, and three cups shaped like almond blossoms, each with calyx and petals, on the other branch—so for the six branches going out of the lampstand. [20]On the lampstand itself there were four cups shaped like almond blossoms, each with its calyxes and petals. [21]There was a calyx of one piece with it under the first pair of branches, a calyx of one piece with it under the next pair of branches, and a calyx of one piece with it under the last pair of branches. [22]Their calyxes and their branches were of one piece with it, the whole of it one hammered piece of pure gold. [23]He made its seven lamps and its snuffers and its trays of pure gold. [24]He made it and all its utensils of a talent of pure gold.

Making the Altar of Incense

25 He made the altar of incense of acacia wood, one cubit long, and one cubit wide; it was square, and was two cubits high; its horns were of one piece with it. [26]He overlaid it with pure gold, its top, and its sides all around, and its horns; and he made for it a molding of gold all around, [27]and made two golden rings for it under its molding, on two opposite sides of it, to hold the poles with which to carry it. [28]And he made the poles of acacia wood, and overlaid them with gold.

Making the Anointing Oil and the Incense

29 He made the holy anointing oil also, and the pure fragrant incense, blended as by the perfumer.

Making the Altar of Burnt Offering

38 He made the altar of burnt offering also of acacia wood; it was five cubits long, and

five cubits wide; it was square, and three cubits high. [2]He made horns for it on its four corners; its horns were of one piece with it, and he overlaid it with bronze. [3]He made all the utensils of the altar, the pots, the shovels, the basins, the forks, and the firepans: all its utensils he made of bronze. [4]He made for the altar a grating, a network of bronze, under its ledge, extending halfway down. [5]He cast four rings on the four corners of the bronze grating to hold the poles; [6]he made the poles of acacia wood, and overlaid them with bronze. [7]And he put the poles through the rings on the sides of the altar, to carry it with them; he made it hollow, with boards.

8 He made the basin of bronze with its stand of bronze, from the mirrors of the women who served at the entrance to the tent of meeting.

Making the Court of the Tabernacle

9 He made the court; for the south side the hangings of the court were of fine twisted linen,

38.9–13 Tabernacle Layout

Unlike a church or synagogue, neither the tabernacle nor temple functioned as a gathering place for public meetings. Worshipers entered a large, open courtyard area to present their offerings and sacrifices. After receiving the offerings, the priests approached the holy place, which contained some of the sacred furniture. Only the high priest could go further, into the most holy place where the ark of the covenant stayed, and he did so only once a year, on the day of atonement.

one hundred cubits long; [10]its twenty pillars and their twenty bases were of bronze, but the hooks of the pillars and their bands were of silver. [11]For the north side there were hangings one hundred cubits long; its twenty pillars and their twenty bases were of bronze, but the hooks of the pillars and their bands were of silver. [12]For the west side there were hangings fifty cubits long, with ten pillars and ten bases; the hooks of the pillars and their bands were of silver. [13]And for the front to the east, fifty cubits. [14]The hangings for one side of the gate were fifteen cubits, with three pillars and three bases. [15]And so for the other side; on each side of the gate of the court were hangings of fifteen cubits, with three pillars and three bases. [16]All the hangings around the court were of fine twisted linen. [17]The bases for the pillars were of bronze, but the hooks of the pillars and their bands were of silver; the overlaying of their capitals was also of silver, and all the pillars of the court were banded with silver. [18]The screen for the entrance to the court was embroidered with needlework in blue, purple, and crimson yarns and fine twisted linen. It was twenty cubits long and, along the width of it, five cubits high, corresponding to the hangings of the court. 19There were four pillars; their four bases were of bronze, their hooks of silver, and the overlaying of their capitals and their bands of silver. 20All the pegs for the tabernacle and for the court all around were of bronze.

Materials of the Tabernacle

21 These are the records of the tabernacle, the tabernacle of the covenant,[o] which were drawn up at the commandment of Moses, the work of the Levites being under the direction of Ithamar son of the priest Aaron. 22Bezalel son of Uri son of Hur, of the tribe of Judah, made all that the LORD commanded Moses; 23and with him was Oholiab son of Ahisamach, of the tribe of Dan, engraver, designer, and embroiderer in blue, purple, and crimson yarns, and in fine linen.

24 All the gold that was used for the work, in all the construction of the sanctuary, the gold from the offering, was twenty-nine talents and seven hundred thirty shekels, measured by the sanctuary shekel. 25The silver from those of the congregation who were counted was one hundred talents and one thousand seven hundred seventy-five shekels, measured by the sanctuary shekel; 26a beka a head (that is, half a shekel, measured by the sanctuary shekel), for everyone who was counted in the census, from twenty years old and upward, for six hundred three thousand, five hundred fifty men. 27The hundred talents of silver were for casting the bases of the sanctuary, and the bases of the curtain; one hundred bases for the hundred talents, a talent for a base. 28Of the thousand seven hundred seventy-five shekels he made hooks for the pillars, and overlaid their capitals and made bands for them. 29The bronze that was contributed was seventy talents, and two thousand four hundred shekels; 30with it he made the bases for the entrance of the tent of meeting, the bronze altar and the bronze grating for it and all the utensils of the altar, 31the bases all around the court, and the bases of the gate of the court, all the pegs of the tabernacle, and all the pegs around the court.

Making the Vestments for the Priesthood

39 Of the blue, purple, and crimson yarns they made finely worked vestments, for ministering in the holy place; they made the sacred vestments for Aaron; as the LORD had commanded Moses.

2 He made the ephod of gold, of blue, purple, and crimson yarns, and of fine twisted linen. 3Gold leaf was hammered out and cut into threads to work into the blue, purple, and crimson yarns and into the fine twisted linen, in skilled design. 4They made for the ephod shoulder-pieces, joined to it at its two edges. 5The decorated band on it was of the same materials and workmanship, of gold, of blue, purple, and crimson yarns, and of fine twisted linen; as the LORD had commanded Moses.

6 The onyx stones were prepared, enclosed in settings of gold filigree and engraved like the engravings of a signet, according to the names of the sons of Israel. 7He set them on the shoulder-pieces of the ephod, to be stones of remembrance for the sons of Israel; as the LORD had commanded Moses.

8 He made the breastpiece, in skilled work, like the work of the ephod, of gold, of blue, purple, and crimson yarns, and of fine twisted linen. 9It was square; the breastpiece was made double, a span in length and a span in width when doubled. 10They set in it four rows of stones. A row of carnelian,[p] chrysolite, and emerald was the first row; 11and the second row, a turquoise, a sapphire,[q] and a moonstone; 12and the third row, a jacinth, an agate, and an amethyst; 13and the fourth row, a beryl, an onyx, and a jasper; they were enclosed in settings of gold filigree. 14There were twelve stones with names corresponding to the names of the sons of Israel; they were like signets, each engraved with its name, for the twelve tribes. 15They made on the breastpiece chains of pure gold, twisted like cords; 16and they made two settings of gold filigree and two gold rings, and put the two rings on the two edges of the breastpiece; 17and they put the two cords of gold in the two rings at the edges of the breastpiece. 18Two ends of the two cords they had attached to the two settings of filigree; in this way they attached it in front to the shoulder-pieces of the ephod. 19Then they made two rings of gold, and put them at the two ends of the breastpiece, on its inside edge next to the ephod. 20They made two rings of gold, and attached them in front to the lower part of the two shoulder-pieces of the ephod, at its joining above the decorated band of the ephod. 21They bound the breastpiece by its rings to the rings of the ephod with a blue cord, so that it should lie on the decorated band of the ephod, and that the breastpiece should not come loose from the ephod; as the LORD had commanded Moses.

22 He also made the robe of the ephod woven all of blue yarn; 23and the opening of the robe in the middle of it was like the opening in a coat of mail,[r] with a binding around the opening, so that it might not be torn. 24On the lower hem of the robe they made pomegranates of blue, purple, and crimson yarns, and of fine twisted linen. 25They also made bells of pure gold, and put the

[o] Or *treaty*, or *testimony*; Heb *eduth* [p] The identification of several of these stones is uncertain [q] Or *lapis lazuli*
[r] Meaning of Heb uncertain

bells between the pomegranates on the lower hem of the robe all around, between the pomegranates; 26a bell and a pomegranate, a bell and a pomegranate all around on the lower hem of the robe for ministering; as the LORD had commanded Moses.

27 They also made the tunics, woven of fine linen, for Aaron and his sons, 28and the turban of fine linen, and the headdresses of fine linen, and the linen undergarments of fine twisted linen, 29and the sash of fine twisted linen, and of blue, purple, and crimson yarns, embroidered with needlework; as the LORD had commanded Moses.

30 They made the rosette of the holy diadem of pure gold, and wrote on it an inscription, like the engraving of a signet, "Holy to the LORD." 31They tied to it a blue cord, to fasten it on the turban above; as the LORD had commanded Moses.

The Work Completed

32 In this way all the work of the tabernacle of the tent of meeting was finished; the Israelites had done everything just as the LORD had commanded Moses. 33Then they brought the tabernacle to

39.32 Following Orders

The last few chapters of Exodus repeat almost verbatim what has gone before; they simply record that the Israelites followed all of God's prior instructions for building the tabernacle. The phrase "as the LORD had commanded" resonates like a drumbeat through this section. A people not known for following orders took the tabernacle project very seriously. It became for them not just a symbol, but the actual reality of God living in their midst. The tabernacle was the focal point of worship for 300 years, until the temple was built. Later, the apostle Paul used this imagery when he called believers God's "temple," or dwelling place.

Moses, the tent and all its utensils, its hooks, its frames, its bars, its pillars, and its bases; 34the covering of tanned rams' skins and the covering of fine leather,s and the curtain for the screen; 35the ark of the covenantt with its poles and the mercy seat;u 36the table with all its utensils, and the bread of the Presence; 37the pure lampstand with its lamps set on it and all its utensils, and the oil for the light; 38the golden altar, the anointing oil and the fragrant incense, and the screen for the entrance of the tent; 39the bronze altar, and its grating of bronze, its poles, and all its utensils; the basin with its stand; 40the hangings of the court, its pillars, and its bases, and the screen for the gate of the court, its cords, and its pegs; and all the

utensils for the service of the tabernacle, for the tent of meeting; 41the finely worked vestments for ministering in the holy place, the sacred vestments for the priest Aaron, and the vestments of his sons to serve as priests. 42The Israelites had done all of the work just as the LORD had commanded Moses. 43When Moses saw that they had done all the work just as the LORD had commanded, he blessed them.

The Tabernacle Erected and Its Equipment Installed

40 The LORD spoke to Moses: 2On the first day of the first month you shall set up the tabernacle of the tent of meeting. 3You shall put in it the ark of the covenant,t and you shall screen the ark with the curtain. 4You shall bring in the table, and arrange its setting; and you shall bring in the lampstand, and set up its lamps. 5You shall put the golden altar for incense before the ark of the covenant,t and set up the screen for the entrance of the tabernacle. 6You shall set the altar of burnt offering before the entrance of the tabernacle of the tent of meeting, 7and place the basin between the tent of meeting and the altar, and put water in it. 8You shall set up the court all around, and hang up the screen for the gate of the court. 9Then you shall take the anointing oil, and anoint the tabernacle and all that is in it, and consecrate it and all its furniture, so that it shall become holy. 10You shall also anoint the altar of burnt offering and all its utensils, and consecrate the altar, so that the altar shall be most holy. 11You shall also anoint the basin with its stand, and consecrate it. 12Then you shall bring Aaron and his sons to the entrance of the tent of meeting, and shall wash them with water, 13and put on Aaron the sacred vestments, and you shall anoint him and consecrate him, so that he may serve me as priest. 14You shall bring his sons also and put tunics on them, 15and anoint them, as you anointed their father, that they may serve me as priests: and their anointing shall admit them to a perpetual priesthood throughout all generations to come.

16 Moses did everything just as the LORD had commanded him. 17In the first month in the second year, on the first day of the month, the tabernacle was set up. 18Moses set up the tabernacle; he laid its bases, and set up its frames, and put in its poles, and raised up its pillars; 19and he spread the tent over the tabernacle, and put the covering of the tent over it; as the LORD had commanded Moses. 20He took the covenantt and put it into the ark, and put the poles on the ark, and set the mercy seatu above the ark; 21and he brought the ark into the tabernacle, and set up the curtain for screening, and screened the ark of the covenant;t as the LORD had commanded Moses. 22He put the

---

s Meaning of Heb uncertain   t Or *treaty*, or *testimony*; Heb *eduth*   u Or *the cover*

table in the tent of meeting, on the north side of the tabernacle, outside the curtain, ²³and set the bread in order on it before the LORD; as the LORD had commanded Moses. ²⁴He put the lampstand in the tent of meeting, opposite the table on the south side of the tabernacle, ²⁵and set up the lamps before the LORD; as the LORD had commanded Moses. ²⁶He put the golden altar in the tent of meeting before the curtain, ²⁷and offered fragrant incense on it; as the LORD had commanded Moses. ²⁸He also put in place the screen for the entrance of the tabernacle. ²⁹He set the altar of burnt offering at the entrance of the tabernacle of the tent of meeting, and offered on it the burnt offering and the grain offering as the LORD had commanded Moses. ³⁰He set the basin between the tent of meeting and the altar, and put water in it for washing, ³¹with which Moses and Aaron and his sons washed their hands and their feet. ³²When they went into the tent of meeting, and when they approached the altar, they washed; as the LORD had commanded Moses. ³³He set up the court around the tabernacle and the altar, and put up the screen at the gate of the court. So Moses finished the work.

The Cloud and the Glory

34 Then the cloud covered the tent of meeting, and the glory of the LORD filled the tabernacle. ³⁵Moses was not able to enter the tent of meeting because the cloud settled upon it, and the glory of the LORD filled the tabernacle. ³⁶Whenever the cloud was taken up from the tabernacle, the Israelites would set out on each stage of their journey; ³⁷but if the cloud was not taken up, then they did not set out until the day that it was taken up. ³⁸For the cloud of the LORD was on the tabernacle by day, and fire was in the cloudᵛ by night, before the eyes of all the house of Israel at each stage of their journey.

ᵛ Heb *it*

LEVITICUS

Living with Fire
Dangerous material more powerful than the atom

L EVITICUS SEEMS MIGHTY STRANGE TO the modern world. Unlike most of the Bible, it has few personalities and stories, and no poetry. Instead, it is crammed full of detailed rules and procedures.

Its painstaking ritual is, however, strikingly similar to the procedures surrounding nuclear technology. The specialized clothing, the concern for purification, the precise handling of crucial materials—both nuclear workers and Old Testament priests share these. This similarity gives an important clue to understanding Leviticus.

> I will place my dwelling in your midst, and I shall not abhor you. And I will walk among you, and will be your God, and you shall be my people.
> 26.11–12

Cleaning Up a Nuclear Spill

At the Hanford plutonium separation plant in eastern Washington, plutonium and U-235 are kept in a special high-security vault, in brass cans wrapped three times in plastic. To move the radioactive material, specially trained handlers don white protection overalls and special breather masks. They never touch the materials except through a sealed "glove box."

If an accident occurs, such as a small fire ignited by the "hot" material, the entire area must be cleansed through laborious scrubbing with soap and water. Carefully trained workers dispose of the dirty water in a specially protected toxic waste area. Anyone contaminated must also be "cleansed" from the exposure. In extreme cases, she or he must stay away from other people for months.

These rigid rules grew out of hard experience. For decades no one knew the dangers of radioactivity. Workers who used radioactive materials to hand-paint the first "glow in the dark" watches licked their paintbrushes to get a fine tip; their supervisors said they would gain sex appeal. Instead, they got cancer. The introduction of nuclear weapons and nuclear power plants increased the amount of radioactive material being handled. Gradually scientists realized: If you are going to use the atom, you must adopt procedures to fit its power.

The Intimate Presence of God

Leviticus reads something like a training manual for atomic plant workers. Its "dangerous material," however, is more powerful than the atom. Leviticus gives exhaustive detail on how to live with God.

A pamphlet on "how to survive a nuclear accident" may be dull if read on vacation, but it's gripping if read in a vibrating nuclear reactor. Similarly, Leviticus is dull if you do not realize the wonderful news behind it: God, the Creator of the universe, has entered the life of a small and insignificant tribe. The Israelites could not merely fit this God into their lives. They needed to restructure their lives—food, sex, economics—to fit with his. It was essential not just for priests, but for everyone.

Ignoring the operations manual could be deadly. It was for Aaron's two sons (chapter 10).

Free from Contamination

Today, because of Jesus Christ, we don't live in the world of Leviticus. Jesus' perfect self-sacrifice made the daily sacrifice of animals unnecessary. He replaced the high priest as our representative before God. Jesus cleanses the real source of contamination, our sinful nature. Leviticus was meant to teach people some basic truths about God, and when their lessons were complete, they could go on to bigger and better things. (The New Testament book of Hebrews spells out this graduation.)

Yet we need to be reminded of the principles Leviticus taught. It tells us that God was then, as he is today, "a consuming fire" (Hebrews 12.29). He has taught us how to live with that fire, not because we deserved to know, but because he wanted our company. We dare not treat him lightly.

How to Read Leviticus

Many well-intentioned readers, determined to read the Bible from beginning to end, bog down in Leviticus. It's a lawbook, a procedural manual for getting along with a holy and powerful God. Sheer detail can bore you, especially if you miss the point behind it.

When you read the Bible, careful attention to detail is usually a key to understanding. In Leviticus, however, you will get more from looking at the big picture than from studying the details. Some laws we simply don't understand. But Leviticus as a whole shows what kind of people God wanted the Israelites to be. As you read, keep your mind on the big picture. Pay special attention to the explanatory notes. Try to imagine how these laws affected everyday life. Keep asking yourself: How would these laws make the Israelites different from other people—and why were those differences important to God?

3-TRACK READING PLAN

For an explanation and complete listing of the 3-track reading plan, turn to page 7.

TRACK 1: *Two-Week Courses on the Bible*
See page 8 for information on these courses.

TRACK 2: *An Overview of Leviticus in 1 Day*
☐ Day 1. Read the Introduction to Leviticus and chapter 26, which summarizes the purpose of God's laws. Scan through the sectional headings of the book to get an idea of what subjects it covers.

Now turn to page 9 for your next Track 2 reading project.

TRACK 3: *All of Leviticus in 26 Days*
After you have read through Leviticus, turn to pages 10–14 for your next Track 3 reading project.

☐1 ☐2 ☐3 ☐4 ☐5 ☐6 ☐7 ☐8
☐9 ☐10 ☐11–12 ☐13 ☐14 ☐15 ☐16 ☐17
☐18 ☐19 ☐20 ☐21 ☐22 ☐23 ☐24 ☐25
☐26 ☐27

The Burnt Offering

1 The LORD summoned Moses and spoke to him from the tent of meeting, saying: ²Speak to the people of Israel and say to them: When any of you bring an offering of livestock to the LORD, you shall bring your offering from the herd or from the flock.

3 If the offering is a burnt offering from the herd, you shall offer a male without blemish; you shall bring it to the entrance of the tent of meeting, for acceptance in your behalf before the LORD. ⁴You shall lay your hand on the head of the burnt offering, and it shall be acceptable in your behalf as atonement for you. ⁵The bull shall be slaughtered before the LORD; and Aaron's sons the priests shall offer the blood, dashing the blood against all sides of the altar that is at the entrance of the tent of meeting. ⁶The burnt offering shall be flayed and cut up into its parts. ⁷The sons of the priest Aaron shall put fire on the altar and arrange wood on the fire. ⁸Aaron's sons the priests shall arrange the parts, with the head and the suet, on the wood that is on the fire on the altar; ⁹but its entrails and its legs shall be washed with water.

Then the priest shall turn the whole into smoke on the altar as a burnt offering, an offering by fire of pleasing odor to the LORD.

10 If your gift for a burnt offering is from the

1.9 Original Holocaust

The word "holocaust," which simply means "burnt whole," derives from the Israelite practice of offering up the entire animal, including legs, head, and inner parts. Later the word stood for a great devastation, especially by fire. After World War II, Jews began referring to Hitler's mass destruction of their race in gas chambers and ovens as "The Holocaust."

flock, from the sheep or goats, your offering shall be a male without blemish. ¹¹It shall be slaughtered on the north side of the altar before the LORD, and Aaron's sons the priests shall dash its blood against all sides of the altar. ¹²It shall be cut up into its parts, with its head and its suet, and the priest shall arrange them on the wood that is on the fire on the altar; [13]but the entrails and the legs shall be washed with water. Then the priest shall offer the whole and turn it into smoke on the altar; it is a burnt offering, an offering by fire of pleasing odor to the LORD.

14 If your offering to the LORD is a burnt offering of birds, you shall choose your offering from turtledoves or pigeons. [15]The priest shall bring it to the altar and wring off its head, and turn it into smoke on the altar; and its blood shall be drained out against the side of the altar. [16]He shall remove its crop with its contents[a] and throw it at the east side of the altar, in the place for ashes. [17]He shall tear it open by its wings without severing it. Then the priest shall turn it into smoke on the altar, on the wood that is on the fire; it is a burnt offering, an offering by fire of pleasing odor to the LORD.

Grain Offerings

2 When anyone presents a grain offering to the LORD, the offering shall be of choice flour; the worshiper shall pour oil on it, and put frankincense on it, [2]and bring it to Aaron's sons the priests. After taking from it a handful of the choice flour and oil, with all its frankincense, the priest shall turn this token portion into smoke on the altar, an offering by fire of pleasing odor to the LORD. [3]And what is left of the grain offering shall be for Aaron and his sons, a most holy part of the offerings by fire to the LORD.

4 When you present a grain offering baked in the oven, it shall be of choice flour: unleavened cakes mixed with oil, or unleavened wafers spread with oil. [5]If your offering is grain prepared on a griddle, it shall be of choice flour mixed with oil, unleavened; [6]break it in pieces, and pour oil on it; it is a grain offering. [7]If your offering is grain prepared in a pan, it shall be made of choice flour in oil. [8]You shall bring to the LORD the grain offering that is prepared in any of these ways; and when it is presented to the priest, he shall take it to the altar. [9]The priest shall remove from the grain offering its token portion and turn this into smoke on the altar, an offering by fire of pleasing odor to the LORD. [10]And what is left of the grain offering shall be for Aaron and his sons; it is a most holy part of the offerings by fire to the LORD.

11 No grain offering that you bring to the LORD shall be made with leaven, for you must not turn any leaven or honey into smoke as an offering by fire to the LORD. [12]You may bring them to the LORD as an offering of choice products, but they shall not be offered on the altar for a pleasing odor. [13]You shall not omit from your grain offerings the salt of the covenant with your God; with all your offerings you shall offer salt.

14 If you bring a grain offering of first fruits to the LORD, you shall bring as the grain offering of your first fruits coarse new grain from fresh ears, parched with fire. [15]You shall add oil to it and lay frankincense on it; it is a grain offering. [16]And the priest shall turn a token portion of it into smoke—some of the coarse grain and oil with all its frankincense; it is an offering by fire to the LORD.

Offerings of Well-Being

3 If the offering is a sacrifice of well-being, if you offer an animal of the herd, whether male or female, you shall offer one without blemish before the LORD. [2]You shall lay your hand on the head of the offering and slaughter it at the entrance of the tent of meeting; and Aaron's sons the priests shall dash the blood against all sides of the altar. [3]You shall offer from the sacrifice of well-being, as an offering by fire to the LORD, the fat that covers the entrails and all the fat that is around the entrails; [4]the two kidneys with the fat that is on them at the loins, and the appendage of the liver, which he shall remove with the kidneys. [5]Then Aaron's sons shall turn these into smoke on the altar, with the burnt offering that is on the wood on the fire, as an offering by fire of pleasing odor to the LORD.

6 If your offering for a sacrifice of well-being to the LORD is from the flock, male or female, you shall offer one without blemish. [7]If you present a sheep as your offering, you shall bring it before the LORD [8]and lay your hand on the head of the offering. It shall be slaughtered before the tent of meeting, and Aaron's sons shall dash its blood against all sides of the altar. [9]You shall present its fat from the sacrifice of well-being, as an offering by fire to the LORD: the whole broad tail, which shall be removed close to the backbone, the fat that covers the entrails, and all the fat that is around the entrails; [10]the two kidneys with the fat that is on them at the loins, and the appendage of the liver, which you shall remove with the kidneys. [11]Then the priest shall turn these into smoke on the altar as a food offering by fire to the LORD.

12 If your offering is a goat, you shall bring it before the LORD [13]and lay your hand on its head; it shall be slaughtered before the tent of meeting; and the sons of Aaron shall dash its blood against all sides of the altar. [14]You shall present as your offering from it, as an offering by fire to the LORD, the fat that covers the entrails, and all the fat that is around the entrails; [15]the two kidneys with the fat that is on them at the loins, and the appendage of the liver, which you shall remove with the kidneys. [16]Then the priest shall turn these into smoke on the altar as a food offering by fire for a pleasing odor.

All fat is the LORD's. [17]It shall be a perpetual statute throughout your generations, in all

---

[a] Meaning of Heb uncertain

your settlements: you must not eat any fat or any blood.

Sin Offerings

4 The LORD spoke to Moses, saying, ²Speak to the people of Israel, saying: When anyone sins unintentionally in any of the LORD's commandments about things not to be done, and does any one of them:

3 If it is the anointed priest who sins, thus bringing guilt on the people, he shall offer for the sin that he has committed a bull of the herd without blemish as a sin offering to the LORD. ⁴He

4.3 The One for the Many

For his sin, a priest had to sacrifice one bull—the same sacrifice required for a sin by the whole community (verses 13–14). The two sins were, in a sense, equal, for the high priest represented the whole community before God. The belief that a single purified individual can stand up for a nation prepared the way for Jesus, whose sinless obedience stands before God in our place.

shall bring the bull to the entrance of the tent of meeting before the LORD and lay his hand on the head of the bull; the bull shall be slaughtered before the LORD. ⁵The anointed priest shall take some of the blood of the bull and bring it into the tent of meeting. ⁶The priest shall dip his finger in the blood and sprinkle some of the blood seven times before the LORD in front of the curtain of the sanctuary. ⁷The priest shall put some of the blood on the horns of the altar of fragrant incense that is in the tent of meeting before the LORD; and the rest of the blood of the bull he shall pour out at the base of the altar of burnt offering, which is at the entrance of the tent of meeting. ⁸He shall remove all the fat from the bull of sin offering: the fat that covers the entrails and all the fat that is around the entrails; ⁹the two kidneys with the fat that is on them at the loins; and the appendage of the liver, which he shall remove with the kidneys, ¹⁰just as these are removed from the ox of the sacrifice of well-being. The priest shall turn them into smoke upon the altar of burnt offering. ¹¹But the skin of the bull and all its flesh, as well as its head, its legs, its entrails, and its dung— ¹²all the rest of the bull—he shall carry out to a clean place outside the camp, to the ash heap, and shall burn it on a wood fire; at the ash heap it shall be burned.

13 If the whole congregation of Israel errs unintentionally and the matter escapes the notice of the assembly, and they do any one of the things that by the LORD's commandments ought not to be done and incur guilt; ¹⁴when the sin that they

have committed becomes known, the assembly shall offer a bull of the herd for a sin offering and bring it before the tent of meeting. ¹⁵The elders of the congregation shall lay their hands on the head

4.13 Ignorance Isn't Bliss

"I didn't know the speed limit had dropped to 30, officer. How can you give me a ticket?" Under the law, ignorance provides no excuse. This chapter and the next cover many instances of unintentional sin. Although held accountable for such wrongdoing, the Israelites could overcome their guilt by offering the prescribed sacrifices.

of the bull before the LORD, and the bull shall be slaughtered before the LORD. ¹⁶The anointed priest shall bring some of the blood of the bull into the tent of meeting, ¹⁷and the priest shall dip his finger in the blood and sprinkle it seven times before the LORD, in front of the curtain. ¹⁸He shall put some of the blood on the horns of the altar that is before the LORD in the tent of meeting; and the rest of the blood he shall pour out at the base of the altar of burnt offering that is at the entrance of the tent of meeting. ¹⁹He shall remove all its fat and turn it into smoke on the altar. ²⁰He shall do with the bull just as is done with the bull of sin offering; he shall do the same with this. The priest shall make atonement for them, and they shall be forgiven. ²¹He shall carry the bull outside the camp, and burn it as he burned the first bull; it is the sin offering for the assembly.

22 When a ruler sins, doing unintentionally any one of all the things that by commandments of the LORD his God ought not to be done and incurs guilt, ²³once the sin that he has committed is made known to him, he shall bring as his offering a male goat without blemish. ²⁴He shall lay his hand on the head of the goat; it shall be slaughtered at the spot where the burnt offering is slaughtered before the LORD; it is a sin offering. ²⁵The priest shall take some of the blood of the sin offering with his finger and put it on the horns of the altar of burnt offering, and pour out the rest of its blood at the base of the altar of burnt offering. ²⁶All its fat he shall turn into smoke on the altar, like the fat of the sacrifice of well-being. Thus the priest shall make atonement on his behalf for his sin, and he shall be forgiven.

27 If anyone of the ordinary people among you sins unintentionally in doing any one of the things that by the LORD's commandments ought not to be done and incurs guilt, ²⁸when the sin that you have committed is made known to you, you shall bring a female goat without blemish as your offering, for the sin that you have committed. ²⁹You shall lay your hand on the head of the

sin offering; and the sin offering shall be slaughtered at the place of the burnt offering. 30The priest shall take some of its blood with his finger and put it on the horns of the altar of burnt offering, and he shall pour out the rest of its blood at the base of the altar. 31He shall remove all its fat, as the fat is removed from the offering of well-being, and the priest shall turn it into smoke on the altar for a pleasing odor to the LORD. Thus the priest shall make atonement on your behalf, and you shall be forgiven.

32 If the offering you bring as a sin offering is a sheep, you shall bring a female without blemish. 33You shall lay your hand on the head of the sin offering; and it shall be slaughtered as a sin offering at the spot where the burnt offering is slaughtered. 34The priest shall take some of the blood of the sin offering with his finger and put it on the horns of the altar of burnt offering, and pour out the rest of its blood at the base of the altar. 35You shall remove all its fat, as the fat of the sheep is removed from the sacrifice of well-being, and the priest shall turn it into smoke on the altar, with the offerings by fire to the LORD. Thus the priest shall make atonement on your behalf for the sin that you have committed, and you shall be forgiven.

5 When any of you sin in that you have heard a public adjuration to testify and—though able to testify as one who has seen or learned of the matter—do not speak up, you are subject to punishment. 2Or when any of you touch any unclean thing—whether the carcass of an unclean beast or the carcass of unclean livestock or the carcass of an unclean swarming thing—and are unaware of it, you have become unclean, and are guilty. 3Or when you touch human uncleanness—any uncleanness by which one can become unclean—and are unaware of it, when you come to know it, you shall be guilty. 4Or when any of you utter aloud a rash oath for a bad or a good purpose, whatever people utter in an oath, and are unaware of it, when you come to know it, you shall in any of these be guilty. 5When you realize your guilt in any of these, you shall confess the sin that you have committed. 6And you shall bring to the LORD, as your penalty for the sin that you have committed, a female from the flock, a sheep or a goat, as a sin offering; and the priest shall make atonement on your behalf for your sin.

7 But if you cannot afford a sheep, you shall bring to the LORD, as your penalty for the sin that you have committed, two turtledoves or two pigeons, one for a sin offering and the other for a burnt offering. 8You shall bring them to the priest, who shall offer first the one for the sin offering, wringing its head at the nape without severing it. 9He shall sprinkle some of the blood of the sin offering on the side of the altar, while the rest of the blood shall be drained out at the base of the altar; it is a sin offering. 10And the second he shall offer for a burnt offering according to the regulation. Thus the priest shall make atonement on your behalf for the sin that you have committed, and you shall be forgiven.

11 But if you cannot afford two turtledoves or two pigeons, you shall bring as your offering for the sin that you have committed one-tenth of an ephah of choice flour for a sin offering; you shall not put oil on it or lay frankincense on it, for it is a sin offering. 12You shall bring it to the priest, and the priest shall scoop up a handful of it as its memorial portion, and turn this into smoke on the altar, with the offerings by fire to the LORD; it is a sin offering. 13Thus the priest shall make atonement on your behalf for whichever of these sins you have committed, and you shall be forgiven. Like the grain offering, the rest shall be for the priest.

Offerings with Restitution

14 The LORD spoke to Moses, saying: 15When any of you commit a trespass and sin unintentionally in any of the holy things of the LORD, you shall bring, as your guilt offering to the LORD, a ram without blemish from the flock, convertible into silver by the sanctuary shekel; it is a guilt offering. 16And you shall make restitution for the holy thing in which you were remiss, and shall add one-fifth to it and give it to the priest. The priest shall make atonement on your behalf with the ram of the guilt offering, and you shall be forgiven.

17 If any of you sin without knowing it, doing any of the things that by the LORD's commandments ought not to be done, you have incurred guilt, and are subject to punishment. 18You shall bring to the priest a ram without blemish from the flock, or the equivalent, as a guilt offering; and the priest shall make atonement on your behalf for the error that you committed unintentionally, and you shall be forgiven. 19It is a guilt offering; you have incurred guilt before the LORD.

6 b The LORD spoke to Moses, saying: 2When any of you sin and commit a trespass against the LORD by deceiving a neighbor in a matter of a deposit or a pledge, or by robbery, or if you have defrauded a neighbor, 3or have found something lost and lied about it—if you swear falsely regarding any of the various things that one may do and sin thereby— 4when you have sinned and realize your guilt, and would restore what you took by robbery or by fraud or the deposit that was committed to you, or the lost thing that you found, 5or anything else about which you have sworn falsely, you shall repay the principal amount and shall add one-fifth to it. You shall pay it to its

b Ch 5.20 in Heb

owner when you realize your guilt. ⁶And you shall bring to the priest, as your guilt offering to the LORD, a ram without blemish from the flock, or its equivalent, for a guilt offering. ⁷The priest shall make atonement on your behalf before the LORD, and you shall be forgiven for any of the things that one may do and incur guilt thereby.

Instructions concerning Sacrifices

8ᶜ The LORD spoke to Moses, saying: ⁹Command Aaron and his sons, saying: This is the

ritual of the burnt offering. The burnt offering itself shall remain on the hearth upon the altar all night until the morning, while the fire on the altar shall be kept burning. ¹⁰The priest shall put on his linen vestments after putting on his linen undergarments next to his body; and he shall take up the ashes to which the fire has reduced the burnt offering on the altar, and place them beside the altar. ¹¹Then he shall take off his vestments and put on other garments, and carry the ashes out to a clean place outside the camp. ¹²The fire on the

ᶜ Ch 6.1 in Heb

The Reason for Sacrifice
Justice: Someone has to pay

WHEN YOU COMMIT A CRIME, you don't get off in court just by saying "Sorry, I'll try not to do it again." Justice requires that you pay for what you did.

The Israelites, therefore, could not just march into God's presence to fellowship with him. They had to bring sacrifices to pay, or "atone," for their inadequacies.

These sacrifices cost dearly. To subsistence farmers, a bull or goat represented a sizable contribution. Very poor people could give less—a pair of doves, or some flour. But, in all cases, a person would feel the cost, cost in terms of something he had worked for, something grown on his own farm.

Thus the priest shall make atonement on your behalf for the sin that you have committed, and you shall be forgiven.
4.35

Up in Smoke

A good portion of the national economy went up in smoke each year: hundreds of animals and a lot of manpower to gather wood, keep the fire lit, and offer sacrifices. Since the tent of meeting stood at the center of the camp, the smell of the two-a-day sacrifices always hung over the Israelites. They rarely could afford meat, but every day they smelled the aroma of barbecue dedicated to God.

Offerings fell into three broad types. The guilt and sin offerings were usually offered first: they cleansed people from sin. Then came the burnt offerings, in which whole animals were burnt to ashes. Made at least twice a day, these sacrifices evidently expressed complete dedication to God. The final sacrifice was the fellowship offering, essentially a family meal shared in the presence of God. (The grain offerings were usually given along with one of the other offerings.)

The sequence of the offerings—forgiveness of sins, then total dedication, then fellowship—shows that their goal was fellowship with God. To reach that goal, forgiveness of sin and complete dedication to God were necessary.

Leviticus, however, does not explain this underlying philosophy; it reads more like an instruction manual on how to make sacrifices exactly the way God wanted. The exactness helped produce a proper attitude. You couldn't approach God carelessly. You had to be very careful to do just what he said, to obey him in every detail.

Can an Animal Really Pay?

The whole scene—with its concern for blood, priests, ritual—is strange to modern people. Just how can killing a goat make things right between God and people? Is the sacrifice of an animal really enough to "pay for" our mistakes? We may forget that throughout history, people have intuitively felt that sacrifice was needed to satisfy God. Many religions around the world still sacrifice today.

For us these sacrifices seem outmoded primarily because one great sacrifice—that of God's own Son—outdid them all. The animal sacrifices were not enough, ultimately, to pay for human sin. They prepared the way for a sacrifice that was.

The cost of an animal was substantial, but the true cost, even for us, is infinitely greater. Yet we don't have to pay the cost. Jesus paid it all.

Life Questions: Do you think of God as requiring sacrifice? How does the picture of God in Leviticus fit with your ideas about God?

altar shall be kept burning; it shall not go out. Every morning the priest shall add wood to it, lay out the burnt offering on it, and turn into smoke the fat pieces of the offerings of well-being. ¹³A perpetual fire shall be kept burning on the altar; it shall not go out.

6.5–7 Double Jeopardy

An Israelite who committed a crime against another person (such as stealing) had two parties to reckon with. First, the offender had to make full restitution, along with a 20 percent penalty, to the person cheated. Second, he or she had to bring a special offering to God. A crime against another person also counted as a sin against God.

14 This is the ritual of the grain offering: The sons of Aaron shall offer it before the LORD, in front of the altar. ¹⁵They shall take from it a handful of the choice flour and oil of the grain offering, with all the frankincense that is on the offering, and they shall turn its memorial portion into smoke on the altar as a pleasing odor to the LORD. ¹⁶Aaron and his sons shall eat what is left of it; it shall be eaten as unleavened cakes in a holy place; in the court of the tent of meeting they shall eat it. ¹⁷It shall not be baked with leaven. I have given it as their portion of my offerings by fire; it is most holy, like the sin offering and the guilt offering. ¹⁸Every male among the descendants of Aaron shall eat of it, as their perpetual due throughout your generations, from the LORD's offerings by fire; anything that touches them shall become holy.

19 The LORD spoke to Moses, saying: ²⁰This is the offering that Aaron and his sons shall offer to the LORD on the day when he is anointed: one-tenth of an ephah of choice flour as a regular offering, half of it in the morning and half in the evening. ²¹It shall be made with oil on a griddle; you shall bring it well soaked, as a grain offering of baked[d] pieces, and you shall present it as a pleasing odor to the LORD. ²²And so the priest, anointed from among Aaron's descendants as a successor, shall prepare it; it is the LORD's—a perpetual due—to be turned entirely into smoke. ²³Every grain offering of a priest shall be wholly burned; it shall not be eaten.

24 The LORD spoke to Moses, saying: ²⁵Speak to Aaron and his sons, saying: This is the ritual of the sin offering. The sin offering shall be slaughtered before the LORD at the spot where the burnt offering is slaughtered; it is most holy. ²⁶The priest who offers it as a sin offering shall eat of it; it shall be eaten in a holy place, in the court of the tent of meeting. ²⁷Whatever touches its flesh shall become holy; and when any of its blood is spattered on a garment, you shall wash the bespattered part in a holy place. ²⁸An earthen vessel in which it was boiled shall be broken; but if it is boiled in a bronze vessel, that shall be scoured and rinsed in water. ²⁹Every male among the priests shall eat of it; it is most holy. ³⁰But no sin offering shall be eaten from which any blood is brought into the tent of meeting for atonement in the holy place; it shall be burned with fire.

7 This is the ritual of the guilt offering. It is most holy; ²at the spot where the burnt offering is slaughtered, they shall slaughter the guilt offering, and its blood shall be dashed against all sides of the altar. ³All its fat shall be offered: the broad tail, the fat that covers the entrails, ⁴the two kidneys with the fat that is on them at the loins, and the appendage of the liver, which shall be removed with the kidneys. ⁵The priest shall turn them into smoke on the altar as an offering by fire to the LORD; it is a guilt offering. ⁶Every male among the priests shall eat of it; it shall be eaten in a holy place; it is most holy.

7 The guilt offering is like the sin offering, there is the same ritual for them; the priest who makes atonement with it shall have it. ⁸So, too, the priest who offers anyone's burnt offering shall keep the skin of the burnt offering that he has offered. ⁹And every grain offering baked in the oven, and all that is prepared in a pan or on a griddle, shall belong to the priest who offers it. ¹⁰But every other grain offering, mixed with oil or dry, shall belong to all the sons of Aaron equally.

Further Instructions

11 This is the ritual of the sacrifice of the offering of well-being that one may offer to the LORD. ¹²If you offer it for thanksgiving, you shall offer with the thank offering unleavened cakes mixed with oil, unleavened wafers spread with oil, and cakes of choice flour well soaked in oil. ¹³With your thanksgiving sacrifice of well-being you shall bring your offering with cakes of leavened bread. ¹⁴From this you shall offer one cake from each offering, as a gift to the LORD; it shall belong to the priest who dashes the blood of the offering of well-being. ¹⁵And the flesh of your thanksgiving sacrifice of well-being shall be eaten on the day it is offered; you shall not leave any of it until morning. ¹⁶But if the sacrifice you offer is a votive offering or a freewill offering, it shall be eaten on the day that you offer your sacrifice, and what is left of it shall be eaten the next day; ¹⁷but what is left of the flesh of the sacrifice shall be burned up on the third day. ¹⁸If any of the flesh of your sacrifice of well-being is eaten on the

d Meaning of Heb uncertain

third day, it shall not be acceptable, nor shall it be credited to the one who offers it; it shall be an abomination, and the one who eats of it shall incur guilt.

19 Flesh that touches any unclean thing shall not be eaten; it shall be burned up. As for other flesh, all who are clean may eat such flesh. 20But those who eat flesh from the LORD's sacrifice of well-being while in a state of uncleanness shall be cut off from their kin. 21When any one of you touches any unclean thing—human uncleanness or an unclean animal or any unclean creature—and then eats flesh from the LORD's sacrifice of well-being, you shall be cut off from your kin.

22 The LORD spoke to Moses, saying: 23Speak to the people of Israel, saying: You shall eat no fat of ox or sheep or goat. 24The fat of an animal that died or was torn by wild animals may be put to any other use, but you must not eat it. 25If any one of you eats the fat from an animal of which an offering by fire may be made to the LORD, you who eat it shall be cut off from your kin. 26You must not eat any blood whatever, either of bird or of animal, in any of your settlements. 27Any one of you who eats any blood shall be cut off from your kin.

28 The LORD spoke to Moses, saying: 29Speak to the people of Israel, saying: Any one of you who would offer to the LORD your sacrifice of well-being must yourself bring to the LORD your offering from your sacrifice of well-being. 30Your own hands shall bring the LORD's offering by fire; you shall bring the fat with the breast, so that the breast may be raised as an elevation offering before the LORD. 31The priest shall turn the fat into smoke on the altar, but the breast shall belong to Aaron and his sons. 32And the right thigh from your sacrifices of well-being you shall give to the priest as an offering; 33the one among the sons of Aaron who offers the blood and fat of the offering of well-being shall have the right thigh for a portion. 34For I have taken the breast of the elevation offering, and the thigh that is offered, from the people of Israel, from their sacrifices of well-being, and have given them to Aaron the priest

and to his sons, as a perpetual due from the people of Israel. 35This is the portion allotted to Aaron and to his sons from the offerings made by fire to the LORD, once they have been brought forward to serve the LORD as priests; 36these the LORD commanded to be given them, when he anointed them, as a perpetual due from the people of Israel throughout their generations.

37 This is the ritual of the burnt offering, the grain offering, the sin offering, the guilt offering, the offering of ordination, and the sacrifice of well-being, 38which the LORD commanded Moses on Mount Sinai, when he commanded the people of Israel to bring their offerings to the LORD, in the wilderness of Sinai.

The Rites of Ordination

8 The LORD spoke to Moses, saying: 2Take Aaron and his sons with him, the vestments, the anointing oil, the bull of sin offering, the two

8.2 The First High Priest

God had set apart the tribe of Levi to perform religious duties for the entire nation. In this scene Moses' brother Aaron assumed the new office of high priest. The impressive public ceremony lasted eight days in all and culminated in a dramatic display of God's approval (9.24). From then on, the priesthood remained in Aaron's family.

rams, and the basket of unleavened bread; 3and assemble the whole congregation at the entrance of the tent of meeting. 4And Moses did as the LORD commanded him. When the congregation was assembled at the entrance of the tent of meeting, 5Moses said to the congregation, "This is what the LORD has commanded to be done."

6 Then Moses brought Aaron and his sons forward, and washed them with water. 7He put the tunic on him, fastened the sash around him, clothed him with the robe, and put the ephod on him. He then put the decorated band of the ephod around him, tying the ephod to him with it. 8He placed the breastpiece on him, and in the breastpiece he put the Urim and the Thummim. 9And he set the turban on his head, and on the turban, in front, he set the golden ornament, the holy crown, as the LORD commanded Moses.

10 Then Moses took the anointing oil and anointed the tabernacle and all that was in it, and consecrated them. 11He sprinkled some of it on the altar seven times, and anointed the altar and all its utensils, and the basin and its base, to consecrate them. 12He poured some of the anointing oil on Aaron's head and anointed him, to consecrate him. 13And Moses brought forward Aaron's sons, and clothed them with tunics, and fastened sashes around them, and tied headdresses on them, as the LORD commanded Moses.

7.34 Priestly Privileges

Priests enjoyed certain privileges, such as exemption from military duty and the right to keep portions of the offerings as food. Yet the priests were not "holier than thou." They had to offer regular sacrifices for their own sins as well as for the sins of the people (9.7–12). The New Testament book of Hebrews uses this fact to underscore Christ's superiority: sinless, he offered a perfect, once-for-all sacrifice for the sake of others.

14 He led forward the bull of sin offering; and Aaron and his sons laid their hands upon the head of the bull of sin offering, 15and it was slaughtered. Moses took the blood and with his finger put some on each of the horns of the altar, purifying the altar; then he poured out the blood at the base of the altar. Thus he consecrated it, to make atonement for it. 16Moses took all the fat that was around the entrails, and the appendage of the liver, and the two kidneys with their fat, and turned them into smoke on the altar. 17But the bull itself, its skin and flesh and its dung, he burned with fire outside the camp, as the LORD commanded Moses.

18 Then he brought forward the ram of burnt offering. Aaron and his sons laid their hands on the head of the ram, 19and it was slaughtered. Moses dashed the blood against all sides of the altar. 20The ram was cut into its parts, and Moses turned into smoke the head and the parts and the suet. 21And after the entrails and the legs were washed with water, Moses turned into smoke the whole ram on the altar; it was a burnt offering for a pleasing odor, an offering by fire to the LORD, as the LORD commanded Moses.

22 Then he brought forward the second ram, the ram of ordination. Aaron and his sons laid their hands on the head of the ram, 23and it was slaughtered. Moses took some of its blood and put it on the lobe of Aaron's right ear and on the thumb of his right hand and on the big toe of his right foot. 24After Aaron's sons were brought forward, Moses put some of the blood on the lobes of their right ears and on the thumbs of their right hands and on the big toes of their right feet; and Moses dashed the rest of the blood against all sides of the altar. 25He took the fat—the broad tail, all the fat that was around the entrails, the appendage of the liver, and the two kidneys with their fat—and the right thigh. 26From the basket of unleavened bread that was before the LORD, he took one cake of unleavened bread, one cake of bread with oil, and one wafer, and placed them on the fat and on the right thigh. 27He placed all these on the palms of Aaron and on the palms of his sons, and raised them as an elevation offering before the LORD. 28Then Moses took them from their hands and turned them into smoke on the altar with the burnt offering. This was an ordination offering for a pleasing odor, an offering by fire to the LORD. 29Moses took the breast and raised it as an elevation offering before the LORD; it was Moses' portion of the ram of ordination, as the LORD commanded Moses.

30 Then Moses took some of the anointing oil and some of the blood that was on the altar and sprinkled them on Aaron and his vestments, and also on his sons and their vestments. Thus he consecrated Aaron and his vestments, and also his sons and their vestments.

31 And Moses said to Aaron and his sons, "Boil the flesh at the entrance of the tent of meeting, and eat it there with the bread that is in the basket of ordination offerings, as I was commanded, 'Aaron and his sons shall eat it'; 32and what remains of the flesh and the bread you shall burn with fire. 33You shall not go outside the entrance of the tent of meeting for seven days, until the day when your period of ordination is completed. For it will take seven days to ordain you; 34as has been done today, the LORD has commanded to be done to make atonement for you. 35You shall remain at the entrance of the tent of meeting day and night for seven days, keeping the LORD's charge so that you do not die; for so I am commanded." 36Aaron and his sons did all the things that the LORD commanded through Moses.

Aaron's Priesthood Inaugurated

9 On the eighth day Moses summoned Aaron and his sons and the elders of Israel. 2He said to Aaron, "Take a bull calf for a sin offering and a ram for a burnt offering, without blemish, and offer them before the LORD. 3And say to the people of Israel, 'Take a male goat for a sin offering; a calf and a lamb, yearlings without blemish, for a burnt offering; 4and an ox and a ram for an offering of well-being to sacrifice before the LORD; and a grain offering mixed with oil. For today the LORD will appear to you.'" 5They brought what Moses commanded to the front of the tent of meeting; and the whole congregation drew near and stood before the LORD. 6And Moses said, "This is the thing that the LORD commanded you to do, so that the glory of the LORD may appear to you." 7Then Moses said to Aaron, "Draw near to the altar and sacrifice your sin offering and your burnt offering, and make atonement for yourself and for the people; and sacrifice the offering of the people, and make atonement for them; as the LORD has commanded."

8 Aaron drew near to the altar, and slaughtered the calf of the sin offering, which was for himself. 9The sons of Aaron presented the blood to him, and he dipped his finger in the blood and put it on the horns of the altar; and the rest of the blood he poured out at the base of the altar. 10But the fat, the kidneys, and the appendage of the liver from the sin offering he turned into smoke on the altar, as the LORD commanded Moses; 11and the flesh and the skin he burned with fire outside the camp.

12 Then he slaughtered the burnt offering. Aaron's sons brought him the blood, and he dashed it against all sides of the altar. 13And they brought him the burnt offering piece by piece, and the head, which he turned into smoke on the altar. 14He washed the entrails and the legs and, with the burnt offering, turned them into smoke on the altar.

15 Next he presented the people's offering. He took the goat of the sin offering that was for

the people, and slaughtered it, and presented it as a sin offering like the first one. [16]He presented the burnt offering, and sacrificed it according to regulation. [17]He presented the grain offering, and, taking a handful of it, he turned it into smoke on the altar, in addition to the burnt offering of the morning.

18 He slaughtered the ox and the ram as a sacrifice of well-being for the people. Aaron's sons brought him the blood, which he dashed against all sides of the altar, [19]and the fat of the ox and of the ram—the broad tail, the fat that covers the entrails, the two kidneys and the fat on them,[e] and the appendage of the liver. [20]They first laid the fat on the breasts, and the fat was turned into smoke on the altar; [21]and the breasts and the right thigh Aaron raised as an elevation offering before the LORD, as Moses had commanded.

22 Aaron lifted his hands toward the people and blessed them; and he came down after sacrificing the sin offering, the burnt offering, and the offering of well-being. [23]Moses and Aaron entered the tent of meeting, and then came out and blessed the people; and the glory of the LORD

9.23 The Glory of the LORD

Israelites were familiar with the brilliant glory of the Lord, but they had seen it only from a distance, on Mount Sinai. Even from that distance it had frightened them (Exodus 19.16–22). Now this glory had come to the tent of meeting itself, in the camp's center. They were indeed "close to God."

appeared to all the people. [24]Fire came out from the LORD and consumed the burnt offering and the fat on the altar; and when all the people saw it, they shouted and fell on their faces.

Nadab and Abihu

10 Now Aaron's sons, Nadab and Abihu, each took his censer, put fire in it, and laid incense on it; and they offered unholy fire before the LORD, such as he had not commanded them. [2]And fire came out from the presence of the LORD and consumed them, and they died before the LORD. [3]Then Moses said to Aaron, "This is what the LORD meant when he said,

'Through those who are near me
 I will show myself holy,
and before all the people
 I will be glorified.'"
And Aaron was silent.

4 Moses summoned Mishael and Elzaphan, sons of Uzziel the uncle of Aaron, and said to them, "Come forward, and carry your kinsmen away from the front of the sanctuary to a place outside the camp." [5]They came forward and carried them by their tunics out of the camp, as

10.2 Fatal Error

At first Aaron and his sons did everything according to God's instructions, and God honored them (8.36; 9.24). But in very short order some of the first official priests got careless about following God's explicit orders. The severe punishment sent out a strong message to other priests: they were there to carry out God's plan, not their own.

Moses had ordered. [6]And Moses said to Aaron and to his sons Eleazar and Ithamar, "Do not dishevel your hair, and do not tear your vestments, or you will die and wrath will strike all the congregation; but your kindred, the whole house of Israel, may mourn the burning that the LORD has sent. [7]You shall not go outside the entrance of the tent of meeting, or you will die; for the anointing oil of the LORD is on you." And they did as Moses had ordered.

8 And the LORD spoke to Aaron: [9]Drink no wine or strong drink, neither you nor your sons, when you enter the tent of meeting, that you may not die; it is a statute forever throughout your generations. [10]You are to distinguish between the holy and the common, and between the unclean and the clean; [11]and you are to teach the people of Israel all the statutes that the LORD has spoken to them through Moses.

12 Moses spoke to Aaron and to his remaining sons, Eleazar and Ithamar: Take the grain offering that is left from the LORD's offerings by fire, and eat it unleavened beside the altar, for it is most holy; [13]you shall eat it in a holy place, because it is your due and your sons' due, from the offerings by fire to the LORD; for so I am commanded. [14]But the breast that is elevated and the thigh that is raised, you and your sons and daughters as well may eat in any clean place; for they have been assigned to you and your children from the sacrifices of the offerings of well-being of the people of Israel. [15]The thigh that is raised and the breast that is elevated they shall bring, together with the offerings by fire of the fat, to raise for an elevation offering before the LORD; they are to be your due and that of your children forever, as the LORD has commanded.

e Gk: Heb *the broad tail, and that which covers, and the kidneys*

16 Then Moses made inquiry about the goat of the sin offering, and—it had already been burned! He was angry with Eleazar and Ithamar, Aaron's remaining sons, and said, 17"Why did you not eat the sin offering in the sacred area? For it is most holy, and God*f* has given it to you that you may remove the guilt of the congregation, to make atonement on their behalf before the LORD. 18Its blood was not brought into the inner part of the sanctuary. You should certainly have eaten it in the sanctuary, as I commanded." 19And Aaron spoke to Moses, "See, today they offered their sin offering and their burnt offering before the LORD; and yet such things as these have befallen me! If I had eaten the sin offering today, would it have been agreeable to the LORD?" 20And when Moses heard that, he agreed.

Clean and Unclean Foods

11 The LORD spoke to Moses and Aaron, saying to them: 2Speak to the people of Israel, saying:

From among all the land animals, these are the creatures that you may eat. 3Any animal that has divided hoofs and is cleft-footed and chews the cud—such you may eat. 4But among those that chew the cud or have divided hoofs, you shall not eat the following: the camel, for even though it chews the cud, it does not have divided hoofs; it is unclean for you. 5The rock badger, for even though it chews the cud, it does not have divided

f Heb *he*

An Invisible Danger
Taking precautions: like a surgeon preparing to operate

> Make a distinction between the unclean and the clean.
> 11.47

FOR MANY YEARS SURGERY REMAINED a desperate last resort for the hopelessly ill. Surgeons knew nothing about germs. Without washing, they would don operating garb, usually an old coat caked with blood and pus from numerous operations. They would pick up the scalpel, wiped clean with an old rag after the last operation, and go to work. Half of those operated on died.

One pioneer after another stumbled on the correct sterile techniques. But each was scorned and humiliated by fellow doctors. Professor Samuel Semmelweis, for one, discovered that making doctors wash their hands could dramatically cut the death rate in maternity wards. Yet his colleagues opposed Semmelweis strenuously, and though he argued for handwashing throughout his life, he died without seeing his ideas take hold.

Why So Slow?

Why were doctors so slow to adopt sterile techniques? The answer is simple: Germs had not yet been discovered. Doctors could not see—and reformers like Semmelweis could not give them—any reason why washing hands should make a difference.

Then Louis Pasteur discovered micro-organisms under his microscope. Sterile procedures began to make sense: they made war on germs. Even so, each reform, from rubber gloves to gauze masks, was accepted only grudgingly and with considerable opposition. It was as though doctors had a hard time remembering that something invisible could be so devastating. Fifty years of constant education and reform were necessary before "sterile technique" became a routine part of surgery, and germs became "real" to most medical minds.

Why All the Rules?

As germs are to a surgeon, "uncleanness" is to Leviticus. Chapters 11–15 describe elaborate precautions—what animals to avoid and how to treat "unclean" skin disease, mildewed clothing or walls, and bodily emissions.

Scholars point out that many clean and unclean rules have good health habits behind them, such as the rule to quarantine a person with an infectious disease or the rule against eating pork (which carries many parasites).

Others say that dietary laws were meant to keep the Israelites apart from their neighbors. Pigs were prominent in Canaanite worship; therefore the Israelites were not to eat pigs. A different dietary standard would keep the two groups from mixing socially, for a meal was always part of Middle Eastern hospitality.

Still other scholars suggest that the uncleanness rules simply fit into what Israelites intuitively thought proper. God was reinforcing a natural sense of repulsion toward creeping insects, scavenger birds, bodily emissions, and skin diseases.

hoofs; it is unclean for you. 6The hare, for even though it chews the cud, it does not have divided hoofs; it is unclean for you. 7The pig, for even though it has divided hoofs and is cleft-footed, it does not chew the cud; it is unclean for you. 8Of their flesh you shall not eat, and their carcasses you shall not touch; they are unclean for you.

9 These you may eat, of all that are in the waters. Everything in the waters that has fins and scales, whether in the seas or in the streams—such you may eat. 10But anything in the seas or the streams that does not have fins and scales, of the swarming creatures in the waters and among all the other living creatures that are in the waters—they are detestable to you 11and detestable they shall remain. Of their flesh you shall not eat, and their carcasses you shall regard as detestable. 12Everything in the waters that does not have fins and scales is detestable to you.

13 These you shall regard as detestable among the birds. They shall not be eaten; they are an abomination: the eagle, the vulture, the osprey, 14the buzzard, the kite of any kind; 15every raven of any kind; 16the ostrich, the nighthawk, the sea gull, the hawk of any kind; 17the little owl, the cormorant, the great owl, 18the water hen, the desert owl,g the carrion vulture, 19the stork, the heron of any kind, the hoopoe, and the bat.h

20 All winged insects that walk upon all fours are detestable to you. 21But among the winged insects that walk on all fours you may eat those that have jointed legs above their feet, with which to leap on the ground. 22Of them you may eat: the locust according to its kind, the bald locust according to its kind, the cricket according to its kind, and the grasshopper according to its kind. 23But all other winged insects that have four feet are detestable to you.

Unclean Animals

24 By these you shall become unclean; whoever touches the carcass of any of them shall be unclean until the evening, 25and whoever carries any part of the carcass of any of them shall wash his clothes and be unclean until the evening. 26Every animal that has divided hoofs but is not cleft-footed or does not chew the cud is unclean for you; everyone who touches one of them shall be unclean. 27All that walk on their paws, among the

g Or *pelican*   h Identification of several of the birds in verses 13-19 is uncertain

---

The Habit of Carefulness

All these explanations have merit, but the underlying basis of clean and unclean was religious. Being unclean was not dangerous or wrong. In fact, you could hardly avoid it. Practically everyone became "unclean" from time to time. But you could not worship God in the tent of meeting while you were unclean, nor bring anything unclean into the presence of God. His holiness would destroy it—and you (15.31).

So Leviticus trains God's people to watch their lives as carefully as surgeons watch their sterile techniques. They must develop the habit of carefulness, even about something they cannot see or feel. They must think about preparing themselves for God, not just do whatever "feels right."

It was not a question of how they felt about God, any more than a surgeon's concern is how he "feels" about germs. Clear, absolute standards laid out what could be acceptable to a God who is perfectly clean, absolute, unchanging. Just as surgeons had to struggle to take germs seriously, so God's people must learn to "purify themselves" for God.

Touching the Unclean

The uncleanness rules of Leviticus are outmoded because of Jesus' declaration that all things are clean (Mark 7.19; see also Acts 10.9–16). But the lessons behind these rules remain valid. God still may not be approached carelessly. Each person must examine his or her life, to be certain that God's purity is not violated.

Until Jesus' day, the slow spread of uncleanness seemed irreversible. You could avoid it, but you could not get rid of it. Contact with anything unclean made you unclean yourself. Naturally, certain diseases, notably leprosy, were twice cursed: they were both dangerous and unclean. You kept away from leprosy, absolutely.

Then Jesus touched a man with leprosy, and he became clean. Jesus touched a woman suffering from internal bleeding, and she was healed. For the first time, cleanness rather than uncleanness spread. The rules of Leviticus tell how to avoid uncleanness. Contact with Jesus, however, changes the unclean to clean.

Life Questions: Suppose sin were visible—small green spots that break out on the skin. Do you think it would help people to take sin more seriously?

animals that walk on all fours, are unclean for you; whoever touches the carcass of any of them shall be unclean until the evening, [28]and the one who carries the carcass shall wash his clothes and be unclean until the evening; they are unclean for you.

29 These are unclean for you among the creatures that swarm upon the earth: the weasel, the mouse, the great lizard according to its kind, [30]the gecko, the land crocodile, the lizard, the sand lizard, and the chameleon. [31]These are unclean for you among all that swarm; whoever touches one of them when they are dead shall be unclean until the evening. [32]And anything upon which any of them falls when they are dead shall be unclean, whether an article of wood or cloth or skin or sacking, any article that is used for any purpose; it shall be dipped into water, and it shall be unclean until the evening, and then it shall be clean. [33]And if any of them falls into any earthen vessel, all that is in it shall be unclean, and you shall break the vessel. [34]Any food that could be eaten shall be unclean if water from any such vessel comes upon it; and any liquid that could be drunk shall be unclean if it was in any such vessel. [35]Everything on which any part of the carcass falls shall be unclean; whether an oven or stove, it shall be broken in pieces; they are unclean, and shall remain unclean for you. [36]But a spring or a cistern holding water shall be clean, while whatever touches the carcass in it shall be unclean. [37]If any part of their carcass falls upon any seed set aside for sowing, it is clean; [38]but if water is put on the seed and any part of their carcass falls on it, it is unclean for you.

39 If an animal of which you may eat dies, anyone who touches its carcass shall be unclean until the evening. [40]Those who eat of its carcass shall wash their clothes and be unclean until the evening; and those who carry the carcass shall wash their clothes and be unclean until the evening.

41 All creatures that swarm upon the earth are detestable; they shall not be eaten. [42]Whatever moves on its belly, and whatever moves on all fours, or whatever has many feet, all the creatures that swarm upon the earth, you shall not eat; for they are detestable. [43]You shall not make yourselves detestable with any creature that swarms; you shall not defile yourselves with them, and so become unclean. [44]For I am the LORD your God; sanctify yourselves therefore, and be holy, for I am holy. You shall not defile yourselves with any swarming creature that moves on the earth. [45]For I am the LORD who brought you up from the land of Egypt, to be your God; you shall be holy, for I am holy.

46 This is the law pertaining to land animal and bird and every living creature that moves through the waters and every creature that swarms upon the earth, [47]to make a distinction between the unclean and the clean, and between the living creature that may be eaten and the living creature that may not be eaten.

Purification of Women after Childbirth

12 The LORD spoke to Moses, saying: [2]Speak to the people of Israel, saying:

If a woman conceives and bears a male child,

11.47 Of Scallops and Rabbits

Scholars have long puzzled over the seemingly arbitrary division between "clean" and "unclean" foods. Why permit the eating of certain fish but not shrimp, and cows but not pigs? "An Invisible Danger," page 132, discusses some of the theories that have been proposed. Probably the best explanation is that God was indeed being arbitrary, in order to form a nation different from any other (see 20.26). In Acts 10 God shows there is nothing intrinsically wrong with the animals labeled "unclean" in Leviticus.

---

she shall be ceremonially unclean seven days; as at the time of her menstruation, she shall be unclean. [3]On the eighth day the flesh of his foreskin shall be circumcised. [4]Her time of blood purification shall be thirty-three days; she shall not touch any holy thing, or come into the sanctuary, until the days of her purification are completed. [5]If she bears a female child, she shall be unclean two weeks, as in her menstruation; her time of blood purification shall be sixty-six days.

6 When the days of her purification are completed, whether for a son or for a daughter, she shall bring to the priest at the entrance of the tent of meeting a lamb in its first year for a burnt offering, and a pigeon or a turtledove for a sin offering. [7]He shall offer it before the LORD, and make atonement on her behalf; then she shall be clean from her flow of blood. This is the law for her who bears a child, male or female. [8]If she cannot afford a sheep, she shall take two turtledoves or two pigeons, one for a burnt offering and the other for a sin offering; and the priest shall make atonement on her behalf, and she shall be clean.

12.8 For Poor People

This alternate offering enabled poor women to live up to their duty to God. Mary offered such a sacrifice after Jesus' birth (see Luke 2.24)—an indication that Jesus' family was not well-off.

Leprosy, Varieties and Symptoms

13 The LORD spoke to Moses and Aaron, saying:

2 When a person has on the skin of his body a swelling or an eruption or a spot, and it turns into a leprous[i] disease on the skin of his body, he shall be brought to Aaron the priest or to one of his sons the priests. ³The priest shall examine the disease on the skin of his body, and if the hair in the diseased area has turned white and the disease appears to be deeper than the skin of his body, it is a leprous[i] disease; after the priest has examined him he shall pronounce him ceremonially unclean. ⁴But if the spot is white in the skin of his body, and appears no deeper than the skin, and the hair in it has not turned white, the priest shall confine the diseased person for seven days. ⁵The priest shall examine him on the seventh day, and if he sees that the disease is checked and the disease has not spread in the skin, then the priest shall confine him seven days more. ⁶The priest shall examine him again on the seventh day, and if the disease has abated and the disease has not spread in the skin, the priest shall pronounce him clean; it is only an eruption; and he shall wash his clothes, and be clean. ⁷But if the eruption spreads in the skin after he has shown himself to the priest for his cleansing, he shall appear again before the priest. ⁸The priest shall make an examination, and if the eruption has spread in the skin, the priest shall pronounce him unclean; it is a leprous[i] disease.

9 When a person contracts a leprous[i] disease, he shall be brought to the priest. ¹⁰The priest shall make an examination, and if there is a white swelling in the skin that has turned the hair white, and there is quick raw flesh in the swelling, ¹¹it is a chronic leprous[i] disease in the skin of his body. The priest shall pronounce him unclean; he shall not confine him, for he is unclean. ¹²But if the disease breaks out in the skin, so that it covers all the skin of the diseased person from head to foot, so far as the priest can see, ¹³then the priest shall make an examination, and if the disease has covered all his body, he shall pronounce him clean of the disease; since it has all turned white, he is clean. ¹⁴But if raw flesh ever appears on him, he shall be unclean; ¹⁵the priest shall examine the raw flesh and pronounce him unclean. Raw flesh is unclean, for it is a leprous[i] disease. ¹⁶But if the raw flesh again turns white, he shall come to the priest; ¹⁷the priest shall examine him, and if the disease has turned white, the priest shall pronounce the diseased person clean. He is clean.

18 When there is on the skin of one's body a boil that has healed, ¹⁹and in the place of the boil there appears a white swelling or a reddish-white spot, it shall be shown to the priest. ²⁰The priest shall make an examination, and if it appears deeper than the skin and its hair has turned white, the priest shall pronounce him unclean; this is a leprous[i] disease, broken out in the boil. ²¹But if the priest examines it and the hair on it is not white, nor is it deeper than the skin but has abated, the priest shall confine him seven days. ²²If it spreads in the skin, the priest shall pronounce him unclean; it is diseased. ²³But if the spot remains in one place and does not spread, it is the scar of the boil; the priest shall pronounce him clean.

24 Or, when the body has a burn on the skin and the raw flesh of the burn becomes a spot, reddish-white or white, ²⁵the priest shall examine it. If the hair in the spot has turned white and it appears deeper than the skin, it is a leprous[i] disease; it has broken out in the burn, and the priest shall pronounce him unclean. This is a leprous[i] disease. ²⁶But if the priest examines it and the hair in the spot is not white, and it is no deeper than the skin but has abated, the priest shall confine him seven days. ²⁷The priest shall examine him the seventh day; if it is spreading in the skin, the priest shall pronounce him unclean. This is a leprous[i] disease. ²⁸But if the spot remains in one place and does not spread in the skin but has abated, it is a swelling from the burn, and the priest shall pronounce him clean; for it is the scar of the burn.

29 When a man or woman has a disease on the head or in the beard, ³⁰the priest shall examine the disease. If it appears deeper than the skin and the hair in it is yellow and thin, the priest shall pronounce him unclean; it is an itch, a leprous[i] disease of the head or the beard. ³¹If the priest examines the itching disease, and it appears no deeper than the skin and there is no black hair in it, the priest shall confine the person with the itching disease for seven days. ³²On the seventh day the priest shall examine the itch; if the itch has not spread, and there is no yellow hair in it, and the itch appears to be no deeper than the skin, ³³he shall shave, but the itch he shall not shave. The priest shall confine the person with the itch for seven days more. ³⁴On the seventh day the priest shall examine the itch; if the itch has not spread in the skin and it appears to be no deeper than the skin, the priest shall pronounce him clean. He shall wash his clothes and be clean. ³⁵But if the itch spreads in the skin after he was pronounced clean, ³⁶the priest shall examine him. If the itch has spread in the skin, the priest need not seek for the yellow hair; he is unclean. ³⁷But if in his eyes the itch is checked, and black hair has grown in it, the itch is healed, he is clean; and the priest shall pronounce him clean.

38 When a man or a woman has spots on the

---

[i] A term for several skin diseases; precise meaning uncertain

skin of the body, white spots, ³⁹the priest shall make an examination, and if the spots on the skin of the body are of a dull white, it is a rash that has broken out on the skin; he is clean.

40 If anyone loses the hair from his head, he is bald but he is clean. ⁴¹If he loses the hair from his forehead and temples, he has baldness of the forehead but he is clean. ⁴²But if there is on the bald head or the bald forehead a reddish-white diseased spot, it is a leprousʲ disease breaking out on his bald head or his bald forehead. ⁴³The priest shall examine him; if the diseased swelling is reddish-white on his bald head or on his bald forehead, which resembles a leprousʲ disease in the skin of the body, ⁴⁴he is leprous,ʲ he is unclean. The priest shall pronounce him unclean; the disease is on his head.

45 The person who has the leprousʲ disease shall wear torn clothes and let the hair of his head be disheveled; and he shall cover his upper lip and cry out, "Unclean, unclean." ⁴⁶He shall remain unclean as long as he has the disease; he is unclean. He shall live alone; his dwelling shall be outside the camp.

47 Concerning clothing: when a leprousʲ disease appears in it, in woolen or linen cloth, ⁴⁸in warp or woof of linen or wool, or in a skin or in anything made of skin, ⁴⁹if the disease shows greenish or reddish in the garment, whether in warp or woof or in skin or in anything made of skin, it is a leprousʲ disease and shall be shown to the priest. ⁵⁰The priest shall examine the disease, and put the diseased article aside for seven days. ⁵¹He shall examine the disease on the seventh day. If the disease has spread in the cloth, in warp or woof, or in the skin, whatever be the use of the skin, this is a spreading leprousʲ disease; it is unclean. ⁵²He shall burn the clothing, whether diseased in warp or woof, woolen or linen, or anything of skin, for it is a spreading leprousʲ disease; it shall be burned in fire.

53 If the priest makes an examination, and the disease has not spread in the clothing, in warp or woof or in anything of skin, ⁵⁴the priest shall command them to wash the article in which the disease appears, and he shall put it aside seven days more. ⁵⁵The priest shall examine the diseased article after it has been washed. If the diseased spot has not changed color, though the disease has not spread, it is unclean; you shall burn it in fire, whether the leprousʲ spot is on the inside or on the outside.

56 If the priest makes an examination, and the disease has abated after it is washed, he shall tear the spot out of the cloth, in warp or woof, or out of skin. ⁵⁷If it appears again in the garment, in warp or woof, or in anything of skin, it is spreading; you shall burn with fire that in which the disease appears. ⁵⁸But the cloth, warp or woof,

or anything of skin from which the disease disappears when you have washed it, shall then be washed a second time, and it shall be clean.

59 This is the ritual for a leprousʲ disease in a cloth of wool or linen, either in warp or woof, or in anything of skin, to decide whether it is clean or unclean.

Purification of Lepers and Leprous Houses

14 The LORD spoke to Moses, saying: ²This shall be the ritual for the leprousʲ person at the time of his cleansing:

He shall be brought to the priest; ³the priest shall go out of the camp, and the priest shall make an examination. If the disease is healed in the leprousʲ person, ⁴the priest shall command that two living clean birds and cedarwood and crimson yarn and hyssop be brought for the one who is to be cleansed. ⁵The priest shall command that one of the birds be slaughtered over fresh water in an earthen vessel. ⁶He shall take the living bird with the cedarwood and the crimson yarn and the hyssop, and dip them and the living bird in the blood of the bird that was slaughtered over the fresh water. ⁷He shall sprinkle it seven times upon the one who is to be cleansed of the leprousʲ disease; then he shall pronounce him clean, and he shall let the living bird go into the open

14.7 A Bird Set Free

It is difficult to assign definite symbolic meaning to all the details in this ceremony for the cleansing of skin diseases. Many scholars suggest that the bird that was killed represented purification by sacrifice, while the bird set free represented new liberty after a long quarantine. When Jesus healed a man with leprosy (Matthew 8.4), he told him to follow these instructions.

field. ⁸The one who is to be cleansed shall wash his clothes, and shave off all his hair, and bathe himself in water, and he shall be clean. After that he shall come into the camp, but shall live outside his tent seven days. ⁹On the seventh day he shall shave all his hair: of head, beard, eyebrows; he shall shave all his hair. Then he shall wash his clothes, and bathe his body in water, and he shall be clean.

10 On the eighth day he shall take two male lambs without blemish, and one ewe lamb in its first year without blemish, and a grain offering of three-tenths of an ephah of choice flour mixed with oil, and one logᵏ of oil. ¹¹The priest who cleanses shall set the person to be cleansed, along

---

ʲ A term for several skin diseases; precise meaning uncertain

with these things, before the LORD, at the entrance of the tent of meeting. [12]The priest shall take one of the lambs, and offer it as a guilt offering, along with the log[k] of oil, and raise them as an elevation offering before the LORD. [13]He shall slaughter the lamb in the place where the sin offering and the burnt offering are slaughtered in the holy place; for the guilt offering, like the sin offering, belongs to the priest: it is most holy. [14]The priest shall take some of the blood of the guilt offering and put it on the lobe of the right ear of the one to be cleansed, and on the thumb of the right hand, and on the big toe of the right foot. [15]The priest shall take some of the log[k] of oil and pour it into the palm of his own left hand, [16]and dip his right finger in the oil that is in his left hand and sprinkle some oil with his finger seven times before the LORD. [17]Some of the oil that remains in his hand the priest shall put on the lobe of the right ear of the one to be cleansed, and on the thumb of the right hand, and on the big toe of the right foot, on top of the blood of the guilt offering. [18]The rest of the oil that is in the priest's hand he shall put on the head of the one to be cleansed. Then the priest shall make atonement on his behalf before the LORD; [19]the priest shall offer the sin offering, to make atonement for the one to be cleansed from his uncleanness. Afterward he shall slaughter the burnt offering; [20]and the priest shall offer the burnt offering and the grain offering on the altar. Thus the priest shall make atonement on his behalf and he shall be clean.

21 But if he is poor and cannot afford so much, he shall take one male lamb for a guilt offering to be elevated, to make atonement on his behalf, and one-tenth of an ephah of choice flour mixed with oil for a grain offering and a log[k] of oil; [22]also two turtledoves or two pigeons, such as he can afford, one for a sin offering and the other for a burnt offering. [23]On the eighth day he shall bring them for his cleansing to the priest, to the entrance of the tent of meeting, before the LORD; [24]and the priest shall take the lamb of the guilt offering and the log[k] of oil, and the priest shall raise them as an elevation offering before the LORD. [25]The priest shall slaughter the lamb of the guilt offering and shall take some of the blood of the guilt offering, and put it on the lobe of the right ear of the one to be cleansed, and on the thumb of the right hand, and on the big toe of the right foot. [26]The priest shall pour some of the oil into the palm of his own left hand, [27]and shall sprinkle with his right finger some of the oil that is in his left hand seven times before the LORD. [28]The priest shall put some of the oil that is in his hand on the lobe of the right ear of the one to be

cleansed, and on the thumb of the right hand, and the big toe of the right foot, where the blood of the guilt offering was placed. [29]The rest of the oil that is in the priest's hand he shall put on the head of the one to be cleansed, to make atonement on his behalf before the LORD. [30]And he shall offer, of the turtledoves or pigeons such as he can afford, [31]one[l] for a sin offering and the other for a burnt offering, along with a grain offering; and the priest shall make atonement before the LORD on behalf of the one being cleansed. [32]This is the ritual for the one who has a leprous[m] disease, who cannot afford the offerings for his cleansing.

33 The LORD spoke to Moses and Aaron, saying:

34 When you come into the land of Canaan, which I give you for a possession, and I put a leprous[m] disease in a house in the land of your possession, [35]the owner of the house shall come and tell the priest, saying, "There seems to me to be some sort of disease in my house." [36]The priest shall command that they empty the house before the priest goes to examine the disease, or all that is in the house will become unclean; and afterward the priest shall go in to inspect the house. [37]He shall examine the disease; if the disease is in the walls of the house with greenish or reddish spots, and if it appears to be deeper than the surface, [38]the priest shall go outside to the door of the house and shut up the house seven days. [39]The priest shall come again on the seventh day and make an inspection; if the disease has spread in the walls of the house, [40]the priest shall command that the stones in which the disease appears be taken out and thrown into an unclean place outside the city. [41]He shall have the inside of the house scraped thoroughly, and the plaster that is scraped off shall be dumped in an unclean place outside the city. [42]They shall take other stones and put them in the place of those stones, and take other plaster and plaster the house.

43 If the disease breaks out again in the house, after he has taken out the stones and scraped the house and plastered it, [44]the priest shall go and make inspection; if the disease has spread in the house, it is a spreading leprous[m] disease in the house; it is unclean. [45]He shall have the house torn down, its stones and timber and all the plaster of the house, and taken outside the city to an unclean place. [46]All who enter the house while it is shut up shall be unclean until the evening; [47]and all who sleep in the house shall wash their clothes; and all who eat in the house shall wash their clothes.

48 If the priest comes and makes an inspection, and the disease has not spread in the house

---

[k] A liquid measure meaning uncertain   [l] Gk Syr: Heb *afford*, [31]*such as he can afford, one*   [m] A term for several skin diseases; precise

after the house was plastered, the priest shall pronounce the house clean; the disease is healed. 49For the cleansing of the house he shall take two birds, with cedarwood and crimson yarn and hyssop, 50and shall slaughter one of the birds over fresh water in an earthen vessel, 51and shall take the cedarwood and the hyssop and the crimson yarn, along with the living bird, and dip them in the blood of the slaughtered bird and the fresh water, and sprinkle the house seven times. 52Thus he shall cleanse the house with the blood of the bird, and with the fresh water, and with the living bird, and with the cedarwood and hyssop and crimson yarn; 53and he shall let the living bird go out of the city into the open field; so he shall make atonement for the house, and it shall be clean.

54 This is the ritual for any leprous[n] disease: for an itch, 55for leprous[n] diseases in clothing and houses, 56and for a swelling or an eruption or a spot, 57to determine when it is unclean and when it is clean. This is the ritual for leprous[n] diseases.

Concerning Bodily Discharges

15 The LORD spoke to Moses and Aaron, saying: 2Speak to the people of Israel and say to them:

When any man has a discharge from his member,[o] his discharge makes him ceremonially unclean. 3The uncleanness of his discharge is this:

15.2 Sex Rules

Some of the rules regarding sex and bodily discharges mystify modern readers, but the Israelites took for granted that God had dominion over the most private aspects of their lives. The Bible does not provide a detailed rationale for these regulations. Some relate to health and hygiene: following the rules would help the Israelites avoid the venereal diseases that plagued their neighbors. Also, pagan religions commonly employed temple prostitutes, and God clearly intended for the Israelites to keep worship and sex separate.

whether his member[o] flows with his discharge, or his member[o] is stopped from discharging, it is uncleanness for him. 4Every bed on which the one with the discharge lies shall be unclean; and everything on which he sits shall be unclean. 5Anyone who touches his bed shall wash his clothes, and bathe in water, and be unclean until the evening. 6All who sit on anything on which the one with the discharge has sat shall wash their clothes, and bathe in water, and be unclean until the evening. 7All who touch the body of the one with the discharge shall wash their clothes, and bathe in

water, and be unclean until the evening. 8If the one with the discharge spits on persons who are clean, then they shall wash their clothes, and bathe in water, and be unclean until the evening. 9Any saddle on which the one with the discharge rides shall be unclean. 10All who touch anything that was under him shall be unclean until the evening, and all who carry such a thing shall wash their clothes, and bathe in water, and be unclean until the evening. 11All those whom the one with the discharge touches without his having rinsed his hands in water shall wash their clothes, and bathe in water, and be unclean until the evening. 12Any earthen vessel that the one with the discharge touches shall be broken; and every vessel of wood shall be rinsed in water.

13 When the one with a discharge is cleansed of his discharge, he shall count seven days for his cleansing; he shall wash his clothes and bathe his body in fresh water, and he shall be clean. 14On the eighth day he shall take two turtledoves or two pigeons and come before the LORD to the entrance of the tent of meeting and give them to the priest. 15The priest shall offer them, one for a sin offering and the other for a burnt offering; and the priest shall make atonement on his behalf before the LORD for his discharge.

16 If a man has an emission of semen, he shall bathe his whole body in water, and be unclean until the evening. 17Everything made of cloth or of skin on which the semen falls shall be washed with water, and be unclean until the evening. 18If a man lies with a woman and has an emission of semen, both of them shall bathe in water, and be unclean until the evening.

19 When a woman has a discharge of blood that is her regular discharge from her body, she shall be in her impurity for seven days, and whoever touches her shall be unclean until the evening. 20Everything upon which she lies during her impurity shall be unclean; everything also upon which she sits shall be unclean. 21Whoever touches her bed shall wash his clothes, and bathe in water, and be unclean until the evening. 22Whoever touches anything upon which she sits shall wash his clothes, and bathe in water, and be unclean until the evening; 23whether it is the bed or anything upon which she sits, when he touches it he shall be unclean until the evening. 24If any man lies with her, and her impurity falls on him, he shall be unclean seven days; and every bed on which he lies shall be unclean.

25 If a woman has a discharge of blood for many days, not at the time of her impurity, or if she has a discharge beyond the time of her impurity, all the days of the discharge she shall continue in uncleanness; as in the days of her impurity, she shall be unclean. 26Every bed on which she lies during all the days of her discharge shall be treat-

---

[n] A term for several skin diseases; precise meaning uncertain   [o] Heb *flesh*

ed as the bed of her impurity; and everything on
which she sits shall be unclean, as in the uncleanness of her impurity. 27Whoever touches these
things shall be unclean, and shall wash his clothes,
and bathe in water, and be unclean until the evening. 28If she is cleansed of her discharge, she shall
count seven days, and after that she shall be clean.
29On the eighth day she shall take two turtledoves
or two pigeons and bring them to the priest at the
entrance of the tent of meeting. 30The priest shall
offer one for a sin offering and the other for a
burnt offering; and the priest shall make atonement on her behalf before the LORD for her unclean discharge.

31 Thus you shall keep the people of Israel
separate from their uncleanness, so that they do
not die in their uncleanness by defiling my tabernacle that is in their midst.

32 This is the ritual for those who have a discharge: for him who has an emission of semen,
becoming unclean thereby, 33for her who is in the
infirmity of her period, for anyone, male or female, who has a discharge, and for the man who
lies with a woman who is unclean.

The Day of Atonement

16 The LORD spoke to Moses after the death of
the two sons of Aaron, when they drew
near before the LORD and died. 2The LORD said to
Moses:

Tell your brother Aaron not to come just at
any time into the sanctuary inside the curtain
before the mercy seat[p] that is upon the ark, or he
will die; for I appear in the cloud upon the mercy
seat.[p] 3Thus shall Aaron come into the holy
place: with a young bull for a sin offering and a
ram for a burnt offering. 4He shall put on the holy
linen tunic, and shall have the linen undergarments next to his body, fasten the linen sash, and
wear the linen turban; these are the holy vestments. He shall bathe his body in water, and then
put them on. 5He shall take from the congregation of the people of Israel two male goats for a
sin offering, and one ram for a burnt offering.

6 Aaron shall offer the bull as a sin offering
for himself, and shall make atonement for himself
and for his house. 7He shall take the two goats
and set them before the LORD at the entrance of
the tent of meeting; 8and Aaron shall cast lots on
the two goats, one lot for the LORD and the other
lot for Azazel.[q] 9Aaron shall present the goat on
which the lot fell for the LORD, and offer it as a sin
offering; 10but the goat on which the lot fell for
Azazel[q] shall be presented alive before the LORD
to make atonement over it, that it may be sent
away into the wilderness to Azazel.[q]

11 Aaron shall present the bull as a sin offering for himself, and shall make atonement for
himself and for his house; he shall slaughter the
bull as a sin offering for himself. 12He shall take a
censer full of coals of fire from the altar before the
LORD, and two handfuls of crushed sweet incense,
and he shall bring it inside the curtain 13and put
the incense on the fire before the LORD, that the
cloud of the incense may cover the mercy seat[p]
that is upon the covenant,[r] or he will die. 14He
shall take some of the blood of the bull, and
sprinkle it with his finger on the front of the
mercy seat,[p] and before the mercy seat[p] he shall
sprinkle the blood with his finger seven times.

15 He shall slaughter the goat of the sin offering that is for the people and bring its blood
inside the curtain, and do with its blood as he did
with the blood of the bull, sprinkling it upon the
mercy seat[p] and before the mercy seat.[p] 16Thus
he shall make atonement for the sanctuary, because of the uncleannesses of the people of Israel,
and because of their transgressions, all their sins;
and so he shall do for the tent of meeting, which
remains with them in the midst of their uncleannesses. 17No one shall be in the tent of meeting
from the time he enters to make atonement in
the sanctuary until he comes out and has made
atonement for himself and for his house and for
all the assembly of Israel. 18Then he shall go out
to the altar that is before the LORD and make
atonement on its behalf, and shall take some of
the blood of the bull and of the blood of the goat,
and put it on each of the horns of the altar. 19He
shall sprinkle some of the blood on it with his
finger seven times, and cleanse it and hallow it
from the uncleannesses of the people of Israel.

20 When he has finished atoning for the holy
place and the tent of meeting and the altar, he
shall present the live goat. 21Then Aaron shall lay
both his hands on the head of the live goat, and
confess over it all the iniquities of the people of
Israel, and all their transgressions, all their sins,
putting them on the head of the goat, and sending
it away into the wilderness by means of someone
designated for the task.[s] 22The goat shall bear on
itself all their iniquities to a barren region; and the
goat shall be set free in the wilderness.

23 Then Aaron shall enter the tent of meeting,
and shall take off the linen vestments that he put

16.20 Scapegoat

The English word scapegoat (escape goat) was formed to capture the essence of this crucial ceremony in which a goat symbolically carried all the sins of Israel into the desert. Today the word is applied to anyone who takes the blame for something other people did.

[p] Or *the cover* [q] Traditionally rendered *a scapegoat* [r] Or *treaty*, or *testament*; Heb *eduth* [s] Meaning of Heb uncertain

on when he went into the holy place, and shall leave them there. 24He shall bathe his body in water in a holy place, and put on his vestments; then he shall come out and offer his burnt offering and the burnt offering of the people, making atonement for himself and for the people. 25The fat of the sin offering he shall turn into smoke on the altar. 26The one who sets the goat free for Azazel[t] shall wash his clothes and bathe his body in water, and afterward may come into the camp. 27The bull of the sin offering and the goat of the sin offering, whose blood was brought in to make atonement in the holy place, shall be taken outside the camp; their skin and their flesh and their dung shall be consumed in fire. 28The one who burns them shall wash his clothes and bathe his body in water, and afterward may come into the camp.

29 This shall be a statute to you forever: In the seventh month, on the tenth day of the month, you shall deny yourselves,[u] and shall do no work, neither the citizen nor the alien who resides among you. 30For on this day atonement shall be made for you, to cleanse you; from all your sins you shall be clean before the LORD. 31It is a sabbath of complete rest to you, and you shall deny yourselves;[u] it is a statute forever. 32The priest who is anointed and consecrated as priest in his father's place shall make atonement, wearing the linen vestments, the holy vestments. 33He shall make atonement for the sanctuary, and he shall make atonement for the tent of meeting and for the altar, and he shall make atonement for the priests and for all the people of the assembly. 34This shall be an everlasting statute for you, to make atonement for the people of Israel once in the year for all their sins. And Moses did as the LORD had commanded him.

The Slaughtering of Animals

17 The LORD spoke to Moses: 2 Speak to Aaron and his sons and to all the people of Israel and say to them: This is what the LORD has commanded. 3If anyone of the house of Israel slaughters an ox or a lamb or a goat in the camp, or slaughters it outside the camp, 4and does not bring it to the entrance of the tent of meeting, to present it as an offering to the LORD before the tabernacle of the LORD, he shall be held guilty of bloodshed; he has shed blood, and he shall be cut off from the people. 5This is in order that the people of Israel may bring their sacrifices that they offer in the open field, that they may bring them to the LORD, to the priest at the entrance of the tent of meeting, and offer them as sacrifices of well-being to the LORD. 6The priest shall dash the blood against the altar of the LORD at the entrance of the tent of meeting, and turn the fat into smoke as a pleasing odor to

the LORD, 7so that they may no longer offer their sacrifices for goat-demons, to whom they prostitute themselves. This shall be a statute forever to them throughout their generations.

8 And say to them further: Anyone of the house of Israel or of the aliens who reside among them who offers a burnt offering or sacrifice, 9and does not bring it to the entrance of the tent of meeting, to sacrifice it to the LORD, shall be cut off from the people.

Eating Blood Prohibited

10 If anyone of the house of Israel or of the aliens who reside among them eats any blood, I will set my face against that person who eats blood, and will cut that person off from the people. 11For the life of the flesh is in the blood; and

17.10 Kosher

To this day many Jews avoid meat unless it has been carefully drained of blood. Blood, which represented the life of living creatures, was to make atonement for, or to "cover up," sins. Thus Jesus' blood, signifying his death, has special significance to Christians. It is the blood of the ultimate sacrifice for sin.

The first Christians debated how much of the law should be required of non-Jews who became Christians (Acts 15). Of the four requirements they settled on, two were "kosher."

I have given it to you for making atonement for your lives on the altar; for, as life, it is the blood that makes atonement. 12Therefore I have said to the people of Israel: No person among you shall eat blood, nor shall any alien who resides among you eat blood. 13And anyone of the people of Israel, or of the aliens who reside among them, who hunts down an animal or bird that may be eaten shall pour out its blood and cover it with earth.

14 For the life of every creature—its blood is its life; therefore I have said to the people of Israel: You shall not eat the blood of any creature, for the life of every creature is its blood; whoever eats it shall be cut off. 15All persons, citizens or aliens, who eat what dies of itself or what has been torn by wild animals, shall wash their clothes, and bathe themselves in water, and be unclean until the evening; then they shall be clean. 16But if they do not wash themselves or bathe their body, they shall bear their guilt.

Sexual Relations

18 The LORD spoke to Moses, saying: 2 Speak to the people of Israel and say to

---

[t] Traditionally rendered *a scapegoat*   [u] Or *shall fast*

them: I am the LORD your God. ³You shall not do as they do in the land of Egypt, where you lived, and you shall not do as they do in the land of Canaan, to which I am bringing you. You shall not follow their statutes. ⁴My ordinances you shall observe and my statutes you shall keep, following them: I am the LORD your God. ⁵You shall keep my statutes and my ordinances; by doing so one shall live: I am the LORD.

6 None of you shall approach anyone near of kin to uncover nakedness: I am the LORD. ⁷You shall not uncover the nakedness of your father, which is the nakedness of your mother; she is your mother, you shall not uncover her nakedness. ⁸You shall not uncover the nakedness of your father's wife; it is the nakedness of your father. ⁹You shall not uncover the nakedness of your sister, your father's daughter or your mother's daughter, whether born at home or born abroad. ¹⁰You shall not uncover the nakedness of your son's daughter or of your daughter's daughter, for their nakedness is your own nakedness. ¹¹You shall not uncover the nakedness of your father's wife's daughter, begotten by your father, since she is your sister. ¹²You shall not uncover the nakedness of your father's sister; she is your father's flesh. ¹³You shall not uncover the nakedness of your mother's sister, for she is your mother's flesh. ¹⁴You shall not uncover the nakedness of your father's brother, that is, you shall not approach his wife; she is your aunt. ¹⁵You shall not uncover the nakedness of your daughter-in-law: she is your son's wife; you shall not uncover her nakedness. ¹⁶You shall not uncover the nakedness of your brother's wife; it is your brother's nakedness. ¹⁷You shall not uncover the nakedness of a woman and her daughter, and you shall not take*v* her son's daughter or her daughter's daughter to uncover her nakedness; they are your*w* flesh; it is depravity. ¹⁸And you shall not take*v* a woman as a rival to her sister, uncovering her nakedness while her sister is still alive.

19 You shall not approach a woman to uncover her nakedness while she is in her menstrual uncleanness. ²⁰You shall not have sexual relations with your kinsman's wife, and defile yourself with her. ²¹You shall not give any of your offspring to sacrifice them*x* to Molech, and so profane the name of your God: I am the LORD. ²²You shall not lie with a male as with a woman; it is an abomination. ²³You shall not have sexual relations with any animal and defile yourself with it, nor shall any woman give herself to an animal to have sexual relations with it: it is perversion.

24 Do not defile yourselves in any of these ways, for by all these practices the nations I am casting out before you have defiled themselves. ²⁵Thus the land became defiled; and I punished it for its iniquity, and the land vomited out its in-habitants. ²⁶But you shall keep my statutes and my ordinances and commit none of these abominations, either the citizen or the alien who resides among you ²⁷(for the inhabitants of the land, who

18.21 Child Sacrifice and Sex

This warning against child sacrifice (repeated and expanded in 20.1–5) seems out of place in the middle of a chapter on rules about sex. Yet, for the Israelites, there was a connection. Their neighbors, who sacrificed their children as a part of their religion, also practiced temple prostitution as a way of worship. To them, sex was a way to get in touch with their gods. God's warnings against various sexual practices begin and end with warnings to behave differently from these neighbors (verses 3,24).

were before you, committed all of these abominations, and the land became defiled); ²⁸otherwise the land will vomit you out for defiling it, as it vomited out the nation that was before you. ²⁹For whoever commits any of these abominations shall be cut off from their people. ³⁰So keep my charge not to commit any of these abominations that were done before you, and not to defile yourselves by them: I am the LORD your God.

Ritual and Moral Holiness

19 The LORD spoke to Moses, saying:
2 Speak to all the congregation of the people of Israel and say to them: You shall be holy, for I the LORD your God am holy. ³You shall each revere your mother and father, and you shall keep my sabbaths: I am the LORD your God. ⁴Do not turn to idols or make cast images for yourselves: I am the LORD your God.

5 When you offer a sacrifice of well-being to the LORD, offer it in such a way that it is acceptable in your behalf. ⁶It shall be eaten on the same day you offer it, or on the next day; and anything left over until the third day shall be consumed in fire. ⁷If it is eaten at all on the third day, it is an abomination; it will not be acceptable. ⁸All who eat it shall be subject to punishment, because they have profaned what is holy to the LORD; and any such person shall be cut off from the people.

9 When you reap the harvest of your land, you shall not reap to the very edges of your field, or gather the gleanings of your harvest. ¹⁰You shall not strip your vineyard bare, or gather the fallen grapes of your vineyard; you shall leave them for the poor and the alien: I am the LORD your God.

11 You shall not steal; you shall not deal falsely; and you shall not lie to one another. ¹²And you

---

v Or *marry*   *w* Gk: Heb lacks *your*   *x* Heb *to pass them over* shall not swear falsely by my name, profaning the name of your God: I am the LORD.

13 You shall not defraud your neighbor; you shall not steal; and you shall not keep for yourself

19.9 A Form of Welfare

God's law was persistently concerned with the welfare of the poor. Everyday farming was to be done in such a way that poor and foreign people could fend for themselves. The reasons for such care are given: we are to imitate the holy character of God (verse 2), who cares for the poor, and to love our neighbor as ourselves (verse 18).

the wages of a laborer until morning. ¹⁴You shall not revile the deaf or put a stumbling block before the blind; you shall fear your God: I am the LORD.

15 You shall not render an unjust judgment; you shall not be partial to the poor or defer to the great: with justice you shall judge your neighbor. ¹⁶You shall not go around as a slanderer*y* among your people, and you shall not profit by the blood*z* of your neighbor: I am the LORD.

17 You shall not hate in your heart anyone of your kin; you shall reprove your neighbor, or you will incur guilt yourself. ¹⁸You shall not take vengeance or bear a grudge against any of your people, but you shall love your neighbor as yourself: I am the LORD.

19 You shall keep my statutes. You shall not let your animals breed with a different kind; you shall not sow your field with two kinds of seed; nor shall you put on a garment made of two different materials.

20 If a man has sexual relations with a woman who is a slave, designated for another man but not ransomed or given her freedom, an inquiry shall be held. They shall not be put to death, since she has not been freed; ²¹but he shall bring a guilt offering for himself to the LORD, at the entrance of the tent of meeting, a ram as guilt offering. ²²And the priest shall make atonement for him with the ram of guilt offering before the LORD for his sin that he committed; and the sin he committed shall be forgiven him.

23 When you come into the land and plant all kinds of trees for food, then you shall regard their fruit as forbidden;*a* three years it shall be forbidden*b* to you, it must not be eaten. ²⁴In the fourth year all their fruit shall be set apart for rejoicing in the LORD. ²⁵But in the fifth year you may eat of their fruit, that their yield may be increased for you: I am the LORD your God.

26 You shall not eat anything with its blood. You shall not practice augury or witchcraft. ²⁷You

shall not round off the hair on your temples or mar the edges of your beard. ²⁸You shall not make any gashes in your flesh for the dead or tattoo any marks upon you: I am the LORD.

29 Do not profane your daughter by making her a prostitute, that the land not become prostituted and full of depravity. ³⁰You shall keep my sabbaths and reverence my sanctuary: I am the LORD.

31 Do not turn to mediums or wizards; do not seek them out, to be defiled by them: I am the LORD your God.

32 You shall rise before the aged, and defer to the old; and you shall fear your God: I am the LORD.

33 When an alien resides with you in your land, you shall not oppress the alien. ³⁴The alien who resides with you shall be to you as the citizen among you; you shall love the alien as yourself, for you were aliens in the land of Egypt: I am the LORD your God.

35 You shall not cheat in measuring length, weight, or quantity. ³⁶You shall have honest balances, honest weights, an honest ephah, and an honest hin: I am the LORD your God, who brought you out of the land of Egypt. ³⁷You shall keep all my statutes and all my ordinances, and observe them: I am the LORD.

Penalties for Violations of Holiness

20 The LORD spoke to Moses, saying: ²Say further to the people of Israel:

Any of the people of Israel, or of the aliens who reside in Israel, who give any of their offspring to Molech shall be put to death; the people of the land shall stone them to death. ³I myself will set my face against them, and will cut them off from the people, because they have given of their offspring to Molech, defiling my sanctuary and profaning my holy name. ⁴And if the people of the land should ever close their eyes to them, when they give of their offspring to Molech, and do not put them to death, ⁵I myself will set my face against them and against their family, and will cut them off from among their people, them and all who follow them in prostituting themselves to Molech.

6 If any turn to mediums and wizards, prostituting themselves to them, I will set my face against them, and will cut them off from the people. ⁷Consecrate yourselves therefore, and be holy; for I am the LORD your God. ⁸Keep my statutes, and observe them; I am the LORD; I sanctify you. ⁹All who curse father or mother shall be put to death; having cursed father or mother, their blood is upon them.

10 If a man commits adultery with the wife of*c* his neighbor, both the adulterer and the adul-

---

y Meaning of Heb uncertain   *z* Heb *stand against the blood*   *a* Heb *as their uncircumcision*
b Heb *uncircumcision*   *c* Heb repeats *if a man commits adultery with the wife of*

teress shall be put to death. [11]The man who lies with his father's wife has uncovered his father's nakedness; both of them shall be put to death; their blood is upon them. [12]If a man lies with his daughter-in-law, both of them shall be put to death; they have committed perversion, their blood is upon them. [13]If a man lies with a male as with a woman, both of them have committed an abomination; they shall be put to death; their blood is upon them. [14]If a man takes a wife and her mother also, it is depravity; they shall be burned to death, both he and they, that there may be no depravity among you. [15]If a man has sexual relations with an animal, he shall be put to death; and you shall kill the animal. [16]If a woman approaches any animal and has sexual relations with

A National Law Library
Setting Israel apart from its neighbors

> You shall be holy to me; for I the LORD am holy, and I have separated you from the other peoples to be mine. 20.26

THE LAWS OF THE UNITED States would fill a library. Elaborate indexes guide lawyers where to look when dealing with a particular issue. No one person can know even a fraction of all the federal, state, and local laws.

If the Old Testament laws recorded in Leviticus (and Exodus, Numbers, and Deuteronomy) seem dull and long-winded, keep them in perspective. These—just over 600 in all—were the entire set of laws for a nation, as far as we know. Their most striking feature, to a lawyer, is brevity and simplicity. You don't have to go to law school to understand them.

The laws are listed in no particular order. A law against witchcraft is followed by a law against improper haircuts, which is followed by a law against tattoos, which in turn is followed by a law against making your daughter into a prostitute. This mixing reveals an important feature of Old Testament thinking. Life is not analyzed in separate components, but seen as a whole.

For the Israelites, separation of church and state did not exist. Every aspect of life—politics, family life, diet, economics—concerned God. Even the Ten Commandments (in Exodus 20) show this, for they include laws regarding our relationship to both God and our neighbor. The two cannot be separated.

Remarkable Features

In comparison with laws from other countries at that time, the Old Testament made a considerable advance. (Indeed, these laws have greatly influenced laws for our day.) Some of the remarkable features:

People were more important than property. For instance, there was never a death penalty for a crime against someone's property. Also, slaves were treated as human beings, not property. This was not true of many other legal codes of that time.

There was no class system. In many ancient countries, a noble was treated far differently from a commoner. Not so in Israel: Everybody stood on the same level before the law. Even a foreigner had clearly defined rights.

The punishment fit the crime. No "cruel and unusual punishment" was allowed. "Eye for eye" (24.20) ensured that no privileged character was "let off" for a crime, while at the same time it limited revenge.

Sexuality mattered. In most countries, the law cared little whether you slept with your neighbor's wife. In Israel, sexual immorality got stern treatment.

The poor and weak had protection. Specific provisions protected their rights from the powerful and wealthy. "Welfare" offered them a way to stay alive, such as the right to "glean the fields." In 19.9,13–14,32–33, God gave protection to various groups that could not defend themselves.

Attitudes, as well as actions, mattered. For instance, Leviticus 19.18 contains the famous law to "love your neighbor as yourself." Living up to the letter of the law was not enough. The law aimed to develop loving relationships.

Designed to Be Different

While we do not understand the reasons for some of the laws (many may have been designed simply to keep the Israelites "different" from their pagan neighbors), their overall impact is clear. These rules were intended to form a nation of compassionate, consistent, fair-minded people. They insisted that each person act positively and lovingly toward his or her neighbor—and particularly toward those in need. The reason? God lived with them. Since he is both just and merciful, his people must be too.

Life Questions: Everybody has a code to live by. Does your personal rulebook show as much concern for the poor and defenseless as Leviticus's?

it, you shall kill the woman and the animal; they shall be put to death, their blood is upon them.

17 If a man takes his sister, a daughter of his father or a daughter of his mother, and sees her

20.7–8 The Bottom Line

These verses, along with verse 26, sum up the underlying reason for many of the laws outlined in Leviticus: God wanted the Israelites to be different. The New Testament makes clear that some of these regulations—eating forbidden animals, touching unclean persons— do not apply for all time. But at this moment, as God's people entered their new land, God wanted them to stand out from the nations around them (verses 22–24). Sadly, before long the Israelites were mimicking almost all the practices of their pagan neighbors.

nakedness, and she sees his nakedness, it is a disgrace, and they shall be cut off in the sight of their people; he has uncovered his sister's nakedness, he shall be subject to punishment. ¹⁸If a man lies with a woman having her sickness and uncovers her nakedness, he has laid bare her flow and she has laid bare her flow of blood; both of them shall be cut off from their people. ¹⁹You shall not uncover the nakedness of your mother's sister or of your father's sister, for that is to lay bare one's own flesh; they shall be subject to punishment. ²⁰If a man lies with his uncle's wife, he has uncovered his uncle's nakedness; they shall be subject to punishment; they shall die childless. ²¹If a man takes his brother's wife, it is impurity; he has uncovered his brother's nakedness; they shall be childless.

22 You shall keep all my statutes and all my ordinances, and observe them, so that the land to which I bring you to settle in may not vomit you out. ²³You shall not follow the practices of the nation that I am driving out before you. Because they did all these things, I abhorred them. ²⁴But I have said to you: You shall inherit their land, and I will give it to you to possess, a land flowing with milk and honey. I am the LORD your God; I have separated you from the peoples. ²⁵You shall therefore make a distinction between the clean animal and the unclean, and between the unclean bird and the clean; you shall not bring abomination on yourselves by animal or by bird or by anything with which the ground teems, which I have set apart for you to hold unclean. ²⁶You shall be holy to me; for I the LORD am holy, and I have separated you from the other peoples to be mine.

27 A man or a woman who is a medium or a wizard shall be put to death; they shall be stoned to death, their blood is upon them.

The Holiness of Priests

21 The LORD said to Moses: Speak to the priests, the sons of Aaron, and say to them: No one shall defile himself for a dead person among his relatives, ²except for his nearest kin: his mother, his father, his son, his daughter, his brother; ³likewise, for a virgin sister, close to him because she has had no husband, he may defile himself for her. ⁴But he shall not defile himself as a husband among his people and so profane himself. ⁵They shall not make bald spots upon their heads, or shave off the edges of their beards, or make any gashes in their flesh. ⁶They shall be holy to their God, and not profane the name of their God; for they offer the LORD's offerings by fire, the food of their God; therefore they shall be holy. ⁷They shall not marry a prostitute or a woman who has been defiled; neither shall they marry a woman divorced from her husband. For they are holy to their God, ⁸and you shall treat them as holy, since they offer the food of your God; they shall be holy to you, for I the LORD, I who sanctify you, am holy. ⁹When the daughter of a priest profanes herself through prostitution, she profanes her father; she shall be burned to death.

10 The priest who is exalted above his fellows, on whose head the anointing oil has been poured and who has been consecrated to wear the vestments, shall not dishevel his hair, nor tear his vestments. ¹¹He shall not go where there is a dead body; he shall not defile himself even for his father or mother. ¹²He shall not go outside the sanctuary and thus profane the sanctuary of his God; for the consecration of the anointing oil of his God is upon him: I am the LORD. ¹³He shall marry only a woman who is a virgin. ¹⁴A widow, or a divorced woman, or a woman who has been defiled, a prostitute, these he shall not marry. He shall marry a virgin of his own kin, ¹⁵that he may not profane his offspring among his kin; for I am the LORD; I sanctify him.

16 The LORD spoke to Moses, saying: ¹⁷Speak to Aaron and say: No one of your offspring throughout their generations who has a blemish may approach to offer the food of his God. ¹⁸For no one who has a blemish shall draw near, one who is blind or lame, or one who has a mutilated face or a limb too long, ¹⁹or one who has a broken foot or a broken hand, ²⁰or a hunchback, or a dwarf, or a man with a blemish in his eyes or an itching disease or scabs or crushed testicles. ²¹No descendant of Aaron the priest who has a blemish shall come near to offer the LORD's offerings by fire; since he has a blemish, he shall not come near to offer the food of his God. ²²He may eat the food of his God, of the most holy as well as of the holy. ²³But he shall not come near the curtain or approach the altar, because he has a blemish, that he may not profane my sanctuaries; for I am the LORD; I sanctify them. ²⁴Thus Moses spoke to

Aaron and to his sons and to all the people of Israel.

The Use of Holy Offerings

22 The LORD spoke to Moses, saying: ²Direct Aaron and his sons to deal carefully with the sacred donations of the people of Israel, which they dedicate to me, so that they may not profane my holy name; I am the LORD. ³Say to them: If anyone among all your offspring throughout your generations comes near the sacred donations, which the people of Israel dedicate to the LORD, while he is in a state of uncleanness, that person shall be cut off from my presence: I am the LORD. ⁴No one of Aaron's offspring who has a leprous*d* disease or suffers a discharge may eat of the sacred donations until he is clean. Whoever touches anything made unclean by a corpse or a man who has had an emission of semen, ⁵and whoever touches any swarming thing by which he may be made unclean or any human being by whom he may be made unclean—whatever his uncleanness may be— ⁶the person who touches any such shall be unclean until evening and shall not eat of the sacred donations unless he has washed his body in water. ⁷When the sun sets he shall be clean; and afterward he may eat of the sacred donations, for they are his food. ⁸That which died or was torn by wild animals he shall not eat, becoming unclean by it: I am the LORD. ⁹They shall keep my charge, so that they may not incur guilt and die in the sanctuary*e* for having profaned it: I am the LORD; I sanctify them.

10 No lay person shall eat of the sacred donations. No bound or hired servant of the priest shall eat of the sacred donations; ¹¹but if a priest acquires anyone by purchase, the person may eat of them; and those that are born in his house may eat of his food. ¹²If a priest's daughter marries a layman, she shall not eat of the offering of the sacred donations; ¹³but if a priest's daughter is widowed or divorced, without offspring, and returns to her father's house, as in her youth, she may eat of her father's food. No lay person shall eat of it. ¹⁴If a man eats of the sacred donation unintentionally, he shall add one-fifth of its value to it, and give the sacred donation to the priest. ¹⁵No one shall profane the sacred donations of the people of Israel, which they offer to the LORD, ¹⁶causing them to bear guilt requiring a guilt offering, by eating their sacred donations: for I am the LORD; I sanctify them.

Acceptable Offerings

17 The LORD spoke to Moses, saying: ¹⁸Speak to Aaron and his sons and all the people of Israel and say to them: When anyone of the house of Israel or of the aliens residing in Israel presents an offering, whether in payment of a vow or as a freewill offering that is offered to the LORD as a burnt offering, ¹⁹to be acceptable in your behalf it shall be a male without blemish, of the cattle or the sheep or the goats. ²⁰You shall not offer anything that has a blemish, for it will not be acceptable in your behalf.

22.19 The Very Best for God

For the Israelite farmers, a farm animal represented a considerable contribution. It would have been tempting to cull out their weakest animals. Instead, they were commanded to give their very best. Similarly, at every harvest they were to bring their very first grain to the Lord (23.10). These practices reminded them again and again of God's place in their lives.

21 When anyone offers a sacrifice of well-being to the LORD, in fulfillment of a vow or as a freewill offering, from the herd or from the flock, to be acceptable it must be perfect; there shall be no blemish in it. ²²Anything blind, or injured, or maimed, or having a discharge or an itch or scabs—these you shall not offer to the LORD or put any of them on the altar as offerings by fire to the LORD. ²³An ox or a lamb that has a limb too long or too short you may present for a freewill offering; but it will not be accepted for a vow. ²⁴Any animal that has its testicles bruised or crushed or torn or cut, you shall not offer to the LORD; such you shall not do within your land, ²⁵nor shall you accept any such animals from a foreigner to offer as food to your God; since they are mutilated, with a blemish in them, they shall not be accepted in your behalf.

26 The LORD spoke to Moses, saying: ²⁷When an ox or a sheep or a goat is born, it shall remain seven days with its mother, and from the eighth day on it shall be acceptable as the LORD's offering by fire. ²⁸But you shall not slaughter, from the herd or the flock, an animal with its young on the same day. ²⁹When you sacrifice a thanksgiving offering to the LORD, you shall sacrifice it so that it may be acceptable in your behalf. ³⁰It shall be eaten on the same day; you shall not leave any of it until morning: I am the LORD.

31 Thus you shall keep my commandments and observe them: I am the LORD. ³²You shall not profane my holy name, that I may be sanctified among the people of Israel: I am the LORD; I sanctify you, ³³I who brought you out of the land of Egypt to be your God: I am the LORD.

Appointed Festivals

23 The LORD spoke to Moses, saying: ²Speak to the people of Israel and say to them:

---

d A term for several skin diseases; precise meaning uncertain *e* Vg: Heb *incur guilt for it and die in it*

These are the appointed festivals of the LORD that you shall proclaim as holy convocations, my appointed festivals.

The Sabbath, Passover, and Unleavened Bread

3 Six days shall work be done; but the seventh day is a sabbath of complete rest, a holy convocation; you shall do no work: it is a sabbath to the LORD throughout your settlements.

4 These are the appointed festivals of the LORD, the holy convocations, which you shall celebrate at the time appointed for them. ⁵In the first month, on the fourteenth day of the month, at twilight,ᶠ there shall be a passover offering to

ᶠ Heb *between the two evenings*

the LORD, ⁶and on the fifteenth day of the same month is the festival of unleavened bread to the LORD; seven days you shall eat unleavened bread. ⁷On the first day you shall have a holy convocation; you shall not work at your occupations. ⁸For seven days you shall present the LORD's offerings by fire; on the seventh day there shall be a holy convocation: you shall not work at your occupations.

The Offering of First Fruits

9 The LORD spoke to Moses: ¹⁰Speak to the people of Israel and say to them: When you enter the land that I am giving you and you reap its harvest, you shall bring the sheaf of the first fruits

In Celebration of God
Jewish holidays focused on one thing

> *Rejoice before the LORD your God for seven days.* 23.40

ANTHROPOLOGISTS STUDYING REMOTE TRIBES ROUTINELY describe their feast days, for these show the people's common values. What would stand out to an anthropologist studying the United States?

Undoubtedly he would notice that our celebration of Christmas, Thanksgiving, and the Fourth of July emphasize family, food, and gifts—the more the better.

What about the Israelites? Leviticus describes five feasts, all focusing on God. Each was marked by special sacrifices to God and a sacred assembly in the tent of meeting where God had "pitched his tent." Rather than giving gifts to each other, the Israelites gave gifts to God.

Sometimes they rejoiced: During the festival of booths everyone camped out to "rejoice before the LORD" for a solid week (23.40). On other occasions, such as the day of atonement, they were sober and solemn (chapter 16, 23.26–32). But always their orientation was God-directed.

God over Money

Nobody worked on Israelite feast days, but their "days off" had a different motive than ours. An Israelite farmer never got a paid holiday. In fact, a holiday could cost him—it might fall on a day perfect for harvesting. But God took priority over work. The weekly sabbath day reinforced the same idea. You had to stop working to worship.

God mattered more than wealth. This fundamental belief showed itself even more in the sabbath year and in the year of jubilee (chapter 25). Every seventh year, people did not farm at all. They lived off whatever the land produced by itself, and dedicated themselves to God. This would be like our closing all businesses and factories for a year.

After 49 years—seven sabbath years—the year of jubilee came. This time, people went for two years straight without planting. All land bought or sold during the previous 49 years went back to its original family ownership. Since the land had originally been equally distributed, this meant that no family would ever become either totally destitute or overwhelmingly rich. Any Israelites who had sold themselves as slaves would also be freed in that year.

Prosperity Came from God

Hard work and the resulting abundance were never scorned in Israel. But prosperity always came ultimately from God, not from hard work or clever dealings alone. The feasts and sabbaths, set aside as special days, helped people remember and praise the God who had given them so much.

So far as we know, no year of jubilee was ever actually practiced. Some of the feasts were forgotten for long periods of time. But such failure is not surprising. After all, think what we have done to the holy day of Christmas! The feast days described in Leviticus give us a good idea of what God wanted Israel to be. Sadly, reality did not often match the ideal.

Life Questions: If someone examined the way you spend your holidays and weekends, what would he or she conclude about your priorities?

of your harvest to the priest. [11]He shall raise the sheaf before the LORD, that you may find acceptance; on the day after the sabbath the priest shall raise it. [12]On the day when you raise the sheaf, you shall offer a lamb a year old, without blemish, as a burnt offering to the LORD. [13]And the grain offering with it shall be two-tenths of an ephah of choice flour mixed with oil, an offering by fire of pleasing odor to the LORD; and the drink offering with it shall be of wine, one-fourth of a hin. [14]You shall eat no bread or parched grain or fresh ears until that very day, until you have brought the offering of your God: it is a statute forever throughout your generations in all your settlements.

The Festival of Weeks

15 And from the day after the sabbath, from the day on which you bring the sheaf of the elevation offering, you shall count off seven weeks; they shall be complete. [16]You shall count until the day after the seventh sabbath, fifty days; then you shall present an offering of new grain to the LORD. [17]You shall bring from your settlements two loaves of bread as an elevation offering, each made of two-tenths of an ephah; they shall be of choice flour, baked with leaven, as first fruits to the LORD. [18]You shall present with the bread seven lambs a year old without blemish, one young bull, and two rams; they shall be a burnt offering to the LORD, along with their grain offering and their drink offerings, an offering by fire of pleasing odor to the LORD. [19]You shall also offer one male goat for a sin offering, and two male lambs a year old as a sacrifice of well-being. [20]The priest shall raise them with the bread of the first fruits as an elevation offering before the LORD, together with the two lambs; they shall be holy to the LORD for the priest. [21]On that same day you shall make proclamation; you shall hold a holy convocation; you shall not work at your occupations. This is a statute forever in all your settlements throughout your generations.

22 When you reap the harvest of your land, you shall not reap to the very edges of your field, or gather the gleanings of your harvest; you shall leave them for the poor and for the alien: I am the LORD your God.

The Festival of Trumpets

23 The LORD spoke to Moses, saying: [24]Speak to the people of Israel, saying: In the seventh month, on the first day of the month, you shall observe a day of complete rest, a holy convocation commemorated with trumpet blasts. [25]You shall not work at your occupations; and you shall present the LORD's offering by fire.

The Day of Atonement

26 The LORD spoke to Moses, saying: [27]Now, the tenth day of this seventh month is the day of atonement; it shall be a holy convocation for you: you shall deny yourselves[g] and present the LORD's offering by fire; [28]and you shall do no work during that entire day; for it is a day of atonement, to make atonement on your behalf before the LORD your God. [29]For anyone who does not practice self-denial[h] during that entire day shall be cut off from the people. [30]And anyone who does any work during that entire day, such a one I will destroy from the midst of the people. [31]You shall do no work: it is a statute forever throughout your generations in all your settlements. [32]It shall be to you a sabbath of complete rest, and you shall deny yourselves;[g] on the ninth day of the month at evening, from evening to evening you shall keep your sabbath.

The Festival of Booths

33 The LORD spoke to Moses, saying: [34]Speak to the people of Israel, saying: On the fifteenth day of this seventh month, and lasting seven days, there shall be the festival of booths[i] to the LORD. [35]The first day shall be a holy convocation; you shall not work at your occupations. [36]Seven days you shall present the LORD's offerings by fire; on the eighth day you shall observe a holy convocation and present the LORD's offerings by fire; it is a solemn assembly; you shall not work at your occupations.

37 These are the appointed festivals of the LORD, which you shall celebrate as times of holy convocation, for presenting to the LORD offerings by fire—burnt offerings and grain offerings, sacrifices and drink offerings, each on its proper day— [38]apart from the sabbaths of the LORD, and apart from your gifts, and apart from all your votive offerings, and apart from all your freewill offerings, which you give to the LORD.

39 Now, the fifteenth day of the seventh month, when you have gathered in the produce of the land, you shall keep the festival of the LORD, lasting seven days; a complete rest on the first day, and a complete rest on the eighth day. [40]On the first day you shall take the fruit of majestic[j] trees, branches of palm trees, boughs of leafy

23.40 Seven Days of Rejoicing

Though the worship of God was a serious business, it was also joyful. Every year, for instance, the Israelites were to hold this week-long campout and celebration, filled with rejoicing.

trees, and willows of the brook; and you shall rejoice before the LORD your God for seven days. ⁴¹You shall keep it as a festival to the LORD seven days in the year; you shall keep it in the seventh month as a statute forever throughout your generations. ⁴²You shall live in booths for seven days; all that are citizens in Israel shall live in booths, ⁴³so that your generations may know that I made the people of Israel live in booths when I brought them out of the land of Egypt: I am the LORD your God.

44 Thus Moses declared to the people of Israel the appointed festivals of the LORD.

The Lamp

24 The LORD spoke to Moses, saying: ²Command the people of Israel to bring you pure oil of beaten olives for the lamp, that a light may be kept burning regularly. ³Aaron shall set it up in the tent of meeting, outside the curtain of the covenant,ᵏ to burn from evening to morning before the LORD regularly; it shall be a statute forever throughout your generations. ⁴He shall set up the lamps on the lampstand of pure goldˡ before the LORD regularly.

The Bread for the Tabernacle

5 You shall take choice flour, and bake twelve loaves of it; two-tenths of an ephah shall be in each loaf. ⁶You shall place them in two rows, six in a row, on the table of pure gold.ᵐ ⁷You shall put pure frankincense with each row, to be a token offering for the bread, as an offering by fire to the LORD. ⁸Every sabbath day Aaron shall set them in order before the LORD regularly as a commitment of the people of Israel, as a covenant forever. ⁹They shall be for Aaron and his descendants, who shall eat them in a holy place, for they are most holy portions for him from the offerings by fire to the LORD, a perpetual due.

Blasphemy and Its Punishment

10 A man whose mother was an Israelite and whose father was an Egyptian came out among the people of Israel; and the Israelite woman's son and a certain Israelite began fighting in the camp. ¹¹The Israelite woman's son blasphemed the Name in a curse. And they brought him to Moses—now his mother's name was Shelomith, daughter of Dibri, of the tribe of Dan— ¹²and they put him in custody, until the decision of the LORD should be made clear to them.

13 The LORD said to Moses, saying: ¹⁴Take the blasphemer outside the camp; and let all who were within hearing lay their hands on his head, and let the whole congregation stone him. ¹⁵And speak to the people of Israel, saying: Anyone who curses God shall bear the sin. ¹⁶One who blasphemes the name of the LORD shall be put to

death; the whole congregation shall stone the blasphemer. Aliens as well as citizens, when they blaspheme the Name, shall be put to death. ¹⁷Anyone who kills a human being shall be put to death. ¹⁸Anyone who kills an animal shall make restitution for it, life for life. ¹⁹Anyone who maims another shall suffer the same injury in return: ²⁰fracture for fracture, eye for eye, tooth for tooth; the injury inflicted is the injury to be

24.20 An Eye for an Eye

Jesus, speaking of this law in Matthew 5.38, told his followers not to resist evil people. Apparently people had been taking "eye for eye" as a basis for private vengeance—as some do today. The law's original intent, however, was to set a standard for punishment in court. It limited vengeance and made certain that both rich and poor, native and foreigner, would pay the same price for their crimes.

suffered. ²¹One who kills an animal shall make restitution for it; but one who kills a human being shall be put to death. ²²You shall have one law for the alien and for the citizen: for I am the LORD your God. ²³Moses spoke thus to the people of Israel; and they took the blasphemer outside the camp, and stoned him to death. The people of Israel did as the LORD had commanded Moses.

The Sabbatical Year

25 The LORD spoke to Moses on Mount Sinai, saying: ²Speak to the people of Israel and say to them: When you enter the land that I am giving you, the land shall observe a sabbath for the LORD. ³Six years you shall sow your field, and six years you shall prune your vineyard, and gather in their yield; ⁴but in the seventh year there shall be a sabbath of complete rest for the land, a sabbath for the LORD: you shall not sow your field or prune your vineyard. ⁵You shall not reap the aftergrowth of your harvest or gather the grapes of your unpruned vine: it shall be a year of complete rest for the land. ⁶You may eat what the land yields during its sabbath—you, your male and female slaves, your hired and your bound laborers who live with you; ⁷for your livestock also, and for the wild animals in your land all its yield shall be for food.

The Year of Jubilee

8 You shall count off seven weeksⁿ of years, seven times seven years, so that the period of seven weeks of years gives forty-nine years. ⁹Then you shall have the trumpet sounded loud; on the tenth day of the seventh month—on the day of atonement—you shall have the trumpet sounded

---

ᵏ Or *treaty*, or *testament*; Heb *eduth*   ˡ Heb *pure lampstand*   ᵐ Heb *pure table*   ⁿ Or *sabbaths*

throughout all your land. ¹⁰And you shall hallow the fiftieth year and you shall proclaim liberty throughout the land to all its inhabitants. It shall be a jubilee for you: you shall return, every one of you, to your property and every one of you to your family. ¹¹That fiftieth year shall be a jubilee for you: you shall not sow, or reap the after-growth, or harvest the unpruned vines. ¹²For it is a jubilee; it shall be holy to you: you shall eat only what the field itself produces.

13 In this year of jubilee you shall return, every one of you, to your property. ¹⁴When you make a sale to your neighbor or buy from your neighbor, you shall not cheat one another. ¹⁵When you buy from your neighbor, you shall pay only for the number of years since the jubilee; the seller shall charge you only for the remaining crop years. ¹⁶If the years are more, you shall increase the price, and if the years are fewer, you shall diminish the price; for it is a certain number of harvests that are being sold to you. ¹⁷You shall not cheat one another, but you shall fear your God; for I am the LORD your God.

18 You shall observe my statutes and faithfully keep my ordinances, so that you may live on the land securely. ¹⁹The land will yield its fruit, and you will eat your fill and live on it securely. ²⁰Should you ask, "What shall we eat in the seventh year, if we may not sow or gather in our crop?" ²¹I will order my blessing for you in the sixth year, so that it will yield a crop for three years. ²²When you sow in the eighth year, you will be eating from the old crop; until the ninth year, when its produce comes in, you shall eat the old. ²³The land shall not be sold in perpetuity, for the land is mine; with me you are but aliens and tenants. ²⁴Throughout the land that you hold, you shall provide for the redemption of the land.

25 If anyone of your kin falls into difficulty and sells a piece of property, then the next of kin shall come and redeem what the relative has sold. ²⁶If the person has no one to redeem it, but then prospers and finds sufficient means to do so, ²⁷the years since its sale shall be computed and the difference shall be refunded to the person to whom it was sold, and the property shall be returned. ²⁸But if there are not sufficient means to recover it, what was sold shall remain with the purchaser until the year of jubilee; in the jubilee it shall be released, and the property shall be returned.

29 If anyone sells a dwelling house in a walled city, it may be redeemed until a year has elapsed since its sale; the right of redemption shall be one year. ³⁰If it is not redeemed before a full year has elapsed, a house that is in a walled city shall pass in perpetuity to the purchaser, throughout the generations; it shall not be released in the jubilee. ³¹But houses in villages that have no walls around

them shall be classed as open country; they may be redeemed, and they shall be released in the jubilee. ³²As for the cities of the Levites, the Levites shall forever have the right of redemption of the houses in the cities belonging to them. ³³Such property as may be redeemed from the Levites—

25.28 Property Rights

God's law provided for a kind of redistribution of wealth every 50 years, when all land would revert to its original owners. The tendency for the rich to buy up all the property (which originally had been divided equally among families) was reversed in the year of jubilee. In essence, you could not sell your land—only lease it out.

houses sold in a city belonging to them—shall be released in the jubilee; because the houses in the cities of the Levites are their possession among the people of Israel. ³⁴But the open land around their cities may not be sold; for that is their possession for all time.

35 If any of your kin fall into difficulty and become dependent on you,ᵒ you shall support them; they shall live with you as though resident aliens. ³⁶Do not take interest in advance or otherwise make a profit from them, but fear your God; let them live with you. ³⁷You shall not lend them your money at interest taken in advance, or provide them food at a profit. ³⁸I am the LORD your God, who brought you out of the land of Egypt, to give you the land of Canaan, to be your God.

39 If any who are dependent on you become so impoverished that they sell themselves to you, you shall not make them serve as slaves. ⁴⁰They shall remain with you as hired or bound laborers. They shall serve with you until the year of the jubilee. ⁴¹Then they and their children with them shall be free from your authority; they shall go back to their own family and return to their ancestral property. ⁴²For they are my servants, whom I brought out of the land of Egypt; they shall not be sold as slaves are sold. ⁴³You shall not rule over them with harshness, but shall fear your God. ⁴⁴As for the male and female slaves whom you may have, it is from the nations around you that you may acquire male and female slaves. ⁴⁵You may also acquire them from among the aliens residing with you, and from their families that are with you, who have been born in your land; and they may be your property. ⁴⁶You may keep them as a possession for your children after you, for them to inherit as property. These you may treat as slaves, but as for your fellow Israelites, no one shall rule over the other with harshness.

ᵒ Meaning of Heb uncertain

47 If resident aliens among you prosper, and if any of your kin fall into difficulty with one of them and sell themselves to an alien, or to a branch of the alien's family, 48after they have sold themselves they shall have the right of redemption; one of their brothers may redeem them, 49or their uncle or their uncle's son may redeem them, or anyone of their family who is of their own flesh may redeem them; or if they prosper they may redeem themselves. 50They shall compute with the purchaser the total from the year when they sold themselves to the alien until the jubilee year; the price of the sale shall be applied to the number of years: the time they were with the owner shall be rated as the time of a hired laborer. 51If many years remain, they shall pay for their redemption in proportion to the purchase price; 52and if few years remain until the jubilee year, they shall compute thus: according to the years involved they shall make payment for their redemption. 53As a laborer hired by the year they shall be under the alien's authority, who shall not, however, rule with harshness over them in your sight. 54And if they have not been redeemed in any of these ways, they and their children with them shall go free in the jubilee year. 55For to me the people of Israel are servants; they are my servants whom I brought out from the land of Egypt: I am the LORD your God.

Rewards for Obedience

26 You shall make for yourselves no idols and erect no carved images or pillars, and you shall not place figured stones in your land, to worship at them; for I am the LORD your God. 2You shall keep my sabbaths and reverence my sanctuary: I am the LORD.

3 If you follow my statutes and keep my commandments and observe them faithfully, 4I will give you your rains in their season, and the land shall yield its produce, and the trees of the field shall yield their fruit. 5Your threshing shall overtake the vintage, and the vintage shall overtake the sowing; you shall eat your bread to the full, and live securely in your land. 6And I will grant peace in the land, and you shall lie down, and no one shall make you afraid; I will remove dangerous animals from the land, and no sword shall go through your land. 7You shall give chase to your enemies, and they shall fall before you by the sword. 8Five of you shall give chase to a hundred, and a hundred of you shall give chase to ten thousand; your enemies shall fall before you by the sword. 9I will look with favor upon you and make you fruitful and multiply you; and I will maintain my covenant with you. 10You shall eat old grain long stored, and you shall have to clear out the old to make way for the new. 11I will place my dwelling in your midst, and I shall not abhor you. 12And I will walk among you, and will be your God, and you shall be my people. 13I am the LORD your God who brought you out of the land of Egypt, to be their slaves no more; I have broken the bars of your yoke and made you walk erect.

Penalties for Disobedience

14 But if you will not obey me, and do not observe all these commandments, 15if you spurn my statutes, and abhor my ordinances, so that you will not observe all my commandments, and you break my covenant, 16I in turn will do this to you: I will bring terror on you; consumption and fever that waste the eyes and cause life to pine away. You shall sow your seed in vain, for your enemies shall eat it. 17I will set my face against you, and you shall be struck down by your enemies; your foes shall rule over you, and you shall flee though no one pursues you. 18And if in spite of this you will not obey me, I will continue to punish you sevenfold for your sins. 19I will break your proud glory, and I will make your sky like iron and your earth like copper. 20Your strength shall be spent to no purpose: your land shall not yield its produce, and the trees of the land shall not yield their fruit.

21 If you continue hostile to me, and will not obey me, I will continue to plague you sevenfold for your sins. 22I will let loose wild animals against you, and they shall bereave you of your children and destroy your livestock; they shall make you few in number, and your roads shall be deserted.

23 If in spite of these punishments you have not turned back to me, but continue hostile to me, 24then I too will continue hostile to you: I myself will strike you sevenfold for your sins. 25I will bring the sword against you, executing vengeance for the covenant; and if you withdraw within your cities, I will send pestilence among you, and you shall be delivered into enemy hands. 26When I break your staff of bread, ten women shall bake your bread in a single oven, and they shall dole out your bread by weight; and though you eat, you shall not be satisfied.

27 But if, despite this, you disobey me, and continue hostile to me, 28I will continue hostile to you in fury; I in turn will punish you myself sevenfold for your sins. 29You shall eat the flesh of your sons, and you shall eat the flesh of your daughters. 30I will destroy your high places and cut down your incense altars; I will heap your carcasses on the carcasses of your idols. I will abhor you. 31I will lay your cities waste, will make your sanctuaries desolate, and I will not smell your pleasing odors. 32I will devastate the land, so that your enemies who come to settle in it shall be appalled at it. 33And you I will scatter among the nations, and I will unsheathe the sword against you; your land shall be a desolation, and your cities a waste.

34 Then the land shall enjoy[P] its sabbath years as long as it lies desolate, while you are in the land of your enemies; then the land shall rest, and enjoy[P] its sabbath years. 35As long as it lies

26.34 Revenge of the Land

There is little evidence that the Israelites ever followed the rules on sabbath years and jubilee. Nevertheless, as ominously foretold here, the land eventually did get its rest. For 70 years the Babylonians held the Israelites hostage, far away from their homeland. And the land had rest.

desolate, it shall have the rest it did not have on your sabbaths when you were living on it. 36And as for those of you who survive, I will send faintness into their hearts in the lands of their enemies; the sound of a driven leaf shall put them to flight, and they shall flee as one flees from the sword, and they shall fall though no one pursues. 37They shall stumble over one another, as if to escape a sword, though no one pursues; and you shall have no power to stand against your enemies. 38You shall perish among the nations, and the land of your enemies shall devour you. 39And those of you who survive shall languish in the land of your enemies because of their iniquities; also they shall languish because of the iniquities of their ancestors.

40 But if they confess their iniquity and the iniquity of their ancestors, in that they committed treachery against me and, moreover, that they continued hostile to me— 41so that I, in turn, continued hostile to them and brought them into the land of their enemies; if then their uncircum-

26.41 Uncircumcised Hearts

Circumcision was the ritual that made a man into a Jew, so to speak. But this reference to uncircumcised hearts shows that, right from the beginning, the inward attitude, as well as the physical operation, was crucial. Six hundred years later Jeremiah accused the Israelites of being uncircumcised in heart (Jeremiah 9.26); another 600 years after him Stephen made the same complaint (Acts 7.51). On this basis Paul wrote, "a person is not a Jew who is one outwardly . . . Rather, a person is a Jew who is one inwardly, and real circumcision is a matter of the heart—it is spiritual and not literal" (Romans 2.28–29). Leviticus offered more than a legal system; these laws appealed to a person's relationship with God.

cised heart is humbled and they make amends for their iniquity, 42then will I remember my covenant with Jacob; I will remember also my covenant with Isaac and also my covenant with Abraham, and I will remember the land. 43For the land shall be deserted by them, and enjoy[P] its sabbath years by lying desolate without them, while they shall make amends for their iniquity, because they dared to spurn my ordinances, and they abhorred my statutes. 44Yet for all that, when they are in the land of their enemies, I will not spurn them, or abhor them so as to destroy them utterly and break my covenant with them; for I am the LORD their God; 45but I will remember in their favor the covenant with their ancestors whom I brought out of the land of Egypt in the sight of the nations, to be their God: I am the LORD.

46 These are the statutes and ordinances and laws that the LORD established between himself and the people of Israel on Mount Sinai through Moses.

Votive Offerings

27 The LORD spoke to Moses, saying: 2Speak to the people of Israel and say to them: When a person makes an explicit vow to the LORD concerning the equivalent for a human being, 3the equivalent for a male shall be: from twenty to sixty years of age the equivalent shall be fifty shekels of silver by the sanctuary shekel. 4If the person is a female, the equivalent is thirty shekels. 5If the age is from five to twenty years of age, the equivalent is twenty shekels for a male and ten shekels for a female. 6If the age is from one month to five years, the equivalent for a male is five shekels of silver, and for a female the equivalent is three shekels of silver. 7And if the person is sixty years old or over, then the equivalent for a male is fifteen shekels, and for a female ten shekels. 8If any cannot afford the equivalent, they shall be brought before the priest and the priest shall assess them; the priest shall assess them according to what each one making a vow can afford.

9 If it concerns an animal that may be brought as an offering to the LORD, any such that may be given to the LORD shall be holy. 10Another shall not be exchanged or substituted for it, either good for bad or bad for good; and if one animal is substituted for another, both that one and its substitute shall be holy. 11If it concerns any unclean animal that may not be brought as an offering to the LORD, the animal shall be presented before the priest. 12The priest shall assess it: whether good or bad, according to the assessment of the priest, so it shall be. 13But if it is to be redeemed, one-fifth must be added to the assessment.

14 If a person consecrates a house to the LORD, the priest shall assess it: whether good or bad, as the priest assesses it, so it shall stand. [15]And if the one who consecrates the house wishes to redeem it, one-fifth shall be added to its assessed value, and it shall revert to the original owner.

16 If a person consecrates to the LORD any inherited landholding, its assessment shall be in accordance with its seed requirements: fifty shekels of silver to a homer of barley seed. [17]If the person consecrates the field as of the year of jubilee, that assessment shall stand; [18]but if the field is consecrated after the jubilee, the priest shall compute the price for it according to the years that remain until the year of jubilee, and the assessment shall be reduced. [19]And if the one who consecrates the field wishes to redeem it, then one-fifth shall be added to its assessed value, and it shall revert to the original owner; [20]but if the field is not redeemed, or if it has been sold to someone else, it shall no longer be redeemable. [21]But when the field is released in the jubilee, it shall be holy to the LORD as a devoted field; it becomes the priest's holding. [22]If someone consecrates to the LORD a field that has been purchased, which is not a part of the inherited landholding, [23]the priest shall compute for it the proportionate assessment up to the year of jubilee, and the assessment shall be paid as of that day, a sacred donation to the LORD. [24]In the year of jubilee the field shall return to the one from whom it was bought, whose holding the land is. [25]All assessments shall be by the sanctuary shekel: twenty gerahs shall make a shekel.

26 A firstling of animals, however, which as a firstling belongs to the LORD, cannot be consecrated by anyone; whether ox or sheep, it is the LORD's. [27]If it is an unclean animal, it shall be ransomed at its assessment, with one-fifth added; if it is not redeemed, it shall be sold at its assessment.

28 Nothing that a person owns that has been devoted to destruction for the LORD, be it human or animal, or inherited landholding, may be sold or redeemed; every devoted thing is most holy to the LORD. [29]No human beings who have been devoted to destruction can be ransomed; they shall be put to death.

30 All tithes from the land, whether the seed from the ground or the fruit from the tree, are the LORD's; they are holy to the LORD. [31]If persons wish to redeem any of their tithes, they must add one-fifth to them. [32]All tithes of herd and flock, every tenth one that passes under the shepherd's staff, shall be holy to the LORD. [33]Let no one inquire whether it is good or bad, or make substitution for it; if one makes substitution for it, then both it and the substitute shall be holy and cannot be redeemed.

34 These are the commandments that the LORD gave to Moses for the people of Israel on Mount Sinai.

NUMBERS

Forty Years of Misery
A joyous adventure comes to a tragic end

A S NUMBERS OPENS, THE ISRAELITES are gearing up for a great adventure. Free at last from the chains of slavery, they are headed for the promised land. Yet the book that begins with a bang ends with a whimper. Weeks, months, and then years in a hostile desert have seemed to melt the spirit of adventure. The Israelites act like people who have lost their moorings. In relentless detail, Numbers records a whole sequence of grumblings and rebellions.

> Now when the people complained in the hearing of the LORD about their misfortunes, the LORD heard it and his anger was kindled.
> 11.1

Forty-Year Detour

Stomachs complained first, as the Israelites began to long for the spices of Egypt. Soon, the great mob of people simply unraveled. At least ten times they lashed out in despair or rose up in open rebellion. They plotted against their leaders and denounced God. Revolt spread to the priests, to the top military scouts, to Moses' family, and finally to Moses himself.

The original Hebrew title of this book was not "Numbers" but rather "In the desert," and this cryptic phrase expresses a little of the Israelites' futility. Surrounded by hostile nations, they had to march under the broiling sun in a desert plagued by snakes, scorpions, and drought. Even today, visitors to the Sinai Desert marvel that an entire nation wandered that ground for so long.

A march through the desert should have taken about two weeks. Instead, it took almost 40 years. Numbers spans the years of wandering and ends where the trek began: at the very spot (Kadesh) where the Israelites' faith had failed. Of the many thousands who left Egypt, only two adults, Joshua and Caleb, would make it into the promised land.

A Different Kind of History

Most ancient histories sound very different from this book. They tell of heroic exploits by mighty warriors and unblemished leaders. With an almost numbing monotony, Numbers presents a far more realistic picture. It shows the early symptoms, the full progression, and the tragic end of grumbling and unbelief.

The Israelites lost faith not only in themselves, but in their God. Because of that, a whole generation of them lies buried in the peninsula known as Sinai.

References to the "desert wanderings" crop up again and again in the Bible. The period of rebellion left an indelible mark on the Jewish people. Exactly what went wrong? The book of Numbers is given to tell us. The apostle Paul points out that these failures "happened to them to serve as an example, and they were written down to instruct us, on whom the ends of the ages have come. So, if you think you are standing, watch out that you do not fall" (1 Corinthians 10.11–12).

How to Read Numbers

P eople who read straight through Numbers very often come away confused or discouraged. The book begins with a long description of a census and proceeds into lists of laws and rituals. These were the official records of a nation, and each word had great significance for the Israelites. (Imagine how our Yellow Pages or Congressional Record would appear to people 3,000 years from now.)

Yet, unlike Leviticus, Numbers does not consist mainly of these long descriptions. Rather, it focuses on stories, with laws and rituals sprinkled in at various points. The stories are exciting, and some, such as the story of Balaam, are quite remarkable.

The action in Numbers takes place in three different settings: (1) Chapters 1–14 begin in the same place Exodus ended: at the foot of Mount Sinai. (2) Chapters 15–19 cover a period of 37 years, the time of the desert wanderings. Moses' summary in chapter 33 lists 42 stops in the desert, but Numbers details very few of them. (3) Chapters 20–36 concern a whole new generation of Israelites, who were making final preparations before the invasion.

As you read Numbers, it will help to have a major theme in mind, such as grumbling and rebellion. Work through the book, looking at examples of this problem. Major outbreaks occur in chapters 11, 12, 13, 14, 16, 20, and 21—at least ten incidents in all. Notice the cause of each rebellion, and also God's response. Can you see parallels to the Israelites' experience in your own life?

Numbers also offers insight into the leadership of Moses by showing his response to each crisis. One illustration of his prominence: Over 80 times the book says that "the LORD said to Moses." Look for the qualities, both positive and negative, that made him an effective leader.

Other parts of the Bible often refer to Numbers. Some of the historical psalms, such as Psalms 78, 105, and 136, recast these events in poetry.

PEOPLE YOU'LL MEET IN NUMBERS

MIRIAM (p. 168)
AARON (p. 170)
BALAAM (p. 180)

3-TRACK READING PLAN

For an explanation and complete listing of the 3-track reading plan, turn to page 7.

TRACK 1:   *Two-Week Courses on the Bible*
See page 7 for information on these courses.

TRACK 2:   *An Overview of Numbers in 2 Days*
☐ Day 1. Read the Introduction to Numbers and then chapter 11, which shows a typical Israelite response to hardship.
☐ Day 2. Read chapter 14, the hinge chapter of Numbers.

Now turn to page 9 for your next Track 2 reading project.

TRACK 3:   *All of Numbers in 35 Days*
After you have read through Numbers, turn to pages 10–14 for your next Track 3 reading project.

☐1–2	☐3	☐4	☐5	☐6	☐7	☐8	☐9
☐10	☐11	☐12	☐13	☐14	☐15	☐16	☐17
☐18	☐19	☐20	☐21	☐22	☐23	☐24	☐25
☐26	☐27	☐28	☐29	☐30	☐31	☐32	☐33
☐34	☐35	☐36					

The First Census of Israel

1 The LORD spoke to Moses in the wilderness of Sinai, in the tent of meeting, on the first day of the second month, in the second year after they had come out of the land of Egypt, saying: ²Take a census of the whole congregation of Israelites, in their clans, by ancestral houses, according to the number of names, every male individually; ³from twenty years old and upward, everyone in Israel able to go to war. You and Aaron shall enroll them, company by company. ⁴A man from each tribe shall be with you, each man the head of his ancestral house. ⁵These are the names of the men who shall assist you:

From Reuben, Elizur son of Shedeur.
⁶ From Simeon, Shelumiel son of Zurishaddai.
⁷ From Judah, Nahshon son of Amminadab.
⁸ From Issachar, Nethanel son of Zuar.
⁹ From Zebulun, Eliab son of Helon.
¹⁰ From the sons of Joseph:
from Ephraim, Elishama son of Ammihud;

from Manasseh, Gamaliel son of
Pedahzur.

11 From Benjamin, Abidan son of Gideoni.
12 From Dan, Ahiezer son of Ammishaddai.
13 From Asher, Pagiel son of Ochran.
14 From Gad, Eliasaph son of Deuel.
15 From Naphtali, Ahira son of Enan.

16These were the ones chosen from the congregation, the leaders of their ancestral tribes, the heads of the divisions of Israel.

17 Moses and Aaron took these men who had been designated by name, 18and on the first day of the second month they assembled the whole congregation together. They registered themselves in their clans, by their ancestral houses, according to the number of names from twenty years old and upward, individually, 19as the LORD commanded Moses. So he enrolled them in the wilderness of Sinai.

20 The descendants of Reuben, Israel's firstborn, their lineage, in their clans, by their ancestral houses, according to the number of names, individually, every male from twenty years old and upward, everyone able to go to war: 21those enrolled of the tribe of Reuben were forty-six thousand five hundred.

22 The descendants of Simeon, their lineage, in their clans, by their ancestral houses, those of them that were numbered, according to the number of names, individually, every male from twenty years old and upward, everyone able to go to war: 23those enrolled of the tribe of Simeon were fifty-nine thousand three hundred.

24 The descendants of Gad, their lineage, in their clans, by their ancestral houses, according to the number of the names, from twenty years old and upward, everyone able to go to war: 25those enrolled of the tribe of Gad were forty-five thousand six hundred fifty.

26 The descendants of Judah, their lineage, in their clans, by their ancestral houses, according to the number of names, from twenty years old and upward, everyone able to go to war: 27those enrolled of the tribe of Judah were seventy-four thousand six hundred.

28 The descendants of Issachar, their lineage, in their clans, by their ancestral houses, according to the number of names, from twenty years old and upward, everyone able to go to war: 29those enrolled of the tribe of Issachar were fifty-four thousand four hundred.

30 The descendants of Zebulun, their lineage, in their clans, by their ancestral houses, according to the number of names, from twenty years old and upward, everyone able to go to war: 31those enrolled of the tribe of Zebulun were fifty-seven thousand four hundred.

32 The descendants of Joseph, namely, the descendants of Ephraim, their lineage, in their clans, by their ancestral houses, according to the number of names, from twenty years old and up-

ward, everyone able to go to war: 33those enrolled of the tribe of Ephraim were forty thousand five hundred.

34 The descendants of Manasseh, their lineage, in their clans, by their ancestral houses, according to the number of names, from twenty

1.32 Two for One

Although Joseph was only one of the twelve brothers who formed the tribes of Israel, his father Israel (Jacob) had adopted Joseph's two sons, Ephraim and Manasseh, as his own (see Genesis 48.5–6). Thus Joseph got a double share of the family inheritance, and there are really thirteen tribes of Israel.

The tribe of Levi were often treated separately, however, because of their special role in worship. This census, for example, taken primarily to prepare a roster for military purposes, excluded the tribe of Levi. As caretakers of God's tabernacle, Levites were ineligible for the draft.

years old and upward, everyone able to go to war: 35those enrolled of the tribe of Manasseh were thirty-two thousand two hundred.

36 The descendants of Benjamin, their lineage, in their clans, by their ancestral houses, according to the number of names, from twenty years old and upward, everyone able to go to war: 37those enrolled of the tribe of Benjamin were thirty-five thousand four hundred.

38 The descendants of Dan, their lineage, in their clans, by their ancestral houses, according to the number of names, from twenty years old and upward, everyone able to go to war: 39those enrolled of the tribe of Dan were sixty-two thousand seven hundred.

40 The descendants of Asher, their lineage, in their clans, by their ancestral houses, according to the number of names, from twenty years old and upward, everyone able to go to war: 41those enrolled of the tribe of Asher were forty-one thousand five hundred.

42 The descendants of Naphtali, their lineage, in their clans, by their ancestral houses, according to the number of names, from twenty years old and upward, everyone able to go to war: 43those enrolled of the tribe of Naphtali were fifty-three thousand four hundred.

44 These are those who were enrolled, whom Moses and Aaron enrolled with the help of the leaders of Israel, twelve men, each representing his ancestral house. 45So the whole number of the Israelites, by their ancestral houses, from twenty years old and upward, everyone able to go to war in Israel— 46their whole number was six hundred

three thousand five hundred fifty. [47]The Levites, however, were not numbered by their ancestral tribe along with them.

48 The LORD had said to Moses: [49]Only the tribe of Levi you shall not enroll, and you shall not take a census of them with the other Israelites. [50]Rather you shall appoint the Levites over the tabernacle of the covenant,[a] and over all its equipment, and over all that belongs to it; they are to carry the tabernacle and all its equipment, and they shall tend it, and shall camp around the tabernacle. [51]When the tabernacle is to set out, the Levites shall take it down; and when the tabernacle is to be pitched, the Levites shall set it up. And any outsider who comes near shall be put to death. [52]The other Israelites shall camp in their respective regimental camps, by companies; [53]but the Levites shall camp around the tabernacle of the covenant,[a] that there may be no wrath on the congregation of the Israelites; and the Levites shall perform the guard duty of the tabernacle of the covenant.[a] [54]The Israelites did so; they did just as the LORD commanded Moses.

The Order of Encampment and Marching

2 The LORD spoke to Moses and Aaron, saying: [2]The Israelites shall camp each in their respective regiments, under ensigns by their ancestral houses; they shall camp facing the tent of

2.2 A Place for Everyone

The Israelites did not wander through the desert as an undisciplined mob. On the contrary, each tribe had an assigned place to camp. At the center of their camp was the tent of meeting (the tabernacle)—a visual reminder, each time they pitched their tents, of what should be at the center of their lives.

meeting on every side. [3]Those to camp on the east side toward the sunrise shall be of the regimental encampment of Judah by companies. The leader of the people of Judah shall be Nahshon son of Amminadab, [4]with a company as enrolled of seventy-four thousand six hundred. [5]Those to camp next to him shall be the tribe of Issachar. The leader of the Issacharites shall be Nethanel son of Zuar, [6]with a company as enrolled of fifty-four thousand four hundred. [7]Then the tribe of Zebulun: The leader of the Zebulunites shall be Eliab son of Helon, [8]with a company as enrolled of fifty-seven thousand four hundred. [9]The total enrollment of the camp of Judah, by companies, is one hundred eighty-six thousand four hundred. They shall set out first on the march.

10 On the south side shall be the regimental encampment of Reuben by companies. The leader of the Reubenites shall be Elizur son of Shedeur, [11]with a company as enrolled of forty-six thousand five hundred. [12]And those to camp next to him shall be the tribe of Simeon. The leader of the Simeonites shall be Shelumiel son of Zurishaddai, [13]with a company as enrolled of fifty-nine thousand three hundred. [14]Then the tribe of Gad: The leader of the Gadites shall be Eliasaph son of Reuel, [15]with a company as enrolled of forty-five thousand six hundred fifty. [16]The total enrollment of the camp of Reuben, by companies, is one hundred fifty-one thousand four hundred fifty. They shall set out second.

17 The tent of meeting, with the camp of the Levites, shall set out in the center of the camps; they shall set out just as they camp, each in position, by their regiments.

18 On the west side shall be the regimental encampment of Ephraim by companies. The leader of the people of Ephraim shall be Elishama son of Ammihud, [19]with a company as enrolled of forty thousand five hundred. [20]Next to him shall be the tribe of Manasseh. The leader of the people of Manasseh shall be Gamaliel son of Pedahzur, [21]with a company as enrolled of thirty-two thousand two hundred. [22]Then the tribe of Benjamin: The leader of the Benjaminites shall be Abidan son of Gideoni, [23]with a company as enrolled of thirty-five thousand four hundred. [24]The total enrollment of the camp of Ephraim, by companies, is one hundred eight thousand one hundred. They shall set out third on the march.

25 On the north side shall be the regimental encampment of Dan by companies. The leader of the Danites shall be Ahiezer son of Ammishaddai, [26]with a company as enrolled of sixty-two thousand seven hundred. [27]Those to camp next to him shall be the tribe of Asher. The leader of the Asherites shall be Pagiel son of Ochran, [28]with a company as enrolled of forty-one thousand five hundred. [29]Then the tribe of Naphtali: The leader of the Naphtalites shall be Ahira son of Enan, [30]with a company as enrolled of fifty-three thousand four hundred. [31]The total enrollment of the camp of Dan is one hundred fifty-seven thousand six hundred. They shall set out last, by companies.[b]

32 This was the enrollment of the Israelites by their ancestral houses; the total enrollment in the camps by their companies was six hundred three thousand five hundred fifty. [33]Just as the LORD had commanded Moses, the Levites were not enrolled among the other Israelites.

34 The Israelites did just as the LORD had commanded Moses: They camped by regiments, and they set out the same way, everyone by clans, according to ancestral houses.

---

[a] Or *treaty*, or *testimony*; Heb *eduth* [b] Compare verses 9, 16, 24: Heb *by their regiments*

The Sons of Aaron

3 This is the lineage of Aaron and Moses at the time when the LORD spoke with Moses on Mount Sinai. ²These are the names of the sons of

> ### 2.32 How Many Israelites?
>
> Debate has raged among scholars about the vast numbers of Israelites reported in the censuses of Numbers. Could two-and-a-half million people (counting women and children) have left Egypt in one day and then survived for 40 years in a desolate desert? Those who defend the large numbers point out that climatic conditions might have been very different in those days when, for example, Egypt was the granary of the world. (Also, the Bible gives many indications of God's miraculous supply of food and water.) Opposing scholars note that the Hebrews had different means of counting, and that the word translated "thousand" could have other meanings, resulting in much smaller figures. Regardless, both positions admit to a very large band of people wandering around a desert for a very long time.

Aaron: Nadab the firstborn, and Abihu, Eleazar, and Ithamar; ³these are the names of the sons of Aaron, the anointed priests, whom he ordained to minister as priests. ⁴Nadab and Abihu died before the LORD when they offered unholy fire before the LORD in the wilderness of Sinai, and they had no children. Eleazar and Ithamar served as priests in the lifetime of their father Aaron.

The Duties of the Levites

5 Then the LORD spoke to Moses, saying: ⁶Bring the tribe of Levi near, and set them before Aaron the priest, so that they may assist him. ⁷They shall perform duties for him and for the whole congregation in front of the tent of meeting, doing service at the tabernacle; ⁸they shall be in charge of all the furnishings of the tent of meeting, and attend to the duties for the Israelites as they do service at the tabernacle. ⁹You shall give the Levites to Aaron and his descendants; they are unreservedly given to him from among the Israelites. ¹⁰But you shall make a register of Aaron and his descendants; it is they who shall attend to the priesthood, and any outsider who comes near shall be put to death.

11 Then the LORD spoke to Moses, saying: ¹²I hereby accept the Levites from among the Israelites as substitutes for all the firstborn that open the womb among the Israelites. The Levites shall be mine, ¹³for all the firstborn are mine; when I killed all the firstborn in the land of Egypt, I consecrated for my own all the firstborn in Israel,

both human and animal; they shall be mine. I am the LORD.

A Census of the Levites

14 Then the LORD spoke to Moses in the wilderness of Sinai, saying: ¹⁵Enroll the Levites by ancestral houses and by clans. You shall enroll every male from a month old and upward. ¹⁶So Moses enrolled them according to the word of the LORD, as he was commanded. ¹⁷The following were the sons of Levi, by their names: Gershon, Kohath, and Merari. ¹⁸These are the names of the sons of Gershon by their clans: Libni and Shimei. ¹⁹The sons of Kohath by their clans: Amram, Izhar, Hebron, and Uzziel. ²⁰The sons of Merari by their clans: Mahli and Mushi. These are the clans of the Levites, by their ancestral houses.

21 To Gershon belonged the clan of the Libnites and the clan of the Shimeites; these were the clans of the Gershonites. ²²Their enrollment, counting all the males from a month old and upward, was seven thousand five hundred. ²³The clans of the Gershonites were to camp behind the tabernacle on the west, ²⁴with Eliasaph son of Lael as head of the ancestral house of the Gershonites. ²⁵The responsibility of the sons of Gershon in the tent of meeting was to be the tabernacle, the tent with its covering, the screen for the entrance of the tent of meeting, ²⁶the hangings of the court, the screen for the entrance of the court that is around the tabernacle and the altar, and its cords—all the service pertaining to these.

27 To Kohath belonged the clan of the Amramites, the clan of the Izharites, the clan of the Hebronites, and the clan of the Uzzielites; these are the clans of the Kohathites. ²⁸Counting all the males, from a month old and upward, there were eight thousand six hundred, attending to the duties of the sanctuary. ²⁹The clans of the Kohathites were to camp on the south side of the tabernacle, ³⁰with Elizaphan son of Uzziel as head of the ancestral house of the clans of the Kohathites. ³¹Their responsibility was to be the ark, the table, the lampstand, the altars, the vessels of the sanctuary with which the priests minister, and the screen—all the service pertaining to these. ³²Eleazar son of Aaron the priest was to be chief over the leaders of the Levites, and to have oversight of those who had charge of the sanctuary.

33 To Merari belonged the clan of the Mahlites and the clan of the Mushites: these are the clans of Merari. ³⁴Their enrollment, counting all the males from a month old and upward, was six thousand two hundred. ³⁵The head of the ancestral house of the clans of Merari was Zuriel son of Abihail; they were to camp on the north side of the tabernacle. ³⁶The responsibility assigned to the sons of Merari was to be the frames of the tabernacle, the bars, the pillars, the bases, and all their accessories—all the service pertaining to

these; 37also the pillars of the court all around, with their bases and pegs and cords.

38 Those who were to camp in front of the tabernacle on the east—in front of the tent of meeting toward the east—were Moses and Aaron and Aaron's sons, having charge of the rites within the sanctuary, whatever had to be done for the Israelites; and any outsider who came near was to be put to death. 39The total enrollment of the Levites whom Moses and Aaron enrolled at the commandment of the LORD, by their clans, all the males from a month old and upward, was twenty-two thousand.

The Redemption of the Firstborn

40 Then the LORD said to Moses: Enroll all the firstborn males of the Israelites, from a month old and upward, and count their names. 41But you shall accept the Levites for me—I am the LORD— as substitutes for all the firstborn among the Israelites, and the livestock of the Levites as substitutes for all the firstborn among the livestock of the Israelites. 42So Moses enrolled all the firstborn among the Israelites, as the LORD commanded him. 43The total enrollment, all the firstborn males from a month old and upward, counting the number of names, was twenty-two thousand two hundred seventy-three.

44 Then the LORD spoke to Moses, saying: 45Accept the Levites as substitutes for all the firstborn among the Israelites, and the livestock of the Levites as substitutes for their livestock; and the Levites shall be mine. I am the LORD. 46As

3.45 Designated Firstborn

At the first passover (Exodus 13.2) God established the firstborn principle, which held that every firstborn male, human or animal, must be dedicated to him. Here, in careful accounting, the Levites are accepted as "designated firstborn" offerings to God. Just as a "designated hitter" in baseball is appointed to bat in place of the pitcher, so here a whole tribe is named to take the place of firstborn members from every family.

the price of redemption of the two hundred seventy-three of the firstborn of the Israelites, over and above the number of the Levites, 47you shall accept five shekels apiece, reckoning by the shekel of the sanctuary, a shekel of twenty gerahs. 48Give to Aaron and his sons the money by which the excess number of them is redeemed. 49So Moses took the redemption money from those who were over and above those redeemed by the Levites; 50from the firstborn of the Israelites he took the money, one thousand three hundred sixty-five shekels, reckoned by the shekel of the sanctuary; 51and Moses gave the redemption money to Aaron and his sons, according to the word of the LORD, as the LORD had commanded Moses.

The Kohathites

4 The LORD spoke to Moses and Aaron, saying: 2Take a census of the Kohathites separate from the other Levites, by their clans and their ancestral houses, 3from thirty years old up to fifty years old, all who qualify to do work relating to the tent of meeting. 4The service of the Kohathites relating to the tent of meeting concerns the most holy things.

5 When the camp is to set out, Aaron and his sons shall go in and take down the screening curtain, and cover the ark of the covenantc with it; 6then they shall put on it a covering of fine leather,d and spread over that a cloth all of blue, and shall put its poles in place. 7Over the table of the bread of the Presence they shall spread a blue cloth, and put on it the plates, the dishes for incense, the bowls, and the flagons for the drink offering; the regular bread also shall be on it; 8then they shall spread over them a crimson cloth, and cover it with a covering of fine leather,d and shall put its poles in place. 9They shall take a blue cloth, and cover the lampstand for the light, with its lamps, its snuffers, its trays, and all the vessels for oil with which it is supplied; 10and they shall put it with all its utensils in a covering of fine leather,d and put it on the carrying frame. 11Over the golden altar they shall spread a blue cloth, and cover it with a covering of fine leather,d and shall put its poles in place; 12and they shall take all the utensils of the service that are used in the sanctuary, and put them in a blue cloth, and cover them with a covering of fine leather,d and put them on the carrying frame. 13They shall take away the ashes from the altar, and spread a purple cloth over it; 14and they shall put on it all the utensils of the altar, which are used for the service there, the firepans, the forks, the shovels, and the basins, all the utensils of the altar; and they shall spread on it a covering of fine leather,d and shall put its poles in place. 15When Aaron and his sons have finished covering the sanctuary and all the furnishings of the sanctuary, as the camp sets out, after that the Kohathites shall come to carry these, but they must not touch the holy things, or they will die. These are the things of the tent of meeting that the Kohathites are to carry.

16 Eleazar son of Aaron the priest shall have charge of the oil for the light, the fragrant incense, the regular grain offering, and the anointing oil, the oversight of all the tabernacle and all that is in it, in the sanctuary and in its utensils.

17 Then the LORD spoke to Moses and Aaron, saying: 18You must not let the tribe of the clans of

c Or *treaty*, or *testimony*; Heb *eduth*   d Meaning of Heb uncertain

the Kohathites be destroyed from among the Levites. [19]This is how you must deal with them in order that they may live and not die when they come near to the most holy things: Aaron and his

4.15 Touch and Die

The precise instructions for moving the holy things reflected the awe and respect that were due God alone. Years later, King David's men flagrantly ignored these instructions and one man, Uzzah, died as a result (see "Why Did Uzzah Die?" page 430). Earlier in Numbers, two of Aaron's sons had died while trying out their own version of worship, ignoring God's directions (3.4, also Leviticus 10.1–5). In the Bible, these drastic punishments tend to occur as God's people enter a new phase of their history (see Joshua 7; 2 Samuel 6.7; Acts 5.1–11). There is no compromising God's holiness.

sons shall go in and assign each to a particular task or burden. [20]But the Kohathites[e] must not go in to look on the holy things even for a moment; otherwise they will die.

The Gershonites and Merarites

21 Then the LORD spoke to Moses, saying: [22]Take a census of the Gershonites also, by their ancestral houses and by their clans; [23]from thirty years old up to fifty years old you shall enroll them, all who qualify to do work in the tent of meeting. [24]This is the service of the clans of the Gershonites, in serving and bearing burdens: [25]They shall carry the curtains of the tabernacle, and the tent of meeting with its covering, and the outer covering of fine leather[f] that is on top of it, and the screen for the entrance of the tent of meeting, [26]and the hangings of the court, and the screen for the entrance of the gate of the court that is around the tabernacle and the altar, and their cords, and all the equipment for their service; and they shall do all that needs to be done with regard to them. [27]All the service of the Gershonites shall be at the command of Aaron and his sons, in all that they are to carry, and in all that they have to do; and you shall assign to their charge all that they are to carry. [28]This is the service of the clans of the Gershonites relating to the tent of meeting, and their responsibilities are to be under the oversight of Ithamar son of Aaron the priest.

29 As for the Merarites, you shall enroll them by their clans and their ancestral houses; [30]from thirty years old up to fifty years old you shall enroll them, everyone who qualifies to do the work of the tent of meeting. [31]This is what they

are charged to carry, as the whole of their service in the tent of meeting: the frames of the tabernacle, with its bars, pillars, and bases, [32]and the pillars of the court all around with their bases, pegs, and cords, with all their equipment and all their related service; and you shall assign by name the objects that they are required to carry. [33]This is the service of the clans of the Merarites, the whole of their service relating to the tent of meeting, under the hand of Ithamar son of Aaron the priest.

Census of the Levites

34 So Moses and Aaron and the leaders of the congregation enrolled the Kohathites, by their clans and their ancestral houses, [35]from thirty years old up to fifty years old, everyone who qualified for work relating to the tent of meeting; [36]and their enrollment by clans was two thousand seven hundred fifty. [37]This was the enrollment of the clans of the Kohathites, all who served at the tent of meeting, whom Moses and Aaron enrolled according to the commandment of the LORD by Moses.

38 The enrollment of the Gershonites, by their clans and their ancestral houses, [39]from thirty years old up to fifty years old, everyone who qualified for work relating to the tent of meeting— [40]their enrollment by their clans and their ancestral houses was two thousand six hundred thirty. [41]This was the enrollment of the clans of the Gershonites, all who served at the tent of meeting, whom Moses and Aaron enrolled according to the commandment of the LORD.

42 The enrollment of the clans of the Merarites, by their clans and their ancestral houses, [43]from thirty years old up to fifty years old, everyone who qualified for work relating to the tent of meeting— [44]their enrollment by their clans was three thousand two hundred. [45]This is the enrollment of the clans of the Merarites, whom Moses and Aaron enrolled according to the commandment of the LORD by Moses.

46 All those who were enrolled of the Levites, whom Moses and Aaron and the leaders of Israel enrolled, by their clans and their ancestral houses, [47]from thirty years old up to fifty years old, everyone who qualified to do the work of service and the work of bearing burdens relating to the tent of meeting, [48]their enrollment was eight thousand five hundred eighty. [49]According to the commandment of the LORD through Moses they were appointed to their several tasks of serving or carrying; thus they were enrolled by him, as the LORD commanded Moses.

Unclean Persons

5 The LORD spoke to Moses, saying: [2]Command the Israelites to put out of the camp

---

e Heb *they*   *f* Meaning of Heb uncertain

everyone who is leprous,g or has a discharge, and everyone who is unclean through contact with a corpse; ³you shall put out both male and female, putting them outside the camp; they must not defile their camp, where I dwell among them. ⁴The Israelites did so, putting them outside the camp; as the LORD had spoken to Moses, so the Israelites did.

Confession and Restitution

5 The LORD spoke to Moses, saying: ⁶Speak to the Israelites: When a man or a woman wrongs another, breaking faith with the LORD, that person incurs guilt ⁷and shall confess the sin that has been committed. The person shall make full restitution for the wrong, adding one-fifth to it, and giving it to the one who was wronged. ⁸If the injured party has no next of kin to whom restitution may be made for the wrong, the restitution for wrong shall go to the LORD for the priest, in addition to the ram of atonement with which atonement is made for the guilty party. ⁹Among all the sacred donations of the Israelites, every gift that they bring to the priest shall be his. ¹⁰The sacred donations of all are their own; whatever anyone gives to the priest shall be his.

Concerning an Unfaithful Wife

11 The LORD spoke to Moses, saying: ¹²Speak to the Israelites and say to them: If any man's wife goes astray and is unfaithful to him, ¹³if a man has had intercourse with her but it is hidden from her husband, so that she is undetected though she has defiled herself, and there is no witness against her since she was not caught in the act; ¹⁴if a spirit of jealousy comes on him, and he is jealous of his wife who has defiled herself; or if a spirit of jealousy comes on him, and he is jealous of his wife, though she has not defiled herself; ¹⁵then the man shall bring his wife to the priest. And he shall bring the offering required for her, one-tenth of an ephah of barley flour. He shall pour no oil on it and put no frankincense on it, for it is a grain offering of jealousy, a grain offering of remembrance, bringing iniquity to remembrance.

16 Then the priest shall bring her near, and set her before the LORD; ¹⁷the priest shall take holy water in an earthen vessel, and take some of the dust that is on the floor of the tabernacle and put it into the water. ¹⁸The priest shall set the woman before the LORD, dishevel the woman's hair, and place in her hands the grain offering of remembrance, which is the grain offering of jealousy. In his own hand the priest shall have the water of bitterness that brings the curse. ¹⁹Then the priest shall make her take an oath, saying, "If no man has lain with you, if you have not turned aside to uncleanness while under your husband's authority, be immune to this water of bitterness that

brings the curse. ²⁰But if you have gone astray while under your husband's authority, if you have defiled yourself and some man other than your husband has had intercourse with you," ²¹—let

5.16 Test for Adultery

The strange test for adultery described here resembles other "trials by ordeal" common then in the Middle East. Presumably, either the emotional reactions of the guilty woman would give her away physiologically (much as a lie detector may), or God would reveal true results through the outcome of the ordeal. The public trial may have helped to clear the reputation of wives who had been falsely accused by their husbands. There is no Biblical record of the procedure actually being used, and the trial described is the only one like it in the Bible.

the priest make the woman take the oath of the curse and say to the woman—"the LORD make you an execration and an oath among your people, when the LORD makes your uterus drop, your womb discharge; ²²now may this water that brings the curse enter your bowels and make your womb discharge, your uterus drop!" And the woman shall say, "Amen. Amen."

23 Then the priest shall put these curses in writing, and wash them off into the water of bitterness. ²⁴He shall make the woman drink the water of bitterness that brings the curse, and the water that brings the curse shall enter her and cause bitter pain. ²⁵The priest shall take the grain offering of jealousy out of the woman's hand, and shall elevate the grain offering before the LORD and bring it to the altar; ²⁶and the priest shall take a handful of the grain offering, as its memorial portion, and turn it into smoke on the altar, and afterward shall make the woman drink the water. ²⁷When he has made her drink the water, then, if she has defiled herself and has been unfaithful to her husband, the water that brings the curse shall enter into her and cause bitter pain, and her womb shall discharge, her uterus drop, and the woman shall become an execration among her people. ²⁸But if the woman has not defiled herself and is clean, then she shall be immune and be able to conceive children.

29 This is the law in cases of jealousy, when a wife, while under her husband's authority, goes astray and defiles herself, ³⁰or when a spirit of jealousy comes on a man and he is jealous of his wife; then he shall set the woman before the LORD, and the priest shall apply this entire law to her. ³¹The man shall be free from iniquity, but the woman shall bear her iniquity.

---

g A term for several skin diseases; precise meaning uncertain

The Nazirites

6 The LORD spoke to Moses, saying: ²Speak to the Israelites and say to them: When either men or women make a special vow, the vow of a nazirite,[h] to separate themselves to the LORD, ³they shall separate themselves from wine and strong drink; they shall drink no wine vinegar or other vinegar, and shall not drink any grape juice or eat grapes, fresh or dried. ⁴All their days as nazirites[i] they shall eat nothing that is produced by the grapevine, not even the seeds or the skins.

5 All the days of their nazirite vow no razor shall come upon the head; until the time is completed for which they separate themselves to the LORD, they shall be holy; they shall let the locks of the head grow long.

6 All the days that they separate themselves to the LORD they shall not go near a corpse. ⁷Even if their father or mother, brother or sister, should die, they may not defile themselves; because their consecration to God is upon the head. ⁸All their days as nazirites[i] they are holy to the LORD.

9 If someone dies very suddenly nearby, defiling the consecrated head, then they shall shave the head on the day of their cleansing; on the seventh day they shall shave it. ¹⁰On the eighth day they shall bring two turtledoves or two young pigeons to the priest at the entrance of the tent of meeting, ¹¹and the priest shall offer one as a sin offering and the other as a burnt offering, and make atonement for them, because they incurred guilt by reason of the corpse. They shall sanctify the head that same day, ¹²and separate themselves to the LORD for their days as nazirites,[i] and bring a male lamb a year old as a guilt offering. The former time shall be void, because the consecrated head was defiled.

6.6 Types of Uncleanness

In its emphasis on purity, Numbers lists three types of unclean persons: victims of certain diseases, people with "a discharge" (including sexual ones), and those in contact with dead bodies. Besides offering obvious health benefits, these rules served to draw a sharp contrast between the Israelites and those who practiced other religions: Egyptians who virtually worshiped the dead, and Phoenicians and others who made sex an important part of religious rites.

An unclean person went into a period of quarantine (5.1–4). When Miriam got leprosy, she was kept away from camp for seven days (12.15). Soldiers, too, went through the same cleansing ritual if they had killed anyone or touched anyone who had died (31.19).

13 This is the law for the nazirites[i] when the time of their consecration has been completed: they shall be brought to the entrance of the tent of meeting, ¹⁴and they shall offer their gift to the LORD, one male lamb a year old without blemish as a burnt offering, one ewe lamb a year old without blemish as a sin offering, one ram without blemish as an offering of well-being, ¹⁵and a basket of unleavened bread, cakes of choice flour mixed with oil and unleavened wafers spread with oil, with their grain offering and their drink offerings. ¹⁶The priest shall present them before the LORD and offer their sin offering and burnt offering, ¹⁷and shall offer the ram as a sacrifice of well-being to the LORD, with the basket of unleavened bread; the priest also shall make the accompanying grain offering and drink offering. ¹⁸Then the nazirites[i] shall shave the consecrated head at the entrance of the tent of meeting, and shall take the hair from the consecrated head and put it on

6.18 Well-known Nazirites

Samson and John the Baptist are two of the most famous nazirites in the Bible. The apostle Paul took a nazirite vow in Jerusalem (Acts 21.21–29) to demonstrate his conformity to Jewish law.

the fire under the sacrifice of well-being. ¹⁹The priest shall take the shoulder of the ram, when it is boiled, and one unleavened cake out of the basket, and one unleavened wafer, and shall put them in the palms of the nazirites,[i] after they have shaved the consecrated head. ²⁰Then the priest shall elevate them as an elevation offering before the LORD; they are a holy portion for the priest, together with the breast that is elevated and the thigh that is offered. After that the nazirites[i] may drink wine.

21 This is the law for the nazirites[i] who take a vow. Their offering to the LORD must be in accordance with the nazirite[h] vow, apart from what else they can afford. In accordance with whatever vow they take, so they shall do, following the law for their consecration.

The Priestly Benediction

22 The LORD spoke to Moses, saying: ²³Speak to Aaron and his sons, saying, Thus you shall bless the Israelites: You shall say to them,
24 The LORD bless you and keep you;
25 the LORD make his face to shine upon
    you, and be gracious to you;
26 the LORD lift up his countenance upon
    you, and give you peace.

---

[h] That is *one separated* or *one consecrated*   [i] That is *those separated* or *those consecrated*

27 So they shall put my name on the Israelites, and I will bless them.

Offerings of the Leaders

7 On the day when Moses had finished setting up the tabernacle, and had anointed and consecrated it with all its furnishings, and had anointed and consecrated the altar with all its utensils, 2the leaders of Israel, heads of their ancestral houses, the leaders of the tribes, who were over those who were enrolled, made offerings. 3They brought their offerings before the LORD, six covered wagons and twelve oxen, a wagon for every two of the leaders, and for each one an ox; they presented them before the tabernacle. 4Then the LORD said to Moses: 5Accept these from them, that they may be used in doing the service of the tent of meeting, and give them to the Levites, to each according to his service. 6So Moses took the wagons and the oxen, and gave them to the Levites. 7Two wagons and four oxen he gave to the Gershonites, according to their service; 8and four wagons and eight oxen he gave to the Merarites, according to their service, under the direction of Ithamar son of Aaron the priest. 9But to the Kohathites he gave none, because they were charged with the care of the holy things that had to be carried on the shoulders.

10 The leaders also presented offerings for the dedication of the altar at the time when it was anointed; the leaders presented their offering before the altar. 11The LORD said to Moses: They shall present their offerings, one leader each day, for the dedication of the altar.

12 The one who presented his offering the first day was Nahshon son of Amminadab, of the tribe of Judah; 13his offering was one silver plate weighing one hundred thirty shekels, one silver basin weighing seventy shekels, according to the shekel of the sanctuary, both of them full of choice flour mixed with oil for a grain offering; 14one golden dish weighing ten shekels, full of incense; 15one young bull, one ram, one male lamb a year old, for a burnt offering; 16one male goat for a sin offering; 17and for the sacrifice of well-being, two oxen, five rams, five male goats, and five male lambs a year old. This was the offering of Nahshon son of Amminadab.

18 On the second day Nethanel son of Zuar, the leader of Issachar, presented an offering; 19he presented for his offering one silver plate weighing one hundred thirty shekels, one silver basin weighing seventy shekels, according to the shekel of the sanctuary, both of them full of choice flour mixed with oil for a grain offering; 20one golden dish weighing ten shekels, full of incense; 21one young bull, one ram, one male lamb a year old, as a burnt offering; 22one male goat as a sin offering; 23and for the sacrifice of well-being, two oxen, five rams, five male goats, and five male lambs a

year old. This was the offering of Nethanel son of Zuar.

24 On the third day Eliab son of Helon, the leader of the Zebulunites: 25his offering was one silver plate weighing one hundred thirty shekels, one silver basin weighing seventy shekels, according to the shekel of the sanctuary, both of them full of choice flour mixed with oil for a grain offering; 26one golden dish weighing ten shekels, full of incense; 27one young bull, one ram, one male lamb a year old, for a burnt offering; 28one male goat for a sin offering; 29and for the sacrifice of well-being, two oxen, five rams, five male goats, and five male lambs a year old. This was the offering of Eliab son of Helon.

30 On the fourth day Elizur son of Shedeur, the leader of the Reubenites: 31his offering was one silver plate weighing one hundred thirty shekels, one silver basin weighing seventy shekels, according to the shekel of the sanctuary, both of them full of choice flour mixed with oil for a grain offering; 32one golden dish weighing ten shekels, full of incense; 33one young bull, one ram, one male lamb a year old, for a burnt offering; 34one male goat for a sin offering; 35and for the sacrifice of well-being, two oxen, five rams, five male goats, and five male lambs a year old. This was the offering of Elizur son of Shedeur.

36 On the fifth day Shelumiel son of Zurishaddai, the leader of the Simeonites: 37his offering was one silver plate weighing one hundred thirty shekels, one silver basin weighing seventy shekels, according to the shekel of the sanctuary, both of them full of choice flour mixed with oil for a grain offering; 38one golden dish weighing ten shekels, full of incense; 39one young bull, one ram, one male lamb a year old, for a burnt offering; 40one male goat for a sin offering; 41and for the sacrifice of well-being, two oxen, five rams, five male goats, and five male lambs a year old. This was the offering of Shelumiel son of Zurishaddai.

42 On the sixth day Eliasaph son of Deuel, the leader of the Gadites: 43his offering was one silver plate weighing one hundred thirty shekels, one silver basin weighing seventy shekels, according to the shekel of the sanctuary, both of them full of choice flour mixed with oil for a grain offering; 44one golden dish weighing ten shekels, full of incense; 45one young bull, one ram, one male lamb a year old, for a burnt offering; 46one male goat for a sin offering; 47and for the sacrifice of well-being, two oxen, five rams, five male goats, and five male lambs a year old. This was the offering of Eliasaph son of Deuel.

48 On the seventh day Elishama son of Ammihud, the leader of the Ephraimites: 49his offering was one silver plate weighing one hundred thirty shekels, one silver basin weighing seventy shekels, according to the shekel of the sanctuary, both of them full of choice flour mixed with oil

for a grain offering; [50]one golden dish weighing ten shekels, full of incense; [51]one young bull, one ram, one male lamb a year old, for a burnt offering; [52]one male goat for a sin offering; [53]and for the sacrifice of well-being, two oxen, five rams, five male goats, and five male lambs a year old. This was the offering of Elishama son of Ammihud.

[54] On the eighth day Gamaliel son of Pedahzur, the leader of the Manassites: [55]his offering was one silver plate weighing one hundred thirty shekels, one silver basin weighing seventy shekels, according to the shekel of the sanctuary, both of them full of choice flour mixed with oil for a grain

7.55 Gold and Silver Dishes

The plates and bowls used in Israelite worship have a history of their own. Some of these originals, perhaps all, were lost during the dark years of the judges. David produced more, which his son Solomon installed in the temple (2 Chronicles 5.1); all were taken as captured goods when the Babylonians destroyed Jerusalem (2 Kings 25.15). At last they were returned to Jerusalem when the Persian king Cyrus let the Jews return (Ezra 1.9–10).

offering; [56]one golden dish weighing ten shekels, full of incense; [57]one young bull, one ram, one male lamb a year old, for a burnt offering; [58]one male goat for a sin offering; [59]and for the sacrifice of well-being, two oxen, five rams, five male goats, and five male lambs a year old. This was the offering of Gamaliel son of Pedahzur.

[60] On the ninth day Abidan son of Gideoni, the leader of the Benjaminites: [61]his offering was one silver plate weighing one hundred thirty shekels, one silver basin weighing seventy shekels, according to the shekel of the sanctuary, both of them full of choice flour mixed with oil for a grain offering; [62]one golden dish weighing ten shekels, full of incense; [63]one young bull, one ram, one male lamb a year old, for a burnt offering; [64]one male goat for a sin offering; [65]and for the sacrifice of well-being, two oxen, five rams, five male goats, and five male lambs a year old. This was the offering of Abidan son of Gideoni.

[66] On the tenth day Ahiezer son of Ammishaddai, the leader of the Danites: [67]his offering was one silver plate weighing one hundred thirty shekels, one silver basin weighing seventy shekels, according to the shekel of the sanctuary, both of them full of choice flour mixed with oil for a grain offering; [68]one golden dish weighing ten shekels, full of incense; [69]one young bull, one ram, one male lamb a year old, for a burnt offering; [70]one male goat for a sin offering; [71]and for the sacrifice

of well-being, two oxen, five rams, five male goats, and five male lambs a year old. This was the offering of Ahiezer son of Ammishaddai.

[72] On the eleventh day Pagiel son of Ochran, the leader of the Asherites: [73]his offering was one silver plate weighing one hundred thirty shekels, one silver basin weighing seventy shekels, according to the shekel of the sanctuary, both of them full of choice flour mixed with oil for a grain offering; [74]one golden dish weighing ten shekels, full of incense; [75]one young bull, one ram, one male lamb a year old, for a burnt offering; [76]one male goat for a sin offering; [77]and for the sacrifice of well-being, two oxen, five rams, five male goats, and five male lambs a year old. This was the offering of Pagiel son of Ochran.

[78] On the twelfth day Ahira son of Enan, the leader of the Naphtalites: [79]his offering was one silver plate weighing one hundred thirty shekels, one silver basin weighing seventy shekels, according to the shekel of the sanctuary, both of them full of choice flour mixed with oil for a grain offering; [80]one golden dish weighing ten shekels, full of incense; [81]one young bull, one ram, one male lamb a year old, for a burnt offering; [82]one male goat for a sin offering; [83]and for the sacrifice of well-being, two oxen, five rams, five male goats, and five male lambs a year old. This was the offering of Ahira son of Enan.

[84] This was the dedication offering for the altar, at the time when it was anointed, from the leaders of Israel: twelve silver plates, twelve silver basins, twelve golden dishes, [85]each silver plate weighing one hundred thirty shekels and each basin seventy, all the silver of the vessels two thousand four hundred shekels according to the shekel of the sanctuary, [86]the twelve golden dishes, full of incense, weighing ten shekels apiece according to the shekel of the sanctuary, all the gold of the dishes being one hundred twenty shekels; [87]all the livestock for the burnt offering twelve bulls, twelve rams, twelve male lambs a year old, with their grain offering; and twelve male goats for a sin offering; [88]and all the livestock for the sacrifice of well-being twenty-four bulls, the rams sixty, the male goats sixty, the male lambs a year old sixty. This was the dedication offering for the altar, after it was anointed.

[89] When Moses went into the tent of meeting to speak with the LORD,[j] he would hear the voice speaking to him from above the mercy seat[k] that was on the ark of the covenant[l] from between the two cherubim; thus it spoke to him.

The Seven Lamps

8 The LORD spoke to Moses, saying: [2]Speak to Aaron and say to him: When you set up the lamps, the seven lamps shall give light in front of the lampstand. [3]Aaron did so; he set up its lamps

---

j Heb *him*   *k* Or *the cover*   *l* Or *treaty*, or *testimony*; Heb *eduth*

to give light in front of the lampstand, as the LORD had commanded Moses. 4Now this was how the lampstand was made, out of hammered work of gold. From its base to its flowers, it was hammered work; according to the pattern that the

LORD had shown Moses, so he made the lampstand.

Consecration and Service of the Levites

5 The LORD spoke to Moses, saying: 6Take the Levites from among the Israelites and cleanse them. 7Thus you shall do to them, to cleanse them: sprinkle the water of purification on them, have them shave their whole body with a razor and wash their clothes, and so cleanse themselves. 8Then let them take a young bull and its grain offering of choice flour mixed with oil, and you shall take another young bull for a sin offering. 9You shall bring the Levites before the tent of meeting, and assemble the whole congregation of the Israelites. 10When you bring the Levites before the LORD, the Israelites shall lay their hands on the Levites, 11and Aaron shall present the Levites before the LORD as an elevation offering from the Israelites, that they may do the service of the LORD. 12The Levites shall lay their hands on the heads of the bulls, and he shall offer the one for a sin offering and the other for a burnt offering to the LORD, to make atonement for the Levites. 13Then you shall have the Levites stand before Aaron and his sons, and you shall present them as an elevation offering to the LORD.

14 Thus you shall separate the Levites from among the other Israelites, and the Levites shall be mine. 15Thereafter the Levites may go in to do service at the tent of meeting, once you have

National Reminders
Built-in object lessons for the Israelites

ALTHOUGH PARTS OF NUMBERS MAY seem strange to a modern reader, it clearly expresses two of the Israelites' chief values: purity and holiness. They had to become pure before they could approach God. And they were called to demonstrate God's holiness before other nations. The need for purity and holiness was reflected in what the Israelites ate and wore, and how they acted each day.

Aaron shall present the Levites before the LORD as an elevation offering from the Israelites, that they may do the service of the LORD. 8.11

Visual Reminders

God set aside certain groups of people as a visual reminder of purity and holiness. The Levites, who somewhat parallel the full-time clergy of our day, took care of formal religious duties (chapters 3, 4, 8). One of their clans packed up the holy objects for moving, while other clans carried the tabernacle curtains and covers and structural parts.

Numbers describes a second group: the Nazirites (chapter 6). These ordinary laypeople dedicated themselves to an extra regimen of purity. They drank no wine and let their hair grow long. Much as Amish people do today, they stood out from the majority in their dress and style.

Holiness was not left to special groups, though. Every Israelite participated in the daily offerings, sacrifices, and occasional festivals. When a family brought a whole bull and saw it skinned, butchered, and then burned on the altar, they were forced to reflect. Sin was serious, and a great gulf was fixed between them and God. In some way, either through story, ritual, or visual symbol, Numbers expresses that separateness on almost every page. In approaching God, the Israelites had to use great care.

Bridging the Gulf

The style of life described in this book differs from our own era of casual dress, informal worship, and talk of "friendship" with God. Later, the New Testament would spell out a God who is our Father, who can be approached at any time, who is interested in the personal details of our individual lives. But Numbers serves as an important background to that kind of relationship. It shows graphically just how great was the gulf between people and God, and helps us fully appreciate all that Jesus Christ did in providing a way across that gulf.

Life Questions: Words like *holiness* and *purity* are not heard in many churches today. Do you think we take God for granted and approach him too casually?

cleansed them and presented them as an elevation offering. [16]For they are unreservedly given to me from among the Israelites; I have taken them for myself, in place of all that open the womb, the firstborn of all the Israelites. [17]For all the firstborn among the Israelites are mine, both human and animal. On the day that I struck down all the firstborn in the land of Egypt I consecrated them for myself, [18]but I have taken the Levites in place of all the firstborn among the Israelites. [19]Moreover, I have given the Levites as a gift to Aaron and his sons from among the Israelites, to do the service for the Israelites at the tent of meeting, and to make atonement for the Israelites, in order that there may be no plague among the Israelites for coming too close to the sanctuary.

20 Moses and Aaron and the whole congregation of the Israelites did with the Levites accordingly; the Israelites did with the Levites just as the LORD had commanded Moses concerning them. [21]The Levites purified themselves from sin and washed their clothes; then Aaron presented them as an elevation offering before the LORD, and Aaron made atonement for them to cleanse them. [22]Thereafter the Levites went in to do their service in the tent of meeting in attendance on Aaron and his sons. As the LORD had commanded Moses concerning the Levites, so they did with them.

23 The LORD spoke to Moses, saying: [24]This applies to the Levites: from twenty-five years old and upward they shall begin to do duty in the service of the tent of meeting; [25]and from the age of fifty years they shall retire from the duty of the service and serve no more. [26]They may assist their brothers in the tent of meeting in carrying out their duties, but they shall perform no service. Thus you shall do with the Levites in assigning their duties.

The Passover at Sinai

9 The LORD spoke to Moses in the wilderness of Sinai, in the first month of the second year after they had come out of the land of Egypt, saying: [2]Let the Israelites keep the passover at its appointed time. [3]On the fourteenth day of this month, at twilight,[m] you shall keep it at its appointed time; according to all its statutes and all its regulations you shall keep it. [4]So Moses told the Israelites that they should keep the passover. [5]They kept the passover in the first month, on the fourteenth day of the month, at twilight,[m] in the wilderness of Sinai. Just as the LORD had commanded Moses, so the Israelites did. [6]Now there were certain people who were unclean through touching a corpse, so that they could not keep the passover on that day. They came before Moses and Aaron on that day, [7]and said to him, "Although we are unclean through touching a corpse, why must we be kept from presenting the

LORD's offering at its appointed time among the Israelites?" [8]Moses spoke to them, "Wait, so that I may hear what the LORD will command concerning you."

9 The LORD spoke to Moses, saying: [10]Speak to the Israelites, saying: Anyone of you or your descendants who is unclean through touching a corpse, or is away on a journey, shall still keep the passover to the LORD. [11]In the second month on the fourteenth day, at twilight,[m] they shall keep it; they shall eat it with unleavened bread and bitter herbs. [12]They shall leave none of it until morning, nor break a bone of it; according to all the statute for the passover they shall keep it. [13]But anyone who is clean and is not on a journey, and yet refrains from keeping the passover, shall be cut off from the people for not presenting the LORD's offering at its appointed time; such a one shall bear the consequences for the sin. [14]Any alien residing among you who wishes to keep the passover to the LORD shall do so according to the statute of the passover and according to its regulation; you shall have one statute for both the resident alien and the native.

The Cloud and the Fire

15 On the day the tabernacle was set up, the cloud covered the tabernacle, the tent of the covenant;[n] and from evening until morning it was over the tabernacle, having the appearance of fire. [16]It was always so: the cloud covered it by day[o] and the appearance of fire by night. [17]Whenever the cloud lifted from over the tent, then the Israelites would set out; and in the place where the cloud settled down, there the Israelites would camp. [18]At the command of the LORD the Israelites would set out, and at the command of the LORD they would camp. As long as the cloud rested over the tabernacle, they would remain in camp. [19]Even when the cloud continued over the tabernacle many days, the Israelites would keep the charge of the LORD, and would not set out.

9.19 Unmistakable Guidance

This passage describes a remarkable fact of the desert experience: the Israelites knew exactly whether and how far God wanted them to move each day. Although they disobeyed God in almost every other way, they usually followed his specific guidance on location.

[20]Sometimes the cloud would remain a few days over the tabernacle, and according to the command of the LORD they would remain in camp; then according to the command of the LORD they would set out. [21]Sometimes the cloud would remain from evening until morning; and when the

cloud lifted in the morning, they would set out, or
if it continued for a day and a night, when the
cloud lifted they would set out. 22 Whether it was
two days, or a month, or a longer time, that the
cloud continued over the tabernacle, resting upon
it, the Israelites would remain in camp and would
not set out; but when it lifted they would set out.
23 At the command of the LORD they would camp,
and at the command of the LORD they would set
out. They kept the charge of the LORD, at the
command of the LORD by Moses.

The Silver Trumpets

10 The LORD spoke to Moses, saying: 2 Make
two silver trumpets; you shall make them
of hammered work; and you shall use them for
summoning the congregation, and for breaking
camp. 3 When both are blown, the whole congregation shall assemble before you at the entrance
of the tent of meeting. 4 But if only one is blown,
then the leaders, the heads of the tribes of Israel,
shall assemble before you. 5 When you blow an
alarm, the camps on the east side shall set out;
6 when you blow a second alarm, the camps on the
south side shall set out. An alarm is to be blown
whenever they are to set out. 7 But when the assembly is to be gathered, you shall blow, but you
shall not sound an alarm. 8 The sons of Aaron, the
priests, shall blow the trumpets; this shall be a
perpetual institution for you throughout your
generations. 9 When you go to war in your land
against the adversary who oppresses you, you
shall sound an alarm with the trumpets, so that
you may be remembered before the LORD your
God and be saved from your enemies. 10 Also on
your days of rejoicing, at your appointed festivals,
and at the beginnings of your months, you shall
blow the trumpets over your burnt offerings and
over your sacrifices of well-being; they shall serve
as a reminder on your behalf before the LORD
your God: I am the LORD your God.

Departure from Sinai

11 In the second year, in the second month,
on the twentieth day of the month, the cloud
lifted from over the tabernacle of the covenant.[p]
12 Then the Israelites set out by stages from the
wilderness of Sinai, and the cloud settled down in
the wilderness of Paran. 13 They set out for the first
time at the command of the LORD by Moses.
14 The standard of the camp of Judah set out first,
company by company, and over the whole company was Nahshon son of Amminadab. 15 Over
the company of the tribe of Issachar was Nethanel
son of Zuar; 16 and over the company of the tribe
of Zebulun was Eliab son of Helon.
17 Then the tabernacle was taken down, and
the Gershonites and the Merarites, who carried
the tabernacle, set out. 18 Next the standard of the
camp of Reuben set out, company by company;
and over the whole company was Elizur son of
Shedeur. 19 Over the company of the tribe of Simeon was Shelumiel son of Zurishaddai, 20 and over
the company of the tribe of Gad was Eliasaph son
of Deuel.
21 Then the Kohathites, who carried the holy
things, set out; and the tabernacle was set up before their arrival. 22 Next the standard of the
Ephraimite camp set out, company by company,
and over the whole company was Elishama son of
Ammihud. 23 Over the company of the tribe of
Manasseh was Gamaliel son of Pedahzur, 24 and
over the company of the tribe of Benjamin was
Abidan son of Gideoni.
25 Then the standard of the camp of Dan,
acting as the rear guard of all the camps, set out,
company by company, and over the whole company was Ahiezer son of Ammishaddai. 26 Over
the company of the tribe of Asher was Pagiel son
of Ochran, 27 and over the company of the tribe of
Naphtali was Ahira son of Enan. 28 This was the
order of march of the Israelites, company by
company, when they set out.
29 Moses said to Hobab son of Reuel the
Midianite, Moses' father-in-law, "We are setting
out for the place of which the LORD said, 'I will
give it to you'; come with us, and we will treat you
well; for the LORD has promised good to Israel."
30 But he said to him, "I will not go, but I will go
back to my own land and to my kindred." 31 He
said, "Do not leave us, for you know where we
should camp in the wilderness, and you will serve
as eyes for us. 32 Moreover, if you go with us,
whatever good the LORD does for us, the same we
will do for you."
33 So they set out from the mount of the
LORD three days' journey with the ark of the covenant of the LORD going before them three days'
journey, to seek out a resting place for them, 34 the
cloud of the LORD being over them by day when
they set out from the camp.
35 Whenever the ark set out, Moses would
say,

"Arise, O LORD, let your enemies be
scattered,
and your foes flee before you."

36 And whenever it came to rest, he would say,

"Return, O LORD of the ten thousand
thousands of Israel."[q]

Complaining in the Desert

11 Now when the people complained in the
hearing of the LORD about their misfortunes, the LORD heard it and his anger was kindled. Then the fire of the LORD burned against
them, and consumed some outlying parts of the
camp. 2 But the people cried out to Moses; and
Moses prayed to the LORD, and the fire abated.

[p] Or *treaty*, or *testimony*; Heb *eduth* [q] Meaning of Heb uncertain

³So that place was called Taberah,ʳ because the fire of the LORD burned against them.

4 The rabble among them had a strong craving; and the Israelites also wept again, and said,

---

10.36 Famous Prayers

Moses' prayer is still repeated in Jewish services when the scroll of the law is removed from its container. Another prayer from Numbers, the blessing of 6.24–26, is quoted both in Jewish and Christian services. In ancient thought, a person's name stood for his character, including all his virtues and powers, and the benediction in 6.27 showed God "putting his name on" the Israelites.

"If only we had meat to eat! ⁵We remember the fish we used to eat in Egypt for nothing, the cucumbers, the melons, the leeks, the onions, and the garlic; ⁶but now our strength is dried up, and there is nothing at all but this manna to look at."

7 Now the manna was like coriander seed, and its color was like the color of gum resin. ⁸The people went around and gathered it, ground it in mills or beat it in mortars, then boiled it in pots and made cakes of it; and the taste of it was like the taste of cakes baked with oil. ⁹When the dew fell on the camp in the night, the manna would fall with it.

10 Moses heard the people weeping throughout their families, all at the entrances of their tents. Then the LORD became very angry, and Moses was displeased. ¹¹So Moses said to the LORD, "Why have you treated your servant so badly? Why have I not found favor in your sight, that you lay the burden of all this people on me? ¹²Did I conceive all this people? Did I give birth to them, that you should say to me, 'Carry them in your bosom, as a nurse carries a sucking child,' to the land that you promised on oath to their ancestors? ¹³Where am I to get meat to give to all this people? For they come weeping to me and say, 'Give us meat to eat!' ¹⁴I am not able to carry all this people alone, for they are too heavy for me. ¹⁵If this is the way you are going to treat me, put me to death at once—if I have found favor in your sight—and do not let me see my misery."

The Seventy Elders

16 So the LORD said to Moses, "Gather for me seventy of the elders of Israel, whom you know to be the elders of the people and officers over them; bring them to the tent of meeting, and have them take their place there with you. ¹⁷I will come down and talk with you there; and I will take some of the spirit that is on you and put it on them; and they shall bear the burden of the people along with you so that you will not bear it all by yourself. ¹⁸And say to the people: Consecrate yourselves for tomorrow, and you shall eat meat; for you have wailed in the hearing of the LORD, saying, 'If only we had meat to eat! Surely it was better for us in Egypt.' Therefore the LORD will give you meat, and you shall eat. ¹⁹You shall eat not only one day, or two days, or five days, or ten days, or twenty days, ²⁰but for a whole month— until it comes out of your nostrils and becomes loathsome to you—because you have rejected the LORD who is among you, and have wailed before him, saying, 'Why did we ever leave Egypt?'" ²¹But Moses said, "The people I am with number six hundred thousand on foot; and you say, 'I will give them meat, that they may eat for a whole month'! ²²Are there enough flocks and herds to slaughter for them? Are there enough fish in the sea to catch for them?" ²³The LORD said to Moses, "Is the LORD's power limited?ˢ Now you shall see whether my word will come true for you or not."

24 So Moses went out and told the people the words of the LORD; and he gathered seventy elders of the people, and placed them all around the tent. ²⁵Then the LORD came down in the cloud and spoke to him, and took some of the spirit that was on him and put it on the seventy elders; and when the spirit rested upon them, they prophesied. But they did not do so again.

26 Two men remained in the camp, one named Eldad, and the other named Medad, and the spirit rested on them; they were among those registered, but they had not gone out to the tent, and so they prophesied in the camp. ²⁷And a young man ran and told Moses, "Eldad and Medad are prophesying in the camp." ²⁸And Joshua son of Nun, the assistant of Moses, one of his chosen men,ᵗ said, "My lord Moses, stop them!" ²⁹But Moses said to him, "Are you jealous for my sake? Would that all the LORD's people were prophets, and that the LORD would put his spirit on them!" ³⁰And Moses and the elders of Israel returned to the camp.

11.29 Burdens of Leadership

In this striking conversation with God, Moses confessed the terrible burden involved in leading a whining, complaining band of "rabble." Although his patience neared the breaking point, he still showed mercy toward rivals. His response to other prophets here resembles Jesus' attitude toward other workers (Mark 9.38–41), as well as Paul's (Philippians 1.18).

ʳ That is *Burning*   ˢ Heb *LORD's hand too short?*   ᵗ Or *of Moses from his youth*

The Quails

31 Then a wind went out from the LORD, and it brought quails from the sea and let them fall beside the camp, about a day's journey on this side and a day's journey on the other side, all around the camp, about two cubits deep on the ground. [32]So the people worked all that day and night and all the next day, gathering the quails; the least anyone gathered was ten homers; and they spread them out for themselves all around the camp. [33]But while the meat was still between their teeth, before it was consumed, the anger of the LORD was kindled against the people, and the LORD struck the people with a very great plague. [34]So that place was called Kibroth-hattaavah,[u] because there they buried the people who had the craving. [35]From Kibroth-hattaavah the people journeyed to Hazeroth.

Aaron and Miriam Jealous of Moses

12 While they were at Hazeroth, Miriam and Aaron spoke against Moses because of the Cushite woman whom he had married (for he had indeed married a Cushite woman); [2]and they said, "Has the LORD spoken only through Moses? Has he not spoken through us also?" And the LORD heard it. [3]Now the man Moses was very humble,[v] more so than anyone else on the face of the earth. [4]Suddenly the LORD said to Moses, Aaron, and Miriam, "Come out, you three, to the tent of meeting." So the three of them came out. [5]Then the LORD came down in a pillar of cloud, and stood at the entrance of the tent, and called Aaron and Miriam; and they both came forward. [6]And he said, "Hear my words:

When there are prophets among you,
    I the LORD make myself known to
        them in visions;

I speak to them in dreams.
7 Not so with my servant Moses;
    he is entrusted with all my house.
8 With him I speak face to face—clearly,
    not in riddles;
    and he beholds the form of the LORD.

12.2 Family Jealousy

Miriam, Moses' older sister, had helped save his life when he was a baby (Exodus 2.7). But she and her brother Aaron felt some sibling rivalry for their kid brother. Irked by his foreign wife, they began undercutting his leadership by asking whether he had a monopoly on God's will.

Moses apparently did not defend himself, but God came to his defense with scathing words that made clear their special relationship. Hebrews 3.1–6 refers to God's homage to Moses, showing that as close as Moses was to God, Jesus deserved even more honor.

Why then were you not afraid to speak against my servant Moses?" [9]And the anger of the LORD was kindled against them, and he departed.

10 When the cloud went away from over the tent, Miriam had become leprous,[w] as white as snow. And Aaron turned towards Miriam and saw that she was leprous. [11]Then Aaron said to Moses, "Oh, my lord, do not punish us[x] for a sin that we have so foolishly committed. [12]Do not let her be like one stillborn, whose flesh is half consumed when it comes out of its mother's womb." [13]And Moses cried to the LORD, "O God, please heal her." [14]But the LORD said to Moses, "If her father had but spit in her face, would she not bear

---

[u] That is *Graves of craving*   [v] Or *devout*   [w] A term for several skin diseases; precise meaning uncertain
[x] Heb *do not lay sin upon us*

MIRIAM *Jealous Sister*

AMONG LIFE'S MOST DIFFICULT TASKS is enjoying the success of a brother or sister who outdoes you. Certainly Moses' sister Miriam found it difficult.

At Moses' birth she was the hero, watching over her baby brother and cleverly jumping in to outwit Pharaoh's daughter (Exodus 2.7). She took the spotlight again when the Israelites crossed the Red Sea, leading the women in a wild song of triumph (Exodus 15.20). As a prophetess, she played an important leadership role alongside Moses, who carried the chief responsibilities.

Then jealousy crept in. Miriam and her brother Aaron, another strong leader, began to grumble. They objected to Moses' wife, a foreigner, and they felt they ought to have equal spiritual status with Moses. "Has the LORD spoken only through Moses?" they asked. "Has he not spoken through us also?" (12.2).

In essence, God responded with a fierce "How dare you?" He singled out Miriam, apparently the leader of the two, for punishment. He would not tolerate jealousy among the leaders of his people—especially jealousy aimed at the humble man whom he had chosen.

Life Questions: What makes you jealous? How can you best handle those feelings?

her shame for seven days? Let her be shut out of the camp for seven days, and after that she may be brought in again." [15]So Miriam was shut out of the camp for seven days; and the people did not set out on the march until Miriam had been brought in again. [16]After that the people set out from Hazeroth, and camped in the wilderness of Paran.

Spies Sent into Canaan

13 The LORD said to Moses, [2]"Send men to spy out the land of Canaan, which I am giving to the Israelites; from each of their ancestral tribes you shall send a man, every one a leader among them." [3]So Moses sent them from the wilderness of Paran, according to the command of the LORD, all of them leading men among the Israelites. [4]These were their names: From the tribe of Reuben, Shammua son of Zaccur; [5]from the tribe of Simeon, Shaphat son of Hori; [6]from the tribe of Judah, Caleb son of Jephunneh; [7]from the tribe of Issachar, Igal son of Joseph; [8]from the tribe of Ephraim, Hoshea son of Nun; [9]from the tribe of Benjamin, Palti son of Raphu; [10]from the tribe of Zebulun, Gaddiel son of Sodi; [11]from the tribe of Joseph (that is, from the tribe of Manasseh), Gaddi son of Susi; [12]from the tribe of Dan, Ammiel son of Gemalli; [13]from the tribe of Asher, Sethur son of Michael; [14]from the tribe of Naphtali, Nahbi son of Vophsi; [15]from the tribe of Gad, Geuel son of Machi. [16]These were the names of the men whom Moses sent to spy out the land. And Moses changed the name of Hoshea son of Nun to Joshua.

[17] Moses sent them to spy out the land of Canaan, and said to them, "Go up there into the Negeb, and go up into the hill country, [18]and see what the land is like, and whether the people who live in it are strong or weak, whether they are few or many, [19]and whether the land they live in is good or bad, and whether the towns that they live in are unwalled or fortified, [20]and whether the land is rich or poor, and whether there are trees in it or not. Be bold, and bring some of the fruit of the land." Now it was the season of the first ripe grapes.

[21] So they went up and spied out the land from the wilderness of Zin to Rehob, near Lebo-hamath. [22]They went up into the Negeb, and came to Hebron; and Ahiman, Sheshai, and Talmai, the Anakites, were there. (Hebron was built seven years before Zoan in Egypt.) [23]And they came to the Wadi Eshcol, and cut down from there a branch with a single cluster of grapes, and they carried it on a pole between two of them. They also brought some pomegranates and figs. [24]That place was called the Wadi Eshcol,[y] because of the cluster that the Israelites cut down from there.

The Report of the Spies

[25] At the end of forty days they returned from spying out the land. [26]And they came to Moses and Aaron and to all the congregation of the Israelites in the wilderness of Paran, at Kadesh; they brought back word to them and to all the congregation, and showed them the fruit of the land. [27]And they told him, "We came to the land to which you sent us; it flows with milk and honey, and this is its fruit. [28]Yet the people who live in the land are strong, and the towns are fortified and very large; and besides, we saw the descendants of Anak there. [29]The Amalekites live in the land of the Negeb; the Hittites, the Jebusites, and the Amorites live in the hill country; and the Canaanites live by the sea, and along the Jordan."

[30] But Caleb quieted the people before Moses, and said, "Let us go up at once and occupy it, for we are well able to overcome it." [31]Then the men who had gone up with him said, "We are not able to go up against this people, for they are stronger than we." [32]So they brought to the Israelites an unfavorable report of the land that they had spied out, saying, "The land that we have gone through as spies is a land that devours its inhabitants; and all the people that we saw in it are of great size. [33]There we saw the Nephilim (the Anakites come from the Nephilim); and to ourselves we seemed like grasshoppers, and so we seemed to them."

The People Rebel

14 Then all the congregation raised a loud cry, and the people wept that night. [2]And all the

14.1 The Worst Rebellion

Chapter 14 records the tragic watershed of Numbers. Despite numerous proofs of God's power on their behalf, the Israelites cowered at the spies' report from Canaan. Fear led to open rebellion, and the nation plotted mutiny against Moses. At the very border of the promised land, theirs for the taking, they lost faith and turned away. In the face of such rebellion, God decided to wait for a whole new generation of Israelites; the original slaves would not cross into the promised land. All of them over the age of 20—except for Caleb and Joshua—were destined to fall as carcasses in the desert.

Israelites complained against Moses and Aaron; the whole congregation said to them, "Would that we had died in the land of Egypt! Or would that we had died in this wilderness! [3]Why is the

y That is Cluster

LORD bringing us into this land to fall by the sword? Our wives and our little ones will become booty; would it not be better for us to go back to Egypt?" ⁴So they said to one another, "Let us choose a captain, and go back to Egypt."

5 Then Moses and Aaron fell on their faces before all the assembly of the congregation of the Israelites. ⁶And Joshua son of Nun and Caleb son of Jephunneh, who were among those who had spied out the land, tore their clothes ⁷and said to all the congregation of the Israelites, "The land that we went through as spies is an exceedingly good land. ⁸If the LORD is pleased with us, he will bring us into this land and give it to us, a land that flows with milk and honey. ⁹Only, do not rebel against the LORD; and do not fear the people of the land, for they are no more than bread for us; their protection is removed from them, and the LORD is with us; do not fear them." ¹⁰But the whole congregation threatened to stone them.

Then the glory of the LORD appeared at the tent of meeting to all the Israelites. ¹¹And the LORD said to Moses, "How long will this people despise me? And how long will they refuse to believe in me, in spite of all the signs that I have done among them? ¹²I will strike them with pestilence and disinherit them, and I will make of you a nation greater and mightier than they."

Moses Intercedes for the People

13 But Moses said to the LORD, "Then the Egyptians will hear of it, for in your might you brought up this people from among them, ¹⁴and they will tell the inhabitants of this land. They have heard that you, O LORD, are in the midst of this people; for you, O LORD, are seen face to face, and your cloud stands over them and you go in front of them, in a pillar of cloud by day and in a pillar of fire by night. ¹⁵Now if you kill this people all at one time, then the nations who have heard about you will say, ¹⁶'It is because the LORD was not able to bring this people into the land he swore to give them that he has slaughtered them in the wilderness.' ¹⁷And now, therefore, let the power of the LORD be great in the way that you promised when you spoke, saying,
¹⁸ 'The LORD is slow to anger,
   and abounding in steadfast love,
   forgiving iniquity and transgression,
   but by no means clearing the guilty,
   visiting the iniquity of the parents
   upon the children
   to the third and the fourth generation.'
¹⁹Forgive the iniquity of this people according to the greatness of your steadfast love, just as you have pardoned this people, from Egypt even until now."

20 Then the LORD said, "I do forgive, just as you have asked; ²¹nevertheless—as I live, and as all the earth shall be filled with the glory of the LORD— ²²none of the people who have seen my glory and the signs that I did in Egypt and in the wilderness, and yet have tested me these ten times and have not obeyed my voice, ²³shall see the land that I swore to give to their ancestors; none of those who despised me shall see it. ²⁴But my servant Caleb, because he has a different spirit and has followed me wholeheartedly, I will bring into the land into which he went, and his descendants shall possess it. ²⁵Now, since the Amalekites and the Canaanites live in the valleys, turn tomorrow

AARON *Working Together . . . and Apart*

EXODUS 1 INTRODUCES US TO one of the Bible's most famous families: Two devout parents from the tribe of Levi and their children Aaron, Miriam and Moses. Surprisingly it was Moses, the younger brother, who got the Bible's star assignments, while the elder Aaron gained fame mainly as a substitute. For example, when God called Moses to free Israel from slavery, Moses shook like a coward. In response, God proposed teamwork. Moses' older brother Aaron would join Moses and make up for his weaknesses (Exodus 4.10–16).

The two worked side by side confronting Pharaoh, leading the Israelites out of Egypt, and calming the ornery people they were supposed to lead. Aaron's gifts in public speaking made up for Moses' stumbling speech, and so Aaron often accompanied Moses to meetings and did the talking. When God gave Moses the Law governing the new nation of Israel, Aaron and his sons were appointed priests. They and only they could lead in worship at the newly built tabernacle in the center of the camp (28.1).

Twice, however, Aaron thwarted teamwork, with disastrous results. While Moses was meeting with God on Mount Sinai, the people grew restless. Aaron came up with the idea of fashioning a golden idol for them to worship (chapter 32). On another occasion, Aaron and his sister openly carped about Moses' foreign-born wife and conspired to challenge his leadership (Numbers 12). Each time, God grew very angry at Aaron.

Aaron was an effective team player, but when he tried to go out on his own he got into trouble.

Life Questions: On what "teams" do you participate? What role do you usually play—starring or substitute?

and set out for the wilderness by the way to the Red Sea."z

An Attempted Invasion is Repulsed

26 And the LORD spoke to Moses and to Aaron, saying: 27How long shall this wicked congregation complain against me? I have heard the complaints of the Israelites, which they complain against me. 28Say to them, "As I live," says the LORD, "I will do to you the very things I heard you say: 29your dead bodies shall fall in this very wilderness; and of all your number, included in the census, from twenty years old and upward, who have complained against me, 30not one of you shall come into the land in which I swore to settle you, except Caleb son of Jephunneh and Joshua son of Nun. 31But your little ones, who you said would become booty, I will bring in, and they shall know the land that you have despised. 32But as for you, your dead bodies shall fall in this wilderness. 33And your children shall be shepherds in the wilderness for forty years, and shall suffer for your faithlessness, until the last of your dead bodies lies in the wilderness. 34According to the number of the days in which you spied out the land, forty days, for every day a year, you shall bear your iniquity, forty years, and you shall know my displeasure." 35I the LORD have spoken; surely I will do thus to all this wicked congregation gathered together against me: in this wilderness they shall come to a full end, and there they shall die.

36 And the men whom Moses sent to spy out the land, who returned and made all the congregation complain against him by bringing a bad report about the land— 37the men who brought an unfavorable report about the land died by a plague before the LORD. 38But Joshua son of Nun and Caleb son of Jephunneh alone remained alive, of those men who went to spy out the land.

39 When Moses told these words to all the

14.39 Imperfect Timing

When the Israelites heard how God would punish them for disobeying, they suddenly found the courage to go up and fight. God sought obedience, though, not courage, and obedience meant following directions immediately. Though Moses warned the Israelites that their courage came too late, and that God would not support them, they went anyway—and were soundly beaten.

Israelites, the people mourned greatly. 40They rose early in the morning and went up to the heights of the hill country, saying, "Here we are. We will go up to the place that the LORD has promised, for we have sinned." 41But Moses said, "Why do you continue to transgress the command of the LORD? That will not succeed. 42Do not go up, for the LORD is not with you; do not let yourselves be struck down before your enemies. 43For the Amalekites and the Canaanites will confront you there, and you shall fall by the sword; because you have turned back from following the LORD, the LORD will not be with you." 44But they presumed to go up to the heights of the hill country, even though the ark of the covenant of the LORD, and Moses, had not left the camp. 45Then the Amalekites and the Canaanites who lived in that hill country came down and defeated them, pursuing them as far as Hormah.

Various Offerings

15 The LORD spoke to Moses, saying: 2Speak to the Israelites and say to them: When you come into the land you are to inhabit, which I am giving you, 3and you make an offering by fire to the LORD from the herd or from the flock— whether a burnt offering or a sacrifice, to fulfill a vow or as a freewill offering or at your appointed festivals—to make a pleasing odor for the LORD, 4then whoever presents such an offering to the LORD shall present also a grain offering, one-tenth of an ephah of choice flour, mixed with one-fourth of a hin of oil. 5Moreover, you shall offer one-fourth of a hin of wine as a drink offering with the burnt offering or the sacrifice, for each lamb. 6For a ram, you shall offer a grain offering, two-tenths of an ephah of choice flour mixed with one-third of a hin of oil; 7and as a drink offering you shall offer one-third of a hin of wine, a pleasing odor to the LORD. 8When you offer a bull as a burnt offering or a sacrifice, to fulfill a vow or as an offering of well-being to the LORD, 9then you shall present with the bull a grain offering, three-tenths of an ephah of choice flour, mixed with half a hin of oil, 10and you shall present as a drink offering half a hin of wine, as an offering by fire, a pleasing odor to the LORD.

11 Thus it shall be done for each ox or ram, or for each of the male lambs or the kids. 12According to the number that you offer, so you shall do with each and every one. 13Every native Israelite shall do these things in this way, in presenting an offering by fire, a pleasing odor to the LORD. 14An alien who lives with you, or who takes up permanent residence among you, and wishes to offer an offering by fire, a pleasing odor to the LORD, shall do as you do. 15As for the assembly, there shall be for both you and the resident alien a single statute, a perpetual statute throughout your generations; you and the alien shall be alike before the LORD. 16You and the alien who resides with you shall have the same law and the same ordinance.

z Or *Sea of Reeds*

17 The LORD spoke to Moses, saying: [18]Speak to the Israelites and say to them: After you come into the land to which I am bringing you, [19]whenever you eat of the bread of the land, you shall present a donation to the LORD. [20]From your first batch of dough you shall present a loaf as a donation; you shall present it just as you present a donation from the threshing floor. [21]Throughout your generations you shall give to the LORD a donation from the first of your batch of dough.

22 But if you unintentionally fail to observe all these commandments that the LORD has spoken to Moses— [23]everything that the LORD has commanded you by Moses, from the day the LORD gave commandment and thereafter, throughout your generations— [24]then if it was done unintentionally without the knowledge of the congregation, the whole congregation shall offer one young bull for a burnt offering, a pleasing odor to the LORD, together with its grain offering and its drink offering, according to the ordinance, and one male goat for a sin offering. [25]The priest shall make atonement for all the congregation of the Israelites, and they shall be forgiven; it was unintentional, and they have brought their offering, an offering by fire to the LORD, and their sin offering before the LORD, for their error. [26]All the congregation of the Israelites shall be forgiven, as well as the aliens residing among them, because the whole people was involved in the error.

27 An individual who sins unintentionally shall present a female goat a year old for a sin offering. [28]And the priest shall make atonement before the LORD for the one who commits an error, when it is unintentional, to make atonement for the person, who then shall be forgiven. [29]For both the native among the Israelites and the alien residing among them—you shall have the same law for anyone who acts in error. [30]But whoever acts high-handedly, whether a native or an alien, affronts the LORD, and shall be cut off from among the people. [31]Because of having despised the word of the LORD and broken his commandment, such a person shall be utterly cut off and bear the guilt.

Penalty for Violating the Sabbath

32 When the Israelites were in the wilderness, they found a man gathering sticks on the sabbath day. [33]Those who found him gathering sticks brought him to Moses, Aaron, and to the whole congregation. [34]They put him in custody, because it was not clear what should be done to him. [35]Then the LORD said to Moses, "The man shall be put to death; all the congregation shall stone him outside the camp." [36]The whole congregation brought him outside the camp and stoned him to death, just as the LORD had commanded Moses.

Fringes on Garments

37 The LORD said to Moses: [38]Speak to the Israelites, and tell them to make fringes on the corners of their garments throughout their generations and to put a blue cord on the fringe at each

15.38 A Safeguard Against Lust

The Israelites had large reminders of God—such as the pillar of fire—and small ones: they wore tassels and blue cords on the corners of clothing to remind them of the Lord's commands. God specifically mentions this practice as a safeguard against lust—a reminder impossible to avoid for one tempted to adultery.

corner. [39]You have the fringe so that, when you see it, you will remember all the commandments of the LORD and do them, and not follow the lust of your own heart and your own eyes. [40]So you shall remember and do all my commandments, and you shall be holy to your God. [41]I am the LORD your God, who brought you out of the land of Egypt, to be your God: I am the LORD your God.

Revolt of Korah, Dathan, and Abiram

16 Now Korah son of Izhar son of Kohath son of Levi, along with Dathan and Abiram sons of Eliab, and On son of Peleth—descendants of Reuben—took [2]two hundred fifty Israelite men, leaders of the congregation, chosen from the assembly, well-known men,[a] and they confronted Moses. [3]They assembled against Moses and against Aaron, and said to them, "You have gone too far! All the congregation are holy, every one of them, and the LORD is among them. So why then do you exalt yourselves above the assembly of the LORD?" [4]When Moses heard it, he fell on his

16.3 Open Revolt

Two hundred and fifty well-known council members, led by Korah, Dathan, and Abiram, rebelled against Moses' leadership. They apparently wanted more people recognized as priests. But in a dramatic test, Moses showed that he was the leader God had chosen.

This rebellion and a second one immediately afterwards (verse 41) are the only two major events that the Bible mentions during the Israelites' 37 years of wandering in the desert. Deuteronomy, however (2.7; 8.4; 29.5–6), indicates the people were well cared for.

[a] Cn: Heb *and they confronted Moses, and two hundred fifty men . . . well-known men*

face. ⁵Then he said to Korah and all his company, "In the morning the LORD will make known who is his, and who is holy, and who will be allowed to approach him; the one whom he will choose he will allow to approach him. ⁶Do this: take censers, Korah and all your*b* company, ⁷and tomorrow put fire in them, and lay incense on them before the LORD; and the man whom the LORD chooses shall be the holy one. You Levites have gone too far!" ⁸Then Moses said to Korah, "Hear now, you Levites! ⁹Is it too little for you that the God of Israel has separated you from the congregation of Israel, to allow you to approach him in order to perform the duties of the LORD's tabernacle, and to stand before the congregation and serve them? ¹⁰He has allowed you to approach him, and all your brother Levites with you; yet you seek the priesthood as well! ¹¹Therefore you and all your company have gathered together against the LORD. What is Aaron that you rail against him?"

12 Moses sent for Dathan and Abiram sons of Eliab; but they said, "We will not come! ¹³Is it too little that you have brought us up out of a land flowing with milk and honey to kill us in the wilderness, that you must also lord it over us? ¹⁴It is clear you have not brought us into a land flowing with milk and honey, or given us an inheritance of fields and vineyards. Would you put out the eyes of these men? We will not come!"

15 Moses was very angry and said to the LORD, "Pay no attention to their offering. I have not taken one donkey from them, and I have not harmed any one of them." ¹⁶And Moses said to Korah, "As for you and all your company, be present tomorrow before the LORD, you and they and Aaron; ¹⁷and let each one of you take his censer, and put incense on it, and each one of you present his censer before the LORD, two hundred fifty censers; you also, and Aaron, each his censer." ¹⁸So each man took his censer, and they put fire in the censers and laid incense on them, and they stood at the entrance of the tent of meeting with Moses and Aaron. ¹⁹Then Korah assembled the whole congregation against them at the entrance of the tent of meeting. And the glory of the LORD appeared to the whole congregation.

20 Then the LORD spoke to Moses and to Aaron, saying: ²¹Separate yourselves from this congregation, so that I may consume them in a moment. ²²They fell on their faces, and said, "O God, the God of the spirits of all flesh, shall one person sin and you become angry with the whole congregation?"

23 And the LORD spoke to Moses, saying: ²⁴Say to the congregation: Get away from the dwellings of Korah, Dathan, and Abiram. ²⁵So Moses got up and went to Dathan and Abiram; the elders of Israel followed him. ²⁶He said to the congregation, "Turn away from the tents of these wicked men, and touch nothing of theirs, or you will be swept away for all their sins." ²⁷So they got away from the dwellings of Korah, Dathan, and Abiram; and Dathan and Abiram came out and stood at the entrance of their tents, together with their wives, their children, and their little ones. ²⁸And Moses said, "This is how you shall know that the LORD has sent me to do all these works; it has not been of my own accord: ²⁹If these people die a natural death, or if a natural fate comes on them, then the LORD has not sent me. ³⁰But if the LORD creates something new, and the ground opens its mouth and swallows them up, with all that belongs to them, and they go down alive into Sheol, then you shall know that these men have despised the LORD."

31 As soon as he finished speaking all these words, the ground under them was split apart. ³²The earth opened its mouth and swallowed them up, along with their households—everyone who belonged to Korah and all their goods. ³³So they with all that belonged to them went down alive into Sheol; the earth closed over them, and they perished from the midst of the assembly. ³⁴All Israel around them fled at their outcry, for they said, "The earth will swallow us too!" ³⁵And fire came out from the LORD and consumed the two hundred fifty men offering the incense.

36*c* Then the LORD spoke to Moses, saying: ³⁷Tell Eleazar son of Aaron the priest to take the censers out of the blaze; then scatter the fire far and wide. ³⁸For the censers of these sinners have become holy at the cost of their lives. Make them into hammered plates as a covering for the altar, for they presented them before the LORD and they became holy. Thus they shall be a sign to the Israelites. ³⁹So Eleazar the priest took the bronze censers that had been presented by those who were burned; and they were hammered out as a covering for the altar— ⁴⁰a reminder to the Israelites that no outsider, who is not of the descendants of Aaron, shall approach to offer incense before the LORD, so as not to become like Korah and his company—just as the LORD had said to him through Moses.

41 On the next day, however, the whole congregation of the Israelites rebelled against Moses and against Aaron, saying, "You have killed the people of the LORD." ⁴²And when the congregation had assembled against them, Moses and Aaron turned toward the tent of meeting; the cloud had covered it and the glory of the LORD appeared. ⁴³Then Moses and Aaron came to the front of the tent of meeting, ⁴⁴and the LORD spoke to Moses, saying, ⁴⁵"Get away from this congregation, so that I may consume them in a moment." And they fell on their faces. ⁴⁶Moses said to Aaron, "Take your censer, put fire on it from the altar and lay incense on it, and carry it quickly to the

b Heb *his*   *c* Ch 17.1 in Heb

congregation and make atonement for them. For wrath has gone out from the LORD; the plague has begun." 47So Aaron took it as Moses had ordered, and ran into the middle of the assembly, where the plague had already begun among the people. He put on the incense, and made atonement for the people. 48He stood between the dead and the living; and the plague was stopped. 49Those who died by the plague were fourteen thousand seven hundred, besides those who died in the affair of Korah. 50When the plague was stopped, Aaron returned to Moses at the entrance of the tent of meeting.

The Budding of Aaron's Rod

17 *d* The LORD spoke to Moses, saying: 2Speak to the Israelites, and get twelve staffs from them, one for each ancestral house, from all the leaders of their ancestral houses. Write each man's name on his staff, 3and write Aaron's name on the staff of Levi. For there shall be one staff for the head of each ancestral house. 4Place them in the tent of meeting before the covenant,*e* where I meet with you. 5And the staff of the man whom I choose shall sprout; thus I will put a stop to the complaints of the Israelites that they continually make against you. 6Moses spoke to the Israelites; and all their leaders gave him staffs, one for each leader, according to their ancestral houses, twelve staffs; and the staff of Aaron was among theirs. 7So Moses placed the staffs before the LORD in the tent of the covenant.*e*

8 When Moses went into the tent of the covenant*e* on the next day, the staff of Aaron for the house of Levi had sprouted. It put forth buds, produced blossoms, and bore ripe almonds. 9Then Moses brought out all the staffs from before the LORD to all the Israelites; and they looked, and each man took his staff. 10And the LORD said to Moses, "Put back the staff of Aaron before the covenant,*e* to be kept as a warning to rebels, so that you may make an end of their complaints

17.10 What's In the Ark

The ark of the covenant was the holiest sign of God's presence. In or near it were placed a few highly significant mementos of the journey to the promised land: the stone tablets of the law of Moses (Exodus 25.16), a jar of the miraculous manna (Exodus 16.33–34), and Aaron's sprouted staff. As a visible proof that God had chosen Aaron to be priest, the miraculous staff could help deter future rebellions.

against me, or else they will die." 11Moses did so; just as the LORD commanded him, so he did.

12 The Israelites said to Moses, "We are per-ishing; we are lost, all of us are lost! 13Everyone who approaches the tabernacle of the LORD will die. Are we all to perish?"

Responsibility of Priests and Levites

18 The LORD said to Aaron: You and your sons and your ancestral house with you shall bear responsibility for offenses connected with the sanctuary, while you and your sons alone shall bear responsibility for offenses connected with the priesthood. 2So bring with you also your brothers of the tribe of Levi, your ancestral tribe, in order that they may be joined to you, and serve you while you and your sons with you are in front of the tent of the covenant.*e* 3They shall perform duties for you and for the whole tent. But they must not approach either the utensils of the sanctuary or the altar, otherwise both they and you will die. 4They are attached to you in order to perform the duties of the tent of meeting, for all the service of the tent; no outsider shall approach you. 5You yourselves shall perform the duties of the sanctuary and the duties of the altar, so that wrath may never again come upon the Israelites. 6It is I who now take your brother Levites from among the Israelites; they are now yours as a gift, dedicated to the LORD, to perform the service of the tent of meeting. 7But you and your sons with you shall diligently perform your priestly duties in all that concerns the altar and the area behind the curtain. I give your priesthood as a gift; *f* any outsider who approaches shall be put to death.

The Priests' Portion

8 The LORD spoke to Aaron: I have given you charge of the offerings made to me, all the holy gifts of the Israelites; I have given them to you and your sons as a priestly portion due you in perpetuity. 9This shall be yours from the most holy things, reserved from the fire: every offering of theirs that they render to me as a most holy thing, whether grain offering, sin offering, or guilt offering, shall belong to you and your sons. 10As a most holy thing you shall eat it; every male may eat it; it shall be holy to you. 11This also is yours: I have given to you, together with your sons and daughters, as a perpetual due, whatever is set aside from the gifts of all the elevation offerings of the Israelites; everyone who is clean in your house may eat them. 12All the best of the oil and all the best of the wine and of the grain, the choice produce that they give to the LORD, I have given to you. 13The first fruits of all that is in their land, which they bring to the LORD, shall be yours; everyone who is clean in your house may eat of it. 14Every devoted thing in Israel shall be yours. 15The first issue of the womb of all creatures, human and animal, which is offered to the LORD, shall be yours; but the firstborn of human beings

---

d Ch 17.16 in Heb   *e* Or *treaty*, or *testimony*; Heb *eduth*   *f* Heb *as a service of gift*

you shall redeem, and the firstborn of unclean animals you shall redeem. ¹⁶Their redemption price, reckoned from one month of age, you shall fix at five shekels of silver, according to the shekel of the sanctuary (that is, twenty gerahs). ¹⁷But the firstborn of a cow, or the firstborn of a sheep, or the firstborn of a goat, you shall not redeem; they are holy. You shall dash their blood on the altar, and shall turn their fat into smoke as an offering by fire for a pleasing odor to the LORD; ¹⁸but their flesh shall be yours, just as the breast that is elevated and as the right thigh are yours. ¹⁹All the holy offerings that the Israelites present to the LORD I have given to you, together with your sons and daughters, as a perpetual due; it is a covenant of salt forever before the LORD for you and your descendants as well. ²⁰Then the LORD said to Aaron: You shall have no allotment in their land, nor shall you have any share among them; I am your share and your possession among the Israelites.

18.20 No Land for Levites

The tribe of Levites got special privileges, but in contrast to the wealthy priestly caste of, say, Egypt, they received no land. God himself was their share and inheritance. For food, they relied largely on offerings from other tribes. Thus the physical survival of "full-time ministers" depended on how faithful the other Israelites were.

21 To the Levites I have given every tithe in Israel for a possession in return for the service that they perform, the service in the tent of meeting. ²²From now on the Israelites shall no longer approach the tent of meeting, or else they will incur guilt and die. ²³But the Levites shall perform the service of the tent of meeting, and they shall bear responsibility for their own offenses; it shall be a perpetual statute throughout your generations. But among the Israelites they shall have no allotment, ²⁴because I have given to the Levites as their portion the tithe of the Israelites, which they set apart as an offering to the LORD. Therefore I have said of them that they shall have no allotment among the Israelites.

25 Then the LORD spoke to Moses, saying: ²⁶You shall speak to the Levites, saying: When you receive from the Israelites the tithe that I have given you from them for your portion, you shall set apart an offering from it to the LORD, a tithe of the tithe. ²⁷It shall be reckoned to you as your gift, the same as the grain of the threshing floor and the fullness of the wine press. ²⁸Thus you also shall set apart an offering to the LORD from all the tithes that you receive from the Israelites; and from them you shall give the LORD's offering to

the priest Aaron. ²⁹Out of all the gifts to you, you shall set apart every offering due to the LORD; the best of all of them is the part to be consecrated. ³⁰Say also to them: When you have set apart the best of it, then the rest shall be reckoned to the Levites as produce of the threshing floor, and as produce of the wine press. ³¹You may eat it in any place, you and your households; for it is your payment for your service in the tent of meeting. ³²You shall incur no guilt by reason of it, when you have offered the best of it. But you shall not profane the holy gifts of the Israelites, on pain of death.

Ceremony of the Red Heifer

19 The LORD spoke to Moses and Aaron, saying: ²This is a statute of the law that the LORD has commanded: Tell the Israelites to bring you a red heifer without defect, in which there is no blemish and on which no yoke has been laid. ³You shall give it to the priest Eleazar, and it shall be taken outside the camp and slaughtered in his presence. ⁴The priest Eleazar shall take some of its blood with his finger and sprinkle it seven times towards the front of the tent of meeting. ⁵Then the heifer shall be burned in his sight; its skin, its flesh, and its blood, with its dung, shall be burned. ⁶The priest shall take cedarwood, hyssop, and crimson material, and throw them into the fire in which the heifer is burning. ⁷Then the priest shall wash his clothes and bathe his body in water, and afterwards he may come into the camp; but the priest shall remain unclean until evening. ⁸The one who burns the heiferᵍ shall wash his clothes in water and bathe his body in water; he shall remain unclean until evening. ⁹Then someone who is clean shall gather up the ashes of the heifer, and deposit them outside the camp in a clean place; and they shall be kept for the congregation of the Israelites for the water for cleansing. It is a purification offering. ¹⁰The one who gathers the ashes of the heifer shall wash his clothes and be unclean until evening.

This shall be a perpetual statute for the Israelites and for the alien residing among them. ¹¹Those who touch the dead body of any human being shall be unclean seven days. ¹²They shall purify themselves with the water on the third day and on the seventh day, and so be clean; but if they do not purify themselves on the third day and on the seventh day, they will not become clean. ¹³All who touch a corpse, the body of a human being who has died, and do not purify themselves, defile the tabernacle of the LORD; such persons shall be cut off from Israel. Since water for cleansing was not dashed on them, they remain unclean; their uncleanness is still on them.

14 This is the law when someone dies in a tent: everyone who comes into the tent, and ev-

g Heb it

eryone who is in the tent, shall be unclean seven days. [15] And every open vessel with no cover fastened on it is unclean. [16] Whoever in the open field touches one who has been killed by a sword, or who has died naturally,[h] or a human bone, or a grave, shall be unclean seven days. [17] For the unclean they shall take some ashes of the burnt purification offering, and running water shall be added in a vessel; [18] then a clean person shall take hyssop, dip it in the water, and sprinkle it on the tent, on all the furnishings, on the persons who were there, and on whoever touched the bone, the slain, the corpse, or the grave. [19] The clean person shall sprinkle the unclean ones on the third day and on the seventh day, thus purifying them on the seventh day. Then they shall wash their clothes and bathe themselves in water, and at evening they shall be clean. [20] Any who are unclean but do not purify themselves, those persons shall be cut off from the assembly, for they have defiled the sanctuary of the LORD. Since the water for cleansing has not been dashed on them, they are unclean.

21 It shall be a perpetual statute for them. The one who sprinkles the water for cleansing shall wash his clothes, and whoever touches the water for cleansing shall be unclean until evening. [22] Whatever the unclean person touches shall be unclean, and anyone who touches it shall be unclean until evening.

The Waters of Meribah

20 The Israelites, the whole congregation, came into the wilderness of Zin in the first month, and the people stayed in Kadesh. Miriam died there, and was buried there.

2 Now there was no water for the congregation; so they gathered together against Moses and against Aaron. [3] The people quarreled with Moses and said, "Would that we had died when our kindred died before the LORD! [4] Why have you brought the assembly of the LORD into this wilderness for us and our livestock to die here? [5] Why have you brought us up out of Egypt, to bring us to this wretched place? It is no place for grain, or figs, or vines, or pomegranates; and there is no water to drink." [6] Then Moses and Aaron went away from the assembly to the entrance of the tent of meeting; they fell on their faces, and the glory of the LORD appeared to them. [7] The LORD spoke to Moses, saying: [8] Take the staff, and assemble the congregation, you and your brother Aaron, and command the rock before their eyes to yield its water. Thus you shall bring water out of the rock for them; thus you shall provide drink for the congregation and their livestock.

9 So Moses took the staff from before the LORD, as he had commanded him. [10] Moses and Aaron gathered the assembly together before the rock, and he said to them, "Listen, you rebels, shall we bring water for you out of this rock?" [11] Then Moses lifted up his hand and struck the rock twice with his staff; water came out abundantly, and the congregation and their livestock drank. [12] But the LORD said to Moses and Aaron, "Because you did not trust in me, to show my holiness before the eyes of the Israelites, therefore you shall not bring this assembly into the land

20.12 Moses' Sin

After so many displays of loyalty and courage, Moses faltered. Numbers does not specify exactly what Moses did that upset God. Was it striking the rock rather than speaking to it as God commanded? Regardless, Moses lashed out angrily against the Israelites and was faulted for his lack of trust in God. In Deuteronomy, God tells Moses, "you broke faith with me . . . by failing to maintain my holiness among the Israelites" (32.51).

The scene at Meribah brought a tragic end to a great man's career: Moses, footsore and weary, was told he too would die in the desert, before the Israelites crossed into the promised land. Deuteronomy 3.23–27 adds a postscript: Moses pleaded with God to reverse the punishment, and, when that failed, he threw the blame back on the Israelites.

that I have given them." [13] These are the waters of Meribah,[i] where the people of Israel quarreled with the LORD, and by which he showed his holiness.

Passage through Edom Refused

14 Moses sent messengers from Kadesh to the king of Edom, "Thus says your brother Israel: You know all the adversity that has befallen us: [15] how our ancestors went down to Egypt, and we lived in Egypt a long time; and the Egyptians oppressed us and our ancestors; [16] and when we

20.21 Blood Feud

Israel asked politely for the right to pass through Edom, offering to pay for water rights. Since the Edomites were distant relatives, descendants of Jacob's brother Esau, Israel expected a favorable response. Instead, Edom's refusal meant a long, hard detour. Moses warned the Israelites not to hate the Edomites, their kin (Deuteronomy 23.7–8). But for the rest of biblical history, there were wars and hatred between the two nations.

---

[h] Heb lacks *naturally*   [i] That is *Quarrel*

cried to the LORD, he heard our voice, and sent an angel and brought us out of Egypt; and here we are in Kadesh, a town on the edge of your territory. [17]Now let us pass through your land. We will not pass through field or vineyard, or drink water from any well; we will go along the King's Highway, not turning aside to the right hand or to the left until we have passed through your territory."

18 But Edom said to him, "You shall not pass through, or we will come out with the sword against you." [19]The Israelites said to him, "We will stay on the highway; and if we drink of your water, we and our livestock, then we will pay for it. It is only a small matter; just let us pass through on foot." [20]But he said, "You shall not pass through." And Edom came out against them with a large force, heavily armed. [21]Thus Edom refused to give Israel passage through their territory; so Israel turned away from them.

The Death of Aaron

22 They set out from Kadesh, and the Israelites, the whole congregation, came to Mount Hor. [23]Then the LORD said to Moses and Aaron at Mount Hor, on the border of the land of Edom, [24]"Let Aaron be gathered to his people. For he shall not enter the land that I have given to the Israelites, because you rebelled against my command at the waters of Meribah. [25]Take Aaron and his son Eleazar, and bring them up Mount Hor; [26]strip Aaron of his vestments, and put them on his son Eleazar. But Aaron shall be gathered to his people,[j] and shall die there." [27]Moses did as the LORD had commanded; they went up Mount Hor in the sight of the whole congregation. [28]Moses stripped Aaron of his vestments, and put them on his son Eleazar; and Aaron died there on the top of the mountain. Moses and Eleazar came down from the mountain. [29]When all the congregation saw that Aaron had died, all the house of Israel mourned for Aaron thirty days.

The Bronze Serpent

21 When the Canaanite, the king of Arad, who lived in the Negeb, heard that Israel was coming by the way of Atharim, he fought against Israel and took some of them captive. [2]Then Israel made a vow to the LORD and said, "If you will indeed give this people into our hands, then we will utterly destroy their towns." [3]The LORD listened to the voice of Israel, and handed over the Canaanites; and they utterly destroyed them and their towns; so the place was called Hormah.[k]

4 From Mount Hor they set out by the way to the Red Sea,[l] to go around the land of Edom; but the people became impatient on the way. [5]The people spoke against God and against Moses, "Why have you brought us up out of Egypt to die in the wilderness? For there is no food and no water, and we detest this miserable food." [6]Then the LORD sent poisonous[m] serpents among the people, and they bit the people, so that many Israelites died. [7]The people came to Moses and said, "We have sinned by speaking against the LORD and against you; pray to the LORD to take away the serpents from us." So Moses prayed for the people. [8]And the LORD said to Moses, "Make a poisonous[n] serpent, and set it on a pole; and everyone who is bitten shall look at it and live." [9]So Moses made a serpent of bronze, and put it upon a pole; and whenever a serpent bit someone, that person would look at the serpent of bronze and live.

21.9 Bronze Snake

Jesus chose this incident as one of the examples from Old Testament history that illustrates his own person and work (John 3.14). Through the snake and through Jesus, God provided a way of escape that required only faith from the people. In typical style, the Israelites corrupted the meaning by keeping the bronze snake as an idol to worship. Centuries later, King Hezekiah destroyed this image (2 Kings 18.4).

The Journey to Moab

10 The Israelites set out, and camped in Oboth. [11]They set out from Oboth, and camped at Iye-abarim, in the wilderness bordering Moab toward the sunrise. [12]From there they set out, and camped in the Wadi Zered. [13]From there they set out, and camped on the other side of the Arnon, in[o] the wilderness that extends from the boundary of the Amorites; for the Arnon is the boundary of Moab, between Moab and the Amorites. [14]Wherefore it is said in the Book of the Wars of the LORD,

"Waheb in Suphah and the wadis.

21.14 Out of Print

This quotation comes from a book no longer in existence. The Bible makes many mentions of such vanished books. Joshua 10.13 and 2 Samuel 1.18, for example, name the Book of Jashar. There are references to the works of various prophets or seers (Gad, Ahijah, Shemaiah) and many references to royal annals such as the book of the kings of Israel (1 Chronicles 9.1). Israel must have had a sizable library.

---

j Heb lacks *to his people*   *k* Heb *Destruction*   *l* Or *Sea of Reeds*   *m* Or *fiery*; Heb *seraphim*   *n* Or *fiery*; Heb *seraph*   *o* Gk: Heb *which is in*

The Arnon [15]and the slopes of the wadis
　that extend to the seat of Ar,
　and lie along the border of Moab." [p]
16 From there they continued to Beer;[q] that
is the well of which the LORD said to Moses,
"Gather the people together, and I will give them
water." [17]Then Israel sang this song:
　"Spring up, O well!—Sing to it!—
18 　the well that the leaders sank,
　that the nobles of the people dug,
　with the scepter, with the staff."
From the wilderness to Mattanah, [19]from Mattanah to Nahaliel, from Nahaliel to Bamoth, [20]and
from Bamoth to the valley lying in the region of
Moab by the top of Pisgah that overlooks the
wasteland.[r]

King Sihon Defeated

21 Then Israel sent messengers to King Sihon
of the Amorites, saying, [22]"Let me pass through
your land; we will not turn aside into field or
vineyard; we will not drink the water of any well;
we will go by the King's Highway until we have
passed through your territory." [23]But Sihon
would not allow Israel to pass through his territory. Sihon gathered all his people together, and
went out against Israel to the wilderness; he came
to Jahaz, and fought against Israel. [24]Israel put
him to the sword, and took possession of his land
from the Arnon to the Jabbok, as far as to the
Ammonites; for the boundary of the Ammonites
was strong. [25]Israel took all these towns, and Israel settled in all the towns of the Amorites, in
Heshbon, and in all its villages. [26]For Heshbon
was the city of King Sihon of the Amorites, who
had fought against the former king of Moab and
captured all his land as far as the Arnon. [27]There-
fore the ballad singers say,
　"Come to Heshbon, let it be built;
　　let the city of Sihon be established.
28 　For fire came out from Heshbon,
　　flame from the city of Sihon.
　It devoured Ar of Moab,
　　and swallowed up[s] the heights of the
　　　Arnon.
29 　Woe to you, O Moab!
　　You are undone, O people of
　　　Chemosh!
　He has made his sons fugitives,
　　and his daughters captives,
　　to an Amorite king, Sihon.
30 　So their posterity perished
　　from Heshbon[t] to Dibon,
　　and we laid waste until fire spread to
　　　Medeba."[u]
31 Thus Israel settled in the land of the Amorites. [32]Moses sent to spy out Jazer; and they cap-

tured its villages, and dispossessed the Amorites
who were there.

King Og Defeated

33 Then they turned and went up the road to
Bashan; and King Og of Bashan came out against
them, he and all his people, to battle at Edrei.
[34]But the LORD said to Moses, "Do not be afraid
of him; for I have given him into your hand, with
all his people, and all his land. You shall do to him
as you did to King Sihon of the Amorites, who
ruled in Heshbon." [35]So they killed him, his sons,
and all his people, until there was no survivor left;
and they took possession of his land.

Balak Summons Balaam to Curse Israel

22 The Israelites set out, and camped in the
plains of Moab across the Jordan from Jericho. [2]Now Balak son of Zippor saw all that Israel
had done to the Amorites. [3]Moab was in great
dread of the people, because they were so numerous; Moab was overcome with fear of the people
of Israel. [4]And Moab said to the elders of Midian,
"This horde will now lick up all that is around us,
as an ox licks up the grass of the field." Now Balak
son of Zippor was king of Moab at that time. [5]He
sent messengers to Balaam son of Beor at Pethor,
which is on the Euphrates, in the land of Amaw,[v]
to summon him, saying, "A people has come out
of Egypt; they have spread over the face of the
earth, and they have settled next to me. [6]Come
now, curse this people for me, since they are
stronger than I; perhaps I shall be able to defeat
them and drive them from the land; for I know
that whomever you bless is blessed, and whomever you curse is cursed."
7 So the elders of Moab and the elders of
Midian departed with the fees for divination in
their hand; and they came to Balaam, and gave
him Balak's message. [8]He said to them, "Stay here
tonight, and I will bring back word to you, just as
the LORD speaks to me"; so the officials of Moab
stayed with Balaam. [9]God came to Balaam and
said, "Who are these men with you?" [10]Balaam
said to God, "King Balak son of Zippor of Moab,
has sent me this message: [11]'A people has come
out of Egypt and has spread over the face of the
earth; now come, curse them for me; perhaps I
shall be able to fight against them and drive them
out.'" [12]God said to Balaam, "You shall not go
with them; you shall not curse the people, for they
are blessed." [13]So Balaam rose in the morning,
and said to the officials of Balak, "Go to your own
land, for the LORD has refused to let me go with
you." [14]So the officials of Moab rose and went
to Balak, and said, "Balaam refuses to come
with us."
15 Once again Balak sent officials, more nu-

---

[p] Meaning of Heb uncertain　　[q] That is Well　　[r] Or Jeshimon　　[s] Gk: Heb and the lords of　　[t] Gk: Heb we have
shot at them; Heshbon has perished　　[u] Compare Sam Gk: Meaning of MT uncertain　　[v] Or land of his kinsfolk

merous and more distinguished than these.
[16]They came to Balaam and said to him, "Thus
says Balak son of Zippor: 'Do not let anything
hinder you from coming to me; [17]for I will surely
do you great honor, and whatever you say to me
I will do; come, curse this people for me.'" [18]But
Balaam replied to the servants of Balak, "Although Balak were to give me his house full of
silver and gold, I could not go beyond the command of the LORD my God, to do less or more.
[19]You remain here, as the others did, so that I
may learn what more the LORD may say to me."
[20]That night God came to Balaam and said to
him, "If the men have come to summon you, get
up and go with them; but do only what I tell you
to do." [21]So Balaam got up in the morning, saddled his donkey, and went with the officials of
Moab.

Balaam, the Donkey, and the Angel

22 God's anger was kindled because he was
going, and the angel of the LORD took his stand in
the road as his adversary. Now he was riding on
the donkey, and his two servants were with him.
[23]The donkey saw the angel of the LORD standing
in the road, with a drawn sword in his hand; so
the donkey turned off the road, and went into the
field; and Balaam struck the donkey, to turn it
back onto the road. [24]Then the angel of the LORD
stood in a narrow path between the vineyards,
with a wall on either side. [25]When the donkey saw
the angel of the LORD, it scraped against the wall,
and scraped Balaam's foot against the wall; so he
struck it again. [26]Then the angel of the LORD went
ahead, and stood in a narrow place, where there
was no way to turn either to the right or to the
left. [27]When the donkey saw the angel of the
LORD, it lay down under Balaam; and Balaam's
anger was kindled, and he struck the donkey with
his staff. [28]Then the LORD opened the mouth of
the donkey, and it said to Balaam, "What have I
done to you, that you have struck me these three
times?" [29]Balaam said to the donkey, "Because
you have made a fool of me! I wish I had a sword
in my hand! I would kill you right now!" [30]But the
donkey said to Balaam, "Am I not your donkey,
which you have ridden all your life to this day?
Have I been in the habit of treating you this way?"
And he said, "No."

31 Then the LORD opened the eyes of Balaam,
and he saw the angel of the LORD standing in the
road, with his drawn sword in his hand; and he
bowed down, falling on his face. [32]The angel of
the LORD said to him, "Why have you struck your
donkey these three times? I have come out as an
adversary, because your way is perverse[w] before
me. [33]The donkey saw me, and turned away from
me these three times. If it had not turned away
from me, surely just now I would have killed you

and let it live." [34]Then Balaam said to the angel of
the LORD, "I have sinned, for I did not know that
you were standing in the road to oppose me. Now
therefore, if it is displeasing to you, I will return
home." [35]The angel of the LORD said to Balaam,
"Go with the men; but speak only what I tell you
to speak." So Balaam went on with the officials of
Balak.

36 When Balak heard that Balaam had come,
he went out to meet him at Ir-moab, on the
boundary formed by the Arnon, at the farthest
point of the boundary. [37]Balak said to Balaam,
"Did I not send to summon you? Why did you
not come to me? Am I not able to honor you?"
[38]Balaam said to Balak, "I have come to you now,
but do I have power to say just anything? The
word God puts in my mouth, that is what I must
say." [39]Then Balaam went with Balak, and they
came to Kiriath-huzoth. [40]Balak sacrificed oxen
and sheep, and sent them to Balaam and to the
officials who were with him.

Balaam's First Oracle

41 On the next day Balak took Balaam and
brought him up to Bamoth-baal; and from there
he could see part of the people of Israel.[x] [1]Then

23 Balaam said to Balak, "Build me seven
altars here, and prepare seven bulls and
seven rams for me." [2]Balak did as Balaam had
said; and Balak and Balaam offered a bull and a
ram on each altar. [3]Then Balaam said to Balak,
"Stay here beside your burnt offerings while I go
aside. Perhaps the LORD will come to meet me.
Whatever he shows me I will tell you." And he
went to a bare height.

4 Then God met Balaam; and Balaam said to
him, "I have arranged the seven altars, and have
offered a bull and a ram on each altar." [5]The LORD
put a word in Balaam's mouth, and said, "Return
to Balak, and this is what you must say." [6]So he
returned to Balak,[y] who was standing beside his
burnt offerings with all the officials of Moab.
[7]Then Balaam[z] uttered his oracle, saying:

"Balak has brought me from Aram,
 the king of Moab from the eastern
  mountains:
'Come, curse Jacob for me;
 Come, denounce Israel!'
8 How can I curse whom God has not
  cursed?
 How can I denounce those whom the
  LORD has not denounced?
9 For from the top of the crags I see him,
  from the hills I behold him;
 Here is a people living alone,
  and not reckoning itself among the
   nations!
10 Who can count the dust of Jacob,
  or number the dust-cloud[a] of Israel?

---

w Meaning of Heb uncertain   x Heb lacks *of Israel*   y Heb *him*   z Heb *he*   a Or *fourth part*

Let me die the death of the upright,
and let my end be like his!"

11 Then Balak said to Balaam, "What have you done to me? I brought you to curse my enemies, but now you have done nothing but bless them." 12He answered, "Must I not take care to say what the LORD puts into my mouth?"

Balaam's Second Oracle

13 So Balak said to him, "Come with me to another place from which you may see them; you shall see only part of them, and shall not see them all; then curse them for me from there." 14So he took him to the field of Zophim, to the top of Pisgah. He built seven altars, and offered a bull and a ram on each altar. 15Balaam said to Balak, "Stand here beside your burnt offerings, while I meet the LORD over there." 16The LORD met Balaam, put a word into his mouth, and said, "Return to Balak, and this is what you shall say." 17When he came to him, he was standing beside his burnt offerings with the officials of Moab. Balak said to him, "What has the LORD said?" 18Then Balaam uttered his oracle, saying:

"Rise, Balak, and hear;
listen to me, O son of Zippor:
19 God is not a human being, that he should lie,

Whose Side Is Balaam On?

A balky prophet, a talking donkey, and a furious king

NUMBERS 22–24 CONTAINS ONE OF the most bizarre stories in the entire Bible. It features a donkey speaking fluent Hebrew and showing more insight than a prophet. One man is at the center of the story, the mysterious character named Balaam.

Balaam was evidently a professional magician of a nomadic clan somewhat like the gypsies. He had an impressive reputation: Nearby kings alarmed by the Israelites hired him to work magic and get the gods on their side.

> Balak said to Balaam, "What have you done to me? I brought you to curse my enemies, but now you have done nothing but bless them." 23.11

Prophet for Hire

Numbers gives enough detail to paint a colorful, dramatic story, but even so, Balaam is cloaked in a fog of mystery. Clearly, God chose to speak through him—he communicated directly to Balaam seven times. Just as clearly, Balaam proved a reluctant prophet, subject to ambition and a handsome bribe. Even his own donkey rebuked him, in the only biblical account of an animal speaking. An angel gave not Balaam, but the donkey, high praise.

Balaam appeared at a solemn occasion designed to curse the Israelites, but instead he pronounced blessings on them and curses on their enemies. He gave four stirring messages, far different in content from what his employer wanted to hear.

"How can I curse whom God has not cursed?" Balaam asked (23.8). His magnificent prophecies shine out from scenes of comic irony. Balaam grew bolder and bolder, changing from a sorcerer into a prophet with backbone.

Prophet or Traitor?

Numbers 22–24 presents Balaam as an apparent convert. Tragically, the changes in him were only temporary. Balaam next appears in Numbers 31.8, the slain victim of an Israelite raid. Outright condemnations in 2 Peter 2.15, Jude 11, and Revelation 2.14 indicate that Balaam quickly returned to his treacherous ways. Having failed to manipulate the Israelites' God for his purposes, he resorted to manipulating the Israelites themselves. He convinced other nations to seduce them with sex and the worship of false gods. His actions led to the deaths of 24,000 people (25.9).

Some have called Balaam the Judas of the Old Testament, and certain parallels do emerge. Both men came close enough to truth to appear sincere and faithful. For a time, both seemed to serve the true God. But, motivated by ambition and greed, they renounced God and turned against him, with catastrophic results.

Part of a Bigger Battle

Seven books of the Bible refer to Balaam. The importance given to his story implies that it stood as a key event in the Israelites' relationship to pagan cultures. The Israelites were about to enter a land where magic and sorcery were used as national weapons. In a stroke of irony, God selected a spokesman who was both magician and pagan. Through him God rebuked those nations and their false gods.

Life Questions: Have you ever been used by God despite your own reluctance?

or a mortal, that he should change his
　　mind.
Has he promised, and will he not do it?
　　Has he spoken, and will he not fulfill
　　it?
20　See, I received a command to bless;
　　he has blessed, and I cannot revoke it.
21　He has not beheld misfortune in Jacob;
　　nor has he seen trouble in Israel.
The LORD their God is with them,
　　acclaimed as a king among them.
22　God, who brings them out of Egypt,
　　is like the horns of a wild ox for them.
23　Surely there is no enchantment against
　　　　Jacob,
　　no divination against Israel;
　　now it shall be said of Jacob and Israel,
　　'See what God has done!'
24　Look, a people rising up like a lioness,
　　and rousing itself like a lion!
　　It does not lie down until it has eaten the
　　　　prey
　　and drunk the blood of the slain.'"

25　Then Balak said to Balaam, "Do not curse
them at all, and do not bless them at all." 26But
Balaam answered Balak, "Did I not tell you,
'Whatever the LORD says, that is what I must
do'?"

27　So Balak said to Balaam, "Come now, I
will take you to another place; perhaps it will
please God that you may curse them for me from
there." 28So Balak took Balaam to the top of Peor,
which overlooks the wasteland.*b* 29Balaam said to
Balak, "Build me seven altars here, and prepare
seven bulls and seven rams for me." 30So Balak
did as Balaam had said, and offered a bull and a
ram on each altar.

Balaam's Third Oracle

24 Now Balaam saw that it pleased the LORD
　　to bless Israel, so he did not go, as at other
times, to look for omens, but set his face toward
the wilderness. 2Balaam looked up and saw Israel
camping tribe by tribe. Then the spirit of God
came upon him, 3and he uttered his oracle, saying:
"The oracle of Balaam son of Beor,
　　the oracle of the man whose eye is
　　　　clear,*c*
4　the oracle of one who hears the words of
　　　　God,
　　who sees the vision of the Almighty,*d*
　　who falls down, but with eyes
　　　　uncovered:
5　how fair are your tents, O Jacob,
　　your encampments, O Israel!
6　Like palm groves that stretch far away,
　　like gardens beside a river,

like aloes that the LORD has planted,
　　like cedar trees beside the waters.
7　Water shall flow from his buckets,
　　and his seed shall have abundant water,
his king shall be higher than Agag,
　　and his kingdom shall be exalted.
8　God who brings him out of Egypt,
　　is like the horns of a wild ox for him;
he shall devour the nations that are his
　　　　foes
　　and break their bones.
He shall strike with his arrows.*e*
9　He crouched, he lay down like a lion,
　　and like a lioness; who will rouse him
　　　　up?
Blessed is everyone who blesses you,
　　and cursed is everyone who curses you."

10　Then Balak's anger was kindled against
Balaam, and he struck his hands together. Balak
said to Balaam, "I summoned you to curse my
enemies, but instead you have blessed them these
three times. 11Now be off with you! Go home! I
said, 'I will reward you richly,' but the LORD has
denied you any reward." 12And Balaam said to
Balak, "Did I not tell your messengers whom you
sent to me, 13'If Balak should give me his house
full of silver and gold, I would not be able to go
beyond the word of the LORD, to do either good
or bad of my own will; what the LORD says, that
is what I will say'? 14So now, I am going to my
people; let me advise you what this people will do
to your people in days to come."

Balaam's Fourth Oracle

15　So he uttered his oracle, saying:
"The oracle of Balaam son of Beor,
　　the oracle of the man whose eye is
　　　　clear,*c*
16　the oracle of one who hears the words of
　　　　God,
　　and knows the knowledge of the Most
　　　　High,*f*
who sees the vision of the Almighty,*d*
　　who falls down, but with his eyes
　　　　uncovered:
17　I see him, but not now;
　　I behold him, but not near—
a star shall come out of Jacob,
　　and a scepter shall rise out of Israel;

24.17 Balaam's Prophecy

*This prediction delivered by Balaam came true
during the reign of King David, who crushed
the nations of Moab and Edom (2 Samuel
8.2,14).*

---

b Or *overlooks Jeshimon*　　*c* Or *closed* or *open*　　*d* Traditional rendering of Heb *Shaddai*　　*e* Meaning of Heb
uncertain　　*f* Or *of Elyon*

it shall crush the borderlands^g of Moab,
and the territory^h of all the Shethites.
18 Edom will become a possession,
Seir a possession of its enemies,^{i}
while Israel does valiantly.
19 One out of Jacob shall rule,
and destroy the survivors of Ir."
20 Then he looked on Amalek, and uttered
his oracle, saying:
"First among the nations was Amalek,
but its end is to perish forever."
21 Then he looked on the Kenite, and uttered
his oracle, saying:
"Enduring is your dwelling place,
and your nest is set in the rock;
22 yet Kain is destined for burning.
How long shall Asshur take you away
captive?"
23 Again he uttered his oracle, saying:
"Alas, who shall live when God does this?
24 But ships shall come from Kittim
and shall afflict Asshur and Eber;
and he also shall perish forever."
25 Then Balaam got up and went back to his
place, and Balak also went his way.

Worship of Baal of Peor

25 While Israel was staying at Shittim, the
people began to have sexual relations with

25.1 Sexual Seduction

*Militarily, Israel was doing well. Their enemies
were terrified (22.3), and the man summoned
to put a curse on Israel had instead spoken
God's blessing (24.8–9). But the Israelites were
vulnerable to sexual temptation. Moabite
women offered sexual favors, then invited the
foreigners to local religious services. (Numbers
31.16 reports that Balaam suggested the tactic.)
It is an old method of subverting God's people,
and it still works.*

the women of Moab. 2These invited the people to
the sacrifices of their gods, and the people ate and
bowed down to their gods. 3Thus Israel yoked
itself to the Baal of Peor, and the LORD's anger was
kindled against Israel. 4The LORD said to Moses,
"Take all the chiefs of the people, and impale
them in the sun before the LORD, in order that the
fierce anger of the LORD may turn away from
Israel." 5And Moses said to the judges of Israel,
"Each of you shall kill any of your people who
have yoked themselves to the Baal of Peor."
6 Just then one of the Israelites came and
brought a Midianite woman into his family, in the
sight of Moses and in the sight of the whole congregation of the Israelites, while they were weeping at the entrance of the tent of meeting. 7When
Phinehas son of Eleazar, son of Aaron the priest,
saw it, he got up and left the congregation. Taking
a spear in his hand, 8he went after the Israelite
man into the tent, and pierced the two of them,
the Israelite and the woman, through the belly. So
the plague was stopped among the people of Israel. 9Nevertheless those that died by the plague
were twenty-four thousand.
10 The LORD spoke to Moses, saying: 11"Phinehas son of Eleazar, son of Aaron the priest, has
turned back my wrath from the Israelites by man-
ifesting such zeal among them on my behalf that
in my jealousy I did not consume the Israelites.
12Therefore say, 'I hereby grant him my covenant
of peace. 13It shall be for him and for his descendants after him a covenant of perpetual priesthood, because he was zealous for his God, and
made atonement for the Israelites.'"
14 The name of the slain Israelite man, who
was killed with the Midianite woman, was Zimri
son of Salu, head of an ancestral house belonging
to the Simeonites. 15The name of the Midianite
woman who was killed was Cozbi daughter of
Zur, who was the head of a clan, an ancestral
house in Midian.
16 The LORD said to Moses, 17"Harass the
Midianites, and defeat them; 18for they have harassed you by the trickery with which they deceived you in the affair of Peor, and in the affair
of Cozbi, the daughter of a leader of Midian, their
sister; she was killed on the day of the plague that
resulted from Peor."

A Census of the New Generation

26 After the plague the LORD said to Moses
and to Eleazar son of Aaron the priest,
2"Take a census of the whole congregation of the
Israelites, from twenty years old and upward, by
their ancestral houses, everyone in Israel able to
go to war." 3Moses and Eleazar the priest spoke
with them in the plains of Moab by the Jordan
opposite Jericho, saying, 4"Take a census of the
people,^{j} from twenty years old and upward," as
the LORD commanded Moses.
The Israelites, who came out of the land of
Egypt, were:
5 Reuben, the firstborn of Israel. The descendants of Reuben: of Hanoch, the clan of the Ha-
nochites; of Pallu, the clan of the Palluites; 6of
Hezron, the clan of the Hezronites; of Carmi, the
clan of the Carmites. 7These are the clans of the
Reubenites; the number of those enrolled was
forty-three thousand seven hundred thirty. 8And
the descendants of Pallu: Eliab. 9The descendants
of Eliab: Nemuel, Dathan, and Abiram. These are

---

^{g} Or *forehead* ^{h} Some Mss read *skull* ^{i} Heb *Seir, its enemies, a possession* ^{j} Heb lacks *take a census of the people*:
Compare verse 2

the same Dathan and Abiram, chosen from the congregation, who rebelled against Moses and Aaron in the company of Korah, when they rebelled against the LORD, [10]and the earth opened its mouth and swallowed them up along with Korah, when that company died, when the fire devoured two hundred fifty men; and they became a warning. [11]Notwithstanding, the sons of Korah did not die.

12 The descendants of Simeon by their clans: of Nemuel, the clan of the Nemuelites; of Jamin, the clan of the Jaminites; of Jachin, the clan of the Jachinites; [13]of Zerah, the clan of the Zerahites; of Shaul, the clan of the Shaulites.[k] [14]These are the clans of the Simeonites, twenty-two thousand two hundred.

15 The children of Gad by their clans: of Zephon, the clan of the Zephonites; of Haggi, the clan of the Haggites; of Shuni, the clan of the Shunites; [16]of Ozni, the clan of the Oznites; of Eri, the clan of the Erites; [17]of Arod, the clan of the Arodites; of Areli, the clan of the Arelites. [18]These are the clans of the Gadites: the number of those enrolled was forty thousand five hundred.

19 The sons of Judah: Er and Onan; Er and Onan died in the land of Canaan. [20]The descendants of Judah by their clans were: of Shelah, the clan of the Shelanites; of Perez, the clan of the Perezites; of Zerah, the clan of the Zerahites. [21]The descendants of Perez were: of Hezron, the clan of the Hezronites; of Hamul, the clan of the Hamulites. [22]These are the clans of Judah: the number of those enrolled was seventy-six thousand five hundred.

23 The descendants of Issachar by their clans: of Tola, the clan of the Tolaites; of Puvah, the clan of the Punites; [24]of Jashub, the clan of the Jashubites; of Shimron, the clan of the Shimronites. [25]These are the clans of Issachar: sixty-four thousand three hundred enrolled.

26 The descendants of Zebulun by their clans: of Sered, the clan of the Seredites; of Elon, the clan of the Elonites; of Jahleel, the clan of the Jahleelites. [27]These are the clans of the Zebulunites; the number of those enrolled was sixty thousand five hundred.

28 The sons of Joseph by their clans: Manasseh and Ephraim. [29]The descendants of Manasseh: of Machir, the clan of the Machirites; and Machir was the father of Gilead; of Gilead, the clan of the Gileadites. [30]These are the descendants of Gilead: of Iezer, the clan of the Iezerites; of Helek, the clan of the Helekites; [31]and of Asriel, the clan of the Asrielites; and of Shechem, the clan of the Shechemites; [32]and of Shemida, the clan of the Shemidaites; and of Hepher, the clan of the Hepherites. [33]Now Zelophehad son of Hepher had no sons, but daughters: and the names of the daughters of Zelophehad were Mahlah, Noah, Hoglah, Milcah, and Tirzah. [34]These are the clans of Manasseh; the number of those enrolled was fifty-two thousand seven hundred.

35 These are the descendants of Ephraim according to their clans: of Shuthelah, the clan of the Shuthelahites; of Becher, the clan of the Becherites; of Tahan, the clan of the Tahanites. [36]And these are the descendants of Shuthelah: of Eran, the clan of the Eranites. [37]These are the clans of the Ephraimites: the number of those enrolled was thirty-two thousand five hundred. These are the descendants of Joseph by their clans.

38 The descendants of Benjamin by their clans: of Bela, the clan of the Belaites; of Ashbel, the clan of the Ashbelites; of Ahiram, the clan of the Ahiramites; [39]of Shephupham, the clan of the Shuphamites; of Hupham, the clan of the Huphamites. [40]And the sons of Bela were Ard and Naaman: of Ard, the clan of the Ardites; of Naaman, the clan of the Naamites. [41]These are the descendants of Benjamin by their clans; the number of those enrolled was forty-five thousand six hundred.

42 These are the descendants of Dan by their clans: of Shuham, the clan of the Shuhamites. These are the clans of Dan by their clans. [43]All the clans of the Shuhamites: sixty-four thousand four hundred enrolled.

44 The descendants of Asher by their families: of Imnah, the clan of the Imnites; of Ishvi, the clan of the Ishvites; of Beriah, the clan of the Berites. [45]Of the descendants of Beriah: of Heber, the clan of the Heberites; of Malchiel, the clan of the Malchielites. [46]And the name of the daughter of Asher was Serah. [47]These are the clans of the Asherites: the number of those enrolled was fifty-three thousand four hundred.

48 The descendants of Naphtali by their clans: of Jahzeel, the clan of the Jahzeelites; of Guni, the clan of the Gunites; [49]of Jezer, the clan of the Jezerites; of Shillem, the clan of the Shillemites. [50]These are the Naphtalites[l] by their clans: the number of those enrolled was forty-five thousand four hundred.

51 This was the number of the Israelites enrolled: six hundred and one thousand seven hundred thirty.

52 The LORD spoke to Moses, saying: [53]To these the land shall be apportioned for inheritance according to the number of names. [54]To a large tribe you shall give a large inheritance, and to a small tribe you shall give a small inheritance; every tribe shall be given its inheritance according to its enrollment. [55]But the land shall be apportioned by lot; according to the names of their ancestral tribes they shall inherit. [56]Their inheritance shall be apportioned according to lot between the larger and the smaller.

---

[k] Or Saul . . . Saulites   [l] Heb clans of Naphtali

57 This is the enrollment of the Levites by their clans: of Gershon, the clan of the Gershonites; of Kohath, the clan of the Kohathites; of Merari, the clan of the Merarites. 58These are the clans of Levi: the clan of the Libnites, the clan of the Hebronites, the clan of the Mahlites, the clan of the Mushites, the clan of the Korahites. Now Kohath was the father of Amram. 59The name of Amram's wife was Jochebed daughter of Levi, who was born to Levi in Egypt; and she bore to Amram: Aaron, Moses, and their sister Miriam. 60To Aaron were born Nadab, Abihu, Eleazar, and Ithamar. 61But Nadab and Abihu died when they offered unholy fire before the LORD. 62The number of those enrolled was twenty-three thousand, every male one month old and upward; for they were not enrolled among the Israelites because there was no allotment given to them among the Israelites.

63 These were those enrolled by Moses and Eleazar the priest, who enrolled the Israelites in the plains of Moab by the Jordan opposite Jericho. 64Among these there was not one of those enrolled by Moses and Aaron the priest, who had enrolled the Israelites in the wilderness of Sinai. 65For the LORD had said of them, "They shall die in the wilderness." Not one of them was left, except Caleb son of Jephunneh and Joshua son of Nun.

The Daughters of Zelophehad

27 Then the daughters of Zelophehad came forward. Zelophehad was son of Hepher son of Gilead son of Machir son of Manasseh son of Joseph, a member of the Manassite clans. The names of his daughters were: Mahlah, Noah, Hoglah, Milcah, and Tirzah. 2They stood before Moses, Eleazar the priest, the leaders, and all the congregation, at the entrance of the tent of meeting, and they said, 3"Our father died in the wilderness; he was not among the company of those who gathered themselves together against the LORD in the company of Korah, but died for his own sin; and he had no sons. 4Why should the name of our father be taken away from his clan because he had no son? Give to us a possession among our father's brothers."

5 Moses brought their case before the LORD. 6And the LORD spoke to Moses, saying: 7The daughters of Zelophehad are right in what they are saying; you shall indeed let them possess an inheritance among their father's brothers and pass the inheritance of their father on to them. 8You shall also say to the Israelites, "If a man dies, and has no son, then you shall pass his inheritance on to his daughter. 9If he has no daughter, then you shall give his inheritance to his brothers. 10If he has no brothers, then you shall give his inheritance to his father's brothers. 11And if his father has no brothers, then you shall give his inheritance to the nearest kinsman of his clan, and he shall possess it. It shall be for the Israelites a statute and ordinance, as the LORD commanded Moses."

Joshua Appointed Moses' Successor

12 The LORD said to Moses, "Go up this mountain of the Abarim range, and see the land that I have given to the Israelites. 13When you have seen it, you also shall be gathered to your people, as your brother Aaron was, 14because you rebelled against my word in the wilderness of Zin when the congregation quarreled with me.*m* You did not show my holiness before their eyes at the waters." (These are the waters of Meribath-kadesh in the wilderness of Zin.) 15Moses spoke to the LORD, saying, 16"Let the LORD, the God of the spirits of all flesh, appoint someone over the congregation 17who shall go out before them and come in before them, who shall lead them out and bring them in, so that the congregation of the LORD may not be like sheep without a shepherd." 18So the LORD said to Moses, "Take Joshua son of Nun, a man in whom is the spirit, and lay your hand upon him; 19have him stand before Eleazar the priest and all the congregation, and commission him in their sight. 20You shall give him some

26.51 Recount

The two censuses in Numbers (chapter 1 and here) stand like bookends, marking the hopeful beginning and tragic end of the vast numbers of Israelites heading toward freedom. After 40 years, the totals were nearly the same— 600,000 men—but only two of the original pilgrims would cross the Jordan River. The nation renewed itself like a human body, which looks the same but replaces all its cells every few years.

27.14 Moses Stayed Out

Because Moses had disobeyed God (the scene is described in 20.1–13), he was not allowed to enter the promised land. In this account he seems to accept his punishment without complaint, quietly turning over his leadership to Joshua. But in his great final speech, recorded in Deuteronomy, he bitterly raised the topic three times (Deuteronomy 1.37, 3.23–27, 4.21–24). The punishment was not forever; Moses did "get in" hundreds of years after his death, in the company of Jesus (Mark 9.4).

m Heb lacks *with me*

of your authority, so that all the congregation of the Israelites may obey. ²¹But he shall stand before Eleazar the priest, who shall inquire for him by the decision of the Urim before the LORD; at his word they shall go out, and at his word they shall come in, both he and all the Israelites with him, the whole congregation." ²²So Moses did as the LORD commanded him. He took Joshua and had him stand before Eleazar the priest and the whole congregation; ²³he laid his hands on him and commissioned him—as the LORD had directed through Moses.

Daily Offerings

28 The LORD spoke to Moses, saying: ²Command the Israelites, and say to them: My offering, the food for my offerings by fire, my pleasing odor, you shall take care to offer to me at its appointed time. ³And you shall say to them, This is the offering by fire that you shall offer to the LORD: two male lambs a year old without blemish, daily, as a regular offering. ⁴One lamb you shall offer in the morning, and the other lamb you shall offer at twilight;ⁿ ⁵also one-tenth of an ephah of choice flour for a grain offering, mixed with one-fourth of a hin of beaten oil. ⁶It is a regular burnt offering, ordained at Mount Sinai for a pleasing odor, an offering by fire to the LORD. ⁷Its drink offering shall be one-fourth of a hin for each lamb; in the sanctuary you shall pour out a drink offering of strong drink to the LORD. ⁸The other lamb you shall offer at twilightⁿ with a grain offering and a drink offering like the one in the morning; you shall offer it as an offering by fire, a pleasing odor to the LORD.

Sabbath Offerings

9 On the sabbath day: two male lambs a year old without blemish, and two-tenths of an ephah of choice flour for a grain offering, mixed with oil, and its drink offering— ¹⁰this is the burnt offering for every sabbath, in addition to the regular burnt offering and its drink offering.

Monthly Offerings

11 At the beginnings of your months you shall offer a burnt offering to the LORD: two young bulls, one ram, seven male lambs a year old without blemish; ¹²also three-tenths of an ephah of choice flour for a grain offering, mixed with oil, for each bull; and two-tenths of choice flour for a grain offering, mixed with oil, for the one ram; ¹³and one-tenth of choice flour mixed with oil as a grain offering for every lamb—a burnt offering of pleasing odor, an offering by fire to the LORD. ¹⁴Their drink offerings shall be half a hin of wine for a bull, one-third of a hin for a ram, and one-fourth of a hin for a lamb. This is the burnt offer-

ing of every month throughout the months of the year. ¹⁵And there shall be one male goat for a sin offering to the LORD; it shall be offered in addition to the regular burnt offering and its drink offering.

Offerings at Passover

16 On the fourteenth day of the first month there shall be a passover offering to the LORD. ¹⁷And on the fifteenth day of this month is a festival; seven days shall unleavened bread be eaten. ¹⁸On the first day there shall be a holy convocation. You shall not work at your occupations. ¹⁹You shall offer an offering by fire, a burnt offering to the LORD: two young bulls, one ram, and seven male lambs a year old; see that they are without blemish. ²⁰Their grain offering shall be of choice flour mixed with oil: three-tenths of an ephah shall you offer for a bull, and two-tenths for a ram; ²¹one-tenth shall you offer for each of the seven lambs; ²²also one male goat for a sin offering, to make atonement for you. ²³You shall offer these in addition to the burnt offering of the morning, which belongs to the regular burnt offering. ²⁴In the same way you shall offer daily, for seven days, the food of an offering by fire, a pleasing odor to the LORD; it shall be offered in addition to the regular burnt offering and its drink offering. ²⁵And on the seventh day you shall have a holy convocation; you shall not work at your occupations.

Offerings at the Festival of Weeks

26 On the day of the first fruits, when you offer a grain offering of new grain to the LORD at your festival of weeks, you shall have a holy convocation; you shall not work at your occupations. ²⁷You shall offer a burnt offering, a pleasing odor to the LORD: two young bulls, one ram, seven male lambs a year old. ²⁸Their grain offering shall be of choice flour mixed with oil, three-tenths of an ephah for each bull, two-tenths for one ram, ²⁹one-tenth for each of the seven lambs; ³⁰with one male goat, to make atonement for you. ³¹In addition to the regular burnt offering with its grain offering, you shall offer them and their drink offering. They shall be without blemish.

Offerings at the Festival of Trumpets

29 On the first day of the seventh month you shall have a holy convocation; you shall not work at your occupations. It is a day for you to blow the trumpets, ²and you shall offer a burnt offering, a pleasing odor to the LORD: one young bull, one ram, seven male lambs a year old without blemish. ³Their grain offering shall be of choice flour mixed with oil, three-tenths of one ephah for the bull, two-tenths for the ram, ⁴and

---

ⁿ Heb *between the two evenings*

one-tenth for each of the seven lambs; [5]with one male goat for a sin offering, to make atonement for you. [6]These are in addition to the burnt offering of the new moon and its grain offering, and

29.1 Interruptions of the Story

Numbers periodically interrupts its history with lists of rules or rituals, such as in this section, chapters 28–30. Usually, they relate to what appears just before or afterward. The instructions here were not new, but God saw a need to review them just as the nation was about to enter the promised land.

the regular burnt offering and its grain offering, and their drink offerings, according to the ordinance for them, a pleasing odor, an offering by fire to the LORD.

Offerings on the Day of Atonement

7 On the tenth day of this seventh month you shall have a holy convocation, and deny yourselves;[o] you shall do no work. [8]You shall offer a burnt offering to the LORD, a pleasing odor: one young bull, one ram, seven male lambs a year old. They shall be without blemish. [9]Their grain offering shall be of choice flour mixed with oil, three-tenths of an ephah for the bull, two-tenths for the one ram, [10]one-tenth for each of the seven lambs; [11]with one male goat for a sin offering, in addition to the sin offering of atonement, and the regular burnt offering and its grain offering, and their drink offerings.

Offerings at the Festival of Booths

12 On the fifteenth day of the seventh month you shall have a holy convocation; you shall not work at your occupations. You shall celebrate a festival to the LORD seven days. [13]You shall offer a burnt offering, an offering by fire, a pleasing odor to the LORD: thirteen young bulls, two rams, fourteen male lambs a year old. They shall be without blemish. [14]Their grain offering shall be of choice flour mixed with oil, three-tenths of an ephah for each of the thirteen bulls, two-tenths for each of the two rams, [15]and one-tenth for each of the fourteen lambs; [16]also one male goat for a sin offering, in addition to the regular burnt offering, its grain offering and its drink offering.

17 On the second day: twelve young bulls, two rams, fourteen male lambs a year old without blemish, [18]with the grain offering and the drink offerings for the bulls, for the rams, and for the lambs, as prescribed in accordance with their number; [19]also one male goat for a sin offering,

in addition to the regular burnt offering and its grain offering, and their drink offerings.

20 On the third day: eleven bulls, two rams, fourteen male lambs a year old without blemish, [21]with the grain offering and the drink offerings for the bulls, for the rams, and for the lambs, as prescribed in accordance with their number; [22]also one male goat for a sin offering, in addition to the regular burnt offering and its grain offering and its drink offering.

23 On the fourth day: ten bulls, two rams, fourteen male lambs a year old without blemish, [24]with the grain offering and the drink offerings for the bulls, for the rams, and for the lambs, as prescribed in accordance with their number; [25]also one male goat for a sin offering, in addition to the regular burnt offering, its grain offering and its drink offering.

26 On the fifth day: nine bulls, two rams, fourteen male lambs a year old without blemish, [27]with the grain offering and the drink offerings for the bulls, for the rams, and for the lambs, as prescribed in accordance with their number; [28]also one male goat for a sin offering, in addition to the regular burnt offering and its grain offering and its drink offering.

29 On the sixth day: eight bulls, two rams, fourteen male lambs a year old without blemish, [30]with the grain offering and the drink offerings for the bulls, for the rams, and for the lambs, as prescribed in accordance with their number; [31]also one male goat for a sin offering, in addition to the regular burnt offering, its grain offering, and its drink offerings.

32 On the seventh day: seven bulls, two rams, fourteen male lambs a year old without blemish, [33]with the grain offering and the drink offerings for the bulls, for the rams, and for the lambs, as prescribed in accordance with their number; [34]also one male goat for a sin offering, besides the regular burnt offering, its grain offering, and its drink offering.

35 On the eighth day you shall have a solemn assembly; you shall not work at your occupations. [36]You shall offer a burnt offering, an offering by fire, a pleasing odor to the LORD: one bull, one ram, seven male lambs a year old without blemish, [37]and the grain offering and the drink offerings for the bull, for the ram, and for the lambs, as prescribed in accordance with their number; [38]also one male goat for a sin offering, in addition to the regular burnt offering and its grain offering and its drink offering.

39 These you shall offer to the LORD at your appointed festivals, in addition to your votive offerings and your freewill offerings, as your burnt offerings, your grain offerings, your drink offerings, and your offerings of well-being.

o Or and fast

40[p] So Moses told the Israelites everything just as the LORD had commanded Moses.

Vows Made by Women

30 Then Moses said to the heads of the tribes of the Israelites: This is what the LORD has commanded. [2]When a man makes a vow to the LORD, or swears an oath to bind himself by a pledge, he shall not break his word; he shall do according to all that proceeds out of his mouth.

3 When a woman makes a vow to the LORD, or binds herself by a pledge, while within her father's house, in her youth, [4]and her father hears of her vow or her pledge by which she has bound herself, and says nothing to her; then all her vows shall stand, and any pledge by which she has bound herself shall stand. [5]But if her father expresses disapproval to her at the time that he hears of it, no vow of hers, and no pledge by which she has bound herself, shall stand; and the LORD will forgive her, because her father had expressed to her his disapproval.

6 If she marries, while obligated by her vows or any thoughtless utterance of her lips by which she has bound herself, [7]and her husband hears of it and says nothing to her at the time that he hears, then her vows shall stand, and her pledges by which she has bound herself shall stand. [8]But if, at the time that her husband hears of it, he expresses disapproval to her, then he shall nullify the vow by which she was obligated, or the thoughtless utterance of her lips, by which she bound herself; and the LORD will forgive her. [9](But every vow of a widow or of a divorced woman, by which she has bound herself, shall be binding upon her.) [10]And if she made a vow in her husband's house, or bound herself by a pledge with an oath, [11]and her husband heard it and said nothing to her, and did not express disapproval to her, then all her vows shall stand, and any pledge by which she bound herself shall stand. [12]But if her husband nullifies them at the time that he hears them, then whatever proceeds out of her lips concerning her vows, or concerning her pledge of herself, shall not stand. Her husband has nullified them, and the LORD will forgive her. [13]Any vow or any binding oath to deny herself,[q] her husband may allow to stand, or her husband may nullify. [14]But if her husband says nothing to her from day to day,[r] then he validates all her vows, or all her pledges, by which she is obligated; he has validated them, because he said nothing to her at the time that he heard of them. [15]But if he nullifies them some time after he has heard of them, then he shall bear her guilt.

16 These are the statutes that the LORD commanded Moses concerning a husband and his wife, and a father and his daughter while she is still young and in her father's house.

War against Midian

31 The LORD spoke to Moses, saying, [2]"Avenge the Israelites on the Midianites; afterward you shall be gathered to your people." [3]So Moses said to the people, "Arm some of your number for the war, so that they may go against Midian, to execute the LORD's vengeance on Midian. [4]You shall send a thousand from each of the tribes of Israel to the war." [5]So out of the thousands of Israel, a thousand from each tribe were conscripted, twelve thousand armed for battle. [6]Moses sent them to the war, a thousand from each tribe, along with Phinehas son of Eleazar the priest,[s] with the vessels of the sanctuary and the trumpets for sounding the alarm in his hand. [7]They did battle against Midian, as the LORD had commanded Moses, and killed every male. [8]They killed the kings of Midian: Evi, Rekem, Zur, Hur, and Reba, the five kings of Midian, in addition to others who were slain by them; and they also killed Balaam son of Beor with the sword. [9]The Israelites took the women of Midian and their little ones captive; and they took all their cattle, their flocks, and all their goods as booty. [10]All their towns where they had settled, and all their encampments, they burned, [11]but they took all the spoil and all the booty, both people and animals. [12]Then they brought the captives and the booty and the spoil to Moses, to Eleazar the priest, and to the congregation of the Israelites, at the camp on the plains of Moab by the Jordan at Jericho.

Return from the War

13 Moses, Eleazar the priest, and all the leaders of the congregation went to meet them outside the camp. [14]Moses became angry with the officers of the army, the commanders of thousands and the commanders of hundreds, who had come from service in the war. [15]Moses said to them, "Have you allowed all the women to live? [16]These women here, on Balaam's advice, made the Israelites act treacherously against the LORD in the affair of Peor, so that the plague came among the congregation of the LORD. [17]Now therefore, kill every male among the little ones, and kill every woman who has known a man by sleeping with him. [18]But all the young girls who have not known a man by sleeping with him, keep alive for yourselves. [19]Camp outside the camp seven days; whoever of you has killed any person or touched a corpse, purify yourselves and your captives on the third and on the seventh day. [20]You shall purify every garment, every article of skin, everything made of goats' hair, and every article of wood."

21 Eleazar the priest said to the troops who had gone to battle: "This is the statute of the law that the LORD has commanded Moses: [22]gold, silver, bronze, iron, tin, and lead— [23]everything

[p] Ch 30.1 in Heb [q] Or *to fast* [r] Or *from that day to the next* [s] Gk: Heb adds *to the war*

that can withstand fire, shall be passed through fire, and it shall be clean. Nevertheless it shall also be purified with the water for purification; and whatever cannot withstand fire, shall be passed

31.19–24 Acts of War

Many readers struggle with the harsh warfare policies God demanded of the Israelites. Numbers 35.34 summarizes one basic reason why policies were so strict: so that the land itself, set apart by God, would not become defiled (see "Is a War Ever Holy?" page 242). Even so, this passage shows that killing was not taken lightly—even war heroes had to go through the process of purification.

through the water. 24You must wash your clothes on the seventh day, and you shall be clean; afterward you may come into the camp."

Disposition of Captives and Booty

25 The LORD spoke to Moses, saying, 26"You and Eleazar the priest and the heads of the ancestral houses of the congregation make an inventory of the booty captured, both human and animal. 27Divide the booty into two parts, between the warriors who went out to battle and all the congregation. 28From the share of the warriors who went out to battle, set aside as tribute for the LORD, one item out of every five hundred, whether persons, oxen, donkeys, sheep, or goats. 29Take it from their half and give it to Eleazar the priest as an offering to the LORD. 30But from the Israelites' half you shall take one out of every fifty, whether persons, oxen, donkeys, sheep, or goats—all the animals—and give them to the Levites who have charge of the tabernacle of the LORD."

31 Then Moses and Eleazar the priest did as the LORD had commanded Moses:

32 The booty remaining from the spoil that the troops had taken totaled six hundred seventy-five thousand sheep, 33seventy-two thousand oxen, 34sixty-one thousand donkeys, 35and thirty-two thousand persons in all, women who had not known a man by sleeping with him.

36 The half-share, the portion of those who had gone out to war, was in number three hundred thirty-seven thousand five hundred sheep and goats, 37and the LORD's tribute of sheep and goats was six hundred seventy-five. 38The oxen were thirty-six thousand, of which the LORD's tribute was seventy-two. 39The donkeys were thirty thousand five hundred, of which the LORD's tribute was sixty-one. 40The persons were sixteen thousand, of which the LORD's tribute was thirty-two persons. 41Moses gave the tribute, the offer-

ing for the LORD, to Eleazar the priest, as the LORD had commanded Moses.

42 As for the Israelites' half, which Moses separated from that of the troops, 43the congregation's half was three hundred thirty-seven thousand five hundred sheep and goats, 44thirty-six thousand oxen, 45thirty thousand five hundred donkeys, 46and sixteen thousand persons. 47From the Israelites' half Moses took one of every fifty, both of persons and of animals, and gave them to the Levites who had charge of the tabernacle of the LORD; as the LORD had commanded Moses.

48 Then the officers who were over the thousands of the army, the commanders of thousands and the commanders of hundreds, approached Moses, 49and said to Moses, "Your servants have counted the warriors who are under our command, and not one of us is missing. 50And we have brought the LORD's offering, what each of us found, articles of gold, armlets and bracelets, signet rings, earrings, and pendants, to make atonement for ourselves before the LORD." 51Moses and Eleazar the priest received the gold from them, all in the form of crafted articles. 52And all the gold of the offering that they offered to the LORD, from the commanders of thousands and the commanders of hundreds, was sixteen thousand seven hundred fifty shekels. 53(The troops had all taken plunder for themselves.) 54So Moses and Eleazar the priest received the gold from the commanders of thousands and of hundreds, and brought it into the tent of meeting as a memorial for the Israelites before the LORD.

Conquest and Division of Transjordan

32 Now the Reubenites and the Gadites owned a very great number of cattle. When they saw that the land of Jazer and the land of Gilead was a good place for cattle, 2the Gadites and the Reubenites came and spoke to Moses, to Eleazar the priest, and to the leaders of the congregation, saying, 3"Ataroth, Dibon, Jazer, Nimrah, Heshbon, Elealeh, Sebam, Nebo, and Beon— 4the land that the LORD subdued before the congregation of Israel—is a land for cattle; and your servants have cattle." 5They continued, "If we have found favor in your sight, let this land be given to your servants for a possession; do not make us cross the Jordan."

6 But Moses said to the Gadites and to the Reubenites, "Shall your brothers go to war while you sit here? 7Why will you discourage the hearts of the Israelites from going over into the land that the LORD has given them? 8Your fathers did this, when I sent them from Kadesh-barnea to see the land. 9When they went up to the Wadi Eshcol and saw the land, they discouraged the hearts of the Israelites from going into the land that the LORD had given them. 10The LORD's anger was kindled on that day and he swore, saying, 11'Surely none of the people who came up out of Egypt, from

twenty years old and upward, shall see the land that I swore to give to Abraham, to Isaac, and to Jacob, because they have not unreservedly followed me— [12]none except Caleb son of Jephunneh the Kenizzite and Joshua son of Nun, for they have unreservedly followed the LORD.' [13]And the LORD's anger was kindled against Israel, and he made them wander in the wilderness for forty years, until all the generation that had done evil in the sight of the LORD had disappeared. [14]And now you, a brood of sinners, have risen in place of your fathers, to increase the LORD's fierce anger against Israel! [15]If you turn away from following him, he will again abandon them in the wilderness; and you will destroy all this people."

16 Then they came up to him and said, "We will build sheepfolds here for our flocks, and towns for our little ones, [17]but we will take up arms as a vanguard[t] before the Israelites, until we have brought them to their place. Meanwhile our little ones will stay in the fortified towns because of the inhabitants of the land. [18]We will not return to our homes until all the Israelites have obtained their inheritance. [19]We will not inherit with them on the other side of the Jordan and beyond, because our inheritance has come to us on this side of the Jordan to the east."

20 So Moses said to them, "If you do this—if you take up arms to go before the LORD for the war, [21]and all those of you who bear arms cross the Jordan before the LORD, until he has driven out his enemies from before him [22]and the land is subdued before the LORD—then after that you may return and be free of obligation to the LORD and to Israel, and this land shall be your possession before the LORD. [23]But if you do not do this,

32.22 Trouble Ahead

According to Joshua 22.1–6, the two and a half tribes did keep their promise to fight with the others. The land they chose was appealing, with parklike scenery, wide pastures, and lush forests. However, their settlement proved troublesome. With no natural borders, the land was open to enemy attack and easy infiltration.

you have sinned against the LORD; and be sure your sin will find you out. [24]Build towns for your little ones, and folds for your flocks; but do what you have promised."

25 Then the Gadites and the Reubenites said to Moses, "Your servants will do as my lord commands. [26]Our little ones, our wives, our flocks, and all our livestock shall remain there in the towns of Gilead; [27]but your servants will cross

over, everyone armed for war, to do battle for the LORD, just as my lord orders."

28 So Moses gave command concerning them to Eleazar the priest, to Joshua son of Nun, and to the heads of the ancestral houses of the Israelite tribes. [29]And Moses said to them, "If the Gadites and the Reubenites, everyone armed for battle before the LORD, will cross over the Jordan with you and the land shall be subdued before you, then you shall give them the land of Gilead for a possession; [30]but if they will not cross over with you armed, they shall have possessions among you in the land of Canaan." [31]The Gadites and the Reubenites answered, "As the LORD has spoken to your servants, so we will do. [32]We will cross over armed before the LORD into the land of Canaan, but the possession of our inheritance shall remain with us on this side of[u] the Jordan."

33 Moses gave to them—to the Gadites and to the Reubenites and to the half-tribe of Manasseh son of Joseph—the kingdom of King Sihon of the Amorites and the kingdom of King Og of Bashan, the land and its towns, with the territories of the surrounding towns. [34]And the Gadites rebuilt Dibon, Ataroth, Aroer, [35]Atroth-shophan, Jazer, Jogbehah, [36]Beth-nimrah, and Beth-haran, fortified cities, and folds for sheep. [37]And the Reubenites rebuilt Heshbon, Elealeh, Kiriathaim, [38]Nebo, and Baal-meon (some names being changed), and Sibmah; and they gave names to the towns that they rebuilt. [39]The descendants of Machir son of Manasseh went to Gilead, captured it, and dispossessed the Amorites who were there; [40]so Moses gave Gilead to Machir son of Manasseh, and he settled there. [41]Jair son of Manasseh went and captured their villages, and renamed them Havvoth-jair.[v] [42]And Nobah went and captured Kenath and its villages, and renamed it Nobah after himself.

The Stages of Israel's Journey from Egypt

33 These are the stages by which the Israelites went out of the land of Egypt in military formation under the leadership of Moses and Aaron. [2]Moses wrote down their starting points, stage by stage, by command of the LORD; and these are their stages according to their starting places. [3]They set out from Rameses in the first month, on the fifteenth day of the first month; on the day after the passover the Israelites went out boldly in the sight of all the Egyptians, [4]while the Egyptians were burying all their firstborn, whom the LORD had struck down among them. The LORD executed judgments even against their gods.

5 So the Israelites set out from Rameses, and camped at Succoth. [6]They set out from Succoth, and camped at Etham, which is on the edge of the wilderness. [7]They set out from Etham, and turned back to Pi-hahiroth, which faces Baal-zephon;

---

[t] Cn: Heb *hurrying*　　[u] Heb *beyond*　　[v] That is *the villages of Jair*

and they camped before Migdol. [8]They set out from Pi-hahiroth, passed through the sea into the wilderness, went a three days' journey in the wilderness of Etham, and camped at Marah. [9]They set out from Marah and came to Elim; at Elim there were twelve springs of water and seventy palm trees, and they camped there. [10]They set out from Elim and camped by the Red Sea.[w] [11]They set out from the Red Sea[w] and camped in the wilderness of Sin. [12]They set out from the wilderness of Sin and camped at Dophkah. [13]They set out from Dophkah and camped at Alush. [14]They set out from Alush and camped at Rephidim, where there was no water for the people to drink. [15]They set out from Rephidim and camped in the wilderness of Sinai. [16]They set out from the wilderness of Sinai and camped at Kibroth-hattaavah. [17]They set out from Kibroth-hattaavah and camped at Hazeroth. [18]They set out from Hazeroth and camped at Rithmah. [19]They set out from Rithmah and camped at Rimmon-perez. [20]They set out from Rimmon-perez and camped at Libnah. [21]They set out from Libnah and camped at Rissah. [22]They set out from Rissah and camped at Kehelathah. [23]They set out from Kehelathah and camped at Mount Shepher. [24]They set out from Mount Shepher and camped at Haradah. [25]They set out from Haradah and camped at Makheloth. [26]They set out from Makheloth and camped at Tahath. [27]They set out from Tahath and camped at Terah. [28]They set out from Terah and camped at Mithkah. [29]They set out from Mithkah and camped at Hashmonah. [30]They set out from Hashmonah and camped at Moseroth. [31]They set out from Moseroth and camped at Bene-jaakan. [32]They set out from Bene-jaakan and camped at Hor-haggidgad. [33]They set out from Hor-haggidgad and camped at Jotbathah. [34]They set out from Jotbathah and camped at Abronah. [35]They set out from Abronah and camped at Ezion-geber. [36]They set out from Ezion-geber and camped in the wilderness of Zin (that is, Kadesh). [37]They set out from Kadesh and camped at Mount Hor, on the edge of the land of Edom.

38 Aaron the priest went up Mount Hor at the command of the LORD and died there in the fortieth year after the Israelites had come out of the land of Egypt, on the first day of the fifth month. [39]Aaron was one hundred twenty-three years old when he died on Mount Hor.

40 The Canaanite, the king of Arad, who lived in the Negeb in the land of Canaan, heard of the coming of the Israelites.

41 They set out from Mount Hor and camped at Zalmonah. [42]They set out from Zalmonah and camped at Punon. [43]They set out from Punon and camped at Oboth. [44]They set out from Oboth and camped at Iye-abarim, in the territory of Moab. [45]They set out from Iyim and camped at Dibon-gad. [46]They set out from Dibon-gad and camped at Almon-diblathaim. [47]They set out from Almon-diblathaim and camped in the mountains of Abarim, before Nebo. [48]They set out from the mountains of Abarim and camped in the plains of Moab by the Jordan at Jericho; [49]they camped by the Jordan from Beth-jeshimoth as far as Abel-shittim in the plains of Moab.

Directions for the Conquest of Canaan

50 In the plains of Moab by the Jordan at Jericho, the LORD spoke to Moses, saying: [51]Speak to the Israelites, and say to them: When you cross over the Jordan into the land of Canaan, [52]you shall drive out all the inhabitants of the land from before you, destroy all their figured stones, destroy all their cast images, and demolish all their high places. [53]You shall take possession of the land and settle in it, for I have given you the land to possess. [54]You shall apportion the land by lot according to your clans; to a large one you shall give a large inheritance, and to a small one you shall give a small inheritance; the inheritance shall belong to the person on whom the lot falls; according to your ancestral tribes you shall inherit. [55]But if you do not drive out the inhabitants of the land from before you, then those whom you let remain shall be as barbs in your eyes and thorns in your sides; they shall trouble you in the land where you are settling. [56]And I will do to you as I thought to do to them.

33.50–56 Final Warnings

Just before the dramatic crossing into the promised land, God gave a clear statement of his priorities and a warning of what would happen if the Israelites failed to obey. His words would one day come back to haunt them, for they failed to carry out fully any of his orders.

The Boundaries of the Land

34 The LORD spoke to Moses, saying: [2]Command the Israelites, and say to them: When you enter the land of Canaan (this is the land that shall fall to you for an inheritance, the land of Canaan, defined by its boundaries), [3]your south sector shall extend from the wilderness of Zin along the side of Edom. Your southern boundary shall begin from the end of the Dead Sea[x] on the east; [4]your boundary shall turn south of the ascent of Akrabbim, and cross to Zin, and its outer limit shall be south of Kadesh-barnea;

---

w Or *Sea of Reeds*   x Heb *Salt Sea*

then it shall go on to Hazar-addar, and cross to Azmon; ⁵the boundary shall turn from Azmon to the Wadi of Egypt, and its termination shall be at the Sea.

6 For the western boundary, you shall have the Great Sea and its ʸ coast; this shall be your western boundary.

7 This shall be your northern boundary: from the Great Sea you shall mark out your line to Mount Hor; ⁸from Mount Hor you shall mark it out to Lebo-hamath, and the outer limit of the boundary shall be at Zedad; ⁹then the boundary shall extend to Ziphron, and its end shall be at Hazar-enan; this shall be your northern boundary.

10 You shall mark out your eastern boundary from Hazar-enan to Shepham; ¹¹and the boundary shall continue down from Shepham to Riblah on the east side of Ain; and the boundary shall go down, and reach the eastern slope of the sea of Chinnereth; ¹²and the boundary shall go down to the Jordan, and its end shall be at the Dead Sea.ᶻ This shall be your land with its boundaries all around.

13 Moses commanded the Israelites, saying: This is the land that you shall inherit by lot, which the LORD has commanded to give to the nine tribes and to the half-tribe; ¹⁴for the tribe of the Reubenites by their ancestral houses and the tribe of the Gadites by their ancestral houses have taken their inheritance, and also the half-tribe of Manasseh; ¹⁵the two tribes and the half-tribe have taken their inheritance beyond the Jordan at Jericho eastward, toward the sunrise.

Tribal Leaders

16 The LORD spoke to Moses, saying: ¹⁷These are the names of the men who shall apportion the land to you for inheritance: the priest Eleazar and Joshua son of Nun. ¹⁸You shall take one leader of every tribe to apportion the land for inheritance. ¹⁹These are the names of the men: Of the tribe of Judah, Caleb son of Jephunneh. ²⁰Of the tribe of the Simeonites, Shemuel son of Ammihud. ²¹Of the tribe of Benjamin, Elidad son of Chislon. ²²Of the tribe of the Danites a leader, Bukki son of Jogli. ²³Of the Josephites: of the tribe of the Manassites a leader, Hanniel son of Ephod, ²⁴and of the tribe of the Ephraimites a leader, Kemuel son of Shiphtan. ²⁵Of the tribe of the Zebulunites a leader, Eli-zaphan son of Parnach. ²⁶Of the tribe of the Issacharites a leader, Paltiel son of Azzan. ²⁷And of the tribe of the Asherites a leader, Ahihud son of Shelomi. ²⁸Of the tribe of the Naphtalites a leader, Pedahel son of Ammihud. ²⁹These were the ones whom the LORD commanded to apportion the inheritance for the Israelites in the land of Canaan.

Cities for the Levites

35 In the plains of Moab by the Jordan at Jericho, the LORD spoke to Moses, saying: ²Command the Israelites to give, from the inheritance that they possess, towns for the Levites to live in; you shall also give to the Levites pasture lands surrounding the towns. ³The towns shall be theirs to live in, and their pasture lands shall be for their cattle, for their livestock, and for all their animals. ⁴The pasture lands of the towns, which you shall give to the Levites, shall reach from the wall of the town outward a thousand cubits all around. ⁵You shall measure, outside the town, for the east side two thousand cubits, for the south side two thousand cubits, for the west side two thousand cubits, and for the north side two thousand cubits, with the town in the middle; this shall belong to them as pasture land for their towns.

6 The towns that you give to the Levites shall include the six cities of refuge, where you shall permit a slayer to flee, and in addition to them

35.6 Controlling Blood Feuds

Even today some nomadic tribes still follow the principles of blood feuds. If a person is responsible, even accidentally, for another's death, a relative of the victim can in turn kill either the murderer or, as a substitute, one of the murderer's relatives. The cities of refuge put a control on this practice, making allowance for "involuntary manslaughter." The assembly judged whether the killing was accidental or intentional (verse 24).

you shall give forty-two towns. ⁷The towns that you give to the Levites shall total forty-eight, with their pasture lands. ⁸And as for the towns that you shall give from the possession of the Israelites, from the larger tribes you shall take many, and from the smaller tribes you shall take few; each, in proportion to the inheritance that it obtains, shall give of its towns to the Levites.

Cities of Refuge

9 The LORD spoke to Moses, saying: ¹⁰Speak to the Israelites, and say to them: When you cross the Jordan into the land of Canaan, ¹¹then you shall select cities to be cities of refuge for you, so that a slayer who kills a person without intent may flee there. ¹²The cities shall be for you a refuge from the avenger, so that the slayer may not die until there is a trial before the congregation.

13 The cities that you designate shall be six cities of refuge for you: ¹⁴you shall designate three cities beyond the Jordan, and three cities in the

ʸ Syr: Heb lacks *its*   ᶻ Heb *Salt Sea*

land of Canaan, to be cities of refuge. ¹⁵These six cities shall serve as refuge for the Israelites, for the resident or transient alien among them, so that anyone who kills a person without intent may flee there.

Concerning Murder and Blood Revenge

16 But anyone who strikes another with an iron object, and death ensues, is a murderer; the murderer shall be put to death. ¹⁷Or anyone who strikes another with a stone in hand that could cause death, and death ensues, is a murderer; the murderer shall be put to death. ¹⁸Or anyone who strikes another with a weapon of wood in hand that could cause death, and death ensues, is a murderer; the murderer shall be put to death. ¹⁹The avenger of blood is the one who shall put the murderer to death; when they meet, the avenger of blood shall execute the sentence. ²⁰Likewise, if someone pushes another from hatred, or hurls something at another, lying in wait, and death ensues, ²¹or in enmity strikes another with the hand, and death ensues, then the one who struck the blow shall be put to death; that person is a murderer; the avenger of blood shall put the murderer to death, when they meet.

22 But if someone pushes another suddenly without enmity, or hurls any object without lying in wait, ²³or, while handling any stone that could cause death, unintentionally*a* drops it on another and death ensues, though they were not enemies, and no harm was intended, ²⁴then the congregation shall judge between the slayer and the avenger of blood, in accordance with these ordinances; ²⁵and the congregation shall rescue the slayer from the avenger of blood. Then the congregation shall send the slayer back to the original city of refuge. The slayer shall live in it until the death of the high priest who was anointed with the holy oil. ²⁶But if the slayer shall at any time go outside the bounds of the original city of refuge, ²⁷and is found by the avenger of blood outside the bounds of the city of refuge, and is killed by the avenger, no bloodguilt shall be incurred. ²⁸For the slayer must remain in the city of refuge until the death of the high priest; but after the death of the high priest the slayer may return home.

29 These things shall be a statute and ordinance for you throughout your generations wherever you live.

30 If anyone kills another, the murderer shall be put to death on the evidence of witnesses; but no one shall be put to death on the testimony of a single witness. ³¹Moreover you shall accept no ransom for the life of a murderer who is subject to the death penalty; a murderer must be put to death. ³²Nor shall you accept ransom for one who has fled to a city of refuge, enabling the fugitive to return to live in the land before the death of the high priest. ³³You shall not pollute the land in which you live; for blood pollutes the land, and no expiation can be made for the land, for the blood that is shed in it, except by the blood of the one who shed it. ³⁴You shall not defile the land in which you live, in which I also dwell; for I the LORD dwell among the Israelites.

Marriage of Female Heirs

36 The heads of the ancestral houses of the clans of the descendants of Gilead son of Machir son of Manasseh, of the Josephite clans, came forward and spoke in the presence of Moses and the leaders, the heads of the ancestral houses of the Israelites; ²they said, "The LORD commanded my lord to give the land for inheritance by lot to the Israelites; and my lord was commanded by the LORD to give the inheritance of our brother Zelophehad to his daughters. ³But if they are married into another Israelite tribe, then their inheritance will be taken from the inheritance of our ancestors and added to the inheritance of the tribe into which they marry; so it will be taken away from the allotted portion of our inheritance. ⁴And when the jubilee of the Israelites comes, then their inheritance will be added to the inheritance of the tribe into which they have married; and their inheritance will be taken from the inheritance of our ancestral tribe."

5 Then Moses commanded the Israelites according to the word of the LORD, saying, "The descendants of the tribe of Joseph are right in what they are saying. ⁶This is what the LORD commands concerning the daughters of Zelophehad, 'Let them marry whom they think best; only it must be into a clan of their father's tribe that they are married, ⁷so that no inheritance of the Israelites shall be transferred from one tribe to another; for all Israelites shall retain the inheritance of their ancestral tribes. ⁸Every daughter who possesses an inheritance in any tribe of the Israelites shall marry one from the clan of her father's tribe, so that all Israelites may continue to possess their ancestral inheritance. ⁹No inheritance shall be transferred from one tribe to another; for each of the tribes of the Israelites shall retain its own inheritance.'"

10 The daughters of Zelophehad did as the LORD had commanded Moses. ¹¹Mahlah, Tirzah, Hoglah, Milcah, and Noah, the daughters of Zelophehad, married sons of their father's brothers. ¹²They were married into the clans of the descendants of Manasseh son of Joseph, and their inheritance remained in the tribe of their father's clan.

13 These are the commandments and the ordinances that the LORD commanded through Moses to the Israelites in the plains of Moab by the Jordan at Jericho.

---

a Heb *without seeing*

DEUTERONOMY

A Personal Plea

Moses' last chance with the people he loved

POLITICIANS GET THIS ADVICE: "WHEN you deliver a speech, make it seem as if you're having a personal talk in a small room with each one of your listeners." No one took that advice better than Franklin Delano Roosevelt—unless, perhaps, you consider Moses' speeches in Deuteronomy.

When Roosevelt became president of the United States in 1932, he faced a national crisis greater than any since the Civil War. Fifteen million people were unemployed in the Great Depression (a 25 percent unemployment rate), and two million of those wandered around the country, homeless, searching for work and food. In addition, war in Europe was not far away.

> From there you will seek the LORD your God, and you will find him if you search after him with all your heart and soul. 4.29

Fireside Chats

To combat the mood of despair, Roosevelt turned to a powerful new communications weapon: radio. The very first week of his presidency he gave his first "fireside chat" from a homey setting in the White House, and a series of such chats helped him pull the nation through its hard times.

Warm and personal in tone, the book of Deuteronomy resembles just such a fireside chat, delivered by the great leader Moses to his people, the Israelites. He, too, led a nation through dangerous times, and at the end of his life he had many parting words. This book is Moses' State of the Union address, personal diary, and tearful swan song all combined into one.

Poised on the Edge

For their length and emotional power, these speeches have no equal in the Bible. Moses passionately went over and over the same ground, occasionally lashing out, but more often showing the anguish and love of a doting parent. An undercurrent of sadness runs through the speeches: Moses knew he would not join in the triumph of entering Canaan. God had revealed that Moses would die before then.

In Exodus, Moses was marked by a quick temper and a reluctance to speak. His humility and eloquence as seen in Deuteronomy show how far he had come in 40 years.

Deep in his soul, Moses felt that the entire history of the Israelites depended on what happened next. Poised on the banks of the Jordan River, they were about to enter the promised land and face the most crucial test of their lives. How would they react to the new land? Would they keep their covenant with God or reject it for the more immediate pleasures around them?

Desert-bred, the Israelites knew little about the seductions of other cultures: the sensuality, the exotic religions, the glittering wealth. They had spent their lives in near-isolation, sheltered from civilization. Now they were marching into a land full of enticements.

Three Speeches

Moses' first great speech, in chapters 1–3, reviewed God's dealings with Israel. Moses recalled Israel's history through his own eyes, mentioning such details as the irrigation system in Egypt, the abrupt departure, the fearsome desert with its snakes and scorpions, and the amazing miracles of God. He filled the account with personal reflections, like an aging father telling his children what to remember after he is gone.

The longest speech, chapters 4–26, went over the moral and civil code the Israelites had agreed to keep. Even here, a personal tone came through. Moses did not list laws as in a textbook; he discussed and amplified and preached them. Along with the laws, he included reminders, object lessons, personal outbursts.

In chapters 27–33 Moses gave a final summing up, a farewell charge from an old man facing certain death. As clearly as he could, he presented the choices facing the Israelites. He would not be with them as they chose their future. They were on their own; they held their destiny in their own hands.

How to Read Deuteronomy

Early in this century archaeologists began turning up samples of Near Eastern treaties. These "suzerainty treaties" set down in official form the relationship between a powerful king (suzerain) and the people he ruled over. Such treaties shed new light on the book of Deuteronomy, which seems to follow very closely the pattern of such a treaty. Typically, a treaty with a powerful king consisted of the following elements:

1. *A preamble identifying the parties of the treaty,* such as a king and a small cluster of tribes who want his protection.

2. *A capsule history describing previous relations between the two parties.*

3. *Rules defining each party's obligations.* The king may swear to defend some tribes with his armies in return for allegiance, taxes, and a percentage of produce.

4. *Witnesses to the treaties,* including, in many cases, a list of gods.

5. *Curses and blessings specifying what will take place if one of the parties breaks the treaty.* The king may promise the people prosperity and peace if they keep the terms, but invasion, deportation, or death if they break them.

Read Deuteronomy as an example of a treaty between a king and his people. *Treaty* is another word for the one we have been using—*covenant*—to describe the formal agreement between God and the Israelites. With a little work, you can identify various portions of Deuteronomy that parallel the five elements above.

Chapters 1–11 and 27–34 contain the best summary of Moses' speeches to the Israelites. He holds back no emotion as he retells the story of his life. Almost all the action he describes repeats what we've heard before (see Exodus 12–20; 32–34; Numbers 11–17; 20–24), but Deuteronomy provides a much more personal account.

Unlike other ancient books, the Bible gives major emphasis to "nobodies"—poor people, aliens, widows, orphans, the sick. Many of the laws relating to them repeat laws from the three preceding books. But Deuteronomy gives hidden insights into why God has such special concern for nobodies and why the Israelites should also. It also gives intriguing ideas on how such concern can be translated into actual political and economic policies. As you go through the book, mark each passage that relates to such people.

The New Testament quotes Deuteronomy more often than almost any other Old Testament book. Twenty-one of the 27 New Testament books allude to Deuteronomy; some scholars count 90 different citations. Jesus himself drew from it during his temptation (Matthew 4).

3-TRACK READING PLAN

For an explanation and complete listing of the 3-track reading plan, turn to page 7.

TRACK 1: **Two-Week Courses on the Bible**
See page 7 for information on these courses.

TRACK 2: **An Overview of Deuteronomy in 3 Days**
☐ Day 1. Read the Introduction to Deuteronomy and then chapter 4, part of Moses' first emotional speech.
☐ Day 2. Read chapter 8; here, Moses reveals his fears about how success may have a harmful effect on the Israelites.
☐ Day 3. Read chapter 28, which, in vivid, shocking language, sets out before the Israelites the choice between obedience and disobedience.

Now turn to page 9 for your next Track 2 reading project.

TRACK 3: **All of Deuteronomy in 34 Days**
After you have read through Deuteronomy, turn to pages 10–14 for your next Track 3 reading project.

☐1	☐2	☐3	☐4	☐5	☐6	☐7	☐8
☐9	☐10	☐11	☐12	☐13	☐14	☐15	☐16
☐17	☐18	☐19	☐20	☐21	☐22	☐23	☐24
☐25	☐26	☐27	☐28	☐29	☐30	☐31	☐32
☐33	☐34						

Events at Horeb Recalled

1 These are the words that Moses spoke to all Israel beyond the Jordan—in the wilderness, on the plain opposite Suph, between Paran and Tophel, Laban, Hazeroth, and Di-zahab. ²(By the way of Mount Seir it takes eleven days to reach Kadesh-barnea from Horeb.) ³In the fortieth year, on the first day of the eleventh month, Moses spoke to the Israelites just as the LORD had commanded him to speak to them. ⁴This was after he had defeated King Sihon of the Amorites, who reigned in Heshbon, and King Og of Bashan, who reigned in Ashtaroth andᵃ in Edrei. ⁵Beyond the Jordan in the land of Moab, Moses undertook to expound this law as follows:

6 The LORD our God spoke to us at Horeb, saying, "You have stayed long enough at this mountain. ⁷Resume your journey, and go into the hill country of the Amorites as well as into the neighboring regions—the Arabah, the hill country, the Shephelah, the Negeb, and the seacoast—the land of the Canaanites and the Lebanon, as far as the great river, the river Euphrates. ⁸See, I have set the land before you; go in and take possession of the land that Iᵇ swore to your ancestors, to Abraham, to Isaac, and to Jacob, to give to them and to their descendants after them."

Appointment of Tribal Leaders

9 At that time I said to you, "I am unable by myself to bear you. ¹⁰The LORD your God has multiplied you, so that today you are as numerous as the stars of heaven. ¹¹May the LORD, the God of your ancestors, increase you a thousand times more and bless you, as he has promised you! ¹²But how can I bear the heavy burden of your disputes all by myself? ¹³Choose for each of your tribes individuals who are wise, discerning, and reputable to be your leaders." ¹⁴You answered me, "The plan you have proposed is a good one." ¹⁵So I took the leaders of your tribes, wise and reputable individuals, and installed them as leaders over you, commanders of thousands, commanders of hundreds, commanders of fifties, commanders of tens, and officials, throughout your tribes. ¹⁶I charged your judges at that time: "Give the members of your community a fair hearing, and judge rightly between one person and another, whether citizen or resident alien. ¹⁷You must not be partial in judging: hear out the small and the great alike; you shall not be intimidated by anyone, for the judgment is God's. Any case that is too hard for you, bring to me, and I will hear it." ¹⁸So I charged you at that time with all the things that you should do.

Israel's Refusal to Enter the Land

19 Then, just as the LORD our God had ordered us, we set out from Horeb and went through all that great and terrible wilderness that you saw, on the way to the hill country of the Amorites, until we reached Kadesh-barnea. ²⁰I said to you, "You have reached the hill country of the Amorites, which the LORD our God is giving us. ²¹See, the LORD your God has given the land to you; go up, take possession, as the LORD, the God of your ancestors, has promised you; do not fear or be dismayed."

22 All of you came to me and said, "Let us send men ahead of us to explore the land for us and bring back a report to us regarding the route by which we should go up and the cities we will come to." ²³The plan seemed good to me, and I selected twelve of you, one from each tribe. ²⁴They set out and went up into the hill country, and when they reached the Valley of Eshcol they spied it out ²⁵and gathered some of the land's produce, which they brought down to us. They brought back a report to us, and said, "It is a good land that the LORD our God is giving us."

26 But you were unwilling to go up. You rebelled against the command of the LORD your God; ²⁷you grumbled in your tents and said, "It is because the LORD hates us that he has brought us out of the land of Egypt, to hand us over to the Amorites to destroy us. ²⁸Where are we headed? Our kindred have made our hearts melt by reporting, 'The people are stronger and taller than we; the cities are large and fortified up to heaven! We actually saw there the offspring of the Anakim!'" ²⁹I said to you, "Have no dread or fear of them. ³⁰The LORD your God, who goes before you, is the one who will fight for you, just as he did for you in Egypt before your very eyes, ³¹and in the wilderness, where you saw how the LORD your God carried you, just as one carries a child, all the way that you traveled until you reached this place. ³²But in spite of this, you have no trust in the LORD your God, ³³who goes before you on the way to seek out a place for you to camp, in fire by night, and in the cloud by day, to show you the route you should take."

The Penalty for Israel's Rebellion

34 When the LORD heard your words, he was wrathful and swore: ³⁵"Not one of these—not one of this evil generation—shall see the good land that I swore to give to your ancestors, ³⁶except Caleb son of Jephunneh. He shall see it, and to him and to his descendants I will give the land on which he set foot, because of his complete fidelity to the LORD." ³⁷Even with me the LORD was angry on your account, saying, "You also shall not enter there. ³⁸Joshua son of Nun, your assistant, shall enter there; encourage him, for he is the one who will secure Israel's possession of it. ³⁹And as for your little ones, who you thought would become booty, your children, who today

---

ᵃ Gk Syr Vg Compare Josh 12.4: Heb lacks and   ᵇ Sam Gk: MT the LORD

do not yet know right from wrong, they shall enter there; to them I will give it, and they shall take possession of it. [40]But as for you, journey back into the wilderness, in the direction of the Red Sea."[c]

1.37 Distributing Blame

God forbade Moses to enter the promised land because of the incident reported in Numbers 20. In his farewell speech, Moses could not resist expressing his own resentment at the Israelites' part in provoking his punishment. In this verse and in 3.26 and 4.21, he turned the blame back on his countrymen.

[41] You answered me, "We have sinned against the LORD! We are ready to go up and fight, just as the LORD our God commanded us." So all of you strapped on your battle gear, and thought it easy to go up into the hill country. [42]The LORD said to me, "Say to them, 'Do not go up and do not fight, for I am not in the midst of you; otherwise you will be defeated by your enemies.'" [43]Although I told you, you would not listen. You rebelled against the command of the LORD and presumptuously went up into the hill country. [44]The Amorites who lived in that hill country then came out against you and chased you as bees do. They beat you down in Seir as far as Hormah. [45]When you returned and wept before the LORD, the LORD would neither heed your voice nor pay you any attention.

The Desert Years

2 [46] After you had stayed at Kadesh as many days as you did, [1]we journeyed back into the wilderness, in the direction of the Red Sea,[c] as the LORD had told me and skirted Mount Seir for many days. [2]Then the LORD said to me: [3]"You have been skirting this hill country long enough. Head north, [4]and charge the people as follows: You are about to pass through the territory of your kindred, the descendants of Esau, who live in Seir. They will be afraid of you, so, be very careful [5]not to engage in battle with them, for I will not give you even so much as a foot's length of their land, since I have given Mount Seir to Esau as a possession. [6]You shall purchase food from them for money, so that you may eat; and you shall also buy water from them for money, so that you may drink. [7]Surely the LORD your God has blessed you in all your undertakings; he knows your going through this great wilderness. These forty years the LORD your God has been with you; you have lacked nothing." [8]So we passed by our kin, the descendants of Esau who

live in Seir, leaving behind the route of the Arabah, and leaving behind Elath and Ezion-geber. When we had headed out along the route of the wilderness of Moab, [9]the LORD said to me: "Do not harass Moab or engage them in battle, for I will not give you any of its land as a possession, since I have given Ar as a possession to the descendants of Lot." [10](The Emim—a large and numerous people, as tall as the Anakim—had formerly inhabited it. [11]Like the Anakim, they are usually reckoned as Rephaim, though the Moabites call them Emim. [12]Moreover, the Horim had formerly inhabited Seir, but the descendants of Esau dispossessed them, destroying them and settling in their place, as Israel has done in the land that the LORD gave them as a possession.) [13]"Now then, proceed to cross over the Wadi Zered."

So we crossed over the Wadi Zered. [14]And the length of time we had traveled from Kadesh-barnea until we crossed the Wadi Zered was thirty-eight years, until the entire generation of warriors had perished from the camp, as the LORD

2.14 Children of the Desert

As he reviewed the Israelites' history, Moses recalled with bitterness the series of rebellions leading to the 40-year punishment in "that great and terrible wilderness" (1.19). Actually, of course, the people listening to him had been mere children when the decisive rebellions occurred (1.39); their parents were the ones forbidden to enter the promised land. Except for Joshua, Caleb, and Moses' own family, all those listening to Moses had grown up in the desert.

had sworn concerning them. [15]Indeed, the LORD's own hand was against them, to root them out from the camp, until all had perished.

[16] Just as soon as all the warriors had died off from among the people, [17]the LORD spoke to me, saying, [18]"Today you are going to cross the boundary of Moab at Ar. [19]When you approach the frontier of the Ammonites, do not harass them or engage them in battle, for I will not give the land of the Ammonites to you as a possession, because I have given it to the descendants of Lot." [20](It also is usually reckoned as a land of Rephaim. Rephaim formerly inhabited it, though the Ammonites call them Zamzummim, [21]a strong and numerous people, as tall as the Anakim. But the LORD destroyed them from before the Ammonites so that they could dispossess them and settle in their place. [22]He did the same for the descendants of Esau, who live in Seir, by destroying the Horim before them so that they could dispossess them and settle in their place even to

[c] Or *Sea of Reeds*

this day. 23As for the Avvim, who had lived in settlements in the vicinity of Gaza, the Caphtorim, who came from Caphtor, destroyed them and settled in their place.) 24"Proceed on your journey and cross the Wadi Arnon. See, I have handed over to you King Sihon the Amorite of Heshbon, and his land. Begin to take possession by engaging him in battle. 25This day I will begin to put the dread and fear of you upon the peoples everywhere under heaven; when they hear report of you, they will tremble and be in anguish because of you."

Defeat of King Sihon

26 So I sent messengers from the wilderness of Kedemoth to King Sihon of Heshbon with the following terms of peace: 27"If you let me pass through your land, I will travel only along the road; I will turn aside neither to the right nor to the left. 28You shall sell me food for money, so that I may eat, and supply me water for money, so that I may drink. Only allow me to pass through on foot— 29just as the descendants of Esau who live in Seir have done for me and likewise the Moabites who live in Ar—until I cross the Jordan into the land that the LORD our God is giving us." 30But King Sihon of Heshbon was not willing to let us pass through, for the LORD your God had hardened his spirit and made his heart defiant in order to hand him over to you, as he has now done.

31 The LORD said to me, "See, I have begun to give Sihon and his land over to you. Begin now to take possession of his land." 32So when Sihon came out against us, he and all his people for battle at Jahaz, 33the LORD our God gave him over to us; and we struck him down, along with his offspring and all his people. 34At that time we captured all his towns, and in each town we utterly destroyed men, women, and children. We left not a single survivor. 35Only the livestock we kept as spoil for ourselves, as well as the plunder of the towns that we had captured. 36From Aroer on the edge of the Wadi Arnon (including the town that is in the wadi itself) as far as Gilead, there was no citadel too high for us. The LORD our God gave everything to us. 37You did not encroach, however, on the land of the Ammonites, avoiding the whole upper region of the Wadi Jabbok as well as the towns of the hill country, just asd the LORD our God had charged.

Defeat of King Og

3 When we headed up the road to Bashan, King Og of Bashan came out against us, he and all his people, for battle at Edrei. 2The LORD said to me, "Do not fear him, for I have handed him over to you, along with his people and his land. Do to him as you did to King Sihon of the Amorites, who reigned in Heshbon." 3So the LORD our God also handed over to us King Og of Bashan and all his people. We struck him down until not a single survivor was left. 4At that time we captured all his towns; there was no citadel that we did not take from them—sixty towns, the whole region of Argob, the kingdom of Og in Bashan. 5All these were fortress towns with high walls, double gates, and bars, besides a great many villages. 6And we utterly destroyed them, as we had done to King Sihon of Heshbon, in each city utterly destroying men, women, and children. 7But all the livestock and the plunder of the towns we kept as spoil for ourselves.

8 So at that time we took from the two kings of the Amorites the land beyond the Jordan, from the Wadi Arnon to Mount Hermon 9(the Sidonians call Hermon Sirion, while the Amorites call it Senir), 10all the towns of the tableland, the whole of Gilead, and all of Bashan, as far as Salecah and Edrei, towns of Og's kingdom in Bashan. 11(Now only King Og of Bashan was left of the remnant of the Rephaim. In fact his bed, an iron bed, can still be seen in Rabbah of the Ammonites. By the common cubit it is nine cubits long and four cubits wide.) 12As for the land that we took possession of at that time, I gave to the Reubenites and Gadites the territory north of Aroer,e that is on the edge of the Wadi Arnon, as well as half the hill country of Gilead with its towns, 13and I gave to the half-tribe of Manasseh the rest of Gilead and all of Bashan, Og's kingdom. (The whole region of Argob: all that portion of Bashan used to be called a land of Rephaim; 14Jair the Manassite acquired the whole region of Argob as far as the border of the Geshurites and the Maacathites, and he named them—that is, Bashan—after himself, Havvoth-jair,f as it is to this day.) 15To Machir I gave Gilead. 16And to the Reubenites and the Gadites I gave the territory from Gilead as far as the Wadi Arnon, with the middle of the wadi as a boundary, and up to the Jabbok, the wadi being boundary of the Ammonites; 17the Arabah also, with the Jordan and its banks, from Chinnereth down to the sea of the Arabah, the Dead Sea,g with the lower slopes of Pisgah on the east.

18 At that time, I charged you as follows: "Although the LORD your God has given you this land to occupy, all your troops shall cross over armed as the vanguard of your Israelite kin. 19Only your wives, your children, and your livestock—I know that you have much livestock—shall stay behind in the towns that I have given to you. 20When the LORD gives rest to your kindred, as to you, and they too have occupied the land that the LORD your God is giving them beyond the Jordan, then each of you may return to the property that I have given to you." 21And I charged Joshua as well at that time, say-

ing: "Your own eyes have seen everything that the LORD your God has done to these two kings; so the LORD will do to all the kingdoms into which you are about to cross. 22Do not fear them, for it is the LORD your God who fights for you."

Moses Views Canaan from Pisgah

23 At that time, too, I entreated the LORD, saying: 24"O Lord GOD, you have only begun to show your servant your greatness and your might; what god in heaven or on earth can perform deeds and mighty acts like yours! 25Let me cross over to see the good land beyond the Jordan, that good hill country and the Lebanon." 26But the LORD was angry with me on your account and would not heed me. The LORD said to me, "Enough from you! Never speak to me of this matter again! 27Go up to the top of Pisgah and look around you to the west, to the north, to the south, and to the east. Look well, for you shall not cross over this Jordan. 28But charge Joshua, and encourage and strengthen him, because it is he who shall cross over at the head of this people and who shall secure their possession of the land that you will see." 29So we remained in the valley opposite Beth-peor.

Moses Commands Obedience

4 So now, Israel, give heed to the statutes and ordinances that I am teaching you to observe, so that you may live to enter and occupy the land that the LORD, the God of your ancestors, is giving you. 2You must neither add anything to what I command you nor take away anything from it, but keep the commandments of the LORD your

4.2 Do Not Add

People usually remember they are not supposed to "drop" one of God's commands, but it is more subtly tempting to add commands. Religious people of Jesus' time, for example, invented elaborate rules on how far you could walk on the sabbath. Such "legalism" may seem holy, but goes against God's directions.

God with which I am charging you. 3You have seen for yourselves what the LORD did with regard to the Baal of Peor—how the LORD your God destroyed from among you everyone who followed the Baal of Peor, 4while those of you who held fast to the LORD your God are all alive today.

5 See, just as the LORD my God has charged me, I now teach you statutes and ordinances for you to observe in the land that you are about to enter and occupy. 6You must observe them diligently, for this will show your wisdom and dis-

cernment to the peoples, who, when they hear all these statutes, will say, "Surely this great nation is a wise and discerning people!" 7For what other great nation has a god so near to it as the LORD our God is whenever we call to him? 8And what

4.6 Old Testament Evangelism

As he explained various laws to the Israelites, Moses often appealed to their unique calling as a nation. God had chosen them as a "priestly kingdom" and a "treasured possession." This passage describes yet another benefit to keeping the law: what today we would call evangelism. The purity of the Israelites would serve as an example to the nations around them, who would then be attracted to the true God.

other great nation has statutes and ordinances as just as this entire law that I am setting before you today?

9 But take care and watch yourselves closely, so as neither to forget the things that your eyes have seen nor to let them slip from your mind all the days of your life; make them known to your children and your children's children— 10how you once stood before the LORD your God at Horeb, when the LORD said to me, "Assemble the people for me, and I will let them hear my words, so that they may learn to fear me as long as they live on the earth, and may teach their children so"; 11you approached and stood at the foot of the mountain while the mountain was blazing up to the very heavens, shrouded in dark clouds. 12Then the LORD spoke to you out of the fire. You heard the sound of words but saw no form; there was only a voice. 13He declared to you his covenant, which he charged you to observe, that is, the ten commandments;[h] and he wrote them on two stone tablets. 14And the LORD charged me at that time to teach you statutes and ordinances for you to observe in the land that you are about to cross into and occupy.

15 Since you saw no form when the LORD spoke to you at Horeb out of the fire, take care and watch yourselves closely, 16so that you do not act corruptly by making an idol for yourselves, in the form of any figure—the likeness of male or female, 17the likeness of any animal that is on the earth, the likeness of any winged bird that flies in the air, 18the likeness of anything that creeps on the ground, the likeness of any fish that is in the water under the earth. 19And when you look up to the heavens and see the sun, the moon, and the stars, all the host of heaven, do not be led astray and bow down to them and serve them, things that the LORD your God has allotted to all the

---

h Heb *the ten words*

peoples everywhere under heaven. [20]But the LORD has taken you and brought you out of the iron-smelter, out of Egypt, to become a people of his very own possession, as you are now.

21 The LORD was angry with me because of you, and he vowed that I should not cross the Jordan and that I should not enter the good land that the LORD your God is giving for your possession. [22]For I am going to die in this land without crossing over the Jordan, but you are going to cross over to take possession of that good land. [23]So be careful not to forget the covenant that the LORD your God made with you, and not to make for yourselves an idol in the form of anything that the LORD your God has forbidden you. [24]For the LORD your God is a devouring fire, a jealous God.

25 When you have had children and children's children, and become complacent in the land, if you act corruptly by making an idol in the form of anything, thus doing what is evil in the sight of the LORD your God, and provoking him to anger, [26]I call heaven and earth to witness against you today that you will soon utterly perish from the land that you are crossing the Jordan to occupy; you will not live long on it, but will be utterly destroyed. [27]The LORD will scatter you among the peoples; only a few of you will be left among the nations where the LORD will lead you. [28]There you will serve other gods made by human hands, objects of wood and stone that neither see, nor hear, nor eat, nor smell. [29]From there you will seek the LORD your God, and you will find him if you search after him with all your heart and soul. [30]In your distress, when all these things have happened to you in time to come, you will return to the LORD your God and heed him. [31]Because the LORD your God is a merciful God, he will neither abandon you nor destroy you; he will not forget the covenant with your ancestors that he swore to them.

32 For ask now about former ages, long before your own, ever since the day that God created human beings on the earth; ask from one end of heaven to the other: has anything so great as this ever happened or has its like ever been heard of? [33]Has any people ever heard the voice of a god speaking out of a fire, as you have heard, and lived? [34]Or has any god ever attempted to go and take a nation for himself from the midst of another nation, by trials, by signs and wonders, by war, by a mighty hand and an outstretched arm, and by terrifying displays of power, as the LORD your God did for you in Egypt before your very eyes? [35]To you it was shown so that you would acknowledge that the LORD is God; there is no other besides him. [36]From heaven he made you hear his voice to discipline you. On earth he showed you his great fire, while you heard his words coming out of the fire. [37]And because he loved your an-cestors, he chose their descendants after them. He brought you out of Egypt with his own presence, by his great power, [38]driving out before you nations greater and mightier than yourselves, to bring you in, giving you their land for a possession, as it is still today. [39]So acknowledge today

4.35 Experience Teaches

Chapter 4 follows a typical pattern in Deuteronomy: Moses begins with the Israelites' experience and then shows how the laws of the covenant relate directly to that experience. In this chapter, he vividly reminds them of their own encounters with God, especially at Mount Sinai. How did God reveal himself to them? "You saw no form," Moses concludes (verse 15); therefore, idols made with human hands would insult and devalue such a God. Then he describes the unique privilege the Israelites have: to know personally the God who created the universe.

and take to heart that the LORD is God in heaven above and on the earth beneath; there is no other. [40]Keep his statutes and his commandments, which I am commanding you today for your own well-being and that of your descendants after you, so that you may long remain in the land that the LORD your God is giving you for all time.

Cities of Refuge East of the Jordan

41 Then Moses set apart on the east side of the Jordan three cities [42]to which a homicide could flee, someone who unintentionally kills another person, the two not having been at enmity before; the homicide could flee to one of these cities and live: [43]Bezer in the wilderness on the tableland belonging to the Reubenites, Ramoth in Gilead belonging to the Gadites, and Golan in Bashan belonging to the Manassites.

Transition to the Second Address

44 This is the law that Moses set before the Israelites. [45]These are the decrees and the statutes and ordinances that Moses spoke to the Israelites when they had come out of Egypt, [46]beyond the Jordan in the valley opposite Beth-peor, in the land of King Sihon of the Amorites, who reigned at Heshbon, whom Moses and the Israelites defeated when they came out of Egypt. [47]They occupied his land and the land of King Og of Bashan, the two kings of the Amorites on the eastern side of the Jordan: [48]from Aroer, which is on the edge of the Wadi Arnon, as far as Mount Sirion[i] (that is, Hermon), [49]together with all the Arabah on the east side of the Jordan as far as the Sea of the Arabah, under the slopes of Pisgah.

i Syr: Heb Sion

The Ten Commandments

5 Moses convened all Israel, and said to them: Hear, O Israel, the statutes and ordinances that I am addressing to you today; you shall learn them and observe them diligently. [2]The LORD our God made a covenant with us at Horeb. [3]Not with our ancestors did the LORD make this covenant, but with us, who are all of us here alive today. [4]The LORD spoke with you face to face at the mountain, out of the fire. [5](At that time I was standing between the LORD and you to declare to you the words [j] of the LORD; for you were afraid because of the fire and did not go up the mountain.) And he said:

6 I am the LORD your God, who brought you out of the land of Egypt, out of the house of slavery; [7]you shall have no other gods before[k] me.

8 You shall not make for yourself an idol, whether in the form of anything that is in heaven above, or that is on the earth beneath, or that is in the water under the earth. [9]You shall not bow down to them or worship them; for I the LORD your God am a jealous God, punishing children for the iniquity of parents, to the third and fourth generation of those who reject me, [10]but showing steadfast love to the thousandth generation[l] of those who love me and keep my commandments.

11 You shall not make wrongful use of the name of the LORD your God, for the LORD will not acquit anyone who misuses his name.

12 Observe the sabbath day and keep it holy, as the LORD your God commanded you. [13]Six days you shall labor and do all your work. [14]But the seventh day is a sabbath to the LORD your God; you shall not do any work—you, or your son or your daughter, or your male or female slave, or your ox or your donkey, or any of your livestock, or the resident alien in your towns, so that your male and female slave may rest as well as you. [15]Remember that you were a slave in the land of Egypt, and the LORD your God brought you out from there with a mighty hand and an outstretched arm; therefore the LORD your God commanded you to keep the sabbath day.

16 Honor your father and your mother, as the LORD your God commanded you, so that your days may be long and that it may go well with you in the land that the LORD your God is giving you. [17]You shall not murder.[m]

18 Neither shall you commit adultery.

19 Neither shall you steal.

20 Neither shall you bear false witness against your neighbor.

21 Neither shall you covet your neighbor's wife.

Neither shall you desire your neighbor's house, or field, or male or female slave, or ox, or donkey, or anything that belongs to your neighbor.

Moses the Mediator of God's Will

22 These words the LORD spoke with a loud voice to your whole assembly at the mountain, out of the fire, the cloud, and the thick darkness, and he added no more. He wrote them on two stone tablets, and gave them to me. [23]When you heard the voice out of the darkness, while the mountain was burning with fire, you approached me, all the heads of your tribes and your elders; [24]and you said, "Look, the LORD our God has shown us his glory and greatness, and we have heard his voice out of the fire. Today we have seen that God may speak to someone and the person may still live. [25]So now why should we die? For this great fire will consume us; if we hear the voice of the LORD our God any longer, we shall die. [26]For who is there of all flesh that has heard the voice of the living God speaking out of fire, as we have, and remained alive? [27]Go near, you yourself, and hear all that the LORD our God will say. Then tell us everything that the LORD our God tells you, and we will listen and do it."

28 The LORD heard your words when you spoke to me, and the LORD said to me: "I have heard the words of this people, which they have spoken to you; they are right in all that they have spoken. [29]If only they had such a mind as this, to fear me and to keep all my commandments always, so that it might go well with them and with their children forever! [30]Go say to them, 'Return to your tents.' [31]But you, stand here by me, and I will tell you all the commandments, the statutes and the ordinances, that you shall teach them, so that they may do them in the land that I am giving them to possess." [32]You must therefore be careful to do as the LORD your God has commanded you; you shall not turn to the right or to the left. [33]You must follow exactly the path that the LORD your God has commanded you, so that you may live, and that it may go well with you, and that you may live long in the land that you are to possess.

The Great Commandment

6 Now this is the commandment—the statutes and the ordinances—that the LORD your God charged me to teach you to observe in the land that you are about to cross into and occupy, [2]so that you and your children and your children's children may fear the LORD your God all the days of your life, and keep all his decrees and his commandments that I am commanding you, so that your days may be long. [3]Hear therefore, O Israel, and observe them diligently, so that it may go well with you, and so that you may multiply greatly in a land flowing with milk and honey, as the LORD, the God of your ancestors, has promised you.

4 Hear, O Israel: The LORD is our God, the

---

j Q Mss Sam Gk Syr Vg Tg: MT *word*   *k* Or *besides*   *l* Or *to thousands*   *m* Or *kill*

LORD alone."[n] [5]You shall love the LORD your God with all your heart, and with all your soul, and with all your might. [6]Keep these words that I am commanding you today in your heart. [7]Recite them to your children and talk about them when you are at home and when you are away, when you lie down and when you rise. [8]Bind them as a sign on your hand, fix them as an emblem[o] on your forehead, [9]and write them on the doorposts of your house and on your gates.

6.4 Most Quoted Verses

These six verses (4–9) may well be the most quoted portion in the entire Bible. Known as the Shema, they are recited every morning and every evening by orthodox Jews—and have been for hundreds of years. They graphically emphasize the importance of God's laws to the Israelites.

Caution against Disobedience

10 When the LORD your God has brought you into the land that he swore to your ancestors, to Abraham, to Isaac, and to Jacob, to give you—a land with fine, large cities that you did not build, [11]houses filled with all sorts of goods that you did not fill, hewn cisterns that you did not hew, vineyards and olive groves that you did not plant—and when you have eaten your fill, [12]take care that you do not forget the LORD, who brought you out of the land of Egypt, out of the house of slavery. [13]The LORD your God you shall fear; him you shall serve, and by his name alone you shall swear. [14]Do not follow other gods, any of the gods of the peoples who are all around you, [15]because the LORD your God, who is present with you, is a jealous God. The anger of the LORD your God would be kindled against you and he would destroy you from the face of the earth.

16 Do not put the LORD your God to the test, as you tested him at Massah. [17]You must diligently keep the commandments of the LORD your God, and his decrees, and his statutes that he has commanded you. [18]Do what is right and good in the sight of the LORD, so that it may go well with you, and so that you may go in and occupy the good land that the LORD swore to your ancestors to give you, [19]thrusting out all your enemies from before you, as the LORD has promised.

20 When your children ask you in time to come, "What is the meaning of the decrees and the statutes and the ordinances that the LORD our God has commanded you?" [21]then you shall say to your children, "We were Pharaoh's slaves in Egypt, but the LORD brought us out of Egypt with a mighty hand. [22]The LORD displayed before our eyes great and awesome signs and wonders against Egypt, against Pharaoh and all his household. [23]He brought us out from there in order to bring us in, to give us the land that he promised on oath to our ancestors. [24]Then the LORD commanded us to observe all these statutes, to fear the LORD our God, for our lasting good, so as to keep us alive, as is now the case. [25]If we diligently observe this entire commandment before the LORD our God, as he has commanded us, we will be in the right."

A Chosen People

7 When the LORD your God brings you into the land that you are about to enter and occupy, and he clears away many nations before you—the Hittites, the Girgashites, the Amorites, the Canaanites, the Perizzites, the Hivites, and the Jebusites, seven nations mightier and more numerous than you— [2]and when the LORD your God gives them over to you and you defeat them, then you must utterly destroy them. Make no covenant with them and show them no mercy. [3]Do not intermarry with them, giving your daughters to their sons or taking their daughters for your sons, [4]for that would turn away your children from following me, to serve other gods. Then the anger of the LORD would be kindled against you, and he would destroy you quickly. [5]But this is how you must deal with them: break down their altars, smash their pillars, hew down their sacred poles,[p] and burn their idols with fire. [6]For you are a people holy to the LORD your God; the LORD your God has chosen you out of all the peoples on earth to be his people, his treasured possession.

7 It was not because you were more numerous than any other people that the LORD set his heart on you and chose you—for you were the

7.7 Why the Israelites?

Deuteronomy makes clear that God chose Israel out of pure grace. He did not select them for their impressiveness (this verse), their goodness (9.5), or their faithfulness (9.24). Rather, he chose them because he loved them, and he had made absolute promises to their ancestors. Deuteronomy promises the new land to the Israelites 69 times.

fewest of all peoples. [8]It was because the LORD loved you and kept the oath that he swore to your ancestors, that the LORD has brought you out with a mighty hand, and redeemed you from the house of slavery, from the hand of Pharaoh king of Egypt. [9]Know therefore that the LORD your God is

---

[n] Or *The LORD our God is one LORD,* or *The LORD our God, the LORD is one,* or *The LORD is our God, the LORD is one*
[o] Or *as a frontlet*   [p] Heb *Asherim*

God, the faithful God who maintains covenant loyalty with those who love him and keep his commandments, to a thousand generations, [10]and who repays in their own person those who reject him. He does not delay but repays in their own person those who reject him. [11]Therefore, observe diligently the commandment—the statutes and the ordinances—that I am commanding you today.

Blessings for Obedience

12 If you heed these ordinances, by diligently observing them, the LORD your God will maintain with you the covenant loyalty that he swore to your ancestors; [13]he will love you, bless you, and multiply you; he will bless the fruit of your womb and the fruit of your ground, your grain and your wine and your oil, the increase of your cattle and the issue of your flock, in the land that he swore to your ancestors to give you. [14]You shall be the most blessed of peoples, with neither sterility nor barrenness among you or your livestock. [15]The LORD will turn away from you every illness; all the dread diseases of Egypt that you experienced, he will not inflict on you, but he will lay them on all who hate you. [16]You shall devour all the peoples that the LORD your God is giving over to you, showing them no pity; you shall not serve their gods, for that would be a snare to you.

17 If you say to yourself, "These nations are more numerous than I; how can I dispossess them?" [18]do not be afraid of them. Just remember what the LORD your God did to Pharaoh and to all Egypt, [19]the great trials that your eyes saw, the signs and wonders, the mighty hand and the outstretched arm by which the LORD your God brought you out. The LORD your God will do the same to all the peoples of whom you are afraid. [20]Moreover, the LORD your God will send the pestilence[q] against them, until even the survivors and the fugitives are destroyed. [21]Have no dread of them, for the LORD your God, who is present with you, is a great and awesome God. [22]The LORD your God will clear away these nations before you little by little; you will not be able to make a quick end of them, otherwise the wild animals would become too numerous for you. [23]But the LORD your God will give them over to you, and throw them into great panic, until they are destroyed. [24]He will hand their kings over to you and you shall blot out their name from under heaven; no one will be able to stand against you, until you have destroyed them. [25]The images of their gods you shall burn with fire. Do not covet the silver or the gold that is on them and take it for yourself, because you could be ensnared by it; for it is abhorrent to the LORD your God. [26]Do not bring an abhorrent thing into your house, or you will be set apart for destruction like it. You must

utterly detest and abhor it, for it is set apart for destruction.

A Warning Not to Forget God in Prosperity

8 This entire commandment that I command you today you must diligently observe, so that you may live and increase, and go in and occupy the land that the LORD promised on oath to your ancestors. [2]Remember the long way that the LORD your God has led you these forty years in the wilderness, in order to humble you, testing you to know what was in your heart, whether or not you would keep his commandments. [3]He humbled you by letting you hunger, then by feeding you with manna, with which neither you nor your ancestors were acquainted, in order to make you understand that one does not live by bread alone, but by every word that comes from the

---

8.3 Words for the Devil

When tempted by Satan (Luke 4.1–13), Jesus responded with three separate quotations from Deuteronomy: this verse, and Deuteronomy 6.13,16. In the desert, Israelites had learned that God would provide all they needed. Jesus, also in the desert, quoted scripture to forcefully remind Satan of that lesson.

---

mouth of the LORD.[r] [4]The clothes on your back did not wear out and your feet did not swell these forty years. [5]Know then in your heart that as a parent disciplines a child so the LORD your God disciplines you. [6]Therefore keep the commandments of the LORD your God, by walking in his ways and by fearing him. [7]For the LORD your God is bringing you into a good land, a land with flowing streams, with springs and underground waters welling up in valleys and hills, [8]a land of wheat and barley, of vines and fig trees and pomegranates, a land of olive trees and honey, [9]a land where you may eat bread without scarcity, where you will lack nothing, a land whose stones are iron and from whose hills you may mine copper. [10]You shall eat your fill and bless the LORD your God for the good land that he has given you.

11 Take care that you do not forget the LORD your God, by failing to keep his commandments, his ordinances, and his statutes, which I am commanding you today. [12]When you have eaten your fill and have built fine houses and live in them, [13]and when your herds and flocks have multiplied, and your silver and gold is multiplied, and all that you have is multiplied, [14]then do not exalt yourself, forgetting the LORD your God, who brought you out of the land of Egypt, out of the

---

[q] Or *hornets*: Meaning of Heb uncertain   [r] Or *by anything that the LORD decrees*

house of slavery, [15]who led you through the great and terrible wilderness, an arid wasteland with poisonous[s] snakes and scorpions. He made water flow for you from flint rock, [16]and fed you in the wilderness with manna that your ancestors did not know, to humble you and to test you, and in the end to do you good. [17]Do not say to yourself, "My power and the might of my own hand have gotten me this wealth." [18]But remember the LORD your God, for it is he who gives you power to get wealth, so that he may confirm his covenant that he swore to your ancestors, as he is doing today. [19]If you do forget the LORD your God and follow other gods to serve and worship them, I solemnly warn you today that you shall surely perish. [20]Like the nations that the LORD is destroying before you, so shall you perish, because you would not obey the voice of the LORD your God.

The Consequences of Rebelling against God

9 Hear, O Israel! You are about to cross the Jordan today, to go in and dispossess nations larger and mightier than you, great cities, fortified to the heavens, [2]a strong and tall people, the offspring of the Anakim, whom you know. You have heard it said of them, "Who can stand up to the Anakim?" [3]Know then today that the LORD your God is the one who crosses over before you as a devouring fire; he will defeat them and subdue them before you, so that you may dispossess and destroy them quickly, as the LORD has promised you.

4 When the LORD your God thrusts them out before you, do not say to yourself, "It is because of my righteousness that the LORD has brought me in to occupy this land"; it is rather because of the wickedness of these nations that the LORD is dispossessing them before you. [5]It is not because

of your righteousness or the uprightness of your heart that you are going in to occupy their land; but because of the wickedness of these nations the LORD your God is dispossessing them before you, in order to fulfill the promise that the LORD made on oath to your ancestors, to Abraham, to Isaac, and to Jacob.

6 Know, then, that the LORD your God is not giving you this good land to occupy because of your righteousness; for you are a stubborn people. [7]Remember and do not forget how you provoked the LORD your God to wrath in the wilderness; you have been rebellious against the LORD from the day you came out of the land of Egypt until you came to this place.

8 Even at Horeb you provoked the LORD to wrath, and the LORD was so angry with you that he was ready to destroy you. [9]When I went up the mountain to receive the stone tablets, the tablets of the covenant that the LORD made with you, I remained on the mountain forty days and forty nights; I neither ate bread nor drank water. [10]And the LORD gave me the two stone tablets written with the finger of God; on them were all the words that the LORD had spoken to you at the mountain out of the fire on the day of the assembly. [11]At the end of forty days and forty nights the LORD gave me the two stone tablets, the tablets of the covenant. [12]Then the LORD said to me, "Get up, go down quickly from here, for your people whom you have brought from Egypt have acted corruptly. They have been quick to turn from the way that I commanded them; they have cast an image for themselves." [13]Furthermore the LORD said to me, "I have seen that this people is indeed a stubborn people. [14]Let me alone that I may destroy them and blot out their name from under heaven; and I will make of you a nation mightier and more numerous than they."

15 So I turned and went down from the mountain, while the mountain was ablaze; the two tablets of the covenant were in my two hands. [16]Then I saw that you had indeed sinned against the LORD your God, by casting for yourselves an image of a calf; you had been quick to turn from the way that the LORD had commanded you. [17]So I took hold of the two tablets and flung them from my two hands, smashing them before your eyes. [18]Then I lay prostrate before the LORD as before, forty days and forty nights; I neither ate bread nor drank water, because of all the sin you had committed, provoking the LORD by doing what was evil in his sight. [19]For I was afraid that the anger that the LORD bore against you was so fierce that he would destroy you. But the LORD listened to me that time also. [20]The LORD was so angry with Aaron that he was ready to destroy him, but I interceded also on behalf of Aaron at that same time. [21]Then I took the sinful thing you

9.4 Reasons for Warfare

Commands for the Israelites to utterly destroy other nations have caused modern readers of the Old Testament much concern. This passage reveals that God was acting not because of the Israelites' superior moral character, but because of the inhabitants' own wickedness. Chapter 20.16–18 gives yet another rationale for the wars: to keep Israel free from contamination by other nations. The Israelites never followed these commands completely, and their nation was ultimately weakened and destroyed precisely because of such contamination. (See "Is a War Ever Holy?" page 242, for further details.)

[s] Or *fiery*; Heb *seraph*

had made, the calf, and burned it with fire and crushed it, grinding it thoroughly, until it was reduced to dust; and I threw the dust of it into the stream that runs down the mountain.

22 At Taberah also, and at Massah, and at Kibroth-hattaavah, you provoked the LORD to wrath. 23And when the LORD sent you from Kadesh-barnea, saying, "Go up and occupy the land that I have given you," you rebelled against the command of the LORD your God, neither trusting him nor obeying him. 24You have been rebellious against the LORD as long as he has*t known you.

t Sam Gk: MT I have

25 Throughout the forty days and forty nights that I lay prostrate before the LORD when the LORD intended to destroy you, 26I prayed to the LORD and said, "Lord GOD, do not destroy the people who are your very own possession, whom you redeemed in your greatness, whom you brought out of Egypt with a mighty hand. 27Remember your servants, Abraham, Isaac, and Jacob; pay no attention to the stubbornness of this people, their wickedness and their sin, 28otherwise the land from which you have brought us might say, 'Because the LORD was not able to bring them into the land that he promised them,

Healthier, Wealthier, and Wiser
Do only good things happen to good people?

> When your herds and flocks have multiplied, and your silver and gold is multiplied, and all that you have is multiplied, then do not exalt yourself, forgetting the LORD your God, who brought you out of the land of Egypt, out of the house of slavery. 8.13–14

DO CHRISTIANS HAVE CAR ACCIDENTS? Do they get cancer? Are they ever fired from their jobs? The answer to all three questions is, of course, yes. But that answer causes big problems for some new Christians. Doesn't the Bible promise that God will look out for and protect his followers? How can such bad things occur?

People puzzled by such questions often refer to Old Testament books where God clearly promised success and protection to the Israelites. In Deuteronomy, Moses spelled out God's promises in complete detail. Israelite wives would have many babies. All the crops—grain, grapes, olive trees—would produce bountifully. Cattle and sheep would multiply. And Moses even included this extraordinary promise: "The LORD will turn away from you every illness" (7.15).

A Special Arrangement

For the Israelites to receive these benefits, God asked only one thing in return: follow the covenant agreement first set forth in the book of Exodus. Deuteronomy repeats much of the covenant and affirms, "Not with our ancestors did the LORD make this covenant, but with us, who are all of us here alive today" (5.3).

God had a unique relationship with the band of refugees who had been roaming the Sinai for 40 years (10.15; 14.2). Moses, for one, could not seem to get over the arrangement. "Ask from one end of heaven to the other," he said. "Has anything so great as this ever happened, or has its like ever been heard of? Has any god ever attempted to go and take a nation for himself from the midst of another nation . . . as the LORD your God did for you in Egypt before your very eyes?" (4.32,34).

Moses promised that good things would come the Israelites' way if they merely held up their end of the covenant. *If,* he said—underscoring that small but very crucial word. Threads of doubt and anxiety run all through the book. Will the Israelites stick to the terms of the covenant? Will they obey?

Dangers of Success

Moses seemed to fear the coming prosperity even more than the rigors of the desert, and he voiced those fears in chapter 8. In the promised land, a lush country of streams and fruit trees and valuable resources, the Israelites might forget God and begin to take credit for their own success. That, at least, was the danger, and the reason Moses kept urging, "Remember!" Remember the days of slavery in Egypt, and God's acts in liberating you. Remember the trials of the vast and desolate desert, and God's faithfulness there. Remember your special calling as a peculiar treasure of God. Do not forget, as a prosperous nation, what you learned as refugees in the Sinai.

God predicted bluntly, "when I have brought them into the land flowing with milk and honey, which I promised on oath to their ancestors, and they have eaten their fill and grown fat, they will turn to other gods and serve them, despising me and breaking my covenant" (31.20).

and because he hated them, he has brought them out to let them die in the wilderness.' ²⁹For they are the people of your very own possession, whom you brought out by your great power and by your outstretched arm."

The Second Pair of Tablets

10 At that time the LORD said to me, "Carve out two tablets of stone like the former ones, and come up to me on the mountain, and make an ark of wood. ²I will write on the tablets the words that were on the former tablets, which you smashed, and you shall put them in the ark." ³So I made an ark of acacia wood, cut two tablets of stone like the former ones, and went up the mountain with the two tablets in my hand. ⁴Then he wrote on the tablets the same words as before, the ten commandments*ᵘ* that the LORD had spoken to you on the mountain out of the fire on the day of the assembly; and the LORD gave them to me. ⁵So I turned and came down from the mountain, and put the tablets in the ark that I had made; and there they are, as the LORD commanded me.

6 (The Israelites journeyed from Beeroth-bene-jaakan*ᵛ* to Moserah. There Aaron died, and there he was buried; his son Eleazar succeeded him as priest. ⁷From there they journeyed to Gudgodah, and from Gudgodah to Jotbathah, a land with flowing streams. ⁸At that time the LORD set apart the tribe of Levi to carry the ark of the covenant of the LORD, to stand before the LORD to minister to him, and to bless in his name, to this day. ⁹Therefore Levi has no allotment or inheritance with his kindred; the LORD is his inheritance, as the LORD your God promised him.)

10 I stayed on the mountain forty days and forty nights, as I had done the first time. And once again the LORD listened to me. The LORD was unwilling to destroy you. ¹¹The LORD said to me, "Get up, go on your journey at the head of the people, that they may go in and occupy the land that I swore to their ancestors to give them."

The Essence of the Law

12 So now, O Israel, what does the LORD your God require of you? Only to fear the LORD your God, to walk in all his ways, to love him, to serve the LORD your God with all your heart and with all your soul, ¹³and to keep the commandments of the LORD your God*ʷ* and his decrees that I am commanding you today, for your own well-being. ¹⁴Although heaven and the heaven of heav-

10.12 More Than a Feeling

Twelve times Deuteronomy says we are to love God. In fact, Jesus was quoting Deuteronomy 6.5 when he gave the most important commandment as "love the Lord your God with all your heart" (Mark 12.30). How can we love when we don't feel loving? In the Bible, love is more than a feeling; it is a decision to serve another person's interest. Only through God's help can this decision be made with "all your heart."

ᵘ Heb *the ten words*   *ᵛ* Or *the wells of the Bene-jaakan*   *ʷ* Q Ms Gk Syr: MT lacks *your God*

As the books following Deuteronomy record, all that God and Moses feared came true. The covenant was irreparably broken. Ultimately, the Israelites received not wealth and happiness but slavery and suffering.

A Message for Us Today

The promises of Deuteronomy were given to a particular people, the Israelites, in a special covenant relationship—a covenant that God prophesied would be broken. The formula was simple: "Do good, get rewarded; do evil, get punished." But Christians of today cannot simply turn to those flagrant promises of wealth and prosperity and apply them directly. Rather, we must look at this book in light of the new covenant introduced by Jesus Christ and spelled out in the New Testament.

When Jesus came, he promised certain rewards for Christians, but he also predicted poverty, rejection, and even persecution. Rewards on this earth cannot be reduced to such a simple "Do good, get rewarded; do evil, get punished" formula. (See Hebrews 11 and "What Is True Faith?" page 1272.) Jesus' disciples proved faithful to him, and yet most of them lived through poverty and persecution and died martyrs' deaths. For them, full rewards had to wait until heaven.

Deuteronomy may offer a clue to why God does not exempt his followers from every bad thing in life. Ironically, prosperity and health may make it harder to depend on God. Moses' fears came true: The Israelites proved least faithful to God after they moved into the prosperity of the promised land. In the desert, at least, they had been forced to lean on God just for daily survival. But after a very short time in Canaan, they forgot about him. There is a grave danger in finally getting what you want.

Life Questions: When do you think most about God: when things are going well or when you are in trouble?

ens belong to the LORD your God, the earth with all that is in it, [15]yet the LORD set his heart in love on your ancestors alone and chose you, their descendants after them, out of all the peoples, as it is today. [16]Circumcise, then, the foreskin of your heart, and do not be stubborn any longer. [17]For the LORD your God is God of gods and Lord of lords, the great God, mighty and awesome, who is not partial and takes no bribe, [18]who executes justice for the orphan and the widow, and who loves the strangers, providing them food and clothing. [19]You shall also love the stranger, for you were strangers in the land of Egypt. [20]You shall fear the LORD your God; him alone you shall worship; to him you shall hold fast, and by his name you shall swear. [21]He is your praise; he is your God, who has done for you these great and awesome things that your own eyes have seen. [22]Your ancestors went down to Egypt seventy persons; and now the LORD your God has made you as numerous as the stars in heaven.

Rewards for Obedience

11 You shall love the LORD your God, therefore, and keep his charge, his decrees, his ordinances, and his commandments always. [2]Remember today that it was not your children (who have not known or seen the discipline of the LORD your God), but it is you who must acknowledge his greatness, his mighty hand and his outstretched arm, [3]his signs and his deeds that he did in Egypt to Pharaoh, the king of Egypt, and to all his land; [4]what he did to the Egyptian army, to their horses and chariots, how he made the water of the Red Sea[x] flow over them as they pursued you, so that the LORD has destroyed them to this day; [5]what he did to you in the wilderness, until you came to this place; [6]and what he did to Dathan and Abiram, sons of Eliab son of Reuben, how in the midst of all Israel the earth opened its mouth and swallowed them up, along with their households, their tents, and every living being in their company; [7]for it is your own eyes that have seen every great deed that the LORD did.

[8] Keep, then, this entire commandment that I am commanding you today, so that you may have strength to go in and occupy the land that you are crossing over to occupy, [9]and so that you may live long in the land that the LORD swore to your ancestors to give them and to their descendants, a land flowing with milk and honey. [10]For the land that you are about to enter to occupy is not like the land of Egypt, from which you have come, where you sow your seed and irrigate by foot like a vegetable garden. [11]But the land that you are crossing over to occupy is a land of hills and valleys, watered by rain from the sky, [12]a land that the LORD your God looks after. The eyes of the

LORD your God are always on it, from the beginning of the year to the end of the year.

[13] If you will only heed his every commandment[y] that I am commanding you today— loving the LORD your God, and serving him with all your heart and with all your soul— [14]then he[z] will give the rain for your land in its season, the early rain and the later rain, and you will gather in your grain, your wine, and your oil; [15]and he[z] will give grass in your fields for your livestock, and you will eat your fill. [16]Take care, or you will be seduced into turning away, serving other gods and worshiping them, [17]for then the anger of the LORD will be kindled against you and he will shut up the heavens, so that there will be no rain and the land will yield no fruit; then you will perish quickly off the good land that the LORD is giving you.

[18] You shall put these words of mine in your heart and soul, and you shall bind them as a sign on your hand, and fix them as an emblem[a] on

11.18 Laws on the Head

Many commentators, both Jewish and Christian, read these sentences figuratively. But strict Jews take them literally. They wear handwritten portions of the Old Testament (including Deuteronomy 6.4–9 and 11.18–20) in a small box strapped to their foreheads, and they also mount them in a box beside the door to their homes. The boxes are called "phylacteries." Jesus referred to the practice (Matthew 23.5), commenting that it could become a showy way of expressing spiritual pride.

your forehead. [19]Teach them to your children, talking about them when you are at home and when you are away, when you lie down and when you rise. [20]Write them on the doorposts of your house and on your gates, [21]so that your days and the days of your children may be multiplied in the land that the LORD swore to your ancestors to give them, as long as the heavens are above the earth.

[22] If you will diligently observe this entire commandment that I am commanding you, loving the LORD your God, walking in all his ways, and holding fast to him, [23]then the LORD will drive out all these nations before you, and you will dispossess nations larger and mightier than yourselves. [24]Every place on which you set foot shall be yours; your territory shall extend from the wilderness to the Lebanon and from the River, the river Euphrates, to the Western Sea. [25]No one will be able to stand against you; the LORD your God will put the fear and dread of you on all the land on which you set foot, as he promised you.

---

[x] Or *Sea of Reeds*   [y] Compare Gk: Heb *my commandments*   [z] Sam Gk Vg: MT I   [a] Or *as a frontlet*

26 See, I am setting before you today a blessing and a curse: [27]the blessing, if you obey the commandments of the LORD your God that I am commanding you today; [28]and the curse, if you do not obey the commandments of the LORD your God, but turn from the way that I am commanding you today, to follow other gods that you have not known.

29 When the LORD your God has brought you into the land that you are entering to occupy, you shall set the blessing on Mount Gerizim and the curse on Mount Ebal. [30]As you know, they are beyond the Jordan, some distance to the west, in the land of the Canaanites who live in the Arabah, opposite Gilgal, beside the oak[b] of Moreh.

31 When you cross the Jordan to go in to occupy the land that the LORD your God is giving you, and when you occupy it and live in it, [32]you must diligently observe all the statutes and ordinances that I am setting before you today.

Pagan Shrines to Be Destroyed

12 These are the statutes and ordinances that you must diligently observe in the land that the LORD, the God of your ancestors, has given you to occupy all the days that you live on the earth.

2 You must demolish completely all the places where the nations whom you are about to dispossess served their gods, on the mountain heights, on the hills, and under every leafy tree.

12.2 Historic Discovery

The Israelites did not fully follow these instructions on destroying the "high places," which were centers of idol worship. But hundreds of years after this scene with Moses, a dramatic event took place. In the midst of a temple renovation, workers came across an old scroll containing the book of the law. Discovery of the book had an electrifying effect on the nation. When King Josiah heard it read, he wept and tore his robes, then called for all the elders to hear the words. The event ushered in a sweeping spiritual revival that included a campaign against idolatry and the "high places." Many scholars believe Deuteronomy was the book that stirred a kingdom (see 2 Kings 22–23 for the full account).

[3]Break down their altars, smash their pillars, burn their sacred poles[c] with fire, and hew down the idols of their gods, and thus blot out their name from their places. [4]You shall not worship the LORD your God in such ways. [5]But you shall seek the place that the LORD your God will choose out of all your tribes as his habitation to put his name

there. You shall go there, [6]bringing there your burnt offerings and your sacrifices, your tithes and your donations, your votive gifts, your freewill offerings, and the firstlings of your herds and flocks. [7]And you shall eat there in the presence of the LORD your God, you and your households together, rejoicing in all the undertakings in which the LORD your God has blessed you.

8 You shall not act as we are acting here today, all of us according to our own desires, [9]for you have not yet come into the rest and the possession that the LORD your God is giving you. [10]When you cross over the Jordan and live in the land that the LORD your God is allotting to you, and when he gives you rest from your enemies all around so that you live in safety, [11]then you shall bring everything that I command you to the place that the LORD your God will choose as a dwelling for his name: your burnt offerings and your sacrifices, your tithes and your donations, and all your choice votive gifts that you vow to the LORD. [12]And you shall rejoice before the LORD your God, you together with your sons and your daughters, your male and female slaves, and the Levites who reside in your towns (since they have no allotment or inheritance with you).

A Prescribed Place of Worship

13 Take care that you do not offer your burnt offerings at any place you happen to see. [14]But only at the place that the LORD will choose in one of your tribes—there you shall offer your burnt offerings and there you shall do everything I command you.

15 Yet whenever you desire you may slaughter and eat meat within any of your towns, according to the blessing that the LORD your God has given you; the unclean and the clean may eat of it, as they would of gazelle or deer. [16]The blood, however, you must not eat; you shall pour it out on the ground like water. [17]Nor may you eat within your towns the tithe of your grain, your wine, and your oil, the firstlings of your herds and your flocks, any of your votive gifts that you vow, your freewill offerings, or your donations; [18]these you shall eat in the presence of the LORD your God at the place that the LORD your God will choose, you together with your son and your daughter, your male and female slaves, and the Levites resident in your towns, rejoicing in the presence of the LORD your God in all your undertakings. [19]Take care that you do not neglect the Levite as long as you live in your land.

20 When the LORD your God enlarges your territory, as he has promised you, and you say, "I am going to eat some meat," because you wish to eat meat, you may eat meat whenever you have the desire. [21]If the place where the LORD your God

---

[b] Gk Syr: Compare Gen 12.6; Heb *oaks* or *terebinths*   [c] Heb *Asherim*

will choose to put his name is too far from you, and you slaughter as I have commanded you any of your herd or flock that the LORD has given you, then you may eat within your towns whenever you desire. ²²Indeed, just as gazelle or deer is eaten, so you may eat it; the unclean and the clean alike may eat it. ²³Only be sure that you do not eat the blood; for the blood is the life, and you shall not eat the life with the meat. ²⁴Do not eat it; you shall pour it out on the ground like water. ²⁵Do not eat it, so that all may go well with you and your children after you, because you do what is right in the sight of the LORD. ²⁶But the sacred donations that are due from you, and your votive gifts, you shall bring to the place that the LORD will choose. ²⁷You shall present your burnt offerings, both the meat and the blood, on the altar of the LORD your God; the blood of your other sacri-

Who Needs Laws?

Love makes the difference in this rulebook

DEUTERONOMY REPEATS VERBATIM MANY OF the laws given in Exodus, Leviticus, and Numbers. Yet it is far from a rulebook. A different spirit pervades it: the spirit of love. The rules in Deuteronomy read more like a guide on "How to Have a Successful Family" than, say, an automobile maintenance manual. To keep up a car you need only follow the rules. To maintain a close personal relationship you need more—you need love.

> Be careful to obey all these words that I command you today, so that it may go well with you and with your children after you forever, because you will be doing what is good and right in the sight of the LORD your God. 12.28

What Makes Deuteronomy Different

Deuteronomy focuses on motives: *why* people should obey laws. The preceding three books barely mentioned the love of God for his people, but Deuteronomy again and again refers to it (see 4.37; 7.7–8; 10.15; 23.5). The author portrays God as a father with his children, as a mother who gives them life, as an eagle hovering over its young.

In return, God asks for obedience based on love, not on a sense of duty. At least 15 times in the book Moses tells the Israelites to love God and cling to him. God wants not just an outward conformity, but an obedience that comes from the heart. (Later, in summing up the Old Testament, Jesus quoted the first and greatest commandment from Deuteronomy: "Love the Lord your God with all your heart, and with all your soul, and with all your might" [Matthew 22.37; Deuteronomy 6.5].)

Restating the Negatives

Deuteronomy also hints at why laws are needed in the first place. Moses stated the principle directly, "the LORD commanded us to observe all these statutes, to fear the LORD our God, for our lasting good, so as to keep us alive, as is now the case" (6.24). In other words, the laws were given for the Israelites' own good.

Most of the Ten Commandments were given in a negative form, "You shall not." But each of these negative statements protects a privileged relationship between two people or a person and God. For example, "Do not murder" could be restated, "Human life is sacred and has enormous worth. Respect such life as the image of God, and defend it." Other commandments protect marriage, private property, honesty, and the day set aside to worship God.

Never Forget

Moses could not have emphasized the laws more strongly. "Keep these words that I am commanding you today in your heart, " he said. "Recite them to your children and talk about them when you are at home and when you are away, when you lie down and when you rise" (6.6–7).

Moses wanted to make sure the Israelites would not possibly forget the laws. He instructed the priests to gather the whole nation together to hear them read aloud every seven years (31.9–13). Any king of Israel was required, as one of his first acts, to write out the laws by hand (17.18–19).

One last visual reminder served to impress the laws on the Israelites' minds. The priests wrote them in bold letters on stones covered with plaster. As the tribes marched across the Jordan River into the new land, they passed between the writing-covered stones (27.1–8).

No one in Israel could plead ignorance of what God required of them—his rules were carved in stone. As history would prove, obeying the rules was another matter.

Life Questions: Read over the Ten Commandments in Deuteronomy 5. How do they help us? What "rights" are they protecting?

fices shall be poured out beside[d] the altar of the LORD your God, but the meat you may eat.

28 Be careful to obey all these words that I command you today,[e] so that it may go well with you and with your children after you forever, because you will be doing what is good and right in the sight of the LORD your God.

Warning against Idolatry

29 When the LORD your God has cut off before you the nations whom you are about to enter to dispossess them, when you have dispossessed them and live in their land, 30take care that you are not snared into imitating them, after they have been destroyed before you: do not inquire concerning their gods, saying, "How did these nations worship their gods? I also want to do the same." 31You must not do the same for the LORD your God, because every abhorrent thing that the LORD hates they have done for their gods. They would even burn their sons and their daughters in the fire to their gods. 32 f You must diligently observe everything that I command you; do not add to it or take anything from it.

13 g If prophets or those who divine by dreams appear among you and promise you omens

or portents, 2and the omens or the portents declared by them take place, and they say, "Let us follow other gods" (whom you have not known) "and let us serve them," 3you must not heed the words of those prophets or those who divine by dreams; for the LORD your God is testing you, to know whether you indeed love the LORD your God with all your heart and soul. 4The LORD your God you shall follow, him alone you shall fear, his commandments you shall keep, his voice you shall obey, him you shall serve, and to him you shall hold fast. 5But those prophets or those who divine by dreams shall be put to death for having spoken treason against the LORD your God—who brought you out of the land of Egypt and redeemed you from the house of slavery—to turn you from the way in which the LORD your God

commanded you to walk. So you shall purge the evil from your midst.

6 If anyone secretly entices you—even if it is your brother, your father's son or[h] your mother's son, or your own son or daughter, or the wife you embrace, or your most intimate friend—saying, "Let us go worship other gods," whom neither you nor your ancestors have known, 7any of the gods of the peoples that are around you, whether near you or far away from you, from one end of the earth to the other, 8you must not yield to or heed any such persons. Show them no pity or compassion and do not shield them. 9But you shall surely kill them; your own hand shall be first against them to execute them, and afterwards the hand of all the people. 10Stone them to death for trying to turn you away from the LORD your God, who brought you out of the land of Egypt, out of the house of slavery. 11Then all Israel shall hear and be afraid, and never again do any such wickedness.

12 If you hear it said about one of the towns that the LORD your God is giving you to live in, 13that scoundrels from among you have gone out and led the inhabitants of the town astray, saying, "Let us go and worship other gods," whom you have not known, 14then you shall inquire and make a thorough investigation. If the charge is established that such an abhorrent thing has been done among you, 15you shall put the inhabitants of that town to the sword, utterly destroying it and everything in it even putting its livestock to the sword. 16All of its spoil you shall gather into its public square; then burn the town and all its spoil with fire, as a whole burnt offering to the LORD your God. It shall remain a perpetual ruin, never to be rebuilt. 17Do not let anything devoted to destruction stick to your hand, so that the LORD may turn from his fierce anger and show you compassion, and in his compassion multiply you, as he swore to your ancestors, 18if you obey the voice of the LORD your God by keeping all his commandments that I am commanding you today, doing what is right in the sight of the LORD your God.

Pagan Practices Forbidden

14 You are children of the LORD your God. You must not lacerate yourselves or shave your forelocks for the dead. 2For you are a people holy to the LORD your God; it is you the LORD has chosen out of all the peoples on earth to be his people, his treasured possession.

Clean and Unclean Foods

3 You shall not eat any abhorrent thing. 4These are the animals you may eat: the ox, the sheep, the goat, 5the deer, the gazelle, the roebuck,

---

d Or on   e Gk Sam Syr: MT lacks today   f Ch 13.1 in Heb   g Ch 13.2 in Heb   h Sam Gk Compare Tg: MT lacks your father's son or

the wild goat, the ibex, the antelope, and the mountain-sheep. 6Any animal that divides the hoof and has the hoof cleft in two, and chews the cud, among the animals, you eat. 7Yet of those that chew the cud or have the hoof cleft you shall not eat these: the camel, the hare, and the rock badger, because they chew the cud but do not divide the hoof; they are unclean for you. 8And the pig, because it divides the hoof but does not chew the cud, is unclean for you. You shall not eat their meat, and you shall not touch their carcasses.

9 Of all that live in water you may eat these: whatever has fins and scales you may eat. 10And whatever does not have fins and scales you shall not eat; it is unclean for you.

11 You may eat any clean birds. 12But these are the ones that you shall not eat: the eagle, the vulture, the osprey, 13the buzzard, the kite of any kind; 14every raven of any kind; 15the ostrich, the nighthawk, the sea gull, the hawk of any kind; 16the little owl and the great owl, the water hen 17and the desert owl,i the carrion vulture and the cormorant, 18the stork, the heron of any kind; the hoopoe and the bat.j 19And all winged insects are unclean for you; they shall not be eaten. 20You may eat any clean winged creature.

21 You shall not eat anything that dies of itself; you may give it to aliens residing in your towns for them to eat, or you may sell it to a foreigner. For you are a people holy to the LORD your God.

You shall not boil a kid in its mother's milk.

Regulations concerning Tithes

22 Set apart a tithe of all the yield of your seed that is brought in yearly from the field. 23In the presence of the LORD your God, in the place that he will choose as a dwelling for his name, you shall eat the tithe of your grain, your wine, and your oil, as well as the firstlings of your herd and flock, so that you may learn to fear the LORD your God always. 24But if, when the LORD your God has blessed you, the distance is so great that you are unable to transport it, because the place where the LORD your God will choose to set his name is too far away from you, 25then you may turn it into money. With the money secure in hand, go to the place that the LORD your God will choose; 26spend the money for whatever you wish—oxen, sheep, wine, strong drink, or whatever you desire. And you shall eat there in the presence of the LORD your God, you and your household rejoicing together. 27As for the Levites resident in your towns, do not neglect them, because they have no allotment or inheritance with you.

28 Every third year you shall bring out the full tithe of your produce for that year, and store it within your towns; 29the Levites, because they have no allotment or inheritance with you, as well as the resident aliens, the orphans, and the widows in your towns, may come and eat their fill so that the LORD your God may bless you in all the work that you undertake.

14.28–29 Tithe to the Poor

Each year the Israelites presented a tithe of produce as an offering to God. Every third year the tithe would be distributed to needy people. God accepted the gifts to these people as an offering to himself. The principle behind this practice was later powerfully expressed in a parable by Jesus (Matthew 25.31–46), who said, "Truly I tell you, just as you did it to one of the least of these who are members of my family, you did it to me."

Laws concerning the Sabbatical Year

15 Every seventh year you shall grant a remission of debts. 2And this is the manner of the remission: every creditor shall remit the claim that is held against a neighbor, not exacting it of a neighbor who is a member of the community, because the LORD's remission has been proclaimed. 3Of a foreigner you may exact it, but you must remit your claim on whatever any member of your community owes you. 4There will, however, be no one in need among you, because the LORD is sure to bless you in the land that the LORD your God is giving you as a possession to occupy, 5if only you will obey the LORD your God by diligently observing this entire commandment that I command you today. 6When the LORD your God has blessed you, as he promised you, you will lend to many nations, but you will not borrow; you will rule over many nations, but they will not rule over you.

7 If there is among you anyone in need, a member of your community in any of your towns within the land that the LORD your God is giving you, do not be hard-hearted or tight-fisted toward your needy neighbor. 8You should rather open your hand, willingly lending enough to meet the need, whatever it may be. 9Be careful that you do not entertain a mean thought, thinking, "The seventh year, the year of remission, is near," and therefore view your needy neighbor with hostility and give nothing; your neighbor might cry to the LORD against you, and you would incur guilt. 10Give liberally and be ungrudging when you do so, for on this account the LORD your God will bless you in all your work and in all that you undertake. 11Since there will never cease to be some in need on the earth, I therefore command

---

i Or *pelican*   j Identification of several of the birds in verses 12-18 is uncertain

you, "Open your hand to the poor and needy neighbor in your land."

12 If a member of your community, whether a Hebrew man or a Hebrew woman, is sold[k] to

15.11 Any Poor People?

At first glance, this verse seems to contradict verse 4, which says there should be no poor people in Israel. Moses knew the difference between what should happen and what will happen. God's blessings in the promised land ought to have eliminated poverty—if the Israelites had obeyed completely. But since some people always fall short, poverty remains a problem. (Jesus confirmed this in a passing remark in Matthew 26.11.) As a result, in our time as in Moses', generosity is essential.

you and works for you six years, in the seventh year you shall set that person free. 13And when you send a male slave[l] out from you a free person, you shall not send him out empty-handed. 14Provide liberally out of your flock, your threshing floor, and your wine press, thus giving to him some of the bounty with which the LORD your God has blessed you. 15Remember that you were a slave in the land of Egypt, and the LORD your God redeemed you; for this reason I lay this command upon you today. 16But if he says to you, "I will not go out from you," because he loves you and your household, since he is well off with you, 17then you shall take an awl and thrust it through his earlobe into the door, and he shall be your slave[m] forever.

You shall do the same with regard to your female slave.[n]

18 Do not consider it a hardship when you send them out from you free persons, because for six years they have given you services worth the wages of hired laborers; and the LORD your God will bless you in all that you do.

The Firstborn of Livestock

19 Every firstling male born of your herd and flock you shall consecrate to the LORD your God; you shall not do work with your firstling ox nor shear the firstling of your flock. 20You shall eat it, you together with your household, in the presence of the LORD your God year by year at the place that the LORD will choose. 21But if it has any defect—any serious defect, such as lameness or blindness—you shall not sacrifice it to the LORD your God; 22within your towns you may eat it, the unclean and the clean alike, as you would a gazelle or deer. 23Its blood, however, you must not eat; you shall pour it out on the ground like water.

The Passover Reviewed

16 Observe the month[o] of Abib by keeping the passover to the LORD your God, for in the month of Abib the LORD your God brought you out of Egypt by night. 2You shall offer the passover sacrifice to the LORD your God, from the flock and the herd, at the place that the LORD will choose as a dwelling for his name. 3You must not eat with it anything leavened. For seven days you shall eat unleavened bread with it—the bread of affliction—because you came out of the land of Egypt in great haste, so that all the days of your life you may remember the day of your departure from the land of Egypt. 4No leaven shall be seen with you in all your territory for seven days; and none of the meat of what you slaughter on the evening of the first day shall remain until morning. 5You are not permitted to offer the passover sacrifice within any of your towns that the LORD your God is giving you. 6But at the place that the LORD your God will choose as a dwelling for his name, only there shall you offer the passover sacrifice, in the evening at sunset, the time of day when you departed from Egypt. 7You shall cook it and eat it at the place that the LORD your God will choose; the next morning you may go back to your tents. 8For six days you shall continue to eat unleavened bread, and on the seventh day there shall be a solemn assembly for the LORD your God, when you shall do no work.

The Festival of Weeks Reviewed

9 You shall count seven weeks; begin to count the seven weeks from the time the sickle is first put to the standing grain. 10Then you shall keep the festival of weeks to the LORD your God, contributing a freewill offering in proportion to the blessing that you have received from the LORD your God. 11Rejoice before the LORD your God— you and your sons and your daughters, your male and female slaves, the Levites resident in your towns, as well as the strangers, the orphans, and the widows who are among you—at the place that the LORD your God will choose as a dwelling for his name. 12Remember that you were a slave in Egypt, and diligently observe these statutes.

The Festival of Booths Reviewed

13 You shall keep the festival of booths[p] for seven days, when you have gathered in the produce from your threshing floor and your wine press. 14Rejoice during your festival, you and your sons and your daughters, your male and female slaves, as well as the Levites, the strangers, the orphans, and the widows resident in your towns. 15Seven days you shall keep the festival to the LORD your God at the place that the LORD will choose; for the LORD your God will bless you in all

---

k Or sells himself or herself   l Heb him   m Or bondman   n Or bondwoman   o Or new moon
p Or tabernacles; Heb succoth

your produce and in all your undertakings, and you shall surely celebrate.

16 Three times a year all your males shall appear before the LORD your God at the place that he will choose: at the festival of unleavened bread, at the festival of weeks, and at the festival of booths.[q] They shall not appear before the LORD empty-handed; [17]all shall give as they are able, according to the blessing of the LORD your God that he has given you.

Municipal Judges and Officers

18 You shall appoint judges and officials throughout your tribes, in all your towns that the LORD your God is giving you, and they shall render just decisions for the people. [19]You must not distort justice; you must not show partiality; and you must not accept bribes, for a bribe blinds the eyes of the wise and subverts the cause of those who are in the right. [20]Justice, and only justice, you shall pursue, so that you may live and occupy the land that the LORD your God is giving you.

Forbidden Forms of Worship

21 You shall not plant any tree as a sacred pole[r] beside the altar that you make for the LORD your God; [22]nor shall you set up a stone pillar—things that the LORD your God hates.

17 You must not sacrifice to the LORD your God an ox or a sheep that has a defect, anything seriously wrong; for that is abhorrent to the LORD your God.

2 If there is found among you, in one of your towns that the LORD your God is giving you, a man or woman who does what is evil in the sight of the LORD your God, and transgresses his covenant [3]by going to serve other gods and worshiping them—whether the sun or the moon or any of the host of heaven, which I have forbidden—[4]and if it is reported to you or you hear of it, and you make a thorough inquiry, and the charge is proved true that such an abhorrent thing has occurred in Israel, [5]then you shall bring out to your gates that man or that woman who has committed this crime and you shall stone the man or woman to death. [6]On the evidence of two or three witnesses the death sentence shall be executed; a person must not be put to death on the evidence of only one witness. [7]The hands of the witnesses shall be the first raised against the person to execute the death penalty, and afterward the hands of all the people. So you shall purge the evil from your midst.

Legal Decisions by Priests and Judges

8 If a judicial decision is too difficult for you to make between one kind of bloodshed and another, one kind of legal right and another, or one kind of assault and another—any such matters of dispute in your towns—then you shall immediately go up to the place that the LORD your God will choose, [9]where you shall consult with the levitical priests and the judge who is in office in those days; they shall announce to you the decision in the case. [10]Carry out exactly the decision that they announce to you from the place that the LORD will choose, diligently observing everything they instruct you. [11]You must carry out fully the law that they interpret for you or the ruling that they announce to you; do not turn aside from the decision that they announce to you, either to the right or to the left. [12]As for anyone who presumes to disobey the priest appointed to minister there to the LORD your God, or the judge, that person shall die. So you shall purge the evil from Israel. [13]All the people will hear and be afraid, and will not act presumptuously again.

Limitations of Royal Authority

14 When you have come into the land that the LORD your God is giving you, and have taken possession of it and settled in it, and you say, "I will set a king over me, like all the nations that are around me," [15]you may indeed set over you a king whom the LORD your God will choose. One of your own community you may set as king over you; you are not permitted to put a foreigner over

17.15 Prescription for a King

Until now, the Bible has not mentioned the possibility of an Israelite king. But here, long before the nation actually got a king, God lays down his prescription for a good one. The list of qualities hardly fits the normal image of a king—or the kind of person the Israelites' descendants usually got.

you, who is not of your own community. [16]Even so, he must not acquire many horses for himself, or return the people to Egypt in order to acquire more horses, since the LORD has said to you, "You must never return that way again." [17]And he must not acquire many wives for himself, or else his heart will turn away; also silver and gold he must not acquire in great quantity for himself. [18]When he has taken the throne of his kingdom, he shall have a copy of this law written for him in the presence of the levitical priests. [19]It shall remain with him and he shall read in it all the days of his life, so that he may learn to fear the LORD his God, diligently observing all the words of this law and these statutes, [20]neither exalting himself above other members of the community nor turning aside from the commandment, either to the right or to the left, so that he and his descendants may reign long over his kingdom in Israel.

Privileges of Priests and Levites

18 The levitical priests, the whole tribe of Levi, shall have no allotment or inheritance within Israel. They may eat the sacrifices that are the LORD's portion[s] ²but they shall have no inheritance among the other members of the community; the LORD is their inheritance, as he promised them.

3 This shall be the priests' due from the people, from those offering a sacrifice, whether an ox or a sheep: they shall give to the priest the shoulder, the two jowls, and the stomach. ⁴The first fruits of your grain, your wine, and your oil, as well as the first of the fleece of your sheep, you shall give him. ⁵For the LORD your God has chosen Levi[t] out of all your tribes, to stand and minister in the name of the LORD, him and his sons for all time.

6 If a Levite leaves any of your towns, from wherever he has been residing in Israel, and comes to the place that the LORD will choose (and he may come whenever he wishes), ⁷then he may minister in the name of the LORD his God, like all his fellow-Levites who stand to minister there before the LORD. ⁸They shall have equal portions to eat, even though they have income from the sale of family possessions.[s]

Child-Sacrifice, Divination, and Magic Prohibited

9 When you come into the land that the LORD your God is giving you, you must not learn to imitate the abhorrent practices of those nations.

18.9–13 "Abhorrent Practices"

This brief paragraph gives a preview of some of the "abhorrent practices" the Israelites would encounter in the promised land. Child sacrifice was a common part of worship in Canaan. God had already stated that the Israelites' invasion was a form of punishment on the Canaanites for these kinds of practices (9.4).

¹⁰No one shall be found among you who makes a son or daughter pass through fire, or who practices divination, or is a soothsayer, or an augur, or a sorcerer, ¹¹or one who casts spells, or who consults ghosts or spirits, or who seeks oracles from the dead. ¹²For whoever does these things is abhorrent to the LORD; it is because of such abhorrent practices that the LORD your God is driving them out before you. ¹³You must remain completely loyal to the LORD your God. ¹⁴Although

these nations that you are about to dispossess do give heed to soothsayers and diviners, as for you, the LORD your God does not permit you to do so.

A New Prophet Like Moses

15 The LORD your God will raise up for you a prophet[u] like me from among your own people; you shall heed such a prophet.[v] ¹⁶This is what you requested of the LORD your God at Horeb on the day of the assembly when you said: "If I hear the voice of the LORD my God any more, or ever again see this great fire, I will die." ¹⁷Then the LORD replied to me: "They are right in what they have said. ¹⁸I will raise up for them a prophet[u] like you from among their own people; I will put my words in the mouth of the prophet,[w] who shall speak to them everything that I command. ¹⁹Anyone who does not heed the words that the prophet[x] shall speak in my name, I myself will hold accountable. ²⁰But any prophet who speaks in the name of other gods, or who presumes to speak in my name a word that I have not commanded the prophet to speak—that prophet shall die." ²¹You may say to yourself, "How can we recognize a word that the LORD has not spoken?" ²²If a prophet speaks in the name of the LORD but the thing does not take place or prove true, it is a word that the LORD has not spoken. The prophet has spoken it presumptuously; do not be frightened by it.

Laws concerning the Cities of Refuge

19 When the LORD your God has cut off the nations whose land the LORD your God is giving you, and you have dispossessed them and settled in their towns and in their houses, ²you shall set apart three cities in the land that the LORD your God is giving you to possess. ³You shall calculate the distances[y] and divide into three regions the land that the LORD your God gives you as a possession, so that any homicide can flee to one of them.

4 Now this is the case of a homicide who might flee there and live, that is, someone who has killed another person unintentionally when the two had not been at enmity before: ⁵Suppose someone goes into the forest with another to cut wood, and when one of them swings the ax to cut down a tree, the head slips from the handle and strikes the other person who then dies; the killer may flee to one of these cities and live. ⁶But if the distance is too great, the avenger of blood in hot anger might pursue and overtake and put the killer to death, although a death sentence was not deserved, since the two had not been at enmity before. ⁷Therefore I command you: You shall set apart three cities.

8 If the LORD your God enlarges your territo-

s Meaning of Heb uncertain   t Heb him   u Or prophets   v Or such prophets   w Or mouths of the prophets
x Heb he   y Or prepare roads to them

ry, as he swore to your ancestors—and he will give you all the land that he promised your ancestors to give you, 9provided you diligently observe this entire commandment that I command you today, by loving the LORD your God and walking always in his ways—then you shall add three more cities to these three, 10so that the blood of an innocent person may not be shed in the land that the LORD your God is giving you as an inheritance, thereby bringing bloodguilt upon you.

11 But if someone at enmity with another lies in wait and attacks and takes the life of that person, and flees into one of these cities, 12then the elders of the killer's city shall send to have the culprit taken from there and handed over to the avenger of blood to be put to death. 13Show no pity; you shall purge the guilt of innocent blood from Israel, so that it may go well with you.

Property Boundaries

14 You must not move your neighbor's boundary marker, set up by former generations, on the property that will be allotted to you in the land that the LORD your God is giving you to possess.

Law concerning Witnesses

15 A single witness shall not suffice to convict a person of any crime or wrongdoing in connection with any offense that may be committed. Only on the evidence of two or three witnesses shall a charge be sustained. 16If a malicious witness comes forward to accuse someone of wrongdoing, 17then both parties to the dispute shall appear before the LORD, before the priests and the judges who are in office in those days, 18and the judges shall make a thorough inquiry. If the witness is a false witness, having testified falsely against another, 19then you shall do to the false witness just as the false witness had meant to do to the other. So you shall purge the evil from your midst. 20The rest shall hear and be afraid, and a crime such as this shall never again be committed among you. 21Show no pity: life for life, eye for eye, tooth for tooth, hand for hand, foot for foot.

Rules of Warfare

20 When you go out to war against your enemies, and see horses and chariots, an army larger than your own, you shall not be afraid of them; for the LORD your God is with you, who brought you up from the land of Egypt. 2Before you engage in battle, the priest shall come forward and speak to the troops, 3and shall say to them: "Hear, O Israel! Today you are drawing near to do battle against your enemies. Do not lose heart, or be afraid, or panic, or be in dread of them; 4for it is the LORD your God who goes with you, to fight for you against your enemies, to give you victory." 5Then the officials shall address the troops, saying, "Has anyone built a new house

but not dedicated it? He should go back to his house, or he might die in the battle and another dedicate it. 6Has anyone planted a vineyard but not yet enjoyed its fruit? He should go back to his

20.5 Uncommon Military Rules

The Israelites gained a reputation as fierce and bloody fighters. Yet Moses' instructions in this chapter defied normal military practice. Soldiers with new homes, new vineyards, and new fiancées—or even just plain scared soldiers—got exemptions from fighting. And before attacking any city, the army was to make a peace offer.

house, or he might die in the battle and another be first to enjoy its fruit. 7Has anyone become engaged to a woman but not yet married her? He should go back to his house, or he might die in the battle and another marry her." 8The officials shall continue to address the troops, saying, "Is anyone afraid or disheartened? He should go back to his house, or he might cause the heart of his comrades to melt like his own." 9When the officials have finished addressing the troops, then the commanders shall take charge of them.

10 When you draw near to a town to fight against it, offer it terms of peace. 11If it accepts your terms of peace and surrenders to you, then all the people in it shall serve you at forced labor. 12If it does not submit to you peacefully, but makes war against you, then you shall besiege it; 13and when the LORD your God gives it into your hand, you shall put all its males to the sword. 14You may, however, take as your booty the women, the children, livestock, and everything else in the town, all its spoil. You may enjoy the spoil of your enemies, which the LORD your God has given you. 15Thus you shall treat all the towns that are very far from you, which are not towns of the nations here. 16But as for the towns of these peoples that the LORD your God is giving you as an inheritance, you must not let anything that breathes remain alive. 17You shall annihilate them—the Hittites and the Amorites, the Canaanites and the Perizzites, the Hivites and the Jebusites—just as the LORD your God has commanded, 18so that they may not teach you to do all the abhorrent things that they do for their gods, and you thus sin against the LORD your God.

19 If you besiege a town for a long time, making war against it in order to take it, you must not destroy its trees by wielding an ax against them. Although you may take food from them, you must not cut them down. Are trees in the field human beings that they should come under siege from you? 20You may destroy only the trees that

you know do not produce food; you may cut them down for use in building siegeworks against the town that makes war with you, until it falls.

Law concerning Murder by Persons Unknown

21 If, in the land that the LORD your God is giving you to possess, a body is found lying in open country, and it is not known who struck the person down, ²then your elders and your judges shall come out to measure the distances to the towns that are near the body. ³The elders of the town nearest the body shall take a heifer that has never been worked, one that has not pulled in the yoke; ⁴the elders of that town shall bring the heifer down to a wadi with running water, which is neither plowed nor sown, and shall break the heifer's neck there in the wadi. ⁵Then the priests, the sons of Levi, shall come forward, for the LORD your God has chosen them to minister to him and to pronounce blessings in the name of the LORD, and by their decision all cases of dispute and assault shall be settled. ⁶All the elders of that town nearest the body shall wash their hands over the heifer whose neck was broken in the wadi, ⁷and they shall declare: "Our hands did not shed this blood, nor were we witnesses to it. ⁸Absolve, O LORD, your people Israel, whom you redeemed; do not let the guilt of innocent blood remain in the midst of your people Israel." Then they will be absolved of bloodguilt. ⁹So you shall purge the guilt of innocent blood from your midst, because you must do what is right in the sight of the LORD.

Female Captives

10 When you go out to war against your enemies, and the LORD your God hands them over to you and you take them captive, ¹¹suppose you see among the captives a beautiful woman whom you desire and want to marry, ¹²and so you bring her home to your house: she shall shave her head, pare her nails, ¹³discard her captive's garb, and shall remain in your house a full month, mourning for her father and mother; after that you may go in to her and be her husband, and she shall be your wife. ¹⁴But if you are not satisfied with her, you shall let her go free and not sell her for money. You must not treat her as a slave, since you have dishonored her.

The Right of the Firstborn

15 If a man has two wives, one of them loved and the other disliked, and if both the loved and the disliked have borne him sons, the firstborn being the son of the one who is disliked, ¹⁶then on the day when he wills his possessions to his sons, he is not permitted to treat the son of the loved as the firstborn in preference to the son of the disliked, who is the firstborn. ¹⁷He must acknowl-

edge as firstborn the son of the one who is disliked, giving him a double portion^z of all that he has; since he is the first issue of his virility, the right of the firstborn is his.

Rebellious Children

18 If someone has a stubborn and rebellious son who will not obey his father and mother, who does not heed them when they discipline him, ¹⁹then his father and his mother shall take hold of him and bring him out to the elders of his town at the gate of that place. ²⁰They shall say to the elders of his town, "This son of ours is stubborn and rebellious. He will not obey us. He is a glutton and a drunkard." ²¹Then all the men of the town shall stone him to death. So you shall purge the evil from your midst; and all Israel will hear, and be afraid.

Miscellaneous Laws

22 When someone is convicted of a crime punishable by death and is executed, and you hang him on a tree, ²³his corpse must not remain all night upon the tree; you shall bury him that same day, for anyone hung on a tree is under God's curse. You must not defile the land that the LORD your God is giving you for possession.

22 You shall not watch your neighbor's ox or sheep straying away and ignore them; you

22.1–7 Respect for Nature

The laws in Deuteronomy demonstrate God's concern that nature be treated with respect. In his instructions on war, Moses ordered those who laid siege to a city to choose carefully which trees to cut down (20.19). God's concern for the weak and helpless extended into the animal kingdom, for the law protected oxen, donkeys, and even birds (22.1–7).

shall take them back to their owner. ²If the owner does not reside near you or you do not know who the owner is, you shall bring it to your own house, and it shall remain with you until the owner claims it; then you shall return it. ³You shall do the same with a neighbor's donkey; you shall do the same with a neighbor's garment; and you shall do the same with anything else that your neighbor loses and you find. You may not withhold your help.

4 You shall not see your neighbor's donkey or ox fallen on the road and ignore it; you shall help to lift it up.

5 A woman shall not wear a man's apparel, nor shall a man put on a woman's garment; for whoever does such things is abhorrent to the LORD your God.

---

^{z} Heb *two-thirds*

6 If you come on a bird's nest, in any tree or on the ground, with fledglings or eggs, with the mother sitting on the fledglings or on the eggs, you shall not take the mother with the young. 7Let the mother go, taking only the young for yourself, in order that it may go well with you and you may live long.

8 When you build a new house, you shall make a parapet for your roof; otherwise you might have bloodguilt on your house, if anyone should fall from it.

9 You shall not sow your vineyard with a second kind of seed, or the whole yield will have to be forfeited, both the crop that you have sown and the yield of the vineyard itself.

10 You shall not plow with an ox and a donkey yoked together.

11 You shall not wear clothes made of wool and linen woven together.

12 You shall make tassels on the four corners of the cloak with which you cover yourself.

Laws concerning Sexual Relations

13 Suppose a man marries a woman, but after going in to her, he dislikes her 14and makes up charges against her, slandering her by saying, "I married this woman; but when I lay with her, I did not find evidence of her virginity." 15The father of the young woman and her mother shall then submit the evidence of the young woman's virginity to the elders of the city at the gate. 16The father of the young woman shall say to the elders: "I gave my daughter in marriage to this man but he dislikes her; 17now he has made up charges against her, saying, 'I did not find evidence of your daughter's virginity.' But here is the evidence of my daughter's virginity." Then they shall spread out the cloth before the elders of the town. 18The elders of that town shall take the man and punish him; 19they shall fine him one hundred shekels of silver (which they shall give to the young woman's father) because he has slandered a virgin of Israel. She shall remain his wife; he shall not be permitted to divorce her as long as he lives.

20 If, however, this charge is true, that evidence of the young woman's virginity was not found, 21then they shall bring the young woman out to the entrance of her father's house and the men of her town shall stone her to death, because she committed a disgraceful act in Israel by prostituting herself in her father's house. So you shall purge the evil from your midst.

22 If a man is caught lying with the wife of another man, both of them shall die, the man who lay with the woman as well as the woman. So you shall purge the evil from Israel.

23 If there is a young woman, a virgin already engaged to be married, and a man meets her in the town and lies with her, 24you shall bring both of them to the gate of that town and stone them to death, the young woman because she did not cry for help in the town and the man because he violated his neighbor's wife. So you shall purge the evil from your midst.

25 But if the man meets the engaged woman in the open country, and the man seizes her and lies with her, then only the man who lay with her shall die. 26You shall do nothing to the young woman; the young woman has not committed an offense punishable by death, because this case is like that of someone who attacks and murders a neighbor. 27Since he found her in the open country, the engaged woman may have cried for help, but there was no one to rescue her.

28 If a man meets a virgin who is not engaged, and seizes her and lies with her, and they are caught in the act, 29the man who lay with her shall give fifty shekels of silver to the young woman's father, and she shall become his wife. Because he violated her he shall not be permitted to divorce her as long as he lives.

30a A man shall not marry his father's wife, thereby violating his father's rights.b

Those Excluded from the Assembly

23 No one whose testicles are crushed or whose penis is cut off shall be admitted to the assembly of the LORD.

2 Those born of an illicit union shall not be admitted to the assembly of the LORD. Even to the tenth generation, none of their descendants shall be admitted to the assembly of the LORD.

3 No Ammonite or Moabite shall be admitted to the assembly of the LORD. Even to the tenth generation, none of their descendants shall be admitted to the assembly of the LORD, 4because they did not meet you with food and water on your journey out of Egypt, and because they hired against you Balaam son of Beor, from Pethor of Mesopotamia, to curse you. 5(Yet the LORD your God refused to heed Balaam; the LORD your God turned the curse into a blessing for you, because the LORD your God loved you.) 6You shall never promote their welfare or their prosperity as long as you live.

7 You shall not abhor any of the Edomites, for they are your kin. You shall not abhor any of the Egyptians, because you were an alien residing in their land. 8The children of the third generation that are born to them may be admitted to the assembly of the LORD.

Sanitary, Ritual, and Humanitarian Precepts

9 When you are encamped against your enemies you shall guard against any impropriety.

10 If one of you becomes unclean because of

---

a Ch 23.1 in Heb   b Heb uncovering his father's skirt

a nocturnal emission, then he shall go outside the camp; he must not come within the camp. [11]When evening comes, he shall wash himself with water, and when the sun has set, he may come back into the camp.

12 You shall have a designated area outside the camp to which you shall go. [13]With your utensils you shall have a trowel; when you relieve yourself outside, you shall dig a hole with it and then cover up your excrement. [14]Because the LORD your God travels along with your camp, to save you and to hand over your enemies to you, therefore your camp must be holy, so that he may not see anything indecent among you and turn away from you.

15 Slaves who have escaped to you from their owners shall not be given back to them. [16]They shall reside with you, in your midst, in any place they choose in any one of your towns, wherever they please; you shall not oppress them.

17 None of the daughters of Israel shall be a temple prostitute; none of the sons of Israel shall be a temple prostitute. [18]You shall not bring the fee of a prostitute or the wages of a male prostitute[c] into the house of the LORD your God in payment for any vow, for both of these are abhorrent to the LORD your God.

19 You shall not charge interest on loans to another Israelite, interest on money, interest on provisions, interest on anything that is lent. [20]On loans to a foreigner you may charge interest, but on loans to another Israelite you may not charge interest, so that the LORD your God may bless you in all your undertakings in the land that you are about to enter and possess.

21 If you make a vow to the LORD your God, do not postpone fulfilling it; for the LORD your God will surely require it of you, and you would incur guilt. [22]But if you refrain from vowing, you will not incur guilt. [23]Whatever your lips utter you must diligently perform, just as you have freely vowed to the LORD your God with your own mouth.

24 If you go into your neighbor's vineyard, you may eat your fill of grapes, as many as you wish, but you shall not put any in a container. 25 If you go into your neighbor's standing grain, you may pluck the ears with your hand, but you shall not put a sickle to your neighbor's standing grain.

Laws concerning Marriage and Divorce

24 Suppose a man enters into marriage with a woman, but she does not please him because he finds something objectionable about her, and so he writes her a certificate of divorce, puts it in her hand, and sends her out of his house; she then leaves his house [2]and goes off to become another man's wife. [3]Then suppose the second

man dislikes her, writes her a bill of divorce, puts it in her hand, and sends her out of his house (or the second man who married her dies); [4]her first husband, who sent her away, is not permitted to take her again to be his wife after she has been defiled; for that would be abhorrent to the LORD, and you shall not bring guilt on the land that the LORD your God is giving you as a possession.

Miscellaneous Laws

5 When a man is newly married, he shall not go out with the army or be charged with any related duty. He shall be free at home one year, to be happy with the wife whom he has married.

6 No one shall take a mill or an upper millstone in pledge, for that would be taking a life in pledge.

24.6 Respect People, Not Money

Old Testament laws contained many provisions to protect people from exploitation. Israelites could not charge each other interest for loans (Exodus 22.25). And Deuteronomy set limits on the "collateral," or pledge, that secured a loan. Here, the lender could not accept a millstone, for that would threaten the debtor's livelihood. Verses 10–13 show further safeguards. The debtor was allowed to keep everything necessary for living. And the lender could not even enter the debtor's house to get his pledge.

7 If someone is caught kidnaping another Israelite, enslaving or selling the Israelite, then that kidnaper shall die. So you shall purge the evil from your midst.

8 Guard against an outbreak of a leprous[d] skin disease by being very careful; you shall carefully observe whatever the levitical priests instruct you, just as I have commanded them. [9]Remember what the LORD your God did to Miriam on your journey out of Egypt.

10 When you make your neighbor a loan of any kind, you shall not go into the house to take the pledge. [11]You shall wait outside, while the person to whom you are making the loan brings the pledge out to you. [12]If the person is poor, you shall not sleep in the garment given you as[e] the pledge. [13]You shall give the pledge back by sunset, so that your neighbor may sleep in the cloak and bless you; and it will be to your credit before the LORD your God.

14 You shall not withhold the wages of poor and needy laborers, whether other Israelites or aliens who reside in your land in one of your towns. [15]You shall pay them their wages daily before sunset, because they are poor and their livelihood depends on them; otherwise they

---

[c] Heb *a dog*   [d] A term for several skin diseases; precise meaning uncertain   [e] Heb lacks *the garment given you as*

might cry to the LORD against you, and you would incur guilt.

16 Parents shall not be put to death for their children, nor shall children be put to death for their parents; only for their own crimes may persons be put to death.

17 You shall not deprive a resident alien or an orphan of justice; you shall not take a widow's garment in pledge. 18Remember that you were a slave in Egypt and the LORD your God redeemed you from there; therefore I command you to do this.

19 When you reap your harvest in your field and forget a sheaf in the field, you shall not go back to get it; it shall be left for the alien, the orphan, and the widow, so that the LORD your God may bless you in all your undertakings.

24.19 Don't Forget the Poor

Chapter 24 contains some of the regulations expressly designed to protect the poor. One, called gleaning, is still practiced today in a modern form. Certain religious organizations in America contract with farmers to harvest their "wasted" or abandoned crops in order to feed the poor. God's laws built a concern for the poor into the Israelites' daily routine.

20When you beat your olive trees, do not strip what is left; it shall be for the alien, the orphan, and the widow.

21 When you gather the grapes of your vineyard, do not glean what is left; it shall be for the alien, the orphan, and the widow. 22Remember that you were a slave in the land of Egypt; therefore I am commanding you to do this.

25 Suppose two persons have a dispute and enter into litigation, and the judges decide between them, declaring one to be in the right and the other to be in the wrong. 2If the one in the wrong deserves to be flogged, the judge shall make that person lie down and be beaten in his presence with the number of lashes proportionate to the offense. 3Forty lashes may be given but not more; if more lashes than these are given, your neighbor will be degraded in your sight.

4 You shall not muzzle an ox while it is treading out the grain.

Levirate Marriage

5 When brothers reside together, and one of them dies and has no son, the wife of the deceased shall not be married outside the family to a stranger. Her husband's brother shall go in to her, taking her in marriage, and performing the duty of a husband's brother to her, 6and the firstborn whom she bears shall succeed to the name of the deceased brother, so that his name may not be blotted out of Israel. 7But if the man has no desire to marry his brother's widow, then his brother's widow shall go up to the elders at the gate and say, "My husband's brother refuses to perpetuate his brother's name in Israel; he will not perform the duty of a husband's brother to me." 8Then the elders of his town shall summon him and speak to him. If he persists, saying, "I have no desire to marry her," 9then his brother's wife shall go up to him in the presence of the elders, pull his sandal off his foot, spit in his face, and declare, "This is what is done to the man who does not build up his brother's house." 10Throughout Israel his family shall be known as "the house of him whose sandal was pulled off."

Various Commands

11 If men get into a fight with one another, and the wife of one intervenes to rescue her husband from the grip of his opponent by reaching out and seizing his genitals, 12you shall cut off her hand; show no pity.

13 You shall not have in your bag two kinds of weights, large and small. 14You shall not have in your house two kinds of measures, large and small. 15You shall have only a full and honest weight; you shall have only a full and honest measure, so that your days may be long in the land that the LORD your God is giving you. 16For all who do such things, all who act dishonestly, are abhorrent to the LORD your God.

17 Remember what Amalek did to you on your journey out of Egypt, 18how he attacked you on the way, when you were faint and weary, and struck down all who lagged behind you; he did not fear God. 19Therefore when the LORD your God has given you rest from all your enemies on every hand, in the land that the LORD your God is giving you as an inheritance to possess, you shall blot out the remembrance of Amalek from under heaven; do not forget.

First Fruits and Tithes

26 When you have come into the land that the LORD your God is giving you as an inheritance to possess, and you possess it, and settle in it, 2you shall take some of the first of all the fruit of the ground, which you harvest from the land that the LORD your God is giving you, and you shall put it in a basket and go to the place that the LORD your God will choose as a dwelling for his name. 3You shall go to the priest who is in office at that time, and say to him, "Today I declare to the LORD your God that I have come into the land that the LORD swore to our ancestors to give us." 4When the priest takes the basket from your hand and sets it down before the altar of the LORD your God, 5you shall make this response before the LORD your God: "A wandering Aramean was my ancestor; he went down into Egypt and lived there as an alien, few in number, and there

he became a great nation, mighty and populous. ⁶When the Egyptians treated us harshly and afflicted us, by imposing hard labor on us, ⁷we cried to the LORD, the God of our ancestors; the LORD heard our voice and saw our affliction, our toil, and our oppression. ⁸The LORD brought us out of Egypt with a mighty hand and an outstretched arm, with a terrifying display of power, and with signs and wonders; ⁹and he brought us into this place and gave us this land, a land flowing with milk and honey. ¹⁰So now I bring the first of the fruit of the ground that you, O LORD, have given me." You shall set it down before the LORD your God and bow down before the LORD your God. ¹¹Then you, together with the Levites and the aliens who reside among you, shall celebrate with all the bounty that the LORD your God has given to you and to your house.

12 When you have finished paying all the tithe of your produce in the third year (which is the year of the tithe), giving it to the Levites, the aliens, the orphans, and the widows, so that they may eat their fill within your towns, ¹³then you shall say before the LORD your God: "I have removed the sacred portion from the house, and I have given it to the Levites, the resident aliens, the orphans, and the widows, in accordance with your entire commandment that you commanded me; I have neither transgressed nor forgotten any of your commandments: ¹⁴I have not eaten of it while in mourning; I have not removed any of it while I was unclean; and I have not offered any of it to the dead. I have obeyed the LORD my God, doing just as you commanded me. ¹⁵Look down from your holy habitation, from heaven, and bless your people Israel and the ground that you have given us, as you swore to our ancestors—a land flowing with milk and honey."

Concluding Exhortation

16 This very day the LORD your God is commanding you to observe these statutes and ordinances; so observe them diligently with all your

26.16 Law of the Heart

The Old Testament gives many rules and regulations. Deuteronomy makes clear, however, that the law was meant to penetrate a person's heart. Unless the law becomes part of a person's inner attitudes, it will probably make no difference.

heart and with all your soul. ¹⁷Today you have obtained the LORD's agreement: to be your God; and for you to walk in his ways, to keep his statutes, his commandments, and his ordinances,

and to obey him. ¹⁸Today the LORD has obtained your agreement: to be his treasured people, as he promised you, and to keep his commandments; ¹⁹for him to set you high above all nations that he has made, in praise and in fame and in honor; and for you to be a people holy to the LORD your God, as he promised.

The Inscribed Stones and Altar on Mount Ebal

27 Then Moses and the elders of Israel charged all the people as follows: Keep the entire commandment that I am commanding you today. ²On the day that you cross over the Jordan into the land that the LORD your God is giving you, you shall set up large stones and cover them with plaster. ³You shall write on them all the words of this law when you have crossed over, to enter the land that the LORD your God is giving you, a land flowing with milk and honey, as the LORD, the God of your ancestors, promised you. ⁴So when you have crossed over the Jordan, you shall set up these stones, about which I am commanding you today, on Mount Ebal, and you shall cover them with plaster. ⁵And you shall build an altar there to the LORD your God, an altar of stones on which you have not used an iron tool. ⁶You must build the altar of the LORD your God of unhewn*ᶠ* stones. Then offer up burnt offerings on it to the LORD your God, ⁷make sacrifices of well-being, and eat them there, rejoicing before the LORD your God. ⁸You shall write on the stones all the words of this law very clearly.

9 Then Moses and the levitical priests spoke to all Israel, saying: Keep silence and hear, O Israel! This very day you have become the people of the LORD your God. ¹⁰Therefore obey the LORD your God, observing his commandments and his statutes that I am commanding you today.

Twelve Curses

11 The same day Moses charged the people as follows: ¹²When you have crossed over the Jordan, these shall stand on Mount Gerizim for the blessing of the people: Simeon, Levi, Judah, Issachar, Joseph, and Benjamin. ¹³And these shall stand on Mount Ebal for the curse: Reuben, Gad, Asher, Zebulun, Dan, and Naphtali. ¹⁴Then the Levites shall declare in a loud voice to all the Israelites:

15 "Cursed be anyone who makes an idol or casts an image, anything abhorrent to the LORD, the work of an artisan, and sets it up in secret." All the people shall respond, saying, "Amen!"

16 "Cursed be anyone who dishonors father or mother." All the people shall say, "Amen!"

17 "Cursed be anyone who moves a neigh-

ᶠ Heb whole

bor's boundary marker." All the people shall say, "Amen!"

18 "Cursed be anyone who misleads a blind person on the road." All the people shall say, "Amen!"

19 "Cursed be anyone who deprives the alien, the orphan, and the widow of justice." All the people shall say, "Amen!"

20 "Cursed be anyone who lies with his father's wife, because he has violated his father's rights."g All the people shall say, "Amen!"

21 "Cursed be anyone who lies with any animal." All the people shall say, "Amen!"

22 "Cursed be anyone who lies with his sister, whether the daughter of his father or the daughter of his mother." All the people shall say, "Amen!"

23 "Cursed be anyone who lies with his mother-in-law." All the people shall say, "Amen!"

24 "Cursed be anyone who strikes down a neighbor in secret." All the people shall say, "Amen!"

25 "Cursed be anyone who takes a bribe to shed innocent blood." All the people shall say, "Amen!"

26 "Cursed be anyone who does not uphold the words of this law by observing them." All the people shall say, "Amen!"

27.12–26 A Task for Joshua

Joshua carried out Moses' instructions for these blessings and curses, as recorded in Joshua 8.31–35. Mount Ebal had special significance for the Israelites, who believed that Abraham first worshiped God near here after receiving the original promise of the land (Genesis 15).

Blessings for Obedience

28 If you will only obey the LORD your God, by diligently observing all his commandments that I am commanding you today, the LORD your God will set you high above all the nations of the earth; 2all these blessings shall come upon you and overtake you, if you obey the LORD your God:

3 Blessed shall you be in the city, and blessed shall you be in the field.

4 Blessed shall be the fruit of your womb, the fruit of your ground, and the fruit of your livestock, both the increase of your cattle and the issue of your flock.

5 Blessed shall be your basket and your kneading bowl.

6 Blessed shall you be when you come in, and blessed shall you be when you go out.

7 The LORD will cause your enemies who rise against you to be defeated before you; they shall come out against you one way, and flee before you seven ways. 8The LORD will command the blessing upon you in your barns, and in all that you undertake; he will bless you in the land that the LORD your God is giving you. 9The LORD will establish you as his holy people, as he has sworn to you, if you keep the commandments of the LORD your God and walk in his ways. 10All the peoples of the earth shall see that you are called by the name of the LORD, and they shall be afraid of you. 11The LORD will make you abound in prosperity, in the fruit of your womb, in the fruit of your livestock, and in the fruit of your ground in the land that the LORD swore to your ancestors to give you. 12The LORD will open for you his rich storehouse, the heavens, to give the rain of your land in its season and to bless all your undertakings. You will lend to many nations, but you will not borrow. 13The LORD will make you the head, and not the tail; you shall be only at the top, and not at the bottom—if you obey the commandments of the LORD your God, which I am commanding you today, by diligently observing them, 14and if you do not turn aside from any of the words that I am commanding you today, either to the right or to the left, following other gods to serve them.

Warnings against Disobedience

15 But if you will not obey the LORD your God by diligently observing all his commandments and decrees, which I am commanding you today, then all these curses shall come upon you and overtake you:

16 Cursed shall you be in the city, and cursed shall you be in the field.

17 Cursed shall be your basket and your kneading bowl.

18 Cursed shall be the fruit of your womb, the fruit of your ground, the increase of your cattle and the issue of your flock.

19 Cursed shall you be when you come in, and cursed shall you be when you go out.

20 The LORD will send upon you disaster, panic, and frustration in everything you attempt to do, until you are destroyed and perish quickly, on account of the evil of your deeds, because you have forsaken me. 21The LORD will make the pestilence cling to you until it has consumed you off the land that you are entering to possess. 22The LORD will afflict you with consumption, fever, inflammation, with fiery heat and drought, and with blight and mildew; they shall pursue you until you perish. 23The sky over your head shall be bronze, and the earth under you iron. 24The LORD will change the rain of your land into powder, and only dust shall come down upon you from the sky until you are destroyed.

g Heb *uncovered his father's skirt*

25 The LORD will cause you to be defeated before your enemies; you shall go out against them one way and flee before them seven ways. You shall become an object of horror to all the kingdoms of the earth. 26Your corpses shall be food for every bird of the air and animal of the earth, and there shall be no one to frighten them away. 27The LORD will afflict you with the boils of Egypt, with ulcers, scurvy, and itch, of which you cannot be healed. 28The LORD will afflict you with madness, blindness, and confusion of mind; 29you shall grope about at noon as blind people grope in darkness, but you shall be unable to find your way; and you shall be continually abused and robbed, without anyone to help. 30You shall become engaged to a woman, but another man shall lie with her. You shall build a house, but not live in it. You shall plant a vineyard, but not enjoy its fruit. 31Your ox shall be butchered before your eyes, but you shall not eat of it. Your donkey shall be stolen in front of you, and shall not be restored to you. Your sheep shall be given to your enemies, without anyone to help you. 32Your sons and daughters shall be given to another people, while you look on; you will strain your eyes looking for them all day but be powerless to do anything. 33A people whom you do not know shall eat up the fruit of your ground and of all your labors; you shall be continually abused and crushed, 34and driven mad by the sight that your eyes shall see. 35The LORD will strike you on the knees and on the legs with grievous boils of which you cannot be healed, from the sole of your foot to the crown of your head. 36The LORD will bring you, and the king whom you set over you, to a nation that neither you nor your ancestors have known, where you shall serve other gods, of wood and

28.36–37 Scattered Abroad

Moses warned that if the Israelites failed to obey God's law, they would be uprooted from the new land and scattered all over the earth. At least three times in history this kind of dispersion of Jews (called Diaspora) took place on a massive scale. Assyria, Babylon, and finally the Roman empire invaded the homeland of the Jews and scattered them far abroad.

stone. 37You shall become an object of horror, a proverb, and a byword among all the peoples where the LORD will lead you.

38 You shall carry much seed into the field but shall gather little in, for the locust shall consume it. 39You shall plant vineyards and dress them, but you shall neither drink the wine nor gather the grapes, for the worm shall eat them. 40You shall have olive trees throughout all your territory, but you shall not anoint yourself with the oil, for your olives shall drop off. 41You shall have sons and daughters, but they shall not remain yours, for they shall go into captivity. 42All your trees and the fruit of your ground the cicada shall take over. 43Aliens residing among you shall ascend above you higher and higher, while you shall descend lower and lower. 44They shall lend to you but you shall not lend to them; they shall be the head and you shall be the tail.

45 All these curses shall come upon you, pursuing and overtaking you until you are destroyed, because you did not obey the LORD your God, by observing the commandments and the decrees that he commanded you. 46They shall be among you and your descendants as a sign and a portent forever.

47 Because you did not serve the LORD your God joyfully and with gladness of heart for the abundance of everything, 48therefore you shall serve your enemies whom the LORD will send against you, in hunger and thirst, in nakedness and lack of everything. He will put an iron yoke on your neck until he has destroyed you. 49The LORD will bring a nation from far away, from the end of the earth, to swoop down on you like an eagle, a nation whose language you do not understand, 50a grim-faced nation showing no respect to the old or favor to the young. 51It shall consume the fruit of your livestock and the fruit of your ground until you are destroyed, leaving you neither grain, wine, and oil, nor the increase of your cattle and the issue of your flock, until it has made you perish. 52It shall besiege you in all your towns until your high and fortified walls, in which you trusted, come down throughout your land; it shall besiege you in all your towns throughout the land that the LORD your God has given you. 53In the desperate straits to which the enemy siege reduces you, you will eat the fruit of your womb, the flesh of your own sons and daughters whom the LORD your God has given you. 54Even the most refined and gentle of men among you will begrudge food to his own brother, to the wife whom he embraces, and to the last of his remaining children, 55giving to none of them any of the flesh of his children whom he is eating, because nothing else remains to him, in the desperate straits to which the enemy siege will reduce you in all your towns. 56She who is the most refined and gentle among you, so gentle and refined that she does not venture to set the sole of her foot on the ground, will begrudge food to the husband whom she embraces, to her own son, and to her own daughter, 57begrudging even the afterbirth that comes out from between her thighs, and the children that she bears, because she is eating them in secret for lack of anything else, in the desperate straits to which the enemy siege will reduce you in your towns.

58 If you do not diligently observe all the

words of this law that are written in this book, fearing this glorious and awesome name, the LORD your God, 59then the LORD will overwhelm both you and your offspring with severe and lasting afflictions and grievous and lasting maladies. 60He will bring back upon you all the diseases of Egypt, of which you were in dread, and they shall cling to you. 61Every other malady and affliction, even though not recorded in the book of this law, the LORD will inflict on you until you are destroyed. 62Although once you were as numerous as the stars in heaven, you shall be left few in number, because you did not obey the LORD your God. 63And just as the LORD took delight in making you prosperous and numerous, so the LORD will take delight in bringing you to ruin and destruction; you shall be plucked off the land that you are entering to possess. 64The LORD will scatter you among all peoples, from one end of the earth to the other; and there you shall serve other gods, of wood and stone, which neither you nor your ancestors have known. 65Among those nations you shall find no ease, no resting place for the sole of your foot. There the LORD will give you

A Scent of Doom
All were jubilant, except one man

OLD HABITS DIE HARD. DEUTERONOMY underscores that lesson, and a more contemporary character shows that people have not changed much. In 1901 Bill Miner got out of San Quentin Prison, where he had served 33 years in all. It was his third stint, and both previous times he had barely sniffed free air before landing in jail again.

Miner was a Wild West legend. He had robbed his first stagecoach at 16. He is credited with first using the line that has played on thousands of Westerns: "Hands up!" Stagecoach passengers called him the Gentleman Bandit because he never shot anyone and he spoke respectfully, using "Sir" and "Ma'am."

When Bill Miner emerged from prison at age 58, his long hair had turned grey and most of his friends had either died or disappeared. Stepping into a new century, he had a new lease on life. No stagecoaches were left to rob: The Wells Fargo company had sold their horses and invested in something he had never seen, steam trains.

> Because you did not serve the LORD your God joyfully and with gladness of heart for the abundance of everything, therefore you shall serve your enemies whom the LORD will send against you, in hunger and thirst, in nakedness and lack of everything. 28.47–48

A Hint of Doom

Miner tried various odd jobs, but most work seemed degrading and boring to a former stagecoach robber. The old restlessness returned. One afternoon, in a Seattle theatre, he watched the movie *The Great Train Robbery*, and discovered a new career, or at least a new twist on an old one. The Gentleman Bandit, at age 60, became The Grey Fox. He went on to mastermind six train robberies, and probably more, until the Mounties tracked him down in British Columbia.

Three separate times Bill Miner had a chance for a new start. The last time, he had entered a new city, in a new century, with no one around to remind him of his reputation. Yet inevitably he went back to the familiar ways of crime. His life had the scent of doom about it.

The last chapters of Deuteronomy show the Israelites facing a situation much like that met by Bill Miner or any prisoner who emerges into freedom after many years. Four decades in the Desert of Sinai had served as a kind of imprisonment, or probation period. And then the long-awaited day of freedom arrived.

Everyone in the Israelite camp was jubilant—all but one man, Moses. He could see past the joy. When he spoke to the crowd, he spoke with an air of doom. He knew his people too well to think that geography would change their old ways.

Moses Pulls out the Stops

For 40 years Moses had led the cranky assortment of tribes. He had listened to their grumbling, endured their gossip, and survived their insurrections. Now he had one last chance to warn them not to repeat their ways.

You cannot read the last chapters of Deuteronomy without detecting a doleful sense of fatalism in Moses' words. The Israelites' settling down into a life of quiet obedience was about as likely as Bill Miner's becoming a banker. They had failed far too often; they were doomed to fail again.

a trembling heart, failing eyes, and a languishing spirit. 66Your life shall hang in doubt before you; night and day you shall be in dread, with no assurance of your life. 67In the morning you shall say, "If only it were evening!" and at evening you shall say, "If only it were morning!"—because of the dread that your heart shall feel and the sights that your eyes shall see. 68The LORD will bring you back in ships to Egypt, by a route that I promised you would never see again; and there you shall offer yourselves for sale to your enemies as male and female slaves, but there will be no buyer.

29^h These are the words of the covenant that the LORD commanded Moses to make with the Israelites in the land of Moab, in addition to the covenant that he had made with them at Horeb.

The Covenant Renewed in Moab

2ⁱ Moses summoned all Israel and said to them: You have seen all that the LORD did before your eyes in the land of Egypt, to Pharaoh and to all his servants and to all his land, 3the great trials that your eyes saw, the signs, and those great wonders. 4But to this day the LORD has not given you a mind to understand, or eyes to see, or ears to hear. 5I have led you forty years in the wilderness. The clothes on your back have not worn out, and the sandals on your feet have not worn out; 6you have not eaten bread, and you have not

drunk wine or strong drink—so that you may know that I am the LORD your God. 7When you came to this place, King Sihon of Heshbon and King Og of Bashan came out against us for battle,

29.5–6 Miracles in the Desert

The Sinai peninsula was a harsh place, and the Bible records the Israelites' problems with food and water supplies. But, as these two verses show, God cared for his people there, giving them daily food and drink and even making sure their clothes did not wear out.

but we defeated them. 8We took their land and gave it as an inheritance to the Reubenites, the Gadites, and the half-tribe of Manasseh. 9Therefore diligently observe the words of this covenant, in order that you may succeed^j in everything that you do.

10 You stand assembled today, all of you, before the LORD your God—the leaders of your tribes,^k your elders, and your officials, all the men of Israel, 11your children, your women, and the aliens who are in your camp, both those who cut your wood and those who draw your water— 12to enter into the covenant of the LORD your God, sworn by an oath, which the LORD your God is making with you today; 13in order that he may

^h Ch 28.69 in Heb   ⁱ Ch 29.1 in Heb   ⁱ Or *deal wisely*   ^k Gk Syr: Heb *your leaders, your tribes*

Moses pulled out all the stops. He orchestrated a dramatic object lesson that would live in their memories forever. It actually took place after Moses' death, as recorded in Joshua 8.30–35. Representatives from all the tribes climbed two mountains, with a narrow valley in between. These designated speakers shouted out curses and blessings on the Israelites (see 11.26–32; 27–28). As they entered the new land, their ears rang with the dissonance of wonderful blessings and horrific curses.

Future Terrors

Moses starkly summarized the future of the Jewish race. They would, he said, have "a trembling heart, failing eyes, and a languishing spirit. Your life shall hang in doubt before you; night and day you shall be in dread, with no assurance of your life. In the morning you shall say, 'If only it were evening!' and at evening you shall say, 'If only it were morning!'—because of the dread that your heart shall feel and the sights that your eyes shall see" (28.65–67). His descriptions of their future are unmatched for their horror.

Just in case the Israelites didn't get the message, Moses taught them a song given him by God (chapter 32). It became a kind of national anthem, memorized by everyone and sung as they marched into Canaan. But the song is like no other national anthem. It has virtually no words of encouragement or hope, only doom.

Moses knew that even the promised land would not change his people's ingrained habits of disobeying God. They would fail in the promised land, just as they had failed in the desert. He concluded his farewell speech to the people with these words, "This is no trifling matter for you, but rather your very life" (32.47). And then on that same day he ascended a mountain to die. He had been forbidden by God to cross into Canaan because of his own disobedience.

This sad final scene may have made the strongest impression of all. No one could get away with rebellion against God—not even Moses, "whom the LORD knew face to face" (34.10).

Life Questions: Why do you think the Bible includes accounts of big failures like this? Have you ever experienced a repeated failure: a sin or problem that keeps returning, no matter what you do?

establish you today as his people, and that he may be your God, as he promised you and as he swore to your ancestors, to Abraham, to Isaac, and to Jacob. ¹⁴I am making this covenant, sworn by an oath, not only with you who stand here with us today before the LORD our God, ¹⁵but also with those who are not here with us today. ¹⁶You know how we lived in the land of Egypt, and how we came through the midst of the nations through which you passed. ¹⁷You have seen their detestable things, the filthy idols of wood and stone, of silver and gold, that were among them. ¹⁸It may be that there is among you a man or woman, or a family or tribe, whose heart is already turning away from the LORD our God to serve the gods of those nations. It may be that there is among you a root sprouting poisonous and bitter growth. ¹⁹All who hear the words of this oath and bless themselves, thinking in their hearts, "We are safe even though we go our own stubborn ways" (thus bringing disaster on moist and dry alike)ˡ— ²⁰the LORD will be unwilling to pardon them, for the LORD's anger and passion will smoke against them. All the curses written in this book will descend on them, and the LORD will blot out their names from under heaven. ²¹The LORD will single them out from all the tribes of Israel for calamity, in accordance with all the curses of the covenant written in this book of the law. ²²The next generation, your children who rise up after you, as well as the foreigner who comes from a distant country, will see the devastation of that land and the afflictions with which the LORD has afflicted it— ²³all its soil burned out by sulfur and salt, nothing planted, nothing sprouting, unable to support any vegetation, like the destruction of Sodom and Gomorrah, Admah and Zeboiim, which the LORD destroyed in his fierce anger— ²⁴they and indeed all the nations will wonder, "Why has the LORD done thus to this land? What caused this great

---

29.24–29 God's Secrets

*"I don't understand why God is doing this,"
people say. But God hasn't told us everything.
Our finite minds could not possibly grasp some
things, and other information is simply
unnecessary or unhelpful for us to know. What
God has told us (in his law, for instance) he
intends for us to obey.*

---

display of anger?" ²⁵They will conclude, "It is because they abandoned the covenant of the LORD, the God of their ancestors, which he made with them when he brought them out of the land of Egypt. ²⁶They turned and served other gods, worshiping them, gods whom they had not known

and whom he had not allotted to them; ²⁷so the anger of the LORD was kindled against that land, bringing on it every curse written in this book. ²⁸The LORD uprooted them from their land in anger, fury, and great wrath, and cast them into another land, as is now the case." ²⁹The secret things belong to the LORD our God, but the revealed things belong to us and to our children forever, to observe all the words of this law.

God's Fidelity Assured

30 When all these things have happened to you, the blessings and the curses that I have set before you, if you call them to mind among all the nations where the LORD your God has driven you, ²and return to the LORD your God, and you and your children obey him with all your heart and with all your soul, just as I am commanding you today, ³then the LORD your God will restore your fortunes and have compassion on you, gathering you again from all the peoples among whom the LORD your God has scattered you. ⁴Even if you are exiled to the ends of the world,ᵐ from there the LORD your God will gather you, and from there he will bring you back. ⁵The LORD your God will bring you into the land that your ancestors possessed, and you will possess it; he will make you more prosperous and numerous than your ancestors.

6 Moreover, the LORD your God will circumcise your heart and the heart of your descendants, so that you will love the LORD your God with all your heart and with all your soul, in order that you may live. ⁷The LORD your God will put all these curses on your enemies and on the adversaries who took advantage of you. ⁸Then you shall again obey the LORD, observing all his commandments that I am commanding you today, ⁹and the LORD your God will make you abundantly prosperous in all your undertakings, in the fruit of your body, in the fruit of your livestock, and in the fruit of your soil. For the LORD will again take delight in prospering you, just as he delighted in prospering your ancestors, ¹⁰when you obey the LORD your God by observing his commandments and decrees that are written in this book of the law, because you turn to the LORD your God with all your heart and with all your soul.

Exhortation to Choose Life

11 Surely, this commandment that I am commanding you today is not too hard for you, nor is it too far away. ¹²It is not in heaven, that you should say, "Who will go up to heaven for us, and get it for us so that we may hear it and observe it?" ¹³Neither is it beyond the sea, that you should say, "Who will cross to the other side of the sea for us, and get it for us so that we may hear it and observe it?" ¹⁴No, the word is very near to you; it is

---

ˡ Meaning of Heb uncertain   ᵐ Heb *of heaven*

in your mouth and in your heart for you to observe.

15 See, I have set before you today life and prosperity, death and adversity. [16]If you obey the

30.14 Keep It Simple

Sometimes people make a relationship with God sound impossibly difficult. Moses emphasizes its simplicity. You don't have to swim oceans or ascend into heaven; you just have to understand, believe, and obey the word God has given. In a famous New Testament passage, the apostle Paul applied this lesson to confessing faith in Jesus Christ (Romans 10.6–10).

commandments of the LORD your God[n] that I am commanding you today, by loving the LORD your God, walking in his ways, and observing his commandments, decrees, and ordinances, then you shall live and become numerous, and the LORD your God will bless you in the land that you are entering to possess. [17]But if your heart turns away and you do not hear, but are led astray to bow down to other gods and serve them, [18]I declare to you today that you shall perish; you shall not live long in the land that you are crossing the Jordan to enter and possess. [19]I call heaven and earth to witness against you today that I have set before you life and death, blessings and curses. Choose life so that you and your descendants may live, [20]loving the LORD your God, obeying him, and holding fast to him; for that means life to you and length of days, so that you may live in the land that the LORD swore to give to your ancestors, to Abraham, to Isaac, and to Jacob.

Joshua Becomes Moses' Successor

31 When Moses had finished speaking all[o] these words to all Israel, [2]he said to them: "I am now one hundred twenty years old. I am no longer able to get about, and the LORD has told me, 'You shall not cross over this Jordan.' [3]The LORD your God himself will cross over before you. He will destroy these nations before you, and you shall dispossess them. Joshua also will cross over before you, as the LORD promised. [4]The LORD will do to them as he did to Sihon and Og, the kings of the Amorites, and to their land, when he destroyed them. [5]The LORD will give them over to you and you shall deal with them in full accord with the command that I have given to you. [6]Be strong and bold; have no fear or dread of them, because it is the LORD your God who goes with you; he will not fail you or forsake you."

7 Then Moses summoned Joshua and said to him in the sight of all Israel: "Be strong and bold, for you are the one who will go with this people into the land that the LORD has sworn to their ancestors to give them; and you will put them in possession of it. [8]It is the LORD who goes before you. He will be with you; he will not fail you or forsake you. Do not fear or be dismayed."

The Law to Be Read Every Seventh Year

9 Then Moses wrote down this law, and gave it to the priests, the sons of Levi, who carried the ark of the covenant of the LORD, and to all the elders of Israel. [10]Moses commanded them: "Every seventh year, in the scheduled year of remission, during the festival of booths,[p] [11]when all Israel comes to appear before the LORD your God at the place that he will choose, you shall read this law before all Israel in their hearing. [12]Assemble the people—men, women, and children, as well as the aliens residing in your towns—so that they may hear and learn to fear the LORD your God and to observe diligently all the words of this law, [13]and so that their children, who have not known it, may hear and learn to fear the LORD your God, as long as you live in the land that you are crossing over the Jordan to possess."

Moses and Joshua Receive God's Charge

14 The LORD said to Moses, "Your time to die is near; call Joshua and present yourselves in the tent of meeting, so that I may commission him." So Moses and Joshua went and presented themselves in the tent of meeting, [15]and the LORD appeared at the tent in a pillar of cloud; the pillar of cloud stood at the entrance to the tent.

16 The LORD said to Moses, "Soon you will lie down with your ancestors. Then this people will begin to prostitute themselves to the foreign gods in their midst, the gods of the land into which they are going; they will forsake me, breaking my covenant that I have made with them. [17]My anger will be kindled against them in that day. I will forsake them and hide my face from them; they will become easy prey, and many terrible troubles will come upon them. In that day they will say, 'Have not these troubles come upon us because our God is not in our midst?' [18]On that day I will surely hide my face on account of all the evil they have done by turning to other gods. [19]Now therefore write this song, and teach it to the Israelites; put it in their mouths, in order that this song may be a witness for me against the Israelites. [20]For when I have brought them into the land flowing with milk and honey, which I promised on oath to their ancestors, and they have eaten their fill and grown fat, they will turn to other gods and serve them, despising me and breaking my covenant. [21]And when many terrible troubles come

---

[n] Gk: Heb lacks *If you obey the commandments of the LORD your God* [o] Q Ms Gk: MT *Moses went and spoke*
[p] Or *tabernacles*; Heb *succoth*

upon them, this song will confront them as a witness, because it will not be lost from the mouths of their descendants. For I know what they are inclined to do even now, before I have brought them into the land that I promised them on oath." 22That very day Moses wrote this song and taught it to the Israelites.

23 Then the LORD commissioned Joshua son of Nun and said, "Be strong and bold, for you shall bring the Israelites into the land that I promised them; I will be with you."

24 When Moses had finished writing down in a book the words of this law to the very end, 25Moses commanded the Levites who carried the ark of the covenant of the LORD, saying, 26"Take this book of the law and put it beside the ark of the covenant of the LORD your God; let it remain there as a witness against you. 27For I know well how rebellious and stubborn you are. If you already have been so rebellious toward the LORD while I am still alive among you, how much more after my death! 28Assemble to me all the elders of your tribes and your officials, so that I may recite these words in their hearing and call heaven and earth to witness against them. 29For I know that after my death you will surely act corruptly, turning aside from the way that I have commanded you. In time to come trouble will befall you, because you will do what is evil in the sight of the LORD, provoking him to anger through the work of your hands."

The Song of Moses

30 Then Moses recited the words of this song, to the very end, in the hearing of the whole assembly of Israel:

32 Give ear, O heavens, and I will speak;
   let the earth hear the words of my
      mouth.
2 May my teaching drop like the rain,
   my speech condense like the dew;
   like gentle rain on grass,
   like showers on new growth.
3 For I will proclaim the name of the LORD;
   ascribe greatness to our God!

4 The Rock, his work is perfect,
   and all his ways are just.
A faithful God, without deceit,
   just and upright is he;
5 yet his degenerate children have dealt
      falsely with him,q
   a perverse and crooked generation.
6 Do you thus repay the LORD,
   O foolish and senseless people?
Is not he your father, who created you,
   who made you and established you?
7 Remember the days of old,

consider the years long past;
ask your father, and he will inform you;
   your elders, and they will tell you.
8 When the Most Highr apportioned the
      nations,
   when he divided humankind,
he fixed the boundaries of the peoples
   according to the number of the gods;s
9 the LORD's own portion was his people,
   Jacob his allotted share.

10 He sustainedt him in a desert land,
   in a howling wilderness waste;
he shielded him, cared for him,
   guarded him as the apple of his eye.
11 As an eagle stirs up its nest,
   and hovers over its young;
as it spreads its wings, takes them up,
   and bears them aloft on its pinions,

12 the LORD alone guided him;
   no foreign god was with him.
13 He set him atop the heights of the land,
   and fed him withu produce of the
      field;
he nursed him with honey from the crags,
   with oil from flinty rock;
14 curds from the herd, and milk from the
      flock,
   with fat of lambs and rams;
Bashan bulls and goats,
   together with the choicest wheat—
   you drank fine wine from the blood of
      grapes.
15 Jacob ate his fill;v
Jeshurun grew fat, and kicked.
   You grew fat, bloated, and gorged!
He abandoned God who made him,
   and scoffed at the Rock of his
      salvation.
16 They made him jealous with strange gods,
   with abhorrent things they provoked
      him.
17 They sacrificed to demons, not God,
   to deities they had never known,

q Meaning of Heb uncertain   r Traditional rendering of Heb *Elyon*   s Q Ms Compare Gk Tg: MT *the Israelites*
t Sam Gk Compare Tg: MT *found*   u Sam Gk Syr Tg: MT *he ate*   v Q Mss Sam Gk: MT lacks *Jacob ate his fill*

to new ones recently arrived,
whom your ancestors had not feared.
18 You were unmindful of the Rock that
bore you;[w]
you forgot the God who gave you
birth.

19 The LORD saw it, and was jealous;[x]
he spurned[y] his sons and daughters.
20 He said: I will hide my face from them,
I will see what their end will be;
for they are a perverse generation,
children in whom there is no
faithfulness.
21 They made me jealous with what is no
god,
provoked me with their idols.
So I will make them jealous with what is
no people,
provoke them with a foolish nation.
22 For a fire is kindled by my anger,
and burns to the depths of Sheol;
it devours the earth and its increase,
and sets on fire the foundations of the
mountains.
23 I will heap disasters upon them,
spend my arrows against them:
24 wasting hunger,
burning consumption,
bitter pestilence.
The teeth of beasts I will send against
them,
with venom of things crawling in the
dust.
25 In the street the sword shall bereave,
and in the chambers terror,
for young man and woman alike,
nursing child and old gray head.
26 I thought to scatter them[z]
and blot out the memory of them from
humankind;
27 but I feared provocation by the enemy,
for their adversaries might
misunderstand
and say, "Our hand is triumphant;
it was not the LORD who did all this."

28 They are a nation void of sense;
there is no understanding in them.
29 If they were wise, they would understand
this;
they would discern what the end would
be.
30 How could one have routed a thousand,
and two put a myriad to flight,
unless their Rock had sold them,
the LORD had given them up?
31 Indeed their rock is not like our Rock;

our enemies are fools.[z]
32 Their vine comes from the vinestock of
Sodom,
from the vineyards of Gomorrah;
their grapes are grapes of poison,
their clusters are bitter;
33 their wine is the poison of serpents,
the cruel venom of asps.

34 Is not this laid up in store with me,
sealed up in my treasuries?
35 Vengeance is mine, and recompense,
for the time when their foot shall slip;
because the day of their calamity is at
hand,
their doom comes swiftly.

32.35 God's Vengeance

The New Testament quotes this verse twice, in two very different ways. The apostle Paul emphasized that because vengeance is God's business, not ours, we should never seek revenge (Romans 12.19). But the author of Hebrews also cited these words to highlight the seriousness of rejecting God, who will certainly judge his people (Hebrews 10.30).

36 Indeed the LORD will vindicate his people,
have compassion on his servants,
when he sees that their power is gone,
neither bond nor free remaining.
37 Then he will say: Where are their gods,
the rock in which they took refuge,
38 who ate the fat of their sacrifices,
and drank the wine of their libations?
Let them rise up and help you,
let them be your protection!

39 See now that I, even I, am he;
there is no god besides me.
I kill and I make alive;
I wound and I heal;
and no one can deliver from my hand.
40 For I lift up my hand to heaven,
and swear: As I live forever,
41 when I whet my flashing sword,
and my hand takes hold on judgment;
I will take vengeance on my adversaries,
and will repay those who hate me.
42 I will make my arrows drunk with blood,
and my sword shall devour flesh—
with the blood of the slain and the
captives,
from the long-haired enemy.

43 Praise, O heavens,[a] his people,

---

[w] Or *that begot you*   [x] Q Mss Gk: MT lacks *was jealous*   [y] Cn: Heb *he spurned because of provocation*
[z] Gk: Meaning of Heb uncertain   [a] Q Ms Gk: MT *nations*

worship him, all you gods![b]
For he will avenge the blood of his
        children,[c]
    and take vengeance on his adversaries;
    he will repay those who hate him,[b]
    and cleanse the land for his people.[d]

44 Moses came and recited all the words of
this song in the hearing of the people, he and
Joshua[e] son of Nun. 45When Moses had finished
reciting all these words to all Israel, 46he said to
them: "Take to heart all the words that I am giving in witness against you today; give them as a
command to your children, so that they may diligently observe all the words of this law. 47This is
no trifling matter for you, but rather your very
life; through it you may live long in the land that
you are crossing over the Jordan to possess."

Moses' Death Foretold

48 On that very day the LORD addressed Moses as follows: 49"Ascend this mountain of the
Abarim, Mount Nebo, which is in the land of
Moab, across from Jericho, and view the land of
Canaan, which I am giving to the Israelites for a
possession; 50you shall die there on the mountain
that you ascend and shall be gathered to your kin,
as your brother Aaron died on Mount Hor and
was gathered to his kin; 51because both of you
broke faith with me among the Israelites at the
waters of Meribath-kadesh in the wilderness of
Zin, by failing to maintain my holiness among the
Israelites. 52Although you may view the land from
a distance, you shall not enter it—the land that I
am giving to the Israelites."

Moses' Final Blessing on Israel

33 This is the blessing with which Moses, the
man of God, blessed the Israelites before
his death. 2He said:
    The LORD came from Sinai,
        and dawned from Seir upon us;[f]

33.1–29 Dying Words

*Just before he died, Moses gave a final word to
the Israelites, most of whom had lived their
entire adult lives under his leadership. Now
they would no longer have him to lean on. As
they prepared to enter the promised land
without him, he bequeathed to them something
more valuable than money, stronger than
power, deeper than learning: a blessing. Tribe
by tribe, Moses spoke of God's personal care
and salvation for the people of Israel.*

    he shone forth from Mount Paran.
    With him were myriads of holy ones;[g]
        at his right, a host of his own.[h]
3   Indeed, O favorite among[i] peoples,
        all his holy ones were in your charge;
    they marched at your heels,
        accepted direction from you.
4   Moses charged us with the law,
        as a possession for the assembly of
            Jacob.
5   There arose a king in Jeshurun,
        when the leaders of the people
            assembled—
        the united tribes of Israel.

6   May Reuben live, and not die out,
        even though his numbers are few.

7And this he said of Judah:
    O LORD, give heed to Judah,
        and bring him to his people;
    strengthen his hands for him,[j]
        and be a help against his adversaries.

8And of Levi he said:
    Give to Levi[k] your Thummim,
        and your Urim to your loyal one,
    whom you tested at Massah,
        with whom you contended at the
            waters of Meribah;
9   who said of his father and mother,
        "I regard them not";
    he ignored his kin,
        and did not acknowledge his children.
    For they observed your word,
        and kept your covenant.
10 They teach Jacob your ordinances,
        and Israel your law;
    they place incense before you,
        and whole burnt offerings on your
            altar.
11 Bless, O LORD, his substance,
        and accept the work of his hands;
    crush the loins of his adversaries,
        of those that hate him, so that they do
            not rise again.

12Of Benjamin he said:
    The beloved of the LORD rests in safety—
    the High God[l] surrounds him all day
            long—
    the beloved[m] rests between his
            shoulders.

13And of Joseph he said:
    Blessed by the LORD be his land,

---

[b] Q Ms Gk: MT lacks this line   [c] Q Ms Gk: MT *his servants*   [d] Q Ms Sam Gk Vg: MT *his land his people*
[e] Sam Gk Syr Vg: MT *Hoshea*   [f] Gk Syr Vg Compare Tg: Heb *upon them*   [g] Cn Compare Gk Sam
Syr Vg: MT *He came from Riboboth-kodesh,*   [h] Cn Compare Gk: meaning of Heb uncertain   [i] Or *O lover of the*
[j] Cn: Heb *with his hands he contended*   [k] Q Ms Gk: MT lacks *Give to Levi*   [l] Heb *above him*   [m] Heb *he*

with the choice gifts of heaven above,
and of the deep that lies beneath;
[14] with the choice fruits of the sun,
and the rich yield of the months;
[15] with the finest produce of the ancient
mountains,
and the abundance of the everlasting
hills;
[16] with the choice gifts of the earth and its
fullness,
and the favor of the one who dwells on
Sinai.[n]
Let these come on the head of Joseph,
on the brow of the prince among his
brothers.
[17] A firstborn[o] bull—majesty is his!
His horns are the horns of a wild ox;
with them he gores the peoples,
driving them to[p] the ends of the earth;
such are the myriads of Ephraim,
such the thousands of Manasseh.

[18]And of Zebulun he said:
Rejoice, Zebulun, in your going out;
and Issachar, in your tents.
[19] They call peoples to the mountain;
there they offer the right sacrifices;
for they suck the affluence of the seas
and the hidden treasures of the sand.

[20]And of Gad he said:
Blessed be the enlargement of Gad!
Gad lives like a lion;
he tears at arm and scalp.
[21] He chose the best for himself,
for there a commander's allotment was
reserved;
he came at the head of the people,
he executed the justice of the LORD,
and his ordinances for Israel.

[22]And of Dan he said:
Dan is a lion's whelp
that leaps forth from Bashan.

[23]And of Naphtali he said:
O Naphtali, sated with favor,
full of the blessing of the LORD,
possess the west and the south.

[24]And of Asher he said:
Most blessed of sons be Asher;
may he be the favorite of his brothers,
and may he dip his foot in oil.
[25] Your bars are iron and bronze;
and as your days, so is your strength.

[26] There is none like God, O Jeshurun,

who rides through the heavens to your
help,
majestic through the skies.
[27] He subdues the ancient gods,[q]
shatters[r] the forces of old;[s]
he drove out the enemy before you,
and said, "Destroy!"
[28] So Israel lives in safety,
untroubled is Jacob's abode[t]
in a land of grain and wine,
where the heavens drop down dew.
[29] Happy are you, O Israel! Who is like you,
a people saved by the LORD,
the shield of your help,
and the sword of your triumph!
Your enemies shall come fawning to you,
and you shall tread on their backs.

Moses Dies and Is Buried in the Land of Moab

34 Then Moses went up from the plains of Moab to Mount Nebo, to the top of Pisgah, which is opposite Jericho, and the LORD showed him the whole land: Gilead as far as Dan, [2]all Naphtali, the land of Ephraim and Manasseh, all the land of Judah as far as the Western Sea, [3]the Negeb, and the Plain—that is, the valley of Jericho, the city of palm trees—as far as Zoar. [4]The LORD said to him, "This is the land of which I swore to Abraham, to Isaac, and to Jacob, saying, 'I will give it to your descendants'; I have let you see it with your eyes, but you shall not cross over there." [5]Then Moses, the servant of the LORD, died there in the land of Moab, at the

34.5 Moses Gets a Preview

To his great disappointment, Moses could not lead his people into the new land, for reasons mentioned in 32.48–52. But God allowed him a final look over all the promised land. And, in a very unexpected way, Moses did realize his dream of setting foot in the promised land. Over a thousand years later, he returned with the prophet Elijah and visited with Jesus on the Mount of Transfiguration (Matthew 17; Mark 9; Luke 9).

LORD's command. [6]He was buried in a valley in the land of Moab, opposite Beth-peor, but no one knows his burial place to this day. [7]Moses was one hundred twenty years old when he died; his sight was unimpaired and his vigor had not abated. [8]The Israelites wept for Moses in the plains of Moab thirty days; then the period of mourning for Moses was ended.

---

[n] Cn: Heb *in the bush*   [o] Q Ms Gk Syr Vg: MT *His firstborn*   [p] Cn: Heb *the peoples, together*   [q] Or *The eternal*
God is a dwelling place   [r] Cn: Heb *from underneath*   [s] Or *the everlasting arms*   [t] Or *fountain*

9 Joshua son of Nun was full of the spirit of wisdom, because Moses had laid his hands on him; and the Israelites obeyed him, doing as the LORD had commanded Moses.

10 Never since has there arisen a prophet in Israel like Moses, whom the LORD knew face to face. [11]He was unequaled for all the signs and wonders that the LORD sent him to perform in the land of Egypt, against Pharaoh and all his servants and his entire land, [12]and for all the mighty deeds and all the terrifying displays of power that Moses performed in the sight of all Israel.

JOSHUA

The Difference 40 Years Can Make
They faced overwhelming odds with renewed hope

> *"Do not be frightened or dismayed, for the LORD your God is with you wherever you go." 1.9*

O N THE SURFACE, NOT MUCH had changed in 40 years. The band of refugees amassing beside the Jordan River greatly resembled a similar horde from four decades before. They had panicked once. Would they again?

The Israelites still faced overwhelming odds. They had no chariots or even horses. They had only primitive arms, an untested new leader, and long-delayed marching orders from God.

A New Spirit, a New Leader

Yet, in another sense, everything had changed. Older Israelites with fearful, slave mentalities had died off in the desert—all the older generation except Joshua and Caleb, two legendary warriors. The new generation had decided to trust God, no matter what. In stark contrast to the spies in Numbers (13.31–33), Joshua's scouts brought back this report, "Truly the LORD has given all the land into our hands; moreover all the inhabitants of the land melt in fear before us" (2.24).

The book of Joshua contains not a word about rebellion against a leader or grumbling against God. It is a good news book, a welcome relief from the discouraging tone of Numbers and the fatalism of Deuteronomy. What a difference 40 years had made!

As newly appointed leader of the Israelites, Joshua took on two main tasks. First, he was to direct a military campaign to take control of the land God had promised. Then, he would parcel out the conquered land among all the tribes.

Learning to Follow Instructions

Once inside Canaan, the Israelites followed God's instructions precisely, even when doing so must have strained their faith to new limits. The residents of Jericho had shut themselves behind stone walls, awaiting the onslaught of the feared Israelites. But how did the Israelites spend their first week in Canaan? They built a stone monument to God, performed circumcision rituals, and held a Passover celebration. No conquering army had ever behaved in such a manner.

Everything in Joshua seems handpicked to strike home the point that God was really in charge. Covering a period of approximately seven years, Joshua's 24 chapters devote only a few sentences to some extensive military campaigns (see chapters 10–11). But key events, such as the fall of Jericho, get detailed coverage, underscoring that the Israelites succeeded when they relied on God, not on military might. The few negative stories (such as the battle of Ai and the trick of the Gibeonites) show what happened when the Israelites did not seek God's will.

A Book of Hope

The Bible does not give history for its own sake. Rather, it presents practical and spiritual lessons. Fortunately, Joshua's lessons are overwhelmingly positive ones. Guided by God, the nation of Israel met with unprecedented success. In fact, the book concludes that "not one of all the good promises that the LORD had made to the house of Israel had failed; all came to pass" (21.45).

The book of Joshua gives a fresh breeze of hope. Writers of hymns and spirituals have often gone back to it to try to recapture the spirit of success that swept over God's people those first few years in the new land. It *can* work: people can follow God. Joshua shows how.

How to Read Joshua

P hrases in the first two paragraphs of Joshua hint at the tone to follow. "I will not fail you or forsake you," God promised. "Every place that the sole of your foot will tread upon I have given to you." "Act in accordance with all the law that my servant Moses commanded you . . . so that you may be successful wherever you go."

Often the Israelites offer examples of what *not* to do. Already the books of Exodus, Numbers, and Deuteronomy have given negative examples, and the historical books to follow will describe further failures in lurid detail. But the Old Testament does offer a few bright spots of hope, the book of Joshua being one of the brightest.

(The "good news" character of Joshua causes some people to compare it to the New Testament books of Ephesians and Philippians, which share its success-and-triumph tone. You may want to read one of those New Testament books along with Joshua.)

Fast-paced battle action appears in chapters 1–11, "the book of war." The latter chapters, "the book of distribution," mostly concern the parceling out of the land.

You can casually read about the military campaigns of Joshua, but to truly appreciate them you must study a map or Bible atlas. Joshua is a very geographical book. Place-names appear in every chapter, describing the military progress and also the division of the land among the tribes of Israel.

As you read Joshua, keep two major themes in mind: Joshua's leadership and God's direct involvement in history. Study Joshua's life as an example of leadership. What were the reasons behind his few failures, such as those recorded in chapters 7 and 9? You may also want to refer to the background passages on his life in Exodus (17,24,32,33) and Numbers (11,13,26). What lesson did Joshua learn at each of these key moments?

PEOPLE YOU'LL MEET IN JOSHUA

RAHAB *(p. 237)*
JOSHUA *(p. 255)*

3-TRACK READING PLAN

For an explanation and complete listing of the 3-track reading plan, turn to page 7.

TRACK 1:   ***Two-Week Courses on the Bible***
See page 7 for information on these courses.

TRACK 2:   ***An Overview of Joshua in 4 Days***
☐ Day 1. Read the Introduction to Joshua and then chapter 2, the story of Rahab and the spies.
☐ Day 2. Read the story of Jericho in chapter 6; the Israelites practiced very unorthodox military tactics, but learned to rely on God.
☐ Day 3. Success at Jericho immediately preceded a great failure; read about it in chapter 7.
☐ Day 4. Read chapter 24, part of Joshua's stirring farewell speech to the nation he led so well.

Now turn to page 9 for your next Track 2 reading project.

TRACK 3:   ***All of Joshua in 21 Days***
After you have read through Joshua, turn to pages 10–14 for your next Track 3 reading project.

☐1   ☐2   ☐3   ☐4   ☐5   ☐6   ☐7   ☐8
☐9   ☐10   ☐11   ☐12–13 ☐14–15 ☐16–17 ☐18   ☐19
☐20   ☐21   ☐22   ☐23   ☐24

God's Commission to Joshua

1 After the death of Moses the servant of the LORD, the LORD spoke to Joshua son of Nun, Moses' assistant, saying, 2"My servant Moses is dead. Now proceed to cross the Jordan, you and all this people, into the land that I am giving to them, to the Israelites. 3Every place that the sole of your foot will tread upon I have given to you, as I promised to Moses. 4From the wilderness and the Lebanon as far as the great river, the river Euphrates, all the land of the Hittites, to the Great Sea in the west shall be your territory. 5No one shall be able to stand against you all the days of your life. As I was with Moses, so I will be with you; I will not fail you or forsake you. 6Be strong and courageous; for you shall put this people in possession of the land that I swore to their ancestors to give them. 7Only be strong and very courageous, being careful to act in accordance with all the law that my servant Moses commanded you; do not turn from it to the right hand or to the left, so that you may be successful wherever you go. 8This book of the law shall not depart out of your mouth; you shall meditate on it day and night, so that you may be careful to act in accordance with all that is written in it. For then you shall make your way prosperous, and then you

1.8 Secret of Success

Three times in this short speech God urged Joshua to "be strong and courageous." Joshua must have quaked at the prospect of taking over for a great man like Moses. But God promised him the resources he needed: God's own presence (verse 5) and the book of the law, which Joshua was to lean on every day.

shall be successful. 9I hereby command you: Be strong and courageous; do not be frightened or dismayed, for the LORD your God is with you wherever you go."

Preparations for the Invasion

10 Then Joshua commanded the officers of the people, 11"Pass through the camp, and command the people: 'Prepare your provisions; for in three days you are to cross over the Jordan, to go in to take possession of the land that the LORD your God gives you to possess.'"

12 To the Reubenites, the Gadites, and the half-tribe of Manasseh Joshua said, 13"Remember the word that Moses the servant of the LORD commanded you, saying, 'The LORD your God is providing you a place of rest, and will give you this land.' 14Your wives, your little ones, and your livestock shall remain in the land that Moses gave

you beyond the Jordan. But all the warriors among you shall cross over armed before your kindred and shall help them, 15until the LORD gives rest to your kindred as well as to you, and they too take possession of the land that the LORD your God is giving them. Then you shall return to your own land and take possession of it, the land that Moses the servant of the LORD gave you beyond the Jordan to the east."

16 They answered Joshua: "All that you have commanded us we will do, and wherever you send us we will go. 17Just as we obeyed Moses in all things, so we will obey you. Only may the LORD your God be with you, as he was with Moses! 18Whoever rebels against your orders and disobeys your words, whatever you command, shall be put to death. Only be strong and courageous."

Spies Sent to Jericho

2 Then Joshua son of Nun sent two men secretly from Shittim as spies, saying, "Go, view the land, especially Jericho." So they went, and entered the house of a prostitute whose name was Rahab, and spent the night there. 2The king of Jericho was told, "Some Israelites have come here tonight to search out the land." 3Then the king of Jericho sent orders to Rahab, "Bring out the men who have come to you, who entered your house, for they have come only to search out the whole land." 4But the woman took the two men and hid them. Then she said, "True, the men came to me, but I did not know where they came from. 5And when it was time to close the gate at dark, the men went out. Where the men went I do not know. Pursue them quickly, for you can overtake them." 6She had, however, brought them up to the roof and hidden them with the stalks of flax that she had laid out on the roof. 7So the men pursued them on the way to the Jordan as far as the fords. As soon as the pursuers had gone out, the gate was shut.

8 Before they went to sleep, she came up to them on the roof 9and said to the men: "I know that the LORD has given you the land, and that dread of you has fallen on us, and that all the inhabitants of the land melt in fear before you. 10For we have heard how the LORD dried up the water of the Red Sea[a] before you when you came out of Egypt, and what you did to the two kings of the Amorites that were beyond the Jordan, to Sihon and Og, whom you utterly destroyed. 11As soon as we heard it, our hearts melted, and there was no courage left in any of us because of you. The LORD your God is indeed God in heaven above and on earth below. 12Now then, since I have dealt kindly with you, swear to me by the LORD that you in turn will deal kindly with my family. Give me a sign of good faith 13that you will spare my father and mother, my brothers and

---

a Or Sea of Reeds

sisters, and all who belong to them, and deliver our lives from death." ¹⁴The men said to her, "Our life for yours! If you do not tell this business of ours, then we will deal kindly and faithfully with you when the LORD gives us the land."

2.12 Rahab's Future

References to Rahab elsewhere in the Bible show that she gained a unique place in Jewish history. She and her family alone survived the battle of Jericho. By marrying a man named Salmon (possibly a relative of the hero Caleb), she became a direct ancestor of Jesus Christ (Matthew 1.5). The authors of James (2.25) and Hebrews (11.31) hold up Rahab as an example of faith.

15 Then she let them down by a rope through the window, for her house was on the outer side of the city wall and she resided within the wall itself. ¹⁶She said to them, "Go toward the hill country, so that the pursuers may not come upon you. Hide yourselves there three days, until the pursuers have returned; then afterward you may go your way." ¹⁷The men said to her, "We will be released from this oath that you have made us swear to you ¹⁸if we invade the land and you do not tie this crimson cord in the window through which you let us down, and you do not gather into your house your father and mother, your brothers, and all your family. ¹⁹If any of you go out of the doors of your house into the street, they shall be responsible for their own death, and we shall be innocent; but if a hand is laid upon any who are with you in the house, we shall bear the responsibility for their death. ²⁰But if you tell this business of ours, then we shall be released from this oath that you made us swear to you." ²¹She said, "According to your words, so be it." She sent them away and they departed. Then she tied the crimson cord in the window.

22 They departed and went into the hill country and stayed there three days, until the pursuers returned. The pursuers had searched all along the way and found nothing. ²³Then the two men came down again from the hill country. They crossed over, came to Joshua son of Nun, and told him all that had happened to them. ²⁴They said to Joshua, "Truly the LORD has given all the land into our hands; moreover all the inhabitants of the land melt in fear before us."

Israel Crosses the Jordan

3 Early in the morning Joshua rose and set out from Shittim with all the Israelites, and they came to the Jordan. They camped there before crossing over. ²At the end of three days the offi-

cers went through the camp ³and commanded the people, "When you see the ark of the covenant of the LORD your God being carried by the levitical priests, then you shall set out from your place. Follow it, ⁴so that you may know the way you should go, for you have not passed this way before. Yet there shall be a space between you and it, a distance of about two thousand cubits; do not come any nearer to it." ⁵Then Joshua said to the people, "Sanctify yourselves; for tomorrow the LORD will do wonders among you." ⁶To the priests Joshua said, "Take up the ark of the covenant, and pass on in front of the people." So they took up the ark of the covenant and went in front of the people.

7 The LORD said to Joshua, "This day I will begin to exalt you in the sight of all Israel, so that they may know that I will be with you as I was with Moses. ⁸You are the one who shall command the priests who bear the ark of the covenant, 'When you come to the edge of the waters of the Jordan, you shall stand still in the Jordan.'" ⁹Joshua then said to the Israelites, "Draw near and hear the words of the LORD your God." ¹⁰Joshua said, "By this you shall know that among you is the living God who without fail will drive out from before you the Canaanites, Hittites, Hivites, Perizzites, Girgashites, Amorites, and Jebusites: ¹¹the ark of the covenant of the Lord of all the earth is going to pass before you into the Jordan. ¹²So now select twelve men from the tribes of Israel, one from each tribe. ¹³When the soles of the feet of the priests who bear the ark of the LORD, the Lord of all the earth, rest in the waters of the Jordan, the waters of the Jordan flowing from above shall be cut off; they shall stand in a single heap."

14 When the people set out from their tents to cross over the Jordan, the priests bearing the ark of the covenant were in front of the people. ¹⁵Now the Jordan overflows all its banks throughout the time of harvest. So when those who bore the ark had come to the Jordan, and the feet of the priests bearing the ark were dipped in the edge of the water, ¹⁶the waters flowing from above stood still, rising up in a single heap far off at Adam, the city that is beside Zarethan, while those flowing toward the sea of the Arabah, the Dead Sea,ᵇ were wholly cut off. Then the people crossed over opposite Jericho. ¹⁷While all Israel were crossing over on dry ground, the priests who bore the ark of the covenant of the LORD stood on dry ground in the middle of the Jordan, until the entire nation finished crossing over the Jordan.

Twelve Stones Set Up at Gilgal

4 When the entire nation had finished crossing over the Jordan, the LORD said to Joshua: ²"Select twelve men from the people, one from

ᵇ Heb *Salt Sea*

each tribe, ³and command them, 'Take twelve stones from here out of the middle of the Jordan, from the place where the priests' feet stood, carry them over with you, and lay them down in the

3.16 Stopping the Jordan River

A 1927 earthquake caused the 40-foot clay banks of the Jordan River to collapse, totally damming the Jordan for 21 hours. Whatever means God used to allow the Israelites to cross, this miracle in Joshua achieved a similar result during the river's swollen flood stage. The miracle echoed the crossing of the Red Sea 40 years before, helping to establish Joshua as a worthy successor to Moses. Joshua and the Israelites crossed at a location very close to where Jesus was later baptized.

place where you camp tonight.'" ⁴Then Joshua summoned the twelve men from the Israelites, whom he had appointed, one from each tribe. ⁵Joshua said to them, "Pass on before the ark of the LORD your God into the middle of the Jordan, and each of you take up a stone on his shoulder, one for each of the tribes of the Israelites, ⁶so that this may be a sign among you. When your children ask in time to come, 'What do those stones mean to you?' ⁷then you shall tell them that the waters of the Jordan were cut off in front of the ark of the covenant of the LORD. When it crossed over the Jordan, the waters of the Jordan were cut off. So these stones shall be to the Israelites a memorial forever."

8 The Israelites did as Joshua commanded. They took up twelve stones out of the middle of the Jordan, according to the number of the tribes of the Israelites, as the LORD told Joshua, carried them over with them to the place where they camped, and laid them down there. ⁹(Joshua set up twelve stones in the middle of the Jordan, in the place where the feet of the priests bearing the ark of the covenant had stood; and they are there to this day.)

10 The priests who bore the ark remained standing in the middle of the Jordan, until everything was finished that the LORD commanded Joshua to tell the people, according to all that Moses had commanded Joshua. The people crossed over in haste. ¹¹As soon as all the people had finished crossing over, the ark of the LORD, and the priests, crossed over in front of the people. ¹²The Reubenites, the Gadites, and the half-tribe of Manasseh crossed over armed before the Israelites, as Moses had ordered them. ¹³About forty thousand armed for war crossed over before the LORD to the plains of Jericho for battle.

14 On that day the LORD exalted Joshua in the sight of all Israel; and they stood in awe of him, as they had stood in awe of Moses, all the days of his life.

15 The LORD said to Joshua, ¹⁶"Command the priests who bear the ark of the covenant,ᶜ to come up out of the Jordan." ¹⁷Joshua therefore commanded the priests, "Come up out of the Jordan." ¹⁸When the priests bearing the ark of the covenant of the LORD came up from the middle of the Jordan, and the soles of the priests' feet touched dry ground, the waters of the Jordan returned to their place and overflowed all its banks, as before.

19 The people came up out of the Jordan on the tenth day of the first month, and they camped in Gilgal on the east border of Jericho. ²⁰Those twelve stones, which they had taken out of the Jordan, Joshua set up in Gilgal, ²¹saying to the Israelites, "When your children ask their parents in time to come, 'What do these stones mean?' ²²then you shall let your children know, 'Israel crossed over the Jordan here on dry ground.' ²³For the LORD your God dried up the waters of the Jordan for you until you crossed over, as the LORD your God did to the Red Sea,ᵈ which he dried up for us until we crossed over, ²⁴so that all the peoples of the earth may know that the hand of the LORD is mighty, and so that you may fear the LORD your God forever."

The New Generation Circumcised

5 When all the kings of the Amorites beyond the Jordan to the west, and all the kings of the Canaanites by the sea, heard that the LORD had dried up the waters of the Jordan for the Israelites until they had crossed over, their hearts melted, and there was no longer any spirit in them, because of the Israelites.

2 At that time the LORD said to Joshua, "Make flint knives and circumcise the Israelites a second time." ³So Joshua made flint knives, and circumcised the Israelites at Gibeath-haaraloth.ᵉ ⁴This is the reason why Joshua circumcised them: all the males of the people who came out of Egypt, all the warriors, had died during the journey through the wilderness after they had come out of Egypt. ⁵Although all the people who came out had been circumcised, yet all the people born on the journey through the wilderness after they had come out of Egypt had not been circumcised. ⁶For the Israelites traveled forty years in the wilderness, until all the nation, the warriors who came out of Egypt, perished, not having listened to the voice of the LORD. To them the LORD swore that he would not let them see the land that he had sworn to their ancestors to give us, a land flowing with milk and honey. ⁷So it was their children, whom he raised up in their place, that Joshua circum-

---

ᶜ Or *treaty*, or *testimony*; Heb *eduth*   ᵈ Or *Sea of Reeds*   ᵉ That is *the Hill of the Foreskins*

cised; for they were uncircumcised, because they had not been circumcised on the way.

8 When the circumcising of all the nation was done, they remained in their places in the camp until they were healed. ⁹The LORD said to Joshua, "Today I have rolled away from you the disgrace of Egypt." And so that place is called Gilgal*f* to this day.

The Passover at Gilgal

10 While the Israelites were camped in Gilgal they kept the passover in the evening on the fourteenth day of the month in the plains of Jericho. ¹¹On the day after the passover, on that very day, they ate the produce of the land, unleavened cakes and parched grain. ¹²The manna ceased on the day they ate the produce of the land, and the Israelites no longer had manna; they ate the crops of the land of Canaan that year.

5.12 No More Free Lunch

For 40 years God had provided manna, a miraculous food that appeared like dew on the ground every night. In the desert, manna had been necessary for survival. In Palestine, however, the free food stopped. Israelites would be able to grow or gather adequate food for themselves.

Joshua's Vision

13 Once when Joshua was by Jericho, he looked up and saw a man standing before him with a drawn sword in his hand. Joshua went to him and said to him, "Are you one of us, or one of our adversaries?" ¹⁴He replied, "Neither; but as commander of the army of the LORD I have now come." And Joshua fell on his face to the earth and worshiped, and he said to him, "What do you command your servant, my lord?" ¹⁵The commander of the army of the LORD said to Joshua, "Remove the sandals from your feet, for the place where you stand is holy." And Joshua did so.

Jericho Taken and Destroyed

6 Now Jericho was shut up inside and out because of the Israelites; no one came out and no one went in. ²The LORD said to Joshua, "See, I have handed Jericho over to you, along with its king and soldiers. ³You shall march around the city, all the warriors circling the city once. Thus you shall do for six days, ⁴with seven priests bearing seven trumpets of rams' horns before the ark. On the seventh day you shall march around the city seven times, the priests blowing the trumpets.

⁵When they make a long blast with the ram's horn, as soon as you hear the sound of the trumpet, then all the people shall shout with a great shout; and the wall of the city will fall down flat, and all the people shall charge straight ahead." ⁶So Joshua son of Nun summoned the priests and said to them, "Take up the ark of the covenant, and have seven priests carry seven trumpets of rams' horns in front of the ark of the LORD." ⁷To the people he said, "Go forward and march around the city; have the armed men pass on before the ark of the LORD."

8 As Joshua had commanded the people, the seven priests carrying the seven trumpets of rams' horns before the LORD went forward, blowing the trumpets, with the ark of the covenant of the LORD following them. ⁹And the armed men went before the priests who blew the trumpets; the rear guard came after the ark, while the trumpets blew continually. ¹⁰To the people Joshua gave this command: "You shall not shout or let your voice be heard, nor shall you utter a word, until the day I tell you to shout. Then you shall shout." ¹¹So the ark of the LORD went around the city, circling it once; and they came into the camp, and spent the night in the camp.

12 Then Joshua rose early in the morning, and the priests took up the ark of the LORD. ¹³The seven priests carrying the seven trumpets of rams' horns before the ark of the LORD passed on, blowing the trumpets continually. The armed men went before them, and the rear guard came after the ark of the LORD, while the trumpets blew continually. ¹⁴On the second day they marched around the city once and then returned to the camp. They did this for six days.

15 On the seventh day they rose early, at dawn, and marched around the city in the same manner seven times. It was only on that day that they marched around the city seven times. ¹⁶And at the seventh time, when the priests had blown the trumpets, Joshua said to the people, "Shout! For the LORD has given you the city. ¹⁷The city and all that is in it shall be devoted to the LORD for destruction. Only Rahab the prostitute and all who are with her in her house shall live because she hid the messengers we sent. ¹⁸As for you, keep away from the things devoted to destruction, so as not to covet*g* and take any of the devoted things and make the camp of Israel an object for destruction, bringing trouble upon it. ¹⁹But all silver and gold, and vessels of bronze and iron, are sacred to the LORD; they shall go into the treasury of the LORD." ²⁰So the people shouted, and the trumpets were blown. As soon as the people heard the sound of the trumpets, they raised a great shout, and the wall fell down flat; so

---

f Related to Heb *galal* to roll   *g* Gk: Heb *devote to destruction* Compare 7.21

the people charged straight ahead into the city and captured it. ²¹Then they devoted to destruction by the edge of the sword all in the city, both men and women, young and old, oxen, sheep, and donkeys.

22 Joshua said to the two men who had spied out the land, "Go into the prostitute's house, and bring the woman out of it and all who belong to her, as you swore to her." ²³So the young men who had been spies went in and brought Rahab out, along with her father, her mother, her brothers, and all who belonged to her—they brought all her kindred out—and set them outside the camp of Israel. ²⁴They burned down the city, and everything in it; only the silver and gold, and the vessels of bronze and iron, they put into the treasury of the house of the LORD. ²⁵But Rahab the prostitute, with her family and all who belonged to her, Joshua spared. Her family*ʰ* has lived in Israel ever since. For she hid the messengers whom Joshua sent to spy out Jericho.

26 Joshua then pronounced this oath, saying,

"Cursed before the LORD be anyone who tries
        to build this city—this Jericho!

6.26 Cursed City

Joshua's curse was fulfilled literally when a man attempted to rebuild the city of Jericho in the days of King Ahab (see 1 Kings 16.34).

At the cost of his firstborn he shall lay its foundation,
    and at the cost of his youngest he shall set up its gates!"

27 So the LORD was with Joshua; and his fame was in all the land.

ʰ Heb *She*

The Sin of Achan and Its Punishment

7 But the Israelites broke faith in regard to the devoted things: Achan son of Carmi son of Zabdi son of Zerah, of the tribe of Judah, took some of the devoted things; and the anger of the LORD burned against the Israelites.

2 Joshua sent men from Jericho to Ai, which is near Beth-aven, east of Bethel, and said to them, "Go up and spy out the land." And the men went up and spied out Ai. ³Then they returned to Joshua and said to him, "Not all the people need go up; about two or three thousand men should go up and attack Ai. Since they are so few, do not make the whole people toil up there." ⁴So about three thousand of the people went up there; and they fled before the men of Ai. ⁵The men of Ai killed about thirty-six of them, chasing them from outside the gate as far as Shebarim and killing them on the slope. The hearts of the people melted and turned to water.

6 Then Joshua tore his clothes, and fell to the ground on his face before the ark of the LORD until the evening, he and the elders of Israel; and they put dust on their heads. ⁷Joshua said, "Ah, Lord GOD! Why have you brought this people across the Jordan at all, to hand us over to the Amorites so as to destroy us? Would that we had been content to settle beyond the Jordan! ⁸O Lord, what can I say, now that Israel has turned their backs to their enemies! ⁹The Canaanites and all the inhabitants of the land will hear of it, and surround us, and cut off our name from the earth. Then what will you do for your great name?"

10 The LORD said to Joshua, "Stand up! Why have you fallen upon your face? ¹¹Israel has sinned; they have transgressed my covenant that I imposed on them. They have taken some of the devoted things; they have stolen, they have acted

RAHAB *A Prostitute's Faith*

PEOPLE WHO STUDY THE BIBLE are often surprised to find a prostitute held up as an example of faith. In two separate places the New Testament commends the prostitute named Rahab. The writers pass over both her profession and the lie that she told the king of Jericho (2.4–5). Her vision is what they admire. Rahab saw things differently than every one else in her community, and she gambled her future on that vision.

Word of the Israelites' amazing successes had spread. According to Rahab, the residents of Jericho were "melt[ing] in fear" at the news of Israel's triumphs over Egypt and other nations. Yet the people of Jericho determined all the more to dig in and fight. Rahab took the opposite course: She decided to join the opposition. Concluding that Israel's God was the real God, she chose to switch to his side.

Perhaps her social position—a prostitute living on the margins of society—made it easier for Rahab to take a stand against her own people. (Centuries later people on the margins of respectability often accepted Jesus, too.) Regardless, because she risked her neck to save the Israelite spies, they made sure that she and her entire family survived the assault.

Life Questions: Do you know anyone with real vision? If so, what do they see that others don't?

deceitfully, and they have put them among their own belongings. ¹²Therefore the Israelites are unable to stand before their enemies; they turn their backs to their enemies, because they have become

---

7.7 A Crisis of Confidence

Ai stood near the original location where God had promised the land to Abraham hundreds of years before (Genesis 12.8). Military defeat here, coming so quickly after a great victory at Jericho, caused even Joshua to tremble. Without God's protection, the Israelites were militarily vulnerable—trapped without possibility of escape across the flooding Jordan River.

The trouble at Ai came because of a single man who had greedily disobeyed God's battle commands. His punishment was drastic. Evidently the fledgling nation (like the fledgling church of Acts 5.1–10) needed a strong lesson in the consequences of taking God's word lightly.

---

a thing devoted for destruction themselves. I will be with you no more, unless you destroy the devoted things from among you. ¹³Proceed to sanctify the people, and say, 'Sanctify yourselves for tomorrow; for thus says the LORD, the God of Israel, "There are devoted things among you, O Israel; you will be unable to stand before your enemies until you take away the devoted things from among you." ¹⁴In the morning therefore you shall come forward tribe by tribe. The tribe that the LORD takes shall come near by clans, the clan that the LORD takes shall come near by households, and the household that the LORD takes shall come near one by one. ¹⁵And the one who is taken as having the devoted things shall be burned with fire, together with all that he has, for having transgressed the covenant of the LORD, and for having done an outrageous thing in Israel.'"

16 So Joshua rose early in the morning, and brought Israel near tribe by tribe, and the tribe of Judah was taken. ¹⁷He brought near the clans of Judah, and the clan of the Zerahites was taken; and he brought near the clan of the Zerahites, family by family,[i] and Zabdi was taken. ¹⁸And he brought near his household one by one, and Achan son of Carmi son of Zabdi son of Zerah, of the tribe of Judah, was taken. ¹⁹Then Joshua said to Achan, "My son, give glory to the LORD God of Israel and make confession to him. Tell me now what you have done; do not hide it from me." ²⁰And Achan answered Joshua, "It is true; I am the one who sinned against the LORD God of Israel. This is what I did: ²¹when I saw among the

spoil a beautiful mantle from Shinar, and two hundred shekels of silver, and a bar of gold weighing fifty shekels, then I coveted them and took them. They now lie hidden in the ground inside my tent, with the silver underneath."

22 So Joshua sent messengers, and they ran to the tent; and there it was, hidden in his tent with the silver underneath. ²³They took them out of the tent and brought them to Joshua and all the Israelites; and they spread them out before the LORD. ²⁴Then Joshua and all Israel with him took Achan son of Zerah, with the silver, the mantle, and the bar of gold, with his sons and daughters, with his oxen, donkeys, and sheep, and his tent and all that he had; and they brought them up to the Valley of Achor. ²⁵Joshua said, "Why did you bring trouble on us? The LORD is bringing trouble on you today." And all Israel stoned him to death; they burned them with fire, cast stones on them, ²⁶and raised over him a great heap of stones that remains to this day. Then the LORD turned from his burning anger. Therefore that place to this day is called the Valley of Achor.[j]

Ai Captured by a Stratagem and Destroyed

8 Then the LORD said to Joshua, "Do not fear or be dismayed; take all the fighting men with you, and go up now to Ai. See, I have handed over to you the king of Ai with his people, his city, and his land. ²You shall do to Ai and its king as you did to Jericho and its king; only its spoil and its livestock you may take as booty for yourselves. Set an ambush against the city, behind it."

8.2 War Strategy

Joshua used expert military strategy against Israel's many enemies in Canaan. His assignment as one of the original spies had given Joshua valuable knowledge of the topography of the land. Israelite armies entered the middle of Canaan, splitting the country in two and intersecting strategic trade routes. His "flying column" formations, night marches, ambush tactics rather than long sieges, and destruction of key cities showed awareness of advanced military techniques.

---

3 So Joshua and all the fighting men set out to go up against Ai. Joshua chose thirty thousand warriors and sent them out by night ⁴with the command, "You shall lie in ambush against the city, behind it; do not go very far from the city, but all of you stay alert. ⁵I and all the people who are with me will approach the city. When they come out against us, as before, we shall flee from them. ⁶They will come out after us until we have

---

i Mss Syr: MT man by man   *j That is Trouble*

drawn them away from the city; for they will say, 'They are fleeing from us, as before.' While we flee from them, 7you shall rise up from the ambush and seize the city; for the LORD your God will give it into your hand. 8And when you have taken the city, you shall set the city on fire, doing as the LORD has ordered; see, I have commanded you." 9So Joshua sent them out; and they went to the place of ambush, and lay between Bethel and Ai, to the west of Ai; but Joshua spent that night in the camp.*k*

10 In the morning Joshua rose early and mustered the people, and went up, with the elders of Israel, before the people to Ai. 11All the fighting men who were with him went up, and drew near before the city, and camped on the north side of Ai, with a ravine between them and Ai. 12Taking about five thousand men, he set them in ambush between Bethel and Ai, to the west of the city. 13So they stationed the forces, the main encampment that was north of the city and its rear guard west of the city. But Joshua spent that night in the valley. 14When the king of Ai saw this, he and all his people, the inhabitants of the city, hurried out early in the morning to the meeting place facing the Arabah to meet Israel in battle; but he did not know that there was an ambush against him behind the city. 15And Joshua and all Israel made a pretense of being beaten before them, and fled in the direction of the wilderness. 16So all the people who were in the city were called together to pursue them, and as they pursued Joshua they were drawn away from the city. 17There was not a man left in Ai or Bethel who did not go out after Israel; they left the city open, and pursued Israel.

18 Then the LORD said to Joshua, "Stretch out the sword that is in your hand toward Ai; for I will give it into your hand." And Joshua stretched out the sword that was in his hand toward the city. 19As soon as he stretched out his hand, the troops in ambush rose quickly out of their place and rushed forward. They entered the city, took it, and at once set the city on fire. 20So when the men of Ai looked back, the smoke of the city was rising to the sky. They had no power to flee this way or that, for the people who fled to the wilderness turned back against the pursuers. 21When Joshua and all Israel saw that the ambush had taken the city and that the smoke of the city was rising, then they turned back and struck down the men of Ai. 22And the others came out from the city against them; so they were surrounded by Israelites, some on one side, and some on the other; and Israel struck them down until no one was left who survived or escaped. 23But the king of Ai was taken alive and brought to Joshua.

24 When Israel had finished slaughtering all the inhabitants of Ai in the open wilderness where they pursued them, and when all of them to the very last had fallen by the edge of the sword, all Israel returned to Ai, and attacked it with the edge of the sword. 25The total of those who fell that day, both men and women, was twelve thousand—all the people of Ai. 26For Joshua did not draw back his hand, with which he stretched out the sword, until he had utterly destroyed all the inhabitants of Ai. 27Only the livestock and the spoil of that city Israel took as their booty, according to the word of the LORD that he had issued to Joshua. 28So Joshua burned Ai, and made it forever a heap of ruins, as it is to this day. 29And he hanged the king of Ai on a tree until evening; and at sunset Joshua commanded, and they took his body down from the tree, threw it down at the entrance of the gate of the city, and raised over it a great heap of stones, which stands there to this day.

Joshua Renews the Covenant

30 Then Joshua built on Mount Ebal an altar to the LORD, the God of Israel, 31just as Moses the

8.30–34 Blessings and Curses

The scene in this section, which describes the carrying out of Moses' instructions in Deuteronomy 27–28, was a profoundly symbolic event in the history of the Israelites. It elaborately portrayed what would happen if they obeyed the covenant, and if they disobeyed. The two mountains, Ebal and Gerizim, formed a natural amphitheater ideal for such a public ceremony. From their peaks much of the promised land could be seen. (Mount Gerizim eventually became the seat of worship for the Samaritans, which helps explain Jesus' conversation in John 4.)

servant of the LORD had commanded the Israelites, as it is written in the book of the law of Moses, "an altar of unhewn*l* stones, on which no iron tool has been used"; and they offered on it burnt offerings to the LORD, and sacrificed offerings of well-being. 32And there, in the presence of the Israelites, Joshua*m* wrote on the stones a copy of the law of Moses, which he had written. 33All Israel, alien as well as citizen, with their elders and officers and their judges, stood on opposite sides of the ark in front of the levitical priests who carried the ark of the covenant of the LORD, half of them in front of Mount Gerizim and half of them in front of Mount Ebal, as Moses the servant of the LORD had commanded at the first, that they should bless the people of Israel. 34And afterward he read all the words of the law, blessings and curses, according to all that is written in the book of the law. 35There was not a word of all that

---

k Heb *among the people*   *l* Heb *whole*   *m* Heb *he*

Moses commanded that Joshua did not read before all the assembly of Israel, and the women, and the little ones, and the aliens who resided among them.

The Gibeonites Save Themselves by Trickery

9 Now when all the kings who were beyond the Jordan in the hill country and in the lowland all along the coast of the Great Sea toward Lebanon—the Hittites, the Amorites, the Canaanites, the Perizzites, the Hivites, and the Jebusites—heard of this, [2]they gathered together with one accord to fight Joshua and Israel.

3 But when the inhabitants of Gibeon heard what Joshua had done to Jericho and to Ai, [4]they on their part acted with cunning: they went and prepared provisions,[n] and took worn-out sacks for their donkeys, and wineskins, worn-out and torn and mended, [5]with worn-out, patched sandals on their feet, and worn-out clothes; and all their provisions were dry and moldy. [6]They went to Joshua in the camp at Gilgal, and said to him and to the Israelites, "We have come from a far country; so now make a treaty with us." [7]But the Israelites said to the Hivites, "Perhaps you live among us; then how can we make a treaty with you?" [8]They said to Joshua, "We are your servants." And Joshua said to them, "Who are you? And where do you come from?" [9]They said to him, "Your servants have come from a very far country, because of the name of the LORD your God; for we have heard a report of him, of all that he did in Egypt, [10]and of all that he did to the two kings of the Amorites who were beyond the Jordan, King Sihon of Heshbon, and King Og of Bashan who lived in Ashtaroth. [11]So our elders and all the inhabitants of our country said to us, 'Take provisions in your hand for the journey; go to meet them, and say to them, "We are your servants; come now, make a treaty with us."' [12]Here is our bread; it was still warm when we took it from our houses as our food for the journey, on the day we set out to come to you, but now, see, it is dry and moldy; [13]these wineskins were new when we filled them, and see, they are burst; and these garments and sandals of ours are worn out from the very long journey." [14]So the leaders[o] partook of their provisions, and did not ask direction from the LORD. [15]And Joshua made peace with them, guaranteeing their lives by a treaty; and the leaders of the congregation swore an oath to them.

16 But when three days had passed after they had made a treaty with them, they heard that they were their neighbors and were living among them. [17]So the Israelites set out and reached their cities on the third day. Now their cities were Gibeon, Chephirah, Beeroth, and Kiriath-jearim. [18]But the Israelites did not attack them, because the leaders of the congregation had sworn to them by the LORD, the God of Israel. Then all the congregation murmured against the leaders.

9.14 Tricked!

The Gibeonites saved themselves by performing an elaborate deception on the Israelite soldiers, acting as if they had come from far away. The Israelites tried to check their story, but neglected the most important test of all: they "did not ask direction from the LORD." Throughout Joshua, God shows that he is in charge and that following him is the only way to victory.

The Gibeonites' trick saved their lives, but they were forced to become servants. Some of them later converted to Judaism. The book of Nehemiah includes Gibeonites (sometimes called Hivites) among those who helped rebuild the walls of Jerusalem. And at least one of King David's "warriors" was a Gibeonite. (See also the incident recorded in 2 Samuel 21.1–14.) Even so, the Gibeonites often caused trouble for Israel.

[19]But all the leaders said to all the congregation, "We have sworn to them by the LORD, the God of Israel, and now we must not touch them. [20]This is what we will do to them: We will let them live, so that wrath may not come upon us, because of the oath that we swore to them." [21]The leaders said to them, "Let them live." So they became hewers of wood and drawers of water for all the congregation, as the leaders had decided concerning them.

22 Joshua summoned them, and said to them, "Why did you deceive us, saying, 'We are very far from you,' while in fact you are living among us? [23]Now therefore you are cursed, and some of you shall always be slaves, hewers of wood and drawers of water for the house of my God." [24]They answered Joshua, "Because it was told to your servants for a certainty that the LORD your God had commanded his servant Moses to give you all the land, and to destroy all the inhabitants of the land before you; so we were in great fear for our lives because of you, and did this thing. [25]And now we are in your hand: do as it seems good and right in your sight to do to us." [26]This is what he did for them: he saved them from the Israelites; and they did not kill them. [27]But on that day Joshua made them hewers of wood and drawers of water for the congregation and for the altar of the LORD, to continue to this day, in the place that he should choose.

[n] Cn: Meaning of Heb uncertain   [o] Gk: Heb *men*

The Sun Stands Still

10 When King Adoni-zedek of Jerusalem heard how Joshua had taken Ai, and had utterly destroyed it, doing to Ai and its king as he had done to Jericho and its king, and how the inhabitants of Gibeon had made peace with Israel and were among them, ²he*p* became greatly frightened, because Gibeon was a large city, like one of the royal cities, and was larger than Ai, and all its men were warriors. ³So King Adoni-zedek of Jerusalem sent a message to King Hoham of Hebron, to King Piram of Jarmuth, to King Japhia of Lachish, and to King Debir of Eglon, saying, ⁴"Come up and help me, and let us attack Gibeon; for it has made peace with Joshua and with the Israelites." ⁵Then the five kings of the Amorites—the king of Jerusalem, the king of Hebron, the king of Jarmuth, the king of Lachish, and the king of Eglon—gathered their forces, and went up with all their armies and camped against Gibeon, and made war against it.

6 And the Gibeonites sent to Joshua at the camp in Gilgal, saying, "Do not abandon your servants; come up to us quickly, and save us, and help us; for all the kings of the Amorites who live in the hill country are gathered against us." ⁷So Joshua went up from Gilgal, he and all the fighting force with him, all the mighty warriors. ⁸The LORD said to Joshua, "Do not fear them, for I have handed them over to you; not one of them shall stand before you." ⁹So Joshua came upon them suddenly, having marched up all night from Gilgal. ¹⁰And the LORD threw them into a panic before Israel, who inflicted a great slaughter on them at Gibeon, chased them by the way of the ascent of Beth-horon, and struck them down as far as Azekah and Makkedah. ¹¹As they fled before Israel, while they were going down the slope of Beth-horon, the LORD threw down huge stones from heaven on them as far as Azekah, and they died; there were more who died because of the hailstones than the Israelites killed with the sword.

12 On the day when the LORD gave the Amorites over to the Israelites, Joshua spoke to the LORD; and he said in the sight of Israel,

"Sun, stand still at Gibeon,
  and Moon, in the valley of Aijalon."
13 And the sun stood still, and the moon
    stopped,
  until the nation took vengeance on
    their enemies.

Is this not written in the Book of Jashar? The sun stopped in midheaven, and did not hurry to set for about a whole day. ¹⁴There has been no day like it before or since, when the LORD heeded a human voice; for the LORD fought for Israel.

15 Then Joshua returned, and all Israel with him, to the camp at Gilgal.

Five Kings Defeated

16 Meanwhile, these five kings fled and hid themselves in the cave at Makkedah. ¹⁷And it was told Joshua, "The five kings have been found, hidden in the cave at Makkedah." ¹⁸Joshua said, "Roll large stones against the mouth of the cave, and set men by it to guard them; ¹⁹but do not stay there yourselves; pursue your enemies, and attack them from the rear. Do not let them enter their towns, for the LORD your God has given them into your hand." ²⁰When Joshua and the Israelites had finished inflicting a very great slaughter on them, until they were wiped out, and when the survivors had entered into the fortified towns, ²¹all the people returned safe to Joshua in the camp at Makkedah; no one dared to speak*q* against any of the Israelites.

22 Then Joshua said, "Open the mouth of the cave, and bring those five kings out to me from the cave." ²³They did so, and brought the five kings out to him from the cave, the king of Jerusalem, the king of Hebron, the king of Jarmuth, the king of Lachish, and the king of Eglon. ²⁴When they brought the kings out to Joshua, Joshua summoned all the Israelites, and said to the chiefs of the warriors who had gone with him, "Come near, put your feet on the necks of these kings." Then they came near and put their feet on

10.24 Act of Humiliation

This act—stepping on a neck—was the ultimate way to humiliate a king. It expressed utter, enforced submission. Egyptian and Assyrian sculptures frequently portrayed this custom.

their necks. ²⁵And Joshua said to them, "Do not be afraid or dismayed; be strong and courageous; for thus the LORD will do to all the enemies against whom you fight." ²⁶Afterward Joshua struck them down and put them to death, and he hung them on five trees. And they hung on the trees until evening. ²⁷At sunset Joshua commanded, and they took them down from the trees and threw them into the cave where they had hidden themselves; they set large stones against the mouth of the cave, which remain to this very day.

28 Joshua took Makkedah on that day, and struck it and its king with the edge of the sword; he utterly destroyed every person in it; he left no one remaining. And he did to the king of Makkedah as he had done to the king of Jericho.

29 Then Joshua passed on from Makkedah, and all Israel with him, to Libnah, and fought against Libnah. ³⁰The LORD gave it also and its king into the hand of Israel; and he struck it with

---

p Heb *they*   *q* Heb *moved his tongue*

the edge of the sword, and every person in it; he left no one remaining in it; and he did to its king as he had done to the king of Jericho.

31 Next Joshua passed on from Libnah, and all Israel with him, to Lachish, and laid siege to it, and assaulted it. [32]The LORD gave Lachish into the hand of Israel, and he took it on the second day, and struck it with the edge of the sword,

and every person in it, as he had done to Libnah.

33 Then King Horam of Gezer came up to help Lachish; and Joshua struck him and his people, leaving him no survivors.

34 From Lachish Joshua passed on with all Israel to Eglon; and they laid siege to it, and assaulted it; [35]and they took it that day, and struck it with the edge of the sword; and every person in

Is a War Ever Holy?

Why did God order a ruthless military campaign?

HOLY WAR. IRONICALLY, THE TERM applies to the most vicious, bloody wars. And often, far too often, Christians have been at the heart of such holy wars.

There is something irrational and even repulsive about a holy war. It harnesses all the best energies of religion for one of the ugliest acts of human nature. And yet anyone who reads the Bible cannot ignore the holy wars in the Old Testament.

Whole books have been written about the problem, and no brief article can begin to cover the issues. But modern readers need some background to help understand why a fierce holy war is presented in such a good light.

> The LORD said to Joshua, "Do not be afraid of them, for tomorrow at this time I will hand over all of them, slain, to Israel."
> 11.6

A Land Promised to the Israelites

The Israelites' fighting style fit the harsh pattern of warfare in that day. Contemporary Egyptian and Assyrian reports boasted of mass executions, torture, and the systematic razing of cities. But God's involvement raises unique questions. He personally ordered the destruction of seven Canaanite nations, with no survivors. Why?

The Old Testament makes clear that the Canaanites were not being uprooted on a sudden whim. God had promised the land to the Israelites over 400 years before Joshua. He had called one man, Abraham, to found a nation of chosen people. He repeated those promises often (Genesis 12.1–3; 15.5–18; 17.2–8; 26.3,23–24; 28.13–14) and finally called the Israelites out of Egypt to take over the promised land. Almost from the beginning Canaan was a vital part of God's plan.

Delayed Punishment

Israel's inheritance, however, meant kicking out the Canaanites. How could innocent people simply be pushed aside, or killed? In answer to this question, the Bible makes clear that the Canaanites were *not* "innocent." Through their long history of sin, they had forfeited their right to the land.

Four hundred years before Joshua, God had told Abraham that his descendants would not occupy the land until the sin of its inhabitants "is not yet complete" (Genesis 15.16). Later, just days before the onset of Joshua's campaign, Moses stated, "It is not because of your righteousness or the uprightness of your heart that you are going in to occupy their land; but because of the wickedness of these nations the LORD your God is dispossessing them before you" (Deuteronomy 9.5).

Historians have uncovered plenty of evidence of this wickedness. Canaanite temples featured prostitutes, orgies, and human sacrifice. Relics and plaques of exaggerated sex organs hint at the morality that characterized Canaan.

Canaanite gods, such as Baal and his wife Anath, delighted in butchery and sadism. Archaeologists have found great numbers of jars containing the tiny bones of children sacrificed to Baal. Families seeking good luck in a new home practiced "foundation sacrifice." They would kill one of their children and seal the body in the mortar of the wall. In many ways, Canaan had become like Sodom and Gomorrah.

The Bible records that God has patience with decadent societies for a time, but judgment inevitably follows. For Sodom and Gomorrah it took the form of fire and brimstone. For Canaan it came through Joshua's conquering armies. Later, God let his own chosen people be ravaged by invaders as punishment for their sins. The judgment pronounced on Canaan seems severe, but no more severe than what was later inflicted on Israel itself.

The Contamination Problem

The Israelites could not simply settle down as new neighbors among existing Canaanite cities.

it he utterly destroyed that day, as he had done to Lachish.

36 Then Joshua went up with all Israel from Eglon to Hebron; they assaulted it, ³⁷and took it, and struck it with the edge of the sword, and its king and its towns, and every person in it; he left no one remaining, just as he had done to Eglon, and utterly destroyed it with every person in it.

38 Then Joshua, with all Israel, turned back to Debir and assaulted it, ³⁹and he took it with its king and all its towns; they struck them with the edge of the sword, and utterly destroyed every person in it; he left no one remaining; just as he had done to Hebron, and, as he had done to Libnah and its king, so he did to Debir and its king.

40 So Joshua defeated the whole land, the hill country and the Negeb and the lowland and the slopes, and all their kings; he left no one remaining, but utterly destroyed all that breathed, as the LORD God of Israel commanded. ⁴¹And Joshua defeated them from Kadesh-barnea to Gaza, and all the country of Goshen, as far as Gibeon. ⁴²Joshua took all these kings and their land at one time, because the LORD God of Israel fought for Israel. ⁴³Then Joshua returned, and all Israel with him, to the camp at Gilgal.

The United Kings of Northern Canaan Defeated

11 When King Jabin of Hazor heard of this, he sent to King Jobab of Madon, to the king of Shimron, to the king of Achshaph, ²and to the kings who were in the northern hill country, and in the Arabah south of Chinneroth, and in the lowland, and in Naphoth-dor on the west, ³to the Canaanites in the east and the west, the Amorites, the Hittites, the Perizzites, and the Jebusites in the hill country, and the Hivites under Hermon in the land of Mizpah. ⁴They came out, with all their troops, a great army, in number like the sand on the seashore, with very many horses and chariots. ⁵All these kings joined their forces, and came and

---

From the time when the tribes had made a golden calf while Moses was receiving the Ten Commandments (Exodus 32), Israelites had shown a fatal weakness to infection from outside. They seemed particularly susceptible to sins of sex and idolatry, Canaan's national specialties.

Israel's later history offers a negative proof of why God commanded utter destruction of Canaanites. The damning phrase in Joshua, "the Israelites did not drive out the Geshurites or the Maacathites," hints at trouble to come, and the very next book, Judges, tells of the devastating results. The Israelites slid to one of their lowest levels because they had not fulfilled the original mission of cleansing the land of impure elements.

A Struggle beyond Nations

Looking back at this period of time, we tend to see the battles of Joshua as national or racial struggles: the Israelites versus the people of Canaan. But the Bible presents the warfare as a wider struggle: one between those who followed God and those who opposed him.

When God judged groups, as he judged the world in Noah's day or as he judged Sodom and Gomorrah, those few who remained faithful to him found a way of escape. And in Joshua one bright story shines out: the story of Rahab, a non-Israelite. A typical Canaanite who worked as a professional prostitute, she nevertheless learned to fear and then trust the God of Israel. She escaped the fall of Jericho. Furthermore, she went on to marry a leading Israelite and become one of the ancestors of the Messiah himself, Jesus.

Rahab claimed that others in her city of Jericho had quaked in fear for 40 years, waiting for the judgment of the God of Israel (2.9–11). Yet only she took the further step of seeking help. If others in Canaan had repented and turned to God, they might well have escaped punishment, as Rahab did.

Holy Wars Today

One fact about "holy war" is very clear. We cannot argue from a war specifically commanded by God in Joshua to any national situation today. In the Old Testament, God was dealing primarily with one particular nation, the Israelites, for a stated purpose. When the Messiah finally emerged out of that nation, everything changed.

Jesus' followers all lived in the same territory captured by Joshua, the "promised land." But four times, in his very last words, Jesus commanded his disciples to go out, away from Jerusalem, into all the world. Go, he told them, not as conquering armies but rather as bearers of the good news that applies to all people, all races, all nations.

Anyone who looks to the book of Joshua for a rationalization of a holy war must also look ahead to Jesus. Although on a holy crusade, he chose against violent means. In fact, he chose suffering and death. Nothing in the New Testament gives consolation to a religious warrior.

(For a longer discussion of this topic, see *The Goodness of God*, by John Wenham.)

Life Questions: What arguments have you heard Christians use for or against wars?

camped together at the waters of Merom, to fight with Israel.

6 And the LORD said to Joshua, "Do not be afraid of them, for tomorrow at this time I will hand over all of them, slain, to Israel; you shall hamstring their horses, and burn their chariots with fire." 7So Joshua came suddenly upon them with all his fighting force, by the waters of Merom, and fell upon them. 8And the LORD handed them over to Israel, who attacked them and chased them as far as Great Sidon and Misrephoth-maim, and eastward as far as the valley of Mizpeh. They struck them down, until they had left no one remaining. 9And Joshua did to them as the LORD commanded him; he hamstrung their horses, and burned their chariots with fire.

11.9 Advanced Weaponry

If a guerrilla band in Central America captured an F-16 fighter, what could they do with it? Probably nothing, unless they had trained pilots. The Israelites faced a similar situation. War-horses and chariots were advanced weapons of war that the Israelites would not master for hundreds more years. Joshua probably crippled the captured horses to ensure they would not fall into enemy hands again. Militarily and economically, the Israelites were up against people more sophisticated than they.

10 Joshua turned back at that time, and took Hazor, and struck its king down with the sword. Before that time Hazor was the head of all those kingdoms. 11And they put to the sword all who were in it, utterly destroying them; there was no one left who breathed, and he burned Hazor with fire. 12And all the towns of those kings, and all their kings, Joshua took, and struck them with the edge of the sword, utterly destroying them, as Moses the servant of the LORD had commanded. 13But Israel burned none of the towns that stood on mounds except Hazor, which Joshua did burn. 14All the spoil of these towns, and the livestock, the Israelites took for their booty; but all the people they struck down with the edge of the sword, until they had destroyed them, and they did not leave any who breathed. 15As the LORD had commanded his servant Moses, so Moses commanded Joshua, and so Joshua did; he left nothing undone of all that the LORD had commanded Moses.

Summary of Joshua's Conquests

16 So Joshua took all that land: the hill country and all the Negeb and all the land of Goshen and the lowland and the Arabah and the hill country of Israel and its lowland, 17from Mount Halak, which rises toward Seir, as far as Baal-gad in the valley of Lebanon below Mount Hermon. He took all their kings, struck them down, and put them to death. 18Joshua made war a long time with all those kings. 19There was not a town that made peace with the Israelites, except the Hivites, the inhabitants of Gibeon; all were taken in battle. 20For it was the LORD's doing to harden their hearts so that they would come against Israel in battle, in order that they might be utterly destroyed, and might receive no mercy, but be exterminated, just as the LORD had commanded Moses.

21 At that time Joshua came and wiped out the Anakim from the hill country, from Hebron, from Debir, from Anab, and from all the hill country of Judah, and from all the hill country of Israel; Joshua utterly destroyed them with their towns. 22None of the Anakim was left in the land of the Israelites; some remained only in Gaza, in Gath, and in Ashdod. 23So Joshua took the whole land, according to all that the LORD had spoken to Moses; and Joshua gave it for an inheritance to Israel according to their tribal allotments. And the land had rest from war.

11.23 Two Accounts of Warfare

Judges 1 summarizes the incidents recorded in Joshua, but from a different point of view. Joshua presents the campaign as highly successful; Judges shows that many military goals were never achieved. One possible explanation: Joshua presented the wars as a series of raids on territory and did not include the "mopping up" and settlement process. Judges shows that, after they divided up the land, the Israelites proved far less successful in the second phase of conquest.

The Kings Conquered by Moses

12 Now these are the kings of the land, whom the Israelites defeated, whose land they occupied beyond the Jordan toward the east, from the Wadi Arnon to Mount Hermon, with all the Arabah eastward: 2King Sihon of the Amorites who lived at Heshbon, and ruled from Aroer, which is on the edge of the Wadi Arnon, and from the middle of the valley as far as the river Jabbok, the boundary of the Ammonites, that is, half of Gilead, 3and the Arabah to the Sea of Chinneroth eastward, and in the direction of Beth-jeshimoth, to the sea of the Arabah, the Dead Sea,r southward to the foot of the slopes of Pisgah; 4and King Ogs of Bashan, one of the last

---

r Heb *Salt Sea*   s Gk: Heb *the boundary of King Og*

of the Rephaim, who lived at Ashtaroth and at Edrei 5and ruled over Mount Hermon and Salecah and all Bashan to the boundary of the Geshurites and the Maacathites, and over half of Gilead to the boundary of King Sihon of Heshbon. 6Moses, the servant of the LORD, and the Israelites defeated them; and Moses the servant of the LORD gave their land for a possession to the Reubenites and the Gadites and the half-tribe of Manasseh.

The Kings Conquered by Joshua

7 The following are the kings of the land whom Joshua and the Israelites defeated on the west side of the Jordan, from Baal-gad in the valley of Lebanon to Mount Halak, that rises toward Seir (and Joshua gave their land to the tribes of Israel as a possession according to their allotments, 8in the hill country, in the lowland, in the Arabah, in the slopes, in the wilderness, and in the Negeb, the land of the Hittites, Amorites, Canaanites, Perizzites, Hivites, and Jebusites):

9 the king of Jericho	one
the king of Ai, which is next	
to Bethel	one
10 the king of Jerusalem	one
the king of Hebron	one
11 the king of Jarmuth	one
the king of Lachish	one
12 the king of Eglon	one
the king of Gezer	one
13 the king of Debir	one
the king of Geder	one
14 the king of Hormah	one
the king of Arad	one
15 the king of Libnah	one
the king of Adullam	one
16 the king of Makkedah	one
the king of Bethel	one
17 the king of Tappuah	one
the king of Hepher	one
18 the king of Aphek	one
the king of Lasharon	one
19 the king of Madon	one
the king of Hazor	one
20 the king of Shimron-meron	one
the king of Achshaph	one
21 the king of Taanach	one
the king of Megiddo	one
22 the king of Kedesh	one
the king of Jokneam in Carmel	one
23 the king of Dor in Naphath-dor	one
the king of Goiim in Galilee,t	one
24 the king of Tirzah	one

thirty-one kings in all.

The Parts of Canaan Still Unconquered

13 Now Joshua was old and advanced in years; and the LORD said to him, "You are old and advanced in years, and very much of the land still remains to be possessed. 2This is the land that still remains: all the regions of the Philistines, and all those of the Geshurites 3(from the Shihor, which is east of Egypt, northward to the boundary of

13.1 Dividing Up the Land

Chapter 13 introduces an abrupt transition. The rest of Joshua tells about what happened five to seven years after the crossing of the Jordan. Chapters 13–22 give a kind of land-title record for the new nation. Genesis 48–49 and Deuteronomy 33 provide background material. For example, Reuben's tribe forfeited the right to first choice because of a sexual sin, and Simeon and Levi lost their rights because of their violent past.

Ekron, it is reckoned as Canaanite; there are five rulers of the Philistines, those of Gaza, Ashdod, Ashkelon, Gath, and Ekron), and those of the Avvim 4in the south; all the land of the Canaanites, and Mearah that belongs to the Sidonians, to Aphek, to the boundary of the Amorites, 5and the land of the Gebalites, and all Lebanon, toward the east, from Baal-gad below Mount Hermon to Lebo-hamath, 6all the inhabitants of the hill country from Lebanon to Misrephoth-maim, even all the Sidonians. I will myself drive them out from before the Israelites; only allot the land to Israel for an inheritance, as I have commanded you. 7Now therefore divide this land for an inheritance to the nine tribes and the half-tribe of Manasseh."

The Territory East of the Jordan

8 With the other half-tribe of Manassehu the Reubenites and the Gadites received their inheritance, which Moses gave them, beyond the Jordan eastward, as Moses the servant of the LORD gave them: 9from Aroer, which is on the edge of the Wadi Arnon, and the town that is in the middle of the valley, and all the tableland fromv Medeba as far as Dibon; 10and all the cities of King Sihon of the Amorites, who reigned in Heshbon, as far as the boundary of the Ammonites; 11and Gilead, and the region of the Geshurites and Maacathites, and all Mount Hermon, and all Bashan to Salecah; 12all the kingdom of Og in Bashan, who reigned in Ashtaroth and in Edrei (he alone was left of the survivors of the Rephaim); these Moses had defeated and driven out. 13Yet the Israelites did not drive out the Geshurites or the Maacathites; but Geshur and Maacath live within Israel to this day.

14 To the tribe of Levi alone Moses gave no inheritance; the offerings by fire to the LORD God of Israel are their inheritance, as he said to them.

t Gk: Heb Gilgal   u Cn: Heb With it   v Compare Gk: Heb lacks from

The Territory of Reuben

15 Moses gave an inheritance to the tribe of the Reubenites according to their clans. ¹⁶Their territory was from Aroer, which is on the edge of the Wadi Arnon, and the town that is in the middle of the valley, and all the tableland by Medeba; ¹⁷with Heshbon, and all its towns that are in the tableland; Dibon, and Bamoth-baal, and Beth-baal-meon, ¹⁸and Jahaz, and Kedemoth, and Mephaath, ¹⁹and Kiriathaim, and Sibmah, and Zereth-shahar on the hill of the valley, ²⁰and Beth-peor, and the slopes of Pisgah, and Beth-jeshimoth, ²¹that is, all the towns of the tableland, and all the kingdom of King Sihon of the Amorites, who reigned in Heshbon, whom Moses defeated with the leaders of Midian, Evi and Rekem and Zur and Hur and Reba, as princes of Sihon, who lived in the land. ²²Along with the rest of those they put to death, the Israelites also put to the sword Balaam son of Beor, who practiced divination. ²³And the border of the Reubenites was the Jordan and its banks. This was the inheritance of the Reubenites according to their families, with their towns and villages.

The Territory of Gad

24 Moses gave an inheritance also to the tribe of the Gadites, according to their families. ²⁵Their territory was Jazer, and all the towns of Gilead, and half the land of the Ammonites, to Aroer, which is east of Rabbah, ²⁶and from Heshbon to Ramath-mizpeh and Betonim, and from Mahanaim to the territory of Debir,ʷ ²⁷and in the valley Beth-haram, Beth-nimrah, Succoth, and Zaphon, the rest of the kingdom of King Sihon of Heshbon, the Jordan and its banks, as far as the lower end of the Sea of Chinnereth, eastward beyond the Jordan. ²⁸This is the inheritance of the Gadites according to their clans, with their towns and villages.

The Territory of the Half-Tribe of Manasseh (East)

29 Moses gave an inheritance to the half-tribe of Manasseh; it was allotted to the half-tribe of the Manassites according to their families. ³⁰Their territory extended from Mahanaim, through all Bashan, the whole kingdom of King Og of Bashan, and all the settlements of Jair, which are in Bashan, sixty towns, ³¹and half of Gilead, and Ashtaroth, and Edrei, the towns of the kingdom of Og in Bashan; these were allotted to the people of Machir son of Manasseh according to their clans—for half the Machirites.

32 These are the inheritances that Moses distributed in the plains of Moab, beyond the Jordan east of Jericho. ³³But to the tribe of Levi Moses gave no inheritance; the LORD God of Israel is their inheritance, as he said to them.

The Distribution of Territory West of the Jordan

14 These are the inheritances that the Israelites received in the land of Canaan, which the priest Eleazar, and Joshua son of Nun, and the heads of the families of the tribes of the Israelites distributed to them. ²Their inheritance was by lot, as the LORD had commanded Moses for the nine and one-half tribes. ³For Moses had given an inheritance to the two and one-half tribes beyond the Jordan; but to the Levites he gave no inheritance among them. ⁴For the people of Joseph were two tribes, Manasseh and Ephraim; and no portion was given to the Levites in the land, but only towns to live in, with their pasture lands for their flocks and herds. ⁵The Israelites did as the LORD commanded Moses; they allotted the land.

Hebron Allotted to Caleb

6 Then the people of Judah came to Joshua at Gilgal; and Caleb son of Jephunneh the Kenizzite said to him, "You know what the LORD said to Moses the man of God in Kadesh-barnea concerning you and me. ⁷I was forty years old when Moses the servant of the LORD sent me from Kadesh-barnea to spy out the land; and I brought him an honest report. ⁸But my companions who went up with me made the heart of the people melt; yet I wholeheartedly followed the LORD my God. ⁹And Moses swore on that day, saying, 'Surely the land on which your foot has trodden shall be an inheritance for you and your children forever, because you have wholeheartedly followed the LORD my God.' ¹⁰And now, as you see, the LORD has kept me alive, as he said, these forty-five years since the time that the LORD spoke this word to Moses, while Israel was journeying through the wilderness; and here I am today, eighty-five years old. ¹¹I am still as strong today

14.10 Seven-year Fight

Just how long did the capture of Palestine take? The book of Joshua doesn't say, but a little arithmetic shows that the fighting had been going on for about seven years. Caleb was 40 when Moses first sent him to explore the land (verse 7). Israel spent 38 years in the desert after that (Deuteronomy 2.14), making Caleb 78 when they finally invaded. Since he had now reached 85, the last seven years of Caleb's life must have been spent fighting. He was one of the two oldest Israelites; all others of his generation had died in the desert.

ʷ Gk Syr Vg: Heb *Lidebir*

as I was on the day that Moses sent me; my strength now is as my strength was then, for war, and for going and coming. ¹²So now give me this hill country of which the LORD spoke on that day; for you heard on that day how the Anakim were there, with great fortified cities; it may be that the LORD will be with me, and I shall drive them out, as the LORD said."

13 Then Joshua blessed him, and gave Hebron to Caleb son of Jephunneh for an inheritance. ¹⁴So Hebron became the inheritance of Caleb son of Jephunneh the Kenizzite to this day, because he wholeheartedly followed the LORD, the God of Israel. ¹⁵Now the name of Hebron formerly was Kiriath-arba;ˣ this Arba wasʸ the greatest man among the Anakim. And the land had rest from war.

The Territory of Judah

15 The lot for the tribe of the people of Judah according to their families reached southward to the boundary of Edom, to the wilderness of Zin at the farthest south. ²And their south boundary ran from the end of the Dead Sea,ᶻ from the bay that faces southward; ³it goes out southward of the ascent of Akrabbim, passes along to Zin, and goes up south of Kadesh-barnea, along by Hezron, up to Addar, makes a turn to Karka, ⁴passes along to Azmon, goes out by the Wadi of Egypt, and comes to its end at the sea. This shall be your south boundary. ⁵And the east boundary is the Dead Sea,ᶻ to the mouth of the Jordan. And the boundary on the north side runs from the bay of the sea at the mouth of the Jordan; ⁶and the boundary goes up to Beth-hoglah, and passes along north of Beth-arabah; and the boundary goes up to the Stone of Bohan, Reuben's son; ⁷and the boundary goes up to Debir from the Valley of Achor, and so northward, turning toward Gilgal, which is opposite the ascent of Adummim, which is on the south side of the valley; and the boundary passes along to the waters of En-shemesh, and ends at En-rogel; ⁸then the boundary goes up by the valley of the son of Hinnom at the southern slope of the Jebusites (that is, Jerusalem); and the boundary goes up to the top of the mountain that lies over against the valley of Hinnom, on the west, at the northern end of the valley of Rephaim; ⁹then the boundary extends from the top of the mountain to the spring of the Waters of Nephtoah, and from there to the towns of Mount Ephron; then the boundary bends around to Baalah (that is, Kiriath-jearim); ¹⁰and the boundary circles west of Baalah to Mount Seir, passes along to the northern slope of Mount Jearim (that is, Chesalon), and goes down to Beth-shemesh, and passes along by Timnah; ¹¹the boundary goes out to the slope of the hill north of Ekron, then the bounda-

ry bends around to Shikkeron, and passes along to Mount Baalah, and goes out to Jabneel; then the boundary comes to an end at the sea. ¹²And the west boundary was the Mediterranean with its coast. This is the boundary surrounding the people of Judah according to their families.

Caleb Occupies His Portion

13 According to the commandment of the LORD to Joshua, he gave to Caleb son of Jephunneh a portion among the people of Judah, Kiriath-arba,ˣ that is, Hebron (Arba was the father of Anak). ¹⁴And Caleb drove out from there the three sons of Anak: Sheshai, Ahiman, and Talmai, the descendants of Anak. ¹⁵From there he went up against the inhabitants of Debir; now the name of Debir formerly was Kiriath-sepher. ¹⁶And Caleb said, "Whoever attacks Kiriath-sepher and takes it, to him I will give my daughter Achsah as wife." ¹⁷Othniel son of Kenaz, the brother of Caleb, took it; and he gave him his daughter Achsah as wife. ¹⁸When she came to him, she urged him to ask her father for a field. As she dismounted from her donkey, Caleb said to her, "What do you wish?" ¹⁹She said to him, "Give me a present; since you have set me in the land of the Negeb, give me springs of water as well." So Caleb gave her the upper springs and the lower springs.

The Towns of Judah

20 This is the inheritance of the tribe of the people of Judah according to their families. ²¹The towns belonging to the tribe of the people of Judah in the extreme south, toward the boundary of Edom, were Kabzeel, Eder, Jagur, ²²Kinah, Dimonah, Adadah, ²³Kedesh, Hazor, Ithnan, ²⁴Ziph, Telem, Bealoth, ²⁵Hazor-hadattah, Kerioth-hezron (that is, Hazor), ²⁶Amam, Shema, Moladah, ²⁷Hazar-gaddah, Heshmon, Beth-pelet, ²⁸Hazar-shual, Beer-sheba, Biziothiah, ²⁹Baalah, Iim, Ezem, ³⁰Eltolad, Chesil, Hormah, ³¹Ziklag, Madmannah, Sansannah, ³²Lebaoth, Shilhim, Ain, and Rimmon: in all, twenty-nine towns, with their villages.

33 And in the lowland, Eshtaol, Zorah, Ashnah, ³⁴Zanoah, En-gannim, Tappuah, Enam, ³⁵Jarmuth, Adullam, Socoh, Azekah, ³⁶Shaaraim, Adithaim, Gederah, Gederothaim: fourteen towns with their villages.

37 Zenan, Hadashah, Migdal-gad, ³⁸Dilan, Mizpeh, Jokthe-el, ³⁹Lachish, Bozkath, Eglon, ⁴⁰Cabbon, Lahmam, Chitlish, ⁴¹Gederoth, Beth-dagon, Naamah, and Makkedah: sixteen towns with their villages.

42 Libnah, Ether, Ashan, ⁴³Iphtah, Ashnah, Nezib, ⁴⁴Keilah, Achzib, and Mareshah: nine towns with their villages.

45 Ekron, with its dependencies and its vil-

ˣ That is *the city of Arba*   ʸ Heb lacks *this Arba was*   ᶻ Heb *Salt Sea*

lages; 46from Ekron to the sea, all that were near Ashdod, with their villages.

47 Ashdod, its towns and its villages; Gaza, its towns and its villages; to the Wadi of Egypt, and the Great Sea with its coast.

48 And in the hill country, Shamir, Jattir, Socoh, 49Dannah, Kiriath-sannah (that is, Debir), 50Anab, Eshtemoh, Anim, 51Goshen, Holon, and Giloh: eleven towns with their villages.

52 Arab, Dumah, Eshan, 53Janim, Beth-tappuah, Aphekah, 54Humtah, Kiriath-arba (that is, Hebron), and Zior: nine towns with their villages.

55 Maon, Carmel, Ziph, Juttah, 56Jezreel, Jokdeam, Zanoah, 57Kain, Gibeah, and Timnah: ten towns with their villages.

58 Halhul, Beth-zur, Gedor, 59Maarath, Beth-anoth, and Eltekon: six towns with their villages.

60 Kiriath-baal (that is, Kiriath-jearim) and Rabbah: two towns with their villages.

61 In the wilderness, Beth-arabah, Middin, Secacah, 62Nibshan, the City of Salt, and En-gedi: six towns with their villages.

63 But the people of Judah could not drive out the Jebusites, the inhabitants of Jerusalem; so the Jebusites live with the people of Judah in Jerusalem to this day.

15.63 Hints of Failure

In several key places (13.2–7; 16.10; 23.4) and in Judges 1, the Bible indicates that pockets of Canaanites remained in the land. The Israelites did not "drive them out." The unconquered tribes became thorns in Israel's side.

The Territory of Ephraim

16 The allotment of the Josephites went from the Jordan by Jericho, east of the waters of Jericho, into the wilderness, going up from Jericho into the hill country to Bethel; 2then going from Bethel to Luz, it passes along to Ataroth, the territory of the Archites; 3then it goes down westward to the territory of the Japhletites, as far as the territory of Lower Beth-horon, then to Gezer, and it ends at the sea.

4 The Josephites—Manasseh and Ephraim—received their inheritance.

5 The territory of the Ephraimites by their families was as follows: the boundary of their inheritance on the east was Ataroth-addar as far as Upper Beth-horon, 6and the boundary goes from there to the sea; on the north is Michmethath; then on the east the boundary makes a turn toward Taanath-shiloh, and passes along beyond it on the east to Janoah, 7then it goes down from Janoah to Ataroth and to Naarah, and touches Jericho, ending at the Jordan. 8From Tappuah the boundary goes westward to the Wadi Kanah, and

ends at the sea. Such is the inheritance of the tribe of the Ephraimites by their families, 9together with the towns that were set apart for the Ephraimites within the inheritance of the Manassites, all those towns with their villages. 10They did not, however, drive out the Canaanites who lived in Gezer: so the Canaanites have lived within Ephraim to this day but have been made to do forced labor.

The Other Half-Tribe of Manasseh (West)

17 Then allotment was made to the tribe of Manasseh, for he was the firstborn of Joseph. To Machir the firstborn of Manasseh, the father of Gilead, were allotted Gilead and Bashan, because he was a warrior. 2And allotments were made to the rest of the tribe of Manasseh, by their families, Abiezer, Helek, Asriel, Shechem, Hepher, and Shemida; these were the male descendants of Manasseh son of Joseph, by their families.

3 Now Zelophehad son of Hepher son of Gilead son of Machir son of Manasseh had no sons, but only daughters; and these are the names of his daughters: Mahlah, Noah, Hoglah, Milcah, and Tirzah. 4They came before the priest Eleazar and Joshua son of Nun and the leaders, and said, "The LORD commanded Moses to give us an inheritance along with our male kin." So according to the commandment of the LORD he gave them an inheritance among the kinsmen of their father. 5Thus there fell to Manasseh ten portions, besides the land of Gilead and Bashan, which is on the other side of the Jordan, 6because the daughters of Manasseh received an inheritance along with his sons. The land of Gilead was allotted to the rest of the Manassites.

17.4 Daughters' Rights

See Numbers 27.1–11 and Numbers 36 for the historical context to these women's appeal.

7 The territory of Manasseh reached from Asher to Michmethath, which is east of Shechem; then the boundary goes along southward to the inhabitants of En-tappuah. 8The land of Tappuah belonged to Manasseh, but the town of Tappuah on the boundary of Manasseh belonged to the Ephraimites. 9Then the boundary went down to the Wadi Kanah. The towns here, to the south of the wadi, among the towns of Manasseh, belong to Ephraim. Then the boundary of Manasseh goes along the north side of the wadi and ends at the sea. 10The land to the south is Ephraim's and that to the north is Manasseh's, with the sea forming its boundary; on the north Asher is reached, and on the east Issachar. 11Within Issachar and Asher, Manasseh had Beth-shean and its villages, Ibleam

and its villages, the inhabitants of Dor and its villages, the inhabitants of En-dor and its villages, the inhabitants of Taanach and its villages, and the inhabitants of Megiddo and its villages (the third is Naphath).*a* 12Yet the Manassites could not take possession of those towns; but the Canaanites continued to live in that land. 13But when the Israelites grew strong, they put the Canaanites to forced labor, but did not utterly drive them out.

The Tribe of Joseph Protests

14 The tribe of Joseph spoke to Joshua, saying, "Why have you given me but one lot and one portion as an inheritance, since we are a numerous people, whom all along the LORD has blessed?" 15And Joshua said to them, "If you are a numerous people, go up to the forest, and clear ground there for yourselves in the land of the Perizzites and the Rephaim, since the hill country of Ephraim is too narrow for you." 16The tribe of Joseph said, "The hill country is not enough for us; yet all the Canaanites who live in the plain have chariots of iron, both those in Beth-shean and its villages and those in the Valley of Jezreel." 17Then Joshua said to the house of Joseph, to Ephraim and Manasseh, "You are indeed a numerous people, and have great power; you shall not have one lot only, 18but the hill country shall be yours, for though it is a forest, you shall clear it and possess it to its farthest borders; for you shall drive out the Canaanites, though they have chariots of iron, and though they are strong."

The Territories of the Remaining Tribes

18 Then the whole congregation of the Israelites assembled at Shiloh, and set up the tent of meeting there. The land lay subdued before them.
2 There remained among the Israelites seven tribes whose inheritance had not yet been apportioned. 3So Joshua said to the Israelites, "How long will you be slack about going in and taking possession of the land that the LORD, the God of your ancestors, has given you? 4Provide three

18.3 Missing an Opportunity

Such verses as 17.13 and 18.3 imply that the Israelites could have driven out the Canaanites, but chose not to. They were using the Canaanites for forced labor and demanding tribute from them—perhaps they learned to rely too comfortably on these services. Also, some tribes balked at campaigns simply because of fear (17.16).

men from each tribe, and I will send them out that they may begin to go throughout the land, writing a description of it with a view to their inheritances. Then come back to me. 5They shall divide it into seven portions, Judah continuing in its territory on the south, and the house of Joseph in their territory on the north. 6You shall describe the land in seven divisions and bring the description here to me; and I will cast lots for you here before the LORD our God. 7The Levites have no portion among you, for the priesthood of the LORD is their heritage; and Gad and Reuben and the half-tribe of Manasseh have received their inheritance beyond the Jordan eastward, which Moses the servant of the LORD gave them."

8 So the men started on their way; and Joshua charged those who went to write the description of the land, saying, "Go throughout the land and write a description of it, and come back to me; and I will cast lots for you here before the LORD in Shiloh." 9So the men went and traversed the land and set down in a book a description of it by towns in seven divisions; then they came back to Joshua in the camp at Shiloh, 10and Joshua cast lots for them in Shiloh before the LORD; and there Joshua apportioned the land to the Israelites, to each a portion.

The Territory of Benjamin

11 The lot of the tribe of Benjamin according to its families came up, and the territory allotted to it fell between the tribe of Judah and the tribe of Joseph. 12On the north side their boundary began at the Jordan; then the boundary goes up to the slope of Jericho on the north, then up through the hill country westward; and it ends at the wilderness of Beth-aven. 13From there the boundary passes along southward in the direction of Luz, to the slope of Luz (that is, Bethel), then the boundary goes down to Ataroth-addar, on the mountain that lies south of Lower Beth-horon. 14Then the boundary goes in another direction, turning on the western side southward from the mountain that lies to the south, opposite Beth-horon, and it ends at Kiriath-baal (that is, Kiriath-jearim), a town belonging to the tribe of Judah. This forms the western side. 15The southern side begins at the outskirts of Kiriath-jearim; and the boundary goes from there to Ephron,*b* to the spring of the Waters of Nephtoah; 16then the boundary goes down to the border of the mountain that overlooks the valley of the son of Hinnom, which is at the north end of the valley of Rephaim; and it then goes down the valley of Hinnom, south of the slope of the Jebusites, and downward to En-rogel; 17then it bends in a northerly direction going on to En-shemesh, and from there goes to Geliloth, which is opposite the ascent of Adummim; then it goes down to the

---

a Meaning of Heb uncertain   *b* Cn See 15.9. Heb *westward*

Stone of Bohan, Reuben's son; [18]and passing on to the north of the slope of Beth-arabah[c] it goes down to the Arabah; [19]then the boundary passes on to the north of the slope of Beth-hoglah; and the boundary ends at the northern bay of the Dead Sea,[d] at the south end of the Jordan: this is the southern border. [20]The Jordan forms its boundary on the eastern side. This is the inheritance of the tribe of Benjamin, according to its families, boundary by boundary all around.

21 Now the towns of the tribe of Benjamin according to their families were Jericho, Beth-hoglah, Emek-keziz, [22]Beth-arabah, Zemaraim, Bethel, [23]Avvim, Parah, Ophrah, [24]Chephar-ammoni, Ophni, and Geba—twelve towns with their villages: [25]Gibeon, Ramah, Beeroth, [26]Mizpeh, Chephirah, Mozah, [27]Rekem, Irpeel, Taralah, [28]Zela, Haeleph, Jebus[e] (that is, Jerusalem), Gibeah[f] and Kiriath-jearim[g]—fourteen towns with their villages. This is the inheritance of the tribe of Benjamin according to its families.

The Territory of Simeon

19 The second lot came out for Simeon, for the tribe of Simeon, according to its families; its inheritance lay within the inheritance of the tribe of Judah. [2]It had for its inheritance Beer-sheba, Sheba, Moladah, [3]Hazar-shual, Balah, Ezem, [4]Eltolad, Bethul, Hormah, [5]Ziklag, Beth-marcaboth, Hazar-susah, [6]Beth-lebaoth, and Sharuhen—thirteen towns with their villages; [7]Ain, Rimmon, Ether, and Ashan—four towns with their villages; [8]together with all the villages all around these towns as far as Baalath-beer, Ramah of the Negeb. This was the inheritance of the tribe of Simeon according to its families. [9]The inheritance of the tribe of Simeon formed part of the territory of Judah; because the portion of the tribe of Judah was too large for them, the tribe of Simeon obtained an inheritance within their inheritance.

The Territory of Zebulun

10 The third lot came up for the tribe of Zebulun, according to its families. The boundary of its inheritance reached as far as Sarid; [11]then its boundary goes up westward, and on to Maralah, and touches Dabbesheth, then the wadi that is east of Jokneam; [12]from Sarid it goes in the other direction eastward toward the sunrise to the boundary of Chisloth-tabor; from there it goes to Daberath, then up to Japhia; [13]from there it passes along on the east toward the sunrise to Gath-hepher, to Eth-kazin, and going on to Rimmon it bends toward Neah; [14]then on the north the boundary makes a turn to Hannathon, and it ends at the valley of Iphtah-el; [15]and Kattath, Nahalal, Shimron, Idalah, and Bethlehem—

twelve towns with their villages. [16]This is the inheritance of the tribe of Zebulun, according to its families—these towns with their villages.

The Territory of Issachar

17 The fourth lot came out for Issachar, for the tribe of Issachar, according to its families. [18]Its territory included Jezreel, Chesulloth, Shunem, [19]Hapharaim, Shion, Anaharath, [20]Rabbith, Kishion, Ebez, [21]Remeth, En-gannim, En-haddah, Beth-pazzez; [22]the boundary also touches Tabor, Shahazumah, and Beth-shemesh, and its boundary ends at the Jordan—sixteen towns with their villages. [23]This is the inheritance of the tribe of Issachar, according to its families—the towns with their villages.

The Territory of Asher

24 The fifth lot came out for the tribe of Asher according to its families. [25]Its boundary included Helkath, Hali, Beten, Achshaph, [26]Allammelech, Amad, and Mishal; on the west it touches Carmel and Shihor-libnath, [27]then it turns eastward, goes to Beth-dagon, and touches Zebulun and the valley of Iphtah-el northward to Beth-emek and Neiel; then it continues in the north to Cabul, [28]Ebron, Rehob, Hammon, Kanah, as far as Great Sidon; [29]then the boundary turns to Ramah, reaching to the fortified city of Tyre; then the boundary turns to Hosah, and it ends at the sea; Mahalab,[h] Achzib, [30]Ummah, Aphek, and Rehob—twenty-two towns with their villages. [31]This is the inheritance of the tribe of Asher according to its families—these towns with their villages.

The Territory of Naphtali

32 The sixth lot came out for the tribe of Naphtali, for the tribe of Naphtali, according to its families. [33]And its boundary ran from Heleph, from the oak in Zaanannim, and Adami-nekeb, and Jabneel, as far as Lakkum; and it ended at the Jordan; [34]then the boundary turns westward to Aznoth-tabor, and goes from there to Hukkok, touching Zebulun at the south, and Asher on the west, and Judah on the east at the Jordan. [35]The fortified towns are Ziddim, Zer, Hammath, Rakkath, Chinnereth, [36]Adamah, Ramah, Hazor, [37]Kedesh, Edrei, En-hazor, [38]Iron, Migdal-el, Horem, Beth-anath, and Beth-shemesh—nineteen towns with their villages. [39]This is the inheritance of the tribe of Naphtali according to its families—the towns with their villages.

The Territory of Dan

40 The seventh lot came out for the tribe of Dan, according to its families. [41]The territory of its inheritance included Zorah, Eshtaol, Ir-

---

[c] Gk: Heb *to the slope over against the Arabah*   [d] Heb *Salt Sea*   [e] Gk Syr Vg: Heb *the Jebusite*   [f] Heb *Gibeath*
[g] Gk: Heb *Kiriath*   [h] Cn Compare Gk: Heb *Mehebel*

shemesh, 42Shaalabbin, Aijalon, Ithlah, 43Elon, Timnah, Ekron, 44Eltekeh, Gibbethon, Baalath, 45Jehud, Bene-berak, Gath-rimmon, 46Mejarkon, and Rakkon at the border opposite Joppa. 47When the territory of the Danites was lost to them, the Danites went up and fought against Leshem, and after capturing it and putting it to the sword, they took possession of it and settled in it, calling Leshem, Dan, after their ancestor Dan. 48This is the inheritance of the tribe of Dan, according to their families—these towns with their villages.

Joshua's Inheritance

49 When they had finished distributing the several territories of the land as inheritances, the Israelites gave an inheritance among them to Joshua son of Nun. 50By command of the LORD they gave him the town that he asked for, Timnath-serah in the hill country of Ephraim; he rebuilt the town, and settled in it.

51 These are the inheritances that the priest Eleazar and Joshua son of Nun and the heads of the families of the tribes of the Israelites distributed by lot at Shiloh before the LORD, at the entrance of the tent of meeting. So they finished dividing the land.

The Cities of Refuge

20 Then the LORD spoke to Joshua, saying, 2"Say to the Israelites, 'Appoint the cities of refuge, of which I spoke to you through Moses,

20.2 Cities of Refuge

The cities of refuge were designed to aid a person who caused an accidental death or "involuntary manslaughter." They provided a sanctuary from revenge. They did not, however, shelter a person who had committed a premeditated, intentional murder. (See Numbers 35.6 and Deuteronomy 4.41–43; 19.1–21.)

3so that anyone who kills a person without intent or by mistake may flee there; they shall be for you a refuge from the avenger of blood. 4The slayer shall flee to one of these cities and shall stand at the entrance of the gate of the city, and explain the case to the elders of that city; then the fugitive shall be taken into the city, and given a place, and shall remain with them. 5And if the avenger of blood is in pursuit, they shall not give up the slayer, because the neighbor was killed by mistake, there having been no enmity between them before. 6The slayer shall remain in that city until there is a trial before the congregation, until the death of the one who is high priest at the time:

then the slayer may return home, to the town in which the deed was done.'"

7 So they set apart Kedesh in Galilee in the hill country of Naphtali, and Shechem in the hill country of Ephraim, and Kiriath-arba (that is, Hebron) in the hill country of Judah. 8And beyond the Jordan east of Jericho, they appointed Bezer in the wilderness on the tableland, from the tribe of Reuben, and Ramoth in Gilead, from the tribe of Gad, and Golan in Bashan, from the tribe of Manasseh. 9These were the cities designated for all the Israelites, and for the aliens residing among them, that anyone who killed a person without intent could flee there, so as not to die by the hand of the avenger of blood, until there was a trial before the congregation.

Cities Allotted to the Levites

21 Then the heads of the families of the Levites came to the priest Eleazar and to Joshua son of Nun and to the heads of the families of the tribes of the Israelites; 2they said to them at Shiloh in the land of Canaan, "The LORD commanded through Moses that we be given towns to live in, along with their pasture lands for our livestock." 3So by command of the LORD the Israelites gave to the Levites the following towns and pasture lands out of their inheritance.

4 The lot came out for the families of the Kohathites. So those Levites who were descendants of Aaron the priest received by lot thirteen towns from the tribes of Judah, Simeon, and Benjamin.

5 The rest of the Kohathites received by lot ten towns from the families of the tribe of Ephraim, from the tribe of Dan, and the half-tribe of Manasseh.

6 The Gershonites received by lot thirteen towns from the families of the tribe of Issachar, from the tribe of Asher, from the tribe of Naphtali, and from the half-tribe of Manasseh in Bashan.

7 The Merarites according to their families received twelve towns from the tribe of Reuben, the tribe of Gad, and the tribe of Zebulun.

8 These towns and their pasture lands the Israelites gave by lot to the Levites, as the LORD had commanded through Moses.

21.8 Towns for the Levites

As part of their calling to serve God, the Levites got no land in Canaan. Rather, they received 48 towns scattered in the other tribes' lands—four towns from each tribe. This forced them to depend not on their inheritance of the land, but on God (see Numbers 18.20). It dispersed the priests among all the people and enabled them to instruct the tribes in the law and to lead worship.

9 Out of the tribe of Judah and the tribe of Simeon they gave the following towns mentioned by name, [10]which went to the descendants of Aaron, one of the families of the Kohathites who belonged to the Levites, since the lot fell to them first. [11]They gave them Kiriath-arba (Arba being the father of Anak), that is Hebron, in the hill country of Judah, along with the pasture lands around it. [12]But the fields of the town and its villages had been given to Caleb son of Jephunneh as his holding.

13 To the descendants of Aaron the priest they gave Hebron, the city of refuge for the slayer, with its pasture lands, Libnah with its pasture lands, [14]Jattir with its pasture lands, Eshtemoa with its pasture lands, [15]Holon with its pasture lands, Debir with its pasture lands, [16]Ain with its pasture lands, Juttah with its pasture lands, and Beth-shemesh with its pasture lands—nine towns out of these two tribes. [17]Out of the tribe of Benjamin: Gibeon with its pasture lands, Geba with its pasture lands, [18]Anathoth with its pasture lands, and Almon with its pasture lands—four towns. [19]The towns of the descendants of Aaron—the priests—were thirteen in all, with their pasture lands.

20 As to the rest of the Kohathites belonging to the Kohathite families of the Levites, the towns allotted to them were out of the tribe of Ephraim. [21]To them were given Shechem, the city of refuge for the slayer, with its pasture lands in the hill country of Ephraim, Gezer with its pasture lands, [22]Kibzaim with its pasture lands, and Beth-horon with its pasture lands—four towns. [23]Out of the tribe of Dan: Elteke with its pasture lands, Gibbethon with its pasture lands, [24]Aijalon with its pasture lands, Gath-rimmon with its pasture lands—four towns. [25]Out of the half-tribe of Manasseh: Taanach with its pasture lands, and Gath-rimmon with its pasture lands—two towns. [26]The towns of the families of the rest of the Kohathites were ten in all, with their pasture lands.

27 To the Gershonites, one of the families of the Levites, were given out of the half-tribe of Manasseh, Golan in Bashan with its pasture lands, the city of refuge for the slayer, and Beeshterah with its pasture lands—two towns. [28]Out of the tribe of Issachar: Kishion with its pasture lands, Daberath with its pasture lands, [29]Jarmuth with its pasture lands, En-gannim with its pasture lands—four towns. [30]Out of the tribe of Asher: Mishal with its pasture lands, Abdon with its pasture lands, [31]Helkath with its pasture lands, and Rehob with its pasture lands—four towns. [32]Out of the tribe of Naphtali: Kedesh in Galilee with its pasture lands, the city of refuge for the slayer, Hammoth-dor with its pasture lands, and Kartan with its pasture lands—three towns. [33]The towns of the several families of the Gershonites were in all thirteen, with their pasture lands.

34 To the rest of the Levites—the Merarite families—were given out of the tribe of Zebulun: Jokneam with its pasture lands, Kartah with its pasture lands, [35]Dimnah with its pasture lands, Nahalal with its pasture lands—four towns. [36]Out of the tribe of Reuben: Bezer with its pasture lands, Jahzah with its pasture lands, [37]Kedemoth with its pasture lands, and Mephaath with its pasture lands—four towns. [38]Out of the tribe of Gad: Ramoth in Gilead with its pasture lands, the city of refuge for the slayer, Mahanaim with its pasture lands, [39]Heshbon with its pasture lands, Jazer with its pasture lands—four towns in all. [40]As for the towns of the several Merarite families, that is, the remainder of the families of the Levites, those allotted to them were twelve in all.

41 The towns of the Levites within the holdings of the Israelites were in all forty-eight towns with their pasture lands. [42]Each of these towns had its pasture lands around it; so it was with all these towns.

43 Thus the LORD gave to Israel all the land that he swore to their ancestors that he would give them; and having taken possession of it, they settled there. [44]And the LORD gave them rest on every side just as he had sworn to their ancestors; not one of all their enemies had withstood them, for the LORD had given all their enemies into their hands. [45]Not one of all the good promises that the LORD had made to the house of Israel had failed; all came to pass.

The Eastern Tribes Return to Their Territory

22 Then Joshua summoned the Reubenites, the Gadites, and the half-tribe of Manasseh, [2]and said to them, "You have observed all that Moses the servant of the LORD commanded you, and have obeyed me in all that I have commanded you; [3]you have not forsaken your kindred these many days, down to this day, but have been careful to keep the charge of the LORD your God. [4]And now the LORD your God has given rest to your kindred, as he promised them; therefore turn and go to your tents in the land where your possession lies, which Moses the servant of the LORD gave you on the other side of the Jordan. [5]Take good care to observe the commandment and instruction that Moses the servant of the LORD commanded you, to love the LORD your God, to walk in all his ways, to keep his commandments, and to hold fast to him, and to serve him with all your heart and with all your soul." [6]So Joshua blessed them and sent them away, and they went to their tents.

7 Now to the one half of the tribe of Manasseh Moses had given a possession in Bashan; but to the other half Joshua had given a possession beside their fellow Israelites in the land west of the Jordan. And when Joshua sent them away to their tents and blessed them, [8]he said to them, "Go back to your tents with much wealth, and with

very much livestock, with silver, gold, bronze, and iron, and with a great quantity of clothing; divide the spoil of your enemies with your kindred." ⁹So the Reubenites and the Gadites and the half-tribe of Manasseh returned home, parting from the Israelites at Shiloh, which is in the land of Canaan, to go to the land of Gilead, their own land of which they had taken possession by command of the LORD through Moses.

A Memorial Altar East of the Jordan

10 When they came to the region^i near the Jordan that lies in the land of Canaan, the Reubenites and the Gadites and the half-tribe of Manasseh built there an altar by the Jordan, an altar

22.10–30 Explosive Quarrel

Chapter 22 records a misunderstanding that could have led to civil war. Several Israelite tribes built a large altar. This inflamed the other tribes. Weren't the builders grossly violating God's law by erecting an altar, a function only priests should perform? Were these tribes so soon abandoning the rules of worship Moses and Joshua had laid down? Or, perhaps, had they provocatively built their altar on the western side of the Jordan River to stake a claim to others' land? The western tribes soon learned the truth: the easterners had built not an altar, but a monument to commemorate their national unity with the western tribes. A civil war was averted after some heated exchanges. The incident reveals the intensity of religious feeling in the new nation.

of great size. ¹¹The Israelites heard that the Reubenites and the Gadites and the half-tribe of Manasseh had built an altar at the frontier of the land of Canaan, in the region^j near the Jordan, on the side that belongs to the Israelites. ¹²And when the people of Israel heard of it, the whole assembly of the Israelites gathered at Shiloh, to make war against them.

13 Then the Israelites sent the priest Phinehas son of Eleazar to the Reubenites and the Gadites and the half-tribe of Manasseh, in the land of Gilead, ¹⁴and with him ten chiefs, one from each of the tribal families of Israel, every one of them the head of a family among the clans of Israel. ¹⁵They came to the Reubenites, the Gadites, and the half-tribe of Manasseh, in the land of Gilead, and they said to them, ¹⁶"Thus says the whole congregation of the LORD, 'What is this treachery that you have committed against the God of Israel in turning away today from following the LORD, by building yourselves an altar today in rebellion

against the LORD? ¹⁷Have we not had enough of the sin at Peor from which even yet we have not cleansed ourselves, and for which a plague came upon the congregation of the LORD, ¹⁸that you must turn away today from following the LORD! If you rebel against the LORD today, he will be angry with the whole congregation of Israel tomorrow. ¹⁹But now, if your land is unclean, cross over into the LORD's land where the LORD's tabernacle now stands, and take for yourselves a possession among us; only do not rebel against the LORD, or rebel against us^k by building yourselves an altar other than the altar of the LORD our God. ²⁰Did not Achan son of Zerah break faith in the matter of the devoted things, and wrath fell upon all the congregation of Israel? And he did not perish alone for his iniquity!'"

21 Then the Reubenites, the Gadites, and the half-tribe of Manasseh said in answer to the heads of the families of Israel, ²²"The LORD, God of gods! The LORD, God of gods! He knows; and let Israel itself know! If it was in rebellion or in breach of faith toward the LORD, do not spare us today ²³for building an altar to turn away from following the LORD; or if we did so to offer burnt offerings or grain offerings or offerings of well-being on it, may the LORD himself take vengeance. ²⁴No! We did it from fear that in time to come your children might say to our children, 'What have you to do with the LORD, the God of Israel? ²⁵For the LORD has made the Jordan a boundary between us and you, you Reubenites and Gadites; you have no portion in the LORD.' So your children might make our children cease to worship the LORD. ²⁶Therefore we said, 'Let us now build an altar, not for burnt offering, nor for sacrifice, ²⁷but to be a witness between us and you, and between the generations after us, that we do perform the service of the LORD in his presence with our burnt offerings and sacrifices and offerings of well-being; so that your children may never say to our children in time to come, "You have no portion in the LORD."' ²⁸And we thought, If this should be said to us or to our descendants in time to come, we could say, 'Look at this copy of the altar of the LORD, which our ancestors made, not for burnt offerings, nor for sacrifice, but to be a witness between us and you.' ²⁹Far be it from us that we should rebel against the LORD, and turn away this day from following the LORD by building an altar for burnt offering, grain offering, or sacrifice, other than the altar of the LORD our God that stands before his tabernacle!"

30 When the priest Phinehas and the chiefs of the congregation, the heads of the families of Israel who were with him, heard the words that the Reubenites and the Gadites and the Manassites spoke, they were satisfied. ³¹The priest Phinehas son of Eleazar said to the Reubenites and the

---

^{i} Or *to Geliloth* ^{j} Or *at Geliloth* ^{k} Or *make rebels of us*

Gadites and the Manassites, "Today we know that the LORD is among us, because you have not committed this treachery against the LORD; now you have saved the Israelites from the hand of the LORD."

32 Then the priest Phinehas son of Eleazar and the chiefs returned from the Reubenites and the Gadites in the land of Gilead to the land of Canaan, to the Israelites, and brought back word to them. 33The report pleased the Israelites; and the Israelites blessed God and spoke no more of making war against them, to destroy the land where the Reubenites and the Gadites were settled. 34The Reubenites and the Gadites called the altar Witness;[l] "For," said they, "it is a witness between us that the LORD is God."

Joshua Exhorts the People

23 A long time afterward, when the LORD had given rest to Israel from all their enemies all around, and Joshua was old and well advanced in years, 2Joshua summoned all Israel, their elders and heads, their judges and officers, and said to them, "I am now old and well advanced in years; 3and you have seen all that the LORD your God has done to all these nations for your sake, for it is the LORD your God who has fought for you. 4I have allotted to you as an inheritance for your tribes those nations that remain, along with all the nations that I have already cut off, from the Jordan to the Great Sea in the west. 5The LORD your God will push them back before you, and drive them out of your sight; and you shall possess their land, as the LORD your God promised you. 6Therefore be very steadfast to observe and do all that is written in the book of the law of Moses, turning aside from it neither to the right nor to the left, 7so that you may not be mixed with these nations left here among you, or make mention of the names of their gods, or swear by them, or serve them, or bow yourselves down to them, 8but hold fast to the LORD your God, as you have done to this day. 9For the LORD has driven out before you great and strong nations; and as for you, no one has been able to withstand you to this day. 10One of you puts to flight a thousand, since it is the LORD your God who fights for you, as he promised you. 11Be very careful, therefore, to love the LORD your God. 12For if you turn back, and join the survivors of these nations left here among you, and intermarry with them, so that you marry their women and they yours, 13know assuredly that the LORD your God will not continue to drive out these nations before you; but they shall be a snare and a trap for you, a scourge on your sides, and thorns in your eyes, until you perish from this good land that the LORD your God has given you.

14 "And now I am about to go the way of all the earth, and you know in your hearts and souls, all of you, that not one thing has failed of all the good things that the LORD your God promised concerning you; all have come to pass for you, not one of them has failed. 15But just as all the good things that the LORD your God promised concerning you have been fulfilled for you, so the LORD will bring upon you all the bad things, until he has destroyed you from this good land that the LORD your God has given you. 16If you transgress the covenant of the LORD your God, which he enjoined on you, and go and serve other gods and bow down to them, then the anger of the LORD will be kindled against you, and you shall perish quickly from the good land that he has given to you."

The Tribes Renew the Covenant

24 Then Joshua gathered all the tribes of Israel to Shechem, and summoned the elders, the heads, the judges, and the officers of Israel; and they presented themselves before God. 2And Joshua said to all the people, "Thus says the LORD, the God of Israel: Long ago your ancestors— Terah and his sons Abraham and Nahor—lived beyond the Euphrates and served other gods.

24.2 Joshua's Farewell

Joshua's final speech has many similarities to the much longer speeches given by Moses in Deuteronomy. Both follow the pattern of a treaty between a ruler and his people. Joshua used the occasion to renew the covenant between God and the Israelites (verses 25–27). For more details, see the description of "suzerainty treaties" in "How to Read Deuteronomy," page 194.

3Then I took your father Abraham from beyond the River and led him through all the land of Canaan and made his offspring many. I gave him Isaac; 4and to Isaac I gave Jacob and Esau. I gave Esau the hill country of Seir to possess, but Jacob and his children went down to Egypt. 5Then I sent Moses and Aaron, and I plagued Egypt with what I did in its midst; and afterwards I brought you out. 6When I brought your ancestors out of Egypt, you came to the sea; and the Egyptians pursued your ancestors with chariots and horsemen to the Red Sea.[m] 7When they cried out to the LORD, he put darkness between you and the Egyptians, and made the sea come upon them and cover them; and your eyes saw what I did to Egypt. Afterwards you lived in the wilderness a long time. 8Then I brought you to the land of the Amorites, who lived on the other side of the Jordan; they fought with you, and I handed them

---

[l] Cn Compare Syr: Heb lacks *Witness*   [m] Or *Sea of Reeds*

Filling Moses' Shoes
Joshua could follow orders as well as give them

Israel served the
LORD all the days of
Joshua. 24.31

LIKE ALL THE ISRAELITES, JOSHUA began in humble surroundings. He was born a slave in Egypt and followed Moses across the Red Sea to freedom. He first appears in the Bible as a military commander.

Soon after escaping from Egypt, the Israelites confronted a new enemy, and Moses turned to Joshua to lead their very first battle (Exodus 17.9–15).

A month later, when Moses climbed craggy Mount Sinai to meet with God, Joshua was at his side. He first reported to Moses the strange sounds coming from the camp, sounds that turned out to be the Israelites' great spiritual rebellion (Exodus 32.17). Joshua rose to become Moses' trusted number-two man, an aide who served him at almost every major crisis. Moses changed his name from Hoshea, which meant "help," or "salvation," to Joshua, meaning "The LORD saves." (The Greek form of Joshua is *Jesus*.)

Becoming Number One

On the verge of entering Canaan, Moses turned to Joshua again, choosing him as one of 12 spies sent to collect information about the land. Ten came back frightened, with predictions of doom. Only Joshua and Caleb had faith that God would keep his promises to the Israelites despite the military odds.

Joshua learned about the hazards of leadership from that spy trip: on his return, thousands of angry Israelites called for his public stoning (Numbers 14). But he stood firm, and God rewarded him. Of all the Israelites who left Egypt, only he and Caleb were allowed to enter the promised land—not even Moses had that honor. As Moses' death neared, God and Moses made Joshua their uncontested choice for a new leader for Israel. It was time for number two to become number one.

Joshua made a remarkably smooth transition into leadership. In fact, Joshua's life had many parallels to that of Moses. The miracle of crossing the Jordan River poignantly replayed Moses' crossing of the Red Sea. Moses encountered God directly at the burning bush; Joshua met God's special representative, the "commander of the army of the LORD," and likewise took off his shoes at the meeting (5.13–15).

Both Moses and Joshua wrote the law onto stones: Moses creating a permanent record for Israel, and Joshua erecting a monument for the nation to pass by on the way into the new land (8.32). Both leaders pleaded with God on behalf of their people. And both ended their terms with stirring speeches that reviewed history and challenged the people toward a critical choice.

Well-rounded Leader

Moses, who grew up in the courts of Pharaoh, obviously received a better education than Joshua. He showed a philosophical bent. Joshua, on the other hand, was action-oriented and pragmatic, a perfect military man. He had the rare combination of knowing how to follow orders as well as how to give them.

The Bible, never guilty of glossing over its heroes' flaws, reveals some of Joshua's mistakes. In one incident in the desert, he was rash (Numbers 11.26–30). During the first battle of Ai and the treaty negotiations with the Gibeonites, he acted impulsively, without first seeking God's advice. And, faced with his first major defeat at Ai, he uncharacteristically dissolved in fright, earning God's stern rebuke: "Stand up! Why have you fallen upon your face?" (7.6–12).

Apart from these few incidents, Joshua's life was marked by unusual faith and obedience. Joshua never let the press of military action interfere with worship and the renewal of the covenant. When he divided up the land (an immense bureaucratic burden that takes up the last half of this book), he did so with wisdom and fairness, selecting his own portion only after all others had chosen.

The Bible records this simple legacy: "Israel served the LORD all the days of Joshua" (24.31). History would show how rarely that occurred in the life of a troublesome nation.

Life Questions: Often when a popular leader—a pastor, a politician, a teacher—retires from office, something slips. What made Joshua such an effective replacement?

over to you, and you took possession of their land, and I destroyed them before you. ⁹Then King Balak son of Zippor of Moab, set out to fight against Israel. He sent and invited Balaam son of Beor to curse you, ¹⁰but I would not listen to Balaam; therefore he blessed you; so I rescued you out of his hand. ¹¹When you went over the Jordan and came to Jericho, the citizens of Jericho fought against you, and also the Amorites, the Perizzites, the Canaanites, the Hittites, the Girgashites, the Hivites, and the Jebusites; and I handed them over to you. ¹²I sent the hornet[n] ahead of you, which drove out before you the two kings of the Amorites; it was not by your sword or by your bow. ¹³I gave you a land on which you had not labored, and towns that you had not built, and you live in them; you eat the fruit of vineyards and oliveyards that you did not plant.

14 "Now therefore revere the LORD, and serve him in sincerity and in faithfulness; put away the gods that your ancestors served beyond the River and in Egypt, and serve the LORD. ¹⁵Now if you are unwilling to serve the LORD, choose this day whom you will serve, whether the gods your ancestors served in the region beyond the River or the gods of the Amorites in whose land you are living; but as for me and my household, we will serve the LORD."

24.15 Free Choice

After all God had done for them, the Israelites still faced a fundamental choice. They could worship the gods their ancestors had served in Egypt or Mesopotamia, they could follow the religious practices of the new land they had entered—or they could follow the God who had freed them from slavery. The choice seems obvious, and Joshua knew exactly which direction he and his family would take. But as the book of Judges shows, many of the Israelites exercised their free will to enslave themselves to foreign gods.

16 Then the people answered, "Far be it from us that we should forsake the LORD to serve other gods; ¹⁷for it is the LORD our God who brought us and our ancestors up from the land of Egypt, out of the house of slavery, and who did those great signs in our sight. He protected us along all the way that we went, and among all the peoples through whom we passed; ¹⁸and the LORD drove out before us all the peoples, the Amorites who lived in the land. Therefore we also will serve the LORD, for he is our God."

19 But Joshua said to the people, "You cannot serve the LORD, for he is a holy God. He is a jealous God; he will not forgive your transgressions or your sins. ²⁰If you forsake the LORD and serve foreign gods, then he will turn and do you harm, and consume you, after having done you good." ²¹And the people said to Joshua, "No, we will serve the LORD!" ²²Then Joshua said to the people, "You are witnesses against yourselves that you have chosen the LORD, to serve him." And they said, "We are witnesses." ²³He said, "Then put away the foreign gods that are among you, and incline your hearts to the LORD, the God of Israel." ²⁴The people said to Joshua, "The LORD our God we will serve, and him we will obey." ²⁵So Joshua made a covenant with the people that day, and made statutes and ordinances for them at Shechem. ²⁶Joshua wrote these words in the book of the law of God; and he took a large stone, and set it up there under the oak in the sanctuary

24.26 Monuments

The Israelites established at least seven memorials to remind future generations of what God had done for them. (Other stone monuments are described in chapters 4,7,8,10,22.) Even if people forgot their debt to God, the land would speak its own story.

of the LORD. ²⁷Joshua said to all the people, "See, this stone shall be a witness against us; for it has heard all the words of the LORD that he spoke to us; therefore it shall be a witness against you, if you deal falsely with your God." ²⁸So Joshua sent the people away to their inheritances.

Death of Joshua and Eleazar

29 After these things Joshua son of Nun, the servant of the LORD, died, being one hundred ten years old. ³⁰They buried him in his own inheritance at Timnath-serah, which is in the hill country of Ephraim, north of Mount Gaash.

31 Israel served the LORD all the days of Joshua, and all the days of the elders who outlived Joshua and had known all the work that the LORD did for Israel.

32 The bones of Joseph, which the Israelites had brought up from Egypt, were buried at Shechem, in the portion of ground that Jacob had bought from the children of Hamor, the father of Shechem, for one hundred pieces of money;[o] it became an inheritance of the descendants of Joseph.

33 Eleazar son of Aaron died; and they buried him at Gibeah, the town of his son Phinehas, which had been given him in the hill country of Ephraim.

---

[n] Meaning of Heb uncertain   [o] Heb *one hundred qesitah*

JUDGES

Freedom Fighters
These "judges" took up arms to defend their homeland

T HE "JUDGES" OF THIS BOOK might be called guerrillas or freedom fighters today. These men (and one woman) were renowned not for court cases, but for their military campaigns against foreign invaders. Like all military leaders, they sometimes settled disputes; but the book of Judges, however, is preoccupied not with legal matters, but with the excitement of fighting for freedom.

Israel's judges certainly did not stick to "the rules of proper warfare." Judge Ehud tricked his opponent into a private conference; behind closed doors he pulled out a knife and plunged it into the enemy king's belly (3.12–30). Judge Gideon won a surprise victory in the middle of the night. His small band so confused the occupying army with noise and lights that the enemy soldiers stabbed each other and fled in the darkness (chapter 7). Samson never led an army; his battle tricks have been compared to the pranks of an overgrown juvenile delinquent (chapters 14–16).

Most of the time the Israelites hid in the hills while their enemies, with superior weapons, controlled the plains. (Chariots, like tanks, were devastating in level country, but almost useless in muddy or rugged terrain.) Outnumbered, the Israelites relied on ambushes and sneak attacks. They knew every gully, for they were fighting for their homeland. Strategy made up for lack of strength.

> Whenever the LORD raised up judges for them, the LORD was with the judge, and he delivered them from the hand of their enemies all the days of the judge.
> 2.18

Ugliest Stories of the Bible

As a book about early Jewish military heroes, Judges inspires and fascinates. But you can't make the whole book fit that description. If you read strictly looking for heroes, you'd have to ignore half of Judges—and you would miss its most important point about God's work with Israel.

For one thing, Judges' "heroes" were badly flawed. Samson was pitifully vulnerable to his lust for women. Gideon won a battle, then led the nation into idolatry. Jephthah, a former outlaw, apparently knew very little about the God he was supposed to serve.

Add to this the "non-heroic" material: Abimelech, Gideon's son, who slaughtered 70 half brothers so he could be named king; Jephthah and Gideon, who massacred fellow Israelites who had failed to support them; and the sad characters of the last five chapters of Judges. These contain some of the ugliest stories in the Bible—tales of homosexual assault, idolatry, civil war, thievery, rape, and murder. The book of Judges runs downhill, from bad to worse. You may end up wondering what such material is doing in the Bible.

Every picture has shadows; every suspenseful novel has chapters that look truly dark. In the story of God and his people, Judges is that kind of chapter. Heroes appear sporadically, but humanity remains terribly unheroic.

Enthusiasm Fades

God wanted better things for his people than he got in Judges. He had rescued Israel from slavery in Egypt. He had given them a rich land and presented them with a grand system of worship and government centering on him. He would be no distant God in the heavens—he would live with them.

But after some initial enthusiasm, the Israelites didn't continue the way God had pointed. Instead, they learned to live with the sophisticated people they found as their neighbors—people whose faults included worshiping idols through sex orgies and child sacrifice.

The Israelites held the mountains, but the foreign-held valleys, cutting through the land, separated the tribes. Soon each group of isolated Israelites began operating independently. The next generation lost its sense of national identity. The people worshiped the idol Baal alongside the Lord. Though descended from 12 brothers, they spent more time fighting each other than the foreign oppressors.

They violated virtually every moral standard. The last verse of Judges sums it up: "All the people did what was right in their own eyes." What they saw as right, wasn't.

The Secret of Their Survival

The foreign invasions were no accident, Judges says: They came from God just as surely as the heroic rescuers did. A pattern developed. God allowed suffering as a consequence of the Israelites' disobedience. When things grew really terrible, their attention would turn back to God. He would respond by sending a judge to rescue them. But soon they would fail again. This pattern repeated itself time and again. The Israelites always forgot their need for God, and the dreary cycle ground on.

The secret of Israel's survival was not, then, military heroes or guerrilla tactics. It was the persistent, unwearied love of God himself. Though they forgot him, he did not forget them. He gave innumerable new beginnings. Again and again he sent "judges" to rescue them. He would not let them go. God is the real hero of Judges.

How to Read Judges

You can read Judges as a collection of heroic stories, the most famous of which are Gideon's and Samson's. But together the tales tell a less heroic story.

Read Judges, therefore, on two levels at once. On one level focus on the new beginning God repeatedly offered by sending a judge to rescue Israel. These are character stories with great fascination. You can gain a great deal by studying the strengths and weaknesses of the individual judges.

On another level, read of the deterioration of a nation that quickly forgot what God had done for it. This will help you understand why, in the next stage of Israel's history, God gave the Israelites a king. For background on this change of government, read "The First King," page 300. Another interesting study is the book of Ruth, a lovely story from the time of Judges that shows a softer, more hopeful side.

PEOPLE YOU'LL MEET IN JUDGES

DEBORAH (p. 262)
GIDEON (p. 265)
SAMSON (p. 274)

3-TRACK READING PLAN

For an explanation and complete listing of the 3-track reading plan, turn to page 7.

TRACK 1: *Two-Week Courses on the Bible*
See page 8 for information on these courses.

TRACK 2: *An Overview of Judges in 3 Days*
☐ Day 1. Read the Introduction to Judges and chapter 6, in which God calls Gideon to lead a guerrilla army.
☐ Day 2. Read chapter 7, Gideon's victory in battle.
☐ Day 3. Read chapter 16, the story of Samson and Delilah, and Samson's death.

Now turn to page 9 for your next Track 2 reading project.

TRACK 3: *All of Judges in 21 Days*
After you have read through Judges, turn to pages 10–14 for your next Track 3 reading project.

☐1 ☐2 ☐3 ☐4 ☐5 ☐6 ☐7 ☐8
☐9 ☐10 ☐11 ☐12 ☐13 ☐14 ☐15 ☐16
☐17 ☐18 ☐19 ☐20 ☐21

Israel's Failure to Complete the Conquest of Canaan

After the death of Joshua, the Israelites inquired of the LORD, "Who shall go up first for us against the Canaanites, to fight against them?" [2]The LORD said, "Judah shall go up. I hereby give the land into his hand." [3]Judah said to his brother Simeon, "Come up with me into the territory allotted to me, that we may fight against the Canaanites; then I too will go with you into the territory allotted to you." So Simeon went with him. [4]Then Judah went up and the LORD gave the Canaanites and the Perizzites into their hand; and they defeated ten thousand of them at Bezek. [5]They came upon Adoni-bezek at Bezek, and fought against him, and defeated the Canaanites and the Perizzites. [6]Adoni-bezek fled; but they pursued him, and caught him, and cut off his thumbs and big toes. [7]Adoni-bezek said, "Seventy kings with their thumbs and big toes cut off used to pick up scraps under my table; as I have done, so God has paid me back." They brought him to Jerusalem, and he died there.

1.7 Thumbs and Big Toes

A person lacking thumbs and big toes could not grip a weapon or run quickly. So cutting off those appendages guaranteed that a captured enemy would never fight again.

[8] Then the people of Judah fought against Jerusalem and took it. They put it to the sword and set the city on fire. [9]Afterward the people of Judah went down to fight against the Canaanites who lived in the hill country, in the Negeb, and in the lowland. [10]Judah went against the Canaanites who lived in Hebron (the name of Hebron was formerly Kiriath-arba); and they defeated Sheshai and Ahiman and Talmai.

[11] From there they went against the inhabitants of Debir (the name of Debir was formerly Kiriath-sepher). [12]Then Caleb said, "Whoever attacks Kiriath-sepher and takes it, I will give him my daughter Achsah as wife." [13]And Othniel son of Kenaz, Caleb's younger brother, took it; and he gave him his daughter Achsah as wife. [14]When she came to him, she urged him to ask her father for a field. As she dismounted from her donkey, Caleb said to her, "What do you wish?" [15]She said to him, "Give me a present; since you have set me in the land of the Negeb, give me also Gulloth-mayim."[a] So Caleb gave her Upper Gulloth and Lower Gulloth.

[16] The descendants of Hobab[b] the Kenite, Moses' father-in-law, went up with the people of Judah from the city of palms into the wilderness of Judah, which lies in the Negeb near Arad. Then they went and settled with the Amalekites.[c] [17]Judah went with his brother Simeon, and they defeated the Canaanites who inhabited Zephath, and devoted it to destruction. So the city was called Hormah. [18]Judah took Gaza with its territory, Ashkelon with its territory, and Ekron with its territory. [19]The LORD was with Judah, and he took possession of the hill country, but could not drive out the inhabitants of the plain, because

1.19 Military Setbacks

Why did the Israelites fail to take all the territory allotted them? One reason was stubborn military opposition. The Israelites had never developed the sophistication to use chariots, the equivalent of modern-day tanks. Israel controlled the hills where chariots were unwieldy, but could not win the plains. The Israelites also failed to conquer Jerusalem (verse 21); its mountainous setting made that city almost impregnable.

they had chariots of iron. [20]Hebron was given to Caleb, as Moses had said; and he drove out from it the three sons of Anak. [21]But the Benjaminites did not drive out the Jebusites who lived in Jerusalem; so the Jebusites have lived in Jerusalem among the Benjaminites to this day.

[22] The house of Joseph also went up against Bethel; and the LORD was with them. [23]The house of Joseph sent out spies to Bethel (the name of the city was formerly Luz). [24]When the spies saw a man coming out of the city, they said to him, "Show us the way into the city, and we will deal kindly with you." [25]So he showed them the way into the city; and they put the city to the sword, but they let the man and all his family go. [26]So the man went to the land of the Hittites and built a city, and named it Luz; that is its name to this day.

[27] Manasseh did not drive out the inhabitants of Beth-shean and its villages, or Taanach and its villages, or the inhabitants of Dor and its villages, or the inhabitants of Ibleam and its villages, or the inhabitants of Megiddo and its villages; but the Canaanites continued to live in that land. [28]When Israel grew strong, they put the Canaanites to forced labor, but did not in fact drive them out.

[29] And Ephraim did not drive out the Canaanites who lived in Gezer; but the Canaanites lived among them in Gezer.

[30] Zebulun did not drive out the inhabitants of Kitron, or the inhabitants of Nahalol; but the Canaanites lived among them, and became subject to forced labor.

[31] Asher did not drive out the inhabitants of Acco, or the inhabitants of Sidon, or of Ahlab, or

---

[a] That is *Basins of Water*   [b] Gk: Heb lacks *Hobab*   [c] See 1 Sam 15.6: Heb *people*

of Achzib, or of Helbah, or of Aphik, or of Rehob; ³²but the Asherites lived among the Canaanites, the inhabitants of the land; for they did not drive them out.

33 Naphtali did not drive out the inhabitants of Beth-shemesh, or the inhabitants of Beth-anath, but lived among the Canaanites, the inhabitants of the land; nevertheless the inhabitants of Beth-shemesh and of Beth-anath became subject to forced labor for them.

34 The Amorites pressed the Danites back into the hill country; they did not allow them to come down to the plain. ³⁵The Amorites continued to live in Har-heres, in Aijalon, and in Shaalbim, but the hand of the house of Joseph rested heavily on them, and they became subject to forced labor. ³⁶The border of the Amorites ran from the ascent of Akrabbim, from Sela and upward.

Israel's Disobedience

2 Now the angel of the LORD went up from Gilgal to Bochim, and said, "I brought you up from Egypt, and brought you into the land that I had promised to your ancestors. I said, 'I will never break my covenant with you. ²For your part, do not make a covenant with the inhabitants of this land; tear down their altars.' But you have not obeyed my command. See what you have done! ³So now I say, I will not drive them out before you; but they shall become adversaries[d] to you, and their gods shall be a snare to you." ⁴When the angel of the LORD spoke these words to all the Israelites, the people lifted up their voices, and wept. ⁵So they named that place Bochim,[e] and there they sacrificed to the LORD.

Death of Joshua

6 When Joshua dismissed the people, the Israelites all went to their own inheritances to take possession of the land. ⁷The people worshiped the LORD all the days of Joshua, and all the days of the elders who outlived Joshua, who had seen all the great work that the LORD had done for Israel. ⁸Joshua son of Nun, the servant of the LORD, died at the age of one hundred ten years. ⁹So they buried him within the bounds of his inheritance in Timnath-heres, in the hill country of Ephraim, north of Mount Gaash. ¹⁰Moreover, that whole generation was gathered to their ancestors, and another generation grew up after them, who did not know the LORD or the work that he had done for Israel.

Israel's Unfaithfulness

11 Then the Israelites did what was evil in the sight of the LORD and worshiped the Baals; ¹²and they abandoned the LORD, the God of their ancestors, who had brought them out of the land of Egypt; they followed other gods, from among the gods of the peoples who were all around them, and bowed down to them; and they provoked the LORD to anger. ¹³They abandoned the LORD, and

2.13 Fertility Gods

Israel's neighbors worshiped Baal and Ashtoreth, male and female gods of fertility. Followers practiced ritual sex at the shrines, believing that sex with sacred prostitutes led to good crops and many children. Sometimes, too, worshipers sacrificed their children to the gods. The Israelites' attraction to these foreign religions continued for most of their history as a nation.

worshiped Baal and the Astartes. ¹⁴So the anger of the LORD was kindled against Israel, and he gave them over to plunderers who plundered them, and he sold them into the power of their enemies all around, so that they could no longer withstand their enemies. ¹⁵Whenever they marched out, the hand of the LORD was against them to bring misfortune, as the LORD had warned them and sworn to them; and they were in great distress.

16 Then the LORD raised up judges, who delivered them out of the power of those who plundered them. ¹⁷Yet they did not listen even to their judges; for they lusted after other gods and bowed down to them. They soon turned aside from the way in which their ancestors had walked, who had obeyed the commandments of the LORD; they did not follow their example. ¹⁸Whenever the LORD raised up judges for them, the LORD was with the judge, and he delivered them from the hand of their enemies all the days of the judge; for the LORD would be moved to pity by their groaning because of those who persecuted and oppressed them. ¹⁹But whenever the judge died, they would relapse and behave worse than their ancestors, following other gods, worshiping them and bowing down to them. They would not drop any of their practices or their stubborn ways. ²⁰So the anger of the LORD was kindled against Israel; and he said, "Because this people have transgressed my covenant that I commanded their ancestors, and have not obeyed my voice, ²¹I will no longer drive out before them any of the nations that Joshua left when he died." ²²In order to test Israel, whether or not they would take care to walk in the way of the LORD as their ancestors did, ²³the LORD had left those nations, not driving them out at once, and had not handed them over to Joshua.

Nations Remaining in the Land

3 Now these are the nations that the LORD left to test all those in Israel who had no experi-

---

[d] OL Vg Compare Gk: Heb *sides*   [e] That is *Weepers*

ence of any war in Canaan ²(it was only that successive generations of Israelites might know war, to teach those who had no experience of it before): ³the five lords of the Philistines, and all the Canaanites, and the Sidonians, and the Hivites who lived on Mount Lebanon, from Mount Baal-hermon as far as Lebo-hamath. ⁴They were for the testing of Israel, to know whether Israel would obey the commandments of the LORD, which he commanded their ancestors by Moses. ⁵So the Israelites lived among the Canaanites, the Hittites, the Amorites, the Perizzites, the Hivites, and the Jebusites; ⁶and they took their daughters as wives for themselves, and their own daughters they gave to their sons; and they worshiped their gods.

3.6 Intermarriage

This passage shows why the Old Testament opposed mixed marriages, which were common in the period of the judges. Ethnic differences were not the main issue. In fact, during the period of the judges Ruth, a non-Jew, married into a Jewish family with full acceptance (see the book of Ruth). But Ruth had accepted the God of Israel. When mixed marriages meant mixed religions, they diluted faith in God.

Othniel

7 The Israelites did what was evil in the sight of the LORD, forgetting the LORD their God, and worshiping the Baals and the Asherahs. ⁸Therefore the anger of the LORD was kindled against Israel, and he sold them into the hand of King Cushan-rishathaim of Aram-naharaim; and the Israelites served Cushan-rishathaim eight years. ⁹But when the Israelites cried out to the LORD, the LORD raised up a deliverer for the Israelites, who delivered them, Othniel son of Kenaz, Caleb's younger brother. ¹⁰The spirit of the LORD came upon him, and he judged Israel; he went out to war, and the LORD gave King Cushan-rishathaim of Aram into his hand; and his hand prevailed over Cushan-rishathaim. ¹¹So the land had rest forty years. Then Othniel son of Kenaz died.

Ehud

12 The Israelites again did what was evil in the sight of the LORD; and the LORD strengthened King Eglon of Moab against Israel, because they had done what was evil in the sight of the LORD. ¹³In alliance with the Ammonites and the Ama-

lekites, he went and defeated Israel; and they took possession of the city of palms. ¹⁴So the Israelites served King Eglon of Moab eighteen years.

15 But when the Israelites cried out to the LORD, the LORD raised up for them a deliverer, Ehud son of Gera, the Benjaminite, a left-handed man. The Israelites sent tribute by him to King Eglon of Moab. ¹⁶Ehud made for himself a sword with two edges, a cubit in length; and he fastened it on his right thigh under his clothes. ¹⁷Then he presented the tribute to King Eglon of Moab. Now Eglon was a very fat man. ¹⁸When Ehud had finished presenting the tribute, he sent the people who carried the tribute on their way. ¹⁹But he himself turned back at the sculptured stones near Gilgal, and said, "I have a secret message for you, O king." So the king said,ᶠ "Silence!" and all his attendants went out from his presence. ²⁰Ehud came to him, while he was sitting alone in his cool roof chamber, and said, "I have a message from God for you." So he rose from his seat. ²¹Then Ehud reached with his left hand, took the sword from his right thigh, and thrust it into Eglon'sᵍ belly; ²²the hilt also went in after the blade, and the fat closed over the blade, for he did not draw the sword out of his belly; and the dirt came out.ʰ ²³Then Ehud went out into the vestibule,ⁱ and closed the doors of the roof chamber on him, and locked them.

24 After he had gone, the servants came. When they saw that the doors of the roof chamber were locked, they thought, "He must be relieving himselfʲ in the cool chamber." ²⁵So they waited until they were embarrassed. When he still did not open the doors of the roof chamber, they took the key and opened them. There was their lord lying dead on the floor.

26 Ehud escaped while they delayed, and passed beyond the sculptured stones, and escaped to Seirah. ²⁷When he arrived, he sounded the trumpet in the hill country of Ephraim; and the Israelites went down with him from the hill country, having him at their head. ²⁸He said to them, "Follow after me; for the LORD has given your enemies the Moabites into your hand." So they went down after him, and seized the fords of the Jordan against the Moabites, and allowed no one to cross over. ²⁹At that time they killed about ten thousand of the Moabites, all strong, able-bodied men; no one escaped. ³⁰So Moab was subdued that day under the hand of Israel. And the land had rest eighty years.

Shamgar

31 After him came Shamgar son of Anath, who killed six hundred of the Philistines with an oxgoad. He too delivered Israel.

ᶠ Heb *he said*   ᵍ Heb *his*   ʰ With Tg Vg: Meaning of Heb uncertain   ⁱ Meaning of Heb uncertain
ʲ Heb *covering his feet*

Deborah and Barak

4 The Israelites again did what was evil in the sight of the LORD, after Ehud died. ²So the LORD sold them into the hand of King Jabin of Canaan, who reigned in Hazor; the commander of his army was Sisera, who lived in Harosheth-ha-goiim. ³Then the Israelites cried out to the LORD for help; for he had nine hundred chariots of iron, and had oppressed the Israelites cruelly twenty years.

4 At that time Deborah, a prophetess, wife of Lappidoth, was judging Israel. ⁵She used to sit under the palm of Deborah between Ramah and Bethel in the hill country of Ephraim; and the Israelites came up to her for judgment. ⁶She sent and summoned Barak son of Abinoam from Kedesh in Naphtali, and said to him, "The LORD, the God of Israel, commands you, 'Go, take position at Mount Tabor, bringing ten thousand from the tribe of Naphtali and the tribe of Zebulun. ⁷I will draw out Sisera, the general of Jabin's army, to meet you by the Wadi Kishon with his chariots and his troops; and I will give him into your hand.'" ⁸Barak said to her, "If you will go with me, I will go; but if you will not go with me, I will not go." ⁹And she said, "I will surely go with you; nevertheless, the road on which you are going will not lead to your glory, for the LORD will sell Sisera into the hand of a woman." Then Deborah got up and went with Barak to Kedesh. ¹⁰Barak summoned Zebulun and Naphtali to Kedesh; and ten thousand warriors went up behind him; and Deborah went up with him.

11 Now Heber the Kenite had separated from the other Kenites,ᵏ that is, the descendants of Hobab the father-in-law of Moses, and had encamped as far away as Elon-bezaanannim, which is near Kedesh.

12 When Sisera was told that Barak son of Abinoam had gone up to Mount Tabor, ¹³Sisera called out all his chariots, nine hundred chariots of iron, and all the troops who were with him, from Harosheth-ha-goiim to the Wadi Kishon. ¹⁴Then Deborah said to Barak, "Up! For this is the day on which the LORD has given Sisera into your hand. The LORD is indeed going out before you." So Barak went down from Mount Tabor with ten thousand warriors following him. ¹⁵And the LORD threw Sisera and all his chariots and all his army into a panicˡ before Barak; Sisera got down from his chariot and fled away on foot, ¹⁶while Barak pursued the chariots and the army to Harosheth-ha-goiim. All the army of Sisera fell by the sword; no one was left.

17 Now Sisera had fled away on foot to the tent of Jael wife of Heber the Kenite; for there was peace between King Jabin of Hazor and the clan of Heber the Kenite. ¹⁸Jael came out to meet Sisera, and said to him, "Turn aside, my lord, turn aside to me; have no fear." So he turned aside to her into the tent, and she covered him with a rug. ¹⁹Then he said to her, "Please give me a little water to drink; for I am thirsty." So she opened a skin of milk and gave him a drink and covered him. ²⁰He said to her, "Stand at the entrance of the tent, and if anybody comes and asks you, 'Is anyone here?' say, 'No.'" ²¹But Jael wife of Heber took a tent peg, and took a hammer in her hand, and went softly to him and drove the peg into his temple, until it went down into the ground—he

---

ᵏ Heb *from the Kain*   ˡ Heb adds *to the sword*; compare verse 16

DEBORAH *Multi-talented Woman*

WOMEN OFTEN GET OVERLOOKED IN the Old Testament, but Deborah is one spectacular exception. As a military leader, poet, prophet and judge, she used her talents to inspire Israel during a dark time.

Deborah won her fame leading a desperate nation to victory. With Israel under the thumb of a cruel foreign ruler, she gave orders for Barak to lead a revolt. He refused to go unless brave Deborah accompanied him to battle. With her giving the orders, Israel's ten thousand troops routed a better-equipped enemy. Deborah's triumph led to forty years of peace.

It is hard to think of an area in which Deborah did not excel. She was a mother and wife. Her wisdom was so renowned that people brought their disputes to her as she sat under a large palm tree, the Palm of Deborah. As a prophet, she had the ability to understand God's message and relay it to his people. When she sent Barak into battle, she stated it this way: "The LORD, the God of Israel, commands you . . ." (4.6).

Finally, Deborah was an accomplished poet, as chapter 5 demonstrates. One of the oldest and most expressive poems in the Bible, it was sung as a duet by Barak and Deborah, but the words give Deborah proper credit (5.7).

Throughout the Bible we can hardly find a more well-rounded leader, male or female, than Deborah.

Life Questions: In what areas could you strengthen your talents to become more well-rounded?

was lying fast asleep from weariness—and he died. 22Then, as Barak came in pursuit of Sisera, Jael went out to meet him, and said to him, "Come, and I will show you the man whom you are seeking." So he went into her tent; and there was Sisera lying dead, with the tent peg in his temple.

23 So on that day God subdued King Jabin of Canaan before the Israelites. 24Then the hand of the Israelites bore harder and harder on King Jabin of Canaan, until they destroyed King Jabin of Canaan.

The Song of Deborah

5 Then Deborah and Barak son of Abinoam sang on that day, saying:

2 "When locks are long in Israel,
     when the people offer themselves
          willingly—
     bless ^{m} the LORD!

3 "Hear, O kings; give ear, O princes;
     to the LORD I will sing,
     I will make melody to the LORD, the
          God of Israel.

4 "LORD, when you went out from Seir,
     when you marched from the region of
          Edom,
     the earth trembled,
     and the heavens poured,
     the clouds indeed poured water.
5 The mountains quaked before the LORD,
     the One of Sinai,
     before the LORD, the God of Israel.

6 "In the days of Shamgar son of Anath,
     in the days of Jael, caravans ceased
     and travelers kept to the byways.
7 The peasantry prospered in Israel,
     they grew fat on plunder,
     because you arose, Deborah,
     arose as a mother in Israel.
8 When new gods were chosen,
     then war was in the gates.
     Was shield or spear to be seen
     among forty thousand in Israel?
9 My heart goes out to the commanders of
          Israel
     who offered themselves willingly among
          the people.
     Bless the LORD.

10 "Tell of it, you who ride on white
          donkeys,
     you who sit on rich carpets ^{n}
     and you who walk by the way.

11 To the sound of musicians ^{n} at the
          watering places,
     there they repeat the triumphs of the
          LORD,
     the triumphs of his peasantry in Israel.

"Then down to the gates marched the
     people of the LORD.

12 "Awake, awake, Deborah!
     Awake, awake, utter a song!
     Arise, Barak, lead away your captives,
     O son of Abinoam.
13 Then down marched the remnant of the
          noble;
     the people of the LORD marched down
     for him ^{o} against the mighty.
14 From Ephraim they set out ^{p} into the
          valley, ^{q}
     following you, Benjamin, with your
          kin;
     from Machir marched down the
          commanders,
     and from Zebulun those who bear the
          marshal's staff;
15 the chiefs of Issachar came with Deborah,
     and Issachar faithful to Barak;
     into the valley they rushed out at his
          heels.
     Among the clans of Reuben
     there were great searchings of heart.
16 Why did you tarry among the sheepfolds,
     to hear the piping for the flocks?
     Among the clans of Reuben
     there were great searchings of heart.
17 Gilead stayed beyond the Jordan;
     and Dan, why did he abide with the
          ships?
     Asher sat still at the coast of the sea,
     settling down by his landings.
18 Zebulun is a people that scorned death;
     Naphtali too, on the heights of the
          field.

19 "The kings came, they fought;
     then fought the kings of Canaan,
     at Taanach, by the waters of Megiddo;
     they got no spoils of silver.
20 The stars fought from heaven,
     from their courses they fought against
          Sisera.
21 The torrent Kishon swept them away,
     the onrushing torrent, the torrent
          Kishon.
     March on, my soul, with might!

22 "Then loud beat the horses' hoofs

---

^{m} Or You who offer yourselves willingly among the people, bless ^{n} Meaning of Heb uncertain ^{o} Gk: Heb me
^{p} Cn: Heb From Ephraim their root ^{q} Gk: Heb in Amalek

with the galloping, galloping of his
steeds.

23 "Curse Meroz, says the angel of the LORD,
curse bitterly its inhabitants,
because they did not come to the help of
the LORD,
to the help of the LORD against the
mighty.

24 "Most blessed of women be Jael,
the wife of Heber the Kenite,
of tent-dwelling women most blessed.
25 He asked water and she gave him milk,
she brought him curds in a lordly
bowl.
26 She put her hand to the tent peg
and her right hand to the workmen's
mallet;
she struck Sisera a blow,
she crushed his head,
she shattered and pierced his temple.
27 He sank, he fell,
he lay still at her feet;
at her feet he sank, he fell;
where he sank, there he fell dead.

28 "Out of the window she peered,
the mother of Sisera gazed[r] through
the lattice:
'Why is his chariot so long in coming?
Why tarry the hoofbeats of his
chariots?'
29 Her wisest ladies make answer,
indeed, she answers the question
herself:
30 'Are they not finding and dividing the
spoil?—
A girl or two for every man;
spoil of dyed stuffs for Sisera,
spoil of dyed stuffs embroidered,
two pieces of dyed work embroidered
for my neck as spoil?'

31 "So perish all your enemies, O LORD!
But may your friends be like the sun as
it rises in its might."

And the land had rest forty years.

The Midianite Oppression

6 The Israelites did what was evil in the sight of
the LORD, and the LORD gave them into the
hand of Midian seven years. 2The hand of Midian
prevailed over Israel; and because of Midian the
Israelites provided for themselves hiding places
in the mountains, caves and strongholds. 3For
whenever the Israelites put in seed, the Midianites
and the Amalekites and the people of the east

would come up against them. 4They would encamp against them and destroy the produce of
the land, as far as the neighborhood of Gaza, and
leave no sustenance in Israel, and no sheep or ox
or donkey. 5For they and their livestock would
come up, and they would even bring their tents,
as thick as locusts; neither they nor their camels
could be counted; so they wasted the land as they

6.5 Camel Power

This is the earliest mention in the Bible of
camels used for military purposes. Midianite
marauders let the Israelites raise their crops,
then swept in and took everything when the
crops were ripe. With no effective defense, the
Israelites hid out in caves and other remote
spots.

came in. 6Thus Israel was greatly impoverished
because of Midian; and the Israelites cried out to
the LORD for help.

7 When the Israelites cried to the LORD on
account of the Midianites, 8the LORD sent a
prophet to the Israelites; and he said to them,
"Thus says the LORD, the God of Israel: I led you
up from Egypt, and brought you out of the house
of slavery; 9and I delivered you from the hand of
the Egyptians, and from the hand of all who oppressed you, and drove them out before you, and
gave you their land; 10and I said to you, 'I am the
LORD your God; you shall not pay reverence to
the gods of the Amorites, in whose land you live.'
But you have not given heed to my voice."

The Call of Gideon

11 Now the angel of the LORD came and sat
under the oak at Ophrah, which belonged to Joash the Abiezrite, as his son Gideon was beating
out wheat in the wine press, to hide it from the
Midianites. 12The angel of the LORD appeared to
him and said to him, "The LORD is with you, you
mighty warrior." 13Gideon answered him, "But
sir, if the LORD is with us, why then has all this
happened to us? And where are all his wonderful
deeds that our ancestors recounted to us, saying,
'Did not the LORD bring us up from Egypt?' But
now the LORD has cast us off, and given us into
the hand of Midian." 14Then the LORD turned to
him and said, "Go in this might of yours and
deliver Israel from the hand of Midian; I hereby
commission you." 15He responded, "But sir, how
can I deliver Israel? My clan is the weakest in
Manasseh, and I am the least in my family." 16The
LORD said to him, "But I will be with you, and you
shall strike down the Midianites, every one of
them." 17Then he said to him, "If now I have

r Gk Compare Tg: Heb exclaimed

found favor with you, then show me a sign that it is you who speak with me. [18]Do not depart from here until I come to you, and bring out my present, and set it before you." And he said, "I will stay until you return."

19 So Gideon went into his house and prepared a kid, and unleavened cakes from an ephah of flour; the meat he put in a basket, and the broth he put in a pot, and brought them to him under the oak and presented them. [20]The angel of God said to him, "Take the meat and the unleavened cakes, and put them on this rock, and pour out the broth." And he did so. [21]Then the angel of the LORD reached out the tip of the staff that was in his hand, and touched the meat and the unleavened cakes; and fire sprang up from the rock

and consumed the meat and the unleavened cakes; and the angel of the LORD vanished from his sight. [22]Then Gideon perceived that it was the angel of the LORD; and Gideon said, "Help me, Lord GOD! For I have seen the angel of the LORD face to face." [23]But the LORD said to him, "Peace be to you; do not fear, you shall not die." [24]Then Gideon built an altar there to the LORD, and called it, The LORD is peace. To this day it still stands at Ophrah, which belongs to the Abiezrites.

25 That night the LORD said to him, "Take your father's bull, the second bull seven years old, and pull down the altar of Baal that belongs to your father, and cut down the sacred pole[s] that is beside it; [26]and build an altar to the LORD your God on the top of the stronghold here, in proper

s Heb *Asherah*

Unlikely Leaders
God drew out Gideon's hidden potential

> The LORD said to him, "Peace be to you; do not fear, you shall not die." 6.23

GIDEON MADE AN UNLIKELY FIGHTER—HESITANT and fearful. We first meet him as he furtively threshed wheat in a winepress. To thresh wheat openly was to invite the occupying Midianite army to confiscate it. The Midianites dominated Israel so thoroughly that Israelites could rarely harvest crops; some lived in caves.

Gideon was planning no heroics until the angel of the Lord came to him with a battle commission. "Who, me?" Gideon seemed to ask, trembling.

In view of the facts, his doubts were justified. His family and village worshiped Baal, not the Lord. He himself was subject to paralyzing fears, even on the eve of battle. Gideon kept demanding miraculous proof that God really was with him—and one miracle was not enough.

At the same time, God seemed to make Gideon's job more formidable. He reduced his army from 32,000 to a pitiful 300. If an army so outnumbered were to win, that would prove beyond a doubt that God was in charge.

God knew Gideon's potential and patiently brought Gideon to the point of courage. He encouraged him, directed him, transformed him. Overnight Gideon became a strong and decisive general. He used noise and lights for scare tactics, enabling his small band to scatter the enemy. Thorough mopping-up operations followed. The little army devastated the scattered Midianites, and Gideon, triumphant, brought in an era of freedom. Perhaps no one was as surprised as he.

Cast-off Material

The selection of Gideon shows a pattern. At a time when women were regarded as second-class citizens (see 9.54; 19.24), God chose Deborah to lead. Jephthah, another judge, had been a social outcast, the leader of a gang of outlaws, before God chose him to lead.

And the pattern is found not only in Judges. Throughout the Bible, God used cast-off material. Israel was not chosen because of its great size or sophistication. (In fact, archaeologists report a drop in the culture of a city after the Israelites captured it.) God did not seek the most capable people, nor the most naturally "good." He chose a small, weak slave tribe, uncultured, with a short memory for his kindness to them. Time and again the Israelites proved themselves faulty. So did their leaders. With this unlikely material God did great things so the world could see that the glory was his and his alone.

Paul took up this theme when he wrote, over a thousand years later, "Consider your own call, brothers and sisters: not many of you were wise by human standards, not many were powerful, not many were of noble birth. But God chose what is foolish in the world to shame the wise; God chose what is weak in the world to shame the strong . . . in order that, as it is written, 'Let the one who boasts, boast in the Lord' " (1 Corinthians 1.26–31).

Life Questions: Do you picture yourself as a leader? Why or why not? What would God have to change to make you a leader?

order; then take the second bull, and offer it as a burnt offering with the wood of the sacred pole[t] that you shall cut down." 27So Gideon took ten of his servants, and did as the LORD had told him; but because he was too afraid of his family and the townspeople to do it by day, he did it by night.

Gideon Destroys the Altar of Baal

28 When the townspeople rose early in the morning, the altar of Baal was broken down, and the sacred pole[t] beside it was cut down, and the second bull was offered on the altar that had been built. 29So they said to one another, "Who has done this?" After searching and inquiring, they were told, "Gideon son of Joash did it." 30Then the townspeople said to Joash, "Bring out your son, so that he may die, for he has pulled down the altar of Baal and cut down the sacred pole[t]

6.30 Topsy-turvy

Israel had turned God's commands upside down. According to Deuteronomy 13.6–10, those who worshiped idols should be stoned. But here Israelites were ready to execute Gideon for destroying their idols.

beside it." 31But Joash said to all who were arrayed against him, "Will you contend for Baal? Or will you defend his cause? Whoever contends for him shall be put to death by morning. If he is a god, let him contend for himself, because his altar has been pulled down." 32Therefore on that day Gideon[u] was called Jerubbaal, that is to say, "Let Baal contend against him," because he pulled down his altar.

33 Then all the Midianites and the Amalekites and the people of the east came together, and crossing the Jordan they encamped in the Valley of Jezreel. 34But the spirit of the LORD took possession of Gideon; and he sounded the trumpet, and the Abiezrites were called out to follow him. 35He sent messengers throughout all Manasseh, and they too were called out to follow him. He also sent messengers to Asher, Zebulun, and Naphtali, and they went up to meet them.

The Sign of the Fleece

36 Then Gideon said to God, "In order to see whether you will deliver Israel by my hand, as you have said, 37I am going to lay a fleece of wool on the threshing floor; if there is dew on the fleece alone, and it is dry on all the ground, then I shall know that you will deliver Israel by my hand, as you have said." 38And it was so. When he rose early next morning and squeezed the fleece, he wrung enough dew from the fleece to fill a bowl

with water. 39Then Gideon said to God, "Do not let your anger burn against me, let me speak one more time; let me, please, make trial with the fleece just once more; let it be dry only on the

6.37 Putting Out a Fleece

How much proof of God's will does one person need? Though the angel of the Lord had assured Gideon of success, he took fright and wanted to double-check, then triple-check, by asking for miracles. In some circles today, "putting out a fleece" has come to mean asking God to do something unusual to confirm his guidance. However, Gideon's action seems more like a lack of faith than a model of seeking God's guidance.

fleece, and on all the ground let there be dew." 40And God did so that night. It was dry on the fleece only, and on all the ground there was dew.

Gideon Surprises and Routs the Midianites

7 Then Jerubbaal (that is, Gideon) and all the troops that were with him rose early and encamped beside the spring of Harod; and the camp of Midian was north of them, below[v] the hill of Moreh, in the valley.

2 The LORD said to Gideon, "The troops with you are too many for me to give the Midianites into their hand. Israel would only take the credit away from me, saying, 'My own hand has delivered me.' 3Now therefore proclaim this in the hearing of the troops, 'Whoever is fearful and trembling, let him return home.'" Thus Gideon sifted them out;[w] twenty-two thousand returned, and ten thousand remained.

4 Then the LORD said to Gideon, "The troops are still too many; take them down to the water and I will sift them out for you there. When I say, 'This one shall go with you,' he shall go with you; and when I say, 'This one shall not go with you,' he shall not go." 5So he brought the troops down to the water; and the LORD said to Gideon, "All those who lap the water with their tongues, as a dog laps, you shall put to one side; all those who kneel down to drink, putting their hands to their mouths,[x] you shall put to the other side." 6The number of those that lapped was three hundred; but all the rest of the troops knelt down to drink water. 7Then the LORD said to Gideon, "With the three hundred that lapped I will deliver you, and give the Midianites into your hand. Let all the others go to their homes." 8So he took the jars of

---

[t] Heb *Asherah*   [u] Heb *he*   [v] Heb *from*   [w] Cn: Heb *home, and depart from Mount Gilead'*   [x] Heb places the words *putting their hands to their mouths* after the word *lapped* in verse 6

the troops from their hands,[y] and their trumpets; and he sent all the rest of Israel back to their own tents, but retained the three hundred. The camp of Midian was below him in the valley.

9 That same night the LORD said to him, "Get up, attack the camp; for I have given it into your hand. [10]But if you fear to attack, go down to the camp with your servant Purah; [11]and you shall hear what they say, and afterward your hands shall be strengthened to attack the camp." Then he went down with his servant Purah to the outposts of the armed men that were in the camp. [12]The Midianites and the Amalekites and all the people of the east lay along the valley as thick as locusts; and their camels were without number, countless as the sand on the seashore. [13]When Gideon arrived, there was a man telling a dream to his comrade; and he said, "I had a dream, and in it a cake of barley bread tumbled into the camp of Midian, and came to the tent, and struck it so that it fell; it turned upside down, and the tent collapsed." [14]And his comrade answered, "This is no other than the sword of Gideon son of Joash, a man of Israel; into his hand God has given Midian and all the army."

15 When Gideon heard the telling of the dream and its interpretation, he worshiped; and he returned to the camp of Israel, and said, "Get up; for the LORD has given the army of Midian into your hand." [16]After he divided the three hundred men into three companies, and put trumpets into the hands of all of them, and empty jars, with torches inside the jars, [17]he said to them, "Look at me, and do the same; when I come to the outskirts of the camp, do as I do. [18]When I blow the trumpet, I and all who are with me, then you also blow the trumpets around the whole camp, and shout, 'For the LORD and for Gideon!'"

19 So Gideon and the hundred who were with him came to the outskirts of the camp at the beginning of the middle watch, when they had just set the watch; and they blew the trumpets and smashed the jars that were in their hands. [20]So the three companies blew the trumpets and broke the jars, holding in their left hands the torches, and in their right hands the trumpets to blow; and they cried, "A sword for the LORD and for Gideon!" [21]Every man stood in his place all around the camp, and all the men in camp ran; they cried out and fled. [22]When they blew the three hundred trumpets, the LORD set every man's sword against his fellow and against all the army; and the army fled as far as Beth-shittah toward Zererah,[z] as far as the border of Abel-meholah, by Tabbath. [23]And the men of Israel were called out from Naphtali and from Asher and from all Manasseh, and they pursued after the Midianites.

24 Then Gideon sent messengers throughout all the hill country of Ephraim, saying, "Come down against the Midianites and seize the waters against them, as far as Beth-barah, and also the Jordan." So all the men of Ephraim were called out, and they seized the waters as far as Beth-barah, and also the Jordan. [25]They captured the two captains of Midian, Oreb and Zeeb; they killed Oreb at the rock of Oreb, and Zeeb they killed at the wine press of Zeeb, as they pursued the Midianites. They brought the heads of Oreb and Zeeb to Gideon beyond the Jordan.

Gideon's Triumph and Vengeance

8 Then the Ephraimites said to him, "What have you done to us, not to call us when you went to fight against the Midianites?" And they upbraided him violently. [2]So he said to them, "What have I done now in comparison with you? Is not the gleaning of the grapes of Ephraim better than the vintage of Abiezer? [3]God has given into your hands the captains of Midian, Oreb and Zeeb; what have I been able to do in comparison with you?" When he said this, their anger against him subsided.

4 Then Gideon came to the Jordan and crossed over, he and the three hundred who were with him, exhausted and famished.[a] [5]So he said to the people of Succoth, "Please give some loaves of bread to my followers, for they are exhausted, and I am pursuing Zebah and Zalmunna, the kings of Midian." [6]But the officials of Succoth said, "Do you already have in your possession the hands of Zebah and Zalmunna, that we should give bread to your army?" [7]Gideon replied, "Well then, when the LORD has given Zebah and Zalmunna into my hand, I will trample your flesh on the thorns of the wilderness and on briers." [8]From there he went up to Penuel, and made the same request of them; and the people of Penuel answered him as the people of Succoth had answered. [9]So he said to the people of Penuel, "When I come back victorious, I will break down this tower."

10 Now Zebah and Zalmunna were in Karkor with their army, about fifteen thousand men, all who were left of all the army of the people of the east; for one hundred twenty thousand men bearing arms had fallen. [11]So Gideon went up by the caravan route east of Nobah and Jogbehah, and attacked the army; for the army was off its guard. [12]Zebah and Zalmunna fled; and he pursued them and took the two kings of Midian, Zebah and Zalmunna, and threw all the army into a panic.

13 When Gideon son of Joash returned from the battle by the ascent of Heres, [14]he caught a young man, one of the people of Succoth, and questioned him; and he listed for him the officials and elders of Succoth, seventy-seven people. [15]Then he came to the people of Succoth, and said, "Here are Zebah and Zalmunna, about

---

[y] Cn: Heb *So the people took provisions in their hands*   [z] Another reading is *Zeredah*   [a] Gk: Heb *pursuing*

whom you taunted me, saying, 'Do you already have in your possession the hands of Zebah and Zalmunna, that we should give bread to your troops who are exhausted?'" [16]So he took the elders of the city and he took thorns of the wilderness and briers and with them he trampled[b] the people of Succoth. [17]He also broke down the tower of Penuel, and killed the men of the city.

18 Then he said to Zebah and Zalmunna, "What about the men whom you killed at Tabor?" They answered, "As you are, so were they, every one of them; they resembled the sons of a king." [19]And he replied, "They were my brothers, the sons of my mother; as the LORD lives, if you had saved them alive, I would not kill you." [20]So he said to Jether his firstborn, "Go kill them!" But the boy did not draw his sword, for he was afraid, because he was still a boy. [21]Then Zebah and Zalmunna said, "You come and kill us; for as the man is, so is his strength." So Gideon proceeded to kill Zebah and Zalmunna; and he took the crescents that were on the necks of their camels.

Gideon's Idolatry

22 Then the Israelites said to Gideon, "Rule over us, you and your son and your grandson also; for you have delivered us out of the hand of Midian." [23]Gideon said to them, "I will not rule over you, and my son will not rule over you; the LORD will rule over you." [24]Then Gideon said to them, "Let me make a request of you; each of you

8.14 Early Literacy

Some scholars argue that much of the Old Testament was handed down by word of mouth and only written at a much later time. This brief mention of a young man's ability to write suggests that literacy was widespread even at this early date—and thus that the Old Testament books could have been written soon after the events they describe.

8.23 No King

Unlike most nations of this time, Israel had no king. Gideon, declining an opportunity to rule, explains why: God alone must rule. Generations later, when Israel insisted on royal leadership, Samuel interpreted the move as a rejection of God (1 Samuel 10.19).

Even after Israel gained a king, the king's power had limits; rulers answered to God, the ultimate ruler. That was a novel idea in an era when people worshiped kings as gods.

give me an earring he has taken as booty." (For the enemy[c] had golden earrings, because they were Ishmaelites.) [25]"We will willingly give them," they answered. So they spread a garment, and each threw into it an earring he had taken as booty. [26]The weight of the golden earrings that he requested was one thousand seven hundred shekels of gold (apart from the crescents and the pendants and the purple garments worn by the kings of Midian, and the collars that were on the necks of their camels). [27]Gideon made an ephod of it and put it in his town, in Ophrah; and all Israel prostituted themselves to it there, and it became a snare to Gideon and to his family. [28]So Midian was subdued before the Israelites, and they lifted up their heads no more. So the land had rest forty years in the days of Gideon.

Death of Gideon

29 Jerubbaal son of Joash went to live in his own house. [30]Now Gideon had seventy sons, his own offspring, for he had many wives. [31]His concubine who was in Shechem also bore him a son, and he named him Abimelech. [32]Then Gideon son of Joash died at a good old age, and was buried in the tomb of his father Joash at Ophrah of the Abiezrites.

33 As soon as Gideon died, the Israelites relapsed and prostituted themselves with the Baals, making Baal-berith their god. [34]The Israelites did not remember the LORD their God, who had rescued them from the hand of all their enemies on every side; [35]and they did not exhibit loyalty to the house of Jerubbaal (that is, Gideon) in return for all the good that he had done to Israel.

Abimelech Attempts to Establish a Monarchy

9 Now Abimelech son of Jerubbaal went to Shechem to his mother's kinsfolk and said to them and to the whole clan of his mother's family, [2]"Say in the hearing of all the lords of Shechem, 'Which is better for you, that all seventy of the sons of Jerubbaal rule over you, or that one rule over you?' Remember also that I am your bone and your flesh." [3]So his mother's kinsfolk spoke all these words on his behalf in the hearing of all the lords of Shechem; and their hearts inclined to follow Abimelech, for they said, "He is our brother." [4]They gave him seventy pieces of silver out of the temple of Baal-berith with which Abimelech hired worthless and reckless fellows, who followed him. [5]He went to his father's house at Ophrah, and killed his brothers the sons of Jerubbaal, seventy men, on one stone; but Jotham, the youngest son of Jerubbaal, survived, for he hid himself. [6]Then all the lords of Shechem and all Beth-millo came together, and they went and made Abimelech king, by the oak of the pillar[d] at Shechem.

---

[b] With verse 7, Compare Gk: Heb *he taught*   [c] Heb *they*   [d] Cn: Meaning of Heb uncertain

The Parable of the Trees

7 When it was told to Jotham, he went and stood on the top of Mount Gerizim, and cried aloud and said to them, "Listen to me, you lords of Shechem, so that God may listen to you.

8 The trees once went out
> to anoint a king over themselves.
> So they said to the olive tree,
> 'Reign over us.'

9 The olive tree answered them,
> 'Shall I stop producing my rich
> oil
> by which gods and mortals
> are honored,
> and go to sway over the trees?'

10 Then the trees said to the fig tree,
> 'You come and reign over us.'

11 But the fig tree answered them,
> 'Shall I stop producing my sweetness
> and my delicious fruit,
> and go to sway over the trees?'

12 Then the trees said to the vine,
> 'You come and reign over us.'

13 But the vine said to them,
> 'Shall I stop producing my wine
> that cheers gods and mortals,
> and go to sway over the trees?'

14 So all the trees said to the bramble,
> 'You come and reign over us.'

15 And the bramble said to the trees,
> 'If in good faith you are anointing me
> king over you,
> then come and take refuge in my
> shade;
> but if not, let fire come out of the
> bramble
> and devour the cedars of Lebanon.'

16 "Now therefore, if you acted in good faith and honor when you made Abimelech king, and if you have dealt well with Jerubbaal and his house, and have done to him as his actions deserved— 17for my father fought for you, and risked his life, and rescued you from the hand of Midian; 18but you have risen up against my father's house this day, and have killed his sons, seventy men on one stone, and have made Abimelech, the son of his slave woman, king over the lords of Shechem, because he is your kinsman— 19if, I say, you have acted in good faith and honor with Jerubbaal and with his house this day, then rejoice in Abimelech, and let him also rejoice in you; 20but if not, let fire come out from Abimelech, and devour the lords of Shechem, and Beth-millo; and let fire come out from the lords of Shechem, and from Beth-millo, and devour Abimelech." 21Then Jotham ran away and fled, going to Beer, where he remained for fear of his brother Abimelech.

The Downfall of Abimelech

22 Abimelech ruled over Israel three years. 23But God sent an evil spirit between Abimelech and the lords of Shechem; and the lords of Shechem dealt treacherously with Abimelech. 24This happened so that the violence done to the seventy

9.23 Evil Spirit

The "evil spirit" God sent was not necessarily a supernatural being. "Spirit" means literally "wind" or "breath" in the Bible, and this comment might be translated, "God sent an ill wind." Perhaps an attitude of bitterness or distrust grew up between Abimelech and the people of Shechem. Characteristically, the Bible attributes this development to God, though human causes were probably involved as well.

sons of Jerubbaal might be avenged[e] and their blood be laid on their brother Abimelech, who killed them, and on the lords of Shechem, who strengthened his hands to kill his brothers. 25So, out of hostility to him, the lords of Shechem set ambushes on the mountain tops. They robbed all who passed by them along that way; and it was reported to Abimelech.

26 When Gaal son of Ebed moved into Shechem with his kinsfolk, the lords of Shechem put confidence in him. 27They went out into the field and gathered the grapes from their vineyards, trod them, and celebrated. Then they went into the temple of their god, ate and drank, and ridiculed Abimelech. 28Gaal son of Ebed said, "Who is Abimelech, and who are we of Shechem, that we should serve him? Did not the son of Jerubbaal and Zebul his officer serve the men of Hamor father of Shechem? Why then should we serve him? 29If only this people were under my command! Then I would remove Abimelech; I would say[f] to him, 'Increase your army, and come out.'"

30 When Zebul the ruler of the city heard the words of Gaal son of Ebed, his anger was kindled. 31He sent messengers to Abimelech at Arumah,[g] saying, "Look, Gaal son of Ebed and his kinsfolk have come to Shechem, and they are stirring up[h] the city against you. 32Now therefore, go by night, you and the troops that are with you, and lie in wait in the fields. 33Then early in the morning, as soon as the sun rises, get up and rush on the city; and when he and the troops that are with him come out against you, you may deal with them as best you can."

34 So Abimelech and all the troops with him got up by night and lay in wait against Shechem in four companies. 35When Gaal son of Ebed

e Heb *might come* f Gk: Heb *and he said* g Cn See 9.41. Heb *Tormah* h Cn: Heb *are besieging*

went out and stood in the entrance of the gate of the city, Abimelech and the troops with him rose from the ambush. ³⁶And when Gaal saw them, he said to Zebul, "Look, people are coming down from the mountain tops!" And Zebul said to him, "The shadows on the mountains look like people to you." ³⁷Gaal spoke again and said, "Look, people are coming down from Tabbur-erez, and one company is coming from the direction of Elon-meonenim."ⁱ ³⁸Then Zebul said to him, "Where is your boastʲ now, you who said, 'Who is Abimelech, that we should serve him?' Are not these the troops you made light of? Go out now and fight with them." ³⁹So Gaal went out at the head of the lords of Shechem, and fought with Abimelech. ⁴⁰Abimelech chased him, and he fled before him. Many fell wounded, up to the entrance of the gate. ⁴¹So Abimelech resided at Arumah; and Zebul drove out Gaal and his kinsfolk, so that they could not live on at Shechem.

42 On the following day the people went out into the fields. When Abimelech was told, ⁴³he took his troops and divided them into three companies, and lay in wait in the fields. When he looked and saw the people coming out of the city, he rose against them and killed them. ⁴⁴Abimelech and the company that wasᵏ with him rushed forward and stood at the entrance of the gate of the city, while the two companies rushed on all who were in the fields and killed them. ⁴⁵Abimelech fought against the city all that day; he took the city, and killed the people that were in it; and he razed the city and sowed it with salt.

46 When all the lords of the Tower of Shechem heard of it, they entered the stronghold of the temple of El-berith. ⁴⁷Abimelech was told that all the lords of the Tower of Shechem were gathered together. ⁴⁸So Abimelech went up to Mount Zalmon, he and all the troops that were with him. Abimelech took an ax in his hand, cut down a bundle of brushwood, and took it up and laid it on his shoulder. Then he said to the troops with him, "What you have seen me do, do quickly, as I have done." ⁴⁹So every one of the troops cut down a bundle and following Abimelech put it against the stronghold, and they set the stronghold on fire over them, so that all the people of the Tower of Shechem also died, about a thousand men and women.

50 Then Abimelech went to Thebez, and encamped against Thebez, and took it. ⁵¹But there was a strong tower within the city, and all the men and women and all the lords of the city fled to it and shut themselves in; and they went to the roof of the tower. ⁵²Abimelech came to the tower, and fought against it, and came near to the entrance of the tower to burn it with fire. ⁵³But a certain woman threw an upper millstone on Abimelech's head, and crushed his skull. ⁵⁴Immediately he

called to the young man who carried his armor and said to him, "Draw your sword and kill me, so people will not say about me, 'A woman killed him.'" So the young man thrust him through,

9.54 Sexist Attitudes

Abimelech preferred dying immediately to having it said that a woman killed him. Sexist attitudes clearly prevailed in the time of the judges, but nevertheless women made their marks, both good and bad. Here and in the story of Jael (4.21), women used domestic implements to kill dangerous men. (Grinding grain with millstones and setting up tents with pegs were traditionally considered "women's work.") Deborah, a judge and general, and Delilah, who seduced Samson, used their wits for good and evil, respectively.

and he died. ⁵⁵When the Israelites saw that Abimelech was dead, they all went home. ⁵⁶Thus God repaid Abimelech for the crime he committed against his father in killing his seventy brothers; ⁵⁷and God also made all the wickedness of the people of Shechem fall back on their heads, and on them came the curse of Jotham son of Jerubbaal.

Tola and Jair

10 After Abimelech, Tola son of Puah son of Dodo, a man of Issachar, who lived at Shamir in the hill country of Ephraim, rose to deliver Israel. ²He judged Israel twenty-three years. Then he died, and was buried at Shamir.

3 After him came Jair the Gileadite, who judged Israel twenty-two years. ⁴He had thirty sons who rode on thirty donkeys; and they had thirty towns, which are in the land of Gilead, and are called Havvoth-jair to this day. ⁵Jair died, and was buried in Kamon.

Oppression by the Ammonites

6 The Israelites again did what was evil in the sight of the LORD, worshiping the Baals and the Astartes, the gods of Aram, the gods of Sidon, the gods of Moab, the gods of the Ammonites, and the gods of the Philistines. Thus they abandoned the LORD, and did not worship him. ⁷So the anger of the LORD was kindled against Israel, and he sold them into the hand of the Philistines and into the hand of the Ammonites, ⁸and they crushed and oppressed the Israelites that year. For eighteen years they oppressed all the Israelites that were beyond the Jordan in the land of the Amorites, which is in Gilead. ⁹The Ammonites also crossed the Jordan to fight against Judah and

ⁱ That is *Diviners' Oak*   ʲ Heb *mouth*   ᵏ Vg and some Gk Mss: Heb *companies that were*

against Benjamin and against the house of Ephraim; so that Israel was greatly distressed.

10 So the Israelites cried to the LORD, saying, "We have sinned against you, because we have abandoned our God and have worshiped the Baals." 11And the LORD said to the Israelites, "Did I not deliver you*l* from the Egyptians and from the Amorites, from the Ammonites and from the Philistines? 12The Sidonians also, and the Amalekites, and the Maonites, oppressed you; and you cried to me, and I delivered you out of their hand. 13Yet you have abandoned me and worshiped other gods; therefore I will deliver you no more. 14Go and cry to the gods whom you have chosen; let them deliver you in the time of your distress." 15And the Israelites said to the LORD, "We have sinned; do to us whatever seems good to you; but deliver us this day!" 16So they put away the foreign gods from among them and worshiped the LORD; and he could no longer bear to see Israel suffer.

17 Then the Ammonites were called to arms, and they encamped in Gilead; and the Israelites came together, and they encamped at Mizpah. 18The commanders of the people of Gilead said to one another, "Who will begin the fight against the Ammonites? He shall be head over all the inhabitants of Gilead."

Jephthah

11 Now Jephthah the Gileadite, the son of a prostitute, was a mighty warrior. Gilead was the father of Jephthah. 2Gilead's wife also bore him sons; and when his wife's sons grew up, they drove Jephthah away, saying to him, "You shall not inherit anything in our father's house; for you are the son of another woman." 3Then Jephthah fled from his brothers and lived in the land of Tob. Outlaws collected around Jephthah and went raiding with him.

4 After a time the Ammonites made war against Israel. 5And when the Ammonites made war against Israel, the elders of Gilead went to bring Jephthah from the land of Tob. 6They said to Jephthah, "Come and be our commander, so that we may fight with the Ammonites." 7But Jephthah said to the elders of Gilead, "Are you not the very ones who rejected me and drove me out of my father's house? So why do you come to me now when you are in trouble?" 8The elders of Gilead said to Jephthah, "Nevertheless, we have now turned back to you, so that you may go with us and fight with the Ammonites, and become head over us, over all the inhabitants of Gilead." 9Jephthah said to the elders of Gilead, "If you bring me home again to fight with the Ammonites, and the LORD gives them over to me, I will be your head." 10And the elders of Gilead said to Jephthah, "The LORD will be witness between us;

we will surely do as you say." 11So Jephthah went with the elders of Gilead, and the people made him head and commander over them; and Jephthah spoke all his words before the LORD at Mizpah.

11.6 A Man Like David

Jephthah, like King David to come, was an outlaw who gained leadership experience at the head of a small band of adventurers. Israel turned to him when they needed military leadership, as they later would turn to David. Yet Jephthah's reputation never equaled David's, and the reason must have had something to do with his lack of wisdom. His rash vow to God (verse 31) and his harsh answer to a complaint (12.3) each had destructive results.

12 Then Jephthah sent messengers to the king of the Ammonites and said, "What is there between you and me, that you have come to me to fight against my land?" 13The king of the Ammonites answered the messengers of Jephthah, "Because Israel, on coming from Egypt, took away my land from the Arnon to the Jabbok and to the Jordan; now therefore restore it peaceably." 14Once again Jephthah sent messengers to the king of the Ammonites 15and said to him: "Thus says Jephthah: Israel did not take away the land of Moab or the land of the Ammonites, 16but when they came up from Egypt, Israel went through the wilderness to the Red Sea*m* and came to Kadesh. 17Israel then sent messengers to the king of Edom, saying, 'Let us pass through your land'; but the king of Edom would not listen. They also sent to the king of Moab, but he would not consent. So Israel remained at Kadesh. 18Then they journeyed through the wilderness, went around the land of Edom and the land of Moab, arrived on the east side of the land of Moab, and camped on the other side of the Arnon. They did not enter the territory of Moab, for the Arnon was the boundary of Moab. 19Israel then sent messengers to King Sihon of the Amorites, king of Heshbon; and Israel said to him, 'Let us pass through your land to our country.' 20But Sihon did not trust Israel to pass through his territory; so Sihon gathered all his people together, and encamped at Jahaz, and fought with Israel. 21Then the LORD, the God of Israel, gave Sihon and all his people into the hand of Israel, and they defeated them; so Israel occupied all the land of the Amorites, who inhabited that country. 22They occupied all the territory of the Amorites from the Arnon to the Jabbok and from the wilderness to the Jordan. 23So now the LORD, the God of Israel, has conquered the Amo-

---

l Heb lacks *Did I not deliver you*   *m* Or *Sea of Reeds* rites for the benefit of his people Israel. Do you intend to take their place? 24Should you not possess what your god Chemosh gives you to possess? And should we not be the ones to possess everything that the LORD our God has conquered for our benefit? 25Now are you any better than King Balak son of Zippor of Moab? Did he ever enter into conflict with Israel, or did he ever go to war with them? 26While Israel lived in Heshbon and its villages, and in Aroer and its villages, and in all the towns that are along the Arnon, three hundred years, why did you not recover them within that time? 27It is not I who have sinned against you, but you are the one who does me wrong by making war on me. Let the LORD, who is judge, decide today for the Israelites or for the Ammonites." 28But the king of the Ammonites did not heed the message that Jephthah sent him.

Jephthah's Vow

29 Then the spirit of the LORD came upon Jephthah, and he passed through Gilead and Manasseh. He passed on to Mizpah of Gilead, and from Mizpah of Gilead he passed on to the Ammonites. 30And Jephthah made a vow to the LORD, and said, "If you will give the Ammonites into my hand, 31then whoever comes out of the doors of my house to meet me, when I return victorious from the Ammonites, shall be the LORD's, to be offered up by me as a burnt offering." 32So Jephthah crossed over to the Ammonites to fight against them; and the LORD gave them into his hand. 33He inflicted a massive defeat on them from Aroer to the neighborhood of Minnith, twenty towns, and as far as Abel-keramim. So the Ammonites were subdued before the people of Israel.

Jephthah's Daughter

34 Then Jephthah came to his home at Mizpah; and there was his daughter coming out to meet him with timbrels and with dancing. She was his only child; he had no son or daughter except her. 35When he saw her, he tore his clothes, and said, "Alas, my daughter! You have brought me very low; you have become the cause of great trouble to me. For I have opened my mouth to the LORD, and I cannot take back my vow." 36She said to him, "My father, if you have opened your mouth to the LORD, do to me according to what has gone out of your mouth, now that the LORD has given you vengeance against your enemies, the Ammonites." 37And she said to her father, "Let this thing be done for me: Grant me two months, so that I may go and wander[n] on the mountains, and bewail my virginity, my companions and I." 38"Go," he said and sent her away for two months. So she departed, she and her com-

panions, and bewailed her virginity on the mountains. 39At the end of two months, she returned to her father, who did with her according to the vow he had made. She had never slept with a man. So there arose an Israelite custom that 40for four days every year the daughters of Israel would go out to lament the daughter of Jephthah the Gileadite.

Intertribal Dissension

12 The men of Ephraim were called to arms, and they crossed to Zaphon and said to Jephthah, "Why did you cross over to fight against the Ammonites, and did not call us to go with you? We will burn your house down over

12.1 A Soft Answer

"A soft answer turns away wrath," says Proverbs 15.1. Compare Jephthah's answer to the men of Ephraim with Gideon's softer response to the same complaint in Judges 8.1–3. In Gideon's case, anger subsided. In this, civil war resulted, and 42,000 Israelites died.

you!" 2Jephthah said to them, "My people and I were engaged in conflict with the Ammonites who oppressed us[o] severely. But when I called you, you did not deliver me from their hand. 3When I saw that you would not deliver me, I took my life in my hand, and crossed over against the Ammonites, and the LORD gave them into my hand. Why then have you come up to me this day, to fight against me?" 4Then Jephthah gathered all the men of Gilead and fought with Ephraim; and the men of Gilead defeated Ephraim, because they said, "You are fugitives from Ephraim, you Gileadites—in the heart of Ephraim and Manasseh."[p] 5Then the Gileadites took the fords of the Jordan against the Ephraimites. Whenever one of the fugitives of Ephraim said, "Let me go over," the men of Gilead would say to him, "Are you an Ephraimite?" When he said, "No," 6they said to him, "Then say Shibboleth," and he said, "Sibboleth," for he could not pronounce it right. Then they seized him and killed him at the fords of the Jordan. Forty-two thousand of the Ephraimites fell at that time.

7 Jephthah judged Israel six years. Then Jephthah the Gileadite died, and was buried in his town in Gilead.[q]

Ibzan, Elon, and Abdon

8 After him Ibzan of Bethlehem judged Israel. 9He had thirty sons. He gave his thirty daughters in marriage outside his clan and brought in thirty young women from outside for his sons. He

---

[n] Cn: Heb *go down because . . . Manasseh*   [o] Gk OL, Syr H: Heb lacks *who oppressed us*   [p] Meaning of Heb uncertain: Gk omits
[q] Gk: Heb *in the towns of Gilead*

judged Israel seven years. ¹⁰Then Ibzan died, and was buried at Bethlehem.

11 After him Elon the Zebulunite judged Israel; and he judged Israel ten years. ¹²Then Elon the Zebulunite died, and was buried at Aijalon in the land of Zebulun.

13 After him Abdon son of Hillel the Pirathonite judged Israel. ¹⁴He had forty sons and thirty grandsons, who rode on seventy donkeys; he judged Israel eight years. ¹⁵Then Abdon son of Hillel the Pirathonite died, and was buried at Pirathon in the land of Ephraim, in the hill country of the Amalekites.

The Birth of Samson

13 The Israelites again did what was evil in the sight of the LORD, and the LORD gave them into the hand of the Philistines forty years.

2 There was a certain man of Zorah, of the tribe of the Danites, whose name was Manoah. His wife was barren, having borne no children. ³And the angel of the LORD appeared to the woman and said to her, "Although you are barren, having borne no children, you shall conceive and bear a son. ⁴Now be careful not to drink wine or strong drink, or to eat anything unclean, ⁵for you shall conceive and bear a son. No razor is to come on his head, for the boy shall be a nazirite^r to God from birth. It is he who shall begin to deliver Israel from the hand of the Philistines." ⁶Then the woman came and told her husband, "A man of God came to me, and his appearance was like that of an angel^s of God, most awe-inspiring; I did not ask him where he came from, and he did not tell me his name; ⁷but he said to me, 'You shall conceive and bear a son. So then drink no wine or strong drink, and eat nothing unclean, for the boy shall be a nazirite^r to God from birth to the day of his death.'"

8 Then Manoah entreated the LORD, and said, "O LORD, I pray, let the man of God whom you sent come to us again and teach us what we are to do concerning the boy who will be born." ⁹God listened to Manoah, and the angel of God came again to the woman as she sat in the field; but her husband Manoah was not with her. ¹⁰So the woman ran quickly and told her husband, "The man who came to me the other day has appeared to me." ¹¹Manoah got up and followed his wife, and came to the man and said to him, "Are you the man who spoke to this woman?" And he said, "I am." ¹²Then Manoah said, "Now when your words come true, what is to be the boy's rule of life; what is he to do?" ¹³The angel of the LORD said to Manoah, "Let the woman give heed to all that I said to her. ¹⁴She may not eat of anything that comes from the vine. She is not to drink wine or strong drink, or eat any unclean thing. She is to observe everything that I commanded her."

15 Manoah said to the angel of the LORD, "Allow us to detain you, and prepare a kid for you." ¹⁶The angel of the LORD said to Manoah, "If you detain me, I will not eat your food; but if you want to prepare a burnt offering, then offer it to the LORD." (For Manoah did not know that he was the angel of the LORD.) ¹⁷Then Manoah said to the angel of the LORD, "What is your name, so that we may honor you when your words come true?" ¹⁸But the angel of the LORD said to him, "Why do you ask my name? It is too wonderful."

19 So Manoah took the kid with the grain offering, and offered it on the rock to the LORD, to him who works^t wonders.^u ²⁰When the flame went up toward heaven from the altar, the angel of the LORD ascended in the flame of the altar while Manoah and his wife looked on; and they fell on their faces to the ground. ²¹The angel of the LORD did not appear again to Manoah and his wife. Then Manoah realized that it was the angel of the LORD. ²²And Manoah said to his wife, "We shall surely die, for we have seen God." ²³But his wife said to him, "If the LORD had meant to kill us, he would not have accepted a burnt offering and a grain offering at our hands, or shown us all these things, or now announced to us such things as these."

24 The woman bore a son, and named him Samson. The boy grew, and the LORD blessed him. ²⁵The spirit of the LORD began to stir him in Mahaneh-dan, between Zorah and Eshtaol.

Samson's Marriage

14 Once Samson went down to Timnah, and at Timnah he saw a Philistine woman.

14.1 The First Sign of Trouble

Timnah was only four miles across the valley from Samson's hometown. Apparently, the Philistines and Israelites moved freely back and forth, and not all Israelites opposed the Philistines (see 15.11). Samson, making the short stroll, was attracted to a young Philistine woman. His lack of concern for differences of religion and his lack of submission to his parents were ominous signs pointing toward Samson's future troubles.

²Then he came up, and told his father and mother, "I saw a Philistine woman at Timnah; now get her for me as my wife." ³But his father and mother said to him, "Is there not a woman among your kin, or among all our^v people, that you must go

---

^r That is *one separated* or *one consecrated*   ^s Or *the angel*   ^t Gk Vg: Heb *and working*   ^u Heb *wonders, while*
Manoah and his wife looked on   ^v Cn: Heb *my*

to take a wife from the uncircumcised Philistines?" But Samson said to his father, "Get her for me, because she pleases me." 4His father and mother did not know that this was from the LORD; for he was seeking a pretext to act against the Philistines. At that time the Philistines had dominion over Israel.

5 Then Samson went down with his father and mother to Timnah. When he came to the vineyards of Timnah, suddenly a young lion roared at him. 6The spirit of the LORD rushed on him, and he tore the lion apart barehanded as one might tear apart a kid. But he did not tell his father or his mother what he had done. 7Then he went down and talked with the woman, and she pleased Samson. 8After a while he returned to marry her, and he turned aside to see the carcass of the lion, and there was a swarm of bees in the body of the lion, and honey. 9He scraped it out into his hands, and went on, eating as he went.

When he came to his father and mother, he gave some to them, and they ate it. But he did not tell them that he had taken the honey from the carcass of the lion.

10 His father went down to the woman, and Samson made a feast there as the young men were accustomed to do. 11When the people saw him, they brought thirty companions to be with him. 12Samson said to them, "Let me now put a riddle to you. If you can explain it to me within the seven days of the feast, and find it out, then I will give you thirty linen garments and thirty festal garments. 13But if you cannot explain it to me, then you shall give me thirty linen garments and thirty festal garments." So they said to him, "Ask your riddle; let us hear it." 14He said to them,

"Out of the eater came something to eat.

Out of the strong came something sweet."

But for three days they could not explain the riddle.

Samson: A Weakness for Women
The strongest man of his generation never lived up to his promise

> "I saw a Philistine woman . . . now get her for me as my wife." 14.2

SAMSON, THE STRONGEST MAN OF his generation, was tragically unable to control his lust. When he saw an attractive woman, he wanted her. He first fell for a young woman he saw in a Philistine village just across the valley from his home. His parents tried to dissuade him, since her religion and culture were unacceptable, but he would not listen. Desire was his only rule. The marriage ended in a matter of days and resulted in dozens of deaths.

The famous Delilah was at least the third woman who dallied with Samson, according to Judges. She, like his first love, was a Philistine living near his home. Where thousands of men had failed to overcome Samson, a wheedling woman succeeded. Thanks to her, he was captured, blinded, and set to work pushing a grinding machine. His final triumph was ironically fitting: Blind and bound, brought out like a freak for a hooting crowd's amusement, he destroyed himself while wreaking vengeance on the crowd. At his death, as throughout his life, it was hard to say who suffered most from Samson's hot temper: the Philistines or Samson.

Needed: A Leader

When you think of what God meant Samson to be, his life appears particularly tragic. Israel desperately needed a strong, confident leader, for the Philistines were moving in as masters, and many Israelites were willing to let them. God intended Samson for great things. Of all the judges, only Samson was announced by an angel before he was born (13.3). He was assigned to that special class of people known as nazirites (described in Numbers 6), whose lives were specially devoted to God. Nazirites never drank wine, went near a dead body, or cut their hair.

Samson never lived up to his promise. Rule 3 was probably the only part of the nazirite vow he kept—it required little self-discipline to let hair grow.

Despite all of Samson's weaknesses, God used him. He is mentioned in the Bible "Hall of Fame" (Hebrews 11.32) as a hero of faith along with Gideon, Barak, and Jephthah, all from Judges. Barely conscious of what it meant to live for God, and given to fits of lust and temper, Samson still had great physical strength, which came supernaturally from God. With it, he pushed back the Philistines—more by accident than by intention—and kept Israel intact.

Samson seems like a train whose engineer has fallen out of the cab, an oversized accident smashing into everything it meets. But for God, there are no accidents. He used the tragedy of Samson's life for good.

Life Questions: Which might best be said of you: "Oh, what he/she might have been!" or "He/she made the best of his/her abilities"?

15 On the fourth[w] day they said to Samson's wife, "Coax your husband to explain the riddle to us, or we will burn you and your father's house with fire. Have you invited us here to impoverish us?" [16]So Samson's wife wept before him, saying, "You hate me; you do not really love me. You have asked a riddle of my people, but you have not explained it to me." He said to her, "Look, I have not told my father or my mother. Why should I tell you?" [17]She wept before him the seven days that their feast lasted; and because she nagged him, on the seventh day he told her. Then she explained the riddle to her people. [18]The men of the town said to him on the seventh day before the sun went down,

"What is sweeter than honey?
What is stronger than a lion?"
And he said to them,
"If you had not plowed with my heifer,
you would not have found out my
riddle."

[19]Then the spirit of the LORD rushed on him, and he went down to Ashkelon. He killed thirty men of the town, took their spoil, and gave the festal garments to those who had explained the riddle. In hot anger he went back to his father's house. [20]And Samson's wife was given to his companion, who had been his best man.

Samson Defeats the Philistines

15 After a while, at the time of the wheat harvest, Samson went to visit his wife, bringing along a kid. He said, "I want to go into my wife's room." But her father would not allow him to go in. [2]Her father said, "I was sure that you had rejected her; so I gave her to your companion. Is not her younger sister prettier than she? Why not take her instead?" [3]Samson said to them, "This time, when I do mischief to the Philistines, I will be without blame." [4]So Samson went and caught three hundred foxes, and took some torches; and he turned the foxes[x] tail to tail, and put a torch between each pair of tails. [5]When he had set fire to the torches, he let the foxes go into the standing grain of the Philistines, and burned up the shocks and the standing grain, as well as the vineyards and[y] olive groves. [6]Then the Philistines asked, "Who has done this?" And they said, "Samson, the son-in-law of the Timnite, because he has taken Samson's wife and given her to his companion." So the Philistines came up, and burned her and her father. [7]Samson said to them, "If this is what you do, I swear I will not stop until I have taken revenge on you." [8]He struck them down hip and thigh with great slaughter; and he went down and stayed in the cleft of the rock of Etam.

9 Then the Philistines came up and encamped in Judah, and made a raid on Lehi. [10]The men of Judah said, "Why have you come up against us?" They said, "We have come up to bind Samson, to do to him as he did to us." [11]Then three thousand men of Judah went down to the cleft of the rock of Etam, and they said to Samson, "Do you not know that the Philistines are rulers over us? What then have you done to us?" He replied, "As they did to me, so I have done to them." [12]They said to him, "We have come down to bind you, so that we may give you into the hands of the Philistines." Samson answered them, "Swear to me that you yourselves will not attack me." [13]They said to him, "No, we will only bind you and give you into their hands; we will not kill you." So they bound him with two new ropes, and brought him up from the rock.

14 When he came to Lehi, the Philistines came shouting to meet him; and the spirit of the LORD rushed on him, and the ropes that were on his arms became like flax that has caught fire, and

15.14 The Spirit and Samson

Four times (see also 13.25; 14.6,19) Judges comments that "the spirit of the LORD" came on Samson. The same comment is made of other judges, though less frequently. But the spirit only gave Samson great strength, as far as we can see; fruit of the spirit like love and self-control seem lacking from his life.

his bonds melted off his hands. [15]Then he found a fresh jawbone of a donkey, reached down and took it, and with it he killed a thousand men. [16]And Samson said,

"With the jawbone of a donkey,
heaps upon heaps,
with the jawbone of a donkey
I have slain a thousand men."

[17]When he had finished speaking, he threw away the jawbone; and that place was called Ramath-lehi.[z]

18 By then he was very thirsty, and he called on the LORD, saying, "You have granted this great victory by the hand of your servant. Am I now to die of thirst, and fall into the hands of the uncircumcised?" [19]So God split open the hollow place that is at Lehi, and water came from it. When he drank, his spirit returned, and he revived. Therefore it was named En-hakkore,[a] which is at Lehi to this day. [20]And he judged Israel in the days of the Philistines twenty years.

Samson and Delilah

16 Once Samson went to Gaza, where he saw a prostitute and went in to her. [2]The Gazites were told,[b] "Samson has come here." So

---

[w] Gk Syr: Heb *seventh*   [x] Heb *them*   [y] Gk Tg Vg: Heb lacks *and*   [z] That is *The Hill of the Jawbone*
[a] That is *The Spring of the One who Called*   [b] Gk: Heb lacks *were told*

they circled around and lay in wait for him all night at the city gate. They kept quiet all night, thinking, "Let us wait until the light of the morning; then we will kill him." ³But Samson lay only until midnight. Then at midnight he rose up, took hold of the doors of the city gate and the two posts, pulled them up, bar and all, put them on his shoulders, and carried them to the top of the hill that is in front of Hebron.

4 After this he fell in love with a woman in the valley of Sorek, whose name was Delilah. ⁵The lords of the Philistines came to her and said to her, "Coax him, and find out what makes his strength so great, and how we may overpower him, so that we may bind him in order to subdue him; and we will each give you eleven hundred pieces of silver." ⁶So Delilah said to Samson, "Please tell me what makes your strength so great, and how you could be bound, so that one could subdue you." ⁷Samson said to her, "If they bind me with seven fresh bowstrings that are not dried out, then I shall become weak, and be like anyone else." ⁸Then the lords of the Philistines brought her seven fresh bowstrings that had not dried out, and she bound him with them. ⁹While men were lying in wait in an inner chamber, she said to him, "The Philistines are upon you, Samson!" But he snapped the bowstrings, as a strand of fiber snaps when it touches the fire. So the secret of his strength was not known.

10 Then Delilah said to Samson, "You have mocked me and told me lies; please tell me how you could be bound." ¹¹He said to her, "If they bind me with new ropes that have not been used, then I shall become weak, and be like anyone else." ¹²So Delilah took new ropes and bound him with them, and said to him, "The Philistines are upon you, Samson!" (The men lying in wait were in an inner chamber.) But he snapped the ropes off his arms like a thread.

13 Then Delilah said to Samson, "Until now you have mocked me and told me lies; tell me how you could be bound." He said to her, "If you weave the seven locks of my head with the web and make it tight with the pin, then I shall become weak, and be like anyone else." ¹⁴So while he slept, Delilah took the seven locks of his head and wove them into the web,ᶜ and made them tight with the pin. Then she said to him, "The Philistines are upon you, Samson!" But he awoke from his sleep, and pulled away the pin, the loom, and the web.

15 Then she said to him, "How can you say, 'I love you,' when your heart is not with me? You have mocked me three times now and have not told me what makes your strength so great." ¹⁶Finally, after she had nagged him with her words day after day, and pestered him, he was tired to death. ¹⁷So he told her his whole secret, and said to her, "A razor has never come upon my head; for I have been a naziriteᵈ to God from my mother's womb. If my head were shaved, then my strength would leave me; I would become weak, and be like anyone else."

18 When Delilah realized that he had told her his whole secret, she sent and called the lords of the Philistines, saying, "This time come up, for he has told his whole secret to me." Then the lords of the Philistines came up to her, and brought the money in their hands. ¹⁹She let him fall asleep on her lap; and she called a man, and had him shave off the seven locks of his head. He began to weaken,ᵉ and his strength left him. ²⁰Then she said, "The Philistines are upon you, Samson!" When he awoke from his sleep, he thought, "I will go out as at other times, and shake myself free." But he did not know that the LORD had left him. ²¹So the Philistines seized him and gouged out his eyes. They brought him down to Gaza and bound him with bronze shackles; and he ground at the mill in the prison. ²²But the hair of his head began to grow again after it had been shaved.

Samson's Death

23 Now the lords of the Philistines gathered to offer a great sacrifice to their god Dagon, and to rejoice; for they said, "Our god has given Samson our enemy into our hand." ²⁴When the people saw him, they praised their god; for they said, "Our god has given our enemy into our hand, the ravager of our country, who has killed many of us." ²⁵And when their hearts were merry, they said, "Call Samson, and let him entertain us." So they called Samson out of the prison, and he performed for them. They made him stand between the pillars; ²⁶and Samson said to the attendant who held him by the hand, "Let me feel the pillars on which the house rests, so that I may lean against them." ²⁷Now the house was full of men and women; all the lords of the Philistines were there, and on the roof there were about three

16.30 Bring the House Down

Archaeologists have excavated temples from Samson's period. Typically, wooden pillars were set close together to support a roof, which sometimes included a covered area for spectators. Quite possibly this structure was already creaking under the weight of 3,000 people, who would have crowded to one side to see Samson perform. Samson managed to push the pillars off their stone bases, and the roof collapsed.

ᶜ Compare Gk: in verses 13-14, Heb lacks *and make it tight . . . into the web*   ᵈ That is *one separated* or *one consecrated*
ᵉ Gk: Heb *She began to torment him*

thousand men and women, who looked on while Samson performed.

28 Then Samson called to the LORD and said, "Lord GOD, remember me and strengthen me only this once, O God, so that with this one act of revenge I may pay back the Philistines for my two eyes."f 29And Samson grasped the two middle pillars on which the house rested, and he leaned his weight against them, his right hand on the one and his left hand on the other. 30Then Samson said, "Let me die with the Philistines." He strained with all his might; and the house fell on the lords and all the people who were in it. So those he killed at his death were more than those he had killed during his life. 31Then his brothers

and all his family came down and took him and brought him up and buried him between Zorah and Eshtaol in the tomb of his father Manoah. He had judged Israel twenty years.

Micah and the Levite

17 There was a man in the hill country of Ephraim whose name was Micah. 2He said to his mother, "The eleven hundred pieces of silver that were taken from you, about which you uttered a curse, and even spoke it in my hearing,—that silver is in my possession; I took it; but now I will return it to you."g And his mother said, "May my son be blessed by the LORD!" 3Then he returned the eleven hundred

f Or so that I may be avenged upon the Philistines for one of my two eyes are transposed from the end of verse 3 in Heb

g The words but now I will return it to you

Hanging by a Thread
Theft, rape, murder, idolatry: Israel was destroying itself

A TIME COMES WHEN YOU CAN no longer blame your problems on other people. In the comic strip character Pogo's immortal words, "We have met the enemy, and he is us."

So it is at the end of Judges. The camera zooms in for a close-up, focusing on internal violence. Foreign enemies are no longer in view: The enemy is Israel itself.

> *In those days there was no king in Israel; all the people did what was right in their own eyes.*
> *17.6*

They make ugly portraits, these last five chapters. Pointless and violent, they begin with a son stealing from his mother and end with parents agreeing to let their daughters be kidnapped. In between are homosexual and heterosexual gang rape, murder, idolatry, armed robbery, mass slaughter. No enemy does all this: Israelites do it to each other. Clearly, the exalted nation of Israel, God's chosen people, has lost all sense of direction.

Who Can Rescue Them Now?

The first 16 chapters of Judges tell of repeated enemy invasions that moved Israel to call out to God. Hearing his people, God would send a freedom fighter to save them.

In the last five chapters, by contrast, God sends no freedom fighters. No military leader could rescue them from themselves. These chapters instead repeat the solemn words: "In those days there was no king in Israel; all the people did what was right in their own eyes."

"All the people did what was right in their own eyes" may not sound very negative in our era, which places high value on individualism and personal freedom. But God prizes something more: unity. He wants his people united in love for him and each other. God's law had bound his people to a common worship in the tabernacle and to a common standard of caring for each other. For this the Israelites substituted do-as-you-please religion and a fractured society, where each family or group fought for its own rights alone. The result? These chapters tell the dismal story.

Israel's Worst Enemy

By the end of Judges, Israelites are reduced to fighting themselves. They have adopted their enemies' customs. They worship idols. They are sexually immoral. They lack respect for parents. They cannot remember the pattern of life God had set out. It is hard to say, by the end of Judges, why God should save Israel from their enemies. It is hard to say whether Israelites are the least bit different from their enemies. Israel has become, in fact, its own worst enemy.

Only one glimmer of hope appears: the Israelites' shock at the Benjamites' gang rape. They can still get together to punish such outrages, and they still consult the Lord about them. But they are a far cry from the hopeful people Joshua led into the promised land.

Life Questions: Do your troubles come more from your circumstances or from your own internal weaknesses? What kind of help do you need from God?

pieces of silver to his mother; and his mother said, "I consecrate the silver to the LORD from my hand for my son, to make an idol of cast metal." [4]So when he returned the money to his mother, his mother took two hundred pieces of silver, and gave it to the silversmith, who made it into an idol of cast metal; and it was in the house of Micah. [5]This man Micah had a shrine, and he made an ephod and teraphim, and installed one of his sons, who became his priest. [6]In those days there was no king in Israel; all the people did what was right in their own eyes.

17.6 A State of Anarchy

Four times the final chapters of Judges mention there was "no king." Twice Judges adds that "all the people did what was right in their own eyes." This editorial remark was probably made later, after the monarchy had begun under Saul and David; a king unified the nation. Some problems of this period are evident in verse 5: idolatry and the installation of a priest who did not come from the priestly family. The story that follows shows one group of Israelites raiding another, as though they were enemies, not relatives.

7 Now there was a young man of Bethlehem in Judah, of the clan of Judah. He was a Levite residing there. [8]This man left the town of Bethlehem in Judah, to live wherever he could find a place. He came to the house of Micah in the hill country of Ephraim to carry on his work.[h] [9]Micah said to him, "From where do you come?" He replied, "I am a Levite of Bethlehem in Judah, and I am going to live wherever I can find a place." [10]Then Micah said to him, "Stay with me, and be to me a father and a priest, and I will give you ten pieces of silver a year, a set of clothes, and your living."[i] [11]The Levite agreed to stay with the man; and the young man became to him like one of his sons. [12]So Micah installed the Levite, and the young man became his priest, and was in the house of Micah. [13]Then Micah said, "Now I know that the LORD will prosper me, because the Levite has become my priest."

The Migration of Dan

18 In those days there was no king in Israel. And in those days the tribe of the Danites was seeking for itself a territory to live in; for until then no territory among the tribes of Israel had been allotted to them. [2]So the Danites sent five valiant men from the whole number of their clan, from Zorah and from Eshtaol, to spy out the land

and to explore it; and they said to them, "Go, explore the land." When they came to the hill country of Ephraim, to the house of Micah, they stayed there. [3]While they were at Micah's house, they recognized the voice of the young Levite; so they went over and asked him, "Who brought you here? What are you doing in this place? What is your business here?" [4]He said to them, "Micah did such and such for me, and he hired me, and I have become his priest." [5]Then they said to him, "Inquire of God that we may know whether the mission we are undertaking will succeed." [6]The priest replied, "Go in peace. The mission you are on is under the eye of the LORD."

7 The five men went on, and when they came to Laish, they observed the people who were there living securely, after the manner of the Sidonians, quiet and unsuspecting, lacking[j] nothing on earth, and possessing wealth.[k] Furthermore, they were far from the Sidonians and had no dealings with Aram.[l] [8]When they came to their kinsfolk at Zorah and Eshtaol, they said to them, "What do you report?" [9]They said, "Come, let us go up against them; for we have seen the land, and it is very good. Will you do nothing? Do not be slow to go, but enter in and possess the land. [10]When you go, you will come to an unsuspecting people. The land is broad—God has indeed given it into your hands—a place where there is no lack of anything on earth."

11 Six hundred men of the Danite clan, armed with weapons of war, set out from Zorah and Eshtaol, [12]and went up and encamped at Kiriath-jearim in Judah. On this account that place is called Mahaneh-dan[m] to this day; it is west of Kiriath-jearim. [13]From there they passed on to the hill country of Ephraim, and came to the house of Micah.

14 Then the five men who had gone to spy out the land (that is, Laish) said to their comrades, "Do you know that in these buildings there are an ephod, teraphim, and an idol of cast metal? Now therefore consider what you will do." [15]So they turned in that direction and came to the house of the young Levite, at the home of Micah, and greeted him. [16]While the six hundred men of the Danites, armed with their weapons of war, stood by the entrance of the gate, [17]the five men who had gone to spy out the land proceeded to enter and take the idol of cast metal, the ephod, and the teraphim.[n] The priest was standing by the entrance of the gate with the six hundred men armed with weapons of war. [18]When the men went into Micah's house and took the idol of cast metal, the ephod, and the teraphim, the priest said to them, "What are you doing?" [19]They said to him, "Keep quiet! Put your hand over your

---

[h] Or *Ephraim, continuing his journey*   [i] Heb *living, and the Levite went*   [j] Cn Compare 18.10: Meaning of Heb uncertain   [k] Meaning of Heb uncertain   [l] Symmachus: Heb *with anyone*   [m] That is *Camp of Dan*
[n] Compare 17.4, 5; 18.14: Heb *teraphim and the cast metal*

mouth, and come with us, and be to us a father and a priest. Is it better for you to be priest to the house of one person, or to be priest to a tribe and clan in Israel?" [20]Then the priest accepted the offer. He took the ephod, the teraphim, and the idol, and went along with the people.

21 So they resumed their journey, putting the little ones, the livestock, and the goods in front of them. [22]When they were some distance from the home of Micah, the men who were in the houses near Micah's house were called out, and they overtook the Danites. [23]They shouted to the Danites, who turned around and said to Micah, "What is the matter that you come with such a company?" [24]He replied, "You take my gods that I made, and the priest, and go away, and what have I left? How then can you ask me, 'What is

18.24 Sad Commentary

Micah's outraged cry offers a sad commentary on the state of Israel. Even though his stolen gods were obviously unable to protect themselves, let alone him, Micah knew no other refuge. Anarchy ruled, as did idolatry.

the matter?'" [25]And the Danites said to him, "You had better not let your voice be heard among us or else hot-tempered fellows will attack you, and you will lose your life and the lives of your household." [26]Then the Danites went their way. When Micah saw that they were too strong for him, he turned and went back to his home.

The Danites Settle in Laish

27 The Danites, having taken what Micah had made, and the priest who belonged to him, came to Laish, to a people quiet and unsuspecting, put them to the sword, and burned down the city. [28]There was no deliverer, because it was far from Sidon and they had no dealings with Aram.[o] It was in the valley that belongs to Beth-rehob. They rebuilt the city, and lived in it. [29]They named the city Dan, after their ancestor Dan, who was born to Israel; but the name of the city was formerly Laish. [30]Then the Danites set up the idol for themselves. Jonathan son of Gershom, son of Moses,[p] and his sons were priests to the tribe of the Danites until the time the land went into captivity. [31]So they maintained as their own Micah's idol that he had made, as long as the house of God was at Shiloh.

The Levite's Concubine

19 In those days, when there was no king in Israel, a certain Levite, residing in the re-

mote parts of the hill country of Ephraim, took to himself a concubine from Bethlehem in Judah. [2]But his concubine became angry with[q] him, and she went away from him to her father's house at Bethlehem in Judah, and was there some four months. [3]Then her husband set out after her, to speak tenderly to her and bring her back. He had with him his servant and a couple of donkeys. When he reached[r] her father's house, the girl's father saw him and came with joy to meet him. [4]His father-in-law, the girl's father, made him stay, and he remained with him three days; so they ate and drank, and he[s] stayed there. [5]On the fourth day they got up early in the morning, and he prepared to go; but the girl's father said to his son-in-law, "Fortify yourself with a bit of food, and after that you may go." [6]So the two men sat and ate and drank together; and the girl's father said to the man, "Why not spend the night and enjoy yourself?" [7]When the man got up to go, his father-in-law kept urging him until he spent the night there again. [8]On the fifth day he got up early in the morning to leave; and the girl's father said, "Fortify yourself." So they lingered[t] until the day declined, and the two of them ate and drank.[u] [9]When the man with his concubine and his servant got up to leave, his father-in-law, the girl's father, said to him, "Look, the day has worn on until it is almost evening. Spend the night. See, the day has drawn to a close. Spend the night here and enjoy yourself. Tomorrow you can get up early in the morning for your journey, and go home."

10 But the man would not spend the night; he got up and departed, and arrived opposite Jebus (that is, Jerusalem). He had with him a couple of saddled donkeys, and his concubine was with him. [11]When they were near Jebus, the day was far spent, and the servant said to his master, "Come now, let us turn aside to this city of the Jebusites, and spend the night in it." [12]But his master said to him, "We will not turn aside into a city of foreigners, who do not belong to the people of Israel; but we will continue on to Gibeah." [13]Then he said to his servant, "Come, let us try to reach one of these places, and spend the night at Gibeah or at Ramah." [14]So they passed on and went their way; and the sun went down on them near Gibeah, which belongs to Benjamin. [15]They turned aside there, to go in and spend the night at Gibeah. He went in and sat down in the open square of the city, but no one took them in to spend the night.

16 Then at evening there was an old man coming from his work in the field. The man was from the hill country of Ephraim, and he was residing in Gibeah. (The people of the place were

---

[o] Cn Compare verse 7: Heb *with anyone against*   [r] Gk: Heb *she brought him*   [p] Another reading is *son of Manasseh*   [s] Compare verse 7 and Gk: Heb *they*   [q] Gk OL: Heb *prostituted herself*   [t] Cn: Heb *Linger*   [u] Gk: Heb *lacks and drank*

Benjaminites.) ¹⁷When the old man looked up and saw the wayfarer in the open square of the city, he said, "Where are you going and where do you come from?" ¹⁸He answered him, "We are

19.15 A Breach of Hospitality

In the ancient Middle East, people took hospitality very seriously. When the Levite sat down in the city square of an Israelite city, he expected the townspeople (his relatives) to offer him a place to stay. But only an old man from his home area offered the Levite lodging—the locals were inhospitable, an ominous sign.

The old man obviously took hospitality seriously. Unfortunately, he took women much less seriously. In fact, he urged the hostile mob to rape his daughter and his guest's concubine as a substitute for the guest himself. His response was nearly identical to Lot's on the eve of Sodom's destruction (Genesis 19.6–8). The story suggests that Israel had become as bad as Sodom.

passing from Bethlehem in Judah to the remote parts of the hill country of Ephraim, from which I come. I went to Bethlehem in Judah; and I am going to my home.ᵛ Nobody has offered to take me in. ¹⁹We your servants have straw and fodder for our donkeys, with bread and wine for me and the woman and the young man along with us. We need nothing more." ²⁰The old man said, "Peace be to you. I will care for all your wants; only do not spend the night in the square." ²¹So he brought him into his house, and fed the donkeys; they washed their feet, and ate and drank.

Gibeah's Crime

22　While they were enjoying themselves, the men of the city, a perverse lot, surrounded the house, and started pounding on the door. They said to the old man, the master of the house, "Bring out the man who came into your house, so that we may have intercourse with him." ²³And the man, the master of the house, went out to them and said to them, "No, my brothers, do not act so wickedly. Since this man is my guest, do not do this vile thing. ²⁴Here are my virgin daughter and his concubine; let me bring them out now. Ravish them and do whatever you want to them; but against this man do not do such a vile thing." ²⁵But the men would not listen to him. So the man seized his concubine, and put her out to them. They wantonly raped her, and abused her all through the night until the morning. And as the dawn began to break, they let her go. ²⁶As morning appeared, the woman came and fell

down at the door of the man's house where her master was, until it was light.

27　In the morning her master got up, opened the doors of the house, and when he went out to go on his way, there was his concubine lying at the door of the house, with her hands on the threshold. ²⁸"Get up," he said to her, "we are going." But there was no answer. Then he put her on the donkey; and the man set out for his home. ²⁹When he had entered his house, he took a knife, and grasping his concubine he cut her into twelve pieces, limb by limb, and sent her throughout all the territory of Israel. ³⁰Then he commanded the men whom he sent, saying, "Thus shall you say to all the Israelites, 'Has such a thing ever happenedʷ since the day that the Israelites came up from the land of Egypt until this day? Consider it, take counsel, and speak out.'"

The Other Tribes Attack Benjamin

20　Then all the Israelites came out, from Dan to Beer-sheba, including the land of Gilead, and the congregation assembled in one body before the LORD at Mizpah. ²The chiefs of all the people, of all the tribes of Israel, presented themselves in the assembly of the people of God, four hundred thousand foot-soldiers bearing arms. ³(Now the Benjaminites heard that the people of Israel had gone up to Mizpah.) And the Israelites said, "Tell us, how did this criminal act come about?" ⁴The Levite, the husband of the woman who was murdered, answered, "I came to Gibeah that belongs to Benjamin, I and my concubine, to spend the night. ⁵The lords of Gibeah rose up against me, and surrounded the house at night. They intended to kill me, and they raped my concubine until she died. ⁶Then I took my concubine and cut her into pieces, and sent her throughout the whole extent of Israel's territory; for they have committed a vile outrage in Israel. ⁷So now, you Israelites, all of you, give your advice and counsel here."

8　All the people got up as one, saying, "We will not any of us go to our tents, nor will any of us return to our houses. ⁹But now this is what we will do to Gibeah: we will go upˣ against it by lot. ¹⁰We will take ten men of a hundred throughout all the tribes of Israel, and a hundred of a thousand, and a thousand of ten thousand, to bring provisions for the troops, who are going to repayʸ Gibeah of Benjamin for all the disgrace that they have done in Israel." ¹¹So all the men of Israel gathered against the city, united as one.

12　The tribes of Israel sent men through all the tribe of Benjamin, saying, "What crime is this that has been committed among you? ¹³Now then, hand over those scoundrels in Gibeah, so that we may put them to death, and purge the evil

---

ᵛ Gk Compare 19.29. Heb *to the house of the LORD*　ʷ Compare Gk: Heb ³⁰*And all who saw it said, "Such a thing has not happened or been seen*　ˣ Gk: Heb lacks *we will go up*　ʸ Compare Gk: Meaning of Heb uncertain

from Israel." But the Benjaminites would not listen to their kinsfolk, the Israelites. ¹⁴The Benjaminites came together out of the towns to Gibeah, to go out to battle against the Israelites. ¹⁵On that day the Benjaminites mustered twenty-six thousand armed men from their towns, besides the inhabitants of Gibeah. ¹⁶Of all this force, there were seven hundred picked men who were left-handed; every one could sling a stone at a hair, and not miss. ¹⁷And the Israelites, apart from Benjamin, mustered four hundred thousand armed men, all of them warriors.

18 The Israelites proceeded to go up to Bethel, where they inquired of God, "Which of us shall go up first to battle against the Benjaminites?" And the LORD answered, "Judah shall go up first."

19 Then the Israelites got up in the morning, and encamped against Gibeah. ²⁰The Israelites went out to battle against Benjamin; and the Israelites drew up the battle line against them at Gibeah. ²¹The Benjaminites came out of Gibeah, and struck down on that day twenty-two thousand of the Israelites. ²³ ᶻ The Israelites went up and wept before the LORD until the evening; and they inquired of the LORD, "Shall we again draw near to battle against our kinsfolk the Benjaminites?" And the LORD said, "Go up against them." ²²The Israelites took courage, and again formed the battle line in the same place where they had formed it on the first day.

24 So the Israelites advanced against the Benjaminites the second day. ²⁵Benjamin moved out against them from Gibeah the second day, and struck down eighteen thousand of the Israelites, all of them armed men. ²⁶Then all the Israelites, the whole army, went back to Bethel and wept, sitting there before the LORD; they fasted that day until evening. Then they offered burnt offerings and sacrifices of well-being before the LORD. ²⁷And the Israelites inquired of the LORD (for the ark of the covenant of God was there in those days, ²⁸and Phinehas son of Eleazar, son of Aaron, ministered before it in those days), saying, "Shall we go out once more to battle against our kinsfolk the Benjaminites, or shall we desist?" The LORD answered, "Go up, for tomorrow I will give them into your hand."

29 So Israel stationed men in ambush around Gibeah. ³⁰Then the Israelites went up against the Benjaminites on the third day, and set themselves in array against Gibeah, as before. ³¹When the Benjaminites went out against the army, they were drawn away from the city. As before they began to inflict casualties on the troops, along the main roads, one of which goes up to Bethel and the other to Gibeah, as well as in the open country, killing about thirty men of Israel. ³²The Benjaminites thought, "They are being routed before us, as previously." But the Israelites said, "Let us retreat and draw them away from the city toward the roads." ³³The main body of the Israelites drew back its battle line to Baal-tamar, while those Israelites who were in ambush rushed out of their place west ᵃ of Geba. ³⁴There came against Gibeah ten thousand picked men out of all Israel, and the battle was fierce. But the Benjaminites did not realize that disaster was close upon them.

35 The LORD defeated Benjamin before Israel; and the Israelites destroyed twenty-five thousand one hundred men of Benjamin that day, all of them armed.

36 Then the Benjaminites saw that they were defeated.ᵇ

The Israelites gave ground to Benjamin, because they trusted to the troops in ambush that they had stationed against Gibeah. ³⁷The troops in ambush rushed quickly upon Gibeah. Then they put the whole city to the sword. ³⁸Now the agreement between the main body of Israel and the men in ambush was that when they sent up a cloud of smoke out of the city ³⁹the main body of Israel should turn in battle. But Benjamin had begun to inflict casualties on the Israelites, killing about thirty of them; so they thought, "Surely they are defeated before us, as in the first battle." ⁴⁰But when the cloud, a column of smoke, began to rise out of the city, the Benjaminites looked behind them—and there was the whole city going up in smoke toward the sky! ⁴¹Then the main body of Israel turned, and the Benjaminites were dismayed, for they saw that disaster was close upon them. ⁴²Therefore they turned away from the Israelites in the direction of the wilderness; but the battle overtook them, and those who came out of the cityᶜ were slaughtering them in between.ᵈ ⁴³Cutting downᵉ the Benjaminites, they pursued them from Nohahᶠ and trod them down as far as a place east of Gibeah. ⁴⁴Eighteen thousand Benjaminites fell, all of them courageous fighters. ⁴⁵When they turned and fled toward the wilderness to the rock of Rimmon, five thousand of them were cut down on the main roads, and they were pursued as far as Gidom, and two thousand of them were slain. ⁴⁶So all who fell that day of Benjamin were twenty-five thousand arms-bearing men, all of them courageous fighters. ⁴⁷But six hundred turned and fled toward the wilderness to the rock of Rimmon, and remained at the rock of Rimmon for four months. ⁴⁸Meanwhile, the Israelites turned back against the Benjaminites, and put them to the sword—the city, the people, the animals, and all that remained. Also the remaining towns they set on fire.

ᶻ Verses 22 and 23 are transposed   ᵃ Gk Vg: Heb in the plain   ᵇ This sentence is continued by verse 45.
ᶜ Compare Vg and some Gk Mss: Heb cities   ᵈ Compare Syr: Meaning of Heb uncertain   ᵉ Gk: Heb Surrounding
ᶠ Gk: Heb pursued them at their resting place

The Benjaminites Saved from Extinction

21 Now the Israelites had sworn at Mizpah, "No one of us shall give his daughter in marriage to Benjamin." ²And the people came to Bethel, and sat there until evening before God, and they lifted up their voices and wept bitterly. ³They said, "O LORD, the God of Israel, why has it come to pass that today there should be one tribe lacking in Israel?" ⁴On the next day, the people got up early, and built an altar there, and offered burnt offerings and sacrifices of well-being. ⁵Then the Israelites said, "Which of all the tribes of Israel did not come up in the assembly to the LORD?" For a solemn oath had been taken concerning whoever did not come up to the LORD to Mizpah, saying, "That one shall be put to death." ⁶But the Israelites had compassion for Benjamin their kin, and said, "One tribe is cut off from Israel this day. ⁷What shall we do for wives for those who are left, since we have sworn by the LORD that we will not give them any of our daughters as wives?"

8 Then they said, "Is there anyone from the tribes of Israel who did not come up to the LORD to Mizpah?" It turned out that no one from Jabesh-gilead had come to the camp, to the assembly. ⁹For when the roll was called among the people, not one of the inhabitants of Jabesh-gilead was there. ¹⁰So the congregation sent twelve thousand soldiers there and commanded them, "Go, put the inhabitants of Jabesh-gilead to the sword, including the women and the little ones. ¹¹This is what you shall do; every male and every woman that has lain with a male you shall devote to destruction." ¹²And they found among the inhabitants of Jabesh-gilead four hundred young virgins who had never slept with a man and brought them to the camp at Shiloh, which is in the land of Canaan.

13 Then the whole congregation sent word to the Benjaminites who were at the rock of Rim-mon, and proclaimed peace to them. ¹⁴Benjamin returned at that time; and they gave them the women whom they had saved alive of the women of Jabesh-gilead; but they did not suffice for them.

15 The people had compassion on Benjamin because the LORD had made a breach in the tribes of Israel. ¹⁶So the elders of the congregation said, "What shall we do for wives for those who are left, since there are no women left in Benjamin?" ¹⁷And they said, "There must be heirs for the survivors of Benjamin, in order that a tribe may not be blotted out from Israel. ¹⁸Yet we cannot give any of our daughters to them as wives." For the Israelites had sworn, "Cursed be anyone who gives a wife to Benjamin." ¹⁹So they said, "Look, the yearly festival of the LORD is taking place at Shiloh, which is north of Bethel, on the east of the highway that goes up from Bethel to Shechem, and south of Lebonah." ²⁰And they instructed the Benjaminites, saying, "Go and lie in wait in the vineyards, ²¹and watch; when the young women of Shiloh come out to dance in the dances, then come out of the vineyards and each of you carry off a wife for himself from the young women of Shiloh, and go to the land of Benjamin. ²²Then if their fathers or their brothers come to complain to us, we will say to them, 'Be generous and allow us to have them; because we did not capture in battle a wife for each man. But neither did you incur guilt by giving your daughters to them.'" ²³The Benjaminites did so; they took wives for each of them from the dancers whom they abducted. Then they went and returned to their territory, and rebuilt the towns, and lived in them. ²⁴So the Israelites departed from there at that time by tribes and families, and they went out from there to their own territories.

25 In those days there was no king in Israel; all the people did what was right in their own eyes.

RUTH

A Rare Bond of Love
Ruth and Naomi lost everything, except their care for each other

R UTH AND NAOMI WERE UNLIKELY friends: a generation apart, one young and strong, the other past middle age. Stranger still, one was the other's mother-in-law and came from a completely different ethnic and religious background. Who would have put them together?

They had lost everything when their husbands died. With no man to rely on, their lives were at risk in those rough times. No one else would come to their defense: They had only each other.

> *Where you go, I will go; where you lodge, I will lodge; your people shall be my people, and your God my God . . . May the LORD do thus and so to me, and more as well, if even death parts me from you! 1.16–17*

The Woman's Initiative

The book of Ruth is not "two women against the world." Rather, it shows the women taking initiative to find, by God's help, a man who would care for them.

A woman's initiative rarely gets so direct as in Ruth. At her mother-in-law's direction Ruth located where Boaz, a relative, was camping out. She waited until dark, then crept to his feet and lay down. When Boaz woke and found her, he didn't have to be told what was on her mind. She wanted him for a husband. Flattered, he didn't let another sun set before making the legal arrangements for marriage.

Society the way God had designed it encouraged men like Boaz to help the needy. For instance, by Old Testament law a farmer had to leave some of his grain behind so that poor people like Ruth could harvest it. And, also by law, a helpless widow had to be taken into the home of her husband's family. This was the law by which Boaz claimed Ruth (4.1–12).

God's Invisible Presence

Behind the eloquent story of Ruth looms an invisible helper—God. He didn't intervene in the events, so far as the story tells. But nobody in Ruth doubted that life proceeded under God's direction. It was the Lord by whom Ruth swore when declaring her love to Naomi (1.17), and the Lord whom Naomi credited for bringing Ruth to Boaz's field (2.20). God's law brought Boaz and Ruth into marriage. Finally, the Lord gave them a son, in whom mother, father, and "grandmother" found deep satisfaction.

The last verses of Ruth show, furthermore, that God's plan extended beyond Ruth and Naomi's personal problems. Ruth was a member of the despised Moabites—enemies of Israel. Yet God not only accepted her into his family, but also used her to produce Israel's greatest king. Ruth's great-grandson turned out to be David. To anyone who thought that God's love was for Israelites only, Ruth's life made a striking contradiction.

How to Read Ruth

R uth, brief enough to read in 15 minutes, is a delight. The German poet Goethe called it "the loveliest complete work on a small scale." But because Ruth's author didn't hammer his points home, it is possible to overlook his deeper meaning. As you read, concentrate on the loving bond between Ruth and Naomi. This love, which thrived in suffering, is the root of the book. It offers hope for other people in hard circumstances.

The author of Ruth assumed that readers understood the cultural and historical background of Ruth's time. You may wish to read about it for deeper understanding.

Deuteronomy 25.5–10 describes the background on marriage for a widow with a member of her husband's family, the "next-of-kin." Leviticus 25.23–28 gives background on a poor person's property. The Introduction to Judges offers historical perspective, for the book of Judges is an overview of the brutal times Ruth lived in.

PEOPLE YOU'LL MEET IN RUTH

RUTH *(p. 286)*

3-TRACK READING PLAN

For an explanation and complete listing of the 3-track reading plan, turn to page 7.

TRACK 1: *Two-Week Courses on the Bible*
See page 8 for information on these courses.

TRACK 2: *An Overview of Ruth in 1 Day*
☐ Day 1. Read the Introduction to Ruth and chapter 1, which describes an unusual friendship developing under the unkindest of conditions.
Now turn to page 9 for your next Track 2 reading project.

TRACK 3: *All of Ruth in 4 Days*
After you have read through Ruth, turn to pages 10–14 for your next Track 3 reading project.
☐1   ☐2   ☐3   ☐4

Elimelech's Family Goes to Moab

1 In the days when the judges ruled, there was a famine in the land, and a certain man of Bethlehem in Judah went to live in the country of Moab, he and his wife and two sons. ²The name of the man was Elimelech and the name of his wife Naomi, and the names of his two sons were Mahlon and Chilion; they were Ephrathites from Bethlehem in Judah. They went into the country of Moab and remained there. ³But Elimelech, the husband of Naomi, died, and she was left with her two sons. ⁴These took Moabite wives; the name of the one was Orpah and the name of the other Ruth. When they had lived there about ten years, ⁵both Mahlon and Chilion also died, so that the woman was left without her two sons and her husband.

Naomi and Her Moabite Daughters-in-Law

6 Then she started to return with her daughters-in-law from the country of Moab, for she had heard in the country of Moab that the LORD had considered his people and given them food. ⁷So she set out from the place where she had been living, she and her two daughters-in-law, and they went on their way to go back to the land of Judah. ⁸But Naomi said to her two daughters-in-law, "Go back each of you to your mother's house. May the LORD deal kindly with you, as you have dealt with the dead and with me. ⁹The LORD grant that you may find security, each of you in the house of your husband." Then she kissed them, and they wept aloud. ¹⁰They said to her, "No, we will return with you to your people." ¹¹But Naomi said, "Turn back, my daughters, why will you go with me? Do I still have sons in my womb that they may become your husbands? ¹²Turn back, my daughters, go your way, for I am too old to have a husband. Even if I thought there was hope for me, even if I should have a husband tonight and bear sons, ¹³would you then wait until they were grown? Would you then refrain from marrying? No, my daughters, it has been far more bitter for me than for you, because the hand of the LORD has turned against me." ¹⁴Then they wept aloud again. Orpah kissed her mother-in-law, but Ruth clung to her.

15 So she said, "See, your sister-in-law has gone back to her people and to her gods; return after your sister-in-law." ¹⁶But Ruth said,

"Do not press me to leave you
    or to turn back from following you!
Where you go, I will go;
    where you lodge, I will lodge;
your people shall be my people,
    and your God my God.
¹⁷ Where you die, I will die—
    there will I be buried.
May the LORD do thus and so to me,

and more as well,
if even death parts me from you!"
[18]When Naomi saw that she was determined to go with her, she said no more to her.

19 So the two of them went on until they came to Bethlehem. When they came to Bethlehem, the whole town was stirred because of them; and the women said, "Is this Naomi?" [20]She said to them,

"Call me no longer Naomi,[a]
call me Mara,[b]
for the Almighty[c] has dealt bitterly
with me.
21 I went away full,
but the LORD has brought me back
empty;
why call me Naomi
when the LORD has dealt harshly with[d]
me,
and the Almighty[c] has brought
calamity upon me?"

22 So Naomi returned together with Ruth the Moabite, her daughter-in-law, who came back with her from the country of Moab. They came to Bethlehem at the beginning of the barley harvest.

1.22 The Worst of Times

The author stresses that Ruth was a Moabitess, a fact that would have greatly impressed the original readers. Moab and Israel were bitter enemies, and Ruth took a risk by emigrating to a land that might treat her as a despised foreigner. This story of family love and loyalty took place during the time of the judges, when murder, immorality, and general anarchy prevailed.

Ruth Meets Boaz

2 Now Naomi had a kinsman on her husband's side, a prominent rich man, of the family of Elimelech, whose name was Boaz. [2]And Ruth the Moabite said to Naomi, "Let me go to the field and glean among the ears of grain, behind someone in whose sight I may find favor." She said to her, "Go, my daughter." [3]So she went. She came and gleaned in the field behind the reapers. As it happened, she came to the part of the field belonging to Boaz, who was of the family of Elimelech. [4]Just then Boaz came from Bethlehem. He said to the reapers, "The LORD be with you." They answered, "The LORD bless you." [5]Then Boaz said to his servant who was in charge of the reapers, "To whom does this young woman belong?" [6]The servant who was in charge of the reapers answered, "She is the Moabite who came back with

Naomi from the country of Moab. [7]She said, 'Please, let me glean and gather among the sheaves behind the reapers.' So she came, and she has been on her feet from early this morning until now, without resting even for a moment."[e]

2.3 Caring for the Poor

In the Old Testament God used several welfare programs to help poor people. One, reflected in this passage, was the command to leave some of the harvest in the field for the poor to gather. Poor people didn't beg for handouts, but worked for what they got. (Leviticus 19.9–10 and Deuteronomy 24.19–22 give the directions.)

Gleaning was humiliating and sometimes dangerous work. Ruth, a single woman and a foreigner, showed courage by working in the fields, and her diligence soon attracted the foreman's attention.

8 Then Boaz said to Ruth, "Now listen, my daughter, do not go to glean in another field or leave this one, but keep close to my young women. [9]Keep your eyes on the field that is being reaped, and follow behind them. I have ordered the young men not to bother you. If you get thirsty, go to the vessels and drink from what the young men have drawn." [10]Then she fell prostrate, with her face to the ground, and said to him, "Why have I found favor in your sight, that you should take notice of me, when I am a foreigner?" [11]But Boaz answered her, "All that you have done for your mother-in-law since the death of your husband has been fully told me, and how you left your father and mother and your native land and came to a people that you did not know before. [12]May the LORD reward you for your deeds, and may you have a full reward from the LORD, the God of Israel, under whose wings you have come for refuge!" [13]Then she said, "May I continue to find favor in your sight, my lord, for you have comforted me and spoken kindly to your servant, even though I am not one of your servants."

14 At mealtime Boaz said to her, "Come here, and eat some of this bread, and dip your morsel in the sour wine." So she sat beside the reapers, and he heaped up for her some parched grain. She ate until she was satisfied, and she had some left over. [15]When she got up to glean, Boaz instructed his young men, "Let her glean even among the standing sheaves, and do not reproach her. [16]You must also pull out some handfuls for her from the bundles, and leave them for her to glean, and do not rebuke her."

17 So she gleaned in the field until evening.

---

[a] That is *Pleasant*   [b] That is *Bitter*   [c] Traditional rendering of Heb *Shaddai*   [d] Or *has testified against*
[e] Compare Gk Vg: Meaning of Heb uncertain

Then she beat out what she had gleaned, and it was about an ephah of barley. ¹⁸She picked it up and came into the town, and her mother-in-law saw how much she had gleaned. Then she took out and gave her what was left over after she herself had been satisfied. ¹⁹Her mother-in-law said to her, "Where did you glean today? And where have you worked? Blessed be the man who took notice of you." So she told her mother-in-law with whom she had worked, and said, "The name of the man with whom I worked today is Boaz." ²⁰Then Naomi said to her daughter-in-law, "Blessed be he by the LORD, whose kindness has not forsaken the living or the dead!" Naomi also said to her, "The man is a relative of ours, one of our nearest kin."ᶠ ²¹Then Ruth the Moabite said, "He even said to me, 'Stay close by my servants, until they have finished all my harvest.'" ²²Naomi said to Ruth, her daughter-in-law, "It is better, my daughter, that you go out with his young women, otherwise you might be bothered in another field." ²³So she stayed close to the young women of Boaz, gleaning until the end of the barley and wheat harvests; and she lived with her mother-in-law.

Ruth and Boaz at the Threshing Floor

3 Naomi her mother-in-law said to her, "My daughter, I need to seek some security for you, so that it may be well with you. ²Now here is our kinsman Boaz, with whose young women you have been working. See, he is winnowing barley tonight at the threshing floor. ³Now wash and anoint yourself, and put on your best clothes and go down to the threshing floor; but do not make yourself known to the man until he has finished eating and drinking. ⁴When he lies down, observe the place where he lies; then, go and uncover his feet and lie down; and he will tell you what to do." ⁵She said to her, "All that you tell me I will do."

6 So she went down to the threshing floor and did just as her mother-in-law had instructed her. ⁷When Boaz had eaten and drunk, and he was in a contented mood, he went to lie down at the end of the heap of grain. Then she came stealthily and uncovered his feet, and lay down. ⁸At midnight the man was startled, and turned over, and there, lying at his feet, was a woman! ⁹He said, "Who are you?" And she answered, "I am Ruth, your servant; spread your cloak over your servant, for you are next-of-kin."ᶠ ¹⁰He said, "May you be blessed by the LORD, my daughter; this last instance of your loyalty is better than the first; you have not gone after young men, whether poor or rich. ¹¹And now, my daughter, do not be afraid, I will do for you all that you ask, for all the assembly of my people know that you are a worthy woman. ¹²But now, though it is true that I am a near kinsman, there is another kinsman more closely related than I. ¹³Remain this night, and in the morning, if he will act as next-of-kinᶠ for you, good; let him do it. If he is not willing to act as next-of-kinᶠ for you, then, as the LORD lives, I will act as next-of-kinᶠ for you. Lie down until the morning."

14 So she lay at his feet until morning, but got up before one person could recognize another; for he said, "It must not be known that the woman came to the threshing floor." ¹⁵Then he said, "Bring the cloak you are wearing and hold it out." So she held it, and he measured out six measures of barley, and put it on her back; then he went into the city. ¹⁶She came to her mother-in-law,

ᶠ Or *one with the right to redeem*

RUTH *Character Counts*

SHE ARRIVED IN ISRAEL PENNILESS, a foreigner and a widow, with her mother-in-law as her only friend. Considering that her home country Moab was often at war with Israel, and that the two nations worshiped different gods, the immigrant named Ruth hardly figured to thrive in Israel. Yet she went to work without delay.

Even though she was a foreigner, Ruth showed herself a model Israelite woman: modest, hard-working and deeply loyal to those she loved. (Her speech to Naomi is one of the world's great love poems [1.16–17]). Ruth never complained about hardship; rather, she responded with gratitude when anyone showed kindness to her. In the end she proved that character counts more than circumstances.

As this gem of a love story recounts, Ruth caught the eye of a very good man. The two married, began a new life together and had a son. Ultimately, through that son, Ruth the refugee became an ancestor of Israel's greatest king.

Ruth's life makes a lovely story in itself, but it has a larger significance. She contradicts a common assumption about the God of the Old Testament—that only members of one special tribe could be his chosen people. Ruth was fully accepted among God's people because she chose to follow the true God, despite her foreign background. Anyone could join in worshiping God, just as Ruth did.

Life Questions: Do you find it hard to accept and admire those who come from outside your group? What "qualifications" do you set up?

who said, "How did things go with you,^{g} my daughter?" Then she told her all that the man had done for her, ^{17}saying, "He gave me these six measures of barley, for he said, 'Do not go back to your mother-in-law empty-handed.'" ^{18}She replied, "Wait, my daughter, until you learn how the matter turns out, for the man will not rest, but will settle the matter today."

The Marriage of Boaz and Ruth

4 No sooner had Boaz gone up to the gate and sat down there than the next-of-kin,^{h} of whom Boaz had spoken, came passing by. So Boaz said, "Come over, friend; sit down here."

4.1 Expensive Bride

In order to marry Ruth, Boaz had to go through a complicated legal procedure at the town gate, a public gathering place. The laws were designed to keep property in the family and to protect family members who might have suffered financial or other setbacks. As a distant relative, Boaz could purchase, or "redeem," Naomi's family property, but only after a closer relative, the "next-of-kin" had declined. Along with the property, Boaz acquired marriage rights to Ruth, Naomi's relative.

And he went over and sat down. ^{2}Then Boaz took ten men of the elders of the city, and said, "Sit down here"; so they sat down. ^{3}He then said to the next-of-kin,^{h} "Naomi, who has come back from the country of Moab, is selling the parcel of land that belonged to our kinsman Elimelech. ^{4}So I thought I would tell you of it, and say: Buy it in the presence of those sitting here, and in the presence of the elders of my people. If you will redeem it, redeem it; but if you will not, tell me, so that I may know; for there is no one prior to you to redeem it, and I come after you." So he said, "I will redeem it." ^{5}Then Boaz said, "The day you acquire the field from the hand of Naomi, you are also acquiring Ruth^i the Moabite, the widow of the dead man, to maintain the dead man's name on his inheritance." ^{6}At this, the next-of-kin^h said, "I cannot redeem it for myself without damaging my own inheritance. Take my right of redemption yourself, for I cannot redeem it."

7 Now this was the custom in former times in Israel concerning redeeming and exchanging: to confirm a transaction, the one took off a sandal and gave it to the other; this was the manner of attesting in Israel. ^{8}So when the next-of-kin^h said to Boaz, "Acquire it for yourself," he took off his sandal. ^{9}Then Boaz said to the elders and all the people, "Today you are witnesses that I have acquired from the hand of Naomi all that belonged to Elimelech and all that belonged to Chilion and Mahlon. ^{10}I have also acquired Ruth the Moabite, the wife of Mahlon, to be my wife, to maintain the dead man's name on his inheritance, in order that the name of the dead may not be cut off from his kindred and from the gate of his native place; today you are witnesses." ^{11}Then all the people who were at the gate, along with the elders, said, "We are witnesses. May the LORD make the woman who is coming into your house like Rachel and Leah, who together built up the house of Israel. May you produce children in Ephrathah and bestow a name in Bethlehem; ^{12}and, through the children that the LORD will give you by this young woman, may your house be like the house of Perez, whom Tamar bore to Judah."

The Genealogy of David

13 So Boaz took Ruth and she became his wife. When they came together, the LORD made her conceive, and she bore a son. ^{14}Then the women said to Naomi, "Blessed be the LORD, who has not left you this day without next-of-kin;^{h} and may his name be renowned in Israel! ^{15}He shall be to you a restorer of life and a nourisher of your old age; for your daughter-in-law who loves you, who is more to you than seven sons, has borne him." ^{16}Then Naomi took the child and laid him in her bosom, and became his nurse. ^{17}The women of the neighborhood gave him a name, saying, "A son has been born to Naomi." They named him Obed; he became the father of Jesse, the father of David.

18 Now these are the descendants of Perez: Perez became the father of Hezron, ^{19}Hezron of Ram, Ram of Amminadab, ^{20}Amminadab of Nahshon, Nahshon of Salmon, ^{21}Salmon of Boaz, Boaz of Obed, ^{22}Obed of Jesse, and Jesse of David.

---

g Or "Who are you, h Or one with the right to redeem i OL Vg: Heb from the hand of Naomi and from Ruth

1 SAMUEL

What Leadership Requires
Israel, fighting for survival, needed a leader

> For not by might does one prevail. The LORD! His adversaries shall be shattered.
> 2.9–10

NO COUNTRY, NO ORGANIZATION, NO family is great without great leadership. But how do you get it? Israel was forced to ask that question during a critical, do-or-die period. Three men rose to the highest power: Samuel, Saul, and David. All were attractive, powerful figures who commanded admiration and respect. Two, David and Samuel, made very successful leaders. The other, Saul, had a promising beginning but ended as a failure.

Fighting for Survival

Israel was fighting for survival. The Philistines had migrated to the region about the same time Israel had escaped from Egypt. Now, from their cities near the Mediterranean coast, they were gradually pushing deeper into the mountains of Israel. They had superior weapons—chariots, in particular. Though less populous than Israel, they were apparently better organized.

Israel had neither central administration nor a regular army. A loose confederation of 12 tribes, Israelites called on each other for help only in emergencies. Occasional inspired leaders—"judges"—took charge of military defense when necessary. The nation had worked that way for well over 100 years, and the tribes seemed too independent to change. But the Philistines were pressing them. A crisis of leadership—a crisis testing the very existence of Israel—was building.

Why Begin with Hannah?

Surprisingly, 1 Samuel opens not with a battle or even with the leadership crisis, but with a very private family problem. Two bitterly jealous wives had a long-standing quarrel, one taunting the other because of her infertility. Hannah, the childless woman, turned to God in desperation, praying and promising to dedicate a son to him. The result was a little boy named Samuel.

Hannah kept her vow to God, and Samuel grew into one of the greatest leaders Israel had ever known. He had a triple role: He served as a prophet who could discern God's will, as a priest who led Israel to worship, and as a military leader. He chose, under God's direction, Israel's first two kings. Samuel's strong personality undergirds the entire book of 1 Samuel, even though he officially retired at the end of chapter 15.

Why begin 1 Samuel with Hannah? Hannah's struggles are Israel's, in miniature. Her frustration forced her to look to God, and as a result her son Samuel served in the tabernacle instead of following in his father's footsteps as a farmer. Hannah's story shows that from bitter pain may come great promise, if that pain leads you to God. The Israelites, who were going to experience a great many more troubles in their history, needed Hannah's example.

God Chooses His Own Leaders

Hannah's story also reminds us that God's leaders don't necessarily come through regulation channels. Ordinarily, Eli's corrupt sons would have carried on national leadership. But God wanted no part of them. Instead, he blessed a woman who had turned to him in her troubles, and he blessed her son as long as that son trusted in him for help. God chose a leader to suit himself, a leader who listened to him. "The LORD declares . . . 'Those who honor me I will honor, and those who despise me shall be treated with contempt' " (2.30).

Samuel never forgot that lesson. He anointed Saul as the first king, and then, when Saul failed to honor God, stripped him of his authority. Passing over many impressive men, Samuel chose David, a young shepherd, to replace Saul. Under David, Israel would be transformed into a wealthy, secure kingdom. Was this because David had such natural leadership qualities? First Samuel suggests a different perspective: David succeeded because God chose him for the job, and because David persistently turned to God for his direction. The best leadership, ultimately, belongs to God.

How to Read 1 Samuel

Some of the stories of 1 Samuel—David and Goliath, for instance—are justly famous as great adventures. But you should read for more than excitement. Look for insights into the character required for leadership. Samuel and David were great leaders. Saul, on the other hand, was a miserable failure.

These men led Israel during a crucial, bloody period. Israel had been dominated by a foreign power and, partly because of this, was changing its government to a monarchy. This change in governmental institutions, along with tribal tensions, form the background for the book. A good commentary can help explain this, but you can get much of it for yourself by asking, as you read, three questions: What are the most important national problems facing Israel? What kind of leadership is needed? How do these three leaders (and numerous smaller figures) respond to these needs?

PEOPLE YOU'LL MEET IN 1 SAMUEL

HANNAH (p. 291)   **SAMUEL** (p. 296)   **JONATHAN** (p. 311)
ELI (p. 293)   **SAUL** (p. 305)   **ABIGAIL** (p. 317)

3-TRACK READING PLAN

For an explanation and complete listing of the 3-track reading plan, turn to page 7.

TRACK 1: **Two-Week Courses on the Bible**
The Track 1 reading program includes one chapter from 1 Samuel. See page 8 for a complete listing of this course.

TRACK 2: **An Overview of 1 Samuel in 4 Days**
☐ Day 1. Read the Introduction to 1 Samuel and chapter 3, God's call of Samuel when he was very young.
☐ Day 2. Read chapter 16 to see how God chose David, and why.
☐ Day 3. Read chapter 17 for the exciting story of David's victory over Goliath, noting the qualities David showed.
☐ Day 4. Read chapter 20 for a glimpse of a model friendship between David and Jonathan.

Now turn to page 9 for your next Track 2 reading project.

TRACK 3: **All of 1 Samuel in 31 Days**
After you have read through 1 Samuel, turn to pages 10–14 for your next Track 3 reading project.

☐1	☐2	☐3	☐4	☐5	☐6	☐7	☐8
☐9	☐10	☐11	☐12	☐13	☐14	☐15	☐16
☐17	☐18	☐19	☐20	☐21	☐22	☐23	☐24
☐25	☐26	☐27	☐28	☐29	☐30	☐31	

Samuel's Birth and Dedication

1 There was a certain man of Ramathaim, a Zuphite[a] from the hill country of Ephraim, whose name was Elkanah son of Jeroham son of Elihu son of Tohu son of Zuph, an Ephraimite. [2]He had two wives; the name of the one was Hannah, and the name of the other Peninnah. Peninnah had children, but Hannah had no children.

3 Now this man used to go up year by year from his town to worship and to sacrifice to the LORD of hosts at Shiloh, where the two sons of Eli, Hophni and Phinehas, were priests of the LORD. [4]On the day when Elkanah sacrificed, he would give portions to his wife Peninnah and to all her sons and daughters; [5]but to Hannah he gave a double portion,[b] because he loved her, though the LORD had closed her womb. [6]Her rival used to provoke her severely, to irritate her, because the LORD had closed her womb. [7]So it went on year by

a Compare Gk and 1 Chr 6.35-36: Heb *Ramathaim-zophim*   b Syr: Meaning of Heb uncertain

year; as often as she went up to the house of the LORD, she used to provoke her. Therefore Hannah wept and would not eat. [8]Her husband Elkanah said to her, "Hannah, why do you weep? Why do you not eat? Why is your heart sad? Am I not more to you than ten sons?"

9 After they had eaten and drunk at Shiloh, Hannah rose and presented herself before the LORD.[c] Now Eli the priest was sitting on the seat beside the doorpost of the temple of the LORD. [10]She was deeply distressed and prayed to the LORD, and wept bitterly. [11]She made this vow: "O LORD of hosts, if only you will look on the misery of your servant, and remember me, and not forget your servant, but will give to your servant a male child, then I will set him before you as a nazirite[d] until the day of his death. He shall drink neither wine nor intoxicants,[e] and no razor shall touch his head."

12 As she continued praying before the LORD, Eli observed her mouth. [13]Hannah was praying silently; only her lips moved, but her voice was not heard; therefore Eli thought she was drunk.

1.13 Sad, Not Drunk

Eli's mistaken assumption suggests that people sometimes came to the tabernacle drunk. Perhaps in these troubled times drunkenness was more common than heartfelt prayer. Hannah prayed with great anguish because she had no children. She is one of several barren women in the Bible whom God helped; others include Sarah (Genesis 11.30), Rebekah (Genesis 25.21), Rachel (Genesis 29.31), and Elizabeth (Luke 1.7).

[14]So Eli said to her, "How long will you make a drunken spectacle of yourself? Put away your wine." [15]But Hannah answered, "No, my lord, I am a woman deeply troubled; I have drunk neither wine nor strong drink, but I have been pouring out my soul before the LORD. [16]Do not regard your servant as a worthless woman, for I have been speaking out of my great anxiety and vexation all this time." [17]Then Eli answered, "Go in peace; the God of Israel grant the petition you have made to him." [18]And she said, "Let your servant find favor in your sight." Then the woman went to her quarters,[f] ate and drank with her husband,[g] and her countenance was sad no longer.[h]

19 They rose early in the morning and worshiped before the LORD; then they went back to their house at Ramah. Elkanah knew his wife Hannah, and the LORD remembered her. [20]In due time Hannah conceived and bore a son. She named him Samuel, for she said, "I have asked him of the LORD."

21 The man Elkanah and all his household went up to offer to the LORD the yearly sacrifice, and to pay his vow. [22]But Hannah did not go up, for she said to her husband, "As soon as the child is weaned, I will bring him, that he may appear in the presence of the LORD, and remain there forever; I will offer him as a nazirite[d] for all time."[i] [23]Her husband Elkanah said to her, "Do what seems best to you, wait until you have weaned him; only—may the LORD establish his word."[j] So the woman remained and nursed her son, until she weaned him. [24]When she had weaned him, she took him up with her, along with a three-year-old bull,[k] an ephah of flour, and a skin of wine. She brought him to the house of the LORD at Shiloh; and the child was young. [25]Then they slaughtered the bull, and they brought the child to Eli. [26]And she said, "Oh, my lord! As you live, my lord, I am the woman who was standing here in your presence, praying to the LORD. [27]For this child I prayed; and the LORD has granted me the petition that I made to him. [28]Therefore I have lent him to the LORD; as long as he lives, he is given to the LORD."

She left him there for[l] the LORD.

Hannah's Prayer

2 Hannah prayed and said,
"My heart exults in the LORD;
   my strength is exalted in my God.[m]
My mouth derides my enemies,
   because I rejoice in my[n] victory.

[2] "There is no Holy One like the LORD,
   no one besides you;
   there is no Rock like our God.
[3] Talk no more so very proudly,
   let not arrogance come from your
      mouth;
for the LORD is a God of knowledge,
   and by him actions are weighed.
[4] The bows of the mighty are broken,
   but the feeble gird on strength.
[5] Those who were full have hired
      themselves out for bread,
   but those who were hungry are fat with
      spoil.
The barren has borne seven,
   but she who has many children is
      forlorn.

---

[c] Gk: Heb lacks *and presented herself before the LORD*   [d] That is *one separated* or *one consecrated*   [e] Cn Compare Gk Q Ms 1.22: MT *then I will give him to the LORD all the days of his life*   [f] Gk: Heb *went her way*   [g] Gk: Heb lacks *and drank with her husband*   [h] Gk: Meaning of Heb uncertain   [i] Cn Compare Q Ms: MT lacks *I will offer him as a nazirite for all time*   [j] MT: Q Ms Gk Compare Syr *that which goes out of your mouth*   [k] Q Ms Gk Syr: MT *three bulls*   [l] Gk (Compare Q Ms) and Gk at 2.11: MT *And he* (that is, Elkanah) *worshiped there before*   [m] Gk: Heb *the LORD*   [n] Q Ms: MT *your*

6 The LORD kills and brings to life;
he brings down to Sheol and raises up.
7 The LORD makes poor and makes rich;
he brings low, he also exalts.
8 He raises up the poor from the dust;
he lifts the needy from the ash heap,
to make them sit with princes
and inherit a seat of honor.*o*
For the pillars of the earth are the LORD's,
and on them he has set the world.

9 "He will guard the feet of his faithful
ones,
but the wicked shall be cut off in
darkness;
for not by might does one prevail.
10 The LORD! His adversaries shall be
shattered;
the Most High*p* will thunder in
heaven.
The LORD will judge the ends of the earth;
he will give strength to his king,
and exalt the power of his anointed."

Eli's Wicked Sons

11 Then Elkanah went home to Ramah, while the boy remained to minister to the LORD, in the presence of the priest Eli.

12 Now the sons of Eli were scoundrels; they had no regard for the LORD 13or for the duties of the priests to the people. When anyone offered sacrifice, the priest's servant would come, while the meat was boiling, with a three-pronged fork in his hand, 14and he would thrust it into the pan, or kettle, or caldron, or pot; all that the fork brought up the priest would take for himself.*q* This is what they did at Shiloh to all the Israelites who came there. 15Moreover, before the fat was burned, the priest's servant would come and say

to the one who was sacrificing, "Give meat for the priest to roast; for he will not accept boiled meat from you, but only raw." 16And if the man said to him, "Let them burn the fat first, and then take whatever you wish," he would say, "No, you must give it now; if not, I will take it by force." 17Thus the sin of the young men was very great in the sight of the LORD; for they treated the offerings of the LORD with contempt.

The Child Samuel at Shiloh

18 Samuel was ministering before the LORD, a boy wearing a linen ephod. 19His mother used to make for him a little robe and take it to him each year, when she went up with her husband to offer the yearly sacrifice. 20Then Eli would bless Elkanah and his wife, and say, "May the LORD repay*r* you with children by this woman for the gift that she made to*s* the LORD"; and then they would return to their home.

21 And*t* the LORD took note of Hannah; she conceived and bore three sons and two daughters. And the boy Samuel grew up in the presence of the LORD.

Prophecy against Eli's Household

22 Now Eli was very old. He heard all that his sons were doing to all Israel, and how they lay with the women who served at the entrance to the tent of meeting. 23He said to them, "Why do you do such things? For I hear of your evil dealings from all these people. 24No, my sons; it is not a good report that I hear the people of the LORD spreading abroad. 25If one person sins against another, someone can intercede for the sinner with the LORD;*u* but if someone sins against the LORD, who can make intercession?" But they would not listen to the voice of their father; for it was the will of the LORD to kill them.

o Gk (Compare Q Ms) adds *He grants the vow of the one who vows, and blesses the years of the just*   *p* Cn Heb *against him he*   *q* Gk Syr Vg: Heb *with it*   *r* Q Ms Gk: MT *give*   *s* Q Ms Gk: MT *for the petition that she asked of*   *t* Q Ms Gk: MT *When*   *u* Gk Compare Q Ms: MT *another, God will mediate for him*

HANNAH *Deepest Longing*

OTHER WOMEN MIGHT ENVY HANNAH. She had, at least, a kind husband who obviously loved her. Yet for Hannah, one deep, unfulfilled longing made life miserable. Hannah wanted a child. (It hardly helped that a rival wife, Peninnah, brought the subject up at every opportunity.)

The longing for children may be the strongest in life. Today, infertile couples spend thousands of dollars in search of a medical remedy. For Hannah, who had no such recourse, her longing outweighed every blessing. Hannah wept, felt bitter and poured out her woes to God.

When God answered Hannah's prayer and gave her a son, Samuel, she poured out her joy to God as well. Remarkably, for a woman who had waited so long for a son, she took Samuel to God's tabernacle as soon as he reached an appropriate age. There she placed him in the priest's care.

Hannah certainly loved her child and never forgot him. Every year she made a garment for him—a huge expenditure in an age when cloth and even thread had to be made by hand. Yet she did not cling to her blessing any more than she had clung to her woes. She gave both to God.

Life Questions: Is some unfulfilled longing making you miserable? How can you take it to God?

26 Now the boy Samuel continued to grow both in stature and in favor with the LORD and with the people.

27 A man of God came to Eli and said to him,

2.25 God in Charge

Eli's sons disobeyed, the Bible says, because God wanted to put them to death. Does this mean that God took away their free choice? To Old Testament writers this "contradiction" seemed less troubling than to us. To them every event occurred only because, ultimately, God let it. Within his overall control people acted freely. In this case, Eli's sons were free to obey or disobey. The author wants us to know, however, that their disobedience was not beyond God's power: He planned to judge their evil activities.

"Thus the LORD has said, 'I revealed[v] myself to the family of your ancestor in Egypt when they were slaves[w] to the house of Pharaoh. [28]I chose him out of all the tribes of Israel to be my priest, to go up to my altar, to offer incense, to wear an ephod before me; and I gave to the family of your ancestor all my offerings by fire from the people of Israel. [29]Why then look with greedy eye[x] at my sacrifices and my offerings that I commanded, and honor your sons more than me by fattening yourselves on the choicest parts of every offering of my people Israel?' [30]Therefore the LORD the God of Israel declares: 'I promised that your family and the family of your ancestor should go in and out before me forever'; but now the LORD declares: 'Far be it from me; for those who honor me I will honor, and those who despise me shall

2.30 Bad News for Eli

For Eli, this pronouncement came as bad news. He was held responsible for his sons' disgraceful behavior in the tabernacle. Eli rebuked them, but "did not restrain them" (3.13). As the priest in charge of the tabernacle, it was his job to stop any abuse there.

be treated with contempt. [31]See, a time is coming when I will cut off your strength and the strength of your ancestor's family, so that no one in your family will live to old age. [32]Then in distress you will look with greedy eye[y] on all the prosperity that shall be bestowed upon Israel; and no one in your family shall ever live to old age. [33]The only one of you whom I shall not cut off from my altar

shall be spared to weep out his[z] eyes and grieve his[a] heart; all the members of your household shall die by the sword.[b] [34]The fate of your two sons, Hophni and Phinehas, shall be the sign to you—both of them shall die on the same day. [35]I will raise up for myself a faithful priest, who shall do according to what is in my heart and in my mind. I will build him a sure house, and he shall go in and out before my anointed one forever. [36]Everyone who is left in your family shall come to implore him for a piece of silver or a loaf of bread, and shall say, Please put me in one of the priest's places, that I may eat a morsel of bread.'"

Samuel's Calling and Prophetic Activity

3 Now the boy Samuel was ministering to the LORD under Eli. The word of the LORD was rare in those days; visions were not widespread. 2 At that time Eli, whose eyesight had begun to grow dim so that he could not see, was lying down in his room; [3]the lamp of God had not yet gone out, and Samuel was lying down in the temple of the LORD, where the ark of God was. [4]Then the LORD called, "Samuel! Samuel!"[c] and he said, "Here I am!" [5]and ran to Eli, and said, "Here I am, for you called me." But he said, "I did not call; lie down again." So he went and lay down. [6]The LORD called again, "Samuel!" Samuel got up and went to Eli, and said, "Here I am, for you called me." But he said, "I did not call, my son; lie down again." [7]Now Samuel did not yet know the LORD, and the word of the LORD had not yet been revealed to him. [8]The LORD called Samuel again, a third time. And he got up and went to Eli, and said, "Here I am, for you called me." Then Eli perceived that the LORD was calling the boy. [9]Therefore Eli said to Samuel, "Go, lie down; and if he calls you, you shall say, 'Speak, LORD, for your servant is listening.'" So Samuel went and lay down in his place.

10 Now the LORD came and stood there, calling as before, "Samuel! Samuel!" And Samuel said, "Speak, for your servant is listening." [11]Then the LORD said to Samuel, "See, I am about to do something in Israel that will make both ears of anyone who hears of it tingle. [12]On that day I will fulfill against Eli all that I have spoken concerning his house, from beginning to end. [13]For I have told him that I am about to punish his house forever, for the iniquity that he knew, because his sons were blaspheming God,[d] and he did not restrain them. [14]Therefore I swear to the house of Eli that the iniquity of Eli's house shall not be expiated by sacrifice or offering forever."

15 Samuel lay there until morning; then he opened the doors of the house of the LORD. Samuel was afraid to tell the vision to Eli. [16]But Eli

---

[v] Gk Tg Syr: Heb *Did I reveal*   [w] Q Ms Gk: MT lacks *slaves*   [x] Q Ms Gk: MT *then kick*   [y] Q Ms Gk: MT *will kick*
[z] Q Ms Gk: MT *your*   [a] Q Ms Gk: Heb *your*   [b] Q Ms See Gk: MT *die like mortals*   [c] Q Ms Gk See 3.10: MT
the LORD called Samuel   [d] Another reading is *for themselves*

called Samuel and said, "Samuel, my son." He said, "Here I am." [17]Eli said, "What was it that he told you? Do not hide it from me. May God do so to you and more also, if you hide anything from me of all that he told you." [18]So Samuel told him everything and hid nothing from him. Then he said, "It is the LORD; let him do what seems good to him."

19 As Samuel grew up, the LORD was with him and let none of his words fall to the ground.

3.19 Still a Boy

While still a boy, Samuel heard God speak. He delivered God's message even though it rebuked Eli, the man who had raised him from childhood. This was one indication that Samuel was a genuine prophet, for false prophets usually delivered only good news. Samuel's message agreed with the prophecy given earlier by a man of God (2.27–36), confirming that God had indeed spoken to him.

[20]And all Israel from Dan to Beer-sheba knew that Samuel was a trustworthy prophet of the LORD. [21]The LORD continued to appear at Shiloh, for the LORD revealed himself to Samuel at Shiloh by the word of the LORD. [1]And the word of Samuel came to all Israel.

The Ark of God Captured

In those days the Philistines mustered for war against Israel,[e] and Israel went out to battle against them;[f] they encamped at Ebenezer, and the Philistines encamped at Aphek. [2]The Philis-tines drew up in line against Israel, and when the battle was joined,[g] Israel was defeated by the Philistines, who killed about four thousand men on the field of battle. [3]When the troops came to the camp, the elders of Israel said, "Why has the LORD put us to rout today before the Philistines? Let us bring the ark of the covenant of the LORD here from Shiloh, so that he may come among us and save us from the power of our enemies." [4]So the people sent to Shiloh, and brought from there the ark of the covenant of the LORD of hosts, who is enthroned on the cherubim. The two sons of Eli, Hophni and Phinehas, were there with the ark of the covenant of God.

5 When the ark of the covenant of the LORD came into the camp, all Israel gave a mighty shout, so that the earth resounded. [6]When the Philistines heard the noise of the shouting, they said, "What does this great shouting in the camp of the Hebrews mean?" When they learned that the ark of the LORD had come to the camp, [7]the Philistines were afraid; for they said, "Gods have[h] come into the camp." They also said, "Woe to us! For nothing like this has happened before. [8]Woe to us! Who can deliver us from the power of these mighty gods? These are the gods who struck the Egyptians with every sort of plague in the wilderness. [9]Take courage, and be men, O Philistines, in order not to become slaves to the Hebrews as they have been to you; be men and fight."

10 So the Philistines fought; Israel was defeated, and they fled, everyone to his home. There was a very great slaughter, for there fell of Israel thirty thousand foot soldiers. [11]The ark of God was captured; and the two sons of Eli, Hophni and Phinehas, died.

e Gk: Heb lacks *In those days the Philistines mustered for war against Israel*   *f* Gk: Heb *against the Philistines*
g Meaning of Heb uncertain   *h* Or *A god has*

ELI *An End and a Beginning*

ELI'S SONS ARE THE WORST example of stereotypically rebellious "preacher's kids." They greedily grabbed from the offerings people brought to the tabernacle, and slept with the female assistants. Though they followed their father into a career as priests, they played God's tent of worship like carnival barkers, bringing contempt on the worship service.

Eli knew about his sons' antics. He talked to them and scolded them, yet he never took firm action. According to the Bible, he honored his sons more than God. As a result, God brought judgment on Eli and his family. Not only would his sons die, but his whole family line would also lose the right to serve as priests.

This tragic message came from the lips of a little boy, Samuel, who had been brought to the tabernacle for Eli to raise. While Eli's biological sons were being cursed, God blessed Eli's foster child. In the same tabernacle that Eli's sons had dishonored, a boy learned to hear God's word from the old, worn-down priest.

Samuel would go on to be the greatest leader Israel had known since Joshua. Although Eli's family legacy died out, through Samuel his best qualities lived on.

Life Questions: Often from the ruins of one era, a new one springs to life. Can you see this cycle of decay and revival in any of the families you know? In your own life?

Death of Eli

12 A man of Benjamin ran from the battle line, and came to Shiloh the same day, with his clothes torn and with earth upon his head.

4.12 The End of Shiloh

The Philistine victory may have led to Shiloh's capture, for the next time we encounter Eli's family, they have moved as a group to Nob. Several Bible passages mention Shiloh's destruction as a punishment for sin (Jeremiah 7.12,14; 26.6,9; Psalm 78.60). If Shiloh did fall at this time, its capture must have added greatly to Israel's general sense of despair, for the city was an important site for worship.

13When he arrived, Eli was sitting upon his seat by the road watching, for his heart trembled for the ark of God. When the man came into the city and told the news, all the city cried out. 14When Eli heard the sound of the outcry, he said, "What is this uproar?" Then the man came quickly and told Eli. 15Now Eli was ninety-eight years old and his eyes were set, so that he could not see. 16The man said to Eli, "I have just come from the battle; I fled from the battle today." He said, "How did it go, my son?" 17The messenger replied, "Israel has fled before the Philistines, and there has also been a great slaughter among the troops; your two sons also, Hophni and Phinehas, are dead, and the ark of God has been captured." 18When he mentioned the ark of God, Eli*i* fell over backward from his seat by the side of the gate; and his neck was broken and he died, for he was an old man, and heavy. He had judged Israel forty years.

19 Now his daughter-in-law, the wife of Phinehas, was pregnant, about to give birth. When she heard the news that the ark of God was captured, and that her father-in-law and her husband were dead, she bowed and gave birth; for her labor pains overwhelmed her. 20As she was about to die, the women attending her said to her, "Do not be afraid, for you have borne a son." But she did not answer or give heed. 21She named the child Ichabod, meaning, "The glory has departed from Israel," because the ark of God had been captured and because of her father-in-law and her husband. 22She said, "The glory has departed from Israel, for the ark of God has been captured."

The Philistines and the Ark

5 When the Philistines captured the ark of God, they brought it from Ebenezer to Ash-

dod; 2then the Philistines took the ark of God and brought it into the house of Dagon and placed it beside Dagon. 3When the people of Ashdod rose early the next day, there was Dagon, fallen on his face to the ground before the ark of the LORD. So they took Dagon and put him back in his place. 4But when they rose early on the next morning, Dagon had fallen on his face to the ground before the ark of the LORD, and the head of Dagon and both his hands were lying cut off upon the threshold; only the trunk of*j* Dagon was left to him. 5This is why the priests of Dagon and all who enter the house of Dagon do not step on the threshold of Dagon in Ashdod to this day.

6 The hand of the LORD was heavy upon the people of Ashdod, and he terrified and struck them with tumors, both in Ashdod and in its territory. 7And when the inhabitants of Ashdod saw how things were, they said, "The ark of the God of Israel must not remain with us; for his hand is heavy on us and on our god Dagon." 8So they sent and gathered together all the lords of the Philistines, and said, "What shall we do with the ark of the God of Israel?" The inhabitants of Gath replied, "Let the ark of God be moved on to us."*k* So they moved the ark of the God of Israel to Gath.*l* 9But after they had brought it to Gath,*m* the hand of the LORD was against the city, causing a very great panic; he struck the inhabitants of the city, both young and old, so that tumors broke out on them. 10So they sent the ark of the God of Israel*n* to Ekron. But when the ark of God came to Ekron, the people of Ekron cried out, "Why*o* have they brought around to us*p* the ark of the God of Israel to kill us*p* and our*q* people?" 11They sent therefore and gathered together all the lords of the Philistines, and said, "Send away the ark of the God of Israel, and let it return to its own place, that it may not kill us and our people." For there was a deathly panic*r* throughout the whole city. The hand of God was very heavy there; 12those who did not die were stricken with tumors, and the cry of the city went up to heaven.

The Ark Returned to Israel

6 The ark of the LORD was in the country of the Philistines seven months. 2Then the Philistines called for the priests and the diviners and said, "What shall we do with the ark of the LORD? Tell us what we should send with it to its place." 3They said, "If you send away the ark of the God of Israel, do not send it empty, but by all means return him a guilt offering. Then you will be healed and will be ransomed;*s* will not his hand then turn from you?" 4And they said, "What is the guilt offering that we shall return to him?"

---

i Heb *he*   *j* Heb lacks *the trunk of*   *k* Gk Compare Q Ms: MT *They answered, "Let the ark of the God of Israel be brought around to Gath."*   *l* Gk: Heb lacks *to Gath*   *m* Q Ms: MT lacks *to Gath*   *n* Q Ms Gk: MT lacks *of Israel*
o Q Ms Gk: MT lacks *Why*   *p* Heb *me*   *q* Heb *my*   *r* Q Ms reads *a panic from the LORD*   *s* Q Ms Gk: MT *and it will be known to you*

They answered, "Five gold tumors and five gold mice, according to the number of the lords of the Philistines; for the same plague was upon all of you and upon your lords. ⁵So you must make images of your tumors and images of your mice that ravage the land, and give glory to the God of Israel; perhaps he will lighten his hand on you

6.5 Magic

The Philistine strategy shows traditional magical thinking, still common in some occult or voodoo rites. By sending gold models of the tumors and rats out of the country, the Philistines hoped to send the originals out of the country too. This is similar to the voodoo practice of sticking pins into wax models of one's enemies.

The Israelites, instead of looking for a magical technique, appealed to the overwhelming power of a personal God, who could not be manipulated with magic.

and your gods and your land. ⁶Why should you harden your hearts as the Egyptians and Pharaoh hardened their hearts? After he had made fools of them, did they not let the people go, and they departed? ⁷Now then, get ready a new cart and two milch cows that have never borne a yoke, and yoke the cows to the cart, but take their calves home, away from them. ⁸Take the ark of the LORD and place it on the cart, and put in a box at its side the figures of gold, which you are returning to him as a guilt offering. Then send it off, and let it go its way. ⁹And watch; if it goes up on the way to its own land, to Beth-shemesh, then it is he who has done us this great harm; but if not, then we shall know that it is not his hand that struck us; it happened to us by chance."

10 The men did so; they took two milch cows and yoked them to the cart, and shut up their calves at home. ¹¹They put the ark of the LORD on the cart, and the box with the gold mice and the images of their tumors. ¹²The cows went straight in the direction of Beth-shemesh along one highway, lowing as they went; they turned neither to the right nor to the left, and the lords of the Philistines went after them as far as the border of Beth-shemesh.

13 Now the people of Beth-shemesh were reaping their wheat harvest in the valley. When they looked up and saw the ark, they went with rejoicing to meet it.ᵗ ¹⁴The cart came into the field of Joshua of Beth-shemesh, and stopped there. A large stone was there; so they split up the wood of the cart and offered the cows as a burnt offering to the LORD. ¹⁵The Levites took down the

ark of the LORD and the box that was beside it, in which were the gold objects, and set them upon the large stone. Then the people of Beth-shemesh offered burnt offerings and presented sacrifices on that day to the LORD. ¹⁶When the five lords of the Philistines saw it, they returned that day to Ekron.

17 These are the gold tumors, which the Philistines returned as a guilt offering to the LORD: one for Ashdod, one for Gaza, one for Ashkelon, one for Gath, one for Ekron; ¹⁸also the gold mice, according to the number of all the cities of the Philistines belonging to the five lords, both fortified cities and unwalled villages. The great stone, beside which they set down the ark of the LORD, is a witness to this day in the field of Joshua of Beth-shemesh.

The Ark at Kiriath-jearim

19 The descendants of Jeconiah did not rejoice with the people of Beth-shemesh when they greetedᵘ the ark of the LORD; and he killed seventy men of them.ᵛ The people mourned because the LORD had made a great slaughter among the people. ²⁰Then the people of Beth-shemesh said, "Who is able to stand before the LORD, this holy God? To whom shall he go so that we may be rid of him?" ²¹So they sent messengers to the inhabitants of Kiriath-jearim, saying, "The Philistines have returned the ark of the LORD. Come down

7 and take it up to you." ¹And the people of Kiriath-jearim came and took up the ark of the LORD, and brought it to the house of Abinadab on the hill. They consecrated his son, Eleazar, to have charge of the ark of the LORD.

2 From the day that the ark was lodged at Kiriath-jearim, a long time passed, some twenty years, and all the house of Israel lamentedʷ after the LORD.

Samuel as Judge

3 Then Samuel said to all the house of Israel, "If you are returning to the LORD with all your heart, then put away the foreign gods and the Astartes from among you. Direct your heart to the LORD, and serve him only, and he will deliver you out of the hand of the Philistines." ⁴So Israel put away the Baals and the Astartes, and they served the LORD only.

5 Then Samuel said, "Gather all Israel at Mizpah, and I will pray to the LORD for you." ⁶So they gathered at Mizpah, and drew water and poured it out before the LORD. They fasted that day, and said, "We have sinned against the LORD." And Samuel judged the people of Israel at Mizpah.

7 When the Philistines heard that the people of Israel had gathered at Mizpah, the lords of the Philistines went up against Israel. And when the

---

ᵗ Gk: Heb *rejoiced to see it*   ᵘ Gk: Heb *And he killed some of the people of Beth-shemesh, because they looked into*
ᵛ Heb *killed seventy men, fifty thousand men*   ʷ Meaning of Heb uncertain

people of Israel heard of it they were afraid of the Philistines. ⁸The people of Israel said to Samuel, "Do not cease to cry out to the LORD our God for us, and pray that he may save us from the hand of the Philistines." ⁹So Samuel took a sucking lamb and offered it as a whole burnt offering to the LORD; Samuel cried out to the LORD for Israel, and the LORD answered him. ¹⁰As Samuel was offering up the burnt offering, the Philistines drew near to attack Israel; but the LORD thundered with a mighty voice that day against the Philistines and threw them into confusion; and they were routed before Israel. ¹¹And the men of Israel went out of Mizpah and pursued the Philistines, and struck them down as far as beyond Beth-car.

12 Then Samuel took a stone and set it up between Mizpah and Jeshanah,ˣ and named it Ebenezer;ʸ for he said, "Thus far the LORD has helped us." ¹³So the Philistines were subdued and did not again enter the territory of Israel; the hand of the LORD was against the Philistines all the days of Samuel. ¹⁴The towns that the Philistines had taken from Israel were restored to Israel, from Ekron to Gath; and Israel recovered their territory from the hand of the Philistines. There was peace also between Israel and the Amorites.

15 Samuel judged Israel all the days of his life. ¹⁶He went on a circuit year by year to Bethel, Gilgal, and Mizpah; and he judged Israel in all these places. ¹⁷Then he would come back to Ramah, for his home was there; he administered

justice there to Israel, and built there an altar to the LORD.

Israel Demands a King

8 When Samuel became old, he made his sons judges over Israel. ²The name of his firstborn son was Joel, and the name of his second, Abijah; they were judges in Beer-sheba. ³Yet his sons did not follow in his ways, but turned aside after gain; they took bribes and perverted justice.

4 Then all the elders of Israel gathered together and came to Samuel at Ramah, ⁵and said to him, "You are old and your sons do not follow in your ways; appoint for us, then, a king to govern us, like other nations." ⁶But the thing displeased Samuel when they said, "Give us a king to govern us." Samuel prayed to the LORD, ⁷and the LORD said to Samuel, "Listen to the voice of the people in all that they say to you; for they have not rejected you, but they have rejected me from being king over them. ⁸Just as they have done to me,ᶻ from the day I brought them up out of Egypt to this day, forsaking me and serving other gods, so also they are doing to you. ⁹Now then, listen to their voice; only—you shall solemnly warn them, and show them the ways of the king who shall reign over them."

10 So Samuel reported all the words of the LORD to the people who were asking him for a king. ¹¹He said, "These will be the ways of the king who will reign over you: he will take your sons and appoint them to his chariots and to be

---

ˣ Gk Syr: Heb *Shen* ʸ That is *Stone of Help* ᶻ Gk: Heb lacks *to me*

SAMUEL *Faithful Leadership*

TIMES OF CRISIS REQUIRE EXCEPTIONAL leadership. That's why George Washington made so great a President. In order to survive, the fledgling United States needed his flawless reputation, his decisive leadership and his wide-ranging talents.

Samuel, similarly, ruled during a difficult transition. The last judge in Israel, Eli, had failed, and Philistine armies were pressing in. With everything in flux, the Israelites needed someone worthy of their trust. Samuel was the leader for the times. He oversaw the change from a loose tribal federation to a monarchy. He anointed Israel's first two kings, wrote down the rules kings were to live by and then deposed one king, Saul, who did not measure up. Samuel ended his long career without a single black mark on his record, and the entire country mourned his death.

Samuel showed remarkable versatility. A lifelong judge, he settled disputes in a regular circuit of Israelite towns. He also gained fame as a prophet, alert to hear God's word and quick to proclaim it clearly—especially when God entrusted him with key information about the future. Finally, he functioned as a priest, presenting sacrifices and prayers on behalf of God's people. He considered prayer one of his basic duties as a leader (12.23).

Like any good leader, Samuel sometimes had to bring bad news. When he was just a boy, he heard God's message of judgment against his foster father Eli (3.11–14). Samuel also gave stern warnings about a king's potential abuses of power, abuses he later had to denounce in Saul. Yet the nation remembered him more for his positive contributions. Taking over the helm when the nation was near disaster, Samuel steered the course faithfully until he could deliver leadership to David, a young man who would become Israel's greatest king.

Life Questions: What leader do you respect most? What qualities does he or she show?

his horsemen, and to run before his chariots; [12]and he will appoint for himself commanders of thousands and commanders of fifties, and some to plow his ground and to reap his harvest, and to make his implements of war and the equipment of his chariots. [13]He will take your daughters to be perfumers and cooks and bakers. [14]He will take the best of your fields and vineyards and olive orchards and give them to his courtiers. [15]He will take one-tenth of your grain and of your vineyards and give it to his officers and his courtiers. [16]He will take your male and female slaves, and the best of your cattle[a] and donkeys, and put them to his work. [17]He will take one-tenth of your flocks, and you shall be his slaves. [18]And in that day you will cry out because of your king, whom you have chosen for yourselves; but the LORD will not answer you in that day."

8.18 Why Not a King?

Considering the disorganized state of the Israelite nation, their request for a new form of government—a monarchy—seems understandable. A king would centralize power, making the nation more efficient in defending itself. However, both Samuel and God opposed the idea, particularly because of the Israelites' motive: They wanted "a king to govern us, like other nations" (8.5). Israel was supposed to be different from the other nations. Whatever the form of their government, they were to trust in God as their leader.

Israel's Request for a King Granted

19 But the people refused to listen to the voice of Samuel; they said, "No! but we are determined to have a king over us, [20]so that we also may be like other nations, and that our king may govern us and go out before us and fight our battles." [21]When Samuel had heard all the words of the people, he repeated them in the ears of the LORD. [22]The LORD said to Samuel, "Listen to their voice and set a king over them." Samuel then said to the people of Israel, "Each of you return home."

Saul Chosen to Be King

9 There was a man of Benjamin whose name was Kish son of Abiel son of Zeror son of Becorath son of Aphiah, a Benjaminite, a man of wealth. [2]He had a son whose name was Saul, a handsome young man. There was not a man among the people of Israel more handsome than he; he stood head and shoulders above everyone else.

3 Now the donkeys of Kish, Saul's father, had strayed. So Kish said to his son Saul, "Take one of the boys with you; go and look for the donkeys." [4]He passed through the hill country of Ephraim and passed through the land of Shalishah, but they did not find them. And they passed through

9.3 A Donkey Hunt

Saul, hunting for donkeys, certainly was not looking for a chance to become king. He was so politically unaware he didn't even know about the great man Samuel. Similarly, Samuel was a small boy when God called him (chapter 3), and David was anointed king while tending sheep (16.11–13). The leaders God appoints are not necessarily those seeking power.

the land of Shaalim, but they were not there. Then he passed through the land of Benjamin, but they did not find them.

5 When they came to the land of Zuph, Saul said to the boy who was with him, "Let us turn back, or my father will stop worrying about the donkeys and worry about us." [6]But he said to him, "There is a man of God in this town; he is a man held in honor. Whatever he says always comes true. Let us go there now; perhaps he will tell us about the journey on which we have set out." [7]Then Saul replied to the boy, "But if we go, what can we bring the man? For the bread in our sacks is gone, and there is no present to bring to the man of God. What have we?" [8]The boy answered Saul again, "Here, I have with me a quarter shekel of silver; I will give it to the man of God, to tell us our way." [9](Formerly in Israel, anyone who went to inquire of God would say, "Come, let us go to the seer"; for the one who is now called a prophet was formerly called a seer.) [10]Saul said to the boy, "Good; come, let us go." So they went to the town where the man of God was.

11 As they went up the hill to the town, they met some girls coming out to draw water, and said to them, "Is the seer here?" [12]They answered, "Yes, there he is just ahead of you. Hurry; he has come just now to the town, because the people have a sacrifice today at the shrine. [13]As soon as you enter the town, you will find him, before he goes up to the shrine to eat. For the people will not eat until he comes, since he must bless the sacrifice; afterward those eat who are invited. Now go up, for you will meet him immediately." [14]So they went up to the town. As they were entering the town, they saw Samuel coming out toward them on his way up to the shrine.

15 Now the day before Saul came, the LORD had revealed to Samuel: [16]"Tomorrow about this time I will send to you a man from the land of Benjamin, and you shall anoint him to be ruler over my people Israel. He shall save my people

[a] Gk: Heb young men

from the hand of the Philistines; for I have seen the suffering of[b] my people, because their outcry has come to me." [17]When Samuel saw Saul, the LORD told him, "Here is the man of whom I spoke to you. He it is who shall rule over my people." [18]Then Saul approached Samuel inside the gate, and said, "Tell me, please, where is the house of the seer?" [19]Samuel answered Saul, "I am the seer; go up before me to the shrine, for today you shall eat with me, and in the morning I will let you go and will tell you all that is on your mind. [20]As for your donkeys that were lost three days ago, give no further thought to them, for they have been found. And on whom is all Israel's desire fixed, if not on you and on all your ancestral house?" [21]Saul answered, "I am only a Benjaminite, from the least of the tribes of Israel, and my family is the humblest of all the families of the tribe of Benjamin. Why then have you spoken to me in this way?"

22 Then Samuel took Saul and his servant-boy and brought them into the hall, and gave them a place at the head of those who had been invited, of whom there were about thirty. [23]And Samuel said to the cook, "Bring the portion I gave you, the one I asked you to put aside." [24]The cook took up the thigh and what went with it[c] and set them before Saul. Samuel said, "See, what was kept is set before you. Eat; for it is set[d] before you at the appointed time, so that you might eat with the guests."[e]

So Saul ate with Samuel that day. [25]When they came down from the shrine into the town, a bed was spread for Saul[f] on the roof, and he lay down to sleep.[g] [26]Then at the break of dawn[h] Samuel called to Saul upon the roof, "Get up, so that I may send you on your way." Saul got up, and both he and Samuel went out into the street.

Samuel Anoints Saul

27 As they were going down to the outskirts of the town, Samuel said to Saul, "Tell the boy to go on before us, and when he has passed on, stop here yourself for a while, that I may make known **10** to you the word of God." [1]Samuel took a vial of oil and poured it on his head, and kissed him; he said, "The LORD has anointed you ruler over his people Israel. You shall reign over the people of the LORD and you will save them from the hand of their enemies all around. Now this shall be the sign to you that the LORD has anointed you ruler[i] over his heritage: [2]When you depart from me today you will meet two men by Rachel's tomb in the territory of Benjamin at Zelzah; they will say to you, 'The donkeys that you went to seek are found, and now your father has stopped worrying about them and is worrying about you, saying: What shall I do about my son?' [3]Then you shall go on from there further and come to the oak of Tabor; three men going up to God at Bethel will meet you there, one carrying three kids, another carrying three loaves of bread, and another carrying a skin of wine. [4]They will greet you and give you two loaves of bread, which you shall accept from them. [5]After that you shall come to Gibeath-elohim,[j] at the place where the Philistine garrison is; there, as you come to the town, you will meet a band of prophets coming down from the shrine with harp, tambourine, flute, and lyre playing in front of them; they will

> ## 10.5 Musical Prophets
>
> *This is one of the earliest references to prophets in the Bible. Under the kings, prophets became much more significant, possibly because they so often spoke out against the kings. The description of the prophets' musical procession is intriguing, though we can only guess what exactly they were doing. Unquestionably, the spirit's powerful effect on Saul made a startling change in him (verse 11).*

be in a prophetic frenzy. [6]Then the spirit of the LORD will possess you, and you will be in a prophetic frenzy along with them and be turned into a different person. [7]Now when these signs meet you, do whatever you see fit to do, for God is with you. [8]And you shall go down to Gilgal ahead of me; then I will come down to you to present burnt offerings and offer sacrifices of well-being. Seven days you shall wait, until I come to you and show you what you shall do."

Saul Prophesies

9 As he turned away to leave Samuel, God gave him another heart; and all these signs were fulfilled that day. [10]When they were going from there[k] to Gibeah,[l] a band of prophets met him; and the spirit of God possessed him, and he fell into a prophetic frenzy along with them. [11]When all who knew him before saw how he prophesied with the prophets, the people said to one another, "What has come over the son of Kish? Is Saul also among the prophets?" [12]A man of the place answered, "And who is their father?" Therefore it became a proverb, "Is Saul also among the prophets?" [13]When his prophetic frenzy had ended, he went home.[m]

14 Saul's uncle said to him and to the boy,

---

[b] Gk: Heb lacks *the suffering of*   [c] Meaning of Heb uncertain   [d] Q Ms Gk: MT *it was kept*   [e] Cn: Heb *it was kept for you, saying, I have invited the people*   [f] Gk: Heb *and he spoke with Saul*   [g] Gk: Heb lacks *and he lay down to sleep*   [h] Gk: Heb *and they arose early and at break of dawn*   [i] Gk: Heb lacks *over his people Israel. You shall . . . anointed you ruler*   [j] Or *the Hill of God*   [k] Gk: Heb *they came there*   [l] Or *the hill*   [m] Cn: Heb *he came to the shrine*

"Where did you go?" And he replied, "To seek the donkeys; and when we saw they were not to be found, we went to Samuel." [15]Saul's uncle said, "Tell me what Samuel said to you." [16]Saul said to his uncle, "He told us that the donkeys had been found." But about the matter of the kingship, of which Samuel had spoken, he did not tell him anything.

Saul Proclaimed King

17　Samuel summoned the people to the LORD at Mizpah [18]and said to them,[n] "Thus says the LORD, the God of Israel, 'I brought up Israel out of Egypt, and I rescued you from the hand of the Egyptians and from the hand of all the kingdoms that were oppressing you.' [19]But today you have rejected your God, who saves you from all your calamities and your distresses; and you have said, 'No! but set a king over us.' Now therefore present yourselves before the LORD by your tribes and by your clans."

20　Then Samuel brought all the tribes of Israel near, and the tribe of Benjamin was taken by lot. [21]He brought the tribe of Benjamin near by its families, and the family of the Matrites was taken by lot. Finally he brought the family of the Matrites near man by man,[o] and Saul the son of Kish was taken by lot. But when they sought him, he could not be found. [22]So they inquired again of the LORD, "Did the man come here?"[p] and the LORD said, "See, he has hidden himself among the baggage." [23]Then they ran and brought him from there. When he took his stand among the people, he was head and shoulders taller than any of them. [24]Samuel said to all the people, "Do you see the one whom the LORD has chosen? There is no one like him among all the people." And all the people shouted, "Long live the king!"

25　Samuel told the people the rights and duties of the kingship; and he wrote them in a book and laid it up before the LORD. Then Samuel sent

10.25 Limits on the King

Though Samuel reluctantly designated Saul as the first king, he insisted on safeguards. Much as the United States government rests on a document, the Constitution, so Saul's kingship was defined and limited by certain rules, which Samuel wrote down and placed in the tabernacle as a permanent record.

all the people back to their homes. [26]Saul also went to his home at Gibeah, and with him went warriors whose hearts God had touched. [27]But some worthless fellows said, "How can this man

save us?" They despised him and brought him no present. But he held his peace.

Now Nahash, king of the Ammonites, had been grievously oppressing the Gadites and the Reubenites. He would gouge out the right eye of each of them and would not grant Israel a deliverer. No one was left of the Israelites across the Jordan whose right eye Nahash, king of the Ammonites, had not gouged out. But there were seven thousand men who had escaped from the Ammonites and had entered Jabesh-gilead.[q]

Saul Defeats the Ammonites

11 About a month later,[r] Nahash the Ammonite went up and besieged Jabesh-gilead; and all the men of Jabesh said to Nahash, "Make a treaty with us, and we will serve you." [2]But Nahash the Ammonite said to them, "On this condition I will make a treaty with you, namely that I gouge out everyone's right eye, and thus put disgrace upon all Israel." [3]The elders of Jabesh said to him, "Give us seven days' respite that we may send messengers through all the territory of Israel. Then, if there is no one to save us, we will give ourselves up to you." [4]When the messengers came to Gibeah of Saul, they reported the matter in the hearing of the people; and all the people wept aloud.

5　Now Saul was coming from the field behind the oxen; and Saul said, "What is the matter with the people, that they are weeping?" So they told him the message from the inhabitants of Jabesh. [6]And the spirit of God came upon Saul in power when he heard these words, and his anger was greatly kindled. [7]He took a yoke of oxen, and cut them in pieces and sent them throughout all the territory of Israel by messengers, saying, "Whoever does not come out after Saul and Samuel, so shall it be done to his oxen!" Then the dread of the LORD fell upon the people, and they came out as one. [8]When he mustered them at Bezek, those from Israel were three hundred thousand, and those from Judah seventy[s] thousand. [9]They said to the messengers who had come, "Thus shall you say to the inhabitants of Jabesh-gilead: 'Tomorrow, by the time the sun is hot, you shall have deliverance.'" When the messengers came and told the inhabitants of Jabesh, they rejoiced. [10]So the inhabitants of Jabesh said, "Tomorrow we will give ourselves up to you, and you may do to us whatever seems good to you." [11]The next day Saul put the people in three companies. At the morning watch they came into the camp and cut down the Ammonites until the heat of the day; and those who survived were scattered, so that no two of them were left together.

12　The people said to Samuel, "Who is it that

---

[n] Heb *to the people of Israel*　　[o] Gk: Heb lacks *Finally . . . man by man*　　[p] Gk: Heb *Is there yet a man to come here?*
[q] Q Ms Compare Josephus, *Antiquities* VI.v.1 (68-71): MT lacks *Now Nahash . . . entered Jabesh-gilead.*　　[r] Q Ms Gk:
MT lacks *About a month later*　　[s] Q Ms Gk: MT *thirty*

The First King

Every other nation had one—why not Israel?

"If both you and the king who reigns over you will follow the LORD your God, it will be well; but if you will not heed the voice of the LORD, . . . then the hand of the LORD will be against you and your king."
12.14–15

MAKING A SINGLE NATION OUT of a dozen tribes was not easy. Unity came hard for Israel; it also came hard for the United States. U.S. history may shed light on 1 Samuel's story.

Most people think George Washington was the first president of the United States, but that honor actually belongs to Samuel Huntington. He never achieved fame because the states he presided over weren't united. They had no Constitution, only Articles of Confederation that made them 13 independent nations loosely linked together.

Congress under Siege

Two years after Huntington took office, on June 21, 1783, 500 unpaid federal soldiers laid siege to Congress in Philadelphia, breaking windows and shouting threats because Congress, which was supposed to pay them, had no money. The jealously independent states had given them none. Driven out of town by the soldiers, Congress became nomadic, meeting in Princeton, Annapolis, Trenton, and New York City. That same June, George Washington wrote, "It is yet to be decided whether the Revolution must ultimately be considered a blessing or a curse."

Troubles continued. In Shays's Rebellion, 1,500 hostile farmers surrounded courtrooms, refusing to let courts meet. The army should have quickly dispersed them, but the national army consisted of only 700 men. Shays's Rebellion made obvious the need for a stronger central government. The next year a constitutional convention met in Philadelphia to hammer out the document that still unifies Americans. Washington was elected president.

Why Israel Needed a King

The 12 tribes of Israel, like the 13 states, were a nation in name only. They had no central government at all. Since conquering Palestine, they had worked together only during emergencies, when inspired "judges"—military heroes like Gideon, Deborah, and Samson—came forward to lead them into battle.

In Samuel's time, though, the Philistines' military threat wouldn't go away. Israel needed superior leadership, but Samuel was an old man. His sons made unappealing successors. What could be done? Looking around them, the tribes noticed that virtually every other country had a king. A king offered two advantages: first, he provided central government; second, since his sons would normally succeed a king, the nation did not have a crisis of leadership every time its leader got old. So the leaders of Israel asked Samuel to appoint a king (8.4–5).

Against God's Will

The idea seems to have been popular with everyone except Samuel and God. Samuel may have been displeased that he and his sons were being rejected. God had a deeper objection: Israel was rejecting his leadership. God told Samuel to warn the elders that a king would oppress his own citizens. Samuel warned of the military draft, of high taxation, of the king's power to make people into slaves (8.10–18).

Was God against a king? Some scholars see the monarchy as a marvelous example of God's use of a choice made against his will. God counseled Israel against the very institution that ultimately produced King David, and through him Jesus, King of kings.

Others suggest that God only opposed the motive behind the request. (Deuteronomy 17.14–20 had assumed that the Israelites would eventually want and get a king.) The key is the phrase the elders used: "So that we also may be like other nations" (8.20). God did not want them to be like all the other nations.

The King Was a Servant

Yet God gave in to their request, bad motives and all. He not only allowed the Israelites a king, he picked out their man. He accepted the monarchy on condition that Israel still consider the Lord as its ultimate ruler (12.14).

Apparently, Israel's king didn't answer to a parliament or court system, but he did answer to God. In short order the first king, Saul, was rejected because he disobeyed God. God rebuked and punished his replacement, David. Most nations' kings held absolute power. In Israel only God was absolute, and the king was his servant.

Life Questions: Have you ever seen God take a bad request made with bad motives and use it for his own purposes?

said, 'Shall Saul reign over us?' Give them to us so that we may put them to death." [13]But Saul said, "No one shall be put to death this day, for today the LORD has brought deliverance to Israel."

14 Samuel said to the people, "Come, let us go to Gilgal and there renew the kingship." [15]So all the people went to Gilgal, and there they made Saul king before the LORD in Gilgal. There they sacrificed offerings of well-being before the LORD, and there Saul and all the Israelites rejoiced greatly.

Samuel's Farewell Address

12 Samuel said to all Israel, "I have listened to you in all that you have said to me, and have set a king over you. [2]See, it is the king who leads you now; I am old and gray, but my sons are with you. I have led you from my youth until this day. [3]Here I am; testify against me before the LORD and before his anointed. Whose ox have I taken? Or whose donkey have I taken? Or whom have I defrauded? Whom have I oppressed? Or from whose hand have I taken a bribe to blind my eyes with it? Testify against me[t] and I will restore it to you." [4]They said, "You have not defrauded us or oppressed us or taken anything from the

12.4 Accuse Me!

Unlike some political and religious leaders who get caught in financial scandals, Samuel considered himself publicly accountable. He began his farewell speech by offering an opportunity for anyone to stand up and testify that he, Samuel, had been dishonest or had taken advantage of his leadership position. Before going on, he asked those present to witness aloud to his honesty.

hand of anyone." [5]He said to them, "The LORD is witness against you, and his anointed is witness this day, that you have not found anything in my hand." And they said, "He is witness."

6 Samuel said to the people, "The LORD is witness, who[u] appointed Moses and Aaron and brought your ancestors up out of the land of Egypt. [7]Now therefore take your stand, so that I may enter into judgment with you before the LORD, and I will declare to you[v] all the saving deeds of the LORD that he performed for you and for your ancestors. [8]When Jacob went into Egypt and the Egyptians oppressed them,[w] then your ancestors cried to the LORD and the LORD sent Moses and Aaron, who brought forth your ances-

tors out of Egypt, and settled them in this place. [9]But they forgot the LORD their God; and he sold them into the hand of Sisera, commander of the army of King Jabin of[x] Hazor, and into the hand of the Philistines, and into the hand of the king of Moab; and they fought against them. [10]Then they cried to the LORD, and said, 'We have sinned, because we have forsaken the LORD, and have served the Baals and the Astartes; but now rescue us out of the hand of our enemies, and we will serve you.' [11]And the LORD sent Jerubbaal and Barak,[y] and Jephthah, and Samson,[z] and rescued you out of the hand of your enemies on every side; and you lived in safety. [12]But when you saw that King Nahash of the Ammonites came against you, you said to me, 'No, but a king shall reign over us,' though the LORD your God was your king. [13]See, here is the king whom you have chosen, for whom you have asked; see, the LORD has set a king over you. [14]If you will fear the LORD and serve him and heed his voice and not rebel against the commandment of the LORD, and if both you and the king who reigns over you will follow the LORD your God, it will be well; [15]but if you will not heed the voice of the LORD, but rebel against the commandment of the LORD, then the hand of the LORD will be against you and your king.[a] [16]Now therefore take your stand and see this great thing that the LORD will do before your eyes. [17]Is it not the wheat harvest today? I will call upon the LORD, that he may send thunder and rain; and you shall know and see that the wickedness that you have done in the sight of the LORD is great in demanding a king for yourselves." [18]So Samuel called upon the LORD, and the LORD sent thunder and rain that day; and all the people greatly feared the LORD and Samuel.

19 All the people said to Samuel, "Pray to the LORD your God for your servants, so that we may not die; for we have added to all our sins the evil of demanding a king for ourselves." [20]And Samuel said to the people, "Do not be afraid; you have done all this evil, yet do not turn aside from following the LORD, but serve the LORD with all your heart; [21]and do not turn aside after useless things that cannot profit or save, for they are useless. [22]For the LORD will not cast away his people, for his great name's sake, because it has pleased the LORD to make you a people for himself. [23]Moreover as for me, far be it from me that I should sin against the LORD by ceasing to pray for you; and I will instruct you in the good and the right way. [24]Only fear the LORD, and serve him faithfully with all your heart; for consider what great things he has done for you. [25]But if you still do wickedly, you shall be swept away, both you and your king."

[t] Gk: Heb lacks *Testify against me*   [u] Gk: Heb lacks *is witness, who*   [v] Gk: Heb lacks *and I will declare to you*
[w] Gk: Heb lacks *and the Egyptians oppressed them*   [x] Gk: Heb lacks *King Jabin of*   [y] Gk Syr: Heb *Bedan*
[z] Gk: Heb *Samuel*   [a] Gk: Heb *and your ancestors*

Saul's Unlawful Sacrifice

13 Saul was ...[b] years old when he began to reign; and he reigned ... and two[c] years over Israel.

2 Saul chose three thousand out of Israel; two thousand were with Saul in Michmash and the hill country of Bethel, and a thousand were with Jonathan in Gibeah of Benjamin; the rest of the people he sent home to their tents. ³Jonathan defeated the garrison of the Philistines that was at Geba; and the Philistines heard of it. And Saul blew the trumpet throughout all the land, saying, "Let the Hebrews hear!" ⁴When all Israel heard that Saul had defeated the garrison of the Philistines, and also that Israel had become odious to the Philistines, the people were called out to join Saul at Gilgal.

5 The Philistines mustered to fight with Israel, thirty thousand chariots, and six thousand horsemen, and troops like the sand on the seashore in multitude; they came up and encamped at Michmash, to the east of Beth-aven. ⁶When the Israelites saw that they were in distress (for the troops were hard pressed), the people hid themselves in caves and in holes and in rocks and in tombs and in cisterns. ⁷Some Hebrews crossed the Jordan to the land of Gad and Gilead. Saul was still at Gilgal, and all the people followed him trembling.

8 He waited seven days, the time appointed by Samuel; but Samuel did not come to Gilgal, and the people began to slip away from Saul.[d] ⁹So Saul said, "Bring the burnt offering here to me, and the offerings of well-being." And he offered the burnt offering. ¹⁰As soon as he had finished offering the burnt offering, Samuel arrived; and Saul went out to meet him and salute him. ¹¹Samuel said, "What have you done?" Saul replied, "When I saw that the people were slipping away from me, and that you did not come within the days appointed, and that the Philistines were mustering at Michmash, ¹²I said, 'Now the Philistines will come down upon me at Gilgal, and I have not entreated the favor of the LORD'; so I forced myself, and offered the burnt offering." ¹³Samuel said to Saul, "You have done foolishly; you have not kept the commandment of the LORD your God, which he commanded you. The LORD would have established your kingdom over Israel forever, ¹⁴but now your kingdom will not continue; the LORD has sought out a man after his own heart; and the LORD has appointed him to be ruler over his people, because you have not kept what the LORD commanded you." ¹⁵And Samuel left and went on his way from Gilgal.[e] The rest of the people followed Saul to join the army; they went up from Gilgal toward Gibeah of Benjamin.[f]

Preparations for Battle

Saul counted the people who were present with him, about six hundred men. ¹⁶Saul, his son Jonathan, and the people who were present with them stayed in Geba of Benjamin; but the Philistines encamped at Michmash. ¹⁷And raiders came out of the camp of the Philistines in three companies; one company turned toward Ophrah, to the land of Shual, ¹⁸another company turned toward Beth-horon, and another company turned toward the mountain[g] that looks down upon the valley of Zeboim toward the wilderness.

19 Now there was no smith to be found throughout all the land of Israel; for the Philistines said, "The Hebrews must not make swords

13.19 Military Dominance

Samuel's leadership had kept the Philistines from occupying Israel (see 7.13). However, nobody could question the Philistines' military dominance. They had outposts in several central Israelite towns (10.5; 13.3) and, most important, kept a monopoly on iron weapons by outlawing local blacksmiths. Only the royal family of Israel possessed a sword or a spear (verse 22), presumably weapons that had been smuggled in and hidden.

or spears for themselves"; ²⁰so all the Israelites went down to the Philistines to sharpen their plowshares, mattocks, axes, or sickles;[h] ²¹The charge was two-thirds of a shekel[i] for the plowshares and for the mattocks, and one-third of a shekel for sharpening the axes and for setting the goads.[j] ²²So on the day of the battle neither sword nor spear was to be found in the possession of any of the people with Saul and Jonathan; but Saul and his son Jonathan had them.

Jonathan Surprises and Routs the Philistines

23 Now a garrison of the Philistines had gone out to the pass of Michmash. **14** ¹One day Jonathan son of Saul said to the young man who carried his armor, "Come, let us go over to the Philistine garrison on the other side." But he did not tell his father. ²Saul was staying in the outskirts of Gibeah under the pomegranate tree that is at Migron; the troops that were with him were about six hundred men, ³along with Ahijah son of Ahitub, Ichabod's brother, son of Phinehas son of Eli, the priest of the LORD in Shiloh, carrying an ephod. Now the people did not know that Jonathan had gone. ⁴In the pass,[k] by which Jona-

---

[b] The number is lacking in the Heb text (the verse is lacking in the Septuagint).   [c] Two is not the entire number; something has dropped out.   [d] Heb him   [e] Gk: Heb went up from Gilgal to Gibeah of Benjamin   [f] Gk: Heb lacks The rest ... of Benjamin   [g] Cn Compare Gk: Heb toward the border   [h] Gk: Heb plowshare   [i] Heb was a pim   [j] Cn: Meaning of Heb uncertain   [k] Heb Between the passes

than tried to go over to the Philistine garrison, there was a rocky crag on one side and a rocky crag on the other; the name of the one was Bozez, and the name of the other Seneh. 5One crag rose on the north in front of Michmash, and the other on the south in front of Geba.

6 Jonathan said to the young man who carried his armor, "Come, let us go over to the garrison of these uncircumcised; it may be that the LORD will act for us; for nothing can hinder the LORD from saving by many or by few." 7His armor-bearer said to him, "Do all that your mind inclines to.*l* I am with you; as your mind is, so is mine."*m* 8Then Jonathan said, "Now we will cross over to those men and will show ourselves to them. 9If they say to us, 'Wait until we come to you,' then we will stand still in our place, and we will not go up to them. 10But if they say, 'Come up to us,' then we will go up; for the LORD has given them into our hand. That will be the sign for us." 11So both of them showed themselves to the garrison of the Philistines; and the Philistines said, "Look, Hebrews are coming out of the holes where they have hidden themselves." 12The men of the garrison hailed Jonathan and his armor-bearer, saying, "Come up to us, and we will show you something." Jonathan said to his armor-bearer, "Come up after me; for the LORD has given them into the hand of Israel." 13Then Jonathan climbed up on his hands and feet, with his armor-bearer following after him. The Philistines*n* fell before Jonathan, and his armor-bearer, coming after him, killed them. 14In that first slaughter Jonathan and his armor-bearer killed about twenty men within an area about half a furrow long in an acre*o* of land. 15There was a panic in the camp, in the field, and among all the people; the garrison and even the raiders trembled; the earth quaked; and it became a very great panic.

16 Saul's lookouts in Gibeah of Benjamin were watching as the multitude was surging back and forth.*p* 17Then Saul said to the troops that were with him, "Call the roll and see who has gone from us." When they had called the roll, Jonathan and his armor-bearer were not there. 18Saul said to Ahijah, "Bring the ark*q* of God here." For at that time the ark*q* of God went with the Israelites. 19While Saul was talking to the priest, the tumult in the camp of the Philistines increased more and more; and Saul said to the priest, "Withdraw your hand." 20Then Saul and all the people who were with him rallied and went into the battle; and every sword was against the other, so that there was very great confusion. 21Now the Hebrews who previously had been with the Philistines and had gone up with them into the camp turned and joined the Israelites who were with Saul and Jonathan. 22Likewise,

when all the Israelites who had gone into hiding in the hill country of Ephraim heard that the Philistines were fleeing, they too followed closely after them in the battle. 23So the LORD gave Israel the victory that day.

The battle passed beyond Beth-aven, and the troops with Saul numbered altogether about ten thousand men. The battle spread out over the hill country of Ephraim.

Saul's Rash Oath

24 Now Saul committed a very rash act on that day.*r* He had laid an oath on the troops, saying, "Cursed be anyone who eats food before it is evening and I have been avenged on my

14.24 Big Ego

Saul's problems surface here in two ways. First, he impulsively pronounced a curse (a very solemn vow) without thinking it through. This rash vow made his hungry army less effective, and led to trouble for his own son. Second, Saul apparently saw the battle as a personal vendetta in which he was avenging himself on his enemies. A wiser leader would have understood that God's honor and the security of his people were the issues.

enemies." So none of the troops tasted food. 25All the troops*s* came upon a honeycomb; and there was honey on the ground. 26When the troops came upon the honeycomb, the honey was dripping out; but they did not put their hands to their mouths, for they feared the oath. 27But Jonathan had not heard his father charge the troops with the oath; so he extended the staff that was in his hand, and dipped the tip of it in the honeycomb, and put his hand to his mouth; and his eyes brightened. 28Then one of the soldiers said, "Your father strictly charged the troops with an oath, saying, 'Cursed be anyone who eats food this day.' And so the troops are faint." 29Then Jonathan said, "My father has troubled the land; see how my eyes have brightened because I tasted a little of this honey. 30How much better if today the troops had eaten freely of the spoil taken from their enemies; for now the slaughter among the Philistines has not been great."

31 After they had struck down the Philistines that day from Michmash to Aijalon, the troops were very faint; 32so the troops flew upon the spoil, and took sheep and oxen and calves, and slaughtered them on the ground; and the troops ate them with the blood. 33Then it was reported to Saul, "Look, the troops are sinning against the LORD by eating with the blood." And he said,

---

l Gk: Heb *Do all that is in your mind. Turn*   *m* Gk: Heb lacks *so is mine*   *n* Heb *They*   *o* Heb *yoke*
p Gk: Heb *they went and there*   *q* Gk *the ephod*   *r* Gk: Heb *The Israelites were distressed that day*   *s* Heb *land*

"You have dealt treacherously; roll a large stone before me here."[t] [34]Saul said, "Disperse yourselves among the troops, and say to them, 'Let all bring their oxen or their sheep, and slaughter them here, and eat; and do not sin against the LORD by eating with the blood.'" So all of the troops brought their oxen with them that night, and slaughtered them there. [35]And Saul built an altar to the LORD; it was the first altar that he built to the LORD.

Jonathan in Danger of Death

36 Then Saul said, "Let us go down after the Philistines by night and despoil them until the morning light; let us not leave one of them." They said, "Do whatever seems good to you." But the priest said, "Let us draw near to God here." [37]So Saul inquired of God, "Shall I go down after the Philistines? Will you give them into the hand of Israel?" But he did not answer him that day. [38]Saul said, "Come here, all you leaders of the people; and let us find out how this sin has arisen today. [39]For as the LORD lives who saves Israel, even if it is in my son Jonathan, he shall surely die!" But there was no one among all the people who answered him. [40]He said to all Israel, "You shall be on one side, and I and my son Jonathan will be on the other side." The people said to Saul, "Do what seems good to you." [41]Then Saul said, "O LORD God of Israel, why have you not answered your servant today? If this guilt is in me or in my son Jonathan, O LORD God of Israel, give Urim; but if this guilt is in your people Israel,[u] give Thummim." And Jonathan and Saul were indicated by the lot, but the people were cleared. [42]Then Saul said, "Cast the lot between me and my son Jonathan." And Jonathan was taken.

43 Then Saul said to Jonathan, "Tell me what you have done." Jonathan told him, "I tasted a little honey with the tip of the staff that was in my hand; here I am, I will die." [44]Saul said, "God do so to me and more also; you shall surely die, Jonathan!" [45]Then the people said to Saul, "Shall Jonathan die, who has accomplished this great victory in Israel? Far from it! As the LORD lives, not one hair of his head shall fall to the ground; for he has worked with God today." So the people ransomed Jonathan, and he did not die. [46]Then Saul withdrew from pursuing the Philistines; and the Philistines went to their own place.

Saul's Continuing Wars

47 When Saul had taken the kingship over Israel, he fought against all his enemies on every side—against Moab, against the Ammonites, against Edom, against the kings of Zobah, and against the Philistines; wherever he turned he routed them. [48]He did valiantly, and struck down the Amalekites, and rescued Israel out of the hands of those who plundered them.

49 Now the sons of Saul were Jonathan, Ishvi, and Malchishua; and the names of his two daughters were these: the name of the firstborn was Merab, and the name of the younger, Michal. [50]The name of Saul's wife was Ahinoam daughter of Ahimaaz. And the name of the commander of his army was Abner son of Ner, Saul's uncle; [51]Kish was the father of Saul, and Ner the father of Abner was the son of Abiel.

52 There was hard fighting against the Philistines all the days of Saul; and when Saul saw any strong or valiant warrior, he took him into his service.

Saul Defeats the Amalekites but Spares Their King

15 Samuel said to Saul, "The LORD sent me to anoint you king over his people Israel; now therefore listen to the words of the LORD. [2]Thus says the LORD of hosts, 'I will punish the Amalekites for what they did in opposing the Israelites

15.2 Old Enemies

The Israelites had first encountered the Amalekites, a semi-nomadic group of pitiless raiders, on their way out of Egypt. Due to the Amalekites' unprovoked attack, Moses had declared that God wanted Amalek wiped out (Exodus 17.8–16; Deuteronomy 25.17–19). The hostility continued. Typically, the Amalekites would sweep into unprotected towns and villages on the edge of the southern desert, killing and looting, leaving the survivors without food. Though Samuel's order to Saul is hard to understand, knowing the Amalekites' reputation makes it easier to sympathize with. For a more general explanation of holy war, see "Is a War Ever Holy?" page 242.

when they came up out of Egypt. [3]Now go and attack Amalek, and utterly destroy all that they have; do not spare them, but kill both man and woman, child and infant, ox and sheep, camel and donkey.'"

4 So Saul summoned the people, and numbered them in Telaim, two hundred thousand foot soldiers, and ten thousand soldiers of Judah. [5]Saul came to the city of the Amalekites and lay in wait in the valley. [6]Saul said to the Kenites, "Go! Leave! Withdraw from among the Amalekites, or I will destroy you with them; for you showed kindness to all the people of Israel when they came up out of Egypt." So the Kenites withdrew from the Amalekites. [7]Saul defeated the Amalekites, from Havilah as far as Shur, which is

---

[t] Gk: Heb *me this day*   [u] Vg Compare Gk: Heb [41]*Saul said to the LORD, the God of Israel*

Why Saul Was Rejected
A leader who failed under pressure

SAUL HAD EVERYTHING GOING FOR him. Tall and handsome, he struck people with his appearance. God chose him as the first king in the history of Israel. Soon after he was secretly anointed, God's spirit came on him—an encounter with God that affected his entire personality.

Almost immediately Saul led a successful rescue operation, saving the people of a besieged city from mutilation. He was then publicly crowned king, even though he himself did no politicking for the office. (In fact, he hid during the selection.) He wisely refrained from allowing his opponents to be punished. Instead, he united all 12 tribes behind him, even though he himself came from a small, minority tribe.

Saul chose the best young men to serve in his army. One of them, David, was not only a skilled general, but also a loyal follower who would never oppose Saul—even when he had good reason. David married Saul's daughter, and Saul's oldest son, Jonathan, became David's best friend. This should have cemented an alliance, sealing Saul's success.

Deterioration under Pressure

Yet Saul's life went tragically wrong. The first sign of trouble, as 1 Samuel tells the story, came not long after he became king. While preparing for a campaign against the Philistines, Saul grew impatient. Samuel, scheduled to lead in the proper spiritual preparation for battle, was seven days late. Saul's men began to desert, and Saul decided he could wait no longer. He himself began to make the religious sacrifices that Samuel, as priest, was supposed to make. Just then Samuel arrived. He blasted Saul (13.13–14). Saul's hastiness, insignificant though it may seem, showed an inner weakness: his willingness to compromise God's directions under pressure.

The battle came soon afterwards, and Israel won miraculously. But in the victory Saul acted sometimes indecisively, sometimes rashly. He could not decide to attack. Then he made a boastful vow that disrupted the Israelite army, allowing the Philistines to escape.

Attempted Murder

Sometime later Saul compromised again in a high-pressure situation, not following the precise instructions God had given for a military campaign (15.3). Again, Samuel caught him in the act. This time he accused Saul of rebelling against God. Samuel's words must have rung in Saul's head the rest of his life: "Because you have rejected the word of the LORD, he has also rejected you from being king" (15.23).

Without God's and Samuel's support, Saul lost his sense of confidence. An evil spirit began to torment him. Instead of building an alliance with David, Saul drove David away, causing him to run for his life in the desert. Eventually fear reduced Saul to a quivering, helpless jellyfish, incapable of leadership. In that condition he and his army lost a historic battle to the Philistines, allowing them to regain control. In the battle, both Saul and Jonathan were killed.

Why Saul Failed

The book of 1 Samuel doesn't psychoanalyze Saul; it merely reports what happened. The facts do point to a moral, though. Saul had begun with all the opportunity in the world. He only lacked, it seems, a strong compulsion to obey God no matter what. Under pressure he bent the rules. He lost God's backing. He grew fearful, rash, and jealous.

Saul's poor leadership left Israel worse off than at the beginning. The kingdom David inherited from Saul was again under Philistine military domination, and it was divided between north and south. Saul shows the unique tragedy of a poor leader. He fails not just himself. Inevitably he drags others down with him.

Life Questions: When you are put in the role of leader, how do you respond to pressure? Are Saul's weaknesses your weaknesses?

east of Egypt. ⁸He took King Agag of the Amalekites alive, but utterly destroyed all the people with the edge of the sword. ⁹Saul and the people spared Agag, and the best of the sheep and of the cattle and of the fatlings, and the lambs, and all that was valuable, and would not utterly destroy them; all that was despised and worthless they utterly destroyed.

Saul Rejected as King

10 The word of the LORD came to Samuel: ¹¹"I regret that I made Saul king, for he has turned back from following me, and has not carried out my commands." Samuel was angry; and he cried out to the LORD all night. ¹²Samuel rose early in the morning to meet Saul, and Samuel was told, "Saul went to Carmel, where he set up a monument for himself, and on returning he passed on down to Gilgal." ¹³When Samuel came to Saul, Saul said to him, "May you be blessed by the LORD; I have carried out the command of the LORD." ¹⁴But Samuel said, "What then is this bleating of sheep in my ears, and the lowing of cattle that I hear?" ¹⁵Saul said, "They have brought them from the Amalekites; for the people spared the best of the sheep and the cattle, to sacrifice to the LORD your God; but the rest we have utterly destroyed." ¹⁶Then Samuel said to Saul, "Stop! I will tell you what the LORD said to me last night." He replied, "Speak."

17 Samuel said, "Though you are little in your own eyes, are you not the head of the tribes of Israel? The LORD anointed you king over Israel. ¹⁸And the LORD sent you on a mission, and said, 'Go, utterly destroy the sinners, the Amalekites, and fight against them until they are consumed.' ¹⁹Why then did you not obey the voice of the LORD? Why did you swoop down on the spoil, and do what was evil in the sight of the LORD?" ²⁰Saul said to Samuel, "I have obeyed the voice of the LORD, I have gone on the mission on which the LORD sent me, I have brought Agag the king of Amalek, and I have utterly destroyed the Amalekites. ²¹But from the spoil the people took sheep and cattle, the best of the things devoted to destruction, to sacrifice to the LORD your God in Gilgal." ²²And Samuel said,

"Has the LORD as great delight in burnt
        offerings and sacrifices,
    as in obedience to the voice of the
        LORD?
Surely, to obey is better than sacrifice,
    and to heed than the fat of rams.
23 For rebellion is no less a sin than
        divination,
    and stubbornness is like iniquity and
        idolatry.

Because you have rejected the word of the
        LORD,
    he has also rejected you from being
        king."

24 Saul said to Samuel, "I have sinned; for I have transgressed the commandment of the LORD and your words, because I feared the people and obeyed their voice. ²⁵Now therefore, I pray, pardon my sin, and return with me, so that I may worship the LORD." ²⁶Samuel said to Saul, "I will not return with you; for you have rejected the word of the LORD, and the LORD has rejected you from being king over Israel." ²⁷As Samuel turned to go away, Saul caught hold of the hem of his robe, and it tore. ²⁸And Samuel said to him, "The LORD has torn the kingdom of Israel from you this very day, and has given it to a neighbor of yours, who is better than you. ²⁹Moreover the Glory of Israel will not recant*ᵛ* or change his mind; for he is not a mortal, that he should change his mind." ³⁰Then Saul*ʷ* said, "I have sinned; yet honor me now before the elders of my people and before Israel, and return with me, so that I may worship the LORD your God." ³¹So Samuel turned back after Saul; and Saul worshiped the LORD.

32 Then Samuel said, "Bring Agag king of the Amalekites here to me." And Agag came to him haltingly.*ˣ* Agag said, "Surely this is the bitterness of death."*ʸ* ³³But Samuel said,

"As your sword has made women
        childless,
    so your mother shall be childless
        among women."

And Samuel hewed Agag in pieces before the LORD in Gilgal.

34 Then Samuel went to Ramah; and Saul went up to his house in Gibeah of Saul. ³⁵Samuel did not see Saul again until the day of his death, but Samuel grieved over Saul. And the LORD was sorry that he had made Saul king over Israel.

David Anointed as King

16 The LORD said to Samuel, "How long will you grieve over Saul? I have rejected him from being king over Israel. Fill your horn with oil and set out; I will send you to Jesse the Bethlehemite, for I have provided for myself a king among his sons." ²Samuel said, "How can I go? If Saul hears of it, he will kill me." And the LORD said, "Take a heifer with you, and say, 'I have come to sacrifice to the LORD.' ³Invite Jesse to the sacrifice, and I will show you what you shall do; and you shall anoint for me the one whom I name to you." ⁴Samuel did what the LORD commanded, and came to Bethlehem. The elders of the city came to meet him trembling, and said, "Do you come peaceably?" ⁵He said, "Peaceably; I have

---

ᵛ Q Ms Gk: MT *deceive*   *ʷ* Heb *he*   *ˣ* Cn Compare Gk: Meaning of Heb uncertain   *ʸ* Q Ms Gk: MT *Surely the bitterness of death is past*

come to sacrifice to the LORD; sanctify yourselves and come with me to the sacrifice." And he sanctified Jesse and his sons and invited them to the sacrifice.

6 When they came, he looked on Eliab and thought, "Surely the LORD's anointed is now before the LORD."z 7But the LORD said to Samuel, "Do not look on his appearance or on the height of his stature, because I have rejected him; for the LORD does not see as mortals see; they look on the outward appearance, but the LORD looks on

16.7 What God Values

What qualified David to be king? Apparently he did not make an overpowering first impression, but God valued hidden qualities far more. Throughout his life David would demonstrate that he loved and trusted God with all his heart, as the law in Deuteronomy 6.4–6 demanded.

the heart." 8Then Jesse called Abinadab, and made him pass before Samuel. He said, "Neither has the LORD chosen this one." 9Then Jesse made Shammah pass by. And he said, "Neither has the LORD chosen this one." 10Jesse made seven of his sons pass before Samuel, and Samuel said to Jesse, "The LORD has not chosen any of these." 11Samuel said to Jesse, "Are all your sons here?" And he said, "There remains yet the youngest, but he is keeping the sheep." And Samuel said to Jesse, "Send and bring him; for we will not sit down until he comes here." 12He sent and brought him in. Now he was ruddy, and had beautiful eyes, and was handsome. The LORD said, "Rise and anoint him; for this is the one." 13Then Samuel took the horn of oil, and anointed him in the presence of his brothers; and the spirit of the LORD came mightily upon David from that day forward. Samuel then set out and went to Ramah.

David Plays the Lyre for Saul

14 Now the spirit of the LORD departed from Saul, and an evil spirit from the LORD tormented him. 15And Saul's servants said to him, "See now, an evil spirit from God is tormenting you. 16Let our lord now command the servants who attend you to look for someone who is skillful in playing the lyre; and when the evil spirit from God is upon you, he will play it, and you will feel better." 17So Saul said to his servants, "Provide for me someone who can play well, and bring him to me." 18One of the young men answered, "I have seen a son of Jesse the Bethlehemite who is skillful in playing, a man of valor, a warrior, prudent in speech, and a man of good presence; and the

LORD is with him." 19So Saul sent messengers to Jesse, and said, "Send me your son David who is with the sheep." 20Jesse took a donkey loaded with bread, a skin of wine, and a kid, and sent them by his son David to Saul. 21And David came to Saul, and entered his service. Saul loved him greatly, and he became his armor-bearer. 22Saul sent to Jesse, saying, "Let David remain in my service, for he has found favor in my sight." 23And whenever the evil spirit from God came upon Saul, David took the lyre and played it with his hand, and Saul would be relieved and feel better, and the evil spirit would depart from him.

David and Goliath

17 Now the Philistines gathered their armies for battle; they were gathered at Socoh, which belongs to Judah, and encamped between Socoh and Azekah, in Ephes-dammim. 2Saul and the Israelites gathered and encamped in the valley of Elah, and formed ranks against the Philistines. 3The Philistines stood on the mountain on the one side, and Israel stood on the mountain on the other side, with a valley between them. 4And there came out from the camp of the Philistines a champion named Goliath, of Gath, whose height

17.4 Everyone Watched Goliath

Wars in ancient times were sometimes decided by "representative combat": champions from each side would fight, and the results of their combat would determine the battle's result. People believed the outcome of the fight was controlled by the warriors' gods more than by the two sides' military strength.

Saul lacked confidence in God's support. His terror demoralized the Israelite army. David, by contrast, was as confident in his God as Goliath was scornful of God's people.

was sixa cubits and a span. 5He had a helmet of bronze on his head, and he was armed with a coat of mail; the weight of the coat was five thousand shekels of bronze. 6He had greaves of bronze on his legs and a javelin of bronze slung between his shoulders. 7The shaft of his spear was like a weaver's beam, and his spear's head weighed six hundred shekels of iron; and his shield-bearer went before him. 8He stood and shouted to the ranks of Israel, "Why have you come out to draw up for battle? Am I not a Philistine, and are you not servants of Saul? Choose a man for yourselves, and let him come down to me. 9If he is able to fight with me and kill me, then we will be your servants; but if I prevail against him and kill him, then you shall be our servants and serve us." 10And the Philistine said, "Today I defy the ranks

z Heb *him*   a MT: Q Ms Gk *four*

of Israel! Give me a man, that we may fight together." [11]When Saul and all Israel heard these words of the Philistine, they were dismayed and greatly afraid.

12 Now David was the son of an Ephrathite of Bethlehem in Judah, named Jesse, who had eight sons. In the days of Saul the man was already old and advanced in years.[b] [13]The three eldest sons of Jesse had followed Saul to the battle; the names of his three sons who went to the battle were Eliab the firstborn, and next to him Abinadab, and the third Shammah. [14]David was the youngest; the three eldest followed Saul, [15]but David went back and forth from Saul to feed his father's sheep at Bethlehem. [16]For forty days the Philistine came forward and took his stand, morning and evening.

17 Jesse said to his son David, "Take for your brothers an ephah of this parched grain and these ten loaves, and carry them quickly to the camp to your brothers; [18]also take these ten cheeses to the commander of their thousand. See how your brothers fare, and bring some token from them."

19 Now Saul, and they, and all the men of Israel, were in the valley of Elah, fighting with the Philistines. [20]David rose early in the morning, left the sheep with a keeper, took the provisions, and went as Jesse had commanded him. He came to the encampment as the army was going forth to the battle line, shouting the war cry. [21]Israel and the Philistines drew up for battle, army against army. [22]David left the things in charge of the keeper of the baggage, ran to the ranks, and went and greeted his brothers. [23]As he talked with them, the champion, the Philistine of Gath, Goliath by name, came up out of the ranks of the Philistines, and spoke the same words as before. And David heard him.

24 All the Israelites, when they saw the man, fled from him and were very much afraid. [25]The Israelites said, "Have you seen this man who has come up? Surely he has come up to defy Israel. The king will greatly enrich the man who kills him, and will give him his daughter and make his family free in Israel." [26]David said to the men who stood by him, "What shall be done for the man who kills this Philistine, and takes away the reproach from Israel? For who is this uncircumcised Philistine that he should defy the armies of the living God?" [27]The people answered him in the same way, "So shall it be done for the man who kills him."

28 His eldest brother Eliab heard him talking to the men; and Eliab's anger was kindled against David. He said, "Why have you come down? With whom have you left those few sheep in the wilderness? I know your presumption and the evil of your heart; for you have come down just to see the battle." [29]David said, "What have I done now?

It was only a question." [30]He turned away from him toward another and spoke in the same way; and the people answered him again as before.

31 When the words that David spoke were heard, they repeated them before Saul; and he sent for him. [32]David said to Saul, "Let no one's heart fail because of him; your servant will go and fight with this Philistine." [33]Saul said to David, "You are not able to go against this Philistine to fight with him; for you are just a boy, and he has been a warrior from his youth." [34]But David said to Saul, "Your servant used to keep sheep for his father; and whenever a lion or a bear came, and took a lamb from the flock, [35]I went after it and struck it down, rescuing the lamb from its mouth; and if it turned against me, I would catch it by the jaw, strike it down, and kill it. [36]Your servant has killed both lions and bears; and this uncircumcised Philistine shall be like one of them, since he has defied the armies of the living God." [37]David said, "The LORD, who saved me from the paw of the lion and from the paw of the bear, will save me from the hand of this Philistine." So Saul said to David, "Go, and may the LORD be with you!"

38 Saul clothed David with his armor; he put a bronze helmet on his head and clothed him with a coat of mail. [39]David strapped Saul's sword over the armor, and he tried in vain to walk, for he was not used to them. Then David said to Saul, "I cannot walk with these; for I am not used to them." So David removed them. [40]Then he took his staff in his hand, and chose five smooth stones from the wadi, and put them in his shepherd's bag, in the pouch; his sling was in his hand, and he drew near to the Philistine.

17.40 Deadly Rocks

The "five smooth stones" that David took from the stream were each probably bigger than a baseball. Someone skilled with a sling could hurl them at close to 100 miles per hour.

41 The Philistine came on and drew near to David, with his shield-bearer in front of him. [42]When the Philistine looked and saw David, he disdained him, for he was only a youth, ruddy and handsome in appearance. [43]The Philistine said to David, "Am I a dog, that you come to me with sticks?" And the Philistine cursed David by his gods. [44]The Philistine said to David, "Come to me, and I will give your flesh to the birds of the air and to the wild animals of the field." [45]But David said to the Philistine, "You come to me with sword and spear and javelin; but I come to you in the name of the LORD of hosts, the God of the armies of Israel, whom you have defied. [46]This

---

b Gk Syr: Heb *among men*

very day the LORD will deliver you into my hand, and I will strike you down and cut off your head; and I will give the dead bodies of the Philistine army this very day to the birds of the air and to the wild animals of the earth, so that all the earth may know that there is a God in Israel, ⁴⁷and that all this assembly may know that the LORD does not save by sword and spear; for the battle is the LORD's and he will give you into our hand."

48 When the Philistine drew nearer to meet David, David ran quickly toward the battle line to meet the Philistine. ⁴⁹David put his hand in his bag, took out a stone, slung it, and struck the Philistine on his forehead; the stone sank into his forehead, and he fell face down on the ground.

50 So David prevailed over the Philistine with a sling and a stone, striking down the Philistine and killing him; there was no sword in David's hand. ⁵¹Then David ran and stood over the Philistine; he grasped his sword, drew it out of its sheath, and killed him; then he cut off his head with it.

When the Philistines saw that their champion was dead, they fled. ⁵²The troops of Israel and Judah rose up with a shout and pursued the Philistines as far as Gath*ᶜ* and the gates of Ekron, so that the wounded Philistines fell on the way from Shaaraim as far as Gath and Ekron. ⁵³The Israelites came back from chasing the Philistines, and they plundered their camp. ⁵⁴David took the head of the Philistine and brought it to Jerusalem; but he put his armor in his tent.

55 When Saul saw David go out against the Philistine, he said to Abner, the commander of the army, "Abner, whose son is this young man?" Abner said, "As your soul lives, O king, I do not know." ⁵⁶The king said, "Inquire whose son the stripling is." ⁵⁷On David's return from killing the Philistine, Abner took him and brought him before Saul, with the head of the Philistine in his hand. ⁵⁸Saul said to him, "Whose son are you, young man?" And David answered, "I am the son of your servant Jesse the Bethlehemite."

Jonathan's Covenant with David

18 When David*ᵈ* had finished speaking to Saul, the soul of Jonathan was bound to the soul of David, and Jonathan loved him as his own soul. ²Saul took him that day and would not let him return to his father's house. ³Then Jonathan made a covenant with David, because he loved him as his own soul. ⁴Jonathan stripped himself of the robe that he was wearing, and gave it to David, and his armor, and even his sword and his bow and his belt. ⁵David went out and was successful wherever Saul sent him; as a result, Saul set him over the army. And all the people, even the servants of Saul, approved.

6 As they were coming home, when David returned from killing the Philistine, the women came out of all the towns of Israel, singing and dancing, to meet King Saul, with tambourines, with songs of joy, and with musical instruments.*ᵉ* ⁷And the women sang to one another as they made merry,

"Saul has killed his thousands,
    and David his ten thousands."

⁸Saul was very angry, for this saying displeased him. He said, "They have ascribed to David ten thousands, and to me they have ascribed thousands; what more can he have but the kingdom?" ⁹So Saul eyed David from that day on.

Saul Tries to Kill David

10 The next day an evil spirit from God rushed upon Saul, and he raved within his house, while David was playing the lyre, as he did day by day. Saul had his spear in his hand; ¹¹and Saul threw the spear, for he thought, "I will pin David to the wall." But David eluded him twice.

12 Saul was afraid of David, because the LORD was with him but had departed from Saul. ¹³So Saul removed him from his presence, and made him a commander of a thousand; and David marched out and came in, leading the army. ¹⁴David had success in all his undertakings; for the LORD was with him. ¹⁵When Saul saw that he had great success, he stood in awe of him. ¹⁶But all Israel and Judah loved David; for it was he who marched out and came in leading them.

David Marries Michal

17 Then Saul said to David, "Here is my elder daughter Merab; I will give her to you as a wife; only be valiant for me and fight the LORD's battles." For Saul thought, "I will not raise a hand against him; let the Philistines deal with him." ¹⁸David said to Saul, "Who am I and who are my kinsfolk, my father's family in Israel, that I should be son-in-law to the king?" ¹⁹But at the time when Saul's daughter Merab should have been given to David, she was given to Adriel the Meholathite as a wife.

20 Now Saul's daughter Michal loved David. Saul was told, and the thing pleased him. ²¹Saul thought, "Let me give her to him that she may be a snare for him and that the hand of the Philistines may be against him." Therefore Saul said to David a second time,*ᶠ* "You shall now be my son-in-law." ²²Saul commanded his servants, "Speak to David in private and say, 'See, the king is delighted with you, and all his servants love you; now then, become the king's son-in-law.'" ²³So Saul's servants reported these words to David in private. And David said, "Does it seem to you a little thing to become the king's son-in-law, seeing that I am a poor man and of no repute?" ²⁴The servants of Saul told him, "This is what

ᶜ Gk Syr: Heb Gai   ᵈ Heb he   ᵉ Or triangles, or three-stringed instruments   ᶠ Heb by two

David said." 25Then Saul said, "Thus shall you say to David, 'The king desires no marriage present except a hundred foreskins of the Philistines, that he may be avenged on the king's enemies.'" Now Saul planned to make David fall by the hand of the Philistines. 26When his servants told David these words, David was well pleased to be the king's son-in-law. Before the time had expired, 27David rose and went, along with his men, and killed one hundred*g* of the Philistines; and David brought their foreskins, which were given in full number to the king, that he might become the king's son-in-law. Saul gave him his daughter

18.27 "Scalps"

This bloody prize, something like the scalps that native Americans and white settlers collected in battles, proved that David's battle claims were not exaggerated. Foreskins would come from Philistines, since other tribes of the area, like Israel, practiced circumcision.

Michal as a wife. 28But when Saul realized that the LORD was with David, and that Saul's daughter Michal loved him, 29Saul was still more afraid of David. So Saul was David's enemy from that time forward.

30 Then the commanders of the Philistines came out to battle; and as often as they came out, David had more success than all the servants of Saul, so that his fame became very great.

Jonathan Intercedes for David

19 Saul spoke with his son Jonathan and with all his servants about killing David. But Saul's son Jonathan took great delight in David. 2Jonathan told David, "My father Saul is trying to kill you; therefore be on guard tomorrow morning; stay in a secret place and hide yourself. 3I will go out and stand beside my father in the field where you are, and I will speak to my father about you; if I learn anything I will tell you." 4Jonathan spoke well of David to his father Saul, saying to him, "The king should not sin against his servant David, because he has not sinned against you, and because his deeds have been of good service to you; 5for he took his life in his hand when he attacked the Philistine, and the LORD brought about a great victory for all Israel. You saw it, and rejoiced; why then will you sin against an innocent person by killing David without cause?" 6Saul heeded the voice of Jonathan; Saul swore, "As the LORD lives, he shall not be put to death." 7So Jonathan called David and related all these

things to him. Jonathan then brought David to Saul, and he was in his presence as before.

Michal Helps David Escape from Saul

8 Again there was war, and David went out to fight the Philistines. He launched a heavy attack on them, so that they fled before him. 9Then an evil spirit from the LORD came upon Saul, as he sat in his house with his spear in his hand, while David was playing music. 10Saul sought to pin David to the wall with the spear; but he eluded Saul, so that he struck the spear into the wall. David fled and escaped that night.

11 Saul sent messengers to David's house to keep watch over him, planning to kill him in the morning. David's wife Michal told him, "If you do not save your life tonight, tomorrow you will be killed." 12So Michal let David down through the window; he fled away and escaped. 13Michal took an idol*h* and laid it on the bed; she put a net*i* of goats' hair on its head, and covered it with the clothes. 14When Saul sent messengers to take David, she said, "He is sick." 15Then Saul sent the messengers to see David for themselves. He said, "Bring him up to me in the bed, that I may kill him." 16When the messengers came in, the idol*j* was in the bed, with the covering*i* of goats' hair on its head. 17Saul said to Michal, "Why have you deceived me like this, and let my enemy go, so that he has escaped?" Michal answered Saul, "He said to me, 'Let me go; why should I kill you?'"

David Joins Samuel in Ramah

18 Now David fled and escaped; he came to Samuel at Ramah, and told him all that Saul had done to him. He and Samuel went and settled at Naioth. 19Saul was told, "David is at Naioth in Ramah." 20Then Saul sent messengers to take David. When they saw the company of the prophets in a frenzy, with Samuel standing in charge of*i* them, the spirit of God came upon the messengers of Saul, and they also fell into a prophetic frenzy. 21When Saul was told, he sent other messengers, and they also fell into a frenzy. Saul sent messengers again the third time, and they also fell into a frenzy. 22Then he himself went to Ramah. He came to the great well that is in Secu;*k* he asked, "Where are Samuel and David?" And someone said, "They are at Naioth in Ramah." 23He went there, toward Naioth in Ramah; and the spirit of God came upon him. As he was going, he fell into a prophetic frenzy, until he came to Naioth in Ramah. 24He too stripped off his clothes, and he too fell into a frenzy before Samuel. He lay naked all that day and all that night. Therefore it is said, "Is Saul also among the prophets?"

---

g Gk Compare 2 Sam 3.14: Heb *two hundred*   *h* Heb *took the teraphim*   *i* Meaning of Heb uncertain   *j* Heb *the teraphim*   *k* Gk reads *to the well of the threshing floor on the bare height*

The Friendship of David and Jonathan

20 David fled from Naioth in Ramah. He came before Jonathan and said, "What have I done? What is my guilt? And what is my sin against your father that he is trying to take my life?" ²He said to him, "Far from it! You shall not die. My father does nothing either great or small without disclosing it to me; and why should my father hide this from me? Never!" ³But David also swore, "Your father knows well that you like me; and he thinks, 'Do not let Jonathan know this, or he will be grieved.' But truly, as the LORD lives and as you yourself live, there is but a step between me and death." ⁴Then Jonathan said to David, "Whatever you say, I will do for you." ⁵David said to Jonathan, "Tomorrow is the new moon, and I should not fail to sit with the king at the meal; but let me go, so that I may hide in the field until the third evening. ⁶If your father misses me at all, then say, 'David earnestly asked leave of me to run to Bethlehem his city; for there is a yearly sacrifice there for all the family.' ⁷If he says,

'Good!' it will be well with your servant; but if he is angry, then know that evil has been determined by him. ⁸Therefore deal kindly with your servant, for you have brought your servant into a sacred covenant[l] with you. But if there is guilt in me, kill me yourself; why should you bring me to your father?" ⁹Jonathan said, "Far be it from you! If I knew that it was decided by my father that evil should come upon you, would I not tell you?" ¹⁰Then David said to Jonathan, "Who will tell me if your father answers you harshly?" ¹¹Jonathan replied to David, "Come, let us go out into the field." So they both went out into the field.

12 Jonathan said to David, "By the LORD, the God of Israel! When I have sounded out my father, about this time tomorrow, or on the third day, if he is well disposed toward David, shall I not then send and disclose it to you? ¹³But if my father intends to do you harm, the LORD do so to Jonathan, and more also, if I do not disclose it to you, and send you away, so that you may go in safety. May the LORD be with you, as he has been with my father. ¹⁴If I am still alive, show me the faithful love of the LORD; but if I die,[m] ¹⁵never cut off your faithful love from my house, even if the LORD were to cut off every one of the enemies of David from the face of the earth." ¹⁶Thus Jonathan made a covenant with the house of David, saying, "May the LORD seek out the enemies of David." ¹⁷Jonathan made David swear again by his love for him; for he loved him as he loved his own life.

18 Jonathan said to him, "Tomorrow is the new moon; you will be missed, because your place will be empty. ¹⁹On the day after tomorrow, you

19.23 Out of Control

Prophets are usually pictured as somber figures. First Samuel reveals a different side: prophecy accompanying ecstatic worship. Saul had met a musical band of such prophets soon after he was anointed king (10.5–11). Now that he was planning evil, however, meeting the spirit of God made him utterly lose control.

---

l Heb *a covenant of the LORD*   *m* Meaning of Heb uncertain

---

JONATHAN *Friends First*

JEALOUS FRIENDS SOMETIMES FORCE US to choose. "Who is your best friend?" they demand, when we'd prefer not to rank them. Jonathan faced that kind of loyalty dilemma with his father, who grew insanely jealous of his son's friendship with David.

Palace intrigues in those days resembled the plot of a Shakespearean play. Insecure and guilt-ridden over past misdeeds, Saul feared that young David would take away his crown. (Indeed, Samuel had secretly anointed David as Israel's future king, but David fought bravely in Saul's service and never tried to usurp the throne.)

Though Jonathan tried to stay loyal to both father and friend, his father made it impossible. Soon Jonathan realized that Saul would kill David if he caught him. Once, in a blind rage, Saul hurled a spear at his own son for standing up for David (20.32–33).

One major factor further complicated Jonathan's choice: As Saul's son, he stood next in line for the throne. By siding with David, he would ultimately harm himself. Even so, at the risk of his own neck, Jonathan chose to help David escape. He told David he would happily follow his friend as his number-two man (23.17).

Tragically, the two friends never got the chance to rule together. In a battle against the Philistines, Jonathan fought at his father's side and was killed (31.2). David, mourning his dearest friend, sang a poignant song in tribute (2 Samuel 1.17–27). Their loyalty and love make for one of the most beautiful stories of friendship ever told.

Life Questions: What friend is most loyal to you? What does that loyalty mean to you?

shall go a long way down; go to the place where you hid yourself earlier, and remain beside the stone there.[n] 20I will shoot three arrows to the side of it, as though I shot at a mark. 21Then I will send the boy, saying, 'Go, find the arrows.' If I say to the boy, 'Look, the arrows are on this side of you, collect them,' then you are to come, for, as the LORD lives, it is safe for you and there is no danger. 22But if I say to the young man, 'Look, the arrows are beyond you,' then go; for the LORD has sent you away. 23As for the matter about which you and I have spoken, the LORD is witness[o] between you and me forever."

24 So David hid himself in the field. When the new moon came, the king sat at the feast to eat. 25The king sat upon his seat, as at other times, upon the seat by the wall. Jonathan stood, while Abner sat by Saul's side; but David's place was empty.

26 Saul did not say anything that day; for he thought, "Something has befallen him; he is not clean, surely he is not clean." 27But on the second day, the day after the new moon, David's place was empty. And Saul said to his son Jonathan, "Why has the son of Jesse not come to the feast, either yesterday or today?" 28Jonathan answered Saul, "David earnestly asked leave of me to go to Bethlehem; 29he said, 'Let me go; for our family is holding a sacrifice in the city, and my brother has commanded me to be there. So now, if I have found favor in your sight, let me get away, and see my brothers.' For this reason he has not come to the king's table."

30 Then Saul's anger was kindled against Jonathan. He said to him, "You son of a perverse, rebellious woman! Do I not know that you have chosen the son of Jesse to your own shame, and to the shame of your mother's nakedness? 31For as long as the son of Jesse lives upon the earth, neither you nor your kingdom shall be established. Now send and bring him to me, for he shall surely die." 32Then Jonathan answered his father Saul, "Why should he be put to death? What has he done?" 33But Saul threw his spear at him to strike him; so Jonathan knew that it was the decision of his father to put David to death. 34Jonathan rose from the table in fierce anger and ate no food on the second day of the month, for he was grieved for David, and because his father had disgraced him.

35 In the morning Jonathan went out into the field to the appointment with David, and with him was a little boy. 36He said to the boy, "Run and find the arrows that I shoot." As the boy ran, he shot an arrow beyond him. 37When the boy came to the place where Jonathan's arrow had fallen, Jonathan called after the boy and said, "Is the arrow not beyond you?" 38Jonathan called after the boy, "Hurry, be quick, do not linger." So Jonathan's boy gathered up the arrows and came to his master. 39But the boy knew nothing; only Jonathan and David knew the arrangement. 40Jonathan gave his weapons to the boy and said to him, "Go and carry them to the city." 41As soon as the boy had gone, David rose from beside the stone heap[p] and prostrated himself with his face to the ground. He bowed three times, and they kissed each other, and wept with each other; David wept the more.[q] 42Then Jonathan said to David, "Go in peace, since both of us have sworn in the name of the LORD, saying, 'The LORD shall be between me and you, and between my descendants and your descendants, forever.'" He got up and left; and Jonathan went into the city.[r]

David and the Holy Bread

21 [s] David came to Nob to the priest Ahimelech. Ahimelech came trembling to meet David, and said to him, "Why are you alone, and no one with you?" 2David said to the priest Ahimelech, "The king has charged me with a matter, and said to me, 'No one must know anything of the matter about which I send you, and with which I have charged you.' I have made an appointment[t] with the young men for such and such a place. 3Now then, what have you at hand? Give me five loaves of bread, or whatever is here." 4The priest answered David, "I have no ordinary bread at hand, only holy bread—provided that the young men have kept themselves from women." 5David answered the priest, "Indeed women

21.4 Disobeying the Law

David was desperate when he reached Nob. He did not even have food. He lied about his situation. Then he ate consecrated bread that was supposed to be reserved for the priests. (A thousand years later Jesus raised the issue of the consecrated bread, suggesting that keeping the ritual laws mattered less than David's survival [Matthew 12.3–4].)

David later admitted that he had been wrong to go to Nob and endanger the priests. Saul, suspicious of their involvement, slaughtered them (22.17–18).

have been kept from us as always when I go on an expedition; the vessels of the young men are holy even when it is a common journey; how much more today will their vessels be holy?" 6So the priest gave him the holy bread; for there was no bread there except the bread of the Presence,

[n] Meaning of Heb uncertain   [o] Gk: Heb lacks *witness*   [p] Gk: Heb *from beside the south*   [q] Vg: Meaning of Heb uncertain   [r] This sentence is 21.1 in Heb   [s] Ch 21.2 in Heb   [t] Q Ms Vg Compare Gk: Meaning of MT uncertain

which is removed from before the LORD, to be replaced by hot bread on the day it is taken away.

7 Now a certain man of the servants of Saul was there that day, detained before the LORD; his name was Doeg the Edomite, the chief of Saul's shepherds.

8 David said to Ahimelech, "Is there no spear or sword here with you? I did not bring my sword or my weapons with me, because the king's business required haste." ⁹The priest said, "The sword of Goliath the Philistine, whom you killed in the valley of Elah, is here wrapped in a cloth behind the ephod; if you will take that, take it, for there is none here except that one." David said, "There is none like it; give it to me."

David Flees to Gath

10 David rose and fled that day from Saul; he went to King Achish of Gath. ¹¹The servants of Achish said to him, "Is this not David the king of the land? Did they not sing to one another of him in dances,

'Saul has killed his thousands,
and David his ten thousands'?"

¹²David took these words to heart and was very much afraid of King Achish of Gath. ¹³So he changed his behavior before them; he pretended to be mad when in their presence.ᵘ He scratched marks on the doors of the gate, and let his spittle run down his beard. ¹⁴Achish said to his servants, "Look, you see the man is mad; why then have you brought him to me? ¹⁵Do I lack madmen, that you have brought this fellow to play the madman in my presence? Shall this fellow come into my house?"

David and His Followers at Adullam

22 David left there and escaped to the cave of Adullam; when his brothers and all his father's house heard of it, they went down there to him. ²Everyone who was in distress, and everyone who was in debt, and everyone who was discontented gathered to him; and he became captain over them. Those who were with him numbered about four hundred.

3 David went from there to Mizpeh of Moab. He said to the king of Moab, "Please let my father

22.3 Long-lost Relatives

Afraid that Saul would hold his family hostage, David took his parents to the neighboring kingdom of Moab for safekeeping. Why Moab? Possibly because he had distant relatives there. His great-grandmother, Ruth, had come from Moab.

and mother comeᵛ to you, until I know what God will do for me." ⁴He left them with the king of Moab, and they stayed with him all the time that David was in the stronghold. ⁵Then the prophet Gad said to David, "Do not remain in the stronghold; leave, and go into the land of Judah." So David left, and went into the forest of Hereth.

Saul Slaughters the Priests at Nob

6 Saul heard that David and those who were with him had been located. Saul was sitting at Gibeah, under the tamarisk tree on the height, with his spear in his hand, and all his servants were standing around him. ⁷Saul said to his servants who stood around him, "Hear now, you Benjaminites; will the son of Jesse give every one of you fields and vineyards, will he make you all commanders of thousands and commanders of hundreds? ⁸Is that why all of you have conspired against me? No one discloses to me when my son makes a league with the son of Jesse, none of you is sorry for me or discloses to me that my son has stirred up my servant against me, to lie in wait, as he is doing today." ⁹Doeg the Edomite, who was in charge of Saul's servants, answered, "I saw the son of Jesse coming to Nob, to Ahimelech son of Ahitub; ¹⁰he inquired of the LORD for him, gave him provisions, and gave him the sword of Goliath the Philistine."

11 The king sent for the priest Ahimelech son of Ahitub and for all his father's house, the priests who were at Nob; and all of them came to the king. ¹²Saul said, "Listen now, son of Ahitub." He answered, "Here I am, my lord." ¹³Saul said to him, "Why have you conspired against me, you and the son of Jesse, by giving him bread and a sword, and by inquiring of God for him, so that he has risen against me, to lie in wait, as he is doing today?"

14 Then Ahimelech answered the king, "Who among all your servants is so faithful as David? He is the king's son-in-law, and is quickʷ to do your bidding, and is honored in your house. ¹⁵Is today the first time that I have inquired of God for him? By no means! Do not let the king impute anything to his servant or to any member of my father's house; for your servant has known nothing of all this, much or little." ¹⁶The king said, "You shall surely die, Ahimelech, you and all your father's house." ¹⁷The king said to the guard who stood around him, "Turn and kill the priests of the LORD, because their hand also is with David; they knew that he fled, and did not disclose it to me." But the servants of the king would not raise their hand to attack the priests of the LORD. ¹⁸Then the king said to Doeg, "You, Doeg, turn and attack the priests." Doeg the Edomite turned and attacked the priests; on that day he killed eighty-five who wore the linen ephod. ¹⁹Nob, the

---

ᵘ Heb *in their hands*   ᵛ Syr Vg: Heb *come out*   ʷ Heb *and turns aside*

city of the priests, he put to the sword; men and women, children and infants, oxen, donkeys, and sheep, he put to the sword.

20 But one of the sons of Ahimelech son of Ahitub, named Abiathar, escaped and fled after David. 21Abiathar told David that Saul had killed the priests of the LORD. 22David said to Abiathar, "I knew on that day, when Doeg the Edomite was there, that he would surely tell Saul. I am responsiblex for the lives of all your father's house. 23Stay with me, and do not be afraid; for the one who seeks my life seeks your life; you will be safe with me."

David Saves the City of Keilah

23 Now they told David, "The Philistines are fighting against Keilah, and are robbing the threshing floors." 2David inquired of the LORD, "Shall I go and attack these Philistines?" The LORD said to David, "Go and attack the Philistines and save Keilah." 3But David's men said to him, "Look, we are afraid here in Judah; how much more then if we go to Keilah against the armies of the Philistines?" 4Then David inquired of the LORD again. The LORD answered him, "Yes, go down to Keilah; for I will give the Philistines into your hand." 5So David and his men went to Keilah, fought with the Philistines, brought away their livestock, and dealt them a heavy defeat. Thus David rescued the inhabitants of Keilah.

6 When Abiathar son of Ahimelech fled to David at Keilah, he came down with an ephod in his hand. 7Now it was told Saul that David had come to Keilah. And Saul said, "God has giveny him into my hand; for he has shut himself in by entering a town that has gates and bars." 8Saul summoned all the people to war, to go down to Keilah, to besiege David and his men. 9When David learned that Saul was plotting evil against him, he said to the priest Abiathar, "Bring the ephod here." 10David said, "O LORD, the God of Israel, your servant has heard that Saul seeks to come to Keilah, to destroy the city on my account. 11And now, willz Saul come down as your servant has heard? O LORD, the God of Israel, I beseech you, tell your servant." The LORD said, "He will come down." 12Then David said, "Will the men of Keilah surrender me and my men into the hand of Saul?" The LORD said, "They will surrender you." 13Then David and his men, who were about six hundred, set out and left Keilah; they wandered wherever they could go. When Saul was told that David had escaped from Keilah, he gave up the expedition. 14David remained in the strongholds in the wilderness, in the hill country of the Wilderness of Ziph. Saul sought him every day, but the LORD a did not give him into his hand.

David Eludes Saul in the Wilderness

15 David was in the Wilderness of Ziph at Horesh when he learned thatb Saul had come out to seek his life. 16Saul's son Jonathan set out and came to David at Horesh; there he strengthened

> ### 23.16 Final Farewell
> This last, secret meeting between Jonathan and David reveals the essence of their friendship. They had grown to love each other despite Saul's (Jonathan's father's) hatred for David. Now, when David was desperate, Jonathan sought him out and "he strengthened his hand through the LORD." Jonathan expected to become David's right-hand man when David became king, but Jonathan's death soon put an end to that dream (see 31.2).

his hand through the LORD.c 17He said to him, "Do not be afraid; for the hand of my father Saul shall not find you; you shall be king over Israel, and I shall be second to you; my father Saul also knows that this is so." 18Then the two of them made a covenant before the LORD; David remained at Horesh, and Jonathan went home.

19 Then some Ziphites went up to Saul at Gibeah and said, "David is hiding among us in the strongholds of Horesh, on the hill of Hachilah, which is south of Jeshimon. 20Now, O king, whenever you wish to come down, do so; and our part will be to surrender him into the king's hand." 21Saul said, "May you be blessed by the LORD for showing me compassion! 22Go and make sure once more; find out exactly where he is, and who has seen him there; for I am told that he is very cunning. 23Look around and learn all the hiding places where he lurks, and come back to me with sure information. Then I will go with you; and if he is in the land, I will search him out among all the thousands of Judah." 24So they set out and went to Ziph ahead of Saul.

David and his men were in the wilderness of Maon, in the Arabah to the south of Jeshimon. 25Saul and his men went to search for him. When David was told, he went down to the rock and stayed in the wilderness of Maon. When Saul heard that, he pursued David into the wilderness of Maon. 26Saul went on one side of the mountain, and David and his men on the other side of the mountain. David was hurrying to get away from Saul, while Saul and his men were closing in on David and his men to capture them. 27Then a messenger came to Saul, saying, "Hurry and come; for the Philistines have made a raid on the land." 28So Saul stopped pursuing David, and

x Gk Vg: Meaning of Heb uncertain   y Gk Tg: Heb made a stranger of   z Q Ms Compare Gk: MT Will the men of
Keilah surrender me into his hand? Will   a Q Ms Gk: MT God   b Or saw that   c Compare Q Ms Gk: MT God

went against the Philistines; therefore that place was called the Rock of Escape.[d] [29] [e] David then went up from there, and lived in the strongholds of En-gedi.

David Spares Saul's Life

24 When Saul returned from following the Philistines, he was told, "David is in the wilderness of En-gedi." [2] Then Saul took three thousand chosen men out of all Israel, and went to look for David and his men in the direction of the Rocks of the Wild Goats. [3] He came to the sheepfolds beside the road, where there was a cave; and Saul went in to relieve himself.[f] Now David and his men were sitting in the innermost parts of the cave. [4] The men of David said to him,

---

[d] Or *Rock of Division*; Meaning of Heb uncertain   [e] Ch 24.1 in Heb   [f] Heb *to cover his feet*

A Sense of God's Timing
Two leaders locked in a death struggle—with one refusing to fight

> "I have not sinned against you, though you are hunting me to take my life. May the LORD judge between me and you!" 24.11–12

IN THE WINTER OF 1777, America had two armies. One lived in comfortable homes in Philadelphia. The other camped in the snow in the hills to the northwest, at a place called Valley Forge. One showed impeccable discipline. The other tried desperately to keep its untrained recruits from deserting. One was supplied by ship with every luxury. The other fought frostbite because its soldiers had no boots.

In sum, one army had everything it could want to weather a cold winter and a war, while the other hung by a thread. Who could have thought, seeing the two, that within three years the army with nothing would defeat the army with everything?

The impoverished American army could never go head-on against the crack British forces. But it could always outwait them. George Washington's army had the support of the American people, while the British army, for all its strength, was far from home. The British had to win decisively, putting an end to the rebellion. The Americans merely had to survive and outlast them.

Washington was a military genius not at battle tactics, but at a more fundamental necessity: encouraging his men to fight on. One-quarter of them died of cold and disease that bitter winter at Valley Forge. Only his personal strength held the miserable army together. That was the key to victory.

Two Kings in Israel

David and his followers lived in a similar situation. Saul was the right and proper king, living in luxury. David had been secretly anointed as his replacement, but he lived in the desert, scrabbling to survive. Saul had a professional army, David a small band composed of family members and an assortment of outlaws.

Twice Saul accidentally fell into David's hands, but David refused to kill him. He felt that would violate God's will. He would not use his sword to become king. He fought not to win but to survive.

Survival was not easy. You can read between the lines of chapters 21–31 and see a great drama unfolding. Saul is clearly deteriorating. Can David hold on long enough to outlast him?

At first David ran from one place to another, alone and completely vulnerable. Then, when 400 outlaws gathered around him, the local people turned him in twice (23.19; 26.1). Perhaps they feared that Saul would slaughter them the way he had the Nob priests (22.6–23).

David survived and managed to keep his army intact. He even built popular support by providing military protection to his neighbors. But eventually he saw that his position was impossible. "I shall now perish one day by the hand of Saul," he said (27.1). He left Israel and became, with his army, a hired soldier for one of the Philistine kings.

Sooner or later David's double-agent act would have been found out. In fact, when the Philistines planned a major military effort against Israel, David barely escaped having to fight his own people.

Time on His Side

Throughout his desert period, David's position was desperate. David had one precious asset only: God had promised he would be king. David believed this promise even when his situation looked very bad. He would wait for God's timing.

A sense of timing, people say, is essential to leadership. You must know when to act boldly and when to wait patiently; when to bend and when to stand firm. David had that critical sense of timing because he trusted God's control of events.

Life Questions: What makes you impatient? What can you learn about patience from David's life?

"Here is the day of which the LORD said to you, 'I will give your enemy into your hand, and you shall do to him as it seems good to you.'" Then David went and stealthily cut off a corner of Saul's cloak. 5Afterward David was stricken to the heart because he had cut off a corner of Saul's cloak.

24.5 David's Bad Conscience

David's conscience troubled him after he cut off part of Saul's robe. Why? Possibly because, to people of that day, a man looked ridiculous with his clothes cut short. See 2 Samuel 10.4–5 for a case where cutting a garment was a deliberate insult that led to war.

6He said to his men, "The LORD forbid that I should do this thing to my lord, the LORD's anointed, to raise my hand against him; for he is the LORD's anointed." 7So David scolded his men severely and did not permit them to attack Saul. Then Saul got up and left the cave, and went on his way.

8 Afterwards David also rose up and went out of the cave and called after Saul, "My lord the king!" When Saul looked behind him, David bowed with his face to the ground, and did obeisance. 9David said to Saul, "Why do you listen to the words of those who say, 'David seeks to do you harm'? 10This very day your eyes have seen how the LORD gave you into my hand in the cave; and some urged me to kill you, but I spared*g* you. I said, 'I will not raise my hand against my lord; for he is the LORD's anointed.' 11See, my father, see the corner of your cloak in my hand; for by the fact that I cut off the corner of your cloak, and did not kill you, you may know for certain that there is no wrong or treason in my hands. I have not sinned against you, though you are hunting me to take my life. 12May the LORD judge between me and you! May the LORD avenge me on you; but my hand shall not be against you. 13As the ancient proverb says, 'Out of the wicked comes forth wickedness'; but my hand shall not be against you. 14Against whom has the king of Israel come out? Whom do you pursue? A dead dog? A single flea? 15May the LORD therefore be judge, and give sentence between me and you. May he see to it, and plead my cause, and vindicate me against you."

16 When David had finished speaking these words to Saul, Saul said, "Is this your voice, my son David?" Saul lifted up his voice and wept. 17He said to David, "You are more righteous than I; for you have repaid me good, whereas I have repaid you evil. 18Today you have explained how you have dealt well with me, in that you did not

kill me when the LORD put me into your hands. 19For who has ever found an enemy, and sent the enemy safely away? So may the LORD reward you with good for what you have done to me this day. 20Now I know that you shall surely be king, and that the kingdom of Israel shall be established in your hand. 21Swear to me therefore by the LORD that you will not cut off my descendants after me, and that you will not wipe out my name from my father's house." 22So David swore this to Saul. Then Saul went home; but David and his men went up to the stronghold.

24.21 The Survival of a Family

Slaughtering the rival's entire family was normal practice when one would-be king won out over another. Such action tended to lessen the probability that the rival family would compete for the throne again. Jonathan, David's closest friend, is asking David not to follow that course when he becomes king. Because of their relationship, David let Jonathan's son Mephibosheth live (2 Samuel 9).

Death of Samuel

25 Now Samuel died; and all Israel assembled and mourned for him. They buried him at his home in Ramah.

Then David got up and went down to the wilderness of Paran.

David and the Wife of Nabal

2 There was a man in Maon, whose property was in Carmel. The man was very rich; he had three thousand sheep and a thousand goats. He was shearing his sheep in Carmel. 3Now the name of the man was Nabal, and the name of his wife Abigail. The woman was clever and beautiful, but the man was surly and mean; he was a Calebite. 4David heard in the wilderness that Nabal was shearing his sheep. 5So David sent ten young men; and David said to the young men, "Go up to Carmel, and go to Nabal, and greet him in my name. 6Thus you shall salute him: 'Peace be to you, and peace be to your house, and peace be to all that you have. 7I hear that you have shearers; now your shepherds have been with us, and we did them no harm, and they missed nothing, all the time they were in Carmel. 8Ask your young men, and they will tell you. Therefore let my young men find favor in your sight; for we have come on a feast day. Please give whatever you have at hand to your servants and to your son David.'"

9 When David's young men came, they said all this to Nabal in the name of David; and then

g Gk Syr Tg Vg: Heb it (my eye) spared

they waited. ¹⁰But Nabal answered David's servants, "Who is David? Who is the son of Jesse? There are many servants today who are breaking away from their masters. ¹¹Shall I take my bread and my water and the meat that I have butchered for my shearers, and give it to men who come from I do not know where?" ¹²So David's young men turned away, and came back and told him all this. ¹³David said to his men, "Every man strap on his sword!" And every one of them strapped on his sword; David also strapped on his sword; and about four hundred men went up after David, while two hundred remained with the baggage.

14 But one of the young men told Abigail, Nabal's wife, "David sent messengers out of the wilderness to salute our master; and he shouted insults at them. ¹⁵Yet the men were very good to us, and we suffered no harm, and we never missed anything when we were in the fields, as long as we were with them; ¹⁶they were a wall to us both by night and by day, all the while we were with them keeping the sheep. ¹⁷Now therefore know this and consider what you should do; for evil has been decided against our master and against all his house; he is so ill-natured that no one can speak to him."

18 Then Abigail hurried and took two hundred loaves, two skins of wine, five sheep ready dressed, five measures of parched grain, one hundred clusters of raisins, and two hundred cakes of figs. She loaded them on donkeys ¹⁹and said to her young men, "Go on ahead of me; I am coming after you." But she did not tell her husband Nabal. ²⁰As she rode on the donkey and came down under cover of the mountain, David and his men came down toward her; and she met them. ²¹Now David had said, "Surely it was in vain that I protected all that this fellow has in the wilderness, so that nothing was missed of all that belonged to him; but he has returned me evil for good. ²²God do so to David[h] and more also, if by morning I leave so much as one male of all who belong to him."

23 When Abigail saw David, she hurried and alighted from the donkey, and fell before David on her face, bowing to the ground. ²⁴She fell at his feet and said, "Upon me alone, my lord, be the guilt; please let your servant speak in your ears, and hear the words of your servant. ²⁵My lord, do not take seriously this ill-natured fellow, Nabal; for as his name is, so is he; Nabal[i] is his name, and folly is with him; but I, your servant, did not see the young men of my lord, whom you sent.

26 "Now then, my lord, as the LORD lives, and as you yourself live, since the LORD has restrained you from bloodguilt and from taking vengeance with your own hand, now let your enemies and those who seek to do evil to my lord be like Nabal. ²⁷And now let this present that your servant has brought to my lord be given to the young men who follow my lord. ²⁸Please forgive the trespass of your servant; for the LORD will certainly make my lord a sure house, because my lord is fighting the battles of the LORD; and evil shall not be found in you so long as you live. ²⁹If anyone should rise up to pursue you and to seek your life, the life of my lord shall be bound in the bundle of the living under the care of the LORD your God; but the lives of your enemies he shall sling out as from the hollow of a sling. ³⁰When the LORD has

---

[h] Gk Compare Syr: Heb *the enemies of David*   [i] That is *Fool*

ABIGAIL *Beauty and Brains*

ABIGAIL WAS NOT A MAIN player in the history of Israel, but as this story shows, she had an instinctive skill for diplomacy and peace-making. A woman of beauty and brains, Abigail could defuse a dangerous situation between hot-headed men.

It is hard to imagine such a shrewd woman choosing marriage to Nabal, and indeed in those days parents, not lovers, arranged the marriages. Nabal was rich, which probably influenced Abigail's parents. She, however, knew her husband as a fool, and this incident characteristically portrays him as rude, drunk and stupid.

Though Abigail may have been trapped in a bad marriage, she was hardly helpless. When her husband mistreated David, Abigail rushed to take decisive action. She saved the day for her people as well as for David, who had lost his temper and was about to take vengeance he would doubtless regret.

A man of passion, David could lose his temper, but he also had the courage to back down when challenged with good sense. He thanked Abigail warmly and made a mental note about this remarkable woman. When her husband died a short time later, David asked the widow to be his wife. Without hesitation, without tears or mourning, Abigail agreed.

Though David was still an outlaw, Abigail sensed that a great future awaited him. As a result of her wise decisions, she became forever linked to Israel's greatest king.

Life Questions: What can you learn from Abigail's style of dealing with hot-tempered people?

done to my lord according to all the good that he has spoken concerning you, and has appointed you prince over Israel, ³¹my lord shall have no cause of grief, or pangs of conscience, for having shed blood without cause or for having saved himself. And when the LORD has dealt well with my lord, then remember your servant."

32 David said to Abigail, "Blessed be the LORD, the God of Israel, who sent you to meet me today! ³³Blessed be your good sense, and blessed be you, who have kept me today from bloodguilt and from avenging myself by my own hand! ³⁴For as surely as the LORD the God of Israel lives, who has restrained me from hurting you, unless you had hurried and come to meet me, truly by morning there would not have been left to Nabal so much as one male." ³⁵Then David received from her hand what she had brought him; he said to her, "Go up to your house in peace; see, I have heeded your voice, and I have granted your petition."

36 Abigail came to Nabal; he was holding a feast in his house, like the feast of a king. Nabal's heart was merry within him, for he was very drunk; so she told him nothing at all until the morning light. ³⁷In the morning, when the wine had gone out of Nabal, his wife told him these things, and his heart died within him; he became like a stone. ³⁸About ten days later the LORD struck Nabal, and he died.

39 When David heard that Nabal was dead, he said, "Blessed be the LORD who has judged the case of Nabal's insult to me, and has kept back his servant from evil; the LORD has returned the evildoing of Nabal upon his own head." Then David sent and wooed Abigail, to make her his wife. ⁴⁰When David's servants came to Abigail at Carmel, they said to her, "David has sent us to you to take you to him as his wife." ⁴¹She rose and bowed down, with her face to the ground, and said, "Your servant is a slave to wash the feet of the servants of my lord." ⁴²Abigail got up hurriedly and rode away on a donkey; her five maids attended her. She went after the messengers of David and became his wife.

43 David also married Ahinoam of Jezreel; both of them became his wives. ⁴⁴Saul had given his daughter Michal, David's wife, to Palti son of Laish, who was from Gallim.

David Spares Saul's Life a Second Time

26 Then the Ziphites came to Saul at Gibeah, saying, "David is in hiding on the hill of Hachilah, which is opposite Jeshimon."ʲ ²So Saul rose and went down to the Wilderness of Ziph, with three thousand chosen men of Israel, to seek David in the Wilderness of Ziph. ³Saul encamped on the hill of Hachilah, which is opposite Jeshimonʲ beside the road. But David remained in the wilderness. When he learned that Saul had come after him into the wilderness, ⁴David sent out spies, and learned that Saul had indeed arrived. ⁵Then David set out and came to the place where Saul had encamped; and David saw the place where Saul lay, with Abner son of Ner, the commander of his army. Saul was lying within the encampment, while the army was encamped around him.

6 Then David said to Ahimelech the Hittite, and to Joab's brother Abishai son of Zeruiah, "Who will go down with me into the camp to Saul?" Abishai said, "I will go down with you." ⁷So David and Abishai went to the army by night; there Saul lay sleeping within the encampment, with his spear stuck in the ground at his head; and Abner and the army lay around him. ⁸Abishai said to David, "God has given your enemy into your hand today; now therefore let me pin him to the ground with one stroke of the spear; I will not strike him twice." ⁹But David said to Abishai, "Do not destroy him; for who can raise his hand against the LORD's anointed, and be guiltless?" ¹⁰David said, "As the LORD lives, the LORD will strike him down; or his day will come to die; or he will go down into battle and perish. ¹¹The LORD forbid that I should raise my hand against the LORD's anointed; but now take the spear that is at his head, and the water jar, and let us go." ¹²So David took the spear that was at Saul's head and the water jar, and they went away. No one saw it, or knew it, nor did anyone awake; for they were all asleep, because a deep sleep from the LORD had fallen upon them.

13 Then David went over to the other side, and stood on top of a hill far away, with a great distance between them. ¹⁴David called to the army and to Abner son of Ner, saying, "Abner! Will you not answer?" Then Abner replied, "Who are you that calls to the king?" ¹⁵David said to Abner, "Are you not a man? Who is like you in Israel? Why then have you not kept watch over your lord the king? For one of the people came in to destroy your lord the king. ¹⁶This thing that you have done is not good. As the LORD lives, you deserve to die, because you have not kept watch over your lord, the LORD's anointed. See now, where is the king's spear, or the water jar that was at his head?"

17 Saul recognized David's voice, and said, "Is this your voice, my son David?" David said, "It is my voice, my lord, O king." ¹⁸And he added, "Why does my lord pursue his servant? For what have I done? What guilt is on my hands? ¹⁹Now therefore let my lord the king hear the words of his servant. If it is the LORD who has stirred you up against me, may he accept an offering; but if it is mortals, may they be cursed before the LORD, for they have driven me out today from

---

ʲ Or opposite the wasteland

my share in the heritage of the LORD, saying, 'Go, serve other gods.' [20]Now therefore, do not let my blood fall to the ground, away from the presence of the LORD; for the king of Israel has come out to seek a single flea, like one who hunts a partridge in the mountains."

21 Then Saul said, "I have done wrong; come back, my son David, for I will never harm you again, because my life was precious in your sight today; I have been a fool, and have made a great mistake." [22]David replied, "Here is the spear, O king! Let one of the young men come over and get it. [23]The LORD rewards everyone for his righteousness and his faithfulness; for the LORD gave you into my hand today, but I would not raise my hand against the LORD's anointed. [24]As your life was precious today in my sight, so may my life be precious in the sight of the LORD, and may he rescue me from all tribulation." [25]Then Saul said to David, "Blessed be you, my son David! You will do many things and will succeed in them." So David went his way, and Saul returned to his place.

David Serves King Achish of Gath

27 David said in his heart, "I shall now perish one day by the hand of Saul; there is nothing better for me than to escape to the land of the Philistines; then Saul will despair of seeking me any longer within the borders of Israel, and I shall escape out of his hand." [2]So David set out and went over, he and the six hundred men who were with him, to King Achish son of Maoch of Gath. [3]David stayed with Achish at Gath, he and his troops, every man with his household, and David with his two wives, Ahinoam of Jezreel, and Abigail of Carmel, Nabal's widow. [4]When Saul was told that David had fled to Gath, he no longer sought for him.

5 Then David said to Achish, "If I have found favor in your sight, let a place be given me in one of the country towns, so that I may live there; for why should your servant live in the royal city with you?" [6]So that day Achish gave him Ziklag; therefore Ziklag has belonged to the kings of Judah to this day. [7]The length of time that David lived in the country of the Philistines was one year and four months.

8 Now David and his men went up and made raids on the Geshurites, the Girzites, and the Amalekites; for these were the landed settlements from Telam[k] on the way to Shur and on to the land of Egypt. [9]David struck the land, leaving neither man nor woman alive, but took away the sheep, the oxen, the donkeys, the camels, and the clothing, and came back to Achish. [10]When Achish asked, "Against whom[l] have you made a raid today?" David would say, "Against the Negeb of Judah," or "Against the Negeb of the Jerahme-

elites," or, "Against the Negeb of the Kenites." [11]David left neither man nor woman alive to be brought back to Gath, thinking, "They might tell about us, and say, 'David has done so and so.'"

27.8 David's Double Game

The Philistines accepted David because they thought he would fight against his own people. Had they known that he retained his Israelite loyalty, they would never have trusted him. So David had to pretend that he was raiding the Israelites, while actually he raided Israel's nomadic enemies. To keep his game secret, he took no prisoners, for it might be noticed that none of them were Israelites.

Such was his practice all the time he lived in the country of the Philistines. [12]Achish trusted David, thinking, "He has made himself utterly abhorrent to his people Israel; therefore he shall always be my servant."

28 In those days the Philistines gathered their forces for war, to fight against Israel. Achish said to David, "You know, of course, that you and your men are to go out with me in the army." [2]David said to Achish, "Very well, then you shall know what your servant can do." Achish said to David, "Very well, I will make you my bodyguard for life."

Saul Consults a Medium

3 Now Samuel had died, and all Israel had mourned for him and buried him in Ramah, his own city. Saul had expelled the mediums and the wizards from the land. [4]The Philistines assembled, and came and encamped at Shunem. Saul gathered all Israel, and they encamped at Gilboa.

28.4 Battle Strategy

For their massive assault from Shunem, the Philistines tried a new tactic. They had fought previous battles in the mountains, rough terrain where their chariots were next to useless. Now they chose strategically important level ground that Israel had to defend. The Valley of Jezreel is the only part of Palestine where you can go from west to east without crossing mountains. A Philistine victory here would cut Israel in half.

[5]When Saul saw the army of the Philistines, he was afraid, and his heart trembled greatly. [6]When Saul inquired of the LORD, the LORD did not answer him, not by dreams, or by Urim, or by

---

[k] Compare Gk 15.4: Heb *from of old*   [l] Q Ms Gk Vg: MT lacks *whom*

prophets. 7Then Saul said to his servants, "Seek out for me a woman who is a medium, so that I may go to her and inquire of her." His servants said to him, "There is a medium at Endor."

8 So Saul disguised himself and put on other clothes and went there, he and two men with him. They came to the woman by night. And he said, "Consult a spirit for me, and bring up for me the one whom I name to you." 9The woman said to him, "Surely you know what Saul has done, how he has cut off the mediums and the wizards from the land. Why then are you laying a snare for my life to bring about my death?" 10But Saul swore to her by the LORD, "As the LORD lives, no punishment shall come upon you for this thing." 11Then the woman said, "Whom shall I bring up for you?" He answered, "Bring up Samuel for me." 12When the woman saw Samuel, she cried out with a loud voice; and the woman said to Saul, "Why have you deceived me? You are Saul!"

28.12 The Witch of Endor

Consulting a medium or spiritist was forbidden (Leviticus 20.6,27; Deuteronomy 18.10–12), as Saul knew well. Earlier, he had banned mediums in the kingdom. But through his disobedience Saul had lost contact with God, and was desperate to know the future. Whether Samuel actually appeared or whether the woman faked it, the results were the same: Saul left more fearful than when he came.

13The king said to her, "Have no fear; what do you see?" The woman said to Saul, "I see a divine being*m* coming up out of the ground." 14He said to her, "What is his appearance?" She said, "An old man is coming up; he is wrapped in a robe." So Saul knew that it was Samuel, and he bowed with his face to the ground, and did obeisance.

15 Then Samuel said to Saul, "Why have you disturbed me by bringing me up?" Saul answered, "I am in great distress, for the Philistines are warring against me, and God has turned away from me and answers me no more, either by prophets or by dreams; so I have summoned you to tell me what I should do." 16Samuel said, "Why then do you ask me, since the LORD has turned from you and become your enemy? 17The LORD has done to you just as he spoke by me; for the LORD has torn the kingdom out of your hand, and given it to your neighbor, David. 18Because you did not obey the voice of the LORD, and did not carry out his fierce wrath against Amalek, therefore the LORD has done this thing to you today. 19Moreover the LORD will give Israel along with you into the hands of the Philistines; and tomorrow you and your sons shall be with me; the LORD will also give

the army of Israel into the hands of the Philistines."

20 Immediately Saul fell full length on the ground, filled with fear because of the words of Samuel; and there was no strength in him, for he had eaten nothing all day and all night. 21The woman came to Saul, and when she saw that he was terrified, she said to him, "Your servant has listened to you; I have taken my life in my hand, and have listened to what you have said to me. 22Now therefore, you also listen to your servant; let me set a morsel of bread before you. Eat, that you may have strength when you go on your way." 23He refused, and said, "I will not eat." But his servants, together with the woman, urged him; and he listened to their words. So he got up from the ground and sat on the bed. 24Now the woman had a fatted calf in the house. She quickly slaughtered it, and she took flour, kneaded it, and baked unleavened cakes. 25She put them before Saul and his servants, and they ate. Then they rose and went away that night.

The Philistines Reject David

29 Now the Philistines gathered all their forces at Aphek, while the Israelites were encamped by the fountain that is in Jezreel. 2As the lords of the Philistines were passing on by hundreds and by thousands, and David and his men were passing on in the rear with Achish, 3the commanders of the Philistines said, "What are these Hebrews doing here?" Achish said to the commanders of the Philistines, "Is this not David, the servant of King Saul of Israel, who has been with me now for days and years? Since he deserted to me I have found no fault in him to this day." 4But the commanders of the Philistines were angry with him; and the commanders of the Philistines said to him, "Send the man back, so that he may return to the place that you have assigned to him; he shall not go down with us to battle, or else he may become an adversary to us in the battle. For how could this fellow reconcile himself to his lord? Would it not be with the heads of the men here? 5Is this not David, of whom they sing to one another in dances,

'Saul has killed his thousands,
    and David his ten thousands'?"

6 Then Achish called David and said to him, "As the LORD lives, you have been honest, and to me it seems right that you should march out and in with me in the campaign; for I have found nothing wrong in you from the day of your coming to me until today. Nevertheless the lords do not approve of you. 7So go back now; and go peaceably; do nothing to displease the lords of the Philistines." 8David said to Achish, "But what have I done? What have you found in your servant from the day I entered your service until

---

m Or *a god*; or *gods*

now, that I should not go and fight against the enemies of my lord the king?" [9]Achish replied to David, "I know that you are as blameless in my sight as an angel of God; nevertheless, the commanders of the Philistines have said, 'He shall not

29.8 Faking It

For the sake of survival, David had become a mercenary in the Philistine army. But he had not yet fought against his own people, and it is doubtful that he would have done so. Now, dismissed from service because he wasn't trusted in the upcoming battle, David acted distressed. Was he genuinely upset? It's quite possible he had hoped to turn the tables against the Philistines by attacking them from behind their own lines. The Philistine commanders made a shrewd move in sending him off.

go up with us to the battle.' [10]Now then rise early in the morning, you and the servants of your lord who came with you, and go to the place that I appointed for you. As for the evil report, do not take it to heart, for you have done well before me.[n] Start early in the morning, and leave as soon as you have light." [11]So David set out with his men early in the morning, to return to the land of the Philistines. But the Philistines went up to Jezreel.

David Avenges the Destruction of Ziklag

30 Now when David and his men came to Ziklag on the third day, the Amalekites had made a raid on the Negeb and on Ziklag. They had attacked Ziklag, burned it down, [2]and taken captive the women and all[o] who were in it, both small and great; they killed none of them, but carried them off, and went their way. [3]When David and his men came to the city, they found it burned down, and their wives and sons and daughters taken captive. [4]Then David and the people who were with him raised their voices and wept, until they had no more strength to weep. [5]David's two wives also had been taken captive, Ahinoam of Jezreel, and Abigail the widow of Nabal of Carmel. [6]David was in great danger; for the people spoke of stoning him, because all the people were bitter in spirit for their sons and daughters. But David strengthened himself in the LORD his God.

[7] David said to the priest Abiathar son of Ahimelech, "Bring me the ephod." So Abiathar brought the ephod to David. [8]David inquired of the LORD, "Shall I pursue this band? Shall I overtake them?" He answered him, "Pursue; for you shall surely overtake and shall surely rescue." [9]So

David set out, he and the six hundred men who were with him. They came to the Wadi Besor, where those stayed who were left behind. [10]But David went on with the pursuit, he and four hundred men; two hundred stayed behind, too exhausted to cross the Wadi Besor.

[11] In the open country they found an Egyptian, and brought him to David. They gave him bread and he ate; they gave him water to drink; [12]they also gave him a piece of fig cake and two clusters of raisins. When he had eaten, his spirit revived; for he had not eaten bread or drunk water for three days and three nights. [13]Then David said to him, "To whom do you belong? Where are you from?" He said, "I am a young man of Egypt, servant to an Amalekite. My master left me behind because I fell sick three days ago. [14]We had made a raid on the Negeb of the Cherethites and on that which belongs to Judah and on the Negeb of Caleb; and we burned Ziklag down." [15]David said to him, "Will you take me down to this raiding party?" He said, "Swear to me by God that you will not kill me, or hand me over to my master, and I will take you down to them."

[16] When he had taken him down, they were spread out all over the ground, eating and drinking and dancing, because of the great amount of spoil they had taken from the land of the Philistines and from the land of Judah. [17]David attacked them from twilight until the evening of the next day. Not one of them escaped, except four hundred young men, who mounted camels and fled. [18]David recovered all that the Amalekites had taken; and David rescued his two wives. [19]Nothing was missing, whether small or great, sons or daughters, spoil or anything that had been taken; David brought back everything. [20]David also captured all the flocks and herds, which were driven ahead of the other cattle; people said, "This is David's spoil."

[21] Then David came to the two hundred men who had been too exhausted to follow David, and who had been left at the Wadi Besor. They went out to meet David and to meet the people who were with him. When David drew near to the people he saluted them. [22]Then all the corrupt and worthless fellows among the men who had gone with David said, "Because they did not go with us, we will not give them any of the spoil that we have recovered, except that each man may take his wife and children, and leave." [23]But David said, "You shall not do so, my brothers, with what the LORD has given us; he has preserved us and handed over to us the raiding party that attacked us. [24]Who would listen to you in this matter? For the share of the one who goes down into the battle shall be the same as the share of the one who stays by the baggage; they shall share alike." [25]From that day forward he made it a statute and

---

[n] Gk: Heb lacks *and go to the place . . . done well before me*   [o] Gk: Heb lacks *and all*

an ordinance for Israel; it continues to the present
day.
26 When David came to Ziklag, he sent part
of the spoil to his friends, the elders of Judah,
saying, "Here is a present for you from the spoil
of the enemies of the LORD"; [27]it was for those in
Bethel, in Ramoth of the Negeb, in Jattir, [28]in
Aroer, in Siphmoth, in Eshtemoa, [29]in Racal, in
the towns of the Jerahmeelites, in the towns of the
Kenites, [30]in Hormah, in Bor-ashan, in Athach,
[31]in Hebron, all the places where David and his
men had roamed.

The Death of Saul and His Sons

31 Now the Philistines fought against Israel;
and the men of Israel fled before the Philistines, and many fell[p] on Mount Gilboa. [2]The
Philistines overtook Saul and his sons; and the
Philistines killed Jonathan and Abinadab and
Malchishua, the sons of Saul. [3]The battle pressed
hard upon Saul; the archers found him, and he
was badly wounded by them. [4]Then Saul said to
his armor-bearer, "Draw your sword and thrust
me through with it, so that these uncircumcised
may not come and thrust me through, and make
sport of me." But his armor-bearer was unwilling;
for he was terrified. So Saul took his own sword
and fell upon it. [5]When his armor-bearer saw that
Saul was dead, he also fell upon his sword and
died with him. [6]So Saul and his three sons and his
armor-bearer and all his men died together on
the same day. [7]When the men of Israel who were
on the other side of the valley and those beyond
the Jordan saw that the men of Israel had fled and
that Saul and his sons were dead, they forsook
their towns and fled; and the Philistines came and
occupied them.
8 The next day, when the Philistines came to
strip the dead, they found Saul and his three sons
fallen on Mount Gilboa. [9]They cut off his head,
stripped off his armor, and sent messengers
throughout the land of the Philistines to carry the
good news to the houses of their idols and to the
people. [10]They put his armor in the temple of
Astarte;[q] and they fastened his body to the wall
of Beth-shan. [11]But when the inhabitants of
Jabesh-gilead heard what the Philistines had done
to Saul, [12]all the valiant men set out, traveled all
night long, and took the body of Saul and the
bodies of his sons from the wall of Beth-shan.
They came to Jabesh and burned them there.
[13]Then they took their bones and buried them
under the tamarisk tree in Jabesh, and fasted sev-
en days.

31.11 Loyal Friends in Death

Saul's first military action as king had been the rescue of Jabesh Gilead (chapter 11). Through all these years its citizens had not forgotten. When they heard of the disgraceful display of Saul's and his sons' bodies, they undertook a dangerous night mission to steal the bodies and give them proper burial.

[p] Heb *and they fell slain* [q] Heb plural

2 SAMUEL

The Life of King David
From herding sheep to ruling a nation

T HE BIBLE IS FILLED WITH strong personalities, but none leads David in the parade. His life was a whirlwind, from which striking images flash. We see him playing his harp, writing poems, fighting battles, faking insanity, dancing jubilantly in praise of God. We watch his tear-streaked face when he learns of his closest friend's death. We see him on his rooftop, gazing down lustfully on Bathsheba's bath. We see Nathan point his finger at him, accusing him of adultery and murder. We hear David's guilty, anguished voice crying to God for the life of his infant child. We see David's bowed head as he stumbles out of Jerusalem, pursued by his murderous son.

I took you from the pasture, from following the sheep to be prince over my people Israel. 7.8

David survived the crises of a dozen lives. Somehow he always bounced back. Somehow he maintained a passionate trust in God. First and Second Samuel don't paint him as a flawless character, nor as a perfect model of strength and courage. David had striking weaknesses. Yet he appeals to us as he did to the Israelites: He was completely, passionately alive. Whatever he did, right or wrong, he did with his whole heart. In his love for God, he held nothing back.

Healing the Wounds of War

While 1 Samuel tells of David's youth and his long exile, 2 Samuel focuses on David as king, leading, uniting, inspiring his people. His time in the desert was over. Different qualities of leadership were required in a king.

David inherited a country in tatters. His fellow southerners recognized him as the new king. But Saul's son, backed by a powerful general, launched a civil war for the throne. Ugly infighting followed: intrigue, murder, and treachery.

Even after David's rivals were eliminated, peace was uneasy. Unless David could heal the wounds of war, resentment might smolder in the hearts of the northerners. David's decisive action showed wisdom and firmness. He justly punished murderers who expected his gratitude. He showed respect for his enemies by mourning their deaths. From his first day in office David behaved as the king of all the people, not just his loyal followers. The northern tribes soon came over to him, submitting to his leadership (5.1–3).

David's next move was to capture Jerusalem. People said it couldn't be done; mountainous Jerusalem was impregnable. David did it, and made Jerusalem his new political and religious capital. Located on the border between north and south, Jerusalem symbolized a new national unity based on trust in God.

That was just the beginning. David led the unified tribes to do what they had barely dreamed of: They defeated the dreaded Philistines once and for all. Almost overnight the tiny, threatened nation of Israel became safe. Secure borders encouraged expanded trade, and Israel boomed. (David's son Solomon reaped most of the wealth from this.) Naturally, David's popularity increased.

A Murderer and an Adulterer

But David's reign held ironic tragedies, too. Second Samuel makes no effort to hide them. David could lead a nation but not his own children. His ineffective parenting nearly destroyed all he had done, when his heartless son Absalom led a rebellion. Second Samuel portrays David without retouching his blemishes: He was a murderer and an adulterer and a leader capable of cruelty.

Nevertheless, he was Israel's greatest king. Even at his lowest points, his great strength of character showed. He was never vengeful with his enemies. He took full responsibility for his mistakes. He managed to remember that he had started out as a mere shepherd. He held power only by the grace of God—and he believed that God had every right to take power away.

Through his love for God and his sense of astonished gratefulness for what God had done for him,

David became a living embodiment of the Israel God wanted. Like all truly great leaders, he made his country thrive not just by what he did, but by who he was.

How to Read 2 Samuel

Second Samuel continues, without a break, the story begun in 1 Samuel—the two were originally one book. The difference is that David, who once sought only to survive, now seeks to unify a badly divided country. His greater responsibilities put extra stress on his leadership qualities. You can study his life with leadership in mind. You can also study chapters 11–20 to see the cancerous effects of a leader's private sins and poor family leadership.

Chapters 21–24 seem to be an appendix, bringing in other important events and facts of David's reign. Much of 2 Samuel's story is also told in 1 Chronicles 11–21, often word for word the same.

PEOPLE YOU'LL MEET IN 2 SAMUEL

DAVID (p. 323)
ABNER (p. 327)
NATHAN (p. 331)

BATHSHEBA (p. 334)
ABSALOM (p. 339)

3-TRACK READING PLAN

For an explanation and complete listing of the 3-track reading plan, turn to page 7.

TRACK 1: *Two-Week Courses on the Bible*
The Track 1 reading program on the Old Testament includes two chapters from 2 Samuel. See page 8 for a complete listing of this course.

TRACK 2: *An Overview of 2 Samuel in 3 Days*
☐ Day 1. Read the Introduction to 2 Samuel and chapter 6, in which the ark of the covenant was brought to Jerusalem and David danced before the Lord.
☐ Day 2. Read chapter 11, in which David's adultery with Bathsheba led to murder.
☐ Day 3. Read chapter 12 for the dramatic account of the prophet Nathan coming to confront David.

Now turn to page 9 for your next Track 2 reading project.

TRACK 3: *All of 2 Samuel in 24 Days*
After you have read through 2 Samuel, turn to pages 10–14 for your next Track 3 reading project.

☐1 ☐2 ☐3 ☐4 ☐5 ☐6 ☐7 ☐8
☐9 ☐10 ☐11 ☐12 ☐13 ☐14 ☐15 ☐16
☐17 ☐18 ☐19 ☐20 ☐21 ☐22 ☐23 ☐24

David Mourns for Saul and Jonathan

1 After the death of Saul, when David had returned from defeating the Amalekites, David remained two days in Ziklag. ²On the third day, a man came from Saul's camp, with his clothes torn and dirt on his head. When he came to David, he fell to the ground and did obeisance. ³David said to him, "Where have you come from?" He said to him, "I have escaped from the camp of Israel." ⁴David said to him, "How did things go? Tell me!" He answered, "The army fled from the battle, but also many of the army fell and died; and Saul and his son Jonathan also died." ⁵Then David asked the young man who was reporting to him, "How do you know that Saul and his son Jonathan died?" ⁶The young man reporting to him said, "I happened to be on Mount Gilboa; and there was Saul leaning on his spear, while the chariots and the horsemen drew close to him. ⁷When he looked behind him, he saw me, and called to me. I answered, 'Here sir.' ⁸And he said to me, 'Who are you?' I answered him, 'I am an Amalekite.' ⁹He said to me, 'Come, stand over me and kill me; for convulsions have seized me, and

yet my life still lingers.' ¹⁰So I stood over him, and killed him, for I knew that he could not live after he had fallen. I took the crown that was on his head and the armlet that was on his arm, and I have brought them here to my lord."

11 Then David took hold of his clothes and tore them; and all the men who were with him did the same. ¹²They mourned and wept, and fasted until evening for Saul and for his son Jonathan, and for the army of the LORD and for the house of Israel, because they had fallen by the sword. ¹³David said to the young man who had reported to him, "Where do you come from?" He answered, "I am the son of a resident alien, an Amalekite." ¹⁴David said to him, "Were you not afraid to lift your hand to destroy the LORD's anointed?" ¹⁵Then David called one of the young men and said, "Come here and strike him down." So he struck him down and he died. ¹⁶David said to him, "Your blood be on your head; for your own mouth has testified against you, saying, 'I have killed the LORD's anointed.'"

17 David intoned this lamentation over Saul and his son Jonathan. ¹⁸(He ordered that The Song of the Bow*a* be taught to the people of Judah; it is written in the Book of Jashar.) He said:
¹⁹ Your glory, O Israel, lies slain upon your
    high places!
  How the mighty have fallen!
²⁰ Tell it not in Gath,
    proclaim it not in the streets of
      Ashkelon;
  or the daughters of the Philistines will
    rejoice,
  the daughters of the uncircumcised will
    exult.

²¹ You mountains of Gilboa,
    let there be no dew or rain upon you,
    nor bounteous fields!*b*
  For there the shield of the mighty was
    defiled,
  the shield of Saul, anointed with oil no
    more.

²² From the blood of the slain,
    from the fat of the mighty,
  the bow of Jonathan did not turn back,
    nor the sword of Saul return empty.

²³ Saul and Jonathan, beloved and lovely!
    In life and in death they were not
      divided;
  they were swifter than eagles,
    they were stronger than lions.

²⁴ O daughters of Israel, weep over Saul,
    who clothed you with crimson, in
      luxury,

  who put ornaments of gold on your
    apparel.

²⁵ How the mighty have fallen
    in the midst of the battle!

Jonathan lies slain upon your high places.
²⁶ I am distressed for you, my brother
    Jonathan;
  greatly beloved were you to me;
    your love to me was wonderful,
    passing the love of women.

²⁷ How the mighty have fallen,
    and the weapons of war perished!

David Anointed King of Judah

2 After this David inquired of the LORD, "Shall I go up into any of the cities of Judah?" The LORD said to him, "Go up." David said, "To which shall I go up?" He said, "To Hebron." ²So David went up there, along with his two wives, Ahinoam of Jezreel, and Abigail the widow of Nabal of Carmel. ³David brought up the men who were with him, every one with his household; and they settled in the towns of Hebron. ⁴Then the people of Judah came, and there they anointed David king over the house of Judah.

When they told David, "It was the people of Jabesh-gilead who buried Saul," ⁵David sent messengers to the people of Jabesh-gilead, and said to them, "May you be blessed by the LORD, because you showed this loyalty to Saul your lord, and

2.5 Potential Rivals

For their own security, dictators try to eliminate all competitors. In the ancient world, rulers did the same: A new king customarily killed the former king's relatives, since they were potential rivals. Not David! He executed the man who claimed to have killed his old enemy King Saul (1.14–15), he sang a painful lament over Saul's and Jonathan's deaths, and he blessed the people of Jabesh Gilead for their kindness in giving Saul a decent burial. David never abandoned his love for Saul's family.

buried him! ⁶Now may the LORD show steadfast love and faithfulness to you! And I too will reward you because you have done this thing. ⁷Therefore let your hands be strong, and be valiant; for Saul your lord is dead, and the house of Judah has anointed me king over them."

Ishbaal King of Israel

8 But Abner son of Ner, commander of Saul's

---

a Heb *that The Bow*   *b* Meaning of Heb uncertain

army, had taken Ishbaal[c] son of Saul, and brought him over to Mahanaim. [9]He made him king over Gilead, the Ashurites, Jezreel, Ephraim, Benjamin, and over all Israel. [10]Ishbaal,[c] Saul's son, was forty years old when he began to reign over Israel, and he reigned two years. But the house of Judah followed David. [11]The time that David was king in Hebron over the house of Judah was seven years and six months.

The Battle of Gibeon

12 Abner son of Ner, and the servants of Ishbaal[c] son of Saul, went out from Mahanaim to Gibeon. [13]Joab son of Zeruiah, and the servants of David, went out and met them at the pool of Gibeon. One group sat on one side of the pool, while the other sat on the other side of the pool. [14]Abner said to Joab, "Let the young men come forward and have a contest before us." Joab said, "Let them come forward." [15]So they came forward and were counted as they passed by, twelve for Benjamin and Ishbaal[c] son of Saul, and twelve of the servants of David. [16]Each grasped his opponent by the head, and thrust his sword in his opponent's side; so they fell down together. Therefore that place was called Helkath-hazzurim,[d] which is at Gibeon. [17]The battle was very fierce that day; and Abner and the men of Israel were beaten by the servants of David.

18 The three sons of Zeruiah were there, Joab, Abishai, and Asahel. Now Asahel was as swift of foot as a wild gazelle. [19]Asahel pursued Abner, turning neither to the right nor to the left as he followed him. [20]Then Abner looked back and said, "Is it you, Asahel?" He answered, "Yes, it is." [21]Abner said to him, "Turn to your right or to your left, and seize one of the young men, and take his spoil." But Asahel would not turn away from following him. [22]Abner said again to Asahel, "Turn away from following me; why should I strike you to the ground? How then could I show my face to your brother Joab?" [23]But he refused to turn away. So Abner struck him in the stomach with the butt of his spear, so that the spear came out at his back. He fell there, and died where he lay. And all those who came to the place where Asahel had fallen and died, stood still.

24 But Joab and Abishai pursued Abner. As the sun was going down they came to the hill of Ammah, which lies before Giah on the way to the wilderness of Gibeon. [25]The Benjaminites rallied around Abner and formed a single band; they took their stand on the top of a hill. [26]Then Abner called to Joab, "Is the sword to keep devouring forever? Do you not know that the end will be bitter? How long will it be before you order your people to turn from the pursuit of their kinsmen?" [27]Joab said, "As God lives, if you had not

spoken, the people would have continued to pursue their kinsmen, not stopping until morning." [28]Joab sounded the trumpet and all the people stopped; they no longer pursued Israel or engaged in battle any further.

29 Abner and his men traveled all that night through the Arabah; they crossed the Jordan, and, marching the whole forenoon,[e] they came to Mahanaim. [30]Joab returned from the pursuit of Abner; and when he had gathered all the people together, there were missing of David's servants nineteen men besides Asahel. [31]But the servants of David had killed of Benjamin three hundred sixty of Abner's men. [32]They took up Asahel and buried him in the tomb of his father, which was at Bethlehem. Joab and his men marched all night, and the day broke upon them at Hebron.

Abner Defects to David

3 There was a long war between the house of Saul and the house of David; David grew stronger and stronger, while the house of Saul became weaker and weaker.

2 Sons were born to David at Hebron: his firstborn was Amnon, of Ahinoam of Jezreel; [3]his second, Chileab, of Abigail the widow of Nabal of Carmel; the third, Absalom son of Maacah, daughter of King Talmai of Geshur; [4]the fourth, Adonijah son of Haggith; the fifth, Shephatiah son of Abital; [5]and the sixth, Ithream, of David's wife Eglah. These were born to David in Hebron.

6 While there was war between the house of Saul and the house of David, Abner was making himself strong in the house of Saul. [7]Now Saul had a concubine whose name was Rizpah daughter of Aiah. And Ishbaal[f] said to Abner, "Why

3.7 Women in Politics

In David's time, women were political symbols. Abner's sleeping with Saul's concubine would have suggested that he had his eyes on becoming king himself. Later, when Absalom drove his father David out of Jerusalem, he slept with David's concubines in public, demonstrating to all eyes that he had taken over from his father (16.22).

David sometimes may have married for political benefit. One wife, Absalom's mother (verse 3), was a princess from a neighboring country; the marriage undoubtedly promoted good foreign relations. David's request that Michal be returned to him (though she had remarried, verses 14–16) made political sense: an alliance with Saul's daughter would tie Saul's family to the palace.

---

[c] Gk Compare 1 Chr 8.33; 9.39: Heb *Ish-bosheth*, "man of shame" Heb uncertain   [f] Heb *And he*   [d] That is *Field of Sword-edges*   [e] Meaning of

have you gone in to my father's concubine?" [8]The words of Ishbaal[g] made Abner very angry; he said, "Am I a dog's head for Judah? Today I keep showing loyalty to the house of your father Saul, to his brothers, and to his friends, and have not given you into the hand of David; and yet you charge me now with a crime concerning this woman. [9]So may God do to Abner and so may he add to it! For just what the LORD has sworn to David, that will I accomplish for him, [10]to transfer the kingdom from the house of Saul, and set up the throne of David over Israel and over Judah, from Dan to Beer-sheba." [11]And Ishbaal[h] could not answer Abner another word, because he feared him.

12 Abner sent messengers to David at Hebron,[i] saying, "To whom does the land belong? Make your covenant with me, and I will give you my support to bring all Israel over to you." [13]He said, "Good; I will make a covenant with you. But one thing I require of you: you shall never appear in my presence unless you bring Saul's daughter Michal when you come to see me." [14]Then David sent messengers to Saul's son Ishbaal,[j] saying, "Give me my wife Michal, to whom I became engaged at the price of one hundred foreskins of the Philistines." [15]Ishbaal[j] sent and took her from her husband Paltiel the son of Laish. [16]But her husband went with her, weeping as he walked behind her all the way to Bahurim. Then Abner said to him, "Go back home!" So he went back.

17 Abner sent word to the elders of Israel, saying, "For some time past you have been seeking David as king over you. [18]Now then bring it about; for the LORD has promised David:

Through my servant David I will save my people Israel from the hand of the Philistines, and from all their enemies." [19]Abner also spoke directly to the Benjaminites; then Abner went to tell David at Hebron all that Israel and the whole house of Benjamin were ready to do.

20 When Abner came with twenty men to David at Hebron, David made a feast for Abner and the men who were with him. [21]Abner said to David, "Let me go and rally all Israel to my lord the king, in order that they may make a covenant with you, and that you may reign over all that your heart desires." So David dismissed Abner, and he went away in peace.

Abner Is Killed by Joab

22 Just then the servants of David arrived with Joab from a raid, bringing much spoil with them. But Abner was not with David at Hebron, for David[k] had dismissed him, and he had gone away in peace. [23]When Joab and all the army that was with him came, it was told Joab, "Abner son of Ner came to the king, and he has dismissed him, and he has gone away in peace." [24]Then Joab went to the king and said, "What have you done? Abner came to you; why did you dismiss him, so that he got away? [25]You know that Abner son of Ner came to deceive you, and to learn your comings and goings and to learn all that you are doing."

26 When Joab came out from David's presence, he sent messengers after Abner, and they brought him back from the cistern of Sirah; but David did not know about it. [27]When Abner returned to Hebron, Joab took him aside in the

g Gk Compare 1 Chr 8.33; 9.39; Heb Ish-bosheth, "man of shame"   h Heb And he   i Gk: Heb where he was
j Heb Ish-bosheth   k Heb he

ABNER *On the Wrong Side*

WAR IS NEVER PRETTY, AND neither are most of the soldiers who fight it. Famous generals such as Rommel, Sherman, Lee or Patton do not always stand for great causes or great morals. They earn respect for their ability to lead men into battle, to kill and to triumph.

Abner was a fine general who fought most of his life for a bad king. Though he introduced David to King Saul (1 Samuel 17.55–58) and commanded David during his early campaigns, Abner ultimately followed Saul's orders and fought against David. During the years when David's band of outlaws was roaming the hills, Abner led the hunt to track them down. Along the way he and David won mutual respect as honorable enemies.

Even after Saul died, Abner remained loyal to the forces arrayed against David. He installed Saul's son as king and fought a long civil war against David's side. Abner died not from battle but from treachery. Joab, David's general, had never forgiven Abner for killing his brother. When Abner finally came to make peace with David, Joab saw his opportunity for revenge. Pretending to conference with Abner, he stuck a knife in him (3.27).

David denounced this act of treachery and gave his former enemy a state funeral. Abner, he said, was a "prince and a great man" (3.38). Israel would need more such soldiers, people who combined war-making skill with loyalty to their king.

Life Questions: Can you think of any sincere men or women today who are passionately fighting on the wrong side of an important cause?

gateway to speak with him privately, and there he stabbed him in the stomach. So he died for shedding[l] the blood of Asahel, Joab's[m] brother. [28]Afterward, when David heard of it, he said, "I and my kingdom are forever guiltless before the LORD for the blood of Abner son of Ner. [29]May the guilt[n] fall on the head of Joab, and on all his father's house; and may the house of Joab never be without one who has a discharge, or who is leprous,[o] or who holds a spindle, or who falls by the sword, or who lacks food!" [30]So Joab and his brother Abishai murdered Abner because he had killed their brother Asahel in the battle at Gibeon.

3.30 Easy on Joab

Though General Douglas MacArthur had been popular and effective during World War II, he opposed the President's Korean War policy, and finally Harry Truman fired him. David faced a similar dilemma, but made a different decision. After David had made peace with Abner, a former enemy, David's commander Joab tricked and murdered Abner. This undercut David's policy of bringing harmony to a divided land. Although David cursed Joab, he didn't punish him or strip away his power. Why not? Perhaps he needed Joab's abilities, and feared what Joab might do if alienated. Many years later, when David lay dying, he instructed Solomon to punish Joab for the crime (1 Kings 2.5–6).

[31] Then David said to Joab and to all the people who were with him, "Tear your clothes, and put on sackcloth, and mourn over Abner." And King David followed the bier. [32]They buried Abner at Hebron. The king lifted up his voice and wept at the grave of Abner, and all the people wept. [33]The king lamented for Abner, saying,

"Should Abner die as a fool dies?
[34] Your hands were not bound,
    your feet were not fettered;
as one falls before the wicked
    you have fallen."

And all the people wept over him again. [35]Then all the people came to persuade David to eat something while it was still day; but David swore, saying, "So may God do to me, and more, if I taste bread or anything else before the sun goes down!" [36]All the people took notice of it, and it pleased them; just as everything the king did pleased all the people. [37]So all the people and all Israel understood that day that the king had no part in the killing of Abner son of Ner. [38]And the king said to his servants, "Do you not know that a prince and a great man has fallen this day in Israel? [39]Today I am powerless, even though anointed king; these men, the sons of Zeruiah, are too violent for me. The LORD pay back the one who does wickedly in accordance with his wickedness!"

Ishbaal Assassinated

4 When Saul's son Ishbaal[p] heard that Abner had died at Hebron, his courage failed, and all Israel was dismayed. [2]Saul's son had two captains of raiding bands; the name of the one was Baanah, and the name of the other Rechab. They were sons of Rimmon a Benjaminite from Beeroth—for Beeroth is considered to belong to Benjamin. [3](Now the people of Beeroth had fled to Gittaim and are there as resident aliens to this day).

[4] Saul's son Jonathan had a son who was crippled in his feet. He was five years old when the news about Saul and Jonathan came from Jezreel. His nurse picked him up and fled; and, in her haste to flee, it happened that he fell and became lame. His name was Mephibosheth.[q]

[5] Now the sons of Rimmon the Beerothite, Rechab and Baanah, set out, and about the heat of the day they came to the house of Ishbaal,[r] while he was taking his noonday rest. [6]They came inside the house as though to take wheat, and they struck him in the stomach; then Rechab and his brother Baanah escaped.[s] [7]Now they had come into the house while he was lying on his couch in his bedchamber; they attacked him, killed him, and beheaded him. Then they took his head and traveled by way of the Arabah all night long. [8]They brought the head of Ishbaal[r] to David at Hebron and said to the king, "Here is the head of Ishbaal,[r] son of Saul, your enemy, who sought your life; the LORD has avenged my lord the king this day on Saul and on his offspring."

[9] David answered Rechab and his brother Baanah, the sons of Rimmon the Beerothite, "As the LORD lives, who has redeemed my life out of every adversity, [10]when the one who told me, 'See, Saul is dead,' thought he was bringing good news, I seized him and killed him at Ziklag—this was the reward I gave him for his news. [11]How much more then, when wicked men have killed a righteous man on his bed in his own house! And now shall I not require his blood at your hand, and destroy you from the earth?" [12]So David commanded the young men, and they killed them; they cut off their hands and feet, and hung their bodies beside the pool at Hebron. But the head of Ishbaal[r] they took and buried in the tomb of Abner at Hebron.

---

[l] Heb lacks *shedding*   [m] Heb *his*   [n] Heb *May it*   [o] A term for several skin diseases; precise meaning uncertain
[p] Heb lacks *Ishbaal* uncertain   [q] In 1 Chr 8.34 and 9.40, *Merib-baal*   [r] Heb *Ish-bosheth*   [s] Meaning of Heb of verse 6

David Anointed King of All Israel

5 Then all the tribes of Israel came to David at Hebron, and said, "Look, we are your bone and flesh. ²For some time, while Saul was king over us, it was you who led out Israel and brought it in. The LORD said to you: It is you who shall be shepherd of my people Israel, you who shall be ruler over Israel." ³So all the elders of Israel came to the king at Hebron; and King David made a covenant with them at Hebron before the LORD, and they anointed David king over Israel. ⁴David was thirty years old when he began to reign, and he reigned forty years. ⁵At Hebron he reigned over Judah seven years and six months; and at Jerusalem he reigned over all Israel and Judah thirty-three years.

Jerusalem Made Capital of the United Kingdom

6 The king and his men marched to Jerusalem against the Jebusites, the inhabitants of the land, who said to David, "You will not come in here, even the blind and the lame will turn you back"—

5.6 Choosing a Capital

In trying to unify the northern and southern tribes, David wanted a capital that offended neither side. He found it in Jerusalem, on the border between North and South and belonging to neither. Its choice can be compared to the U.S. capital, Washington, D.C., a compromise between North and South.

thinking, "David cannot come in here." ⁷Nevertheless David took the stronghold of Zion, which is now the city of David. ⁸David had said on that day, "Whoever would strike down the Jebusites, let him get up the water shaft to attack the lame and the blind, those whom David hates."ᵗ Therefore it is said, "The blind and the lame shall not come into the house." ⁹David occupied the stronghold, and named it the city of David. David built the city all around from the Millo inward. ¹⁰And David became greater and greater, for the LORD, the God of hosts, was with him.

11 King Hiram of Tyre sent messengers to David, along with cedar trees, and carpenters and masons who built David a house. ¹²David then perceived that the LORD had established him king over Israel, and that he had exalted his kingdom for the sake of his people Israel.

13 In Jerusalem, after he came from Hebron, David took more concubines and wives; and more sons and daughters were born to David. ¹⁴These are the names of those who were born to

him in Jerusalem: Shammua, Shobab, Nathan, Solomon, ¹⁵Ibhar, Elishua, Nepheg, Japhia, ¹⁶Elishama, Eliada, and Eliphelet.

Philistine Attack Repulsed

17 When the Philistines heard that David had been anointed king over Israel, all the Philistines went up in search of David; but David heard about it and went down to the stronghold. ¹⁸Now the Philistines had come and spread out in the valley of Rephaim. ¹⁹David inquired of the LORD, "Shall I go up against the Philistines? Will you give them into my hand?" The LORD said to David, "Go up; for I will certainly give the Philistines

5.19 Seeking Guidance

Most ancient kings sought signs from God. David went well beyond that practice, regularly asking God for guidance about military and governmental decisions. David's faith wasn't impersonal; he had a close, practical, and deep relationship with God.

into your hand." ²⁰So David came to Baal-perazim, and David defeated them there. He said, "The LORD has burst forth againstᵘ my enemies before me, like a bursting flood." Therefore that place is called Baal-perazim.ᵛ ²¹The Philistines abandoned their idols there, and David and his men carried them away.

22 Once again the Philistines came up, and were spread out in the valley of Rephaim. ²³When David inquired of the LORD, he said, "You shall not go up; go around to their rear, and come upon them opposite the balsam trees. ²⁴When you hear the sound of marching in the tops of the balsam trees, then be on the alert; for then the LORD has gone out before you to strike down the army of the Philistines." ²⁵David did just as the LORD had commanded him; and he struck down the Philistines from Geba all the way to Gezer.

David Brings the Ark to Jerusalem

6 David again gathered all the chosen men of Israel, thirty thousand. ²David and all the people with him set out and went from Baale-judah, to bring up from there the ark of God, which is called by the name of the LORD of hosts who is enthroned on the cherubim. ³They carried the ark of God on a new cart, and brought it out of the house of Abinadab, which was on the hill. Uzzah and Ahio,ʷ the sons of Abinadab, were driving the new cart ⁴with the ark of God;ˣ and Ahioʷ went in front of the ark. ⁵David and all the house of Israel were dancing before the LORD with

---

ᵗ Another reading is *those who hate David*　　ᵘ Heb *paraz*　　ᵛ That is *Lord of Bursting Forth*　　ʷ Or *and his brother*
ˣ Compare Gk: Heb *and brought it out of the house of Abinadab, which was on the hill with the ark of God*

all their might, with songs[y] and lyres and harps and tambourines and castanets and cymbals.

6 When they came to the threshing floor of Nacon, Uzzah reached out his hand to the ark of God and took hold of it, for the oxen shook it. [7]The anger of the LORD was kindled against Uzzah; and God struck him there because he reached out his hand to the ark;[z] and he died there beside the ark of God. [8]David was angry because the LORD had burst forth with an outburst upon Uzzah; so that place is called Perezuzzah,[a] to this day. [9]David was afraid of the LORD that day; he said, "How can the ark of the LORD come into my care?" [10]So David was unwilling to take the ark of the LORD into his care in the city of David; instead David took it to the house of Obed-edom the Gittite. [11]The ark of the LORD remained in the house of Obed-edom the Gittite three months; and the LORD blessed Obed-edom and all his household.

12 It was told King David, "The LORD has blessed the household of Obed-edom and all that belongs to him, because of the ark of God." So David went and brought up the ark of God from the house of Obed-edom to the city of David with rejoicing; [13]and when those who bore the ark of the LORD had gone six paces, he sacrificed an ox and a fatling. [14]David danced before the LORD with all his might; David was girded with a linen ephod. [15]So David and all the house of Israel brought up the ark of the LORD with shouting, and with the sound of the trumpet.

16 As the ark of the LORD came into the city of David, Michal daughter of Saul looked out of the window, and saw King David leaping and dancing before the LORD; and she despised him in her heart.

17 They brought in the ark of the LORD, and set it in its place, inside the tent that David had pitched for it; and David offered burnt offerings and offerings of well-being before the LORD. [18]When David had finished offering the burnt offerings and the offerings of well-being, he blessed the people in the name of the LORD of hosts, [19]and distributed food among all the people, the whole multitude of Israel, both men and women, to each a cake of bread, a portion of meat,[b] and a cake of raisins. Then all the people went back to their homes.

20 David returned to bless his household. But Michal the daughter of Saul came out to meet David, and said, "How the king of Israel honored himself today, uncovering himself today before the eyes of his servants' maids, as any vulgar fellow might shamelessly uncover himself!" [21]David said to Michal, "It was before the LORD, who chose me in place of your father and all his house-

hold, to appoint me as prince over Israel, the people of the LORD, that I have danced before the LORD. [22]I will make myself yet more contemptible than this, and I will be abased in my own eyes; but by the maids of whom you have spoken, by them I shall be held in honor." [23]And Michal the daughter of Saul had no child to the day of her death.

God's Covenant with David

7 Now when the king was settled in his house, and the LORD had given him rest from all his enemies around him, [2]the king said to the prophet Nathan, "See now, I am living in a house of cedar, but the ark of God stays in a tent." [3]Nathan said to the king, "Go, do all that you have in mind; for the LORD is with you."

4 But that same night the word of the LORD came to Nathan: [5]Go and tell my servant David: Thus says the LORD: Are you the one to build me a house to live in? [6]I have not lived in a house since the day I brought up the people of Israel from Egypt to this day, but I have been moving about in a tent and a tabernacle. [7]Wherever I have moved about among all the people of Israel, did I ever speak a word with any of the tribal leaders[c] of Israel, whom I commanded to shepherd my people Israel, saying, "Why have you not built me a house of cedar?" [8]Now therefore thus you shall say to my servant David: Thus says the LORD of hosts: I took you from the pasture, from following the sheep to be prince over my people Israel; [9]and I have been with you wherever you went, and have cut off all your enemies from before you; and I will make for you a great name, like the name of the great ones of the earth. [10]And I will appoint a place for my people Israel and will plant them, so that they may live in their own place, and be disturbed no more; and evildoers shall afflict them no more, as formerly, [11]from the time that I appointed judges over my people Israel; and I will give you rest from all your enemies. Moreover the LORD declares to you that the LORD will make you a house. [12]When your days are fulfilled and you lie down with your ancestors, I will raise up your offspring after you, who shall come forth from your body, and I will establish his kingdom. [13]He shall build a house for my name, and I will establish the throne of his kingdom forever. [14]I will be a father to him, and he shall be a son to me. When he commits iniquity, I will punish him with a rod such as mortals use, with blows inflicted by human beings. [15]But I will not take[d] my steadfast love from him, as I took it from Saul, whom I put away from before you. [16]Your house and your kingdom shall be made sure forever before me;[e] your throne shall be

established forever. [17]In accordance with all these words and with all this vision, Nathan spoke to David.

David's Prayer

18 Then King David went in and sat before the LORD, and said, "Who am I, O Lord GOD, and what is my house, that you have brought me thus far? [19]And yet this was a small thing in your eyes,

---

7.16 God's Great Promise

The Lord's promise that "your house and your kingdom shall be made sure forever" suggested that Israel would never lack the leadership they needed. This promise was one of a series of covenants between God and his people—with Abraham (Genesis 12), with Moses at Sinai (Exodus 20), and now with David. The New Testament sees this promise fulfilled in Jesus, a son of David, and King of kings forever (Luke 1.32–33).

O Lord GOD; you have spoken also of your servant's house for a great while to come. May this be instruction for the people,[f] O Lord GOD! [20]And what more can David say to you? For you know your servant, O Lord GOD! [21]Because of your promise, and according to your own heart,

you have wrought all this greatness, so that your servant may know it. [22]Therefore you are great, O LORD God; for there is no one like you, and there is no God besides you, according to all that we have heard with our ears. [23]Who is like your people, like Israel? Is there another[g] nation on earth whose God went to redeem it as a people, and to make a name for himself, doing great and awesome things for them,[h] by driving out[i] before his people nations and their gods?[j] [24]And you established your people Israel for yourself to be your people forever; and you, O LORD, became their God. [25]And now, O LORD God, as for the word that you have spoken concerning your servant and concerning his house, confirm it forever; do as you have promised. [26]Thus your name will be magnified forever in the saying, 'The LORD of hosts is God over Israel'; and the house of your servant David will be established before you. [27]For you, O LORD of hosts, the God of Israel, have made this revelation to your servant, saying, 'I will build you a house'; therefore your servant has found courage to pray this prayer to you. [28]And now, O Lord GOD, you are God, and your words are true, and you have promised this good thing to your servant; [29]now therefore may it please you to bless the house of your servant, so that it may continue forever before you; for you, O Lord GOD, have spoken, and with your blessing shall the house of your servant be blessed forever."

---

f Meaning of Heb uncertain   g Gk: Heb *one*   h Heb *you*   i Gk 1 Chr 17.21; Heb *for your land*   j Cn: Heb *before your people, whom you redeemed for yourself from Egypt, nations and its gods*

NATHAN   *The King's Conscience*

"LET YOUR CONSCIENCE BE YOUR guide." That's good advice only if your conscience doesn't cheat. Most people find ways to soothe their consciences by rationalizing whatever they want to do. That's why it's best to check with trustworthy people for advice.

Ancient rulers had an additional problem. Since few people had the courage to contradict an all-powerful king, such kings tended to get favorable advice even if they were doing something dead wrong. As one Roman senator said to Tiberius Caesar, "But if you speak first no one will want to refute you, and if you speak last, we will not want to have spoken against your position."

Only a few brave souls dared to be different. The prophet Nathan, for example, told the king the truth, pleasant or not. Nathan burst David's bubble by informing him that God did not want him to build the temple (7.5–16). He also spoke up to remind David of his neglected promise to crown Solomon as his successor (1 Kings 1.24–30).

Most memorably, Nathan accused David of sinning against God by committing adultery with Bathsheba and murdering her husband (2 Samuel 12). Nathan did so artfully, trapping the king with a powerful story that aroused the king's fury—until Nathan drove home the point. Nathan could have died for bringing this message, but it was a measure of David's character that he listened to Nathan even when his own conscience had gone numb. When David repented, Nathan stood beside him, assuring him of God's forgiveness.

Nathan was a true prophet. Though Biblical prophets sometimes predicted the future (as Nathan did in describing the punishments David would suffer) they were best known for telling the truth—especially the unpleasant truth that no one wanted to hear.

Life Questions: Who helps your conscience? Who can you count on to tell you the unpleasant truth about yourself?

David's Wars

8 Some time afterward, David attacked the Philistines and subdued them; David took Metheg-ammah out of the hand of the Philistines.

2 He also defeated the Moabites and, making them lie down on the ground, measured them off with a cord; he measured two lengths of cord for those who were to be put to death, and one length[k] for those who were to be spared. And the Moabites became servants to David and brought tribute.

3 David also struck down King Hadadezer son of Rehob of Zobah, as he went to restore his monument[l] at the river Euphrates. [4]David took from him one thousand seven hundred horsemen, and twenty thousand foot soldiers. David hamstrung all the chariot horses, but left enough

8.4 Not Ready for Chariots

Chariots were as great an innovation in weaponry as were guns centuries later. However, chariots required trained charioteers. Since David hamstrung all but 100 chariot horses, he may have lacked such trained personnel. Israel could defend the mountains, where chariots were of little use, but they were not ready to take on big armies on the surrounding plains.

for a hundred chariots. [5]When the Arameans of Damascus came to help King Hadadezer of Zobah, David killed twenty-two thousand men of the Arameans. [6]Then David put garrisons among the Arameans of Damascus; and the Arameans became servants to David and brought tribute. The LORD gave victory to David wherever he went. [7]David took the gold shields that were carried by the servants of Hadadezer, and brought them to Jerusalem. [8]From Betah and from Berothai, towns of Hadadezer, King David took a great amount of bronze.

9 When King Toi of Hamath heard that David had defeated the whole army of Hadadezer, [10]Toi sent his son Joram to King David, to greet him and to congratulate him because he had fought against Hadadezer and defeated him. Now Hadadezer had often been at war with Toi. Joram brought with him articles of silver, gold, and bronze; [11]these also King David dedicated to the LORD, together with the silver and gold that he dedicated from all the nations he subdued, [12]from Edom, Moab, the Ammonites, the Philistines, Amalek, and from the spoil of King Hadadezer son of Rehob of Zobah.

13 David won a name for himself. When he returned, he killed eighteen thousand Edomites[m] in the Valley of Salt. [14]He put garrisons in Edom; throughout all Edom he put garrisons, and all the Edomites became David's servants. And the LORD gave victory to David wherever he went.

David's Officers

15 So David reigned over all Israel; and David administered justice and equity to all his people. [16]Joab son of Zeruiah was over the army; Jehoshaphat son of Ahilud was recorder; [17]Zadok son of Ahitub and Ahimelech son of Abiathar were priests; Seraiah was secretary; [18]Benaiah son of Jehoiada was over[n] the Cherethites and the Pelethites; and David's sons were priests.

David's Kindness to Mephibosheth

9 David asked, "Is there still anyone left of the house of Saul to whom I may show kindness for Jonathan's sake?" [2]Now there was a servant of the house of Saul whose name was Ziba, and he was summoned to David. The king said to him, "Are you Ziba?" And he said, "At your service!" [3]The king said, "Is there anyone remaining of the house of Saul to whom I may show the kindness of God?" Ziba said to the king, "There remains a son of Jonathan; he is crippled in his feet." [4]The king said to him, "Where is he?" Ziba said to the king, "He is in the house of Machir son of Ammiel, at Lo-debar." [5]Then King David sent and brought him from the house of Machir son of Ammiel, at Lo-debar. [6]Mephibosheth[o] son of Jonathan son of Saul came to David, and fell on his face and did obeisance. David said, "Mephibosheth!"[o] He answered, "I am your servant." [7]David said to him, "Do not be afraid, for I will show you kindness for the sake of your father Jonathan; I will restore to you all the land of your grandfather Saul, and you yourself shall eat at my

9.7 Saul's Lame Grandson

Although Saul had been David's worst enemy, David consistently showed kindness and generosity to his family. In other kingdoms of that day, Mephibosheth would have been killed. David sought him out, restored his land, and welcomed him as a permanent guest at the royal table—a considerable honor. Later, when Mephibosheth suspiciously failed to join David in fleeing from Absalom's insurrection, David gave him the benefit of the doubt (19.24–30).

table always." [8]He did obeisance and said, "What is your servant, that you should look upon a dead dog such as I?"

9 Then the king summoned Saul's servant

---

[k] Heb *one full length*   [l] Compare 1 Sam 15.12 and 2 Sam 18.18   [m] Gk: Heb *returned from striking down eighteen*
thousand Arameans   [n] Syr Tg Vg 20.23; 1 Chr 18.17: Heb lacks *was over*   [o] Or *Merib-baal*: See 4.4 note

Ziba, and said to him, "All that belonged to Saul
and to all his house I have given to your master's
grandson. 10You and your sons and your servants
shall till the land for him, and shall bring in the
produce, so that your master's grandson may
have food to eat; but your master's grandson Mephibosheth[p] shall always eat at my table." Now
Ziba had fifteen sons and twenty servants. 11Then
Ziba said to the king, "According to all that my
lord the king commands his servant, so your servant will do." Mephibosheth[p] ate at David's[q]
table, like one of the king's sons. 12Mephibo-
sheth[p] had a young son whose name was Mica.
And all who lived in Ziba's house became Mephibosheth's[r] servants. 13Mephibosheth[p] lived
in Jerusalem, for he always ate at the king's table.
Now he was lame in both his feet.

The Ammonites and Arameans Are Defeated

10 Some time afterward, the king of the Ammonites died, and his son Hanun succeeded him. 2David said, "I will deal loyally with Hanun son of Nahash, just as his father dealt loyally
with me." So David sent envoys to console him
concerning his father. When David's envoys came
into the land of the Ammonites, 3the princes of
the Ammonites said to their lord Hanun, "Do you
really think that David is honoring your father
just because he has sent messengers with condo-
lences to you? Has not David sent his envoys to
you to search the city, to spy it out, and to overthrow it?" 4So Hanun seized David's envoys,
shaved off half the beard of each, cut off their
garments in the middle at their hips, and sent
them away. 5When David was told, he sent to
meet them, for the men were greatly ashamed.
The king said, "Remain at Jericho until your
beards have grown, and then return."

6 When the Ammonites saw that they had
become odious to David, the Ammonites sent
and hired the Arameans of Beth-rehob and the
Arameans of Zobah, twenty thousand foot soldiers, as well as the king of Maacah, one thousand
men, and the men of Tob, twelve thousand men.
7When David heard of it, he sent Joab and all the
army with the warriors. 8The Ammonites came
out and drew up in battle array at the entrance of
the gate; but the Arameans of Zobah and of Rehob, and the men of Tob and Maacah, were by
themselves in the open country.

9 When Joab saw that the battle was set
against him both in front and in the rear, he chose
some of the picked men of Israel, and arrayed
them against the Arameans; 10the rest of his men
he put in the charge of his brother Abishai, and he
arrayed them against the Ammonites. 11He said,
"If the Arameans are too strong for me, then you
shall help me; but if the Ammonites are too
strong for you, then I will come and help you.
12Be strong, and let us be courageous for the sake
of our people, and for the cities of our God; and
may the LORD do what seems good to him." 13So
Joab and the people who were with him moved
forward into battle against the Arameans; and
they fled before him. 14When the Ammonites saw
that the Arameans fled, they likewise fled before
Abishai, and entered the city. Then Joab returned
from fighting against the Ammonites, and came
to Jerusalem.

15 But when the Arameans saw that they had
been defeated by Israel, they gathered themselves
together. 16Hadadezer sent and brought out the
Arameans who were beyond the Euphrates; and
they came to Helam, with Shobach the commander of the army of Hadadezer at their head.
17When it was told David, he gathered all Israel
together, and crossed the Jordan, and came to
Helam. The Arameans arrayed themselves against
David and fought with him. 18The Arameans fled
before Israel; and David killed of the Arameans
seven hundred chariot teams, and forty thousand
horsemen,[s] and wounded Shobach the commander of their army, so that he died there.
19When all the kings who were servants of Hadadezer saw that they had been defeated by Israel,
they made peace with Israel, and became subject
to them. So the Arameans were afraid to help the
Ammonites any more.

David Commits Adultery with Bathsheba

11 In the spring of the year, the time when
kings go out to battle, David sent Joab with
his officers and all Israel with him; they ravaged
the Ammonites, and besieged Rabbah. But David
remained at Jerusalem.

2 It happened, late one afternoon, when David rose from his couch and was walking about on
the roof of the king's house, that he saw from the
roof a woman bathing; the woman was very beautiful. 3David sent someone to inquire about the
woman. It was reported, "This is Bathsheba
daughter of Eliam, the wife of Uriah the Hittite."
4So David sent messengers to get her, and she
came to him, and he lay with her. (Now she was
purifying herself after her period.) Then she returned to her house. 5The woman conceived; and
she sent and told David, "I am pregnant."

6 So David sent word to Joab, "Send me Uriah the Hittite." And Joab sent Uriah to David.
7When Uriah came to him, David asked how Joab
and the people fared, and how the war was going.
8Then David said to Uriah, "Go down to your
house, and wash your feet." Uriah went out of the

[p] Or *Merib-baal*: See 4.4 note [q] Gk: Heb *my* [r] Or *Merib-baal's*: See 4.4 note [s] 1 Chr 19.18 and some Gk Mss read *foot soldiers*

king's house, and there followed him a present from the king. ⁹But Uriah slept at the entrance of the king's house with all the servants of his lord, and did not go down to his house. ¹⁰When they told David, "Uriah did not go down to his house," David said to Uriah, "You have just come from a journey. Why did you not go down to your house?" ¹¹Uriah said to David, "The ark and Israel and Judah remain in booths;ᵗ and my lord Joab and the servants of my lord are camping in the open field; shall I then go to my house, to eat and to drink, and to lie with my wife? As you live, and as your soul lives, I will not do such a thing."

11.11 A Military Hero

Israelite soldiers had no sexual relations while they were preparing for battle. (See, for instance, 1 Samuel 21.5.) Uriah refused to sleep with Bathsheba because he remembered duty before pleasure. He is mentioned (in 23.39) as one of the Thirty, a group of leading warriors under David.

¹²Then David said to Uriah, "Remain here today also, and tomorrow I will send you back." So Uriah remained in Jerusalem that day. On the next day, ¹³David invited him to eat and drink in his presence and made him drunk; and in the evening he went out to lie on his couch with the servants of his lord, but he did not go down to his house.

ᵗ Or *at Succoth*   ᵘ Gk Syr Judg 7.1: Heb *Jerubbesheth*

David Has Uriah Killed

14 In the morning David wrote a letter to Joab, and sent it by the hand of Uriah. ¹⁵In the letter he wrote, "Set Uriah in the forefront of the hardest fighting, and then draw back from him, so that he may be struck down and die." ¹⁶As Joab was besieging the city, he assigned Uriah to the place where he knew there were valiant warriors. ¹⁷The men of the city came out and fought with Joab; and some of the servants of David among the people fell. Uriah the Hittite was killed as well. ¹⁸Then Joab sent and told David all the news about the fighting; ¹⁹and he instructed the messenger, "When you have finished telling the king all the news about the fighting, ²⁰then, if the king's anger rises, and if he says to you, 'Why did you go so near the city to fight? Did you not know that they would shoot from the wall? ²¹Who killed Abimelech son of Jerubbaal?ᵘ Did not a woman throw an upper millstone on him from the wall, so that he died at Thebez? Why did you go so near the wall?' then you shall say, 'Your servant Uriah the Hittite is dead too.'"

22 So the messenger went, and came and told David all that Joab had sent him to tell. ²³The messenger said to David, "The men gained an advantage over us, and came out against us in the field; but we drove them back to the entrance of the gate. ²⁴Then the archers shot at your servants from the wall; some of the king's servants are dead; and your servant Uriah the Hittite is dead also." ²⁵David said to the messenger, "Thus you shall say to Joab, 'Do not let this matter trouble

BATHSHEBA *Only Following Orders*

AFTER WORLD WAR II, NAZI soldiers made a classic defense for their war crimes: "We were only following orders." Then and ever since courts have struck down that defense. A person who knowingly does wrong is responsible, regardless of the circumstances.

Still, many people feel sympathy for the person who commits a crime under pressure or coercion. Perhaps Bathsheba fits this category. She could hardly help being beautiful, and in all probability she was bathing quite innocently when she caught David's eye (houses then had no bathrooms). To complicate matters, the king—not just anybody—summoned her to sleep with him. The king's word was law, and had Bathsheba refused him she might have expected severe penalties—perhaps even death.

Certainly, Bathsheba suffered for what she did. She lost her husband and her child. Did she join with David in his repentance? The Bible does not say. After bearing another child, Solomon, she received no further mention in Scripture until the very end of David's life, when she supported Solomon's bid for the throne. The one really notable thing Bathsheba accomplished in life was the wrong thing—her affair with the king.

The way the Bible tells the story, David bore the chief responsibility for this national scandal. He initiated the adultery, followed it up with murder, and suffered the consequences throughout the rest of his life. When we consider how the repercussions of David's actions affected the entire nation, however, we can see why "I was only following orders" is no defense. Although Bathsheba was in some ways a victim, her failure to resist a sinful situation made David's sin possible.

Life Questions: Are there any situations in which you are tempted to "just go along" with sin because of pressure?

you, for the sword devours now one and now another; press your attack on the city, and overthrow it.' And encourage him."

26 When the wife of Uriah heard that her husband was dead, she made lamentation for him. ²⁷When the mourning was over, David sent and brought her to his house, and she became his wife, and bore him a son.

Nathan Condemns David

12 But the thing that David had done displeased the LORD, ¹and the LORD sent Nathan to David. He came to him, and said to him, "There were two men in a certain city, the one rich and the other poor. ²The rich man had very many flocks and herds; ³but the poor man had nothing but one little ewe lamb, which he had bought. He brought it up, and it grew up with him and with his children; it used to eat of his meager fare, and drink from his cup, and lie in his bosom, and it was like a daughter to him. ⁴Now there came a traveler to the rich man, and he was loath to take one of his own flock or herd to prepare for the wayfarer who had come to him, but he took the poor man's lamb, and prepared that for the guest who had come to him." ⁵Then David's anger was greatly kindled against the man. He said to Nathan, "As the LORD lives, the man who has done this deserves to die; ⁶he shall restore the lamb fourfold, because he did this thing, and because he had no pity."

7 Nathan said to David, "You are the man! Thus says the LORD, the God of Israel: I anointed you king over Israel, and I rescued you from the hand of Saul; ⁸I gave you your master's house, and your master's wives into your bosom, and gave you the house of Israel and of Judah; and if that had been too little, I would have added as much more. ⁹Why have you despised the word of the LORD, to do what is evil in his sight? You have struck down Uriah the Hittite with the sword, and have taken his wife to be your wife, and have killed him with the sword of the Ammonites. ¹⁰Now therefore the sword shall never depart from your house, for you have despised me, and have taken the wife of Uriah the Hittite to be your wife. ¹¹Thus says the LORD: I will raise up trouble against you from within your own house; and I will take your wives before your eyes, and give them to your neighbor, and he shall lie with your wives in the sight of this very sun. ¹²For you did it secretly; but I will do this thing before all Israel, and before the sun." ¹³David said to Nathan, "I have sinned against the LORD." Nathan said to David, "Now the LORD has put away your sin; you shall not die. ¹⁴Nevertheless, because by this deed you have utterly scorned the LORD,ᵛ the child that is born to you shall die." ¹⁵Then Nathan went to his house.

Bathsheba's Child Dies

The LORD struck the child that Uriah's wife bore to David, and it became very ill. ¹⁶David therefore pleaded with God for the child; David fasted, and went in and lay all night on the ground. ¹⁷The elders of his house stood beside him, urging him to rise from the ground; but he would not, nor did he eat food with them. ¹⁸On the seventh day the child died. And the servants of David were afraid to tell him that the child was dead; for they said, "While the child was still alive, we spoke to him, and he did not listen to us; how then can we tell him the child is dead? He may do himself some harm." ¹⁹But when David saw that his servants were whispering together, he perceived that the child was dead; and David said to his servants, "Is the child dead?" They said, "He is dead."

20 Then David rose from the ground, washed, anointed himself, and changed his clothes. He went into the house of the LORD, and worshiped; he then went to his own house; and when he asked, they set food before him and he ate. ²¹Then his servants said to him, "What is this thing that you have done? You fasted and wept for the child while it was alive; but when the child died, you rose and ate food." ²²He said, "While the child was still alive, I fasted and wept; for I said, 'Who knows? The LORD may be gracious to me, and the child may live.' ²³But now he is dead; why should I fast? Can I bring him back again? I shall go to him, but he will not return to me."

12.13 David's Finest Moment

David, who possessed absolute power, could have had Nathan killed for his daring public confrontation. Or, he could have laughed him off and thrown him out of the palace. But David knew Nathan spoke for God, and in what may have been the greatest moment of his life, he admitted, "I have sinned against the LORD." David showed what made him a man after God's own heart; though he was king, he humbled himself before the King of kings.

Solomon Is Born

24 Then David consoled his wife Bathsheba, and went to her, and lay with her; and she bore a son, and he named him Solomon. The LORD loved him, ²⁵and sent a message by the prophet Nathan; so he named him Jedidiah,ʷ because of the LORD.

The Ammonites Crushed

26 Now Joab fought against Rabbah of the Ammonites, and took the royal city. ²⁷Joab sent messengers to David, and said, "I have fought

ᵛ Ancient scribal tradition: Compare 1 Sam 25.22 note: Heb *scorned the enemies of the LORD*   ʷ That is *Beloved of the LORD*

against Rabbah; moreover, I have taken the water city. ²⁸Now, then, gather the rest of the people together, and encamp against the city, and take it; or I myself will take the city, and it will be called by my name." ²⁹So David gathered all the people together and went to Rabbah, and fought against it and took it. ³⁰He took the crown of Milcomˣ from his head; the weight of it was a talent of gold, and in it was a precious stone; and it was placed on David's head. He also brought forth the spoil of the city, a very great amount. ³¹He brought out the people who were in it, and set them to work with saws and iron picks and iron axes, or sent them to the brickworks. Thus he did to all the cities of the Ammonites. Then David and all the people returned to Jerusalem.

Amnon and Tamar

13 Some time passed. David's son Absalom had a beautiful sister whose name was Tamar; and David's son Amnon fell in love with her. ²Amnon was so tormented that he made himself ill because of his sister Tamar, for she was a virgin and it seemed impossible to Amnon to do anything to her. ³But Amnon had a friend whose name was Jonadab, the son of David's brother Shimeah; and Jonadab was a very crafty man. ⁴He said to him, "O son of the king, why are you so

ˣ Gk See 1 Kings 11.5, 33: Heb *their kings*

Adultery and Murder
The king could do as he pleased—or so he thought

AN ANCIENT AND ENDURING TRADITION teaches that the people on top make the rules—they don't have to live by them. Lots of leaders in history have followed this course, taking the women they wanted, the money they wanted, the privileges they wanted.

Nobody, therefore, challenged David's right to sleep with another man's wife. David saw Bathsheba, lusted for her, and sent for her. As far as we know, neither his servants nor Bathsheba lodged a protest. Only when she got pregnant did a problem arise. Then David, who had had no thought of marrying Bathsheba, found himself in a jam. He called her husband, Uriah, home on leave from the army, hoping that Uriah would sleep with his wife and later be unable to prove the child belonged to another father.

Uriah's single-minded devotion to duty spoiled David's plan. David rewarded Uriah with murder. Again, not a word of protest was filed: What the king wanted the king got, no questions asked. The murder of Uriah took other good men with him, but David showed no regrets. He was at his worst: cold as iron, arrogant in his power.

After a mourning period, Bathsheba came into his house and he married her. A good many people must have known what had happened—the servants knew, at any rate—but the Bible doesn't report that any of them were displeased. It only says, "The thing that David had done displeased the LORD" (11.27).

> David's anger was greatly kindled against the man. He said to Nathan, "As the LORD lives, the man who has done this deserves to die;" . . . Nathan said to David, "You are the man!"
> 12.5,7

Who Will Challenge the King?

Who would have the courage—or the authority—to challenge the king? In most nations, no one. But Israel had this distinctive: its ultimate king was not David, but God. And God had his spokesmen, the prophets. He sent Nathan to David.

Nathan cleverly captivated David with a heartrending story about a rich man who had abused his power. He offered the case to David, the highest judge in Israel. David knew exactly how to judge such a case: The man deserved death! When he said so, Nathan turned David's own judgment around: "You are the man!"

In this dramatic scene David's greatness showed itself. He could easily have had Nathan killed. Or he could have laughed and shown him out of the palace. Instead, "David said to Nathan, 'I have sinned against the LORD' " (12.13). David recognized that God was the true king of Israel.

Nathan's confrontation with David set the standard for centuries of conflict between kings and prophets. Time and again an Old Testament prophet went to the palace—sometimes risking his life— and told the king that God would punish him for what he was doing. The kings, rich and powerful by birth, did not have to listen. In fact, they rarely did. David was a great king partly because he did not act with the normal pride of a king. When confronted with the truth, he repented.

Life Questions: What determines your choices? Your own desires? Or your understanding of God's will? Think of some recent decisions you have made and apply this question to them.

haggard morning after morning? Will you not tell me?" Amnon said to him, "I love Tamar, my brother Absalom's sister." 5Jonadab said to him, "Lie down on your bed, and pretend to be ill; and when your father comes to see you, say to him, 'Let my sister Tamar come and give me something to eat, and prepare the food in my sight, so that I may see it and eat it from her hand.'" 6So Amnon lay down, and pretended to be ill; and when the king came to see him, Amnon said to the king, "Please let my sister Tamar come and make a couple of cakes in my sight, so that I may eat from her hand."

7 Then David sent home to Tamar, saying, "Go to your brother Amnon's house, and prepare food for him." 8So Tamar went to her brother Amnon's house, where he was lying down. She took dough, kneaded it, made cakes in his sight, and baked the cakes. 9Then she took the pan and set them*y* out before him, but he refused to eat. Amnon said, "Send out everyone from me." So everyone went out from him. 10Then Amnon said to Tamar, "Bring the food into the chamber, so that I may eat from your hand." So Tamar took the cakes she had made, and brought them into the chamber to Amnon her brother. 11But when she brought them near him to eat, he took hold of her, and said to her, "Come, lie with me, my sister." 12She answered him, "No, my brother, do not force me; for such a thing is not done in Israel; do not do anything so vile! 13As for me, where could I carry my shame? And as for you, you would be as one of the scoundrels in Israel. Now therefore, I beg you, speak to the king; for he will not withhold me from you." 14But he would not listen to her; and being stronger than she, he forced her and lay with her.

15 Then Amnon was seized with a very great loathing for her; indeed, his loathing was even greater than the lust he had felt for her. Amnon said to her, "Get out!" 16But she said to him, "No, my brother;*z* for this wrong in sending me away is greater than the other that you did to me." But he would not listen to her. 17He called the young man who served him and said, "Put this woman out of my presence, and bolt the door after her." 18(Now she was wearing a long robe with sleeves; for this is how the virgin daughters of the king were clothed in earlier times.*a*) So his servant put her out, and bolted the door after her. 19But Tamar put ashes on her head, and tore the long robe that she was wearing; she put her hand on her head, and went away, crying aloud as she went.

20 Her brother Absalom said to her, "Has Amnon your brother been with you? Be quiet for now, my sister; he is your brother; do not take this to heart." So Tamar remained, a desolate

woman, in her brother Absalom's house. 21When King David heard of all these things, he became very angry, but he would not punish his son Amnon, because he loved him, for he was his firstborn.*b* 22But Absalom spoke to Amnon neither good nor bad; for Absalom hated Amnon, because he had raped his sister Tamar.

Absalom Avenges the Violation of His Sister

23 After two full years Absalom had sheepshearers at Baal-hazor, which is near Ephraim, and Absalom invited all the king's sons. 24Absalom came to the king, and said, "Your servant has sheepshearers; will the king and his servants please go with your servant?" 25But the king said to Absalom, "No, my son, let us not all go, or else we will be burdensome to you." He pressed him, but he would not go but gave him his blessing. 26Then Absalom said, "If not, please let my brother Amnon go with us." The king said to him, "Why should he go with you?" 27But Absalom pressed him until he let Amnon and all the king's sons go with him. Absalom made a feast like a king's feast.*c* 28Then Absalom commanded his servants, "Watch when Amnon's heart is merry with wine, and when I say to you, 'Strike Amnon,' then kill him. Do not be afraid; have I not myself commanded you? Be courageous and valiant." 29So the servants of Absalom did to Amnon as Absalom had commanded. Then all the king's sons rose, and each mounted his mule and fled.

13.29 Vicious Children

What went wrong with David's children? Amnon raped his sister Tamar. Absalom killed Amnon in revenge. Ultimately Absalom plotted a coup against his father, driving David from Jerusalem. All through these events—rape, murder, rebellion—David failed to discipline his children. According to the law they deserved severe punishment, but David let them off with hardly a word. Perhaps his own guilt over Bathsheba had undercut his sense of moral authority.

30 While they were on the way, the report came to David that Absalom had killed all the king's sons, and not one of them was left. 31The king rose, tore his garments, and lay on the ground; and all his servants who were standing by tore their garments. 32But Jonadab, the son of David's brother Shimeah, said, "Let not my lord suppose that they have killed all the young men the king's sons; Amnon alone is dead. This has

---

y Heb *and poured*   *z* Cn Compare Gk Vg: Meaning of Heb uncertain   *a* Cn: Heb *were clothed in robes*   *b* Q Ms Gk: MT lacks *but he would not punish . . . firstborn*   *c* Gk Compare Q Ms: MT lacks *Absalom made a feast like a king's feast*

been determined by Absalom from the day Amnon[d] raped his sister Tamar. [33]Now therefore, do not let my lord the king take it to heart, as if all the king's sons were dead; for Amnon alone is dead."

34 But Absalom fled. When the young man who kept watch looked up, he saw many people coming from the Horonaim road[e] by the side of the mountain. [35]Jonadab said to the king, "See, the king's sons have come; as your servant said, so it has come about." [36]As soon as he had finished speaking, the king's sons arrived, and raised their voices and wept; and the king and all his servants also wept very bitterly.

37 But Absalom fled, and went to Talmai son of Ammihud, king of Geshur. David mourned for his son day after day. [38]Absalom, having fled to

13.38 A Refuge with His Family

Absalom ran to Geshur, a neighboring kingdom, probably because his mother was a daughter of Geshur's king. He could be assured of safety there.

Geshur, stayed there three years. [39]And the heart of[f] the king went out, yearning for Absalom; for he was now consoled over the death of Amnon.

Absalom Returns to Jerusalem

14 Now Joab son of Zeruiah perceived that the king's mind was on Absalom. [2]Joab sent to Tekoa and brought from there a wise woman. He said to her, "Pretend to be a mourner; put on mourning garments, do not anoint yourself with oil, but behave like a woman who has been mourning many days for the dead. [3]Go to the king and speak to him as follows." And Joab put the words into her mouth.

4 When the woman of Tekoa came to the king, she fell on her face to the ground and did obeisance, and said, "Help, O king!" [5]The king asked her, "What is your trouble?" She answered, "Alas, I am a widow; my husband is dead. [6]Your servant had two sons, and they fought with one another in the field; there was no one to part them, and one struck the other and killed him. [7]Now the whole family has risen against your servant. They say, 'Give up the man who struck his brother, so that we may kill him for the life of his brother whom he murdered, even if we destroy the heir as well.' Thus they would quench my one remaining ember, and leave to my husband neither name nor remnant on the face of the earth."

8 Then the king said to the woman, "Go to your house, and I will give orders concerning

you." [9]The woman of Tekoa said to the king, "On me be the guilt, my lord the king, and on my father's house; let the king and his throne be guiltless." [10]The king said, "If anyone says anything to you, bring him to me, and he shall never touch you again." [11]Then she said, "Please, may the king keep the LORD your God in mind, so that the avenger of blood may kill no more, and my son not be destroyed." He said, "As the LORD lives, not one hair of your son shall fall to the ground."

12 Then the woman said, "Please let your servant speak a word to my lord the king." He said, "Speak." [13]The woman said, "Why then have you planned such a thing against the people of God? For in giving this decision the king convicts himself, inasmuch as the king does not bring his banished one home again. [14]We must all die; we are like water spilled on the ground, which cannot be gathered up. But God will not take away a life; he will devise plans so as not to keep an outcast banished forever from his presence.[g] [15]Now I have come to say this to my lord the king because the people have made me afraid; your servant thought, 'I will speak to the king; it may be that the king will perform the request of his servant. [16]For the king will hear, and deliver his servant from the hand of the man who would cut both me and my son off from the heritage of God.' [17]Your servant thought, 'The word of my lord the king will set me at rest'; for my lord the king is like the angel of God, discerning good and evil. The LORD your God be with you!"

18 Then the king answered the woman, "Do not withhold from me anything I ask you." The woman said, "Let my lord the king speak." [19]The king said, "Is the hand of Joab with you in all this?" The woman answered and said, "As surely as you live, my lord the king, one cannot turn right or left from anything that my lord the king has said. For it was your servant Joab who commanded me; it was he who put all these words into the mouth of your servant. [20]In order to change the course of affairs your servant Joab did this. But my lord has wisdom like the wisdom of the angel of God to know all things that are on the earth."

21 Then the king said to Joab, "Very well, I grant this; go, bring back the young man Absalom." [22]Joab prostrated himself with his face to the ground and did obeisance, and blessed the king; and Joab said, "Today your servant knows that I have found favor in your sight, my lord the king, in that the king has granted the request of his servant." [23]So Joab set off, went to Geshur, and brought Absalom to Jerusalem. [24]The king said, "Let him go to his own house; he is not to come into my presence." So Absalom went to his

---

d Heb *he*   *e* Cn Compare Gk: Heb *the road behind him* uncertain   *f* Q Ms Gk: MT *And David*   *g* Meaning of Heb

own house, and did not come into the king's presence.

David Forgives Absalom

25 Now in all Israel there was no one to be praised so much for his beauty as Absalom; from the sole of his foot to the crown of his head there was no blemish in him. 26When he cut the hair of his head (for at the end of every year he used to cut it; when it was heavy on him, he cut it), he weighed the hair of his head, two hundred shekels by the king's weight. 27There were born to Absalom three sons, and one daughter whose name was Tamar; she was a beautiful woman.

28 So Absalom lived two full years in Jerusalem, without coming into the king's presence. 29Then Absalom sent for Joab to send him to the king; but Joab would not come to him. He sent a second time, but Joab would not come. 30Then he said to his servants, "Look, Joab's field is next to mine, and he has barley there; go and set it on fire." So Absalom's servants set the field on fire. 31Then Joab rose and went to Absalom at his house, and said to him, "Why have your servants set my field on fire?" 32Absalom answered Joab, "Look, I sent word to you: Come here, that I may send you to the king with the question, 'Why have I come from Geshur? It would be better for me to be there still.' Now let me go into the king's presence; if there is guilt in me, let him kill me!" 33Then Joab went to the king and told him; and he summoned Absalom. So he came to the king and prostrated himself with his face to the ground before the king; and the king kissed Absalom.

Absalom Usurps the Throne

15 After this Absalom got himself a chariot and horses, and fifty men to run ahead of him. 2Absalom used to rise early and stand beside the road into the gate; and when anyone brought a suit before the king for judgment, Absalom would call out and say, "From what city are you?" When the person said, "Your servant is of such and such a tribe in Israel," 3Absalom would say, "See, your claims are good and right; but there is no one deputed by the king to hear you." 4Absalom said moreover, "If only I were judge in the land! Then all who had a suit or cause might come to me, and I would give them justice." 5Whenever people came near to do obeisance to him, he would put out his hand and take hold of them, and kiss them. 6Thus Absalom did to every Israelite who came to the king for judgment; so Absalom stole the hearts of the people of Israel.

7 At the end of four[h] years Absalom said to the king, "Please let me go to Hebron and pay the vow that I have made to the LORD. 8For your servant made a vow while I lived at Geshur in Aram: If the LORD will indeed bring me back to Jerusalem, then I will worship the LORD in Hebron."[i] 9The king said to him, "Go in peace." So he got up, and went to Hebron. 10But Absalom sent secret messengers throughout all the tribes of Israel, saying, "As soon as you hear the sound of the trumpet, then shout: Absalom has become king at Hebron!" 11Two hundred men from Jerusalem went with Absalom; they were invited guests, and they went in their innocence, knowing nothing of the matter. 12While Absalom was offering the sacrifices, he sent for[j] Ahithophel

[h] Gk Syr: Heb forty   [i] Gk Mss: Heb lacks in Hebron   [j] Or he sent

ABSALOM *All That Glitters*

HE WAS THE MOST HANDSOME man of his day, a royal prince with plenty of charisma thrown in for good measure. When people had needs, Absalom seemed to care: In this way he "stole the hearts of the people of Israel" (15.6). We first meet him sheltering his sister after she had been raped (13.20). Two years later, Absalom got murderous revenge in defense of his sister's honor. Unlike his father David, he refused to let such a crime go unpunished.

Nevertheless, Absalom's glittering surface did not reveal a golden heart. As time went on it became clear that Absalom cared mainly for himself. Absalom was a tragic figure, a symbol of David's failures as a parent. For five years father and son did not speak to one another, and this simmering family feud only hardened Absalom further.

Absalom tended to act like a spoiled brat, whether getting Joab's attention by burning his barley field, or gaining the honor he thought he deserved by driving his own father out of town. Like many egotists, however, Absalom overestimated his strength and popularity.

During the bloody revolt one of David's advisers, pretending to have switched to Absalom's side, shrewdly advised a delay. David gained time to assemble his own seasoned fighters, who quickly put down Absalom's uprising. The king's son died as vainly as he had lived: While escaping on a mule, he caught his long, handsome hair in a tree and was killed by Joab and his men.

Life Questions: If someone is good-looking, gifted or naturally likable, how can such a person guard against egotism?

the Gilonite, David's counselor, from his city Giloh. The conspiracy grew in strength, and the people with Absalom kept increasing.

David Flees from Jerusalem

13 A messenger came to David, saying, "The hearts of the Israelites have gone after Absalom." [14]Then David said to all his officials who were with him at Jerusalem, "Get up! Let us flee, or there will be no escape for us from Absalom. Hurry, or he will soon overtake us, and bring disaster down upon us, and attack the city with the edge of the sword." [15]The king's officials said to the king, "Your servants are ready to do whatever our lord the king decides." [16]So the king left, followed by all his household, except ten concubines whom he left behind to look after the house. [17]The king left, followed by all the people; and they stopped at the last house. [18]All his officials passed by him; and all the Cherethites, and all the Pelethites, and all the six hundred Gittites who had followed him from Gath, passed on before the king.

19 Then the king said to Ittai the Gittite, "Why are you also coming with us? Go back, and stay with the king; for you are a foreigner, and also an exile from your home. [20]You came only yesterday, and shall I today make you wander about with us, while I go wherever I can? Go back, and take your kinsfolk with you; and may the LORD show[k] steadfast love and faithfulness to you." [21]But Ittai answered the king, "As the LORD lives, and as my lord the king lives, wherever my lord the king may be, whether for death or for life, there also your servant will be." [22]David said to Ittai, "Go then, march on." So Ittai the Gittite marched on, with all his men and all the little ones

15.22 Mercenaries

David's army included more than just loyal Israelites; he had added mercenaries (hired soldiers). The Gittites came from the Philistine city of Gath. David had probably recruited them during his stay there (1 Samuel 27.2), and they had loyally followed him ever since.

who were with him. [23]The whole country wept aloud as all the people passed by; the king crossed the Wadi Kidron, and all the people moved on toward the wilderness.

24 Abiathar came up, and Zadok also, with all the Levites, carrying the ark of the covenant of God. They set down the ark of God, until the people had all passed out of the city. [25]Then the king said to Zadok, "Carry the ark of God back into the city. If I find favor in the eyes of the LORD,

he will bring me back and let me see both it and the place where it stays. [26]But if he says, 'I take no pleasure in you,' here I am, let him do to me what seems good to him." [27]The king also said to the priest Zadok, "Look,[l] go back to the city in peace, you and Abiathar,[m] with your two sons, Ahimaaz your son, and Jonathan son of Abiathar. [28]See, I will wait at the fords of the wilderness until word comes from you to inform me." [29]So Zadok and Abiathar carried the ark of God back to Jerusalem, and they remained there.

30 But David went up the ascent of the Mount of Olives, weeping as he went, with his head covered and walking barefoot; and all the people who were with him covered their heads and went up, weeping as they went. [31]David was told that Ahithophel was among the conspirators with Absalom. And David said, "O LORD, I pray you, turn the counsel of Ahithophel into foolishness."

Hushai Becomes David's Spy

32 When David came to the summit, where God was worshiped, Hushai the Archite came to meet him with his coat torn and earth on his head. [33]David said to him, "If you go on with me, you will be a burden to me. [34]But if you return to the city and say to Absalom, 'I will be your servant, O king; as I have been your father's servant in time past, so now I will be your servant,' then you will defeat for me the counsel of Ahithophel. [35]The priests Zadok and Abiathar will be with you there. So whatever you hear from the king's house, tell it to the priests Zadok and Abiathar. [36]Their two sons are with them there, Zadok's son Ahimaaz and Abiathar's son Jonathan; and by them you shall report to me everything you hear." [37]So Hushai, David's friend, came into the city, just as Absalom was entering Jerusalem.

David's Adversaries

16 When David had passed a little beyond the summit, Ziba the servant of Mephibosheth[n] met him, with a couple of donkeys saddled, carrying two hundred loaves of bread, one hundred bunches of raisins, one hundred of summer fruits, and one skin of wine. [2]The king said to Ziba, "Why have you brought these?" Ziba answered, "The donkeys are for the king's household to ride, the bread and summer fruit for the young men to eat, and the wine is for those to drink who faint in the wilderness." [3]The king said, "And where is your master's son?" Ziba said to the king, "He remains in Jerusalem; for he said, 'Today the house of Israel will give me back my grandfather's kingdom.'" [4]Then the king said to Ziba, "All that belonged to Mephibosheth[n] is

---

[k] Gk Compare 2.6: Heb lacks *may the LORD show* Abiathar   [l] Gk: Heb *Are you a seer* or *Do you see?*   [m] Cn: Heb lacks *and* [n] Or *Merib-baal*: See 4.4 note

now yours." Ziba said, "I do obeisance; let me find favor in your sight, my lord the king."

Shimei Curses David

5 When King David came to Bahurim, a man of the family of the house of Saul came out whose name was Shimei son of Gera; he came out cursing. 6He threw stones at David and at all the servants of King David; now all the people and all the warriors were on his right and on his left. 7Shimei shouted while he cursed, "Out! Out! Murderer! Scoundrel! 8The LORD has avenged on all of you the blood of the house of Saul, in whose place you have reigned; and the LORD has given the kingdom into the hand of your son Absalom. See, disaster has overtaken you; for you are a man of blood."

9 Then Abishai son of Zeruiah said to the king, "Why should this dead dog curse my lord the king? Let me go over and take off his head." 10But the king said, "What have I to do with you, you sons of Zeruiah? If he is cursing because the LORD has said to him, 'Curse David,' who then shall say, 'Why have you done so?'" 11David said to Abishai and to all his servants, "My own son seeks my life; how much more now may this Benjaminite! Let him alone, and let him curse; for the LORD has bidden him. 12It may be that the LORD will look on my distress,o and the LORD will repay me with good for this cursing of me today." 13So David and his men went on the road, while Shimei went along on the hillside opposite him and cursed as he went, throwing stones and flinging dust at him. 14The king and all the people who were with him arrived weary at the Jordan;p and there he refreshed himself.

The Counsel of Ahithophel

15 Now Absalom and all the Israelitesq came to Jerusalem; Ahithophel was with him. 16When Hushai the Archite, David's friend, came to Absalom, Hushai said to Absalom, "Long live the king! Long live the king!" 17Absalom said to Hushai, "Is this your loyalty to your friend? Why did you not go with your friend?" 18Hushai said to Absalom, "No; but the one whom the LORD and this people and all the Israelites have chosen, his I will be, and with him I will remain. 19Moreover, whom should I serve? Should it not be his son? Just as I have served your father, so I will serve you."

20 Then Absalom said to Ahithophel, "Give us your counsel; what shall we do?" 21Ahithophel said to Absalom, "Go in to your father's concubines, the ones he has left to look after the house; and all Israel will hear that you have made yourself odious to your father, and the hands of all who are with you will be strengthened." 22So they pitched a tent for Absalom upon the roof; and

Absalom went in to his father's concubines in the sight of all Israel. 23Now in those days the counsel that Ahithophel gave was as if one consulted the oracler of God; so all the counsel of Ahithophel was esteemed, both by David and by Absalom.

16.22 No Way Back

Absalom publicly slept with his father's concubines for political reasons. It made clear his claim to the throne (see 3.6 for a similar case) and was extremely offensive to David. Israelites who had held back their allegiance, thinking that father and son would reconcile their differences, knew now that the breach was permanent. They had to take sides.

17 Moreover Ahithophel said to Absalom, "Let me choose twelve thousand men, and I will set out and pursue David tonight. 2I will come upon him while he is weary and discouraged, and throw him into a panic; and all the people who are with him will flee. I will strike down only the king, 3and I will bring all the people back to you as a bride comes home to her husband. You seek the life of only one man,s and all the people will be at peace." 4The advice pleased Absalom and all the elders of Israel.

The Counsel of Hushai

5 Then Absalom said, "Call Hushai the Archite also, and let us hear too what he has to say." 6When Hushai came to Absalom, Absalom said to him, "This is what Ahithophel has said; shall we do as he advises? If not, you tell us." 7Then Hushai said to Absalom, "This time the counsel that Ahithophel has given is not good." 8Hushai continued, "You know that your father and his men are warriors, and that they are enraged, like a bear robbed of her cubs in the field. Besides, your father is expert in war; he will not spend the night with the troops. 9Even now he has hidden himself in one of the pits, or in some other place. And when some of our troopst fall at the first attack, whoever hears it will say, 'There has been a slaughter among the troops who follow Absalom.' 10Then even the valiant warrior, whose heart is like the heart of a lion, will utterly melt with fear; for all Israel knows that your father is a warrior, and that those who are with him are valiant warriors. 11But my counsel is that all Israel be gathered to you, from Dan to Beer-sheba, like the sand by the sea for multitude, and that you go to battle in person. 12So we shall come upon him in whatever place he may be found, and we shall light on him as the dew falls on the ground; and he will not survive, nor will any of those with him.

---

o Gk Vg: Heb *iniquity*   p Gk: Heb lacks *at the Jordan*   q Gk: Heb *all the people, the men of Israel*   r Heb *word*
s Gk: Heb *like the return of the whole (is) the man whom you seek*   t Gk Mss: Heb *some of them*

[13]If he withdraws into a city, then all Israel will bring ropes to that city, and we shall drag it into the valley, until not even a pebble is to be found there." [14]Absalom and all the men of Israel said,

17.11 Flattering Advice

Hushai, one of David's top advisers, slipped into Absalom's camp pretending to have deserted David. He deliberately gave bad advice, cleverly phrasing it to flatter Absalom. Hushai suggested that if Absalom delayed his pursuit of David, Absalom (who had never fought in battle) could gather a gigantic army to lead. Absalom fell for it, and the delay gave David enough time to consolidate his support.

"The counsel of Hushai the Archite is better than the counsel of Ahithophel." For the LORD had ordained to defeat the good counsel of Ahithophel, so that the LORD might bring ruin on Absalom.

Hushai Warns David to Escape

15   Then Hushai said to the priests Zadok and Abiathar, "Thus and so did Ahithophel counsel Absalom and the elders of Israel; and thus and so I have counseled. [16]Therefore send quickly and tell David, 'Do not lodge tonight at the fords of the wilderness, but by all means cross over; otherwise the king and all the people who are with him will be swallowed up.'" [17]Jonathan and Ahimaaz were waiting at En-rogel; a servant-girl used to go and tell them, and they would go and tell King David; for they could not risk being seen entering the city. [18]But a boy saw them, and told Absalom; so both of them went away quickly, and came to the house of a man at Bahurim, who had a well in his courtyard; and they went down into it. [19]The man's wife took a covering, stretched it over the well's mouth, and spread out grain on it; and nothing was known of it. [20]When Absalom's servants came to the woman at the house, they said, "Where are Ahimaaz and Jonathan?" The woman said to them, "They have crossed over the brook[u] of water." And when they had searched and could not find them, they returned to Jerusalem.

21   After they had gone, the men came up out of the well, and went and told King David. They said to David, "Go and cross the water quickly; for thus and so has Ahithophel counseled against you." [22]So David and all the people who were with him set out and crossed the Jordan; by daybreak not one was left who had not crossed the Jordan.

23   When Ahithophel saw that his counsel was not followed, he saddled his donkey and went off home to his own city. He set his house in order, and hanged himself; he died and was buried in the tomb of his father.

24   Then David came to Mahanaim, while Absalom crossed the Jordan with all the men of Israel. [25]Now Absalom had set Amasa over the army in the place of Joab. Amasa was the son of a man named Ithra the Ishmaelite,[v] who had married Abigal daughter of Nahash, sister of Zeruiah, Joab's mother. [26]The Israelites and Absalom encamped in the land of Gilead.

27   When David came to Mahanaim, Shobi son of Nahash from Rabbah of the Ammonites, and Machir son of Ammiel from Lo-debar, and Barzillai the Gileadite from Rogelim, [28]brought beds, basins, and earthen vessels, wheat, barley, meal, parched grain, beans and lentils,[w] [29]honey and curds, sheep, and cheese from the herd, for David and the people with him to eat; for they said, "The troops are hungry and weary and thirsty in the wilderness."

The Defeat and Death of Absalom

18   Then David mustered the men who were with him, and set over them commanders of thousands and commanders of hundreds. [2]And David divided the army into three groups:[x] one third under the command of Joab, one third under the command of Abishai son of Zeruiah, Joab's brother, and one third under the command of Ittai the Gittite. The king said to the men, "I myself will also go out with you." [3]But the men said, "You shall not go out. For if we flee, they will not care about us. If half of us die, they will not care about us. But you are worth ten thousand of us;[y] therefore it is better that you send us help from the city." [4]The king said to them, "Whatever seems best to you I will do." So the king stood at the side of the gate, while all the army marched out by hundreds and by thousands. [5]The king ordered Joab and Abishai and Ittai, saying, "Deal gently for my sake with the young man Absalom." And all the people heard when the king gave orders to all the commanders concerning Absalom.

6   So the army went out into the field against Israel; and the battle was fought in the forest of Ephraim. [7]The men of Israel were defeated there by the servants of David, and the slaughter there was great on that day, twenty thousand men. [8]The battle spread over the face of all the country; and the forest claimed more victims that day than the sword.

9   Absalom happened to meet the servants of David. Absalom was riding on his mule, and the mule went under the thick branches of a great oak. His head caught fast in the oak, and he was left hanging[z] between heaven and earth, while

---

[u] Meaning of Heb uncertain   [v] 1 Chr 2.17: Heb *Israelite*   [w] Heb *and lentils and parched grain*   [x] Gk: Heb *sent forth the army*   [y] Gk Vg Symmachus: Heb *for now there are ten thousand such as we*   [z] Gk Syr Tg: Heb *was put*

Sin As a Cancer
First David, then his family, then a nation

> "O my son Absalom, my son, my son Absalom! Would I had died instead of you, O Absalom, my son, my son!"
> 18.33

SINS: MANY PEOPLE THINK OF them as parking tickets. If you get too many, the cops may track you down or give your car "the boot." However, one or two here and there won't make a big difference.

The Bible views sins more as cancer cells. One or two here and there do make a difference— often the difference between life and death. Because cancer cells grow, multiply, and take over, major surgery may be needed to save your life.

Second Samuel 11–20 reads like a history of a spreading cancer. In the beginning, David was on top of the world—and so was Israel. The civil war was over, the land was at peace, and Israel was entering an era of unprecedented prosperity. God had promised to ensure David's descendants a continuous reign forever. What more could David hope for? The rest of life appeared as one long celebration.

The Cancer Grows

That celebration never began. One night David caught a glimpse of Bathsheba's beautiful, naked body and impulsively sent for her. The cover-up required a murder. Nobody could deny it was an ugly business: Even David admitted it when Nathan confronted him. However, it was soon over. He repented. He married Bathsheba. He did not intend to fall to that temptation again.

But the consequences of the sin were far from over. Unknown to David, cancer was growing in his own household. David's oldest son Amnon had an eye for women too. He tricked his half sister Tamar into his bedroom, then raped her. Afterwards, filled with disgust, he threw her out.

David was furious. But, maybe because he felt his own sin had robbed him of moral authority, he did nothing to punish his son. According to the law (Leviticus 18.9,29), Amnon deserved exile, but he got off free. David apparently wanted the matter forgotten.

A Cold-blooded Character

It merely disappeared from view. Absalom waited two full years to avenge his sister's rape. Then he murdered Amnon in cold blood. Again David was long on regret, short on punishment. He wept over Amnon's death but perhaps recognized his own responsibility for it. After three years David let Absalom return to Jerusalem unpunished; two years later, when Absalom angrily demanded either a murder trial or full acceptance back into the palace (14.32), David kissed and made up completely.

Again the cancer disappeared from view. But it was not gone; it grew. Now an arrogant Absalom started a program of public relations designed to make him look better than his aging father. At the end of four years, having become quite popular, he set his coup in motion. Taken completely by surprise, David was driven out of Jerusalem, into the desert.

The shock seemed to awaken David. Though dazed and weeping as he left the city, he had enough sense to make some clever plans. When the battle came at last, David's army won, and Absalom was captured and killed.

Weeping for His Son

For David the king, Absalom's defeat was a great triumph. For David the father, it was a horrible tragedy. The worst thing that can happen to a father had happened to him. His own son had tried to kill him, and in trying, had been killed. David could not stop weeping over his son's death until Joab, his general, warned him that he was insulting the troops who had fought for him.

David pulled himself together. Piece by piece, he put his kingdom back in order. He sent conciliatory words to the rebellious leaders of his own tribe. He rewarded his supporters. He took no revenge on any rebel faction, but showed remarkable fairness. A second rebellion broke out but was soon put down. The cancer seemed finally to have run its course.

Yet it had not. David had no more trouble with rebellion in his lifetime, but after his death Solomon killed a brother who he thought was scheming for the throne (1 Kings 2.25). After Solomon's reign, the old tribal tensions rose again, and the North and the South, which David had so carefully knit together, split for good (1 Kings 12). Such may be the consequences when a leader sins. His cancer not only poisons him; it grows to affect all those he leads—and it undermines his work.

Life Questions: Many people will, at some point, see their well-run lives disintegrate. What enables someone to pick up the pieces, as David did?

the mule that was under him went on. [10]A man saw it, and told Joab, "I saw Absalom hanging in an oak." [11]Joab said to the man who told him, "What, you saw him! Why then did you not strike him there to the ground? I would have been glad to give you ten pieces of silver and a belt." [12]But the man said to Joab, "Even if I felt in my hand the weight of a thousand pieces of silver, I would not raise my hand against the king's son; for in our hearing the king commanded you and Abishai and Ittai, saying: For my sake protect the young man Absalom! [13]On the other hand, if I had dealt treacherously against his life[a] (and there is nothing hidden from the king), then you yourself would have stood aloof." [14]Joab said, "I will not waste time like this with you." He took three spears in his hand, and thrust them into the heart of Absalom, while he was still alive in the oak. [15]And ten young men, Joab's armor-bearers, surrounded Absalom and struck him, and killed him.

16 Then Joab sounded the trumpet, and the troops came back from pursuing Israel, for Joab restrained the troops. [17]They took Absalom, threw him into a great pit in the forest, and raised over him a very great heap of stones. Meanwhile all the Israelites fled to their homes. [18]Now Absalom in his lifetime had taken and set up for himself a pillar that is in the King's Valley, for he said, "I have no son to keep my name in remembrance"; he called the pillar by his own name. It is called Absalom's Monument to this day.

David Hears of Absalom's Death

19 Then Ahimaaz son of Zadok said, "Let me run, and carry tidings to the king that the LORD has delivered him from the power of his enemies." [20]Joab said to him, "You are not to carry tidings today; you may carry tidings another day, but today you shall not do so, because the king's son is dead." [21]Then Joab said to a Cushite, "Go, tell the king what you have seen." The Cushite bowed before Joab, and ran. [22]Then Ahimaaz son of Zadok said again to Joab, "Come what may, let me also run after the Cushite." And Joab said, "Why will you run, my son, seeing that you have no reward[b] for the tidings?" [23]"Come what may," he said, "I will run." So he said to him, "Run." Then Ahimaaz ran by the way of the Plain, and outran the Cushite.

24 Now David was sitting between the two gates. The sentinel went up to the roof of the gate by the wall, and when he looked up, he saw a man running alone. [25]The sentinel shouted and told the king. The king said, "If he is alone, there are tidings in his mouth." He kept coming, and drew near. [26]Then the sentinel saw another man running; and the sentinel called to the gatekeeper and said, "See, another man running alone!" The king said, "He also is bringing tidings." [27]The sentinel said, "I think the running of the first one is like the running of Ahimaaz son of Zadok." The king said, "He is a good man, and comes with good tidings."

28 Then Ahimaaz cried out to the king, "All is well!" He prostrated himself before the king with his face to the ground, and said, "Blessed be the LORD your God, who has delivered up the men who raised their hand against my lord the king." [29]The king said, "Is it well with the young man Absalom?" Ahimaaz answered, "When Joab sent your servant,[c] I saw a great tumult, but I do not know what it was." [30]The king said, "Turn aside, and stand here." So he turned aside, and stood still.

31 Then the Cushite came; and the Cushite said, "Good tidings for my lord the king! For the LORD has vindicated you this day, delivering you from the power of all who rose up against you." [32]The king said to the Cushite, "Is it well with the young man Absalom?" The Cushite answered, "May the enemies of my lord the king, and all who rise up to do you harm, be like that young man."

David Mourns for Absalom

33[d] The king was deeply moved, and went up to the chamber over the gate, and wept; and as he went, he said, "O my son Absalom, my son, my son Absalom! Would I had died instead of you, O Absalom, my son, my son!"

18.33 Absalom, Absalom!

David's cry is one of the most poignant in all literature. Yet here again, David's love for his children collided with his effectiveness as a leader. He wept so excessively over Absalom that it demoralized the troops who had just risked their necks for the king (19.3).

19 It was told Joab, "The king is weeping and mourning for Absalom." [2]So the victory that day was turned into mourning for all the troops; for the troops heard that day, "The king is grieving for his son." [3]The troops stole into the city that day as soldiers steal in who are ashamed when they flee in battle. [4]The king covered his face, and the king cried with a loud voice, "O my son Absalom, O Absalom, my son, my son!" [5]Then Joab came into the house to the king, and said, "Today you have covered with shame the faces of all your officers who have saved your life today, and the lives of your sons and your daughters, and the lives of your wives and your concu-

---

[a] Another reading is *at the risk of my life*   [b] Meaning of Heb uncertain   [c] Heb *the king's servant, your servant*
[d] Ch 19.1 in Heb

bines, [6]for love of those who hate you and for hatred of those who love you. You have made it clear today that commanders and officers are nothing to you; for I perceive that if Absalom were alive and all of us were dead today, then you would be pleased. [7]So go out at once and speak kindly to your servants; for I swear by the LORD, if you do not go, not a man will stay with you this night; and this will be worse for you than any disaster that has come upon you from your youth until now." [8]Then the king got up and took his seat in the gate. The troops were all told, "See, the king is sitting in the gate"; and all the troops came before the king.

David Recalled to Jerusalem

Meanwhile, all the Israelites had fled to their homes. [9]All the people were disputing throughout all the tribes of Israel, saying, "The king delivered us from the hand of our enemies, and saved us from the hand of the Philistines; and now he has fled out of the land because of Absalom. [10]But Absalom, whom we anointed over us, is dead in battle. Now therefore why do you say nothing about bringing the king back?"

11 King David sent this message to the priests Zadok and Abiathar, "Say to the elders of Judah, 'Why should you be the last to bring the king back to his house? The talk of all Israel has come to the king.[e] [12]You are my kin, you are my bone and my flesh; why then should you be the last to bring back the king?' [13]And say to Amasa, 'Are you not my bone and my flesh? So may God do to me, and more, if you are not the commander of my army from now on, in place of Joab.'" [14]Amasa[f] swayed the hearts of all the people of Judah as one, and they sent word to the king, "Return, both you and all your servants." [15]So the king came back to the Jordan; and Judah came to Gilgal to meet the king and to bring him over the Jordan.

16 Shimei son of Gera, the Benjaminite, from Bahurim, hurried to come down with the people of Judah to meet King David; [17]with him were a thousand people from Benjamin. And Ziba, the servant of the house of Saul, with his fifteen sons and his twenty servants, rushed down to the Jordan ahead of the king, [18]while the crossing was taking place,[g] to bring over the king's household, and to do his pleasure.

David's Mercy to Shimei

Shimei son of Gera fell down before the king, as he was about to cross the Jordan, [19]and said to the king, "May my lord not hold me guilty or remember how your servant did wrong on the day my lord the king left Jerusalem; may the king not bear it in mind. [20]For your servant knows that I have sinned; therefore, see, I have come this day, the first of all the house of Joseph to come down to meet my lord the king." [21]Abishai son of Zeruiah answered, "Shall not Shimei be put to death for this, because he cursed the LORD's anointed?" [22]But David said, "What have I to do with you, you sons of Zeruiah, that you should today become an adversary to me? Shall anyone be put to death in Israel this day? For do I not know that I am this day king over Israel?" [23]The king said to Shimei, "You shall not die." And the king gave him his oath.

David and Mephibosheth Meet

24 Mephibosheth[h] grandson of Saul came down to meet the king; he had not taken care of his feet, or trimmed his beard, or washed his clothes, from the day the king left until the day he

19.24 The "Traitor's" Story

Mephibosheth's servant Ziba had told David that Mephibosheth was a traitor with dreams that he, as Saul's grandson, would be made king (16.1–4). Hearing this, David had given Ziba all of Mephibosheth's property.

Now we hear Mephibosheth's side of the story. He claimed that Ziba had betrayed him, presumably by taking his donkey so he, a cripple, could not follow David. More convincing than his words was his appearance. He had not washed himself or trimmed his mustache. He looked as though he had been mourning, not grooming himself for the throne.

Did David believe him? Perhaps not completely. He ordered Ziba to give back half, but not all, of the property.

came back in safety. [25]When he came from Jerusalem to meet the king, the king said to him, "Why did you not go with me, Mephibosheth?"[h] [26]He answered, "My lord, O king, my servant deceived me; for your servant said to him, 'Saddle a donkey for me,[i] so that I may ride on it and go with the king.' For your servant is lame. [27]He has slandered your servant to my lord the king. But my lord the king is like the angel of God; do therefore what seems good to you. [28]For all my father's house were doomed to death before my lord the king; but you set your servant among those who eat at your table. What further right have I, then, to appeal to the king?" [29]The king said to him, "Why speak any more of your affairs? I have decided: you and Ziba shall divide the land." [30]Mephibosheth[h] said to the king, "Let

---

[e] Gk: Heb *to the king, to his house*   [f] Heb *He*   [g] Cn: Heb *the ford crossed*   [h] Or *Merib-baal:* See 4.4 note
[i] Gk Syr Vg: Heb *said, 'I will saddle a donkey for myself*

him take it all, since my lord the king has arrived home safely."

David's Kindness to Barzillai

31 Now Barzillai the Gileadite had come down from Rogelim; he went on with the king to the Jordan, to escort him over the Jordan. ³²Barzillai was a very aged man, eighty years old. He had provided the king with food while he stayed at Mahanaim, for he was a very wealthy man. ³³The king said to Barzillai, "Come over with me, and I will provide for you in Jerusalem at my side." ³⁴But Barzillai said to the king, "How many years have I still to live, that I should go up with the king to Jerusalem? ³⁵Today I am eighty years old; can I discern what is pleasant and what is not? Can your servant taste what he eats or what he drinks? Can I still listen to the voice of singing men and singing women? Why then should your servant be an added burden to my lord the king? ³⁶Your servant will go a little way over the Jordan with the king. Why should the king recompense me with such a reward? ³⁷Please let your servant return, so that I may die in my own town, near the graves of my father and my mother. But here is your servant Chimham; let him go over with my lord the king; and do for him whatever seems good to you." ³⁸The king answered, "Chimham shall go over with me, and I will do for him whatever seems good to you; and all that you desire of me I will do for you." ³⁹Then all the people crossed over the Jordan, and the king crossed over; the king kissed Barzillai and blessed him, and he returned to his own home. ⁴⁰The king went on to Gilgal, and Chimham went on with him; all the people of Judah, and also half the people of Israel, brought the king on his way.

41 Then all the people of Israel came to the king, and said to him, "Why have our kindred the people of Judah stolen you away, and brought the king and his household over the Jordan, and all David's men with him?" ⁴²All the people of Judah answered the people of Israel, "Because the king is near of kin to us. Why then are you angry over this matter? Have we eaten at all at the king's expense? Or has he given us any gift?" ⁴³But the people of Israel answered the people of Judah, "We have ten shares in the king, and in David also we have more than you. Why then did you despise us? Were we not the first to speak of bringing back our king?" But the words of the people of Judah were fiercer than the words of the people of Israel.

The Rebellion of Sheba

20 Now a scoundrel named Sheba son of Bichri, a Benjaminite, happened to be there. He sounded the trumpet and cried out,

"We have no portion in David,
     no share in the son of Jesse!
Everyone to your tents, O Israel!"

²So all the people of Israel withdrew from David and followed Sheba son of Bichri; but the people of Judah followed their king steadfastly from the Jordan to Jerusalem.

20.2 North Versus South

Ethnic tension crackled between North ("Israel") and South ("Judah"). Saul came from the tribe of Benjamin in the north; David was a southerner. David worked hard to heal these divisions, but this rebellion shows that many in the north remained dissatisfied. David and his son Solomon managed to keep the two regions together, but after Solomon's death they broke apart for good.

3 David came to his house at Jerusalem; and the king took the ten concubines whom he had left to look after the house, and put them in a house under guard, and provided for them, but did not go in to them. So they were shut up until the day of their death, living as if in widowhood.

4 Then the king said to Amasa, "Call the men of Judah together to me within three days, and be here yourself." ⁵So Amasa went to summon Judah; but he delayed beyond the set time that had been appointed him. ⁶David said to Abishai, "Now Sheba son of Bichri will do us more harm than Absalom; take your lord's servants and pursue him, or he will find fortified cities for himself, and escape from us." ⁷Joab's men went out after him, along with the Cherethites, the Pelethites, and all the warriors; they went out from Jerusalem to pursue Sheba son of Bichri. ⁸When they were at the large stone that is in Gibeon, Amasa came to meet them. Now Joab was wearing a soldier's garment and over it was a belt with a sword in its sheath fastened at his waist; as he went forward it fell out. ⁹Joab said to Amasa, "Is it well with you, my brother?" And Joab took Amasa by the beard with his right hand to kiss him. ¹⁰But Amasa did not notice the sword in Joab's hand; Joab struck him in the belly so that his entrails poured out on the ground, and he died. He did not strike a second blow.

Then Joab and his brother Abishai pursued Sheba son of Bichri. ¹¹And one of Joab's men took his stand by Amasa, and said, "Whoever favors Joab, and whoever is for David, let him follow Joab." ¹²Amasa lay wallowing in his blood on the highway, and the man saw that all the people were stopping. Since he saw that all who came by him were stopping, he carried Amasa from the highway into a field, and threw a garment over him. ¹³Once he was removed from the highway, all the people went on after Joab to pursue Sheba son of Bichri.

14 Sheba[j] passed through all the tribes of Israel to Abel of Beth-maacah;[k] and all the Bichrites[l] assembled, and followed him inside. [15]Joab's forces[m] came and besieged him in Abel of Beth-maacah; they threw up a siege ramp against the city, and it stood against the rampart. Joab's forces were battering the wall to break it down. [16]Then a wise woman called from the city, "Listen! Listen! Tell Joab, 'Come here, I want to speak to you.'" [17]He came near her; and the woman said, "Are you Joab?" He answered, "I am." Then she said to him, "Listen to the words of your servant." He answered, "I am listening." [18]Then she said, "They used to say in the old days, 'Let them inquire at Abel'; and so they would settle a matter. [19]I am one of those who are peaceable and faithful in Israel; you seek to destroy a city that is a mother in Israel; why will you swallow up the heritage of the LORD?" [20]Joab answered, "Far be it from me, far be it, that I should swallow up or destroy! [21]That is not the case! But a man of the hill country of Ephraim, called Sheba son of Bichri, has lifted up his hand against King David; give him up alone, and I will withdraw from the city." The woman said to Joab, "His head shall be thrown over the wall to you." [22]Then the woman went to all the people with her wise plan. And they cut off the head of Sheba son of Bichri, and threw it out to Joab. So he blew the trumpet, and they dispersed from the city, and all went to their homes, while Joab returned to Jerusalem to the king.

23 Now Joab was in command of all the army of Israel;[n] Benaiah son of Jehoiada was in command of the Cherethites and the Pelethites; [24]Adoram was in charge of the forced labor; Jehoshaphat son of Ahilud was the recorder; [25]Sheva was secretary; Zadok and Abiathar were priests; [26]and Ira the Jairite was also David's priest.

David Avenges the Gibeonites

21 Now there was a famine in the days of David for three years, year after year; and David inquired of the LORD. The LORD said, "There is bloodguilt on Saul and on his house, because he put the Gibeonites to death." [2]So the king called the Gibeonites and spoke to them. (Now the Gibeonites were not of the people of Israel, but of the remnant of the Amorites; although the people of Israel had sworn to spare them, Saul had tried to wipe them out in his zeal for the people of Israel and Judah.) [3]David said to the Gibeonites, "What shall I do for you? How shall I make expiation, that you may bless the heritage of the LORD?" [4]The Gibeonites said to him, "It is not a matter of silver or gold between us and Saul or his house;

neither is it for us to put anyone to death in Israel." He said, "What do you say that I should do for you?" [5]They said to the king, "The man who consumed us and planned to destroy us, so that we should have no place in all the territory of Israel— [6]let seven of his sons be handed over to us, and we will impale them before the LORD at Gibeon on the mountain of the LORD."[o] The king said, "I will hand them over."

21.6 Needless Deaths

Is there any excuse for David's agreeing to the execution of Saul's descendants? Perhaps. One must remember that David had certain legal responsibilities as king of Israel. Having offered compensation to the Gibeonites for their mistreatment under Saul, he may have been under legal obligation to cooperate with their demand for blood. In Old Testament times, a family was considered responsible for the crimes of any individual in his family. By modern standards, however, these executions seem needless and cruel.

7 But the king spared Mephibosheth,[p] the son of Saul's son Jonathan, because of the oath of the LORD that was between them, between David and Jonathan son of Saul. [8]The king took the two sons of Rizpah daughter of Aiah, whom she bore to Saul, Armoni and Mephibosheth;[p] and the five sons of Merab[q] daughter of Saul, whom she bore to Adriel son of Barzillai the Meholathite; [9]he gave them into the hands of the Gibeonites, and they impaled them on the mountain before the LORD. The seven of them perished together. They were put to death in the first days of harvest, at the beginning of barley harvest.

10 Then Rizpah the daughter of Aiah took sackcloth, and spread it on a rock for herself, from the beginning of harvest until rain fell on them from the heavens; she did not allow the birds of the air to come on the bodies[r] by day, or the wild animals by night. [11]When David was told what Rizpah daughter of Aiah, the concubine of Saul, had done, [12]David went and took the bones of Saul and the bones of his son Jonathan from the people of Jabesh-gilead, who had stolen them from the public square of Beth-shan, where the Philistines had hung them up, on the day the Philistines killed Saul on Gilboa. [13]He brought up from there the bones of Saul and the bones of his son Jonathan; and they gathered the bones of those who had been impaled. [14]They buried the bones of Saul and of his son Jonathan in the land of Benjamin in Zela, in the tomb of his father

---

[j] Heb *He*   [k] Compare 20.15: Heb *and Beth-maacah*   [l] Compare Gk Vg: Heb *Berites*   [m] Heb *They*
[n] Cn: Heb *Joab to all the army, Israel*   [o] Cn Compare Gk and 21.9: Heb *at Gibeah of Saul, the chosen of the* LORD
[p] Or *Merib-baal*: See 4.4 note   [q] Two Heb Mss Syr Compare Gk: MT *Michal*   [r] Heb *them*

Kish; they did all that the king commanded. After that, God heeded supplications for the land.

Exploits of David's Men

15 The Philistines went to war again with Israel, and David went down together with his servants. They fought against the Philistines, and David grew weary. [16]Ishbi-benob, one of the descendants of the giants, whose spear weighed three hundred shekels of bronze, and who was fitted out with new weapons,[s] said he would kill David. [17]But Abishai son of Zeruiah came to his aid, and attacked the Philistine and killed him. Then David's men swore to him, "You shall not go out with us to battle any longer, so that you do not quench the lamp of Israel."

18 After this a battle took place with the Philistines, at Gob; then Sibbecai the Hushathite killed Saph, who was one of the descendants of the giants. [19]Then there was another battle with the Philistines at Gob; and Elhanan son of Jaare-oregim, the Bethlehemite, killed Goliath the Gittite, the shaft of whose spear was like a weaver's beam. [20]There was again war at Gath, where there was a man of great size, who had six fingers on each hand, and six toes on each foot, twenty-four in number; he too was descended from the giants. [21]When he taunted Israel, Jonathan son of David's brother Shimei, killed him. [22]These four were descended from the giants in Gath; they fell by the hands of David and his servants.

David's Song of Thanksgiving

22 David spoke to the LORD the words of this song on the day when the LORD delivered him from the hand of all his enemies, and from the hand of Saul. [2]He said:
> The LORD is my rock, my fortress, and
>   my deliverer,
[3] my God, my rock, in whom I take
>   refuge,
> my shield and the horn of my salvation,
>   my stronghold and my refuge,
>   my savior; you save me from violence.
[4] I call upon the LORD, who is worthy to be
>   praised,
>   and I am saved from my enemies.

[5] For the waves of death encompassed me,
>   the torrents of perdition assailed me;
[6] the cords of Sheol entangled me,
>   the snares of death confronted me.

[7] In my distress I called upon the LORD;
>   to my God I called.
> From his temple he heard my voice,
>   and my cry came to his ears.

[8] Then the earth reeled and rocked;

> the foundations of the heavens
>   trembled
> and quaked, because he was angry.
[9] Smoke went up from his nostrils,

22.1 David's Psalms

This song of praise was included in the book of Psalms as Psalm 18. Many psalms are credited to David, and some have titles suggesting the events that inspired them. You can read these as a spiritual and emotional commentary on key events in David's life:
Psalm 3. When he fled from his son Absalom (2 Samuel 15.13)
Psalm 18. When the Lord delivered him from his enemies and Saul (1 Samuel 19–31)
Psalm 51. After Nathan confronted David over Bathsheba (2 Samuel 12)
Psalm 52. When Doeg turned in the high priest for helping David (1 Samuel 22.9–10)
Psalm 54. When the Ziphites told Saul that David was hiding in their territory (1 Samuel 23.19–20; 26.1–25)
Psalm 56. When the Philistines seized David in Gath (1 Samuel 21.10–15)
Psalm 57. When David fled from Saul into the cave (1 Samuel 22.1–2)
Psalm 59. When Saul sent men to watch David's house in order to kill him (1 Samuel 19.11)
Psalm 60. After an important battle
Psalm 63. When he was in the Desert of Judah
Psalm 142. When he was in the cave, hiding from Saul

> and devouring fire from his mouth;
>   glowing coals flamed forth from him.
[10] He bowed the heavens, and came down;
>   thick darkness was under his feet.
[11] He rode on a cherub, and flew;
>   he was seen upon the wings of the
>   wind.
[12] He made darkness around him a canopy,
>   thick clouds, a gathering of water.
[13] Out of the brightness before him
>   coals of fire flamed forth.
[14] The LORD thundered from heaven;
>   the Most High uttered his voice.
[15] He sent out arrows, and scattered them
>   —lightning, and routed them.
[16] Then the channels of the sea were seen,
>   the foundations of the world were laid
>   bare
> at the rebuke of the LORD,
>   at the blast of the breath of his nostrils.

[17] He reached from on high, he took me,
>   he drew me out of mighty waters.

---

[s] Heb *was belted anew*

18 He delivered me from my strong enemy,
    from those who hated me;
    for they were too mighty for me.
19 They came upon me in the day of my
    calamity,
    but the LORD was my stay.
20 He brought me out into a broad place;
    he delivered me, because he delighted
    in me.

21 The LORD rewarded me according to my
    righteousness;
    according to the cleanness of my hands
    he recompensed me.
22 For I have kept the ways of the LORD,
    and have not wickedly departed from
    my God.
23 For all his ordinances were before me,
    and from his statutes I did not turn
    aside.
24 I was blameless before him,
    and I kept myself from guilt.
25 Therefore the LORD has recompensed me
    according to my righteousness,
    according to my cleanness in his sight.

26 With the loyal you show yourself loyal;
    with the blameless you show yourself
    blameless;
27 with the pure you show yourself pure,
    and with the crooked you show
    yourself perverse.
28 You deliver a humble people,
    but your eyes are upon the haughty to
    bring them down.
29 Indeed, you are my lamp, O LORD,
    the LORD lightens my darkness.
30 By you I can crush a troop,
    and by my God I can leap over a wall.
31 This God—his way is perfect;
    the promise of the LORD proves true;
    he is a shield for all who take refuge in
    him.

32 For who is God, but the LORD?
    And who is a rock, except our God?
33 The God who has girded me with
    strength[t]
    has opened wide my path.[u]
34 He made my[v] feet like the feet of deer,
    and set me secure on the heights.
35 He trains my hands for war,
    so that my arms can bend a bow of
    bronze.
36 You have given me the shield of your
    salvation,
    and your help[w] has made me great.
37 You have made me stride freely,

    and my feet do not slip;
38 I pursued my enemies and destroyed
    them,
    and did not turn back until they were
    consumed.
39 I consumed them; I struck them down, so
    that they did not rise;
    they fell under my feet.
40 For you girded me with strength for the
    battle;
    you made my assailants sink under me.
41 You made my enemies turn their backs to
    me,
    those who hated me, and I destroyed
    them.
42 They looked, but there was no one to
    save them;
    they cried to the LORD, but he did not
    answer them.
43 I beat them fine like the dust of the earth,
    I crushed them and stamped them
    down like the mire of the streets.

44 You delivered me from strife with the
    peoples;[x]
    you kept me as the head of the
    nations;
    people whom I had not known served
    me.
45 Foreigners came cringing to me;
    as soon as they heard of me, they
    obeyed me.
46 Foreigners lost heart,
    and came trembling out of their
    strongholds.

47 The LORD lives! Blessed be my rock,
    and exalted be my God, the rock of my
    salvation,
48 the God who gave me vengeance
    and brought down peoples under me,
49 who brought me out from my enemies;
    you exalted me above my adversaries,
    you delivered me from the violent.

50 For this I will extol you, O LORD, among
    the nations,
    and sing praises to your name.
51 He is a tower of salvation for his king,
    and shows steadfast love to his
    anointed,
    to David and his descendants forever.

The Last Words of David

23 Now these are the last words of David:
    The oracle of David, son of Jesse,

---

[t] Q Ms Gk Syr Vg Compare Ps 18.32: MT *God is my strong refuge*
reading is *his*   [w] Q Ms: MT *your answering*   [x] Gk: Heb *from strife with my people*

[u] Meaning of Heb uncertain   [v] Another

the oracle of the man whom God
  exalted,^{y}
the anointed of the God of Jacob,
  the favorite of the Strong One of Israel:

23.1 Final Words

People hold on to a loved one's last words, for
they sometimes sum up his or her life. This,
David's final poem, shows David's deep
concern to be a king who pleases God. He
insists that a leader in tune with God will
always be a blessing to God's people, and
recalls God's promise that his descendants will
always rule. A memorial to David's "mighty
men" follows this psalm, honoring those who
fought alongside him with unusual courage.
Uriah the Hittite, whom David had murdered,
makes the list. The vindictive Joab does not.

2 The spirit of the LORD speaks through me,
  his word is upon my tongue.
3 The God of Israel has spoken,
  the Rock of Israel has said to me:
One who rules over people justly,
  ruling in the fear of God,
4 is like the light of morning,
  like the sun rising on a cloudless
    morning,
  gleaming from the rain on the grassy
    land.

5 Is not my house like this with God?
  For he has made with me an
    everlasting covenant,
  ordered in all things and secure.
Will he not cause to prosper
  all my help and my desire?
6 But the godless are^z all like thorns that
    are thrown away;
  for they cannot be picked up with the
    hand;
7 to touch them one uses an iron bar
  or the shaft of a spear.
And they are entirely consumed in fire
  on the spot.^{a}

David's Mighty Men

8 These are the names of the warriors whom
David had: Josheb-basshebeth a Tahchemonite;
he was chief of the Three;^{b} he wielded his spear^c
against eight hundred whom he killed at one
time.
9 Next to him among the three warriors was
Eleazar son of Dodo son of Ahohi. He was with
David when they defied the Philistines who were
gathered there for battle. The Israelites withdrew,
^{10}but he stood his ground. He struck down the
Philistines until his arm grew weary, though his
hand clung to the sword. The LORD brought
about a great victory that day. Then the people
came back to him—but only to strip the dead.
11 Next to him was Shammah son of Agee,
the Hararite. The Philistines gathered together at
Lehi, where there was a plot of ground full of
lentils; and the army fled from the Philistines.
^{12}But he took his stand in the middle of the plot,
defended it, and killed the Philistines; and the
LORD brought about a great victory.
13 Towards the beginning of harvest three of
the thirty^d chiefs went down to join David at the
cave of Adullam, while a band of Philistines was
encamped in the valley of Rephaim. ^{14}David was
then in the stronghold; and the garrison of the
Philistines was then at Bethlehem. ^{15}David said
longingly, "O that someone would give me water
to drink from the well of Bethlehem that is by the
gate!" ^{16}Then the three warriors broke through
the camp of the Philistines, drew water from the
well of Bethlehem that was by the gate, and
brought it to David. But he would not drink of it;
he poured it out to the LORD, ^{17}for he said, "The
LORD forbid that I should do this. Can I drink the
blood of the men who went at the risk of their
lives?" Therefore he would not drink it. The three
warriors did these things.
18 Now Abishai son of Zeruiah, the brother
of Joab, was chief of the Thirty.^{e} With his spear
he fought against three hundred men and killed
them, and won a name beside the Three. ^{19}He was
the most renowned of the Thirty,^{f} and became
their commander; but he did not attain to the
Three.
20 Benaiah son of Jehoiada was a valiant war-
rior^g from Kabzeel, a doer of great deeds; he
struck down two sons of Ariel^h of Moab. He also
went down and killed a lion in a pit on a day
when snow had fallen. ^{21}And he killed an Egyptian, a handsome man. The Egyptian had a spear
in his hand; but Benaiah went against him with
a staff, snatched the spear out of the Egyptian's
hand, and killed him with his own spear. ^{22}Such
were the things Benaiah son of Jehoiada did, and
won a name beside the three warriors. ^{23}He was
renowned among the Thirty, but he did not attain
to the Three. And David put him in charge of his
bodyguard.
24 Among the Thirty were Asahel brother
of Joab; Elhanan son of Dodo of Bethlehem;
^{25}Shammah of Harod; Elika of Harod; ^{26}Helez the
Paltite; Ira son of Ikkesh of Tekoa; ^{27}Abiezer of

y Q Ms: MT *who was raised on high* z Heb *But worthlessness* a Heb *in sitting* b Gk Vg Compare 1 Chr 11.11:
Meaning of Heb uncertain c 1 Chr 11.11: Meaning of Heb uncertain d Heb adds *head* e Two Heb Mss Syr:
MT *Three* f Syr Compare 1 Chr 11.25: Heb *Was he the most renowned of the Three?* g Another reading is *the son
of Ish-hai* h Gk: Heb lacks *sons of*

Anathoth; Mebunnai the Hushathite; 28Zalmon the Ahohite; Maharai of Netophah; 29Heleb son of Baanah of Netophah; Ittai son of Ribai of Gibeah of the Benjaminites; 30Benaiah of Pirathon; Hiddai of the torrents of Gaash; 31Abi-albon the Arbathite; Azmaveth of Bahurim; 32Eliahba of Shaalbon; the sons of Jashen: Jonathan 33son of[i] Shammah the Hararite; Ahiam son of Sharar the Hararite; 34Eliphelet son of Ahasbai of Maacah; Eliam son of Ahithophel the Gilonite; 35Hezro[j] of Carmel; Paarai the Arbite; 36Igal son of Nathan of Zobah; Bani the Gadite; 37Zelek the Ammonite; Naharai of Beeroth, the armor-bearer of Joab son of Zeruiah; 38Ira the Ithrite; Gareb the Ithrite; 39Uriah the Hittite—thirty-seven in all.

David's Census of Israel and Judah

24 Again the anger of the Lord was kindled against Israel, and he incited David against them, saying, "Go, count the people of Israel and Judah." 2So the king said to Joab and the commanders of the army,[k] who were with him, "Go through all the tribes of Israel, from Dan to Beersheba, and take a census of the people, so that I may know how many there are." 3But Joab said to the king, "May the Lord your God increase the number of the people a hundredfold, while the eyes of my lord the king can still see it! But why does my lord the king want to do this?" 4But the king's word prevailed against Joab and the commanders of the army. So Joab and the commanders of the army went out from the presence of the king to take a census of the people of Israel. 5They crossed the Jordan, and began from[l] Aroer and from the city that is in the middle of the valley, toward Gad and on to Jazer. 6Then they came to Gilead, and to Kadesh in the land of the Hittites;[m] and they came to Dan, and from Dan[n] they went around to Sidon, 7and came to the fortress of Tyre and to all the cities of the Hivites and Ca-

24.1 Satan or the Lord?

In a parallel account, 1 Chronicles 21.1 says that Satan incited David to take a census. Who was it—Satan or the Lord? One explanation is that both are true. The Lord, as the ultimate power, allowed the census, and as is typical in the Old Testament, he gets full credit here. The Chronicles version is more concerned about being precise: Because the census was clearly evil (David confessed it as a sin, verse 10), Satan was more directly responsible. As is so often true of evil, people (and Satan) meant it for evil, but God used it for his own purposes.

naanites; and they went out to the Negeb of Judah at Beer-sheba. 8So when they had gone through all the land, they came back to Jerusalem at the end of nine months and twenty days. 9Joab reported to the king the number of those who had been recorded: in Israel there were eight hundred thousand soldiers able to draw the sword, and those of Judah were five hundred thousand.

Judgment on David's Sin

10 But afterward, David was stricken to the heart because he had numbered the people. David said to the Lord, "I have sinned greatly in what I have done. But now, O Lord, I pray you, take away the guilt of your servant; for I have done very foolishly." 11When David rose in the morning, the word of the Lord came to the prophet Gad, David's seer, saying, 12"Go and say to David: Thus says the Lord: Three things I offer[o] you; choose one of them, and I will do it to you." 13So Gad came to David and told him; he asked him, "Shall three[p] years of famine come to you on your land? Or will you flee three months before your foes while they pursue you? Or shall there be three days' pestilence in your land? Now consider, and decide what answer I shall return to the one who sent me." 14Then David said to Gad, "I am in great distress; let us fall into the hand of the Lord, for his mercy is great; but let me not fall into human hands."

15 So the Lord sent a pestilence on Israel from that morning until the appointed time; and seventy thousand of the people died, from Dan to Beer-sheba. 16But when the angel stretched out his hand toward Jerusalem to destroy it, the Lord relented concerning the evil, and said to the angel who was bringing destruction among the people, "It is enough; now stay your hand." The angel of the Lord was then by the threshing floor of Araunah the Jebusite. 17When David saw the angel who was destroying the people, he said to the Lord, "I alone have sinned, and I alone have done wickedly; but these sheep, what have they done? Let your hand, I pray, be against me and against my father's house."

David's Altar on the Threshing Floor

18 That day Gad came to David and said to him, "Go up and erect an altar to the Lord on the threshing floor of Araunah the Jebusite." 19Following Gad's instructions, David went up, as the Lord had commanded. 20When Araunah looked down, he saw the king and his servants coming toward him; and Araunah went out and prostrated himself before the king with his face to the ground. 21Araunah said, "Why has my lord the king come to his servant?" David said, "To buy

---

i Gk: Heb lacks *son of*   *j* Another reading is *Hezrai*   *k* 1 Chr 21.2 Gk: Heb *to Joab the commander of the army*
l Gk Mss: Heb *encamped in Aroer south of*   *m* Gk: Heb *to the land of Tahtim-hodshi*   *n* Cn Compare Gk: Heb *they*
came to Dan-jaan and   *o* Or *hold over*   *p* 1 Chr 21.12 Gk: Heb *seven*

the threshing floor from you in order to build an altar to the LORD, so that the plague may be averted from the people." 22Then Araunah said to David, "Let my lord the king take and offer up what seems good to him; here are the oxen for the burnt offering, and the threshing sledges and the yokes of the oxen for the wood. 23All this, O king, Araunah gives to the king." And Araunah said to the king, "May the LORD your God respond favorably to you."

24 But the king said to Araunah, "No, but I will buy them from you for a price; I will not offer burnt offerings to the LORD my God that cost me nothing." So David bought the threshing floor and the oxen for fifty shekels of silver. 25David built there an altar to the LORD, and offered burnt offerings and offerings of well-being. So the LORD answered his supplication for the land, and the plague was averted from Israel.

24.24 The Cost of True Worship

David's response is timeless: He sees that worship which costs nothing is not true worship at all. It is typical of David that even after falling into sin, he was not blinded to spiritual concerns. Feeling guilty already, he might have thought "one more compromise" would make no difference. Instead he stuck to his principle.

1 KINGS

The Man Who Had Everything
The richest, wisest, most successful person of his time

THE FIRST HALF OF 1 Kings describes a man who got life handed to him on a silver platter. The son of King David and Queen Bathsheba, young Solomon grew up in the royal palace. Early on, he astounded others with his talent for songwriting and natural history. He composed 1,005 songs and spun off 3,000 proverbs (a sampling of which were collected in the biblical book of Proverbs).

Solomon became king of Israel and received from God the special gift of wisdom. He was called the wisest man in the world, and kings and queens traveled hundreds of miles to meet him. They went away dazzled by the genius of Israel's king and by the prosperity of his nation.

The Best Years Ever

Israel reached its Golden Age under King Solomon, a time forever remembered with nostalgia by Jews. Almost all the promised land lay in Israel's hands, and the nation was at peace. Literature and culture flourished. Of the people, the Bible records simply that "they ate and drank and were happy" (4.20). "The king made silver as common in Jerusalem as stones" (10.27).

Of all Solomon's accomplishments, one stands out above the others. He built the temple of God, the finest building in the world of that day. Almost 200,000 men labored for seven years to complete it.

Despite the successes of Solomon's reign, however, later in his life the king had a dramatic downturn. His fall eventually brought the kingdom crashing down around him, and the second half of 1 Kings describes the grim process of dismemberment.

What Went Wrong?

How did it happen? How could the liveliest, wealthiest, most contented nation of its day slide so disastrously in one generation?

As 1 Kings tells it, Solomon seemed unable to control his excesses. Reared in a palace, he loved luxury. When Israel launched its first maritime expeditions, he used them to gather such exotica as gold, ivory, apes, peacocks, and silver. He plated the floor of the temple with gold, wastefully gilded over fine cedar and precious ivory, and fashioned militarily useless shields out of gold. First Kings describes the seven-year construction of the temple in elaborate detail. But then it pointedly notes that the construction of Solomon's palace—twice the temple's size—took 13 years (7.1).

Solomon showed similar extravagance in his love life. First, he married the daughter of the Egyptian pharaoh (perhaps indicating he was relying on military alliances, not on God, for the defense of his country). Then, disobeying God's specific orders, he married the princesses of Moab, Ammon, Edom, Sidon, and other nations. Seven hundred wives in all, and 300 concubines! The entire complexion of the court changed. It became un-Jewish, foreign. To please his wives, Solomon took a final, terrible step: he built altars to all their gods. The one who had built the Israelites' greatest monument to God had fallen to worshiping idols.

Rumblings of Discontent in the Land

To pay for the building projects, Solomon instituted Israel's first national taxation system. He drafted workers for employment and kept them as virtual slaves. When bills mounted, he went so far as to cede certain northern towns in the promised land to another king (9.10–14). Resentment opened up between Israel's North and South.

But the gulf separating Israel from God was even more dangerous. Previously, the people of Israel had looked to God as their leader. Now, however, the focus shifted from God in heaven to the king in Jerusalem. Solomon had even made himself the unofficial religious leader of the country, and when he slid badly, the nation soon followed.

Solomon started out with every advantage of wealth, power, and wisdom. But 1 Kings gives this tragic conclusion: "So Solomon did what was evil in the sight of the LORD, and did not completely follow the LORD, as his father David had done" (11.6).

Solomon seemed obsessed with a desire to outdo anyone who had ever lived. Along the way, he failed to make God the center of his life. He achieved lasting fame in history, but as a negative example. Jesus Christ himself rendered the final verdict on Solomon and his striving for glory when he pointed to a lily growing wild in the field. "Even Solomon in all his glory," he said, "was not clothed like one of these" (Matthew 6.29).

How to Read 1 Kings

First and Second Kings were originally one book: The same Hebrew scroll contained both. Hebrew, having no vowels, is a very compact language, and when the book of Kings was translated into the wordier Greek and Latin, more space was needed. Translators arbitrarily split Kings. The two books, however, should be read as one.

First Kings divides neatly almost in half, with mostly good news in the first half. It tells of Israel's Golden Age, when King Solomon brought peace and prosperity to the nation. But he also sowed the seed for the calamities to follow. Chapter 12 marks the beginning of a civil war that ruptured Israel into two nations: Israel in the North and Judah in the South. The rest of 1, 2 Kings describes, ruler by ruler, the reigns of 19 kings in the North and 19 kings and one queen in the South.

Another book, 2 Chronicles, covers the exact same historical period as 1, 2 Kings. In some cases, 2 Chronicles adds more detail, so if a story interests you, read the parallel account there. These books of history form the background for 17 other books of the Bible: the Prophets. Famous prophets such as Isaiah, Jeremiah, Hosea, and Amos preached during the time of Kings.

Keeping 39 rulers straight can seem hopeless, especially since the books jump back and forth between two countries. Remember:

> Israel was the Northern Kingdom, with its capital in Samaria. Its kings were all unfaithful to God.
> Judah was the Southern Kingdom, with its capital in Jerusalem. Almost half of its rulers remained somewhat faithful to God; the others proved disobedient.

On pages 1349–1357, you will find a lineup of all the rulers, tracing the rise and fall of both the Northern and Southern Kingdoms. Use this handy reference as you read the history. You may find it helpful to underline the various rulers' names, using different colored marking pens (for example, red for Judah and blue for Israel). Add a star by those kings cited as doing "what was right in the sight of the LORD." First Kings mentions two such kings: Asa and Jehoshaphat. By marking the kings and queen with some visual scheme, you can quickly refer back to them when you read references to them in the books of the prophets.

PEOPLE YOU'LL MEET IN 1 KINGS

SOLOMON (p. 353)
ABIATHAR (p. 358)
JEROBOAM (p. 369)

ELIJAH (p. 376)
AHAB (p. 383)

3-TRACK READING PLAN

For an explanation and complete listing of the 3-track reading plan, turn to page 7.

TRACK 1: *Two-Week Courses on the Bible*
The Track 1 reading program on the Old Testament includes one chapter from 1 Kings. See page 8 for a complete listing of this course.

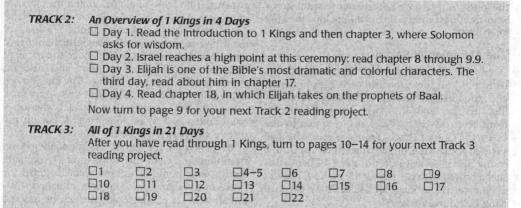

Now turn to page 9 for your next Track 2 reading project.

The Struggle for the Succession

1 King David was old and advanced in years; and although they covered him with clothes, he could not get warm. [2]So his servants said to him, "Let a young virgin be sought for my lord the king, and let her wait on the king, and be his attendant; let her lie in your bosom, so that my lord the king may be warm." [3]So they searched for a beautiful girl throughout all the territory of Israel, and found Abishag the Shunammite, and brought her to the king. [4]The girl was very beautiful. She became the king's attendant and served him, but the king did not know her sexually.

5 Now Adonijah son of Haggith exalted himself, saying, "I will be king"; he prepared for himself chariots and horsemen, and fifty men to run before him. [6]His father had never at any time displeased him by asking, "Why have you done thus and so?" He was also a very handsome man, and he was born next after Absalom. [7]He conferred with Joab son of Zeruiah and with the priest Abiathar, and they supported Adonijah. [8]But the priest Zadok, and Benaiah son of Jehoiada, and the prophet Nathan, and Shimei, and Rei, and David's own warriors did not side with Adonijah.

9 Adonijah sacrificed sheep, oxen, and fatted cattle by the stone Zoheleth, which is beside En-rogel, and he invited all his brothers, the king's sons, and all the royal officials of Judah, [10]but he did not invite the prophet Nathan or Benaiah or the warriors or his brother Solomon.

11 Then Nathan said to Bathsheba, Solomon's mother, "Have you not heard that Adonijah son of Haggith has become king and our lord David does not know it? [12]Now therefore come, let me give you advice, so that you may save your own life and the life of your son Solomon. [13]Go in at once to King David, and say to him, 'Did you not, my lord the king, swear to your servant, say-ing: Your son Solomon shall succeed me as king, and he shall sit on my throne? Why then is Adonijah king?' [14]Then while you are still there speaking with the king, I will come in after you and confirm your words."

15 So Bathsheba went to the king in his room. The king was very old; Abishag the Shunammite was attending the king. [16]Bathsheba bowed and did obeisance to the king, and the king said, "What do you wish?" [17]She said to him, "My lord, you swore to your servant by the LORD your God, saying: Your son Solomon shall succeed me as king, and he shall sit on my throne. [18]But now suddenly Adonijah has become king, though you, my lord the king, do not know it. [19]He has sacrificed oxen, fatted cattle, and sheep in abundance, and has invited all the children of the king, the priest Abiathar, and Joab the commander of the army; but your servant Solomon he has not invited. [20]But you, my lord the king—the eyes of all Israel are on you to tell them who shall sit on the throne of my lord the king after him. [21]Otherwise it will come to pass, when my lord the king sleeps with his ancestors, that my son Solomon and I will be counted offenders."

22 While she was still speaking with the king, the prophet Nathan came in. [23]The king was told, "Here is the prophet Nathan." When he came in before the king, he did obeisance to the king, with his face to the ground. [24]Nathan said, "My lord the king, have you said, 'Adonijah shall succeed me as king, and he shall sit on my throne'? [25]For today he has gone down and has sacrificed oxen, fatted cattle, and sheep in abundance, and has invited all the king's children, Joab the commander[a] of the army, and the priest Abiathar, who are now eating and drinking before him, and saying, 'Long live King Adonijah!' [26]But he did not invite me, your servant, and the priest Zadok, and Benaiah son of Jehoiada, and your servant Solomon. [27]Has this thing been brought about by my lord

---

[a] Gk: Heb the commanders

the king and you have not let your servants know who should sit on the throne of my lord the king after him?"

The Accession of Solomon

28   King David answered, "Summon Bathsheba to me." So she came into the king's presence, and stood before the king. 29The king swore, saying, "As the LORD lives, who has saved my life from every adversity, 30as I swore to you by the LORD, the God of Israel, 'Your son Solomon shall succeed me as king, and he shall sit on my throne in my place,' so will I do this day." 31Then Bathsheba bowed with her face to the ground, and did obeisance to the king, and said, "May my lord King David live forever!"

32   King David said, "Summon to me the priest Zadok, the prophet Nathan, and Benaiah son of Jehoiada." When they came before the king, 33the king said to them, "Take with you the servants of your lord, and have my son Solomon ride on my own mule, and bring him down to Gihon. 34There let the priest Zadok and the prophet Nathan anoint him king over Israel; then blow the trumpet, and say, 'Long live King Solomon!' 35You shall go up following him. Let him enter and sit on my throne; he shall be king in my place; for I have appointed him to be ruler over Israel and over Judah." 36Benaiah son of Jehoiada answered the king, "Amen! May the LORD, the God of my lord the king, so ordain. 37As the LORD has been with my lord the king, so may he be with Solomon, and make his throne greater than the throne of my lord King David."

38   So the priest Zadok, the prophet Nathan, and Benaiah son of Jehoiada, and the Cherethites and the Pelethites, went down and had Solomon ride on King David's mule, and led him to Gihon. 39There the priest Zadok took the horn of oil from the tent and anointed Solomon. Then they blew the trumpet, and all the people said, "Long live King Solomon!" 40And all the people went up following him, playing on pipes and rejoicing with great joy, so that the earth quaked at their noise.

41   Adonijah and all the guests who were with him heard it as they finished feasting. When Joab heard the sound of the trumpet, he said, "Why is the city in an uproar?" 42While he was still speaking, Jonathan son of the priest Abiathar arrived. Adonijah said, "Come in, for you are a worthy man and surely you bring good news." 43Jonathan answered Adonijah, "No, for our lord King David has made Solomon king; 44the king has sent with him the priest Zadok, the prophet Nathan, and Benaiah son of Jehoiada, and the Cherethites and the Pelethites; and they had him ride on the king's mule; 45the priest Zadok and the prophet Nathan have anointed him king at Gihon; and they have gone up from there rejoicing, so that the city is in an uproar. This is the noise that you heard. 46Solomon now sits on the royal throne. 47Moreover the king's servants came to congratulate our lord King David, saying, 'May God make the name of Solomon more famous than yours, and make his throne greater than your throne.' The king bowed in worship on the bed 48and went on to pray thus, 'Blessed be the LORD, the God of Israel, who today has granted one of my offspring*b* to sit on my throne and permitted me to witness it.'"

49   Then all the guests of Adonijah got up trembling and went their own ways. 50Adonijah, fearing Solomon, got up and went to grasp the horns of the altar. 51Solomon was informed, "Adonijah is afraid of King Solomon; see, he has laid hold of the horns of the altar, saying, 'Let King Solomon swear to me first that he will not kill his servant with the sword.'" 52So Solomon responded, "If he proves to be a worthy man, not one of his hairs shall fall to the ground; but if wickedness is found in him, he shall die." 53Then King Solomon sent to have him brought down from the altar. He came to do obeisance to King Solomon; and Solomon said to him, "Go home."

David's Instruction to Solomon

2   When David's time to die drew near, he charged his son Solomon, saying: 2"I am about to go the way of all the earth. Be strong, be courageous, 3and keep the charge of the LORD your God, walking in his ways and keeping his statutes, his commandments, his ordinances, and his testimonies, as it is written in the law of Moses, so that you may prosper in all that you do and wherever you turn. 4Then the LORD will establish his word that he spoke concerning me: 'If your heirs take heed to their way, to walk before me in faithfulness with all their heart and with all their soul, there shall not fail you a successor on the throne of Israel.'

5   "Moreover you know also what Joab son of Zeruiah did to me, how he dealt with the two commanders of the armies of Israel, Abner son of Ner, and Amasa son of Jether, whom he murdered, retaliating in time of peace for blood that had been shed in war, and putting the blood of war on the belt around his waist, and on the

2.5 Paying Back Joab

For the background to David's comments about Joab, see 2 Samuel 3.17–30; 20.4–11.

sandals on his feet. 6Act therefore according to your wisdom, but do not let his gray head go down to Sheol in peace. 7Deal loyally, however,

b Gk: Heb *one*

with the sons of Barzillai the Gileadite, and let them be among those who eat at your table; for with such loyalty they met me when I fled from your brother Absalom. [8]There is also with you Shimei son of Gera, the Benjaminite from Bahurim, who cursed me with a terrible curse on the day when I went to Mahanaim; but when he came down to meet me at the Jordan, I swore to him by the LORD, 'I will not put you to death with the sword.' [9]Therefore do not hold him guiltless, for you are a wise man; you will know what you ought to do to him, and you must bring his gray head down with blood to Sheol."

Death of David

10 Then David slept with his ancestors, and was buried in the city of David. [11]The time that David reigned over Israel was forty years; he reigned seven years in Hebron, and thirty-three years in Jerusalem. [12]So Solomon sat on the throne of his father David; and his kingdom was firmly established.

Solomon Consolidates His Reign

13 Then Adonijah son of Haggith came to Bathsheba, Solomon's mother. She asked, "Do you come peaceably?" He said, "Peaceably." [14]Then he said, "May I have a word with you?" She said, "Go on." [15]He said, "You know that the kingdom was mine, and that all Israel expected me to reign; however, the kingdom has turned about and become my brother's, for it was his from the LORD. [16]And now I have one request to make of you; do not refuse me." She said to him, "Go on." [17]He said, "Please ask King Solomon—he will not refuse you—to give me Abishag the

2.17 After More than a Wife?

Solomon had a rather harsh response (verse 23) to Adonijah's request to marry King David's companion. But asking for her may have been Adonijah's veiled attempt to regain the throne lost to Solomon. In the ancient Middle East, a person who married any of the late king's wives or concubines publicly claimed the rights of the former king (see 2 Samuel 12.8 and 16.21–22 for examples). Adonijah might have been cunningly hatching another conspiracy; Solomon, at least, seemed to think so.

Shunammite as my wife." [18]Bathsheba said, "Very well; I will speak to the king on your behalf."

19 So Bathsheba went to King Solomon, to speak to him on behalf of Adonijah. The king rose to meet her, and bowed down to her; then he sat on his throne, and had a throne brought for the king's mother, and she sat on his right. [20]Then she said, "I have one small request to make of you; do not refuse me." And the king said to her,

"Make your request, my mother; for I will not refuse you." [21]She said, "Let Abishag the Shunammite be given to your brother Adonijah as his wife." [22]King Solomon answered his mother, "And why do you ask Abishag the Shunammite for Adonijah? Ask for him the kingdom as well! For he is my elder brother; ask not only for him but also for the priest Abiathar and for Joab son of Zeruiah!" [23]Then King Solomon swore by the LORD, "So may God do to me, and more also, for Adonijah has devised this scheme at the risk of his life! [24]Now therefore as the LORD lives, who has established me and placed me on the throne of my father David, and who has made me a house as he promised, today Adonijah shall be put to death." [25]So King Solomon sent Benaiah son of Jehoiada; he struck him down, and he died.

26 The king said to the priest Abiathar, "Go to Anathoth, to your estate; for you deserve death. But I will not at this time put you to death, because you carried the ark of the Lord GOD before my father David, and because you shared in all the hardships my father endured." [27]So Solomon banished Abiathar from being priest to the LORD, thus fulfilling the word of the LORD that he had spoken concerning the house of Eli in Shiloh.

28 When the news came to Joab—for Joab had supported Adonijah though he had not supported Absalom—Joab fled to the tent of the LORD and grasped the horns of the altar. [29]When it was told King Solomon, "Joab has fled to the tent of the LORD and now is beside the altar," Solomon sent Benaiah son of Jehoiada, saying, "Go, strike him down." [30]So Benaiah came to the tent of the LORD and said to him, "The king commands, 'Come out.'" But he said, "No, I will die here." Then Benaiah brought the king word again, saying, "Thus said Joab, and thus he answered me." [31]The king replied to him, "Do as he has said, strike him down and bury him; and thus take away from me and from my father's house the guilt for the blood that Joab shed without cause. [32]The LORD will bring back his bloody deeds on his own head, because, without the knowledge of my father David, he attacked and killed with the sword two men more righteous and better than himself, Abner son of Ner, commander of the army of Israel, and Amasa son of Jether, commander of the army of Judah. [33]So shall their blood come back on the head of Joab and on the head of his descendants forever; but to David, and to his descendants, and to his house, and to his throne, there shall be peace from the LORD forevermore." [34]Then Benaiah son of Jehoiada went up and struck him down and killed him; and he was buried at his own house near the wilderness. [35]The king put Benaiah son of Jehoiada over the army in his place, and the king put the priest Zadok in the place of Abiathar.

36 Then the king sent and summoned Shimei, and said to him, "Build yourself a house in

Jerusalem, and live there, and do not go out from there to any place whatever. 37For on the day you go out, and cross the Wadi Kidron, know for certain that you shall die; your blood shall be on your own head." 38And Shimei said to the king, "The sentence is fair; as my lord the king has said, so will your servant do." So Shimei lived in Jerusalem many days.

39 But it happened at the end of three years that two of Shimei's slaves ran away to King Achish son of Maacah of Gath. When it was told Shimei, "Your slaves are in Gath," 40Shimei arose and saddled a donkey, and went to Achish in Gath, to search for his slaves; Shimei went and brought his slaves from Gath. 41When Solomon was told that Shimei had gone from Jerusalem to Gath and returned, 42the king sent and summoned Shimei, and said to him, "Did I not make you swear by the LORD, and solemnly adjure you, saying, 'Know for certain that on the day you go out and go to any place whatever, you shall die'? And you said to me, 'The sentence is fair; I accept.' 43Why then have you not kept your oath to the LORD and the commandment with which I charged you?" 44The king also said to Shimei, "You know in your own heart all the evil that you did to my father David; so the LORD will bring back your evil on your own head. 45But King Solomon shall be blessed, and the throne of David shall be established before the LORD forever." 46Then the king commanded Benaiah son of Jehoiada; and he went out and struck him down, and he died.

So the kingdom was established in the hand of Solomon.

Solomon's Prayer for Wisdom

3 Solomon made a marriage alliance with Pharaoh king of Egypt; he took Pharaoh's daughter and brought her into the city of David,

2.46 Wise Yet Ruthless

Chapters 2 and 3 show conflicting personality traits in Solomon. In the power struggles of chapter 2 he proved more ruthless than his father David had ever been. This tendency stirred up resentment among the northern tribes of Israel and eventually led to civil war. But chapter 3 shows Solomon could also be faithful, wise, and even humble. Tragically, he gave in to his darker side more and more as his reign wore on.

until he had finished building his own house and the house of the LORD and the wall around Jerusalem. 2The people were sacrificing at the high places, however, because no house had yet been built for the name of the LORD.

3 Solomon loved the LORD, walking in the statutes of his father David; only, he sacrificed and offered incense at the high places. 4The king went to Gibeon to sacrifice there, for that was the principal high place; Solomon used to offer a thousand burnt offerings on that altar. 5At Gibeon the LORD appeared to Solomon in a dream by night; and God said, "Ask what I should give you." 6And Solomon said, "You have shown great and steadfast love to your servant my father David, because he walked before you in faithfulness,

ABIATHAR *Outlaw Priest*

GENERATIONS BEFORE, A PROPHET HAD predicted that Israel's chief family of priests would be destroyed (1 Samuel 2.31–36), Abiathar witnessed the horrible fulfillment of that prediction. All the men in his extended family—85 in all—were lined up and slaughtered. Abiathar's whole village—women, children, babies, even animals—perished, all because they were suspected of helping David escape from King Saul (1 Samuel 22.18).

Abiathar somehow got away and straggled into David's outlaw camp, the lone survivor bearing news of the massacre. He brought with him the ephod: the priest's garment containing the Urim and Thummim, sacred objects used to determine God's will.

From that day on David relied on Abiathar and his ephod to gain direction from God. Somewhat like Friar Tuck in Robin Hood's band, Abiathar became official priest to the outlaw band. When King Saul died and David and his guerrilla army finally came to power, David made Abiathar the nation's high priest in the new sanctuary at Jerusalem.

Abiathar's harrowing moments did not end even after he joined the power structure. When David's son Absalom led a rebellion, Abiathar remained loyal to David, returning to the conquered city as a spy (2 Samuel 15.24–29). When David grew old and feeble, Abiathar backed the wrong son to succeed the king. The aging priest might have been executed—others were—but Solomon showed mercy and banished him instead. Abiathar thus ended his career as he began: as an outcast (1 Kings 2.26).

Life Questions: Do you know anyone like Abiathar, someone who has suffered stunning losses? How can you—or someone else—be like David to him or her?

in righteousness, and in uprightness of heart toward you; and you have kept for him this great and steadfast love, and have given him a son to sit on his throne today. [7]And now, O LORD my God, you have made your servant king in place of my father David, although I am only a little child; I do not know how to go out or come in. [8]And your servant is in the midst of the people whom you have chosen, a great people, so numerous they cannot be numbered or counted. [9]Give your servant therefore an understanding mind to govern your people, able to discern between good and evil; for who can govern this your great people?"

3.9 Solomon's Wish

By requesting the wisdom to be a good king, Solomon showed that he possessed much wisdom already. Pleased at Solomon's unselfish request, God gave Solomon even more. Unfortunately, the humility displayed in this scene did not stay with Solomon throughout his career.

[10]It pleased the Lord that Solomon had asked this. [11]God said to him, "Because you have asked this, and have not asked for yourself long life or riches, or for the life of your enemies, but have asked for yourself understanding to discern what is right, [12]I now do according to your word. Indeed I give you a wise and discerning mind; no one like you has been before you and no one like you shall arise after you. [13]I give you also what you have not asked, both riches and honor all your life; no other king shall compare with you. [14]If you will walk in my ways, keeping my statutes and my commandments, as your father David walked, then I will lengthen your life."

[15]Then Solomon awoke; it had been a dream. He came to Jerusalem where he stood before the ark of the covenant of the LORD. He offered up burnt offerings and offerings of well-being, and provided a feast for all his servants.

Solomon's Wisdom in Judgment

[16]Later, two women who were prostitutes came to the king and stood before him. [17]The one woman said, "Please, my lord, this woman and I live in the same house; and I gave birth while she was in the house. [18]Then on the third day after I gave birth, this woman also gave birth. We were together; there was no one else with us in the house, only the two of us were in the house. [19]Then this woman's son died in the night, because she lay on him. [20]She got up in the middle of the night and took my son from beside me while your servant slept. She laid him at her breast, and laid her dead son at my breast. [21]When I rose in the morning to nurse my son, I saw that he was dead; but when I looked at him closely in the morning, clearly it was not the son I had borne." [22]But the other woman said, "No, the living son is mine, and the dead son is yours." The first said, "No, the dead son is yours, and the living son is mine." So they argued before the king.

[23]Then the king said, "The one says, 'This is my son that is alive, and your son is dead'; while the other says, 'Not so! Your son is dead, and my son is the living one.'" [24]So the king said, "Bring me a sword," and they brought a sword before the king. [25]The king said, "Divide the living boy in two; then give half to the one, and half to the other." [26]But the woman whose son was alive said to the king—because compassion for her son burned within her—"Please, my lord, give her the living boy; certainly do not kill him!" The other said, "It shall be neither mine nor yours; divide it." [27]Then the king responded: "Give the first woman the living boy; do not kill him. She is his mother." [28]All Israel heard of the judgment that the king had rendered; and they stood in awe of the king, because they perceived that the wisdom of God was in him, to execute justice.

Solomon's Administrative Officers

4 King Solomon was king over all Israel, [2]and these were his high officials: Azariah son of Zadok was the priest; [3]Elihoreph and Ahijah sons of Shisha were secretaries; Jehoshaphat son of Ahilud was recorder; [4]Benaiah son of Jehoiada was in command of the army; Zadok and Abiathar were priests; [5]Azariah son of Nathan was over the officials; Zabud son of Nathan was priest and king's friend; [6]Ahishar was in charge of the palace; and Adoniram son of Abda was in charge of the forced labor.

[7]Solomon had twelve officials over all Israel, who provided food for the king and his household; each one had to make provision for one month in the year. [8]These were their names: Ben-hur, in the hill country of Ephraim; [9]Ben-deker, in Makaz, Shaalbim, Beth-shemesh, and Elon-beth-hanan; [10]Ben-hesed, in Arubboth (to him belonged Socoh and all the land of Hepher); [11]Ben-abinadab, in all Naphath-dor (he had Taphath, Solomon's daughter, as his wife); [12]Baana son of Ahilud, in Taanach, Megiddo, and all Beth-shean, which is beside Zarethan below Jezreel, and from Beth-shean to Abel-meholah, as far as the other side of Jokmeam; [13]Ben-geber, in Ramoth-gilead (he had the villages of Jair son of Manasseh, which are in Gilead, and he had the region of Argob, which is in Bashan, sixty great cities with walls and bronze bars); [14]Ahinadab son of Iddo, in Mahanaim; [15]Ahimaaz, in Naphtali (he had taken Basemath, Solomon's daughter, as his wife); [16]Baana son of Hushai, in Asher and Bealoth; [17]Jehoshaphat son of Paruah, in Issachar; [18]Shimei son of Ela, in Benjamin; [19]Geber son of

Uri, in the land of Gilead, the country of King Sihon of the Amorites and of King Og of Bashan. And there was one official in the land of Judah.

Magnificence of Solomon's Rule

20 Judah and Israel were as numerous as the sand by the sea; they ate and drank and were happy. 21 c Solomon was sovereign over all the kingdoms from the Euphrates to the land of the Philistines, even to the border of Egypt; they brought tribute and served Solomon all the days of his life.

4.21 How Large Was Israel?

Under the reigns of David and Solomon, Israel stretched from the border of Egypt to the border of Babylonia. It was approximately three times the size of the modern nation of Israel, encompassing land that now belongs to Jordan, Syria, and Lebanon.

22 Solomon's provision for one day was thirty cors of choice flour, and sixty cors of meal, 23ten fat oxen, and twenty pasture-fed cattle, one hundred sheep, besides deer, gazelles, roebucks, and fatted fowl. 24For he had dominion over all the region west of the Euphrates from Tiphsah to Gaza, over all the kings west of the Euphrates; and he had peace on all sides. 25During Solomon's lifetime Judah and Israel lived in safety, from Dan even to Beer-sheba, all of them under their vines and fig trees. 26Solomon also had forty thousand stalls of horses for his chariots, and twelve thousand horsemen. 27Those officials supplied provisions for King Solomon and for all who came to King Solomon's table, each one in his month; they let nothing be lacking. 28They also brought to the required place barley and straw for the horses and swift steeds, each according to his charge.

Fame of Solomon's Wisdom

29 God gave Solomon very great wisdom, discernment, and breadth of understanding as vast as the sand on the seashore, 30so that Solomon's wisdom surpassed the wisdom of all the people of the east, and all the wisdom of Egypt. 31He was wiser than anyone else, wiser than Ethan the Ezrahite, and Heman, Calcol, and Darda, children of Mahol; his fame spread throughout all the surrounding nations. 32He composed three thousand proverbs, and his songs numbered a thousand and five. 33He would speak of trees, from the cedar that is in the Lebanon to the hyssop that grows in the wall; he would speak of animals, and birds, and reptiles, and fish. 34People came from all the nations to hear the wisdom of Solomon;

they came from all the kings of the earth who had heard of his wisdom.

Preparations and Materials for the Temple

5 d Now King Hiram of Tyre sent his servants to Solomon, when he heard that they had anointed him king in place of his father; for Hiram had always been a friend to David. 2Solomon sent word to Hiram, saying, 3"You know that my father David could not build a house for the name of the LORD his God because of the warfare with which his enemies surrounded him, until the LORD put them under the soles of his feet.e 4But now the LORD my God has given me rest on every side; there is neither adversary nor misfortune. 5So I intend to build a house for the name of the LORD my God, as the LORD said to my father David, 'Your son, whom I will set on your throne in your place, shall build the house for my name.' 6Therefore command that cedars from the Lebanon be cut for me. My servants will join your servants, and I will give you whatever wages you set for your servants; for you know that there is no one among us who knows how to cut timber like the Sidonians."

7 When Hiram heard the words of Solomon, he rejoiced greatly, and said, "Blessed be the LORD today, who has given to David a wise son to be over this great people." 8Hiram sent word to Solomon, "I have heard the message that you have sent to me; I will fulfill all your needs in the matter of cedar and cypress timber. 9My servants shall bring it down to the sea from the Lebanon; I will make it into rafts to go by sea to the place you indicate. I will have them broken up there for you to take away. And you shall meet my needs by providing food for my household." 10So Hiram supplied Solomon's every need for timber of cedar and cypress. 11Solomon in turn gave Hiram twenty thousand cors of wheat as food for his household, and twenty cors of fine oil. Solomon gave this to Hiram year by year. 12So the LORD gave Solomon wisdom, as he promised him. There was peace between Hiram and Solomon; and the two of them made a treaty.

13 King Solomon conscripted forced labor out of all Israel; the levy numbered thirty thousand men. 14He sent them to the Lebanon, ten thousand a month in shifts; they would be a month in the Lebanon and two months at home; Adoniram was in charge of the forced labor. 15Solomon also had seventy thousand laborers and eighty thousand stonecutters in the hill country, 16besides Solomon's three thousand three hundred supervisors who were over the work, having charge of the people who did the work. 17At the king's command, they quarried out great, costly stones in order to lay the foundation of the house with dressed stones. 18So Solomon's build-

ers and Hiram's builders and the Gebalites did the stonecutting and prepared the timber and the stone to build the house.

Solomon Builds the Temple

6 In the four hundred eightieth year after the Israelites came out of the land of Egypt, in the fourth year of Solomon's reign over Israel, in the month of Ziv, which is the second month, he began to build the house of the LORD. ²The house that King Solomon built for the LORD was sixty cubits long, twenty cubits wide, and thirty cubits high. ³The vestibule in front of the nave of the house was twenty cubits wide, across the width of the house. Its depth was ten cubits in

6.3 History of the Temple

The Bible describes the temple architecture in some detail, though, notably, it does not record detailed instructions from God—in contrast to the very specific commands given for the tabernacle. Solomon's temple lasted about 380 years, occasionally falling into disrepair. Destroyed by Babylon's King Nebuchadnezzar, it was partially rebuilt under the leadership of Ezra and Nehemiah, and then reconstructed by King Herod in Jesus' day. Jesus walked in the temple on "Solomon's Porch." The early church met on the temple grounds, Peter preached there, and Ananias and Sapphira probably died there (Acts 5). Currently the temple site is occupied by a Muslim mosque.

front of the house. ⁴ For the house he made windows with recessed frames.*ᶠ* ⁵He also built a structure against the wall of the house, running around the walls of the house, both the nave and the inner sanctuary; and he made side chambers all around. ⁶The lowest story*ᵍ* was five cubits wide, the middle one was six cubits wide, and the third was seven cubits wide; for around the outside of the house he made offsets on the wall in order that the supporting beams should not be inserted into the walls of the house.

7 The house was built with stone finished at the quarry, so that neither hammer nor ax nor any tool of iron was heard in the temple while it was being built.

8 The entrance for the middle story was on the south side of the house: one went up by winding stairs to the middle story, and from the middle story to the third. ⁹So he built the house, and finished it; he roofed the house with beams and planks of cedar. ¹⁰He built the structure against the whole house, each story*ʰ* five cubits high, and it was joined to the house with timbers of cedar.

11 Now the word of the LORD came to Solo-

mon, ¹²"Concerning this house that you are building, if you will walk in my statutes, obey my ordinances, and keep all my commandments by walking in them, then I will establish my promise with you, which I made to your father David. ¹³I will dwell among the children of Israel, and will not forsake my people Israel."

14 So Solomon built the house, and finished it. ¹⁵He lined the walls of the house on the inside with boards of cedar; from the floor of the house to the rafters of the ceiling, he covered them on the inside with wood; and he covered the floor of the house with boards of cypress. ¹⁶He built twenty cubits of the rear of the house with boards of cedar from the floor to the rafters, and he built this within as an inner sanctuary, as the most holy place. ¹⁷The house, that is, the nave in front of the inner sanctuary, was forty cubits long. ¹⁸The cedar within the house had carvings of gourds and open flowers; all was cedar, no stone was seen. ¹⁹The inner sanctuary he prepared in the innermost part of the house, to set there the ark of the covenant of the LORD. ²⁰The interior of the inner sanctuary was twenty cubits long, twenty cubits wide, and twenty cubits high; he overlaid it with pure gold. He also overlaid the altar with cedar.*ⁱ* ²¹Solomon overlaid the inside of the house with pure gold, then he drew chains of gold across, in front of the inner sanctuary, and overlaid it with gold. ²²Next he overlaid the whole house with gold, in order that the whole house might be perfect; even the whole altar that belonged to the inner sanctuary he overlaid with gold.

The Furnishings of the Temple

23 In the inner sanctuary he made two cherubim of olivewood, each ten cubits high. ²⁴Five cubits was the length of one wing of the cherub, and five cubits the length of the other wing of the cherub; it was ten cubits from the tip of one wing to the tip of the other. ²⁵The other cherub also measured ten cubits; both cherubim had the same measure and the same form. ²⁶The height of one cherub was ten cubits, and so was that of the other cherub. ²⁷He put the cherubim in the innermost part of the house; the wings of the cherubim were spread out so that a wing of one was touching the one wall, and a wing of the other cherub was touching the other wall; their other wings toward the center of the house were touching wing to wing. ²⁸He also overlaid the cherubim with gold.

29 He carved the walls of the house all around about with carved engravings of cherubim, palm trees, and open flowers, in the inner and outer rooms. ³⁰The floor of the house he overlaid with gold, in the inner and outer rooms.

31 For the entrance to the inner sanctuary he made doors of olivewood; the lintel and the door-

---

ᶠ Gk: Meaning of Heb uncertain   *ᵍ* Gk: Heb *structure*   *ʰ* Heb lacks *each story*   *ⁱ* Meaning of Heb uncertain

posts were five-sided.*j* ³²He covered the two doors of olivewood with carvings of cherubim, palm trees, and open flowers; he overlaid them with gold, and spread gold on the cherubim and on the palm trees.

33 So also he made for the entrance to the nave doorposts of olivewood, four-sided each, ³⁴and two doors of cypress wood; the two leaves of the one door were folding, and the two leaves of the other door were folding. ³⁵He carved cherubim, palm trees, and open flowers, overlaying them with gold evenly applied upon the carved work. ³⁶He built the inner court with three courses of dressed stone to one course of cedar beams.

37 In the fourth year the foundation of the house of the LORD was laid, in the month of Ziv. ³⁸In the eleventh year, in the month of Bul, which is the eighth month, the house was finished in all its parts, and according to all its specifications. He was seven years in building it.

Solomon's Palace and Other Buildings

7 Solomon was building his own house thirteen years, and he finished his entire house.

7.1 Prosperity under Solomon

The magnificent temple and palace built by Solomon came to symbolize Israel's Golden Age. Solomon built many leading cities, assuming control of vital trade routes. He fortified Jerusalem, the capital, with a wall so thick that parts of it still stand. He modernized the Israelite army with 12,000 horses and the first chariot brigades, and made shrewd alliances with neighboring countries.

2 He built the House of the Forest of the Lebanon one hundred cubits long, fifty cubits wide, and thirty cubits high, built on four rows of cedar pillars, with cedar beams on the pillars. ³It was roofed with cedar on the forty-five rafters, fifteen in each row, which were on the pillars. ⁴There were window frames in the three rows, facing each other in the three rows. ⁵All the doorways and doorposts had four-sided frames, opposite, facing each other in the three rows.

6 He made the Hall of Pillars fifty cubits long and thirty cubits wide. There was a porch in front with pillars, and a canopy in front of them.

7 He made the Hall of the Throne where he was to pronounce judgment, the Hall of Justice, covered with cedar from floor to floor.

8 His own house where he would reside, in the other court back of the hall, was of the same construction. Solomon also made a house like this hall for Pharaoh's daughter, whom he had taken in marriage.

9 All these were made of costly stones, cut according to measure, sawed with saws, back and front, from the foundation to the coping, and from outside to the great court. ¹⁰The foundation was of costly stones, huge stones, stones of eight and ten cubits. ¹¹There were costly stones above, cut to measure, and cedarwood. ¹²The great court had three courses of dressed stone to one layer of cedar beams all around; so had the inner court of the house of the LORD, and the vestibule of the house.

Products of Hiram the Bronzeworker

13 Now King Solomon invited and received Hiram from Tyre. ¹⁴He was the son of a widow of the tribe of Naphtali, whose father, a man of Tyre, had been an artisan in bronze; he was full of skill, intelligence, and knowledge in working bronze. He came to King Solomon, and did all his work.

15 He cast two pillars of bronze. Eighteen cubits was the height of the one, and a cord of twelve cubits would encircle it; the second pillar was the same.*k* ¹⁶He also made two capitals of molten bronze, to set on the tops of the pillars; the height of the one capital was five cubits, and the height of the other capital was five cubits. ¹⁷There were nets of checker work with wreaths of chain work for the capitals on the tops of the pillars; seven*l* for the one capital, and seven*l* for the other capital. ¹⁸He made the columns with two rows around each latticework to cover the capitals that were above the pomegranates; he did the same with the other capital. ¹⁹Now the capitals that were on the tops of the pillars in the vestibule were of lily-work, four cubits high. ²⁰The capitals were on the two pillars and also above the rounded projection that was beside the latticework; there were two hundred pomegranates in rows all around; and so with the other capital. ²¹He set up the pillars at the vestibule of the temple; he set up the pillar on the south and called it Jachin; and he set up the pillar on the north and called it Boaz. ²²On the tops of the pillars was lily-work. Thus the work of the pillars was finished.

23 Then he made the molten sea; it was round, ten cubits from brim to brim, and five cubits high. A line of thirty cubits would encircle it completely. ²⁴Under its brim were panels all around it, each of ten cubits, surrounding the sea; there were two rows of panels, cast when it was cast. ²⁵It stood on twelve oxen, three facing north, three facing west, three facing south, and three facing east; the sea was set on them. The hindquarters of each were toward the inside. ²⁶Its thickness was a handbreadth; its brim was made

---

j Meaning of Heb uncertain   *k* Cn: Heb *and a cord of twelve cubits encircled the second pillar*; Compare Jer 52.21
l Heb: Gk *a net*

like the brim of a cup, like the flower of a lily; it held two thousand baths.*m*

27 He also made the ten stands of bronze; each stand was four cubits long, four cubits wide, and three cubits high. 28This was the construction of the stands: they had borders; the borders were within the frames; 29on the borders that were set in the frames were lions, oxen, and cherubim. On the frames, both above and below the lions and oxen, there were wreaths of beveled work. 30Each stand had four bronze wheels and axles of bronze; at the four corners were supports for a basin. The supports were cast with wreaths at the side of each. 31Its opening was within the crown whose height was one cubit; its opening was round, as a pedestal is made; it was a cubit and a half wide. At its opening there were carvings; its borders were four-sided, not round. 32The four wheels were underneath the borders; the axles of the wheels were in the stands; and the height of a wheel was a cubit and a half. 33The wheels were made like a chariot wheel; their axles, their rims, their spokes, and their hubs were all cast. 34There were four supports at the four corners of each stand; the supports were of one piece with the stands. 35On the top of the stand there was a round band half a cubit high; on the top of the stand, its stays and its borders were of one piece with it. 36On the surfaces of its stays and on its borders he carved cherubim, lions, and palm trees, where each had space, with wreaths all around. 37In this way he made the ten stands; all of them were cast alike, with the same size and the same form.

38 He made ten basins of bronze; each basin held forty baths,*m* each basin measured four cubits; there was a basin for each of the ten stands. 39He set five of the stands on the south side of the house, and five on the north side of the house; he set the sea on the southeast corner of the house.

40 Hiram also made the pots, the shovels, and the basins. So Hiram finished all the work that he did for King Solomon on the house of the LORD: 41the two pillars, the two bowls of the capitals that were on the tops of the pillars, the two latticeworks to cover the two bowls of the capitals that were on the tops of the pillars; 42the four hundred pomegranates for the two latticeworks, two rows of pomegranates for each latticework, to cover the two bowls of the capitals that were on the pillars; 43the ten stands, the ten basins on the stands; 44the one sea, and the twelve oxen underneath the sea.

45 The pots, the shovels, and the basins, all these vessels that Hiram made for King Solomon for the house of the LORD were of burnished bronze. 46In the plain of the Jordan the king cast them, in the clay ground between Succoth and Zarethan. 47Solomon left all the vessels un-weighed, because there were so many of them; the weight of the bronze was not determined.

48 So Solomon made all the vessels that were in the house of the LORD: the golden altar, the golden table for the bread of the Presence, 49the lampstands of pure gold, five on the south side and five on the north, in front of the inner sanctuary; the flowers, the lamps, and the tongs, of gold; 50the cups, snuffers, basins, dishes for incense, and firepans, of pure gold; the sockets for the doors of the innermost part of the house, the most holy place, and for the doors of the nave of the temple, of gold.

51 Thus all the work that King Solomon did on the house of the LORD was finished. Solomon brought in the things that his father David had dedicated, the silver, the gold, and the vessels, and stored them in the treasuries of the house of the LORD.

Dedication of the Temple

8 Then Solomon assembled the elders of Israel and all the heads of the tribes, the leaders of the ancestral houses of the Israelites, before King Solomon in Jerusalem, to bring up the ark of the covenant of the LORD out of the city of David, which is Zion. 2All the people of Israel assembled to King Solomon at the festival in the month Ethanim, which is the seventh month. 3And all the elders of Israel came, and the priests carried the ark. 4So they brought up the ark of the LORD, the tent of meeting, and all the holy vessels that were in the tent; the priests and the Levites brought them up. 5King Solomon and all the congregation of Israel, who had assembled before him, were with him before the ark, sacrificing so many sheep and oxen that they could not be counted or numbered. 6Then the priests brought the ark of the covenant of the LORD to its place, in the inner sanctuary of the house, in the most holy place, underneath the wings of the cherubim. 7For the cherubim spread out their wings over the place of the ark, so that the cherubim made a covering above the ark and its poles. 8The poles were so long that the ends of the poles were seen from the holy place in front of the inner sanctuary; but they could not be seen from outside; they are there to this day. 9There was nothing in the ark except the two tablets of stone that Moses had placed there at Horeb, where the LORD made a covenant with the Israelites, when they came out of the land of Egypt. 10And when the priests came out of the holy place, a cloud filled the house of the LORD, 11so that the priests could not stand to minister because of the cloud; for the glory of the LORD filled the house of the LORD.

12 Then Solomon said,
"The LORD has said that he would dwell
in thick darkness.

---

m A Heb measure of volume

13 I have built you an exalted house,
   a place for you to dwell in forever."

Solomon's Speech

14 Then the king turned around and blessed

8.11 Off-limits for People

Much of the temple stayed off-limits to the general public; only priests went in. Not even priests ventured into the most holy place, except on very special occasions. Solomon had not intended the building for humans—he wanted a place suitable for God to dwell. And on the memorable day described here, the awesome glory of the Lord did indeed fill the temple.

all the assembly of Israel, while all the assembly of Israel stood. 15He said, "Blessed be the LORD, the God of Israel, who with his hand has fulfilled what he promised with his mouth to my father David, saying, 16'Since the day that I brought my people Israel out of Egypt, I have not chosen a city from any of the tribes of Israel in which to build a house, that my name might be there; but I chose David to be over my people Israel.' 17My father David had it in mind to build a house for the name of the LORD, the God of Israel. 18But the LORD said to my father David, 'You did well to consider building a house for my name; 19nevertheless you shall not build the house, but your son who shall be born to you shall build the house for my name.' 20Now the LORD has upheld the promise that he made; for I have risen in the place of my father David; I sit on the throne of Israel, as the LORD promised, and have built the house for the name of the LORD, the God of Israel. 21There I have provided a place for the ark, in which is the covenant of the LORD that he made with our ancestors when he brought them out of the land of Egypt."

Solomon's Prayer of Dedication

22 Then Solomon stood before the altar of the LORD in the presence of all the assembly of Israel, and spread out his hands to heaven. 23He said, "O LORD, God of Israel, there is no God like you in heaven above or on earth beneath, keeping covenant and steadfast love for your servants who walk before you with all their heart, 24the covenant that you kept for your servant my father David as you declared to him; you promised with your mouth and have this day fulfilled with your hand. 25Therefore, O LORD, God of Israel, keep for your servant my father David that which you promised him, saying, 'There shall never fail you a successor before me to sit on the throne of

Israel, if only your children look to their way, to walk before me as you have walked before me.' 26Therefore, O God of Israel, let your word be confirmed, which you promised to your servant my father David.

27 "But will God indeed dwell on the earth? Even heaven and the highest heaven cannot contain you, much less this house that I have built!

8.27 Where God Dwells

King Solomon was at his most eloquent in the great speech and prayer of chapter 8. He made it clear that the Lord of the universe could not fully dwell in a building. Nevertheless, God's presence, or his "Name," would indeed live there. For that reason, Solomon began the practice of praying toward Jerusalem, a practice still followed by many Jews today (verse 29).

28Regard your servant's prayer and his plea, O LORD my God, heeding the cry and the prayer that your servant prays to you today; 29that your eyes may be open night and day toward this house, the place of which you said, 'My name shall be there,' that you may heed the prayer that your servant prays toward this place. 30Hear the plea of your servant and of your people Israel when they pray toward this place; O hear in heaven your dwelling place; heed and forgive.

31 "If someone sins against a neighbor and is given an oath to swear, and comes and swears before your altar in this house, 32then hear in heaven, and act, and judge your servants, condemning the guilty by bringing their conduct on their own head, and vindicating the righteous by rewarding them according to their righteousness.

33 "When your people Israel, having sinned against you, are defeated before an enemy but turn again to you, confess your name, pray and plead with you in this house, 34then hear in heaven, forgive the sin of your people Israel, and bring them again to the land that you gave to their ancestors.

35 "When heaven is shut up and there is no rain because they have sinned against you, and then they pray toward this place, confess your name, and turn from their sin, because you punish[n] them, 36then hear in heaven, and forgive the sin of your servants, your people Israel, when you teach them the good way in which they should walk; and grant rain on your land, which you have given to your people as an inheritance.

37 "If there is famine in the land, if there is plague, blight, mildew, locust, or caterpillar; if their enemy besieges them in any[o] of their cities; whatever plague, whatever sickness there is;

---

n Or when you answer   *o Gk Syr: Heb in the land*

[38]whatever prayer, whatever plea there is from any individual or from all your people Israel, all knowing the afflictions of their own hearts so that they stretch out their hands toward this house; [39]then hear in heaven your dwelling place, forgive, act, and render to all whose hearts you know—according to all their ways, for only you know what is in every human heart— [40]so that they may fear you all the days that they live in the land that you gave to our ancestors.

41 "Likewise when a foreigner, who is not of your people Israel, comes from a distant land because of your name [42]—for they shall hear of your great name, your mighty hand, and your outstretched arm—when a foreigner comes and prays toward this house, [43]then hear in heaven your dwelling place, and do according to all that the foreigner calls to you, so that all the peoples of the earth may know your name and fear you, as do your people Israel, and so that they may know that your name has been invoked on this house that I have built.

44 "If your people go out to battle against their enemy, by whatever way you shall send them, and they pray to the LORD toward the city that you have chosen and the house that I have built for your name, [45]then hear in heaven their prayer and their plea, and maintain their cause.

46 "If they sin against you—for there is no one who does not sin—and you are angry with them and give them to an enemy, so that they are carried away captive to the land of the enemy, far off or near; [47]yet if they come to their senses in the land to which they have been taken captive, and repent, and plead with you in the land of their captors, saying, 'We have sinned, and have done wrong; we have acted wickedly'; [48]if they repent with all their heart and soul in the land of their enemies, who took them captive, and pray to you toward their land, which you gave to their ancestors, the city that you have chosen, and the house that I have built for your name; [49]then hear in heaven your dwelling place their prayer and their plea, maintain their cause [50]and forgive your people who have sinned against you, and all their transgressions that they have committed against you; and grant them compassion in the sight of their captors, so that they may have compassion on them [51](for they are your people and heritage, which you brought out of Egypt, from the midst of the iron-smelter). [52]Let your eyes be open to the plea of your servant, and to the plea of your people Israel, listening to them whenever they call to you. [53]For you have separated them from among all the peoples of the earth, to be your heritage, just as you promised through Moses, your servant, when you brought our ancestors out of Egypt, O Lord GOD."

Solomon Blesses the Assembly

54 Now when Solomon finished offering all this prayer and this plea to the LORD, he arose from facing the altar of the LORD, where he had knelt with hands outstretched toward heaven; [55]he stood and blessed all the assembly of Israel with a loud voice:

56 "Blessed be the LORD, who has given rest to his people Israel according to all that he promised; not one word has failed of all his good promise, which he spoke through his servant Moses. [57]The LORD our God be with us, as he was with our ancestors; may he not leave us or abandon us, [58]but incline our hearts to him, to walk in all his ways, and to keep his commandments, his statutes, and his ordinances, which he commanded our ancestors. [59]Let these words of mine, with which I pleaded before the LORD, be near to the LORD our God day and night, and may he maintain the cause of his servant and the cause of his people Israel, as each day requires; [60]so that all the peoples of the earth may know that the LORD is God; there is no other. [61]Therefore devote yourselves completely to the LORD our God, walking in his statutes and keeping his commandments, as at this day."

Solomon Offers Sacrifices

62 Then the king, and all Israel with him, offered sacrifice before the LORD. [63]Solomon offered as sacrifices of well-being to the LORD twenty-two thousand oxen and one hundred twenty thousand sheep. So the king and all the people of Israel dedicated the house of the LORD. [64]The same day the king consecrated the middle of the court that was in front of the house of the LORD; for there he offered the burnt offerings and the grain offerings and the fat pieces of the sacrifices of well-being, because the bronze altar that was before the LORD was too small to receive the burnt offerings and the grain offerings and the fat pieces of the sacrifices of well-being.

65 So Solomon held the festival at that time, and all Israel with him—a great assembly, people from Lebo-hamath to the Wadi of Egypt—before the LORD our God, seven days.[p] [66]On the eighth day he sent the people away; and they blessed the king, and went to their tents, joyful and in good spirits because of all the goodness that the LORD had shown to his servant David and to his people Israel.

God Appears Again to Solomon

9 When Solomon had finished building the house of the LORD and the king's house and all that Solomon desired to build, [2]the LORD appeared to Solomon a second time, as he had ap-

p Compare Gk: Heb seven days and seven days, fourteen days

peared to him at Gibeon. 3The LORD said to him,
"I have heard your prayer and your plea, which
you made before me; I have consecrated this
house that you have built, and put my name there
forever; my eyes and my heart will be there for all
time. 4As for you, if you will walk before me, as
David your father walked, with integrity of heart
and uprightness, doing according to all that I
have commanded you, and keeping my statutes
and my ordinances, 5then I will establish your
royal throne over Israel forever, as I promised
your father David, saying, 'There shall not fail you
a successor on the throne of Israel.'
6 "If you turn aside from following me, you
or your children, and do not keep my commandments and my statutes that I have set before you,
but go and serve other gods and worship them,
7then I will cut Israel off from the land that I have
given them; and the house that I have consecrated
for my name I will cast out of my sight; and Israel
will become a proverb and a taunt among all
peoples. 8This house will become a heap of ruins;[q] everyone passing by it will be astonished,
and will hiss; and they will say, 'Why has the LORD
done such a thing to this land and to this house?'
9Then they will say, 'Because they have forsaken
the LORD their God, who brought their ancestors
out of the land of Egypt, and embraced other
gods, worshiping them and serving them; therefore the LORD has brought this disaster upon
them.'"
10 At the end of twenty years, in which Solomon had built the two houses, the house of the
LORD and the king's house, 11King Hiram of Tyre
having supplied Solomon with cedar and cypress
timber and gold, as much as he desired, King
Solomon gave to Hiram twenty cities in the land
of Galilee. 12But when Hiram came from Tyre to
see the cities that Solomon had given him, they
did not please him. 13Therefore he said, "What
kind of cities are these that you have given me,
my brother?" So they are called the land of Cabul[r] to this day. 14But Hiram had sent to the king
one hundred twenty talents of gold.

9.13 Good-for-nothing Towns

Solomon gave away part of God's promised land to a foreigner, an act that may have stirred up the resentment of northern tribes against the South. King Hiram, unimpressed with the 20 Galilean towns Solomon gave him as payment for services, called them "Cabul" (good-for-nothing). Interestingly, Jesus chose this very area as the early focal point of his ministry on earth.

Other Acts of Solomon

15 This is the account of the forced labor that
King Solomon conscripted to build the house
of the LORD and his own house, the Millo and
the wall of Jerusalem, Hazor, Megiddo, Gezer
16(Pharaoh king of Egypt had gone up and captured Gezer and burned it down, had killed the
Canaanites who lived in the city, and had given it
as dowry to his daughter, Solomon's wife; 17so
Solomon rebuilt Gezer), Lower Beth-horon, 18Ba-
alath, Tamar in the wilderness, within the land,
19as well as all of Solomon's storage cities, the
cities for his chariots, the cities for his cavalry, and
whatever Solomon desired to build, in Jerusalem,
in Lebanon, and in all the land of his dominion.
20All the people who were left of the Amorites, the
Hittites, the Perizzites, the Hivites, and the Jebusites, who were not of the people of Israel—
21their descendants who were still left in the land,
whom the Israelites were unable to destroy
completely—these Solomon conscripted for slave
labor, and so they are to this day. 22But of the
Israelites Solomon made no slaves; they were the
soldiers, they were his officials, his commanders,
his captains, and the commanders of his chariotry
and cavalry.
23 These were the chief officers who were
over Solomon's work: five hundred fifty, who had
charge of the people who carried on the work.
24 But Pharaoh's daughter went up from the
city of David to her own house that Solomon had
built for her; then he built the Millo.
25 Three times a year Solomon used to offer
up burnt offerings and sacrifices of well-being on
the altar that he built for the LORD, offering incense[s] before the LORD. So he completed the
house.

Solomon's Commercial Activity

26 King Solomon built a fleet of ships at
Ezion-geber, which is near Eloth on the shore of
the Red Sea,[t] in the land of Edom. 27Hiram sent
his servants with the fleet, sailors who were familiar with the sea, together with the servants of
Solomon. 28They went to Ophir, and imported
from there four hundred twenty talents of gold,
which they delivered to King Solomon.

Visit of the Queen of Sheba

10 When the queen of Sheba heard of the
fame of Solomon (fame due to[u] the name
of the LORD), she came to test him with hard
questions. 2She came to Jerusalem with a very
great retinue, with camels bearing spices, and very
much gold, and precious stones; and when she
came to Solomon, she told him all that was on her
mind. 3Solomon answered all her questions; there
was nothing hidden from the king that he could

[q] Syr Old Latin: Heb *will become high it that was* [r] Perhaps meaning *a land good for nothing* [s] Gk: Heb *offering incense with* [t] Or *Sea of Reeds* [u] Meaning of Heb uncertain

not explain to her. ⁴When the queen of Sheba had observed all the wisdom of Solomon, the house that he had built, ⁵the food of his table, the seating of his officials, and the attendance of his servants, their clothing, his valets, and his burnt offerings that he offered at the house of the LORD, there was no more spirit in her.

6 So she said to the king, "The report was true that I heard in my own land of your accomplishments and of your wisdom, ⁷but I did not believe the reports until I came and my own eyes had seen it. Not even half had been told me; your wisdom and prosperity far surpass the report that I had heard. ⁸Happy are your wives!ᵛ Happy are these your servants, who continually attend you and hear your wisdom! ⁹Blessed be the LORD your God, who has delighted in you and set you on the throne of Israel! Because the LORD loved Israel forever, he has made you king to execute justice and righteousness." ¹⁰Then she gave the king one hundred twenty talents of gold, a great quantity of spices, and precious stones; never again did spices come in such quantity as that which the queen of Sheba gave to King Solomon.

11 Moreover, the fleet of Hiram, which carried gold from Ophir, brought from Ophir a great quantity of almug wood and precious stones. ¹²From the almug wood the king made supports for the house of the LORD, and for the king's house, lyres also and harps for the singers; no such almug wood has come or been seen to this day.

13 Meanwhile King Solomon gave to the queen of Sheba every desire that she expressed, as well as what he gave her out of Solomon's royal bounty. Then she returned to her own land, with her servants.

14 The weight of gold that came to Solomon in one year was six hundred sixty-six talents of

10.14 A King of Excess

This passage (10.14–29) graphically illustrates how far Solomon had strayed from God's ideal. The book of Deuteronomy cites Moses' forthright warnings about what kind of king should rule over Israel (Deuteronomy 17.14–20). Solomon defied those warnings by acquiring huge numbers of horses, getting involved in foreign trade, taking many wives, and accumulating silver and gold.

gold, ¹⁵besides that which came from the traders and from the business of the merchants, and from all the kings of Arabia and the governors of the land. ¹⁶King Solomon made two hundred large shields of beaten gold; six hundred shekels of gold went into each large shield. ¹⁷He made three hun-

dred shields of beaten gold; three minas of gold went into each shield; and the king put them in the House of the Forest of Lebanon. ¹⁸The king also made a great ivory throne, and overlaid it with the finest gold. ¹⁹The throne had six steps. The top of the throne was rounded in the back, and on each side of the seat were arm rests and two lions standing beside the arm rests, ²⁰while twelve lions were standing, one on each end of a step on the six steps. Nothing like it was ever made in any kingdom. ²¹All King Solomon's drinking vessels were of gold, and all the vessels of the House of the Forest of Lebanon were of pure gold; none were of silver—it was not considered as anything in the days of Solomon. ²²For the king had a fleet of ships of Tarshish at sea with the fleet of Hiram. Once every three years the fleet of ships of Tarshish used to come bringing gold, silver, ivory, apes, and peacocks.ʷ

23 Thus King Solomon excelled all the kings of the earth in riches and in wisdom. ²⁴The whole earth sought the presence of Solomon to hear his wisdom, which God had put into his mind. ²⁵Every one of them brought a present, objects of silver and gold, garments, weaponry, spices, horses, and mules, so much year by year.

26 Solomon gathered together chariots and horses; he had fourteen hundred chariots and twelve thousand horses, which he stationed in the chariot cities and with the king in Jerusalem. ²⁷The king made silver as common in Jerusalem as stones, and he made cedars as numerous as the sycamores of the Shephelah. ²⁸Solomon's import of horses was from Egypt and Kue, and the king's traders received them from Kue at a price. ²⁹A chariot could be imported from Egypt for six hundred shekels of silver, and a horse for one hundred fifty; so through the king's traders they were exported to all the kings of the Hittites and the kings of Aram.

Solomon's Errors

11 King Solomon loved many foreign women along with the daughter of Pharaoh: Moabite, Ammonite, Edomite, Sidonian, and Hittite women, ²from the nations concerning which the LORD had said to the Israelites, "You shall not enter into marriage with them, neither shall they with you; for they will surely incline your heart to follow their gods"; Solomon clung to these in love. ³Among his wives were seven hundred princesses and three hundred concubines; and his wives turned away his heart. ⁴For when Solomon was old, his wives turned away his heart after other gods; and his heart was not true to the LORD his God, as was the heart of his father David. ⁵For Solomon followed Astarte the goddess of the Sidonians, and Milcom the abomination of the Ammonites. ⁶So Solomon did what was evil in the

ᵛ Gk Syr: Heb *men*   ʷ Or *baboons*

sight of the LORD, and did not completely follow the LORD, as his father David had done. ⁷Then Solomon built a high place for Chemosh the abomination of Moab, and for Molech the abomination of the Ammonites, on the mountain east

11.3 So Many Women

Solomon's 700 wives were foreigners who worshiped other gods and had different standards of right and wrong. He probably married them as part of treaty arrangements with surrounding nations; a royal marriage was supposed to cement a bond between peoples. These marriages violated God's law (Deuteronomy 7.3–4; 17.17) and ultimately led Solomon away from God. Because of his wives' religions, he built shrines and encouraged pagan worship right in Jerusalem.

of Jerusalem. ⁸He did the same for all his foreign wives, who offered incense and sacrificed to their gods.

9 Then the LORD was angry with Solomon, because his heart had turned away from the LORD, the God of Israel, who had appeared to him twice, ¹⁰and had commanded him concerning this matter, that he should not follow other gods; but he did not observe what the LORD commanded. ¹¹Therefore the LORD said to Solomon, "Since this has been your mind and you have not kept my covenant and my statutes that I have commanded you, I will surely tear the kingdom from you and give it to your servant. ¹²Yet for the sake of your father David I will not do it in your lifetime; I will tear it out of the hand of your son. ¹³I will not, however, tear away the entire kingdom; I will give one tribe to your son, for the sake of my servant David and for the sake of Jerusalem, which I have chosen."

Adversaries of Solomon

14 Then the LORD raised up an adversary against Solomon, Hadad the Edomite; he was of the royal house in Edom. ¹⁵For when David was in Edom, and Joab the commander of the army went up to bury the dead, he killed every male in Edom ¹⁶(for Joab and all Israel remained there six months, until he had eliminated every male in Edom); ¹⁷but Hadad fled to Egypt with some Edomites who were servants of his father. He was a young boy at that time. ¹⁸They set out from Midian and came to Paran; they took people with them from Paran and came to Egypt, to Pharaoh king of Egypt, who gave him a house, assigned him an allowance of food, and gave him land. ¹⁹Hadad found great favor in the sight of Pharaoh, so that he gave him his sister-in-law for a

wife, the sister of Queen Tahpenes. ²⁰The sister of Tahpenes gave birth by him to his son Genubath, whom Tahpenes weaned in Pharaoh's house; Genubath was in Pharaoh's house among the children of Pharaoh. ²¹When Hadad heard in Egypt that David slept with his ancestors and that Joab the commander of the army was dead, Hadad said to Pharaoh, "Let me depart, that I may go to my own country." ²²But Pharaoh said to him, "What do you lack with me that you now seek to go to your own country?" And he said, "No, do let me go."

23 God raised up another adversary against Solomon,ˣ Rezon son of Eliada, who had fled from his master, King Hadadezer of Zobah. ²⁴He gathered followers around him and became leader of a marauding band, after the slaughter by David; they went to Damascus, settled there, and made him king in Damascus. ²⁵He was an adversary of Israel all the days of Solomon, making trouble as Hadad did; he despised Israel and reigned over Aram.

Jeroboam's Rebellion

26 Jeroboam son of Nebat, an Ephraimite of Zeredah, a servant of Solomon, whose mother's name was Zeruah, a widow, rebelled against the king. ²⁷The following was the reason he rebelled against the king. Solomon built the Millo, and closed up the gap in the wallʸ of the city of his father David. ²⁸The man Jeroboam was very able, and when Solomon saw that the young man was industrious he gave him charge over all the forced labor of the house of Joseph. ²⁹About that time, when Jeroboam was leaving Jerusalem, the prophet Ahijah the Shilonite found him on the road. Ahijah had clothed himself with a new garment. The two of them were alone in the open country ³⁰when Ahijah laid hold of the new garment he was wearing and tore it into twelve pieces. ³¹He then said to Jeroboam: Take for yourself ten pieces; for thus says the LORD, the God of Israel, "See, I am about to tear the kingdom from the hand of Solomon, and will give you ten tribes. ³²One tribe will remain his, for the sake of my servant David and for the sake of Jerusalem, the city that I have chosen out of all the tribes of Israel. ³³This is because he hasᶻ forsaken me, worshiped Astarte the goddess of the Sidonians, Chemosh the god of Moab, and Milcom the god of the Ammonites, and hasᶻ not walked in my ways, doing what is right in my sight and keeping my statutes and my ordinances, as his father David did. ³⁴Nevertheless I will not take the whole kingdom away from him but will make him ruler all the days of his life, for the sake of my servant David whom I chose and who did keep my commandments and my statutes; ³⁵but I will take the kingdom away from his son and give it to you—

that is, the ten tribes. [36]Yet to his son I will give one tribe, so that my servant David may always have a lamp before me in Jerusalem, the city where I have chosen to put my name. [37]I will take you, and you shall reign over all that your soul desires; you shall be king over Israel. [38]If you will listen to all that I command you, walk in my ways, and do what is right in my sight by keeping my statutes and my commandments, as David my servant did, I will be with you, and will build you an enduring house, as I built for David, and I will give Israel to you. [39]For this reason I will punish the descendants of David, but not forever." [40]Solomon sought therefore to kill Jeroboam; but Jeroboam promptly fled to Egypt, to King Shishak of Egypt, and remained in Egypt until the death of Solomon.

Death of Solomon

41 Now the rest of the acts of Solomon, all that he did as well as his wisdom, are they not written in the Book of the Acts of Solomon? [42]The time that Solomon reigned in Jerusalem over all Israel was forty years. [43]Solomon slept with his ancestors and was buried in the city of his father David; and his son Rehoboam succeeded him.

The Northern Tribes Secede

12 Rehoboam went to Shechem, for all Israel had come to Shechem to make him king. [2]When Jeroboam son of Nebat heard of it (for he

[a] Gk Vg Compare 2 Chr 10.2: Heb lived in

was still in Egypt, where he had fled from King Solomon), then Jeroboam returned from[a] Egypt. [3]And they sent and called him; and Jeroboam and all the assembly of Israel came and said to Rehoboam, [4]"Your father made our yoke heavy. Now therefore lighten the hard service of your father and his heavy yoke that he placed on us, and we

---

11.41 Using Other Sources

The author makes liberal use of other historical records, most of which have not survived. This verse refers to "the Book of the Acts of Solomon." Elsewhere, 1 Kings relies on accounts of the kings of Judah (22.45) or of Israel (15.31). In all, the two books of Kings make 34 references to other sources.

---

will serve you." [5]He said to them, "Go away for three days, then come again to me." So the people went away.

6 Then King Rehoboam took counsel with the older men who had attended his father Solomon while he was still alive, saying, "How do you advise me to answer this people?" [7]They answered him, "If you will be a servant to this people today and serve them, and speak good words to them when you answer them, then they will be your servants forever." [8]But he disregarded the advice

---

JEROBOAM *Blown Opportunity*

POLITICIANS WHO RUN ON A platform of reform often, when they attain power, act depressingly like the corrupt leaders they have just replaced. Such is the story of Jeroboam, a decent man who had a unique chance to stop the Israel's slide into corruption.

Jeroboam came to power by the back door. On his way out of Jerusalem, where he worked as a top official for King Solomon, Jeroboam met a prophet named Ahijah. The prophet took off the cloak he was wearing and ripped the brand-new garment into twelve pieces. Then he handed ten pieces to Jeroboam and delivered the message behind the object lesson: Because of King Solomon's failures, God would rip the kingdom of Israel apart. The bureaucrat Jeroboam would soon inherit leadership over ten of the twelve tribes.

This dramatic prophecy launched a fierce struggle for power. At first, fearing for his life, Jeroboam fled the country. Years later he came back from exile to make peace with Solomon's son, but found the son stupidly harsher than the old man. (See "Rehoboam: a Fool's Answer," p. 453.) The fed-up northern tribes rebelled, and Jeroboam became king of a new nation. God's people were irrevocably split into two camps.

Jeroboam's rule may have begun with God's approval, but the bureaucrat who would be king never lived up to God's call. Fearing that his citizens would gradually be won back to the south—they had to travel to Jerusalem to worship in the temple—Jeroboam made a clever but terrible choice. He started his own, competing religion in the north.

By outward standards the new religion succeeded, enduring as long as Israel did. God, however, who had brought Jeroboam to power, reacted with outrage. He predicted and then carried out the total destruction of Jeroboam's family (15.27–30).

Life Questions: Do you find it easier to criticize leaders than to lead? How do you usually respond when you're placed in a leadership position?

that the older men gave him, and consulted with the young men who had grown up with him and now attended him. ⁹He said to them, "What do you advise that we answer this people who have said to me, 'Lighten the yoke that your father put on us'?" ¹⁰The young men who had grown up with him said to him, "Thus you should say to this people who spoke to you, 'Your father made our yoke heavy, but you must lighten it for us'; thus you should say to them, 'My little finger is thicker than my father's loins. ¹¹Now, whereas my father laid on you a heavy yoke, I will add to your yoke. My father disciplined you with whips, but I will discipline you with scorpions.'"

12 So Jeroboam and all the people came to Rehoboam the third day, as the king had said, "Come to me again the third day." ¹³The king answered the people harshly. He disregarded the advice that the older men had given him ¹⁴and spoke to them according to the advice of the young men, "My father made your yoke heavy, but I will add to your yoke; my father disciplined you with whips, but I will discipline you with scorpions." ¹⁵So the king did not listen to the people, because it was a turn of affairs brought about by the LORD that he might fulfill his word, which the LORD had spoken by Ahijah the Shilonite to Jeroboam son of Nebat.

16 When all Israel saw that the king would not listen to them, the people answered the king,

"What share do we have in David?
　We have no inheritance in the son of
　　Jesse.
To your tents, O Israel!
　Look now to your own house,
　　O David."

So Israel went away to their tents. ¹⁷But Rehoboam reigned over the Israelites who were living in the towns of Judah. ¹⁸When King Rehoboam sent Adoram, who was taskmaster over the forced labor, all Israel stoned him to death. King Rehoboam then hurriedly mounted his chariot to flee to Jerusalem. ¹⁹So Israel has been in rebellion against the house of David to this day.

First Dynasty: Jeroboam Reigns over Israel

20 When all Israel heard that Jeroboam had returned, they sent and called him to the assembly and made him king over all Israel. There was no one who followed the house of David, except the tribe of Judah alone.

21 When Rehoboam came to Jerusalem, he assembled all the house of Judah and the tribe of Benjamin, one hundred eighty thousand chosen troops to fight against the house of Israel, to restore the kingdom to Rehoboam son of Solomon. ²²But the word of God came to Shemaiah the man of God: ²³Say to King Rehoboam of Judah, son of Solomon, and to all the house of Judah and Benjamin, and to the rest of the people, ²⁴"Thus says the LORD, You shall not go up or fight against your kindred the people of Israel. Let everyone go home, for this thing is from me." So they heeded the word of the LORD and went home again, according to the word of the LORD.

Jeroboam's Golden Calves

25 Then Jeroboam built Shechem in the hill country of Ephraim, and resided there; he went out from there and built Penuel. ²⁶Then Jeroboam said to himself, "Now the kingdom may well revert to the house of David. ²⁷If this people continues to go up to offer sacrifices in the house of the LORD at Jerusalem, the heart of this people will turn again to their master, King Rehoboam of Judah; they will kill me and return to King Rehoboam of Judah." ²⁸So the king took counsel, and made two calves of gold. He said to the people,ᵇ "You have gone up to Jerusalem long enough. Here are your gods, O Israel, who brought you up out of the land of Egypt." ²⁹He set one in Bethel, and the other he put in Dan. ³⁰And this thing became a sin, for the people went to worship before the one at Bethel and before the other as far as Dan.ᶜ ³¹He also made housesᵈ on high places, and appointed priests from among all the people, who were not Levites. ³²Jeroboam appointed a festival on the fifteenth day of the eighth month like the festival that was in Judah, and he offered sacrifices on the altar; so he did in Bethel, sacrificing to the calves that he had made. And he placed in Bethel the priests of the high places that he had made. ³³He went up to the altar that he had made in Bethel on the fifteenth day in the eighth month, in the month that he alone had devised; he appointed a festival for the people of Israel, and he went up to the altar to offer incense.

A Man of God from Judah

13 While Jeroboam was standing by the altar to offer incense, a man of God came out of Judah by the word of the LORD to Bethel ²and proclaimed against the altar by the word of the LORD, and said, "O altar, altar, thus says the LORD: 'A son shall be born to the house of David, Josiah by name; and he shall sacrifice on you the priests of the high places who offer incense on you, and human bones shall be burned on you.'" ³He gave a sign the same day, saying, "This is the sign that the LORD has spoken: 'The altar shall be torn down, and the ashes that are on it shall be poured out.'" ⁴When the king heard what the man of God cried out against the altar at Bethel, Jeroboam stretched out his hand from the altar, saying, "Seize him!" But the hand that he stretched out against him withered so that he could not draw it back to himself. ⁵The altar also was torn down, and the ashes poured out from

---

ᵇ Gk: Heb *to them*   ᶜ Compare Gk: Heb *went to the one as far as Dan*   ᵈ Gk Vg Compare 13.32: Heb *a house*

the altar, according to the sign that the man of God had given by the word of the LORD. ⁶The king said to the man of God, "Entreat now the favor of the LORD your God, and pray for me, so that my hand may be restored to me." So the man of God entreated the LORD; and the king's hand was restored to him, and became as it was before. ⁷Then the king said to the man of God, "Come home with me and dine, and I will give you a

13.7–10 Standing Up to the King

Afraid that temple worship in Jerusalem would lure his northern supporters back to the South, Jeroboam lifted a page from Israel's past (Exodus 32.1–4) and put up two golden calves for worship (see 12.32). An anonymous man of God prophesied against this idol worship in the strongest terms.

Jeroboam's offer of a gift to the prophet reflects the kings' tendencies to keep "court prophets," paid to tell the kings what they wanted to hear. The anonymous man of God would have nothing to do with Jeroboam's hospitality. He had come to protest Jeroboam's new religion, and would not be bought.

gift." ⁸But the man of God said to the king, "If you give me half your kingdom, I will not go in with you; nor will I eat food or drink water in this place. ⁹For thus I was commanded by the word of the LORD: You shall not eat food, or drink water, or return by the way that you came." ¹⁰So he went another way, and did not return by the way that he had come to Bethel.

11 Now there lived an old prophet in Bethel. One of his sons came and told him all that the man of God had done that day in Bethel; the words also that he had spoken to the king, they told to their father. ¹²Their father said to them, "Which way did he go?" And his sons showed him the way that the man of God who came from Judah had gone. ¹³Then he said to his sons, "Saddle a donkey for me." So they saddled a donkey for him, and he mounted it. ¹⁴He went after the man of God, and found him sitting under an oak tree. He said to him, "Are you the man of God who came from Judah?" He answered, "I am." ¹⁵Then he said to him, "Come home with me and eat some food." ¹⁶But he said, "I cannot return with you, or go in with you; nor will I eat food or drink water with you in this place; ¹⁷for it was said to me by the word of the LORD: You shall not eat food or drink water there, or return by the way that you came." ¹⁸Then the otherᵉ said to him, "I also am a prophet as you are, and an angel spoke to me by the word of the LORD: Bring him back with you into your house so that he may eat food

and drink water." But he was deceiving him. ¹⁹Then the man of Godᵉ went back with him, and ate food and drank water in his house.

20 As they were sitting at the table, the word of the LORD came to the prophet who had brought him back; ²¹and he proclaimed to the man of God who came from Judah, "Thus says the LORD: Because you have disobeyed the word of the LORD, and have not kept the commandment that the LORD your God commanded you, ²²but have come back and have eaten food and drunk water in the place of which he said to you, 'Eat no food, and drink no water,' your body shall not come to your ancestral tomb." ²³After the man of Godᵉ had eaten food and had drunk, they saddled for him a donkey belonging to the prophet who had brought him back. ²⁴Then as he went away, a lion met him on the road and killed him. His body was thrown in the road, and the donkey stood beside it; the lion also stood beside the body. ²⁵People passed by and saw the body thrown in the road, with the lion standing by the body. And they came and told it in the town where the old prophet lived.

26 When the prophet who had brought him back from the way heard of it, he said, "It is the man of God who disobeyed the word of the LORD; therefore the LORD has given him to the lion, which has torn him and killed him according to the word that the LORD spoke to him." ²⁷Then he said to his sons, "Saddle a donkey for me." So they saddled one, ²⁸and he went and found the body thrown in the road, with the donkey and the lion standing beside the body. The lion had not eaten the body or attacked the donkey. ²⁹The prophet took up the body of the man of God, laid it on the donkey, and brought it back to the city,ᶠ to mourn and to bury him. ³⁰He laid the body in his own grave; and they mourned over him, saying, "Alas, my brother!" ³¹After he had buried him, he said to his sons, "When I die, bury me in the grave in which the man of God is buried; lay my bones beside his bones. ³²For the saying that he proclaimed by the word of the LORD against the altar in Bethel, and against all the houses of the high places that are in the cities of Samaria, shall surely come to pass."

33 Even after this event Jeroboam did not turn from his evil way, but made priests for the high places again from among all the people; any who wanted to be priests he consecrated for the high places. ³⁴This matter became sin to the house of Jeroboam, so as to cut it off and to destroy it from the face of the earth.

Judgment on the House of Jeroboam

14 At that time Abijah son of Jeroboam fell sick. ²Jeroboam said to his wife, "Go, disguise yourself, so that it will not be known that

ᵉ Heb *he*   ᶠ Gk: Heb *he came to the town of the old prophet*

The Nation Splits Apart
A rebellion leads to civil war

CHAPTER 12 OF 1 KINGS MARKS a decisive turning point in the nation of Israel. For 120 years Saul, David, and Solomon had consolidated power, expanded borders, and built a strong government. But immediately after Solomon's death everything began to unravel. Simmering hostility in the North boiled over at last, and the northern tribes seceded to form their own nation.

> There was war ... continually.
> 14.30

Two Nations out of One

Ten tribes joined together under Jeroboam to form a nation in the North called Israel. Only two tribes, Judah and Benjamin, remained loyal to Solomon's heir in Jerusalem. These southerners took on the name Judah and made Jerusalem, home of the temple, their capital. From that time forward, the united nation of Israel ceased to exist.

The northern rebellion brought a terrible civil war to Israel, a war that dragged on for 50 years. Despite a peace treaty, war kept breaking out.

The book of Kings records the histories of both nations. Action shifts back and forth between Israel in the North and Judah in the South. The effect resembles an account of America during Civil War years, first describing events in the North and then shifting to what was simultaneously taking place in the South.

This book does not attempt to give a full history of both nations. Rather, it focuses on their kings and queens. As guardian of the covenant with God, the king or queen came to symbolize the spiritual health of the nation. As that monarch went, so went the nation. Each ruler gets a capsule summary and usually a one-sentence rating. He or she either performed like David, who "had done what was right in the sight of the LORD," or like the northern king Jeroboam, who "caused Israel to commit" sin.

The North: A Perpetual Slide Downward

Ironically, the northern tribes seceded as part of a reform movement, to correct some of the excesses of Solomon's reign. But starting with the first king, Jeroboam, no king of Israel did what was right in God's eyes. The books of 1, 2 Kings condemn all the northern kings.

Northern kings brought idolatry into their religion and corruption into their politics. They adopted all the oppressive ways that had sparked the original rebellion: harsh taxation, repression of prophets, abuse of power. Of 19 northern kings, eight either were murdered or committed suicide. One king, Zimri, lasted only seven days.

The worst rulers, King Ahab and Queen Jezebel, introduced the terrible practice of Baal worship (see "Why All the Fuss about Idols?" page 405). Israel hit its spiritual low point, and Ahab replaced Jeroboam as a symbol of evil. Kings to follow were called "Ahabs" much as a ruthless tyrant today is compared with Hitler. Israel's future destruction became certain; after Ahab and Jezebel, the nation was merely marking time.

The South: A Surprising Twist

While Israel—which began as a reform movement—slid toward disaster, the two tribes in the South, Judah, proved more faithful to God. They produced at least a handful of good kings. Even when other nations took advantage of Judah's weakness and plundered Jerusalem, the nation still held together.

Idolatry plagued Judah also, but not to the same extent as in the North. The temple remained a powerful symbol of worship of the true God. And every few generations a sincere, committed king arose to sweep away his predecessors' dangerous practices. The authors pointedly note that these good kings usually outlived the bad rulers.

Within 250 years the Northern Kingdom, Israel, was obliterated. Judah survived another 135 years before likewise falling to foreign invaders. In a sense, their fate was sealed from the time of the original secession. The prophet Isaiah would remember the schism as the worst disaster that had befallen his people (Isaiah 7.17).

Life Questions: Have you seen rebellion lead to "civil war" in families? Churches? Schools? When you don't like what the leaders are doing, are there alternatives to outright rebellion?

you are the wife of Jeroboam, and go to Shiloh; for the prophet Ahijah is there, who said of me that I should be king over this people. ³Take with you ten loaves, some cakes, and a jar of honey, and go to him; he will tell you what shall happen to the child."

4 Jeroboam's wife did so; she set out and went to Shiloh, and came to the house of Ahijah. Now Ahijah could not see, for his eyes were dim because of his age. ⁵But the LORD said to Ahijah, "The wife of Jeroboam is coming to inquire of you concerning her son; for he is sick. Thus and thus you shall say to her."

When she came, she pretended to be another woman. ⁶But when Ahijah heard the sound of her feet, as she came in at the door, he said, "Come in, wife of Jeroboam; why do you pretend to be another? For I am charged with heavy tidings for you. ⁷Go, tell Jeroboam, 'Thus says the LORD, the God of Israel: Because I exalted you from among the people, made you leader over my people Israel, ⁸and tore the kingdom away from the house of David to give it to you; yet you have not been like my servant David, who kept my commandments and followed me with all his heart, doing only that which was right in my sight, ⁹but you have done evil above all those who were before you and have gone and made for yourself other gods, and cast images, provoking me to anger, and have thrust me behind your back; ¹⁰therefore, I will bring evil upon the house of Jeroboam. I will cut off from Jeroboam every male, both bond and free in Israel, and will consume the house of Jeroboam, just as one burns up dung until it is all gone. ¹¹Anyone belonging to Jeroboam who dies in the city, the dogs shall eat; and anyone who dies in the open country, the birds of the air shall eat; for the LORD has spoken.' ¹²Therefore set out, go to your house. When your feet enter the city, the child shall die. ¹³All Israel shall mourn for him and bury him; for he alone of Jeroboam's family shall come to the grave, because in him there is found something pleasing to the LORD, the God of Israel, in the house of Jeroboam. ¹⁴Moreover the LORD will raise up for himself a king over Israel, who shall cut off the house of Jeroboam today, even right now!ᵍ

15 "The LORD will strike Israel, as a reed is shaken in the water; he will root up Israel out of this good land that he gave to their ancestors, and scatter them beyond the Euphrates, because they have made their sacred poles,ʰ provoking the LORD to anger. ¹⁶He will give Israel up because of the sins of Jeroboam, which he sinned and which he caused Israel to commit."

17 Then Jeroboam's wife got up and went away, and she came to Tirzah. As she came to the threshold of the house, the child died. ¹⁸All Israel buried him and mourned for him, according to the word of the LORD, which he spoke by his servant the prophet Ahijah.

Death of Jeroboam

19 Now the rest of the acts of Jeroboam, how he warred and how he reigned, are written in the Book of the Annals of the Kings of Israel. ²⁰The time that Jeroboam reigned was twenty-two years; then he slept with his ancestors, and his son Nadab succeeded him.

Rehoboam Reigns over Judah

21 Now Rehoboam son of Solomon reigned in Judah. Rehoboam was forty-one years old when he began to reign, and he reigned seventeen years in Jerusalem, the city that the LORD had chosen out of all the tribes of Israel, to put his name there. His mother's name was Naamah the Ammonite. ²²Judah did what was evil in the sight of the LORD; they provoked him to jealousy with their sins that they committed, more than all that their ancestors had done. ²³For they also built for themselves high places, pillars, and sacred polesʰ on every high hill and under every green tree;

14.23 Notorious Asherah Poles

Introduced in the reign of Rehoboam, Asherah poles became a regular feature of Judah's landscape for hundreds of years. They were dedicated to a mother-goddess and often erected alongside altars on the high places devoted to God. They came to represent Judah's slide into idolatry. When judging the failures of various kings, the authors often comment, "the high places were not taken away."

²⁴there were also male temple prostitutes in the land. They committed all the abominations of the nations that the LORD drove out before the people of Israel.

25 In the fifth year of King Rehoboam, King Shishak of Egypt came up against Jerusalem; ²⁶he took away the treasures of the house of the LORD and the treasures of the king's house; he took everything. He also took away all the shields of gold that Solomon had made; ²⁷so King Rehoboam made shields of bronze instead, and committed them to the hands of the officers of the guard, who kept the door of the king's house. ²⁸As often as the king went into the house of the LORD, the guard carried them and brought them back to the guardroom.

29 Now the rest of the acts of Rehoboam, and all that he did, are they not written in the Book of the Annals of the Kings of Judah? ³⁰There was war between Rehoboam and Jeroboam continually.

ᵍ Meaning of Heb uncertain   ʰ Heb Asherim

³¹Rehoboam slept with his ancestors and was buried with his ancestors in the city of David. His mother's name was Naamah the Ammonite. His son Abijam succeeded him.

Abijam Reigns over Judah: Idolatry and War

15 Now in the eighteenth year of King Jeroboam son of Nebat, Abijam began to reign over Judah. ²He reigned for three years in Jerusalem. His mother's name was Maacah daughter of Abishalom. ³He committed all the sins that his father did before him; his heart was not true to the LORD his God, like the heart of his father David. ⁴Nevertheless for David's sake the LORD his God gave him a lamp in Jerusalem, setting up his son after him, and establishing Jerusalem; ⁵because David did what was right in the sight of the LORD, and did not turn aside from anything that he commanded him all the days of his life, except in the matter of Uriah the Hittite. ⁶The war begun between Rehoboam and Jeroboam continued all the days of his life. ⁷The rest of the acts of Abijam, and all that he did, are they not written in the Book of the Annals of the Kings of Judah? There was war between Abijam and Jeroboam. ⁸Abijam slept with his ancestors, and they buried him in the city of David. Then his son Asa succeeded him.

Asa Reigns over Judah

9 In the twentieth year of King Jeroboam of Israel, Asa began to reign over Judah; ¹⁰he reigned forty-one years in Jerusalem. His mother's name was Maacah daughter of Abishalom. ¹¹Asa did what was right in the sight of the LORD, as his father David had done. ¹²He put away the male temple prostitutes out of the land, and removed all the idols that his ancestors had made. ¹³He also removed his mother Maacah from being queen mother, because she had made an abominable image for Asherah; Asa cut down her image and burned it at the Wadi Kidron. ¹⁴But the high places were not taken away. Nevertheless the heart of Asa was true to the LORD all his days. ¹⁵He brought into the house of the LORD the votive gifts of his father and his own votive gifts— silver, gold, and utensils.

Alliance with Aram against Israel

16 There was war between Asa and King Baasha of Israel all their days. ¹⁷King Baasha of Israel went up against Judah, and built Ramah, to prevent anyone from going out or coming in to King Asa of Judah. ¹⁸Then Asa took all the silver and the gold that were left in the treasures of the house of the LORD and the treasures of the king's house, and gave them into the hands of his servants. King Asa sent them to King Ben-hadad son of Tabrimmon son of Hezion of Aram, who resided in Damascus, saying, ¹⁹"Let there be an alliance between me and you, like that between my father and your father: I am sending you a present of silver and gold; go, break your alliance with King Baasha of Israel, so that he may withdraw from me." ²⁰Ben-hadad listened to King Asa, and sent the commanders of his armies against the cities of Israel. He conquered Ijon, Dan, Abel-beth-maacah, and all Chinneroth, with all the land of Naphtali. ²¹When Baasha heard of it, he stopped building Ramah and lived in Tirzah. ²²Then King Asa made a proclamation to all Judah, none was exempt: they carried away the stones of Ramah and its timber, with which Baasha had been building; with them King Asa built Geba of Benjamin and Mizpah. ²³Now the rest of all the acts of Asa, all his power, all that he did, and the cities that he built, are they not written in the Book of the Annals of the Kings of Judah? But in his old age he was diseased in his feet. ²⁴Then Asa slept with his ancestors, and was buried with his ancestors in the city of his father David; his son Jehoshaphat succeeded him.

Nadab Reigns over Israel

25 Nadab son of Jeroboam began to reign over Israel in the second year of King Asa of Judah; he reigned over Israel two years. ²⁶He did what was evil in the sight of the LORD, walking in the way of his ancestor and in the sin that he caused Israel to commit.

27 Baasha son of Ahijah, of the house of Issachar, conspired against him; and Baasha struck him down at Gibbethon, which belonged to the Philistines; for Nadab and all Israel were laying siege to Gibbethon. ²⁸So Baasha killed Nadab*i* in the third year of King Asa of Judah, and succeeded him. ²⁹As soon as he was king, he killed all the house of Jeroboam; he left to the house of Jeroboam not one that breathed, until he had destroyed it, according to the word of the LORD that he spoke by his servant Ahijah the Shilonite— ³⁰because of the sins of Jeroboam that he committed and that he caused Israel to commit, and because of the anger to which he provoked the LORD, the God of Israel.

31 Now the rest of the acts of Nadab, and all that he did, are they not written in the Book of the Annals of the Kings of Israel? ³²There was war between Asa and King Baasha of Israel all their days.

Second Dynasty: Baasha Reigns over Israel

33 In the third year of King Asa of Judah, Baasha son of Ahijah began to reign over all Israel at Tirzah; he reigned twenty-four years. ³⁴He did what was evil in the sight of the LORD, walking in

i Heb *him*

the way of Jeroboam and in the sin that he caused Israel to commit.

16 The word of the LORD came to Jehu son of Hanani against Baasha, saying, 2"Since I exalted you out of the dust and made you leader over my people Israel, and you have walked in the way of Jeroboam, and have caused my people Israel to sin, provoking me to anger with their sins, 3therefore, I will consume Baasha and his house, and I will make your house like the house of Jeroboam son of Nebat. 4Anyone belonging to Baasha who dies in the city the dogs shall eat; and anyone of his who dies in the field the birds of the air shall eat."

5 Now the rest of the acts of Baasha, what he did, and his power, are they not written in the Book of the Annals of the Kings of Israel? 6Baasha slept with his ancestors, and was buried at Tirzah; and his son Elah succeeded him. 7Moreover the word of the LORD came by the prophet Jehu son of Hanani against Baasha and his house, both because of all the evil that he did in the sight of the LORD, provoking him to anger with the work of his hands, in being like the house of Jeroboam, and also because he destroyed it.

Elah Reigns over Israel

8 In the twenty-sixth year of King Asa of Judah, Elah son of Baasha began to reign over Israel in Tirzah; he reigned two years. 9But his servant Zimri, commander of half his chariots, conspired against him. When he was at Tirzah, drinking himself drunk in the house of Arza, who was in charge of the palace at Tirzah, 10Zimri came in and struck him down and killed him, in the twenty-seventh year of King Asa of Judah, and succeeded him.

11 When he began to reign, as soon as he had seated himself on his throne, he killed all the house of Baasha; he did not leave him a single male of his kindred or his friends. 12Thus Zimri destroyed all the house of Baasha, according to the word of the LORD, which he spoke against Baasha by the prophet Jehu— 13because of all the sins of Baasha and the sins of his son Elah that they committed, and that they caused Israel to commit, provoking the LORD God of Israel to anger with their idols. 14Now the rest of the acts of Elah, and all that he did, are they not written in the Book of the Annals of the Kings of Israel?

Third Dynasty: Zimri Reigns over Israel

15 In the twenty-seventh year of King Asa of Judah, Zimri reigned seven days in Tirzah. Now the troops were encamped against Gibbethon, which belonged to the Philistines, 16and the troops who were encamped heard it said, "Zimri has conspired, and he has killed the king"; therefore all Israel made Omri, the commander of the army, king over Israel that day in the camp. 17So Omri went up from Gibbethon, and all Israel with

him, and they besieged Tirzah. 18When Zimri saw that the city was taken, he went into the citadel of the king's house; he burned down the king's house over himself with fire, and died— 19because of the sins that he committed, doing evil in the sight of the LORD, walking in the way of Jeroboam, and for the sin that he committed, causing Israel to sin. 20Now the rest of the acts of Zimri, and the conspiracy that he made, are they not written in the Book of the Annals of the Kings of Israel?

Fourth Dynasty: Omri Reigns over Israel

21 Then the people of Israel were divided into two parts; half of the people followed Tibni son of Ginath, to make him king, and half followed

16.21–28 A Strong, Weak King

King Omri gets a grand total of eight verses in 1 Kings, even though secular historians regard him as one of Israel's most powerful kings. After his firm rule, Israel was called Omriland in Assyrian records. He built the capital city of Samaria in a location that guarded all routes north and south. Yet he also started the religious heresies that led to his nation's extinction. Politically shrewd, he married off his son to a neighboring king's daughter (Jezebel). The books of 1, 2 Kings, however, are concerned with the rulers' spiritual health, and Omri scores very poorly.

Omri. 22But the people who followed Omri overcame the people who followed Tibni son of Ginath; so Tibni died, and Omri became king. 23In the thirty-first year of King Asa of Judah, Omri began to reign over Israel; he reigned for twelve years, six of them in Tirzah.

Samaria the New Capital

24 He bought the hill of Samaria from Shemer for two talents of silver; he fortified the hill, and called the city that he built, Samaria, after the name of Shemer, the owner of the hill.

25 Omri did what was evil in the sight of the LORD; he did more evil than all who were before him. 26For he walked in all the way of Jeroboam son of Nebat, and in the sins that he caused Israel to commit, provoking the LORD, the God of Israel, to anger by their idols. 27Now the rest of the acts of Omri that he did, and the power that he showed, are they not written in the Book of the Annals of the Kings of Israel? 28Omri slept with his ancestors, and was buried in Samaria; his son Ahab succeeded him.

Ahab Reigns over Israel

29 In the thirty-eighth year of King Asa of Judah, Ahab son of Omri began to reign over

Israel; Ahab son of Omri reigned over Israel in Samaria twenty-two years. ³⁰Ahab son of Omri did evil in the sight of the LORD more than all who were before him.

Ahab Marries Jezebel and Worships Baal

31 And as if it had been a light thing for him to walk in the sins of Jeroboam son of Nebat, he took as his wife Jezebel daughter of King Ethbaal of the Sidonians, and went and served Baal, and worshiped him. ³²He erected an altar for Baal in the house of Baal, which he built in Samaria. ³³Ahab also made a sacred pole.ʲ Ahab did more to provoke the anger of the LORD, the God of Israel, than had all the kings of Israel who were before him. ³⁴In his days Hiel of Bethel built Jericho; he laid its foundation at the cost of Abiram his firstborn, and set up its gates at the cost of his youngest son Segub, according to the word of the LORD, which he spoke by Joshua son of Nun.

16.34 A Curse from Joshua

Joshua 6.26 records the solemn pronouncement of what would happen to anyone who attempted to rebuild Jericho. The curse had tragic consequences for Hiel.

Elijah Predicts a Drought

17 Now Elijah the Tishbite, of Tishbeᵏ in Gilead, said to Ahab, "As the LORD the God of Israel lives, before whom I stand, there shall be neither dew nor rain these years, except by my word." ²The word of the LORD came to him, saying, ³"Go from here and turn eastward, and hide yourself by the Wadi Cherith, which is east of the Jordan. ⁴You shall drink from the wadi, and I have commanded the ravens to feed you there." ⁵So he went and did according to the word of the LORD; he went and lived by the Wadi Cherith, which is east of the Jordan. ⁶The ravens brought him bread and meat in the morning, and bread and meat in the evening; and he drank from the wadi. ⁷But after a while the wadi dried up, because there was no rain in the land.

The Widow of Zarephath

8 Then the word of the LORD came to him, saying, ⁹"Go now to Zarephath, which belongs to Sidon, and live there; for I have commanded a widow there to feed you." ¹⁰So he set out and went to Zarephath. When he came to the gate of the town, a widow was there gathering sticks; he called to her and said, "Bring me a little water in a vessel, so that I may drink." ¹¹As she was going to bring it, he called to her and said, "Bring me a morsel of bread in your hand." ¹²But she said, "As the LORD your God lives, I have nothing baked, only a handful of meal in a jar, and a little oil in a jug; I am now gathering a couple of sticks, so that I may go home and prepare it for myself and my son, that we may eat it, and die." ¹³Elijah said to her, "Do not be afraid; go and do as you have said; but first make me a little cake of it and bring it to me, and afterwards make something for yourself and your son. ¹⁴For thus says the LORD the God of Israel: The jar of meal will not be emptied and the jug of oil will not fail until the day that the LORD sends rain on the earth." ¹⁵She went and did as Elijah said, so that she as well as he and her household ate for many days. ¹⁶The jar of meal was not emptied, neither did the jug of oil fail, according to the word of the LORD that he spoke by Elijah.

ʲ Heb *Asherah*   ᵏ Gk: Heb *of the settlers*

ELIJAH *Miracle Worker*

WHEN WE SPEAK OF MIRACLES in the Bible, three names stand out: Moses, Elijah and Jesus. Those three, in fact, are the ones who met on the Mount of Transfiguration to talk about Jesus' departure from earth (Luke 9.30–31). In their lifetimes, all three saw the power—and also the limitations—of miracles.

First and Second Kings record eight amazing miracles God worked through Elijah. Some, like his contest with the prophets of Baal (1 Kings 18.16–39), were performed before a large audience. Others, like his restoration of the widow's son (17.17–24), were more private. Ironically, Elijah's experience shows the limits of miracles in encouraging faith. Right after his greatest miracle—the contest with Baal—Elijah grew depressed and afraid. It was then that God revealed his presence not through demonstrations of power, but in "a sound of sheer silence" (19.12).

The prophet Malachi predicted that a visit by Elijah would precede the Messiah's arrival—a prediction Jesus said that John the Baptist fulfilled (Matthew 17.9–13). All the Jews of Jesus' day—including Jesus—held Elijah in highest esteem. Even today during certain holidays Orthodox Jews leave a place at the table for Elijah, worker of wonders.

Life Questions: Have you ever witnessed a miracle? If so, how did it affect you?

Elijah Revives the Widow's Son

17 After this the son of the woman, the mistress of the house, became ill; his illness was so severe that there was no breath left in him. 18She

then said to Elijah, "What have you against me, O man of God? You have come to me to bring my sin to remembrance, and to cause the death of my son!" 19But he said to her, "Give me your son." He took him from her bosom, carried him up into the upper chamber where he was lodging, and laid him on his own bed. 20He cried out to the LORD, "O LORD my God, have you brought calamity even upon the widow with whom I am staying, by killing her son?" 21Then he stretched himself upon the child three times, and cried out to the LORD, "O LORD my God, let this child's life come into him again." 22The LORD listened to the voice of Elijah; the life of the child came into him again, and he revived. 23Elijah took the child, brought him down from the upper chamber into the house, and gave him to his mother; then Elijah said, "See, your son is alive." 24So the woman said to Elijah, "Now I know that you are a man of God, and that the word of the LORD in your mouth is truth."

Elijah's Message to Ahab

18 After many days the word of the LORD came to Elijah, in the third year of the drought,*l* saying, "Go, present yourself to Ahab; I will send rain on the earth." 2So Elijah went to present himself to Ahab. The famine was severe in Samaria. 3Ahab summoned Obadiah, who was in charge of the palace. (Now Obadiah revered the LORD greatly; 4when Jezebel was killing off the prophets of the LORD, Obadiah took a hundred prophets, hid them fifty to a cave, and provided them with bread and water.) 5Then Ahab said to Obadiah, "Go through the land to all the springs of water and to all the wadis; perhaps we may find grass to keep the horses and mules alive, and not

lose some of the animals." 6So they divided the land between them to pass through it; Ahab went in one direction by himself, and Obadiah went in another direction by himself.

7 As Obadiah was on the way, Elijah met him; Obadiah recognized him, fell on his face, and said, "Is it you, my lord Elijah?" 8He answered him, "It is I. Go, tell your lord that Elijah is here." 9And he said, "How have I sinned, that you would hand your servant over to Ahab, to kill me? 10As the LORD your God lives, there is no nation or kingdom to which my lord has not sent to seek you; and when they would say, 'He is not here,' he would require an oath of the kingdom or nation, that they had not found you. 11But now you say, 'Go, tell your lord that Elijah is here.' 12As soon as I have gone from you, the spirit of the LORD will carry you I know not where; so, when I come and tell Ahab and he cannot find you, he will kill me, although I your servant have revered the LORD from my youth. 13Has it not been told my lord what I did when Jezebel killed the prophets of the LORD, how I hid a hundred of the LORD's prophets fifty to a cave, and provided them with bread and water? 14Yet now you say, 'Go, tell your lord that Elijah is here'; he will surely kill me." 15Elijah said, "As the LORD of hosts lives, before whom I stand, I will surely show myself to him today." 16So Obadiah went to meet Ahab, and told him; and Ahab went to meet Elijah.

17 When Ahab saw Elijah, Ahab said to him, "Is it you, you troubler of Israel?" 18He answered, "I have not troubled Israel; but you have, and your father's house, because you have forsaken the commandments of the LORD and followed the Baals. 19Now therefore have all Israel assemble for me at Mount Carmel, with the four hundred fifty prophets of Baal and the four hundred prophets of Asherah, who eat at Jezebel's table."

Elijah's Triumph over the Priests of Baal

20 So Ahab sent to all the Israelites, and assembled the prophets at Mount Carmel. 21Elijah then came near to all the people, and said, "How long will you go limping with two different opinions? If the LORD is God, follow him; but if Baal, then follow him." The people did not answer him a word. 22Then Elijah said to the people, "I, even I only, am left a prophet of the LORD; but Baal's prophets number four hundred fifty. 23Let two bulls be given to us; let them choose one bull for themselves, cut it in pieces, and lay it on the wood, but put no fire to it; I will prepare the other bull and lay it on the wood, but put no fire to it. 24Then you call on the name of your god and I will call on the name of the LORD; the god who answers by fire is indeed God." All the people answered, "Well spoken!" 25Then Elijah said to the prophets of Baal, "Choose for yourselves one

l Heb lacks *of the drought*

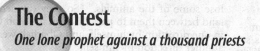

The Contest
One lone prophet against a thousand priests

FEW SCENES IN THE BIBLE are more dramatic than this one. The forces of evil and the forces of good collided head on. In books like J.R.R. Tolkien's *Lord of the Rings* or television shows such as the "Star Trek" series, mythmakers dream up cosmic confrontations. But the incident in 1 Kings 18 is no myth. On that day, a bedraggled desert prophet single-handedly took on a king and nearly a thousand powerful priests.

Elijah had made a grand entrance three years before. Like a wild, startling apparition, he came out of nowhere to stalk the terraced streets of affluent Samaria. Clothed in black camel's hair, he made a striking contrast to the priests of Baal in their white linen robes and high-pointed bonnets. He had a simple, unpopular message of doom: "There shall be neither dew nor rain these years, except by my word" (17.1). It was a direct affront to followers of Baal, who believed their god could control the weather.

> Elijah then came near to all the people, and said, "How long will you go limping with two different opinions? If the LORD is God, follow him; but if Baal, then follow him." 18.21

Having delivered his message, Elijah disappeared. For three years he was the most wanted fugitive in Israel, for he alone had the power to bring rain. And then, in the scene reported in chapter 18, the prophet Elijah returned to Samaria.

Elijah's Contest

Israel was at a crossroads. Other kings had introduced idolatry into Israelite religion, but King Ahab and the notorious Queen Jezebel were going much further. They wanted to wipe out all worship of the true God.

The prophet Elijah proved a worthy adversary. His very name meant "The LORD is my God." He proposed a showdown, the ultimate contest to prove who was the true God. First Kings presents the scene in full color, complete with the priests' desperate contortions and Elijah's mocking, taunting commentary. In the final analysis, it was no contest at all. God unleashed a spectacular display of raw power.

Elijah was one of the most colorful of all Israel's prophets. He suffered from bouts of depression and self-doubt, but during times of crisis he showed amazing courage. The Mount Carmel showdown was merely one sign of the high drama going on. Elijah lived during one of the greatest outbreaks of miracles in biblical history. God was sounding a final warning to Israel.

Israel's Real Heroes

The author of the book of 1 Kings starts out by recording the history of God's anointed leaders. But as the rulers and then priests grow more and more corrupt, this book trains the spotlight on prophets like Elijah. They emerge as Israel's real heroes.

The prophets were not, to Israel, merely preachers or poets. They were channels of God's power, through word and deed. They served on the front line of the struggle between good and evil. Over time, the prophets' significance overtook and even surpassed that of kings. Kings came and went, but the message of the prophets endured.

Voices in the Desert

Whether they served in the government or wandered in occasionally from the desert, the true prophets remained accountable only to God. They decried other, "false," prophets, employed by the king, who generally told the king whatever he wished to hear.

Not all prophets left written messages (Elijah and Elisha, for example, did not). But those prophetic writings that did survive form 17 books of the Old Testament, most of them stemming from the time period described in 1 and 2 Kings.

The prophets told of a God who worked in history to accomplish his will in the world. Sometimes he seemed silent. Sometimes he worked slowly and mysteriously. But occasionally God did step in directly, spectacularly, with a display of power. And when he did, a prophet was usually right in the middle of things—like Elijah on Mount Carmel.

Life Questions: Who serves the role of "prophet" today?

bull and prepare it first, for you are many; then call on the name of your god, but put no fire to it." ²⁶So they took the bull that was given them, prepared it, and called on the name of Baal from morning until noon, crying, "O Baal, answer us!" But there was no voice, and no answer. They limped about the altar that they had made. ²⁷At noon Elijah mocked them, saying, "Cry aloud! Surely he is a god; either he is meditating, or he has wandered away, or he is on a journey, or perhaps he is asleep and must be awakened." ²⁸Then they cried aloud and, as was their custom, they cut themselves with swords and lances until the blood gushed out over them. ²⁹As midday passed, they raved on until the time of the offering of the oblation, but there was no voice, no answer, and no response.

30 Then Elijah said to all the people, "Come closer to me"; and all the people came closer to him. First he repaired the altar of the LORD that had been thrown down; ³¹Elijah took twelve stones, according to the number of the tribes of the sons of Jacob, to whom the word of the LORD came, saying, "Israel shall be your name"; ³²with the stones he built an altar in the name of the LORD. Then he made a trench around the altar, large enough to contain two measures of seed. ³³Next he put the wood in order, cut the bull in pieces, and laid it on the wood. He said, "Fill four jars with water and pour it on the burnt offering

18.33 Elijah Rubs It In

Elijah designed the contest to expose Baal, the alleged god of weather, who was often depicted carrying a thunderbolt. Elijah doused his own altar with 12 large jars of water—a precious commodity after three years of drought—before calling on God. Fire from heaven burned up the sacrifice, the wood, the stones, the soil, and even licked up the water in the trench.

and on the wood." ³⁴Then he said, "Do it a second time"; and they did it a second time. Again he said, "Do it a third time"; and they did it a third time, ³⁵so that the water ran all around the altar, and filled the trench also with water.

36 At the time of the offering of the oblation, the prophet Elijah came near and said, "O LORD, God of Abraham, Isaac, and Israel, let it be known this day that you are God in Israel, that I am your servant, and that I have done all these things at your bidding. ³⁷Answer me, O LORD, answer me, so that this people may know that you, O LORD, are God, and that you have turned their hearts back." ³⁸Then the fire of the LORD fell and consumed the burnt offering, the wood, the stones, and the dust, and even licked up the water

that was in the trench. ³⁹When all the people saw it, they fell on their faces and said, "The LORD indeed is God; the LORD indeed is God." ⁴⁰Elijah said to them, "Seize the prophets of Baal; do not let one of them escape." Then they seized them; and Elijah brought them down to the Wadi Kishon, and killed them there.

The Drought Ends

41 Elijah said to Ahab, "Go up, eat and drink; for there is a sound of rushing rain." ⁴²So Ahab went up to eat and to drink. Elijah went up to the top of Carmel; there he bowed himself down upon the earth and put his face between his knees. ⁴³He said to his servant, "Go up now, look toward the sea." He went up and looked, and said, "There is nothing." Then he said, "Go again seven times." ⁴⁴At the seventh time he said, "Look, a little cloud no bigger than a person's hand is rising out of the sea." Then he said, "Go say to Ahab, 'Harness your chariot and go down before the rain stops you.'" ⁴⁵In a little while the heavens grew black with clouds and wind; there was a heavy rain. Ahab rode off and went to Jezreel. ⁴⁶But the hand of the LORD was on Elijah; he girded up his loins and ran in front of Ahab to the entrance of Jezreel.

Elijah Flees from Jezebel

19 Ahab told Jezebel all that Elijah had done, and how he had killed all the prophets with the sword. ²Then Jezebel sent a messenger to Elijah, saying, "So may the gods do to me, and more also, if I do not make your life like the life of one of them by this time tomorrow." ³Then he was afraid; he got up and fled for his life, and came to Beer-sheba, which belongs to Judah; he left his servant there.

19.3 Wicked Queen Jezebel

Queen Jezebel's reputation was such that Elijah ran from her in fear even after God had triumphantly displayed his power on Mount Carmel. The Roman historian Josephus records her family history. Her father, who had served as high priest in a pagan temple in Tyre, murdered the king and ruled there for 32 years. His reign was characterized by murderous idolatries and a reckless contempt for human rights.

Jezebel followed in her father's footsteps. Married to Ahab as part of a political alliance, she installed 950 prophets of Baal and ordered the wholesale slaughter of any prophets of God who opposed her. Ahab fell under her sway. Alone, he could be brave, chivalrous, and even conscientious. But his weakness and Jezebel's influence led him to become the most wicked king of Israel.

4 But he himself went a day's journey into the wilderness, and came and sat down under a solitary broom tree. He asked that he might die: "It is enough; now, O LORD, take away my life, for I am no better than my ancestors." 5Then he lay down under the broom tree and fell asleep. Suddenly an angel touched him and said to him, "Get up and eat." 6He looked, and there at his head was a cake baked on hot stones, and a jar of water. He ate and drank, and lay down again. 7The angel of the LORD came a second time, touched him, and said, "Get up and eat, otherwise the journey will be too much for you." 8He got up, and ate and drank; then he went in the strength of that food forty days and forty nights to Horeb the mount of God. 9At that place he came to a cave, and spent the night there.

Then the word of the LORD came to him, saying, "What are you doing here, Elijah?" 10He answered, "I have been very zealous for the LORD, the God of hosts; for the Israelites have forsaken your covenant, thrown down your altars, and killed your prophets with the sword. I alone am left, and they are seeking my life, to take it away."

Elijah Meets God at Horeb

11 He said, "Go out and stand on the mountain before the LORD, for the LORD is about to pass by." Now there was a great wind, so strong that it was splitting mountains and breaking rocks in pieces before the LORD, but the LORD was not in the wind; and after the wind an earthquake, but the LORD was not in the earthquake; 12and after the earthquake a fire, but the LORD was not in the fire; and after the fire a sound of sheer silence. 13When Elijah heard it, he wrapped his face in his mantle and went out and stood at the entrance of the cave. Then there came a voice to him that said, "What are you doing here, Elijah?" 14He answered, "I have been very zealous for the LORD, the God of hosts; for the Israelites have forsaken your covenant, thrown down your altars, and killed your prophets with the sword. I alone am left, and they are seeking my life, to take it away." 15Then the LORD said to him, "Go, return on your way to the wilderness of Damascus; when you arrive, you shall anoint Hazael as king over Aram. 16Also you shall anoint Jehu son of Nimshi as king over Israel; and you shall anoint Elisha son of Shaphat of Abel-meholah as prophet in your place. 17Whoever escapes from the sword of Hazael, Jehu shall kill; and whoever escapes from the sword of Jehu, Elisha shall kill. 18Yet I will leave seven thousand in Israel, all the knees that have not bowed to Baal, and every mouth that has not kissed him."

Elisha Becomes Elijah's Disciple

19 So he set out from there, and found Elisha son of Shaphat, who was plowing. There were twelve yoke of oxen ahead of him, and he was with the twelfth. Elijah passed by him and threw his mantle over him. 20He left the oxen, ran after Elijah, and said, "Let me kiss my father and my mother, and then I will follow you." Then Elijah*m* said to him, "Go back again; for what have I done to you?" 21He returned from following him, took the yoke of oxen, and slaughtered them; using the equipment from the oxen, he boiled their flesh, and gave it to the people, and they ate. Then he set out and followed Elijah, and became his servant.

Ahab's Wars with the Arameans

20 King Ben-hadad of Aram gathered all his army together; thirty-two kings were with him, along with horses and chariots. He marched against Samaria, laid siege to it, and attacked it. 2Then he sent messengers into the city to King Ahab of Israel, and said to him: "Thus says Ben-hadad: 3Your silver and gold are mine; your fairest wives and children also are mine." 4The king of Israel answered, "As you say, my lord, O king, I am yours, and all that I have." 5The messengers came again and said: "Thus says Ben-hadad: I sent to you, saying, 'Deliver to me your silver and gold, your wives and children'; 6nevertheless I will send my servants to you tomorrow about this time, and they shall search your house and the houses of your servants, and lay hands on whatever pleases them,*n* and take it away."

7 Then the king of Israel called all the elders of the land, and said, "Look now! See how this man is seeking trouble; for he sent to me for my wives, my children, my silver, and my gold; and I did not refuse him." 8Then all the elders and all the people said to him, "Do not listen or consent." 9So he said to the messengers of Ben-hadad, "Tell my lord the king: All that you first demanded of your servant I will do; but this thing I cannot do." The messengers left and brought him word again. 10Ben-hadad sent to him and said, "The gods do so to me, and more also, if the dust of Samaria will provide a handful for each of the people who follow me." 11The king of Israel answered, "Tell him: One who puts on armor should not brag like one who takes it off." 12When Ben-hadad heard this message—now he had been drinking with the kings in the booths—he said to his men, "Take your positions!" And they took their positions against the city.

Prophetic Opposition to Ahab

13 Then a certain prophet came up to King Ahab of Israel and said, "Thus says the LORD, Have you seen all this great multitude? Look, I will give it into your hand today; and you shall know that I am the LORD." 14Ahab said, "By

m Heb *he*   *n* Gk Syr Vg: Heb *you*

whom?" He said, "Thus says the LORD, By the young men who serve the district governors." Then he said, "Who shall begin the battle?" He answered, "You." [15]Then he mustered the young men who served the district governors, two hundred thirty-two; after them he mustered all the people of Israel, seven thousand.

16 They went out at noon, while Ben-hadad was drinking himself drunk in the booths, he and the thirty-two kings allied with him. [17]The young men who served the district governors went out first. Ben-hadad had sent out scouts,[o] and they reported to him, "Men have come out from Samaria." [18]He said, "If they have come out for peace, take them alive; if they have come out for war, take them alive."

19 But these had already come out of the city: the young men who served the district governors, and the army that followed them. [20]Each killed his man; the Arameans fled and Israel pursued them, but King Ben-hadad of Aram escaped on a horse with the cavalry. [21]The king of Israel went out, attacked the horses and chariots, and defeated the Arameans with a great slaughter.

22 Then the prophet approached the king of Israel and said to him, "Come, strengthen yourself, and consider well what you have to do; for in the spring the king of Aram will come up against you."

The Arameans Are Defeated

23 The servants of the king of Aram said to him, "Their gods are gods of the hills, and so they were stronger than we; but let us fight against them in the plain, and surely we shall be stronger than they. [24]Also do this: remove the kings, each from his post, and put commanders in place of them; [25]and muster an army like the army that you have lost, horse for horse, and chariot for chariot; then we will fight against them in the plain, and surely we shall be stronger than they." He heeded their voice, and did so.

26 In the spring Ben-hadad mustered the Arameans and went up to Aphek to fight against Israel. [27]After the Israelites had been mustered and provisioned, they went out to engage them; the people of Israel encamped opposite them like two little flocks of goats, while the Arameans filled the country. [28]A man of God approached and said to the king of Israel, "Thus says the LORD: Because the Arameans have said, 'The LORD is a god of the hills but he is not a god of the valleys,' therefore I will give all this great multitude into your hand, and you shall know that I am the LORD." [29]They encamped opposite one another seven days. Then on the seventh day the battle began; the Israelites killed one hundred thousand Aramean foot soldiers in one day. [30]The rest fled into the city of Aphek; and the wall fell on twenty-seven thousand men that were left.

Ben-hadad also fled, and entered the city to hide. [31]His servants said to him, "Look, we have heard that the kings of the house of Israel are merciful kings; let us put sackcloth around our waists and ropes on our heads, and go out to the king of Israel; perhaps he will spare your life." [32]So they tied sackcloth around their waists, put ropes on their heads, went to the king of Israel, and said, "Your servant Ben-hadad says, 'Please let me live.'" And he said, "Is he still alive? He is my brother." [33]Now the men were watching for an omen; they quickly took it up from him and said, "Yes, Ben-hadad is your brother." Then he said, "Go and bring him." So Ben-hadad came out to him; and he had him come up into the chariot. [34]Ben-hadad[p] said to him, "I will restore the towns that my father took from your father; and you may establish bazaars for yourself in Damascus, as my father did in Samaria." The king of Israel responded,[q] "I will let you go on those terms." So he made a treaty with him and let him go.

A Prophet Condemns Ahab

35 At the command of the LORD a certain member of a company of prophets[r] said to another, "Strike me!" But the man refused to strike him. [36]Then he said to him, "Because you have not obeyed the voice of the LORD, as soon as you have left me, a lion will kill you." And when he had left him, a lion met him and killed him. [37]Then he found another man and said, "Strike me!" So the man hit him, striking and wounding him. [38]Then the prophet departed, and waited for the king along the road, disguising himself with a bandage over his eyes. [39]As the king passed by, he cried to the king and said, "Your servant went out into the thick of the battle; then a soldier turned and brought a man to me, and said, 'Guard this man; if he is missing, your life shall be given for his life, or else you shall pay a talent of silver.' [40]While your servant was busy here and there, he was gone." The king of Israel said to him, "So shall your judgment be; you yourself have decided it." [41]Then he quickly took the bandage away from his eyes. The king of Israel recognized him as one of the prophets. [42]Then he said to him, "Thus says the LORD, 'Because you have let the man go whom I had devoted to destruction, therefore your life shall be for his life, and your people for his people.'" [43]The king of Israel set out toward home, resentful and sullen, and came to Samaria.

Naboth's Vineyard

21 Later the following events took place: Naboth the Jezreelite had a vineyard in Jezreel,

[o] Heb lacks *scouts* [p] Heb *He* [q] Heb lacks *The king of Israel responded* [r] Heb *of the sons of the prophets*

beside the palace of King Ahab of Samaria. ²And Ahab said to Naboth, "Give me your vineyard, so that I may have it for a vegetable garden, because it is near my house; I will give you a better vineyard for it; or, if it seems good to you, I will give

21.1 A Stolen Vineyard

The incident of Naboth's vineyard shows the selective way in which Old Testament authors wove history together. In one sense, the theft was a minor incident in King Ahab's reign. Yet 1 Kings devotes more space to it than to the entire reigns of some kings. It showed the kings' abuse of power and disrespect for God's covenant. Every Israelite had the right to possess a piece of the promised land—not even a king could legally usurp that right. In fact, selling the land would break a law God gave Moses (Leviticus 25.23–31). Ahab's greed and Jezebel's intrigue led to murder and ultimately spelled doom for the kingdom.

you its value in money." ³But Naboth said to Ahab, "The LORD forbid that I should give you my ancestral inheritance." ⁴Ahab went home resentful and sullen because of what Naboth the Jezreelite had said to him; for he had said, "I will not give you my ancestral inheritance." He lay down on his bed, turned away his face, and would not eat.

5 His wife Jezebel came to him and said, "Why are you so depressed that you will not eat?" ⁶He said to her, "Because I spoke to Naboth the Jezreelite and said to him, 'Give me your vineyard for money; or else, if you prefer, I will give you another vineyard for it'; but he answered, 'I will not give you my vineyard.'" ⁷His wife Jezebel said to him, "Do you now govern Israel? Get up, eat some food, and be cheerful; I will give you the vineyard of Naboth the Jezreelite."

8 So she wrote letters in Ahab's name and sealed them with his seal; she sent the letters to the elders and the nobles who lived with Naboth in his city. ⁹She wrote in the letters, "Proclaim a fast, and seat Naboth at the head of the assembly; ¹⁰seat two scoundrels opposite him, and have them bring a charge against him, saying, 'You have cursed God and the king.' Then take him out, and stone him to death." ¹¹The men of his city, the elders and the nobles who lived in his city, did as Jezebel had sent word to them. Just as it was written in the letters that she had sent to them, ¹²they proclaimed a fast and seated Naboth at the head of the assembly. ¹³The two scoundrels came in and sat opposite him; and the scoundrels brought a charge against Naboth, in the presence of the people, saying, "Naboth cursed God and

the king." So they took him outside the city, and stoned him to death. ¹⁴Then they sent to Jezebel, saying, "Naboth has been stoned; he is dead."

15 As soon as Jezebel heard that Naboth had been stoned and was dead, Jezebel said to Ahab, "Go, take possession of the vineyard of Naboth the Jezreelite, which he refused to give you for money; for Naboth is not alive, but dead." ¹⁶As soon as Ahab heard that Naboth was dead, Ahab set out to go down to the vineyard of Naboth the Jezreelite, to take possession of it.

Elijah Pronounces God's Sentence

17 Then the word of the LORD came to Elijah the Tishbite, saying: ¹⁸Go down to meet King Ahab of Israel, who rules⁵ in Samaria; he is now in the vineyard of Naboth, where he has gone to take possession. ¹⁹You shall say to him, "Thus says the LORD: Have you killed, and also taken possession?" You shall say to him, "Thus says the LORD: In the place where dogs licked up the blood of Naboth, dogs will also lick up your blood."

20 Ahab said to Elijah, "Have you found me, O my enemy?" He answered, "I have found you. Because you have sold yourself to do what is evil in the sight of the LORD, ²¹I will bring disaster on you; I will consume you, and will cut off from Ahab every male, bond or free, in Israel; ²²and I will make your house like the house of Jeroboam son of Nebat, and like the house of Baasha son of Ahijah, because you have provoked me to anger and have caused Israel to sin. ²³Also concerning Jezebel the LORD said, 'The dogs shall eat Jezebel within the bounds of Jezreel.' ²⁴Anyone belonging to Ahab who dies in the city the dogs shall eat; and anyone of his who dies in the open country the birds of the air shall eat."

25 (Indeed, there was no one like Ahab, who sold himself to do what was evil in the sight of the LORD, urged on by his wife Jezebel. ²⁶He acted most abominably in going after idols, as the Amorites had done, whom the LORD drove out before the Israelites.)

27 When Ahab heard those words, he tore his clothes and put sackcloth over his bare flesh; he fasted, lay in the sackcloth, and went about dejectedly. ²⁸Then the word of the LORD came to Elijah the Tishbite: ²⁹"Have you seen how Ahab has humbled himself before me? Because he has humbled himself before me, I will not bring the disaster in his days; but in his son's days I will bring the disaster on his house."

Joint Campaign with Judah against Aram

22 For three years Aram and Israel continued without war. ²But in the third year King Jehoshaphat of Judah came down to the king of Israel. ³The king of Israel said to his servants, "Do you know that Ramoth-gilead belongs to us, yet

---

⁵ Heb *who is*

we are doing nothing to take it out of the hand of the king of Aram?" [4]He said to Jehoshaphat, "Will you go with me to battle at Ramoth-gilead?" Jehoshaphat replied to the king of Israel, "I am as you are; my people are your people, my horses are your horses."

22.4 Unholy Alliance

After years of warfare, peace was finally arranged between Israel and Judah. Ironically, it joined Israel's worst king, Ahab, with one of Judah's best, King Jehoshaphat. The unholy alliance with Ahab led to a fateful battle against Aram that almost cost Jehoshaphat his life (verses 29–33). Judah's king spurned later offers of cooperation (verse 49), but his son married King Ahab's daughter. This unwise marriage exposed Judah to the evil practices of the North and ultimately led to a royal bloodbath.

5 But Jehoshaphat also said to the king of Israel, "Inquire first for the word of the LORD." [6]Then the king of Israel gathered the prophets together, about four hundred of them, and said to them, "Shall I go to battle against Ramoth-gilead, or shall I refrain?" They said, "Go up; for the LORD will give it into the hand of the king." [7]But Jehoshaphat said, "Is there no other prophet of the LORD here of whom we may inquire?" [8]The king of Israel said to Jehoshaphat, "There is still one other by whom we may inquire of the LORD, Micaiah son of Imlah; but I hate him, for he never

t Heb he

prophesies anything favorable about me, but only disaster." Jehoshaphat said, "Let the king not say such a thing." [9]Then the king of Israel summoned an officer and said, "Bring quickly Micaiah son of Imlah." [10]Now the king of Israel and King Jehoshaphat of Judah were sitting on their thrones, arrayed in their robes, at the threshing floor at the entrance of the gate of Samaria; and all the prophets were prophesying before them. [11]Zedekiah son of Chenaanah made for himself horns of iron, and he said, "Thus says the LORD: With these you shall gore the Arameans until they are destroyed." [12]All the prophets were prophesying the same and saying, "Go up to Ramoth-gilead and triumph; the LORD will give it into the hand of the king."

Micaiah Predicts Failure

13 The messenger who had gone to summon Micaiah said to him, "Look, the words of the prophets with one accord are favorable to the king; let your word be like the word of one of them, and speak favorably." [14]But Micaiah said, "As the LORD lives, whatever the LORD says to me, that I will speak."

15 When he had come to the king, the king said to him, "Micaiah, shall we go to Ramoth-gilead to battle, or shall we refrain?" He answered him, "Go up and triumph; the LORD will give it into the hand of the king." [16]But the king said to him, "How many times must I make you swear to tell me nothing but the truth in the name of the LORD?" [17]Then Micaiah[r] said, "I saw all Israel scattered on the mountains, like sheep that have no shepherd; and the LORD said, 'These have no master; let each one go home in peace.'" [18]The

AHAB *Worst King Yet*

IMAGINE THE UPROAR IF A U.S. president suddenly decided to demolish all church buildings and replace every Christian pastor with a Hindu priest. Something like that happened in King Ahab's day. True, Ahab inherited a bad situation: a divided kingdom in which religious faith was in free fall. Yet somehow he made it worse, doing evil in the sight of the LORD more than all who were before him" (16.30).

The Bible lays much of the blame for Ahab's performance on a bad marriage. To forge a political alliance he married Jezebel, the daughter of a neighboring king. When she brought along her idols of Baal, Ahab joined in, building a temple to Baal right in his capital. Jezebel then tried to hunt down and destroy all remnants of true Israelite faith, replacing God's prophets with her own imported substitutes.

While Ahab may seem like the passive partner in crime, he bore his share of responsibility as well. The prophet Elijah might have been his salvation; Ahab saw him instead as an enemy and a troublemaker (18.17; 21.20). Time after time Ahab rejected good and godly advice.

By secular standards of prosperity and military strength, Ahab achieved success. He built a fine palace inlaid with ivory. (Archaeologists have found ivory plaques from homes of this period.) He drove back invaders from Syria. From the Bible's point of view, however, these achievements meant nothing compared to his failures of faith and morality. As a traitor to God, Ahab was the worst king yet.

Life Questions: In today's world, how do political leaders affect a country's overall moral and spiritual climate? Should they do more?

king of Israel said to Jehoshaphat, "Did I not tell you that he would not prophesy anything favorable about me, but only disaster?"

19 Then Micaiah[u] said, "Therefore hear the word of the LORD: I saw the LORD sitting on his throne, with all the host of heaven standing beside him to the right and to the left of him. 20And the LORD said, 'Who will entice Ahab, so that he may go up and fall at Ramoth-gilead?' Then one said one thing, and another said another, 21until a spirit came forward and stood before the LORD, saying, 'I will entice him.' 22'How?' the LORD asked him. He replied, 'I will go out and be a lying spirit in the mouth of all his prophets.' Then the LORD[u] said, 'You are to entice him, and you shall succeed; go out and do it.' 23So you see, the LORD has put a lying spirit in the mouth of all these your prophets; the LORD has decreed disaster for you."

24 Then Zedekiah son of Chenaanah came up to Micaiah, slapped him on the cheek, and said, "Which way did the spirit of the LORD pass from me to speak to you?" 25Micaiah replied, "You will find out on that day when you go in to hide in an inner chamber." 26The king of Israel then ordered, "Take Micaiah, and return him to Amon the governor of the city and to Joash the king's son, 27and say, 'Thus says the king: Put this fellow in prison, and feed him on reduced rations of bread and water until I come in peace.'" 28Micaiah said, "If you return in peace, the LORD has not spoken by me." And he said, "Hear, you peoples, all of you!"

Defeat and Death of Ahab

29 So the king of Israel and King Jehoshaphat of Judah went up to Ramoth-gilead. 30The king of Israel said to Jehoshaphat, "I will disguise myself and go into battle, but you wear your robes." So the king of Israel disguised himself and went into battle. 31Now the king of Aram had commanded the thirty-two captains of his chariots, "Fight with no one small or great, but only with the king of Israel." 32When the captains of the chariots saw Jehoshaphat, they said, "It is surely the king of Israel." So they turned to fight against him; and Jehoshaphat cried out. 33When the captains of the chariots saw that it was not the king of Israel, they turned back from pursuing him. 34But a certain man drew his bow and unknowingly struck the king of Israel between the scale armor and the breastplate; so he said to the driver of his chariot, "Turn around, and carry me out of the battle, for I am wounded." 35The battle grew hot that day, and the king was propped up in his chariot facing the Arameans, until at evening he died; the blood

from the wound had flowed into the bottom of the chariot. 36Then about sunset a shout went through the army, "Every man to his city, and every man to his country!"

37 So the king died, and was brought to Samaria; they buried the king in Samaria. 38They washed the chariot by the pool of Samaria; the dogs licked up his blood, and the prostitutes washed themselves in it,[v] according to the word of the LORD that he had spoken. 39Now the rest of the acts of Ahab, and all that he did, and the ivory house that he built, and all the cities that he built, are they not written in the Book of the Annals of the Kings of Israel? 40So Ahab slept with his ancestors; and his son Ahaziah succeeded him.

Jehoshaphat Reigns over Judah

41 Jehoshaphat son of Asa began to reign over Judah in the fourth year of King Ahab of Israel. 42Jehoshaphat was thirty-five years old when he began to reign, and he reigned twenty-five years in Jerusalem. His mother's name was Azubah daughter of Shilhi. 43He walked in all the way of his father Asa; he did not turn aside from it, doing what was right in the sight of the LORD; yet the high places were not taken away, and the people still sacrificed and offered incense on the high places. 44Jehoshaphat also made peace with the king of Israel.

45 Now the rest of the acts of Jehoshaphat, and his power that he showed, and how he waged war, are they not written in the Book of the Annals of the Kings of Judah? 46The remnant of the male temple prostitutes who were still in the land in the days of his father Asa, he exterminated.

47 There was no king in Edom; a deputy was king. 48Jehoshaphat made ships of the Tarshish type to go to Ophir for gold; but they did not go, for the ships were wrecked at Ezion-geber. 49Then Ahaziah son of Ahab said to Jehoshaphat, "Let my servants go with your servants in the ships," but Jehoshaphat was not willing. 50Jehoshaphat slept with his ancestors and was buried with his ancestors in the city of his father David; his son Jehoram succeeded him.

Ahaziah Reigns over Israel

51 Ahaziah son of Ahab began to reign over Israel in Samaria in the seventeenth year of King Jehoshaphat of Judah; he reigned two years over Israel. 52He did what was evil in the sight of the LORD, and walked in the way of his father and mother, and in the way of Jeroboam son of Nebat, who caused Israel to sin. 53He served Baal and worshiped him; he provoked the LORD, the God of Israel, to anger, just as his father had done.

---

[u] Heb *he*   [v] Heb lacks *in it*

2 KINGS

The Great Wars of Israel
The promised land turns into a bloody battlefield

THE BOOK OF 2 KINGS tells of dark days in the promised land. First, the Northern Kingdom, Israel, fell to outside invaders. Then Judah, the Southern Kingdom, was conquered. To appreciate what those two events meant in Jewish history, consider our century's two great wars.

In 1918 the bloodiest war of all time came to an end. The entire planet had chosen sides. In all, nine million soldiers died. Survivors thought nothing could ever again match The Great War's ferocity and destruction. "The war to end all wars," they called it.

Yet, in a mere 20 years, a man named Adolf Hitler brought war again. In World War II, global violence stretched from London in the West to Japan in the East. The war finally closed with a blinding mushroom cloud, an ominous portent for the future.

> The LORD said, "I will remove Judah also out of my sight, as I have removed Israel; and I will reject this city that I have chosen, Jerusalem, and the house of which I said, My name shall be there." 23.27

Two Large Blots in History

No matter what else happens, the 20th century has been permanently stained by those two large blots: World War I and World War II. Everything else—art, literature, advances in science and medicine—fades into the background.

As 2 Kings tells it, something very similar occurred in the Biblical nation of Israel. Two large blots spread across the land: successive invasions by foreign giants. In the long, turbulent history of the Jews, these two invasions stand out as the Great Wars, overshadowing nearly everything else.

Israel Falls First

The kingdom had already split into two—1 Kings tells that story. Its sequel, 2 Kings, describes ever-increasing tragedy.

From the very first chapters you can sense the pending crisis in the North. Not one northern king followed the ways of God. National politics slipped into an endless cycle of intrigue and bloody revolt. Meanwhile, Elijah and Elisha intensified their attacks on the kings, and miracles broke out with unusual frequency.

Assyria's campaigns—the "World War I" in Israel's history—are reported in 2 Kings 15–18. Other records of the period tell of vicious fighting. Samaria, Israel's capital, made one final heroic stand against a two-year siege. Finally, the starving survivors surrendered, and the people of Israel were carried away into captivity.

Only two Israelite tribes remained in the promised land, holding out in the tiny Southern Kingdom of Judah. Ultimately, King Sennacherib of Assyria turned against Judah also, penetrating all the way to the gates of Jerusalem. Contemporary accounts record that he leveled 46 walled cities and carried away 200,150 people, young and old, along with all their horses, mules, cattle, and possessions. He scornfully dismissed King Hezekiah as "a bird in a cage."

A Brief Comeback

Could the tiny nation of Judah survive such an onslaught? Somehow the "caged bird" (Hezekiah) made a remarkable comeback, and Judah did survive for another 135 years. Still, Judah did not learn from the dramatic object lesson of Israel's destruction in the North. Most of the kings who followed Hezekiah failed dismally to obey God. Another foreign invader, Babylon, finally leveled Jerusalem in the "World War II" of that era.

The book of Kings ends with a bleak picture: refugees picking through the rubble of Jerusalem, and the Israelites enslaved by foreign powers. The temple itself, God's house, lay in ruins, its treasures carted off to Babylon. When the dust settled around 600 B.C., the Israelites were scattered across the earth, not to be reunited as an independent nation for 25 centuries.

All along, prophets had given eloquent warnings of what would happen to a nation that turned its back on God. But nothing makes a bigger impact than the object lesson of history itself. Ever since, Jews have looked back on their history and seen two indelible stains. Those were the dark days of Assyria and Babylon, when everything came apart.

How to Read 2 Kings

The first eight chapters of 2 Kings, full of excitement and adventure, read easily. They focus on the last days of the prophet Elijah and on the long life of his successor Elisha. But beginning with chapter 9, the book can become very confusing. It switches back and forth between two histories: that of Israel in the North and Judah in the South.

Israel was strong initially, with 10 of the 12 tribes united there. But it proved less faithful to God and was ultimately destroyed by Assyria. Chapters 18–25 cover the period after the Assyrian invasion, when only Judah existed.

Use the boldface sectional headings in this Bible for orientation: They clearly mark whether a king or queen ruled over Judah or Israel. Also, a lineup of all the rulers appears on pages 1349–1357, giving an overview of the history of each country.

One important reason for studying the books of Kings and Chronicles is that they give historical background on the prophets. Elijah and Elisha appeared at a crucial turning point in the history of the Northern Kingdom, just as Ahab was changing the official religion from worship of God to worship of Baal. Other prophets, who wrote books of the Bible, were also active during this time.

Amos and Hosea concentrated their work in the Northern Kingdom of Israel. The following prophets lived and preached in the Southern Kingdom of Judah: Obadiah, Joel, Isaiah, Micah, Nahum, Zephaniah, Jeremiah, and Habakkuk. More prophets came later, when the Israelites were still captive in Babylon or after they had returned to their homeland. The How to Read section of each book of the prophets gives a brief summary of when and where each author worked (see An Overview of the Bible, pages 17–20, for a list of the books of the prophets).

Second Kings, like its companion books, makes brief and sweeping judgments of each king or queen. As you read, look for what pleased God and what displeased him. The 39 rulers comprise a fine study of leadership of all kinds, from the inspiring to the degenerate.

PEOPLE YOU'LL MEET IN 2 KINGS

ELISHA *(p. 389)*
JEZEBEL *(p. 397)*
JOSIAH *(p. 412)*
ZEDEKIAH *(p. 415)*

3-TRACK READING PLAN

For an explanation and complete listing of the 3-track reading plan, turn to page 7.

TRACK 1: *Two-Week Courses on the Bible*
See page 7 for information on these courses.

TRACK 2: *An Overview of 2 Kings in 3 Days*
☐ Day 1. Read the Introduction to 2 Kings and then chapter 5 on Elisha's miracle of healing an enemy from Aram.
☐ Day 2. Read chapter 17, which gives a final summary of the decline and utter devastation of the Northern Kingdom of Israel.
☐ Day 3. One of the high points in 2 Kings occurred during the reign of the boy-king Josiah. Read about the beginning of his reforms in chapter 22 and the first three verses of chapter 23.

Now turn to page 9 for your next Track 2 reading project.

TRACK 3: **All of 2 Kings in 25 Days**
After you have read through 2 Kings, turn to pages 10–14 for your next Track 3 reading project.

☐1 ☐2 ☐3 ☐4 ☐5 ☐6 ☐7 ☐8
☐9 ☐10 ☐11 ☐12 ☐13 ☐14 ☐15 ☐16
☐17 ☐18 ☐19 ☐20 ☐21 ☐22 ☐23 ☐24
☐25

Elijah Denounces Ahaziah

1 After the death of Ahab, Moab rebelled against Israel.

2 Ahaziah had fallen through the lattice in his upper chamber in Samaria, and lay injured; so he sent messengers, telling them, "Go, inquire of Baal-zebub, the god of Ekron, whether I shall recover from this injury." ³But the angel of the LORD said to Elijah the Tishbite, "Get up, go to meet the messengers of the king of Samaria, and say to them, 'Is it because there is no God in Israel that you are going to inquire of Baal-zebub, the god of Ekron?' ⁴Now therefore thus says the LORD, 'You shall not leave the bed to which you have gone, but you shall surely die.'" So Elijah went.

5 The messengers returned to the king, who said to them, "Why have you returned?" ⁶They answered him, "There came a man to meet us, who said to us, 'Go back to the king who sent you, and say to him: Thus says the LORD: Is it because there is no God in Israel that you are sending to inquire of Baal-zebub, the god of Ekron? Therefore you shall not leave the bed to which you have gone, but shall surely die.'" ⁷He said to them, "What sort of man was he who came to meet you and told you these things?" ⁸They answered him, "A hairy man, with a leather belt around his waist." He said, "It is Elijah the Tishbite."

9 Then the king sent to him a captain of fifty with his fifty men. He went up to Elijah, who was sitting on the top of a hill, and said to him, "O man of God, the king says, 'Come down.'" ¹⁰But Elijah answered the captain of fifty, "If I am a man of God, let fire come down from heaven and consume you and your fifty." Then fire came down from heaven, and consumed him and his fifty.

11 Again the king sent to him another captain of fifty with his fifty. He went up[a] and said to him, "O man of God, this is the king's order: Come down quickly!" ¹²But Elijah answered them, "If I am a man of God, let fire come down from heaven and consume you and your fifty." Then the fire of God came down from heaven and consumed him and his fifty.

13 Again the king sent the captain of a third fifty with his fifty. So the third captain of fifty went up, and came and fell on his knees before Elijah, and entreated him, "O man of God, please let my life, and the life of these fifty servants of yours, be precious in your sight. ¹⁴Look, fire came down from heaven and consumed the two former captains of fifty men with their fifties; but now let my life be precious in your sight." ¹⁵Then the angel of the LORD said to Elijah, "Go down with him; do not be afraid of him." So he set out and went down with him to the king, ¹⁶and said to him, "Thus says the LORD: Because you have sent messengers to inquire of Baal-zebub, the god of Ekron,—is it because there is no God in Israel to inquire of his word?—therefore you shall not leave the bed to which you have gone, but you shall surely die."

Death of Ahaziah

17 So he died according to the word of the LORD that Elijah had spoken. His brother,[b] Jehoram succeeded him as king in the second year of King Jehoram son of Jehoshaphat of Judah, because Ahaziah had no son. ¹⁸Now the rest of the acts of Ahaziah that he did, are they not written in the Book of the Annals of the Kings of Israel?

Elijah Ascends to Heaven

2 Now when the LORD was about to take Elijah up to heaven by a whirlwind, Elijah and Elisha were on their way from Gilgal. ²Elijah said to Elisha, "Stay here; for the LORD has sent me as far as Bethel." But Elisha said, "As the LORD lives, and as you yourself live, I will not leave you." So they went down to Bethel. ³The company of prophets[c] who were in Bethel came out to Elisha, and said to him, "Do you know that today the LORD will take your master away from you?" And he said, "Yes, I know; keep silent."

4 Elijah said to him, "Elisha, stay here; for the LORD has sent me to Jericho." But he said, "As the LORD lives, and as you yourself live, I will not leave you." So they came to Jericho. ⁵The company of prophets[c] who were at Jericho drew near to Elisha, and said to him, "Do you know that today the LORD will take your master away from you?" And he answered, "Yes, I know; be silent."

6 Then Elijah said to him, "Stay here; for the LORD has sent me to the Jordan." But he said, "As

---

a Gk Compare verses 9, 13: Heb *He answered*   b Gk Syr: Heb lacks *His brother*   c Heb *sons of the prophets* the LORD lives, and as you yourself live, I will not leave you." So the two of them went on. ⁷Fifty men of the company of prophets*d* also went, and stood at some distance from them, as they both were standing by the Jordan. ⁸Then Elijah took his mantle and rolled it up, and struck the water; the water was parted to the one side and to the other, until the two of them crossed on dry ground.

9 When they had crossed, Elijah said to Elisha, "Tell me what I may do for you, before I am taken from you." Elisha said, "Please let me inherit a double share of your spirit." ¹⁰He responded, "You have asked a hard thing; yet, if you see me as I am being taken from you, it will be granted you; if not, it will not." ¹¹As they continued walking and talking, a chariot of fire and horses of fire separated the two of them, and Elijah ascended in a whirlwind into heaven. ¹²Elisha kept watching and crying out, "Father, father! The chariots of Israel and its horsemen!" But when he could no longer see him, he grasped his own clothes and tore them in two pieces.

2.12 An Obscure Compliment

Elisha's last words to Elijah were obviously a compliment, but what did they mean? Most likely they referred to Elijah's power, indicating he was worth more to the nation of Israel than a company of chariots and horsemen. Interestingly, a king of Israel said these exact words to Elisha himself as he lay dying (13.14).

Elisha Succeeds Elijah

13 He picked up the mantle of Elijah that had fallen from him, and went back and stood on the bank of the Jordan. ¹⁴He took the mantle of Elijah that had fallen from him, and struck the water, saying, "Where is the LORD, the God of Elijah?" When he had struck the water, the water was parted to the one side and to the other, and Elisha went over.

15 When the company of prophets*d* who were at Jericho saw him at a distance, they declared, "The spirit of Elijah rests on Elisha." They came to meet him and bowed to the ground before him. ¹⁶They said to him, "See now, we have fifty strong men among your servants; please let them go and seek your master; it may be that the spirit of the LORD has caught him up and thrown him down on some mountain or into some valley." He responded, "No, do not send them." ¹⁷But when they urged him until he was ashamed, he said, "Send them." So they sent fifty men who searched for three days but did not find him. ¹⁸When they came back to him (he had remained at Jericho), he said to them, "Did I not say to you, Do not go?"

Elisha Performs Miracles

19 Now the people of the city said to Elisha, "The location of this city is good, as my lord sees; but the water is bad, and the land is unfruitful." ²⁰He said, "Bring me a new bowl, and put salt in it." So they brought it to him. ²¹Then he went to the spring of water and threw the salt into it, and said, "Thus says the LORD, I have made this water wholesome; from now on neither death nor miscarriage shall come from it." ²²So the water has been wholesome to this day, according to the word that Elisha spoke.

23 He went up from there to Bethel; and while he was going up on the way, some small boys came out of the city and jeered at him, saying, "Go away, baldhead! Go away, baldhead!"

2.23 Background on the Bears

At first reading, the brief account in these three verses is very troubling. A prophet calling on bears to maul children? But, in this instance, historical background and a precise translation help cast the event in a different light. Bethel was a hotbed of Baal worship, and its residents were engaged in a life-and-death struggle with the true prophets of God. When the youths called out, "Go away, baldhead!" they were likely referring to what had just happened to the prophet Elijah—they were calling for Elisha to vanish into the sky, or in other words, to die. Furthermore, the word translated youths usually refers to young people in their late teens. In actuality, a large gang of teenagers was threatening a prophet's life. Elisha cursed them, but there is no indication he actually called for a bear attack.

²⁴When he turned around and saw them, he cursed them in the name of the LORD. Then two she-bears came out of the woods and mauled forty-two of the boys. ²⁵From there he went on to Mount Carmel, and then returned to Samaria.

Jehoram Reigns over Israel

3 In the eighteenth year of King Jehoshaphat of Judah, Jehoram son of Ahab became king over Israel in Samaria; he reigned twelve years. ²He did what was evil in the sight of the LORD, though not like his father and mother, for he removed the pillar of Baal that his father had made. ³Nevertheless he clung to the sin of Jeroboam son of Nebat, which he caused Israel to commit; he did not depart from it.

---

d Heb *sons of the prophets*

War with Moab

4 Now King Mesha of Moab was a sheep breeder, who used to deliver to the king of Israel one hundred thousand lambs, and the wool of one hundred thousand rams. ⁵But when Ahab died, the king of Moab rebelled against the king of Israel. ⁶So King Jehoram marched out of Samaria at that time and mustered all Israel. ⁷As he went he sent word to King Jehoshaphat of Judah, "The king of Moab has rebelled against me; will you go with me to battle against Moab?" He answered, "I will; I am with you, my people are your people, my horses are your horses." ⁸Then he asked, "By which way shall we march?" Jehoram answered, "By the way of the wilderness of Edom."

Replacing a Legend
Who could follow the great Elijah?

WHEN A PROPHET LIKE ELIJAH leaves the scene, who will dare to take his place? As time came to choose a successor, Elijah looked to find someone out of a different mold. He settled on his most faithful companion, a farmer named Elisha.

> When they had crossed, Elijah said to Elisha, "Tell me what I may do for you, before I am taken from you." Elisha said, "Please let me inherit a double share of your spirit." 2.9

Similar Names but Different Styles

The slight variance in the two men's names expresses their difference in style. Elijah, whose name meant "The LORD is my God," dueled a king and the priests of Baal in dramatic confrontations of power. He lived apart from the people and preached judgment and the need for repentance.

Elisha ("God is salvation") shifted the emphasis. He lived among people, preferring the poor and outcast, and stressed life, hope, and God's grace. All social classes had access to Elisha, from lowly widows to foreign kings. His colorful life included work as a spy, a miracle worker, an adviser to the king, a leader of a school of prophets, and an anointer of revolutionaries.

Elisha traveled widely, and his bald head and wooden walking staff became his trademarks. News of his miracles spread, making him a famous national figure for 50 years. As Elisha lay on his deathbed, the distraught king of Israel knelt beside him, asking for one last word of advice.

Serving the People and the Kingdom

Elisha's exploits fall roughly into two categories, and the Bible seems to group them that way. One set of stories concerns people with evident needs. Elisha showed a deep sensitivity for the suffering and distressed, and sometimes helped them in miraculous ways: providing food, healing diseases, even raising a young boy from the dead. He dealt far more gently with the poor and downtrodden than with kings and generals.

Another group of stories relates to the nation. Israel was reeling from the corruption brought in during King Ahab's reign (see page 1351). Politically, Israel was at the mercy of the neighboring state of Aram (the area known today as Syria), which launched periodic raids across the border.

Sometimes Elisha helped out Israel's army, using his special insight to detect bands of raiders. Twice, miracles he predicted allowed Israel's army to break out of an impossible situation and rout the enemy. Yet he refused to become a "court prophet" serving the king's whims. On at least one occasion, he blatantly insulted a king of Israel (3.13–14). Another time, he anointed a general to overthrow the king in an outright revolution.

A Dying Breed

Incidents from Elisha's life—the healing of Naaman, the chariots of fire, the widow's oil—have become among the most familiar of Old Testament stories. In a sense, Elijah and Elisha represent the last of a breed. Prophets who followed them relied less on spectacular displays and more on the power of verbal messages from God.

Elijah and Elisha used both words and dramatic events to convey their message. Everyone knew their power, especially the kings who sometimes sought them out for advice and other times tried to kill them. In a great irony, the kings and political leaders—who thought themselves the center of history at the time—all faded away. Meanwhile the stories and words of Israel's prophets live on, expressing a message as forceful today as ever.

Life Questions: Elijah and Elisha show how God uses quite different personalities to get his message across. From the description above, which of the two prophets do you more closely identify with?

9 So the king of Israel, the king of Judah, and the king of Edom set out; and when they had made a roundabout march of seven days, there was no water for the army or for the animals that were with them. ¹⁰Then the king of Israel said, "Alas! The LORD has summoned us, three kings, only to be handed over to Moab." ¹¹But Jehoshaphat said, "Is there no prophet of the LORD here, through whom we may inquire of the LORD?" Then one of the servants of the king of Israel answered, "Elisha son of Shaphat, who used to pour water on the hands of Elijah, is here." ¹²Jehoshaphat said, "The word of the LORD is with him." So the king of Israel and Jehoshaphat and the king of Edom went down to him.

13 Elisha said to the king of Israel, "What have I to do with you? Go to your father's prophets or to your mother's." But the king of Israel said to him, "No; it is the LORD who has summoned us, three kings, only to be handed over to Moab." ¹⁴Elisha said, "As the LORD of hosts lives, whom I serve, were it not that I have regard for King Jehoshaphat of Judah, I would give you neither a look nor a glance. ¹⁵But get me a musician." And then, while the musician was playing, the power of the LORD came on him. ¹⁶And he said, "Thus says the LORD, 'I will make this wadi full of pools.' ¹⁷For thus says the LORD, 'You shall see neither wind nor rain, but the wadi shall be filled with water, so that you shall drink, you, your cattle, and your animals.' ¹⁸This is only a trifle in the sight of the LORD, for he will also hand Moab over to you. ¹⁹You shall conquer every fortified city and every choice city; every good tree you shall fell, all springs of water you shall stop up, and every good piece of land you shall ruin with stones." ²⁰The next day, about the time of the morning offering, suddenly water began to flow from the direction of Edom, until the country was filled with water.

21 When all the Moabites heard that the kings had come up to fight against them, all who were able to put on armor, from the youngest to the oldest, were called out and were drawn up at the frontier. ²²When they rose early in the morning, and the sun shone upon the water, the Moabites saw the water opposite them as red as blood. ²³They said, "This is blood; the kings must have fought together, and killed one another. Now then, Moab, to the spoil!" ²⁴But when they came to the camp of Israel, the Israelites rose up and attacked the Moabites, who fled before them; as they entered Moab they continued the attack.ᵉ ²⁵The cities they overturned, and on every good piece of land everyone threw a stone, until it was covered; every spring of water they stopped up, and every good tree they felled. Only at Kirhareseth did the stone walls remain, until the slingers surrounded and attacked it. ²⁶When the

king of Moab saw that the battle was going against him, he took with him seven hundred swordsmen to break through, opposite the king of Edom; but they could not. ²⁷Then he took his firstborn son who was to succeed him, and offered him as a burnt offering on the wall. And great wrath came upon Israel, so they withdrew from him and returned to their own land.

Elisha and the Widow's Oil

4 Now the wife of a member of the company of prophetsᶠ cried to Elisha, "Your servant my husband is dead; and you know that your servant feared the LORD, but a creditor has come to take my two children as slaves." ²Elisha said to her, "What shall I do for you? Tell me, what do you have in the house?" She answered, "Your servant has nothing in the house, except a jar of oil." ³He said, "Go outside, borrow vessels from all your neighbors, empty vessels and not just a few. ⁴Then go in, and shut the door behind you and your children, and start pouring into all these vessels; when each is full, set it aside." ⁵So she left him and shut the door behind her and her children; they kept bringing vessels to her, and she kept pouring. ⁶When the vessels were full, she said to her son, "Bring me another vessel." But he said to her, "There are no more." Then the oil stopped flowing. ⁷She came and told the man of God, and he said, "Go sell the oil and pay your debts, and you and your children can live on the rest."

Elisha Raises the Shunammite's Son

8 One day Elisha was passing through Shunem, where a wealthy woman lived, who urged him to have a meal. So whenever he passed that

4.8 Elisha's Miracles

Elisha had asked for a double share of Elijah's spirit (2.9), and the Bible pointedly records about twice as many miracles performed by Elisha. Many of these miracles, especially those in chapter 4, have great similarities to the miracles Jesus himself would later perform; they show God caring for the needs of ordinary people. Although Elisha was very famous in his own time, his name appears only once outside the book of Kings (Luke 4.27). In contrast, Elijah is often mentioned, and John the Baptist is frequently compared to him.

way, he would stop there for a meal. ⁹She said to her husband, "Look, I am sure that this man who regularly passes our way is a holy man of God. ¹⁰Let us make a small roof chamber with walls, and put there for him a bed, a table, a chair, and

ᵉ Compare Gk Syr: Meaning of Heb uncertain   ᶠ Heb *the sons of the prophets*

a lamp, so that he can stay there whenever he comes to us."

11 One day when he came there, he went up to the chamber and lay down there. [12]He said to his servant Gehazi, "Call the Shunammite woman." When he had called her, she stood before him. [13]He said to him, "Say to her, Since you have taken all this trouble for us, what may be done for you? Would you have a word spoken on your behalf to the king or to the commander of the army?" She answered, "I live among my own people." [14]He said, "What then may be done for her?" Gehazi answered, "Well, she has no son, and her husband is old." [15]He said, "Call her." When he had called her, she stood at the door. [16]He said, "At this season, in due time, you shall embrace a son." She replied, "No, my lord, O man of God; do not deceive your servant."

17 The woman conceived and bore a son at that season, in due time, as Elisha had declared to her.

18 When the child was older, he went out one day to his father among the reapers. [19]He complained to his father, "Oh, my head, my head!" The father said to his servant, "Carry him to his mother." [20]He carried him and brought him to his mother; the child sat on her lap until noon, and he died. [21]She went up and laid him on the bed of the man of God, closed the door on him, and left. [22]Then she called to her husband, and said, "Send me one of the servants and one of the donkeys, so that I may quickly go to the man of God and come back again." [23]He said, "Why go to him today? It is neither new moon nor sabbath." She said, "It will be all right." [24]Then she saddled the donkey and said to her servant, "Urge the animal on; do not hold back for me unless I tell you." [25]So she set out, and came to the man of God at Mount Carmel.

When the man of God saw her coming, he said to Gehazi his servant, "Look, there is the Shunammite woman; [26]run at once to meet her, and say to her, Are you all right? Is your husband all right? Is the child all right?" She answered, "It is all right." [27]When she came to the man of God at the mountain, she caught hold of his feet. Gehazi approached to push her away. But the man of God said, "Let her alone, for she is in bitter distress; the LORD has hidden it from me and has not told me." [28]Then she said, "Did I ask my lord for a son? Did I not say, Do not mislead me?" [29]He said to Gehazi, "Gird up your loins, and take my staff in your hand, and go. If you meet anyone, give no greeting, and if anyone greets you, do not answer; and lay my staff on the face of the child." [30]Then the mother of the child said, "As the LORD lives, and as you yourself live, I will not leave without you." So he rose up and followed her.

[31]Gehazi went on ahead and laid the staff on the face of the child, but there was no sound or sign of life. He came back to meet him and told him, "The child has not awakened."

32 When Elisha came into the house, he saw the child lying dead on his bed. [33]So he went in and closed the door on the two of them, and prayed to the LORD. [34]Then he got up on the bed[g] and lay upon the child, putting his mouth upon his mouth, his eyes upon his eyes, and his hands upon his hands; and while he lay bent over him, the flesh of the child became warm. [35]He got down, walked once to and fro in the room, then got up again and bent over him; the child sneezed seven times, and the child opened his eyes. [36]Elisha[h] summoned Gehazi and said, "Call the Shunammite woman." So he called her. When she came to him, he said, "Take your son." [37]She came and fell at his feet, bowing to the ground; then she took her son and left.

Elisha Purifies the Pot of Stew

38 When Elisha returned to Gilgal, there was a famine in the land. As the company of prophets was[i] sitting before him, he said to his servant, "Put the large pot on, and make some stew for the company of prophets."[j] [39]One of them went out into the field to gather herbs; he found a wild vine and gathered from it a lapful of wild gourds, and came and cut them up into the pot of stew, not knowing what they were. [40]They served some for the men to eat. But while they were eating the stew, they cried out, "O man of God, there is death in the pot!" They could not eat it. [41]He said, "Then bring some flour." He threw it into the pot, and said, "Serve the people and let them eat." And there was nothing harmful in the pot.

Elisha Feeds One Hundred Men

42 A man came from Baal-shalishah, bringing food from the first fruits to the man of God: twenty loaves of barley and fresh ears of grain in his sack. Elisha said, "Give it to the people and let them eat." [43]But his servant said, "How can I set this before a hundred people?" So he repeated, "Give it to the people and let them eat, for thus says the LORD, 'They shall eat and have some left.'" [44]He set it before them, they ate, and had some left, according to the word of the LORD.

The Healing of Naaman

5 Naaman, commander of the army of the king of Aram, was a great man and in high favor with his master, because by him the LORD had given victory to Aram. The man, though a mighty warrior, suffered from leprosy.[k] [2]Now the Arameans on one of their raids had taken a young girl captive from the land of Israel, and she served

---

g Heb lacks *on the bed*   h Heb *he*   i Heb *sons of the prophets were*   j Heb *sons of the prophets*   k A term for several skin diseases; precise meaning uncertain

Naaman's wife. [3]She said to her mistress, "If only my lord were with the prophet who is in Samaria! He would cure him of his leprosy."[l] [4]So Naaman[m] went in and told his lord just what the girl

5.3 A Captive's Compassion

She had been captured in a raid, taken to a foreign country, and made a slave. Yet instead of bitterness, she showed compassion toward her master. She wanted him healed, and she believed her God would do it. God used this girl's tragedy to heal and convert her enemy—a wonderful example of love reaching out.

from the land of Israel had said. [5]And the king of Aram said, "Go then, and I will send along a letter to the king of Israel."

He went, taking with him ten talents of silver, six thousand shekels of gold, and ten sets of garments. [6]He brought the letter to the king of Israel, which read, "When this letter reaches you, know that I have sent to you my servant Naaman, that you may cure him of his leprosy."[l] [7]When the king of Israel read the letter, he tore his clothes and said, "Am I God, to give death or life, that this man sends word to me to cure a man of his leprosy?[l] Just look and see how he is trying to pick a quarrel with me."

8 But when Elisha the man of God heard that the king of Israel had torn his clothes, he sent a message to the king, "Why have you torn your clothes? Let him come to me, that he may learn that there is a prophet in Israel." [9]So Naaman came with his horses and chariots, and halted at the entrance of Elisha's house. [10]Elisha sent a messenger to him, saying, "Go, wash in the Jordan seven times, and your flesh shall be restored

5.10–16 Harder on the Rich

Elisha's treatment of the general Naaman here, and of the king of Israel elsewhere, contrasts sharply with his mild manner around the poor and oppressed. Elisha's prescribed cure obviously offended Naaman's pride. And Elisha pointedly refused to accept payment from the wealthy general, who was used to paying his way. In this incident, and in another (8.7–15), Elisha was serving the kingdom of Aram, an enemy of Israel.

and you shall be clean." [11]But Naaman became angry and went away, saying, "I thought that for me he would surely come out, and stand and call

on the name of the LORD his God, and would wave his hand over the spot, and cure the leprosy![l] [12]Are not Abana[n] and Pharpar, the rivers of Damascus, better than all the waters of Israel? Could I not wash in them, and be clean?" He turned and went away in a rage. [13]But his servants approached and said to him, "Father, if the prophet had commanded you to do something difficult, would you not have done it? How much more, when all he said to you was, 'Wash, and be clean'?" [14]So he went down and immersed himself seven times in the Jordan, according to the word of the man of God; his flesh was restored like the flesh of a young boy, and he was clean.

15 Then he returned to the man of God, he and all his company; he came and stood before him and said, "Now I know that there is no God in all the earth except in Israel; please accept a present from your servant." [16]But he said, "As the LORD lives, whom I serve, I will accept nothing!" He urged him to accept, but he refused. [17]Then Naaman said, "If not, please let two mule-loads of earth be given to your servant; for your servant will no longer offer burnt offering or sacrifice to any god except the LORD. [18]But may the LORD pardon your servant on one count: when my master goes into the house of Rimmon to worship there, leaning on my arm, and I bow down in the house of Rimmon, when I do bow down in the house of Rimmon, may the LORD pardon your servant on this one count." [19]He said to him, "Go in peace."

Gehazi's Greed

But when Naaman had gone from him a short distance, [20]Gehazi, the servant of Elisha the man of God, thought, "My master has let that Aramean Naaman off too lightly by not accepting from him what he offered. As the LORD lives, I will run after him and get something out of him." [21]So Gehazi went after Naaman. When Naaman saw someone running after him, he jumped down from the chariot to meet him and said, "Is everything all right?" [22]He replied, "Yes, but my master has sent me to say, 'Two members of a company of prophets[o] have just come to me from the hill country of Ephraim; please give them a talent of silver and two changes of clothing.'" [23]Naaman said, "Please accept two talents." He urged him, and tied up two talents of silver in two bags, with two changes of clothing, and gave them to two of his servants, who carried them in front of Gehazi.[p] [24]When he came to the citadel, he took the bags[q] from them, and stored them inside; he dismissed the men, and they left.

25 He went in and stood before his master; and Elisha said to him, "Where have you been, Gehazi?" He answered, "Your servant has not

---

[l] A term for several skin diseases; precise meaning uncertain [m] Heb *he* [n] Another reading is *Amana*
[o] Heb *sons of the prophets* [p] Heb *him* [q] Heb lacks *the bags*

gone anywhere at all." 26But he said to him, "Did I not go with you in spirit when someone left his chariot to meet you? Is this a time to accept money and to accept clothing, olive orchards and vineyards, sheep and oxen, and male and female slaves? 27Therefore the leprosy*r* of Naaman shall cling to you, and to your descendants forever." So he left his presence leprous,*r* as white as snow.

The Miracle of the Ax Head

6 Now the company of prophets*s* said to Elisha, "As you see, the place where we live under your charge is too small for us. 2Let us go to the Jordan, and let us collect logs there, one for each of us, and build a place there for us to live." He answered, "Do so." 3Then one of them said, "Please come with your servants." And he answered, "I will." 4So he went with them. When they came to the Jordan, they cut down trees. 5But as one was felling a log, his ax head fell into the water; he cried out, "Alas, master! It was borrowed." 6Then the man of God said, "Where did it fall?" When he showed him the place, he cut off a stick, and threw it in there, and made the iron float. 7He said, "Pick it up." So he reached out his hand and took it.

The Aramean Attack Is Thwarted

8 Once when the king of Aram was at war with Israel, he took counsel with his officers. He said, "At such and such a place shall be my camp." 9But the man of God sent word to the king of Israel, "Take care not to pass this place, because the Arameans are going down there." 10The king of Israel sent word to the place of which the man of God spoke. More than once or twice he warned such a place*t* so that it was on the alert.

11 The mind of the king of Aram was greatly perturbed because of this; he called his officers and said to them, "Now tell me who among us sides with the king of Israel?" 12Then one of his officers said, "No one, my lord king. It is Elisha, the prophet in Israel, who tells the king of Israel the words that you speak in your bedchamber." 13He said, "Go and find where he is; I will send and seize him." He was told, "He is in Dothan." 14So he sent horses and chariots there and a great army; they came by night, and surrounded the city.

15 When an attendant of the man of God rose early in the morning and went out, an army with horses and chariots was all around the city. His servant said, "Alas, master! What shall we do?" 16He replied, "Do not be afraid, for there are more with us than there are with them." 17Then Elisha prayed: "O LORD, please open his eyes that he may see." So the LORD opened the eyes of the

servant, and he saw; the mountain was full of horses and chariots of fire all around Elisha. 18When the Arameans*u* came down against him, Elisha prayed to the LORD, and said, "Strike this people, please, with blindness." So he struck them

6.17 Chariots of Fire

Surrounded by an army, Elisha's servant cried, "What shall we do?" But when Elisha prayed, the servant could suddenly see that God's forces, invisible to everyone else, far outnumbered the enemy. The story offers a rare glimpse of the "invisible world" of supernatural forces. God has resources to help that we cannot see.

with blindness as Elisha had asked. 19Elisha said to them, "This is not the way, and this is not the city; follow me, and I will bring you to the man whom you seek." And he led them to Samaria.

20 As soon as they entered Samaria, Elisha said, "O LORD, open the eyes of these men so that they may see." The LORD opened their eyes, and they saw that they were inside Samaria. 21When the king of Israel saw them he said to Elisha, "Father, shall I kill them? Shall I kill them?" 22He answered, "No! Did you capture with your sword and your bow those whom you want to kill? Set food and water before them so that they may eat and drink; and let them go to their master." 23So he prepared for them a great feast; after they ate and drank, he sent them on their way, and they went to their master. And the Arameans no longer came raiding into the land of Israel.

Ben-hadad's Siege of Samaria

24 Some time later King Ben-hadad of Aram mustered his entire army; he marched against Samaria and laid siege to it. 25As the siege continued, famine in Samaria became so great that a donkey's head was sold for eighty shekels of silver, and one-fourth of a kab of dove's dung for five shekels of silver. 26Now as the king of Israel was walking on the city wall, a woman cried out to him, "Help, my lord king!" 27He said, "No! Let the LORD help you. How can I help you? From the threshing floor or from the wine press?" 28But then the king asked her, "What is your complaint?" She answered, "This woman said to me, 'Give up your son; we will eat him today, and we will eat my son tomorrow.' 29So we cooked my son and ate him. The next day I said to her, 'Give up your son and we will eat him.' But she has hidden her son." 30When the king heard the words of the woman he tore his clothes—now since he was walking on the city wall, the people

---

r A term for several skin diseases; precise meaning uncertain   *s* Heb *sons of the prophets*   *t* Heb *warned it*
u Heb *they*

could see that he had sackcloth on his body underneath— [31]and he said, "So may God do to me, and more, if the head of Elisha son of Shaphat stays on his shoulders today." [32]So he dispatched a man from his presence.

6.31 The Prophet and Politics

Elisha's long career spanned the reigns of six kings and included some dramatic ups and downs with them. On one occasion Elisha outright insulted a king (3.14). But, as this chapter shows, he could also be an invaluable military resource, serving as a virtual spy. At Elisha's deathbed, the reigning king of Israel knelt beside him, weeping (13.14).

Now Elisha was sitting in his house, and the elders were sitting with him. Before the messenger arrived, Elisha said to the elders, "Are you aware that this murderer has sent someone to take off my head? When the messenger comes, see that you shut the door and hold it closed against him. Is not the sound of his master's feet behind him?" [33]While he was still speaking with them, the king[v] came down to him and said, "This trouble is from the LORD! Why should I hope in the LORD 7 any longer?" [1]But Elisha said, "Hear the word of the LORD: thus says the LORD, Tomorrow about this time a measure of choice meal shall be sold for a shekel, and two measures of barley for a shekel, at the gate of Samaria." [2]Then the captain on whose hand the king leaned said to the man of God, "Even if the LORD were to make windows in the sky, could such a thing happen?" But he said, "You shall see it with your own eyes, but you shall not eat from it."

The Arameans Flee

3 Now there were four leprous[w] men outside the city gate, who said to one another, "Why should we sit here until we die? [4]If we say, 'Let us enter the city,' the famine is in the city, and we shall die there; but if we sit here, we shall also die. Therefore, let us desert to the Aramean camp; if they spare our lives, we shall live; and if they kill us, we shall but die." [5]So they arose at twilight to go to the Aramean camp; but when they came to the edge of the Aramean camp, there was no one there at all. [6]For the Lord had caused the Aramean army to hear the sound of chariots, and of horses, the sound of a great army, so that they said to one another, "The king of Israel has hired the kings of the Hittites and the kings of Egypt to fight against us." [7]So they fled away in the twilight and abandoned their tents, their horses, and their donkeys leaving the camp just as it was, and fled

for their lives. [8]When these leprous[w] men had come to the edge of the camp, they went into a tent, ate and drank, carried off silver, gold, and clothing, and went and hid them. Then they came back, entered another tent, carried off things from it, and went and hid them.

9 Then they said to one another, "What we are doing is wrong. This is a day of good news; if we are silent and wait until the morning light, we will be found guilty; therefore let us go and tell the king's household." [10]So they came and called to the gatekeepers of the city, and told them, "We went to the Aramean camp, but there was no one to be seen or heard there, nothing but the horses tied, the donkeys tied, and the tents as they were." [11]Then the gatekeepers called out and proclaimed it to the king's household. [12]The king got up in the night, and said to his servants, "I will tell you what the Arameans have prepared against us. They know that we are starving; so they have left the camp to hide themselves in the open country, thinking, 'When they come out of the city, we shall take them alive and get into the city.'" [13]One of his servants said, "Let some men take five of the remaining horses, since those left here will suffer the fate of the whole multitude of Israel that have perished already;[x] let us send and find out." [14]So they took two mounted men, and the king sent them after the Aramean army, saying, "Go and find out." [15]So they went after them as far as the Jordan; the whole way was littered with garments and equipment that the Arameans had thrown away in their haste. So the messengers returned, and told the king.

16 Then the people went out, and plundered the camp of the Arameans. So a measure of choice meal was sold for a shekel, and two measures of barley for a shekel, according to the word of the LORD. [17]Now the king had appointed the captain on whose hand he leaned to have charge of the gate; the people trampled him to death in the gate, just as the man of God had said when the king came down to him. [18]For when the man of God had said to the king, "Two measures of barley shall be sold for a shekel, and a measure of choice meal for a shekel, about this time tomorrow in the gate of Samaria," [19]the captain had answered the man of God, "Even if the LORD were to make windows in the sky, could such a thing happen?" And he had answered, "You shall see it with your own eyes, but you shall not eat from it." [20]It did indeed happen to him; the people trampled him to death in the gate.

The Shunammite Woman's Land Restored

8 Now Elisha had said to the woman whose son he had restored to life, "Get up and go with your household, and settle wherever you can; for

---

[v] See 7.2: Heb *messenger* Meaning of Heb uncertain   [w] A term for several skin diseases; precise meaning uncertain   [x] Compare Gk Syr Vg:

the LORD has called for a famine, and it will come on the land for seven years." [2]So the woman got up and did according to the word of the man of God; she went with her household and settled in the land of the Philistines seven years. [3]At the end of the seven years, when the woman returned from the land of the Philistines, she set out to appeal to the king for her house and her land. [4]Now the king was talking with Gehazi the servant of the man of God, saying, "Tell me all the great things that Elisha has done." [5]While he was telling the king how Elisha had restored a dead person to life, the woman whose son he had restored to life appealed to the king for her house and her land. Gehazi said, "My lord king, here is the woman, and here is her son whom Elisha restored to life." [6]When the king questioned the woman, she told him. So the king appointed an official for her, saying, "Restore all that was hers, together with all the revenue of the fields from the day that she left the land until now."

Death of Ben-hadad

7 Elisha went to Damascus while King Ben-hadad of Aram was ill. When it was told him, "The man of God has come here," [8]the king said to Hazael, "Take a present with you and go to meet the man of God. Inquire of the LORD through him, whether I shall recover from this illness." [9]So Hazael went to meet him, taking a present with him, all kinds of goods of Damascus, forty camel loads. When he entered and stood before him, he said, "Your son King Ben-hadad of Aram has sent me to you, saying, 'Shall I recover from this illness?'" [10]Elisha said to him, "Go, say to him, 'You shall certainly recover'; but the LORD has shown me that he shall certainly die." [11]He fixed his gaze and stared at him, until he was ashamed. Then the man of God wept. [12]Hazael asked, "Why does my lord weep?" He answered, "Because I know the evil that you will do to the people of Israel; you will set their fortresses on fire, you will kill their young men with the sword, dash in pieces their little ones, and rip up their pregnant women." [13]Hazael said, "What is your servant, who is a mere dog, that he should do this great thing?" Elisha answered, "The LORD has shown me that you are to be king over Aram." [14]Then he left Elisha, and went to his master Ben-hadad,[y] who said to him, "What did Elisha say to you?" And he answered, "He told me that you would certainly recover." [15]But the next day he took the bed-cover and dipped it in water and spread it over the king's face, until he died. And Hazael succeeded him.

Jehoram Reigns over Judah

16 In the fifth year of King Joram son of Ahab of Israel,[z] Jehoram son of King Jehoshaphat of Judah began to reign. [17]He was thirty-two years old when he became king, and he reigned eight years in Jerusalem. [18]He walked in the way of the kings of Israel, as the house of Ahab had done, for

8.16 Two Kings, One Name

It's difficult enough to keep 39 rulers straight. When two of them from neighboring countries have the same name, the plot thickens. Joram, a son of Ahab, ruled Israel at the same time Jehoram (sometimes spelled Joram also) took over Judah's throne. Both were wicked. Jehoram's marriage to Ahab's daughter ushered in a terrible period in Judah's history. (2 Chronicles 21 gives much more detail on this king.) In addition, both Judah and Israel had a king named Ahaziah.

the daughter of Ahab was his wife. He did what was evil in the sight of the LORD. [19]Yet the LORD would not destroy Judah, for the sake of his servant David, since he had promised to give a lamp to him and to his descendants forever.

20 In his days Edom revolted against the rule of Judah, and set up a king of their own. [21]Then Joram crossed over to Zair with all his chariots. He set out by night and attacked the Edomites and their chariot commanders who had surrounded him;[a] but his army fled home. [22]So Edom has been in revolt against the rule of Judah to this day. Libnah also revolted at the same time. [23]Now the rest of the acts of Joram, and all that he did, are they not written in the Book of the Annals of the Kings of Judah? [24]So Joram slept with his ancestors, and was buried with them in the city of David; his son Ahaziah succeeded him.

Ahaziah Reigns over Judah

25 In the twelfth year of King Joram son of Ahab of Israel, Ahaziah son of King Jehoram of Judah began to reign. [26]Ahaziah was twenty-two years old when he began to reign; he reigned one year in Jerusalem. His mother's name was Athaliah, a granddaughter of King Omri of Israel. [27]He also walked in the way of the house of Ahab, doing what was evil in the sight of the LORD, as the house of Ahab had done, for he was son-in-law to the house of Ahab.

28 He went with Joram son of Ahab to wage war against King Hazael of Aram at Ramoth-gilead, where the Arameans wounded Joram. [29]King Joram returned to be healed in Jezreel of the wounds that the Arameans had inflicted on him at Ramah, when he fought against King Hazael of Aram. King Ahaziah son of Jehoram of Judah went down to see Joram son of Ahab in Jezreel, because he was wounded.

---

y Heb lacks *Ben-hadad*   *z* Gk Syr: Heb adds *Jehoshaphat being king of Judah,*   *a* Meaning of Heb uncertain

Anointing of Jehu

9 Then the prophet Elisha called a member of the company of prophets[b] and said to him, "Gird up your loins; take this flask of oil in your

8.27 Political Marriages

Ahab shrewdly arranged marriages to cement alliances with Israel's neighbors. His wife Jezebel, for example, hailed from Phoenicia, which thus became an ally of Israel. Ahab also married off his daughter to the king of Judah, bringing peace to the two warring neighbors. Later, when Jehu revolted and slaughtered all of Ahab's family members, he aroused the ire of those allies and threw Israel's foreign policy into disarray.

hand, and go to Ramoth-gilead. ²When you arrive, look there for Jehu son of Jehoshaphat, son of Nimshi; go in and get him to leave his companions, and take him into an inner chamber. ³Then take the flask of oil, pour it on his head, and say, 'Thus says the LORD: I anoint you king over Israel.' Then open the door and flee; do not linger."

4 So the young man, the young prophet, went to Ramoth-gilead. ⁵He arrived while the commanders of the army were in council, and he announced, "I have a message for you, commander." "For which one of us?" asked Jehu. "For you, commander." ⁶So Jehu[c] got up and went inside; the young man poured the oil on his head, saying to him, "Thus says the LORD the God of Israel: I anoint you king over the people of the LORD, over Israel. ⁷You shall strike down the house of your master Ahab, so that I may avenge on Jezebel the blood of my servants the prophets, and the blood of all the servants of the LORD. ⁸For the whole house of Ahab shall perish; I will cut off from Ahab every male, bond or free, in Israel. ⁹I will make the house of Ahab like the house of Jeroboam son of Nebat, and like the house of Baasha son of Ahijah. ¹⁰The dogs shall eat Jezebel in the territory of Jezreel, and no one shall bury her." Then he opened the door and fled.

11 When Jehu came back to his master's officers, they said to him, "Is everything all right? Why did that madman come to you?" He answered them, "You know the sort and how they babble." ¹²They said, "Liar! Come on, tell us!" So he said, "This is just what he said to me: 'Thus says the LORD, I anoint you king over Israel.'" ¹³Then hurriedly they all took their cloaks and spread them for him on the bare[d] steps; and they blew the trumpet, and proclaimed, "Jehu is king."

Joram of Israel Killed

14 Thus Jehu son of Jehoshaphat son of Nimshi conspired against Joram. Joram with all Israel had been on guard at Ramoth-gilead against King Hazael of Aram; ¹⁵but King Joram had returned to be healed in Jezreel of the wounds that the Arameans had inflicted on him, when he fought against King Hazael of Aram. So Jehu said, "If this is your wish, then let no one slip out of the city to go and tell the news in Jezreel." ¹⁶Then Jehu mounted his chariot and went to Jezreel, where Joram was lying ill. King Ahaziah of Judah had come down to visit Joram.

17 In Jezreel, the sentinel standing on the tower spied the company of Jehu arriving, and said, "I see a company." Joram said, "Take a horseman; send him to meet them, and let him say, 'Is it peace?'" ¹⁸So the horseman went to meet him; he said, "Thus says the king, 'Is it peace?'" Jehu responded, "What have you to do with peace? Fall in behind me." The sentinel reported, saying, "The messenger reached them, but he is not coming back." ¹⁹Then he sent out a second horseman, who came to them and said, "Thus says the king, 'Is it peace?'" Jehu answered, "What have you to do with peace? Fall in behind me." ²⁰Again the sentinel reported, "He reached them, but he is not coming back. It looks like the driving of Jehu son of Nimshi; for he drives like a maniac."

21 Joram said, "Get ready." And they got his chariot ready. Then King Joram of Israel and King Ahaziah of Judah set out, each in his chariot, and went to meet Jehu; they met him at the property of Naboth the Jezreelite. ²²When Joram saw Jehu, he said, "Is it peace, Jehu?" He answered, "What peace can there be, so long as the many whoredoms and sorceries of your mother Jezebel continue?" ²³Then Joram reined about and fled, saying to Ahaziah, "Treason, Ahaziah!" ²⁴Jehu drew his bow with all his strength, and shot Joram between the shoulders, so that the arrow pierced his heart; and he sank in his chariot. ²⁵Jehu said to his aide Bidkar, "Lift him out, and throw him on the plot of ground belonging to Naboth the Jezreelite; for remember, when you and I rode side by side behind his father Ahab how the LORD uttered this oracle against him: ²⁶'For the blood of Naboth and for the blood of his children that I saw yesterday, says the LORD, I swear I will repay you on this very plot of ground.' Now therefore lift him out and throw him on the plot of ground, in accordance with the word of the LORD."

Ahaziah of Judah Killed

27 When King Ahaziah of Judah saw this, he fled in the direction of Beth-haggan. Jehu pursued him, saying, "Shoot him also!" And they

---

[b] Heb *sons of the prophets*   [c] Heb *he*   [d] Meaning of Heb uncertain

shot him[e] in the chariot at the ascent to Gur, which is by Ibleam. Then he fled to Megiddo, and died there. [28]His officers carried him in a chariot to Jerusalem, and buried him in his tomb with his ancestors in the city of David.

29 In the eleventh year of Joram son of Ahab, Ahaziah began to reign over Judah.

Jezebel's Violent Death

30 When Jehu came to Jezreel, Jezebel heard of it; she painted her eyes, and adorned her head, and looked out of the window. [31]As Jehu entered the gate, she said, "Is it peace, Zimri, murderer of your master?" [32]He looked up to the window and said, "Who is on my side? Who?" Two or three eunuchs looked out at him. [33]He said, "Throw her down." So they threw her down; some of her blood spattered on the wall and on the horses, which trampled on her. [34]Then he went in and ate and drank; he said, "See to that cursed woman and bury her; for she is a king's daughter." [35]But when they went to bury her, they found no more of her than the skull and the feet and the palms of her hands. [36]When they came back and told him, he said, "This is the word of the LORD, which he spoke by his servant Elijah the Tishbite, 'In the territory of Jezreel the dogs shall eat the flesh of Jezebel; [37]the corpse of Jezebel shall be like dung on the field in the territory of Jezreel, so that no one can say, This is Jezebel.'"

Massacre of Ahab's Descendants

10 Now Ahab had seventy sons in Samaria. So Jehu wrote letters and sent them to Samaria, to the rulers of Jezreel,[f] to the elders, and to the guardians of the sons of[g] Ahab, saying, [2]"Since your master's sons are with you and you have at your disposal chariots and horses, a fortified city, and weapons, [3]select the son of your master who is the best qualified, set him on his father's throne, and fight for your master's house." [4]But they were utterly terrified and said, "Look, two kings could not withstand him; how then can we stand?" [5]So the steward of the palace, and the governor of the city, along with the elders and the guardians, sent word to Jehu: "We are your servants; we will do anything you say. We will not make anyone king; do whatever you think right." [6]Then he wrote them a second letter, saying, "If you are on my side, and if you are ready to obey me, take the heads of your master's sons and come to me at Jezreel tomorrow at this time." Now the king's sons, seventy persons, were with the leaders of the city, who were charged with their upbringing. [7]When the letter reached them, they took the king's sons and killed them, seventy persons; they put their heads in baskets and sent them to him at Jezreel. [8]When the messenger came and told him, "They have brought the heads of the king's sons," he said, "Lay them in two heaps at the entrance of the gate until the

[e] Syr Vg Compare Gk: Heb lacks *and they shot him sons of*   [f] Or *of the city*; Vg Compare Gk   [g] Gk: Heb lacks *of the*

JEZEBEL *Wild and Wicked*

JEZEBEL WAS SUCH A REMARKABLE woman that her name came to define a type of person. "An impudent, shameless or abandoned woman," says the dictionary listing for jezebel. No modern jezebel ever exceeded the original, however. The proud, determined daughter of a king, Jezebel set out single-handedly to force Israel into paganism—and she nearly succeeded.

She came from Sidon on the Mediterranean coast, where her father reigned over the Phoenicians. Her royal wedding to Ahab, king of Israel, cemented an alliance between the two kingdoms. Other Israelite kings, such as Solomon, had also flouted God's law by marrying foreign wives. Typically, these women brought their religion with them (which explains why God forbade foreign marriage in the first place).

Jezebel went far beyond other foreign wives, however. Not content to worship Baal by herself, she insisted that all Israelites worship with her. She convinced Ahab to build a temple for Baal in the capital, and imported hundreds of foreign priests to work in that temple. She set out to exterminate the worship of Israel's God, killing anyone who stood in her way.

Only one man dared to oppose Jezebel publicly: the prophet Elijah. Yet even his amazing triumph on Mount Carmel (1 Kings 18) failed to faze her. God's unmistakable display of power only made her want to kill Elijah, not convert.

Jezebel died as she lived, cutting a memorable figure. When her luck ran out, she didn't beg for mercy. Like a Hollywood vamp she dressed up for the showdown and waited at the window to taunt the man who had come to deal with her. A woman who inspired no loyalty, she was tossed out the window by her own servants. As Elijah had prophesied (1 Kings 21.23), the town dogs devoured her body.

Life Questions: Some people say it doesn't matter what you believe, as long as you believe it with all your heart. What would Jezebel say to this? What would Elijah?

morning." [9]Then in the morning when he went out, he stood and said to all the people, "You are innocent. It was I who conspired against my master and killed him; but who struck down all these? [10]Know then that there shall fall to the earth nothing of the word of the LORD, which the LORD spoke concerning the house of Ahab; for the LORD has done what he said through his servant Elijah." [11]So Jehu killed all who were left of the house of Ahab in Jezreel, all his leaders, close friends, and priests, until he left him no survivor.

12 Then he set out and went to Samaria. On the way, when he was at Beth-eked of the Shepherds, [13]Jehu met relatives of King Ahaziah of Judah and said, "Who are you?" They answered, "We are kin of Ahaziah; we have come down to visit the royal princes and the sons of the queen mother." [14]He said, "Take them alive." They took them alive, and slaughtered them at the pit of Beth-eked, forty-two in all; he spared none of them.

10.14 Jehu's Slaughters

Jehu's bold attacks against the princes of Judah had serious consequences. To protect Israel against revenge from Judah and its friends, Jehu had to pay Assyria tribute. In fact, he is the only king of Israel whose picture has survived. A carving on an archaeological relic, the Black Obelisk, shows him paying tribute to Assyria. Although God had chosen Jehu to purge Israel, the Bible makes clear that his violence went far beyond his original assignment. God himself condemns Jehu in Hosea 1.4.

15 When he left there, he met Jehonadab son of Rechab coming to meet him; he greeted him, and said to him, "Is your heart as true to mine as mine is to yours?"[h] Jehonadab answered, "It is." Jehu said,[i] "If it is, give me your hand." So he gave him his hand. Jehu took him up with him into the chariot. [16]He said, "Come with me, and see my zeal for the LORD." So he[j] had him ride in his chariot. [17]When he came to Samaria, he killed all who were left to Ahab in Samaria, until he had wiped them out, according to the word of the LORD that he spoke to Elijah.

Slaughter of Worshipers of Baal

18 Then Jehu assembled all the people and said to them, "Ahab offered Baal small service; but Jehu will offer much more. [19]Now therefore summon to me all the prophets of Baal, all his worshipers, and all his priests; let none be missing, for I have a great sacrifice to offer to Baal;

whoever is missing shall not live." But Jehu was acting with cunning in order to destroy the worshipers of Baal. [20]Jehu decreed, "Sanctify a solemn assembly for Baal." So they proclaimed it. [21]Jehu sent word throughout all Israel; all the worshipers of Baal came, so that there was no one left who did not come. They entered the temple of Baal, until the temple of Baal was filled from wall to wall. [22]He said to the keeper of the wardrobe, "Bring out the vestments for all the worshipers of Baal." So he brought out the vestments for them. [23]Then Jehu entered the temple of Baal with Jehonadab son of Rechab; he said to the worshipers of Baal, "Search and see that there is no worshiper of the LORD here among you, but only worshipers of Baal." [24]Then they proceeded to offer sacrifices and burnt offerings.

Now Jehu had stationed eighty men outside, saying, "Whoever allows any of those to escape whom I deliver into your hands shall forfeit his life." [25]As soon as he had finished presenting the burnt offering, Jehu said to the guards and to the officers, "Come in and kill them; let no one escape." So they put them to the sword. The guards and the officers threw them out, and then went into the citadel of the temple of Baal. [26]They brought out the pillar[k] that was in the temple of Baal, and burned it. [27]Then they demolished the pillar of Baal, and destroyed the temple of Baal, and made it a latrine to this day.

28 Thus Jehu wiped out Baal from Israel. [29]But Jehu did not turn aside from the sins of Jeroboam son of Nebat, which he caused Israel to commit—the golden calves that were in Bethel and in Dan. [30]The LORD said to Jehu, "Because you have done well in carrying out what I consider right, and in accordance with all that was in my heart have dealt with the house of Ahab, your sons of the fourth generation shall sit on the throne of Israel." [31]But Jehu was not careful to follow the law of the LORD the God of Israel with all his heart; he did not turn from the sins of Jeroboam, which he caused Israel to commit.

Death of Jehu

32 In those days the LORD began to trim off parts of Israel. Hazael defeated them throughout the territory of Israel: [33]from the Jordan eastward, all the land of Gilead, the Gadites, the Reubenites, and the Manassites, from Aroer, which is by the Wadi Arnon, that is, Gilead and Bashan. [34]Now the rest of the acts of Jehu, all that he did, and all his power, are they not written in the Book of the Annals of the Kings of Israel? [35]So Jehu slept with his ancestors, and they buried him in Samaria. His son Jehoahaz succeeded him. [36]The time that Jehu reigned over Israel in Samaria was twenty-eight years.

---

[h] Gk: Heb *Is it right with your heart, as my heart is with your heart?*   [i] Gk: Heb lacks *Jehu said*   [j] Gk Syr Tg: Heb *they*   [k] Gk Vg Syr Tg: Heb *pillars*

Athaliah Reigns over Judah

11 Now when Athaliah, Ahaziah's mother, saw that her son was dead, she set about to destroy all the royal family. [2]But Jehosheba, King Joram's daughter, Ahaziah's sister, took Joash son of Ahaziah, and stole him away from among the king's children who were about to be killed; she put[l] him and his nurse in a bedroom. Thus she[m] hid him from Athaliah, so that he was not killed;

11.2 Preserving the Royal Line

Queen Athaliah came within one baby of wiping out the royal line descending from King David. The prophets predicted that Jesus the Messiah would come from David's line, so in a sense the entire future of God's plan rested with the family's success in hiding Joash and returning him to the throne.

[3]he remained with her six years, hidden in the house of the LORD, while Athaliah reigned over the land.

Jehoiada Anoints the Child Joash

4 But in the seventh year Jehoiada summoned the captains of the Carites and of the guards and had them come to him in the house of the LORD. He made a covenant with them and put them under oath in the house of the LORD; then he showed them the king's son. [5]He commanded them, "This is what you are to do: one-third of you, those who go off duty on the sabbath and guard the king's house [6](another third being at the gate Sur and a third at the gate behind the guards), shall guard the palace; [7]and your two divisions that come on duty in force on the sabbath and guard the house of the LORD[n] [8]shall surround the king, each with weapons in hand; and whoever approaches the ranks is to be killed. Be with the king in his comings and goings."

9 The captains did according to all that the priest Jehoiada commanded; each brought his men who were to go off duty on the sabbath, with those who were to come on duty on the sabbath, and came to the priest Jehoiada. [10]The priest delivered to the captains the spears and shields that had been King David's, which were in the house of the LORD; [11]the guards stood, every man with his weapons in his hand, from the south side of the house to the north side of the house, around the altar and the house, to guard the king on every side. [12]Then he brought out the king's son, put the crown on him, and gave him the covenant;[o] they proclaimed him king, and anointed

him; they clapped their hands and shouted, "Long live the king!"

Death of Athaliah

13 When Athaliah heard the noise of the guard and of the people, she went into the house of the LORD to the people; [14]when she looked, there was the king standing by the pillar, according to custom, with the captains and the trumpeters beside the king, and all the people of the land rejoicing and blowing trumpets. Athaliah tore her clothes and cried, "Treason! Treason!" [15]Then the priest Jehoiada commanded the captains who were set over the army, "Bring her out between the ranks, and kill with the sword anyone who follows her." For the priest said, "Let her not be killed in the house of the LORD." [16]So they laid hands on her; she went through the horses' entrance to the king's house, and there she was put to death.

17 Jehoiada made a covenant between the LORD and the king and people, that they should be the LORD's people; also between the king and the people. [18]Then all the people of the land went to the house of Baal, and tore it down; his altars and his images they broke in pieces, and they killed Mattan, the priest of Baal, before the altars. The priest posted guards over the house of the LORD. [19]He took the captains, the Carites, the guards, and all the people of the land; then they brought the king down from the house of the LORD, marching through the gate of the guards to the king's house. He took his seat on the throne of the kings. [20]So all the people of the land rejoiced; and the city was quiet after Athaliah had been killed with the sword at the king's house.

21[p] Jehoash[q] was seven years old when he began to reign.

The Temple Repaired

12 In the seventh year of Jehu, Jehoash began to reign; he reigned forty years in Jerusalem. His mother's name was Zibiah of Beersheba. [2]Jehoash did what was right in the sight of the LORD all his days, because the priest Jehoiada instructed him. [3]Nevertheless the high places were not taken away; the people continued to sacrifice and make offerings on the high places.

4 Jehoash said to the priests, "All the money offered as sacred donations that is brought into the house of the LORD, the money for which each person is assessed—the money from the assessment of persons—and the money from the voluntary offerings brought into the house of the LORD, [5]let the priests receive from each of the donors; and let them repair the house wherever any need of repairs is discovered." [6]But by the twenty-third year of King Jehoash the priests had

---

[l] With 2 Chr 22.11: Heb lacks *she put*　　[m] Gk Syr Vg Compare 2 Chr 22.11: Heb *they*　　[n] Heb the LORD *to the king*
[o] Or *treaty* or *testimony*; Heb *eduth*　　[p] Ch 12.1 in Heb　　[q] Another spelling is *Joash*; see verse 19

made no repairs on the house. [7]Therefore King Jehoash summoned the priest Jehoiada with the other priests and said to them, "Why are you not repairing the house? Now therefore do not accept any more money from your donors but hand it over for the repair of the house." [8]So the priests agreed that they would neither accept more money from the people nor repair the house.

9 Then the priest Jehoiada took a chest, made a hole in its lid, and set it beside the altar on the right side as one entered the house of the LORD; the priests who guarded the threshold put in it all the money that was brought into the house of the LORD. [10]Whenever they saw that there was a great deal of money in the chest, the king's secretary and the high priest went up, counted the money that was found in the house of the LORD, and tied it up in bags. [11]They would give the money that was weighed out into the hands of the workers who had the oversight of the house of the LORD; then they paid it out to the carpenters and the builders who worked on the house of the LORD, [12]to the masons and the stonecutters, as well as to buy timber and quarried stone for making repairs on the house of the LORD, as well as for any outlay for repairs of the house. [13]But for the house of the LORD no basins of silver, snuffers, bowls, trumpets, or any vessels of gold, or of silver, were made from the money that was brought into the house of the LORD, [14]for that was given to the workers who were repairing the house of the LORD with it. [15]They did not ask an accounting from those into whose hand they delivered the money to pay out to the workers, for they dealt honestly. [16]The money from the guilt offerings and the money from the sin offerings was not brought into the house of the LORD; it belonged to the priests.

Hazael Threatens Jerusalem

17 At that time King Hazael of Aram went up, fought against Gath, and took it. But when Hazael set his face to go up against Jerusalem, [18]King Jehoash of Judah took all the votive gifts that Jehoshaphat, Jehoram, and Ahaziah, his ancestors, the kings of Judah, had dedicated, as well as his own votive gifts, all the gold that was found in the treasuries of the house of the LORD and of the king's house, and sent these to King Hazael of Aram. Then Hazael withdrew from Jerusalem.

Death of Joash

19 Now the rest of the acts of Joash, and all that he did, are they not written in the Book of the Annals of the Kings of Judah? [20]His servants arose, devised a conspiracy, and killed Joash in the house of Millo, on the way that goes down to Silla. [21]It was Jozacar son of Shimeath and Jehozabad son of Shomer, his servants, who struck him down, so that he died. He was buried with his ancestors in the city of David; then his son Amaziah succeeded him.

Jehoahaz Reigns over Israel

13 In the twenty-third year of King Joash son of Ahaziah of Judah, Jehoahaz son of Jehu began to reign over Israel in Samaria; he reigned seventeen years. [2]He did what was evil in the sight of the LORD, and followed the sins of Jeroboam son of Nebat, which he caused Israel to sin; he did not depart from them. [3]The anger of the LORD was kindled against Israel, so that he gave them repeatedly into the hand of King Hazael of Aram, then into the hand of Ben-hadad son of Hazael. [4]But Jehoahaz entreated the LORD, and the LORD heeded him; for he saw the oppression of Israel,

13.4 Turnaround

Like so many kings of Israel, Jehoahaz started out doing "evil in the sight of the LORD." Unlike so many kings of Israel, he repented. God, never eager to punish and always willing to relent, accepted his change of heart. Unfortunately, Jehoahaz's repentance didn't rub off. The Israelites continued their idol worship, in direct disobedience of God's command.

how the king of Aram oppressed them. [5]Therefore the LORD gave Israel a savior, so that they escaped from the hand of the Arameans; and the people of Israel lived in their homes as formerly. [6]Nevertheless they did not depart from the sins of the house of Jeroboam, which he caused Israel to sin, but walked[r] in them; the sacred pole[s] also remained in Samaria. [7]So Jehoahaz was left with an army of not more than fifty horsemen, ten chariots and ten thousand footmen; for the king of Aram had destroyed them and made them like the dust at threshing. [8]Now the rest of the acts of Jehoahaz and all that he did, including his might, are they not written in the Book of the Annals of the Kings of Israel? [9]So Jehoahaz slept with his ancestors, and they buried him in Samaria; then his son Joash succeeded him.

Jehoash Reigns over Israel

10 In the thirty-seventh year of King Joash of Judah, Jehoash son of Jehoahaz began to reign over Israel in Samaria; he reigned sixteen years. [11]He also did what was evil in the sight of the LORD; he did not depart from all the sins of Jeroboam son of Nebat, which he caused Israel to sin, but he walked in them. [12]Now the rest of the acts of Joash, and all that he did, as well as the might with which he fought against King Amaziah of Judah, are they not written in the Book of the

---

[r] Gk Syr Tg Vg: Heb *he walked*   [s] Heb *Asherah*

Annals of the Kings of Israel? [13]So Joash slept with his ancestors, and Jeroboam sat upon his throne; Joash was buried in Samaria with the kings of Israel.

Death of Elisha

14 Now when Elisha had fallen sick with the illness of which he was to die, King Joash of Israel went down to him, and wept before him, crying, "My father, my father! The chariots of Israel and its horsemen!" [15]Elisha said to him, "Take a bow and arrows"; so he took a bow and arrows. [16]Then he said to the king of Israel, "Draw the bow"; and he drew it. Elisha laid his hands on the king's hands. [17]Then he said, "Open the window eastward"; and he opened it. Elisha said, "Shoot"; and he shot. Then he said, "The LORD's arrow of victory, the arrow of victory over Aram! For you shall fight the Arameans in Aphek until you have made an end of them." [18]He continued, "Take the arrows"; and he took them. He said to the king of Israel, "Strike the ground with them"; he struck three times, and stopped. [19]Then the man of God was angry with him, and said, "You should have struck five or six times; then you would have struck down Aram until you had made an end of it, but now you will strike down Aram only three times."

20 So Elisha died, and they buried him. Now bands of Moabites used to invade the land in the

13.20 Troublesome Neighbors

Moab and Aram (Syria) often make an appearance in the books of 1, 2 Kings. They were small kingdoms much like Judah and Israel. Sometimes they fought against Israel or Judah, and sometimes they joined together in alliances to oppose a larger threat. On the world scene, constant threats came from Egypt and Assyria. Assyria cut a huge swath through history before its empire declined. Later, Babylon became the giant of the region.

spring of the year. [21]As a man was being buried, a marauding band was seen and the man was thrown into the grave of Elisha; as soon as the man touched the bones of Elisha, he came to life and stood on his feet.

Israel Recaptures Cities from Aram

22 Now King Hazael of Aram oppressed Israel all the days of Jehoahaz. [23]But the LORD was gracious to them and had compassion on them; he turned toward them, because of his covenant with Abraham, Isaac, and Jacob, and would not destroy them; nor has he banished them from his presence until now.

24 When King Hazael of Aram died, his son Ben-hadad succeeded him. [25]Then Jehoash son of

Jehoahaz took again from Ben-hadad son of Hazael the towns that he had taken from his father Jehoahaz in war. Three times Joash defeated him and recovered the towns of Israel.

Amaziah Reigns over Judah

14 In the second year of King Joash son of Joahaz of Israel, King Amaziah son of Joash of Judah, began to reign. [2]He was twenty-five years old when he began to reign, and he reigned twenty-nine years in Jerusalem. His mother's name was Jehoaddin of Jerusalem. [3]He did what was right in the sight of the LORD, yet not like his ancestor David; in all things he did as his father Joash had done. [4]But the high places were not removed; the people still sacrificed and made offerings on the high places. [5]As soon as the royal power was firmly in his hand he killed his servants who had murdered his father the king. [6]But he did not put to death the children of the murderers; according to what is written in the book of the law of Moses, where the LORD commanded, "The parents shall not be put to death for the children, or the children be put to death for the parents; but all shall be put to death for their own sins."

7 He killed ten thousand Edomites in the Valley of Salt and took Sela by storm; he called it Jokthe-el, which is its name to this day.

8 Then Amaziah sent messengers to King Jehoash son of Jehoahaz, son of Jehu, of Israel, saying, "Come, let us look one another in the face." [9]King Jehoash of Israel sent word to King Amaziah of Judah, "A thornbush on Lebanon sent to a cedar on Lebanon, saying, 'Give your daughter to my son for a wife'; but a wild animal of Lebanon passed by and trampled down the thornbush. [10]You have indeed defeated Edom, and your heart has lifted you up. Be content with your glory, and stay at home; for why should you provoke trouble so that you fall, you and Judah with you?"

11 But Amaziah would not listen. So King Jehoash of Israel went up; he and King Amaziah of Judah faced one another in battle at Bethshemesh, which belongs to Judah. [12]Judah was defeated by Israel; everyone fled home. [13]King Jehoash of Israel captured King Amaziah of Judah son of Jehoash, son of Ahaziah, at Beth-shemesh; he came to Jerusalem, and broke down the wall of Jerusalem from the Ephraim Gate to the Corner Gate, a distance of four hundred cubits. [14]He seized all the gold and silver, and all the vessels that were found in the house of the LORD and in the treasuries of the king's house, as well as hostages; then he returned to Samaria.

15 Now the rest of the acts that Jehoash did, his might, and how he fought with King Amaziah of Judah, are they not written in the Book of the Annals of the Kings of Israel? [16]Jehoash slept with his ancestors, and was buried in Samaria with the

kings of Israel; then his son Jeroboam succeeded him.

17 King Amaziah son of Joash of Judah lived fifteen years after the death of King Jehoash son of Jehoahaz of Israel. 18Now the rest of the deeds of Amaziah, are they not written in the Book of the Annals of the Kings of Judah? 19They made a conspiracy against him in Jerusalem, and he fled to Lachish. But they sent after him to Lachish, and killed him there. 20They brought him on horses; he was buried in Jerusalem with his ancestors in the city of David. 21All the people of Judah took Azariah, who was sixteen years old, and made him king to succeed his father Amaziah. 22He rebuilt Elath and restored it to Judah, after King Amaziah*t* slept with his ancestors.

Jeroboam II Reigns over Israel

23 In the fifteenth year of King Amaziah son of Joash of Judah, King Jeroboam son of Joash of Israel began to reign in Samaria; he reigned forty-

14.23 Unfair Credit?

Secular historians report that Omri and Jeroboam were the strongest kings of Israel. Under them, the nation gained new heights of power and prestige. But consistently the books of 1, 2 Kings give little notice to political strength. They judge kings on the basis of spirituality, and thus both Omri and Jeroboam II are dismissed in a few paragraphs.

The wealthy-but-corrupt state of the nation during this time can be seen in the books by Amos and Hosea, both of whom prophesied in the beautiful city of Samaria. (Jonah also lived then—verse 25—but he prophesied in Nineveh, the capital city of Assyria.) Israel scoffed at these prophets' words of doom, but within 30 years all their dire predictions had come true.

one years. 24He did what was evil in the sight of the LORD; he did not depart from all the sins of Jeroboam son of Nebat, which he caused Israel to sin. 25He restored the border of Israel from Lebo-hamath as far as the Sea of the Arabah, according to the word of the LORD, the God of Israel, which he spoke by his servant Jonah son of Amittai, the prophet, who was from Gath-hepher. 26For the LORD saw that the distress of Israel was very bitter; there was no one left, bond or free, and no one to help Israel. 27But the LORD had not said that he would blot out the name of Israel from under heaven, so he saved them by the hand of Jeroboam son of Joash.

28 Now the rest of the acts of Jeroboam, and all that he did, and his might, how he fought, and how he recovered for Israel Damascus and Ha-

math, which had belonged to Judah, are they not written in the Book of the Annals of the Kings of Israel? 29Jeroboam slept with his ancestors, the kings of Israel; his son Zechariah succeeded him.

Azariah Reigns over Judah

15 In the twenty-seventh year of King Jeroboam of Israel King Azariah son of Amaziah of Judah began to reign. 2He was sixteen years old when he began to reign, and he reigned fifty-two years in Jerusalem. His mother's name was Jecoliah of Jerusalem. 3He did what was right in the sight of the LORD, just as his father Amaziah had done. 4Nevertheless the high places were not taken away; the people still sacrificed and made offerings on the high places. 5The LORD struck the king, so that he was leprous*u* to the day of his death, and lived in a separate house. Jotham the king's son was in charge of the palace, governing the people of the land. 6Now the rest of the acts of Azariah, and all that he did, are they not written in the Book of the Annals of the Kings of Judah? 7Azariah slept with his ancestors; they buried him with his ancestors in the city of David; his son Jotham succeeded him.

Zechariah Reigns over Israel

8 In the thirty-eighth year of King Azariah of Judah, Zechariah son of Jeroboam reigned over Israel in Samaria six months. 9He did what was evil in the sight of the LORD, as his ancestors had done. He did not depart from the sins of Jeroboam son of Nebat, which he caused Israel to sin. 10Shallum son of Jabesh conspired against him, and struck him down in public and killed him, and reigned in place of him. 11Now the rest of the deeds of Zechariah are written in the Book of the Annals of the Kings of Israel. 12This was the promise of the LORD that he gave to Jehu, "Your sons shall sit on the throne of Israel to the fourth generation." And so it happened.

Shallum Reigns over Israel

13 Shallum son of Jabesh began to reign in the thirty-ninth year of King Uzziah of Judah; he reigned one month in Samaria. 14Then Menahem son of Gadi came up from Tirzah and came to Samaria; he struck down Shallum son of Jabesh in Samaria and killed him; he reigned in place of him. 15Now the rest of the deeds of Shallum, including the conspiracy that he made, are written in the Book of the Annals of the Kings of Israel. 16At that time Menahem sacked Tiphsah, all who were in it and its territory from Tirzah on; because they did not open it to him, he sacked it. He ripped open all the pregnant women in it.

Menahem Reigns over Israel

17 In the thirty-ninth year of King Azariah of

---

t Heb *the king*   *u* A term for several skin diseases; precise meaning uncertain

Judah, Menahem son of Gadi began to reign over Israel; he reigned ten years in Samaria. [18]He did what was evil in the sight of the LORD; he did not depart all his days from any of the sins of Jeroboam son of Nebat, which he caused Israel to sin. [19]King Pul of Assyria came against the land; Menahem gave Pul a thousand talents of silver, so that he might help him confirm his hold on the royal power. [20]Menahem exacted the money from Israel, that is, from all the wealthy, fifty shekels of silver from each one, to give to the king of Assyria. So the king of Assyria turned back, and did not stay there in the land. [21]Now the rest of the deeds of Menahem, and all that he did, are they not written in the Book of the Annals of the Kings of Israel? [22]Menahem slept with his ancestors, and his son Pekahiah succeeded him.

Pekahiah Reigns over Israel

[23] In the fiftieth year of King Azariah of Judah, Pekahiah son of Menahem began to reign over Israel in Samaria; he reigned two years. [24]He did what was evil in the sight of the LORD; he did not turn away from the sins of Jeroboam son of Nebat, which he caused Israel to sin. [25]Pekah son of Remaliah, his captain, conspired against him with fifty of the Gileadites, and attacked him in Samaria, in the citadel of the palace along with Argob and Arieh; he killed him, and reigned in place of him. [26]Now the rest of the deeds of Pekahiah, and all that he did, are written in the Book of the Annals of the Kings of Israel.

Pekah Reigns over Israel

[27] In the fifty-second year of King Azariah of Judah, Pekah son of Remaliah began to reign over Israel in Samaria; he reigned twenty years. [28]He did what was evil in the sight of the LORD; he did not depart from the sins of Jeroboam son of Nebat, which he caused Israel to sin. [29] In the days of King Pekah of Israel, King Tiglath-pileser of Assyria came and captured Ijon, Abel-beth-maacah, Janoah, Kedesh, Hazor, Gilead, and Galilee, all the land of Naphtali; and he carried the people captive to Assyria. [30]Then Hoshea son of Elah made a conspiracy against Pekah son of Remaliah, attacked him, and killed him; he reigned in place of him, in the twentieth year of Jotham son of Uzziah. [31]Now the rest of the acts of Pekah, and all that he did, are written in the Book of the Annals of the Kings of Israel.

Jotham Reigns over Judah

[32] In the second year of King Pekah son of Remaliah of Israel, King Jotham son of Uzziah of Judah began to reign. [33]He was twenty-five years old when he began to reign and reigned sixteen years in Jerusalem. His mother's name was Jerusha daughter of Zadok. [34]He did what was right in the sight of the LORD, just as his father Uzziah had done. [35]Nevertheless the high places were not removed; the people still sacrificed and made offerings on the high places. He built the upper gate of the house of the LORD. [36]Now the rest of the acts of Jotham, and all that he did, are they not written in the Book of the Annals of the Kings of Judah? [37]In those days the LORD began to send King Rezin of Aram and Pekah son of Remaliah against Judah. [38]Jotham slept with his ancestors, and was buried with his ancestors in the city of David, his ancestor; his son Ahaz succeeded him.

Ahaz Reigns over Judah

16 In the seventeenth year of Pekah son of Remaliah, King Ahaz son of Jotham of Judah began to reign. [2]Ahaz was twenty years old

16.1 Ahaz's Fateful Decisions

King Ahaz figured large in the histories of Israel and Judah. When Israel theatened his kingdom of Judah, he purchased military aid from Assyria. In response, Assyria obliterated Israel and made Judah a virtual puppet. Worse, Ahaz copied the pagan religions of his conquered territories, even to the extent of sacrificing his son in the fire.

when he began to reign; he reigned sixteen years in Jerusalem. He did not do what was right in the sight of the LORD his God, as his ancestor David had done, [3]but he walked in the way of the kings of Israel. He even made his son pass through fire, according to the abominable practices of the nations whom the LORD drove out before the people of Israel. [4]He sacrificed and made offerings on the high places, on the hills, and under every green tree.

[5] Then King Rezin of Aram and King Pekah son of Remaliah of Israel came up to wage war on Jerusalem; they besieged Ahaz but could not conquer him. [6]At that time the king of Edom[v] recovered Elath for Edom,[w] and drove the Judeans from Elath; and the Edomites came to Elath, where they live to this day. [7]Ahaz sent messengers to King Tiglath-pileser of Assyria, saying, "I am your servant and your son. Come up, and rescue me from the hand of the king of Aram and from the hand of the king of Israel, who are attacking me." [8]Ahaz also took the silver and gold found in the house of the LORD and in the treasures of the king's house, and sent a present to the king of Assyria. [9]The king of Assyria listened to him; the king of Assyria marched up against Damascus, and took it, carrying its people captive to Kir; then he killed Rezin.

[10] When King Ahaz went to Damascus to

[v] Cn: Heb *King Rezin of Aram*   [w] Cn: Heb *Aram*

meet King Tiglath-pileser of Assyria, he saw the altar that was at Damascus. King Ahaz sent to the priest Uriah a model of the altar, and its pattern, exact in all its details. [11]The priest Uriah built the altar; in accordance with all that King Ahaz had sent from Damascus, just so did the priest Uriah build it, before King Ahaz arrived from Damascus. [12]When the king came from Damascus, the king viewed the altar. Then the king drew near to the altar, went up on it, [13]and offered his burnt offering and his grain offering, poured his drink offering, and dashed the blood of his offerings of well-being against the altar. [14]The bronze altar that was before the LORD he removed from the front of the house, from the place between his altar and the house of the LORD, and put it on the north side of his altar. [15]King Ahaz commanded the priest Uriah, saying, "Upon the great altar offer the morning burnt offering, and the evening grain offering, and the king's burnt offering, and his grain offering, with the burnt offering of all the people of the land, their grain offering, and their drink offering; then dash against it all the blood of the burnt offering, and all the blood of the sacrifice; but the bronze altar shall be for me to inquire by." [16]The priest Uriah did everything that King Ahaz commanded.

17 Then King Ahaz cut off the frames of the stands, and removed the laver from them; he removed the sea from the bronze oxen that were under it, and put it on a pediment of stone. [18]The covered portal for use on the sabbath that had been built inside the palace, and the outer entrance for the king he removed from[x] the house of the LORD. He did this because of the king of Assyria. [19]Now the rest of the acts of Ahaz that he did, are they not written in the Book of the Annals of the Kings of Judah? [20]Ahaz slept with his ancestors, and was buried with his ancestors in the city of David; his son Hezekiah succeeded him.

Hoshea Reigns over Israel

17 In the twelfth year of King Ahaz of Judah, Hoshea son of Elah began to reign in Samaria over Israel; he reigned nine years. [2]He did what was evil in the sight of the LORD, yet not like the kings of Israel who were before him. [3]King Shalmaneser of Assyria came up against him; Hoshea became his vassal, and paid him tribute. [4]But the king of Assyria found treachery in Hoshea; for he had sent messengers to King So of Egypt, and offered no tribute to the king of Assyria, as he had done year by year; therefore the king of Assyria confined him and imprisoned him.

Israel Carried Captive to Assyria

5 Then the king of Assyria invaded all the land and came to Samaria; for three years he besieged it. [6]In the ninth year of Hoshea the king of Assyria captured Samaria; he carried the Israelites away to Assyria. He placed them in Halah, on the Habor, the river of Gozan, and in the cities of the Medes.

7 This occurred because the people of Israel had sinned against the LORD their God, who had brought them up out of the land of Egypt from under the hand of Pharaoh king of Egypt. They had worshiped other gods [8]and walked in the customs of the nations whom the LORD drove out before the people of Israel, and in the customs that the kings of Israel had introduced.[y] [9]The people of Israel secretly did things that were not right against the LORD their God. They built for themselves high places at all their towns, from watchtower to fortified city; [10]they set up for themselves pillars and sacred poles[z] on every high hill and under every green tree; [11]there they made offerings on all the high places, as the nations did whom the LORD carried away before them. They did wicked things, provoking the LORD to anger; [12]they served idols, of which the LORD had said to them, "You shall not do this." [13]Yet the LORD warned Israel and Judah by every prophet and every seer, saying, "Turn from your evil ways and keep my commandments and my statutes, in accordance with all the law that I commanded your ancestors and that I sent to you by my servants the prophets." [14]They would not listen but were stubborn, as their ancestors had been, who did not believe in the LORD their God. [15]They despised his statutes, and his covenant that he made with their ancestors, and the warnings that he gave them. They went after false idols and became false; they followed the nations that were around them, concerning whom the LORD had commanded them that they should not do as they did. [16]They rejected all the commandments of the LORD their God and made for themselves cast images of two calves; they made a sacred pole,[a] worshiped all the host of heaven, and served Baal. [17]They made their sons and their daughters pass through fire; they used divination and augury; and they sold themselves to do evil in the sight of the LORD, provoking him to anger. [18]Therefore the LORD was very angry with Israel and removed them out of his sight; none was left but the tribe of Judah alone.

19 Judah also did not keep the commandments of the LORD their God but walked in the customs that Israel had introduced. [20]The LORD rejected all the descendants of Israel; he punished them and gave them into the hand of plunderers, until he had banished them from his presence.

21 When he had torn Israel from the house of David, they made Jeroboam son of Nebat king. Jeroboam drove Israel from following the LORD and made them commit great sin. [22]The people

x Cn: Heb lacks *from*   y Meaning of Heb uncertain   z Heb *Asherim*   a Heb *Asherah*

Why All the Fuss about Idols?

The strange practice that led to a kingdom's fall

They went after false idols and became false.

17.15

YOU CANNOT READ VERY FAR in the Old Testament without encountering idols, for idolatry ranks as perhaps the most common topic in the Bible. A nagging question haunts these pages: Why did the Israelites keep deserting the God who had delivered them from Egypt for the sake of carved tree trunks and bronze statues? What was the big attraction?

Idolatry seems especially strange to us in modern times. Today, idols may show up as exotic props in a movie, but does anyone truly believe in them anymore? Why do they merit so much attention in the Old Testament?

Responses to Idols Today

Actually, idols still thrive in such places as Africa and Asia, and their effect on the people there sheds light on Old Testament idolatry. In India, for example, each city and village has its own favorite god—over 1,000 different gods are worshiped. Portable idols stand on street corners of the major cities.

For devout Hindus, idolatry adds a dimension of magic to life. Hindus believe the gods control all events, including such disasters as monsoons, floods, diseases, and traffic accidents. These powerful gods must be kept happy at all costs.

But what pleases a god depends on the god's character, and gods can be fearsome and violent. Some Indians worship idols in the form of a snake; others worship the smallpox goddess. The largest city in India, Calcutta, has adopted the murderous goddess Kali, who wears a garland of gruesome heads around her waist. Devotion to such gods can easily lead to a paralyzing fear. If Kali isn't kept happy, her followers believe, she will cruelly punish them.

Other Hindus, less devout, take a different approach. They treat their gods almost as good-luck charms. A taxi driver mounts a tiny statue of a monkey god on the dashboard of his car, occasionally draping it with flowers for decoration. If you ask, he'll say he prays to the god for safety—but you know about the traffic in India, he adds with a laugh.

A Good-Luck Charm or an Evil Cult

Idolatry had similar effects on the ancient Israelites. Some Israelites took the same spirit as the Indian taxi driver: Maybe an idol will help you out, maybe not, but why not play along? They drifted carelessly from god to god, adopting the religion of whatever group seemed to be having the most success with its agriculture or armies.

No attitude could be further from that demanded by the true God. He had chosen the Israelites as a kingdom of priests, a treasured possession set apart for him. As Lord of the universe, he wanted not a casual faith, but total allegiance. He was not a good-luck charm.

Far too often, however, idols in Israel took on a more sinister form, resembling the evil goddess of Calcutta. Legends about Baal, for example, celebrated his drunkenness and debauchery. Followers worshiped him by having sex in the temple with prostitutes or even by sacrificing human babies.

Worshiping Baal meant a complete rejection of God's special relationship with the Israelites—a crime very much like adultery, as the prophets often pointed out. Baal worship could not possibly coexist with the worship of God.

What Was the Appeal?

Why did Baal and the other idols prove so appealing to the Israelites? Like peasants gawking at big-city life, the Israelites moved from 40 years of wilderness wanderings into a land of cities and more advanced technology. They had been landless nomads and shepherds. When they settled down to a new occupation of farming, they looked to a Canaanite god, Baal, as a possible means of guaranteeing good crops. In other words, they sought a shortcut through magic.

Similarly, when a mighty army threatened their borders, they smuggled in a few of that army's favorite idols, hedging their bets in case their own religion did not bring them military success. Idols became a phantom source of power, an alternative place to invest faith and hope.

Idolatry made such inroads into Israel and Judah that God had to tear apart both kingdoms in order to root it out. Second Kings clearly blames idolatry as the chief sin leading to both nations' collapse. History records that the punishment ultimately worked. After the Assyrian and Babylonian invasions, never again did the Israelites dabble in idolatry.

Life Questions: Idolatry need not involve images of wood or stone; it's possible to worship such things as money, another person, or fame. What are some "idols" you might be tempted to worship?

of Israel continued in all the sins that Jeroboam committed; they did not depart from them ²³until the LORD removed Israel out of his sight, as he had foretold through all his servants the prophets.

17.17 A Higher Standard

To the casual eye, it seemed unfair. God let the Assyrians, a much crueler people, conquer Israel and take the whole nation into exile. Why? Israel was judged by a higher standard, on the basis of the great advantages God had given them. As Jesus would say hundreds of years later, "From the one to whom much has been entrusted, even more will be demanded" (Luke 12.48).

A hair-raising list of Israel's sins (verses 7–23) shows why they deserved judgment: they adopted their neighbors' fertility religion, even offering their own children as human sacrifices. Assyria lacked Israel's advantages, but they would be judged too—which explains why the powerful nation of Assyria no longer exists.

So Israel was exiled from their own land to Assyria until this day.

Assyria Resettles Samaria

24 The king of Assyria brought people from Babylon, Cuthah, Avva, Hamath, and Sepharvaim, and placed them in the cities of Samaria in place of the people of Israel; they took possession

17.24 Scorched-Earth Policy

In early wars Assyrian conquerors followed a cruel policy of genocide. They exterminated their enemies and destroyed their land and property. But in later years they adopted a new technique: deporting their victims to Assyria and other countries and replacing them with foreigners from other conquered territories. In this way, they disrupted cultures and made sure the conquered peoples would never regroup and rise up as a new threat. This verse shows the origin of Samaritans, a group that still existed in New Testament times and, in fact, can still be found in modern Israel. They combined their own religions with some reverence for the true God.

of Samaria, and settled in its cities. ²⁵When they first settled there, they did not worship the LORD; therefore the LORD sent lions among them, which killed some of them. ²⁶So the king of Assyria was told, "The nations that you have carried away and placed in the cities of Samaria do not know the law of the god of the land; therefore he has sent lions among them; they are killing them, because they do not know the law of the god of the land." ²⁷Then the king of Assyria commanded, "Send there one of the priests whom you carried away from there; let him[b] go and live there, and teach them the law of the god of the land." ²⁸So one of the priests whom they had carried away from Samaria came and lived in Bethel; he taught them how they should worship the LORD.

29 But every nation still made gods of its own and put them in the shrines of the high places that the people of Samaria had made, every nation in the cities in which they lived; ³⁰the people of Babylon made Succoth-benoth, the people of Cuth made Nergal, the people of Hamath made Ashima; ³¹the Avvites made Nibhaz and Tartak; the Sepharvites burned their children in the fire to Adrammelech and Anammelech, the gods of Sepharvaim. ³²They also worshiped the LORD and appointed from among themselves all sorts of people as priests of the high places, who sacrificed for them in the shrines of the high places. ³³So they worshiped the LORD but also served their own gods, after the manner of the nations from among whom they had been carried away. ³⁴To this day they continue to practice their former customs.

They do not worship the LORD and they do not follow the statutes or the ordinances or the law or the commandment that the LORD commanded the children of Jacob, whom he named Israel. ³⁵The LORD had made a covenant with them and commanded them, "You shall not worship other gods or bow yourselves to them or serve them or sacrifice to them, ³⁶but you shall worship the LORD, who brought you out of the land of Egypt with great power and with an outstretched arm; you shall bow yourselves to him, and to him you shall sacrifice. ³⁷The statutes and the ordinances and the law and the commandment that he wrote for you, you shall always be careful to observe. You shall not worship other gods; ³⁸you shall not forget the covenant that I have made with you. You shall not worship other gods, ³⁹but you shall worship the LORD your God; he will deliver you out of the hand of all your enemies." ⁴⁰They would not listen, however, but they continued to practice their former custom.

41 So these nations worshiped the LORD, but also served their carved images; to this day their children and their children's children continue to do as their ancestors did.

Hezekiah's Reign over Judah

18 In the third year of King Hoshea son of Elah of Israel, Hezekiah son of King Ahaz of Judah began to reign. ²He was twenty-five

---

b Syr Vg: Heb them

years old when he began to reign; he reigned twenty-nine years in Jerusalem. His mother's name was Abi daughter of Zechariah. ³He did what was right in the sight of the LORD just as his ancestor David had done. ⁴He removed the high places, broke down the pillars, and cut down the sacred pole.ᶜ He broke in pieces the bronze serpent that Moses had made, for until those days the people of Israel had made offerings to it; it was called Nehushtan. ⁵He trusted in the LORD the God of Israel; so that there was no one like him among all the kings of Judah after him, or among those who were before him. ⁶For he held fast to the LORD; he did not depart from following him but kept the commandments that the LORD commanded Moses. ⁷The LORD was with him; wherever he went, he prospered. He rebelled against the king of Assyria and would not serve him. ⁸He attacked the Philistines as far as Gaza and its territory, from watchtower to fortified city.

9 In the fourth year of King Hezekiah, which was the seventh year of King Hoshea son of Elah of Israel, King Shalmaneser of Assyria came up against Samaria, besieged it, ¹⁰and at the end of three years, took it. In the sixth year of Hezekiah, which was the ninth year of King Hoshea of Israel, Samaria was taken. ¹¹The king of Assyria carried the Israelites away to Assyria, settled them in Halah, on the Habor, the river of Gozan, and in the cities of the Medes, ¹²because they did not obey the voice of the LORD their God but transgressed his covenant—all that Moses the servant of the LORD had commanded; they neither listened nor obeyed.

Sennacherib Invades Judah

13 In the fourteenth year of King Hezekiah, King Sennacherib of Assyria came up against all the fortified cities of Judah and captured them. ¹⁴King Hezekiah of Judah sent to the king of Assyria at Lachish, saying, "I have done wrong; withdraw from me; whatever you impose on me I will bear." The king of Assyria demanded of King Hezekiah of Judah three hundred talents of silver and thirty talents of gold. ¹⁵Hezekiah gave him all the silver that was found in the house of the LORD and in the treasuries of the king's house. ¹⁶At that time Hezekiah stripped the gold from the doors of the temple of the LORD, and from the doorposts that King Hezekiah of Judah had overlaid and gave it to the king of Assyria. ¹⁷The king of Assyria sent the Tartan, the Rabsaris, and the Rabshakeh with a great army from Lachish to King Hezekiah at Jerusalem. They went up and came to Jerusalem. When they arrived, they came and stood by the conduit of the upper pool, which is on the highway to the Fuller's Field. ¹⁸When they called for the king, there came out to them Eliakim son of Hilkiah, who was in charge of the

palace, and Shebnah the secretary, and Joah son of Asaph, the recorder.

19 The Rabshakeh said to them, "Say to Hezekiah: Thus says the great king, the king of Assyria: On what do you base this confidence of yours?

18.16 King of Contradictions

Overall, Hezekiah made a good king, trusting in God. But his life contained a mixture of wisdom and folly, vice and virtue. On the good side, Hezekiah "trusted in the LORD" (verse 5), cleansed Judah from idol worship, and won independence from the powerful nations around. When he prayed for healing, he was granted an unprecedented extension of his life (20.1–11).

On the bad side, Hezekiah foolishly tried to bribe the Assyrians with gold stripped from the temple. Later, when representatives from Babylon came (20.13), he boastfully showed them all his treasures. And when the prophet Isaiah warned that Babylon would come back to take those treasures and more, Hezekiah blithely contented himself that there would be "peace and security in my days" (20.19).

²⁰Do you think that mere words are strategy and power for war? On whom do you now rely, that you have rebelled against me? ²¹See, you are relying now on Egypt, that broken reed of a staff, which will pierce the hand of anyone who leans on it. Such is Pharaoh king of Egypt to all who rely on him. ²²But if you say to me, 'We rely on the LORD our God,' is it not he whose high places and altars Hezekiah has removed, saying to Judah and to Jerusalem, 'You shall worship before this altar in Jerusalem'? ²³Come now, make a wager with my master the king of Assyria: I will give you two thousand horses, if you are able on your part to set riders on them. ²⁴How then can you repulse a single captain among the least of my master's servants, when you rely on Egypt for chariots and for horsemen? ²⁵Moreover, is it without the LORD that I have come up against this place to destroy it? The LORD said to me, Go up against this land, and destroy it."

26 Then Eliakim son of Hilkiah, and Shebnah, and Joah said to the Rabshakeh, "Please speak to your servants in the Aramaic language, for we understand it; do not speak to us in the language of Judah within the hearing of the people who are on the wall." ²⁷But the Rabshakeh said to them, "Has my master sent me to speak these words to your master and to you, and not to the people sitting on the wall, who are doomed with you to eat their own dung and to drink their own urine?"

ᶜ Heb *Asherah*

28 Then the Rabshakeh stood and called out in a loud voice in the language of Judah, "Hear the word of the great king, the king of Assyria! 29Thus says the king: 'Do not let Hezekiah deceive you, for he will not be able to deliver you out of my hand. 30Do not let Hezekiah make you rely on the LORD by saying, The LORD will surely deliver us, and this city will not be given into the hand of the king of Assyria.' 31Do not listen to Hezekiah; for thus says the king of Assyria: 'Make your peace with me and come out to me; then every one of you will eat from your own vine and your own fig tree, and drink water from your own cistern, 32until I come and take you away to a land like your own land, a land of grain and wine, a land of bread and vineyards, a land of olive oil and honey, that you may live and not die. Do not listen to Hezekiah when he misleads you by saying, The LORD will deliver us. 33Has any of the gods of the nations ever delivered its land out of the hand of the king of Assyria? 34Where are the gods of Hamath and Arpad? Where are the gods of Sepharvaim, Hena, and Ivvah? Have they delivered Samaria out of my hand? 35Who among all the gods of the countries have delivered their countries out of my hand, that the LORD should deliver Jerusalem out of my hand?'"

36 But the people were silent and answered him not a word, for the king's command was, "Do not answer him." 37Then Eliakim son of Hilkiah, who was in charge of the palace, and Shebna the secretary, and Joah son of Asaph, the recorder, came to Hezekiah with their clothes torn and told him the words of the Rabshakeh.

Hezekiah Consults Isaiah

19 When King Hezekiah heard it, he tore his clothes, covered himself with sackcloth, and went into the house of the LORD. 2And he sent Eliakim, who was in charge of the palace, and Shebna the secretary, and the senior priests, covered with sackcloth, to the prophet Isaiah son of Amoz. 3They said to him, "Thus says Hezekiah, This day is a day of distress, of rebuke, and of disgrace; children have come to the birth, and there is no strength to bring them forth. 4It may be that the LORD your God heard all the words of the Rabshakeh, whom his master the king of Assyria has sent to mock the living God, and will rebuke the words that the LORD your God has heard; therefore lift up your prayer for the remnant that is left." 5When the servants of King Hezekiah came to Isaiah, 6Isaiah said to them, "Say to your master, 'Thus says the LORD: Do not be afraid because of the words that you have heard, with which the servants of the king of Assyria have reviled me. 7I myself will put a spirit in him, so that he shall hear a rumor and return to his own land; I will cause him to fall by the sword in his own land.'"

Sennacherib's Threat

8 The Rabshakeh returned, and found the king of Assyria fighting against Libnah; for he had heard that the king had left Lachish. 9When the king[d] heard concerning King Tirhakah of Ethiopia,[e] "See, he has set out to fight against you," he sent messengers again to Hezekiah, saying, 10"Thus shall you speak to King Hezekiah of Judah: Do not let your God on whom you rely deceive you by promising that Jerusalem will not be given into the hand of the king of Assyria. 11See, you have heard what the kings of Assyria have done to all lands, destroying them utterly. Shall you be delivered? 12Have the gods of the nations delivered them, the nations that my predecessors destroyed, Gozan, Haran, Rezeph, and the people of Eden who were in Telassar? 13Where is the king of Hamath, the king of Arpad, the king of the city of Sepharvaim, the king of Hena, or the king of Ivvah?"

Hezekiah's Prayer

14 Hezekiah received the letter from the hand of the messengers and read it; then Hezekiah went up to the house of the LORD and spread it before the LORD. 15And Hezekiah prayed before the LORD, and said: "O LORD the God of Israel, who are enthroned above the cherubim, you are God, you alone, of all the kingdoms of the earth; you have made heaven and earth. 16Incline your ear, O LORD, and hear; open your eyes, O LORD, and see; hear the words of Sennacherib, which he has sent to mock the living God. 17Truly, O LORD, the kings of Assyria have laid waste the nations and their lands, 18and have hurled their gods into the fire, though they were no gods but the work of human hands—wood and stone—and so they were destroyed. 19So now, O LORD our God, save us, I pray you, from his hand, so that all the kingdoms of the earth may know that you, O LORD, are God alone."

20 Then Isaiah son of Amoz sent to Hezekiah, saying, "Thus says the LORD, the God of Israel: I have heard your prayer to me about King Sennacherib of Assyria. 21This is the word that the LORD has spoken concerning him:

She despises you, she scorns you—
  virgin daughter Zion;
she tosses her head—behind your back,
  daughter Jerusalem.

22 "Whom have you mocked and reviled?
  Against whom have you raised your
      voice
  and haughtily lifted your eyes?
  Against the Holy One of Israel!

---

d Heb *he*   *e* Or *Nubia*; Heb *Cush*

23 By your messengers you have mocked the
  Lord,
  and you have said, 'With my many
    chariots
  I have gone up the heights of the
    mountains,
  to the far recesses of Lebanon;
  I felled its tallest cedars,
    its choicest cypresses;
  I entered its farthest retreat,
    its densest forest.
24 I dug wells
    and drank foreign waters,
  I dried up with the sole of my foot
    all the streams of Egypt.'

25 "Have you not heard
    that I determined it long ago?
  I planned from days of old
    what now I bring to pass,
  that you should make fortified cities
    crash into heaps of ruins,
26 while their inhabitants, shorn of strength,
    are dismayed and confounded;
  they have become like plants of the field
    and like tender grass,
  like grass on the housetops,
    blighted before it is grown.

27 "But I know your rising*f* and your
    sitting,
  your going out and coming in,
    and your raging against me.
28 Because you have raged against me
    and your arrogance has come to my
      ears,
  I will put my hook in your nose
    and my bit in your mouth;
  I will turn you back on the way
    by which you came.

29 "And this shall be the sign for you: This
year you shall eat what grows of itself, and in the
second year what springs from that; then in the
third year sow, reap, plant vineyards, and eat their
fruit. 30The surviving remnant of the house of
Judah shall again take root downward, and bear
fruit upward; 31for from Jerusalem a remnant
shall go out, and from Mount Zion a band of
survivors. The zeal of the LORD of hosts will do
this.

32 "Therefore thus says the LORD concerning
the king of Assyria: He shall not come into this
city, shoot an arrow there, come before it with a
shield, or cast up a siege ramp against it. 33By the
way that he came, by the same he shall return; he
shall not come into this city, says the LORD. 34For
I will defend this city to save it, for my own sake
and for the sake of my servant David."

Sennacherib's Defeat and Death

35 That very night the angel of the LORD set
out and struck down one hundred eighty-five
thousand in the camp of the Assyrians; when

19.31 Deliverance for Jerusalem

*Jerusalem appeared to be a doomed city
during the dark days of Assyria's siege. But two
things happened to fulfill this prophecy. First, a
great plague struck the Assyrians (verse 35), a
plague also recorded by the historian
Herodotus. Later, the murder of Assyria's
leader brought internal chaos to that country,
canceling out the Assyrian threat. The
miraculous deliverance convinced some
Israelites that Jerusalem, God's city, was
indestructible— a belief that would later be
proven false.*

morning dawned, they were all dead bodies.
36Then King Sennacherib of Assyria left, went
home, and lived at Nineveh. 37As he was worshiping in the house of his god Nisroch, his sons
Adrammelech and Sharezer killed him with the
sword, and they escaped into the land of Ararat.
His son Esar-haddon succeeded him.

Hezekiah's Illness

20 In those days Hezekiah became sick and
was at the point of death. The prophet
Isaiah son of Amoz came to him, and said to him,
"Thus says the LORD: Set your house in order, for
you shall die; you shall not recover." 2Then Hezekiah turned his face to the wall and prayed to the
LORD: 3"Remember now, O LORD, I implore you,
how I have walked before you in faithfulness with
a whole heart, and have done what is good in
your sight." Hezekiah wept bitterly. 4Before Isaiah
had gone out of the middle court, the word of the
LORD came to him: 5"Turn back, and say to Hezekiah prince of my people, Thus says the LORD, the
God of your ancestor David: I have heard your
prayer, I have seen your tears; indeed, I will heal
you; on the third day you shall go up to the house
of the LORD. 6I will add fifteen years to your life.
I will deliver you and this city out of the hand of
the king of Assyria; I will defend this city for
my own sake and for my servant David's sake."
7Then Isaiah said, "Bring a lump of figs. Let them
take it and apply it to the boil, so that he may
recover."

8 Hezekiah said to Isaiah, "What shall be the
sign that the LORD will heal me, and that I shall go
up to the house of the LORD on the third day?"
9Isaiah said, "This is the sign to you from the
LORD, that the LORD will do the thing that he has

f Gk Compare Isa 37.27 Q Ms: MT lacks *rising*

promised: the shadow has now advanced ten intervals; shall it retreat ten intervals?" [10]Hezekiah answered, "It is normal for the shadow to lengthen ten intervals; rather let the shadow retreat ten intervals." [11]The prophet Isaiah cried to the LORD; and he brought the shadow back the ten intervals, by which the sun[g] had declined on the dial of Ahaz.

Envoys from Babylon

12 At that time King Merodach-baladan son of Baladan of Babylon sent envoys with letters and a present to Hezekiah, for he had heard that Hezekiah had been sick. [13]Hezekiah welcomed them;[h] he showed them all his treasure house, the silver, the gold, the spices, the precious oil, his armory, all that was found in his storehouses; there was nothing in his house or in all his realm that Hezekiah did not show them. [14]Then the prophet Isaiah came to King Hezekiah, and said to him, "What did these men say? From where did they come to you?" Hezekiah answered, "They have come from a far country, from Babylon." [15]He said, "What have they seen in your house?" Hezekiah answered, "They have seen all that is in my house; there is nothing in my storehouses that I did not show them."

16 Then Isaiah said to Hezekiah, "Hear the word of the LORD: [17]Days are coming when all that is in your house, and that which your ancestors have stored up until this day, shall be carried to Babylon; nothing shall be left, says the LORD. [18]Some of your own sons who are born to you shall be taken away; they shall be eunuchs in the palace of the king of Babylon." [19]Then Hezekiah said to Isaiah, "The word of the LORD that you have spoken is good." For he thought, "Why not, if there will be peace and security in my days?"

Death of Hezekiah

20 The rest of the deeds of Hezekiah, all his power, how he made the pool and the conduit and brought water into the city, are they not written in the Book of the Annals of the Kings of Judah? [21]Hezekiah slept with his ancestors; and his son Manasseh succeeded him.

Manasseh Reigns over Judah

21 Manasseh was twelve years old when he began to reign; he reigned fifty-five years in Jerusalem. His mother's name was Hephzibah. [2]He did what was evil in the sight of the LORD, following the abominable practices of the nations that the LORD drove out before the people of Israel. [3]For he rebuilt the high places that his father Hezekiah had destroyed; he erected altars for Baal, made a sacred pole,[i] as King Ahab of Israel had done, worshiped all the host of heaven, and served them. [4]He built altars in the house of the LORD, of which the LORD had said, "In Jerusalem I will put my name." [5]He built altars for all the host of heaven in the two courts of the house of the LORD. [6]He made his son pass through fire; he practiced soothsaying and augury, and dealt with mediums and with wizards. He did much evil in the sight of the LORD, provoking him to anger. [7]The carved image of Asherah that he had made he set in the house of which the LORD said to David and to his son Solomon, "In this house, and in Jerusalem, which I have chosen out of all the tribes of Israel, I will put my name forever; [8]I will not cause the feet of Israel to wander any more out of the land that I gave to their ancestors, if only they will be careful to do according to all that I have commanded them, and according to all the law that my servant Moses commanded them." [9]But they did not listen; Manasseh misled them to do more evil than the nations had done that the LORD destroyed before the people of Israel.

10 The LORD said by his servants the prophets, [11]"Because King Manasseh of Judah has committed these abominations, has done things more wicked than all that the Amorites did, who were before him, and has caused Judah also to sin with his idols; [12]therefore thus says the LORD, the God of Israel, I am bringing upon Jerusalem and Judah such evil that the ears of everyone who hears of it will tingle. [13]I will stretch over Jerusalem the measuring line for Samaria, and the plummet for the house of Ahab; I will wipe Jerusalem as one wipes a dish, wiping it and turning it upside down. [14]I will cast off the remnant of my heritage, and give them into the hand of their enemies; they shall become a prey and a spoil to all their enemies, [15]because they have done what is evil in my sight and have provoked me to anger, since the day their ancestors came out of Egypt, even to this day."

16 Moreover Manasseh shed very much innocent blood, until he had filled Jerusalem from

20.20 A Lifeline Tunnel

The tunnel, one of Hezekiah's major accomplishments, can still be seen in modern Jerusalem. In ancient days, Jerusalem had no source of water within its walls, making it vulnerable to an extended siege. Hezekiah undertook a tremendous engineering feat to bring water from a spring to a reservoir inside Jerusalem. In the late 1800s some boys swimming in the pool of Siloam happened upon a carved record, dating from Hezekiah's time, of how the tunnel had been dug. The marks of pickaxes are still clearly visible.

g Syr See Isa 38.8 and Tg: Heb it   h Gk Vg Syr: Heb *When Hezekiah heard about them*   i Heb *Asherah*

one end to another, besides the sin that he caused Judah to sin so that they did what was evil in the sight of the LORD.

17 Now the rest of the acts of Manasseh, all that he did, and the sin that he committed, are they not written in the Book of the Annals of the Kings of Judah? [18]Manasseh slept with his ancestors, and was buried in the garden of his house, in the garden of Uzza. His son Amon succeeded him.

Amon Reigns over Judah

19 Amon was twenty-two years old when he began to reign; he reigned two years in Jerusalem. His mother's name was Meshullemeth daughter of Haruz of Jotbah. [20]He did what was evil in the sight of the LORD, as his father Manasseh had done. [21]He walked in all the way in which his father walked, served the idols that his father served, and worshiped them; [22]he abandoned the LORD, the God of his ancestors, and did not walk in the way of the LORD. [23]The servants of Amon conspired against him, and killed the king in his house. [24]But the people of the land killed all those who had conspired against King Amon, and the people of the land made his son Josiah king in place of him. [25]Now the rest of the acts of Amon that he did, are they not written in the Book of the Annals of the Kings of Judah? [26]He was buried in his tomb in the garden of Uzza; then his son Josiah succeeded him.

Josiah Reigns over Judah

22 Josiah was eight years old when he began to reign; he reigned thirty-one years in Jerusalem. His mother's name was Jedidah daughter of Adaiah of Bozkath. [2]He did what was right in the sight of the LORD, and walked in all the way of his father David; he did not turn aside to the right or to the left.

Hilkiah Finds the Book of the Law

3 In the eighteenth year of King Josiah, the king sent Shaphan son of Azaliah, son of Meshullam, the secretary, to the house of the LORD, saying, [4]"Go up to the high priest Hilkiah, and have him count the entire sum of the money that has been brought into the house of the LORD, which the keepers of the threshold have collected from the people; [5]let it be given into the hand of the workers who have the oversight of the house of the LORD; let them give it to the workers who are at the house of the LORD, repairing the house, [6]that is, to the carpenters, to the builders, to the masons; and let them use it to buy timber and quarried stone to repair the house. [7]But no accounting shall be asked from them for the money that is delivered into their hand, for they deal honestly."

8 The high priest Hilkiah said to Shaphan the secretary, "I have found the book of the law in the house of the LORD." When Hilkiah gave the book to Shaphan, he read it. [9]Then Shaphan the secretary came to the king, and reported to the king, "Your servants have emptied out the money that was found in the house, and have delivered it into the hand of the workers who have oversight of the house of the LORD." [10]Shaphan the secretary informed the king, "The priest Hilkiah has given me a book." Shaphan then read it aloud to the king.

11 When the king heard the words of the

22.11 Dramatic Discovery

Most scholars believe the book of the law referred to was Deuteronomy—or at least a portion of that book. The find, confirmed by a prophetess, resulted in the most thoroughgoing religious reform Judah had ever seen.

book of the law, he tore his clothes. [12]Then the king commanded the priest Hilkiah, Ahikam son of Shaphan, Achbor son of Micaiah, Shaphan the secretary, and the king's servant Asaiah, saying, [13]"Go, inquire of the LORD for me, for the people, and for all Judah, concerning the words of this book that has been found; for great is the wrath of the LORD that is kindled against us, because our ancestors did not obey the words of this book, to do according to all that is written concerning us."

14 So the priest Hilkiah, Ahikam, Achbor, Shaphan, and Asaiah went to the prophetess Huldah the wife of Shallum son of Tikvah, son of Harhas, keeper of the wardrobe; she resided in Jerusalem in the Second Quarter, where they consulted her. [15]She declared to them, "Thus says the LORD, the God of Israel: Tell the man who sent you to me, [16]Thus says the LORD, I will indeed bring disaster on this place and on its inhabitants—all the words of the book that the king of Judah has read. [17]Because they have abandoned me and have made offerings to other gods, so that they have provoked me to anger with all the work of their hands, therefore my wrath will be kindled against this place, and it will not be quenched. [18]But as to the king of Judah, who sent you to inquire of the LORD, thus shall you say to him, Thus says the LORD, the God of Israel: Regarding the words that you have heard, [19]because your heart was penitent, and you humbled yourself before the LORD, when you heard how I spoke against this place, and against its inhabitants, that they should become a desolation and a curse, and because you have torn your clothes and wept before me, I also have heard you, says the LORD. [20]Therefore, I will gather you to your ancestors, and you shall be gathered to your grave in peace; your eyes shall not see all the disaster that I will bring on this place." They took the message back to the king.

Josiah's Reformation

23 Then the king directed that all the elders of Judah and Jerusalem should be gathered to him. ²The king went up to the house of the LORD, and with him went all the people of Judah, all the inhabitants of Jerusalem, the priests, the prophets, and all the people, both small and great; he read in their hearing all the words of the book of the covenant that had been found in the house of the LORD. ³The king stood by the pillar and made a covenant before the LORD, to follow the LORD, keeping his commandments, his decrees, and his statutes, with all his heart and all his soul, to perform the words of this covenant that were written in this book. All the people joined in the covenant.

4 The king commanded the high priest Hilkiah, the priests of the second order, and the guardians of the threshold, to bring out of the temple of the LORD all the vessels made for Baal, for Asherah, and for all the host of heaven; he burned them outside Jerusalem in the fields of the Kidron, and carried their ashes to Bethel. ⁵He deposed the idolatrous priests whom the kings of Judah had ordained to make offerings in the high places at the cities of Judah and around Jerusalem; those also who made offerings to Baal, to the sun, the moon, the constellations, and all the host of the heavens. ⁶He brought out the image of[j] Asherah from the house of the LORD, outside Jerusalem, to the Wadi Kidron, burned it at the Wadi Kidron, beat it to dust and threw the dust of it upon the graves of the common people. ⁷He

broke down the houses of the male temple prostitutes that were in the house of the LORD, where the women did weaving for Asherah. ⁸He brought all the priests out of the towns of Judah, and defiled the high places where the priests had made offerings, from Geba to Beer-sheba; he broke down the high places of the gates that were at the entrance of the gate of Joshua the governor of the city, which were on the left at the gate of the city. ⁹The priests of the high places, however, did not come up to the altar of the LORD in Jerusalem, but ate unleavened bread among their kindred. ¹⁰He defiled Topheth, which is in the valley of Ben-hinnom, so that no one would make a son or a daughter pass through fire as an offering to Molech. ¹¹He removed the horses that the kings of Judah had dedicated to the sun, at the entrance to the house of the LORD, by the chamber of the eunuch Nathan-melech, which was in the precincts;[k] then he burned the chariots of the sun with fire. ¹²The altars on the roof of the upper chamber of Ahaz, which the kings of Judah had made, and the altars that Manasseh had made in the two courts of the house of the LORD, he pulled down from there and broke in pieces, and threw the rubble into the Wadi Kidron. ¹³The king defiled the high places that were east of Jerusalem, to the south of the Mount of Destruction, which King Solomon of Israel had built for Astarte the abomination of the Sidonians, for Chemosh the abomination of Moab, and for Milcom the abomination of the Ammonites. ¹⁴He broke the pillars in pieces, cut down the sacred poles,[l] and covered the sites with human bones.

---

j Heb lacks image of   k Meaning of Heb uncertain   l Heb Asherim

---

JOSIAH Last Gasp

JOSIAH CAME TO THE THRONE when his father, at age 24, fell to assassins. Josiah himself was a mere child of eight when he was abruptly called to fill a king's shoes. By the time he reached 16, however, the boy-king had begun to find himself.

God's holy city of Jerusalem and his chosen people, the Israelites, had sunk to historic lows. The temple featured idols, male shrine prostitutes, and carved horses dedicated to sun worshipers. In a nearby valley, people burned their children in sacrifice to the god Molech. Other pagan shrines dotted the hilltops around Jerusalem and throughout the land of Judah.

During the long slide away from God, all sacred records had disappeared. The God of Abraham, Isaac and Jacob was just a faint memory.

Perhaps Josiah had heard about his great-grandfather Hezekiah, who while king had purified the temple and restored the Passover celebration. In his youth Josiah set reforms like Hezekiah's in motion again. Then, in the process of cleaning out the temple, priests discovered an old book of Scripture. Josiah took its message to heart, spurred on by his fear of God's judgment against those who failed to obey his law.

Josiah sent to a prophetess, Huldah, for advice. (Both Jeremiah and Zephaniah were prophesying at the time, but Huldah got the call.) The nation would indeed be punished, Huldah confirmed, but because of Josiah's humility the calamity would not occur in his lifetime (22.15–20). Her words came true. After Josiah's tragic death at the age of 39, Judah went quickly downhill to total destruction. Josiah was the Israelites' last, great gasp.

Life Questions: When you see immorality all around you, what can you do to change it?

15 Moreover, the altar at Bethel, the high place erected by Jeroboam son of Nebat, who caused Israel to sin—he pulled down that altar along with the high place. He burned the high place, crushing it to dust; he also burned the sacred pole.*m* 16As Josiah turned, he saw the tombs there on the mount; and he sent and took the bones out of the tombs, and burned them on the altar, and defiled it, according to the word of the LORD that the man of God proclaimed,*n* when Jeroboam stood by the altar at the festival; he turned and looked up at the tomb of the man of God who had predicted these things. 17Then he said, "What is that monument that I see?" The people of the city told him, "It is the tomb of the man of God who came from Judah and predicted these things that you have done against the altar at Bethel." 18He said, "Let him rest; let no one move his bones." So they let his bones alone, with the bones of the prophet who came out of Samaria. 19Moreover, Josiah removed all the shrines of the high places that were in the towns of Samaria, which kings of Israel had made, provoking the LORD to anger; he did to them just as he had done at Bethel. 20He slaughtered on the altars all the priests of the high places who were there, and burned human bones on them. Then he returned to Jerusalem.

The Passover Celebrated

21 The king commanded all the people, "Keep the passover to the LORD your God as prescribed in this book of the covenant." 22No such passover had been kept since the days of the judges who judged Israel, even during all the days of the kings of Israel and of the kings of Judah; 23but in the eighteenth year of King Josiah this passover was kept to the LORD in Jerusalem.

24 Moreover Josiah put away the mediums, wizards, teraphim,*o* idols, and all the abominations that were seen in the land of Judah and in Jerusalem, so that he established the words of the law that were written in the book that the priest Hilkiah had found in the house of the LORD. 25Before him there was no king like him, who turned to the LORD with all his heart, with all his soul, and with all his might, according to all the law of Moses; nor did any like him arise after him.

26 Still the LORD did not turn from the fierceness of his great wrath, by which his anger was kindled against Judah, because of all the provocations with which Manasseh had provoked him. 27The LORD said, "I will remove Judah also out of my sight, as I have removed Israel; and I will reject this city that I have chosen, Jerusalem, and the house of which I said, My name shall be there."

Josiah Dies in Battle

28 Now the rest of the acts of Josiah, and all that he did, are they not written in the Book of the Annals of the Kings of Judah? 29In his days Pharaoh Neco king of Egypt went up to the king of

23.26–28 Too Little Too Late

Josiah became king when he was only eight, and at the age of 26 led a dramatic reform movement. Yet for all this wise king accomplished, the Lord still determined to punish Judah, as verse 26 tells us. Evil had become so deeply ingrained that the best efforts of one good king could not root it out. In fact, as soon as Josiah died, Judah reverted to their previous form.

Assyria to the river Euphrates. King Josiah went to meet him; but when Pharaoh Neco met him at Megiddo, he killed him. 30His servants carried him dead in a chariot from Megiddo, brought him to Jerusalem, and buried him in his own tomb. The people of the land took Jehoahaz son of Josiah, anointed him, and made him king in place of his father.

Reign and Captivity of Jehoahaz

31 Jehoahaz was twenty-three years old when he began to reign; he reigned three months in Jerusalem. His mother's name was Hamutal daughter of Jeremiah of Libnah. 32He did what was evil in the sight of the LORD, just as his ancestors had done. 33Pharaoh Neco confined him at Riblah in the land of Hamath, so that he might not reign in Jerusalem, and imposed tribute on the land of one hundred talents of silver and a talent of gold. 34Pharaoh Neco made Eliakim son of Josiah king in place of his father Josiah, and changed his name to Jehoiakim. But he took Jehoahaz away; he came to Egypt, and died there. 35Jehoiakim gave the silver and the gold to Pharaoh, but he taxed the land in order to meet Pharaoh's demand for money. He exacted the silver and the gold from the people of the land, from all according to their assessment, to give it to Pharaoh Neco.

Jehoiakim Reigns over Judah

36 Jehoiakim was twenty-five years old when he began to reign; he reigned eleven years in Jerusalem. His mother's name was Zebidah daughter of Pedaiah of Rumah. 37He did what was evil in the sight of the LORD, just as all his ancestors had done.

m Heb *Asherah*   *n* Gk: Heb *proclaimed, who had predicted these things*   *o* Or *household gods*

Judah Overrun by Enemies

24 In his days King Nebuchadnezzar of Babylon came up; Jehoiakim became his servant for three years; then he turned and rebelled against him. 2The LORD sent against him bands of the Chaldeans, bands of the Arameans, bands of the Moabites, and bands of the Ammonites; he sent them against Judah to destroy it, according to the word of the LORD that he spoke by his servants the prophets. 3Surely this came upon Judah at the command of the LORD, to remove them out of his sight, for the sins of Manasseh, for all that he had committed, 4and also for the innocent blood that he had shed; for he filled Jerusalem with innocent blood, and the LORD was not willing to pardon. 5Now the rest of the deeds of Jehoiakim, and all that he did, are they not written in the Book of the Annals of the Kings of Judah? 6So Jehoiakim slept with his ancestors; then his son Jehoiachin succeeded him. 7The king of Egypt did not come again out of his land, for the king of Babylon had taken over all that belonged to the king of Egypt from the Wadi of Egypt to the River Euphrates.

> ### 24.1 Jeremiah's Influence
>
> ***The last two chapters, which closely parallel material in Jeremiah 52, reveal the influence of that prophet on the book of Kings. Some scholars have concluded that he wrote this historical record.***

Reign and Captivity of Jehoiachin

8 Jehoiachin was eighteen years old when he began to reign; he reigned three months in Jerusalem. His mother's name was Nehushta daughter of Elnathan of Jerusalem. 9He did what was evil in the sight of the LORD, just as his father had done.

10 At that time the servants of King Nebuchadnezzar of Babylon came up to Jerusalem, and the city was besieged. 11King Nebuchadnezzar of Babylon came to the city, while his servants were besieging it; 12King Jehoiachin of Judah gave himself up to the king of Babylon, himself, his mother, his servants, his officers, and his palace officials. The king of Babylon took him prisoner in the eighth year of his reign.

Capture of Jerusalem

13 He carried off all the treasures of the house of the LORD, and the treasures of the king's house; he cut in pieces all the vessels of gold in the temple of the LORD, which King Solomon of Israel had made, all this as the LORD had foretold. 14He carried away all Jerusalem, all the officials, all the warriors, ten thousand captives, all the artisans and the smiths; no one remained, except the poorest people of the land. 15He carried away Jehoiachin to Babylon; the king's mother, the king's wives, his officials, and the elite of the land, he took into captivity from Jerusalem to Babylon. 16The king of Babylon brought captive to Babylon all the men of valor, seven thousand, the artisans and the smiths, one thousand, all of them strong and fit for war. 17The king of Babylon made Mattaniah, Jehoiachin's uncle, king in his place, and changed his name to Zedekiah.

Zedekiah Reigns over Judah

18 Zedekiah was twenty-one years old when he began to reign; he reigned eleven years in Jerusalem. His mother's name was Hamutal daughter of Jeremiah of Libnah. 19He did what was evil in the sight of the LORD, just as Jehoiakim had done. 20Indeed, Jerusalem and Judah so angered the LORD that he expelled them from his presence.

The Fall and Captivity of Judah

Zedekiah rebelled against the king of Babylon.

25 1And in the ninth year of his reign, in the tenth month, on the tenth day of the month, King Nebuchadnezzar of Babylon came with all his army against Jerusalem, and laid siege to it; they built siegeworks against it all around. 2So the city was besieged until the eleventh year of King Zedekiah. 3On the ninth day of the fourth month the famine became so severe in the city that there was no food for the people of the land. 4Then a breach was made in the city wall;[p] the king with all the soldiers fled[q] by night by the way of the gate between the two walls, by the king's garden, though the Chaldeans were all around the city. They went in the direction of the Arabah. 5But the army of the Chaldeans pursued the king, and overtook him in the plains of Jericho; all his army was scattered, deserting him. 6Then they captured the king and brought him up to the king of Babylon at Riblah, who passed sentence on him. 7They slaughtered the sons of Zedekiah before his eyes, then put out the eyes of Zedekiah; they bound him in fetters and took him to Babylon.

8 In the fifth month, on the seventh day of the month—which was the nineteenth year of King Nebuchadnezzar, king of Babylon—Nebuzaradan, the captain of the bodyguard, a servant of the king of Babylon, came to Jerusalem. 9He burned the house of the LORD, the king's house, and all the houses of Jerusalem; every great house he burned down. 10All the army of the Chaldeans who were with the captain of the guard broke down the walls around Jerusalem. 11Nebuzaradan the captain of the guard carried into exile

[p] Heb lacks *wall* [q] Gk Compare Jer 39.4; 52.7: Heb lacks *the king* and lacks *fled*

the rest of the people who were left in the city and the deserters who had defected to the king of Babylon—all the rest of the population. 12But the captain of the guard left some of the poorest people of the land to be vinedressers and tillers of the soil.

13 The bronze pillars that were in the house of the LORD, as well as the stands and the bronze sea that were in the house of the LORD, the Chaldeans broke in pieces, and carried the bronze to Babylon. 14They took away the pots, the shovels, the snuffers, the dishes for incense, and all the bronze vessels used in the temple service, 15as well as the firepans and the basins. What was made of gold the captain of the guard took away for the gold, and what was made of silver, for the silver. 16As for the two pillars, the one sea, and the stands, which Solomon had made for the house of the LORD, the bronze of all these vessels was beyond weighing. 17The height of the one pillar was eighteen cubits, and on it was a bronze capital; the height of the capital was three cubits; latticework and pomegranates, all of bronze, were on the capital all around. The second pillar had the same, with the latticework.

18 The captain of the guard took the chief priest Seraiah, the second priest Zephaniah, and the three guardians of the threshold; 19from the city he took an officer who had been in command of the soldiers, and five men of the king's council who were found in the city; the secretary who was the commander of the army who mustered the people of the land; and sixty men of the people of the land who were found in the city. 20Nebuzaradan the captain of the guard took them, and brought them to the king of Babylon at Riblah. 21The king of Babylon struck them down and put them to death at Riblah in the land of Hamath. So Judah went into exile out of its land.

Gedaliah Made Governor of Judah

22 He appointed Gedaliah son of Ahikam son of Shaphan as governor over the people who remained in the land of Judah, whom King Nebuchadnezzar of Babylon had left. 23Now when all

25.22 A Kingdom Disappears

Judah's final rebellion against mighty Babylon failed, resulting in an 18-month siege and the destruction of Jerusalem. Survivors were taken away in what became known as the "Babylonian captivity," a tragic moment in Jewish history. God spelled out the reasons for this disaster in 2 Kings 21.10–16.

the captains of the forces and their men heard that the king of Babylon had appointed Gedaliah as governor, they came with their men to Gedaliah at Mizpah, namely, Ishmael son of Nethaniah, Johanan son of Kareah, Seraiah son of Tanhumeth the Netophathite, and Jaazaniah son of the Maacathite. 24Gedaliah swore to them and their men, saying, "Do not be afraid because of the Chaldean officials; live in the land, serve the king of Babylon, and it shall be well with you." 25But in the seventh month, Ishmael son of Nethaniah son of Elishama, of the royal family, came with ten men; they struck down Gedaliah so that he died, along with the Judeans and Chaldeans who were with him at Mizpah. 26Then all the people, high

ZEDEKIAH *The Bitter End*

FOR A VERY LONG TIME the kingdom of Judah had been sliding downhill. Good kings like Hezekiah and Josiah managed to stop the decline temporarily, but as soon as they passed from the scene, immorality and idolatry surged back. Prophets warned again and again of God's judgment, but few heeded them.

Fittingly, Judah endured its bitter end under the weak leadership of Zedekiah, a puppet king put on the throne by Judah's captor, the Babylonian King Nebuchadnezzar. Zedekiah personified all that was wrong with Judah. He took an oath of loyalty to Babylon, then spent his eleven-year reign cheating on it.

The great prophet Jeremiah lived during this same time, offering a strong counterpoint to Zedekiah's weakness. Zedekiah could never make up his mind whether to treat Jeremiah as a prophet of truth or as a trouble-making traitor. When Jeremiah warned against Zedekiah's policies, the king had him beaten and imprisoned. At the same time, he kept bringing Jeremiah in for secret consultations, usually ignoring his advice.

Judah paid cruelly for Zedekiah's poor leadership. Responding to his rebellion, the Babylonians put Jerusalem under a two-year siege, then utterly wrecked the city. They treated Zedekiah as a traitor, executing his sons while he watched, then putting out his eyes so that their deaths would be his last visual memory. Judah's final king was led off to Babylon, blind and in chains.

Life Questions: Under pressure, are you confident or indecisive? What do you need to gain confidence?

and low,ʳ and the captains of the forces set out and went to Egypt; for they were afraid of the Chaldeans.

Jehoiachin Released from Prison

27 In the thirty-seventh year of the exile of King Jehoiachin of Judah, in the twelfth month, on the twenty-seventh day of the month, King Evil-merodach of Babylon, in the year that he began to reign, released King Jehoiachin of Judah from prison; ²⁸he spoke kindly to him, and gave him a seat above the other seats of the kings who were with him in Babylon. ²⁹So Jehoiachin put aside his prison clothes. Every day of his life he dined regularly in the king's presence. ³⁰For his allowance, a regular allowance was given him by the king, a portion every day, as long as he lived.

ʳ Or young and old

1 CHRONICLES

A Family Record
These facts reminded Israelites of their place in God's plan

I N PIONEER DAYS, MANY AMERICAN families prized a huge black family Bible. Often the only book in the house, it served for more than reading. It was also the family memory bank. Every important event—a marriage, a birth, a death—was recorded on its flyleaves. The Bible was passed down from generation to generation, and through it, a family kept track of its past.

The book of 1 Chronicles is something like that—a record of Israel's family history, and particularly of David, Israel's greatest king. In fact, at first glance, 1 Chronicles looks like a rehash of David's life as told in 2 Samuel and 1 Kings. Some of the most dramatic episodes in David's life—his clash with Goliath, his sin with Bathsheba—don't make it into this account. But David's organization of the temple is told in great detail, and long lists and genealogies fill over half the book.

Because of that, few people read 1 Chronicles. Most of us are more interested in personalities than in institutions and genealogies.

> *"Who is like your people Israel, one nation on the earth whom God went to redeem to be his people?"* 17.21

David's Lasting Impact

First Chronicles, however, is far more interested in David's lasting accomplishments than in his ups and downs as an individual. The nation he led was more than a collection of inspired individuals. It was founded on God's unshakable promises to the children of Abraham. He had promised to be with them. He had promised to provide leadership. He had promised to make them a blessing to the world. These promises took shape in enduring institutions—the temple and the monarchy, most notably.

Why a List of Names?

The first nine chapters of 1 Chronicles trace the genealogy of Israel back to Adam. The author brings together more family records than you'll find anywhere else in the Bible. These records helped the Israelites remember their position as members in God's chosen family. God had given them unique ways to follow and worship him. First Chronicles reminded the Israelites—as it reminds us—of how different their family was meant to be.

How to Read 1 Chronicles

F ew will enjoy reading 1 Chronicles's many lists and genealogies straight through. You should approach them more like a puzzle. Don't get lost in the hundreds of names. Instead, try to understand how the different parts of 1 Chronicles fit together. For each section ask, "Why was this included? What did it mean to the original audience—to the Israelites who had returned from exile in Babylon? How did it encourage them as they made a new beginning?"

First Chronicles divides cleanly into two parts. The first nine chapters are mainly lists of names. In these, the Israelites read their family tree and discovered their heritage. Chapters 10 to 29 tell David's story, focusing on the legacy he left behind for future generations—especially the temple. David, a founding father of Israel, transformed the nation in a way that lasted hundreds of years.

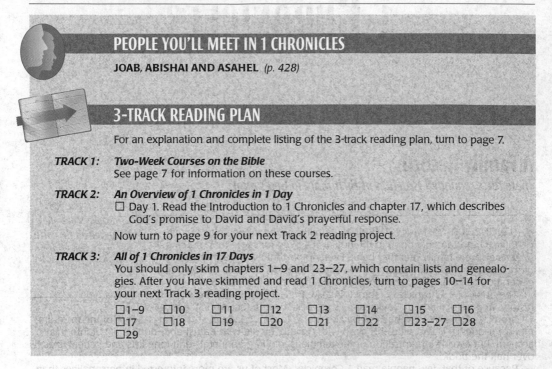

PEOPLE YOU'LL MEET IN 1 CHRONICLES

JOAB, ABISHAI AND ASAHEL *(p. 428)*

3-TRACK READING PLAN

For an explanation and complete listing of the 3-track reading plan, turn to page 7.

TRACK 1: *Two-Week Courses on the Bible*
See page 7 for information on these courses.

TRACK 2: *An Overview of 1 Chronicles in 1 Day*
☐ Day 1. Read the Introduction to 1 Chronicles and chapter 17, which describes God's promise to David and David's prayerful response.

Now turn to page 9 for your next Track 2 reading project.

TRACK 3: *All of 1 Chronicles in 17 Days*
You should only skim chapters 1–9 and 23–27, which contain lists and genealogies. After you have skimmed and read 1 Chronicles, turn to pages 10–14 for your next Track 3 reading project.

☐1–9 ☐10 ☐11 ☐12 ☐13 ☐14 ☐15 ☐16
☐17 ☐18 ☐19 ☐20 ☐21 ☐22 ☐23–27 ☐28
☐29

From Adam to Abraham

1 Adam, Seth, Enosh; ²Kenan, Mahalalel, Jared; ³Enoch, Methuselah, Lamech; ⁴Noah, Shem, Ham, and Japheth.

5 The descendants of Japheth: Gomer, Magog, Madai, Javan, Tubal, Meshech, and Tiras. ⁶The descendants of Gomer: Ashkenaz, Diphath,ᵃ and Togarmah. ⁷The descendants of Javan: Elishah, Tarshish, Kittim, and Rodanim.ᵇ

8 The descendants of Ham: Cush, Egypt, Put, and Canaan. ⁹The descendants of Cush: Seba, Havilah, Sabta, Raama, and Sabteca. The descendants of Raamah: Sheba and Dedan. ¹⁰Cush became the father of Nimrod; he was the first to be a mighty one on the earth.

11 Egypt became the father of Ludim, Anamim, Lehabim, Naphtuhim, ¹²Pathrusim, Casluhim, and Caphtorim, from whom the Philistines come.ᶜ

13 Canaan became the father of Sidon his firstborn, and Heth, ¹⁴and the Jebusites, the Amorites, the Girgashites, ¹⁵the Hivites, the Arkites, the Sinites, ¹⁶the Arvadites, the Zemarites, and the Hamathites.

17 The descendants of Shem: Elam, Asshur, Arpachshad, Lud, Aram, Uz, Hul, Gether, and Meshech.ᵈ ¹⁸Arpachshad became the father of Shelah; and Shelah became the father of Eber. ¹⁹To Eber were born two sons: the name of the one was Peleg (for in his days the earth was divid-

ed), and the name of his brother Joktan. ²⁰Joktan became the father of Almodad, Sheleph, Hazarmaveth, Jerah, ²¹Hadoram, Uzal, Diklah, ²²Ebal, Abimael, Sheba, ²³Ophir, Havilah, and Jobab; all these were the descendants of Joktan.

24 Shem, Arpachshad, Shelah; ²⁵Eber, Peleg, Reu; ²⁶Serug, Nahor, Terah; ²⁷Abram, that is, Abraham.

From Abraham to Jacob

28 The sons of Abraham: Isaac and Ishmael. ²⁹These are their genealogies: the firstborn of Ishmael, Nebaioth; and Kedar, Adbeel, Mibsam, ³⁰Mishma, Dumah, Massa, Hadad, Tema, ³¹Jetur, Naphish, and Kedemah. These are the sons of Ishmael. ³²The sons of Keturah, Abraham's concubine: she bore Zimran, Jokshan, Medan, Midian, Ishbak, and Shuah. The sons of Jokshan: Sheba and Dedan. ³³The sons of Midian: Ephah, Epher, Hanoch, Abida, and Eldaah. All these were the descendants of Keturah.

34 Abraham became the father of Isaac. The sons of Isaac: Esau and Israel. ³⁵The sons of Esau: Eliphaz, Reuel, Jeush, Jalam, and Korah. ³⁶The sons of Eliphaz: Teman, Omar, Zephi, Gatam, Kenaz, Timna, and Amalek. ³⁷The sons of Reuel: Nahath, Zerah, Shammah, and Mizzah.

38 The sons of Seir: Lotan, Shobal, Zibeon, Anah, Dishon, Ezer, and Dishan. ³⁹The sons of Lotan: Hori and Homam; and Lotan's sister was

---

ᵃ Gen 10.3 *Ripath*; See Gk Vg *Caphtorim*; See Am 9.7, Jer 47.4   ᵇ Gen 10.4 *Dodanim*; See Syr Vg   ᵈ *Mash* in Gen 10.23   ᶜ Heb *Casluhim, from which the Philistines come,*

Timna. ⁴⁰The sons of Shobal: Alian, Manahath, Ebal, Shephi, and Onam. The sons of Zibeon: Aiah and Anah. ⁴¹The sons of Anah: Dishon. The sons of Dishon: Hamran, Eshban, Ithran, and Cheran. ⁴²The sons of Ezer: Bilhan, Zaavan, and Jaakan.ᵉ The sons of Dishan:ᶠ Uz and Aran.

1.28 Compressed History

The books of 1 and 2 Chronicles, focusing on the kings of the recent past, do not pretend to give a complete history of the Israelites. But by recording individuals' names all the way back to Adam, the books underscore that God has kept his hand on this line of people from the very beginning. The Gospels complete the list begun here: Matthew traces Jesus' lineage back to Abraham, and Luke traces it back to Adam.

43 These are the kings who reigned in the land of Edom before any king reigned over the Israelites: Bela son of Beor, whose city was called Dinhabah. ⁴⁴When Bela died, Jobab son of Zerah of Bozrah succeeded him. ⁴⁵When Jobab died, Husham of the land of the Temanites succeeded him. ⁴⁶When Husham died, Hadad son of Bedad, who defeated Midian in the country of Moab, succeeded him; and the name of his city was Avith. ⁴⁷When Hadad died, Samlah of Masrekah succeeded him. ⁴⁸When Samlah died, Shaulᵍ of Rehoboth on the Euphrates succeeded him. ⁴⁹When Shaulᵍ died, Baal-hanan son of Achbor succeeded him. ⁵⁰When Baal-hanan died, Hadad succeeded him; the name of his city was Pai, and his wife's name Mehetabel daughter of Matred, daughter of Me-zahab. ⁵¹And Hadad died.

The clansʰ of Edom were: clansʰ Timna, Aliah,ⁱ Jetheth, ⁵²Oholibamah, Elah, Pinon, ⁵³Kenaz, Teman, Mibzar, ⁵⁴Magdiel, and Iram; these are the clansʰ of Edom.

The Sons of Israel and the Descendants of Judah

2 These are the sons of Israel: Reuben, Simeon, Levi, Judah, Issachar, Zebulun, ²Dan, Joseph, Benjamin, Naphtali, Gad, and Asher. ³The sons of Judah: Er, Onan, and Shelah; these three the Canaanite woman Bath-shua bore to him. Now Er, Judah's firstborn, was wicked in the sight of the LORD, and he put him to death. ⁴His daughter-in-law Tamar also bore him Perez and Zerah. Judah had five sons in all.

5 The sons of Perez: Hezron and Hamul. ⁶The sons of Zerah: Zimri, Ethan, Heman, Calcol, and Dara,ʲ five in all. ⁷The sons of Carmi: Achar, the troubler of Israel, who transgressed in the matter of the devoted thing; ⁸and Ethan's son was Azariah.

9 The sons of Hezron, who were born to him: Jerahmeel, Ram, and Chelubai. ¹⁰Ram became the father of Amminadab, and Amminadab became the father of Nahshon, prince of the sons of Judah. ¹¹Nahshon became the father of Salma, Salma of Boaz, ¹²Boaz of Obed, Obed of Jesse. ¹³Jesse became the father of Eliab his firstborn, Abinadab the second, Shimea the third, ¹⁴Nethanel the fourth, Raddai the fifth, ¹⁵Ozem the sixth, David the seventh; ¹⁶and their sisters were Zeruiah and Abigail. The sons of Zeruiah: Abishai, Joab, and Asahel, three. ¹⁷Abigail bore Amasa, and the father of Amasa was Jether the Ishmaelite.

18 Caleb son of Hezron had children by his wife Azubah, and by Jerioth; these were her sons: Jesher, Shobab, and Ardon. ¹⁹When Azubah died, Caleb married Ephrath, who bore him Hur. ²⁰Hur became the father of Uri, and Uri became the father of Bezalel.

21 Afterward Hezron went in to the daughter of Machir father of Gilead, whom he married when he was sixty years old; and she bore him Segub; ²²and Segub became the father of Jair, who had twenty-three towns in the land of Gilead. ²³But Geshur and Aram took from them Havvoth-jair, Kenath and its villages, sixty towns. All these were descendants of Machir, father of Gilead. ²⁴After the death of Hezron, in Caleb-ephrathah, Abijah wife of Hezron bore him Ashhur, father of Tekoa.

25 The sons of Jerahmeel, the firstborn of Hezron: Ram his firstborn, Bunah, Oren, Ozem, and Ahijah. ²⁶Jerahmeel also had another wife, whose name was Atarah; she was the mother of Onam. ²⁷The sons of Ram, the firstborn of Jerahmeel: Maaz, Jamin, and Eker. ²⁸The sons of Onam: Shammai and Jada. The sons of Shammai: Nadab and Abishur. ²⁹The name of Abishur's wife was Abihail, and she bore him Ahban and Molid. ³⁰The sons of Nadab: Seled and Appaim; and Seled died childless. ³¹The sonᵏ of Appaim: Ishi. The sonᵏ of Ishi: Sheshan. The sonᵏ of Sheshan: Ahlai. ³²The sons of Jada, Shammai's brother: Jether and Jonathan; and Jether died childless. ³³The sons of Jonathan: Peleth and Zaza. These were the descendants of Jerahmeel. ³⁴Now Sheshan had no sons, only daughters; but Sheshan had an Egyptian slave, whose name was Jarha. ³⁵So Sheshan gave his daughter in marriage to his slave Jarha; and she bore him Attai. ³⁶Attai became the father of Nathan, and Nathan of Zabad. ³⁷Zabad became the father of Ephlal, and Ephlal of Obed. ³⁸Obed became the father of Jehu, and Jehu of Azariah. ³⁹Azariah became the father of Helez, and Helez of Eleasah. ⁴⁰Eleasah became the father of Sismai, and Sismai of Shallum.

ᵉ Or *and Akan*; See Gen 36.27   ᶠ See 1.38: Heb *Dishon*   ᵍ Or *Saul*   ʰ Or *chiefs*   ⁱ Or *Alvah*; See Gen 36.40
ʲ Or *Darda*; Compare Syr Tg some Gk Mss; See 1 Kings 4.31   ᵏ Heb *sons*

41Shallum became the father of Jekamiah, and Jekamiah of Elishama.

42 The sons of Caleb brother of Jerahmeel: Mesha[l] his firstborn, who was father of Ziph. The sons of Mareshah father of Hebron. 43The sons of Hebron: Korah, Tappuah, Rekem, and Shema. 44Shema became father of Raham, father of Jorkeam; and Rekem became the father of Shammai. 45The son of Shammai: Maon; and Maon was the father of Beth-zur. 46Ephah also, Caleb's concubine, bore Haran, Moza, and Gazez; and Haran became the father of Gazez. 47The sons of Jahdai: Regem, Jotham, Geshan, Pelet, Ephah, and Shaaph. 48Maacah, Caleb's concubine, bore Sheber and Tirhanah. 49She also bore Shaaph father of Madmannah, Sheva father of Machbenah and father of Gibea; and the daughter of Caleb was Achsah. 50These were the descendants of Caleb.

The sons[m] of Hur the firstborn of Ephrathah: Shobal father of Kiriath-jearim, 51Salma father of Bethlehem, and Hareph father of Beth-gader. 52Shobal father of Kiriath-jearim had other sons: Haroeh, half of the Menuhoth. 53And the families of Kiriath-jearim: the Ithrites, the Puthites, the Shumathites, and the Mishraites; from these came the Zorathites and the Eshtaolites. 54The sons of Salma: Bethlehem, the Netophathites, Atroth-beth-joab, and half of the Manahathites, the Zo-rites. 55The families also of the scribes that lived at Jabez: the Tirathites, the Shimeathites, and the Sucathites. These are the Kenites who came from Hammath, father of the house of Rechab.

Descendants of David and Solomon

3 These are the sons of David who were born to him in Hebron: the firstborn Amnon, by Ahinoam the Jezreelite; the second Daniel, by Abigail the Carmelite; 2the third Absalom, son of Maacah, daughter of King Talmai of Geshur; the fourth Adonijah, son of Haggith; 3the fifth Shephatiah, by Abital; the sixth Ithream, by his wife Eglah; 4six were born to him in Hebron, where he reigned for seven years and six months. And he reigned thirty-three years in Jerusalem. 5These

were born to him in Jerusalem: Shimea, Shobab, Nathan, and Solomon, four by Bath-shua, daughter of Ammiel; 6then Ibhar, Elishama, Eliphelet, 7Nogah, Nepheg, Japhia, 8Elishama, Eliada, and Eliphelet, nine. 9All these were David's sons, besides the sons of the concubines; and Tamar was their sister.

10 The descendants of Solomon: Rehoboam, Abijah his son, Asa his son, Jehoshaphat his son, 11Joram his son, Ahaziah his son, Joash his son, 12Amaziah his son, Azariah his son, Jotham his son, 13Ahaz his son, Hezekiah his son, Manasseh his son, 14Amon his son, Josiah his son. 15The sons of Josiah: Johanan the firstborn, the second Jehoiakim, the third Zedekiah, the fourth Shallum. 16The descendants of Jehoiakim: Jeconiah his son, Zedekiah his son; 17and the sons of Jeconiah, the captive: Shealtiel his son, 18Malchiram,

3.17 The Royal Line

Chronicles was written to people who no longer had a king. However, as this section reminds us, they still knew the royal line. God's promise to provide them with kingly leadership forever still held. They could expect a son of David to someday become king again. This is one reason why the New Testament takes the trouble to show that Jesus was descended from David. He was that King.

Pedaiah, Shenazzar, Jekamiah, Hoshama, and Nedabiah; 19The sons of Pedaiah: Zerubbabel and Shimei; and the sons of Zerubbabel: Meshullam and Hananiah, and Shelomith was their sister; 20and Hashubah, Ohel, Berechiah, Hasadiah, and Jushab-hesed, five. 21The sons of Hananiah: Pelatiah and Jeshaiah, his son[n] Rephaiah, his son[n] Arnan, his son[n] Obadiah, his son[n] Shecaniah. 22The son[o] of Shecaniah: Shemaiah. And the sons of Shemaiah: Hattush, Igal, Bariah, Neariah, and Shaphat, six. 23The sons of Neariah: Elioenai, Hizkiah, and Azrikam, three. 24The sons of Elioenai: Hodaviah, Eliashib, Pelaiah, Akkub, Johanan, Delaiah, and Anani, seven.

Descendants of Judah

4 The sons of Judah: Perez, Hezron, Carmi, Hur, and Shobal. 2Reaiah son of Shobal became the father of Jahath, and Jahath became the father of Ahumai and Lahad. These were the families of the Zorathites. 3These were the sons[p] of Etam: Jezreel, Ishma, and Idbash; and the name of their sister was Hazzelelponi, 4and Penuel was the father of Gedor, and Ezer the father of Hushah. These were the sons of Hur, the firstborn of Ephrathah, the father of Bethlehem. 5Ashhur fa-

3.5 Why the Cleanup?

Names like Bathsheba, Absalom, and Tamar all bring to mind unsavory scenes from David's life (see 2 Samuel 11–18). The author certainly would have known about these stories, but chose to omit them. Writing to dispirited refugees, he wanted to inspire them with a model of what the nation could become, not remind them of how it had failed in the past.

---

[l] Gk reads *Mareshah*   [m] Gk Vg: Heb *son*   [n] Gk Compare Syr Vg: Heb *sons of*   [o] Heb *sons*   [p] Gk Compare Vg: Heb *the father*

ther of Tekoa had two wives, Helah and Naarah; [6]Naarah bore him Ahuzzam, Hepher, Temeni, and Haahashtari.[q] These were the sons of Naarah. [7]The sons of Helah: Zereth, Izhar,[r] and Ethnan. [8]Koz became the father of Anub, Zobebah, and the families of Aharhel son of Harum. [9]Jabez was honored more than his brothers; and his mother named him Jabez, saying, "Because I bore him in pain." [10]Jabez called on the God of Israel, saying, "Oh that you would bless me and enlarge my border, and that your hand might be with me, and that you would keep me from hurt and harm!" And God granted what he asked. [11]Chelub the brother of Shuhah became the father of Mehir, who was the father of Eshton. [12]Eshton became the father of Beth-rapha, Paseah, and Tehinnah the father of Ir-nahash. These are the men of Recah. [13]The sons of Kenaz: Othniel and Seraiah; and the sons of Othniel: Hathath and Meonothai.[s] [14]Meonothai became the father of Ophrah; and Seraiah became the father of Joab father of Ge-harashim,[t] so-called because they were artisans. [15]The sons of Caleb son of Jephunneh: Iru, Elah, and Naam; and the son[u] of Elah: Kenaz. [16]The sons of Jehallelel: Ziph, Ziphah, Tiria, and Asarel. [17]The sons of Ezrah: Jether, Mered, Epher, and Jalon. These are the sons of Bithiah, daughter of Pharaoh, whom Mered married;[v] and she conceived and bore[w] Miriam, Shammai, and Ishbah father of Eshtemoa. [18]And his Judean wife bore Jered father of Gedor, Heber father of Soco, and Jekuthiel father of Zanoah. [19]The sons of the wife of Hodiah, the sister of Naham, were the fathers of Keilah the Garmite and Eshtemoa the Maacathite. [20]The sons of Shimon: Amnon, Rinnah, Ben-hanan, and Tilon. The sons of Ishi: Zoheth and Ben-zoheth. [21]The sons of Shelah son of Judah: Er father of Lecah, Laadah father of Mareshah, and the families of the guild of linen workers at Beth-ashbea; [22]and Jokim, and the men of Cozeba, and Joash, and Saraph, who married into Moab but returned to Lehem[x] (now the records[y] are ancient). [23]These were the potters and inhabitants of Netaim and Gederah; they lived there with the king in his service.

Descendants of Simeon

24 The sons of Simeon: Nemuel, Jamin, Jarib, Zerah, Shaul;[z] [25]Shallum was his son, Mibsam his son, Mishma his son. [26]The sons of Mishma: Hammuel his son, Zaccur his son, Shimei his son. [27]Shimei had sixteen sons and six daughters; but his brothers did not have many children, nor did all their family multiply like the Judeans. [28]They lived in Beer-sheba, Moladah, Hazar-shual, [29]Bilhah, Ezem, Tolad, [30]Bethuel, Hormah, Ziklag, [31]Beth-marcaboth, Hazar-susim, Beth-biri, and

Shaaraim. These were their towns until David became king. [32]And their villages were Etam, Ain, Rimmon, Tochen, and Ashan, five towns, [33]along with all their villages that were around these towns as far as Baal. These were their settlements. And they kept a genealogical record.

34 Meshobab, Jamlech, Joshah son of Amaziah, [35]Joel, Jehu son of Joshibiah son of Seraiah son of Asiel, [36]Elioenai, Jaakobah, Jeshohaiah, Asaiah, Adiel, Jesimiel, Benaiah, [37]Ziza son of Shiphi son of Allon son of Jedaiah son of Shimri son of Shemaiah— [38]these mentioned by name were leaders in their families, and their clans increased greatly. [39]They journeyed to the entrance of Gedor, to the east side of the valley, to seek pasture for their flocks, [40]where they found rich, good pasture, and the land was very broad, quiet, and peaceful; for the former inhabitants there belonged to Ham. [41]These, registered by name, came in the days of King Hezekiah of Judah, and attacked their tents and the Meunim who were found there, and exterminated them to this day, and settled in their place, because there was pasture there for their flocks. [42]And some of them, five hundred men of the Simeonites, went to Mount Seir, having as their leaders Pelatiah, Neariah, Rephaiah, and Uzziel, sons of Ishi; [43]they destroyed the remnant of the Amalekites that had escaped, and they have lived there to this day.

Descendants of Reuben

5 The sons of Reuben the firstborn of Israel. (He was the firstborn, but because he defiled his father's bed his birthright was given to the sons of Joseph son of Israel, so that he is not enrolled in the genealogy according to the birthright; [2]though Judah became prominent among his brothers and a ruler came from him, yet the birthright belonged to Joseph.) [3]The sons of Reuben, the firstborn of Israel: Hanoch, Pallu, Hezron, and Carmi. [4]The sons of Joel: Shemaiah his son, Gog his son, Shimei his son, [5]Micah his son, Reaiah his son, Baal his son, [6]Beerah his son, whom King Tilgath-pilneser of Assyria carried away into exile; he was a chieftain of the Reubenites. [7]And his kindred by their families, when the genealogy of their generations was reckoned: the chief, Jeiel, and Zechariah, [8]and Bela son of Azaz, son of Shema, son of Joel, who lived in Aroer, as far as Nebo and Baal-meon. [9]He also lived to the east as far as the beginning of the desert this side of the Euphrates, because their cattle had multiplied in the land of Gilead. [10]And in the days of Saul they made war on the Hagrites, who fell by their hand; and they lived in their tents throughout all the region east of Gilead.

q Or Ahashtari   r Another reading is Zohar   s Gk Vg: Heb lacks and Meonothai   t That is Valley of artisans
u Heb sons   v The clause: These are . . . married is transposed from verse 18   w Heb lacks and bore
x Vg Compare Gk: Heb and Jashubi-lahem   y Or matters   z Or Saul

Descendants of Gad

11 The sons of Gad lived beside them in the land of Bashan as far as Salecah: [12]Joel the chief, Shapham the second, Janai, and Shaphat in Bashan. [13]And their kindred according to their clans: Michael, Meshullam, Sheba, Jorai, Jacan, Zia, and Eber, seven. [14]These were the sons of Abihail son of Huri, son of Jaroah, son of Gilead, son of Michael, son of Jeshishai, son of Jahdo, son of Buz; [15]Ahi son of Abdiel, son of Guni, was chief in their clan; [16]and they lived in Gilead, in Bashan and in its towns, and in all the pasture lands of Sharon to their limits. [17]All of these were enrolled by genealogies in the days of King Jotham of Judah, and in the days of King Jeroboam of Israel.

18 The Reubenites, the Gadites, and the half-tribe of Manasseh had valiant warriors, who carried shield and sword, and drew the bow, expert in war, forty-four thousand seven hundred sixty, ready for service. [19]They made war on the Hagrites, Jetur, Naphish, and Nodab; [20]and when they received help against them, the Hagrites and all who were with them were given into their hands, for they cried to God in the battle, and he granted their entreaty because they trusted in him. [21]They captured their livestock: fifty thousand of their camels, two hundred fifty thousand sheep, two thousand donkeys, and one hundred thousand captives. [22]Many fell slain, because the war was of God. And they lived in their territory until the exile.

The Half-Tribe of Manasseh

23 The members of the half-tribe of Manasseh lived in the land; they were very numerous from Bashan to Baal-hermon, Senir, and Mount Hermon. [24]These were the heads of their clans: Epher,[a] Ishi, Eliel, Azriel, Jeremiah, Hodaviah, and Jahdiel, mighty warriors, famous men, heads of their clans. [25]But they transgressed against the God of their ancestors, and prostituted themselves to the gods of the peoples of the land, whom God had destroyed before them. [26]So the God of Israel stirred up the spirit of King Pul of Assyria, the spirit of King Tilgath-pilneser of Assyria, and he carried them away, namely, the Reubenites, the Gadites, and the half-tribe of Manasseh, and brought them to Halah, Habor, Hara, and the river Gozan, to this day.

Descendants of Levi

6[b] The sons of Levi: Gershom,[c] Kohath, and Merari. [2]The sons of Kohath: Amram, Izhar, Hebron, and Uzziel. [3]The children of Amram: Aaron, Moses, and Miriam. The sons of Aaron: Nadab, Abihu, Eleazar, and Ithamar. [4]Eleazar became the father of Phinehas, Phinehas of Abishua,

[5]Abishua of Bukki, Bukki of Uzzi, [6]Uzzi of Zerahiah, Zerahiah of Meraioth, [7]Meraioth of Amariah, Amariah of Ahitub, [8]Ahitub of Zadok, Zadok of Ahimaaz, [9]Ahimaaz of Azariah, Azariah of Johanan, [10]and Johanan of Azariah (it was he who served as priest in the house that Solomon built in

6.1 Key People

First Chronicles 1–9 form the Bible's most complete genealogical record. These chapters emphasize the two tribes most crucial to God's plans: Judahites, the tribe that David and all the later kings of Judah came from, and Levites, who had responsibility to lead Israel in worship.

It's possible that the Levite priest named Ezra wrote the two books of Chronicles, for they date from his time period. Jewish refugees had returned from exile in Babylon, and leaders like Ezra were trying to inspire the exiles to reestablish their proud nation and rebuild the temple.

Jerusalem). [11]Azariah became the father of Amariah, Amariah of Ahitub, [12]Ahitub of Zadok, Zadok of Shallum, [13]Shallum of Hilkiah, Hilkiah of Azariah, [14]Azariah of Seraiah, Seraiah of Jehozadak; [15]and Jehozadak went into exile when the LORD sent Judah and Jerusalem into exile by the hand of Nebuchadnezzar.

16[d] The sons of Levi: Gershom, Kohath, and Merari. [17]These are the names of the sons of Gershom: Libni and Shimei. [18]The sons of Kohath: Amram, Izhar, Hebron, and Uzziel. [19]The sons of Merari: Mahli and Mushi. These are the clans of the Levites according to their ancestry. [20]Of Gershom: Libni his son, Jahath his son, Zimmah his son, [21]Joah his son, Iddo his son, Zerah his son, Jeatherai his son. [22]The sons of Kohath: Amminadab his son, Korah his son, Assir his son, [23]Elkanah his son, Ebiasaph his son, Assir his son, [24]Tahath his son, Uriel his son, Uzziah his son, and Shaul his son. [25]The sons of Elkanah: Amasai and Ahimoth, [26]Elkanah his son, Zophai his son, Nahath his son, [27]Eliab his son, Jeroham his son, Elkanah his son. [28]The sons of Samuel: Joel[e] his firstborn, the second Abijah.[f] [29]The sons of Merari: Mahli, Libni his son, Shimei his son, Uzzah his son, [30]Shimea his son, Haggiah his son, and Asaiah his son.

Musicians Appointed by David

31 These are the men whom David put in charge of the service of song in the house of the LORD, after the ark came to rest there. [32]They

---

[a] Gk Vg: Heb *and Epher*   [b] Ch 5.27 in Heb   [c] Heb *Gershon*, variant of *Gershom*; See 6.16   [d] Ch 6.1 in Heb
[e] Gk Syr Compare verse 33 and 1 Sam 8.2: Heb lacks *Joel the second* as a proper name   [f] Heb reads *Vashni, and Abijah* for *the second Abijah*, taking

ministered with song before the tabernacle of the tent of meeting, until Solomon had built the house of the LORD in Jerusalem; and they performed their service in due order. 33These are the

> ## 6.31 And Now, the Choir . . .
>
> *The author of 1 Chronicles had a special fondness for musicians. Several times he mentions David's role in establishing guilds of musicians for temple worship, and here he even records their ancestry.*

men who served; and their sons were: Of the Kohathites: Heman, the singer, son of Joel, son of Samuel, 34son of Elkanah, son of Jeroham, son of Eliel, son of Toah, 35son of Zuph, son of Elkanah, son of Mahath, son of Amasai, 36son of Elkanah, son of Joel, son of Azariah, son of Zephaniah, 37son of Tahath, son of Assir, son of Ebiasaph, son of Korah, 38son of Izhar, son of Kohath, son of Levi, son of Israel; 39and his brother Asaph, who stood on his right, namely, Asaph son of Berechiah, son of Shimea, 40son of Michael, son of Baaseiah, son of Malchijah, 41son of Ethni, son of Zerah, son of Adaiah, 42son of Ethan, son of Zimmah, son of Shimei, 43son of Jahath, son of Gershom, son of Levi. 44On the left were their kindred the sons of Merari: Ethan son of Kishi, son of Abdi, son of Malluch, 45son of Hashabiah, son of Amaziah, son of Hilkiah, 46son of Amzi, son of Bani, son of Shemer, 47son of Mahli, son of Mushi, son of Merari, son of Levi; 48and their kindred the Levites were appointed for all the service of the tabernacle of the house of God.

49 But Aaron and his sons made offerings on the altar of burnt offering and on the altar of incense, doing all the work of the most holy place, to make atonement for Israel, according to all that Moses the servant of God had commanded. 50These are the sons of Aaron: Eleazar his son, Phinehas his son, Abishua his son, 51Bukki his son, Uzzi his son, Zerahiah his son, 52Meraioth his son, Amariah his son, Ahitub his son, 53Zadok his son, Ahimaaz his son.

Settlements of the Levites

54 These are their dwelling places according to their settlements within their borders: to the sons of Aaron of the families of Kohathites—for the lot fell to them first— 55to them they gave Hebron in the land of Judah and its surrounding pasture lands, 56but the fields of the city and its villages they gave to Caleb son of Jephunneh. 57To the sons of Aaron they gave the cities of refuge: Hebron, Libnah with its pasture lands, Jattir, Eshtemoa with its pasture lands, 58Hilen g with its

pasture lands, Debir with its pasture lands, 59Ashan with its pasture lands, and Beth-shemesh with its pasture lands. 60From the tribe of Benjamin, Geba with its pasture lands, Alemeth with its pasture lands, and Anathoth with its pasture lands. All their towns throughout their families were thirteen.

61 To the rest of the Kohathites were given by lot out of the family of the tribe, out of the half-tribe, the half of Manasseh, ten towns. 62To the Gershomites according to their families were allotted thirteen towns out of the tribes of Issachar, Asher, Naphtali, and Manasseh in Bashan. 63To the Merarites according to their families were allotted twelve towns out of the tribes of Reuben, Gad, and Zebulun. 64So the people of Israel gave the Levites the towns with their pasture lands. 65They also gave them by lot out of the tribes of Judah, Simeon, and Benjamin these towns that are mentioned by name.

66 And some of the families of the sons of Kohath had towns of their territory out of the tribe of Ephraim. 67They were given the cities of refuge: Shechem with its pasture lands in the hill country of Ephraim, Gezer with its pasture lands, 68Jokmeam with its pasture lands, Beth-horon with its pasture lands, 69Aijalon with its pasture lands, Gath-rimmon with its pasture lands; 70and out of the half-tribe of Manasseh, Aner with its pasture lands, and Bileam with its pasture lands, for the rest of the families of the Kohathites.

71 To the Gershomites: out of the half-tribe of Manasseh: Golan in Bashan with its pasture lands and Ashtaroth with its pasture lands; 72and out of the tribe of Issachar: Kedesh with its pasture lands, Daberath h with its pasture lands, 73Ramoth with its pasture lands, and Anem with its pasture lands; 74out of the tribe of Asher: Mashal with its pasture lands, Abdon with its pasture lands, 75Hukok with its pasture lands, and Rehob with its pasture lands; 76and out of the tribe of Naphtali: Kedesh in Galilee with its pasture lands, Hammon with its pasture lands, and Kiriathaim with its pasture lands. 77To the rest of the Merarites out of the tribe of Zebulun: Rimmono with its pasture lands, Tabor with its pasture lands, 78and across the Jordan from Jericho, on the east side of the Jordan, out of the tribe of Reuben: Bezer in the steppe with its pasture lands, Jahzah with its pasture lands, 79Kedemoth with its pasture lands, and Mephaath with its pasture lands; 80and out of the tribe of Gad: Ramoth in Gilead with its pasture lands, Mahanaim with its pasture lands, 81Heshbon with its pasture lands, and Jazer with its pasture lands.

Descendants of Issachar

7 The sons i of Issachar: Tola, Puah, Jashub, and Shimron, four. 2The sons of Tola: Uzzi,

---

g Other readings *Hilez, Holon*; See Josh 21.15　　h Or *Dobrath*　　i Syr Compare Vg: Heb *And to the sons*

Rephaiah, Jeriel, Jahmai, Ibsam, and Shemuel, heads of their ancestral houses, namely of Tola, mighty warriors of their generations, their number in the days of David being twenty-two thousand six hundred. [3]The son[j] of Uzzi: Izrahiah. And the sons of Izrahiah: Michael, Obadiah, Joel, and Isshiah, five, all of them chiefs; [4]and along with them, by their generations, according to their ancestral houses, were units of the fighting force, thirty-six thousand, for they had many wives and sons. [5]Their kindred belonging to all the families of Issachar were in all eighty-seven thousand mighty warriors, enrolled by genealogy.

Descendants of Benjamin

6 The sons of Benjamin: Bela, Becher, and Jediael, three. [7]The sons of Bela: Ezbon, Uzzi, Uzziel, Jerimoth, and Iri, five, heads of ancestral houses, mighty warriors; and their enrollment by genealogies was twenty-two thousand thirty-four. [8]The sons of Becher: Zemirah, Joash, Eliezer, Elioenai, Omri, Jeremoth, Abijah, Anathoth, and Alemeth. All these were the sons of Becher; [9]and their enrollment by genealogies, according to their generations, as heads of their ancestral houses, mighty warriors, was twenty thousand two hundred. [10]The sons of Jediael: Bilhan. And the sons of Bilhan: Jeush, Benjamin, Ehud, Chenaanah, Zethan, Tarshish, and Ahishahar. [11]All these were the sons of Jediael according to the heads of their ancestral houses, mighty warriors, seventeen thousand two hundred, ready for service in war. [12]And Shuppim and Huppim were the sons of Ir, Hushim the son[j] of Aher.

Descendants of Naphtali

13 The descendants of Naphtali: Jahziel, Guni, Jezer, and Shallum, the descendants of Bilhah.

Descendants of Manasseh

14 The sons of Manasseh: Asriel, whom his Aramean concubine bore; she bore Machir the father of Gilead. [15]And Machir took a wife for Huppim and for Shuppim. The name of his sister was Maacah. And the name of the second was Zelophehad; and Zelophehad had daughters. [16]Maacah the wife of Machir bore a son, and she named him Peresh; the name of his brother was Sheresh; and his sons were Ulam and Rekem. [17]The son[j] of Ulam: Bedan. These were the sons of Gilead son of Machir, son of Manasseh. [18]And his sister Hammolecheth bore Ishhod, Abiezer, and Mahlah. [19]The sons of Shemida were Ahian, Shechem, Likhi, and Aniam.

Descendants of Ephraim

20 The sons of Ephraim: Shuthelah, and Bered his son, Tahath his son, Eleadah his son, Tahath his son, [21]Zabad his son, Shuthelah his son, and Ezer and Elead. Now the people of Gath, who were born in the land, killed them, because they came down to raid their cattle. [22]And their father

7.14 Joseph's Heirs

Joseph, Jacob's son, by rights deserved to have one of the "twelve tribes of Israel" named after him. Instead, Joseph passed that honor to his own sons Ephraim and Manasseh, whose offspring settled one of the largest tracts of land in Palestine and then competed with each other for prestige and influence. Their mention here is significant, for these tribes lived in the Northern Kingdom of Israel; wounds had healed, and the southern leaders in Jerusalem were now beginning to welcome back their estranged relatives.

Ephraim mourned many days, and his brothers came to comfort him. [23]Ephraim[k] went in to his wife, and she conceived and bore a son; and he named him Beriah, because disaster[l] had befallen his house. [24]His daughter was Sheerah, who built both Lower and Upper Beth-horon, and Uzzen-sheerah. [25]Rephah was his son, Resheph his son, Telah his son, Tahan his son, [26]Ladan his son, Ammihud his son, Elishama his son, [27]Nun[m] his son, Joshua his son. [28]Their possessions and settlements were Bethel and its towns, and eastward Naaran, and westward Gezer and its towns, Shechem and its towns, as far as Ayyah and its towns; [29]also along the borders of the Manassites, Beth-shean and its towns, Taanach and its towns, Megiddo and its towns, Dor and its towns. In these lived the sons of Joseph son of Israel.

Descendants of Asher

30 The sons of Asher: Imnah, Ishvah, Ishvi, Beriah, and their sister Serah. [31]The sons of Beriah: Heber and Malchiel, who was the father of Birzaith. [32]Heber became the father of Japhlet, Shomer, Hotham, and their sister Shua. [33]The sons of Japhlet: Pasach, Bimhal, and Ashvath. These are the sons of Japhlet. [34]The sons of Shemer: Ahi, Rohgah, Hubbah, and Aram. [35]The sons of Helem[n] his brother: Zophah, Imna, Shelesh, and Amal. [36]The sons of Zophah: Suah, Harnepher, Shual, Beri, Imrah, [37]Bezer, Hod, Shamma, Shilshah, Ithran, and Beera. [38]The sons of Jether: Jephunneh, Pispa, and Ara. [39]The sons of Ulla: Arah, Hanniel, and Rizia. [40]All of these were men of Asher, heads of ancestral houses, select mighty warriors, chief of the princes. Their number enrolled by genealogies, for service in war, was twenty-six thousand men.

Descendants of Benjamin

8 Benjamin became the father of Bela his firstborn, Ashbel the second, Aharah the third, [2]Nohah the fourth, and Rapha the fifth. [3]And Bela had sons: Addar, Gera, Abihud,[o] [4]Abishua, Naaman, Ahoah, [5]Gera, Shephuphan, and Huram. [6]These are the sons of Ehud (they were heads of ancestral houses of the inhabitants of Geba, and they were carried into exile to Manahath): [7]Naaman,[p] Ahijah, and Gera, that is, Heglam,[q] who became the father of Uzza and Ahihud. [8]And Shaharaim had sons in the country of Moab after he had sent away his wives Hushim and Baara. [9]He had sons by his wife Hodesh: Jobab, Zibia, Mesha, Malcam, [10]Jeuz, Sachia, and Mirmah. These were his sons, heads of ancestral houses. [11]He also had sons by Hushim: Abitub and Elpaal. [12]The sons of Elpaal: Eber, Misham, and Shemed, who built Ono and Lod with its towns, [13]and Beriah and Shema (they were heads of ancestral houses of the inhabitants of Aijalon, who put to flight the inhabitants of Gath); [14]and Ahio, Shashak, and Jeremoth. [15]Zebadiah, Arad, Eder, [16]Michael, Ishpah, and Joha were sons of Beriah. [17]Zebadiah, Meshullam, Hizki, Heber, [18]Ishmerai, Izliah, and Jobab were the sons of Elpaal. [19]Jakim, Zichri, Zabdi, [20]Elienai, Zillethai, Eliel, [21]Adaiah, Beraiah, and Shimrath were the sons of Shimei. [22]Ishpan, Eber, Eliel, [23]Abdon, Zichri, Hanan, [24]Hananiah, Elam, Anthothijah, [25]Iphdeiah, and Penuel were the sons of Shashak. [26]Shamsherai, Shehariah, Athaliah, [27]Jaareshiah, Elijah, and Zichri were the sons of Jeroham. [28]These were the heads of ancestral houses, according to their generations, chiefs. These lived in Jerusalem.

> ### 8.1 Dynasty Rejected
> ***Saul, Israel's first king, came from the tribe of Benjamin. Normally a royal dynasty would have followed him, descending from that same tribe. After Saul's dismal performance, however, God turned instead to the tribe of Judah and selected David, who became one of the ancestors of Jesus the Messiah.***

29 Jeiel[r] the father of Gibeon lived in Gibeon, and the name of his wife was Maacah. [30]His firstborn son: Abdon, then Zur, Kish, Baal,[s] Nadab, [31]Gedor, Ahio, Zecher, [32]and Mikloth, who became the father of Shimeah. Now these also lived opposite their kindred in Jerusalem, with their kindred. [33]Ner became the father of Kish, Kish of Saul,[t] Saul[t] of Jonathan, Malchishua, Abinadab, and Esh-baal; [34]and the son of Jonathan was Merib-baal; and Merib-baal became the father of Micah. [35]The sons of Micah: Pithon, Melech, Tarea, and Ahaz. [36]Ahaz became the father of Jehoaddah; and Jehoaddah became the father of Alemeth, Azmaveth, and Zimri; Zimri became the father of Moza. [37]Moza became the father of Binea; Raphah was his son, Eleasah his son, Azel his son. [38]Azel had six sons, and these are their names: Azrikam, Bocheru, Ishmael, Sheariah, Obadiah, and Hanan; all these were the sons of Azel. [39]The sons of his brother Eshek: Ulam his firstborn, Jeush the second, and Eliphelet the third. [40]The sons of Ulam were mighty warriors, archers, having many children and grandchildren, one hundred fifty. All these were Benjaminites.

9 So all Israel was enrolled by genealogies; and these are written in the Book of the Kings of Israel. And Judah was taken into exile in Babylon because of their unfaithfulness. [2]Now the first to live again in their possessions in their towns were Israelites, priests, Levites, and temple servants.

> ### 9.1 The Source of Genealogies
> ***The author of 1 Chronicles acknowledges that he relied on older documents for his information. In 1 and 2 Chronicles (originally one book) approximately 14 sources are named. During the Israelites' exile in Babylon, historical records had been lost and family information forgotten (see Ezra 2.59). First Chronicles condenses the most important of the genealogical information. It was meant to help the Israelites reestablish their identity as God's people.***

Inhabitants of Jerusalem after the Exile

3 And some of the people of Judah, Benjamin, Ephraim, and Manasseh lived in Jerusalem: [4]Uthai son of Ammihud, son of Omri, son of Imri, son of Bani, from the sons of Perez son of Judah. [5]And of the Shilonites: Asaiah the firstborn, and his sons. [6]Of the sons of Zerah: Jeuel and their kin, six hundred ninety. [7]Of the Benjaminites: Sallu son of Meshullam, son of Hodaviah, son of Hassenuah, [8]Ibneiah son of Jeroham, Elah son of Uzzi, son of Michri, and Meshullam son of Shephatiah, son of Reuel, son of Ibnijah; [9]and their kindred according to their generations, nine hundred fifty-six. All these were heads of families according to their ancestral houses.

Priestly Families

10 Of the priests: Jedaiah, Jehoiarib, Jachin, [11]and Azariah son of Hilkiah, son of Meshullam, son of Zadok, son of Meraioth, son of Ahitub, the

[o] Or *father of Ehud*; see 8.6 [p] Heb *and Naaman* [q] Or *he carried them into exile* [r] Compare 9.35: Heb lacks *Jeiel* [s] Gk Ms adds *Ner*; Compare 8.33 and 9.36 [t] Or *Shaul*

chief officer of the house of God; [12]and Adaiah son of Jeroham, son of Pashhur, son of Malchijah, and Maasai son of Adiel, son of Jahzerah, son of Meshullam, son of Meshillemith, son of Immer; [13]besides their kindred, heads of their ancestral houses, one thousand seven hundred sixty, qualified for the work of the service of the house of God.

Levitical Families

14 Of the Levites: Shemaiah son of Hasshub, son of Azrikam, son of Hashabiah, of the sons of Merari; [15]and Bakbakkar, Heresh, Galal, and Mattaniah son of Mica, son of Zichri, son of Asaph; [16]and Obadiah son of Shemaiah, son of Galal, son of Jeduthun, and Berechiah son of Asa, son of Elkanah, who lived in the villages of the Netophathites.

17 The gatekeepers were: Shallum, Akkub, Talmon, Ahiman; and their kindred Shallum was the chief, [18]stationed previously in the king's gate on the east side. These were the gatekeepers of the camp of the Levites. [19]Shallum son of Kore, son of Ebiasaph, son of Korah, and his kindred of his ancestral house, the Korahites, were in charge of the work of the service, guardians of the thresholds of the tent, as their ancestors had been in charge of the camp of the LORD, guardians of the entrance. [20]And Phinehas son of Eleazar was chief over them in former times; the LORD was with him. [21]Zechariah son of Meshelemiah was gatekeeper at the entrance of the tent of meeting. [22]All these, who were chosen as gatekeepers at the thresholds, were two hundred twelve. They were enrolled by genealogies in their villages. David and the seer Samuel established them in their office of trust. [23]So they and their descendants were in charge of the gates of the house of the LORD, that is, the house of the tent, as guards. [24]The gatekeepers were on the four sides, east, west, north, and south; [25]and their kindred who were in their villages were obliged to come in every seven days, in turn, to be with them; [26]for the four chief gatekeepers, who were Levites, were in charge of the chambers and the treasures of the house of God. [27]And they would spend the night near the house of God; for on them lay the duty of watching, and they had charge of opening it every morning.

28 Some of them had charge of the utensils of service, for they were required to count them when they were brought in and taken out. [29]Others of them were appointed over the furniture, and over all the holy utensils, also over the choice flour, the wine, the oil, the incense, and the spices. [30]Others, of the sons of the priests, prepared the mixing of the spices, [31]and Mattithiah, one of the Levites, the firstborn of Shallum the Korahite, was in charge of making the flat cakes. [32]Also some of their kindred of the Kohathites had charge of the rows of bread, to prepare them for each sabbath.

33 Now these are the singers, the heads of ancestral houses of the Levites, living in the chambers of the temple free from other service, for they were on duty day and night. [34]These were heads of ancestral houses of the Levites, according to their generations; these leaders lived in Jerusalem.

9.2–34 After the Exile

While most of 1 Chronicles deals with the time of David, this short section (2–34) jumps ahead 500 years to the time when a small portion of Israel had returned from exile. (See the books of Ezra, Nehemiah, Haggai, and Zechariah for more information about these returned exiles.)

The Family of King Saul

35 In Gibeon lived the father of Gibeon, Jeiel, and the name of his wife was Maacah. [36]His firstborn son was Abdon, then Zur, Kish, Baal, Ner, Nadab, [37]Gedor, Ahio, Zechariah, and Mikloth; [38]and Mikloth became the father of Shimeam; and these also lived opposite their kindred in Jerusalem, with their kindred. [39]Ner became the father of Kish, Kish of Saul, Saul of Jonathan, Malchishua, Abinadab, and Esh-baal; [40]and the son of Jonathan was Merib-baal; and Merib-baal became the father of Micah. [41]The sons of Micah: Pithon, Melech, Tahrea, and Ahaz;[u] [42]and Ahaz became the father of Jarah, and Jarah of Alemeth, Azmaveth, and Zimri; and Zimri became the father of Moza. [43]Moza became the father of Binea; and Rephaiah was his son, Eleasah his son, Azel his son. [44]Azel had six sons, and these are their names: Azrikam, Bocheru, Ishmael, Sheariah, Obadiah, and Hanan; these were the sons of Azel.

Death of Saul and His Sons

10 Now the Philistines fought against Israel; and the men of Israel fled before the Philistines, and fell slain on Mount Gilboa. [2]The Philistines overtook Saul and his sons; and the Philistines killed Jonathan and Abinadab and Malchishua, sons of Saul. [3]The battle pressed hard on Saul; and the archers found him, and he was wounded by the archers. [4]Then Saul said to his armor-bearer, "Draw your sword, and thrust me through with it, so that these uncircumcised may not come and make sport of me." But his armor-bearer was unwilling, for he was terrified. So Saul took his own sword and fell on it. [5]When his armor-bearer saw that Saul was dead, he also fell on his sword and died. [6]Thus Saul died; he and his three sons and all his house died together.

[u] Compare 8.35: Heb lacks *and Ahaz*

7When all the men of Israel who were in the valley saw that the army[v] had fled and that Saul and his sons were dead, they abandoned their towns and fled; and the Philistines came and occupied them.

8 The next day when the Philistines came to strip the dead, they found Saul and his sons fallen on Mount Gilboa. 9They stripped him and took his head and his armor, and sent messengers throughout the land of the Philistines to carry the good news to their idols and to the people. 10They put his armor in the temple of their gods, and fastened his head in the temple of Dagon. 11But when all Jabesh-gilead heard everything that the Philistines had done to Saul, 12all the valiant warriors got up and took away the body of Saul and the bodies of his sons, and brought them to Jabesh. Then they buried their bones under the oak in Jabesh, and fasted seven days.

13 So Saul died for his unfaithfulness; he was unfaithful to the LORD in that he did not keep the command of the LORD; moreover, he had consulted a medium, seeking guidance, 14and did not

10.13 Moral of the Story

First Chronicles covers much the same history as 1 Samuel, but with a distinctive approach. First Samuel gives more details about Saul's failures, while 1 Chronicles primarily concerns itself with drawing moral lessons from them. For example, 1 Samuel 28 tells the background to Saul's consulting a medium; 1 Chronicles merely alludes to it (most original readers would know the story well) and connects that act of disobedience to Saul's death.

seek guidance from the LORD. Therefore the LORD [w] put him to death and turned the kingdom over to David son of Jesse.

David Anointed King of All Israel

11 Then all Israel gathered together to David at Hebron and said, "See, we are your bone and flesh. 2For some time now, even while Saul was king, it was you who commanded the army of Israel. The LORD your God said to you: It is you who shall be shepherd of my people Israel, you who shall be ruler over my people Israel." 3So all the elders of Israel came to the king at Hebron, and David made a covenant with them at Hebron before the LORD. And they anointed David king over Israel, according to the word of the LORD by Samuel.

Jerusalem Captured

4 David and all Israel marched to Jerusalem, that is Jebus, where the Jebusites were, the inhabitants of the land. 5The inhabitants of Jebus said to David, "You will not come in here." Nevertheless David took the stronghold of Zion, now the city of David. 6David had said, "Whoever attacks the Jebusites first shall be chief and commander." And Joab son of Zeruiah went up first, so he became chief. 7David resided in the stronghold; therefore it was called the city of David. 8He built the city all around, from the Millo in complete circuit; and Joab repaired the rest of the city. 9And David became greater and greater, for the LORD of hosts was with him.

David's Mighty Men and Their Exploits

10 Now these are the chiefs of David's warriors, who gave him strong support in his kingdom, together with all Israel, to make him king, according to the word of the LORD concerning Israel. 11This is an account of David's mighty warriors: Jashobeam, son of Hachmoni,[x] was chief of the Three;[y] he wielded his spear against three hundred whom he killed at one time.

12 And next to him among the three warriors was Eleazar son of Dodo, the Ahohite. 13He was with David at Pas-dammim when the Philistines were gathered there for battle. There was a plot of ground full of barley. Now the people had fled from the Philistines, 14but he and David took their stand in the middle of the plot, defended it, and killed the Philistines; and the LORD saved them by a great victory.

15 Three of the thirty chiefs went down to the rock to David at the cave of Adullam, while the army of Philistines was encamped in the valley of Rephaim. 16David was then in the stronghold; and the garrison of the Philistines was then at Bethlehem. 17David said longingly, "O that someone would give me water to drink from the well of Bethlehem that is by the gate!" 18Then the Three broke through the camp of the Philistines, and drew water from the well of Bethlehem that was by the gate, and they brought it to David. But David would not drink of it; he poured it out to the LORD, 19and said, "My God forbid that I should do this. Can I drink the blood of these men? For at the risk of their lives they brought it." Therefore he would not drink it. The three warriors did these things.

20 Now Abishai,[z] the brother of Joab, was chief of the Thirty.[a] With his spear he fought against three hundred and killed them, and won a name beside the Three. 21He was the most renowned[b] of the Thirty,[a] and became their commander; but he did not attain to the Three.

22 Benaiah son of Jehoiada was a valiant man[c] of Kabzeel, a doer of great deeds; he struck

---

[v] Heb *they* [w] Heb *he* [x] Or *a Hachmonite* [y] Compare 2 Sam 23.8: Heb *Thirty* or *captains* [z] Gk Vg Tg
Compare 2 Sam 23.18: Heb *Abshai* [a] Syr: Heb *Three* [b] Compare 2 Sam 23.19: Heb *more renowned among the two*
[c] Syr: Heb *the son of a valiant man*

down two sons of[d] Ariel of Moab. He also went down and killed a lion in a pit on a day when snow had fallen. 23And he killed an Egyptian, a man of great stature, five cubits tall. The Egyptian had in his hand a spear like a weaver's beam; but Benaiah went against him with a staff, snatched the spear out of the Egyptian's hand, and killed him with his own spear. 24Such were the things Benaiah son of Jehoiada did, and he won a name beside the three warriors. 25He was renowned among the Thirty, but he did not attain to the Three. And David put him in charge of his bodyguard.

26 The warriors of the armies were Asahel brother of Joab, Elhanan son of Dodo of Bethlehem, 27Shammoth of Harod,[e] Helez the Pelonite, 28Ira son of Ikkesh of Tekoa, Abiezer of Anathoth, 29Sibbecai the Hushathite, Ilai the Ahohite, 30Maharai of Netophah, Heled son of Baanah of Netophah, 31Ithai son of Ribai of Gibeah of the Benjaminites, Benaiah of Pirathon, 32Hurai of the wadis of Gaash, Abiel the Arbathite, 33Azmaveth of Baharum, Eliahba of Shaalbon, 34Hashem[f] the Gizonite, Jonathan son of Shagee the Hararite, 35Ahiam son of Sachar the Hararite, Eliphal son of Ur, 36Hepher the Mecherathite, Ahijah the Pelonite, 37Hezro of Carmel, Naarai son of Ezbai, 38Joel the brother of Nathan, Mibhar son of Hagri, 39Zelek the Ammonite, Naharai of Beeroth, the armor-bearer of Joab son of Zeruiah, 40Ira the Ithrite, Gareb the Ithrite, 41Uriah the Hittite, Zabad son of Ahlai, 42Adina son of Shiza the Reubenite, a leader of the Reubenites, and thirty with him, 43Hanan son of Maacah, and Joshaphat the Mithnite, 44Uzzia the Ashterathite, Shama and Jeiel sons of Hotham the Aroerite, 45Jediael son of Shimri, and his brother Joha the Tizite, 46Eliel the Mahavite, and Jeribai and Joshaviah sons of Elnaam, and Ithmah the Moabite, 47Eliel, and Obed, and Jaasiel the Mezobaite.

David's Followers in the Wilderness

12 The following are those who came to David at Ziklag, while he could not move about freely because of Saul son of Kish; they were among the mighty warriors who helped him in war. 2They were archers, and could shoot arrows and sling stones with either the right hand or the left; they were Benjaminites, Saul's kindred. 3The chief was Ahiezer, then Joash, both sons of She-

[d] See 2 Sam 23.20: Heb lacks sons of   [e] Compare 2 Sam 23.25: Heb the Harorite   [f] Compare Gk and 2 Sam 23.32: Heb the sons of Hashem

JOAB, ABISHAI AND ASAHEL *Bloody Brothers*

WAR IS ALWAYS BRUTAL, AND hand-to-hand combat especially so. Allow one instant of pity as you look into your enemy's eyes, and he may stick a knife in your gut. A good warrior must be ruthless, and by that criterion Joab, Abishai and Asahel excelled. They lived violent lives, and at least two of the three died violent deaths.

Relatives of David, the brothers joined up with the future king while he was an outlaw hiding from King Saul. In a famous incident from those days, Abishai and David crept into the enemy camp at night and caught Saul fast asleep. Abishai wanted to kill Saul then and there, but David stopped him. That incident set a pattern: Several times Abishai impulsively sought to slaughter someone, only to be restrained by David.

The three brothers held to a strict code of revenge. When Asahel died in battle, the remaining brothers plotted revenge. The opportunity came some time later, when Saul's chief of the army called a truce to talk peace. Joab pretended to greet Abner and then, in an unguarded moment, stabbed him in the stomach.

David disapproved of the brothers' violent tactics, but he needed such strong and loyal soldiers. Joab proved his mettle by leading David's armies in a rout of powerful enemies. From that point on, Joab's brilliant soldiering became indispensable. David even trusted Joab with his sins: The two collaborated to murder Bathsheba's husband after David's adulterous affair. Significantly, David repented but Joab showed no interest in God or morality. He cared only about winning at war.

The bloody brothers had a fierce loyalty to David, and yet his inability to control them cost him dearly. When David's son Absalom led a rebellion, Joab and Abishai crushed the revolt. Joab caught the rebel son and dispatched him in cold blood, against David's explicit orders to let Absalom live.

Later, when David turned over the army to another general (perhaps because of the disobeyed order), Joab tricked and murdered his new rival. David never seemed capable of controlling Joab.

There is nothing pretty about these brothers and their careers in war. And as their commander-in-chief, David was inevitably drawn into their way of life. That may explain why God said to David, "You shall not build a house for my name, for you are a warrior and have shed blood" (1 Chronicles 28.3).

Life Questions: Have you ever felt yourself being drawn in to another person's way of life, even when you disapprove? What can you do to escape?

maah of Gibeah; also Jeziel and Pelet sons of Az-maveth; Beracah, Jehu of Anathoth, ⁴Ishmaiah of Gibeon, a warrior among the Thirty and a leader over the Thirty; Jeremiah,ᵍ Jahaziel, Johanan,

---

12.2 Accent on Unity

Chronicles bends over backwards to emphasize the need for unity of "all Israel," an important theme for a nation riven by tribalism and civil war. Here the author points out that even Saul's own kinsmen joined David's revolt. Later in the chapter (verses 23–38) he takes pains to mention compatriots from every tribe of Israel.

Jozabad of Gederah, ⁵Eluzai,ʰ Jerimoth, Bealiah, Shemariah, Shephatiah the Haruphite; ⁶Elkanah, Isshiah, Azarel, Joezer, and Jashobeam, the Ko-rahites; ⁷and Joelah and Zebadiah, sons of Jero-ham of Gedor.

8 From the Gadites there went over to David at the stronghold in the wilderness mighty and experienced warriors, expert with shield and spear, whose faces were like the faces of lions, and who were swift as gazelles on the mountains: ⁹Ezer the chief, Obadiah second, Eliab third, ¹⁰Mishmannah fourth, Jeremiah fifth, ¹¹Attai sixth, Eliel seventh, ¹²Johanan eighth, Elzabad ninth, ¹³Jeremiah tenth, Machbannai eleventh. ¹⁴These Gadites were officers of the army, the least equal to a hundred and the greatest to a thousand. ¹⁵These are the men who crossed the Jordan in the first month, when it was overflowing all its banks, and put to flight all those in the valleys, to the east and to the west.

16 Some Benjaminites and Judahites came to the stronghold to David. ¹⁷David went out to meet them and said to them, "If you have come to me in friendship, to help me, then my heart will be knit to you; but if you have come to betray me to my adversaries, though my hands have done no wrong, then may the God of our ancestors see and give judgment." ¹⁸Then the spirit came upon Amasai, chief of the Thirty, and he said,

"We are yours, O David;
    and with you, O son of Jesse!
Peace, peace to you,
    and peace to the one who helps you!
For your God is the one who helps
    you."

Then David received them, and made them officers of his troops.

19 Some of the Manassites deserted to David when he came with the Philistines for the battle against Saul. (Yet he did not help them, for the rulers of the Philistines took counsel and sent him away, saying, "He will desert to his master Saul at the cost of our heads.") ²⁰As he went to Ziklag these Manassites deserted to him: Adnah, Joza-bad, Jediael, Michael, Jozabad, Elihu, and Zille-thai, chiefs of the thousands in Manasseh. ²¹They helped David against the band of raiders,ⁱ for they were all warriors and commanders in the army. ²²Indeed from day to day people kept coming to David to help him, until there was a great army, like an army of God.

David's Army at Hebron

23 These are the numbers of the divisions of the armed troops who came to David in Hebron to turn the kingdom of Saul over to him, according to the word of the LORD. ²⁴The people of Judah bearing shield and spear numbered six thousand eight hundred armed troops. ²⁵Of the Simeonites, mighty warriors, seven thousand one hundred. ²⁶Of the Levites four thousand six hundred. ²⁷Jehoiada, leader of the house of Aaron, and with him three thousand seven hundred. ²⁸Zadok, a young warrior, and twenty-two commanders from his own ancestral house. ²⁹Of the Benjaminites, the kindred of Saul, three thousand, of whom the majority had continued to keep their allegiance to the house of Saul. ³⁰Of the Ephraimites, twenty thousand eight hundred, mighty warriors, notables in their ancestral houses. ³¹Of the half-tribe of Manasseh, eighteen thousand, who were expressly named to come and make David king. ³²Of Issachar, those who had understanding of the times, to know what Israel ought to do, two hundred chiefs, and all their kindred under their command. ³³Of Zebulun, fifty thousand seasoned troops, equipped for battle with all the weapons of war, to help Davidʲ with singleness of purpose. ³⁴Of Naphtali, a thousand commanders, with whom there were thirty-seven thousand armed with shield and spear. ³⁵Of the Danites, twenty-eight thousand six hundred equipped for battle. ³⁶Of Asher, forty thousand seasoned troops ready for battle. ³⁷Of the Reubenites and Gadites and the half-tribe of Manasseh from beyond the Jordan, one hundred twenty thousand armed with all the weapons of war.

38 All these, warriors arrayed in battle order, came to Hebron with full intent to make David king over all Israel; likewise all the rest of Israel were of a single mind to make David king. ³⁹They were there with David for three days, eating and drinking, for their kindred had provided for them. ⁴⁰And also their neighbors, from as far away as Issachar and Zebulun and Naphtali, came bringing food on donkeys, camels, mules, and oxen—abundant provisions of meal, cakes of figs, clusters of raisins, wine, oil, oxen, and sheep, for there was joy in Israel.

ᵍ Heb verse 5   ʰ Heb verse 6   ⁱ Or *as officers of his troops*   ʲ Gk: Heb lacks *David*

The Ark Brought from Kiriath-jearim

13 David consulted with the commanders of the thousands and of the hundreds, with every leader. ²David said to the whole assembly of Israel, "If it seems good to you, and if it is the will of the LORD our God, let us send abroad to our kindred who remain in all the land of Israel, including the priests and Levites in the cities that have pasture lands, that they may come together to us. ³Then let us bring again the ark of our God to us; for we did not turn to it in the days of Saul." ⁴The whole assembly agreed to do so, for the thing pleased all the people.

5 So David assembled all Israel from the Shihor of Egypt to Lebo-hamath, to bring the ark of God from Kiriath-jearim. ⁶And David and all Israel went up to Baalah, that is, to Kiriath-jearim, which belongs to Judah, to bring up from there the ark of God, the LORD, who is enthroned on the cherubim, which is called by his[k] name. ⁷They carried the ark of God on a new cart, from the house of Abinadab, and Uzzah and Ahio[l] were driving the cart. ⁸David and all Israel were dancing before God with all their might, with song and lyres and harps and tambourines and cymbals and trumpets.

9 When they came to the threshing floor of Chidon, Uzzah put out his hand to hold the ark,

13.9 Why Did Uzzah Die?

People who read of Uzzah's death in 2 Samuel 6.6–7 have often puzzled over why he died for trying to keep God's ark from tipping over. In 1 Chronicles the reason is clearer. David explained (15.13) that the Lord had been angry at them for moving the ark in a way disobedient to God's law.

Numbers 4.14–15 and Exodus 37.5 specify that Levites were to carry the ark with poles— and never touch it, on pain of death. Uzzah and his brother, non-Levites, were carrying it on an oxcart—the same vehicle the Philistines had used (1 Samuel 6.7). When the oxen stumbled and Uzzah stepped in to catch the ark, that was the final straw. Uzzah's death resulted from prolonged (though possibly well-intentioned) disobedience to God's direction. God had told them how to honor the ark, a sign of his presence. Their sloppiness revealed a lack of concern for God's honor.

for the oxen shook it. ¹⁰The anger of the LORD was kindled against Uzzah; he struck him down because he put out his hand to the ark; and he died there before God. ¹¹David was angry because the LORD had burst out against Uzzah; so that place

is called Perez-uzzah[m] to this day. ¹²David was afraid of God that day; he said, "How can I bring the ark of God into my care?" ¹³So David did not take the ark into his care into the city of David; he took it instead to the house of Obed-edom the Gittite. ¹⁴The ark of God remained with the household of Obed-edom in his house three months, and the LORD blessed the household of Obed-edom and all that he had.

David Established at Jerusalem

14 King Hiram of Tyre sent messengers to David, along with cedar logs, and masons and carpenters to build a house for him. ²David then perceived that the LORD had established him as king over Israel, and that his kingdom was highly exalted for the sake of his people Israel.

3 David took more wives in Jerusalem, and David became the father of more sons and daughters. ⁴These are the names of the children whom he had in Jerusalem: Shammua, Shobab, and Nathan; Solomon, ⁵Ibhar, Elishua, and Elpelet; ⁶Nogah, Nepheg, and Japhia; ⁷Elishama, Beeliada, and Eliphelet.

Defeat of the Philistines

8 When the Philistines heard that David had been anointed king over all Israel, all the Philistines went up in search of David; and David heard of it and went out against them. ⁹Now the Philistines had come and made a raid in the valley of Rephaim. ¹⁰David inquired of God, "Shall I go up against the Philistines? Will you give them into my hand?" The LORD said to him, "Go up, and I will give them into your hand." ¹¹So he went up to Baal-perazim, and David defeated them there. David said, "God has burst out[n] against my enemies by my hand, like a bursting flood." Therefore that place is called Baal-perazim.[o] ¹²They abandoned their gods there, and at David's command they were burned.

13 Once again the Philistines made a raid in the valley. ¹⁴When David again inquired of God, God said to him, "You shall not go up after them; go around and come on them opposite the balsam trees. ¹⁵When you hear the sound of marching in the tops of the balsam trees, then go out to battle; for God has gone out before you to strike down the army of the Philistines." ¹⁶David did as God had commanded him, and they struck down the Philistine army from Gibeon to Gezer. ¹⁷The fame of David went out into all lands, and the LORD brought the fear of him on all nations.

The Ark Brought to Jerusalem

15 David[p] built houses for himself in the city of David, and he prepared a place for the ark of God and pitched a tent for it. ²Then David

---

[k] Heb lacks *his*   [l] Or *and his brother*   [m] That is *Bursting Out Against Uzzah*   [n] Heb *paraz*   [o] That is *Lord of Bursting Out*   [p] Heb *He*

commanded that no one but the Levites were to carry the ark of God, for the LORD had chosen them to carry the ark of the LORD and to minister to him forever. [3]David assembled all Israel in Jerusalem to bring up the ark of the LORD to its place, which he had prepared for it. [4]Then David gathered together the descendants of Aaron and the Levites: [5]of the sons of Kohath, Uriel the chief, with one hundred twenty of his kindred; [6]of the sons of Merari, Asaiah the chief, with two hundred twenty of his kindred; [7]of the sons of Gershom, Joel the chief, with one hundred thirty of his kindred; [8]of the sons of Elizaphan, Shemaiah the chief, with two hundred of his kindred; [9]of the sons of Hebron, Eliel the chief, with eighty of his kindred; [10]of the sons of Uzziel, Amminadab the chief, with one hundred twelve of his kindred.

15.3 Red-letter Day

Much of Chronicles summarizes and interprets history that is covered more fully in the books of Samuel. But this chapter contains mostly new material, reflecting a central concern of the author. David's bringing the ark to Jerusalem had been a landmark event, signifying the renewed presence of God in the nation (see also Psalm 132). The Chronicler yearned for a similar spirit of renewal among the people of his own time.

11 David summoned the priests Zadok and Abiathar, and the Levites Uriel, Asaiah, Joel, Shemaiah, Eliel, and Amminadab. [12]He said to them, "You are the heads of families of the Levites; sanctify yourselves, you and your kindred, so that you may bring up the ark of the LORD, the God of Israel, to the place that I have prepared for it. [13]Because you did not carry it the first time,[q] the LORD our God burst out against us, because we did not give it proper care." [14]So the priests and the Levites sanctified themselves to bring up the ark of the LORD, the God of Israel. [15]And the Levites carried the ark of God on their shoulders with the poles, as Moses had commanded according to the word of the LORD.

16 David also commanded the chiefs of the Levites to appoint their kindred as the singers to play on musical instruments, on harps and lyres and cymbals, to raise loud sounds of joy. [17]So the Levites appointed Heman son of Joel; and of his kindred Asaph son of Berechiah; and of the sons of Merari, their kindred, Ethan son of Kushaiah; [18]and with them their kindred of the second order, Zechariah, Jaaziel, Shemiramoth, Jehiel, Unni, Eliab, Benaiah, Maaseiah, Mattithiah, Eliphelehu, and Mikneiah, and the gatekeepers Obed-edom and Jeiel. [19]The singers Heman, Asaph, and Ethan were to sound bronze cymbals; [20]Zechariah, Aziel, Shemiramoth, Jehiel, Unni, Eliab, Maaseiah, and Benaiah were to play harps according to Alamoth; [21]but Mattithiah, Eliphelehu, Mikneiah, Obed-edom, Jeiel, and Azaziah were to lead with lyres according to the Sheminith. [22]Chenaniah, leader of the Levites in music, was to direct the music, for he understood it. [23]Berechiah and Elkanah were to be gatekeepers for the ark. [24]Shebaniah, Joshaphat, Nethanel, Amasai, Zechariah, Benaiah, and Eliezer, the priests, were to blow the trumpets before the ark of God. Obed-edom and Jehiah also were to be gatekeepers for the ark.

25 So David and the elders of Israel, and the commanders of the thousands, went to bring up the ark of the covenant of the LORD from the house of Obed-edom with rejoicing. [26]And because God helped the Levites who were carrying the ark of the covenant of the LORD, they sacrificed seven bulls and seven rams. [27]David was clothed with a robe of fine linen, as also were all the Levites who were carrying the ark, and the singers, and Chenaniah the leader of the music of the singers; and David wore a linen ephod. [28]So all Israel brought up the ark of the covenant of the LORD with shouting, to the sound of the horn, trumpets, and cymbals, and made loud music on harps and lyres.

29 As the ark of the covenant of the LORD came to the city of David, Michal daughter of Saul looked out of the window, and saw King David leaping and dancing; and she despised him in her heart.

The Ark Placed in the Tent

16 They brought in the ark of God, and set it inside the tent that David had pitched for it; and they offered burnt offerings and offerings of well-being before God. [2]When David had finished offering the burnt offerings and the offerings of well-being, he blessed the people in the name of the LORD; [3]and he distributed to every person in Israel—man and woman alike—to each a loaf of bread, a portion of meat,[r] and a cake of raisins.

4 He appointed certain of the Levites as ministers before the ark of the LORD, to invoke, to thank, and to praise the LORD, the God of Israel. [5]Asaph was the chief, and second to him Zechariah, Jeiel, Shemiramoth, Jehiel, Mattithiah, Eliab, Benaiah, Obed-edom, and Jeiel, with harps and lyres; Asaph was to sound the cymbals, [6]and the priests Benaiah and Jahaziel were to blow trumpets regularly, before the ark of the covenant of God.

David's Psalm of Thanksgiving

7 Then on that day David first appointed the

[q] Meaning of Heb uncertain [r] Compare Gk Syr Vg: Meaning of Heb uncertain

singing of praises to the Lord by Asaph and his kindred.

8 O give thanks to the Lord, call on his
name,
make known his deeds among the
peoples.
9 Sing to him, sing praises to him,
tell of all his wonderful works.
10 Glory in his holy name;
let the hearts of those who seek the
Lord rejoice.
11 Seek the Lord and his strength,
seek his presence continually.
12 Remember the wonderful works he has
done,
his miracles, and the judgments he
uttered,
13 O offspring of his servant Israel,[s]
children of Jacob, his chosen ones.

14 He is the Lord our God;
his judgments are in all the earth.
15 Remember his covenant forever,
the word that he commanded, for a
thousand generations,
16 the covenant that he made with Abraham,
his sworn promise to Isaac,
17 which he confirmed to Jacob as a statute,
to Israel as an everlasting covenant,
18 saying, "To you I will give the land of
Canaan
as your portion for an inheritance."

19 When they were few in number,
of little account, and strangers in the
land,[t]
20 wandering from nation to nation,
from one kingdom to another people,
21 he allowed no one to oppress them;
he rebuked kings on their account,
22 saying, "Do not touch my anointed ones;
do my prophets no harm."

23 Sing to the Lord, all the earth.
Tell of his salvation from day to day.
24 Declare his glory among the nations,
his marvelous works among all the
peoples.
25 For great is the Lord, and greatly to be
praised;
he is to be revered above all gods.
26 For all the gods of the peoples are idols,
but the Lord made the heavens.
27 Honor and majesty are before him;
strength and joy are in his place.

28 Ascribe to the Lord, O families of the
peoples,

ascribe to the Lord glory and strength.
29 Ascribe to the Lord the glory due his
name;
bring an offering, and come before
him.
Worship the Lord in holy splendor;
30 tremble before him, all the earth.
The world is firmly established; it shall
never be moved.
31 Let the heavens be glad, and let the earth
rejoice,
and let them say among the nations,
"The Lord is king!"
32 Let the sea roar, and all that fills it;
let the field exult, and everything in it.
33 Then shall the trees of the forest sing for
joy
before the Lord, for he comes to judge
the earth.
34 O give thanks to the Lord, for he is good;
for his steadfast love endures forever.

35 Say also:
"Save us, O God of our salvation,
and gather and rescue us from among
the nations,
that we may give thanks to your holy
name,
and glory in your praise.
36 Blessed be the Lord, the God of Israel,
from everlasting to everlasting."
Then all the people said "Amen!" and praised the Lord.

Regular Worship Maintained

37 David left Asaph and his kinsfolk there before the ark of the covenant of the Lord to minister regularly before the ark as each day required, 38and also Obed-edom and his[u] sixty-eight kinsfolk; while Obed-edom son of Jeduthun and Hosah were to be gatekeepers. 39And he left the priest Zadok and his kindred the priests before the tabernacle of the Lord in the high place that was at Gibeon, 40to offer burnt offerings to the Lord on the altar of burnt offering regularly,

16.39 Two Tabernacles

For a number of years, Israel had two tabernacles. David had constructed a new tent for the ark of the covenant when it came to Jerusalem. Yet the old tent, dating from Moses' time, still stood at Gibeon, five miles away. Sacrifices were offered at both locations. When the temple was built under David's son Solomon, worship was centralized at Jerusalem.

---

[s] Another reading is *Abraham* (compare Ps 105.6)   [t] Heb *in it*   [u] Gk Syr Vg: Heb *their*

morning and evening, according to all that is written in the law of the LORD that he commanded Israel. ⁴¹With them were Heman and Jeduthun, and the rest of those chosen and expressly named to render thanks to the LORD, for his steadfast love endures forever. ⁴²Heman and Jeduthun had with them trumpets and cymbals for the music, and instruments for sacred song. The sons of Jeduthun were appointed to the gate.

43 Then all the people departed to their homes, and David went home to bless his household.

God's Covenant with David

17 Now when David settled in his house, David said to the prophet Nathan, "I am living in a house of cedar, but the ark of the covenant of the LORD is under a tent." ²Nathan said to David, "Do all that you have in mind, for God is with you."

3 But that same night the word of the LORD came to Nathan, saying: ⁴Go and tell my servant David: Thus says the LORD: You shall not build me a house to live in. ⁵For I have not lived in a house since the day I brought out Israel to this very day, but I have lived in a tent and a tabernacle.ᵛ ⁶Wherever I have moved about among all Israel, did I ever speak a word with any of the judges of Israel, whom I commanded to shepherd my people, saying, Why have you not built me a house of cedar? ⁷Now therefore thus you shall say to my servant David: Thus says the LORD of hosts: I took you from the pasture, from following the sheep, to be ruler over my people Israel; ⁸and I have been with you wherever you went, and have cut off all your enemies before you; and I will make for you a name, like the name of the great ones of the earth. ⁹I will appoint a place for my people Israel, and will plant them, so that they may live in their own place, and be disturbed no

ᵛ Gk 2 Sam 7.6: Heb *but I have been from tent to tent and from tabernacle*

Hope in a Time of Sorrow
A people starting over need to know God's promises

> "Who am I, O LORD God, and what is my house, that you have brought me thus far?" 17.16

FIRST CHRONICLES WAS WRITTEN FOR Israelites living centuries after David. In those years Israel had gone through tremendous sorrow. None of the kings who followed David had matched him. Israel had deteriorated until God let Babylon capture and destroy Jerusalem, carrying its population into exile.

After half a century as captives, a small proportion of the Israelites returned to their former home. They had lost, in those beaten-down years, their own sense of identity. They were no longer self-governing. They had no king to follow in David's footsteps. Their relatives were scattered all over the Middle East. Chronicles was written to help them get in touch with what Israel had once been and could become again.

After devoting nine chapters to genealogies, 1 Chronicles tells the life of David. In keeping with its goal of encouragement, Chronicles leaves out stories of David's personal sin and failure. Nor does it tell of David's life before he became king. Instead it concentrates on the accomplishments David left behind for future generations.

The Importance of Worship

David emphasized worship as the foundation of Israel. As soon as he conquered Jerusalem, he brought the ark of the covenant there. He made preparations to build the temple and organized the priests and Levites to serve there. He established large corps of musicians to praise God. In response, God promised that a line of leaders would descend from him (17.10–14).

David's days were the high point of Israelite history: prosperous, secure, and, above all, devoted to God. How could the returned exiles recapture that grandeur? What resources could they use to begin again? First Chronicles emphasizes a legacy they still possessed. They had Jerusalem, and they had a new temple built on the site of the old one. They had the priests and Levites, so essential to proper worship. In short, they had the resources necessary to rise again, to be God's people in God's land.

Most important, they had God. They could find strength in worshiping him, as David always had. God had made them great before; he could make them great again, and provide a new leader in David's line. A sorrowful people could start over on the old foundations—foundations that depended on an unchanging God and his unchanging choice of them.

Life Questions: If you were to suffer great personal and material loss, as the Israelites did, what would you cling to?

more; and evildoers shall wear them down no more, as they did formerly, [10]from the time that I appointed judges over my people Israel; and I will subdue all your enemies.

Moreover I declare to you that the LORD will build you a house. [11]When your days are fulfilled to go to be with your ancestors, I will raise up your offspring after you, one of your own sons, and I will establish his kingdom. [12]He shall build a house for me, and I will establish his throne forever. [13]I will be a father to him, and he shall be a son to me. I will not take my steadfast love from him, as I took it from him who was before you, [14]but I will confirm him in my house and in my kingdom forever, and his throne shall be established forever. [15]In accordance with all these words and all this vision, Nathan spoke to David.

David's Prayer

16 Then King David went in and sat before the LORD, and said, "Who am I, O LORD God, and what is my house, that you have brought me thus

17.16 Rare Trait

King David possessed in abundance that rarest of qualities in a powerful ruler: humility. Ever mindful of his modest background, he credited God's grace, not his own merit, for his success. David could have taken offense at Nathan's message; after all, God was rejecting his offer to build a temple. Instead, David accepted the news with meekness and thanksgiving.

far? [17]And even this was a small thing in your sight, O God; you have also spoken of your servant's house for a great while to come. You regard me as someone of high rank,[w] O LORD God! [18]And what more can David say to you for honoring your servant? You know your servant. [19]For your servant's sake, O LORD, and according to your own heart, you have done all these great deeds, making known all these great things. [20]There is no one like you, O LORD, and there is no God besides you, according to all that we have heard with our ears. [21]Who is like your people Israel, one nation on the earth whom God went to redeem to be his people, making for yourself a name for great and terrible things, in driving out nations before your people whom you redeemed from Egypt? [22]And you made your people Israel to be your people forever; and you, O LORD, became their God.

23 "And now, O LORD, as for the word that you have spoken concerning your servant and concerning his house, let it be established forever, and do as you have promised. [24]Thus your name will be established and magnified forever in the

saying, 'The LORD of hosts, the God of Israel, is Israel's God'; and the house of your servant David will be established in your presence. [25]For you, my God, have revealed to your servant that you will build a house for him; therefore your servant has found it possible to pray before you. [26]And now, O LORD, you are God, and you have promised this good thing to your servant; [27]therefore may it please you to bless the house of your servant, that it may continue forever before you. For you, O LORD, have blessed and are blessed[x] forever."

David's Kingdom Established and Extended

18 Some time afterward, David attacked the Philistines and subdued them; he took Gath and its villages from the Philistines.

2 He defeated Moab, and the Moabites became subject to David and brought tribute.

3 David also struck down King Hadadezer of Zobah, toward Hamath,[w] as he went to set up a monument at the river Euphrates. [4]David took from him one thousand chariots, seven thousand cavalry, and twenty thousand foot soldiers. David hamstrung all the chariot horses, but left one hundred of them. [5]When the Arameans of Damascus came to help King Hadadezer of Zobah, David killed twenty-two thousand Arameans. [6]Then David put garrisons[y] in Aram of Damascus; and the Arameans became subject to David, and brought tribute. The LORD gave victory to David wherever he went. [7]David took the gold shields that were carried by the servants of Hadadezer, and brought them to Jerusalem. [8]From Tibhath and from Cun, cities of Hadadezer, David took a vast quantity of bronze; with it Solomon made the bronze sea and the pillars and the vessels of bronze.

9 When King Tou of Hamath heard that David had defeated the whole army of King Hadadezer of Zobah, [10]he sent his son Hadoram to King David, to greet him and to congratulate him, because he had fought against Hadadezer and defeated him. Now Hadadezer had often been at war with Tou. He sent all sorts of articles of gold, of silver, and of bronze; [11]these also King David dedicated to the LORD, together with the silver and gold that he had carried off from all the nations, from Edom, Moab, the Ammonites, the Philistines, and Amalek.

12 Abishai son of Zeruiah killed eighteen thousand Edomites in the Valley of Salt. [13]He put garrisons in Edom; and all the Edomites became subject to David. And the LORD gave victory to David wherever he went.

David's Administration

14 So David reigned over all Israel; and he

---

[w] Meaning of Heb uncertain   [x] Or *and it is blessed*   [y] Gk Vg 2 Sam 8.6 Compare Syr: Heb lacks *garrisons*

administered justice and equity to all his people. [15]Joab son of Zeruiah was over the army; Jehoshaphat son of Ahilud was recorder; [16]Zadok son of Ahitub and Ahimelech son of Abiathar were priests; Shavsha was secretary; [17]Benaiah son of Jehoiada was over the Cherethites and the Pelethites; and David's sons were the chief officials in the service of the king.

Defeat of the Ammonites and Arameans

19 Some time afterward, King Nahash of the Ammonites died, and his son succeeded him. [2]David said, "I will deal loyally with Hanun son of Nahash, for his father dealt loyally with me." So David sent messengers to console him concerning his father. When David's servants came to Hanun in the land of the Ammonites, to console him, [3]the officials of the Ammonites said to Hanun, "Do you think, because David has sent consolers to you, that he is honoring your father? Have not his servants come to you to search and to overthrow and to spy out the land?" [4]So Hanun seized David's servants, shaved them, cut off their garments in the middle at their hips, and sent

19.4 Comedy of Errors

Wars start for the oddest reasons. One modern war in Central America erupted after a poorly refereed soccer match. In this instance the king of Ammon misjudged the motives of a funeral delegation, and David felt obliged to respond to an insult that today seems more humorous than humiliating. The resulting war crushed one of Israel's peskiest enemies, the Ammonites, offspring of the incestuous relations between Lot and his daughter (Genesis 19).

them away; [5]and they departed. When David was told about the men, he sent messengers to them, for they felt greatly humiliated. The king said, "Remain at Jericho until your beards have grown, and then return."

6 When the Ammonites saw that they had made themselves odious to David, Hanun and the Ammonites sent a thousand talents of silver to hire chariots and cavalry from Mesopotamia, from Aram-maacah and from Zobah. [7]They hired thirty-two thousand chariots and the king of Maacah with his army, who came and camped before Medeba. And the Ammonites were mustered from their cities and came to battle. [8]When David heard of it, he sent Joab and all the army of the warriors. [9]The Ammonites came out and drew up in battle array at the entrance of the city,

and the kings who had come were by themselves in the open country.

10 When Joab saw that the line of battle was set against him both in front and in the rear, he chose some of the picked men of Israel and arrayed them against the Arameans; [11]the rest of his troops he put in the charge of his brother Abishai, and they were arrayed against the Ammonites. [12]He said, "If the Arameans are too strong for me, then you shall help me; but if the Ammonites are too strong for you, then I will help you. [13]Be strong, and let us be courageous for our people and for the cities of our God; and may the LORD do what seems good to him." [14]So Joab and the troops who were with him advanced toward the Arameans for battle; and they fled before him. [15]When the Ammonites saw that the Arameans fled, they likewise fled before Abishai, Joab's brother, and entered the city. Then Joab came to Jerusalem.

16 But when the Arameans saw that they had been defeated by Israel, they sent messengers and brought out the Arameans who were beyond the Euphrates, with Shophach the commander of the army of Hadadezer at their head. [17]When David was informed, he gathered all Israel together, crossed the Jordan, came to them, and drew up his forces against them. When David set the battle in array against the Arameans, they fought with him. [18]The Arameans fled before Israel; and David killed seven thousand Aramean charioteers and forty thousand foot soldiers, and also killed Shophach the commander of their army. [19]When the servants of Hadadezer saw that they had been defeated by Israel, they made peace with David, and became subject to him. So the Arameans were not willing to help the Ammonites any more.

Siege and Capture of Rabbah

20 In the spring of the year, the time when kings go out to battle, Joab led out the army, ravaged the country of the Ammonites, and came and besieged Rabbah. But David remained at Jerusalem. Joab attacked Rabbah, and overthrew it. [2]David took the crown of Milcom[z] from his head; he found that it weighed a talent of gold, and in it was a precious stone; and it was placed on David's head. He also brought out the booty of the city, a very great amount. [3]He brought out the people who were in it, and set them to work[a] with saws and iron picks and axes.[b] Thus David did to all the cities of the Ammonites. Then David and all the people returned to Jerusalem.

Exploits against the Philistines

4 After this, war broke out with the Philistines at Gezer; then Sibbecai the Hushathite killed Sip-

---

z Gk Vg See 1 Kings 11.5, 33: MT *of their king*   a Compare 2 Sam 12.31: Heb *and he sawed*   b Compare 2 Sam 12.31: Heb *saws* pai, who was one of the descendants of the giants; and the Philistines were subdued. ⁵Again there was war with the Philistines; and Elhanan son of Jair killed Lahmi the brother of Goliath the Gittite, the shaft of whose spear was like a weaver's beam. ⁶Again there was war at Gath, where there was a man of great size, who had six fingers on each hand, and six toes on each foot, twenty-four in number; he also was descended from the giants. ⁷When he taunted Israel, Jonathan son of Shimea, David's brother, killed him. ⁸These were descended from the giants in Gath; they fell by the hand of David and his servants.

The Census and Plague

21 Satan stood up against Israel, and incited David to count the people of Israel. ²So David said to Joab and the commanders of the army, "Go, number Israel, from Beer-sheba to Dan, and bring me a report, so that I may know their number." ³But Joab said, "May the LORD increase the number of his people a hundredfold! Are they not, my lord the king, all of them my lord's servants? Why then should my lord require this? Why should he bring guilt on Israel?" ⁴But the king's word prevailed against Joab. So Joab departed and went throughout all Israel, and came back to Jerusalem. ⁵Joab gave the total count of the people to David. In all Israel there were one million one hundred thousand men who drew the sword, and in Judah four hundred seventy thousand who drew the sword. ⁶But he did not include Levi and Benjamin in the numbering, for the king's command was abhorrent to Joab.

7 But God was displeased with this thing, and

21.7 Act of Pride

Taking a census was not in itself immoral—God commanded it in the book of Numbers (chapters 1,26). This census, however, came out of David's desire to survey his kingdom, now at peace, in order to glory in its size and its potential military strength. God wanted him to continue relying on divine help and guidance, not on national pride. Even Joab, a top general, sensed the grievous mistake (verse 3). For more details, see "Satan or the Lord?" page 351.

he struck Israel. ⁸David said to God, "I have sinned greatly in that I have done this thing. But now, I pray you, take away the guilt of your servant; for I have done very foolishly." ⁹The LORD spoke to Gad, David's seer, saying, ¹⁰"Go and say to David, 'Thus says the LORD: Three things I offer you; choose one of them, so that I may do it to you.'" ¹¹So Gad came to David and said to him, "Thus says the LORD, 'Take your choice: ¹²either three years of famine; or three months of

devastation by your foes, while the sword of your enemies overtakes you; or three days of the sword of the LORD, pestilence on the land, and the angel of the LORD destroying throughout all the territory of Israel.' Now decide what answer I shall return to the one who sent me." ¹³Then David said to Gad, "I am in great distress; let me fall into the hand of the LORD, for his mercy is very great; but let me not fall into human hands."

14 So the LORD sent a pestilence on Israel; and seventy thousand persons fell in Israel. ¹⁵And God sent an angel to Jerusalem to destroy it; but when he was about to destroy it, the LORD took note and relented concerning the calamity; he said to the destroying angel, "Enough! Stay your hand." The angel of the LORD was then standing by the threshing floor of Ornan the Jebusite. ¹⁶David looked up and saw the angel of the LORD standing between earth and heaven, and in his hand a drawn sword stretched out over Jerusalem. Then David and the elders, clothed in sackcloth, fell on their faces. ¹⁷And David said to God, "Was it not I who gave the command to count the people? It is I who have sinned and done very wickedly. But these sheep, what have they done? Let your hand, I pray, O LORD my God, be against me and against my father's house; but do not let your people be plagued!"

David's Altar and Sacrifice

18 Then the angel of the LORD commanded Gad to tell David that he should go up and erect an altar to the LORD on the threshing floor of Ornan the Jebusite. ¹⁹So David went up following Gad's instructions, which he had spoken in the name of the LORD. ²⁰Ornan turned and saw the angel; and while his four sons who were with him hid themselves, Ornan continued to thresh wheat. ²¹As David came to Ornan, Ornan looked and saw David; he went out from the threshing floor, and did obeisance to David with his face to the ground. ²²David said to Ornan, "Give me the site of the threshing floor that I may build on it an altar to the LORD—give it to me at its full price—so that the plague may be averted from the people." ²³Then Ornan said to David, "Take it; and let my lord the king do what seems good to him; see, I present the oxen for burnt offerings, and the threshing sledges for the wood, and the wheat for a grain offering. I give it all." ²⁴But King David said to Ornan, "No; I will buy them for the full price. I will not take for the LORD what is yours, nor offer burnt offerings that cost me nothing." ²⁵So David paid Ornan six hundred shekels of gold by weight for the site. ²⁶David built there an altar to the LORD and presented burnt offerings and offerings of well-being. He called upon the LORD, and he answered him with fire from heaven on the altar of burnt offering. ²⁷Then the LORD commanded the angel, and he put his sword back into its sheath.

The Place Chosen for the Temple

28 At that time, when David saw that the LORD had answered him at the threshing floor of Ornan the Jebusite, he made his sacrifices there. 29For the tabernacle of the LORD, which Moses had made in the wilderness, and the altar of burnt offering were at that time in the high place at Gibeon; 30but David could not go before it to inquire of God, for he was afraid of the sword of the angel of the LORD. 1Then David said, "Here shall be the house of the LORD God and here the altar of burnt offering for Israel."

22

David Prepares to Build the Temple

2 David gave orders to gather together the aliens who were residing in the land of Israel, and he set stonecutters to prepare dressed stones for building the house of God. 3David also provided great stores of iron for nails for the doors of the gates and for clamps, as well as bronze in quantities beyond weighing, 4and cedar logs without number—for the Sidonians and Tyrians brought great quantities of cedar to David. 5For David said, "My son Solomon is young and inexperienced, and the house that is to be built for the LORD must be exceedingly magnificent, famous and glorified throughout all lands; I will therefore make preparation for it." So David provided materials in great quantity before his death.

David's Charge to Solomon and the Leaders

6 Then he called for his son Solomon and charged him to build a house for the LORD, the God of Israel. 7David said to Solomon, "My son, I had planned to build a house to the name of the LORD my God. 8But the word of the LORD came to me, saying, 'You have shed much blood and have waged great wars; you shall not build a house to my name, because you have shed so much blood

22.8 A Man of Blood

David explained to Solomon that the Lord had not allowed him to build the temple because of his life of bloodshed. This does not suggest that David had been wrong to lead Israel in battle. God had directed him to conduct at least some of the wars. Nonetheless, war and bloodshed, even when necessary, fall short of God's ideal. He wanted the temple built by a man of peace.

in my sight on the earth. 9See, a son shall be born to you; he shall be a man of peace. I will give him peace from all his enemies on every side; for his name shall be Solomon,c and I will give peaced

and quiet to Israel in his days. 10He shall build a house for my name. He shall be a son to me, and I will be a father to him, and I will establish his royal throne in Israel forever.' 11Now, my son, the LORD be with you, so that you may succeed in building the house of the LORD your God, as he has spoken concerning you. 12Only, may the LORD grant you discretion and understanding, so that when he gives you charge over Israel you may keep the law of the LORD your God. 13Then you will prosper if you are careful to observe the statutes and the ordinances that the LORD commanded Moses for Israel. Be strong and of good courage. Do not be afraid or dismayed. 14With great pains I have provided for the house of the LORD one hundred thousand talents of gold, one million talents of silver, and bronze and iron beyond weighing, for there is so much of it; timber and stone too I have provided. To these you must add more. 15You have an abundance of workers: stonecutters, masons, carpenters, and all kinds of artisans without number, skilled in working 16gold, silver, bronze, and iron. Now begin the work, and the LORD be with you."

17 David also commanded all the leaders of Israel to help his son Solomon, saying, 18"Is not the LORD your God with you? Has he not given you peace on every side? For he has delivered the inhabitants of the land into my hand; and the land is subdued before the LORD and his people. 19Now set your mind and heart to seek the LORD your God. Go and build the sanctuary of the LORD God so that the ark of the covenant of the LORD and the holy vessels of God may be brought into a house built for the name of the LORD."

Families of the Levites and Their Functions

23 When David was old and full of days, he made his son Solomon king over Israel.

2 David assembled all the leaders of Israel and the priests and the Levites. 3The Levites, thirty years old and upward, were counted, and the total was thirty-eight thousand. 4"Twenty-four thousand of these," David said, "shall have charge of the work in the house of the LORD, six thousand shall be officers and judges, 5four thousand gatekeepers, and four thousand shall offer praises to the LORD with the instruments that I have made for praise." 6And David organized them in divisions corresponding to the sons of Levi: Gershon,e Kohath, and Merari.

7 The sons of Gershonf were Ladan and Shimei. 8The sons of Ladan: Jehiel the chief, Zetham, and Joel, three. 9The sons of Shimei: Shelomoth, Haziel, and Haran, three. These were the heads of families of Ladan. 10And the sons of Shimei: Jahath, Zina, Jeush, and Beriah. These

c Heb *Shelomoh* d Heb *shalom* e Or *Gershom*; See 1 Chr 6.1, note, and 23.15 f Vg Compare Gk Syr: Heb *to the Gershonite*

four were the sons of Shimei. ¹¹Jahath was the chief, and Zizah the second; but Jeush and Beriah did not have many sons, so they were enrolled as a single family.

23.6 Keeping the Temple

Ever since the time of Moses, the Levites had been in charge of carrying and caring for the tabernacle—the portable tent where God was worshiped. But now that the ark had been placed permanently in Jerusalem, and a temple was to be built, the Levites needed new duties and organization. Chapters 23–26 describe those duties in detail.

12 The sons of Kohath: Amram, Izhar, Hebron, and Uzziel, four. ¹³The sons of Amram: Aaron and Moses. Aaron was set apart to consecrate the most holy things, so that he and his sons forever should make offerings before the LORD, and minister to him and pronounce blessings in his name forever; ¹⁴but as for Moses the man of God, his sons were to be reckoned among the tribe of Levi. ¹⁵The sons of Moses: Gershom and Eliezer. ¹⁶The sons of Gershom: Shebuel the chief. ¹⁷The sons of Eliezer: Rehabiah the chief; Eliezer had no other sons, but the sons of Rehabiah were very numerous. ¹⁸The sons of Izhar: Shelomith the chief. ¹⁹The sons of Hebron: Jeriah the chief, Amariah the second, Jahaziel the third, and Jekameam the fourth. ²⁰The sons of Uzziel: Micah the chief and Isshiah the second.

21 The sons of Merari: Mahli and Mushi. The sons of Mahli: Eleazar and Kish. ²²Eleazar died having no sons, but only daughters; their kindred, the sons of Kish, married them. ²³The sons of Mushi: Mahli, Eder, and Jeremoth, three.

24 These were the sons of Levi by their ancestral houses, the heads of families as they were enrolled according to the number of the names of the individuals from twenty years old and upward who were to do the work for the service of the house of the LORD. ²⁵For David said, "The LORD, the God of Israel, has given rest to his people; and he resides in Jerusalem forever. ²⁶And so the Levites no longer need to carry the tabernacle or any of the things for its service"— ²⁷for according to the last words of David these were the number of the Levites from twenty years old and upward— ²⁸"but their duty shall be to assist the descendants of Aaron for the service of the house of the LORD, having the care of the courts and the chambers, the cleansing of all that is holy, and any work for the service of the house of God; ²⁹to assist also with the rows of bread, the choice flour for the grain offering, the wafers of unleavened bread, the baked offering, the offering mixed with oil, and all measures of quantity or size. ³⁰And they shall

stand every morning, thanking and praising the LORD, and likewise at evening, ³¹and whenever burnt offerings are offered to the LORD on sabbaths, new moons, and appointed festivals, according to the number required of them, regularly before the LORD. ³²Thus they shall keep charge of the tent of meeting and the sanctuary, and shall attend the descendants of Aaron, their kindred, for the service of the house of the LORD."

23.29 Little People

The best way to get volunteers is to guarantee them adequate credit, and 1 Chronicles leaves no volunteer in nation-building overlooked. After focusing on King David for several chapters, the book turns attention to those who performed menial tasks: bailiffs, bureaucrats, bread-bakers, weight-checkers, custodians, accountants, musicians, guards, a recording secretary.

Divisions of the Priests

24 The divisions of the descendants of Aaron were these. The sons of Aaron: Nadab, Abihu, Eleazar, and Ithamar. ²But Nadab and Abihu died before their father, and had no sons; so Eleazar and Ithamar became the priests. ³Along with Zadok of the sons of Eleazar, and Ahimelech of the sons of Ithamar, David organized them according to the appointed duties in their service. ⁴Since more chief men were found among the sons of Eleazar than among the sons of Ithamar, they organized them under sixteen heads of ancestral houses of the sons of Eleazar, and eight of the sons of Ithamar. ⁵They organized them by lot, all alike, for there were officers of the sanctuary and officers of God among both the sons of Eleazar and the sons of Ithamar. ⁶The scribe Shemaiah son of Nethanel, a Levite, recorded them in the presence of the king, and the officers, and Zadok the priest, and Ahimelech son of Abiathar, and the heads of ancestral houses of the priests and of the Levites; one ancestral house being chosen for Eleazar and one chosen for Ithamar.

7 The first lot fell to Jehoiarib, the second to Jedaiah, ⁸the third to Harim, the fourth to Seorim, ⁹the fifth to Malchijah, the sixth to Mijamin, ¹⁰the seventh to Hakkoz, the eighth to Abijah, ¹¹the ninth to Jeshua, the tenth to Shecaniah, ¹²the eleventh to Eliashib, the twelfth to Jakim, ¹³the thirteenth to Huppah, the fourteenth to Jeshebeab, ¹⁴the fifteenth to Bilgah, the sixteenth to Immer, ¹⁵the seventeenth to Hezir, the eighteenth to Happizzez, ¹⁶the nineteenth to Pethahiah, the twentieth to Jehezkel, ¹⁷the twenty-first to Jachin, the twenty-second to Gamul, ¹⁸the twenty-third to

Delaiah, the twenty-fourth to Maaziah. [19]These had as their appointed duty in their service to enter the house of the LORD according to the procedure established for them by their ancestor Aaron, as the LORD God of Israel had commanded him.

Other Levites

20 And of the rest of the sons of Levi: of the sons of Amram, Shubael; of the sons of Shubael, Jehdeiah. [21]Of Rehabiah: of the sons of Rehabiah, Isshiah the chief. [22]Of the Izharites, Shelomoth; of the sons of Shelomoth, Jahath. [23]The sons of Hebron:[g] Jeriah the chief,[h] Amariah the second, Jahaziel the third, Jekameam the fourth. [24]The sons of Uzziel, Micah; of the sons of Micah, Shamir. [25]The brother of Micah, Isshiah; of the sons of Isshiah, Zechariah. [26]The sons of Merari: Mahli and Mushi. The sons of Jaaziah: Beno.[i] [27]The sons of Merari: of Jaaziah, Beno,[i] Shoham, Zaccur, and Ibri. [28]Of Mahli: Eleazar, who had no sons. [29]Of Kish, the sons of Kish: Jerahmeel. [30]The sons of Mushi: Mahli, Eder, and Jerimoth. These were the sons of the Levites according to their ancestral houses. [31]These also cast lots corresponding to their kindred, the descendants of Aaron, in the presence of King David, Zadok, Ahimelech, and the heads of ancestral houses of the priests and of the Levites, the chief as well as the youngest brother.

The Temple Musicians

25 David and the officers of the army also set apart for the service the sons of Asaph, and of Heman, and of Jeduthun, who should prophesy with lyres, harps, and cymbals. The list of those who did the work and of their duties was:

25.1 Church and State

Israel, a theocracy ruled by God through a king, had no "separation of church and state." David even consulted with his military commanders for such decisions as appointing prophets and musicians for worship.

[2]Of the sons of Asaph: Zaccur, Joseph, Nethaniah, and Asarelah, sons of Asaph, under the direction of Asaph, who prophesied under the direction of the king. [3]Of Jeduthun, the sons of Jeduthun: Gedaliah, Zeri, Jeshaiah, Shimei,[j] Hashabiah, and Mattithiah, six, under the direction of their father Jeduthun, who prophesied with the lyre in thanksgiving and praise to the LORD. [4]Of Heman, the sons of Heman: Bukkiah, Mattaniah, Uzziel, Shebuel, and Jerimoth, Hananiah, Hanani, Eliathah, Giddalti, and Romamti-ezer, Joshbekashah,

Mallothi, Hothir, Mahazioth. [5]All these were the sons of Heman the king's seer, according to the promise of God to exalt him; for God had given Heman fourteen sons and three daughters. [6]They were all under the direction of their father for the music in the house of the LORD with cymbals, harps, and lyres for the service of the house of God. Asaph, Jeduthun, and Heman were under the order of the king. [7]They and their kindred, who were trained in singing to the LORD, all of whom were skillful, numbered two hundred eighty-eight. [8]And they cast lots for their duties, small and great, teacher and pupil alike.

9 The first lot fell for Asaph to Joseph; the second to Gedaliah, to him and his brothers and his sons, twelve; [10]the third to Zaccur, his sons and his brothers, twelve; [11]the fourth to Izri, his sons and his brothers, twelve; [12]the fifth to Nethaniah, his sons and his brothers, twelve; [13]the sixth to Bukkiah, his sons and his brothers, twelve; [14]the seventh to Jesarelah,[k] his sons and his brothers, twelve; [15]the eighth to Jeshaiah, his sons and his brothers, twelve; [16]the ninth to Mattaniah, his sons and his brothers, twelve; [17]the tenth to Shimei, his sons and his brothers, twelve; [18]the eleventh to Azarel, his sons and his brothers, twelve; [19]the twelfth to Hashabiah, his sons and his brothers, twelve; [20]to the thirteenth, Shubael, his sons and his brothers, twelve; [21]to the fourteenth, Mattithiah, his sons and his brothers, twelve; [22]to the fifteenth, to Jeremoth, his sons and his brothers, twelve; [23]to the sixteenth, to Hananiah, his sons and his brothers, twelve; [24]to the seventeenth, to Joshbekashah, his sons and his brothers, twelve; [25]to the eighteenth, to Hanani, his sons and his brothers, twelve; [26]to the nineteenth, to Mallothi, his sons and his brothers, twelve; [27]to the twentieth, to Eliathah, his sons and his brothers, twelve; [28]to the twenty-first, to Hothir, his sons and his brothers, twelve; [29]to the twenty-second, to Giddalti, his sons and his brothers, twelve; [30]to the twenty-third, to Mahazioth, his sons and his brothers, twelve; [31]to the twenty-fourth, to Romamti-ezer, his sons and his brothers, twelve.

The Gatekeepers

26 As for the divisions of the gatekeepers: of the Korahites, Meshelemiah son of Kore, of the sons of Asaph. [2]Meshelemiah had sons: Zechariah the firstborn, Jediael the second, Zebadiah the third, Jathniel the fourth, [3]Elam the fifth, Jehohanan the sixth, Eliehoenai the seventh. [4]Obed-edom had sons: Shemaiah the firstborn, Jehozabad the second, Joah the third, Sachar the fourth, Nethanel the fifth, [5]Ammiel the sixth, Issachar the seventh, Peullethai the eighth; for God blessed him. [6]Also to his son Shemaiah sons were

---

g See 23.19: Heb lacks *Hebron*   h See 23.19: Heb lacks *the chief*   i Or *his son*: Meaning of Heb uncertain   j One Ms: Gk: MT lacks *Shimei*   k Or *Asarelah*; see 25.2

born who exercised authority in their ancestral houses, for they were men of great ability. 7The sons of Shemaiah: Othni, Rephael, Obed, and Elzabad, whose brothers were able men, Elihu and

26.1–12 Major Enterprise

To aid in worship, David appointed 4,000 gatekeepers, or temple guards, and 4,000 musicians (23.3–4). The numbers give some indication of the importance attached to worship in national life. David was preparing his nation for the day when his son Solomon would build the temple.

Semachiah. 8All these, sons of Obed-edom with their sons and brothers, were able men qualified for the service; sixty-two of Obed-edom. 9Meshelemiah had sons and brothers, able men, eighteen. 10Hosah, of the sons of Merari, had sons: Shimri the chief (for though he was not the firstborn, his father made him chief), 11Hilkiah the second, Tebaliah the third, Zechariah the fourth: all the sons and brothers of Hosah totaled thirteen.

12 These divisions of the gatekeepers, corresponding to their leaders, had duties, just as their kindred did, ministering in the house of the LORD; 13and they cast lots by ancestral houses, small and great alike, for their gates. 14The lot for the east fell to Shelemiah. They cast lots also for his son Zechariah, a prudent counselor, and his lot came out for the north. 15Obed-edom's came out for the south, and to his sons was allotted the storehouse. 16For Shuppim and Hosah it came out for the west, at the gate of Shallecheth on the ascending road. Guard corresponded to guard. 17On the east there were six Levites each day,*l* on the north four each day, on the south four each day, as well as two and two at the storehouse; 18and for the colonnade*m* on the west there were four at the road and two at the colonnade.*m* 19These were the divisions of the gatekeepers among the Korahites and the sons of Merari.

The Treasurers, Officers, and Judges

20 And of the Levites, Ahijah had charge of the treasuries of the house of God and the treasuries of the dedicated gifts. 21The sons of Ladan, the sons of the Gershonites belonging to Ladan, the heads of families belonging to Ladan the Gershonite: Jehieli.*n*

22 The sons of Jehieli, Zetham and his brother Joel, were in charge of the treasuries of the house of the LORD. 23Of the Amramites, the Izharites, the Hebronites, and the Uzzielites: 24Shebuel son of Gershom, son of Moses, was chief officer

in charge of the treasuries. 25His brothers: from Eliezer were his son Rehabiah, his son Jeshaiah, his son Joram, his son Zichri, and his son Shelomoth. 26This Shelomoth and his brothers were in charge of all the treasuries of the dedicated gifts that King David, and the heads of families, and the officers of the thousands and the hundreds, and the commanders of the army, had dedicated. 27From booty won in battles they dedicated gifts for the maintenance of the house of the LORD. 28Also all that Samuel the seer, and Saul son of Kish, and Abner son of Ner, and Joab son of Zeruiah had dedicated—all dedicated gifts were in the care of Shelomoth*o* and his brothers.

29 Of the Izharites, Chenaniah and his sons were appointed to outside duties for Israel, as officers and judges. 30Of the Hebronites, Hashabiah and his brothers, one thousand seven hundred men of ability, had the oversight of Israel west of the Jordan for all the work of the LORD and for the service of the king. 31Of the Hebronites, Jerijah was chief of the Hebronites. (In the fortieth year of David's reign search was made, of whatever genealogy or family, and men of great ability among them were found at Jazer in Gilead.) 32King David appointed him and his brothers, two thousand seven hundred men of ability, heads of families, to have the oversight of the Reubenites, the Gadites, and the half-tribe of the Manassites for everything pertaining to God and for the affairs of the king.

The Military Divisions

27 This is the list of the people of Israel, the heads of families, the commanders of the thousands and the hundreds, and their officers who served the king in all matters concerning the divisions that came and went, month after month throughout the year, each division numbering twenty-four thousand:

2 Jashobeam son of Zabdiel was in charge of the first division in the first month; in his division were twenty-four thousand. 3He was a descendant of Perez, and was chief of all the commanders of the army for the first month. 4Dodai the Ahohite was in charge of the division of the second month; Mikloth was the chief officer of his division. In his division were twenty-four thousand. 5The third commander, for the third month, was Benaiah son of the priest Jehoiada, as chief; in his division were twenty-four thousand. 6This is the Benaiah who was a mighty man of the Thirty and in command of the Thirty; his son Ammizabad was in charge of his division.*p* 7Asahel brother of Joab was fourth, for the fourth month, and his son Zebadiah after him; in his division were twenty-four thousand. 8The fifth commander, for the fifth month, was Shamhuth,

---

l Gk: Heb lacks *each day*   *m* Heb *parbar*: meaning uncertain   *n* The Hebrew text of verse 21 is confused
o Gk Compare 26.28: Heb *Shelomith*   *p* Gk Vg: Heb *Ammizabad was his division*

the Izrahite; in his division were twenty-four thousand. ⁹Sixth, for the sixth month, was Ira son of Ikkesh the Tekoite; in his division were twenty-four thousand. ¹⁰Seventh, for the seventh month, was Helez the Pelonite, of the Ephraimites; in his division were twenty-four thousand. ¹¹Eighth, for the eighth month, was Sibbecai the Hushathite, of the Zerahites; in his division were twenty-four thousand. ¹²Ninth, for the ninth month, was Abiezer of Anathoth, a Benjaminite; in his division were twenty-four thousand. ¹³Tenth, for the tenth month, was Maharai of Netophah, of the Zerahites; in his division were twenty-four thousand. ¹⁴Eleventh, for the eleventh month, was Benaiah of Pirathon, of the Ephraimites; in his division were twenty-four thousand. ¹⁵Twelfth, for the twelfth month, was Heldai the Netophathite, of Othniel; in his division were twenty-four thousand.

Leaders of Tribes

16 Over the tribes of Israel, for the Reubenites, Eliezer son of Zichri was chief officer; for the Simeonites, Shephatiah son of Maacah; ¹⁷for Levi, Hashabiah son of Kemuel; for Aaron, Zadok; ¹⁸for Judah, Elihu, one of David's brothers; for Issachar, Omri son of Michael; ¹⁹for Zebulun, Ishmaiah son of Obadiah; for Naphtali, Jerimoth son of Azriel; ²⁰for the Ephraimites, Hoshea son of Azaziah; for the half-tribe of Manasseh, Joel son of Pedaiah; ²¹for the half-tribe of Manasseh in Gilead, Iddo son of Zechariah; for Benjamin, Jaasiel son of Abner; ²²for Dan, Azarel son of Jeroham. These were the leaders of the tribes of Israel. ²³David did not count those below twenty years of age, for the LORD had promised to make Israel as numerous as the stars of heaven. ²⁴Joab son of Zeruiah began to count them, but did not finish; yet wrath came upon Israel for this, and the number was not entered into the account of the Annals of King David.

Other Civic Officials

25 Over the king's treasuries was Azmaveth son of Adiel. Over the treasuries in the country, in the cities, in the villages and in the towers, was Jonathan son of Uzziah. ²⁶Over those who did the work of the field, tilling the soil, was Ezri son of Chelub. ²⁷Over the vineyards was Shimei the Ramathite. Over the produce of the vineyards for the wine cellars was Zabdi the Shiphmite. ²⁸Over the olive and sycamore trees in the Shephelah was Baal-hanan the Gederite. Over the stores of oil was Joash. ²⁹Over the herds that pastured in Sharon was Shitrai the Sharonite. Over the herds in the valleys was Shaphat son of Adlai. ³⁰Over the camels was Obil the Ishmaelite. Over the donkeys was Jehdeiah the Meronothite. Over the flocks was Jaziz the Hagrite. ³¹All these were stewards of King David's property.

32 Jonathan, David's uncle, was a counselor, being a man of understanding and a scribe; Jehiel son of Hachmoni attended the king's sons. ³³Ahithophel was the king's counselor, and Hushai the Archite was the king's friend. ³⁴After Ahithophel came Jehoiada son of Benaiah, and Abiathar. Joab was commander of the king's army.

Solomon Instructed to Build the Temple

28 David assembled at Jerusalem all the officials of Israel, the officials of the tribes, the officers of the divisions that served the king, the commanders of the thousands, the commanders of the hundreds, the stewards of all the property and cattle of the king and his sons, together with the palace officials, the mighty warriors, and all the warriors. ²Then King David rose to his feet and said: "Hear me, my brothers and my people. I had planned to build a house of rest for the ark of the covenant of the LORD, for the footstool of our God; and I made preparations for building. ³But God said to me, 'You shall not build a house for my name, for you are a warrior and have shed blood.' ⁴Yet the LORD God of Israel chose me from all my ancestral house to be king over Israel forever; for he chose Judah as leader, and in the house of Judah my father's house, and among my father's sons he took delight in making me king over all Israel. ⁵And of all my sons, for the LORD has given me many, he has chosen my son Solomon to sit upon the throne of the kingdom of the LORD over Israel. ⁶He said to me, 'It is your son Solomon who shall build my house and my courts, for I have chosen him to be a son to me, and I will be a father to him. ⁷I will establish his kingdom forever if he continues resolute in keeping my commandments and my ordinances, as he is today.' ⁸Now therefore in the sight of all Israel, the assembly of the LORD, and in the hearing of our God, observe and search out all the commandments of the LORD your God; that you may possess this good land, and leave it for an inheritance to your children after you forever.

9 "And you, my son Solomon, know the God of your father, and serve him with single mind and willing heart; for the LORD searches every mind, and understands every plan and thought. If you seek him, he will be found by you; but if you forsake him, he will abandon you forever. ¹⁰Take heed now, for the LORD has chosen you to build a house as the sanctuary; be strong, and act."

11 Then David gave his son Solomon the plan of the vestibule of the temple, and of its houses, its treasuries, its upper rooms, and its inner chambers, and of the room for the mercy seat;q ¹²and the plan of all that he had in mind: for the

q Or the cover

courts of the house of the Lord, all the surrounding chambers, the treasuries of the house of God, and the treasuries for dedicated gifts; 13for the divisions of the priests and of the Levites, and all

28.9 Conditional Promise

God's promise to David of unending descendants on the throne was so important to Israel that it was reported, in different forms, several times. (See chapter 17, for instance.) Sometimes it read as though God would bless a line of successful kings regardless of their behavior. Here, though, David explained that God's favor would depend on Solomon's devotion to God.

the work of the service in the house of the Lord; for all the vessels for the service in the house of the Lord, 14the weight of gold for all golden vessels for each service, the weight of silver vessels for each service, 15the weight of the golden lampstands and their lamps, the weight of gold for each lampstand and its lamps, the weight of silver for a lampstand and its lamps, according to the use of each in the service, 16the weight of gold for each table for the rows of bread, the silver for the silver tables, 17and pure gold for the forks, the basins, and the cups; for the golden bowls and the weight of each; for the silver bowls and the weight of each; 18for the altar of incense made of refined gold, and its weight; also his plan for the golden chariot of the cherubim that spread their wings and covered the ark of the covenant of the Lord.

19 "All this, in writing at the Lord's direction, he made clear to me—the plan of all the works."

20 David said further to his son Solomon, "Be strong and of good courage, and act. Do not be afraid or dismayed; for the Lord God, my God, is with you. He will not fail you or forsake you, until all the work for the service of the house of the Lord is finished. 21Here are the divisions of the priests and the Levites for all the service of the house of God; and with you in all the work will be every volunteer who has skill for any kind of service; also the officers and all the people will be wholly at your command."

Offerings for Building the Temple

29 King David said to the whole assembly, "My son Solomon, whom alone God has chosen, is young and inexperienced, and the work is great; for the temple^r will not be for mortals but for the Lord God. 2So I have provided for the house of my God, so far as I was able, the gold for the things of gold, the silver for the things of silver, and the bronze for the things of bronze, the

iron for the things of iron, and wood for the things of wood, besides great quantities of onyx and stones for setting, antimony, colored stones, all sorts of precious stones, and marble in abundance. 3Moreover, in addition to all that I have provided for the holy house, I have a treasure of my own of gold and silver, and because of my devotion to the house of my God I give it to the house of my God: 4three thousand talents of gold, of the gold of Ophir, and seven thousand talents of refined silver, for overlaying the walls of the house, 5and for all the work to be done by artisans, gold for the things of gold and silver for the things of silver. Who then will offer willingly, consecrating themselves today to the Lord?"

6 Then the leaders of ancestral houses made their freewill offerings, as did also the leaders of the tribes, the commanders of the thousands and of the hundreds, and the officers over the king's work. 7They gave for the service of the house of God five thousand talents and ten thousand darics of gold, ten thousand talents of silver, eighteen thousand talents of bronze, and one hundred thousand talents of iron. 8Whoever had precious stones gave them to the treasury of the house of the Lord, into the care of Jehiel the Gershonite. 9Then the people rejoiced because these had given willingly, for with single mind they had offered freely to the Lord; King David also rejoiced greatly.

David's Praise to God

10 Then David blessed the Lord in the presence of all the assembly; David said: "Blessed are you, O Lord, the God of our ancestor Israel, forever and ever. 11Yours, O Lord, are the greatness,

29.10 David's Great Prayer

David's prayer at the beginning of temple construction shows why he was a man after God's own heart. Despite all his achievements, he was deeply humble. He wanted glory to go to God, not himself. This passage would have reminded the original readers of Chronicles, back from exile and without a king, that David's greatest concern was for the temple, where his people could worship and serve God. They, his descendants, did not need a king to carry on David's deepest concerns.

the power, the glory, the victory, and the majesty; for all that is in the heavens and on the earth is yours; yours is the kingdom, O Lord, and you are exalted as head above all. 12Riches and honor come from you, and you rule over all. In your hand are power and might; and it is in your hand to make great and to give strength to all. 13And

^r Heb *fortress*

now, our God, we give thanks to you and praise your glorious name.

14 "But who am I, and what is my people, that we should be able to make this freewill offering? For all things come from you, and of your own have we given you. ¹⁵For we are aliens and transients before you, as were all our ancestors; our days on the earth are like a shadow, and there is no hope. ¹⁶O LORD our God, all this abundance that we have provided for building you a house for your holy name comes from your hand and is all your own. ¹⁷I know, my God, that you search the heart, and take pleasure in uprightness; in the uprightness of my heart I have freely offered all these things, and now I have seen your people, who are present here, offering freely and joyously to you. ¹⁸O LORD, the God of Abraham, Isaac, and Israel, our ancestors, keep forever such purposes and thoughts in the hearts of your people, and direct their hearts toward you. ¹⁹Grant to my son Solomon that with single mind he may keep your commandments, your decrees, and your statutes, performing all of them, and that he may build the temple[s] for which I have made provision."

20 Then David said to the whole assembly, "Bless the LORD your God." And all the assembly blessed the LORD, the God of their ancestors, and bowed their heads and prostrated themselves before the LORD and the king. ²¹On the next day they offered sacrifices and burnt offerings to the LORD, a thousand bulls, a thousand rams, and a thousand lambs, with their libations, and sacrifices in abundance for all Israel; ²²and they ate and drank before the LORD on that day with great joy.

Solomon Anointed King

They made David's son Solomon king a second time; they anointed him as the LORD's prince,

and Zadok as priest. ²³Then Solomon sat on the throne of the LORD, succeeding his father David as king; he prospered, and all Israel obeyed him. ²⁴All the leaders and the mighty warriors, and also

29.24 A Second Coronation

Assuming that his readers were familiar with the family quarrels told of in 1 Kings 1, the author refers to this coronation as the "second time" (verse 22). The first coronation happened when David learned that Solomon's older brother had been conspiring to become king. David immediately called for a private coronation (1 Kings 1.32–40). Only later did this public ceremony occur, when the rebellious brother swore his loyalty. Typically, 1 Chronicles leaves out the nasty politics and emphasizes the positive result.

all the sons of King David, pledged their allegiance to King Solomon. ²⁵The LORD highly exalted Solomon in the sight of all Israel, and bestowed upon him such royal majesty as had not been on any king before him in Israel.

Summary of David's Reign

26 Thus David son of Jesse reigned over all Israel. ²⁷The period that he reigned over Israel was forty years; he reigned seven years in Hebron, and thirty-three years in Jerusalem. ²⁸He died in a good old age, full of days, riches, and honor; and his son Solomon succeeded him. ²⁹Now the acts of King David, from first to last, are written in the records of the seer Samuel, and in the records of the prophet Nathan, and in the records of the seer Gad, ³⁰with accounts of all his rule and his might and of the events that befell him and Israel and all the kingdoms of the earth.

[s] Heb *fortress*

2 CHRONICLES

A Time for Hope
Restoring pride to a group of refugees

I N THE EARLY 1960s, A wave of feeling known as "black pride" swept across America. It started when African-American leaders realized that far more than legal rights had been repressed for 200 years. Everything about the African-American culture, from hair texture to history, had taken a back seat to that of the white majority.

Over time, a dramatic rediscovery of the African-American heritage occurred. Textbook publishers issued new editions that for the first time included the stories of African-Americans: a soldier who rowed George Washington across the Delaware, a scientist who perfected the process of blood transfusion, an educator who founded colleges for African-Americans.

"Black pride" reminded all Americans that a minority race had made giant contributions in many fields. People encountered a heritage they had known little about. Heroes were uncovered. African-Americans everywhere began to see the past in a new light.

> "If my people who are called by my name humble themselves, pray, seek my face, and turn from their wicked ways, then I will hear from heaven, and will forgive their sin and heal their land."
>
> 7.14

Need for a Pep Talk

There was a time when the Israelites, too, desperately needed a new look at the past. Their ancestors had also been torn from home, beaten, and dragged off in chains to serve as slaves in a foreign country. In Babylon, a new generation grew up knowing little of the Israelite past: the covenant with God, the promised line of kings, the magnificent temple in Jerusalem.

When captive Israelites were finally allowed to return home, they found a pile of rubble. In Israel's Golden Age, people had traveled thousands of miles to view the majesty of Jerusalem and its temple. But to the refugees' horror, not one stone of the temple remained standing. The carved beams had all been hacked to pieces, the gold and ivory stripped away, and the furniture auctioned off or destroyed.

Outside the capital, whole villages had disappeared. Vital religious customs had gone uncelebrated for 70 years. Jewish culture was in danger of leaking away.

The book of Chronicles was written to those refugees who returned. For that dispirited group of people, the author recounted the glory days of Israel. He wanted to restore pride in the Israelite past and bring hope to their future.

History in a New Light

Chronicles (both 1 and 2) thus retells history, starting all the way at the beginning, with Adam. Most of the characters are familiar, but Chronicles tells old stories in a new light. Its author isn't just reciting facts. He is delivering a word of bright hope, a pep talk, to just-freed refugees.

Some accuse Chronicles of being a "whitewashed" history, especially in comparison to the Bible's other history books. True, the book barely mentions the Israelites' great failures—it says nothing of David's or Solomon's mistakes, for instance. Presumably, the refugees had heard plenty about the dark side of their nation's recent past: the books of Samuel and Kings, which ruthlessly exposed those failures, had been around for years.

Similarly, Chronicles ignores the chaotic Northern Kingdom of Israel, and the civil war Judah waged against it. Nothing remained of the ten scattered tribes of the North, and the book wastes little space on them. Instead, Chronicles reaches higher, seeking to restore pride in the original ideals of the nation.

A Distant Hope

The good kings of Judah, eight in all, dominate the story: Over two-thirds of 2 Chronicles is devoted to their reigns. Chronicles focuses on God's special relationship with the Israelites, recalling the covenant that had brought about their Golden Age. It reviews the religious reforms led by each king, and, above all, highlights the temple, the house where God's presence came to rest. If God had lived among them in the past, couldn't he do so again?

How to Read 2 Chronicles

Y ou will recognize many of the stories in 2 Chronicles—about half of it closely follows other Bible passages. The author freely admits he has relied on the books of Moses, Samuel, and Kings. He also quotes from Judges, Jeremiah, Psalms, Isaiah, and Lamentations, as well as many books that have been lost to history.

But 2 Chronicles does not merely repeat. It weaves together stories and facts for a specific purpose: a Jewish philosophy of history. Chronicles sheds new light on that history by highlighting rare moments of peace and prosperity. Worship of the true God had made Israel strong. As you read, notice how 2 Chronicles underscores that fact by stressing the temple and the priests.

For comparison, you may want to read companion passages in the book of Kings (for a list, see "A Lineup of Rulers," pages 1349–1357). Read side by side, the two accounts clearly reveal the distinct purpose behind the book of Chronicles.

Look past all the names and events for the few kings who did right. (See "The Great Reformers," pages 460–461) What made them successful? What lessons about faith can we learn from them?

PEOPLE YOU'LL MEET IN 2 CHRONICLES

REHOBOAM (p. 453)
ATHALIAH (p. 463)
HEZEKIAH (p.469)

3-TRACK READING PLAN

For an explanation and complete listing of the 3-track reading plan, turn to page 7.

TRACK 1: *Two-Week Courses on the Bible*
See page 7 for information on these courses.

TRACK 2: *An Overview of 2 Chronicles in 3 Days*
☐ Day 1. Read the Introduction to 2 Chronicles and then chapter 20. It tells of a high point when King Jehoshaphat brought the whole nation together in prayer.
☐ Day 2. Hezekiah had an eventful life, with soaring highs and deep lows. Read about a national high point in chapter 30.
☐ Day 3. Hezekiah lived in treacherous times. Read of his close scrape with disaster in chapter 32.

Now turn to page 9 for your next Track 2 reading project.

TRACK 3: *All of 2 Chronicles in 34 Days*
After you have read through 2 Chronicles, turn to pages 10–14 for your next Track 3 reading project.

☐1 ☐2 ☐3 ☐4 ☐5 ☐6 ☐7 ☐8
☐9 ☐10 ☐11 ☐12 ☐13 ☐14 ☐15 ☐16–17
☐18 ☐19 ☐20 ☐21 ☐22 ☐23 ☐24 ☐25
☐26–27 ☐28 ☐29 ☐30 ☐31 ☐32 ☐33 ☐34
☐35 ☐36

Solomon Requests Wisdom

1 Solomon son of David established himself in his kingdom; the LORD his God was with him and made him exceedingly great.

2 Solomon summoned all Israel, the commanders of the thousands and of the hundreds, the judges, and all the leaders of all Israel, the heads of families. 3Then Solomon, and the whole assembly with him, went to the high place that was at Gibeon; for God's tent of meeting, which Moses the servant of the LORD had made in the wilderness, was there. 4(But David had brought the ark of God up from Kiriath-jearim to the place that David had prepared for it; for he had pitched a tent for it in Jerusalem.) 5Moreover the bronze altar that Bezalel son of Uri, son of Hur, had made, was there in front of the tabernacle of the LORD. And Solomon and the assembly inquired at it. 6Solomon went up there to the bronze altar before the LORD, which was at the tent of meeting, and offered a thousand burnt offerings on it.

7 That night God appeared to Solomon, and said to him, "Ask what I should give you." 8Solomon said to God, "You have shown great and steadfast love to my father David, and have made me succeed him as king. 9O LORD God, let your promise to my father David now be fulfilled, for you have made me king over a people as numerous as the dust of the earth. 10Give me now wisdom and knowledge to go out and come in before this people, for who can rule this great people of yours?" 11God answered Solomon, "Because this was in your heart, and you have not asked for possessions, wealth, honor, or the life of those who hate you, and have not even asked for long life, but have asked for wisdom and knowledge for yourself that you may rule my people over whom I have made you king, 12wisdom and knowledge are granted to you. I will also give you riches, possessions, and honor, such as none of the kings had who were before you, and none after you shall have the like." 13So Solomon came from[a] the high place at Gibeon, from the tent of meeting, to Jerusalem. And he reigned over Israel.

Solomon's Military and Commercial Activity

14 Solomon gathered together chariots and horses; he had fourteen hundred chariots and twelve thousand horses, which he stationed in the chariot cities and with the king in Jerusalem. 15The king made silver and gold as common in Jerusalem as stone, and he made cedar as plentiful as the sycamore of the Shephelah. 16Solomon's horses were imported from Egypt and Kue; the king's traders received them from Kue at the prevailing price. 17They imported from Egypt, and then exported, a chariot for six hundred shekels of silver, and a horse for one hundred fifty; so through them these were exported to all the kings of the Hittites and the kings of Aram.

Preparations for Building the Temple

2 [b] Solomon decided to build a temple for the name of the LORD, and a royal palace for himself. 2 [c] Solomon conscripted seventy thousand laborers and eighty thousand stonecutters in the hill country, with three thousand six hundred to oversee them.

2.2 Solomon's Forced Labor

King Solomon drafted laborers for his construction projects much like an army drafts soldiers. His policy of forced labor sowed dissension in the kingdom, especially among resentful northern tribes. In keeping with its morale-building purpose, 2 Chronicles has little bad to say about Solomon. The author mentions Solomon's wealth (1.14; 9.22–25) without comment, although such excess defied the rules for kings (Deuteronomy 17.15–17). Chronicles also omits reference to Solomon's palace, which Kings had pointedly described as exceeding even the temple in its splendor.

Alliance with Huram of Tyre

3 Solomon sent word to King Huram of Tyre: "Once you dealt with my father David and sent him cedar to build himself a house to live in. 4I am now about to build a house for the name of the LORD my God and dedicate it to him for offering fragrant incense before him, and for the regular offering of the rows of bread, and for burnt offerings morning and evening, on the sabbaths and the new moons and the appointed festivals of the LORD our God, as ordained forever for Israel. 5The house that I am about to build will be great, for our God is greater than other gods. 6But who is able to build him a house, since heaven, even highest heaven, cannot contain him? Who am I to build a house for him, except as a place to make offerings before him? 7So now send me an artisan skilled to work in gold, silver, bronze, and iron, and in purple, crimson, and blue fabrics, trained also in engraving, to join the skilled workers who are with me in Judah and Jerusalem, whom my father David provided. 8Send me also cedar, cypress, and algum timber from Lebanon, for I know that your servants are skilled in cutting Lebanon timber. My servants will work with your servants 9to prepare timber for me in abundance, for the house I am about to build will be great and wonderful. 10I will provide for your servants, those who cut the timber, twenty thousand cors

of crushed wheat, twenty thousand cors of barley, twenty thousand baths*d* of wine, and twenty thousand baths of oil."

11 Then King Huram of Tyre answered in a letter that he sent to Solomon, "Because the LORD loves his people he has made you king over them." 12Huram also said, "Blessed be the LORD God of Israel, who made heaven and earth, who has given King David a wise son, endowed with discretion and understanding, who will build a temple for the LORD, and a royal palace for himself.

13 "I have dispatched Huram-abi, a skilled artisan, endowed with understanding, 14the son of one of the Danite women, his father a Tyrian. He is trained to work in gold, silver, bronze, iron, stone, and wood, and in purple, blue, and crimson fabrics and fine linen, and to do all sorts of engraving and execute any design that may be assigned him, with your artisans, the artisans of my lord, your father David. 15Now, as for the wheat, barley, oil, and wine, of which my lord has spoken, let him send them to his servants. 16We will cut whatever timber you need from Lebanon, and bring it to you as rafts by sea to Joppa; you will take it up to Jerusalem."

17 Then Solomon took a census of all the aliens who were residing in the land of Israel, after the census that his father David had taken; and there were found to be one hundred fifty-three thousand six hundred. 18Seventy thousand of them he assigned as laborers, eighty thousand as stonecutters in the hill country, and three thousand six hundred as overseers to make the people work.

Solomon Builds the Temple

3 Solomon began to build the house of the LORD in Jerusalem on Mount Moriah, where the LORD had appeared to his father David, at the place that David had designated, on the threshing floor of Ornan the Jebusite. 2He began to build on the second day of the second month of the fourth year of his reign. 3These are Solomon's measurements*e* for building the house of God: the length, in cubits of the old standard, was sixty cubits, and the width twenty cubits. 4The vestibule in front of the nave of the house was twenty cubits long, across the width of the house;*f* and its height was one hundred twenty cubits. He overlaid it on the inside with pure gold. 5The nave he lined with cypress, covered it with fine gold, and made palms and chains on it. 6He adorned the house with settings of precious stones. The gold was gold from Parvaim. 7So he lined the house with gold—its beams, its thresholds, its walls, and its doors; and he carved cherubim on the walls.

8 He made the most holy place; its length,

corresponding to the width of the house, was twenty cubits, and its width was twenty cubits; he overlaid it with six hundred talents of fine gold. 9The weight of the nails was fifty shekels of gold. He overlaid the upper chambers with gold.

10 In the most holy place he made two carved cherubim and overlaid*g* them with gold. 11The wings of the cherubim together extended twenty cubits: one wing of the one, five cubits long, touched the wall of the house, and its other wing, five cubits long, touched the wing of the other cherub; 12and of this cherub, one wing, five cubits long, touched the wall of the house, and the other wing, also five cubits long, was joined to the wing of the first cherub. 13The wings of these cherubim extended twenty cubits; the cherubim*h* stood on their feet, facing the nave. 14And Solomon*i* made the curtain of blue and purple and crimson fabrics and fine linen, and worked cherubim into it.

3.14 A Temporary Separation

Just as it had in the tabernacle, a curtain in the temple separated the holy place and most holy place. The curtain symbolized the distance between God and people. Even priests were forbidden to go beyond that curtain into the presence of God, except on the day of atonement. When Jesus died on the cross, this temple curtain miraculously ripped in two. That event also had symbolic meaning: Christ had opened up the way to God (Hebrews 9.7–12).

15 In front of the house he made two pillars thirty-five cubits high, with a capital of five cubits on the top of each. 16He made encircling*j* chains and put them on the tops of the pillars; and he made one hundred pomegranates, and put them on the chains. 17He set up the pillars in front of the temple, one on the right, the other on the left; the one on the right he called Jachin, and the one on the left, Boaz.

Furnishings of the Temple

4 He made an altar of bronze, twenty cubits long, twenty cubits wide, and ten cubits high. 2Then he made the molten sea; it was round, ten cubits from rim to rim, and five cubits high. A line of thirty cubits would encircle it completely. 3Under it were panels all around, each of ten cubits, surrounding the sea; there were two rows of panels, cast when it was cast. 4It stood on twelve oxen, three facing north, three facing west, three facing south, and three facing east; the sea was set on them. The hindquarters of each were toward the inside. 5Its thickness was a handbreadth; its rim was made like the rim of a cup, like the flower

---

d A Hebrew measure of volume   *e* Syr: Heb *foundations*   *f* Compare 1 Kings 6.3: Meaning of Heb uncertain
g Heb *they overlaid*   *h* Heb *they*   *i* Heb *he*   *j* Cn: Heb *in the inner sanctuary*

of a lily; it held three thousand baths.*k* *6*He also made ten basins in which to wash, and set five on the right side, and five on the left. In these they were to rinse what was used for the burnt offering. The sea was for the priests to wash in.

7 He made ten golden lampstands as prescribed, and set them in the temple, five on the south side and five on the north. *8*He also made ten tables and placed them in the temple, five on the right side and five on the left. And he made one hundred basins of gold. *9*He made the court of the priests, and the great court, and doors for the court; he overlaid their doors with bronze. *10*He set the sea at the southeast corner of the house.

11 And Huram made the pots, the shovels, and the basins. Thus Huram finished the work that he did for King Solomon on the house of God: *12*the two pillars, the bowls, and the two capitals on the top of the pillars; and the two latticeworks to cover the two bowls of the capitals that were on the top of the pillars; *13*the four hundred pomegranates for the two latticeworks, two rows of pomegranates for each latticework, to cover the two bowls of the capitals that were on the pillars. *14*He made the stands, the basins on the stands, *15*the one sea, and the twelve oxen underneath it. *16*The pots, the shovels, the forks, and all the equipment for these Huram-abi made of burnished bronze for King Solomon for the house of the LORD. *17*In the plain of the Jordan the king cast them, in the clay ground between Succoth and Zeredah. *18*Solomon made all these things in great quantities, so that the weight of the bronze was not determined.

19 So Solomon made all the things that were in the house of God: the golden altar, the tables for the bread of the Presence, *20*the lampstands and their lamps of pure gold to burn before the inner sanctuary, as prescribed; *21*the flowers, the lamps, and the tongs, of purest gold; *22*the snuffers, basins, ladles, and firepans, of pure gold. As for the entrance to the temple: the inner doors to the most holy place and the doors of the nave of the temple were of gold.

5 Thus all the work that Solomon did for the house of the LORD was finished. Solomon brought in the things that his father David had dedicated, and stored the silver, the gold, and all the vessels in the treasuries of the house of God.

The Ark Brought into the Temple

2 Then Solomon assembled the elders of Israel and all the heads of the tribes, the leaders of the ancestral houses of the people of Israel, in Jerusalem, to bring up the ark of the covenant of the LORD out of the city of David, which is Zion. *3*And all the Israelites assembled before the king at the festival that is in the seventh month. *4*And all the elders of Israel came, and the Levites carried the ark. *5*So they brought up the ark, the tent of meeting, and all the holy vessels that were in the tent; the priests and the Levites brought them up. *6*King Solomon and all the congregation of Israel, who had assembled before him, were before the ark, sacrificing so many sheep and oxen that they could not be numbered or counted. *7*Then the priests brought the ark of the covenant of the LORD to its place, in the inner sanctuary of the house, in the most holy place, underneath the wings of the cherubim. *8*For the cherubim spread out their wings over the place of the ark, so that the cherubim made a covering above the ark and its poles. *9*The poles were so long that the ends of the poles were seen from the holy place in front of the inner sanctuary; but they could not be seen from outside; they are there to this day. *10*There was nothing in the ark except the two tablets that Moses put there at Horeb, where the LORD made a covenant*l* with the people of Israel after they came out of Egypt.

5.10 Proof of the Covenant

Until the invasion by Babylon, the Israelites possessed a visible reminder of God's treaty, or "covenant," with them. It stayed in the most sacred piece of furniture in Israel, the ark. But the ark was lost during the Babylonian captivity— and has never been found.

11 Now when the priests came out of the holy place (for all the priests who were present had sanctified themselves, without regard to their divisions), *12*all the levitical singers, Asaph, Heman, and Jeduthun, their sons and kindred, arrayed in fine linen, with cymbals, harps, and lyres, stood east of the altar with one hundred twenty priests who were trumpeters. *13*It was the duty of the trumpeters and singers to make themselves heard in unison in praise and thanksgiving to the LORD, and when the song was raised, with trumpets and cymbals and other musical instruments, in praise to the LORD,

"For he is good,
for his steadfast love endures forever,"

the house, the house of the LORD, was filled with a cloud, *14*so that the priests could not stand to minister because of the cloud; for the glory of the LORD filled the house of God.

Dedication of the Temple

6 Then Solomon said, "The LORD has said that he would reside in thick darkness. *2*I have built you an exalted house, a place for you to reside in forever."

---

k A Hebrew measure of volume   *l* Heb lacks *a covenant*

3 Then the king turned around and blessed all the assembly of Israel, while all the assembly of Israel stood. 4And he said, "Blessed be the LORD, the God of Israel, who with his hand has fulfilled what he promised with his mouth to my father David, saying, 5'Since the day that I brought my people out of the land of Egypt, I have not chosen a city from any of the tribes of Israel in which to build a house, so that my name might be there, and I chose no one as ruler over my people Israel; 6but I have chosen Jerusalem in order that my name may be there, and I have chosen David to be over my people Israel.' 7My father David had it in mind to build a house for the name of the LORD, the God of Israel. 8But the LORD said to my father David, 'You did well to consider building a house for my name; 9nevertheless you shall not build the house, but your son who shall be born to you shall build the house for my name.' 10Now the LORD has fulfilled his promise that he made; for I have succeeded my father David, and sit on the throne of Israel, as the LORD promised, and have built the house for the name of the LORD, the God of Israel. 11There I have set the ark, in which is the covenant of the LORD that he made with the people of Israel."

Solomon's Prayer of Dedication

12 Then Solomon[m] stood before the altar of the LORD in the presence of the whole assembly of Israel, and spread out his hands. 13Solomon had made a bronze platform five cubits long, five cubits wide, and three cubits high, and had set it in the court; and he stood on it. Then he knelt on his knees in the presence of the whole assembly of Israel, and spread out his hands toward heaven. 14He said, "O LORD, God of Israel, there is no God like you, in heaven or on earth, keeping covenant in steadfast love with your servants who

6.14 Solomon's Peak

This chapter records Solomon's high point as a leader and hints at his lost potential. Thanks to David's conquests, Israel was at peace, and prosperous. Solomon's splendid prayer reveals the depth of his wisdom and spiritual sensitivity. But from this point on, Solomon, potentially the greatest of all Israel's rulers, slid toward selfishness and overindulgence. His failings led the nation into immorality and eventual civil war.

walk before you with all their heart— 15you who have kept for your servant, my father David, what you promised to him. Indeed, you promised with your mouth and this day have fulfilled with your hand. 16Therefore, O LORD, God of Israel, keep

for your servant, my father David, that which you promised him, saying, 'There shall never fail you a successor before me to sit on the throne of Israel, if only your children keep to their way, to walk in my law as you have walked before me.' 17Therefore, O LORD, God of Israel, let your word be confirmed, which you promised to your servant David.

18 "But will God indeed reside with mortals on earth? Even heaven and the highest heaven cannot contain you, how much less this house that I have built! 19Regard your servant's prayer and his plea, O LORD my God, heeding the cry and the prayer that your servant prays to you. 20May your eyes be open day and night toward this house, the place where you promised to set your name, and may you heed the prayer that your servant prays toward this place. 21And hear the plea of your servant and of your people Israel, when they pray toward this place; may you hear from heaven your dwelling place; hear and forgive.

22 "If someone sins against another and is required to take an oath and comes and swears before your altar in this house, 23may you hear from heaven, and act, and judge your servants, repaying the guilty by bringing their conduct on their own head, and vindicating those who are in the right by rewarding them in accordance with their righteousness.

24 "When your people Israel, having sinned against you, are defeated before an enemy but turn again to you, confess your name, pray and plead with you in this house, 25may you hear from heaven, and forgive the sin of your people Israel, and bring them again to the land that you gave to them and to their ancestors.

26 "When heaven is shut up and there is no rain because they have sinned against you, and then they pray toward this place, confess your name, and turn from their sin, because you punish them, 27may you hear in heaven, forgive the sin of your servants, your people Israel, when you teach them the good way in which they should walk; and send down rain upon your land, which you have given to your people as an inheritance.

28 "If there is famine in the land, if there is plague, blight, mildew, locust, or caterpillar; if their enemies besiege them in any of the settlements of the lands; whatever suffering, whatever sickness there is; 29whatever prayer, whatever plea from any individual or from all your people Israel, all knowing their own suffering and their own sorrows so that they stretch out their hands toward this house; 30may you hear from heaven, your dwelling place, forgive, and render to all whose heart you know, according to all their ways, for only you know the human heart. 31Thus may they fear you and walk in your ways all the

---

[m] Heb *he*

days that they live in the land that you gave to our ancestors.

32 "Likewise when foreigners, who are not of your people Israel, come from a distant land because of your great name, and your mighty hand, and your outstretched arm, when they come and pray toward this house, ³³may you hear from heaven your dwelling place, and do whatever the foreigners ask of you, in order that all the peoples of the earth may know your name and fear you, as do your people Israel, and that they may know that your name has been invoked on this house that I have built.

34 "If your people go out to battle against their enemies, by whatever way you shall send them, and they pray to you toward this city that you have chosen and the house that I have built for your name, ³⁵then hear from heaven their prayer and their plea, and maintain their cause.

36 "If they sin against you—for there is no one who does not sin—and you are angry with them and give them to an enemy, so that they are carried away captive to a land far or near; ³⁷then if they come to their senses in the land to which they have been taken captive, and repent, and plead with you in the land of their captivity, saying, 'We have sinned, and have done wrong; we have acted wickedly'; ³⁸if they repent with all their heart and soul in the land of their captivity, to which they were taken captive, and pray toward their land, which you gave to their ancestors, the city that you have chosen, and the house that I have built for your name, ³⁹then hear from heaven your dwelling place their prayer and their pleas, maintain their cause and forgive your people who have sinned against you. ⁴⁰Now, O my God, let your eyes be open and your ears attentive to prayer from this place.

⁴¹ "Now rise up, O LORD God, and go to
    your resting place,
    you and the ark of your might.
Let your priests, O LORD God, be clothed
    with salvation,
    and let your faithful rejoice in your
    goodness.
⁴² O LORD God, do not reject your anointed
    one.
    Remember your steadfast love for your
    servant David."

Solomon Dedicates the Temple

7 When Solomon had ended his prayer, fire came down from heaven and consumed the burnt offering and the sacrifices; and the glory of the LORD filled the temple. ²The priests could not enter the house of the LORD, because the glory of the LORD filled the LORD's house. ³When all the people of Israel saw the fire come down and the glory of the LORD on the temple, they bowed down on the pavement with their faces to the ground, and worshiped and gave thanks to the LORD, saying,

"For he is good,
    for his steadfast love endures forever."

7.1 A High-water Mark

Solomon's prayer in chapter 6 and God's response in chapter 7 marked a high point in Israel's existence as a nation. United, the Israelites gathered before the gleaming new temple. They saw fire come down from heaven and the glory of the Lord fill the temple. Later, when this building was destroyed, Ezra led a drive to build a new temple. But the dramatic scene of God's glory coming down was never duplicated.

4 Then the king and all the people offered sacrifice before the LORD. ⁵King Solomon offered as a sacrifice twenty-two thousand oxen and one hundred twenty thousand sheep. So the king and all the people dedicated the house of God. ⁶The priests stood at their posts; the Levites also, with the instruments for music to the LORD that King David had made for giving thanks to the LORD— for his steadfast love endures forever—whenever David offered praises by their ministry. Opposite them the priests sounded trumpets; and all Israel stood.

7 Solomon consecrated the middle of the court that was in front of the house of the LORD; for there he offered the burnt offerings and the fat of the offerings of well-being because the bronze altar Solomon had made could not hold the burnt offering and the grain offering and the fat parts.

8 At that time Solomon held the festival for seven days, and all Israel with him, a very great congregation, from Lebo-hamath to the Wadi of Egypt. ⁹On the eighth day they held a solemn assembly; for they had observed the dedication of the altar seven days and the festival seven days. ¹⁰On the twenty-third day of the seventh month he sent the people away to their homes, joyful and in good spirits because of the goodness that the LORD had shown to David and to Solomon and to his people Israel.

11 Thus Solomon finished the house of the LORD and the king's house; all that Solomon had planned to do in the house of the LORD and in his own house he successfully accomplished.

God's Second Appearance to Solomon

12 Then the LORD appeared to Solomon in the night and said to him: "I have heard your prayer, and have chosen this place for myself as a house of sacrifice. ¹³When I shut up the heavens so that there is no rain, or command the locust to devour the land, or send pestilence among my people, ¹⁴if my people who are called by my name

humble themselves, pray, seek my face, and turn from their wicked ways, then I will hear from heaven, and will forgive their sin and heal their land. [15]Now my eyes will be open and my ears attentive to the prayer that is made in this place. [16]For now I have chosen and consecrated this house so that my name may be there forever; my eyes and my heart will be there for all time. [17]As for you, if you walk before me, as your father David walked, doing according to all that I have commanded you and keeping my statutes and my ordinances, [18]then I will establish your royal throne, as I made covenant with your father David saying, 'You shall never lack a successor to rule over Israel.'

19 "But if you[n] turn aside and forsake my statutes and my commandments that I have set before you, and go and serve other gods and worship them, [20]then I will pluck you[o] up from the land that I have given you;[o] and this house, which I have consecrated for my name, I will cast out of my sight, and will make it a proverb and a byword among all peoples. [21]And regarding this house, now exalted, everyone passing by will be astonished, and say, 'Why has the LORD done such a thing to this land and to this house?' [22]Then they will say, 'Because they abandoned the LORD the God of their ancestors who brought them out of the land of Egypt, and they adopted other gods, and worshiped them and served them; therefore he has brought all this calamity upon them.'"

Various Activities of Solomon

8 At the end of twenty years, during which Solomon had built the house of the LORD and his own house, [2]Solomon rebuilt the cities that Huram had given to him, and settled the people of Israel in them.

3 Solomon went to Hamath-zobah, and captured it. [4]He built Tadmor in the wilderness and all the storage towns that he built in Hamath. [5]He also built Upper Beth-horon and Lower Beth-horon, fortified cities, with walls, gates, and bars, [6]and Baalath, as well as all Solomon's storage towns, and all the towns for his chariots, the towns for his cavalry, and whatever Solomon desired to build, in Jerusalem, in Lebanon, and in all the land of his dominion. [7]All the people who were left of the Hittites, the Amorites, the Perizzites, the Hivites, and the Jebusites, who were not of Israel, [8]from their descendants who were still left in the land, whom the people of Israel had not destroyed—these Solomon conscripted for forced labor, as is still the case today. [9]But of the people of Israel Solomon made no slaves for his work; they were soldiers, and his officers, the commanders of his chariotry and cavalry. [10]These were the chief officers of King Solomon, two hun-

dred fifty of them, who exercised authority over the people.

11 Solomon brought Pharaoh's daughter from the city of David to the house that he had built for her, for he said, "My wife shall not live in the house of King David of Israel, for the places to which the ark of the LORD has come are holy."

8.11 Inconsistent Ethics

Solomon scrupulously kept Pharaoh's daughter, a Gentile foreigner, apart from the Israelite sacred places. Yet as the book of Kings shows, he eventually allowed his foreign wives to bring in their own idols, which had a disastrous effect on Israel.

12 Then Solomon offered up burnt offerings to the LORD on the altar of the LORD that he had built in front of the vestibule, [13]as the duty of each day required, offering according to the commandment of Moses for the sabbaths, the new moons, and the three annual festivals—the festival of unleavened bread, the festival of weeks, and the festival of booths. [14]According to the ordinance of his father David, he appointed the divisions of the priests for their service, and the Levites for their offices of praise and ministry alongside the priests as the duty of each day required, and the gatekeepers in their divisions for the several gates; for so David the man of God had commanded. [15]They did not turn away from what the king had commanded the priests and Levites regarding anything at all, or regarding the treasuries.

16 Thus all the work of Solomon was accomplished from[p] the day the foundation of the house of the LORD was laid until the house of the LORD was finished completely.

17 Then Solomon went to Ezion-geber and Eloth on the shore of the sea, in the land of Edom. [18]Huram sent him, in the care of his servants, ships and servants familiar with the sea. They went to Ophir, together with the servants of Solomon, and imported from there four hundred fifty talents of gold and brought it to King Solomon.

Visit of the Queen of Sheba

9 When the queen of Sheba heard of the fame of Solomon, she came to Jerusalem to test him with hard questions, having a very great retinue and camels bearing spices and very much gold and precious stones. When she came to Solomon, she discussed with him all that was on her mind. [2]Solomon answered all her questions; there was nothing hidden from Solomon that he could not explain to her. [3]When the queen of Sheba had observed the wisdom of Solomon, the house that he had built, [4]the food of his table, the seating of his officials, and the attendance of his servants, and their clothing, his valets, and their clothing, and his burnt offerings[q] that he offered at the house of the LORD, there was no more spirit left in her.

5 So she said to the king, "The report was true that I heard in my own land of your accomplishments and of your wisdom, [6]but I did not believe the[r] reports until I came and my own eyes saw it. Not even half of the greatness of your wisdom had been told to me; you far surpass the report that I had heard. [7]Happy are your people! Happy are these your servants, who continually attend you and hear your wisdom! [8]Blessed be the LORD your God, who has delighted in you and set you on his throne as king for the LORD your God. Because your God loved Israel and would establish them forever, he has made you king over them, that you may execute justice and righteousness." [9]Then she gave the king one hundred twenty talents of gold, a very great quantity of spices, and precious stones: there were no spices such as those that the queen of Sheba gave to King Solomon.

10 Moreover the servants of Huram and the servants of Solomon who brought gold from Ophir brought algum wood and precious stones. [11]From the algum wood, the king made steps[s] for the house of the LORD and for the king's house, lyres also and harps for the singers; there never was seen the like of them before in the land of Judah.

12 Meanwhile King Solomon granted the queen of Sheba every desire that she expressed, well beyond what she had brought to the king.

9.12 An Unfounded Rumor

The queen of Sheba has mistakenly gone down in legend as one of Solomon's lovers. The king had 700 wives and 300 concubines, but the queen of Sheba was not among them.

The queen's personal visit from hundreds of miles away shows Jerusalem's reputation as the sumptuous showpiece of the Middle East. She was probably on a high-level diplomatic mission. Solomon's kingdom represented a huge threat to her land, which previously had held a trade monopoly over the land route through Israel.

Solomon financed his building projects through iron and copper-smelting industries. He traded these products to Arabia and Africa for gold, silver, ivory, and exotic animals. Evidently, he and the queen reached an agreement.

Then she returned to her own land, with her servants.

Solomon's Great Wealth

13 The weight of gold that came to Solomon in one year was six hundred sixty-six talents of gold, [14]besides that which the traders and merchants brought; and all the kings of Arabia and the governors of the land brought gold and silver to Solomon. [15]King Solomon made two hundred large shields of beaten gold; six hundred shekels of beaten gold went into each large shield. [16]He made three hundred shields of beaten gold; three hundred shekels of gold went into each shield; and the king put them in the House of the Forest of Lebanon. [17]The king also made a great ivory throne, and overlaid it with pure gold. [18]The throne had six steps and a footstool of gold, which were attached to the throne, and on each side of the seat were arm rests and two lions standing beside the arm rests, [19]while twelve lions were standing, one on each end of a step on the six steps. The like of it was never made in any kingdom. [20]All King Solomon's drinking vessels were of gold, and all the vessels of the House of the Forest of Lebanon were of pure gold; silver was not considered as anything in the days of Solomon. [21]For the king's ships went to Tarshish with the servants of Huram; once every three years the ships of Tarshish used to come bringing gold, silver, ivory, apes, and peacocks.[t]

22 Thus King Solomon excelled all the kings of the earth in riches and in wisdom. [23]All the kings of the earth sought the presence of Solomon to hear his wisdom, which God had put into his mind. [24]Every one of them brought a present, objects of silver and gold, garments, weaponry, spices, horses, and mules, so much year by year. [25]Solomon had four thousand stalls for horses and chariots, and twelve thousand horses, which he stationed in the chariot cities and with the king in Jerusalem. [26]He ruled over all the kings from the Euphrates to the land of the Philistines, and to the border of Egypt. [27]The king made silver as common in Jerusalem as stone, and cedar as plentiful as the sycamore of the Shephelah. [28]Horses were imported for Solomon from Egypt and from all lands.

Death of Solomon

29 Now the rest of the acts of Solomon, from first to last, are they not written in the history of the prophet Nathan, and in the prophecy of Ahijah the Shilonite, and in the visions of the seer Iddo concerning Jeroboam son of Nebat? [30]Solomon reigned in Jerusalem over all Israel forty years. [31]Solomon slept with his ancestors and was

q Gk Syr Vg 1 Kings 10.5: Heb ascent   r Heb their   s Gk Vg: Meaning of Heb uncertain   t Or baboons

buried in the city of his father David; and his son Rehoboam succeeded him.

The Revolt against Rehoboam

10 Rehoboam went to Shechem, for all Israel had come to Shechem to make him king. ²When Jeroboam son of Nebat heard of it (for he was in Egypt, where he had fled from King Solomon), then Jeroboam returned from Egypt. ³They sent and called him; and Jeroboam and all Israel came and said to Rehoboam, ⁴"Your father made our yoke heavy. Now therefore lighten the hard service of your father and his heavy yoke that he placed on us, and we will serve you." ⁵He said to them, "Come to me again in three days." So the people went away.

6 Then King Rehoboam took counsel with the older men who had attended his father Solomon while he was still alive, saying, "How do you advise me to answer this people?" ⁷They answered him, "If you will be kind to this people and please them, and speak good words to them, then they will be your servants forever." ⁸But he rejected the advice that the older men gave him, and consulted the young men who had grown up with him and now attended him. ⁹He said to them, "What do you advise that we answer this people who have said to me, 'Lighten the yoke that your father put on us'?" ¹⁰The young men who had grown up with him said to him, "Thus should you speak to the people who said to you, 'Your father made our yoke heavy, but you must lighten it for us'; tell them, 'My little finger is thicker than my father's loins. ¹¹Now, whereas my father laid on you a heavy yoke, I will add to your yoke. My father disciplined you with whips, but I will discipline you with scorpions.'"

12 So Jeroboam and all the people came to Rehoboam the third day, as the king had said, "Come to me again the third day." ¹³The king answered them harshly. King Rehoboam rejected the advice of the older men; ¹⁴he spoke to them in accordance with the advice of the young men, "My father made your yoke heavy, but I will add to it; my father disciplined you with whips, but I will discipline you with scorpions." ¹⁵So the king did not listen to the people, because it was a turn of affairs brought about by God so that the LORD might fulfill his word, which he had spoken by Ahijah the Shilonite to Jeroboam son of Nebat.

16 When all Israel saw that the king would not listen to them, the people answered the king,
"What share do we have in David?
　We have no inheritance in the son of
　　Jesse.
Each of you to your tents, O Israel!
　Look now to your own house,
　　O David."

So all Israel departed to their tents. ¹⁷But Rehoboam reigned over the people of Israel who were living in the cities of Judah. ¹⁸When King Rehoboam sent Hadoram, who was taskmaster over the forced labor, the people of Israel stoned him to death. King Rehoboam hurriedly mounted his chariot to flee to Jerusalem. ¹⁹So Israel has been in rebellion against the house of David to this day.

Judah and Benjamin Fortified

11 When Rehoboam came to Jerusalem, he assembled one hundred eighty thousand chosen troops of the house of Judah and Benjamin to fight against Israel, to restore the kingdom to Rehoboam. ²But the word of the LORD came to Shemaiah the man of God: ³Say to King Rehoboam

---

REHOBOAM *A Fool's Answer*

HIS FATHER SOLOMON HAD ASKED God for wisdom as his reign began (1.10). Evidently the wisdom did not get passed down in the family DNA.

At a coronation ceremony, the northern tribes of Israel were ready to swear allegiance to Rehoboam. They asked only that the new king ease Solomon's harsh taxation and forced labor policies. Rehoboam wisely asked for three days to think about it, and wisely consulted a number of counselors. But then he foolishly followed the very worst advice of some young men he had grown up with. "My father disciplined you with whips," he told the Israelites. "I will discipline you with scorpions" (10.14).

This harsh answer resulted in armed rebellion, the tragic split of Israel into two countries and a "family fight" that continued on and off as long as both nations survived. The twelve tribes of Israel, named for twelve brothers, broke into two warring factions. One man's misplaced bravado caused it all.

Rehoboam was not always so foolish. At times he listened to the right counselors. Yet in general he showed little interest in the godliness that would have strengthened his kingdom: "He did evil, for he did not set his heart to seek the LORD" (12.14). By the Bible's standard, that made him the biggest fool.

Life Questions: When pressed, do you tend to harden your position, or listen carefully to the other side? What can help you avoid a belligerent response?

of Judah, son of Solomon, and to all Israel in Judah and Benjamin, ⁴"Thus says the LORD: You shall not go up or fight against your kindred. Let everyone return home, for this thing is from me."

10.19 Unified Front

Second Chronicles pays little attention to the rebellion of the ten northern tribes against the two tribes in Judah. As the book of Kings shows, the two kingdoms existed side by side, and the North, Israel, often achieved more power than the South. But Chronicles, written to survivors in the South, virtually ignores the history of the North. In fact, in several places it uses the word Israel to refer to the South, Judah.

So they heeded the word of the LORD and turned back from the expedition against Jeroboam.

5 Rehoboam resided in Jerusalem, and he built cities for defense in Judah. ⁶He built up Bethlehem, Etam, Tekoa, ⁷Beth-zur, Soco, Adullam, ⁸Gath, Mareshah, Ziph, ⁹Adoraim, Lachish, Azekah, ¹⁰Zorah, Aijalon, and Hebron, fortified cities that are in Judah and in Benjamin. ¹¹He made the fortresses strong, and put commanders in them, and stores of food, oil, and wine. ¹²He also put large shields and spears in all the cities, and made them very strong. So he held Judah and Benjamin.

Priests and Levites Support Rehoboam

13 The priests and the Levites who were in all Israel presented themselves to him from all their territories. ¹⁴The Levites had left their common lands and their holdings and had come to Judah and Jerusalem, because Jeroboam and his sons had prevented them from serving as priests of the LORD, ¹⁵and had appointed his own priests for the high places, and for the goat-demons, and for the calves that he had made. ¹⁶Those who had set their hearts to seek the LORD God of Israel came after them from all the tribes of Israel to Jerusalem to sacrifice to the LORD, the God of their ancestors. ¹⁷They strengthened the kingdom of Judah, and for three years they made Rehoboam son of Solomon secure, for they walked for three years in the way of David and Solomon.

Rehoboam's Marriages

18 Rehoboam took as his wife Mahalath daughter of Jerimoth son of David, and of Abihail daughter of Eliab son of Jesse. ¹⁹She bore him sons: Jeush, Shemariah, and Zaham. ²⁰After him he took Maacah daughter of Absalom, who bore him Abijah, Attai, Ziza, and Shelomith. ²¹Rehoboam loved Maacah daughter of Absalom more than all his other wives and concubines (he took eighteen wives and sixty concubines, and became the father of twenty-eight sons and sixty daughters). ²²Rehoboam appointed Abijah son of Maacah as chief prince among his brothers, for he intended to make him king. ²³He dealt wisely, and distributed some of his sons through all the districts of Judah and Benjamin, in all the fortified cities; he gave them abundant provisions, and found many wives for them.

Egypt Attacks Judah

12 When the rule of Rehoboam was established and he grew strong, he abandoned the law of the LORD, he and all Israel with him. ²In the fifth year of King Rehoboam, because they had been unfaithful to the LORD, King Shishak of Egypt came up against Jerusalem ³with twelve hundred chariots and sixty thousand cavalry. A countless army came with him from Egypt—Libyans, Sukkiim, and Ethiopians.ᵘ ⁴He took the fortified cities of Judah and came as far as Jerusalem. ⁵Then the prophet Shemaiah came to Rehoboam and to the officers of Judah, who had gathered at Jerusalem because of Shishak, and said to them, "Thus says the LORD: You abandoned me, so I have abandoned you to the hand of Shishak." ⁶Then the officers of Israel and the king humbled themselves and said, "The LORD is in the right." ⁷When the LORD saw that they humbled themselves, the word of the LORD came to Shemaiah, saying: "They have humbled themselves; I will not destroy them, but I will grant them some deliverance, and my wrath shall not be poured out on Jerusalem by the hand of Shishak. ⁸Nevertheless they shall be his servants, so that they may know the difference between serving me and serving the kingdoms of other lands."

9 So King Shishak of Egypt came up against Jerusalem; he took away the treasures of the house of the LORD and the treasures of the king's house; he took everything. He also took away the shields of gold that Solomon had made; ¹⁰but King Rehoboam made in place of them shields of bronze, and committed them to the hands of the officers of the guard, who kept the door of the king's house. ¹¹Whenever the king went into the house of the LORD, the guard would come along bearing them, and would then bring them back to the guardroom. ¹²Because he humbled himself the wrath of the LORD turned from him, so as not to destroy them completely; moreover, conditions were good in Judah.

Death of Rehoboam

13 So King Rehoboam established himself in Jerusalem and reigned. Rehoboam was forty-one years old when he began to reign; he reigned seventeen years in Jerusalem, the city that the

ᵘ Or *Nubians*; Heb *Cushites*

LORD had chosen out of all the tribes of Israel to put his name there. His mother's name was Naamah the Ammonite. [14]He did evil, for he did not set his heart to seek the LORD.

15 Now the acts of Rehoboam, from first to last, are they not written in the records of the prophet Shemaiah and of the seer Iddo, recorded by genealogy? There were continual wars between Rehoboam and Jeroboam. [16]Rehoboam slept with his ancestors and was buried in the city of David; and his son Abijah succeeded him.

Abijah Reigns over Judah

13 In the eighteenth year of King Jeroboam, Abijah began to reign over Judah. [2]He reigned for three years in Jerusalem. His mother's name was Micaiah daughter of Uriel of Gibeah.

Now there was war between Abijah and Jeroboam. [3]Abijah engaged in battle, having an army of valiant warriors, four hundred thousand picked men; and Jeroboam drew up his line of battle against him with eight hundred thousand picked mighty warriors. [4]Then Abijah stood on the slope of Mount Zemaraim that is in the hill country of Ephraim, and said, "Listen to me, Jeroboam and all Israel! [5]Do you not know that the

13.4 A Brighter Outlook

Typically, Chronicles paints a rosy picture of Judah's kings. The account of Abijah in Kings, for example, tells nothing of this speech and dismisses his reign as wicked (1 Kings 15.1–8).

LORD God of Israel gave the kingship over Israel forever to David and his sons by a covenant of salt? [6]Yet Jeroboam son of Nebat, a servant of Solomon son of David, rose up and rebelled against his lord; [7]and certain worthless scoundrels gathered around him and defied Rehoboam son of Solomon, when Rehoboam was young and irresolute and could not withstand them.

8 "And now you think that you can withstand the kingdom of the LORD in the hand of the sons of David, because you are a great multitude and have with you the golden calves that Jeroboam made as gods for you. [9]Have you not driven out the priests of the LORD, the descendants of Aaron, and the Levites, and made priests for yourselves like the peoples of other lands? Whoever comes to be consecrated with a young bull or seven rams becomes a priest of what are no gods. [10]But as for us, the LORD is our God, and we have not abandoned him. We have priests ministering to the LORD who are descendants of Aaron, and Levites for their service. [11]They offer to the LORD every morning and every evening burnt offerings and

fragrant incense, set out the rows of bread on the table of pure gold, and care for the golden lampstand so that its lamps may burn every evening; for we keep the charge of the LORD our God, but you have abandoned him. [12]See, God is with us at our head, and his priests have their battle trumpets to sound the call to battle against you. O Israelites, do not fight against the LORD, the God of your ancestors; for you cannot succeed."

13 Jeroboam had sent an ambush around to come on them from behind; thus his troops[v] were in front of Judah, and the ambush was behind them. [14]When Judah turned, the battle was in front of them and behind them. They cried out to the LORD, and the priests blew the trumpets. [15]Then the people of Judah raised the battle shout. And when the people of Judah shouted, God defeated Jeroboam and all Israel before Abijah and Judah. [16]The Israelites fled before Judah, and God gave them into their hands. [17]Abijah and his army defeated them with great slaughter; five hundred thousand picked men of Israel fell slain. [18]Thus the Israelites were subdued at that time, and the people of Judah prevailed, because they relied on the LORD, the God of their ancestors. [19]Abijah pursued Jeroboam, and took cities from him: Bethel with its villages and Jeshanah with its villages and Ephron[w] with its villages. [20]Jeroboam did not recover his power in the days of Abijah; the LORD struck him down, and he died. [21]But Abijah grew strong. He took fourteen wives, and became the father of twenty-two sons and sixteen daughters. [22]The rest of the acts of Abijah, his behavior and his deeds, are written in the story of the prophet Iddo.

Asa Reigns

14[x] So Abijah slept with his ancestors, and they buried him in the city of David. His son Asa succeeded him. In his days the land had rest for ten years. [2][y] Asa did what was good and right in the sight of the LORD his God. [3]He took away the foreign altars and the high places, broke down the pillars, hewed down the sacred poles,[z] [4]and commanded Judah to seek the LORD, the God of their ancestors, and to keep the law and the commandment. [5]He also removed from all the cities of Judah the high places and the incense altars. And the kingdom had rest under him. [6]He built fortified cities in Judah while the land had rest. He had no war in those years, for the LORD gave him peace. [7]He said to Judah, "Let us build these cities, and surround them with walls and towers, gates and bars; the land is still ours because we have sought the LORD our God; we have sought him, and he has given us peace on every side." So they built and prospered. [8]Asa had an army of three hundred thousand from Judah, armed with large shields and spears, and two hundred eighty

---

v Heb *they*   *w* Another reading is *Ephrain*   *x* Ch 13.23 in Heb   *y* Ch 14.1 in Heb   *z* Heb *Asherim*

thousand troops from Benjamin who carried shields and drew bows; all these were mighty warriors.

Ethiopian Invasion Repulsed

9 Zerah the Ethiopian[a] came out against them with an army of a million men and three hundred chariots, and came as far as Mareshah. [10]Asa went out to meet him, and they drew up their lines of battle in the valley of Zephathah at Mareshah. [11]Asa cried to the LORD his God, "O LORD, there is no difference for you between helping the mighty and the weak. Help us, O LORD our God, for we rely on you, and in your name we have come against this multitude. O LORD, you are our God; let no mortal prevail against you." [12]So the LORD defeated the Ethiopians[b] before Asa and before Judah, and the Ethiopians[b] fled. [13]Asa and the army with him pursued them as far as Gerar, and the Ethiopians[b] fell until no one remained alive; for they were broken before the LORD and his army. The people of Judah[c] carried away a great quantity of booty. [14]They defeated all the cities around Gerar, for the fear of the LORD was on them. They plundered all the cities; for there was much plunder in them. [15]They also attacked the tents of those who had livestock,[d] and carried away sheep and goats in abundance, and camels. Then they returned to Jerusalem.

15 The spirit of God came upon Azariah son of Oded. [2]He went out to meet Asa and said to him, "Hear me, Asa, and all Judah and Benjamin: The LORD is with you, while you are with him. If you seek him, he will be found by you, but if you abandon him, he will abandon you. [3]For a long time Israel was without the true God, and without a teaching priest, and without law; [4]but when in their distress they turned to the LORD, the God of Israel, and sought him, he was found by them. [5]In those times it was not safe for anyone to go or come, for great disturbances afflicted all the inhabitants of the lands. [6]They were broken in pieces, nation against nation and city against city, for God troubled them with every sort of distress. [7]But you, take courage! Do not let your hands be weak, for your work shall be rewarded."

8 When Asa heard these words, the prophecy of Azariah son of Oded,[e] he took courage, and put away the abominable idols from all the land of Judah and Benjamin and from the towns that he had taken in the hill country of Ephraim. He repaired the altar of the LORD that was in front of the vestibule of the house of the LORD.[f] [9]He gathered all Judah and Benjamin, and those from Ephraim, Manasseh, and Simeon who were residing as aliens with them, for great numbers de-

serted to him from Israel when they saw that the LORD his God was with him. [10]They were gathered at Jerusalem in the third month of the fifteenth year of the reign of Asa. [11]They sacrificed

15.9–15 Northern Visitors

For the first 50 years after Jeroboam's rebellion, Israel and Judah fought a civil war. Judah was badly outnumbered, but had one great rallying point: God's temple in the city of Jerusalem. Many of the kings of Israel had built idols on "high places" as alternative worship sites to discourage their citizens from making the pilgrimage to Jerusalem. But when a southern king such as Asa launched a religious revival, members of the northern tribes would sometimes come over to Jerusalem.

to the LORD on that day, from the booty that they had brought, seven hundred oxen and seven thousand sheep. [12]They entered into a covenant to seek the LORD, the God of their ancestors, with all their heart and with all their soul. [13]Whoever would not seek the LORD, the God of Israel, should be put to death, whether young or old, man or woman. [14]They took an oath to the LORD with a loud voice, and with shouting, and with trumpets, and with horns. [15]All Judah rejoiced over the oath; for they had sworn with all their heart, and had sought him with their whole desire, and he was found by them, and the LORD gave them rest all around.

16 King Asa even removed his mother Maacah from being queen mother because she had made an abominable image for Asherah. Asa cut down her image, crushed it, and burned it at the Wadi Kidron. [17]But the high places were not taken out of Israel. Nevertheless the heart of Asa was true all his days. [18]He brought into the house of God the votive gifts of his father and his own votive gifts—silver, gold, and utensils. [19]And there was no more war until the thirty-fifth year of the reign of Asa.

Alliance with Aram Condemned

16 In the thirty-sixth year of the reign of Asa, King Baasha of Israel went up against Judah, and built Ramah, to prevent anyone from going out or coming into the territory of[g] King Asa of Judah. [2]Then Asa took silver and gold from the treasures of the house of the LORD and the king's house, and sent them to King Benhadad of Aram, who resided in Damascus, saying, [3]"Let there be an alliance between me and you, like that between my father and your father; I am sending to you silver and gold; go, break your

---

[a] Or Nubian; Heb Cushite   [b] Or Nubians; Heb Cushites   [c] Heb They   [d] Meaning of Heb uncertain
[e] Compare Syr Vg: Heb the prophecy, the prophet Obed   [f] Heb the vestibule of the LORD   [g] Heb lacks the territory of

alliance with King Baasha of Israel, so that he may withdraw from me." ⁴Ben-hadad listened to King Asa, and sent the commanders of his armies against the cities of Israel. They conquered Ijon, Dan, Abel-maim, and all the store-cities of Naphtali. ⁵When Baasha heard of it, he stopped building Ramah, and let his work cease. ⁶Then King Asa brought all Judah, and they carried away the stones of Ramah and its timber, with which Baasha had been building, and with them he built up Geba and Mizpah.

7 At that time the seer Hanani came to King Asa of Judah, and said to him, "Because you relied on the king of Aram, and did not rely on the LORD your God, the army of the king of Aram has escaped you. ⁸Were not the Ethiopians*h* and the Libyans a huge army with exceedingly many chariots and cavalry? Yet because you relied on the LORD, he gave them into your hand. ⁹For the eyes of the LORD range throughout the entire earth, to strengthen those whose heart is true to him. You have done foolishly in this; for from now on you will have wars." ¹⁰Then Asa was angry with the seer, and put him in the stocks, in prison, for he was in a rage with him because of this. And Asa inflicted cruelties on some of the people at the same time.

Asa's Disease and Death

11 The acts of Asa, from first to last, are written in the Book of the Kings of Judah and Israel. ¹²In the thirty-ninth year of his reign Asa was diseased in his feet, and his disease became severe; yet even in his disease he did not seek the LORD,

16.12 Bad Medical Advice

King Asa suffered from a serious foot disease, which some scholars think was dropsy. The Bible criticizes his consultations with physicians because in those days "physicians" were pagan healers who used rituals that conflicted with the law of God.

but sought help from physicians. ¹³Then Asa slept with his ancestors, dying in the forty-first year of his reign. ¹⁴They buried him in the tomb that he had hewn out for himself in the city of David. They laid him on a bier that had been filled with various kinds of spices prepared by the perfumer's art; and they made a very great fire in his honor.

Jehoshaphat's Reign

17 His son Jehoshaphat succeeded him, and strengthened himself against Israel. ²He placed forces in all the fortified cities of Judah, and set garrisons in the land of Judah, and in the cities of Ephraim that his father Asa had taken. ³The LORD was with Jehoshaphat, because he walked in the earlier ways of his father;*i* he did not seek the Baals, ⁴but sought the God of his father and walked in his commandments, and not according to the ways of Israel. ⁵Therefore the LORD established the kingdom in his hand. All Judah brought tribute to Jehoshaphat, and he had great riches and honor. ⁶His heart was courageous in the ways of the LORD; and furthermore he removed the high places and the sacred poles*j* from Judah.

7 In the third year of his reign he sent his officials, Ben-hail, Obadiah, Zechariah, Nethanel, and Micaiah, to teach in the cities of Judah. ⁸With them were the Levites, Shemaiah, Nethaniah, Zebadiah, Asahel, Shemiramoth, Jehonathan, Adonijah, Tobijah, and Tob-adonijah; and with these Levites, the priests Elishama and Jehoram. ⁹They taught in Judah, having the book of the law of the LORD with them; they went around through all the cities of Judah and taught among the people.

10 The fear of the LORD fell on all the kingdoms of the lands around Judah, and they did not make war against Jehoshaphat. ¹¹Some of the Philistines brought Jehoshaphat presents, and silver for tribute; and the Arabs also brought him seven thousand seven hundred rams and seven thousand seven hundred male goats. ¹²Jehoshaphat grew steadily greater. He built fortresses and storage cities in Judah. ¹³He carried out great works in the cities of Judah. He had soldiers, mighty warriors, in Jerusalem. ¹⁴This was the muster of them by ancestral houses: Of Judah, the commanders of the thousands: Adnah the commander, with three hundred thousand mighty warriors, ¹⁵and next to him Jehohanan the commander, with two hundred eighty thousand, ¹⁶and next to him Amasiah son of Zichri, a volunteer for the service of the LORD, with two hundred thousand mighty warriors. ¹⁷Of Benjamin: Eliada, a mighty warrior, with two hundred thousand armed with bow and shield, ¹⁸and next to him Jehozabad with one hundred eighty thousand armed for war. ¹⁹These were in the service of the king, besides those whom the king had placed in the fortified cities throughout all Judah.

Micaiah Predicts Failure

18 Now Jehoshaphat had great riches and honor; and he made a marriage alliance with Ahab. ²After some years he went down to Ahab in Samaria. Ahab slaughtered an abundance of sheep and oxen for him and for the people who were with him, and induced him to go up against Ramoth-gilead. ³King Ahab of Israel said to King Jehoshaphat of Judah, "Will you go with me to

h Or *Nubians*; Heb *Cushites*   *i* Another reading is *his father David*   *j* Heb *Asherim*

Ramoth-gilead?" He answered him, "I am with you, my people are your people. We will be with you in the war."

4 But Jehoshaphat also said to the king of Israel, "Inquire first for the word of the LORD." 5Then the king of Israel gathered the prophets together, four hundred of them, and said to them, "Shall we go to battle against Ramoth-gilead, or shall I refrain?" They said, "Go up; for God will give it into the hand of the king." 6But Jehoshaphat said, "Is there no other prophet of the LORD

18.6 A True or False Prophet?

Looking back from a modern perspective, it is difficult to imagine the confusion that surrounded ancient prophets. Which ones were true prophets and which were false? In this case, 400 prophets all insisted God said one thing; only one bold man contradicted them. King Jehoshaphat sensed a falseness in the 400 and insisted on listening to the true prophet. Yet, unaccountably, he failed to heed Micaiah's warning. The decision nearly cost him his life. See Deuteronomy 18.17–22 for advice on distinguishing true prophets from false.

here of whom we may inquire?" 7The king of Israel said to Jehoshaphat, "There is still one other by whom we may inquire of the LORD, Micaiah son of Imlah; but I hate him, for he never prophesies anything favorable about me, but only disaster." Jehoshaphat said, "Let the king not say such a thing." 8Then the king of Israel summoned an officer and said, "Bring quickly Micaiah son of Imlah." 9Now the king of Israel and King Jehoshaphat of Judah were sitting on their thrones, arrayed in their robes; and they were sitting at the threshing floor at the entrance of the gate of Samaria; and all the prophets were prophesying before them. 10Zedekiah son of Chenaanah made for himself horns of iron, and he said, "Thus says the LORD: With these you shall gore the Arameans until they are destroyed." 11All the prophets were prophesying the same and saying, "Go up to Ramoth-gilead and triumph; the LORD will give it into the hand of the king."

12 The messenger who had gone to summon Micaiah said to him, "Look, the words of the prophets with one accord are favorable to the king; let your word be like the word of one of them, and speak favorably." 13But Micaiah said, "As the LORD lives, whatever my God says, that I will speak."

14 When he had come to the king, the king said to him, "Micaiah, shall we go to Ramoth-gilead to battle, or shall I refrain?" He answered,

"Go up and triumph; they will be given into your hand." 15But the king said to him, "How many times must I make you swear to tell me nothing but the truth in the name of the LORD?" 16Then Micaiah[k] said, "I saw all Israel scattered on the mountains, like sheep without a shepherd; and the LORD said, 'These have no master; let each one go home in peace.'" 17The king of Israel said to Jehoshaphat, "Did I not tell you that he would not prophesy anything favorable about me, but only disaster?"

18 Then Micaiah[k] said, "Therefore hear the word of the LORD: I saw the LORD sitting on his throne, with all the host of heaven standing to the right and to the left of him. 19And the LORD said, 'Who will entice King Ahab of Israel, so that he may go up and fall at Ramoth-gilead?' Then one said one thing, and another said another, 20until a spirit came forward and stood before the LORD, saying, 'I will entice him.' The LORD asked him, 'How?' 21He replied, 'I will go out and be a lying spirit in the mouth of all his prophets.' Then the LORD[k] said, 'You are to entice him, and you shall succeed; go out and do it.' 22So you see, the LORD has put a lying spirit in the mouth of these your prophets; the LORD has decreed disaster for you."

23 Then Zedekiah son of Chenaanah came up to Micaiah, slapped him on the cheek, and said, "Which way did the spirit of the LORD pass from me to speak to you?" 24Micaiah replied, "You will find out on that day when you go in to hide in an inner chamber." 25The king of Israel then ordered, "Take Micaiah, and return him to Amon the governor of the city and to Joash the king's son; 26and say, 'Thus says the king: Put this fellow in prison, and feed him on reduced rations of bread and water until I return in peace.'" 27Micaiah said, "If you return in peace, the LORD has not spoken by me." And he said, "Hear, you peoples, all of you!"

Defeat and Death of Ahab

28 So the king of Israel and King Jehoshaphat of Judah went up to Ramoth-gilead. 29The king of Israel said to Jehoshaphat, "I will disguise myself and go into battle, but you wear your robes." So the king of Israel disguised himself, and they went into battle. 30Now the king of Aram had commanded the captains of his chariots, "Fight with no one small or great, but only with the king of Israel." 31When the captains of the chariots saw Jehoshaphat, they said, "It is the king of Israel." So they turned to fight against him; and Jehoshaphat cried out, and the LORD helped him. God drew them away from him, 32for when the captains of the chariots saw that it was not the king of Israel, they turned back from pursuing him. 33But a certain man drew his bow and unknowingly struck the king of Israel between the scale

k Heb *he*

armor and the breastplate; so he said to the driver of his chariot, "Turn around, and carry me out of the battle, for I am wounded." ³⁴The battle grew hot that day, and the king of Israel propped himself up in his chariot facing the Arameans until evening; then at sunset he died.

19 King Jehoshaphat of Judah returned in safety to his house in Jerusalem. ²Jehu son of Hanani the seer went out to meet him and said to King Jehoshaphat, "Should you help the wicked and love those who hate the LORD? Because of this, wrath has gone out against you from the LORD. ³Nevertheless, some good is found in you, for you destroyed the sacred poles[l] out of the land, and have set your heart to seek God."

The Reforms of Jehoshaphat

4 Jehoshaphat resided at Jerusalem; then he went out again among the people, from Beer-sheba to the hill country of Ephraim, and brought them back to the LORD, the God of their ancestors. ⁵He appointed judges in the land in all the fortified cities of Judah, city by city, ⁶and said to the judges, "Consider what you are doing, for you judge not on behalf of human beings but on the LORD's behalf; he is with you in giving judgment. ⁷Now, let the fear of the LORD be upon you; take care what you do, for there is no perversion of justice with the LORD our God, or partiality, or taking of bribes."

8 Moreover in Jerusalem Jehoshaphat appointed certain Levites and priests and heads of families of Israel, to give judgment for the LORD and to decide disputed cases. They had their seat at Jerusalem. ⁹He charged them: "This is how you shall act: in the fear of the LORD, in faithfulness, and with your whole heart; ¹⁰whenever a case comes to you from your kindred who live in their cities, concerning bloodshed, law or commandment, statutes or ordinances, then you shall instruct them, so that they may not incur guilt before the LORD and wrath may not come on you and your kindred. Do so, and you will not incur guilt. ¹¹See, Amariah the chief priest is over you in all matters of the LORD; and Zebadiah son of Ishmael, the governor of the house of Judah, in all the king's matters; and the Levites will serve you as officers. Deal courageously, and may the LORD be with the good!"

Invasion from the East

20 After this the Moabites and Ammonites, and with them some of the Meunites,[m] came against Jehoshaphat for battle. ²Messengers[n] came and told Jehoshaphat, "A great multitude is coming against you from Edom,[o] from beyond the sea; already they are at Hazazon-tamar" (that is, En-gedi). ³Jehoshaphat was

afraid; he set himself to seek the LORD, and proclaimed a fast throughout all Judah. ⁴Judah assembled to seek help from the LORD; from all the towns of Judah they came to seek the LORD.

Jehoshaphat's Prayer and Victory

5 Jehoshaphat stood in the assembly of Judah and Jerusalem, in the house of the LORD, before the new court, ⁶and said, "O LORD, God of our ancestors, are you not God in heaven? Do you not rule over all the kingdoms of the nations? In your hand are power and might, so that no one is able

20.6 A Model Prayer

Second Chronicles contains two great prayers: Solomon's in chapter 6 and King Jehoshaphat's here. Commentators often point to this as a model prayer. Jehoshaphat began with adoration of God, reminded him of his promises, set forth a problem, and asked for help. Confident, Jehoshaphat thanked God for the answer even before it came.

to withstand you. ⁷Did you not, O our God, drive out the inhabitants of this land before your people Israel, and give it forever to the descendants of your friend Abraham? ⁸They have lived in it, and in it have built you a sanctuary for your name, saying, ⁹'If disaster comes upon us, the sword, judgment,[p] or pestilence, or famine, we will stand before this house, and before you, for your name is in this house, and cry to you in our distress, and you will hear and save.' ¹⁰See now, the people of Ammon, Moab, and Mount Seir, whom you would not let Israel invade when they came from the land of Egypt, and whom they avoided and did not destroy— ¹¹they reward us by coming to drive us out of your possession that you have given us to inherit. ¹²O our God, will you not execute judgment upon them? For we are powerless against this great multitude that is coming against us. We do not know what to do, but our eyes are on you."

13 Meanwhile all Judah stood before the LORD, with their little ones, their wives, and their children. ¹⁴Then the spirit of the LORD came upon Jahaziel son of Zechariah, son of Benaiah, son of Jeiel, son of Mattaniah, a Levite of the sons of Asaph, in the middle of the assembly. ¹⁵He said, "Listen, all Judah and inhabitants of Jerusalem, and King Jehoshaphat: Thus says the LORD to you: 'Do not fear or be dismayed at this great multitude; for the battle is not yours but God's. ¹⁶Tomorrow go down against them; they will come up by the ascent of Ziz; you will find them at the end of the valley, before the wilderness of

---

l Heb *Asheroth*   *m* Compare 26.7: Heb *Ammonites*   *n* Heb *They*   *o* One Ms: MT *Aram*   *p* Or *the sword of*
judgment

Jeruel. ¹⁷This battle is not for you to fight; take your position, stand still, and see the victory of the LORD on your behalf, O Judah and Jerusalem.' Do not fear or be dismayed; tomorrow go out against them, and the LORD will be with you."

18 Then Jehoshaphat bowed down with his face to the ground, and all Judah and the inhabitants of Jerusalem fell down before the LORD, worshiping the LORD. ¹⁹And the Levites, of the Kohathites and the Korahites, stood up to praise the LORD, the God of Israel, with a very loud voice.

20 They rose early in the morning and went out into the wilderness of Tekoa; and as they went out, Jehoshaphat stood and said, "Listen to me, O Judah and inhabitants of Jerusalem! Believe in the LORD your God and you will be established;

believe his prophets." ²¹When he had taken counsel with the people, he appointed those who were to sing to the LORD and praise him in holy splendor, as they went before the army, saying,
"Give thanks to the LORD,
    for his steadfast love endures forever."
²²As they began to sing and praise, the LORD set an ambush against the Ammonites, Moab, and Mount Seir, who had come against Judah, so that they were routed. ²³For the Ammonites and Moab attacked the inhabitants of Mount Seir, destroying them utterly; and when they had made an end of the inhabitants of Seir, they all helped to destroy one another.

24 When Judah came to the watchtower of the wilderness, they looked toward the multitude; they were corpses lying on the ground; no one

The Great Reformers
Profiles in courage: the heroic kings of Judah

IN 1954 UNITED STATES SENATOR John F. Kennedy knew he would spend at least six months flat on his back. Surgeons were about to begin work on him to correct an old war injury. How could he best spend his time?

Kennedy decided to use those "idle" hours to research the most courageous individuals in American history. The idea for a book was born. *Profiles in Courage* went on to win the Pulitzer Prize and become a best seller. Kennedy's study of courageous people inspired the young senator to model his own life after them.

> "The LORD is with you, while you are with him. If you seek him, he will be found by you, but if you abandon him, he will abandon you." 15.2

Courage in Judah

The book of 2 Chronicles can be seen as a kind of "profiles in courage" for the nation of Judah. The vast majority of kings flunked the courage test. But a few exceptions did stand out, and 2 Chronicles dwells on them.

This book records a form of courage different from what John Kennedy had in mind. Judah was drifting further and further away from the worship of the true God. It took great courage to fight against that trend and call for a return to the law of Moses. Therefore these kings excelled not so much because of military or political strength, but because of their faithfulness to God. All the great reformers described here took over in difficult times. They helped stop, at least temporarily, their nation's tragic slide away from God.

Asa: Cleaning Up the Land (chapters 14–16)

Asa inherited a country full of crime and anarchy. He led a wildfire revival, with the whole nation uniting behind him in a huge celebration in Jerusalem. Yet Asa became cocky in his later years—he jailed a prophet of God and lived out his last days plagued by war and by disease. He did much good, but fell short of the kind of courage that endures a national crisis.

Jehoshaphat: The Organizer (chapters 17–20)

Where Asa inspired the nation, Jehoshaphat organized it. He had an outstanding domestic policy: He educated his citizens in the book of the law and built up a national court system and large army. Curiously, Jehoshaphat's wise judgment failed to carry over into foreign policy, for he made foolish alliances with neighboring Israel's very worst king, Ahab.

Joash: Refurbishing the Temple (chapters 23–24)

Joash stepped onto the throne as a boy of seven. He reigned 40 years and accomplished much

had escaped. [25]When Jehoshaphat and his people came to take the booty from them, they found livestock[q] in great numbers, goods, clothing, and precious things, which they took for themselves until they could carry no more. They spent three days taking the booty, because of its abundance. [26]On the fourth day they assembled in the Valley of Beracah, for there they blessed the LORD; therefore that place has been called the Valley of Beracah[r] to this day. [27]Then all the people of Judah and Jerusalem, with Jehoshaphat at their head, returned to Jerusalem with joy, for the LORD had enabled them to rejoice over their enemies. [28]They came to Jerusalem, with harps and lyres and trumpets, to the house of the LORD. [29]The fear of God came on all the kingdoms of the countries when they heard that the LORD had fought against the enemies of Israel. [30]And the realm of Jehoshaphat was quiet, for his God gave him rest all around.

The End of Jehoshaphat's Reign

[31] So Jehoshaphat reigned over Judah. He was thirty-five years old when he began to reign; he reigned twenty-five years in Jerusalem. His mother's name was Azubah daughter of Shilhi. [32]He walked in the way of his father Asa and did not turn aside from it, doing what was right in the sight of the LORD. [33]Yet the high places were not

removed; the people had not yet set their hearts upon the God of their ancestors.

34 Now the rest of the acts of Jehoshaphat, from first to last, are written in the Annals of Jehu son of Hanani, which are recorded in the Book of the Kings of Israel.

35 After this King Jehoshaphat of Judah joined with King Ahaziah of Israel, who did wickedly. [36]He joined him in building ships to go to Tarshish; they built the ships in Ezion-geber. [37]Then Eliezer son of Dodavahu of Mareshah prophesied against Jehoshaphat, saying, "Because you have joined with Ahaziah, the LORD will destroy what you have made." And the ships were wrecked and were not able to go to Tarshish.

Jehoram's Reign

21 Jehoshaphat slept with his ancestors and was buried with his ancestors in the city of David; his son Jehoram succeeded him. [2]He had brothers, the sons of Jehoshaphat: Azariah, Jehiel, Zechariah, Azariah, Michael, and Shephatiah; all these were the sons of King Jehoshaphat of Judah.[s] [3]Their father gave them many gifts, of silver, gold, and valuable possessions, together with fortified cities in Judah; but he gave the kingdom to Jehoram, because he was the firstborn. [4]When Jehoram had ascended the throne of his father and was established, he put all his brothers to the

q Gk: Heb *among them*   r That is *Blessing*   s Gk Syr: Heb *Israel*

---

good. Second Chronicles focuses mainly on his repairs of the temple, which he tried to restore to former glory.

Jehoiada: Strength behind the Throne (chapters 23–24)

King Joash hardly deserves a compliment without the mention of a priest named Jehoiada. He hid the boy Joash from a murderous queen and led the dramatic revolt against her. When Jehoiada died at a very old age, the nation gave him the extraordinary honor of a burial place alongside kings. After Jehoiada's death, everything went downhill. The boy king who had shown such promise murdered Jehoiada's son, a deed that went down as one of the great crimes of Israelite history. It became clear that the real strength of the kingdom had come from the old priest, not the young king.

Hezekiah: A Day to Remember (chapters 29–32)

Second Chronicles gives more space to the reign of Hezekiah than to that of any other reformer. He sponsored a great religious festival, an idea that first met with scorn and ridicule. But the nation did come together in a remarkable scene of happiness and unity. "There was great joy in Jerusalem," the Bible says, "for since the time of Solomon son of king David of Israel there had been nothing like this in Jerusalem" (30.26).

Josiah: The Complete Reformer (chapters 34–35)

Josiah was perhaps the most reform-conscious of all Judah's kings. When the book of the law (probably Deuteronomy) was discovered, Josiah realized just how far his kingdom had strayed from God's ideal. He tore his robes and wept, and led Judah back toward God. A foolish military campaign brought about Josiah's death and ruined the chances for permanent change in Judah. Known as "the good king Josiah," he was mourned by the whole nation. The prophet Jeremiah composed songs, or laments, in his memory.

Life Questions: These kings demonstrate that one person's faith can affect a great many others. Think of strong leaders you know up close. What makes them effective at inspiring and motivating others?

sword, and also some of the officials of Israel. [5]Jehoram was thirty-two years old when he began to reign; he reigned eight years in Jerusalem. [6]He walked in the way of the kings of Israel, as the house of Ahab had done; for the daughter of Ahab was his wife. He did what was evil in the

21.6 Married Despots

After the benign reign of Jehoshaphat, Judah got one of its worst kings ever, Jehoram. His marriage to Athaliah, daughter of a despised pagan king, undoubtedly stirred up revolt. To eliminate rivals, Jehoram promptly killed off his brothers, along with the "officials of Israel" (possibly leaders of the revolt). Later, Athaliah would become Judah's only reigning queen—and commit even greater atrocities (22.10).

sight of the LORD. [7]Yet the LORD would not destroy the house of David because of the covenant that he had made with David, and since he had promised to give a lamp to him and to his descendants forever.

Revolt of Edom

8 In his days Edom revolted against the rule of Judah and set up a king of their own. [9]Then Jehoram crossed over with his commanders and all his chariots. He set out by night and attacked the Edomites, who had surrounded him and his chariot commanders. [10]So Edom has been in revolt against the rule of Judah to this day. At that time Libnah also revolted against his rule, because he had forsaken the LORD, the God of his ancestors.

Elijah's Letter

11 Moreover he made high places in the hill country of Judah, and led the inhabitants of Jerusalem into unfaithfulness, and made Judah go astray. [12]A letter came to him from the prophet Elijah, saying: "Thus says the LORD, the God of your father David: Because you have not walked in the ways of your father Jehoshaphat or in the ways of King Asa of Judah, [13]but have walked in the way of the kings of Israel, and have led Judah and the inhabitants of Jerusalem into unfaithfulness, as the house of Ahab led Israel into unfaithfulness, and because you also have killed your brothers, members of your father's house, who were better than yourself, [14]see, the LORD will bring a great plague on your people, your children, your wives, and all your possessions, [15]and you yourself will have a severe sickness with a disease of your bowels, until your bowels come out, day after day, because of the disease."

16 The LORD aroused against Jehoram the an-

ger of the Philistines and of the Arabs who are near the Ethiopians.[t] [17]They came up against Judah, invaded it, and carried away all the possessions they found that belonged to the king's house, along with his sons and his wives, so that no son was left to him except Jehoahaz, his youngest son.

Disease and Death of Jehoram

18 After all this the LORD struck him in his bowels with an incurable disease. [19]In course of time, at the end of two years, his bowels came out because of the disease, and he died in great agony. His people made no fire in his honor, like the fires made for his ancestors. [20]He was thirty-two years old when he began to reign; he reigned eight years in Jerusalem. He departed with no one's regret. They buried him in the city of David, but not in the tombs of the kings.

Ahaziah's Reign

22 The inhabitants of Jerusalem made his youngest son Ahaziah king as his successor; for the troops who came with the Arabs to the camp had killed all the older sons. So Ahaziah son of Jehoram reigned as king of Judah. [2]Ahaziah was forty-two years old when he began to reign; he reigned one year in Jerusalem. His mother's name was Athaliah, a granddaughter of Omri. [3]He also walked in the ways of the house of Ahab, for his mother was his counselor in doing wickedly. [4]He did what was evil in the sight of the LORD, as the house of Ahab had done; for after the death of his father they were his counselors, to his ruin. [5]He even followed their advice, and went with Jehoram son of King Ahab of Israel to make war against King Hazael of Aram at Ramoth-gilead. The Arameans wounded Joram, [6]and he returned to be healed in Jezreel of the wounds that he had received at Ramah, when he fought King Hazael of Aram. And Ahaziah son of King Jehoram of Judah went down to see Joram son of Ahab in Jezreel, because he was sick.

7 But it was ordained by God that the downfall of Ahaziah should come about through his going to visit Joram. For when he came there he went out with Jehoram to meet Jehu son of Nimshi, whom the LORD had anointed to destroy the house of Ahab. [8]When Jehu was executing judgment on the house of Ahab, he met the officials of Judah and the sons of Ahaziah's brothers, who attended Ahaziah, and he killed them. [9]He searched for Ahaziah, who was captured while hiding in Samaria and was brought to Jehu, and put to death. They buried him, for they said, "He is the grandson of Jehoshaphat, who sought the LORD with all his heart." And the house of Ahaziah had no one able to rule the kingdom.

---

t Or Nubians; Heb *Cushites*

Athaliah Seizes the Throne

10 Now when Athaliah, Ahaziah's mother, saw that her son was dead, she set about to destroy all the royal family of the house of Judah. ¹¹But Jehoshabeath, the king's daughter, took Joash son of Ahaziah, and stole him away from among the king's children who were about to be killed; she put him and his nurse in a bedroom. Thus Jehoshabeath, daughter of King Jehoram and wife of the priest Jehoiada—because she was a sister of Ahaziah—hid him from Athaliah, so that she did not kill him; ¹²he remained with them six years, hidden in the house of God, while Athaliah reigned over the land.

23 But in the seventh year Jehoiada took courage, and entered into a compact with the commanders of the hundreds, Azariah son of Jeroham, Ishmael son of Jehohanan, Azariah son of Obed, Maaseiah son of Adaiah, and Elishaphat son of Zichri. ²They went around through Judah and gathered the Levites from all the towns of Judah, and the heads of families of Israel, and they came to Jerusalem. ³Then the whole assembly made a covenant with the king in the house of God. Jehoiada*u* said to them, "Here is the king's son! Let him reign, as the LORD promised concerning the sons of David. ⁴This is what you are to do: one-third of you, priests and Levites, who come on duty on the sabbath, shall be gatekeepers, ⁵one-third shall be at the king's house, and one-third at the Gate of the Foundation; and all the people shall be in the courts of the house of the LORD. ⁶Do not let anyone enter the house of the LORD except the priests and ministering Levites; they may enter, for they are holy, but all the other*v* people shall observe the instructions of the LORD. ⁷The Levites shall surround the king, each with his weapons in his hand; and who-

ever enters the house shall be killed. Stay with the king in his comings and goings."

Joash Crowned King

8 The Levites and all Judah did according to

23.7 The Priests Take up Arms

Athaliah, daughter of Jezebel, introduced Baal worship to Judah and very nearly destroyed the entire royal line of David. Conditions in Judah got so bad that a priest, Jehoiada, took the extraordinary step of arming the Levites for a palace coup. They placed the rightful heir, Joash, on the throne.

all that the priest Jehoiada commanded; each brought his men, who were to come on duty on the sabbath, with those who were to go off duty on the sabbath; for the priest Jehoiada did not dismiss the divisions. ⁹The priest Jehoiada delivered to the captains the spears and the large and small shields that had been King David's, which were in the house of God; ¹⁰and he set all the people as a guard for the king, everyone with weapon in hand, from the south side of the house to the north side of the house, around the altar and the house. ¹¹Then he brought out the king's son, put the crown on him, and gave him the covenant;*w* they proclaimed him king, and Jehoiada and his sons anointed him; and they shouted, "Long live the king!"

Athaliah Murdered

12 When Athaliah heard the noise of the people running and praising the king, she went into the house of the LORD to the people; ¹³and when

---

u Heb *He*　　*v* Heb lacks *other*　　*w* Or *treaty*, or *testimony*; Heb *eduth*

ATHALIAH   *Live by the Sword . . .*

IN OLD TESTAMENT TIMES AMBITIOUS women usually exerted themselves through their husbands. Athaliah's wicked mother Jezebel, for example, dominated her husband Ahab, king of Israel.

Athaliah took another route, preferring to go it alone. She reigned eight years as queen to King Jehoram and a year as Queen Mother with their son Ahaziah. But when Ahaziah died a violent death, Mother decided to take charge for herself. Ruthless as Lady Macbeth, Athaliah had all potential rivals—including her own children and grandchildren—put to death. She reigned alone for six years, secure in the throne since she had eliminated all opposition.

Then appeared, in a scene as dramatic as any in the Bible, a royal heir she had overlooked. The seven-year-old boy Joash—her grandson—had been hidden in the temple all those years. This boy was now brought out and displayed on the temple steps. When Athaliah heard the tumultuous response, she went to see what the commotion was about. A revolution was underway. Rebels captured her and put her to death, and not a single person came to her defense.

Life Questions: Which type of people do you think are more likely to cause trouble: "loners," or people who have many friends and allies? Why?

she looked, there was the king standing by his pillar at the entrance, and the captains and the trumpeters beside the king, and all the people of the land rejoicing and blowing trumpets, and the singers with their musical instruments leading in the celebration. Athaliah tore her clothes, and cried, "Treason! Treason!" ¹⁴Then the priest Jehoiada brought out the captains who were set over the army, saying to them, "Bring her out between the ranks; anyone who follows her is to be put to the sword." For the priest said, "Do not put her to death in the house of the LORD." ¹⁵So they laid hands on her; she went into the entrance of the Horse Gate of the king's house, and there they put her to death.

16 Jehoiada made a covenant between himself and all the people and the king that they should be the LORD's people. ¹⁷Then all the people went to the house of Baal, and tore it down; his altars and his images they broke in pieces, and they killed Mattan, the priest of Baal, in front of the altars. ¹⁸Jehoiada assigned the care of the house of the LORD to the levitical priests whom David had organized to be in charge of the house of the LORD, to offer burnt offerings to the LORD, as it is written in the law of Moses, with rejoicing and with singing, according to the order of David. ¹⁹He stationed the gatekeepers at the gates of the house of the LORD so that no one should enter who was in any way unclean. ²⁰And he took the captains, the nobles, the governors of the people, and all the people of the land, and they brought the king down from the house of the LORD, marching through the upper gate to the king's house. They set the king on the royal throne. ²¹So all the people of the land rejoiced, and the city was quiet after Athaliah had been killed with the sword.

Joash Repairs the Temple

24 Joash was seven years old when he began to reign; he reigned forty years in Jerusalem; his mother's name was Zibiah of Beer-sheba. ²Joash did what was right in the sight of the LORD all the days of the priest Jehoiada. ³Jehoiada got two wives for him, and he became the father of sons and daughters.

4 Some time afterward Joash decided to restore the house of the LORD. ⁵He assembled the priests and the Levites and said to them, "Go out to the cities of Judah and gather money from all Israel to repair the house of your God, year by year; and see that you act quickly." But the Levites did not act quickly. ⁶So the king summoned Jehoiada the chief, and said to him, "Why have you not required the Levites to bring in from Judah and Jerusalem the tax levied by Moses, the servant of the LORD, on*x* the congregation of Israel for the tent of the covenant?"*y* ⁷For the children of

Athaliah, that wicked woman, had broken into the house of God, and had even used all the dedicated things of the house of the LORD for the Baals.

8 So the king gave command, and they made a chest, and set it outside the gate of the house of the LORD. ⁹A proclamation was made throughout Judah and Jerusalem to bring in for the LORD the tax that Moses the servant of God laid on Israel in the wilderness. ¹⁰All the leaders and all the people rejoiced and brought their tax and dropped it into the chest until it was full. ¹¹Whenever the chest was brought to the king's officers by the Levites, when they saw that there was a large amount of money in it, the king's secretary and the officer of the chief priest would come and empty the chest and take it and return it to its place. So they did day after day, and collected money in abundance. ¹²The king and Jehoiada gave it to those who had charge of the work of the house of the LORD, and they hired masons and carpenters to restore the house of the LORD, and also workers in iron and bronze to repair the house of the LORD. ¹³So those who were engaged in the work labored, and the repairing went forward at their hands, and they restored the house of God to its proper condition and strengthened it. ¹⁴When they had finished, they brought the rest of the money to the king and Jehoiada, and with it were made utensils for the house of the LORD, utensils for the service and for the burnt offerings, and ladles, and vessels of gold and silver. They offered burnt offerings in the house of the LORD regularly all the days of Jehoiada.

Apostasy of Joash

15 But Jehoiada grew old and full of days, and died; he was one hundred thirty years old at his death. ¹⁶And they buried him in the city of David among the kings, because he had done good in Israel, and for God and his house.

17 Now after the death of Jehoiada the officials of Judah came and did obeisance to the king; then the king listened to them. ¹⁸They abandoned the house of the LORD, the God of their ancestors, and served the sacred poles*z* and the idols. And wrath came upon Judah and Jerusalem for this guilt of theirs. ¹⁹Yet he sent prophets among them to bring them back to the LORD; they testified against them, but they would not listen.

20 Then the spirit of God took possession of*a* Zechariah son of the priest Jehoiada; he stood above the people and said to them, "Thus says God: Why do you transgress the commandments of the LORD, so that you cannot prosper? Because you have forsaken the LORD, he has also forsaken you." ²¹But they conspired against him, and by command of the king they stoned him to death in the court of the house of the LORD. ²²King Joash

---

x Compare Vg: Heb *and*   *y* Or *treaty*, or *testimony*; Heb *eduth*   *z* Heb *Asherim*   *a* Heb *clothed itself with*

did not remember the kindness that Jehoiada, Zechariah's father, had shown him, but killed his son. As he was dying, he said, "May the LORD see and avenge!"

24.21 An Infamous Murder

Joash showed promise in his early years as king. But, like many other kings, he could not tolerate the damning words of one of God's prophets. The murder carried out on his order brought in enemy armies, inspired a conspiracy against Joash, and destroyed his reputation forever. Jesus may have been speaking of this incident when he alluded to a murder hundreds of years later (Luke 11.51; Matthew 23.35).

Death of Joash

23 At the end of the year the army of Aram came up against Joash. They came to Judah and Jerusalem, and destroyed all the officials of the people from among them, and sent all the booty they took to the king of Damascus. 24Although the army of Aram had come with few men, the LORD delivered into their hand a very great army, because they had abandoned the LORD, the God of their ancestors. Thus they executed judgment on Joash.

25 When they had withdrawn, leaving him severely wounded, his servants conspired against him because of the blood of the son*b* of the priest Jehoiada, and they killed him on his bed. So he died; and they buried him in the city of David, but they did not bury him in the tombs of the kings. 26Those who conspired against him were Zabad son of Shimeath the Ammonite, and Jehozabad son of Shimrith the Moabite. 27Accounts of his sons, and of the many oracles against him, and of the rebuilding*c* of the house of God are written in the Commentary on the Book of the Kings. And his son Amaziah succeeded him.

Reign of Amaziah

25 Amaziah was twenty-five years old when he began to reign, and he reigned twenty-nine years in Jerusalem. His mother's name was Jehoaddan of Jerusalem. 2He did what was right in the sight of the LORD, yet not with a true heart. 3As soon as the royal power was firmly in his hand he killed his servants who had murdered his father the king. 4But he did not put their children to death, according to what is written in the law, in the book of Moses, where the LORD commanded, "The parents shall not be put to death for the children, or the children be put to death for the parents; but all shall be put to death for their own sins."

Slaughter of the Edomites

5 Amaziah assembled the people of Judah, and set them by ancestral houses under commanders of the thousands and of the hundreds for all Judah and Benjamin. He mustered those twenty years old and upward, and found that they were three hundred thousand picked troops fit for war, able to handle spear and shield. 6He also hired one hundred thousand mighty warriors from Israel for one hundred talents of silver. 7But a man of God came to him and said, "O king, do not let the army of Israel go with you, for the LORD is not with Israel—all these Ephraimites. 8Rather, go by yourself and act; be strong in battle, or God will fling you down before the enemy; for God has power to help or to overthrow." 9Amaziah said to the man of God, "But what shall we do about the hundred talents that I have given to the army of Israel?" The man of God answered, "The LORD is able to give you much more than this." 10Then Amaziah discharged the army that had come to him from Ephraim, letting them go home again. But they became very angry with Judah, and returned home in fierce anger.

11 Amaziah took courage, and led out his people; he went to the Valley of Salt, and struck down ten thousand men of Seir. 12The people of Judah captured another ten thousand alive, took them to the top of Sela, and threw them down from the top of Sela, so that all of them were dashed to pieces. 13But the men of the army whom Amaziah sent back, not letting them go with him to battle, fell on the cities of Judah from Samaria to Beth-horon; they killed three thousand people in them, and took much booty.

14 Now after Amaziah came from the slaughter of the Edomites, he brought the gods of the people of Seir, set them up as his gods, and worshiped them, making offerings to them. 15The LORD was angry with Amaziah and sent to him a prophet, who said to him, "Why have you resorted to a people's gods who could not deliver their own people from your hand?" 16But as he was speaking the king*d* said to him, "Have we made you a royal counselor? Stop! Why should you be put to death?" So the prophet stopped, but said, "I know that God has determined to destroy you, because you have done this and have not listened to my advice."

Israel Defeats Judah

17 Then King Amaziah of Judah took counsel and sent to King Joash son of Jehoahaz son of Jehu of Israel, saying, "Come, let us look one another in the face." 18King Joash of Israel sent word to King Amaziah of Judah, "A thornbush on Lebanon sent to a cedar on Lebanon, saying, 'Give your daughter to my son for a wife'; but a wild animal of Lebanon passed by and trampled

b Gk Vg: Heb *sons*   *c* Heb *founding*   *d* Heb *he*

down the thornbush. ¹⁹You say, 'See, I have defeated Edom,' and your heart has lifted you up in boastfulness. Now stay at home; why should you provoke trouble so that you fall, you and Judah with you?"

20 But Amaziah would not listen—it was God's doing, in order to hand them over, because they had sought the gods of Edom. ²¹So King Joash of Israel went up; he and King Amaziah of Judah faced one another in battle at Beth-shemesh, which belongs to Judah. ²²Judah was defeated by Israel; everyone fled home. ²³King Joash of Israel captured King Amaziah of Judah, son of Joash, son of Ahaziah, at Beth-shemesh; he brought him to Jerusalem, and broke down the wall of Jerusalem from the Ephraim Gate to the Corner Gate, a distance of four hundred cubits. ²⁴He seized all the gold and silver, and all the vessels that were found in the house of God, and Obed-edom with them; he seized also the treasuries of the king's house, also hostages; then he returned to Samaria.

Death of Amaziah

25 King Amaziah son of Joash of Judah, lived fifteen years after the death of King Joash son of Jehoahaz of Israel. ²⁶Now the rest of the deeds of Amaziah, from first to last, are they not written in the Book of the Kings of Judah and Israel? ²⁷From the time that Amaziah turned away from the LORD they made a conspiracy against him in Jerusalem, and he fled to Lachish. But they sent after him to Lachish, and killed him there. ²⁸They brought him back on horses; he was buried with his ancestors in the city of David.

Reign of Uzziah

26 Then all the people of Judah took Uzziah, who was sixteen years old, and made him king to succeed his father Amaziah. ²He rebuilt Eloth and restored it to Judah, after the king slept with his ancestors. ³Uzziah was sixteen years old when he began to reign, and he reigned fifty-two years in Jerusalem. His mother's name was Jecoliah of Jerusalem. ⁴He did what was right in the sight of the LORD, just as his father Amaziah had done. ⁵He set himself to seek God in the days of Zechariah, who instructed him in the fear of God; and as long as he sought the LORD, God made him prosper.

6 He went out and made war against the Philistines, and broke down the wall of Gath and the wall of Jabneh and the wall of Ashdod; he built cities in the territory of Ashdod and elsewhere among the Philistines. ⁷God helped him against the Philistines, against the Arabs who lived in Gur-baal, and against the Meunites. ⁸The Ammonites paid tribute to Uzziah, and his fame spread even to the border of Egypt, for he became

very strong. ⁹Moreover Uzziah built towers in Jerusalem at the Corner Gate, at the Valley Gate, and at the Angle, and fortified them. ¹⁰He built towers in the wilderness and hewed out many cisterns, for he had large herds, both in the Shephelah and in the plain, and he had farmers and vinedressers in the hills and in the fertile lands, for he loved the soil. ¹¹Moreover Uzziah had an army of soldiers, fit for war, in divisions according to the numbers in the muster made by the secretary Jeiel and the officer Maaseiah, under the direction of Hananiah, one of the king's commanders. ¹²The whole number of the heads of ancestral houses of mighty warriors was two thousand six hundred. ¹³Under their command was an army of three hundred seven thousand five hundred, who could make war with mighty power, to help the king against the enemy. ¹⁴Uzziah provided for all the army the shields, spears, helmets, coats of mail, bows, and stones for slinging. ¹⁵In Jerusalem he set up machines, invented by skilled workers, on the towers and the corners for shooting arrows and large stones. And his fame spread far, for he was marvelously helped until he became strong.

Pride and Apostasy

16 But when he had become strong he grew proud, to his destruction. For he was false to the LORD his God, and entered the temple of the LORD

26.16 A King's Pride

Archaeological discoveries have verified the prosperity of Judah during Uzziah's reign. However, like many of Judah's kings, he fell victim to the sin of pride. He usurped the role of the priests and suffered ever after from a contagious skin disease.

to make offering on the altar of incense. ¹⁷But the priest Azariah went in after him, with eighty priests of the LORD who were men of valor; ¹⁸they withstood King Uzziah, and said to him, "It is not for you, Uzziah, to make offering to the LORD, but for the priests the descendants of Aaron, who are consecrated to make offering. Go out of the sanctuary; for you have done wrong, and it will bring you no honor from the LORD God." ¹⁹Then Uzziah was angry. Now he had a censer in his hand to make offering, and when he became angry with the priests a leprous*ᵉ* disease broke out on his forehead, in the presence of the priests in the house of the LORD, by the altar of incense. ²⁰When the chief priest Azariah, and all the priests, looked at him, he was leprous*ᵉ* in his forehead. They hurried him out, and he himself hurried to get

ᵉ A term for several skin diseases; precise meaning uncertain out, because the LORD had struck him. [21]King Uzziah was leprous[f] to the day of his death, and being leprous[f] lived in a separate house, for he was excluded from the house of the LORD. His son Jotham was in charge of the palace of the king, governing the people of the land.

22 Now the rest of the acts of Uzziah, from first to last, the prophet Isaiah son of Amoz wrote. [23]Uzziah slept with his ancestors; they buried him near his ancestors in the burial field that belonged to the kings, for they said, "He is leprous."[f] His son Jotham succeeded him.

Reign of Jotham

27 Jotham was twenty-five years old when he began to reign; he reigned sixteen years in Jerusalem. His mother's name was Jerushah daughter of Zadok. [2]He did what was right in the sight of the LORD just as his father Uzziah had done—only he did not invade the temple of the LORD. But the people still followed corrupt practices. [3]He built the upper gate of the house of the LORD, and did extensive building on the wall of Ophel. [4]Moreover he built cities in the hill country of Judah, and forts and towers on the wooded hills. [5]He fought with the king of the Ammonites and prevailed against them. The Ammonites gave him that year one hundred talents of silver, ten thousand cors of wheat and ten thousand of barley. The Ammonites paid him the same amount in the second and the third years. [6]So Jotham became strong because he ordered his ways before the LORD his God. [7]Now the rest of the acts of Jotham, and all his wars and his ways, are written in the Book of the Kings of Israel and Judah. [8]He was twenty-five years old when he began to reign; he reigned sixteen years in Jerusalem. [9]Jotham slept with his ancestors, and they buried him in the city of David; and his son Ahaz succeeded him.

Reign of Ahaz

28 Ahaz was twenty years old when he began to reign; he reigned sixteen years in Jerusalem. He did not do what was right in the sight of the LORD, as his ancestor David had done, [2]but he walked in the ways of the kings of Israel. He even made cast images for the Baals; [3]and he made offerings in the valley of the son of Hinnom, and made his sons pass through fire, according to the abominable practices of the nations whom the LORD drove out before the people of Israel. [4]He sacrificed and made offerings on the high places, on the hills, and under every green tree.

Aram and Israel Defeat Judah

5 Therefore the LORD his God gave him into the hand of the king of Aram, who defeated him and took captive a great number of his people and brought them to Damascus. He was also given into the hand of the king of Israel, who defeated him with great slaughter. [6]Pekah son of Remaliah killed one hundred twenty thousand in Judah in one day, all of them valiant warriors, because they had abandoned the LORD, the God of their ancestors. [7]And Zichri, a mighty warrior of Ephraim, killed the king's son Maaseiah, Azrikam the commander of the palace, and Elkanah the next in authority to the king.

Intervention of Oded

8 The people of Israel took captive two hundred thousand of their kin, women, sons, and daughters; they also took much booty from them and brought the booty to Samaria. [9]But a prophet of the LORD was there, whose name was Oded; he went out to meet the army that came to Samaria, and said to them, "Because the LORD, the God of your ancestors, was angry with Judah, he gave them into your hand, but you have killed them in

28.9 Limits of a Just War

Advocates of a "just war" theory sometimes cite the fascinating story in this chapter. God sanctioned Israel's attack on Judah, but the invaders from the North went too far. They slaughtered many civilians and carried away others as captives. A prophet rebuked Israel's army for their crimes committed "in a rage that has reached up to heaven." The Israelites had fought a war with a just end—carrying out God's punishment—but used cruel and unjust means in waging it.

The prophet convinced the Israelites to give up plunder and prisoners and make restitution. They fed the prisoners from Judah, gave them clothes, sandals, and medicine, and put them on donkeys to return home. This scene is one of the few in 2 Chronicles that shows the Northern Kingdom in a favorable light.

a rage that has reached up to heaven. [10]Now you intend to subjugate the people of Judah and Jerusalem, male and female, as your slaves. But what have you except sins against the LORD your God? [11]Now hear me, and send back the captives whom you have taken from your kindred, for the fierce wrath of the LORD is upon you." [12]Moreover, certain chiefs of the Ephraimites, Azariah son of Johanan, Berechiah son of Meshillemoth, Jehizkiah son of Shallum, and Amasa son of Hadlai, stood up against those who were coming from the war, [13]and said to them, "You shall not bring the captives in here, for you propose to bring on us guilt against the LORD in addition to our present sins and guilt. For our guilt is already great, and there

---

[f] A term for several skin diseases; precise meaning uncertain

is fierce wrath against Israel." [14]So the warriors left the captives and the booty before the officials and all the assembly. [15]Then those who were mentioned by name got up and took the captives, and with the booty they clothed all that were naked among them; they clothed them, gave them sandals, provided them with food and drink, and anointed them; and carrying all the feeble among them on donkeys, they brought them to their kindred at Jericho, the city of palm trees. Then they returned to Samaria.

Assyria Refuses to Help Judah

16 At that time King Ahaz sent to the king[g] of Assyria for help. [17]For the Edomites had again invaded and defeated Judah, and carried away captives. [18]And the Philistines had made raids on the cities in the Shephelah and the Negeb of Judah, and had taken Beth-shemesh, Aijalon, Gederoth, Soco with its villages, Timnah with its villages, and Gimzo with its villages; and they settled there. [19]For the LORD brought Judah low because of King Ahaz of Israel, for he had behaved without restraint in Judah and had been faithless to the LORD. [20]So King Tilgath-pilneser of Assyria came against him, and oppressed him instead of strengthening him. [21]For Ahaz plundered the house of the LORD and the houses of the king and of the officials, and gave tribute to the king of Assyria; but it did not help him.

Apostasy and Death of Ahaz

22 In the time of his distress he became yet more faithless to the LORD—this same King Ahaz. [23]For he sacrificed to the gods of Damascus, which had defeated him, and said, "Because the gods of the kings of Aram helped them, I will sacrifice to them so that they may help me." But they were the ruin of him, and of all Israel. [24]Ahaz gathered together the utensils of the house of God, and cut in pieces the utensils of the house of God. He shut up the doors of the house of the LORD and made himself altars in every corner of Jerusalem. [25]In every city of Judah he made high places to make offerings to other gods, provoking to anger the LORD, the God of his ancestors. [26]Now the rest of his acts and all his ways, from first to last, are written in the Book of the Kings of Judah and Israel. [27]Ahaz slept with his ancestors, and they buried him in the city, in Jerusalem; but they did not bring him into the tombs of the kings of Israel. His son Hezekiah succeeded him.

Reign of Hezekiah

29 Hezekiah began to reign when he was twenty-five years old; he reigned twenty-nine years in Jerusalem. His mother's name was Abijah daughter of Zechariah. [2]He did what was right in the sight of the LORD, just as his ancestor David had done.

The Temple Cleansed

3 In the first year of his reign, in the first month, he opened the doors of the house of the LORD and repaired them. [4]He brought in the priests and the Levites and assembled them in the square on the east. [5]He said to them, "Listen to me, Levites! Sanctify yourselves, and sanctify the house of the LORD, the God of your ancestors, and carry out the filth from the holy place. [6]For our ancestors have been unfaithful and have done what was evil in the sight of the LORD our God; they have forsaken him, and have turned away their faces from the dwelling of the LORD, and turned their backs. [7]They also shut the doors of the vestibule and put out the lamps, and have not offered incense or made burnt offerings in the holy place to the God of Israel. [8]Therefore the wrath of the LORD came upon Judah and Jerusalem, and he has made them an object of horror, of astonishment, and of hissing, as you see with your own eyes. [9]Our fathers have fallen by the sword and our sons and our daughters and our wives are in captivity for this. [10]Now it is in my heart to make a covenant with the LORD, the God of Israel, so that his fierce anger may turn away from us. [11]My sons, do not now be negligent, for the LORD has chosen you to stand in his presence to minister to him, and to be his ministers and make offerings to him."

12 Then the Levites arose, Mahath son of Amasai, and Joel son of Azariah, of the sons of the Kohathites; and of the sons of Merari, Kish son of Abdi, and Azariah son of Jehallelel; and of the Gershonites, Joah son of Zimmah, and Eden son of Joah; [13]and of the sons of Elizaphan, Shimri and Jeuel; and of the sons of Asaph, Zechariah and Mattaniah; [14]and of the sons of Heman, Jehuel and Shimei; and of the sons of Jeduthun, Shemaiah and Uzziel. [15]They gathered their brothers, sanctified themselves, and went in as the king had commanded, by the words of the LORD, to cleanse the house of the LORD. [16]The priests went into the inner part of the house of the LORD to cleanse it, and they brought out all the unclean things that they found in the temple of the LORD into the court of the house of the LORD; and the Levites took them and carried them out to the Wadi Kidron. [17]They began to sanctify on the first day of the first month, and on the eighth day of the month they came to the vestibule of the LORD; then for eight days they sanctified the house of the LORD, and on the sixteenth day of the first month they finished. [18]Then they went inside to King Hezekiah and said, "We have cleansed all the house of the LORD, the altar of burnt offering and all its utensils, and the table for the rows of bread

and all its utensils. ¹⁹All the utensils that King Ahaz repudiated during his reign when he was faithless, we have made ready and sanctified; see, they are in front of the altar of the LORD."

Temple Worship Restored

20 Then King Hezekiah rose early, assembled the officials of the city, and went up to the house of the LORD. ²¹They brought seven bulls, seven rams, seven lambs, and seven male goats for a sin offering for the kingdom and for the sanctuary and for Judah. He commanded the priests the descendants of Aaron to offer them on the altar of the LORD. ²²So they slaughtered the bulls, and the priests received the blood and dashed it against the altar; they slaughtered the rams and their blood was dashed against the altar; they also slaughtered the lambs and their blood was dashed against the altar. ²³Then the male goats for the sin offering were brought to the king and the assembly; they laid their hands on them, ²⁴and the priests slaughtered them and made a sin offering with their blood at the altar, to make atonement for all Israel. For the king commanded that the burnt offering and the sin offering should be made for all Israel.

25 He stationed the Levites in the house of the LORD with cymbals, harps, and lyres, according to the commandment of David and of Gad the king's seer and of the prophet Nathan, for the commandment was from the LORD through his prophets. ²⁶The Levites stood with the instruments of David, and the priests with the trumpets. ²⁷Then Hezekiah commanded that the burnt offering be offered on the altar. When the burnt offering began, the song to the LORD began also, and the trumpets, accompanied by the instruments of King David of Israel. ²⁸The whole assembly worshiped, the singers sang, and the trumpeters sounded; all this continued until the burnt offering was finished. ²⁹When the offering was finished, the king and all who were present with him bowed down and worshiped. ³⁰King Hezekiah and the officials commanded the Levites to sing praises to the LORD with the words of David and of the seer Asaph. They sang praises with gladness, and they bowed down and worshiped.

31 Then Hezekiah said, "You have now consecrated yourselves to the LORD; come near, bring sacrifices and thank offerings to the house of the LORD." The assembly brought sacrifices and thank offerings; and all who were of a willing heart brought burnt offerings. ³²The number of the burnt offerings that the assembly brought was seventy bulls, one hundred rams, and two hun-

HEZEKIAH *Cleaning House*

HIS OWN FATHER HAD CLOSED the temple in Jerusalem, imported a pagan altar from Damascus and erected shrines to other gods on every street corner. Inheriting the throne as a young man, Hezekiah saw that his nation was hurtling toward disaster. He watched as the great power of Assyria invaded his sister nation Israel, demolishing its cities and sending its citizens into exile.

Unlike other kings, Hezekiah did not scurry around seeking political alliances to bolster his strength. He listened carefully to the prophet Isaiah and looked instead for God's protection. To reverse the course of his nation, he began by cleaning out God's house—the temple in Jerusalem.

When he began this task, priests and Levites who had been assigned to coordinate temple worship had dwindled away, demoralized. Hezekiah rallied them like an army and gave them marching orders: Clean up yourselves and clean up the temple. It took more than two weeks for them to dump all the idolatrous materials into a nearby ravine and to reconsecrate the temple. Worship recommenced: regular sacrifices to God, singing of the temple music written by David, even a dramatic restaging of the long-neglected Passover festival.

In these policies Hezekiah showed courage and initiative. He took risks, raising dust and probably raising hackles. Even Moses' bronze snake had to go—people were now worshiping it! (2 Kings 18.4) Hezekiah embarked on these reforms out of deep personal commitment. "And every work that he undertook in the service of the house of God, and in accordance with the law and the commandments, to seek his God, he did with all his heart; and he prospered" (31.21).

When the powerful Assyrians camped at his gate, sneering at his God and threatening to destroy him, Hezekiah knew where to turn—to God. The prophet Isaiah prayed with Hezekiah, and Judah was miraculously saved. Later, when Hezekiah himself was close to death, God also answered his prayers for healing, extending his life by 15 years.

Hezekiah had some flaws, but overall he went down as one of the finest rulers in the Old Testament. "There was no one like him among all the kings of Judah after him, or among those who were before him. For he held fast to the LORD; he did not depart from following him but kept the commandments that the LORD commanded Moses" (2 Kings 18.5–6).

Life Questions: Where do you think house cleaning most needs to occur? In your life? In your church? Among your friends? In your city, state or nation?

dred lambs; all these were for a burnt offering to the LORD. [33]The consecrated offerings were six hundred bulls and three thousand sheep. [34]But the priests were too few and could not skin all the burnt offerings, so, until other priests had sanctified themselves, their kindred, the Levites, helped them until the work was finished—for the Levites were more conscientious[h] than the priests in sanctifying themselves. [35]Besides the great number of burnt offerings there was the fat of the offerings of well-being, and there were the drink offerings for the burnt offerings. Thus the service of the house of the LORD was restored. [36]And Hezekiah and all the people rejoiced because of what God had done for the people; for the thing had come about suddenly.

The Great Passover

30 Hezekiah sent word to all Israel and Judah, and wrote letters also to Ephraim and Manasseh, that they should come to the house of the LORD at Jerusalem, to keep the passover to the

30.1 Delayed Passover

By moving the passover date back one month, Hezekiah allowed extra time for priests to prepare and for pilgrims to make travel plans. Pointedly, Hezekiah invited tribes from the ravaged Northern Kingdom. For the first time in 200 years, the entire nation celebrated a religious festival together.

LORD the God of Israel. [2]For the king and his officials and all the assembly in Jerusalem had taken counsel to keep the passover in the second month [3](for they could not keep it at its proper time because the priests had not sanctified themselves in sufficient number, nor had the people assembled in Jerusalem). [4]The plan seemed right to the king and all the assembly. [5]So they decreed to make a proclamation throughout all Israel, from Beer-sheba to Dan, that the people should come and keep the passover to the LORD the God of Israel, at Jerusalem; for they had not kept it in great numbers as prescribed. [6]So couriers went throughout all Israel and Judah with letters from the king and his officials, as the king had commanded, saying, "O people of Israel, return to the LORD, the God of Abraham, Isaac, and Israel, so that he may turn again to the remnant of you who have escaped from the hand of the kings of Assyria. [7]Do not be like your ancestors and your kindred, who were faithless to the LORD God of their ancestors, so that he made them a desolation, as you see. [8]Do not now be stiff-necked as your ancestors were, but yield yourselves to the LORD

and come to his sanctuary, which he has sanctified forever, and serve the LORD your God, so that his fierce anger may turn away from you. [9]For as you return to the LORD, your kindred and your children will find compassion with their captors, and return to this land. For the LORD your God is gracious and merciful, and will not turn away his face from you, if you return to him."

10 So the couriers went from city to city through the country of Ephraim and Manasseh, and as far as Zebulun; but they laughed them to scorn, and mocked them. [11]Only a few from Asher, Manasseh, and Zebulun humbled themselves and came to Jerusalem. [12]The hand of God was also on Judah to give them one heart to do what the king and the officials commanded by the word of the LORD.

13 Many people came together in Jerusalem to keep the festival of unleavened bread in the second month, a very large assembly. [14]They set to work and removed the altars that were in Jerusalem, and all the altars for offering incense they took away and threw into the Wadi Kidron. [15]They slaughtered the passover lamb on the fourteenth day of the second month. The priests and the Levites were ashamed, and they sanctified themselves and brought burnt offerings into the house of the LORD. [16]They took their accustomed posts according to the law of Moses the man of God; the priests dashed the blood that they received[i] from the hands of the Levites. [17]For there were many in the assembly who had not sanctified themselves; therefore the Levites had to slaughter the passover lamb for everyone who was not clean, to make it holy to the LORD. [18]For a multitude of the people, many of them from Ephraim, Manasseh, Issachar, and Zebulun, had not cleansed themselves, yet they ate the passover otherwise than as prescribed. But Hezekiah prayed for them, saying, "The good LORD pardon all [19]who set their hearts to seek God, the LORD the God of their ancestors, even though not in accordance with the sanctuary's rules of cleanness." [20]The LORD heard Hezekiah, and healed the people. [21]The people of Israel who were present at Jerusalem kept the festival of unleavened bread seven days with great gladness; and the Levites and the priests praised the LORD day by day, accompanied by loud instruments for the LORD. [22]Hezekiah spoke encouragingly to all the Levites who showed good skill in the service of the LORD. So the people ate the food of the festival for seven days, sacrificing offerings of well-being and giving thanks to the LORD the God of their ancestors.

23 Then the whole assembly agreed together to keep the festival for another seven days; so they kept it for another seven days with gladness. [24]For King Hezekiah of Judah gave the assembly a thousand bulls and seven thousand sheep for

---

[h] Heb *upright in heart*   [i] Heb lacks *that they received*

offerings, and the officials gave the assembly a thousand bulls and ten thousand sheep. The priests sanctified themselves in great numbers. [25]The whole assembly of Judah, the priests and the Levites, and the whole assembly that came out of Israel, and the resident aliens who came out of the land of Israel, and the resident aliens who lived in Judah, rejoiced. [26]There was great joy in Jerusalem, for since the time of Solomon son of King David of Israel there had been nothing like this in Jerusalem. [27]Then the priests and the Levites stood up and blessed the people, and their voice was heard; their prayer came to his holy dwelling in heaven.

Pagan Shrines Destroyed

31 Now when all this was finished, all Israel who were present went out to the cities of Judah and broke down the pillars, hewed down the sacred poles,[j] and pulled down the high places and the altars throughout all Judah and Benjamin, and in Ephraim and Manasseh, until they had destroyed them all. Then all the people of Israel returned to their cities, all to their individual properties.

[2] Hezekiah appointed the divisions of the priests and of the Levites, division by division, everyone according to his service, the priests and the Levites, for burnt offerings and offerings of well-being, to minister in the gates of the camp of the LORD and to give thanks and praise. [3]The contribution of the king from his own possessions was for the burnt offerings: the burnt offerings of morning and evening, and the burnt offerings for the sabbaths, the new moons, and the appointed festivals, as it is written in the law of the LORD. [4]He commanded the people who lived in Jerusalem to give the portion due to the priests and the Levites, so that they might devote themselves to the law of the LORD. [5]As soon as the word spread, the people of Israel gave in abundance the first fruits of grain, wine, oil, honey, and of all the produce of the field; and they brought in abundantly the tithe of everything. [6]The people of Israel and Judah who lived in the cities of Judah also brought in the tithe of cattle and sheep, and the tithe of the dedicated things that had been consecrated to the LORD their God, and laid them in heaps. [7]In the third month they began to pile up the heaps, and finished them in the seventh month. [8]When Hezekiah and the officials came and saw the heaps, they blessed the LORD and his people Israel. [9]Hezekiah questioned the priests and the Levites about the heaps. [10]The chief priest Azariah, who was of the house of Zadok, answered him, "Since they began to bring the contributions into the house of the LORD, we have had enough to eat and have plenty to spare; for

the LORD has blessed his people, so that we have this great supply left over."

Reorganization of Priests and Levites

[11] Then Hezekiah commanded them to prepare store-chambers in the house of the LORD; and they prepared them. [12]Faithfully they brought in the contributions, the tithes and the dedicated things. The chief officer in charge of them was Conaniah the Levite, with his brother Shimei as second; [13]while Jehiel, Azaziah, Nahath, Asahel, Jerimoth, Jozabad, Eliel, Ismachiah, Mahath, and Benaiah were overseers assisting Conaniah and his brother Shimei, by the appointment of King Hezekiah and of Azariah the chief officer of the house of God. [14]Kore son of Imnah the Levite, keeper of the east gate, was in charge of the freewill offerings to God, to apportion the contribution reserved for the LORD and the most holy offerings. [15]Eden, Miniamin, Jeshua, Shemaiah, Amariah, and Shecaniah were faithfully assisting him in the cities of the priests, to distribute the portions to their kindred, old and young alike, by divisions, [16]except those enrolled by genealogy, males from three years old and upwards, all who entered the house of the LORD as the duty of each day required, for their service according to their offices, by their divisions. [17]The enrollment of the priests was according to their ancestral houses; that of the Levites from twenty years old and upwards was according to their offices, by their divisions. [18]The priests were enrolled with all their little children, their wives, their sons, and their daughters, the whole multitude; for they were faithful in keeping themselves holy. [19]And for the descendants of Aaron, the priests, who were in the fields of common land belonging to their towns, town by town, the people designated by name were to distribute portions to every male among the priests and to everyone among the Levites who was enrolled.

[20] Hezekiah did this throughout all Judah; he did what was good and right and faithful before the LORD his God. [21]And every work that he undertook in the service of the house of God, and in accordance with the law and the commandments, to seek his God, he did with all his heart; and he prospered.

Sennacherib's Invasion

32 After these things and these acts of faithfulness, King Sennacherib of Assyria came and invaded Judah and encamped against the fortified cities, thinking to win them for himself. [2]When Hezekiah saw that Sennacherib had come and intended to fight against Jerusalem, [3]he planned with his officers and his warriors to stop the flow of the springs that were outside the city; and they helped him. [4]A great many people were

gathered, and they stopped all the springs and the wadi that flowed through the land, saying, "Why should the Assyrian kings come and find water in abundance?" ⁵Hezekiah*ᵏ* set to work resolutely and built up the entire wall that was broken down, and raised towers on it,*ˡ* and outside it he built another wall; he also strengthened the Millo in the city of David, and made weapons and shields in abundance. ⁶He appointed combat commanders over the people, and gathered them together to him in the square at the gate of the city and spoke encouragingly to them, saying, ⁷"Be strong and of good courage. Do not be afraid or dismayed before the king of Assyria and all the horde that is with him; for there is one greater with us than with him. ⁸With him is an arm of flesh; but with us is the LORD our God, to help us and to fight our battles." The people were encouraged by the words of King Hezekiah of Judah.

9 After this, while King Sennacherib of Assyria was at Lachish with all his forces, he sent his servants to Jerusalem to King Hezekiah of Judah and to all the people of Judah that were in Jerusalem, saying, ¹⁰"Thus says King Sennacherib of Assyria: On what are you relying, that you undergo the siege of Jerusalem? ¹¹Is not Hezekiah mis-

ᵏ Heb *He*   *ˡ* Vg: Heb *and raised on the towers*

Lessons from the Battlefield
What made Judah win some wars and lose others?

> "Do not be afraid or dismayed before the king of Assyria and all the horde that is with him; for there is one greater with us than with him." 32.7

NO KING OF JUDAH HAD a wholly peaceful reign. As a result, much of the action in 2 Chronicles takes place on a battlefield. And, in a nutshell, here is the book's philosophy of war: "Humble yourself and rely totally on God—regardless of the odds against you. If you rely on your own military might or that of powerful neighbors, you will lose."

Listening to the Prophets

Chapter 12, for example, tells of a grave crisis facing Judah's very first king. Five years into Rehoboam's reign, a huge military machine from Egypt rolled in with chariots and battering rams. Surrounded, Rehoboam wanted a word of hope from a prophet. Instead, he got a rebuke: "Thus says the LORD: 'You abandoned me, so I have abandoned you to the hand of Shishak'" (12.5).

God was using the armies of Egypt to punish Judah for its errors. This first invasion set a pattern: Whenever an immoral king corrupted the nation, God sent an invading army as punishment.

Often the kings of Judah ignored their prophets' hard advice. But in this first case, King Rehoboam repented and humbled himself, saving his country from even greater devastation.

A Wrong Way and a Right Way

Few kings had the faith to believe in God alone at moments of great peril. Even the best of them reached into the royal treasury and purchased help from neighboring nations. When they did, Judah usually ended up weaker than before. But 2 Chronicles concentrates on the good moments, when kings turned to God.

King Jehoshaphat was a textbook example of the proper response. He called the entire nation together in a giant prayer meeting (20.4–28). When the time came for battle, he sent a choir in front of his army to sing praises to God. Judah's enemies all turned on each other and Jehoshaphat's armies marched home victorious.

Hezekiah's Faith

Perhaps the greatest single example of a king following his prophet's advice occurred during the reign of Hezekiah. The Bible reports the incident in three places: 2 Chronicles 32, 2 Kings 18–19, and Isaiah 36–37. At the time, Judah's situation looked hopeless. Mighty Assyria had taken 27 cities and villages in Judah and was now laying siege to Jerusalem.

Hezekiah showed his true moral strength by joining together with the prophet Isaiah to humble himself in prayer. God granted a miracle that drove off the Assyrian army.

Second Chronicles stressed incidents like these as a lesson to its first readers, who had inherited a land in ruins. Looking back over their history, they could see what had gone wrong: The nation had forgotten to rely on God. To rebuild their nation they would have to relearn the simple faith that had brought them victory in the past.

Life Questions: What does it mean to trust God completely today?

leading you, handing you over to die by famine and by thirst, when he tells you, 'The LORD our God will save us from the hand of the king of Assyria'? ¹²Was it not this same Hezekiah who

32.1–21 Invasion

Sennacherib's campaign is well-documented, for he kept scrupulous records of his military ventures. Invading Palestine in 701 B.C., his armies captured 46 cities in Judah and then laid siege to Jerusalem. The Bible includes three different accounts of this major event: here, in 2 Kings 18, and in Isaiah 36.

took away his high places and his altars and commanded Judah and Jerusalem, saying, 'Before one altar you shall worship, and upon it you shall make your offerings'? ¹³Do you not know what I and my ancestors have done to all the peoples of other lands? Were the gods of the nations of those lands at all able to save their lands out of my hand? ¹⁴Who among all the gods of those nations that my ancestors utterly destroyed was able to save his people from my hand, that your God should be able to save you from my hand? ¹⁵Now therefore do not let Hezekiah deceive you or mislead you in this fashion, and do not believe him, for no god of any nation or kingdom has been able to save his people from my hand or from the hand of my ancestors. How much less will your God save you out of my hand!"

16 His servants said still more against the Lord GOD and against his servant Hezekiah. ¹⁷He also wrote letters to throw contempt on the LORD the God of Israel and to speak against him, saying, "Just as the gods of the nations in other lands did not rescue their people from my hands, so the God of Hezekiah will not rescue his people from my hand." ¹⁸They shouted it with a loud voice in the language of Judah to the people of Jerusalem who were on the wall, to frighten and terrify them, in order that they might take the city. ¹⁹They spoke of the God of Jerusalem as if he were like the gods of the peoples of the earth, which are the work of human hands.

Sennacherib's Defeat and Death

20 Then King Hezekiah and the prophet Isaiah son of Amoz prayed because of this and cried to heaven. ²¹And the LORD sent an angel who cut off all the mighty warriors and commanders and officers in the camp of the king of Assyria. So he returned in disgrace to his own land. When he came into the house of his god, some of his own sons struck him down there with the sword. ²²So the LORD saved Hezekiah and the inhabitants of

Jerusalem from the hand of King Sennacherib of Assyria and from the hand of all his enemies; he gave them rest*m* on every side. ²³Many brought gifts to the LORD in Jerusalem and precious things to King Hezekiah of Judah, so that he was exalted in the sight of all nations from that time onward.

Hezekiah's Sickness

24 In those days Hezekiah became sick and was at the point of death. He prayed to the LORD, and he answered him and gave him a sign. ²⁵But Hezekiah did not respond according to the benefit done to him, for his heart was proud. Therefore wrath came upon him and upon Judah and Jerusalem. ²⁶Then Hezekiah humbled himself for the pride of his heart, both he and the inhabitants of Jerusalem, so that the wrath of the LORD did not come upon them in the days of Hezekiah.

Hezekiah's Prosperity and Achievements

27 Hezekiah had very great riches and honor; and he made for himself treasuries for silver, for gold, for precious stones, for spices, for shields, and for all kinds of costly objects; ²⁸storehouses also for the yield of grain, wine, and oil; and stalls for all kinds of cattle, and sheepfolds.*n* ²⁹He likewise provided cities for himself, and flocks and herds in abundance; for God had given him very great possessions. ³⁰This same Hezekiah closed the upper outlet of the waters of Gihon and directed them down to the west side of the city of David. Hezekiah prospered in all his works. ³¹So also in the matter of the envoys of the officials of Babylon, who had been sent to him to inquire about the sign that had been done in the land, God left him to himself, in order to test him and to know all that was in his heart.

32 Now the rest of the acts of Hezekiah, and his good deeds, are written in the vision of the prophet Isaiah son of Amoz in the Book of the Kings of Judah and Israel. ³³Hezekiah slept with his ancestors, and they buried him on the ascent to the tombs of the descendants of David; and all Judah and the inhabitants of Jerusalem did him honor at his death. His son Manasseh succeeded him.

Reign of Manasseh

33 Manasseh was twelve years old when he began to reign; he reigned fifty-five years in Jerusalem. ²He did what was evil in the sight of the LORD, according to the abominable practices of the nations whom the LORD drove out before the people of Israel. ³For he rebuilt the high places that his father Hezekiah had pulled down, and erected altars to the Baals, made sacred poles,*o* worshiped all the host of heaven, and served them. ⁴He built altars in the house of the LORD, of which the LORD had said, "In Jerusalem shall my

m Gk Vg: Heb *guided them*   *n* Gk Vg: Heb *flocks for folds*   *o* Heb *Asheroth*

name be forever." [5]He built altars for all the host
of heaven in the two courts of the house of the
LORD. [6]He made his son pass through fire in the
valley of the son of Hinnom, practiced soothsaying and augury and sorcery, and dealt with mediums and with wizards. He did much evil in the
sight of the LORD, provoking him to anger. [7]The
carved image of the idol that he had made he set
in the house of God, of which God said to David
and to his son Solomon, "In this house, and in
Jerusalem, which I have chosen out of all the
tribes of Israel, I will put my name forever; [8]I will
never again remove the feet of Israel from the
land that I appointed for your ancestors, if only
they will be careful to do all that I have commanded them, all the law, the statutes, and the
ordinances given through Moses." [9]Manasseh
misled Judah and the inhabitants of Jerusalem, so
that they did more evil than the nations whom the
LORD had destroyed before the people of Israel.

Manasseh Restored after Repentance

10 The LORD spoke to Manasseh and to his
people, but they gave no heed. [11]Therefore the
LORD brought against them the commanders of
the army of the king of Assyria, who took Manasseh captive in manacles, bound him with fetters,
and brought him to Babylon. [12]While he was in
distress he entreated the favor of the LORD his
God and humbled himself greatly before the God
of his ancestors. [13]He prayed to him, and God
received his entreaty, heard his plea, and restored
him again to Jerusalem and to his kingdom. Then
Manasseh knew that the LORD indeed was God.

33.13 A Tardy Change of Mind

Unlike the other history books, Chronicles records great moments of faith, even when they have no lasting consequences for the nation as a whole. Second Chronicles characteristically adds a new perspective on the reign of Manasseh, one of Judah's worst kings. While acknowledging his weaknesses, it adds this account of his amazing turnabout late in life. This brief episode gave an object lesson to the nation on what happens when even a wicked king repents.

14 Afterward he built an outer wall for the
city of David west of Gihon, in the valley, reaching the entrance at the Fish Gate; he carried it
around Ophel, and raised it to a very great height.
He also put commanders of the army in all the
fortified cities in Judah. [15]He took away the foreign gods and the idol from the house of the
LORD, and all the altars that he had built on the
mountain of the house of the LORD and in Jerusalem, and he threw them out of the city. [16]He also
restored the altar of the LORD and offered on it
sacrifices of well-being and of thanksgiving; and
he commanded Judah to serve the LORD the God
of Israel. [17]The people, however, still sacrificed at
the high places, but only to the LORD their God.

Death of Manasseh

18 Now the rest of the acts of Manasseh, his
prayer to his God, and the words of the seers who
spoke to him in the name of the LORD God of
Israel, these are in the Annals of the Kings of
Israel. [19]His prayer, and how God received his
entreaty, all his sin and his faithlessness, the sites
on which he built high places and set up the sacred poles[p] and the images, before he humbled
himself, these are written in the records of the
seers.[q] [20]So Manasseh slept with his ancestors,
and they buried him in his house. His son Amon
succeeded him.

Amon's Reign and Death

21 Amon was twenty-two years old when he
began to reign; he reigned two years in Jerusalem.
[22]He did what was evil in the sight of the LORD, as
his father Manasseh had done. Amon sacrificed to
all the images that his father Manasseh had made,
and served them. [23]He did not humble himself
before the LORD, as his father Manasseh had humbled himself, but this Amon incurred more and
more guilt. [24]His servants conspired against him
and killed him in his house. [25]But the people of
the land killed all those who had conspired
against King Amon; and the people of the land
made his son Josiah king to succeed him.

Reign of Josiah

34 Josiah was eight years old when he began
to reign; he reigned thirty-one years in Jerusalem. [2]He did what was right in the sight of the
LORD, and walked in the ways of his ancestor
David; he did not turn aside to the right or to the
left. [3]For in the eighth year of his reign, while he
was still a boy, he began to seek the God of his
ancestor David, and in the twelfth year he began
to purge Judah and Jerusalem of the high places,
the sacred poles,[p] and the carved and the cast
images. [4]In his presence they pulled down the
altars of the Baals; he demolished the incense altars that stood above them. He broke down the
sacred poles[p] and the carved and the cast images;
he made dust of them and scattered it over the
graves of those who had sacrificed to them. [5]He
also burned the bones of the priests on their altars, and purged Judah and Jerusalem. [6]In the
towns of Manasseh, Ephraim, and Simeon, and as
far as Naphtali, in their ruins[r] all around, [7]he
broke down the altars, beat the sacred poles[p] and
the images into powder, and demolished all the

[p] Heb *Asherim* [q] One Ms Gk: MT *of Hozai* [r] Meaning of Heb uncertain

incense altars throughout all the land of Israel. Then he returned to Jerusalem.

Discovery of the Book of the Law

8 In the eighteenth year of his reign, when he had purged the land and the house, he sent Shaphan son of Azaliah, Maaseiah the governor of the city, and Joah son of Joahaz, the recorder, to repair the house of the LORD his God. ⁹They came to the high priest Hilkiah and delivered the money that had been brought into the house of God, which the Levites, the keepers of the threshold, had collected from Manasseh and Ephraim and from all the remnant of Israel and from all Judah and Benjamin and from the inhabitants of Jerusalem. ¹⁰They delivered it to the workers who had the oversight of the house of the LORD, and the workers who were working in the house of the LORD gave it for repairing and restoring the house. ¹¹They gave it to the carpenters and the builders to buy quarried stone, and timber for binders, and beams for the buildings that the kings of Judah had let go to ruin. ¹²The people did the work faithfully. Over them were appointed the Levites Jahath and Obadiah, of the sons of Merari, along with Zechariah and Meshullam, of the sons of the Kohathites, to have oversight. Other Levites, all skillful with instruments of music, ¹³were over the burden bearers and directed all who did work in every kind of service; and some of the Levites were scribes, and officials, and gatekeepers.

14 While they were bringing out the money that had been brought into the house of the LORD, the priest Hilkiah found the book of the law of the LORD given through Moses. ¹⁵Hilkiah said to the secretary Shaphan, "I have found the book of the law in the house of the LORD"; and Hilkiah gave the book to Shaphan. ¹⁶Shaphan brought the book to the king, and further reported to the king, "All that was committed to your servants they are doing. ¹⁷They have emptied out the money that was found in the house of the LORD and have delivered it into the hand of the overseers and the workers." ¹⁸The secretary Shaphan informed the king, "The priest Hilkiah has given me a book." Shaphan then read it aloud to the king.

19 When the king heard the words of the law he tore his clothes. ²⁰Then the king commanded Hilkiah, Ahikam son of Shaphan, Abdon son of Micah, the secretary Shaphan, and the king's servant Asaiah: ²¹"Go, inquire of the LORD for me and for those who are left in Israel and in Judah, concerning the words of the book that has been found; for the wrath of the LORD that is poured out on us is great, because our ancestors did not keep the word of the LORD, to act in accordance with all that is written in this book."

The Prophet Huldah Consulted

22 So Hilkiah and those whom the king had sent went to the prophet Huldah, the wife of Shallum son of Tokhath son of Hasrah, keeper of the wardrobe (who lived in Jerusalem in the Second Quarter) and spoke to her to that effect. ²³She declared to them, "Thus says the LORD, the God of Israel: Tell the man who sent you to me, ²⁴Thus says the LORD: I will indeed bring disaster upon this place and upon its inhabitants, all the curses that are written in the book that was read before the king of Judah. ²⁵Because they have forsaken me and have made offerings to other gods, so that they have provoked me to anger with all the works of their hands, my wrath will be poured out on this place and will not be quenched. ²⁶But as to the king of Judah, who sent you to inquire of the LORD, thus shall you say to him: Thus says the LORD, the God of Israel: Regarding the words that you have heard, ²⁷because your heart was penitent and you humbled yourself before God when you heard his words against this place and its inhabitants, and you have humbled yourself before me, and have torn your clothes and wept before me, I also have heard you, says the LORD. ²⁸I will gather you to your ancestors and you shall be gathered to your grave in peace; your eyes shall not see all the disaster that I will bring on this place and its inhabitants." They took the message back to the king.

The Covenant Renewed

29 Then the king sent word and gathered together all the elders of Judah and Jerusalem. ³⁰The king went up to the house of the LORD, with all the people of Judah, the inhabitants of Jerusalem, the priests and the Levites, all the people both great and small; he read in their hearing all the words of the book of the covenant that had been found in the house of the LORD. ³¹The king stood in his place and made a covenant before the LORD, to follow the LORD, keeping his commandments, his decrees, and his statutes, with all his heart and all his soul, to perform the words of the covenant that were written in this book. ³²Then he made all who were present in Jerusalem and in Benjamin pledge themselves to it. And the inhabitants of Jerusalem acted according to the covenant of God, the God of their ancestors. ³³Josiah took away all the abominations from all the territory that belonged to the people of Israel, and made all who were in Israel worship the LORD their God. All his days they did not turn away from following the LORD the God of their ancestors.

Celebration of the Passover

35 Josiah kept a passover to the LORD in Jerusalem; they slaughtered the passover lamb on the fourteenth day of the first month. ²He appointed the priests to their offices and encouraged them in the service of the house of the LORD. ³He said to the Levites who taught all Israel and who were holy to the LORD, "Put the holy ark in the house that Solomon son of David, king of Israel, built; you need no longer carry it on your shoulders. Now serve the LORD your God and his people Israel. 4Make preparations by your ancestral houses by your divisions, following the written directions of King David of Israel and the written directions of his son Solomon. 5Take position in the holy place according to the groupings of the ancestral houses of your kindred the people, and let there be Levites for each division of an ancestral house.s 6Slaughter the passover lamb, sanctify yourselves, and on behalf of your kindred make preparations, acting according to the word of the LORD by Moses."

7 Then Josiah contributed to the people, as passover offerings for all that were present, lambs and kids from the flock to the number of thirty thousand, and three thousand bulls; these were from the king's possessions. 8His officials contributed willingly to the people, to the priests, and to the Levites. Hilkiah, Zechariah, and Jehiel, the chief officers of the house of God, gave to the priests for the passover offerings two thousand six hundred lambs and kids and three hundred bulls. 9Conaniah also, and his brothers Shemaiah and Nethanel, and Hashabiah and Jeiel and Jozabad, the chiefs of the Levites, gave to the Levites for the passover offerings five thousand lambs and kids and five hundred bulls.

10 When the service had been prepared for, the priests stood in their place, and the Levites in their divisions according to the king's command. 11They slaughtered the passover lamb, and the priests dashed the blood that they receivedt from them, while the Levites did the skinning. 12They set aside the burnt offerings so that they might distribute them according to the groupings of the ancestral houses of the people, to offer to the LORD, as it is written in the book of Moses. And they did the same with the bulls. 13They roasted the passover lamb with fire according to the ordinance; and they boiled the holy offerings in pots, in caldrons, and in pans, and carried them quickly to all the people. 14Afterward they made preparations for themselves and for the priests, because the priests the descendants of Aaron were occupied in offering the burnt offerings and the fat parts until night; so the Levites made preparations for themselves and for the priests, the descendants of Aaron. 15The singers, the descendants of Asaph, were in their place according to the command of David, and Asaph, and Heman, and the king's seer Jeduthun. The gatekeepers were at each gate; they did not need to interrupt their service, for their kindred the Levites made preparations for them.

16 So all the service of the LORD was prepared

that day, to keep the passover and to offer burnt offerings on the altar of the LORD, according to the command of King Josiah. 17The people of Israel who were present kept the passover at that time, and the festival of unleavened bread seven days. 18No passover like it had been kept in Israel since the days of the prophet Samuel; none of the kings of Israel had kept such a passover as was kept by Josiah, by the priests and the Levites, by all Judah and Israel who were present, and by the inhabitants of Jerusalem. 19In the eighteenth year of the reign of Josiah this passover was kept.

Defeat by Pharaoh Neco and Death of Josiah

20 After all this, when Josiah had set the temple in order, King Neco of Egypt went up to fight at Carchemish on the Euphrates, and Josiah went out against him. 21But Necou sent envoys to him, saying, "What have I to do with you, king of Judah? I am not coming against you today, but against the house with which I am at war; and God has commanded me to hurry. Cease opposing God, who is with me, so that he will not destroy you." 22But Josiah would not turn away from him, but disguised himself in order to fight with him. He did not listen to the words of Neco from the mouth of God, but joined battle in the

35.22 A Bloody Battlefield

Some historians estimate that the valley of Megiddo has seen more fighting and bloodshed than any other spot on earth. Sitting astride the chief north-south trade route in Canaan, it has great strategic significance. The book of Revelation records that the last battle of the age, Harmagedon, will take place here (Revelation 16.16).

plain of Megiddo. 23The archers shot King Josiah; and the king said to his servants, "Take me away, for I am badly wounded." 24So his servants took him out of the chariot and carried him in his second chariotv and brought him to Jerusalem. There he died, and was buried in the tombs of his ancestors. All Judah and Jerusalem mourned for Josiah. 25Jeremiah also uttered a lament for Josiah, and all the singing men and singing women have spoken of Josiah in their laments to this day. They made these a custom in Israel; they are recorded in the Laments. 26Now the rest of the acts of Josiah and his faithful deeds in accordance with what is written in the law of the LORD, 27and his acts, first and last, are written in the Book of the Kings of Israel and Judah.

---

s Meaning of Heb uncertain   t Heb lacks *that they received*   u Heb he   v Or *the chariot of his deputy*

Reign of Jehoahaz

36 The people of the land took Jehoahaz son of Josiah and made him king to succeed his father in Jerusalem. ²Jehoahaz was twenty-three years old when he began to reign; he reigned three months in Jerusalem. ³Then the king of Egypt deposed him in Jerusalem and laid on the land a tribute of one hundred talents of silver and one talent of gold. ⁴The king of Egypt made his brother Eliakim king over Judah and Jerusalem, and changed his name to Jehoiakim; but Neco took his brother Jehoahaz and carried him to Egypt.

Reign and Captivity of Jehoiakim

5 Jehoiakim was twenty-five years old when he began to reign; he reigned eleven years in Jerusalem. He did what was evil in the sight of the LORD his God. ⁶Against him King Nebuchadnezzar of Babylon came up, and bound him with fetters to take him to Babylon. ⁷Nebuchadnezzar also carried some of the vessels of the house of the LORD to Babylon and put them in his palace in Babylon. ⁸Now the rest of the acts of Jehoiakim, and the abominations that he did, and what was found against him, are written in the Book of the Kings of Israel and Judah; and his son Jehoiachin succeeded him.

Reign and Captivity of Jehoiachin

9 Jehoiachin was eight years old when he began to reign; he reigned three months and ten days in Jerusalem. He did what was evil in the sight of the LORD. ¹⁰In the spring of the year King Nebuchadnezzar sent and brought him to Babylon, along with the precious vessels of the house of the LORD, and made his brother Zedekiah king over Judah and Jerusalem.

Reign of Zedekiah

11 Zedekiah was twenty-one years old when he began to reign; he reigned eleven years in Jerusalem. ¹²He did what was evil in the sight of the LORD his God. He did not humble himself before the prophet Jeremiah who spoke from the mouth of the LORD. ¹³He also rebelled against King Nebuchadnezzar, who had made him swear by God; he stiffened his neck and hardened his heart against turning to the LORD, the God of Israel. ¹⁴All the leading priests and the people also were exceedingly unfaithful, following all the abominations of the nations; and they polluted the house of the LORD that he had consecrated in Jerusalem.

The Fall of Jerusalem

15 The LORD, the God of their ancestors, sent persistently to them by his messengers, because he had compassion on his people and on his dwelling place; ¹⁶but they kept mocking the messengers of God, despising his words, and scoffing at his prophets, until the wrath of the LORD against his people became so great that there was no remedy.

17 Therefore he brought up against them the king of the Chaldeans, who killed their youths with the sword in the house of their sanctuary, and had no compassion on young man or young woman, the aged or the feeble; he gave them all into his hand. ¹⁸All the vessels of the house of God, large and small, and the treasures of the house of the LORD, and the treasures of the king and of his officials, all these he brought to Babylon. ¹⁹They burned the house of God, broke down the wall of Jerusalem, burned all its palaces with fire, and destroyed all its precious vessels.

36.19 Between the Temples

For about 70 years the Jews had no temple. The first local synagogues probably developed during this time, as gathering places where Jews could hear readings from the Old Testament and offer prayers. The last few verses of Chronicles hint that a more hopeful time is coming when the temple will be rebuilt. These verses are repeated at the beginning of Ezra. Most scholars believe Chronicles, Ezra, and Nehemiah were originally connected in one book.

²⁰He took into exile in Babylon those who had escaped from the sword, and they became servants to him and to his sons until the establishment of the kingdom of Persia, ²¹to fulfill the word of the LORD by the mouth of Jeremiah, until the land had made up for its sabbaths. All the days that it lay desolate it kept sabbath, to fulfill seventy years.

Cyrus Proclaims Liberty for the Exiles

22 In the first year of King Cyrus of Persia, in fulfillment of the word of the LORD spoken by Jeremiah, the LORD stirred up the spirit of King Cyrus of Persia so that he sent a herald throughout all his kingdom and also declared in a written edict: ²³"Thus says King Cyrus of Persia: The LORD, the God of heaven, has given me all the kingdoms of the earth, and he has charged me to build him a house at Jerusalem, which is in Judah. Whoever is among you of all his people, may the LORD his God be with him! Let him go up."

EZRA

Beginning Again

For the exiles from Babylon, news almost too good to be true

E ZRA BEGINS WITH EXILES RETURNING to a ruined city—a brush-covered ghost town burned and pillaged nearly 50 years before by an overpowering Babylonian army. Would Jerusalem now have a new beginning?

Psalm 126 captures the returning exiles' feelings: "We were like those who dream. Then our mouth was filled with laughter, and our tongue with shouts of joy." The Persian empire had conquered mighty Babylon and, under the emperor Cyrus, offered all Jews a chance to return to their land. It was too good to believe.

> *Many of the priests and Levites and heads of families, old people who had seen the first house on its foundations, wept with a loud voice . . . though many shouted aloud for joy. 3.12*

A New Start with God

One poet in exile had written, "If I forget you, O Jerusalem, let my right hand wither!" (Psalm 137.5). These returned exiles were the minority who, decades afterwards, had not forgotten. They treasured their spiritual heritage more than the houses and businesses they had built in Babylon. They wanted to live and worship in the place God had given his people. Any sacrifice was worth this opportunity. Their first impulse when they arrived was to rebuild the temple, God's home.

The tolerant Persians (whose official policy was to encourage the local religion in every area they governed) had even brought out the silver and gold temple articles, carefully preserved in a Babylonian temple as though waiting on God's timing. When the returned exiles laid the foundation to the new temple, the sound of their shouting (and noisy weeping) could be heard from far away (3.13). The temple, after all, was the place where they would meet God. It symbolized a new start with him.

The Problems of Beginning Again

God had opened the way, but the exiles needed determination to follow it. The book of Ezra divides into three parts, each one dealing with an obstacle that arose. The first part tells how, immediately after the return of the exiles, their neighbors in the surrounding countryside became hostile. After their deceptive offer of "help" was turned down, these neighbors began a campaign of opposition. They managed to stop further progress on the temple.

The temple lay in ruins for nearly 20 more years, until the prophets Haggai and Zechariah (whose messages are recorded in the books named after them) again stirred up interest in building. This "second push" is described in chapters 5 and 6. When opposition arose this time, the Jews managed to push through—again with the assistance of a Persian king.

Another problem preoccupies the final four chapters. Ezra, the man after whom this book is named, actually arrived in Jerusalem during this period, 80 years after the first party. The temple had by then been up for half a century. But the "new beginning" stood in severe jeopardy again. The Jews had begun to mingle (and compromise their faith) with the hostile people around them. Ezra's leadership, which came from deep biblical faith and genuine sorrow over sin, forced a radical, painful solution.

Ezra Leads Up to Jesus

The book of Ezra introduces an entirely new period in Israel's history—a period in which they became more like a church than a nation. Israelites before the exile had given much of their energy to fighting enemy armies. Now they focused on fighting sin and spiritual compromise.

The minority who returned could build a temple only with the permission of a foreign government in Persia. They had lost political independence, yet they clung to their religion, especially to the Old Testament Scriptures and temple worship. They feared repeating the mistakes that had sent them into exile. True, they did flirt with spiritual compromise. Yet when God's prophets spoke, people responded.

As those who had chosen a ruined Jerusalem over a prosperous Babylon, the returned Jews looked to God instead of to government for help. Still they dreamed, more than ever, of the powerful Messiah the prophets promised. This dream, and their strong determination to obey the law of God, continued right up until the time of Jesus, about 450 years after Ezra's last words.

How to Read Ezra

The book of Ezra describes several highly emotional events. Yet it reads like a historical report, citing official documents, letters, and lists written over an 80-year span. You are often left to imagine for yourself the feelings of the returning exiles. The book can, therefore, seem confusing and dry unless you take time to imagine how the scenes must have looked and to reflect on how people must have felt.

The three distinct periods Ezra deals with all have the same theme: a new beginning for God's people. In each situation God gave opportunity and the outside world threatened it. God's people drifted back and forth in their response. Carefully take note of the "messages" from both God and the world, and how the Israelites responded. Examine Ezra's model, as an unwavering man of the law as well as of deep personal faith.

To understand how Ezra fits into Israel's long-term pattern of response to God and the world, read some historical background. Articles on "Ezra," "Haggai" or "Israel, History of" in a Bible dictionary may offer the best summary. The short book of Haggai zeroes in on the crucial months described in Ezra 5.1−2 and makes a valuable companion to any study of Ezra.

PEOPLE YOU'LL MEET IN EZRA

EZRA (p. 485)
ARTAXERXES (p. 486)

3-TRACK READING PLAN

For an explanation and complete listing of the 3-track reading plan, turn to page 7.

TRACK 1: *Two-Week Courses on the Bible*
See page 7 for information on these courses.

TRACK 2: *An Overview of Ezra in 1 Day*
☐ Day 1. Read the Introduction to Ezra and chapter 3 for the emotional story of how the returned exiles laid the foundation for the new temple.
Now turn to page 9 for your next Track 2 reading project.

TRACK 3: *All of Ezra in 9 Days*
After you have read through Ezra, turn to pages 10–14 for your next Track 3 reading project.
☐1–2 ☐3 ☐4 ☐5 ☐6 ☐7 ☐8 ☐9
☐10

End of the Babylonian Captivity

1 In the first year of King Cyrus of Persia, in order that the word of the LORD by the mouth of Jeremiah might be accomplished, the LORD stirred up the spirit of King Cyrus of Persia so that he sent a herald throughout all his kingdom, and also in a written edict declared:

2 "Thus says King Cyrus of Persia: The LORD, the God of heaven, has given me all the kingdoms of the earth, and he has charged me to build him a house at Jerusalem in Judah. ³Any of those among you who are of his people—may their God be with them!—are now permitted to go up to Jerusalem in Judah, and rebuild the house of the LORD, the God of Israel—he is the God who is in Jerusalem; ⁴and let all survivors, in whatever place they reside, be assisted by the people of their place with silver and gold, with goods and with animals, besides freewill offerings for the house of God in Jerusalem."

5 The heads of the families of Judah and Benjamin, and the priests and the Levites—everyone

whose spirit God had stirred—got ready to go up and rebuild the house of the LORD in Jerusalem. 6All their neighbors aided them with silver vessels, with gold, with goods, with animals, and with valuable gifts, besides all that was freely offered.

1.2 Prediction Fulfilled

The fulfilled prophecy was probably Jeremiah 29.10, God's promise to bring Israel back to Jerusalem after 70 years. Additionally, Isaiah 44.28 and 45.1,13 had named Cyrus of Persia as God's agent to see Jerusalem and the temple rebuilt. This is not evidence that Cyrus worshiped Israel's God. He had a policy of religious tolerance and contributed to the rebuilding of several nations' temples.

7King Cyrus himself brought out the vessels of the house of the LORD that Nebuchadnezzar had carried away from Jerusalem and placed in the house of his gods. 8King Cyrus of Persia had them released into the charge of Mithredath the treasurer, who counted them out to Sheshbazzar the prince of Judah. 9And this was the inventory: gold basins, thirty; silver basins, one thousand; knives,[a] twenty-nine; 10gold bowls, thirty; other silver bowls, four hundred ten; other vessels, one thousand; 11the total of the gold and silver vessels was five thousand four hundred. All these Sheshbazzar brought up, when the exiles were brought up from Babylonia to Jerusalem.

List of the Returned Exiles

2 Now these were the people of the province who came from those captive exiles whom King Nebuchadnezzar of Babylon had carried captive to Babylonia; they returned to Jerusalem and Judah, all to their own towns. 2They came with Zerubbabel, Jeshua, Nehemiah, Seraiah, Re-

2.1 A People Preserved

Lists of names, whether in the Bible or the telephone book, make dull reading. But the way these names are grouped reveals God's care for the people of Israel. They had not lost track of their Israelite identity during two generations in Babylon. They knew their family record, and they could place themselves according to Israelite families, Israelite towns, and Israelite religious duties in the temple. Like the temple articles, carefully stored in readiness (1.7), these were a people preserved to serve God again.

elaiah, Mordecai, Bilshan, Mispar, Bigvai, Rehum, and Baanah.

The number of the Israelite people: 3the descendants of Parosh, two thousand one hundred seventy-two. 4Of Shephatiah, three hundred seventy-two. 5Of Arah, seven hundred seventy-five. 6Of Pahath-moab, namely the descendants of Jeshua and Joab, two thousand eight hundred twelve. 7Of Elam, one thousand two hundred fifty-four. 8Of Zattu, nine hundred forty-five. 9Of Zaccai, seven hundred sixty. 10Of Bani, six hundred forty-two. 11Of Bebai, six hundred twenty-three. 12Of Azgad, one thousand two hundred twenty-two. 13Of Adonikam, six hundred sixty-six. 14Of Bigvai, two thousand fifty-six. 15Of Adin, four hundred fifty-four. 16Of Ater, namely of Hezekiah, ninety-eight. 17Of Bezai, three hundred twenty-three. 18Of Jorah, one hundred twelve. 19Of Hashum, two hundred twenty-three. 20Of Gibbar, ninety-five. 21Of Bethlehem, one hundred twenty-three. 22The people of Netophah, fifty-six. 23Of Anathoth, one hundred twenty-eight. 24The descendants of Azmaveth, forty-two. 25Of Kiriatharim, Chephirah, and Beeroth, seven hundred forty-three. 26Of Ramah and Geba, six hundred twenty-one. 27The people of Michmas, one hundred twenty-two. 28Of Bethel and Ai, two hundred twenty-three. 29The descendants of Nebo, fifty-two. 30Of Magbish, one hundred fifty-six. 31Of the other Elam, one thousand two hundred fifty-four. 32Of Harim, three hundred twenty. 33Of Lod, Hadid, and Ono, seven hundred twenty-five. 34Of Jericho, three hundred forty-five. 35Of Senaah, three thousand six hundred thirty.

36 The priests: the descendants of Jedaiah, of the house of Jeshua, nine hundred seventy-three. 37Of Immer, one thousand fifty-two. 38Of Pashhur, one thousand two hundred forty-seven. 39Of Harim, one thousand seventeen.

40 The Levites: the descendants of Jeshua and Kadmiel, of the descendants of Hodaviah, seventy-four. 41The singers: the descendants of Asaph, one hundred twenty-eight. 42The descendants of the gatekeepers: of Shallum, of Ater, of Talmon, of Akkub, of Hatita, and of Shobai, in all one hundred thirty-nine.

43 The temple servants: the descendants of Ziha, Hasupha, Tabbaoth, 44Keros, Siaha, Padon, 45Lebanah, Hagabah, Akkub, 46Hagab, Shamlai, Hanan, 47Giddel, Gahar, Reaiah, 48Rezin, Nekoda, Gazzam, 49Uzza, Paseah, Besai, 50Asnah, Meunim, Nephisim, 51Bakbuk, Hakupha, Harhur, 52Bazluth, Mehida, Harsha, 53Barkos, Sisera, Temah, 54Neziah, and Hatipha.

55 The descendants of Solomon's servants: Sotai, Hassophereth, Peruda, 56Jaalah, Darkon, Giddel, 57Shephatiah, Hattil, Pochereth-hazzebaim, and Ami.

[a] Vg: Meaning of Heb uncertain

58 All the temple servants and the descendants of Solomon's servants were three hundred ninety-two.

59 The following were those who came up from Tel-melah, Tel-harsha, Cherub, Addan, and Immer, though they could not prove their families or their descent, whether they belonged to Israel: ⁶⁰the descendants of Delaiah, Tobiah, and Nekoda, six hundred fifty-two. ⁶¹Also, of the descendants of the priests: the descendants of Habaiah, Hakkoz, and Barzillai (who had married one of the daughters of Barzillai the Gileadite, and was called by their name). ⁶²These looked for their entries in the genealogical records, but they were not found there, and so they were excluded from the priesthood as unclean; ⁶³the governor told them that they were not to partake of the most holy food, until there should be a priest to consult Urim and Thummim.

2.63 The Need for Guidance

The Urim and Thummim were probably something like dice. Priests in the Old Testament used them to determine God's will. Until the Urim and Thummim could be employed, the families whose records were lost (verse 62) had no way to establish themselves as genuine priests. For a people determined to follow God's word precisely, this mattered tremendously. God had said that only Aaron's descendants could touch the holy things in the sanctuary, on pain of death (Numbers 18.1–7).

64 The whole assembly together was forty-two thousand three hundred sixty, ⁶⁵besides their male and female servants, of whom there were seven thousand three hundred thirty-seven; and they had two hundred male and female singers. ⁶⁶They had seven hundred thirty-six horses, two hundred forty-five mules, ⁶⁷four hundred thirty-five camels, and six thousand seven hundred twenty donkeys.

68 As soon as they came to the house of the LORD in Jerusalem, some of the heads of families made freewill offerings for the house of God, to erect it on its site. ⁶⁹According to their resources they gave to the building fund sixty-one thousand darics of gold, five thousand minas of silver, and one hundred priestly robes.

70 The priests, the Levites, and some of the people lived in Jerusalem and its vicinity;ᵇ and the singers, the gatekeepers, and the temple servants lived in their towns, and all Israel in their towns.

Worship Restored at Jerusalem

3 When the seventh month came, and the Israelites were in the towns, the people gathered together in Jerusalem. ²Then Jeshua son of Jozadak, with his fellow priests, and Zerubbabel son of Shealtiel with his kin set out to build the altar of the God of Israel, to offer burnt offerings on it, as prescribed in the law of Moses the man of God. ³They set up the altar on its foundation, because they were in dread of the neighboring peoples, and they offered burnt offerings upon it to the LORD, morning and evening. ⁴And they kept the festival of booths,ᶜ as prescribed, and offered the daily burnt offerings by number according to the ordinance, as required for each day, ⁵and after that the regular burnt offerings, the offerings at the new moon and at all the sacred festivals of the LORD, and the offerings of everyone who made a freewill offering to the LORD. ⁶From the first day of the seventh month they began to offer burnt offerings to the LORD. But the foundation of the temple of the LORD was not yet laid. ⁷So they gave money to the masons and the carpenters, and food, drink, and oil to the Sidonians and the Tyrians to bring cedar trees from Lebanon to the sea, to Joppa, according to the grant that they had from King Cyrus of Persia.

Foundation Laid for the Temple

8 In the second year after their arrival at the house of God at Jerusalem, in the second month, Zerubbabel son of Shealtiel and Jeshua son of Jozadak made a beginning, together with the rest of their people, the priests and the Levites and all who had come to Jerusalem from the captivity. They appointed the Levites, from twenty years old and upward, to have the oversight of the work on the house of the LORD. ⁹And Jeshua with his sons and his kin, and Kadmiel and his sons, Binnui and Hodaviahᵈ along with the sons of Henadad, the Levites, their sons and kin, together took charge of the workers in the house of God.

10 When the builders laid the foundation of the temple of the LORD, the priests in their vestments were stationed to praise the LORD with trumpets, and the Levites, the sons of Asaph, with cymbals, according to the directions of King David of Israel; ¹¹and they sang responsively, praising and giving thanks to the LORD,

"For he is good,
    for his steadfast love endures forever
        toward Israel."

And all the people responded with a great shout when they praised the LORD, because the foundation of the house of the LORD was laid. ¹²But many of the priests and Levites and heads of families, old people who had seen the first house on its foundations, wept with a loud voice when they

---

ᵇ 1 Esdras 5.46: Heb lacks *lived in Jerusalem and its vicinity* Neh 7.43; 1 Esdras 5.58: Heb *sons of Judah*   ᶜ Or *tabernacles*; Heb *succoth*   ᵈ Compare 2.40;

saw this house, though many shouted aloud for joy, [13]so that the people could not distinguish the sound of the joyful shout from the sound of the people's weeping, for the people shouted so loudly that the sound was heard far away.

Resistance to Rebuilding the Temple

4 When the adversaries of Judah and Benjamin heard that the returned exiles were building a

4.1 How to Stop God's Work

Chapter 4 describes three different strategies used to hinder God's people: 1) Offer help that will lead to compromises or even a complete takeover of the project by unbelievers (verses 1–3). 2) Discourage, frighten, and frustrate God's people (verses 4–5). 3) Use official power to force them to stop (verses 23–24). Now as then, governments and opposition groups use these strategies to stop the work of believers.

temple to the LORD, the God of Israel, [2]they approached Zerubbabel and the heads of families and said to them, "Let us build with you, for we worship your God as you do, and we have been sacrificing to him ever since the days of King Esar-haddon of Assyria who brought us here." [3]But Zerubbabel, Jeshua, and the rest of the heads of families in Israel said to them, "You shall have no part with us in building a house to our God; but we alone will build to the LORD, the God of Israel, as King Cyrus of Persia has commanded us."

4 Then the people of the land discouraged the people of Judah, and made them afraid to build, [5]and they bribed officials to frustrate their plan throughout the reign of King Cyrus of Persia and until the reign of King Darius of Persia.

Rebuilding of Jerusalem Opposed

6 In the reign of Ahasuerus, in his accession year, they wrote an accusation against the inhabitants of Judah and Jerusalem.

7 And in the days of Artaxerxes, Bishlam and Mithredath and Tabeel and the rest of their associates wrote to King Artaxerxes of Persia; the letter was written in Aramaic and translated.[e] [8]Rehum the royal deputy and Shimshai the scribe wrote a letter against Jerusalem to King Artaxerxes as follows [9](then Rehum the royal deputy, Shimshai the scribe, and the rest of their associates, the judges, the envoys, the officials, the Persians, the people of Erech, the Babylonians, the people of Susa, that is, the Elamites, [10]and the rest of the nations whom the great and noble Osnappar deported and settled in the cities of Samaria

and in the rest of the province Beyond the River wrote—and now [11]this is a copy of the letter that they sent):

"To King Artaxerxes: Your servants, the people of the province Beyond the River, send greeting. And now [12]may it be known to the king that the Jews who came up from you to us have gone to Jerusalem. They are rebuilding that rebellious and wicked city; they are finishing the walls and repairing the foundations. [13]Now may it be known to the king that, if this city is rebuilt and the walls finished, they will not pay tribute, custom, or toll, and the royal revenue will be reduced. [14]Now because we share the salt of the palace and it is not fitting for us to witness the king's dishonor, therefore we send and inform the king, [15]so that a search may be made in the annals of your ancestors. You will discover in the annals that this is a rebellious city, hurtful to kings and provinces, and that sedition was stirred up in it from long ago. On that account this city was laid waste. [16]We make known to the king that, if this city is rebuilt and its walls finished, you will then have no possession in the province Beyond the River."

4.6–23 A Flash Forward

This section is a glance forward in history. The Israelites would continue to feel opposition from their neighbors even long after the temple was successfully completed. The quarrel described here, during Ahasuerus' and Artaxerxes' reigns, was not over the temple but the defensive wall to be built around Jerusalem—a wall Nehemiah, with Ezra's help, completed years later.

17 The king sent an answer: "To Rehum the royal deputy and Shimshai the scribe and the rest of their associates who live in Samaria and in the rest of the province Beyond the River, greeting. And now [18]the letter that you sent to us has been read in translation before me. [19]So I made a decree, and someone searched and discovered that this city has risen against kings from long ago, and that rebellion and sedition have been made in it. [20]Jerusalem has had mighty kings who ruled over the whole province Beyond the River, to whom tribute, custom, and toll were paid. [21]Therefore issue an order that these people be made to cease, and that this city not be rebuilt, until I make a decree. [22]Moreover, take care not to be slack in this matter; why should damage grow to the hurt of the king?"

23 Then when the copy of King Artaxerxes' letter was read before Rehum and the scribe

---

[e] Heb adds *in Aramaic,* indicating that 4.8-6.18 is in Aramaic. Another interpretation is *The letter was written in the Aramaic script and set forth in the Aramaic language*

Shimshai and their associates, they hurried to the Jews in Jerusalem and by force and power made them cease. 24At that time the work on the house of God in Jerusalem stopped and was discontinued until the second year of the reign of King Darius of Persia.

Restoration of the Temple Resumed

5 Now the prophets, Haggai[f] and Zechariah son of Iddo, prophesied to the Jews who were in Judah and Jerusalem, in the name of the God of Israel who was over them. 2Then Zerubbabel son of Shealtiel and Jeshua son of Jozadak set out to rebuild the house of God in Jerusalem; and with them were the prophets of God, helping them.

3 At the same time Tattenai the governor of the province Beyond the River and Shethar-bozenai and their associates came to them and spoke to them thus, "Who gave you a decree to build this house and to finish this structure?" 4They[g] also asked them this, "What are the names of the men who are building this building?" 5But the eye of their God was upon the elders of the Jews, and they did not stop them until a report reached Darius and then answer was returned by letter in reply to it.

6 The copy of the letter that Tattenai the governor of the province Beyond the River and Shethar-bozenai and his associates the envoys who were in the province Beyond the River sent to King Darius; 7they sent him a report, in which was written as follows: "To Darius the king, all peace! 8May it be known to the king that we went to the province of Judah, to the house of the great God. It is being built of hewn stone, and timber is laid in the walls; this work is being done diligently and prospers in their hands. 9Then we spoke to those elders and asked them, 'Who gave you a decree to build this house and to finish this structure?' 10We also asked them their names, for your information, so that we might write down the names of the men at their head. 11This was their reply to us: 'We are the servants of the God of heaven and earth, and we are rebuilding the house that was built many years ago, which a great king of Israel built and finished. 12But because our ancestors had angered the God of heaven, he gave them into the hand of King Nebuchadnezzar of Babylon, the Chaldean, who destroyed this house and carried away the people to Babylonia. 13However, King Cyrus of Babylon, in the first year of his reign, made a decree that this house of God should be rebuilt. 14Moreover, the gold and silver vessels of the house of God, which Nebuchadnezzar had taken out of the temple in Jerusalem and had brought into the temple of Babylon, these King Cyrus took out of the temple of Babylon, and they were delivered to a man named Sheshbazzar, whom he had made governor. 15He said to him, "Take these vessels; go and put them in the temple in Jerusalem, and let the house of God be rebuilt on its site." 16Then this Sheshbazzar came and laid the foundations of the house of God in Jerusalem; and from that time until now it has been under construction, and it is not yet finished.' 17And now, if it seems good to the king, have a search made in the royal archives there in Babylon, to see whether a decree was issued by King Cyrus for the rebuilding of this house of God in Jerusalem. Let the king send us his pleasure in this matter."

The Decree of Darius

6 Then King Darius made a decree, and they searched the archives where the documents were stored in Babylon. 2But it was in Ecbatana, the capital in the province of Media, that a scroll was found on which this was written: "A record.

6.2 The Ring of Truth

In a made-up legend, there is no need for insignificant, divergent details. All the loose ends tie up neatly. Real life, however, is messier. Ezra records a typical example: a document was searched for in Babylon, but it unexpectedly turned up in remote Ecbatana, where (history records) Cyrus spent the summer of his first year as king. Such details suggest that Ezra is based on accurate and detailed historical sources.

3In the first year of his reign, King Cyrus issued a decree: Concerning the house of God at Jerusalem, let the house be rebuilt, the place where sacrifices are offered and burnt offerings are brought;[h] its height shall be sixty cubits and its width sixty cubits, 4with three courses of hewn stones and one course of timber; let the cost be paid from the royal treasury. 5Moreover, let the gold and silver vessels of the house of God, which Nebuchadnezzar took out of the temple in Jerusalem and brought to Babylon, be restored and brought back to the temple in Jerusalem, each to its place; you shall put them in the house of God."

6 "Now you, Tattenai, governor of the province Beyond the River, Shethar-bozenai, and you, their associates, the envoys in the province Beyond the River, keep away; 7let the work on this house of God alone; let the governor of the Jews and the elders of the Jews rebuild this house of God on its site. 8Moreover I make a decree regarding what you shall do for these elders of the Jews for the rebuilding of this house of God: the cost is to be paid to these people, in full and without delay, from the royal revenue, the tribute

---

f Aram adds *the prophet*   g Gk Syr: Aram *We*   h Meaning of Aram uncertain

of the province Beyond the River. 9Whatever is needed—young bulls, rams, or sheep for burnt offerings to the God of heaven, wheat, salt, wine, or oil, as the priests in Jerusalem require—let that be given to them day by day without fail, 10so that they may offer pleasing sacrifices to the God of heaven, and pray for the life of the king and his children. 11Furthermore I decree that if anyone alters this edict, a beam shall be pulled out of the house of the perpetrator, who then shall be impaled on it. The house shall be made a dunghill.

6.11 Ironic Outcome

Governor Tattenai had written the central government in order to harass the Jews who sought to rebuild the temple (5.7–17). As it turned out, his strategy backfired. He and his local government were ordered to pay all the Jews' expenses or be impaled on their own roof beams.

12May the God who has established his name there overthrow any king or people that shall put forth a hand to alter this, or to destroy this house of God in Jerusalem. I, Darius, make a decree; let it be done with all diligence."

Completion and Dedication of the Temple

13 Then, according to the word sent by King Darius, Tattenai, the governor of the province Beyond the River, Shethar-bozenai, and their associates did with all diligence what King Darius had ordered. 14So the elders of the Jews built and prospered, through the prophesying of the prophet Haggai and Zechariah son of Iddo. They finished their building by command of the God of Israel and by decree of Cyrus, Darius, and King Artaxerxes of Persia; 15and this house was finished on the third day of the month of Adar, in the sixth year of the reign of King Darius.

16 The people of Israel, the priests and the Levites, and the rest of the returned exiles, celebrated the dedication of this house of God with joy. 17They offered at the dedication of this house of God one hundred bulls, two hundred rams, four hundred lambs, and as a sin offering for all Israel, twelve male goats, according to the number of the tribes of Israel. 18Then they set the priests in their divisions and the Levites in their courses for the service of God at Jerusalem, as it is written in the book of Moses.

The Passover Celebrated

19 On the fourteenth day of the first month the returned exiles kept the passover. 20For both the priests and the Levites had purified themselves; all of them were clean. So they killed the passover lamb for all the returned exiles, for their fellow priests, and for themselves. 21It was eaten by the people of Israel who had returned from exile, and also by all who had joined them and separated themselves from the pollutions of the nations of the land to worship the LORD, the God of Israel. 22With joy they celebrated the festival of unleavened bread seven days; for the LORD had made them joyful, and had turned the heart of the king of Assyria to them, so that he aided them in the work on the house of God, the God of Israel.

The Coming and Work of Ezra

7 After this, in the reign of King Artaxerxes of Persia, Ezra son of Seraiah, son of Azariah, son of Hilkiah, 2son of Shallum, son of Zadok, son of Ahitub, 3son of Amariah, son of Azariah, son of Meraioth, 4son of Zerahiah, son of Uzzi, son of Bukki, 5son of Abishua, son of Phinehas, son of Eleazar, son of the chief priest Aaron— 6this Ezra went up from Babylonia. He was a scribe skilled in the law of Moses that the LORD the God of Israel had given; and the king granted him all that he asked, for the hand of the LORD his God was upon him.

7 Some of the people of Israel, and some of the priests and Levites, the singers and gatekeepers, and the temple servants also went up to Jerusalem, in the seventh year of King Artaxerxes. 8They came to Jerusalem in the fifth month, which was in the seventh year of the king. 9On the first day of the first month the journey up from Babylon was begun, and on the first day of the fifth month he came to Jerusalem, for the gracious hand of his God was upon him. 10For Ezra had set his heart to study the law of the LORD, and to do it, and to teach the statutes and ordinances in Israel.

The Letter of Artaxerxes to Ezra

11 This is a copy of the letter that King Artaxerxes gave to the priest Ezra, the scribe, a scholar of the text of the commandments of the LORD and his statutes for Israel: 12"Artaxerxes, king of kings, to the priest Ezra, the scribe of the law of the God of heaven: Peace.*i* And now 13I decree that any of the people of Israel or their priests or Levites in my kingdom who freely offers to go to Jerusalem may go with you. 14For you are sent by the king and his seven counselors to make inquiries about Judah and Jerusalem according to the law of your God, which is in your hand, 15and also to convey the silver and gold that the king and his counselors have freely offered to the God of Israel, whose dwelling is in Jerusalem, 16with all the silver and gold that you shall find in the whole province of Babylonia, and with the freewill offerings of the people and the priests, given willingly for the house of their God in Jerusalem. 17With this money, then, you shall with all diligence buy bulls, rams, and lambs, and their grain offerings

---

i Syr Vg 1 Esdras 8.9: Aram *Perfect*

and their drink offerings, and you shall offer them on the altar of the house of your God in Jerusalem. [18]Whatever seems good to you and your colleagues to do with the rest of the silver and gold, you may do, according to the will of your God. [19]The vessels that have been given you for the service of the house of your God, you shall deliver before the God of Jerusalem. [20]And whatever else is required for the house of your God, which you are responsible for providing, you may provide out of the king's treasury.

21 "I, King Artaxerxes, decree to all the treasurers in the province Beyond the River: Whatever the priest Ezra, the scribe of the law of the God of heaven, requires of you, let it be done with all diligence, [22]up to one hundred talents of silver, one hundred cors of wheat, one hundred baths[j] of wine, one hundred baths[j] of oil, and unlimited salt. [23]Whatever is commanded by the God of heaven, let it be done with zeal for the house of the God of heaven, or wrath will come upon the realm of the king and his heirs. [24]We also notify you that it shall not be lawful to impose tribute, custom, or toll on any of the priests, the Levites,

[j] A Heb measure of volume

Ezra, a Man of the Heart
He applied God's word to himself before preaching it to others

EZRA KNEW HOW TO GET things done. He had the political savvy to win a Persian king's support for the trip back to Jerusalem, the salesmanship to convince Jewish family leaders to go along, and the organizational know-how to mount the long, complicated, and dangerous expedition. (There were no Holiday Inns.)

At the same time, Ezra was a priest who depended on God. He set aside days for fasting and prayer. He knew and lived by the Old Testament law, but used it as a path to a profound relationship with God. When he studied scripture, he applied it to himself before applying it to others (7.10).

*While Ezra prayed and made confession, weeping and throwing himself down before the house of God, a very great assembly of men, women and children gathered to him out of Israel.
10.1*

A Strong Negative Reaction

Ezra's party got to Jerusalem 80 years after the first exiles had returned. Yet within four months the Jewish leaders were asking this latecomer for advice on the most sensitive matters.

They told Ezra that Israelites were marrying their idolatrous neighbors. At the news, Ezra completely lost his composure, tore his clothes, and sat down stunned (9.3). His grief-filled prayer of repentance inspired a large crowd to join him in bitter weeping. Then and there they resolved to break up the marriages. The women and children were to be sent away. Ezra, a practical man even in his emotional condition, put the machinery into operation and saw it done.

Why did Ezra react so negatively to these marriages? How could he allow children to be sent away from their fathers, families split? Some people see proof that he was racially oriented, bound to exclude non-Jews from Israel.

But racial purity was not Ezra's worry. Non-Jews like Rahab and Ruth, who converted to Judaism, had long been accepted into Israel. Ezra 6.21 suggests that outsiders who sought the Lord were still welcomed. Ezra's concern was that intermarriage represented a compromised faith that threatened the future existence of Israel.

Tossing Away One Last Chance

Marriage in those days was more than a personal matter. It created a political and religious alliance between two families. These mixed marriages were tying Israelites to other faiths—for Israel's neighbors worshiped idols, an act God hated. Ezra knew that his God must hold the only place in his people's hearts. They must be a special people with a sense of their unique destiny. The law told them not to intermarry (Exodus 34.15–16; Deuteronomy 7.3–6). (In a related situation Paul instructed Christians not to be "mismatched with unbelievers" [2 Corinthians 6.14], though he told Christians already married to non-Christians not to divorce [1 Corinthians 7.12–16].)

Ezra's prayer shows that petty technicalities of the law were far from his mind. His concerns involved the heart. He saw his people falling into the same pattern of compromise that had led God to give them up to the Babylonians years before. Had they learned nothing from their long exile? They were tossing away one last remarkable chance to start over.

Life Questions: Ezra saw intermarriage as a compromise in people's faith. Do people today make other compromises that have the same impact on their faith?

the singers, the doorkeepers, the temple servants, or other servants of this house of God. 25 "And you, Ezra, according to the God-given wisdom you possess, appoint magistrates and judges who may judge all the people in the province Beyond the River who know the laws of your God; and you shall teach those who do not know them. 26All who will not obey the law of your God and the law of the king, let judgment be strictly executed on them, whether for death or for banishment or for confiscation of their goods or for imprisonment."

27 Blessed be the LORD, the God of our ancestors, who put such a thing as this into the heart of the king to glorify the house of the LORD in Jerusalem, 28and who extended to me steadfast love before the king and his counselors, and before all the king's mighty officers. I took courage, for the hand of the LORD my God was upon me, and I gathered leaders from Israel to go up with me.

Heads of Families Who Returned with Ezra

8 These are their family heads, and this is the genealogy of those who went up with me from Babylonia, in the reign of King Artaxerxes: 2Of the descendants of Phinehas, Gershom. Of Ithamar, Daniel. Of David, Hattush, 3of the descendants of Shecaniah. Of Parosh, Zechariah, with whom were registered one hundred fifty males. 4Of the descendants of Pahath-moab, Elie-hoenai son of Zerahiah, and with him two hundred males. 5Of the descendants of Zattu,k Shecaniah son of Jahaziel, and with him three hundred males. 6Of the descendants of Adin, Ebed son of Jonathan, and with him fifty males. 7Of the de-

scendants of Elam, Jeshaiah son of Athaliah, and with him seventy males. 8Of the descendants of Shephatiah, Zebadiah son of Michael, and with him eighty males. 9Of the descendants of Joab, Obadiah son of Jehiel, and with him two hundred eighteen males. 10Of the descendants of Bani,l Shelomith son of Josiphiah, and with him one hundred sixty males. 11Of the descendants of Bebai, Zechariah son of Bebai, and with him twenty-eight males. 12Of the descendants of Azgad, Johanan son of Hakkatan, and with him one hundred ten males. 13Of the descendants of Adonikam, those who came later, their names being Eliphelet, Jeuel, and Shemaiah, and with them sixty males. 14Of the descendants of Bigvai, Uthai and Zaccur, and with them seventy males.

Servants for the Temple

15 I gathered them by the river that runs to Ahava, and there we camped three days. As I reviewed the people and the priests, I found there none of the descendants of Levi. 16Then I sent for Eliezer, Ariel, Shemaiah, Elnathan, Jarib, Elnathan, Nathan, Zechariah, and Meshullam, who were leaders, and for Joiarib and Elnathan, who were wise, 17and sent them to Iddo, the leader at the place called Casiphia, telling them what to say to Iddo and his colleagues the temple servants at Casiphia, namely, to send us ministers for the house of our God. 18Since the gracious hand of our God was upon us, they brought us a man of discretion, of the descendants of Mahli son of Levi son of Israel, namely Sherebiah, with his sons and kin, eighteen; 19also Hashabiah and with him Jeshaiah of the descendants of Merari, with his kin and their sons, twenty; 20besides two hun-

---

k Gk 1 Esdras 8.32: Heb lacks *of Zattu*   l Gk 1 Esdras 8.36: Heb lacks *Bani*

ARTAXERXES *Friendly Foreigner*

THROUGHOUT HISTORY, STRONG GOVERNMENTS HAVE had a love-hate relationship with religion. Some encourage faith and try to manipulate it for political gain. Others, such as Communist China or Albania, pass harsh laws against religion and persecute the faithful. Only rarely does a totalitarian regime let religion go its own way.

After domination by the brutal regimes of Assyria and Babylon, the Persian Empire must have seemed like a relief to the Jews. They especially welcomed the Persians' tolerant, even friendly attitude toward other nations' religions. Not only did Persia's King Artaxerxes allow Ezra to return to Jerusalem, he wrote a remarkable letter of support for Ezra's mission.

Other despots, like the Pharaoh of Egypt, saw Israel's God as a threat to their unrestricted power. Artaxerxes apparently hoped to win God's favor. He provided material support, safe passage to Jews wanting to return to their land and freedom from taxation for all temple employees. In effect, this secular regime subsidized Judaism.

Later, Artaxerxes encouraged Nehemiah to go to Jerusalem for a potentially risky task: rebuilding the walls of the city so it could be militarily defended (Nehemiah 2.1–9). As one of his top officials, Nehemiah had evidently given Artaxerxes assurance that a strong Israelite nation would not cause trouble.

Life Questions: Is it good for churches to receive help—financial or otherwise—as the Jews did from Artaxerxes? What would be the dangers in such an approach?

dred twenty of the temple servants, whom David and his officials had set apart to attend the Levites. These were all mentioned by name.

Fasting and Prayer for Protection

21 Then I proclaimed a fast there, at the river Ahava, that we might deny ourselves[m] before our God, to seek from him a safe journey for ourselves, our children, and all our possessions. 22For I was ashamed to ask the king for a band of soldiers and cavalry to protect us against the enemy on our way, since we had told the king that the hand of our God is gracious to all who seek him, but his power and his wrath are against all

8.22 Risk of Faith

Like gold shipments in the old Wild West, Ezra's consignment of treasure made for a dangerous journey through lawless Palestine. A military escort would surely have helped. But, having told the king that God would protect the settlers, Ezra was ashamed to ask for help that would seem to contradict his statement. His faith on the line, he determined to rely on prayer rather than soldiers.

who forsake him. 23So we fasted and petitioned our God for this, and he listened to our entreaty.

Gifts for the Temple

24 Then I set apart twelve of the leading priests: Sherebiah, Hashabiah, and ten of their kin with them. 25And I weighed out to them the silver and the gold and the vessels, the offering for the house of our God that the king, his counselors, his lords, and all Israel there present had offered; 26I weighed out into their hand six hundred fifty talents of silver, and one hundred silver vessels worth … talents,[n] and one hundred talents of gold, 27twenty gold bowls worth a thousand darics, and two vessels of fine polished bronze as precious as gold. 28And I said to them, "You are holy to the LORD, and the vessels are holy; and the silver and the gold are a freewill offering to the LORD, the God of your ancestors. 29Guard them and keep them until you weigh them before the chief priests and the Levites and the heads of families in Israel at Jerusalem, within the chambers of the house of the LORD." 30So the priests and the Levites took over the silver, the gold, and the vessels as they were weighed out, to bring them to Jerusalem, to the house of our God.

The Return to Jerusalem

31 Then we left the river Ahava on the twelfth day of the first month, to go to Jerusalem; the hand of our God was upon us, and he delivered

us from the hand of the enemy and from ambushes along the way. 32We came to Jerusalem and remained there three days. 33On the fourth day, within the house of our God, the silver, the gold, and the vessels were weighed into the hands of the priest Meremoth son of Uriah, and with him was Eleazar son of Phinehas, and with them were the Levites, Jozabad son of Jeshua and Noadiah son of Binnui. 34The total was counted and weighed, and the weight of everything was recorded.

35 At that time those who had come from captivity, the returned exiles, offered burnt offerings to the God of Israel, twelve bulls for all Israel, ninety-six rams, seventy-seven lambs, and as a sin offering twelve male goats; all this was a burnt offering to the LORD. 36They also delivered the king's commissions to the king's satraps and to the governors of the province Beyond the River; and they supported the people and the house of God.

Denunciation of Mixed Marriages

9 After these things had been done, the officials approached me and said, "The people of Israel, the priests, and the Levites have not separated themselves from the peoples of the lands with their abominations, from the Canaanites, the Hittites, the Perizzites, the Jebusites, the Ammonites, the Moabites, the Egyptians, and the Amorites. 2For they have taken some of their daughters as wives for themselves and for their sons. Thus the holy seed has mixed itself with the peoples of the lands, and in this faithlessness the officials and leaders have led the way." 3When I heard this, I tore my garment and my mantle, and pulled hair from my head and beard, and sat appalled. 4Then all who trembled at the words of the God of Israel, because of the faithlessness of the returned exiles, gathered around me while I sat appalled until the evening sacrifice.

Ezra's Prayer

5 At the evening sacrifice I got up from my fasting, with my garments and my mantle torn, and fell on my knees, spread out my hands to the LORD my God, 6and said,

"O my God, I am too ashamed and embarrassed to lift my face to you, my God, for our iniquities have risen higher than our heads, and our guilt has mounted up to the heavens. 7From the days of our ancestors to this day we have been deep in guilt, and for our iniquities we, our kings, and our priests have been handed over to the kings of the lands, to the sword, to captivity, to plundering, and to utter shame, as is now the case. 8But now for a brief moment favor has been shown by the LORD our God, who has left us a remnant, and given us a stake in his holy place, in

---

m Or *might fast*   n The number of talents is lacking

order that he[o] may brighten our eyes and grant us a little sustenance in our slavery. [9]For we are slaves; yet our God has not forsaken us in our slavery, but has extended to us his steadfast love before the kings of Persia, to give us new life to set up the house of our God, to repair its ruins, and to give us a wall in Judea and Jerusalem.

10 "And now, our God, what shall we say after this? For we have forsaken your commandments, [11]which you commanded by your servants the prophets, saying, 'The land that you are entering to possess is a land unclean with the pollutions of the peoples of the lands, with their abominations. They have filled it from end to end with their uncleanness. [12]Therefore do not give your daughters to their sons, neither take their daughters for your sons, and never seek their peace or prosperity, so that you may be strong and eat the good of the land and leave it for an inheritance to your children forever.' [13]After all that has come upon us for our evil deeds and for our great guilt, seeing that you, our God, have punished us less than our iniquities deserved and have given us such a remnant as this, [14]shall we break your commandments again and intermarry with the peoples who practice these abominations? Would you not be angry with us until you destroy us without remnant or survivor? [15]O LORD, God of Israel, you are just, but we have escaped as a remnant, as is now the case. Here we are before you in our guilt, though no one can face you because of this."

The People's Response

10 While Ezra prayed and made confession, weeping and throwing himself down before the house of God, a very great assembly of men, women, and children gathered to him out of Israel; the people also wept bitterly. [2]Shecaniah son of Jehiel, of the descendants of Elam, addressed Ezra, saying, "We have broken faith with our God and have married foreign women from the peoples of the land, but even now there is hope for Israel in spite of this. [3]So now let us make a covenant with our God to send away all these wives and their children, according to the counsel of my lord and of those who tremble at the commandment of our God; and let it be done according to the law. [4]Take action, for it is your duty, and we are with you; be strong, and do it." [5]Then Ezra stood up and made the leading priests, the Levites, and all Israel swear that they would do as had been said. So they swore.

10.1 Unprecedented Response

Ezra's grief over Israel's spiritual compromise was similar to that of many prophets. But the people's response to Ezra was unprecedented. Pre-exile prophets like Amos or Jeremiah never saw such heartfelt repentance. Evidently the exile really had purified Israel.

Foreign Wives and Their Children Rejected

6 Then Ezra withdrew from before the house of God, and went to the chamber of Jehohanan son of Eliashib, where he spent the night.[p] He did not eat bread or drink water, for he was mourning over the faithlessness of the exiles. [7]They made a proclamation throughout Judah and Jerusalem to all the returned exiles that they should assemble at Jerusalem, [8]and that if any did not come within three days, by order of the officials and the elders all their property should be forfeited, and they themselves banned from the congregation of the exiles.

9 Then all the people of Judah and Benjamin assembled at Jerusalem within the three days; it was the ninth month, on the twentieth day of the month. All the people sat in the open square before the house of God, trembling because of this matter and because of the heavy rain. [10]Then Ezra the priest stood up and said to them, "You have trespassed and married foreign women, and so increased the guilt of Israel. [11]Now make confession to the LORD the God of your ancestors, and do his will; separate yourselves from the peoples of the land and from the foreign wives." [12]Then all the assembly answered with a loud voice, "It is so; we must do as you have said. [13]But the people are many, and it is a time of heavy rain; we cannot stand in the open. Nor is this a task for one day or for two, for many of us have transgressed in this matter. [14]Let our officials represent the whole assembly, and let all in our towns who have taken foreign wives come at appointed times, and with them the elders and judges of every town, until the fierce wrath of our God on this account is averted from us." [15]Only Jonathan son of Asahel and Jahzeiah son of Tikvah opposed this, and Meshullam and Shabbethai the Levites supported them.

16 Then the returned exiles did so. Ezra the priest selected men,[q] heads of families, according to their families, each of them designated by name. On the first day of the tenth month they sat down to examine the matter. [17]By the first day of the first month they had come to the end of all the men who had married foreign women.

18 There were found of the descendants of the priests who had married foreign women, of the descendants of Jeshua son of Jozadak and his brothers: Maaseiah, Eliezer, Jarib, and Gedaliah. [19]They pledged themselves to send away their

[o] Heb *our God* [p] 1 Esdras 9.2: Heb *where he went* [q] 1 Esdras 9.16: Syr: Heb *And there were selected Ezra,*

wives, and their guilt offering was a ram of the flock for their guilt. [20]Of the descendants of Immer: Hanani and Zebadiah. [21]Of the descendants of Harim: Maaseiah, Elijah, Shemaiah, Jehiel, and

10.17 Corrupt Leaders

The problem Ezra had evidently expected to solve in a day (verse 13) took, in fact, two months to sort out. Intermarriage must have been more widespread than he realized. The list of those involved shows that the priests and Levites, who were the religious leaders, had a higher proportion of intermarriage than the rest of the people.

Uzziah. [22]Of the descendants of Pashhur: Elioenai, Maaseiah, Ishmael, Nethanel, Jozabad, and Elasah.

23 Of the Levites: Jozabad, Shimei, Kelaiah (that is, Kelita), Pethahiah, Judah, and Eliezer. [24]Of the singers: Eliashib. Of the gatekeepers: Shallum, Telem, and Uri.

25 And of Israel: of the descendants of Parosh: Ramiah, Izziah, Malchijah, Mijamin, Elea-

zar, Hashabiah,[r] and Benaiah. [26]Of the descendants of Elam: Mattaniah, Zechariah, Jehiel, Abdi, Jeremoth, and Elijah. [27]Of the descendants of Zattu: Elioenai, Eliashib, Mattaniah, Jeremoth, Zabad, and Aziza. [28]Of the descendants of Bebai: Jehohanan, Hananiah, Zabbai, and Athlai. [29]Of the descendants of Bani: Meshullam, Malluch, Adaiah, Jashub, Sheal, and Jeremoth. [30]Of the descendants of Pahath-moab: Adna, Chelal, Benaiah, Maaseiah, Mattaniah, Bezalel, Binnui, and Manasseh. [31]Of the descendants of Harim: Eliezer, Isshijah, Malchijah, Shemaiah, Shimeon, [32]Benjamin, Malluch, and Shemariah. [33]Of the descendants of Hashum: Mattenai, Mattattah, Zabad, Eliphelet, Jeremai, Manasseh, and Shimei. [34]Of the descendants of Bani: Maadai, Amram, Uel, [35]Benaiah, Bedeiah, Cheluhi, [36]Vaniah, Meremoth, Eliashib, [37]Mattaniah, Mattenai, and Jaasu. [38]Of the descendants of Binnui:[s] Shimei, [39]Shelemiah, Nathan, Adaiah, [40]Machnadebai, Shashai, Sharai, [41]Azarel, Shelemiah, Shemariah, [42]Shallum, Amariah, and Joseph. [43]Of the descendants of Nebo: Jeiel, Mattithiah, Zabad, Zebina, Jaddai, Joel, and Benaiah. [44]All these had married foreign women, and they sent them away with their children.[t]

---

[r] 1 Esdras 9.26 Gk: Heb *Malchijah*   [s] Gk: Heb *Bani, Binnui*   [t] 1 Esdras 9.36; Meaning of Heb uncertain

NEHEMIAH

A Man of Action
He set out to build a wall, but left an enduring legacy of leadership

> "Do not be afraid of them. Remember the LORD, who is great and awesome, and fight." 4.14

I N THE BOOK OF NEHEMIAH we peek inside the personal memoirs of a great leader. You can't mistake his style. He was an organizer, a pragmatic leader. That, no doubt, is why he had made his way to a top position in the Persian empire, one of the grandest in the history of the world.

Yet his heart was elsewhere—in Jerusalem, a small, troublesome place far from the center of power. When he heard of the difficulties his people were experiencing there, he took his career— and probably his life—in his hands and spoke to the king about it. Shortly thereafter he was touring, by night, the broken-down walls of a city he probably had never seen before.

Nearly 100 years had passed since his people had returned to Jerusalem from exile. Though the temple had been rebuilt, the city was barely occupied. More Jews lived in the outlying villages and towns than in the holy city. They mixed with all kinds of foreigners. They were in danger of losing their identity. Why? Partly because the city lacked a wall.

What's in a Wall?

Compared to many concerns, building a wall may not seem terribly important. But think of it this way—what if the border between Mexico and the United States was wide open, so that anyone could cross and live on either side at will? One thing is certain: The distinction between Mexico and Texas would soon dissolve.

For lack of a wall the Jews were facing assimilation into the culture of their neighbors. In those days a city without a wall was easy pickings for any robber band. Jews, concerned for security, had scattered among other nationalities in small villages outside Jerusalem. There they were intermarrying and gradually losing their own language, culture and—most important—their own religion. A wall would give them a chance to make Jerusalem a truly Jewish city, keeping it safe and controlling who came and went.

Waiting for a Leader

What had kept them from doing anything about the broken-down wall for nearly 100 years? One obstacle was local resistance: powerful politicians were determined to keep the Jews down. Perhaps another reason was the lack of a leader like Nehemiah. In his memoirs, which fill most of this book, he shows remarkable qualities of leadership: impassioned speech, prayer, organization, resolve, trust in God, quick and determined response to problems, unselfishness. Perhaps his years in the Persian court had been preparing him. Organizing a difficult building project and handling fierce opposition seemed to come easily to him.

Nehemiah was more than a good business manager. He was a man of God. He did not act without prayer, and he did not pray without acting. His prayers punctuate the book. He recognized God's role in all that happened and never forgot to give him credit. He was not looking for earthly status—if he had been, he never would have left Persia.

How to Read Nehemiah

Nehemiah's personality is the outstanding quality of the book that bears his name. No other biblical character gives such clear information about how to "practice the presence of God" while carrying a leadership role. As you read, take note of the qualities that made Nehemiah successful as a leader and man of God. You may also wish to contrast his leadership with Ezra's. They worked in tandem but had very different styles. Nehemiah was an activist, Ezra a student; Nehemiah was outspoken, Ezra more withdrawn. Yet both faced similar problems and had similar success—and the two worked smoothly together.

The books of Ezra and Nehemiah both tell how the disgraced and chastened Jews returned from exile to rebuild their country. As history, Nehemiah includes some long lists of different family groups, as well as a detailed description of who built which parts of the Jerusalem wall. Unless you are an advanced student, you should skim these lists mainly to get an understanding of why they were kept. Concentrate more on how the Israelites had been transformed and purified by exile, making them ready to meet new challenges when they returned home.

PEOPLE YOU'LL MEET IN NEHEMIAH

NEHEMIAH (p. 490)

3-TRACK READING PLAN

For an explanation and complete listing of the 3-track reading plan, turn to page 7.

TRACK 1: *Two-Week Courses on the Bible*
See page 7 for information on these courses.

TRACK 2: *An Overview of Nehemiah in 2 Days*
☐ Day 1. Read the Introduction to Nehemiah and chapter 2, which tells how Nehemiah began his work on the wall.
☐ Day 2. Read chapter 8, showing the power of God's Word read aloud.
Now turn to page 9 for your next Track 2 reading project.

TRACK 3: *All of Nehemiah in 12 Days*
After you have read through Nehemiah, turn to pages 10–14 for your next Track 3 reading project.
☐1　☐2–3　☐4　☐5　☐6　☐7　☐8　☐9
☐10　☐11　☐12　☐13

Nehemiah Prays for His People

1 The words of Nehemiah son of Hacaliah. In the month of Chislev, in the twentieth year, while I was in Susa the capital, ²one of my brothers, Hanani, came with certain men from Judah; and I asked them about the Jews that survived, those who had escaped the captivity, and about Jerusalem. ³They replied, "The survivors there in the province who escaped captivity are in great trouble and shame; the wall of Jerusalem is broken down, and its gates have been destroyed by fire."

4 When I heard these words I sat down and wept, and mourned for days, fasting and praying before the God of heaven. ⁵I said, "O LORD God of heaven, the great and awesome God who keeps covenant and steadfast love with those who love

him and keep his commandments; ⁶let your ear be attentive and your eyes open to hear the prayer of your servant that I now pray before you day and night for your servants, the people of Israel, confessing the sins of the people of Israel, which we have sinned against you. Both I and my family have sinned. ⁷We have offended you deeply, failing to keep the commandments, the statutes, and the ordinances that you commanded your servant Moses. ⁸Remember the word that you commanded your servant Moses, 'If you are unfaithful, I will scatter you among the peoples; ⁹but if you return to me and keep my commandments and do them, though your outcasts are under the farthest skies, I will gather them from there and bring them to the place at which I have chosen to establish my name.' ¹⁰They are your servants and your people, whom you redeemed by your great power and your strong hand. [11]O Lord, let your ear be attentive to the prayer of your servant, and to the prayer of your servants who delight in revering your name. Give success to your servant today, and grant him mercy in the sight of this man!"

At the time, I was cupbearer to the king.

Nehemiah Sent to Judah

2 In the month of Nisan, in the twentieth year of King Artaxerxes, when wine was served him, I carried the wine and gave it to the king. Now, I had never been sad in his presence before. [2]So the king said to me, "Why is your face sad, since you are not sick? This can only be sadness of the heart." Then I was very much afraid. [3]I said to the king, "May the king live forever! Why should my face not be sad, when the city, the place of my ancestors' graves, lies waste, and its gates have been destroyed by fire?" [4]Then the king said to me, "What do you request?" So I

2.4 The "Arrow Prayer"

Nehemiah characteristically prayed to God while he went about his duties. He even "shot an arrow" to God, silently asking him for help in the middle of this crucial conversation with the king. He spontaneously inserted prayers as he wrote his memoirs. Some other examples: 1.5–11; 4.4–5; 5.19; 6.9,14; 13.14,22,31.

prayed to the God of heaven. [5]Then I said to the king, "If it pleases the king, and if your servant has found favor with you, I ask that you send me to Judah, to the city of my ancestors' graves, so that I may rebuild it." [6]The king said to me (the queen also was sitting beside him), "How long will you be gone, and when will you return?" So it pleased the king to send me, and I set him a date. [7]Then I said to the king, "If it pleases the king, let letters be given me to the governors of the province Beyond the River, that they may grant me passage until I arrive in Judah; [8]and a letter to Asaph, the keeper of the king's forest, directing him to give me timber to make beams for the gates of the temple fortress, and for the wall of the city, and for the house that I shall occupy." And the king granted me what I asked, for the gracious hand of my God was upon me.

[9] Then I came to the governors of the province Beyond the River, and gave them the king's letters. Now the king had sent officers of the army and cavalry with me. [10]When Sanballat the Horonite and Tobiah the Ammonite official heard this, it displeased them greatly that someone had come to seek the welfare of the people of Israel.

Nehemiah's Inspection of the Walls

[11] So I came to Jerusalem and was there for three days. [12]Then I got up during the night, I and a few men with me; I told no one what my God

2.10 Powerful Opponents

Both Sanballat and Tobiah were influential local politicians. Sanballat's family governed Samaria and had managed to marry into the high priest's family (see 13.28). Tobiah, an official in Ammon (a small country east of Judah), had family ties and influence among the top Jewish families (see 6.17–19; 13.4–5). There is some evidence both men were from Jewish backgrounds, though they preferred the political status quo in which Jewish identity was diluted.

had put into my heart to do for Jerusalem. The only animal I took was the animal I rode. [13]I went out by night by the Valley Gate past the Dragon's Spring and to the Dung Gate, and I inspected the walls of Jerusalem that had been broken down and its gates that had been destroyed by fire. [14]Then I went on to the Fountain Gate and to the King's Pool; but there was no place for the animal I was riding to continue. [15]So I went up by way of the valley by night and inspected the wall. Then I turned back and entered by the Valley Gate, and so returned. [16]The officials did not know where I had gone or what I was doing; I had not yet told the Jews, the priests, the nobles, the officials, and the rest that were to do the work.

Decision to Restore the Walls

[17] Then I said to them, "You see the trouble we are in, how Jerusalem lies in ruins with its gates burned. Come, let us rebuild the wall of Jerusalem, so that we may no longer suffer disgrace." [18]I told them that the hand of my God had been gracious upon me, and also the words that the king had spoken to me. Then they said, "Let us start building!" So they committed themselves to the common good. [19]But when Sanballat the Horonite and Tobiah the Ammonite official, and Geshem the Arab heard of it, they mocked and ridiculed us, saying, "What is this that you are doing? Are you rebelling against the king?" [20]Then I replied to them, "The God of heaven is the one who will give us success, and we his servants are going to start building; but you have no share or claim or historic right in Jerusalem."

Organization of the Work

3 Then the high priest Eliashib set to work with his fellow priests and rebuilt the Sheep Gate. They consecrated it and set up its doors; they consecrated it as far as the Tower of the Hundred

and as far as the Tower of Hananel. [2]And the men of Jericho built next to him. And next to them[a] Zaccur son of Imri built.

3 The sons of Hassenaah built the Fish Gate;

3.1–32 Lasting Credit

Archaeologists love this chapter for its valuable clues to the design of ancient Jerusalem. Other readers may find these details less inspiring, but they do give evidence of Nehemiah's organizational genius. Somehow he motivated skilled craftsmen to work alongside ordinary laborers, and he even got children to pitch in. For added motivation, he assigned families repair projects just outside their own homes. This chapter, like a brass plaque listing "Important Contributors," assured that they would receive lasting credit for their efforts.

---

they laid its beams and set up its doors, its bolts, and its bars. [4]Next to them Meremoth son of Uriah son of Hakkoz made repairs. Next to them Meshullam son of Berechiah son of Meshezabel made repairs. Next to them Zadok son of Baana made repairs. [5]Next to them the Tekoites made repairs; but their nobles would not put their shoulders to the work of their Lord.[b]

6 Joiada son of Paseah and Meshullam son of Besodeiah repaired the Old Gate; they laid its beams and set up its doors, its bolts, and its bars. [7]Next to them repairs were made by Melatiah the Gibeonite and Jadon the Meronothite—the men of Gibeon and of Mizpah—who were under the jurisdiction of[c] the governor of the province Beyond the River. [8]Next to them Uzziel son of Harhaiah, one of the goldsmiths, made repairs. Next to him Hananiah, one of the perfumers, made repairs; and they restored Jerusalem as far as the Broad Wall. [9]Next to them Rephaiah son of Hur, ruler of half the district of[d] Jerusalem, made repairs. [10]Next to them Jedaiah son of Harumaph made repairs opposite his house; and next to him Hattush son of Hashabneiah made repairs. [11]Malchijah son of Harim and Hasshub son of Pahathmoab repaired another section and the Tower of the Ovens. [12]Next to him Shallum son of Hallohesh, ruler of half the district of[d] Jerusalem, made repairs, he and his daughters.

13 Hanun and the inhabitants of Zanoah repaired the Valley Gate; they rebuilt it and set up its doors, its bolts, and its bars, and repaired a thousand cubits of the wall, as far as the Dung Gate.

14 Malchijah son of Rechab, ruler of the district of[e] Beth-haccherem, repaired the Dung Gate; he rebuilt it and set up its doors, its bolts, and its bars.

15 And Shallum son of Col-hozeh, ruler of the district of[e] Mizpah, repaired the Fountain Gate; he rebuilt it and covered it and set up its doors, its bolts, and its bars; and he built the wall of the Pool of Shelah of the king's garden, as far as the stairs that go down from the City of David. [16]After him Nehemiah son of Azbuk, ruler of half the district of[d] Beth-zur, repaired from a point opposite the graves of David, as far as the artificial pool and the house of the warriors. [17]After him the Levites made repairs: Rehum son of Bani; next to him Hashabiah, ruler of half the district of[d] Keilah, made repairs for his district. [18]After him their kin made repairs: Binnui,[f] son of Henadad, ruler of half the district of[d] Keilah; [19]next to him Ezer son of Jeshua, ruler[g] of Mizpah, repaired another section opposite the ascent to the armory at the Angle. [20]After him Baruch son of Zabbai repaired another section from the Angle to the door of the house of the high priest Eliashib. [21]After him Meremoth son of Uriah son of Hakkoz repaired another section from the door of the house of Eliashib to the end of the house of Eliashib. [22]After him the priests, the men of the surrounding area, made repairs. [23]After them Benjamin and Hasshub made repairs opposite their house. After them Azariah son of Maaseiah son of Ananiah made repairs beside his own house. [24]After him Binnui son of Henadad repaired another section, from the house of Azariah to the Angle and to the corner. [25]Palal son of Uzai repaired opposite the Angle and the tower projecting from the upper house of the king at the court of the guard. After him Pedaiah son of Parosh [26]and the temple servants living[h] on Ophel made repairs up to a point opposite the Water Gate on the east and the projecting tower. [27]After him the Tekoites repaired another section opposite the great projecting tower as far as the wall of Ophel.

28 Above the Horse Gate the priests made repairs, each one opposite his own house. [29]After them Zadok son of Immer made repairs opposite his own house. After him Shemaiah son of Shecaniah, the keeper of the East Gate, made repairs. [30]After him Hananiah son of Shelemiah and Hanun sixth son of Zalaph repaired another section. After him Meshullam son of Berechiah made repairs opposite his living quarters. [31]After him Malchijah, one of the goldsmiths, made repairs as far as the house of the temple servants and of the merchants, opposite the Muster Gate,[i] and to the upper room of the corner. [32]And between the upper room of the corner and the Sheep Gate the goldsmiths and the merchants made repairs.

---

[a] Heb *him*   [b] Or *lords*   [c] Meaning of Heb uncertain   [d] Or *supervisor of half the portion assigned to*
[e] Or *supervisor of the portion assigned to*   [f] Gk Syr Compare verse 24, 10.9: Heb *Bavvai*   [g] Or *supervisor*
[h] Cn: Heb *were living*   [i] Or *Hammiphkad Gate*

Hostile Plots Thwarted

4 [j] Now when Sanballat heard that we were building the wall, he was angry and greatly enraged, and he mocked the Jews. [2]He said in the presence of his associates and of the army of Samaria, "What are these feeble Jews doing? Will they restore things? Will they sacrifice? Will they finish it in a day? Will they revive the stones out of the heaps of rubbish—and burned ones at that?" [3]Tobiah the Ammonite was beside him, and he said, "That stone wall they are building—any fox going up on it would break it down!" [4]Hear, O our God, for we are despised; turn their taunt back on their own heads, and give them over as plunder in a land of captivity. [5]Do not cover their guilt, and do not let their sin be blotted out from your sight; for they have hurled insults in the face of the builders.

6 So we rebuilt the wall, and all the wall was joined together to half its height; for the people had a mind to work.

7 [k] But when Sanballat and Tobiah and the Arabs and the Ammonites and the Ashdodites heard that the repairing of the walls of Jerusalem was going forward and the gaps were beginning to be closed, they were very angry, [8]and all plotted together to come and fight against Jerusalem and to cause confusion in it. [9]So we prayed to our God, and set a guard as a protection against them day and night.

4.9 Praise the Lord and Fight

Nehemiah felt no difficulty combining prayer and action, as this verse shows: "We prayed to our God and set a guard." Verse 14 gives another unembarrassed combination of spiritual and military tactics: "Remember the LORD . . . and fight."

10 But Judah said, "The strength of the burden bearers is failing, and there is too much rubbish so that we are unable to work on the wall." [11]And our enemies said, "They will not know or see anything before we come upon them and kill them and stop the work." [12]When the Jews who lived near them came, they said to us ten times, "From all the places where they live[l] they will come up against us."[m] [13]So in the lowest parts of the space behind the wall, in open places, I stationed the people according to their families,[n] with their swords, their spears, and their bows. [14]After I looked these things over, I stood up and said to the nobles and the officials and the rest of the people, "Do not be afraid of them. Remember the LORD, who is great and awesome, and fight for

your kin, your sons, your daughters, your wives, and your homes."

15 When our enemies heard that their plot was known to us, and that God had frustrated it, we all returned to the wall, each to his work. [16]From that day on, half of my servants worked on construction, and half held the spears, shields, bows, and body-armor; and the leaders posted themselves behind the whole house of Judah, [17]who were building the wall. The burden bearers carried their loads in such a way that each labored on the work with one hand and with the other held a weapon. [18]And each of the builders had his sword strapped at his side while he built. The man who sounded the trumpet was beside me. [19]And I said to the nobles, the officials, and the rest of the people, "The work is great and widely spread out, and we are separated far from one another on the wall. [20]Rally to us wherever you hear the sound of the trumpet. Our God will fight for us."

21 So we labored at the work, and half of them held the spears from break of dawn until the stars came out. [22]I also said to the people at that time, "Let every man and his servant pass the night inside Jerusalem, so that they may be a guard for us by night and may labor by day." [23]So neither I nor my brothers nor my servants nor the men of the guard who followed me ever took off our clothes; each kept his weapon in his right hand.[o]

Nehemiah Deals with Oppression

5 Now there was a great outcry of the people and of their wives against their Jewish kin. [2]For there were those who said, "With our sons and our daughters, we are many; we must get grain, so that we may eat and stay alive." [3]There were also those who said, "We are having to pledge our fields, our vineyards, and our houses in order to get grain during the famine." [4]And there were those who said, "We are having to borrow money on our fields and vineyards to pay the king's tax. [5]Now our flesh is the same as that of our kindred; our children are the same as their children; and yet we are forcing our sons and daughters to be slaves, and some of our daughters have been ravished; we are powerless, and our fields and vineyards now belong to others."

6 I was very angry when I heard their outcry and these complaints. [7]After thinking it over, I brought charges against the nobles and the officials; I said to them, "You are all taking interest from your own people." And I called a great assembly to deal with them, [8]and said to them, "As far as we were able, we have bought back our Jewish kindred who had been sold to other nations; but now you are selling your own kin, who must then be bought back by us!" They were

---

[j] Ch 3.33 in Heb   [k] Ch 4.1 in Heb   [l] Cn: Heb *you return*   [m] Compare Gk Syr: Meaning of Heb uncertain
[n] Meaning of Heb uncertain   [o] Cn: Heb *each his weapon the water*

silent, and could not find a word to say. [9]So I said, "The thing that you are doing is not good. Should you not walk in the fear of our God, to prevent the taunts of the nations our enemies? [10]Moreover I and my brothers and my servants are lending them money and grain. Let us stop this taking of interest. [11]Restore to them, this very day, their fields, their vineyards, their olive orchards, and their houses, and the interest on money, grain, wine, and oil that you have been exacting from them." [12]Then they said, "We will restore everything and demand nothing more from them. We will do as you say." And I called the priests, and made them take an oath to do as they had promised. [13]I also shook out the fold of my garment and said, "So may God shake out everyone from house and from property who does not perform this promise. Thus may they be shaken out and emptied." And all the assembly said, "Amen," and praised the LORD. And the people did as they had promised.

The Generosity of Nehemiah

14 Moreover from the time that I was appointed to be their governor in the land of Judah, from the twentieth year to the thirty-second year of King Artaxerxes, twelve years, neither I nor my brothers ate the food allowance of the governor.

5.14 Politician Without Greed

Nehemiah faced a daunting task similar to that confronting many leaders of developing countries today. The land was devastated, with all wealth concentrated in the hands of a few powerful families. Jews were mortgaging their property and even selling their children into slavery in order to raise money to pay taxes. Nehemiah, who apparently came from wealth, could have profited further from his political position. Instead, he set a sterling example of generosity and self-sacrifice that made a profound impression on his oppressed countrymen.

[15]The former governors who were before me laid heavy burdens on the people, and took food and wine from them, besides forty shekels of silver. Even their servants lorded it over the people. But I did not do so, because of the fear of God. [16]Indeed, I devoted myself to the work on this wall, and acquired no land; and all my servants were gathered there for the work. [17]Moreover there were at my table one hundred fifty people, Jews and officials, besides those who came to us from the nations around us. [18]Now that which was prepared for one day was one ox and six choice sheep; also fowls were prepared for me, and every ten days skins of wine in abundance; yet with all this I did not demand the food allowance of the governor, because of the heavy burden of labor on the people. [19]Remember for my good, O my God, all that I have done for this people.

Intrigues of Enemies Foiled

6 Now when it was reported to Sanballat and Tobiah and to Geshem the Arab and to the rest of our enemies that I had built the wall and that there was no gap left in it (though up to that time I had not set up the doors in the gates), [2]Sanballat and Geshem sent to me, saying, "Come and let us meet together in one of the villages in the plain of Ono." But they intended to do me harm. [3]So I sent messengers to them, saying, "I am doing a great work and I cannot come down. Why should the work stop while I leave it to come down to you?" [4]They sent to me four times in this way, and I answered them in the same manner. [5]In the same way Sanballat for the fifth time sent his servant to me with an open letter in his hand.

6.5 Psychological Warfare

After fending off ridicule and threats of violence from his enemies (chapter 4), Nehemiah suddenly faced a new scare tactic. The author points out that this accusatory letter came "open" to public view. Ordinarily, letters were rolled up, tied, sealed with wax, and delivered in a silk bag to guarantee privacy. Opponents were doubtless trying to intimidate Nehemiah by openly spreading rumors to arouse the suspicion of his Persian overseers. As usual, he was not easily intimidated.

[6]In it was written, "It is reported among the nations—and Geshem[p] also says it—that you and the Jews intend to rebel; that is why you are building the wall; and according to this report you wish to become their king. [7]You have also set up prophets to proclaim in Jerusalem concerning you, 'There is a king in Judah!' And now it will be reported to the king according to these words. So come, therefore, and let us confer together." [8]Then I sent to him, saying, "No such things as you say have been done; you are inventing them out of your own mind" [9]—for they all wanted to frighten us, thinking, "Their hands will drop from the work, and it will not be done." But now, O God, strengthen my hands.

10 One day when I went into the house of Shemaiah son of Delaiah son of Mehetabel, who was confined to his house, he said, "Let us meet together in the house of God, within the temple, and let us close the doors of the temple, for they

p Heb Gashmu

are coming to kill you; indeed, tonight they are coming to kill you." [11]But I said, "Should a man like me run away? Would a man like me go into the temple to save his life? I will not go in!" [12]Then I perceived and saw that God had not sent him at all, but he had pronounced the prophecy against me because Tobiah and Sanballat had hired him. [13]He was hired for this purpose, to intimidate me and make me sin by acting in this way, and so they could give me a bad name, in order to taunt me. [14]Remember Tobiah and Sanballat, O my God, according to these things that they did, and also the prophetess Noadiah and the rest of the prophets who wanted to make me afraid.

The Wall Completed

15 So the wall was finished on the twenty-fifth day of the month Elul, in fifty-two days. [16]And when all our enemies heard of it, all the nations around us were afraid[q] and fell greatly in their own esteem; for they perceived that this work had been accomplished with the help of our God. [17]Moreover in those days the nobles of Judah sent many letters to Tobiah, and Tobiah's letters came to them. [18]For many in Judah were bound by oath to him, because he was the son-in-law of Shecaniah son of Arah: and his son Jehohanan had married the daughter of Meshullam son of Berechiah. [19]Also they spoke of his good deeds in my presence, and reported my words to him. And Tobiah sent letters to intimidate me.

7 Now when the wall had been built and I had set up the doors, and the gatekeepers, the singers, and the Levites had been appointed, [2]I gave my brother Hanani charge over Jerusalem, along with Hananiah the commander of the citadel—for he was a faithful man and feared God more than many. [3]And I said to them, "The gates of Jerusalem are not to be opened until the sun is hot; while the gatekeepers[r] are still standing guard, let them shut and bar the doors. Appoint guards from among the inhabitants of Jerusalem, some at their watch posts, and others before their own houses." [4]The city was wide and large, but the people within it were few and no houses had been built.

Lists of the Returned Exiles

5 Then my God put it into my mind to assemble the nobles and the officials and the people to be enrolled by genealogy. And I found the book of the genealogy of those who were the first to come back, and I found the following written in it:

6 These are the people of the province who came up out of the captivity of those exiles whom King Nebuchadnezzar of Babylon had carried into exile; they returned to Jerusalem and Judah, each to his town. [7]They came with Zerubbabel, Jeshua, Nehemiah, Azariah, Raamiah, Nahamani, Mordecai, Bilshan, Mispereth, Bigvai, Nehum, Baanah.

7.6 Remembering Our Past

Because their cultural identity was threatened, the Jews in Ezra and Nehemiah kept careful track of their roots. All Jews wanted to trace their family lineage back to Abraham's grandson Israel (Jacob) in order to prove their Jewishness. In addition, descendants of Levi the priest and David the king took great pains to establish their heritage. The process had been vastly complicated by Nebuchadnezzar's burning of Jerusalem, which destroyed many records (see verses 61,64). This list (verses 8–73) almost exactly repeats the one found in Ezra 2.

The number of the Israelite people: [8]the descendants of Parosh, two thousand one hundred seventy-two. [9]Of Shephatiah, three hundred seventy-two. [10]Of Arah, six hundred fifty-two. [11]Of Pahath-moab, namely the descendants of Jeshua and Joab, two thousand eight hundred eighteen. [12]Of Elam, one thousand two hundred fifty-four. [13]Of Zattu, eight hundred forty-five. [14]Of Zaccai, seven hundred sixty. [15]Of Binnui, six hundred forty-eight. [16]Of Bebai, six hundred twenty-eight. [17]Of Azgad, two thousand three hundred twenty-two. [18]Of Adonikam, six hundred sixty-seven. [19]Of Bigvai, two thousand sixty-seven. [20]Of Adin, six hundred fifty-five. [21]Of Ater, namely of Hezekiah, ninety-eight. [22]Of Hashum, three hundred twenty-eight. [23]Of Bezai, three hundred twenty-four. [24]Of Hariph, one hundred twelve. [25]Of Gibeon, ninety-five. [26]The people of Bethlehem and Netophah, one hundred eighty-eight. [27]Of Anathoth, one hundred twenty-eight. [28]Of Beth-azmaveth, forty-two. [29]Of Kiriath-jearim, Chephirah, and Beeroth, seven hundred forty-three. [30]Of Ramah and Geba, six hundred twenty-one. [31]Of Michmas, one hundred twenty-two. [32]Of Bethel and Ai, one hundred twenty-three. [33]Of the other Nebo, fifty-two. [34]The descendants of the other Elam, one thousand two hundred fifty-four. [35]Of Harim, three hundred twenty. [36]Of Jericho, three hundred forty-five. [37]Of Lod, Hadid, and Ono, seven hundred twenty-one. [38]Of Senaah, three thousand nine hundred thirty.

39 The priests: the descendants of Jedaiah, namely the house of Jeshua, nine hundred seventy-three. [40]Of Immer, one thousand fifty-

two. [41]Of Pashhur, one thousand two hundred forty-seven. [42]Of Harim, one thousand seventeen.

43 The Levites: the descendants of Jeshua, namely of Kadmiel of the descendants of Hodevah, seventy-four. [44]The singers: the descendants of Asaph, one hundred forty-eight. [45]The gatekeepers: the descendants of Shallum, of Ater, of Talmon, of Akkub, of Hatita, of Shobai, one hundred thirty-eight.

46 The temple servants: the descendants of Ziha, of Hasupha, of Tabbaoth, [47]of Keros, of Sia, of Padon, [48]of Lebana, of Hagaba, of Shalmai, [49]of Hanan, of Giddel, of Gahar, [50]of Reaiah, of Rezin, of Nekoda, [51]of Gazzam, of Uzza, of Paseah, [52]of Besai, of Meunim, of Nephushesim, [53]of Bakbuk, of Hakupha, of Harhur, [54]of Bazlith, of Mehida, of Harsha, [55]of Barkos, of Sisera, of Temah, [56]of Neziah, of Hatipha.

57 The descendants of Solomon's servants: of Sotai, of Sophereth, of Perida, [58]of Jaala, of Darkon, of Giddel, [59]of Shephatiah, of Hattil, of Pochereth-hazzebaim, of Amon.

60 All the temple servants and the descendants of Solomon's servants were three hundred ninety-two.

61 The following were those who came up from Tel-melah, Tel-harsha, Cherub, Addon, and Immer, but they could not prove their ancestral houses or their descent, whether they belonged to Israel: [62]the descendants of Delaiah, of Tobiah, of Nekoda, six hundred forty-two. [63]Also, of the priests: the descendants of Hobaiah, of Hakkoz, of Barzillai (who had married one of the daughters of Barzillai the Gileadite and was called by their name). [64]These sought their registration among those enrolled in the genealogies, but it was not found there, so they were excluded from the priesthood as unclean; [65]the governor told them that they were not to partake of the most holy food, until a priest with Urim and Thummim should come.

66 The whole assembly together was forty-two thousand three hundred sixty, [67]besides their male and female slaves, of whom there were seven thousand three hundred thirty-seven; and they had two hundred forty-five singers, male and female. [68]They had seven hundred thirty-six horses, two hundred forty-five mules,[s] [69]four hundred thirty-five camels, and six thousand seven hundred twenty donkeys.

70 Now some of the heads of ancestral houses contributed to the work. The governor gave to the treasury one thousand darics of gold, fifty basins, and five hundred thirty priestly robes. [71]And some of the heads of ancestral houses gave into the building fund twenty thousand darics of gold and two thousand two hundred minas of silver. [72]And what the rest of the people gave was twenty thousand darics of gold, two thousand minas of silver, and sixty-seven priestly robes.

73 So the priests, the Levites, the gatekeepers, the singers, some of the people, the temple servants, and all Israel settled in their towns.

Ezra Summons the People to Obey the Law

8 When the seventh month came—the people of Israel being settled in their towns— [1]all the people gathered together into the square before the Water Gate. They told the scribe Ezra to bring the book of the law of Moses, which the LORD had given to Israel. [2]Accordingly, the priest Ezra brought the law before the assembly, both men and women and all who could hear with understanding. This was on the first day of the seventh month. [3]He read from it facing the square before the Water Gate from early morning until midday, in the presence of the men and the women and those who could understand; and the ears of all the people were attentive to the book of the law. [4]The scribe Ezra stood on a wooden platform that had been made for the purpose; and beside him stood Mattithiah, Shema, Anaiah, Uriah, Hilkiah, and Maaseiah on his right hand; and Pedaiah, Mishael, Malchijah, Hashum, Hashbaddanah, Zechariah, and Meshullam on his left hand. [5]And Ezra opened the book in the sight of all the people, for he was standing above all the people; and when he opened it, all the people stood up. [6]Then Ezra blessed the LORD, the great God, and all the people answered, "Amen, Amen," lifting up their hands. Then they bowed their heads and worshiped the LORD with their faces to the ground. [7]Also Jeshua, Bani, Sherebiah, Jamin, Akkub, Shabbethai, Hodiah, Maaseiah, Kelita, Azariah, Jozabad, Hanan, Pelaiah, the Levites,[t] helped the people to understand the law, while the people remained in their places. [8]So they read from the book, from the law of God, with interpretation. They gave the sense, so that the people understood the reading.

9 And Nehemiah, who was the governor, and Ezra the priest and scribe, and the Levites who

8.9 The Joy of the Lord

People sometimes think of the Old Testament as gloomy. Here, however (verses 9–12), Israel's leaders urged the people to stop weeping. Sadness, they said, did not suit a sacred day. As they discovered the next day, the law they mourned over commanded not weeping, but an eight-day celebration and campout.

[s] Ezra 2.66 and the margins of some Hebrew Mss: MT lacks *They had ... forty-five mules*   [t] 1 Esdras 9.48 Vg: Heb *and the Levites*

taught the people said to all the people, "This day is holy to the LORD your God; do not mourn or weep." For all the people wept when they heard the words of the law. [10]Then he said to them, "Go your way, eat the fat and drink sweet wine and send portions of them to those for whom nothing is prepared, for this day is holy to our LORD; and do not be grieved, for the joy of the LORD is your strength." [11]So the Levites stilled all the people, saying, "Be quiet, for this day is holy; do not be grieved." [12]And all the people went their way to eat and drink and to send portions and to make great rejoicing, because they had understood the words that were declared to them.

The Festival of Booths Celebrated

13 On the second day the heads of ancestral houses of all the people, with the priests and the Levites, came together to the scribe Ezra in order to study the words of the law. [14]And they found it written in the law, which the LORD had commanded by Moses, that the people of Israel

A People of the Book
Ezra stood on a wooden platform, reading from a simple scroll

The priest Ezra brought the law before the assembly... He read from it . . . from early morning until mid-day. 8.2–3

PICTURE IT: A VAST, HUSHED crowd watching as Ezra ascends a newly built platform in the square. As he opens the book, they stand up. They praise God, hands lifted high; then they bow down, faces in the dirt. Ezra begins to read. His helpers circulate in the crowd, explaining and interpreting what God's Word says. The people listen attentively. And then a strange sound begins to rise, spreading through the multitude. It is the sound of weeping.

The law Ezra read was very ancient, but that day marked something new. The Jews were becoming, in a way they had never been before, a people of the book. They were being rebuilt, with material as strong as the stones in their newly built city wall.

Throughout their history, they had drawn strength from two sources besides the law. One was the temple, where they worshiped God. It was a magnificently beautiful building in which they met God. The other was their leadership—first Moses, then Joshua, then the judges, and finally David and his offspring, the kings.

The Disappointing Reality

But these realities had not saved them from disgrace. The temple? For all its splendor it had become a meaningless symbol to most Jews. They had even put idols in it. God had finally allowed the Babylonians to burn the temple down.

After the exile the Jews had made rebuilding the temple their first priority (see Ezra 1–6). But it was no longer an automatic insurance policy. They could never again see the building as a substitute for real devotion to God.

Their leaders? Not one king, over hundreds of years, had come close to matching God's ideal. Most kings had been scoundrels—descendants of David in name only. After the exile, Israel had no king of its own. The Israelites were under the thumb of a Persian, who was determined to keep all power himself.

The Power of the Word

They turned to another source of power: the word of God. The great gathering of chapter 8 stands in contrast to temples and kings. The splendor of jewels and crowns is replaced by a single man atop a wooden platform, reading from a simple scroll. Yet the words he reads, carefully explained to all, show their power in the way they affect those who hear them. The people are moved to praise God, to weep over their sins, to change their behavior, and to make renewed promises to God.

From this time on, the Jews were known as the people of the book. They lived under foreign domination, so their political leadership became secondary. Their temple, while important, was never again a guarantee of God's presence. Increasingly they studied God's law and tried to obey it. A new kind of leader emerged, following Ezra—the scribe, a student of scripture. The nation we see at the end of Nehemiah looks very much like the nation we find, after 400 years of scriptural silence, when Jesus appears. Israelites found their unique strength neither in government nor in worship rituals, but in reverence for God's written word.

Life Questions: Can you point to ways in which God's Word has been powerful in your life? How has it changed you?

should live in booths[u] during the festival of the seventh month, 15and that they should publish and proclaim in all their towns and in Jerusalem as follows, "Go out to the hills and bring branches of olive, wild olive, myrtle, palm, and other leafy trees to make booths,[u] as it is written." 16So the people went out and brought them, and made booths[u] for themselves, each on the roofs of their houses, and in their courts and in the courts of the house of God, and in the square at the Water Gate and in the square at the Gate of Ephraim. 17And all the assembly of those who had returned from the captivity made booths[u] and lived in them; for from the days of Jeshua son of Nun to that day the people of Israel had not done so. And there was very great rejoicing. 18And day by day, from the first day to the last day, he read from the book of the law of God. They kept the festival seven days; and on the eighth day there was a solemn assembly, according to the ordinance.

National Confession

9 Now on the twenty-fourth day of this month the people of Israel were assembled with fasting and in sackcloth, and with earth on their heads.[v] 2Then those of Israelite descent separated themselves from all foreigners, and stood and confessed their sins and the iniquities of their ancestors. 3They stood up in their place and read from the book of the law of the LORD their God for a fourth part of the day, and for another fourth they made confession and worshiped the LORD their God. 4Then Jeshua, Bani, Kadmiel, Shebaniah, Bunni, Sherebiah, Bani, and Chenani stood on the stairs of the Levites and cried out with a loud voice to the LORD their God. 5Then the Levites, Jeshua, Kadmiel, Bani, Hashabneiah, Sherebiah, Hodiah, Shebaniah, and Pethahiah, said, "Stand up and bless the LORD your God from everlasting to everlasting. Blessed be your glorious name, which is exalted above all blessing and praise."

6 And Ezra said:[w] "You are the LORD, you alone; you have made heaven, the heaven of heavens, with all their host, the earth and all that is on it, the seas and all that is in them. To all of them you give life, and the host of heaven worships you. 7You are the LORD, the God who chose Abram and brought him out of Ur of the Chaldeans and gave him the name Abraham; 8and you found his heart faithful before you, and made with him a covenant to give to his descendants the land of the Canaanite, the Hittite, the Amorite, the Perizzite, the Jebusite, and the Girgashite; and you have fulfilled your promise, for you are righteous.

9 "And you saw the distress of our ancestors in Egypt and heard their cry at the Red Sea.[x] 10You performed signs and wonders against Pharaoh and all his servants and all the people of his land, for you knew that they acted insolently against our ancestors. You made a name for yourself, which remains to this day. 11And you divided

the sea before them, so that they passed through the sea on dry land, but you threw their pursuers into the depths, like a stone into mighty waters. 12Moreover, you led them by day with a pillar of cloud, and by night with a pillar of fire, to give them light on the way in which they should go. 13You came down also upon Mount Sinai, and spoke with them from heaven, and gave them right ordinances and true laws, good statutes and commandments, 14and you made known your holy sabbath to them and gave them commandments and statutes and a law through your servant Moses. 15For their hunger you gave them bread from heaven, and for their thirst you brought water for them out of the rock, and you told them to go in to possess the land that you swore to give them.

16 "But they and our ancestors acted presumptuously and stiffened their necks and did not obey your commandments; 17they refused to obey, and were not mindful of the wonders that you performed among them; but they stiffened their necks and determined to return to their slavery in Egypt. But you are a God ready to forgive, gracious and merciful, slow to anger and abounding in steadfast love, and you did not forsake them. 18Even when they had cast an image of a calf for themselves and said, 'This is your God who brought you up out of Egypt,' and had committed great blasphemies, 19you in your great mercies did not forsake them in the wilderness; the pillar of cloud that led them in the way did not leave them by day, nor the pillar of fire by night that gave them light on the way by which they should go. 20You gave your good spirit to instruct them, and did not withhold your manna from their mouths, and gave them water for their thirst. 21Forty years you sustained them in the wilder-

9.6 Stained-Glass Prayer

In cathedrals of medieval Europe, stained-glass windows served a dual purpose: 1) the artists designed them as aids to the worship of God; and 2) for a nonliterate society, scenes depicted in glass made it easier to learn biblical history. Old Testament Jews prohibited all images, but often their prayers served a similar purpose: they expressed worship and reminded the listeners of their providential past. This beautiful example reviews essential lessons from all of human history—an important guide for a people beginning a new life.

---

[u] Or *tabernacles*; Heb *succoth*   [v] Heb *on them*   [w] Gk: Heb lacks *And Ezra said*   [x] Or *Sea of Reeds*

ness so that they lacked nothing; their clothes did not wear out and their feet did not swell. ²²And you gave them kingdoms and peoples, and allotted to them every corner,ʸ so they took possession of the land of King Sihon of Heshbon and the land of King Og of Bashan. ²³You multiplied their descendants like the stars of heaven, and brought them into the land that you had told their ancestors to enter and possess. ²⁴So the descendants went in and possessed the land, and you subdued before them the inhabitants of the land, the Canaanites, and gave them into their hands, with their kings and the peoples of the land, to do with them as they pleased. ²⁵And they captured fortress cities and a rich land, and took possession of houses filled with all sorts of goods, hewn cisterns, vineyards, olive orchards, and fruit trees in abundance; so they ate, and were filled and became fat, and delighted themselves in your great goodness.

26 "Nevertheless they were disobedient and rebelled against you and cast your law behind their backs and killed your prophets, who had warned them in order to turn them back to you, and they committed great blasphemies. ²⁷Therefore you gave them into the hands of their enemies, who made them suffer. Then in the time of their suffering they cried out to you and you heard them from heaven, and according to your great mercies you gave them saviors who saved them from the hands of their enemies. ²⁸But after they had rest, they again did evil before you, and you abandoned them to the hands of their enemies, so that they had dominion over them; yet when they turned and cried to you, you heard from heaven, and many times you rescued them according to your mercies. ²⁹And you warned them in order to turn them back to your law. Yet they acted presumptuously and did not obey your commandments, but sinned against your ordinances, by the observance of which a person shall live. They turned a stubborn shoulder and stiffened their neck and would not obey. ³⁰Many years you were patient with them, and warned them by your spirit through your prophets; yet they would not listen. Therefore you handed them over to the peoples of the lands. ³¹Nevertheless, in your great mercies you did not make an end of them or forsake them, for you are a gracious and merciful God.

32 "Now therefore, our God—the great and mighty and awesome God, keeping covenant and steadfast love—do not treat lightly all the hardship that has come upon us, upon our kings, our officials, our priests, our prophets, our ancestors, and all your people, since the time of the kings of Assyria until today. ³³You have been just in all that has come upon us, for you have dealt faithfully and we have acted wickedly; ³⁴our kings, our

officials, our priests, and our ancestors have not kept your law or heeded the commandments and the warnings that you gave them. ³⁵Even in their own kingdom, and in the great goodness you bestowed on them, and in the large and rich land that you set before them, they did not serve you and did not turn from their wicked works. ³⁶Here we are, slaves to this day—slaves in the land that you gave to our ancestors to enjoy its fruit and its good gifts. ³⁷Its rich yield goes to the kings whom you have set over us because of our sins; they have power also over our bodies and over our livestock at their pleasure, and we are in great distress."

Those Who Signed the Covenant

38ᶻ Because of all this we make a firm agreement in writing, and on that sealed document are inscribed the names of our officials, our Levites, and our priests.

10ᵃ Upon the sealed document are the names of Nehemiah the governor, son of Hacaliah, and Zedekiah; ²Seraiah, Azariah, Jeremiah, ³Pashhur, Amariah, Malchijah, ⁴Hattush, Shebaniah, Malluch, ⁵Harim, Meremoth, Obadiah, ⁶Daniel, Ginnethon, Baruch, ⁷Meshullam, Abijah, Mijamin, ⁸Maaziah, Bilgai, Shemaiah; these are the priests. ⁹And the Levites: Jeshua son of Azaniah, Binnui of the sons of Henadad, Kadmiel; ¹⁰and their associates, Shebaniah, Hodiah, Kelita, Pelaiah, Hanan, ¹¹Mica, Rehob, Hashabiah, ¹²Zaccur, Sherebiah, Shebaniah, ¹³Hodiah, Bani, Beninu. ¹⁴The leaders of the people: Parosh, Pahath-moab, Elam, Zattu, Bani, ¹⁵Bunni, Azgad, Bebai, ¹⁶Adonijah, Bigvai, Adin, ¹⁷Ater, Hezekiah, Azzur, ¹⁸Hodiah, Hashum, Bezai, ¹⁹Hariph, Anathoth, Nebai, ²⁰Magpiash, Meshullam, Hezir, ²¹Meshezabel, Zadok, Jaddua, ²²Pelatiah, Hanan, Anaiah, ²³Hoshea, Hananiah, Hasshub, ²⁴Hallohesh, Pilha, Shobek, ²⁵Rehum, Hashabnah, Maaseiah, ²⁶Ahiah, Hanan, Anan, ²⁷Malluch, Harim, and Baanah.

Summary of the Covenant

28 The rest of the people, the priests, the Levites, the gatekeepers, the singers, the temple servants, and all who have separated themselves from the peoples of the lands to adhere to the law of God, their wives, their sons, their daughters, all who have knowledge and understanding, ²⁹join with their kin, their nobles, and enter into a curse and an oath to walk in God's law, which was given by Moses the servant of God, and to observe and do all the commandments of the LORD our Lord and his ordinances and his statutes. ³⁰We will not give our daughters to the peoples of the land or take their daughters for our sons; ³¹and if the peoples of the land bring in merchandise or any grain on the sabbath day to sell, we will not buy

---

ʸ Meaning of Heb uncertain   ᶻ Ch 10.1 in Heb   ᵃ Ch 10.2 in Heb it from them on the sabbath or on a holy day; and we will forego the crops of the seventh year and the exaction of every debt.

32　We also lay on ourselves the obligation to

10.31 A Year of Freedom

According to God's law, Jews were supposed to take every seventh day—the sabbath—off from work. Not only that, but every seventh year was a holiday from farming and a time when all debts were canceled (see Leviticus 25.1–7; Deuteronomy 15.1–11). But these rules for the seventh year were seldom if ever followed; "business as usual" generally prevailed.

charge ourselves yearly one-third of a shekel for the service of the house of our God: ³³for the rows of bread, the regular grain offering, the regular burnt offering, the sabbaths, the new moons, the appointed festivals, the sacred donations, and the sin offerings to make atonement for Israel, and for all the work of the house of our God. ³⁴We have also cast lots among the priests, the Levites, and the people, for the wood offering, to bring it into the house of our God, by ancestral houses, at appointed times, year by year, to burn on the altar of the Lord our God, as it is written in the law. ³⁵We obligate ourselves to bring the first fruits of our soil and the first fruits of all fruit of every tree, year by year, to the house of the Lord; ³⁶also to bring to the house of our God, to the priests who minister in the house of our God, the firstborn of our sons and of our livestock, as it is written in the law, and the firstlings of our herds and of our flocks; ³⁷and to bring the first of our dough, and our contributions, the fruit of every tree, the wine and the oil, to the priests, to the chambers of the house of our God; and to bring to the Levites the tithes from our soil, for it is the Levites who collect the tithes in all our rural towns. ³⁸And the priest, the descendant of Aaron, shall be with the Levites when the Levites receive the tithes; and the Levites shall bring up a tithe of the tithes to the house of our God, to the chambers of the storehouse. ³⁹For the people of Israel and the sons of Levi shall bring the contribution of grain, wine, and oil to the storerooms where the vessels of the sanctuary are, and where the priests that minister, and the gatekeepers and the singers are. We will not neglect the house of our God.

Population of the City Increased

11 Now the leaders of the people lived in Jerusalem; and the rest of the people cast lots to bring one out of ten to live in the holy city Jerusalem, while nine-tenths remained in the other towns. ²And the people blessed all those who willingly offered to live in Jerusalem.

3　These are the leaders of the province who lived in Jerusalem; but in the towns of Judah all lived on their property in their towns: Israel, the priests, the Levites, the temple servants, and the descendants of Solomon's servants. ⁴And in Jerusalem lived some of the Judahites and of the Benjaminites. Of the Judahites: Athaiah son of Uzziah son of Zechariah son of Amariah son of Shephatiah son of Mahalalel, of the descendants of Perez; ⁵and Maaseiah son of Baruch son of Col-hozeh son of Hazaiah son of Adaiah son of Joiarib son of Zechariah son of the Shilonite. ⁶All the descendants of Perez who lived in Jerusalem were four hundred sixty-eight valiant warriors.

11.1 City Fright

The 1990 U.S. census revealed that for the first time a majority of Americans lived in cities having more than a million in population. Worldwide, people are flocking to mega-cities such as Tokyo, London, and Mexico City. Not so in Nehemiah's day. The Israelites had learned that big cities like Jerusalem made prime targets for invading armies. In order to repopulate the city, leaders had to resort to a lottery system. (Characteristically, Nehemiah made sure the new settlers got proper credit.)

7　And these are the Benjaminites: Sallu son of Meshullam son of Joed son of Pedaiah son of Kolaiah son of Maaseiah son of Ithiel son of Jeshaiah. ⁸And his brothers*ᵇ* Gabbai, Sallai: nine hundred twenty-eight. ⁹Joel son of Zichri was their overseer; and Judah son of Hassenuah was second in charge of the city.

10　Of the priests: Jedaiah son of Joiarib, Jachin, ¹¹Seraiah son of Hilkiah son of Meshullam son of Zadok son of Meraioth son of Ahitub, officer of the house of God, ¹²and their associates who did the work of the house, eight hundred twenty-two; and Adaiah son of Jeroham son of Pelaliah son of Amzi son of Zechariah son of Pashhur son of Malchijah, ¹³and his associates, heads of ancestral houses, two hundred forty-two; and Amashsai son of Azarel son of Ahzai son of Meshillemoth son of Immer, ¹⁴and their associates, valiant warriors, one hundred twenty-eight; their overseer was Zabdiel son of Haggedolim.

15　And of the Levites: Shemaiah son of Hasshub son of Azrikam son of Hashabiah son of Bunni; ¹⁶and Shabbethai and Jozabad, of the leaders of the Levites, who were over the outside work of the house of God; ¹⁷and Mattaniah son of Mica son of Zabdi son of Asaph, who was the leader to begin the thanksgiving in prayer, and Bakbukiah,

ᵇ Gk Mss: Heb And after him

the second among his associates; and Abda son of Shammua son of Galal son of Jeduthun. [18]All the Levites in the holy city were two hundred eighty-four.

19 The gatekeepers, Akkub, Talmon and their associates, who kept watch at the gates, were one hundred seventy-two. [20]And the rest of Israel, and of the priests and the Levites, were in all the towns of Judah, all of them in their inheritance. [21]But the temple servants lived on Ophel; and Ziha and Gishpa were over the temple servants.

22 The overseer of the Levites in Jerusalem was Uzzi son of Bani son of Hashabiah son of Mattaniah son of Mica, of the descendants of Asaph, the singers, in charge of the work of the house of God. [23]For there was a command from the king concerning them, and a settled provision for the singers, as was required every day. [24]And Pethahiah son of Meshezabel, of the descendants of Zerah son of Judah, was at the king's hand in all matters concerning the people.

Villages outside Jerusalem

25 And as for the villages, with their fields, some of the people of Judah lived in Kiriath-arba and its villages, and in Dibon and its villages, and in Jekabzeel and its villages, [26]and in Jeshua and in Moladah and Beth-pelet, [27]in Hazar-shual, in Beer-sheba and its villages, [28]in Ziklag, in Meconah and its villages, [29]in En-rimmon, in Zorah, in Jarmuth, [30]Zanoah, Adullam, and their villages, Lachish and its fields, and Azekah and its villages. So they camped from Beer-sheba to the valley of Hinnom. [31]The people of Benjamin also lived from Geba onward, at Michmash, Aija, Bethel and its villages, [32]Anathoth, Nob, Ananiah, [33]Hazor, Ramah, Gittaim, [34]Hadid, Zeboim, Neballat, [35]Lod, and Ono, the valley of artisans. [36]And certain divisions of the Levites in Judah were joined to Benjamin.

A List of Priests and Levites

12 These are the priests and the Levites who came up with Zerubbabel son of Shealtiel, and Jeshua: Seraiah, Jeremiah, Ezra, [2]Amariah, Malluch, Hattush, [3]Shecaniah, Rehum, Meremoth, [4]Iddo, Ginnethoi, Abijah, [5]Mijamin, Maadiah, Bilgah, [6]Shemaiah, Joiarib, Jedaiah, [7]Sallu, Amok, Hilkiah, Jedaiah. These were the leaders of the priests and of their associates in the days of Jeshua.

8 And the Levites: Jeshua, Binnui, Kadmiel, Sherebiah, Judah, and Mattaniah, who with his associates was in charge of the songs of thanksgiving. [9]And Bakbukiah and Unno their associates stood opposite them in the service. [10]Jeshua was the father of Joiakim, Joiakim the father of Eliashib, Eliashib the father of Joiada, [11]Joiada the father of Jonathan, and Jonathan the father of Jaddua.

12 In the days of Joiakim the priests, heads of ancestral houses, were: of Seraiah, Meraiah; of Jeremiah, Hananiah; [13]of Ezra, Meshullam; of Amariah, Jehohanan; [14]of Malluchi, Jonathan; of Shebaniah, Joseph; [15]of Harim, Adna; of Meraioth, Helkai; [16]of Iddo, Zechariah; of Ginnethon, Meshullam; [17]of Abijah, Zichri; of Miniamin, of Moadiah, Piltai; [18]of Bilgah, Shammua; of Shemaiah, Jehonathan; [19]of Joiarib, Mattenai; of Jedaiah, Uzzi; [20]of Sallai, Kallai; of Amok, Eber; [21]of Hilkiah, Hashabiah; of Jedaiah, Nethanel.

22 As for the Levites, in the days of Eliashib, Joiada, Johanan, and Jaddua, there were recorded the heads of ancestral houses; also the priests until the reign of Darius the Persian. [23]The Levites, heads of ancestral houses, were recorded in the Book of the Annals until the days of Johanan son of Eliashib. [24]And the leaders of the Levites: Hashabiah, Sherebiah, and Jeshua son of Kadmiel, with their associates over against them, to praise and to give thanks, according to the commandment of David the man of God, section opposite to section. [25]Mattaniah, Bakbukiah, Obadiah, Meshullam, Talmon, and Akkub were gatekeepers standing guard at the storehouses of the gates. [26]These were in the days of Joiakim son of Jeshua son of Jozadak, and in the days of the governor Nehemiah and of the priest Ezra, the scribe.

Dedication of the City Wall

27 Now at the dedication of the wall of Jerusalem they sought out the Levites in all their places, to bring them to Jerusalem to celebrate the dedication with rejoicing, with thanksgivings and with singing, with cymbals, harps, and lyres.

12.27 Victory Party

Ezra, a religious leader, tried for a decade to get the wall rebuilt. Nehemiah, more pragmatic and action-oriented, managed to get the job done in 52 days (6.15). When the huge task was finished, he orchestrated a giant celebration featuring two choirs that circled the wall in opposite directions. Ezra led one of the choirs; Nehemiah, in an act of humility, brought up the rear of the other. When they met in the middle, near the temple area, they held a worship service such as Jerusalem had not seen in more than a century.

[28]The companies of the singers gathered together from the circuit around Jerusalem and from the villages of the Netophathites; [29]also from Beth-gilgal and from the region of Geba and Azmaveth; for the singers had built for themselves villages around Jerusalem. [30]And the priests and the Levites purified themselves; and they purified the people and the gates and the wall.

31 Then I brought the leaders of Judah up

onto the wall, and appointed two great companies that gave thanks and went in procession. One went to the right on the wall to the Dung Gate; [32]and after them went Hoshaiah and half the officials of Judah, [33]and Azariah, Ezra, Meshullam, [34]Judah, Benjamin, Shemaiah, and Jeremiah, [35]and some of the young priests with trumpets: Zechariah son of Jonathan son of Shemaiah son of Mattaniah son of Micaiah son of Zaccur son of Asaph; [36]and his kindred, Shemaiah, Azarel, Milalai, Gilalai, Maai, Nethanel, Judah, and Hanani, with the musical instruments of David the man of God; and the scribe Ezra went in front of them. [37]At the Fountain Gate, in front of them, they went straight up by the stairs of the city of David, at the ascent of the wall, above the house of David, to the Water Gate on the east.

38 The other company of those who gave thanks went to the left,[c] and I followed them with half of the people on the wall, above the Tower of the Ovens, to the Broad Wall, [39]and above the Gate of Ephraim, and by the Old Gate, and by the Fish Gate and the Tower of Hananel and the Tower of the Hundred, to the Sheep Gate; and they came to a halt at the Gate of the Guard. [40]So both companies of those who gave thanks stood in the house of God, and I and half of the officials with me; [41]and the priests Eliakim, Maaseiah, Miniamin, Micaiah, Elioenai, Zechariah, and Hananiah, with trumpets; [42]and Maaseiah, Shemaiah, Eleazar, Uzzi, Jehohanan, Malchijah, Elam, and Ezer. And the singers sang with Jezrahiah as their leader. [43]They offered great sacrifices that day and rejoiced, for God had made them rejoice with great joy; the women and children also rejoiced. The joy of Jerusalem was heard far away.

Temple Responsibilities

44 On that day men were appointed over the chambers for the stores, the contributions, the first fruits, and the tithes, to gather into them the portions required by the law for the priests and for the Levites from the fields belonging to the towns; for Judah rejoiced over the priests and the Levites who ministered. [45]They performed the service of their God and the service of purification, as did the singers and the gatekeepers, according to the command of David and his son Solomon. [46]For in the days of David and Asaph long ago there was a leader of the singers, and there were songs of praise and thanksgiving to God. [47]In the days of Zerubbabel and in the days of Nehemiah all Israel gave the daily portions for the singers and the gatekeepers. They set apart that which was for the Levites; and the Levites set apart that which was for the descendants of Aaron.

Foreigners Separated from Israel

13 On that day they read from the book of Moses in the hearing of the people; and in it was found written that no Ammonite or Moabite should ever enter the assembly of God, [2]because they did not meet the Israelites with bread and water, but hired Balaam against them to curse them—yet our God turned the curse into a blessing. [3]When the people heard the law, they separated from Israel all those of foreign descent.

The Reforms of Nehemiah

4 Now before this, the priest Eliashib, who was appointed over the chambers of the house of our God, and who was related to Tobiah, [5]prepared for Tobiah a large room where they had previously put the grain offering, the frankincense, the vessels, and the tithes of grain, wine, and oil, which were given by commandment to the Levites, singers, and gatekeepers, and the contributions for the priests. [6]While this was taking place I was not in Jerusalem, for in the thirty-second year of King Artaxerxes of Babylon I went to the king. After some time I asked leave of the king [7]and returned to Jerusalem. I then discovered the wrong that Eliashib had done on behalf of Tobiah, preparing a room for him in the courts of the house of God. [8]And I was very angry, and I threw all the household furniture of Tobiah out of the room. [9]Then I gave orders and they cleansed the chambers, and I brought back the vessels of the house of God, with the grain offering and the frankincense.

10 I also found out that the portions of the Levites had not been given to them; so that the Levites and the singers, who had conducted the service, had gone back to their fields. [11]So I remonstrated with the officials and said, "Why is the house of God forsaken?" And I gathered them together and set them in their stations. [12]Then all Judah brought the tithe of the grain, wine, and oil into the storehouses. [13]And I appointed as treasurers over the storehouses the priest Shelemiah, the scribe Zadok, and Pedaiah of the Levites, and as their assistant Hanan son of Zaccur son of Mattaniah, for they were considered faithful; and their duty was to distribute to their associates. [14]Remember me, O my God, concerning this, and do not wipe out my good deeds that I have done for the house of my God and for his service.

Sabbath Reforms Begun

15 In those days I saw in Judah people treading wine presses on the sabbath, and bringing in heaps of grain and loading them on donkeys; and also wine, grapes, figs, and all kinds of burdens, which they brought into Jerusalem on the sabbath day; and I warned them at that time against selling food. [16]Tyrians also, who lived in the city,

brought in fish and all kinds of merchandise and sold them on the sabbath to the people of Judah, and in Jerusalem. [17]Then I remonstrated with the nobles of Judah and said to them, "What is this evil thing that you are doing, profaning the sabbath day? [18]Did not your ancestors act in this way, and did not our God bring all this disaster on us and on this city? Yet you bring more wrath on Israel by profaning the sabbath."

19 When it began to be dark at the gates of Jerusalem before the sabbath, I commanded that the doors should be shut and gave orders that they should not be opened until after the sabbath. And I set some of my servants over the gates, to prevent any burden from being brought in on the

13.19 Never-ending Task

Fairy tales end, "and they lived happily ever after," but real life never does. Pointedly, Nehemiah's book does not close with the triumph of chapter 12, but with a preview of the continuing hassles of leadership. Old problems recurred, new problems sprang up, and Nehemiah tackled both kinds with courage and wisdom.

sabbath day. [20]Then the merchants and sellers of all kinds of merchandise spent the night outside Jerusalem once or twice. [21]But I warned them and said to them, "Why do you spend the night in front of the wall? If you do so again, I will lay hands on you." From that time on they did not come on the sabbath. [22]And I commanded the Levites that they should purify themselves and

come and guard the gates, to keep the sabbath day holy. Remember this also in my favor, O my God, and spare me according to the greatness of your steadfast love.

Mixed Marriages Condemned

23 In those days also I saw Jews who had married women of Ashdod, Ammon, and Moab; [24]and half of their children spoke the language of Ashdod, and they could not speak the language of Judah, but spoke the language of various peoples. [25]And I contended with them and cursed them and beat some of them and pulled out their hair; and I made them take an oath in the name of God, saying, "You shall not give your daughters to their sons, or take their daughters for your sons or for yourselves. [26]Did not King Solomon of Israel sin on account of such women? Among the many nations there was no king like him, and he was beloved by his God, and God made him king over all Israel; nevertheless, foreign women made even him to sin. [27]Shall we then listen to you and do all this great evil and act treacherously against our God by marrying foreign women?"

28 And one of the sons of Jehoiada, son of the high priest Eliashib, was the son-in-law of Sanballat the Horonite; I chased him away from me. [29]Remember them, O my God, because they have defiled the priesthood, the covenant of the priests and the Levites.

30 Thus I cleansed them from everything foreign, and I established the duties of the priests and Levites, each in his work; [31]and I provided for the wood offering, at appointed times, and for the first fruits. Remember me, O my God, for good.

ESTHER

A Profile of Courage
Heroes act while others stand and watch

W HAT MAKES A HERO? ASK one, and you may find a surprising nonchalance: "I'm sure other people would have done exactly the same thing," they say. "I was just in the right place at the right time."

People become heroes because they take quick action at that "right time," while others stand watching in horror. The true hero recognizes the crisis and moves to meet it. This kind of courage made Esther great—worthy of a book in the Bible.

> *"I will go to the king, though it is against the law; and if I perish, I perish."* 4.16

A Queen Risks Her Life

 By the "accident" of her beauty and the "accident" of the former queen's dismissal, Esther found herself queen of one of the greatest powers of the world. Then, when all seemed smooth, her crucial moment came.

This moment has been echoed many times since. As a successful racial minority in the Persian empire, Esther's people, the Jews, had not melted into their surroundings. Others were jealous of their success and separatism. A vengeful prime minister, Haman, made up his mind to destroy them. He issued an edict of government-sponsored genocide.

Would Queen Esther intervene? Doing so would risk her life. And what difference could she make? She was a powerless sex partner to a king who strongly preferred women who never interfered with his wishes. She came only when he called, and he had not called her for a month. And yet she alone, of all the Jews, had access to the king.

Esther's cousin Mordecai reminded her of her unique place. "Who knows? Perhaps you have come to royal dignity for just such a time as this." Esther responded with action. Her courageous words are a classic statement of heroism: "I will go to the king, though it is against the law; and if I perish, I perish" (4.16).

Coincidence or Plan?

The book of Esther shows, though indirectly, God's heroic concern for the Jews. The story runs on a series of extraordinary coincidences. Esther just "happened" to be chosen as the new queen. The king just "happened" to be unable to sleep, and, when he picked up some reading, just "happened" across an account of a good deed Esther's cousin Mordecai had done. The evil Haman just "happened" along at that crucial moment. These coincidences, along with Esther's courage, tilted terrible events toward the Jews' favor.

Were these really mere coincidences? Or was God behind them? The book of Esther doesn't say directly: God is not mentioned even once, and sometimes seems deliberately left out. But believing readers, whether Jews or Christians, can have no doubt. All of life is under God's command. Nothing just happens. These "coincidences" were part of God's plan to save the Jews.

God protected his people because he loved them—because he had chosen them from the beginning. Even their enemies knew the "luck" of the Jews. (See Esther 6.13, for instance.) Esther's story is another chapter in the amazing story of God's perpetual love for the Jews. Though sometimes far from his will, this tiny, often hated minority has survived and thrived down the centuries.

From Haman to Hitler, vindictive leaders have hated the Jews. Yet while no other group has been so hated, no other group has shown the Jews' ability to overcome adversity. Nor can any other ethnic group alive today point to such continuity with their ancestors. They have endured as a unique and great people. How? Esther shows that God's exquisite timing—combined with the courage of individuals who "happened" to be in the right place at the right time—made his chosen people prosper.

How to Read Esther

Esther makes such suspenseful reading that most people will find it hard to quit. As in a detective story, every detail folds into another. You don't know, from one page to the next, how the drama will turn out.

The essence of Esther lies in its characters. Study Esther, Mordecai, Haman, and King Ahasuerus. What kind of people were they? What were their ambitions? What were their strengths and weaknesses? What crucial moment showed the true character of each? What do you learn from them that can help you rise to the challenge when you are "the right person at the right place at the right time"?

Knowing the historical setting for Esther's story can enrich your study. A good commentary or Bible dictionary (under "Esther") will illuminate many of the details that make Esther such a convincing historical document.

PEOPLE YOU'LL MEET IN ESTHER

ESTHER *(p. 505)*
MORDECAI *(p. 509)*

3-TRACK READING PLAN

For an explanation and complete listing of the 3-track reading plan, turn to page 7.

TRACK 1: *Two-Week Courses on the Bible*
See page 7 for information on these courses.

TRACK 2: *An Overview of Esther in 1 Day*
☐ Day 1. Read the Introduction to Esther and chapter 4, in which Esther learns that her people are in dire straits and decides to take action.

Now turn to page 9 for your next Track 2 reading project.

TRACK 3: *All of Esther in 8 Days*
After you have read through Esther, turn to pages 10–14 for your next Track 3 reading project.

☐1   ☐2   ☐3   ☐4   ☐5   ☐6–7   ☐8   ☐9–10

King Ahasuerus Deposes Queen Vashti

1 This happened in the days of Ahasuerus, the same Ahasuerus who ruled over one hundred twenty-seven provinces from India to Ethiopia.[a] ²In those days when King Ahasuerus sat on his royal throne in the citadel of Susa, ³in the third year of his reign, he gave a banquet for all his officials and ministers. The army of Persia and Media and the nobles and governors of the provinces were present, ⁴while he displayed the great wealth of his kingdom and the splendor and pomp of his majesty for many days, one hundred eighty days in all.

5 When these days were completed, the king gave for all the people present in the citadel of Susa, both great and small, a banquet lasting for seven days, in the court of the garden of the king's palace. ⁶There were white cotton curtains and blue hangings tied with cords of fine linen and purple to silver rings[b] and marble pillars. There were couches of gold and silver on a mosaic pavement of porphyry, marble, mother-of-pearl, and colored stones. ⁷Drinks were served in golden goblets, goblets of different kinds, and the royal wine was lavished according to the bounty of the king. ⁸Drinking was by flagons, without restraint; for the king had given orders to all the officials of his palace to do as each one desired. ⁹Furthermore, Queen Vashti gave a banquet for the women in the palace of King Ahasuerus.

10 On the seventh day, when the king was merry with wine, he commanded Mehuman, Biztha, Harbona, Bigtha and Abagtha, Zethar and Carkas, the seven eunuchs who attended him, ¹¹to bring Queen Vashti before the king, wearing the royal crown, in order to show the peoples and the officials her beauty; for she was fair to behold. ¹²But Queen Vashti refused to come at the king's

a Or *Nubia;* Heb *Cush*   *b* Or *rods*

command conveyed by the eunuchs. At this the king was enraged, and his anger burned within him.

13 Then the king consulted the sages who knew the laws[c] (for this was the king's procedure

1.7 The Influence of Wine

Other historical sources bear out the accuracy of this verse. Greek historian Herodotus wrote that the Persians "are very fond of wine, and drink it in large quantities . . . It is also their general practice to deliberate upon affairs of weight when they are drunk . . . Sometimes, however, they are sober at their first deliberation, but in this case they always reconsider the matter under the influence of wine."

toward all who were versed in law and custom, [14]and those next to him were Carshena, Shethar, Admatha, Tarshish, Meres, Marsena, and Memucan, the seven officials of Persia and Media, who had access to the king, and sat first in the kingdom): [15]"According to the law, what is to be done to Queen Vashti because she has not performed the command of King Ahasuerus conveyed by the eunuchs?" [16]Then Memucan said in the presence of the king and the officials, "Not only has Queen Vashti done wrong to the king, but also to all the officials and all the peoples who are in all the provinces of King Ahasuerus. [17]For this deed of the queen will be made known to all women, causing them to look with contempt on their husbands, since they will say, 'King Ahasuerus commanded Queen Vashti to be brought before him, and she did not come.' [18]This very day the noble ladies of Persia and Media who have heard of the queen's behavior will rebel against[d] the king's officials, and there will be no end of contempt and wrath! [19]If it pleases the king, let a royal order go out from him, and let it be written among the laws of the Persians and the Medes so that it may not be altered, that Vashti is never again to come before King Ahasuerus; and let the king give her royal position to another who is better than she. [20]So when the decree made by the king is proclaimed throughout all his kingdom, vast as it is, all women will give honor to their husbands, high and low alike."

21 This advice pleased the king and the officials, and the king did as Memucan proposed; [22]he sent letters to all the royal provinces, to every province in its own script and to every people in its own language, declaring that every man should be master in his own house.[e]

Esther Becomes Queen

2 After these things, when the anger of King Ahasuerus had abated, he remembered Vashti and what she had done and what had been decreed against her. [2]Then the king's servants who attended him said, "Let beautiful young virgins be sought out for the king. [3]And let the king appoint commissioners in all the provinces of his kingdom to gather all the beautiful young virgins to the harem in the citadel of Susa under custody of Hegai, the king's eunuch, who is in charge of the women; let their cosmetic treatments be given them. [4]And let the girl who pleases the king be queen instead of Vashti." This pleased the king, and he did so.

5 Now there was a Jew in the citadel of Susa whose name was Mordecai son of Jair son of Shimei son of Kish, a Benjaminite. [6]Kish[f] had been carried away from Jerusalem among the captives carried away with King Jeconiah of Judah, whom King Nebuchadnezzar of Babylon had

2.6 Those Who Stayed Behind

Ezra and Nehemiah, the books preceding Esther, tell the inspiring story of Jews returning to Jerusalem after years of captivity. Actually, only 50,000 Jews came back to their plundered land, however. Many more—among them Mordecai's family—stayed behind, and some of these prospered. The story of Esther takes place in that foreign setting, ruled by the Persian empire. Modern-day communities of Jews in Iraq and Iran have descended from these ancient exiles.

carried away. [7]Mordecai[g] had brought up Hadassah, that is Esther, his cousin, for she had neither father nor mother; the girl was fair and beautiful, and when her father and her mother died, Mordecai adopted her as his own daughter. [8]So when the king's order and his edict were proclaimed, and when many young women were gathered in the citadel of Susa in custody of Hegai, Esther also was taken into the king's palace and put in custody of Hegai, who had charge of the women. [9]The girl pleased him and won his favor, and he quickly provided her with her cosmetic treatments and her portion of food, and with seven chosen maids from the king's palace, and advanced her and her maids to the best place in the harem. [10]Esther did not reveal her people or kindred, for Mordecai had charged her not to tell. [11]Every day Mordecai would walk around in front of the court of the harem, to learn how Esther was and how she fared.

12 The turn came for each girl to go in to

---

[c] Cn: Heb *times*   [d] Cn: Heb *will tell*   [e] Heb adds *and speak according to the language of his people*   [f] Heb *a*
Benjamite [6]who   [g] Heb *He*

King Ahasuerus, after being twelve months under the regulations for the women, since this was the regular period of their cosmetic treatment, six months with oil of myrrh and six months with perfumes and cosmetics for women. 13When the girl went in to the king she was given whatever she asked for to take with her from the harem to the king's palace. 14In the evening she went in; then in the morning she came back to the second harem in custody of Shaashgaz, the king's eunuch, who was in charge of the concubines; she did not go in to the king again, unless the king delighted in her and she was summoned by name.

15 When the turn came for Esther daughter of Abihail the uncle of Mordecai, who had adopted her as his own daughter, to go in to the king, she asked for nothing except what Hegai the king's eunuch, who had charge of the women, advised. Now Esther was admired by all who saw her. 16When Esther was taken to King Ahasuerus in his royal palace in the tenth month, which is the month of Tebeth, in the seventh year of his

2.16 Off at War

Between Queen Vashti's dismissal (chapter 1) and Esther's acceptance as the new queen, four years passed. Why did Ahasuerus wait so long? Historians say that during these four years he was off fighting, unsuccessfully trying to conquer Greece. The six-month conference described in chapter 1 was, most likely, a consultation to prepare the invasion.

reign, 17the king loved Esther more than all the other women; of all the virgins she won his favor and devotion, so that he set the royal crown on her head and made her queen instead of Vashti. 18Then the king gave a great banquet to all his officials and ministers—"Esther's banquet." He also granted a holiday[h] to the provinces, and gave gifts with royal liberality.

Mordecai Discovers a Plot

19 When the virgins were being gathered together,[i] Mordecai was sitting at the king's gate. 20Now Esther had not revealed her kindred or her people, as Mordecai had charged her; for Esther obeyed Mordecai just as when she was brought up by him. 21In those days, while Mordecai was sitting at the king's gate, Bigthan and Teresh, two of the king's eunuchs, who guarded the threshold, became angry and conspired to assassinate[j] King Ahasuerus. 22But the matter came to the knowledge of Mordecai, and he told it to Queen Esther, and Esther told the king in the name of Mordecai. 23When the affair was investigated and found to

be so, both the men were hanged on the gallows. It was recorded in the book of the annals in the presence of the king.

Haman Undertakes to Destroy the Jews

3 After these things King Ahasuerus promoted Haman son of Hammedatha the Agagite, and advanced him and set his seat above all the officials who were with him. 2And all the king's servants who were at the king's gate bowed down and did obeisance to Haman; for the king had so commanded concerning him. But Mordecai did not bow down or do obeisance. 3Then the king's servants who were at the king's gate said to Mordecai, "Why do you disobey the king's command?" 4When they spoke to him day after day and he would not listen to them, they told Haman, in order to see whether Mordecai's words would avail; for he had told them that he was a Jew. 5When Haman saw that Mordecai did not bow down or do obeisance to him, Haman was infuriated. 6But he thought it beneath him to lay hands on Mordecai alone. So, having been told who Mordecai's people were, Haman plotted to destroy all the Jews, the people of Mordecai, throughout the whole kingdom of Ahasuerus.

7 In the first month, which is the month of Nisan, in the twelfth year of King Ahasuerus, they cast Pur—which means "the lot"—before Haman for the day and for the month, and the lot fell on the thirteenth day[k] of the twelfth month, which is the month of Adar. 8Then Haman said to King Ahasuerus, "There is a certain people scattered and separated among the peoples in all the provinces of your kingdom; their laws are different from those of every other people, and they do not keep the king's laws, so that it is not appropriate for the king to tolerate them. 9If it pleases the king, let a decree be issued for their destruction, and I will pay ten thousand talents of silver into the hands of those who have charge of the king's business, so that they may put it into the king's treasuries." 10So the king took his signet ring from his hand and gave it to Haman son of Hammedatha the Agagite, the enemy of the Jews. 11The king said to Haman, "The money is given to you, and the people as well, to do with them as it seems good to you."

12 Then the king's secretaries were summoned on the thirteenth day of the first month, and an edict, according to all that Haman commanded, was written to the king's satraps and to the governors over all the provinces and to the officials of all the peoples, to every province in its own script and every people in its own language; it was written in the name of King Ahasuerus and sealed with the king's ring. 13Letters were sent by couriers to all the king's provinces, giving orders

---

h Or *an amnesty*   *i* Heb adds *a second time*   *j* Heb *to lay hands on*   *k* Cn Compare Gk and verse 13 below: Heb
the twelfth month

to destroy, to kill, and to annihilate all Jews, young and old, women and children, in one day, the thirteenth day of the twelfth month, which is the month of Adar, and to plunder their goods.

3.13 Pony Express

Persia boasted one of the first efficient communication systems. The king kept men and horses stationed a day's journey apart on all major highways. Each messenger rode for a day and relayed the message on to the next station. "Nothing mortal travels so fast as these Persian messengers," wrote the historian Herodotus. Their efficiency made it essential for Mordecai and Esther to overturn the king's edict as soon as possible.

[14]A copy of the document was to be issued as a decree in every province by proclamation, calling on all the peoples to be ready for that day. [15]The couriers went quickly by order of the king, and the decree was issued in the citadel of Susa. The king and Haman sat down to drink; but the city of Susa was thrown into confusion.

Esther Agrees to Help the Jews

4 When Mordecai learned all that had been done, Mordecai tore his clothes and put on sackcloth and ashes, and went through the city, wailing with a loud and bitter cry; [2]he went up to the entrance of the king's gate, for no one might enter the king's gate clothed with sackcloth. [3]In every province, wherever the king's command

and his decree came, there was great mourning among the Jews, with fasting and weeping and lamenting, and most of them lay in sackcloth and ashes.

[4]When Esther's maids and her eunuchs came and told her, the queen was deeply distressed; she sent garments to clothe Mordecai, so that he might take off his sackcloth; but he would not accept them. [5]Then Esther called for Hathach, one of the king's eunuchs, who had been appointed to attend her, and ordered him to go to Mordecai to learn what was happening and why. [6]Hathach went out to Mordecai in the open square of the city in front of the king's gate, [7]and Mordecai told him all that had happened to him, and the exact sum of money that Haman had promised to pay into the king's treasuries for the destruction of the Jews. [8]Mordecai also gave him a copy of the written decree issued in Susa for their destruction, that he might show it to Esther, explain it to her, and charge her to go to the king to make supplication to him and entreat him for her people.

[9]Hathach went and told Esther what Mordecai had said. [10]Then Esther spoke to Hathach and gave him a message for Mordecai, saying, [11]"All the king's servants and the people of the king's provinces know that if any man or woman goes to the king inside the inner court without being called, there is but one law—all alike are to be put to death. Only if the king holds out the golden scepter to someone, may that person live. I myself have not been called to come in to the king for thirty days." [12]When they told Mordecai what Esther had said, [13]Mordecai told them to reply to Esther, "Do not think that in the king's palace you

MORDECAI *Standing Tall*

HIS FAMILY HAD COME TO Persia as virtual slaves, captives of Jerusalem's last stand against the Babylonians. Yet even in enemy territory Mordecai succeeded in business. His relative, Esther, found more success; she was selected from all the beautiful women in the land as King Ahasuerus' queen.

With his connections inside the palace, Mordecai probably had high ambitions. He would have to hide his background, though, and he strongly advised Esther to keep her Jewish heritage a secret as well.

Yet when a crisis came Mordecai stood tall, showing extraordinary courage. The king had named the evil Haman his second-in-command, and everyone bowed before him—everyone except Mordecai, who stayed on his feet. His motive? Perhaps he knew of Haman's character, and of his hatred for Jews.

When Haman set out to annihilate all Jews in the empire, Mordecai urged Esther to "come out" completely, even at the risk of her life. Clearly, loyalty to their people came before success or safety.

Mordecai's stand and Esther's courage led to a dramatic turnaround for the whole community of Jewish exiles. King Ahasuerus rewarded Mordecai with a high position in his court. More importantly, his own community honored him, "for he sought the good of his people and interceded for the welfare of all his descendants" (10.3).

The feast of Purim, still celebrated by Jews today, commemorates these amazing events. Against history's dark background of anti-Semitism, Mordecai's triumph shines.

Life Questions: Whom do you speak up for? For what group would you willingly risk your life or your reputation?

will escape any more than all the other Jews. [14]For if you keep silence at such a time as this, relief and deliverance will rise for the Jews from another quarter, but you and your father's family will perish. Who knows? Perhaps you have come to royal

4.13 One Safe Jew?

Esther, ensconced in the safety and luxury of the palace, was possibly the only Jew in Persia who had not heard of the extermination plans. Most likely she would have been spared, but, as Mordecai warned, the king might just as easily turn against her. Mordecai had a sophisticated view of God's providence that never lapsed into fatalism. He believed that God would somehow preserve his people; yet he also knew that God might accomplish that goal through the courageous actions of people like himself and Esther.

dignity for just such a time as this." [15]Then Esther said in reply to Mordecai, [16]"Go, gather all the Jews to be found in Susa, and hold a fast on my behalf, and neither eat nor drink for three days, night or day. I and my maids will also fast as you do. After that I will go to the king, though it is against the law; and if I perish, I perish." [17]Mordecai then went away and did everything as Esther had ordered him.

Esther's Banquet

5 On the third day Esther put on her royal robes and stood in the inner court of the king's palace, opposite the king's hall. The king was sitting on his royal throne inside the palace opposite the entrance to the palace. [2]As soon as the king saw Queen Esther standing in the court, she won his favor and he held out to her the golden scepter that was in his hand. Then Esther approached and touched the top of the scepter. [3]The king said to her, "What is it, Queen Esther? What is your request? It shall be given you, even to the half of my kingdom." [4]Then Esther said, "If it pleases the king, let the king and Haman come today to a banquet that I have prepared for the king." [5]Then the king said, "Bring Haman quickly, so that we may do as Esther desires." So the king and Haman came to the banquet that Esther had prepared. [6]While they were drinking wine, the king said to Esther, "What is your petition? It shall be granted you. And what is your request? Even to the half of my kingdom, it shall be fulfilled." [7]Then Esther said, "This is my petition and request: [8]If I have won the king's favor, and if it pleases the king to grant my petition and fulfill my request, let the king and Haman come

tomorrow to the banquet that I will prepare for them, and then I will do as the king has said."

Haman Plans to Have Mordecai Hanged

[9] Haman went out that day happy and in good spirits. But when Haman saw Mordecai in the king's gate, and observed that he neither rose nor trembled before him, he was infuriated with Mordecai; [10]nevertheless Haman restrained himself and went home. Then he sent and called for his friends and his wife Zeresh, [11]and Haman recounted to them the splendor of his riches, the number of his sons, all the promotions with which the king had honored him, and how he had advanced him above the officials and the ministers of the king. [12]Haman added, "Even Queen Esther let no one but myself come with the king to the banquet that she prepared. Tomorrow also I am invited by her, together with the king. [13]Yet all this does me no good so long as I see the Jew Mordecai sitting at the king's gate." [14]Then his wife Zeresh and all his friends said to him, "Let a gallows fifty cubits high be made, and in the morning tell the king to have Mordecai hanged on it; then go with the king to the banquet in good spirits." This advice pleased Haman, and he had the gallows made.

The King Honors Mordecai

6 On that night the king could not sleep, and he gave orders to bring the book of records,

6.1 Ahasuerus: A Wild Man

Other historical sources portray Ahasuerus as a dangerously impulsive king. When a bridge he had ordered built was destroyed in a storm, he commanded that the sea receive 300 lashes, and then had the bridge builders beheaded. When one of his loyal subjects contributed a huge sum toward a military expedition, Ahasuerus was so enraptured that he returned the money, along with a handsome gift of his own. But when the same man asked Ahasuerus to let just one of his sons go free from the draft, Ahasuerus, enraged, ordered the son cut into two and the army to march between the pieces.

the annals, and they were read to the king. [2]It was found written how Mordecai had told about Bigthana and Teresh, two of the king's eunuchs, who guarded the threshold, and who had conspired to assassinate[l] King Ahasuerus. [3]Then the king said, "What honor or distinction has been bestowed on Mordecai for this?" The king's servants who attended him said, "Nothing has been done for him." [4]The king said, "Who is in the court?" Now Haman had just entered the outer court of

l Heb *to lay hands on*

the king's palace to speak to the king about having Mordecai hanged on the gallows that he had prepared for him. [5]So the king's servants told him, "Haman is there, standing in the court." The king said, "Let him come in." [6]So Haman came in, and the king said to him, "What shall be done for the man whom the king wishes to honor?" Haman said to himself, "Whom would the king wish to honor more than me?" [7]So Haman said to the king, "For the man whom the king wishes to honor, [8]let royal robes be brought, which the king has worn, and a horse that the king has ridden, with a royal crown on its head. [9]Let the robes and the horse be handed over to one of the king's most noble officials; let him[m] robe the man whom the king wishes to honor, and let him[m] conduct the man on horseback through the open square of the city, proclaiming before him: 'Thus shall it be done for the man whom the king wishes to honor.'" [10]Then the king said to Haman, "Quickly, take the robes and the horse, as you have said, and do so to the Jew Mordecai who sits at the king's gate. Leave out nothing that you have mentioned." [11]So Haman took the robes and the horse and robed Mordecai and led him riding through the open square of the city, proclaiming, "Thus shall it be done for the man whom the king wishes to honor."

12 Then Mordecai returned to the king's gate, but Haman hurried to his house, mourning and with his head covered. [13]When Haman told his wife Zeresh and all his friends everything that had happened to him, his advisers and his wife Zeresh said to him, "If Mordecai, before whom your downfall has begun, is of the Jewish people, you will not prevail against him, but will surely fall before him."

Haman's Downfall and Mordecai's Advancement

14 While they were still talking with him, the king's eunuchs arrived and hurried Haman off to the banquet that Esther had prepared. [1]So the king and Haman went in to feast with Queen Esther. [2]On the second day, as they were drinking wine, the king again said to Esther, "What is your petition, Queen Esther? It shall be granted you. And what is your request? Even to the half of my kingdom, it shall be fulfilled." [3]Then Queen Esther answered, "If I have won your favor, O king, and if it pleases the king, let my life be given me—that is my petition—and the lives of my people—that is my request. [4]For we have been sold, I and my people, to be destroyed, to be killed, and to be annihilated. If we had been sold merely as slaves, men and women, I would have held my peace; but no enemy can compensate for this damage to the king."[n] [5]Then King Ahasuerus said to Queen Esther, "Who is he, and where

is he, who has presumed to do this?" [6]Esther said, "A foe and enemy, this wicked Haman!" Then Haman was terrified before the king and the queen. [7]The king rose from the feast in wrath and

7.1 Subtle Approach

Esther knew well the perils of standing up to autocratic Ahasuerus: she had gotten her job because of the king's furious response to a queen's brashness (1.12—2.7). Esther's "banquet plot" shows that she had mastered the wiles necessary to soften the king. She grew increasingly bold and more direct, finally convincing the king to issue another decree, countering the one against the Jews—a rare turnabout for a Persian ruler (8.8).

went into the palace garden, but Haman stayed to beg his life from Queen Esther, for he saw that the king had determined to destroy him. [8]When the king returned from the palace garden to the banquet hall, Haman had thrown himself on the couch where Esther was reclining; and the king said, "Will he even assault the queen in my presence, in my own house?" As the words left the mouth of the king, they covered Haman's face. [9]Then Harbona, one of the eunuchs in attendance on the king, said, "Look, the very gallows that Haman has prepared for Mordecai, whose word saved the king, stands at Haman's house, fifty cubits high." And the king said, "Hang him on that." [10]So they hanged Haman on the gallows that he had prepared for Mordecai. Then the anger of the king abated.

Esther Saves the Jews

8 On that day King Ahasuerus gave to Queen Esther the house of Haman, the enemy of the Jews; and Mordecai came before the king, for Esther had told what he was to her. [2]Then the king took off his signet ring, which he had taken from Haman, and gave it to Mordecai. So Esther set Mordecai over the house of Haman.

3 Then Esther spoke again to the king; she fell at his feet, weeping and pleading with him to avert the evil design of Haman the Agagite and the plot that he had devised against the Jews. [4]The king held out the golden scepter to Esther, [5]and Esther rose and stood before the king. She said, "If it pleases the king, and if I have won his favor, and if the thing seems right before the king, and I have his approval, let an order be written to revoke the letters devised by Haman son of Hammedatha the Agagite, which he wrote giving orders to destroy the Jews who are in all the provinces of the king. [6]For how can I bear to see the calamity that is coming on my people? Or how

---

[m] Heb *them*   [n] Meaning of Heb uncertain

can I bear to see the destruction of my kindred?" [7]Then King Ahasuerus said to Queen Esther and to the Jew Mordecai, "See, I have given Esther the house of Haman, and they have hanged him on the gallows, because he plotted to lay hands on the Jews. [8]You may write as you please with regard to the Jews, in the name of the king, and seal it with the king's ring; for an edict written in the name of the king and sealed with the king's ring cannot be revoked."

9 The king's secretaries were summoned at that time, in the third month, which is the month of Sivan, on the twenty-third day; and an edict was written, according to all that Mordecai commanded, to the Jews and to the satraps and the governors and the officials of the provinces from India to Ethiopia,[o] one hundred twenty-seven provinces, to every province in its own script and to every people in its own language, and also to the Jews in their script and their language. [10]He wrote letters in the name of King Ahasuerus, sealed them with the king's ring, and sent them by mounted couriers riding on fast steeds bred from the royal herd.[p] [11]By these letters the king allowed the Jews who were in every city to assemble and defend their lives, to destroy, to kill, and to annihilate any armed force of any people or province that might attack them, with their children

8.11–17 What about God?

Why is God's name not mentioned in Esther—especially in obvious places like this one? Scholars suggest several answers to this riddle. Some, reading between the lines, suggest that Esther and Mordecai were not outstanding examples of faith. They were even willing to hide Esther's Jewish background. Esther showed no reluctance to be married to a pagan king and become part of his harem. Most critically, she and Mordecai (along with all the other Jews in Esther) had chosen not to return to Jerusalem with the first wave of Jews nearly half a century before. (The story of that return is told in Ezra 1–6.) Those who stayed in Persia presumably cared more about their finances than about God's plans for the Jews to return to Jerusalem from exile. Perhaps because of this, Esther is told as a secular story, to illustrate God's care over even "secularized" Jews.

and women, and to plunder their goods [12]on a single day throughout all the provinces of King Ahasuerus, on the thirteenth day of the twelfth month, which is the month of Adar. [13]A copy of the writ was to be issued as a decree in every province and published to all peoples, and the Jews were to be ready on that day to take revenge

on their enemies. [14]So the couriers, mounted on their swift royal steeds, hurried out, urged by the king's command. The decree was issued in the citadel of Susa.

15 Then Mordecai went out from the presence of the king, wearing royal robes of blue and white, with a great golden crown and a mantle of fine linen and purple, while the city of Susa shouted and rejoiced. [16]For the Jews there was light and gladness, joy and honor. [17]In every province and in every city, wherever the king's command and his edict came, there was gladness and joy among the Jews, a festival and a holiday. Furthermore, many of the peoples of the country professed to be Jews, because the fear of the Jews had fallen upon them.

Destruction of the Enemies of the Jews

9 Now in the twelfth month, which is the month of Adar, on the thirteenth day, when the king's command and edict were about to be executed, on the very day when the enemies of the Jews hoped to gain power over them, but which had been changed to a day when the Jews would gain power over their foes, [2]the Jews gathered in their cities throughout all the provinces of King Ahasuerus to lay hands on those who had sought their ruin; and no one could withstand them, because the fear of them had fallen upon all peoples. [3]All the officials of the provinces, the satraps and the governors, and the royal officials were supporting the Jews, because the fear of Mordecai had fallen upon them. [4]For Mordecai was powerful in the king's house, and his fame spread throughout all the provinces as the man Mordecai grew more and more powerful. [5]So the Jews struck down all their enemies with the sword, slaughtering, and destroying them, and did as they pleased to those who hated them. [6]In the citadel of Susa the Jews killed and destroyed five hundred people. [7]They killed Parshandatha, Dalphon, Aspatha, [8]Poratha, Adalia, Aridatha, [9]Parmashta, Arisai, Aridai, Vaizatha, [10]the ten sons of Haman son of Hammedatha, the enemy of the Jews; but they did not touch the plunder.

11 That very day the number of those killed in the citadel of Susa was reported to the king. [12]The king said to Queen Esther, "In the citadel of Susa the Jews have killed five hundred people and also the ten sons of Haman. What have they done in the rest of the king's provinces? Now what is your petition? It shall be granted you. And what further is your request? It shall be fulfilled." [13]Esther said, "If it pleases the king, let the Jews who are in Susa be allowed tomorrow also to do according to this day's edict, and let the ten sons of Haman be hanged on the gallows." [14]So the king commanded this to be done; a decree was issued in Susa, and the ten sons of Haman were hanged.

[15]The Jews who were in Susa gathered also on the fourteenth day of the month of Adar and they killed three hundred persons in Susa; but they did not touch the plunder.

16 Now the other Jews who were in the king's provinces also gathered to defend their lives, and gained relief from their enemies, and killed seventy-five thousand of those who hated them; but they laid no hands on the plunder. [17]This was on the thirteenth day of the month of Adar, and on the fourteenth day they rested and made that a day of feasting and gladness.

The Feast of Purim Inaugurated

18 But the Jews who were in Susa gathered on the thirteenth day and on the fourteenth, and rested on the fifteenth day, making that a day of feasting and gladness. [19]Therefore the Jews of the villages, who live in the open towns, hold the fourteenth day of the month of Adar as a day for gladness and feasting, a holiday on which they send gifts of food to one another.

9.19 A Day to Remember

Just as Christians retell the Christmas story each December, acting it out in church plays and manger scenes, the Jews commemorate great moments from their history. Jewish families read the book of Esther aloud on the day of Purim. The festival got its name from the casting of lots (like dice) against the Jews (3.7), a gamble that eventually backfired against Haman. The author explains the origin of celebrating Purim on two different days; even today, Jews observe Purim on the 14th everywhere except in Jerusalem, which schedules it on the 15th.

20 Mordecai recorded these things, and sent letters to all the Jews who were in all the provinces of King Ahasuerus, both near and far, [21]enjoining them that they should keep the fourteenth day of the month Adar and also the fifteenth day of the same month, year by year, [22]as the days on which the Jews gained relief from their enemies, and as the month that had been turned for them from sorrow into gladness and from mourning into a holiday; that they should make them days of feasting and gladness, days for sending gifts of food to one another and presents to the poor. [23]So the Jews adopted as a custom what they had begun to do, as Mordecai had written to them.

24 Haman son of Hammedatha the Agagite, the enemy of all the Jews, had plotted against the Jews to destroy them, and had cast Pur—that is "the lot"—to crush and destroy them; [25]but when Esther came before the king, he gave orders in writing that the wicked plot that he had devised

against the Jews should come upon his own head, and that he and his sons should be hanged on the gallows. [26]Therefore these days are called Purim, from the word Pur. Thus because of all that was written in this letter, and of what they had faced in this matter, and of what had happened to them, [27]the Jews established and accepted as a custom for themselves and their descendants and all who joined them, that without fail they would continue to observe these two days every year, as it was written and at the time appointed. [28]These days should be remembered and kept throughout every generation, in every family, province, and city; and these days of Purim should never fall into disuse among the Jews, nor should the commemoration of these days cease among their descendants.

29 Queen Esther daughter of Abihail, along with the Jew Mordecai, gave full written authority, confirming this second letter about Purim. [30]Letters were sent wishing peace and security to all the Jews, to the one hundred twenty-seven provinces of the kingdom of Ahasuerus, [31]and giving orders that these days of Purim should be observed at their appointed seasons, as the Jew Mordecai and Queen Esther enjoined on the Jews, just as they had laid down for themselves and for their descendants regulations concerning their fasts and their lamentations. [32]The command of Queen Esther fixed these practices of Purim, and it was recorded in writing.

10.2 Is Esther Accurate?

Because of the many coincidences in Esther, some have considered it "just a story," having little or no historical validity. Yet as archaeologists have learned more about ancient Persian history, the details of Esther have proven remarkably reliable. Certainly the book presents itself as history: here the author confidently asserts that readers can check the facts in the historical records. These records are lost—but evidently they were known to the early readers of Esther.

10 King Ahasuerus laid tribute on the land and on the islands of the sea. [2]All the acts of his power and might, and the full account of the high honor of Mordecai, to which the king advanced him, are they not written in the annals of the kings of Media and Persia? [3]For Mordecai the Jew was next in rank to King Ahasuerus, and he was powerful among the Jews and popular with his many kindred, for he sought the good of his people and interceded for the welfare of all his descendants.

JOB

When Bad Things Happened to a Good Person
Nobody suffered more; nobody deserved it less

H OW COULD IT HAPPEN? ALL at once the world came crashing down on a single innocent man, a man named Job. It was the ultimate in unfairness. First, raiders stole his belongings and slaughtered his servants. Then fire from the sky burned up his sheep, and a mighty wind destroyed his house and killed his sons and daughters. Finally, Job came down with a horrible, painful disease. *What did I do to deserve such suffering?*, he wailed.

> *"Have you considered my servant Job? There is no one like him on the earth, a blameless and upright man who fears God and turns away from evil." 1.8*

A Cosmic Contest

The book of Job reads like a detective story in which the readers know far more than the central characters. The very first chapter answers Job's main question: He had done nothing to deserve such suffering. We, the readers, know that, but nobody tells Job and his friends.

Unknown to him, Job was involved in a cosmic test, a contest proposed in heaven but staged on earth. In this extreme test of faith, the best man on earth suffered the worst calamities. Satan had claimed that people like Job love God only because of the good things he provides. Remove those good things, Satan challenged, and Job's faith would melt away along with his riches and health.

God's reputation was on the line. Would Job continue to trust him, even while his life was falling apart? This is the crucial question of the book: Would Job turn against God?

Job's wife mocked him, "Do you still persist in your integrity? Curse God, and die" (2.9). His friends were even crueler: They argued that Job was being punished, that he fully deserved the tragedies crashing into his life. For his part, Job struggled to do what seemed impossible: to keep on believing in a loving, fair God even though all the evidence pointed against such a God.

Job on Trial

It helps to think of this book as a courtroom drama, full of long, eloquent speeches. For most of the book, Job sits in the defendant's chair listening to his friends' harangues. He knows no airtight refutations; what they say about suffering as punishment seems to make sense. Yet he also knows, deep in his soul, that they are wrong. He does not deserve the treatment he is getting. There has to be some other explanation.

Like all grieving persons, Job went through emotional cycles. He whined, exploded, cajoled, and collapsed into self-pity. He agreed with his friends, then shifted positions and contradicted himself. And occasionally he came up with a statement of brilliant hope.

Mainly, Job asked for one thing: an appearance by the one Person who could explain his miserable fate. He wanted to meet God himself, face to face. Eventually Job got his wish; God did show up in person. And when God finally spoke, no one—not Job, nor any of his friends—was prepared for what he had to say.

When We Feel Like Job

Sooner or later we all find ourselves in a position somewhat like Job's. Our world seems to crumble. Nothing makes sense any more. God seems distant and silent.

At such moments of great crisis, each one of us is put on trial. In a sense we become actors in a contest like the one Job went through. This book records every step in that process with unflinching honesty. Job's life stands as an example to every person who must go through great suffering.

How to Read Job

The book of Job is regarded as one of the world's truly great literary masterpieces. It contains some of the finest, most expressive poetry in the Bible. Yet first-time readers of Job can easily get lost because the complete "story line" is found in the first two chapters and the last one. Everything in between consists of a series of speeches.

The boldface sectional headings and the phrases that follow, such as "Job again took up his discourse" and "Then Eliphaz the Temanite answered," serve as markers or signposts throughout the book. Rather than reading large sections of the book, read one entire speech by Job, or a speech by Job and a rebuttal from one of his friends.

It may help if you try to summarize the statement behind each speech in one sentence and write that sentence in the margin (for example, "Job protests that he's innocent"). Speakers of that day impressed their audience more by eloquence than by rigorous logic, so the speeches may seem flowery. The issues Job and his friends address, however, are life-and-death ones.

As you read the speeches of Job's friends, remember that their views do not necessarily reflect God's. The book of Job merely records the friends' viewpoints; it does not endorse them.

PEOPLE YOU'LL MEET IN JOB

JOB *(p. 514)*

3-TRACK READING PLAN

For an explanation and complete listing of the 3-track reading plan, turn to page 7.

TRACK 1: *Two-Week Courses on the Bible*
The Track 1 reading program on the Old Testament includes one chapter from Job. See page 8 for a complete listing of this course.

TRACK 2: *An Overview of Job in 3 Days*
□ Day 1. Read the Introduction to Job and then two short chapters, 1 and 2, which give background for the entire book.
□ Day 2. Read chapter 38, which opens God's great speech to Job.
□ Day 3. Read chapter 42, completing the "plot" of Job.

Now turn to page 9 for your next Track 2 reading project.

TRACK 3: *All of Job in 41 Days*
After you have read through Job, turn to pages 10–14 for your next Track 3 reading project.

□1	□2	□3	□4	□5	□6	□7	□8
□9	□10	□11	□12	□13	□14	□15	□16
□17	□18	□19	□20	□21	□22	□23	□24
□25–26	□27	□28	□29	□30	□31	□32	□33
□34	□35	□36	□37	□38	□39	□40	□41
□42							

Job and His Family

1 There was once a man in the land of Uz whose name was Job. That man was blameless and upright, one who feared God and turned away from evil. ²There were born to him seven sons and three daughters. ³He had seven thousand sheep, three thousand camels, five hundred yoke of oxen, five hundred donkeys, and very many servants; so that this man was the greatest of all the people of the east. ⁴His sons used to go and hold feasts in one another's houses in turn; and they would send and invite their three sisters to eat and drink with them. ⁵And when the feast days had run their course, Job would send and sanctify them, and he would rise early in the morning and offer burnt offerings according to the number of them all; for Job said, "It may be that my children have sinned, and cursed God in their hearts." This is what Job always did.

Attack on Job's Character

6 One day the heavenly beings[a] came to present themselves before the LORD, and Satan[b] also came among them. ⁷The LORD said to Satan,[b] "Where have you come from?" Satan[b] answered the LORD, "From going to and fro on the earth, and from walking up and down on it." ⁸The LORD said to Satan,[b] "Have you considered my servant Job? There is no one like him on the earth, a blameless and upright man who fears God and turns away from evil." ⁹Then Satan[b] answered the LORD, "Does Job fear God for nothing? ¹⁰Have you not put a fence around him and his house and all that he has, on every side? You have blessed the work of his hands, and his possessions have increased in the land. ¹¹But stretch out your hand now, and touch all that he has, and he will curse you to your face." ¹²The LORD said to Satan,[b] "Very well, all that he has is in your power; only do not stretch out your hand against him!" So Satan[b] went out from the presence of the LORD.

1.12—2.6 The Extent of Satan's Power

Job's portrayal of Satan echoes the story in Genesis 3: Satan has supernatural power to oppress people, but is restrained by God. As John Newton said, "Satan can only go to the end of his chain." The Bible records at least one other instance where Satan specifically asked permission to attack an individual: Luke 22.31–32.

Job Loses Property and Children

13 One day when his sons and daughters were eating and drinking wine in the eldest brother's house, ¹⁴a messenger came to Job and said, "The oxen were plowing and the donkeys were feeding beside them, ¹⁵and the Sabeans fell on them and carried them off, and killed the servants with the edge of the sword; I alone have escaped to tell you." ¹⁶While he was still speaking, another came and said, "The fire of God fell from heaven and burned up the sheep and the servants, and consumed them; I alone have escaped to tell you." ¹⁷While he was still speaking, another came and said, "The Chaldeans formed three columns, made a raid on the camels and carried them off, and killed the servants with the edge of the sword; I alone have escaped to tell you." ¹⁸While he was still speaking, another came and said, "Your sons and daughters were eating and drinking wine in their eldest brother's house, ¹⁹and suddenly a great wind came across the desert, struck the four corners of the house, and it fell on the young people, and they are dead; I alone have escaped to tell you."

20 Then Job arose, tore his robe, shaved his head, and fell on the ground and worshiped. ²¹He said, "Naked I came from my mother's womb, and naked shall I return there; the LORD gave, and the LORD has taken away; blessed be the name of the LORD."

22 In all this Job did not sin or charge God with wrongdoing.

Attack on Job's Health

2 One day the heavenly beings[a] came to present themselves before the LORD, and Satan[b] also came among them to present himself before the LORD. ²The LORD said to Satan,[b] "Where have you come from?" Satan[c] answered the LORD, "From going to and fro on the earth, and from walking up and down on it." ³The LORD said to Satan,[b] "Have you considered my servant Job? There is no one like him on the earth, a blameless and upright man who fears God and turns away from evil. He still persists in his integrity, although you incited me against him, to destroy him for no reason." ⁴Then Satan[b] answered the LORD, "Skin for skin! All that people have they will give to save their lives.[d] ⁵But stretch out your hand now and touch his bone and his flesh, and he will curse you to your face." ⁶The LORD said to Satan,[b] "Very well, he is in your power; only spare his life."

7 So Satan[b] went out from the presence of the LORD, and inflicted loathsome sores on Job from the sole of his foot to the crown of his head. ⁸Job[e] took a potsherd with which to scrape himself, and sat among the ashes.

ᵃ Heb *sons of God* ᵇ Or *the Accuser*; Heb *ha-satan* ᶜ Or *The Accuser*; Heb *ha-satan* ᵈ Or *All that the man has*
he will give for his life ᵉ Heb *He*

9 Then his wife said to him, "Do you still persist in your integrity? Curse[f] God, and die." [10]But he said to her, "You speak as any foolish woman would speak. Shall we receive the good at the hand of God, and not receive the bad?" In all this Job did not sin with his lips.

Job's Three Friends

11 Now when Job's three friends heard of all these troubles that had come upon him, each of them set out from his home—Eliphaz the Temanite, Bildad the Shuhite, and Zophar the Naamathite. They met together to go and console and comfort him. [12]When they saw him from a distance, they did not recognize him, and they raised their voices and wept aloud; they tore their robes and threw dust in the air upon their heads. [13]They sat with him on the ground seven days and seven nights, and no one spoke a word to him, for they saw that his suffering was very great.

2.13 Keeping Quiet

The term "Job's comforter" has come to describe how not to act around a suffering person. These three friends proved of scant help to Job and were dismissed by God himself in the end. This verse, though, reveals the depth of their feeling for Job: They sat with him for a full week in shared, silent grief. As it turned out, compassionate silence was the most profound help they imparted to Job—a good lesson to remember for anyone who works with suffering people.

Job Curses the Day He Was Born

3 After this Job opened his mouth and cursed the day of his birth. [2]Job said:
3 "Let the day perish in which I was born,
  and the night that said,
  'A man-child is conceived.'
4 Let that day be darkness!
  May God above not seek it,
  or light shine on it.
5 Let gloom and deep darkness claim it.
  Let clouds settle upon it;
  let the blackness of the day terrify it.
6 That night—let thick darkness seize it!
  let it not rejoice among the days of the year;
  let it not come into the number of the months.
7 Yes, let that night be barren;
  let no joyful cry be heard[g] in it.
8 Let those curse it who curse the Sea,[h]
  those who are skilled to rouse up Leviathan.

9 Let the stars of its dawn be dark;
  let it hope for light, but have none;
  may it not see the eyelids of the morning—
10 because it did not shut the doors of my mother's womb,
  and hide trouble from my eyes.

11 "Why did I not die at birth,
  come forth from the womb and expire?
12 Why were there knees to receive me,
  or breasts for me to suck?
13 Now I would be lying down and quiet;
  I would be asleep; then I would be at rest
14 with kings and counselors of the earth
  who rebuild ruins for themselves,
15 or with princes who have gold,
  who fill their houses with silver.
16 Or why was I not buried like a stillborn child,
  like an infant that never sees the light?
17 There the wicked cease from troubling,
  and there the weary are at rest.
18 There the prisoners are at ease together;
  they do not hear the voice of the taskmaster.
19 The small and the great are there,
  and the slaves are free from their masters.

20 "Why is light given to one in misery,
  and life to the bitter in soul,
21 who long for death, but it does not come,
  and dig for it more than for hidden treasures;
22 who rejoice exceedingly,
  and are glad when they find the grave?
23 Why is light given to one who cannot see the way,
  whom God has fenced in?
24 For my sighing comes like[i] my bread,
  and my groanings are poured out like water.
25 Truly the thing that I fear comes upon me,
  and what I dread befalls me.
26 I am not at ease, nor am I quiet;
  I have no rest; but trouble comes."

Eliphaz Speaks: Job Has Sinned

4 Then Eliphaz the Temanite answered:
2 "If one ventures a word with you, will you be offended?
  But who can keep from speaking?
3 See, you have instructed many;
  you have strengthened the weak hands.
4 Your words have supported those who were stumbling,

---

f Heb *Bless*   g Heb *come*   h Cn: Heb *day*   i Heb *before*

and you have made firm the feeble
   knees.
5 But now it has come to you, and you are
      impatient;
   it touches you, and you are dismayed.
6 Is not your fear of God your confidence,
   and the integrity of your ways your
      hope?

7 "Think now, who that was innocent ever
      perished?
   Or where were the upright cut off?
8 As I have seen, those who plow iniquity
   and sow trouble reap the same.
9 By the breath of God they perish,
   and by the blast of his anger they are
      consumed.
10 The roar of the lion, the voice of the
      fierce lion,
   and the teeth of the young lions are
      broken.
11 The strong lion perishes for lack of prey,
   and the whelps of the lioness are
      scattered.

12 "Now a word came stealing to me,
   my ear received the whisper of it.
13 Amid thoughts from visions of the night,
   when deep sleep falls on mortals,

4.13 Appealing to a Vision

The book of Job includes parallels to most modern-day responses to people in pain. To impress the other listeners with his religious authority, Eliphaz appealed to a mysterious vision in which a "spirit" restated Eliphaz's own line of argument. In the next chapter, he hints that Job should turn to God for a miracle (5.8–10).

14 dread came upon me, and trembling,
   which made all my bones shake.
15 A spirit glided past my face;
   the hair of my flesh bristled.
16 It stood still,
   but I could not discern its appearance.
   A form was before my eyes;
   there was silence, then I heard a voice:
17 'Can mortals be righteous before[j] God?
   Can human beings be pure before[j]
      their Maker?
18 Even in his servants he puts no trust,
   and his angels he charges with error;
19 how much more those who live in houses
      of clay,
   whose foundation is in the dust,

who are crushed like a moth.
20 Between morning and evening they are
      destroyed;
   they perish forever without any
      regarding it.
21 Their tent-cord is plucked up within
      them,
   and they die devoid of wisdom.'

Job Is Corrected by God

5 "Call now; is there anyone who will answer
      you?
   To which of the holy ones will you turn?
2 Surely vexation kills the fool,
   and jealousy slays the simple.
3 I have seen fools taking root,
   but suddenly I cursed their dwelling.
4 Their children are far from safety,
   they are crushed in the gate,
   and there is no one to deliver them.
5 The hungry eat their harvest,
   and they take it even out of the
      thorns;[k]
   and the thirsty[l] pant after their wealth.
6 For misery does not come from the earth,
   nor does trouble sprout from the
      ground;
7 but human beings are born to trouble
   just as sparks[m] fly upward.

8 "As for me, I would seek God,
   and to God I would commit my cause.
9 He does great things and unsearchable,
   marvelous things without number.
10 He gives rain on the earth
   and sends waters on the fields;
11 he sets on high those who are lowly,
   and those who mourn are lifted to
      safety.
12 He frustrates the devices of the crafty,
   so that their hands achieve no success.
13 He takes the wise in their own craftiness;
   and the schemes of the wily are
      brought to a quick end.
14 They meet with darkness in the daytime,
   and grope at noonday as in the night.
15 But he saves the needy from the sword of
      their mouth,
   from the hand of the mighty.
16 So the poor have hope,
   and injustice shuts its mouth.

17 "How happy is the one whom God
      reproves;
   therefore do not despise the discipline
      of the Almighty.[n]
18 For he wounds, but he binds up;
   he strikes, but his hands heal.

---

j Or *more than*   *k* Meaning of Heb uncertain   *l* Aquila Symmachus Syr Vg: Heb *snare*   *m* Or *birds*; Heb *sons of Resheph*   *n* Traditional rendering of Heb *Shaddai*

19 He will deliver you from six troubles;
 in seven no harm shall touch you.
20 In famine he will redeem you from death,
 and in war from the power of the
 sword.

5.17 Pain as Punishment

Job's friends sound so pious and eloquent that it's easy to accept their words as all-encompassing truth. Some Christians have quoted this verse like a proverb, applying it indiscriminately to instances of suffering. In reality, Eliphaz was dead wrong in his theory that God was disciplining Job. God had already held up Job as a model of goodness (1.9).

21 You shall be hidden from the scourge of
 the tongue,
 and shall not fear destruction when it
 comes.
22 At destruction and famine you shall
 laugh,
 and shall not fear the wild animals of
 the earth.
23 For you shall be in league with the stones
 of the field,
 and the wild animals shall be at peace
 with you.
24 You shall know that your tent is safe,
 you shall inspect your fold and miss
 nothing.
25 You shall know that your descendants will
 be many,
 and your offspring like the grass of the
 earth.
26 You shall come to your grave in ripe old
 age,
 as a shock of grain comes up to the
 threshing floor in its season.
27 See, we have searched this out; it is true.
 Hear, and know it for yourself."

Job Replies: My Complaint Is Just

6 Then Job answered:
2 "O that my vexation were weighed,
 and all my calamity laid in the
 balances!
3 For then it would be heavier than the
 sand of the sea;
 therefore my words have been rash.
4 For the arrows of the Almighty*o* are in
 me;
 my spirit drinks their poison;
 the terrors of God are arrayed against
 me.
5 Does the wild ass bray over its grass,

 or the ox low over its fodder?
6 Can that which is tasteless be eaten
 without salt,
 or is there any flavor in the juice of
 mallows?*P*
7 My appetite refuses to touch them;
 they are like food that is loathsome to
 me.*P*

8 "O that I might have my request,
 and that God would grant my desire;
9 that it would please God to crush me,
 that he would let loose his hand and
 cut me off!

6.9 Why Keep on Living?

Job steadfastly refused to curse God, but he did curse the day he was born. In this speech he asked for a quick death, realizing he could not hold out trusting in God forever. If he died soon, at least he would die still believing. His speeches contain some of the most profound expressions of pain and despair in all of literature.

10 This would be my consolation;
 I would even exult*P* in unrelenting
 pain;
 for I have not denied the words of the
 Holy One.
11 What is my strength, that I should wait?
 And what is my end, that I should be
 patient?
12 Is my strength the strength of stones,
 or is my flesh bronze?
13 In truth I have no help in me,
 and any resource is driven from me.

14 "Those who withhold*q* kindness from a
 friend
 forsake the fear of the Almighty.*o*
15 My companions are treacherous like a
 torrent-bed,
 like freshets that pass away,
16 that run dark with ice,
 turbid with melting snow.
17 In time of heat they disappear;
 when it is hot, they vanish from their
 place.
18 The caravans turn aside from their course;
 they go up into the waste, and perish.
19 The caravans of Tema look,
 the travelers of Sheba hope.
20 They are disappointed because they were
 confident;
 they come there and are confounded.

o Traditional rendering of Heb *Shaddai*   *P* Meaning of Heb uncertain   *q* Syr Vg Compare Tg: Meaning of Heb uncertain

21 Such you have now become to me;[r]
  you see my calamity, and are afraid.
22 Have I said, 'Make me a gift'?
  Or, 'From your wealth offer a bribe for
    me'?
23 Or, 'Save me from an opponent's hand'?
  Or, 'Ransom me from the hand of
    oppressors'?

24 "Teach me, and I will be silent;
  make me understand how I have gone
    wrong.
25 How forceful are honest words!
  But your reproof, what does it reprove?
26 Do you think that you can reprove words,
  as if the speech of the desperate were
    wind?

[r] Cn Compare Gk Syr: Meaning of Heb uncertain

What Not to Say to a Hurting Person
Job's friends only made it worse

YOU ARE SITTING IN A hospital room, where the faint smell of antiseptic lingers and the sound of lowered voices rustles all around you. The medical prognosis of your friend is bleak. You've listened to your friend's anger and despair, and a jumble of other emotions. Now it's your turn to reply. Everyone in the room waits for your response.

> "How forceful are honest words! But your reproof, what does it reprove?"
> 6.25

What do you say to a suffering person? The book of Job gives page after page of examples. Job's three friends, finding him in despair, filled the air with high-sounding advice. But unfortunately they offer models of what *not* to say. Their main argument only made Job feel worse, and at the end God dismissed them all with a scowl.

Who Were Job's Friends?

This book gives few details on time and place, but it presents Job as a very wealthy "sheik" of the Middle East. His three friends, from neighboring lands, were also prosperous and well respected. When they first saw Job, they wept aloud and sat with him on the ground, silent, for seven days and nights, overcome with grief (2.13).

After Job finally broke the silence, each friend delivered a flowery speech on Job's dilemma. There are three cycles of speeches in all, with Eliphaz, Bildad, and Zophar taking turns, allowing Job to respond to each. Eliphaz, who led off, had strong and noble ideas. Bildad was briefer and slightly less sympathetic. Zophar (who did not speak in the third cycle) showed passion and fire.

The friends seemed to crescendo in emotional intensity. In the first cycle (chapters 4–14), they showed hope of winning Job over to their point of view. In the second cycle (chapters 15–21), the speeches grew more severe and threatening. And by the time of the concluding speeches (chapters 22–25), Job's friends were making direct accusations against him.

A Flawed Theory about Suffering

Job's friends believed in a God of love and fairness; their arguments started from that fact. Surely a just God would not allow an *innocent* man to suffer so much, they reasoned. Most of their comments boil down to one simple theory: Job must have committed some great crime for which God was punishing him. All three believed that good people prosper and bad people suffer; therefore, suffering must betray some hidden sin.

"God will not reject a blameless person, nor take the hand of evildoers," they said to Job (8.20). Repent, they admonished him, and God will forgive and restore you. Their words got this response from Job: "You whitewash with lies; all of you are worthless physicians." (13.4). Job also believed in a loving God, but he knew he was innocent.

When God finally made his appearance, he dismissed the three friends in one sentence to Eliphaz, "My wrath is kindled against you and against your two friends; for you have not spoken of me what is right, as my servant Job has" (42.7).

Although the Bible elsewhere gives examples of suffering that resulted from a person's sin, Job clearly shows that such a theory cannot be applied in every case. (For a related discussion, see "Healthier, Wealthier, and Wiser," page 204.) It is not for us to try to reason out the specific cause of a person's suffering; God reserves that knowledge for himself.

Life Questions: What is the most "unfair" thing that has ever happened to you? How did it affect the way you thought about God?

27 You would even cast lots over the orphan,
and bargain over your friend.

28 "But now, be pleased to look at me;
for I will not lie to your face.
29 Turn, I pray, let no wrong be done.
Turn now, my vindication is at stake.
30 Is there any wrong on my tongue?
Cannot my taste discern calamity?

Job: My Suffering Is without End

7 "Do not human beings have a hard service
on earth,
and are not their days like the days of
a laborer?
2 Like a slave who longs for the shadow,
and like laborers who look for their
wages,
3 so I am allotted months of emptiness,
and nights of misery are apportioned
to me.
4 When I lie down I say, 'When shall I
rise?'
But the night is long,
and I am full of tossing until dawn.
5 My flesh is clothed with worms and dirt;
my skin hardens, then breaks out
again.
6 My days are swifter than a weaver's
shuttle,
and come to their end without hope. [s]

7 "Remember that my life is a breath;
my eye will never again see good.
8 The eye that beholds me will see me no
more;
while your eyes are upon me, I shall be
gone.
9 As the cloud fades and vanishes,
so those who go down to Sheol do not
come up;
10 they return no more to their houses,
nor do their places know them any
more.

11 "Therefore I will not restrain my mouth;
I will speak in the anguish of my spirit;
I will complain in the bitterness of my
soul.
12 Am I the Sea, or the Dragon,
that you set a guard over me?
13 When I say, 'My bed will comfort me,
my couch will ease my complaint,'
14 then you scare me with dreams
and terrify me with visions,
15 so that I would choose strangling
and death rather than this body.
16 I loathe my life; I would not live forever.
Let me alone, for my days are a breath.

17 What are human beings, that you make
so much of them,
that you set your mind on them,
18 visit them every morning,
test them every moment?
19 Will you not look away from me for a
while,
let me alone until I swallow my spittle?
20 If I sin, what do I do to you, you watcher
of humanity?
Why have you made me your target?
Why have I become a burden to you?
21 Why do you not pardon my transgression
and take away my iniquity?
For now I shall lie in the earth;
you will seek me, but I shall not be."

Bildad Speaks: Job Should Repent

8 Then Bildad the Shuhite answered:
2 "How long will you say these things,
and the words of your mouth be a
great wind?
3 Does God pervert justice?
Or does the Almighty [t] pervert the
right?
4 If your children sinned against him,
he delivered them into the power of
their transgression.

8.4 A Mixture of True and False

*Although God rejected the overall force of their
arguments, Job's three friends said some
things that were totally false and others that
were true. In this case, Bildad appealed to
common sense, ("God will not reject a
blameless person," verse 20), implying that Job
sinned to deserve his suffering. But God
specifically had called Job "blameless and
upright" (2.3). Elsewhere, a statement by
Eliphaz (5.11–13) is quoted approvingly in the
New Testament (1 Corinthians 3.19).*

5 If you will seek God
and make supplication to the
Almighty, [t]
6 if you are pure and upright,
surely then he will rouse himself for
you
and restore to you your rightful place.
7 Though your beginning was small,
your latter days will be very great.

8 "For inquire now of bygone generations,
and consider what their ancestors have
found;
9 for we are but of yesterday, and we know
nothing,

s Or *as the thread runs out*   t Traditional rendering of Heb *Shaddai*

for our days on earth are but a
    shadow.
10 Will they not teach you and tell you
    and utter words out of their
        understanding?

11 "Can papyrus grow where there is no
        marsh?
    Can reeds flourish where there is no
        water?
12 While yet in flower and not cut down,
    they wither before any other plant.
13 Such are the paths of all who forget God;
    the hope of the godless shall perish.
14 Their confidence is gossamer,
    a spider's house their trust.
15 If one leans against its house, it will not
        stand;
    if one lays hold of it, it will not endure.
16 The wicked thrive[u] before the sun,
    and their shoots spread over the
        garden.
17 Their roots twine around the stoneheap;
    they live among the rocks.[v]
18 If they are destroyed from their place,
    then it will deny them, saying, 'I have
        never seen you.'
19 See, these are their happy ways,[w]
    and out of the earth still others will
        spring.

20 "See, God will not reject a blameless
        person,
    nor take the hand of evildoers.
21 He will yet fill your mouth with laughter,
    and your lips with shouts of joy.
22 Those who hate you will be clothed with
        shame,
    and the tent of the wicked will be no
        more."

Job Replies: There Is No Mediator

9 Then Job answered:
2 "Indeed I know that this is so;
    but how can a mortal be just before
        God?
3 If one wished to contend with him,
    one could not answer him once in a
        thousand.
4 He is wise in heart, and mighty in
        strength
    —who has resisted him, and
        succeeded?—
5 he who removes mountains, and they do
        not know it,
    when he overturns them in his anger;
6 who shakes the earth out of its place,
    and its pillars tremble;

7 who commands the sun, and it does not
        rise;
    who seals up the stars;
8 who alone stretched out the heavens

9.4 Arms Too Short

*A gospel musical based on the book of Job took
the title "Arms Too Short to Box with God."
From the beginning Job knew he didn't stand a
chance in a dispute with God. Moreover, he
wasn't sure what to dispute—much of the time
Job demonstrated a better grasp of theology
than his friends. (For example, his words in this
chapter bear striking resemblance to what God
says at the end of the book.) But good insights
did not relieve Job's sense of being abandoned
by God. His crisis of faith was more personal
than intellectual.*

and trampled the waves of the Sea;[x]
9 who made the Bear and Orion,
    the Pleiades and the chambers of the
        south;
10 who does great things beyond
        understanding,
    and marvelous things without number.
11 Look, he passes by me, and I do not see
        him;
    he moves on, but I do not perceive
        him.
12 He snatches away; who can stop him?
    Who will say to him, 'What are you
        doing?'

13 "God will not turn back his anger;
    the helpers of Rahab bowed beneath
        him.
14 How then can I answer him,
    choosing my words with him?
15 Though I am innocent, I cannot answer
        him;
    I must appeal for mercy to my
        accuser.[y]
16 If I summoned him and he answered me,
    I do not believe that he would listen to
        my voice.
17 For he crushes me with a tempest,
    and multiplies my wounds without
        cause;
18 he will not let me get my breath,
    but fills me with bitterness.
19 If it is a contest of strength, he is the
        strong one!
    If it is a matter of justice, who can
        summon him?[z]

---

[u] Heb *He thrives*   [v] Gk Vg: Meaning of Heb uncertain   [w] Meaning of Heb uncertain   [x] Or *trampled the back of*
the sea dragon   [y] Or *for my right*   [z] Compare Gk: Heb *me*

20 Though I am innocent, my own mouth
  would condemn me;
  though I am blameless, he would prove
  me perverse.
21 I am blameless; I do not know myself;
  I loathe my life.
22 It is all one; therefore I say,
  he destroys both the blameless and the
  wicked.
23 When disaster brings sudden death,
  he mocks at the calamity[a] of the
  innocent.
24 The earth is given into the hand of the
  wicked;
  he covers the eyes of its judges—
  if it is not he, who then is it?

25 "My days are swifter than a runner;
  they flee away, they see no good.
26 They go by like skiffs of reed,
  like an eagle swooping on the prey.
27 If I say, 'I will forget my complaint;
  I will put off my sad countenance and
  be of good cheer,'
28 I become afraid of all my suffering,
  for I know you will not hold me
  innocent.
29 I shall be condemned;
  why then do I labor in vain?
30 If I wash myself with soap
  and cleanse my hands with lye,
31 yet you will plunge me into filth,
  and my own clothes will abhor me.
32 For he is not a mortal, as I am, that I
  might answer him,
  that we should come to trial together.
33 There is no umpire[b] between us,
  who might lay his hand on us both.

9.33–35 Looking for an Arbitrator

Job recognized the enormous gulf between God and people. He poignantly asked for an arbitrator "who might lay his hand on us both." A few such comments of Job, expressing great longing for an advocate, found their full realization in Jesus, who was called the "one mediator between God and humankind" (1 Timothy 2.5).

34 If he would take his rod away from me,
  and not let dread of him terrify me,
35 then I would speak without fear of him,
  for I know I am not what I am
  thought to be.[c]

Job: I Loathe My Life

10 "I loathe my life;
  I will give free utterance to my
  complaint;
  I will speak in the bitterness of my
  soul.
2 I will say to God, Do not condemn me;
  let me know why you contend against
  me.
3 Does it seem good to you to oppress,
  to despise the work of your hands
  and favor the schemes of the wicked?
4 Do you have eyes of flesh?
  Do you see as humans see?
5 Are your days like the days of mortals,
  or your years like human years,
6 that you seek out my iniquity
  and search for my sin,
7 although you know that I am not guilty,
  and there is no one to deliver out of
  your hand?
8 Your hands fashioned and made me;
  and now you turn and destroy me.[d]

10.8 Fond Memories

Author Joseph Bayly, who watched three of his sons die in their youth, said, "Don't forget in the darkness what you've learned in the light." Job lived by this same principle. Even though he could not understand God at the moment, he never belittled the blessings he had already received. In a fit of anger, a divorcée might say, "Oh, I never really loved him anyway"; Job never once turned his back on God in that way.

9 Remember that you fashioned me like
  clay;
  and will you turn me to dust again?
10 Did you not pour me out like milk
  and curdle me like cheese?
11 You clothed me with skin and flesh,
  and knit me together with bones and
  sinews.
12 You have granted me life and steadfast
  love,
  and your care has preserved my spirit.
13 Yet these things you hid in your heart;
  I know that this was your purpose.
14 If I sin, you watch me,
  and do not acquit me of my iniquity.
15 If I am wicked, woe to me!
  If I am righteous, I cannot lift up my
  head,
  for I am filled with disgrace
  and look upon my affliction.

a Meaning of Heb uncertain   b Another reading is *Would that there were an umpire*   c Cn: Heb *for I am not so in myself*   d Cn Compare Gk Syr: Heb *made me together all around, and you destroy me*

16 Bold as a lion you hunt me;
  you repeat your exploits against me.
17 You renew your witnesses against me,
  and increase your vexation toward me;
  you bring fresh troops against me.*e*

18 "Why did you bring me forth from the
    womb?
  Would that I had died before any eye
    had seen me,
19 and were as though I had not been,
  carried from the womb to the grave.
20 Are not the days of my life few?*f*
  Let me alone, that I may find a little
    comfort*g*
21 before I go, never to return,
  to the land of gloom and deep
    darkness,
22 the land of gloom*h* and chaos,
  where light is like darkness."

Zophar Speaks: Job's Guilt Deserves Punishment

11 Then Zophar the Naamathite answered:
2 "Should a multitude of words go
    unanswered,
  and should one full of talk be
    vindicated?
3 Should your babble put others to silence,
  and when you mock, shall no one
    shame you?
4 For you say, 'My conduct*i* is pure,
  and I am clean in God's*j* sight.'
5 But O that God would speak,
  and open his lips to you,
6 and that he would tell you the secrets of
    wisdom!
  For wisdom is many-sided.*k*
  Know then that God exacts of you less
    than your guilt deserves.

7 "Can you find out the deep things of
    God?
  Can you find out the limit of the
    Almighty?*l*
3 It is higher than heaven*m*—what can you
    do?
  Deeper than Sheol—what can you
    know?
9 Its measure is longer than the earth,
  and broader than the sea.
10 If he passes through, and imprisons,
  and assembles for judgment, who can
    hinder him?
11 For he knows those who are worthless;

when he sees iniquity, will he not
    consider it?
12 But a stupid person will get
    understanding,
  when a wild ass is born human.*k*

13 "If you direct your heart rightly,
  you will stretch out your hands toward
    him.
14 If iniquity is in your hand, put it far
    away,
  and do not let wickedness reside in
    your tents.

11.14 Unfair Accusation

*Zophar, the least tactful of the three friends,
made direct accusations against Job, repeating
the common refrain that Job was being
punished for some sin. In a speech recorded in
chapter 12, Job agreed in principle that God
rewards the righteous and punishes the
wicked. But in his own case he knew he was
innocent. No matter how convincing their
arguments, he had to protest against them.*

15 Surely then you will lift up your face
    without blemish;
  you will be secure, and will not fear.
16 You will forget your misery;
  you will remember it as waters that
    have passed away.
17 And your life will be brighter than the
    noonday;
  its darkness will be like the morning.
18 And you will have confidence, because
    there is hope;
  you will be protected*n* and take your
    rest in safety.
19 You will lie down, and no one will make
    you afraid;
  many will entreat your favor.
20 But the eyes of the wicked will fail;
  all way of escape will be lost to them,
  and their hope is to breathe their last."

Job Replies: I Am a Laughingstock

12 Then Job answered:
2 "No doubt you are the people,
  and wisdom will die with you.
3 But I have understanding as well as you;
  I am not inferior to you.
  Who does not know such things as
    these?
4 I am a laughingstock to my friends;

---

e Cn Compare Gk: Heb *toward me; changes and a troop are with me*   *f* Cn Compare Gk Syr: Heb *Are not my days few?*
Let him cease!   *g* Heb *that I may brighten up a little*   *h* Heb *gloom as darkness, deep darkness*   *i* Gk: Heb
teaching   *j* Heb *your*   *k* Meaning of Heb uncertain   *l* Traditional rendering of Heb *Shaddai*   *m* Heb *The
heights of heaven*   *n* Or *you will look around*

I, who called upon God and he
　answered me,
a just and blameless man, I am a
　laughingstock.
5 Those at ease have contempt for
　misfortune,*o*
　but it is ready for those whose feet are
　unstable.

12.5 Contempt, not Sympathy

After his release from a Siberian prison, Alexander Solzhenitsyn gained overnight fame as a novelist. One day he was summoned to the opulent office of an admiring Soviet official. In those comfortable surroundings, the agony of the Soviet prison camps seemed very far away. "It is impossible for a man who is warm to understand one who is cold," he concluded. Job accused his friends—and even God—of the same lack of sympathy. His complaint against God would be answered finally by the Incarnation, when God voluntarily subjected himself to cold, hunger, and every other human misfortune.

6 The tents of robbers are at peace,
　and those who provoke God are
　　secure,
　who bring their god in their hands.*p*

7 "But ask the animals, and they will teach
　　you;
　the birds of the air, and they will tell
　　you;
8 ask the plants of the earth,*q* and they will
　　teach you;
　and the fish of the sea will declare to
　　you.
9 Who among all these does not know
　that the hand of the LORD has done
　　this?
10 In his hand is the life of every living thing
　and the breath of every human being.
11 Does not the ear test words
　as the palate tastes food?
12 Is wisdom with the aged,
　and understanding in length of days?

13 "With God*r* are wisdom and strength;
　he has counsel and understanding.
14 If he tears down, no one can rebuild;
　if he shuts someone in, no one can
　　open up.
15 If he withholds the waters, they dry up;
　if he sends them out, they overwhelm
　　the land.

16 With him are strength and wisdom;
　the deceived and the deceiver are his.
17 He leads counselors away stripped,
　and makes fools of judges.
18 He looses the sash of kings,
　and binds a waistcloth on their loins.
19 He leads priests away stripped,
　and overthrows the mighty.
20 He deprives of speech those who are
　　trusted,
　and takes away the discernment of the
　　elders.
21 He pours contempt on princes,
　and looses the belt of the strong.
22 He uncovers the deeps out of darkness,
　and brings deep darkness to light.
23 He makes nations great, then destroys
　　them;
　he enlarges nations, then leads them
　　away.
24 He strips understanding from the
　　leaders*s* of the earth,
　and makes them wander in a pathless
　　waste.
25 They grope in the dark without light;
　he makes them stagger like a drunkard.

13 "Look, my eye has seen all this,
　my ear has heard and understood it.
2 What you know, I also know;
　I am not inferior to you.
3 But I would speak to the Almighty,*t*
　and I desire to argue my case with
　　God.
4 As for you, you whitewash with lies;
　all of you are worthless physicians.
5 If you would only keep silent,
　that would be your wisdom!
6 Hear now my reasoning,
　and listen to the pleadings of my lips.
7 Will you speak falsely for God,
　and speak deceitfully for him?
8 Will you show partiality toward him,
　will you plead the case for God?
9 Will it be well with you when he searches
　　you out?
　Or can you deceive him, as one person
　　deceives another?
10 He will surely rebuke you
　if in secret you show partiality.
11 Will not his majesty terrify you,
　and the dread of him fall upon you?
12 Your maxims are proverbs of ashes,
　your defenses are defenses of clay.
13 "Let me have silence, and I will speak,
　and let come on me what may.
14 I will take my flesh in my teeth,

and put my life in my hand.[u]
15 See, he will kill me; I have no hope;[v]
    but I will defend my ways to his face.
16 This will be my salvation,

13.15 A Desperate Hope

This statement more than any other shows the depth of Job's faith, and the reason he made good on God's challenge against Satan. He valued his faith in God even above his own life. He asked only for a "day in court," a chance to confront God personally and hear an explanation.

---

    that the godless shall not come before
        him.
17 Listen carefully to my words,
    and let my declaration be in your ears.
18 I have indeed prepared my case;
    I know that I shall be vindicated.
19 Who is there that will contend with me?
    For then I would be silent and die.

Job's Despondent Prayer

20 Only grant two things to me,
    then I will not hide myself from your
        face:
21 withdraw your hand far from me,
    and do not let dread of you terrify me.
22 Then call, and I will answer;
    or let me speak, and you reply to me.
23 How many are my iniquities and my sins?
    Make me know my transgression and
        my sin.
24 Why do you hide your face,
    and count me as your enemy?
25 Will you frighten a windblown leaf
    and pursue dry chaff?
26 For you write bitter things against me,
    and make me reap[w] the iniquities of
        my youth.
27 You put my feet in the stocks,
    and watch all my paths;
    you set a bound to the soles of my
        feet.
28 One wastes away like a rotten thing,
    like a garment that is moth-eaten.

14 "A mortal, born of woman, few of days
    and full of trouble,
2   comes up like a flower and withers,
    flees like a shadow and does not last.
3 Do you fix your eyes on such a one?
    Do you bring me into judgment with
        you?

4 Who can bring a clean thing out of an
        unclean?
    No one can.
5 Since their days are determined,
    and the number of their months is
        known to you,
    and you have appointed the bounds
        that they cannot pass,
6 look away from them, and desist,[x]
    that they may enjoy, like laborers, their
        days.

7 "For there is hope for a tree,
    if it is cut down, that it will sprout
        again,
    and that its shoots will not cease.
8 Though its root grows old in the earth,
    and its stump dies in the ground,
9 yet at the scent of water it will bud
    and put forth branches like a young
        plant.
10 But mortals die, and are laid low;
    humans expire, and where are they?
11 As waters fail from a lake,
    and a river wastes away and dries up,
12 so mortals lie down and do not rise again;
    until the heavens are no more, they
        will not awake
    or be roused out of their sleep.
13 O that you would hide me in Sheol,
    that you would conceal me until your
        wrath is past,
    that you would appoint me a set time,
        and remember me!
14 If mortals die, will they live again?
    All the days of my service I would wait
    until my release should come.
15 You would call, and I would answer you;
    you would long for the work of your
        hands.
16 For then you would not[y] number my
        steps,
    you would not keep watch over my sin;
17 my transgression would be sealed up in a
        bag,
    and you would cover over my iniquity.

18 "But the mountain falls and crumbles
        away,
    and the rock is removed from its place;
19 the waters wear away the stones;
    the torrents wash away the soil of the
        earth;
    so you destroy the hope of mortals.
20 You prevail forever against them, and
        they pass away;
    you change their countenance, and
        send them away.

---

[u] Gk: Heb Why should I take . . . in my hand?   [v] Or Though he kill me, yet I will trust in him   [w] Heb inherit
[x] Cn: Heb that they may desist   [y] Syr: Heb lacks not

21 Their children come to honor, and they
do not know it;
they are brought low, and it goes
unnoticed.
22 They feel only the pain of their own
bodies,
and mourn only for themselves."

Eliphaz Speaks: Job Undermines Religion

15 Then Eliphaz the Temanite answered:
2 "Should the wise answer with windy
knowledge,
and fill themselves with the east wind?
3 Should they argue in unprofitable talk,
or in words with which they can do no
good?
4 But you are doing away with the fear of
God,
and hindering meditation before God.

15.4 A Shocking Lack of Piety

*Job minced no words in his complaints against
God. As a result, his friends criticized him for
undermining piety and hindering devotion to
God. Notably, in his summing-up speech God
did not condemn Job's varying moods; he
instead dismissed the pious words of Job's
friends.*

*Counselors know that repressed feelings of
anger or disappointment don't just disappear;
they usually fester inside, and grow even more
toxic. Job expressed his feeling openly, much to
his friends' dismay.*

---

5 For your iniquity teaches your mouth,
and you choose the tongue of the
crafty.
6 Your own mouth condemns you, and
not I;
your own lips testify against you.

7 "Are you the firstborn of the human race?
Were you brought forth before the
hills?
8 Have you listened in the council of God?
And do you limit wisdom to yourself?
9 What do you know that we do not know?
What do you understand that is not
clear to us?
10 The gray-haired and the aged are on our
side,
those older than your father.
11 Are the consolations of God too small for
you,
or the word that deals gently with you?
12 Why does your heart carry you away,

and why do your eyes flash,[z]
13 so that you turn your spirit against God,
and let such words go out of your
mouth?
14 What are mortals, that they can be clean?
Or those born of woman, that they can
be righteous?
15 God puts no trust even in his holy ones,
and the heavens are not clean in his
sight;
16 how much less one who is abominable
and corrupt,
one who drinks iniquity like water!

17 "I will show you; listen to me;
what I have seen I will declare—
18 what sages have told,
and their ancestors have not hidden,
19 to whom alone the land was given,
and no stranger passed among them.
20 The wicked writhe in pain all their days,
through all the years that are laid up
for the ruthless.
21 Terrifying sounds are in their ears;
in prosperity the destroyer will come
upon them.
22 They despair of returning from darkness,
and they are destined for the sword.
23 They wander abroad for bread, saying,
'Where is it?'
They know that a day of darkness is
ready at hand;
24 distress and anguish terrify them;
they prevail against them, like a king
prepared for battle.
25 Because they stretched out their hands
against God,
and bid defiance to the Almighty,[a]
26 running stubbornly against him
with a thick-bossed shield;
27 because they have covered their faces with
their fat,
and gathered fat upon their loins,
28 they will live in desolate cities,
in houses that no one should inhabit,
houses destined to become heaps of
ruins;
29 they will not be rich, and their wealth will
not endure,
nor will they strike root in the earth;[b]
30 they will not escape from darkness;
the flame will dry up their shoots,
and their blossom[c] will be swept
away[d] by the wind.
31 Let them not trust in emptiness, deceiving
themselves;
for emptiness will be their recompense.
32 It will be paid in full before their time,

---

z Meaning of Heb uncertain   a Traditional rendering of Heb *Shaddai*   b Vg: Meaning of Heb uncertain
c Gk: Heb *mouth*   d Cn: Heb *will depart*

and their branch will not be green.
33 They will shake off their unripe grape,
like the vine,
and cast off their blossoms, like the
olive tree.
34 For the company of the godless is barren,
and fire consumes the tents of bribery.
35 They conceive mischief and bring forth
evil
and their heart prepares deceit."

Job Reaffirms His Innocence

16 Then Job answered:
2 "I have heard many such things;
miserable comforters are you all.
3 Have windy words no limit?
Or what provokes you that you keep
on talking?
4 I also could talk as you do,
if you were in my place;
I could join words together against you,
and shake my head at you.
5 I could encourage you with my mouth,
and the solace of my lips would
assuage your pain.

6 "If I speak, my pain is not assuaged,
and if I forbear, how much of it leaves
me?
7 Surely now God has worn me out;
he has^e made desolate all my
company.
8 And he has^e shriveled me up,
which is a witness against me;
my leanness has risen up against me,
and it testifies to my face.
9 He has torn me in his wrath, and hated
me;
he has gnashed his teeth at me;
my adversary sharpens his eyes against
me.

16.9 When God Seems Angry

*In his trauma, Job could not help feeling that he
was the object of God's anger. Many people
who undergo great pain feel the same. In Job's
case, however, we know that God was not
angry with him. God had held him up before
Satan as a "man who fears God and turns
away from evil" (1.8).*

10 They have gaped at me with their mouths;
they have struck me insolently on the
cheek;
they mass themselves together against
me.

11 God gives me up to the ungodly,
and casts me into the hands of the
wicked.
12 I was at ease, and he broke me in two;
he seized me by the neck and dashed
me to pieces;
he set me up as his target;
13 his archers surround me.
He slashes open my kidneys, and shows
no mercy;
he pours out my gall on the ground.
14 He bursts upon me again and again;
he rushes at me like a warrior.
15 I have sewed sackcloth upon my skin,
and have laid my strength in the dust.
16 My face is red with weeping,
and deep darkness is on my eyelids,
17 though there is no violence in my hands,
and my prayer is pure.

18 "O earth, do not cover my blood;
let my outcry find no resting place.
19 Even now, in fact, my witness is in
heaven,
and he that vouches for me is on high.
20 My friends scorn me;
my eye pours out tears to God,
21 that he would maintain the right of a
mortal with God,
as^f one does for a neighbor.
22 For when a few years have come,
I shall go the way from which I shall
not return.

Job Prays for Relief

17 My spirit is broken, my days are extinct,
the grave is ready for me.
2 Surely there are mockers around me,
and my eye dwells on their
provocation.

3 "Lay down a pledge for me with yourself;
who is there that will give surety for
me?
4 Since you have closed their minds to
understanding,
therefore you will not let them
triumph.
5 Those who denounce friends for
reward—
the eyes of their children will fail.

6 "He has made me a byword of the
peoples,
and I am one before whom people spit.
7 My eye has grown dim from grief,
and all my members are like a shadow.
8 The upright are appalled at this,

e Heb *you have*   f Syr Vg Tg: Heb *and*

and the innocent stir themselves up
    against the godless.
9 Yet the righteous hold to their way,
    and they that have clean hands grow
        stronger and stronger.
10 But you, come back now, all of you,
    and I shall not find a sensible person
        among you.
11 My days are past, my plans are broken
        off,
    the desires of my heart.
12 They make night into day;
    'The light,' they say, 'is near to the
        darkness.'g
13 If I look for Sheol as my house,
    if I spread my couch in darkness,
14 if I say to the Pit, 'You are my father,'
    and to the worm, 'My mother,' or 'My
        sister,'
15 where then is my hope?
    Who will see my hope?
16 Will it go down to the bars of Sheol?
    Shall we descend together into the
        dust?"

17.12–16 A Wrong Time for Cheer

*Falsely cheerful advice can actually make a
suffering person even more discouraged. Job's
sentiments here are echoed in a verse from
Proverbs: "Like vinegar on a wound, is one who
sings songs to a heavy heart" (25.20).*

Bildad Speaks: God Punishes the Wicked

18 Then Bildad the Shuhite answered:
2 "How long will you hunt for words?
    Consider, and then we shall speak.
3 Why are we counted as cattle?
    Why are we stupid in your sight?
4 You who tear yourself in your anger—
    shall the earth be forsaken because of
        you,
    or the rock be removed out of its
        place?

5 "Surely the light of the wicked is put out,
    and the flame of their fire does not
        shine.
6 The light is dark in their tent,
    and the lamp above them is put out.
7 Their strong steps are shortened,
    and their own schemes throw them
        down.
8 For they are thrust into a net by their
        own feet,
    and they walk into a pitfall.

9 A trap seizes them by the heel;
    a snare lays hold of them.
10 A rope is hid for them in the ground,
    a trap for them in the path.
11 Terrors frighten them on every side,
    and chase them at their heels.
12 Their strength is consumed by hunger,h
    and calamity is ready for their
        stumbling.
13 By disease their skin is consumed,i
    the firstborn of Death consumes their
        limbs.

18.13 Battle of Words

*After Job lashed out at his friends (see
17.10–12), Bildad retorted in kind, followed by
Zophar in chapter 20. These two speeches,
among the nastiest in the book, show the
danger of bitter argument about anything,
including theology. Friends who were
overwhelmed with compassion when they first
visited Job are now seen cruelly heaping more
grief upon him—just to defend their (faulty)
theological point.*

14 They are torn from the tent in which they
        trusted,
    and are brought to the king of terrors.
15 In their tents nothing remains;
    sulfur is scattered upon their
        habitations.
16 Their roots dry up beneath,
    and their branches wither above.
17 Their memory perishes from the earth,
    and they have no name in the street.
18 They are thrust from light into darkness,
    and driven out of the world.
19 They have no offspring or descendant
        among their people,
    and no survivor where they used to
        live.
20 They of the west are appalled at their fate,
    and horror seizes those of the east.
21 Surely such are the dwellings of the
        ungodly,
    such is the place of those who do not
        know God."

Job Replies: I Know That My Redeemer Lives

19 Then Job answered:
2 "How long will you torment me,
    and break me in pieces with words?
3 These ten times you have cast reproach
        upon me;
    are you not ashamed to wrong me?
4 And even if it is true that I have erred,

my error remains with me.
5 If indeed you magnify yourselves against
me,
and make my humiliation an argument
against me,
6 know then that God has put me in the
wrong,
and closed his net around me.
7 Even when I cry out, 'Violence!' I am not
answered;
I call aloud, but there is no justice.
8 He has walled up my way so that I
cannot pass,
and he has set darkness upon my
paths.
9 He has stripped my glory from me,
and taken the crown from my head.
10 He breaks me down on every side, and I
am gone,
he has uprooted my hope like a tree.
11 He has kindled his wrath against me,
and counts me as his adversary.
12 His troops come on together;
they have thrown up siegeworks[j]
against me,
and encamp around my tent.

13 "He has put my family far from me,
and my acquaintances are wholly
estranged from me.
14 My relatives and my close friends have
failed me;
15 the guests in my house have forgotten
me;
my serving girls count me as a stranger;
I have become an alien in their eyes.
16 I call to my servant, but he gives me no
answer;
I must myself plead with him.
17 My breath is repulsive to my wife;
I am loathsome to my own family.
18 Even young children despise me;
when I rise, they talk against me.
19 All my intimate friends abhor me,
and those whom I loved have turned
against me.
20 My bones cling to my skin and to my
flesh,
and I have escaped by the skin of my
teeth.
21 Have pity on me, have pity on me, O you
my friends,
for the hand of God has touched me!
22 Why do you, like God, pursue me,
never satisfied with my flesh?

23 "O that my words were written down!
O that they were inscribed in a book!

24 O that with an iron pen and with lead
they were engraved on a rock forever!
25 For I know that my Redeemer[k] lives,
and that at the last he[l] will stand
upon the earth;[m]

19.25 An Outburst of Hope

In the midst of his deepest agony, Job expressed astonishing words of hope. This prophecy expands on two other flashes of hope (9.33; 16.19–21). Job did not try to hide his despair and anguish, but, as this verse shows, the trials never crushed all of his hope.

26 and after my skin has been thus
destroyed,
then in[n] my flesh I shall see God,[o]
27 whom I shall see on my side,[p]
and my eyes shall behold, and not
another.
My heart faints within me!
28 If you say, 'How we will persecute him!'
and, 'The root of the matter is found
in him';
29 be afraid of the sword,
for wrath brings the punishment of the
sword,
so that you may know there is a
judgment."

Zophar Speaks: Wickedness Receives Just Retribution

20 Then Zophar the Naamathite answered:
2 "Pay attention! My thoughts urge
me to answer,
because of the agitation within me.
3 I hear censure that insults me,
and a spirit beyond my understanding
answers me.
4 Do you not know this from of old,
ever since mortals were placed on
earth,
5 that the exulting of the wicked is short,
and the joy of the godless is but for a
moment?
6 Even though they mount up high as the
heavens,
and their head reaches to the clouds,
7 they will perish forever like their own
dung;
those who have seen them will say,
'Where are they?'
8 They will fly away like a dream, and not
be found;

---

j Cn: Heb *their way*   k Or *Vindicator*   l Or *that he the Last*   m Heb *dust*   n Or *without*   o Meaning of
Heb of this verse uncertain   p Or *for myself*

they will be chased away like a vision
of the night.
9 The eye that saw them will see them no
more,
nor will their place behold them any
longer.
10 Their children will seek the favor of the
poor,
and their hands will give back their
wealth.
11 Their bodies, once full of youth,
will lie down in the dust with them.

12 "Though wickedness is sweet in their
mouth,
though they hide it under their
tongues,
13 though they are loath to let it go,
and hold it in their mouths;
14 yet their food is turned in their stomachs;
it is the venom of asps within them.
15 They swallow down riches and vomit
them up again;
God casts them out of their bellies.
16 They will suck the poison of asps;
the tongue of a viper will kill them.
17 They will not look on the rivers,
the streams flowing with honey and
curds.
18 They will give back the fruit of their toil,
and will not swallow it down;
from the profit of their trading
they will get no enjoyment.
19 For they have crushed and abandoned the
poor,
they have seized a house that they did
not build.

20 "They knew no quiet in their bellies;
in their greed they let nothing escape.
21 There was nothing left after they had
eaten;
therefore their prosperity will not
endure.
22 In full sufficiency they will be in distress;
all the force of misery will come upon
them.
23 To fill their belly to the full
God⁹ will send his fierce anger into
them,
and rain it upon them as their food.ʳ
24 They will flee from an iron weapon;
a bronze arrow will strike them
through.
25 It is drawn forth and comes out of their
body,
and the glittering point comes out of
their gall;
terrors come upon them.

26 Utter darkness is laid up for their
treasures;
a fire fanned by no one will devour
them;
what is left in their tent will be
consumed.
27 The heavens will reveal their iniquity,
and the earth will rise up against them.
28 The possessions of their house will be
carried away,
dragged off in the day of God'sˢ
wrath.
29 This is the portion of the wicked from
God,
the heritage decreed for them by God."

Job Replies: The Wicked Often Go Unpunished

21 Then Job answered:
2 "Listen carefully to my words,
and let this be your consolation.
3 Bear with me, and I will speak;
then after I have spoken, mock on.
4 As for me, is my complaint addressed to
mortals?
Why should I not be impatient?
5 Look at me, and be appalled,
and lay your hand upon your mouth.
6 When I think of it I am dismayed,
and shuddering seizes my flesh.
7 Why do the wicked live on,
reach old age, and grow mighty in
power?

21.7–15 Wicked People Prosper

In most of his speeches Job accepted the general principle that evil people suffer punishment in this life. But in this speech he began to question that theory. He cited examples of wicked people who lived comfortable, successful lives. His meandering thoughts proved so convincing to him that he concluded his friends' advice was "empty nothings" (verse 34).

8 Their children are established in their
presence,
and their offspring before their eyes.
9 Their houses are safe from fear,
and no rod of God is upon them.
10 Their bull breeds without fail;
their cow calves and never miscarries.
11 They send out their little ones like a flock,
and their children dance around.
12 They sing to the tambourine and the lyre,
and rejoice to the sound of the pipe.
13 They spend their days in prosperity,

q Heb *he*   r Cn: Meaning of Heb uncertain   s Heb *his*

and in peace they go down to Sheol.

14 They say to God, 'Leave us alone!
We do not desire to know your ways.

15 What is the Almighty,[t] that we should
serve him?
And what profit do we get if we pray
to him?'

16 Is not their prosperity indeed their own
achievement?[u]
The plans of the wicked are repugnant
to me.

17 "How often is the lamp of the wicked put
out?
How often does calamity come upon
them?
How often does God[v] distribute pains
in his anger?

18 How often are they like straw before the
wind,
and like chaff that the storm carries
away?

19 You say, 'God stores up their iniquity for
their children.'
Let it be paid back to them, so that
they may know it.

20 Let their own eyes see their destruction,
and let them drink of the wrath of the
Almighty.[t]

21 For what do they care for their household
after them,
when the number of their months is
cut off?

22 Will any teach God knowledge,
seeing that he judges those that are on
high?

23 One dies in full prosperity,
being wholly at ease and secure,

24 his loins full of milk
and the marrow of his bones moist.

25 Another dies in bitterness of soul,
never having tasted of good.

26 They lie down alike in the dust,
and the worms cover them.

27 "Oh, I know your thoughts,
and your schemes to wrong me.

28 For you say, 'Where is the house of the
prince?
Where is the tent in which the wicked
lived?'

29 Have you not asked those who travel the
roads,
and do you not accept their testimony,

30 that the wicked are spared in the day of
calamity,
and are rescued in the day of wrath?

31 Who declares their way to their face,
and who repays them for what they
have done?

32 When they are carried to the grave,
a watch is kept over their tomb.

33 The clods of the valley are sweet to them;
everyone will follow after,
and those who went before are
innumerable.

34 How then will you comfort me with
empty nothings?
There is nothing left of your answers
but falsehood."

Eliphaz Speaks: Job's Wickedness Is Great

22 Then Eliphaz the Temanite answered:
2 "Can a mortal be of use to God?
Can even the wisest be of service to
him?

3 Is it any pleasure to the Almighty[t] if you
are righteous,
or is it gain to him if you make your
ways blameless?

4 Is it for your piety that he reproves you,
and enters into judgment with you?

5 Is not your wickedness great?
There is no end to your iniquities.

6 For you have exacted pledges from your
family for no reason,
and stripped the naked of their
clothing.

22.6 The Attacks Get Personal

*Unable to convince Job through philosophizing,
Eliphaz shifted to more personal attacks
against Job's behavior. These arguments were
perhaps the unkindest of all, and Job
specifically refuted each one in his closing
speech (chapters 29–31).*

7 You have given no water to the weary to
drink,
and you have withheld bread from the
hungry.

8 The powerful possess the land,
and the favored live in it.

9 You have sent widows away
empty-handed,
and the arms of the orphans you have
crushed.[w]

10 Therefore snares are around you,
and sudden terror overwhelms you,

11 or darkness so that you cannot see;
a flood of water covers you.

---

[t] Traditional rendering of Heb *Shaddai*   [u] Heb *in their hand*   [v] Heb *he*   [w] Gk Syr Tg Vg: Heb *were crushed*

12 "Is not God high in the heavens?
See the highest stars, how lofty they
are!
13 Therefore you say, 'What does God
know?
Can he judge through the deep
darkness?
14 Thick clouds enwrap him, so that he does
not see,
and he walks on the dome of heaven.'
15 Will you keep to the old way
that the wicked have trod?
16 They were snatched away before their
time;
their foundation was washed away by a
flood.
17 They said to God, 'Leave us alone,'
and 'What can the Almighty[x] do to
us?'[y]
18 Yet he filled their houses with good
things—
but the plans of the wicked are
repugnant to me.
19 The righteous see it and are glad;
the innocent laugh them to scorn,
20 saying, 'Surely our adversaries are cut off,
and what they left, the fire has
consumed.'

21 "Agree with God,[z] and be at peace;
in this way good will come to you.
22 Receive instruction from his mouth,
and lay up his words in your heart.
23 If you return to the Almighty,[x] you will
be restored,
if you remove unrighteousness from
your tents,
24 if you treat gold like dust,
and gold of Ophir like the stones of
the torrent-bed,
25 and if the Almighty[x] is your gold
and your precious silver,
26 then you will delight yourself in the
Almighty,[x]
and lift up your face to God.
27 You will pray to him, and he will hear
you,
and you will pay your vows.
28 You will decide on a matter, and it will be
established for you,
and light will shine on your ways.
29 When others are humiliated, you say it is
pride;
for he saves the humble.
30 He will deliver even those who are guilty;
they will escape because of the
cleanness of your hands."[a]

Job Replies: My Complaint Is Bitter

23 Then Job answered:
2 "Today also my complaint is
bitter;[b]
his[c] hand is heavy despite my
groaning.
3 Oh, that I knew where I might find him,
that I might come even to his dwelling!
4 I would lay my case before him,
and fill my mouth with arguments.
5 I would learn what he would answer me,
and understand what he would say to
me.
6 Would he contend with me in the
greatness of his power?
No; but he would give heed to me.
7 There an upright person could reason
with him,
and I should be acquitted forever by
my judge.

8 "If I go forward, he is not there;
or backward, I cannot perceive him;
9 on the left he hides, and I cannot behold
him;
I turn[d] to the right, but I cannot see
him.
10 But he knows the way that I take;
when he has tested me, I shall come
out like gold.
11 My foot has held fast to his steps;
I have kept his way and have not
turned aside.
12 I have not departed from the
commandment of his lips;
I have treasured in[e] my bosom the
words of his mouth.
13 But he stands alone and who can dissuade
him?
What he desires, that he does.
14 For he will complete what he appoints for
me;
and many such things are in his mind.

23.13 Unstable Ground

*Job's friends hammered away at consistent
themes whereas Job, like most people in pain,
found himself shifting back and forth, unsure
what to believe. In the first paragraph of
chapter 23, he is ready to take God on; in the
second, he wonders if he'll ever find God to
state his case; in the third, he trembles to think
what might happen if he actually does locate
God!*

15 Therefore I am terrified at his presence;
  when I consider, I am in dread of him.
16 God has made my heart faint;
  the Almighty[f] has terrified me;
17 If only I could vanish in darkness,
  and thick darkness would cover my
    face![g]

Job Complains of Violence on the Earth

24 "Why are times not kept by the
    Almighty,[f]
  and why do those who know him
    never see his days?
2 The wicked[h] remove landmarks;
  they seize flocks and pasture them.
3 They drive away the donkey of the
    orphan;
  they take the widow's ox for a pledge.
4 They thrust the needy off the road;
  the poor of the earth all hide
    themselves.
5 Like wild asses in the desert
  they go out to their toil,
  scavenging in the wasteland
    food for their young.
6 They reap in a field not their own
  and they glean in the vineyard of the
    wicked.
7 They lie all night naked, without clothing,
  and have no covering in the cold.
8 They are wet with the rain of the
    mountains,
  and cling to the rock for want of
    shelter.

9 "There are those who snatch the orphan
    child from the breast,
  and take as a pledge the infant of the
    poor.
10 They go about naked, without clothing;
  though hungry, they carry the sheaves;
11 between their terraces[i] they press out oil;
  they tread the wine presses, but suffer
    thirst.
12 From the city the dying groan,
  and the throat of the wounded cries for
    help;
  yet God pays no attention to their
    prayer.

13 "There are those who rebel against the
    light,
  who are not acquainted with its ways,
  and do not stay in its paths.
14 The murderer rises at dusk
  to kill the poor and needy,
  and in the night is like a thief.

15 The eye of the adulterer also waits for the
    twilight,
  saying, 'No eye will see me';
  and he disguises his face.
16 In the dark they dig through houses;
  by day they shut themselves up;
  they do not know the light.
17 For deep darkness is morning to all of
    them;
  for they are friends with the terrors of
    deep darkness.

18 "Swift are they on the face of the waters;
  their portion in the land is cursed;
  no treader turns toward their
    vineyards.
19 Drought and heat snatch away the snow
    waters;
  so does Sheol those who have sinned.
20 The womb forgets them;
  the worm finds them sweet;
  they are no longer remembered;
  so wickedness is broken like a tree.
21 "They harm[j] the childless woman,
  and do no good to the widow.
22 Yet God[k] prolongs the life of the mighty
    by his power;
  they rise up when they despair of life.
23 He gives them security, and they are
    supported;
  his eyes are upon their ways.
24 They are exalted a little while, and then
    are gone;
  they wither and fade like the mallow;[l]
  they are cut off like the heads of grain.
25 If it is not so, who will prove me a liar,
  and show that there is nothing in what
    I say?"

Bildad Speaks: How Can a Mortal Be Righteous Before God?

25 Then Bildad the Shuhite answered:
2 "Dominion and fear are with
    God;[m]
  he makes peace in his high heaven.
3 Is there any number to his armies?
  Upon whom does his light not arise?
4 How then can a mortal be righteous
    before God?
  How can one born of woman be pure?
5 If even the moon is not bright
  and the stars are not pure in his sight,
6 how much less a mortal, who is a maggot,
  and a human being, who is a worm!"

---

[f] Traditional rendering of Heb *Shaddai*   [g] Or *But I am not destroyed by the darkness; he has concealed the thick*
darkness from me   [h] Gk: Heb *they*   [i] Meaning of Heb uncertain   [j] Gk Tg: Heb *feed on* or *associate with*
[k] Heb *he*   [l] Gk: Heb *like all others*   [m] Heb *him*

Job Replies: God's Majesty Is Unsearchable

26 Then Job answered:
² "How you have helped one who
has no power!

How you have assisted the arm that
has no strength!
³ How you have counseled one who has no
wisdom,
and given much good advice!
⁴ With whose help have you uttered words,
and whose spirit has come forth from
you?
⁵ The shades below tremble,
the waters and their inhabitants.
⁶ Sheol is naked before God,
and Abaddon has no covering.
⁷ He stretches out Zaphon[n] over the void,
and hangs the earth upon nothing.
⁸ He binds up the waters in his thick
clouds,
and the cloud is not torn open by
them.
⁹ He covers the face of the full moon,
and spreads over it his cloud.
¹⁰ He has described a circle on the face of
the waters,
at the boundary between light and
darkness.
¹¹ The pillars of heaven tremble,

and are astounded at his rebuke.
¹² By his power he stilled the Sea;
by his understanding he struck down
Rahab.
¹³ By his wind the heavens were made fair;
his hand pierced the fleeing serpent.
¹⁴ These are indeed but the outskirts of his
ways;
and how small a whisper do we hear of
him!
But the thunder of his power who can
understand?"

Job Maintains His Integrity

27 Job again took up his discourse and said:
² "As God lives, who has taken away
my right,
and the Almighty,[o] who has made my
soul bitter,
³ as long as my breath is in me
and the spirit of God is in my nostrils,
⁴ my lips will not speak falsehood,
and my tongue will not utter deceit.
⁵ Far be it from me to say that you are
right;
until I die I will not put away my
integrity from me.
⁶ I hold fast my righteousness, and will not
let it go;
my heart does not reproach me for any
of my days.

⁷ "May my enemy be like the wicked,
and may my opponent be like the
unrighteous.
⁸ For what is the hope of the godless when
God cuts them off,
when God takes away their lives?
⁹ Will God hear their cry
when trouble comes upon them?
¹⁰ Will they take delight in the Almighty?[o]
Will they call upon God at all times?
¹¹ I will teach you concerning the hand of
God;
that which is with the Almighty[o] I will
not conceal.
¹² All of you have seen it yourselves;
why then have you become altogether
vain?

¹³ "This is the portion of the wicked with
God,
and the heritage that oppressors receive
from the Almighty:[o]
¹⁴ If their children are multiplied, it is for
the sword;
and their offspring have not enough to
eat.

[n] Or *the North*   [o] Traditional rendering of Heb *Shaddai*

15 Those who survive them the pestilence
buries,
and their widows make no lamentation.
16 Though they heap up silver like dust,
and pile up clothing like clay—
17 they may pile it up, but the just will wear
it,
and the innocent will divide the silver.
18 They build their houses like nests,
like booths made by sentinels of the
vineyard.
19 They go to bed with wealth, but will do
so no more;
they open their eyes, and it is gone.
20 Terrors overtake them like a flood;
in the night a whirlwind carries them
off.
21 The east wind lifts them up and they are
gone;
it sweeps them out of their place.
22 It*p* hurls at them without pity;
they flee from its*q* power in headlong
flight.
23 It*p* claps its*q* hands at them,
and hisses at them from its*q* place.

Interlude: Where Wisdom Is Found

28 "Surely there is a mine for silver,
and a place for gold to be refined.

28.1 A Poem on Wisdom

*In the midst of one of his most beautiful
speeches, Job included a self-contained poem
on wisdom. It uses the analogy of mining
precious metals to make the point that wisdom
cannot be found by any amount of searching
(verses 1–19). God alone knows where it
dwells. In the rest of the poem, Job admitted
some things were beyond his understanding,
then lapsed into a reminiscence of what life
was like before his time of trials.*

2 Iron is taken out of the earth,
and copper is smelted from ore.
3 Miners put*r* an end to darkness,
and search out to the farthest bound
the ore in gloom and deep darkness.
4 They open shafts in a valley away from
human habitation;
they are forgotten by travelers,
they sway suspended, remote from
people.
5 As for the earth, out of it comes bread;
but underneath it is turned up as by
fire.

6 Its stones are the place of sapphires,*s*
and its dust contains gold.

7 "That path no bird of prey knows,
and the falcon's eye has not seen it.
8 The proud wild animals have not trodden
it;
the lion has not passed over it.

9 "They put their hand to the flinty rock,
and overturn mountains by the roots.
10 They cut out channels in the rocks,
and their eyes see every precious thing.
11 The sources of the rivers they probe;*t*
hidden things they bring to light.

12 "But where shall wisdom be found?
And where is the place of
understanding?
13 Mortals do not know the way to it,*u*
and it is not found in the land of the
living.
14 The deep says, 'It is not in me,'
and the sea says, 'It is not with me.'
15 It cannot be gotten for gold,
and silver cannot be weighed out as its
price.
16 It cannot be valued in the gold of Ophir,
in precious onyx or sapphire.*s*
17 Gold and glass cannot equal it,
nor can it be exchanged for jewels of
fine gold.
18 No mention shall be made of coral or of
crystal;
the price of wisdom is above pearls.
19 The chrysolite of Ethiopia*v* cannot
compare with it,
nor can it be valued in pure gold.

20 "Where then does wisdom come from?
And where is the place of
understanding?
21 It is hidden from the eyes of all living,
and concealed from the birds of the
air.
22 Abaddon and Death say,
'We have heard a rumor of it with our
ears.'

23 "God understands the way to it,
and he knows its place.
24 For he looks to the ends of the earth,
and sees everything under the heavens.
25 When he gave to the wind its weight,
and apportioned out the waters by
measure;
26 when he made a decree for the rain,
and a way for the thunderbolt;

---

p Or *He* (that is God)   *q* Or *his*   *r* Heb *He puts*   *s* Or *lapis lazuli*   *t* Gk Vg: Heb *bind*   *u* Gk: Heb *its price*
v Or *Nubia*; Heb *Cush*

27 then he saw it and declared it;
  he established it, and searched it out.
28 And he said to humankind,
  'Truly, the fear of the Lord, that is
      wisdom;
  and to depart from evil is
      understanding.'"

Job Finishes His Defense

29 Job again took up his discourse and said:
  2 "O that I were as in the months of
      old,
  as in the days when God watched over
      me;
  3 when his lamp shone over my head,
    and by his light I walked through
        darkness;
  4 when I was in my prime,
    when the friendship of God was upon
        my tent;
  5 when the Almighty[w] was still with me,
    when my children were around me;
  6 when my steps were washed with milk,
    and the rock poured out for me
        streams of oil!
  7 When I went out to the gate of the city,
    when I took my seat in the square,
  8 the young men saw me and withdrew,
    and the aged rose up and stood;
  9 the nobles refrained from talking,
    and laid their hands on their mouths;
  10 the voices of princes were hushed,
     and their tongues stuck to the roof of
         their mouths.
  11 When the ear heard, it commended me,
     and when the eye saw, it approved;

29.11 The Good Old Days

Tenderly, Job reminisces about the "months of old" (verse 2), before his trials began. Job could think of no reason why he might "deserve" such treatment—the point of the book of Job exactly. His recollections of life in those days refute his friends' accusations against him. He had shown concern for the poor and oppressed—a fact that must have increased his puzzlement over the unfair treatment he was receiving.

  12 because I delivered the poor who cried,
     and the orphan who had no helper.
  13 The blessing of the wretched came upon
         me,
     and I caused the widow's heart to sing
         for joy.
  14 I put on righteousness, and it clothed me;

my justice was like a robe and a
    turban.
15 I was eyes to the blind,
   and feet to the lame.
16 I was a father to the needy,
   and I championed the cause of the
       stranger.
17 I broke the fangs of the unrighteous,
   and made them drop their prey from
       their teeth.
18 Then I thought, 'I shall die in my nest,
   and I shall multiply my days like the
       phoenix;[x]
19 my roots spread out to the waters,
   with the dew all night on my branches;
20 my glory was fresh with me,
   and my bow ever new in my hand.'

21 "They listened to me, and waited,
   and kept silence for my counsel.
22 After I spoke they did not speak again,
   and my word dropped upon them like
       dew.[y]
23 They waited for me as for the rain;
   they opened their mouths as for the
       spring rain.
24 I smiled on them when they had no
       confidence;
   and the light of my countenance they
       did not extinguish.[z]
25 I chose their way, and sat as chief,
   and I lived like a king among his
       troops,
   like one who comforts mourners.

30 "But now they make sport of me,
  those who are younger than I,
whose fathers I would have disdained
    to set with the dogs of my flock.
  2 What could I gain from the strength of
        their hands?
    All their vigor is gone.
  3 Through want and hard hunger
    they gnaw the dry and desolate ground,
  4 they pick mallow and the leaves of
        bushes,
    and to warm themselves the roots of
        broom.
  5 They are driven out from society;
    people shout after them as after a thief.
  6 In the gullies of wadis they must live,
    in holes in the ground, and in the
        rocks.
  7 Among the bushes they bray;
    under the nettles they huddle together.
  8 A senseless, disreputable brood,
    they have been whipped out of the
        land.

---

[w] Traditional rendering of Heb *Shaddai*   [x] Or *like sand*   [y] Heb lacks *like dew*   [z] Meaning of Heb uncertain

9 "And now they mock me in song;
  I am a byword to them.
10 They abhor me, they keep aloof from me;
  they do not hesitate to spit at the sight
  of me.
11 Because God has loosed my bowstring
  and humbled me,
  they have cast off restraint in my
  presence.
12 On my right hand the rabble rise up;
  they send me sprawling,
  and build roads for my ruin.
13 They break up my path,
  they promote my calamity;
  no one restrains*a* them.
14 As through a wide breach they come;
  amid the crash they roll on.
15 Terrors are turned upon me;
  my honor is pursued as by the wind,
  and my prosperity has passed away like
  a cloud.

16 "And now my soul is poured out within
  me;
  days of affliction have taken hold of
  me.
17 The night racks my bones,
  and the pain that gnaws me takes no
  rest.
18 With violence he seizes my garment;*b*
  he grasps me by*c* the collar of my
  tunic.
19 He has cast me into the mire,
  and I have become like dust and ashes.
20 I cry to you and you do not answer me;
  I stand, and you merely look at me.
21 You have turned cruel to me;
  with the might of your hand you
  persecute me.
22 You lift me up on the wind, you make
  me ride on it,
  and you toss me about in the roar of
  the storm.
23 I know that you will bring me to death,
  and to the house appointed for all
  living.

24 "Surely one does not turn against the
  needy,*d*
  when in disaster they cry for help.*e*
25 Did I not weep for those whose day was
  hard?
  Was not my soul grieved for the poor?
26 But when I looked for good, evil came;
  and when I waited for light, darkness
  came.
27 My inward parts are in turmoil, and are
  never still;

days of affliction come to meet me.
28 I go about in sunless gloom;
  I stand up in the assembly and cry for
  help.
29 I am a brother of jackals,
  and a companion of ostriches.
30 My skin turns black and falls from me,
  and my bones burn with heat.
31 My lyre is turned to mourning,
  and my pipe to the voice of those who
  weep.

31 "I have made a covenant with my eyes;
  how then could I look upon a virgin?

31.1 Binding Oaths

*This chapter, Job's final line of defense, is
written in a form that had legal significance to
his hearers. Job was solemnly swearing his
innocence in response to a whole series of
accusations. He called down curses on himself
if he could be proved wrong. The oaths were
somewhat like our modern custom of swearing
on the Bible "to tell the truth, the whole truth
and nothing but the truth." Job's oaths
impressed his three friends and effectively
ended the debate. Then a new character, Elihu,
joined in.*

2 What would be my portion from God
  above,
  and my heritage from the Almighty*f*
  on high?
3 Does not calamity befall the unrighteous,
  and disaster the workers of iniquity?
4 Does he not see my ways,
  and number all my steps?

5 "If I have walked with falsehood,
  and my foot has hurried to deceit—
6 let me be weighed in a just balance,
  and let God know my integrity!—
7 if my step has turned aside from the way,
  and my heart has followed my eyes,
  and if any spot has clung to my hands;
8 then let me sow, and another eat;
  and let what grows for me be rooted
  out.

9 "If my heart has been enticed by a
  woman,
  and I have lain in wait at my
  neighbor's door;
10 then let my wife grind for another,
  and let other men kneel over her.
11 For that would be a heinous crime;

---

a Cn: Heb *helps*   *b* Gk: Heb *my garment is disfigured*   *c* Heb *like*   *d* Heb *ruin*   *e* Cn: Meaning of Heb
uncertain   *f* Traditional rendering of Heb *Shaddai*

that would be a criminal offense;
12 for that would be a fire consuming down
to Abaddon,
and it would burn to the root all my
harvest.

13 "If I have rejected the cause of my male
or female slaves,
when they brought a complaint against
me;
14 what then shall I do when God rises up?
When he makes inquiry, what shall I
answer him?
15 Did not he who made me in the womb
make them?
And did not one fashion us in the
womb?

16 "If I have withheld anything that the poor
desired,
or have caused the eyes of the widow
to fail,
17 or have eaten my morsel alone,
and the orphan has not eaten from
it—

g Heb *him*   *h* Heb *her*

18 for from my youth I reared the orphan*g*
like a father,
and from my mother's womb I guided
the widow*h*—

> ### 31.16 A Habit of Trust
>
> *This chapter gives insights into Job's life of spiritual discipline. He had developed the habit of obeying God. Now, with all the props knocked out, he still turned to God for strength, even though God seemed utterly absent. It was as if he had a resource bank of trust in God: the trust he had accumulated in more comfortable times helped him survive his time of hardship.*

19 if I have seen anyone perish for lack of
clothing,
or a poor person without covering,
20 whose loins have not blessed me,
and who was not warmed with the
fleece of my sheep;
21 if I have raised my hand against the
orphan,

A Silent Friend Decides to Speak Up

Elihu, out of nowhere, proposes new ideas about suffering

UP TO THIS POINT IN Job, the action has revolved around Job and his three friends. The debate among them, growing ever more heated, finally breaks off. They have reached a standoff. Job will not admit to any sin deserving of terrible punishment, and his three friends will not back down from their ideas about suffering.

> *"There was . . . no one that confuted Job, no one among you that answered his words." 32.12*

Suddenly, a new voice is heard. Elihu, a young man, has been listening in silence all this time. He can restrain himself no longer. He flares up, first at Job for being so self-righteous and then at the three friends for not coming up with an answer to Job's questions. He refutes all four of them, turning their own words against them.

Is Elihu Right?

Elihu is shocked at Job's vigorous self-defense. Surely God cannot be unjust, he insists. Submit to the pain, even if you don't understand it. Don't blame God; praise him. God has shown too much of his wisdom and perfection, especially in nature, for anyone to doubt him.

Elihu offers a new explanation for Job's pain. Perhaps, he suggests, God gave suffering to Job not as punishment but as a purifying influence. God can use suffering to improve a person, if it is received in the right spirit.

Where did Elihu come from? Who is he? Are his theories right? Mystery surrounds the man. His speeches stand alone, and no one responds to them. As a result, the book of Job gives no clue on whether Elihu expressed a worthy point of view.

Some readers believe Elihu forms a bridge between the flawed theories of Job's three friends and God's own speech. Perhaps his speeches prepare the way for God's. Others see him as repeating the same fine-sounding, but not-quite-true, advice of Job's three friends.

When God does make an entrance, he dismisses Job's friends and has some mild criticism for Job. But he ignores Elihu entirely. Elihu remains a mysterious figure.

Life Questions: Do Elihu's arguments sound familiar? What do you think of friends who have similar thoughts about others who suffer?

because I saw I had supporters at the gate;

22 then let my shoulder blade fall from my shoulder,
and let my arm be broken from its socket.

23 For I was in terror of calamity from God,
and I could not have faced his majesty.

24 "If I have made gold my trust,
or called fine gold my confidence;

25 if I have rejoiced because my wealth was great,
or because my hand had gotten much;

26 if I have looked at the sun[i] when it shone,
or the moon moving in splendor,

27 and my heart has been secretly enticed,
and my mouth has kissed my hand;

28 this also would be an iniquity to be punished by the judges,
for I should have been false to God above.

29 "If I have rejoiced at the ruin of those who hated me,
or exulted when evil overtook them—

30 I have not let my mouth sin
by asking for their lives with a curse—

31 if those of my tent ever said,
'O that we might be sated with his flesh!'[j]—

32 the stranger has not lodged in the street;
I have opened my doors to the traveler—

33 if I have concealed my transgressions as others do,[k]
by hiding my iniquity in my bosom,

34 because I stood in great fear of the multitude,
and the contempt of families terrified me,
so that I kept silence, and did not go out of doors—

35 O that I had one to hear me!
(Here is my signature! Let the Almighty[l] answer me!)
O, that I had the indictment written by my adversary!

36 Surely I would carry it on my shoulder;
I would bind it on me like a crown;

37 I would give him an account of all my steps;
like a prince I would approach him.

38 "If my land has cried out against me,

and its furrows have wept together;

39 if I have eaten its yield without payment,
and caused the death of its owners;

40 let thorns grow instead of wheat,
and foul weeds instead of barley."

The words of Job are ended.

Elihu Rebukes Job's Friends

32 So these three men ceased to answer Job, because he was righteous in his own eyes. [2]Then Elihu son of Barachel the Buzite, of the family of Ram, became angry. He was angry at Job because he justified himself rather than God; [3]he was angry also at Job's three friends because they had found no answer, though they had declared Job to be in the wrong.[m] [4]Now Elihu had waited to speak to Job, because they were older than he. [5]But when Elihu saw that there was no answer in the mouths of these three men, he became angry.

6 Elihu son of Barachel the Buzite answered:
"I am young in years,
and you are aged;
therefore I was timid and afraid
to declare my opinion to you.

7 I said, 'Let days speak,
and many years teach wisdom.'

8 But truly it is the spirit in a mortal,
the breath of the Almighty,[l] that
makes for understanding.

9 It is not the old[n] that are wise,
nor the aged that understand what is right.

10 Therefore I say, 'Listen to me;
let me also declare my opinion.'

11 "See, I waited for your words,
I listened for your wise sayings,
while you searched out what to say.

12 I gave you my attention,
but there was in fact no one that confuted Job,
no one among you that answered his words.

13 Yet do not say, 'We have found wisdom;
God may vanquish him, not a human.'

14 He has not directed his words against me,
and I will not answer him with your speeches.

15 "They are dismayed, they answer no more;
they have not a word to say.

16 And am I to wait, because they do not speak,
because they stand there, and answer no more?

---

[i] Heb *the light*   [j] Meaning of Heb uncertain   [k] Or *as Adam did*   [l] Traditional rendering of Heb *Shaddai*
[m] Another ancient tradition reads *answer, and had put God in the wrong*   [n] Gk Syr Vg: Heb *many*

17 I also will give my answer;
    I also will declare my opinion.
18 For I am full of words;
    the spirit within me constrains me.
19 My heart is indeed like wine that has no
        vent;
    like new wineskins, it is ready to burst.
20 I must speak, so that I may find relief;
    I must open my lips and answer.
21 I will not show partiality to any person
    or use flattery toward anyone.
22 For I do not know how to flatter—
    or my Maker would soon put an end
        to me!

Elihu Rebukes Job

33 "But now, hear my speech, O Job,
    and listen to all my words.
2 See, I open my mouth;
    the tongue in my mouth speaks.
3 My words declare the uprightness of my
        heart,
    and what my lips know they speak
        sincerely.
4 The spirit of God has made me,
    and the breath of the Almighty[o] gives
        me life.
5 Answer me, if you can;
    set your words in order before me;
        take your stand.
6 See, before God I am as you are;
    I too was formed from a piece of clay.
7 No fear of me need terrify you;
    my pressure will not be heavy on you.

8 "Surely, you have spoken in my hearing,
    and I have heard the sound of your
        words.
9 You say, 'I am clean, without
        transgression;
    I am pure, and there is no iniquity in
        me.
10 Look, he finds occasions against me,
    he counts me as his enemy;
11 he puts my feet in the stocks,
    and watches all my paths.'
12 "But in this you are not right. I will
        answer you:
    God is greater than any mortal.
13 Why do you contend against him,
    saying, 'He will answer none of my[p]
        words'?
14 For God speaks in one way,
    and in two, though people do not
        perceive it.
15 In a dream, in a vision of the night,
    when deep sleep falls on mortals,
    while they slumber on their beds,

16 then he opens their ears,
    and terrifies them with warnings,
17 that he may turn them aside from their
        deeds,
    and keep them from pride,
18 to spare their souls from the Pit,
    their lives from traversing the River.
19 They are also chastened with pain upon
        their beds,
    and with continual strife in their bones,

33.19 Kinder, Gentler Friend

Evidently, Elihu had sat in silence throughout the discussions to this point (in deference to the other speakers' age, as he explains). That fact alone shows his calmer nature: he refused to jump into very heated arguments. Although Elihu introduces some new ideas, he also follows the general line of reasoning—"You're being punished for your sins, Job" (see verses 17–22)—that God corrects in the end.

20 so that their lives loathe bread,
    and their appetites dainty food.
21 Their flesh is so wasted away that it
        cannot be seen;
    and their bones, once invisible, now
        stick out.
22 Their souls draw near the Pit,
    and their lives to those who bring
        death.
23 Then, if there should be for one of them
        an angel,
    a mediator, one of a thousand,
    one who declares a person upright,
24 and he is gracious to that person, and
        says,
    'Deliver him from going down into the
        Pit;
    I have found a ransom;
25 let his flesh become fresh with youth;
    let him return to the days of his
        youthful vigor';
26 then he prays to God, and is accepted by
        him,
    he comes into his presence with joy,
    and God[q] repays him for his
        righteousness.
27 That person sings to others and says,
    'I sinned, and perverted what was right,
    and it was not paid back to me.
28 He has redeemed my soul from going
        down to the Pit,
    and my life shall see the light.'

29 "God indeed does all these things,
    twice, three times, with mortals,

[o] Traditional rendering of Heb *Shaddai*   [p] Compare Gk: Heb *his*   [q] Heb *he*

30 to bring back their souls from the Pit,
   so that they may see the light of life.ʳ
31 Pay heed, Job, listen to me;
   be silent, and I will speak.

33.30 Pain as a Warning

*Elihu did not defend Job as innocent. But his
arguments shifted the emphasis of suffering
from punishment to warning. Perhaps, he
suggested, God allows a man to suffer in order
"to bring back their souls from the Pit."
Primarily, however, Elihu defended God's
actions. "God will not do wickedly, and the
Almighty will not pervert justice" (34.12).*

32 If you have anything to say, answer me;
   speak, for I desire to justify you.
33 If not, listen to me;
   be silent, and I will teach you wisdom."

Elihu Proclaims God's Justice

34 Then Elihu continued and said:
2 "Hear my words, you wise men,
   and give ear to me, you who know;
3 for the ear tests words
   as the palate tastes food.
4 Let us choose what is right;
   let us determine among ourselves what
     is good.
5 For Job has said, 'I am innocent,
   and God has taken away my right;
6 in spite of being right I am counted a liar;
   my wound is incurable, though I am
     without transgression.'
7 Who is there like Job,
   who drinks up scoffing like water,
8 who goes in company with evildoers
   and walks with the wicked?
9 For he has said, 'It profits one nothing
   to take delight in God.'

10 "Therefore, hear me, you who have sense,
   far be it from God that he should do
     wickedness,
   and from the Almightyˢ that he
     should do wrong.
11 For according to their deeds he will repay
     them,
   and according to their ways he will
     make it befall them.
12 Of a truth, God will not do wickedly,
   and the Almightyˢ will not pervert
     justice.
13 Who gave him charge over the earth
   and who laid on himᵗ the whole
     world?

14 If he should take back his spiritᵘ to
     himself,
   and gather to himself his breath,
15 all flesh would perish together,
   and all mortals return to dust.

16 "If you have understanding, hear this;
   listen to what I say.
17 Shall one who hates justice govern?
   Will you condemn one who is
     righteous and mighty,
18 who says to a king, 'You scoundrel!'
   and to princes, 'You wicked men!';
19 who shows no partiality to nobles,
   nor regards the rich more than the
     poor,
   for they are all the work of his hands?
20 In a moment they die;
   at midnight the people are shaken and
     pass away,
   and the mighty are taken away by no
     human hand.

21 "For his eyes are upon the ways of
     mortals,
   and he sees all their steps.
22 There is no gloom or deep darkness
   where evildoers may hide themselves.
23 For he has not appointed a timeᵛ for
     anyone
   to go before God in judgment.
24 He shatters the mighty without
     investigation,
   and sets others in their place.
25 Thus, knowing their works,
   he overturns them in the night, and
     they are crushed.
26 He strikes them for their wickedness
   while others look on,
27 because they turned aside from following
     him,
   and had no regard for any of his ways,
28 so that they caused the cry of the poor to
     come to him,
   and he heard the cry of the afflicted—
29 When he is quiet, who can condemn?
   When he hides his face, who can
     behold him,
   whether it be a nation or an
     individual?—
30 so that the godless should not reign,
   or those who ensnare the people.

31 "For has anyone said to God,
   'I have endured punishment; I will not
     offend any more;
32 teach me what I do not see;

ʳ Syr: Heb *to be lighted with the light of life*   ˢ Traditional rendering of Heb *Shaddai*   ᵗ Heb lacks *on him*
ᵘ Heb *his heart his spirit*   ᵛ Cn: Heb *yet*

if I have done iniquity, I will do it no
more'?
33 Will he then pay back to suit you,
because you reject it?
For you must choose, and not I;
therefore declare what you know.[w]
34 Those who have sense will say to me,
and the wise who hear me will say,
35 'Job speaks without knowledge,
his words are without insight.'
36 Would that Job were tried to the limit,
because his answers are those of the
wicked.
37 For he adds rebellion to his sin;
he claps his hands among us,
and multiplies his words against God."

Elihu Condemns Self-Righteousness

35 Elihu continued and said:
2 "Do you think this to be just?
You say, 'I am in the right before
God.'
3 If you ask, 'What advantage have I?
How am I better off than if I had
sinned?'
4 I will answer you
and your friends with you.
5 Look at the heavens and see;
observe the clouds, which are higher
than you.
6 If you have sinned, what do you
accomplish against him?
And if your transgressions are
multiplied, what do you do to
him?
7 If you are righteous, what do you give to
him;
or what does he receive from your
hand?
8 Your wickedness affects others like you,
and your righteousness, other human
beings.

9 "Because of the multitude of oppressions
people cry out;
they call for help because of the arm of
the mighty.
10 But no one says, 'Where is God my
Maker,
who gives strength in the night,
11 who teaches us more than the animals of
the earth,
and makes us wiser than the birds of
the air?'
12 There they cry out, but he does not
answer,
because of the pride of evildoers.

13 Surely God does not hear an empty cry,
nor does the Almighty[x] regard it.
14 How much less when you say that you do
not see him,
that the case is before him, and you
are waiting for him!

35.14 Is God Really Listening?

*Readers differ on how true Elihu's words were.
But in this chapter he seems to say Job had no
right to argue before God or to ask for a
personal appearance. Why should God be
concerned about one man's wickedness or
righteousness? he asks (verse 8). The opening
chapters of the book, however, revealed how
much hung on Job's responses. And ultimately
God did step in and reveal himself. In fact, he
made an entrance just as Elihu was explaining
why God would not appear.*

15 And now, because his anger does not
punish,
and he does not greatly heed
transgression,[y]
16 Job opens his mouth in empty talk,
he multiplies words without
knowledge."

Elihu Exalts God's Goodness

36 Elihu continued and said:
2 "Bear with me a little, and I will
show you,
for I have yet something to say on
God's behalf.
3 I will bring my knowledge from far away,
and ascribe righteousness to my Maker.
4 For truly my words are not false;
one who is perfect in knowledge is
with you.
5 "Surely God is mighty and does not
despise any;
he is mighty in strength of
understanding.
6 He does not keep the wicked alive,
but gives the afflicted their right.
7 He does not withdraw his eyes from the
righteous,
but with kings on the throne
he sets them forever, and they are
exalted.
8 And if they are bound in fetters
and caught in the cords of affliction,
9 then he declares to them their work
and their transgressions, that they are
behaving arrogantly.

[w] Meaning of Heb of verses 29-33 uncertain [x] Traditional rendering of Heb *Shaddai* [y] Theodotion Symmachus
Compare Vg: Meaning of Heb uncertain

10 He opens their ears to instruction,
and commands that they return from
iniquity.
11 If they listen, and serve him,
they complete their days in prosperity,
and their years in pleasantness.
12 But if they do not listen, they shall perish
by the sword,
and die without knowledge.

13 "The godless in heart cherish anger;
they do not cry for help when he binds
them.
14 They die in their youth,
and their life ends in shame.ᶻ
15 He delivers the afflicted by their affliction,
and opens their ear by adversity.
16 He also allured you out of distress

ᶻ Heb *ends among the temple prostitutes*

into a broad place where there was no
constraint,
and what was set on your table was full
of fatness.

17 "But you are obsessed with the case of the
wicked;
judgment and justice seize you.
18 Beware that wrath does not entice you
into scoffing,
and do not let the greatness of the
ransom turn you aside.
19 Will your cry avail to keep you from
distress,
or will all the force of your strength?
20 Do not long for the night,
when peoples are cut off in their place.
21 Beware! Do not turn to iniquity;

What Job Teaches about Suffering
The problem of pain and the book of Job

> "He delivers the afflicted by their affliction, and opens their ear by adversity." 36.15

"WHY ME?" ALMOST EVERYONE ASKS this question when terrible suffering strikes. An automobile accident, a diagnosis of cancer, a long-term disease like arthritis—each of these raises intense questions about why God allows pain.

Over the centuries, suffering Christians have gained help and comfort from studying the book of Job. The book gives no compact theory of why good people suffer. Nevertheless, the following insights into the problem of suffering do come out of the book of Job.

Principles from Job

1. *Some suffering is caused by Satan.* Chapters 1 and 2 make the important distinction that God did not cause Job's problems. He allowed them, but Satan actually caused the pain.

2. *God is all-powerful and good.* Nowhere does the book of Job suggest that God lacks power or goodness. Some people say that God is weak and powerless to prevent human suffering. Others, called deists, assume he runs the world at a distance, without personal involvement. But in Job, God's power is never questioned; only his fairness. And in his final summation speech, God used splendid illustrations from nature to prove his power.

3. *Suffering doesn't always come as a result of sin.* The Bible supports the general principle that "you reap whatever you sow," even in this life (Galatians 6.7; see Psalms 1.3; 37.25). But other people have no right to apply that *general* principle to a *particular* person. Job's friends tried with all their persuasive power. However, when God rendered the final verdict, he said simply, "You have not spoken of me what is right, as my servant Job has" (42.7). The Old Testament includes other examples of people who suffered through no fault of their own, such as Abel (Genesis 4) and Uriah (2 Samuel 11). And Jesus spoke out against the notion that suffering implies sin (see John 9.1–5 and Luke 13.1–5).

4. *God will reward and punish fairly in a final judgment after death.* Job's friends, along with most Old Testament folk, did not have a clearly formed belief in an afterlife. Therefore, they expected that God's fairness—his approval or disapproval of people—had to be shown in this life. Other parts of the Bible teach that God will reward and punish fairly after death.

5. *God does not condemn doubt and despair.* God did not condemn Job's anguished responses, only his ignorance. Job did not take his pain meekly; he cried out in anguish to God. His strong remarks scandalized his friends (see, for example, 15.1–16), but not God. Ironically, despite his bitter speeches, Job earned God's praise, while his pious friends were soundly rebuked.

6. *No one person has all the facts about suffering.* Neither Job nor his friends had enough facts. Job concluded God was unfair, treating him like an enemy. His friends maintained that God opposed Job

because of that you have been tried by
affliction.
22 See, God is exalted in his power;
who is a teacher like him?
23 Who has prescribed for him his way,
or who can say, 'You have done
wrong'?

Elihu Proclaims God's Majesty

24 "Remember to extol his work,
of which mortals have sung.
25 All people have looked on it;
everyone watches it from far away.
26 Surely God is great, and we do not know
him;
the number of his years is
unsearchable.
27 For he draws up the drops of water;
he distills*a* his mist in rain,
28 which the skies pour down
and drop upon mortals abundantly.
29 Can anyone understand the spreading of
the clouds,
the thunderings of his pavilion?
30 See, he scatters his lightning around him
and covers the roots of the sea.
31 For by these he governs peoples;
he gives food in abundance.

32 He covers his hands with the lightning,
and commands it to strike the mark.
33 Its crashing*b* tells about him;
he is jealous*b* with anger against
iniquity.

37 "At this also my heart trembles,
and leaps out of its place.
2 Listen, listen to the thunder of his voice
and the rumbling that comes from his
mouth.
3 Under the whole heaven he lets it loose,
and his lightning to the corners of the
earth.
4 After it his voice roars;
he thunders with his majestic voice
and he does not restrain the
lightnings*c* when his voice is
heard.
5 God thunders wondrously with his voice;
he does great things that we cannot
comprehend.
6 For to the snow he says, 'Fall on the
earth';
and the shower of rain, his heavy
shower of rain,
7 serves as a sign on everyone's hand,

---

a Cn: Heb *they distill*   *b* Meaning of Heb uncertain   *c* Heb *them*

---

because of his sin. All of them later learned they had been viewing the situation from a very limited perspective, blind to the real struggle being waged in heaven.

7. *God is never totally silent.* Elihu made that point convincingly, reminding Job of dreams, visions, past blessings, even the daily works of God in nature (chapter 33). God also appealed to nature as giving evidence of his wisdom and power. Although he may seem silent, some evidence of him can be found. One contemporary author expressed that truth this way, "Remember in the darkness what you have learned in the light."

8. *Well-intentioned advice can sometimes do more harm than good.* Job's friends were classic examples of people who let their pride and sense of being right interfere with their compassion. They repeated pious phrases and argued theology with Job. His response: "If you would only keep silent, that would be your wisdom!" (13.5).

9. *God asks for faith.* God refocused the central issue from the *cause* of Job's suffering to his *response.* Mysteriously, God never gave an explanation for the problem of suffering. He did not even inform Job of the reason behind it: the contest recorded in chapters 1 and 2. He concentrated instead on Job's response. The real issue at stake was Job's faith—whether he would continue to trust God even when everything went wrong.

10. *Suffering can be used for a higher good.* In Job's case, God used a time of very great pain to win an important, even cosmic, victory over Satan. Looking backward, but only looking backward, we can see the "advantage" Job gained by continuing to trust God. Job is often cited as an Old Testament picture of Jesus Christ, who lived a perfectly innocent life but endured great pain and death. The terrible event of Christ's death was also transformed into a great victory.

Thousands of years later, Job's questions have not gone away. People who suffer still find themselves borrowing Job's own words as they cry out against God's seeming lack of concern. But Job affirms that God is not deaf to our cries and is in control of this world no matter how it looks. God did not answer all Job's questions, but his very appearance caused Job's doubts to melt away. Job learned that God cared about him and that God rules the world. It was enough.

Life Questions: Do these principles from Job match up with what you have heard about suffering from other Christians?

so that all whom he has made may
    know it.[d]

8 Then the animals go into their lairs
    and remain in their dens.

37.7 The Message of a Blizzard

*Anyone who has lived in a northern city can
identify with Elihu's comment about a
snowstorm. A blizzard "serves as a sign on
everyone's hand," as schools, businesses, and
buses shut down. It's a reminder, says Elihu, of
God's undeniable power.*

9 From its chamber comes the whirlwind,
    and cold from the scattering winds.
10 By the breath of God ice is given,
    and the broad waters are frozen fast.
11 He loads the thick cloud with moisture;
    the clouds scatter his lightning.
12 They turn round and round by his
        guidance,
    to accomplish all that he commands
        them
    on the face of the habitable world.
13 Whether for correction, or for his land,
    or for love, he causes it to happen.

14 "Hear this, O Job;
    stop and consider the wondrous works
        of God.
15 Do you know how God lays his
        command upon them,
    and causes the lightning of his cloud to
        shine?
16 Do you know the balancings of the
        clouds,
    the wondrous works of the one whose
        knowledge is perfect,
17 you whose garments are hot
    when the earth is still because of the
        south wind?
18 Can you, like him, spread out the skies,
    hard as a molten mirror?
19 Teach us what we shall say to him;
    we cannot draw up our case because of
        darkness.
20 Should he be told that I want to speak?
    Did anyone ever wish to be swallowed
        up?
21 Now, no one can look on the light
    when it is bright in the skies,
    when the wind has passed and cleared
        them.
22 Out of the north comes golden splendor;
    around God is awesome majesty.
23 The Almighty[e]—we cannot find him;

he is great in power and justice,
    and abundant righteousness he will not
        violate.
24 Therefore mortals fear him;
    he does not regard any who are wise in
        their own conceit."

The LORD Answers Job

38 Then the LORD answered Job out of the
    whirlwind:
2 "Who is this that darkens counsel by
        words without knowledge?
3 Gird up your loins like a man,
    I will question you, and you shall
        declare to me.

4 "Where were you when I laid the
        foundation of the earth?
    Tell me, if you have understanding.
5 Who determined its measurements—
        surely you know!
    Or who stretched the line upon it?
6 On what were its bases sunk,
    or who laid its cornerstone
7 when the morning stars sang together
    and all the heavenly beings[f] shouted
        for joy?

8 "Or who shut in the sea with doors
    when it burst out from the womb?—
9 when I made the clouds its garment,
    and thick darkness its swaddling band,
10 and prescribed bounds for it,
    and set bars and doors,
11 and said, 'Thus far shall you come, and
        no farther,
    and here shall your proud waves be
        stopped'?

12 "Have you commanded the morning since
        your days began,
    and caused the dawn to know its place,
13 so that it might take hold of the skirts of
        the earth,
    and the wicked be shaken out of it?
14 It is changed like clay under the seal,
    and it is dyed[g] like a garment.
15 Light is withheld from the wicked,
    and their uplifted arm is broken.

16 "Have you entered into the springs of the
        sea,
    or walked in the recesses of the deep?
17 Have the gates of death been revealed to
        you,
    or have you seen the gates of deep
        darkness?

---

[d] Meaning of Heb of verse 7 uncertain   [e] Traditional rendering of Heb *Shaddai*   [f] Heb *sons of God*   [g] Cn: Heb
and they stand forth

18 Have you comprehended the expanse of
the earth?
Declare, if you know all this.

19 "Where is the way to the dwelling of
light,
and where is the place of darkness,
20 that you may take it to its territory
and that you may discern the paths to
its home?
21 Surely you know, for you were born then,
and the number of your days is great!

38.21 God Pulls Out the Stops

*God is not above using sarcasm, as this barb
directed at Job clearly shows. His entire speech
stresses the vast difference between a God of
all creation and one puny man like Job. "Have
you an arm like God?" he asks (40.9).*

22 "Have you entered the storehouses of the
snow,
or have you seen the storehouses of the
hail,
23 which I have reserved for the time of
trouble,
for the day of battle and war?
24 What is the way to the place where the
light is distributed,
or where the east wind is scattered
upon the earth?
25 "Who has cut a channel for the torrents
of rain,
and a way for the thunderbolt,
26 to bring rain on a land where no one
lives,
on the desert, which is empty of
human life,
27 to satisfy the waste and desolate land,
and to make the ground put forth
grass?
28 "Has the rain a father,
or who has begotten the drops of dew?
29 From whose womb did the ice come
forth,
and who has given birth to the
hoarfrost of heaven?
30 The waters become hard like stone,
and the face of the deep is frozen.
31 "Can you bind the chains of the Pleiades,
or loose the cords of Orion?
32 Can you lead forth the Mazzaroth in their
season,

or can you guide the Bear with its
children?
33 Do you know the ordinances of the
heavens?
Can you establish their rule on the
earth?
34 "Can you lift up your voice to the clouds,
so that a flood of waters may cover you?
35 Can you send forth lightnings, so that
they may go
and say to you, 'Here we are'?
36 Who has put wisdom in the inward
parts,[h]
or given understanding to the mind?[h]
37 Who has the wisdom to number the
clouds?
Or who can tilt the waterskins of the
heavens,
38 when the dust runs into a mass
and the clods cling together?
39 "Can you hunt the prey for the lion,
or satisfy the appetite of the young
lions,
40 when they crouch in their dens,
or lie in wait in their covert?
41 Who provides for the raven its prey,
when its young ones cry to God,
and wander about for lack of food?

39

"Do you know when the mountain goats
give birth?
Do you observe the calving of the deer?
2 Can you number the months that they
fulfill,
and do you know the time when they
give birth,
3 when they crouch to give birth to their
offspring,
and are delivered of their young?
4 Their young ones become strong, they
grow up in the open;
they go forth, and do not return to
them.
5 "Who has let the wild ass go free?
Who has loosed the bonds of the swift
ass,
6 to which I have given the steppe for its
home,
the salt land for its dwelling place?
7 It scorns the tumult of the city;
it does not hear the shouts of the
driver.
8 It ranges the mountains as its pasture,
and it searches after every green thing.

[h] Meaning of Heb uncertain

9 "Is the wild ox willing to serve you?
  Will it spend the night at your crib?
10 Can you tie it in the furrow with ropes,
  or will it harrow the valleys after you?
11 Will you depend on it because its strength
  is great,
  and will you hand over your labor to it?
12 Do you have faith in it that it will return,

and bring your grain to your threshing
  floor?[i]

13 "The ostrich's wings flap wildly,
  though its pinions lack plumage.[j]
14 For it leaves its eggs to the earth,
  and lets them be warmed on the
  ground,

[i] Heb *your grain and your threshing floor*   [j] Meaning of Heb uncertain

God Speaks to Job
At last, Job gets what he demanded

"*Shall a faultfinder contend with the Almighty? Anyone who argues with God must respond.*"
40.2

IN THE SPAN OF A few days Job experienced more tragedy than most people encounter in a lifetime. He scratched himself with shards of pottery and mourned the day he was born. He could not even suffer with dignity; he had to endure his wife's taunts and his friends' ramblings. Nothing anyone said helped him.

Through it all, Job steadfastly refused to turn his back on God. He had only one request. He wanted to hear from God in person. He wanted an explanation straight from the Source.

At last Job got his wish. God answered Job with a speech often quoted for its majesty and beauty. In a touch of irony, God made his entrance just as Elihu was explaining why Job could not expect a direct answer from him.

Not the Expected Message

Job had saved up a long list of questions, but it was God who asked the questions, not Job. "Gird up your loins like a man," he began. "I will question you, and you declare to me."

Author Frederick Buechner sums up what follows: "God doesn't explain. He explodes. He asks Job who he thinks he is anyway. He says that to try to explain the kind of things Job wants explained would be like trying to explain Einstein to a little-neck clam." God did not need Job's or anyone else's advice on how to run the world.

God's reply resembled a nature lesson more than an explanation of the problem of suffering. He pointed out, one by one, all the creations that gave him greatest pride. In short, God asked Job, "Do you want to try running the universe for a while? Go ahead, try designing an ostrich, or a mountain goat, or even a snowflake."

Astonishingly, the question of suffering itself did not even come up. Yet somehow Job seemed satisfied—humiliated, actually. "Therefore I have uttered what I did not understand," he confessed, "things too wonderful for me, which I did not know" (42.3).

Job Passes the Test

Job had endured his terrible sufferings in the dark. When he needed God most, God had stayed silent. And that was exactly the point of the contest begun at the beginning of the book, back in chapter 1. Satan had promised God that Job would "curse you to your face." He lost the challenge. Despite everything that happened, Job did not curse God. He clung to his belief in a just God, even when everything in his experience seemed to contradict it.

God had some words of correction for Job. No one, not Job and especially not his friends, had the evidence needed to make judgments about how he runs the world. But mainly, God had praise for Job. He called him "my servant," and, in an ironic twist, told the three friends to go to Job and ask for his mercy (42.7–8). Much later, in the book of Ezekiel (14.14), God included Job in a list of the finest human examples of righteousness.

The book of Job ends on a note of surprise. Job's friends, who had spouted all the right pieties and clichés, ask for forgiveness. Job, who had raged and cried out, is given twice as much as he ever had before. "And Job died, old and full of days" (42.17).

Life Questions: In Job's place, what kind of answer would you have wanted from God? Does God's reply to Job surprise you?

15 forgetting that a foot may crush them,
   and that a wild animal may trample
   them.
16 It deals cruelly with its young, as if they
   were not its own;
   though its labor should be in vain, yet
   it has no fear;

39.9 The Wildness of Animals

*God seems to take special delight in animals
with a streak of wildness: mountain goats,
lions, wild donkeys, hawks, wild oxen. They
serve as reminders that people are not as
fully in control of the world as they might
think.*

17 because God has made it forget wisdom,
   and given it no share in understanding.
18 When it spreads its plumes aloft,[j]
   it laughs at the horse and its rider.

19 "Do you give the horse its might?
   Do you clothe its neck with mane?
20 Do you make it leap like the locust?
   Its majestic snorting is terrible.
21 It paws[k] violently, exults mightily;
   it goes out to meet the weapons.
22 It laughs at fear, and is not dismayed;
   it does not turn back from the sword.
23 Upon it rattle the quiver,
   the flashing spear, and the javelin.
24 With fierceness and rage it swallows the
   ground;
   it cannot stand still at the sound of the
   trumpet.
25 When the trumpet sounds, it says 'Aha!'
   From a distance it smells the battle,
   the thunder of the captains, and the
   shouting.

26 "Is it by your wisdom that the hawk
   soars,
   and spreads its wings toward the
   south?
27 Is it at your command that the eagle
   mounts up
   and makes its nest on high?
28 It lives on the rock and makes its home
   in the fastness of the rocky crag.
29 From there it spies the prey;
   its eyes see it from far away.
30 Its young ones suck up blood;
   and where the slain are, there it is."

40 And the LORD said to Job:
2 "Shall a faultfinder contend with
   the Almighty?[l]
   Anyone who argues with God must
   respond."

Job's Response to God

3 Then Job answered the LORD:
4 "See, I am of small account; what shall I
   answer you?
   I lay my hand on my mouth.
5 I have spoken once, and I will not
   answer;
   twice, but will proceed no further."

God's Challenge to Job

6 Then the LORD answered Job out of the
whirlwind:
7 "Gird up your loins like a man;
   I will question you, and you declare to
   me.
8 Will you even put me in the wrong?
   Will you condemn me that you may be
   justified?
9 Have you an arm like God,
   and can you thunder with a voice like
   his?

10 "Deck yourself with majesty and dignity;
   clothe yourself with glory and splendor.
11 Pour out the overflowings of your anger,
   and look on all who are proud, and
   abase them.
12 Look on all who are proud, and bring
   them low;
   tread down the wicked where they
   stand.
13 Hide them all in the dust together;
   bind their faces in the world below.[m]
14 Then I will also acknowledge to you
   that your own right hand can give you
   victory.

15 "Look at Behemoth,
   which I made just as I made you;
   it eats grass like an ox.

40.15 Behemoth and Leviathan?

*No one is quite sure what is meant by these two
words, so the English Bible leaves them
untranslated. The behemoth resembles a
hippopotamus or elephant. The leviathan (41.1)
has some features of a crocodile and some of a
dragon. In other places, the Bible refers to the
leviathan as either a whale-like creature
(Psalm 104.26) or a serpent or monster of the
sea (Isaiah 27.1). God used the leviathan as a
symbol of something powerful and
uncontrollable. Job got the message: If you
can't take on one of God's fearsome creatures,
don't attempt to take on God.*

---

j Meaning of Heb uncertain k Gk Syr Vg: Heb *they dig* l Traditional rendering of Heb *Shaddai*
m Heb *the hidden place*

16 Its strength is in its loins,
and its power in the muscles of its
belly.
17 It makes its tail stiff like a cedar;
the sinews of its thighs are knit
together.
18 Its bones are tubes of bronze,
its limbs like bars of iron.

19 "It is the first of the great acts of God—
only its Maker can approach it with the
sword.
20 For the mountains yield food for it
where all the wild animals play.
21 Under the lotus plants it lies,
in the covert of the reeds and in the
marsh.
22 The lotus trees cover it for shade;
the willows of the wadi surround it.
23 Even if the river is turbulent, it is not
frightened;
it is confident though Jordan rushes
against its mouth.
24 Can one take it with hooks[n]
or pierce its nose with a snare?

41 [o] "Can you draw out Leviathan[p] with a
fishhook,
or press down its tongue with a cord?
2 Can you put a rope in its nose,
or pierce its jaw with a hook?
3 Will it make many supplications to you?
Will it speak soft words to you?
4 Will it make a covenant with you
to be taken as your servant forever?
5 Will you play with it as with a bird,
or will you put it on leash for your
girls?
6 Will traders bargain over it?
Will they divide it up among the
merchants?
7 Can you fill its skin with harpoons,
or its head with fishing spears?
8 Lay hands on it;
think of the battle; you will not do it
again!
9[q] Any hope of capturing it[r] will be
disappointed;
were not even the gods[s] overwhelmed
at the sight of it?
10 No one is so fierce as to dare to stir it up.
Who can stand before it?[t]
11 Who can confront it[t] and be safe?[u]
—under the whole heaven, who?[v]

12 "I will not keep silence concerning its
limbs,

or its mighty strength, or its splendid
frame.
13 Who can strip off its outer garment?
Who can penetrate its double coat of
mail?[w]
14 Who can open the doors of its face?
There is terror all around its teeth.
15 Its back[x] is made of shields in rows,
shut up closely as with a seal.
16 One is so near to another
that no air can come between them.
17 They are joined one to another;
they clasp each other and cannot be
separated.
18 Its sneezes flash forth light,
and its eyes are like the eyelids of the
dawn.
19 From its mouth go flaming torches;
sparks of fire leap out.
20 Out of its nostrils comes smoke,
as from a boiling pot and burning
rushes.
21 Its breath kindles coals,
and a flame comes out of its mouth.
22 In its neck abides strength,
and terror dances before it.
23 The folds of its flesh cling together;
it is firmly cast and immovable.
24 Its heart is as hard as stone,
as hard as the lower millstone.
25 When it raises itself up the gods are
afraid;
at the crashing they are beside
themselves.
26 Though the sword reaches it, it does not
avail,
nor does the spear, the dart, or the
javelin.
27 It counts iron as straw,
and bronze as rotten wood.
28 The arrow cannot make it flee;
slingstones, for it, are turned to chaff.
29 Clubs are counted as chaff;
it laughs at the rattle of javelins.
30 Its underparts are like sharp potsherds;
it spreads itself like a threshing sledge
on the mire.
31 It makes the deep boil like a pot;
it makes the sea like a pot of ointment.
32 It leaves a shining wake behind it;
one would think the deep to be
white-haired.
33 On earth it has no equal,
a creature without fear.
34 It surveys everything that is lofty;
it is king over all that are proud."

---

n Cn: Heb *in his eyes*   o Ch 40.25 in Heb   p Or *the crocodile*   q Ch 41.1 in Heb   r Heb *of it*
s Cn Compare Symmachus Syr: Heb *one is*   t Heb *me*   u Gk: Heb *that I shall repay*   v Heb *to me*
w Gk: Heb *bridle*   x Cn Compare Gk Vg: Heb *pride*

Job Is Humbled and Satisfied

42 Then Job answered the LORD:
2 "I know that you can do all things,
and that no purpose of yours can be
thwarted.

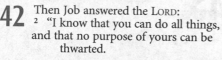

42.2–5 A Visit for All Time

*A personal visit from God utterly silenced all
Job's questions about unfairness. Once he saw
God, he had nothing more to say. Few people in
history have had such a direct, visible
encounter with God, but the book of Job
foreshadows a time when God paid a much
longer personal visit to earth. In Jesus, God
came not in power and majesty, but in poverty
and pain. Job stands as the clearest Old
Testament example of unfairness: an upright
man who suffered greatly. Jesus stands as the
New Testament example: a perfect man who
suffered even more. Both hint at a happy
ending after all.*

3 'Who is this that hides counsel without
knowledge?'
Therefore I have uttered what I did not
understand,
things too wonderful for me, which I
did not know.
4 'Hear, and I will speak;
I will question you, and you declare to
me.'
5 I had heard of you by the hearing of the
ear,
but now my eye sees you;
6 therefore I despise myself,
and repent in dust and ashes."

Job's Friends Are Humiliated

7 After the LORD had spoken these words to
Job, the LORD said to Eliphaz the Temanite: "My
wrath is kindled against you and against your two
friends; for you have not spoken of me what is
right, as my servant Job has. 8Now therefore take
seven bulls and seven rams, and go to my servant
Job, and offer up for yourselves a burnt offering;
and my servant Job shall pray for you, for I will
accept his prayer not to deal with you according
to your folly; for you have not spoken of me what
is right, as my servant Job has done." 9So Eliphaz
the Temanite and Bildad the Shuhite and Zophar
the Naamathite went and did what the LORD had
told them; and the LORD accepted Job's prayer.

Job's Fortunes Are Restored Twofold

10 And the LORD restored the fortunes of Job
when he had prayed for his friends; and the LORD
gave Job twice as much as he had before. 11Then
there came to him all his brothers and sisters and
all who had known him before, and they ate bread
with him in his house; they showed him sympathy
and comforted him for all the evil that the LORD
had brought upon him; and each of them gave

42.10 Seeing in the Dark

*Significantly, Job spoke his contrite words
(verse 6) before any of his losses had been
restored, while still sitting in a pile of ashes,
naked and covered with sores. Because he had
seen God, he had learned to believe God even
in the midst of suffering, with no certainty of
relief.*

him a piece of money[y] and a gold ring. 12The
LORD blessed the latter days of Job more than his
beginning; and he had fourteen thousand sheep,
six thousand camels, a thousand yoke of oxen,
and a thousand donkeys. 13He also had seven
sons and three daughters. 14He named the first
Jemimah, the second Keziah, and the third
Keren-happuch. 15In all the land there were no
women so beautiful as Job's daughters; and their
father gave them an inheritance along with their
brothers. 16After this Job lived one hundred and
forty years, and saw his children, and his children's children, four generations. 17And Job died,
old and full of days.

PSALMS

Cries from the Heart
Songs for sorrow as well as joy

> You are a hiding place for me; you preserve me from trouble; you surround me with glad cries of deliverance.
> 32.7

HERE AT THE VERY CENTER of the Bible are songs, rising up like a tune from its heart. They capture the innermost thoughts and prayers of Old Testament people—and they still speak directly to our needs.

For every emotion and mood you can find a psalm to match. The psalms wrestle with the deepest sorrow and ask God the hardest questions about suffering and injustice. Their voice is refreshingly spontaneous. They do not tip flowery compliments toward God; they cry out to him, or shout for joy before him.

After you read these poems, you can't think of the Old Testament as dry and rule-bound. Nor is the Old Testament God distant and impersonal. In almost every psalm you find the presence of God, not as a philosophical principle, but as an active, strong, and loving ruler—a God who makes a difference in life.

How Did the Psalms Come Together?

While almost half of the psalms are credited to David, at least one was written 500 years after his birth. A number of poets and writers contributed, and about a third of the psalms are completely anonymous.

How did the psalms come together? They seem to have been compiled as a hymnbook for use in temple worship. Some psalms were written from an individual's experiences, but were adapted for congregational use. Directions for musicians were added, along with a few verses to widen the psalms' meaning to everybody.

The psalms show tremendous variation, reflecting the many personalities who contributed their poems and prayers over several centuries. Yet readers have found an inner consistency in the whole book, so they can move from one psalm to the next without being particularly aware that one poem is centuries older than another. Some have called the psalms a Bible within the Bible—different books telling a single story.

Others have compared the book of Psalms to a beautiful cathedral built over centuries. Each wing and each window show the individual genius of its designers, yet all the parts are somehow harmonious. This harmony comes not merely from a common sense of style, but from unity of purpose: The whole cathedral is made for the worship of one and the same God. Just so, the psalms reflect, in a hundred moods and experiences, the never-changing reality of a strong and loving God who cares for his people.

The Presence of Real Enemies

God is not the only reality in the psalms. Equally persistent are enemies who sneer and hurt and plot violence. They, too, appear in nearly every psalm. For the psalmists, faith in God was a struggle against powerful forces that often seemed more real than God.

The psalm writers frequently asked, "Where are you, God? Why don't you help me?" Despite their love for God, they often felt abandoned, misused, betrayed. They found no guarantee of safety in their closeness to God. The joy and praise that saturate these prayers came not from an absence of problems, but from a deep conviction that a great God would overcome them.

Jesus, dying on the cross, twice expressed himself in the words of psalms (22.1 and 31.5), and his disciples, in trying to explain his life, quoted from Psalms more than any other book. They appear to have meditated on the psalms often as they considered the meaning of Jesus' life. In the psalms they could see that even the best men—even David, the great king—suffer agony and feel abandoned.

Living by faith is not easy. It was not for David; it was not for Jesus either. These powerful poems of praise and worship, some of the most beautiful ever written, offer no magical formulas to make troubles go away. Yet, while real-life questions, struggles, and discouragements have a strong voice in these poems, more powerful still is the voice of joy and security in the strength and fortress of Israel: the Lord himself.

How to Read Psalms

The best way to read the psalms is also the most common way: to make these ancient prayers your own and speak them directly to God. So many of the poems catch such deep human feelings that you can't help being moved by them.

But not all the psalms seem attractive. Some sound harsh, self-congratulatory, or boring. You will not find it easy to pray these until you understand them.

And there are so many psalms! This is the longest book in the Bible. To compensate, many people read only selected psalms, skimming over the others. But then they miss the deeper messages found there, including the messages that the New Testament writers saw when they quoted Psalms more than any other Old Testament book. The richest lessons from Psalms may come from particularly difficult poems you must read again and again until you begin to see what the author had in mind.

The original Hebrew of these poems probably used no rhyme or strict rhythm as traditional English poems do. Instead, the psalmists wrote with parallelism, following one thought by a "rhyming" thought or by its opposite. (For more on this, see "Hebrew Poetry," page 657.) Fortunately, this kind of poetry can be translated into almost any language without loss.

Readers may be confused by the psalms' frequent change of voice. In a single poem the psalmist may talk to God, then talk about him, and then return to talking to him, all in rapid succession. This would be strange English prose, but was common in Hebrew poetry.

Because so many of the psalm titles refer to David, you may find it helpful to refer to his life story. It is found in 1 Samuel 16–31, the whole book of 2 Samuel, and the first two chapters of 1 Kings. However, most of the psalms can make perfect sense without reference to any outside information. They merely ask—and reward—time and close attention. Read and reread them. They grow richer with careful study.

PEOPLE YOU'LL MEET IN PSALMS

MELCHIZEDEK *(p. 625)*

3-TRACK READING PLAN

For an explanation and complete listing of the 3-track reading plan, turn to page 7.

TRACK 1: *Two-Week Courses on the Bible*
The Track 1 reading program on the Old Testament includes one chapter from Psalms. See page 8 for a complete listing of this course.

TRACK 2: *An Overview of Psalms in 7 Days*
☐ Day 1. Read the Introduction to Psalms and Psalm 19: Perfect Harmony.
☐ Day 2. Read Psalm 23: The Shepherd Song.
☐ Day 3. Read Psalm 27: Confidence in Trouble.
☐ Day 4. Read Psalm 51: The Great Confession.
☐ Day 5. Read Psalm 84: The Delight of Worshiping God.
☐ Day 6. Read Psalm 103: God's Benefits.
☐ Day 7. Read Psalm 139: God's Care.

Now turn to page 9 for your next Track 2 reading project.

TRACK 3: *All of Psalms in Two Two-Month Periods (122 days)*
After you have read through Psalms, turn to pages 10–14 for your next Track 3 reading project.

Part I
☐1–2 ☐3–4 ☐5 ☐6 ☐7 ☐8 ☐9 ☐10 ☐11–12 ☐13–14
☐15–16 ☐17 ☐18 ☐19 ☐20–21 ☐22 ☐23–24 ☐25 ☐26 ☐27
☐28–29 ☐30 ☐31 ☐32 ☐33 ☐34 ☐35 ☐36 ☐37 ☐38
☐39 ☐40 ☐41 ☐42–43 ☐44 ☐45 ☐46–47 ☐48 ☐49 ☐50
☐51 ☐52 ☐53–54 ☐55 ☐56 ☐57 ☐58 ☐59 ☐60–61 ☐62
☐63–64 ☐65 ☐66 ☐67 ☐68 ☐69 ☐70 ☐71 ☐72 ☐73
☐74 ☐75

BOOK I

(Psalms 1–41)

Psalm 1

The Two Ways

1 Happy are those
    who do not follow the advice of the
        wicked,
or take the path that sinners tread,
    or sit in the seat of scoffers;
2 but their delight is in the law of the LORD,
    and on his law they meditate day and
        night.
3 They are like trees
    planted by streams of water,
which yield their fruit in its season,
    and their leaves do not wither.
In all that they do, they prosper.

4 The wicked are not so,
    but are like chaff that the wind drives
        away.
5 Therefore the wicked will not stand in the
        judgment,
    nor sinners in the congregation of the
        righteous;
6 for the LORD watches over the way of the
        righteous,
    but the way of the wicked will perish.

Psalm 2

God's Promise to His Anointed

1 Why do the nations conspire,
    and the peoples plot in vain?
2 The kings of the earth set themselves,
    and the rulers take counsel together,
    against the LORD and his anointed,
        saying,
3 "Let us burst their bonds asunder,
    and cast their cords from us."

4 He who sits in the heavens laughs;
    the LORD has them in derision.
5 Then he will speak to them in his wrath,
    and terrify them in his fury, saying,

6 "I have set my king on Zion, my holy
    hill."

7 I will tell of the decree of the LORD:
He said to me, "You are my son;
    today I have begotten you.
8 Ask of me, and I will make the nations
    your heritage,

1.4 Blowing in the Wind

The opposite of "trees planted by streams" (verse 3) should be a tree withered by drought—and so it is in Jeremiah 17.5–8, which paints a similar contrast between good and bad people. This image of the wicked as "chaff," however, is far more absolute—for chaff, utterly worthless even for a fire, disappears in the wind. God's judgment day is what finally makes the wicked seem like chaff.

    and the ends of the earth your
        possession.
9 You shall break them with a rod of iron,
    and dash them in pieces like a potter's
        vessel."

10 Now therefore, O kings, be wise;
    be warned, O rulers of the earth.
11 Serve the LORD with fear,

2.2 The Messiah in the Psalms

Israelite kings and priests were anointed with oil when they took office. "His anointed" probably originally meant "king." It came, however, to stand for more. The Hebrew word is masiah, which became Messiah and translated into Greek as Christos or Christ. This psalm was understood in the New Testament as referring to Jesus—for no Old Testament king ever gained the control of the nations implied here. You can find quotations in Acts 4.25–26; 13.33; Hebrews 1.5; 5.5; and Revelation 2.27; 12.5; and 19.15.

with trembling [12]kiss his feet,[a]
or he will be angry, and you will perish in
the way;
for his wrath is quickly kindled.

Happy are all who take refuge in him.

Psalm 3

Trust in God under Adversity

*A Psalm of David, when he fled from
his son Absalom.*

[1] O LORD, how many are my foes!
Many are rising against me;
[2] many are saying to me,
"There is no help for you[b] in God."
Selah

[3] But you, O LORD, are a shield around me,
my glory, and the one who lifts up my
head.
[4] I cry aloud to the LORD,
and he answers me from his holy hill.
Selah

[5] I lie down and sleep;
I wake again, for the LORD sustains me.
[6] I am not afraid of ten thousands of
people
who have set themselves against me all
around.

[7] Rise up, O LORD!
Deliver me, O my God!
For you strike all my enemies on the
cheek;
you break the teeth of the wicked.

[8] Deliverance belongs to the LORD;
may your blessing be on your people!
Selah

Psalm 4

Confident Plea for Deliverance
from Enemies

*To the leader: with stringed instruments.
A Psalm of David.*

[1] Answer me when I call, O God of my
right!
You gave me room when I was in
distress.
Be gracious to me, and hear my prayer.

[2] How long, you people, shall my honor
suffer shame?

How long will you love vain words,
and seek after lies?
Selah
[3] But know that the LORD has set apart the
faithful for himself;
the LORD hears when I call to him.

[4] When you are disturbed,[c] do not sin;
ponder it on your beds, and be silent.
Selah

4.4 Angry Inside

*Is anger sinful? No, though it can certainly lead
to sin. This prayer depicts anger springing from
anxiety, which proves especially troublesome
on sleepless nights. The psalm suggests that,
rather than venting your worry in outbursts
against others, you should examine your own
heart. Paul applied this verse to another
situation: difficult personal relationships
(Ephesians 4.26).*

[5] Offer right sacrifices,
and put your trust in the LORD.

[6] There are many who say, "O that we
might see some good!
Let the light of your face shine on us,
O LORD!"
[7] You have put gladness in my heart
more than when their grain and wine
abound.

[8] I will both lie down and sleep in peace;
for you alone, O LORD, make me lie
down in safety.

Psalm 5

Trust in God for Deliverance
from Enemies

To the leader: for the flutes. A Psalm of David.

[1] Give ear to my words, O LORD;
give heed to my sighing.
[2] Listen to the sound of my cry,
my King and my God,
for to you I pray.
[3] O LORD, in the morning you hear my
voice;
in the morning I plead my case to you,
and watch.

[4] For you are not a God who delights in
wickedness;
evil will not sojourn with you.
[5] The boastful will not stand before your
eyes;

---

[a] Cn: Meaning of Heb of verses 11b and 12a is uncertain   [b] Syr: Heb *him*   [c] Or *are angry*

you hate all evildoers.
6 You destroy those who speak lies;
the LORD abhors the bloodthirsty and
deceitful.

7 But I, through the abundance of your
steadfast love,
will enter your house,
I will bow down toward your holy temple
in awe of you.
8 Lead me, O LORD, in your righteousness
because of my enemies;
make your way straight before me.

9 For there is no truth in their mouths;
their hearts are destruction;
their throats are open graves;
they flatter with their tongues.

5.9 Evil Everywhere

Renowned for their beautiful pictures of God's love, the psalms present equally heartfelt portraits of evil. They often describe people who deeply deserve God's punishment. In Romans 3.10–18, Paul quotes from a number of different psalms like this one, making his case that evil infects all people, everywhere.

10 Make them bear their guilt, O God;
let them fall by their own counsels;
because of their many transgressions cast
them out,
for they have rebelled against you.

11 But let all who take refuge in you rejoice;
let them ever sing for joy.
Spread your protection over them,
so that those who love your name may
exult in you.
12 For you bless the righteous, O LORD;
you cover them with favor as with a
shield.

Psalm 6

Prayer for Recovery from Grave Illness

To the leader: with stringed instruments;
according to The Sheminith. A Psalm of David.

1 O LORD, do not rebuke me in your anger,
or discipline me in your wrath.
2 Be gracious to me, O LORD, for I am
languishing;
O LORD, heal me, for my bones are
shaking with terror.
3 My soul also is struck with terror,
while you, O LORD—how long?

4 Turn, O LORD, save my life;
deliver me for the sake of your
steadfast love.
5 For in death there is no remembrance of
you;
in Sheol who can give you praise?

6 I am weary with my moaning;
every night I flood my bed with tears;
I drench my couch with my weeping.
7 My eyes waste away because of grief;
they grow weak because of all my foes.

8 Depart from me, all you workers of evil,
for the LORD has heard the sound of
my weeping.
9 The LORD has heard my supplication;
the LORD accepts my prayer.
10 All my enemies shall be ashamed and
struck with terror;
they shall turn back, and in a moment
be put to shame.

Psalm 7

Plea for Help against Persecutors

A Shiggaion of David, which he sang to the
LORD concerning Cush, a Benjaminite.

1 O LORD my God, in you I take refuge;
save me from all my pursuers, and
deliver me,
2 or like a lion they will tear me apart;
they will drag me away, with no one to
rescue.

3 O LORD my God, if I have done this,
if there is wrong in my hands,
4 if I have repaid my ally with harm
or plundered my foe without cause,
5 then let the enemy pursue and overtake
me,
trample my life to the ground,
and lay my soul in the dust.   *Selah*

6 Rise up, O LORD, in your anger;
lift yourself up against the fury of my
enemies;
awake, O my God;[d] you have
appointed a judgment.
7 Let the assembly of the peoples be
gathered around you,
and over it take your seat[e] on high.
8 The LORD judges the peoples;
judge me, O LORD, according to my
righteousness
and according to the integrity that is in
me.

d Or *awake for me*   e Cn: Heb *return*

⁹ O let the evil of the wicked come to an
       end,
   but establish the righteous,
 you who test the minds and hearts,
       O righteous God.
¹⁰ God is my shield,
   who saves the upright in heart.
¹¹ God is a righteous judge,
   and a God who has indignation every
       day.

¹² If one does not repent, God*f* will whet
       his sword;
   he has bent and strung his bow;
¹³ he has prepared his deadly weapons,
   making his arrows fiery shafts.
¹⁴ See how they conceive evil,
   and are pregnant with mischief,
   and bring forth lies.
¹⁵ They make a pit, digging it out,
   and fall into the hole that they have
       made.
¹⁶ Their mischief returns upon their own
       heads,
   and on their own heads their violence
       descends.

¹⁷ I will give to the LORD the thanks due to
       his righteousness,
   and sing praise to the name of the
       LORD, the Most High.

Psalm 8

Divine Majesty and Human Dignity

To the leader: according to The Gittith.
A Psalm of David.

¹ O LORD, our Sovereign,
   how majestic is your name in all the
       earth!

   You have set your glory above the
       heavens.
² Out of the mouths of babes and infants
 you have founded a bulwark because of
       your foes,
   to silence the enemy and the avenger.

8.2 Children's Power

*An almighty God needs no great powers to
back him. He shuts up his enemies through
little children and their spontaneous praise.
That is exactly what happened in Jesus' time
(Matthew 21.16).*

³ When I look at your heavens, the work of
       your fingers,
   the moon and the stars that you have
       established;
⁴ what are human beings that you are
       mindful of them,
   mortals*g* that you care for them?

⁵ Yet you have made them a little lower
       than God,*h*
   and crowned them with glory and
       honor.
⁶ You have given them dominion over the
       works of your hands;
   you have put all things under their feet,
⁷ all sheep and oxen,
   and also the beasts of the field,
⁸ the birds of the air, and the fish of the
       sea,
   whatever passes along the paths of the
       seas.

⁹ O LORD, our Sovereign,
   how majestic is your name in all the
       earth!

Psalm 9

God's Power and Justice

To the leader: according to Muth-labben.
A Psalm of David.

¹ I will give thanks to the LORD with my
       whole heart;
   I will tell of all your wonderful deeds.
² I will be glad and exult in you;
   I will sing praise to your name,
       O Most High.

³ When my enemies turned back,
   they stumbled and perished before you.
⁴ For you have maintained my just cause;
   you have sat on the throne giving
       righteous judgment.

⁵ You have rebuked the nations, you have
       destroyed the wicked;
   you have blotted out their name
       forever and ever.
⁶ The enemies have vanished in everlasting
       ruins;
   their cities you have rooted out;
   the very memory of them has perished.

⁷ But the LORD sits enthroned forever,
   he has established his throne for
       judgment.
⁸ He judges the world with righteousness;
   he judges the peoples with equity.

---

f Heb *he*   *g* Heb *ben adam*, lit. *son of man*   *h* Or *than the divine beings* or *angels*: Heb *elohim*

9 The LORD is a stronghold for the
    oppressed,
  a stronghold in times of trouble.
10 And those who know your name put their
    trust in you,
  for you, O LORD, have not forsaken
    those who seek you.

11 Sing praises to the LORD, who dwells in
    Zion.
  Declare his deeds among the peoples.
12 For he who avenges blood is mindful of
    them;
  he does not forget the cry of the
    afflicted.

13 Be gracious to me, O LORD.
  See what I suffer from those who hate
    me;
  you are the one who lifts me up from
    the gates of death,
14 so that I may recount all your praises,
  and, in the gates of daughter Zion,
    rejoice in your deliverance.

15 The nations have sunk in the pit that they
    made;
  in the net that they hid has their own
    foot been caught.
16 The LORD has made himself known, he
    has executed judgment;
  the wicked are snared in the work of
    their own hands. *Higgaion. Selah*

17 The wicked shall depart to Sheol,
  all the nations that forget God.

18 For the needy shall not always be
    forgotten,
  nor the hope of the poor perish
    forever.

19 Rise up, O LORD! Do not let mortals
    prevail;
  let the nations be judged before you.
20 Put them in fear, O LORD;
  let the nations know that they are only
    human.   *Selah*

Psalm 10

Prayer for Deliverance from Enemies

1 Why, O LORD, do you stand far off?
  Why do you hide yourself in times of
    trouble?
2 In arrogance the wicked persecute the
    poor—
  let them be caught in the schemes they
    have devised.

3 For the wicked boast of the desires of
    their heart,
  those greedy for gain curse and
    renounce the LORD.
4 In the pride of their countenance the
    wicked say, "God will not seek it
    out";
  all their thoughts are, "There is no
    God."

5 Their ways prosper at all times;
  your judgments are on high, out of
    their sight;
  as for their foes, they scoff at them.
6 They think in their heart, "We shall not
    be moved;
  throughout all generations we shall not
    meet adversity."

7 Their mouths are filled with cursing and
    deceit and oppression;
  under their tongues are mischief and
    iniquity.
8 They sit in ambush in the villages;
  in hiding places they murder the
    innocent.

  Their eyes stealthily watch for the
    helpless;
9 they lurk in secret like a lion in its
    covert;
  they lurk that they may seize the poor;
  they seize the poor and drag them off
    in their net.

10 They stoop, they crouch,
  and the helpless fall by their might.
11 They think in their heart, "God has
    forgotten,
  he has hidden his face, he will never
    see it."

12 Rise up, O LORD; O God, lift up your
    hand;
  do not forget the oppressed.
13 Why do the wicked renounce God,
  and say in their hearts, "You will not
    call us to account"?

14 But you do see! Indeed you note trouble
    and grief,
  that you may take it into your hands;
  the helpless commit themselves to you;
  you have been the helper of the
    orphan.

15 Break the arm of the wicked and
    evildoers;
  seek out their wickedness until you
    find none.

16 The LORD is king forever and ever;
      the nations shall perish from his land.

17 O LORD, you will hear the desire of the
      meek;
   you will strengthen their heart, you will
      incline your ear
18 to do justice for the orphan and the
      oppressed,
   so that those from earth may strike
      terror no more.*i*

Psalm 11

Song of Trust in God

To the leader. Of David.

1 In the LORD I take refuge; how can you
      say to me,
   "Flee like a bird to the mountains;*j*
2 for look, the wicked bend the bow,
      they have fitted their arrow to the
         string,
   to shoot in the dark at the upright in
      heart.
3 If the foundations are destroyed,
      what can the righteous do?"

4 The LORD is in his holy temple;
      the LORD's throne is in heaven.
   His eyes behold, his gaze examines
      humankind.
5 The LORD tests the righteous and the
      wicked,
   and his soul hates the lover of violence.
6 On the wicked he will rain coals of fire
      and sulfur;
   a scorching wind shall be the portion
      of their cup.
7 For the LORD is righteous;
   he loves righteous deeds;
      the upright shall behold his face.

Psalm 12

Plea for Help in Evil Times

To the leader: according to The Sheminith.
A Psalm of David.

1 Help, O LORD, for there is no longer
      anyone who is godly;
   the faithful have disappeared from
      humankind.
2 They utter lies to each other;
      with flattering lips and a double heart
         they speak.

3 May the LORD cut off all flattering lips,
      the tongue that makes great boasts,
4 those who say, "With our tongues we will
      prevail;
   our lips are our own—who is our
      master?"

12.4 Who Owns Your Lips?

*Repeatedly the Bible stresses that talk can do
tremendous good or evil. One key distinctive is
suggested here: Wicked people use words to
build themselves up over others. They insist
that no one has the right to tell them what to
say.*

5 "Because the poor are despoiled, because
      the needy groan,
   I will now rise up," says the LORD;
   "I will place them in the safety for
      which they long."
6 The promises of the LORD are promises
      that are pure,
   silver refined in a furnace on the
      ground,
   purified seven times.

7 You, O LORD, will protect us;
      you will guard us from this generation
         forever.
8 On every side the wicked prowl,
      as vileness is exalted among
         humankind.

Psalm 13

Prayer for Deliverance from Enemies

To the leader. A Psalm of David.

1 How long, O LORD? Will you forget me
      forever?
   How long will you hide your face from
      me?
2 How long must I bear pain*k* in my soul,
      and have sorrow in my heart all day
         long?
   How long shall my enemy be exalted over
      me?

3 Consider and answer me, O LORD my
      God!
   Give light to my eyes, or I will sleep
      the sleep of death,
4 and my enemy will say, "I have
      prevailed";
   my foes will rejoice because I am
      shaken.

---

i Meaning of Heb uncertain   *j* Gk Syr Jerome Tg: Heb *flee to your mountain, O bird*   *k* Syr: Heb *hold counsels*

5 But I trusted in your steadfast love;
  my heart shall rejoice in your salvation.
6 I will sing to the LORD,
  because he has dealt bountifully with
    me.

Psalm 14

Denunciation of Godlessness

To the leader. Of David.

1 Fools say in their hearts, "There is no
    God."
  They are corrupt, they do abominable
    deeds;
  there is no one who does good.

2 The LORD looks down from heaven on
    humankind
  to see if there are any who are wise,
  who seek after God.

3 They have all gone astray, they are all
    alike perverse;
  there is no one who does good,
  no, not one.

14.3 Who Seeks God?

Though David was called a "man after God's own heart," he is credited with this chilling assessment of humankind—including himself. In God's eyes, nobody—not even David—is good. Paul quoted this in a crucial New Testament passage, Romans 3.10–12.

4 Have they no knowledge, all the evildoers
  who eat up my people as they eat
    bread,
  and do not call upon the LORD?

5 There they shall be in great terror,
  for God is with the company of the
    righteous.
6 You would confound the plans of the
    poor,
  but the LORD is their refuge.

7 O that deliverance for Israel would come
    from Zion!
  When the LORD restores the fortunes of
    his people,
  Jacob will rejoice; Israel will be glad.

Psalm 15

Who Shall Abide in God's Sanctuary?

A Psalm of David.

1 O LORD, who may abide in your tent?
  Who may dwell on your holy hill?

2 Those who walk blamelessly, and do what
    is right,
  and speak the truth from their heart;
3 who do not slander with their tongue,
  and do no evil to their friends,
  nor take up a reproach against their
    neighbors;
4 in whose eyes the wicked are despised,
  but who honor those who fear the
    LORD;
  who stand by their oath even to their
    hurt;
5 who do not lend money at interest,
  and do not take a bribe against the
    innocent.

Those who do these things shall never be
  moved.

Psalm 16

Song of Trust and Security in God

A Miktam of David.

1 Protect me, O God, for in you I take
    refuge.
2 I say to the LORD, "You are my Lord;
  I have no good apart from you."[l]

3 As for the holy ones in the land, they are
    the noble,
  in whom is all my delight.

4 Those who choose another god multiply
    their sorrows;[m]
  their drink offerings of blood I will not
    pour out
  or take their names upon my lips.

5 The LORD is my chosen portion and my
    cup;
  you hold my lot.
6 The boundary lines have fallen for me in
    pleasant places;
  I have a goodly heritage.

7 I bless the LORD who gives me counsel;
  in the night also my heart instructs me.
8 I keep the LORD always before me;
  because he is at my right hand, I shall
    not be moved.

---

l Jerome Tg: Meaning of Heb uncertain   m Cn: Meaning of Heb uncertain

9 Therefore my heart is glad, and my soul
rejoices;
my body also rests secure.
10 For you do not give me up to Sheol,
or let your faithful one see the Pit.

11 You show me the path of life.
In your presence there is fullness of
joy;
in your right hand are pleasures
forevermore.

Psalm 17

Prayer for Deliverance from Persecutors

A Prayer of David.

1 Hear a just cause, O LORD; attend to my
cry;
give ear to my prayer from lips free of
deceit.
2 From you let my vindication come;
let your eyes see the right.

3 If you try my heart, if you visit me by
night,
if you test me, you will find no
wickedness in me;
my mouth does not transgress.
4 As for what others do, by the word of
your lips
I have avoided the ways of the violent.
5 My steps have held fast to your paths;
my feet have not slipped.

6 I call upon you, for you will answer me,
O God;
incline your ear to me, hear my words.
7 Wondrously show your steadfast love,
O savior of those who seek refuge
from their adversaries at your right
hand.

8 Guard me as the apple of the eye;
hide me in the shadow of your wings,

9 from the wicked who despoil me,
my deadly enemies who surround me.
10 They close their hearts to pity;
with their mouths they speak
arrogantly.
11 They track me down;*n* now they
surround me;
they set their eyes to cast me to the
ground.
12 They are like a lion eager to tear,
like a young lion lurking in ambush.

13 Rise up, O LORD, confront them,
overthrow them!
By your sword deliver my life from the
wicked,
14 from mortals—by your hand, O LORD—
from mortals whose portion in life is in
this world.
May their bellies be filled with what you
have stored up for them;
may their children have more than
enough;
may they leave something over to their
little ones.

15 As for me, I shall behold your face in
righteousness;
when I awake I shall be satisfied,
beholding your likeness.

Psalm 18

Royal Thanksgiving for Victory

To the leader. A Psalm of David the servant of
the LORD, who addressed the words of this song
to the LORD on the day when the LORD delivered
him from the hand of all his enemies, and from
the hand of Saul. He said:

1 I love you, O LORD, my strength.
2 The LORD is my rock, my fortress, and
my deliverer,
my God, my rock in whom I take
refuge,
my shield, and the horn of my
salvation, my stronghold.

n One Ms Compare Syr: MT *Our steps*

3 I call upon the LORD, who is worthy to be
  praised,
    so I shall be saved from my enemies.

4 The cords of death encompassed me;
    the torrents of perdition assailed me;
5 the cords of Sheol entangled me;
    the snares of death confronted me.

6 In my distress I called upon the LORD;
    to my God I cried for help.
  From his temple he heard my voice,
    and my cry to him reached his ears.

7 Then the earth reeled and rocked;
    the foundations also of the mountains
      trembled
    and quaked, because he was angry.
8 Smoke went up from his nostrils,
    and devouring fire from his mouth;
    glowing coals flamed forth from him.
9 He bowed the heavens, and came down;
    thick darkness was under his feet.
10 He rode on a cherub, and flew;

he came swiftly upon the wings of the
  wind.
11 He made darkness his covering around
  him,
    his canopy thick clouds dark with
      water.
12 Out of the brightness before him
    there broke through his clouds
    hailstones and coals of fire.
13 The LORD also thundered in the heavens,
    and the Most High uttered his voice.°
14 And he sent out his arrows, and scattered
      them;
    he flashed forth lightnings, and routed
      them.
15 Then the channels of the sea were seen,
    and the foundations of the world were
      laid bare
  at your rebuke, O LORD,
    at the blast of the breath of your
      nostrils.

16 He reached down from on high, he took
      me;
    he drew me out of mighty waters.

° Gk See 2 Sam 22.14: Heb adds *hailstones and coals of fire*

Life after Death
When you die, will it all be over?

> You do not give me
> up to Sheol, or let
> your faithful one
> see the Pit. *16.10*

WHAT HAPPENS TO YOU AFTER you die? People have always wanted an answer to that question, and the psalmists were no different. They lived in an age without effective medicine, in an age when wars were fought hand-to-hand. Dead bodies were a familiar reality. Yet death, however familiar, remained mysterious and frightening to them.

Israelites called the dark and shadowy place where dead people go "Sheol." When you got there, your life seemed thoroughly finished. The psalmists emphatically did not want to go there, and they asked God, when praying for his help, what possible good there might be in death. "Are your wonders known in the darkness, or your saving help in the land of forgetfulness?" (88.12). Sheol was the great leveler: it meant the end of plans, of worship, of a relationship with God (30.9; 88.5; 146.4). The dead were found there, not the living.

God's Power over Death

Yet some psalms also hint at a happier view. They hold such a strong view of God's authority that they show—vaguely, but unmistakably—God's power over the grave. For instance, God is *in* Sheol (139.8). He—and only he—can redeem a person from there (49.7–9,15). God will not let his "faithful one" see decay—a claim that both Peter and Paul saw as a clear prediction of Jesus' resurrection from the dead (16.10, quoted in Acts 2.27; 13.35).

What did they expect life after death to be like, if God's power redeemed someone from Sheol? You won't find a clearly defined picture of heaven here—only hints. The psalmists' thoughts center on God's face and his presence. For God is the only unchangeable reality: Wherever you are, in life or in death, he will be there. He is the ultimate reward to those who love him.

The expectation of God's face shows through in Psalms 16.8–11; 17.15; 49.15; 73.23–26. But for a clearer perspective on life after death, you must read, in the Old Testament, Isaiah 26.19 and Daniel 12.1–3, and in the New Testament, 2 Corinthians 5.1–10, among many other passages.

Life Questions: Describe what you believe happens after you die. Is this a frightening or an encouraging picture to you?

17 He delivered me from my strong enemy,
    and from those who hated me;
    for they were too mighty for me.
18 They confronted me in the day of my
      calamity;
    but the LORD was my support.
19 He brought me out into a broad place;
    he delivered me, because he delighted
      in me.

20 The LORD rewarded me according to my
      righteousness;
    according to the cleanness of my hands
      he recompensed me.
21 For I have kept the ways of the LORD,
    and have not wickedly departed from
      my God.
22 For all his ordinances were before me,
    and his statutes I did not put away
      from me.
23 I was blameless before him,
    and I kept myself from guilt.
24 Therefore the LORD has recompensed me
      according to my righteousness,
    according to the cleanness of my hands
      in his sight.

25 With the loyal you show yourself loyal;
    with the blameless you show yourself
      blameless;
26 with the pure you show yourself pure;
    and with the crooked you show
      yourself perverse.
27 For you deliver a humble people,
    but the haughty eyes you bring down.
28 It is you who light my lamp;
    the LORD, my God, lights up my
      darkness.
29 By you I can crush a troop,
    and by my God I can leap over a
      wall.
30 This God—his way is perfect;
    the promise of the LORD proves true;
    he is a shield for all who take refuge in
      him.

31 For who is God except the LORD?
    And who is a rock besides our God?—
32 the God who girded me with strength,
    and made my way safe.
33 He made my feet like the feet of a deer,
    and set me secure on the heights.
34 He trains my hands for war,
    so that my arms can bend a bow of
      bronze.
35 You have given me the shield of your
      salvation,

and your right hand has supported
      me;
    your help *p* has made me great.
36 You gave me a wide place for my steps
      under me,
    and my feet did not slip.
37 I pursued my enemies and overtook
      them;
    and did not turn back until they were
      consumed.
38 I struck them down, so that they were not
      able to rise;
    they fell under my feet.
39 For you girded me with strength for the
      battle;
    you made my assailants sink under
      me.
40 You made my enemies turn their backs
      to me,
    and those who hated me I destroyed.
41 They cried for help, but there was no one
      to save them;
    they cried to the LORD, but he did not
      answer them.
42 I beat them fine, like dust before the
      wind;
    I cast them out like the mire of the
      streets.

43 You delivered me from strife with the
      peoples;*q*
    you made me head of the nations;
    people whom I had not known served
      me.
44 As soon as they heard of me they obeyed
      me;
    foreigners came cringing to me.
45 Foreigners lost heart,
    and came trembling out of their
      strongholds.

46 The LORD lives! Blessed be my rock,
    and exalted be the God of my
      salvation,
47 the God who gave me vengeance
    and subdued peoples under me;
48 who delivered me from my enemies;
    indeed, you exalted me above my
      adversaries;
    you delivered me from the violent.

49 For this I will extol you, O LORD, among
      the nations,
    and sing praises to your name.
50 Great triumphs he gives to his king,
    and shows steadfast love to his
      anointed,
    to David and his descendants forever.

p Or *gentleness*   *q* Gk Tg: Heb *people*

Psalm 19

God's Glory in Creation and the Law

To the leader. A Psalm of David.

1 The heavens are telling the glory of God;
and the firmament[r] proclaims his
handiwork.

18.49 Going Public

For the psalmists, praising God was more than a personal matter between the believer and his God. They praised God publicly—even in front of unbelievers—often inviting their audience to join in. Such public praise anticipated New Testament evangelism, the spreading of good news to the entire world. Paul quoted this verse in Romans 15.9 to stress that God had always meant his love to reach out from the Jews to the rest of humanity.

---

2 Day to day pours forth speech,
and night to night declares knowledge.
3 There is no speech, nor are there words;
their voice is not heard;
4 yet their voice[s] goes out through all the
earth,
and their words to the end of the
world.

In the heavens[t] he has set a tent for the
sun,
5 which comes out like a bridegroom from
his wedding canopy,
and like a strong man runs its course
with joy.
6 Its rising is from the end of the heavens,
and its circuit to the end of them;
and nothing is hid from its heat.

7 The law of the LORD is perfect,
reviving the soul;
the decrees of the LORD are sure,
making wise the simple;
8 the precepts of the LORD are right,
rejoicing the heart;
the commandment of the LORD is clear,
enlightening the eyes;
9 the fear of the LORD is pure,
enduring forever;
the ordinances of the LORD are true
and righteous altogether.
10 More to be desired are they than gold,
even much fine gold;
sweeter also than honey,
and drippings of the honeycomb.

11 Moreover by them is your servant
warned;
in keeping them there is great reward.
12 But who can detect their errors?
Clear me from hidden faults.
13 Keep back your servant also from the
insolent;[u]
do not let them have dominion over
me.
Then I shall be blameless,
and innocent of great transgression.

14 Let the words of my mouth and the
meditation of my heart
be acceptable to you,
O LORD, my rock and my redeemer.

19.7–14 The Names of God

After describing the skies as a reflection of God's glory in the first six verses, Psalm 19 switches gears. From the sun, moon, and stars it turns to consider the beauty of God's law. Reflecting that change, the poem in Hebrew uses a different, more personal name for God. The first six verses refer to God with a general name that anyone, of any religion, might use—just like our English word God. But from verse seven on, God is called "the LORD" (a translation of the Hebrew Yahweh)—the personal name God revealed to Moses from the burning bush (Exodus 3.15). The heavens declare the glory of God, but God's law reveals even more—his personal voice to his chosen people. He introduces himself to them by his first name, as it were.

Psalm 20

Prayer for Victory

To the leader. A Psalm of David.

1 The LORD answer you in the day of
trouble!
The name of the God of Jacob protect
you!
2 May he send you help from the sanctuary,
and give you support from Zion.
3 May he remember all your offerings,
and regard with favor your burnt
sacrifices. *Selah*

4 May he grant you your heart's desire,
and fulfill all your plans.
5 May we shout for joy over your victory,

---

r Or dome   *s Gk Jerome Compare Syr: Heb line*   *t Heb In them*   *u Or from proud thoughts*

and in the name of our God set up our
banners.
May the LORD fulfill all your petitions.

6 Now I know that the LORD will help his
anointed;
he will answer him from his holy
heaven
with mighty victories by his right hand.
7 Some take pride in chariots, and some in
horses,
but our pride is in the name of the
LORD our God.
8 They will collapse and fall,
but we shall rise and stand upright.

9 Give victory to the king, O LORD;
answer us when we call.ᵛ

Psalm 21

Thanksgiving for Victory

To the leader. A Psalm of David.

1 In your strength the king rejoices,
O LORD,
and in your help how greatly he exults!
2 You have given him his heart's desire,
and have not withheld the request of
his lips.   Selah
3 For you meet him with rich blessings;
you set a crown of fine gold on his
head.
4 He asked you for life; you gave it to
him—
length of days forever and ever.
5 His glory is great through your help;
splendor and majesty you bestow on
him.
6 You bestow on him blessings forever;
you make him glad with the joy of
your presence.
7 For the king trusts in the LORD,
and through the steadfast love of the
Most High he shall not be
moved.

8 Your hand will find out all your enemies;
your right hand will find out those
who hate you.
9 You will make them like a fiery furnace
when you appear.
The LORD will swallow them up in his
wrath,
and fire will consume them.
10 You will destroy their offspring from the
earth,
and their children from among
humankind.

11 If they plan evil against you,
if they devise mischief, they will not
succeed.
12 For you will put them to flight;
you will aim at their faces with your
bows.

13 Be exalted, O LORD, in your strength!
We will sing and praise your power.

Psalm 22

Plea for Deliverance from Suffering and Hostility

To the leader: according to The Deer
of the Dawn. A Psalm of David.

1 My God, my God, why have you forsaken
me?
Why are you so far from helping me,
from the words of my groaning?
2 O my God, I cry by day, but you do not
answer;
and by night, but find no rest.

3 Yet you are holy,
enthroned on the praises of Israel.
4 In you our ancestors trusted;
they trusted, and you delivered them.
5 To you they cried, and were saved;
in you they trusted, and were not put
to shame.

6 But I am a worm, and not human;
scorned by others, and despised by the
people.
7 All who see me mock at me;
they make mouths at me, they shake
their heads;
8 "Commit your cause to the LORD; let him
deliver—
let him rescue the one in whom he
delights!"

9 Yet it was you who took me from the
womb;
you kept me safe on my mother's
breast.
10 On you I was cast from my birth,
and since my mother bore me you
have been my God.
11 Do not be far from me,
for trouble is near
and there is no one to help.

12 Many bulls encircle me,
strong bulls of Bashan surround me;
13 they open wide their mouths at me,
like a ravening and roaring lion.

ᵛ Gk: Heb give victory, O LORD; let the King answer us when we call

14 I am poured out like water,
and all my bones are out of joint;
my heart is like wax;
it is melted within my breast;
15 my mouth[w] is dried up like a potsherd,
and my tongue sticks to my jaws;
you lay me in the dust of death.

16 For dogs are all around me;
a company of evildoers encircles me.
My hands and feet have shriveled;[x]
17 I can count all my bones.
They stare and gloat over me;
18 they divide my clothes among themselves,
and for my clothing they cast lots.

19 But you, O LORD, do not be far away!
O my help, come quickly to my aid!
20 Deliver my soul from the sword,
my life[y] from the power of the dog!
21 Save me from the mouth of the lion!

From the horns of the wild oxen you
have rescued[z] me.
22 I will tell of your name to my brothers
and sisters;[a]
in the midst of the congregation I will
praise you:
23 You who fear the LORD, praise him!
All you offspring of Jacob, glorify
him;

---

w Cn: Heb *strength*   x Meaning of Heb uncertain   y Heb *my only one*   z Heb *answered*   a Or *kindred*

The Song of the Cross
Even the best people sometimes suffer

SUPERFICIALLY, THE OLD TESTAMENT CAN sometimes read like it's taken from old movies. The good guys are the Israelites, and they fight with the bad guys from nations around them. The Israelites have moments when they get off track, worshiping idols and acting like their "bad guy" neighbors. But when they turn back to God, they invariably win, and win big. The ending, in story after story, is happy. God *is* on their side.

> They divide my clothes among themselves, and for my clothing they cast lots. 22.18

Yet, in Psalm 22 and a few other places, the "good guy" story doesn't fit at all. This poem, credited to David, the great king and man "after God's own heart," tells of tremendous suffering with no relief from God. It sounds like a mob scene, a lynching. The "good guy's" enemies have him. They surround him, jeering, like a pack of dogs. He is helpless and exhausted. All he can do is cry to God.

The psalmist wavers back and forth, first crying out in misery, then taking stock of God's wonderful character, then describing his misery again. The whole poem is a prayer to God. Although this cry has gone up day and night (verse 2), God remains silent.

Whose Humiliations?

Then, at verse 22, the poem takes a dramatic turn, switching from grief to jubilation. Somehow, God has saved the sufferer, who, in great excitement, tells others about it. He sees more than his own good fortune: He foresees this deliverance spilling over into the whole world. He predicts the story of God's help told to future generations forever. God will be worshiped by the entire world.

A person might read Psalm 22 as an extravagantly poetic description of David's troubles. But Jesus and the writers of the New Testament saw something more in it. When Jesus was dying on the cross, he had this psalm on his lips (Matthew 27.46). Afterwards, when his disciples wanted to explain Jesus' life and sufferings, they turned to this psalm and others like it.

In them the disciples saw a pattern and a foreshadowing. The pattern is redemptive suffering. If good guys do not always win, if God seems actually to desert them—if David himself, the great leader and true man of God, knew these pains—then surely no one is exempt. And this suffering has a point. After it (and because of it) come victory and power, and the salvation of the world. This pattern helped Jesus' followers appreciate why Jesus, along with his followers, had to suffer.

A Fulfillment of Prophecy

Psalm 22 also helped the New Testament writers to see Jesus' life as a fulfillment of Old Testament prophecy. Jews had expected a Warrior-Messiah, a son of David who, like David, would lead his people to victory through battle. In Psalm 22 they saw that David had left another legacy: victory through suffering. The Messiah would lead his followers in suffering. Only Isaiah had put it more clearly, in his famous "servant" passages (Isaiah 42.1–9; 49.1–7; 50.4–9; 52.13–53.12). Psalm 22 stretches beyond the time of David; Jesus fits it perfectly.

Life Questions: Have you ever seen good come out of suffering for your friends or family?

stand in awe of him, all you offspring
of Israel!
24 For he did not despise or abhor
the affliction of the afflicted;
he did not hide his face from me,[b]
but heard when I[c] cried to him.

25 From you comes my praise in the great
congregation;
my vows I will pay before those who
fear him.
26 The poor[d] shall eat and be satisfied;
those who seek him shall praise the
LORD.
May your hearts live forever!

27 All the ends of the earth shall remember
and turn to the LORD;
and all the families of the nations
shall worship before him.[e]
28 For dominion belongs to the LORD,
and he rules over the nations.

29 To him,[f] indeed, shall all who sleep in[g]
the earth bow down;
before him shall bow all who go down
to the dust,
and I shall live for him.[h]
30 Posterity will serve him;
future generations will be told about
the Lord,
31 and[i] proclaim his deliverance to a people
yet unborn,
saying that he has done it.

Psalm 23

The Divine Shepherd

A Psalm of David.

1 The LORD is my shepherd, I shall not
want.
2 He makes me lie down in green
pastures;
he leads me beside still waters;[j]
3 he restores my soul.[k]
He leads me in right paths[l]
for his name's sake.

4 Even though I walk through the darkest
valley,[m]
I fear no evil;
for you are with me;
your rod and your staff—
they comfort me.

5 You prepare a table before me
in the presence of my enemies;
you anoint my head with oil;
my cup overflows.
6 Surely[n] goodness and mercy[o] shall
follow me
all the days of my life,
and I shall dwell in the house of the LORD
my whole life long.[p]

Psalm 24

Entrance into the Temple

Of David. A Psalm.

1 The earth is the LORD's and all that is
in it,
the world, and those who live in it;
2 for he has founded it on the seas,
and established it on the rivers.

3 Who shall ascend the hill of the LORD?
And who shall stand in his holy place?
4 Those who have clean hands and pure
hearts,
who do not lift up their souls to what
is false,
and do not swear deceitfully.
5 They will receive blessing from the LORD,
and vindication from the God of their
salvation.
6 Such is the company of those who seek
him,
who seek the face of the God of
Jacob.[q]   Selah

7 Lift up your heads, O gates!
and be lifted up, O ancient doors!
that the King of glory may come in.
8 Who is the King of glory?
The LORD, strong and mighty,
the LORD, mighty in battle.
9 Lift up your heads, O gates!
and be lifted up, O ancient doors!
that the King of glory may come in.
10 Who is this King of glory?
The LORD of hosts,
he is the King of glory.   Selah

Psalm 25

Prayer for Guidance and for Deliverance

Of David.

1 To you, O LORD, I lift up my soul.
2 O my God, in you I trust;

---

[b] Heb him   [c] Heb he   [d] Or afflicted   [e] Gk Syr Jerome: Heb you   [f] Cn: Heb They have eaten and
[g] Cn: Heb all the fat ones   [h] Compare Gk Syr Vg: Heb and he who cannot keep himself alive   [i] Compare Gk: Heb
it will be told about the Lord to the generation, 31they will come and   [j] Heb waters of rest   [k] Or life   [l] Or paths
of righteousness   [m] Or the valley of the shadow of death   [n] Or Only   [o] Or kindness   [p] Heb for length of days
[q] Gk Syr: Heb your face, O Jacob

do not let me be put to shame;
do not let my enemies exult over me.
3 Do not let those who wait for you be put
to shame;
let them be ashamed who are wantonly
treacherous.

4 Make me to know your ways, O LORD;
teach me your paths.
5 Lead me in your truth, and teach me,
for you are the God of my salvation;
for you I wait all day long.

6 Be mindful of your mercy, O LORD, and
of your steadfast love,
for they have been from of old.
7 Do not remember the sins of my youth
or my transgressions;
according to your steadfast love
remember me,
for your goodness' sake, O LORD!

8 Good and upright is the LORD;
therefore he instructs sinners in the
way.
9 He leads the humble in what is right,
and teaches the humble his way.
10 All the paths of the LORD are steadfast
love and faithfulness,
for those who keep his covenant and
his decrees.

11 For your name's sake, O LORD,
pardon my guilt, for it is great.
12 Who are they that fear the LORD?
He will teach them the way that they
should choose.
13 They will abide in prosperity,
and their children shall possess the
land.
14 The friendship of the LORD is for those
who fear him,
and he makes his covenant known to
them.
15 My eyes are ever toward the LORD,
for he will pluck my feet out of the
net.

16 Turn to me and be gracious to me,
for I am lonely and afflicted.
17 Relieve the troubles of my heart,
and bring me[r] out of my distress.
18 Consider my affliction and my trouble,
and forgive all my sins.
19 Consider how many are my foes,
and with what violent hatred they hate
me.

20 O guard my life, and deliver me;
do not let me be put to shame, for I
take refuge in you.
21 May integrity and uprightness preserve
me,
for I wait for you.

22 Redeem Israel, O God,
out of all its troubles.

Psalm 26

Plea for Justice and Declaration of Righteousness

Of David.

1 Vindicate me, O LORD,
for I have walked in my integrity,
and I have trusted in the LORD without
wavering.
2 Prove me, O LORD, and try me;
test my heart and mind.
3 For your steadfast love is before my eyes,
and I walk in faithfulness to you.[s]

4 I do not sit with the worthless,
nor do I consort with hypocrites;
5 I hate the company of evildoers,
and will not sit with the wicked.

6 I wash my hands in innocence,
and go around your altar, O LORD,
7 singing aloud a song of thanksgiving,
and telling all your wondrous deeds.

8 O LORD, I love the house in which you
dwell,
and the place where your glory abides.
9 Do not sweep me away with sinners,
nor my life with the bloodthirsty,
10 those in whose hands are evil devices,
and whose right hands are full of
bribes.

11 But as for me, I walk in my integrity;
redeem me, and be gracious to me.
12 My foot stands on level ground;
in the great congregation I will bless
the LORD.

Psalm 27

Triumphant Song of Confidence

Of David.

1 The LORD is my light and my salvation;
whom shall I fear?
The LORD is the stronghold[t] of my life;
of whom shall I be afraid?

r Or The troubles of my heart are enlarged; bring me   s Or in your faithfulness   t Or refuge

2 When evildoers assail me
   to devour my flesh—
my adversaries and foes—
   they shall stumble and fall.

26.11 Self-righteous?

This claim to be blameless or righteous—repeated many times in other psalms—should not be stretched too far. Whenever the psalmists examined themselves before God, they acknowledged their deep need for forgiveness (see 19.12; 32.1–5; 130.3; and 143.2).

Here, though, the issue is God's fairness. Knowing little about life after death, the psalmists expected that good people would do better in this life than bad people. They were deeply puzzled when they did not. Didn't God control every event? In calling for justice, they emphasized that they had been more faithful to God than their enemies.

Compared to the people plotting murder and betrayal against him, the psalmist was blameless. In a wholehearted, sincere way he had followed God. He was no hypocrite. He responds like a person swearing in court about his traffic accident: "My driving is blameless." He doesn't mean he never makes a mistake. He means only that he doesn't deserve punishment.

3 Though an army encamp against me,
   my heart shall not fear;
though war rise up against me,
   yet I will be confident.

4 One thing I asked of the LORD,
   that will I seek after:
to live in the house of the LORD
   all the days of my life,
to behold the beauty of the LORD,
   and to inquire in his temple.

5 For he will hide me in his shelter
   in the day of trouble;
he will conceal me under the cover of his
   tent;
   he will set me high on a rock.

6 Now my head is lifted up
   above my enemies all around me,
and I will offer in his tent
   sacrifices with shouts of joy;
I will sing and make melody to the LORD.

7 Hear, O LORD, when I cry aloud,
   be gracious to me and answer me!
8 "Come," my heart says, "seek his face!"

   Your face, LORD, do I seek.
9   Do not hide your face from me.

Do not turn your servant away in anger,
   you who have been my help.
Do not cast me off, do not forsake me,
   O God of my salvation!
10 If my father and mother forsake me,
   the LORD will take me up.

11 Teach me your way, O LORD,
   and lead me on a level path
   because of my enemies.
12 Do not give me up to the will of
     my adversaries,
for false witnesses have risen against
   me,
   and they are breathing out violence.

13 I believe that I shall see the goodness of
     the LORD
   in the land of the living.
14 Wait for the LORD;
   be strong, and let your heart take
     courage;
   wait for the LORD!

Psalm 28

Prayer for Help and Thanksgiving for It

Of David

1 To you, O LORD, I call;
   my rock, do not refuse to hear me,
for if you are silent to me,
   I shall be like those who go down to
     the Pit.
2 Hear the voice of my supplication,
   as I cry to you for help,
as I lift up my hands
   toward your most holy sanctuary.*u*

3 Do not drag me away with the wicked,
   with those who are workers of evil,
who speak peace with their neighbors,
   while mischief is in their hearts.
4 Repay them according to their work,
   and according to the evil of their
     deeds;
repay them according to the work of their
     hands;
   render them their due reward.
5 Because they do not regard the works of
     the LORD,
   or the work of his hands,
he will break them down and build them
     up no more.

6 Blessed be the LORD,

---

u Heb *your innermost sanctuary*

for he has heard the sound of my
   pleadings.
7 The LORD is my strength and my shield;
   in him my heart trusts;
so I am helped, and my heart exults,
   and with my song I give thanks to
   him.

8 The LORD is the strength of his people;
   he is the saving refuge of his anointed.
9 O save your people, and bless your
   heritage;
be their shepherd, and carry them
   forever.

Psalm 29

The Voice of God in a Great Storm

A Psalm of David.

1 Ascribe to the LORD, O heavenly beings,[v]
   ascribe to the LORD glory and strength.
2 Ascribe to the LORD the glory of his
   name;
worship the LORD in holy splendor.

3 The voice of the LORD is over the waters;
   the God of glory thunders,
   the LORD, over mighty waters.
4 The voice of the LORD is powerful;
   the voice of the LORD is full of majesty.

5 The voice of the LORD breaks the cedars;
   the LORD breaks the cedars of Lebanon.
6 He makes Lebanon skip like a calf,
   and Sirion like a young wild ox.

7 The voice of the LORD flashes forth flames
   of fire.
8 The voice of the LORD shakes the
   wilderness;
the LORD shakes the wilderness of
   Kadesh.

9 The voice of the LORD causes the oaks to
   whirl,[w]
and strips the forest bare;
   and in his temple all say, "Glory!"

10 The LORD sits enthroned over the flood;
   the LORD sits enthroned as king
   forever.
11 May the LORD give strength to his people!
   May the LORD bless his people with
   peace!

Psalm 30

Thanksgiving for Recovery from Grave Illness

*A Psalm. A Song at the dedication of the
temple. Of David.*

1 I will extol you, O LORD, for you have
   drawn me up,
   and did not let my foes rejoice over
   me.
2 O LORD my God, I cried to you for help,
   and you have healed me.
3 O LORD, you brought up my soul from
   Sheol,
   restored me to life from among those
   gone down to the Pit.[x]

4 Sing praises to the LORD, O you his
   faithful ones,
   and give thanks to his holy name.
5 For his anger is but for a moment;
   his favor is for a lifetime.
Weeping may linger for the night,
   but joy comes with the morning.

30.5 One-night Guest

*The Bible never ignores the emotions of the
moment. Here, the psalmist acknowledges the
tough times that come with living as God's
child. But the Bible also insists on a long-range
perspective. Difficulties don't last; God's care
does. This psalm pictures "weeping" as a guest
who comes to stay for just a single night.*

6 As for me, I said in my prosperity,
   "I shall never be moved."
7 By your favor, O LORD,
   you had established me as a strong
   mountain;
you hid your face;
   I was dismayed.

8 To you, O LORD, I cried,
   and to the LORD I made supplication:
9 "What profit is there in my death,
   if I go down to the Pit?
Will the dust praise you?
   Will it tell of your faithfulness?
10 Hear, O LORD, and be gracious to me!
   O LORD, be my helper!"

11 You have turned my mourning into
   dancing;
you have taken off my sackcloth
   and clothed me with joy,

---

v Heb *sons of gods*   w Or *causes the deer to calve*   x Or *that I should not go down to the Pit*

12 so that my soul[y] may praise you and not
    be silent.
  O Lord my God, I will give thanks to
    you forever.

Psalm 31

Prayer and Praise for Deliverance
from Enemies

To the leader. A Psalm of David.

1 In you, O Lord, I seek refuge;
    do not let me ever be put to shame;
    in your righteousness deliver me.
2 Incline your ear to me;
    rescue me speedily.
  Be a rock of refuge for me,
    a strong fortress to save me.

3 You are indeed my rock and my fortress;
    for your name's sake lead me and
      guide me,
4 take me out of the net that is hidden for
      me,
    for you are my refuge.
5 Into your hand I commit my spirit;
    you have redeemed me, O Lord,
      faithful God.

6 You hate[z] those who pay regard to
      worthless idols,
    but I trust in the Lord.
7 I will exult and rejoice in your steadfast
      love,
    because you have seen my affliction;
    you have taken heed of my adversities,
8 and have not delivered me into the hand
      of the enemy;
    you have set my feet in a broad place.

9 Be gracious to me, O Lord, for I am in
      distress;
    my eye wastes away from grief,
    my soul and body also.
10 For my life is spent with sorrow,
    and my years with sighing;
  my strength fails because of my misery,[a]
    and my bones waste away.

11 I am the scorn of all my adversaries,
    a horror[b] to my neighbors,
  an object of dread to my acquaintances;
    those who see me in the street flee
      from me.
12 I have passed out of mind like one who is
      dead;
    I have become like a broken vessel.
13 For I hear the whispering of many—

terror all around!—
  as they scheme together against me,
    as they plot to take my life.

14 But I trust in you, O Lord;
    I say, "You are my God."
15 My times are in your hand;
    deliver me from the hand of my
      enemies and persecutors.
16 Let your face shine upon your servant;
    save me in your steadfast love.
17 Do not let me be put to shame, O Lord,
    for I call on you;
  let the wicked be put to shame;
    let them go dumbfounded to Sheol.
18 Let the lying lips be stilled
    that speak insolently against the
      righteous
    with pride and contempt.

19 O how abundant is your goodness
    that you have laid up for those who
      fear you,
  and accomplished for those who take
      refuge in you,
    in the sight of everyone!
20 In the shelter of your presence you hide
      them
    from human plots;
  you hold them safe under your shelter
    from contentious tongues.

21 Blessed be the Lord,
    for he has wondrously shown his
      steadfast love to me
    when I was beset as a city under siege.
22 I had said in my alarm,
    "I am driven far[c] from your sight."
  But you heard my supplications
    when I cried out to you for help.

23 Love the Lord, all you his saints.
    The Lord preserves the faithful,
    but abundantly repays the one who
      acts haughtily.
24 Be strong, and let your heart take
      courage,
    all you who wait for the Lord.

Psalm 32

The Joy of Forgiveness

Of David. A Maskil.

1 Happy are those whose transgression is
      forgiven,
    whose sin is covered.

---

y Heb *that glory*   *z* One Heb Ms Gk Syr Jerome: MT *I hate*   *a* Gk Syr: Heb *my iniquity*   *b* Cn: Heb *exceedingly*
c Another reading is *cut off*

2 Happy are those to whom the Lord
 imputes no iniquity,
 and in whose spirit there is no
  deceit.

3 While I kept silence, my body wasted
 away

32.2 The Benefits of Faith

**Paul quoted this verse in Romans 4.6–8, while
making his case that we do not earn status in
God's eyes: God must credit righteousness on
the basis of faith.**

 through my groaning all day long.
4 For day and night your hand was heavy
 upon me;
 my strength was dried up[d] as by the
  heat of summer.   *Selah*

5 Then I acknowledged my sin to you,
 and I did not hide my iniquity;
 I said, "I will confess my transgressions to
  the Lord,"
 and you forgave the guilt of my sin.
       Selah

6 Therefore let all who are faithful
 offer prayer to you;
 at a time of distress,[e] the rush of mighty
  waters
 shall not reach them.
7 You are a hiding place for me;
 you preserve me from trouble;
 you surround me with glad cries of
  deliverance.   *Selah*

8 I will instruct you and teach you the way
 you should go;
 I will counsel you with my eye upon
  you.
9 Do not be like a horse or a mule, without
 understanding,
 whose temper must be curbed with bit
  and bridle,
 else it will not stay near you.

10 Many are the torments of the wicked,
 but steadfast love surrounds those who
  trust in the Lord.
11 Be glad in the Lord and rejoice,
 O righteous,

and shout for joy, all you upright in
 heart.

Psalm 33

The Greatness and Goodness of God

1 Rejoice in the Lord, O you righteous.
 Praise befits the upright.
2 Praise the Lord with the lyre;
 make melody to him with the harp of
  ten strings.
3 Sing to him a new song;
 play skillfully on the strings, with loud
  shouts.

4 For the word of the Lord is upright,
 and all his work is done in faithfulness.
5 He loves righteousness and justice;
 the earth is full of the steadfast love of
  the Lord.

6 By the word of the Lord the heavens
 were made,
 and all their host by the breath of his
  mouth.
7 He gathered the waters of the sea as in a
 bottle;
 he put the deeps in storehouses.

8 Let all the earth fear the Lord;
 let all the inhabitants of the world
  stand in awe of him.
9 For he spoke, and it came to be;
 he commanded, and it stood firm.

10 The Lord brings the counsel of the
 nations to nothing;
 he frustrates the plans of the peoples.
11 The counsel of the Lord stands forever,
 the thoughts of his heart to all
  generations.
12 Happy is the nation whose God is the
 Lord,
 the people whom he has chosen as his
  heritage.

13 The Lord looks down from heaven;
 he sees all humankind.
14 From where he sits enthroned he
 watches
 all the inhabitants of the earth—
15 he who fashions the hearts of them
 all,
 and observes all their deeds.
16 A king is not saved by his great army;
 a warrior is not delivered by his great
  strength.

d Meaning of Heb uncertain e Cn: Heb *at a time of finding only*

17 The war horse is a vain hope for victory,
and by its great might it cannot save.

18 Truly the eye of the LORD is on those who
fear him,
on those who hope in his steadfast
love,

19 to deliver their soul from death,
and to keep them alive in famine.

20 Our soul waits for the LORD;
he is our help and shield.

21 Our heart is glad in him,
because we trust in his holy name.

22 Let your steadfast love, O LORD, be upon
us,
even as we hope in you.

Psalm 34
Praise for Deliverance from Trouble

*Of David, when he feigned madness before
Abimelech, so that he drove him out, and he
went away.*

1 I will bless the LORD at all times;
his praise shall continually be in my
mouth.

2 My soul makes its boast in the LORD;
let the humble hear and be glad.

3 O magnify the LORD with me,
and let us exalt his name together.

4 I sought the LORD, and he answered me,
and delivered me from all my fears.

5 Look to him, and be radiant;

Lyrics for the Living God
The psalms were meant to be sung—and shouted

> Sing to him a new song; play skillfully on the strings, with loud shouts. 33.3

WILLIAM BOOTH, BELIEVING THE 19TH-CENTURY English church had become too refined to reach the cities' poor, took the gospel into the streets. He organized his workers into a "salvation army," complete with uniforms and military rank.

With hecklers and drunks abounding, the "army" didn't always find preaching easy or safe. A local builder, Charles William Fry, offered himself and his three sons as bodyguards. As it happened all four played brass instruments, which they carried along to accompany singing.

Booth's rowdier supporters were soon dragging along concertinas, bells, hunting horns, banjos, tambourines, and drums to praise the Lord. Said one leader, "It sounds as if a brass band's gone out of its mind."

Salvation Army recruits did not stick to traditional hymns but invented their own words for rousing popular tunes. "Here's to Good Old Whiskey" became "Storm the Forts of Darkness." Booth had his doubts about this trend until one night, hearing a beautiful rendition of "Bless His Name, He Sets Me Free," he asked about the tune. "Why, Mr. Booth, that's 'Champagne Charlie Is My Name,'" the embarrassed singer replied.

"That settles it," Booth said. "Why *should* the devil have all the best tunes?" Soon 400 bands were crashing about England, playing hit tunes with Christian words.

The Best Music Available

David and his people would have liked that spirit. Many of the psalms were meant to be sung, and sung joyfully. Modern church formality seems far removed from their frequent command: "Sing for joy! Shout aloud!" Their instruments included cymbals, tambourines, trumpets, ram's horns, harps, and lyres. Sometimes dancing erupted. The world, in the psalmist's imagination, can't contain the delight God inspires. A *new* song must be sung. "Make a joyful noise to the LORD, all the earth; break forth into joyous song and sing praises" (98.4).

First Chronicles 15.16 and 23.5 report that David appointed 4,000 professional musicians to provide their services to the temple. They offered the best music available, and the congregation joined in. Nobody knows exactly what it sounded like, but scholars doubt it was all soft and soothing. Musicians improvised. Most of the instruments used suggest rousing, rhythmic sound.

Every generation of Christians renews the discovery of this "new song," sometimes through the music of their forebears, sometimes in a form that shocks their solemn elders. The Salvation Army did, as did the Jesus Movement in the 60s and Christian rock music in the 80s and 90s. David would not have been surprised. He jolted his own wife with spontaneous dancing (see 1 Chronicles 15.29). When people know God, they come to life with a jubilant song on their lips.

Life Questions: When you sing to God, what kind of emotions do you hope to feel? What kind of music contributes to that?

so your[f] faces shall never be ashamed.
6 This poor soul cried, and was heard by
the Lord,
and was saved from every trouble.
7 The angel of the Lord encamps
around those who fear him, and
delivers them.
8 O taste and see that the Lord is good;
happy are those who take refuge in
him.
9 O fear the Lord, you his holy ones,
for those who fear him have no want.

34.9 Is God Frightening?

"Fear of the Lord" is a phrase we find frequently in the Old Testament. Does it mean that we should be frightened of God? Apparently not. "Fear of the Lord" gradually became a standard phrase for a good relationship with God. A good relationship begins with a reverent sense that God is so powerful and righteous that we dare not take him lightly. But it goes on from awe to a sense of deep security, as this psalm fully demonstrates.

10 The young lions suffer want and hunger,
but those who seek the Lord lack no
good thing.

11 Come, O children, listen to me;
I will teach you the fear of the Lord.
12 Which of you desires life,
and covets many days to enjoy good?
13 Keep your tongue from evil,
and your lips from speaking deceit.
14 Depart from evil, and do good;
seek peace, and pursue it.

15 The eyes of the Lord are on the
righteous,
and his ears are open to their cry.
16 The face of the Lord is against evildoers,
to cut off the remembrance of them
from the earth.
17 When the righteous cry for help, the
Lord hears,
and rescues them from all their
troubles.
18 The Lord is near to the brokenhearted,
and saves the crushed in spirit.

19 Many are the afflictions of the righteous,
but the Lord rescues them from them
all.
20 He keeps all their bones;
not one of them will be broken.
21 Evil brings death to the wicked,

and those who hate the righteous will
be condemned.
22 The Lord redeems the life of his servants;
none of those who take refuge in him
will be condemned.

Psalm 35

Prayer for Deliverance from Enemies

Of David.

1 Contend, O Lord, with those who
contend with me;
fight against those who fight against
me!
2 Take hold of shield and buckler,
and rise up to help me!
3 Draw the spear and javelin
against my pursuers;
say to my soul,
"I am your salvation."

4 Let them be put to shame and dishonor
who seek after my life.
Let them be turned back and confounded
who devise evil against me.
5 Let them be like chaff before the wind,
with the angel of the Lord driving
them on.
6 Let their way be dark and slippery,
with the angel of the Lord pursuing
them.

7 For without cause they hid their net[g] for
me;
without cause they dug a pit[h] for my
life.
8 Let ruin come on them unawares.
And let the net that they hid ensnare
them;
let them fall in it—to their ruin.

9 Then my soul shall rejoice in the Lord,
exulting in his deliverance.
10 All my bones shall say,
"O Lord, who is like you?
You deliver the weak
from those too strong for them,
the weak and needy from those who
despoil them."

11 Malicious witnesses rise up;
they ask me about things I do not
know.
12 They repay me evil for good;
my soul is forlorn.
13 But as for me, when they were sick,
I wore sackcloth;
I afflicted myself with fasting.

---

[f] Gk Syr Jerome: Heb *their*   [g] Heb *a pit, their net*   [h] The word *pit* is transposed from the preceding line

I prayed with head bowed[i] on my
bosom,
14 as though I grieved for a friend or a
brother;
I went about as one who laments for a
mother,
bowed down and in mourning.

15 But at my stumbling they gathered in
glee,
they gathered together against me;
ruffians whom I did not know
tore at me without ceasing;
16 they impiously mocked more and more,[j]
gnashing at me with their teeth.

17 How long, O LORD, will you look on?
Rescue me from their ravages,
my life from the lions!
18 Then I will thank you in the great
congregation;
in the mighty throng I will praise you.

19 Do not let my treacherous enemies rejoice
over me,
or those who hate me without cause
wink the eye.
20 For they do not speak peace,
but they conceive deceitful words
against those who are quiet in the land.
21 They open wide their mouths against me;
they say, "Aha, Aha,
our eyes have seen it."

22 You have seen, O LORD; do not be silent!
O Lord, do not be far from me!
23 Wake up! Bestir yourself for my defense,
for my cause, my God and my Lord!
24 Vindicate me, O LORD, my God,
according to your righteousness,
and do not let them rejoice over me.
25 Do not let them say to themselves,
"Aha, we have our heart's desire."
Do not let them say, "We have swallowed
you[k] up."

26 Let all those who rejoice at my calamity
be put to shame and confusion;
let those who exalt themselves against me
be clothed with shame and dishonor.

27 Let those who desire my vindication
shout for joy and be glad,
and say evermore,
"Great is the LORD,
who delights in the welfare of his
servant."

28 Then my tongue shall tell of your
righteousness
and of your praise all day long.

Psalm 36

Human Wickedness and Divine Goodness

*To the leader. Of David, the servant
of the LORD.*

1 Transgression speaks to the wicked
deep in their hearts;
there is no fear of God
before their eyes.
2 For they flatter themselves in their own
eyes
that their iniquity cannot be found out
and hated.
3 The words of their mouths are mischief
and deceit;
they have ceased to act wisely and do
good.
4 They plot mischief while on their beds;
they are set on a way that is not good;
they do not reject evil.

5 Your steadfast love, O LORD, extends to
the heavens,
your faithfulness to the clouds.
6 Your righteousness is like the mighty
mountains,
your judgments are like the great deep;
you save humans and animals alike,
O LORD.

7 How precious is your steadfast love,
O God!
All people may take refuge in the
shadow of your wings.
8 They feast on the abundance of your
house,
and you give them drink from the river
of your delights.
9 For with you is the fountain of life;
in your light we see light.

36.9 Light Makes Light

*By itself, light is invisible; and yet everything
is invisible until light strikes it. So it is with
God: we can't see him, but "in his light" (under
his loving influence) we see and understand
his love in all that surrounds us. God's
overwhelming generosity stands in complete
contrast to the self-important plotting of
wicked human beings (verses 1–4).*

---

i Or *My prayer turned back*   *j* Cn Compare Gk: Heb *like the profanest of mockers of a cake*   *k* Heb *him*

10 O continue your steadfast love to those
            who know you,
      and your salvation to the upright of
            heart!
11 Do not let the foot of the arrogant tread
            on me,
      or the hand of the wicked drive me
            away.
12 There the evildoers lie prostrate;
      they are thrust down, unable to rise.

Psalm 37

Exhortation to Patience and Trust

Of David.

1 Do not fret because of the wicked;
      do not be envious of wrongdoers,
2 for they will soon fade like the grass,
      and wither like the green herb.

3 Trust in the LORD, and do good;
      so you will live in the land, and enjoy
            security.
4 Take delight in the LORD,
      and he will give you the desires of your
            heart.

5 Commit your way to the LORD;
      trust in him, and he will act.
6 He will make your vindication shine like
            the light,
      and the justice of your cause like the
            noonday.

7 Be still before the LORD, and wait
            patiently for him;
      do not fret over those who prosper in
            their way,
      over those who carry out evil devices.

8 Refrain from anger, and forsake wrath.
      Do not fret—it leads only to evil.
9 For the wicked shall be cut off,
      but those who wait for the LORD shall
            inherit the land.

10 Yet a little while, and the wicked will be
            no more;
      though you look diligently for their
            place, they will not be there.
11 But the meek shall inherit the land,
      and delight themselves in abundant
            prosperity.

12 The wicked plot against the righteous,
      and gnash their teeth at them;
13 but the LORD laughs at the wicked,
      for he sees that their day is coming.

14 The wicked draw the sword and bend
            their bows
      to bring down the poor and needy,
      to kill those who walk uprightly;
15 their sword shall enter their own heart,
      and their bows shall be broken.

16 Better is a little that the righteous person
            has
      than the abundance of many wicked.
17 For the arms of the wicked shall be
            broken,
      but the LORD upholds the righteous.

18 The LORD knows the days of the
            blameless,
      and their heritage will abide forever;
19 they are not put to shame in evil times,
      in the days of famine they have
            abundance.

20 But the wicked perish,
      and the enemies of the LORD are like
            the glory of the pastures;
      they vanish—like smoke they vanish
            away.

21 The wicked borrow, and do not pay back,
      but the righteous are generous and
            keep giving;
22 for those blessed by the LORD shall inherit
            the land,
      but those cursed by him shall be cut
            off.

23 Our steps[l] are made firm by the LORD,
      when he delights in our[m] way;
24 though we stumble,[n] we[o] shall not fall
            headlong,
      for the LORD holds us[p] by the hand.

25 I have been young, and now am old,
      yet I have not seen the righteous
            forsaken
      or their children begging bread.

37.25 Never Abandoned

Is life unfair? Psalm 37 ponders that perplexing question. Its basic conclusion: The success of wicked people won't last, while in the long run people who do right will flourish. The psalmist adds this observation, based on experience: Through a lifetime of troubles and anxieties, he has yet to see the righteous abandoned by God and unable to provide the basics of life for their children. Their generosity doesn't bankrupt them.

l Heb A man's steps   m Heb his   n Heb he stumbles   o Heb he   p Heb him

²⁶ They are ever giving liberally and lending,
and their children become a blessing.

²⁷ Depart from evil, and do good;
so you shall abide forever.
²⁸ For the LORD loves justice;
he will not forsake his faithful ones.

The righteous shall be kept safe forever,
but the children of the wicked shall be
cut off.
²⁹ The righteous shall inherit the land,
and live in it forever.

³⁰ The mouths of the righteous utter
wisdom,
and their tongues speak justice.
³¹ The law of their God is in their hearts;
their steps do not slip.

³² The wicked watch for the righteous,
and seek to kill them.
³³ The LORD will not abandon them to their
power,
or let them be condemned when they
are brought to trial.

³⁴ Wait for the LORD, and keep to his way,
and he will exalt you to inherit the
land;
you will look on the destruction of the
wicked.

³⁵ I have seen the wicked oppressing,
and towering like a cedar of Lebanon.^q
³⁶ Again I^r passed by, and they were no
more;
though I sought them, they could not
be found.

³⁷ Mark the blameless, and behold the
upright,
for there is posterity for the peaceable.
³⁸ But transgressors shall be altogether
destroyed;
the posterity of the wicked shall be cut
off.

³⁹ The salvation of the righteous is from the
LORD;
he is their refuge in the time of
trouble.
⁴⁰ The LORD helps them and rescues them;
he rescues them from the wicked, and
saves them,
because they take refuge in him.

Psalm 38

A Penitent Sufferer's Plea for Healing

A Psalm of David, for the memorial offering.

¹ O LORD, do not rebuke me in your anger,
or discipline me in your wrath.
² For your arrows have sunk into me,
and your hand has come down on me.

³ There is no soundness in my flesh
because of your indignation;
there is no health in my bones
because of my sin.
⁴ For my iniquities have gone over my
head;
they weigh like a burden too heavy for
me.

⁵ My wounds grow foul and fester
because of my foolishness;
⁶ I am utterly bowed down and prostrate;
all day long I go around mourning.
⁷ For my loins are filled with burning,
and there is no soundness in my flesh.
⁸ I am utterly spent and crushed;
I groan because of the tumult of my
heart.

⁹ O Lord, all my longing is known to you;
my sighing is not hidden from you.
¹⁰ My heart throbs, my strength fails me;
as for the light of my eyes—it also has
gone from me.
¹¹ My friends and companions stand aloof
from my affliction,
and my neighbors stand far off.

¹² Those who seek my life lay their snares;
those who seek to hurt me speak of
ruin,
and meditate treachery all day long.

¹³ But I am like the deaf, I do not hear;
like the mute, who cannot speak.
¹⁴ Truly, I am like one who does not hear,
and in whose mouth is no retort.

¹⁵ But it is for you, O LORD, that I wait;
it is you, O Lord my God, who will
answer.
¹⁶ For I pray, "Only do not let them rejoice
over me,
those who boast against me when my
foot slips."

¹⁷ For I am ready to fall,
and my pain is ever with me.
¹⁸ I confess my iniquity;

q Gk: Meaning of Heb uncertain   r Gk Syr Jerome: Heb he

I am sorry for my sin.
19 Those who are my foes without cause[s]
    are mighty,
and many are those who hate me
    wrongfully.
20 Those who render me evil for good
    are my adversaries because I follow
    after good.

21 Do not forsake me, O Lord;
    O my God, do not be far from me;
22 make haste to help me,
    O Lord, my salvation.

Psalm 39

Prayer for Wisdom and Forgiveness

To the leader: to Jeduthun. A Psalm of David.

1 I said, "I will guard my ways
    that I may not sin with my tongue;
I will keep a muzzle on my mouth
    as long as the wicked are in my
        presence."
2 I was silent and still;
    I held my peace to no avail;
my distress grew worse,
3   my heart became hot within me.
While I mused, the fire burned;
    then I spoke with my tongue:

4 "Lord, let me know my end,
    and what is the measure of my days;
let me know how fleeting my life is.
5 You have made my days a few
        handbreadths,
    and my lifetime is as nothing in your
        sight.
Surely everyone stands as a mere breath.
                                    Selah
6   Surely everyone goes about like a
        shadow.
Surely for nothing they are in turmoil;
    they heap up, and do not know who
        will gather.

7 "And now, O Lord, what do I wait for?
    My hope is in you.
8 Deliver me from all my transgressions.
    Do not make me the scorn of the fool.
9 I am silent; I do not open my mouth,
    for it is you who have done it.
10 Remove your stroke from me;
    I am worn down by the blows[t] of
        your hand.

11 "You chastise mortals
    in punishment for sin,
consuming like a moth what is dear to
        them;
surely everyone is a mere breath.   Selah

12 "Hear my prayer, O Lord,
    and give ear to my cry;
    do not hold your peace at my tears.
For I am your passing guest,
    an alien, like all my forebears.

39.10 Wrestling with God

Not all the psalms are happy. Some, such as this one and Psalms 44 and 88, are intensely sad. They try to make sense out of suffering, and fail. They ask God for help and receive none. The Bible's inclusion of such hopeless cries eloquently testifies to God's acceptance of human struggles. These psalms are not the final word on suffering. They show, however, that wrestling with God has value even when we fail to find answers.

13 Turn your gaze away from me, that I may
        smile again,
    before I depart and am no more."

Psalm 40

Thanksgiving for Deliverance and Prayer for Help

To the leader. Of David. A Psalm.

1 I waited patiently for the Lord;
    he inclined to me and heard my cry.
2 He drew me up from the desolate pit,[u]
    out of the miry bog,
and set my feet upon a rock,
    making my steps secure.
3 He put a new song in my mouth,
    a song of praise to our God.
Many will see and fear,
    and put their trust in the Lord.

4 Happy are those who make
        the Lord their trust,
who do not turn to the proud,
    to those who go astray after false gods.
5 You have multiplied, O Lord my God,
    your wondrous deeds and your
        thoughts toward us;
    none can compare with you.
Were I to proclaim and tell of them,
    they would be more than can be
        counted.

6 Sacrifice and offering you do not desire,
    but you have given me an open ear.[v]

---

[s] Q Ms: MT *my living foes*   [t] Heb *hostility*   [u] Cn: Heb *pit of tumult*   [v] Heb *ears you have dug for me*

Burnt offering and sin offering
you have not required.
7 Then I said, "Here I am;
in the scroll of the book it is written of
me.ʷ

40.6 A Better Sacrifice

While the Old Testament law prescribed animal and grain sacrifices to deal with the problem of sin, Old Testament writers made clear that God really wanted obedient lives, not ritual performances. Hebrews 10.5–9 quotes these verses (6–8) in explaining that Jesus' sacrifice made all the animal sacrifices obsolete. Only Jesus' sacrifice has the power to actually forgive sins and change lives.

8 I delight to do your will, O my God;
your law is within my heart."

9 I have told the glad news of deliverance
in the great congregation;
see, I have not restrained my lips,
as you know, O LORD.
10 I have not hidden your saving help within
my heart,
I have spoken of your faithfulness and
your salvation;
I have not concealed your steadfast love
and your faithfulness
from the great congregation.

11 Do not, O LORD, withhold
your mercy from me;
let your steadfast love and your
faithfulness
keep me safe forever.
12 For evils have encompassed me
without number;
my iniquities have overtaken me,
until I cannot see;
they are more than the hairs of my head,
and my heart fails me.

13 Be pleased, O LORD, to deliver me;
O LORD, make haste to help me.
14 Let all those be put to shame and
confusion
who seek to snatch away my life;
let those be turned back and brought to
dishonor
who desire my hurt.
15 Let those be appalled because of their
shame
who say to me, "Aha, Aha!"

16 But may all who seek you

rejoice and be glad in you;
may those who love your salvation
say continually, "Great is the LORD!"
17 As for me, I am poor and needy,
but the Lord takes thought for me.
You are my help and my deliverer;
do not delay, O my God.

Psalm 41

Assurance of God's Help and a Plea for Healing

To the leader. A Psalm of David.

1 Happy are those who consider the poor;ˣ
the LORD delivers them in the day of
trouble.

41.1 A Key Characteristic

The psalmist was severely ill. Enemies and rivals—and even a close friend, verse 9—whispered that he was dying. What made him so confident that God would heal him? He knew that God helps those who "consider the poor." Because he had shown integrity in this, he confidently expected God to show mercy to him. Jesus reflected this value when he said, "Blessed are the merciful, for they will receive mercy" (Matthew 5.7).

2 The LORD protects them and keeps them
alive;
they are called happy in the land.
You do not give them up to the will of
their enemies.
3 The LORD sustains them on their sickbed;
in their illness you heal all their
infirmities.ʸ

4 As for me, I said, "O LORD, be gracious to
me;
heal me, for I have sinned against
you."
5 My enemies wonder in malice
when I will die, and my name perish.
6 And when they come to see me, they
utter empty words,
while their hearts gather mischief;
when they go out, they tell it abroad.
7 All who hate me whisper together about
me;
they imagine the worst for me.

8 They think that a deadly thing has
fastened on me,
that I will not rise again from where I
lie.

ʷ Meaning of Heb uncertain   ˣ Or *weak*   ʸ Heb *you change all his bed*

9 Even my bosom friend in whom I trusted,
who ate of my bread, has lifted the
heel against me.
10 But you, O LORD, be gracious to me,
and raise me up, that I may repay
them.

11 By this I know that you are pleased with
me;
because my enemy has not triumphed
over me.
12 But you have upheld me because of my
integrity,
and set me in your presence forever.

13 Blessed be the LORD, the God of Israel,
from everlasting to everlasting.
Amen and Amen.

BOOK II
(Psalms 42–72)

Psalm 42

Longing for God and His Help in Distress

To the leader. A Maskil of the Korahites.

1 As a deer longs for flowing streams,
so my soul longs for you, O God.
2 My soul thirsts for God,
for the living God.
When shall I come and behold
the face of God?
3 My tears have been my food
day and night,
while people say to me continually,
"Where is your God?"

4 These things I remember,
as I pour out my soul:
how I went with the throng,z
and led them in procession to the
house of God,
with glad shouts and songs of
thanksgiving,
a multitude keeping festival.
5 Why are you cast down, O my soul,
and why are you disquieted within me?
Hope in God; for I shall again praise him,
my help 6and my God.

My soul is cast down within me;
therefore I remember you
from the land of Jordan and of Hermon,
from Mount Mizar.
7 Deep calls to deep
at the thunder of your cataracts;
all your waves and your billows
have gone over me.

8 By day the LORD commands his steadfast
love,
and at night his song is with me,
a prayer to the God of my life.

9 I say to God, my rock,
"Why have you forgotten me?
Why must I walk about mournfully
because the enemy oppresses me?"
10 As with a deadly wound in my body,
my adversaries taunt me,
while they say to me continually,
"Where is your God?"

11 Why are you cast down, O my soul,
and why are you disquieted within me?
Hope in God; for I shall again praise him,
my help and my God.

Psalm 43

Prayer to God in Time of Trouble

1 Vindicate me, O God, and defend my
cause
against an ungodly people;
from those who are deceitful and unjust
deliver me!
2 For you are the God in whom I take
refuge;
why have you cast me off?
Why must I walk about mournfully
because of the oppression of the
enemy?

3 O send out your light and your truth;
let them lead me;
let them bring me to your holy hill
and to your dwelling.
4 Then I will go to the altar of God,
to God my exceeding joy;
and I will praise you with the harp,
O God, my God.

5 Why are you cast down, O my soul,
and why are you disquieted within me?
Hope in God; for I shall again praise him,
my help and my God.

Psalm 44

National Lament and Prayer for Help

To the leader. Of the Korahites. A Maskil.

1 We have heard with our ears, O God,
our ancestors have told us,
what deeds you performed in their days,
in the days of old:
2 you with your own hand drove out the
nations,

z Meaning of Heb uncertain

but them you planted;
you afflicted the peoples,
but them you set free;
3 for not by their own sword did they win
the land,
nor did their own arm give them
victory;
but your right hand, and your arm,
and the light of your countenance,
for you delighted in them.

4 You are my King and my God;
you command[a] victories for Jacob.
5 Through you we push down our foes;
through your name we tread down our
assailants.
6 For not in my bow do I trust,
nor can my sword save me.
7 But you have saved us from our foes,
and have put to confusion those who
hate us.
8 In God we have boasted continually,
and we will give thanks to your name
forever.   *Selah*

9 Yet you have rejected us and abased us,
and have not gone out with our
armies.
10 You made us turn back from the foe,
and our enemies have gotten spoil.
11 You have made us like sheep for
slaughter,
and have scattered us among
the nations.
12 You have sold your people for a trifle,
demanding no high price for them.
13 You have made us the taunt of our
neighbors,
the derision and scorn of those around
us.
14 You have made us a byword among the
nations,
a laughingstock[b] among the peoples.
15 All day long my disgrace is before me,
and shame has covered my face
16 at the words of the taunters and revilers,
at the sight of the enemy and the
avenger.

17 All this has come upon us,
yet we have not forgotten you,
or been false to your covenant.
18 Our heart has not turned back,
nor have our steps departed from your
way,
19 yet you have broken us in the haunt of
jackals,
and covered us with deep darkness.

20 If we had forgotten the name of our God,
or spread out our hands to a strange
god,
21 would not God discover this?
For he knows the secrets of the heart.
22 Because of you we are being killed all day
long,
and accounted as sheep for the
slaughter.

44.22 No Happy Ending

This psalm, while beginning with distant memories of what God did in the past, ends with a poignant plea for help. Prayers and faith in God have not produced any results. Is God asleep?

Yet God works in bigger patterns than we can see. The apostle Paul, considering the place of suffering in a Christian's life, quoted this verse to remind his readers that suffering was nothing new for believers (Romans 8.36). He asked, "Who will separate us from the love of Christ?" His response: "No one! Nothing!" He would have loved to go back in time and tell the suffering psalmist about all the good things in store for God's people.

23 Rouse yourself! Why do you sleep,
O Lord?
Awake, do not cast us off forever!
24 Why do you hide your face?
Why do you forget our affliction and
oppression?
25 For we sink down to the dust;
our bodies cling to the ground.
26 Rise up, come to our help.
Redeem us for the sake of your
steadfast love.

Psalm 45

Ode for a Royal Wedding

To the leader: according to Lilies.
Of the Korahites. A Maskil. A love song.

1 My heart overflows with a goodly theme;
I address my verses to the king;
my tongue is like the pen of a ready
scribe.

2 You are the most handsome of men;
grace is poured upon your lips;
therefore God has blessed you forever.
3 Gird your sword on your thigh, O mighty
one,
in your glory and majesty.

---

[a] Gk Syr: Heb *You are my King, O God; command*   [b] Heb *a shaking of the head*

4 In your majesty ride on victoriously
    for the cause of truth and to defend[c]
      the right;
    let your right hand teach you dread
      deeds.
5 Your arrows are sharp
    in the heart of the king's enemies;
    the peoples fall under you.

6 Your throne, O God,[d] endures forever
    and ever.
    Your royal scepter is a scepter of
      equity;
7 you love righteousness and hate
    wickedness.
    Therefore God, your God, has anointed
      you
    with the oil of gladness beyond your
      companions;

8 your robes are all fragrant with myrrh
    and aloes and cassia.
    From ivory palaces stringed instruments
      make you glad;
9   daughters of kings are among your
      ladies of honor;
    at your right hand stands the queen in
      gold of Ophir.

10 Hear, O daughter, consider and incline
    your ear;
    forget your people and your father's
      house,
11   and the king will desire your beauty.
    Since he is your lord, bow to him;
12   the people[e] of Tyre will seek your
      favor with gifts,
    the richest of the people 13with all
      kinds of wealth.

[c] Cn: Heb *and the meekness of*   [d] Or *Your throne is a throne of God, it*   [e] Heb *daughter*

A Wedding Fit for a King

Why should this poem be found in a book of prayers?

> Your throne, O God,
> endures forever and
> ever. 45.6

IN THE MIDDLE OF A book of heartfelt prayers, a wedding poem suddenly appears. Does Psalm 45 belong here? Its "goodly theme" (verse 1) is not God's kindness, but the excellence of his majesty the king as he prepares to take a bride. While most of the psalms express an intimacy with God that could have been written yesterday, thrones, scepters, and royal robes make us think of an old Hollywood epic.

To understand why this psalm was included we need to know, first, that the king in biblical times was more than just a symbol. He was the president and the commanding general and the chief justice of the Supreme Court, all rolled into one. An unjust or cowardly king could cost his people their lives. A clever, successful king, on the other hand, could assure them of prosperity.

When the Israelites wished the king well, therefore, they wished themselves well. Seeing their king decked out in finery was like looking at a picture of their own success. And when their king made a happy and fruitful marriage, it assured them of stable leadership for years to come. The king's welfare represented the welfare of God's people.

The Promise to David

David was the first good king Israel had known. God had told David that his "house" would endure forever (2 Samuel 7.16). This meant that Israel would endure, too. When David's people combined this promise with the other benefits God had promised to Abraham and Moses, they could foresee a great future for their small, poor, war-weary nation.

Yet David's descendants disappointed these hopes. Israel remained a small, hemmed-in nation. Gradually, Israelites began to expect another king who would live up to the Bible's praises and promises. They called him "the anointed" (for kings and priests took office through an official anointing with oil, like our swearing in). When they read psalms that mentioned the king, they thought of this coming ruler.

As the years went by and Israel's kings failed miserably, Israel's longing grew stronger and stronger. People looked for "the consolation of Israel" (Luke 2.25). The word for "the anointed" became *Messiah*, or (in Greek) *Christ*.

Only when "the anointed" came—in Jesus—did the extravagant language of Psalm 45.6–7 (along with unusual descriptions in Psalms 2 and 110) make sense. These verses were quoted in Hebrews 1.8–9 to show that the king the Jews had long expected could be no ordinary man. The king turned out to *be* God—as verse 6 had suggested. The poem that seemed to be only about a king's marriage turned out, in the end, to be about God's marriage to humanity.

The princess is decked in her chamber
    with gold-woven robes;*f*

14 in many-colored robes she is led to the
    king;
    behind her the virgins, her
        companions, follow.

15 With joy and gladness they are led along
    as they enter the palace of the king.

16 In the place of ancestors you, O king,*g*
    shall have sons;
    you will make them princes in all the
        earth.

17 I will cause your name to be celebrated in
    all generations;
    therefore the peoples will praise you
        forever and ever.

Psalm 46

God's Defense of His City and People

To the leader. Of the Korahites.
According to Alamoth. A Song.

1 God is our refuge and strength,
    a very present*h* help in trouble.

2 Therefore we will not fear, though the
        earth should change,
    though the mountains shake in the
        heart of the sea;

3 though its waters roar and foam,
    though the mountains tremble with its
        tumult.   *Selah*

4 There is a river whose streams make glad
    the city of God,
    the holy habitation of the Most High.

5 God is in the midst of the city;*i* it shall
    not be moved;
    God will help it when the morning
        dawns.

6 The nations are in an uproar, the
        kingdoms totter;
    he utters his voice, the earth melts.

7 The LORD of hosts is with us;
    the God of Jacob is our refuge.*j*   *Selah*

8 Come, behold the works of the LORD;
    see what desolations he has brought on
        the earth.

9 He makes wars cease to the end of the
        earth;
    he breaks the bow, and shatters the
        spear;
    he burns the shields with fire.

10 "Be still, and know that I am God!
    I am exalted among the nations,
    I am exalted in the earth."

11 The LORD of hosts is with us;
    the God of Jacob is our refuge.*j*   *Selah*

Psalm 47

God's Rule over the Nations

To the leader. Of the Korahites. A Psalm.

1 Clap your hands, all you peoples;
    shout to God with loud songs of joy.

2 For the LORD, the Most High, is awesome,
    a great king over all the earth.

3 He subdued peoples under us,
    and nations under our feet.

4 He chose our heritage for us,
    the pride of Jacob whom he loves.   *Selah*

5 God has gone up with a shout,
    the LORD with the sound of a trumpet.

6 Sing praises to God, sing praises;
    sing praises to our King, sing praises.

7 For God is the king of all the earth;
    sing praises with a psalm.*k*

47.7–9 Who Are God's People?

While the Israelites often thought of themselves as exclusively God's people, Psalms contains frequent references to a day when "the peoples"—that is, all ethnic groups—will exultantly praise God. In this psalm they not only join in, they do so as "the people of the God of Abraham"—that is, as insiders included in God's covenant with the Israelites.

8 God is king over the nations;
    God sits on his holy throne.

9 The princes of the peoples gather
    as the people of the God of Abraham.
For the shields of the earth belong to
        God;
    he is highly exalted.

Psalm 48

The Glory and Strength of Zion

A Song. A Psalm of the Korahites.

1 Great is the LORD and greatly to be
    praised
    in the city of our God.
His holy mountain, 2beautiful in elevation,
    is the joy of all the earth,
Mount Zion, in the far north,
    the city of the great King.

---

f Or *people.* *13All glorious is the princess within, gold embroidery is her clothing*   *g* Heb lacks *O king*   *h* Or *well proved*
i Heb *of it*   *j* Or *fortress*   *k* Heb *Maskil*

3 Within its citadels God
has shown himself a sure defense.

4 Then the kings assembled,
they came on together.
5 As soon as they saw it, they were
astounded;
they were in panic, they took to flight;
6 trembling took hold of them there,
pains as of a woman in labor,
7 as when an east wind shatters
the ships of Tarshish.
8 As we have heard, so have we seen
in the city of the LORD of hosts,
in the city of our God,
which God establishes forever.   *Selah*

9 We ponder your steadfast love, O God,
in the midst of your temple.
10 Your name, O God, like your praise,
reaches to the ends of the earth.
Your right hand is filled with victory.
11 Let Mount Zion be glad,
let the towns*l* of Judah rejoice
because of your judgments.

12 Walk about Zion, go all around it,
count its towers,
13 consider well its ramparts;
go through its citadels,
that you may tell the next generation
14 that this is God,
our God forever and ever.
He will be our guide forever.

Psalm 49

The Folly of Trust in Riches

To the leader. Of the Korahites. A Psalm.

1 Hear this, all you peoples;
give ear, all inhabitants of the world,
2 both low and high,
rich and poor together.
3 My mouth shall speak wisdom;
the meditation of my heart shall be
understanding.
4 I will incline my ear to a proverb;
I will solve my riddle to the music of
the harp.

5 Why should I fear in times of trouble,
when the iniquity of my persecutors
surrounds me,
6 those who trust in their wealth
and boast of the abundance of their
riches?

7 Truly, no ransom avails for one's life,*m*
there is no price one can give to God
for it.
8 For the ransom of life is costly,
and can never suffice,

49.5–20 Money Can't Buy Life

How do you make sense of a world in which bad people get rich and actually oppress good people? This psalm ponders this riddle and finds the answer on the other side of death. Money can do many things, but it simply cannot buy an escape from the grave. "No ransom avails for one's life . . . the ransom can never suffice that one should live on forever" (verses 7–9). But "God will ransom my soul from the power of Sheol," says verse 15; "he will receive me."

9 that one should live on forever
and never see the grave.*n*

10 When we look at the wise, they die;
fool and dolt perish together
and leave their wealth to others.
11 Their graves*o* are their homes forever,
their dwelling places to all generations,
though they named lands their own.
12 Mortals cannot abide in their pomp;
they are like the animals that perish.

13 Such is the fate of the foolhardy,
the end of those*p* who are pleased with
their lot.   *Selah*
14 Like sheep they are appointed for Sheol;
Death shall be their shepherd;
straight to the grave they descend,*q*
and their form shall waste away;
Sheol shall be their home.*r*
15 But God will ransom my soul from the
power of Sheol,
for he will receive me.   *Selah*

16 Do not be afraid when some become rich,
when the wealth of their houses
increases.
17 For when they die they will carry nothing
away;
their wealth will not go down after
them.
18 Though in their lifetime they count
themselves happy
—for you are praised when you do
well for yourself—

---

l Heb *daughters*   *m* Another reading is *no one can ransom a brother*   *n* Heb *the pit*   *o* Gk Syr Compare Tg: Heb
their inward (thought)   *p* Tg: Heb *after them*   *q* Cn: Heb *the upright shall have dominion over them in the morning*
r Meaning of Heb uncertain

19 they[s] will go to the company of their
    ancestors,
  who will never again see the light.
20 Mortals cannot abide in their pomp;
  they are like the animals that perish.

Psalm 50

The Acceptable Sacrifice

A Psalm of Asaph.

1 The mighty one, God the LORD,
  speaks and summons the earth
  from the rising of the sun to its setting.
2 Out of Zion, the perfection of beauty,
  God shines forth.

3 Our God comes and does not keep
    silence,
  before him is a devouring fire,
  and a mighty tempest all around him.
4 He calls to the heavens above
  and to the earth, that he may judge his
    people:
5 "Gather to me my faithful ones,
  who made a covenant with me by
    sacrifice!"
6 The heavens declare his righteousness,
  for God himself is judge.   Selah

7 "Hear, O my people, and I will speak,
  O Israel, I will testify against you.
  I am God, your God.
8 Not for your sacrifices do I rebuke you;
  your burnt offerings are continually
    before me.
9 I will not accept a bull from your house,
  or goats from your folds.
10 For every wild animal of the forest is
    mine,
  the cattle on a thousand hills.

11 I know all the birds of the air,[t]
  and all that moves in the field is mine.

12 "If I were hungry, I would not tell you,
  for the world and all that is in it is
    mine.
13 Do I eat the flesh of bulls,
  or drink the blood of goats?
14 Offer to God a sacrifice of thanksgiving,[u]
  and pay your vows to the Most High.
15 Call on me in the day of trouble;
  I will deliver you, and you shall glorify
    me."

16 But to the wicked God says:
  "What right have you to recite my
    statutes,
  or take my covenant on your lips?
17 For you hate discipline,
  and you cast my words behind you.
18 You make friends with a thief when you
    see one,
  and you keep company with adulterers.

19 "You give your mouth free rein for evil,
  and your tongue frames deceit.
20 You sit and speak against your kin;
  you slander your own mother's child.
21 These things you have done and I have
    been silent;
  you thought that I was one just like
    yourself.
But now I rebuke you, and lay the charge
    before you.

22 "Mark this, then, you who forget God,
  or I will tear you apart, and there will
    be no one to deliver.
23 Those who bring thanksgiving as their
    sacrifice honor me;
  to those who go the right way[v]
  I will show the salvation of God."

Psalm 51

Prayer for Cleansing and Pardon

To the leader. A Psalm of David, when the
prophet Nathan came to him, after he had gone
in to Bathsheba.

1 Have mercy on me, O God,
  according to your steadfast love;
according to your abundant mercy
  blot out my transgressions.
2 Wash me thoroughly from my iniquity,
  and cleanse me from my sin.

3 For I know my transgressions,
  and my sin is ever before me.

50.9–12 Does God Need Our Gifts?

People often try to bargain with God, thinking that by their good deeds they can get God to do what they want. Old Testament people sometimes viewed their animal sacrifices this way: not as an act of commitment and fellowship with God, but as a way to manipulate God into putting his stamp of approval on their plans. These majestic words from God scorn such a view. He is rich beyond their dreams; he has no need of their offerings. What matters to him is the attitude they take toward him.

---

[s] Cn: Heb *you*   [t] Gk Syr Tg: Heb *mountains*   [u] Or *make thanksgiving your sacrifice to God*   [v] Heb *who set a way*

4 Against you, you alone, have I sinned,
    and done what is evil in your sight,
  so that you are justified in your sentence
    and blameless when you pass
      judgment.
5 Indeed, I was born guilty,
    a sinner when my mother conceived
      me.

6 You desire truth in the inward being;[w]
    therefore teach me wisdom in my
      secret heart.
7 Purge me with hyssop, and I shall be
      clean;
    wash me, and I shall be whiter than
      snow.
8 Let me hear joy and gladness;
    let the bones that you have crushed
      rejoice.
9 Hide your face from my sins,
    and blot out all my iniquities.

10 Create in me a clean heart, O God,
    and put a new and right[x] spirit within
      me.

11 Do not cast me away from your presence,
    and do not take your holy spirit from
      me.
12 Restore to me the joy of your salvation,
    and sustain in me a willing[y] spirit.

13 Then I will teach transgressors your ways,
    and sinners will return to you.
14 Deliver me from bloodshed, O God,
    O God of my salvation,
    and my tongue will sing aloud of your
      deliverance.
15 O Lord, open my lips,
    and my mouth will declare your praise.
16 For you have no delight in sacrifice;
    if I were to give a burnt offering, you
      would not be pleased.
17 The sacrifice acceptable to God[z] is a
      broken spirit;
    a broken and contrite heart, O God,
      you will not despise.

18 Do good to Zion in your good pleasure;
    rebuild the walls of Jerusalem,

w Meaning of Heb uncertain   x Or steadfast   y Or generous   z Or My sacrifice, O God,

David Caught in the Act
Israel had a strange way to remember its heroes

DAVID FOUND A PLACE IN the hearts of Israelites something like the one Abraham Lincoln found in the hearts of Americans. Both men led their nations through dark hours with courage, wisdom, and deep faith.

Against you, you alone, have I sinned, and done what is evil in your sight. 51.4

But there are essential differences in the way they are remembered. Suppose, for example, that Abraham Lincoln had been caught in the act of adultery. Would his private outpouring of grief before God have been included in America's July 4th celebration? Hardly: America tends to cover up the faults of its heroes, and even invent stories about their spotless honesty.

Yet, for David, no cover-up was attempted. Just the opposite: Psalm 51 publishes David's anguished reaction when he was caught in sin. The story behind the psalm is told in 2 Samuel 11 and 12—a sordid tale of adultery, intrigue, and murder. David, the greatest king in Israel's history, acted like the worst.

David apparently thought nothing of his crime until the prophet Nathan accused him to his face. Then, in tears, David confessed—and this poem was one result. It was recorded (along with the story of David's deeds) in the holy scriptures. It may well have been used in worship services, as a guide for others' confession.

David's Greatest Legacy

All nations have heroes. Israel may have been alone in making heroic literature about its heroes' failings. In confessing his failures openly, David was certainly unique among all leaders of his day. He knew his place before God, and this humility made him an example for his people.

Ultimately Israel remembered David more for his devotion to God than for his military achievements. In centuries to come, Israel looked for a "son of David" to come and save them. They wanted a truly strong leader—one humble enough to know that God must lead the leaders.

Life Questions: When you fail, what is your response—to cover up your failure, or to publicize your confession?

19 then you will delight in right sacrifices,
  in burnt offerings and whole burnt
    offerings;
  then bulls will be offered on your altar.

Psalm 52

Judgment on the Deceitful

> To the leader. A Maskil of David, when Doeg
> the Edomite came to Saul and said to him,
> "David has come to the house of Ahimelech."

1 Why do you boast, O mighty one,
  of mischief done against the godly?[a]
  All day long 2you are plotting
    destruction.
  Your tongue is like a sharp razor,
  you worker of treachery.
3 You love evil more than good,
  and lying more than speaking the
    truth.   *Selah*
4 You love all words that devour,
  O deceitful tongue.

5 But God will break you down forever;
  he will snatch and tear you from your
    tent;
  he will uproot you from the land of the
    living.   *Selah*
6 The righteous will see, and fear,
  and will laugh at the evildoer,[b] saying,
7 "See the one who would not take
    refuge in God,
  but trusted in abundant riches,
  and sought refuge in wealth!"[c]

8 But I am like a green olive tree
  in the house of God.
  I trust in the steadfast love of God
  forever and ever.
9 I will thank you forever,
  because of what you have done.
  In the presence of the faithful
  I will proclaim[d] your name, for it is
    good.

Psalm 53

Denunciation of Godlessness

> To the leader: according to Mahalath. A Maskil
> of David.

1 Fools say in their hearts, "There is no
    God."
  They are corrupt, they commit
    abominable acts;
  there is no one who does good.

2 God looks down from heaven on
    humankind
  to see if there are any who are wise,
  who seek after God.

3 They have all fallen away, they are all
    alike perverse;
  there is no one who does good,
  no, not one.

53.3 Sound Familiar?

*Psalm 53 is nearly identical to Psalm 14.
Scholars think the book of Psalms bundled
together several different collections of hymns;
this duplication is one reason they believe so.*

---

4 Have they no knowledge, those evildoers,
  who eat up my people as they eat
    bread,
  and do not call upon God?

5 There they shall be in great terror,
  in terror such as has not been.
  For God will scatter the bones of the
    ungodly;[e]
  they will be put to shame,[f] for God
    has rejected them.

6 O that deliverance for Israel would come
    from Zion!
  When God restores the fortunes of his
    people,
  Jacob will rejoice; Israel will be glad.

Psalm 54

Prayer for Vindication

> To the leader: with stringed instruments.
> A Maskil of David, when the Ziphites went and
> told Saul, "David is in hiding among us."

1 Save me, O God, by your name,
  and vindicate me by your might.
2 Hear my prayer, O God;
  give ear to the words of my mouth.

3 For the insolent have risen against me,
  the ruthless seek my life;
  they do not set God before them. *Selah*

4 But surely, God is my helper;
  the Lord is the upholder of[g] my life.
5 He will repay my enemies for their evil.
  In your faithfulness, put an end to
    them.

---

a Cn Compare Syr: Heb *the kindness of God*   b Heb *him*   c Syr Tg: Heb *in his destruction*   d Cn: Heb *wait for*
e Cn Compare Gk Syr: Heb *him who encamps against you*   f Gk: Heb *you have put (them) to shame*   g Gk Syr
Jerome: Heb *is of those who uphold* or *is with those who uphold*

6 With a freewill offering I will sacrifice to
    you;
  I will give thanks to your name,
    O LORD, for it is good.
7 For he has delivered me from every
    trouble,
  and my eye has looked in triumph on
    my enemies.

Psalm 55

Complaint about a Friend's Treachery

*To the leader: with stringed instruments.
A Maskil of David.*

1 Give ear to my prayer, O God;
  do not hide yourself from my
    supplication.
2 Attend to me, and answer me;
  I am troubled in my complaint.
I am distraught ³by the noise of the
    enemy,
  because of the clamor of the wicked.
For they bring[h] trouble upon me,
  and in anger they cherish enmity
    against me.

4 My heart is in anguish within me,
  the terrors of death have fallen upon
    me.
5 Fear and trembling come upon me,
  and horror overwhelms me.
6 And I say, "O that I had wings like a
    dove!
  I would fly away and be at rest;
7 truly, I would flee far away;
  I would lodge in the wilderness;   *Selah*
8 I would hurry to find a shelter for myself
  from the raging wind and tempest."

9 Confuse, O Lord, confound their speech;
  for I see violence and strife in the city.
10 Day and night they go around it
  on its walls,
and iniquity and trouble are within it;
11   ruin is in its midst;
oppression and fraud
  do not depart from its marketplace.

12 It is not enemies who taunt me—
  I could bear that;
it is not adversaries who deal insolently
    with me—
  I could hide from them.
13 But it is you, my equal,
  my companion, my familiar friend,
14 with whom I kept pleasant company;
  we walked in the house of God with
    the throng.

15 Let death come upon them;
  let them go down alive to Sheol;
  for evil is in their homes and in their
    hearts.

55.14 Betrayed by a Friend

It is hard enough to deal with enemies, but far harder to face the fact of betrayal by a close friend. Feeling that he can no longer trust anyone, the psalmist turns to God for help. God, he knows, will never betray him.

16 But I call upon God,
  and the LORD will save me.
17 Evening and morning and at noon
  I utter my complaint and moan,
  and he will hear my voice.
18 He will redeem me unharmed
  from the battle that I wage,
  for many are arrayed against me.
19 God, who is enthroned from of old,   *Selah*
  will hear, and will humble them—
because they do not change,
  and do not fear God.

20 My companion laid hands on a friend
  and violated a covenant with me[i]
21 with speech smoother than butter,
  but with a heart set on war;
with words that were softer than oil,
  but in fact were drawn swords.

22 Cast your burden[j] on the LORD,
  and he will sustain you;
he will never permit
  the righteous to be moved.

23 But you, O God, will cast them down
  into the lowest pit;
the bloodthirsty and treacherous
  shall not live out half their days.
But I will trust in you.

Psalm 56

Trust in God under Persecution

*To the leader: according to The Dove
on Far-off Terebinths. Of David. A Miktam,
when the Philistines seized him in Gath.*

1 Be gracious to me, O God, for people
    trample on me;
  all day long foes oppress me;
2 my enemies trample on me all day long,
  for many fight against me.
O Most High, ³when I am afraid,
  I put my trust in you.

---

[h] Cn Compare Gk: Heb *they cause to totter*   [i] Heb lacks *with me*   [j] Or *Cast what he has given you*

4 In God, whose word I praise,
     in God I trust; I am not afraid;
     what can flesh do to me?

5 All day long they seek to injure my cause;
     all their thoughts are against me for
          evil.
6 They stir up strife, they lurk,
     they watch my steps.
   As they hoped to have my life,
7   so repay[k] them for their crime;
     in wrath cast down the peoples,
          O God!

8 You have kept count of my tossings;
     put my tears in your bottle.
   Are they not in your record?
9 Then my enemies will retreat
     in the day when I call.
   This I know, that[l] God is for me.
10 In God, whose word I praise,
     in the LORD, whose word I praise,
11 in God I trust; I am not afraid.
   What can a mere mortal do to me?

12 My vows to you I must perform, O God;
     I will render thank offerings to you.
13 For you have delivered my soul from
          death,
     and my feet from falling,
   so that I may walk before God
     in the light of life.

Psalm 57

Praise and Assurance under Persecution

To the leader: Do Not Destroy. Of David.
A Miktam, when he fled from Saul, in the cave.

1 Be merciful to me, O God, be merciful to
          me,
     for in you my soul takes refuge;
   in the shadow of your wings I will take
          refuge,
     until the destroying storms pass by.
2 I cry to God Most High,
     to God who fulfills his purpose for me.
3 He will send from heaven and save me,
     he will put to shame those who
          trample on me.   Selah
   God will send forth his steadfast love and
     his faithfulness.

4 I lie down among lions
     that greedily devour[m] human prey;
   their teeth are spears and arrows,
     their tongues sharp swords.

5 Be exalted, O God, above the heavens.
     Let your glory be over all the earth.

6 They set a net for my steps;
     my soul was bowed down.
   They dug a pit in my path,
     but they have fallen into it themselves.
                                        Selah
7 My heart is steadfast, O God,
     my heart is steadfast.
   I will sing and make melody.
8   Awake, my soul!
   Awake, O harp and lyre!
     I will awake the dawn.
9 I will give thanks to you, O Lord, among
          the peoples;
     I will sing praises to you among the
          nations.
10 For your steadfast love is as high as the
          heavens;
     your faithfulness extends to the clouds.

11 Be exalted, O God, above the heavens.
     Let your glory be over all the earth.

Psalm 58

Prayer for Vengeance

To the leader: Do Not Destroy. Of David.
A Miktam.

1 Do you indeed decree what is right, you
          gods?[n]
     Do you judge people fairly?
2 No, in your hearts you devise wrongs;
     your hands deal out violence on earth.

3 The wicked go astray from the womb;
     they err from their birth, speaking lies.
4 They have venom like the venom of a
          serpent,
     like the deaf adder that stops its ear,
5 so that it does not hear the voice of
          charmers
     or of the cunning enchanter.

6 O God, break the teeth in their mouths;
     tear out the fangs of the young lions,
          O LORD!
7 Let them vanish like water that runs away;
     like grass let them be trodden down[o]
          and wither.
8 Let them be like the snail that dissolves
          into slime;
     like the untimely birth that never sees
          the sun.
9 Sooner than your pots can feel the heat of
          thorns,

k Cn: Heb *rescue*   l Or *because*   m Cn: Heb *are aflame for*
uncertain   n Or *mighty lords*   o Cn: Meaning of Heb

whether green or ablaze, may he sweep
them away!

10 The righteous will rejoice when they see
vengeance done;

58.8 Rough Words

The psalmist's white-hot anger is never more obvious than in these ardent words asking God to punish wicked people. His demand for retribution is a far cry from Jesus' command to love your enemies; no Christian should make this a model of prayer. We ought to remember, though, that the psalmist is asking God for justice—not planning how he will bring it about himself. For more on this subject, see "What about Curses?" page 642.

they will bathe their feet in the blood
of the wicked.
11 People will say, "Surely there is a reward
for the righteous;
surely there is a God who judges on
earth."

Psalm 59

Prayer for Deliverance from Enemies

To the leader: Do Not Destroy. Of David.
A Miktam, when Saul ordered his house to be
watched in order to kill him.

1 Deliver me from my enemies, O my God;
protect me from those who rise up
against me.
2 Deliver me from those who work evil;
from the bloodthirsty save me.

3 Even now they lie in wait for my life;
the mighty stir up strife against me.
For no transgression or sin of mine,
O LORD,
4 for no fault of mine, they run and
make ready.

Rouse yourself, come to my help and see!
5 You, LORD God of hosts, are God of
Israel.
Awake to punish all the nations;
spare none of those who treacherously
plot evil. *Selah*

6 Each evening they come back,
howling like dogs
and prowling about the city.
7 There they are, bellowing with their
mouths,

with sharp words[p] on their lips—
for "Who," they think,[q] "will hear us?"

8 But you laugh at them, O LORD;
you hold all the nations in derision.
9 O my strength, I will watch for you;
for you, O God, are my fortress.
10 My God in his steadfast love will meet
me;
my God will let me look in triumph on
my enemies.

11 Do not kill them, or my people may
forget;
make them totter by your power, and
bring them down,
O Lord, our shield.
12 For the sin of their mouths, the words of
their lips,
let them be trapped in their pride.
For the cursing and lies that they utter,
13 consume them in wrath;
consume them until they are no more.
Then it will be known to the ends of the
earth
that God rules over Jacob. *Selah*

14 Each evening they come back,
howling like dogs
and prowling about the city.
15 They roam about for food,
and growl if they do not get their fill.

16 But I will sing of your might;
I will sing aloud of your steadfast love
in the morning.
For you have been a fortress for me
and a refuge in the day of my distress.
17 O my strength, I will sing praises to you,
for you, O God, are my fortress,
the God who shows me steadfast love.

Psalm 60

Prayer for National Victory after Defeat

To the leader: according to the Lily
of the Covenant. A Miktam of David;
for instruction; when he struggled
with Aram-naharaim and with Aram-zobah,
and when Joab on his return killed twelve
thousand Edomites in the Valley of Salt.

1 O God, you have rejected us, broken our
defenses;
you have been angry; now restore us!
2 You have caused the land to quake; you
have torn it open;
repair the cracks in it, for it is
tottering.

p Heb *with swords*   q Heb lacks *they think*

3 You have made your people suffer hard
  things;
    you have given us wine to drink that
    made us reel.
4 You have set up a banner for those who
  fear you,
    to rally to it out of bowshot.[r]   *Selah*
5 Give victory with your right hand, and
  answer us,[s]
    so that those whom you love may be
    rescued.

6 God has promised in his sanctuary:[t]
  "With exultation I will divide up
  Shechem,
    and portion out the Vale of Succoth.
7 Gilead is mine, and Manasseh is mine;
    Ephraim is my helmet;
    Judah is my scepter;
8 Moab is my washbasin;
    on Edom I hurl my shoe;
    over Philistia I shout in triumph."

9 Who will bring me to the fortified city?
    Who will lead me to Edom?
10 Have you not rejected us, O God?
    You do not go out, O God, with our
    armies.
11 O grant us help against the foe,
    for human help is worthless.
12 With God we shall do valiantly;
    it is he who will tread down our foes.

Psalm 61

Assurance of God's Protection

To the leader: with stringed instruments.
Of David.

1 Hear my cry, O God;
    listen to my prayer.
2 From the end of the earth I call to you,
    when my heart is faint.

Lead me to the rock
    that is higher than I;
3 for you are my refuge,
    a strong tower against the enemy.

4 Let me abide in your tent forever,
    find refuge under the shelter of your
    wings.   *Selah*
5 For you, O God, have heard my vows;
    you have given me the heritage of
    those who fear your name.

6 Prolong the life of the king;

may his years endure to all
generations!
7 May he be enthroned forever before God;
    appoint steadfast love and faithfulness
    to watch over him!

8 So I will always sing praises to your
  name,
    as I pay my vows day after day.

Psalm 62

Song of Trust in God Alone

To the leader: according to Jeduthun. A Psalm
of David.

1 For God alone my soul waits in silence;
    from him comes my salvation.
2 He alone is my rock and my salvation,
    my fortress; I shall never be shaken.

3 How long will you assail a person,
    will you batter your victim, all of you,
    as you would a leaning wall, a tottering
    fence?
4 Their only plan is to bring down a person
    of prominence.
  They take pleasure in falsehood;
they bless with their mouths,
    but inwardly they curse.   *Selah*

5 For God alone my soul waits in silence,
    for my hope is from him.
6 He alone is my rock and my salvation,
    my fortress; I shall not be shaken.
7 On God rests my deliverance and my
  honor;
    my mighty rock, my refuge is in God.

62.7 The Hideout

*In the years when David was an outlaw from
King Saul, his hideouts included a "rock" in the
desert (1 Samuel 23.25–28), as well as a
"stronghold" (1 Samuel 22.4). As an
experienced fighter, David knew the value of
such defenses. He recognized, however, that he
owed his safety to God, his true rock and
fortress.*

8 Trust in him at all times, O people;
    pour out your heart before him;
    God is a refuge for us.   *Selah*

9 Those of low estate are but a breath,
    those of high estate are a delusion;
in the balances they go up;
    they are together lighter than a breath.

---

[r] Gk Syr Jerome: Heb *because of the truth*   [s] Another reading is *me*   [t] Or *by his holiness*

10 Put no confidence in extortion,
and set no vain hopes on robbery;
if riches increase, do not set your heart
on them.

11 Once God has spoken;
twice have I heard this:
that power belongs to God,
12 and steadfast love belongs to you,
O Lord.
For you repay to all
according to their work.

Psalm 63

Comfort and Assurance in God's Presence

*A Psalm of David, when he was
in the Wilderness of Judah.*

1 O God, you are my God, I seek you,
my soul thirsts for you;
my flesh faints for you,
as in a dry and weary land where there
is no water.
2 So I have looked upon you in the
sanctuary,
beholding your power and glory.
3 Because your steadfast love is better than
life,
my lips will praise you.
4 So I will bless you as long as I live;
I will lift up my hands and call on
your name.

5 My soul is satisfied as with a rich feast,*u*
and my mouth praises you with joyful
lips
6 when I think of you on my bed,
and meditate on you in the watches of
the night;
7 for you have been my help,
and in the shadow of your wings I sing
for joy.
8 My soul clings to you;
your right hand upholds me.

9 But those who seek to destroy my life
shall go down into the depths of the
earth;
10 they shall be given over to the power of
the sword,
they shall be prey for jackals.
11 But the king shall rejoice in God;
all who swear by him shall exult,
for the mouths of liars will be stopped.

Psalm 64

Prayer for Protection from Enemies

To the leader. A Psalm of David.

1 Hear my voice, O God, in my complaint;
preserve my life from the dread enemy.
2 Hide me from the secret plots of the
wicked,
from the scheming of evildoers,
3 who whet their tongues like swords,
who aim bitter words like arrows,
4 shooting from ambush at the blameless;
they shoot suddenly and without fear.
5 They hold fast to their evil purpose;
they talk of laying snares secretly,
thinking, "Who can see us?*v*
6 Who can search out our crimes?*w*
We have thought out a cunningly
conceived plot."
For the human heart and mind are
deep.

7 But God will shoot his arrow at them;
they will be wounded suddenly.
8 Because of their tongue he will bring
them to ruin;*x*
all who see them will shake with
horror.
9 Then everyone will fear;
they will tell what God has brought
about,
and ponder what he has done.

10 Let the righteous rejoice in the LORD
and take refuge in him.
Let all the upright in heart glory.

Psalm 65

Thanksgiving for Earth's Bounty

To the leader. A Psalm of David. A Song.

1 Praise is due to you,
O God, in Zion;
and to you shall vows be performed,
2 O you who answer prayer!
To you all flesh shall come.
3 When deeds of iniquity overwhelm us,
you forgive our transgressions.
4 Happy are those whom you choose and
bring near
to live in your courts.
We shall be satisfied with the goodness of
your house,
your holy temple.

u Heb *with fat and fatness*   *v* Syr: Heb *them*   *w* Cn: Heb *They search out crimes*   *x* Cn: Heb *They will bring him*
to ruin, their tongue being against them

⁵ By awesome deeds you answer us with
    deliverance,
    O God of our salvation;
you are the hope of all the ends of the
    earth
    and of the farthest seas.
⁶ By your*y* strength you established the
    mountains;
    you are girded with might.
⁷ You silence the roaring of the seas,
    the roaring of their waves,
    the tumult of the peoples.
⁸ Those who live at earth's farthest bounds
    are awed by your signs;
you make the gateways of the morning
    and the evening shout for joy.

65.8 God Reaches Out

*God's Old Testament people primarily came
from a specially chosen ethnic group. Some
outsiders joined them in their faith (Ruth, for
instance), but the Israelites didn't issue blanket
invitations. Nevertheless, they recognized that
God's love extended to people over the horizon.
His care for the earth, so beautifully described
here, called for a response everywhere, not just
in Israel.*

⁹ You visit the earth and water it,
    you greatly enrich it;
the river of God is full of water;
    you provide the people with grain,
    for so you have prepared it.
¹⁰ You water its furrows abundantly,
    settling its ridges,
softening it with showers,
    and blessing its growth.
¹¹ You crown the year with your bounty;
    your wagon tracks overflow with
    richness.
¹² The pastures of the wilderness overflow,
    the hills gird themselves with joy,
¹³ the meadows clothe themselves with
    flocks,
    the valleys deck themselves with grain,
they shout and sing together for joy.

Psalm 66

Praise for God's Goodness to Israel

To the leader. A Song. A Psalm.

¹ Make a joyful noise to God, all the earth;
²   sing the glory of his name;
    give to him glorious praise.

³ Say to God, "How awesome are your
    deeds!
    Because of your great power, your
    enemies cringe before you.
⁴ All the earth worships you;
    they sing praises to you,
    sing praises to your name."   *Selah*

⁵ Come and see what God has done:
    he is awesome in his deeds among
    mortals.
⁶ He turned the sea into dry land;
    they passed through the river on foot.
There we rejoiced in him,
⁷   who rules by his might forever,
whose eyes keep watch on the nations—
    let the rebellious not exalt themselves.
           Selah

⁸ Bless our God, O peoples,
    let the sound of his praise be heard,
⁹ who has kept us among the living,
    and has not let our feet slip.
¹⁰ For you, O God, have tested us;
    you have tried us as silver is tried.
¹¹ You brought us into the net;
    you laid burdens on our backs;
¹² you let people ride over our heads;
    we went through fire and through
    water;
yet you have brought us out to a spacious
    place.*z*

¹³ I will come into your house with burnt
    offerings;
    I will pay you my vows,
¹⁴ those that my lips uttered
    and my mouth promised when I was
    in trouble.
¹⁵ I will offer to you burnt offerings of
    fatlings,
    with the smoke of the sacrifice of rams;
I will make an offering of bulls and goats.
           Selah

¹⁶ Come and hear, all you who fear God,
    and I will tell what he has done for me.
¹⁷ I cried aloud to him,
    and he was extolled with my tongue.
¹⁸ If I had cherished iniquity in my heart,
    the Lord would not have listened.
¹⁹ But truly God has listened;
    he has given heed to the words of my
    prayer.
²⁰ Blessed be God,
    because he has not rejected my prayer
    or removed his steadfast love from me.

y Gk Jerome: Heb *his*   *z* Cn Compare Gk Syr Jerome Tg: Heb *to a saturation*

Psalm 67

The Nations Called to Praise God

To the leader: with stringed instruments.
A Psalm. A Song.

1 May God be gracious to us and bless us
  and make his face to shine upon us,
                                        Selah
2 that your way may be known upon earth,
  your saving power among all nations.
3 Let the peoples praise you, O God;
  let all the peoples praise you.

4 Let the nations be glad and sing for joy,
  for you judge the peoples with equity
  and guide the nations upon earth.
                                        Selah

5 Let the peoples praise you, O God;
  let all the peoples praise you.

6 The earth has yielded its increase;
  God, our God, has blessed us.
7 May God continue to bless us;
  let all the ends of the earth revere him.

Psalm 68

Praise and Thanksgiving

To the leader. Of David. A Psalm. A Song.

1 Let God rise up, let his enemies be
    scattered;
  let those who hate him flee before him.
2 As smoke is driven away, so drive them
    away;
  as wax melts before the fire,
  let the wicked perish before God.
3 But let the righteous be joyful;
  let them exult before God;
  let them be jubilant with joy.

4 Sing to God, sing praises to his name;
  lift up a song to him who rides upon
    the clouds[a]—
  his name is the LORD—
  be exultant before him.

5 Father of orphans and protector of
    widows
  is God in his holy habitation.
6 God gives the desolate a home to live in;
  he leads out the prisoners to
    prosperity,
  but the rebellious live in a parched
    land.

7 O God, when you went out before your
    people,

when you marched through the
    wilderness,   *Selah*
8 the earth quaked, the heavens poured
    down rain
  at the presence of God, the God of
    Sinai,
  at the presence of God, the God of
    Israel.
9 Rain in abundance, O God, you showered
    abroad;
  you restored your heritage when it
    languished;
10 your flock found a dwelling in it;
  in your goodness, O God, you
    provided for the needy.

11 The Lord gives the command;
  great is the company of those[b] who
    bore the tidings:
12 "The kings of the armies, they flee,
    they flee!"
  The women at home divide the spoil,
13   though they stay among the
    sheepfolds—
  the wings of a dove covered with silver,
    its pinions with green gold.
14 When the Almighty[c] scattered kings
    there,
  snow fell on Zalmon.

15 O mighty mountain, mountain of Bashan;
  O many-peaked mountain, mountain
    of Bashan!
16 Why do you look with envy,
  O many-peaked mountain,
  at the mount that God desired for his
    abode,
  where the LORD will reside forever?

17 With mighty chariotry, twice ten
    thousand,
  thousands upon thousands,
  the Lord came from Sinai into the holy
    place.[d]
18 You ascended the high mount,
  leading captives in your train
  and receiving gifts from people,
  even from those who rebel against the
    LORD God's abiding there.
19 Blessed be the Lord,
  who daily bears us up;
  God is our salvation.   *Selah*
20 Our God is a God of salvation,
  and to GOD, the Lord, belongs escape
    from death.

21 But God will shatter the heads of his
    enemies,

---

a Or *cast up a highway for him who rides through the deserts*   b Or *company of the women*   c Traditional rendering
of Heb *Shaddai*   d Cn: Heb *The Lord among them Sinai in the holy* (place)

the hairy crown of those who walk in
their guilty ways.
22 The Lord said,
"I will bring them back from Bashan,
I will bring them back from the depths of
the sea,
23 so that you may bathe[e] your feet in
blood,
so that the tongues of your dogs may
have their share from the foe."

24 Your solemn processions are seen,[f]
O God,
the processions of my God, my King,
into the sanctuary—

68.24 The Way They Worshiped

*Many of the psalms were sung in the temple, to
worship God. Exactly how people worshiped,
however, is difficult to know. This verse offers
unmistakable clues to how this psalm was
used—in a procession leading to the temple. It
may have first been sung when David brought
the ark—the sign of God's actual presence—into
Jerusalem (2 Samuel 6; 1 Chronicles 15–16). Or
it may have been used in one of the annual
festivals that drew Israelites from all over to
the capital.*

25 the singers in front, the musicians last,
between them girls playing
tambourines:
26 "Bless God in the great congregation,
the LORD, O you who are of Israel's
fountain!"
27 There is Benjamin, the least of them, in
the lead,
the princes of Judah in a body,
the princes of Zebulun, the princes of
Naphtali.

28 Summon your might, O God;
show your strength, O God, as you
have done for us before.
29 Because of your temple at Jerusalem
kings bear gifts to you.
30 Rebuke the wild animals that live among
the reeds,
the herd of bulls with the calves of the
peoples.
Trample[g] under foot those who lust after
tribute;
scatter the peoples who delight in
war.[h]
31 Let bronze be brought from Egypt;

let Ethiopia[i] hasten to stretch out its
hands to God.
32 Sing to God, O kingdoms of the earth;
sing praises to the Lord,   *Selah*
33 O rider in the heavens, the ancient
heavens;
listen, he sends out his voice, his
mighty voice.
34 Ascribe power to God,
whose majesty is over Israel;
and whose power is in the skies.
35 Awesome is God in his[j] sanctuary,
the God of Israel;
he gives power and strength to his
people.

Blessed be God!

Psalm 69

Prayer for Deliverance from Persecution

To the leader: according to Lilies. Of David.

1 Save me, O God,
for the waters have come up to my
neck.
2 I sink in deep mire,
where there is no foothold;
I have come into deep waters,
and the flood sweeps over me.
3 I am weary with my crying;
my throat is parched.
My eyes grow dim
with waiting for my God.

4 More in number than the hairs of my
head
are those who hate me without cause;
many are those who would destroy me,
my enemies who accuse me falsely.
What I did not steal
must I now restore?
5 O God, you know my folly;
the wrongs I have done are not hidden
from you.

6 Do not let those who hope in you be put
to shame because of me,
O Lord GOD of hosts;
do not let those who seek you be
dishonored because of me,
O God of Israel.
7 It is for your sake that I have borne
reproach,
that shame has covered my face.
8 I have become a stranger to my kindred,
an alien to my mother's children.

---

e Gk Syr Tg: Heb *shatter*   *f* Or *have been seen*   *g* Cn: Heb *Trampling*   *h* Meaning of Heb of verse 30 is uncertain
i Or *Nubia*; Heb *Cush*   *j* Gk: Heb *from your*

9 It is zeal for your house that has
consumed me;
the insults of those who insult you
have fallen on me.

69.9 Foreshadowing Jesus

*Psalm 69 was quoted repeatedly by New
Testament writers, who identify Jesus as the
righteous sufferer. "It is zeal for your house
that has consumed me" was quoted in John
2.17, for instance, when Jesus drove out the
money changers, and Romans 15.3 quoted the
second half of that verse, referring to Jesus'
self-sacrificial attitude.*

*Why did the New Testament writers see
Jesus in this psalm? The psalm was attributed
to David, the great king. Yet it is not David's
greatness and majesty that are described here.
Instead, the psalm is a cry of suffering from a
righteous man, alienated even from his family
because of his zeal for God. It is strange:
Israel's greatest hero is portrayed as a helpless
victim because of his faith in God. Yet Jesus
filled this pattern completely. He did not,
however, follow every part of the psalm:
Instead of the curses this psalm directs toward
enemies, Jesus prayed that God would forgive
the men murdering him.*

10 When I humbled my soul with fasting,[k]
they insulted me for doing so.
11 When I made sackcloth my clothing,
I became a byword to them.
12 I am the subject of gossip for those who
sit in the gate,
and the drunkards make songs about
me.

13 But as for me, my prayer is to you,
O LORD.
At an acceptable time, O God,
in the abundance of your steadfast
love, answer me.
With your faithful help [14]rescue me
from sinking in the mire;
let me be delivered from my enemies
and from the deep waters.
15 Do not let the flood sweep over me,
or the deep swallow me up,
or the Pit close its mouth over me.

16 Answer me, O LORD, for your steadfast
love is good;
according to your abundant mercy,
turn to me.
17 Do not hide your face from your servant,

for I am in distress—make haste to
answer me.
18 Draw near to me, redeem me,
set me free because of my enemies.

19 You know the insults I receive,
and my shame and dishonor;
my foes are all known to you.
20 Insults have broken my heart,
so that I am in despair.
I looked for pity, but there was none;
and for comforters, but I found none.
21 They gave me poison for food,
and for my thirst they gave me vinegar
to drink.

22 Let their table be a trap for them,
a snare for their allies.
23 Let their eyes be darkened so that they
cannot see,
and make their loins tremble
continually.
24 Pour out your indignation upon them,
and let your burning anger overtake
them.
25 May their camp be a desolation;
let no one live in their tents.
26 For they persecute those whom you have
struck down,
and those whom you have wounded,
they attack still more.[l]
27 Add guilt to their guilt;
may they have no acquittal from you.
28 Let them be blotted out of the book of
the living;
let them not be enrolled among the
righteous.
29 But I am lowly and in pain;
let your salvation, O God, protect me.

30 I will praise the name of God with a song;
I will magnify him with thanksgiving.
31 This will please the LORD more than an
ox
or a bull with horns and hoofs.
32 Let the oppressed see it and be glad;
you who seek God, let your hearts
revive.
33 For the LORD hears the needy,
and does not despise his own that are
in bonds.

34 Let heaven and earth praise him,
the seas and everything that moves in
them.
35 For God will save Zion
and rebuild the cities of Judah;

---

k Gk Syr: Heb *I wept, with fasting my soul,* or *I made my soul mourn with fasting*   l Gk Syr: Heb *recount the pain of*

and his servants shall live[m] there and
 possess it;
36 the children of his servants shall inherit
 it,
 and those who love his name shall live
 in it.

Psalm 70

Prayer for Deliverance from Enemies

*To the leader. Of David, for the
memorial offering.*

1 Be pleased, O God, to deliver me.
 O LORD, make haste to help me!
2 Let those be put to shame and confusion
 who seek my life.
 Let those be turned back and brought to
 dishonor
 who desire to hurt me.
3 Let those who say, "Aha, Aha!"
 turn back because of their shame.

4 Let all who seek you
 rejoice and be glad in you.
 Let those who love your salvation
 say evermore, "God is great!"
5 But I am poor and needy;
 hasten to me, O God!
 You are my help and my deliverer;
 O LORD, do not delay!

Psalm 71

Prayer for Lifelong Protection and Help

1 In you, O LORD, I take refuge;
 let me never be put to shame.
2 In your righteousness deliver me and
 rescue me;
 incline your ear to me and save me.
3 Be to me a rock of refuge,
 a strong fortress,[n] to save me,
 for you are my rock and my fortress.

4 Rescue me, O my God, from the hand of
 the wicked,
 from the grasp of the unjust and cruel.
5 For you, O Lord, are my hope,
 my trust, O LORD, from my youth.
6 Upon you I have leaned from my birth;
 it was you who took me from my
 mother's womb.
 My praise is continually of you.

7 I have been like a portent to many,
 but you are my strong refuge.
8 My mouth is filled with your praise,
 and with your glory all day long.

9 Do not cast me off in the time of old age;
 do not forsake me when my strength is
 spent.
10 For my enemies speak concerning me,
 and those who watch for my life
 consult together.
11 They say, "Pursue and seize that person
 whom God has forsaken,
 for there is no one to deliver."

12 O God, do not be far from me;
 O my God, make haste to help me!
13 Let my accusers be put to shame and
 consumed;
 let those who seek to hurt me
 be covered with scorn and disgrace.
14 But I will hope continually,
 and will praise you yet more and more.
15 My mouth will tell of your righteous acts,
 of your deeds of salvation all day long,
 though their number is past my
 knowledge.
16 I will come praising the mighty deeds of
 the Lord GOD,
 I will praise your righteousness, yours
 alone.

17 O God, from my youth you have taught
 me,
 and I still proclaim your wondrous
 deeds.
18 So even to old age and gray hairs,
 O God, do not forsake me,
until I proclaim your might
 to all the generations to come.[o]

71.18 A View from Old Age

*Older people have a peculiar privilege: the
chance to see God's faithfulness over a lifetime.
Their troubles do not grow smaller as the years
go by (see verses 9–11), but their experiences
can strengthen confidence that God will deliver
as he always has (verses 20–21).*

Your power [19]and your righteousness,
 O God,
 reach the high heavens.

You who have done great things,
 O God, who is like you?
20 You who have made me see many
 troubles and calamities
 will revive me again;
from the depths of the earth
 you will bring me up again.

---

[m] Syr: Heb *and they shall live*   [n] Gk Compare 31.3: Heb *to come continually you have commanded*   [o] Gk Compare
Syr: Heb *to a generation, to all that come*

21 You will increase my honor,
  and comfort me once again.

22 I will also praise you with the harp
  for your faithfulness, O my God;
  I will sing praises to you with the lyre,
  O Holy One of Israel.
23 My lips will shout for joy
  when I sing praises to you;
  my soul also, which you have rescued.
24 All day long my tongue will talk of your
  righteous help,
  for those who tried to do me harm
  have been put to shame, and disgraced.

Psalm 72

Prayer for Guidance and Support for the King

Of Solomon.

1 Give the king your justice, O God,
  and your righteousness to a king's son.
2 May he judge your people with
  righteousness,
  and your poor with justice.
3 May the mountains yield prosperity for
  the people,
  and the hills, in righteousness.
4 May he defend the cause of the poor of
  the people,
  give deliverance to the needy,
  and crush the oppressor.

5 May he live*p* while the sun endures,
  and as long as the moon, throughout
  all generations.
6 May he be like rain that falls on the
  mown grass,
  like showers that water the earth.
7 In his days may righteousness flourish
  and peace abound, until the moon is
  no more.

8 May he have dominion from sea to sea,
  and from the River to the ends of the
  earth.
9 May his foes*q* bow down before him,
  and his enemies lick the dust.
10 May the kings of Tarshish and of the isles
  render him tribute,
  may the kings of Sheba and Seba
  bring gifts.
11 May all kings fall down before him,
  all nations give him service.

12 For he delivers the needy when they call,
  the poor and those who have no
  helper.
13 He has pity on the weak and the needy,
  and saves the lives of the needy.
14 From oppression and violence he redeems
  their life;
  and precious is their blood in his sight.

15 Long may he live!
  May gold of Sheba be given to him.
  May prayer be made for him continually,
  and blessings invoked for him all day
  long.
16 May there be abundance of grain in the
  land;
  may it wave on the tops of the
  mountains;
  may its fruit be like Lebanon;
  and may people blossom in the cities
  like the grass of the field.
17 May his name endure forever,
  his fame continue as long as the sun.
  May all nations be blessed in him;*r*
  may they pronounce him happy.

18 Blessed be the LORD, the God of Israel,
  who alone does wondrous things.
19 Blessed be his glorious name forever;
  may his glory fill the whole earth.
  Amen and Amen.

20 The prayers of David son of Jesse are
  ended.

BOOK III

(Psalms 73–89)

Psalm 73

Plea for Relief from Oppressors

A Psalm of Asaph.

1 Truly God is good to the upright,*s*
  to those who are pure in heart.
2 But as for me, my feet had almost
  stumbled;
  my steps had nearly slipped.
3 For I was envious of the arrogant;
  I saw the prosperity of the wicked.

4 For they have no pain;
  their bodies are sound and sleek.
5 They are not in trouble as others are;
  they are not plagued like other people.
6 Therefore pride is their necklace;
  violence covers them like a garment.
7 Their eyes swell out with fatness;
  their hearts overflow with follies.

p Gk: Heb *may they fear you*   *q* Cn: Heb *those who live in the wilderness*   *r* Or *bless themselves by him*
s Or *good to Israel*

8 They scoff and speak with malice;
    loftily they threaten oppression.
9 They set their mouths against heaven,
    and their tongues range over the earth.

73.1 The Five Books

Psalms was probably made into one big book from five separate collections. These are set off in our Bible as Book I, Book II, and so on, each book ending with a concluding line of praise. The contents sometimes overlap: Psalm 14 in Book I turns up again as Psalm 53 in Book II. Part of Psalm 40 (Book I) becomes Psalm 70 (Book II), and parts of Psalms 57 and 60 make up Psalm 108 (Book IV). Other less noticeable differences stand out between the books. But perhaps the most eloquent proof that all these psalms were not originally collected together is found at the end of Psalm 72, "The prayers of David son of Jesse are ended." Since 18 more "psalms of David" appear in Psalms, it seems very likely that Psalm 72.20 originally concluded a songbook. Later, this collection was incorporated into the book of Psalms.

10 Therefore the people turn and praise
    them,[t]
    and find no fault in them.[u]
11 And they say, "How can God know?
    Is there knowledge in the Most High?"
12 Such are the wicked;
    always at ease, they increase in riches.
13 All in vain I have kept my heart clean
    and washed my hands in innocence.
14 For all day long I have been plagued,
    and am punished every morning.

15 If I had said, "I will talk on in this way,"
    I would have been untrue to the circle
        of your children.
16 But when I thought how to understand
        this,
    it seemed to me a wearisome task,
17 until I went into the sanctuary of God;
    then I perceived their end.

73.3–20 Short-Run Rewards

Some people are deeply disturbed when they see evil people living without a care. Does a bad life always make you unhappy? Not in the short run, according to this description. In fact, the life of the wicked sometimes looks enviable. Only in the light of eternity is godly living always more rewarding.

18 Truly you set them in slippery places;
    you make them fall to ruin.
19 How they are destroyed in a moment,
    swept away utterly by terrors!
20 They are[v] like a dream when one awakes;
    on awaking you despise their
        phantoms.

21 When my soul was embittered,
    when I was pricked in heart,
22 I was stupid and ignorant;
    I was like a brute beast toward you.
23 Nevertheless I am continually with you;
    you hold my right hand.
24 You guide me with your counsel,
    and afterward you will receive me with
        honor.[w]
25 Whom have I in heaven but you?
    And there is nothing on earth that I
        desire other than you.
26 My flesh and my heart may fail,
    but God is the strength[x] of my heart
        and my portion forever.
27 Indeed, those who are far from you will
        perish;
    you put an end to those who are false
        to you.
28 But for me it is good to be near God;
    I have made the Lord GOD my refuge,
    to tell of all your works.

Psalm 74

Plea for Help in Time of National Humiliation

A Maskil of Asaph.

1 O God, why do you cast us off forever?
    Why does your anger smoke against
        the sheep of your pasture?
2 Remember your congregation, which you
        acquired long ago,
    which you redeemed to be the tribe of
        your heritage.
    Remember Mount Zion, where you
        came to dwell.
3 Direct your steps to the perpetual ruins;
    the enemy has destroyed everything in
        the sanctuary.

4 Your foes have roared within your holy
        place;
    they set up their emblems there.
5 At the upper entrance they hacked
    the wooden trellis with axes.[y]
6 And then, with hatchets and hammers,
    they smashed all its carved work.

---

[t] Cn: Heb *his people return here*   [u] Cn: Heb *abundant waters are drained by them*   [v] Cn: Heb *Lord*   [w] Or *to glory*   [x] Heb *rock*   [y] Cn Compare Gk Syr: Meaning of Heb uncertain

7 They set your sanctuary on fire;
  they desecrated the dwelling place of
    your name,
  bringing it to the ground.
8 They said to themselves, "We will utterly
    subdue them";
  they burned all the meeting places of
    God in the land.

9 We do not see our emblems;
  there is no longer any prophet,
  and there is no one among us who
    knows how long.
10 How long, O God, is the foe to scoff?
  Is the enemy to revile your name
    forever?
11 Why do you hold back your hand;
  why do you keep your hand in*z* your
    bosom?

12 Yet God my King is from of old,
  working salvation in the earth.
13 You divided the sea by your might;
  you broke the heads of the dragons in
    the waters.
14 You crushed the heads of Leviathan;
  you gave him as food*a* for the
    creatures of the wilderness.
15 You cut openings for springs and
    torrents;
  you dried up ever-flowing streams.
16 Yours is the day, yours also the night;
  you established the luminaries*b* and
    the sun.
17 You have fixed all the bounds of the
    earth;
  you made summer and winter.

18 Remember this, O LORD, how the enemy
    scoffs,
  and an impious people reviles your
    name.
19 Do not deliver the soul of your dove to
    the wild animals;
  do not forget the life of your poor
    forever.

20 Have regard for your*c* covenant,
  for the dark places of the land are full
    of the haunts of violence.
21 Do not let the downtrodden be put to
    shame;
  let the poor and needy praise your
    name.
22 Rise up, O God, plead your cause;
  remember how the impious scoff at
    you all day long.
23 Do not forget the clamor of your foes,

the uproar of your adversaries that
  goes up continually.

Psalm 75

Thanksgiving for God's Wondrous Deeds

To the leader: Do Not Destroy. A Psalm
  of Asaph. A Song.

1 We give thanks to you, O God;
  we give thanks; your name is near.
People tell of your wondrous deeds.

2 At the set time that I appoint
  I will judge with equity.
3 When the earth totters, with all its
    inhabitants,
  it is I who keep its pillars steady.   *Selah*
4 I say to the boastful, "Do not boast,"
  and to the wicked, "Do not lift up your
    horn;
5 do not lift up your horn on high,
  or speak with insolent neck."

6 For not from the east or from the west
  and not from the wilderness comes
    lifting up;
7 but it is God who executes judgment,
  putting down one and lifting up
    another.
8 For in the hand of the LORD there is a
    cup
  with foaming wine, well mixed;
he will pour a draught from it,
  and all the wicked of the earth
  shall drain it down to the dregs.
9 But I will rejoice*d* forever;
  I will sing praises to the God of Jacob.

10 All the horns of the wicked I will cut off,
  but the horns of the righteous shall be
    exalted.

Psalm 76

Israel's God—Judge of All the Earth

To the leader: with stringed instruments.
  A Psalm of Asaph. A Song.

1 In Judah God is known,
  his name is great in Israel.
2 His abode has been established in Salem,
  his dwelling place in Zion.
3 There he broke the flashing arrows,
  the shield, the sword, and the weapons
    of war.   *Selah*

4 Glorious are you, more majestic
  than the everlasting mountains.*e*

---

z Cn: Heb *do you consume your right hand from*   *a* Heb *food for the people*   *b* Or *moon*; Heb *light*   *c* Gk Syr:
Heb *the*   *d* Gk: Heb *declare*   *e* Gk: Heb *the mountains of prey*

5 The stouthearted were stripped of their
   spoil;
   they sank into sleep;
none of the troops
   was able to lift a hand.
6 At your rebuke, O God of Jacob,
   both rider and horse lay stunned.

7 But you indeed are awesome!
   Who can stand before you
   when once your anger is roused?
8 From the heavens you uttered judgment;
   the earth feared and was still
9 when God rose up to establish judgment,
   to save all the oppressed of the earth.
                                    Selah

10 Human wrath serves only to praise you,
    when you bind the last bit of your*f*
       wrath around you.
11 Make vows to the LORD your God, and
       perform them;
    let all who are around him bring gifts
    to the one who is awesome,
12 who cuts off the spirit of princes,
    who inspires fear in the kings of the
       earth.

Psalm 77

God's Mighty Deeds Recalled

To the leader: according to Jeduthun. Of Asaph.
A Psalm.

1 I cry aloud to God,
   aloud to God, that he may hear me.
2 In the day of my trouble I seek the Lord;
   in the night my hand is stretched out
      without wearying;
   my soul refuses to be comforted.
3 I think of God, and I moan;
   I meditate, and my spirit faints.   *Selah*

77.3–12 Sleepless Nights

*Sleeplessness afflicts millions, and this psalm
shows it is nothing new. Anxiety tormented the
psalmist while he lay awake at night. What to
do? He deliberately turned his thoughts to the
past, remembering what God had done for him
and for his people.*

4 You keep my eyelids from closing;
   I am so troubled that I cannot speak.
5 I consider the days of old,
   and remember the years of long ago.
6 I commune*g* with my heart in the night;
   I meditate and search my spirit:*h*

7 "Will the Lord spurn forever,
   and never again be favorable?
8 Has his steadfast love ceased forever?
   Are his promises at an end for all
      time?
9 Has God forgotten to be gracious?
   Has he in anger shut up his
      compassion?"   *Selah*
10 And I say, "It is my grief
    that the right hand of the Most High
       has changed."

11 I will call to mind the deeds of the LORD;
    I will remember your wonders of old.
12 I will meditate on all your work,
    and muse on your mighty deeds.
13 Your way, O God, is holy.
    What god is so great as our God?
14 You are the God who works wonders;
    you have displayed your might among
       the peoples.
15 With your strong arm you redeemed your
       people,
    the descendants of Jacob and Joseph.
                                       Selah

16 When the waters saw you, O God,
    when the waters saw you, they were
       afraid;
    the very deep trembled.
17 The clouds poured out water;
    the skies thundered;
    your arrows flashed on every side.
18 The crash of your thunder was in the
       whirlwind;
    your lightnings lit up the world;
    the earth trembled and shook.
19 Your way was through the sea,
    your path, through the mighty waters;
    yet your footprints were unseen.
20 You led your people like a flock
    by the hand of Moses and Aaron.

Psalm 78

God's Goodness and Israel's Ingratitude

A Maskil of Asaph.

1 Give ear, O my people, to my teaching;
   incline your ears to the words of my
      mouth.
2 I will open my mouth in a parable;
   I will utter dark sayings from of old,
3 things that we have heard and known,
   that our ancestors have told us.
4 We will not hide them from their
      children;
   we will tell to the coming generation

---

f Heb lacks *your*   *g* Gk Syr: Heb *My music*   *h* Syr Jerome: Heb *my spirit searches*

the glorious deeds of the LORD, and his
might,
and the wonders that he has done.

5 He established a decree in Jacob,
and appointed a law in Israel,
which he commanded our ancestors
to teach to their children;
6 that the next generation might know
them,
the children yet unborn,
and rise up and tell them to their
children,
7 so that they should set their hope in
God,
and not forget the works of God,
but keep his commandments;

i Heb *armed with shooting*

8 and that they should not be like their
ancestors,
a stubborn and rebellious generation,
a generation whose heart was not
steadfast,
whose spirit was not faithful to God.
9 The Ephraimites, armed with[i] the bow,
turned back on the day of battle.
10 They did not keep God's covenant,
but refused to walk according to his
law.
11 They forgot what he had done,
and the miracles that he had shown
them.
12 In the sight of their ancestors he worked
marvels
in the land of Egypt, in the fields of Zoan.

Remembering Back
The past can give you hope for the future

> I will call to mind
> the deeds of the
> LORD. 77.11

MARRIED PEOPLE MAKE IT THEIR business to remember how love began. Anniversaries recall their wedding day, year after year. Wedding rings remind them of their commitment. Wedding photos capture the moment when "two become one." In remembering the beginning of their love, couples often find new hope for the future.

Forgetting, on the other hand, amounts to treason. If one person forgets the all-important anniversary, tears and anger may follow.

An Anniversary Day

The book of Psalms remembers too. When things get bad, these poems often refer to the past—particularly to the great events when, under Moses, the Israelite nation began. God freed the Israelites from Egyptian slavery, carried them through the Red Sea, gave them directions for living, and ushered them into the promised land. This miraculous beginning was as significant to Jews as the cross is to Christians.

The Israelites even had an "anniversary day"—known as passover—to remember it. Every spring passover reminded them of their escape from Egypt. It's no accident that Easter often falls on the same week. Both days celebrate liberation from slavery.

The memories weren't all positive. The Israelites could, in fact, be brutally frank about their early failings. Even as they remembered how persistently wonderful God had been, they also remembered how rebellious, complaining, and forgetful they had been. Yet they had one great, happy reason to celebrate: God had kept his promise to love them.

Hope in a Time of Despair

Psalm 77 is a "remembering" poem. It starts with deep despair. "Will the Lord spurn forever, and never again be favorable? Has God forgotten to be gracious? Has he in anger shut up his compassion?" (77.7,9). Imagine a wife asking such questions about her husband.

Then thoughts turn, deliberately, to the past. Remember the turmoil at the banks of the Red Sea? Could anything be worse? But in that turbulent water they had seen the Lord's power: God had led them through to safety. He would do the same again.

The historical psalms (77, 78, 105, 106) invite us, along with the Israelites, to relive history. Like married couples remembering back, we can recall God's work—his powerful victories recorded all through scripture, his promises and proofs of love toward his people. And we can refer to God's history with us as individuals, too. Who cannot count some blessings, some undeserved favors? Through such remembering we are strengthened to face the future, and to recommit ourselves to trusting God's care.

Life Questions: If you were to refer to a single past event for encouragement, what would it be?

13 He divided the sea and let them pass
        through it,
    and made the waters stand like a heap.
14 In the daytime he led them with a cloud,
    and all night long with a fiery light.
15 He split rocks open in the wilderness,
    and gave them drink abundantly as
        from the deep.
16 He made streams come out of the rock,
    and caused waters to flow down like
        rivers.

78.2 Speaking in Parables

*Matthew saw this verse as foreshadowing
Jesus' teaching style (Matthew 13.35). A
"parable" or "proverb" (the Hebrew word is the
same) simply compares one thing with
another. This psalm compares the present to
the past. By going over the great things God
has done—and the great indifference God's
people have often shown—the psalmist warns
against making the same mistakes again.*

17 Yet they sinned still more against him,
    rebelling against the Most High in the
        desert.
18 They tested God in their heart
    by demanding the food they craved.
19 They spoke against God, saying,
    "Can God spread a table in the
        wilderness?
20 Even though he struck the rock so that
        water gushed out
    and torrents overflowed,
    can he also give bread,
    or provide meat for his people?"

21 Therefore, when the LORD heard, he was
        full of rage;
    a fire was kindled against Jacob,
    his anger mounted against Israel,
22 because they had no faith in God,
    and did not trust his saving power.
23 Yet he commanded the skies above,
    and opened the doors of heaven;
24 he rained down on them manna to eat,
    and gave them the grain of heaven.
25 Mortals ate of the bread of angels;
    he sent them food in abundance.
26 He caused the east wind to blow in the
        heavens,
    and by his power he led out the south
        wind;
27 he rained flesh upon them like dust,
    winged birds like the sand of the seas;
28 he let them fall within their camp,
    all around their dwellings.

29 And they ate and were well filled,
    for he gave them what they craved.
30 But before they had satisfied their craving,
    while the food was still in their
        mouths,
31 the anger of God rose against them
    and he killed the strongest of them,
    and laid low the flower of Israel.

32 In spite of all this they still sinned;
    they did not believe in his wonders.
33 So he made their days vanish like a
        breath,
    and their years in terror.
34 When he killed them, they sought for
        him;
    they repented and sought God
        earnestly.
35 They remembered that God was their
        rock,
    the Most High God their redeemer.
36 But they flattered him with their mouths;
    they lied to him with their tongues.
37 Their heart was not steadfast toward him;
    they were not true to his covenant.
38 Yet he, being compassionate,
    forgave their iniquity,
    and did not destroy them;
    often he restrained his anger,
    and did not stir up all his wrath.
39 He remembered that they were but flesh,
    a wind that passes and does not come
        again.
40 How often they rebelled against him in
        the wilderness
    and grieved him in the desert!
41 They tested God again and again,
    and provoked the Holy One of Israel.
42 They did not keep in mind his power,
    or the day when he redeemed them
        from the foe;
43 when he displayed his signs in Egypt,
    and his miracles in the fields of Zoan.
44 He turned their rivers to blood,
    so that they could not drink of their
        streams.
45 He sent among them swarms of flies,
    which devoured them,
    and frogs, which destroyed them.
46 He gave their crops to the caterpillar,
    and the fruit of their labor to the
        locust.
47 He destroyed their vines with hail,
    and their sycamores with frost.
48 He gave over their cattle to the hail,
    and their flocks to thunderbolts.
49 He let loose on them his fierce anger,
    wrath, indignation, and distress,
    a company of destroying angels.

50 He made a path for his anger;
   he did not spare them from death,
   but gave their lives over to the plague.
51 He struck all the firstborn in Egypt,
   the first issue of their strength in the
   tents of Ham.
52 Then he led out his people like sheep,
   and guided them in the wilderness like
   a flock.
53 He led them in safety, so that they were
   not afraid;
   but the sea overwhelmed their enemies.
54 And he brought them to his holy hill,
   to the mountain that his right hand
   had won.
55 He drove out nations before them;
   he apportioned them for a possession
   and settled the tribes of Israel in their
   tents.

56 Yet they tested the Most High God,
   and rebelled against him.
   They did not observe his decrees,
57 but turned away and were faithless like
   their ancestors;
   they twisted like a treacherous bow.
58 For they provoked him to anger with
   their high places;
   they moved him to jealousy with their
   idols.
59 When God heard, he was full of wrath,
   and he utterly rejected Israel.
60 He abandoned his dwelling at Shiloh,
   the tent where he dwelt among
   mortals,
61 and delivered his power to captivity,
   his glory to the hand of the foe.
62 He gave his people to the sword,
   and vented his wrath on his heritage.
63 Fire devoured their young men,
   and their girls had no marriage
   song.
64 Their priests fell by the sword,
   and their widows made no
   lamentation.
65 Then the Lord awoke as from sleep,

78.64 The Bad Old Days

*From the time they entered the promised land
to the time when Saul was named their first
king, Israelites had no central government.
Instead they were governed by "judges,"
colorful volunteer leaders like Deborah, Gideon,
and Samson. Israel had few nostalgic
memories of those days. Psalm 78 portrays
them as a time when Israel abandoned God—
and God rejected Israel. These verses (59–64)
draw from the events described in 1 Samuel 4.*

like a warrior shouting because of
   wine.
66 He put his adversaries to rout;
   he put them to everlasting disgrace.

67 He rejected the tent of Joseph,
   he did not choose the tribe of
   Ephraim;
68 but he chose the tribe of Judah,
   Mount Zion, which he loves.
69 He built his sanctuary like the high
   heavens,
   like the earth, which he has founded
   forever.
70 He chose his servant David,
   and took him from the sheepfolds;
71 from tending the nursing ewes he brought
   him
   to be the shepherd of his people Jacob,
   of Israel, his inheritance.
72 With upright heart he tended them,
   and guided them with skillful hand.

Psalm 79

Plea for Mercy for Jerusalem

A Psalm of Asaph.

1 O God, the nations have come into your
   inheritance;
   they have defiled your holy temple;
   they have laid Jerusalem in ruins.
2 They have given the bodies of your
   servants
   to the birds of the air for food,
   the flesh of your faithful to the wild
   animals of the earth.
3 They have poured out their blood like
   water
   all around Jerusalem,
   and there was no one to bury them.
4 We have become a taunt to our
   neighbors,
   mocked and derided by those around
   us.

5 How long, O LORD? Will you be angry
   forever?
   Will your jealous wrath burn like fire?
6 Pour out your anger on the nations
   that do not know you,
   and on the kingdoms
   that do not call on your name.
7 For they have devoured Jacob
   and laid waste his habitation.

8 Do not remember against us the iniquities
   of our ancestors;
   let your compassion come speedily to
   meet us,
   for we are brought very low.

9 Help us, O God of our salvation,
   for the glory of your name;
   deliver us, and forgive our sins,
   for your name's sake.
10 Why should the nations say,
   "Where is their God?"
   Let the avenging of the outpoured blood
   of your servants
   be known among the nations before
   our eyes.

11 Let the groans of the prisoners come
   before you;
   according to your great power preserve
   those doomed to die.
12 Return sevenfold into the bosom of our
   neighbors
   the taunts with which they taunted
   you, O Lord!
13 Then we your people, the flock of your
   pasture,
   will give thanks to you forever;
   from generation to generation we will
   recount your praise.

Psalm 80

Prayer for Israel's Restoration

To the leader: on Lilies, a Covenant. Of Asaph.
A Psalm.

1 Give ear, O Shepherd of Israel,
   you who lead Joseph like a flock!
   You who are enthroned upon the
   cherubim, shine forth
2 before Ephraim and Benjamin and
   Manasseh.
   Stir up your might,
   and come to save us!

3 Restore us, O God;
   let your face shine, that we may be
   saved.

4 O LORD God of hosts,
   how long will you be angry with your
   people's prayers?
5 You have fed them with the bread of
   tears,
   and given them tears to drink in full
   measure.
6 You make us the scorn[j] of our
   neighbors;
   our enemies laugh among themselves.

7 Restore us, O God of hosts;
   let your face shine, that we may be
   saved.

8 You brought a vine out of Egypt;
   you drove out the nations and planted
   it.
9 You cleared the ground for it;
   it took deep root and filled the land.
10 The mountains were covered with its
   shade,
   the mighty cedars with its branches;
11 it sent out its branches to the sea,
   and its shoots to the River.
12 Why then have you broken down its
   walls,
   so that all who pass along the way
   pluck its fruit?
13 The boar from the forest ravages it,
   and all that move in the field feed on
   it.

14 Turn again, O God of hosts;
   look down from heaven, and see;
   have regard for this vine,

80.14 Grapevines

The Old Testament often portrays God's people as a vineyard. Jesus, too, used the image (see Mark 12.1–9; John 15.1–5). Raising grapes was as familiar to Israelites as playing baseball is to Americans. Many sermon illustrations have been made from both.

15   the stock that your right hand
      planted.[k]
16 They have burned it with fire, they have
   cut it down;[l]
   may they perish at the rebuke of your
   countenance.
17 But let your hand be upon the one at
   your right hand,
   the one whom you made strong for
   yourself.
18 Then we will never turn back from you;
   give us life, and we will call on your
   name.

19 Restore us, O LORD God of hosts;
   let your face shine, that we may be
   saved.

Psalm 81

God's Appeal to Stubborn Israel

To the leader: according to The Gittith.
Of Asaph.

1 Sing aloud to God our strength;
   shout for joy to the God of Jacob.

---

j Syr: Heb *strife*   *k* Heb adds from verse 17 *and upon the one whom you made strong for yourself*   *l* Cn: Heb *it is cut down*

2 Raise a song, sound the tambourine,
   the sweet lyre with the harp.
3 Blow the trumpet at the new moon,
   at the full moon, on our festal day.
4 For it is a statute for Israel,
   an ordinance of the God of Jacob.
5 He made it a decree in Joseph,
   when he went out over[m] the land of
      Egypt.

I hear a voice I had not known:
6 "I relieved your[n] shoulder of the burden;
   your[n] hands were freed from the
      basket.
7 In distress you called, and I rescued you;
   I answered you in the secret place of
      thunder;
   I tested you at the waters of Meribah.
                                      Selah
8 Hear, O my people, while I admonish
      you;
   O Israel, if you would but listen to me!
9 There shall be no strange god among you;
   you shall not bow down to a foreign
      god.
10 I am the LORD your God,
   who brought you up out of the land of
      Egypt.
   Open your mouth wide and I will fill
      it.

11 "But my people did not listen to my
      voice;
   Israel would not submit to me.
12 So I gave them over to their stubborn
      hearts,
   to follow their own counsels.
13 O that my people would listen to me,
   that Israel would walk in my ways!
14 Then I would quickly subdue their
      enemies,
   and turn my hand against their foes.
15 Those who hate the LORD would cringe
      before him,
   and their doom would last forever.
16 I would feed you[o] with the finest of the
      wheat,
   and with honey from the rock I would
      satisfy you."

Psalm 82

A Plea for Justice

A Psalm of Asaph.

1 God has taken his place in the divine
      council;
   in the midst of the gods he holds
      judgment:

2 "How long will you judge unjustly
   and show partiality to the wicked?
                                      Selah
3 Give justice to the weak and the orphan;
   maintain the right of the lowly and the
      destitute.

82.1 Among "the Gods"

Human beings like to think of themselves as godlike—able to do whatever they like. Many commentators believe this psalm's snort of disdain is aimed at human judges and "powers that be" who set themselves up as little gods. What will become of their arrogance if they defy God? They will "die like mortals" (verse 7). The grave is a perfect answer to their pretensions.

When Jesus was accused of blasphemy for claiming to be God's Son, he referred his critics to this psalm (John 10.35). If scripture could apply such lofty terminology to sinful human beings, was it not possible that a perfect man could be God's own Son?

4 Rescue the weak and the needy;
   deliver them from the hand of the
      wicked."

5 They have neither knowledge nor
      understanding,
   they walk around in darkness;
   all the foundations of the earth are
      shaken.

6 I say, "You are gods,
   children of the Most High, all of you;
7 nevertheless, you shall die like mortals,
   and fall like any prince."[p]

8 Rise up, O God, judge the earth;
   for all the nations belong to you!

Psalm 83

Prayer for Judgment on Israel's Foes

A Song. A Psalm of Asaph.

1 O God, do not keep silence;
   do not hold your peace or be still,
      O God!
2 Even now your enemies are in tumult;
   those who hate you have raised their
      heads.
3 They lay crafty plans against your people;
   they consult together against those you
      protect.

---

[m] Or *against*   [n] Heb *his*   [o] Cn Compare verse 16b: Heb *he would feed him*   [p] Or *fall as one man, O princes*

4 They say, "Come, let us wipe them out as
      a nation;
   let the name of Israel be remembered
      no more."
5 They conspire with one accord;
   against you they make a covenant—
6 the tents of Edom and the Ishmaelites,
   Moab and the Hagrites,
7 Gebal and Ammon and Amalek,
   Philistia with the inhabitants of Tyre;
8 Assyria also has joined them;
   they are the strong arm of the children
      of Lot.   Selah

9 Do to them as you did to Midian,
   as to Sisera and Jabin at the Wadi
      Kishon,
10 who were destroyed at En-dor,
   who became dung for the ground.
11 Make their nobles like Oreb and Zeeb,
   all their princes like Zebah and
      Zalmunna,
12 who said, "Let us take the pastures of
      God
   for our own possession."

13 O my God, make them like whirling
      dust,q
   like chaff before the wind.
14 As fire consumes the forest,
   as the flame sets the mountains ablaze,
15 so pursue them with your tempest
   and terrify them with your hurricane.
16 Fill their faces with shame,
   so that they may seek your name,
      O LORD.
17 Let them be put to shame and dismayed
      forever;
   let them perish in disgrace.
18 Let them know that you alone,
   whose name is the LORD,
   are the Most High over all the earth.

Psalm 84

The Joy of Worship in the Temple

   To the leader: according to The Gittith.
   Of the Korahites. A Psalm.

1 How lovely is your dwelling place,
   O LORD of hosts!
2 My soul longs, indeed it faints
   for the courts of the LORD;
   my heart and my flesh sing for joy
   to the living God.

3 Even the sparrow finds a home,
   and the swallow a nest for herself,
   where she may lay her young,

at your altars, O LORD of hosts,
   my King and my God.
4 Happy are those who live in your house,
   ever singing your praise.   Selah

5 Happy are those whose strength is in you,
   in whose heart are the highways to
      Zion.r
6 As they go through the valley of Baca
   they make it a place of springs;
   the early rain also covers it with pools.
7 They go from strength to strength;
   the God of gods will be seen in Zion.

8 O LORD God of hosts, hear my prayer;
   give ear, O God of Jacob!   Selah
9 Behold our shield, O God;
   look on the face of your anointed.

10 For a day in your courts is better
   than a thousand elsewhere.
   I would rather be a doorkeeper in the
      house of my God
   than live in the tents of wickedness.

84.10 Homecoming

*"Home Sweet Home" probably adorns more
plaques than any other motto. Home is a place
where you can lay down your tired body and
bruised ego in safety. Psalm 84 contains the
same idea, but with a dramatic difference.
Home is in God's house, a place that brings
comfort right down into your bones. You'd
rather spend one day near God, praising him,
than a thousand days anywhere else.*

11 For the LORD God is a sun and shield;
   he bestows favor and honor.
   No good thing does the LORD withhold
   from those who walk uprightly.
12 O LORD of hosts,
   happy is everyone who trusts in you.

Psalm 85

Prayer for the Restoration of God's Favor

   To the leader. Of the Korahites. A Psalm.

1 LORD, you were favorable to your land;
   you restored the fortunes of Jacob.
2 You forgave the iniquity of your people;
   you pardoned all their sin.   Selah
3 You withdrew all your wrath;
   you turned from your hot anger.

4 Restore us again, O God of our salvation,

q Or a tumbleweed   r Heb lacks to Zion

and put away your indignation toward
us.
5 Will you be angry with us forever?
Will you prolong your anger to all
generations?
6 Will you not revive us again,
so that your people may rejoice in you?
7 Show us your steadfast love, O LORD,
and grant us your salvation.

8 Let me hear what God the LORD will
speak,
for he will speak peace to his people,
to his faithful, to those who turn to
him in their hearts.ˢ
9 Surely his salvation is at hand for those
who fear him,
that his glory may dwell in our land.

10 Steadfast love and faithfulness will meet;
righteousness and peace will kiss each
other.
11 Faithfulness will spring up from the
ground,
and righteousness will look down from
the sky.
12 The LORD will give what is good,
and our land will yield its increase.
13 Righteousness will go before him,
and will make a path for his steps.

Psalm 86

Supplication for Help against Enemies

A Prayer of David.

1 Incline your ear, O LORD, and answer me,
for I am poor and needy.
2 Preserve my life, for I am devoted to you;
save your servant who trusts in you.
You are my God; ³be gracious to me,
O Lord,
for to you do I cry all day long.
4 Gladden the soul of your servant,
for to you, O Lord, I lift up my soul.
5 For you, O Lord, are good and forgiving,
abounding in steadfast love to all who
call on you.
6 Give ear, O LORD, to my prayer;
listen to my cry of supplication.
7 In the day of my trouble I call on you,
for you will answer me.

8 There is none like you among the gods,
O Lord,
nor are there any works like yours.
9 All the nations you have made shall come
and bow down before you, O Lord,
and shall glorify your name.

10 For you are great and do wondrous
things;
you alone are God.
11 Teach me your way, O LORD,
that I may walk in your truth;
give me an undivided heart to revere
your name.

86.11 Heart Surgery

*David prays for an undivided heart, in order to
give all of it to God in his praise. "Heart" in the
Bible doesn't refer merely to emotions, but to
the whole person. David's prayer means, "Help
me aim myself in a single direction!"*

12 I give thanks to you, O Lord my God,
with my whole heart,
and I will glorify your name forever.
13 For great is your steadfast love toward
me;
you have delivered my soul from the
depths of Sheol.

14 O God, the insolent rise up against me;
a band of ruffians seeks my life,
and they do not set you before them.
15 But you, O Lord, are a God merciful and
gracious,
slow to anger and abounding in
steadfast love and faithfulness.
16 Turn to me and be gracious to me;
give your strength to your servant;
save the child of your serving girl.
17 Show me a sign of your favor,
so that those who hate me may see it
and be put to shame,
because you, LORD, have helped me
and comforted me.

Psalm 87

The Joy of Living in Zion

Of the Korahites. A Psalm. A Song.

1 On the holy mount stands the city he
founded;
2 the LORD loves the gates of Zion
more than all the dwellings of Jacob.
3 Glorious things are spoken of you,
O city of God. *Selah*

4 Among those who know me I mention
Rahab and Babylon;
Philistia too, and Tyre, with
Ethiopiaᵗ—
"This one was born there," they say.

ˢ Gk: Heb *but let them not turn back to folly* ᵗ Or *Nubia*; Heb *Cush*

⁵ And of Zion it shall be said,
  "This one and that one were born in
    it";
  for the Most High himself will establish
    it.
⁶ The LORD records, as he registers the
    peoples,
  "This one was born there."   *Selah*

⁷ Singers and dancers alike say,
  "All my springs are in you."

Psalm 88

Prayer for Help in Despondency

  A Song. A Psalm of the Korahites.
To the leader: according to Mahalath Leannoth.
  A Maskil of Heman the Ezrahite.

¹ O LORD, God of my salvation,
  when, at night, I cry out in your
    presence,

88.1 Bad Father, Good Kids

*Psalm 88 is the last of 12 psalms ascribed to
"the Korahites." Korah, a rebel against Moses'
leadership, died in his rebellion (Numbers 16).
His children were spared, and many years later
David chose their clan to found a temple choir
(1 Chronicles 6.31–37). Apparently these
psalms were part of a musical collection they
used.*

² let my prayer come before you;
  incline your ear to my cry.

³ For my soul is full of troubles,
  and my life draws near to Sheol.
⁴ I am counted among those who go down
    to the Pit;
  I am like those who have no help,
⁵ like those forsaken among the dead,
  like the slain that lie in the grave,
  like those whom you remember no more,
    for they are cut off from your hand.
⁶ You have put me in the depths of the Pit,
  in the regions dark and deep.
⁷ Your wrath lies heavy upon me,
  and you overwhelm me with all your
    waves.   *Selah*

⁸ You have caused my companions to shun
    me;
  you have made me a thing of horror to
    them.
  I am shut in so that I cannot escape;
⁹   my eye grows dim through sorrow.

Every day I call on you, O LORD;
  I spread out my hands to you.
¹⁰ Do you work wonders for the dead?
  Do the shades rise up to praise you?
      Selah
¹¹ Is your steadfast love declared in the
    grave,
  or your faithfulness in Abaddon?
¹² Are your wonders known in the darkness,
  or your saving help in the land of
    forgetfulness?

¹³ But I, O LORD, cry out to you;
  in the morning my prayer comes
    before you.
¹⁴ O LORD, why do you cast me off?
  Why do you hide your face from
    me?
¹⁵ Wretched and close to death from my
    youth up,
  I suffer your terrors; I am desperate.ᵘ
¹⁶ Your wrath has swept over me;
  your dread assaults destroy me.
¹⁷ They surround me like a flood all day
    long;
  from all sides they close in on me.
¹⁸ You have caused friend and neighbor to
    shun me;
  my companions are in darkness.

Psalm 89

God's Covenant with David

  A Maskil of Ethan the Ezrahite.

¹ I will sing of your steadfast love,
    O LORD,ᵛ forever;
  with my mouth I will proclaim your
    faithfulness to all generations.
² I declare that your steadfast love is
    established forever;
  your faithfulness is as firm as the
    heavens.

³ You said, "I have made a covenant with
    my chosen one,
  I have sworn to my servant David:
⁴ 'I will establish your descendants forever,
  and build your throne for all
    generations.'"   *Selah*

⁵ Let the heavens praise your wonders,
    O LORD,
  your faithfulness in the assembly of the
    holy ones.
⁶ For who in the skies can be compared to
    the LORD?

ᵘ Meaning of Heb uncertain   ᵛ Gk: Heb *the steadfast love of the LORD*

Who among the heavenly beings is like
   the LORD,
7 a God feared in the council of the holy
   ones,
   great and awesome[w] above all that are
      around him?
8 O LORD God of hosts,
   who is as mighty as you, O LORD?
   Your faithfulness surrounds you.
9 You rule the raging of the sea;
   when its waves rise, you still them.
10 You crushed Rahab like a carcass;
   you scattered your enemies with your
      mighty arm.
11 The heavens are yours, the earth also is
   yours;
   the world and all that is in it—you
      have founded them.
12 The north and the south[x]—you created
   them;
   Tabor and Hermon joyously praise
      your name.
13 You have a mighty arm;
   strong is your hand, high your right
      hand.
14 Righteousness and justice are the
      foundation of your throne;
   steadfast love and faithfulness go before
      you.
15 Happy are the people who know the festal
      shout,
   who walk, O LORD, in the light of your
      countenance;
16 they exult in your name all day long,
   and extol[y] your righteousness.
17 For you are the glory of their strength;
   by your favor our horn is exalted.
18 For our shield belongs to the LORD,
   our king to the Holy One of Israel.

19 Then you spoke in a vision to your
      faithful one, and said:
   "I have set the crown[z] on one who is
      mighty,
   I have exalted one chosen from the
      people.
20 I have found my servant David;
   with my holy oil I have anointed him;
21 my hand shall always remain with him;
   my arm also shall strengthen him.
22 The enemy shall not outwit him,
   the wicked shall not humble him.
23 I will crush his foes before him
   and strike down those who hate him.
24 My faithfulness and steadfast love shall be
      with him;
   and in my name his horn shall be
      exalted.

25 I will set his hand on the sea
   and his right hand on the rivers.
26 He shall cry to me, 'You are my
      Father,
   my God, and the Rock of my
      salvation!'
27 I will make him the firstborn,
   the highest of the kings of the earth.
28 Forever I will keep my steadfast love for
      him,
   and my covenant with him will stand
      firm.
29 I will establish his line forever,
   and his throne as long as the heavens
      endure.
30 If his children forsake my law
   and do not walk according to my
      ordinances,

89.30–49 Shame Forever?

God, as this psalm notes, had made tremendous promises to David and to his descendants (see 2 Samuel 7.4–17). But what do you do when God's promises don't match your experience? This psalm was probably written after the Babylonians had deported the young king Jehoiachin (see here and 2 Kings 24.8,15) and torn down Jerusalem (see verse 40 and 2 Kings 25.10). It gives no explanation of how God's promises fit with this humiliation and suffering. But it offers a model of how to respond, taking the problem straight to God in the frankest terms. Only when Jesus came centuries later did Israel see God fulfill these promises to honor and love a "son of David" as his own Son (verses 26–29).

31 if they violate my statutes
   and do not keep my commandments,
32 then I will punish their transgression with
      the rod
   and their iniquity with scourges;
33 but I will not remove from him my
      steadfast love,
   or be false to my faithfulness.
34 I will not violate my covenant,
   or alter the word that went forth from
      my lips.
35 Once and for all I have sworn by my
      holiness;
   I will not lie to David.
36 His line shall continue forever,
   and his throne endure before me like
      the sun.

---

[w] Gk Syr: Heb *greatly awesome*   [x] Or *Zaphon and Yamin*   [y] Cn: Heb *are exalted in*   [z] Cn: Heb *help*

37 It shall be established forever like the
    moon,
      an enduring witness in the skies." *Selah*

38 But now you have spurned and rejected
    him;
      you are full of wrath against your
      anointed.
39 You have renounced the covenant with
    your servant;
      you have defiled his crown in the
      dust.
40 You have broken through all his walls;
    you have laid his strongholds in ruins.
41 All who pass by plunder him;
    he has become the scorn of his
      neighbors.
42 You have exalted the right hand of his
    foes;
      you have made all his enemies rejoice.
43 Moreover, you have turned back the edge
    of his sword,
      and you have not supported him in
      battle.
44 You have removed the scepter from his
    hand,*a*
      and hurled his throne to the ground.
45 You have cut short the days of his youth;
    you have covered him with shame.
                Selah

46 How long, O Lord? Will you hide
    yourself forever?
      How long will your wrath burn like
      fire?
47 Remember how short my time is—*b*
    for what vanity you have created all
      mortals!
48 Who can live and never see death?
    Who can escape the power of Sheol?
                Selah

49 Lord, where is your steadfast love of old,
    which by your faithfulness you swore
      to David?
50 Remember, O Lord, how your servant is
    taunted;
      how I bear in my bosom the insults of
      the peoples,*c*
51 with which your enemies taunt, O Lord,
    with which they taunted the footsteps
      of your anointed.

52 Blessed be the Lord forever.
      Amen and Amen.

BOOK IV
(*Psalms 90–106*)

Psalm 90

God's Eternity and Human Frailty

A Prayer of Moses, the man of God.

1 Lord, you have been our dwelling place*d*
    in all generations.
2 Before the mountains were brought forth,
    or ever you had formed the earth and
      the world,
    from everlasting to everlasting you are
      God.

3 You turn us*e* back to dust,
    and say, "Turn back, you mortals."
4 For a thousand years in your sight
    are like yesterday when it is past,
    or like a watch in the night.

5 You sweep them away; they are like a
    dream,
    like grass that is renewed in the
      morning;
6 in the morning it flourishes and is
    renewed;
    in the evening it fades and withers.

7 For we are consumed by your anger;
    by your wrath we are overwhelmed.
8 You have set our iniquities before you,
    our secret sins in the light of your
      countenance.

9 For all our days pass away under your
    wrath;
    our years come to an end*f* like a sigh.
10 The days of our life are seventy years,
    or perhaps eighty, if we are strong;
    even then their span*g* is only toil and
      trouble;
    they are soon gone, and we fly away.

11 Who considers the power of your anger?
    Your wrath is as great as the fear that
      is due you.
12 So teach us to count our days
    that we may gain a wise heart.

13 Turn, O Lord! How long?
    Have compassion on your servants!
14 Satisfy us in the morning with your
    steadfast love,
    so that we may rejoice and be glad all
      our days.

---

a Cn: Heb *removed his cleanness*   *b* Meaning of Heb uncertain   *c* Cn: Heb *bosom all of many peoples*   *d* Another
reading is *our refuge*   *e* Heb *humankind*   *f* Syr: Heb *we bring our years to an end*   *g* Cn Compare Gk Syr
Jerome Tg: Heb *pride*

15 Make us glad as many days as you have
  afflicted us,
  and as many years as we have seen
  evil.
16 Let your work be manifest to your
  servants,
  and your glorious power to their
  children.
17 Let the favor of the Lord our God be
  upon us,
  and prosper for us the work of our
  hands—
  O prosper the work of our hands!

Psalm 91

Assurance of God's Protection

1 You who live in the shelter of the Most
  High,
  who abide in the shadow of the
  Almighty, [h]
2 will say to the LORD, "My refuge and my
  fortress;
  my God, in whom I trust."
3 For he will deliver you from the snare of
  the fowler
  and from the deadly pestilence;
4 he will cover you with his pinions,
  and under his wings you will find
  refuge;
  his faithfulness is a shield and buckler.
5 You will not fear the terror of the night,
  or the arrow that flies by day,
6 or the pestilence that stalks in darkness,
  or the destruction that wastes at
  noonday.

7 A thousand may fall at your side,
  ten thousand at your right hand,
  but it will not come near you.
8 You will only look with your eyes
  and see the punishment of the wicked.

9 Because you have made the LORD your
  refuge, [i]
  the Most High your dwelling place,
10 no evil shall befall you,
  no scourge come near your tent.

11 For he will command his angels
  concerning you
  to guard you in all your ways.
12 On their hands they will bear you up,
  so that you will not dash your foot
  against a stone.
13 You will tread on the lion and the adder,
  the young lion and the serpent you will
  trample under foot.

14 Those who love me, I will deliver;
  I will protect those who know my
  name.
15 When they call to me, I will answer them;

> **91.12 Satan and the Bible**
>
> *Satan knows Scripture. He quoted this promise
> to Jesus when tempting him to spiritual
> arrogance (see Matthew 4.6). Jesus recognized
> that Satan had twisted its meaning. The
> magnificent assurances in this psalm
> encourage us to rest in God, not test him.*

  I will be with them in trouble,
  I will rescue them and honor them.
16 With long life I will satisfy them,
  and show them my salvation.

Psalm 92

Thanksgiving for Vindication

  A Psalm. A Song for the Sabbath Day.

1 It is good to give thanks to the LORD,
  to sing praises to your name, O Most
  High;
2 to declare your steadfast love in the
  morning,
  and your faithfulness by night,
3 to the music of the lute and the harp,
  to the melody of the lyre.
4 For you, O LORD, have made me glad by
  your work;
  at the works of your hands I sing for
  joy.

5 How great are your works, O LORD!
  Your thoughts are very deep!
6 The dullard cannot know,
  the stupid cannot understand this:
7 though the wicked sprout like grass
  and all evildoers flourish,
  they are doomed to destruction forever,
8 but you, O LORD, are on high forever.
9 For your enemies, O LORD,
  for your enemies shall perish;
  all evildoers shall be scattered.

10 But you have exalted my horn like that of
  the wild ox;
  you have poured over me [j] fresh oil.
11 My eyes have seen the downfall of my
  enemies;
  my ears have heard the doom of my
  evil assailants.

[h] Traditional rendering of Heb *Shaddai*   [i] Cn: Heb *Because you, LORD, are my refuge; you have made*
[j] Syr: Meaning of Heb uncertain

12 The righteous flourish like the palm tree,
and grow like a cedar in Lebanon.
13 They are planted in the house of the
LORD;
they flourish in the courts of our God.
14 In old age they still produce fruit;
they are always green and full of sap,
15 showing that the LORD is upright;
he is my rock, and there is no
unrighteousness in him.

Psalm 93

The Majesty of God's Rule

1 The LORD is king, he is robed in majesty;
the LORD is robed, he is girded with
strength.
He has established the world; it shall
never be moved;
2 your throne is established from of old;
you are from everlasting.

3 The floods have lifted up, O LORD,
the floods have lifted up their voice;
the floods lift up their roaring.
4 More majestic than the thunders of
mighty waters,
more majestic than the waves[k] of the
sea,
majestic on high is the LORD!

5 Your decrees are very sure;
holiness befits your house,
O LORD, forevermore.

Psalm 94

God the Avenger of the Righteous

1 O LORD, you God of vengeance,
you God of vengeance, shine forth!
2 Rise up, O judge of the earth;
give to the proud what they deserve!
3 O LORD, how long shall the wicked,
how long shall the wicked exult?

4 They pour out their arrogant words;
all the evildoers boast.
5 They crush your people, O LORD,
and afflict your heritage.
6 They kill the widow and the stranger,
they murder the orphan,
7 and they say, "The LORD does not see;
the God of Jacob does not perceive."

8 Understand, O dullest of the people;
fools, when will you be wise?
9 He who planted the ear, does he not
hear?
He who formed the eye, does he not see?

10 He who disciplines the nations,
he who teaches knowledge to humankind,
does he not chastise?
11 The LORD knows our thoughts,[l]
that they are but an empty breath.

12 Happy are those whom you discipline,
O LORD,
and whom you teach out of your law,
13 giving them respite from days of trouble,
until a pit is dug for the wicked.
14 For the LORD will not forsake his people;
he will not abandon his heritage;
15 for justice will return to the righteous,
and all the upright in heart will follow
it.

16 Who rises up for me against the wicked?
Who stands up for me against
evildoers?
17 If the LORD had not been my help,
my soul would soon have lived in the
land of silence.
18 When I thought, "My foot is slipping,"
your steadfast love, O LORD, held me
up.
19 When the cares of my heart are many,
your consolations cheer my soul.
20 Can wicked rulers be allied with you,
those who contrive mischief by statute?
21 They band together against the life of the
righteous,
and condemn the innocent to death.
22 But the LORD has become my stronghold,
and my God the rock of my refuge.
23 He will repay them for their iniquity
and wipe them out for their
wickedness;
the LORD our God will wipe them out.

Psalm 95

A Call to Worship and Obedience

1 O come, let us sing to the LORD;
let us make a joyful noise to the rock
of our salvation!
2 Let us come into his presence with
thanksgiving;
let us make a joyful noise to him with
songs of praise!
3 For the LORD is a great God,
and a great King above all gods.
4 In his hand are the depths of the earth;
the heights of the mountains are his
also.
5 The sea is his, for he made it,
and the dry land, which his hands have
formed.

k Cn: Heb *majestic are the waves*   l Heb *the thoughts of humankind*

6 O come, let us worship and bow down,
    let us kneel before the LORD,
        our Maker!
7 For he is our God,
    and we are the people of his pasture,
    and the sheep of his hand.

O that today you would listen to his
        voice!
8 Do not harden your hearts, as at
        Meribah,
    as on the day at Massah in the
        wilderness,

95.8 Rebellion

*One of Israel's worst memories involved a place
known as Massah and Meribah. There, on their
way to the promised land, the Israelites ran out
of water (Exodus 17.1–7) and rebelled against
Moses and God. Because of their lack of faith,
God made them wander the wilderness for 40
years.*

*Now, hundreds of years later, Psalm 95
warns another generation of Israelites not to
repeat the mistake that had made their
forebears miss "God's rest." In the New
Testament, Hebrews 4.1–13 argues that "God's
rest" means not merely the promised land of
Israel, but a state of peaceful unity with God.
The warning still applies.*

9 when your ancestors tested me,
    and put me to the proof, though they
        had seen my work.
10 For forty years I loathed that generation
    and said, "They are a people whose
        hearts go astray,
    and they do not regard my ways."
11 Therefore in my anger I swore,
    "They shall not enter my rest."

Psalm 96

Praise to God Who Comes in Judgment

1 O sing to the LORD a new song;
    sing to the LORD, all the earth.
2 Sing to the LORD, bless his name;
    tell of his salvation from day to day.
3 Declare his glory among the nations,
    his marvelous works among all the
        peoples.
4 For great is the LORD, and greatly to be
        praised;
    he is to be revered above all gods.
5 For all the gods of the peoples are idols,
    but the LORD made the heavens.
6 Honor and majesty are before him;

strength and beauty are in his
        sanctuary.

7 Ascribe to the LORD, O families of the
        peoples,
    ascribe to the LORD glory and strength.
8 Ascribe to the LORD the glory due his
        name;
    bring an offering, and come into his
        courts.
9 Worship the LORD in holy splendor;
    tremble before him, all the earth.

10 Say among the nations, "The LORD is
        king!
    The world is firmly established; it shall
        never be moved.
    He will judge the peoples with equity."
11 Let the heavens be glad, and let the earth
        rejoice;
    let the sea roar, and all that fills it;
12 let the field exult, and everything in it.
    Then shall all the trees of the forest sing
        for joy
13 before the LORD; for he is coming,
    for he is coming to judge the earth.
    He will judge the world with
        righteousness,
    and the peoples with his truth.

Psalm 97

The Glory of God's Reign

1 The LORD is king! Let the earth rejoice;
    let the many coastlands be glad!
2 Clouds and thick darkness are all around
        him;
    righteousness and justice are the
        foundation of his throne.
3 Fire goes before him,
    and consumes his adversaries on every
        side.
4 His lightnings light up the world;
    the earth sees and trembles.
5 The mountains melt like wax before the
        LORD,
    before the Lord of all the earth.

6 The heavens proclaim his righteousness;
    and all the peoples behold his glory.
7 All worshipers of images are put
        to shame,
    those who make their boast in
        worthless idols;
    all gods bow down before him.
8 Zion hears and is glad,
    and the towns*m* of Judah rejoice,
    because of your judgments, O God.

m Heb *daughters*

9 For you, O LORD, are most high over all
   the earth;
      you are exalted far above all gods.

10 The LORD loves those who hate[n] evil;
      he guards the lives of his faithful;
      he rescues them from the hand of the
         wicked.
11 Light dawns[o] for the righteous,
      and joy for the upright in heart.
12 Rejoice in the LORD, O you righteous,
      and give thanks to his holy name!

Psalm 98

Praise the Judge of the World

A Psalm.

1 O sing to the LORD a new song,
      for he has done marvelous things.
   His right hand and his holy arm
      have gotten him victory.
2 The LORD has made known his victory;
      he has revealed his vindication in the
         sight of the nations.
3 He has remembered his steadfast love and
         faithfulness
      to the house of Israel.
   All the ends of the earth have seen
      the victory of our God.

4 Make a joyful noise to the LORD, all the
      earth;
      break forth into joyous song and sing
         praises.
5 Sing praises to the LORD with the lyre,
      with the lyre and the sound of melody.
6 With trumpets and the sound of the horn
      make a joyful noise before the King,
         the LORD.

7 Let the sea roar, and all that fills it;
      the world and those who live in it.
8 Let the floods clap their hands;
      let the hills sing together for joy
9 at the presence of the LORD, for he is
      coming

98.8 Ecological Choir

*Seas, rivers, and mountains crown this psalm
with their praise. God's salvation doesn't just
affect human beings. When rebellion against
God finally ends, nature itself will celebrate.
Romans 8.18–22 takes up this theme as part of
the wonderful salvation God offers to all
people.*

to judge the earth.
He will judge the world with
      righteousness,
      and the peoples with equity.

Psalm 99

Praise to God for His Holiness

1 The LORD is king; let the peoples tremble!
   He sits enthroned upon the cherubim;
      let the earth quake!
2 The LORD is great in Zion;
      he is exalted over all the peoples.
3 Let them praise your great and awesome
         name.
   Holy is he!

4 Mighty King,[p] lover of justice,
      you have established equity;
   you have executed justice
      and righteousness in Jacob.
5 Extol the LORD our God;
      worship at his footstool.
   Holy is he!

6 Moses and Aaron were among his priests,
      Samuel also was among those who
         called on his name.
   They cried to the LORD, and he
         answered them.
7 He spoke to them in the pillar of cloud;
      they kept his decrees,
      and the statutes that he gave them.

8 O LORD our God, you answered them;
      you were a forgiving God to them,
      but an avenger of their wrongdoings.
9 Extol the LORD our God,
      and worship at his holy mountain;
      for the LORD our God is holy.

Psalm 100

All Lands Summoned to Praise God

A Psalm of thanksgiving.

1 Make a joyful noise to the LORD, all the
      earth.
2 Worship the LORD with gladness;
      come into his presence with singing.

3 Know that the LORD is God.
      It is he that made us, and we are his;[q]
   we are his people, and the sheep of his
         pasture.

4 Enter his gates with thanksgiving,

---

[n] Cn: Heb *You who love the LORD hate*   [o] Gk Syr Jerome: Heb *is sown*   [p] Cn: Heb *And a king's strength*
[q] Another reading is *and not we ourselves*

and his courts with praise.
Give thanks to him, bless his name.

5 For the LORD is good;
    his steadfast love endures forever,
    and his faithfulness to all generations.

Psalm 101

A Sovereign's Pledge of Integrity and Justice

Of David. A Psalm.

1 I will sing of loyalty and of justice;
    to you, O LORD, I will sing.
2 I will study the way that is blameless.
    When shall I attain it?

I will walk with integrity of heart
    within my house;
3 I will not set before my eyes
    anything that is base.

I hate the work of those who fall away;
    it shall not cling to me.
4 Perverseness of heart shall be far from
        me;
    I will know nothing of evil.

5 One who secretly slanders a neighbor
    I will destroy.
A haughty look and an arrogant heart
    I will not tolerate.

6 I will look with favor on the faithful in
        the land,
    so that they may live with me;
whoever walks in the way that is
        blameless
    shall minister to me.

7 No one who practices deceit
    shall remain in my house;
no one who utters lies
    shall continue in my presence.

8 Morning by morning I will destroy

101.7 The Company You Keep

Some friends build you up, others tear you down. That's true for people in influential positions as well. "Politics makes strange bedfellows," they say, because a politician must work with people from various political factions, whether he or she admires them or not. But here David, the head of state, pledges to steer clear of all shady alliances. He wants a clean administration, from the top down.

all the wicked in the land,
cutting off all evildoers
    from the city of the LORD.

Psalm 102

Prayer to the Eternal King for Help

*A prayer of one afflicted, when faint and
    pleading before the LORD.*

1 Hear my prayer, O LORD;
    let my cry come to you.
2 Do not hide your face from me
    in the day of my distress.
Incline your ear to me;
    answer me speedily in the day when I
        call.

3 For my days pass away like smoke,
    and my bones burn like a furnace.
4 My heart is stricken and withered like
        grass;
    I am too wasted to eat my bread.
5 Because of my loud groaning
    my bones cling to my skin.
6 I am like an owl of the wilderness,
    like a little owl of the waste places.
7 I lie awake;
    I am like a lonely bird on the
        housetop.
8 All day long my enemies taunt me;
    those who deride me use my name for
        a curse.
9 For I eat ashes like bread,
    and mingle tears with my drink,
10 because of your indignation and anger;
    for you have lifted me up and thrown
        me aside.
11 My days are like an evening shadow;
    I wither away like grass.

12 But you, O LORD, are enthroned forever;
    your name endures to all generations.
13 You will rise up and have compassion on
        Zion,
    for it is time to favor it;
    the appointed time has come.
14 For your servants hold its stones dear,
    and have pity on its dust.
15 The nations will fear the name of the
        LORD,
    and all the kings of the earth your
        glory.
16 For the LORD will build up Zion;
    he will appear in his glory.
17 He will regard the prayer of the destitute,
    and will not despise their prayer.

18 Let this be recorded for a generation to
        come,

so that a people yet unborn may praise
the LORD:
19 that he looked down from his holy height,
from heaven the LORD looked at the
earth,
20 to hear the groans of the prisoners,
to set free those who were doomed to
die;
21 so that the name of the LORD may be
declared in Zion,
and his praise in Jerusalem,
22 when peoples gather together,
and kingdoms, to worship the LORD.

23 He has broken my strength in midcourse;
he has shortened my days.
24 "O my God," I say, "do not take
me away
at the midpoint of my life,
you whose years endure
throughout all generations."

25 Long ago you laid the foundation of the
earth,
and the heavens are the work of your
hands.
26 They will perish, but you endure;
they will all wear out like a garment.
You change them like clothing, and they
pass away;

102.26 Outlasting the Universe

Is a diamond forever? Not according to the psalmist, who predicts that the universe, which God made, will wear out like old clothes. But God remains the same forever—and he will preserve his people, whom he is committed to far more than to his universe.

27 but you are the same, and your years
have no end.
28 The children of your servants shall live
secure;
their offspring shall be established in
your presence.

Psalm 103

Thanksgiving for God's Goodness

Of David.

1 Bless the LORD, O my soul,
and all that is within me,
bless his holy name.
2 Bless the LORD, O my soul,
and do not forget all his benefits—

3 who forgives all your iniquity,
who heals all your diseases,
4 who redeems your life from the Pit,
who crowns you with steadfast love
and mercy,
5 who satisfies you with good as long as
you live[r]
so that your youth is renewed like the
eagle's.

6 The LORD works vindication
and justice for all who are oppressed.
7 He made known his ways to Moses,
his acts to the people of Israel.
8 The LORD is merciful and gracious,
slow to anger and abounding in
steadfast love.
9 He will not always accuse,
nor will he keep his anger forever.
10 He does not deal with us according to
our sins,
nor repay us according to our
iniquities.
11 For as the heavens are high above the
earth,
so great is his steadfast love toward
those who fear him;
12 as far as the east is from the west,
so far he removes our transgressions
from us.
13 As a father has compassion for his
children,
so the LORD has compassion for those
who fear him.
14 For he knows how we were made;
he remembers that we are dust.

15 As for mortals, their days are like grass;
they flourish like a flower of the field;
16 for the wind passes over it, and it is gone,
and its place knows it no more.
17 But the steadfast love of the LORD is from
everlasting to everlasting
on those who fear him,
and his righteousness to children's
children,
18 to those who keep his covenant
and remember to do his
commandments.

19 The LORD has established his throne in
the heavens,
and his kingdom rules over all.
20 Bless the LORD, O you his angels,
you mighty ones who do his bidding,
obedient to his spoken word.
21 Bless the LORD, all his hosts,
his ministers that do his will.

r Meaning of Heb uncertain

22 Bless the Lord, all his works,
   in all places of his dominion.
   Bless the Lord, O my soul.

Psalm 104

God the Creator and Provider

1 Bless the Lord, O my soul.
   O Lord my God, you are very great.
   You are clothed with honor and majesty,
2   wrapped in light as with a garment.
   You stretch out the heavens like a tent,
3   you set the beams of your[s] chambers
         on the waters,
   you make the clouds your[s] chariot,
      you ride on the wings of the wind,
4   you make the winds your[s] messengers,

[s] Heb *his*

   fire and flame your[s] ministers.
5 You set the earth on its foundations,
      so that it shall never be shaken.
6 You cover it with the deep as with a
         garment;
   the waters stood above the mountains.
7 At your rebuke they flee;
      at the sound of your thunder they take
         to flight.
8 They rose up to the mountains, ran down
         to the valleys
   to the place that you appointed for
         them.
9 You set a boundary that they may not
         pass,
   so that they might not again cover the
         earth.

Ecology Plus
Creation sings God's praise

> O Lord, how manifold are your works! In wisdom you have made them all.
> 104.24

IN 1962 BIOLOGIST RACHEL CARSON published *Silent Spring*, a book tracing the effects of pesticides—DDT in particular. Until then, DDT had been treated like a wonder chemical, sprayed almost at random to kill pests. Carson showed how it worked its way up the food chain, killing larger animals—like songbirds. If no birds were left to sing, we would have an ominously "silent spring."

Until then, *ecology* had been a word known only to specialists. But with Carson's book, ordinary people began to take an interest in what only biologists had known: the delicate balance of nature, in which each creature is intertwined with every other. The ecology movement had begun.

The Value in "Useless" Creatures

Ecology was new, but its ideas were old. You could have learned its basic principles from Psalm 104. It shows appreciation for every aspect of nature, even creatures like wild goats, lions, and the "Leviathan," the crocodile or sea monster. The Israelites, as herders and farmers, had no romantic idealization of the outdoors. Nobody who herds sheep thinks of them as soft and fluffy pets. But to the poet who wrote Psalm 104, creatures that are of no "use" to anyone still have intrinsic worth—especially to God.

The author saw how the world fits together, everything in its proper sphere. At night wild animals hunt; at daybreak humans go out to work. The rain falls, nourishing crops for people and grass for cattle, but also watering the forest to provide a place for birds to nest.

Ecology Is God's Work

The intertwining of nature is not, for the psalmist, like a complex machine, dangerously sensitive. Things fit together because an intimate, personal God watches over his creation. Animals eat on schedule not just because their habitat contains adequate food, but because God gives them their food "in due season." Every breath of life depends on his will. So do the weather, the winds and clouds, the water supply, the very stability of the earth. The psalmist doesn't just marvel over the complexity and beauty of nature; in it he sees the work of God.

When modern people think of ecology, they are preoccupied with the fear of overcrowding and of poisoning the planet with landfills, oil spills, and toxic chemicals. The psalms show no such fear, for overcrowding and pollution were not major problems in that preindustrial civilization. Yet interestingly enough, this psalm ends with a wish that God would clean up the earth—cleanse it of sinners, who mar its perfection by their rejection of God's will. The beauty of the earth, made by God, calls out for purity—purity of the heart.

Life Questions: How does nature affect you? How do you affect it?

10 You make springs gush forth in the
valleys;
  they flow between the hills,
11 giving drink to every wild animal;
  the wild asses quench their thirst.
12 By the streams[t] the birds of the air have
their habitation;
  they sing among the branches.
13 From your lofty abode you water the
mountains;
  the earth is satisfied with the fruit of
your work.

14 You cause the grass to grow for the cattle,
and plants for people to use,[u]
to bring forth food from the earth,
15 and wine to gladden the human heart,
oil to make the face shine,
  and bread to strengthen the human
heart.
16 The trees of the LORD are watered
abundantly,
  the cedars of Lebanon that he planted.
17 In them the birds build their nests;
  the stork has its home in the fir trees.
18 The high mountains are for the wild
goats;
  the rocks are a refuge for the coneys.
19 You have made the moon to mark the
seasons;
  the sun knows its time for setting.
20 You make darkness, and it is night,
  when all the animals of the forest come
creeping out.
21 The young lions roar for their prey,
  seeking their food from God.
22 When the sun rises, they withdraw
  and lie down in their dens.
23 People go out to their work
  and to their labor until the evening.

24 O LORD, how manifold are your works!
  In wisdom you have made them all;
  the earth is full of your creatures.
25 Yonder is the sea, great and wide,
  creeping things innumerable are there,
  living things both small and great.
26 There go the ships,
  and Leviathan that you formed to sport
in it.

27 These all look to you
  to give them their food in due season;
28 when you give to them, they gather it up;
  when you open your hand, they are
filled with good things.
29 When you hide your face, they are
dismayed;

when you take away their breath, they
die
  and return to their dust.
30 When you send forth your spirit,[v] they
are created;
  and you renew the face of the ground.

104.26 Just for Fun

*What good is a Leviathan (possibly a whale,
but to the landlocked Israelites a frightening
sea monster)? Why would God make such a
creature? Simply "to sport." God makes and
delights in each creature for its own sake.*

31 May the glory of the LORD endure forever;
  may the LORD rejoice in his works—
32 who looks on the earth and it trembles,
  who touches the mountains and they
smoke.
33 I will sing to the LORD as long as I live;
  I will sing praise to my God while I
have being.
34 May my meditation be pleasing to him,
  for I rejoice in the LORD.
35 Let sinners be consumed from the earth,
  and let the wicked be no more.
Bless the LORD, O my soul.
Praise the LORD!

Psalm 105

God's Faithfulness to Israel

1 O give thanks to the LORD, call on his
name,
  make known his deeds among the
peoples.
2 Sing to him, sing praises to him;
  tell of all his wonderful works.
3 Glory in his holy name;
  let the hearts of those who seek the
LORD rejoice.
4 Seek the LORD and his strength;
  seek his presence continually.
5 Remember the wonderful works he has
done,
  his miracles, and the judgments he has
uttered,
6 O offspring of his servant Abraham,[w]
  children of Jacob, his chosen ones.

7 He is the LORD our God;
  his judgments are in all the earth.
8 He is mindful of his covenant forever,
  of the word that he commanded, for a
thousand generations,
9 the covenant that he made with Abraham,

---

[t] Heb *By them* [u] Or *to cultivate* [v] Or *your breath* [w] Another reading is *Israel* (compare 1 Chr 16.13)

his sworn promise to Isaac,
10 which he confirmed to Jacob as a statute,
to Israel as an everlasting covenant,
11 saying, "To you I will give the land of
Canaan
as your portion for an inheritance."

12 When they were few in number,
of little account, and strangers in it,
13 wandering from nation to nation,
from one kingdom to another people,
14 he allowed no one to oppress them;
he rebuked kings on their account,
15 saying, "Do not touch my anointed ones;
do my prophets no harm."

16 When he summoned famine against the
land,
and broke every staff of bread,
17 he had sent a man ahead of them,
Joseph, who was sold as a slave.
18 His feet were hurt with fetters,
his neck was put in a collar of iron;
19 until what he had said came to pass,
the word of the LORD kept testing him.
20 The king sent and released him;
the ruler of the peoples set him free.
21 He made him lord of his house,
and ruler of all his possessions,
22 to instruct[x] his officials at his pleasure,
and to teach his elders wisdom.

23 Then Israel came to Egypt;
Jacob lived as an alien in the land of
Ham.
24 And the LORD made his people very
fruitful,
and made them stronger than their
foes,
25 whose hearts he then turned to hate his
people,
to deal craftily with his servants.

26 He sent his servant Moses,
and Aaron whom he had chosen.
27 They performed his signs among them,
and miracles in the land of Ham.
28 He sent darkness, and made the land
dark;
they rebelled[y] against his words.
29 He turned their waters into blood,
and caused their fish to die.
30 Their land swarmed with frogs,
even in the chambers of their kings.
31 He spoke, and there came swarms of flies,
and gnats throughout their country.
32 He gave them hail for rain,
and lightning that flashed through their
land.

33 He struck their vines and fig trees,
and shattered the trees of their country.
34 He spoke, and the locusts came,
and young locusts without number;
35 they devoured all the vegetation in their
land,
and ate up the fruit of their ground.
36 He struck down all the firstborn in their
land,
the first issue of all their strength.

37 Then he brought Israel[z] out with silver
and gold,
and there was no one among their
tribes who stumbled.
38 Egypt was glad when they departed,
for dread of them had fallen upon it.
39 He spread a cloud for a covering,
and fire to give light by night.
40 They asked, and he brought quails,
and gave them food from heaven in
abundance.
41 He opened the rock, and water gushed
out;
it flowed through the desert like a
river.
42 For he remembered his holy promise,
and Abraham, his servant.

43 So he brought his people out with joy,
his chosen ones with singing.
44 He gave them the lands of the nations,
and they took possession of the wealth
of the peoples,
45 that they might keep his statutes
and observe his laws.
Praise the LORD!

Psalm 106

A Confession of Israel's Sins

1 Praise the LORD!
O give thanks to the LORD, for he is
good;
for his steadfast love endures forever.
2 Who can utter the mighty doings of the
LORD,
or declare all his praise?
3 Happy are those who observe justice,
who do righteousness at all times.

4 Remember me, O LORD, when you show
favor to your people;
help me when you deliver them;
5 that I may see the prosperity of your
chosen ones,
that I may rejoice in the gladness of
your nation,
that I may glory in your heritage.

---

x Gk Syr Jerome: Heb *to bind*   y Cn Compare Gk Syr: Heb *they did not rebel*   z Heb *them*

6 Both we and our ancestors have sinned;
  we have committed iniquity, have done
    wickedly.
7 Our ancestors, when they were in Egypt,
  did not consider your wonderful
    works;
  they did not remember the abundance of
    your steadfast love,
  but rebelled against the Most High[a] at
    the Red Sea.[b]
8 Yet he saved them for his name's sake,
  so that he might make known his
    mighty power.
9 He rebuked the Red Sea,[b] and it became
    dry;
  he led them through the deep as
    through a desert.
10 So he saved them from the hand of the
    foe,
  and delivered them from the hand of
    the enemy.
11 The waters covered their adversaries;
  not one of them was left.
12 Then they believed his words;
  they sang his praise.

106.12 The Turning Point

*When the Israelites praised God, their thoughts
turned naturally back to the time when God
(through Moses) freed them from slavery and
gave them a country all their own. In it they
saw God's pure graciousness. They had done
nothing to win their freedom; God had done it
all. Similarly, Christians look back to Jesus'
death and resurrection, which freed them from
sin's slavery.*

13 But they soon forgot his works;
  they did not wait for his counsel.
14 But they had a wanton craving in the
    wilderness,
  and put God to the test in the desert;
15 he gave them what they asked,
  but sent a wasting disease among them.

16 They were jealous of Moses in the camp,
  and of Aaron, the holy one of
    the LORD.
17 The earth opened and swallowed
    up Dathan,
  and covered the faction of Abiram.
18 Fire also broke out in their company;
  the flame burned up the wicked.

19 They made a calf at Horeb
  and worshiped a cast image.

20 They exchanged the glory of God[c]
  for the image of an ox that eats grass.
21 They forgot God, their Savior,
  who had done great things in Egypt,
22 wondrous works in the land of Ham,
  and awesome deeds by the Red Sea.[b]
23 Therefore he said he would destroy
    them—
  had not Moses, his chosen one,
  stood in the breach before him,
  to turn away his wrath from destroying
    them.

24 Then they despised the pleasant land,
  having no faith in his promise.
25 They grumbled in their tents,
  and did not obey the voice of
    the LORD.
26 Therefore he raised his hand and swore to
    them
  that he would make them fall in the
    wilderness,
27 and would disperse[d] their descendants
    among the nations,
  scattering them over the lands.

28 Then they attached themselves to the Baal
    of Peor,
  and ate sacrifices offered to the dead;
29 they provoked the LORD to anger with
    their deeds,
  and a plague broke out among them.
30 Then Phinehas stood up and interceded,
  and the plague was stopped.
31 And that has been reckoned to him as
    righteousness
  from generation to generation forever.

32 They angered the LORD[e] at the waters of
    Meribah,
  and it went ill with Moses on their
    account;
33 for they made his spirit bitter,
  and he spoke words that were rash.

34 They did not destroy the peoples,
  as the LORD commanded them,
35 but they mingled with the nations
  and learned to do as they did.
36 They served their idols,
  which became a snare to them.
37 They sacrificed their sons
  and their daughters to the demons;
38 they poured out innocent blood,
  the blood of their sons and daughters,
  whom they sacrificed to the idols of
    Canaan;
  and the land was polluted with blood.

a Cn Compare 78.17, 56: Heb *rebelled at the sea*   b Or *Sea of Reeds*   c Compare Gk Mss: Heb *exchanged their glory*
d Syr Compare Ezek 20.23: Heb *cause to fall*   e Heb *him*

39 Thus they became unclean by their acts,
       and prostituted themselves in their
          doings.

40 Then the anger of the LORD was kindled
          against his people,
       and he abhorred his heritage;
41 he gave them into the hand of the
          nations,
       so that those who hated them ruled
          over them.
42 Their enemies oppressed them,
       and they were brought into subjection
          under their power.
43 Many times he delivered them,
       but they were rebellious in their
          purposes,
       and were brought low through their
          iniquity.
44 Nevertheless he regarded their distress
       when he heard their cry.
45 For their sake he remembered his
          covenant,
       and showed compassion according to
          the abundance of his steadfast
          love.
46 He caused them to be pitied
       by all who held them captive.

47 Save us, O LORD our God,
       and gather us from among the nations,
    that we may give thanks to your holy
          name
       and glory in your praise.

48 Blessed be the LORD, the God of Israel,
       from everlasting to everlasting.
    And let all the people say, "Amen."
    Praise the LORD!

BOOK V
(Psalms 107–150)

Psalm 107

Thanksgiving for Deliverance from Many Troubles

1 O give thanks to the LORD, for he is good;
       for his steadfast love endures forever.
2 Let the redeemed of the LORD say so,
       those he redeemed from trouble
3 and gathered in from the lands,
       from the east and from the west,
       from the north and from the south.f

4 Some wandered in desert wastes,
       finding no way to an inhabited town;
5 hungry and thirsty,

their soul fainted within them.
6 Then they cried to the LORD in their
          trouble,
       and he delivered them from their
          distress;
7 he led them by a straight way,
       until they reached an inhabited town.
8 Let them thank the LORD for his steadfast
          love,
       for his wonderful works to humankind.
9 For he satisfies the thirsty,
       and the hungry he fills with good
          things.

10 Some sat in darkness and in gloom,
        prisoners in misery and in irons,
11 for they had rebelled against the words of
          God,
        and spurned the counsel of the Most
          High.
12 Their hearts were bowed down with hard
          labor;
        they fell down, with no one to help.
13 Then they cried to the LORD in their
          trouble,
        and he saved them from their distress;
14 he brought them out of darkness and
          gloom,
        and broke their bonds asunder.
15 Let them thank the LORD for his steadfast
          love,
        for his wonderful works to humankind.
16 For he shatters the doors of bronze,
        and cuts in two the bars of iron.

17 Some were sickg through their sinful
          ways,
        and because of their iniquities endured
          affliction;
18 they loathed any kind of food,
        and they drew near to the gates of
          death.
19 Then they cried to the LORD in their
          trouble,
        and he saved them from their distress;
20 he sent out his word and healed them,
        and delivered them from destruction.
21 Let them thank the LORD for his steadfast
          love,
        for his wonderful works to humankind.
22 And let them offer thanksgiving sacrifices,
        and tell of his deeds with songs of joy.

23 Some went down to the sea in ships,
        doing business on the mighty waters;
24 they saw the deeds of the LORD,
        his wondrous works in the deep.
25 For he commanded and raised the stormy
          wind,

f Cn: Heb sea   g Cn: Heb fools

which lifted up the waves of the sea.
26 They mounted up to heaven, they went
down to the depths;
their courage melted away in their
calamity;
27 they reeled and staggered like drunkards,
and were at their wits' end.

107.27 Worst Case

No problem is too great for God. This psalm imagines the worst calamities a Jew could think of: homelessness and starvation (verses 4–5), imprisonment (10–12), self-inflicted disease (17–18), and—the ultimate—imminent shipwreck (23–27). (Since Israel was landlocked, Jews had little experience with turbulent seas—and they dreaded them.) In all these cases, God was able to rescue those who called for his help.

28 Then they cried to the LORD in their
trouble,
and he brought them out from their
distress;
29 he made the storm be still,
and the waves of the sea were hushed.
30 Then they were glad because they had
quiet,
and he brought them to their desired
haven.
31 Let them thank the LORD for his steadfast
love,
for his wonderful works to humankind.
32 Let them extol him in the congregation of
the people,
and praise him in the assembly of the
elders.

33 He turns rivers into a desert,
springs of water into thirsty ground,
34 a fruitful land into a salty waste,
because of the wickedness of its
inhabitants.
35 He turns a desert into pools of water,
a parched land into springs of water.
36 And there he lets the hungry live,
and they establish a town to live in;
37 they sow fields, and plant vineyards,
and get a fruitful yield.
38 By his blessing they multiply greatly,
and he does not let their cattle
decrease.

39 When they are diminished and brought
low
through oppression, trouble,
and sorrow,

40 he pours contempt on princes
and makes them wander in trackless
wastes;
41 but he raises up the needy out of distress,
and makes their families like flocks.
42 The upright see it and are glad;
and all wickedness stops its mouth.
43 Let those who are wise give heed to these
things,
and consider the steadfast love of the
LORD.

Psalm 108

Praise and Prayer for Victory

A Song. A Psalm of David.

1 My heart is steadfast, O God, my heart is
steadfast;[h]
I will sing and make melody.
Awake, my soul![i]
2 Awake, O harp and lyre!
I will awake the dawn.
3 I will give thanks to you, O LORD, among
the peoples,
and I will sing praises to you among
the nations.
4 For your steadfast love is higher than the
heavens,
and your faithfulness reaches to the
clouds.

5 Be exalted, O God, above the heavens,
and let your glory be over all the
earth.
6 Give victory with your right hand, and
answer me,
so that those whom you love may be
rescued.

7 God has promised in his sanctuary:[j]
"With exultation I will divide up
Shechem,
and portion out the Vale of Succoth.
8 Gilead is mine; Manasseh is mine;
Ephraim is my helmet;
Judah is my scepter.
9 Moab is my washbasin;
on Edom I hurl my shoe;
over Philistia I shout in triumph."

10 Who will bring me to the fortified city?
Who will lead me to Edom?
11 Have you not rejected us, O God?
You do not go out, O God, with our
armies.
12 O grant us help against the foe,
for human help is worthless.

---

h Heb Mss Gk Syr: MT lacks *my heart is steadfast*   i Compare 57.8: Heb *also my soul*   j Or *by his holiness*

13 With God we shall do valiantly;
　　it is he who will tread down our
　　　foes.

Psalm 109

Prayer for Vindication and Vengeance

To the leader. Of David. A Psalm.

1 Do not be silent, O God of my praise.
2 For wicked and deceitful mouths are
　　opened against me,
　　speaking against me with lying tongues.
3 They beset me with words of hate,
　　and attack me without cause.
4 In return for my love they accuse me,
　　even while I make prayer for them.[k]
5 So they reward me evil for good,
　　and hatred for my love.

6 They say,[l] "Appoint a wicked man
　　　against him;
　　let an accuser stand on his right.
7 When he is tried, let him be found guilty;
　　let his prayer be counted as sin.
8 May his days be few;
　　may another seize his position.

109.8 The Judas Principle

*Peter applied this verse to Judas (Acts 1.20).
The New Testament writers saw David's life as
the pattern and foreshadowing of the Messiah,
David's son. The savage betrayal recorded in
this poem shows, as do many psalms, that
unexplained suffering comes to the most
devoted of God's people: first David, then Jesus.*

9 May his children be orphans,
　　and his wife a widow.
10 May his children wander about and beg;
　　may they be driven out of[m] the ruins
　　　they inhabit.
11 May the creditor seize all that he has;
　　may strangers plunder the fruits of his
　　　toil.
12 May there be no one to do him a
　　　kindness,
　　nor anyone to pity his orphaned
　　　children.
13 May his posterity be cut off;
　　may his name be blotted out in the
　　　second generation.
14 May the iniquity of his father[n] be
　　remembered before the LORD,

and do not let the sin of his mother be
　　blotted out.
15 Let them be before the LORD continually,
　　and may his[o] memory be cut off from
　　　the earth.
16 For he did not remember to show
　　　kindness,
　　but pursued the poor and needy
　　and the brokenhearted to their death.
17 He loved to curse; let curses come on
　　　him.
　　He did not like blessing; may it be far
　　　from him.
18 He clothed himself with cursing as his
　　　coat,
　　may it soak into his body like water,
　　like oil into his bones.
19 May it be like a garment that he wraps
　　　around himself,
　　like a belt that he wears every day."

20 May that be the reward of my accusers
　　　from the LORD,
　　of those who speak evil against my life.
21 But you, O LORD my Lord,
　　act on my behalf for your name's sake;
　　because your steadfast love is good,
　　　deliver me.
22 For I am poor and needy,
　　and my heart is pierced within me.
23 I am gone like a shadow at evening;
　　I am shaken off like a locust.
24 My knees are weak through fasting;
　　my body has become gaunt.
25 I am an object of scorn to my accusers;
　　when they see me, they shake their
　　　heads.

26 Help me, O LORD my God!
　　Save me according to your steadfast
　　　love.
27 Let them know that this is your hand;
　　you, O LORD, have done it.
28 Let them curse, but you will bless.
　　Let my assailants be put to shame;[p]
　　may your servant be glad.
29 May my accusers be clothed with
　　　dishonor;
　　may they be wrapped in their own
　　　shame as in a mantle.

30 With my mouth I will give great thanks
　　　to the LORD;
　　I will praise him in the midst of the
　　　throng.
31 For he stands at the right hand of the
　　　needy,
　　to save them from those who would
　　　condemn them to death.

k Syr: Heb *I prayer*　　*l* Heb lacks *They say*　　*m* Gk: Heb *and seek*　　*n* Cn: Heb *fathers*　　*o* Gk: Heb *their*
p Gk: Heb *They have risen up and have been put to shame*

Psalm 110

Assurance of Victory for God's Priest-King

Of David. A Psalm.

¹ The LORD says to my lord,
  "Sit at my right hand
  until I make your enemies your footstool."

² The LORD sends out from Zion
    your mighty scepter.
    Rule in the midst of your foes.
³ Your people will offer themselves willingly
    on the day you lead your forces
    on the holy mountains.*q*
  From the womb of the morning,
    like dew, your youth*r* will come to
    you.

q Another reading is *in holy splendor*   *r* Cn: Heb *the dew of your youth*

The Twelfth Man

He came "out of nowhere" to win great respect

> "You are a priest forever according to the order of Melchizedek."
> 110.4

IN DALLAS, TEXAS, ON JANUARY 1, 1922, Texas A&M fought it out in the first bowl game ever played in the Southwest. Coach Dana Bible watched helplessly as, one by one, his running backs limped off the field with injuries. As the game neared halftime, he had only one reserve left.

What to do? He remembered a small, wiry back who had not made the traveling team. He had told Coach Bible, "I'll be in the stands if you need me." Bible sent a messenger to search for the young player, King Gill, and get him to suit up for the second half. The Texas A&M tradition of "the twelfth man" began.

Since then, a series of "twelfth men" have come from the student body to help Texas A&M teams. At some schools football players are a breed apart. But Texas A&M, with its "twelfth man" tradition, remembers that a football player may come "out of nowhere." Help doesn't always arrive in the proper uniform.

Mystery Man

The Bible has a kind of twelfth man, a shadowy figure who is mentioned only three times, yet has great importance. Melchizedek came "out of nowhere" in Genesis 14.18–20 as a priest whom Abraham honored. Melchizedek never reappeared. But Psalm 110 mentions him in referring to the Messiah, the conquering king whom Israelites expected. And in the New Testament, the book of Hebrews devotes more than a chapter to Melchizedek's significance. Why so? The answer has to do with Israel's longing for great leadership.

Much as the United States government recognizes three branches of government, Israel had three important kinds of leaders: prophets, priests, and kings. Prophets told the truth, revealing God's righteousness. Kings were to put righteousness into effect, as head of the government. Priests were to see that God met his people in worship: they represented God to the people, and the people to God. According to the God-given Israelite constitution, kings and priests always came from different tribes: a priest from the family of Levi and a king from the family of Judah. Ordinarily, a king could not be a priest.

Total Leadership

The Messiah, however, must be a total leader: a perfect king governing justly, a perfect prophet revealing God's truth, a perfect priest bringing God and people together. But how could he be all three, when priests and kings were supposed to come from different families? Wouldn't that violate God's law?

Psalm 110 suggests (and Hebrews 7 amplifies) the answer. Just as a football player need not necessarily come from the athletic dorm, so Melchizedek's example proves that a priest need not necessarily come from the proper family. Melchizedek was not even an Israelite, let alone from the Levite family. He knew nothing about the temple or the Old Testament law, for these came after his time. Yet his spiritual power impressed Abraham. Melchizedek showed the kind of leadership Christ was to bring. He was both a priest and a king.

Psalm 110's brief praise provides a thread between the Old and New Testaments. It hints that the Messiah would be greater than David, while David's descendant. And by tracing the Messiah's roots to Melchizedek, it established his credibility as both priest and king.

Life Questions: What are the "proper channels" you expect to see spiritual leadership come from? Has God ever led you through someone outside those channels?

4 The LORD has sworn and will not change
    his mind,
  "You are a priest forever according to
    the order of Melchizedek."[s]

110.1 The Son of God

Jesus quoted this verse in Mark 12.35–37 to show that the Messiah would not be merely a human military leader, as many Jews expected. Here David refers to the coming King (David's descendant) as "my lord." If the Messiah were strictly his human descendant, David would not address him so respectfully.

5 The Lord is at your right hand;
  he will shatter kings on the day of his
    wrath.
6 He will execute judgment among the
    nations,
  filling them with corpses;
  he will shatter heads
    over the wide earth.
7 He will drink from the stream by the
    path;
  therefore he will lift up his head.

Psalm 111

Praise for God's Wonderful Works

1 Praise the LORD!
  I will give thanks to the LORD with my
    whole heart,
  in the company of the upright, in the
    congregation.
2 Great are the works of the LORD,
  studied by all who delight in them.
3 Full of honor and majesty is his work,
  and his righteousness endures forever.
4 He has gained renown by his wonderful
    deeds;
  the LORD is gracious and merciful.
5 He provides food for those who fear
    him;
  he is ever mindful of his covenant.
6 He has shown his people the power of
    his works,
  in giving them the heritage of the
    nations.
7 The works of his hands are faithful and
    just;
  all his precepts are trustworthy.
8 They are established forever and
    ever,

  to be performed with faithfulness and
    uprightness.
9 He sent redemption to his people;
  he has commanded his covenant
    forever.
  Holy and awesome is his name.
10 The fear of the LORD is the beginning of
    wisdom;
  all those who practice it[t] have a good
    understanding.
  His praise endures forever.

Psalm 112

Blessings of the Righteous

1 Praise the LORD!
  Happy are those who fear the LORD,
  who greatly delight in his
    commandments.
2 Their descendants will be mighty in the
    land;
  the generation of the upright will be
    blessed.
3 Wealth and riches are in their houses,
  and their righteousness endures
    forever.
4 They rise in the darkness as a light for the
    upright;
  they are gracious, merciful, and
    righteous.
5 It is well with those who deal generously
    and lend,
  who conduct their affairs with justice.
6 For the righteous will never be moved;
  they will be remembered forever.
7 They are not afraid of evil tidings;
  their hearts are firm, secure in the
    LORD.
8 Their hearts are steady, they will not be
    afraid;
  in the end they will look in triumph on
    their foes.
9 They have distributed freely, they have
    given to the poor;
  their righteousness endures forever;
  their horn is exalted in honor.
10 The wicked see it and are angry;
  they gnash their teeth and melt away;
  the desire of the wicked comes
    to nothing.

Psalm 113

God the Helper of the Needy

1 Praise the LORD!
  Praise, O servants of the LORD;
  praise the name of the LORD.

---

[s] Or *forever, a rightful king by my edict*   [t] Gk Syr: Heb *them*

2 Blessed be the name of the LORD
   from this time on and forevermore.
3 From the rising of the sun to its setting
   the name of the LORD is to be praised.
4 The LORD is high above all nations,
   and his glory above the heavens.

113.1 Psalms of the Last Supper

Psalms 113 to 118 were traditionally sung at the passover meal—the first two before the meal, the last four after. These were probably the last songs Jesus sang with his disciples before his death (Mark 14.26).

5 Who is like the LORD our God,
   who is seated on high,
6 who looks far down
   on the heavens and the earth?
7 He raises the poor from the dust,
   and lifts the needy from the ash
      heap,
8 to make them sit with princes,
   with the princes of his people.
9 He gives the barren woman a home,
   making her the joyous mother of
      children.
   Praise the LORD!

Psalm 114

God's Wonders at the Exodus

1 When Israel went out from Egypt,
   the house of Jacob from a people of
      strange language,
2 Judah became God's*u* sanctuary,
   Israel his dominion.

3 The sea looked and fled;
   Jordan turned back.
4 The mountains skipped like rams,
   the hills like lambs.

5 Why is it, O sea, that you flee?
   O Jordan, that you turn back?
6 O mountains, that you skip like rams?
   O hills, like lambs?

7 Tremble, O earth, at the presence of the
      LORD,
   at the presence of the God of Jacob,
8 who turns the rock into a pool of water,
   the flint into a spring of water.

Psalm 115

The Impotence of Idols and the Greatness of God

1 Not to us, O LORD, not to us, but to your
      name give glory,
   for the sake of your steadfast love and
      your faithfulness.
2 Why should the nations say,
   "Where is their God?"

3 Our God is in the heavens;
   he does whatever he pleases.
4 Their idols are silver and gold,
   the work of human hands.
5 They have mouths, but do not speak;
   eyes, but do not see.
6 They have ears, but do not hear;
   noses, but do not smell.
7 They have hands, but do not feel;
   feet, but do not walk;
   they make no sound in their throats.
8 Those who make them are like them;
   so are all who trust in them.

9 O Israel, trust in the LORD!
   He is their help and their shield.
10 O house of Aaron, trust in the LORD!
   He is their help and their shield.
11 You who fear the LORD, trust in the LORD!
   He is their help and their shield.

12 The LORD has been mindful of us; he will
      bless us;
   he will bless the house of Israel;
   he will bless the house of Aaron;
13 he will bless those who fear the LORD,
   both small and great.

14 May the LORD give you increase,
   both you and your children.
15 May you be blessed by the LORD,
   who made heaven and earth.

16 The heavens are the LORD's heavens,
   but the earth he has given to human
      beings.
17 The dead do not praise the LORD,
   nor do any that go down into silence.
18 But we will bless the LORD
   from this time on and forevermore.
   Praise the LORD!

Psalm 116

Thanksgiving for Recovery from Illness

1 I love the LORD, because he has heard
   my voice and my supplications.
2 Because he inclined his ear to me,

u Heb his

therefore I will call on him as long as I
live.
3 The snares of death encompassed me;
the pangs of Sheol laid hold on me;
I suffered distress and anguish.
4 Then I called on the name of the LORD:
"O LORD, I pray, save my life!"

5 Gracious is the LORD, and righteous;
our God is merciful.
6 The LORD protects the simple;
when I was brought low, he saved me.
7 Return, O my soul, to your rest,
for the LORD has dealt bountifully with
you.

8 For you have delivered my soul from
death,
my eyes from tears,
my feet from stumbling.
9 I walk before the LORD
in the land of the living.
10 I kept my faith, even when I said,
"I am greatly afflicted";
11 I said in my consternation,
"Everyone is a liar."

12 What shall I return to the LORD
for all his bounty to me?
13 I will lift up the cup of salvation
and call on the name of the LORD,
14 I will pay my vows to the LORD
in the presence of all his people.
15 Precious in the sight of the LORD
is the death of his faithful ones.

116.15 Precious Death

*This verse, often read at funerals, in no way
implies that God enjoys the death of his people.
Instead, it means that he carefully watches
over their death, and that it matters deeply to
him. The whole psalm praises God for saving
from death. Psalm 72.14 uses a similar phrase
in a similar way: "precious is their blood in his
sight."*

16 O LORD, I am your servant;
I am your servant, the child of your
serving girl.
You have loosed my bonds.
17 I will offer to you a thanksgiving sacrifice
and call on the name of the LORD.
18 I will pay my vows to the LORD
in the presence of all his people,
19 in the courts of the house of the LORD,
in your midst, O Jerusalem.
Praise the LORD!

Psalm 117

Universal Call to Worship

1 Praise the LORD, all you nations!
Extol him, all you peoples!
2 For great is his steadfast love toward us,
and the faithfulness of the LORD
endures forever.
Praise the LORD!

Psalm 118

A Song of Victory

1 O give thanks to the LORD, for he is good;
his steadfast love endures forever!

2 Let Israel say,
"His steadfast love endures forever."
3 Let the house of Aaron say,
"His steadfast love endures forever."
4 Let those who fear the LORD say,
"His steadfast love endures forever."

5 Out of my distress I called on the LORD;
the LORD answered me and set me in a
broad place.
6 With the LORD on my side I do not fear.
What can mortals do to me?
7 The LORD is on my side to help me;
I shall look in triumph on those who
hate me.
8 It is better to take refuge in the LORD
than to put confidence in mortals.
9 It is better to take refuge in the LORD
than to put confidence in princes.

10 All nations surrounded me;
in the name of the LORD I cut them
off!
11 They surrounded me, surrounded me on
every side;
in the name of the LORD I cut them
off!
12 They surrounded me like bees;
they blazed[v] like a fire of thorns;
in the name of the LORD I cut them
off!
13 I was pushed hard,[w] so that I was falling,
but the LORD helped me.
14 The LORD is my strength and my might;
he has become my salvation.

15 There are glad songs of victory in the
tents of the righteous:
"The right hand of the LORD does
valiantly;
16 the right hand of the LORD is exalted;
the right hand of the LORD does
valiantly."

v Gk: Heb *were extinguished*   w Gk Syr Jerome: Heb *You pushed me hard*

17 I shall not die, but I shall live,
and recount the deeds of the LORD.
18 The LORD has punished me severely,
but he did not give me over to death.

19 Open to me the gates of righteousness,
that I may enter through them
and give thanks to the LORD.

20 This is the gate of the LORD;
the righteous shall enter through it.

21 I thank you that you have answered me
and have become my salvation.
22 The stone that the builders rejected
has become the chief cornerstone.

118.22 Last-place Winner

God has a habit of reversing people's status. The poor and needy end up satisfied, while the rich and arrogant lose their position. As Jesus said, "many who are first will be last, and the last will be first" (Matthew 19.30). This psalm expresses the concept with an image: A stone builders considered unusable ends up holding the whole building together. Jesus applied it to himself, and it was quoted by Peter as a prophecy fulfilled by Jesus' death and resurrection (see Matthew 21.42; 1 Peter 2.7; and Acts 4.11).

23 This is the LORD's doing;
it is marvelous in our eyes.
24 This is the day that the LORD has made;
let us rejoice and be glad in it.ˣ
25 Save us, we beseech you, O LORD!
O LORD, we beseech you, give us
success!

26 Blessed is the one who comes in the name
of the LORD.ʸ
We bless you from the house of the
LORD.
27 The LORD is God,
and he has given us light.
Bind the festal procession with branches,
up to the horns of the altar.ᶻ

28 You are my God, and I will give thanks
to you;
you are my God, I will extol you.

29 O give thanks to the LORD, for he is good,
for his steadfast love endures forever.

Psalm 119

The Glories of God's Law

1 Happy are those whose way is blameless,
who walk in the law of the LORD.
2 Happy are those who keep his decrees,
who seek him with their whole heart,
3 who also do no wrong,
but walk in his ways.
4 You have commanded your precepts
to be kept diligently.
5 O that my ways may be steadfast
in keeping your statutes!
6 Then I shall not be put to shame,
having my eyes fixed on all your
commandments.
7 I will praise you with an upright heart,
when I learn your righteous
ordinances.
8 I will observe your statutes;
do not utterly forsake me.

9 How can young people keep their way
pure?
By guarding it according to your word.
10 With my whole heart I seek you;
do not let me stray from your
commandments.
11 I treasure your word in my heart,
so that I may not sin against you.
12 Blessed are you, O LORD;
teach me your statutes.
13 With my lips I declare
all the ordinances of your mouth.
14 I delight in the way of your decrees
as much as in all riches.
15 I will meditate on your precepts,
and fix my eyes on your ways.
16 I will delight in your statutes;
I will not forget your word.

17 Deal bountifully with your servant,
so that I may live and observe your
word.
18 Open my eyes, so that I may behold
wondrous things out of your law.
19 I live as an alien in the land;
do not hide your commandments from
me.
20 My soul is consumed with longing
for your ordinances at all times.
21 You rebuke the insolent, accursed ones,
who wander from your
commandments;
22 take away from me their scorn and
contempt,
for I have kept your decrees.
23 Even though princes sit plotting against
me,

ˣ Or *in him*   ʸ Or *Blessed in the name of the LORD is the one who comes*   ᶻ Meaning of Heb uncertain

your servant will meditate on your
statutes.
24 Your decrees are my delight,
they are my counselors.

25 My soul clings to the dust;
revive me according to your word.
26 When I told of my ways, you answered
me;
teach me your statutes.
27 Make me understand the way of your
precepts,
and I will meditate on your wondrous
works.
28 My soul melts away for sorrow;
strengthen me according to your word.
29 Put false ways far from me;
and graciously teach me your law.
30 I have chosen the way of faithfulness;
I set your ordinances before me.
31 I cling to your decrees, O LORD;
let me not be put to shame.
32 I run the way of your commandments,
for you enlarge my understanding.

33 Teach me, O LORD, the way of your
statutes,
and I will observe it to the end.
34 Give me understanding, that I may keep
your law
and observe it with my whole heart.
35 Lead me in the path of your
commandments,
for I delight in it.
36 Turn my heart to your decrees,
and not to selfish gain.
37 Turn my eyes from looking at vanities;
give me life in your ways.
38 Confirm to your servant your promise,
which is for those who fear you.
39 Turn away the disgrace that I dread,
for your ordinances are good.
40 See, I have longed for your precepts;
in your righteousness give me life.

41 Let your steadfast love come to me,
O LORD,
your salvation according to your
promise.
42 Then I shall have an answer for those
who taunt me,
for I trust in your word.
43 Do not take the word of truth utterly out
of my mouth,
for my hope is in your ordinances.
44 I will keep your law continually,
forever and ever.
45 I shall walk at liberty,
for I have sought your precepts.

46 I will also speak of your decrees before
kings,
and shall not be put to shame;
47 I find my delight in your commandments,
because I love them.
48 I revere your commandments, which I
love,
and I will meditate on your statutes.

49 Remember your word to your servant,
in which you have made me hope.
50 This is my comfort in my distress,
that your promise gives me life.
51 The arrogant utterly deride me,
but I do not turn away from your law.
52 When I think of your ordinances from of
old,
I take comfort, O LORD.
53 Hot indignation seizes me because of the
wicked,
those who forsake your law.
54 Your statutes have been my songs
wherever I make my home.
55 I remember your name in the night,
O LORD,
and keep your law.

119.55 Lying in Bed

*The psalms consider every aspect of life—even
the thoughts that come while lying in bed at
night. You can easily become obsessed with
other people's wrongs against you. But you
can also turn your thoughts to God and quiet
your anxieties while strengthening your
commitment. Other psalms that refer to such
nighttime thoughts, good and bad, are these:
4.4; 6.6; 16.7; 17.3; 63.6; 77.2; 102.7; and
119.62,148.*

56 This blessing has fallen to me,
for I have kept your precepts.

57 The LORD is my portion;
I promise to keep your words.
58 I implore your favor with all my heart;
be gracious to me according to your
promise.
59 When I think of your ways,
I turn my feet to your decrees;
60 I hurry and do not delay
to keep your commandments.
61 Though the cords of the wicked ensnare
me,
I do not forget your law.
62 At midnight I rise to praise you,
because of your righteous ordinances.
63 I am a companion of all who fear you,
of those who keep your precepts.

⁶⁴ The earth, O LORD, is full of your
steadfast love;
teach me your statutes.

⁶⁵ You have dealt well with your servant,
O LORD, according to your word.
⁶⁶ Teach me good judgment and knowledge,
for I believe in your commandments.
⁶⁷ Before I was humbled I went astray,

but now I keep your word.
⁶⁸ You are good and do good;
teach me your statutes.
⁶⁹ The arrogant smear me with lies,
but with my whole heart I keep your
precepts.
⁷⁰ Their hearts are fat and gross,
but I delight in your law.
⁷¹ It is good for me that I was humbled,

A Love Poem to God's Law
How could Scripture inspire such poetry?

> *I revere your commandments, which I love. 119.48*

FOR ALL THE HUNDREDS OF books written about William Shakespeare, he remains a mysterious figure. His "dark lady" prompts endless guesses. He wrote 26 passionate poems to her, yet we do not even know her name. Numerous books try to guess it, "proving" that one lady or another must have been the one.

One thing we do know: She had captivated Shakespeare. Seldom has love produced such writhing emotion as his sonnets express. Helplessly ravished by her unfashionable "black (brunette) beauty," Shakespeare longed to forget her, to escape her evil character. Yet he was uncontrollably drawn.

> *My thoughts and my discourse as madman's are . . .*
> *For I have sworn thee fair, and thought thee bright,*
> *Who art as black as hell, as dark as night.*

But what an oddity to express such fevered emotion in sonnets! The sonnets require discipline: precisely 14 lines, an exact rhyming scheme, and iambic pentameter rhythm. How can a raging storm be reflected in such a small, still pond? Yet the evidence of the poems is unmistakable. The discipline gave wild emotion a backbone.

A Love Poem to the Law

Psalm 119 contains even greater oddities. As emotional as Shakespeare's sonnets, this poem also takes a very systematic form: the acrostic, where each line of each stanza begins with a letter from the Hebrew alphabet, *A* in the first stanza, *B* in the second, and so on, through all 22 letters of the Hebrew alphabet.

But the subject is the biggest surprise. Psalm 119 is a long, passionate love poem about God's law.

How do you fall in love with law? Most people admit that rules are necessary, and appreciate them grudgingly. But no one writes love poems to the federal drug abuse statutes.

The word translated "law" doesn't merely mean rules. It expresses the totality of God's written instructions. The poet sees life full of uncertainties, of enemies, of pain. But God has given a reliable guide for living—like pavement underfoot after you have been stuck in mud. Obeying God's law, to the psalmist, is no slavery—rather it is freedom. "I run the way of your commandments, for you enlarge my understanding" (verse 32).

On the Edge of Death

Psalm 119 is not written from an ivory tower. The poet has apparently been near death (verse 87), and even as he writes, "the wicked lie in wait to destroy" him (verse 95). But in this dangerous situation he has learned to hang on to God's wisdom. The lesson is so valuable he has become grateful for his sufferings: "It is good for me that I was humbled, so that I might learn your statutes" (verse 71).

The psalmist simply does not see God's law as a dusty, rigid rulebook. He hears God's loving voice in it. "The earth, O LORD is full of your steadfast love; teach me your statutes" (verse 64). "Your decrees . . . are the joy of my heart" (verse 111).

God's laws channel God's love into the poet's life. They protect him from doing wrong and give him wisdom to understand his situation. They make new life flow into him. No wonder he writes with such thankfulness. In God's word he finds more than direction. He finds God himself.

Life Questions: Do you ever feel with the psalmist that life has become frighteningly out of control? How can God's law help you regain confidence?

so that I might learn your statutes.
72 The law of your mouth is better to me
than thousands of gold and silver
pieces.

73 Your hands have made and fashioned me;
give me understanding that I may learn
your commandments.
74 Those who fear you shall see me and
rejoice,
because I have hoped in your word.
75 I know, O LORD, that your judgments are
right,
and that in faithfulness you have
humbled me.
76 Let your steadfast love become my
comfort
according to your promise to your
servant.
77 Let your mercy come to me, that I may
live;
for your law is my delight.
78 Let the arrogant be put to shame,
because they have subverted me with
guile;
as for me, I will meditate on your
precepts.
79 Let those who fear you turn to me,
so that they may know your decrees.
80 May my heart be blameless in your
statutes,
so that I may not be put to shame.

81 My soul languishes for your salvation;
I hope in your word.
82 My eyes fail with watching for your
promise;
I ask, "When will you comfort me?"
83 For I have become like a wineskin in the
smoke,
yet I have not forgotten your statutes.
84 How long must your servant endure?
When will you judge those who
persecute me?
85 The arrogant have dug pitfalls for me;
they flout your law.
86 All your commandments are enduring;
I am persecuted without cause; help
me!
87 They have almost made an end of me on
earth;
but I have not forsaken your precepts.
88 In your steadfast love spare my life,
so that I may keep the decrees of your
mouth.

89 The LORD exists forever;
your word is firmly fixed in heaven.
90 Your faithfulness endures to all
generations;

you have established the earth, and it
stands fast.
91 By your appointment they stand today,
for all things are your servants.
92 If your law had not been my delight,
I would have perished in my misery.
93 I will never forget your precepts,
for by them you have given me life.
94 I am yours; save me,
for I have sought your precepts.
95 The wicked lie in wait to destroy me,
but I consider your decrees.
96 I have seen a limit to all perfection,
but your commandment is exceedingly
broad.

119.96 Free At Last

*People often wonder if following God's law will
restrict them, but actual experience shows that
God's law liberates—by freeing us from the
destructive impact of sinful behavior, and by
introducing us to the mind-expanding realm of
God's wisdom. Like the author of Ecclesiastes,
the psalmist had looked around and seen
limits to everything. Only in following God's
commands, he sees, can a person escape this
frustrating sense of boundaries.*

97 Oh, how I love your law!
It is my meditation all day long.
98 Your commandment makes me wiser
than my enemies,
for it is always with me.
99 I have more understanding than all my
teachers,
for your decrees are my meditation.
100 I understand more than the aged,
for I keep your precepts.
101 I hold back my feet from every evil way,
in order to keep your word.
102 I do not turn away from your
ordinances,
for you have taught me.
103 How sweet are your words to my taste,
sweeter than honey to my mouth!
104 Through your precepts I get
understanding;
therefore I hate every false way.

105 Your word is a lamp to my feet
and a light to my path.
106 I have sworn an oath and confirmed it,
to observe your righteous ordinances.
107 I am severely afflicted;
give me life, O LORD, according to
your word.
108 Accept my offerings of praise, O LORD,
and teach me your ordinances.

109 I hold my life in my hand continually,
  but I do not forget your law.
110 The wicked have laid a snare for me,
  but I do not stray from your precepts.
111 Your decrees are my heritage forever;
  they are the joy of my heart.
112 I incline my heart to perform your
    statutes
  forever, to the end.

113 I hate the double-minded,
  but I love your law.
114 You are my hiding place and my shield;
  I hope in your word.
115 Go away from me, you evildoers,
  that I may keep the commandments
    of my God.
116 Uphold me according to your promise,
    that I may live,
  and let me not be put to shame in my
    hope.
117 Hold me up, that I may be safe
  and have regard for your statutes
    continually.
118 You spurn all who go astray from your
    statutes;
  for their cunning is in vain.
119 All the wicked of the earth you count as
    dross;
  therefore I love your decrees.
120 My flesh trembles for fear of you,
  and I am afraid of your judgments.

121 I have done what is just and right;
  do not leave me to my oppressors.
122 Guarantee your servant's well-being;
  do not let the godless oppress me.
123 My eyes fail from watching for your
    salvation,
  and for the fulfillment of your
    righteous promise.
124 Deal with your servant according to your
    steadfast love,
  and teach me your statutes.
125 I am your servant; give me
    understanding,
  so that I may know your decrees.
126 It is time for the LORD to act,
  for your law has been broken.
127 Truly I love your commandments
  more than gold, more than fine gold.
128 Truly I direct my steps by all your
    precepts;[a]
  I hate every false way.

129 Your decrees are wonderful;
  therefore my soul keeps them.
130 The unfolding of your words gives light;

it imparts understanding to the
    simple.
131 With open mouth I pant,
  because I long for your
    commandments.
132 Turn to me and be gracious to me,
  as is your custom toward those who
    love your name.
133 Keep my steps steady according to your
    promise,
  and never let iniquity have dominion
    over me.
134 Redeem me from human oppression,
  that I may keep your precepts.
135 Make your face shine upon your servant,
  and teach me your statutes.
136 My eyes shed streams of tears
  because your law is not kept.

137 You are righteous, O LORD,
  and your judgments are right.
138 You have appointed your decrees in
    righteousness
  and in all faithfulness.
139 My zeal consumes me
  because my foes forget your words.
140 Your promise is well tried,
  and your servant loves it.
141 I am small and despised,
  yet I do not forget your precepts.
142 Your righteousness is an everlasting
    righteousness,
  and your law is the truth.
143 Trouble and anguish have come
    upon me,
  but your commandments are my
    delight.
144 Your decrees are righteous forever;
  give me understanding that I may live.

145 With my whole heart I cry; answer me,
    O LORD.
  I will keep your statutes.
146 I cry to you; save me,
  that I may observe your decrees.
147 I rise before dawn and cry for help;
  I put my hope in your words.
148 My eyes are awake before each watch of
    the night,
  that I may meditate on your promise.
149 In your steadfast love hear my voice;
  O LORD, in your justice preserve my
    life.
150 Those who persecute me with evil
    purpose draw near;
  they are far from your law.
151 Yet you are near, O LORD,
  and all your commandments are true.

a Gk Jerome: Meaning of Heb uncertain

152 Long ago I learned from your decrees
　　that you have established them
　　　forever.

153 Look on my misery and rescue me,
　　for I do not forget your law.

119.151 Near and Nearer

The psalmist doesn't claim that God makes problem people disappear. He merely points out that while they are near, so is God. Big problems gain a different perspective when we remember the nearness of a bigger God.

154 Plead my cause and redeem me;
　　give me life according to your
　　　promise.
155 Salvation is far from the wicked,
　　for they do not seek your statutes.
156 Great is your mercy, O LORD;
　　give me life according to your justice.
157 Many are my persecutors and my
　　　adversaries,
　　yet I do not swerve from your
　　　decrees.
158 I look at the faithless with disgust,
　　because they do not keep your
　　　commands.
159 Consider how I love your precepts;
　　preserve my life according to your
　　　steadfast love.
160 The sum of your word is truth;
　　and every one of your righteous
　　　ordinances endures forever.

161 Princes persecute me without cause,
　　but my heart stands in awe of your
　　　words.
162 I rejoice at your word
　　like one who finds great spoil.
163 I hate and abhor falsehood,
　　but I love your law.
164 Seven times a day I praise you
　　for your righteous ordinances.
165 Great peace have those who love your
　　　law;
　　nothing can make them stumble.
166 I hope for your salvation, O LORD,
　　and I fulfill your commandments.
167 My soul keeps your decrees;
　　I love them exceedingly.
168 I keep your precepts and decrees,
　　for all my ways are before you.

169 Let my cry come before you, O LORD;
　　give me understanding according to
　　　your word.

170 Let my supplication come before you;
　　deliver me according to your promise.
171 My lips will pour forth praise,
　　because you teach me your statutes.
172 My tongue will sing of your promise,
　　for all your commandments are right.
173 Let your hand be ready to help me,
　　for I have chosen your precepts.
174 I long for your salvation, O LORD,
　　and your law is my delight.
175 Let me live that I may praise you,
　　and let your ordinances help me.
176 I have gone astray like a lost sheep; seek
　　　out your servant,
　　for I do not forget your
　　　commandments.

Psalm 120

Prayer for Deliverance from Slanderers

A Song of Ascents.

1 In my distress I cry to the LORD,
　　that he may answer me:
2 "Deliver me, O LORD,
　　from lying lips,
　　from a deceitful tongue."

3 What shall be given to you?
　　And what more shall be done to you,
　　you deceitful tongue?
4 A warrior's sharp arrows,
　　with glowing coals of the broom tree!

5 Woe is me, that I am an alien in
　　　Meshech,
　　that I must live among the tents of
　　　Kedar.
6 Too long have I had my dwelling
　　among those who hate peace.
7 I am for peace;
　　but when I speak,
　　they are for war.

Psalm 121

Assurance of God's Protection

A Song of Ascents.

1 I lift up my eyes to the hills—
　　from where will my help come?
2 My help comes from the LORD,
　　who made heaven and earth.

3 He will not let your foot be moved;
　　he who keeps you will not slumber.
4 He who keeps Israel
　　will neither slumber nor sleep.

5 The LORD is your keeper;
   the LORD is your shade at your right
     hand.
6 The sun shall not strike you by day,
   nor the moon by night.

7 The LORD will keep you from all evil;
   he will keep your life.
8 The LORD will keep
   your going out and your coming in
   from this time on and forevermore.

Psalm 122

Song of Praise and Prayer for Jerusalem

A Song of Ascents. Of David.

1 I was glad when they said to me,
   "Let us go to the house of the LORD!"
2 Our feet are standing
   within your gates, O Jerusalem.

3 Jerusalem—built as a city
   that is bound firmly together.
4 To it the tribes go up,
   the tribes of the LORD,
 as was decreed for Israel,
   to give thanks to the name of
     the LORD.
5 For there the thrones for judgment were
     set up,
   the thrones of the house of David.

6 Pray for the peace of Jerusalem:
   "May they prosper who love you.
7 Peace be within your walls,
   and security within your towers."
8 For the sake of my relatives and friends
   I will say, "Peace be within you."
9 For the sake of the house of the LORD our
     God,
   I will seek your good.

Psalm 123

Supplication for Mercy

A Song of Ascents.

1 To you I lift up my eyes,
   O you who are enthroned in the
     heavens!
2 As the eyes of servants
   look to the hand of their master,
 as the eyes of a maid
   to the hand of her mistress,
 so our eyes look to the LORD our God,
   until he has mercy upon us.

3 Have mercy upon us, O LORD, have
     mercy upon us,
   for we have had more than enough of
     contempt.
4 Our soul has had more than its fill
   of the scorn of those who are at ease,
   of the contempt of the proud.

Psalm 124

Thanksgiving for Israel's Deliverance

A Song of Ascents. Of David.

1 If it had not been the LORD who was on
     our side
   —let Israel now say—
2 if it had not been the LORD who was on
     our side,
   when our enemies attacked us,
3 then they would have swallowed us up
     alive,
   when their anger was kindled against
     us;
4 then the flood would have swept us away,
   the torrent would have gone over us;
5 then over us would have gone
   the raging waters.

6 Blessed be the LORD,
   who has not given us
   as prey to their teeth.
7 We have escaped like a bird
   from the snare of the fowlers;
 the snare is broken,
   and we have escaped.

8 Our help is in the name of the LORD,
   who made heaven and earth.

124.7 Deeper and Deeper

Some trouble is quick—bang and it's over. If you get caught speeding, for instance, you pay your fine and that ends the whole affair. But with other trouble, trying to escape only gets you more deeply entangled. Spreading gossip, for instance, may lead you into all kinds of unexpected consequences as the gossip spreads. If you try to undo the damage, you only make it worse.

That's exactly the picture of "the snare of the fowlers." The bird that caught its neck in the noose only tightened the snare's choke-hold by struggling. The bird could not get out by its own effort. But this time, says David, the snare has miraculously broken, and the bird has flown to safety. When you escape that way, there's only one person to thank: the Lord.

Psalm 125

The Security of God's People

A Song of Ascents.

1 Those who trust in the LORD are like
      Mount Zion,
  which cannot be moved, but abides
      forever.
2 As the mountains surround Jerusalem,
  so the LORD surrounds his people,
      from this time on and forevermore.
3 For the scepter of wickedness shall not
      rest
  on the land allotted to the righteous,
  so that the righteous might not stretch
      out
      their hands to do wrong.
4 Do good, O LORD, to those who are good,
  and to those who are upright in their
      hearts.
5 But those who turn aside to their own
      crooked ways
  the LORD will lead away with evildoers.
      Peace be upon Israel!

Psalm 126

A Harvest of Joy

A Song of Ascents.

1 When the LORD restored the fortunes of
      Zion,[b]
  we were like those who dream.
2 Then our mouth was filled with laughter,
  and our tongue with shouts of joy;
  then it was said among the nations,
      "The LORD has done great things for
      them."
3 The LORD has done great things for us,
  and we rejoiced.

4 Restore our fortunes, O LORD,
  like the watercourses in the Negeb.
5 May those who sow in tears
  reap with shouts of joy.
6 Those who go out weeping,
  bearing the seed for sowing,
  shall come home with shouts of joy,
      carrying their sheaves.

Psalm 127

God's Blessings in the Home

A Song of Ascents. Of Solomon.

1 Unless the LORD builds the house,
  those who build it labor in vain.
  Unless the LORD guards the city,

the guard keeps watch in vain.
2 It is in vain that you rise up early
  and go late to rest,
  eating the bread of anxious toil;
      for he gives sleep to his beloved.[c]

3 Sons are indeed a heritage from the LORD,
  the fruit of the womb a reward.
4 Like arrows in the hand of a warrior
  are the sons of one's youth.
5 Happy is the man who has
  his quiver full of them.
  He shall not be put to shame
      when he speaks with his enemies in the
      gate.

Psalm 128

The Happy Home of the Faithful

A Song of Ascents.

1 Happy is everyone who fears the LORD,
  who walks in his ways.
2 You shall eat the fruit of the labor of your
      hands;
  you shall be happy, and it shall go well
      with you.

3 Your wife will be like a fruitful vine
  within your house;
  your children will be like olive shoots
      around your table.
4 Thus shall the man be blessed
  who fears the LORD.

5 The LORD bless you from Zion.
  May you see the prosperity of
      Jerusalem
  all the days of your life.
6 May you see your children's children.
  Peace be upon Israel!

Psalm 129

Prayer for the Downfall
of Israel's Enemies

A Song of Ascents.

1 "Often have they attacked me from my
      youth"
      —let Israel now say—
2 "often have they attacked me from my
      youth,
  yet they have not prevailed against me.
3 The plowers plowed on my back;
  they made their furrows long."
4 The LORD is righteous;
  he has cut the cords of the wicked.
5 May all who hate Zion

---

[b] Or brought back those who returned to Zion   [c] Or for he provides for his beloved during sleep

be put to shame and turned backward.
⁶ Let them be like the grass on the
housetops
that withers before it grows up,

129.3 The Right Words

You can't improve on the vivid images used in great poetry. If someone asks you, "What's it about?" you can only quote the poem. The psalms are full of such unforgettable language. "The plowers plowed on my back; they made their furrows long" makes you grit your teeth with the sense of oppression. "Let them be like the grass on the housetops that withers before it grows up" (verse 6) says it better than any alternate phrase like, "Let their successes amount to nothing."

⁷ with which reapers do not fill their hands
or binders of sheaves their arms,
⁸ while those who pass by do not say,
"The blessing of the LORD be upon
you!
We bless you in the name of the
LORD!"

Psalm 130

Waiting for Divine Redemption

A Song of Ascents.

¹ Out of the depths I cry to you, O LORD.
² Lord, hear my voice!
Let your ears be attentive
to the voice of my supplications!

³ If you, O LORD, should mark iniquities,
Lord, who could stand?
⁴ But there is forgiveness with you,
so that you may be revered.

⁵ I wait for the LORD, my soul waits,
and in his word I hope;
⁶ my soul waits for the Lord
more than those who watch for the
morning,
more than those who watch for the
morning.

⁷ O Israel, hope in the LORD!
For with the LORD there is steadfast
love,
and with him is great power to redeem.
⁸ It is he who will redeem Israel
from all its iniquities.

Psalm 131

Song of Quiet Trust

A Song of Ascents. Of David.

¹ O LORD, my heart is not lifted up,
my eyes are not raised too high;
I do not occupy myself with things
too great and too marvelous for me.
² But I have calmed and quieted my soul,
like a weaned child with its mother;
my soul is like the weaned child that is
with me. *d*

³ O Israel, hope in the LORD
from this time on and forevermore.

131.2 A Child with Its Mother

How trusting is a baby? Not very, some would say, for babies cry violently as soon as they feel the slightest hunger. It is the weaned child, a little older, who has learned to trust its mother, to fret less and simply ask for food instead of wailing. The profound simplicity of this patience is David's model for how he, and all Israel, should wait on the Lord. The apostle Paul comments similarly, "I have learned to be content with whatever I have . . . I can do all things through him who strengthens me" (Philippians 4.11–13).

Psalm 132

The Eternal Dwelling of God in Zion

A Song of Ascents.

¹ O LORD, remember in David's favor
all the hardships he endured;
² how he swore to the LORD
and vowed to the Mighty One of Jacob,
³ "I will not enter my house
or get into my bed;
⁴ I will not give sleep to my eyes
or slumber to my eyelids,
⁵ until I find a place for the LORD,
a dwelling place for the Mighty One of
Jacob."

⁶ We heard of it in Ephrathah;
we found it in the fields of Jaar.
⁷ "Let us go to his dwelling place;
let us worship at his footstool."

⁸ Rise up, O LORD, and go to your resting
place,
you and the ark of your might.

---

d Or my soul within me is like a weaned child

9 Let your priests be clothed with
righteousness,
and let your faithful shout for joy.
10 For your servant David's sake
do not turn away the face of your
anointed one.

11 The LORD swore to David a sure oath
from which he will not turn back:
"One of the sons of your body
I will set on your throne.

132.11–18 Promise to David

*God's covenant with David promised that he
and his descendants would always reign over
Israel. For Israel, this promise meant that God
would never let the nation disintegrate, that he
would always provide a leader. Over the
centuries, when Israel chafed under the
domination of other nations, Jews remembered
this promise and looked for a "Messiah" or
"anointed one" (a king) who would provide this
leadership. That is why the New Testament
often refers to Jesus as a "son of David."*

12 If your sons keep my covenant
and my decrees that I shall teach them,
their sons also, forevermore,
shall sit on your throne."

13 For the LORD has chosen Zion;
he has desired it for his habitation:
14 "This is my resting place forever;
here I will reside, for I have desired it.
15 I will abundantly bless its provisions;
I will satisfy its poor with bread.
16 Its priests I will clothe with salvation,
and its faithful will shout for joy.
17 There I will cause a horn to sprout up for
David;
I have prepared a lamp for my
anointed one.
18 His enemies I will clothe with disgrace,
but on him, his crown will gleam."

Psalm 133

The Blessedness of Unity

A Song of Ascents.

1 How very good and pleasant it is
when kindred live together in unity!
2 It is like the precious oil on the head,
running down upon the beard,
on the beard of Aaron,
running down over the collar of his
robes.
3 It is like the dew of Hermon,
which falls on the mountains of Zion.

For there the LORD ordained his blessing,
life forevermore.

Psalm 134

Praise in the Night

A Song of Ascents.

1 Come, bless the LORD, all you servants of
the LORD,
who stand by night in the house of the
LORD!
2 Lift up your hands to the holy place,
and bless the LORD.

3 May the LORD, maker of heaven and
earth,
bless you from Zion.

Psalm 135

Praise for God's Goodness and Might

1 Praise the LORD!
Praise the name of the LORD;
give praise, O servants of the LORD,
2 you that stand in the house of the LORD,
in the courts of the house of our God.
3 Praise the LORD, for the LORD is good;
sing to his name, for he is gracious.
4 For the LORD has chosen Jacob for
himself,
Israel as his own possession.

5 For I know that the LORD is great;
our Lord is above all gods.
6 Whatever the LORD pleases he does,
in heaven and on earth,
in the seas and all deeps.
7 He it is who makes the clouds rise at the
end of the earth;
he makes lightnings for the rain
and brings out the wind from his
storehouses.

8 He it was who struck down the firstborn
of Egypt,
both human beings and animals;
9 he sent signs and wonders
into your midst, O Egypt,
against Pharaoh and all his servants.
10 He struck down many nations
and killed mighty kings—
11 Sihon, king of the Amorites,
and Og, king of Bashan,
and all the kingdoms of Canaan—
12 and gave their land as a heritage,
a heritage to his people Israel.

13 Your name, O LORD, endures forever,
your renown, O LORD, throughout all
ages.

14 For the LORD will vindicate his people,
 and have compassion on his servants.

15 The idols of the nations are silver and
 gold,
 the work of human hands.
16 They have mouths, but they do not speak;
 they have eyes, but they do not see;
17 they have ears, but they do not hear,
 and there is no breath in their mouths.
18 Those who make them
 and all who trust them
 shall become like them.

19 O house of Israel, bless the LORD!
 O house of Aaron, bless the LORD!
20 O house of Levi, bless the LORD!
 You that fear the LORD, bless the LORD!
21 Blessed be the LORD from Zion,
 he who resides in Jerusalem.
 Praise the LORD!

Psalm 136

God's Work in Creation and in History

1 O give thanks to the LORD, for he is good,
 for his steadfast love endures forever.

136.1 Call and Response

Scholars think most of the psalms were used in temple worship, but they are unsure how they were sung. This psalm seems like an example of what is known in African-American music as "call and response." A leader sings out a story, and the congregation shouts back a rhythmic refrain.

2 O give thanks to the God of gods,
 for his steadfast love endures forever.
3 O give thanks to the Lord of lords,
 for his steadfast love endures forever;

4 who alone does great wonders,
 for his steadfast love endures forever;
5 who by understanding made the heavens,
 for his steadfast love endures forever;
6 who spread out the earth on the waters,
 for his steadfast love endures forever;
7 who made the great lights,
 for his steadfast love endures forever;
8 the sun to rule over the day,
 for his steadfast love endures forever;
9 the moon and stars to rule over the night,
 for his steadfast love endures forever;

10 who struck Egypt through their firstborn,
 for his steadfast love endures forever;
11 and brought Israel out from among them,
 for his steadfast love endures forever;
12 with a strong hand and an outstretched
 arm,
 for his steadfast love endures forever;
13 who divided the Red Sea*e* in two,
 for his steadfast love endures forever;
14 and made Israel pass through the midst of
 it,
 for his steadfast love endures forever;
15 but overthrew Pharaoh and his army in
 the Red Sea,*e*
 for his steadfast love endures forever;
16 who led his people through the
 wilderness,
 for his steadfast love endures forever;
17 who struck down great kings,
 for his steadfast love endures forever;
18 and killed famous kings,
 for his steadfast love endures forever;
19 Sihon, king of the Amorites,
 for his steadfast love endures forever;
20 and Og, king of Bashan,
 for his steadfast love endures forever;
21 and gave their land as a heritage,
 for his steadfast love endures forever;
22 a heritage to his servant Israel,
 for his steadfast love endures forever.

23 It is he who remembered us in our low
 estate,
 for his steadfast love endures forever;
24 and rescued us from our foes,
 for his steadfast love endures forever;
25 who gives food to all flesh,
 for his steadfast love endures forever.

26 O give thanks to the God of heaven,
 for his steadfast love endures forever.

Psalm 137

Lament over the Destruction of Jerusalem

1 By the rivers of Babylon—
 there we sat down and there we wept
 when we remembered Zion.
2 On the willows*f* there
 we hung up our harps.
3 For there our captors
 asked us for songs,
 and our tormentors asked for mirth,
 saying,
 "Sing us one of the songs of Zion!"

4 How could we sing the LORD's song
 in a foreign land?
5 If I forget you, O Jerusalem,
 let my right hand wither!

e Or *Sea of Reeds*   *f* Or *poplars*

6 Let my tongue cling to the roof of my
    mouth,
  if I do not remember you,
  if I do not set Jerusalem
    above my highest joy.

7 Remember, O LORD, against the Edomites
    the day of Jerusalem's fall,
  how they said, "Tear it down! Tear it
    down!
  Down to its foundations!"
8 O daughter Babylon, you devastator!*g*
  Happy shall they be who pay you back
    what you have done to us!
9 Happy shall they be who take your little
    ones
  and dash them against the rock!

Psalm 138

Thanksgiving and Praise

Of David.

1 I give you thanks, O LORD, with my
    whole heart;
  before the gods I sing your praise;
2 I bow down toward your holy temple
  and give thanks to your name for your
    steadfast love and your
    faithfulness;
  for you have exalted your name and
    your word
  above everything.*h*
3 On the day I called, you answered me,
  you increased my strength of soul.*i*

4 All the kings of the earth shall praise you,
    O LORD,
  for they have heard the words of your
    mouth.
5 They shall sing of the ways of the LORD,
  for great is the glory of the LORD.
6 For though the LORD is high, he regards
    the lowly;
  but the haughty he perceives from far
    away.

7 Though I walk in the midst of trouble,
  you preserve me against the wrath of
    my enemies;
  you stretch out your hand,
  and your right hand delivers me.
8 The LORD will fulfill his purpose for me;
  your steadfast love, O LORD, endures
    forever.
  Do not forsake the work of your
    hands.

Psalm 139

The Inescapable God

To the leader. Of David. A Psalm.

1 O LORD, you have searched me and
    known me.
2 You know when I sit down and when I
    rise up;
  you discern my thoughts from
    far away.
3 You search out my path and my lying
    down,
  and are acquainted with all my ways.
4 Even before a word is on my tongue,
  O LORD, you know it completely.
5 You hem me in, behind and before,
  and lay your hand upon me.
6 Such knowledge is too wonderful for me;
  it is so high that I cannot attain it.

7 Where can I go from your spirit?
  Or where can I flee from your
    presence?
8 If I ascend to heaven, you are there;
  if I make my bed in Sheol, you are
    there.
9 If I take the wings of the morning
  and settle at the farthest limits of the
    sea,
10 even there your hand shall lead me,
  and your right hand shall hold me fast.
11 If I say, "Surely the darkness shall cover
    me,
  and the light around me become
    night,"
12 even the darkness is not dark to you;
  the night is as bright as the day,
  for darkness is as light to you.

13 For it was you who formed my inward
    parts;
  you knit me together in my mother's
    womb.
14 I praise you, for I am fearfully and
    wonderfully made.

139.13–16 Love Before Birth

Does life begin at conception, or at birth? This psalm doesn't directly answer that question, but it does make clear that God's loving involvement with our lives starts long before birth. Nothing can escape God's concern, according to this psalm—no person, no thought, no place, no time.

---

g Or *you who are devastated*   *h* Cn: Heb *you have exalted your word above all your name*   *i* Syr Compare Gk Tg:
Heb *you made me arrogant in my soul with strength*

Wonderful are your works;
that I know very well.

15 My frame was not hidden from you,
when I was being made in secret,
intricately woven in the depths of the
earth.

16 Your eyes beheld my unformed substance.
In your book were written
all the days that were formed for me,
when none of them as yet existed.

17 How weighty to me are your thoughts,
O God!
How vast is the sum of them!

18 I try to count them—they are more than
the sand;
I come to the end[j]—I am still with
you.

19 O that you would kill the wicked, O God,
and that the bloodthirsty would depart
from me—

20 those who speak of you maliciously,
and lift themselves up against you for
evil![k]

21 Do I not hate those who hate you,
O LORD?
And do I not loathe those who rise up
against you?

22 I hate them with perfect hatred;
I count them my enemies.

23 Search me, O God, and know my heart;
test me and know my thoughts.

24 See if there is any wicked[l] way in me,
and lead me in the way everlasting.[m]

Psalm 140

Prayer for Deliverance from Enemies

To the leader. A Psalm of David.

1 Deliver me, O LORD, from evildoers;
protect me from those who are violent,

2 who plan evil things in their minds
and stir up wars continually.

3 They make their tongue sharp as a
snake's,
and under their lips is the venom of
vipers. *Selah*

4 Guard me, O LORD, from the hands of the
wicked;
protect me from the violent
who have planned my downfall.

5 The arrogant have hidden a trap for me,

and with cords they have spread a
net,[n]
along the road they have set snares for
me. *Selah*

6 I say to the LORD, "You are my God;
give ear, O LORD, to the voice of my
supplications."

7 O LORD, my Lord, my strong deliverer,
you have covered my head in the day
of battle.

8 Do not grant, O LORD, the desires of the
wicked;
do not further their evil plot.[o] *Selah*

9 Those who surround me lift up their
heads;[p]
let the mischief of their lips overwhelm
them!

10 Let burning coals fall on them!
Let them be flung into pits, no more to
rise!

11 Do not let the slanderer be established in
the land;
let evil speedily hunt down the violent!

12 I know that the LORD maintains the cause
of the needy,
and executes justice for the poor.

140.12 Justice for the Poor

In ancient societies (and in most of the world today) poor people lose all status. Nobody of influence will listen to them or take up their cause. In the Bible, though, God emphasizes his concern for the poor. He will see that they get just treatment. Naturally he expects his followers to do the same.

13 Surely the righteous shall give thanks to
your name;
the upright shall live in your presence.

Psalm 141

Prayer for Preservation from Evil

A Psalm of David.

1 I call upon you, O LORD; come quickly to
me;
give ear to my voice when I call to
you.

---

[j] Or *I awake*   [k] Cn: Meaning of Heb uncertain   [l] Heb *hurtful*   [m] Or *the ancient way.* Compare Jer 6.16
[n] Or *they have spread cords as a net*   [o] Heb adds *they are exalted are uplifted in head*; Heb divides verses 8 and 9 differently   [p] Cn Compare Gk: Heb *those who surround me*

2 Let my prayer be counted as incense
  before you,
  and the lifting up of my hands as an
  evening sacrifice.

3 Set a guard over my mouth, O LORD;
  keep watch over the door of my lips.
4 Do not turn my heart to any evil,
  to busy myself with wicked deeds
  in company with those who work
  iniquity;
  do not let me eat of their delicacies.

5 Let the righteous strike me;
  let the faithful correct me.
  Never let the oil of the wicked anoint my
  head,[q]
  for my prayer is continually[r] against
  their wicked deeds.

6 When they are given over to those who
  shall condemn them,
  then they shall learn that my words
  were pleasant.
7 Like a rock that one breaks apart and
  shatters on the land,
  so shall their bones be strewn at the
  mouth of Sheol.[s]

8 But my eyes are turned toward you,
  O GOD, my Lord;
  in you I seek refuge; do not leave me
  defenseless.
9 Keep me from the trap that they have
  laid for me,
  and from the snares of evildoers.
10 Let the wicked fall into their own
  nets,
  while I alone escape.

q Gk: Meaning of Heb uncertain   r Cn: Heb *for continually and my prayer*   s Meaning of Heb of verses 5-7 is uncertain

What about Curses?
Bitter emotions expressed in sorrow

> Happy shall they be who take your little ones and dash them against the rock!
> 137.9

THE SO-CALLED "CURSING PSALMS" COME as a shock. Psalm 137 is the most famous example. In a gorgeous lament from exile, the poet crescendoes to wish that God would bless anyone who knocks a Babylonian baby's brains out.

To many people, this wish seems too bitter to belong in the Bible. Aren't Christians supposed to love their enemies and pray for those who persecute them (Matthew 5.44)? Even in the Old Testament, enemies were not to be treated unkindly (Exodus 23.4). How does this outburst fit into God's Word?

A Cry for Justice

To answer we must go to the courtroom, where more and more judges are allowing the victims of a crime to testify during sentencing. A mother who has lost her child to a murderer may spout wild and even vindictive emotions as she stands to demand the death sentence. Still the court needs to hear her. She alone knows fully what was lost. She alone feels the full outrage of the crime.

The cursing psalms voice such "victim testimony" to God, the judge. They always assume that the punishment they ask for is deserved. For example, Psalm 109 calls down curses on a man who "pursued the poor and needy and the brokenhearted to their death. He loved to curse; let curses come on him" (109.16–17).

Psalm 137 was written out of similar anguish. As a nation, Babylon had callously murdered, earning punishment. The Bible says that God hears the cries of the innocent. He promises to punish those who have hurt them.

With all his teaching on forgiving enemies, Jesus did not change this idea of justice. He taught that justice will be done by God after death. (See, for instance, Matthew 25.31–46.) But Old Testament Israelites had only vague ideas about life after death. For them, justice had to be done in this life, before their eyes. They asked for it in the cursing psalms.

Mercy for Your Enemies

What about mercy? Isn't our duty to forgive our enemies, and love them? How do the cursing psalms fit with that?

Three things must be said. First, while no mercy shows through in the cursing psalms, that doesn't mean the people who wrote them were wholly unmerciful. David, credited with some of the strongest cursing psalms, showed extraordinary mercy toward Saul, his vengeful enemy. The cursing psalms are

Psalm 142

Prayer for Deliverance from Persecutors

*A Maskil of David. When he was in the cave.
A Prayer.*

1 With my voice I cry to the LORD;
  with my voice I make supplication to
    the LORD.
2 I pour out my complaint before him;
  I tell my trouble before him.
3 When my spirit is faint,
  you know my way.

In the path where I walk
  they have hidden a trap for me.
4 Look on my right hand and see—
  there is no one who takes notice of me;
no refuge remains to me;
  no one cares for me.

5 I cry to you, O LORD;
  I say, "You are my refuge,
  my portion in the land of the living."
6 Give heed to my cry,
  for I am brought very low.

Save me from my persecutors,
  for they are too strong for me.
7 Bring me out of prison,
  so that I may give thanks to your
    name.

The righteous will surround me,
  for you will deal bountifully with me.

Psalm 143

Prayer for Deliverance from Enemies

A Psalm of David.

1 Hear my prayer, O LORD;
  give ear to my supplications in your
    faithfulness;
  answer me in your righteousness.
2 Do not enter into judgment with your
    servant,
  for no one living is righteous before
    you.

3 For the enemy has pursued me,
  crushing my life to the ground,
  making me sit in darkness like those
    long dead.
4 Therefore my spirit faints within me;
  my heart within me is appalled.
5 I remember the days of old,
  I think about all your deeds,
  I meditate on the works of your hands.
6 I stretch out my hands to you;
  my soul thirsts for you like a parched
    land.   *Selah*

7 Answer me quickly, O LORD;

---

unbridled cries of agony. They honestly reflect the way people felt. Their authors' lives sometimes balanced this cry with compassion.

Second, the psalmists wrote before Jesus offered forgiveness to all by dying, as God's Son, in people's place. Even today many people find it difficult to accept Jesus' teaching on forgiving enemies, for it means forgiving rapists, child molesters, mass murderers. We can only forgive them because Jesus paid the price for their crimes. The psalmists lived before that payment.

Third, the cursing psalms prepared the way for forgiveness. You can only be genuinely merciful if you start with a full appreciation of guilt. The judge who carelessly lets a criminal off on a technicality is not showing mercy. Maybe he or she just lacks sympathy for the crime's victim. True mercy comes when victims themselves turn and forgive the people who hurt them, releasing them to liberty.

Jesus the Victim

The cursing psalms express the hideousness of violence and injustice. Unless you feel the depth of this, you cannot understand the depth of God's forgiveness, offered freely to anyone who pleads for mercy. God is not merely letting people off on a legal technicality. He hears the cry of their victims, and more: He shares it. In Jesus, God was the victim, beaten, cursed, killed.

The New Testament actually quoted two of the cursing psalms, referring to Judas's betrayal of Jesus. These psalms speak of bitter injustice, and Jesus suffered the ultimate injustice. But the final word comes from Jesus himself: "Father, forgive them; for they do not know what they are doing."

If we follow Jesus' example, we dare not mouth the cursing psalms when we think of our enemies. These psalms are not for us to borrow from, as are other psalms. Yet these cursing psalms remind us of the bitter suffering many experience, and reading them can impel us to fight for justice. More, they remind us to forgive. For God, hearing such cries from the victim, having suffered as they suffer, forgives. So can we.

Life Questions: What is the worst injustice you have ever experienced? Did you feel some of the anger expressed in the cursing psalms? Were you able to forgive?

my spirit fails.
Do not hide your face from me,
    or I shall be like those who go down to
        the Pit.
8 Let me hear of your steadfast love in the
        morning,
    for in you I put my trust.
Teach me the way I should go,
    for to you I lift up my soul.

9 Save me, O LORD, from my enemies;
    I have fled to you for refuge.[t]
10 Teach me to do your will,
    for you are my God.
Let your good spirit lead me
    on a level path.

11 For your name's sake, O LORD, preserve
        my life.
    In your righteousness bring me out of
        trouble.
12 In your steadfast love cut off my enemies,
    and destroy all my adversaries,
        for I am your servant.

Psalm 144

Prayer for National Deliverance and Security

Of David.

1 Blessed be the LORD, my rock,
    who trains my hands for war, and my
        fingers for battle;
2 my rock[u] and my fortress,
    my stronghold and my deliverer,
my shield, in whom I take refuge,
    who subdues the peoples[v] under me.

3 O LORD, what are human beings that you
        regard them,
    or mortals that you think of them?
4 They are like a breath;
    their days are like a passing shadow.

5 Bow your heavens, O LORD, and come
        down;
    touch the mountains so that they
        smoke.
6 Make the lightning flash and scatter them;
    send out your arrows and rout them.
7 Stretch out your hand from on high;
    set me free and rescue me from the
        mighty waters,
from the hand of aliens,
8 whose mouths speak lies,
    and whose right hands are false.

9 I will sing a new song to you, O God;
    upon a ten-stringed harp I will play to
        you,
10 the one who gives victory to kings,
    who rescues his servant David.
11 Rescue me from the cruel sword,
    and deliver me from the hand of
        aliens,
whose mouths speak lies,
    and whose right hands are false.

12 May our sons in their youth
    be like plants full grown,
our daughters like corner pillars,
    cut for the building of a palace.
13 May our barns be filled,
    with produce of every kind;
may our sheep increase by thousands,
    by tens of thousands in our fields,
14   and may our cattle be heavy with
        young.
May there be no breach in the walls,[w] no
        exile,
    and no cry of distress in our streets.

15 Happy are the people to whom such
        blessings fall;
    happy are the people whose God is the
        LORD.

Psalm 145

The Greatness and the Goodness of God

Praise. Of David.

1 I will extol you, my God and King,
    and bless your name forever and ever.
2 Every day I will bless you,
    and praise your name forever and ever.
3 Great is the LORD, and greatly to be
        praised;
    his greatness is unsearchable.

4 One generation shall laud your works to
        another,
    and shall declare your mighty acts.
5 On the glorious splendor of your majesty,
    and on your wondrous works, I will
        meditate.
6 The might of your awesome deeds shall
        be proclaimed,
    and I will declare your greatness.
7 They shall celebrate the fame of your
        abundant goodness,
    and shall sing aloud of your
        righteousness.

8 The LORD is gracious and merciful,

---

t One Heb Ms Gk: MT to you I have hidden   u With 18.2 and 2 Sam 22.2: Heb my steadfast love   v Heb Mss Syr
Aquila Jerome: MT my people   w Heb lacks in the walls

slow to anger and abounding in
steadfast love.
9 The LORD is good to all,
and his compassion is over all that he
has made.

10 All your works shall give thanks to you,
O LORD,
and all your faithful shall bless you.
11 They shall speak of the glory of your
kingdom,
and tell of your power,
12 to make known to all people your[x]
mighty deeds,
and the glorious splendor of your[y]
kingdom.
13 Your kingdom is an everlasting kingdom,
and your dominion endures
throughout all generations.

The LORD is faithful in all his words,
and gracious in all his deeds.[z]
14 The LORD upholds all who are falling,
and raises up all who are bowed down.
15 The eyes of all look to you,
and you give them their food in due
season.
16 You open your hand,
satisfying the desire of every living
thing.
17 The LORD is just in all his ways,
and kind in all his doings.
18 The LORD is near to all who call on him,
to all who call on him in truth.
19 He fulfills the desire of all who fear him;
he also hears their cry, and saves them.
20 The LORD watches over all who love him,
but all the wicked he will destroy.

21 My mouth will speak the praise of the
LORD,
and all flesh will bless his holy name
forever and ever.

Psalm 146

Praise for God's Help

1 Praise the LORD!
Praise the LORD, O my soul!
2 I will praise the LORD as long as I live;
I will sing praises to my God all my
life long.

3 Do not put your trust in princes,
in mortals, in whom there is no help.
4 When their breath departs, they return to
the earth;
on that very day their plans perish.

5 Happy are those whose help is the God of
Jacob,
whose hope is in the LORD their God,
6 who made heaven and earth,
the sea, and all that is in them;
who keeps faith forever;
7 who executes justice for the oppressed;
who gives food to the hungry.

The LORD sets the prisoners free;
8 the LORD opens the eyes of the blind.
The LORD lifts up those who are bowed
down;
the LORD loves the righteous.
9 The LORD watches over the strangers;
he upholds the orphan and the widow,
but the way of the wicked he brings to
ruin.

10 The LORD will reign forever,
your God, O Zion, for all generations.
Praise the LORD!

Psalm 147

Praise for God's Care for Jerusalem

1 Praise the LORD!
How good it is to sing praises to our
God;
for he is gracious, and a song of praise
is fitting.
2 The LORD builds up Jerusalem;
he gathers the outcasts of Israel.
3 He heals the brokenhearted,
and binds up their wounds.
4 He determines the number of the stars;
he gives to all of them their names.
5 Great is our Lord, and abundant
in power;
his understanding is beyond measure.
6 The LORD lifts up the downtrodden;
he casts the wicked to the ground.

7 Sing to the LORD with thanksgiving;
make melody to our God on the lyre.
8 He covers the heavens with clouds,
prepares rain for the earth,
makes grass grow on the hills.
9 He gives to the animals their food,
and to the young ravens when they
cry.
10 His delight is not in the strength of the
horse,
nor his pleasure in the speed of
a runner;[a]
11 but the LORD takes pleasure in those who
fear him,
in those who hope in his steadfast love.

---

[x] Gk Jerome Syr: Heb *his*   [y] Heb *his*   [z] These two lines supplied by Q Ms Gk Syr   [a] Heb *legs of a person*

¹² Praise the LORD, O Jerusalem!
  Praise your God, O Zion!
¹³ For he strengthens the bars of your gates;
  he blesses your children within you.

147.11 God's Great Concern

The Lord is a God of strength, as this song amply demonstrates. But power doesn't delight him (verse 10). More than anything he loves to be in a close relationship to people who respond to his love.

¹⁴ He grants peace[b] within your borders;
  he fills you with the finest of wheat.
¹⁵ He sends out his command to the earth;
  his word runs swiftly.
¹⁶ He gives snow like wool;
  he scatters frost like ashes.
¹⁷ He hurls down hail like crumbs—
  who can stand before his cold?
¹⁸ He sends out his word, and melts them;
  he makes his wind blow, and the
    waters flow.
¹⁹ He declares his word to Jacob,
  his statutes and ordinances to Israel.
²⁰ He has not dealt thus with any other
    nation;
  they do not know his ordinances.
Praise the LORD!

Psalm 148

Praise for God's Universal Glory

¹ Praise the LORD!
  Praise the LORD from the heavens;
    praise him in the heights!
² Praise him, all his angels;
  praise him, all his host!

³ Praise him, sun and moon;
  praise him, all you shining stars!
⁴ Praise him, you highest heavens,
  and you waters above the heavens!

⁵ Let them praise the name of the LORD,
  for he commanded and they
    were created.
⁶ He established them forever and ever;
  he fixed their bounds, which cannot be
    passed.[c]

⁷ Praise the LORD from the earth,
  you sea monsters and all deeps,
⁸ fire and hail, snow and frost,
  stormy wind fulfilling his command!

⁹ Mountains and all hills,
  fruit trees and all cedars!
¹⁰ Wild animals and all cattle,
  creeping things and flying birds!
¹¹ Kings of the earth and all peoples,
  princes and all rulers of the earth!
¹² Young men and women alike,
  old and young together!

¹³ Let them praise the name of the LORD,
  for his name alone is exalted;
    his glory is above earth and heaven.
¹⁴ He has raised up a horn for his people,
  praise for all his faithful,
    for the people of Israel who are close
      to him.
Praise the LORD!

Psalm 149

Praise for God's Goodness to Israel

¹ Praise the LORD!
  Sing to the LORD a new song,
    his praise in the assembly of the
      faithful.
² Let Israel be glad in its Maker;
  let the children of Zion rejoice in their
    King.
³ Let them praise his name with dancing,
  making melody to him with
    tambourine and lyre.
⁴ For the LORD takes pleasure in his
    people;
  he adorns the humble with victory.
⁵ Let the faithful exult in glory;
  let them sing for joy on their couches.
⁶ Let the high praises of God be in their
    throats
  and two-edged swords in their hands,
⁷ to execute vengeance on the nations
  and punishment on the peoples,
⁸ to bind their kings with fetters
  and their nobles with chains of iron,
⁹ to execute on them the judgment decreed.
  This is glory for all his faithful ones.
Praise the LORD!

Psalm 150

Praise for God's Surpassing Greatness

¹ Praise the LORD!
  Praise God in his sanctuary;
    praise him in his mighty firmament![d]
² Praise him for his mighty deeds;
  praise him according to his surpassing
    greatness!

---

b Or *prosperity*   *c* Or *he set a law that cannot pass away*   *d* Or *dome*

³ Praise him with trumpet sound;
  praise him with lute and harp!
⁴ Praise him with tambourine and
  dance;
  praise him with strings and pipe!

⁵ Praise him with clanging cymbals;
  praise him with loud clashing cymbals!
⁶ Let everything that breathes praise the
  LORD!
Praise the LORD!

PROVERBS

Uncommon Sense
A most down-to-earth book

"SESAME STREET," THE EDUCATIONAL TV show, has changed a lot of people's ideas about education. It offers a kaleidoscopic mix of gentle fun that seems to have nothing to do with education at all. One episode may start with a band of puppet rock stars—the Beetles—singing an ode entitled "Letter B" (to a tune that sounds surprisingly like the Beatles' "Let It Be"). Then the picture cuts to Big Bird asking Oscar the Grouch to help him write a letter to his uncle—Uncle Bird, whose name just happens to start with the letter B. Five minutes later, a cartoon letter B is jumping in front of various letter combinations while a voice intones the words spelled out: "B-b-boy." "B-b-bathtub." "B-b-bicycle."

"Sesame Street" showed that teaching kids doesn't always mean forcing them to sit down and memorize lists. By watching Big Bird, Cookie Monster, and Oscar the Grouch, children painlessly learn the letter B as well as colors, shapes, and a lot more.

> If you indeed cry out for insight, and raise your voice for understanding; if you seek it like silver, and search for it as for hidden treasures—then you will understand the fear of the LORD and find the knowledge of God. 2.3–5

The book of Proverbs does for wisdom what "Sesame Street" does for the ABCs. Much of Proverbs reads like a collection of one-liners, moving quickly (and apparently illogically) from one subject to another. A proverb pleases the ear much as "Sesame Street" pleases the eye, using "shortness, sense and salt" to compress life into a handful of memorable words. But just as with the TV program, Proverbs has an overall objective behind its disorder. If you spend enough time in Proverbs, you will gain a subtle and practical understanding of life.

A Father's Guidance

Proverbs is probably the most down-to-earth book in the Bible. Its education prepares you for the street and the marketplace, not the schoolroom. (1.20–21 expresses this poetically.) The book offers the warm advice you get by growing up in a good family: practical guidance for successfully making your way in the world. It covers small questions as well as large: talking too much, visiting neighbors too often, being unbearably cheerful too early in the morning.

The first nine chapters, which explain the purpose of Proverbs's wisdom, are spoken from father to child. Fifteen times the fatherly voice says, "My child." Some of the advice seems particularly well suited to young people: warnings against joining gangs, for instance, or urgent cautions against sex outside marriage. But the central message of Proverbs applies to anyone, old or young: "Get wisdom at all costs." It is a plea to strain your mind and your ears searching for the wise way to live.

Virtue Is Not Its Only Reward

Anybody with a brain can find exceptions to Proverbs's generalities. For instance, Proverbs 28.19 proclaims that "Anyone who tills the land will have plenty of bread, but one who follows worthless pursuits will have plenty of poverty." Yet farmers who work hard go hungry in a drought, and dreamers win $10 million in a lottery.

Proverbs simply tells how life works most of the time. You can worry about the exceptions after you have learned the rule. Try to live by the exceptions, and you court disaster.

The rule is that the godly, moral, hardworking, and wise will reap many rewards. Those who learn the practical and godly wisdom of Proverbs not only sleep better, they succeed and become able to help their family and friends. Fools and scoffers, though they appear successful, will eventually pay the cost of their lifestyle.

Much of Proverbs's practical advice makes no mention of God, and its concern for success may therefore seem quite secular. But if you take the book as a whole, it becomes obvious that the lifestyle Proverbs teaches depends on a healthy respect for God (1.7) affecting every aspect of life (3.5–7).

Proverbs frankly concedes that the wise path will not be chosen by many; it is easier to live carelessly and godlessly. But those who choose to live by Proverbs will get success and safety, and more: they will get to know God himself. "Then you will understand the fear of the LORD and find the knowledge of God" (2.5).

How to Read Proverbs

People love to quote proverbs. Often they express truth about life in an elegant, witty kernel. You'll find more humor in Proverbs than anywhere else in the Bible.

Yet Proverbs may well be the most abused book in the Bible. People often quote the proverbs as though they were absolute promises from God or rigid rules for living. In fact, few of the proverbs should be read that way. And some proverbs, read alone, would give you a distorted point of view.

To understand Proverbs, you should not hunt through it for proverbs you like. You should study the whole book to get its overall point of view. This takes time, for Proverbs covers dozens of subjects in subtle detail.

Each of the more than 500 proverbs is a tough nut you have to crack before you get the inner meat. Read Proverbs slowly, but not for too long at one sitting.

Some people like to read a small number of proverbs each day in addition to their regular Bible readings. Others concentrate on memorizing proverbs, so they can run them through their heads as they go on about the day. Whatever technique you use, keep two things in mind: Think carefully about each proverb, and try to put each into the bigger context of the teachings of all of Proverbs. To help you see the total picture of Proverbs's teaching on some key subjects, ten Insights scattered thoughout Proverbs briefly introduce ten subjects and list relevant proverbs.

The book of Proverbs is divided into two main parts: an introduction in the first nine chapters and the proverbs themselves in the remaining 22 chapters. If you skip the introduction, you won't understand the point of Proverbs as a book. It introduces "Lady Wisdom," and explains what she can do for you.

3-TRACK READING PLAN

For an explanation and complete listing of the 3-track reading plan, turn to page 7.

TRACK 1: *Two-Week Courses on the Bible*
See page 7 for information on these courses.

TRACK 2: *An Overview of Proverbs in 3 Days*
☐ Day 1. Read the Introduction to Proverbs and chapter 4, which gives an introduction to the importance of wisdom and the style of life you need to pursue it.
☐ Day 2. Read chapter 10, which covers a fairly typical range of subject matter.
☐ Day 3. Read all the proverbs listed in "Verbal Dynamite," on page 664.

Now turn to page 9 for your next Track 2 reading project.

TRACK 3: *All of Proverbs in 31 Days*
After you have read through Proverbs, turn to pages 10–14 for your next Track 3 reading project.

☐1 ☐2 ☐3 ☐4 ☐5 ☐6 ☐7 ☐8
☐9 ☐10 ☐11 ☐12 ☐13 ☐14 ☐15 ☐16
☐17 ☐18 ☐19 ☐20 ☐21 ☐22 ☐23 ☐24
☐25 ☐26 ☐27 ☐28 ☐29 ☐30 ☐31

1

The proverbs of Solomon son of David, king of Israel:

Prologue

2 For learning about wisdom and
        instruction,
    for understanding words of insight,
3 for gaining instruction in wise dealing,
    righteousness, justice, and equity;
4 to teach shrewdness to the simple,
    knowledge and prudence to the
        young—
5 let the wise also hear and gain in learning,
    and the discerning acquire skill,
6 to understand a proverb and a figure,
    the words of the wise and their riddles.

7 The fear of the LORD is the beginning of
        knowledge;
    fools despise wisdom and instruction.

Warnings against Evil Companions

8 Hear, my child, your father's instruction,
    and do not reject your mother's
        teaching;
9 for they are a fair garland for your head,
    and pendants for your neck.
10 My child, if sinners entice you,
    do not consent.
11 If they say, "Come with us, let us lie in
        wait for blood;
    let us wantonly ambush the innocent;
12 like Sheol let us swallow them alive
    and whole, like those who go down to
        the Pit.
13 We shall find all kinds of costly things;
    we shall fill our houses with booty.
14 Throw in your lot among us;
    we will all have one purse"—
15 my child, do not walk in their way,
    keep your foot from their paths;
16 for their feet run to evil,
    and they hurry to shed blood.
17 For in vain is the net baited
    while the bird is looking on;
18 yet they lie in wait—to kill themselves!
    and set an ambush—for their own
        lives!
19 Such is the end*a* of all who are greedy
        for gain;
    it takes away the life of its possessors.

The Call of Wisdom

20 Wisdom cries out in the street;
    in the squares she raises her voice.
21 At the busiest corner she cries out;

at the entrance of the city gates she
        speaks:
22 "How long, O simple ones, will you love
        being simple?
    How long will scoffers delight in their
        scoffing
    and fools hate knowledge?

1.22 Three Problem People

Scoffers, fools, the simple: Proverbs keeps using these words to define the "bad characters" we should stay away from. What kind of people are they? The "simple" are the least harmful group: they live without thinking and are too lazy to change. But they, like the others, will end up sorry. "Fools" have more smarts but have made a conscious decision to live by their own wits, independent of God and independent of advice. "Scoffers," worst of all, are rebels against God who make their prideful position known to everyone. They mock God, but God will mock them in the end (verse 26).

23 Give heed to my reproof;
    I will pour out my thoughts to you;
    I will make my words known to you.
24 Because I have called and you refused,
    have stretched out my hand and no
        one heeded,
25 and because you have ignored all my
        counsel
    and would have none of my reproof,
26 I also will laugh at your calamity;
    I will mock when panic strikes you,
27 when panic strikes you like a storm,
    and your calamity comes like a
        whirlwind,
    when distress and anguish come upon
        you.
28 Then they will call upon me, but I will
        not answer;
    they will seek me diligently, but will
        not find me.
29 Because they hated knowledge
    and did not choose the fear of the
        LORD,
30 would have none of my counsel,
    and despised all my reproof,
31 therefore they shall eat the fruit of their
        way
    and be sated with their own devices.
32 For waywardness kills the simple,
    and the complacency of fools destroys
        them;
33 but those who listen to me will be secure
    and will live at ease, without dread of
        disaster."

a Gk: Heb *are the ways*

The Value of Wisdom

2 My child, if you accept my words
  and treasure up my commandments
    within you,
² making your ear attentive to wisdom
  and inclining your heart to
    understanding;
³ if you indeed cry out for insight,
  and raise your voice for understanding;
⁴ if you seek it like silver,
  and search for it as for hidden
    treasures—
⁵ then you will understand the fear of the
    LORD
  and find the knowledge of God.
⁶ For the LORD gives wisdom;
  from his mouth come knowledge and
    understanding;
⁷ he stores up sound wisdom for the
    upright;
  he is a shield to those who walk
    blamelessly,
⁸ guarding the paths of justice
  and preserving the way of his faithful
    ones.
⁹ Then you will understand righteousness
    and justice
  and equity, every good path;
¹⁰ for wisdom will come into your heart,
  and knowledge will be pleasant to your
    soul;
¹¹ prudence will watch over you;
  and understanding will guard you.
¹² It will save you from the way of evil,
  from those who speak perversely,
¹³ who forsake the paths of uprightness
  to walk in the ways of darkness,
¹⁴ who rejoice in doing evil
  and delight in the perverseness of evil;
¹⁵ those whose paths are crooked,
  and who are devious in their ways.

¹⁶ You will be saved from the loose*b*
    woman,
  from the adulteress with her smooth
    words,
¹⁷ who forsakes the partner of her youth
  and forgets her sacred covenant;
¹⁸ for her way*c* leads down to death,
  and her paths to the shades;
¹⁹ those who go to her never come back,
  nor do they regain the paths of life.

²⁰ Therefore walk in the way of the good,
  and keep to the paths of the just.
²¹ For the upright will abide in the land,
  and the innocent will remain in it;
²² but the wicked will be cut off from the
    land,

and the treacherous will be rooted out
  of it.

Admonition to Trust and Honor God

3 My child, do not forget my teaching,
  but let your heart keep my
    commandments;
² for length of days and years of life
  and abundant welfare they will give
    you.

³ Do not let loyalty and faithfulness forsake
    you;
  bind them around your neck,
  write them on the tablet of your heart.
⁴ So you will find favor and good repute
  in the sight of God and of people.

⁵ Trust in the LORD with all your heart,
  and do not rely on your own insight.
⁶ In all your ways acknowledge him,
  and he will make straight your paths.

3.6 Walking with God

In the original Hebrew, "in all your ways acknowledge him" is more literally "in all your ways know him." This fundamental statement of how to relate to God implies more than mere reverence. Nodding in God's direction is not enough: You must know him by living closely with him, relating to him personally in every aspect of your life.

⁷ Do not be wise in your own eyes;
  fear the LORD, and turn away from evil.
⁸ It will be a healing for your flesh
  and a refreshment for your body.

⁹ Honor the LORD with your substance
  and with the first fruits of all your
    produce;
¹⁰ then your barns will be filled with plenty,
  and your vats will be bursting with
    wine.

¹¹ My child, do not despise the LORD's
    discipline
  or be weary of his reproof,
¹² for the LORD reproves the one he loves,
  as a father the son in whom he
    delights.

The True Wealth

¹³ Happy are those who find wisdom,
  and those who get understanding,
¹⁴ for her income is better than silver,
  and her revenue better than gold.

b Heb *strange*   *c* Cn: Heb *house*

15 She is more precious than jewels,
   and nothing you desire can compare
      with her.
16 Long life is in her right hand;
   in her left hand are riches and honor.
17 Her ways are ways of pleasantness,
   and all her paths are peace.
18 She is a tree of life to those who lay hold
      of her;
   those who hold her fast are called
      happy.

God's Wisdom in Creation

19 The LORD by wisdom founded the earth;
   by understanding he established the
      heavens;
20 by his knowledge the deeps broke open,
   and the clouds drop down the dew.

The True Security

21 My child, do not let these escape from
      your sight:
   keep sound wisdom and prudence,
22 and they will be life for your soul
   and adornment for your neck.
23 Then you will walk on your way securely
   and your foot will not stumble.
24 If you sit down,*d* you will not be afraid;
   when you lie down, your sleep will be
      sweet.
25 Do not be afraid of sudden panic,
   or of the storm that strikes the wicked;
26 for the LORD will be your confidence
   and will keep your foot from being
      caught.

27 Do not withhold good from those to
      whom it is due,*e*
   when it is in your power to do it.
28 Do not say to your neighbor, "Go, and
      come again,
   tomorrow I will give it"—when you
      have it with you.
29 Do not plan harm against your neighbor
   who lives trustingly beside you.
30 Do not quarrel with anyone without
      cause,
   when no harm has been done to you.
31 Do not envy the violent
   and do not choose any of their ways;
32 for the perverse are an abomination to
      the LORD,
   but the upright are in his confidence.
33 The LORD's curse is on the house of the
      wicked,
   but he blesses the abode of the
      righteous.
34 Toward the scorners he is scornful,
   but to the humble he shows favor.

35 The wise will inherit honor,
   but stubborn fools, disgrace.

Parental Advice

4 Listen, children, to a father's instruction,
   and be attentive, that you may gain*f*
      insight;
2 for I give you good precepts:
   do not forsake my teaching.
3 When I was a son with my father,
   tender, and my mother's favorite,
4 he taught me, and said to me,
   "Let your heart hold fast my words;
   keep my commandments, and live.
5 Get wisdom; get insight: do not forget,
   nor turn away
   from the words of my mouth.
6 Do not forsake her, and she will keep
      you;
   love her, and she will guard you.
7 The beginning of wisdom is this: Get
      wisdom,
   and whatever else you get, get insight.

4.7 A Lifelong Quest

A father's advice can easily degenerate into, "Don't do this, don't do that." But the fatherly advice of Proverbs isn't preoccupied with rules. Instead, this father tries to help his son develop a love for the best things in life—just as his father did for him. This love for the best—and most of all for wisdom—begins with listening to your father's advice, but it goes beyond taking instructions. The love of wisdom becomes a lifelong quest that may make you wiser than your father.

8 Prize her highly, and she will exalt you;
   she will honor you if you embrace her.
9 She will place on your head a fair garland;
   she will bestow on you a beautiful
      crown."

Admonition to Keep to the Right Path

10 Hear, my child, and accept my words,
   that the years of your life may
      be many.
11 I have taught you the way of wisdom;
   I have led you in the paths of
      uprightness.
12 When you walk, your step will not be
      hampered;
   and if you run, you will not stumble.
13 Keep hold of instruction; do not let go;
   guard her, for she is your life.
14 Do not enter the path of the wicked,

d Gk: Heb *lie down*   *e* Heb *from its owners*   *f* Heb *know*

and do not walk in the way of
    evildoers.
15 Avoid it; do not go on it;
    turn away from it and pass on.
16 For they cannot sleep unless they have
    done wrong;
    they are robbed of sleep unless they
    have made someone stumble.
17 For they eat the bread of wickedness
    and drink the wine of violence.
18 But the path of the righteous is like the
    light of dawn,
    which shines brighter and brighter until
    full day.
19 The way of the wicked is like deep
    darkness;
    they do not know what they stumble
    over.
20 My child, be attentive to my words;
    incline your ear to my sayings.
21 Do not let them escape from your sight;
    keep them within your heart.
22 For they are life to those who find them,
    and healing to all their flesh.
23 Keep your heart with all vigilance,
    for from it flow the springs of life.
24 Put away from you crooked speech,
    and put devious talk far from you.
25 Let your eyes look directly forward,
    and your gaze be straight before you.
26 Keep straight the path of your feet,
    and all your ways will be sure.
27 Do not swerve to the right or to the left;
    turn your foot away from evil.

Warning against Impurity and Infidelity

5 My child, be attentive to my wisdom;
    incline your ear to my understanding,
2 so that you may hold on to prudence,
    and your lips may guard knowledge.
3 For the lips of a loose*g* woman drip
    honey,
    and her speech is smoother than oil;
4 but in the end she is bitter as wormwood,
    sharp as a two-edged sword.
5 Her feet go down to death;
    her steps follow the path to Sheol.
6 She does not keep straight to the path of
    life;
    her ways wander, and she does not
    know it.

7 And now, my child,*h* listen to me,
    and do not depart from the words of
    my mouth.
8 Keep your way far from her,
    and do not go near the door of her
    house;

9 or you will give your honor to others,
    and your years to the merciless,
10 and strangers will take their fill of your
    wealth,
    and your labors will go to the house of
    an alien;
11 and at the end of your life you will groan,
    when your flesh and body are
    consumed,
12 and you say, "Oh, how I hated discipline,
    and my heart despised reproof!
13 I did not listen to the voice of my
    teachers
    or incline my ear to my instructors.
14 Now I am at the point of utter ruin
    in the public assembly."

15 Drink water from your own cistern,
    flowing water from your own well.
16 Should your springs be scattered abroad,
    streams of water in the streets?
17 Let them be for yourself alone,
    and not for sharing with strangers.
18 Let your fountain be blessed,
    and rejoice in the wife of your youth,
19 a lovely deer, a graceful doe.
    May her breasts satisfy you at all times;
    may you be intoxicated always by her
    love.
20 Why should you be intoxicated, my son,
    by another woman
    and embrace the bosom of an
    adulteress?
21 For human ways are under the eyes of the
    LORD,
    and he examines all their paths.
22 The iniquities of the wicked ensnare
    them,
    and they are caught in the toils of their
    sin.
23 They die for lack of discipline,
    and because of their great folly they are
    lost.

Practical Admonitions

6 My child, if you have given your pledge to
    your neighbor,
    if you have bound yourself to
    another,*i*
2 you are snared by the utterance of your
    lips,*j*
    caught by the words of your mouth.
3 So do this, my child, and save yourself,
    for you have come into your
    neighbor's power:
    go, hurry,*k* and plead with your
    neighbor.
4 Give your eyes no sleep

---

g Heb *strange*   *h* Gk Vg: Heb *children*   *i* Or *a stranger*   *j* Cn Compare Gk Syr: Heb *the words of your mouth*
k Or *humble yourself*

and your eyelids no slumber;
5 save yourself like a gazelle from the
hunter,[l]
like a bird from the hand of the fowler.

6.1–3 Danger in Debt

Proverbs warns against giving "your pledge" for a neighbor—something like co-signing a loan for a friend who doesn't otherwise qualify. Proverbs supports generosity, but not open-ended charity in which the amount you must give and the timing are determined by circumstances beyond your control. Too often it leads to disaster. (See also 11.15; 17.18; 22.26–27.)

6 Go to the ant, you lazybones;
consider its ways, and be wise.
7 Without having any chief
or officer or ruler,
8 it prepares its food in summer,
and gathers its sustenance in harvest.
9 How long will you lie there, O lazybones?
When will you rise from your sleep?
10 A little sleep, a little slumber,
a little folding of the hands to rest,
11 and poverty will come upon you like a
robber,
and want, like an armed warrior.

12 A scoundrel and a villain
goes around with crooked speech,
13 winking the eyes, shuffling the feet,
pointing the fingers,
14 with perverted mind devising evil,
continually sowing discord;
15 on such a one calamity will descend
suddenly;
in a moment, damage beyond repair.

16 There are six things that the LORD hates,
seven that are an abomination to him:
17 haughty eyes, a lying tongue,
and hands that shed innocent blood,
18 a heart that devises wicked plans,
feet that hurry to run to evil,
19 a lying witness who testifies falsely,
and one who sows discord in a family.

20 My child, keep your father's
commandment,
and do not forsake your mother's
teaching.
21 Bind them upon your heart always;
tie them around your neck.
22 When you walk, they[m] will lead you;

when you lie down, they[m] will watch
over you;
and when you awake, they[m] will talk
with you.
23 For the commandment is a lamp and the
teaching a light,
and the reproofs of discipline are the
way of life,
24 to preserve you from the wife of
another,[n]
from the smooth tongue of the
adulteress.
25 Do not desire her beauty in your heart,
and do not let her capture you with
her eyelashes;
26 for a prostitute's fee is only a loaf of
bread,[o]
but the wife of another stalks a man's
very life.
27 Can fire be carried in the bosom
without burning one's clothes?
28 Or can one walk on hot coals
without scorching the feet?
29 So is he who sleeps with his neighbor's
wife;
no one who touches her will go
unpunished.
30 Thieves are not despised who steal only
to satisfy their appetite when they are
hungry.
31 Yet if they are caught, they will pay
sevenfold;
they will forfeit all the goods of their
house.
32 But he who commits adultery has no
sense;
he who does it destroys himself.
33 He will get wounds and dishonor,
and his disgrace will not be wiped
away.
34 For jealousy arouses a husband's fury,
and he shows no restraint when he
takes revenge.
35 He will accept no compensation,
and refuses a bribe no matter how
great.

The False Attractions of Adultery

7 My child, keep my words
and store up my commandments with
you;
2 keep my commandments and live,
keep my teachings as the apple of your
eye;
3 bind them on your fingers,
write them on the tablet of your heart.
4 Say to wisdom, "You are my sister,"
and call insight your intimate friend,

---

[l] Cn: Heb *from the hand of a harlot to a piece of bread*   [m] Heb *it*   [n] Gk: MT *the evil woman*   [o] Cn Compare Gk Syr Vg Tg: Heb *for because*

5 that they may keep you from the loose[p]
  woman,
  from the adulteress with her smooth
  words.

6 For at the window of my house
  I looked out through my lattice,
7 and I saw among the simple ones,
  I observed among the youths,
  a young man without sense,
8 passing along the street near her corner,
  taking the road to her house
9 in the twilight, in the evening,
  at the time of night and darkness.

10 Then a woman comes toward him,
  decked out like a prostitute, wily of
  heart.[q]
11 She is loud and wayward;
  her feet do not stay at home;
12 now in the street, now in the squares,
  and at every corner she lies in wait.
13 She seizes him and kisses him,
  and with impudent face she says to
  him:
14 "I had to offer sacrifices,
  and today I have paid my vows;
15 so now I have come out to meet you,
  to seek you eagerly, and I have found
  you!
16 I have decked my couch with coverings,
  colored spreads of Egyptian linen;
17 I have perfumed my bed with myrrh,
  aloes, and cinnamon.
18 Come, let us take our fill of love until
  morning;
  let us delight ourselves with love.
19 For my husband is not at home;
  he has gone on a long journey.
20 He took a bag of money with him;
  he will not come home until full
  moon."

21 With much seductive speech she
  persuades him;

with her smooth talk she compels him.
22 Right away he follows her,
  and goes like an ox to the slaughter,
  or bounds like a stag toward the trap[r]
23 until an arrow pierces its entrails.
  He is like a bird rushing into a snare,
  not knowing that it will cost him his
  life.

24 And now, my children, listen to me,
  and be attentive to the words of my
  mouth.
25 Do not let your hearts turn aside to her
  ways;
  do not stray into her paths.
26 for many are those she has laid low,
  and numerous are her victims.
27 Her house is the way to Sheol,
  going down to the chambers of death.

The Gifts of Wisdom

8 Does not wisdom call,
  and does not understanding raise her
  voice?
2 On the heights, beside the way,
  at the crossroads she takes her stand;
3 beside the gates in front of the town,
  at the entrance of the portals she cries
  out:
4 "To you, O people, I call,
  and my cry is to all that live.
5 O simple ones, learn prudence;
  acquire intelligence, you who lack it.
6 Hear, for I will speak noble things,
  and from my lips will come what is
  right;
7 for my mouth will utter truth;
  wickedness is an abomination to my
  lips.
8 All the words of my mouth are righteous;
  there is nothing twisted or crooked in
  them.
9 They are all straight to one who
  understands
  and right to those who find knowledge.
10 Take my instruction instead of silver,
  and knowledge rather than choice gold;
11 for wisdom is better than jewels,
  and all that you may desire cannot
  compare with her.
12 I, wisdom, live with prudence,[q]
  and I attain knowledge and discretion.
13 The fear of the LORD is hatred of evil.
  Pride and arrogance and the way of evil
  and perverted speech I hate.
14 I have good advice and sound wisdom;
  I have insight, I have strength.
15 By me kings reign,
  and rulers decree what is just;

16 by me rulers rule,
and nobles, all who govern rightly.
17 I love those who love me,
and those who seek me diligently find
me.

8.13 The Fear of the Lord

The phrase "fear of the LORD" doesn't mean fright or terror. It means "a good relationship with God," based on reverence and respect for him and his commands. Here, for instance, the fear of the Lord means righteous living.

18 Riches and honor are with me,
enduring wealth and prosperity.
19 My fruit is better than gold, even fine
gold,
and my yield than choice silver.
20 I walk in the way of righteousness,
along the paths of justice,
21 endowing with wealth those who love me,
and filling their treasuries.

Wisdom's Part in Creation

22 The LORD created me at the beginning[s]
of his work,[t]
the first of his acts of long ago.
23 Ages ago I was set up,
at the first, before the beginning of the
earth.
24 When there were no depths I was brought
forth,
when there were no springs abounding
with water.
25 Before the mountains had been shaped,
before the hills, I was brought forth—
26 when he had not yet made earth and
fields,[u]
or the world's first bits of soil.
27 When he established the heavens, I was
there,
when he drew a circle on the face of
the deep,
28 when he made firm the skies above,
when he established the fountains of
the deep,
29 when he assigned to the sea its limit,
so that the waters might not transgress
his command,
when he marked out the foundations of
the earth,
30 then I was beside him, like a master
worker;[v]
and I was daily his[w] delight,
rejoicing before him always,

31 rejoicing in his inhabited world
and delighting in the human race.

32 "And now, my children, listen to me:
happy are those who keep my ways.
33 Hear instruction and be wise,
and do not neglect it.
34 Happy is the one who listens to me,
watching daily at my gates,
waiting beside my doors.
35 For whoever finds me finds life
and obtains favor from the LORD;
36 but those who miss me injure themselves;
all who hate me love death."

Wisdom's Feast

9 Wisdom has built her house,
she has hewn her seven pillars.
2 She has slaughtered her animals, she has
mixed her wine,
she has also set her table.
3 She has sent out her servant-girls, she
calls
from the highest places in the town,
4 "You that are simple, turn in here!"
To those without sense she says,
5 "Come, eat of my bread
and drink of the wine I have mixed.
6 Lay aside immaturity,[x] and live,
and walk in the way of insight."

General Maxims

7 Whoever corrects a scoffer wins abuse;
whoever rebukes the wicked gets hurt.
8 A scoffer who is rebuked will only hate
you;
the wise, when rebuked, will love you.
9 Give instruction[y] to the wise, and they
will become wiser still;
teach the righteous and they will gain
in learning.
10 The fear of the LORD is the beginning of
wisdom,
and the knowledge of the Holy One is
insight.
11 For by me your days will be multiplied,
and years will be added to your life.
12 If you are wise, you are wise for yourself;
if you scoff, you alone will bear it.

Folly's Invitation and Promise

13 The foolish woman is loud;
she is ignorant and knows nothing.
14 She sits at the door of her house,
on a seat at the high places of the
town,
15 calling to those who pass by,
who are going straight on their way,

---

[s] Or *me as the beginning*   [t] Heb *way*   [u] Meaning of Heb uncertain   [v] Another reading is *little child*
[w] Gk: Heb lacks *his*   [x] Or *simpleness*   [y] Heb lacks *instruction*

16 "You who are simple, turn in here!"
  And to those without sense she says,
17 "Stolen water is sweet,
  and bread eaten in secret is pleasant."
18 But they do not know that the dead*z* are
    there,
  that her guests are in the depths of
    Sheol.

Wise Sayings of Solomon

10 The proverbs of Solomon.

A wise child makes a glad father,
  but a foolish child is a mother's grief.
2 Treasures gained by wickedness do not
    profit,
  but righteousness delivers from death.
3 The LORD does not let the righteous go
    hungry,
  but he thwarts the craving of the
    wicked.
4 A slack hand causes poverty,
  but the hand of the diligent makes
    rich.
5 A child who gathers in summer is
    prudent,
  but a child who sleeps in harvest brings
    shame.
6 Blessings are on the head of the righteous,
  but the mouth of the wicked conceals
    violence.

z Heb *shades*

7 The memory of the righteous is a
    blessing,
  but the name of the wicked will rot.
8 The wise of heart will heed
    commandments,
  but a babbling fool will come to ruin.
9 Whoever walks in integrity walks
    securely,

10.1 Hebrew Poetry

"Parallelism" is a technical term for the form of Hebrew poetry that repeats a thought in slightly different ways. "Synonymous parallelism" is found in Proverbs 15.30, "The light of the eyes rejoices the heart, and good news refreshes the body." "Antithetical parallelism," in which a thought is followed by its opposite, is found in 14.30, "A tranquil mind gives life to the flesh, but passion makes the bones rot."

In studying parallelism the trick is to compare each part with its pair in the other half of the proverb. For instance, in 14.30 "a tranquil mind" pairs with its opposite, "passion," and "makes the bones rot" is the opposite of "gives life to the flesh." Sometimes these comparisons bare subtle shades of meaning.

God and "How-to-Succeed"
Does Proverbs care more for success than for God?

> The fear of the LORD is the beginning of wisdom. 9.10

BOOKSTORES ARE FULL OF "HOW-TO" books, each promising to teach you how to make a success of yourself by just following a few simple rules. Is Proverbs an ancient "how-to" book? It seems, at first look, more interested in success and prosperity than in God. Many of the proverbs can be adopted by those who have no love for God.

But if you look at Proverbs as a book, rather than a collection of unrelated fragments, you will find that its "how-tos" of wise living can't be separated from God. While some proverbs observe the hard facts of life—that bribes are effective, for instance, or that money does buy friends of a kind—the book never for a moment endorses success techniques that involve immorality. More important, a deep sense of people's sin and their utter dependence on God pervades Proverbs. Wisdom, that fundamental tool for living, starts with the fear of God and leads to a knowledge of him.

The words LORD or God are actually mentioned nearly 100 times, so a complete study of God's place in Proverbs takes you through virtually the entire book.
Proverbs on God's relationship to wisdom: 1.7; 2.5–9; 8.22–31; 9.10; 22.17–19.
Proverbs on sin: 15.8; 16.6; 20.9; 24.11–12; 28.9,13.
Proverbs on trust in God: 3.5–12; 14.26–27; 16.20; 18.10; 19.21; 21.31; 29.25–26; 30.5–9.
Proverbs on God's blessing: 10.22,27,29; 15.16.
Other proverbs of particular interest: 11.1; 17.3; 19.3; 20.12; 21.3; 28.5.

Life Questions: What are your plans for success? Is God's will the basis of your plans, or is it an afterthought?

but whoever follows perverse ways will be found out.

10 Whoever winks the eye causes trouble,
  but the one who rebukes boldly makes peace.[a]

11 The mouth of the righteous is a fountain of life,
  but the mouth of the wicked conceals violence.

12 Hatred stirs up strife,
  but love covers all offenses.

10.12 Love Is the Greatest

If you think of love as restricted to the New Testament, Proverbs will surprise you. Here love is the all-purpose cure, covering all wrongs. It is worth searching for. It should be expressed openly.

Some of the proverbs on love are found in the following passages: 3.3–4; 9.8; 10.12; 14.22; 15.17; 16.6; 17.9; 19.22; 20.6,28; 21.21; 27.5.

---

13 On the lips of one who has understanding wisdom is found,
  but a rod is for the back of one who lacks sense.

14 The wise lay up knowledge,
  but the babbling of a fool brings ruin near.

15 The wealth of the rich is their fortress;
  the poverty of the poor is their ruin.

16 The wage of the righteous leads to life,
  the gain of the wicked to sin.

17 Whoever heeds instruction is on the path to life,
  but one who rejects a rebuke goes astray.

18 Lying lips conceal hatred,
  and whoever utters slander is a fool.

19 When words are many, transgression is not lacking,
  but the prudent are restrained in speech.

20 The tongue of the righteous is choice silver;
  the mind of the wicked is of little worth.

21 The lips of the righteous feed many,
  but fools die for lack of sense.

22 The blessing of the LORD makes rich,
  and he adds no sorrow with it.[b]

23 Doing wrong is like sport to a fool,
  but wise conduct is pleasure to a person of understanding.

24 What the wicked dread will come upon them,
  but the desire of the righteous will be granted.

25 When the tempest passes, the wicked are no more,
  but the righteous are established forever.

26 Like vinegar to the teeth, and smoke to the eyes,
  so are the lazy to their employers.

27 The fear of the LORD prolongs life,

[a] Gk: Heb but a babbling fool will come to ruin   [b] Or and toil adds nothing to it

---

What Makes People Poor?
A clear-eyed view of wealth and poverty

> The wealth of the rich is their fortress; the poverty of the poor is their ruin.
> 10.15

"POOR PEOPLE ARE LAZY," SAYS one person. Someone else claims the opposite: "They are poor because the rich control the system." People tend to oversimplify when they discuss wealth and poverty. Curiously, both sides may quote Proverbs to prove their point.

You have to read all of Proverbs to get its subtle view. It says people are poor for various reasons: because of laziness and drunkenness, but also because the rich oppress them. People get rich for various reasons too: because of hard work, because of the Lord's blessing, because they cheated.

Proverbs gives an evenhanded view of what money does for people. Wealth brings benefits, including eager friends, Proverbs says; but it also brings worries and troubles. Proverbs strongly urges the rich and powerful to be generous and fair to poor people. It remains remarkably clear-eyed about the tangled causes of poverty and about the dangers and benefits of wealth.

Proverbs on money: 10.4,15,22; 11.4,16,28; 13.8,18,22–23; 14.20,23,31; 15.16; 18.23; 19.1,4,17; 20.13; 21.5,17; 22.1–2,4,7,9,16,22–23; 23.5; 28.3,6,8,11,19,20,22,27; 29.7,14; 30.7–9.

Life Questions: Think of the richest and the poorest people you know. Have stereotypes about wealth and poverty affected your attitude toward them?

but the years of the wicked will be
　　short.

28 The hope of the righteous ends in
　　gladness,
　　but the expectation of the wicked
　　　comes to nothing.
29 The way of the LORD is a stronghold for
　　the upright,
　　but destruction for evildoers.
30 The righteous will never be removed,
　　but the wicked will not remain in the
　　　land.
31 The mouth of the righteous brings forth
　　wisdom,
　　but the perverse tongue will be cut off.
32 The lips of the righteous know what is
　　acceptable,
　　but the mouth of the wicked what is
　　　perverse.

11 A false balance is an abomination to the
　　LORD,
　　but an accurate weight is his delight.
2 When pride comes, then comes disgrace;
　　but wisdom is with the humble.
3 The integrity of the upright guides them,
　　but the crookedness of the treacherous
　　　destroys them.
4 Riches do not profit in the day of wrath,
　　but righteousness delivers from death.
5 The righteousness of the blameless keeps
　　their ways straight,
　　but the wicked fall by their own
　　　wickedness.
6 The righteousness of the upright saves
　　them,
　　but the treacherous are taken captive
　　　by their schemes.
7 When the wicked die, their hope perishes,
　　and the expectation of the godless
　　　comes to nothing.
8 The righteous are delivered from trouble,
　　and the wicked get into it instead.
9 With their mouths the godless would
　　destroy their neighbors,
　　but by knowledge the righteous are
　　　delivered.
10 When it goes well with the righteous, the
　　city rejoices;
　　and when the wicked perish, there is
　　　jubilation.
11 By the blessing of the upright a city is
　　exalted,
　　but it is overthrown by the mouth of
　　　the wicked.
12 Whoever belittles another lacks sense,
　　but an intelligent person remains silent.
13 A gossip goes about telling secrets,
　　but one who is trustworthy in spirit
　　　keeps a confidence.

14 Where there is no guidance, a nation[c]
　　falls,
　　but in an abundance of counselors
　　　there is safety.
15 To guarantee loans for a stranger brings
　　trouble,
　　but there is safety in refusing to do so.
16 A gracious woman gets honor,
　　but she who hates virtue is covered
　　　with shame.[d]
　　The timid become destitute,[e]
　　but the aggressive gain riches.
17 Those who are kind reward themselves,
　　but the cruel do themselves harm.
18 The wicked earn no real gain,
　　but those who sow righteousness get a
　　　true reward.
19 Whoever is steadfast in righteousness will
　　live,
　　but whoever pursues evil will die.
20 Crooked minds are an abomination to the
　　LORD,
　　but those of blameless ways are his
　　　delight.
21 Be assured, the wicked will not go
　　unpunished,
　　but those who are righteous will
　　　escape.
22 Like a gold ring in a pig's snout
　　is a beautiful woman without good
　　　sense.

11.22 Skin-deep Beauty

*Throughout Proverbs, character is what counts.
When not matched by inward beauty, good
looks seem ridiculous, as this saying
humorously suggests.*

23 The desire of the righteous ends only in
　　good;
　　the expectation of the wicked in wrath.
24 Some give freely, yet grow all the richer;
　　others withhold what is due, and only
　　　suffer want.
25 A generous person will be enriched,
　　and one who gives water will get
　　　water.
26 The people curse those who hold back
　　grain,
　　but a blessing is on the head of those
　　　who sell it.
27 Whoever diligently seeks good seeks
　　favor,
　　but evil comes to the one who searches
　　　for it.

---

c Or *an army*　　d Compare Gk Syr: Heb lacks *but she ... shame*　　e Gk: Heb lacks *The timid ... destitute*

28 Those who trust in their riches will
wither,*f*
but the righteous will flourish like
green leaves.
29 Those who trouble their households will
inherit wind,
and the fool will be servant to the wise.
30 The fruit of the righteous is a tree of life,
but violence*g* takes lives away.
31 If the righteous are repaid on earth,
how much more the wicked and the
sinner!

12 Whoever loves discipline loves
knowledge,
but those who hate to be rebuked are
stupid.
2 The good obtain favor from the LORD,
but those who devise evil he
condemns.
3 No one finds security by wickedness,
but the root of the righteous will never
be moved.
4 A good wife is the crown of her husband,
but she who brings shame is like
rottenness in his bones.
5 The thoughts of the righteous are just;
the advice of the wicked is treacherous.
6 The words of the wicked are a deadly
ambush,
but the speech of the upright delivers
them.
7 The wicked are overthrown and are no
more,
but the house of the righteous will
stand.
8 One is commended for good sense,
but a perverse mind is despised.
9 Better to be despised and have a servant,
than to be self-important and lack
food.
10 The righteous know the needs of their
animals,
but the mercy of the wicked is cruel.
11 Those who till their land will have plenty
of food,
but those who follow worthless pursuits
have no sense.
12 The wicked covet the proceeds of
wickedness,*h*
but the root of the righteous bears
fruit.
13 The evil are ensnared by the transgression
of their lips,
but the righteous escape from trouble.
14 From the fruit of the mouth one is filled
with good things,
and manual labor has its reward.

15 Fools think their own way is right,
but the wise listen to advice.
16 Fools show their anger at once,
but the prudent ignore an insult.
17 Whoever speaks the truth gives honest
evidence,
but a false witness speaks deceitfully.

12.17 Deeper Meanings

Some proverbs, disarmingly obvious at first glance, offer deep truth when chewed on. For instance, verse 17 seems to merely repeat the obvious. But its underlying meaning is that a person's character determines his or her actions. You can reflect at length on what this implies about why you do what you do.

18 Rash words are like sword thrusts,
but the tongue of the wise brings
healing.
19 Truthful lips endure forever,
but a lying tongue lasts only a
moment.
20 Deceit is in the mind of those who plan
evil,
but those who counsel peace have joy.
21 No harm happens to the righteous,
but the wicked are filled with trouble.
22 Lying lips are an abomination to the
LORD,
but those who act faithfully are his
delight.
23 One who is clever conceals knowledge,
but the mind of a fool*i* broadcasts
folly.
24 The hand of the diligent will rule,
while the lazy will be put to forced
labor.
25 Anxiety weighs down the human heart,
but a good word cheers it up.
26 The righteous gives good advice
to friends,*j*
but the way of the wicked leads astray.
27 The lazy do not roast*k* their game,
but the diligent obtain precious
wealth.*k*
28 In the path of righteousness there is life,
in walking its path there is no death.

13 A wise child loves discipline,*l*
but a scoffer does not listen to rebuke.
2 From the fruit of their words good
persons eat good things,
but the desire of the treacherous is for
wrongdoing.

f Cn: Heb *fall*   *g* Cn Compare Gk Syr: Heb *a wise man*   *h* Or *covet the catch of the wicked*   *i* Heb *the heart of
fools*   *j* Syr: Meaning of Heb uncertain   *k* Meaning of Heb uncertain   *l* Cn: Heb *A wise child the discipline of his
father*

3 Those who guard their mouths preserve
their lives;
those who open wide their lips come to
ruin.
4 The appetite of the lazy craves, and gets
nothing,
while the appetite of the diligent is
richly supplied.
5 The righteous hate falsehood,
but the wicked act shamefully and
disgracefully.
6 Righteousness guards one whose way is
upright,
but sin overthrows the wicked.
7 Some pretend to be rich, yet have
nothing;
others pretend to be poor, yet have
great wealth.
8 Wealth is a ransom for a person's life,
but the poor get no threats.
9 The light of the righteous rejoices,
but the lamp of the wicked goes out.
10 By insolence the heedless make strife,
but wisdom is with those who take
advice.
11 Wealth hastily gotten[m] will dwindle,
but those who gather little by little will
increase it.
12 Hope deferred makes the heart sick,
but a desire fulfilled is a tree of life.
13 Those who despise the word bring
destruction on themselves,
but those who respect the
commandment will be rewarded.

14 The teaching of the wise is a fountain of
life,
so that one may avoid the snares of
death.
15 Good sense wins favor,
but the way of the faithless is their
ruin.[n]
16 The clever do all things intelligently,
but the fool displays folly.
17 A bad messenger brings trouble,
but a faithful envoy, healing.
18 Poverty and disgrace are for the one who
ignores instruction,
but one who heeds reproof is honored.
19 A desire realized is sweet to the soul,
but to turn away from evil is an
abomination to fools.
20 Whoever walks with the wise becomes
wise,
but the companion of fools suffers
harm.
21 Misfortune pursues sinners,
but prosperity rewards the righteous.
22 The good leave an inheritance to their
children's children,
but the sinner's wealth is laid up for
the righteous.
23 The field of the poor may yield much
food,
but it is swept away through injustice.
24 Those who spare the rod hate their
children,
but those who love them are diligent to
discipline them.

[m] Gk Vg: Heb *from vanity*   [n] Cn Compare Gk Syr Vg Tg: Heb *is enduring*

The Supreme Gift of Wisdom
First, learn to listen

> Whoever walks with
> the wise becomes
> wise, but the com-
> panion of fools suf-
> fers harm. 13.20

PROVERBS JUDGES EVERY THOUGHT OR action by one stan-
dard: "Is this wise?" The word *wisdom* brings up pictures of gray-haired
old men muttering obscure philosophic maxims. But that is almost the
opposite of what Proverbs means by the word. Wisdom is above all practical
and down to earth. Young people as well as old can and should have it. Wisdom teaches you how to live. It combines understanding with discipline—the
kind of discipline an athlete needs in training. It also adds a healthy dose of good common sense—
except that common sense isn't, and never has been, common.

How do you become a wise person? You must first begin to listen. Wisdom is freely available to
those who will stop talking and start paying attention—to God and his word, to parents, to wise counselors. Anybody can become wise, Proverbs says. Wisdom is not reserved for a brainy elite. But becoming wise requires self-discipline to study and humbly seek wisdom at every opportunity.
Proverbs on becoming a wise person: 2.1–6; 9.1–10; 10.1,5,8,14,19,23; 11.2; 12.18; 13.10,20; 14.8;
15.7,31; 16.23; 17.24; 18.15; 19.11,20; 20.1; 21.11,20,30; 23.4; 29.3,8,11,15; 30.5–6.

Life Questions: Think over the last two years of your life. To whom do you listen? Who has the greatest
influence on you?

25 The righteous have enough to satisfy their
        appetite,
    but the belly of the wicked is empty.

14 The wise woman[o] builds her house,
    but the foolish tears it down with her
        own hands.
2 Those who walk uprightly fear the LORD,
    but one who is devious in conduct
        despises him.
3 The talk of fools is a rod for their backs,[p]
    but the lips of the wise preserve them.
4 Where there are no oxen, there is no
        grain;
    abundant crops come by the strength
        of the ox.
5 A faithful witness does not lie,
    but a false witness breathes out lies.
6 A scoffer seeks wisdom in vain,
    but knowledge is easy for one who
        understands.
7 Leave the presence of a fool,
    for there you do not find words of
        knowledge.
8 It is the wisdom of the clever to
        understand where they go,
    but the folly of fools misleads.
9 Fools mock at the guilt offering,[q]
    but the upright enjoy God's favor.
10 The heart knows its own bitterness,
    and no stranger shares its joy.
11 The house of the wicked is destroyed,
    but the tent of the upright flourishes.
12 There is a way that seems right to a
        person,
    but its end is the way to death.[r]
13 Even in laughter the heart is sad,

and the end of joy is grief.
14 The perverse get what their ways deserve,
    and the good, what their deeds
        deserve.[s]
15 The simple believe everything,
    but the clever consider their steps.

14.12 Be Careful

*Proverbs offers common sense, but doesn't
encourage simply trusting your own sense.
Choices that seem perfectly right may end up
destroying you. That is precisely why people
need to cultivate wisdom: What looks good
often isn't.*

16 The wise are cautious and turn away from
        evil,
    but the fool throws off restraint and is
        careless.
17 One who is quick-tempered acts foolishly,
    and the schemer is hated.
18 The simple are adorned with[t] folly,
    but the clever are crowned with
        knowledge.
19 The evil bow down before the good,
    the wicked at the gates of the
        righteous.
20 The poor are disliked even by their
        neighbors,
    but the rich have many friends.
21 Those who despise their neighbors are
        sinners,
    but happy are those who are kind to
        the poor.

o Heb *Wisdom of women*   p Cn: Heb *a rod of pride*   q Meaning of Heb uncertain   r Heb *ways of death*
s Cn: Heb *from upon him*   t Or *inherit*

A Matter of Life and Death
More than mere survival

PROVERBS FREQUENTLY TALKS ABOUT LIFE and death. Wise
living, it says, tends to make you live longer, while foolish living will
push you into an early grave.
    If you take this observation at face value, you'll have a problem: Plenty
of people who live foolishly survive into old age. But the concept of life and
death in Proverbs includes much more than physical survival. By life, Proverbs
means "real living" full of peace and joy and wisdom. By death, it means spiritual as well as physical
decay. A person who misses the way of wisdom may be as good as dead, even though he or she is
still walking around.
    Proverbs on "real living": 3.18,21–22; 4.23; 8.34–36; 10.11,16; 12.28; 13.12; 14.27,30; 15.4,27; 18.21;
        19.23; 21.21; 28.16.
    Proverbs on "real dying": 2.16–18; 5.3–6,22–23; 10.21; 14.12,32; 15.10; 19.16; 21.25; 27.20.

> There is a way that
> seems right to a
> person, but its end
> is the way to death.
> 14.12

Life Questions: Can you remember a specific experience that represents, for you, "real living"? How
about "real dying"?

22 Do they not err that plan evil?
   Those who plan good find loyalty and
      faithfulness.
23 In all toil there is profit,

14.20 Lucky Rich

*Rich people have many friends, whereas the
poor often get ignored. That's the way life is.
But, according to the next proverb (verse 21),
life isn't meant to be "the way it is." Verse 31
goes on to show God himself closely involved
in the way we treat poor people.*

   but mere talk leads only to poverty.
24 The crown of the wise is their wisdom,ᵘ
   but folly is the garlandᵛ of fools.
25 A truthful witness saves lives,
   but one who utters lies is a betrayer.
26 In the fear of the LORD one has strong
      confidence,
   and one's children will have a refuge.
27 The fear of the LORD is a fountain of life,
   so that one may avoid the snares of
      death.
28 The glory of a king is a multitude of
      people;
   without people a prince is ruined.
29 Whoever is slow to anger has great
      understanding,
   but one who has a hasty temper exalts
      folly.
30 A tranquil mind gives life to the flesh,
   but passion makes the bones rot.
31 Those who oppress the poor insult their
      Maker,
   but those who are kind to the needy
      honor him.
32 The wicked are overthrown by their
      evildoing,
   but the righteous find a refuge in their
      integrity.ʷ
33 Wisdom is at home in the mind of one
      who has understanding,
   but it is notˣ known in the heart of
      fools.
34 Righteousness exalts a nation,
   but sin is a reproach to any people.
35 A servant who deals wisely has the king's
      favor,
   but his wrath falls on one who acts
      shamefully.

15 A soft answer turns away wrath,
   but a harsh word stirs up anger.
2 The tongue of the wise dispenses
      knowledge,ʸ
   but the mouths of fools pour out folly.

3 The eyes of the LORD are in every place,
   keeping watch on the evil and the
      good.
4 A gentle tongue is a tree of life,
   but perverseness in it breaks the spirit.
5 A fool despises a parent's instruction,
   but the one who heeds admonition is
      prudent.
6 In the house of the righteous there is
      much treasure,
   but trouble befalls the income of the
      wicked.
7 The lips of the wise spread knowledge;
   not so the minds of fools.
8 The sacrifice of the wicked is an
      abomination to the LORD,
   but the prayer of the upright is his
      delight.
9 The way of the wicked is an abomination
      to the LORD,
   but he loves the one who pursues
      righteousness.
10 There is severe discipline for one who
      forsakes the way,
   but one who hates a rebuke will die.
11 Sheol and Abaddon lie open before the
      LORD,
   how much more human hearts!
12 Scoffers do not like to be rebuked;
   they will not go to the wise.
13 A glad heart makes a cheerful
      countenance,
   but by sorrow of heart the spirit is
      broken.
14 The mind of one who has understanding
      seeks knowledge,
   but the mouths of fools feed on folly.
15 All the days of the poor are hard,
   but a cheerful heart has a continual
      feast.
16 Better is a little with the fear of the LORD
   than great treasure and trouble with it.
17 Better is a dinner of vegetables where love
      is
   than a fatted ox and hatred with it.
18 Those who are hot-tempered stir up
      strife,
   but those who are slow to anger calm
      contention.
19 The way of the lazy is overgrown with
      thorns,
   but the path of the upright is a level
      highway.
20 A wise child makes a glad father,
   but the foolish despise their mothers.
21 Folly is a joy to one who has no sense,
   but a person of understanding walks
      straight ahead.

ᵘ Cn Compare Gk: Heb *riches*   ᵛ Cn: Heb *is the folly*   ʷ Gk Syr: Heb *in their death*   ˣ Gk Syr: Heb lacks *not*
ʸ Cn: Heb *makes knowledge good*

22 Without counsel, plans go wrong,
    but with many advisers they succeed.
23 To make an apt answer is a joy to
        anyone,
    and a word in season, how good it is!
24 For the wise the path of life leads
        upward,
    in order to avoid Sheol below.
25 The LORD tears down the house of the
        proud,
    but maintains the widow's boundaries.

15.25 Poor and Helpless

In Old Testament society the most helpless person was the widow. With no one to protect her, she could only watch as her late husband's land was grabbed by bullying neighbors. But a widow was never completely helpless. The Lord was on her side. In the final analysis her condition was more secure than that of her proud, rich neighbor.

26 Evil plans are an abomination to the
        LORD,
    but gracious words are pure.
27 Those who are greedy for unjust gain
        make trouble for their
        households,
    but those who hate bribes will live.
28 The mind of the righteous ponders how
        to answer,
    but the mouth of the wicked pours out
        evil.
29 The LORD is far from the wicked,

but he hears the prayer of the
        righteous.
30 The light of the eyes rejoices the heart,
    and good news refreshes the body.
31 The ear that heeds wholesome admonition
    will lodge among the wise.
32 Those who ignore instruction despise
        themselves,
    but those who heed admonition gain
        understanding.
33 The fear of the LORD is instruction in
        wisdom,
    and humility goes before honor.

16 The plans of the mind belong to mortals,
    but the answer of the tongue is from
        the LORD.
2 All one's ways may be pure in one's own
        eyes,
    but the LORD weighs the spirit.
3 Commit your work to the LORD,
    and your plans will be established.
4 The LORD has made everything for its
        purpose,
    even the wicked for the day of trouble.
5 All those who are arrogant are an
        abomination to the LORD;
    be assured, they will not go
        unpunished.
6 By loyalty and faithfulness iniquity is
        atoned for,
    and by the fear of the LORD one avoids
        evil.
7 When the ways of people please the LORD,
    he causes even their enemies to be at
        peace with them.
8 Better is a little with righteousness

Verbal Dynamite
Even truthful words can damage other people

WHAT COULD BE WRONG WITH just talking, as long as you don't actually lie? Proverbs sees plenty of danger. Words are dynamite; they can destroy people. They should be carefully weighed before they are spoken. Even truthful words can damage. Yet they can also save a friend from going wrong. Proverbs speaks strongly about both the danger of gossip and the good done when someone justly rebukes his or her friend.

A perverse person spreads strife, and a whisperer separates close friends. 16.28

"Death and life are in the power of the tongue," Proverbs 18.21 says, "and those who love it will eat its fruits." Proverbs teaches the skill of speaking so as to give life.
Proverbs on the importance of words: 10.11,20; 12.14; 15.4; 17.10; 18.21; 25.11.
Proverbs on the wrong way to speak: 6.16–19; 11.9,12–13; 12.18; 13.3; 16.27–28; 18.8,13; 26.23–28; 29.5.
Proverbs on the right way to speak: 10.14,21,32; 12.25; 15.1,23,28; 16.13,23–24; 17.27–28; 25.12,15; 27.5–6; 28.23.
Proverbs on the dangers of words: 10.19; 14.23.

Life Questions: Have you said anything recently that you wish you could take back? What are the most life-giving words you've spoken lately?

than large income with injustice.

9 The human mind plans the way,
   but the LORD directs the steps.

10 Inspired decisions are on the lips of a
   king;
   his mouth does not sin in judgment.

11 Honest balances and scales are the LORD's;
   all the weights in the bag are his work.

12 It is an abomination to kings to do evil,
   for the throne is established by
   righteousness.

13 Righteous lips are the delight of a king,
   and he loves those who speak what is
   right.

14 A king's wrath is a messenger of death,
   and whoever is wise will appease it.

15 In the light of a king's face there is life,
   and his favor is like the clouds that
   bring the spring rain.

16 How much better to get wisdom than
   gold!
   To get understanding is to be chosen
   rather than silver.

17 The highway of the upright avoids evil;
   those who guard their way preserve
   their lives.

18 Pride goes before destruction,
   and a haughty spirit before a fall.

19 It is better to be of a lowly spirit among
   the poor
   than to divide the spoil with the proud.

20 Those who are attentive to a matter will
   prosper,
   and happy are those who trust in the
   LORD.

21 The wise of heart is called perceptive,
   and pleasant speech increases
   persuasiveness.

22 Wisdom is a fountain of life to one who
   has it,
   but folly is the punishment of fools.

23 The mind of the wise makes their speech
   judicious,
   and adds persuasiveness to their lips.

24 Pleasant words are like a honeycomb,
   sweetness to the soul and health to the
   body.

25 Sometimes there is a way that seems to be
   right,
   but in the end it is the way to death.

26 The appetite of workers works for them;
   their hunger urges them on.

27 Scoundrels concoct evil,
   and their speech is like a scorching fire.

28 A perverse person spreads strife,
   and a whisperer separates close friends.

29 The violent entice their neighbors,
   and lead them in a way that is not
   good.

30 One who winks the eyes plans[z] perverse
   things;
   one who compresses the lips brings evil
   to pass.

31 Gray hair is a crown of glory;
   it is gained in a righteous life.

32 One who is slow to anger is better than
   the mighty,
   and one whose temper is controlled
   than one who captures a city.

33 The lot is cast into the lap,
   but the decision is the LORD's alone.

17 Better is a dry morsel with quiet
   than a house full of feasting with strife.

2 A slave who deals wisely will rule over a
   child who acts shamefully,
   and will share the inheritance as one of
   the family.

3 The crucible is for silver, and the furnace
   is for gold,
   but the LORD tests the heart.

4 An evildoer listens to wicked lips;
   and a liar gives heed to a mischievous
   tongue.

5 Those who mock the poor insult their
   Maker;
   those who are glad at calamity will not
   go unpunished.

6 Grandchildren are the crown of the aged,
   and the glory of children is their
   parents.

7 Fine speech is not becoming to a fool;
   still less is false speech to a ruler.[a]

8 A bribe is like a magic stone in the eyes
   of those who give it;
   wherever they turn they prosper.

17.8 Bribery Works Wonders!

*Proverbs is utterly realistic about the hard facts
of life. One is that bribery works. A complete
education ought to include that fact! But does
that make bribery right? No—just a few verses
later (verse 23), Proverbs condemns bribery.*

9 One who forgives an affront fosters
   friendship,
   but one who dwells on disputes will
   alienate a friend.

10 A rebuke strikes deeper into a discerning
   person
   than a hundred blows into a fool.

11 Evil people seek only rebellion,
   but a cruel messenger will be sent
   against them.

12 Better to meet a she-bear robbed of its
   cubs

---

[z] Gk Syr Vg Tg: Heb *to plan*   [a] Or *a noble person*

than to confront a fool immersed in
folly.
13 Evil will not depart from the house
of one who returns evil for good.
14 The beginning of strife is like letting out
water;
so stop before the quarrel breaks out.
15 One who justifies the wicked and one
who condemns the righteous
are both alike an abomination to the
LORD.
16 Why should fools have a price in hand
to buy wisdom, when they have no
mind to learn?
17 A friend loves at all times,
and kinsfolk are born to share
adversity.

17.17 How to Be a Good Friend

*The Old Testament puts great emphasis on
close family relationships. Surprisingly,
Proverbs rates a good friend even higher, for
he or she "sticks closer than one's nearest kin"
(18.24). Fair-weather friends are common
(14.20), and the wrong kind of companions will
bring you trouble. But a true friend loves you at
all times, even when things are bad.*

*Some key proverbs on being a good friend
and neighbor can be found in the following
passages: 3.27–28; 11.12; 12.26; 17.9,17; 18.24;
22.24–25; 25.20; 26.18–19; 27.6,9–10,14,17;
28.23; 29.5.*

18 It is senseless to give a pledge,
to become surety for a neighbor.
19 One who loves transgression loves strife;
one who builds a high threshold invites
broken bones.
20 The crooked of mind do not prosper,
and the perverse of tongue fall into
calamity.
21 The one who begets a fool gets trouble;
the parent of a fool has no joy.
22 A cheerful heart is a good medicine,
but a downcast spirit dries up
the bones.
23 The wicked accept a concealed bribe
to pervert the ways of justice.
24 The discerning person looks to wisdom,
but the eyes of a fool to the ends of
the earth.
25 Foolish children are a grief to their father
and bitterness to her who bore them.
26 To impose a fine on the innocent is not
right,
or to flog the noble for their integrity.
27 One who spares words is knowledgeable;

one who is cool in spirit has
understanding.
28 Even fools who keep silent are considered
wise;
when they close their lips, they are
deemed intelligent.

18 The one who lives alone is self-indulgent,
showing contempt for all who have
sound judgment.[b]
2 A fool takes no pleasure in
understanding,
but only in expressing personal
opinion.
3 When wickedness comes, contempt comes
also;
and with dishonor comes disgrace.
4 The words of the mouth are deep waters;
the fountain of wisdom is a gushing
stream.
5 It is not right to be partial to the guilty,
or to subvert the innocent in judgment.
6 A fool's lips bring strife,
and a fool's mouth invites a flogging.
7 The mouths of fools are their ruin,
and their lips a snare to themselves.
8 The words of a whisperer are like
delicious morsels;
they go down into the inner parts of
the body.
9 One who is slack in work
is close kin to a vandal.
10 The name of the LORD is a strong tower;
the righteous run into it and are safe.
11 The wealth of the rich is their strong city;
in their imagination it is like a high
wall.
12 Before destruction one's heart is haughty,
but humility goes before honor.
13 If one gives answer before hearing,
it is folly and shame.
14 The human spirit will endure sickness;
but a broken spirit—who can bear?
15 An intelligent mind acquires knowledge,
and the ear of the wise seeks
knowledge.
16 A gift opens doors;
it gives access to the great.
17 The one who first states a case seems
right,
until the other comes and
cross-examines.
18 Casting the lot puts an end to disputes
and decides between powerful
contenders.
19 An ally offended is stronger than a city;[c]
such quarreling is like the bars of a
castle.
20 From the fruit of the mouth one's
stomach is satisfied;

---

b Meaning of Heb uncertain   c Gk Syr Vg Tg: Meaning of Heb uncertain

the yield of the lips brings satisfaction.
21 Death and life are in the power of the
   tongue,
   and those who love it will eat its fruits.
22 He who finds a wife finds a good thing,
   and obtains favor from the LORD.
23 The poor use entreaties,
   but the rich answer roughly.
24 Some*d* friends play at friendship*e*
   but a true friend sticks closer than
   one's nearest kin.

19 Better the poor walking in integrity
   than one perverse of speech who is a
   fool.
2 Desire without knowledge is not good,
   and one who moves too hurriedly
   misses the way.
3 One's own folly leads to ruin,
   yet the heart rages against the LORD.
4 Wealth brings many friends,
   but the poor are left friendless.
5 A false witness will not go unpunished,
   and a liar will not escape.
6 Many seek the favor of the generous,
   and everyone is a friend to a giver of
   gifts.
7 If the poor are hated even by their kin,
   how much more are they shunned by
   their friends!
   When they call after them, they are not
   there.*f*
8 To get wisdom is to love oneself;
   to keep understanding is to prosper.
9 A false witness will not go unpunished,
   and the liar will perish.
10 It is not fitting for a fool to live in luxury,
   much less for a slave to rule over
   princes.
11 Those with good sense are slow to anger,
   and it is their glory to overlook an
   offense.
12 A king's anger is like the growling of a
   lion,
   but his favor is like dew on the grass.
13 A stupid child is ruin to a father,
   and a wife's quarreling is a continual
   dripping of rain.
14 House and wealth are inherited from
   parents,
   but a prudent wife is from the LORD.
15 Laziness brings on deep sleep;
   an idle person will suffer hunger.
16 Those who keep the commandment will
   live;
   those who are heedless of their ways
   will die.
17 Whoever is kind to the poor lends to the
   LORD,
   and will be repaid in full.

18 Discipline your children while there is
   hope;
   do not set your heart on their
   destruction.
19 A violent tempered person will pay the
   penalty;
   if you effect a rescue, you will only
   have to do it again.*f*
20 Listen to advice and accept instruction,
   that you may gain wisdom for the
   future.
21 The human mind may devise many plans,
   but it is the purpose of the LORD that
   will be established.
22 What is desirable in a person is loyalty,
   and it is better to be poor than a liar.
23 The fear of the LORD is life indeed;
   filled with it one rests secure
   and suffers no harm.
24 The lazy person buries a hand in the dish,
   and will not even bring it back to the
   mouth.
25 Strike a scoffer, and the simple will learn
   prudence;
   reprove the intelligent, and they will
   gain knowledge.
26 Those who do violence to their father and
   chase away their mother
   are children who cause shame and
   bring reproach.
27 Cease straying, my child, from the words
   of knowledge,
   in order that you may hear instruction.
28 A worthless witness mocks at justice,
   and the mouth of the wicked devours
   iniquity.
29 Condemnation is ready for scoffers,
   and flogging for the backs of fools.

20 Wine is a mocker, strong drink a
   brawler,
   and whoever is led astray by it is not
   wise.
2 The dread anger of a king is like the
   growling of a lion;
   anyone who provokes him to anger
   forfeits life itself.
3 It is honorable to refrain from strife,
   but every fool is quick to quarrel.
4 The lazy person does not plow in season;
   harvest comes, and there is nothing to
   be found.
5 The purposes in the human mind are like
   deep water,
   but the intelligent will draw them out.
6 Many proclaim themselves loyal,
   but who can find one worthy of trust?
7 The righteous walk in integrity—
   happy are the children who follow
   them!

d Syr Tg: Heb *A man of*   *e* Cn Compare Syr Vg Tg: Meaning of Heb uncertain   *f* Meaning of Heb uncertain

8 A king who sits on the throne of
    judgment
    winnows all evil with his eyes.
9 Who can say, "I have made my heart
    clean;
    I am pure from my sin"?
10 Diverse weights and diverse measures
    are both alike an abomination to the
    LORD.
11 Even children make themselves known by
    their acts,
    by whether what they do is pure and
    right.
12 The hearing ear and the seeing eye—
    the LORD has made them both.
13 Do not love sleep, or else you will come
    to poverty;
    open your eyes, and you will have
    plenty of bread.
14 "Bad, bad," says the buyer,
    then goes away and boasts.
15 There is gold, and abundance of costly
    stones;
    but the lips informed by knowledge are
    a precious jewel.
16 Take the garment of one who has given
    surety for a stranger;
    seize the pledge given as surety for
    foreigners.
17 Bread gained by deceit is sweet,
    but afterward the mouth will be full of
    gravel.
18 Plans are established by taking advice;
    wage war by following wise guidance.
19 A gossip reveals secrets;
    therefore do not associate with a
    babbler.
20 If you curse father or mother,
    your lamp will go out in utter
    darkness.
21 An estate quickly acquired in the
    beginning
    will not be blessed in the end.
22 Do not say, "I will repay evil";
    wait for the LORD, and he will help
    you.
23 Differing weights are an abomination to
    the LORD,
    and false scales are not good.
24 All our steps are ordered by the LORD;
    how then can we understand our own
    ways?
25 It is a snare for one to say rashly, "It is
    holy,"
    and begin to reflect only after making
    a vow.
26 A wise king winnows the wicked,
    and drives the wheel over them.

27 The human spirit is the lamp of the LORD,
    searching every inmost part.
28 Loyalty and faithfulness preserve the king,
    and his throne is upheld by
    righteousness.*g*
29 The glory of youths is their strength,
    but the beauty of the aged is their gray
    hair.
30 Blows that wound cleanse away evil;
    beatings make clean the innermost
    parts.

21 The king's heart is a stream of water in
    the hand of the LORD;
    he turns it wherever he will.
2 All deeds are right in the sight of the
    doer,
    but the LORD weighs the heart.
3 To do righteousness and justice
    is more acceptable to the LORD than
    sacrifice.
4 Haughty eyes and a proud heart—
    the lamp of the wicked—are sin.
5 The plans of the diligent lead surely to
    abundance,
    but everyone who is hasty comes only
    to want.
6 The getting of treasures by a lying tongue
    is a fleeting vapor and a snare*h* of
    death.
7 The violence of the wicked will sweep
    them away,
    because they refuse to do what is just.
8 The way of the guilty is crooked,
    but the conduct of the pure is right.
9 It is better to live in a corner of the
    housetop
    than in a house shared with a
    contentious wife.
10 The souls of the wicked desire evil;
    their neighbors find no mercy in their
    eyes.
11 When a scoffer is punished, the simple
    become wiser;
    when the wise are instructed, they
    increase in knowledge.
12 The Righteous One observes the house of
    the wicked;

21.11 Learning the Easy Way

*"The simple"—those who live without thinking—
are rarely persuaded to change, because they
don't listen. One lesson may get through to
them, though: seeing a troublemaker—the
"scoffer"—get punished. Wise people learn in a
much less painful way. When told something,
they pay attention.*

g Gk: Heb *loyalty*   *h* Gk: Heb *seekers*

he casts the wicked down to ruin.
13 If you close your ear to the cry of the
      poor,
   you will cry out and not be heard.
14 A gift in secret averts anger;
   and a concealed bribe in the bosom,
      strong wrath.
15 When justice is done, it is a joy to the
      righteous,
   but dismay to evildoers.
16 Whoever wanders from the way of
      understanding
   will rest in the assembly of the dead.
17 Whoever loves pleasure will suffer want;
   whoever loves wine and oil will not be
      rich.
18 The wicked is a ransom for the righteous,
   and the faithless for the upright.
19 It is better to live in a desert land
   than with a contentious and fretful
      wife.
20 Precious treasure remains[i] in the house
      of the wise,
   but the fool devours it.
21 Whoever pursues righteousness and
      kindness
   will find life[j] and honor.
22 One wise person went up against a city of
      warriors
   and brought down the stronghold in
      which they trusted.
23 To watch over mouth and tongue
   is to keep out of trouble.

24 The proud, haughty person, named
      "Scoffer,"
   acts with arrogant pride.
25 The craving of the lazy person is fatal,
   for lazy hands refuse to labor.
26 All day long the wicked covet,[k]
   but the righteous give and do not hold
      back.
27 The sacrifice of the wicked is an
      abomination;
   how much more when brought with
      evil intent.
28 A false witness will perish,
   but a good listener will testify
      successfully.
29 The wicked put on a bold face,
   but the upright give thought to[l] their
      ways.
30 No wisdom, no understanding, no
      counsel,
   can avail against the LORD.
31 The horse is made ready for the day of
      battle,
   but the victory belongs to the LORD.

22 A good name is to be chosen rather
      than great riches,
   and favor is better than silver or gold.
2 The rich and the poor have this in
      common:
   the LORD is the maker of them all.
3 The clever see danger and hide;
   but the simple go on, and suffer
      for it.

_i_ Gk: Heb _and oil_   _j_ Gk: Heb _life and righteousness_   _k_ Gk: Heb _all day long one covets covetously_   _l_ Another
reading is _establish_

Whom Should You Marry?
A good partner can make or break your life

IN ANCIENT TIMES WOMEN WERE often viewed as men's
property, good for bearing children and not much more. Proverbs,
addressed to young men approaching the age of marriage, takes a different view. It holds up marriage as a crucial choice, to be made with great
care.

> _Better to live in a corner of the house-top than in a house shared with a contentious wife. 21.9_

A wife (or husband, we can assume) will make or break her partner's life.
Her duties lay the foundation for her family's welfare (14.1; 31.10–31). She shares with her husband the
most significant task of teaching their children the way of wisdom (1.8–9; 6.20). Therefore, her character matters far more than her physical beauty.

Not that Proverbs ignores the physical side of love. It urges marriage partners to rejoice in their
love, to be captivated by it (5.18–19). It warns young people against sexual sin precisely because this
wastes sexuality on unsatisfying, unloving relationships. Sex ought to be saved for the long-lasting,
productive joy of marriage.

Proverbs on sexual sin: 2.16–19; 5.1–23; 6.20–35; 7.6–27; 23.26–28.
Proverbs on marriage: 5.15–19; 12.4; 14.1; 18.22; 19.13–14; 21.9,19; 27.15–16; 31.10–31.

Life Questions: What do you look for in a mate? How does your list compare with Proverbs's rating of
attributes such as physical attractiveness?

4 The reward for humility and fear of the
   LORD
  is riches and honor and life.
5 Thorns and snares are in the way of the
   perverse;
  the cautious will keep far from them.
6 Train children in the right way,
  and when old, they will not stray.

22.6 Good Parenting

An individual proverb shouldn't be read as either an invariable rule or a binding promise from God. Proverbs 10.4 generalizes truthfully, "the hand of the diligent makes rich," but you would not have to look too far to find an exception to the rule. Verse 6, a famous proverb, reinforces the importance of early training in forming a person's lifelong character. But you can find individuals who, though well brought up, choose to reject their training. Proverbs studies life the way it normally works. The general rule is this: Good parents raise good children.

7 The rich rule over the poor,
  and the borrower is the slave of the
   lender.
8 Whoever sows injustice will reap calamity,
  and the rod of anger will fail.
9 Those who are generous are blessed,
  for they share their bread with the
   poor.
10 Drive out a scoffer, and strife goes out;
  quarreling and abuse will cease.

11 Those who love a pure heart and are
   gracious in speech
  will have the king as a friend.
12 The eyes of the LORD keep watch over
   knowledge,
  but he overthrows the words of the
   faithless.
13 The lazy person says, "There is a lion
   outside!
  I shall be killed in the streets!"
14 The mouth of a loose[m] woman is a deep
   pit;
  he with whom the LORD is angry falls
   into it.
15 Folly is bound up in the heart of a boy,
  but the rod of discipline drives it far
   away.
16 Oppressing the poor in order to enrich
   oneself,
  and giving to the rich, will lead only to
   loss.

Sayings of the Wise

17   The words of the wise:

  Incline your ear and hear my words,[n]
  and apply your mind to my teaching;
18 for it will be pleasant if you keep them
   within you,
  if all of them are ready on your lips.
19 So that your trust may be in the LORD,
  I have made them known to you
   today—yes, to you.
20 Have I not written for you thirty sayings
  of admonition and knowledge,
21 to show you what is right and true,

[m] Heb *strange*   [n] Cn Compare Gk: Heb *Incline your ear, and hear the words of the wise*

How to Raise Children
Family members should be allies, not adversaries

> Train children in the right way, and when old, they will not stray. **22.6**

"SPARE THE ROD AND SPOIL the child" may be the most famous of the Bible's proverbs. Proverbs calls punishment a form of love and says that parents who won't discipline their children are in danger of ruining them (29.15). But that much-quoted maxim is only a small part of what Proverbs has to offer on the subject of bringing up children.

The overwhelming emphasis of Proverbs is on verbal encouragement and teaching. The whole book is framed as a father's words to his son, teaching him those "facts of life" that have nothing to do with biology. Again and again he pleads, "Hear, my child." Mother has equally important words (1.8; 6.20). The parent-child conversation is a warm one, and Proverbs 17.6 bears out what the whole book implies: Parents and children are not meant to be adversaries, but allies in life who are proud of each other.

Proverbs on parent-child relationships: 3.11−12; 10.1,5; 13.1,24; 14.26; 15.20; 17.6,21; 19.18,26−27; 20.20; 22.6,15; 23.13−16,22−25; 27.11; 29.15,17; 31.28.

Life Questions: In your upbringing, which had the most effect: punishment and discipline, or verbal instruction and encouragement?

so that you may give a true answer to
those who sent you?

22 Do not rob the poor because they are
poor,
or crush the afflicted at the gate;
23 for the LORD pleads their cause
and despoils of life those who despoil
them.
24 Make no friends with those given to
anger,
and do not associate with hotheads,
25 or you may learn their ways
and entangle yourself in a snare.
26 Do not be one of those who give pledges,
who become surety for debts.
27 If you have nothing with which to pay,
why should your bed be taken from
under you?
28 Do not remove the ancient landmark
that your ancestors set up.
29 Do you see those who are skillful in their
work?
They will serve kings;
they will not serve common people.

23 When you sit down to eat with a ruler,
observe carefully what[o] is before you,
2 and put a knife to your throat
if you have a big appetite.
3 Do not desire the ruler's[p] delicacies,
for they are deceptive food.
4 Do not wear yourself out to get rich;
be wise enough to desist.
5 When your eyes light upon it, it is gone;
for suddenly it takes wings to itself,
flying like an eagle toward heaven.
6 Do not eat the bread of the stingy;
do not desire their delicacies;
7 for like a hair in the throat, so are they.[q]
"Eat and drink!" they say to you;
but they do not mean it.
8 You will vomit up the little you have
eaten,
and you will waste your pleasant
words.
9 Do not speak in the hearing of a fool,
who will only despise the wisdom of
your words.
10 Do not remove an ancient landmark
or encroach on the fields of orphans,
11 for their redeemer is strong;
he will plead their cause against you.
12 Apply your mind to instruction
and your ear to words of knowledge.
13 Do not withhold discipline from your
children;
if you beat them with a rod, they will
not die.

14 If you beat them with the rod,
you will save their lives from Sheol.
15 My child, if your heart is wise,
my heart too will be glad.
16 My soul will rejoice
when your lips speak what is right.
17 Do not let your heart envy sinners,
but always continue in the fear of the
LORD.
18 Surely there is a future,
and your hope will not be cut off.

19 Hear, my child, and be wise,
and direct your mind in the way.
20 Do not be among winebibbers,
or among gluttonous eaters of meat;
21 for the drunkard and the glutton will
come to poverty,
and drowsiness will clothe them with
rags.

22 Listen to your father who begot you,
and do not despise your mother when
she is old.
23 Buy truth, and do not sell it;
buy wisdom, instruction, and
understanding.
24 The father of the righteous will greatly
rejoice;
he who begets a wise son will be glad
in him.
25 Let your father and mother be glad;
let her who bore you rejoice.

26 My child, give me your heart,
and let your eyes observe[r] my ways.
27 For a prostitute is a deep pit;
an adulteress[s] is a narrow well.
28 She lies in wait like a robber
and increases the number of the
faithless.

29 Who has woe? Who has sorrow?
Who has strife? Who has complaining?
Who has wounds without cause?
Who has redness of eyes?
30 Those who linger late over wine,
those who keep trying mixed wines.
31 Do not look at wine when it is red,
when it sparkles in the cup
and goes down smoothly.
32 At the last it bites like a serpent,
and stings like an adder.
33 Your eyes will see strange things,
and your mind utter perverse things.
34 You will be like one who lies down in the
midst of the sea,
like one who lies on the top of
a mast.[q]

---

o Or *who*   p Heb *his*   q Meaning of Heb uncertain   r Another reading is *delight in*   s Heb *an alien woman*

35 "They struck me," you will say,[t] "but I
       was not hurt;
   they beat me, but I did not feel it.
   When shall I awake?
   I will seek another drink."

23.35 The Dangers of Wine

Wine was common in biblical times, but its dangers were recognized. Proverbs contains some of the Bible's strongest warnings against overindulgence: 20.1; 21.17; 23.20–21, 30–35; 31.4–7.

24 Do not envy the wicked,
    nor desire to be with them;
2 for their minds devise violence,
   and their lips talk of mischief.

3 By wisdom a house is built,
   and by understanding it is established;
4 by knowledge the rooms are filled
   with all precious and pleasant riches.
5 Wise warriors are mightier than strong
     ones,[u]
   and those who have knowledge than
     those who have strength;
6 for by wise guidance you can wage your
     war,
   and in abundance of counselors there
     is victory.
7 Wisdom is too high for fools;
   in the gate they do not open
     their mouths.

8 Whoever plans to do evil
   will be called a mischief-maker.
9 The devising of folly is sin,
   and the scoffer is an abomination to
     all.

10 If you faint in the day of adversity,
   your strength being small;
11 if you hold back from rescuing those
     taken away to death,
   those who go staggering to the
     slaughter;
12 if you say, "Look, we did not
     know this"—
   does not he who weighs the heart
     perceive it?
   Does not he who keeps watch over your
     soul know it?
   And will he not repay all according to
     their deeds?

13 My child, eat honey, for it is good,
   and the drippings of the honeycomb
     are sweet to your taste.
14 Know that wisdom is such to your soul;
   if you find it, you will find a future,
   and your hope will not be cut off.

15 Do not lie in wait like an outlaw against
     the home of the righteous;
   do no violence to the place where the
     righteous live;
16 for though they fall seven times, they will
     rise again;
   but the wicked are overthrown by
     calamity.

[t] Gk Syr Vg Tg: Heb lacks *you will say*   [u] Gk Compare Syr Tg: Heb *A wise man is strength*

The Problem with Laziness
Becoming a sluggard requires little effort

THE "SLUGGARD" IS LAZIER THAN a pig on vacation. His only exercise is turning on his bed; Proverbs says he is *hinged* to it. Any far-fetched excuse—"there is a lion in the road!"—will keep him from going to work. Proverbs laughs at the sluggard a little, but uses him to teach serious lessons. You can be like him very easily, for it doesn't require much: "A little sleep, a little slumber, a little folding of the hands to rest." Putting things off, making excuses, sleeping in—who doesn't sometimes fall victim to these tendencies?

A little sleep, a little slumber, a little folding of the hands to rest, and poverty will come upon you like a robber. 24.33-34

The result of such a life? Poverty, frustration, broken relationships. The sluggard still wants the luxuries hard work earns, but he never gets them. "The craving of the lazy person is fatal" (21.25).

Proverbs on laziness: 6.6–11; 10.4,26; 12.24,27; 13.4; 15.19; 19.15,24; 20.4; 21.25; 22.13; 24.30–34; 26.13–16.

Life Questions: What attributes of a sluggard do you recognize in yourself? Do you think of these as serious?

¹⁷ Do not rejoice when your enemies fall,
and do not let your heart be glad when
they stumble,
¹⁸ or else the LORD will see it and be
displeased,
and turn away his anger from them.

¹⁹ Do not fret because of evildoers.
Do not envy the wicked;
²⁰ for the evil have no future;
the lamp of the wicked will go out.

²¹ My child, fear the LORD and the king,
and do not disobey either of them;ᵛ
²² for disaster comes from them suddenly,
and who knows the ruin that both can
bring?

Further Sayings of the Wise

²³ These also are sayings of the wise:

Partiality in judging is not good.
²⁴ Whoever says to the wicked, "You are
innocent,"
will be cursed by peoples, abhorred by
nations;
²⁵ but those who rebuke the wicked will
have delight,
and a good blessing will come upon
them.
²⁶ One who gives an honest answer
gives a kiss on the lips.

²⁷ Prepare your work outside,
get everything ready for you in the
field;
and after that build your house.

²⁸ Do not be a witness against your
neighbor without cause,
and do not deceive with your lips.
²⁹ Do not say, "I will do to others as they
have done to me;
I will pay them back for what they
have done."

³⁰ I passed by the field of one who was lazy,
by the vineyard of a stupid person;
³¹ and see, it was all overgrown with thorns;
the ground was covered with nettles,
and its stone wall was broken down.
³² Then I saw and considered it;
I looked and received instruction.
³³ A little sleep, a little slumber,
a little folding of the hands to rest,
³⁴ and poverty will come upon you like a
robber,
and want, like an armed warrior.

Further Wise Sayings of Solomon

25 These are other proverbs of Solomon that
the officials of King Hezekiah of Judah
copied.

25.1 Good Government

*Proverbs lists three kings in its credits:
Solomon (1.1; 10.1), Hezekiah (25.1), and
Lemuel (31.1). So, naturally, it shows concern
for what makes good government. The
qualities needed in a king still apply to
governmental heads today. Proverbs doesn't
mention political philosophy or administrative
efficiency. Justice and fairness matter most.
    Proverbs on good government include the
following: 14.35; 16.10,12–13; 20.26; 22.11;
25.4–5; 29.4,14; 31.3–5.*

² It is the glory of God to conceal things,
but the glory of kings is to search
things out.
³ Like the heavens for height, like the earth
for depth,
so the mind of kings is unsearchable.
⁴ Take away the dross from the silver,
and the smith has material for a vessel;
⁵ take away the wicked from the presence
of the king,
and his throne will be established in
righteousness.
⁶ Do not put yourself forward in the king's
presence
or stand in the place of the great;
⁷ for it is better to be told, "Come
up here,"
than to be put lower in the presence of
a noble.

What your eyes have seen
⁸   do not hastily bring into court;
forʷ what will you do in the end,
when your neighbor puts you to
shame?
⁹ Argue your case with your neighbor
directly,
and do not disclose another's secret;
¹⁰ or else someone who hears you will bring
shame upon you,
and your ill repute will have no end.

¹¹ A word fitly spoken
is like apples of gold in a setting of
silver.
¹² Like a gold ring or an ornament of gold
is a wise rebuke to a listening ear.

ᵛ Gk: Heb *do not associate with those who change*   ʷ Cn: Heb *or else*

13 Like the cold of snow in the time
        of harvest
    are faithful messengers to those who
        send them;
    they refresh the spirit of their masters.
14 Like clouds and wind without rain
    is one who boasts of a gift never given.
15 With patience a ruler may be persuaded,
    and a soft tongue can break bones.
16 If you have found honey, eat only enough
        for you,
    or else, having too much, you will
        vomit it.
17 Let your foot be seldom in your
        neighbor's house,
    otherwise the neighbor will become
        weary of you and hate you.
18 Like a war club, a sword, or a sharp
        arrow
    is one who bears false witness against a
        neighbor.
19 Like a bad tooth or a lame foot
    is trust in a faithless person in time of
        trouble.
20 Like vinegar on a wound*x*
    is one who sings songs to a heavy
        heart.
    Like a moth in clothing or a worm in
        wood,
    sorrow gnaws at the human heart.*y*
21 If your enemies are hungry, give them
        bread to eat;
    and if they are thirsty, give them water
        to drink;
22 for you will heap coals of fire on their
        heads,

and the LORD will reward you.
23 The north wind produces rain,
    and a backbiting tongue, angry looks.
24 It is better to live in a corner of the
        housetop
    than in a house shared with a
        contentious wife.
25 Like cold water to a thirsty soul,
    so is good news from a far country.
26 Like a muddied spring or a polluted
        fountain
    are the righteous who give way before
        the wicked.
27 It is not good to eat much honey,
    or to seek honor on top of honor.
28 Like a city breached, without walls,
    is one who lacks self-control.

26 Like snow in summer or rain in harvest,
    so honor is not fitting for a fool.
2 Like a sparrow in its flitting, like a
        swallow in its flying,
    an undeserved curse goes nowhere.
3 A whip for the horse, a bridle for the
        donkey,
    and a rod for the back of fools.
4 Do not answer fools according to their
        folly,
    or you will be a fool yourself.
5 Answer fools according to their folly,
    or they will be wise in their own eyes.
6 It is like cutting off one's foot and
        drinking down violence,
    to send a message by a fool.
7 The legs of a disabled person hang limp;
    so does a proverb in the mouth of a
        fool.

x Gk: Heb *Like one who takes off a garment on a cold day, like vinegar on lye*   *y* Gk Syr Tg: Heb lacks *Like a moth . . .*
human heart

The Making of a Fool
Even a genius can be one

> *Like a dog that
> returns to its vomit
> is a fool that reverts
> to his folly. 26.11*

FOOLS, IN MODERN ENGLISH, ARE people who lack brains. But the word has a different meaning in the Bible. Fools may have high IQs. People may admire their reputation for success. Yet a wise person views them as a disaster.

One of the Bible's worst insults is "You fool!" People become fools by ignoring the wisdom God offers them, preferring to follow the crowd or their own conceited opinions. They may think themselves very clever, but their cleverness will land them in trouble.

Proverbs aims its sharpest warnings, not against acting immorally, but against becoming a fool. If you develop such a character, no set of rules can keep you out of trouble. A wise person ought to learn to recognize a fool from far away, and stay out of his or her path.

Poignant proverbs on foolishness: 1.7; 10.8; 12.15–16,23; 14.8–9,16,24; 15.14; 17.10,12,16; 18.2,6; 20.3; 26.3,11; 27.22; 28.26; 29.11.

Life Questions: Do you know anyone whom Proverbs would call a fool? If so, how should you relate to him or her?

8 It is like binding a stone in a sling
to give honor to a fool.
9 Like a thornbush brandished by the hand
of a drunkard
is a proverb in the mouth of a fool.
10 Like an archer who wounds everybody
is one who hires a passing fool or
drunkard.[z]
11 Like a dog that returns to its vomit
is a fool who reverts to his folly.
12 Do you see persons wise in their own
eyes?
There is more hope for fools than for
them.
13 The lazy person says, "There is a lion in
the road!
There is a lion in the streets!"

26.13 Excuses of a Lazy Person

*At first glance some proverbs, like this one,
appear incomplete and pointless. But this
proverb cleverly pinpoints a lazy person's habit
of seeing dangerous obstacles to every plan
and making incredible excuses. Such a person
will not go anywhere (on a road) or even get
out of the house (into the streets) because their
imagination conjures up all the things that
could go wrong.*

14 As a door turns on its hinges,
so does a lazy person in bed.
15 The lazy person buries a hand in the dish,
and is too tired to bring it back to the
mouth.
16 The lazy person is wiser in self-esteem
than seven who can answer discreetly.
17 Like somebody who takes a passing dog
by the ears
is one who meddles in the quarrel of
another.
18 Like a maniac who shoots deadly
firebrands and arrows,
19 so is one who deceives a neighbor
and says, "I am only joking!"
20 For lack of wood the fire goes out,
and where there is no whisperer,
quarreling ceases.
21 As charcoal is to hot embers and wood to
fire,
so is a quarrelsome person for kindling
strife.
22 The words of a whisperer are like
delicious morsels;
they go down into the inner parts of
the body.
23 Like the glaze[a] covering an earthen vessel

are smooth[b] lips with an evil heart.
24 An enemy dissembles in speaking
while harboring deceit within;
25 when an enemy speaks graciously, do not
believe it,
for there are seven abominations
concealed within;
26 though hatred is covered with guile,
the enemy's wickedness will be exposed
in the assembly.
27 Whoever digs a pit will fall into it,
and a stone will come back on the one
who starts it rolling.
28 A lying tongue hates its victims,
and a flattering mouth works ruin.

27 Do not boast about tomorrow,
for you do not know what a day may
bring.
2 Let another praise you, and not your own
mouth—
a stranger, and not your own lips.
3 A stone is heavy, and sand is weighty,
but a fool's provocation is heavier than
both.
4 Wrath is cruel, anger is overwhelming,
but who is able to stand before
jealousy?
5 Better is open rebuke
than hidden love.
6 Well meant are the wounds a friend
inflicts,
but profuse are the kisses of an enemy.
7 The sated appetite spurns honey,
but to a ravenous appetite even the
bitter is sweet.
8 Like a bird that strays from its nest
is one who strays from home.
9 Perfume and incense make the heart glad,
but the soul is torn by trouble.[c]
10 Do not forsake your friend or the friend
of your parent;
do not go to the house of your kindred
in the day of your calamity.
Better is a neighbor who is nearby
than kindred who are far away.
11 Be wise, my child, and make my heart
glad,
so that I may answer whoever
reproaches me.
12 The clever see danger and hide;
but the simple go on, and suffer for it.
13 Take the garment of one who has given
surety for a stranger;
seize the pledge given as surety for
foreigners.[d]
14 Whoever blesses a neighbor with a loud
voice,
rising early in the morning,

will be counted as cursing.

15 A continual dripping on a rainy day
   and a contentious wife are alike;
16 to restrain her is to restrain the wind
   or to grasp oil in the right hand.*e*
17 Iron sharpens iron,
   and one person sharpens the wits*f* of
      another.
18 Anyone who tends a fig tree will eat its
      fruit,
   and anyone who takes care of a master
      will be honored.
19 Just as water reflects the face,
   so one human heart reflects another.
20 Sheol and Abaddon are never satisfied,
   and human eyes are never satisfied.
21 The crucible is for silver, and the furnace
      is for gold,
   so a person is tested*g* by being
      praised.
22 Crush a fool in a mortar with a pestle
      along with crushed grain,
   but the folly will not be driven out.

23 Know well the condition of your flocks,
   and give attention to your herds;
24 for riches do not last forever,
   nor a crown for all generations.
25 When the grass is gone, and new growth
      appears,
   and the herbage of the mountains is
      gathered,
26 the lambs will provide your clothing,
   and the goats the price of a field;
27 there will be enough goats' milk for your
      food,
   for the food of your household
   and nourishment for your servant-girls.

28 The wicked flee when no one pursues,
   but the righteous are as bold as a lion.
2 When a land rebels
   it has many rulers;
   but with an intelligent ruler
      there is lasting order.*e*
3 A ruler*h* who oppresses the poor
   is a beating rain that leaves no food.
4 Those who forsake the law praise the
      wicked,
   but those who keep the law struggle
      against them.
5 The evil do not understand justice,
   but those who seek the LORD
      understand it completely.
6 Better to be poor and walk in integrity
   than to be crooked in one's ways even
      though rich.
7 Those who keep the law are wise children,

but companions of gluttons shame
   their parents.
8 One who augments wealth by exorbitant
      interest
   gathers it for another who is kind to
      the poor.
9 When one will not listen to the law,
   even one's prayers are an abomination.
10 Those who mislead the upright into evil
      ways
   will fall into pits of their own making,
   but the blameless will have a goodly
      inheritance.
11 The rich is wise in self-esteem,
   but an intelligent poor person sees
      through the pose.
12 When the righteous triumph, there is
      great glory,
   but when the wicked prevail, people go
      into hiding.
13 No one who conceals transgressions will
      prosper,
   but one who confesses and forsakes
      them will obtain mercy.
14 Happy is the one who is never without
      fear,
   but one who is hard-hearted will fall
      into calamity.
15 Like a roaring lion or a charging bear
   is a wicked ruler over a poor people.
16 A ruler who lacks understanding is a cruel
      oppressor;
   but one who hates unjust gain will
      enjoy a long life.
17 If someone is burdened with the blood of
      another,
   let that killer be a fugitive until death;
   let no one offer assistance.
18 One who walks in integrity will be safe,
   but whoever follows crooked ways will
      fall into the Pit.*i*
19 Anyone who tills the land will have plenty
      of bread,
   but one who follows worthless pursuits
      will have plenty of poverty.
20 The faithful will abound with blessings,
   but one who is in a hurry to be rich
      will not go unpunished.
21 To show partiality is not good—
   yet for a piece of bread a person may
      do wrong.
22 The miser is in a hurry to get rich
   and does not know that loss is sure to
      come.
23 Whoever rebukes a person will afterward
      find more favor
   than one who flatters with the tongue.
24 Anyone who robs father or mother

---

e Meaning of Heb uncertain   *f* Heb *face*   *g* Heb lacks *is tested*   *h* Cn: Heb *A poor person*   *i* Syr: Heb *fall all*
at once

and says, "That is no crime,"
is partner to a thug.
25 The greedy person stirs up strife,
but whoever trusts in the LORD will be
enriched.
26 Those who trust in their own wits are
fools;
but those who walk in wisdom come
through safely.
27 Whoever gives to the poor will lack
nothing,
but one who turns a blind eye will get
many a curse.
28 When the wicked prevail, people go into
hiding;
but when they perish, the righteous
increase.

29 One who is often reproved, yet remains
stubborn,
will suddenly be broken beyond
healing.
2 When the righteous are in authority, the
people rejoice;
but when the wicked rule, the people
groan.
3 A child who loves wisdom makes a parent
glad,
but to keep company with prostitutes
is to squander one's substance.
4 By justice a king gives stability to the
land,
but one who makes heavy exactions
ruins it.
5 Whoever flatters a neighbor
is spreading a net for the neighbor's
feet.
6 In the transgression of the evil there is a
snare,
but the righteous sing and rejoice.
7 The righteous know the rights of the
poor;
the wicked have no such
understanding.

8 Scoffers set a city aflame,
but the wise turn away wrath.
9 If the wise go to law with fools,
there is ranting and ridicule without
relief.

29.5 Dangerous Flattery

*"Flattery can get you anywhere," some say. But
flattery—the art of making someone feel good
by stretching the truth—can be downright
harmful. It can leave a trusting friend
unprepared for troubles ahead. Instead of
flattering, we should warn a friend where he or
she is headed (see 28.23).*

10 The bloodthirsty hate the blameless,
and they seek the life of the upright.
11 A fool gives full vent to anger,
but the wise quietly holds it back.
12 If a ruler listens to falsehood,
all his officials will be wicked.
13 The poor and the oppressor have this in
common:
the LORD gives light to the eyes of
both.
14 If a king judges the poor with equity,
his throne will be established forever.
15 The rod and reproof give wisdom,
but a mother is disgraced by a
neglected child.
16 When the wicked are in authority,
transgression increases,
but the righteous will look upon their
downfall.
17 Discipline your children, and they will
give you rest;
they will give delight to your heart.
18 Where there is no prophecy, the people
cast off restraint,
but happy are those who keep the law.

Five Dangerous Responses
Inner attitudes can destroy you

> *A fool gives full vent
> to anger, but the
> wise quietly holds it
> back. 29.11*

ANGER WILL DESTROY YOU BEFORE it destroys anyone else.
Control your temper! Read Proverbs 14.17; 14.29; 15.18; 19.19; 22.24–25;
29.11; 29.22.
  Pride will lead to your downfall. Humility is far more rewarding. See
Proverbs 3.34; 11.2; 13.10; 16.5,18–19; 18.12; 21.4.
  Jealousy grows like a cancer. Read Proverbs 14.30; 23.17; 24.1; 27.4.
  Fear of people is unnecessary if you trust God. See Proverbs 3.25–26; 29.25.
  Conceit is ugly. A conceited person forgets God's place in his or her life. Read Proverbs 16.2; 25.27;
26.12; 27.2; 28.11,13.

Life Questions: Which of these responses tempts you most? Why?

19 By mere words servants are not
        disciplined,
    for though they understand, they will
        not give heed.
20 Do you see someone who is hasty
        in speech?
    There is more hope for a fool than for
        anyone like that.
21 A slave pampered from childhood
        will come to a bad end.*j*
22 One given to anger stirs up strife,
    and the hothead causes much
        transgression.
23 A person's pride will bring humiliation,
    but one who is lowly in spirit will
        obtain honor.
24 To be a partner of a thief is to hate one's
        own life;
    one hears the victim's curse, but
        discloses nothing.*k*
25 The fear of others*l* lays a snare,
    but one who trusts in the LORD
        is secure.
26 Many seek the favor of a ruler,
    but it is from the LORD that one gets
        justice.
27 The unjust are an abomination to the
        righteous,
    but the upright are an abomination to
        the wicked.

Sayings of Agur

30 The words of Agur son of Jakeh. An ora-
    cle.

    Thus says the man: I am weary, O God,
    I am weary, O God. How can I
        prevail?*m*
2 Surely I am too stupid to be human;
    I do not have human understanding.
3 I have not learned wisdom,
    nor have I knowledge of the
        holy ones.*n*
4 Who has ascended to heaven and come
        down?
    Who has gathered the wind in the
        hollow of the hand?
    Who has wrapped up the waters in a
        garment?
    Who has established all the ends of the
        earth?
    What is the person's name?
    And what is the name of the person's
        child?
    Surely you know!

5 Every word of God proves true;

he is a shield to those who take refuge
        in him.
6 Do not add to his words,
    or else he will rebuke you, and you will
        be found a liar.
7 Two things I ask of you;
    do not deny them to me before I die:
8 Remove far from me falsehood and lying;
    give me neither poverty nor riches;
    feed me with the food that I need,
9 or I shall be full, and deny you,
    and say, "Who is the LORD?"
    or I shall be poor, and steal,
    and profane the name of my God.

10 Do not slander a servant to a master,
    or the servant will curse you, and you
        will be held guilty.

11 There are those who curse their fathers
    and do not bless their mothers.
12 There are those who are pure in their
        own eyes
    yet are not cleansed of their filthiness.
13 There are those—how lofty are their eyes,
    how high their eyelids lift!—
14 there are those whose teeth are swords,
    whose teeth are knives,
    to devour the poor from off the earth,
    the needy from among mortals.

15 The leech*k* has two daughters;
    "Give, give," they cry.
    Three things are never satisfied;
    four never say, "Enough":
16 Sheol, the barren womb,
    the earth ever thirsty for water,
    and the fire that never says,
        "Enough."*k*

17 The eye that mocks a father
    and scorns to obey a mother
    will be pecked out by the ravens of the
        valley
    and eaten by the vultures.

18 Three things are too wonderful for me;
    four I do not understand:
19 the way of an eagle in the sky,
    the way of a snake on a rock,
    the way of a ship on the high seas,
    and the way of a man with a girl.

20 This is the way of an adulteress:
    she eats, and wipes her mouth,
    and says, "I have done no wrong."

---

j Vg: Meaning of Heb uncertain   *k* Meaning of Heb uncertain   *l* Or *human fear*   *m* Or *I am spent.* Meaning of
Heb uncertain   *n* Or *Holy One*

21 Under three things the earth trembles;
    under four it cannot bear up:
22 a slave when he becomes king,
    and a fool when glutted with food;
23 an unloved woman when she gets
        a husband,
    and a maid when she succeeds her
        mistress.

24 Four things on earth are small,
    yet they are exceedingly wise:
25 the ants are a people without strength,
    yet they provide their food in
        the summer;
26 the badgers are a people without power,
    yet they make their homes in
        the rocks;
27 the locusts have no king,
    yet all of them march in rank;
28 the lizard*o* can be grasped in the hand,
    yet it is found in kings' palaces.

29 Three things are stately in their stride;
    four are stately in their gait:
30 the lion, which is mightiest among wild
        animals
    and does not turn back before any;
31 the strutting rooster,*p* the he-goat,
    and a king striding before*q* his people.

32 If you have been foolish, exalting yourself,
    or if you have been devising evil,
    put your hand on your mouth.
33 For as pressing milk produces curds,
    and pressing the nose produces blood,
    so pressing anger produces strife.

The Teaching of King Lemuel's Mother

31 The words of King Lemuel. An oracle that
   his mother taught him:

2 No, my son! No, son of my womb!
    No, son of my vows!
3 Do not give your strength to women,
    your ways to those who destroy kings.
4 It is not for kings, O Lemuel,
    it is not for kings to drink wine,
    or for rulers to desire*r* strong drink;
5 or else they will drink and forget what has
        been decreed,
    and will pervert the rights of all the
        afflicted.
6 Give strong drink to one who is
        perishing,
    and wine to those in bitter distress;
7 let them drink and forget their poverty,
    and remember their misery no more.
8 Speak out for those who cannot speak,

    for the rights of all the destitute.*s*
9 Speak out, judge righteously,
    defend the rights of the poor
        and needy.

31.8 For the Voiceless

*The German pastor Dietrich Bonhoeffer
frequently quoted this verse in the years before
World War II. He was urging his fellow
Christians to speak up for Hitler's victims,
particularly Jews who had been stripped of
their civil rights.*

Ode to a Capable Wife

10 A capable wife who can find?
    She is far more precious than jewels.
11 The heart of her husband trusts in her,
    and he will have no lack of gain.
12 She does him good, and not harm,
    all the days of her life.
13 She seeks wool and flax,
    and works with willing hands.
14 She is like the ships of the merchant,
    she brings her food from far away.
15 She rises while it is still night
    and provides food for her household
    and tasks for her servant-girls.
16 She considers a field and buys it;
    with the fruit of her hands she plants a
        vineyard.
17 She girds herself with strength,
    and makes her arms strong.
18 She perceives that her merchandise is
        profitable.
    Her lamp does not go out at night.
19 She puts her hands to the distaff,
    and her hands hold the spindle.
20 She opens her hand to the poor,
    and reaches out her hands to
        the needy.
21 She is not afraid for her household when
        it snows,
    for all her household are clothed in
        crimson.
22 She makes herself coverings;
    her clothing is fine linen and purple.
23 Her husband is known in the city gates,
    taking his seat among the elders of the
        land.
24 She makes linen garments and sells them;
    she supplies the merchant with sashes.
25 Strength and dignity are her clothing,
    and she laughs at the time to come.
26 She opens her mouth with wisdom,

---

o Or *spider*   *p* Gk Syr Tg Compare Vg: Meaning of Heb uncertain   *q* Meaning of Heb uncertain   *r* Cn: Heb
where   *s* Heb *all children of passing away*

and the teaching of kindness is on her
    tongue.
27 She looks well to the ways of her
    household,
  and does not eat the bread of idleness.
28 Her children rise up and call her happy;
    her husband too, and he praises
      her:

29 "Many women have done excellently,
    but you surpass them all."
30 Charm is deceitful, and beauty is vain,
  but a woman who fears the LORD is to
    be praised.
31 Give her a share in the fruit of her hands,
  and let her works praise her in the city
    gates.

ECCLESIASTES

When Life Seems Senseless
A book for our time

> *Vanity of vanities,*
> *says the Teacher,*
> *vanity of vanities!*
> *All is vanity. 1.2*

"I N THIS WORLD THERE ARE only two tragedies," said Irish writer Oscar Wilde. "One is not getting what one wants, and the other is getting it." This paradoxical proverb has often proved true. Consider a larger-than-life character from the 20th century, a man named Howard Hughes.

World's Richest Man

At age 45 Hughes was one of the most glamorous men in America. He courted actresses, piloted exotic test aircraft, and worked on top-secret CIA contracts. He owned a string of hotels around the world, and even an airline—TWA—to carry him on global jaunts.

Twenty years later, at 65, Howard Hughes still had plenty of money—$2.3 billion, to be exact. But the world's richest man had become one of its most pathetic. He lived in small, dark rooms atop his hotels, without sun and without joy. He was unkempt: A scraggly beard had grown waist-length, his hair fell well down his back, and his fingernails were two inches long. His once-powerful 6'4" frame had shrunk to about 100 pounds.

This famous man spent most of his time watching movies over and over, with the same movie showing as many as 150 times. He lay naked in bed, deathly afraid of germs. Life held no meaning for him. Finally, emaciated and hooked on drugs, he died at age 67, for lack of a medical device his own company had helped to develop.

A King's Charmed Life

Howard Hughes is an extreme example of a syndrome that can afflict the rich and famous. His attitude toward life closely followed the thoughts of another successful man, a great king who ruled Israel long ago. This book, Ecclesiastes, records what happened to that man who had everything.

The author of Ecclesiastes had tasted just about everything life has to offer. Wealth? No one could exceed him in luxurious lifestyle (2.4–9). Wisdom? His was world-renowned (1.13–18). Fame? He was king, the most famous man of his time (1.12). Systematically, he sampled all of life's powers and pleasures, yet all ultimately disappointed him. All proved meaningless.

What is the point of life? he asked. You work hard, and someone else gets all the credit. You struggle to be good, and evil people take advantage of you. You accumulate money, and it just goes to spoiled heirs. You seek pleasure, and it turns sour on you. And everyone—rich or poor, good or evil—meets the same end. We all die. There is only one word to describe this life: meaningless!

Life Under the Sun

Ecclesiastes strikes a responsive chord in our age. Its words show up in folk songs and at presidential inaugurations. No century has seen such progress, and yet such despair. What is the purpose of life anyway? Is there any ultimate meaning? "Is that all there is?" asked one songwriter after listing life's pleasures.

A key phrase in this book, "under the sun," describes the world lived on one level, apart from God and without any belief in the afterlife. If you live on that level, you may well conclude that life is meaningless.

Ecclesiastes gives some words of hope, including the final summary: "Fear God, and keep his commandments; for that is the whole duty of everyone" (12.13). That's the positive message, the "lesson" of Ecclesiastes. But such positive words are almost overwhelmed by the author's powerful negative example. You could summarize his whole life in Jesus' one statement, "For what will it profit them if they gain the whole world but forfeit their life?" (Matthew 16.26).

How to Read Ecclesiastes

Ecclesiastes attracts extreme reactions. For several hundred years, Jewish scholars fiercely debated whether the book should even be included in the Old Testament. Yet American novelist Thomas Wolfe said of it, "Ecclesiastes is the greatest single piece of writing I have ever known, and the wisdom expressed in it the most lasting and profound."

Because of the book's unique nature, it is important to keep certain principles in mind while reading it. Consider Ecclesiastes as a whole. The Teacher was exploring various philosophies of life. During his search, he tried different approaches, including hedonism, the unrestrained pursuit of pleasure. The book honestly records the author's search without endorsing it.

At times the author concludes with despairing statements that directly contradict other parts of the Bible (for example, the recurring phrase, "All is vanity"). Read such individual statements in their context. Just as the book of Job contains arguments that God directly refuted later, so Ecclesiastes contains many isolated statements that contradict its final conclusion.

Ecclesiastes performs two very valuable functions. First, it should stimulate compassion for those who are trapped in despair and live in a meaningless world, alone, without God. The author brilliantly captures the futility and meaninglessness of that world, expressing a philosophy of life widespread in the 20th century.

But the book includes more than despair. It also blends in proverbs about how life should be lived, pungent observations that can be easily overlooked. Look for these nuggets of wisdom, especially toward the end of the book. (You may also find it helpful to balance out Ecclesiastes with the more confident advice of Proverbs.)

By asking questions, the author of Ecclesiastes helped prepare for the answers God ultimately provided. The Teacher concluded, "All is vanity" under the sun, but when Jesus Christ came, he promised life "abundantly" (John 10.10).

3-TRACK READING PLAN

For an explanation and complete listing of the 3-track reading plan, turn to page 7.

TRACK 1: **Two-Week Courses on the Bible**
See page 7 for information on these courses.

TRACK 2: **An Overview of Ecclesiastes in 1 Day**
☐ Day 1. Read the Introduction to Ecclesiastes and then chapter 3, perhaps the most enduring portion of the book's poetry. Folksinger Pete Seeger used the first part verbatim in a famous song, and former United States president John F. Kennedy had these words read at his inauguration.

Now turn to page 9 for your next Track 2 reading project.

TRACK 3: **All of Ecclesiastes in 12 Days**
After you have read through Ecclesiastes, turn to pages 10–14 for your next Track 3 reading project.
☐1　　☐2　　☐3　　☐4　　☐5　　☐6　　☐7　　☐8
☐9　　☐10　　☐11　　☐12

Reflections of a Royal Philosopher

1 The words of the Teacher,[a] the son of David,
   king in Jerusalem.
² Vanity of vanities, says the Teacher,[a]
   vanity of vanities! All is vanity.
³ What do people gain from all the toil
   at which they toil under the sun?
⁴ A generation goes, and a generation comes,
   but the earth remains forever.
⁵ The sun rises and the sun goes down,
   and hurries to the place where it rises.
⁶ The wind blows to the south,
   and goes around to the north;
   round and round goes the wind,
   and on its circuits the wind returns.
⁷ All streams run to the sea,
   but the sea is not full;

---

[a] Heb *Qoheleth*, traditionally rendered *Preacher*

to the place where the streams flow,
    there they continue to flow.
8 All things[b] are wearisome;
    more than one can express;
the eye is not satisfied with seeing,
    or the ear filled with hearing.
9 What has been is what will be,
    and what has been done is what will be
        done;
    there is nothing new under the sun.
10 Is there a thing of which it is said,
    "See, this is new"?
It has already been,
    in the ages before us.
11 The people of long ago are not
        remembered,
    nor will there be any remembrance
of people yet to come
    by those who come after them.

The Futility of Seeking Wisdom

12 I, the Teacher,[c] when king over Israel in
Jerusalem, [13]applied my mind to seek and to
search out by wisdom all that is done under heav-
en; it is an unhappy business that God has given
to human beings to be busy with. [14]I saw all the
deeds that are done under the sun; and see, all is
vanity and a chasing after wind.[d]
15 What is crooked cannot be made straight,
    and what is lacking cannot be counted.

16 I said to myself, "I have acquired great
wisdom, surpassing all who were over Jerusalem
before me; and my mind has had great experience
of wisdom and knowledge." [17]And I applied my
mind to know wisdom and to know madness and
folly. I perceived that this also is but a chasing
after wind.[d]
18 For in much wisdom is much vexation,
    and those who increase knowledge
        increase sorrow.

The Futility of Self-Indulgence

2 I said to myself, "Come now, I will make a
    test of pleasure; enjoy yourself." But again,
this also was vanity. [2]I said of laughter, "It is
mad," and of pleasure, "What use is it?" [3]I
searched with my mind how to cheer my body
with wine—my still guiding me with
wisdom—and how to lay hold on folly, until I
might see what was good for mortals to do under
heaven during the few days of their life. [4]I made
great works; I built houses and planted vineyards
for myself; [5]I made myself gardens and parks, and
planted in them all kinds of fruit trees. [6]I made
myself pools from which to water the forest of
growing trees. [7]I bought male and female slaves,
and had slaves who were born in my house; I also

had great possessions of herds and flocks, more
than any who had been before me in Jerusalem.
[8]I also gathered for myself silver and gold and the
treasure of kings and of the provinces; I got singers, both men and women, and delights of the
flesh, and many concubines.[e]

2.1 Outside the Palace

*The first two chapters of Ecclesiastes tell of "the
Teacher's" own experience of despair and
meaninglessness. The life described in this
autobiographical section resembles that of
King Solomon. In the rest of the book, the
Teacher examines the world around him to see
if others have found answers to life "under the
sun." To his disappointment, he finds the same
pattern repeated over and over.*

9 So I became great and surpassed all who
were before me in Jerusalem; also my wisdom
remained with me. [10]Whatever my eyes desired I
did not keep from them; I kept my heart from no
pleasure, for my heart found pleasure in all my
toil, and this was my reward for all my toil.
[11]Then I considered all that my hands had done
and the toil I had spent in doing it, and again, all
was vanity and a chasing after wind,[d] and there
was nothing to be gained under the sun.

Wisdom and Joy Given to One Who Pleases God

12 So I turned to consider wisdom and madness and folly; for what can the one do who comes
after the king? Only what has already been done.
[13]Then I saw that wisdom excels folly as light
excels darkness.
14 The wise have eyes in their head,
    but fools walk in darkness.
Yet I perceived that the same fate befalls all of
them. [15]Then I said to myself, "What happens to
the fool will happen to me also; why then have I
been so very wise?" And I said to myself that this
also is vanity. [16]For there is no enduring remembrance of the wise or of fools, seeing that in the
days to come all will have been long forgotten.
How can the wise die just like fools? [17]So I hated
life, because what is done under the sun was
grievous to me; for all is vanity and a chasing after
wind.[d]

18 I hated all my toil in which I had toiled
under the sun, seeing that I must leave it to those
who come after me [19]—and who knows whether
they will be wise or foolish? Yet they will be master of all for which I toiled and used my wisdom
under the sun. This also is vanity. [20]So I turned

---

[b] Or *words*   [c] Heb *Qoheleth*, traditionally rendered *Preacher*   [d] Or *a feeding on wind.* See Hos 12.1   [e] *Meaning*
of Heb uncertain

and gave my heart up to despair concerning all the toil of my labors under the sun, 21because sometimes one who has toiled with wisdom and knowledge and skill must leave all to be enjoyed by another who did not toil for it. This also is vanity and a great evil. 22What do mortals get from all the toil and strain with which they toil under the sun? 23For all their days are full of pain, and their work is a vexation; even at night their minds do not rest. This also is vanity.

24 There is nothing better for mortals than to eat and drink, and find enjoyment in their toil. This also, I saw, is from the hand of God; 25for apart from him*f* who can eat or who can have enjoyment? 26For to the one who pleases him God gives wisdom and knowledge and joy; but to the sinner he gives the work of gathering and heaping, only to give to one who pleases God. This also is vanity and a chasing after wind.*g*

Everything Has Its Time

3 For everything there is a season, and a time for every matter under heaven:

2 a time to be born, and a time to die;
   a time to plant, and a time to pluck up
      what is planted;
3 a time to kill, and a time to heal;
   a time to break down, and a time to build
      up;
4 a time to weep, and a time to laugh;
   a time to mourn, and a time to dance;

3.4 Change or No Change?

At first the Teacher complained that nothing ever changes (1.10–14). Now in this passage—made famous by a popular song in the 1960s—he indicates that life is full of changes. The French proverb, "The more things change, the more they stay the same," expresses this same paradox. For someone in despair who can see no meaning in life, everything that happens seems like an endless, repetitive cycle of futility.

5 a time to throw away stones, and a time
      to gather stones together;
   a time to embrace, and a time to refrain
      from embracing;
6 a time to seek, and a time to lose;
   a time to keep, and a time to throw away;
7 a time to tear, and a time to sew;
   a time to keep silence, and a time to
      speak;
8 a time to love, and a time to hate;
   a time for war, and a time for peace.

The God-Given Task

9 What gain have the workers from their toil?

10I have seen the business that God has given to everyone to be busy with. 11He has made everything suitable for its time; moreover he has put a sense of past and future into their minds, yet they cannot find out what God has done from the beginning to the end. 12I know that there is nothing better for them than to be happy and enjoy themselves as long as they live; 13moreover, it is God's gift that all should eat and drink and take pleasure in all their toil. 14I know that whatever God does endures forever; nothing can be added to it, nor anything taken from it; God has done this, so that all should stand in awe before him. 15That which is, already has been; that which is to be, already is; and God seeks out what has gone by.*h*

Judgment and the Future Belong to God

16 Moreover I saw under the sun that in the place of justice, wickedness was there, and in the place of righteousness, wickedness was there as well. 17I said in my heart, God will judge the righteous and the wicked, for he has appointed a time for every matter, and for every work. 18I said in my heart with regard to human beings that God is testing them to show that they are but animals. 19For the fate of humans and the fate of animals is the same; as one dies, so dies the other. They all have the same breath, and humans have no advantage over the animals; for all is vanity. 20All go to one place; all are from the dust, and all turn to dust again. 21Who knows whether the human spirit goes upward and the spirit of animals goes downward to the earth? 22So I saw that there is nothing better than that all should enjoy their work, for that is their lot; who can bring them to see what will be after them?

3.20 Is There an Afterlife?

Old Testament writers said very little about the afterlife. Not until Jesus' coming did God reveal details about heaven and hell. In this passage, the author wonders aloud whether death will be the end of everything. Yet he also adds some intriguing hints about the future. God "has put a sense of past and future into their minds," he declares (verse 11). He also refers to a time of future judgment (verse 17).

4 Again I saw all the oppressions that are practiced under the sun. Look, the tears of the oppressed—with no one to comfort them! On the side of their oppressors there was power—with no one to comfort them. 2And I thought the dead, who have already died, more fortunate than the living, who are still alive; 3but better than both is

---

f Gk Syr: Heb *apart from me*   *g* Or *a feeding on wind.* See Hos 12.1   *h* Heb *what is pursued*

the one who has not yet been, and has not seen the evil deeds that are done under the sun.

4 Then I saw that all toil and all skill in work come from one person's envy of another. This also is vanity and a chasing after wind.[i]

5 Fools fold their hands
and consume their own flesh.

6 Better is a handful with quiet
than two handfuls with toil,
and a chasing after wind.[i]

7 Again, I saw vanity under the sun: [8]the case of solitary individuals, without sons or brothers; yet there is no end to all their toil, and their eyes are never satisfied with riches. "For whom am I toiling," they ask, "and depriving myself of pleasure?" This also is vanity and an unhappy business.

The Value of a Friend

9 Two are better than one, because they have a good reward for their toil. [10]For if they fall, one will lift up the other; but woe to one who is alone and falls and does not have another to help. [11]Again, if two lie together, they keep warm; but how can one keep warm alone? [12]And though one might prevail against another, two will withstand one. A threefold cord is not quickly broken.

13 Better is a poor but wise youth than an old but foolish king, who will no longer take advice. [14]One can indeed come out of prison to reign, even though born poor in the kingdom. [15]I saw all the living who, moving about under the sun, follow that[j] youth who replaced the king;[k] [16]there was no end to all those people whom he led. Yet those who come later will not rejoice in him. Surely this also is vanity and a chasing after wind.[i]

Reverence, Humility, and Contentment

5 [l] Guard your steps when you go to the house of God; to draw near to listen is better than the sacrifice offered by fools; for they do not know how to keep from doing evil.[m] [2] [n] Never be rash with your mouth, nor let your heart be quick to utter a word before God, for God is in heaven, and you upon earth; therefore let your words be few.

3 For dreams come with many cares, and a fool's voice with many words.

4 When you make a vow to God, do not delay fulfilling it; for he has no pleasure in fools. Fulfill what you vow. [5]It is better that you should not vow than that you should vow and not fulfill it. [6]Do not let your mouth lead you into sin, and do not say before the messenger that it was a mistake; why should God be angry at your words, and destroy the work of your hands?

7 With many dreams come vanities and a multitude of words;[o] but fear God.

8 If you see in a province the oppression of the poor and the violation of justice and right, do not be amazed at the matter; for the high official is watched by a higher, and there are yet higher ones over them. [9]But all things considered, this is an advantage for a land: a king for a plowed field.[o]

10 The lover of money will not be satisfied with money; nor the lover of wealth, with gain. This also is vanity.

5.10 Never Enough

Someone asked John D. Rockefeller, the richest man of his time, how much money is enough. He replied with a perfect definition of greed: "Just a little bit more." A real estate tycoon said something similar: "I don't want all the land in the world, just whatever touches mine."

11 When goods increase, those who eat them increase; and what gain has their owner but to see them with his eyes?

12 Sweet is the sleep of laborers, whether they eat little or much; but the surfeit of the rich will not let them sleep.

13 There is a grievous ill that I have seen under the sun: riches were kept by their owners to their hurt, [14]and those riches were lost in a bad venture; though they are parents of children, they have nothing in their hands. [15]As they came from their mother's womb, so they shall go again, naked as they came; they shall take nothing for their toil, which they may carry away with their hands. [16]This also is a grievous ill: just as they came, so shall they go; and what gain do they have from toiling for the wind? [17]Besides, all their days they eat in darkness, in much vexation and sickness and resentment.

18 This is what I have seen to be good: it is fitting to eat and drink and find enjoyment in all the toil with which one toils under the sun the few days of the life God gives us; for this is our lot. [19]Likewise all to whom God gives wealth and possessions and whom he enables to enjoy them, and to accept their lot and find enjoyment in their toil—this is the gift of God. [20]For they will scarcely brood over the days of their lives, because God keeps them occupied with the joy of their hearts.

The Frustration of Desires

6 There is an evil that I have seen under the sun, and it lies heavy upon humankind: [2]those to whom God gives wealth, possessions, and honor, so that they lack nothing of all that

---

[i] Or *a feeding on wind.* See Hos 12.1   [j] Heb *the second*   [k] Heb *him*   [l] Ch 4.17 in Heb   [m] Cn: Heb *they do not know how to do evil*   [n] Ch 5.1 in Heb   [o] Meaning of Heb uncertain

they desire, yet God does not enable them to enjoy these things, but a stranger enjoys them. This is vanity; it is a grievous ill. ³A man may beget a hundred children, and live many years;

5.18 Good for Something

As he tasted various attractions in life—work, food, drink, success—the Teacher decided that all are "vanity." None gave ultimate satisfaction. But in passages like this one, he admits that such good things are gifts from God and have a temporary value. Some possessions are better than none, wisdom is better than ignorance, life is better than death.

but however many are the days of his years, if he does not enjoy life's good things, or has no burial, I say that a stillborn child is better off than he. ⁴For it comes into vanity and goes into darkness, and in darkness its name is covered; ⁵moreover it has not seen the sun or known anything; yet it finds rest rather than he. ⁶Even though he should live a thousand years twice over, yet enjoy no good—do not all go to one place?

7 All human toil is for the mouth, yet the appetite is not satisfied. ⁸For what advantage have the wise over fools? And what do the poor have who know how to conduct themselves before the living? ⁹Better is the sight of the eyes than the wandering of desire; this also is vanity and a chasing after wind.ᵖ

10 Whatever has come to be has already been named, and it is known what human beings are, and that they are not able to dispute with those who are stronger. ¹¹The more words, the more vanity, so how is one the better? ¹²For who knows what is good for mortals while they live the few days of their vain life, which they pass like a shadow? For who can tell them what will be after them under the sun?

A Disillusioned View of Life

7 A good name is better than precious
    ointment,
    and the day of death, than the day of
    birth.
² It is better to go to the house of
    mourning
    than to go to the house of feasting;
    for this is the end of everyone,
    and the living will lay it to heart.
³ Sorrow is better than laughter,
    for by sadness of countenance the
    heart is made glad.
⁴ The heart of the wise is in the house of
    mourning;

but the heart of fools is in the house of
    mirth.
⁵ It is better to hear the rebuke of the wise
    than to hear the song of fools.
⁶ For like the crackling of thorns under a
    pot,
    so is the laughter of fools;
    this also is vanity.
⁷ Surely oppression makes the wise foolish,
    and a bribe corrupts the heart.
⁸ Better is the end of a thing than its
    beginning;
    the patient in spirit are better than the
    proud in spirit.
⁹ Do not be quick to anger,
    for anger lodges in the bosom of fools.
¹⁰ Do not say, "Why were the former days
    better than these?"
    For it is not from wisdom that you ask
    this.
¹¹ Wisdom is as good as an inheritance,
    an advantage to those who see the sun.
¹² For the protection of wisdom is like the
    protection of money,
    and the advantage of knowledge is that
    wisdom gives life to the one who
    possesses it.
¹³ Consider the work of God;
    who can make straight what he has
    made crooked?

14 In the day of prosperity be joyful, and in the day of adversity consider; God has made the one as well as the other, so that mortals may not find out anything that will come after them.

The Riddles of Life

15 In my vain life I have seen everything; there are righteous people who perish in their righteousness, and there are wicked people who

7.15 Companion Book

Passages in Ecclesiastes sound eerily like the book of Job. Both books are "philosophical," asking the hardest questions about life. Both authors battled despair, but for opposite reasons: Job was overwhelmed by tragedy and pain while the Teacher was jaded by luxury and success. No matter what their status in life, everyone has to face the same basic issues: Is there a God? Is life unfair? Does it have meaning?

prolong their life in their evildoing. ¹⁶Do not be too righteous, and do not act too wise; why should you destroy yourself? ¹⁷Do not be too wicked, and do not be a fool; why should you die before your time? ¹⁸It is good that you should

ᵖ Or *a feeding on wind.* See Hos 12.1

take hold of the one, without letting go of the other; for the one who fears God shall succeed with both.

19 Wisdom gives strength to the wise more than ten rulers that are in a city.

20 Surely there is no one on earth so righteous as to do good without ever sinning.

21 Do not give heed to everything that people say, or you may hear your servant cursing you; 22your heart knows that many times you have yourself cursed others.

23 All this I have tested by wisdom; I said, "I will be wise," but it was far from me. 24That which is, is far off, and deep, very deep; who can find it out? 25I turned my mind to know and to search out and to seek wisdom and the sum of things, and to know that wickedness is folly and that foolishness is madness. 26I found more bitter than death the woman who is a trap, whose heart is snares and nets, whose hands are fetters; one who pleases God escapes her, but the sinner is taken by her. 27See, this is what I found, says the Teacher,q adding one thing to another to find the sum, 28which my mind has sought repeatedly, but I have not found. One man among a thousand I found, but a woman among all these I have not found. 29See, this alone I found, that God made human beings straightforward, but they have devised many schemes.

Obey the King and Enjoy Yourself

8 Who is like the wise man?
    And who knows the interpretation of a
        thing?
Wisdom makes one's face shine,
    and the hardness of one's countenance
        is changed.

2 Keepr the king's command because of your sacred oath. 3Do not be terrified; go from his presence, do not delay when the matter is unpleasant, for he does whatever he pleases. 4For the word of the king is powerful, and who can say to him, "What are you doing?" 5Whoever obeys a command will meet no harm, and the wise mind will know the time and way. 6For every matter has its time and way, although the troubles of mortals lie heavy upon them. 7Indeed, they do not know what is to be, for who can tell them how it will be? 8No one has power over the winds to restrain the wind,s or power over the day of death; there is no discharge from the battle, nor does wickedness deliver those who practice it. 9All this I observed, applying my mind to all that is done under the sun, while one person exercises authority over another to the other's hurt.

God's Ways Are Inscrutable

10 Then I saw the wicked buried; they used to

go in and out of the holy place, and were praised in the city where they had done such things.t This also is vanity. 11Because sentence against an evil deed is not executed speedily, the human heart is fully set to do evil. 12Though sinners do evil a hundred times and prolong their lives, yet I know that it will be well with those who fear God, because they stand in fear before him, 13but it will not be well with the wicked, neither will they prolong their days like a shadow, because they do not stand in fear before God.

14 There is a vanity that takes place on earth, that there are righteous people who are treated according to the conduct of the wicked, and there are wicked people who are treated according to the conduct of the righteous. I said that this also is vanity. 15So I commend enjoyment, for there is nothing better for people under the sun than to eat, and drink, and enjoy themselves, for this will go with them in their toil through the days of life that God gives them under the sun.

16 When I applied my mind to know wisdom, and to see the business that is done on earth, how one's eyes see sleep neither day nor night, 17then I saw all the work of God, that no one can find out what is happening under the sun. However much they may toil in seeking, they will not find it out; even though those who are wise claim to know, they cannot find it out.

8.17 God's Fault?

Despite their similarities, Job and Ecclesiastes reveal important differences. As this verse shows, the Teacher never really expected to solve life's riddles; his attitude of resignation contrasts with Job's combativeness. Also, in his anguish, Job sometimes questioned the character of God himself, demanding a personal explanation. At no time did the Teacher blame God for the unfairness and meaninglessness he saw around him. "God made human beings straightforward," he concludes, "but they have devised many schemes" (7.29).

Take Life as It Comes

9 All this I laid to heart, examining it all, how the righteous and the wise and their deeds are in the hand of God; whether it is love or hate one does not know. Everything that confronts them 2is vanity,u since the same fate comes to all, to the righteous and the wicked, to the good and the evil,v to the clean and the unclean, to those who sacrifice and those who do not sacrifice. As are the good, so are the sinners; those who swear are like those who shun an oath. 3This is an evil in all

---

q Qoheleth, traditionally rendered Preacher   r Heb I keep   s Or breath   t Meaning of Heb uncertain
u Syr Compare Gk: Heb Everything that confronts them 2is everything   v Gk Syr Vg: Heb lacks and the evil

that happens under the sun, that the same fate comes to everyone. Moreover, the hearts of all are full of evil; madness is in their hearts while they live, and after that they go to the dead. 4But whoever is joined with all the living has hope, for a living dog is better than a dead lion. 5The living know that they will die, but the dead know nothing; they have no more reward, and even the memory of them is lost. 6Their love and their hate and their envy have already perished; never again will they have any share in all that happens under the sun.

7 Go, eat your bread with enjoyment, and drink your wine with a merry heart; for God has long ago approved what you do. 8Let your garments always be white; do not let oil be lacking on your head. 9Enjoy life with the wife whom you love, all the days of your vain life that are given you under the sun, because that is your portion in life and in your toil at which you toil under the sun. 10Whatever your hand finds to do, do with your might; for there is no work or thought or knowledge or wisdom in Sheol, to which you are going.

11 Again I saw that under the sun the race is not to the swift, nor the battle to the strong, nor bread to the wise, nor riches to the intelligent, nor favor to the skillful; but time and chance happen

9.11 Life Is Unfair

Chapters 8 and 9 eloquently voice the unfairness of life. People don't get what they deserve, claims the Teacher. Good people suffer while wicked people prosper. Everything seems determined only by time and chance. The Teacher's doubts about the afterlife (see 3.20) affected all his thinking, because he saw the utter unfairness of life around him. In contrast, New Testament authors, with a solid belief in the afterlife, showed confidence that God would ultimately judge all people with fairness.

to them all. 12For no one can anticipate the time of disaster. Like fish taken in a cruel net, and like birds caught in a snare, so mortals are snared at a time of calamity, when it suddenly falls upon them.

Wisdom Superior to Folly

13 I have also seen this example of wisdom under the sun, and it seemed great to me. 14There was a little city with few people in it. A great king came against it and besieged it, building great siegeworks against it. 15Now there was found in it a poor wise man, and he by his wisdom delivered the city. Yet no one remembered that poor man. 16So I said, "Wisdom is better than might; yet the

poor man's wisdom is despised, and his words are not heeded."

17 The quiet words of the wise are more to
be heeded
than the shouting of a ruler among
fools.
18 Wisdom is better than weapons of war,
but one bungler destroys much good.

Miscellaneous Observations

10 Dead flies make the perfumer's ointment
give off a foul odor;
so a little folly outweighs wisdom and
honor.
2 The heart of the wise inclines to the right,
but the heart of a fool to the left.
3 Even when fools walk on the road, they
lack sense,
and show to everyone that they are
fools.
4 If the anger of the ruler rises against you,
do not leave your post,
for calmness will undo great offenses.

5 There is an evil that I have seen under the sun, as great an error as if it proceeded from the ruler: 6folly is set in many high places, and the rich sit in a low place. 7I have seen slaves on horseback, and princes walking on foot like slaves.

8 Whoever digs a pit will fall into it;
and whoever breaks through a wall will
be bitten by a snake.
9 Whoever quarries stones will be hurt by
them;
and whoever splits logs will be
endangered by them.
10 If the iron is blunt, and one does not
whet the edge,
then more strength must be exerted;
but wisdom helps one to succeed.
11 If the snake bites before it is charmed,
there is no advantage in a charmer.

12 Words spoken by the wise bring them
favor,
but the lips of fools consume them.
13 The words of their mouths begin in
foolishness,
and their talk ends in wicked madness;
14 yet fools talk on and on.
No one knows what is to happen,
and who can tell anyone what the
future holds?
15 The toil of fools wears them out,
for they do not even know the way to
town.

16 Alas for you, O land, when your king is a
servant,w

w Or a child

and your princes feast in the morning!

17 Happy are you, O land, when your king
is a nobleman,
and your princes feast at the proper
time—
for strength, and not for drunkenness!

18 Through sloth the roof sinks in,
and through indolence the house
leaks.

19 Feasts are made for laughter;
wine gladdens life,
and money meets every need.

20 Do not curse the king, even in your
thoughts,
or curse the rich, even in your
bedroom;
for a bird of the air may carry your
voice,
or some winged creature tell
the matter.

The Value of Diligence

11 Send out your bread upon the waters,
for after many days you will get it
back.

2 Divide your means seven ways, or even
eight,
for you do not know what disaster may
happen on earth.

3 When clouds are full,
they empty rain on the earth;
whether a tree falls to the south or to the
north,
in the place where the tree falls, there it
will lie.

4 Whoever observes the wind will not sow;
and whoever regards the clouds will
not reap.

5 Just as you do not know how the breath
comes to the bones in the mother's womb, so you
do not know the work of God, who makes everything.

6 In the morning sow your seed, and at evening do not let your hands be idle; for you do not
know which will prosper, this or that, or whether
both alike will be good.

Youth and Old Age

7 Light is sweet, and it is pleasant for the eyes
to see the sun.

8 Even those who live many years should rejoice in them all; yet let them remember that the
days of darkness will be many. All that comes is
vanity.

9 Rejoice, young man, while you are young,
and let your heart cheer you in the days of your
youth. Follow the inclination of your heart and
the desire of your eyes, but know that for all these
things God will bring you into judgment.

10 Banish anxiety from your mind, and put
away pain from your body; for youth and the
dawn of life are vanity.

12.13 The Gamble

*Having tried everything life has to offer, the
Teacher circles back to this uncomplicated
formula for making sense of our time on earth.
Although Ecclesiastes displays little of the
confidence of the book of Proverbs preceding it,
both arrive at exactly the same conclusion (see
Proverbs 1.7).*

*The 17th-century mathematician and
philosopher Blaise Pascal, who similarly
struggled with issues of meaninglessness,
concluded that faith sometimes resembles a
wager. He told his friends, "If I believe in God
and life after death and you do not, and if there
is no God, we both lose when we die. However,
if there is a God, you still lose and I gain
everything."*

11.5 Beyond Understanding

*Even the Teacher, a man who possessed
brilliant powers of wisdom and observation,
had to conclude some things are beyond
understanding. Failing in his attempt to "figure
out" life, he fell back on simple advice: Fear God
and obey him, no matter how things seem to
you. In essence, he concluded in favor of a life
of faith. For him, an old man, much of life had
already passed; in eloquent poetry he
describes the decay that was already at work
in his body (12.1–7). Thus he stressed,
"Remember your creator in the days of your
youth" (12.1).*

12 Remember your creator in the days of your
youth, before the days of trouble come, and
the years draw near when you will say, "I have no
pleasure in them"; 2before the sun and the light
and the moon and the stars are darkened and the
clouds return with[x] the rain; 3in the day when the
guards of the house tremble, and the strong men
are bent, and the women who grind cease working because they are few, and those who look
through the windows see dimly; 4when the doors
on the street are shut, and the sound of the grinding is low, and one rises up at the sound of a bird,
and all the daughters of song are brought low;
5when one is afraid of heights, and terrors are in
the road; the almond tree blossoms, the grasshopper drags itself along[y] and desire fails; because all

x Or *after*; Heb *'ahar*   y Or *is a burden*

must go to their eternal home, and the mourners will go about the streets; [6]before the silver cord is snapped,[z] and the golden bowl is broken, and the pitcher is broken at the fountain, and the wheel broken at the cistern, [7]and the dust returns to the earth as it was, and the breath[a] returns to God who gave it. [8]Vanity of vanities, says the Teacher;[b] all is vanity.

Epilogue

9 Besides being wise, the Teacher[b] also taught the people knowledge, weighing and studying and arranging many proverbs. [10]The Teacher[b]

sought to find pleasing words, and he wrote words of truth plainly.

11 The sayings of the wise are like goads, and like nails firmly fixed are the collected sayings that are given by one shepherd.[c] [12]Of anything beyond these, my child, beware. Of making many books there is no end, and much study is a weariness of the flesh.

13 The end of the matter; all has been heard. Fear God, and keep his commandments; for that is the whole duty of everyone. [14]For God will bring every deed into judgment, including[d] every secret thing, whether good or evil.

SONG OF SOLOMON

An Intoxicating Love
A poem about love the way it's meant to be

S
NAP THE RADIO ON, ZIP to any station, and what are you likely to hear?
Love songs. Songs of new love, songs of disappointed love, songs of grateful love, songs of crazy love. Times change, but through history the flow of
love songs is a constant.

> *Many waters cannot quench love, neither can floods drown it.*
> 8.7

Plenty of people are shocked to find an explicit love song in the Bible—complete with erotic lyrics.
But Song of Solomon is exactly that. It shows no embarrassment about lovers enjoying each other's
bodies, and talking about it. Consequently, intermittent attempts have been made to rule Song of
Solomon out of the Bible or to make it for "Adults Only." In 16th-century Spain, for instance, professor
Fray Luis de Leon was dragged out of his classroom and imprisoned for four years. His crime? He
translated Song of Solomon into Spanish.

Allegorical Interpretation

More often, Song of Solomon has been read as though it had nothing to do with lovers at all. Many
have interpreted it as an allegory of love between God and his people. Some of these interpretations
identify every poetic detail with some corresponding facet of our relationship to God. For instance, the
bride's hair may be interpreted as non-Jewish nations who come to Christ. The famous 12th-century
monk Saint Bernard of Clairvaux, using this allegorical approach, wrote 86 sermons on the first two
chapters of Song of Solomon.

Nowadays, few follow that kind of interpretation. Most scholars believe that the poem was
intended to celebrate love between a newly married couple. God values love between a man and a
woman. That's why he placed this song in his holy Bible. It may have been sung first at a wedding.

Naked and Unashamed

These lovers love to look at each other. They love to tell each other what they feel. They revel in
the sensuous: the beauty of nature, the scent of perfumes and spices. They are openly erotic.

Their intoxication with love sounds quite up-to-date, not so different from what you hear on the
radio. Yet Song of Solomon conveys a very different atmosphere from most modern love songs. The
explicit lyrics never become even slightly dirty. This love comes from the Garden of Eden, when both
man and woman were naked and unashamed. It is tender, filled with delight, natural. You sense no
shame or guilt; you feel that God is with the two as they love.

The lovers act as equals. Both woman and man take the initiative in praising each other. They don't
flirt or play games: they say what they mean.

Yet they show caution and dignity in their love. While at the peak of joy, the lovers repeatedly warn
others not to stir up love prematurely (2.7; 3.5; 8.4). They recognize the dangerously explosive side of
love. "For love is strong as death, passion fierce as the grave. Its flashes are flashes of fire, a raging
flame" (8.6).

How to Read Song of Solomon

S
ince love songs are always popular, many people approach Song of Solomon with
great expectations. However, readers often find the book different from what they
had expected.

Two main problems may hinder today's reader. One is the poetic imagery. No modern lover would say, "Your hair is like a flock of goats" (4.1), or, "Your nose is like the tower of Lebanon" (7.4). While some images in Song of Solomon appeal—"His intention toward me was love" (2.4) or "Love is strong as death" (8.6)—the majority of the book's metaphors sound strange to our ears.

Most of the comparisons aren't visual, but emotional. For instance, when the lover tells his beloved that "your two breasts are like two fawns" (4.5), he isn't saying that her breasts look like deer. He is saying that they bring out the same tender feelings baby deer do. When you read strange-sounding metaphors in Song of Solomon, don't ask, "What did these things (pomegranates, myrrh, a flock of sheep) look like?" but ask, "What did the lovers *feel* when they thought of them?"

A second problem: Song of Solomon is hard to follow. One part doesn't seem connected to the next. Think of it as a series of snapshots of a couple in love—snapshots not necessarily in order. Put together in one photo album, they show the profound feelings of newly married lovers.

Though Song of Solomon is primarily about love on the human level, many Christians and Jews have read it as a book about God's love. This was probably not the author's original intent, but it is a legitimate and inspiring way to look at the book. After all, God made human love, and other parts of the Bible suggest its similarity to God's love. (See Hosea 1—3 and Ephesians 5.22–33.) Song of Solomon never makes this connection, but it does present a love so rich, so full, so unashamed that it's natural to think of God and his love for us.

3-TRACK READING PLAN

For an explanation and complete listing of the 3-track reading plan, turn to page 7.

TRACK 1: **Two-Week Courses on the Bible**
See page 7 for information on these courses.

TRACK 2: **An Overview of Song of Solomon in 1 Day**
☐ Day 1. Read the Introduction to Song of Solomon and chapter 2, a beautiful love poem.

Now turn to page 9 for your next Track 2 reading project.

TRACK 3: **All of Song of Solomon in 8 Days**
After you have read through Song of Solomon, turn to pages 10–14 for your next Track 3 reading project.
☐1   ☐2   ☐3   ☐4   ☐5   ☐6   ☐7   ☐8

---

1 The Song of Songs, which is Solomon's.

Colloquy of Bride and Friends

2 Let him kiss me with the kisses of his
        mouth!
For your love is better than wine,
3   your anointing oils are fragrant,
your name is perfume poured out;
        therefore the maidens love you.
4 Draw me after you, let us make haste.
        The king has brought me into his
        chambers.
We will exult and rejoice in you;
    we will extol your love more
        than wine;
    rightly do they love you.

5 I am black and beautiful,
        O daughters of Jerusalem,
like the tents of Kedar,
        like the curtains of Solomon.
6 Do not gaze at me because I am dark,
        because the sun has gazed on me.
My mother's sons were angry with me;
        they made me keeper of the vineyards,
        but my own vineyard I have not kept!
7 Tell me, you whom my soul loves,
        where you pasture your flock,
        where you make it lie down at noon;
for why should I be like one who is
        veiled
        beside the flocks of your companions?

8 If you do not know,
        O fairest among women,
follow the tracks of the flock,
        and pasture your kids
        beside the shepherds' tents.

Colloquy of Bridegroom, Friends, and Bride

9 I compare you, my love,
   to a mare among Pharaoh's chariots.
10 Your cheeks are comely with ornaments,
   your neck with strings of jewels.
11 We will make you ornaments of gold,
   studded with silver.

1.6 Tan Lines

Modern Americans, who lavish millions of dollars on tanning lotions and tanning salons, consider a suntan desirable, despite its health risks. Not so in Victorian times—or in Solomon's time. Soft white skin marked a more refined person who had not been required to work outdoors.

12 While the king was on his couch,
   my nard gave forth its fragrance.
13 My beloved is to me a bag of myrrh
   that lies between my breasts.
14 My beloved is to me a cluster of henna
      blossoms
   in the vineyards of En-gedi.

15 Ah, you are beautiful, my love;
   ah, you are beautiful;
   your eyes are doves.
16 Ah, you are beautiful, my beloved,
   truly lovely.
   Our couch is green;
17   the beams of our house are cedar,
   our rafters*a* are pine.

2 I am a rose*b* of Sharon,
   a lily of the valleys.

2 As a lily among brambles,
   so is my love among maidens.

3 As an apple tree among the trees of the
      wood,
   so is my beloved among young men.
   With great delight I sat in his shadow,
   and his fruit was sweet to my taste.
4 He brought me to the banqueting house,
   and his intention toward me was love.
5 Sustain me with raisins,
   refresh me with apples;
   for I am faint with love.
6 O that his left hand were under my head,
   and that his right hand embraced me!
7 I adjure you, O daughters of Jerusalem,
   by the gazelles or the wild does:

do not stir up or awaken love
   until it is ready!

Springtime Rhapsody

8 The voice of my beloved!
   Look, he comes,
   leaping upon the mountains,
   bounding over the hills.
9 My beloved is like a gazelle
   or a young stag.
   Look, there he stands
   behind our wall,
   gazing in at the windows,
   looking through the lattice.
10 My beloved speaks and says to me:
   "Arise, my love, my fair one,
   and come away;
11 for now the winter is past,
   the rain is over and gone.
12 The flowers appear on the earth;
   the time of singing has come,
   and the voice of the turtledove
   is heard in our land.
13 The fig tree puts forth its figs,
   and the vines are in blossom;
   they give forth fragrance.
   Arise, my love, my fair one,
   and come away.
14 O my dove, in the clefts of the rock,
   in the covert of the cliff,
   let me see your face,
   let me hear your voice;
   for your voice is sweet,
   and your face is lovely.
15 Catch us the foxes,
   the little foxes,
   that ruin the vineyards—
   for our vineyards are in blossom."

16 My beloved is mine and I am his;
   he pastures his flock among the lilies.
17 Until the day breathes
   and the shadows flee,
   turn, my beloved, be like a gazelle
   or a young stag on the cleft
      mountains.*c*

Love's Dream

3 Upon my bed at night
   I sought him whom my soul loves;
   I sought him, but found him not;
   I called him, but he gave no answer.*d*
2 "I will rise now and go about the city,
   in the streets and in the squares;
   I will seek him whom my soul loves."
   I sought him, but found him not.
3 The sentinels found me,
   as they went about in the city.

a Meaning of Heb uncertain   *b* Heb *crocus*   *c* Or *on the mountains of Bether*: meaning of Heb uncertain
d Gk: Heb lacks this line

"Have you seen him whom my soul
loves?"
4 Scarcely had I passed them,
when I found him whom my soul
loves.
I held him, and would not let him go
until I brought him into my mother's
house,
and into the chamber of her that
conceived me.
5 I adjure you, O daughters of Jerusalem,
by the gazelles or the wild does:
do not stir up or awaken love
until it is ready!

3.5 Let Love Sleep

If love is so wonderful, as this poem beautifully sings, shouldn't people pursue it recklessly? Yet the beloved warns them not to. Three times she urges others not to force love, but to let it develop at its own rate. Love should wait for its proper time.

The Groom and His Party Approach

6 What is that coming up from the
wilderness,
like a column of smoke,
perfumed with myrrh and frankincense,
with all the fragrant powders of the
merchant?
7 Look, it is the litter of Solomon!
Around it are sixty mighty men
of the mighty men of Israel,
8 all equipped with swords
and expert in war,
each with his sword at his thigh
because of alarms by night.
9 King Solomon made himself a palanquin
from the wood of Lebanon.
10 He made its posts of silver,
its back of gold, its seat of purple;
its interior was inlaid with love.*e*
Daughters of Jerusalem,
11 come out.
Look, O daughters of Zion,
at King Solomon,
at the crown with which his mother
crowned him
on the day of his wedding,
on the day of the gladness of his heart.

The Bride's Beauty Extolled

4 How beautiful you are, my love,
how very beautiful!
Your eyes are doves
behind your veil.

Your hair is like a flock of goats,
moving down the slopes of Gilead.
2 Your teeth are like a flock of shorn ewes
that have come up from the washing,
all of which bear twins,
and not one among them is bereaved.
3 Your lips are like a crimson thread,
and your mouth is lovely.
Your cheeks are like halves of a
pomegranate
behind your veil.
4 Your neck is like the tower of David,
built in courses;
on it hang a thousand bucklers,
all of them shields of warriors.
5 Your two breasts are like two fawns,
twins of a gazelle,
that feed among the lilies.
6 Until the day breathes
and the shadows flee,
I will hasten to the mountain of myrrh
and the hill of frankincense.
7 You are altogether beautiful, my love;
there is no flaw in you.
8 Come with me from Lebanon, my bride;
come with me from Lebanon.
Depart*f* from the peak of Amana,
from the peak of Senir and Hermon,
from the dens of lions,
from the mountains of leopards.

9 You have ravished my heart, my sister,
my bride,
you have ravished my heart with a
glance of your eyes,
with one jewel of your necklace.
10 How sweet is your love, my sister, my
bride!
how much better is your love than
wine,
and the fragrance of your oils than any
spice!
11 Your lips distill nectar, my bride;
honey and milk are under your tongue;
the scent of your garments is like the
scent of Lebanon.
12 A garden locked is my sister, my bride,
a garden locked, a fountain sealed.
13 Your channel*e* is an orchard of
pomegranates
with all choicest fruits,
henna with nard,
14 nard and saffron, calamus and cinnamon,
with all trees of frankincense,
myrrh and aloes,
with all chief spices—
15 a garden fountain, a well of living water,
and flowing streams from Lebanon.

e Meaning of Heb uncertain   *f* Or *Look*

¹⁶ Awake, O north wind,
and come, O south wind!
Blow upon my garden
that its fragrance may be wafted
abroad.
Let my beloved come to his garden,
and eat its choicest fruits.

5 I come to my garden, my sister, my bride;
I gather my myrrh with my spice,
I eat my honeycomb with my honey,
I drink my wine with my milk.

Eat, friends, drink,
and be drunk with love.

Another Dream

² I slept, but my heart was awake.
Listen! my beloved is knocking.
"Open to me, my sister, my love,
my dove, my perfect one;
for my head is wet with dew,
my locks with the drops of the night."

5.2–8 A Nightmare

This short passage and the first five verses of chapter 3 are strange and troubling interludes. Many scholars think they are dream sequences, nightmares showing that the beauty of love also brings an increased vulnerability to pain and fear. Here, the beloved is slow to get out of bed to welcome her lover. As a result, he is gone when she reaches the door.

³ I had put off my garment;
how could I put it on again?
I had bathed my feet;
how could I soil them?
⁴ My beloved thrust his hand into the
opening,
and my inmost being yearned for him.
⁵ I arose to open to my beloved,
and my hands dripped with myrrh,
my fingers with liquid myrrh,
upon the handles of the bolt.
⁶ I opened to my beloved,
but my beloved had turned and was
gone.
My soul failed me when he spoke.
I sought him, but did not find him;
I called him, but he gave no answer.
⁷ Making their rounds in the city
the sentinels found me;
they beat me, they wounded me,
they took away my mantle,
those sentinels of the walls.

⁸ I adjure you, O daughters of Jerusalem,
if you find my beloved,
tell him this:
I am faint with love.

Colloquy of Friends and Bride

⁹ What is your beloved more than another
beloved,
O fairest among women?
What is your beloved more than another
beloved,
that you thus adjure us?

¹⁰ My beloved is all radiant and ruddy,
distinguished among ten thousand.
¹¹ His head is the finest gold;
his locks are wavy,
black as a raven.
¹² His eyes are like doves
beside springs of water,
bathed in milk,
fitly set.^g
¹³ His cheeks are like beds of spices,
yielding fragrance.
His lips are lilies,
distilling liquid myrrh.
¹⁴ His arms are rounded gold,
set with jewels.
His body is ivory work,^g
encrusted with sapphires.^h
¹⁵ His legs are alabaster columns,
set upon bases of gold.
His appearance is like Lebanon,
choice as the cedars.
¹⁶ His speech is most sweet,
and he is altogether desirable.
This is my beloved and this is my friend,
O daughters of Jerusalem.

6 Where has your beloved gone,
O fairest among women?
Which way has your beloved turned,
that we may seek him with you?

² My beloved has gone down to his garden,
to the beds of spices,
to pasture his flock in the gardens,
and to gather lilies.
³ I am my beloved's and my beloved is
mine;
he pastures his flock among the lilies.

The Bride's Matchless Beauty

⁴ You are beautiful as Tirzah, my love,
comely as Jerusalem,
terrible as an army with banners.
⁵ Turn away your eyes from me,
for they overwhelm me!
Your hair is like a flock of goats,

moving down the slopes of Gilead.
6 Your teeth are like a flock of ewes,
that have come up from the washing;
all of them bear twins,
and not one among them is bereaved.
7 Your cheeks are like halves of a
pomegranate
behind your veil.
8 There are sixty queens and eighty
concubines,
and maidens without number.
9 My dove, my perfect one, is the only one,
the darling of her mother,
flawless to her that bore her.
The maidens saw her and called her
happy;
the queens and concubines also, and
they praised her.
10 "Who is this that looks forth like the
dawn,
fair as the moon, bright as the sun,
terrible as an army with banners?"

11 I went down to the nut orchard,
to look at the blossoms of the valley,
to see whether the vines had budded,
whether the pomegranates were in
bloom.
12 Before I was aware, my fancy set me
in a chariot beside my prince.[i]

13[j] Return, return, O Shulammite!
Return, return, that we may look upon
you.

Why should you look upon the
Shulammite,
as upon a dance before two armies?[k]

Expressions of Praise

7 How graceful are your feet in sandals,
O queenly maiden!
Your rounded thighs are like jewels,
the work of a master hand.
2 Your navel is a rounded bowl
that never lacks mixed wine.
Your belly is a heap of wheat,
encircled with lilies.
3 Your two breasts are like two fawns,
twins of a gazelle.
4 Your neck is like an ivory tower.
Your eyes are pools in Heshbon,
by the gate of Bath-rabbim.
Your nose is like a tower of Lebanon,
overlooking Damascus.
5 Your head crowns you like Carmel,

and your flowing locks are like purple;
a king is held captive in the tresses.[l]

6 How fair and pleasant you are,
O loved one, delectable maiden![m]
7 You are stately[n] as a palm tree,
and your breasts are like its clusters.
8 I say I will climb the palm tree
and lay hold of its branches.
O may your breasts be like clusters of the
vine,
and the scent of your breath like
apples,
9 and your kisses[o] like the best wine
that goes down[p] smoothly,
gliding over lips and teeth.[q]

10 I am my beloved's,
and his desire is for me.
11 Come, my beloved,
let us go forth into the fields,
and lodge in the villages;
12 let us go out early to the vineyards,
and see whether the vines have
budded,
whether the grape blossoms have opened
and the pomegranates are in bloom.
There I will give you my love.
13 The mandrakes give forth fragrance,
and over our doors are all choice
fruits,
new as well as old,
which I have laid up for you, O my
beloved.

8 O that you were like a brother to me,
who nursed at my mother's breast!
If I met you outside, I would kiss you,
and no one would despise me.

8.1 A Brotherly Kiss

In oriental culture, even a married couple could not express their love publicly. Only a brother and sister could openly kiss. The beloved is wishing she had the right to show their love to the world.

2 I would lead you and bring you
into the house of my mother,
and into the chamber of the one who
bore me.[r]
I would give you spiced wine to drink,
the juice of my pomegranates.
3 O that his left hand were under my head,
and that his right hand embraced me!
4 I adjure you, O daughters of Jerusalem,

---

[i] Cn: Meaning of Heb uncertain   [j] Ch 7.1 in Heb   [k] Or *dance of Mahanaim*   [l] Meaning of Heb uncertain
[m] Syr: Heb *in delights*   [n] Heb *This your stature is*   [o] Heb *palate*   [p] Heb *down for my lover*   [q] Gk Syr Vg:
Heb *lips of sleepers*   [r] Gk Syr: Heb *my mother; she* (or *you*) *will teach me*

do not stir up or awaken love
until it is ready!

Homecoming

5 Who is that coming up from the
wilderness,
leaning upon her beloved?

Under the apple tree I awakened you.
There your mother was in labor with you;
there she who bore you was in labor.

6 Set me as a seal upon your heart,
as a seal upon your arm;
for love is strong as death,
passion fierce as the grave.
Its flashes are flashes of fire,
a raging flame.

8.6 Love and Death

*Death sweeps everything away. It yields to no
one, and once you are in its power you cannot
escape. So with love: It takes control of your
life, and like a gigantic fire, it cannot be doused.
Love must be treated with the greatest caution
and respect.*

7 Many waters cannot quench love,
neither can floods drown it.
If one offered for love
all the wealth of one's house,
it would be utterly scorned.

8 We have a little sister,
and she has no breasts.
What shall we do for our sister,
on the day when she is spoken for?

9 If she is a wall,
we will build upon her a battlement of
silver;
but if she is a door,
we will enclose her with boards of
cedar.

10 I was a wall,
and my breasts were like towers;
then I was in his eyes
as one who brings[s] peace.

11 Solomon had a vineyard at Baal-hamon;
he entrusted the vineyard to keepers;
each one was to bring for its fruit a
thousand pieces of silver.

12 My vineyard, my very own, is for myself;
you, O Solomon, may have the
thousand,
and the keepers of the fruit two
hundred!

13 O you who dwell in the gardens,
my companions are listening for your
voice;
let me hear it.

14 Make haste, my beloved,
and be like a gazelle
or a young stag
upon the mountains of spices!

---

[s] Or *finds*

ISAIAH

Prophet, Poet, and Politician
His nation at a crossroads, Isaiah rose to meet the challenge

THE PROPHET ISAIAH WAS A giant of Jewish history. He was the Shakespeare of Hebrew literature, and the New Testament quotes him more than all the other prophets combined. No other biblical author can match his rich vocabulary and use of imagery.

He expected justice, but saw bloodshed; righteousness, but heard a cry! 5.7

And yet Isaiah spent his days not in an ivory tower, but in the corridors of power. He served as adviser to the kings of Judah and helped set the course of his nation.

Days of Crisis

Isaiah lived at a crucial time, midway between the founding of the kingdom under Saul and David and its eventual destruction. A civil war had split the Israelites into North (Israel) and South (Judah), and Isaiah lived in the more pious Southern Kingdom.

When Isaiah began his work, the nation seemed strong and wealthy. But Isaiah saw signs of grave danger. People were using their power to harass the poor. Men went around drunk; women cared more about their clothes than about their neighbors' hunger. People gave lip service to God and kept up the outward appearance of religion but did little more.

Outside dangers loomed even larger. The armies of neighboring Israel were rattling swords and spears at the border. On all sides, monster empires were growing, especially Egypt and Assyria. Judah was caught in a pincers. Should the nation choose one of the empires as an ally?

Harsh Words from an Uncompromising Prophet

The nation of Judah, said Isaiah, stood at a crossroads: It could either regain its footing or begin a dangerous slide downward. The prophet did not temper his message for the sake of popular opinion. He had harsh and unyielding words about what changes must take place.

Although he moved in royal circles, Isaiah was hardly a yes-man in politics. Sometimes he stood alone against a tide of optimism. His very name meant "The LORD saves," and he warned kings that relying on military power or wealth or any force other than God would lead to disaster.

Isaiah outlasted four kings, but he finally offended one beyond repair. King Manasseh (notorious for practicing infant sacrifice) found Isaiah's strong words too much to bear. Tradition records that he had Isaiah killed by fastening him between two planks of wood and sawing his body in half.

Manasseh has long since disappeared into obscurity. But Isaiah, through this book, endures as one of the great authors of all time. Sometimes the pen *is* mightier than the sword.

How to Read Isaiah

In the eighth century B.C., about the time Homer was writing *The Iliad* and *The Odyssey*, Isaiah wrote the book that bears his name. It is arguably the most eloquent book in the Old Testament, and you will likely recognize many verses and phrases.

Isaiah is full of profound insights into the nature of God and his plan for the earth. Due to its length and its peculiar organization, however, the book may seem hard to grasp.

Remember that Isaiah consists of a collection of many messages on various topics, pulled together into groupings. To understand Isaiah, it helps to think of "road markers" that set off the major groupings. Here is a summary of them:

Isaiah 1–12:	Isaiah's call and messages of warning to Judah during the prosperous days of the kingdom. (These came mostly in the reigns of Jotham and Ahaz: see "A Lineup of Rulers," pages 1349–1357.)
Isaiah 13–23:	Isaiah's messages to all the nations around Judah—including enemies and close allies.
Isaiah 24–35:	A view of the earth's future (24–27) and specific messages to the people of Judah as they faced Assyria's imminent invasion.
Isaiah 36–39:	An interlude telling of great crises faced by King Hezekiah. The focus of the book moves from Assyria to Babylon.
Isaiah 40–48:	Prophecies addressed to a very different situation, 200 years into the future. Now Babylon, not Assyria, is the great enemy.
Isaiah 49–55:	A word of hope about final deliverance through the "suffering servant."
Isaiah 56–66:	General warnings to Judah, and a view of the future.

PEOPLE YOU'LL MEET IN ISAIAH

ISAIAH *(p. 698)*
CYRUS *(p. 743)*

3-TRACK READING PLAN

For an explanation and complete listing of the 3-track reading plan, turn to page 7.

TRACK 1: *Two-Week Courses on the Bible*
The Track 1 reading program on the Old Testament includes one chapter from Isaiah. See page 8 for a complete listing of this course.

TRACK 2: *An Overview of Isaiah in 6 Days*
☐ Day 1. Read the Introduction to Isaiah and also chapter 6. This chapter describes Isaiah's dramatic call.
☐ Day 2. Read chapter 25, a song of praise.
☐ Day 3. Read chapter 40, a great description of God and his power over the whole earth.
☐ Day 4. Read chapter 52, which gives detailed descriptions of God's ultimate plan.
☐ Day 5. Read chapter 53, a remarkable prophecy quoted at least ten times in the New Testament.
☐ Day 6. Read chapter 55, a word of great comfort from God.

Now turn to page 9 for your next Track 2 reading project.

TRACK 3: *All of Isaiah in 63 Days*
After you have read through Isaiah, turn to pages 10–14 for your next Track 3 reading project.

☐1	☐2	☐3	☐4–5	☐6	☐7	☐8	☐9
☐10	☐11	☐12	☐13	☐14	☐15	☐16	☐17
☐18	☐19–20	☐21	☐22	☐23	☐24	☐25	☐26
☐27	☐28	☐29	☐30	☐31	☐32	☐33	☐34
☐35	☐36	☐37	☐38–39	☐40	☐41	☐42	☐43
☐44	☐45	☐46	☐47	☐48	☐49	☐50	☐51
☐52	☐53	☐54	☐55	☐56	☐57	☐58	☐59
☐60	☐61	☐62	☐63	☐64	☐65	☐66	

1 The vision of Isaiah son of Amoz, which he saw concerning Judah and Jerusalem in the days of Uzziah, Jotham, Ahaz, and Hezekiah, kings of Judah.

The Wickedness of Judah

2 Hear, O heavens, and listen, O earth;
　　for the Lord has spoken:
I reared children and brought them up,
　　but they have rebelled against me.
3 The ox knows its owner,
　　and the donkey its master's crib;
but Israel does not know,
　　my people do not understand.

4 Ah, sinful nation,
　　people laden with iniquity,
offspring who do evil,
　　children who deal corruptly,
who have forsaken the Lord,
　　who have despised the Holy One of
　　　　Israel,
　　who are utterly estranged!

5 Why do you seek further beatings?
　　Why do you continue to rebel?
The whole head is sick,
　　and the whole heart faint.
6 From the sole of the foot even to the
　　　　head,
　　there is no soundness in it,
but bruises and sores
　　and bleeding wounds;
they have not been drained, or bound up,
　　or softened with oil.

7 Your country lies desolate,
　　your cities are burned with fire;
in your very presence
　　aliens devour your land;
　　it is desolate, as overthrown by
　　　　foreigners.
8 And daughter Zion is left
　　like a booth in a vineyard,
like a shelter in a cucumber field,
　　like a besieged city.
9 If the Lord of hosts
　　had not left us a few survivors,
we would have been like Sodom,
　　and become like Gomorrah.

10 Hear the word of the Lord,
　　you rulers of Sodom!
Listen to the teaching of our God,
　　you people of Gomorrah!
11 What to me is the multitude of your
　　　　sacrifices?
　　says the Lord;

I have had enough of burnt offerings of
　　　　rams
　　and the fat of fed beasts;
I do not delight in the blood of bulls,
　　or of lambs, or of goats.

12 When you come to appear before me,[a]
　　who asked this from your hand?
　　Trample my courts no more;
13 bringing offerings is futile;
　　incense is an abomination to me.
New moon and sabbath and calling of
　　　　convocation—
　　I cannot endure solemn assemblies
　　　　with iniquity.
14 Your new moons and your appointed
　　　　festivals
　　my soul hates;
they have become a burden to me,
　　I am weary of bearing them.

1.14 The New Sodom

Is God finished with Israel? He denounces them as "Sodom and Gomorrah" (verse 10), judging their worship worthless, and their prayers an insult. But just when his tirade reaches its peak, God invites the Israelites to "come . . . argue" with him. Sins "like scarlet" shall be "like snow" (verse 18). God judges his people not to destroy them, but to bring them to repentance, forgiveness, and redemption.

15 When you stretch out your hands,
　　I will hide my eyes from you;
even though you make many prayers,
　　I will not listen;
　　your hands are full of blood.
16 Wash yourselves; make yourselves clean;
　　remove the evil of your doings
　　　　from before my eyes;
cease to do evil,
17 　　learn to do good;
seek justice,
　　rescue the oppressed,
defend the orphan,
　　plead for the widow.

18 Come now, let us argue it out,
　　says the Lord:
though your sins are like scarlet,
　　they shall be like snow;
though they are red like crimson,
　　they shall become like wool.
19 If you are willing and obedient,
　　you shall eat the good of the land;
20 but if you refuse and rebel,

you shall be devoured by the sword;
for the mouth of the LORD has spoken.

The Degenerate City

21 How the faithful city
has become a whore!
She that was full of justice,
righteousness lodged in her—
but now murderers!
22 Your silver has become dross,
your wine is mixed with water.
23 Your princes are rebels
and companions of thieves.
Everyone loves a bribe
and runs after gifts.
They do not defend the orphan,
and the widow's cause does not come
before them.

1.23 Justice, Not Religion

*Isaiah 1 paints a striking picture of conditions
in Judah. Descriptions of luxury indicate the
nation was prospering economically. There
was no shortage of offerings, prayers, and
religious celebrations (verses 11–17). But Isaiah
condemned Judah for not putting religion into
practice by defending weak people, such as
widows and the fatherless. The country's
prosperity had come at the poor's expense.*

24 Therefore says the Sovereign, the LORD of
hosts, the Mighty One of Israel:
Ah, I will pour out my wrath on my
enemies,
and avenge myself on my foes!
25 I will turn my hand against you;
I will smelt away your dross as with lye
and remove all your alloy.
26 And I will restore your judges as at the
first,
and your counselors as at the
beginning.
Afterward you shall be called the city of
righteousness,
the faithful city.

27 Zion shall be redeemed by justice,
and those in her who repent, by
righteousness.
28 But rebels and sinners shall be destroyed
together,
and those who forsake the LORD shall
be consumed.
29 For you shall be ashamed of the oaks
in which you delighted;
and you shall blush for the gardens
that you have chosen.

30 For you shall be like an oak
whose leaf withers,
and like a garden without water.
31 The strong shall become like tinder,
and their work[b] like a spark;
they and their work shall burn together,
with no one to quench them.

The Future House of God

2 The word that Isaiah son of Amoz saw concerning Judah and Jerusalem.

2 In days to come
the mountain of the LORD's house
shall be established as the highest of the
mountains,
and shall be raised above the hills;
all the nations shall stream to it.
3 Many peoples shall come and say,
"Come, let us go up to the mountain of
the LORD,
to the house of the God of Jacob;
that he may teach us his ways
and that we may walk in his paths."
For out of Zion shall go forth instruction,
and the word of the LORD from
Jerusalem.
4 He shall judge between the nations,
and shall arbitrate for many peoples;
they shall beat their swords into
plowshares,
and their spears into pruning hooks;
nation shall not lift up sword against
nation,
neither shall they learn war any more.

Judgment Pronounced on Arrogance

5 O house of Jacob,
come, let us walk
in the light of the LORD!
6 For you have forsaken the ways of[c] your
people,
O house of Jacob.
Indeed they are full of diviners[d] from the
east
and of soothsayers like the Philistines,
and they clasp hands with foreigners.
7 Their land is filled with silver and gold,
and there is no end to their treasures;
their land is filled with horses,
and there is no end to their chariots.
8 Their land is filled with idols;
they bow down to the work of their
hands,
to what their own fingers have made.
9 And so people are humbled,
and everyone is brought low—
do not forgive them!
10 Enter into the rock,

---

b Or *its makers*   *c* Heb lacks *the ways of*   *d* Cn: Heb lacks *of diviners*

and hide in the dust
from the terror of the LORD,
and from the glory of his majesty.
11 The haughty eyes of people shall be
brought low,
and the pride of everyone shall be
humbled;
and the LORD alone will be exalted on
that day.
12 For the LORD of hosts has a day
against all that is proud and lofty,
against all that is lifted up and high;*e*
13 against all the cedars of Lebanon,
lofty and lifted up;
and against all the oaks of Bashan;
14 against all the high mountains,
and against all the lofty hills;
15 against every high tower,
and against every fortified wall;
16 against all the ships of Tarshish,
and against all the beautiful craft.*f*
17 The haughtiness of people shall be
humbled,
and the pride of everyone shall be
brought low;
and the LORD alone will be exalted on
that day.
18 The idols shall utterly pass away.
19 Enter the caves of the rocks
and the holes of the ground,
from the terror of the LORD,
and from the glory of his majesty,
when he rises to terrify the earth.
20 On that day people will throw away
to the moles and to the bats
their idols of silver and their idols of gold,
which they made for themselves to
worship,
21 to enter the caverns of the rocks
and the clefts in the crags,
from the terror of the LORD,
and from the glory of his majesty,
when he rises to terrify the earth.
22 Turn away from mortals,
who have only breath in their nostrils,
for of what account are they?

3 For now the Sovereign, the LORD of hosts,
is taking away from Jerusalem and
from Judah
support and staff—
all support of bread,
and all support of water—
2 warrior and soldier,
judge and prophet,
diviner and elder,
3 captain of fifty
and dignitary,
counselor and skillful magician
and expert enchanter.

4 And I will make boys their princes,
and babes shall rule over them.
5 The people will be oppressed,
everyone by another
and everyone by a neighbor;
the youth will be insolent to the elder,
and the base to the honorable.

6 Someone will even seize a relative,
a member of the clan, saying,
"You have a cloak;
you shall be our leader,
and this heap of ruins
shall be under your rule."

3.6 Total Anarchy

*Isaiah foresees a time of judgment on Judah,
when total anarchy will prevail. Leaders will be
chosen at random, and the nation's supply of
young men will be decimated by war (verse
25). The vivid passage on the haughty women
of Zion (3.16–4.1) shows why this book is
admired for its writing style.*

7 But the other will cry out on that day,
saying,
"I will not be a healer;
in my house there is neither bread nor
cloak;
you shall not make me
leader of the people."
8 For Jerusalem has stumbled
and Judah has fallen,
because their speech and their deeds are
against the LORD,
defying his glorious presence.

9 The look on their faces bears witness
against them;
they proclaim their sin like Sodom,
they do not hide it.
Woe to them!
For they have brought evil on
themselves.
10 Tell the innocent how fortunate they are,
for they shall eat the fruit of their
labors.
11 Woe to the guilty! How unfortunate they
are,
for what their hands have done shall be
done to them.
12 My people—children are their oppressors,
and women rule over them.
O my people, your leaders mislead you,
and confuse the course of your paths.

e Cn Compare Gk: Heb *low*   *f* Compare Gk: Meaning of Heb uncertain

13 The LORD rises to argue his case;
    he stands to judge the peoples.
14 The LORD enters into judgment
    with the elders and princes of his
        people:
It is you who have devoured the vineyard;
    the spoil of the poor is in your houses.
15 What do you mean by crushing my
        people,
    by grinding the face of the poor? says
        the Lord GOD of hosts.

16 The LORD said:
Because the daughters of Zion are
        haughty
    and walk with outstretched necks,
    glancing wantonly with their eyes,
mincing along as they go,
    tinkling with their feet;
17 the Lord will afflict with scabs
    the heads of the daughters of Zion,
    and the LORD will lay bare their secret
        parts.

18 In that day the Lord will take away the finery of the anklets, the headbands, and the crescents; 19the pendants, the bracelets, and the scarfs; 20the headdresses, the armlets, the sashes, the perfume boxes, and the amulets; 21the signet rings and nose rings; 22the festal robes, the mantles, the cloaks, and the handbags; 23the garments of gauze, the linen garments, the turbans, and the veils.
24 Instead of perfume there will be a stench;
    and instead of a sash, a rope;
and instead of well set hair, baldness;
    and instead of a rich robe, a binding of
        sackcloth;
    instead of beauty, shame.g
25 Your men shall fall by the sword
    and your warriors in battle.
26 And her gates shall lament and mourn;
    ravaged, she shall sit upon the ground.

4 Seven women shall take hold of one man in that day, saying,
"We will eat our own bread and wear our
        own clothes;
just let us be called by your name;
    take away our disgrace."

The Future Glory of the Survivors in Zion

2 On that day the branch of the LORD shall be beautiful and glorious, and the fruit of the land shall be the pride and glory of the survivors of Israel. 3Whoever is left in Zion and remains in Jerusalem will be called holy, everyone who has been recorded for life in Jerusalem, 4once the Lord has washed away the filth of the daughters of Zion and cleansed the bloodstains of Jerusalem

from its midst by a spirit of judgment and by a spirit of burning. 5Then the LORD will create over the whole site of Mount Zion and over its places of assembly a cloud by day and smoke and the shining of a flaming fire by night. Indeed over all the glory there will be a canopy. 6It will serve as a pavilion, a shade by day from the heat, and a refuge and a shelter from the storm and rain.

The Song of the Unfruitful Vineyard

5 Let me sing for my beloved
    my love-song concerning his vineyard:
My beloved had a vineyard
    on a very fertile hill.
2 He dug it and cleared it of stones,
    and planted it with choice vines;
he built a watchtower in the midst of it,
    and hewed out a wine vat in it;
he expected it to yield grapes,
    but it yielded wild grapes.

3 And now, inhabitants of Jerusalem
    and people of Judah,
judge between me
    and my vineyard.
4 What more was there to do for my
        vineyard
    that I have not done in it?
When I expected it to yield grapes,
    why did it yield wild grapes?

5.4 What Can God Do?

The "Song of the Unfruitful Vineyard" beautifully summarizes God's message to Judah. Although he had done everything possible to care for the nation, his "vineyard"—the house of Israel—had produced only wild grapes. What else could he do but allow it to grow wild and uncultivated? Jesus used a related analogy in some of his parables (Matthew 20.1–16; 21.33–46; Mark 12.1–12; Luke 13.6–9; 20.9–19).

5 And now I will tell you
    what I will do to my vineyard.
I will remove its hedge,
    and it shall be devoured;
I will break down its wall,
    and it shall be trampled down.
6 I will make it a waste;
    it shall not be pruned or hoed,
    and it shall be overgrown with briers
        and thorns;
I will also command the clouds
    that they rain no rain upon it.

7 For the vineyard of the LORD of hosts

g Q Ms: MT lacks *shame*

is the house of Israel,
and the people of Judah
are his pleasant planting;
he expected justice,
but saw bloodshed;
righteousness,
but heard a cry!

Social Injustice Denounced

8 Ah, you who join house to house,
who add field to field,
until there is room for no one but you,
and you are left to live alone
in the midst of the land!
9 The LORD of hosts has sworn in my
hearing:
Surely many houses shall be desolate,
large and beautiful houses, without
inhabitant.
10 For ten acres of vineyard shall yield but
one bath,
and a homer of seed shall yield a mere
ephah.*h*

11 Ah, you who rise early in the morning
in pursuit of strong drink,
who linger in the evening
to be inflamed by wine,
12 whose feasts consist of lyre and harp,
tambourine and flute and wine,
but who do not regard the deeds of the
LORD,
or see the work of his hands!
13 Therefore my people go into exile without
knowledge;
their nobles are dying of hunger,
and their multitude is parched with
thirst.

14 Therefore Sheol has enlarged its appetite
and opened its mouth beyond measure;
the nobility of Jerusalem*i* and her
multitude go down,
her throng and all who exult in her.
15 People are bowed down, everyone is
brought low,
and the eyes of the haughty are
humbled.
16 But the LORD of hosts is exalted
by justice,
and the Holy God shows himself holy
by righteousness.
17 Then the lambs shall graze as in their
pasture,
fatlings and kids*j* shall feed among the
ruins.

18 Ah, you who drag iniquity along with
cords of falsehood,

who drag sin along as with cart ropes,
19 who say, "Let him make haste,
let him speed his work
that we may see it;
let the plan of the Holy One of Israel
hasten to fulfillment,
that we may know it!"
20 Ah, you who call evil good
and good evil,
who put darkness for light
and light for darkness,
who put bitter for sweet
and sweet for bitter!
21 Ah, you who are wise in your own eyes,
and shrewd in your own sight!
22 Ah, you who are heroes in drinking wine
and valiant at mixing drink,
23 who acquit the guilty for a bribe,
and deprive the innocent of their
rights!

Foreign Invasion Predicted

24 Therefore, as the tongue of fire devours
the stubble,
and as dry grass sinks down in the
flame,
so their root will become rotten,
and their blossom go up like dust;
for they have rejected the instruction of
the LORD of hosts,
and have despised the word of the
Holy One of Israel.

25 Therefore the anger of the LORD was
kindled against his people,
and he stretched out his hand against
them and struck them;
the mountains quaked,
and their corpses were like refuse
in the streets.
For all this his anger has not turned away,
and his hand is stretched out still.

26 He will raise a signal for a nation far
away,
and whistle for a people at the ends of
the earth;
Here they come, swiftly, speedily!
27 None of them is weary, none stumbles,
none slumbers or sleeps,
not a loincloth is loose,
not a sandal-thong broken;
28 their arrows are sharp,
all their bows bent,
their horses' hoofs seem like flint,
and their wheels like the whirlwind.
29 Their roaring is like a lion,
like young lions they roar;
they growl and seize their prey,

---

h The Heb *bath*, *homer*, and *ephah* are measures of quantity   *i* Heb *her nobility*   *j* Cn Compare Gk: Heb *aliens*

they carry it off, and no one
can rescue.
30 They will roar over it on that day,
like the roaring of the sea.
And if one look to the land—
only darkness and distress;
and the light grows dark with clouds.

A Vision of God in the Temple

6 In the year that King Uzziah died, I saw the
Lord sitting on a throne, high and lofty; and
the hem of his robe filled the temple. 2Seraphs
were in attendance above him; each had six
wings: with two they covered their faces, and with

6.2 A Message from God

*Isaiah experienced a dramatic call from God
to become a prophet. The message was
personally delivered by seraphs, a term that
appears only here and means "something
burning and dazzling." Evidently, seraphs were
angels who acted as spokesmen for God.*

---

two they covered their feet, and with two they
flew. 3And one called to another and said:

"Holy, holy, holy is the LORD of hosts;
the whole earth is full of his glory."

4The pivots[k] on the thresholds shook at the
voices of those who called, and the house filled
with smoke. 5And I said: "Woe is me! I am lost,
for I am a man of unclean lips, and I live among
a people of unclean lips; yet my eyes have seen the
King, the LORD of hosts!"

6 Then one of the seraphs flew to me, holding
a live coal that had been taken from the altar with
a pair of tongs. 7The seraph[l] touched my mouth
with it and said: "Now that this has touched your
lips, your guilt has departed and your sin is blotted out." 8Then I heard the voice of the Lord
saying, "Whom shall I send, and who will go for
us?" And I said, "Here am I; send me!" 9And he
said, "Go and say to this people:

'Keep listening, but do not comprehend;
keep looking, but do not understand.'

10 Make the mind of this people dull,
and stop their ears,
and shut their eyes,
so that they may not look with their eyes,
and listen with their ears,
and comprehend with their minds,
and turn and be healed."

11 Then I said, "How long, O Lord?" And he
said:

"Until cities lie waste
without inhabitant,
and houses without people,

and the land is utterly desolate;
12 until the LORD sends everyone far away,
and vast is the emptiness in the midst
of the land.
13 Even if a tenth part remain in it,
it will be burned again,
like a terebinth or an oak
whose stump remains standing
when it is felled."[k]
The holy seed is its stump.

Isaiah Reassures King Ahaz

7 In the days of Ahaz son of Jotham son of
Uzziah, king of Judah, King Rezin of Aram
and King Pekah son of Remaliah of Israel went up
to attack Jerusalem, but could not mount an attack against it. 2When the house of David heard
that Aram had allied itself with Ephraim, the
heart of Ahaz[m] and the heart of his people shook
as the trees of the forest shake before the wind.

3 Then the LORD said to Isaiah, Go out to
meet Ahaz, you and your son Shear-jashub,[n] at
the end of the conduit of the upper pool on the
highway to the Fuller's Field, 4and say to him,
Take heed, be quiet, do not fear, and do not let
your heart be faint because of these two smoldering stumps of firebrands, because of the fierce
anger of Rezin and Aram and the son of Remaliah. 5Because Aram—with Ephraim and the son
of Remaliah—has plotted evil against you, saying, 6Let us go up against Judah and cut off Jerusalem[o] and conquer it for ourselves and make
the son of Tabeel king in it; 7therefore thus says
the Lord GOD:

It shall not stand,
and it shall not come to pass.
8 For the head of Aram is Damascus,
and the head of Damascus is Rezin.

(Within sixty-five years Ephraim will be shattered, no longer a people.)

9 The head of Ephraim is Samaria,
and the head of Samaria is the son of
Remaliah.
If you do not stand firm in faith,
you shall not stand at all.

Isaiah Gives Ahaz the Sign of Immanuel

10 Again the LORD spoke to Ahaz, saying,
11Ask a sign of the LORD your God; let it be deep
as Sheol or high as heaven. 12But Ahaz said, I will
not ask, and I will not put the LORD to the test.
13Then Isaiah[p] said: "Hear then, O house of David! Is it too little for you to weary mortals, that
you weary my God also? 14Therefore the Lord
himself will give you a sign. Look, the young
woman[q] is with child and shall bear a son, and
shall name him Immanuel.[r] 15He shall eat curds
and honey by the time he knows how to refuse the

---

k Meaning of Heb uncertain   l Heb He   m Heb his heart   n That is A remnant shall return   o Heb cut it off
p Heb he   q Gk the virgin   r That is God is with us

evil and choose the good. [16]For before the child knows how to refuse the evil and choose the good, the land before whose two kings you are in dread will be deserted. [17]The LORD will bring on you and

7.14 A Famous Sign

Like so many prophecies, this one probably had two meanings: one for Isaiah's time and another much later. Isaiah urged King Ahaz to seek a sign from God about Judah's safety from its neighbors. Ahaz, notoriously stubborn and ungodly, refused.

Isaiah told of the sign anyway: A young boy would be born, and before he grew out of childhood Judah's feared enemies would be destroyed. Only 12 years after this prediction, the Northern Kingdom of Israel fell. The New Testament sees a further meaning in this prophecy, applying it to the birth of Jesus Christ (Matthew 1.23).

on your people and on your ancestral house such days as have not come since the day that Ephraim departed from Judah—the king of Assyria."

18 On that day the LORD will whistle for the fly that is at the sources of the streams of Egypt, and for the bee that is in the land of Assyria. [19]And they will all come and settle in the steep ravines, and in the clefts of the rocks, and on all the thornbushes, and on all the pastures.

20 On that day the Lord will shave with a razor hired beyond the River—with the king of Assyria—the head and the hair of the feet, and it will take off the beard as well.

21 On that day one will keep alive a young cow and two sheep, [22]and will eat curds because of the abundance of milk that they give; for everyone that is left in the land shall eat curds and honey.

23 On that day every place where there used to be a thousand vines, worth a thousand shekels of silver, will become briers and thorns. [24]With bow and arrows one will go there, for all the land will be briers and thorns; [25]and as for all the hills that used to be hoed with a hoe, you will not go there for fear of briers and thorns; but they will become a place where cattle are let loose and where sheep tread.

Isaiah's Son a Sign of the Assyrian Invasion

8 Then the LORD said to me, Take a large tablet and write on it in common characters, "Belonging to Maher-shalal-hash-baz,"[s] [2]and have it attested[t] for me by reliable witnesses, the priest Uriah and Zechariah son of Jeberechiah. [3]And I

went to the prophetess, and she conceived and bore a son. Then the LORD said to me, Name him Maher-shalal-hash-baz; [4]for before the child knows how to call "My father" or "My mother," the wealth of Damascus and the spoil of Samaria will be carried away by the king of Assyria.

5 The LORD spoke to me again: [6]Because this people has refused the waters of Shiloah that flow gently, and melt in fear before[u] Rezin and the son of Remaliah; [7]therefore, the Lord is bringing up against it the mighty flood waters of the River, the king of Assyria and all his glory; it will rise above all its channels and overflow all its banks; [8]it will sweep on into Judah as a flood, and, pouring over, it will reach up to the neck; and its outspread wings will fill the breadth of your land, O Immanuel.

9 Band together, you peoples, and be
          dismayed;
     listen, all you far countries;
gird yourselves and be dismayed;
     gird yourselves and be dismayed!
10 Take counsel together, but it shall be
          brought to naught;
     speak a word, but it will not stand,
     for God is with us.[v]

11 For the LORD spoke thus to me while his hand was strong upon me, and warned me not to walk in the way of this people, saying: [12]Do not call conspiracy all that this people calls conspiracy, and do not fear what it fears, or be in dread. [13]But the LORD of hosts, him you shall regard as holy; let him be your fear, and let him be your dread. [14]He will become a sanctuary, a stone one strikes against; for both houses of Israel he will become a rock one stumbles over—a trap and a snare for the inhabitants of Jerusalem. [15]And many among them shall stumble; they shall fall and be broken; they shall be snared and taken.

Disciples of Isaiah

16 Bind up the testimony, seal the teaching among my disciples. [17]I will wait for the LORD, who is hiding his face from the house of Jacob, and I will hope in him. [18]See, I and the children whom the LORD has given me are signs and portents in Israel from the LORD of hosts, who dwells on Mount Zion. [19]Now if people say to you, "Consult the ghosts and the familiar spirits that chirp and mutter; should not a people consult their gods, the dead on behalf of the living, [20]for teaching and for instruction?" surely, those who speak like this will have no dawn! [21]They will pass through the land,[w] greatly distressed and hungry; when they are hungry, they will be enraged and will curse[x] their king and their gods. They will turn their faces upward, [22]or they will look to the

---

[s] That is *The spoil speeds, the prey hastens*   [t] Q Ms Gk Syr: MT *and I caused to be attested*   [u] Cn: Meaning of Heb uncertain   [v] Heb *immanu el*   [w] Heb *it*   [x] Or *curse by*

earth, but will see only distress and darkness, the gloom of anguish; and they will be thrust into thick darkness.*y*

The Righteous Reign of the Coming King

9 *z* But there will be no gloom for those who were in anguish. In the former time he brought into contempt the land of Zebulun and the land of Naphtali, but in the latter time he will make glorious the way of the sea, the land beyond the Jordan, Galilee of the nations.

2*a* The people who walked in darkness
      have seen a great light;
   those who lived in a land of deep
            darkness—
      on them light has shined.
3 You have multiplied the nation,
      you have increased its joy;
   they rejoice before you
      as with joy at the harvest,
      as people exult when dividing plunder.
4 For the yoke of their burden,
      and the bar across their shoulders,
      the rod of their oppressor,
      you have broken as on the day of
            Midian.
5 For all the boots of the tramping warriors
      and all the garments rolled in blood
      shall be burned as fuel for the fire.
6 For a child has been born for us,
      a son given to us;
   authority rests upon his shoulders;
      and he is named
   Wonderful Counselor, Mighty God,
      Everlasting Father, Prince of Peace.

9.6 A Child Is Born

Isaiah includes many direct predictions of the coming Messiah, including this passage, which established that the Messiah will come from Galilee (verse 1). The lands Isaiah mentions as "brought into contempt" in verse 1 are the very regions devastated by Assyria's armies (2 Kings 15.29). Thus Isaiah offers a word of distant hope for those parts of his nation most affected by war.

7 His authority shall grow continually,
      and there shall be endless peace
   for the throne of David and his kingdom.
   He will establish and uphold it
   with justice and with righteousness
      from this time onward and
            forevermore.
   The zeal of the LORD of hosts will do this.

Judgment on Arrogance and Oppression

8 The Lord sent a word against Jacob,
      and it fell on Israel;
9 and all the people knew it—
      Ephraim and the inhabitants of
            Samaria—
   but in pride and arrogance of heart
      they said:
10 "The bricks have fallen,
      but we will build with dressed stones;
   the sycamores have been cut down,
      but we will put cedars in their place."
11 So the LORD raised adversaries*b* against
            them,
      and stirred up their enemies,
12 the Arameans on the east and the
            Philistines on the west,
      and they devoured Israel with open
            mouth.
   For all this his anger has not turned away;
      his hand is stretched out still.

13 The people did not turn to him who
            struck them,
      or seek the LORD of hosts.
14 So the LORD cut off from Israel head and
            tail,
      palm branch and reed in one day—
15 elders and dignitaries are the head,
      and prophets who teach lies are the
            tail;
16 for those who led this people led them
            astray,
      and those who were led by them were
            left in confusion.
17 That is why the Lord did not have pity
            on*c* their young people,
      or compassion on their orphans and
            widows;
   for everyone was godless and an evildoer,
      and every mouth spoke folly.
   For all this his anger has not turned away;
      his hand is stretched out still.

18 For wickedness burned like a fire,
      consuming briers and thorns;
   it kindled the thickets of the forest,
      and they swirled upward in a column
            of smoke.
19 Through the wrath of the LORD of hosts
      the land was burned,
   and the people became like fuel for the
            fire;
      no one spared another.
20 They gorged on the right, but still were
            hungry,
      and they devoured on the left, but were
            not satisfied;

---

y Meaning of Heb uncertain   *z* Ch 8.23 in Heb   *a* Ch 9.1 in Heb   *b* Cn: Heb *the adversaries of Rezin*
c Q Ms: MT *rejoice over*

they devoured the flesh of their own
    kindred;[d]
21 Manasseh devoured Ephraim, and
    Ephraim Manasseh,
    and together they were against Judah.
For all this his anger has not turned away;
    his hand is stretched out still.

10

Ah, you who make iniquitous decrees,
    who write oppressive statutes,
2 to turn aside the needy from justice
    and to rob the poor of my people of
      their right,
that widows may be your spoil,
    and that you may make the orphans
      your prey!
3 What will you do on the day of
      punishment,
    in the calamity that will come from far
      away?
To whom will you flee for help,
    and where will you leave your wealth,
4 so as not to crouch among the prisoners
    or fall among the slain?
For all this his anger has not turned away;
    his hand is stretched out still.

Arrogant Assyria Also Judged

5 Ah, Assyria, the rod of my anger—
    the club in their hands is my fury!
6 Against a godless nation I send him,
    and against the people of my wrath I
      command him,
to take spoil and seize plunder,
    and to tread them down like the mire
      of the streets.
7 But this is not what he intends,
    nor does he have this in mind;
but it is in his heart to destroy,
    and to cut off nations not a few.

10.7 God's Hand in History

*In this comment, God reveals how he works
through history in hidden, indirect ways. The
pagan empire Assyria had no idea it was being
used by the true God—it dealt with Jerusalem
just as it dealt with any nation and its idols
(verse 11). Nevertheless, Assyria would serve
God's purpose, and would one day be punished
for its own pride and greed (verse 12).*

8 For he says:
    "Are not my commanders all kings?
9 Is not Calno like Carchemish?
    Is not Hamath like Arpad?

Is not Samaria like Damascus?
10 As my hand has reached to the kingdoms
      of the idols
    whose images were greater than those
      of Jerusalem and Samaria,
11 shall I not do to Jerusalem and her idols
    what I have done to Samaria and her
      images?"

12 When the Lord has finished all his work
on Mount Zion and on Jerusalem, he[e] will punish the arrogant boasting of the king of Assyria
and his haughty pride. 13For he says:
    "By the strength of my hand I have done
      it,
    and by my wisdom, for I have
      understanding;
I have removed the boundaries of
      peoples,
    and have plundered their treasures;
    like a bull I have brought down those
      who sat on thrones.
14 My hand has found, like a nest,
    the wealth of the peoples;
and as one gathers eggs that have been
      forsaken,
    so I have gathered all the earth;
and there was none that moved a wing,
    or opened its mouth, or chirped."

15 Shall the ax vaunt itself over the one who
      wields it,
    or the saw magnify itself against the
      one who handles it?
As if a rod should raise the one who lifts
      it up,
    or as if a staff should lift the one who
      is not wood!
16 Therefore the Sovereign, the LORD of
      hosts,
    will send wasting sickness among his
      stout warriors,
and under his glory a burning will be
      kindled,
    like the burning of fire.
17 The light of Israel will become a fire,
    and his Holy One a flame;
and it will burn and devour
    his thorns and briers in one day.
18 The glory of his forest and his fruitful
      land
    the LORD will destroy, both soul and
      body,
    and it will be as when an invalid wastes
      away.
19 The remnant of the trees of his forest will
      be so few
    that a child can write them down.

---

[d] Or *arm*   [e] Heb *I*

The Repentant Remnant of Israel

20 On that day the remnant of Israel and the survivors of the house of Jacob will no more lean on the one who struck them, but will lean on the LORD, the Holy One of Israel, in truth. 21A remnant will return, the remnant of Jacob, to the mighty God. 22For though your people Israel were like the sand of the sea, only a remnant of them will return. Destruction is decreed, overflowing with righteousness. 23For the Lord GOD of hosts will make a full end, as decreed, in all the earth.ᶠ

24 Therefore thus says the Lord GOD of hosts: O my people, who live in Zion, do not be afraid of the Assyrians when they beat you with a rod and lift up their staff against you as the Egyptians did. 25For in a very little while my indignation will come to an end, and my anger will be directed to their destruction. 26The LORD of hosts will wield a whip against them, as when he struck Midian at the rock of Oreb; his staff will be over the sea, and he will lift it as he did in Egypt. 27On that day his burden will be removed from your shoulder, and his yoke will be destroyed from your neck.

28 He has gone up from Rimmon,ᵍ
he has come to Aiath;
he has passed through Migron,
at Michmash he stores his baggage;
29 they have crossed over the pass,
at Geba they lodge for the night;
Ramah trembles,
Gibeah of Saul has fled.
30 Cry aloud, O daughter Gallim!
Listen, O Laishah!
Answer her, O Anathoth!
31 Madmenah is in flight,
the inhabitants of Gebim flee for safety.
32 This very day he will halt at Nob,
he will shake his fist
at the mount of daughter Zion,
the hill of Jerusalem.

33 Look, the Sovereign, the LORD of hosts,
will lop the boughs with terrifying
power;
the tallest trees will be cut down,
and the lofty will be brought low.
34 He will hack down the thickets of the
forest with an ax,
and Lebanon with its majestic treesʰ
will fall.

The Peaceful Kingdom

11 A shoot shall come out from the stump of
Jesse,
and a branch shall grow out of his
roots.

2 The spirit of the LORD shall rest on him,
the spirit of wisdom and
understanding,
the spirit of counsel and might,
the spirit of knowledge and the fear of
the LORD.

11.1–16 The Good Old Days

To express his message of hope to the Israelite people, Isaiah appealed to their fondest memories. This chapter borrows images from three of the greatest events from the past: the prosperous dynasty of David when Israel was united (verse 1); the Garden of Eden (verses 6–9); and the miracles of the exodus from Egypt (verse 15). Whatever the state of "the good old days," the future time of peace will exceed it.

3 His delight shall be in the fear of the
LORD.

He shall not judge by what his eyes see,
or decide by what his ears hear;
4 but with righteousness he shall judge the
poor,
and decide with equity for the meek of
the earth;
he shall strike the earth with the rod of
his mouth,
and with the breath of his lips he shall
kill the wicked.
5 Righteousness shall be the belt around his
waist,
and faithfulness the belt around his
loins.

6 The wolf shall live with the lamb,
the leopard shall lie down with the kid,
the calf and the lion and the fatling
together,
and a little child shall lead them.
7 The cow and the bear shall graze,
their young shall lie down together;
and the lion shall eat straw like the ox.
8 The nursing child shall play over the hole
of the asp,
and the weaned child shall put its hand
on the adder's den.
9 They will not hurt or destroy
on all my holy mountain;
for the earth will be full of the knowledge
of the LORD
as the waters cover the sea.

ᶠ Or land   ᵍ Cn: Heb and his yoke from your neck, and a yoke will be destroyed because of fatness   ʰ Cn Compare
Gk Vg: Heb with a majestic one

Return of the Remnant of Israel and Judah

10 On that day the root of Jesse shall stand as a signal to the peoples; the nations shall inquire of him, and his dwelling shall be glorious.

11 On that day the Lord will extend his hand yet a second time to recover the remnant that is left of his people, from Assyria, from Egypt, from Pathros, from Ethiopia,ⁱ from Elam, from Shinar, from Hamath, and from the coastlands of the sea.

12 He will raise a signal for the nations,
    and will assemble the outcasts of Israel,
and gather the dispersed of Judah
    from the four corners of the earth.
13 The jealousy of Ephraim shall depart,
    the hostility of Judah shall be cut off;
Ephraim shall not be jealous of Judah,
    and Judah shall not be hostile towards
        Ephraim.
14 But they shall swoop down on the backs
        of the Philistines in the west,
    together they shall plunder the people
        of the east.
They shall put forth their hand against
        Edom and Moab,
    and the Ammonites shall obey them.
15 And the Lord will utterly destroy
    the tongue of the sea of Egypt;
and will wave his hand over the River
    with his scorching wind;
and will split it into seven channels,
    and make a way to cross on foot;
16 so there shall be a highway from Assyria
    for the remnant that is left of
        his people,
as there was for Israel
    when they came up from the land of
        Egypt.

Thanksgiving and Praise

12 You will say in that day:
I will give thanks to you, O Lord,
    for though you were angry with me,
your anger turned away,
    and you comforted me.

2 Surely God is my salvation;
    I will trust, and will not be afraid,
for the Lord God ^j is my strength and
        my might;
    he has become my salvation.

3 With joy you will draw water from the wells of salvation. ⁴And you will say in that day:
    Give thanks to the Lord,
        call on his name;

make known his deeds among the
        nations;
    proclaim that his name is exalted.

5 Sing praises to the Lord, for he has done
        gloriously;
    let this be known^k in all the earth.
6 Shout aloud and sing for joy, O royal^l
        Zion,
    for great in your midst is the Holy One
        of Israel.

12.6 A Key Phrase

The first 12 chapters contain specific messages to Judah. But now Isaiah shifts his focus to surrounding nations. He ends the first section with a reference to the "Holy One of Israel," a key phrase that hints at the special relationship between God and his covenant nation. The phrase appears only five times in the rest of the Old Testament, but 26 times in Isaiah.

Proclamation against Babylon

13 The oracle concerning Babylon that Isaiah son of Amoz saw.

2 On a bare hill raise a signal,
    cry aloud to them;
wave the hand for them to enter
    the gates of the nobles.
3 I myself have commanded my consecrated
        ones,
    have summoned my warriors, my
        proudly exulting ones,
    to execute my anger.

4 Listen, a tumult on the mountains
    as of a great multitude!
Listen, an uproar of kingdoms,
    of nations gathering together!
The Lord of hosts is mustering
    an army for battle.
5 They come from a distant land,
    from the end of the heavens,
the Lord and the weapons of his
        indignation,
    to destroy the whole earth.

6 Wail, for the day of the Lord is near;
    it will come like destruction from the
        Almighty!^m
7 Therefore all hands will be feeble,
    and every human heart will melt,
8   and they will be dismayed.
Pangs and agony will seize them;

i Or *Nubia*; Heb *Cush*   j Heb *for Yah, the* LORD   k Or *this is made known*   l Or *O inhabitant of*
m Traditional rendering of Heb *Shaddai*

they will be in anguish like a woman in
labor.
They will look aghast at one another;
their faces will be aflame.
9 See, the day of the LORD comes,
cruel, with wrath and fierce anger,
to make the earth a desolation,
and to destroy its sinners from it.
10 For the stars of the heavens and their
constellations
will not give their light;
the sun will be dark at its rising,
and the moon will not shed its light.
11 I will punish the world for its evil,
and the wicked for their iniquity;
I will put an end to the pride of
the arrogant,
and lay low the insolence of tyrants.
12 I will make mortals more rare than fine
gold,
and humans than the gold of Ophir.
13 Therefore I will make the heavens
tremble,
and the earth will be shaken out of its
place,
at the wrath of the LORD of hosts
in the day of his fierce anger.
14 Like a hunted gazelle,
or like sheep with no one to gather
them,
all will turn to their own people,
and all will flee to their own lands.
15 Whoever is found will be thrust through,
and whoever is caught will fall by the
sword.
16 Their infants will be dashed to pieces
before their eyes;
their houses will be plundered,
and their wives ravished.
17 See, I am stirring up the Medes against
them,
who have no regard for silver
and do not delight in gold.
18 Their bows will slaughter the young men;
they will have no mercy on the fruit of
the womb;
their eyes will not pity children.
19 And Babylon, the glory of kingdoms,
the splendor and pride of the
Chaldeans,
will be like Sodom and Gomorrah
when God overthrew them.
20 It will never be inhabited
or lived in for all generations;
Arabs will not pitch their tents there,
shepherds will not make their flocks lie
down there.
21 But wild animals will lie down there,

and its houses will be full of howling
creatures;
there ostriches will live,
and there goat-demons will dance.
22 Hyenas will cry in its towers,
and jackals in the pleasant palaces;
its time is close at hand,
and its days will not be prolonged.

Restoration of Judah

14 But the LORD will have compassion on Jacob and will again choose Israel, and will
set them in their own land; and aliens will join
them and attach themselves to the house of Jacob.
2And the nations will take them and bring them
to their place, and the house of Israel will possess
the nations[n] as male and female slaves in the
LORD's land; they will take captive those who were
their captors, and rule over those who oppressed
them.

Downfall of the King of Babylon

3 When the LORD has given you rest from
your pain and turmoil and the hard service with
which you were made to serve, 4you will take up
this taunt against the king of Babylon:
How the oppressor has ceased!
How his insolence[o] has ceased!
5 The LORD has broken the staff of the
wicked,
the scepter of rulers,
6 that struck down the peoples in wrath
with unceasing blows,
that ruled the nations in anger
with unrelenting persecution.
7 The whole earth is at rest and quiet;
they break forth into singing.
8 The cypresses exult over you,
the cedars of Lebanon, saying,
"Since you were laid low,
no one comes to cut us down."
9 Sheol beneath is stirred up
to meet you when you come;
it rouses the shades to greet you,
all who were leaders of the earth;
it raises from their thrones
all who were kings of the nations.
10 All of them will speak
and say to you:
"You too have become as weak as we!
You have become like us!"
11 Your pomp is brought down to Sheol,
and the sound of your harps;
maggots are the bed beneath you,
and worms are your covering.

12 How you are fallen from heaven,
O Day Star, son of Dawn!
How you are cut down to the ground,

---

n Heb *them*   o Q Ms Compare Gk Syr Vg: Meaning of MT uncertain

you who laid the nations low!

13 You said in your heart,
   "I will ascend to heaven;
   I will raise my throne
      above the stars of God;
   I will sit on the mount of assembly
      on the heights of Zaphon;ᵖ

14 I will ascend to the tops of the clouds,

I will make myself like the Most High."

15 But you are brought down to Sheol,
   to the depths of the Pit.

16 Those who see you will stare at you,
   and ponder over you:
   "Is this the man who made the earth
      tremble,
   who shook kingdoms,

ᵖ Or *assembly in the far north*

Faith in God or the Military?
Where does a weak nation turn for help?

IN 1944, WILD CHEERING GREETED the Russian tanks that rolled into Poland. The Russians were freeing Poland from the Nazis, and grateful Poles showered the liberating soldiers with fresh flowers.

But 45 years later, Russian troops had worn out their welcome, and the Polish government asked them to leave. The Polish experience offers living proof of a painful lesson of history: Military help from great powers usually comes with strings attached.

> *This is the plan that is planned concerning the whole earth; and this is the hand that is stretched out over all the nations.*
> 14.26

A Small Nation Seeks Help

What can a small nation do when facing a military giant? Judah found itself in that predicament early in Isaiah's career. When two neighboring nations invaded, the tiny kingdom suffered heavy losses. King Ahaz and the people of Judah were shaken, "as the trees of the forest shake before the wind" (7.2). Panicked, Ahaz sought Isaiah's advice.

Isaiah had received a "call" to ministry as dramatic as any recorded in the Bible (chapter 6). King Ahaz knew that Isaiah would deliver a message straight from God, no matter how unpopular. Still, Ahaz was hardly prepared for what Isaiah said: Stay calm, don't worry, simply trust God.

The attacking kings were mere "smoldering stumps of firebrands," Isaiah declared (7.4). Whatever happens, don't seek help from an empire like Assyria; if you do, you will invite in the very army that will one day destroy you.

The Long Slide Begins

But Ahaz, reeling from the invasion, wanted quick relief. Ignoring Isaiah's warnings, he negotiated a treaty with mighty Assyria, using as a bribe the treasury of the temple in Jerusalem.

In the short term, Ahaz's decision brought results. No army of that day could match the Assyrian war machine, and all Judah's enemies fell to the onslaught. Israel, to the north, was wiped off the map. At last Judah had peace. But at what cost?

Perhaps as part of the treaty with Assyria, Ahaz began corrupting Judah's religion. He first closed the doors of the temple to worship, and later replaced the sacred altar to God with a foreign one. He officially adopted Assyria's state religion, going so far as to make a human sacrifice of his sons in a fire. In every way King Ahaz became a puppet king, under the thumb of Assyria. Foreign armies stayed in Judah. Indeed, Assyria's help had come with strings attached.

Messages for Then and Now

The prophet Isaiah was furious. He had grown up in a boom time in Judah, under a good king. Suddenly he saw his country become a mere pawn of Assyria, trading away even its great religious heritage.

Chapters 7—19 record his passionate words, not only against Judah, but against her neighbors also. He told of a reckoning day, when each nation would be punished for its sin and rebellion. The immediate future looked very bleak, and Isaiah minced no words in describing it.

But Isaiah did not stop there. He went on to project far into the future, in familiar words that still stir up hope and longing. This section begins with a question from a king about where to turn for help. It ends with a grand sweep of all of history.

Life Questions: What do you think Isaiah would say if he were writing today about such superpower countries as the United States and Russia?

17 who made the world like a desert
and overthrew its cities,
who would not let his prisoners go
home?"

14.12 Fall of the Day Star

A name used of Satan—"Lucifer," or "Day Star,"—comes from this verse. The word Lucifer refers to Venus, one of the brightest objects in the sky. Yet, when the sun rises, the light of even the brightest morning star is totally eclipsed.

In context, Isaiah was describing the cruelly oppressive king of Babylon, who swelled with pride but would be brought down to defeat. However, Isaiah may be hinting at a force behind the human king: Satan himself. Isaiah's metaphor of the faded morning star aptly describes the eclipse of the haughty king of Babylon—and of Satan.

18 All the kings of the nations lie in glory,
each in his own tomb;
19 but you are cast out, away from your
grave,
like loathsome carrion,q
clothed with the dead, those pierced by
the sword,
who go down to the stones of the Pit,
like a corpse trampled underfoot.
20 You will not be joined with them
in burial,
because you have destroyed your land,
you have killed your people.

May the descendants of evildoers
nevermore be named!
21 Prepare slaughter for his sons
because of the guilt of their father.r
Let them never rise to possess the earth
or cover the face of the world with
cities.

22 I will rise up against them, says the LORD of hosts, and will cut off from Babylon name and remnant, offspring and posterity, says the LORD. 23And I will make it a possession of the hedgehog, and pools of water, and I will sweep it with the broom of destruction, says the LORD of hosts.

An Oracle concerning Assyria

24 The LORD of hosts has sworn:
As I have designed,
so shall it be;
and as I have planned,
so shall it come to pass:

25 I will break the Assyrian in my land,
and on my mountains trample him
under foot;
his yoke shall be removed from them,
and his burden from their shoulders.
26 This is the plan that is planned
concerning the whole earth;
and this is the hand that is stretched out
over all the nations.
27 For the LORD of hosts has planned,
and who will annul it?
His hand is stretched out,
and who will turn it back?

An Oracle concerning Philistia

28In the year that King Ahaz died this oracle
came:

29 Do not rejoice, all you Philistines,
that the rod that struck you is broken,
for from the root of the snake will come
forth an adder,
and its fruit will be a flying
fiery serpent.
30 The firstborn of the poor will graze,
and the needy lie down in safety;
but I will make your root die of famine,
and your remnant Is will kill.
31 Wail, O gate; cry, O city;
melt in fear, O Philistia, all of you!
For smoke comes out of the north,
and there is no straggler in its ranks.

32 What will one answer the messengers of
the nation?
"The LORD has founded Zion,
and the needy among his people
will find refuge in her."

An Oracle concerning Moab

15 An oracle concerning Moab.

Because Ar is laid waste in a night,
Moab is undone;
because Kir is laid waste in a night,
Moab is undone.
2 Dibont has gone up to the temple,
to the high places to weep;
over Nebo and over Medeba
Moab wails.
On every head is baldness,
every beard is shorn;
3 in the streets they bind on sackcloth;
on the housetops and in the squares
everyone wails and melts in tears.
4 Heshbon and Elealeh cry out,
their voices are heard as far as Jahaz;
therefore the loins of Moab quiver;u

q Cn Compare Gk: Heb *like a loathed branch*   r Syr Compare Gk: Heb *fathers*   s Q Ms Vg: MT *he*   t Cn: Heb
the house and Dibon   u Cn Compare Gk Syr: Heb *the armed men of Moab cry aloud*

his soul trembles.
5 My heart cries out for Moab;
  his fugitives flee to Zoar,
  to Eglath-shelishiyah.
For at the ascent of Luhith
  they go up weeping;
on the road to Horonaim
  they raise a cry of destruction;
6 the waters of Nimrim
  are a desolation;
the grass is withered, the new growth fails,
  the verdure is no more.
7 Therefore the abundance they have gained
  and what they have laid up
they carry away
  over the Wadi of the Willows.
8 For a cry has gone
  around the land of Moab;
the wailing reaches to Eglaim,
  the wailing reaches to Beer-elim.
9 For the waters of Dibon[v] are full
    of blood;
  yet I will bring upon Dibon[v] even
    more—
a lion for those of Moab who escape,
  for the remnant of the land.

16 Send lambs
  to the ruler of the land,
from Sela, by way of the desert,
  to the mount of daughter Zion.
2 Like fluttering birds,
  like scattered nestlings,
so are the daughters of Moab
  at the fords of the Arnon.
3 "Give counsel,
  grant justice;
make your shade like night
  at the height of noon;
hide the outcasts,
  do not betray the fugitive;
4 let the outcasts of Moab
  settle among you;
be a refuge to them
  from the destroyer."

When the oppressor is no more,
  and destruction has ceased,
and marauders have vanished from the
    land,
5 then a throne shall be established in
    steadfast love
  in the tent of David,
and on it shall sit in faithfulness
a ruler who seeks justice
  and is swift to do what is right.

6 We have heard of the pride of Moab
  —how proud he is!—

of his arrogance, his pride, and his
    insolence;
  his boasts are false.
7 Therefore let Moab wail,
  let everyone wail for Moab.
Mourn, utterly stricken,
  for the raisin cakes of Kir-hareseth.

8 For the fields of Heshbon languish,
  and the vines of Sibmah,
whose clusters once made drunk
  the lords of the nations,
reached to Jazer
  and strayed to the desert;
their shoots once spread abroad
  and crossed over the sea.
9 Therefore I weep with the weeping of
    Jazer
  for the vines of Sibmah;
I drench you with my tears,
  O Heshbon and Elealeh;
for the shout over your fruit harvest
  and your grain harvest has ceased.

16.9 A Prophet's Pain

Although Isaiah often delivered bad news to the nations around him, he never took pleasure in it. Remarkably, he often deeply identified with the pain of other, non-Israelite nations such as Moab (see 15.5). Chapters 15–16 were likely used as sources for Jeremiah 48. (Jeremiah was another prophet who suffered greatly.)

10 Joy and gladness are taken away
  from the fruitful field;
and in the vineyards no songs are sung,
  no shouts are raised;
no treader treads out wine in the presses;
  the vintage-shout is hushed.[w]
11 Therefore my heart throbs like a harp for
    Moab,
  and my very soul for Kir-heres.
12 When Moab presents himself, when he
wearies himself upon the high place, when he
comes to his sanctuary to pray, he will not prevail.
13 This was the word that the LORD spoke
concerning Moab in the past. 14But now the LORD
says, In three years, like the years of a hired worker, the glory of Moab will be brought into contempt, in spite of all its great multitude; and those
who survive will be very few and feeble.

An Oracle concerning Damascus

17 An oracle concerning Damascus.

See, Damascus will cease to be a city,

---

v Q Ms Vg Compare Syr: MT *Dimon*   w Gk: Heb *I have hushed*

and will become a heap of ruins.
2 Her towns will be deserted forever;[x]
  they will be places for flocks,
  which will lie down, and no one will
    make them afraid.
3 The fortress will disappear from Ephraim,
  and the kingdom from Damascus;
and the remnant of Aram will be
  like the glory of the children of Israel,
                    says the LORD of hosts.

4 On that day
  the glory of Jacob will be brought low,
  and the fat of his flesh will grow lean.
5 And it shall be as when reapers gather
    standing grain
  and their arms harvest the ears,
and as when one gleans the ears of grain
  in the Valley of Rephaim.
6 Gleanings will be left in it,
  as when an olive tree is beaten—
two or three berries
  in the top of the highest bough,
four or five
  on the branches of a fruit tree,
                    says the LORD God of Israel.

7 On that day people will regard their Maker, and their eyes will look to the Holy One of Israel; [8]they will not have regard for the altars, the work of their hands, and they will not look to what their own fingers have made, either the sacred poles[y] or the altars of incense.

9 On that day their strong cities will be like the deserted places of the Hivites and the Amorites,[z] which they deserted because of the children of Israel, and there will be desolation.

10 For you have forgotten the God of your
    salvation,
  and have not remembered the Rock of
    your refuge;
therefore, though you plant pleasant
    plants
  and set out slips of an alien god,
11 though you make them grow on the day
    that you plant them,
  and make them blossom in the
    morning that you sow;
yet the harvest will flee away
  in a day of grief and incurable pain.

12 Ah, the thunder of many peoples,
  they thunder like the thundering of the
    sea!
Ah, the roar of nations,
  they roar like the roaring of mighty
    waters!

13 The nations roar like the roaring of many
    waters,
  but he will rebuke them, and they will
    flee far away,
chased like chaff on the mountains before
    the wind
  and whirling dust before the storm.
14 At evening time, lo, terror!
  Before morning, they are no more.
This is the fate of those who despoil us,
  and the lot of those who plunder us.

An Oracle concerning Ethiopia

18 Ah, land of whirring wings
  beyond the rivers of Ethiopia,[a]
2 sending ambassadors by the Nile
  in vessels of papyrus on the waters!
Go, you swift messengers,
  to a nation tall and smooth,
to a people feared near and far,
  a nation mighty and conquering,
  whose land the rivers divide.

18.2 Foreign Policy

Isaiah never balked at direct political involvement. He consistently lobbied against alliances with any foreign powers. Here, he warned against the "ambassadors by the Nile" coming from Cush, a region near Ethiopia or Sudan. Judah's king was often tempted to make alliances with Ethiopia or Egypt, but according to Isaiah, both nations would meet disaster.

3 All you inhabitants of the world,
  you who live on the earth,
when a signal is raised on the mountains,
    look!
  When a trumpet is blown, listen!
4 For thus the LORD said to me:
I will quietly look from my dwelling
  like clear heat in sunshine,
  like a cloud of dew in the heat
    of harvest.
5 For before the harvest, when the blossom
    is over
  and the flower becomes a ripening
    grape,
he will cut off the shoots with pruning
    hooks,
  and the spreading branches he will hew
    away.
6 They shall all be left
  to the birds of prey of the mountains
  and to the animals of the earth.

---

[x] Cn Compare Gk: Heb *the cities of Aroer are deserted and the highest bough*   [a] Or *Nubia*; Heb *Cush*   [y] Heb *Asherim*   [z] Cn Compare Gk: Heb *places of the wood*

And the birds of prey will summer on
them,
and all the animals of the earth will
winter on them.

7 At that time gifts will be brought to the
LORD of hosts from[b] a people tall and smooth,
from a people feared near and far, a nation
mighty and conquering, whose land the rivers
divide, to Mount Zion, the place of the name of
the LORD of hosts.

An Oracle concerning Egypt

19 An oracle concerning Egypt.

See, the LORD is riding on a swift cloud
and comes to Egypt;
the idols of Egypt will tremble at his
presence,
and the heart of the Egyptians will melt
within them.
2 I will stir up Egyptians against Egyptians,
and they will fight, one against the
other,
neighbor against neighbor,
city against city, kingdom against
kingdom;
3 the spirit of the Egyptians within them
will be emptied out,
and I will confound their plans;
they will consult the idols and the spirits
of the dead
and the ghosts and the familiar spirits;
4 I will deliver the Egyptians
into the hand of a hard master;
a fierce king will rule over them,
says the Sovereign, the LORD of hosts.

5 The waters of the Nile will be dried up,
and the river will be parched and dry;
6 its canals will become foul,
and the branches of Egypt's Nile will
diminish and dry up,
reeds and rushes will rot away.
7 There will be bare places by the Nile,
on the brink of the Nile;
and all that is sown by the Nile will dry
up,
be driven away, and be no more.
8 Those who fish will mourn;
all who cast hooks in the Nile will
lament,
and those who spread nets on the
water will languish.
9 The workers in flax will be in despair,
and the carders and those at the loom
will grow pale.
10 Its weavers will be dismayed,

and all who work for wages will be
grieved.

11 The princes of Zoan are utterly foolish;
the wise counselors of Pharaoh give
stupid counsel.
How can you say to Pharaoh,
"I am one of the sages,
a descendant of ancient kings"?
12 Where now are your sages?
Let them tell you and make known
what the LORD of hosts has planned
against Egypt.
13 The princes of Zoan have become fools,
and the princes of Memphis
are deluded;
those who are the cornerstones of its
tribes
have led Egypt astray.
14 The LORD has poured into them[c]
a spirit of confusion;
and they have made Egypt stagger in all
its doings
as a drunkard staggers around
in vomit.
15 Neither head nor tail, palm branch or
reed,
will be able to do anything for Egypt.

16 On that day the Egyptians will be like
women, and tremble with fear before the hand
that the LORD of hosts raises against them. 17And
the land of Judah will become a terror to the
Egyptians; everyone to whom it is mentioned will
fear because of the plan that the LORD of hosts is
planning against them.

Egypt, Assyria, and Israel Blessed

18 On that day there will be five cities in the
land of Egypt that speak the language of Canaan
and swear allegiance to the LORD of hosts. One of
these will be called the City of the Sun.
19 On that day there will be an altar to the
LORD in the center of the land of Egypt, and a
pillar to the LORD at its border. 20It will be a sign
and a witness to the LORD of hosts in the land of
Egypt; when they cry to the LORD because of oppressors, he will send them a savior, and will defend and deliver them. 21The LORD will make
himself known to the Egyptians; and the Egyptians will know the LORD on that day, and will
worship with sacrifice and burnt offering, and
they will make vows to the LORD and perform
them. 22The LORD will strike Egypt, striking and
healing; they will return to the LORD, and he will
listen to their supplications and heal them.
23 On that day there will be a highway from
Egypt to Assyria, and the Assyrian will come into

b Q Ms Gk Vg: MT of   c Gk Compare Tg: Heb it

Egypt, and the Egyptian into Assyria, and the Egyptians will worship with the Assyrians.

24 On that day Israel will be the third with Egypt and Assyria, a blessing in the midst of the earth, 25whom the LORD of hosts has blessed, saying, "Blessed be Egypt my people, and Assyria the work of my hands, and Israel my heritage."

Isaiah Dramatizes the Conquest of Egypt and Ethiopia

20 In the year that the commander-in-chief, who was sent by King Sargon of Assyria, came to Ashdod and fought against it and took it— 2at that time the LORD had spoken to Isaiah son of Amoz, saying, "Go, and loose the sackcloth from your loins and take your sandals off your feet," and he had done so, walking naked and

20.2 A Dramatic Object Lesson

Isaiah was an educated and urbane prophet, at home in the corridors of power. His reputation must have made this object lesson very shocking: For three years he walked around stripped and barefoot, in the guise of a slave, to protest a planned alliance with Egypt and Cush. He had originally opposed an alliance with Assyria. Now he opposed a treaty with other nations as well.

barefoot. 3Then the LORD said, "Just as my servant Isaiah has walked naked and barefoot for three years as a sign and a portent against Egypt and Ethiopia,d 4so shall the king of Assyria lead away the Egyptians as captives and the Ethiopianse as exiles, both the young and the old, naked and barefoot, with buttocks uncovered, to the shame of Egypt. 5And they shall be dismayed and confounded because of Ethiopiad their hope and of Egypt their boast. 6In that day the inhabitants of this coastland will say, 'See, this is what has happened to those in whom we hoped and to whom we fled for help and deliverance from the king of Assyria! And we, how shall we escape?'"

Oracles concerning Babylon, Edom, and Arabia

21 The oracle concerning the wilderness of the sea.

As whirlwinds in the Negeb sweep on,
  it comes from the desert,
  from a terrible land.
2 A stern vision is told to me;
  the betrayer betrays,
  and the destroyer destroys.
Go up, O Elam,

lay siege, O Media;
all the sighing she has caused
  I bring to an end.
3 Therefore my loins are filled with anguish;
  pangs have seized me,
  like the pangs of a woman in labor;
I am bowed down so that I cannot hear,
  I am dismayed so that I cannot see.
4 My mind reels, horror has appalled me;
  the twilight I longed for
  has been turned for me into trembling.
5 They prepare the table,
  they spread the rugs,
  they eat, they drink.
Rise up, commanders,
  oil the shield!
6 For thus the Lord said to me:
"Go, post a lookout,
  let him announce what he sees.
7 When he sees riders, horsemen in pairs,
  riders on donkeys, riders on camels,
let him listen diligently,
  very diligently."
8 Then the watcherf called out:
"Upon a watchtower I stand, O Lord,
  continually by day,
and at my post I am stationed
  throughout the night.
9 Look, there they come, riders,
  horsemen in pairs!"
Then he responded,
  "Fallen, fallen is Babylon;
and all the images of her gods
  lie shattered on the ground."
10 O my threshed and winnowed one,
  what I have heard from the LORD of
    hosts,
  the God of Israel, I announce to you.

11 The oracle concerning Dumah.

One is calling to me from Seir,
  "Sentinel, what of the night?
  Sentinel, what of the night?"
12 The sentinel says:
"Morning comes, and also the night.
  If you will inquire, inquire;
  come back again."

13 The oracle concerning the desert plain.

In the scrub of the desert plain you will
    lodge,
  O caravans of Dedanites.
14 Bring water to the thirsty,
  meet the fugitive with bread,
  O inhabitants of the land of Tema.
15 For they have fled from the swords,
  from the drawn sword,

d Or Nubia; Heb Cush   e Or Nubians; Heb Cushites   f Q Ms: MT a lion

from the bent bow,
　and from the stress of battle.
16 For thus the Lord said to me: Within a
year, according to the years of a hired worker, all
the glory of Kedar will come to an end; [17]and the
remaining bows of Kedar's warriors will be few;
for the LORD, the God of Israel, has spoken.

A Warning of Destruction of Jerusalem

22 The oracle concerning the valley of vision.

What do you mean that you have gone
　up,
all of you, to the housetops,
2 you that are full of shoutings,
　tumultuous city, exultant town?
Your slain are not slain by the sword,
　nor are they dead in battle.
3 Your rulers have all fled together;

they were captured without the use of
　a bow.[g]
All of you who were found were captured,
　though they had fled far away.[h]
4 Therefore I said:
Look away from me,
　let me weep bitter tears;
do not try to comfort me
　for the destruction of my
　　beloved people.

5 For the Lord GOD of hosts has a day
　of tumult and trampling and confusion
in the valley of vision,
a battering down of walls
　and a cry for help to the mountains.
6 Elam bore the quiver
　with chariots and cavalry,[i]
　and Kir uncovered the shield.

g Or *without their bows*　　h Gk Syr Vg: Heb *fled from far away*　　i Meaning of Heb uncertain

Catastrophes Through God's Eyes
An endless cycle of war and death—what did it mean?

THERE IS ONE EASY WAY to picture the Middle East of Isaiah's
day: Simply follow today's newspaper headlines and project backward in
time. Then, as now, one nation would invade its neighbor, leveling cities
and devastating the land and its people. The prophet Isaiah longed for an
end to the cycle, much as modern-day residents of Lebanon or Israel do
today.

Isaiah looked at the world with a kind of split vision. Around him he saw
spiritual decay and the dreary cycle of war and death. Yet God had given him a
clear vision of what his nation could one day become: a pure people, faithful to
God, living in peace with "war no more."

*Therefore my loins
are filled with
anguish; pangs
have seized me, like
the pangs of a
woman in labor; I
am bowed down so
that I cannot hear, I
am dismayed so
that I cannot see.
21.3*

A Kingdom for a Purpose

With God's view of the future shining brightly before him, Isaiah went
about reinterpreting history. Others in Judah looked upon military invasions as terrible catastrophes. In
contrast, Isaiah—though he felt anguish over the events—saw glimpses of a higher purpose.

Isaiah said that Judah had to endure pain and suffering in order to be purified. He counseled
against making political alliances to forestall the punishment. God's people had to go through the fire,
and from the trials a *remnant*—a small remaining number of persons—would emerge that God could
then use to accomplish his work. Isaiah went so far as to name his own son "a remnant shall return" as
a walking object lesson of his message to Judah (see 7.3 and footnote).

Why had the Jews been called by God in the first place? They were to be a "light to the nations,"
Isaiah said, a nation used by God to bring his truth to other nations. And out of the land of Judah God
would raise up a great Prince who would rule over all the earth.

Who Is in Charge?

In short, God had not discarded his people, no matter how bleak things looked. The Israelites
would ultimately become a missionary nation, pointing others to God.

Above all messages, Isaiah stressed this one: God is in charge of history. To Judah—surrounded by
enemies, staggering from invasion, weary of bloodshed—God seemed far away and distant. Isaiah
assured them that the great powers of earth were mere tools in God's hands; he would use them and
fling them aside.

Life Questions: Isaiah described people who felt afraid and abandoned by God. Have you ever felt like
that? How does Isaiah's message offer hope for us today?

⁷ Your choicest valleys were full of chariots,
and the cavalry took their stand at the
gates.
⁸ He has taken away the covering of Judah.

On that day you looked to the weapons of the
House of the Forest, ⁹and you saw that there were
many breaches in the city of David, and you collected the waters of the lower pool. ¹⁰You counted
the houses of Jerusalem, and you broke down the
houses to fortify the wall. ¹¹You made a reservoir
between the two walls for the water of the old
pool. But you did not look to him who did it, or
have regard for him who planned it long ago.

¹² In that day the Lord GOD of hosts
called to weeping and mourning,
to baldness and putting on sackcloth;

22.12 Smiles Instead of Tears

*This chapter may refer to Jerusalem's
deliverance recorded in Isaiah 36–37. Isaiah
was distressed because, although great
devastation was prophesied, Jerusalem was
celebrating, not mourning. People had
reinforced walls and built water reservoirs to
prepare for war, but had not turned to God for
help (verse 11). Israelites at that time had a
certain cockiness about the city of Jerusalem,
believing that God would never allow it to fall
into enemy hands.*

¹³ but instead there was joy and festivity,
killing oxen and slaughtering sheep,
eating meat and drinking wine.
"Let us eat and drink,
for tomorrow we die."
¹⁴ The LORD of hosts has revealed himself in
my ears:
Surely this iniquity will not be forgiven
you until you die,
says the Lord GOD of hosts.

Denunciation of Self-Seeking Officials

15 Thus says the Lord GOD of hosts: Come,
go to this steward, to Shebna, who is master of the
household, and say to him: ¹⁶What right do you
have here? Who are your relatives here, that you
have cut out a tomb here for yourself, cutting a
tomb on the height, and carving a habitation for
yourself in the rock? ¹⁷The LORD is about to hurl
you away violently, my fellow. He will seize firm
hold on you, ¹⁸whirl you round and round, and
throw you like a ball into a wide land; there you
shall die, and there your splendid chariots shall
lie, O you disgrace to your master's house! ¹⁹I will

thrust you from your office, and you will be
pulled down from your post.
20 On that day I will call my servant Eliakim
son of Hilkiah, ²¹and will clothe him with your
robe and bind your sash on him. I will commit
your authority to his hand, and he shall be a
father to the inhabitants of Jerusalem and to the
house of Judah. ²²I will place on his shoulder the
key of the house of David; he shall open, and no
one shall shut; he shall shut, and no one shall
open. ²³I will fasten him like a peg in a secure
place, and he will become a throne of honor to his
ancestral house. ²⁴And they will hang on him the
whole weight of his ancestral house, the offspring
and issue, every small vessel, from the cups to all
the flagons. ²⁵On that day, says the LORD of hosts,
the peg that was fastened in a secure place will
give way; it will be cut down and fall, and the load
that was on it will perish, for the LORD has spoken.

An Oracle concerning Tyre

23 The oracle concerning Tyre.

Wail, O ships of Tarshish,
for your fortress is destroyed.ʲ
When they came in from Cyprus
they learned of it.

23.1 The Decline of Tyre

*In Isaiah's day the city of Tyre was a major
power, dominating the sea trade in the eastern
Mediterranean. Her many colonies included the
island of Cyprus, and her merchants traveled
as far as the Indian Ocean and the English
Channel. But not long after this prophecy
Assyria conquered the city, and Tyre's king fled
to Cyprus.*

² Be still, O inhabitants of the coast,
O merchants of Sidon,
your messengers crossed over the seaᵏ
³ and were on the mighty waters;
your revenue was the grain of Shihor,
the harvest of the Nile;
you were the merchant of the nations.
⁴ Be ashamed, O Sidon, for the sea has
spoken,
the fortress of the sea, saying:
"I have neither labored nor given birth,
I have neither reared young men
nor brought up young women."
⁵ When the report comes to Egypt,
they will be in anguish over the report
about Tyre.
⁶ Cross over to Tarshish—
wail, O inhabitants of the coast!
⁷ Is this your exultant city

ʲ Cn Compare verse 14: Heb *for it is destroyed, without houses*

ᵏ Q Ms: MT *crossing over the sea, they replenished you*

whose origin is from days of old,
whose feet carried her
to settle far away?
8 Who has planned this
against Tyre, the bestower of crowns,
whose merchants were princes,
whose traders were the honored of
the earth?
9 The LORD of hosts has planned it—
to defile the pride of all glory,
to shame all the honored of the earth.
10 Cross over to your own land,
O ships of[l] Tarshish;
this is a harbor[m] no more.
11 He has stretched out his hand over the
sea,
he has shaken the kingdoms;
the LORD has given command concerning
Canaan
to destroy its fortresses.
12 He said:
You will exult no longer,
O oppressed virgin daughter Sidon;
rise, cross over to Cyprus—
even there you will have no rest.

13 Look at the land of the Chaldeans! This is
the people; it was not Assyria. They destined Tyre
for wild animals. They erected their siege towers,
they tore down her palaces, they made her a
ruin.[n]
14 Wail, O ships of Tarshish,
for your fortress is destroyed.
15From that day Tyre will be forgotten for seventy
years, the lifetime of one king. At the end of seventy years, it will happen to Tyre as in the song
about the prostitute:
16 Take a harp,
go about the city,
you forgotten prostitute!
Make sweet melody,
sing many songs,
that you may be remembered.
17At the end of seventy years, the LORD will visit
Tyre, and she will return to her trade, and will
prostitute herself with all the kingdoms of the
world on the face of the earth. 18Her merchandise
and her wages will be dedicated to the LORD; her
profits[o] will not be stored or hoarded, but her
merchandise will supply abundant food and fine
clothing for those who live in the presence of the
LORD.

Impending Judgment on the Earth

24 Now the LORD is about to lay waste the
earth and make it desolate,
and he will twist its surface and scatter
its inhabitants.

2 And it shall be, as with the people, so
with the priest;
as with the slave, so with his master;
as with the maid, so with her mistress;
as with the buyer, so with the seller;
as with the lender, so with the
borrower;
as with the creditor, so with the debtor.
3 The earth shall be utterly laid waste and
utterly despoiled;
for the LORD has spoken this word.

4 The earth dries up and withers,
the world languishes and withers;
the heavens languish together with the
earth.
5 The earth lies polluted
under its inhabitants;
for they have transgressed laws,
violated the statutes,
broken the everlasting covenant.
6 Therefore a curse devours the earth,
and its inhabitants suffer for their guilt;
therefore the inhabitants of the earth
dwindled,
and few people are left.
7 The wine dries up,
the vine languishes,
all the merry-hearted sigh.
8 The mirth of the timbrels is stilled,
the noise of the jubilant has ceased,
the mirth of the lyre is stilled.
9 No longer do they drink wine with
singing;
strong drink is bitter to those who
drink it.
10 The city of chaos is broken down,
every house is shut up so that no one
can enter.
11 There is an outcry in the streets for lack
of wine;
all joy has reached its eventide;
the gladness of the earth is banished.
12 Desolation is left in the city,
the gates are battered into ruins.
13 For thus it shall be on the earth
and among the nations,
as when an olive tree is beaten,
as at the gleaning when the grape
harvest is ended.

14 They lift up their voices, they sing for joy;
they shout from the west over the
majesty of the LORD.
15 Therefore in the east give glory to the
LORD;
in the coastlands of the sea glorify the
name of the LORD, the God of
Israel.

---

[l] Cn Compare Gk: Heb *like the Nile, daughter*   [m] Cn: Heb *restraint*   [n] Meaning of Heb uncertain   [o] Heb *it*

16 From the ends of the earth we hear songs
 of praise,
 of glory to the Righteous One.
But I say, I pine away,
 I pine away. Woe is me!
For the treacherous deal treacherously,
 the treacherous deal very treacherously.

17 Terror, and the pit, and the snare
 are upon you, O inhabitant of the
 earth!
18 Whoever flees at the sound of the terror
 shall fall into the pit;
and whoever climbs out of the pit
 shall be caught in the snare.
For the windows of heaven are opened,
 and the foundations of the earth
 tremble.
19 The earth is utterly broken,
 the earth is torn asunder,
 the earth is violently shaken.
20 The earth staggers like a drunkard,
 it sways like a hut;
its transgression lies heavy upon it,
 and it falls, and will not rise again.

21 On that day the LORD will punish
 the host of heaven in heaven,
 and on earth the kings of the earth.
22 They will be gathered together
 like prisoners in a pit;
they will be shut up in a prison,
 and after many days they will be
 punished.
23 Then the moon will be abashed,
 and the sun ashamed;
for the LORD of hosts will reign
 on Mount Zion and in Jerusalem,
and before his elders he will manifest his
 glory.

Praise for Deliverance from Oppression

25 O LORD, you are my God;
 I will exalt you, I will praise your
 name;
for you have done wonderful things,
 plans formed of old, faithful and sure.
2 For you have made the city a heap,
 the fortified city a ruin;
the palace of aliens is a city no more,
 it will never be rebuilt.
3 Therefore strong peoples will glorify you;
 cities of ruthless nations will fear you.
4 For you have been a refuge to the poor,
 a refuge to the needy in their distress,
 a shelter from the rainstorm and a
 shade from the heat.
When the blast of the ruthless was like a
 winter rainstorm,

5 the noise of aliens like heat in a dry
 place,
you subdued the heat with the shade of
 clouds;
the song of the ruthless was stilled.

6 On this mountain the LORD of hosts will
 make for all peoples
 a feast of rich food, a feast of well-aged
 wines,
 of rich food filled with marrow, of
 well-aged wines strained clear.

25.6 A Promise of Eternal Life

The Old Testament includes only a few hints about resurrection and the afterlife, and this is one of the strongest. Isaiah follows a devastating chapter on God's judgment of the whole earth (chapter 24) with a bright promise of a future life. Then, death and pain will be abolished (see verses 7–8 and 26.19), and God will reign with perfect justice.

7 And he will destroy on this mountain
 the shroud that is cast over all peoples,
 the sheet that is spread over all nations;
8 he will swallow up death forever.
Then the Lord GOD will wipe away the
 tears from all faces,
 and the disgrace of his people he will
 take away from all the earth,
for the LORD has spoken.
9 It will be said on that day,
 Lo, this is our God; we have waited for
 him, so that he might save us.
 This is the LORD for whom we have
 waited;
 let us be glad and rejoice in his
 salvation.
10 For the hand of the LORD will rest on this
 mountain.

The Moabites shall be trodden down in
 their place
 as straw is trodden down in a
 dung-pit.
11 Though they spread out their hands in
 the midst of it,
 as swimmers spread out their hands to
 swim,
 their pride will be laid low despite the
 struggle *p* of their hands.
12 The high fortifications of his walls will be
 brought down,
 laid low, cast to the ground, even to
 the dust.

p Meaning of Heb uncertain

Judah's Song of Victory

26 On that day this song will be sung in the land of Judah:

We have a strong city;
    he sets up victory
    like walls and bulwarks.
2 Open the gates,
    so that the righteous nation that keeps
        faith
    may enter in.
3 Those of steadfast mind you keep
    in peace—
    in peace because they trust in you.

26.3 Perfect Peace

Isaiah, who lived in a time of tremendous turmoil, predicted more of the same. Godly people would suffer along with everybody else, he said. How should believers cope? Isaiah urged them to focus on a reality greater than their current troubles: to keep their minds steady on God, who never loses control over events.

4 Trust in the LORD forever,
    for in the LORD GOD *q*
    you have an everlasting rock.
5 For he has brought low
    the inhabitants of the height;
    the lofty city he lays low.
He lays it low to the ground,
    casts it to the dust.
6 The foot tramples it,
    the feet of the poor,
    the steps of the needy.

7 The way of the righteous is level;
    O Just One, you make smooth the path
        of the righteous.
8 In the path of your judgments,
    O LORD, we wait for you;
your name and your renown
    are the soul's desire.
9 My soul yearns for you in the night,
    my spirit within me earnestly seeks
        you.
For when your judgments are in the
        earth,
    the inhabitants of the world learn
        righteousness.
10 If favor is shown to the wicked,
    they do not learn righteousness;
in the land of uprightness they deal
        perversely

and do not see the majesty of
    the LORD.
11 O LORD, your hand is lifted up,
    but they do not see it.
Let them see your zeal for your people,
    and be ashamed.
    Let the fire for your adversaries
    consume them.
12 O LORD, you will ordain peace for us,
    for indeed, all that we have done, you
        have done for us.
13 O LORD our God,
    other lords besides you have ruled over
        us,
    but we acknowledge your name alone.
14 The dead do not live;
    shades do not rise—
because you have punished and destroyed
        them,
    and wiped out all memory of them.
15 But you have increased the nation,
        O LORD,
    you have increased the nation; you are
        glorified;
you have enlarged all the borders of
    the land.
16 O LORD, in distress they sought you,
    they poured out a prayer *r*
    when your chastening was on them.
17 Like a woman with child,
    who writhes and cries out in her pangs
    when she is near her time,
so were we because of you, O LORD;
18   we were with child, we writhed,
    but we gave birth only to wind.
We have won no victories on earth,
    and no one is born to inhabit
        the world.
19 Your dead shall live, their corpses *s* shall
    rise.
    O dwellers in the dust, awake and sing
    for joy!
For your dew is a radiant dew,
    and the earth will give birth to those
        long dead. *t*

20 Come, my people, enter your chambers,
    and shut your doors behind you;
hide yourselves for a little while
    until the wrath is past.
21 For the LORD comes out from his place
    to punish the inhabitants of the earth
        for their iniquity;
the earth will disclose the blood shed on
    it,
    and will no longer cover its slain.

---

q Heb *in Yah, the* LORD   *r* Meaning of Heb uncertain   *s* Cn Compare Syr Tg: Heb *my corpse*
t Heb *to the shades*

Israel's Redemption

27 On that day the LORD with his cruel and great and strong sword will punish Leviathan the fleeing serpent, Leviathan the twisting serpent, and he will kill the dragon that is in the sea.

27.1 A Prophecy for the World

Most of Isaiah 1–39 concerns specific nations in the prophet's own time. But chapters 24 to 27 form a unit that seems to sum up all world history. Those chapters contain some of Isaiah's strongest imagery.

2 On that day:
A pleasant vineyard, sing about it!
3 I, the LORD, am its keeper;
every moment I water it.
I guard it night and day
so that no one can harm it;
4 I have no wrath.
If it gives me thorns and briers,
I will march to battle against it.
I will burn it up.
5 Or else let it cling to me for protection,
let it make peace with me,
let it make peace with me.

6 In days to come[u] Jacob shall take root,
Israel shall blossom and put
forth shoots,
and fill the whole world with fruit.

7 Has he struck them down as he struck
down those who struck them?
Or have they been killed as their killers
were killed?
8 By expulsion,[v] by exile you struggled
against them;
with his fierce blast he removed them
in the day of the east wind.
9 Therefore by this the guilt of Jacob will be
expiated,
and this will be the full fruit of the
removal of his sin:
when he makes all the stones of the altars
like chalkstones crushed to pieces,
no sacred poles[w] or incense altars will
remain standing.
10 For the fortified city is solitary,
a habitation deserted and forsaken, like
the wilderness;
the calves graze there,
there they lie down, and strip its
branches.

11 When its boughs are dry, they
are broken;
women come and make a fire of them.
For this is a people without
understanding;
therefore he that made them will not
have compassion on them,
he that formed them will show them
no favor.

12 On that day the LORD will thresh from the channel of the Euphrates to the Wadi of Egypt, and you will be gathered one by one, O people of Israel. 13 And on that day a great trumpet will be blown, and those who were lost in the land of Assyria and those who were driven out to the land of Egypt will come and worship the LORD on the holy mountain at Jerusalem.

Judgment on Corrupt Rulers, Priests, and Prophets

28 Ah, the proud garland of the drunkards
of Ephraim,
and the fading flower of its glorious
beauty,
which is on the head of those bloated
with rich food, of those overcome
with wine!
2 See, the Lord has one who is mighty and
strong;
like a storm of hail, a destroying
tempest,
like a storm of mighty, overflowing
waters;
with his hand he will hurl them down
to the earth.
3 Trampled under foot will be
the proud garland of the drunkards of
Ephraim.
4 And the fading flower of its glorious
beauty,
which is on the head of those bloated
with rich food,
will be like a first-ripe fig before the
summer;
whoever sees it, eats it up
as soon as it comes to hand.

5 In that day the LORD of hosts will be a
garland of glory,
and a diadem of beauty, to the
remnant of his people;
6 and a spirit of justice to the one who sits
in judgment,
and strength to those who turn back
the battle at the gate.

7 These also reel with wine
and stagger with strong drink;

---

[u] Heb *Those to come*   [v] Meaning of Heb uncertain   [w] Heb *Asherim*

the priest and the prophet reel with
    strong drink,
they are confused with wine,
they stagger with strong drink;
they err in vision,
they stumble in giving judgment.
8 All tables are covered with filthy vomit;
    no place is clean.

9 "Whom will he teach knowledge,
    and to whom will he explain
        the message?
Those who are weaned from milk,
    those taken from the breast?
10 For it is precept upon precept, precept
        upon precept,
    line upon line, line upon line,
    here a little, there a little."ˣ

11 Truly, with stammering lip
    and with alien tongue
he will speak to this people,
12   to whom he has said,
"This is rest;
    give rest to the weary;
and this is repose";
    yet they would not hear.
13 Therefore the word of the LORD will be to
        them,
    "Precept upon precept, precept upon
        precept,
    line upon line, line upon line,
    here a little, there a little;"ˣ
in order that they may go, and fall
        backward,
    and be broken, and snared, and taken.

14 Therefore hear the word of the LORD, you
        scoffers
    who rule this people in Jerusalem.
15 Because you have said, "We have made a
        covenant with death,
    and with Sheol we have an agreement;
when the overwhelming scourge passes
        through
    it will not come to us;
for we have made lies our refuge,
    and in falsehood we have taken
        shelter";
16 therefore thus says the Lord GOD,
See, I am laying in Zion a foundation
        stone,
    a tested stone,
a precious cornerstone, a sure foundation:
    "One who trusts will not panic."
17 And I will make justice the line,
    and righteousness the plummet;
hail will sweep away the refuge of lies,
    and waters will overwhelm the shelter.

18 Then your covenant with death will be
        annulled,
    and your agreement with Sheol will not
        stand;
when the overwhelming scourge passes
        through
    you will be beaten down by it.
19 As often as it passes through, it will take
        you;
    for morning by morning it will pass
        through,
    by day and by night;
and it will be sheer terror to understand
        the message.
20 For the bed is too short to stretch oneself
        on it,
    and the covering too narrow to wrap
        oneself in it.
21 For the LORD will rise up as on Mount
        Perazim,
    he will rage as in the valley of Gibeon
to do his deed—strange is his deed!—
    and to work his work—alien is his
        work!
22 Now therefore do not scoff,
    or your bonds will be made stronger;
for I have heard a decree of destruction
    from the Lord GOD of hosts upon the
        whole land.

23 Listen, and hear my voice;
    Pay attention, and hear my speech.
24 Do those who plow for sowing plow
        continually?
    Do they continually open and harrow
        their ground?

28.24 Like a Wise Farmer

*Drawing an analogy from farming, Isaiah
shows that God varies his treatment of nations,
depending on conditions. Just as different
crops—grain, barley, caraway, cummin—
require different farming techniques, so each
nation requires individual treatment. Those
who readily repent need only light punishment,
while stubborn nations need further discipline.*

25 When they have leveled its surface,
    do they not scatter dill, sow cummin,
and plant wheat in rows
    and barley in its proper place,
    and spelt as the border?
26 For they are well instructed;
    their God teaches them.

27 Dill is not threshed with a threshing
        sledge,

ˣ Meaning of Heb of this verse uncertain

nor is a cart wheel rolled over cummin;
   but dill is beaten out with a stick,
   and cummin with a rod.
28 Grain is crushed for bread,
   but one does not thresh it forever;
   one drives the cart wheel and horses over
      it,
   but does not pulverize it.
29 This also comes from the LORD of hosts;
   he is wonderful in counsel,
   and excellent in wisdom.

The Siege of Jerusalem

29 Ah, Ariel, Ariel,
   the city where David encamped!
Add year to year;
   let the festivals run their round.
2 Yet I will distress Ariel,
   and there shall be moaning and
      lamentation,
   and Jerusalem*y* shall be to me like an
      Ariel.*z*
3 And like David*a* I will encamp against
      you;
   I will besiege you with towers
   and raise siegeworks against you.
4 Then deep from the earth you shall speak,
   from low in the dust your words shall
      come;
   your voice shall come from the ground
      like the voice of a ghost,
   and your speech shall whisper out of
      the dust.

5 But the multitude of your foes*b* shall be
      like small dust,
   and the multitude of tyrants like flying
      chaff.
   And in an instant, suddenly,
6   you will be visited by the LORD of hosts
   with thunder and earthquake and great
      noise,
   with whirlwind and tempest, and the
      flame of a devouring fire.
7 And the multitude of all the nations that
      fight against Ariel,
   all that fight against her and her
      stronghold, and who distress her,
   shall be like a dream, a vision
      of the night.
8 Just as when a hungry person dreams of
      eating
   and wakes up still hungry,
   or a thirsty person dreams of drinking
   and wakes up faint, still thirsty,
   so shall the multitude of all the nations be
   that fight against Mount Zion.

9 Stupefy yourselves and be in a stupor,
   blind yourselves and be blind!
   Be drunk, but not from wine;
   stagger, but not from strong drink!
10 For the LORD has poured out upon you
   a spirit of deep sleep;
   he has closed your eyes, you prophets,
   and covered your heads, you seers.

11 The vision of all this has become for you like the words of a sealed document. If it is given to those who can read, with the command, "Read this," they say, "We cannot, for it is sealed." 12 And if it is given to those who cannot read, saying, "Read this," they say, "We cannot read."

13 The Lord said:
   Because these people draw near with their
      mouths
   and honor me with their lips,
   while their hearts are far from me,
   and their worship of me is a human
      commandment learned by rote;

29.13 Hypocrites

Again and again, Isaiah blasts the Israelites for a superficial faith—all words and no heart. Hundreds of years later, Jesus quoted this verse, saying that it applied precisely to people of his day (Mark 7.6–7).

14 so I will again do
   amazing things with this people,
   shocking and amazing.
   The wisdom of their wise shall perish,
   and the discernment of the discerning
      shall be hidden.

15 Ha! You who hide a plan too deep for the
      LORD,
   whose deeds are in the dark,
   and who say, "Who sees us? Who
      knows us?"
16 You turn things upside down!
   Shall the potter be regarded as the
      clay?
   Shall the thing made say of its maker,
      "He did not make me";
   or the thing formed say of the one who
      formed it,
      "He has no understanding"?

Hope for the Future

17 Shall not Lebanon in a very little while
   become a fruitful field,

---

y Heb *she*   *z* Probable meaning, *altar hearth*; compare Ezek 43.15   *a* Gk: Meaning of Heb uncertain
b Cn: Heb *strangers*

and the fruitful field be regarded as a
forest?

18 On that day the deaf shall hear
the words of a scroll,
and out of their gloom and darkness
the eyes of the blind shall see.

19 The meek shall obtain fresh joy in the
LORD,
and the neediest people shall exult in
the Holy One of Israel.

20 For the tyrant shall be no more,
and the scoffer shall cease to be;
all those alert to do evil shall be cut
off—

21 those who cause a person to lose a
lawsuit,
who set a trap for the arbiter in the
gate,
and without grounds deny justice to
the one in the right.

22 Therefore thus says the LORD, who redeemed Abraham, concerning the house of Jacob:
No longer shall Jacob be ashamed,
no longer shall his face grow pale.

23 For when he sees his children,
the work of my hands, in his midst,
they will sanctify my name;
they will sanctify the Holy One of Jacob,
and will stand in awe of the God of
Israel.

24 And those who err in spirit will come to
understanding,
and those who grumble will accept
instruction.

The Futility of Reliance on Egypt

30 Oh, rebellious children, says the LORD,
who carry out a plan, but not mine;
who make an alliance, but against my
will,
adding sin to sin;

2 who set out to go down to Egypt
without asking for my counsel,
to take refuge in the protection of
Pharaoh,
and to seek shelter in the shadow of
Egypt;

3 Therefore the protection of Pharaoh shall
become your shame,
and the shelter in the shadow of Egypt
your humiliation.

4 For though his officials are at Zoan
and his envoys reach Hanes,

5 everyone comes to shame
through a people that cannot profit
them,
that brings neither help nor profit,
but shame and disgrace.

6 An oracle concerning the animals of the
Negeb.
Through a land of trouble and distress,
of lioness and roaring[c] lion,
of viper and flying serpent,

30.1 Isaiah in His Prime

*Isaiah delivered the messages of chapters
28–35 at the peak of his ministry, under
Hezekiah. He unleashed six great "woes," or
warnings: (1) to drunken, scoffing politicians,
28.1; (2) to those who carry on the form of
religion, without true faith, 29.1; (3) to those
who hide their plans from God (possibly
referring to secret political intrigues), 29.15; (4)
to the pro-Egyptian party lobbying for a
political alliance, 30.1; (5) to those who trust in
military power (horses and chariots) instead of
God, 31.1; and (6) to the Assyrian destroyer,
33.1. Seemingly invincible at the time, the
Assyrian empire would face a judgment day.*

they carry their riches on the backs of
donkeys,
and their treasures on the humps of
camels,
to a people that cannot profit them.

7 For Egypt's help is worthless and empty,
therefore I have called her,
"Rahab who sits still."[d]

A Rebellious People

8 Go now, write it before them on a tablet,
and inscribe it in a book,
so that it may be for the time to come
as a witness forever.

9 For they are a rebellious people,
faithless children,
children who will not hear
the instruction of the LORD;

10 who say to the seers, "Do not see";
and to the prophets, "Do not prophesy
to us what is right;
speak to us smooth things,
prophesy illusions,

11 leave the way, turn aside from the path,
let us hear no more about the Holy
One of Israel."

12 Therefore thus says the Holy One of
Israel:
Because you reject this word,
and put your trust in oppression and
deceit,
and rely on them;

13 therefore this iniquity shall become for
you

c Cn: Heb *from them*   d Meaning of Heb uncertain

like a break in a high wall, bulging out,
and about to collapse,
whose crash comes suddenly, in an
instant;
14 its breaking is like that of a potter's vessel
that is smashed so ruthlessly
that among its fragments not a sherd is
found
for taking fire from the hearth,
or dipping water out of the cistern.

15 For thus said the Lord GOD, the Holy
One of Israel:
In returning and rest you shall be saved;
in quietness and in trust shall be your
strength.
But you refused 16and said,
"No! We will flee upon horses"—
therefore you shall flee!
and, "We will ride upon swift steeds"—
therefore your pursuers shall be swift!
17 A thousand shall flee at the threat of one,
at the threat of five you shall flee,
until you are left
like a flagstaff on the top of
a mountain,
like a signal on a hill.

God's Promise to Zion

18 Therefore the LORD waits to be gracious
to you;
therefore he will rise up to show mercy
to you.
For the LORD is a God of justice;
blessed are all those who wait for him.

19 Truly, O people in Zion, inhabitants of Jerusalem, you shall weep no more. He will surely
be gracious to you at the sound of your cry; when
he hears it, he will answer you. 20Though the Lord
may give you the bread of adversity and the water
of affliction, yet your Teacher will not hide himself any more, but your eyes shall see your Teacher. 21And when you turn to the right or when you
turn to the left, your ears shall hear a word behind
you, saying, "This is the way; walk in it." 22Then
you will defile your silver-covered idols and your
gold-plated images. You will scatter them like
filthy rags; you will say to them, "Away with you!"

23 He will give rain for the seed with which
you sow the ground, and grain, the produce of the
ground, which will be rich and plenteous. On that
day your cattle will graze in broad pastures; 24and
the oxen and donkeys that till the ground will eat
silage, which has been winnowed with shovel and
fork. 25On every lofty mountain and every high
hill there will be brooks running with water—on
a day of the great slaughter, when the towers fall.
26Moreover the light of the moon will be like the
light of the sun, and the light of the sun will be

sevenfold, like the light of seven days, on the day
when the LORD binds up the injuries of his people,
and heals the wounds inflicted by his blow.

Judgment on Assyria

27 See, the name of the LORD comes from far
away,
burning with his anger, and in thick
rising smoke;e
his lips are full of indignation,
and his tongue is like a devouring fire;

30.27 An End to Punishment

*Isaiah minces no words in his fierce
descriptions of the punishment awaiting Judah.
But as this chapter shows, the punishment will
reach an end, and then God will turn on the
surrounding evil nations. The fire of judgment
will culminate in Topheth (verse 33), a valley
near Jerusalem where human sacrifices were
offered to the god Molech.*

28 his breath is like an overflowing stream
that reaches up to the neck—
to sift the nations with the sieve of
destruction,
and to place on the jaws of the peoples
a bridle that leads them astray.

29 You shall have a song as in the night when
a holy festival is kept; and gladness of heart, as
when one sets out to the sound of the flute to go
to the mountain of the LORD, to the Rock of Israel.
30And the LORD will cause his majestic voice to be
heard and the descending blow of his arm to be
seen, in furious anger and a flame of devouring
fire, with a cloudburst and tempest and hailstones. 31The Assyrian will be terror-stricken at
the voice of the LORD, when he strikes with his
rod. 32And every stroke of the staff of punishment
that the LORD lays upon him will be to the sound
of timbrels and lyres; battling with brandished
arm he will fight with him. 33For his burning
placef has long been prepared; truly it is made
ready for the king,g its pyre made deep and wide,
with fire and wood in abundance; the breath of
the LORD, like a stream of sulfur, kindles it.

Alliance with Egypt Is Futile

31 Alas for those who go down to Egypt for
help
and who rely on horses,
who trust in chariots because they are
many
and in horsemen because they are very
strong,
but do not look to the Holy One of Israel

e Meaning of Heb uncertain   f Or Topheth   g Or Molech

or consult the LORD!

2 Yet he too is wise and brings disaster;
  he does not call back his words,
but will rise against the house of the
    evildoers,
and against the helpers of those who
    work iniquity.

3 The Egyptians are human, and not God;
  their horses are flesh, and not spirit.
When the LORD stretches out his hand,
  the helper will stumble, and the one
    helped will fall,
and they will all perish together.

4 For thus the LORD said to me,
As a lion or a young lion growls over its
    prey,
  and—when a band of shepherds is
    called out against it—
is not terrified by their shouting
  or daunted at their noise,
so the LORD of hosts will come down
  to fight upon Mount Zion and upon its
    hill.

5 Like birds hovering overhead, so the LORD
    of hosts
  will protect Jerusalem;

A Time of Crisis
Defeat seemed certain to everyone but Isaiah

> "The Assyrian shall fall by a sword, not of mortals." 31.8

AFTER TWO DISMAL DECADES UNDER King Ahaz, Judah finally saw a ray of hope when Hezekiah ascended the throne. Second Kings summarizes his reign this way: "There was no one like him among all the kings of Judah after him, or among those who were before him" (2 Kings 18.5).

Isaiah reached the peak of his ministry under King Hezekiah, who often sought his advice. The king needed Isaiah's help; he had inherited a kingdom in mortal danger from Assyria.

Protesting a Foolish Rebellion

How could Judah break free from Assyrian domination? Like other kings before him, Hezekiah thought of joining with other countries. Both Egypt and a rising Babylon seemed eager to court Judah as an ally.

Isaiah, however, said no. He urged Hezekiah to trust only in God. To dramatize his point, the court prophet did a shocking thing: he stalked around stripped and barefoot for three years as a protest against the pro-Egypt lobby (20.1–6). This protest forms the background for some of the strongest speeches in Isaiah's book (chapters 18–20; 30–31).

Isaiah's protest failed, however. Not even Hezekiah could resist the temptation to oppose Assyria. First, he shored up the defenses of Jerusalem and built up the city's water supplies. Then he formed an alliance of small kingdoms and led an outright rebellion against Assyria.

Revenge of an Empire

Assyria lowered the boom. Its armies smashed into Judah, leveling 46 walled cities and carrying away 200,150 captives. The Assyrian king demanded huge sums of money from Hezekiah, whom he mockingly described as "a bird in a cage."

Hezekiah, cowering under siege in Jerusalem, once more turned to Isaiah for advice. Should he surrender? Assyrian soldiers were already pressing in around the walls, hurling insults at the demoralized citizens inside.

Isaiah avoided an "I told you so" attitude. Against all odds, he again recommended prayer and reliance on the power of God. Have faith, he said; don't surrender, don't fear. Assyria will return home, wounded (37.5–7).

Isaiah's deep courage and optimism raised the morale of all Jerusalem. And in a spectacular way (37.36; also 2 Kings 19), God took care of the Assyrian army.

An Authentic Hero

Chapters 18–35 contain Isaiah's messages from this period, including many of the very words that stirred a desperate nation to faith. Without his inspiring example, Jerusalem might have surrendered.

Many of the prophets of Israel and Judah were loners, voices "crying in the desert." Isaiah was an exception. He had the king's ear at a critical moment in Judah's history. Because of his effectiveness, Isaiah went down in history as a great statesman and hero.

Life Questions: In your life, what experience has called for the most courage and faith? How did you respond at the time?

he will protect and deliver it,
he will spare and rescue it.

6 Turn back to him whom you[h] have deeply
betrayed, O people of Israel. [7]For on that day all
of you shall throw away your idols of silver and
idols of gold, which your hands have sinfully
made for you.
8 "Then the Assyrian shall fall by a sword,
not of mortals;
and a sword, not of humans, shall
devour him;
he shall flee from the sword,
and his young men shall be put to
forced labor.
9 His rock shall pass away in terror,
and his officers desert the standard in
panic,"
says the LORD, whose fire is in Zion,
and whose furnace is in Jerusalem.

Government with Justice Predicted

32 See, a king will reign in righteousness,
and princes will rule with justice.

32.1–20 Shifting Stance in Time

*Isaiah's writings often shift confusingly,
describing the present surroundings and then
moving on to predict the future. At times Isaiah
even projects himself into the future, writing in
the past tense about events that have not yet
happened. Note the shifting time sequence in
this chapter.*

---

2 Each will be like a hiding place from the
wind,
a covert from the tempest,
like streams of water in a dry place,
like the shade of a great rock in a
weary land.
3 Then the eyes of those who have sight
will not be closed,
and the ears of those who have hearing
will listen.
4 The minds of the rash will have good
judgment,
and the tongues of stammerers will
speak readily and distinctly.
5 A fool will no longer be called noble,
nor a villain said to be honorable.
6 For fools speak folly,
and their minds plot iniquity:
to practice ungodliness,
to utter error concerning the LORD,
to leave the craving of the hungry
unsatisfied,

and to deprive the thirsty of drink.
7 The villainies of villains are evil;
they devise wicked devices
to ruin the poor with lying words,
even when the plea of the needy is
right.
8 But those who are noble plan noble
things,
and by noble things they stand.

Complacent Women Warned of Disaster

9 Rise up, you women who are at ease, hear
my voice;
you complacent daughters, listen to my
speech.
10 In little more than a year
you will shudder, you complacent ones;
for the vintage will fail,
the fruit harvest will not come.
11 Tremble, you women who are at ease,
shudder, you complacent ones;
strip, and make yourselves bare,
and put sackcloth on your loins.
12 Beat your breasts for the pleasant fields,
for the fruitful vine,
13 for the soil of my people
growing up in thorns and briers;
yes, for all the joyous houses
in the jubilant city.
14 For the palace will be forsaken,
the populous city deserted;
the hill and the watchtower
will become dens forever,
the joy of wild asses,
a pasture for flocks;
15 until a spirit from on high is poured out
on us,
and the wilderness becomes a fruitful
field,
and the fruitful field is deemed a forest.

The Peace of God's Reign

16 Then justice will dwell in the wilderness,
and righteousness abide in the fruitful
field.
17 The effect of righteousness will be peace,
and the result of righteousness,
quietness and trust forever.
18 My people will abide in a peaceful
habitation,
in secure dwellings, and in quiet resting
places.
19 The forest will disappear completely,[i]
and the city will be utterly laid low.
20 Happy will you be who sow beside every
stream,
who let the ox and the donkey range
freely.

---

[h] Heb *they*   [i] Cn: Heb *And it will hail when the forest comes down*

A Prophecy of Deliverance from Foes

33 Ah, you destroyer,
who yourself have not been destroyed;
you treacherous one,
with whom no one has dealt
treacherously!
When you have ceased to destroy,
you will be destroyed;
and when you have stopped dealing
treacherously,
you will be dealt with treacherously.

2 O Lord, be gracious to us; we wait for
you.
Be our arm every morning,
our salvation in the time of trouble.
3 At the sound of tumult, peoples fled;
before your majesty, nations scattered.
4 Spoil was gathered as the caterpillar
gathers;
as locusts leap, they leaped*j* upon it.
5 The Lord is exalted, he dwells on high;
he filled Zion with justice and
righteousness;
6 he will be the stability of your times,
abundance of salvation, wisdom, and
knowledge;
the fear of the Lord is Zion's
treasure.*k*

7 Listen! the valiant*j* cry in the streets;
the envoys of peace weep bitterly.
8 The highways are deserted,
travelers have quit the road.
The treaty is broken,
its oaths*l* are despised,
its obligation*m* is disregarded.
9 The land mourns and languishes;
Lebanon is confounded and withers
away;
Sharon is like a desert;
and Bashan and Carmel shake off their
leaves.

10 "Now I will arise," says the Lord,
"now I will lift myself up;
now I will be exalted.
11 You conceive chaff, you bring
forth stubble;
your breath is a fire that will consume
you.
12 And the peoples will be as if burned to
lime,
like thorns cut down, that are burned
in the fire."

13 Hear, you who are far away, what I have
done;
and you who are near, acknowledge
my might.
14 The sinners in Zion are afraid;
trembling has seized the godless:
"Who among us can live with the
devouring fire?
Who among us can live with
everlasting flames?"
15 Those who walk righteously and speak
uprightly,
who despise the gain of oppression,
who wave away a bribe instead of
accepting it,
who stop their ears from hearing of
bloodshed
and shut their eyes from looking on
evil,
16 they will live on the heights;
their refuge will be the fortresses of
rocks;
their food will be supplied, their water
assured.

The Land of the Majestic King

17 Your eyes will see the king in his beauty;
they will behold a land that stretches
far away.
18 Your mind will muse on the terror:
"Where is the one who counted?
Where is the one who weighed the
tribute?
Where is the one who counted the
towers?"
19 No longer will you see the insolent
people,
the people of an obscure speech that
you cannot comprehend,
stammering in a language that you
cannot understand.
20 Look on Zion, the city of our appointed
festivals!
Your eyes will see Jerusalem,
a quiet habitation, an immovable tent,
whose stakes will never be pulled up,
and none of whose ropes will
be broken.
21 But there the Lord in majesty will be for
us
a place of broad rivers and streams,
where no galley with oars can go,
nor stately ship can pass.
22 For the Lord is our judge, the Lord is
our ruler,
the Lord is our king; he will save us.

23 Your rigging hangs loose;
it cannot hold the mast firm in its
place,
or keep the sail spread out.

---

j Meaning of Heb uncertain   *k* Heb *his treasure*; meaning of Heb uncertain   *l* Q Ms: MT *cities*   *m* Or *everyone*

Then prey and spoil in abundance will be
divided;
even the lame will fall to plundering.
24 And no inhabitant will say, "I am sick";
the people who live there will be
forgiven their iniquity.

Judgment on the Nations

34 Draw near, O nations, to hear;
O peoples, give heed!
Let the earth hear, and all that fills it;
the world, and all that comes from it.

34.1 Isaiah the Historian

Isaiah's book includes many references to nations and leaders of his day. Perhaps more than any other prophet, Isaiah had a deep sense of history. In fact, he wrote an account of the life of King Uzziah and a record of the rulers of Israel and Judah (see 2 Chronicles 26.22; 32.32). Although neither of these books has survived, the one that bears his name gives a blow-by-blow analysis of all the nations of his time.

2 For the LORD is enraged against all the
nations,
and furious against all their hordes;
he has doomed them, has given them
over for slaughter.
3 Their slain shall be cast out,
and the stench of their corpses shall
rise;
the mountains shall flow with their
blood.
4 All the host of heaven shall rot away,
and the skies roll up like a scroll.
All their host shall wither
like a leaf withering on a vine,
or fruit withering on a fig tree.

5 When my sword has drunk its fill in the
heavens,
lo, it will descend upon Edom,
upon the people I have doomed to
judgment.
6 The LORD has a sword; it is sated with
blood,
it is gorged with fat,
with the blood of lambs and goats,
with the fat of the kidneys of rams.
For the LORD has a sacrifice in Bozrah,
a great slaughter in the land of Edom.
7 Wild oxen shall fall with them,
and young steers with the mighty bulls.
Their land shall be soaked with blood,
and their soil made rich with fat.

8 For the LORD has a day of vengeance,
a year of vindication by Zion's cause.*n*
9 And the streams of Edom*o* shall be
turned into pitch,
and her soil into sulfur;
her land shall become burning pitch.
10 Night and day it shall not be quenched;
its smoke shall go up forever.
From generation to generation it shall lie
waste;
no one shall pass through it forever
and ever.
11 But the hawk*p* and the hedgehog*p* shall
possess it;
the owl*p* and the raven shall live in it.
He shall stretch the line of confusion over
it,
and the plummet of chaos over*q* its
nobles.
12 They shall name it No Kingdom There,
and all its princes shall be nothing.
13 Thorns shall grow over its strongholds,
nettles and thistles in its fortresses.
It shall be the haunt of jackals,
an abode for ostriches.
14 Wildcats shall meet with hyenas,
goat-demons shall call to each other;
there too Lilith shall repose,
and find a place to rest.
15 There shall the owl nest
and lay and hatch and brood in its
shadow;
there too the buzzards shall gather,
each one with its mate.
16 Seek and read from the book of the LORD:
Not one of these shall be missing;
none shall be without its mate.
For the mouth of the LORD has
commanded,
and his spirit has gathered them.
17 He has cast the lot for them,
his hand has portioned it out to them
with the line;
they shall possess it forever,
from generation to generation they
shall live in it.

The Return of the Redeemed to Zion

35 The wilderness and the dry land shall be
glad,
the desert shall rejoice and blossom;
like the crocus 2it shall blossom
abundantly,
and rejoice with joy and singing.
The glory of Lebanon shall be given to it,
the majesty of Carmel and Sharon.
They shall see the glory of the LORD,
the majesty of our God.

---

n Or *of recompense by Zion's defender*   *o* Heb *her streams*   *p* Identification uncertain   *q* Heb lacks *over*

³ Strengthen the weak hands,
and make firm the feeble knees.
⁴ Say to those who are of a fearful heart,
"Be strong, do not fear!
Here is your God.
He will come with vengeance,
with terrible recompense.
He will come and save you."

⁵ Then the eyes of the blind shall
be opened,
and the ears of the deaf unstopped;
⁶ then the lame shall leap like a deer,
and the tongue of the speechless sing
for joy.
For waters shall break forth in the
wilderness,
and streams in the desert;
⁷ the burning sand shall become a pool,
and the thirsty ground springs
of water;
the haunt of jackals shall become
a swamp,*r*
the grass shall become reeds and
rushes.

⁸ A highway shall be there,
and it shall be called the Holy Way;
the unclean shall not travel on it,*s*
but it shall be for God's people;*t*
no traveler, not even fools, shall go
astray.
⁹ No lion shall be there,
nor shall any ravenous beast come up
on it;
they shall not be found there,
but the redeemed shall walk there.
¹⁰ And the ransomed of the LORD shall
return,
and come to Zion with singing;
everlasting joy shall be upon their heads;
they shall obtain joy and gladness,
and sorrow and sighing shall flee away.

Sennacherib Threatens Jerusalem

36 In the fourteenth year of King Hezekiah, King Sennacherib of Assyria came up against all the fortified cities of Judah and captured them. ²The king of Assyria sent the Rabshakeh from Lachish to King Hezekiah at Jerusalem, with a great army. He stood by the conduit of the upper pool on the highway to the Fuller's Field. ³And there came out to him Eliakim son of Hilkiah, who was in charge of the palace, and Shebna the secretary, and Joah son of Asaph, the recorder.

4 The Rabshakeh said to them, "Say to Hezekiah: Thus says the great king, the king of Assyria: On what do you base this confidence of yours?

⁵Do you think that mere words are strategy and power for war? On whom do you now rely, that you have rebelled against me? ⁶See, you are relying on Egypt, that broken reed of a staff, which

36.1 Bridge Chapters

After a beautiful poem describing the renewed world God will make, Isaiah plunges into a historical account of Judah's troubles with the superpower Assyria. These next four historical chapters (which closely follow 2 Kings 18.13–20.19) form a bridge between problems with Assyria (chapters 1–35) and those with Babylon (chapters 40–66). They record some of the greatest crises in Isaiah's and King Hezekiah's lives, beginning with Assyria's final assault on Jerusalem and ending with Hezekiah's biggest blunder. That blunder led to Isaiah's prediction that Babylon would someday destroy Judah.

will pierce the hand of anyone who leans on it. Such is Pharaoh king of Egypt to all who rely on him. ⁷But if you say to me, 'We rely on the LORD our God,' is it not he whose high places and altars Hezekiah has removed, saying to Judah and to Jerusalem, 'You shall worship before this altar'? ⁸Come now, make a wager with my master the king of Assyria: I will give you two thousand horses, if you are able on your part to set riders on them. ⁹How then can you repulse a single captain among the least of my master's servants, when you rely on Egypt for chariots and for horsemen? ¹⁰Moreover, is it without the LORD that I have come up against this land to destroy it? The LORD said to me, Go up against this land, and destroy it."

11 Then Eliakim, Shebna, and Joah said to the Rabshakeh, "Please speak to your servants in Aramaic, for we understand it; do not speak to us in the language of Judah within the hearing of the people who are on the wall." ¹²But the Rabshakeh said, "Has my master sent me to speak these words to your master and to you, and not to the

36.11 Fear in the City

The Assyrian commander showed great skill in demoralizing the besieged residents of Jerusalem. King Hezekiah's own officials were terrified (36.22–37.4). Only Isaiah stood firm in believing that God could save the city. Earlier (see 22.15–25), God had expressed through Isaiah utter contempt for these very officials of Hezekiah.

r Cn: Heb *in the haunt of jackals is her resting place*   *s* Or *pass it by*   *t* Cn: Heb *for them*

people sitting on the wall, who are doomed with you to eat their own dung and drink their own urine?"

13 Then the Rabshakeh stood and called out in a loud voice in the language of Judah, "Hear the words of the great king, the king of Assyria! [14]Thus says the king: 'Do not let Hezekiah deceive you, for he will not be able to deliver you. [15]Do not let Hezekiah make you rely on the LORD by saying, The LORD will surely deliver us; this city will not be given into the hand of the king of Assyria.' [16]Do not listen to Hezekiah; for thus says the king of Assyria: 'Make your peace with me and come out to me; then everyone of you will eat from your own vine and your own fig tree and drink water from your own cistern, [17]until I come and take you away to a land like your own land, a land of grain and wine, a land of bread and vineyards. [18]Do not let Hezekiah mislead you by saying, The LORD will save us. Has any of the gods of the nations saved their land out of the hand of the king of Assyria? [19]Where are the gods of Hamath and Arpad? Where are the gods of Sepharvaim? Have they delivered Samaria out of my hand? [20]Who among all the gods of these countries have saved their countries out of my hand, that the LORD should save Jerusalem out of my hand?'"

21 But they were silent and answered him not a word, for the king's command was, "Do not answer him." [22]Then Eliakim son of Hilkiah, who was in charge of the palace, and Shebna the secretary, and Joah son of Asaph, the recorder, came to Hezekiah with their clothes torn, and told him the words of the Rabshakeh.

Hezekiah Consults Isaiah

37 When King Hezekiah heard it, he tore his clothes, covered himself with sackcloth, and went into the house of the LORD. [2]And he sent Eliakim, who was in charge of the palace, and Shebna the secretary, and the senior priests, covered with sackcloth, to the prophet Isaiah son of Amoz. [3]They said to him, "Thus says Hezekiah, This day is a day of distress, of rebuke, and of disgrace; children have come to the birth, and there is no strength to bring them forth. [4]It may be that the LORD your God heard the words of the Rabshakeh, whom his master the king of Assyria has sent to mock the living God, and will rebuke the words that the LORD your God has heard; therefore lift up your prayer for the remnant that is left."

5 When the servants of King Hezekiah came to Isaiah, [6]Isaiah said to them, "Say to your master, 'Thus says the LORD: Do not be afraid because of the words that you have heard, with which the servants of the king of Assyria have reviled me. [7]I myself will put a spirit in him, so that he shall hear

a rumor, and return to his own land; I will cause him to fall by the sword in his own land.'"

8 The Rabshakeh returned, and found the king of Assyria fighting against Libnah; for he had heard that the king had left Lachish. [9]Now the king[u] heard concerning King Tirhakah of Ethiopia,[v] "He has set out to fight against you." When he heard it, he sent messengers to Hezekiah, saying, [10]"Thus shall you speak to King Hezekiah of Judah: Do not let your God on whom you rely deceive you by promising that Jerusalem will not be given into the hand of the king of Assyria. [11]See, you have heard what the kings of Assyria have done to all lands, destroying them utterly. Shall you be delivered? [12]Have the gods of the nations delivered them, the nations that my predecessors destroyed, Gozan, Haran, Rezeph, and the people of Eden who were in Telassar? [13]Where is the king of Hamath, the king of Arpad, the king of the city of Sepharvaim, the king of Hena, or the king of Ivvah?"

Hezekiah's Prayer

14 Hezekiah received the letter from the hand of the messengers and read it; then Hezekiah went up to the house of the LORD and spread it before the LORD. [15]And Hezekiah prayed to the LORD, saying: [16]"O LORD of hosts, God of Israel, who are enthroned above the cherubim, you are God, you alone, of all the kingdoms of the earth; you have made heaven and earth. [17]Incline your ear, O LORD, and hear; open your eyes, O LORD, and see; hear all the words of Sennacherib, which he has sent to mock the living God. [18]Truly, O LORD, the kings of Assyria have laid waste all the nations and their lands, [19]and have hurled their gods into the fire, though they were no gods, but the work of human hands—wood and stone—and so they were destroyed. [20]So now, O LORD our God, save us from his hand, so that all the kingdoms of the earth may know that you alone are the LORD."

21 Then Isaiah son of Amoz sent to Hezekiah, saying: "Thus says the LORD, the God of Israel: Because you have prayed to me concerning King Sennacherib of Assyria, [22]this is the word that the LORD has spoken concerning him:

She despises you, she scorns you—
    virgin daughter Zion;
she tosses her head—behind your back,
    daughter Jerusalem.

23 "Whom have you mocked and reviled?
    Against whom have you raised your
        voice
and haughtily lifted your eyes?
    Against the Holy One of Israel!
24 By your servants you have mocked the
        Lord,

and you have said, 'With my many
    chariots
I have gone up the heights of the
    mountains,
    to the far recesses of Lebanon;
I felled its tallest cedars,
    its choicest cypresses;
I came to its remotest height,
    its densest forest.
25 I dug wells
    and drank waters,
I dried up with the sole of my foot
    all the streams of Egypt.'

26 "Have you not heard
    that I determined it long ago?
I planned from days of old
    what now I bring to pass,
that you should make fortified cities
    crash into heaps of ruins,
27 while their inhabitants, shorn of strength,
    are dismayed and confounded;
they have become like plants of the field
    and like tender grass,
like grass on the housetops,
    blighted[w] before it is grown.

28 "I know your rising up[x] and your sitting
    down,
    your going out and coming in,
    and your raging against me.
29 Because you have raged against me
    and your arrogance has come to my
    ears,
I will put my hook in your nose
    and my bit in your mouth;
I will turn you back on the way
    by which you came.

30 "And this shall be the sign for you: This year eat what grows of itself, and in the second year what springs from that; then in the third year sow, reap, plant vineyards, and eat their fruit. 31The surviving remnant of the house of Judah shall again take root downward, and bear fruit upward; 32for from Jerusalem a remnant shall go out, and from Mount Zion a band of survivors. The zeal of the LORD of hosts will do this.

33 "Therefore thus says the LORD concerning the king of Assyria: He shall not come into this city, shoot an arrow there, come before it with a shield, or cast up a siege ramp against it. 34By the way that he came, by the same he shall return; he shall not come into this city, says the LORD. 35For I will defend this city to save it, for my own sake and for the sake of my servant David."

Sennacherib's Defeat and Death

36 Then the angel of the LORD set out and struck down one hundred eighty-five thousand in the camp of the Assyrians; when morning dawned, they were all dead bodies. 37Then King Sennacherib of Assyria left, went home, and lived at Nineveh. 38As he was worshiping in the house of his god Nisroch, his sons Adrammelech and Sharezer killed him with the sword, and they escaped into the land of Ararat. His son Esarhaddon succeeded him.

Hezekiah's Illness

38 In those days Hezekiah became sick and was at the point of death. The prophet Isaiah son of Amoz came to him, and said to him, "Thus says the LORD: Set your house in order, for

38.1 Fifteen More Years

When the doctor solemnly pronounces a disease terminal, who doesn't crave a second chance? After Isaiah announced to Hezekiah that his disease would be fatal, Hezekiah did not give up. He wept bitterly and asked God to remember his devotion. In response, God sent Isaiah back with an amazing message: He had granted Hezekiah fifteen additional years. Here, as so often in the Bible, God changes events because of prayer.

you shall die; you shall not recover." 2Then Hezekiah turned his face to the wall, and prayed to the LORD: 3"Remember now, O LORD, I implore you, how I have walked before you in faithfulness with a whole heart, and have done what is good in your sight." And Hezekiah wept bitterly.

4 Then the word of the LORD came to Isaiah: 5"Go and say to Hezekiah, Thus says the LORD, the God of your ancestor David: I have heard your prayer, I have seen your tears; I will add fifteen years to your life. 6I will deliver you and this city out of the hand of the king of Assyria, and defend this city.

7 "This is the sign to you from the LORD, that the LORD will do this thing that he has promised: 8See, I will make the shadow cast by the declining sun on the dial of Ahaz turn back ten steps." So the sun turned back on the dial the ten steps by which it had declined.[y]

9 A writing of King Hezekiah of Judah, after he had been sick and had recovered from his sickness:
10 I said: In the noontide of my days
    I must depart;
I am consigned to the gates of Sheol
    for the rest of my years.
11 I said, I shall not see the LORD
    in the land of the living;

---

w With 2 Kings 19.26: Heb *field*   x Q Ms Gk: MT lacks *your rising up*   y Meaning of Heb uncertain

I shall look upon mortals no more
    among the inhabitants of the world.

12 My dwelling is plucked up and removed
      from me
    like a shepherd's tent;
like a weaver I have rolled up my life;
    he cuts me off from the loom;
from day to night you bring me to an
      end;*z*

13 I cry for help*a* until morning;
like a lion he breaks all my bones;
    from day to night you bring me to an
      end.*z*

14 Like a swallow or a crane*z* I clamor,
    I moan like a dove.
My eyes are weary with looking upward.
    O Lord, I am oppressed; be my
      security!

15 But what can I say? For he has spoken to
    me,
    and he himself has done it.
All my sleep has fled*b*
    because of the bitterness of my soul.

16 O Lord, by these things people live,
    and in all these is the life of
      my spirit.*z*
    Oh, restore me to health and make me
      live!

17 Surely it was for my welfare
    that I had great bitterness;
but you have held back*c* my life
    from the pit of destruction,
for you have cast all my sins
    behind your back.

18 For Sheol cannot thank you,
    death cannot praise you;
those who go down to the Pit cannot
      hope
    for your faithfulness.

19 The living, the living, they thank you,
    as I do this day;
fathers make known to children
    your faithfulness.

20 The Lord will save me,
    and we will sing to stringed
      instruments*d*
all the days of our lives,
    at the house of the Lord.

21 Now Isaiah had said, "Let them take a lump of figs, and apply it to the boil, so that he may recover." 22Hezekiah also had said, "What is the sign that I shall go up to the house of the Lord?"

Envoys from Babylon Welcomed

39 At that time King Merodach-baladan son of Baladan of Babylon sent envoys with letters and a present to Hezekiah, for he heard that he had been sick and had recovered. 2Hezekiah welcomed them; he showed them his treasure house, the silver, the gold, the spices, the precious oil, his whole armory, all that was found in his storehouses. There was nothing in his house or in all his realm that Hezekiah did not show them. 3Then the prophet Isaiah came to King Hezekiah and said to him, "What did these men say? From where did they come to you?" Hezekiah answered, "They have come to me from a far country, from Babylon." 4He said, "What have they seen in your house?" Hezekiah answered, "They have seen all that is in my house; there is nothing in my storehouses that I did not show them."

5 Then Isaiah said to Hezekiah, "Hear the word of the Lord of hosts: 6Days are coming when all that is in your house, and that which your ancestors have stored up until this day, shall be carried to Babylon; nothing shall be left, says the Lord. 7Some of your own sons who are born to you shall be taken away; they shall be eunuchs in the palace of the king of Babylon." 8Then Hezekiah said to Isaiah, "The word of the Lord that you have spoken is good." For he thought, "There will be peace and security in my days."

God's People Are Comforted

40 Comfort, O comfort my people,
    says your God.
2 Speak tenderly to Jerusalem,
    and cry to her
that she has served her term,
    that her penalty is paid,
that she has received from the Lord's
      hand
    double for all her sins.

3 A voice cries out:
"In the wilderness prepare the way of the
      Lord,
    make straight in the desert a highway
      for our God.
4 Every valley shall be lifted up,
    and every mountain and hill be made
      low;
the uneven ground shall become level,
    and the rough places a plain.
5 Then the glory of the Lord shall
      be revealed,
    and all people shall see it together,
for the mouth of the Lord has
      spoken."

6 A voice says, "Cry out!"

---

z Meaning of Heb uncertain   *a* Cn: Meaning of Heb uncertain   *b* Cn Compare Syr: Heb *I will walk slowly all my years*   *c* Cn Compare Gk Vg: Heb *loved*   *d* Heb *my stringed instruments*

A New Song

A dramatic change in tone: comfort and hope for the worst of times

YOU CAN SENSE THE CHANGE in the very first words of chapter 40. "Comfort, O comfort my people, says your God. Speak tenderly to Jerusalem, and cry to her that she has served her term." Soft, reassuring words replace the harsh warnings of Isaiah's earlier chapters.

During much of Isaiah's life, Judah was confident and strong. But the prophecies beginning in chapter 40 project forward to a radically different scene. The land of Judah has been devastated, and the Jews have been taken captive. Jerusalem lies in ruins. Some 200 years separate what is described in the first part of Isaiah from the latter part. (Many scholars believe these later prophecies were given by another prophet.)

> Those who wait for the LORD shall renew their strength, they shall mount up with wings like eagles, they shall run and not be weary, they shall walk and not faint. 40:31

What Happened in the Meantime

To understand the rest of the book of Isaiah, you need to understand what happened in those 200 years. The confident nation Isaiah once knew slid further and further downward. At the same time a new empire, Babylon, gained strength. This new enemy invaded Judah.

The armies of Babylon did something no army had accomplished since King David's time: they conquered Jerusalem itself. Siege engines breached the walls. Judah's king was led out of Jerusalem, blinded. Their homes destroyed, most of the city's inhabitants followed their king in chains. The dark period of Babylonian captivity began.

Prophets of this period, and those who prophesied in advance about the coming catastrophes, faced huge questions. Was God abandoning his "eternal" throne of David? How could he watch in silence as his own nation—his own temple—was ripped to shreds by pagan armies?

Three Great Hopes

Reflecting the change in circumstances, Isaiah 40—66 shifts into a new key. Gone are the bleak predictions of judgment on the Jews. Instead, a majestic message of hope and joy and light breaks in, beginning with the opening words of comfort. The prophet sets out to reestablish faith in God.

What happened to Judah, Isaiah teaches, was not God's defeat. God had in mind a new thing, a plan far more grand than anything seen before.

The author of Isaiah expresses the plan as a series of wonderful reasons for hope. First, he says, will come deliverance from the Babylonian captivity. A new star, a ruler named Cyrus, will arise in the east and set the Jews free. He will allow them to return to Jerusalem to begin the long task of rebuilding a city and a nation. Chapters 40—48 detail God's confident predictions about Cyrus and the relief he would give captive Jews.

Indeed, just such a ruler did ascend to the throne in ancient Persia (present-day Iran). Cyrus smashed Babylon's armies in one decisive battle. As recorded in Ezra 1:1—4, he granted the Jews permission to return to their city and rebuild.

In words that have become very familiar, the book of Isaiah tells of two further hopes for the future. A mysterious figure called "the servant" appears in chapter 49. That servant, through his suffering, would provide a way to rescue the entire world. Finally, in conclusion, the prophet turns to a far-away time, when God will usher in peace for all in a new heaven and new earth. "The Holy One of Israel" (one of Isaiah's favorite names for God) will rule as the God of the whole earth.

Surviving Tough Times

Isaiah 40—66 had immense practical value for the people who first heard it. The Jews, facing a series of great crises, needed the prophet's message of hope: Forgiveness was on the way; the Jews, though scattered, would one day be gathered "one by one."

Further, Isaiah teaches that no matter how difficult the circumstances, God can use them for our benefit. Again and again in the Israelites' history, good times led to decadence. In contrast, times of suffering tested and refined the true people of God. Ultimately, suffering would lead to the salvation of all the world.

Life Questions: Try to put yourself in the circumstances of the Jews back then. Would you have found the prophet's words comforting?

And I said, "What shall I cry?"
All people are grass,
    their constancy is like the flower of the
        field.

40.3 Voice in the Wilderness

Beginning here, Isaiah's emphasis shifts away from judgment and toward comfort. The comfort will ultimately come through God's glorious arrival, which God's people should prepare for by building a "highway" for God to travel on. In the New Testament, John the Baptist identified himself as the "voice" calling for this preparation (John 1.23). The "earthmoving" he demanded was repentance from sin, a preparation for Jesus' arrival.

7 The grass withers, the flower fades,
    when the breath of the LORD blows
        upon it;
    surely the people are grass.
8 The grass withers, the flower fades;
    but the word of our God will stand
        forever.
9 Get you up to a high mountain,
    O Zion, herald of good tidings;*e*
lift up your voice with strength,
    O Jerusalem, herald of good tidings,*f*
    lift it up, do not fear;
say to the cities of Judah,
    "Here is your God!"
10 See, the Lord GOD comes with might,
    and his arm rules for him;
his reward is with him,
    and his recompense before him.
11 He will feed his flock like a shepherd;
    he will gather the lambs in his arms,
and carry them in his bosom,
    and gently lead the mother sheep.

12 Who has measured the waters in the
        hollow of his hand
    and marked off the heavens with a
        span,
enclosed the dust of the earth in
        a measure,
    and weighed the mountains in scales
    and the hills in a balance?
13 Who has directed the spirit of the LORD,
    or as his counselor has instructed him?
14 Whom did he consult for his
        enlightenment,
    and who taught him the path of
        justice?
Who taught him knowledge,
    and showed him the way of
        understanding?

15 Even the nations are like a drop from a
        bucket,
    and are accounted as dust on
        the scales;
    see, he takes up the isles like fine dust.
16 Lebanon would not provide fuel enough,
    nor are its animals enough for a burnt
        offering.
17 All the nations are as nothing before him;
    they are accounted by him as less than
        nothing and emptiness.

18 To whom then will you liken God,
    or what likeness compare with him?
19 An idol? —A workman casts it,
    and a goldsmith overlays it with gold,
    and casts for it silver chains.
20 As a gift one chooses mulberry wood*g*
    —wood that will not rot—
then seeks out a skilled artisan
    to set up an image that will not topple.

21 Have you not known? Have you
        not heard?
Has it not been told you from the
        beginning?
Have you not understood from the
        foundations of the earth?
22 It is he who sits above the circle of the
        earth,
    and its inhabitants are like
        grasshoppers;
who stretches out the heavens like a
        curtain,
    and spreads them like a tent to live in;
23 who brings princes to naught,
    and makes the rulers of the earth as
        nothing.

24 Scarcely are they planted, scarcely sown,
    scarcely has their stem taken root in
        the earth,
when he blows upon them, and they
        wither,
    and the tempest carries them off like
        stubble.

25 To whom then will you compare me,
    or who is my equal? says the Holy
        One.
26 Lift up your eyes on high and see:
    Who created these?
He who brings out their host and
        numbers them,
    calling them all by name;
because he is great in strength,
    mighty in power,
    not one is missing.

---

e Or O herald of good tidings to Zion   *f Or O herald of good tidings to Jerusalem*   *g Meaning of Heb uncertain*

27 Why do you say, O Jacob,
and speak, O Israel,
"My way is hidden from the LORD,
and my right is disregarded by my
God"?
28 Have you not known? Have you
not heard?
The LORD is the everlasting God,
the Creator of the ends of the earth.
He does not faint or grow weary;
his understanding is unsearchable.
29 He gives power to the faint,
and strengthens the powerless.
30 Even youths will faint and be weary,
and the young will fall exhausted;
31 but those who wait for the LORD shall
renew their strength,
they shall mount up with wings like
eagles,
they shall run and not be weary,
they shall walk and not faint.

Israel Assured of God's Help

41 Listen to me in silence, O coastlands;
let the peoples renew their strength;
let them approach, then let them speak;
let us together draw near for judgment.

2 Who has roused a victor from the east,
summoned him to his service?
He delivers up nations to him,
and tramples kings under foot;
he makes them like dust with his sword,
like driven stubble with his bow.
3 He pursues them and passes on safely,
scarcely touching the path with his feet.
4 Who has performed and done this,
calling the generations from the
beginning?

41.4 How to Understand God

Chapters 40–46 echo the majestic chapters at the end of Job. God shows himself as master of the universe. Before him, nations are like a drop in a bucket (40.15) and people are like grasshoppers (40.22). He taunts all other so-called "gods": such idols are carved of the same tree used to cook supper! (44.12–20). The true God, the God of the Israelites, is the One who created the universe (45.12,18), who called Abraham (41.8), who rescued the Israelites from slavery in Egypt. For the dispirited Jewish survivors of Babylon's invasion, this exalted view of God was a reminder that God had neither vanished nor rejected them.

I, the LORD, am first,
and will be with the last.
5 The coastlands have seen and are afraid,
the ends of the earth tremble;
they have drawn near and come.
6 Each one helps the other,
saying to one another, "Take courage!"
7 The artisan encourages the goldsmith,
and the one who smooths with the
hammer encourages the one who
strikes the anvil,
saying of the soldering, "It is good";
and they fasten it with nails so that it
cannot be moved.
8 But you, Israel, my servant,
Jacob, whom I have chosen,
the offspring of Abraham, my friend;
9 you whom I took from the ends of the
earth,
and called from its farthest corners,
saying to you, "You are my servant,
I have chosen you and not cast you
off";
10 do not fear, for I am with you,
do not be afraid, for I am your God;
I will strengthen you, I will help you,
I will uphold you with my victorious
right hand.

11 Yes, all who are incensed against you
shall be ashamed and disgraced;
those who strive against you
shall be as nothing and shall perish.
12 You shall seek those who contend with
you,
but you shall not find them;
those who war against you
shall be as nothing at all.
13 For I, the LORD your God,
hold your right hand;
it is I who say to you, "Do not fear,
I will help you."
14 Do not fear, you worm Jacob,
you insect[h] Israel!
I will help you, says the LORD;
your Redeemer is the Holy One of
Israel.
15 Now, I will make of you a threshing
sledge,
sharp, new, and having teeth;
you shall thresh the mountains and crush
them,
and you shall make the hills like chaff.
16 You shall winnow them and the wind
shall carry them away,
and the tempest shall scatter them.
Then you shall rejoice in the LORD;
in the Holy One of Israel you shall
glory.

[h] Syr: Heb *men of*

17 When the poor and needy seek water,
  and there is none,
  and their tongue is parched with thirst,
I the LORD will answer them,
  I the God of Israel will not forsake
    them.
18 I will open rivers on the bare heights,[i]
  and fountains in the midst of
    the valleys;
I will make the wilderness a pool
  of water,
  and the dry land springs of water.
19 I will put in the wilderness the cedar,
  the acacia, the myrtle, and the olive;
I will set in the desert the cypress,
  the plane and the pine together,
20 so that all may see and know,
  all may consider and understand,
that the hand of the LORD has done this,
  the Holy One of Israel has created it.

The Futility of Idols

21 Set forth your case, says the LORD;
  bring your proofs, says the King of
    Jacob.
22 Let them bring them, and tell us
  what is to happen.
Tell us the former things, what they are,
  so that we may consider them,
and that we may know their outcome;
  or declare to us the things to come.
23 Tell us what is to come hereafter,
  that we may know that you are gods;
do good, or do harm,
  that we may be afraid and terrified.
24 You, indeed, are nothing
  and your work is nothing at all;
  whoever chooses you is an
    abomination.

25 I stirred up one from the north, and he
    has come,
  from the rising of the sun he was
    summoned by name.[j]
He shall trample[k] on rulers as on mortar,
  as the potter treads clay.
26 Who declared it from the beginning, so
    that we might know,
  and beforehand, so that we might say,
    "He is right"?
There was no one who declared it, none
    who proclaimed,
  none who heard your words.
27 I first have declared it to Zion,[l]
  and I give to Jerusalem a herald of
    good tidings.
28 But when I look there is no one;
  among these there is no counselor

who, when I ask, gives an answer.
29 No, they are all a delusion;
  their works are nothing;
  their images are empty wind.

The Servant, a Light to the Nations

42 Here is my servant, whom I uphold,
  my chosen, in whom my soul delights;
I have put my spirit upon him;
  he will bring forth justice to the
    nations.

42.1 The Solution

Having described shocking injustice, Isaiah now gives the solution: God's servant, who in a quiet, gentle, steady way will bring justice not only to Israel but to "the nations"—that is, the entire earth. Matthew 12.18–21, quoting this passage, identifies the servant as Jesus.

2 He will not cry or lift up his voice,
  or make it heard in the street;
3 a bruised reed he will not break,
  and a dimly burning wick he will not
    quench;
he will faithfully bring forth justice.
4 He will not grow faint or be crushed
  until he has established justice in the
    earth;
  and the coastlands wait for his
    teaching.

5 Thus says God, the LORD,
  who created the heavens and stretched
    them out,
  who spread out the earth and what
    comes from it,
who gives breath to the people upon it
  and spirit to those who walk in it:
6 I am the LORD, I have called you in
    righteousness,
  I have taken you by the hand and kept
    you;
I have given you as a covenant to the
    people,[m]
  a light to the nations,
7   to open the eyes that are blind,
to bring out the prisoners from the
    dungeon,
  from the prison those who sit in
    darkness.
8 I am the LORD, that is my name;
  my glory I give to no other,
  nor my praise to idols.
9 See, the former things have come to pass,
  and new things I now declare;

---

*i Or trails   j Cn Compare Q Ms Gk: MT and he shall call on my name   k Cn: Heb come   l Cn: Heb First to
Zion—Behold, behold them   m Meaning of Heb uncertain*

before they spring forth,
  I tell you of them.

A Hymn of Praise

10 Sing to the LORD a new song,
    his praise from the end of the earth!
  Let the sea roar[n] and all that fills it,
    the coastlands and their inhabitants.
11 Let the desert and its towns lift up their
      voice,
    the villages that Kedar inhabits;
  let the inhabitants of Sela sing for joy,
    let them shout from the tops of the
      mountains.
12 Let them give glory to the LORD,
    and declare his praise in the coastlands.
13 The LORD goes forth like a soldier,
    like a warrior he stirs up his fury;
  he cries out, he shouts aloud,
    he shows himself mighty against his
      foes.

14 For a long time I have held my peace,
    I have kept still and restrained myself;
  now I will cry out like a woman in labor,
    I will gasp and pant.

42.14 Does God Care?

After telling of his power, God goes on to
describe the depth of his feelings for his people.
He uses tender and sometimes shocking
language, especially in this comparison of his
pain to that of childbirth.

15 I will lay waste mountains and hills,
    and dry up all their herbage;
  I will turn the rivers into islands,
    and dry up the pools.
16 I will lead the blind
    by a road they do not know,
  by paths they have not known
    I will guide them.
  I will turn the darkness before them into
      light,
    the rough places into level ground.
  These are the things I will do,
    and I will not forsake them.
17 They shall be turned back and utterly put
      to shame—
    those who trust in carved images,
  who say to cast images,
    "You are our gods."

18 Listen, you that are deaf;

and you that are blind, look up and
      see!
19 Who is blind but my servant,
    or deaf like my messenger whom I
      send?
  Who is blind like my dedicated one,
    or blind like the servant of the LORD?
20 He sees many things, but does[o] not
      observe them;
    his ears are open, but he does
      not hear.

Israel's Disobedience

21 The LORD was pleased, for the sake of his
      righteousness,
    to magnify his teaching and make it
      glorious.
22 But this is a people robbed and
      plundered,
    all of them are trapped in holes
      and hidden in prisons;
  they have become a prey with no one to
      rescue,
    a spoil with no one to say, "Restore!"
23 Who among you will give heed to this,
    who will attend and listen for the time
      to come?
24 Who gave up Jacob to the spoiler,
    and Israel to the robbers?
  Was it not the LORD, against whom we
      have sinned,
    in whose ways they would not walk,
    and whose law they would not obey?
25 So he poured upon him the heat of his
      anger
    and the fury of war;
  it set him on fire all around, but he did
      not understand;
    it burned him, but he did not take it to
      heart.

Restoration and Protection Promised

43 But now thus says the LORD,
    he who created you, O Jacob,
  he who formed you, O Israel:
  Do not fear, for I have redeemed you;
    I have called you by name, you are
      mine.
2 When you pass through the waters, I will
      be with you;
    and through the rivers, they shall not
      overwhelm you;
  when you walk through fire you shall not
      be burned,
    and the flame shall not consume you.
3 For I am the LORD your God,
    the Holy One of Israel, your Savior.
  I give Egypt as your ransom,

---

[n] Cn Compare Ps 96.11; 98.7: Heb *Those who go down to the sea*   [o] Heb *You see many things but do*

Ethiopia*p* and Seba in exchange for
you.
4 Because you are precious in my sight,
and honored, and I love you,

43.3 Ransom for the Captives

*God speaks of providing the nations of Egypt,
Cush, and Seba as a ransom or reward for
allowing the Jews to return to their land.
Historically, Cyrus of Persia permitted the Jews
to resettle in the sixth century B.C. Shortly after
that, Persia conquered the territories
mentioned here.*

I give people in return for you,
nations in exchange for your life.
5 Do not fear, for I am with you;
I will bring your offspring from the
east,
and from the west I will gather you;
6 I will say to the north, "Give them up,"
and to the south, "Do not withhold;
bring my sons from far away
and my daughters from the end of the
earth—
7 everyone who is called by my name,
whom I created for my glory,
whom I formed and made."

8 Bring forth the people who are blind, yet
have eyes,
who are deaf, yet have ears!
9 Let all the nations gather together,
and let the peoples assemble.
Who among them declared this,
and foretold to us the former things?
Let them bring their witnesses to justify
them,
and let them hear and say, "It is true."
10 You are my witnesses, says the LORD,
and my servant whom I have chosen,
so that you may know and believe me
and understand that I am he.

43.10 Courtroom Drama

*Isaiah pictures a courtlike drama, in which the
world assembles to decide who is really God. As
each would-be god calls witnesses in turn, the
God of Israel calls his people to witness for him.
They had heard God's prediction that he would
bring back his people, scattered all over the
Middle East, to reestablish their nation. As his
witnesses, they need only testify that he has
done what he promised.*

Before me no god was formed,
nor shall there be any after me.
11 I, I am the LORD,
and besides me there is no savior.
12 I declared and saved and proclaimed,
when there was no strange god among
you;
and you are my witnesses, says the
LORD.
13 I am God, and also henceforth I am He;
there is no one who can deliver from
my hand;
I work and who can hinder it?

14 Thus says the LORD,
your Redeemer, the Holy One of Israel:
For your sake I will send to Babylon
and break down all the bars,
and the shouting of the Chaldeans will
be turned to lamentation.*q*
15 I am the LORD, your Holy One,
the Creator of Israel, your King.
16 Thus says the LORD,
who makes a way in the sea,
a path in the mighty waters,
17 who brings out chariot and horse,
army and warrior;
they lie down, they cannot rise,
they are extinguished, quenched like a
wick:
18 Do not remember the former things,
or consider the things of old.
19 I am about to do a new thing;
now it springs forth, do you not
perceive it?
I will make a way in the wilderness
and rivers in the desert.
20 The wild animals will honor me,
the jackals and the ostriches;
for I give water in the wilderness,
rivers in the desert,
to give drink to my chosen people,
21 the people whom I formed for myself
so that they might declare my praise.

22 Yet you did not call upon me, O Jacob;
but you have been weary of me,
O Israel!
23 You have not brought me your sheep for
burnt offerings,
or honored me with your sacrifices.
I have not burdened you with offerings,
or wearied you with frankincense.
24 You have not bought me sweet cane with
money,
or satisfied me with the fat of your
sacrifices.
But you have burdened me with your
sins;

---

p Or *Nubia*; Heb *Cush*   *q* Meaning of Heb uncertain

you have wearied me with your
    iniquities.

25 I, I am He
    who blots out your transgressions for
        my own sake,
    and I will not remember your sins.
26 Accuse me, let us go to trial;
    set forth your case, so that you may be
        proved right.
27 Your first ancestor sinned,
    and your interpreters transgressed
        against me.
28 Therefore I profaned the princes of the
        sanctuary,
    I delivered Jacob to utter destruction,
    and Israel to reviling.

God's Blessing on Israel

44 But now hear, O Jacob my servant,
    Israel whom I have chosen!
2 Thus says the LORD who made you,
    who formed you in the womb and will
        help you:
    Do not fear, O Jacob my servant,
    Jeshurun whom I have chosen.
3 For I will pour water on the thirsty land,
    and streams on the dry ground;
    I will pour my spirit upon your
        descendants,
    and my blessing on your offspring.
4 They shall spring up like a green
        tamarisk,
    like willows by flowing streams.
5 This one will say, "I am the LORD's,"
    another will be called by the name of
        Jacob,
    yet another will write on the hand, "The
        LORD's,"
    and adopt the name of Israel.

6 Thus says the LORD, the King of Israel,
    and his Redeemer, the LORD of hosts:
    I am the first and I am the last;
    besides me there is no god.
7 Who is like me? Let them proclaim it,
    let them declare and set it forth before
        me.
    Who has announced from of old the
        things to come?[r]
    Let them tell us[s] what is yet to be.
8 Do not fear, or be afraid;
    have I not told you from of old and
        declared it?
    You are my witnesses!
    Is there any god besides me?
    There is no other rock; I know not
        one.

The Absurdity of Idol Worship

9 All who make idols are nothing, and the
things they delight in do not profit; their witnesses neither see nor know. And so they will be
put to shame. [10]Who would fashion a god or cast
an image that can do no good? [11]Look, all its
devotees shall be put to shame; the artisans too
are merely human. Let them all assemble, let them
stand up; they shall be terrified, they shall all be
put to shame.

12 The ironsmith fashions it[t] and works it
over the coals, shaping it with hammers, and
forging it with his strong arm; he becomes hungry
and his strength fails, he drinks no water and is
faint. [13]The carpenter stretches a line, marks it out
with a stylus, fashions it with planes, and marks it
with a compass; he makes it in human form, with
human beauty, to be set up in a shrine. [14]He cuts
down cedars or chooses a holm tree or an oak and
lets it grow strong among the trees of the forest.
He plants a cedar and the rain nourishes it.
[15]Then it can be used as fuel. Part of it he takes
and warms himself; he kindles a fire and bakes
bread. Then he makes a god and worships it,
makes it a carved image and bows down before it.
[16]Half of it he burns in the fire; over this half he
roasts meat, eats it and is satisfied. He also warms
himself and says, "Ah, I am warm, I can feel the
fire!" [17]The rest of it he makes into a god, his idol,
bows down to it and worships it; he prays to it
and says, "Save me, for you are my god!"

18 They do not know, nor do they comprehend; for their eyes are shut, so that they cannot
see, and their minds as well, so that they cannot
understand. [19]No one considers, nor is there
knowledge or discernment to say, "Half of it I
burned in the fire; I also baked bread on its coals,
I roasted meat and have eaten. Now shall I make
the rest of it an abomination? Shall I fall down
before a block of wood?" [20]He feeds on ashes; a
deluded mind has led him astray, and he cannot
save himself or say, "Is not this thing in my right
hand a fraud?"

Israel Is Not Forgotten

21 Remember these things, O Jacob,
    and Israel, for you are my servant;
    I formed you, you are my servant;
    O Israel, you will not be forgotten by
        me.
22 I have swept away your transgressions like
        a cloud,
    and your sins like mist;
    return to me, for I have redeemed you.

23 Sing, O heavens, for the LORD has done it;
    shout, O depths of the earth;
    break forth into singing, O mountains,
    O forest, and every tree in it!

r Cn: Heb *from my placing an eternal people and things to come*   s Tg: Heb *them*   t Cn: Heb *an ax*

For the LORD has redeemed Jacob,
and will be glorified in Israel.

24 Thus says the LORD, your Redeemer,
who formed you in the womb:
I am the LORD, who made all things,
who alone stretched out the heavens,
who by myself spread out the earth;
25 who frustrates the omens of liars,
and makes fools of diviners;
who turns back the wise,
and makes their knowledge foolish;
26 who confirms the word of his servant,
and fulfills the prediction of his
messengers;
who says of Jerusalem, "It shall be
inhabited,"
and of the cities of Judah, "They shall
be rebuilt,
and I will raise up their ruins";
27 who says to the deep, "Be dry—
I will dry up your rivers";
28 who says of Cyrus, "He is my shepherd,
and he shall carry out all my purpose";
and who says of Jerusalem, "It shall be
rebuilt,"
and of the temple, "Your foundation
shall be laid."

Cyrus, God's Instrument

45 Thus says the LORD to his anointed, to
Cyrus,
whose right hand I have grasped
to subdue nations before him
and strip kings of their robes,

to open doors before him—
and the gates shall not be closed:
2 I will go before you
and level the mountains,[u]
I will break in pieces the doors of bronze
and cut through the bars of iron,
3 I will give you the treasures of darkness
and riches hidden in secret places,
so that you may know that it is I, the
LORD,
the God of Israel, who call you by your
name.
4 For the sake of my servant Jacob,
and Israel my chosen,
I call you by your name,
I surname you, though you do not
know me.
5 I am the LORD, and there is no other;
besides me there is no god.
I arm you, though you do not know
me,
6 so that they may know, from the rising of
the sun
and from the west, that there is no one
besides me;
I am the LORD, and there is no other.
7 I form light and create darkness,
I make weal and create woe;
I the LORD do all these things.

8 Shower, O heavens, from above,
and let the skies rain down
righteousness;
let the earth open, that salvation may
spring up,[v]

[u] Q Ms Gk: MT *the swellings*   [v] Q Ms: MT *that they may bring forth salvation*

CYRUS *Good Shepherd?*

GOD REFERRED TO HIM AS "my shepherd," delegated to him the rebuilding of Jerusalem and the temple (44.28), summoned him by name and bestowed on him a "surname," or title of honor (45.4). Who was this ruler so favored by God? Surprisingly, Cyrus was not one of God's faithful followers at all. He was a foreigner, the emperor and founder of the great Persian Empire. A political and military genius, Cyrus had melded the Medes and the Persians into a unified nation and used his power to overthrow the cruel Babylonians.

Cyrus introduced a genuinely fresh idea onto the world stage: tolerance. Rather than smashing small countries, killing or deporting their people and destroying their religion and identity, Cyrus began a policy of encouraging ethnic minorities. He let them return to their homelands and helped them reestablish their places of worship.

The Jews benefited greatly from this policy (as the book of Ezra recounts in detail). Cyrus allowed the captive Jews to return to Jerusalem and rebuild their temple. Some 42,360 made the long trek home. Amazingly, Cyrus restored to the Jews the temple vessels stolen by the Babylonians and even contributed financially to the Jewish cause.

From the story of Cyrus, Isaiah draws the strong lesson that God has complete control over human history. He can use anybody to accomplish his work, even a great emperor who does not acknowledge him. All people of the earth belong to God, whether they know it or not.

Life Questions: Do you think God is using powerful leaders today to accomplish his will? How?

and let it cause righteousness to sprout
up also;
I the LORD have created it.

9 Woe to you who strive with your Maker,
earthen vessels with the potter!*w*
Does the clay say to the one who fashions
it, "What are you making"?
or "Your work has no handles"?

45.9 Quarrels with God

*Quarreling with your Maker goes far beyond
the spirited dialogue that Moses, Job, and
Jeremiah engaged in. Isaiah is describing an
insolent assault on God's competence. Not only
is it wrong, it is ridiculous—as ridiculous as a
pot complaining about the shape the potter
gives it. In Romans 9.20, Paul applies this
analogy to complaints that God had treated the
Jews unfairly.*

10 Woe to anyone who says to a father,
"What are you begetting?"
or to a woman, "With what are you in
labor?"
11 Thus says the LORD,
the Holy One of Israel, and its Maker:
Will you question me*x* about my
children,
or command me concerning the work
of my hands?
12 I made the earth,
and created humankind upon it;
it was my hands that stretched out the
heavens,
and I commanded all their host.
13 I have aroused Cyrus*y* in righteousness,
and I will make all his paths straight;
he shall build my city
and set my exiles free,
not for price or reward,
says the LORD of hosts.
14 Thus says the LORD:
The wealth of Egypt and the merchandise
of Ethiopia,*z*
and the Sabeans, tall of stature,
shall come over to you and be yours,
they shall follow you;
they shall come over in chains and
bow down to you.
They will make supplication to you,
saying,
"God is with you alone, and there is
no other;
there is no god besides him."
15 Truly, you are a God who hides himself,

O God of Israel, the Savior.
16 All of them are put to shame and
confounded,
the makers of idols go in confusion
together.
17 But Israel is saved by the LORD
with everlasting salvation;
you shall not be put to shame or
confounded
to all eternity.

18 For thus says the LORD,
who created the heavens
(he is God!),
who formed the earth and made it
(he established it;
he did not create it a chaos,
he formed it to be inhabited!):
I am the LORD, and there is no other.
19 I did not speak in secret,
in a land of darkness;
I did not say to the offspring of Jacob,
"Seek me in chaos."
I the LORD speak the truth,
I declare what is right.

Idols Cannot Save Babylon

20 Assemble yourselves and come together,
draw near, you survivors of the
nations!
They have no knowledge—
those who carry about their wooden
idols,
and keep on praying to a god
that cannot save.
21 Declare and present your case;
let them take counsel together!
Who told this long ago?
Who declared it of old?
Was it not I, the LORD?
There is no other god besides me,
a righteous God and a Savior;
there is no one besides me.

22 Turn to me and be saved,
all the ends of the earth!

45.21 Foretelling the Future

*Isaiah contains many predictions of future
events. These chapters tell of Cyrus's rise from
the east. Elsewhere, the prophet gives specific
predictions about the coming Messiah and
about events near the end of time. God uses
these predictions as proof of his power and
knowledge, challenging the pagan gods to
foretell anything (41.23).*

w Cn: Heb *with the potsherds,* or *with the potters*   *x* Cn: Heb *Ask me of things to come*   *y* Heb *him*   *z* Or Nubia;
Heb *Cush*

For I am God, and there is no other.
23 By myself I have sworn,
  from my mouth has gone forth in
    righteousness
  a word that shall not return:
  "To me every knee shall bow,
    every tongue shall swear."

24 Only in the LORD, it shall be said of me,
  are righteousness and strength;
  all who were incensed against him
  shall come to him and be ashamed.
25 In the LORD all the offspring of Israel
  shall triumph and glory.

46 Bel bows down, Nebo stoops,
  their idols are on beasts and cattle;
  these things you carry are loaded
  as burdens on weary animals.
2 They stoop, they bow down together;
  they cannot save the burden,
  but themselves go into captivity.

3 Listen to me, O house of Jacob,
  all the remnant of the house of Israel,
  who have been borne by me from your
    birth,
  carried from the womb;
4 even to your old age I am he,
  even when you turn gray I will carry
    you.
  I have made, and I will bear;
  I will carry and will save.

46.4 I Carried You

*Is religion a burden? For idol worshipers,
certainly, in the most literal sense: Their
helpless gods had to be carried around on carts
(verse 1). In contrast, God carries his people,
and has done so from the time of their
conception and birth. He won't stop; he will
sustain and rescue them in their old age.*

5 To whom will you liken me and make me
    equal,
  and compare me, as though we were
    alike?
6 Those who lavish gold from the purse,
  and weigh out silver in the scales—
  they hire a goldsmith, who makes it into
    a god;
  then they fall down and worship!
7 They lift it to their shoulders, they carry
    it,
  they set it in its place, and it stands
    there;

it cannot move from its place.
If one cries out to it, it does not answer
  or save anyone from trouble.

8 Remember this and consider,[a]
  recall it to mind, you transgressors,
9   remember the former things of old;
  for I am God, and there is no other;
  I am God, and there is no one like me,
10 declaring the end from the beginning
  and from ancient times things not yet
    done,
  saying, "My purpose shall stand,
    and I will fulfill my intention,"
11 calling a bird of prey from the east,
  the man for my purpose from a far
    country.
  I have spoken, and I will bring it to pass;
  I have planned, and I will do it.

12 Listen to me, you stubborn of heart,
  you who are far from deliverance:
13 I bring near my deliverance, it is not far
    off,
  and my salvation will not tarry;
  I will put salvation in Zion,
  for Israel my glory.

The Humiliation of Babylon

47 Come down and sit in the dust,
  virgin daughter Babylon!
Sit on the ground without a throne,
  daughter Chaldea!
For you shall no more be called
  tender and delicate.
2 Take the millstones and grind meal,
    remove your veil,
  strip off your robe, uncover your legs,
    pass through the rivers.
3 Your nakedness shall be uncovered,
  and your shame shall be seen.
  I will take vengeance,
  and I will spare no one.
4 Our Redeemer—the LORD of hosts is his
    name—
  is the Holy One of Israel.

5 Sit in silence, and go into darkness,
  daughter Chaldea!
For you shall no more be called
  the mistress of kingdoms.
6 I was angry with my people,
  I profaned my heritage;
  I gave them into your hand,
  you showed them no mercy;
  on the aged you made your yoke
    exceedingly heavy.
7 You said, "I shall be mistress forever,"

[a] Meaning of Heb uncertain

so that you did not lay these things to
heart
or remember their end.

8 Now therefore hear this, you lover of
pleasures,
who sit securely,
who say in your heart,
"I am, and there is no one besides me;
I shall not sit as a widow
or know the loss of children"—

47.7 An Evil Queen

*Over the centuries, Babylon became a byword
for evil among the Jews, for she was the nation
that had destroyed Jerusalem and its temple.
Psalm 137, composed by captive Jews in
Babylon, expresses their anguish. But in this
chapter God predicts that the great queen will
become a prostitute, surprised by a sudden
catastrophe. The same theme is echoed in
the book of Revelation, which applies the
symbolism of "Babylon the great" to another
evil empire (Revelation 18).*

9 both these things shall come upon you
in a moment, in one day:
the loss of children and widowhood
shall come upon you in full measure,
in spite of your many sorceries
and the great power of your
enchantments.

10 You felt secure in your wickedness;
you said, "No one sees me."
Your wisdom and your knowledge
led you astray,
and you said in your heart,
"I am, and there is no one besides
me."
11 But evil shall come upon you,
which you cannot charm away;
disaster shall fall upon you,
which you will not be able to ward off;
and ruin shall come on you suddenly,
of which you know nothing.

12 Stand fast in your enchantments
and your many sorceries,
with which you have labored from
your youth;
perhaps you may be able to succeed,
perhaps you may inspire terror.
13 You are wearied with your many
consultations;
let those who study[b] the heavens
stand up and save you,

those who gaze at the stars,
and at each new moon predict
what[c] shall befall you.

14 See, they are like stubble,
the fire consumes them;
they cannot deliver themselves
from the power of the flame.
No coal for warming oneself is this,
no fire to sit before!
15 Such to you are those with whom you
have labored,
who have trafficked with you from
your youth;
they all wander about in their own paths;
there is no one to save you.

God the Creator and Redeemer

48 Hear this, O house of Jacob,
who are called by the name of Israel,
and who came forth from the loins[d] of
Judah;
who swear by the name of the LORD,
and invoke the God of Israel,
but not in truth or right.
2 For they call themselves after the holy
city,
and lean on the God of Israel;
the LORD of hosts is his name.

3 The former things I declared long ago,
they went out from my mouth and I
made them known;
then suddenly I did them and they
came to pass.
4 Because I know that you are obstinate,
and your neck is an iron sinew
and your forehead brass,
5 I declared them to you from long ago,
before they came to pass I announced
them to you,
so that you would not say, "My idol did
them,
my carved image and my cast image
commanded them."

6 You have heard; now see all this;
and will you not declare it?
From this time forward I make you hear
new things,
hidden things that you have not
known.
7 They are created now, not long ago;
before today you have never heard of
them,
so that you could not say, "I already
knew them."
8 You have never heard, you have never
known,

---

b Meaning of Heb uncertain   c Gk Syr Compare Vg: Heb *from what*   d Cn: Heb *waters*

from of old your ear has not been
  opened.
For I knew that you would deal very
    treacherously,
  and that from birth you were called a
    rebel.

9 For my name's sake I defer my anger,
  for the sake of my praise I restrain it
    for you,
  so that I may not cut you off.
10 See, I have refined you, but not like*e*
    silver;
  I have tested you in the furnace of
    adversity.
11 For my own sake, for my own sake, I do
    it,
  for why should my name*f* be
    profaned?
  My glory I will not give to another.

12 Listen to me, O Jacob,
  and Israel, whom I called:
  I am He; I am the first,
  and I am the last.
13 My hand laid the foundation of the earth,
  and my right hand spread out
    the heavens;
  when I summon them,
  they stand at attention.

14 Assemble, all of you, and hear!
  Who among them has declared these
    things?
  The LORD loves him;
  he shall perform his purpose on
    Babylon,
  and his arm shall be against the
    Chaldeans.
15 I, even I, have spoken and called him,
  I have brought him, and he will
    prosper in his way.
16 Draw near to me, hear this!
  From the beginning I have not spoken
    in secret,
  from the time it came to be I have
    been there.
  And now the Lord GOD has sent me and
    his spirit.

17 Thus says the LORD,
  your Redeemer, the Holy One of Israel:
  I am the LORD your God,
  who teaches you for your own good,
  who leads you in the way you should
    go.
18 O that you had paid attention to my
    commandments!

Then your prosperity would have been
    like a river,
  and your success like the waves of the
    sea;
19 your offspring would have been like the
    sand,
  and your descendants like its grains;
  their name would never be cut off
  or destroyed from before me.

20 Go out from Babylon, flee from Chaldea,
    declare this with a shout of joy,
      proclaim it,
  send it forth to the end of the earth;
    say, "The LORD has redeemed his
      servant Jacob!"
21 They did not thirst when he led them
      through the deserts;
  he made water flow for them from the
      rock;
  he split open the rock and the water
      gushed out.

22 "There is no peace," says the LORD, "for
    the wicked."

The Servant's Mission

49 Listen to me, O coastlands,
  pay attention, you peoples from far
    away!
  The LORD called me before I was born,
    while I was in my mother's womb he
    named me.
2 He made my mouth like a sharp sword,
  in the shadow of his hand he hid me;
  he made me a polished arrow,
  in his quiver he hid me away.
3 And he said to me, "You are my servant,
  Israel, in whom I will be glorified."
4 But I said, "I have labored in vain,
  I have spent my strength for nothing
    and vanity;
  yet surely my cause is with the LORD,
  and my reward with my God."

5 And now the LORD says,
  who formed me in the womb to be his
    servant,
  to bring Jacob back to him,
  and that Israel might be gathered to
    him,
  for I am honored in the sight of
    the LORD,
  and my God has become my
    strength—
6 he says,
  "It is too light a thing that you should be
    my servant
  to raise up the tribes of Jacob

e Cn: Heb *with*   *f* Gk Old Latin: Heb *for why should it*

and to restore the survivors of Israel;
I will give you as a light to the nations,
    that my salvation may reach to the end
        of the earth."

49.6 Israel's Final Destiny

*The book of Isaiah spells out Israel's ultimate
destiny: to be a light for the Gentiles and to
bring salvation to the ends of the earth. Isaiah
is not introducing a brand-new thought—God
had made clear his intentions in the original
covenant (Genesis 22.18). But, along the way,
Israel and Judah's desire for political greatness
had obscured their original calling.*

7 Thus says the LORD,
    the Redeemer of Israel and his Holy
        One,
to one deeply despised, abhorred by the
        nations,
    the slave of rulers,
"Kings shall see and stand up,
    princes, and they shall prostrate
        themselves,
because of the LORD, who is faithful,
    the Holy One of Israel, who has chosen
        you."

Zion's Children to Be Brought Home

8 Thus says the LORD:
In a time of favor I have answered you,
    on a day of salvation I have helped
        you;
I have kept you and given you
    as a covenant to the people,*g*
to establish the land,
    to apportion the desolate heritages;
9 saying to the prisoners, "Come out,"
    to those who are in darkness, "Show
        yourselves."
They shall feed along the ways,
    on all the bare heights*h* shall be their
        pasture;
10 they shall not hunger or thirst,
    neither scorching wind nor sun shall
        strike them down,
for he who has pity on them will lead
        them,
    and by springs of water will guide
        them.
11 And I will turn all my mountains into
        a road,
    and my highways shall be raised
        up.
12 Lo, these shall come from far away,

and lo, these from the north and from
        the west,
    and these from the land of Syene.*i*

13 Sing for joy, O heavens, and exult,
        O earth;
    break forth, O mountains, into singing!
For the LORD has comforted his people,
    and will have compassion on his
        suffering ones.

14 But Zion said, "The LORD has forsaken
        me,
    my Lord has forgotten me."
15 Can a woman forget her nursing child,
    or show no compassion for the child of
        her womb?
Even these may forget,
    yet I will not forget you.
16 See, I have inscribed you on the palms of
        my hands;
    your walls are continually before me.
17 Your builders outdo your destroyers,*j*
    and those who laid you waste go away
        from you.
18 Lift up your eyes all around and see;
    they all gather, they come to you.
As I live, says the LORD,
    you shall put all of them on like an
        ornament,
    and like a bride you shall bind them
        on.

19 Surely your waste and your desolate
        places
    and your devastated land—
surely now you will be too crowded for
        your inhabitants,
    and those who swallowed you up will
        be far away.
20 The children born in the time of your
        bereavement
    will yet say in your hearing:
"The place is too crowded for me;
    make room for me to settle."
21 Then you will say in your heart,
    "Who has borne me these?
I was bereaved and barren,
    exiled and put away—
    so who has reared these?
I was left all alone—
    where then have these come from?"

22 Thus says the Lord GOD:
I will soon lift up my hand to the nations,
    and raise my signal to the peoples;
and they shall bring your sons in their
        bosom,

---

g Meaning of Heb uncertain   *h* Or *the trails*   *i* Q Ms: MT *Sinim*   *j* Or *Your children come swiftly; your destroyers*

and your daughters shall be carried on
 their shoulders.
23 Kings shall be your foster fathers,
 and their queens your nursing mothers.
With their faces to the ground they shall
  bow down to you,
 and lick the dust of your feet.
Then you will know that I am the LORD;
 those who wait for me shall not be put
  to shame.

24 Can the prey be taken from the mighty,
 or the captives of a tyrant[k] be rescued?
25 But thus says the LORD:
Even the captives of the mighty shall be
  taken,
 and the prey of the tyrant be rescued;
for I will contend with those who contend
  with you,
 and I will save your children.
26 I will make your oppressors eat their own
  flesh,
 and they shall be drunk with their own
  blood as with wine.
Then all flesh shall know
 that I am the LORD your Savior,
 and your Redeemer, the Mighty One of
  Jacob.

50 Thus says the LORD:
Where is your mother's bill of divorce
 with which I put her away?
Or which of my creditors is it
 to whom I have sold you?
No, because of your sins you were sold,
 and for your transgressions your
  mother was put away.
2 Why was no one there when I came?
 Why did no one answer when I called?
Is my hand shortened, that it cannot
  redeem?
 Or have I no power to deliver?
By my rebuke I dry up the sea,
 I make the rivers a desert;
their fish stink for lack of water,
 and die of thirst.[l]
3 I clothe the heavens with blackness,
 and make sackcloth their covering.

The Servant's Humiliation and Vindication

4 The Lord GOD has given me
 the tongue of a teacher,[m]
that I may know how to sustain
 the weary with a word.
Morning by morning he wakens—
 wakens my ear
to listen as those who are taught.

5 The Lord GOD has opened my ear,
 and I was not rebellious,
 I did not turn backward.
6 I gave my back to those who struck me,
 and my cheeks to those who pulled out
  the beard;
I did not hide my face
 from insult and spitting.

7 The Lord GOD helps me;
 therefore I have not been disgraced;
therefore I have set my face like flint,
 and I know that I shall not be put to
  shame;
8 he who vindicates me is near.
Who will contend with me?
 Let us stand up together.
Who are my adversaries?
 Let them confront me.
9 It is the Lord GOD who helps me;
 who will declare me guilty?
All of them will wear out like a garment;
 the moth will eat them up.

10 Who among you fears the LORD
 and obeys the voice of his servant,
who walks in darkness
 and has no light,
yet trusts in the name of the LORD
 and relies upon his God?
11 But all of you are kindlers of fire,
 lighters of firebrands.[n]
Walk in the flame of your fire,
 and among the brands that you have
  kindled!
This is what you shall have from my
  hand:
 you shall lie down in torment.

Blessings in Store for God's People

51 Listen to me, you that pursue
 righteousness,
 you that seek the LORD.
Look to the rock from which you were
  hewn,
 and to the quarry from which
  you were dug.
2 Look to Abraham your father
 and to Sarah who bore you;
for he was but one when I called him,
 but I blessed him and made him many.
3 For the LORD will comfort Zion;
 he will comfort all her waste places,
and will make her wilderness like Eden,
 her desert like the garden of the LORD;
joy and gladness will be found in her,
 thanksgiving and the voice of song.

---

k Q Ms Syr Vg: MT *of a righteous person* l Or *die on the thirsty ground* m Cn: Heb *of those who are taught*
n Syr: Heb *you gird yourselves with firebrands*

4 Listen to me, my people,
 and give heed to me, my nation;
for a teaching will go out from me,
 and my justice for a light to
  the peoples.
5 I will bring near my deliverance swiftly,
 my salvation has gone out
 and my arms will rule the peoples;
the coastlands wait for me,
 and for my arm they hope.
6 Lift up your eyes to the heavens,
 and look at the earth beneath;
for the heavens will vanish like smoke,
 the earth will wear out like a garment,
 and those who live on it will die like
  gnats;[o]
but my salvation will be forever,
 and my deliverance will never
  be ended.

7 Listen to me, you who know
  righteousness,
 you people who have my teaching in
  your hearts;
do not fear the reproach of others,
 and do not be dismayed when they
  revile you.
8 For the moth will eat them up like a
  garment,
 and the worm will eat them like wool;
but my deliverance will be forever,
 and my salvation to all generations.

9 Awake, awake, put on strength,
 O arm of the LORD!
Awake, as in days of old,
 the generations of long ago!
Was it not you who cut Rahab in pieces,
 who pierced the dragon?

51.9 Rahab the Monster

*The Rahab in Isaiah (here and in 30.7) should
not be confused with the Rahab who helped
Joshua's spies in Jericho (Joshua 2). Rather, the
word refers to a sea-monster that appears in
much Middle Eastern mythology. Because the
mythological monster lived in the Nile River
region, Rahab can stand for the nation of
Egypt, as it does here.*

10 Was it not you who dried up the sea,
 the waters of the great deep;
who made the depths of the sea a way
 for the redeemed to cross over?
11 So the ransomed of the LORD shall return,
 and come to Zion with singing;
everlasting joy shall be upon their heads;

 they shall obtain joy and gladness,
 and sorrow and sighing shall flee away.

12 I, I am he who comforts you;
 why then are you afraid of a mere
  mortal who must die,
 a human being who fades like grass?
13 You have forgotten the LORD, your
  Maker,
 who stretched out the heavens
 and laid the foundations of the earth.
You fear continually all day long
 because of the fury of the oppressor,
who is bent on destruction.
 But where is the fury of the oppressor?
14 The oppressed shall speedily be released;
 they shall not die and go down to the
  Pit,
 nor shall they lack bread.
15 For I am the LORD your God,
 who stirs up the sea so that its waves
  roar—
 the LORD of hosts is his name.
16 I have put my words in your mouth,
 and hidden you in the shadow of my
  hand,
stretching out[p] the heavens
 and laying the foundations of the earth,
 and saying to Zion, "You are my
  people."

17 Rouse yourself, rouse yourself!
 Stand up, O Jerusalem,
you who have drunk at the hand of the
  LORD
 the cup of his wrath,
who have drunk to the dregs
 the bowl of staggering.
18 There is no one to guide her
 among all the children she has borne;
there is no one to take her by the hand
 among all the children she has brought
  up.
19 These two things have befallen you
 —who will grieve with you?—
devastation and destruction, famine and
  sword—
 who will comfort you?[q]
20 Your children have fainted,
 they lie at the head of every street
 like an antelope in a net;
they are full of the wrath of the LORD,
 the rebuke of your God.

21 Therefore hear this, you who are
  wounded,[r]
 who are drunk, but not with wine:
22 Thus says your Sovereign, the LORD,

---

[o] Or *in like manner*   [p] Syr: Heb *planting*   [q] Q Ms Gk Syr Vg: MT *how may I comfort you?*   [r] Or *humbled*

your God who pleads the cause of his
people:
See, I have taken from your hand the cup
of staggering;
you shall drink no more
from the bowl of my wrath.
23 And I will put it into the hand of your
tormentors,
who have said to you,
"Bow down, that we may walk
on you";
and you have made your back like the
ground
and like the street for them to walk on.

Let Zion Rejoice

52 Awake, awake,
put on your strength, O Zion!
Put on your beautiful garments,
O Jerusalem, the holy city;
for the uncircumcised and the unclean
shall enter you no more.
2 Shake yourself from the dust, rise up,
O captives Jerusalem;
loose the bonds from your neck,
O captive daughter Zion!

3 For thus says the LORD: You were sold for
nothing, and you shall be redeemed without
money. 4For thus says the Lord GOD: Long ago,
my people went down into Egypt to reside there
as aliens; the Assyrian, too, has oppressed them
without cause. 5Now therefore what am I doing
here, says the LORD, seeing that my people are
taken away without cause? Their rulers howl, says
the LORD, and continually, all day long, my name
is despised. 6Therefore my people shall know my
name; therefore in that day they shall know that
it is I who speak; here am I.

7 How beautiful upon the mountains
are the feet of the messenger who
announces peace,
who brings good news,
who announces salvation,

52.7 Beautiful Feet

*Isaiah portrays the joy of carrying good news
to those desperately hoping for it—perhaps a
city waiting for news of a battle in which all
their young men were at risk. But Isaiah's news
is not of war; it is of God's people returning
from exile, with the Lord himself leading the
way. In Romans 10.15, Paul applied this joyful
cheer to the messengers who, like himself, bore
the good news of Jesus Christ.*

who says to Zion, "Your God reigns."
8 Listen! Your sentinels lift up their voices,
together they sing for joy;
for in plain sight they see
the return of the LORD to Zion.
9 Break forth together into singing,
you ruins of Jerusalem;
for the LORD has comforted his people,
he has redeemed Jerusalem.
10 The LORD has bared his holy arm
before the eyes of all the nations;
and all the ends of the earth shall see
the salvation of our God.

11 Depart, depart, go out from there!
Touch no unclean thing;
go out from the midst of it, purify
yourselves,
you who carry the vessels of the LORD.
12 For you shall not go out in haste,
and you shall not go in flight;
for the LORD will go before you,
and the God of Israel will be your rear
guard.

The Suffering Servant

13 See, my servant shall prosper;
he shall be exalted and lifted up,
and shall be very high.
14 Just as there were many who were
astonished at himt
—so marred was his appearance,
beyond human semblance,
and his form beyond that of mortals—
15 so he shall startleu many nations;
kings shall shut their mouths because
of him;
for that which had not been told them
they shall see,
and that which they had not heard
they shall contemplate.

53 Who has believed what we have heard?
And to whom has the arm of the LORD
been revealed?
2 For he grew up before him like a young
plant,
and like a root out of dry ground;
he had no form or majesty that we should
look at him,
nothing in his appearance that we
should desire him.
3 He was despised and rejected by others;
a man of sufferingv and acquainted
with infirmity;
and as one from whom others hide their
facesw
he was despised, and we held him of
no account.

---

s Cn: Heb *rise up, sit*   t Syr Tg: Heb *you*   u Meaning of Heb uncertain   v Or *a man of sorrows*   w Or *as one
who hides his face from us*

4 Surely he has borne our infirmities
   and carried our diseases;
yet we accounted him stricken,
   struck down by God, and afflicted.
5 But he was wounded for our
      transgressions,
   crushed for our iniquities;
upon him was the punishment that made
      us whole,
   and by his bruises we are healed.
6 All we like sheep have gone astray;

we have all turned to our own
      way,
and the LORD has laid on him
   the iniquity of us all.

7 He was oppressed, and he was afflicted,
   yet he did not open his mouth;
like a lamb that is led to the slaughter,
   and like a sheep that before its shearers
      is silent,
   so he did not open his mouth.

The Suffering Servant
A great victory looked at first like defeat

CHAPTERS 49–55 OF ISAIAH TELL of a "suffering servant" who will come from Israel to bring light to all nations. Who is this suffering servant?

Jewish scholars puzzled over these passages for centuries. Many considered them the most significant part of the entire Old Testament, and yet they could not agree on exactly what the prophet meant. (Four passages especially are called the "servant songs": 42.1–9; 49.1–13; 50.4–9; 52.13–53.12.)

> He was despised and rejected by others; a man of suffering and acquainted with infirmity.
> 53.3

A Nation or a Person?

Sometimes the verses speak about the nation of Israel as a whole: "You are my servant, Israel, in whom I will be glorified" (49.3). But in other places the servant seems to refer to a specific individual, a great leader who suffers terribly.

Isaiah presents the servant as the deliverer of all humankind. And yet it portrays him more as a tragic figure than as a hero: "He had no form or majesty that we should look at him. . . . He was oppressed, and he was afflicted, yet he did not open his mouth; like a lamb that is led to the slaughter" (53.2,7).

Some Jewish scholars guessed the prophet was describing himself or another prophet, such as Jeremiah. Still others focused their hopes on a Messiah to come. They expected a king from very humble origins, whose power would depend not on swords, but on the spirits of people committed to him.

An Answer from the New Testament

The idea of the suffering servant did not really catch on among the Jewish nation. They longed for a victorious Messiah, not a suffering one. The image of the suffering servant went underground, as it were, lying dormant for centuries.

Then, in a very dramatic scene early in his ministry, Jesus quoted from one of the servant passages in Isaiah (Luke 4.18–19). "And he rolled up the scroll, gave it back to the attendant and sat down. The eyes of everyone in the synagogue were fixed on him. Then he began to say to them, 'Today this scripture has been fulfilled in your hearing' " (Luke 4.20–21).

Following his example, the New Testament writers named Jesus as the servant, at least ten times. In one instance, Philip corrected an Ethiopian official who had wondered if the suffering servant referred to an ancient prophet (Acts 8.26–35).

The Final Sacrifice

Isaiah 49–55 includes vivid scenes of the servant's sufferings, predictions that found their fulfillment in Jesus' death on the cross. Written like an eyewitness account, they were actually composed centuries before Christ's death.

According to Isaiah, the servant died for a very specific purpose: "He was wounded for our transgressions" (53.5). Through his wounds, the suffering servant won a great victory. His death made possible a future when all that is wrong on earth will be set right. Significantly, the book of Isaiah does not end with the suffering servant image. It goes on to describe a wonderful life in a new heaven and new earth made possible by the servant's death.

Life Questions: If you had been a Jew in Jesus' day, would you have been disappointed in the Messiah? Why did Jesus choose to come as a suffering servant rather than, say, a triumphant army general?

8 By a perversion of justice he was taken
away.
Who could have imagined his future?
For he was cut off from the land of the
living,

53.5 Healing Wounds

*Throughout the New Testament, the Suffering
Servant described here is understood to be
Jesus. This astounding verse claims that his
wounds heal us. Peter explained it this way:
when Jesus died on the cross, his suffering and
death "healed" us of our sins, enabling us to
live for righteousness (1 Peter 2.24).*

stricken for the transgression of my
people.
9 They made his grave with the wicked
and his tomb[x] with the rich,[y]
although he had done no violence,
and there was no deceit in his mouth.

10 Yet it was the will of the LORD to crush
him with pain.[z]
When you make his life an offering for
sin,[a]
he shall see his offspring, and shall
prolong his days;
through him the will of the LORD shall
prosper.
11 Out of his anguish he shall see light;[b]
he shall find satisfaction through his
knowledge.
The righteous one,[c] my servant, shall
make many righteous,
and he shall bear their iniquities.
12 Therefore I will allot him a portion with
the great,
and he shall divide the spoil with the
strong;
because he poured out himself to death,
and was numbered with the
transgressors;
yet he bore the sin of many,
and made intercession for the
transgressors.

The Eternal Covenant of Peace

54 Sing, O barren one who did not bear;
burst into song and shout,
you who have not been in labor!
For the children of the desolate woman
will be more
than the children of her that is
married, says the LORD.

2 Enlarge the site of your tent,
and let the curtains of your habitations
be stretched out;
do not hold back; lengthen your cords
and strengthen your stakes.
3 For you will spread out to the right and
to the left,
and your descendants will possess the
nations
and will settle the desolate towns.

4 Do not fear, for you will not be ashamed;
do not be discouraged, for you will not
suffer disgrace;
for you will forget the shame of your
youth,
and the disgrace of your widowhood
you will remember no more.
5 For your Maker is your husband,
the LORD of hosts is his name;
the Holy One of Israel is your Redeemer,
the God of the whole earth he is called.
6 For the LORD has called you
like a wife forsaken and grieved in
spirit,
like the wife of a man's youth when she is
cast off,
says your God.

54.6 Jerusalem's Future

*The book of Isaiah insists that God will not
permanently divorce the nation of Israel. It
foretells a time when the ruined capital city will
be rebuilt and achieve a greatness it has never
known. Yet the description in these chapters
goes far beyond what has ever been realized in
Jerusalem. It merges into a vision of the future,
when sin and sorrow will be no more and
people will live in final peace with God.*

7 For a brief moment I abandoned you,
but with great compassion I will gather
you.
8 In overflowing wrath for a moment
I hid my face from you,
but with everlasting love I will have
compassion on you,
says the LORD, your Redeemer.

9 This is like the days of Noah to me:
Just as I swore that the waters of Noah
would never again go over the earth,
so I have sworn that I will not be angry
with you
and will not rebuke you.

x Q Ms: MT *and in his death*   y Cn: Heb *with a rich person*   z Or *by disease*; meaning of Heb uncertain
a Meaning of Heb uncertain   b Q Mss: MT lacks *light*   c Or *and he shall find satisfaction. Through his knowledge,*
the righteous one

10 For the mountains may depart
　　and the hills be removed,
　but my steadfast love shall not depart
　　　from you,
　　and my covenant of peace shall not be
　　　removed,
　　says the LORD, who has compassion on
　　　you.

11 O afflicted one, storm-tossed, and not
　　　comforted,
　　I am about to set your stones in
　　　antimony,
　　and lay your foundations with
　　　sapphires.^{d}
12 I will make your pinnacles of rubies,
　　your gates of jewels,
　　and all your wall of precious stones.
13 All your children shall be taught by the
　　　LORD,
　　and great shall be the prosperity of
　　　your children.
14 In righteousness you shall be established;
　　you shall be far from oppression, for
　　　you shall not fear;
　　and from terror, for it shall not come
　　　near you.
15 If anyone stirs up strife,
　　it is not from me;
　whoever stirs up strife with you
　　shall fall because of you.
16 See it is I who have created the smith
　　who blows the fire of coals,
　　and produces a weapon fit for
　　　its purpose;
　I have also created the ravager to destroy.
17 No weapon that is fashioned against
　　　you shall prosper,
　　and you shall confute every tongue that
　　　rises against you in judgment.
　This is the heritage of the servants of the
　　　LORD
　　and their vindication from me, says the
　　　LORD.

An Invitation to Abundant Life

55 Ho, everyone who thirsts,
　　come to the waters;
　and you that have no money,
　　come, buy and eat!
　Come, buy wine and milk
　　without money and without price.
2 Why do you spend your money for that
　　　which is not bread,
　　and your labor for that which does not
　　　satisfy?
　Listen carefully to me, and eat what is
　　　good,
　　and delight yourselves in rich food.

3 Incline your ear, and come to me;
　　listen, so that you may live.
　I will make with you an everlasting
　　　covenant,
　　my steadfast, sure love for David.

55.1 Who Can Be Saved?

*God, through Isaiah, issues an open invitation
to "everyone who thirsts." Anyone can eat and
drink this meal, free of charge. The only
requirement is that they come. In verse 6 Isaiah
urges everyone to take this opportunity for
forgiveness while it is so freely available.*

4 See, I made him a witness to the peoples,
　　a leader and commander for
　　　the peoples.
5 See, you shall call nations that you do not
　　　know,
　　and nations that do not know you shall
　　　run to you,
　because of the LORD your God, the Holy
　　　One of Israel,
　　for he has glorified you.

6 Seek the LORD while he may be found,
　　call upon him while he is near;
7 let the wicked forsake their way,
　　and the unrighteous their thoughts;
　let them return to the LORD, that he may
　　　have mercy on them,
　　and to our God, for he will abundantly
　　　pardon.
8 For my thoughts are not your thoughts,
　　nor are your ways my ways, says the
　　　LORD.
9 For as the heavens are higher than the
　　　earth,
　　so are my ways higher than your ways
　　and my thoughts than your thoughts.

10 For as the rain and the snow come down
　　　from heaven,
　　and do not return there until they have
　　　watered the earth,
　making it bring forth and sprout,
　　giving seed to the sower and bread to
　　　the eater,
11 so shall my word be that goes out from
　　　my mouth;
　　it shall not return to me empty,
　but it shall accomplish that which I
　　　purpose,
　　and succeed in the thing for which I
　　　sent it.

^{d} Or *lapis lazuli*

12 For you shall go out in joy,
    and be led back in peace;
the mountains and the hills before you
    shall burst into song,
and all the trees of the field shall clap
    their hands.
13 Instead of the thorn shall come up the
        cypress;
    instead of the brier shall come up the
        myrtle;
and it shall be to the LORD for a
        memorial,
    for an everlasting sign that shall not be
        cut off.

The Covenant Extended to All Who Obey

56 Thus says the LORD:
    Maintain justice, and do what is right,
for soon my salvation will come,
    and my deliverance be revealed.

2 Happy is the mortal who does this,
    the one who holds it fast,
who keeps the sabbath, not profaning it,
    and refrains from doing any evil.

3 Do not let the foreigner joined to the
        LORD say,
    "The LORD will surely separate me
        from his people";
and do not let the eunuch say,
    "I am just a dry tree."
4 For thus says the LORD:
To the eunuchs who keep my sabbaths,
    who choose the things that please me
        and hold fast my covenant,
5 I will give, in my house and within my
        walls,
    a monument and a name
    better than sons and daughters;
I will give them an everlasting name
    that shall not be cut off.

6 And the foreigners who join themselves to
        the LORD,
    to minister to him, to love the name of
        the LORD,
    and to be his servants,
all who keep the sabbath, and do not
        profane it,
    and hold fast my covenant—
7 these I will bring to my holy mountain,
    and make them joyful in my house of
        prayer;
their burnt offerings and their sacrifices
    will be accepted on my altar;
for my house shall be called a house of
        prayer
    for all peoples.

8 Thus says the Lord GOD,
    who gathers the outcasts of Israel,
I will gather others to them
    besides those already gathered.[e]

56.7 House of Prayer

Traditionally, foreigners and eunuchs were excluded from worshiping God (see Exodus 12.43; Deuteronomy 23.1,3,7–8). But now God promises to welcome all those once excluded. The New Testament church welcomed foreigners and eunuchs into God's family; in contrast, the temple in Jerusalem never made non-Jews welcome. Jesus complained that rather than creating a "house of prayer for all the nations," merchants had turned it into a "den of robbers" (Mark 11.17).

The Corruption of Israel's Rulers

9 All you wild animals,
    all you wild animals in the forest, come
        to devour!
10 Israel's[f] sentinels are blind,
    they are all without knowledge;
they are all silent dogs
    that cannot bark;
dreaming, lying down,
    loving to slumber.

56.10–11 Doglike Prophets

This passage gives one of the most scathing denunciations of Israel's corrupt spiritual leaders in the entire Bible.

11 The dogs have a mighty appetite;
    they never have enough.
The shepherds also have no
        understanding;
    they have all turned to their own way,
    to their own gain, one and all.
12 "Come," they say, "let us[g] get wine;
    let us fill ourselves with strong drink.
And tomorrow will be like today,
    great beyond measure."

Israel's Futile Idolatry

57 The righteous perish,
    and no one takes it to heart;
the devout are taken away,
    while no one understands.
For the righteous are taken away from
        calamity,
2   and they enter into peace;
those who walk uprightly

e Heb *besides his gathered ones*   *f* Heb *His*   *g* Q Ms Syr Vg Tg: MT *me*

will rest on their couches.
3 But as for you, come here,
  you children of a sorceress,
  you offspring of an adulterer and a
    whore.*h*
4 Whom are you mocking?
  Against whom do you open your
    mouth wide
  and stick out your tongue?
  Are you not children of transgression,
    the offspring of deceit—
5 you that burn with lust among the oaks,
    under every green tree;
  you that slaughter your children in the
    valleys,
    under the clefts of the rocks?
6 Among the smooth stones of the valley is
    your portion;
  they, they, are your lot;
  to them you have poured out a drink
    offering,
  you have brought a grain offering.
  Shall I be appeased for these things?
7 Upon a high and lofty mountain
  you have set your bed,
  and there you went up to offer
    sacrifice.
8 Behind the door and the doorpost
  you have set up your symbol;
  for, in deserting me,*i* you have
    uncovered your bed,
  you have gone up to it,
  you have made it wide;
  and you have made a bargain for yourself
    with them,
  you have loved their bed,
  you have gazed on their nakedness.*j*
9 You journeyed to Molech*k* with oil,
  and multiplied your perfumes;
  you sent your envoys far away,
  and sent down even to Sheol.
10 You grew weary from your many
    wanderings,
  but you did not say, "It is useless."
  You found your desire rekindled,
  and so you did not weaken.

11 Whom did you dread and fear
  so that you lied,
  and did not remember me
  or give me a thought?
  Have I not kept silent and closed my
    eyes,*l*
  and so you do not fear me?
12 I will concede your righteousness and
    your works,
  but they will not help you.

13 When you cry out, let your collection of
    idols deliver you!
  The wind will carry them off,
  a breath will take them away.
  But whoever takes refuge in me shall
    possess the land
  and inherit my holy mountain.

A Promise of Help and Healing

14 It shall be said,
  "Build up, build up, prepare the way,
  remove every obstruction from my
    people's way."
15 For thus says the high and lofty one
  who inhabits eternity, whose name is
    Holy:
  I dwell in the high and holy place,
  and also with those who are contrite
    and humble in spirit,
  to revive the spirit of the humble,
  and to revive the heart of the contrite.
16 For I will not continually accuse,
  nor will I always be angry;
  for then the spirits would grow faint
    before me,
  even the souls that I have made.
17 Because of their wicked covetousness I
    was angry;
  I struck them, I hid and was angry;
  but they kept turning back to their
    own ways.
18 I have seen their ways, but I will heal
    them;
  I will lead them and repay them with
    comfort,
  creating for their mourners the fruit of
    the lips.*i*
19 Peace, peace, to the far and the near, says
    the LORD;
  and I will heal them.
20 But the wicked are like the tossing sea
  that cannot keep still;
  its waters toss up mire and mud.
21 There is no peace, says my God, for the
    wicked.

False and True Worship

58 Shout out, do not hold back!
  Lift up your voice like a trumpet!
  Announce to my people their rebellion,
  to the house of Jacob their sins.
2 Yet day after day they seek me
  and delight to know my ways,
  as if they were a nation that practiced
    righteousness
  and did not forsake the ordinance of
    their God;
  they ask of me righteous judgments,

---

h Heb *an adulterer and she plays the whore*   *i* Meaning of Heb uncertain   *j* Or *their phallus*; Heb *the hand*
k Or *the king*   *l* Gk Vg: Heb *silent even for a long time*

they delight to draw near to God.
3 "Why do we fast, but you do not see?
  Why humble ourselves, but you do not
      notice?"
Look, you serve your own interest on
      your fast day,
  and oppress all your workers.
4 Look, you fast only to quarrel and to fight
  and to strike with a wicked fist.
Such fasting as you do today
  will not make your voice heard on
      high.
5 Is such the fast that I choose,
  a day to humble oneself?
Is it to bow down the head like a bulrush,
  and to lie in sackcloth and ashes?
Will you call this a fast,
  a day acceptable to the LORD?

6 Is not this the fast that I choose:
  to loose the bonds of injustice,
  to undo the thongs of the yoke,
to let the oppressed go free,
  and to break every yoke?

58.6 Religion at Its Best

*The book of Isaiah begins in chapter 1 by
exposing false religion that had the right form
and ritual, but no true sincerity. This chapter
gives the other side: the spiritual work God
prefers. The book of James includes a similar
perspective (1.27).*

7 Is it not to share your bread with the
      hungry,
  and bring the homeless poor into your
      house;
when you see the naked, to cover them,
  and not to hide yourself from your
      own kin?
8 Then your light shall break forth like the
      dawn,
  and your healing shall spring
      up quickly;
your vindicator[m] shall go before you,
  the glory of the LORD shall be your rear
      guard.
9 Then you shall call, and the LORD will
      answer;
  you shall cry for help, and he will say,
      Here I am.

If you remove the yoke from among you,
  the pointing of the finger, the speaking
      of evil,
10 if you offer your food to the hungry

and satisfy the needs of the afflicted,
then your light shall rise in the darkness
  and your gloom be like the noonday.
11 The LORD will guide you continually,
  and satisfy your needs in parched
      places,
  and make your bones strong;
and you shall be like a watered garden,
  like a spring of water,
  whose waters never fail.
12 Your ancient ruins shall be rebuilt;
  you shall raise up the foundations of
      many generations;
you shall be called the repairer of the
      breach,
  the restorer of streets to live in.

13 If you refrain from trampling the sabbath,
  from pursuing your own interests on
      my holy day;
if you call the sabbath a delight
  and the holy day of the LORD
      honorable;
if you honor it, not going your own ways,
  serving your own interests, or pursuing
      your own affairs;[n]
14 then you shall take delight in the LORD,
  and I will make you ride upon the
      heights of the earth;
I will feed you with the heritage of your
      ancestor Jacob,
  for the mouth of the LORD has spoken.

Injustice and Oppression to Be Punished

59 See, the LORD's hand is not too short to
      save,
  nor his ear too dull to hear.
2 Rather, your iniquities have been barriers
      between you and your God,
and your sins have hidden his face from
      you
  so that he does not hear.
3 For your hands are defiled with blood,
  and your fingers with iniquity;
your lips have spoken lies,
  your tongue mutters wickedness.
4 No one brings suit justly,
  no one goes to law honestly;
they rely on empty pleas, they speak lies,
  conceiving mischief and begetting
      iniquity.
5 They hatch adders' eggs,
  and weave the spider's web;
whoever eats their eggs dies,
  and the crushed egg hatches out a
      viper.
6 Their webs cannot serve as clothing;
  they cannot cover themselves with what
      they make.

---

m Or *vindication*   *n* Heb or *speaking words*

Their works are works of iniquity,
and deeds of violence are in their
hands.
7 Their feet run to evil,
and they rush to shed innocent blood;
their thoughts are thoughts of iniquity,
desolation and destruction are in
their highways.
8 The way of peace they do not know,
and there is no justice in their paths.
Their roads they have made crooked;
no one who walks in them knows
peace.

9 Therefore justice is far from us,
and righteousness does not reach us;
we wait for light, and lo! there is
darkness;
and for brightness, but we walk in
gloom.
10 We grope like the blind along a wall,
groping like those who have no eyes;
we stumble at noon as in the twilight,
among the vigorous° as though we
were dead.
11 We all growl like bears;
like doves we moan mournfully.
We wait for justice, but there is none;
for salvation, but it is far from us.
12 For our transgressions before you are
many,
and our sins testify against us.
Our transgressions indeed are with us,
and we know our iniquities:
13 transgressing, and denying the LORD,
and turning away from following our
God,
talking oppression and revolt,
conceiving lying words and uttering
them from the heart.
14 Justice is turned back,
and righteousness stands at a distance;
for truth stumbles in the public square,
and uprightness cannot enter.
15 Truth is lacking,
and whoever turns from evil is
despoiled.

The LORD saw it, and it displeased him
that there was no justice.
16 He saw that there was no one,
and was appalled that there was no one
to intervene;
so his own arm brought him victory,
and his righteousness upheld him.
17 He put on righteousness like a breastplate,
and a helmet of salvation on his head;
he put on garments of vengeance for
clothing,

and wrapped himself in fury as in a
mantle.
18 According to their deeds, so will he repay;
wrath to his adversaries, requital to his
enemies;
to the coastlands he will render
requital.
19 So those in the west shall fear the name
of the LORD,
and those in the east, his glory;
for he will come like a pent-up stream
that the wind of the LORD drives on.

20 And he will come to Zion as Redeemer,
to those in Jacob who turn from
transgression, says the LORD.
21And as for me, this is my covenant with them,
says the LORD: my spirit that is upon you, and my
words that I have put in your mouth, shall not
depart out of your mouth, or out of the mouths
of your children, or out of the mouths of your
children's children, says the LORD, from now on
and forever.

The Ingathering of the Dispersed

60 Arise, shine; for your light has come,
and the glory of the LORD has risen
upon you.
2 For darkness shall cover the earth,
and thick darkness the peoples;
but the LORD will arise upon you,
and his glory will appear over you.
3 Nations shall come to your light,
and kings to the brightness of your
dawn.

4 Lift up your eyes and look around;
they all gather together, they come to
you;
your sons shall come from far away,
and your daughters shall be carried on
their nurses' arms.
5 Then you shall see and be radiant;
your heart shall thrill and rejoice,ᵖ
because the abundance of the sea shall be
brought to you,
the wealth of the nations shall come to
you.
6 A multitude of camels shall cover you,
the young camels of Midian and
Ephah;
all those from Sheba shall come.
They shall bring gold and frankincense,
and shall proclaim the praise of the
LORD.
7 All the flocks of Kedar shall be gathered
to you,
the rams of Nebaioth shall minister to
you;

---

o Meaning of Heb uncertain   p Heb be enlarged

they shall be acceptable on my altar,
and I will glorify my glorious house.

8 Who are these that fly like a cloud,
and like doves to their windows?
9 For the coastlands shall wait for me,
the ships of Tarshish first,
to bring your children from far away,
their silver and gold with them,
for the name of the LORD your God,
and for the Holy One of Israel,
because he has glorified you.
10 Foreigners shall build up your walls,
and their kings shall minister to you;
for in my wrath I struck you down,
but in my favor I have had mercy on
you.
11 Your gates shall always be open;
day and night they shall not be shut,
so that nations shall bring you their
wealth,
with their kings led in procession.
12 For the nation and kingdom
that will not serve you shall perish;
those nations shall be utterly
laid waste.
13 The glory of Lebanon shall come to you,
the cypress, the plane, and the pine,
to beautify the place of my sanctuary;
and I will glorify where my feet rest.
14 The descendants of those who oppressed
you
shall come bending low to you,
and all who despised you
shall bow down at your feet;
they shall call you the City of the LORD,
the Zion of the Holy One of Israel.
15 Whereas you have been forsaken and
hated,
with no one passing through,
I will make you majestic forever,
a joy from age to age.
16 You shall suck the milk of nations,
you shall suck the breasts of kings;
and you shall know that I, the LORD, am
your Savior
and your Redeemer, the Mighty One of
Jacob.

17 Instead of bronze I will bring gold,
instead of iron I will bring silver;
instead of wood, bronze,
instead of stones, iron.
I will appoint Peace as your overseer
and Righteousness as your taskmaster.
18 Violence shall no more be heard in your
land,
devastation or destruction within your
borders;

you shall call your walls Salvation,
and your gates Praise.

God the Glory of Zion

19 The sun shall no longer be
your light by day,
nor for brightness shall the moon
give light to you by night;*q*
but the LORD will be your everlasting
light,
and your God will be your glory.
20 Your sun shall no more go down,
or your moon withdraw itself;
for the LORD will be your everlasting light,
and your days of mourning shall be
ended.
21 Your people shall all be righteous;
they shall possess the land forever.
They are the shoot that I planted, the
work of my hands,
so that I might be glorified.
22 The least of them shall become a clan,
and the smallest one a mighty nation;
I am the LORD;
in its time I will accomplish it quickly.

The Good News of Deliverance

61 The spirit of the Lord GOD is upon me,
because the LORD has anointed me;
he has sent me to bring good news to the
oppressed,
to bind up the brokenhearted,
to proclaim liberty to the captives,
and release to the prisoners;

61.1 Jesus Began Here

*When Jesus was ready to announce himself
and his mission, he began with a dramatic
quotation of this passage (Luke 4.18–19).
Notably, he stopped in mid-sentence, before he
reached the phrase "the day of vengeance of
our God." Jesus taught that this day of
vengeance would indeed take place, but at the
time of his second coming, not his first.*

2 to proclaim the year of the LORD's favor,
and the day of vengeance of our God;
to comfort all who mourn;
3 to provide for those who mourn in
Zion—
to give them a garland instead of ashes,
the oil of gladness instead of mourning,
the mantle of praise instead of a faint
spirit.
They will be called oaks of righteousness,
the planting of the LORD, to display his
glory.

q Q Ms Gk Old Latin Tg: MT lacks *by night*

4 They shall build up the ancient ruins,
    they shall raise up the former
        devastations;
they shall repair the ruined cities,
    the devastations of many generations.

5 Strangers shall stand and feed your flocks,
    foreigners shall till your land and dress
        your vines;
6 but you shall be called priests of the
    LORD,
    you shall be named ministers of our
        God;
you shall enjoy the wealth of the nations,
    and in their riches you shall glory.
7 Because their[r] shame was double,
    and dishonor was proclaimed as their
        lot,
therefore they shall possess a double
        portion;
    everlasting joy shall be theirs.

8 For I the LORD love justice,
    I hate robbery and wrongdoing;[s]
I will faithfully give them their
        recompense,
    and I will make an everlasting covenant
        with them.
9 Their descendants shall be known among
        the nations,
    and their offspring among the peoples;
all who see them shall acknowledge
    that they are a people whom the LORD
        has blessed.
10 I will greatly rejoice in the LORD,
    my whole being shall exult in my God;
for he has clothed me with the garments
        of salvation,
he has covered me with the robe of
        righteousness,
as a bridegroom decks himself with a
        garland,
    and as a bride adorns herself with her
        jewels.
11 For as the earth brings forth its shoots,
    and as a garden causes what is sown in
        it to spring up,
so the Lord GOD will cause righteousness
        and praise
    to spring up before all the nations.

The Vindication and Salvation of Zion

62 For Zion's sake I will not keep silent,
    and for Jerusalem's sake I will not rest,
until her vindication shines out like the
        dawn,
    and her salvation like a burning torch.
2 The nations shall see your vindication,

and all the kings your glory;
and you shall be called by a new name
    that the mouth of the LORD will give.
3 You shall be a crown of beauty in the
        hand of the LORD,
    and a royal diadem in the hand of
        your God.
4 You shall no more be termed Forsaken,[t]
    and your land shall no more be termed
        Desolate;[u]
but you shall be called My Delight Is in
        Her,[v]
    and your land Married;[w]
for the LORD delights in you,
    and your land shall be married.
5 For as a young man marries a young
        woman,
    so shall your builder[x] marry you,
and as the bridegroom rejoices over the
        bride,
    so shall your God rejoice over you.
6 Upon your walls, O Jerusalem,
    I have posted sentinels;
all day and all night
    they shall never be silent.
You who remind the LORD,
    take no rest,
7 and give him no rest
    until he establishes Jerusalem
    and makes it renowned throughout the
        earth.
8 The LORD has sworn by his right hand
    and by his mighty arm:
I will not again give your grain
    to be food for your enemies,
and foreigners shall not drink the wine
    for which you have labored;
9 but those who garner it shall eat it
    and praise the LORD,
and those who gather it shall drink it
    in my holy courts.

10 Go through, go through the gates,
    prepare the way for the people;
build up, build up the highway,
    clear it of stones,
lift up an ensign over the peoples.
11 The LORD has proclaimed
    to the end of the earth:
Say to daughter Zion,
    "See, your salvation comes;
his reward is with him,
    and his recompense before him."
12 They shall be called, "The Holy People,
    The Redeemed of the LORD";
and you shall be called, "Sought Out,
    A City Not Forsaken."

---

r Heb your   s Or robbery with a burnt offering   t Heb Azubah   u Heb Shemamah   v Heb Hephzibah
w Heb Beulah   x Cn: Heb your sons

Vengeance on Edom

63 "Who is this that comes from Edom,
from Bozrah in garments stained
crimson?
Who is this so splendidly robed,
marching in his great might?"

"It is I, announcing vindication,
mighty to save."

2 "Why are your robes red,
and your garments like theirs who
tread the wine press?"

3 "I have trodden the wine press alone,
and from the peoples no one was with
me;
I trod them in my anger
and trampled them in my wrath;
their juice spattered on my garments,
and stained all my robes.
4 For the day of vengeance was in my
heart,

and the year for my redeeming work
had come.
5 I looked, but there was no helper;
I stared, but there was no one to
sustain me;
so my own arm brought me victory,
and my wrath sustained me.
6 I trampled down peoples in my anger,
I crushed them in my wrath,
and I poured out their lifeblood on the
earth."

God's Mercy Remembered

7 I will recount the gracious deeds of the
LORD,
the praiseworthy acts of the LORD,
because of all that the LORD has done for
us,
and the great favor to the house of
Israel
that he has shown them according to his
mercy,
according to the abundance of his
steadfast love.

A Glimpse of Things to Come
When all our best dreams will come true

EVERYBODY WANTS A GLIMPSE INTO the future, and the last part of Isaiah gives just that. It tells what will happen at the end of our age on earth. The account is not easy to decipher, however, because the prophet shifts back and forth between his own time and the final events on earth.

> I am about to create new heavens and a new earth; the former things shall not be remembered or come to mind.
> 65.17

A Missionary Book

To the original audience of Israelites, Isaiah makes one thing clear: God would not permanently divorce Israel. "For a brief moment I abandoned you," says God, "but with great compassion I will gather you" (54.7). There is a future for his chosen people.

Isaiah declares that Israel's future involves other nations. Foreigners will flock to Jerusalem: "My house shall be called a house of prayer for all peoples" (56.7). Word about God will go out to nations nearby and far away, and to distant islands that have never heard of him (66.18–21).

Thus the last part of Isaiah, addressed to a people facing deep despair, opens the door for the Jews to become a gift to all people. This prophecy saw fulfillment in Jesus, who recruited disciples to take his message to everyone. Through his life and death, the suffering servant indeed introduced the gospel to the entire world.

What Isaiah Says to Us

The book of Isaiah goes on to describe a new beginning, a time of final triumph and peace. In that day, there will be no need for tears. Wild animals will tamely lie down together. The sun and moon will fade, overwhelmed by the brightness of God's glory.

In chapters 60 and 65, the prophet describes the future with such eloquence that New Testament books like Revelation could not improve on the language; they merely quoted Isaiah. Even today some of these phrases—"beat their swords into plowshares," for example—surface in popular language, expressing our deepest longings for peace.

We dream of a time of peace, without pain or fear or disease or death. Isaiah assures us that one day those dreams will come true.

Life Questions: What would you most like to see changed about your world? Does Isaiah speak to that change?

8 For he said, "Surely they are my people,
     children who will not deal falsely";
   and he became their savior
9   in all their distress.
   It was no messenger[y] or angel
     but his presence that saved them;[z]
   in his love and in his pity he redeemed
       them;
     he lifted them up and carried them all
       the days of old.

63.9–17 A Lesson from History

The Babylonian captivity brought a grave crisis to the Israelites. To them, God's own integrity was at stake. They had a treaty, or covenant, with him. Had he abandoned them? In this chapter, the prophet reviews all the good things God has done for the Israelites and says that, even in the worst times, "he became their savior in all their distress." If God had been with them in the past, then he would be with them in the future. Then he turns to God directly and makes an impassioned appeal for help: "O, that you would tear open the heavens and come down" (64.1).

10 But they rebelled
     and grieved his holy spirit;
   therefore he became their enemy;
     he himself fought against them.
11 Then they[a] remembered the days of old,
     of Moses his servant.[b]
   Where is the one who brought them up
       out of the sea
     with the shepherds of his flock?
   Where is the one who put within them
       his holy spirit,
12 who caused his glorious arm
     to march at the right hand of Moses,
   who divided the waters before them
     to make for himself an everlasting
       name,
13   who led them through the depths?
   Like a horse in the desert,
     they did not stumble.
14 Like cattle that go down into the valley,
     the spirit of the LORD gave them rest.
   Thus you led your people,
     to make for yourself a glorious name.

A Prayer of Penitence

15 Look down from heaven and see,
     from your holy and glorious habitation.
   Where are your zeal and your might?
     The yearning of your heart and your
       compassion?
   They are withheld from me.
16 For you are our father,
     though Abraham does not know us
     and Israel does not acknowledge us;
   you, O LORD, are our father;
     our Redeemer from of old is
       your name.
17 Why, O LORD, do you make us stray from
       your ways
     and harden our heart, so that we do
       not fear you?
   Turn back for the sake of your servants,
     for the sake of the tribes that are your
       heritage.
18 Your holy people took possession for a
       little while;
     but now our adversaries have trampled
       down your sanctuary.
19 We have long been like those whom you
       do not rule,
     like those not called by your name.

64 O that you would tear open the heavens
       and come down,
     so that the mountains would quake at
       your presence—
2[c] as when fire kindles brushwood
       and the fire causes water to boil—
   to make your name known to your
       adversaries,
     so that the nations might tremble at
       your presence!
3 When you did awesome deeds that we
       did not expect,
     you came down, the mountains quaked
       at your presence.
4 From ages past no one has heard,
     no ear has perceived,
   no eye has seen any God besides you,
     who works for those who wait for him.
5 You meet those who gladly do right,
     those who remember you in your ways.
   But you were angry, and we sinned;
     because you hid yourself we
       transgressed.[d]
6 We have all become like one who is
       unclean,
     and all our righteous deeds are like a
       filthy cloth.
   We all fade like a leaf,
     and our iniquities, like the wind, take
       us away.
7 There is no one who calls on your name,
     or attempts to take hold of you;
   for you have hidden your face from us,

---

y Gk: Heb *anguish*   *z* Or *savior.* *9In all their distress he was distressed; the angel of his presence saved them;*
a Heb *he*   *b* Cn: Heb *his people*   *c* Ch 64.1 in Heb   *d* Meaning of Heb uncertain

and have delivered[e] us into the hand
of our iniquity.
8 Yet, O LORD, you are our Father;
we are the clay, and you are
our potter;
we are all the work of your hand.
9 Do not be exceedingly angry, O LORD,
and do not remember iniquity forever.
Now consider, we are all your people.
10 Your holy cities have become a
wilderness,
Zion has become a wilderness,
Jerusalem a desolation.
11 Our holy and beautiful house,
where our ancestors praised you,
has been burned by fire,
and all our pleasant places have
become ruins.
12 After all this, will you restrain yourself,
O LORD?
Will you keep silent, and punish us so
severely?

The Righteousness of God's Judgment

65 I was ready to be sought out by those
who did not ask,
to be found by those who did not seek
me.
I said, "Here I am, here I am,"
to a nation that did not call on my
name.
2 I held out my hands all day long
to a rebellious people,
who walk in a way that is not good,
following their own devices;
3 a people who provoke me
to my face continually,
sacrificing in gardens
and offering incense on bricks;

65.3 Provoking God

*In this speech, God is directly attacking the
most repulsive practices of Judah, notably its
idolatry. "Gardens" refers to the gardens that
usually surrounded pagan shrines. Verse 4
mentions the superstitious practice of sitting in
cemeteries to seek help from the dead. And the
"swine's flesh" was eaten in a sacrificial meal
for a pagan god—faithful Jews did not eat pork.*

4 who sit inside tombs,
and spend the night in secret places;
who eat swine's flesh,
with broth of abominable things in
their vessels;
5 who say, "Keep to yourself,

do not come near me, for I am too
holy for you."
These are a smoke in my nostrils,
a fire that burns all day long.
6 See, it is written before me:
I will not keep silent, but I will repay;
I will indeed repay into their laps
7 their[f] iniquities and their[f] ancestors'
iniquities together,
says the LORD;
because they offered incense on the
mountains
and reviled me on the hills,
I will measure into their laps
full payment for their actions.
8 Thus says the LORD:
As the wine is found in the cluster,
and they say, "Do not destroy it,
for there is a blessing in it,"
so I will do for my servants' sake,
and not destroy them all.
9 I will bring forth descendants[g] from
Jacob,
and from Judah inheritors[h] of my
mountains;
my chosen shall inherit it,
and my servants shall settle there.
10 Sharon shall become a pasture for flocks,
and the Valley of Achor a place for
herds to lie down,
for my people who have sought me.
11 But you who forsake the LORD,
who forget my holy mountain,
who set a table for Fortune
and fill cups of mixed wine for
Destiny;
12 I will destine you to the sword,
and all of you shall bow down to the
slaughter;
because, when I called, you did
not answer,
when I spoke, you did not listen,
but you did what was evil in my sight,
and chose what I did not delight in.
13 Therefore thus says the Lord GOD:
My servants shall eat,
but you shall be hungry;
my servants shall drink,
but you shall be thirsty;
my servants shall rejoice,
but you shall be put to shame;
14 my servants shall sing for gladness of
heart,
but you shall cry out for pain of heart,
and shall wail for anguish of spirit.
15 You shall leave your name to my chosen
to use as a curse,
and the Lord GOD will put you
to death;

---

[e] Gk Syr Old Latin Tg: Heb *melted*   [f] Gk Syr: Heb *your*   [g] Or *a descendant*   [h] Or *an inheritor*

but to his servants he will give a
    different name.
16 Then whoever invokes a blessing in the
    land
  shall bless by the God of faithfulness,
and whoever takes an oath in the land
  shall swear by the God of faithfulness;
because the former troubles are forgotten
  and are hidden from my sight.

The Glorious New Creation

17 For I am about to create new heavens
    and a new earth;
the former things shall not be
    remembered
    or come to mind.

65.17 New Earth

*Human beings have always longed for a
utopia. Isaiah repeatedly promises just that,
here and in chapters 11 and 35. He has in mind
a whole new earth, in which people will build
and farm, work and raise children—but without
frustration. The violence and sadness that
mark our earth will vanish. The key to that
new era will be an intimate relationship with
God. "Before they call I will answer, while they
are yet speaking I will hear" (verse 24).*

18 But be glad and rejoice forever
    in what I am creating;
for I am about to create Jerusalem as a
    joy,
  and its people as a delight.
19 I will rejoice in Jerusalem,
    and delight in my people;
no more shall the sound of weeping be
    heard in it,
    or the cry of distress.
20 No more shall there be in it
    an infant that lives but a few days,
    or an old person who does not live out
    a lifetime;
for one who dies at a hundred years will
    be considered a youth,
    and one who falls short of a hundred
    will be considered accursed.
21 They shall build houses and inhabit them;
    they shall plant vineyards and eat their
    fruit.
22 They shall not build and another inhabit;
    they shall not plant and another eat;
for like the days of a tree shall the days of
    my people be,
    and my chosen shall long enjoy the
    work of their hands.
23 They shall not labor in vain,

or bear children for calamity;[i]
for they shall be offspring blessed by the
    LORD—
  and their descendants as well.
24 Before they call I will answer,
    while they are yet speaking I will hear.
25 The wolf and the lamb shall feed together,
    the lion shall eat straw like the ox;
    but the serpent—its food shall be dust!
They shall not hurt or destroy
    on all my holy mountain,
        says the LORD.

The Worship God Demands

66 Thus says the LORD:
Heaven is my throne
    and the earth is my footstool;
what is the house that you would build
    for me,
    and what is my resting place?
2 All these things my hand has made,
    and so all these things are mine,[j]
        says the LORD.
But this is the one to whom I will look,
    to the humble and contrite in spirit,
    who trembles at my word.

3 Whoever slaughters an ox is like one who
    kills a human being;
  whoever sacrifices a lamb, like one who
    breaks a dog's neck;
whoever presents a grain offering, like one
    who offers swine's blood;[k]
  whoever makes a memorial offering of
    frankincense, like one who blesses
    an idol.
These have chosen their own ways,
    and in their abominations they take
    delight;
4 I also will choose to mock[l] them,
    and bring upon them what they fear;
because, when I called, no one answered,
    when I spoke, they did not listen;
but they did what was evil in my sight,
    and chose what did not please me.

The LORD Vindicates Zion

5 Hear the word of the LORD,
    you who tremble at his word:
Your own people who hate you
    and reject you for my name's sake
have said, "Let the LORD be glorified,
    so that we may see your joy";
  but it is they who shall be put
    to shame.

6 Listen, an uproar from the city!
    A voice from the temple!

---

i Or *sudden terror*   *j* Gk Syr: Heb *these things came to be*   *k* Meaning of Heb uncertain   *l* Or *to punish*

The voice of the LORD,
dealing retribution to his enemies!

7 Before she was in labor
she gave birth;
before her pain came upon her
she delivered a son.
8 Who has heard of such a thing?
Who has seen such things?
Shall a land be born in one day?
Shall a nation be delivered in one
moment?
Yet as soon as Zion was in labor
she delivered her children.
9 Shall I open the womb and not deliver?
says the LORD;
shall I, the one who delivers, shut the
womb?
says your God.

66.9 Pain with a Purpose

*Nowhere does the book of Isaiah minimize the
pain Israel went through; the prophet shared
the nation's agony. But God makes clear that
the pain was not arbitrary and purposeless.
Like childbirth, this pain will lead to something
happy and good. "As a mother comforts her
child, so I will comfort you" (verse 13). In one
last word of triumph, God reaffirms that the
suffering of the Israelites will one day lead to a
great missionary outreach among all humanity
(verses 19,23).*

10 Rejoice with Jerusalem, and be glad for
her,
all you who love her;
rejoice with her in joy,
all you who mourn over her—
11 that you may nurse and be satisfied
from her consoling breast;
that you may drink deeply with delight
from her glorious bosom.

12 For thus says the LORD:
I will extend prosperity to her like a river,
and the wealth of the nations like an
overflowing stream;
and you shall nurse and be carried on her
arm,
and dandled on her knees.
13 As a mother comforts her child,
so I will comfort you;
you shall be comforted in Jerusalem.

The Reign and Indignation of God

14 You shall see, and your heart shall rejoice;

your bodies[m] shall flourish like the
grass;
and it shall be known that the hand of
the LORD is with his servants,
and his indignation is against
his enemies.
15 For the LORD will come in fire,
and his chariots like the whirlwind,
to pay back his anger in fury,
and his rebuke in flames of fire.
16 For by fire will the LORD execute
judgment,
and by his sword, on all flesh;
and those slain by the LORD shall be
many.

17 Those who sanctify and purify themselves
to go into the gardens, following the one in the
center, eating the flesh of pigs, vermin, and ro-
dents, shall come to an end together, says the
LORD.

18 For I know[n] their works and their
thoughts, and I am[o] coming to gather all nations
and tongues; and they shall come and shall see my
glory, 19and I will set a sign among them. From
them I will send survivors to the nations, to Tarshish, Put,[p] and Lud—which draw the bow—to
Tubal and Javan, to the coastlands far away that
have not heard of my fame or seen my glory; and
they shall declare my glory among the nations.
20They shall bring all your kindred from all the
nations as an offering to the LORD, on horses, and
in chariots, and in litters, and on mules, and on
dromedaries, to my holy mountain Jerusalem,
says the LORD, just as the Israelites bring a grain
offering in a clean vessel to the house of the LORD.
21And I will also take some of them as priests and
as Levites, says the LORD.

22 For as the new heavens and the new
earth,
which I will make,
shall remain before me, says the LORD;
so shall your descendants and your
name remain.
23 From new moon to new moon,
and from sabbath to sabbath,
all flesh shall come to worship before me,
says the LORD.

24 And they shall go out and look at the dead
bodies of the people who have rebelled against
me; for their worm shall not die, their fire shall
not be quenched, and they shall be an abhorrence
to all flesh.

---

m Heb *bones*   *n* Gk Syr: Heb lacks *know*   *o* Gk Syr Vg Tg: Heb *it is*   *p* Gk: Heb *Pul*

JEREMIAH

God's Reluctant Messenger

Jeremiah felt frightened and insecure—but he burned with a message

JEREMIAH LIVED ONE OF THE most dramatic lives in the Bible, and that is saying something. But he never learned to like his role. Through all the excitement he remained reluctant, insecure, and often unhappy.

> *"Do not be afraid of them, for I am with you to deliver you, says the LORD." 1.8*

God chose him to be "over nations and over kingdoms, to pluck up and to pull down, to destroy and to overthrow, to build and to plant" (1.10). To accomplish that, Jeremiah had only one resource—his mouth. How did he respond to such an awesome challenge? "Ah, Lord GOD! Truly I do not know how to speak, for I am only a boy" (1.6). He didn't stride forward; he barely hung on. He wanted out of the job.

His only encouragement was God's promise: "I for my part have made you today a fortified city, an iron pillar, and a bronze wall, against the whole land" (1.18). For 40 years Jeremiah gave top officials a warning they hated to hear and refused to heed. Several times they arrested and imprisoned him; they nearly killed him.

His message? With God's approval, the savage Babylonians would sweep down into Judah. Clever alliances with other powers like Egypt would not help, said Jeremiah. Neither would Judah's half-hearted religion. Judah's only hope lay in renewing an alliance with the living God.

A Disturbing Glimpse of Jeremiah's Mind

The book of Jeremiah stands out not for beautiful poetry or great ideas. Its power comes from its disturbing glimpse of Jeremiah's mind. Jeremiah talked like a man who has awakened from a nightmare, convinced that the nightmare is coming true. His words were sledgehammer blows designed to crack the hardest, most indifferent skull. Though he wished to keep quiet, he found that God's word was "like a burning fire shut up in my bones" (20.9).

No prophet exposed his feelings more than Jeremiah. His relationship with God was streaked with quarrels, reproaches, and outbursts. He told God he wished he were dead (20.14–18). He accused God of being unreliable (15.18). But God offered no sympathy. Rather, he promised more of the same, reminding Jeremiah of his promise to stand by him (12.5–6; 15.19–20). Their relationship, doubts and all, forms one of the best examples in the Bible of what it means to follow God in spite of everything.

Reason to Fear

Jeremiah frankly feared death. He wearied of ridicule. He hated standing alone against the crowd. He told God how he felt. Yet he obeyed God, and in the end his message proved true. He stands as a far greater man than the kings in their luxurious palaces who imprisoned him and burned his writings.

He spoke a gloomy message in a gloomy time, and as a result his words are not always pleasant to read. He reminds us, in an era of artificial cheer and television smiles, that God's message is not always comforting and encouraging. People who disregard God will have reason to fear. For a world that defies him, he plans judgment. And no one, not even his chosen messengers, will escape suffering. God's presence will make them strong enough to face it.

How to Read Jeremiah

Suppose you find, in an old trunk, a thick packet of letters written by your great uncle. You soon realize they are all out of order. One he wrote from the trenches of France during World War I. The next also refers to a war, but from the references to British prime minister Winston Churchill you soon recognize it as World War II, over 20 years later.

Those letters might contain the whole of your uncle's life, but to get his story straight, you'd have to read the whole packet. A reader of Jeremiah finds a very similar situation. The book is an anthology of prophecies given at different times. They jump forward and backward in history, and if you imagine that the book is in chronological order, you will become very confused. Fortunately, it is not hard to reconstruct the order of the main events of Jeremiah's life.

Jeremiah spoke to a nation about to be destroyed by war. Three hundred years before him, the Israelites had split into two countries, Israel in the North and Judah in the South. About 100 years before Jeremiah, Assyria had conquered the Northern Kingdom. This disaster was "World War I" in Old Testament history.

Now, during Jeremiah's life, World War II threatened. Another fierce kingdom, Babylon, assembled troops against the remaining Southern Kingdom. Would God save his chosen people? Jeremiah loudly insisted for more than 20 years that God would punish Judah just as he had Israel, by letting Babylon take them into captivity. He lived to see his predictions come true.

Many passages in Jeremiah refer to the five kings he knew. When you see their names, use them as a reference point in figuring out the order of events:

Josiah (17 years)
Jehoahaz (3 months)
Jehoiakim (12 years)
Jehoiachin (3 months)
Zedekiah (11 years)

Second Kings 23–25 or 2 Chronicles 34–36 gives an overall historical summary of their reigns. You can read a brief synopsis in "A Lineup of Rulers," pages 1349–1357. The better you grasp the historical situation Jeremiah lived in, the more insight you will have into his words.

To capture the full emotion of Jeremiah, you may want to read the first few chapters out loud.

PEOPLE YOU'LL MEET IN JEREMIAH

JEREMIAH *(p. 766)*

3-TRACK READING PLAN

For an explanation and complete listing of the 3-track reading plan, turn to page 7.

TRACK 1: *Two-Week Courses on the Bible*
See page 7 for information on these courses.

TRACK 2: *An Overview of Jeremiah in 4 Days*
☐ Day 1. Read the Introduction to Jeremiah and chapter 2, for God's passionate indictment of his people.
☐ Day 2. Read chapter 15, part of an emotional dialogue between Jeremiah and God.
☐ Day 3. Read chapter 31, God's promise of restoration and a new covenant.
☐ Day 4. Read chapter 38, for Jeremiah's dramatic skirmishes with death in the last days of Jerusalem.

Now turn to page 9 for your next Track 2 reading project.

TRACK 3: *All of Jeremiah in 51 Days*
After you have read through Jeremiah, turn to pages 10–14 for your next Track 3 reading project.

☐1	☐2	☐3	☐4	☐5	☐6	☐7	☐8
☐9	☐10	☐11	☐12	☐13	☐14	☐15	☐16
☐17	☐18	☐19	☐20	☐21	☐22	☐23	☐24
☐25	☐26	☐27	☐28	☐29	☐30	☐31	☐32
☐33	☐34	☐35	☐36	☐37	☐38	☐39	☐40
☐41	☐42	☐43	☐44–45	☐46	☐47	☐48	☐49
☐50	☐51	☐52					

1 The words of Jeremiah son of Hilkiah, of the priests who were in Anathoth in the land of Benjamin, ²to whom the word of the LORD came in the days of King Josiah son of Amon of Judah, in the thirteenth year of his reign. ³It came also in the days of King Jehoiakim son of Josiah of Judah, and until the end of the eleventh year of King Zedekiah son of Josiah of Judah, until the captivity of Jerusalem in the fifth month.

Jeremiah's Call and Commission

4 Now the word of the LORD came to me saying,

5 "Before I formed you in the womb I
        knew you,
and before you were born I consecrated
        you;
I appointed you a prophet to the
        nations."

⁶Then I said, "Ah, Lord GOD! Truly I do not know how to speak, for I am only a boy." ⁷But the LORD said to me,

"Do not say, 'I am only a boy';
for you shall go to all to whom I send
        you,
and you shall speak whatever I command
        you.
8 Do not be afraid of them,
for I am with you to deliver you,
                says the LORD."

⁹Then the LORD put out his hand and touched my mouth; and the LORD said to me,

"Now I have put my words in your
        mouth.
10 See, today I appoint you over nations and
        over kingdoms,
to pluck up and to pull down,
to destroy and to overthrow,
to build and to plant."

11 The word of the LORD came to me, saying, "Jeremiah, what do you see?" And I said, "I see a branch of an almond tree."ᵃ ¹²Then the LORD said to me, "You have seen well, for I am watchingᵇ over my word to perform it." ¹³The word of the LORD came to me a second time, saying, "What do you see?" And I said, "I see a boiling pot, tilted away from the north." ¹⁴Then the LORD said to me: Out of the north disaster shall break out on all the inhabitants of the land. ¹⁵For now I am calling all the tribes of the kingdoms of the north, says the LORD; and they shall come and all of them shall set their thrones at the entrance of the gates of Jerusalem, against all its surrounding walls and against all the cities of Judah. ¹⁶And I will utter my judgments against them, for all their wickedness in forsaking me; they have made offerings to other gods, and worshiped the works of their own hands. ¹⁷But you, gird up your loins; stand up and tell them everything that I command you. Do not break down before them, or I will break you before them. ¹⁸And I for my part have made you today a fortified city, an iron pillar, and a bronze wall, against the whole land—against the kings of Judah, its princes, its priests, and the people of the

1.18 Too Young?

Like Moses before him, Jeremiah responded reluctantly to God's call. "I am only a boy," he protested, feeling too inexperienced to carry such responsibility (verse 6). But God contradicted him. Age and experience did not matter; God's presence did (verse 8). In the face of powerful opposition, God would make Jeremiah as strong as iron.

land. ¹⁹They will fight against you; but they shall not prevail against you, for I am with you, says the LORD, to deliver you.

God Pleads with Israel to Repent

2 The word of the LORD came to me, saying: ²Go and proclaim in the hearing of Jerusalem, Thus says the LORD:

I remember the devotion of your youth,
        your love as a bride,
how you followed me in the wilderness,
        in a land not sown.
3 Israel was holy to the LORD,
        the first fruits of his harvest.
All who ate of it were held guilty;
        disaster came upon them,
                        says the LORD.

4 Hear the word of the LORD, O house of Jacob, and all the families of the house of Israel. ⁵Thus says the LORD:

What wrong did your ancestors find in
        me
        that they went far from me,
and went after worthless things, and
        became worthless themselves?
6 They did not say, "Where is the LORD
        who brought us up from the land of
                Egypt,
who led us in the wilderness,
        in a land of deserts and pits,
in a land of drought and deep darkness,
        in a land that no one passes through,
        where no one lives?"
7 I brought you into a plentiful land
        to eat its fruits and its good things.
But when you entered you defiled my
        land,
        and made my heritage an abomination.

ᵃ Heb *shaqed*   ᵇ Heb *shoqed*

8 The priests did not say, "Where is the
LORD?"
Those who handle the law did not
know me;
the rulers[c] transgressed against me;
the prophets prophesied by Baal,
and went after things that do
not profit.

9 Therefore once more I accuse you,
says the LORD,
and I accuse your children's children.
10 Cross to the coasts of Cyprus and look,
send to Kedar and examine with care;
see if there has ever been such a thing.
11 Has a nation changed its gods,
even though they are no gods?
But my people have changed their glory
for something that does not profit.
12 Be appalled, O heavens, at this,
be shocked, be utterly desolate,
says the LORD,
13 for my people have committed two evils:
they have forsaken me,
the fountain of living water,
and dug out cisterns for themselves,
cracked cisterns
that can hold no water.

2.13 An Astounding Trade

*Jeremiah piles image on top of image,
searching for a way to express the astounding
fact that Israelites had traded the living God for
the idols of their neighbors. Here he compares
the deed to exchanging a spring of living water
for a leaky cistern. In verse 20 he graphically
compares idolatry to sexual promiscuity. In an
interesting twist, Jesus offered "living water" to
a sexually promiscuous Samaritan woman in
John 4.10.*

14 Is Israel a slave? Is he a homeborn
servant?
Why then has he become plunder?
15 The lions have roared against him,
they have roared loudly.
They have made his land a waste;
his cities are in ruins, without
inhabitant.
16 Moreover, the people of Memphis and
Tahpanhes
have broken the crown of your head.
17 Have you not brought this upon yourself
by forsaking the LORD your God,
while he led you in the way?
18 What then do you gain by going
to Egypt,
to drink the waters of the Nile?
Or what do you gain by going to Assyria,
to drink the waters of the Euphrates?
19 Your wickedness will punish you,
and your apostasies will convict you.
Know and see that it is evil and bitter
for you to forsake the LORD your God;
the fear of me is not in you,
says the Lord GOD of hosts.

20 For long ago you broke your yoke
and burst your bonds,
and you said, "I will not serve!"
On every high hill
and under every green tree
you sprawled and played the whore.
21 Yet I planted you as a choice vine,
from the purest stock.
How then did you turn degenerate
and become a wild vine?
22 Though you wash yourself with lye
and use much soap,
the stain of your guilt is still before me,
says the Lord GOD.
23 How can you say, "I am not defiled,
I have not gone after the Baals"?
Look at your way in the valley;
know what you have done—
a restive young camel interlacing her
tracks,
24 a wild ass at home in the wilderness,
in her heat sniffing the wind!
Who can restrain her lust?
None who seek her need weary
themselves;
in her month they will find her.
25 Keep your feet from going unshod
and your throat from thirst.
But you said, "It is hopeless,
for I have loved strangers,
and after them I will go."

26 As a thief is shamed when caught,
so the house of Israel shall be
shamed—
they, their kings, their officials,
their priests, and their prophets,
27 who say to a tree, "You are my father,"
and to a stone, "You gave me birth."
For they have turned their backs to me,
and not their faces.
But in the time of their trouble they say,
"Come and save us!"
28 But where are your gods
that you made for yourself?
Let them come, if they can save you,
in your time of trouble;
for you have as many gods
as you have towns, O Judah.

c Heb *shepherds*

29 Why do you complain against me?
     You have all rebelled against me,
                              says the LORD.
30 In vain I have struck down your children;
     they accepted no correction.
   Your own sword devoured your prophets
     like a ravening lion.
31 And you, O generation, behold the word
                        of the LORD![d]
   Have I been a wilderness to Israel,
     or a land of thick darkness?
   Why then do my people say, "We are
                              free,
     we will come to you no more"?
32 Can a girl forget her ornaments,
     or a bride her attire?
   Yet my people have forgotten me,
     days without number.

33 How well you direct your course
     to seek lovers!
   So that even to wicked women
     you have taught your ways.
34 Also on your skirts is found
     the lifeblood of the innocent poor,
   though you did not catch them breaking
                              in.
   Yet in spite of all these things[d]
35 you say, "I am innocent;
     surely his anger has turned from me."
   Now I am bringing you to judgment
     for saying, "I have not sinned."
36 How lightly you gad about,
     changing your ways!
   You shall be put to shame by Egypt
     as you were put to shame by Assyria.
37 From there also you will come away
     with your hands on your head;
   for the LORD has rejected those in whom
                              you trust,
     and you will not prosper through
                              them.

Unfaithful Israel

3 If[e] a man divorces his wife
     and she goes from him
   and becomes another man's wife,
     will he return to her?
   Would not such a land be greatly
                              polluted?
   You have played the whore with many
                              lovers;
     and would you return to me?
                              says the LORD.
2 Look up to the bare heights,[f] and see!
     Where have you not been lain with?
   By the waysides you have sat waiting for
                              lovers,
     like a nomad in the wilderness.

You have polluted the land
     with your whoring and wickedness.
3 Therefore the showers have been
                              withheld,
     and the spring rain has not come;

3.2 Ritual Sex

Today, the news that a minister or priest has committed adultery sends shock waves through the community. But Israel's neighbors in ancient times actually incorporated adultery into their religious rites. Pagans worshiped their gods through cultic prostitution, believing sex would put them in tune with divine power. This ritual sex went on at religious shrines located on the "high places" (hilltops). When Israel joined in their neighbors' worship, God properly called it adultery—both physical and spiritual. Israel was going out with every god in town.

---

yet you have the forehead of a whore,
     you refuse to be ashamed.
4 Have you not just now called to me,
     "My Father, you are the friend of my
                              youth—
5 will he be angry forever,
     will he be indignant to the end?"
   This is how you have spoken,
     but you have done all the evil that you
                              could.

A Call to Repentance

6 The LORD said to me in the days of King Josiah: Have you seen what she did, that faithless one, Israel, how she went up on every high hill and under every green tree, and played the whore there? [7]And I thought, "After she has done all this she will return to me"; but she did not return, and her false sister Judah saw it. [8]She[g] saw that for all the adulteries of that faithless one, Israel, I had sent her away with a decree of divorce; yet her false sister Judah did not fear, but she too went

---

3.10 A Superficial Change

King Josiah, one of the few good kings in Judah's history, led a massive religious reform (see 2 Kings 22 and 23). While Josiah was unquestionably sincere, Jeremiah saw that the nation's return to God wasn't. Jeremiah's accusation was borne out after King Josiah's death: Judah returned quickly to her former ways.

---

[d] Meaning of Heb uncertain   [e] Q Ms Gk Syr: MT *Saying, If*   [f] Or *the trails*   [g] Q Ms Gk Mss Syr: MT *I*

and played the whore. ⁹Because she took her whoredom so lightly, she polluted the land, committing adultery with stone and tree. ¹⁰Yet for all this her false sister Judah did not return to me with her whole heart, but only in pretense, says the LORD.

11 Then the LORD said to me: Faithless Israel has shown herself less guilty than false Judah. ¹²Go, and proclaim these words toward the north, and say:

Return, faithless Israel,
            says the LORD.
I will not look on you in anger,
    for I am merciful,
            says the LORD;
I will not be angry forever.
¹³ Only acknowledge your guilt,

that you have rebelled against the LORD
        your God,
and scattered your favors among strangers
        under every green tree,
and have not obeyed my voice,
            says the LORD.
¹⁴ Return, O faithless children,
            says the LORD,
    for I am your master;
I will take you, one from a city and two
        from a family,
and I will bring you to Zion.

15 I will give you shepherds after my own heart, who will feed you with knowledge and understanding. ¹⁶And when you have multiplied and increased in the land, in those days, says the LORD, they shall no longer say, "The ark of the

A Lover's Quarrel
The violent emotions of a scorned lover

THE CALL COMES LATE, AFTER midnight, to a police officer who grimaces and shakes his head. Then, siren screaming, he races toward the house. Neighbors heard a woman's cries. Someone saw a man threatening her with a knife. As the police officer pulls up to the house, he hears her high-pitched shrieks. She is begging for mercy—from her husband.

Such cases are called "domestic disturbances." They happen nearly every night, and particularly on weekends. The police usually dislike getting called in. Both husband and wife can turn on the person who is "interfering."

Lovers' quarrels may seem silly to outsiders, but they are deadly serious to those involved. Some turn violent, even murderous. The most precious, desired gift anyone can offer has been abused. Love has been betrayed. Lovers react to that with violent emotions.

> You have played the whore with many lovers; and would you return to me? says the LORD. 3.1

Words that Tear His Heart

It is a lovers' quarrel that Jeremiah exposes in chapters 2 and 3, and the emotions are violent and helpless. Again and again God makes his charge against Judah. Of all the nations, he had picked her; he had tenderly offered his protection and care. But she keeps sleeping with other men. He warns her again and again, but she ignores him. She saw how he divorced her sister Israel. Doesn't she know he will do the same to her?

God's words bleed pain. He accuses as though he cannot help himself, although his words tear his own heart. First, he is tender, full of memories: "I remember . . . your love as a bride, how you followed me in the wilderness" (2.2). But then you "burst your bonds, and you said, 'I will not serve!' On every high hill and under every green tree you sprawled and played the whore" (2.20). In disgust God compares Judah to a donkey in heat, "in her heat sniffing the wind! . . . None who seek her need weary themselves" (2.24). But the comparison hurts him more than her. His love, not hers, is scorned.

Married to a Whore

The prophet Hosea was the first to draw the picture of God married to a prostitute. Jeremiah amplifies it. The comparison cries out both the passionate love God feels for his people and the terrible, wounded pain he feels at their betrayal. Jeremiah's imagery is violent and dark, but underneath it, something wonderful shines out: the tender and personal love of God for his people.

The "adultery" Jeremiah wrote about focuses on the worship of idols. Most modern people find it hard to understand why Israelites felt any impulse to kneel before wooden or metal statues, or why their doing so made God furious. But when Jeremiah refers to it as adultery, God's hatred of idolatry becomes understandable. God meant his people to have only one true love in their lives—God himself. God the lover will not take second place; he refuses to share his bride.

Life Questions: Have you ever fought with God? What issues were you fighting about?

covenant of the LORD." It shall not come to mind, or be remembered, or missed; nor shall another one be made. ¹⁷At that time Jerusalem shall be called the throne of the LORD, and all nations shall gather to it, to the presence of the LORD in Jerusalem, and they shall no longer stubbornly follow their own evil will. ¹⁸In those days the house of Judah shall join the house of Israel, and together they shall come from the land of the north to the land that I gave your ancestors for a heritage.

¹⁹ I thought
  how I would set you among
      my children,
and give you a pleasant land,
  the most beautiful heritage of all the
      nations.
And I thought you would call me, My
      Father,
  and would not turn from following me.
²⁰ Instead, as a faithless wife leaves her
      husband,
  so you have been faithless to me,
      O house of Israel,
                    says the LORD.

²¹ A voice on the bare heights^h is heard,
  the plaintive weeping of Israel's
      children,
because they have perverted their way,
  they have forgotten the LORD their
      God:
²² Return, O faithless children,
  I will heal your faithlessness.

"Here we come to you;
  for you are the LORD our God.
²³ Truly the hills are^i a delusion,
  the orgies on the mountains.
Truly in the LORD our God
  is the salvation of Israel.

24 "But from our youth the shameful thing has devoured all for which our ancestors had labored, their flocks and their herds, their sons and their daughters. ²⁵Let us lie down in our shame, and let our dishonor cover us; for we have sinned against the LORD our God, we and our ancestors, from our youth even to this day; and we have not obeyed the voice of the LORD our God."

4 If you return, O Israel,
                    says the LORD,
  if you return to me,
if you remove your abominations from
      my presence,
  and do not waver,
² and if you swear, "As the LORD lives!"
  in truth, in justice, and in uprightness,

then nations shall be blessed^j by him,
  and by him they shall boast.

3 For thus says the LORD to the people of Judah and to the inhabitants of Jerusalem:
Break up your fallow ground,
  and do not sow among thorns.
4 Circumcise yourselves to the LORD,
  remove the foreskin of your hearts,
      O people of Judah and inhabitants of
          Jerusalem,
or else my wrath will go forth like fire,
  and burn with no one to quench it,
      because of the evil of your doings.

4.4 Circumcised Hearts

All male Jewish babies underwent circumcision, a sign of their "set-apartness" as God's chosen people. Often, though, circumcision became just a ritual, not reflecting any real difference in the way people lived. Jeremiah used a startling metaphor—"circumcise yourselves"—to remind the Israelites that membership in God's family should make a difference inside, not just on the surface. The apostle Paul wrote that Christ brings about this inner circumcision (Colossians 2.11).

Invasion and Desolation of Judah Threatened

5 Declare in Judah, and proclaim in Jerusalem, and say:
Blow the trumpet through the land;
  shout aloud^k and say,
"Gather together, and let us go
  into the fortified cities!"
6 Raise a standard toward Zion,
  flee for safety, do not delay,
for I am bringing evil from the north,
  and a great destruction.
7 A lion has gone up from its thicket,
  a destroyer of nations has set out;
he has gone out from his place
  to make your land a waste;
your cities will be ruins
  without inhabitant.
8 Because of this put on sackcloth,
  lament and wail:
"The fierce anger of the LORD
  has not turned away from us."

⁹On that day, says the LORD, courage shall fail the king and the officials; the priests shall be appalled and the prophets astounded. ¹⁰Then I said, "Ah, Lord GOD, how utterly you have deceived this

---

^{h} Or *the trails* ^{i} Gk Syr Vg: Heb *Truly from the hills is weapons*: Heb *shout, fill* (your hand) ^{j} Or *shall bless themselves* ^{k} Or *shout, take your*

people and Jerusalem, saying, 'It shall be well with you,' even while the sword is at the throat!"

11 At that time it will be said to this people and to Jerusalem: A hot wind comes from me out of the bare heights[l] in the desert toward my poor people, not to winnow or cleanse— [12]a wind too strong for that. Now it is I who speak in judgment against them.

13 Look! He comes up like clouds,
    his chariots like the whirlwind;
his horses are swifter than eagles—
    woe to us, for we are ruined!
14 O Jerusalem, wash your heart clean of
        wickedness
    so that you may be saved.
How long shall your evil schemes
    lodge within you?
15 For a voice declares from Dan
    and proclaims disaster from Mount
        Ephraim.
16 Tell the nations, "Here they are!"
    Proclaim against Jerusalem,
"Besiegers come from a distant land;
    they shout against the cities of Judah.
17 They have closed in around her like
        watchers of a field,
    because she has rebelled against me,
                        says the LORD.
18 Your ways and your doings
    have brought this upon you.
This is your doom; how bitter it is!
    It has reached your very heart."

Sorrow for a Doomed Nation

19 My anguish, my anguish! I writhe in pain!
    Oh, the walls of my heart!
My heart is beating wildly;
    I cannot keep silent;
for I[m] hear the sound of the trumpet,
    the alarm of war.
20 Disaster overtakes disaster,
    the whole land is laid waste.
Suddenly my tents are destroyed,
    my curtains in a moment.
21 How long must I see the standard,
    and hear the sound of the trumpet?
22 "For my people are foolish,
    they do not know me;
they are stupid children,
    they have no understanding.
They are skilled in doing evil,
    but do not know how to do good."

23 I looked on the earth, and lo, it was waste
        and void;
    and to the heavens, and they had no
        light.

24 I looked on the mountains, and lo, they
        were quaking,
    and all the hills moved to and fro.
25 I looked, and lo, there was no one at all,
    and all the birds of the air had fled.

4.23 Return to the Void

Jeremiah used words from Genesis 1.2 to describe the effect of the Israelites' sin. It was as though the Israelites were carrying the earth back to the chaos before creation, destroying all the beauty and order God had made.

26 I looked, and lo, the fruitful land was a
        desert,
    and all its cities were laid in ruins
    before the LORD, before his fierce
        anger.
27 For thus says the LORD: The whole land shall be a desolation; yet I will not make a full end.
28 Because of this the earth shall mourn,
    and the heavens above grow black;
for I have spoken, I have purposed;
    I have not relented nor will I turn
        back.

29 At the noise of horseman and archer
    every town takes to flight;
they enter thickets; they climb among
        rocks;
    all the towns are forsaken,
    and no one lives in them.
30 And you, O desolate one,
what do you mean that you dress in
        crimson,
    that you deck yourself with ornaments
        of gold,
    that you enlarge your eyes with paint?
In vain you beautify yourself.
    Your lovers despise you;
    they seek your life.
31 For I heard a cry as of a woman in labor,
    anguish as of one bringing forth her
        first child,
the cry of daughter Zion gasping for
        breath,
    stretching out her hands,
"Woe is me! I am fainting before killers!"

The Utter Corruption of God's People

5 Run to and fro through the streets of
        Jerusalem,
    look around and take note!
Search its squares and see
    if you can find one person
who acts justly

---

[l] Or *the trails*   [m] Another reading is *for you, O my soul,*

and seeks truth—
so that I may pardon Jerusalem.[n]
2 Although they say, "As the LORD lives,"
yet they swear falsely.

5.1 Search for an Honest Person

In Genesis 18.22–33, Abraham tried to convince God not to destroy Sodom and Gomorrah if as many as ten righteous people could be found. God agreed, but evidently the ten did not exist. Here, God offers to forgive Jerusalem if a single honest person can be found. God's people had sunk to Sodom's level (23.14).

3 O LORD, do your eyes not look for truth?
You have struck them,
but they felt no anguish;
you have consumed them,
but they refused to take correction.
They have made their faces harder than
rock;
they have refused to turn back.

4 Then I said, "These are only the poor,
they have no sense;
for they do not know the way of
the LORD,
the law of their God.
5 Let me go to the rich[o]
and speak to them;
surely they know the way of the LORD,
the law of their God."
But they all alike had broken the yoke,
they had burst the bonds.

6 Therefore a lion from the forest shall kill
them,
a wolf from the desert shall destroy
them.
A leopard is watching against their cities;
everyone who goes out of them shall
be torn in pieces—
because their transgressions are many,
their apostasies are great.

7 How can I pardon you?
Your children have forsaken me,
and have sworn by those who are no
gods.
When I fed them to the full,
they committed adultery
and trooped to the houses of
prostitutes.
8 They were well-fed lusty stallions,
each neighing for his neighbor's wife.

9 Shall I not punish them for these things?
says the LORD;
and shall I not bring retribution
on a nation such as this?

10 Go up through her vine-rows
and destroy,
but do not make a full end;
strip away her branches,
for they are not the LORD's.
11 For the house of Israel and the house of
Judah
have been utterly faithless to me,
says the LORD.
12 They have spoken falsely of the LORD,
and have said, "He will do nothing.
No evil will come upon us,
and we shall not see sword or famine."

5.12 Don't Worry, Be Happy

Nobody likes bad news, and if you can find a way to shrug it off, you probably will. So the people of Judah treated Jeremiah's gloomy prophecies as so much hot air. To protect their comfortable lifestyles, they pictured a God who was uninvolved, either unable or unwilling to interfere.

13 The prophets are nothing but wind,
for the word is not in them.
Thus shall it be done to them!

14 Therefore thus says the LORD, the God of
hosts:
Because they[p] have spoken this word,
I am now making my words in your
mouth a fire,
and this people wood, and the fire shall
devour them.
15 I am going to bring upon you
a nation from far away, O house of
Israel,
says the LORD.
It is an enduring nation,
it is an ancient nation,
a nation whose language you do
not know,
nor can you understand what they say.
16 Their quiver is like an open tomb;
all of them are mighty warriors.
17 They shall eat up your harvest and your
food;
they shall eat up your sons and your
daughters;
they shall eat up your flocks and your
herds;

---

[n] Heb *it*   [o] Or *the great*   [p] Heb *you*

they shall eat up your vines and your
fig trees;
they shall destroy with the sword
your fortified cities in which you trust.

18 But even in those days, says the LORD, I
will not make a full end of you. 19 And when your
people say, "Why has the LORD our God done all
these things to us?" you shall say to them, "As you
have forsaken me and served foreign gods in your
land, so you shall serve strangers in a land that is
not yours."

20 Declare this in the house of Jacob,
proclaim it in Judah:
21 Hear this, O foolish and senseless people,
who have eyes, but do not see,
who have ears, but do not hear.
22 Do you not fear me? says the LORD;
Do you not tremble before me?
I placed the sand as a boundary for the
sea,
a perpetual barrier that it cannot pass;
though the waves toss, they cannot
prevail,
though they roar, they cannot pass
over it.
23 But this people has a stubborn and
rebellious heart;
they have turned aside and gone away.
24 They do not say in their hearts,
"Let us fear the LORD our God,
who gives the rain in its season,
the autumn rain and the spring rain,
and keeps for us
the weeks appointed for the harvest."
25 Your iniquities have turned these away,
and your sins have deprived you of
good.
26 For scoundrels are found among
my people;
they take over the goods of others.
Like fowlers they set a trap;[q]
they catch human beings.
27 Like a cage full of birds,
their houses are full of treachery;
therefore they have become great and
rich,
28 they have grown fat and sleek.
They know no limits in deeds of
wickedness;
they do not judge with justice
the cause of the orphan, to make
it prosper,
and they do not defend the rights of
the needy.
29 Shall I not punish them for these things?
says the LORD,
and shall I not bring retribution
on a nation such as this?

30 An appalling and horrible thing
has happened in the land:
31 the prophets prophesy falsely,
and the priests rule as the prophets
direct;[r]
my people love to have it so,
but what will you do when the end
comes?

The Imminence and Horror of the Invasion

6 Flee for safety, O children of Benjamin,
from the midst of Jerusalem!
Blow the trumpet in Tekoa,
and raise a signal on Beth-haccherem;
for evil looms out of the north,
and great destruction.
2 I have likened daughter Zion
to the loveliest pasture.[s]
3 Shepherds with their flocks shall come
against her.
They shall pitch their tents around her;
they shall pasture, all in their places.
4 "Prepare war against her;
up, and let us attack at noon!"
"Woe to us, for the day declines,
the shadows of evening lengthen!"
5 "Up, and let us attack by night,
and destroy her palaces!"
6 For thus says the LORD of hosts:
Cut down her trees;
cast up a siege ramp against Jerusalem.
This is the city that must be punished;[t]
there is nothing but oppression within
her.
7 As a well keeps its water fresh,
so she keeps fresh her wickedness;
violence and destruction are heard within
her;
sickness and wounds are ever before
me.
8 Take warning, O Jerusalem,
or I shall turn from you in disgust,
and make you a desolation,
an uninhabited land.

9 Thus says the LORD of hosts:
Glean[u] thoroughly as a vine
the remnant of Israel;
like a grape-gatherer, pass your hand
again
over its branches.

10 To whom shall I speak and give warning,
that they may hear?

[q] Meaning of Heb uncertain [r] Or *rule by their own authority* [s] Or *I will destroy daughter Zion, the loveliest pasture*
[t] Or *the city of license* [u] Cn: Heb *They shall glean*

See, their ears are closed,[v]
    they cannot listen.
The word of the LORD is to them an
        object of scorn;
    they take no pleasure in it.
11 But I am full of the wrath of the LORD;
    I am weary of holding it in.

Pour it out on the children in the street,
    and on the gatherings of young men as
        well;
both husband and wife shall be taken,
    the old folk and the very aged.
12 Their houses shall be turned over to
        others,
    their fields and wives together;
for I will stretch out my hand
    against the inhabitants of the land,
                  says the LORD.

13 For from the least to the greatest of them,
    everyone is greedy for unjust gain;
and from prophet to priest,
    everyone deals falsely.
14 They have treated the wound of my
        people carelessly,
    saying, "Peace, peace,"
    when there is no peace.

6.14 Greedy Doctors

A good doctor sometimes has to convey bad tidings, delivering a diagnosis of cancer, for example. But in Judah the spiritual "doctors" (prophets and priests) only gave out good news. They covered up serious wounds with a Band-Aid.

15 They acted shamefully, they committed
        abomination;
    yet they were not ashamed,
    they did not know how to blush.
Therefore they shall fall among those who
        fall;
    at the time that I punish them, they
        shall be overthrown,
                  says the LORD.
16 Thus says the LORD:
Stand at the crossroads, and look,
    and ask for the ancient paths,
where the good way lies; and walk in it,
    and find rest for your souls.
But they said, "We will not walk in it."
17 Also I raised up sentinels for you:
    "Give heed to the sound of the
        trumpet!"
But they said, "We will not give heed."

18 Therefore hear, O nations,
    and know, O congregation, what will
        happen to them.
19 Hear, O earth; I am going to bring
        disaster on this people,
    the fruit of their schemes,
because they have not given heed to my
        words;
    and as for my teaching, they have
        rejected it.
20 Of what use to me is frankincense that
        comes from Sheba,
    or sweet cane from a distant land?
Your burnt offerings are not acceptable,
    nor are your sacrifices pleasing to me.
21 Therefore thus says the LORD:
See, I am laying before this people
    stumbling blocks against which they
        shall stumble;
parents and children together,
    neighbor and friend shall perish.

22 Thus says the LORD:
See, a people is coming from the land of
        the north,
    a great nation is stirring from the
        farthest parts of the earth.
23 They grasp the bow and the javelin,
    they are cruel and have no mercy,
    their sound is like the roaring sea;
they ride on horses,
    equipped like a warrior for battle,
    against you, O daughter Zion!

24 "We have heard news of them,
    our hands fall helpless;
anguish has taken hold of us,
    pain as of a woman in labor.
25 Do not go out into the field,
    or walk on the road;
for the enemy has a sword,
    terror is on every side."

26 O my poor people, put on sackcloth,
    and roll in ashes;
make mourning as for an only child,
    most bitter lamentation:
for suddenly the destroyer
    will come upon us.

27 I have made you a tester and a refiner[w]
    among my people
    so that you may know and test their
        ways.
28 They are all stubbornly rebellious,
    going about with slanders;
they are bronze and iron,
    all of them act corruptly.
29 The bellows blow fiercely,

---

[v] Heb *are uncircumcised*   [w] Or *a fortress*

the lead is consumed by the fire;
in vain the refining goes on,
for the wicked are not removed.
30 They are called "rejected silver,"
for the LORD has rejected them.

Jeremiah Proclaims God's Judgment on the Nation

7 The word that came to Jeremiah from the LORD: 2Stand in the gate of the LORD's house, and proclaim there this word, and say, Hear the word of the LORD, all you people of Judah, you that enter these gates to worship the LORD. 3Thus says the LORD of hosts, the God of Israel: Amend your ways and your doings, and let me dwell with you[x] in this place. 4Do not trust in these deceptive words: "This is[y] the temple of the LORD, the temple of the LORD, the temple of the LORD."

5 For if you truly amend your ways and your doings, if you truly act justly one with another, 6if you do not oppress the alien, the orphan, and the widow, or shed innocent blood in this place, and if you do not go after other gods to your own hurt, 7then I will dwell with you in this place, in the land that I gave of old to your ancestors forever and ever.

8 Here you are, trusting in deceptive words to no avail. 9Will you steal, murder, commit adultery, swear falsely, make offerings to Baal, and go after other gods that you have not known, 10and then come and stand before me in this house, which is called by my name, and say, "We are safe!"—only to go on doing all these abominations? 11Has this house, which is called by my name, become a den of robbers in your sight? You know, I too am watching, says the LORD.

7.11 A Den of Robbers

Israelites of Jeremiah's time felt they were safe from invasion as long as they had the temple. After all, they thought, God would not let his home be destroyed (verse 4). But the Lord, through Jeremiah, said that the temple had become "a den of robbers" and would be demolished. In Jeremiah's lifetime this prediction came true. Jesus quoted a reference to a den of robbers when driving out money changers from the rebuilt temple (Mark 11.17).

12Go now to my place that was in Shiloh, where I made my name dwell at first, and see what I did to it for the wickedness of my people Israel. 13And now, because you have done all these things, says the LORD, and when I spoke to you persistently, you did not listen, and when I called you, you did not answer, 14therefore I will do to the house that

is called by my name, in which you trust, and to the place that I gave to you and to your ancestors, just what I did to Shiloh. 15And I will cast you out of my sight, just as I cast out all your kinsfolk, all the offspring of Ephraim.

The People's Disobedience

16 As for you, do not pray for this people, do not raise a cry or prayer on their behalf, and do not intercede with me, for I will not hear you. 17Do you not see what they are doing in the towns of Judah and in the streets of Jerusalem? 18The children gather wood, the fathers kindle fire, and the women knead dough, to make cakes for the queen of heaven; and they pour out drink offerings to other gods, to provoke me to anger. 19Is it I whom they provoke? says the LORD. Is it not themselves, to their own hurt? 20Therefore thus says the Lord GOD: My anger and my wrath shall be poured out on this place, on human beings and animals, on the trees of the field and the fruit of the ground; it will burn and not be quenched.

21 Thus says the LORD of hosts, the God of Israel: Add your burnt offerings to your sacrifices, and eat the flesh. 22For in the day that I brought your ancestors out of the land of Egypt, I did not speak to them or command them concerning burnt offerings and sacrifices. 23But this command I gave them, "Obey my voice, and I will be your God, and you shall be my people; and walk only in the way that I command you, so that it may be well with you." 24Yet they did not obey or incline their ear, but, in the stubbornness of their evil will, they walked in their own counsels, and looked backward rather than forward. 25From the day that your ancestors came out of the land of Egypt until this day, I have persistently sent all my servants the prophets to them, day after day; 26yet they did not listen to me, or pay attention, but they stiffened their necks. They did worse than their ancestors did.

27 So you shall speak all these words to them, but they will not listen to you. You shall call to them, but they will not answer you. 28You shall say to them: This is the nation that did not obey the voice of the LORD their God, and did not accept discipline; truth has perished; it is cut off from their lips.

29 Cut off your hair and throw it away;
raise a lamentation on the bare
heights,[z]
for the LORD has rejected and forsaken
the generation that provoked his wrath.

30 For the people of Judah have done evil in my sight, says the LORD; they have set their abominations in the house that is called by my name, defiling it. 31And they go on building the high place[a] of Topheth, which is in the valley of the son of Hinnom, to burn their sons and their

---

x Or *and I will let you dwell*   y Heb *They are*   z Or *the trails*   a Gk Tg: Heb *high places*

daughters in the fire—which I did not command, nor did it come into my mind. [32]Therefore, the days are surely coming, says the LORD, when it will no more be called Topheth, or the valley of the son of Hinnom, but the valley of Slaughter: for they will bury in Topheth until there is no more room. [33]The corpses of this people will be food for the birds of the air, and for the animals of the earth; and no one will frighten them away. [34]And I will bring to an end the sound of mirth and gladness, the voice of the bride and bridegroom in the cities of Judah and in the streets of Jerusalem; for the land shall become a waste.

8 At that time, says the LORD, the bones of the kings of Judah, the bones of its officials, the bones of the priests, the bones of the prophets, and the bones of the inhabitants of Jerusalem shall be brought out of their tombs; [2]and they shall be spread before the sun and the moon and all the host of heaven, which they have loved and served, which they have followed, and which they have inquired of and worshiped; and they shall not be gathered or buried; they shall be like dung on the surface of the ground. [3]Death shall be preferred to life by all the remnant that remains of this evil family in all the places where I have driven them, says the LORD of hosts.

The Blind Perversity of the Whole Nation

[4] You shall say to them, Thus says the
  LORD:
When people fall, do they not get up
  again?
  If they go astray, do they not turn
  back?
[5] Why then has this people[b] turned away
  in perpetual backsliding?
They have held fast to deceit,
  they have refused to return.
[6] I have given heed and listened,
  but they do not speak honestly;
no one repents of wickedness,
  saying, "What have I done!"
All of them turn to their own course,
  like a horse plunging headlong into
  battle.
[7] Even the stork in the heavens
  knows its times;
and the turtledove, swallow, and crane[c]
  observe the time of their coming;
but my people do not know
  the ordinance of the LORD.

[8] How can you say, "We are wise,
  and the law of the LORD is with us,"
when, in fact, the false pen of the scribes
  has made it into a lie?
[9] The wise shall be put to shame,

they shall be dismayed and taken;
since they have rejected the word of the
  LORD,
  what wisdom is in them?
[10] Therefore I will give their wives to others
  and their fields to conquerors,
because from the least to the greatest
  everyone is greedy for unjust gain;
from prophet to priest
  everyone deals falsely.
[11] They have treated the wound of my
  people carelessly,
  saying, "Peace, peace,"
  when there is no peace.
[12] They acted shamefully, they committed
  abomination;
  yet they were not at all ashamed,
  they did not know how to blush.
Therefore they shall fall among those who
  fall;
  at the time when I punish them, they
  shall be overthrown,
                    says the LORD.
[13] When I wanted to gather them, says the
  LORD,
  there are[d] no grapes on the vine,
  nor figs on the fig tree;
  even the leaves are withered,
  and what I gave them has passed away
  from them.[c]

[14] Why do we sit still?
Gather together, let us go into the
  fortified cities
  and perish there;
for the LORD our God has doomed us to
  perish,
  and has given us poisoned water to
  drink,
  because we have sinned against the
  LORD.
[15] We look for peace, but find no good,
  for a time of healing, but there is terror
  instead.

[16] The snorting of their horses is heard from
  Dan;
  at the sound of the neighing of their
  stallions
  the whole land quakes.
They come and devour the land and all
  that fills it,
  the city and those who live in it.
[17] See, I am letting snakes loose among you,
  adders that cannot be charmed,
  and they shall bite you,
                    says the LORD.

---

[b] One Ms Gk: MT this people, Jerusalem,   [c] Meaning of Heb uncertain   [d] Or I will make an end of them, says the
LORD. There are

The Prophet Mourns for the People

18 My joy is gone, grief is upon me,
    my heart is sick.
19 Hark, the cry of my poor people
    from far and wide in the land:
  "Is the LORD not in Zion?
    Is her King not in her?"
  ("Why have they provoked me to anger
        with their images,
    with their foreign idols?")
20 "The harvest is past, the summer
        is ended,
    and we are not saved."
21 For the hurt of my poor people I am
        hurt,
    I mourn, and dismay has taken hold of
        me.

22 Is there no balm in Gilead?
    Is there no physician there?
  Why then has the health of my poor
        people
    not been restored?

9 *e* O that my head were a spring of water,
    and my eyes a fountain of tears,
  so that I might weep day and night
    for the slain of my poor people!

9.1 A Fountain of Tears

Jeremiah never stood aside like a stern moralist, enjoying others' well-deserved sufferings. He felt the bitterness of the judgment he announced. "For the hurt of my poor people I am hurt, I mourn, and dismay has taken hold of me" (8.21). In the end, Jeremiah swallowed the bitter medicine of exile like the others.

Jeremiah reminds us of another "man of suffering." Like Jesus, Jeremiah wept over Jerusalem. Like Jesus, he was rejected by his own hometown (11.18–23). Jeremiah even compared himself to a lamb led to the slaughter (11.19), language that would later be applied to Jesus' sacrifice for our sins.

2 *f* O that I had in the desert
    a traveler's lodging place,
  that I might leave my people
    and go away from them!
  For they are all adulterers,
    a band of traitors.
3 They bend their tongues like bows;
    they have grown strong in the land for
        falsehood, and not for truth;

for they proceed from evil to evil,
    and they do not know me, says the
        LORD.

4 Beware of your neighbors,
    and put no trust in any of your kin; *g*
  for all your kin *h* are supplanters,
    and every neighbor goes around like a
        slanderer.
5 They all deceive their neighbors,
    and no one speaks the truth;
  they have taught their tongues to speak
        lies;
    they commit iniquity and are too
        weary to repent. *i*
6 Oppression upon oppression, deceit *j*
        upon deceit!
    They refuse to know me, says
        the LORD.

7 Therefore thus says the LORD of hosts:
  I will now refine and test them,
    for what else can I do with my sinful
        people? *k*
8 Their tongue is a deadly arrow;
    it speaks deceit through the mouth.
  They all speak friendly words to their
        neighbors,
    but inwardly are planning to lay an
        ambush.
9 Shall I not punish them for these things?
        says the LORD;
    and shall I not bring retribution
  on a nation such as this?

10 Take up *l* weeping and wailing for the
        mountains,
    and a lamentation for the pastures of
        the wilderness,
  because they are laid waste so that no one
        passes through,
    and the lowing of cattle is not heard;
  both the birds of the air and the animals
        have fled and are gone.
11 I will make Jerusalem a heap of ruins,
    a lair of jackals;
  and I will make the towns of Judah a
        desolation,
    without inhabitant.

12 Who is wise enough to understand this? To whom has the mouth of the LORD spoken, so that they may declare it? Why is the land ruined and laid waste like a wilderness, so that no one passes through? 13 And the LORD says: Because they have forsaken my law that I set before them,

e Ch 8.23 in Heb   *f* Ch 9.1 in Heb   *g* Heb *in a brother*   *h* Heb *for every brother*   *i* Cn Compare Gk: Heb *they weary themselves with iniquity.* 6 *Your dwelling*   *j* Cn: Heb *Your dwelling in the midst of deceit*   *k* Or *my poor people*   *l* Gk Syr: Heb *I will take up*

and have not obeyed my voice, or walked in accordance with it, [14]but have stubbornly followed their own hearts and have gone after the Baals, as their ancestors taught them. [15]Therefore thus says the LORD of hosts, the God of Israel: I am feeding this people with wormwood, and giving them poisonous water to drink. [16]I will scatter them among nations that neither they nor their ancestors have known; and I will send the sword after them, until I have consumed them.

The People Mourn in Judgment

17 Thus says the LORD of hosts:
Consider, and call for the mourning
women to come;
send for the skilled women to come;
18 let them quickly raise a dirge over us,
so that our eyes may run down with
tears,
and our eyelids flow with water.
19 For a sound of wailing is heard from
Zion:
"How we are ruined!
We are utterly shamed,
because we have left the land,
because they have cast down our
dwellings."

20 Hear, O women, the word of the LORD,
and let your ears receive the word of
his mouth;
teach to your daughters a dirge,
and each to her neighbor a lament.
21 "Death has come up into our windows,
it has entered our palaces,
to cut off the children from the streets
and the young men from the squares."
22 Speak! Thus says the LORD:
"Human corpses shall fall
like dung upon the open field,
like sheaves behind the reaper,
and no one shall gather them."

23 Thus says the LORD: Do not let the wise boast in their wisdom, do not let the mighty boast in their might, do not let the wealthy boast in their wealth; [24]but let those who boast boast in this, that they understand and know me, that I am the LORD; I act with steadfast love, justice, and righteousness in the earth, for in these things I delight, says the LORD.

25 The days are surely coming, says the LORD, when I will attend to all those who are circumcised only in the foreskin: [26]Egypt, Judah, Edom, the Ammonites, Moab, and all those with shaven temples who live in the desert. For all these nations are uncircumcised, and all the house of Israel is uncircumcised in heart.

Idolatry Has Brought Ruin on Israel

10 Hear the word that the LORD speaks to you,
O house of Israel. [2]Thus says the LORD:
Do not learn the way of the nations,
or be dismayed at the signs of the
heavens;
for the nations are dismayed at them.
3 For the customs of the peoples are false:
a tree from the forest is cut down,
and worked with an ax by the hands of
an artisan;

9.24 Bragging on God

In dire circumstances like those Jeremiah predicts, what has value? Wisdom? Strength? Money? In the midst of a devastating invasion, these will get you nothing. Only one thing will count: a living, confident relationship with God. If you have that, it's worth boasting about. Paul quoted this verse in writing to the Corinthians (1 Corinthians 1.31); he said God seems to prefer to work through weak and poor people, those who have little else to brag about.

4 people deck it with silver and gold;
they fasten it with hammer and nails
so that it cannot move.
5 Their idols[m] are like scarecrows in a
cucumber field,
and they cannot speak;
they have to be carried,
for they cannot walk.
Do not be afraid of them,
for they cannot do evil,
nor is it in them to do good.

6 There is none like you, O LORD;
you are great, and your name is great
in might.
7 Who would not fear you, O King of the
nations?
For that is your due;
among all the wise ones of the nations
and in all their kingdoms
there is no one like you.
8 They are both stupid and foolish;
the instruction given by idols
is no better than wood![n]
9 Beaten silver is brought from Tarshish,
and gold from Uphaz.
They are the work of the artisan and of
the hands of the goldsmith;
their clothing is blue and purple;
they are all the product of skilled
workers.
10 But the LORD is the true God;

[m] Heb *They*   [n] Meaning of Heb uncertain

he is the living God and the everlasting
King.
At his wrath the earth quakes,
and the nations cannot endure his
indignation.

11 Thus shall you say to them: The gods who
did not make the heavens and the earth shall
perish from the earth and from under the heavens.*o*

12 It is he who made the earth by his power,
who established the world by
his wisdom,
and by his understanding stretched out
the heavens.
13 When he utters his voice, there is a
tumult of waters in the heavens,
and he makes the mist rise from the
ends of the earth.
He makes lightnings for the rain,
and he brings out the wind from his
storehouses.
14 Everyone is stupid and without
knowledge;
goldsmiths are all put to shame by
their idols;
for their images are false,
and there is no breath in them.
15 They are worthless, a work of delusion;
at the time of their punishment they
shall perish.
16 Not like these is the LORD,*p* the portion
of Jacob,
for he is the one who formed
all things,
and Israel is the tribe of his inheritance;
the LORD of hosts is his name.

The Coming Exile

17 Gather up your bundle from the ground,
O you who live under siege!
18 For thus says the LORD:
I am going to sling out the inhabitants of
the land
at this time,
and I will bring distress on them,
so that they shall feel it.

19 Woe is me because of my hurt!
My wound is severe.
But I said, "Truly this is my punishment,
and I must bear it."
20 My tent is destroyed,
and all my cords are broken;
my children have gone from me,
and they are no more;
there is no one to spread my tent again,
and to set up my curtains.

21 For the shepherds are stupid,
and do not inquire of the LORD;
therefore they have not prospered,
and all their flock is scattered.

22 Hear, a noise! Listen, it is coming—
a great commotion from the land of
the north
to make the cities of Judah a desolation,
a lair of jackals.

23 I know, O LORD, that the way of human
beings is not in their control,
that mortals as they walk cannot direct
their steps.
24 Correct me, O LORD, but in just measure;
not in your anger, or you will bring
me to nothing.

25 Pour out your wrath on the nations that
do not know you,
and on the peoples that do not call on
your name;
for they have devoured Jacob;
they have devoured him and consumed
him,
and have laid waste his habitation.

Israel and Judah Have Broken the Covenant

11 The word that came to Jeremiah from the
LORD: 2Hear the words of this covenant, and
speak to the people of Judah and the inhabitants
of Jerusalem. 3You shall say to them, Thus says
the LORD, the God of Israel: Cursed be anyone
who does not heed the words of this covenant,
4which I commanded your ancestors when I
brought them out of the land of Egypt, from the
iron-smelter, saying, Listen to my voice, and do
all that I command you. So shall you be my people, and I will be your God, 5that I may perform
the oath that I swore to your ancestors, to give
them a land flowing with milk and honey, as at
this day. Then I answered, "So be it, LORD."

6 And the LORD said to me: Proclaim all these
words in the cities of Judah, and in the streets of
Jerusalem: Hear the words of this covenant and
do them. 7For I solemnly warned your ancestors
when I brought them up out of the land of Egypt,
warning them persistently, even to this day, saying, Obey my voice. 8Yet they did not obey or
incline their ear, but everyone walked in the stubbornness of an evil will. So I brought upon them
all the words of this covenant, which I commanded them to do, but they did not.

9 And the LORD said to me: Conspiracy exists
among the people of Judah and the inhabitants of
Jerusalem. 10They have turned back to the iniquities of their ancestors of old, who refused to heed

---

o This verse is in Aramaic   *p* Heb lacks *the LORD*

my words; they have gone after other gods to serve them; the house of Israel and the house of Judah have broken the covenant that I made with their ancestors. [11]Therefore, thus says the LORD,

11.8 Day of Reckoning

If you sign a note to buy a house, you have to follow through. Miss too many payments, and the bank will evict you. So it was with Israel. Hundreds of years before Jeremiah's time, God had made a "covenant" with them—a treaty binding him to be their God, in exchange for their obedience (see "The Covenant," page 98). This was formally ratified, along with a series of "blessings" and "curses"—good consequences for obedience, bad consequences for disobedience—as recorded in Deuteronomy 28. Now, God announces, because the covenant has been broken, severe punishment must follow.

assuredly I am going to bring disaster upon them that they cannot escape; though they cry out to me, I will not listen to them. [12]Then the cities of Judah and the inhabitants of Jerusalem will go and cry out to the gods to whom they make offerings, but they will never save them in the time of their trouble. [13]For your gods have become as many as your towns, O Judah; and as many as the streets of Jerusalem are the altars to shame you have set up, altars to make offerings to Baal.

14 As for you, do not pray for this people, or lift up a cry or prayer on their behalf, for I will not listen when they call to me in the time of their trouble. [15]What right has my beloved in my house, when she has done vile deeds? Can vows*q* and sacrificial flesh avert your doom? Can you then exult? [16]The LORD once called you, "A green olive tree, fair with goodly fruit"; but with the roar of a great tempest he will set fire to it, and its branches will be consumed. [17]The LORD of hosts, who planted you, has pronounced evil against you, because of the evil that the house of Israel and the house of Judah have done, provoking me to anger by making offerings to Baal.

Jeremiah's Life Threatened

18 It was the LORD who made it known to
     me, and I knew;
        then you showed me their evil deeds.
19 But I was like a gentle lamb
        led to the slaughter.
     And I did not know it was against me
        that they devised schemes, saying,
     "Let us destroy the tree with its fruit,
        let us cut him off from the land of the
           living,

so that his name will no longer be
     remembered!"
20 But you, O LORD of hosts, who judge
     righteously,
        who try the heart and the mind,
     let me see your retribution upon them,
        for to you I have committed my cause.
21 Therefore thus says the LORD concerning the people of Anathoth, who seek your life, and say, "You shall not prophesy in the name of the LORD, or you will die by our hand"— [22]therefore thus says the LORD of hosts: I am going to punish them; the young men shall die by the sword; their sons and their daughters shall die by famine; [23]and not even a remnant shall be left of them. For I will bring disaster upon the people of Anathoth, the year of their punishment.

11.23 Hometown Enemies

Jeremiah's life was endangered several times because of his message. On this occasion, men from his hometown were plotting against him. Though Jeremiah was completely unprepared for their attack, God protected him. Other prophets, however, had been killed (2.30).

Jeremiah Complains to God

12 You will be in the right, O LORD,
        when I lay charges against you;
        but let me put my case to you.
     Why does the way of the guilty prosper?
        Why do all who are treacherous thrive?
2   You plant them, and they take root;
        they grow and bring forth fruit;
     you are near in their mouths
        yet far from their hearts.
3   But you, O LORD, know me;
     You see me and test me—my heart is
           with you.
     Pull them out like sheep for the slaughter,
        and set them apart for the day
           of slaughter.
4   How long will the land mourn,
        and the grass of every field wither?
     For the wickedness of those who live in it
        the animals and the birds are swept
           away,
     and because people said, "He is blind
        to our ways."*r*

God Replies to Jeremiah

5   If you have raced with foot-runners and
        they have wearied you,
     how will you compete with horses?
     And if in a safe land you fall down,

q Gk: Heb *Can many*   *r* Gk: Heb *to our future*

how will you fare in the thickets of the
Jordan?
6 For even your kinsfolk and your own
family,
even they have dealt treacherously with
you;
they are in full cry after you;
do not believe them,
though they speak friendly words to
you.

7 I have forsaken my house,
I have abandoned my heritage;
I have given the beloved of my heart
into the hands of her enemies.
8 My heritage has become to me
like a lion in the forest;
she has lifted up her voice against me—
therefore I hate her.
9 Is the hyena greedy[s] for my heritage at
my command?
Are the birds of prey all around her?
Go, assemble all the wild animals;
bring them to devour her.
10 Many shepherds have destroyed
my vineyard,
they have trampled down my portion,
they have made my pleasant portion
a desolate wilderness.
11 They have made it a desolation;
desolate, it mourns to me.
The whole land is made desolate,
but no one lays it to heart.
12 Upon all the bare heights[t] in the desert
spoilers have come;
for the sword of the LORD devours
from one end of the land to the other;
no one shall be safe.
13 They have sown wheat and have reaped
thorns,
they have tired themselves out but
profit nothing.
They shall be ashamed of their[u] harvests
because of the fierce anger of the LORD.

14 Thus says the LORD concerning all my evil
neighbors who touch the heritage that I have giv-
en my people Israel to inherit: I am about to
pluck them up from their land, and I will pluck
up the house of Judah from among them. 15And
after I have plucked them up, I will again have
compassion on them, and I will bring them again
to their heritage and to their land, everyone of
them. 16And then, if they will diligently learn the
ways of my people, to swear by my name, "As the
LORD lives," as they taught my people to swear by
Baal, then they shall be built up in the midst of my
people. 17But if any nation will not listen, then I

will completely uproot it and destroy it, says the
LORD.

The Linen Loincloth

13 Thus said the LORD to me, "Go and buy
yourself a linen loincloth, and put it on

> ### 12.16 Hope for the Gentiles
> *Through most of the Old Testament, Israel's
> Gentile neighbors seem to have no part in
> God's plan. Here, though, God clearly promises
> them his salvation.*

your loins, but do not dip it in water." 2So I
bought a loincloth according to the word of the
LORD, and put it on my loins. 3And the word
of the LORD came to me a second time, saying,
4"Take the loincloth that you bought and are
wearing, and go now to the Euphrates,[v] and hide
it there in a cleft of the rock." 5So I went, and hid
it by the Euphrates,[w] as the LORD commanded
me. 6And after many days the LORD said to me,
"Go now to the Euphrates,[v] and take from there
the loincloth that I commanded you to hide
there." 7Then I went to the Euphrates,[v] and dug,
and I took the loincloth from the place where I
had hidden it. But now the loincloth was ruined;
it was good for nothing.

8 Then the word of the LORD came to me:
9Thus says the LORD: Just so I will ruin the pride
of Judah and the great pride of Jerusalem. 10This
evil people, who refuse to hear my words, who
stubbornly follow their own will and have gone
after other gods to serve them and worship them,
shall be like this loincloth, which is good for nothing. 11For as the loincloth clings to one's loins, so
I made the whole house of Israel and the whole
house of Judah cling to me, says the LORD, in
order that they might be for me a people, a name,
a praise, and a glory. But they would not listen.

Symbol of the Wine-Jars

12 You shall speak to them this word: Thus
says the LORD, the God of Israel: Every wine-jar
should be filled with wine. And they will say to
you, "Do you think we do not know that every
wine-jar should be filled with wine?" 13Then you
shall say to them: Thus says the LORD: I am about
to fill all the inhabitants of this land—the kings
who sit on David's throne, the priests, the prophets, and all the inhabitants of Jerusalem—with
drunkenness. 14And I will dash them one against
another, parents and children together, says the
LORD. I will not pity or spare or have compassion
when I destroy them.

---

s Cn: Heb *Is the hyena, the bird of prey*   t Or *the trails*   u Heb *your*   v Or *to Parah*; Heb *perath*
w Or *by Parah*; Heb *perath*

Exile Threatened

15 Hear and give ear; do not be haughty,
　　for the LORD has spoken.
16 Give glory to the LORD your God
　　before he brings darkness,
and before your feet stumble
　　on the mountains at twilight;
while you look for light,
　　he turns it into gloom
　　and makes it deep darkness.
17 But if you will not listen,
　　my soul will weep in secret for your
　　　　pride;
my eyes will weep bitterly and run down
　　　　with tears,
　　because the LORD's flock has been
　　　　taken captive.

18 Say to the king and the queen mother:
　　"Take a lowly seat,
for your beautiful crown
　　has come down from your head."ˣ
19 The towns of the Negeb are shut up
　　with no one to open them;
all Judah is taken into exile,
　　wholly taken into exile.

20 Lift up your eyes and see
　　those who come from the north.
Where is the flock that was given you,
　　your beautiful flock?
21 What will you say when they set as head
　　　　over you
　　those whom you have trained
　　to be your allies?
Will not pangs take hold of you,
　　like those of a woman in labor?
22 And if you say in your heart,
　　"Why have these things come upon
　　　　me?"
it is for the greatness of your iniquity
　　that your skirts are lifted up,
　　and you are violated.
23 Can Ethiopiansʸ change their skin
　　or leopards their spots?
Then also you can do good
　　who are accustomed to do evil.
24 I will scatter youᶻ like chaff
　　driven by the wind from the desert.
25 This is your lot,
　　the portion I have measured out to
　　　　you, says the LORD,
because you have forgotten me
　　and trusted in lies.
26 I myself will lift up your skirts over your
　　　　face,
　　and your shame will be seen.
27 I have seen your abominations,

your adulteries and neighings, your
　　　　shameless prostitutions
on the hills of the countryside.
Woe to you, O Jerusalem!
　　How long will it be
　　before you are made clean?

The Great Drought

14 The word of the LORD that came to Jeremi-
　　ah concerning the drought:
2 Judah mourns
　　and her gates languish;
they lie in gloom on the ground,
　　and the cry of Jerusalem goes up.
3 Her nobles send their servants for water;
　　they come to the cisterns,
they find no water,
　　they return with their vessels empty.
They are ashamed and dismayed
　　and cover their heads,
4 because the ground is cracked.
　　Because there has been no rain on the
　　　　land
the farmers are dismayed;
　　they cover their heads.
5 Even the doe in the field forsakes her
　　　　newborn fawn
because there is no grass.
6 The wild asses stand on the bare
　　　　heights,ᵃ
　　they pant for air like jackals;
their eyes fail
　　because there is no herbage.

7 Although our iniquities testify against us,
　　act, O LORD, for your name's sake;
our apostasies indeed are many,
　　and we have sinned against you.
8 O hope of Israel,
　　its savior in time of trouble,
why should you be like a stranger in the
　　　　land,
　　like a traveler turning aside for the
　　　　night?
9 Why should you be like someone
　　　　confused,
　　like a mighty warrior who cannot give
　　　　help?
Yet you, O LORD, are in the midst of us,
　　and we are called by your name;
　　do not forsake us!

10 Thus says the LORD concerning
　　　　this people:
Truly they have loved to wander,
　　they have not restrained their feet;
therefore the LORD does not accept them,
　　now he will remember their iniquity
　　and punish their sins.

ˣ Gk Syr Vg: Meaning of Heb uncertain　　ʸ Or Nubians; Heb Cushites　　ᶻ Heb them　　ᵃ Or the trails

11 The Lord said to me: Do not pray for the welfare of this people. [12]Although they fast, I do not hear their cry, and although they offer burnt offering and grain offering, I do not accept them; but by the sword, by famine, and by pestilence I consume them.

14.11 God's Patience Exhausted

God gave Jeremiah these dreaded instructions, repeated nowhere else in the Bible: "Do not pray for this people . . . for I will not listen" (11.14). He repeated that message twice (7.16; 14.11). He told Jeremiah, "Though Moses and Samuel stood before me, yet my heart would not turn toward this people. Send them out of my sight!" (15.1).

Denunciation of Lying Prophets

13 Then I said: "Ah, Lord God! Here are the prophets saying to them, 'You shall not see the sword, nor shall you have famine, but I will give you true peace in this place.'" [14]And the Lord said to me: The prophets are prophesying lies in my name; I did not send them, nor did I command them or speak to them. They are prophesying to you a lying vision, worthless divination, and the deceit of their own minds. [15]Therefore thus says the Lord concerning the prophets who prophesy in my name though I did not send them, and who say, "Sword and famine shall not come on this land": By sword and famine those prophets shall be consumed. [16]And the people to whom they prophesy shall be thrown out into the streets of Jerusalem, victims of famine and sword. There shall be no one to bury them—themselves, their wives, their sons, and their daughters. For I will pour out their wickedness upon them.

17 You shall say to them this word:
Let my eyes run down with tears night
and day,
and let them not cease,
for the virgin daughter—my people—is
struck down with a crushing
blow,
with a very grievous wound.
18 If I go out into the field,
look—those killed by the sword!
And if I enter the city,
look—those sick with[b] famine!
For both prophet and priest ply their
trade throughout the land,
and have no knowledge.

The People Plead for Mercy

19 Have you completely rejected Judah?

Does your heart loathe Zion?
Why have you struck us down
so that there is no healing for us?
We look for peace, but find no good;
for a time of healing, but there is terror
instead.
20 We acknowledge our wickedness, O Lord,
the iniquity of our ancestors,
for we have sinned against you.
21 Do not spurn us, for your name's sake;
do not dishonor your glorious throne;
remember and do not break your
covenant with us.
22 Can any idols of the nations bring rain?
Or can the heavens give showers?
Is it not you, O Lord our God?
We set our hope on you,
for it is you who do all this.

Punishment Is Inevitable

15 Then the Lord said to me: Though Moses and Samuel stood before me, yet my heart would not turn toward this people. Send them out of my sight, and let them go! [2]And when they say to you, "Where shall we go?" you shall say to them: Thus says the Lord:
Those destined for pestilence, to
pestilence,
and those destined for the sword, to
the sword;
those destined for famine, to famine,
and those destined for captivity, to
captivity.
[3]And I will appoint over them four kinds of destroyers, says the Lord: the sword to kill, the dogs to drag away, and the birds of the air and the wild animals of the earth to devour and destroy. [4]I will make them a horror to all the kingdoms of the earth because of what King Manasseh son of Hezekiah of Judah did in Jerusalem.

5 Who will have pity on you, O Jerusalem,
or who will bemoan you?
Who will turn aside
to ask about your welfare?
6 You have rejected me, says the Lord,
you are going backward;
so I have stretched out my hand against
you and destroyed you—
I am weary of relenting.
7 I have winnowed them with a winnowing
fork
in the gates of the land;
I have bereaved them, I have destroyed
my people;
they did not turn from their ways.
8 Their widows became more numerous
than the sand of the seas;

b Heb look—the sicknesses of

I have brought against the mothers of
>   youths
>   a destroyer at noonday;
I have made anguish and terror
>   fall upon her suddenly.
9 She who bore seven has languished;
>   she has swooned away;
her sun went down while it was yet day;
>   she has been shamed and disgraced.
And the rest of them I will give to the
>   sword
>   before their enemies,
>   says the LORD.

Jeremiah Complains Again and Is Reassured

10 Woe is me, my mother, that you ever bore me, a man of strife and contention to the whole land! I have not lent, nor have I borrowed, yet all of them curse me. 11The LORD said: Surely I have intervened in your life[c] for good, surely I have imposed enemies on you in a time of trouble and in a time of distress.[d] 12Can iron and bronze break iron from the north?

13 Your wealth and your treasures I will give as plunder, without price, for all your sins, throughout all your territory. 14I will make you serve your enemies in a land that you do not know, for in my anger a fire is kindled that shall burn forever.

15 O LORD, you know;
>   remember me and visit me,
>   and bring down retribution for me on
>   my persecutors.
In your forbearance do not take me away;
>   know that on your account I suffer
>   insult.
16 Your words were found, and I ate them,
>   and your words became to me a joy
>   and the delight of my heart;
for I am called by your name,
>   O LORD, God of hosts.
17 I did not sit in the company of
>   merrymakers,
>   nor did I rejoice;
under the weight of your hand I
>   sat alone,
>   for you had filled me with indignation.
18 Why is my pain unceasing,
>   my wound incurable,
>   refusing to be healed?
Truly, you are to me like a deceitful
>   brook,
>   like waters that fail.

19 Therefore thus says the LORD:
>   If you turn back, I will take you back,
>   and you shall stand before me.

If you utter what is precious, and not
>   what is worthless,
>   you shall serve as my mouth.
It is they who will turn to you,
>   not you who will turn to them.
20 And I will make you to this people
>   a fortified wall of bronze;
they will fight against you,
>   but they shall not prevail over you,
for I am with you
>   to save you and deliver you,
>   says the LORD.
21 I will deliver you out of the hand of the
>   wicked,
>   and redeem you from the grasp of the
>   ruthless.

Jeremiah's Celibacy and Message

16 The word of the LORD came to me: 2You shall not take a wife, nor shall you have sons or daughters in this place. 3For thus says the LORD concerning the sons and daughters who are born in this place, and concerning the mothers who bear them and the fathers who beget them in this land: 4They shall die of deadly diseases. They shall not be lamented, nor shall they be buried; they shall become like dung on the surface of the ground. They shall perish by the sword and by famine, and their dead bodies shall become food for the birds of the air and for the wild animals of the earth.

5 For thus says the LORD: Do not enter the house of mourning, or go to lament, or bemoan them; for I have taken away my peace from this people, says the LORD, my steadfast love and mercy. 6Both great and small shall die in this land; they shall not be buried, and no one shall lament for them; there shall be no gashing, no shaving of the head for them. 7No one shall break bread[e] for the mourner, to offer comfort for the dead; nor shall anyone give them the cup of consolation to drink for their fathers or their mothers. 8You shall not go into the house of feasting to sit with them, to eat and drink. 9For thus says the LORD of hosts, the God of Israel: I am going to banish from this place, in your days and before your eyes, the voice of mirth and the voice of gladness, the voice of the bridegroom and the voice of the bride.

10 And when you tell this people all these words, and they say to you, "Why has the LORD pronounced all this great evil against us? What is our iniquity? What is the sin that we have committed against the LORD our God?" 11then you shall say to them: It is because your ancestors have forsaken me, says the LORD, and have gone after other gods and have served and worshiped them, and have forsaken me and have not kept my law; 12and because you have behaved worse than your ancestors, for here you are, every one

---

c Heb *intervened with you*   d Meaning of Heb uncertain   e Two Mss Gk: MT *break for them*

of you, following your stubborn evil will, refusing to listen to me. 13Therefore I will hurl you out of this land into a land that neither you nor your ancestors have known, and there you shall serve other gods day and night, for I will show you no favor.

God Will Restore Israel

14 Therefore, the days are surely coming, says the LORD, when it shall no longer be said, "As the LORD lives who brought the people of Israel up out of the land of Egypt," 15but "As the LORD lives who brought the people of Israel up out of the land of the north and out of all the lands where he had driven them." For I will bring them back to their own land that I gave to their ancestors. 16 I am now sending for many fishermen, says the LORD, and they shall catch them; and afterward I will send for many hunters, and they shall hunt them from every mountain and every hill, and out of the clefts of the rocks. 17For my eyes are on all their ways; they are not hidden from my presence, nor is their iniquity concealed from my sight. 18And*f* I will doubly repay their iniquity and their sin, because they have polluted my land with the carcasses of their detestable idols, and have filled my inheritance with their abominations.

19 O LORD, my strength and my stronghold,
     my refuge in the day of trouble,
to you shall the nations come
     from the ends of the earth and say:
Our ancestors have inherited nothing but
          lies,
     worthless things in which there is no
          profit.
20 Can mortals make for themselves gods?
     Such are no gods!

21 "Therefore I am surely going to teach them, this time I am going to teach them my power and my might, and they shall know that my name is the LORD."

Judah's Sin and Punishment

17 The sin of Judah is written with an iron pen; with a diamond point it is engraved on the tablet of their hearts, and on the horns of their altars, 2while their children remember their altars and their sacred poles,*g* beside every green tree, and on the high hills, 3on the mountains in the open country. Your wealth and all your treasures I will give for spoil as the price of your sin*h* throughout all your territory. 4By your own act you shall lose the heritage that I gave you, and I will make you serve your enemies in a land that you do not know, for in my anger a fire is kindled*i* that shall burn forever.

5 Thus says the LORD:
   Cursed are those who trust in
          mere mortals
     and make mere flesh their strength,
     whose hearts turn away from the LORD.
6 They shall be like a shrub in the desert,
     and shall not see when relief comes.
   They shall live in the parched places of
          the wilderness,
     in an uninhabited salt land.

7 Blessed are those who trust in the LORD,
     whose trust is the LORD.
8 They shall be like a tree planted by water,
     sending out its roots by the stream.
   It shall not fear when heat comes,
     and its leaves shall stay green;
   in the year of drought it is not anxious,
     and it does not cease to bear fruit.
9 The heart is devious above all else;
     it is perverse—
   who can understand it?
10 I the LORD test the mind
     and search the heart,

f Gk: Heb *And first*   *g* Heb *Asherim*   *h* Cn: Heb *spoil your high places for sin*   *i* Two Mss Theodotion: *you*
kindled

to give to all according to their ways,
according to the fruit of their doings.

11 Like the partridge hatching what it did
not lay,
so are all who amass wealth unjustly;
in mid-life it will leave them,
and at their end they will prove to be
fools.

12 O glorious throne, exalted from the
beginning,
shrine of our sanctuary!
13 O hope of Israel! O LORD!
All who forsake you shall be put to
shame;
those who turn away from you^j shall be
recorded in the underworld,^{k}
for they have forsaken the fountain of
living water, the LORD.

Jeremiah Prays for Vindication

14 Heal me, O LORD, and I shall be healed;
save me, and I shall be saved;
for you are my praise.
15 See how they say to me,
"Where is the word of the LORD?
Let it come!"
16 But I have not run away from being a
shepherd^l in your service,
nor have I desired the fatal day.
You know what came from my lips;
it was before your face.
17 Do not become a terror to me;
you are my refuge in the day
of disaster;
18 Let my persecutors be shamed,
but do not let me be shamed;
let them be dismayed,
but do not let me be dismayed;
bring on them the day of disaster;
destroy them with double destruction!

Hallow the Sabbath Day

19 Thus said the LORD to me: Go and stand in
the People's Gate, by which the kings of Judah
enter and by which they go out, and in all the
gates of Jerusalem, 20and say to them: Hear the
word of the LORD, you kings of Judah, and all
Judah, and all the inhabitants of Jerusalem, who
enter by these gates. 21Thus says the LORD: For the
sake of your lives, take care that you do not bear
a burden on the sabbath day or bring it in by the
gates of Jerusalem. 22And do not carry a burden
out of your houses on the sabbath or do any
work, but keep the sabbath day holy, as I commanded your ancestors. 23Yet they did not listen
or incline their ear; they stiffened their necks and
would not hear or receive instruction.

24 But if you listen to me, says the LORD, and
bring in no burden by the gates of this city on the
sabbath day, but keep the sabbath day holy and
do no work on it, 25then there shall enter by the
gates of this city kings^m who sit on the throne of
David, riding in chariots and on horses, they and
their officials, the people of Judah and the inhabitants of Jerusalem; and this city shall be inhabited
forever. 26And people shall come from the towns
of Judah and the places around Jerusalem, from
the land of Benjamin, from the Shephelah, from
the hill country, and from the Negeb, bringing
burnt offerings and sacrifices, grain offerings and
frankincense, and bringing thank offerings to the
house of the LORD. 27But if you do not listen to
me, to keep the sabbath day holy, and to carry in
no burden through the gates of Jerusalem on the
sabbath day, then I will kindle a fire in its gates;
it shall devour the palaces of Jerusalem and shall
not be quenched.

The Potter and the Clay

18 The word that came to Jeremiah from the
LORD: 2"Come, go down to the potter's
house, and there I will let you hear my words."
3So I went down to the potter's house, and there
he was working at his wheel. 4The vessel he was
making of clay was spoiled in the potter's hand,
and he reworked it into another vessel, as seemed
good to him.

5 Then the word of the LORD came to me:
6Can I not do with you, O house of Israel, just as
this potter has done? says the LORD. Just like the
clay in the potter's hand, so are you in my hand,

18.6 The Potter and the Clay

*God is in control—a message vividly portrayed
to Jeremiah as he watched a potter start over
on a pot that did not take the shape he wanted
it to take. Israelites had gradually come to
think that God, because he had chosen them as
his people, was obliged to protect them. But
their unnatural behavior toward him had
brought God to the point of "starting over." In
Romans 9.21, Paul returned to this metaphor to
answer people who were claiming God was
unjust.*

O house of Israel. 7At one moment I may declare
concerning a nation or a kingdom, that I will
pluck up and break down and destroy it, 8but
if that nation, concerning which I have spoken,
turns from its evil, I will change my mind about
the disaster that I intended to bring on it. 9And at
another moment I may declare concerning a nation or a kingdom that I will build and plant it,
10but if it does evil in my sight, not listening to my

^{j} Heb *me* ^{k} Or *in the earth* ^{l} Meaning of Heb uncertain ^{m} Cn: Heb *kings and officials*

voice, then I will change my mind about the good that I had intended to do to it. [11]Now, therefore, say to the people of Judah and the inhabitants of Jerusalem: Thus says the LORD: Look, I am a potter shaping evil against you and devising a plan against you. Turn now, all of you from your evil way, and amend your ways and your doings.

Israel's Stubborn Idolatry

12 But they say, "It is no use! We will follow our own plans, and each of us will act according to the stubbornness of our evil will."

13 Therefore thus says the LORD:
Ask among the nations:
Who has heard the like of this?
The virgin Israel has done
a most horrible thing.
14 Does the snow of Lebanon leave
the crags of Sirion?[n]
Do the mountain[o] waters run dry,[p]
the cold flowing streams?
15 But my people have forgotten me,
they burn offerings to a delusion;
they have stumbled[q] in their ways,
in the ancient roads,
and have gone into bypaths,
not the highway,
16 making their land a horror,
a thing to be hissed at forever.
All who pass by it are horrified
and shake their heads.
17 Like the wind from the east,
I will scatter them before the enemy.
I will show them my back, not my face,
in the day of their calamity.

A Plot against Jeremiah

18 Then they said, "Come, let us make plots against Jeremiah—for instruction shall not perish from the priest, nor counsel from the wise, nor the word from the prophet. Come, let us bring charges against him,[r] and let us not heed any of his words."

19 Give heed to me, O LORD,
and listen to what my adversaries say!
20 Is evil a recompense for good?
Yet they have dug a pit for my life.
Remember how I stood before you
to speak good for them,
to turn away your wrath from them.
21 Therefore give their children over to
famine;
hurl them out to the power of
the sword,
let their wives become childless and
widowed.

May their men meet death by
pestilence,
their youths be slain by the sword in
battle.
22 May a cry be heard from their houses,
when you bring the marauder suddenly
upon them!
For they have dug a pit to catch me,
and laid snares for my feet.
23 Yet you, O LORD, know
all their plotting to kill me.
Do not forgive their iniquity,
do not blot out their sin from your
sight.
Let them be tripped up before you;
deal with them while you are angry.

The Broken Earthenware Jug

19 Thus said the LORD: Go and buy a potter's earthenware jug. Take with you[s] some of the elders of the people and some of the senior priests, [2]and go out to the valley of the son of Hinnom at the entry of the Potsherd Gate, and proclaim there the words that I tell you. [3]You shall say: Hear the word of the LORD, O kings of Judah and inhabitants of Jerusalem. Thus says the LORD of hosts, the God of Israel: I am going to bring such disaster upon this place that the ears of everyone who hears of it will tingle. [4]Because the people have forsaken me, and have profaned this place by making offerings in it to other gods whom neither they nor their ancestors nor the kings of Judah have known, and because they have filled this place with the blood of the innocent, [5]and gone on building the high places of Baal to burn their children in the fire as burnt offerings to Baal, which I did not command or decree, nor did it enter my mind; [6]therefore the days are surely coming, says the LORD, when this place shall no more be called Topheth, or the valley of the son of Hinnom, but the valley of Slaughter. [7]And in this place I will make void the plans of Judah and Jerusalem, and will make them fall by the sword before their enemies, and by the hand of those who seek their life. I will give their dead bodies for food to the birds of the air and to the wild animals of the earth. [8]And I will make this city a horror, a thing to be hissed at; everyone who passes by it will be horrified and will hiss because of all its disasters. [9]And I will make them eat the flesh of their sons and the flesh of their daughters, and all shall eat the flesh of their neighbors in the siege, and in the distress with which their enemies and those who seek their life afflict them.

10 Then you shall break the jug in the sight of those who go with you, [11]and shall say to them: Thus says the LORD of hosts: So will I break this

---

[n] Cn: Heb of the field   [o] Cn: Heb foreign   [p] Cn: Heb Are . . . plucked up?   [q] Gk Syr Vg: Heb they made them
stumble   [r] Heb strike him with the tongue   [s] Syr Tg Compare Gk: Heb lacks take with you

people and this city, as one breaks a potter's vessel, so that it can never be mended. In Topheth they shall bury until there is no more room to bury. ¹²Thus will I do to this place, says the LORD, and to its inhabitants, making this city like Topheth. ¹³And the houses of Jerusalem and the houses of the kings of Judah shall be defiled like the place of Topheth—all the houses upon whose roofs offerings have been made to the whole host of heaven, and libations have been poured out to other gods.

14 When Jeremiah came from Topheth, where the LORD had sent him to prophesy, he stood in the court of the LORD's house and said to

Idolatry
It still flourishes, even without statues

> The people have forsaken me, and have profaned this place. 19.4

SUPPOSE YOU FOUND A FRIEND carving a small statue out of a piece of wood. "What are you going to do with that?" you ask. "I'm going to worship it," he says. "I've got a nice spot in my bedroom where I can kneel down and ask it for things."

Or imagine people on a suburban street pooling their wedding rings and other jewelry to make a statue they can put in the park. They plan to kill animals and leave the meat out in front of the statue.

To moderns, idolatry is as weird as cannibalism; we're not tempted to try it. But since a great part of the Old Testament is concerned with idolatry, we need to get some idea of what people saw in it—and why God condemned it.

Mixing Religions

In Jeremiah's day, practically everybody practiced idolatry. Israelites had a hard time seeing that a few statues interfered with their relationship with the one true God. They worshiped the God of Abraham, but mixed in the gods of countries surrounding them. They had idols right in the Jerusalem temple (7.30). They could go to worship God right after burning incense to Baal (7.9–10).

They had built shrines on top of many hills—the "high places"—and under the tallest trees so that worship could be carried out conveniently, without a trip to Jerusalem. They ignored the prophets' warnings that God hated this "mixed" religion.

Judah's neighbors believed in many gods, each having its sphere of influence. The Jews themselves had begun to wonder: Why should their God be so different? Why should he want to knock out all competition? If idols were a fraud, mere carvings (10.4), why should God worry about them?

The Evils Idols Stood For

Idols were far from innocent, however. They stood for vile, angry gods who could hurt you unless you bartered for peace. The highest sacrifice? Slaughter your own son. The Israelites had adopted this practice (19.5).

According to these idol-worshiping religions, success came through the fertile power of nature and the gods. You could tune in to such power by having sex with temple prostitutes, either male or female. The Israelites also borrowed this (2 Kings 23.7). These ideas disgusted the God of Israel. By mixing such practices with their devotion to him, God's people were becoming confused about his true character. (For more on idolatry, see "Why All the Fuss about Idols?" page 405.)

Idolatry Today

The New Testament broadens the definition of idolatry so that it applies to us, even though we worship no statues. Paul said that greed is idolatry (Ephesians 5.5; Colossians 3.5). The things people get greedy for—money, sex, power, even food—can function as little gods. When we feel depressed, we turn to them for comfort. When we're happy, we give them the credit. We gradually become their slaves. But this is exactly the place for God in our lives, and God alone. If something else takes his place, we are as guilty of idolatry as the people Jeremiah spoke to. God cannot share us. He is either the only God, or he is not God at all.

Jealousy is an ugly emotion, but in some situations it is the only appropriate response. A father is jealous of his children; he will fight never to give them up to another family. A husband is jealous of his wife; he will not share her most intimate love with anyone else. So God feels about his people. They belong to him, and to him alone.

Life Questions: Where do you turn when you're troubled? Do money, success, popularity, or other factors serve as substitutes for God?

all the people: ¹⁵Thus says the LORD of hosts, the God of Israel: I am now bringing upon this city and upon all its towns all the disaster that I have pronounced against it, because they have stiffened their necks, refusing to hear my words.

Jeremiah Persecuted by Pashhur

20 Now the priest Pashhur son of Immer, who was chief officer in the house of the LORD, heard Jeremiah prophesying these things. ²Then Pashhur struck the prophet Jeremiah, and put him in the stocks that were in the upper Benjamin Gate of the house of the LORD. ³The next morning when Pashhur released Jeremiah from the stocks, Jeremiah said to him, The LORD has named you not Pashhur but "Terror-all-around." ⁴For thus says the LORD: I am making you a terror to yourself and to all your friends; and they shall fall by the sword of their enemies while you look on. And I will give all Judah into the hand of the king of Babylon; he shall carry them captive to Babylon, and shall kill them with the sword. ⁵I will give all the wealth of this city, all its gains, all its prized belongings, and all the treasures of the kings of Judah into the hand of their enemies, who shall plunder them, and seize them, and carry them to Babylon. ⁶And you, Pashhur, and all who live in your house, shall go into captivity, and to Babylon you shall go; there you shall die, and there you shall be buried, you and all your friends, to whom you have prophesied falsely.

Jeremiah Denounces His Persecutors

⁷ O LORD, you have enticed me,
   and I was enticed;
you have overpowered me,
   and you have prevailed.
I have become a laughingstock all day
      long;
   everyone mocks me.
⁸ For whenever I speak, I must cry out,
   I must shout, "Violence and
      destruction!"
For the word of the LORD has become for
      me
   a reproach and derision all day long.
⁹ If I say, "I will not mention him,
   or speak any more in his name,"
then within me there is something like a
      burning fire
   shut up in my bones;
I am weary with holding it in,
   and I cannot.
¹⁰ For I hear many whispering:
   "Terror is all around!
Denounce him! Let us denounce him!"
   All my close friends
   are watching for me to stumble.
"Perhaps he can be enticed,
   and we can prevail against him,

and take our revenge on him."
¹¹ But the LORD is with me like a dread
      warrior;
   therefore my persecutors will stumble,

> ## 20.9 Fire in His Bones
>
> *When Jeremiah spoke to God, he often complained angrily about the role God had given him. Here he claimed that God "overpowered" him into carrying a message that people ridiculed (verse 7). Jeremiah cursed his own birth, wishing he had been stillborn (verses 14–18). Just how did God "overpower" Jeremiah? God's message was like fire in his bones, so powerful that he could not resist telling it. The "force" God used on Jeremiah was the power of truth.*

   and they will not prevail.
They will be greatly shamed,
   for they will not succeed.
Their eternal dishonor
   will never be forgotten.
¹² O LORD of hosts, you test the righteous,
   you see the heart and the mind;
let me see your retribution upon them,
   for to you I have committed my cause.

¹³ Sing to the LORD;
   praise the LORD!
For he has delivered the life of the needy
   from the hands of evildoers.

¹⁴ Cursed be the day
   on which I was born!
The day when my mother bore me,
   let it not be blessed!
¹⁵ Cursed be the man
   who brought the news to my father,
      saying,
"A child is born to you, a son,"
   making him very glad.
¹⁶ Let that man be like the cities
   that the LORD overthrew without pity;
let him hear a cry in the morning
   and an alarm at noon,
¹⁷ because he did not kill me in the womb;
   so my mother would have been my
      grave,
   and her womb forever great.
¹⁸ Why did I come forth from the womb
   to see toil and sorrow,
   and spend my days in shame?

Jerusalem Will Fall to Nebuchadrezzar

21 This is the word that came to Jeremiah from the LORD, when King Zedekiah sent to him Pashhur son of Malchiah and the priest Zephaniah son of Maaseiah, saying, ²"Please inquire of the LORD on our behalf, for King Nebuchadrezzar of Babylon is making war against us; perhaps the LORD will perform a wonderful deed for us, as he has often done, and will make him withdraw from us."

3 Then Jeremiah said to them: [4]Thus you shall say to Zedekiah: Thus says the LORD, the God of Israel: I am going to turn back the weapons of war that are in your hands and with which you are fighting against the king of Babylon and against the Chaldeans who are besieging you outside the walls; and I will bring them together into the center of this city. [5]I myself will fight against you with outstretched hand and mighty arm, in anger, in fury, and in great wrath. [6]And I will strike down the inhabitants of this city, both human beings and animals; they shall die of a great pestilence. [7]Afterward, says the LORD, I will give King Zedekiah of Judah, and his servants, and the people in this city—those who survive the pestilence, sword, and famine—into the hands of King Nebuchadrezzar of Babylon, into the hands of their enemies, into the hands of those who seek their lives. He shall strike them down with the edge of the sword; he shall not pity them, or spare them, or have compassion.

21.7 God's Answer: No

Prayer changes things, but the results depend on who's asking and what their motives are. Faced with a crisis, King Zedekiah asked Jeremiah to pray to God on his behalf. He hoped for a miracle, but the answer Jeremiah received was anything but good news. Not only would God not help, he would fight against Zedekiah and his people. Why was God's response so negative? Because nobody had paid attention to his warnings. Judah wanted to be rescued—not to alter its behavior.

8 And to this people you shall say: Thus says the LORD: See, I am setting before you the way of life and the way of death. [9]Those who stay in this city shall die by the sword, by famine, and by pestilence; but those who go out and surrender to the Chaldeans who are besieging you shall live and shall have their lives as a prize of war. [10]For I have set my face against this city for evil and not for good, says the LORD: it shall be given into the hands of the king of Babylon, and he shall burn it with fire.

Message to the House of David

11 To the house of the king of Judah say: Hear the word of the LORD, [12]O house of David! Thus says the LORD:
Execute justice in the morning,

and deliver from the hand of the
    oppressor
anyone who has been robbed,
or else my wrath will go forth like fire,
    and burn, with no one to quench it,
    because of your evil doings.

13 See, I am against you, O inhabitant of the
    valley,
    O rock of the plain,
               says the LORD;
you who say, "Who can come down
    against us,
    or who can enter our places of refuge?"
14 I will punish you according to the fruit of
    your doings,
               says the LORD;
I will kindle a fire in its forest,
    and it shall devour all that is around it.

Exhortation to Repent

22 Thus says the LORD: Go down to the house of the king of Judah, and speak there this word, [2]and say: Hear the word of the LORD, O King of Judah sitting on the throne of David—you, and your servants, and your people who enter these gates. [3]Thus says the LORD: Act with justice and righteousness, and deliver from the hand of the oppressor anyone who has been robbed. And do no wrong or violence to the alien, the orphan, and the widow, or shed innocent blood in this place. [4]For if you will indeed obey this word, then through the gates of this house shall enter kings who sit on the throne of David, riding in chariots and on horses, they, and their servants, and their people. [5]But if you will not heed these words, I swear by myself, says the LORD, that this house shall become a desolation. [6]For thus says the LORD concerning the house of the king of Judah:
You are like Gilead to me,
    like the summit of Lebanon;
but I swear that I will make you a desert,
    an uninhabited city.[l]
7 I will prepare destroyers against you,
    all with their weapons;
they shall cut down your choicest cedars
    and cast them into the fire.

8 And many nations will pass by this city, and all of them will say one to another, "Why has the LORD dealt in this way with that great city?" [9]And they will answer, "Because they abandoned the covenant of the LORD their God, and worshiped other gods and served them."

10 Do not weep for him who is dead,
    nor bemoan him;
weep rather for him who goes away,

---

[l] Cn: Heb *uninhabited cities*

for he shall return no more
to see his native land.

Message to the Sons of Josiah

11 For thus says the LORD concerning Shallum son of King Josiah of Judah, who succeeded his father Josiah, and who went away from this place: He shall return here no more, 12but in the place where they have carried him captive he shall die, and he shall never see this land again.

13 Woe to him who builds his house by
        unrighteousness,
    and his upper rooms by injustice;
who makes his neighbors work for
        nothing,
    and does not give them their wages;
14 who says, "I will build myself a spacious
        house
    with large upper rooms,"
and who cuts out windows for it,
    paneling it with cedar,
    and painting it with vermilion.
15 Are you a king
    because you compete in cedar?
Did not your father eat and drink
    and do justice and righteousness?
    Then it was well with him.
16 He judged the cause of the poor
        and needy;
    then it was well.
Is not this to know me?
    says the LORD.
17 But your eyes and heart
    are only on your dishonest gain,
for shedding innocent blood,
    and for practicing oppression and
        violence.

18 Therefore thus says the LORD concerning King Jehoiakim son of Josiah of Judah:
They shall not lament for him, saying,
    "Alas, my brother!" or "Alas, sister!"
They shall not lament for him, saying,
    "Alas, lord!" or "Alas, his majesty!"
19 With the burial of a donkey he shall be
        buried—
    dragged off and thrown out beyond the
        gates of Jerusalem.

20 Go up to Lebanon, and cry out,
    and lift up your voice in Bashan;
cry out from Abarim,
    for all your lovers are crushed.
21 I spoke to you in your prosperity,
    but you said, "I will not listen."
This has been your way from your youth,
    for you have not obeyed my voice.
22 The wind shall shepherd all your
        shepherds,

and your lovers shall go into captivity;
then you will be ashamed and dismayed
    because of all your wickedness.
23 O inhabitant of Lebanon,
    nested among the cedars,
how you will groan[u] when pangs come
        upon you,
    pain as of a woman in labor!

Judgment on Coniah (Jehoiachin)

24 As I live, says the LORD, even if King Coniah son of Jehoiakim of Judah were the signet ring on my right hand, even from there I would tear you off 25and give you into the hands of those who seek your life, into the hands of those of whom you are afraid, even into the hands of King Nebuchadrezzar of Babylon and into the hands of the Chaldeans. 26I will hurl you and the mother who bore you into another country, where you were not born, and there you shall die. 27But they shall not return to the land to which they long to return.

28 Is this man Coniah a despised broken
        pot,
    a vessel no one wants?
Why are he and his offspring hurled out
    and cast away in a land that they do
        not know?
29 O land, land, land,
    hear the word of the LORD!
30 Thus says the LORD:
Record this man as childless,
    a man who shall not succeed in his
        days;
for none of his offspring shall succeed
    in sitting on the throne of David,
    and ruling again in Judah.

Restoration after Exile

23 Woe to the shepherds who destroy and scatter the sheep of my pasture! says the LORD. 2Therefore thus says the LORD, the God of Israel, concerning the shepherds who shepherd my people: It is you who have scattered my flock, and have driven them away, and you have not attended to them. So I will attend to you for your evil doings, says the LORD. 3Then I myself will gather the remnant of my flock out of all the lands where I have driven them, and I will bring them back to their fold, and they shall be fruitful and multiply. 4I will raise up shepherds over them who will shepherd them, and they shall not fear any longer, or be dismayed, nor shall any be missing, says the LORD.

The Righteous Branch of David

5 The days are surely coming, says the LORD, when I will raise up for David a righteous Branch, and he shall reign as king and deal wisely, and

---

u Gk Vg Syr: Heb will be pitied

shall execute justice and righteousness in the land. [6]In his days Judah will be saved and Israel will live in safety. And this is the name by which he will be called: "The LORD is our righteousness."

23.6 The Messianic Promise

Long before, God had promised David that his descendants would always rule Israel. But the kings who followed David had been more like wolves than shepherds of God's people. Jeremiah predicted that the kings of his day would either be killed or carried into captivity— which in fact occurred. He also predicted that a good king would replace them—the Messiah.

[7] Therefore, the days are surely coming, says the LORD, when it shall no longer be said, "As the LORD lives who brought the people of Israel up out of the land of Egypt," [8]but "As the LORD lives who brought out and led the offspring of the house of Israel out of the land of the north and out of all the lands where he[v] had driven them." Then they shall live in their own land.

False Prophets of Hope Denounced

[9] Concerning the prophets:
My heart is crushed within me,
    all my bones shake;
I have become like a drunkard,
    like one overcome by wine,
because of the LORD
    and because of his holy words.
[10] For the land is full of adulterers;
    because of the curse the land mourns,
    and the pastures of the wilderness are
        dried up.
Their course has been evil,
    and their might is not right.
[11] Both prophet and priest are ungodly;
    even in my house I have found their
        wickedness,
           says the LORD.
[12] Therefore their way shall be to them
    like slippery paths in the darkness,
    into which they shall be driven and fall;
for I will bring disaster upon them
    in the year of their punishment,
           says the LORD.
[13] In the prophets of Samaria
    I saw a disgusting thing:
they prophesied by Baal
    and led my people Israel astray.
[14] But in the prophets of Jerusalem
    I have seen a more shocking thing:
they commit adultery and walk in lies;

they strengthen the hands of evildoers,
    so that no one turns from wickedness;
all of them have become like Sodom to
      me,
    and its inhabitants like Gomorrah.
[15] Therefore thus says the LORD of hosts
    concerning the prophets:
"I am going to make them eat
      wormwood,
    and give them poisoned water to drink;
for from the prophets of Jerusalem
    ungodliness has spread throughout the
      land."

[16] Thus says the LORD of hosts: Do not listen to the words of the prophets who prophesy to you; they are deluding you. They speak visions of their own minds, not from the mouth of the LORD. [17]They keep saying to those who despise the word of the LORD, "It shall be well with you"; and to all who stubbornly follow their own stubborn hearts, they say, "No calamity shall come upon you."

[18] For who has stood in the council of the
    LORD
    so as to see and to hear his word?
    Who has given heed to his word so as
      to proclaim it?
[19] Look, the storm of the LORD!
    Wrath has gone forth,
a whirling tempest;
    it will burst upon the head of
      the wicked.
[20] The anger of the LORD will not turn back
    until he has executed and accomplished
      the intents of his mind.
In the latter days you will understand it
      clearly.

[21] I did not send the prophets,
    yet they ran;
I did not speak to them,
    yet they prophesied.
[22] But if they had stood in my council,
    then they would have proclaimed my
      words to my people,
and they would have turned them from
      their evil way,
    and from the evil of their doings.

[23] Am I a God near by, says the LORD, and not a God far off? [24]Who can hide in secret places so that I cannot see them? says the LORD. Do I not fill heaven and earth? says the LORD. [25]I have heard what the prophets have said who prophesy lies in my name, saying, "I have dreamed, I have dreamed!" [26]How long? Will the hearts of the

prophets ever turn back—those who prophesy lies, and who prophesy the deceit of their own heart? ²⁷They plan to make my people forget my name by their dreams that they tell one another, just as their ancestors forgot my name for Baal. ²⁸Let the prophet who has a dream tell the dream, but let the one who has my word speak my word

23.25 Questionable Dreams

For the casual observer, it must have been difficult to tell real prophets from false prophets in Jeremiah's day. Jeremiah was outnumbered by optimists who claimed God gave them dreams and messages. In reality, their dreams had nothing to do with God's word, and anyone who compared their message with Scripture could have seen the difference. They predicted peace when God had promised severe punishment for his people's sins.

faithfully. What has straw in common with wheat? says the LORD. ²⁹Is not my word like fire, says the LORD, and like a hammer that breaks a rock in pieces? ³⁰See, therefore, I am against the prophets, says the LORD, who steal my words from one another. ³¹See, I am against the prophets, says the LORD, who use their own tongues and say, "Says the LORD." ³²See, I am against those who prophesy lying dreams, says the LORD, and who tell them, and who lead my people astray by their lies and their recklessness, when I did not send them or appoint them; so they do not profit this people at all, says the LORD.

33 When this people, or a prophet, or a priest asks you, "What is the burden of the LORD?" you shall say to them, "You are the burden,ʷ and I will cast you off, says the LORD." ³⁴And as for the prophet, priest, or the people who say, "The burden of the LORD," I will punish them and their households. ³⁵Thus shall you say to one another, among yourselves, "What has the LORD answered?" or "What has the LORD spoken?" ³⁶But "the burden of the LORD" you shall mention no more, for the burden is everyone's own word, and so you pervert the words of the living God, the LORD of hosts, our God. ³⁷Thus you shall ask the prophet, "What has the LORD answered you?" or "What has the LORD spoken?" ³⁸But if you say, "the burden of the LORD," thus says the LORD: Because you have said these words, "the burden of the LORD," when I sent to you, saying, You shall not say, "the burden of the LORD," ³⁹therefore, I will surely lift you upˣ and cast you away from my presence, you and the city that I gave to you and your ancestors. ⁴⁰And I will bring upon you everlasting disgrace and perpetual shame, which shall not be forgotten.

The Good and the Bad Figs

24 The LORD showed me two baskets of figs placed before the temple of the LORD. This was after King Nebuchadrezzar of Babylon had taken into exile from Jerusalem King Jeconiah son of Jehoiakim of Judah, together with the officials of Judah, the artisans, and the smiths, and had brought them to Babylon. ²One basket had very good figs, like first-ripe figs, but the other basket had very bad figs, so bad that they could not be eaten. ³And the LORD said to me, "What do you see, Jeremiah?" I said, "Figs, the good figs very good, and the bad figs very bad, so bad that they cannot be eaten."

4 Then the word of the LORD came to me: ⁵Thus says the LORD, the God of Israel: Like these good figs, so I will regard as good the exiles from Judah, whom I have sent away from this place to the land of the Chaldeans. ⁶I will set my eyes upon them for good, and I will bring them back to this land. I will build them up, and not tear them down; I will plant them, and not pluck them up. ⁷I will give them a heart to know that I am the LORD; and they shall be my people and I will be their God, for they shall return to me with their whole heart.

8 But thus says the LORD: Like the bad figs that are so bad they cannot be eaten, so will I treat King Zedekiah of Judah, his officials, the remnant of Jerusalem who remain in this land, and those who live in the land of Egypt. ⁹I will make them a horror, an evil thing, to all the kingdoms of the earth—a disgrace, a byword, a taunt, and a curse in all the places where I shall drive them. ¹⁰And I will send sword, famine, and pestilence upon them, until they are utterly destroyed from the land that I gave to them and their ancestors.

The Babylonian Captivity Foretold

25 The word that came to Jeremiah concerning all the people of Judah, in the fourth year of King Jehoiakim son of Josiah of Judah (that was the first year of King Nebuchadrezzar of Babylon), ²which the prophet Jeremiah spoke to all the people of Judah and all the inhabitants of Jerusalem: ³For twenty-three years, from the thirteenth year of King Josiah son of Amon of Judah, to this day, the word of the LORD has come to me, and I have spoken persistently to you, but you have not listened. ⁴And though the LORD persistently sent you all his servants the prophets, you have neither listened nor inclined your ears to hear ⁵when they said, "Turn now, everyone of you, from your evil way and wicked doings, and you will remain upon the land that the LORD has given to you and your ancestors from of old and forever; ⁶do not go after other gods to serve and worship them, and do not provoke me to anger with the work of your hands. Then I will do you

---

ʷ Gk Vg: Heb *What burden*   ˣ Heb Mss Gk Vg: MT *forget you*

no harm." [7]Yet you did not listen to me, says the Lord, and so you have provoked me to anger with the work of your hands to your own harm.

8 Therefore thus says the Lord of hosts: Because you have not obeyed my words, [9]I am going to send for all the tribes of the north, says the Lord, even for King Nebuchadrezzar of Babylon, my servant, and I will bring them against this land and its inhabitants, and against all these nations around; I will utterly destroy them, and make them an object of horror and of hissing, and an everlasting disgrace.[y] [10]And I will banish from them the sound of mirth and the sound of gladness, the voice of the bridegroom and the voice of the bride, the sound of the millstones and the light of the lamp. [11]This whole land shall become a ruin and a waste, and these nations shall serve

25.11–12 Gone, But Not Forever

Seventy years of captivity, God predicted. This probably represents a rounded-off number; the precise length of the captivity can be calculated in different ways, since several waves of captives were taken away and several waves of exiles returned. The number 70 has a deeper significance, though: It says that the punishment, though long and severe (at least two generations would die far from home), will not last forever. Unlike other nations taken into captivity, Israel will return. God's judgment is limited, but his mercy is forever.

the king of Babylon seventy years. [12]Then after seventy years are completed, I will punish the king of Babylon and that nation, the land of the Chaldeans, for their iniquity, says the Lord, making the land an everlasting waste. [13]I will bring upon that land all the words that I have uttered against it, everything written in this book, which Jeremiah prophesied against all the nations. [14]For many nations and great kings shall make slaves of them also; and I will repay them according to their deeds and the work of their hands.

The Cup of God's Wrath

15 For thus the Lord, the God of Israel, said to me: Take from my hand this cup of the wine of wrath, and make all the nations to whom I send you drink it. [16]They shall drink and stagger and go out of their minds because of the sword that I am sending among them.

17 So I took the cup from the Lord's hand, and made all the nations to whom the Lord sent me drink it: [18]Jerusalem and the towns of Judah, its kings and officials, to make them a desolation and a waste, an object of hissing and of cursing,

as they are today; [19]Pharaoh king of Egypt, his servants, his officials, and all his people; [20]all the mixed people;[z] all the kings of the land of Uz; all the kings of the land of the Philistines— Ashkelon, Gaza, Ekron, and the remnant of Ashdod; [21]Edom, Moab, and the Ammonites; [22]all the kings of Tyre, all the kings of Sidon, and the kings of the coastland across the sea; [23]Dedan, Tema, Buz, and all who have shaven temples; [24]all the kings of Arabia and all the kings of the mixed peoples[z] that live in the desert; [25]all the kings of Zimri, all the kings of Elam, and all the kings of Media; [26]all the kings of the north, far and near, one after another, and all the kingdoms of the world that are on the face of the earth. And after them the king of Sheshach[a] shall drink.

27 Then you shall say to them, Thus says the Lord of hosts, the God of Israel: Drink, get drunk and vomit, fall and rise no more, because of the sword that I am sending among you.

28 And if they refuse to accept the cup from your hand to drink, then you shall say to them: Thus says the Lord of hosts: You must drink! [29]See, I am beginning to bring disaster on the city that is called by my name, and how can you possibly avoid punishment? You shall not go unpunished, for I am summoning a sword against all the inhabitants of the earth, says the Lord of hosts.

30 You, therefore, shall prophesy against them all these words, and say to them:

The Lord will roar from on high,
    and from his holy habitation utter his
        voice;
he will roar mightily against his fold,
    and shout, like those who tread grapes,
    against all the inhabitants of the earth.
[31] The clamor will resound to the ends of
      the earth,
    for the Lord has an indictment against
      the nations;
he is entering into judgment with all flesh,
    and the guilty he will put to the sword,
            says the Lord.

32 Thus says the Lord of hosts:
See, disaster is spreading
    from nation to nation,
and a great tempest is stirring
    from the farthest parts of the earth!
33 Those slain by the Lord on that day shall extend from one end of the earth to the other. They shall not be lamented, or gathered, or buried; they shall become dung on the surface of the ground.
34 Wail, you shepherds, and cry out;
    roll in ashes, you lords of the flock,
for the days of your slaughter have
      come—and your dispersions,[z]

---

[y] Gk Compare Syr: Heb *and everlasting desolations*   [z] Meaning of Heb uncertain   [a] *Sheshach* is a cryptogram for Babel, Babylon

and you shall fall like a choice vessel.
35 Flight shall fail the shepherds,
 and there shall be no escape for the
  lords of the flock.
36 Hark! the cry of the shepherds,
 and the wail of the lords of the flock!
For the LORD is despoiling their pasture,
37 and the peaceful folds are devastated,
 because of the fierce anger of the LORD.
38 Like a lion he has left his covert;
 for their land has become a waste
because of the cruel sword,
 and because of his fierce anger.

Jeremiah's Prophecies in the Temple

26 At the beginning of the reign of King Jehoiakim son of Josiah of Judah, this word came from the LORD: ²Thus says the LORD: Stand in the court of the LORD's house, and speak to all the cities of Judah that come to worship in the house of the LORD; speak to them all the words that I command you; do not hold back a word. ³It may be that they will listen, all of them, and will turn from their evil way, that I may change my mind about the disaster that I intend to bring on them because of their evil doings. ⁴You shall say to them: Thus says the LORD: If you will not listen to me, to walk in my law that I have set before you, ⁵and to heed the words of my servants the prophets whom I send to you urgently—though you have not heeded— ⁶then I will make this house like Shiloh, and I will make this city a curse for all the nations of the earth.

7 The priests and the prophets and all the people heard Jeremiah speaking these words in the house of the LORD. ⁸And when Jeremiah had finished speaking all that the LORD had commanded him to speak to all the people, then the priests and the prophets and all the people laid hold of him, saying, "You shall die! ⁹Why have you prophesied in the name of the LORD, saying, 'This house shall be like Shiloh, and this city shall be desolate, without inhabitant'?" And all the people gathered around Jeremiah in the house of the LORD.

10 When the officials of Judah heard these things, they came up from the king's house to the house of the LORD and took their seat in the entry of the New Gate of the house of the LORD. ¹¹Then the priests and the prophets said to the officials and to all the people, "This man deserves the sentence of death because he has prophesied against this city, as you have heard with your own ears."

12 Then Jeremiah spoke to all the officials and all the people, saying, "It is the LORD who sent me to prophesy against this house and this city all the words you have heard. ¹³Now therefore amend your ways and your doings, and obey the voice of the LORD your God, and the LORD will change his mind about the disaster that he has pronounced against you. ¹⁴But as for me, here I am in your hands. Do with me as seems good and right to you. ¹⁵Only know for certain that if you put me to death, you will be bringing innocent blood upon yourselves and upon this city and its inhabitants, for in truth the LORD sent me to you to speak all these words in your ears."

16 Then the officials and all the people said to the priests and the prophets, "This man does not deserve the sentence of death, for he has spoken to us in the name of the LORD our God." ¹⁷And some of the elders of the land arose and said to all the assembled people, ¹⁸"Micah of Moresheth, who prophesied during the days of King Hezekiah of Judah, said to all the people of Judah: 'Thus says the LORD of hosts,

 Zion shall be plowed as a field;
  Jerusalem shall become a heap of ruins,
  and the mountain of the house a
   wooded height.'
¹⁹Did King Hezekiah of Judah and all Judah actually put him to death? Did he not fear the LORD and entreat the favor of the LORD, and did not the LORD change his mind about the disaster that he had pronounced against them? But we are about to bring great disaster on ourselves!"

26.19 Scripture Saves a Life

Jeremiah's scorn for the temple was considered sacrilege and might have cost him his life. (Another prophet, Uriah, was assassinated for the same message—see verses 20–23.) But some of the elders remembered the treatment given Micah years before. Hezekiah—a good king—had listened to Micah. Based on this precedent, Jeremiah was allowed to live.

20 There was another man prophesying in the name of the LORD, Uriah son of Shemaiah from Kiriath-jearim. He prophesied against this city and against this land in words exactly like those of Jeremiah. ²¹And when King Jehoiakim, with all his warriors and all the officials, heard his words, the king sought to put him to death; but when Uriah heard of it, he was afraid and fled and escaped to Egypt. ²²Then King Jehoiakim sent*b* Elnathan son of Achbor and men with him to Egypt, ²³and they took Uriah from Egypt and brought him to King Jehoiakim, who struck him down with the sword and threw his dead body into the burial place of the common people.

24 But the hand of Ahikam son of Shaphan was with Jeremiah so that he was not given over into the hands of the people to be put to death.

b Heb adds *men to Egypt*

The Sign of the Yoke

27 In the beginning of the reign of King Zedekiah^c son of Josiah of Judah, this word came to Jeremiah from the LORD. ²Thus the LORD said to me: Make yourself a yoke of straps and bars, and put them on your neck. ³Send word^d to the king of Edom, the king of Moab, the king of the Ammonites, the king of Tyre, and the king of Sidon by the hand of the envoys who have come to Jerusalem to King Zedekiah of Judah. ⁴Give them this charge for their masters: Thus says the LORD of hosts, the God of Israel: This is what you shall say to your masters: ⁵It is I who by my great power and my outstretched arm have made the earth, with the people and animals that are on the earth, and I give it to whomever I please. ⁶Now I have given all these lands into the hand of King Nebuchadnezzar of Babylon, my servant, and I have given him even the wild animals of the field to serve him. ⁷All the nations shall serve him and his son and his grandson, until the time of his own land comes; then many nations and great kings shall make him their slave.

8 But if any nation or kingdom will not serve this king, Nebuchadnezzar of Babylon, and put its neck under the yoke of the king of Babylon, then I will punish that nation with the sword, with famine, and with pestilence, says the LORD, until I have completed its^e destruction by his hand. ⁹You, therefore, must not listen to your prophets, your diviners, your dreamers,^f your soothsayers, or your sorcerers, who are saying to you, "You shall not serve the king of Babylon." ¹⁰For they are prophesying a lie to you, with the result that you will be removed far from your land; I will drive you out, and you will perish. ¹¹But any nation that will bring its neck under the yoke of the king of Babylon and serve him, I will leave on its own land, says the LORD, to till it and live there.

12 I spoke to King Zedekiah of Judah in the same way: Bring your necks under the yoke of the king of Babylon, and serve him and his people, and live. ¹³Why should you and your people die

by the sword, by famine, and by pestilence, as the LORD has spoken concerning any nation that will not serve the king of Babylon? ¹⁴Do not listen to the words of the prophets who are telling you not to serve the king of Babylon, for they are prophesying a lie to you. ¹⁵I have not sent you, says the LORD, but they are prophesying falsely in my name, with the result that I will drive you out and you will perish, you and the prophets who are prophesying to you.

16 Then I spoke to the priests and to all this people, saying, Thus says the LORD: Do not listen to the words of your prophets who are prophesying to you, saying, "The vessels of the LORD's house will soon be brought back from Babylon," for they are prophesying a lie to you. ¹⁷Do not listen to them; serve the king of Babylon and live. Why should this city become a desolation? ¹⁸If indeed they are prophets, and if the word of the LORD is with them, then let them intercede with the LORD of hosts, that the vessels left in the house of the LORD, in the house of the king of Judah, and in Jerusalem may not go to Babylon. ¹⁹For thus says the LORD of hosts concerning the pillars, the sea, the stands, and the rest of the vessels that are left in this city, ²⁰which King Nebuchadnezzar of Babylon did not take away when he took into exile from Jerusalem to Babylon King Jeconiah son of Jehoiakim of Judah, and all the nobles of Judah and Jerusalem— ²¹thus says the LORD of hosts, the God of Israel, concerning the vessels left in the house of the LORD, in the house of the king of Judah, and in Jerusalem: ²²They shall be carried to Babylon, and there they shall stay, until the day when I give attention to them, says the LORD. Then I will bring them up and restore them to this place.

Hananiah Opposes Jeremiah and Dies

28 In that same year, at the beginning of the reign of King Zedekiah of Judah, in the fifth month of the fourth year, the prophet Hananiah son of Azzur, from Gibeon, spoke to me in the house of the LORD, in the presence of the priests and all the people, saying, ²"Thus says the LORD of hosts, the God of Israel: I have broken the yoke of the king of Babylon. ³Within two years I will bring back to this place all the vessels of the LORD's house, which King Nebuchadnezzar of Babylon took away from this place and carried to Babylon. ⁴I will also bring back to this place King Jeconiah son of Jehoiakim of Judah, and all the exiles from Judah who went to Babylon, says the LORD, for I will break the yoke of the king of Babylon."

5 Then the prophet Jeremiah spoke to the prophet Hananiah in the presence of the priests and all the people who were standing in the house of the LORD; ⁶and the prophet Jeremiah said,

27.12 Counseling Surrender

By the time Zedekiah took office, Israel had twice surrendered to Babylon. Two groups of Israelites had already been exiled, including in their number King Jehoiachin. The desire for independence did not die easily, however. Zedekiah, who had been put into office as a puppet king, soon began scheming for revolution. Jeremiah persistently counseled submission to Babylon—unpopular advice that nearly cost him his life when he was accused of treason.

---

^c Another reading is *Jehoiakim*   ^d Cn: Heb *send them*   ^e Heb *their*   ^f Gk Syr Vg: Heb *dreams*

"Amen! May the LORD do so; may the LORD fulfill the words that you have prophesied, and bring back to this place from Babylon the vessels of the house of the LORD, and all the exiles. ⁷But listen now to this word that I speak in your hearing and in the hearing of all the people. ⁸The prophets who preceded you and me from ancient times prophesied war, famine, and pestilence against many countries and great kingdoms. ⁹As for the prophet who prophesies peace, when the word of that prophet comes true, then it will be known that the LORD has truly sent the prophet."

10 Then the prophet Hananiah took the yoke from the neck of the prophet Jeremiah, and broke it. ¹¹And Hananiah spoke in the presence of all the people, saying, "Thus says the LORD: This is how I will break the yoke of King Nebuchadnezzar of Babylon from the neck of all the nations within two years." At this, the prophet Jeremiah went his way.

12 Sometime after the prophet Hananiah had broken the yoke from the neck of the prophet Jeremiah, the word of the LORD came to Jeremiah: ¹³Go, tell Hananiah, Thus says the LORD: You have broken wooden bars only to forge iron bars in place of them! ¹⁴For thus says the LORD of hosts, the God of Israel: I have put an iron yoke on the neck of all these nations so that they may serve King Nebuchadnezzar of Babylon, and they shall indeed serve him; I have even given him the wild animals. ¹⁵And the prophet Jeremiah said to the prophet Hananiah, "Listen, Hananiah, the LORD has not sent you, and you made this people trust in a lie. ¹⁶Therefore thus says the LORD: I am going to send you off the face of the earth. Within this year you will be dead, because you have spoken rebellion against the LORD."

17 In that same year, in the seventh month, the prophet Hananiah died.

Jeremiah's Letter to the Exiles in Babylon

29 These are the words of the letter that the prophet Jeremiah sent from Jerusalem to the remaining elders among the exiles, and to the priests, the prophets, and all the people, whom Nebuchadnezzar had taken into exile from Jerusalem to Babylon. ²This was after King Jeconiah, and the queen mother, the court officials, the leaders of Judah and Jerusalem, the artisans, and the smiths had departed from Jerusalem. ³The letter was sent by the hand of Elasah son of Shaphan and Gemariah son of Hilkiah, whom King Zedekiah of Judah sent to Babylon to King Nebuchadnezzar of Babylon. It said: ⁴Thus says the LORD of hosts, the God of Israel, to all the exiles whom I have sent into exile from Jerusalem to Babylon: ⁵Build houses and live in them; plant gardens and eat what they produce. ⁶Take wives and have sons and daughters; take wives for your sons, and give your daughters in marriage, that they may bear sons and daughters; multiply there, and do not decrease. ⁷But seek the welfare of the city where I have sent you into exile, and pray to the LORD on its behalf, for in its welfare you will find your welfare. ⁸For thus says the LORD of

29.5 Writing to Ezekiel

During the last years of Jeremiah's work, a sizable community of exiles were already living in Babylon. Among them were Daniel, a young man who would rise to tremendous power in court, and the prophet Ezekiel. Ezekiel was preaching at the same time as Jeremiah, and their messages are similar in many ways. Since neither one mentions the other, however, we can't be sure whether they were acquainted.

hosts, the God of Israel: Do not let the prophets and the diviners who are among you deceive you, and do not listen to the dreams that they dream,ᵍ ⁹for it is a lie that they are prophesying to you in my name; I did not send them, says the LORD.

10 For thus says the LORD: Only when Babylon's seventy years are completed will I visit you, and I will fulfill to you my promise and bring you back to this place. ¹¹For surely I know the plans I have for you, says the LORD, plans for your welfare and not for harm, to give you a future with hope. ¹²Then when you call upon me and come and pray to me, I will hear you. ¹³When you search for me, you will find me; if you seek me with all your heart, ¹⁴I will let you find me, says the LORD, and I will restore your fortunes and gather you from all the nations and all the places where I have driven you, says the LORD, and I will bring you back to the place from which I sent you into exile.

15 Because you have said, "The LORD has raised up prophets for us in Babylon,"— ¹⁶Thus says the LORD concerning the king who sits on the throne of David, and concerning all the people who live in this city, your kinsfolk who did not go out with you into exile: ¹⁷Thus says the LORD of hosts, I am going to let loose on them sword, famine, and pestilence, and I will make them like rotten figs that are so bad they cannot be eaten. ¹⁸I will pursue them with the sword, with famine, and with pestilence, and will make them a horror to all the kingdoms of the earth, to be an object of cursing, and horror, and hissing, and a derision among all the nations where I have driven them, ¹⁹because they did not heed my words, says the LORD, when I persistently sent to you my servants the prophets, but theyʰ would not listen, says the LORD. ²⁰But now, all you exiles whom I sent away from Jerusalem to Babylon, hear the word of the

---

g Cn: Heb *your dreams that you cause to dream*   *h* Syr: Heb *you*

LORD: 21Thus says the LORD of hosts, the God of Israel, concerning Ahab son of Kolaiah and Zedekiah son of Maaseiah, who are prophesying a lie to you in my name: I am going to deliver them into the hand of King Nebuchadrezzar of Babylon, and he shall kill them before your eyes. 22And on account of them this curse shall be used by all the exiles from Judah in Babylon: "The LORD make you like Zedekiah and Ahab, whom the king of Babylon roasted in the fire," 23because they have perpetrated outrage in Israel and have committed adultery with their neighbors' wives, and have spoken in my name lying words that I did not command them; I am the one who knows and bears witness, says the LORD.

The Letter of Shemaiah

24 To Shemaiah of Nehelam you shall say: 25Thus says the LORD of hosts, the God of Israel: In your own name you sent a letter to all the people who are in Jerusalem, and to the priest Zephaniah son of Maaseiah, and to all the priests, saying, 26The LORD himself has made you priest instead of the priest Jehoiada, so that there may be officers in the house of the LORD to control any madman who plays the prophet, to put him in the stocks and the collar. 27So now why have you not rebuked Jeremiah of Anathoth who plays the prophet for you? 28For he has actually sent to us in Babylon, saying, "It will be a long time; build houses and live in them, and plant gardens and eat what they produce."

29 The priest Zephaniah read this letter in the hearing of the prophet Jeremiah. 30Then the word of the LORD came to Jeremiah: 31Send to all the exiles, saying, Thus says the LORD concerning Shemaiah of Nehelam: Because Shemaiah has prophesied to you, though I did not send him, and has led you to trust in a lie, 32therefore thus says the LORD: I am going to punish Shemaiah of Nehelam and his descendants; he shall not have anyone living among this people to see[i] the good that I am going to do to my people, says the LORD, for he has spoken rebellion against the LORD.

Restoration Promised for Israel and Judah

30 The word that came to Jeremiah from the LORD: 2Thus says the LORD, the God of Israel: Write in a book all the words that I have spoken to you. 3For the days are surely coming, says the LORD, when I will restore the fortunes of my people, Israel and Judah, says the LORD, and I will bring them back to the land that I gave to their ancestors and they shall take possession of it.

4 These are the words that the LORD spoke concerning Israel and Judah:

5 Thus says the LORD:
  We have heard a cry of panic,

of terror, and no peace.
6 Ask now, and see,
    can a man bear a child?
  Why then do I see every man
    with his hands on his loins like a
      woman in labor?
  Why has every face turned pale?
7 Alas! that day is so great
    there is none like it;
  it is a time of distress for Jacob;
    yet he shall be rescued from it.

8 On that day, says the LORD of hosts, I will break the yoke from off his[j] neck, and I will burst his[j] bonds, and strangers shall no more make a servant of him. 9But they shall serve the LORD their God and David their king, whom I will raise up for them.

10 But as for you, have no fear, my servant
      Jacob, says the LORD,
    and do not be dismayed, O Israel;
  for I am going to save you from far away,
    and your offspring from the land of
      their captivity.
  Jacob shall return and have quiet and
      ease,
    and no one shall make him afraid.
11 For I am with you, says the LORD, to save
      you;
  I will make an end of all the nations
    among which I scattered you,
    but of you I will not make an end.
  I will chastise you in just measure,
    and I will by no means leave you
      unpunished.

30.11 Free Again

Though Jeremiah mainly spoke of God's judgment, he also offered hope beyond judgment. Someday, Israel would be free again. The prophecy of this verse has been fulfilled: not one of the powerful cultures surrounding Israel has endured, but the Jews have survived with their language, customs, and religion intact.

12 For thus says the LORD:
  Your hurt is incurable,
    your wound is grievous.
13 There is no one to uphold your cause,
    no medicine for your wound,
    no healing for you.
14 All your lovers have forgotten you;
    they care nothing for you;
  for I have dealt you the blow of
    an enemy,

---

[i] Gk: Heb *and he shall not see*   [j] Cn: Heb *your*

The People Who Refuse to Die

Their powerful neighbors have disappeared—but the Jews live on

IF YOU GET LOST IN Brooklyn, New York, and wander into the section called Williamsburg, prepare to do a double take. Boys playing baseball look odd: long, uncut curls of hair trail from above their ears down to their chests. Men in black, with long, untrimmed beards, coach from the sidelines. All the women you see wear wigs because they've shaved their heads completely. Is this a new cult from California? The latest punk fashion from London?

You've stumbled into a community of Hasidic Jews. They live, not by the latest fad, but by ancient rules based on Old Testament laws. They follow complicated dietary regulations. They keep one set of bowls for meat, and another for dairy products. Young men devote long hours of study to the Hebrew Old Testament. Though they are Americans living in New York, their cultural compass points to Mount Sinai, where God gave Moses the law.

> I am going to save you from far away, and your offspring from the land of their captivity. Jacob shall return and have quiet and ease, and no one shall make him afraid. 30.10

Jews Outlived Their Enemies

The Jewish people have survived, astonishingly. Who in Jeremiah's time could have predicted their persistence, when they were hemmed in and threatened with total destruction? The Babylonians conquered and carried them into exile. But where are the Babylonians today? They have vanished. Desert sand covers their capital.

The story of the Jews is a long chronicle of discrimination, exile, punishment, and slaughter. Against no other people have such destructive measures been taken. Yet they have survived, and thrived. Their language endures. Their book, the Old Testament, is part of the great best seller of all time. They have rebuilt their nation.

Even more remarkably, this durability was predicted in writing 2,500 years ago. God promised in the clearest terms that he would never reject his people.

The New Covenant

Jeremiah, known for his stinging denunciations and repeated predictions of savage destruction, also brought word of God's eternal faithfulness and of a new covenant replacing the old, broken one. The new covenant would improve generously on the old one, Jeremiah said. God would no longer simply list rules for his people to obey. He would plant those rules in their hearts, so they would want to obey (31.33). Each individual would know the Lord personally. God would offer forgiveness for sins.

Jeremiah promised more than that. He said a new king from David's line would come to rule. He would be called "The LORD is our righteousness" (23.5–8). Israel would return from exile to their land. They would farm there again. They would rebuild Jerusalem and again worship God there. Jeremiah wrote these rosy words in the face of Israel's worst catastrophe.

Jeremiah didn't just deliver these messages. He acted them out. He made what was either one of the stupidest financial investments of all time, or a remarkable act of faith. He bought property from a relative at the height of the Babylonian siege (chapter 32). God had promised Jeremiah that someday the property would be worth money again to his family. He believed and invested in that distant prospect. He bet on the survival of Israel.

The Fulfillment of Prophecy

Christians agree that the new king Jeremiah predicted was Jesus. They agree that Jesus brought the new covenant, which puts the law into people's hearts and enables them to know God. But on the restoration of Israel Christians hold different opinions. Some feel that the modern nation of Israel is, at least partly, the reincarnated nation Jeremiah wrote about. Others feel that the New Testament teaches that Christians of all races form Jeremiah's "new nation" of God's people, and that the promises apply allegorically to them.

All agree, though, that what Jesus set out to do is not yet finished. Someday he will destroy the forces of evil and fully establish his new kingdom.

Life Questions: Jeremiah bought a field as a sign of his faith in the future of Israel. By what "investments" can you demonstrate practical faith in God's kingdom?

the punishment of a merciless foe,
because your guilt is great,
because your sins are so numerous.
15 Why do you cry out over your hurt?
Your pain is incurable.
Because your guilt is great,
because your sins are so numerous,
I have done these things to you.
16 Therefore all who devour you shall be
devoured,
and all your foes, everyone of them,
shall go into captivity;
those who plunder you shall be
plundered,
and all who prey on you I will make a
prey.
17 For I will restore health to you,
and your wounds I will heal,
                    says the LORD,
because they have called you an outcast:
"It is Zion; no one cares for her!"

18 Thus says the LORD:
I am going to restore the fortunes of the
tents of Jacob,
and have compassion on his dwellings;
the city shall be rebuilt upon its mound,
and the citadel set on its rightful site.
19 Out of them shall come thanksgiving,
and the sound of merrymakers.
I will make them many, and they shall
not be few;
I will make them honored, and they
shall not be disdained.
20 Their children shall be as of old,
their congregation shall be established
before me;
and I will punish all who oppress
them.
21 Their prince shall be one of their own,
their ruler shall come from their midst;
I will bring him near, and he shall
approach me,
for who would otherwise dare to
approach me?
                    says the LORD.
22 And you shall be my people,
and I will be your God.

23 Look, the storm of the LORD!
Wrath has gone forth,
a whirling^k tempest;
it will burst upon the head of
the wicked.
24 The fierce anger of the LORD will not turn
back
until he has executed and accomplished

the intents of his mind.
In the latter days you will understand this.

The Joyful Return of the Exiles

31 At that time, says the LORD, I will be the
God of all the families of Israel, and they
shall be my people.
2 Thus says the LORD:
The people who survived the sword
found grace in the wilderness;
when Israel sought for rest,
3 the LORD appeared to him^l from far
away.^{m}
I have loved you with an everlasting love;
therefore I have continued my
faithfulness to you.
4 Again I will build you, and you shall be
built,
O virgin Israel!
Again you shall take^n your tambourines,
and go forth in the dance of the
merrymakers.
5 Again you shall plant vineyards
on the mountains of Samaria;
the planters shall plant,
and shall enjoy the fruit.
6 For there shall be a day when sentinels
will call
in the hill country of Ephraim:
"Come, let us go up to Zion,
to the LORD our God."

7 For thus says the LORD:
Sing aloud with gladness for Jacob,
and raise shouts for the chief of the
nations;
proclaim, give praise, and say,
"Save, O LORD, your people,
the remnant of Israel."
8 See, I am going to bring them from the
land of the north,
and gather them from the farthest parts
of the earth,
among them the blind and the lame,
those with child and those in labor,
together;
a great company, they shall return
here.
9 With weeping they shall come,
and with consolations^o I will lead
them back,
I will let them walk by brooks of water,
in a straight path in which they shall
not stumble;
for I have become a father to Israel,
and Ephraim is my firstborn.

10 Hear the word of the LORD, O nations,

---

^{k} One Ms: Meaning of MT uncertain ^{l} Gk: Heb me ^{m} Or to him long ago ^{n} Or adorn yourself with
^{o} Gk Compare Vg Tg: Heb supplications

and declare it in the coastlands far
away;
say, "He who scattered Israel will gather
him,
and will keep him as a shepherd a
flock."
11 For the LORD has ransomed Jacob,
and has redeemed him from hands too
strong for him.
12 They shall come and sing aloud on the
height of Zion,
and they shall be radiant over the
goodness of the LORD,
over the grain, the wine, and the oil,
and over the young of the flock and
the herd;
their life shall become like a watered
garden,
and they shall never languish again.
13 Then shall the young women rejoice in
the dance,
and the young men and the old shall
be merry.
I will turn their mourning into joy,
I will comfort them, and give them
gladness for sorrow.
14 I will give the priests their fill of fatness,
and my people shall be satisfied with
my bounty,
says the LORD.

15 Thus says the LORD:
A voice is heard in Ramah,
lamentation and bitter weeping.
Rachel is weeping for her children;
she refuses to be comforted for her
children,
because they are no more.

31.15 Pain in Redemption

*The Babylonians used Ramah, a town north of
Jerusalem, as a collection point for the captives
they were about to exile. Rachel, the "mother of
Israel," was buried near there, and she is
portrayed as weeping over the exiles. But the
Lord's voice answers hers, offering hope for
their return. Matthew related this verse to King
Herod's slaughter of all baby boys in the
vicinity of Bethlehem (Matthew 2.18). In
deepest grief, God is not absent: He is planning
redemption.*

16 Thus says the LORD:
Keep your voice from weeping,
and your eyes from tears;
for there is a reward for your work,
says the LORD:

they shall come back from the land of
the enemy;
17 there is hope for your future,
says the LORD:
your children shall come back to their
own country.

18 Indeed I heard Ephraim pleading:
"You disciplined me, and I took the
discipline;
I was like a calf untrained.
Bring me back, let me come back,
for you are the LORD my God.
19 For after I had turned away I repented;
and after I was discovered, I struck my
thigh;
I was ashamed, and I was dismayed
because I bore the disgrace of my
youth."
20 Is Ephraim my dear son?
Is he the child I delight in?
As often as I speak against him,
I still remember him.
Therefore I am deeply moved for him;
I will surely have mercy on him,
says the LORD.

21 Set up road markers for yourself,
make yourself guideposts;
consider well the highway,
the road by which you went.
Return, O virgin Israel,
return to these your cities.
22 How long will you waver,
O faithless daughter?
For the LORD has created a new thing on
the earth:
a woman encompasses*p* a man.

23 Thus says the LORD of hosts, the God of
Israel: Once more they shall use these words in
the land of Judah and in its towns when I restore
their fortunes:
"The LORD bless you, O abode of
righteousness,
O holy hill!"
24And Judah and all its towns shall live there together, and the farmers and those who wander*q*
with their flocks.
25 I will satisfy the weary,
and all who are faint I will replenish.
26 Thereupon I awoke and looked, and my
sleep was pleasant to me.

Individual Retribution

27 The days are surely coming, says the LORD,
when I will sow the house of Israel and the house
of Judah with the seed of humans and the seed of
animals. 28And just as I have watched over them

p Meaning of Heb uncertain   *q* Cn Compare Syr Vg Tg: Heb *and they shall wander*

to pluck up and break down, to overthrow, destroy, and bring evil, so I will watch over them to build and to plant, says the LORD. ²⁹In those days they shall no longer say:

> "The parents have eaten sour grapes,
>   and the children's teeth are set on
>   edge."

³⁰But all shall die for their own sins; the teeth of everyone who eats sour grapes shall be set on edge.

A New Covenant

31   The days are surely coming, says the LORD, when I will make a new covenant with the house of Israel and the house of Judah. ³²It will not be like the covenant that I made with their ancestors when I took them by the hand to bring them out of the land of Egypt—a covenant that they broke, though I was their husband,ʳ says the LORD. ³³But this is the covenant that I will make with the house of Israel after those days, says the LORD: I will put my law within them, and I will write it on their hearts; and I will be their God, and they shall

31.33–34 Law in Their Hearts

The book of Hebrews quotes this passage (Hebrews 8.8–12) in explaining why Christians no longer live by Old Testament regulations. The written law was useful, and God-given. But as the history of Israel proved, it didn't have the power to transform people's inner attitudes. Something more was needed. God would have to change his people from the inside out, putting his law into their hearts through his Holy Spirit.

be my people. ³⁴No longer shall they teach one another, or say to each other, "Know the LORD," for they shall all know me, from the least of them to the greatest, says the LORD; for I will forgive their iniquity, and remember their sin no more.

35   Thus says the LORD,
        who gives the sun for light by day
            and the fixed order of the moon and
                the stars for light by night,
        who stirs up the sea so that its waves
            roar—
        the LORD of hosts is his name:
36   If this fixed order were ever to cease
            from my presence, says the LORD,
        then also the offspring of Israel would
                cease
            to be a nation before me forever.

37   Thus says the LORD:
        If the heavens above can be measured,

and the foundations of the earth below
        can be explored,
    then I will reject all the offspring of Israel
        because of all they have done,
                                    says the LORD.

Jerusalem to Be Enlarged

38   The days are surely coming, says the LORD, when the city shall be rebuilt for the LORD from the tower of Hananel to the Corner Gate. ³⁹And the measuring line shall go out farther, straight to the hill Gareb, and shall then turn to Goah. ⁴⁰The whole valley of the dead bodies and the ashes, and all the fields as far as the Wadi Kidron, to the corner of the Horse Gate toward the east, shall be sacred to the LORD. It shall never again be uprooted or overthrown.

Jeremiah Buys a Field During the Siege

32   The word that came to Jeremiah from the LORD in the tenth year of King Zedekiah of Judah, which was the eighteenth year of Nebuchadrezzar. ²At that time the army of the king of Babylon was besieging Jerusalem, and the prophet Jeremiah was confined in the court of the guard that was in the palace of the king of Judah, ³where King Zedekiah of Judah had confined him. Zedekiah had said, "Why do you prophesy and say: Thus says the LORD: I am going to give this city into the hand of the king of Babylon, and he shall take it; ⁴King Zedekiah of Judah shall not escape out of the hands of the Chaldeans, but shall surely be given into the hands of the king of Babylon, and shall speak with him face to face and see him eye to eye; ⁵and he shall take Zedekiah to Babylon, and there he shall remain until I attend to him, says the LORD; though you fight against the Chaldeans, you shall not succeed?"

6   Jeremiah said, The word of the LORD came to me: ⁷Hanamel son of your uncle Shallum is going to come to you and say, "Buy my field that is at Anathoth, for the right of redemption by purchase is yours." ⁸Then my cousin Hanamel

32.7 Bargain Hunting

Jerusalem, under siege from the most powerful army in the world, hardly looked like a prime market for real estate. Nevertheless, God told Jeremiah to buy up family property that was presently occupied by Babylonians. Though worthless in the short run, it would grow valuable when Jeremiah's heirs returned from exile. Through his outrageous investment, Jeremiah put his money where his mouth was. He showed practical faith that God would bring his people back.

ʳ Or *master*

came to me in the court of the guard, in accordance with the word of the LORD, and said to me, "Buy my field that is at Anathoth in the land of Benjamin, for the right of possession and redemption is yours; buy it for yourself." Then I knew that this was the word of the LORD.

9 And I bought the field at Anathoth from my cousin Hanamel, and weighed out the money to him, seventeen shekels of silver. ¹⁰I signed the deed, sealed it, got witnesses, and weighed the money on scales. ¹¹Then I took the sealed deed of purchase, containing the terms and conditions, and the open copy; ¹²and I gave the deed of purchase to Baruch son of Neriah son of Mahseiah, in the presence of my cousin Hanamel, in the presence of the witnesses who signed the deed of purchase, and in the presence of all the Judeans who were sitting in the court of the guard. ¹³In their presence I charged Baruch, saying, ¹⁴Thus says the LORD of hosts, the God of Israel: Take these deeds, both this sealed deed of purchase and this open deed, and put them in an earthenware jar, in order that they may last for a long time. ¹⁵For thus says the LORD of hosts, the God of Israel: Houses and fields and vineyards shall again be bought in this land.

Jeremiah Prays for Understanding

16 After I had given the deed of purchase to Baruch son of Neriah, I prayed to the LORD, saying: ¹⁷Ah Lord GOD! It is you who made the heavens and the earth by your great power and by your outstretched arm! Nothing is too hard for you. ¹⁸You show steadfast love to the thousandth generation,⁵ but repay the guilt of parents into the laps of their children after them, O great and mighty God whose name is the LORD of hosts, ¹⁹great in counsel and mighty in deed; whose eyes are open to all the ways of mortals, rewarding all according to their ways and according to the fruit of their doings. ²⁰You showed signs and wonders in the land of Egypt, and to this day in Israel and among all humankind, and have made yourself a name that continues to this very day. ²¹You brought your people Israel out of the land of Egypt with signs and wonders, with a strong hand and outstretched arm, and with great terror; ²²and you gave them this land, which you swore to their ancestors to give them, a land flowing with milk and honey; ²³and they entered and took possession of it. But they did not obey your voice or follow your law; of all you commanded them to do, they did nothing. Therefore you have made all these disasters come upon them. ²⁴See, the siege ramps have been cast up against the city to take it, and the city, faced with sword, famine, and pestilence, has been given into the hands of the Chaldeans who are fighting against it. What you spoke has happened, as you yourself can see.

²⁵Yet you, O Lord GOD, have said to me, "Buy the field for money and get witnesses"—though the city has been given into the hands of the Chaldeans.

God's Assurance of the People's Return

26 The word of the LORD came to Jeremiah: ²⁷See, I am the LORD, the God of all flesh; is anything too hard for me? ²⁸Therefore, thus says the LORD: I am going to give this city into the hands of the Chaldeans and into the hand of King Nebuchadrezzar of Babylon, and he shall take it. ²⁹The Chaldeans who are fighting against this city shall come, set it on fire, and burn it, with the houses on whose roofs offerings have been made to Baal and libations have been poured out to other gods, to provoke me to anger. ³⁰For the people of Israel and the people of Judah have done nothing but evil in my sight from their youth; the people of Israel have done nothing but provoke me to anger by the work of their hands, says the LORD. ³¹This city has aroused my anger and wrath, from the day it was built until this day, so that I will remove it from my sight ³²because of all the evil of the people of Israel and the people of Judah that they did to provoke me to anger—they, their kings and their officials, their priests and their prophets, the citizens of Judah and the inhabitants of Jerusalem. ³³They have turned their backs to me, not their faces; though I have taught them persistently, they would not listen and accept correction. ³⁴They set up their abominations in the house that bears my name, and defiled it. ³⁵They built the high places of Baal in the valley of the son of Hinnom, to offer up their sons and daughters to Molech, though I did not command them, nor did it enter my mind that they should do this abomination, causing Judah to sin.

36 Now therefore thus says the LORD, the God of Israel, concerning this city of which you say, "It is being given into the hand of the king of Babylon by the sword, by famine, and by pestilence": ³⁷See, I am going to gather them from all the lands to which I drove them in my anger and my wrath and in great indignation; I will bring them back to this place, and I will settle them in safety. ³⁸They shall be my people, and I will be their God. ³⁹I will give them one heart and one way, that they may fear me for all time, for their own good and the good of their children after them. ⁴⁰I will make an everlasting covenant with them, never to draw back from doing good to them; and I will put the fear of me in their hearts, so that they may not turn from me. ⁴¹I will rejoice in doing good to them, and I will plant them in this land in faithfulness, with all my heart and all my soul.

42 For thus says the LORD: Just as I have brought all this great disaster upon this people, so I will bring upon them all the good fortune that

⁵ Or to thousands

I now promise them. ⁴³Fields shall be bought in this land of which you are saying, It is a desolation, without human beings or animals; it has been given into the hands of the Chaldeans.

32.40 A New Covenant

The foundation of Israel was its covenant with God. It bound both sides together on the basis of clear-cut expectations (see "The Covenant," page 98). Israel had never really lived up to the covenant, however. Here (and in 31.31–34) God promised a new covenant, far better than the old one. It would change the people's thinking. Paul amplified the contrast in 2 Corinthians 2.12–3.18. The new covenant came in Christ.

⁴⁴Fields shall be bought for money, and deeds shall be signed and sealed and witnessed, in the land of Benjamin, in the places around Jerusalem, and in the cities of Judah, of the hill country, of the Shephelah, and of the Negeb; for I will restore their fortunes, says the LORD.

Healing after Punishment

33 The word of the LORD came to Jeremiah a second time, while he was still confined in the court of the guard: ²Thus says the LORD who made the earth,^t the LORD who formed it to establish it—the LORD is his name: ³Call to me and I will answer you, and will tell you great and hidden things that you have not known. ⁴For thus says the LORD, the God of Israel, concerning the houses of this city and the houses of the kings of Judah that were torn down to make a defense against the siege ramps and before the sword:^u ⁵The Chaldeans are coming in to fight^v and to fill them with the dead bodies of those whom I shall strike down in my anger and my wrath, for I have hidden my face from this city because of all their wickedness. ⁶I am going to bring it recovery and healing; I will heal them and reveal to them abundance^u of prosperity and security. ⁷I will restore the fortunes of Judah and the fortunes of Israel, and rebuild them as they were at first. ⁸I will cleanse them from all the guilt of their sin against me, and I will forgive all the guilt of their sin and rebellion against me. ⁹And this city^w shall be to me a name of joy, a praise and a glory before all the nations of the earth who shall hear of all the good that I do for them; they shall fear and tremble because of all the good and all the prosperity I provide for it.

10 Thus says the LORD: In this place of which you say, "It is a waste without human beings or animals," in the towns of Judah and the streets of Jerusalem that are desolate, without inhabitants,

human or animal, there shall once more be heard ¹¹the voice of mirth and the voice of gladness, the voice of the bridegroom and the voice of the bride, the voices of those who sing, as they bring thank offerings to the house of the LORD:

"Give thanks to the LORD of hosts,
   for the LORD is good,
   for his steadfast love endures forever!"

For I will restore the fortunes of the land as at first, says the LORD.

12 Thus says the LORD of hosts: In this place that is waste, without human beings or animals, and in all its towns there shall again be pasture for shepherds resting their flocks. ¹³In the towns of the hill country, of the Shephelah, and of the Negeb, in the land of Benjamin, the places around Jerusalem, and in the towns of Judah, flocks shall again pass under the hands of the one who counts them, says the LORD.

The Righteous Branch and the Covenant with David

14 The days are surely coming, says the LORD, when I will fulfill the promise I made to the house of Israel and the house of Judah. ¹⁵In those days and at that time I will cause a righteous Branch to spring up for David; and he shall execute justice and righteousness in the land. ¹⁶In those days Judah will be saved and Jerusalem will live in safety. And this is the name by which it will be called: "The LORD is our righteousness."

17 For thus says the LORD: David shall never lack a man to sit on the throne of the house of Israel, ¹⁸and the levitical priests shall never lack a man in my presence to offer burnt offerings, to make grain offerings, and to make sacrifices for all time.

33.18 Unchanged Promises

Jerusalem lay in rubble, and survivors must surely have wondered whether God's covenants had been irrevocably broken. In this message through Jeremiah, God says that his promises still stand. Israel will always have an heir of David to provide leadership, and priests to lead in worship. The New Testament, and particularly the book of Hebrews, teaches that these promises are fulfilled forever in Jesus, who is both priest and king.

19 The word of the LORD came to Jeremiah: ²⁰Thus says the LORD: If any of you could break my covenant with the day and my covenant with the night, so that day and night would not come at their appointed time, ²¹only then could my covenant with my servant David be broken, so

---

^t Gk: Heb *it*   ^u Meaning of Heb uncertain   ^v Cn: Heb *They are coming in to fight against the Chaldeans*
^w Heb *And it*

that he would not have a son to reign on his throne, and my covenant with my ministers the Levites. ²²Just as the host of heaven cannot be numbered and the sands of the sea cannot be measured, so I will increase the offspring of my servant David, and the Levites who minister to me.

23 The word of the LORD came to Jeremiah: ²⁴Have you not observed how these people say, "The two families that the LORD chose have been rejected by him," and how they hold my people in such contempt that they no longer regard them as a nation? ²⁵Thus says the LORD: Only if I had not established my covenant with day and night and the ordinances of heaven and earth, ²⁶would I reject the offspring of Jacob and of my servant David and not choose any of his descendants as rulers over the offspring of Abraham, Isaac, and Jacob. For I will restore their fortunes, and will have mercy upon them.

Death in Captivity Predicted for Zedekiah

34 The word that came to Jeremiah from the LORD, when King Nebuchadrezzar of Babylon and all his army and all the kingdoms of the earth and all the peoples under his dominion were fighting against Jerusalem and all its cities: ²Thus says the LORD, the God of Israel: Go and speak to King Zedekiah of Judah and say to him: Thus says the LORD: I am going to give this city into the hand of the king of Babylon, and he shall burn it with fire. ³And you yourself shall not escape from his hand, but shall surely be captured and handed over to him; you shall see the king of Babylon eye to eye and speak with him face to face; and you shall go to Babylon. ⁴Yet hear the word of the LORD, O King Zedekiah of Judah! Thus says the LORD concerning you: You shall not die by the sword; ⁵you shall die in peace. And as spices were burned˟ for your ancestors, the earlier kings who preceded you, so they shall burn spicesʸ for you and lament for you, saying, "Alas, lord!" For I have spoken the word, says the LORD.

6 Then the prophet Jeremiah spoke all these words to Zedekiah king of Judah, in Jerusalem, ⁷when the army of the king of Babylon was fighting against Jerusalem and against all the cities of Judah that were left, Lachish and Azekah; for these were the only fortified cities of Judah that remained.

Treacherous Treatment of Slaves

8 The word that came to Jeremiah from the LORD, after King Zedekiah had made a covenant with all the people in Jerusalem to make a proclamation of liberty to them— ⁹that all should set free their Hebrew slaves, male and female, so that no one should hold another Judean in slavery. ¹⁰And they obeyed, all the officials and all the people who had entered into the covenant that all would set free their slaves, male or female, so that they would not be enslaved again; they obeyed and set them free. ¹¹But afterward they turned around and took back the male and female slaves they had set free, and brought them again into subjection as slaves. ¹²The word of the LORD came to Jeremiah from the LORD: ¹³Thus says the LORD, the God of Israel: I myself made a covenant with your ancestors when I brought them out of the land of Egypt, out of the house of slavery, saying, ¹⁴"Every seventh year each of you must set free any Hebrews who have been sold to you and have served you six years; you must set them free from your service." But your ancestors did not listen to me or incline their ears to me. ¹⁵You yourselves recently repented and did what was right in my sight by proclaiming liberty to one another, and you made a covenant before me in the house that is called by my name; ¹⁶but then you turned around and profaned my name when each of you took back your male and female slaves, whom you had set free according to their desire, and you brought them again into subjection to be your slaves. ¹⁷Therefore, thus says the LORD: You have not obeyed me by granting a release to your neighbors and friends; I am going to grant a release to you, says the LORD—a release to the sword, to pestilence, and to famine. I will make you a horror to all the kingdoms of the earth. ¹⁸And those who transgressed my covenant and did not keep the terms of the covenant that they made before me, I will make likeᶻ the calf when they cut it in two and passed between its parts: ¹⁹the officials of Judah, the officials of Jerusalem, the eunuchs, the priests, and all the people of the land who passed between the parts of the calf ²⁰shall be handed over to their enemies and to those who seek their lives. Their corpses shall become food for the birds of the air and the wild animals of the earth. ²¹And as for King Zedekiah of Judah and his officials, I will hand them over to their enemies and to those who seek their lives, to the army of the king of Babylon, which has withdrawn from you. ²²I am going to command, says the LORD, and will bring them back to this city; and they will fight against it, and take it, and burn it with fire. The towns of Judah I will make a desolation without inhabitant.

The Rechabites Commended

35 The word that came to Jeremiah from the LORD in the days of King Jehoiakim son of Josiah of Judah: ²Go to the house of the Rechabites, and speak with them, and bring them to the house of the LORD, into one of the chambers; then offer them wine to drink. ³So I took Jaazaniah son of Jeremiah son of Habazziniah, and his brothers, and all his sons, and the whole house of the Rech-

---

˟ Heb *as there was burning*   ʸ Heb *shall burn*   ᶻ Cn: Heb lacks *like*

abites. ⁴I brought them to the house of the LORD into the chamber of the sons of Hanan son of Igdaliah, the man of God, which was near the chamber of the officials, above the chamber of Maaseiah son of Shallum, keeper of the threshold. ⁵Then I set before the Rechabites pitchers full of wine, and cups; and I said to them, "Have some wine." ⁶But they answered, "We will drink no wine, for our ancestor Jonadab son of Rechab commanded us, 'You shall never drink wine, neither you nor your children; ⁷nor shall you ever build a house, or sow seed; nor shall you plant a vineyard, or even own one; but you shall live in tents all your days, that you may live many days in the land where you reside.' ⁸We have obeyed the charge of our ancestor Jonadab son of Rechab in all that he commanded us, to drink no wine all our days, ourselves, our wives, our sons, or our daughters, ⁹and not to build houses to live in. We have no vineyard or field or seed; ¹⁰but we have lived in tents, and have obeyed and done all that our ancestor Jonadab commanded us. ¹¹But when King Nebuchadrezzar of Babylon came up against the land, we said, 'Come, and let us go to Jerusa-lem for fear of the army of the Chaldeans and the army of the Arameans.' That is why we are living in Jerusalem."

12 Then the word of the LORD came to Jeremiah: ¹³Thus says the LORD of hosts, the God of Israel: Go and say to the people of Judah and the inhabitants of Jerusalem, Can you not learn a lesson and obey my words? says the LORD. ¹⁴The command has been carried out that Jonadab son of Rechab gave to his descendants to drink no wine; and they drink none to this day, for they have obeyed their ancestor's command. But I myself have spoken to you persistently, and you have not obeyed me. ¹⁵I have sent to you all my servants the prophets, sending them persistently, saying, "Turn now everyone of you from your evil way, and amend your doings, and do not go after other gods to serve them, and then you shall live in the land that I gave to you and your ancestors." But you did not incline your ear or obey me. ¹⁶The descendants of Jonadab son of Rechab have carried out the command that their ancestor gave them, but this people has not obeyed me. ¹⁷Therefore, thus says the LORD, the God of hosts,

Living Parables
Jeremiah's bizarre protests

> You did not incline your ear or obey me.
> 35.15

OCCASIONALLY THE EVENING NEWS BRINGS us word of someone's bizarre protest. Anti-military demonstrators pour pigs' blood on a sidewalk. Monks set themselves on fire. Environmental activists chain themselves to trees to protest logging. Marchers block the entrance to a nuclear power station. Such protests leave many people feeling uneasy. We can't easily imagine a serious political figure, or a respectable pastor, acting that way.

But Jeremiah's life was full of such protests, at the express command of God. He made an ox yoke and wore it everywhere until the false prophet Hananiah took it off and broke it in the temple one day. (Jeremiah prophesied Hananiah's death, and within two months he was gone.) Jeremiah's point? He wanted to emphasize the yoke of captivity the king of Babylon would put on Judah's shoulders. The story is in chapters 27–28.

On another occasion (chapter 35) Jeremiah invited a group of well-known nondrinkers into a room in the temple and offered them wine. They refused, and that made another sermon. If they could remember their vows not to drink, then why couldn't the people of Judah and Jerusalem remember the words of the living God?

Nothing Was Too Undignified

Jeremiah bought a beautiful linen sash and buried it in a hole until it was ruined (chapter 13). He invited the rulers of Jerusalem on a trip outside the city, and in the midst of a sermon about God's anger smashed a pot to smithereens (chapter 19). And in his most famous "enacted parable," Jeremiah bought a farm while the Babylonian army was knocking at Jerusalem's door (chapter 32). He might as well have been a Jew buying property within a German concentration camp during World War II, for all the hope he had of using it. But his action demonstrated bold hope. Someday his family would farm there again.

Why such weird activity? It says less about Jeremiah than it does about the God who gave the orders. God would not let go of his people until he had done all in his power to turn them around. Nothing was too undignified; no carnival ploy was too corny. So long as he had the slightest hope of breaking through to them, he would keep shouting.

Life Questions: How does God get through to you? Does he use dramatic means like Jeremiah's or quieter methods?

the God of Israel: I am going to bring on Judah and on all the inhabitants of Jerusalem every disaster that I have pronounced against them; because I have spoken to them and they have not listened, I have called to them and they have not answered.

35.14 Teetotalers

The Rechabites had a family tradition of not drinking, and nothing Jeremiah said or did could budge them from it. He made their tenacity the basis of a sermon. If family traditions are carried on for generations, why not God's traditions?

18 But to the house of the Rechabites Jeremiah said: Thus says the LORD of hosts, the God of Israel: Because you have obeyed the command of your ancestor Jonadab, and kept all his precepts, and done all that he commanded you, ¹⁹therefore thus says the LORD of hosts, the God of Israel: Jonadab son of Rechab shall not lack a descendant to stand before me for all time.

The Scroll Read in the Temple

36 In the fourth year of King Jehoiakim son of Josiah of Judah, this word came to Jeremiah from the LORD: ²Take a scroll and write on it all the words that I have spoken to you against Israel and Judah and all the nations, from the day I spoke to you, from the days of Josiah until today. ³It may be that when the house of Judah hears of all the disasters that I intend to do to them, all of them may turn from their evil ways, so that I may forgive their iniquity and their sin.

4 Then Jeremiah called Baruch son of Neriah, and Baruch wrote on a scroll at Jeremiah's dictation all the words of the LORD that he had spoken to him. ⁵And Jeremiah ordered Baruch, saying, "I am prevented from entering the house of the LORD; ⁶so you go yourself, and on a fast day in the hearing of the people in the LORD's house you shall read the words of the LORD from the scroll that you have written at my dictation. You shall read them also in the hearing of all the people of Judah who come up from their towns. ⁷It may be that their plea will come before the LORD, and that all of them will turn from their evil ways, for great is the anger and wrath that the LORD has pronounced against this people." ⁸And Baruch son of Neriah did all that the prophet Jeremiah ordered him about reading from the scroll the words of the LORD in the LORD's house.

9 In the fifth year of King Jehoiakim son of Josiah of Judah, in the ninth month, all the people in Jerusalem and all the people who came from the towns of Judah to Jerusalem proclaimed a fast before the LORD. ¹⁰Then, in the hearing of all the people, Baruch read the words of Jeremiah from the scroll, in the house of the LORD, in the chamber of Gemariah son of Shaphan the secretary, which was in the upper court, at the entry of the New Gate of the LORD's house.

The Scroll Read in the Palace

11 When Micaiah son of Gemariah son of Shaphan heard all the words of the LORD from the scroll, ¹²he went down to the king's house, into the secretary's chamber; and all the officials were sitting there: Elishama the secretary, Delaiah son of Shemaiah, Elnathan son of Achbor, Gemariah son of Shaphan, Zedekiah son of Hananiah, and all the officials. ¹³And Micaiah told them all the words that he had heard, when Baruch read the scroll in the hearing of the people. ¹⁴Then all the officials sent Jehudi son of Nethaniah son of Shelemiah son of Cushi to say to Baruch, "Bring the scroll that you read in the hearing of the people, and come." So Baruch son of Neriah took the scroll in his hand and came to them. ¹⁵And they said to him, "Sit down and read it to us." So Baruch read it to them. ¹⁶When they heard all the words, they turned to one another in alarm, and said to Baruch, "We certainly must report all these words to the king." ¹⁷Then they questioned Baruch, "Tell us now, how did you write all these words? Was it at his dictation?" ¹⁸Baruch answered them, "He dictated all these words to me, and I wrote them with ink on the scroll." ¹⁹Then the officials said to Baruch, "Go and hide, you and Jeremiah, and let no one know where you are."

Jehoiakim Burns the Scroll

20 Leaving the scroll in the chamber of Elishama the secretary, they went to the court of the king; and they reported all the words to the king. ²¹Then the king sent Jehudi to get the scroll, and he took it from the chamber of Elishama the secretary; and Jehudi read it to the king and all the officials who stood beside the king. ²²Now the king was sitting in his winter apartment (it was the ninth month), and there was a fire burning in the brazier before him. ²³As Jehudi read three or four columns, the king[a] would cut them off with a penknife and throw them into the fire in the brazier, until the entire scroll was consumed in the fire that was in the brazier. ²⁴Yet neither the king, nor any of his servants who heard all these words, was alarmed, nor did they tear their garments. ²⁵Even when Elnathan and Delaiah and Gemariah urged the king not to burn the scroll, he would not listen to them. ²⁶And the king commanded Jerahmeel the king's son and Seraiah son of Azriel and Shelemiah son of Abdeel to arrest

a Heb he

the secretary Baruch and the prophet Jeremiah. But the LORD hid them.

Jeremiah Dictates Another

27 Now, after the king had burned the scroll with the words that Baruch wrote at Jeremiah's dictation, the word of the LORD came to Jeremiah: 28Take another scroll and write on it all the former words that were in the first scroll, which King Jehoiakim of Judah has burned. 29And concerning King Jehoiakim of Judah you shall say: Thus says the LORD, You have dared to burn this scroll, saying, Why have you written in it that the king of Babylon will certainly come and destroy this land, and will cut off from it human beings and animals? 30Therefore thus says the LORD concerning King Jehoiakim of Judah: He shall have no one to sit upon the throne of David, and his dead body shall be cast out to the heat by day and the frost by night. 31And I will punish him and his offspring and his servants for their iniquity; I will bring on them, and on the inhabitants of Jerusalem, and on the people of Judah, all the disasters with which I have threatened them—but they would not listen.

32 Then Jeremiah took another scroll and gave it to the secretary Baruch son of Neriah, who wrote on it at Jeremiah's dictation all the words of the scroll that King Jehoiakim of Judah had burned in the fire; and many similar words were added to them.

Zedekiah's Vain Hope

37 Zedekiah son of Josiah, whom King Nebuchadrezzar of Babylon made king in the land of Judah, succeeded Coniah son of Jehoiakim. 2But neither he nor his servants nor the people of the land listened to the words of the LORD that he spoke through the prophet Jeremiah.

3 King Zedekiah sent Jehucal son of Shelemiah and the priest Zephaniah son of Maaseiah to the prophet Jeremiah saying, "Please pray for us to the LORD our God." 4Now Jeremiah was still going in and out among the people, for he had not yet been put in prison. 5Meanwhile, the army of Pharaoh had come out of Egypt; and when the Chaldeans who were besieging Jerusalem heard news of them, they withdrew from Jerusalem.

6 Then the word of the LORD came to the prophet Jeremiah: 7Thus says the LORD, God of Israel: This is what the two of you shall say to the king of Judah, who sent you to me to inquire of me: Pharaoh's army, which set out to help you, is going to return to its own land, to Egypt. 8And the Chaldeans shall return and fight against this city; they shall take it and burn it with fire. 9Thus says the LORD: Do not deceive yourselves, saying, "The Chaldeans will surely go away from us," for they will not go away. 10Even if you defeated the

whole army of Chaldeans who are fighting against you, and there remained of them only wounded men in their tents, they would rise up and burn this city with fire.

Jeremiah Is Imprisoned

11 Now when the Chaldean army had withdrawn from Jerusalem at the approach of Pharaoh's army, 12Jeremiah set out from Jerusalem to go to the land of Benjamin to receive his share of property[b] among the people there. 13When he reached the Benjamin Gate, a sentinel there

37.5 The Siege Lifted

Israel was a small nation, hemmed in by bigger powers such as Egypt and Babylon. Israelite kings often attempted to keep their independence by playing off the big powers against each other. King Zedekiah tried to get Egypt to intervene against Babylon, and during this brief period it seemed he had succeeded. Because the Egyptian army marched out, Nebuchadnezzar lifted his siege of Jerusalem. Jeremiah, who had warned that this foreign policy must ultimately fail, was arrested for treason.

named Irijah son of Shelemiah son of Hananiah arrested the prophet Jeremiah saying, "You are deserting to the Chaldeans." 14And Jeremiah said, "That is a lie; I am not deserting to the Chaldeans." But Irijah would not listen to him, and arrested Jeremiah and brought him to the officials. 15The officials were enraged at Jeremiah, and they beat him and imprisoned him in the house of the secretary Jonathan, for it had been made a prison. 16Thus Jeremiah was put in the cistern house, in the cells, and remained there many days.

17 Then King Zedekiah sent for him, and received him. The king questioned him secretly in his house, and said, "Is there any word from the LORD?" Jeremiah said, "There is!" Then he said, "You shall be handed over to the king of Babylon." 18Jeremiah also said to King Zedekiah, "What wrong have I done to you or your servants or this people, that you have put me in prison? 19Where are your prophets who prophesied to you, saying, 'The king of Babylon will not come against you and against this land'? 20Now please hear me, my lord king: be good enough to listen to my plea, and do not send me back to the house of the secretary Jonathan to die there." 21So King Zedekiah gave orders, and they committed Jeremiah to the court of the guard; and a loaf of bread was given him daily from the bakers' street, until all the bread of the city was gone. So Jeremiah remained in the court of the guard.

[b] Meaning of Heb uncertain

Jeremiah in the Cistern

38 Now Shephatiah son of Mattan, Gedaliah son of Pashhur, Jucal son of Shelemiah, and Pashhur son of Malchiah heard the words that Jeremiah was saying to all the people, ²Thus says the LORD, Those who stay in this city shall die by the sword, by famine, and by pestilence; but those who go out to the Chaldeans shall live; they shall have their lives as a prize of war, and live. ³Thus says the LORD, This city shall surely be handed over to the army of the king of Babylon and be taken. ⁴Then the officials said to the king, "This man ought to be put to death, because he is discouraging the soldiers who are left in this city, and all the people, by speaking such words to them. For this man is not seeking the welfare of this people, but their harm." ⁵King Zedekiah said, "Here he is; he is in your hands; for the king is powerless against you." ⁶So they took Jeremiah and threw him into the cistern of Malchiah, the king's son, which was in the court of the guard, letting Jeremiah down by ropes. Now there was no water in the cistern, but only mud, and Jeremiah sank in the mud.

Jeremiah Is Rescued by Ebed-melech

7 Ebed-melech the Ethiopian,ᶜ a eunuch in the king's house, heard that they had put Jeremiah into the cistern. The king happened to be sitting at the Benjamin Gate, ⁸So Ebed-melech left the king's house and spoke to the king, ⁹"My lord king, these men have acted wickedly in all they did to the prophet Jeremiah by throwing him into the cistern to die there of hunger, for there is no

38.9 Close to Death

Jeremiah was arrested during the long, final siege of Jerusalem—a time when food became so short some Israelites resorted to cannibalism. Imprisoned at the bottom of an empty cistern, the prophet could easily have starved to death. Interestingly, only a foreigner cared enough to go to the king and convince him to let Jeremiah out. For this, Ebed-melech received a special message from God (39.15–18).

bread left in the city." ¹⁰Then the king commanded Ebed-melech the Ethiopian,ᶜ "Take three men with you from here, and pull the prophet Jeremiah up from the cistern before he dies." ¹¹So Ebed-melech took the men with him and went to the house of the king, to a wardrobe ofᵈ the storehouse, and took from there old rags and worn-out clothes, which he let down to Jeremiah in the cistern by ropes. ¹²Then Ebed-melech the Ethiopianᶜ said to Jeremiah, "Just put the rags and clothes between your armpits and the ropes." Jeremiah did so. ¹³Then they drew Jeremiah up by the ropes and pulled him out of the cistern. And Jeremiah remained in the court of the guard.

Zedekiah Consults Jeremiah Again

14 King Zedekiah sent for the prophet Jeremiah and received him at the third entrance of the temple of the LORD. The king said to Jeremiah, "I have something to ask you; do not hide anything from me." ¹⁵Jeremiah said to Zedekiah, "If I tell you, you will put me to death, will you not? And if I give you advice, you will not listen to me." ¹⁶So King Zedekiah swore an oath in secret to Jeremiah, "As the LORD lives, who gave us our lives, I will not put you to death or hand you over to these men who seek your life."

17 Then Jeremiah said to Zedekiah, "Thus says the LORD, the God of hosts, the God of Israel, If you will only surrender to the officials of the king of Babylon, then your life shall be spared, and this city shall not be burned with fire, and you and your house shall live. ¹⁸But if you do not surrender to the officials of the king of Babylon, then this city shall be handed over to the Chaldeans, and they shall burn it with fire, and you yourself shall not escape from their hand." ¹⁹King Zedekiah said to Jeremiah, "I am afraid of the Judeans who have deserted to the Chaldeans, for I might be handed over to them and they would abuse me." ²⁰Jeremiah said, "That will not happen. Just obey the voice of the LORD in what I say to you, and it shall go well with you, and your life shall be spared. ²¹But if you are determined not to surrender, this is what the LORD has shown me—
²²a vision of all the women remaining in the house of the king of Judah being led out to the officials of the king of Babylon and saying,

'Your trusted friends have seduced you
    and have overcome you;
Now that your feet are stuck in the mud,
    they desert you.'
²³All your wives and your children shall be led out to the Chaldeans, and you yourself shall not escape from their hand, but shall be seized by the king of Babylon; and this city shall be burned with fire."

24 Then Zedekiah said to Jeremiah, "Do not let anyone else know of this conversation, or you will die. ²⁵If the officials should hear that I have spoken with you, and they should come and say to you, 'Just tell us what you said to the king; do not conceal it from us, or we will put you to death. What did the king say to you?' ²⁶then you shall say to them, 'I was presenting my plea to the king not to send me back to the house of Jonathan to die there.'" ²⁷All the officials did come to Jeremiah and questioned him; and he answered

ᶜ Or *Nubian*; Heb *Cushite*   ᵈ Cn: Heb *to under*

them in the very words the king had commanded. So they stopped questioning him, for the conversation had not been overheard. ²⁸And Jeremiah remained in the court of the guard until the day that Jerusalem was taken.

The Fall of Jerusalem

39 In the ninth year of King Zedekiah of Judah, in the tenth month, King Nebuchadrezzar of Babylon and all his army came against Jerusalem and besieged it; ²in the eleventh year of Zedekiah, in the fourth month, on the ninth day of the month, a breach was made in the city. ³When Jerusalem was taken,ᵉ all the officials of the king of Babylon came and sat in the middle gate: Nergal-sharezer, Samgar-nebo, Sarsechim the Rabsaris, Nergal-sharezer the Rabmag, with all the rest of the officials of the king of Babylon. ⁴When King Zedekiah of Judah and all the soldiers saw them, they fled, going out of the city at night by way of the king's garden through the gate between the two walls; and they went toward the Arabah. ⁵But the army of the Chaldeans pursued them, and overtook Zedekiah in the plains of Jericho; and when they had taken him, they brought him up to King Nebuchadrezzar of Babylon, at Riblah, in the land of Hamath; and he passed sentence on him. ⁶The king of Babylon slaughtered the sons of Zedekiah at Riblah before his eyes; also the king of Babylon slaughtered all the nobles of Judah. ⁷He put out the eyes of Zedekiah, and bound him in fetters to take him to Babylon. ⁸The Chaldeans burned the king's house and the houses of the people, and broke down the walls of Jerusalem. ⁹Then Nebuzaradan the captain of the guard exiled to Babylon the rest of the people who were left in the city, those who had deserted to him, and the people who remained. ¹⁰Nebuzaradan the captain of the guard left in the land of Judah some of the poor people who owned nothing, and gave them vineyards and fields at the same time.

Jeremiah, Set Free, Remembers Ebed-melech

11 King Nebuchadrezzar of Babylon gave command concerning Jeremiah through Nebuzaradan, the captain of the guard, saying, ¹²"Take him, look after him well and do him no harm, but deal with him as he may ask you." ¹³So Nebuzaradan the captain of the guard, Nebushazban the Rabsaris, Nergal-sharezer the Rabmag, and all the chief officers of the king of Babylon sent ¹⁴and took Jeremiah from the court of the guard. They entrusted him to Gedaliah son of Ahikam son of Shaphan to be brought home. So he stayed with his own people.

15 The word of the LORD came to Jeremiah while he was confined in the court of the guard:

¹⁶Go and say to Ebed-melech the Ethiopian:ᶠ Thus says the LORD of hosts, the God of Israel: I am going to fulfill my words against this city for evil and not for good, and they shall be accomplished in your presence on that day. ¹⁷But I will

39.12 Influential Prisoner

Jeremiah's message of doom made him unpopular in Jerusalem but evidently impressed the conquering Babylonians. The highest officials knew about the prophet and gave explicit instructions to see that he was not hurt. Later they offered him his freedom (40.4).

save you on that day, says the LORD, and you shall not be handed over to those whom you dread. ¹⁸For I will surely save you, and you shall not fall by the sword; but you shall have your life as a prize of war, because you have trusted in me, says the LORD.

Jeremiah with Gedaliah the Governor

40 The word that came to Jeremiah from the LORD after Nebuzaradan the captain of the guard had let him go from Ramah, when he took him bound in fetters along with all the captives of Jerusalem and Judah who were being exiled to Babylon. ²The captain of the guard took Jeremiah and said to him, "The LORD your God threatened this place with this disaster; ³and now the LORD has brought it about, and has done as he said, because all of you sinned against the LORD and did not obey his voice. Therefore this thing has come upon you. ⁴Now look, I have just released you today from the fetters on your hands. If you wish to come with me to Babylon, come, and I will take good care of you; but if you do not wish to come with me to Babylon, you need not come. See, the whole land is before you; go wherever you think it good and right to go. ⁵If you remain,ᵍ then return to Gedaliah son of Ahikam son of Shaphan, whom the king of Babylon appointed governor of the towns of Judah, and stay with him among the people; or go wherever you think it right to go." So the captain of the guard gave him an allowance of food and a present, and let him go. ⁶Then Jeremiah went to Gedaliah son of Ahikam at Mizpah, and stayed with him among the people who were left in the land.

7 When all the leaders of the forces in the open country and their troops heard that the king of Babylon had appointed Gedaliah son of Ahikam governor in the land, and had committed to him men, women, and children, those of the poorest of the land who had not been taken into exile to Babylon, ⁸they went to Gedaliah at

---

ᵉ This clause has been transposed from 38.28   ᶠ Or *Nubian*; Heb *Cushite*   ᵍ Syr: Meaning of Heb uncertain

Mizpah—Ishmael son of Nethaniah, Johanan son of Kareah, Seraiah son of Tanhumeth, the sons of Ephai the Netophathite, Jezaniah son of the Maacathite, they and their troops. [9]Gedaliah son of Ahikam son of Shaphan swore to them and their troops, saying, "Do not be afraid to serve the Chaldeans. Stay in the land and serve the king of Babylon, and it shall go well with you. [10]As for me, I am staying at Mizpah to represent you before the Chaldeans who come to us; but as for you, gather wine and summer fruits and oil, and store them in your vessels, and live in the towns that you have taken over." [11]Likewise, when all the Judeans who were in Moab and among the Ammonites and in Edom and in other lands heard that the king of Babylon had left a remnant in Judah and had appointed Gedaliah son of Ahikam son of Shaphan as governor over them, [12]then all the Judeans returned from all the places to which they had been scattered and came to the land of Judah, to Gedaliah at Mizpah; and they gathered wine and summer fruits in great abundance.

40.12 False Hopes

The Babylonians, once they had captured rebel Jerusalem, left some of the common people behind under a governor. When other Jews scattered in the region heard news of this, they came home and gathered an excellent harvest—undoubtedly from fields the exiles had left behind. But even this small nucleus of Jews was to be scattered—this time due to local political infighting.

13 Now Johanan son of Kareah and all the leaders of the forces in the open country came to Gedaliah at Mizpah [14]and said to him, "Are you at all aware that Baalis king of the Ammonites has sent Ishmael son of Nethaniah to take your life?" But Gedaliah son of Ahikam would not believe them. [15]Then Johanan son of Kareah spoke secretly to Gedaliah at Mizpah, "Please let me go and kill Ishmael son of Nethaniah, and no one else will know. Why should he take your life, so that all the Judeans who are gathered around you would be scattered, and the remnant of Judah would perish?" [16]But Gedaliah son of Ahikam said to Johanan son of Kareah, "Do not do such a thing, for you are telling a lie about Ishmael."

Insurrection against Gedaliah

41 In the seventh month, Ishmael son of Nethaniah son of Elishama, of the royal family, one of the chief officers of the king, came with ten men to Gedaliah son of Ahikam, at Mizpah. As they ate bread together there at Mizpah, [2]Ishmael son of Nethaniah and the ten men with him got up and struck down Gedaliah son of Ahikam son of Shaphan with the sword and killed him, because the king of Babylon had appointed him governor in the land. [3]Ishmael also killed all the Judeans who were with Gedaliah at Mizpah, and the Chaldean soldiers who happened to be there.

4 On the day after the murder of Gedaliah, before anyone knew of it, [5]eighty men arrived from Shechem and Shiloh and Samaria, with their beards shaved and their clothes torn, and their bodies gashed, bringing grain offerings and incense to present at the temple of the LORD. [6]And Ishmael son of Nethaniah came out from Mizpah to meet them, weeping as he came. As he met them, he said to them, "Come to Gedaliah son of Ahikam." [7]When they reached the middle of the city, Ishmael son of Nethaniah and the men with him slaughtered them, and threw them[h] into a cistern. [8]But there were ten men among them who said to Ishmael, "Do not kill us, for we have stores of wheat, barley, oil, and honey hidden in the fields." So he refrained, and did not kill them along with their companions.

9 Now the cistern into which Ishmael had thrown all the bodies of the men whom he had struck down was the large cistern[i] that King Asa had made for defense against King Baasha of Israel; Ishmael son of Nethaniah filled that cistern with those whom he had killed. [10]Then Ishmael took captive all the rest of the people who were in Mizpah, the king's daughters and all the people who were left at Mizpah, whom Nebuzaradan, the captain of the guard, had committed to Gedaliah son of Ahikam. Ishmael son of Nethaniah took them captive and set out to cross over to the Ammonites.

11 But when Johanan son of Kareah and all the leaders of the forces with him heard of all the crimes that Ishmael son of Nethaniah had done, [12]they took all their men and went to fight against Ishmael son of Nethaniah. They came upon him at the great pool that is in Gibeon. [13]And when all the people who were with Ishmael saw Johanan son of Kareah and all the leaders of the forces with him, they were glad. [14]So all the people whom Ishmael had carried away captive from Mizpah turned around and came back, and went to Johanan son of Kareah. [15]But Ishmael son of Nethaniah escaped from Johanan with eight men, and went to the Ammonites. [16]Then Johanan son of Kareah and all the leaders of the forces with him took all the rest of the people whom Ishmael son of Nethaniah had carried away captive[j] from Mizpah after he had slain Gedaliah son of Ahikam—soldiers, women, children, and eunuchs, whom Johanan brought back from Gibe-

---

h Syr: Heb lacks *and threw them*; compare verse 9   *i* Gk: Heb *whom he had killed by the hand of Gedaliah*
j Cn: Heb *whom he recovered from Ishmael son of Nethaniah*

on.*k* ¹⁷And they set out, and stopped at Geruth Chimham near Bethlehem, intending to go to Egypt ¹⁸because of the Chaldeans; for they were afraid of them, because Ishmael son of Nethaniah had killed Gedaliah son of Ahikam, whom the king of Babylon had made governor over the land.

Jeremiah Advises Survivors Not to Migrate

42 Then all the commanders of the forces, and Johanan son of Kareah and Azariah*l* son of Hoshaiah, and all the people from the least to the greatest, approached ²the prophet Jeremiah and said, "Be good enough to listen to our plea, and pray to the LORD your God for us—for all this remnant. For there are only a few of us left out of many, as your eyes can see. ³Let the LORD your God show us where we should go and what we should do." ⁴The prophet Jeremiah said to them, "Very well: I am going to pray to the LORD your God as you request, and whatever the LORD answers you I will tell you; I will keep nothing back from you." ⁵They in their turn said to Jeremiah, "May the LORD be a true and faithful witness against us if we do not act according to everything that the LORD your God sends us through you. ⁶Whether it is good or bad, we will obey the voice of the LORD our God to whom we are sending you, in order that it may go well with us when we obey the voice of the LORD our God."

7 At the end of ten days the word of the LORD came to Jeremiah. ⁸Then he summoned Johanan son of Kareah and all the commanders of the forces who were with him, and all the people from the least to the greatest, ⁹and said to them, "Thus says the LORD, the God of Israel, to whom you sent me to present your plea before him: ¹⁰If you will only remain in this land, then I will build you up and not pull you down; I will plant you, and not pluck you up; for I am sorry for the disaster that I have brought upon you. ¹¹Do not be afraid of the king of Babylon, as you have been; do not be afraid of him, says the LORD, for I am with you, to save you and to rescue you from his hand. ¹²I will grant you mercy, and he will have mercy on you and restore you to your native soil. ¹³But if you continue to say, 'We will not stay in this land,' thus disobeying the voice of the LORD your God ¹⁴and saying, 'No, we will go to the land of Egypt, where we shall not see war, or hear the sound of the trumpet, or be hungry for bread, and there we will stay,' ¹⁵then hear the word of the LORD, O remnant of Judah. Thus says the LORD of hosts, the God of Israel: If you are determined to enter Egypt and go to settle there, ¹⁶then the sword that you fear shall overtake you there, in the land of Egypt; and the famine that you dread shall follow close after you into Egypt; and there you shall die. ¹⁷All the people who have determined to go to Egypt to settle there shall die by the sword, by famine, and by pestilence; they shall have no remnant or survivor from the disaster that I am bringing upon them.

18 "For thus says the LORD of hosts, the God of Israel: Just as my anger and my wrath were poured out on the inhabitants of Jerusalem, so my wrath will be poured out on you when you go to Egypt. You shall become an object of execration and horror, of cursing and ridicule. You shall see this place no more. ¹⁹The LORD has said to you, O remnant of Judah, Do not go to Egypt. Be well aware that I have warned you today ²⁰that you have made a fatal mistake. For you yourselves sent me to the LORD your God, saying, 'Pray for us to the LORD our God, and whatever the LORD our God says, tell us and we will do it.' ²¹So I have told you today, but you have not obeyed the voice of the LORD your God in anything that he sent me to tell you. ²²Be well aware, then, that you shall die by the sword, by famine, and by pestilence in the place where you desire to go and settle."

Taken to Egypt, Jeremiah Warns of Judgment

43 When Jeremiah finished speaking to all the people all these words of the LORD their God, with which the LORD their God had sent him to them, ²Azariah son of Hoshaiah and Johanan son of Kareah and all the other insolent men said to Jeremiah, "You are telling a lie. The LORD our God did not send you to say, 'Do not go to Egypt to settle there'; ³but Baruch son of Neriah is inciting you against us, to hand us over to the Chaldeans, in order that they may kill us or take us into

43.3 Closed Minds

Jeremiah was kidnapped by the few Israelites remaining in Jerusalem. Fearful that the Babylonians would blame them for the governor's murder, they took Jeremiah with them as they headed for Egypt. They stopped near Bethlehem to ask Jeremiah if they were doing the right thing. When he told them God wanted them to go back, they called him a liar. Jeremiah was disbelieved from the beginning to the end of his ministry, even by those who had seen some of his predictions come true.

exile in Babylon." ⁴So Johanan son of Kareah and all the commanders of the forces and all the people did not obey the voice of the LORD, to stay in the land of Judah. ⁵But Johanan son of Kareah and all the commanders of the forces took all the remnant of Judah who had returned to settle in the land of Judah from all the nations to which they had been driven— ⁶the men, the women, the

---

k Meaning of Heb uncertain   *l* Gk: Heb *Jezaniah*

children, the princesses, and everyone whom Nebuzaradan the captain of the guard had left with Gedaliah son of Ahikam son of Shaphan; also the prophet Jeremiah and Baruch son of Neriah. 7And they came into the land of Egypt, for they did not obey the voice of the LORD. And they arrived at Tahpanhes.

8 Then the word of the LORD came to Jeremiah in Tahpanhes: 9Take some large stones in your hands, and bury them in the clay pavement*m* that is at the entrance to Pharaoh's palace in Tahpanhes. Let the Judeans see you do it, 10and say to them, Thus says the LORD of hosts, the God of Israel: I am going to send and take my servant King Nebuchadrezzar of Babylon, and he*n* will set his throne above these stones that I have buried, and he will spread his royal canopy over them. 11He shall come and ravage the land of Egypt, giving

those who are destined for pestilence, to pestilence,
and those who are destined for captivity, to captivity,
and those who are destined for the sword, to the sword.

12He*o* shall kindle a fire in the temples of the gods of Egypt; and he shall burn them and carry them away captive; and he shall pick clean the land of Egypt, as a shepherd picks his cloak clean of vermin; and he shall depart from there safely. 13He shall break the obelisks of Heliopolis, which is in the land of Egypt; and the temples of the gods of Egypt he shall burn with fire.

Denunciation of Persistent Idolatry

44 The word that came to Jeremiah for all the Judeans living in the land of Egypt, at Migdol, at Tahpanhes, at Memphis and in the land of Pathros, 2Thus says the LORD of hosts, the God of Israel: You yourselves have seen all the disaster that I have brought on Jerusalem and on all the towns of Judah. Look at them; today they are a desolation, without an inhabitant in them, 3because of the wickedness that they committed, provoking me to anger, in that they went to make offerings and serve other gods that they had not known, neither they, nor you, nor your ancestors. 4Yet I persistently sent to you all my servants the prophets, saying, "I beg you not to do this abominable thing that I hate!" 5But they did not listen or incline their ear, to turn from their wickedness and make no offerings to other gods. 6So my wrath and my anger were poured out and kindled in the towns of Judah and in the streets of Jerusalem; and they became a waste and a desolation, as they still are today. 7And now thus says the LORD God of hosts, the God of Israel: Why are you doing such great harm to yourselves, to cut off

man and woman, child and infant, from the midst of Judah, leaving yourselves without a remnant? 8Why do you provoke me to anger with the works of your hands, making offerings to other gods in the land of Egypt where you have come to settle? Will you be cut off and become an object of cursing and ridicule among all the nations of the earth? 9Have you forgotten the crimes of your ancestors, of the kings of Judah, of their*p* wives, your own crimes and those of your wives, which they committed in the land of Judah and in the streets of Jerusalem? 10They have shown no contrition or fear to this day, nor have they walked in my law and my statutes that I set before you and before your ancestors.

11 Therefore thus says the LORD of hosts, the God of Israel: I am determined to bring disaster on you, to bring all Judah to an end. 12I will take the remnant of Judah who are determined to come to the land of Egypt to settle, and they shall perish, everyone; in the land of Egypt they shall fall; by the sword and by famine they shall perish; from the least to the greatest, they shall die by the sword and by famine; and they shall become an object of execration and horror, of cursing and ridicule. 13I will punish those who live in the land of Egypt, as I have punished Jerusalem, with the sword, with famine, and with pestilence, 14so that none of the remnant of Judah who have come to settle in the land of Egypt shall escape or survive or return to the land of Judah. Although they long to go back to live there, they shall not go back, except some fugitives.

15 Then all the men who were aware that their wives had been making offerings to other gods, and all the women who stood by, a great assembly, all the people who lived in Pathros in the land of Egypt, answered Jeremiah: 16"As for the word that you have spoken to us in the name of the LORD, we are not going to listen to you. 17Instead, we will do everything that we have vowed, make offerings to the queen of heaven and pour out libations to her, just as we and our ancestors, our kings and our officials, used to do in the towns of Judah and in the streets of Jerusalem. We used to have plenty of food, and prospered, and saw no misfortune. 18But from the time we stopped making offerings to the queen of heaven and pouring out libations to her, we have lacked everything and have perished by the sword and by famine." 19And the women said,*q* "Indeed we will go on making offerings to the queen of heaven and pouring out libations to her; do you think that we made cakes for her, marked with her image, and poured out libations to her without our husbands' being involved?"

20 Then Jeremiah said to all the people, men and women, all the people who were giving him

m Meaning of Heb uncertain   *n* Gk Syr: Heb I   *o* Gk Syr Vg: Heb I   *p* Heb *his*
And the women said   *q* Compare Syr: Heb lacks

this answer: [21]"As for the offerings that you made in the towns of Judah and in the streets of Jerusalem, you and your ancestors, your kings and your officials, and the people of the land, did not the

44.18 Queen of Heaven

"Queen of heaven" was a title for Ishtar, a Babylonian goddess of fertility. Israelites—women especially—had worshiped her for a very long time, until the revival sparked by King Josiah put a stop to the practice (2 Kings 22). Now, about 35 years after Josiah's campaign, Israelites blamed their downfall on his reform. Jeremiah tried to set the record straight: It was persistence in pagan worship that had led to their destruction.

LORD remember them? Did it not come into his mind? [22]The LORD could no longer bear the sight of your evil doings, the abominations that you committed; therefore your land became a desolation and a waste and a curse, without inhabitant, as it is to this day. [23]It is because you burned offerings, and because you sinned against the LORD and did not obey the voice of the LORD or walk in his law and in his statutes and in his decrees, that this disaster has befallen you, as is still evident today."

[24] Jeremiah said to all the people and all the women, "Hear the word of the LORD, all you Judeans who are in the land of Egypt, [25]Thus says the LORD of hosts, the God of Israel: You and your wives have accomplished in deeds what you declared in words, saying, 'We are determined to perform the vows that we have made, to make offerings to the queen of heaven and to pour out libations to her.' By all means, keep your vows and make your libations! [26]Therefore hear the word of the LORD, all you Judeans who live in the land of Egypt: Lo, I swear by my great name, says the LORD, that my name shall no longer be pronounced on the lips of any of the people of Judah in all the land of Egypt, saying, 'As the Lord GOD lives.' [27]I am going to watch over them for harm and not for good; all the people of Judah who are in the land of Egypt shall perish by the sword and by famine, until not one is left. [28]And those who escape the sword shall return from the land of Egypt to the land of Judah, few in number; and all the remnant of Judah, who have come to the land of Egypt to settle, shall know whose words will stand, mine or theirs! [29]This shall be the sign to you, says the LORD, that I am going to punish you in this place, in order that you may know that my words against you will surely be carried out: [30]Thus says the LORD, I am going to give Pharaoh Hophra, king of Egypt, into the hands of his enemies, those who seek his life, just as I gave King

Zedekiah of Judah into the hand of King Nebuchadrezzar of Babylon, his enemy who sought his life."

A Word of Comfort to Baruch

45 The word that the prophet Jeremiah spoke to Baruch son of Neriah, when he wrote these words in a scroll at the dictation of Jeremiah, in the fourth year of King Jehoiakim son of Josiah of Judah: [2]Thus says the LORD, the God of Israel, to you, O Baruch: [3]You said, "Woe is me! The LORD has added sorrow to my pain; I am weary with my groaning, and I find no rest." [4]Thus you shall say to him, "Thus says the LORD: I am going to break down what I have built, and pluck up what I have planted—that is, the whole land. [5]And you, do you seek great things for yourself? Do not seek them; for I am going to bring disaster upon all flesh, says the LORD; but I will give you your life as a prize of war in every place to which you may go."

Judgment on Egypt

46 The word of the LORD that came to the prophet Jeremiah concerning the nations.

2 Concerning Egypt, about the army of Pharaoh Neco, king of Egypt, which was by the river Euphrates at Carchemish and which King Nebuchadrezzar of Babylon defeated in the fourth year of King Jehoiakim son of Josiah of Judah:

3   Prepare buckler and shield,
    and advance for battle!
4   Harness the horses;
    mount the steeds!
  Take your stations with your helmets,
    whet your lances,
    put on your coats of mail!
5   Why do I see them terrified?
    They have fallen back;
  their warriors are beaten down,
    and have fled in haste.
  They do not look back—
    terror is all around!
                says the LORD.
6   The swift cannot flee away,
    nor can the warrior escape;
  in the north by the river Euphrates
    they have stumbled and fallen.

7   Who is this, rising like the Nile,
    like rivers whose waters surge?
8   Egypt rises like the Nile,
    like rivers whose waters surge.
  It said, Let me rise, let me cover the
    earth,
    let me destroy cities and their
      inhabitants.
9   Advance, O horses,
    and dash madly, O chariots!
  Let the warriors go forth:

Ethiopia[r] and Put who carry
the shield,
the Ludim, who draw[s] the bow.
10 That day is the day of the Lord GOD of
hosts,
a day of retribution,
to gain vindication from his foes.
The sword shall devour and be sated,
and drink its fill of their blood.
For the Lord GOD of hosts holds
a sacrifice
in the land of the north by the river
Euphrates.
11 Go up to Gilead, and take balm,
O virgin daughter Egypt!
In vain you have used many medicines;
there is no healing for you.
12 The nations have heard of your shame,
and the earth is full of your cry;
for warrior has stumbled against warrior;
both have fallen together.

Babylonia Will Strike Egypt

13 The word that the LORD spoke to the
prophet Jeremiah about the coming of King Neb-

uchadrezzar of Babylon to attack the land of
Egypt:
14 Declare in Egypt, and proclaim in Migdol;
proclaim in Memphis and Tahpanhes;
Say, "Take your stations and be ready,
for the sword shall devour those
around you."
15 Why has Apis fled?[t]
Why did your bull not stand?
—because the LORD thrust him down.
16 Your multitude stumbled[u] and fell,
and one said to another,[v]
"Come, let us go back to our own people
and to the land of our birth,
because of the destroying sword."
17 Give Pharaoh, king of Egypt, the name
"Braggart who missed his chance."

18 As I live, says the King,
whose name is the LORD of hosts,
one is coming
like Tabor among the mountains,
and like Carmel by the sea.
19 Pack your bags for exile,
sheltered daughter Egypt!

r Or Nubia; Heb Cush   s Cn: Heb who grasp, who draw   t Gk: Heb Why was it swept away   u Gk: Meaning of
Heb uncertain   v Gk: Heb and fell one to another and they said

World at War
While nations battle, God is in control

FLIP ON THE TV NEWS. Scenes from around the world flash
across the screen. In the Middle East, a bomb explodes and a building
collapses. Bodies lie in the gutter. Women howl with anguish over their
dead.

> The sword shall
> devour and be
> sated, and drink its
> fill of their blood.
> 46.10

Seconds later you are in Africa. Revolutionaries, rifles brandished over
their heads, march through captured streets. The camera zeroes in on the crum-
pled body of their former president.

The scene shifts to a Central American capital. Sirens scream around a burning restaurant while
stretcher-bearers carry out the moaning victims of a drug-lord attack. Next, in Africa again, starving
children grimace at you, too far gone to beg for food. Then you see snatches of violence in United
States ghettoes, scenes of ethnic unrest in Europe, and political protests in Tibet and India. The world is
whirling out of control. Your mind cannot take it in; one disaster muddles with another.

God Is in Control

In chapters 46 to 50, Jeremiah gives a similar portrait of the world. We flash by imagination from
one country to the next. We smell the rotting bodies; we hear the exultant cries of conquerors. Jeremiah shows, in vivid color, a world as frightening as ours.

But there is a difference. TV news leaves viewers with a dizzy feeling that chaos reigns. But Jeremiah's vision shows, paradoxically, that God is in control. Through these disasters God punishes those
who have opposed his will. As Israel's neighbors are destroyed, exiled Jews are freed to return to their
land. History is not just "one thing after another." God gives it a sense of direction.

Jeremiah delivered his longest and most biting message to Babylon, Judah's conqueror. Their
sheer arrogance, their assumption that they could do whatever they liked, drew God's fury. To a lesser
degree, other countries followed the same pattern. God did not judge them by his law, because they
never knew it. He judged them for their pride. They ought to have shown humility before God.

Life Questions: Can you discern any pattern or purpose to the violence in the world today?

For Memphis shall become a waste,
    a ruin, without inhabitant.

20 A beautiful heifer is Egypt—
    a gadfly from the north lights upon
        her.
21 Even her mercenaries in her midst
    are like fatted calves;
they too have turned and fled together,
    they did not stand;
for the day of their calamity has come
        upon them,
    the time of their punishment.

22 She makes a sound like a snake gliding
        away;
    for her enemies march in force,
and come against her with axes,
    like those who fell trees.
23 They shall cut down her forest,
                says the LORD,
    though it is impenetrable,
because they are more numerous
    than locusts;
    they are without number.
24 Daughter Egypt shall be put to shame;
    she shall be handed over to a people
        from the north.

25 The LORD of hosts, the God of Israel, said:
See, I am bringing punishment upon Amon of
Thebes, and Pharaoh, and Egypt and her gods
and her kings, upon Pharaoh and those who trust
in him. 26I will hand them over to those who seek
their life, to King Nebuchadrezzar of Babylon and
his officers. Afterward Egypt shall be inhabited as
in the days of old, says the LORD.

God Will Save Israel

27 But as for you, have no fear, my servant
    Jacob,
    and do not be dismayed, O Israel;
for I am going to save you from far away,
    and your offspring from the land of
        their captivity.
Jacob shall return and have quiet and
        ease,
    and no one shall make him afraid.
28 As for you, have no fear, my servant
    Jacob,
               says the LORD,
    for I am with you.
I will make an end of all the nations
    among which I have banished you,
but I will not make an end of you!
I will chastise you in just measure,
    and I will by no means leave you
        unpunished.

Judgment on the Philistines

47 The word of the LORD that came to the
    prophet Jeremiah concerning the Philis-
tines, before Pharaoh attacked Gaza:
2 Thus says the LORD:
See, waters are rising out of the north
    and shall become an overflowing
        torrent;
they shall overflow the land and all that
    fills it,
    the city and those who live in it.
People shall cry out,
    and all the inhabitants of the land shall
        wail.
3 At the noise of the stamping of the hoofs
    of his stallions,
    at the clatter of his chariots, at the
        rumbling of their wheels,
parents do not turn back for children,
    so feeble are their hands,
4 because of the day that is coming
    to destroy all the Philistines,
to cut off from Tyre and Sidon
    every helper that remains.
For the LORD is destroying the Philistines,
    the remnant of the coastland
        of Caphtor.
5 Baldness has come upon Gaza,
    Ashkelon is silenced.
O remnant of their power!w
    How long will you gash yourselves?
6 Ah, sword of the LORD!
    How long until you are quiet?
Put yourself into your scabbard,
    rest and be still!
7 How can itx be quiet,
    when the LORD has given it an order?
Against Ashkelon and against the
        seashore—
    there he has appointed it.

Judgment on Moab

48 Concerning Moab.

Thus says the LORD of hosts, the God of Israel:
Alas for Nebo, it is laid waste!
    Kiriathaim is put to shame, it is taken;
    the fortress is put to shame and broken
        down;
2   the renown of Moab is no more.
In Heshbon they planned evil against her:
    "Come, let us cut her off from being a
        nation!"
You also, O Madmen, shall be brought to
        silence;y
    the sword shall pursue you.
3 Hark! a cry from Horonaim,
    "Desolation and great destruction!"

---

w Gk: Heb *their valley*   x Gk Vg: Heb *you*   y The place-name *Madmen* sounds like the Hebrew verb *to be silent*

4 "Moab is destroyed!"
    her little ones cry out.
5 For at the ascent of Luhith
    they go[z] up weeping bitterly;
for at the descent of Horonaim
    they have heard the distressing cry of
        anguish.
6 Flee! Save yourselves!
    Be like a wild ass[a] in the desert!

7 Surely, because you trusted in your
        strongholds[b] and your treasures,
    you also shall be taken;
Chemosh shall go out into exile,
    with his priests and his attendants.

48.7 An Exiled God

*The gods of the Middle East tended to occupy a
certain territory—thus each city had its own
god. Chemosh, the chief god of Moab, was
worshiped through child sacrifice (2 Kings
3.27). Here Jeremiah predicts that not only
would the Moabites go into exile—their god
would too. These gods were powerless before
the God of Israel.*

8 The destroyer shall come upon every
        town,
    and no town shall escape;
the valley shall perish,
    and the plain shall be destroyed,
    as the LORD has spoken.

9 Set aside salt for Moab,
    for she will surely fall;
her towns shall become a desolation,
    with no inhabitant in them.

10 Accursed is the one who is slack in doing
the work of the LORD; and accursed is the one
who keeps back the sword from bloodshed.

11 Moab has been at ease from his youth,
    settled like wine[c] on its dregs;
he has not been emptied from vessel to
        vessel,
    nor has he gone into exile;
therefore his flavor has remained
    and his aroma is unspoiled.
12 Therefore, the time is surely coming, says
the LORD, when I shall send to him decanters to
decant him, and empty his vessels, and break
his[d] jars in pieces. 13Then Moab shall be ashamed
of Chemosh, as the house of Israel was ashamed
of Bethel, their confidence.

14 How can you say, "We are heroes
    and mighty warriors"?
15 The destroyer of Moab and his towns has
        come up,
    and the choicest of his young men
        have gone down to slaughter,
    says the King, whose name is the LORD
        of hosts.
16 The calamity of Moab is near at hand
    and his doom approaches swiftly.
17 Mourn over him, all you his neighbors,
    and all who know his name;
say, "How the mighty scepter is broken,
    the glorious staff!"

18 Come down from glory,
    and sit on the parched ground,
    enthroned daughter Dibon!
For the destroyer of Moab has come up
        against you;
    he has destroyed your strongholds.
19 Stand by the road and watch,
    you inhabitant of Aroer!
Ask the man fleeing and the woman
        escaping;
    say, "What has happened?"
20 Moab is put to shame, for it is broken
        down;
    wail and cry!
Tell it by the Arnon,
    that Moab is laid waste.

21 Judgment has come upon the tableland,
upon Holon, and Jahzah, and Mephaath, 22and
Dibon, and Nebo, and Beth-diblathaim, 23and
Kiriathaim, and Beth-gamul, and Beth-meon,
24and Kerioth, and Bozrah, and all the towns of
the land of Moab, far and near. 25The horn of
Moab is cut off, and his arm is broken, says the
LORD.
26 Make him drunk, because he magnified
himself against the LORD; let Moab wallow in his
vomit; he too shall become a laughingstock. 27Is-
rael was a laughingstock for you, though he was
not caught among thieves; but whenever you
spoke of him you shook your head!

28 Leave the towns, and live on the rock,
    O inhabitants of Moab!
Be like the dove that nests
    on the sides of the mouth of a gorge.
29 We have heard of the pride of Moab—
    he is very proud—
of his loftiness, his pride, and his
        arrogance,
    and the haughtiness of his heart.
30 I myself know his insolence, says the
    LORD;

---

[z] Cn: Heb *he goes*   [a] Gk Aquila: Heb *like Aroer*   [b] Gk: Heb *works*   [c] Heb lacks *like wine*
[d] Gk Aquila: Heb *their*

his boasts are false,
his deeds are false.
31 Therefore I wail for Moab;
I cry out for all Moab;
for the people of Kir-heres I mourn.
32 More than for Jazer I weep for you,
O vine of Sibmah!
Your branches crossed over the sea,
reached as far as Jazer;*e*
upon your summer fruits and
your vintage
the destroyer has fallen.
33 Gladness and joy have been taken away
from the fruitful land of Moab;
I have stopped the wine from the wine
presses;
no one treads them with shouts of joy;
the shouting is not the shout of joy.

34 Heshbon and Elealeh cry out;*f* as far as
Jahaz they utter their voice, from Zoar to Horonaim and Eglath-shelishiyah. For even the waters
of Nimrim have become desolate. 35And I will
bring to an end in Moab, says the LORD, those
who offer sacrifice at a high place and make offerings to their gods. 36Therefore my heart moans
for Moab like a flute, and my heart moans like a
flute for the people of Kir-heres; for the riches
they gained have perished.
37 For every head is shaved and every beard
cut off; on all the hands there are gashes, and on
the loins sackcloth. 38On all the housetops of
Moab and in the squares there is nothing but
lamentation; for I have broken Moab like a vessel
that no one wants, says the LORD. 39How it is
broken! How they wail! How Moab has turned his
back in shame! So Moab has become a derision
and a horror to all his neighbors.
40 For thus says the LORD:
Look, he shall swoop down like an eagle,
and spread his wings against Moab;
41 the towns*g* shall be taken
and the strongholds seized.
The hearts of the warriors of Moab, on
that day,
shall be like the heart of a woman in
labor.
42 Moab shall be destroyed as a people,
because he magnified himself against
the LORD.
43 Terror, pit, and trap
are before you, O inhabitants of Moab!
says the LORD.
44 Everyone who flees from the terror
shall fall into the pit,
and everyone who climbs out of the pit
shall be caught in the trap.
For I will bring these things*h* upon Moab

in the year of their punishment,
says the LORD.
45 In the shadow of Heshbon
fugitives stop exhausted;

48.43 Well-turned Phrase

*Some of Jeremiah's language eludes
translation, especially when, as here, he
chooses Hebrew words for the sake of sound.
"Terror, pit, trap" are translations of "pahad,
pahat, pah." Isaiah (or some poet before him)
had already minted the phrase, generations
before Jeremiah (see Isaiah 24.17).*

for a fire has gone out from Heshbon,
a flame from the house of Sihon;
it has destroyed the forehead of Moab,
the scalp of the people of tumult.*i*
46 Woe to you, O Moab!
The people of Chemosh have perished,
for your sons have been taken captive,
and your daughters into captivity.
47 Yet I will restore the fortunes of Moab
in the latter days, says the LORD.
Thus far is the judgment on Moab.

Judgment on the Ammonites

49 Concerning the Ammonites.

Thus says the LORD:
Has Israel no sons?
Has he no heir?
Why then has Milcom dispossessed Gad,
and his people settled in its towns?
2 Therefore, the time is surely coming,
says the LORD,
when I will sound the battle alarm
against Rabbah of the Ammonites;
it shall become a desolate mound,
and its villages shall be burned with
fire;
then Israel shall dispossess those who
dispossessed him,
says the LORD.

3 Wail, O Heshbon, for Ai is laid waste!
Cry out, O daughters*j* of Rabbah!
Put on sackcloth,
lament, and slash yourselves with
whips!*k*
For Milcom shall go into exile,
with his priests and his attendants.
4 Why do you boast in your strength?
Your strength is ebbing,
O faithless daughter.

---

e Two Mss and Isa 16.8: MT *the sea of Jazer*   *f* Cn: Heb *From the cry of Heshbon to Elealeh*   *g* Or *Kerioth*
h Gk Syr: Heb *bring upon it*   *i* Or *of Shaon*   *j* Or *villages*   *k* Cn: Meaning of Heb uncertain

You trusted in your treasures, saying,
"Who will attack me?"
5 I am going to bring terror upon you,
says the Lord GOD of hosts,
from all your neighbors,
and you will be scattered, each headlong,
with no one to gather the fugitives.

6 But afterward I will restore the fortunes of the Ammonites, says the LORD.

Judgment on Edom

7 Concerning Edom.

Thus says the LORD of hosts:
Is there no longer wisdom in Teman?
Has counsel perished from
the prudent?
Has their wisdom vanished?
8 Flee, turn back, get down low,
inhabitants of Dedan!
For I will bring the calamity of Esau upon
him,
the time when I punish him.
9 If grape-gatherers came to you,
would they not leave gleanings?
If thieves came by night,
even they would pillage only what they
wanted.
10 But as for me, I have stripped Esau bare,
I have uncovered his hiding places,
and he is not able to conceal himself.
His offspring are destroyed, his kinsfolk
and his neighbors; and he is no more.
11 Leave your orphans, I will keep them
alive;
and let your widows trust in me.
12 For thus says the LORD: If those who do not deserve to drink the cup still have to drink it, shall you be the one to go unpunished? You shall not go unpunished; you must drink it. 13For by myself I have sworn, says the LORD, that Bozrah shall become an object of horror and ridicule, a waste, and an object of cursing; and all her towns shall be perpetual wastes.
14 I have heard tidings from the LORD,
and a messenger has been sent among
the nations:
"Gather yourselves together and come
against her,
and rise up for battle!"
15 For I will make you least among the
nations,
despised by humankind.
16 The terror you inspire
and the pride of your heart have
deceived you,
you who live in the clefts of the rock,[l]
who hold the height of the hill.

Although you make your nest as high as
the eagle's,
from there I will bring you down,
says the LORD.
17 Edom shall become an object of horror; everyone who passes by it will be horrified and will hiss because of all its disasters. 18As when Sodom and Gomorrah and their neighbors were overthrown, says the LORD, no one shall live there, nor shall anyone settle in it. 19Like a lion coming up from the thickets of the Jordan against a perennial pasture, I will suddenly chase Edom[m] away from it; and I will appoint over it whomever I choose.[n] For who is like me? Who can summon me? Who is the shepherd who can stand before me? 20Therefore hear the plan that the LORD has made against Edom and the purposes that he has formed against the inhabitants of Teman: Surely the little ones of the flock shall be dragged away; surely their fold shall be appalled at their fate. 21At the sound of their fall the earth shall tremble; the sound of their cry shall be heard at the Red Sea.[o] 22Look, he shall mount up and swoop down like an eagle, and spread his wings against Bozrah, and the heart of the warriors of Edom in that day shall be like the heart of a woman in labor.

Judgment on Damascus

23 Concerning Damascus.

Hamath and Arpad are confounded,
for they have heard bad news;
they melt in fear, they are troubled like
the sea[p]
that cannot be quiet.
24 Damascus has become feeble, she turned
to flee,
and panic seized her;
anguish and sorrows have taken hold of
her,
as of a woman in labor.
25 How the famous city is forsaken,[q]
the joyful town![r]
26 Therefore her young men shall fall in her
squares,
and all her soldiers shall be destroyed
in that day,
says the LORD of hosts.
27 And I will kindle a fire at the wall of
Damascus,
and it shall devour the strongholds of
Ben-hadad.

Judgment on Kedar and Hazor

28 Concerning Kedar and the kingdoms of Hazor that King Nebuchadrezzar of Babylon defeated.

---

l Or of Sela   m Heb him   n Or and I will single out the choicest of his rams: Meaning of Heb uncertain   o Or Sea
of Reeds   p Cn: Heb there is trouble in the sea   q Vg: Heb is not forsaken   r Syr Vg Tg: Heb the town of my joy

Thus says the LORD:
Rise up, advance against Kedar!
Destroy the people of the east!
29 Take their tents and their flocks,
their curtains and all their goods;
carry off their camels for yourselves,
and a cry shall go up: "Terror is all
around!"
30 Flee, wander far away, hide in
deep places,
O inhabitants of Hazor!
says the LORD.
For King Nebuchadrezzar of Babylon
has made a plan against you
and formed a purpose against you.

31 Rise up, advance against a nation at ease,
that lives secure,
says the LORD,
that has no gates or bars,
that lives alone.
32 Their camels shall become booty,
their herds of cattle a spoil.
I will scatter to every wind
those who have shaven temples,
and I will bring calamity
against them from every side,
says the LORD.
33 Hazor shall become a lair of jackals,
an everlasting waste;
no one shall live there,
nor shall anyone settle in it.

Judgment on Elam

34 The word of the LORD that came to the prophet Jeremiah concerning Elam, at the beginning of the reign of King Zedekiah of Judah.
35 Thus says the LORD of hosts: I am going to break the bow of Elam, the mainstay of their might; 36and I will bring upon Elam the four winds from the four quarters of heaven; and I will scatter them to all these winds, and there shall be no nation to which the exiles from Elam shall not come. 37I will terrify Elam before their enemies, and before those who seek their life; I will bring disaster upon them, my fierce anger, says the LORD. I will send the sword after them, until I have consumed them; 38and I will set my throne in Elam, and destroy their king and officials, says the LORD.
39 But in the latter days I will restore the fortunes of Elam, says the LORD.

Judgment on Babylon

50 The word that the LORD spoke concerning Babylon, concerning the land of the Chaldeans, by the prophet Jeremiah:
2 Declare among the nations and proclaim,
set up a banner and proclaim,

do not conceal it, say:
Babylon is taken,
Bel is put to shame,
Merodach is dismayed.
Her images are put to shame,
her idols are dismayed.

50.1–3 None Escape

Chapters 46–50 record a virtual catalog of Israel's enemies. Jeremiah begins with Egypt, goes on to Israel's immediate (small) neighbors, and ends with archenemy Babylon. No nation is exempt from God's justice.

3 For out of the north a nation has come up against her; it shall make her land a desolation, and no one shall live in it; both human beings and animals shall flee away.

4 In those days and in that time, says the LORD, the people of Israel shall come, they and the people of Judah together; they shall come weeping as they seek the LORD their God. 5They shall ask the way to Zion, with faces turned toward it, and they shall come and join[s] themselves to the LORD by an everlasting covenant that will never be forgotten.

6 My people have been lost sheep; their shepherds have led them astray, turning them away on the mountains; from mountain to hill they have gone, they have forgotten their fold. 7All who found them have devoured them, and their enemies have said, "We are not guilty, because they have sinned against the LORD, the true pasture, the LORD, the hope of their ancestors."

8 Flee from Babylon, and go out of the land of the Chaldeans, and be like male goats leading the flock. 9For I am going to stir up and bring against Babylon a company of great nations from the land of the north; and they shall array themselves against her; from there she shall be taken. Their arrows are like the arrows of a skilled warrior who does not return empty-handed. 10Chaldea shall be plundered; all who plunder her shall be sated, says the LORD.

11 Though you rejoice, though you exult,
O plunderers of my heritage,
though you frisk about like a heifer on
the grass,
and neigh like stallions,
12 your mother shall be utterly shamed,
and she who bore you shall
be disgraced.

s Gk: Heb *toward it. Come! They shall join*

Lo, she shall be the last of the nations,
a wilderness, dry land, and a desert.
13 Because of the wrath of the LORD she shall
not be inhabited,
but shall be an utter desolation;
everyone who passes by Babylon shall be
appalled
and hiss because of all her wounds.
14 Take up your positions around Babylon,
all you that bend the bow;
shoot at her, spare no arrows,
for she has sinned against the LORD.
15 Raise a shout against her from all sides,
"She has surrendered;
her bulwarks have fallen,
her walls are thrown down."
For this is the vengeance of the LORD:
take vengeance on her,
do to her as she has done.
16 Cut off from Babylon the sower,
and the wielder of the sickle in time of
harvest;
because of the destroying sword
all of them shall return to their own
people,
and all of them shall flee to their own
land.

17 Israel is a hunted sheep driven away by lions. First the king of Assyria devoured it, and now at the end King Nebuchadrezzar of Babylon has gnawed its bones. 18Therefore, thus says the LORD of hosts, the God of Israel: I am going to punish the king of Babylon and his land, as I punished the king of Assyria. 19I will restore Israel to its pasture, and it shall feed on Carmel and in Bashan, and on the hills of Ephraim and in Gilead its hunger shall be satisfied. 20In those days and at that time, says the LORD, the iniquity of Israel shall be sought, and there shall be none; and the sins of Judah, and none shall be found; for I will pardon the remnant that I have spared.

50.20 An End to Guilt

For 50 chapters the book of Jeremiah hammers away at Israel's guilt. Because of it, punishment was bound to come. Yet the forgiveness to come from God will be as absolute as the guilt: A search for Israel's sins will not uncover a single one.

21 Go up to the land of Merathaim;*t*
go up against her,
and attack the inhabitants of Pekod*u*
and utterly destroy the last of them,*v*
says the LORD;

do all that I have commanded you.
22 The noise of battle is in the land,
and great destruction!
23 How the hammer of the whole earth
is cut down and broken!
How Babylon has become
a horror among the nations!
24 You set a snare for yourself and you were
caught, O Babylon,
but you did not know it;
you were discovered and seized,
because you challenged the LORD.
25 The LORD has opened his armory,
and brought out the weapons of his
wrath,
for the Lord GOD of hosts has a task to
do
in the land of the Chaldeans.
26 Come against her from every quarter;
open her granaries;
pile her up like heaps of grain, and
destroy her utterly;
let nothing be left of her.
27 Kill all her bulls,
let them go down to the slaughter.
Alas for them, their day has come,
the time of their punishment!

28 Listen! Fugitives and refugees from the land of Babylon are coming to declare in Zion the vengeance of the LORD our God, vengeance for his temple.

29 Summon archers against Babylon, all who bend the bow. Encamp all around her; let no one escape. Repay her according to her deeds; just as she has done, do to her—for she has arrogantly defied the LORD, the Holy One of Israel. 30Therefore her young men shall fall in her squares, and all her soldiers shall be destroyed on that day, says the LORD.

31 I am against you, O arrogant one,
says the Lord GOD of hosts;
for your day has come,
the time when I will punish you.
32 The arrogant one shall stumble and fall,
with no one to raise him up,
and I will kindle a fire in his cities,
and it will devour everything around
him.

33 Thus says the LORD of hosts: The people of Israel are oppressed, and so too are the people of Judah; all their captors have held them fast and refuse to let them go. 34Their Redeemer is strong; the LORD of hosts is his name. He will surely plead their cause, that he may give rest to the earth, but unrest to the inhabitants of Babylon.

t Or *of Double Rebellion*   *u* Or *of Punishment*   *v* Tg: Heb *destroy after them*

35 A sword against the Chaldeans, says the
        LORD,
    and against the inhabitants of Babylon,
    and against her officials and her sages!
36 A sword against the diviners,
    so that they may become fools!
    A sword against her warriors,
    so that they may be destroyed!
37 A sword against her[w] horses and against
        her[w] chariots,
    and against all the foreign troops in
        her midst,
    so that they may become women!
    A sword against all her treasures,
    that they may be plundered!
38 A drought[x] against her waters,
    that they may be dried up!
    For it is a land of images,
    and they go mad over idols.

39 Therefore wild animals shall live with hyenas in Babylon,[y] and ostriches shall inhabit her;
she shall never again be peopled, or inhabited for
all generations. 40As when God overthrew Sodom
and Gomorrah and their neighbors, says the
LORD, so no one shall live there, nor shall anyone
settle in her.

41 Look, a people is coming from the north;
    a mighty nation and many kings
    are stirring from the farthest parts of
        the earth.
42 They wield bow and spear,
    they are cruel and have no mercy.
    The sound of them is like the roaring sea;
    they ride upon horses,
    set in array as a warrior for battle,
    against you, O daughter Babylon!

43 The king of Babylon heard news of them,
    and his hands fell helpless;
    anguish seized him,
    pain like that of a woman in labor.

44 Like a lion coming up from the thickets of
the Jordan against a perennial pasture, I will suddenly chase them away from her; and I will appoint over her whomever I choose.[z] For who is
like me? Who can summon me? Who is the shepherd who can stand before me? 45Therefore hear
the plan that the LORD has made against Babylon,
and the purposes that he has formed against the
land of the Chaldeans: Surely the little ones of the
flock shall be dragged away; surely their[a] fold
shall be appalled at their fate. 46At the sound of
the capture of Babylon the earth shall tremble,
and her cry shall be heard among the nations.

51 Thus says the LORD:
    I am going to stir up a destructive
        wind[b]
    against Babylon
    and against the inhabitants of
        Leb-qamai;[c]
2 and I will send winnowers to Babylon,
    and they shall winnow her.
    They shall empty her land
    when they come against her from every
        side
    on the day of trouble.
3 Let not the archer bend his bow,
    and let him not array himself in his
        coat of mail.
    Do not spare her young men;
    utterly destroy her entire army.
4 They shall fall down slain in the land of
        the Chaldeans,
    and wounded in her streets.
5 Israel and Judah have not been forsaken
    by their God, the LORD of hosts,
    though their land is full of guilt
    before the Holy One of Israel.

6 Flee from the midst of Babylon,
    save your lives, each of you!
    Do not perish because of her guilt,
    for this is the time of the LORD's
        vengeance;
    he is repaying her what is due.
7 Babylon was a golden cup in the LORD's
        hand,
    making all the earth drunken;
    the nations drank of her wine,
    and so the nations went mad.
8 Suddenly Babylon has fallen and
        is shattered;
    wail for her!
    Bring balm for her wound;
    perhaps she may be healed.
9 We tried to heal Babylon,
    but she could not be healed.
    Forsake her, and let each of us go
    to our own country;
    for her judgment has reached up
        to heaven
    and has been lifted up even to the
        skies.
10 The LORD has brought forth our
        vindication;
    come, let us declare in Zion
    the work of the LORD our God.

11 Sharpen the arrows!
    Fill the quivers!
The LORD has stirred up the spirit of the kings of

w Cn: Heb his   x Another reading is A sword   y Heb lacks in Babylon   z Or and I will single out the choicest of
her rams: Meaning of Heb uncertain   a Syr Gk Tg Compare 49.20: Heb lacks their   b Or stir up the spirit of a
destroyer   c Leb-qamai is a cryptogram for Kasdim, Chaldea

the Medes, because his purpose concerning Babylon is to destroy it, for that is the vengeance of the LORD, vengeance for his temple.

12 Raise a standard against the walls of
      Babylon;
  make the watch strong;
post sentinels;
  prepare the ambushes;
for the LORD has both planned and done
  what he spoke concerning the
      inhabitants of Babylon.
13 You who live by mighty waters,
  rich in treasures,
your end has come,
  the thread of your life is cut.

51.13 Waters of Babylon

Water has always been precious in the Middle East, and Babylon's mighty Euphrates River, complemented by a magnificent system of irrigation canals, was a major source of wealth and security in times of drought. The modern-day nations of Iraq, Iran, and Turkey still argue—and sometimes fight—over this resource.

14 The LORD of hosts has sworn by himself:
  Surely I will fill you with troops like a
      swarm of locusts,
  and they shall raise a shout of victory
      over you.

15 It is he who made the earth by his power,
  who established the world by
      his wisdom,
and by his understanding stretched out
      the heavens.
16 When he utters his voice there is a tumult
      of waters in the heavens,
  and he makes the mist rise from the
      ends of the earth.
He makes lightnings for the rain,
  and he brings out the wind from his
      storehouses.
17 Everyone is stupid and without
      knowledge;
  goldsmiths are all put to shame by
      their idols;
for their images are false,
  and there is no breath in them.
18 They are worthless, a work of delusion;
  at the time of their punishment they
      shall perish.
19 Not like these is the LORD,[d] the portion
      of Jacob,
  for he is the one who formed
      all things,

and Israel is the tribe of his inheritance;
  the LORD of hosts is his name.

Israel the Creator's Instrument

20 You are my war club, my weapon of
      battle:
with you I smash nations;
  with you I destroy kingdoms;
21 with you I smash the horse and its rider;
  with you I smash the chariot and the
      charioteer;
22 with you I smash man and woman;
  with you I smash the old man and the
      boy;
with you I smash the young man and the
      girl;
23 with you I smash shepherds and their
      flocks;
with you I smash farmers and their teams;
  with you I smash governors and
      deputies.

The Doom of Babylon

24 I will repay Babylon and all the inhabitants of Chaldea before your very eyes for all the wrong that they have done in Zion, says the LORD.

25 I am against you, O destroying mountain,
                        says the LORD,
  that destroys the whole earth;
I will stretch out my hand against you,
  and roll you down from the crags,
  and make you a burned-out mountain.
26 No stone shall be taken from you for a
      corner
  and no stone for a foundation,
but you shall be a perpetual waste,
  says the LORD.

27 Raise a standard in the land,
  blow the trumpet among the nations;
prepare the nations for war against her,
  summon against her the kingdoms,
  Ararat, Minni, and Ashkenaz;
appoint a marshal against her,
  bring up horses like bristling locusts.
28 Prepare the nations for war against her,
  the kings of the Medes, with their
      governors and deputies,
  and every land under their dominion.
29 The land trembles and writhes,
  for the LORD's purposes against
      Babylon stand,
to make the land of Babylon a desolation,
  without inhabitant.
30 The warriors of Babylon have given up
      fighting,
  they remain in their strongholds;
their strength has failed,

---

d Heb lacks *the* LORD

they have become women;
her buildings are set on fire,
her bars are broken.
31 One runner runs to meet another,
and one messenger to meet another,
to tell the king of Babylon
that his city is taken from end to end:
32 the fords have been seized,
the marshes have been burned with
fire,
and the soldiers are in panic.
33 For thus says the LORD of hosts, the God
of Israel:
Daughter Babylon is like a threshing floor
at the time when it is trodden;
yet a little while
and the time of her harvest will come.

34 "King Nebuchadrezzar of Babylon has
devoured me,
he has crushed me;
he has made me an empty vessel,
he has swallowed me like a monster;
he has filled his belly with my delicacies,
he has spewed me out.
35 May my torn flesh be avenged on
Babylon,"
the inhabitants of Zion shall say.
"May my blood be avenged on the
inhabitants of Chaldea,"
Jerusalem shall say.
36 Therefore thus says the LORD:
I am going to defend your cause
and take vengeance for you.
I will dry up her sea
and make her fountain dry;
37 and Babylon shall become a heap
of ruins,
a den of jackals,
an object of horror and of hissing,
without inhabitant.

38 Like lions they shall roar together;
they shall growl like lions' whelps.
39 When they are inflamed, I will set out
their drink
and make them drunk, until they
become merry
and then sleep a perpetual sleep
and never wake, says the LORD.
40 I will bring them down like lambs to the
slaughter,
like rams and goats.

41 How Sheshach[e] is taken,
the pride of the whole earth seized!
How Babylon has become
an object of horror among the nations!
42 The sea has risen over Babylon;

she has been covered by its tumultuous
waves.
43 Her cities have become an object
of horror,
a land of drought and a desert,
a land in which no one lives,
and through which no mortal passes.
44 I will punish Bel in Babylon,
and make him disgorge what he has
swallowed.
The nations shall no longer stream to
him;
the wall of Babylon has fallen.

45 Come out of her, my people!
Save your lives, each of you,
from the fierce anger of the LORD!
46 Do not be fainthearted or fearful
at the rumors heard in the land—
one year one rumor comes,
the next year another,
rumors of violence in the land
and of ruler against ruler.
47 Assuredly, the days are coming
when I will punish the images
of Babylon;
her whole land shall be put to shame,
and all her slain shall fall in her midst.
48 Then the heavens and the earth,
and all that is in them,
shall shout for joy over Babylon;
for the destroyers shall come against
them out of the north,
says the LORD.
49 Babylon must fall for the slain of Israel,
as the slain of all the earth have fallen
because of Babylon.

50 You survivors of the sword,
go, do not linger!
Remember the LORD in a distant land,
and let Jerusalem come into your
mind:
51 We are put to shame, for we have heard
insults;
dishonor has covered our face,
for aliens have come
into the holy places of the
LORD's house.

52 Therefore the time is surely coming, says
the LORD,
when I will punish her idols,
and through all her land
the wounded shall groan.
53 Though Babylon should mount up to
heaven,

---

e Sheshach is a cryptogram for Babel, Babylon

and though she should fortify her
strong height,
from me destroyers would come upon
her,
says the LORD.

51.53 Apocalyptic Arrogance

The arrogance of Babylon—her sense of absolute, untouchable power—became an emblem of the forces God will ultimately destroy. Jeremiah probably was thinking only of Babylon's towering ziggurat (or temple) and double wall defenses. But Babylon's "reaching for the sky" suggested an image of a nation trying to compete with God. Revelation 18— written long after Jeremiah's Babylon had been destroyed—described the fall of another proud and wealthy "Babylon" at the end of the age.

54 Listen!—a cry from Babylon!
A great crashing from the land of the
Chaldeans!
55 For the LORD is laying Babylon waste,
and stilling her loud clamor.
Their waves roar like mighty waters,
the sound of their clamor resounds;
56 for a destroyer has come against her,
against Babylon;
her warriors are taken,
their bows are broken;
for the LORD is a God of recompense,
he will repay in full.
57 I will make her officials and her sages
drunk,
also her governors, her deputies, and
her warriors;
they shall sleep a perpetual sleep and
never wake,
says the King, whose name is the LORD
of hosts.

58 Thus says the LORD of hosts:
The broad wall of Babylon
shall be leveled to the ground,
and her high gates
shall be burned with fire.
The peoples exhaust themselves for
nothing,
and the nations weary themselves only
for fire.f

Jeremiah's Command to Seraiah

59 The word that the prophet Jeremiah commanded Seraiah son of Neriah son of Mahseiah, when he went with King Zedekiah of Judah to Babylon, in the fourth year of his reign. Seraiah was the quartermaster. 60Jeremiah wrote in ag scroll all the disasters that would come on Babylon, all these words that are written concerning Babylon. 61And Jeremiah said to Seraiah: "When you come to Babylon, see that you read all these words, 62and say, 'O LORD, you yourself threatened to destroy this place so that neither human beings nor animals shall live in it, and it shall be desolate forever.' 63When you finish reading this scroll, tie a stone to it, and throw it into the middle of the Euphrates, 64and say, 'Thus shall Babylon sink, to rise no more, because of the disasters that I am bringing on her.'"h

Thus far are the words of Jeremiah.

The Destruction of Jerusalem Reviewed

52 Zedekiah was twenty-one years old when he began to reign; he reigned eleven years in Jerusalem. His mother's name was Hamutal daughter of Jeremiah of Libnah. 2He did what was evil in the sight of the LORD, just as Jehoiakim had done. 3Indeed, Jerusalem and Judah so angered the LORD that he expelled them from his presence.

Zedekiah rebelled against the king of Babylon. 4And in the ninth year of his reign, in the tenth month, on the tenth day of the month, King Nebuchadrezzar of Babylon came with all his army against Jerusalem, and they laid siege to it; they built siegeworks against it all around. 5So the city was besieged until the eleventh year of King Zedekiah. 6On the ninth day of the fourth month the famine became so severe in the city that there was no food for the people of the land. 7Then a breach was made in the city wall;i and all the soldiers fled and went out from the city by night by the way of the gate between the two walls, by the king's garden, though the Chaldeans were all around the city. They went in the direction of the Arabah. 8But the army of the Chaldeans pursued the king, and overtook Zedekiah in the plains of Jericho; and all his army was scattered, deserting him. 9Then they captured the king, and brought him up to the king of Babylon at Riblah in the land of Hamath, and he passed sentence on him. 10The king of Babylon killed the sons of Zedekiah before his eyes, and also killed all the officers of Judah at Riblah. 11He put out the eyes of Zedekiah, and bound him in fetters, and the king of Babylon took him to Babylon, and put him in prison until the day of his death.

12 In the fifth month, on the tenth day of the month—which was the nineteenth year of King Nebuchadrezzar, king of Babylon—Nebuzaradan the captain of the bodyguard who served the king of Babylon, entered Jerusalem. 13He burned the house of the LORD, the king's house, and all the houses of Jerusalem; every great house he burned down. 14All the army of the Chaldeans, who were

---

f Gk Syr Compare Hab 2.13: Heb *and the nations for fire, and they are weary they shall weary themselves* i Heb lacks *wall* g Or *one* h Gk: Heb *on her. And*

with the captain of the guard, broke down all the walls around Jerusalem. [15]Nebuzaradan the captain of the guard carried into exile some of the poorest of the people and the rest of the people

52.13 Total Destruction

A small but subtle change telegraphs a huge turnabout. Verse 4 gives the date in terms of (Israelite) King Zedekiah's reign; verse 12 gives it in terms of (Babylonian) King Nebuchadrezzar. From this point on in history, Israel survived only on the periphery of other nations' empires. Instead of reckoning years in terms of their own leaders' time in office, Israel would base their calendar on the empires that ruled them.

who were left in the city and the deserters who had defected to the king of Babylon, together with the rest of the artisans. [16]But Nebuzaradan the captain of the guard left some of the poorest people of the land to be vinedressers and tillers of the soil.

17 The pillars of bronze that were in the house of the LORD, and the stands and the bronze sea that were in the house of the LORD, the Chaldeans broke in pieces, and carried all the bronze to Babylon. [18]They took away the pots, the shovels, the snuffers, the basins, the ladles, and all the vessels of bronze used in the temple service. [19]The captain of the guard took away the small bowls also, the firepans, the basins, the pots, the lampstands, the ladles, and the bowls for libation, both those of gold and those of silver. [20]As for the two pillars, the one sea, the twelve bronze bulls that were under the sea, and the stands,[j] which King Solomon had made for the house of the LORD, the bronze of all these vessels was beyond weighing. [21]As for the pillars, the height of the one pillar was eighteen cubits, its circumference was twelve cubits; it was hollow and its thickness was four fingers. [22]Upon it was a capital of bronze; the height of the capital was five cubits; latticework and

pomegranates, all of bronze, encircled the top of the capital. And the second pillar had the same, with pomegranates. [23]There were ninety-six pomegranates on the sides; all the pomegranates encircling the latticework numbered one hundred.

24 The captain of the guard took the chief priest Seraiah, the second priest Zephaniah, and the three guardians of the threshold; [25]and from the city he took an officer who had been in command of the soldiers, and seven men of the king's council who were found in the city; the secretary of the commander of the army who mustered the people of the land; and sixty men of the people of the land who were found inside the city. [26]Then Nebuzaradan the captain of the guard took them, and brought them to the king of Babylon at Riblah. [27]And the king of Babylon struck them down, and put them to death at Riblah in the land of Hamath. So Judah went into exile out of its land.

28 This is the number of the people whom Nebuchadrezzar took into exile: in the seventh year, three thousand twenty-three Judeans; [29]in the eighteenth year of Nebuchadrezzar he took into exile from Jerusalem eight hundred thirty-two persons; [30]in the twenty-third year of Nebuchadrezzar, Nebuzaradan the captain of the guard took into exile of the Judeans seven hundred forty-five persons; all the persons were four thousand six hundred.

Jehoiachin Favored in Captivity

31 In the thirty-seventh year of the exile of King Jehoiachin of Judah, in the twelfth month, on the twenty-fifth day of the month, King Evilmerodach of Babylon, in the year he began to reign, showed favor to King Jehoiachin of Judah and brought him out of prison; [32]he spoke kindly to him, and gave him a seat above the seats of the other kings who were with him in Babylon. [33]So Jehoiachin put aside his prison clothes, and every day of his life he dined regularly at the king's table. [34]For his allowance, a regular daily allowance was given him by the king of Babylon, as long as he lived, up to the day of his death.

---

j Cn: Heb that were under the stands

LAMENTATIONS

A City in Ruins
There was nothing left to do but weep

Is it nothing to you, all you who pass by? 1.12

EVERY YEAR THE WORLD PAUSES to remember one awful day in Hiroshima, Japan, when the power of the atom came out of the sky. Opinions vary over whether an atom bomb was necessary to end World War II. Necessary or not, however, Hiroshima was a horrible tragedy. Though the survivors have gone on with their lives, they cannot forget. Nor can the rest of the world. Hiroshima's shadow stretches through to our time.

Five Poems of Grief

Lamentations offers five poems written from a state of dazed grief worthy of Hiroshima. A whole city has been destroyed. Brothers, sisters, children, friends are all gone. Men the town admired wander the body-littered streets, their skins shriveled and their faces barely recognizable. Starvation has even compelled women to cook their own children (4.10).

And so the author mourns. He carefully reviews everything he has seen and felt, his pain darkening every line. He writes the first four poems in an acrostic style, following the Hebrew alphabet, one letter for each stanza. Perhaps this system helps him to pursue the subject thoroughly and not to break down in spasms of emotion. When he thinks of the starving children, he nearly does (2.11).

God Caused the Carnage

The author of Lamentations—tradition ascribes it to Jeremiah—evidently had seen the siege and destruction of Jerusalem in 586 B.C., when the Babylonian army burned and destroyed all the principal buildings and carried most of the surviving inhabitants into exile. Lamentations conducts a kind of postmortem on the death of Jerusalem, examining the body in clinical detail.

Like a doctor, Lamentations's author seeks to know the cause of death. He has no final doubt: Though the Babylonians did the work, ultimately God was responsible. But could God willingly create such misery? The author seems stunned that God has actually destroyed his own people, though he admits they richly deserved the punishment. "The Lord has become like an enemy," he cries in astonishment (2.5). "Though I call and cry for help, he shuts out my prayer" (3.8). "He led me off the way and tore me to pieces; he has made me desolate" (3.11). "He has made my teeth grind on gravel" (3.16).

But, though astonished and grief-stricken, the author never doubts God's justice. Jerusalem's destruction came as a result of sin (1.5). This fact prompts quiet hope, based on the character of God. "Although he causes grief, he will have compassion according to the abundance of his steadfast love; for he does not willingly afflict or grieve anyone" (3.32–33). When sin is eliminated, the Lord acts quickly to forgive and heal.

Looking for Recovery

Though the grief of Lamentations is as deep and heavy as any ever written, hope lies at the bottom. The author does not say "Cheer up!" to himself or anyone else. He mourns passionately and fully. But in mourning he looks to recovery. Lamentations ends with a prayer to God, asking him to restore his people, "unless you have utterly rejected us, and are angry with us beyond measure"(5.22). Behind that "unless" lies confidence. God can never be angry without limits.

The author of Lamentations doesn't soften his words to God for fear of offending him. He expresses the full and dreadful horror of what he has seen, and he gives God full responsibility. But, remembering that the Lord is a loving God, he counts on God to heal Israel's wounds. This time of mourning will be followed by another time, a time to dance.

How to Read Lamentations

Lamentations is poetry, one poem per chapter. Its main purpose is not to describe events, nor to teach lessons, though it does both. Its intent is to express grief, to pour out before God the horror and bitterness of what has happened to Jerusalem. These five poems can help you to understand what it meant for Jews to see Jerusalem destroyed. They can also help you learn to deal appropriately with grief, your own or others'. Read them expressively, preferably out loud, so that you catch the deep emotion. Note that the author does not rush to express his hope in God, but fully grieves for the tragedy he was involved in.

Lamentations is not difficult to understand, though some of the poetical allusions may become clearer if you use a Bible dictionary or a commentary. For a summary of the destruction that inspired Lamentations, read 2 Kings 25.

3-TRACK READING PLAN

For an explanation and complete listing of the 3-track reading plan, turn to page 7.

TRACK 1: **Two-Week Courses on the Bible**
See page 7 for information on these courses.

TRACK 2: **An Overview of Lamentations in 1 Day**
☐ Day 1. Read the Introduction to Lamentations and chapter 3, which contains both bitter grief and quiet hope.
Now turn to page 9 for your next Track 2 reading project.

TRACK 3: **All of Lamentations in 5 Days**
After you have read through Lamentations, turn to pages 10–14 for your next Track 3 reading project.
☐1   ☐2   ☐3   ☐4   ☐5

The Deserted City

1 How lonely sits the city
    that once was full of people!
How like a widow she has become,
    she that was great among the nations!
She that was a princess among the
            provinces
    has become a vassal.

2 She weeps bitterly in the night,
    with tears on her cheeks;
among all her lovers
    she has no one to comfort her;
all her friends have dealt treacherously
            with her,
    they have become her enemies.

3 Judah has gone into exile with suffering
    and hard servitude;
she lives now among the nations,
    and finds no resting place;
her pursuers have all overtaken her
    in the midst of her distress.

4 The roads to Zion mourn,
for no one comes to the festivals;
all her gates are desolate,
    her priests groan;
her young girls grieve,[a]
    and her lot is bitter.

5 Her foes have become the masters,
    her enemies prosper,
because the LORD has made her suffer
    for the multitude of her transgressions;
her children have gone away,
    captives before the foe.

6 From daughter Zion has departed
    all her majesty.
Her princes have become like stags
    that find no pasture;
they fled without strength
    before the pursuer.

7 Jerusalem remembers,
    in the days of her affliction and
            wandering,
all the precious things
    that were hers in days of old.

─────────────

a Meaning of Heb uncertain

When her people fell into the hand of the
    foe,
  and there was no one to help her,
the foe looked on mocking
    over her downfall.

1.4–5 Structured Passion

*Middle Easterners often commemorated
catastrophes in poetry and song, as a kind of
dirge in memory of the event. (See Psalm 137
for another example.) Lamentations, a
response to the destruction of Jerusalem,
contains as much passion as any book in the
Bible. Yet, remarkably, the author has poured
his passion into a highly structured form of
poetry. Note that each chapter contains exactly
22 verses, or "stanzas," except for chapter 3,
which has 66 verses (3 times 22). There were
22 letters in the Hebrew alphabet, and all but
one of these poems follow an acrostic form,
with each stanza beginning with a different
letter of the alphabet.*

8 Jerusalem sinned grievously,
    so she has become a mockery;
all who honored her despise her,
    for they have seen her nakedness;
she herself groans,
    and turns her face away.

9 Her uncleanness was in her skirts;
    she took no thought of her future;
her downfall was appalling,
    with none to comfort her.
"O Lord, look at my affliction,
    for the enemy has triumphed!"

10 Enemies have stretched out their hands
    over all her precious things;
she has even seen the nations

1.10 The Temple Destroyed

*Non-Jews were barred from the holy places of
the temple. But when the Babylonians
conquered Jerusalem, they not only entered the
temple; they looted and burned it. This shook
devout Jews deeply; more than anything else it
showed that God had given them up. Even
today Orthodox Jews observe the anniversary
of the temple's destruction by reading the book
of Lamentations aloud, and pilgrims daily
recite its prayers at the Wailing Wall in
Jerusalem.*

invade her sanctuary,
  those whom you forbade
    to enter your congregation.

11 All her people groan
    as they search for bread;
they trade their treasures for food
    to revive their strength.
Look, O Lord, and see
    how worthless I have become.

12 Is it nothing to you,[b] all you who pass
    by?
  Look and see
if there is any sorrow like my sorrow,
    which was brought upon me,
which the Lord inflicted
    on the day of his fierce anger.

13 From on high he sent fire;
    it went deep into my bones;
he spread a net for my feet;
    he turned me back;
he has left me stunned,
    faint all day long.

14 My transgressions were bound[b] into a
    yoke;
  by his hand they were fastened
      together;
they weigh on my neck,
    sapping my strength;
the Lord handed me over
    to those whom I cannot withstand.

15 The Lord has rejected
    all my warriors in the midst of me;
he proclaimed a time against me
    to crush my young men;
the Lord has trodden as in a wine press
    the virgin daughter Judah.

16 For these things I weep;
    my eyes flow with tears;
for a comforter is far from me,
    one to revive my courage;
my children are desolate,
    for the enemy has prevailed.

17 Zion stretches out her hands,
    but there is no one to comfort her;
the Lord has commanded against Jacob
    that his neighbors should become his
      foes;
Jerusalem has become
    a filthy thing among them.

18 The Lord is in the right,
    for I have rebelled against his word;

b Meaning of Heb uncertain

but hear, all you peoples,
  and behold my suffering;
my young women and young men
  have gone into captivity.

19 I called to my lovers
  but they deceived me;
my priests and elders
  perished in the city
while seeking food
  to revive their strength.

20 See, O LORD, how distressed I am;
  my stomach churns,
my heart is wrung within me,
  because I have been very rebellious.
In the street the sword bereaves;
  in the house it is like death.

21 They heard how I was groaning,
  with no one to comfort me.
All my enemies heard of my trouble;
  they are glad that you have done it.
Bring on the day you have announced,
  and let them be as I am.

22 Let all their evil doing come before you;
  and deal with them
as you have dealt with me
  because of all my transgressions;
for my groans are many
  and my heart is faint.

God's Warnings Fulfilled

2 How the Lord in his anger
  has humiliated[c] daughter Zion!
He has thrown down from heaven to
    earth
  the splendor of Israel;
he has not remembered his footstool
  in the day of his anger.

2 The Lord has destroyed without mercy
  all the dwellings of Jacob;
in his wrath he has broken down
  the strongholds of daughter Judah;
he has brought down to the ground in
    dishonor
  the kingdom and its rulers.

3 He has cut down in fierce anger
  all the might of Israel;
he has withdrawn his right hand from
    them
  in the face of the enemy;
he has burned like a flaming fire in Jacob,
  consuming all around.

4 He has bent his bow like an enemy,

with his right hand set like a foe;
he has killed all in whom we took pride
  in the tent of daughter Zion;
he has poured out his fury like fire.

5 The Lord has become like an enemy;
  he has destroyed Israel.
He has destroyed all its palaces,
  laid in ruins its strongholds,
and multiplied in daughter Judah
  mourning and lamentation.

6 He has broken down his booth like a
    garden,
  he has destroyed his tabernacle;
the LORD has abolished in Zion
  festival and sabbath,
and in his fierce indignation has spurned
  king and priest.

7 The Lord has scorned his altar,
  disowned his sanctuary;
he has delivered into the hand of the
    enemy
  the walls of her palaces;
a clamor was raised in the house of the
    LORD
  as on a day of festival.

8 The LORD determined to lay in ruins
  the wall of daughter Zion;
he stretched the line;
  he did not withhold his hand from
    destroying;
he caused rampart and wall to lament;
  they languish together.

9 Her gates have sunk into the ground;
  he has ruined and broken her bars;
her king and princes are among
    the nations;
  guidance is no more,
and her prophets obtain
  no vision from the LORD.

10 The elders of daughter Zion
  sit on the ground in silence;
they have thrown dust on their heads
  and put on sackcloth;
the young girls of Jerusalem
  have bowed their heads to the ground.

11 My eyes are spent with weeping;
  my stomach churns;
my bile is poured out on the ground
  because of the destruction of
    my people,
because infants and babes faint
  in the streets of the city.

c Meaning of Heb uncertain

12 They cry to their mothers,
  "Where is bread and wine?"
as they faint like the wounded
  in the streets of the city,
as their life is poured out
  on their mothers' bosom.

2.12 Pity the Children

Everyone suffered in the destruction of Jerusalem, rich and poor, young and old, male and female. Lamentations grieves for them all, but especially for the children, who were dying of hunger. During the long siege, hunger grew so fierce that mothers ate their own children (2.20; 4.10). Compassion for children had disappeared (4.3–4).

13 What can I say for you, to what compare you,
  O daughter Jerusalem?
To what can I liken you, that I may comfort you,
  O virgin daughter Zion?
For vast as the sea is your ruin;
  who can heal you?

14 Your prophets have seen for you
  false and deceptive visions;
they have not exposed your iniquity
  to restore your fortunes,
but have seen oracles for you
  that are false and misleading.

15 All who pass along the way
  clap their hands at you;
they hiss and wag their heads
  at daughter Jerusalem;
"Is this the city that was called
  the perfection of beauty,
  the joy of all the earth?"

16 All your enemies
  open their mouths against you;
they hiss, they gnash their teeth,
  they cry: "We have devoured her!
Ah, this is the day we longed for;
  at last we have seen it!"

17 The LORD has done what he purposed,
  he has carried out his threat;
as he ordained long ago,
  he has demolished without pity;
he has made the enemy rejoice over you,
  and exalted the might of your foes.

18 Cry aloud[d] to the Lord!

O wall of daughter Zion!
Let tears stream down like a torrent
  day and night!
Give yourself no rest,
  your eyes no respite!

19 Arise, cry out in the night,
  at the beginning of the watches!
Pour out your heart like water
  before the presence of the Lord!
Lift your hands to him
  for the lives of your children,
who faint for hunger
  at the head of every street.

20 Look, O LORD, and consider!
  To whom have you done this?
Should women eat their offspring,
  the children they have borne?
Should priest and prophet be killed
  in the sanctuary of the Lord?

21 The young and the old are lying
  on the ground in the streets;
my young women and my young men
  have fallen by the sword;
in the day of your anger you have killed them,
  slaughtering without mercy.

22 You invited my enemies from all around
  as if for a day of festival;
and on the day of the anger of the LORD
  no one escaped or survived;
those whom I bore and reared
  my enemy has destroyed.

God's Steadfast Love Endures

3 I am one who has seen affliction
  under the rod of God's[e] wrath;
2 he has driven and brought me
  into darkness without any light;

3.1 Autobiography of Pain

Ancient traditions say that Jeremiah wrote the book of Lamentations, and if so, this chapter records that doleful prophet's autobiography of pain. He was persecuted by enemies, thrown in a well, dragged captive, and jailed. Jeremiah knew, of course, that the people who did those things were God's enemies too, and he had delivered strong pronouncements against them. Yet to a person in pain—like Job, like Jeremiah—it often feels as if God himself has turned his back.

d Cn: Heb *Their heart cried*   e Heb *his*

3 against me alone he turns his hand,
again and again, all day long.

4 He has made my flesh and my skin waste
away,
and broken my bones;
5 he has besieged and enveloped me
with bitterness and tribulation;
6 he has made me sit in darkness
like the dead of long ago.

7 He has walled me about so that I cannot
escape;
he has put heavy chains on me;
8 though I call and cry for help,
he shuts out my prayer;
9 he has blocked my ways with hewn
stones,
he has made my paths crooked.

10 He is a bear lying in wait for me,
a lion in hiding;
11 he led me off my way and tore me to
pieces;
he has made me desolate;
12 he bent his bow and set me
as a mark for his arrow.

13 He shot into my vitals
the arrows of his quiver;
14 I have become the laughingstock of all my
people,
the object of their taunt-songs all day
long.
15 He has filled me with bitterness,
he has sated me with wormwood.

16 He has made my teeth grind on gravel,
and made me cower in ashes;
17 my soul is bereft of peace;
I have forgotten what happiness is;
18 so I say, "Gone is my glory,
and all that I had hoped for from the
LORD."

19 The thought of my affliction and my
homelessness
is wormwood and gall!
20 My soul continually thinks of it
and is bowed down within me.
21 But this I call to mind,
and therefore I have hope:

22 The steadfast love of the LORD never
ceases,*f*
his mercies never come to an end;
23 they are new every morning;
great is your faithfulness.

24 "The LORD is my portion," says my soul,
"therefore I will hope in him."

25 The LORD is good to those who wait for
him,
to the soul that seeks him.
26 It is good that one should wait quietly
for the salvation of the LORD.
27 It is good for one to bear
the yoke in youth,
28 to sit alone in silence
when the Lord has imposed it,
29 to put one's mouth to the dust
(there may yet be hope),
30 to give one's cheek to the smiter,
and be filled with insults.

31 For the Lord will not
reject forever.
32 Although he causes grief, he will have
compassion
according to the abundance of his
steadfast love;
33 for he does not willingly afflict
or grieve anyone.

3.33 Hope for the Grieving

Lamentations bares the full horror of suffering, yet offers hope based on the character of God. He has let some survive (verse 22), and he is not a God to be angry with them forever. Their duty is to accept fully their grief, and quietly meditate on its meaning while waiting for the Lord.

34 When all the prisoners of the land
are crushed under foot,
35 when human rights are perverted
in the presence of the Most High,
36 when one's case is subverted
—does the Lord not see it?

37 Who can command and have it done,
if the Lord has not ordained it?
38 Is it not from the mouth of the Most
High
that good and bad come?
39 Why should any who draw breath
complain
about the punishment of their sins?

40 Let us test and examine our ways,
and return to the LORD.
41 Let us lift up our hearts as well as our
hands
to God in heaven.

f Syr Tg: Heb LORD, we are not cut off

42 We have transgressed and rebelled,
    and you have not forgiven.

43 You have wrapped yourself with anger
        and pursued us,
    killing without pity;
44 you have wrapped yourself with a cloud
    so that no prayer can pass through.
45 You have made us filth and rubbish
    among the peoples.

46 All our enemies
    have opened their mouths against us;
47 panic and pitfall have come upon us,
    devastation and destruction.
48 My eyes flow with rivers of tears
    because of the destruction of
        my people.

49 My eyes will flow without ceasing,
        without respite,
50 until the LORD from heaven
    looks down and sees.
51 My eyes cause me grief
    at the fate of all the young women in
        my city.

52 Those who were my enemies without
        cause
    have hunted me like a bird;
53 they flung me alive into a pit
    and hurled stones on me;
54 water closed over my head;
    I said, "I am lost."

55 I called on your name, O LORD,
    from the depths of the pit;
56 you heard my plea, "Do not close your
        ear
    to my cry for help, but give me relief!"
57 You came near when I called on you;
    you said, "Do not fear!"

58 You have taken up my cause, O Lord,
    you have redeemed my life.
59 You have seen the wrong done to me,
        O LORD;
    judge my cause.
60 You have seen all their malice,
    all their plots against me.

61 You have heard their taunts, O LORD,
    all their plots against me.
62 The whispers and murmurs of my
        assailants
    are against me all day long.
63 Whether they sit or rise—see,
    I am the object of their taunt-songs.

64 Pay them back for their deeds, O LORD,
    according to the work of their hands!
65 Give them anguish of heart;
    your curse be on them!
66 Pursue them in anger and destroy them
    from under the LORD's heavens.

The Punishment of Zion

4 How the gold has grown dim,
    how the pure gold is changed!
The sacred stones lie scattered
    at the head of every street.

2 The precious children of Zion,
    worth their weight in fine gold—
how they are reckoned as earthen pots,
    the work of a potter's hands!

3 Even the jackals offer the breast
    and nurse their young,
but my people has become cruel,
    like the ostriches in the wilderness.

4 The tongue of the infant sticks
    to the roof of its mouth for thirst;
the children beg for food,
    but no one gives them anything.

4.4 Starving to Death

Horrible scenes of starvation, like those shown in documentaries of African famines in recent times, were seen in the streets of Jerusalem during the Babylonian invasion. Foreign armies encircled the city for two years, cutting off all sources of food. The residents of this once-proud city resorted to eating their own children (verse 10) just to stay alive.

5 Those who feasted on delicacies
    perish in the streets;
those who were brought up in purple
    cling to ash heaps.

6 For the chastisement[g] of my people has
        been greater
    than the punishment[h] of Sodom,
which was overthrown in a moment,
    though no hand was laid on it.[i]

7 Her princes were purer than snow,
    whiter than milk;
their bodies were more ruddy than coral,
    their hair[i] like sapphire.[j]

8 Now their visage is blacker than soot;
    they are not recognized in the streets.

g Or *iniquity*   h Or *sin*   i Meaning of Heb uncertain   j Or *lapis lazuli*

Their skin has shriveled on their bones;
it has become as dry as wood.

9 Happier were those pierced by the sword
than those pierced by hunger,
whose life drains away, deprived
of the produce of the field.

10 The hands of compassionate women
have boiled their own children;
they became their food
in the destruction of my people.

11 The LORD gave full vent to his wrath;
he poured out his hot anger,
and kindled a fire in Zion
that consumed its foundations.

12 The kings of the earth did not believe,
nor did any of the inhabitants of the
world,
that foe or enemy could enter
the gates of Jerusalem.

13 It was for the sins of her prophets
and the iniquities of her priests,
who shed the blood of the righteous
in the midst of her.

14 Blindly they wandered through the streets,
so defiled with blood
that no one was able
to touch their garments.

15 "Away! Unclean!" people shouted
at them;
"Away! Away! Do not touch!"
So they became fugitives and wanderers;
it was said among the nations,
"They shall stay here no longer."

16 The LORD himself has scattered them,
he will regard them no more;
no honor was shown to the priests,
no favor to the elders.

17 Our eyes failed, ever watching
vainly for help;
we were watching eagerly
for a nation that could not save.

18 They dogged our steps
so that we could not walk in
our streets;
our end drew near; our days were
numbered;
for our end had come.

19 Our pursuers were swifter

than the eagles in the heavens;
they chased us on the mountains,
they lay in wait for us in the
wilderness.

20 The LORD's anointed, the breath of our
life,
was taken in their pits—
the one of whom we said, "Under his
shadow
we shall live among the nations."

4.17 False Hope

In the last decades before Jerusalem was conquered, Judah's kings frequently tried to play Egypt, another superpower, against Babylon. Right to the end they expected Egypt's armies to rescue them. But as Jeremiah had warned, Egypt proved to be an unreliable ally (Jeremiah 2.36–37; 37.5–8).

21 Rejoice and be glad, O daughter Edom,
you that live in the land of Uz;
but to you also the cup shall pass;
you shall become drunk and strip
yourself bare.

22 The punishment of your iniquity,
O daughter Zion, is
accomplished,
he will keep you in exile no longer;
but your iniquity, O daughter Edom, he
will punish,
he will uncover your sins.

A Plea for Mercy

5 Remember, O LORD, what has befallen us;
look, and see our disgrace!
2 Our inheritance has been turned over to
strangers,
our homes to aliens.
3 We have become orphans, fatherless;
our mothers are like widows.
4 We must pay for the water we drink;
the wood we get must be bought.
5 With a yoke[k] on our necks we are hard
driven;
we are weary, we are given no rest.
6 We have made a pact with[l] Egypt and
Assyria,
to get enough bread.
7 Our ancestors sinned; they are no more,
and we bear their iniquities.
8 Slaves rule over us;

---

k Symmachus: Heb lacks *With a yoke*   l Heb *have given the hand to*

there is no one to deliver us from their
  hand.
9 We get our bread at the peril of our lives,
  because of the sword in the wilderness.
10 Our skin is black as an oven
  from the scorching heat of famine.
11 Women are raped in Zion,
  virgins in the towns of Judah.
12 Princes are hung up by their hands;
  no respect is shown to the elders.
13 Young men are compelled to grind,
  and boys stagger under loads of wood.
14 The old men have left the city gate,
  the young men their music.
15 The joy of our hearts has ceased;
  our dancing has been turned
    to mourning.
16 The crown has fallen from our head;

woe to us, for we have sinned!
17 Because of this our hearts are sick,
  because of these things our eyes have
    grown dim:
18 because of Mount Zion, which
    lies desolate;
  jackals prowl over it.

19 But you, O LORD, reign forever;
  your throne endures to all generations.
20 Why have you forgotten us completely?
  Why have you forsaken us these many
    days?
21 Restore us to yourself, O LORD, that we
    may be restored;
  renew our days as of old—
22 unless you have utterly rejected us,
  and are angry with us beyond measure.

EZEKIEL

Seeing the Unseen God
God showed himself to Ezekiel in unearthly radiance

EZEKIEL BEGINS WITH A DESCRIPTION so unearthly that some have suggested the prophet saw a UFO. Indeed, there are similarities: glowing lights, quick movements, inhuman figures shrouded with fire. But at least one critical difference sets Ezekiel's story apart. UFOs typically appear in remote places and then mysteriously zoom off, never to be heard from again. The majestic being Ezekiel described was not rushing off to disappear. He wanted to be known—by everyone.

Like the bow in a cloud on a rainy day, such was the appearance of the splendor all around . . . When I saw it, I fell on my face. 1.28

For Ezekiel was quite sure that he had seen and heard the God of the Bible. While few have been privileged to see him as Ezekiel did, this God had been speaking plainly for generations. His words were on record.

Before such splendor Ezekiel felt utterly weak and inadequate, just as Isaiah had during a similar vision (Isaiah 6). He fell on his face, repeatedly. But God raised Ezekiel to his feet and gave him a message to deliver.

A Stunning Portrait of God

In describing his call by God, Ezekiel groped for words. He portrayed a God of stunning grandeur, above and beyond our world. Yet this supernatural God was inescapably near and real. He demanded complete obedience. Surprisingly, he appeared to Ezekiel in Babylon—the last place an Israelite expected to see him. This God could not be locked in by national or geographical boxes. He ruled the earth.

Ezekiel repeated this classic message over 60 times: "Then they shall know that I am the LORD." God said it when promising the destruction of Jerusalem in the first 24 chapters. He said it when predicting the downfall of Israel's neighbors in chapters 25 through 32. And, after Jerusalem had fallen, God said it when promising a great future in the last 16 chapters. God did not want to remain vague or far off. He wanted his people to know him. More, Ezekiel's God wanted to live with his people. He wanted to make his home in the center of their city.

A Strange Book

Ezekiel has a reputation for strangeness, partly because of the unearthly visions with which his book begins and ends, and partly because Ezekiel acted out God's messages through some bizarre behavior. (For instance, for months at a time he lay in public on his side, bound by ropes, facing a clay model of Jerusalem.) Strange? When a car is speeding down a road unaware of a bridge washout, you may take strange measures to get the driver's attention. You may scream and gesture so wildly people think you are insane. So it was with Ezekiel. His message came in the most vivid form possible, meant to force people to pay attention.

Ezekiel lived in perhaps the most tragic period of his people's existence. They had been tempting fate for generations, ignoring God's messengers (prophets like Micah, Amos, Isaiah) who warned that if they didn't listen to God, they would be destroyed. Finally, Babylonian armies swept through Judah, deporting large groups of citizens.

Ezekiel had gone into exile in one of the first groups, as had Daniel. Ezekiel became God's messenger as a captive in Babylon. His voice blended in stereo with Jeremiah's, still in Jerusalem. Both prophets warned their people (who kept plotting ways to break free of Babylon) that the captives were going to be in Babylon for a long time. They predicted that Babylon's oppression would grow heavier: Jerusalem and the temple would be destroyed. Since Judah had ignored God's repeated warnings, God would use another means to get their attention: suffering.

A New Jerusalem

Yet even while punishing them, God's aim remained the same: to make himself known. God had warned Ezekiel that the Israelites were unlikely to listen (3.7), even from captivity. They preferred idols to the living God. Yet Ezekiel's messages and dramas and visions continued to come, year after year. It's as though God were saying through him, "Some way, some day, I will get through to them. If the message doesn't reach their hearts one way, I'll try another."

Ezekiel ends with hope. The final chapters show a new Jerusalem rising from the ruins of the old. The renewed city would never die, for it would be built on an unshifting reality: "They shall know that I am the LORD." The burning vision of God that Ezekiel had seen would become accessible to all. God would make himself at home there forever. Ezekiel's last verse says it all: "And the name of the city from that time on shall be, The LORD is There."

How to Read Ezekiel

The special difficulty in reading Ezekiel is the dizzying variety of forms he used to get his message across. The book is like a multimedia package—a mix of visions, messages, dramas, poems. But three remarkable visions of God bracket the package, beginning, middle, and end (1.1–3.15; 8.1–6 and 11.16–25; 40.1–4 and 43.1–9). And throughout, one line is repeated: "Then they shall know that I am the LORD." All God's messages are meant to shock his people into restoring a living relationship with him.

As you read Ezekiel, note down when each prophecy was made and its dominant image—Jerusalem as a prostitute, as a spreading grapevine, as a shaved head, etc. (For insight into why Ezekiel sometimes acted out his message in bizarre fashion, read "Living Parables," page 808.) Don't skip ahead too fast as you read—take time to think about the message in each section. Remember that the book of Ezekiel compresses messages God gave over 22 years. Try to imagine the impact of each message on the people who first heard or saw it.

Most of what Ezekiel said in Babylonia concerned a dramatic military situation hundreds of miles away in Jerusalem. His message changed from doom to hope in chapter 33; the turning point came with news of Jerusalem's fall. You can get to know the historical situation by reading 2 Kings 23.36–25.12. "A Lineup of Rulers," page 1349–1357, can help you place Ezekiel in Israel's history.

A fascinating though difficult study is the design of the renewed temple, which Ezekiel described in chapters 40–43. A commentary on Ezekiel or a Bible dictionary (under "Ezekiel" or "temple") can help immensely in understanding these visions.

PEOPLE YOU'LL MEET IN EZEKIEL

EZEKIEL *(p. 842)*

3-TRACK READING PLAN

For an explanation and complete listing of the 3-track reading plan, turn to page 7.

TRACK 1: ***Two-Week Courses on the Bible***
See page 7 for information on these courses.

TRACK 2: ***An Overview of Ezekiel in 4 Days***
☐ Day 1. Read the Introduction to Ezekiel and chapter 1, the majestic vision of a living God who appeared to Ezekiel.
☐ Day 2. Read chapters 2–3, which tell how God called Ezekiel to deliver a difficult message.
☐ Day 3. Read chapter 4, one of the most dramatic of the "enacted parables" Ezekiel performed.
☐ Day 4. Read chapter 37, a message of hope and resurrection for a defeated people.

Now turn to page 9 for your next Track 2 reading project.

TRACK 3: **All of Ezekiel in 47 Days**
After you have read through Ezekiel, turn to pages 10–14 for your next Track 3 reading project.

☐1 ☐2–3 ☐4 ☐5 ☐6 ☐7 ☐8 ☐9
☐10 ☐11 ☐12 ☐13 ☐14 ☐15 ☐16 ☐17
☐18 ☐19 ☐20 ☐21 ☐22 ☐23 ☐24 ☐25
☐26 ☐27 ☐28 ☐29 ☐30 ☐31 ☐32 ☐33
☐34 ☐35 ☐36 ☐37 ☐38 ☐39 ☐40 ☐41
☐42 ☐43 ☐44 ☐45 ☐46 ☐47 ☐48

The Vision of the Chariot

1 In the thirtieth year, in the fourth month, on the fifth day of the month, as I was among the exiles by the river Chebar, the heavens were opened, and I saw visions of God. ²On the fifth day of the month (it was the fifth year of the exile of King Jehoiachin), ³the word of the LORD came to the priest Ezekiel son of Buzi, in the land of the Chaldeans by the river Chebar; and the hand of the LORD was on him there.

1.3 Foreign Appearance

Most ancient religions worshiped tribal gods, whose rule extended only within the tribal territory. As an exile, Ezekiel may have wondered whether the God of Israel would still speak so far from home. But it was in Babylon that God appeared. The terrifying vision in a windstorm revealed a God who ruled over the entire world, awesome, magnificent, exalted, far more powerful than the Babylonian armies.

4 As I looked, a stormy wind came out of the north: a great cloud with brightness around it and fire flashing forth continually, and in the middle of the fire, something like gleaming amber. ⁵In the middle of it was something like four living creatures. This was their appearance: they were of human form. ⁶Each had four faces, and each of them had four wings. ⁷Their legs were straight, and the soles of their feet were like the sole of a calf's foot; and they sparkled like burnished bronze. ⁸Under their wings on their four sides they had human hands. And the four had their faces and their wings thus: ⁹their wings touched one another; each of them moved straight ahead, without turning as they moved. ¹⁰As for the appearance of their faces: the four had the face of a human being, the face of a lion on the right side, the face of an ox on the left side, and the face of an eagle; ¹¹such were their faces. Their wings were spread out above; each creature had two wings, each of which touched the wing of another, while two covered their bodies. ¹²Each moved straight ahead; wherever the spirit would go, they went, without turning as they went. ¹³In the middle of[a] the living creatures there was something that looked like burning coals of fire, like torches moving to and fro among the living creatures; the fire was bright, and lightning issued from the fire. ¹⁴The living creatures darted to and fro, like a flash of lightning.

15 As I looked at the living creatures, I saw a wheel on the earth beside the living creatures, one for each of the four of them.[b] ¹⁶As for the appearance of the wheels and their construction: their appearance was like the gleaming of beryl; and the four had the same form, their construction being something like a wheel within a wheel. ¹⁷When they moved, they moved in any of the four directions without veering as they moved. ¹⁸Their rims were tall and awesome, for the rims of all four were full of eyes all around. ¹⁹When the living creatures moved, the wheels moved beside them; and when the living creatures rose from the earth, the wheels rose. ²⁰Wherever the spirit would go, they went, and the wheels rose along with them; for the spirit of the living creatures was in the wheels. ²¹When they moved, the others moved; when they stopped, the others stopped; and when they rose from the earth, the wheels rose along with them; for the spirit of the living creatures was in the wheels.

22 Over the heads of the living creatures there was something like a dome, shining like crystal,[c] spread out above their heads. ²³Under the dome their wings were stretched out straight, one toward another; and each of the creatures had two wings covering its body. ²⁴When they moved, I heard the sound of their wings like the sound of mighty waters, like the thunder of the Almighty,[d] a sound of tumult like the sound of an army; when they stopped, they let down their wings. ²⁵And there came a voice from above the dome over their heads; when they stopped, they let down their wings.

26 And above the dome over their heads there was something like a throne, in appearance like sapphire;[e] and seated above the likeness of a

---

[a] Gk OL: Heb *And the appearance of*   [b] Heb *of their faces*   [c] Gk: Heb *like the awesome crystal*   [d] Traditional rendering of Heb *Shaddai*   [e] Or *lapis lazuli*

throne was something that seemed like a human form. [27]Upward from what appeared like the loins I saw something like gleaming amber, something that looked like fire enclosed all around; and downward from what looked like the loins I saw something that looked like fire, and there was a splendor all around. [28]Like the bow in a cloud on a rainy day, such was the appearance of the splendor all around. This was the appearance of the likeness of the glory of the LORD.

When I saw it, I fell on my face, and I heard the voice of someone speaking.

The Vision of the Scroll

2 He said to me: O mortal,[f] stand up on your feet, and I will speak with you. [2]And when he spoke to me, a spirit entered into me and set me on my feet; and I heard him speaking to me. [3]He said to me, Mortal, I am sending you to the people of Israel, to a nation[g] of rebels who have rebelled against me; they and their ancestors have transgressed against me to this very day. [4]The descendants are impudent and stubborn. I am sending you to them, and you shall say to them, "Thus says the Lord GOD." [5]Whether they hear or refuse to hear (for they are a rebellious house), they shall know that there has been a prophet among them. [6]And you, O mortal, do not be afraid of them, and do not be afraid of their words, though briers and thorns surround you and you live among scorpions; do not be afraid of their words, and do not be dismayed at their looks, for they are a rebellious house. [7]You shall speak my words to them, whether they hear or refuse to hear; for they are a rebellious house.

8 But you, mortal, hear what I say to you; do not be rebellious like that rebellious house; open your mouth and eat what I give you. [9]I looked, and a hand was stretched out to me, and a written scroll was in it. [10]He spread it before me; it had writing on the front and on the back, and written on it were words of lamentation and mourning and woe.

3 He said to me, O mortal, eat what is offered to you; eat this scroll, and go, speak to the house of Israel. [2]So I opened my mouth, and he gave me the scroll to eat. [3]He said to me, Mortal, eat this scroll that I give you and fill your stomach with it. Then I ate it; and in my mouth it was as sweet as honey.

4 He said to me: Mortal, go to the house of Israel and speak my very words to them. [5]For you are not sent to a people of obscure speech and difficult language, but to the house of Israel— [6]not to many peoples of obscure speech and difficult language, whose words you cannot understand. Surely, if I sent you to them, they would

3.3 Eat the Scroll

The scroll with words of woe looked inedible, but tasted sweet as honey to Ezekiel. Most of God's prophets gave bitter messages of warning, but God's word sustained and strengthened them as they served him. (See also Jeremiah's experience, in Jeremiah 15.16.) Similarly, the book of Revelation tells of a scroll being eaten (Revelation 10.9–11). Many of Ezekiel's images are paralleled in that book.

listen to you. [7]But the house of Israel will not listen to you, for they are not willing to listen to me; because all the house of Israel have a hard forehead and a stubborn heart. [8]See, I have made your face hard against their faces, and your forehead hard against their foreheads. [9]Like the hardest stone, harder than flint, I have made your forehead; do not fear them or be dismayed at their looks, for they are a rebellious house. [10]He said to me: Mortal, all my words that I shall speak to you receive in your heart and hear with your ears; [11]then go to the exiles, to your people, and speak to them. Say to them, "Thus says the Lord GOD"; whether they hear or refuse to hear.

Ezekiel at the River Chebar

12 Then the spirit lifted me up, and as the glory of the LORD rose[h] from its place, I heard behind me the sound of loud rumbling; [13]it was the sound of the wings of the living creatures brushing against one another, and the sound of the wheels beside them, that sounded like a loud rumbling. [14]The spirit lifted me up and bore me away; I went in bitterness in the heat of my spirit, the hand of the LORD being strong upon me. [15]I came to the exiles at Tel-abib, who lived by the river Chebar.[i] And I sat there among them, stunned, for seven days.

16 At the end of seven days, the word of the LORD came to me: [17]Mortal, I have made you a sentinel for the house of Israel; whenever you hear a word from my mouth, you shall give them warning from me. [18]If I say to the wicked, "You shall surely die," and you give them no warning, or speak to warn the wicked from their wicked way, in order to save their life, those wicked persons shall die for their iniquity; but their blood I will require at your hand. [19]But if you warn the wicked, and they do not turn from their wickedness, or from their wicked way, they shall die for their iniquity; but you will have saved your life. [20]Again, if the righteous turn from their righteousness and commit iniquity, and I lay a stum-

---

f Or *son of man*; Heb *ben adam* (and so throughout the book when Ezekiel is addressed)   g Syr: Heb *to nations*
h Cn: Heb *and blessed be the glory of the LORD*   i Two Mss Syr: Heb *Chebar, and to where they lived*. Another reading is *Chebar, and I sat where they sat*

bling block before them, they shall die; because you have not warned them, they shall die for their sin, and their righteous deeds that they have done shall not be remembered; but their blood I will require at your hand. 21If, however, you warn the righteous not to sin, and they do not sin, they shall surely live, because they took warning; and you will have saved your life.

Ezekiel Isolated and Silenced

22 Then the hand of the LORD was upon me there; and he said to me, Rise up, go out into the valley, and there I will speak with you. 23So I rose up and went out into the valley; and the glory of the LORD stood there, like the glory that I had seen by the river Chebar; and I fell on my face. 24The spirit entered into me, and set me on my feet; and he spoke with me and said to me: Go, shut yourself inside your house. 25As for you, mortal, cords shall be placed on you, and you shall be bound with them, so that you cannot go out among the people; 26and I will make your tongue cling to the roof of your mouth, so that you shall be speechless and unable to reprove them; for they are a rebellious house. 27But when I speak with you, I will open your mouth, and you shall say to them, "Thus says the Lord GOD"; let those who will hear, hear; and let those who refuse to hear, refuse; for they are a rebellious house.

The Siege of Jerusalem Portrayed

4 And you, O mortal, take a brick and set it before you. On it portray a city, Jerusalem; 2and put siegeworks against it, and build a siege wall against it, and cast up a ramp against it; set camps also against it, and plant battering rams against it all around. 3Then take an iron plate and place it as an iron wall between you and the city; set your face toward it, and let it be in a state of siege, and press the siege against it. This is a sign for the house of Israel.

4 Then lie on your left side, and place the punishment of the house of Israel upon it; you shall bear their punishment for the number of the days that you lie there. 5For I assign to you a number of days, three hundred ninety days, equal to the number of the years of their punishment; and so you shall bear the punishment of the house of Israel. 6When you have completed these, you shall lie down a second time, but on your right side, and bear the punishment of the house of Judah; forty days I assign you, one day for each year. 7You shall set your face toward the siege of Jerusalem, and with your arm bared you shall prophesy against it. 8See, I am putting cords on you so that you cannot turn from one side to the other until you have completed the days of your siege.

9 And you, take wheat and barley, beans and lentils, millet and spelt; put them into one vessel, and make bread for yourself. During the number of days that you lie on your side, three hundred ninety days, you shall eat it. 10The food that you eat shall be twenty shekels a day by weight; at fixed times you shall eat it. 11And you shall drink water by measure, one-sixth of a hin; at fixed

EZEKIEL *Radical Priest*

SOME GREAT HISTORICAL FIGURES ARE known only by their accomplishments. The artists who created the great European cathedrals, for example—in most cases we do not even know their names. They fashioned beautiful monuments to God, not to themselves.

In some ways Ezekiel fits this pattern. He created a major book of the Bible and acted as God's messenger in some hinge moments of history. We know what he did, yet we know next to nothing about *him:* his personality, his background, his family life. Ezekiel recounted his calling as a prophet in detail and mentioned his work as a priest, but otherwise his book includes only a few shreds of personal information (such as the fact that he was married). His work swallowed up his life.

Ezekiel's story begins with King Nebuchadnezzar taking him captive from Jerusalem to Babylon—the site of present-day Iraq. No doubt the foreign setting made him feel lonely and homesick. He was a priest far from God's temple, as fruitless a combination as a basketball coach without a gym. What could Ezekiel do?

Complicating Ezekiel's life, God told him to deliver a very unpopular message—that God would continue to punish his people because they had not repented from their sin. Moreover, God instructed Ezekiel to dramatize that message in bizarre ways. At various times he ate a book, shaved his head, cooked with cow manure, and lay outdoors beside a model of Jerusalem. Looking back, some of Ezekiel's "object lessons" seem downright weird.

For one short period, when his predictions came true, Ezekiel enjoyed popularity and acceptance (33.30–32). More often, though, he needed God's prodding and encouragement: "Do not be afraid of them, and do not be afraid of their words, though briers and thorns surround you and you live among scorpions" (2.6). God had vital work for him to do. For Ezekiel, that made for a worthy life, regardless of the cost.

Life Questions: If you were to die today, what "monument" would you leave behind?

times you shall drink. ¹²You shall eat it as a barley-cake, baking it in their sight on human dung. ¹³The LORD said, "Thus shall the people of Israel eat their bread, unclean, among the nations to which I will drive them." ¹⁴Then I said, "Ah Lord GOD! I have never defiled myself; from my youth up until now I have never eaten what died of itself or was torn by animals, nor has carrion flesh come into my mouth." ¹⁵Then he said to me, "See, I will let you have cow's dung instead of human dung, on which you may prepare your bread."

16 Then he said to me, Mortal, I am going to break the staff of bread in Jerusalem; they shall eat bread by weight and with fearfulness; and they shall drink water by measure and in dismay. ¹⁷Lacking bread and water, they will look at one another in dismay, and waste away under their punishment.

A Sword against Jerusalem

5 And you, O mortal, take a sharp sword; use it as a barber's razor and run it over your head and your beard; then take balances for weighing, and divide the hair. ²One third of the hair you shall burn in the fire inside the city, when the days of the siege are completed; one third you shall take and strike with the sword all around the city;ʲ and one third you shall scatter to the wind, and I will unsheathe the sword after them. ³Then you shall take from these a small number, and bind them in the skirts of your robe. ⁴From these, again, you shall take some, throw them into the fire and burn them up; from there a fire will come out against all the house of Israel.

5 Thus says the Lord GOD: This is Jerusalem; I have set her in the center of the nations, with

5.5 Navel of the Universe

Maps dating from the Middle Ages often showed Jerusalem and Israel as the center of a flat world. The practice probably stemmed from several verses like this one, referring to Jerusalem as "the center of the nations." Geography was not what God had in mind, however. Jerusalem was at the center of his love. A lover might say something similar: "You're the center of my universe."

countries all around her. ⁶But she has rebelled against my ordinances and my statutes, becoming more wicked than the nations and the countries all around her, rejecting my ordinances and not following my statutes. ⁷Therefore thus says the Lord GOD: Because you are more turbulent than the nations that are all around you, and have not

followed my statutes or kept my ordinances, but have acted according to the ordinances of the nations that are all around you; ⁸therefore thus says the Lord GOD: I, I myself, am coming against you; I will execute judgments among you in the sight of the nations. ⁹And because of all your abominations, I will do to you what I have never yet done, and the like of which I will never do again. ¹⁰Surely, parents shall eat their children in your midst, and children shall eat their parents; I will execute judgments on you, and any of you who survive I will scatter to every wind. ¹¹Therefore, as I live, says the Lord GOD, surely, because you have defiled my sanctuary with all your detestable things and with all your abominations— therefore I will cut you down;ᵏ my eye will not spare, and I will have no pity. ¹²One third of you shall die of pestilence or be consumed by famine among you; one third shall fall by the sword around you; and one third I will scatter to every wind and will unsheathe the sword after them.

13 My anger shall spend itself, and I will vent my fury on them and satisfy myself; and they shall know that I, the LORD, have spoken in my jealousy, when I spend my fury on them. ¹⁴Moreover I will make you a desolation and an object of mocking among the nations around you, in the sight of all that pass by. ¹⁵You shall beˡ a mockery and a taunt, a warning and a horror, to the nations around you, when I execute judgments on you in anger and fury, and with furious punishments—I, the LORD, have spoken— ¹⁶when I loose against youᵐ my deadly arrows of famine, arrows for destruction, which I will let loose to destroy you, and when I bring more and more famine upon you, and break your staff of bread. ¹⁷I will send famine and wild animals against you, and they will rob you of your children; pestilence and bloodshed shall pass through you; and I will bring the sword upon you. I, the LORD, have spoken.

Judgment on Idolatrous Israel

6 The word of the LORD came to me: ²O mortal, set your face toward the mountains of Israel, and prophesy against them, ³and say, You mountains of Israel, hear the word of the Lord GOD! Thus says the Lord GOD to the mountains and the hills, to the ravines and the valleys: I, I myself will bring a sword upon you, and I will destroy your high places. ⁴Your altars shall become desolate, and your incense stands shall be broken; and I will throw down your slain in front of your idols. ⁵I will lay the corpses of the people of Israel in front of their idols; and I will scatter your bones around your altars. ⁶Wherever you live, your towns shall be waste and your high places ruined, so that your altars will be waste and

---

ʲ Heb it   ᵏ Another reading is *I will withdraw*   ˡ Gk Syr Vg Tg: Heb *It shall be*   ᵐ Heb *them*

ruined,[n] your idols broken and destroyed, your incense stands cut down, and your works wiped out. [7]The slain shall fall in your midst; then you shall know that I am the LORD.

8 But I will spare some. Some of you shall escape the sword among the nations and be scattered through the countries. [9]Those of you who escape shall remember me among the nations where they are carried captive, how I was crushed by their wanton heart that turned away from me, and their wanton eyes that turned after their idols. Then they will be loathsome in their own sight for the evils that they have committed, for all their

6.9 A Dim View of Idolatry

Ezekiel said little about exploitation and injustice. He concentrated on Israel's rejection of a relationship with the living God; they preferred idols instead. The Hebrew word translated "idols" here is used 38 times in Ezekiel, nine in the rest of the Old Testament. Some scholars believe the word is derived from "pellet of dung," indicating Ezekiel's scorn.

abominations. [10]And they shall know that I am the LORD; I did not threaten in vain to bring this disaster upon them.

11 Thus says the Lord GOD: Clap your hands and stamp your foot, and say, Alas for all the vile abominations of the house of Israel! For they shall fall by the sword, by famine, and by pestilence. [12]Those far off shall die of pestilence; those nearby shall fall by the sword; and any who are left and are spared shall die of famine. Thus I will spend my fury upon them. [13]And you shall know that I am the LORD, when their slain lie among their idols around their altars, on every high hill, on all the mountain tops, under every green tree, and under every leafy oak, wherever they offered pleasing odor to all their idols. [14]I will stretch out my hand against them, and make the land desolate and waste, throughout all their settlements, from the wilderness to Riblah.[o] Then they shall know that I am the LORD.

Impending Disaster

7 The word of the LORD came to me: [2]You, O mortal, thus says the Lord GOD to the land of Israel:
An end! The end has come
   upon the four corners of the land.
[3] Now the end is upon you,
   I will let loose my anger upon you;
   I will judge you according to your ways,
   I will punish you for all your
      abominations.

[4] My eye will not spare you, I will have no
      pity.
   I will punish you for your ways,
      while your abominations are among
         you.
Then you shall know that I am the LORD.
5 Thus says the Lord GOD:
   Disaster after disaster! See, it comes.
[6]   An end has come, the end has come.
   It has awakened against you; see,
      it comes!
[7] Your doom[p] has come to you,
   O inhabitant of the land.
The time has come, the day is near—
   of tumult, not of reveling on the
      mountains.
[8] Soon now I will pour out my wrath upon
      you;
   I will spend my anger against you.
I will judge you according to your ways,
   and punish you for all your
      abominations.
[9] My eye will not spare; I will have no pity.
   I will punish you according to your
      ways,
   while your abominations are among
      you.
Then you shall know that it is I the LORD who strike.
[10] See, the day! See, it comes!
   Your doom[p] has gone out.
The rod has blossomed, pride has
   budded.
[11]   Violence has grown into a rod
      of wickedness.
None of them shall remain,
   not their abundance, not their wealth;
   no pre-eminence among them.[p]
12 The time has come, the day draws near;
   let not the buyer rejoice, nor the seller
      mourn,
   for wrath is upon all their multitude.
[13]For the sellers shall not return to what has been sold as long as they remain alive. For the vision concerns all their multitude; it shall not be revoked. Because of their iniquity, they cannot maintain their lives.[p]
14 They have blown the horn and made
      everything ready,
   but no one goes to battle,
   for my wrath is upon all their
      multitude.
[15] The sword is outside, pestilence and
      famine are inside;
   those in the field die by the sword;
   those in the city—famine and
      pestilence devour them.
[16] If any survivors escape,
   they shall be found on the mountains

---

[n] Syr Vg Tg: Heb *and be made guilty*   [o] Another reading is *Diblah*   [p] Meaning of Heb uncertain

like doves of the valleys,
  all of them moaning over their iniquity.
17 All hands shall grow feeble,
  all knees turn to water.
18 They shall put on sackcloth,
  horror shall cover them.
Shame shall be on all faces,
  baldness on all their heads.
19 They shall fling their silver into the
  streets,
  their gold shall be treated as unclean.
Their silver and gold cannot save them on the day of the wrath of the LORD. They shall not satisfy their hunger or fill their stomachs with it. For it was the stumbling block of their iniquity. 20From their*q* beautiful ornament, in which they took pride, they made their abominable images, their detestable things; therefore I will make of it an unclean thing to them.
21 I will hand it over to strangers as booty,
  to the wicked of the earth as plunder;
  they shall profane it.
22 I will avert my face from them,
  so that they may profane my
  treasured*r* place;
the violent shall enter it,
  they shall profane it.
23 Make a chain!*s*
For the land is full of bloody crimes;
  the city is full of violence.
24 I will bring the worst of the nations
  to take possession of their houses.
I will put an end to the arrogance of the
  strong,
  and their holy places shall be profaned.
25 When anguish comes, they will seek
  peace,
  but there shall be none.
26 Disaster comes upon disaster,
  rumor follows rumor;
they shall keep seeking a vision from the
  prophet;
  instruction shall perish from the priest,
  and counsel from the elders.
27 The king shall mourn,
  the prince shall be wrapped in despair,
  and the hands of the people of the
  land shall tremble.
According to their way I will deal with
  them;
  according to their own judgments I will
  judge them.
And they shall know that I am the LORD.

Abominations in the Temple

8 In the sixth year, in the sixth month, on the fifth day of the month, as I sat in my house, with the elders of Judah sitting before me, the hand of the Lord GOD fell upon me there. 2I

looked, and there was a figure that looked like a human being;*t* below what appeared to be its loins it was fire, and above the loins it was like the appearance of brightness, like gleaming amber. 3It stretched out the form of a hand, and took me by a lock of my head; and the spirit lifted me up between earth and heaven, and brought me in visions of God to Jerusalem, to the entrance of the gateway of the inner court that faces north, to the seat of the image of jealousy, which provokes to jealousy. 4And the glory of the God of Israel was there, like the vision that I had seen in the valley.

5 Then God*u* said to me, "O mortal, lift up your eyes now in the direction of the north." So I lifted up my eyes toward the north, and there, north of the altar gate, in the entrance, was this image of jealousy. 6He said to me, "Mortal, do you see what they are doing, the great abominations that the house of Israel are committing here, to drive me far from my sanctuary? Yet you will see still greater abominations."

8.6 Detestable Things

Ezekiel, a priest, had a special concern about the abuses going on in the temple. Here, in a vision, he sees painful details of these practices, notably idol worship (verses 5,10) and sun worship (verse 16). The leaders of Israel had lost faith in their God, and were desperately trying alternatives. Here and elsewhere Ezekiel accuses leaders by name; his original audience would have known them well.

7 And he brought me to the entrance of the court; I looked, and there was a hole in the wall. 8Then he said to me, "Mortal, dig through the wall"; and when I dug through the wall, there was an entrance. 9He said to me, "Go in, and see the vile abominations that they are committing here." 10So I went in and looked; there, portrayed on the wall all around, were all kinds of creeping things, and loathsome animals, and all the idols of the house of Israel. 11Before them stood seventy of the elders of the house of Israel, with Jaazaniah son of Shaphan standing among them. Each had his censer in his hand, and the fragrant cloud of incense was ascending. 12Then he said to me, "Mortal, have you seen what the elders of the house of Israel are doing in the dark, each in his room of images? For they say, 'The LORD does not see us, the LORD has forsaken the land.'" 13He said also to me, "You will see still greater abominations that they are committing."

14 Then he brought me to the entrance of the north gate of the house of the LORD; women were sitting there weeping for Tammuz. 15Then he said

---

q Syr Symmachus: Heb *its*   *r* Or *secret*   *s* Meaning of Heb uncertain   *t* Gk: Heb *like fire*   *u* Heb *he* to me, "Have you seen this, O mortal? You will see still greater abominations than these."

16 And he brought me into the inner court of the house of the LORD; there, at the entrance of the temple of the LORD, between the porch and the altar, were about twenty-five men, with their backs to the temple of the LORD, and their faces toward the east, prostrating themselves to the sun toward the east. [17]Then he said to me, "Have you seen this, O mortal? Is it not bad enough that the house of Judah commits the abominations done here? Must they fill the land with violence, and provoke my anger still further? See, they are putting the branch to their nose! [18]Therefore I will act in wrath; my eye will not spare, nor will I have pity; and though they cry in my hearing with a loud voice, I will not listen to them."

The Slaughter of the Idolaters

9 Then he cried in my hearing with a loud voice, saying, "Draw near, you executioners of the city, each with his destroying weapon in his hand." [2]And six men came from the direction of the upper gate, which faces north, each with his weapon for slaughter in his hand; among them was a man clothed in linen, with a writing case at his side. They went in and stood beside the bronze altar.

3 Now the glory of the God of Israel had gone up from the cherub on which it rested to the threshold of the house. The LORD called to the man clothed in linen, who had the writing case at his side; [4]and said to him, "Go through the city, through Jerusalem, and put a mark on the foreheads of those who sigh and groan over all the

9.4 The Saving Mark

The man in linen marked those to be saved with a taw, the final letter in the Hebrew alphabet, written in the oldest script as "x"— a cross, as Christians have noted.

abominations that are committed in it." [5]To the others he said in my hearing, "Pass through the city after him, and kill; your eye shall not spare, and you shall show no pity. [6]Cut down old men, young men and young women, little children and women, but touch no one who has the mark. And begin at my sanctuary." So they began with the elders who were in front of the house. [7]Then he said to them, "Defile the house, and fill the courts with the slain. Go!" So they went out and killed in the city. [8]While they were killing, and I was left alone, I fell prostrate on my face and cried out, "Ah Lord GOD! will you destroy all who remain of Israel as you pour out your wrath upon

Jerusalem?" [9]He said to me, "The guilt of the house of Israel and Judah is exceedingly great; the land is full of bloodshed and the city full of perversity; for they say, 'The LORD has forsaken the land, and the LORD does not see.' [10]As for me, my eye will not spare, nor will I have pity, but I will bring down their deeds upon their heads."

11 Then the man clothed in linen, with the writing case at his side, brought back word, saying, "I have done as you commanded me."

God's Glory Leaves Jerusalem

10 Then I looked, and above the dome that was over the heads of the cherubim there appeared above them something like a sapphire,[v] in form resembling a throne. [2]He said to the man clothed in linen, "Go within the wheelwork underneath the cherubim; fill your hands with burning coals from among the cherubim, and scatter them over the city." He went in as I looked on. [3]Now the cherubim were standing on the south side of the house when the man went in; and a cloud filled the inner court. [4]Then the glory of the LORD rose up from the cherub to the threshold of the house; the house was filled with the cloud, and the court was full of the brightness of the glory of the LORD. [5]The sound of the wings of the cherubim was heard as far as the outer court, like the voice of God Almighty[w] when he speaks.

6 When he commanded the man clothed in linen, "Take fire from within the wheelwork, from among the cherubim," he went in and stood beside a wheel. [7]And a cherub stretched out his hand from among the cherubim to the fire that was among the cherubim, took some of it and put it into the hands of the man clothed in linen, who took it and went out. [8]The cherubim appeared to have the form of a human hand under their wings.

9 I looked, and there were four wheels beside the cherubim, one beside each cherub; and the appearance of the wheels was like gleaming beryl. [10]And as for their appearance, the four looked alike, something like a wheel within a wheel. [11]When they moved, they moved in any of the four directions without veering as they moved; but in whatever direction the front wheel faced, the others followed without veering as they moved. [12]Their entire body, their rims, their spokes, their wings, and the wheels—the wheels of the four of them—were full of eyes all around. [13]As for the wheels, they were called in my hearing "the wheelwork." [14]Each one had four faces: the first face was that of the cherub, the second face was that of a human being, the third that of a lion, and the fourth that of an eagle.

15 The cherubim rose up. These were the living creatures that I saw by the river Chebar. [16]When the cherubim moved, the wheels moved

v Or *lapis lazuli*   w Traditional rendering of Heb *El Shaddai*

beside them; and when the cherubim lifted up their wings to rise up from the earth, the wheels at their side did not veer. [17]When they stopped, the others stopped, and when they rose up, the others rose up with them; for the spirit of the living creatures was in them.

18 Then the glory of the LORD went out from the threshold of the house and stopped above the

10.18 Good-bye, God

What would it mean if the President of the United States grew so disgusted with the government that he moved out of the White House—and vanished? It would mean spectacular news, and trouble for the nation. Ezekiel's vision indicates even bigger problems for the Israelites. God—the same powerful God who appeared to Ezekiel in Babylon (chapter 1) —leaves the temple. Sick of his people's corruption, he simply moves out.

cherubim. [19]The cherubim lifted up their wings and rose up from the earth in my sight as they went out with the wheels beside them. They stopped at the entrance of the east gate of the house of the LORD; and the glory of the God of Israel was above them.

20 These were the living creatures that I saw underneath the God of Israel by the river Chebar; and I knew that they were cherubim. [21]Each had four faces, each four wings, and underneath their wings something like human hands. [22]As for what their faces were like, they were the same faces whose appearance I had seen by the river Chebar. Each one moved straight ahead.

Judgment on Wicked Counselors

11 The spirit lifted me up and brought me to the east gate of the house of the LORD, which faces east. There, at the entrance of the gateway, were twenty-five men; among them I saw Jaazaniah son of Azzur, and Pelatiah son of Benaiah, officials of the people. [2]He said to me, "Mortal, these are the men who devise iniquity and who give wicked counsel in this city; [3]they say, 'The time is not near to build houses; this city is the pot, and we are the meat.' [4]Therefore prophesy against them; prophesy, O mortal."

5 Then the spirit of the LORD fell upon me, and he said to me, "Say, Thus says the LORD: This is what you think, O house of Israel; I know the things that come into your mind. [6]You have killed many in this city, and have filled its streets with the slain. [7]Therefore thus says the Lord GOD: The slain whom you have placed within it are the

meat, and this city is the pot; but you shall be taken out of it. [8]You have feared the sword; and I will bring the sword upon you, says the Lord GOD. [9]I will take you out of it and give you over to the hands of foreigners, and execute judgments upon you. [10]You shall fall by the sword; I will judge you at the border of Israel. And you shall know that I am the LORD. [11]This city shall not be your pot, and you shall not be the meat inside it; I will judge you at the border of Israel. [12]Then you shall know that I am the LORD, whose statutes you have not followed, and whose ordinances you have not kept, but you have acted according to the ordinances of the nations that are around you."

13 Now, while I was prophesying, Pelatiah son of Benaiah died. Then I fell down on my face, cried with a loud voice, and said, "Ah Lord GOD! will you make a full end of the remnant of Israel?"

God Will Restore Israel

14 Then the word of the LORD came to me: [15]Mortal, your kinsfolk, your own kin, your fellow exiles,[x] the whole house of Israel, all of them, are those of whom the inhabitants of Jerusalem have said, "They have gone far from the LORD; to us this land is given for a possession." [16]Therefore say: Thus says the Lord GOD: Though I removed them far away among the nations, and though I scattered them among the countries, yet I have been a sanctuary to them for a little while[y] in the countries where they have gone. [17]Therefore say: Thus says the Lord GOD: I will gather you from the peoples, and assemble you out of the countries where you have been scattered, and I will give you the land of Israel. [18]When they come there, they will remove from it all its detestable things and all its abominations. [19]I will give them one[z] heart, and put a new spirit within them; I will remove the heart of stone from their flesh and give them a heart of flesh, [20]so that they may follow my statutes and keep my ordinances and obey them. Then they shall be my people, and I will be their God. [21]But as for those whose heart goes after their detestable things and their abominations,[a] I will bring their deeds upon their own heads, says the Lord GOD.

22 Then the cherubim lifted up their wings, with the wheels beside them; and the glory of the God of Israel was above them. [23]And the glory of the LORD ascended from the middle of the city, and stopped on the mountain east of the city. [24]The spirit lifted me up and brought me in a vision by the spirit of God into Chaldea, to the exiles. Then the vision that I had seen left me. [25]And I told the exiles all the things that the LORD had shown me.

---

[x] Gk Syr: Heb *people of your kindred*   [y] Or *to some extent*   [z] Another reading is *a new*   [a] Cn: Heb *And to the heart of their detestable things and their abominations their heart goes*

Judah's Captivity Portrayed

12 The word of the LORD came to me: ²Mortal, you are living in the midst of a rebellious house, who have eyes to see but do not see, who have ears to hear but do not hear; ³for they are a rebellious house. Therefore, mortal, prepare for yourself an exile's baggage, and go into exile by day in their sight; you shall go like an exile from your place to another place in their sight. Perhaps they will understand, though they are a rebellious house. ⁴You shall bring out your baggage by day in their sight, as baggage for exile; and you shall go out yourself at evening in their sight, as those do who go into exile. ⁵Dig through the wall in their sight, and carry the baggage through it. ⁶In their sight you shall lift the baggage on your shoulder, and carry it out in the dark; you shall cover your face, so that you may not see the land; for I have made you a sign for the house of Israel.

7 I did just as I was commanded. I brought out my baggage by day, as baggage for exile, and in the evening I dug through the wall with my own hands; I brought it out in the dark, carrying it on my shoulder in their sight.

8 In the morning the word of the LORD came to me: ⁹Mortal, has not the house of Israel, the rebellious house, said to you, "What are you doing?" ¹⁰Say to them, "Thus says the Lord GOD: This oracle concerns the prince in Jerusalem and all the house of Israel in it." ¹¹Say, "I am a sign for you: as I have done, so shall it be done to them; they shall go into exile, into captivity." ¹²And the prince who is among them shall lift his baggage on his shoulder in the dark, and shall go out; he*ᵇ* shall dig through the wall and carry it through; he shall cover his face, so that he may not see the

---

12.12 Out Through the Hole

Ezekiel's prediction of Jerusalem's leader leaving through a hole in the wall was literally fulfilled. You can read about it in 2 Kings 25.4–7 or Jeremiah 39.4–7.

---

land with his eyes. ¹³I will spread my net over him, and he shall be caught in my snare; and I will bring him to Babylon, the land of the Chaldeans, yet he shall not see it; and he shall die there. ¹⁴I will scatter to every wind all who are around him, his helpers and all his troops; and I will unsheathe the sword behind them. ¹⁵And they shall know that I am the LORD, when I disperse them among the nations and scatter them through the countries. ¹⁶But I will let a few of them escape from the sword, from famine and pestilence, so that they may tell of all their abominations among the nations where they go; then they shall know that I am the LORD.

Judgment Not Postponed

17 The word of the LORD came to me: ¹⁸Mortal, eat your bread with quaking, and drink your water with trembling and with fearfulness; ¹⁹and say to the people of the land, Thus says the Lord GOD concerning the inhabitants of Jerusalem in the land of Israel: They shall eat their bread with fearfulness, and drink their water in dismay, because their land shall be stripped of all it contains, on account of the violence of all those who live in it. ²⁰The inhabited cities shall be laid waste, and the land shall become a desolation; and you shall know that I am the LORD.

21 The word of the LORD came to me: ²²Mortal, what is this proverb of yours about the land of Israel, which says, "The days are prolonged, and every vision comes to nothing"? ²³Tell them therefore, "Thus says the Lord GOD: I will put an end to this proverb, and they shall use it no more as a proverb in Israel." But say to them, The days are near, and the fulfillment of every vision. ²⁴For there shall no longer be any false vision or flattering divination within the house of Israel. ²⁵But I the LORD will speak the word that I speak, and it will be fulfilled. It will no longer be delayed; but in your days, O rebellious house, I will speak the word and fulfill it, says the Lord GOD.

26 The word of the LORD came to me: ²⁷Mortal, the house of Israel is saying, "The vision that he sees is for many years ahead; he prophesies for distant times." ²⁸Therefore say to them, Thus says the Lord GOD: None of my words will be delayed any longer, but the word that I speak will be fulfilled, says the Lord GOD.

False Prophets Condemned

13 The word of the LORD came to me: ²Mortal, prophesy against the prophets of Israel who are prophesying; say to those who prophesy out of their own imagination: "Hear the word of the LORD!" ³Thus says the Lord GOD, Alas for the senseless prophets who follow their own spirit, and have seen nothing! ⁴Your prophets have been like jackals among ruins, O Israel. ⁵You have not gone up into the breaches, or repaired a wall for the house of Israel, so that it might stand in battle on the day of the LORD. ⁶They have envisioned falsehood and lying divination; they say, "Says the LORD," when the LORD has not sent them, and yet they wait for the fulfillment of their word! ⁷Have you not seen a false vision or uttered a lying divination, when you have said, "Says the LORD," even though I did not speak?

8 Therefore thus says the Lord GOD: Because you have uttered falsehood and envisioned lies, I am against you, says the Lord GOD. ⁹My hand will

---

ᵇ Gk Syr: Heb they

be against the prophets who see false visions and utter lying divinations; they shall not be in the council of my people, nor be enrolled in the register of the house of Israel, nor shall they enter the land of Israel; and you shall know that I am the Lord God. ¹⁰Because, in truth, because they have misled my people, saying, "Peace," when there is no peace; and because, when the people build a wall, these prophets*c* smear whitewash on it.

13.10–16 Whitewash

The Hebrew word translated "whitewash" means "to plaster over." The picture is of a poorly constructed wall that is carefully plastered so it looks well built. False prophets, wanting everyone to be happy, spoke cheerfully about the future. But they were only covering up the surface of fundamental problems. A storm, God warns, will strip off their coat of whitewash, and the flawed wall will collapse. In contrast, real prophets were unafraid of exposing the truth, however bad, for only then could problems be remedied.

Ezekiel 13.6–9 asserts that the false prophets thought up messages, then attributed them to God. Ezekiel, on the other hand, was repeatedly seized by a supernatural power. See, for examples, Ezekiel 8.1–5; 10.1–2; 24.1–2; and 33.21–22.

---

¹¹Say to those who smear whitewash on it that it shall fall. There will be a deluge of rain,*d* great hailstones will fall, and a stormy wind will break out. ¹²When the wall falls, will it not be said to you, "Where is the whitewash you smeared on it?" ¹³Therefore thus says the Lord God: In my wrath I will make a stormy wind break out, and in my anger there shall be a deluge of rain, and hailstones in wrath to destroy it. ¹⁴I will break down the wall that you have smeared with whitewash, and bring it to the ground, so that its foundation will be laid bare; when it falls, you shall perish within it; and you shall know that I am the Lord. ¹⁵Thus I will spend my wrath upon the wall, and upon those who have smeared it with whitewash; and I will say to you, The wall is no more, nor those who smeared it— ¹⁶the prophets of Israel who prophesied concerning Jerusalem and saw visions of peace for it, when there was no peace, says the Lord God.

17 As for you, mortal, set your face against the daughters of your people, who prophesy out of their own imagination; prophesy against them ¹⁸and say, Thus says the Lord God: Woe to the women who sew bands on all wrists, and make veils for the heads of persons of every height, in the hunt for human lives! Will you hunt down lives among my people, and maintain your own lives? ¹⁹You have profaned me among my people for handfuls of barley and for pieces of bread, putting to death persons who should not die and keeping alive persons who should not live, by your lies to my people, who listen to lies.

20 Therefore thus says the Lord God: I am against your bands with which you hunt lives;*e* I will tear them from your arms, and let the lives go free, the lives that you hunt down like birds. ²¹I will tear off your veils, and save my people from your hands; they shall no longer be prey in your hands; and you shall know that I am the Lord. ²²Because you have disheartened the righteous falsely, although I have not disheartened them, and you have encouraged the wicked not to turn from their wicked way and save their lives; ²³therefore you shall no longer see false visions or practice divination; I will save my people from your hand. Then you will know that I am the Lord.

God's Judgments Justified

14 Certain elders of Israel came to me and sat down before me. ²And the word of the Lord came to me: ³Mortal, these men have taken their idols into their hearts, and placed their iniquity as a stumbling block before them; shall I let myself be consulted by them? ⁴Therefore speak to them, and say to them, Thus says the Lord God: Any of those of the house of Israel who take their idols into their hearts and place their iniquity as a stumbling block before them, and yet come to the prophet—I the Lord will answer those who come with the multitude of their idols, ⁵in order that I may take hold of the hearts of the house of Israel, all of whom are estranged from me through their idols.

6 Therefore say to the house of Israel, Thus says the Lord God: Repent and turn away from your idols; and turn away your faces from all your abominations. ⁷For any of those of the house of Israel, or of the aliens who reside in Israel, who separate themselves from me, taking their idols into their hearts and placing their iniquity as a stumbling block before them, and yet come to a prophet to inquire of me by him, I the Lord will answer them myself. ⁸I will set my face against them; I will make them a sign and a byword, and cut them off from the midst of my people; and you shall know that I am the Lord.

9 If a prophet is deceived and speaks a word, I, the Lord, have deceived that prophet, and I will stretch out my hand against him, and will destroy him from the midst of my people Israel. ¹⁰And they shall bear their punishment—the punishment of the inquirer and the punishment of the prophet shall be the same— ¹¹so that the house of Israel may no longer go astray from me, nor

---

c Heb *they* 　*d* Heb *rain and you* 　*e* Gk Syr: Heb *lives for birds*

defile themselves any more with all their transgressions. Then they shall be my people, and I will be their God, says the Lord GOD.

12 The word of the LORD came to me: [13]Mortal, when a land sins against me by acting faithlessly, and I stretch out my hand against it, and break its staff of bread and send famine upon it, and cut off from it human beings and animals, [14]even if Noah, Daniel,[f] and Job, these three, were in it, they would save only their own lives by their righteousness, says the Lord GOD. [15]If I send wild animals through the land to ravage it, so that it is made desolate, and no one may pass through because of the animals; [16]even if these three men were in it, as I live, says the Lord GOD, they would save neither sons nor daughters; they alone would be saved, but the land would be desolate. [17]Or if I bring a sword upon that land and say, "Let a sword pass through the land," and I cut off human beings and animals from it; [18]though these three men were in it, as I live, says the Lord GOD, they would save neither sons nor daughters, but they alone would be saved. [19]Or if I send a pestilence into that land, and pour out my wrath upon it with blood, to cut off humans and animals from it; [20]even if Noah, Daniel,[f] and Job were in it, as I live, says the Lord GOD, they would save neither son nor daughter; they would save only their own lives by their righteousness.

21 For thus says the Lord GOD: How much more when I send upon Jerusalem my four deadly acts of judgment, sword, famine, wild animals, and pestilence, to cut off humans and animals from it! [22]Yet, survivors shall be left in it, sons and daughters who will be brought out; they will come out to you. When you see their ways and their deeds, you will be consoled for the evil that I have brought upon Jerusalem, for all that I have brought upon it. [23]They shall console you, when you see their ways and their deeds; and you shall know that it was not without cause that I did all that I have done in it, says the Lord GOD.

The Useless Vine

15 The word of the LORD came to me:
2   O mortal, how does the wood of
      the vine surpass all other wood—
      the vine branch that is among the trees
          of the forest?
3   Is wood taken from it to make anything?
      Does one take a peg from it on which
          to hang any object?
4   It is put in the fire for fuel;
      when the fire has consumed both ends
          of it
      and the middle of it is charred,
      is it useful for anything?

5   When it was whole it was used
          for nothing;
      how much less—when the fire has
          consumed it,
      and it is charred—
      can it ever be used for anything!
6   Therefore thus says the Lord GOD: Like the wood of the vine among the trees of the forest, which I have given to the fire for fuel, so I will give up the inhabitants of Jerusalem. [7]I will set my face against them; although they escape from the fire, the fire shall still consume them; and you shall know that I am the LORD, when I set my face against them. [8]And I will make the land desolate, because they have acted faithlessly, says the Lord GOD.

God's Faithless Bride

16 The word of the LORD came to me: [2]Mortal, make known to Jerusalem her abominations, [3]and say, Thus says the Lord GOD to Jerusalem: Your origin and your birth were in the land of the Canaanites; your father was an Amorite, and your mother a Hittite. [4]As for your birth, on the day you were born your navel cord was not cut, nor were you washed with water to cleanse you, nor rubbed with salt, nor wrapped in cloths. [5]No eye pitied you, to do any of these things for you out of compassion for you; but you were thrown out in the open field, for you were abhorred on the day you were born.

6 I passed by you, and saw you flailing about in your blood. As you lay in your blood, I said to you, "Live! [7]and grow up[g] like a plant of the field." You grew up and became tall and arrived at full womanhood;[h] your breasts were formed, and your hair had grown; yet you were naked and bare.

8 I passed by you again and looked on you; you were at the age for love. I spread the edge of my cloak over you, and covered your nakedness: I pledged myself to you and entered into a covenant with you, says the Lord GOD, and you became mine. [9]Then I bathed you with water and washed off the blood from you, and anointed you with oil. [10]I clothed you with embroidered cloth and with sandals of fine leather; I bound you in fine linen and covered you with rich fabric.[i] [11]I adorned you with ornaments: I put bracelets on your arms, a chain on your neck, [12]a ring on your nose, earrings in your ears, and a beautiful crown upon your head. [13]You were adorned with gold and silver, while your clothing was of fine linen, rich fabric,[i] and embroidered cloth. You had choice flour and honey and oil for food. You grew exceedingly beautiful, fit to be a queen. [14]Your fame spread among the nations on account of your beauty, for it was perfect because of my

---

[f] Or, as otherwise read, *Danel*   [g] Gk Syr: Heb *Live! I made you a myriad*   [h] Cn: Heb *ornament of ornaments*
[i] Meaning of Heb uncertain

splendor that I had bestowed on you, says the Lord GOD.

15 But you trusted in your beauty, and played the whore because of your fame, and lavished your whorings on any passer-by.*j* 16You took some of your garments, and made for yourself colorful shrines, and on them played the whore; nothing like this has ever been or ever shall be.*k* 17You also took your beautiful jewels of my gold and my silver that I had given you, and made for yourself male images, and with them played the whore; 18and you took your embroidered garments to cover them, and set my oil and my incense before them. 19Also my bread that I gave you—I fed you with choice flour and oil and honey—you set it before them as a pleasing odor; and so it was, says the Lord GOD. 20You took your sons and your daughters, whom you had borne to me, and these you sacrificed to them to be devoured. As if your whorings were not enough! 21You slaughtered my children and delivered them up as an offering to them. 22And in all your abominations and your whorings you did not remember the days of your youth, when you were naked and bare, flailing about in your blood.

23 After all your wickedness (woe, woe to you! says the Lord GOD), 24you built yourself a platform and made yourself a lofty place in every square; 25at the head of every street you built your lofty place and prostituted your beauty, offering yourself to every passer-by, and multiplying your whoring. 26You played the whore with the Egyptians, your lustful neighbors, multiplying your

16.26 Worse than a Whore

In this graphic allegory, Ezekiel compares Jerusalem to an abandoned baby whom God rescues and raises with great tenderness. (Female children, often unwanted, were sometimes left to die.) Yet she rebels, preferring life on the wild side. She becomes a prostitute, then sinks even lower. Rather than being paid for her services, she actually pays for sex (verse 34). Ezekiel is depicting Israel's eagerness to adopt the religious practices of her neighbors.

whoring, to provoke me to anger. 27Therefore I stretched out my hand against you, reduced your rations, and gave you up to the will of your enemies, the daughters of the Philistines, who were ashamed of your lewd behavior. 28You played the whore with the Assyrians, because you were insatiable; you played the whore with them, and still you were not satisfied. 29You multiplied your whoring with Chaldea, the land of merchants; and even with this you were not satisfied.

30 How sick is your heart, says the Lord GOD,

that you did all these things, the deeds of a brazen whore; 31building your platform at the head of every street, and making your lofty place in every square! Yet you were not like a whore, because you scorned payment. 32Adulterous wife, who receives strangers instead of her husband! 33Gifts are given to all whores; but you gave your gifts to all your lovers, bribing them to come to you from all around for your whorings. 34So you were different from other women in your whorings: no one solicited you to play the whore; and you gave payment, while no payment was given to you; you were different.

35 Therefore, O whore, hear the word of the LORD: 36Thus says the Lord GOD, Because your lust was poured out and your nakedness uncovered in your whoring with your lovers, and because of all your abominable idols, and because of the blood of your children that you gave to them, 37therefore, I will gather all your lovers, with whom you took pleasure, all those you loved and all those you hated; I will gather them against you from all around, and will uncover your nakedness to them, so that they may see all your nakedness. 38I will judge you as women who commit adultery and shed blood are judged, and bring blood upon you in wrath and jealousy. 39I will deliver you into their hands, and they shall throw down your platform and break down your lofty places; they shall strip you of your clothes and take your beautiful objects and leave you naked and bare. 40They shall bring up a mob against you, and they shall stone you and cut you to pieces with their swords. 41They shall burn your houses and execute judgments on you in the sight of many women; I will stop you from playing the whore, and you shall also make no more payments. 42So I will satisfy my fury on you, and my jealousy shall turn away from you; I will be calm, and will be angry no longer. 43Because you have not remembered the days of your youth, but have enraged me with all these things; therefore, I have returned your deeds upon your head, says the Lord GOD.

Have you not committed lewdness beyond all your abominations? 44See, everyone who uses proverbs will use this proverb about you, "Like mother, like daughter." 45You are the daughter of your mother, who loathed her husband and her children; and you are the sister of your sisters, who loathed their husbands and their children. Your mother was a Hittite and your father an Amorite. 46Your elder sister is Samaria, who lived with her daughters to the north of you; and your younger sister, who lived to the south of you, is Sodom with her daughters. 47You not only followed their ways, and acted according to their abominations; within a very little time you were more corrupt than they in all your ways. 48As I live, says the Lord GOD, your sister Sodom and

j Heb adds *let it be his*   *k* Meaning of Heb uncertain

her daughters have not done as you and your daughters have done. ⁴⁹This was the guilt of your sister Sodom: she and her daughters had pride, excess of food, and prosperous ease, but did not

---

16.49 The Sin of Sodom

Why had God destroyed Sodom and Gomorrah? The Genesis 19 account suggests sexual perversion and violence as the cause. Ezekiel here adds an interesting aspect: arrogant, uncaring wealth. The attempt at homosexual gang rape, chronicled in Genesis, was only part of a bigger problem.

---

aid the poor and needy. ⁵⁰They were haughty, and did abominable things before me; therefore I removed them when I saw it. ⁵¹Samaria has not committed half your sins; you have committed more abominations than they, and have made your sisters appear righteous by all the abominations that you have committed. ⁵²Bear your disgrace, you also, for you have brought about for your sisters a more favorable judgment; because of your sins in which you acted more abominably than they, they are more in the right than you. So be ashamed, you also, and bear your disgrace, for you have made your sisters appear righteous.

53 I will restore their fortunes, the fortunes of Sodom and her daughters and the fortunes of Samaria and her daughters, and I will restore your own fortunes along with theirs, ⁵⁴in order that you may bear your disgrace and be ashamed of all that you have done, becoming a consolation to them. ⁵⁵As for your sisters, Sodom and her daughters shall return to their former state, Samaria and her daughters shall return to their former state, and you and your daughters shall return to your former state. ⁵⁶Was not your sister Sodom a byword in your mouth in the day of your pride, ⁵⁷before your wickedness was uncovered? Now you are a mockery to the daughters of Aram*l* and all her neighbors, and to the daughters of the Philistines, those all around who despise you. ⁵⁸You must bear the penalty of your lewdness and your abominations, says the LORD.

An Everlasting Covenant

59 Yes, thus says the Lord GOD: I will deal with you as you have done, you who have despised the oath, breaking the covenant; ⁶⁰yet I will remember my covenant with you in the days of your youth, and I will establish with you an everlasting covenant. ⁶¹Then you will remember your ways, and be ashamed when I*m* take your sisters, both your elder and your younger, and give them to you as daughters, but not on account of my*n*

covenant with you. ⁶²I will establish my covenant with you, and you shall know that I am the LORD, ⁶³in order that you may remember and be confounded, and never open your mouth again because of your shame, when I forgive you all that you have done, says the Lord GOD.

The Two Eagles and the Vine

17 The word of the LORD came to me: ²O mortal, propound a riddle, and speak an allegory to the house of Israel. ³Say: Thus says the Lord GOD:

A great eagle, with great wings and long
　　pinions,
　rich in plumage of many colors,
　　came to the Lebanon.
He took the top of the cedar,
⁴　broke off its topmost shoot;
　he carried it to a land of trade,
　　set it in a city of merchants.
⁵　Then he took a seed from the land,
　　placed it in fertile soil;
　a plant*o* by abundant waters,
　　he set it like a willow twig.
⁶　It sprouted and became a vine
　　spreading out, but low;
　its branches turned toward him,
　　its roots remained where it stood.
　So it became a vine;
　　it brought forth branches,
　　put forth foliage.

⁷　There was another great eagle,
　　with great wings and much plumage.
　And see! This vine stretched out
　　its roots toward him;
　it shot out its branches toward him,
　　so that he might water it.
　From the bed where it was planted
⁸　　it was transplanted
　to good soil by abundant waters,
　　so that it might produce branches
　　and bear fruit
　　and become a noble vine.
⁹Say: Thus says the Lord GOD:
　Will it prosper?
　Will he not pull up its roots,
　　cause its fruit to rot*o* and wither,
　　its fresh sprouting leaves to fade?
　No strong arm or mighty army will be
　　needed
　　to pull it from its roots.
¹⁰　When it is transplanted, will it thrive?
　When the east wind strikes it,
　　will it not utterly wither,
　　wither on the bed where it grew?

11 Then the word of the LORD came to me: ¹²Say now to the rebellious house: Do you not know what these things mean? Tell them: The

---

l Another reading is *Edom* 　*m* Syr: Heb *you* 　*n* Heb lacks *my* 　*o* Meaning of Heb uncertain

king of Babylon came to Jerusalem, took its king and its officials, and brought them back with him to Babylon. 13He took one of the royal offspring and made a covenant with him, putting him under oath (he had taken away the chief men of the land), 14so that the kingdom might be humble and not lift itself up, and that by keeping his covenant it might stand. 15But he rebelled against him by sending ambassadors to Egypt, in order that they might give him horses and a large army. Will he succeed? Can one escape who does such things? Can he break the covenant and yet escape? 16As I live, says the Lord GOD, surely in the place where the king resides who made him king, whose oath he despised, and whose covenant with him he broke—in Babylon he shall die. 17Pharaoh with his mighty army and great company will not help him in war, when ramps are cast up and siege walls built to cut off many lives. 18Because he despised the oath and broke the covenant, because he gave his hand and yet did all these things, he shall not escape. 19Therefore thus says the Lord GOD: As I live, I will surely return upon his head my oath that he despised, and my covenant that he broke. 20I will spread my net over him, and he shall be caught in my snare; I will bring him to Babylon and enter into judgment with him there for the treason he has committed against me. 21All the pick*p* of his troops shall fall by the sword, and the survivors shall be scattered to every wind; and you shall know that I, the LORD, have spoken.

Israel Exalted at Last

22 Thus says the Lord GOD:
   I myself will take a sprig
      from the lofty top of a cedar;
   I will set it out.
   I will break off a tender one
      from the topmost of its young twigs;
   I myself will plant it
      on a high and lofty mountain.
23 On the mountain height of Israel
      I will plant it,
   in order that it may produce boughs and
         bear fruit,
      and become a noble cedar.
   Under it every kind of bird will live;
      in the shade of its branches will nest
      winged creatures of every kind.
24 All the trees of the field shall know
      that I am the LORD.
   I bring low the high tree,
      I make high the low tree;
   I dry up the green tree
      and make the dry tree flourish.
   I the LORD have spoken;
      I will accomplish it.

Individual Retribution

18 The word of the LORD came to me: 2What do you mean by repeating this proverb concerning the land of Israel, "The parents have eaten sour grapes, and the children's teeth are set

18.2 Jeremiah and Ezekiel

This proverb, which suggests the way children pay for their parents' sins, was also quoted by Jeremiah (Jeremiah 31.29). While Ezekiel did his work in Babylon, Jeremiah carried out a parallel work in Jerusalem. Neither mentions the other, but their messages carry many similarities. Note particularly Jeremiah 1.14–19; 3.6–13; 6.27–30; 8.10–11; 15.1–2; 16.5–8; 23.16–40; 24; 29; 31.27–34; 39—all passages that have close parallels in Ezekiel.

on edge"? 3As I live, says the Lord GOD, this proverb shall no more be used by you in Israel. 4Know that all lives are mine; the life of the parent as well as the life of the child is mine: it is only the person who sins that shall die.

5 If a man is righteous and does what is lawful and right— 6if he does not eat upon the mountains or lift up his eyes to the idols of the house of Israel, does not defile his neighbor's wife or approach a woman during her menstrual period, 7does not oppress anyone, but restores to the debtor his pledge, commits no robbery, gives his bread to the hungry and covers the naked with a garment, 8does not take advance or accrued interest, withholds his hand from iniquity, executes true justice between contending parties, 9follows my statutes, and is careful to observe my ordinances, acting faithfully—such a one is righteous; he shall surely live, says the Lord GOD.

10 If he has a son who is violent, a shedder of blood, 11who does any of these things (though his father*q* does none of them), who eats upon the mountains, defiles his neighbor's wife, 12oppresses the poor and needy, commits robbery, does not restore the pledge, lifts up his eyes to the idols, commits abomination, 13takes advance or accrued interest; shall he then live? He shall not. He has done all these abominable things; he shall surely die; his blood shall be upon himself.

14 But if this man has a son who sees all the sins that his father has done, considers, and does not do likewise, 15who does not eat upon the mountains or lift up his eyes to the idols of the house of Israel, does not defile his neighbor's wife, 16does not wrong anyone, exacts no pledge, commits no robbery, but gives his bread to the hungry and covers the naked with a garment, 17withholds his hand from iniquity,*r* takes no

p Another reading is *fugitives*   *q* Heb *he*   *r* Gk: Heb *the poor*

advance or accrued interest, observes my ordi-nances, and follows my statutes; he shall not die for his father's iniquity; he shall surely live. [18]As for his father, because he practiced extortion, robbed his brother, and did what is not good among his people, he dies for his iniquity.

19 Yet you say, "Why should not the son suf-fer for the iniquity of the father?" When the son has done what is lawful and right, and has been careful to observe all my statutes, he shall surely live. [20]The person who sins shall die. A child shall not suffer for the iniquity of a parent, nor a parent suffer for the iniquity of a child; the righteousness of the righteous shall be his own, and the wicked-ness of the wicked shall be his own.

21 But if the wicked turn away from all their sins that they have committed and keep all my statutes and do what is lawful and right, they shall surely live; they shall not die. [22]None of the trans-gressions that they have committed shall be re-membered against them; for the righteousness that they have done they shall live. [23]Have I any pleasure in the death of the wicked, says the Lord God, and not rather that they should turn from their ways and live? [24]But when the righteous turn away from their righteousness and commit iniq-uity and do the same abominable things that the wicked do, shall they live? None of the righteous deeds that they have done shall be remembered; for the treachery of which they are guilty and the sin they have committed, they shall die.

25 Yet you say, "The way of the Lord is un-fair." Hear now, O house of Israel: Is my way

18.25 God Is Unfair?

"The way of the Lord is unfair" probably was less a complaint than a fatalistic sigh, much like our saying, "Life isn't fair." People had lost any sense that they were suffering because of their sins. They were saying that it made no difference how they acted. Determined to break down this attitude, God guaranteed forgiveness for those who turn away from their sins.

unfair? Is it not your ways that are unfair? [26]When the righteous turn away from their righteousness and commit iniquity, they shall die for it; for the iniquity that they have committed they shall die. [27]Again, when the wicked turn away from the wickedness they have committed and do what is lawful and right, they shall save their life. [28]Be-cause they considered and turned away from all the transgressions that they had committed, they shall surely live; they shall not die. [29]Yet the house of Israel says, "The way of the Lord is unfair."

O house of Israel, are my ways unfair? Is it not your ways that are unfair?

30 Therefore I will judge you, O house of Is-rael, all of you according to your ways, says the Lord God. Repent and turn from all your trans-gressions; otherwise iniquity will be your ruin.[s] [31]Cast away from you all the transgressions that you have committed against me, and get your-selves a new heart and a new spirit! Why will you die, O house of Israel? [32]For I have no pleasure in the death of anyone, says the Lord God. Turn, then, and live.

Israel Degraded

19 As for you, raise up a lamentation for the princes of Israel, [2]and say:
What a lioness was your mother
    among lions!
She lay down among young lions,
    rearing her cubs.
[3] She raised up one of her cubs;
    he became a young lion,
and he learned to catch prey;
    he devoured humans.
[4] The nations sounded an alarm against
        him;
    he was caught in their pit;
and they brought him with hooks
    to the land of Egypt.
[5] When she saw that she was thwarted,
    that her hope was lost,
she took another of her cubs
    and made him a young lion.
[6] He prowled among the lions;
    he became a young lion,
and he learned to catch prey;
    he devoured people.
[7] And he ravaged their strongholds,[t]
    and laid waste their towns;
the land was appalled, and all in it,
    at the sound of his roaring.
[8] The nations set upon him
    from the provinces all around;
they spread their net over him;
    he was caught in their pit.
[9] With hooks they put him in a cage,
    and brought him to the king
        of Babylon;
    they brought him into custody,
so that his voice should be heard no more
    on the mountains of Israel.
[10] Your mother was like a vine in
        a vineyard[u]
    transplanted by the water,
fruitful and full of branches
    from abundant water.
[11] Its strongest stem became
    a ruler's scepter;[v]

---

[s] Or *so that they shall not be a stumbling block of iniquity to you*   [t] Heb *his widows*   [u] Cn: Heb *in your blood*
[v] Heb *Its strongest stems became rulers' scepters*

it towered aloft
  among the thick boughs;
it stood out in its height
  with its mass of branches.
12 But it was plucked up in fury,
  cast down to the ground;
the east wind dried it up;
  its fruit was stripped off,
its strong stem was withered;
  the fire consumed it.
13 Now it is transplanted into the wilderness,
  into a dry and thirsty land.
14 And fire has gone out from its stem,
  has consumed its branches and fruit,
so that there remains in it no strong stem,
  no scepter for ruling.

This is a lamentation, and it is used as a lamentation.

Israel's Continuing Rebellion

20 In the seventh year, in the fifth month, on the tenth day of the month, certain elders of Israel came to consult the LORD, and sat down before me. 2And the word of the LORD came to me: 3Mortal, speak to the elders of Israel, and say to them: Thus says the Lord GOD: Why are you coming? To consult me? As I live, says the Lord

20.3 Don't Ask God

Does God always want people to pray? According to this passage, time sometimes runs out on prayer. When elders came to Ezekiel to ask God for direction, God said: Don't bother. What is the use, when he has told them over and over what the problem is? He has nothing more to say.

GOD, I will not be consulted by you. 4Will you judge them, mortal, will you judge them? Then let them know the abominations of their ancestors, 5and say to them: Thus says the Lord GOD: On the day when I chose Israel, I swore to the offspring of the house of Jacob—making myself known to them in the land of Egypt—I swore to them, saying, I am the LORD your God. 6On that day I swore to them that I would bring them out of the land of Egypt into a land that I had searched out for them, a land flowing with milk and honey, the most glorious of all lands. 7And I said to them, Cast away the detestable things your eyes feast on, every one of you, and do not defile yourselves with the idols of Egypt; I am the LORD your God. 8But they rebelled against me and would not listen to me; not one of them cast away the detestable things their eyes feasted on, nor did they forsake the idols of Egypt.

Then I thought I would pour out my wrath upon them and spend my anger against them in the midst of the land of Egypt. 9But I acted for the sake of my name, that it should not be profaned in the sight of the nations among whom they lived, in whose sight I made myself known to them in bringing them out of the land of Egypt. 10So I led them out of the land of Egypt and brought them into the wilderness. 11I gave them my statutes and showed them my ordinances, by whose observance everyone shall live. 12Moreover I gave them my sabbaths, as a sign between me and them, so that they might know that I the LORD sanctify them. 13But the house of Israel rebelled against me in the wilderness; they did not observe my statutes but rejected my ordinances, by whose observance everyone shall live; and my sabbaths they greatly profaned.

Then I thought I would pour out my wrath upon them in the wilderness, to make an end of them. 14But I acted for the sake of my name, so that it should not be profaned in the sight of the nations, in whose sight I had brought them out. 15Moreover I swore to them in the wilderness that I would not bring them into the land that I had given them, a land flowing with milk and honey, the most glorious of all lands, 16because they rejected my ordinances and did not observe my statutes, and profaned my sabbaths; for their heart went after their idols. 17Nevertheless my eye spared them, and I did not destroy them or make an end of them in the wilderness.

18 I said to their children in the wilderness, Do not follow the statutes of your parents, nor observe their ordinances, nor defile yourselves with their idols. 19I the LORD am your God; follow my statutes, and be careful to observe my ordinances, 20and hallow my sabbaths that they may be a sign between me and you, so that you may know that I the LORD am your God. 21But the children rebelled against me; they did not follow my statutes, and were not careful to observe my ordinances, by whose observance everyone shall live; they profaned my sabbaths.

Then I thought I would pour out my wrath upon them and spend my anger against them in the wilderness. 22But I withheld my hand, and acted for the sake of my name, so that it should not be profaned in the sight of the nations, in whose sight I had brought them out. 23Moreover I swore to them in the wilderness that I would scatter them among the nations and disperse them through the countries, 24because they had not executed my ordinances, but had rejected my statutes and profaned my sabbaths, and their eyes were set on their ancestors' idols. 25Moreover I gave them statutes that were not good and ordinances by which they could not live. 26I defiled them through their very gifts, in their offering up all their firstborn, in order that I might horrify them, so that they might know that I am the LORD.

27 Therefore, mortal, speak to the house of Israel and say to them, Thus says the Lord GOD: In this again your ancestors blasphemed me, by dealing treacherously with me. 28For when I had brought them into the land that I swore to give them, then wherever they saw any high hill or any leafy tree, there they offered their sacrifices and presented the provocation of their offering; there they sent up their pleasing odors, and there they poured out their drink offerings. 29(I said to them, What is the high place to which you go? So it is called Bamahʷ to this day.) 30Therefore say to the house of Israel, Thus says the Lord GOD: Will you defile yourselves after the manner of your ancestors and go astray after their detestable things? 31When you offer your gifts and make your children pass through the fire, you defile yourselves with all your idols to this day. And shall I be consulted by you, O house of Israel? As I live, says the Lord GOD, I will not be consulted by you. 32 What is in your mind shall never happen—the thought, "Let us be like the nations, like the tribes of the countries, and worship wood and stone."

20.32 Like Everybody Else

"Everybody does it!" children sometimes whine to their parents. Good parents aren't swayed, however. They want their children to live up to their own potential, not mimic everybody else.

Like those children, Israelites grew tired of their calling. They wanted to relax and live like other nations. But God swears he will never let it happen. He will remain strict, even putting them through another desert experience to purify them, but he absolutely refuses to let them conform.

God Will Restore Israel

33 As I live, says the Lord GOD, surely with a mighty hand and an outstretched arm, and with wrath poured out, I will be king over you. 34I will bring you out from the peoples and gather you out of the countries where you are scattered, with a mighty hand and an outstretched arm, and with wrath poured out; 35and I will bring you into the wilderness of the peoples, and there I will enter into judgment with you face to face. 36As I entered into judgment with your ancestors in the wilderness of the land of Egypt, so I will enter into judgment with you, says the Lord GOD. 37I will make you pass under the staff, and will bring you within the bond of the covenant. 38I will purge out the rebels among you, and those who transgress against me; I will bring them out of the land where they reside as aliens, but they shall not enter the land of Israel. Then you shall know that I am the LORD.

39 As for you, O house of Israel, thus says the Lord GOD: Go serve your idols, everyone of you now and hereafter, if you will not listen to me; but my holy name you shall no more profane with your gifts and your idols.

40 For on my holy mountain, the mountain height of Israel, says the Lord GOD, there all the house of Israel, all of them, shall serve me in the land; there I will accept them, and there I will require your contributions and the choicest of your gifts, with all your sacred things. 41As a pleasing odor I will accept you, when I bring you out from the peoples, and gather you out of the countries where you have been scattered; and I will manifest my holiness among you in the sight of the nations. 42You shall know that I am the LORD, when I bring you into the land of Israel, the country that I swore to give to your ancestors. 43There you shall remember your ways and all the deeds by which you have polluted yourselves; and you shall loathe yourselves for all the evils that you have committed. 44And you shall know that I am the LORD, when I deal with you for my name's sake, not according to your evil ways, or corrupt deeds, O house of Israel, says the Lord GOD.

A Prophecy against the Negeb

45ˣ The word of the LORD came to me: 46Mortal, set your face toward the south, preach against the south, and prophesy against the forest land in the Negeb; 47say to the forest of the Negeb, Hear the word of the LORD: Thus says the Lord GOD, I will kindle a fire in you, and it shall devour every green tree in you and every dry tree; the blazing flame shall not be quenched, and all faces from south to north shall be scorched by it. 48All flesh shall see that I the LORD have kindled it; it shall not be quenched. 49Then I said, "Ah Lord GOD! they are saying of me, 'Is he not a maker of allegories?'"

The Drawn Sword of God

21 ʸ The word of the LORD came to me: 2Mortal, set your face toward Jerusalem and preach against the sanctuaries; prophesy against the land of Israel 3and say to the land of Israel, Thus says the LORD: I am coming against you, and will draw my sword out of its sheath, and will cut off from you both righteous and wicked. 4Because I will cut off from you both righteous and wicked, therefore my sword shall go out of its sheath against all flesh from south to north; 5and all flesh shall know that I the LORD have drawn my sword out of its sheath; it shall not be sheathed again. 6Moan therefore, mortal; moan with breaking heart and bitter grief before their eyes. 7And when

---

ʷ That is *High Place*   ˣ Ch 21.1 in Heb   ʸ Ch 21.6 in Heb

they say to you, "Why do you moan?" you shall say, "Because of the news that has come. Every heart will melt and all hands will be feeble, every spirit will faint and all knees will turn to water. See, it comes and it will be fulfilled," says the Lord GOD.

8 And the word of the LORD came to me: 9Mortal, prophesy and say: Thus says the Lord; Say:

A sword, a sword is sharpened,
 it is also polished;
10 it is sharpened for slaughter,
 honed to flash like lightning!
How can we make merry?
 You have despised the rod,
 and all discipline.z
11 The sworda is given to be polished,
 to be grasped in the hand;
it is sharpened, the sword is polished,
 to be placed in the slayer's hand.
12 Cry and wail, O mortal,
 for it is against my people;
it is against all Israel's princes;
 they are thrown to the sword,
 together with my people.
Ah! Strike the thigh!
13For consider: What! If you despise the rod, will it not happen?z says the Lord GOD.
14 And you, mortal, prophesy;
 strike hand to hand.
Let the sword fall twice, thrice;
 it is a sword for killing.
A sword for great slaughter—
 it surrounds them;
15 therefore hearts melt
 and many stumble.
At all their gates I have set
 the pointz of the sword.
Ah! It is made for flashing,
 it is polishedb for slaughter.
16 Attack to the right!
 Engage to the left!
 —wherever your edge is directed.
17 I too will strike hand to hand,
 I will satisfy my fury;
 I the LORD have spoken.

18 The word of the LORD came to me: 19Mortal, mark out two roads for the sword of the king of Babylon to come; both of them shall issue from the same land. And make a signpost, make it for a fork in the road leading to a city; 20mark out the road for the sword to come to Rabbah of the Ammonites or to Judah and toc Jerusalem the fortified. 21For the king of Babylon stands at the parting of the way, at the fork in the two roads, to use divination; he shakes the arrows, he consults the teraphim,d he inspects the liver. 22Into his right hand comes the lot for Jerusalem,

to set battering rams, to call out for slaughter, for raising the battle cry, to set battering rams against the gates, to cast up ramps, to build siege towers. 23But to them it will seem like a false divination;

21.21 Liver-Gazing

This verse shows how an ancient Babylonian king might seek direction from his gods. Casting lots with arrows apparently meant marking arrows with various alternatives, putting them in a quiver, and drawing one out. Consulting idols would mean praying to them, perhaps hoping for a dream or an omen. The livers of animals, like tea leaves today, were often studied in ancient times; their shape or color was supposed to tell the future.

---

they have sworn solemn oaths; but he brings their guilt to remembrance, bringing about their capture.

24 Therefore thus says the Lord GOD: Because you have brought your guilt to remembrance, in that your transgressions are uncovered, so that in all your deeds your sins appear—because you have come to remembrance, you shall be taken in hand.e
25 As for you, vile, wicked prince of Israel,
 you whose day has come,
 the time of final punishment,
26 thus says the Lord GOD:
Remove the turban, take off the crown;
 things shall not remain as they are.
Exalt that which is low,
 abase that which is high.
27 A ruin, a ruin, a ruin
 I will make it!
(Such has never occurred.)
Until he comes whose right it is;
 to him I will give it.

28 As for you, mortal, prophesy, and say, Thus says the Lord GOD concerning the Ammonites, and concerning their reproach; say:
A sword, a sword! Drawn for slaughter,
 polished to consume,f to flash like
 lightning.
29 Offering false visions for you,
 divining lies for you,
they place you over the necks
 of the vile, wicked ones—
those whose day has come,
 the time of final punishment.
30 Return it to its sheath!
In the place where you were created,
 in the land of your origin,
 I will judge you.
31 I will pour out my indignation upon you,

---

z Meaning of Heb uncertain a Heb *It* b Tg: Heb *wrapped up* c Gk Syr: Heb *Judah in* d Or *the household gods* e Or *be taken captive* f Cn: Heb *to contain*

with the fire of my wrath
 I will blow upon you.
I will deliver you into brutish hands,
 those skillful to destroy.
32 You shall be fuel for the fire,
 your blood shall enter the earth;
you shall be remembered no more,
 for I the LORD have spoken.

The Bloody City

22 The word of the LORD came to me: [2]You, mortal, will you judge, will you judge the bloody city? Then declare to it all its abominable deeds. [3]You shall say, Thus says the Lord GOD: A city! Shedding blood within itself; its time has come; making its idols, defiling itself. [4]You have become guilty by the blood that you have shed, and defiled by the idols that you have made; you have brought your day near, the appointed time of your years has come. Therefore I have made you a disgrace before the nations, and a mockery to all the countries. [5]Those who are near and those who are far from you will mock you, you infamous one, full of tumult.

6 The princes of Israel in you, everyone according to his power, have been bent on shedding blood. [7]Father and mother are treated with contempt in you; the alien residing within you suffers extortion; the orphan and the widow are wronged in you. [8]You have despised my holy things, and profaned my sabbaths. [9]In you are those who slander to shed blood, those in you who eat upon the mountains, who commit lewdness in your midst. [10]In you they uncover their fathers' nakedness; in you they violate women in their menstrual periods. [11]One commits abomination with his neighbor's wife; another lewdly defiles his daughter-in-law; another in you defiles his sister, his father's daughter. [12]In you, they take bribes to shed blood; you take both advance interest and accrued interest, and make gain of your neighbors by extortion; and you have forgotten me, says the Lord GOD.

13 See, I strike my hands together at the dishonest gain you have made, and at the blood that has been shed within you. [14]Can your courage endure, or can your hands remain strong in the days when I shall deal with you? I the LORD have spoken, and I will do it. [15]I will scatter you among the nations and disperse you through the countries, and I will purge your filthiness out of you. [16]And I[g] shall be profaned through you in the sight of the nations; and you shall know that I am the LORD.

17 The word of the LORD came to me: [18]Mortal, the house of Israel has become dross to me; all of them, silver,[h] bronze, tin, iron, and lead. In the smelter they have become dross. [19]Therefore thus

says the Lord GOD: Because you have all become dross, I will gather you into the midst of Jerusalem. [20]As one gathers silver, bronze, iron, lead, and tin into a smelter, to blow the fire upon them in order to melt them; so I will gather you in my anger and in my wrath, and I will put you in and melt you. [21]I will gather you and blow upon you with the fire of my wrath, and you shall be melted within it. [22]As silver is melted in a smelter, so you shall be melted in it; and you shall know that I the LORD have poured out my wrath upon you.

23 The word of the LORD came to me: [24]Mortal, say to it: You are a land that is not cleansed, not rained upon in the day of indignation. [25]Its princes[i] within it are like a roaring lion tearing the prey; they have devoured human lives; they have taken treasure and precious things; they have made many widows within it. [26]Its priests have done violence to my teaching and have profaned my holy things; they have made no distinction between the holy and the common, neither have they taught the difference between the unclean and the clean, and they have disregarded my sabbaths, so that I am profaned among them. [27]Its officials within it are like wolves tearing the prey, shedding blood, destroying lives to get dishonest gain. [28]Its prophets have smeared whitewash on their behalf, seeing false visions and divining lies for them, saying, "Thus says the Lord GOD," when the LORD has not spoken. [29]The people of the land have practiced extortion and committed robbery; they have oppressed the poor and needy, and have extorted from the alien without redress. [30]And I sought for anyone among them who would repair the wall and stand in the breach before me on behalf of the land, so that I would not destroy it; but I found no one. [31]Therefore I have poured out my indignation upon them; I have consumed them with the fire of my wrath; I have returned their conduct upon their heads, says the Lord GOD.

Oholah and Oholibah

23 The word of the LORD came to me: [2]Mortal, there were two women, the daughters of one mother; [3]they played the whore in Egypt; they played the whore in their youth; their breasts were caressed there, and their virgin bosoms were fondled. [4]Oholah was the name of the elder and Oholibah the name of her sister. They became mine, and they bore sons and daughters. As for their names, Oholah is Samaria, and Oholibah is Jerusalem.

5 Oholah played the whore while she was mine; she lusted after her lovers the Assyrians, warriors[j] [6]clothed in blue, governors and commanders, all of them handsome young men, mounted horsemen. [7]She bestowed her favors

---

g Gk Syr Vg: Heb you *conspiracy of its prophets*   h Transposed from the end of the verse; compare verse 20   i Gk: Heb *indignation*. 25A   j Meaning of Heb uncertain

upon them, the choicest men of Assyria all of them; and she defiled herself with all the idols of everyone for whom she lusted. [8]She did not give up her whorings that she had practiced since Egypt; for in her youth men had lain with her and fondled her virgin bosom and poured out their lust upon her. [9]Therefore I delivered her into the hands of her lovers, into the hands of the Assyrians, for whom she lusted. [10]These uncovered her nakedness; they seized her sons and her daughters; and they killed her with the sword. Judgment was executed upon her, and she became a byword among women.

11 Her sister Oholibah saw this, yet she was more corrupt than she in her lusting and in her whorings, which were worse than those of her sister. [12]She lusted after the Assyrians, governors and commanders, warriors[k] clothed in full armor, mounted horsemen, all of them handsome young men. [13]And I saw that she was defiled; they both took the same way. [14]But she carried her whorings further; she saw male figures carved on the wall, images of the Chaldeans portrayed in vermilion, [15]with belts around their waists, with flowing turbans on their heads, all of them looking like officers—a picture of Babylonians whose native land was Chaldea. [16]When she saw them she lusted after them, and sent messengers to them in Chaldea. [17]And the Babylonians came to her into the bed of love, and they defiled her with their lust; and after she defiled herself with them, she turned from them in disgust. [18]When she carried on her whorings so openly and flaunted her nakedness, I turned in disgust from her, as I had turned from her sister. [19]Yet she increased her whorings, remembering the days of her youth, when she played the whore in the land of Egypt [20]and lusted after her paramours there, whose members were like those of donkeys, and whose emission was like that of stallions. [21]Thus you longed for the lewdness of your youth, when the Egyptians[l] fondled your bosom and caressed[m] your young breasts.

22 Therefore, O Oholibah, thus says the Lord

---

[k] Meaning of Heb uncertain   [l] Two Mss: MT *from Egypt*   [m] Cn: Heb *for the sake of*

The Runaways
A story meant to make you sick

> *They carry on their sexual acts with her.*
> 23.43

THIS STORY, WHICH USES SEXUALLY explicit language, turns you off, not on. It tells of two sisters who choose promiscuous sex. Once they are involved, nothing satisfies them. They go from one man to the next. God calls them prostitutes, but they don't do it for the money. They do it because they like to live perversely.

Finally, in grief and frustration, God turns them over to their chosen lovers, who treat them like trash. God seems to take angry satisfaction in this. Love makes him angry—angry enough to weep.

An Allegory of Love

Ezekiel doesn't pretend that these two sisters are real people. From the beginning he identifies them with the capitals of the two halves of Israel—Samaria in the North, which the Assyrians had wiped out over 100 years before, and Jerusalem in the South. Samaria was properly rewarded for her prostitution, Ezekiel says, and Jerusalem will be too. The story of the two sisters is, in a sense, one more graphic way of saying that God has been patient with Jerusalem long enough. (A similar story is told in Ezekiel 16.)

A Drastic Dose of Reality

God had promised the Israelites everything their hearts desired if they would stick by him. But they were always cozying up to other nations whose prosperity and power they envied. In those days, a little nation like Israel couldn't just sign a friendship pact with a big power. Political alliances meant accepting the big power's religion and worshiping its gods alongside your own. God warned Israel against this repeatedly, but they ignored the warning. Therefore, Ezekiel says, they will get their wish. They will experience firsthand the care and concern of their Babylonian "lovers."

God responds like a father who has finally given up trying to regulate his daughter's bad habits. He tells her, "Get out! Find out for yourself what life is like on the street!" God says, "You shall drink your sister's cup, deep and wide; you shall be scorned and derided, it holds so much.... You shall drink it and drain it out; and gnaw its sherds, and tear out your breasts" (23.32–34). He says it in anger, but also in hope that such bitter grief will awaken Israel to the disastrous choices she made in rejecting God's care.

Life Questions: Have you ever loved someone who didn't love you back? What emotions did you feel?

GOD: I will rouse against you your lovers from whom you turned in disgust, and I will bring them against you from every side: [23]the Babylonians and all the Chaldeans, Pekod and Shoa and Koa, and all the Assyrians with them, handsome young men, governors and commanders all of them, officers and warriors,[n] all of them riding on horses. [24]They shall come against you from the north[o] with chariots and wagons and a host of peoples; they shall set themselves against you on every side with buckler, shield, and helmet, and I will commit the judgment to them, and they shall judge you according to their ordinances. [25]I will direct my indignation against you, in order that they may deal with you in fury. They shall cut off your nose and your ears, and your survivors shall fall by the sword. They shall seize your sons and your daughters, and your survivors shall be devoured by fire. [26]They shall also strip you of your clothes and take away your fine jewels. [27]So I will put an end to your lewdness and your whoring brought from the land of Egypt; you shall not long for them, or remember Egypt any more. [28]For thus says the Lord GOD: I will deliver you into the hands of those whom you hate, into the hands of those from whom you turned in disgust; [29]and they shall deal with you in hatred, and take away all the fruit of your labor, and leave you naked and bare, and the nakedness of your whorings shall be exposed. Your lewdness and your whorings [30]have brought this upon you, because you played the whore with the nations, and polluted yourself with their idols. [31]You have gone the way of your sister; therefore I will give her cup into your hand. [32]Thus says the Lord GOD:

You shall drink your sister's cup,
    deep and wide;
you shall be scorned and derided,
    it holds so much.
[33] You shall be filled with drunkenness and
        sorrow.
A cup of horror and desolation
    is the cup of your sister Samaria;
[34] you shall drink it and drain it out,
    and gnaw its sherds,
    and tear out your breasts;

for I have spoken, says the Lord GOD. [35]Therefore thus says the Lord GOD: Because you have forgotten me and cast me behind your back, therefore bear the consequences of your lewdness and whorings.

36 The LORD said to me: Mortal, will you judge Oholah and Oholibah? Then declare to them their abominable deeds. [37]For they have committed adultery, and blood is on their hands; with their idols they have committed adultery; and they have even offered up to them for food the children whom they had borne to me. [38]Moreover this they have done to me: they have defiled my sanctuary on the same day and profaned my sabbaths. [39]For when they had slaughtered their children for their idols, on the same day they came into my sanctuary to profane it. This is what they did in my house.

40 They even sent for men to come from far away, to whom a messenger was sent, and they came. For them you bathed yourself, painted your eyes, and decked yourself with ornaments; [41]you sat on a stately couch, with a table spread before it on which you had placed my incense and my oil. [42]The sound of a raucous multitude was around her, with many of the rabble brought in drunken from the wilderness; and they put bracelets on the arms[p] of the women, and beautiful crowns upon their heads.

43 Then I said, Ah, she is worn out with adulteries, but they carry on their sexual acts with her. [44]For they have gone in to her, as one goes in to a whore. Thus they went in to Oholah and to Oholibah, wanton women. [45]But righteous judges shall declare them guilty of adultery and of bloodshed; because they are adulteresses and blood is on their hands.

46 For thus says the Lord GOD: Bring up an assembly against them, and make them an object of terror and of plunder. [47]The assembly shall stone them and with their swords they shall cut them down; they shall kill their sons and their daughters, and burn up their houses. [48]Thus will I put an end to lewdness in the land, so that all women may take warning and not commit lewdness as you have done. [49]They shall repay you for your lewdness, and you shall bear the penalty for your sinful idolatry; and you shall know that I am the Lord GOD.

The Boiling Pot

24 In the ninth year, in the tenth month, on the tenth day of the month, the word of the LORD came to me: [2]Mortal, write down the name of this day, this very day. The king of Babylon has laid siege to Jerusalem this very day.

24.2 Prophet's Proof

With Ezekiel living in Babylon, news from Israel took months to reach him. By recording the date when God told him the final siege of Jerusalem had begun, Ezekiel would have evidence that he was genuinely a prophet of God.

[3]And utter an allegory to the rebellious house and say to them, Thus says the Lord GOD:

    Set on the pot, set it on,
        pour in water also;

---

[n] Compare verses 6 and 12: Heb *officers and called ones*   [o] Gk: Meaning of Heb uncertain   [p] Heb *hands*

⁴ put in it the pieces,
　all the good pieces, the thigh and the
　　shoulder;
fill it with choice bones.
⁵ Take the choicest one of the flock,
　pile the logs*q* under it;
boil its pieces,*r*
seethe*s* also its bones in it.

6　Therefore thus says the Lord GOD:
Woe to the bloody city,
　the pot whose rust is in it,
whose rust has not gone out of it!
Empty it piece by piece,
　making no choice at all.*t*
⁷ For the blood she shed is inside it;
　she placed it on a bare rock;
she did not pour it out on the ground,
　to cover it with earth.
⁸ To rouse my wrath, to take vengeance,
　I have placed the blood she shed
　　on a bare rock,
so that it may not be covered.
⁹Therefore thus says the Lord GOD:
Woe to the bloody city!
　I will even make the pile great.
10　Heap up the logs, kindle the fire;
　boil the meat well, mix in the spices,
　let the bones be burned.
11　Stand it empty upon the coals,
　so that it may become hot, its copper
　　glow,
　its filth melt in it, its rust
　　be consumed.
12　In vain I have wearied myself;*u*
　its thick rust does not depart.
To the fire with its rust!*v*
13　Yet, when I cleansed you in your filthy
　　lewdness,
　you did not become clean from your
　　filth;
you shall not again be cleansed
　until I have satisfied my fury upon
　　you.
14I the LORD have spoken; the time is coming, I
will act. I will not refrain, I will not spare, I will
not relent. According to your ways and your doings I will judge you, says the Lord GOD.

Ezekiel's Bereavement

15　The word of the LORD came to me: 16Mor-
tal, with one blow I am about to take away from
you the delight of your eyes; yet you shall not
mourn or weep, nor shall your tears run down.
17Sigh, but not aloud; make no mourning for the
dead. Bind on your turban, and put your sandals
on your feet; do not cover your upper lip or eat

the bread of mourners.*w* 18So I spoke to the people in the morning, and at evening my wife died.
And on the next morning I did as I was commanded.

19　Then the people said to me, "Will you not
tell us what these things mean for us, that you are
acting this way?" 20Then I said to them: The word
of the LORD came to me: 21Say to the house of
Israel, Thus says the Lord GOD: I will profane my
sanctuary, the pride of your power, the delight of
your eyes, and your heart's desire; and your sons
and your daughters whom you left behind shall
fall by the sword. 22And you shall do as I have
done; you shall not cover your upper lip or eat the
bread of mourners.*w* 23Your turbans shall be on
your heads and your sandals on your feet; you
shall not mourn or weep, but you shall pine away
in your iniquities and groan to one another.
24Thus Ezekiel shall be a sign to you; you shall do
just as he has done. When this comes, then you
shall know that I am the Lord GOD.

25　And you, mortal, on the day when I take
from them their stronghold, their joy and glory,
the delight of their eyes and their heart's affection,
and also*x* their sons and their daughters, 26on
that day, one who has escaped will come to you
to report to you the news. 27On that day your
mouth shall be opened to the one who has escaped, and you shall speak and no longer be silent. So you shall be a sign to them; and they shall
know that I am the LORD.

Proclamation against Ammon

25 The word of the LORD came to me: 2Mor-
　　tal, set your face toward the Ammonites
and prophesy against them. 3Say to the Ammonites, Hear the word of the Lord GOD: Thus says
the Lord GOD, Because you said, "Aha!" over my
sanctuary when it was profaned, and over the
land of Israel when it was made desolate, and over
the house of Judah when it went into exile; 4there-
fore I am handing you over to the people of the
east for a possession. They shall set their encampments among you and pitch their tents in your
midst; they shall eat your fruit, and they shall
drink your milk. 5I will make Rabbah a pasture
for camels and Ammon a fold for flocks. Then
you shall know that I am the LORD. 6For thus says
the Lord GOD: Because you have clapped your
hands and stamped your feet and rejoiced with all
the malice within you against the land of Israel,
7therefore I have stretched out my hand against
you, and will hand you over as plunder to the
nations. I will cut you off from the peoples; I will
make you perish out of the countries; I will
destroy you. Then you shall know that I am the
LORD.

---

q Compare verse 10: Heb *the bones*　　*r* Two Mss: Heb *its boilings*　　*s* Cn: Heb *its bones seethe*　　*t* Heb *piece, no lot
has fallen on it*　　*u* Cn: Meaning of Heb uncertain　　*v* Meaning of Heb uncertain　　*w* Vg Tg: Heb *of men*
x Heb lacks *and also*

Proclamation against Moab

8 Thus says the Lord GOD: Because Moab[y] said, The house of Judah is like all the other nations, [9]therefore I will lay open the flank of Moab from the towns[z] on its frontier, the glory of the country, Beth-jeshimoth, Baal-meon, and Kiriathaim. [10]I will give it along with Ammon to the people of the east as a possession. Thus Ammon shall be remembered no more among the nations,

[11]and I will execute judgments upon Moab. Then they shall know that I am the LORD.

Proclamation against Edom

12 Thus says the Lord GOD: Because Edom acted revengefully against the house of Judah and has grievously offended in taking vengeance upon them, [13]therefore thus says the Lord GOD, I will stretch out my hand against Edom, and cut off

[y] Gk Old Latin: Heb *Moab and Seir*   [z] Heb *towns from its towns*

Just What They Deserved
God will judge every nation in the world

> I will execute great vengeance on them with wrathful punishments. Then they shall know that I am the LORD. 25.17

WORLD WAR II ENDED IN Europe with the surrender of the German army. People danced in the streets.

But the victorious allies could not simply pack and go home. They had captured thousands of Nazis. Among them were some of the most brutal murderers the world has ever known—monsters, really, who had enriched themselves with the gold and jewelry of the millions of Jews they had exterminated.

A question came up: Under what law could the Nazis be tried? American, British, or French law didn't apply in Germany. Faced with this dilemma, the Allies invented something new: the Nuremberg trials for war crimes. Judgments were based on a belief in a higher law—an international code of right and wrong that applies to every person, regardless of country. Under this unwritten law many Nazi leaders were condemned to death.

Nations on Trial

Ezekiel introduces a similar concept of justice, beginning in chapter 25. In the first 24 chapters he had spoken harsh words to the Israelites, who had repeatedly broken the law God had given them. But now Ezekiel's vision expands to nations who never had that law. Ezekiel marches through Ammon, Moab, Edom, Philistia—four nations that, on the small scale of Palestinian geography, could be seen with the naked eye from Jerusalem.

Each nation has its moment in court, and each is condemned for its inhumane malice against Israel. (The sentences Ezekiel gave were soon carried out historically. The nations listed vanished from the face of the earth, victims of the same violence they had used against Israel.)

Ezekiel goes on to Tyre, 100 miles up the coast. Tyre's soul was profit; its merchants controlled trade for the whole Mediterranean. Because of their wealth and success, they considered themselves virtual gods (28.2,6). They had callously rejoiced in Jerusalem's downfall, seeing it as a chance for increased trade (26.2). For such unfeeling arrogance, God would sentence them. Nebuchadnezzar began this punishment in Ezekiel's era, and centuries later Alexander the Great finished it off by razing the city. Tyre became, as Ezekiel had predicted, "a bare rock . . . a place for spreading nets" (26.14).

A Comic Condemnation

Pausing briefly to give a judgment against Sidon, Ezekiel travels on to Egypt. His words might have seemed comic. Who does he think he is, passing judgment on one of the great powers of his day? Ezekiel, a captive from a two-bit country about to be overrun, sounds rather like a refugee from Haiti shaking his fist at the United States. Yet Ezekiel confidently asserts that Egypt can start mourning now. As it happened, Egypt, a great power for many centuries, lost its dominance and has never regained it (29.15).

Perhaps, in taking up these nations' fates, Ezekiel intended to build suspense for the climactic tragedy of Jerusalem's fall. But certainly this trial of the nations demonstrated that Jerusalem had not been singled out for justice. Every nation would be judged by the standard of right and wrong that they knew. If God was harder on Judah, it was only because Judah knew so much more about God and his expectations.

Life Questions: Do you believe in universal standards of right and wrong? What "code of conduct" applies to everybody, regardless of their upbringing?

from it humans and animals, and I will make it desolate; from Teman even to Dedan they shall fall by the sword. [14]I will lay my vengeance upon Edom by the hand of my people Israel; and they shall act in Edom according to my anger and according to my wrath; and they shall know my vengeance, says the Lord GOD.

Proclamation against Philistia

15 Thus says the Lord GOD: Because with unending hostilities the Philistines acted in vengeance, and with malice of heart took revenge in destruction; [16]therefore thus says the Lord GOD, I will stretch out my hand against the Philistines, cut off the Cherethites, and destroy the rest of the seacoast. [17]I will execute great vengeance on them with wrathful punishments. Then they shall know that I am the LORD, when I lay my vengeance on them.

Proclamation against Tyre

26 In the eleventh year, on the first day of the month, the word of the LORD came to me: [2]Mortal, because Tyre said concerning Jerusalem, "Aha, broken is the gateway of
  the peoples;
    it has swung open to me;
I shall be replenished,
  now that it is wasted,"
[3]therefore, thus says the Lord GOD:
  See, I am against you, O Tyre!
  I will hurl many nations against you,
    as the sea hurls its waves.
[4] They shall destroy the walls of Tyre
    and break down its towers.
  I will scrape its soil from it
    and make it a bare rock.
[5] It shall become, in the midst of the sea,
    a place for spreading nets.
I have spoken, says the Lord GOD.
  It shall become plunder for the nations,
[6]   and its daughter-towns in the country
    shall be killed by the sword.
Then they shall know that I am the LORD.

7 For thus says the Lord GOD: I will bring against Tyre from the north King Nebuchadrezzar of Babylon, king of kings, together with horses, chariots, cavalry, and a great and powerful army.
[8] Your daughter-towns in the country
    he shall put to the sword.
  He shall set up a siege wall against you,
    cast up a ramp against you,
    and raise a roof of shields against you.
[9] He shall direct the shock of his battering
    rams against your walls
  and break down your towers with his
    axes.

[10] His horses shall be so many
    that their dust shall cover you.
  At the noise of cavalry, wheels,
    and chariots
  your very walls shall shake,
    when he enters your gates
    like those entering a breached city.
[11] With the hoofs of his horses
    he shall trample all your streets.
  He shall put your people to the sword,
    and your strong pillars shall fall to the
      ground.
[12] They will plunder your riches
    and loot your merchandise;
  they shall break down your walls
    and destroy your fine houses.
  Your stones and timber and soil
    they shall cast into the water.
[13] I will silence the music of your songs;
    the sound of your lyres shall be heard
      no more.
[14] I will make you a bare rock;
    you shall be a place for spreading nets.
  You shall never again be rebuilt,
    for I the LORD have spoken,
    says the Lord GOD.

26.14 Alexander the Great

Tyre, a city on the Mediterranean coast, included two rocky offshore islands. Nebuchadrezzar captured the mainland city in 572 B.C., just 12 years after the fall of Jerusalem. But the islands were not taken until Alexander the Great destroyed them two centuries later. True to this prophecy, the city has never been rebuilt.

15 Thus says the Lord GOD to Tyre: Shall not the coastlands shake at the sound of your fall, when the wounded groan, when slaughter goes on within you? [16]Then all the princes of the sea shall step down from their thrones; they shall remove their robes and strip off their embroidered garments. They shall clothe themselves with trembling, and shall sit on the ground; they shall tremble every moment, and be appalled at you. [17]And they shall raise a lamentation over you, and say to you:
  How you have vanished[a] from the seas,
    O city renowned,
  once mighty on the sea,
    you and your inhabitants,[b]
  who imposed your[c] terror
    on all the mainland![d]
[18] Now the coastlands tremble
    on the day of your fall;

---

[a] Gk OL Aquila: Heb *have vanished, O inhabited one,* inhabitants   [b] Heb *it and its inhabitants*   [c] Heb *their*   [d] Cn: Heb *its*

the coastlands by the sea
are dismayed at your passing.

19 For thus says the Lord GOD: When I make
you a city laid waste, like cities that are not inhabited, when I bring up the deep over you, and the
great waters cover you, ²⁰then I will thrust you
down with those who descend into the Pit, to the
people of long ago, and I will make you live in the
world below, among primeval ruins, with those
who go down to the Pit, so that you will not be
inhabited or have a place[e] in the land of the
living. ²¹I will bring you to a dreadful end, and
you shall be no more; though sought for, you will
never be found again, says the Lord GOD.

Lamentation over Tyre

27 The word of the LORD came to me: ²Now
you, mortal, raise a lamentation over Tyre,
³and say to Tyre, which sits at the entrance to the
sea, merchant of the peoples on many coastlands,
Thus says the Lord GOD:

O Tyre, you have said,
"I am perfect in beauty."
⁴ Your borders are in the heart of the seas;
your builders made perfect
your beauty.
⁵ They made all your planks
of fir trees from Senir;
they took a cedar from Lebanon
to make a mast for you.
⁶ From oaks of Bashan
they made your oars;
they made your deck of pines[f]
from the coasts of Cyprus,
inlaid with ivory.
⁷ Of fine embroidered linen from Egypt
was your sail,
serving as your ensign;
blue and purple from the coasts
of Elishah
was your awning.
⁸ The inhabitants of Sidon and Arvad
were your rowers;
skilled men of Zemer[g] were within you,
they were your pilots.
⁹ The elders of Gebal and its artisans were
within you,
caulking your seams;
all the ships of the sea with their mariners
were within you,
to barter for your wares.
¹⁰ Paras[h] and Lud and Put
were in your army,
your mighty warriors;
they hung shield and helmet in you;
they gave you splendor.
¹¹ Men of Arvad and Helech[i]

were on your walls all around;
men of Gamad were at your towers.
They hung their quivers all around your
walls;
they made perfect your beauty.

12 Tarshish did business with you out of the
abundance of your great wealth; silver, iron, tin,
and lead they exchanged for your wares. ¹³Javan,
Tubal, and Meshech traded with you; they exchanged human beings and vessels of bronze for
your merchandise. ¹⁴Beth-togarmah exchanged
for your wares horses, war horses, and mules.
¹⁵The Rhodians[j] traded with you; many coast-
lands were your own special markets; they
brought you in payment ivory tusks and ebony.
¹⁶Edom[k] did business with you because of your
abundant goods; they exchanged for your wares
turquoise, purple, embroidered work, fine linen,
coral, and rubies. ¹⁷Judah and the land of Israel
traded with you; they exchanged for your merchandise wheat from Minnith, millet,[l] honey, oil,
and balm. ¹⁸Damascus traded with you for your
abundant goods—because of your great wealth of
every kind—wine of Helbon, and white wool.
¹⁹Vedan and Javan from Uzal[l] entered into trade
for your wares; wrought iron, cassia, and sweet
cane were bartered for your merchandise. ²⁰De-
dan traded with you in saddlecloths for riding.
²¹Arabia and all the princes of Kedar were your
favored dealers in lambs, rams, and goats; in these
they did business with you. ²²The merchants of
Sheba and Raamah traded with you; they exchanged for your wares the best of all kinds of
spices, and all precious stones, and gold. ²³Haran,
Canneh, Eden, the merchants of Sheba, Asshur,
and Chilmad traded with you. ²⁴These traded
with you in choice garments, in clothes of blue
and embroidered work, and in carpets of colored
material, bound with cords and made secure; in
these they traded with you.[m] ²⁵The ships of Tarshish traveled for you in your trade.

So you were filled and heavily laden
in the heart of the seas.
²⁶ Your rowers have brought you
into the high seas.
The east wind has wrecked you
in the heart of the seas.
²⁷ Your riches, your wares, your
merchandise,
your mariners and your pilots,
your caulkers, your dealers in
merchandise,
and all your warriors within you,
with all the company
that is with you,
sink into the heart of the seas
on the day of your ruin.

---

[e] Gk: Heb *I will give beauty*   [f] Or *boxwood*   [g] Cn Compare Gen 10.18: Heb *your skilled men, O Tyre*
[h] Or *Persia*   [i] Or *and your army*   [j] Gk: Heb *The Dedanites*   [k] Another reading is *Aram*   [l] Meaning of Heb
uncertain   [m] Cn: Heb *in your market*

28 At the sound of the cry of your pilots
　　the countryside shakes,
29 and down from their ships
　　come all that handle the oar.
　　The mariners and all the pilots of the sea
　　stand on the shore
30 and wail aloud over you,
　　and cry bitterly.
　　They throw dust on their heads
　　and wallow in ashes;
31 they make themselves bald for you,
　　and put on sackcloth,
　　and they weep over you in bitterness of
　　　　soul,
　　with bitter mourning.
32 In their wailing they raise a lamentation
　　　　for you,
　　and lament over you:
　　"Who was ever destroyed[n] like Tyre
　　in the midst of the sea?
33 When your wares came from the seas,
　　you satisfied many peoples;
　　with your abundant wealth and
　　　　merchandise
　　you enriched the kings of the earth.
34 Now you are wrecked by the seas,
　　in the depths of the waters;
　　your merchandise and all your crew
　　have sunk with you.
35 All the inhabitants of the coastlands
　　are appalled at you;
　　and their kings are horribly afraid,
　　their faces are convulsed.
36 The merchants among the peoples hiss at
　　　　you;
　　you have come to a dreadful end
　　and shall be no more forever."

Proclamation against the King of Tyre

28 The word of the LORD came to me: [2]Mortal, say to the prince of Tyre, Thus says the Lord GOD:
　　Because your heart is proud
　　and you have said, "I am a god;
　　I sit in the seat of the gods,
　　in the heart of the seas,"
　　yet you are but a mortal, and no god,
　　though you compare your mind
　　with the mind of a god.
3 You are indeed wiser than Daniel;[o]
　　no secret is hidden from you;
4 by your wisdom and your understanding
　　you have amassed wealth for yourself,
　　and have gathered gold and silver
　　into your treasuries.
5 By your great wisdom in trade
　　you have increased your wealth,
　　and your heart has become proud in
　　　　your wealth.

6 Therefore thus says the Lord GOD:
　　Because you compare your mind
　　with the mind of a god,
7 therefore, I will bring strangers against
　　　　you,
　　the most terrible of the nations;

28.3 Different Daniel

This Daniel, also mentioned in 14.14, is probably not the prophet Daniel, but an earlier patriarch revered for his wisdom. The prophet Daniel, Ezekiel's fellow exile in Babylon, would not likely have gained such renown so soon. Also, his name is spelled slightly differently in Hebrew.

　　they shall draw their swords against the
　　　　beauty of your wisdom
　　and defile your splendor.
8 They shall thrust you down to the Pit,
　　and you shall die a violent death
　　in the heart of the seas.
9 Will you still say, "I am a god,"
　　in the presence of those who kill you,
　　though you are but a mortal, and no god,
　　in the hands of those who wound you?
10 You shall die the death of the
　　　　uncircumcised
　　by the hand of foreigners;
　　for I have spoken, says the Lord GOD.

Lamentation over the King of Tyre

11 Moreover the word of the LORD came to me: [12]Mortal, raise a lamentation over the king of Tyre, and say to him, Thus says the Lord GOD:
　　You were the signet of perfection,[p]
　　full of wisdom and perfect in beauty.
13 You were in Eden, the garden of God;
　　every precious stone was your covering,
　　carnelian, chrysolite, and moonstone,
　　beryl, onyx, and jasper,
　　sapphire,[q] turquoise, and emerald;
　　and worked in gold were your settings
　　and your engravings.[p]
　　On the day that you were created
　　they were prepared.
14 With an anointed cherub as guardian I
　　　　placed you;[p]
　　you were on the holy mountain
　　　　of God;
　　you walked among the stones of fire.
15 You were blameless in your ways
　　from the day that you were created,
　　until iniquity was found in you.
16 In the abundance of your trade

---

[n] Tg Vg: Heb *like silence*　　[o] Or, as otherwise read, *Danel*　　[p] Meaning of Heb uncertain　　[q] Or *lapis lazuli*

you were filled with violence, and you
    sinned;
so I cast you as a profane thing from the
    mountain of God,
and the guardian cherub drove you out
    from among the stones of fire.

17 Your heart was proud because of your
    beauty;
you corrupted your wisdom for the
    sake of your splendor.
I cast you to the ground;
    I exposed you before kings,
to feast their eyes on you.

18 By the multitude of your iniquities,
    in the unrighteousness of your trade,
    you profaned your sanctuaries.
So I brought out fire from within you;
    it consumed you,
and I turned you to ashes on the earth
    in the sight of all who saw you.

19 All who know you among the peoples
    are appalled at you;
you have come to a dreadful end
    and shall be no more forever.

Proclamation against Sidon

20 The word of the LORD came to me: 21Mor-
tal, set your face toward Sidon, and prophesy
against it, 22and say, Thus says the Lord GOD:
I am against you, O Sidon,
    and I will gain glory in your midst.
They shall know that I am the LORD
    when I execute judgments in it,
    and manifest my holiness in it;
23 for I will send pestilence into it,
    and bloodshed into its streets;
and the dead shall fall in its midst,
    by the sword that is against it on every
      side.
And they shall know that I am the LORD.

24 The house of Israel shall no longer find a
pricking brier or a piercing thorn among all their
neighbors who have treated them with contempt.
And they shall know that I am the Lord GOD.

Future Blessing for Israel

25 Thus says the Lord GOD: When I gather
the house of Israel from the peoples among
whom they are scattered, and manifest my holiness in them in the sight of the nations, then they
shall settle on their own soil that I gave to my
servant Jacob. 26They shall live in safety in it, and
shall build houses and plant vineyards. They shall
live in safety, when I execute judgments upon all
their neighbors who have treated them with contempt. And they shall know that I am the LORD
their God.

Proclamation against Egypt

29 In the tenth year, in the tenth month, on
the twelfth day of the month, the word
of the LORD came to me: 2Mortal, set your face
against Pharaoh king of Egypt, and prophesy
against him and against all Egypt; 3speak, and say,
Thus says the Lord GOD:
I am against you,
    Pharaoh king of Egypt,
the great dragon sprawling
    in the midst of its channels,
saying, "My Nile is my own;
    I made it for myself."

4 I will put hooks in your jaws,
    and make the fish of your channels
      stick to your scales.
I will draw you up from your channels,
    with all the fish of your channels
    sticking to your scales.

5 I will fling you into the wilderness,
    you and all the fish of your channels;
you shall fall in the open field,
    and not be gathered and buried.
To the animals of the earth and to the
      birds of the air
    I have given you as food.

6 Then all the inhabitants of Egypt shall
      know
    that I am the LORD
because your were a staff of reed
    to the house of Israel;

7 when they grasped you with the hand,
      you broke,
    and tore all their shoulders;
and when they leaned on you, you broke,
    and made all their legs unsteady.s

29.7 Unreliable Egypt

*When threatened by another superpower
(Babylon or Assyria), Israel often turned to
Egypt for help. Each time that nation let Israel
down. Right up until the final destruction of
Jerusalem, the Israelites expected Egypt to
come to their rescue, but its mighty armies
never appeared.*

8 Therefore, thus says the Lord GOD: I will
bring a sword upon you, and will cut off from you
human being and animal; 9and the land of Egypt
shall be a desolation and a waste. Then they shall
know that I am the LORD.
Because yout said, "The Nile is mine, and I
made it," 10therefore, I am against you, and
against your channels, and I will make the land of
Egypt an utter waste and desolation, from Migdol
to Syene, as far as the border of Ethiopia.u 11No

r Gk Syr Vg: Heb *they*   s Syr: Heb *stand*   t Gk Syr Vg: Heb *he*   u Or *Nubia;* Heb *Cush*

human foot shall pass through it, and no animal foot shall pass through it; it shall be uninhabited forty years. [12]I will make the land of Egypt a desolation among desolated countries; and her cities shall be a desolation forty years among cities that are laid waste. I will scatter the Egyptians among the nations, and disperse them among the countries.

13 Further, thus says the Lord GOD: At the end of forty years I will gather the Egyptians from the peoples among whom they were scattered; [14]and I will restore the fortunes of Egypt, and bring them back to the land of Pathros, the land of their origin; and there they shall be a lowly kingdom. [15]It shall be the most lowly of the kingdoms, and never again exalt itself above the nations; and I will make them so small that they will never again rule over the nations. [16]The Egyptians[v] shall never again be the reliance of the house of Israel; they will recall their iniquity, when they turned to them for aid. Then they shall know that I am the Lord GOD.

Babylonia Will Plunder Egypt

17 In the twenty-seventh year, in the first month, on the first day of the month, the word of the LORD came to me: [18]Mortal, King Nebuchadrezzar of Babylon made his army labor hard against Tyre; every head was made bald and every shoulder was rubbed bare; yet neither he nor his army got anything from Tyre to pay for the labor that he had expended against it. [19]Therefore thus says the Lord GOD: I will give the land of Egypt to King Nebuchadrezzar of Babylon; and he shall carry off its wealth and despoil it and plunder it; and it shall be the wages for his army. [20]I have given him the land of Egypt as his payment for which he labored, because they worked for me, says the Lord GOD.

21 On that day I will cause a horn to sprout up for the house of Israel, and I will open your lips among them. Then they shall know that I am the LORD.

Lamentation for Egypt

30 The word of the LORD came to me: [2]Mortal, prophesy, and say, Thus says the Lord GOD:
Wail, "Alas for the day!"
[3] For a day is near,
the day of the LORD is near;
it will be a day of clouds,
a time of doom[w] for the nations.
[4] A sword shall come upon Egypt,
and anguish shall be in Ethiopia,[x]
when the slain fall in Egypt,
and its wealth is carried away,
and its foundations are torn down.

[5]Ethiopia,[x] and Put, and Lud, and all Arabia, and Libya,[y] and the people of the allied land[z] shall fall with them by the sword.

[6] Thus says the LORD:
Those who support Egypt shall fall,
and its proud might shall come down;
from Migdol to Syene
they shall fall within it by the sword,
says the Lord GOD.
[7] They shall be desolated among other
desolated countries,
and their cities shall lie among cities
laid waste.
[8] Then they shall know that I am the LORD,
when I have set fire to Egypt,
and all who help it are broken.

9 On that day, messengers shall go out from me in ships to terrify the unsuspecting Ethiopians;[a] and anguish shall come upon them on the day of Egypt's doom;[b] for it is coming!

[10] Thus says the Lord GOD:
I will put an end to the hordes of Egypt,
by the hand of King Nebuchadrezzar of
Babylon.
[11] He and his people with him, the most
terrible of the nations,
shall be brought in to destroy the land;
and they shall draw their swords against
Egypt,
and fill the land with the slain.

30.11 Most Ruthless

Babylonians had a well-deserved reputation for cruelty. When they finally took Jerusalem at the end of a two-and-a-half-year siege, they executed all of King Zedekiah's sons while he watched. Then they put out his eyes and carted him off to Babylon (see 2 Kings 25.7).

[12] I will dry up the channels,
and will sell the land into the hand of
evildoers;
I will bring desolation upon the land and
everything in it
by the hand of foreigners;
I the LORD have spoken.

[13] Thus says the Lord GOD:
I will destroy the idols
and put an end to the images
in Memphis;
there shall no longer be a prince in the
land of Egypt;
so I will put fear in the land of Egypt.

---

[v] Heb *It* uncertain [w] Heb lacks *of doom* [a] Or *Nubians*; Heb *Cush* [x] Or *Nubia*; Heb *Cush* [b] Heb *the day of Egypt* [y] Compare Gk Syr Vg: Heb *Cub* [z] Meaning of Heb

14 I will make Pathros a desolation,
    and will set fire to Zoan,
    and will execute acts of judgment on
        Thebes.
15 I will pour my wrath upon Pelusium,
    the stronghold of Egypt,
    and cut off the hordes of Thebes.
16 I will set fire to Egypt;
    Pelusium shall be in great agony;
Thebes shall be breached,
    and Memphis face adversaries by day.
17 The young men of On and of Pi-beseth
        shall fall by the sword;
    and the cities themselves[c] shall go into
        captivity.
18 At Tehaphnehes the day shall be dark,
    when I break there the dominion of
        Egypt,
    and its proud might shall come to an end;
    the city[d] shall be covered by a cloud,
    and its daughter-towns shall go into
        captivity.
19 Thus I will execute acts of judgment on
        Egypt.
    Then they shall know that I am the
        LORD.

Proclamation against Pharaoh

20 In the eleventh year, in the first month, on the seventh day of the month, the word of the LORD came to me: [21]Mortal, I have broken the arm of Pharaoh king of Egypt; it has not been bound up for healing or wrapped with a bandage, so that it may become strong to wield the sword. [22]Therefore thus says the Lord GOD: I am against Pharaoh king of Egypt, and will break his arms, both the strong arm and the one that was broken; and I will make the sword fall from his hand. [23]I will scatter the Egyptians among the nations, and disperse them throughout the lands. [24]I will strengthen the arms of the king of Babylon, and put my sword in his hand; but I will break the arms of Pharaoh, and he will groan before him with the groans of one mortally wounded. [25]I will strengthen the arms of the king of Babylon, but the arms of Pharaoh shall fall. And they shall know that I am the LORD, when I put my sword into the hand of the king of Babylon. He shall stretch it out against the land of Egypt, [26]and I will scatter the Egyptians among the nations and disperse them throughout the countries. Then they shall know that I am the LORD.

The Lofty Cedar

31 In the eleventh year, in the third month, on the first day of the month, the word of the LORD came to me: [2]Mortal, say to Pharaoh king of Egypt and to his hordes:
    Whom are you like in your greatness?

3   Consider Assyria, a cedar of Lebanon,
    with fair branches and forest shade,
        and of great height,
        its top among the clouds.[e]
4   The waters nourished it,
        the deep made it grow tall,
    making its rivers flow[f]
        around the place it was planted,
    sending forth its streams
        to all the trees of the field.
5   So it towered high
        above all the trees of the field;
    its boughs grew large
        and its branches long,
        from abundant water in its shoots.
6   All the birds of the air
        made their nests in its boughs;
    under its branches all the animals of the
            field
        gave birth to their young;
    and in its shade
        all great nations lived.
7   It was beautiful in its greatness,
        in the length of its branches;
    for its roots went down
        to abundant water.
8   The cedars in the garden of God could
            not rival it,
        nor the fir trees equal its boughs;
    the plane trees were as nothing
        compared with its branches;
    no tree in the garden of God
        was like it in beauty.
9   I made it beautiful
        with its mass of branches,
    the envy of all the trees of Eden
        that were in the garden of God.

10 Therefore thus says the Lord GOD: Because it[g] towered high and set its top among the clouds,[e] and its heart was proud of its height, [11]I gave it into the hand of the prince of the nations; he has dealt with it as its wickedness deserves. I have cast it out. [12]Foreigners from the most terrible of the nations have cut it down and left it. On the mountains and in all the valleys its branches have fallen, and its boughs lie broken in all the watercourses of the land; and all the peoples of the earth went away from its shade and left it.
13 On its fallen trunk settle
        all the birds of the air,
    and among its boughs lodge
        all the wild animals.
[14]All this is in order that no trees by the waters may grow to lofty height or set their tops among the clouds,[e] and that no trees that drink water may reach up to them in height.
    For all of them are handed over to death,
        to the world below;

---

c Heb and they   d Heb she   e Gk: Heb thick boughs   f Gk: Heb rivers going   g Syr Vg: Heb you

along with all mortals,
    with those who go down to the Pit.

15 Thus says the Lord GOD: On the day it
went down to Sheol I closed the deep over it and
covered it; I restrained its rivers, and its mighty
waters were checked. I clothed Lebanon in gloom
for it, and all the trees of the field fainted because
of it. [16]I made the nations quake at the sound of
its fall, when I cast it down to Sheol with those
who go down to the Pit; and all the trees of Eden,
the choice and best of Lebanon, all that were
well watered, were consoled in the world below.
[17]They also went down to Sheol with it, to those
killed by the sword, along with its allies,[h] those
who lived in its shade among the nations.

18 Which among the trees of Eden was like
you in glory and in greatness? Now you shall be
brought down with the trees of Eden to the world
below; you shall lie among the uncircumcised,
with those who are killed by the sword. This is
Pharaoh and all his horde, says the Lord GOD.

Lamentation over Pharaoh and Egypt

32 In the twelfth year, in the twelfth month,
on the first day of the month, the word of
the LORD came to me: [2]Mortal, raise a lamentation over Pharaoh king of Egypt, and say to him:
  You consider yourself a lion among the
      nations,
  but you are like a dragon in the seas;
you thrash about in your streams,
  trouble the water with your feet,
  and foul your[i] streams.
3 Thus says the Lord GOD:
  In an assembly of many peoples
  I will throw my net over you;
  and I[j] will haul you up in my dragnet.
4 I will throw you on the ground,
  on the open field I will fling you,
and will cause all the birds of the air to
      settle on you,
  and I will let the wild animals of the
      whole earth gorge themselves with
      you.
5 I will strew your flesh on the mountains,
  and fill the valleys with your carcass.[k]
6 I will drench the land with your flowing
      blood
  up to the mountains,
and the watercourses will be filled with
      you.
7 When I blot you out, I will cover the
      heavens,
  and make their stars dark;
I will cover the sun with a cloud,
  and the moon shall not give its light.
8 All the shining lights of the heavens
  I will darken above you,

and put darkness on your land,
      says the Lord GOD.
9 I will trouble the hearts of many peoples,
  as I carry you captive[l] among the
      nations,
  into countries you have not known.
10 I will make many peoples appalled at you;
  their kings shall shudder because of
      you.
When I brandish my sword before them,
  they shall tremble every moment
for their lives, each one of them,
  on the day of your downfall.
11 For thus says the Lord GOD:
The sword of the king of Babylon shall
      come against you.
12 I will cause your hordes to fall
  by the swords of mighty ones,
  all of them most terrible among the
      nations.
They shall bring to ruin the pride of
      Egypt,
  and all its hordes shall perish.
13 I will destroy all its livestock
  from beside abundant waters;
and no human foot shall trouble them
      any more,
  nor shall the hoofs of cattle trouble
      them.
14 Then I will make their waters clear,
  and cause their streams to run like oil,
      says the Lord GOD.
15 When I make the land of Egypt desolate
  and when the land is stripped of all
      that fills it,
when I strike down all who live in it,
  then they shall know that I am the
      LORD.
16 This is a lamentation; it shall be chanted.
  The women of the nations shall chant
      it.
Over Egypt and all its hordes they shall
      chant it,
  says the Lord GOD.

Dirge over Egypt

17 In the twelfth year, in the first month,[m] on
the fifteenth day of the month, the word of the
LORD came to me:
18 Mortal, wail over the hordes of Egypt,
  and send them down,
with Egypt[n] and the daughters of
      majestic nations,
to the world below,
  with those who go down to the Pit.
19 "Whom do you surpass in beauty?
  Go down! Be laid to rest with the
      uncircumcised!"

---

h Heb *its arms*   i Heb *their*   j Gk Vg: Heb *they*   k Symmachus Syr Vg: Heb *your height*   l Gk: Heb *bring*
your destruction   m Gk: Heb lacks *in the first month*   n Heb *it*

20They shall fall among those who are killed by the sword. Egypt*o* has been handed over to the sword; carry away both it and its hordes. 21The mighty chiefs shall speak of them, with their helpers, out of the midst of Sheol: "They have come down, they lie still, the uncircumcised, killed by the sword."

32.21 The Afterlife

Though eternal life shines through a few Old Testament passages (see "Life after Death," page 562), life after death was extremely vague in most of the Old Testament. The grave was represented by a place called "Sheol." The fate of the nations described here as "out of the midst of Sheol" gives a vivid, eerie sense of death.

22 Assyria is there, and all its company, their graves all around it, all of them killed, fallen by the sword. 23Their graves are set in the uttermost parts of the Pit. Its company is all around its grave, all of them killed, fallen by the sword, who spread terror in the land of the living.

24 Elam is there, and all its hordes around its grave; all of them killed, fallen by the sword, who went down uncircumcised into the world below, who spread terror in the land of the living. They bear their shame with those who go down to the Pit. 25They have made Elam*p* a bed among the slain with all its hordes, their graves all around it, all of them uncircumcised, killed by the sword; for terror of them was spread in the land of the living, and they bear their shame with those who go down to the Pit; they are placed among the slain.

26 Meshech and Tubal are there, and all their multitude, their graves all around them, all of them uncircumcised, killed by the sword; for they spread terror in the land of the living. 27And they do not lie with the fallen warriors of long ago*q* who went down to Sheol with their weapons of war, whose swords were laid under their heads, and whose shields*r* are upon their bones; for the terror of the warriors was in the land of the living. 28So you shall be broken and lie among the uncircumcised, with those who are killed by the sword.

29 Edom is there, its kings and all its princes, who for all their might are laid with those who are killed by the sword; they lie with the uncircumcised, with those who go down to the Pit.

30 The princes of the north are there, all of them, and all the Sidonians, who have gone down in shame with the slain, for all the terror that they caused by their might; they lie uncircumcised with those who are killed by the sword, and bear their shame with those who go down to the Pit.

31 When Pharaoh sees them, he will be consoled for all his hordes—Pharaoh and all his army, killed by the sword, says the Lord GOD. 32For he*s* spread terror in the land of the living; therefore he shall be laid to rest among the uncircumcised, with those who are slain by the sword—Pharaoh and all his multitude, says the Lord GOD.

Ezekiel Israel's Sentry

33 The word of the LORD came to me: 2O Mortal, speak to your people and say to them, If I bring the sword upon a land, and the people of the land take one of their number as their sentinel; 3and if the sentinel sees the sword coming upon the land and blows the trumpet and warns the people; 4then if any who hear the sound of the trumpet do not take warning, and the sword comes and takes them away, their blood shall be upon their own heads. 5They heard the sound of the trumpet and did not take warning; their blood shall be upon themselves. But if they had taken warning, they would have saved their lives. 6But if the sentinel sees the sword coming and does not blow the trumpet, so that the people are not warned, and the sword comes and takes any of them, they are taken away in their iniquity, but their blood I will require at the sentinel's hand.

7 So you, mortal, I have made a sentinel for the house of Israel; whenever you hear a word from my mouth, you shall give them warning

33.7 Watch Out

You don't hire a watchman to fight off robbers single-handed; he is responsible for sounding the alarm. God assigns Ezekiel the watchman's role, here and earlier (3.18). It's tragic when someone dies for his or her sins, but when he or she dies without being warned, that is inexcusable—for the watchman was assigned to offer a chance to repent.

from me. 8If I say to the wicked, "O wicked ones, you shall surely die," and you do not speak to warn the wicked to turn from their ways, the wicked shall die in their iniquity, but their blood I will require at your hand. 9But if you warn the wicked to turn from their ways, and they do not turn from their ways, the wicked shall die in their iniquity, but you will have saved your life.

God's Justice and Mercy

10 Now you, mortal, say to the house of Israel, Thus you have said: "Our transgressions and our sins weigh upon us, and we waste away be-

o Heb *It*   *p* Heb *it*   *q* Gk Old Latin: Heb *of the uncircumcised*   *r* Cn: Heb *iniquities*   *s* Cn: Heb *I*

cause of them; how then can we live?" ¹¹Say to them, As I live, says the Lord GOD, I have no pleasure in the death of the wicked, but that the wicked turn from their ways and live; turn back, turn back from your evil ways; for why will you die, O house of Israel? ¹²And you, mortal, say to your people, The righteousness of the righteous shall not save them when they transgress; and as for the wickedness of the wicked, it shall not make them stumble when they turn from their wickedness; and the righteous shall not be able to live by their righteousness*ᵗ* when they sin. ¹³Though I

ᵗ Heb *by it*

say to the righteous that they shall surely live, yet if they trust in their righteousness and commit iniquity, none of their righteous deeds shall be remembered; but in the iniquity that they have committed they shall die. ¹⁴Again, though I say to the wicked, "You shall surely die," yet if they turn from their sin and do what is lawful and right— ¹⁵if the wicked restore the pledge, give back what they have taken by robbery, and walk in the statutes of life, committing no iniquity—they shall surely live, they shall not die. ¹⁶None of the sins that they have committed shall be remembered

The Turning Point
From here forward, Ezekiel offers good news

TO THEIR CHILDREN PARENTS CAN seem frighteningly inconsistent. One minute a father is gripping his son's wrist, shouting about something. The next moment, punishment over, he is talking about going camping together next summer. How can he change so drastically? Why so angry one minute and so loving the next?

The sudden change makes sense only if you grasp that most parents hate the role of disciplinarian. They punish in order to correct something they see as harmful. Afterwards, they put punishment behind them as quickly as possible, because they dream of better times in the future.

> *In the twelfth year of our exile . . . someone who had escaped from Jerusalem came to me and said, "The city has fallen." 33.21*

A Happier Life for Ezekiel

Ezekiel portrays just such a drastic change between God and Israel. Until chapter 33 he had offered mostly anger and threats. Suddenly, in verse 21, the news of Jerusalem's fall reached Ezekiel. The punishment, long threatened, had come. From this point on, Ezekiel's message from God became dominated by dreams of the future—happy dreams. Ezekiel's life became happier too. After seven years of virtual silence (3.26–27—he spoke only what God told him to), he opened his mouth freely again.

God, speaking through Ezekiel, began to paint the future with the same vivid colors he had used to promise punishment. He spoke of Israel as a flock of sheep and himself as their loving shepherd (chapter 34). He previewed the mountains of Israel as they will look under his full blessing (chapter 36)—very different from the prediction given those same mountains in chapter 6.

God showed Ezekiel a valley of dry bones rising up and taking life (chapter 37), a vision that has inspired musicians and preachers ever since. He forecast a fantastic battle with evil forces from the north, Gog and Magog, in which God's people would triumph magnificently (chapters 38–39). Then, in his final vision, God showed Ezekiel the nation of Israel restored, with its boundaries extended far into hostile territory, its temple rebuilt in new splendor (chapters 40–48). The Lord would come back to his home, to live with his people.

The Temple's Significance

The temple, to Israel, was a sign of God's love. By taking up a home there, he committed himself to be with them permanently—not to come and go but to be available at any and all times to his people. When he left the temple (10.18) and let it be razed by the Babylonians (2 Kings 25.9), he communicated clearly that Israel had forfeited any right to his care.

So Ezekiel's vision of a rebuilt temple, with God's glory filling it, was a promise of new hope. The temple has never been rebuilt according to the precise description Ezekiel gave (chapters 40–43), and many scholars understand his portrayal as symbolic. But the central beauty of the temple is this: "The LORD is There." The glorious, astonishing God whom Ezekiel first saw in the Babylonian desert will make his home in the center of the land. He will not always be angry. He has great plans for the happiness of his people.

Life Questions: In your relationship with God, are you more concerned with past failures? Or with hopes for the future?

against them; they have done what is lawful and right, they shall surely live.

17 Yet your people say, "The way of the Lord is not just," when it is their own way that is not just. [18]When the righteous turn from their righteousness, and commit iniquity, they shall die for it.[u] [19]And when the wicked turn from their wickedness, and do what is lawful and right, they shall live by it.[u] [20]Yet you say, "The way of the Lord is not just." O house of Israel, I will judge all of you according to your ways!

The Fall of Jerusalem

21 In the twelfth year of our exile, in the tenth month, on the fifth day of the month, someone who had escaped from Jerusalem came to me and said, "The city has fallen." [22]Now the hand of the LORD had been upon me the evening before the fugitive came; but he had opened my mouth by the time the fugitive came to me in the morning; so my mouth was opened, and I was no longer unable to speak.

33.22 End of the Silence

For nearly eight years, since the beginning of his ministry, Ezekiel had been silent except when giving God's words. Now, an exile arrived in Babylon with bad news from Jerusalem: The temple had been burned, the city destroyed. Ezekiel's long silence ended, by God's permission. His message of doom ended too, for his prediction of punishment had come true. From this point on, Ezekiel's prophecies take up a more hopeful theme, of rebuilding a broken people.

The Survivors in Judah

23 The word of the LORD came to me: [24]Mortal, the inhabitants of these waste places in the land of Israel keep saying, "Abraham was only one man, yet he got possession of the land; but we are many; the land is surely given us to possess." [25]Therefore say to them, Thus says the Lord GOD: You eat flesh with the blood, and lift up your eyes to your idols, and shed blood; shall you then possess the land? [26]You depend on your swords, you commit abominations, and each of you defiles his neighbor's wife; shall you then possess the land? [27]Say this to them, Thus says the Lord GOD: As I live, surely those who are in the waste places shall fall by the sword; and those who are in the open field I will give to the wild animals to be devoured; and those who are in strongholds and in caves shall die by pestilence. [28]I will make the land a desolation and a waste, and its proud might shall come to an end; and the mountains of Israel

shall be so desolate that no one will pass through. [29]Then they shall know that I am the LORD, when I have made the land a desolation and a waste because of all their abominations that they have committed.

30 As for you, mortal, your people who talk together about you by the walls, and at the doors of the houses, say to one another, each to a neighbor, "Come and hear what the word is that comes from the LORD." [31]They come to you as people come, and they sit before you as my people, and they hear your words, but they will not obey them. For flattery is on their lips, but their heart is set on their gain. [32]To them you are like a singer of love songs,[v] one who has a beautiful voice and plays well on an instrument; they hear what you

33.32 Prophetic Entertainment

Ezekiel's popularity soared after Jerusalem's fall, for his warnings had all come true. Even so, his audience listened just for entertainment, as they would to music. God reminds Ezekiel that the true purpose of prophecy is to change people's lives, not to draw a crowd.

say, but they will not do it. [33]When this comes— and come it will!—then they shall know that a prophet has been among them.

Israel's False Shepherds

34 The word of the LORD came to me: [2]Mortal, prophesy against the shepherds of Israel: prophesy, and say to them—to the shepherds: Thus says the Lord GOD: Ah, you shepherds of Israel who have been feeding yourselves! Should not shepherds feed the sheep? [3]You eat the fat, you clothe yourselves with the wool, you slaughter the fatlings; but you do not feed the sheep. [4]You have not strengthened the weak, you have not healed the sick, you have not bound up the injured, you have not brought back the strayed, you have not sought the lost, but with force and harshness you have ruled them. [5]So they were scattered, because there was no shepherd; and scattered, they became food for all the wild animals. [6]My sheep were scattered, they wandered over all the mountains and on every high hill; my sheep were scattered over all the face of the earth, with no one to search or seek for them.

7 Therefore, you shepherds, hear the word of the LORD: [8]As I live, says the Lord GOD, because my sheep have become a prey, and my sheep have become food for all the wild animals, since there was no shepherd; and because my shepherds have not searched for my sheep, but the shepherds have fed themselves, and have not fed my sheep;

---

[u] Heb *them*   [v] Cn: Heb *like a love song*

⁹therefore, you shepherds, hear the word of the LORD: ¹⁰Thus says the Lord GOD, I am against the shepherds; and I will demand my sheep at their hand, and put a stop to their feeding the sheep; no longer shall the shepherds feed themselves. I will rescue my sheep from their mouths, so that they may not be food for them.

God, the True Shepherd

11 For thus says the Lord GOD: I myself will search for my sheep, and will seek them out. ¹²As shepherds seek out their flocks when they are among their scattered sheep, so I will seek out my sheep. I will rescue them from all the places to which they have been scattered on a day of clouds and thick darkness. ¹³I will bring them out from the peoples and gather them from the countries, and will bring them into their own land; and I will

feed them on the mountains of Israel, by the watercourses, and in all the inhabited parts of the land. ¹⁴I will feed them with good pasture, and the mountain heights of Israel shall be their pasture; there they shall lie down in good grazing land, and they shall feed on rich pasture on the mountains of Israel. ¹⁵I myself will be the shepherd of my sheep, and I will make them lie down, says the Lord GOD. ¹⁶I will seek the lost, and I will bring back the strayed, and I will bind up the injured, and I will strengthen the weak, but the fat and the strong I will destroy. I will feed them with justice.

17 As for you, my flock, thus says the Lord GOD: I shall judge between sheep and sheep, between rams and goats: ¹⁸Is it not enough for you to feed on the good pasture, but you must tread down with your feet the rest of your pasture? When you drink of clear water, must you foul the

The Sad Truth
Ezekiel became popular overnight—but the praise was empty

GOD WARNED EZEKIEL IT WOULD be a terrible job. Nobody would listen to his message. He would find Israel with a "hard forehead and a stubborn heart" (3.7). And how would God help him? "I have made your face hard against their faces" (3.8).

As a result Ezekiel lived a lonely life. Those few who believed his prophecies expected nothing to happen in their lifetime (12.27). People thought of Ezekiel as someone just telling stories (20.49). They couldn't believe that God would let Jerusalem fall, as Ezekiel was stubbornly predicting.

Then, after years of prophecy, news came that Babylon had conquered Jerusalem (33.21). Suddenly Ezekiel was popular. People talked about him, flocked to hear his words, expressed devotion. But they listened to Ezekiel without changing their hearts. He was just a "singer of love songs" (33.32). The people heard his words but did not put them into practice.

> They sit before you as my people, and they hear your words, but they will not obey them.
> 33.31

A Dreadful Message

In some ways Ezekiel could sympathize with the people's negative attitude. He did not like his message either; sometimes it horrified him. Twice, seeing God's judgment, he fell facedown in horror, crying out (9.8; 11.13). When God told him to cook food over human excrement, a symbol of defilement, he was too shocked to agree (4.14). When his wife, "the delight of his eyes," died, he was not even allowed to weep (24.15–24).

Ezekiel had to subordinate ordinary human emotions to the unpleasant task God had given him: to tell the truth, the whole truth, and nothing but the truth, and to tell it in a way that the Israelites could not ignore. "As I live, says the Lord GOD, I have no pleasure in the death of the wicked, but that the wicked turn from their ways and live; turn back, turn back from your evil ways; for why will you die, O house of Israel?" (33.11).

Phony Optimism

The false prophets, by contrast, tended to be optimists. They overlooked their nation's corruption and predicted that everything would work out. Chapter 13 records Ezekiel's words against them. "Alas for the senseless prophets who follow their own spirit, and have seen nothing!" he said (13.3). They would "whitewash" a bad situation with claims that God could never let Jerusalem be destroyed (13.10–16).

In the end Ezekiel got to deliver genuine good news: the promise of restored life. He saw a vision that still lives in song: scattered, bleached bones coming to life (37.1–14). In another vision, he saw God return to live in Jerusalem (43.1–5). Ezekiel didn't live to see these hopeful predictions fulfilled. But you can be sure he enjoyed making them far more than he enjoyed his predictions of disaster.

Life Questions: Is there any place today for "bad news" of the kind Ezekiel proclaimed?

rest with your feet? [19]And must my sheep eat what you have trodden with your feet, and drink what you have fouled with your feet?

20 Therefore, thus says the Lord GOD to

34.11–16 The Good Shepherd

Ezekiel, who used strong imagery throughout his writing, developed the image of God as a shepherd with more detail than any other author in the Bible. To people who herded sheep for a living, the simile had tremendous impact.

The same comparison is used repeatedly throughout the Bible. One much-loved passage is Psalm 23, which begins, "The LORD is my shepherd." Jesus called himself "the good shepherd" (John 10.11–16) and had compassion on crowds because they were like "sheep without a shepherd" (Mark 6.34). The image of God as a shepherd begins with Jacob (Genesis 48.15) and ends with Revelation 7.17.

them: I myself will judge between the fat sheep and the lean sheep. [21]Because you pushed with flank and shoulder, and butted at all the weak animals with your horns until you scattered them far and wide, [22]I will save my flock, and they shall no longer be ravaged; and I will judge between sheep and sheep.

23 I will set up over them one shepherd, my servant David, and he shall feed them: he shall feed them and be their shepherd. [24]And I, the LORD, will be their God, and my servant David shall be prince among them; I, the LORD, have spoken.

25 I will make with them a covenant of peace and banish wild animals from the land, so that they may live in the wild and sleep in the woods securely. [26]I will make them and the region around my hill a blessing; and I will send down the showers in their season; they shall be showers of blessing. [27]The trees of the field shall yield their fruit, and the earth shall yield its increase. They shall be secure on their soil; and they shall know that I am the LORD, when I break the bars of their yoke, and save them from the hands of those who enslaved them. [28]They shall no more be plunder for the nations, nor shall the animals of the land devour them; they shall live in safety, and no one shall make them afraid. [29]I will provide for them a splendid vegetation so that they shall no more be consumed with hunger in the land, and no longer suffer the insults of the nations. [30]They shall know that I, the LORD their God, am with them, and that they, the house of Israel, are my people, says the Lord GOD. [31]You are my sheep,

the sheep of my pasture[w] and I am your God, says the Lord GOD.

Judgment on Mount Seir

35 The word of the LORD came to me: [2]Mortal, set your face against Mount Seir, and prophesy against it, [3]and say to it, Thus says the Lord GOD:

I am against you, Mount Seir;
 I stretch out my hand against you
 to make you a desolation and a waste.
[4] I lay your towns in ruins;
 you shall become a desolation,
 and you shall know that I am
 the LORD.
[5]Because you cherished an ancient enmity, and gave over the people of Israel to the power of the sword at the time of their calamity, at the time of

35.5 Bad Blood

Ill will between two clans dated from the beginning, when Jacob cheated his brother Esau out of the family inheritance. Over the centuries Esau's descendants became the nation of Edom, and Jacob's became Israel. Bad feelings persisted. To Israelites, however, this incident was the ultimate offense: When Babylon burned down Jerusalem, the Edomites looted the city and egged on the Babylonians.

their final punishment; [6]therefore, as I live, says the Lord GOD, I will prepare you for blood, and blood shall pursue you; since you did not hate bloodshed, bloodshed shall pursue you. [7]I will make Mount Seir a waste and a desolation; and I will cut off from it all who come and go. [8]I will fill its mountains with the slain; on your hills and in your valleys and in all your watercourses those killed with the sword shall fall. [9]I will make you a perpetual desolation, and your cities shall never be inhabited. Then you shall know that I am the LORD.

10 Because you said, "These two nations and these two countries shall be mine, and we will take possession of them,"—although the LORD was there— [11]therefore, as I live, says the Lord GOD, I will deal with you according to the anger and envy that you showed because of your hatred against them; and I will make myself known among you,[x] when I judge you. [12]You shall know that I, the LORD, have heard all the abusive speech that you uttered against the mountains of Israel, saying, "They are laid desolate, they are given us to devour." [13]And you magnified yourselves against me with your mouth, and multiplied your words against me; I heard it. [14]Thus says the Lord GOD: As the whole earth rejoices, I will make you

---

[w] Gk OL: Heb *pasture, you are people*   [x] Gk: Heb *them*

desolate. [15]As you rejoiced over the inheritance of the house of Israel, because it was desolate, so I will deal with you; you shall be desolate, Mount Seir, and all Edom, all of it. Then they shall know that I am the LORD.

Blessing on Israel

36 And you, mortal, prophesy to the mountains of Israel, and say: O mountains of Israel, hear the word of the LORD. [2]Thus says the Lord GOD: Because the enemy said of you, "Aha!" and, "The ancient heights have become our possession," [3]therefore prophesy, and say: Thus says the Lord GOD: Because they made you desolate indeed, and crushed you from all sides, so that you became the possession of the rest of the nations, and you became an object of gossip and slander among the people; [4]therefore, O mountains of Israel, hear the word of the Lord GOD: Thus says the Lord GOD to the mountains and the hills, the watercourses and the valleys, the desolate wastes and the deserted towns, which have become a source of plunder and an object of derision to the rest of the nations all around; [5]therefore thus says the Lord GOD: I am speaking in my hot jealousy against the rest of the nations, and against all Edom, who, with wholehearted joy and utter contempt, took my land as their possession, because of its pasture, to plunder it. [6]Therefore prophesy concerning the land of Israel, and say to the mountains and hills, to the watercourses and valleys, Thus says the Lord GOD: I am speaking in my jealous wrath, because you have suffered the insults of the nations; [7]therefore thus says the Lord GOD: I swear that the nations that are all around you shall themselves suffer insults.

8 But you, O mountains of Israel, shall shoot out your branches, and yield your fruit to my people Israel; for they shall soon come home. [9]See now, I am for you; I will turn to you, and you shall be tilled and sown; [10]and I will multiply your population, the whole house of Israel, all of it; the towns shall be inhabited and the waste places rebuilt; [11]and I will multiply human beings and animals upon you. They shall increase and be fruitful; and I will cause you to be inhabited as in your former times, and will do more good to you than ever before. Then you shall know that I am the LORD. [12]I will lead people upon you—my people Israel—and they shall possess you, and you shall be their inheritance. No longer shall you bereave them of children.

13 Thus says the Lord GOD: Because they say to you, "You devour people, and you bereave your nation of children," [14]therefore you shall no longer devour people and no longer bereave your nation of children, says the Lord GOD; [15]and no longer will I let you hear the insults of the nations, no longer shall you bear the disgrace of the peoples; and no longer shall you cause your nation to stumble, says the Lord GOD.

The Renewal of Israel

16 The word of the LORD came to me: [17]Mortal, when the house of Israel lived on their own soil, they defiled it with their ways and their deeds; their conduct in my sight was like the uncleanness of a woman in her menstrual period. [18]So I poured out my wrath upon them for the blood that they had shed upon the land, and for the idols with which they had defiled it. [19]I scattered them among the nations, and they were dispersed through the countries; in accordance with their conduct and their deeds I judged them. [20]But when they came to the nations, wherever they came, they profaned my holy name, in that it was said of them, "These are the people of the LORD, and yet they had to go out of his land." [21]But I had concern for my holy name, which the house of Israel had profaned among the nations to which they came.

22 Therefore say to the house of Israel, Thus says the Lord GOD: It is not for your sake, O house of Israel, that I am about to act, but for the sake of my holy name, which you have profaned among the nations to which you came. [23]I will sanctify my great name, which has been profaned among the nations, and which you have profaned among them; and the nations shall know that I am the LORD, says the Lord GOD, when through you I display my holiness before their eyes. [24]I will take you from the nations, and gather you from all the countries, and bring you into your own land. [25]I will sprinkle clean water upon you, and you shall be clean from all your uncleannesses, and from all your idols I will cleanse you. [26]A new heart I will give you, and a new spirit I will put within you; and I will remove from your body the heart of stone and give you a heart of flesh. [27]I will put my spirit within you, and make you follow my statutes and be careful

36.27 A New Spirit

Like Jeremiah, Ezekiel realized that Israel needed more than a fresh start. To avoid making the same mistakes all over again, they needed new motivation and orientation. God must work radical surgery on them, to implant a new heart and a new spirit. Jesus' followers believed that this began when the Holy Spirit came at Pentecost (Acts 2.17–21).

to observe my ordinances. [28]Then you shall live in the land that I gave to your ancestors; and you shall be my people, and I will be your God. [29]I will save you from all your uncleannesses, and I will summon the grain and make it abundant and lay no famine upon you. [30]I will make the fruit of the tree and the produce of the field abundant, so that you may never again suffer the disgrace of famine among the nations. [31]Then you shall remember your evil ways, and your dealings that were not good; and you shall loathe yourselves for your iniquities and your abominable deeds. [32]It is not for your sake that I will act, says the Lord GOD; let that be known to you. Be ashamed and dismayed for your ways, O house of Israel.

33 Thus says the Lord GOD: On the day that I cleanse you from all your iniquities, I will cause the towns to be inhabited, and the waste places shall be rebuilt. [34]The land that was desolate shall be tilled, instead of being the desolation that it was in the sight of all who passed by. [35]And they will say, "This land that was desolate has become like the garden of Eden; and the waste and desolate and ruined towns are now inhabited and fortified." [36]Then the nations that are left all around you shall know that I, the LORD, have rebuilt the ruined places, and replanted that which was desolate; I, the LORD, have spoken, and I will do it.

37 Thus says the Lord GOD: I will also let the house of Israel ask me to do this for them: to increase their population like a flock. [38]Like the flock for sacrifices,[y] like the flock at Jerusalem during her appointed festivals, so shall the ruined towns be filled with flocks of people. Then they shall know that I am the LORD.

The Valley of Dry Bones

37 The hand of the LORD came upon me, and he brought me out by the spirit of the LORD and set me down in the middle of a valley; it was full of bones. [2]He led me all around them; there were very many lying in the valley, and they were very dry. [3]He said to me, "Mortal, can these bones live?" I answered, "O Lord GOD, you know." [4]Then he said to me, "Prophesy to these bones, and say to them: O dry bones, hear the word of the LORD. [5]Thus says the Lord GOD to these bones: I will cause breath[z] to enter you, and you shall live. [6]I will lay sinews on you, and will cause flesh to come upon you, and cover you with skin, and put breath[z] in you, and you shall live; and you shall know that I am the LORD."

7 So I prophesied as I had been commanded; and as I prophesied, suddenly there was a noise, a rattling, and the bones came together, bone to its bone. [8]I looked, and there were sinews on them, and flesh had come upon them, and skin had covered them; but there was no breath in them. [9]Then he said to me, "Prophesy to the breath, prophesy, mortal, and say to the breath:[a] Thus says the Lord GOD: Come from the four winds, O breath,[a] and breathe upon these slain, that they may live." [10]I prophesied as he commanded me, and the breath came into them, and they lived, and stood on their feet, a vast multitude.

11 Then he said to me, "Mortal, these bones

are the whole house of Israel. They say, 'Our bones are dried up, and our hope is lost; we are cut off completely.' [12]Therefore prophesy, and say to them, Thus says the Lord GOD: I am going to

37.9 Dry Bones

This marvelous vision, celebrated in a famous song, begins with a collection of bones littering a valley floor. Before Ezekiel's eyes, the bones come together, assembling into skeletons and growing flesh and skin. The bodies stay dead, however, until in a dramatic moment God puts breath into them. The Hebrew for "breath" also means spirit, and the vision would have reminded any Jew of Genesis 2.7, where God breathed life into the first man.

God is reminding Ezekiel that it would take a miracle to bring the remnants of Israel back together from the many locations where they were scattered. But to be truly alive, Israel will need a greater miracle: a new spirit, breathed by God. Only a new creation can resurrect Israel or anyone else.

open your graves, and bring you up from your graves, O my people; and I will bring you back to the land of Israel. [13]And you shall know that I am the LORD, when I open your graves, and bring you up from your graves, O my people. [14]I will put my spirit within you, and you shall live, and I will place you on your own soil; then you shall know that I, the LORD, have spoken and will act, says the LORD."

The Two Sticks

15 The word of the LORD came to me: [16]Mortal, take a stick and write on it, "For Judah, and the Israelites associated with it"; then take another stick and write on it, "For Joseph (the stick of Ephraim) and all the house of Israel associated with it"; [17]and join them together into one stick, so that they may become one in your hand. [18]And when your people say to you, "Will you not show us what you mean by these?" [19]say to them, Thus says the Lord GOD: I am about to take the stick of Joseph (which is in the hand of Ephraim) and the tribes of Israel associated with it; and I will put the stick of Judah upon it,[b] and make them one stick, in order that they may be one in my hand. [20]When the sticks on which you write are in your hand before their eyes, [21]then say to them, Thus says the Lord GOD: I will take the people of Israel from the nations among which they have gone, and will gather them from every quarter, and bring them to their own land. [22]I will make them one nation in the land, on the mountains of Israel; and one king shall be king over them all. Never

---

[y] Heb *flock of holy things*   [z] Or *spirit*   [a] Or *wind* or *spirit*   [b] Heb *I will put them upon it*

again shall they be two nations, and never again shall they be divided into two kingdoms. 23They shall never again defile themselves with their idols and their detestable things, or with any of their

37.22 North and South Reunited

Israel longed to be reunited. The Jews had been split into two nations (sometimes at war) since the days of Solomon, over 300 years before. Yet, like East and West Germany, now united again, and North and South Korea today, they had not forgotten their common origin. God promised to reunite the two—even though one had been in exile, scattered among other nations, for over 100 years.

transgressions. I will save them from all the apostasies into which they have fallen,*c* and will cleanse them. Then they shall be my people, and I will be their God.

24 My servant David shall be king over them; and they shall all have one shepherd. They shall follow my ordinances and be careful to observe my statutes. 25They shall live in the land that I gave to my servant Jacob, in which your ancestors lived; they and their children and their children's children shall live there forever; and my servant David shall be their prince forever. 26I will make a covenant of peace with them; it shall be an everlasting covenant with them; and I will bless*d* them and multiply them, and will set my sanctuary among them forevermore. 27My dwelling place shall be with them; and I will be their God, and they shall be my people. 28Then the nations shall know that I the LORD sanctify Israel, when my sanctuary is among them forevermore.

Invasion by Gog

38 The word of the LORD came to me: 2Mortal, set your face toward Gog, of the land of Magog, the chief prince of Meshech and Tubal. Prophesy against him 3and say: Thus says the Lord GOD: I am against you, O Gog, chief prince of Meshech and Tubal; 4I will turn you around and put hooks into your jaws, and I will lead you out with all your army, horses and horsemen, all of them clothed in full armor, a great company, all of them with shield and buckler, wielding swords. 5Persia, Ethiopia,*e* and Put are with them, all of them with buckler and helmet; 6Gomer and all its troops; Beth-togarmah from the remotest parts of the north with all its troops— many peoples are with you.

7 Be ready and keep ready, you and all the companies that are assembled around you, and hold yourselves in reserve for them. 8After many

days you shall be mustered; in the latter years you shall go against a land restored from war, a land where people were gathered from many nations on the mountains of Israel, which had long lain waste; its people were brought out from the nations and now are living in safety, all of them. 9You shall advance, coming on like a storm; you shall be like a cloud covering the land, you and all your troops, and many peoples with you.

10 Thus says the Lord GOD: On that day thoughts will come into your mind, and you will devise an evil scheme. 11You will say, "I will go up against the land of unwalled villages; I will fall upon the quiet people who live in safety, all of them living without walls, and having no bars or gates"; 12to seize spoil and carry off plunder; to assail the waste places that are now inhabited, and the people who were gathered from the nations, who are acquiring cattle and goods, who live at the center*f* of the earth. 13Sheba and Dedan and the merchants of Tarshish and all its young warriors*g* will say to you, "Have you come to seize spoil? Have you assembled your horde to carry off plunder, to carry away silver and gold, to take away cattle and goods, to seize a great amount of booty?"

14 Therefore, mortal, prophesy, and say to Gog: Thus says the Lord GOD: On that day when my people Israel are living securely, you will rouse yourself*h* 15and come from your place out of the remotest parts of the north, you and many peoples with you, all of them riding on horses, a great horde, a mighty army; 16you will come up against my people Israel, like a cloud covering the earth. In the latter days I will bring you against my land, so that the nations may know me, when through you, O Gog, I display my holiness before their eyes.

Judgment on Gog

17 Thus says the Lord GOD: Are you he of whom I spoke in former days by my servants the prophets of Israel, who in those days prophesied for years that I would bring you against them? 18On that day, when Gog comes against the land of Israel, says the Lord GOD, my wrath shall be aroused. 19For in my jealousy and in my blazing wrath I declare: On that day there shall be a great shaking in the land of Israel; 20the fish of the sea, and the birds of the air, and the animals of the field, and all creeping things that creep on the ground, and all human beings that are on the face of the earth, shall quake at my presence, and the mountains shall be thrown down, and the cliffs shall fall, and every wall shall tumble to the ground. 21I will summon the sword against Gog*i* in*j* all my mountains, says the Lord GOD; the swords of all will be against their comrades.

---

c Another reading is *from all the settlements in which they have sinned*   *d* Tg: Heb *give*   *e* Or *Nubia*; Heb *Cush*
f Heb *navel*   *g* Heb *young lions*   *h* Gk: Heb *will you not know?*   *i* Heb *him*   *j* Heb *to* or *for*

22With pestilence and bloodshed I will enter into judgment with him; and I will pour down torrential rains and hailstones, fire and sulfur, upon him and his troops and the many peoples that are with him. 23So I will display my greatness and my holiness and make myself known in the eyes of many nations. Then they shall know that I am the LORD.

Gog's Armies Destroyed

39 And you, mortal, prophesy against Gog, and say: Thus says the Lord GOD: I am against you, O Gog, chief prince of Meshech and

39.1 Gog and Magog

Who are Gog and Magog? Bible interpreters disagree. At the very least, they represent an evil empire that attacks Israel from the north. More than ordinary enemies, they are a personification of evil—the evil that has fought God's people from the very beginning. These chapters show God delivering his people by destroying Gog. The two names, Gog and Magog, reappear in Revelation 20.8, participating in the final battle with evil.

Tubal! 2I will turn you around and drive you forward, and bring you up from the remotest parts of the north, and lead you against the mountains of Israel. 3I will strike your bow from your left hand, and will make your arrows drop out of your right hand. 4You shall fall upon the mountains of Israel, you and all your troops and the peoples that are with you; I will give you to birds of prey of every kind and to the wild animals to be devoured. 5You shall fall in the open field; for I have spoken, says the Lord GOD. 6I will send fire on Magog and on those who live securely in the coastlands; and they shall know that I am the LORD.

7 My holy name I will make known among my people Israel; and I will not let my holy name be profaned any more; and the nations shall know that I am the LORD, the Holy One in Israel. 8It has come! It has happened, says the Lord GOD. This is the day of which I have spoken.

9 Then those who live in the towns of Israel will go out and make fires of the weapons and burn them—bucklers and shields, bows and arrows, handpikes and spears—and they will make fires of them for seven years. 10They will not need to take wood out of the field or cut down any trees in the forests, for they will make their fires of the weapons; they will despoil those who despoiled them, and plunder those who plundered them, says the Lord GOD.

The Burial of Gog

11 On that day I will give to Gog a place for burial in Israel, the Valley of the Travelers[k] east of the sea; it shall block the path of the travelers, for there Gog and all his horde will be buried; it shall be called the Valley of Hamon-gog.[l] 12Seven months the house of Israel shall spend burying them, in order to cleanse the land. 13All the people of the land shall bury them; and it will bring them honor on the day that I show my glory, says the Lord GOD. 14They will set apart men to pass through the land regularly and bury any invaders[m] who remain on the face of the land, so as to cleanse it; for seven months they shall make their search. 15As the searchers[m] pass through the land, anyone who sees a human bone shall set up a sign by it, until the buriers have buried it in the Valley of Hamon-gog.[l] 16(A city Hamonah[n] is there also.) Thus they shall cleanse the land.

17 As for you, mortal, thus says the Lord GOD: Speak to the birds of every kind and to all the wild animals: Assemble and come, gather from all around to the sacrificial feast that I am preparing for you, a great sacrificial feast on the mountains of Israel, and you shall eat flesh and drink blood. 18You shall eat the flesh of the mighty, and drink the blood of the princes of the earth—of rams, of lambs, and of goats, of bulls, all of them fatlings of Bashan. 19You shall eat fat until you are filled, and drink blood until you are drunk, at the sacrificial feast that I am preparing for you. 20And you shall be filled at my table with horses and charioteers,[o] with warriors and all kinds of soldiers, says the Lord GOD.

Israel Restored to the Land

21 I will display my glory among the nations; and all the nations shall see my judgment that I have executed, and my hand that I have laid on them. 22The house of Israel shall know that I am the LORD their God, from that day forward. 23And the nations shall know that the house of Israel went into captivity for their iniquity, because they dealt treacherously with me. So I hid my face from them and gave them into the hand of their adversaries, and they all fell by the sword. 24I dealt with them according to their uncleanness and their transgressions, and hid my face from them.

25 Therefore thus says the Lord GOD: Now I will restore the fortunes of Jacob, and have mercy on the whole house of Israel; and I will be jealous for my holy name. 26They shall forget[p] their shame, and all the treachery they have practiced against me, when they live securely in their land with no one to make them afraid, 27when I have brought them back from the peoples and gathered them from their enemies' lands, and through them have displayed my holiness in the sight of

---

k Or *of the Abarim*   l That is, *the Horde of Gog*   m Heb *travelers*   n That is *The Horde*   o Heb *chariots*
p Another reading is *They shall bear*

many nations. 28Then they shall know that I am the LORD their God because I sent them into exile among the nations, and then gathered them into their own land. I will leave none of them behind; 29and I will never again hide my face from them, when I pour out my spirit upon the house of Israel, says the Lord GOD.

The Vision of the New Temple

40 In the twenty-fifth year of our exile, at the beginning of the year, on the tenth day of the month, in the fourteenth year after the city was struck down, on that very day, the hand of the LORD was upon me, and he brought me there. 2He brought me, in visions of God, to the land of Israel, and set me down upon a very high mountain, on which was a structure like a city to the south. 3When he brought me there, a man was there, whose appearance shone like bronze, with a linen cord and a measuring reed in his hand; and he was standing in the gateway. 4The man said to me, "Mortal, look closely and listen attentively, and set your mind upon all that I shall show you, for you were brought here in order that I might show it to you; declare all that you see to the house of Israel."

5 Now there was a wall all around the outside of the temple area. The length of the measuring reed in the man's hand was six long cubits, each being a cubit and a handbreadth in length; so he measured the thickness of the wall, one reed; and the height, one reed. 6Then he went into the gateway facing east, going up its steps, and measured the threshold of the gate, one reed deep.[q] There were 7recesses, and each recess was one reed wide and one reed deep; and the space between the recesses, five cubits; and the threshold of the gate by the vestibule of the gate at the inner end was one reed deep. 8Then he measured the inner vestibule of the gateway, one cubit. 9Then he measured the vestibule of the gateway, eight cubits; and its pilasters, two cubits; and the vestibule of the gate was at the inner end. 10There were three recesses on either side of the east gate; the three were of the same size; and the pilasters on either side were of the same size. 11Then he measured the width of the opening of the gateway, ten cubits; and the width of the gateway, thirteen cubits. 12There was a barrier before the recesses, one cubit on either side; and the recesses were six cubits on either side. 13Then he measured the gate from the back[r] of the one recess to the back[r] of the other, a width of twenty-five cubits, from wall to wall.[s] 14He measured[t] also the vestibule, twenty cubits; and the gate next to the pilaster on every side of the court.[u] 15From the front of the gate at the entrance to the end of the inner vestibule of the gate was fifty cubits. 16The recesses and their pilasters had windows, with shutters[u] on the inside of the gateway all around, and the vestibules also had windows on the inside all around; and on the pilasters were palm trees.

17 Then he brought me into the outer court; there were chambers there, and a pavement, all around the court; thirty chambers fronted on the pavement. 18The pavement ran along the side of the gates, corresponding to the length of the gates; this was the lower pavement. 19Then he measured the distance from the inner front of[v] the lower gate to the outer front of the inner court, one hundred cubits.[w]

20 Then he measured the gate of the outer court that faced north—its depth and width. 21Its recesses, three on either side, and its pilasters and its vestibule were of the same size as those of the first gate; its depth was fifty cubits, and its width twenty-five cubits. 22Its windows, its vestibule, and its palm trees were of the same size as those of the gate that faced toward the east. Seven steps led up to it; and its vestibule was on the inside.[x] 23Opposite the gate on the north, as on the east, was a gate to the inner court; he measured from gate to gate, one hundred cubits.

24 Then he led me toward the south, and there was a gate on the south; and he measured its pilasters and its vestibule; they had the same dimensions as the others. 25There were windows all around in it and in its vestibule, like the windows of the others; its depth was fifty cubits, and its width twenty-five cubits. 26There were seven steps leading up to it; its vestibule was on the inside.[x] It had palm trees on its pilasters, one on either side. 27There was a gate on the south of the inner court; and he measured from gate to gate toward the south, one hundred cubits.

28 Then he brought me to the inner court by the south gate, and he measured the south gate; it was of the same dimensions as the others. 29Its

40.5 Taking Measurements

When Moses and Solomon supervised the building of God's dwelling place, they placed great emphasis on exact specifications for its construction. Ezekiel does the same, even though the temple he measured with such care was never constructed. Some scholars see the details as symbolic, emphasizing how important renewed worship in the temple would be. The symmetry and beauty of the new temple witness to the perfection of God's plan for his people.

[q] Heb *deep, and one threshold, one reed deep* [r] Gk: Heb *roof* [s] Heb *opening facing opening* [t] Heb *made* [u] Meaning of Heb uncertain [v] Compare Gk: Heb *from before* [w] Heb adds *the east and the north* [x] Gk: Heb *before them*

recesses, its pilasters, and its vestibule were of the same size as the others; and there were windows all around in it and in its vestibule; its depth was fifty cubits, and its width twenty-five cubits. [30]There were vestibules all around, twenty-five cubits deep and five cubits wide. [31]Its vestibule faced the outer court, and palm trees were on its pilasters, and its stairway had eight steps.

32 Then he brought me to the inner court on the east side, and he measured the gate; it was of the same size as the others. [33]Its recesses, its pilasters, and its vestibule were of the same dimensions as the others; and there were windows all around in it and in its vestibule; its depth was fifty cubits, and its width twenty-five cubits. [34]Its vestibule faced the outer court, and it had palm trees on its pilasters, on either side; and its stairway had eight steps.

35 Then he brought me to the north gate, and he measured it; it had the same dimensions as the others. [36]Its recesses, its pilasters, and its vestibule were of the same size as the others;[y] and it had windows all around. Its depth was fifty cubits, and its width twenty-five cubits. [37]Its vestibule[z] faced the outer court, and it had palm trees on its pilasters, on either side; and its stairway had eight steps.

38 There was a chamber with its door in the vestibule of the gate,[a] where the burnt offering was to be washed. [39]And in the vestibule of the gate were two tables on either side, on which the burnt offering and the sin offering and the guilt offering were to be slaughtered. [40]On the outside of the vestibule[b] at the entrance of the north gate were two tables; and on the other side of the vestibule of the gate were two tables. [41]Four tables were on the inside, and four tables on the outside of the side of the gate, eight tables, on which the sacrifices were to be slaughtered. [42]There were also four tables of hewn stone for the burnt offering, a cubit and a half long, and one cubit and a half wide, and one cubit high, on which the instruments were to be laid with which the burnt offerings and the sacrifices were slaughtered. [43]There were pegs, one handbreadth long, fastened all around the inside. And on the tables the flesh of the offering was to be laid.

44 On the outside of the inner gateway there were chambers for the singers in the inner court, one[c] at the side of the north gate facing south, the other at the side of the east gate facing north. [45]He said to me, "This chamber that faces south is for the priests who have charge of the temple, [46]and the chamber that faces north is for the priests who have charge of the altar; these are the descendants of Zadok, who alone among the descendants of Levi may come near to the LORD to minister to him." [47]He measured the court, one hundred cubits deep, and one hundred cubits wide, a square; and the altar was in front of the temple.

The Temple

48 Then he brought me to the vestibule of the temple and measured the pilasters of the vestibule, five cubits on either side; and the width of the gate was fourteen cubits; and the sidewalls of the gate were three cubits[d] on either side. [49]The depth of the vestibule was twenty cubits, and the width twelve[e] cubits; ten steps led up[f] to it; and there were pillars beside the pilasters on either side.

41 Then he brought me to the nave, and measured the pilasters; on each side six cubits was the width of the pilasters.[g] [2]The width of the entrance was ten cubits; and the sidewalls of the entrance were five cubits on either side. He measured the length of the nave, forty cubits, and its

---

41.2 Seeing the New Temple

You'll find it easier to visualize Ezekiel's temple if you look at a sketch from a Bible dictionary. (Look under "Temple" or "Ezekiel.") Ezekiel's description reveals fascinating insights. For instance, the number of steps up toward the holy place grows greater at each stage, so that a worshiper mounts increasingly higher. But the doorways grow narrower (40.48; 41.2–3)— suggesting that the nearer to God's presence one climbs, the narrower the path he or she must follow.

---

width, twenty cubits. [3]Then he went into the inner room and measured the pilasters of the entrance, two cubits; and the width of the entrance, six cubits; and the sidewalls[h] of the entrance, seven cubits. [4]He measured the depth of the room, twenty cubits, and its width, twenty cubits, beyond the nave. And he said to me, This is the most holy place.

5 Then he measured the wall of the temple, six cubits thick; and the width of the side chambers, four cubits, all around the temple. [6]The side chambers were in three stories, one over another, thirty in each story. There were offsets[i] all around the wall of the temple to serve as supports for the side chambers, so that they should not be supported by the wall of the temple. [7]The passageway[j] of the side chambers widened from

---

[y] One Ms: Compare verses 29 and 33: MT lacks *were of the same size as the others*   [z] Gk Vg Compare verses 26, 31, 34: Heb *pilasters*   [a] Cn: Heb *at the pilasters of the gates*   [b] Cn: Heb *to him who goes up*   [c] Heb lacks *one*   [d] Gk: Heb *and the width of the gate was three cubits*   [e] Gk: Heb *eleven*   [f] Gk: Heb *and by steps that went up*   [g] Compare Gk: Heb *tent*   [h] Gk: Heb *width*   [i] Gk Compare 1 Kings 6.6: Heb *they entered*   [j] Cn: Heb *it was surrounded*

story to story; for the structure was supplied with a stairway all around the temple. For this reason the structure became wider from story to story. One ascended from the bottom story to the uppermost story by way of the middle one. [8]I saw also that the temple had a raised platform all around; the foundations of the side chambers measured a full reed of six long cubits. [9]The thickness of the outer wall of the side chambers was five cubits; and the free space between the side chambers of the temple [10]and the chambers of the court was a width of twenty cubits all around the temple on every side. [11]The side chambers opened onto the area left free, one door toward the north, and another door toward the south; and the width of the part that was left free was five cubits all around.

12 The building that was facing the temple yard on the west side was seventy cubits wide; and the wall of the building was five cubits thick all around, and its depth ninety cubits.

13 Then he measured the temple, one hundred cubits deep; and the yard and the building with its walls, one hundred cubits deep; [14]also the width of the east front of the temple and the yard, one hundred cubits.

15 Then he measured the depth of the building facing the yard at the west, together with its galleries[k] on either side, one hundred cubits.

The nave of the temple and the inner room and the outer[l] vestibule [16]were paneled,[m] and, all around, all three had windows with recessed[n] frames. Facing the threshold the temple was paneled with wood all around, from the floor up to the windows (now the windows were covered), [17]to the space above the door, even to the inner room, and on the outside. And on all the walls all around in the inner room and the nave there was a pattern.[o] [18]It was formed of cherubim and palm trees, a palm tree between cherub and cherub. Each cherub had two faces: [19]a human face turned toward the palm tree on the one side, and the face of a young lion turned toward the palm tree on the other side. They were carved on the whole temple all around; [20]from the floor to the area above the door, cherubim and palm trees were carved on the wall.[p]

21 The doorposts of the nave were square. In front of the holy place was something resembling [22]an altar of wood, three cubits high, two cubits long, and two cubits wide;[q] its corners, its base,[r] and its walls were of wood. He said to me, "This is the table that stands before the LORD." [23]The nave and the holy place had each a double door. [24]The doors had two leaves apiece, two swinging

leaves for each door. [25]On the doors of the nave were carved cherubim and palm trees, such as were carved on the walls; and there was a canopy of wood in front of the vestibule outside. [26]And there were recessed windows and palm trees on either side, on the sidewalls of the vestibule.[s]

The Holy Chambers and the Outer Wall

42 Then he led me out into the outer court, toward the north, and he brought me to the chambers that were opposite the temple yard and opposite the building on the north. [2]The length of the building that was on the north side[t] was[u] one hundred cubits, and the width fifty cubits. [3]Across the twenty cubits that belonged to the inner court, and facing the pavement that belonged to the outer court, the chambers rose[v] gallery[w] by gallery[w] in three stories. [4]In front of the chambers was a passage on the inner side, ten cubits wide and one hundred cubits deep,[x] and its[y] entrances were on the north. [5]Now the upper chambers were narrower, for the galleries[w] took more away from them than from the lower and middle chambers in the building. [6]For they were in three stories, and they had no pillars like the pillars of the outer[z] court; for this reason the upper chambers were set back from the ground more than the lower and the middle ones. [7]There was a wall outside parallel to the chambers, toward the outer court, opposite the chambers, fifty cubits long. [8]For the chambers on the outer court were fifty cubits long, while those opposite the temple were one hundred cubits long. [9]At the foot of these chambers ran a passage that one entered from the east in order to enter them from the outer court. [10]The width of the passage[a] was fixed by the wall of the court.

On the south[b] also, opposite the vacant area and opposite the building, there were chambers [11]with a passage in front of them; they were similar to the chambers on the north, of the same length and width, with the same exits[c] and arrangements and doors. [12]So the entrances of the chambers to the south were entered through the entrance at the head of the corresponding passage, from the east, along the matching wall.[w]

13 Then he said to me, "The north chambers and the south chambers opposite the vacant area are the holy chambers, where the priests who approach the LORD shall eat the most holy offerings; there they shall deposit the most holy offerings— the grain offering, the sin offering, and the guilt offering—for the place is holy. [14]When the priests enter the holy place, they shall not go out of it into the outer court without laying there the vestments

k Cn: Meaning of Heb uncertain   l Gk: Heb of the court   m Gk: Heb the thresholds   n Cn Compare Gk
1 Kings 6.4: Meaning of Heb uncertain   o Heb measures   p Cn Compare verse 25: Heb and the wall   q Gk: Heb
lacks two cubits wide   r Gk: Heb length   s Cn: Heb vestibule. And the side chambers of the temple and the canopies
t Gk: Heb door   u Gk: Heb before the length   v Heb lacks the chambers rose   w Meaning of Heb uncertain
x Gk Syr: Heb a way of one cubit   y Heb their   z Gk: Heb lacks outer   a Heb lacks of the passage   b Gk: Heb
east   c Heb and all their exits

in which they minister, for these are holy; they shall put on other garments before they go near to the area open to the people."

15　When he had finished measuring the interior of the temple area, he led me out by the gate that faces east, and measured the temple area all around. ¹⁶He measured the east side with the measuring reed, five hundred cubits by the measuring reed. ¹⁷Then he turned and measured*d* the north side, five hundred cubits by the measuring reed. ¹⁸Then he turned and measured*d* the south side, five hundred cubits by the measuring reed. ¹⁹Then he turned to the west side and measured, five hundred cubits by the measuring reed. ²⁰He measured it on the four sides. It had a wall around it, five hundred cubits long and five hundred cubits wide, to make a separation between the holy and the common.

The Divine Glory Returns to the Temple

43 Then he brought me to the gate, the gate facing east. ²And there, the glory of the God of Israel was coming from the east; the sound was like the sound of mighty waters; and the earth shone with his glory. ³The*e* vision I saw was like the vision that I had seen when he came to destroy the city, and*f* like the vision that I had seen by the river Chebar; and I fell upon my face. ⁴As the glory of the LORD entered the temple by the

43.4–9 The Glory Returns

Nineteen years had passed since Ezekiel saw the glory of the Lord leave the temple (11.22–23). That temple was now dust and ashes and broken stones: The conquering Babylonians had burnt and destroyed it. The new temple Ezekiel saw in this vision symbolized that God would again live with his renewed people.

gate facing east, ⁵the spirit lifted me up, and brought me into the inner court; and the glory of the LORD filled the temple.

6　While the man was standing beside me, I heard someone speaking to me out of the temple. ⁷He said to me: Mortal, this is the place of my throne and the place for the soles of my feet, where I will reside among the people of Israel forever. The house of Israel shall no more defile my holy name, neither they nor their kings, by their whoring, and by the corpses of their kings at their death.*g* ⁸When they placed their threshold by my threshold and their doorposts beside my doorposts, with only a wall between me and them, they were defiling my holy name by their abominations that they committed; therefore I have

consumed them in my anger. ⁹Now let them put away their idolatry and the corpses of their kings far from me, and I will reside among them forever.

10　As for you, mortal, describe the temple to the house of Israel, and let them measure the pattern; and let them be ashamed of their iniquities. ¹¹When they are ashamed of all that they have done, make known to them the plan of the temple, its arrangement, its exits and its entrances, and its whole form—all its ordinances and its entire plan and all its laws; and write it down in their sight, so that they may observe and follow the entire plan and all its ordinances. ¹²This is the law of the temple: the whole territory on the top of the mountain all around shall be most holy. This is the law of the temple.

The Altar

13　These are the dimensions of the altar by cubits (the cubit being one cubit and a handbreadth): its base shall be one cubit high,*h* and one cubit wide, with a rim of one span around its edge. This shall be the height of the altar: ¹⁴From the base on the ground to the lower ledge, two cubits, with a width of one cubit; and from the smaller ledge to the larger ledge, four cubits, with a width of one cubit; ¹⁵and the altar hearth, four cubits; and from the altar hearth projecting upward, four horns. ¹⁶The altar hearth shall be square, twelve cubits long by twelve wide. ¹⁷The ledge also shall be square, fourteen cubits long by fourteen wide, with a rim around it half a cubit wide, and its surrounding base, one cubit. Its steps shall face east.

18　Then he said to me: Mortal, thus says the Lord GOD: These are the ordinances for the altar: On the day when it is erected for offering burnt offerings upon it and for dashing blood against it, ¹⁹you shall give to the levitical priests of the family of Zadok, who draw near to me to minister to me, says the Lord GOD, a bull for a sin offering. ²⁰And you shall take some of its blood, and put it on the four horns of the altar, and on the four corners of the ledge, and upon the rim all around; thus you shall purify it and make atonement for it. ²¹You shall also take the bull of the sin offering, and it shall be burnt in the appointed place belonging to the temple, outside the sacred area.

22　On the second day you shall offer a male goat without blemish for a sin offering; and the altar shall be purified, as it was purified with the bull. ²³When you have finished purifying it, you shall offer a bull without blemish and a ram from the flock without blemish. ²⁴You shall present them before the LORD, and the priests shall throw salt on them and offer them up as a burnt offering to the LORD. ²⁵For seven days you shall provide

---

d Gk: Heb *measuring reed all around. He measured*　　*e* Gk: Heb *Like the vision*　　*f* Syr: Heb *and the visions*
g Or *on their high places*　　*h* Gk: Heb lacks *high*

daily a goat for a sin offering; also a bull and a ram from the flock, without blemish, shall be provided. [26]Seven days shall they make atonement for the altar and cleanse it, and so consecrate it. [27]When these days are over, then from the eighth day onward the priests shall offer upon the altar your burnt offerings and your offerings of well-being; and I will accept you, says the Lord GOD.

The Closed Gate

44 Then he brought me back to the outer gate of the sanctuary, which faces east; and it was shut. [2]The LORD said to me: This gate shall remain shut; it shall not be opened, and no one shall enter by it; for the LORD, the God of Israel, has entered by it; therefore it shall remain shut. [3]Only the prince, because he is a prince, may sit in it to eat food before the LORD; he shall enter by way of the vestibule of the gate, and shall go out by the same way.

Admission to the Temple

[4] Then he brought me by way of the north gate to the front of the temple; and I looked, and lo! the glory of the LORD filled the temple of the LORD; and I fell upon my face. [5]The LORD said to me: Mortal, mark well, look closely, and listen attentively to all that I shall tell you concerning all the ordinances of the temple of the LORD and all its laws; and mark well those who may be admitted to[i] the temple and all those who are to be excluded from the sanctuary. [6]Say to the rebellious house,[j] to the house of Israel, Thus says the Lord GOD: O house of Israel, let there be an end to all your abominations [7]in admitting foreigners, uncircumcised in heart and flesh, to be in my sanctuary, profaning my temple when you offer to me my food, the fat and the blood. You[k] have broken my covenant with all your abominations. [8]And you have not kept charge of my sacred offerings; but you have appointed foreigners[l] to act for you in keeping my charge in my sanctuary.

[9] Thus says the Lord GOD: No foreigner, uncircumcised in heart and flesh, of all the foreigners who are among the people of Israel, shall enter my sanctuary. [10]But the Levites who went far from me, going astray from me after their idols when Israel went astray, shall bear their punishment. [11]They shall be ministers in my sanctuary, having oversight at the gates of the temple, and serving in the temple; they shall slaughter the burnt offering and the sacrifice for the people, and they shall attend on them and serve them. [12]Because they ministered to them before their idols and made the house of Israel stumble into iniquity, therefore I have sworn concerning them, says the Lord GOD, that they shall bear their punishment. [13]They shall not come near to me, to serve me as priest, nor come near any of my sacred offerings, the things that are most sacred; but they shall bear their shame, and the consequences of the abominations that they have committed. [14]Yet I will appoint them to keep charge of the temple, to do all its chores, all that is to be done in it.

The Levitical Priests

[15] But the levitical priests, the descendants of Zadok, who kept the charge of my sanctuary when the people of Israel went astray from me, shall come near to me to minister to me; and they shall attend me to offer me the fat and the blood, says the Lord GOD. [16]It is they who shall enter my sanctuary, it is they who shall approach my table, to minister to me, and they shall keep my charge. [17]When they enter the gates of the inner court, they shall wear linen vestments; they shall have nothing of wool on them, while they minister at the gates of the inner court, and within. [18]They shall have linen turbans on their heads, and linen undergarments on their loins; they shall not bind themselves with anything that causes sweat. [19]When they go out into the outer court to the people, they shall remove the vestments in which they have been ministering, and lay them in the holy chambers; and they shall put on other garments, so that they may not communicate holiness to the people with their vestments. [20]They shall not shave their heads or let their locks grow long; they shall only trim the hair of their heads. [21]No priest shall drink wine when he enters the inner court. [22]They shall not marry a widow, or a divorced woman, but only a virgin of the stock of the house of Israel, or a widow who is the widow of a priest. [23]They shall teach my people the difference between the holy and the common, and show them how to distinguish between the unclean and the clean. [24]In a controversy they shall act as judges, and they shall decide it according to my judgments. They shall keep my laws and my statutes regarding all my appointed festivals, and they shall keep my sabbaths holy. [25]They shall not defile themselves by going near to a dead person; for father or mother, however, and for son or daughter, and for brother or unmarried sister they may defile themselves. [26]After he has become clean, they shall count seven days for him. [27]On the day that he goes into the holy place, into the inner court, to minister in the holy place, he shall offer his sin offering, says the Lord GOD.

[28] This shall be their inheritance: I am their inheritance; and you shall give them no holding in Israel; I am their holding. [29]They shall eat the grain offering, the sin offering, and the guilt offering; and every devoted thing in Israel shall be theirs. [30]The first of all the first fruits of all kinds, and every offering of all kinds from all your offerings, shall belong to the priests; you shall also give

---

[i] Cn: Heb the entrance of   [j] Gk: Heb lacks house   [k] Gk Syr Vg: Heb They   [l] Heb lacks foreigners

to the priests the first of your dough, in order that a blessing may rest on your house. [31]The priests shall not eat of anything, whether bird or animal, that died of itself or was torn by animals.

The Holy District

45 When you allot the land as an inheritance, you shall set aside for the LORD a portion of the land as a holy district, twenty-five thousand cubits long and twenty[m] thousand cubits wide; it shall be holy throughout its entire extent. [2]Of this, a square plot of five hundred by five hundred cubits shall be for the sanctuary, with fifty cubits for an open space around it. [3]In the holy district you shall measure off a section twenty-five thousand cubits long and ten thousand wide, in which shall be the sanctuary, the most holy place. [4]It shall be a holy portion of the land; it shall be for the priests, who minister in the sanctuary and approach the LORD to minister to him; and it shall be both a place for their houses and a holy place for the sanctuary. [5]Another section, twenty-five thousand cubits long and ten thousand cubits wide, shall be for the Levites who minister at the temple, as their holding for cities to live in.[n]

6 Alongside the portion set apart as the holy district you shall assign as a holding for the city an area five thousand cubits wide, and twenty-five thousand cubits long; it shall belong to the whole house of Israel.

7 And to the prince shall belong the land on both sides of the holy district and the holding of the city, alongside the holy district and the holding of the city, on the west and on the east, corresponding in length to one of the tribal portions, and extending from the western to the eastern boundary [8]of the land. It is to be his property in Israel. And my princes shall no longer oppress my people; but they shall let the house of Israel have the land according to their tribes.

9 Thus says the Lord GOD: Enough, O princes of Israel! Put away violence and oppression, and do what is just and right. Cease your evictions of my people, says the Lord GOD.

Weights and Measures

10 You shall have honest balances, an honest ephah, and an honest bath.[o] [11]The ephah and the bath shall be of the same measure, the bath containing one-tenth of a homer, and the ephah one-tenth of a homer; the homer shall be the standard measure. [12]The shekel shall be twenty gerahs. Twenty shekels, twenty-five shekels, and fifteen shekels shall make a mina for you.

Offerings

13 This is the offering that you shall make: one-sixth of an ephah from each homer of wheat, and one-sixth of an ephah from each homer of barley, [14]and as the fixed portion of oil,[p] one-tenth of a bath from each cor (the cor,[q] like the homer, contains ten baths); [15]and one sheep from

---

45.10 Honest Weight

The Bible, always practical, doesn't bother to define honesty in philosophic terms. It merely says, "Don't cheat on your measures." Such cheating was a common problem in Judah (see, for instance, Micah 6.10–12). Archaeologists have found many weights once used in Hebrew marketplaces, but very few have weighed exactly the weight inscribed on them.

---

every flock of two hundred, from the pastures of Israel. This is the offering for grain offerings, burnt offerings, and offerings of well-being, to make atonement for them, says the Lord GOD. [16]All the people of the land shall join with the prince in Israel in making this offering. [17]But this shall be the obligation of the prince regarding the burnt offerings, grain offerings, and drink offerings, at the festivals, the new moons, and the sabbaths, all the appointed festivals of the house of Israel: he shall provide the sin offerings, grain offerings, the burnt offerings, and the offerings of well-being, to make atonement for the house of Israel.

Festivals

18 Thus says the Lord GOD: In the first month, on the first day of the month, you shall take a young bull without blemish, and purify the sanctuary. [19]The priest shall take some of the blood of the sin offering and put it on the doorposts of the temple, the four corners of the ledge of the altar, and the posts of the gate of the inner court. [20]You shall do the same on the seventh day of the month for anyone who has sinned through error or ignorance; so you shall make atonement for the temple.

21 In the first month, on the fourteenth day of the month, you shall celebrate the festival of the passover, and for seven days unleavened bread shall be eaten. [22]On that day the prince shall provide for himself and all the people of the land a young bull for a sin offering. [23]And during the seven days of the festival he shall provide as a burnt offering to the LORD seven young bulls and seven rams without blemish, on each of the seven days; and a male goat daily for a sin offering. [24]He shall provide as a grain offering an ephah for each bull, an ephah for each ram, and a hin of oil to each ephah. [25]In the seventh month, on the fif-

---

[m] Gk: Heb ten   [n] Gk: Heb as their holding, twenty chambers   [o] A Heb measure of volume   [p] Cn: Heb oil, the
bath the oil   [q] Vg: Heb homer

teenth day of the month and for the seven days of the festival, he shall make the same provision for sin offerings, burnt offerings, and grain offerings, and for the oil.

Miscellaneous Regulations

46 Thus says the Lord GOD: The gate of the inner court that faces east shall remain closed on the six working days; but on the sabbath day it shall be opened and on the day of the new moon it shall be opened. ²The prince shall enter by the vestibule of the gate from outside, and shall take his stand by the post of the gate. The priests shall offer his burnt offering and his offerings of well-being, and he shall bow down at the threshold of the gate. Then he shall go out, but the gate shall not be closed until evening. ³The people of the land shall bow down at the entrance of that gate before the LORD on the sabbaths and on the new moons. ⁴The burnt offering that the prince offers to the LORD on the sabbath day shall be six lambs without blemish and a ram without blemish; ⁵and the grain offering with the ram shall be an ephah, and the grain offering with the lambs shall be as much as he wishes to give, together with a hin of oil to each ephah. ⁶On the day of the new moon he shall offer a young bull without blemish, and six lambs and a ram, which shall be without blemish; ⁷as a grain offering he shall provide an ephah with the bull and an ephah with the ram, and with the lambs as much as he wishes, together with a hin of oil to each ephah. ⁸When the prince enters, he shall come in by the vestibule of the gate, and he shall go out by the same way.

9 When the people of the land come before the LORD at the appointed festivals, whoever enters by the north gate to worship shall go out by the south gate; and whoever enters by the south gate shall go out by the north gate: they shall not return by way of the gate by which they entered, but shall go out straight ahead. ¹⁰When they come in, the prince shall come in with them; and when they go out, he shall go out.

11 At the festivals and the appointed seasons the grain offering with a young bull shall be an ephah, and with a ram an ephah, and with the lambs as much as one wishes to give, together with a hin of oil to an ephah. ¹²When the prince provides a freewill offering, either a burnt offering or offerings of well-being as a freewill offering to the LORD, the gate facing east shall be opened for him; and he shall offer his burnt offering or his offerings of well-being as he does on the sabbath day. Then he shall go out, and after he has gone out the gate shall be closed.

13 He shall provide a lamb, a yearling, without blemish, for a burnt offering to the LORD daily; morning by morning he shall provide it.

¹⁴And he shall provide a grain offering with it morning by morning regularly, one-sixth of an ephah, and one-third of a hin of oil to moisten the choice flour, as a grain offering to the LORD; this is the ordinance for all time. ¹⁵Thus the lamb and the grain offering and the oil shall be provided, morning by morning, as a regular burnt offering.

16 Thus says the Lord GOD: If the prince makes a gift to any of his sons out of his inheritance,ʳ it shall belong to his sons, it is their holding by inheritance. ¹⁷But if he makes a gift out of his inheritance to one of his servants, it shall be his to the year of liberty; then it shall revert to the prince; only his sons may keep a gift from his inheritance. ¹⁸The prince shall not take any of the inheritance of the people, thrusting them out of their holding; he shall give his sons their inheritance out of his own holding, so that none of my people shall be dispossessed of their holding.

19 Then he brought me through the entrance, which was at the side of the gate, to the north row of the holy chambers for the priests; and there I saw a place at the extreme western end of them. ²⁰He said to me, "This is the place where the priests shall boil the guilt offering and the sin offering, and where they shall bake the grain offering, in order not to bring them out into the outer court and so communicate holiness to the people."

21 Then he brought me out to the outer court, and led me past the four corners of the court; and in each corner of the court there was a court— ²²in the four corners of the court were smallˢ courts, forty cubits long and thirty wide; the four were of the same size. ²³On the inside, around each of the four courtsᵗ was a row of masonry, with hearths made at the bottom of the rows all around. ²⁴Then he said to me, "These are the kitchens where those who serve at the temple shall boil the sacrifices of the people."

Water Flowing from the Temple

47 Then he brought me back to the entrance of the temple; there, water was flowing from below the threshold of the temple toward the east (for the temple faced east); and the water was flowing down from below the south end of the threshold of the temple, south of the altar. ²Then he brought me out by way of the north gate, and led me around on the outside to the outer gate that faces toward the east;ᵘ and the water was coming out on the south side.

3 Going on eastward with a cord in his hand, the man measured one thousand cubits, and then led me through the water; and it was ankle-deep. ⁴Again he measured one thousand, and led me through the water; and it was knee-deep. Again

---

ʳ Gk: Heb *it is his inheritance*   ˢ Gk Syr Vg: Meaning of Heb uncertain   ᵗ Heb *the four of them*   ᵘ Meaning of Heb uncertain

he measured one thousand, and led me through the water; and it was up to the waist. 5Again he measured one thousand, and it was a river that I could not cross, for the water had risen; it was deep enough to swim in, a river that could not be crossed. 6He said to me, "Mortal, have you seen this?"

Then he led me back along the bank of the river. 7As I came back, I saw on the bank of the river a great many trees on the one side and on the other. 8He said to me, "This water flows toward the eastern region and goes down into the Arabah; and when it enters the sea, the sea of stagnant waters, the water will become fresh. 9Wherever the river goes,ᵛ every living creature that swarms will live, and there will be very many fish, once these waters reach there. It will become fresh; and everything will live where the river goes. 10People will stand fishing beside the seaʷ from En-gedi to En-eglaim; it will be a place for the spreading of nets; its fish will be of a great many kinds, like the fish of the Great Sea. 11But its swamps and marshes will not become fresh; they are to be left for salt. 12On the banks, on both sides of the river, there will grow all kinds of trees for food. Their leaves will not wither nor their fruit fail, but they will bear fresh fruit every month, because the water for them flows from the sanctuary. Their fruit will be for food, and their leaves for healing."

47.12 River from the Temple

This river, flowing from the temple, had miraculous properties: it reversed the deadly saltiness of the Dead Sea and produced healing fruit on its banks. The early Christians used similar symbolism; in John's vision of a new Jerusalem (Revelation 22), he saw a river of life flowing from the throne of God.

The New Boundaries of the Land

13 Thus says the Lord GOD: These are the boundaries by which you shall divide the land for inheritance among the twelve tribes of Israel. Joseph shall have two portions. 14You shall divide it equally; I swore to give it to your ancestors, and this land shall fall to you as your inheritance.

15 This shall be the boundary of the land: On the north side, from the Great Sea by way of Hethlon to Lebo-hamath, and on to Zedad,ˣ 16Berothah, Sibraim (which lies between the border of Damascus and the border of Hamath), as far as Hazer-hatticon, which is on the border of Hauran. 17So the boundary shall run from the sea

to Hazar-enon, which is north of the border of Damascus, with the border of Hamath to the north.ʸ This shall be the north side.

18 On the east side, between Hauran and Damascus; along the Jordan between Gilead and the land of Israel; to the eastern sea and as far as Tamar.ᶻ This shall be the east side.

19 On the south side, it shall run from Tamar as far as the waters of Meribath-kadesh, from there along the Wadi of Egyptᵃ to the Great Sea. This shall be the south side.

20 On the west side, the Great Sea shall be the boundary to a point opposite Lebo-hamath. This shall be the west side.

21 So you shall divide this land among you according to the tribes of Israel. 22You shall allot it as an inheritance for yourselves and for the aliens who reside among you and have begotten children among you. They shall be to you as citizens of Israel; with you they shall be allotted an inheritance among the tribes of Israel. 23In whatever tribe aliens reside, there you shall assign them their inheritance, says the Lord GOD.

The Tribal Portions

48 These are the names of the tribes: Beginning at the northern border, on the Hethlon road,ᵇ from Lebo-hamath, as far as Hazar-enon (which is on the border of Damascus, with Hamath to the north), andᶜ extending from the east side to the west,ᵈ Dan, one portion. 2Adjoining the territory of Dan, from the east side to the west, Asher, one portion. 3Adjoining the territory of Asher, from the east side to the west, Naphtali, one portion. 4Adjoining the territory of Naphtali, from the east side to the west, Manasseh, one portion. 5Adjoining the territory of Manasseh, from the east side to the west, Ephraim, one portion. 6Adjoining the territory of Ephraim, from the east side to the west, Reuben, one portion. 7Adjoining the territory of Reuben, from the east side to the west, Judah, one portion.

8 Adjoining the territory of Judah, from the east side to the west, shall be the portion that you shall set apart, twenty-five thousand cubits in width, and in length equal to one of the tribal portions, from the east side to the west, with the sanctuary in the middle of it. 9The portion that you shall set apart for the LORD shall be twenty-five thousand cubits in length, and twentyᵉ thousand in width. 10These shall be the allotments of the holy portion: the priests shall have an allotment measuring twenty-five thousand cubits on the northern side, ten thousand cubits in width on the western side, ten thousand in width on the eastern side, and twenty-five thousand in length

---

ᵛ Gk Syr Vg Tg: Heb *the two rivers go* ʷ Heb *it* ˣ Gk: Heb *Lebo-zedad,* ¹⁶*Hamath* ʸ Meaning of Heb uncertain ᶻ Compare Syr: Heb *you shall measure* ᵃ Heb lacks *of Egypt* ᵇ Compare 47.15: Heb *by the side of the way* ᶜ Cn: Heb *and they shall be his* ᵈ Gk Compare verses 2-8: Heb *the east side the west* ᵉ Compare 45.1: Heb *ten*

on the southern side, with the sanctuary of the Lord in the middle of it. [11]This shall be for the consecrated priests, the descendants[f] of Zadok, who kept my charge, who did not go astray when the people of Israel went astray, as the Levites did. [12]It shall belong to them as a special portion from the holy portion of the land, a most holy place, adjoining the territory of the Levites. [13]Alongside the territory of the priests, the Levites shall have an allotment twenty-five thousand cubits in length and ten thousand in width. The whole length shall be twenty-five thousand cubits and the width twenty[g] thousand. [14]They shall not sell or exchange any of it; they shall not transfer this choice portion of the land, for it is holy to the Lord.

15 The remainder, five thousand cubits in width and twenty-five thousand in length, shall be for ordinary use for the city, for dwellings and for open country. In the middle of it shall be the city; [16]and these shall be its dimensions: the north side four thousand five hundred cubits, the south side four thousand five hundred, the east side four thousand five hundred, and the west side four thousand five hundred. [17]The city shall have open land: on the north two hundred fifty cubits, on the south two hundred fifty, on the east two hundred fifty, on the west two hundred fifty. [18]The remainder of the length alongside the holy portion shall be ten thousand cubits to the east, and ten thousand to the west, and it shall be alongside the holy portion. Its produce shall be food for the workers of the city. [19]The workers of the city, from all the tribes of Israel, shall cultivate it. [20]The whole portion that you shall set apart shall be twenty-five thousand cubits square, that is, the holy portion together with the property of the city.

21 What remains on both sides of the holy portion and of the property of the city shall belong to the prince. Extending from the twenty-five thousand cubits of the holy portion to the east border, and westward from the twenty-five thousand cubits to the west border, parallel to the tribal portions, it shall belong to the prince. The holy portion with the sanctuary of the temple in the middle of it, [22]and the property of the Levites and of the city, shall be in the middle of that which belongs to the prince. The portion of the prince shall lie between the territory of Judah and the territory of Benjamin.

23 As for the rest of the tribes: from the east side to the west, Benjamin, one portion. [24]Adjoining the territory of Benjamin, from the east side to the west, Simeon, one portion. [25]Adjoining the territory of Simeon, from the east side to the west, Issachar, one portion. [26]Adjoining the territory of Issachar, from the east side to the west, Zebulun, one portion. [27]Adjoining the territory of Zebulun, from the east side to the west, Gad, one portion. [28]And adjoining the territory of Gad to the south, the boundary shall run from Tamar to the waters of Meribath-kadesh, from there along the Wadi of Egypt[h] to the Great Sea. [29]This is the land that you shall allot as an inheritance among the tribes of Israel, and these are their portions, says the Lord God.

30 These shall be the exits of the city: On the north side, which is to be four thousand five hundred cubits by measure, [31]three gates, the gate of

48.30 Gates to the City

These twelve gates, named after the twelve tribes of Israel, are also described in the new Jerusalem (Revelation 21.12). Other details of Ezekiel's vision are echoed in Revelation 21–22: for example, the view from a high mountain (40.2), the angel guide (40.3), and the healing river (47.12). The most important similarity is reflected in the name of Ezekiel's city: "The Lord is There" (48.35). As Revelation expresses it, "See, the home of God is among mortals. He will dwell with them" (Revelation 21.3).

Reuben, the gate of Judah, and the gate of Levi, the gates of the city being named after the tribes of Israel. [32]On the east side, which is to be four thousand five hundred cubits, three gates, the gate of Joseph, the gate of Benjamin, and the gate of Dan. [33]On the south side, which is to be four thousand five hundred cubits by measure, three gates, the gate of Simeon, the gate of Issachar, and the gate of Zebulun. [34]On the west side, which is to be four thousand five hundred cubits, three gates,[i] the gate of Gad, the gate of Asher, and the gate of Naphtali. [35]The circumference of the city shall be eighteen thousand cubits. And the name of the city from that time on shall be, The Lord is There.

f One Ms Gk: Heb of the descendants   g Gk: Heb ten   h Heb lacks of Egypt   i One Ms Gk Syr: MT their gates three

DANIEL

"Kidnapped"
Even as prime minister, Daniel remained a lonely outsider

> Daniel resolved that he would not defile himself with the royal rations of food and wine; so he asked the palace master to allow him not to defile himself.
> 1.8

A S A YOUNG MAN, DANIEL could have anticipated an outstanding future in Jerusalem. He came from a prominent family, and he had a first-rate mind (1.4). But, when the Babylonian army dragged him captive to a faraway country, they didn't ask about his plans and dreams.

True, the Babylonians recognized Daniel's potential and put him into a top civil service training program. But even the study material was distasteful to a Jew: It covered sorcery, magic, and a pagan, multigod religion. After graduation Daniel was put to work for the Babylonian king, who continued to war against Daniel's people for nearly 20 more years.

Anyone far from home feels lonely. But Daniel was one of those whose lives get lost in the shuffle of history—refugees, captives. He was destined to spend his life as an alien in Babylon. We have no record that he ever married or had family members nearby.

Great Personal Courage

Through his ability and God's blessing he rose to the post of prime minister of Babylon. Yet he remained an outsider. The higher he rose, the more prominent a target he became. Babylonians resented his foreign background and his political success. Their plots put him under pressure to compromise his faith, to fit in, to bend his principles. His life was often at risk.

Daniel's career near the top lasted at least 66 years, so that by the time he was thrown into the lions' den (chapter 6), he must have been in his 80s. Throughout these years he labored with great effectiveness for Babylon. He was respectful and diligent, even though working for pagan kings. Yet he never compromised his faith. He would not bend, even when threatened with death. The Bible gives no better model of how to live with and serve those who don't share or respect your beliefs.

The Shape of the Future

Near the end of Daniel's life God gave him a series of visions, described in chapters 7–12. In graphic images God showed Daniel the pattern of future history. Daniel's people would duplicate his own experience, but on a world stage.

The Jews, Daniel's visions showed, would be caught in a political storm, battered about by a series of world empires. Daniel foresaw nations raging in battle against each other. He foresaw God's people thrown in between these nations, suffering through no fault of their own. They would be helpless until God himself rescued them from their troubles. Daniel foresaw, in the end, all people falling down to worship "one like a human being" (7.13). This was the title Jesus applied to himself when he came, nearly six centuries after Daniel, to bring the good news of salvation for all people.

Spreading the Word

Daniel's people had thought of God in terms of their own small community, their own capital city and the temple there. Not only were the Jews God's chosen people, but (they tended to think) they held exclusive rights to him.

But God had never intended his blessings to stop with the Jews. He had the world in mind. At the time he called Abraham, he had promised that through Abraham's offspring he would bless the whole earth (Genesis 12.3).

The Jews had found it difficult enough to keep their own faith, let alone spread it to others. Only while captives in Babylon, unwillingly dragged far from home, did they begin to convince others that their God deserved honor. The proclamations Nebuchadnezzar and Darius made because of Daniel (4.2–3; 6.26–27) honored God more than anything a king of Judah had done in years.

How to Read Daniel

D aniel breaks into two parts, each quite different from the other. The first six chapters tell the "famous" Daniel stories—including the stories of three men thrown into a fiery furnace and Daniel in the lions' den. Any of these chapters would make a script for a thriller. As you read them, reflect on the principles Daniel lived by, far from home and in dangerous circumstances. Ask yourself what Daniel can teach you about faithfulness to God in similarly "alien" circumstances.

Most people find chapters 7–12 far more difficult: They record Daniel's visions about the future of world history. Such symbolism was a familiar mode of expression in the ancient world, but it reads very strangely now—almost like science fiction. Look for broad impressions of how God's people can live, caught in the jaws of brutal world politics. Let the visual symbols engage your emotions and imagination.

If you seek a more detailed understanding of these visions, a commentary on Daniel will be a great help. In some passages, background information on ancient world history is essential. A good commentary can offer this, along with an interpretation of difficult symbols.

You can place Daniel's message in the context of Israelite history by looking at "A Lineup of Rulers," pages 1349–1357.

PEOPLE YOU'LL MEET IN DANIEL

DANIEL (p. 888)
NEBUCHADNEZZAR (p. 893)

3-TRACK READING PLAN

For an explanation and complete listing of the 3-track reading plan, turn to page 7.

TRACK 1: *Two-Week Courses on the Bible*
The Track 1 reading program on the Old Testament includes one chapter from Daniel. See page 8 for a complete listing of this course.

TRACK 2: *An Overview of Daniel in 4 Days*
☐ Day 1. Read the Introduction to Daniel and chapter 1, which describes Daniel's courage in rejecting compromise. He set a lifelong pattern.
☐ Day 2. Read chapter 3, the famous story of three men thrown into a fiery furnace.
☐ Day 3. Read chapter 5, the "handwriting on the wall" that announced the destruction of a great empire.
☐ Day 4. Read chapter 6, Daniel in the lions' den.

Now turn to page 9 for your next Track 2 reading project.

TRACK 3: *All of Daniel in 12 Days*
After you have read through Daniel, turn to pages 10–14 for your next Track 3 reading project.

☐1 ☐2 ☐3 ☐4 ☐5 ☐6 ☐7 ☐8
☐9 ☐10 ☐11 ☐12

Four Young Israelites at the Babylonian Court

1 In the third year of the reign of King Jehoiakim of Judah, King Nebuchadnezzar of Babylon came to Jerusalem and besieged it. ²The Lord let King Jehoiakim of Judah fall into his power, as well as some of the vessels of the house of God. These he brought to the land of Shinar,ᵃ and placed the vessels in the treasury of his gods.

3 Then the king commanded his palace master Ashpenaz to bring some of the Israelites of the royal family and of the nobility, ⁴young men without physical defect and handsome, versed in every branch of wisdom, endowed with knowledge and insight, and competent to serve in the king's palace; they were to be taught the literature

ᵃ Gk Theodotion: Heb adds *to the house of his own gods*

and language of the Chaldeans. ⁵The king assigned them a daily portion of the royal rations of food and wine. They were to be educated for three years, so that at the end of that time they could be stationed in the king's court. ⁶Among them were Daniel, Hananiah, Mishael, and Azariah, from the tribe of Judah. ⁷The palace master gave them other names: Daniel he called Belteshazzar, Hananiah he called Shadrach, Mishael he called Meshach, and Azariah he called Abednego.

8 But Daniel resolved that he would not defile himself with the royal rations of food and wine; so he asked the palace master to allow him not to defile himself. ⁹Now God allowed Daniel to receive favor and compassion from the palace master. ¹⁰The palace master said to Daniel, "I am afraid of my lord the king; he has appointed your food and your drink. If he should see you in poorer condition than the other young men of your own age, you would endanger my head with the king." ¹¹Then Daniel asked the guard whom the palace master had appointed over Daniel, Hananiah, Mishael, and Azariah: ¹²"Please test your servants for ten days. Let us be given vegetables to eat and water to drink. ¹³You can then compare our appearance with the appearance of the young men who eat the royal rations, and deal with your servants according to what you observe." ¹⁴So he agreed to this proposal and tested them for ten days. ¹⁵At the end of ten days it was observed that they appeared better and fatter than all the young men who had been eating the royal rations. ¹⁶So the guard continued to withdraw their royal rations and the wine they were to drink, and gave them vegetables. ¹⁷To these four young men God gave knowledge and skill in every aspect of literature and wisdom; Daniel also had insight into all visions and dreams.

18 At the end of the time that the king had set for them to be brought in, the palace master brought them into the presence of Nebuchadnezzar, ¹⁹and the king spoke with them. And among them all, no one was found to compare with Daniel, Hananiah, Mishael, and Azariah; therefore they were stationed in the king's court. ²⁰In every matter of wisdom and understanding concerning which the king inquired of them, he found them ten times better than all the magicians and enchanters in his whole kingdom. ²¹And Daniel continued there until the first year of King Cyrus.

Nebuchadnezzar's Dream

2 In the second year of Nebuchadnezzar's reign, Nebuchadnezzar dreamed such dreams that his spirit was troubled and his sleep left him. ²So the king commanded that the magicians, the enchanters, the sorcerers, and the Chaldeans be summoned to tell the king his dreams. When they came in and stood before the king, ³he

said to them, "I have had such a dream that my spirit is troubled by the desire to understand it." ⁴The Chaldeans said to the king (in Aramaic),ᵇ "O king, live forever! Tell your servants the dream, and we will reveal the interpretation."

2.4 A Change in Language

The astrologers spoke in Aramaic, the most common language of the Middle East during this period. From this point through chapter 7, Daniel was written in Aramaic, instead of Hebrew. Only the book of Ezra is similarly split into two languages. Some theorize that these chapters would have been of general interest throughout the Middle East and so were put in a language everyone could understand.

⁵The king answered the Chaldeans, "This is a public decree: if you do not tell me both the dream and its interpretation, you shall be torn limb from limb, and your houses shall be laid in ruins. ⁶But if you do tell me the dream and its interpretation, you shall receive from me gifts and rewards and great honor. Therefore tell me the dream and its interpretation." ⁷They answered a second time, "Let the king first tell his servants the dream, then we can give its interpretation." ⁸The king answered, "I know with certainty that you are trying to gain time, because you see I have firmly decreed: ⁹if you do not tell me the dream, there is but one verdict for you. You have agreed to speak lying and misleading words to me until things take a turn. Therefore, tell me the dream, and I shall know that you can give me its interpretation." ¹⁰The Chaldeans answered the king, "There is no one on earth who can reveal what the king demands! In fact no king, however great and powerful, has ever asked such a thing of any magician or enchanter or Chaldean. ¹¹The thing that the king is asking is too difficult, and no one can reveal it to the king except the gods, whose dwelling is not with mortals."

12 Because of this the king flew into a violent rage and commanded that all the wise men of Babylon be destroyed. ¹³The decree was issued, and the wise men were about to be executed; and they looked for Daniel and his companions, to execute them. ¹⁴Then Daniel responded with prudence and discretion to Arioch, the king's chief executioner, who had gone out to execute the wise men of Babylon; ¹⁵he asked Arioch, the royal official, "Why is the decree of the king so urgent?" Arioch then explained the matter to Daniel. ¹⁶So Daniel went in and requested that the king give him time and he would tell the king the interpretation.

ᵇ The text from this point to the end of chapter 7 is in Aramaic

God Reveals Nebuchadnezzar's Dream

17 Then Daniel went to his home and informed his companions, Hananiah, Mishael, and Azariah, 18and told them to seek mercy from the God of heaven concerning this mystery, so that Daniel and his companions with the rest of the wise men of Babylon might not perish. 19Then the mystery was revealed to Daniel in a vision of the night, and Daniel blessed the God of heaven. 20 Daniel said:

"Blessed be the name of God from age to age,
for wisdom and power are his.

2.20 Revealing Prayer

This brief "psalm" gives insight into Daniel's spiritual life. It begins by expressing absolute confidence in God's control over the world: Daniel clung to such faith even while living in an enemy nation that had just destroyed God's temple in Jerusalem. Also, the prayer shows Daniel's spirit of humility and praise in the midst of crisis: He paused to give God credit before rushing to the king to interpret his dream.

21 He changes times and seasons,
deposes kings and sets up kings;
he gives wisdom to the wise
and knowledge to those who have
understanding.
22 He reveals deep and hidden things;
he knows what is in the darkness,
and light dwells with him.
23 To you, O God of my ancestors,
I give thanks and praise,
for you have given me wisdom
and power,
and have now revealed to me what we
asked of you,
for you have revealed to us what the
king ordered."

Daniel Interprets the Dream

24 Therefore Daniel went to Arioch, whom the king had appointed to destroy the wise men of Babylon, and said to him, "Do not destroy the wise men of Babylon; bring me in before the king, and I will give the king the interpretation." 25 Then Arioch quickly brought Daniel before the king and said to him: "I have found among the exiles from Judah a man who can tell the king the interpretation." 26The king said to Daniel, whose name was Belteshazzar, "Are you able to tell me the dream that I have seen and its interpretation?" 27Daniel answered the king, "No

wise men, enchanters, magicians, or diviners can show to the king the mystery that the king is asking, 28but there is a God in heaven who reveals mysteries, and he has disclosed to King Nebuchadnezzar what will happen at the end of days. Your dream and the visions of your head as you lay in bed were these: 29To you, O king, as you lay in bed, came thoughts of what would be hereafter, and the revealer of mysteries disclosed to you what is to be. 30But as for me, this mystery has not been revealed to me because of any wisdom that I have more than any other living being, but in order that the interpretation may be known to the king and that you may understand the thoughts of your mind.

31 "You were looking, O king, and lo! there was a great statue. This statue was huge, its brilliance extraordinary; it was standing before you, and its appearance was frightening. 32The head of that statue was of fine gold, its chest and arms of silver, its middle and thighs of bronze, 33its legs of iron, its feet partly of iron and partly of clay. 34As you looked on, a stone was cut out, not by human hands, and it struck the statue on its feet of iron and clay and broke them in pieces. 35Then the iron, the clay, the bronze, the silver, and the gold, were all broken in pieces and became like the chaff of the summer threshing floors; and the wind carried them away, so that not a trace of them could be found. But the stone that struck the statue became a great mountain and filled the whole earth.

36 "This was the dream; now we will tell the king its interpretation. 37You, O king, the king of kings—to whom the God of heaven has given the kingdom, the power, the might, and the glory, 38into whose hand he has given human beings, wherever they live, the wild animals of the field, and the birds of the air, and whom he has established as ruler over them all—you are the head of gold. 39After you shall arise another kingdom inferior to yours, and yet a third kingdom of bronze, which shall rule over the whole earth. 40And there shall be a fourth kingdom, strong as iron; just as iron crushes and smashes everything,c it shall crush and shatter all these. 41As you saw the feet and toes partly of potter's clay and partly of iron, it shall be a divided kingdom; but some of the strength of iron shall be in it, as you saw the iron mixed with the clay. 42As the toes of the feet were part iron and part clay, so the kingdom shall be partly strong and partly brittle. 43As you saw the iron mixed with clay, so will they mix with one another in marriage,d but they will not hold together, just as iron does not mix with clay. 44And in the days of those kings the God of heaven will set up a kingdom that shall never be destroyed, nor shall this kingdom be left to another people. It shall crush all these kingdoms

c Gk Theodotion Syr Vg: Aram adds *and like iron that crushes*   d Aram *by human seed*

and bring them to an end, and it shall forever; [45]just as you saw that a stone was cut from the mountain not by hands, and that it crushed the iron, the bronze, the clay, the silver, and the gold. The great God has informed the king what shall be hereafter. The dream is certain, and its interpretation trustworthy."

Daniel and His Friends Promoted

46 Then King Nebuchadnezzar fell on his face, worshiped Daniel, and commanded that a grain offering and incense be offered to him. [47]The king said to Daniel, "Truly, your God is God of gods and Lord of kings and a revealer of mysteries, for you have been able to reveal this mystery!" [48]Then the king promoted Daniel, gave him many great gifts, and made him ruler over the whole province of Babylon and chief prefect

2.48 A Nation of Dreamers

The Babylonians highly valued dream interpretation, for they believed the gods spoke to them through dreams. "If a man cannot remember the dream he saw, his personal god is angry with him," says one Babylonian proverb. That proverb helps explain Nebuchadnezzar's panic over forgetting his dream—and his lavish reward to Daniel for recalling and interpreting it.

over all the wise men of Babylon. [49]Daniel made a request of the king, and he appointed Shadrach, Meshach, and Abednego over the affairs of the province of Babylon. But Daniel remained at the king's court.

The Golden Image

3 King Nebuchadnezzar made a golden statue whose height was sixty cubits and whose width was six cubits; he set it up on the plain of Dura in the province of Babylon. [2]Then King Nebuchadnezzar sent for the satraps, the prefects, and the governors, the counselors, the treasurers, the justices, the magistrates, and all the officials of the provinces, to assemble and come to the dedication of the statue that King Nebuchadnezzar had set up. [3]So the satraps, the prefects, and the governors, the counselors, the treasurers, the justices, the magistrates, and all the officials of the provinces, assembled for the dedication of the statue that King Nebuchadnezzar had set up. When they were standing before the statue that Nebuchadnezzar had set up, [4]the herald proclaimed aloud, "You are commanded, O peoples, nations, and languages, [5]that when you hear the sound of the horn, pipe, lyre, trigon, harp, drum,

and entire musical ensemble, you are to fall down and worship the golden statue that King Nebuchadnezzar has set up. [6]Whoever does not fall down and worship shall immediately be thrown into a furnace of blazing fire." [7]Therefore, as soon as all the peoples heard the sound of the horn, pipe, lyre, trigon, harp, drum, and entire musical ensemble, all the peoples, nations, and languages fell down and worshiped the golden statue that King Nebuchadnezzar had set up.

8 Accordingly, at this time certain Chaldeans came forward and denounced the Jews. [9]They said to King Nebuchadnezzar, "O king, live forever! [10]You, O king, have made a decree, that everyone who hears the sound of the horn, pipe, lyre, trigon, harp, drum, and entire musical ensemble, shall fall down and worship the golden statue, [11]and whoever does not fall down and worship shall be thrown into a furnace of blazing fire. [12]There are certain Jews whom you have appointed over the affairs of the province of Babylon: Shadrach, Meshach, and Abednego. These pay no heed to you, O king. They do not serve your gods and they do not worship the golden statue that you have set up."

13 Then Nebuchadnezzar in furious rage commanded that Shadrach, Meshach, and Abednego be brought in; so they brought those men before the king. [14]Nebuchadnezzar said to them, "Is it true, O Shadrach, Meshach, and Abednego, that you do not serve my gods and you do not worship the golden statue that I have set up? [15]Now if you are ready when you hear the sound of the horn, pipe, lyre, trigon, harp, drum, and entire musical ensemble to fall down and worship the statue that I have made, well and good.[e] But if you do not worship, you shall immediately be thrown into a furnace of blazing fire, and who is the god that will deliver you out of my hands?"

16 Shadrach, Meshach, and Abednego answered the king, "O Nebuchadnezzar, we have no need to present a defense to you in this matter. [17]If our God whom we serve is able to deliver us from the furnace of blazing fire and out of your hand, O king, let him deliver us.[f] [18]But if not, be it known to you, O king, that we will not serve your gods and we will not worship the golden statue that you have set up."

The Fiery Furnace

19 Then Nebuchadnezzar was so filled with rage against Shadrach, Meshach, and Abednego that his face was distorted. He ordered the furnace heated up seven times more than was customary, [20]and ordered some of the strongest guards in his army to bind Shadrach, Meshach, and Abednego and to throw them into the furnace of blazing fire. [21]So the men were bound, still

---

[e] Aram lacks *well and good*   [f] Or *If our God whom we serve is able to deliver us, he will deliver us from the furnace of blazing fire and out of your hand, O king.*

wearing their tunics,[g] their trousers,[g] their hats, and their other garments, and they were thrown into the furnace of blazing fire. 22Because the king's command was urgent and the furnace was

3.18 Whether Rescued or Not

Daniel's three friends illustrated perfectly the quality of faith that is later commended in Hebrews 11. When allegiance to God led them to commit an act of civil disobedience, they were willing to face the consequences whether or not God rescued them. Daniel himself faced a severe test of faith, with a similarly happy ending (see chapter 6). Along with Elijah and Elisha, he was one of the few Old Testament prophets whose ministry was marked by miracles.

so overheated, the raging flames killed the men who lifted Shadrach, Meshach, and Abednego. 23But the three men, Shadrach, Meshach, and Abednego, fell down, bound, into the furnace of blazing fire.

24 Then King Nebuchadnezzar was astonished and rose up quickly. He said to his counselors, "Was it not three men that we threw bound into the fire?" They answered the king, "True, O king." 25He replied, "But I see four men unbound, walking in the middle of the fire, and they are not hurt; and the fourth has the appearance of a god."[h] 26Nebuchadnezzar then approached the

door of the furnace of blazing fire and said, "Shadrach, Meshach, and Abednego, servants of the Most High God, come out! Come here!" So Shadrach, Meshach, and Abednego came out from the fire. 27And the satraps, the prefects, the governors, and the king's counselors gathered together and saw that the fire had not had any power over the bodies of those men; the hair of their heads was not singed, their tunics[g] were not harmed, and not even the smell of fire came from them. 28Nebuchadnezzar said, "Blessed be the God of Shadrach, Meshach, and Abednego, who has sent his angel and delivered his servants who trusted in him. They disobeyed the king's command and yielded up their bodies rather than serve and worship any god except their own God. 29Therefore I make a decree: Any people, nation, or language that utters blasphemy against the God of Shadrach, Meshach, and Abednego shall be torn limb from limb, and their houses laid in ruins; for there is no other god who is able to deliver in this way." 30Then the king promoted Shadrach, Meshach, and Abednego in the province of Babylon.

Nebuchadnezzar's Second Dream

4[i] King Nebuchadnezzar to all peoples, nations, and languages that live throughout the earth: May you have abundant prosperity! 2The signs and wonders that the Most High God has worked for me I am pleased to recount.

3 How great are his signs,
   how mighty his wonders!
His kingdom is an everlasting kingdom,

---

[g] Meaning of Aram word uncertain   [h] Aram *a son of the gods*   [i] Ch 3.31 in Aram

NEBUCHADNEZZAR *Power and Pride*

NEBUCHADNEZZAR, THE WORLD'S MOST POWERFUL man, had reason to be proud. He captained the mighty Babylonian army (based in what is now Iraq) on its march through the Middle East, annihilating all opposition and demanding tribute. No one could withstand him.

The kingdom of Judah, vastly reduced by previous wars, was just one small country among many that sent money and captives to try to appease this tyrant. Ultimately Nebuchadnezzar destroyed Jerusalem and its temple and dragged its remaining citizens into exile. Jews still look back on that time as one of the darkest periods of Jewish history.

On the home front, Nebuchadnezzar went on a lavish building campaign. He decorated the sacred Procession Way with 120 lions flanking its length of nearly a mile. He adorned the Ishtar Gate with enameled brickwork depicting 575 dragons and bulls. He built spectacular palaces and temples and also the "Hanging Gardens of Babylon," one of the Seven Wonders of the Ancient World.

The book of Daniel, however, shows Nebuchadnezzar in a different light: as a vulnerable man who needed to recognize the King of kings. Some of the hapless Jews whom Nebuchadnezzar carried into exile became his trusted officials. Through them, and through a humiliating (but God-given) bout of insanity, Nebuchadnezzar came to terms with his pride. He learned his lesson while living out in the fields like a wild animal, eating grass.

In the end, the mighty Nebuchadnezzar himself wrote of Daniel's God: "He is able to bring low those who walk in pride" (4.37).

Life Questions: Do the most powerful people you know recognize God's "higher power?" What could you do to help them see it?

and his sovereignty is from generation
to generation.

4[j] I, Nebuchadnezzar, was living at ease in my home and prospering in my palace. [5]I saw a dream that frightened me; my fantasies in bed and the visions of my head terrified me. [6]So I made a decree that all the wise men of Babylon should be brought before me, in order that they might tell me the interpretation of the dream. [7]Then the magicians, the enchanters, the Chaldeans, and the diviners came in, and I told them the dream, but they could not tell me its interpretation. [8]At last Daniel came in before me—he who was named Belteshazzar after the name of my god, and who is endowed with a spirit of the holy gods[k]—and I told him the dream:

4.8 The Name of a God

Names were extremely important in Biblical times, for they conveyed something of a person's identity. Thus God sometimes gave a person a new name to indicate a changed life. However, the name the Babylonians presented to Daniel, Belteshazzar, was no gift from God. It was taken from "Bel," a title for the Babylonian god Marduk. Daniel was surrounded by an alien culture and could not avoid every aspect of it.

[9]"O Belteshazzar, chief of the magicians, I know that you are endowed with a spirit of the holy gods[k] and that no mystery is too difficult for you. Hear[l] the dream that I saw; tell me its interpretation.

[10,m] Upon my bed this is what I saw;
there was a tree at the center of the
earth,
and its height was great.
[11] The tree grew great and strong,
its top reached to heaven,
and it was visible to the ends of the
whole earth.
[12] Its foliage was beautiful,
its fruit abundant,
and it provided food for all.
The animals of the field found shade
under it,
the birds of the air nested in
its branches,
and from it all living beings were fed.

[13] "I continued looking, in the visions of my head as I lay in bed, and there was a holy watcher, coming down from heaven. [14]He cried aloud and said:

'Cut down the tree and chop off
its branches,
strip off its foliage and scatter its fruit.
Let the animals flee from beneath it
and the birds from its branches.
[15] But leave its stump and roots in the
ground,
with a band of iron and bronze,
in the tender grass of the field.
Let him be bathed with the dew
of heaven,
and let his lot be with the animals of
the field
in the grass of the earth.
[16] Let his mind be changed from that of a
human,
and let the mind of an animal be given
to him.
And let seven times pass over him.
[17] The sentence is rendered by decree of the
watchers,
the decision is given by order of the
holy ones,
in order that all who live may know
that the Most High is sovereign over
the kingdom of mortals;
he gives it to whom he will
and sets over it the lowliest of human
beings.'

[18] "This is the dream that I, King Nebuchadnezzar, saw. Now you, Belteshazzar, declare the interpretation, since all the wise men of my kingdom are unable to tell me the interpretation. You are able, however, for you are endowed with a spirit of the holy gods."[k]

Daniel Interprets the Second Dream

[19] Then Daniel, who was called Belteshazzar, was severely distressed for a while. His thoughts terrified him. The king said, "Belteshazzar, do not let the dream or the interpretation terrify you." Belteshazzar answered, "My lord, may the dream be for those who hate you, and its interpretation for your enemies! [20]The tree that you saw, which grew great and strong, so that its top reached to heaven and was visible to the end of the whole earth, [21]whose foliage was beautiful and its fruit abundant, and which provided food for all, under which animals of the field lived, and in whose branches the birds of the air had nests— [22]it is you, O king! You have grown great and strong. Your greatness has increased and reaches to heaven, and your sovereignty to the ends of the earth. [23]And whereas the king saw a holy watcher coming down from heaven and saying, 'Cut down the tree and destroy it, but leave its stump and roots in the ground, with a band of iron and bronze, in

---

j Ch 4.1 in Aram   *k* Or *a holy, divine spirit*   *l* Theodotion: Aram *The visions of*   *m* Theodotion Syr Compare Gk:
Aram adds *The visions of my head*

the grass of the field; and let him be bathed with the dew of heaven, and let his lot be with the animals of the field, until seven times pass over him'— [24]this is the interpretation, O king, and it is a decree of the Most High that has come upon my lord the king: [25]You shall be driven away from human society, and your dwelling shall be with the wild animals. You shall be made to eat grass like oxen, you shall be bathed with the dew of heaven, and seven times shall pass over you, until you have learned that the Most High has sovereignty over the kingdom of mortals, and gives it to whom he will. [26]As it was commanded to leave the stump and roots of the tree, your kingdom shall be re-established for you from the time that you learn that Heaven is sovereign. [27]Therefore, O king, may my counsel be acceptable to you: atone for[n] your sins with righteousness, and your iniquities with mercy to the oppressed, so that your prosperity may be prolonged."

Nebuchadnezzar's Humiliation

28 All this came upon King Nebuchadnezzar. [29]At the end of twelve months he was walking on the roof of the royal palace of Babylon, [30]and the king said, "Is this not magnificent Babylon, which I have built as a royal capital by my mighty power and for my glorious majesty?" [31]While the words were still in the king's mouth, a voice came from heaven: "O King Nebuchadnezzar, to you it is declared: The kingdom has departed from you! [32]You shall be driven away from human society, and your dwelling shall be with the animals of the field. You shall be made to eat grass like oxen, and seven times shall pass over you, until you have learned that the Most High has sovereignty over the kingdom of mortals and gives it to whom he will." [33]Immediately the sentence was fulfilled against Nebuchadnezzar. He was driven away from human society, ate grass like oxen, and his body was bathed with the dew of heaven, until his hair grew as long as eagles' feathers and his nails became like birds' claws.

Nebuchadnezzar Praises God

34 When that period was over, I, Nebuchadnezzar, lifted my eyes to heaven, and my reason returned to me.
I blessed the Most High,
and praised and honored the one who
lives forever.
For his sovereignty is an everlasting
sovereignty,
and his kingdom endures from
generation to generation.
[35] All the inhabitants of the earth are
accounted as nothing,
and he does what he wills with the host
of heaven

and the inhabitants of the earth.
There is no one who can stay his hand
or say to him, "What are you doing?"
[36]At that time my reason returned to me; and my majesty and splendor were restored to me for the glory of my kingdom. My counselors and my lords sought me out, I was re-established over my kingdom, and still more greatness was added to me. [37]Now I, Nebuchadnezzar, praise and extol and honor the King of heaven,
for all his works are truth,
and his ways are justice;
and he is able to bring low
those who walk in pride.

Belshazzar's Feast

5 King Belshazzar made a great festival for a thousand of his lords, and he was drinking wine in the presence of the thousand.

5.1 The Throne Room

Modern archaeological excavation has found, in the Babylonian palace, a large room (about 150 feet by 50 feet—one quarter the size of a football field) that has become known as the Throne Room. One wall had a design of blue enameled bricks, but the other three were covered in white plaster (see verse 5).

2 Under the influence of the wine, Belshazzar commanded that they bring in the vessels of gold and silver that his father Nebuchadnezzar had taken out of the temple in Jerusalem, so that the king and his lords, his wives, and his concubines might drink from them. [3]So they brought in the vessels of gold and silver[o] that had been taken out of the temple, the house of God in Jerusalem, and the king and his lords, his wives, and his concubines drank from them. [4]They drank the wine and praised the gods of gold and silver, bronze, iron, wood, and stone.

The Writing on the Wall

5 Immediately the fingers of a human hand appeared and began writing on the plaster of the wall of the royal palace, next to the lampstand. The king was watching the hand as it wrote. [6]Then the king's face turned pale, and his thoughts terrified him. His limbs gave way, and his knees knocked together. [7]The king cried aloud to bring in the enchanters, the Chaldeans, and the diviners; and the king said to the wise men of Babylon, "Whoever can read this writing and tell me its interpretation shall be clothed in purple, have a chain of gold around his neck, and rank third in the kingdom." [8]Then all the king's wise

[n] Aram *break off*   [o] Theodotion Vg: Aram lacks *and silver*

men came in, but they could not read the writing or tell the king the interpretation. 9Then King Belshazzar became greatly terrified and his face turned pale, and his lords were perplexed.

10 The queen, when she heard the discussion of the king and his lords, came into the banqueting hall. The queen said, "O king, live forever! Do not let your thoughts terrify you or your face grow pale. 11There is a man in your kingdom who is endowed with a spirit of the holy gods.p In the days of your father he was found to have enlightenment, understanding, and wisdom like the wisdom of the gods. Your father, King Nebuchadnezzar, made him chief of the magicians, enchanters, Chaldeans, and diviners,q 12because an excellent spirit, knowledge, and understanding to interpret dreams, explain riddles, and solve problems were found in this Daniel, whom the king named Belteshazzar. Now let Daniel be called, and he will give the interpretation."

The Writing on the Wall Interpreted

13 Then Daniel was brought in before the king. The king said to Daniel, "So you are Daniel, one of the exiles of Judah, whom my father the king brought from Judah? 14I have heard of you that a spirit of the godsr is in you, and that enlightenment, understanding, and excellent wisdom are found in you. 15Now the wise men, the enchanters, have been brought in before me to read this writing and tell me its interpretation, but they were not able to give the interpretation of the matter. 16But I have heard that you can give interpretations and solve problems. Now if you are able to read the writing and tell me its interpretation, you shall be clothed in purple, have a chain of gold around your neck, and rank third in the kingdom."

17 Then Daniel answered in the presence of the king, "Let your gifts be for yourself, or give your rewards to someone else! Nevertheless I will read the writing to the king and let him know the interpretation. 18O king, the Most High God gave your father Nebuchadnezzar kingship, greatness, glory, and majesty. 19And because of the greatness that he gave him, all peoples, nations, and languages trembled and feared before him. He killed those he wanted to kill, kept alive those he wanted to keep alive, honored those he wanted to honor, and degraded those he wanted to degrade. 20But when his heart was lifted up and his spirit was hardened so that he acted proudly, he was deposed from his kingly throne, and his glory was stripped from him. 21He was driven from human society, and his mind was made like that of an animal. His dwelling was with the wild asses, he was fed grass like oxen, and his body was bathed with the dew of heaven, until he learned that the Most High God has sovereignty over the kingdom of mortals, and sets over it whomever he will. 22And you, Belshazzar his son, have not humbled your heart, even though you knew all this! 23You have exalted yourself against the Lord of heaven! The vessels of his temple have been brought in before you, and you and your lords, your wives and your concubines have been drinking wine from them. You have praised the gods of silver and gold, of bronze, iron, wood, and stone, which do not see or hear or know; but the God in whose power is your very breath, and to whom belong all your ways, you have not honored.

24 "So from his presence the hand was sent and this writing was inscribed. 25And this is the writing that was inscribed: MENE, MENE, TEKEL, and PARSIN. 26This is the interpretation of the matter: MENE, God has numbered the days ofs your kingdom and brought it to an end; 27TEKEL, you have been weighed on the scales and found wanting; 28PERES,t your kingdom is divided and given to the Medes and Persians."

29 Then Belshazzar gave the command, and Daniel was clothed in purple, a chain of gold was put around his neck, and a proclamation was made concerning him that he should rank third in the kingdom.

30 That very night Belshazzar, the Chaldean king, was killed. 31 u And Darius the Mede received the kingdom, being about sixty-two years old.

5.30 Sneak Attack

Two empires, the Medes and the Persians, joined forces to overthrow Babylon, the dominant power of the day. Invading armies diverted the river Euphrates to another channel, then marched along the dry riverbed underneath the city walls. The site of ancient Babylon lies about fifty miles from modern-day Baghdad, Iraq.

The Plot against Daniel

6 It pleased Darius to set over the kingdom one hundred twenty satraps, stationed throughout the whole kingdom, 2and over them three presidents, including Daniel; to these the satraps gave account, so that the king might suffer no loss. 3Soon Daniel distinguished himself above all the other presidents and satraps because an excellent spirit was in him, and the king planned to appoint him over the whole kingdom. 4So the presidents and the satraps tried to find grounds for complaint against Daniel in connection with the kingdom. But they could find no grounds for

---

p Or a holy, divine spirit   q Aram adds the king your father
t The singular of Parsin   u Ch 6.1 in Aram

r Or a divine spirit   s Aram lacks the days of

complaint or any corruption, because he was faithful, and no negligence or corruption could be found in him. ⁵The men said, "We shall not find any ground for complaint against this Daniel unless we find it in connection with the law of his God."

6 So the presidents and satraps conspired and came to the king and said to him, "O King Darius, live forever! ⁷All the presidents of the kingdom, the prefects and the satraps, the counselors and the governors are agreed that the king should establish an ordinance and enforce an interdict, that whoever prays to anyone, divine or human, for thirty days, except to you, O king, shall be thrown into a den of lions. ⁸Now, O king, establish the interdict and sign the document, so that it cannot be changed, according to the law of the Medes and the Persians, which cannot be revoked." ⁹Therefore King Darius signed the document and interdict.

Daniel in the Lions' Den

10 Although Daniel knew that the document had been signed, he continued to go to his house, which had windows in its upper room open toward Jerusalem, and to get down on his knees three times a day to pray to his God and praise

6.10–11 A Jewish Orientation

Daniel had lost much of his Jewish heritage—even his name had been changed to a Babylonian one (1.7). Certainly he could not worship God in the way God's law commanded, through sacrifices at the temple in Jerusalem. He did, however, point himself toward the promised land three times a day in prayer. Not even the threat of death could make him vary this practice. By this time Daniel had been in Babylon over 60 years; he was probably in his 80s.

him, just as he had done previously. ¹¹The conspirators came and found Daniel praying and seeking mercy before his God. ¹²Then they approached the king and said concerning the interdict, "O king! Did you not sign an interdict, that anyone who prays to anyone, divine or human, within thirty days except to you, O king, shall be thrown into a den of lions?" The king answered, "The thing stands fast, according to the law of the Medes and Persians, which cannot be revoked." ¹³Then they responded to the king, "Daniel, one of the exiles from Judah, pays no attention to you, O king, or to the interdict you have signed, but he is saying his prayers three times a day." ¹⁴ When the king heard the charge, he was very much distressed. He was determined to save Daniel, and until the sun went down he made every effort to rescue him. ¹⁵Then the conspira-

tors came to the king and said to him, "Know, O king, that it is a law of the Medes and Persians that no interdict or ordinance that the king establishes can be changed."

16 Then the king gave the command, and Daniel was brought and thrown into the den of lions. The king said to Daniel, "May your God, whom you faithfully serve, deliver you!" ¹⁷A stone was brought and laid on the mouth of the den, and the king sealed it with his own signet and with the signet of his lords, so that nothing might be changed concerning Daniel. ¹⁸Then the king went to his palace and spent the night fasting; no food was brought to him, and sleep fled from him.

Daniel Saved from the Lions

19 Then, at break of day, the king got up and hurried to the den of lions. ²⁰When he came near the den where Daniel was, he cried out anxiously to Daniel, "O Daniel, servant of the living God, has your God whom you faithfully serve been able to deliver you from the lions?" ²¹Daniel then said to the king, "O king, live forever! ²²My God sent his angel and shut the lions' mouths so that they would not hurt me, because I was found blameless before him; and also before you, O king, I have done no wrong." ²³Then the king was exceedingly glad and commanded that Daniel be taken up out of the den. So Daniel was taken up out of the den, and no kind of harm was found on him, because he had trusted in his God. ²⁴The king gave a command, and those who had accused Daniel were brought and thrown into the den of lions—they, their children, and their wives. Before they reached the bottom of the den the lions overpowered them and broke all their bones in pieces.

25 Then King Darius wrote to all peoples and nations of every language throughout the whole world: "May you have abundant prosperity! ²⁶I make a decree, that in all my royal dominion people should tremble and fear before the God of Daniel:

For he is the living God,
  enduring forever.
His kingdom shall never be destroyed,
  and his dominion has no end.
²⁷ He delivers and rescues,
  he works signs and wonders in heaven
    and on earth;
for he has saved Daniel
  from the power of the lions."

²⁸So this Daniel prospered during the reign of Darius and the reign of Cyrus the Persian.

Visions of the Four Beasts

7 In the first year of King Belshazzar of Babylon, Daniel had a dream and visions of his head as he lay in bed. Then he wrote down the

dream:[v] [2]I,[w] Daniel, saw in my vision by night the four winds of heaven stirring up the great sea, [3]and four great beasts came up out of the sea, different from one another. [4]The first was like a lion and had eagles' wings. Then, as I watched, its wings were plucked off, and it was lifted up from the ground and made to stand on two feet like a human being; and a human mind was given to it. [5]Another beast appeared, a second one, that looked like a bear. It was raised up on one side, had three tusks[x] in its mouth among its teeth and was told, "Arise, devour many bodies!" [6]After this, as I watched, another appeared, like a leopard. The beast had four wings of a bird on its back and four heads; and dominion was given to it. [7]After this I saw in the visions by night a fourth beast, terrifying and dreadful and exceedingly strong. It had great iron teeth and was devouring, breaking in pieces, and stamping what was left with its feet. It was different from all the beasts that preceded it, and it had ten horns. [8]I was considering the horns, when another horn appeared, a little one coming up among them; to make room for it, three of the earlier horns were plucked up by the roots. There were eyes like human eyes in this horn, and a mouth speaking arrogantly.

Judgment before the Ancient One

[9] As I watched,
  thrones were set in place,
    and an Ancient One[y] took his throne,
  his clothing was white as snow,
    and the hair of his head like
      pure wool;
  his throne was fiery flames,
    and its wheels were burning fire.
[10] A stream of fire issued
    and flowed out from his presence.
  A thousand thousands served him,
    and ten thousand times ten thousand
      stood attending him.
  The court sat in judgment,
    and the books were opened.

[11]I watched then because of the noise of the arrogant words that the horn was speaking. And as I watched, the beast was put to death, and its body destroyed and given over to be burned with fire. [12]As for the rest of the beasts, their dominion was taken away, but their lives were prolonged for a season and a time. [13]As I watched in the night visions,
  I saw one like a human being[z]
    coming with the clouds of heaven.
  And he came to the Ancient One[a]

---

[v] Q Ms Theodotion: MT adds *the beginning of the words; he said and said, "I* [x] Or *ribs* [y] Aram *an Ancient of Days* [z] Aram *one like a son of man* [a] Aram *the Ancient*
of Days

[w] Theodotion: Aram *Daniel answered*

Symbols of Power
The bigger the tyrant, the more statues litter the landscape

IT'S NO SURPRISE THAT NEBUCHADNEZZAR erected a gold image for people to worship (chapter 3). Kings and rulers love to display statues or gigantic photos as symbols of their power. The bigger the tyrants, the more of their statues litter the landscape.

It seems reasonable, then, that Daniel's visions depict political realms through statues and symbolic animals. But since each of the visions uses a different set of symbols, you can easily lose track of what the symbols stand for. This chart may help you coordinate Daniel's view of four great empires—and the almighty God who overwhelms their power in the end:

"I saw in the visions by night a fourth beast, terrifying and dreadful and exceedingly strong. It had great iron teeth and was devouring, breaking in pieces." 7.7

	Babylon	Medo-Persia	Greece	Rome	Kingdom of God
Chapter 2	gold	silver	bronze	iron	supernatural rock
Chapter 7	lion	bear	leopard	beast with horns	Ancient One, Son of Man
Chapter 8	—	ram	goat	—	—
Chapter 11	—	—	king of North	—	—

Life Questions: What images "litter the landscape" in our time? Are they symbols of power? If so, how does that power affect you?

and was presented before him.
14 To him was given dominion
and glory and kingship,
that all peoples, nations, and languages
should serve him.
His dominion is an everlasting dominion
that shall not pass away,
and his kingship is one
that shall never be destroyed.

7.13–14 A Son of Man

God's power is given to one "like a son of man" (see footnote) rather than to those like beasts. The contrast suggests God's kingdom has power that is humane, not savage or bestial. Jesus adopted this term for himself.

Daniel's Visions Interpreted

15 As for me, Daniel, my spirit was troubled within me,[b] and the visions of my head terrified me. 16I approached one of the attendants to ask him the truth concerning all this. So he said that he would disclose to me the interpretation of the matter: 17"As for these four great beasts, four kings shall arise out of the earth. 18But the holy ones of the Most High shall receive the kingdom and possess the kingdom forever—forever and ever."

19 Then I desired to know the truth concerning the fourth beast, which was different from all the rest, exceedingly terrifying, with its teeth of iron and claws of bronze, and which devoured and broke in pieces, and stamped what was left with its feet; 20and concerning the ten horns that were on its head, and concerning the other horn, which came up and to make room for which three of them fell out—the horn that had eyes and a mouth that spoke arrogantly, and that seemed greater than the others. 21As I looked, this horn made war with the holy ones and was prevailing over them, 22until the Ancient One[c] came; then judgment was given for the holy ones of the Most High, and the time arrived when the holy ones gained possession of the kingdom.

23 This is what he said: "As for the fourth beast,
there shall be a fourth kingdom on earth
that shall be different from all the
other kingdoms;
it shall devour the whole earth,
and trample it down, and break it to
pieces.
24 As for the ten horns,
out of this kingdom ten kings shall arise,

and another shall arise after them.
This one shall be different from the
former ones,
and shall put down three kings.
25 He shall speak words against the Most
High,
shall wear out the holy ones of the
Most High,
and shall attempt to change the sacred
seasons and the law;
and they shall be given into his power
for a time, two times,[d] and half a
time.
26 Then the court shall sit in judgment,
and his dominion shall be taken away,
to be consumed and totally destroyed.
27 The kingship and dominion
and the greatness of the kingdoms
under the whole heaven
shall be given to the people of the holy
ones of the Most High;
their kingdom shall be an everlasting
kingdom,
and all dominions shall serve and obey
them."

28 Here the account ends. As for me, Daniel, my thoughts greatly terrified me, and my face turned pale; but I kept the matter in my mind.

Vision of a Ram and a Goat

8 In the third year of the reign of King Belshazzar a vision appeared to me, Daniel, after the one that had appeared to me at first. 2In the vision I was looking and saw myself in Susa the capital, in the province of Elam,[e] and I was by the river Ulai.[f] 3I looked up and saw a ram standing beside the river.[g] It had two horns. Both horns were long, but one was longer than the other, and the longer one came up second. 4I saw the ram charging westward and northward and southward. All beasts were powerless to withstand it, and no one could rescue from its power; it did as it pleased and became strong.

5 As I was watching, a male goat appeared from the west, coming across the face of the whole earth without touching the ground. The goat had a horn[h] between its eyes. 6It came toward the ram with the two horns that I had seen standing beside the river,[g] and it ran at it with savage force. 7I saw it approaching the ram. It was enraged against it and struck the ram, breaking its two horns. The ram did not have power to withstand it; it threw the ram down to the ground and trampled upon it, and there was no one who could rescue the ram from its power. 8Then the male goat grew exceedingly great; but at the height of its power, the great horn was broken,

b Aram *troubled in its sheath*   *c* Aram *the Ancient of Days*   *d* Aram *a time, times*   *e* Gk Theodotion: MT Q Ms
repeat *in the vision I was looking*   *f* Or *the Ulai Gate*   *g* Or *gate*   *h* Theodotion: Gk *one horn*; Heb *a horn of*
vision

and in its place there came up four prominent horns toward the four winds of heaven.

9 Out of one of them came another[i] horn, a little one, which grew exceedingly great toward the south, toward the east, and toward the beautiful land. [10]It grew as high as the host of heaven. It threw down to the earth some of the host and some of the stars, and trampled on them. [11]Even against the prince of the host it acted arrogantly; it took the regular burnt offering away from him and overthrew the place of his sanctuary. [12]Because of wickedness, the host was given over to it together with the regular burnt offering;[j] it cast truth to the ground, and kept prospering in what it did. [13]Then I heard a holy one speaking, and another holy one said to the one that spoke, "For how long is this vision concerning the regular burnt offering, the transgression that makes desolate, and the giving over of the sanctuary and host to be trampled?"[j] [14]And he answered him,[k] "For two thousand three hundred evenings and mornings; then the sanctuary shall be restored to its rightful state."

Gabriel Interprets the Vision

15 When I, Daniel, had seen the vision, I tried to understand it. Then someone appeared standing before me, having the appearance of a man, [16]and I heard a human voice by the Ulai, calling, "Gabriel, help this man understand the vision." [17]So he came near where I stood; and when he came, I became frightened and fell prostrate. But he said to me, "Understand, O mortal,[l] that the vision is for the time of the end."

18 As he was speaking to me, I fell into a trance, face to the ground; then he touched me and set me on my feet. [19]He said, "Listen, and I will tell you what will take place later in the period of wrath; for it refers to the appointed time of the end. [20]As for the ram that you saw with the two horns, these are the kings of Media and Persia. [21]The male goat[m] is the king of Greece, and the great horn between its eyes is the first king. [22]As for the horn that was broken, in place of which four others arose, four kingdoms shall arise from his[n] nation, but not with his power.

23 At the end of their rule,
    when the transgressions have reached
        their full measure,
    a king of bold countenance shall arise,
        skilled in intrigue.
24 He shall grow strong in power,[o]
        shall cause fearful destruction,
        and shall succeed in what he does.
    He shall destroy the powerful
        and the people of the holy ones.
25 By his cunning

he shall make deceit prosper under his
        hand,
    and in his own mind he shall be great.
Without warning he shall destroy many
    and shall even rise up against the
        Prince of princes.
    But he shall be broken, and not by
        human hands.
[26]The vision of the evenings and the mornings that has been told is true. As for you, seal up the vision, for it refers to many days from now."

8.26 Long Delay

Twice (here and 12.4) the angel tells Daniel to seal up the vision because it concerns the distant future. Pointedly, in Revelation, the last book of the Bible, an angel tells John, "Do not seal up the words of the prophecy of this book, for the time is near" (Revelation 22.10). Daniel and Revelation, written hundreds of years apart, arrive at the same conclusion: No matter how bad things look, God is in control of history and will one day reclaim the earth.

27 So I, Daniel, was overcome and lay sick for some days; then I arose and went about the king's business. But I was dismayed by the vision and did not understand it.

Daniel's Prayer for the People

9 In the first year of Darius son of Ahasuerus, by birth a Mede, who became king over the realm of the Chaldeans— [2]in the first year of his reign, I, Daniel, perceived in the books the number of years that, according to the word of the LORD to the prophet Jeremiah, must be fulfilled for the devastation of Jerusalem, namely, seventy years.

9.2 Favored by God and Kings

This chapter gives a rare glimpse of one prophet, Daniel, being comforted by the words of another, Jeremiah. Daniel's response shows that, despite his government service to two enemy empires (Babylon and Persia), loyalty to his homeland never faltered. The remarkable prayer that follows expresses well his intimate relationship with God.

3 Then I turned to the Lord God, to seek an answer by prayer and supplication with fasting and sackcloth and ashes. [4]I prayed to the LORD my God and made confession, saying,

---

[i] Cn Compare 7.8: Heb *one*   [j] Meaning of Heb uncertain
[m] Or *shaggy male goat*   [n] Gk Theodotion Vg: Heb *the*
not with his power

[k] Gk Theodotion Syr Vg: Heb *me*   [l] Heb *son of man*
[o] Theodotion and one Gk Ms: Heb repeats (from 8.22) *but*

"Ah, Lord, great and awesome God, keeping
covenant and steadfast love with those who love
you and keep your commandments, [5]we have
sinned and done wrong, acted wickedly and rebelled, turning aside from your commandments
and ordinances. [6]We have not listened to your
servants the prophets, who spoke in your name to
our kings, our princes, and our ancestors, and to
all the people of the land.
7 "Righteousness is on your side, O Lord, but
open shame, as at this day, falls on us, the people
of Judah, the inhabitants of Jerusalem, and all
Israel, those who are near and those who are far
away, in all the lands to which you have driven
them, because of the treachery that they have
committed against you. [8]Open shame, O LORD,
falls on us, our kings, our officials, and our ancestors, because we have sinned against you. [9]To the
Lord our God belong mercy and forgiveness, for
we have rebelled against him, [10]and have not
obeyed the voice of the LORD our God by following his laws, which he set before us by his servants
the prophets.
11 "All Israel has transgressed your law and
turned aside, refusing to obey your voice. So the
curse and the oath written in the law of Moses, the
servant of God, have been poured out upon us,
because we have sinned against you. [12]He has
confirmed his words, which he spoke against us
and against our rulers, by bringing upon us a
calamity so great that what has been done against
Jerusalem has never before been done under the
whole heaven. [13]Just as it is written in the law of
Moses, all this calamity has come upon us. We
did not entreat the favor of the LORD our God,
turning from our iniquities and reflecting on his[p]
fidelity. [14]So the LORD kept watch over this calamity until he brought it upon us. Indeed, the LORD
our God is right in all that he has done; for we
have disobeyed his voice.
15 "And now, O Lord our God, who brought
your people out of the land of Egypt with a
mighty hand and made your name renowned
even to this day—we have sinned, we have done
wickedly. [16]O Lord, in view of all your righteous
acts, let your anger and wrath, we pray, turn away
from your city Jerusalem, your holy mountain;
because of our sins and the iniquities of our ancestors, Jerusalem and your people have become
a disgrace among all our neighbors. [17]Now therefore, O our God, listen to the prayer of your servant and to his supplication, and for your own
sake, Lord,[q] let your face shine upon your desolated sanctuary. [18]Incline your ear, O my God,
and hear. Open your eyes and look at our desolation and the city that bears your name. We do
not present our supplication before you on the
ground of our righteousness, but on the ground
of your great mercies. [19]O Lord, hear; O Lord,
forgive; O Lord, listen and act and do not delay!
For your own sake, O my God, because your city
and your people bear your name!"

The Seventy Weeks

20 While I was speaking, and was praying and
confessing my sin and the sin of my people Israel,
and presenting my supplication before the LORD
my God on behalf of the holy mountain of my
God— [21]while I was speaking in prayer, the man
Gabriel, whom I had seen before in a vision, came
to me in swift flight at the time of the evening
sacrifice. [22]He came[r] and said to me, "Daniel, I
have now come out to give you wisdom and understanding. [23]At the beginning of your supplications a word went out, and I have come to declare
it, for you are greatly beloved. So consider the
word and understand the vision:
24 "Seventy weeks are decreed for your people and your holy city: to finish the transgression,
to put an end to sin, and to atone for iniquity, to
bring in everlasting righteousness, to seal both
vision and prophet, and to anoint a most holy
place.[s] [25]Know therefore and understand: from
the time that the word went out to restore and
rebuild Jerusalem until the time of an anointed
prince, there shall be seven weeks; and for sixty-
two weeks it shall be built again with streets and
moat, but in a troubled time. [26]After the sixty-two
weeks, an anointed one shall be cut off and shall
have nothing, and the troops of the prince who is
to come shall destroy the city and the sanctuary.
Its[t] end shall come with a flood, and to the end
there shall be war. Desolations are decreed. [27]He
shall make a strong covenant with many for one
week, and for half of the week he shall make
sacrifice and offering cease; and in their place[u]
shall be an abomination that desolates, until the
decreed end is poured out upon the desolator."

Conflict of Nations and Heavenly Powers

10 In the third year of King Cyrus of Persia
a word was revealed to Daniel, who was
named Belteshazzar. The word was true, and it
concerned a great conflict. He understood the
word, having received understanding in the vision.
2 At that time I, Daniel, had been mourning
for three weeks. [3]I had eaten no rich food, no
meat or wine had entered my mouth, and I had
not anointed myself at all, for the full three weeks.
[4]On the twenty-fourth day of the first month, as
I was standing on the bank of the great river (that
is, the Tigris), [5]I looked up and saw a man clothed
in linen, with a belt of gold from Uphaz around
his waist. [6]His body was like beryl, his face like
lightning, his eyes like flaming torches, his arms

[p] Heb *your* [q] Theodotion Vg Compare Syr: Heb *for the Lord's sake* [r] Gk Syr: Heb *He made to understand*
[s] Or *thing* or *one* [t] Or *His* [u] Cn: Meaning of Heb uncertain

and legs like the gleam of burnished bronze, and the sound of his words like the roar of a multitude. [7]I, Daniel, alone saw the vision; the people who were with me did not see the vision, though a great trembling fell upon them, and they fled and hid themselves. [8]So I was left alone to see this great vision. My strength left me, and my complexion grew deathly pale, and I retained no strength. [9]Then I heard the sound of his words; and when I heard the sound of his words, I fell into a trance, face to the ground.

10 But then a hand touched me and roused me to my hands and knees. [11]He said to me, "Daniel, greatly beloved, pay attention to the words that I am going to speak to you. Stand on your feet, for I have now been sent to you." So while he was speaking this word to me, I stood up trembling. [12]He said to me, "Do not fear, Daniel, for from the first day that you set your mind to gain understanding and to humble yourself before your God, your words have been heard, and I have come because of your words. [13]But the prince of the kingdom of Persia opposed me twenty-one days. So Michael, one of the chief princes, came to help me, and I left him there with the prince of the kingdom of Persia,[v] [14]and have come to help you understand what is to happen to your people at the end of days. For there is a further vision for those days."

15 While he was speaking these words to me, I turned my face toward the ground and was speechless. [16]Then one in human form touched my lips, and I opened my mouth to speak, and said to the one who stood before me, "My lord, because of the vision such pains have come upon me that I retain no strength. [17]How can my lord's servant talk with my lord? For I am shaking,[w] no strength remains in me, and no breath is left in me."

18 Again one in human form touched me and strengthened me. [19]He said, "Do not fear, greatly beloved, you are safe. Be strong and courageous!" When he spoke to me, I was strengthened and said, "Let my lord speak, for you have strengthened me." [20]Then he said, "Do you know why I have come to you? Now I must return to fight against the prince of Persia, and when I am through with him, the prince of Greece will come.

[21]But I am to tell you what is inscribed in the book of truth. There is no one with me who contends against these princes except Michael, your prince. [1]As for me, in the first year of Darius the Mede, I stood up to support and strengthen him.

11

2 "Now I will announce the truth to you. Three more kings shall arise in Persia. The fourth shall be far richer than all of them, and when he has become strong through his riches, he shall stir up all against the kingdom of Greece. [3]Then a warrior king shall arise, who shall rule with great dominion and take action as he pleases. [4]And while still rising in power, his kingdom shall be broken and divided toward the four winds of heaven, but not to his posterity, nor according to the dominion with which he ruled; for his kingdom shall be uprooted and go to others besides these.

5 "Then the king of the south shall grow strong, but one of his officers shall grow stronger than he and shall rule a realm greater than his own realm. [6]After some years they shall make an alliance, and the daughter of the king of the south shall come to the king of the north to ratify the agreement. But she shall not retain her power, and his offspring shall not endure. She shall be given up, she and her attendants and her child and the one who supported her.

"In those times [7]a branch from her roots shall rise up in his place. He shall come against the army and enter the fortress of the king of the north, and he shall take action against them and prevail. [8]Even their gods, with their idols and with their precious vessels of silver and gold, he shall carry off to Egypt as spoils of war. For some years he shall refrain from attacking the king of the north; [9]then the latter shall invade the realm of the king of the south, but will return to his own land.

10 "His sons shall wage war and assemble a multitude of great forces, which shall advance like a flood and pass through, and again shall carry the war as far as his fortress. [11]Moved with rage, the king of the south shall go out and do battle against the king of the north, who shall muster a great multitude, which shall, however, be defeated by his enemy. [12]When the multitude has been carried off, his heart shall be exalted, and he shall overthrow tens of thousands, but he shall not prevail. [13]For the king of the north shall again raise a multitude, larger than the former, and after some years[x] he shall advance with a great army and abundant supplies.

14 "In those times many shall rise against the king of the south. The lawless among your own people shall lift themselves up in order to fulfill

10.20 Slow to Answer Prayer

These comments come from what seems to be an angelic messenger. They hint at heavenly warfare human beings know little about. When prayers go unanswered for long periods, more may be involved than we ever dream.

[v] Gk Theodotion: Heb *I was left there with the kings of Persia times years* [w] Gk: Heb *from now* [x] Heb *and at the end of the*

the vision, but they shall fail. ¹⁵Then the king of the north shall come and throw up siegeworks, and take a well-fortified city. And the forces of the south shall not stand, not even his picked troops, for there shall be no strength to resist. ¹⁶But he who comes against him shall take the actions he pleases, and no one shall withstand him. He shall take a position in the beautiful land, and all of it shall be in his power. ¹⁷He shall set his mind to come with the strength of his whole kingdom, and he shall bring terms of peace[y] and perform them. In order to destroy the kingdom,[z]

he shall give him a woman in marriage; but it shall not succeed or be to his advantage. ¹⁸Afterward he shall turn to the coastlands, and shall capture many. But a commander shall put an end to his insolence; indeed,[a] he shall turn his insolence back upon him. ¹⁹Then he shall turn back toward the fortresses of his own land, but he shall stumble and fall, and shall not be found.

20 "Then shall arise in his place one who shall send an official for the glory of the kingdom; but within a few days he shall be broken, though not in anger or in battle. ²¹In his place shall arise a

y Gk: Heb kingdom, and upright ones with him   z Heb it   a Meaning of Heb uncertain

In the Hands of Tyrants
Daniel's visions portray history as one bestial empire after another

> "The king shall act as he pleases. He shall exalt himself and consider himself greater than any god, and shall speak horrendous things against the God of gods."
> 11.36

JOSEF STALIN, HEAD OF THE Soviet Union from 1924 to 1953, murdered millions. His supporters knew that the slightest slip would lead them to the executioner. Of 1,966 delegates to one Party Congress, Stalin had 1,108—all Stalin supporters—arrested and killed. Of the 139 Central Committee members, 98 were shot.

In spite of this, the nation virtually worshiped Stalin. He had made himself a god. Every public park displayed his statue. Every newspaper published lavish tributes daily. For one of his birthdays, an entire museum in Moscow was stripped so it could be filled with his birthday presents. He was called Father of the Peoples, the Greatest Genius in History, the Shining Sun of Humanity, the Life-giving Force of Socialism.

He was not the first, nor the last, of his kind. Increasingly, it seems, totalitarian leaders promise everything—and demand everything. They brutally dispose of anyone who opposes them. Hitler, Stalin, Idi Amin, Chairman Mao, the Ayatollah Khomeini, Saddam Hussein . . . the list grows longer.

A Single, Cruel King

Daniel's visions predicted such tyrants. History, in these visions, is one terrible empire after another. Each is stronger but more bestial than the last.

The focus narrows (in 8.23–25 and 11.21–45) to a single, cruel king. Most scholars agree the description matches Antiochus IV of Syria. An obscure tyrant who ruled a century and a half before Jesus, he was the Jews' worst enemy in history, until Hitler.

Antiochus, never totally victorious against archenemy Egypt, took out his frustrations on little Jerusalem. He determined to make that city Greek rather than Jewish by rooting out its religion. He sold the high priest's position to an opportunist and transformed the temple into an altar for the Greek god Zeus. This desecration sparked one of history's earliest guerrilla wars, the Maccabean revolt that began in 168 B.C. Antiochus conquered Jerusalem twice, slaughtering thousands. He outlawed Judaism and proclaimed himself to be God incarnate.

The End of the Tyrant

And yet, for all his power and terror, Antiochus died raving from insanity, and his mark on history has virtually disappeared. Ironically, the religion he sought to destroy has endured and touched the whole world. This is just what you could expect from reading Daniel. Terrible rulers rise up one after another, but they disappear just as quickly. We can expect political terror. But we can count on God.

The New Testament suggests that Antiochus's brutal pattern will culminate someday in the antichrist, an arrogant leader who will dominate the world and persecute God's people as never before. Many scholars believe that the last part of Daniel's final vision refers to this character. Yet despite the antichrist's power, he too will fall in the end. God's justice will rule the earth. Those who believe in such an outcome have reason to be as brave as Daniel.

*Life Questions:*How does Daniel's view of history affect your perspective on world politics? How should a Christian regard the human "powers-that-be"?

contemptible person on whom royal majesty had not been conferred; he shall come in without warning and obtain the kingdom through intrigue. [22]Armies shall be utterly swept away and broken before him, and the prince of the covenant as well. [23]And after an alliance is made with him, he shall act deceitfully and become strong with a small party. [24]Without warning he shall come into the richest parts[b] of the province and do what none of his predecessors had ever done, lavishing plunder, spoil, and wealth on them. He shall devise plans against strongholds, but only for a time. [25]He shall stir up his power and determination against the king of the south with a great army, and the king of the south shall wage war with a much greater and stronger army. But he shall not succeed, for plots shall be devised against him [26]by those who eat of the royal rations. They shall break him, his army shall be swept away, and many shall fall slain. [27]The two kings, their minds bent on evil, shall sit at one table and exchange lies. But it shall not succeed, for there remains an end at the time appointed. [28]He shall return to his land with great wealth, but his heart shall be set against the holy covenant. He shall work his will, and return to his own land.

29 "At the time appointed he shall return and come into the south, but this time it shall not be as it was before. [30]For ships of Kittim shall come against him, and he shall lose heart and withdraw. He shall be enraged and take action against the holy covenant. He shall turn back and pay heed to those who forsake the holy covenant. [31]Forces sent by him shall occupy and profane the temple and fortress. They shall abolish the regular burnt offering and set up the abomination that makes desolate. [32]He shall seduce with intrigue those who violate the covenant; but the people who are loyal to their God shall stand firm and take action. [33]The wise among the people shall give understanding to many; for some days, however, they shall fall by sword and flame, and suffer captivity and plunder. [34]When they fall victim, they shall receive a little help, and many shall join them insincerely. [35]Some of the wise shall fall, so that they may be refined, purified, and cleansed,[c] until the time of the end, for there is still an interval until the time appointed.

36 "The king shall act as he pleases. He shall exalt himself and consider himself greater than any god, and shall speak horrendous things against the God of gods. He shall prosper until the period of wrath is completed, for what is determined shall be done. [37]He shall pay no respect to the gods of his ancestors, or to the one beloved by women; he shall pay no respect to any other god, for he shall consider himself greater than all. [38]He shall honor the god of fortresses instead of these;

a god whom his ancestors did not know he shall honor with gold and silver, with precious stones and costly gifts. [39]He shall deal with the strongest fortresses by the help of a foreign god. Those who acknowledge him he shall make more wealthy, and shall appoint them as rulers over many, and shall distribute the land for a price.

11.37–45 Exalted above the Gods

The tyrant Antiochus IV, whom most commentators believe is described here, minted many coins showing his portrait. The early coins were merely stamped, "King Antiochus." But, as he grew more obsessed with his own importance, he added features to his portrait that made him look like the Greek gods Apollo or Zeus, and to his given name he appended the title "Epiphanes"—"God Manifest." Such behavior earned him the nickname "Antiochus Epimanes"—"crazy Antiochus."

The Time of the End

40 "At the time of the end the king of the south shall attack him. But the king of the north shall rush upon him like a whirlwind, with chariots and horsemen, and with many ships. He shall advance against countries and pass through like a flood. [41]He shall come into the beautiful land, and tens of thousands shall fall victim, but Edom and Moab and the main part of the Ammonites shall escape from his power. [42]He shall stretch out his hand against the countries, and the land of Egypt shall not escape. [43]He shall become ruler of the treasures of gold and of silver, and all the riches of Egypt; and the Libyans and the Ethiopians[d] shall follow in his train. [44]But reports from the east and the north shall alarm him, and he shall go out with great fury to bring ruin and complete destruction to many. [45]He shall pitch his palatial tents between the sea and the beautiful holy mountain. Yet he shall come to his end, with no one to help him.

The Resurrection of the Dead

12 "At that time Michael, the great prince, the protector of your people, shall arise. There shall be a time of anguish, such as has never occurred since nations first came into existence. But at that time your people shall be delivered, everyone who is found written in the book. [2]Many of those who sleep in the dust of the earth[e] shall awake, some to everlasting life, and some to shame and everlasting contempt. [3]Those who are wise shall shine like the brightness of the sky,[f] and those who lead many to righteousness, like

---

[b] Or *among the richest men*   [c] Heb *made them white*   [d] Or Nubians; Heb *Cushites*   [e] Or *the land of dust*
[f] Or *dome*

the stars forever and ever. ⁴But you, Daniel, keep the words secret and the book sealed until the time of the end. Many shall be running back and forth, and evil⁸ shall increase."

5 Then I, Daniel, looked, and two others appeared, one standing on this bank of the stream and one on the other. ⁶One of them said to the man clothed in linen, who was upstream, "How long shall it be until the end of these wonders?" ⁷The man clothed in linen, who was upstream, raised his right hand and his left hand toward

heaven. And I heard him swear by the one who lives forever that it would be for a time, two times, and half a time,ʰ and that when the shattering of the power of the holy people comes to an end, all these things would be accomplished. ⁸I heard but could not understand; so I said, "My lord, what shall be the outcome of these things?" ⁹He said, "Go your way, Daniel, for the words are to remain secret and sealed until the time of the end. ¹⁰Many shall be purified, cleansed, and refined, but the wicked shall continue to act wickedly. None of the wicked shall understand, but those who are wise shall understand. ¹¹From the time that the regular burnt offering is taken away and the abomination that desolates is set up, there shall be one thousand two hundred ninety days. ¹²Happy are those who persevere and attain the thousand three hundred thirty-five days. ¹³But you, go your way,ⁱ and rest; you shall rise for your reward at the end of the days."

---

g Cn Compare Gk: Heb *knowledge*   h Heb *a time, times, and a half*   i Gk Theodotion: Heb adds *to the end*

HOSEA

Tearing God's Heart
Why would he love such a woman?

HOSEA BEGINS WITH A LOVE story—a painful, personal love story, the prophet's very own. Hosea had married a woman who acted like a prostitute. Yet the more she went out on him, the more Hosea loved her. He gave her everything a good wife deserved: his love, his home, his name, his reputation. She responded by sleeping around with other men. He warned her, he pleaded with her, he punished her. She humiliated him until he wanted to cry, yet still he clung to her.

> She ... decked herself with her ring and jewelry, and went after her lovers, and forgot me, says the LORD.
> 2.13

Why did Hosea begin with his personal life? Because God had expressly told him to relate it to another, more tragic love story: the painful love of God for his people. God could have simply declared, "Israel is like a wife to me—an adulterous wife." Instead, he used Hosea to act out the treachery in real life—and to show in living color God's fury, his jealousy, and above all else, his love for his people.

Winding Down to a Bitter End

Virtually every chapter of Hosea talks about the "whoredom" or "adultery" of God's people (1.2; 2.2,4; 3.1; 4.2,10–15,18; 5.3–4; 6.10; 7.4; 8.9; 9.1). Underlying some hard words is a remarkably tender revelation: God doesn't want to be only "master" to his people. He wants to be a husband, giving all of himself in intimate love.

Hosea spoke and acted these messages to the northern part of God's divided country—Israel or "Ephraim," as Hosea sometimes called it. King Jeroboam II's reign was a time of prosperity; the prophet Amos blasted the rich for their greedy injustices toward the poor. But soon after Jeroboam's death the national fabric began to unravel. In just over 20 years six kings took the throne—four of them by murdering the previous king. Hosea probably lived to see the massive Assyrian armies storm the capital and deport all the Israelite citizens to other lands. God's "wife" was carried off, just as he had warned.

God Is a Lover

When most people must have been preoccupied with politics and military matters, Hosea kept his message aimed at idol worship, which he referred to as adultery. He saw that as the root of Israel's problems.

Israel tended to mix religions freely—to think that everybody's religion had a little truth in it, and the more religion you got, the better off you would be. Many prophets attacked Israel's idol worship. Hosea shows that God's concern about idolatry is no fussy, religious matter. It is terribly personal. God, the lover, will not share his bride with anyone else.

God's anger and jealousy, expressed so often throughout the Old Testament, reflect his powerful love. Sin does not merely break God's law, it breaks his heart. He punishes to get his lover's attention. Yet even when she turns her back on him, he sticks with her. He is willing to suffer, in the hope that someday she will change. Hosea shows that God longs not to punish, but to love.

How to Read Hosea

Hosea is one of the most emotional books in the Bible, an outpouring of suffering love from God's heart. This shows in the writing, which jumps impulsively from one thought to the next. Read a chapter dramatically aloud, and you will get this sense. It is almost like listening in on a husband-and-wife fight.

The book divides into two parts. In the first three chapters, the prophet Hosea briefly describes his marriage to an adulterous woman and makes the connection to Israel's unfaithfulness to God. From chapter 4 onward this dramatic, personal beginning is not mentioned again. But it has set the stage. God's deep love, his disappointment and anger, and his determination to persevere with his unfaithful wife pour out in a series of vivid speeches.

For a historical perspective on Hosea's times, read from 2 Kings 14.23 to 17.41, noting that some sections describe Judah, the southern nation, while the rest relate to the deteriorating Israel Hosea knew. This history is summarized in 'A Lineup of Rulers,' pages 1349–1357. The prophet Amos spoke to the North at about the same time as Hosea, but from a noticeably different point of view. Amos concentrated on law and justice, with special concern for the poor, while Hosea concentrated on the broken relationship with God that led to this injustice. Together, these two prophets provide a three-dimensional view of Israel's problems.

Because Hosea is so emotional, he doesn't stop to explain a large number of images or biblical references. A Bible dictionary will help you understand the names and places you aren't familiar with.

3-TRACK READING PLAN

For an explanation and complete listing of the 3-track reading plan, turn to page 7.

TRACK 1: *Two-Week Courses on the Bible*
See page 7 for information on these courses.

TRACK 2: *An Overview of Hosea in 2 Days*
☐ Day 1. Read the Introduction to Hosea and chapters 2 and 3, which compare Hosea's marriage to Israel's relationship with God.
☐ Day 2. Read chapter 11, which shows God's powerful, competing emotions as he thinks of Israel.

Now turn to page 9 for your next Track 2 reading project.

TRACK 3: *All of Hosea in 10 Days*
After you have read through Hosea, turn to pages 10–14 for your next Track 3 reading project.

☐1   ☐2–3   ☐4   ☐5   ☐6–7   ☐8   ☐9   ☐10
☐11–12   ☐13–14

1 The word of the LORD that came to Hosea son of Beeri, in the days of Kings Uzziah, Jotham, Ahaz, and Hezekiah of Judah, and in the days of King Jeroboam son of Joash of Israel.

The Family of Hosea

2 When the LORD first spoke through Hosea, the LORD said to Hosea, "Go, take for yourself a wife of whoredom and have children of whoredom, for the land commits great whoredom by forsaking the LORD." ³So he went and took Gomer daughter of Diblaim, and she conceived and bore him a son.

4 And the LORD said to him, "Name him Jezreel;[a] for in a little while I will punish the house of Jehu for the blood of Jezreel, and I will put an end to the kingdom of the house of Israel. ⁵On that day I will break the bow of Israel in the valley of Jezreel."

6 She conceived again and bore a daughter. Then the LORD said to him, "Name her Loruhamah,[b] for I will no longer have pity on the house of Israel or forgive them. ⁷But I will have pity on the house of Judah, and I will save them by the LORD their God; I will not save them by bow, or by sword, or by war, or by horses, or by horsemen."

8 When she had weaned Lo-ruhamah, she conceived and bore a son. ⁹Then the LORD said, "Name him Lo-ammi,[c] for you are not my people and I am not your God."[d]

The Restoration of Israel

10[e] Yet the number of the people of Israel shall be like the sand of the sea, which can be neither measured nor numbered; and in the place where it was said to them, "You are not my people," it shall be said to them, "Children of the living God." ¹¹The people of Judah and the people of Israel shall be gathered together, and they shall appoint for themselves one head; and they shall

---

[a] That is *God sows*   [b] That is *Not pitied*   [c] That is *Not my people*   [d] Heb *I am not yours*   [e] Ch 2.1 in Heb

take possession of^f the land, for great shall be the day of Jezreel.

2 ^{g} Say to your brother,^{h} Ammi,^{i} and to your sister,^{j} Ruhamah.^{k}

1.4 Children's Strange Names

At God's direction, Hosea named his three children in a way that symbolized God's anger. Their names show God's increasing judgment against Israel's adultery: first comes punishment, then a loss of love, finally total divorce. The first name, Jezreel, refers to a historical incident from 2 Kings 9–10. Jezreel was the place where King Jehu slaughtered a wicked king and all his associates (2 Kings 10.11). Hosea lived to see his prediction of punishment on Jehu's house fulfilled, when the last king in Jehu's line was murdered 2 Kings 15.8–12).

Punishment, however, was not the last word. Jezreel has a double meaning—both to "scatter" and to "sow." In verse 11 and in verses 22–23 of chapter 2, Jezreel takes on the hopeful sense of planting new life. Hosea's other two children's names are similarly turned from curses to blessings. God's anger leads to new life.

Israel's Infidelity, Punishment, and Redemption

2 Plead with your mother, plead—
  for she is not my wife,
  and I am not her husband—
that she put away her whoring from her
  face,
  and her adultery from between her
  breasts,
3 or I will strip her naked
  and expose her as in the day she was
  born,
and make her like a wilderness,
  and turn her into a parched land,
  and kill her with thirst.
4 Upon her children also I will
  have no pity,
  because they are children of
  whoredom.
5 For their mother has played the whore;
  she who conceived them has acted
  shamefully.
For she said, "I will go after my lovers;
  they give me my bread and my water,
  my wool and my flax, my oil and my
  drink."
6 Therefore I will hedge up her^l way with
  thorns;

and I will build a wall against her,
  so that she cannot find her paths.
7 She shall pursue her lovers,
  but not overtake them;
and she shall seek them,
  but shall not find them.
Then she shall say, "I will go
  and return to my first husband,
  for it was better with me then than now."
8 She did not know
  that it was I who gave her
  the grain, the wine, and the oil,
and who lavished upon her silver
  and gold that they used for Baal.
9 Therefore I will take back
  my grain in its time,
  and my wine in its season;
and I will take away my wool and my
  flax,
  which were to cover her nakedness.
10 Now I will uncover her shame
  in the sight of her lovers,
  and no one shall rescue her out of my
  hand.
11 I will put an end to all her mirth,
  her festivals, her new moons, her
  sabbaths,
  and all her appointed festivals.
12 I will lay waste her vines and her fig trees,
  of which she said,
"These are my pay,
  which my lovers have given me."
I will make them a forest,
  and the wild animals shall devour
  them.
13 I will punish her for the festival days of
  the Baals,
  when she offered incense to them
and decked herself with her ring and
  jewelry,
  and went after her lovers,
  and forgot me, says the LORD.

14 Therefore, I will now allure her,
  and bring her into the wilderness,
  and speak tenderly to her.
15 From there I will give her her vineyards,
  and make the Valley of Achor a door
  of hope.
There she shall respond as in the days of
  her youth,
  as at the time when she came out of
  the land of Egypt.
16On that day, says the LORD, you will call me, "My husband," and no longer will you call me, "My Baal."^{m} 17For I will remove the names of the

---

^{f} Heb *rise up from* ^{g} Ch 2.3 in Heb ^{h} Gk: Heb *brothers* ^{i} That is *My people* ^{j} Gk Vg: Heb *sisters*
^{k} That is *Pitied* ^{l} Gk Syr: Heb *your* ^{m} That is, "*My master*"

Baals from her mouth, and they shall be mentioned by name no more. [18]I will make for you[n] a covenant on that day with the wild animals, the birds of the air, and the creeping things of the ground; and I will abolish[o] the bow, the sword, and war from the land; and I will make you lie down in safety. [19]And I will take you for my wife forever; I will take you for my wife in righteousness and in justice, in steadfast love, and in mercy. [20]I will take you for my wife in faithfulness; and you shall know the LORD.

[21] On that day I will answer, says the LORD,
    I will answer the heavens
      and they shall answer the earth;
[22] and the earth shall answer the grain, the
          wine, and the oil,
      and they shall answer Jezreel;[p]
[23]   and I will sow him[q] for myself in the
          land.
    And I will have pity on Lo-ruhamah,[r]
      and I will say to Lo-ammi,[s] "You are
          my people";
    and he shall say, "You are my God."

Further Assurances of God's Redeeming Love

3 The LORD said to me again, "Go, love a woman who has a lover and is an adulteress, just as the LORD loves the people of Israel, though they

3.1 Parable of Love

No other prophet lived out an object lesson with quite the same emotional force as Hosea did. Gomer had sunk so low as to sell herself into slavery, but Hosea purchased her back and reclaimed her as his wife. That remarkable deed, certainly the subject of his countrymen's gossip, symbolized God's undying love for his people. Though they had dragged his name in the mud, still he welcomed them back.

turn to other gods and love raisin cakes." [2]So I bought her for fifteen shekels of silver and a homer of barley and a measure of wine.[t] [3]And I said to her, "You must remain as mine for many days; you shall not play the whore, you shall not have intercourse with a man, nor I with you." [4]For the Israelites shall remain many days without king or prince, without sacrifice or pillar, without ephod or teraphim. [5]Afterward the Israelites shall return and seek the LORD their God, and David their king; they shall come in awe to the LORD and to his goodness in the latter days.

God Accuses Israel

4 Hear the word of the LORD, O people of
      Israel;
    for the LORD has an indictment against
        the inhabitants of the land.
  There is no faithfulness or loyalty,
    and no knowledge of God in the land.
[2] Swearing, lying, and murder,
    and stealing and adultery break out;
    bloodshed follows bloodshed.
[3] Therefore the land mourns,
    and all who live in it languish;
  together with the wild animals
    and the birds of the air,
    even the fish of the sea are perishing.

[4] Yet let no one contend,
    and let none accuse,
  for with you is my contention,
        O priest.[u]
[5] You shall stumble by day;
    the prophet also shall stumble with you
        by night,
    and I will destroy your mother.
[6] My people are destroyed for lack of
        knowledge;
    because you have rejected knowledge,
    I reject you from being a priest to me.
  And since you have forgotten the law of
        your God,
    I also will forget your children.

[7] The more they increased,
    the more they sinned against me;
    they changed[v] their glory into shame.

4.7 Poor Trade

Early in its history, the Northern Kingdom of Israel began appointing its own priests from ineligible tribes (1 Kings 12.31). These priests led the people in the worship of golden calves—idols—instead of in the worship of the God of Abraham and Moses. This verse has an echo in Romans 1.23, where Paul blasts pagans who exchange the glory of immortal God for mere statues of birds, animals, and reptiles.

[8] They feed on the sin of my people;
    they are greedy for their iniquity.
[9] And it shall be like people, like priest;
    I will punish them for their ways,
    and repay them for their deeds.
[10] They shall eat, but not be satisfied;
    they shall play the whore, but not
        multiply;

---

[n] Heb *them*   [o] Heb *break*   [p] That is *God sows*   [q] Cn: Heb *her*   [r] That is *Not pitied*   [s] That is *Not my people*   [t] Gk: Heb *a homer of barley and a lethech of barley*   [u] Cn: Meaning of Heb uncertain   [v] Ancient Heb tradition: MT *I will change*

because they have forsaken the LORD
to devote themselves to [11]whoredom.

The Idolatry of Israel

Wine and new wine
take away the understanding.
12 My people consult a piece of wood,
and their divining rod gives
them oracles.
For a spirit of whoredom has led them
astray,
and they have played the whore,
forsaking their God.
13 They sacrifice on the tops of the
mountains,
and make offerings upon the hills,
under oak, poplar, and terebinth,
because their shade is good.

Therefore your daughters play the whore,
and your daughters-in-law commit
adultery.

4.13 Real Prostitution

*In each of the first nine chapters of his book,
Hosea describes Israel's sin as prostitution or
adultery. This is primarily symbolism meant to
emphasize God's deep, personal love for Israel
and his pain when the Israelites desert him to
go after other gods.*

*But prostitution has a literal meaning also.
The religions Israel pursued taught that human
sexuality was tied to agricultural fertility. To
encourage good crops, believers in these
religions practiced their human fertility. This
meant organized prostitution, done as part of
their worship experience.*

14 I will not punish your daughters when
they play the whore,
nor your daughters-in-law when they
commit adultery;
for the men themselves go aside with
whores,
and sacrifice with temple prostitutes;
thus a people without understanding
comes to ruin.

15 Though you play the whore, O Israel,
do not let Judah become guilty.
Do not enter into Gilgal,
or go up to Beth-aven,
and do not swear, "As the LORD lives."
16 Like a stubborn heifer,
Israel is stubborn;

can the LORD now feed them
like a lamb in a broad pasture?

17 Ephraim is joined to idols—
let him alone.
18 When their drinking is ended, they
indulge in sexual orgies;
they love lewdness more than their
glory.[w]
19 A wind has wrapped them[x] in its wings,
and they shall be ashamed because of
their altars.[y]

Impending Judgment on Israel and Judah

5 Hear this, O priests!
Give heed, O house of Israel!
Listen, O house of the king!
For the judgment pertains to you;
for you have been a snare at Mizpah,
and a net spread upon Tabor,
2 and a pit dug deep in Shittim;[z]
but I will punish all of them.

3 I know Ephraim,
and Israel is not hidden from me;
for now, O Ephraim, you have played the
whore;
Israel is defiled.
4 Their deeds do not permit them
to return to their God.
For the spirit of whoredom is within
them,
and they do not know the LORD.

5 Israel's pride testifies against him;
Ephraim[a] stumbles in his guilt;
Judah also stumbles with them.
6 With their flocks and herds they shall go
to seek the LORD,
but they will not find him;
he has withdrawn from them.
7 They have dealt faithlessly with the LORD;
for they have borne illegitimate
children.
Now the new moon shall devour them
along with their fields.

8 Blow the horn in Gibeah,
the trumpet in Ramah.
Sound the alarm at Beth-aven;
look behind you, Benjamin!
9 Ephraim shall become a desolation
in the day of punishment;
among the tribes of Israel
I declare what is sure.
10 The princes of Judah have become
like those who remove the landmark;
on them I will pour out

---

w Cn Compare Gk: Meaning of Heb uncertain   x Heb *her*   y Gk Syr: Heb *sacrifices*   z Cn: Meaning of Heb
uncertain   a Heb *Israel and Ephraim*

my wrath like water.
11 Ephraim is oppressed, crushed in
judgment,
because he was determined to go after
vanity.*b*
12 Therefore I am like maggots to Ephraim,
and like rottenness to the house of
Judah.
13 When Ephraim saw his sickness,
and Judah his wound,
then Ephraim went to Assyria,
and sent to the great king.*c*
But he is not able to cure you
or heal your wound.
14 For I will be like a lion to Ephraim,
and like a young lion to the house of
Judah.
I myself will tear and go away;
I will carry off, and no one
shall rescue.
15 I will return again to my place
until they acknowledge their guilt and
seek my face.
In their distress they will beg my favor:

A Call to Repentance

6 "Come, let us return to the LORD;
for it is he who has torn, and he will
heal us;
he has struck down, and he will bind
us up.
2 After two days he will revive us;
on the third day he will raise us up,
that we may live before him.
3 Let us know, let us press on to know the
LORD;
his appearing is as sure as the dawn;
he will come to us like the showers,
like the spring rains that water the
earth."

Impenitence of Israel and Judah

4 What shall I do with you, O Ephraim?
What shall I do with you, O Judah?
Your love is like a morning cloud,
like the dew that goes away early.
5 Therefore I have hewn them by the
prophets,
I have killed them by the words of my
mouth,
and my*d* judgment goes forth as the
light.
6 For I desire steadfast love and not
sacrifice,
the knowledge of God rather than
burnt offerings.

7 But at*e* Adam they transgressed the
covenant;
there they dealt faithlessly with me.
8 Gilead is a city of evildoers,
tracked with blood.
9 As robbers lie in wait*f* for someone,
so the priests are banded together;*g*
they murder on the road to Shechem,
they commit a monstrous crime.
10 In the house of Israel I have seen a
horrible thing;
Ephraim's whoredom is there, Israel is
defiled.
11 For you also, O Judah, a harvest
is appointed.

When I would restore the fortunes of my
people,
7 1 when I would heal Israel,
the corruption of Ephraim is revealed,
and the wicked deeds of Samaria;
for they deal falsely,
the thief breaks in,
and the bandits raid outside.
2 But they do not consider
that I remember all their wickedness.
Now their deeds surround them,
they are before my face.
3 By their wickedness they make the king
glad,
and the officials by their treachery.
4 They are all adulterers;
they are like a heated oven,
whose baker does not need to stir the fire,
from the kneading of the dough until it
is leavened.

7.4 Smoldering Passion

In parts of the Middle East, ovens are made of clay and shaped like a large cone or beehive. The baker builds a fire inside and tends it until the clay gets very hot. Then, fire and wood ash can be pulled out and the fresh dough placed inside. It rises due to the heat contained inside the oven, which stays hot long after the fire has been removed. Such was Israel's lust for other gods: It kept on smoldering, like a self-fueling oven (verse 6).

5 On the day of our king the officials
became sick with the heat of wine;
he stretched out his hand with
mockers.
6 For they are kindled*h* like an oven, their
heart burns within them;

---

b Gk: Meaning of Heb uncertain   *c* Cn: Heb *to a king who will contend*   *d* Gk Syr: Heb *your*   *e* Cn: Heb *like*
f Cn: Meaning of Heb uncertain   *g* Syr: Heb *are a company*   *h* Gk Syr: Heb *brought near*

all night their anger smolders;
  in the morning it blazes like a flaming
    fire.
7 All of them are hot as an oven,
    and they devour their rulers.
  All their kings have fallen;
    none of them calls upon me.

8 Ephraim mixes himself with the peoples;
    Ephraim is a cake not turned.
9 Foreigners devour his strength,
    but he does not know it;
  gray hairs are sprinkled upon him,
    but he does not know it.
10 Israel's pride testifies against[i] him;
    yet they do not return to the LORD
      their God,
    or seek him, for all this.

Futile Reliance on the Nations

11 Ephraim has become like a dove,
    silly and without sense;
  they call upon Egypt, they go
    to Assyria.
12 As they go, I will cast my net over them;
    I will bring them down like birds of
      the air;
  I will discipline them according to the
    report made to their assembly.[j]
13 Woe to them, for they have strayed from
      me!
  Destruction to them, for they have
    rebelled against me!
  I would redeem them,
    but they speak lies against me.

14 They do not cry to me from the heart,
    but they wail upon their beds;
  they gash themselves for grain and wine;
    they rebel against me.
15 It was I who trained and strengthened
      their arms,
    yet they plot evil against me.
16 They turn to that which does not profit;[k]
    they have become like a defective bow;
  their officials shall fall by the sword
    because of the rage of their tongue.
  So much for their babbling in the land of
    Egypt.

Israel's Apostasy

8 Set the trumpet to your lips!
    One like a vulture[j] is over the house
      of the LORD,
  because they have broken my covenant,
    and transgressed my law.
2 Israel cries to me,
    "My God, we—Israel—know you!"

3 Israel has spurned the good;
    the enemy shall pursue him.

4 They made kings, but not through me;
    they set up princes, but without my
      knowledge.
  With their silver and gold they made idols
    for their own destruction.
5 Your calf is rejected, O Samaria.
    My anger burns against them.
  How long will they be incapable of
    innocence?
6   For it is from Israel,
  an artisan made it;
    it is not God.
  The calf of Samaria
    shall be broken to pieces.[l]

7 For they sow the wind,
    and they shall reap the whirlwind.
  The standing grain has no heads,
    it shall yield no meal;
  if it were to yield,
    foreigners would devour it.
8 Israel is swallowed up;
    now they are among the nations
      as a useless vessel.
9 For they have gone up to Assyria,
    a wild ass wandering alone;
  Ephraim has bargained for lovers.
10 Though they bargain with the nations,
    I will now gather them up.
  They shall soon writhe
    under the burden of kings and princes.

11 When Ephraim multiplied altars
      to expiate sin,
    they became to him altars for sinning.

8.11 How to Be Religious Without Pleasing God

The Israelites didn't think they were rejecting God. In fact, they became increasingly pious. (See 6.1–3; 8.2,11,13; and 10.1 for their expressions of faith.) But they wanted to worship on their terms, not God's. While their sacrifices to God increased, they kept on worshiping idols as well.

12 Though I write for him the multitude of
      my instructions,
    they are regarded as a strange thing.
13 Though they offer choice sacrifices,[k]
    though they eat flesh,
    the LORD does not accept them.
  Now he will remember their iniquity,
    and punish their sins;

they shall return to Egypt.
14 Israel has forgotten his Maker,
    and built palaces;
and Judah has multiplied fortified cities;
    but I will send a fire upon his cities,
    and it shall devour his strongholds.

Punishment for Israel's Sin

9 Do not rejoice, O Israel!
    Do not exult[m] as other nations do;
for you have played the whore, departing
        from your God.
    You have loved a prostitute's pay
        on all threshing floors.
2 Threshing floor and wine vat shall not
        feed them,
    and the new wine shall fail them.
3 They shall not remain in the land of the
        LORD;
    but Ephraim shall return to Egypt,
    and in Assyria they shall eat unclean
        food.

4 They shall not pour drink offerings of
        wine to the LORD,
    and their sacrifices shall not please
        him.
    Such sacrifices shall be like mourners'
        bread;
    all who eat of it shall be defiled;
for their bread shall be for their hunger
        only;
    it shall not come to the house of the
        LORD.

5 What will you do on the day of appointed
        festival,
    and on the day of the festival of the
        LORD?
6 For even if they escape destruction,
    Egypt shall gather them,
    Memphis shall bury them.
Nettles shall possess their precious things
        of silver;[n]
    thorns shall be in their tents.

7 The days of punishment have come,
    the days of recompense have come;
    Israel cries,[o]
"The prophet is a fool,
    the man of the spirit is mad!"
Because of your great iniquity,
    your hostility is great.
8 The prophet is a sentinel for my God
        over Ephraim,
    yet a fowler's snare is on all his ways,
    and hostility in the house of his God.
9 They have deeply corrupted themselves
    as in the days of Gibeah;

he will remember their iniquity,
    he will punish their sins.

10 Like grapes in the wilderness,
    I found Israel.

9.9 Two Instances of Evil

The "days of Gibeah" evidently refers to the vicious murder of a woman, told in Judges 19–21. This horrifying incident was a version of Sodom and Gomorrah right in Israel. Another incident (verse 10), equally bad in its own way, occurred at Baal Peor (see Numbers 25.1–3). Israelite men en route to the promised land slept with Moabite women and worshiped their gods. From both these incidents, Hosea proves that sin is nothing new to Israel.

Like the first fruit on the fig tree,
    in its first season,
    I saw your ancestors.
But they came to Baal-peor,
    and consecrated themselves to a thing
        of shame,
    and became detestable like the thing
        they loved.
11 Ephraim's glory shall fly away like a
        bird—
    no birth, no pregnancy, no conception!
12 Even if they bring up children,
    I will bereave them until no one is left.
Woe to them indeed
    when I depart from them!
13 Once I saw Ephraim as a young palm
        planted in a lovely meadow,[n]
    but now Ephraim must lead out his
        children for slaughter.
14 Give them, O LORD—
    what will you give?
Give them a miscarrying womb
    and dry breasts.

15 Every evil of theirs began at Gilgal;
    there I came to hate them.
Because of the wickedness of their deeds
    I will drive them out of my house.
I will love them no more;
    all their officials are rebels.

16 Ephraim is stricken,
    their root is dried up,
    they shall bear no fruit.
Even though they give birth,
    I will kill the cherished offspring of
        their womb.
17 Because they have not listened to him,
    my God will reject them;

---

[m] Gk: Heb *To exultation*   [n] Meaning of Heb uncertain   [o] Cn Compare Gk: Heb *shall know*

they shall become wanderers among
the nations.

Israel's Sin and Captivity

10 Israel is a luxuriant vine
that yields its fruit.
The more his fruit increased
the more altars he built;
as his country improved,
he improved his pillars.
2 Their heart is false;
now they must bear their guilt.
The LORD *p* will break down their altars,
and destroy their pillars.

3 For now they will say:
"We have no king,
for we do not fear the LORD,
and a king—what could he do for us?"
4 They utter mere words;
with empty oaths they make covenants;
so litigation springs up like poisonous
weeds
in the furrows of the field.
5 The inhabitants of Samaria tremble
for the calf*q* of Beth-aven.
Its people shall mourn for it,
and its idolatrous priests shall wail*r*
over it,
over its glory that has departed from it.

10.5 The New Golden Calf

*Beth-aven ("house of wickedness") is a
sarcastic reference to Bethel ("house of God"),
which is mentioned more times in the Bible
than any other city except Jerusalem. When
Israel split into North and South, the northern
king, Jeroboam I, made Bethel the chief
religious sanctuary, to replace Jerusalem.
There he put up a golden calf for people to
worship (1 Kings 12.26–30). Mixing worship of
the one true God with the idol worship of Baal
was, according to Hosea, the root of Israel's
trouble.*

6 The thing itself shall be carried to Assyria
as tribute to the great king.*s*
Ephraim shall be put to shame,
and Israel shall be ashamed of his
idol.*t*

7 Samaria's king shall perish
like a chip on the face of the waters.
8 The high places of Aven, the sin of Israel,
shall be destroyed.
Thorn and thistle shall grow up

on their altars.
They shall say to the mountains, Cover
us,
and to the hills, Fall on us.

9 Since the days of Gibeah you have sinned,
O Israel;
there they have continued.
Shall not war overtake them in Gibeah?
10 I will come*u* against the wayward people
to punish them;
and nations shall be gathered against
them
when they are punished*v* for their
double iniquity.
11 Ephraim was a trained heifer
that loved to thresh,
and I spared her fair neck;
but I will make Ephraim break the
ground;
Judah must plow;
Jacob must harrow for himself.
12 Sow for yourselves righteousness;
reap steadfast love;
break up your fallow ground;
for it is time to seek the LORD,
that he may come and rain
righteousness upon you.
13 You have plowed wickedness,
you have reaped injustice,
you have eaten the fruit of lies.
Because you have trusted in your power
and in the multitude of your warriors,
14 therefore the tumult of war shall rise
against your people,
and all your fortresses shall
be destroyed,
as Shalman destroyed Beth-arbel on the
day of battle
when mothers were dashed in pieces
with their children.
15 Thus it shall be done to you, O Bethel,
because of your great wickedness.
At dawn the king of Israel
shall be utterly cut off.

God's Compassion Despite Israel's Ingratitude

11 When Israel was a child, I loved him,
and out of Egypt I called my son.
2 The more I*w* called them,
the more they went from me;*x*
they kept sacrificing to the Baals,
and offering incense to idols.
3 Yet it was I who taught Ephraim to walk,

---

p Heb *he*   *q* Gk Syr: Heb *calves*   *r* Cn: Heb *exult*   *s* Cn: Heb *to a king who will contend*   *t* Cn: Heb *counsel*
u Cn Compare Gk: Heb *In my desire*   *v* Gk: Heb *bound*   *w* Gk: Heb *they*   *x* Gk: Heb *them*

I took them up in my[y] arms;
but they did not know that I healed
them.
4 I led them with cords of human kindness,
with bands of love.
I was to them like those
who lift infants to their cheeks.[z]
I bent down to them and fed them.

11.1 Rebel Son

God has already illustrated his unquenchable love for Israel through the real-life parable of Hosea and his unfaithful wife. Now he introduces yet another picture: a rebellious son. According to the laws of Deuteronomy, a rebel son could be sentenced to death by stoning (Deuteronomy 21.18–21). But God cannot make himself carry out that sentence (verses 8–9). He gives his people one more chance.

5 They shall return to the land of Egypt,
and Assyria shall be their king,
because they have refused to return to
me.
6 The sword rages in their cities,
it consumes their oracle-priests,
and devours because of their schemes.
7 My people are bent on turning away from
me.
To the Most High they call,
but he does not raise them up at all.[a]

8 How can I give you up, Ephraim?
How can I hand you over, O Israel?
How can I make you like Admah?
How can I treat you like Zeboiim?
My heart recoils within me;
my compassion grows warm
and tender.
9 I will not execute my fierce anger;
I will not again destroy Ephraim;
for I am God and no mortal,
the Holy One in your midst,
and I will not come in wrath.[a]

10 They shall go after the LORD,
who roars like a lion;
when he roars,
his children shall come trembling from
the west.
11 They shall come trembling like birds from
Egypt,
and like doves from the land of
Assyria;

and I will return them to their homes,
says the LORD.

12b Ephraim has surrounded me with lies,
and the house of Israel with deceit;
but Judah still walks[c] with God,
and is faithful to the Holy One.

12 Ephraim herds the wind,
and pursues the east wind all day long;
they multiply falsehood and violence;
they make a treaty with Assyria,
and oil is carried to Egypt.

The Long History of Rebellion

2 The LORD has an indictment against
Judah,
and will punish Jacob according to his
ways,
and repay him according to his deeds.

12.2 Jacob, a Man and a Country

"Israel" was a nation named after a man—a man also known as Jacob, whose story is told principally in Genesis 25–35. He was greedy and grasping, and he went into exile for it. Yet he had another side: an eagerness to meet God and he blessed by him, culminating in his nighttime "wrestling with God" (Genesis 32). Though Jacob went into exile, as would Israel, he came back with God's blessing on his future. So, Hosea suggests, could the nation that carried his name.

3 In the womb he tried to supplant his
brother,
and in his manhood he strove with
God.
4 He strove with the angel and prevailed,
he wept and sought his favor;
he met him at Bethel,
and there he spoke with him.[d]
5 The LORD the God of hosts,
the LORD is his name!
6 But as for you, return to your God,
hold fast to love and justice,
and wait continually for your God.

7 A trader, in whose hands are false
balances,
he loves to oppress.
8 Ephraim has said, "Ah, I am rich,
I have gained wealth for myself;
in all of my gain
no offense has been found in me
that would be sin."[a]
9 I am the LORD your God

---

[y] Gk Syr Vg: Heb *his*   [z] Or *who ease the yoke on their jaws*   [a] Meaning of Heb uncertain   [b] Ch 12.1 in Heb
[c] Heb *roams* or *rules*   [d] Gk Syr: Heb *us*

from the land of Egypt;
I will make you live in tents again,
  as in the days of the appointed festival.

10 I spoke to the prophets;
  it was I who multiplied visions,
  and through the prophets I will bring
    destruction.
11 In Gilead[e] there is iniquity,
  they shall surely come to nothing.
In Gilgal they sacrifice bulls,
  so their altars shall be like stone heaps
    on the furrows of the field.
12 Jacob fled to the land of Aram,
  there Israel served for a wife,
  and for a wife he guarded sheep.[f]
13 By a prophet the LORD brought Israel up
    from Egypt,
  and by a prophet he was guarded.
14 Ephraim has given bitter offense,
  so his Lord will bring his crimes down
    on him
  and pay him back for his insults.

Relentless Judgment on Israel

13 When Ephraim spoke, there was
      trembling;
  he was exalted in Israel;
  but he incurred guilt through Baal and
    died.
2 And now they keep on sinning
    and make a cast image for themselves,
  idols of silver made according to their
    understanding,
  all of them the work of artisans.
"Sacrifice to these," they say.[g]
  People are kissing calves!
3 Therefore they shall be like the morning
    mist
  or like the dew that goes away early,
like chaff that swirls from the threshing
    floor
  or like smoke from a window.

4 Yet I have been the LORD your God

ever since the land of Egypt;
you know no God but me,
  and besides me there is no savior.
5 It was I who fed[h] you in the wilderness,
  in the land of drought.
6 When I fed[i] them, they were satisfied;
  they were satisfied, and their heart was
    proud;
  therefore they forgot me.
7 So I will become like a lion to them,
  like a leopard I will lurk beside the
    way.
8 I will fall upon them like a bear robbed of
      her cubs,
  and will tear open the covering
    of their heart;
there I will devour them like a lion,
  as a wild animal would mangle them.

9 I will destroy you, O Israel;
  who can help you?[j]
10 Where now is[k] your king, that he may
      save you?
  Where in all your cities are your rulers,
of whom you said,
  "Give me a king and rulers"?
11 I gave you a king in my anger,
  and I took him away in my wrath.

12 Ephraim's iniquity is bound up;
  his sin is kept in store.
13 The pangs of childbirth come for him,
  but he is an unwise son;
for at the proper time he does not present
    himself
  at the mouth of the womb.

14 Shall I ransom them from the power of
      Sheol?
  Shall I redeem them from Death?
O Death, where are[l] your plagues?
  O Sheol, where is[l] your destruction?
  Compassion is hidden from my eyes.

15 Although he may flourish among rushes,[m]
    the east wind shall come, a blast from
      the LORD,
  rising from the wilderness;
and his fountain shall dry up,
  his spring shall be parched.
It shall strip his treasury
  of every precious thing.
16[n] Samaria shall bear her guilt,
  because she has rebelled against her
      God;
  they shall fall by the sword,

13.3 As Reliable as the Wind

The fruitlessness of Israel's deeds is beautifully expressed in the metaphor of wind: They feed on it, they pursue it all day (12.1), they sow it, and they reap the whirlwind (8.7). Their love is like the morning mist, or dew (6.4), and their lives will be as lasting as the early dew or as chaff or as smoke escaping out of a window (13.3).

---

[e] Compare Syr: Heb *Gilead*   [f] Heb lacks *sheep*   [g] Cn Compare Gk: Heb *To these they say sacrifices of people*
[h] Gk Syr: Heb *knew*   [i] Cn: Heb *according to their pasture*   [j] Gk Syr: Heb *for in me is your help*   [k] Gk Syr Vg:
Heb *I will be*   [l] Gk Syr: Heb *I will be*   [m] Or *among brothers*   [n] Ch 14.1 in Heb

their little ones shall be dashed in
    pieces,
and their pregnant women
    ripped open.

A Plea for Repentance

14 Return, O Israel, to the LORD your God,
    for you have stumbled because of your
    iniquity.
2 Take words with you
    and return to the LORD;
say to him,
    "Take away all guilt;
accept that which is good,
    and we will offer
    the fruit[o] of our lips.
3 Assyria shall not save us;
    we will not ride upon horses;
we will say no more, 'Our God,'
    to the work of our hands.
In you the orphan finds mercy."

Assurance of Forgiveness

4 I will heal their disloyalty;
    I will love them freely,
    for my anger has turned from them.
5 I will be like the dew to Israel;
    he shall blossom like the lily,
he shall strike root like the forests of
    Lebanon.[p]
6 His shoots shall spread out;
    his beauty shall be like the olive tree,
    and his fragrance like that of Lebanon.

7 They shall again live beneath
    my[q] shadow,
they shall flourish as a garden;[r]
they shall blossom like the vine,
    their fragrance shall be like the wine of
    Lebanon.

14.5 New Hope

In its conclusion the book of Hosea, so full of torment, dissolves into a series of serene images of what Israel can become. God compares the nation to a lily (beauty), a cedar (strength), an olive tree (value), a fragrant tree (delight), grain (abundance), a grapevine (fruitfulness). Thus a book dominated by images of unfaithfulness—an adulterous wife, a rebellious son—ends with the firm promise of restoration.

8 O Ephraim, what have I[s] to do with
    idols?
It is I who answer and look after
    you.[t]
I am like an evergreen cypress;
    your faithfulness[u] comes from me.
9 Those who are wise understand these
    things;
    those who are discerning know them.
For the ways of the LORD are right,
    and the upright walk in them,
    but transgressors stumble in them.

---

o Gk Syr: Heb *bulls*   *p* Cn: Heb *like Lebanon*   *q* Heb *his*   *r* Cn: Heb *they shall grow grain*   *s* Or *What more has Ephraim*   *t* Heb *him*   *u* Heb *your fruit*

JOEL

The Meaning of a Natural Disaster
What's behind a devastating locust plague?

> The earth quakes before them, the heavens tremble. The sun and the moon are darkened, and the stars withdraw their shining.
> 2.10

THEIR NUMBER WAS ASTOUNDING; THE whole face of the mountain was black with them. On they came like a living deluge. We dug trenches, and kindled fires, and beat and burned to death 'heaps upon heaps'; but the effort was utterly useless. Wave after wave rolled up the mountainside and poured over rocks, walls, ditches and hedges—those behind covering up and bridging over the masses already killed. It was perfectly appalling to watch this animated river as it flowed up the road and ascended the hill above my house. For four days they continued to pass on toward the east ...."

Eyewitness W. M. Thomson is describing a locust plague. Descriptions of the aftermath sound just as awful. When locusts have passed, the terrain looks as though it has been swept by a scorching fire.

Why Have I Lived?

Many awestruck observers have written accounts of locust swarms, but none more graphically than the prophet Joel. In striking, polished imagery he described the devastation. His people faced starvation. Joel drew a verbal portrait of grief and fear.

Natural disasters provoke questions. Why did God allow this disaster to happen? Why have I lived and others died? Is there a lesson here? For Joel, a plague of locusts led to deep insights into God's universal plan.

Joel had no doubt that God was behind the plague. In fact, he pictured God leading the locusts like an army into battle (2.11). They represented "the day of the LORD," a judgment on Israel. Unlike many of the other prophets, Joel did not devote time to an analysis of Israel's failings. He concentrated, instead, on a cure.

Joel urged the priests to call a nationwide day of prayer and fasting to lead the people back to God. Then God would roll back the damage done by the locusts, and more: "You shall eat in plenty and be satisfied, and praise the name of the LORD your God, who has dealt wondrously with you" (2.26). They would emerge from the experience with new, durable confidence in God's love. So it has often proved for God's people: A disaster has pressed them to a deeper relationship with him.

God's Bigger Plans

Though the locust plague was by far the worst Joel had ever heard of (1.2–3), no historical record of this particular invasion has endured, other than the one Joel left us. The truth is, even the worst natural disasters fade from memory. Joel wanted the disaster to turn people's attention toward something more lasting—toward an eternal God.

Joel wanted God's people to believe that God controlled the locusts, and, even more important, that God shaped the entire course of history to his plan. As terribly as the locusts had destroyed, and as wonderfully as God had rolled back their destruction, these events only foreshadowed far more terrible and wonderful things. Joel saw that God's Spirit would transform his people into those who love him constantly, not just when a disaster catches their attention. After a time of terrible judgment, God would create a renewed, secure city for his people, in which he himself would live.

How to Read Joel

Joel breaks naturally into two parts. Up to 2.28, it talks about a locust invasion and the response of God's people to such a natural disaster. From that verse on, however, Joel's view rises above the local situation and deals with the far-off future.

Joel rarely refers to unfamiliar people, places, or events, so you can read it fairly easily without using any outside reference like a Bible dictionary. The challenge is to connect his understanding of a natural disaster—a locust plague—with his vision of the future.

The Bible often refers to "the day of the LORD" as the time when God will completely take charge of our world. But Joel seems to see "the day of the LORD" partly revealed in the disasters of his day. As you read, try to see the similarities Joel draws between the locust invasion and the final consummation of history. Ask yourself: How do I respond to disaster? How would Joel want me to respond?

3-TRACK READING PLAN

For an explanation and complete listing of the 3-track reading plan, turn to page 7.

TRACK 1: **_Two-Week Courses on the Bible_**
See page 7 for information on these courses.

TRACK 2: **_An Overview of Joel in 1 Day_**
☐ Day 1. Read the Introduction to Joel and chapter 2, which describes the locust plague and its effect on the people's relationship with God.

Now turn to page 9 for your next Track 2 reading project.

TRACK 3: **_All of Joel in 3 Days_**
After you have read through Joel, turn to pages 10–14 for your next Track 3 reading project.
☐1   ☐2   ☐3

1 The word of the LORD that came to Joel son of Pethuel:

Lament over the Ruin of the Country

2 Hear this, O elders,
    give ear, all inhabitants of the land!
Has such a thing happened in your days,
    or in the days of your ancestors?
3 Tell your children of it,
    and let your children tell their children,
    and their children another generation.

4 What the cutting locust left,
    the swarming locust has eaten.
What the swarming locust left,
    the hopping locust has eaten,
and what the hopping locust left,
    the destroying locust has eaten.

5 Wake up, you drunkards, and weep;
    and wail, all you wine-drinkers,
over the sweet wine,
    for it is cut off from your mouth.
6 For a nation has invaded my land,
    powerful and innumerable;
its teeth are lions' teeth,
    and it has the fangs of a lioness.

7 It has laid waste my vines,
    and splintered my fig trees;
it has stripped off their bark and thrown
    it down;
    their branches have turned white.
8 Lament like a virgin dressed in sackcloth
    for the husband of her youth.
9 The grain offering and the drink offering
    are cut off
    from the house of the LORD.
The priests mourn,
    the ministers of the LORD.
10 The fields are devastated,

1.4 Doomsday

Nowadays we tend to think of doomsday in terms of nuclear holocaust. But until recent times the most powerful weapons in the world belonged to nature. Earthquakes, floods, and plagues of illness caused far more destruction than arrows, spears, and swords. Natural disasters were frightening and unpredictable: A plague of locusts, for example, could wipe out an entire food supply overnight.

the ground mourns;
for the grain is destroyed,
the wine dries up,
the oil fails.

11 Be dismayed, you farmers,
wail, you vinedressers,
over the wheat and the barley;
for the crops of the field are ruined.
12 The vine withers,
the fig tree droops.
Pomegranate, palm, and apple—
all the trees of the field are dried up;
surely, joy withers away
among the people.

A Call to Repentance and Prayer

13 Put on sackcloth and lament, you priests;
wail, you ministers of the altar.
Come, pass the night in sackcloth,
you ministers of my God!
Grain offering and drink offering
are withheld from the house of your
God.

14 Sanctify a fast,
call a solemn assembly.
Gather the elders
and all the inhabitants of the land
to the house of the LORD your God,
and cry out to the LORD.

15 Alas for the day!
For the day of the LORD is near,
and as destruction from the Almighty[a]
it comes.
16 Is not the food cut off
before our eyes,
joy and gladness
from the house of our God?

17 The seed shrivels under the clods,[b]
the storehouses are desolate;
the granaries are ruined
because the grain has failed.
18 How the animals groan!
The herds of cattle wander about
because there is no pasture for them;
even the flocks of sheep are dazed.[c]

19 To you, O LORD, I cry.
For fire has devoured
the pastures of the wilderness,
and flames have burned
all the trees of the field.
20 Even the wild animals cry to you
because the watercourses are dried up,
and fire has devoured
the pastures of the wilderness.

2 Blow the trumpet in Zion;
sound the alarm on my holy mountain!
Let all the inhabitants of the land tremble,

1.18 Total Devastation

No wine for the drunkards, no husbands for young brides, no crops for the farmers, no offerings for the priests—the disaster was affecting every part of society. Cattle moaned, sheep wandered in starvation. People had nowhere to turn but God, concluded Joel. So why didn't they?

for the day of the LORD is coming, it is
near—
2 a day of darkness and gloom,
a day of clouds and thick darkness!
Like blackness spread upon the
mountains
a great and powerful army comes;
their like has never been from of old,
nor will be again after them
in ages to come.

3 Fire devours in front of them,
and behind them a flame burns.
Before them the land is like the garden of
Eden,
but after them a desolate wilderness,
and nothing escapes them.

4 They have the appearance of horses,
and like war-horses they charge.
5 As with the rumbling of chariots,
they leap on the tops of the mountains,
like the crackling of a flame of fire
devouring the stubble,
like a powerful army
drawn up for battle.

6 Before them peoples are in anguish,
all faces grow pale.[b]
7 Like warriors they charge,
like soldiers they scale the wall.
Each keeps to its own course,
they do not swerve from[d] their paths.
8 They do not jostle one another,
each keeps to its own track;
they burst through the weapons
and are not halted.
9 They leap upon the city,
they run upon the walls;
they climb up into the houses,
they enter through the windows like a
thief.

---

[a] Traditional rendering of Heb *Shaddai*   [b] Meaning of Heb uncertain   [c] Compare Gk Syr Vg: Meaning of Heb uncertain   [d] Gk Syr Vg: Heb *they do not take a pledge along*

10 The earth quakes before them,
   the heavens tremble.
The sun and the moon are darkened,
   and the stars withdraw their shining.
11 The LORD utters his voice
   at the head of his army;
how vast is his host!
   Numberless are those who obey his
      command.
Truly the day of the LORD is great;
   terrible indeed—who can endure it?

12 Yet even now, says the LORD,
   return to me with all your heart,
with fasting, with weeping, and with
   mourning;
13   rend your hearts and not
      your clothing.
Return to the LORD, your God,
   for he is gracious and merciful,
slow to anger, and abounding in steadfast
   love,
   and relents from punishing.

2.13 Torn Hearts

In the Old Testament, men and women tore their robes as a sign of sorrow and mourning. (Some Middle Easterners do so still.) Jacob, Moses, Joshua, Elijah, David, and Job all tore their clothes as an expression of grief or anguish. In Joel's day, however, God looked for change on the inside, not just another outward show of remorse. He sought broken hearts, not torn garments.

14 Who knows whether he will not turn and
      relent,
   and leave a blessing behind him,
a grain offering and a drink offering
   for the LORD, your God?

15 Blow the trumpet in Zion;
   sanctify a fast;
call a solemn assembly;
16   gather the people.
Sanctify the congregation;
   assemble the aged;
gather the children,
   even infants at the breast.
Let the bridegroom leave his room,
   and the bride her canopy.

17 Between the vestibule and the altar
   let the priests, the ministers of the
      LORD, weep.

Let them say, "Spare your people,
      O LORD,
   and do not make your heritage a
      mockery,
   a byword among the nations.
Why should it be said among the peoples,
   'Where is their God?'"

God's Response and Promise

18 Then the LORD became jealous for his
      land,
   and had pity on his people.
19 In response to his people the LORD said:
I am sending you
   grain, wine, and oil,
   and you will be satisfied;
and I will no more make you
   a mockery among the nations.

20 I will remove the northern army far from
      you,
   and drive it into a parched and
      desolate land,
its front into the eastern sea,
   and its rear into the western sea;
its stench and foul smell will rise up.
   Surely he has done great things!

21 Do not fear, O soil;
   be glad and rejoice,
   for the LORD has done great things!
22 Do not fear, you animals of the field,
   for the pastures of the wilderness are
      green;
the tree bears its fruit,
   the fig tree and vine give their full
      yield.

23 O children of Zion, be glad
   and rejoice in the LORD your God;
for he has given the early rain[e] for your
      vindication,
   he has poured down for you abundant
      rain,
   the early and the later rain, as before.
24 The threshing floors shall be full of grain,
   the vats shall overflow with wine and
      oil.

25 I will repay you for the years
   that the swarming locust has eaten,
the hopper, the destroyer, and the cutter,
   my great army, which I sent against
      you.

26 You shall eat in plenty and be satisfied,
   and praise the name of the LORD your
      God,

e Meaning of Heb uncertain

who has dealt wondrously with you.
And my people shall never again be put
to shame.

27 You shall know that I am in the midst of
Israel,
and that I, the LORD, am your God and
there is no other.
And my people shall never again be put
to shame.

God's Spirit Poured Out

28f Then afterward
I will pour out my spirit on all flesh;
your sons and your daughters shall
prophesy,
your old men shall dream dreams,
and your young men shall see visions.

29 Even on the male and female slaves,
in those days, I will pour out my spirit.

2.29 The Spirit Poured Out

This prophecy was quoted by Peter on the day of Pentecost (Acts 2.17–21). He said it had been fulfilled when the Holy Spirit came on Jesus' disciples. Paul also quoted verse 32 in Romans 10.12–13, making the point that God would respond to Jews and non-Jews without distinction.

30 I will show portents in the heavens and on the earth, blood and fire and columns of smoke. 31The sun shall be turned to darkness, and the moon to blood, before the great and terrible day of the LORD comes. 32Then everyone who calls on the name of the LORD shall be saved; for in Mount Zion and in Jerusalem there shall be those who escape, as the LORD has said, and among the survivors shall be those whom the LORD calls.

3 g For then, in those days and at that time, when I restore the fortunes of Judah and Jerusalem, 2I will gather all the nations and bring them down to the valley of Jehoshaphat, and I will enter into judgment with them there, on account of my people and my heritage Israel, because they have scattered them among the nations. They have divided my land, 3and cast lots for my people, and traded boys for prostitutes, and sold girls for wine, and drunk it down.

4 What are you to me, O Tyre and Sidon, and all the regions of Philistia? Are you paying me back for something? If you are paying me back, I will turn your deeds back upon your own heads swiftly and speedily. 5For you have taken my silver and my gold, and have carried my rich treasures into your temples.h 6You have sold the

people of Judah and Jerusalem to the Greeks, removing them far from their own border. 7But now I will rouse them to leave the places to which

3.3 Gambling Prizes

The Babylonians who invaded Judah fulfilled this prophecy literally: They seized captives as part of the spoils of war, divided them up by casting lots, then traded them for prostitutes and wine. In this section, God promises vengeance on such war crimes.

you have sold them, and I will turn your deeds back upon your own heads. 8I will sell your sons and your daughters into the hand of the people of Judah, and they will sell them to the Sabeans, to a nation far away; for the LORD has spoken.

Judgment in the Valley of Jehoshaphat

9 Proclaim this among the nations:
Prepare war,i
stir up the warriors.
Let all the soldiers draw near,
let them come up.

10 Beat your plowshares into swords,
and your pruning hooks into spears;
let the weakling say, "I am a warrior."

11 Come quickly,j
all you nations all around,
gather yourselves there.
Bring down your warriors, O LORD.

12 Let the nations rouse themselves,
and come up to the valley of
Jehoshaphat;
for there I will sit to judge
all the neighboring nations.

13 Put in the sickle,
for the harvest is ripe.
Go in, tread,
for the wine press is full.
The vats overflow,
for their wickedness is great.

14 Multitudes, multitudes,
in the valley of decision!
For the day of the LORD is near
in the valley of decision.

15 The sun and the moon are darkened,
and the stars withdraw their shining.

16 The LORD roars from Zion,
and utters his voice from Jerusalem,

---

f Ch 3.1 in Heb   g Ch 4.1 in Heb   h Or *palaces*   i Heb *sanctify war*   j Meaning of Heb uncertain

and the heavens and the earth shake.
But the LORD is a refuge for his people,
a stronghold for the people of Israel.

The Glorious Future of Judah

17 So you shall know that I, the LORD your
God,
dwell in Zion, my holy mountain.
And Jerusalem shall be holy,
and strangers shall never again pass
through it.

18 In that day
the mountains shall drip sweet wine,
the hills shall flow with milk,
and all the stream beds of Judah
shall flow with water;
a fountain shall come forth from the
house of the LORD
and water the Wadi Shittim.

19 Egypt shall become a desolation
and Edom a desolate wilderness,
because of the violence done to the
people of Judah,
in whose land they have shed innocent
blood.
20 But Judah shall be inhabited forever,
and Jerusalem to all generations.
21 I will avenge their blood, and I will not
clear the guilty,[k]
for the LORD dwells in Zion.

k Gk Syr: Heb *I will hold innocent their blood that I have not held innocent*

AMOS

Justice!
A simple farmer takes on a materialistic nation

Let justice roll down like waters, and righteousness like an ever-flowing stream. 5.24

BUSINESS HAD NEVER BEEN BETTER. For the first time in generations, Israel faced no military threat. Since they controlled the crucial trade routes, merchants piled up big profits. Luxuries became readily available—new stone houses, ivory-inlaid furniture, top-grade meat and fine wine, the best body lotions.

Amid such peace and prosperity, one lone voice scraped like fingernails on a blackboard. Amos spoke bluntly with a farmer's vocabulary, calling the city socialites "cows" (4.1). A mere shepherd—among the poorest of all professions—he treated luxury with scorn. Worst of all, Amos was a foreigner from the South—from Tekoa, a small town in Judah. Since Israel had split from the South about 170 years before, Israelite leaders did not take kindly to criticism from a southerner.

But to Amos, social acceptance didn't matter. He was no professional prophet, making his living talking smoothly about God (7.14). God had called him to leave his job and carry a message. God had said go, and Amos had obeyed.

God's View of "Religion"

The people Amos addressed had plenty of "religion." They went regularly to shrines for worship. They looked forward to "the day of the LORD," when God would fulfill all their expectations for their country. But Amos brought unexpected bad news from God: "I hate, I despise your festivals" (5.21). God didn't want sacrifice or singing. He demanded justice.

Amos listed all Israel's neighbors, announcing God's judgment for their crimes against humanity. Israelites liked this kind of talk; they felt superior to all these nations. But having caught the Israelites' attention, Amos circled dramatically home. God would judge Israel too. The people, their beautiful homes, their sacred altars—all would be destroyed.

The Character of God

More than any other book in the Bible, Amos concentrates on injustice. Israel had plenty of other faults he might have blasted. Their religious system, for instance, centered on two calf-idols. But Amos wasted little breath on that. He focused on the facts that met his eyes and ears in every marketplace: oppression of the poor, dishonest business, bribery in court, privilege bought with money.

The wealthy Israelites were getting their luxuries at the expense of the poor. They congratulated themselves on their devotion to God with no sense that they had cut the heart out of their relationship to him. They wanted God to fit conveniently into life as an additive. God showed himself through Amos as lordly, absolute, inescapable. He must be master over all of life, including business affairs.

How to Read Amos

Perhaps because he was a farmer, Amos used a plain writing style, filled with strong country language. The organization of his book is clear too: chapters 1–2 line up the Middle Eastern nations for trial, chapters 3–6 give a series of messages from God (usually beginning with "Hear this word"), and the last three chapters convey God's judgment through five graphic visions.

Throughout, Amos sticks close to his main concern: cruelty and inhumanity between people. The injustices Amos condemns often sound familiar today. As you read, ask yourself, "What would Amos say about me and about my people?"

It is a good idea to read Amos and Hosea together, for they give two views of the same situation. A visitor from the South, Amos was shocked by the injustices he saw in every marketplace. Hosea emphasized the inner dimension, an abused relationship to a loving God.

Amos predicted that Israel would be punished, and his prediction proved right. After King Jeroboam, the government deteriorated. Five kings took the throne in the next 13 years; four were assassinated. In 30 years Israel was permanently dismantled by Assyrian armies. For historical background, read 2 Kings 14.23–17.41, noting that the kings of both Israel and Judah are interspersed. For a briefer account, read the summaries of their reigns in "A Lineup of Rulers," pages 1349–1357.

3-TRACK READING PLAN

For an explanation and complete listing of the 3-track reading plan, turn to page 7.

TRACK 1:   *Two-Week Courses on the Bible*
The Track 1 reading program on the Old Testament includes one chapter from Amos. See page 8 for a complete listing of this course.

TRACK 2:   *An Overview of Amos in 1 Day*
☐ Day 1. Read the Introduction to Amos and chapter 4, which sums up God's majestic anger against his people.

Now turn to page 9 for your next Track 2 reading project.

TRACK 3:   *All of Amos in 9 Days*
After you have read through Amos, turn to pages 10–14 for your next Track 3 reading project.
☐1   ☐2   ☐3   ☐4   ☐5   ☐6   ☐7   ☐8
☐9

1 The words of Amos, who was among the shepherds of Tekoa, which he saw concerning Israel in the days of King Uzziah of Judah and in the days of King Jeroboam son of Joash of Israel, two years[a] before the earthquake.

Judgment on Israel's Neighbors

2 And he said:
The LORD roars from Zion,
   and utters his voice from Jerusalem;
the pastures of the shepherds wither,
   and the top of Carmel dries up.

3 Thus says the LORD:
For three transgressions of Damascus,
   and for four, I will not revoke the
      punishment;[b]
because they have threshed Gilead
   with threshing sledges of iron.
4 So I will send a fire on the house
      of Hazael,
   and it shall devour the strongholds of
      Ben-hadad.

5 I will break the gate bars of Damascus,
   and cut off the inhabitants from the
      Valley of Aven,
and the one who holds the scepter from
      Beth-eden;
   and the people of Aram shall go into
      exile to Kir,
                           says the LORD.

6 Thus says the LORD:
For three transgressions of Gaza,
   and for four, I will not revoke the
      punishment;[b]
because they carried into exile entire
      communities,
   to hand them over to Edom.
7 So I will send a fire on the wall of Gaza,
   fire that shall devour its strongholds.
8 I will cut off the inhabitants from
      Ashdod,
   and the one who holds the scepter
      from Ashkelon;
I will turn my hand against Ekron,

---

[a] Or *during two years*   [b] Heb *cause it to return*

and the remnant of the Philistines shall
perish,
                    says the Lord GOD.

9 Thus says the LORD:
For three transgressions of Tyre,
    and for four, I will not revoke the
        punishment;[c]
because they delivered entire communities
    over to Edom,
and did not remember the covenant of
    kinship.

1.9 Atrocities

*Amos began with thundering pronouncements
against the enemies of Israel and Judah. His
local audience must have cheered as he called
down judgment on the blatant misdeeds of
their neighbors: selling slaves, breaking
treaties, ripping open pregnant women,
desecrating the dead. But then Amos turned his
attention to his own countrymen (2.4–16). God
held his people to a far higher standard of
morality. Israelites failed by breaking God's
law; their neighbors were judged guilty of
"crimes against humanity," for breaking laws
of common decency.*

---

10 So I will send a fire on the wall of Tyre,
    fire that shall devour its strongholds.

11 Thus says the LORD:
For three transgressions of Edom,
    and for four, I will not revoke the
        punishment;[c]
because he pursued his brother with the
    sword
    and cast off all pity;
he maintained his anger perpetually,[d]
    and kept his wrath[e] forever.
12 So I will send a fire on Teman,
    and it shall devour the strongholds of
        Bozrah.

13 Thus says the LORD:
For three transgressions of the
        Ammonites,
    and for four, I will not revoke the
        punishment;[c]
because they have ripped open pregnant
    women in Gilead
    in order to enlarge their territory.
14 So I will kindle a fire against the wall of
        Rabbah,
    fire that shall devour its strongholds,
with shouting on the day of battle,

with a storm on the day of the
    whirlwind;
15 then their king shall go into exile,
    he and his officials together,
                    says the LORD.

2 Thus says the LORD:
For three transgressions of Moab,
    and for four, I will not revoke the
        punishment;[c]
because he burned to lime
    the bones of the king of Edom.
2 So I will send a fire on Moab,
    and it shall devour the strongholds of
        Kerioth,
and Moab shall die amid uproar,
    amid shouting and the sound of the
        trumpet;
3 I will cut off the ruler from its midst,
    and will kill all its officials with him,
                    says the LORD.

Judgment on Judah

4 Thus says the LORD:
For three transgressions of Judah,
    and for four, I will not revoke the
        punishment;[c]
because they have rejected the law of the
        LORD,
    and have not kept his statutes,
but they have been led astray by the same
        lies
    after which their ancestors walked.
5 So I will send a fire on Judah,
    and it shall devour the strongholds of
        Jerusalem.

Judgment on Israel

6 Thus says the LORD:
For three transgressions of Israel,
    and for four, I will not revoke the
        punishment;[c]
because they sell the righteous for silver,
    and the needy for a pair of sandals—
7 they who trample the head of the poor
    into the dust of the earth,
    and push the afflicted out of the way;
father and son go in to the same girl,
    so that my holy name is profaned;
8 they lay themselves down beside every
        altar
    on garments taken in pledge;
and in the house of their God they drink
    wine bought with fines they imposed.

9 Yet I destroyed the Amorite before them,
    whose height was like the height of
        cedars,
    and who was as strong as oaks;

---

[c] Heb *cause it to return*   [d] Syr Vg: Heb *and his anger tore perpetually*   [e] Gk Syr Vg: Heb *and his wrath kept*

I destroyed his fruit above,
and his roots beneath.

10 Also I brought you up out of the land of
Egypt,

2.8 Ruthless Bill Collectors

Bankers making loans usually want collateral to back up the promise to repay. In Amos's day poor people resorted to pledging the very clothes on their backs as collateral. Bill collectors who took a debtor's garments flagrantly violated God's law (Exodus 22.25–27). Worse, they were using the clothes as bedding when they went to their shrines to worship God.

and led you forty years in
the wilderness,
to possess the land of the Amorite.

11 And I raised up some of your children to
be prophets
and some of your youths to be
nazirites.*f*
Is it not indeed so, O people of Israel?
says the LORD.

12 But you made the nazirites*f* drink wine,
and commanded the prophets,
saying, "You shall not prophesy."

13 So, I will press you down in your place,
just as a cart presses down
when it is full of sheaves.*g*

14 Flight shall perish from the swift,
and the strong shall not retain their
strength,
nor shall the mighty save their lives;

15 those who handle the bow shall not stand,
and those who are swift of foot shall
not save themselves,
nor shall those who ride horses save
their lives;

16 and those who are stout of heart among
the mighty
shall flee away naked in that day,
says the LORD.

Israel's Guilt and Punishment

3 Hear this word that the LORD has spoken
against you, O people of Israel, against the
whole family that I brought up out of the land of
Egypt:

2 You only have I known
of all the families of the earth;
therefore I will punish you
for all your iniquities.

3 Do two walk together
unless they have made an
appointment?

4 Does a lion roar in the forest,
when it has no prey?
Does a young lion cry out from its den,
if it has caught nothing?

5 Does a bird fall into a snare on the earth,
when there is no trap for it?
Does a snare spring up from the ground,
when it has taken nothing?

6 Is a trumpet blown in a city,
and the people are not afraid?
Does disaster befall a city,
unless the LORD has done it?

7 Surely the Lord GOD does nothing,
without revealing his secret
to his servants the prophets.

8 The lion has roared;
who will not fear?
The Lord GOD has spoken;
who can but prophesy?

9 Proclaim to the strongholds in Ashdod,
and to the strongholds in the land of
Egypt,
and say, "Assemble yourselves on
Mount*h* Samaria,
and see what great tumults are within
it,
and what oppressions are in its midst."

10 They do not know how to do right, says
the LORD,
those who store up violence and
robbery in their strongholds.

11 Therefore thus says the Lord GOD:
An adversary shall surround the land,
and strip you of your defense;
and your strongholds shall be
plundered.

12 Thus says the LORD: As the shepherd rescues from the mouth of the lion two legs, or a
piece of an ear, so shall the people of Israel who
live in Samaria be rescued, with the corner of a
couch and part*g* of a bed.

13 Hear, and testify against the house of
Jacob,
says the Lord GOD, the God of hosts:

14 On the day I punish Israel for its
transgressions,
I will punish the altars of Bethel,
and the horns of the altar shall be cut off
and fall to the ground.

15 I will tear down the winter house as well
as the summer house;
and the houses of ivory shall perish,

f That is, *those separated* or *those consecrated*   *g* Meaning of Heb uncertain   *h* Gk Syr: Heb *the mountains of*

and the great houses[i] shall come to an
end,
says the LORD.

4 Hear this word, you cows of Bashan
who are on Mount Samaria,
who oppress the poor, who crush the
needy,
who say to their husbands, "Bring
something to drink!"

4.1 Prize Cows

*With searing scornfulness, Amos paints a
picture of women living in sheer luxury. These
"cows" thought only of their pleasure, not of
the oppressed poor who made their life of
luxury possible. Amos paints their punishment
just as vividly. The brutal Assyrian armies, who
later captured Israel and took its people into
exile, left monuments portraying their captives
being dragged off with hooks in their mouths.*

2 The Lord GOD has sworn by his holiness:
The time is surely coming upon you,
when they shall take you away with
hooks,
even the last of you with fishhooks.
3 Through breaches in the wall you shall
leave,
each one straight ahead;
and you shall be flung out into
Harmon,[j]
says the LORD.
4 Come to Bethel—and transgress;
to Gilgal—and multiply transgression;
bring your sacrifices every morning,
your tithes every three days;
5 bring a thank offering of leavened bread,
and proclaim freewill offerings, publish
them;
for so you love to do, O people
of Israel!
says the Lord GOD.

Israel Rejects Correction

6 I gave you cleanness of teeth in all your
cities,
and lack of bread in all your places,
yet you did not return to me,
says the LORD.

7 And I also withheld the rain from you
when there were still three months to
the harvest;
I would send rain on one city,
and send no rain on another city;

one field would be rained upon,
and the field on which it did not rain
withered;
8 so two or three towns wandered to one
town
to drink water, and were not satisfied;
yet you did not return to me,
says the LORD.

9 I struck you with blight and mildew;
I laid waste[k] your gardens and your
vineyards;
the locust devoured your fig trees and
your olive trees;
yet you did not return to me,
says the LORD.

10 I sent among you a pestilence after the
manner of Egypt;
I killed your young men with
the sword;
I carried away your horses;[l]
and I made the stench of your camp
go up into your nostrils;
yet you did not return to me,
says the LORD.

11 I overthrew some of you,
as when God overthrew Sodom and
Gomorrah,
and you were like a brand snatched
from the fire;
yet you did not return to me,
says the LORD.

12 Therefore thus I will do to you, O Israel;
because I will do this to you,
prepare to meet your God, O Israel!

4.12 Before It's Too Late

*This is the most famous verse in Amos, thanks
to graffiti artists who write "Prepare to meet
thy God!" in unlikely places. Amos has just
reviewed a series of natural disasters—famine,
drought, blight, plagues, war—any of which
should have been enough to turn the nation to
God. But Israel did not respond, and now Amos
is holding out one last chance for repentance.*

13 For lo, the one who forms the mountains,
creates the wind,
reveals his thoughts to mortals,
makes the morning darkness,
and treads on the heights of
the earth—

---

[i] Or *many houses*   [j] Meaning of Heb uncertain   [k] Cn: Heb *the multitude of*   [l] Heb *with the captivity*
of your horses

the LORD, the God of hosts, is
his name!

A Lament for Israel's Sin

5 Hear this word that I take up over you in
lamentation, O house of Israel:

2 Fallen, no more to rise,
is maiden Israel;
forsaken on her land,
with no one to raise her up.

3 For thus says the Lord GOD:
The city that marched out a thousand
shall have a hundred left,
and that which marched out a hundred
shall have ten left.[m]

4 For thus says the LORD to the house of
Israel:
Seek me and live;

5 but do not seek Bethel,
and do not enter into Gilgal
or cross over to Beer-sheba;
for Gilgal shall surely go into exile,
and Bethel shall come to nothing.

6 Seek the LORD and live,
or he will break out against the house
of Joseph like fire,
and it will devour Bethel, with no one
to quench it.

7 Ah, you that turn justice to wormwood,
and bring righteousness to the ground!

8 The one who made the Pleiades
and Orion,
and turns deep darkness into
the morning,
and darkens the day into night,
who calls for the waters of the sea,
and pours them out on the surface of
the earth,
the LORD is his name,

9 who makes destruction flash out against
the strong,
so that destruction comes upon the
fortress.

10 They hate the one who reproves in the
gate,
and they abhor the one who speaks the
truth.

11 Therefore because you trample on the
poor
and take from them levies of grain,
you have built houses of hewn stone,
but you shall not live in them;
you have planted pleasant vineyards,
but you shall not drink their wine.

12 For I know how many are your
transgressions,
and how great are your sins—
you who afflict the righteous, who take a
bribe,
and push aside the needy in the gate.

13 Therefore the prudent will keep silent in
such a time;
for it is an evil time.

14 Seek good and not evil,
that you may live;
and so the LORD, the God of hosts, will be
with you,
just as you have said.

15 Hate evil and love good,
and establish justice in the gate;
it may be that the LORD, the God of hosts,
will be gracious to the remnant of
Joseph.

16 Therefore thus says the LORD, the God of
hosts, the Lord:
In all the squares there shall be wailing;
and in all the streets they shall say,
"Alas! alas!"
They shall call the farmers to mourning,
and those skilled in lamentation, to
wailing;

17 in all the vineyards there shall be wailing,
for I will pass through the midst of
you,
says the LORD.

The Day of the LORD a Dark Day

18 Alas for you who desire the day of the
LORD!
Why do you want the day of the LORD?
It is darkness, not light;

19 as if someone fled from a lion,
and was met by a bear;
or went into the house and rested a hand
against the wall,
and was bitten by a snake.

20 Is not the day of the LORD darkness, not
light,
and gloom with no brightness in it?

5.20 The Day of the Lord

*In Amos's day as today, some religious people
looked forward to "the day of the LORD," when
God will intervene personally in history and
save his people. Israelites, assuming that "God
is on our side," thought it would be a great day
for them. But Amos contradicted their
expectations. In a few words he depicted "the
day of the LORD" as a nightmare.*

---

[m] Heb adds *to the house of Israel*

21 I hate, I despise your festivals,
  and I take no delight in your solemn
    assemblies.
22 Even though you offer me your burnt
    offerings and grain offerings,
  I will not accept them;
  and the offerings of well-being of your
    fatted animals
  I will not look upon.
23 Take away from me the noise of your
    songs;
  I will not listen to the melody of your
    harps.
24 But let justice roll down like waters,
  and righteousness like an ever-flowing
    stream.

25 Did you bring to me sacrifices and offerings the forty years in the wilderness, O house of Israel? 26You shall take up Sakkuth your king, and Kaiwan your star-god, your images,*n* which you made for yourselves; 27therefore I will take you into exile beyond Damascus, says the LORD, whose name is the God of hosts.

Complacent Self-Indulgence Will Be Punished

6 Alas for those who are at ease in Zion,
  and for those who feel secure on
    Mount Samaria,
  the notables of the first of the nations,
  to whom the house of Israel resorts!

6.1 Soft and Fat

Amos is at his sarcastic best in this message to "the notables of the first of the nations." Consistently, Israel proved much better at handling hardship than success. In prosperous times like Amos's they grew addicted to luxury and power, forgetting all about God. Hundreds of years before, Moses had warned against this very syndrome (Deuteronomy 8.10–20).

2 Cross over to Calneh, and see;
  from there go to Hamath the great;
  then go down to Gath of the
    Philistines.
  Are you better*o* than these kingdoms?
  Or is your*p* territory greater than
    their*q* territory,
3 O you that put far away the evil day,
  and bring near a reign of violence?

4 Alas for those who lie on beds of ivory,
  and lounge on their couches,
  and eat lambs from the flock,
  and calves from the stall;
5 who sing idle songs to the sound
    of the harp,
  and like David improvise on
    instruments of music;
6 who drink wine from bowls,
  and anoint themselves with the finest
    oils,
  but are not grieved over the ruin of
    Joseph!
7 Therefore they shall now be the first to go
    into exile,
  and the revelry of the loungers shall
    pass away.

8 The Lord GOD has sworn by himself
  (says the LORD, the God of hosts):
  I abhor the pride of Jacob
    and hate his strongholds;
  and I will deliver up the city and all
    that is in it.

9 If ten people remain in one house, they shall die. 10And if a relative, one who burns the dead,*r* shall take up the body to bring it out of the house, and shall say to someone in the innermost parts of the house, "Is anyone else with you?" the answer will come, "No." Then the relative*s* shall say, "Hush! We must not mention the name of the LORD."

11 See, the LORD commands,
  and the great house shall be shattered
    to bits,
  and the little house to pieces.
12 Do horses run on rocks?
  Does one plow the sea with oxen?*t*
  But you have turned justice into poison
  and the fruit of righteousness into
    wormwood—
13 you who rejoice in Lo-debar,*u*
  who say, "Have we not by our own
    strength
  taken Karnaim*v* for ourselves?"
14 Indeed, I am raising up against you a
    nation,
  O house of Israel, says the LORD, the
    God of hosts,
  and they shall oppress you from
    Lebo-hamath
  to the Wadi Arabah.

Locusts, Fire, and a Plumb Line

7 This is what the Lord GOD showed me: he was forming locusts at the time the latter growth began to sprout (it was the latter growth

---

n Heb *your images, your star-god*   *o* Or *Are they better for him*   *s* Heb *he*   *t* Or *Does one plow them with oxen*   *p* Heb *their*   *q* Heb *your*   *r* Or *who makes a burning*   *u* Or *in a thing of nothingness*   *v* Or *horns*

after the king's mowings). ²When they had finished eating the grass of the land, I said,

"O Lord GOD, forgive, I beg you!
How can Jacob stand?
He is so small!"
³ The LORD relented concerning this;
"It shall not be," said the LORD.

4 This is what the Lord GOD showed me: the Lord GOD was calling for a shower of fire,ʷ and it devoured the great deep and was eating up the land. ⁵Then I said,

"O Lord GOD, cease, I beg you!
How can Jacob stand?
He is so small!"
⁶ The LORD relented concerning this;
"This also shall not be," said the Lord
GOD.

7 This is what he showed me: the Lord was standing beside a wall built with a plumb line, with a plumb line in his hand. ⁸And the LORD said to me, "Amos, what do you see?" And I said, "A plumb line." Then the Lord said,

"See, I am setting a plumb line
in the midst of my people Israel;
I will never again pass them by;

7.8 A Plumb Line

A plumb line is a weight on the end of a string; builders use it to make certain that their walls stand straight. A wall may look right, but if it doesn't match a plumb line, it is out of kilter. Similarly God will use a plumb line to judge whether Israel is "straight" by his standards.

9 the high places of Isaac shall be made
desolate,
and the sanctuaries of Israel shall be
laid waste,
and I will rise against the house of
Jeroboam with the sword."

Amaziah Complains to the King

10 Then Amaziah, the priest of Bethel, sent to King Jeroboam of Israel, saying, "Amos has conspired against you in the very center of the house of Israel; the land is not able to bear all his words. ¹¹For thus Amos has said,

'Jeroboam shall die by the sword,
and Israel must go into exile
away from his land.'"

¹²And Amaziah said to Amos, "O seer, go, flee away to the land of Judah, earn your bread there, and prophesy there; ¹³but never again prophesy at Bethel, for it is the king's sanctuary, and it is a temple of the kingdom."

14 Then Amos answered Amaziah, "I amˣ no prophet, nor a prophet's son; but I amˣ a herdsman, and a dresser of sycamore trees, ¹⁵and the LORD took me from following the flock, and the LORD said to me, 'Go, prophesy to my people Israel.'
¹⁶ "Now therefore hear the word of the
LORD.
You say, 'Do not prophesy against Israel,
and do not preach against the house of
Isaac.'
¹⁷ Therefore thus says the LORD:
'Your wife shall become a prostitute in
the city,
and your sons and your daughters shall
fall by the sword,
and your land shall be parceled out by
line;
you yourself shall die in an unclean land,
and Israel shall surely go into exile
away from its land.'"

The Basket of Fruit

8 This is what the Lord GOD showed me—a basket of summer fruit.ʸ ²He said, "Amos, what do you see?" And I said, "A basket of summer fruit."ʸ Then the LORD said to me,

"The endᶻ has come upon my people
Israel;
I will never again pass them by.
³ The songs of the templeᵃ shall become
wailings in that day,"
says the Lord GOD;
"the dead bodies shall be many,
cast out in every place. Be silent!"

4 Hear this, you that trample on the needy,
and bring to ruin the poor of the land,
5 saying, "When will the new moon be over
so that we may sell grain;
and the sabbath,
so that we may offer wheat for sale?
We will make the ephah small and the
shekel great,
and practice deceit with false balances,
6 buying the poor for silver
and the needy for a pair of sandals,
and selling the sweepings of
the wheat."

7 The LORD has sworn by the pride
of Jacob:
Surely I will never forget any of their
deeds.
8 Shall not the land tremble on
this account,
and everyone mourn who lives in it,

ʷ Or *for a judgment by fire*   ˣ Or *was*   ʸ Heb *qayits*   ᶻ Heb *qets*   ᵃ Or *palace*

and all of it rise like the Nile,
and be tossed about and sink again,
like the Nile of Egypt?

9 On that day, says the Lord GOD,
I will make the sun go down at noon,
and darken the earth in broad daylight.
10 I will turn your feasts into mourning,
and all your songs into lamentation;
I will bring sackcloth on all loins,
and baldness on every head;
I will make it like the mourning for an
only son,
and the end of it like a bitter day.

11 The time is surely coming, says the Lord
GOD,
when I will send a famine on the land;
not a famine of bread, or a thirst for
water,
but of hearing the words of the LORD.

8.11 Worst of All Famines

*In this chapter, God describes devastations that
will fall upon Israel if they do not repent. One
judgment, however stands out above all
others: The nation will experience the silence of
God, a famine of the words of the Lord. A few
more prophets succeeded Amos, but after
Malachi no prophet appeared in Israel for four
centuries, until John the Baptist came to
announce Jesus.*

12 They shall wander from sea to sea,
and from north to east;
they shall run to and fro, seeking the
word of the LORD,
but they shall not find it.

13 In that day the beautiful young women
and the young men
shall faint for thirst.
14 Those who swear by Ashimah of Samaria,
and say, "As your god lives, O Dan,"
and, "As the way of Beer-sheba lives"—
they shall fall, and never rise again.

The Destruction of Israel

9 I saw the LORD standing beside[b] the altar,
and he said:
Strike the capitals until the thresholds
shake,
and shatter them on the heads of all
the people;[c]

and those who are left I will kill with the
sword;
not one of them shall flee away,
not one of them shall escape.

2 Though they dig into Sheol,
from there shall my hand take them;
though they climb up to heaven,
from there I will bring them down.
3 Though they hide themselves on the top
of Carmel,
from there I will search out and take
them;
and though they hide from my sight at
the bottom of the sea,
there I will command the sea-serpent,
and it shall bite them.
4 And though they go into captivity in front
of their enemies,
there I will command the sword, and it
shall kill them;
and I will fix my eyes on them
for harm and not for good.
5 The Lord, GOD of hosts,
he who touches the earth and it melts,
and all who live in it mourn,
and all of it rises like the Nile,
and sinks again, like the Nile of Egypt;
6 who builds his upper chambers in the
heavens,
and founds his vault upon the earth;
who calls for the waters of the sea,
and pours them out upon the surface
of the earth—
the LORD is his name.

9.4 An Inescapable God

*The beautiful verses of Psalm 139.7–12
describe God's inescapable presence as a
comfort. Here, in similar poetry, Amos gives the
opposite side of that truth. Those whom God
opposes can find no refuge. They may hide on
top of Mount Carmel, or even at the very
bottom of the sea, but God's eye will follow
them.*

7 Are you not like the Ethiopians[d] to me,
O people of Israel? says the LORD.
Did I not bring Israel up from the land of
Egypt,
and the Philistines from Caphtor and
the Arameans from Kir?
8 The eyes of the Lord GOD are upon the
sinful kingdom,

---

b Or *on*   *c* Heb *all of them*   *d* Or *Nubians*; Heb *Cushites*

and I will destroy it from the face of
the earth
—except that I will not utterly destroy
the house of Jacob,
says the LORD.

9 For lo, I will command,
and shake the house of Israel among
all the nations
as one shakes with a sieve,
but no pebble shall fall to the ground.
10 All the sinners of my people shall die by
the sword,
who say, "Evil shall not overtake or
meet us."

The Restoration of David's Kingdom

11 On that day I will raise up
the booth of David that is fallen,
and repair its e breaches,
and raise up its f ruins,
and rebuild it as in the days of old;
12 in order that they may possess the
remnant of Edom

and all the nations who are called by
my name,
says the LORD who does this.

13 The time is surely coming, says the LORD,
when the one who plows shall overtake
the one who reaps,
and the treader of grapes the one who
sows the seed;
the mountains shall drip sweet wine,
and all the hills shall flow with it.
14 I will restore the fortunes of my people
Israel,
and they shall rebuild the ruined cities
and inhabit them;
they shall plant vineyards and drink their
wine,
and they shall make gardens and eat
their fruit.
15 I will plant them upon their land,
and they shall never again be plucked
up
out of the land that I have given them,
says the LORD your God.

e Gk: Heb their   f Gk: Heb his

OBADIAH

Poetic Justice
Obadiah gave the final word on a blood feud

> As you have done, it shall be done to you.
> 15

THE FEUD BEGAN WITH TWIN brothers, Jacob and Esau. Esau, the older by minutes, would have inherited family leadership, but in a moment of hunger he traded it for a meal (Genesis 25.19–34). Jacob went on to become the founding father of the nation of Israel. Esau, a born hunter, moved southeast to desolate mountain country. He founded the nation of Edom.

Their descendants continued the quarrel. Over hundreds of years the two nations battled repeatedly but inconclusively. The Edomites' capital, Sela, sat on a high plateau above a sheer cliff; the only access was by a deep ravine. From that well-protected enclave, the Edomites raided Israel.

Though the Israelites had been commanded, "You shall not abhor any of the Edomites, for they are your kin" (Deuteronomy 23.7), they grew to regard the Edomites as cruel and heartless. Repeatedly the prophets predicted Edom's punishment by God. The final straw came when Babylon dismembered Jerusalem and took its citizens into exile. The Edomites egged on the conquering army, preyed on fleeing Israelites, and helped plunder Jerusalem. Psalm 137, one of the saddest passages in the Bible, records the Israelite bitterness over this. As Esau had cared more for a meal than for the family name, so his descendants cared more for the profit they could get from plunder than for the compassion they owed a brother.

Fair Return for Cruelty

Obadiah predicts poetic justice for proud Edom: their treachery toward Judah (verses 11–12) repaid with treachery from their own allies (7), their robbery (13) repaid with robbery (5–6), their violence (10) with violence (9), their love of destruction (12–14) repaid with utter destruction (10,18). Obadiah predicts that downtrodden Israel will rise again, while Edom will disappear from the face of the earth.

This prediction came precisely true. Edom was destroyed, not by Israel but by a series of foreign invaders. The last remnant of Edomites were destroyed in the Roman siege of Jerusalem in A.D. 70. Ironically, the nation that had tormented Jews in Jerusalem later died defending that city.

Why does this blood feud earn a place in Scripture? It demonstrates God's ongoing protection of his people from their enemies. It also shows that God's standards extend beyond his chosen people. Every nation will be judged, like Edom, by their own standard: "As you have done, it shall be done to you" (15).

How to Read Obadiah

The shortest book in the Old Testament, Obadiah can easily be read and understood in one sitting. Many readers, however, have a hard time seeing the importance of this ongoing border feud between blood relatives.

A Bible dictionary can summarize the centuries of violence. Look under "Edom." Perhaps, though, you can only fully appreciate Israel's feelings by reflecting on your own when a close relative treats you cruelly. A family betrayal is uniquely offensive to God and humanity. Obadiah reminds us that justice will be done.

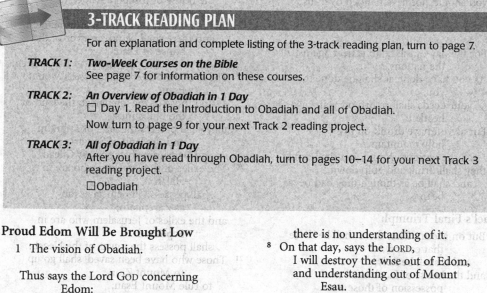

3-TRACK READING PLAN

For an explanation and complete listing of the 3-track reading plan, turn to page 7.

TRACK 1: **_Two-Week Courses on the Bible_**
See page 7 for information on these courses.

TRACK 2: **_An Overview of Obadiah in 1 Day_**
☐ Day 1. Read the Introduction to Obadiah and all of Obadiah.

Now turn to page 9 for your next Track 2 reading project.

TRACK 3: **_All of Obadiah in 1 Day_**
After you have read through Obadiah, turn to pages 10–14 for your next Track 3 reading project.
☐Obadiah

Proud Edom Will Be Brought Low

1 The vision of Obadiah.

Thus says the Lord GOD concerning
        Edom:
We have heard a report from the LORD,
    and a messenger has been sent among
        the nations:
"Rise up! Let us rise against it for battle!"
2 I will surely make you least among the
                nations;
    you shall be utterly despised.
3 Your proud heart has deceived you,
    you that live in the clefts of the rock,[a]
    whose dwelling is in the heights.
You say in your heart,
    "Who will bring me down to
        the ground?"
4 Though you soar aloft like the eagle,
    though your nest is set among the stars,
    from there I will bring you down,
                        says the LORD.

Pillage and Slaughter Will Repay Edom's Cruelty

5 If thieves came to you,
    if plunderers by night
    —how you have been destroyed!—
    would they not steal only what they
        wanted?
If grape-gatherers came to you,
    would they not leave gleanings?
6 How Esau has been pillaged,
    his treasures searched out!
7 All your allies have deceived you,
    they have driven you to the border;
your confederates have prevailed against you;
    those who ate[b] your bread have set a
        trap for you—

there is no understanding of it.
8 On that day, says the LORD,
    I will destroy the wise out of Edom,
    and understanding out of Mount
        Esau.
9 Your warriors shall be shattered,
        O Teman,
    so that everyone from Mount Esau will
        be cut off.

Edom Mistreated His Brother

10 For the slaughter and violence done to
            your brother Jacob,
    shame shall cover you,
    and you shall be cut off forever.
11 On the day that you stood aside,
    on the day that strangers carried off his
        wealth,
and foreigners entered his gates
    and cast lots for Jerusalem,
    you too were like one of them.
12 But you should not have gloated[c] over[d]
            your brother
    on the day of his misfortune;
you should not have rejoiced over the
            people of Judah
    on the day of their ruin;
you should not have boasted
    on the day of distress.
13 You should not have entered the gate of
            my people
    on the day of their calamity;
you should not have joined in the
            gloating over Judah's[e] disaster
    on the day of his calamity;
you should not have looted his goods
    on the day of his calamity.
14 You should not have stood at
            the crossings

_a_ Or _clefts of Sela_   _b_ Cn: Heb lacks _those who ate_   _c_ Heb _But do not gloat_ (and similarly through verse 14)
_d_ Heb _on the day of_   _e_ Heb _his_

to cut off his fugitives;
you should not have handed over his
    survivors
    on the day of distress.

15 For the day of the LORD is near against all
    the nations.
As you have done, it shall be done to
    you;
    your deeds shall return on your own
    head.
16 For as you have drunk on my
    holy mountain,
    all the nations around you shall drink;
they shall drink and gulp down,*f*
    and shall be as though they had never
    been.

Israel's Final Triumph

17 But on Mount Zion there shall be those
    that escape,
    and it shall be holy;
and the house of Jacob shall take
    possession of those who
    dispossessed them.

18 The house of Jacob shall be a fire,
    the house of Joseph a flame,
    and the house of Esau stubble;
they shall burn them and consume them,
    and there shall be no survivor of the
    house of Esau;
        for the LORD has spoken.
19 Those of the Negeb shall possess Mount
    Esau,
    and those of the Shephelah the land of
    the Philistines;
they shall possess the land of Ephraim
    and the land of Samaria,
    and Benjamin shall possess Gilead.
20 The exiles of the Israelites who are in
    Halah*g*
    shall possess*h* Phoenicia as far
    as Zarephath;
and the exiles of Jerusalem who are in
    Sepharad
    shall possess the towns of the Negeb.
21 Those who have been saved*i* shall go up
    to Mount Zion
    to rule Mount Esau;
    and the kingdom shall be the LORD's.

---

f Meaning of Heb uncertain   *g* Cn: Heb *in this army*   *h* Cn: Meaning of Heb uncertain   *i* Or *Saviors*

JONAH

Good News for the Enemy?
Jonah balked at loving the cruel Assyrians

"And should I not be concerned about Nineveh, that great city, in which there are more than a hundred and twenty thousand persons...?" 4.11

JESUS TOLD HIS FOLLOWERS, "LOVE your enemies and pray for those who persecute you" (Matthew 5.44). While everyone talks admiringly about that command, loving your enemies is no easy thing. Many people doubt whether it is even right. Should we forgive the Nazis? Should we make a point to be kind to the Ku Klux Klan? Should we have compassion on dictators like Saddam Hussein?

The book of Jonah tells the story of a man whom God instructed to love his enemies in Nineveh. True to life, the prophet Jonah did just the opposite of what God commanded. He refused to go to the people he hated. Instead, he tried to run away from the Lord.

Nineveh was a large, important city in Assyria, situated on the river Tigris. It posed a grave military threat to tiny Israel. God sent Jonah there, and he responded without hesitation: in Joppa he caught a boat going in the opposite direction. Obviously, Jonah didn't want to warn Nineveh's citizens they were about to be destroyed. He suspected they would repent and God would forgive them.

Why Jonah Didn't Want to Go

We can't be sure why Jonah hated Assyria, but another short Old Testament book, Nahum, gives a clue. This book, also completely dedicated to Nineveh, describes a ruthless, bloodthirsty people. The Assyrians themselves left monuments to their cruelty—long, boastful inscriptions describing their torture and slaughter of people who opposed them.

Israelites had reasons to hate and fear Nineveh. But God *loved* Nineveh. He wanted to save the city, not destroy it. He knew Nineveh was ripe for change. When Jonah finally preached there, the entire city believed his message and repented. Though cruel and hardened, Nineveh was ready to believe God. Israel had never responded to a prophet like these Assyrians did.

An Attitude Like God's

Since God repeatedly warned the Israelites not to intermarry with people of other religions, and even ordered them to drive other nations out of the promised land, some readers conclude that the Old Testament is racially narrow-minded. They say the New Testament gives the first indication that God cares for non-Jewish people.

The book of Jonah contradicts that view. It shows, instead, that God wanted to use Israelites like Jonah as agents of his concern. They would preach doom but always with the hope that the warning would lead to repentance.

Jonah needed to develop an attitude like God's toward his enemies. Insistently, God led Jonah to this understanding of his own mind and heart. The book of Jonah is a story of a miraculous change in Nineveh, but even more a story of miraculous change in Jonah.

How to Read Jonah

Like Esther and Ruth, Jonah is a delightful short narrative by a master writer. Its spiritual implications are powerful and obvious. You can easily read it at one sitting.

As you read Jonah, notice the changes that the city of Nineveh goes through. Try also to trace the changes that occur in Jonah, and observe how God pushes him to make these changes. Then ask yourself: What did this book say to its original Jewish readers? What does it say to me?

You may also be interested in following Nineveh's entire history. Though the Ninevites repented in Jonah's time, they later returned to old patterns. Later prophets (Nahum and Zephaniah) predicted Nineveh's downfall for "endless cruelty" (Nahum 3.19), and in 612 B.C. that city was destroyed, never to be inhabited again. A Bible dictionary can summarize Nineveh's long history as a world power; look under "Assyria." To place Jonah in Israelite history, see "A Lineup of Rulers," pages 1349–1357.

Is Jonah a "fish story"? Interpreters differ over whether it should be read as a parable (not necessarily factual) or as historical fact. At least one reliable account exists of a man swallowed by a sperm whale and later found, alive, in the whale's stomach. Jonah's historical basis cannot be dismissed simply because of the "great fish."

More to the point, Jesus compared himself to Jonah, and the people of his time to the Ninevites (Matthew 12.39–41; Luke 11.29–32). He predicted that "the people of Nineveh will rise up at the judgment with this generation and condemn it, because they repented at the proclamation of Jonah, and see, something greater than Jonah is here!" It is hard to see how fictional characters could stand up at an event Jesus evidently believed would be historical.

3-TRACK READING PLAN

For an explanation and complete listing of the 3-track reading plan, turn to page 7.

TRACK 1: *Two-Week Courses on the Bible*
See page 7 for information on these courses.

TRACK 2: *An Overview of Jonah in 1 Day*
☐ Day 1. Read the Introduction to Jonah and chapters 3 and 4. These two short chapters tell the less familiar part of the story: How Jonah got to Nineveh and became more bitter than before.

Now turn to page 9 for your next Track 2 reading project.

TRACK 3: *All of Jonah in 2 Days*
After you have read through Jonah, turn to pages 10–14 for your next Track 3 reading project.
☐1–2 ☐3–4

Jonah Tries to Run Away from God

1 Now the word of the LORD came to Jonah son of Amittai, saying, 2"Go at once to Nineveh, that great city, and cry out against it; for their wickedness has come up before me." 3But Jonah set out to flee to Tarshish from the presence of the LORD. He went down to Joppa and found a ship going to Tarshish; so he paid his fare and went on board, to go with them to Tarshish, away from the presence of the LORD.

4 But the LORD hurled a great wind upon the sea, and such a mighty storm came upon the sea that the ship threatened to break up. 5Then the mariners were afraid, and each cried to his god. They threw the cargo that was in the ship into the sea, to lighten it for them. Jonah, meanwhile, had gone down into the hold of the ship and had lain down, and was fast asleep. 6The captain came and said to him, "What are you doing sound asleep? Get up, call on your god! Perhaps the god will spare us a thought so that we do not perish."

7 The sailors*a* said to one another, "Come, let us cast lots, so that we may know on whose account this calamity has come upon us." So they cast lots, and the lot fell on Jonah. 8Then they said to him, "Tell us why this calamity has come upon us. What is your occupation? Where do you come from? What is your country? And of what people are you?" 9"I am a Hebrew," he replied. "I worship the LORD, the God of heaven, who made the sea and the dry land." 10Then the men were even more afraid, and said to him, "What is this that you have done!" For the men knew that he was fleeing from the presence of the LORD, because he had told them so.

11 Then they said to him, "What shall we do to you, that the sea may quiet down for us?" For the sea was growing more and more tempestuous. 12He said to them, "Pick me up and throw me into the sea; then the sea will quiet down for you; for I know it is because of me that this great storm

a Heb *They*

has come upon you." [13]Nevertheless the men rowed hard to bring the ship back to land, but they could not, for the sea grew more and more stormy against them. [14]Then they cried out to the LORD, "Please, O LORD, we pray, do not let us perish on account of this man's life. Do not make us guilty of innocent blood; for you, O LORD, have done as it pleased you." [15]So they picked Jonah up and threw him into the sea; and the sea ceased from its raging. [16]Then the men feared the LORD even more, and they offered a sacrifice to the LORD and made vows.

[17][b] But the LORD provided a large fish to swallow up Jonah; and Jonah was in the belly of the fish three days and three nights.

A Psalm of Thanksgiving

2 Then Jonah prayed to the LORD his God from the belly of the fish, [2]saying,

"I called to the LORD out of my distress,
  and he answered me;
out of the belly of Sheol I cried,
  and you heard my voice.
[3] You cast me into the deep,
  into the heart of the seas,
  and the flood surrounded me;
all your waves and your billows
  passed over me.
[4] Then I said, 'I am driven away
  from your sight;
how[c] shall I look again
  upon your holy temple?'
[5] The waters closed in over me;
  the deep surrounded me;
weeds were wrapped around my head
[6] at the roots of the mountains.
I went down to the land
  whose bars closed upon me forever;
yet you brought up my life from the Pit,
  O LORD my God.
[7] As my life was ebbing away,
  I remembered the LORD;
and my prayer came to you,
  into your holy temple.
[8] Those who worship vain idols
  forsake their true loyalty.
[9] But I with the voice of thanksgiving
  will sacrifice to you;
what I have vowed I will pay.
  Deliverance belongs to the LORD!"

[10]Then the LORD spoke to the fish, and it spewed Jonah out upon the dry land.

Conversion of Nineveh

3 The word of the LORD came to Jonah a second time, saying, [2]"Get up, go to Nineveh, that great city, and proclaim to it the message that I tell you." [3]So Jonah set out and went to Nineveh, according to the word of the LORD. Now Nineveh was an exceedingly large city, a three days' walk across. [4]Jonah began to go into the city, going a day's walk. And he cried out, "Forty days more, and Nineveh shall be overthrown!" [5]And the people of Nineveh believed God; they proclaimed a fast, and everyone, great and small, put on sackcloth.

3.3 How Big a City?

Archaeologists who have dug up Nineveh report that at its peak its walls were 7 ¾ miles in circumference. Since it would not take three days to go around a city of that size, most probably the "three days" refers to the administrative district of which Nineveh was the capital. This comprised four cities with a circumference of about 60 miles. Another possibility: Perhaps it took Jonah three days to go to every neighborhood, marketplace, and city gate with his message.

[6] When the news reached the king of Nineveh, he rose from his throne, removed his robe, covered himself with sackcloth, and sat in ashes. [7]Then he had a proclamation made in Nineveh: "By the decree of the king and his nobles: No human being or animal, no herd or flock, shall taste anything. They shall not feed, nor shall they drink water. [8]Human beings and animals shall be covered with sackcloth, and they shall cry mightily to God. All shall turn from their evil ways and from the violence that is in their hands. [9]Who knows? God may relent and change his mind; he may turn from his fierce anger, so that we do not perish."

[10] When God saw what they did, how they turned from their evil ways, God changed his mind about the calamity that he had said he would bring upon them; and he did not do it.

Jonah's Anger

4 But this was very displeasing to Jonah, and he became angry. [2]He prayed to the LORD and said, "O LORD! Is not this what I said while I was still in my own country? That is why I fled to Tarshish at the beginning; for I knew that you are a gracious God and merciful, slow to anger, and abounding in steadfast love, and ready to relent from punishing. [3]And now, O LORD, please take my life from me, for it is better for me to die than to live." [4]And the LORD said, "Is it right for you to be angry?" [5]Then Jonah went out of the city and sat down east of the city, and made a booth for himself there. He sat under it in the shade, waiting to see what would become of the city.

b Ch 2.1 in Heb   *c* Theodotion: Heb *surely*

6 The LORD God appointed a bush,[d] and made it come up over Jonah, to give shade over his head, to save him from his discomfort; so Jonah was very happy about the bush. 7But when dawn came up the next day, God appointed a worm that attacked the bush, so that it withered. 8When the sun rose, God prepared a sultry east wind, and the sun beat down on the head of Jonah so that he was faint and asked that he might die. He said, "It is better for me to die than to live."

4.2 Too Merciful a God?

The poet Robert Frost said, "After Jonah, you could never trust God not to be merciful again." The balky prophet discloses why he ran away from God in the first place: He was afraid God would forgive his archenemies. In fact, God did just that, after Nineveh repented with an eagerness that the Jews themselves often lacked (see Matthew 12.41). Pointedly, the book of Jonah ends with a question. Can anyone put limits on God's mercy and forgiveness?

Jonah Is Reproved

9 But God said to Jonah, "Is it right for you to be angry about the bush?" And he said, "Yes, angry enough to die." 10Then the LORD said, "You are concerned about the bush, for which you did not labor and which you did not grow; it came into being in a night and perished in a night. 11And should I not be concerned about Nineveh, that great city, in which there are more than a hundred and twenty thousand persons who do not know their right hand from their left, and also many animals?"

---

[d] Heb *qiqayon*, possibly *the castor bean plant*

MICAH

Light in a Dark Time
Evil and violence were creeping south toward Jerusalem

COUNTRY BOYS OFTEN LOSE PERSPECTIVE in the big city. They gawk at the tall buildings, the fancy clothes, and the showy symbols of power. Micah was a country boy from Moresheth, a small village in the no-man's-land southwest of Jerusalem. While his contemporary, Isaiah, moved in and out of the king's palace, Micah shows no sign of traveling in such circles.

> And what does the LORD require of you but to do justice, and to love kindness, and to walk humbly with your God? 6.8

Yet this country boy kept his sense of perspective. The blood and violence of his day did not overwhelm him, nor was he intimidated by powerful and wealthy people. He spoke like a person who had seen the world through God's eyes.

Micah lived in one of the darkest times in Israel's history, a time of brutal warfare. The country had long been split into North and South. Micah saw war break out between these sides, with 120,000 deaths on the southern side alone (2 Chronicles 28.6). Then Assyria, the brutal chief power of the day, smashed the Northern Kingdom after a three-year siege of its capital, Samaria. Only a miracle kept those same Assyrian armies out of Jerusalem (2 Chronicles 32). But for how long would the South remain free?

The Sin of the South

Micah had no doubt how to interpret these chaotic events. God had punished the northern nation of Israel for sins summarized in 2 Kings 17.16–17: idolatry, Baal worship, child sacrifice, magic and sorcery. Now these same activities were creeping south into Judah—so much so that Micah referred in disgust to Jerusalem as a "high place," the traditional setting for pagan idol worship (1.5). The same judgment the North had suffered would come to Judah if people continued to disobey God.

Other historical accounts give more details of the South's sins. They describe how King Ahaz set up a foreign altar in God's temple, altering the temple construction "because of the king of Assyria" (2 Kings 16.18). He gave his own children in human sacrifice and shut the Lord's temple, substituting altars on every street corner (2 Chronicles 28.3,24–25). Along with this religious corruption came every other kind of sin: dishonesty (6.10–11), bribery (3.11), injustice (2.2), and distrust that destroyed families (7.5–6).

Beyond the Darkness

Yet Micah saw light ahead. He perceived a majestic God over all events, who punished his people only to purify and restore them. Along with making some of the Bible's frankest predictions of destruction, Micah gave some of the clearest predictions of the Messiah, the leader who would come to save Israel. Micah's perspective encompassed not only the events of his time but events far into the future, when the nations "shall beat their swords into plowshares" (4.3).

Micah looked straight at the darkness of his time and at the darkness yet to come. But his perspective—God's perspective—enabled him to see beyond darkness. "Do not rejoice over me, O my enemy; when I fall, I shall rise; when I sit in darkness, the LORD will be a light to me" (7.8).

How to Read Micah

Micah had the big view of history, and thus he covered a lot of ground. His book, only seven chapters, is loaded with pronouncements on the events of several thousand years. Because so much is jammed into so short a space, reading Micah can be confusing. A fragment may deal with the Messiah, for instance, and without warning the next few verses shift to the battle against Assyria.

To grasp Micah's message, think of his book as a collection of short speeches. One speech doesn't necessarily lead into the next. Instead of reading quickly from start to finish, pause after each short section to see whether you understand what it says. Try to understand who is speaking. Sometimes God speaks, sometimes Micah, sometimes the rebellious people.

In general, Micah follows this outline: chapters 1–3 indict both Northern and Southern Kingdoms, with their leaders; chapters 4 and 5 turn to the wonderful future God is planning; the last two chapters give the trial, punishment, and hope of the guilty nations.

It's very helpful to understand Micah's historical situation. Micah 1.1 names the kings of Judah he worked under. You can read about these kings, and their northern counterparts, in 2 Kings 15.27–20.21 and 2 Chronicles 27–32. For a brief summary, see "A Lineup of Rulers," pages 1349–1357.

3-TRACK READING PLAN

For an explanation and complete listing of the 3-track reading plan, turn to page 7.

TRACK 1: **Two-Week Courses on the Bible**
See page 7 for information on these courses.

TRACK 2: **An Overview of Micah in 1 Day**
☐ Day 1. Read the Introduction to Micah and chapter 6, which includes one of the most succinct statements in the Old Testament of what God wants our lives to be.

Now turn to page 9 for your next Track 2 reading project.

TRACK 3: **All of Micah in 7 Days**
After you have read through Micah, turn to pages 10–14 for your next Track 3 reading project.
☐1   ☐2   ☐3   ☐4   ☐5   ☐6   ☐7

1 The word of the LORD that came to Micah of Moresheth in the days of Kings Jotham, Ahaz, and Hezekiah of Judah, which he saw concerning Samaria and Jerusalem.

Judgment Pronounced against Samaria

2 Hear, you peoples, all of you;
    listen, O earth, and all that is in it;
and let the Lord GOD be a witness against
        you,
    the Lord from his holy temple.
3 For lo, the LORD is coming out of his
        place,
    and will come down and tread upon
        the high places of the earth.
4 Then the mountains will melt under him
    and the valleys will burst open,
like wax near the fire,
    like waters poured down a steep place.
5 All this is for the transgression of Jacob
    and for the sins of the house of Israel.
What is the transgression of Jacob?
    Is it not Samaria?

And what is the high place[a] of Judah?
    Is it not Jerusalem?
6 Therefore I will make Samaria a heap in
        the open country,
    a place for planting vineyards.
I will pour down her stones into
        the valley,
    and uncover her foundations.
7 All her images shall be beaten to pieces,
    all her wages shall be burned with fire,
    and all her idols I will lay waste;
for as the wages of a prostitute she
        gathered them,
    and as the wages of a prostitute they
        shall again be used.

The Doom of the Cities of Judah

8 For this I will lament and wail;
    I will go barefoot and naked;
I will make lamentation like the jackals,
    and mourning like the ostriches.
9 For her wound[b] is incurable.
    It has come to Judah;

---

a Heb what are the high places   b Gk Syr Vg: Heb wounds

it has reached to the gate of my people,
to Jerusalem.

10 Tell it not in Gath,
weep not at all;
in Beth-leaphrah
roll yourselves in the dust.

1.10 A Passion for Punning

Puns stump even the best translators. In verses 10–15 Micah plays on the names of a series of Israelite towns—probably marking the path Assyrian invaders followed. The puns were not meant to be funny. They extracted grief from the place-names of the invasion. Micah's Hebrew puns are virtually untranslatable.

11 Pass on your way,
inhabitants of Shaphir,
in nakedness and shame;
the inhabitants of Zaanan
do not come forth;
Beth-ezel is wailing
and shall remove its support from you.
12 For the inhabitants of Maroth
wait anxiously for good,
yet disaster has come down from the
LORD
to the gate of Jerusalem.
13 Harness the steeds to the chariots,
inhabitants of Lachish;
it was the beginning of sin
to daughter Zion,
for in you were found
the transgressions of Israel.
14 Therefore you shall give parting gifts
to Moresheth-gath;
the houses of Achzib shall be a deception
to the kings of Israel.
15 I will again bring a conqueror upon you,
inhabitants of Mareshah;
the glory of Israel
shall come to Adullam.
16 Make yourselves bald and cut off your
hair
for your pampered children;
make yourselves as bald as the eagle,
for they have gone from you into exile.

Social Evils Denounced

2 Alas for those who devise wickedness
and evil deeds*c* on their beds!
When the morning dawns, they perform
it,
because it is in their power.
2 They covet fields, and seize them;

houses, and take them away;
they oppress householder and house,
people and their inheritance.
3 Therefore thus says the LORD:
Now, I am devising against this family an
evil
from which you cannot remove your
necks;
and you shall not walk haughtily,
for it will be an evil time.
4 On that day they shall take up a taunt
song against you,
and wail with bitter lamentation,
and say, "We are utterly ruined;
the LORD *d* alters the inheritance of my
people;
how he removes it from me!
Among our captors*e* he parcels out
our fields."
5 Therefore you will have no one to cast the
line by lot
in the assembly of the LORD.

6 "Do not preach"—thus they preach—
"one should not preach of such things;
disgrace will not overtake us."
7 Should this be said, O house of Jacob?
Is the LORD's patience exhausted?
Are these his doings?
Do not my words do good
to one who walks uprightly?
8 But you rise up against my people*f* as an
enemy;
you strip the robe from the peaceful,*g*
from those who pass by trustingly
with no thought of war.
9 The women of my people you drive out
from their pleasant houses;
from their young children you take away
my glory forever.
10 Arise and go;
for this is no place to rest,
because of uncleanness that destroys
with a grievous destruction.*h*
11 If someone were to go about uttering
empty falsehoods,
saying, "I will preach to you of wine
and strong drink,"
such a one would be the preacher for
this people!

A Promise for the Remnant of Israel

12 I will surely gather all of you, O Jacob,
I will gather the survivors of Israel;
I will set them together
like sheep in a fold,
like a flock in its pasture;
it will resound with people.

---

c Cn: Heb *work evil*   *d* Heb *he*   *e* Cn: Heb *the rebellious*
from before a garment   *h* Meaning of Heb uncertain

f Cn: Heb *But yesterday my people rose*   *g* Cn: Heb

13 The one who breaks out will go up before
them;
they will break through and pass the
gate,

2.11 Plenty of Beer

*Modern politicians avoid the phrase like
poison: "tax hike." They love to proclaim "a
new day in America," and hate to bring bad
news. Prophets in Micah's time were just the
same. They insisted that Micah stop predicting
bad news (2.6; 3.5) and join their peace
bandwagon. In fact, says Micah sarcastically,
the ideal prophet for feel-good Israel would
predict plenty of wine and beer.*

going out by it.
Their king will pass on before them,
the LORD at their head.

Wicked Rulers and Prophets

3 And I said:
Listen, you heads of Jacob
and rulers of the house of Israel!
Should you not know justice?—
2 you who hate the good and love the
evil,
who tear the skin off my people,[i]
and the flesh off their bones;
3 who eat the flesh of my people,
flay their skin off them,
break their bones in pieces,
and chop them up like meat[j] in a
kettle,
like flesh in a caldron.

4 Then they will cry to the LORD,
but he will not answer them;
he will hide his face from them at that
time,
because they have acted wickedly.

5 Thus says the LORD concerning
the prophets
who lead my people astray,
who cry "Peace"
when they have something to eat,
but declare war against those
who put nothing into their mouths.
6 Therefore it shall be night to you, without
vision,
and darkness to you, without
revelation.
The sun shall go down upon
the prophets,
and the day shall be black over them;
7 the seers shall be disgraced,

and the diviners put to shame;
they shall all cover their lips,
for there is no answer from God.
8 But as for me, I am filled with power,
with the spirit of the LORD,
and with justice and might,
to declare to Jacob his transgression
and to Israel his sin.

9 Hear this, you rulers of the house of
Jacob
and chiefs of the house of Israel,
who abhor justice
and pervert all equity,
10 who build Zion with blood
and Jerusalem with wrong!
11 Its rulers give judgment for a bribe,
its priests teach for a price,
its prophets give oracles for money;
yet they lean upon the LORD and say,
"Surely the LORD is with us!
No harm shall come upon us."
12 Therefore because of you
Zion shall be plowed as a field;
Jerusalem shall become a heap of ruins,
and the mountain of the house a
wooded height.

3.12 Life-saving Prophecy

*One hundred years after this clear prophecy of
its destruction, Jerusalem still stood. By that
time Jeremiah was making similar predictions,
which led to his arrest for treason. Some of the
city leaders, however, quoted Micah's "ancient"
prophecy, pointing out that since Micah had
not been put to death, neither should Jeremiah
be (Jeremiah 26.18–19). Their memory
probably saved Jeremiah's life.*

*Within another 20 years, both Micah's and
Jeremiah's predictions came true and
Jerusalem was reduced to rubble.*

Peace and Security through Obedience

4 In days to come
the mountain of the LORD's house
shall be established as the highest of the
mountains,
and shall be raised up above the hills.
Peoples shall stream to it,
2 and many nations shall come and say:
"Come, let us go up to the mountain of
the LORD,
to the house of the God of Jacob;
that he may teach us his ways
and that we may walk in his paths."
For out of Zion shall go forth instruction,

i Heb *from them*   *j* Gk: Heb *as*

and the word of the Lord
    from Jerusalem.
3 He shall judge between many peoples,
    and shall arbitrate between strong
        nations far away;
they shall beat their swords into
    plowshares,
    and their spears into pruning hooks;
nation shall not lift up sword against
    nation,
neither shall they learn war any more;

4.3 Parallel with Isaiah

Micah 4.1–3, which describes the wonderful future in store for the world, has an almost exact parallel in Isaiah 2.2–4. Isaiah must have quoted Micah, or vice versa, or perhaps both quoted a third unknown prophet. Both prophets spoke in Jerusalem at about the same time.

4 but they shall all sit under their own vines
        and under their own fig trees,
        and no one shall make them afraid;
    for the mouth of the Lord of hosts has
        spoken.

5 For all the peoples walk,
    each in the name of its god,
but we will walk in the name of the Lord
    our God
    forever and ever.

Restoration Promised after Exile

6 In that day, says the Lord,
    I will assemble the lame
and gather those who have been driven
    away,
    and those whom I have afflicted.
7 The lame I will make the remnant,
    and those who were cast off, a strong
        nation;
and the Lord will reign over them in
        Mount Zion
    now and forevermore.

8 And you, O tower of the flock,
    hill of daughter Zion,
to you it shall come,
    the former dominion shall come,
    the sovereignty of daughter Jerusalem.

9 Now why do you cry aloud?
    Is there no king in you?
Has your counselor perished,
    that pangs have seized you like a
        woman in labor?
10 Writhe and groan,[k] O daughter Zion,
    like a woman in labor;
for now you shall go forth from the city
    and camp in the open country;
    you shall go to Babylon.
There you shall be rescued,
    there the Lord will redeem you
    from the hands of your enemies.

11 Now many nations
    are assembled against you,
saying, "Let her be profaned,
    and let our eyes gaze upon Zion."
12 But they do not know
    the thoughts of the Lord;
they do not understand his plan,
    that he has gathered them as sheaves to
        the threshing floor.
13 Arise and thresh,
    O daughter Zion,
for I will make your horn iron
    and your hoofs bronze;
you shall beat in pieces many peoples,
    and shall[l] devote their gain to the
        Lord,
    their wealth to the Lord of the whole
        earth.

5 [m] Now you are walled around with a wall;[n]
    siege is laid against us;
with a rod they strike the ruler of Israel
    upon the cheek.

The Ruler from Bethlehem

2[o] But you, O Bethlehem of Ephrathah,
    who are one of the little clans of Judah,
from you shall come forth for me
    one who is to rule in Israel,
whose origin is from of old,
    from ancient days.
3 Therefore he shall give them up until the
        time

5.2 Messiah's Birthplace

When the Magi came looking for a newborn "king of the Jews," King Herod asked the biblical scholars where to search. They referred him to this passage (see Matthew 2.6), which predicted that the Messiah would come from the small town of Bethlehem. Micah also describes Christ as a shepherd who will not merely bring peace, but be Israel's peace.

---

k Meaning of Heb uncertain   l Gk Syr Tg: Heb *and I will*   m Ch 4.14 in Heb   n Cn Compare Gk: Meaning of Heb uncertain   o Ch 5.1 in Heb

when she who is in labor has brought
forth;
then the rest of his kindred shall return
to the people of Israel.
4 And he shall stand and feed his flock in
the strength of the LORD,
in the majesty of the name of the LORD
his God.
And they shall live secure, for now he
shall be great
to the ends of the earth;
5 and he shall be the one of peace.

If the Assyrians come into our land
and tread upon our soil,*p*
we will raise against them seven shepherds
and eight installed as rulers.
6 They shall rule the land of Assyria with
the sword,
and the land of Nimrod with the
drawn sword;*q*
they*r* shall rescue us from the Assyrians
if they come into our land
or tread within our border.

The Future Role of the Remnant

7 Then the remnant of Jacob,
surrounded by many peoples,
shall be like dew from the LORD,
like showers on the grass,
which do not depend upon people
or wait for any mortal.

8 And among the nations the remnant of
Jacob,
surrounded by many peoples,
shall be like a lion among the animals of
the forest,
like a young lion among the flocks of
sheep,
which, when it goes through, treads down
and tears in pieces, with no one to
deliver.
9 Your hand shall be lifted up over your
adversaries,
and all your enemies shall be cut off.

10 In that day, says the LORD,
I will cut off your horses from among
you
and will destroy your chariots;
11 and I will cut off the cities of your land
and throw down all your strongholds;
12 and I will cut off sorceries from your
hand,
and you shall have no more
soothsayers;
13 and I will cut off your images
and your pillars from among you,
and you shall bow down no more
to the work of your hands;
14 and I will uproot your sacred poles*s*
from among you
and destroy your towns.

p Gk: Heb *in our palaces*   *q* Cn: Heb *in its entrances*   *r* Heb *he*   *s* Heb *Asherim*

Seeing in Two Dimensions
Little distinction between next week and the next thousand years

> They shall beat their swords into plowshares, and their spears into pruning hooks. 4.3

WHEN YOU SEE A MOUNTAIN range from a distance, it's very difficult to tell which peak is highest. Often a smaller mountain looms largest simply because it is much closer to you than another, higher peak.

Micah, and many of the other Old Testament prophets, saw the future like that. They made little distinction between events coming next week and events that would come a thousand years later. They seemed to see the future with limited "depth perception."

In the space of one verse, for instance, Micah shifts from a prediction (3.12) that Jerusalem will become a mound of rubble—a prophecy fulfilled about 100 years later—to a prophecy (4.1) that the same mountain will be lifted up as "highest of the mountains"—something that has yet to be fulfilled today. In Micah 5.2 comes a prediction that Matthew 2.6 records as fulfilled by Jesus' birth in Bethlehem 700 years later.

In Micah, the thousands of years between these fulfillments are unclear. They all seem to be about the same distance into the future. Almost certainly, Micah himself saw them unclearly. First Peter 1.10–11 comments that "the prophets . . . made careful search and inquiry, inquiring about the person or time that the Spirit of Christ within them indicated when it testified in advance to the sufferings destined for Christ and the subsequent glory."

Life Questions: What emotions do you feel knowing that some prophecies have not yet been fulfilled?

15 And in anger and wrath I will execute
vengeance
on the nations that did not obey.

God Challenges Israel

6 Hear what the LORD says:
Rise, plead your case before
the mountains,
and let the hills hear your voice.
2 Hear, you mountains, the controversy of
the LORD,
and you enduring foundations of the
earth;
for the LORD has a controversy with his
people,
and he will contend with Israel.

3 "O my people, what have I done to you?
In what have I wearied you? Answer
me!
4 For I brought you up from the land of
Egypt,
and redeemed you from the house of
slavery;
and I sent before you Moses,
Aaron, and Miriam.
5 O my people, remember now what King
Balak of Moab devised,
what Balaam son of Beor answered
him,

and what happened from Shittim
to Gilgal,
that you may know the saving acts of
the LORD."

What God Requires

6 "With what shall I come before the LORD,
and bow myself before God on high?
Shall I come before him with
burnt offerings,
with calves a year old?
7 Will the LORD be pleased with thousands
of rams,
with ten thousands of rivers of oil?
Shall I give my firstborn for my
transgression,
the fruit of my body for the sin of my
soul?"
8 He has told you, O mortal, what is good;
and what does the LORD require of you
but to do justice, and to love kindness,
and to walk humbly with your God?

6.8 What God Wants

*Micah's most famous pronouncement
summarizes the qualities that matter to God.
Jesus spoke in similar terms to the Pharisees
about their religious hypocrisy: They gave a
tenth of even their spices to God, yet they
neglected justice, mercy, and faithfulness
(Matthew 23.23).*

6.5 Names with Meaning

*Speaking to people who knew their own
history well, Micah needed only to mention
names like Balaam and Balak to recall God's
goodness and humankind's disobedience.
Numbers 22–24 tells the story of Balaam, in
which Balak tried to get Balaam to curse Israel.
Balaam gave this famous reply: "How can I
curse whom God has not cursed?" (Numbers
23.8). The trip from Shittim to Gilgal apparently
refers to Israel's miraculous crossing of the
Jordan River (Joshua 3.1; 4.19–20), the final
stage in their journey from slavery in Egypt to
freedom in the promised land. These events,
which had occurred about 500 years before,
were as real to the Israelites as yesterday.*

*Verse 16 offers a different kind of memory:
"The statutes of Omri and all the works of the
house of Ahab." Omri and his son Ahab were
two of the most notoriously wicked kings in
Israelite history (1 Kings 16.21–33). Ahab went
so far as to marry Jezebel, a Phoenician
princess, and set up a temple for her god, Baal,
in the new capital of Samaria. He sponsored
her massacre of genuine prophets.*

Cheating and Violence to Be Punished

9 The voice of the LORD cries to the city
(it is sound wisdom to fear
your name):
Hear, O tribe and assembly of the city!*t*
10 Can I forget*u* the treasures of
wickedness in the house of the
wicked,
and the scant measure that is accursed?
11 Can I tolerate wicked scales
and a bag of dishonest weights?
12 Your*v* wealthy are full of violence;
your*w* inhabitants speak lies,
with tongues of deceit in their mouths.
13 Therefore I have begun*x* to strike you
down,
making you desolate because of your
sins.
14 You shall eat, but not be satisfied,
and there shall be a gnawing hunger
within you;
you shall put away, but not save,

---

t Cn Compare Gk: Heb *tribe, and who has appointed it yet?*   *u* Cn: Meaning of Heb uncertain   *v* Heb *Whose*
w Heb *whose*   *x* Gk Syr Vg: Heb *have made sick*

and what you save, I will hand over to
the sword.

15 You shall sow, but not reap;
    you shall tread olives, but not anoint
        yourselves with oil;
    you shall tread grapes, but not drink
        wine.

16 For you have kept the statutes of Omri[y]
    and all the works of the house
        of Ahab,
    and you have followed their counsels.
    Therefore I will make you a desolation,
        and your[z] inhabitants an object
            of hissing;
    so you shall bear the scorn of
        my people.

The Total Corruption of the People

7 Woe is me! For I have become like one
    who,
    after the summer fruit has
        been gathered,
    after the vintage has been gleaned,
finds no cluster to eat;
    there is no first-ripe fig for which I
        hunger.

2 The faithful have disappeared from the
        land,
    and there is no one left who is upright;
    they all lie in wait for blood,
    and they hunt each other with nets.

3 Their hands are skilled to do evil;
    the official and the judge ask for a
        bribe,
    and the powerful dictate what they desire;
    thus they pervert justice.[a]

4 The best of them is like a brier,
    the most upright of them a
        thorn hedge.
    The day of their[b] sentinels, of their[b]
        punishment, has come;
    now their confusion is at hand.

5 Put no trust in a friend,
    have no confidence in a loved one;
    guard the doors of your mouth
    from her who lies in your embrace;

6 for the son treats the father with
        contempt,
    the daughter rises up against
        her mother,
    the daughter-in-law against her
        mother-in-law;
    your enemies are members of your
        own household.

7 But as for me, I will look to the LORD,
    I will wait for the God of my salvation;
    my God will hear me.

Penitence and Trust in God

8 Do not rejoice over me, O my enemy;
    when I fall, I shall rise;
    when I sit in darkness,
        the LORD will be a light to me.

9 I must bear the indignation of the LORD,
        because I have sinned against him,
    until he takes my side
        and executes judgment for me.
    He will bring me out to the light;
        I shall see his vindication.

10 Then my enemy will see,
        and shame will cover her who said to
            me,
    "Where is the LORD your God?"
    My eyes will see her downfall;[c]
        now she will be trodden down
        like the mire of the streets.

A Prophecy of Restoration

11 A day for the building of your walls!
        In that day the boundary shall be far
            extended.

12 In that day they will come to you
        from Assyria to[d] Egypt,
    and from Egypt to the River,
        from sea to sea and from mountain to
            mountain.

13 But the earth will be desolate
        because of its inhabitants,
    for the fruit of their doings.

14 Shepherd your people with your staff,
        the flock that belongs to you,
    which lives alone in a forest
        in the midst of a garden land;
    let them feed in Bashan and Gilead
        as in the days of old.

15 As in the days when you came out of the
            land of Egypt,
        show us[e] marvelous things.

16 The nations shall see and be ashamed
        of all their might;
    they shall lay their hands on
            their mouths;
        their ears shall be deaf;

17 they shall lick dust like a snake,

7.18 Nobody Like God

*Theologians use big words to describe God's
unique qualities: transcendence, omnipotence,
omnipresence. Micah marveled even more over
this: God's forgiveness. Unlike the angry gods
of other nations, Israel's God delighted to show
mercy.*

---

y Gk Syr Vg Tg: Heb *the statutes of Omri are kept*   z Heb *its*   a Cn: Heb *they weave it*   b Heb *your*
c Heb lacks *downfall*   d One Ms: MT *Assyria and cities of*   e Cn: Heb *I will show him*

like the crawling things of the earth;
they shall come trembling out of their
fortresses;
they shall turn in dread to the LORD
our God,
and they shall stand in fear of
you.

God's Compassion and Steadfast Love

18 Who is a God like you, pardoning
iniquity
and passing over the transgression
of the remnant of your[f] possession?
He does not retain his anger forever,
because he delights in showing
clemency.
19 He will again have compassion upon us;
he will tread our iniquities under foot.
You will cast all our[g] sins
into the depths of the sea.
20 You will show faithfulness to Jacob
and unswerving loyalty to Abraham,
as you have sworn to our ancestors
from the days of old.

NAHUM

God's Answer to Injustice
A power above the powers

I S LIFE FAIR? IT RARELY seems so, especially in international politics. The most vicious dictators thrive, and raw power is the key ingredient in a successful foreign policy. Weak people get trampled.

Who can stand before his indignation? Who can endure the heat of his anger? 1.6

As a citizen of Judah, the prophet Nahum felt the force of such injustice. His message from God concerned the greatest city of the time, Nineveh. This city, the capital of Assyria, represented raw, brutal power—"endless cruelty," as Nahum put it (3.19). Though Nineveh was hundreds of miles northeast of Judah, Assyrian power dominated the Middle East. In contrast, Judah was a small, fragile state barely clinging to indepedence.

Nahum's Nerve

Judah's sister nation to the north, Israel, had already been defeated by Assyria and carried into exile. Only God's miraculous intervention had saved Judah on that occasion. And now, in Nahum's time, the Assyrians had returned. They dragged off Manasseh, the king, with a hook in his nose (2 Chronicles 33.11). Judah was forced to pay tribute as a vassal state.

Few people can stare into the face of such raw power and come away unimpressed. Nahum did so only because he had seen a far greater power—the power of a God whose wrath could shatter rocks. If God was angry, how could Nineveh stand? Nahum's absolute confidence in God is underlined throughout this book.

It took nerve to stand up and predict the downfall of the most powerful nation in the world. Yet, in this book, Nahum sounds unintimidated, almost lordly. He spoke with confidence because he knew God's character: "The Lord will by no means clear the guilty" (1.3).

Decline and Fall of Nineveh

Within a few years, Nahum's predictions came true. Nineveh did fall, never to rise again. The greatest city in the world became a pile of rubble overgrown with grass. Both Alexander the Great and Napoleon camped near it but had no idea a city had ever been there. The site became known as "the mound of many sheep."

The name *Nahum* means "comfort." Though Nahum describes God's anger, his message offers comfort to those who live with injustice and evil. "The Lord is good," said Nahum, "a stronghold in a day of trouble; he protects those who take refuge in him, even in a rushing flood. He will make a full end of his adversaries, and will pursue his enemies into darkness" (1.7–8). Nineveh is gone, but Nahum's testimony lives on, reminding us that though God's justice may seem slow, nothing can ultimately escape it.

How to Read Nahum

N ahum stands out from the other short prophetic books in two ways. He addressed a foreign city—Nineveh—instead of his own home nation, and he used unusually vivid language.

You can read more background on Judah and its relationship to Nineveh in the following historical accounts: 2 Kings 17–19 and 2 Chronicles 32–33.13. The background will help you understand why God was so angry at Nineveh.

As you read Nahum, pay special attention to the vivid imagery. Some of the best examples are the following:

Descriptions of warfare: 2.3–7; 3.1–3
Nineveh like a pool with its water draining out: 2.8
Nineveh like a lions' den, full of bones: 2.11–12
Nineveh like a prostitute shamed in the streets: 3.5–6
Nineveh's fortresses like fig trees, with fruit shaken into the mouth of their attacker: 3.12
Nineveh's numerous citizens like grasshoppers: prolific, voracious, and quickly disappearing: 3.15–17

3-TRACK READING PLAN

For an explanation and complete listing of the 3-track reading plan, turn to page 7.

TRACK 1: *Two-Week Courses on the Bible*
See page 8 for information on these courses.

TRACK 2: *An Overview of Nahum in 1 Day*
☐ Day 1. Read the Introduction to Nahum and chapter 1, which portrays God's anger against Nineveh's injustice.

Now turn to page 9 for your next Track 2 reading project.

TRACK 3: *All of Nahum in 3 Days*
After you have read through Nahum, turn to pages 10–14 for your next Track 3 reading project.
☐1   ☐2   ☐3

1 An oracle concerning Nineveh. The book of the vision of Nahum of Elkosh.

The Consuming Wrath of God

2 A jealous and avenging God is the LORD,
  the LORD is avenging and wrathful;
the LORD takes vengeance on his
      adversaries
  and rages against his enemies.
3 The LORD is slow to anger but great in
      power,
  and the LORD will by no means clear
      the guilty.

His way is in whirlwind and storm,
  and the clouds are the dust of his feet.
4 He rebukes the sea and makes it dry,
  and he dries up all the rivers;
Bashan and Carmel wither,
  and the bloom of Lebanon fades.
5 The mountains quake before him,
  and the hills melt;
the earth heaves before him,
  the world and all who live in it.

6 Who can stand before his indignation?
  Who can endure the heat of his anger?
His wrath is poured out like fire,
  and by him the rocks are broken in
      pieces.

7 The LORD is good,
  a stronghold in a day of trouble;
he protects those who take refuge in him,
8   even in a rushing flood.
He will make a full end of his adversaries,[a]
  and will pursue his enemies into
      darkness.

1.3 God Is Slow to Anger

God's anger against Nineveh had not appeared overnight. Assyria had been the dominant world power for at least 300 years. Once before, Jonah had carried a message of condemnation to its chief city, Nineveh. As was always true with God's prophets, Jonah's condemnation sounded absolute. Actually, it included an escape clause. In Jeremiah 18.7–10, God spelled it out: "At one moment I may declare concerning a nation or a kingdom, that I will pluck up and break down and destroy it, but if that nation, concerning which I have spoken, turns from its evil, I will change my mind about the disaster that I intended to bring on it." Hearing Jonah, the Ninevites had repented, and God had spared their city.

The repentance had not lasted, however. By Nahum's time, Nineveh had returned to her evil ways. God's anger, while slow to develop, was sure.

a Gk: Heb *of her place*

9 Why do you plot against the LORD?
    He will make an end;
    no adversary will rise up twice.
10 Like thorns they are entangled,
    like drunkards they are drunk;
    they are consumed like dry straw.
11 From you one has gone out
    who plots evil against the LORD,
    one who counsels wickedness.

Good News for Judah

12 Thus says the LORD,
 "Though they are at full strength and
    many,[b]
    they will be cut off and pass away.
 Though I have afflicted you,
    I will afflict you no more.
13 And now I will break off his yoke from
    you
    and snap the bonds that bind you."

14 The LORD has commanded concerning
    you:
 "Your name shall be perpetuated no
    longer;
 from the house of your gods I will cut off
    the carved image and the cast image.
 I will make your grave, for you
    are worthless."

15c Look! On the mountains the feet of one
    who brings good tidings,
    who proclaims peace!
 Celebrate your festivals, O Judah,
    fulfill your vows,
 for never again shall the wicked invade
    you;
    they are utterly cut off.

The Destruction of the Wicked City

2 A shatterer[d] has come up against you.
    Guard the ramparts;
    watch the road;
 gird your loins;
    collect all your strength.

2 (For the LORD is restoring the majesty of
    Jacob,
    as well as the majesty of Israel,
 though ravagers have ravaged them
    and ruined their branches.)

3 The shields of his warriors are red;
    his soldiers are clothed in crimson.
 The metal on the chariots flashes
    on the day when he musters them;
    the chargers[e] prance.
4 The chariots race madly through the streets,

they rush to and fro through
    the squares;
 their appearance is like torches,
    they dart like lightning.
5 He calls his officers;
    they stumble as they come forward;
 they hasten to the wall,
    and the mantelet[b] is set up.

2.5 Battle Tactics

To most people, mighty Nineveh seemed impregnable. A thick protective wall eight miles long encircled the city, and just to reach the wall attackers had to cross a moat 150 feet wide. Behind those fortifications waited the Assyrian troops, renowned for their cruelty. One Assyrian king boasted of erecting a pyramid of chopped-off heads in front of an enemy's city. Even so, Nahum predicted Nineveh's complete downfall.

6 The river gates are opened,
    the palace trembles.
7 It is decreed[b] that the city[f] be exiled,
    its slave women led away,
 moaning like doves
    and beating their breasts.
8 Nineveh is like a pool
    whose waters[g] run away.
 "Halt! Halt!"—
    but no one turns back.
9 "Plunder the silver,
    plunder the gold!
 There is no end of treasure!
    An abundance of every precious
        thing!"

10 Devastation, desolation, and destruction!
    Hearts faint and knees tremble,
 all loins quake,
    all faces grow pale!
11 What became of the lions' den,
    the cave[h] of the young lions,
 where the lion goes,
    and the lion's cubs, with no one to
        disturb them?
12 The lion has torn enough for his whelps
    and strangled prey for his lionesses;
 he has filled his caves with prey
    and his dens with torn flesh.

13 See, I am against you, says the LORD of
hosts, and I will burn your[i] chariots in smoke,
and the sword shall devour your young lions; I

---

b Meaning of Heb uncertain   c Ch 2.1 in Heb   d Cn: Heb scatterer   e Cn Compare Gk Syr: Heb cypresses
f Heb it   g Cn Compare Gk: Heb a pool, from the days that she has become, and they   h Cn: Heb pasture   i Heb her

will cut off your prey from the earth, and the voice of your messengers shall be heard no more.

Ruin Imminent and Inevitable

3 Ah! City of bloodshed,
    utterly deceitful, full of booty—
    no end to the plunder!
2 The crack of whip and rumble of wheel,
    galloping horse and bounding chariot!
3 Horsemen charging,
    flashing sword and glittering spear,
piles of dead,
    heaps of corpses,
dead bodies without end—
    they stumble over the bodies!
4 Because of the countless debaucheries of
        the prostitute,
    gracefully alluring, mistress of sorcery,
who enslaves[j] nations through her
        debaucheries,
    and peoples through her sorcery,
5 I am against you,
    says the LORD of hosts,
    and will lift up your skirts over your
        face;
and I will let nations look on your
        nakedness
    and kingdoms on your shame.
6 I will throw filth at you
    and treat you with contempt,
    and make you a spectacle.
7 Then all who see you will shrink from
        you and say,
"Nineveh is devastated; who will bemoan
        her?"
    Where shall I seek comforters for you?

8 Are you better than Thebes[k]
    that sat by the Nile,
with water around her,
    her rampart a sea,
    water her wall?
9 Ethiopia[l] was her strength,

3.8 Another Powerful City

In approximately 663 B.C. Assyria overwhelmed Thebes, the ancient, wealthy capital of Upper Egypt. This victory seemed to symbolize Assyria's absolute power. To Nahum, however, the battle told a different tale. If Thebes was vulnerable, so was proud Nineveh. About 50 years after capturing Thebes, Nineveh fell to the Babylonians. The mention of Thebes's downfall enables us to date Nahum's message within that 50-year period.

    Egypt too, and that without limit;
    Put and the Libyans were her[m] helpers.
10 Yet she became an exile,
    she went into captivity;
even her infants were dashed in pieces
    at the head of every street;
lots were cast for her nobles,
    all her dignitaries were bound
        in fetters.
11 You also will be drunken,
    you will go into hiding;[n]
you will seek
    a refuge from the enemy.
12 All your fortresses are like fig trees
    with first-ripe figs—
if shaken they fall
    into the mouth of the eater.
13 Look at your troops:
    they are women in your midst.
The gates of your land
    are wide open to your foes;
    fire has devoured the bars of
        your gates.
14 Draw water for the siege,
    strengthen your forts;
trample the clay,
    tread the mortar,
    take hold of the brick mold!
15 There the fire will devour you,
    the sword will cut you off.
It will devour you like the locust.

Multiply yourselves like the locust,
    multiply like the grasshopper!
16 You increased your merchants
    more than the stars of the heavens.
The locust sheds its skin and
        flies away.
17 Your guards are like grasshoppers,
    your scribes like swarms[n] of locusts
settling on the fences
    on a cold day—
when the sun rises, they fly away;
    no one knows where they have gone.
18 Your shepherds are asleep,
    O king of Assyria;
    your nobles slumber.
Your people are scattered on the
        mountains
    with no one to gather them.
19 There is no assuaging your hurt,
    your wound is mortal.
All who hear the news about you
    clap their hands over you.
For who has ever escaped
    your endless cruelty?

---

j Heb *sells*   *k* Heb *No-amon*   *l* Or *Nubia*; Heb *Cush*   *m* Gk: Heb *your*   *n* Meaning of Heb uncertain

HABAKKUK

The Problem of Evil

Habakkuk's question: "Why is God silent while the wicked succeed?"

> The righteous live by their faith. 2.4

THE BOOK OF HABAKKUK BEGINS with a complaint. The prophet saw injustice, violence, and evil in his own country, yet God remained silent and invisible. Why didn't God intervene? Why did he give no answer when Habakkuk called out for help? Habakkuk took these questions directly to God, in prayer.

God answered him, but hardly in the way Habakkuk had anticipated. God said he was sending the Babylonians to punish Judah. God's words described a ruthless, savage army that would tear Israel apart.

So Habakkuk complained again. Could this be justice—punishing Judah through an even more evil nation? Deeply perplexed, Habakkuk waited to see what answer God would give to his second complaint.

How long he had to wait, we do not know. But God did reply, and his answer is perhaps the best explanation we have of God's attitude toward evil. It satisfied Habakkuk, so that his book, which begins with a complaint, ends with one of the most beautiful songs in the Bible.

Two Certainties to Live By

God pointed out two certainties to Habakkuk. First, the violent, proud Babylonians would be paid back with the very weapons they had used on others. Just as they destroyed nations, they would be destroyed. "Is it not from the LORD of hosts that . . . nations weary themselves for nothing?" (2.13). Evil may dominate the earth, but it always wears itself out.

The second certainty was God's character. He may be silent for a time, but not forever. "The earth will be filled with the knowledge of the glory of the LORD, as the waters cover the sea" (2.14). In chapter 3, Habakkuk "saw" this powerful glory, and his heart pounded. It changed his attitude from complaining to joy.

Because the future belongs to God, a believer can cling to the truth embodied in 2.4: "The righteous live by their faith." Habakkuk beautifully expressed this attitude of faith in the last three verses of his book: no matter how hard life might become, he would rejoice and find strength in the Lord.

Living by Faith

Did Habakkuk explain why God allows evil? Not precisely. He did affirm that God has not lost control. Evil is moving toward its own logical end of self-destruction, and God's glory will someday fill the earth. Habakkuk offers no proof of this, merely the record of God's communication to him. A believer can find hope and joy through faith in God, regardless of circumstances. Habakkuk's capsule of faith was quoted at three crucial points in the New Testament: Romans 1.17; Galatians 3.11; and Hebrews 10.38.

Though Habakkuk probably did not live to see it, the Babylonians were destroyed. Today they are merely a memory. Yet we, like Habakkuk, must still wait in faith to see the earth "filled with the knowledge of the glory of the LORD."

How to Read Habakkuk

Other prophets carried messages from God to humankind; Habakkuk addressed God alone. He pondered deep riddles of life while wrestling with two terrible realities: the degeneration of his own nation and the certainty that it was about to be overrun by another, worse nation. How can a just God allow, even use, such evil? To fully delve into

Habakkuk's questions, you may want to read the book of Job and Psalm 73, which explore related issues.

The first two chapters of Habakkuk tell of two questions and two answers. As you read, try to imagine the emotional changes Habakkuk experienced as he talked with God. Then read the joyful psalm of chapter 3 (set to music, either by Habakkuk or someone else) and ask yourself: Where did this joyful confidence come from?

3-TRACK READING PLAN

For an explanation and complete listing of the 3-track reading plan, turn to page 7.

TRACK 1: **Two-Week Courses on the Bible**
See page 8 for information on these courses.

TRACK 2: **An Overview of Habakkuk in 1 Day**
☐ Day 1. Read the Introduction to Habakkuk and chapter 1, which gives you a flavor of the dialogue between God and the prophet.

Now turn to page 9 for your next Track 2 reading project.

TRACK 3: **All of Habakkuk in 3 Days**
After you have read through Habakkuk, turn to pages 10–14 for your next Track 3 reading project.
☐1   ☐2   ☐3

1

The oracle that the prophet Habakkuk saw.

The Prophet's Complaint

2 O LORD, how long shall I cry for help,
    and you will not listen?
Or cry to you "Violence!"
    and you will not save?
3 Why do you make me see wrongdoing
    and look at trouble?
Destruction and violence are before me;
    strife and contention arise.
4 So the law becomes slack
    and justice never prevails.
The wicked surround the righteous—
    therefore judgment comes forth
        perverted.

5 Look at the nations, and see!
    Be astonished! Be astounded!
For a work is being done in your days
    that you would not believe if you were
        told.
6 For I am rousing the Chaldeans,
    that fierce and impetuous nation,
who march through the breadth of the
        earth
    to seize dwellings not their own.
7 Dread and fearsome are they;
    their justice and dignity proceed from
        themselves.
8 Their horses are swifter than leopards,
    more menacing than wolves at dusk;

their horses charge.
Their horsemen come from far away;
    they fly like an eagle swift to devour.
9 They all come for violence,
    with faces pressing[a] forward;
    they gather captives like sand.

1.5 Unbelievable!

To Habakkuk and his fellow Israelites, it seemed unbelievable. How could God hand his own people over to the cruel and arrogant Babylonians? But incredible reversals can happen to people who think they have an automatic entitlement with God. Hundreds of years later the apostle Paul quoted this verse to a synagogue congregation (Acts 13.41), urging them not to let complacency keep them from accepting Jesus.

10 At kings they scoff,
    and of rulers they make sport.
They laugh at every fortress,
    and heap up earth to take it.
11 Then they sweep by like the wind;
    they transgress and become guilty;
    their own might is their god!

12 Are you not from of old,
    O LORD my God, my Holy One?
You[b] shall not die.

---

a Meaning of Heb uncertain   *b* Ancient Heb tradition: MT *We*

O LORD, you have marked them for
    judgment;
and you, O Rock, have established
    them for punishment.

1.11 Worshiping the Military

*The Babylonians had their own gods, but
Habakkuk claimed that they really worshiped
their "net," that is, their military might (verse
16). God described them as "guilty; their own
might is their god" (verse 11).*

13 Your eyes are too pure to behold evil,
    and you cannot look on wrongdoing;
why do you look on the treacherous,
    and are silent when the wicked swallow
    those more righteous than they?
14 You have made people like the fish of the
    sea,
    like crawling things that have no ruler.

15 The enemy*c* brings all of them up with a
    hook;
    he drags them out with his net,
he gathers them in his seine;
    so he rejoices and exults.
16 Therefore he sacrifices to his net
    and makes offerings to his seine;
for by them his portion is lavish,
    and his food is rich.
17 Is he then to keep on emptying his net,
    and destroying nations without mercy?

God's Reply to the Prophet's Complaint

2 I will stand at my watchpost,
    and station myself on the rampart;
I will keep watch to see what he will say
    to me,
    and what he*d* will answer concerning
    my complaint.
2 Then the LORD answered me and said:
Write the vision;
    make it plain on tablets,
    so that a runner may read it.
3 For there is still a vision for the appointed
    time;
it speaks of the end, and does not lie.
If it seems to tarry, wait for it;
    it will surely come, it will not delay.
4 Look at the proud!
    Their spirit is not right in them,
    but the righteous live by their faith.*e*
5 Moreover, wealth*f* is treacherous;
    the arrogant do not endure.
They open their throats wide as Sheol;
    like Death they never have enough.

They gather all nations for themselves,
    and collect all peoples as their own.

The Woes of the Wicked

6 Shall not everyone taunt such people and,
with mocking riddles, say about them,
    "Alas for you who heap up what is not
    your own!"
    How long will you load yourselves with
    goods taken in pledge?
7 Will not your own creditors suddenly rise,
    and those who make you tremble wake
    up?
    Then you will be booty for them.
8 Because you have plundered many
    nations,
    all that survive of the peoples shall
    plunder you—
because of human bloodshed, and
    violence to the earth,
to cities and all who live in them.

2.4 Righteous by Faith

*Has any brief slogan made a bigger impact
than this one? For Habakkuk, "the righteous
live by their faith" meant that righteous people
must patiently trust God in a difficult time. The
New Testament quoted Habakkuk in a wider
context (Romans 1.17; Galatians 3.11; Hebrews
10.38–39), saying not only that believers must
live by faith, but that they are saved by grace
through faith. When Martin Luther read that
quote in Romans, it changed his life, and
"righteousness by faith" became a rallying cry
of the Protestant Reformation.*

9 "Alas for you who get evil gain for your
    house s,
    setting your nest on high
    to be safe from the reach of harm!"
10 You have devised shame for your house
    by cutting off many peoples;
    you have forfeited your life.
11 The very stones will cry out from the
    wall,
    and the plaster*g* will respond from the
    woodwork.

12 "Alas for you who build a town by
    bloodshed,
    and found a city on iniquity!"
13 Is it not from the LORD of hosts
    that peoples labor only to feed the
    flames,
    and nations weary themselves for
    nothing?

---

c Heb *He*   *d* Syr: Heb *I*   *e* Or *faithfulness*   *f* Other Heb Mss read *wine*   *g* Or *beam*

14 But the earth will be filled
   with the knowledge of the glory of the
     Lord,
   as the waters cover the sea.

15 "Alas for you who make your neighbors
     drink,
   pouring out your wrath[h] until they are
     drunk,
   in order to gaze on their nakedness!"
16 You will be sated with contempt instead
     of glory.
   Drink, you yourself, and stagger![i]
   The cup in the Lord's right hand
   will come around to you,
   and shame will come upon your glory!
17 For the violence done to Lebanon will
     overwhelm you;
   the destruction of the animals will
     terrify you—[j]
   because of human bloodshed and violence
     to the earth,
   to cities and all who live in them.

18 What use is an idol
   once its maker has shaped it—
   a cast image, a teacher of lies?
   For its maker trusts in what has been
     made,
   though the product is only an idol that
     cannot speak!
19 Alas for you who say to the wood, "Wake
     up!"
   to silent stone, "Rouse yourself!"
   Can it teach?
   See, it is gold and silver plated,
   and there is no breath in it at all.

20 But the Lord is in his holy temple;
   let all the earth keep silence before
     him!

3 A prayer of the prophet Habakkuk according
   to Shigionoth.

The Prophet's Prayer

2 O Lord, I have heard of your renown,
   and I stand in awe, O Lord, of your
     work.
   In our own time revive it;
   in our own time make it known;
   in wrath may you remember mercy.
3 God came from Teman,
   the Holy One from Mount Paran.
                                    Selah

His glory covered the heavens,
   and the earth was full of his praise.
4 The brightness was like the sun;
   rays came forth from his hand,
   where his power lay hidden.
5 Before him went pestilence,
   and plague followed close behind.
6 He stopped and shook the earth;
   he looked and made the
     nations tremble.
   The eternal mountains were shattered;
   along his ancient pathways
   the everlasting hills sank low.
7 I saw the tents of Cushan under affliction;
   the tent-curtains of the land of Midian
     trembled.
8 Was your wrath against the rivers,[k]
     O Lord?
   Or your anger against the rivers,[k]
   or your rage against the sea,[l]
   when you drove your horses,
   your chariots to victory?
9 You brandished your naked bow,
   sated[m] were the arrows at your
     command.[n]   *Selah*
   You split the earth with rivers.
10 The mountains saw you, and writhed;
   a torrent of water swept by;
   the deep gave forth its voice.
   The sun[o] raised high its hands;
11 the moon[p] stood still in its exalted place,
   at the light of your arrows speeding
     by,
   at the gleam of your flashing spear.
12 In fury you trod the earth,
   in anger you trampled nations.
13 You came forth to save your people,
   to save your anointed.
   You crushed the head of the
     wicked house,
   laying it bare from foundation
     to roof.[n]   *Selah*

3.14 God at Work

"You pierced with his own arrows the head of his warriors" is how Habakkuk sees God overcoming the leader of evil. Earlier (2.6–7), Habakkuk had demonstrated how this would work out: The Babylonians' own enemies would treat them just as they had treated others. Violence turns back on the violent. On the surface, God's power is not always visible, but the person of faith knows God is behind it all.

---

[h] Or *poison*   [i] Q Ms Gk: MT *be uncircumcised*   [j] Gk Syr: Meaning of Heb uncertain   [k] Or *against River*
[l] Or *against Sea*   [m] Cn: Heb *oaths*   [n] Meaning of Heb uncertain   [o] Heb *It*   [p] Heb *sun, moon*

14 You pierced with their own arrows the
  head*q* of his warriors,*r*
  who came like a whirlwind to scatter
  us,*s*
  gloating as if ready to devour the poor
  who were in hiding.
15 You trampled the sea with your horses,
  churning the mighty waters.

16 I hear, and I tremble within;
  my lips quiver at the sound.
  Rottenness enters into my bones,
  and my steps tremble*t* beneath me.
  I wait quietly for the day of calamity
  to come upon the people who attack
  us.

Trust and Joy in the Midst of Trouble

17 Though the fig tree does not blossom,
  and no fruit is on the vines;
  though the produce of the olive fails,
  and the fields yield no food;
  though the flock is cut off from the fold,
  and there is no herd in the stalls,
18 yet I will rejoice in the LORD;
  I will exult in the God of my salvation.
19 GOD, the Lord, is my strength;
  he makes my feet like the feet of a
  deer,
  and makes me tread upon the
  heights.*u*

To the leader: with stringed*v* instruments.

---

q Or *leader*   *r* Vg Compare Gk Syr: Meaning of Heb uncertain   *s* Heb *me*   *t* Cn Compare Gk: Meaning of Heb
uncertain   *u* Heb *my heights*   *v* Heb *my stringed*

ZEPHANIAH

Beyond Darkness
A worldwide catastrophe and a shining light

Z EPHANIAH WROTE NOT LONG AFTER Manasseh had ended his 50-year reign in Judah. One of the worst kings on record, Manasseh had made idol worship and child sacrifice common practice. He had built altars for star worshipers in God's temple and had encouraged male prostitution as part of the religious ritual. He had also "shed very much innocent blood, until he had filled Jerusalem from one end to another" (2 Kings 21.16). His son Amon carried on in the same way during his short reign.

> The LORD . . . will renew you in his love; he will exult over you with loud singing. 3.17

Then came King Josiah, who took the throne at the age of eight, after his father's assassination. The Bible says there was never a king like Josiah (2 Kings 23.25). He led a reform, destroying all the pagan idols and restoring the temple. He organized the first passover celebration in generations.

Zephaniah, who was probably related to the king through his great-great-grandfather King Hezekiah, apparently spoke just before the big changes. The nation's future hung in the balance, and Zephaniah's words may well have helped tip it toward renewal of faith in God.

From Gloom to Exultation

Zephaniah's book begins in deep gloom. Like other prophets, he condemned the sins of his nation and predicted judgment from God. But he went one big step further. He talked repeatedly about "the day of the LORD" and saw that it would be a supernatural event sweeping clean the whole planet. Zephaniah offered no hope that it could be avoided. The Lord had warned and pleaded, but to no avail (3.6–7). Zephaniah saw hope for a minority only. A faithful, humble remnant could be sheltered from disaster if they would seek God.

Beyond the judgment fires Zephaniah saw something remarkably bright. He predicted that a purified remnant of God's people, truthful and humble, would trust in God. He foresaw a remade world learning to worship God.

Therefore this short book, which starts with such gloom, ends with an ecstatic song of joy: an anticipation of the kingdom to come after the judgment. God's blessing will flow freely as every nation worships him. Zephaniah's words may have been influential in encouraging Josiah's reforms, but his vision extended far beyond. The New Testament speaks often, like Zephaniah, of the worldwide judgment and a renewed world to come.

How to Read Zephaniah

Z ephaniah will seem more interesting if you grasp the historical situation in which he wrote. For the decadence that led to King Josiah's reforms, read 2 Kings 21. Josiah's history is told in chapters 22 and 23. Second Chronicles 33–35 tells the same story with slightly different details. You can find a brief summary of these reigns in "A Lineup of Rulers," pages 1349-1357.

Zephaniah is easily understood. It has a clear and symmetrical structure, opening (after a brief introduction) with a warning of judgment for Judah and its capital of Jerusalem, then extending the judgment to Judah's neighbors, and closing in chapter 3 with good news about Jerusalem.

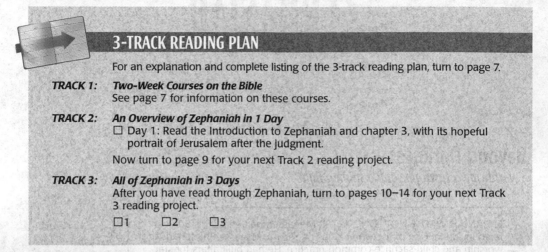

3-TRACK READING PLAN

For an explanation and complete listing of the 3-track reading plan, turn to page 7.

TRACK 1: *Two-Week Courses on the Bible*
See page 7 for information on these courses.

TRACK 2: *An Overview of Zephaniah in 1 Day*
☐ Day 1: Read the Introduction to Zephaniah and chapter 3, with its hopeful portrait of Jerusalem after the judgment.
Now turn to page 9 for your next Track 2 reading project.

TRACK 3: *All of Zephaniah in 3 Days*
After you have read through Zephaniah, turn to pages 10–14 for your next Track 3 reading project.
☐1   ☐2   ☐3

1 The word of the LORD that came to Zephaniah son of Cushi son of Gedaliah son of Amariah son of Hezekiah, in the days of King Josiah son of Amon of Judah.

1.1 Royal Blood

Prophets had to be hand-picked by God. Education or family background didn't qualify them for the job. Zephaniah, however, came from an impressive family. His great-great-grandfather was King Hezekiah. Despite his royal blood, Zephaniah was blunt and uncompromising; he took no white-glove approach to prophecy.

The Coming Judgment on Judah

2 I will utterly sweep away everything
    from the face of the earth, says the
        LORD.
3 I will sweep away humans and animals;
    I will sweep away the birds of the air
    and the fish of the sea.
I will make the wicked stumble.[a]
    I will cut off humanity
    from the face of the earth, says the
        LORD.
4 I will stretch out my hand against Judah,
    and against all the inhabitants of
        Jerusalem;
and I will cut off from this place every
        remnant of Baal
    and the name of the idolatrous
        priests;[b]
5 those who bow down on the roofs
    to the host of the heavens;

those who bow down and swear to the
        LORD,
    but also swear by Milcom;[c]
6 those who have turned back from
        following the LORD,
    who have not sought the LORD or
        inquired of him.

7 Be silent before the Lord GOD!
    For the day of the LORD is at hand;
    the LORD has prepared a sacrifice,
        he has consecrated his guests.
8 And on the day of the LORD's sacrifice
I will punish the officials and the king's
        sons
    and all who dress themselves in foreign
        attire.
9 On that day I will punish
    all who leap over the threshold,
who fill their master's house
    with violence and fraud.

10 On that day, says the LORD,
    a cry will be heard from the Fish Gate,
    a wail from the Second Quarter,
    a loud crash from the hills.
11 The inhabitants of the Mortar wail,
    for all the traders have perished;
    all who weigh out silver are cut off.
12 At that time I will search Jerusalem with
        lamps,
    and I will punish the people
    who rest complacently[d] on their dregs,
        those who say in their hearts,
"The LORD will not do good,
    nor will he do harm."
13 Their wealth shall be plundered,
    and their houses laid waste.

a Cn: Heb *sea, and those who cause the wicked to stumble*   b Compare Gk: Heb *the idolatrous priests with the priests*
c Gk Mss Syr Vg: Heb *Malcam* (or, *their king*)   d Heb *who thicken*

Though they build houses,
they shall not inhabit them;
though they plant vineyards,
they shall not drink wine from them.

1.12 Practical Atheism

The people of Judah did terrible things, such as worshiping Molech (verse 5), the Ammonite god who sometimes required child sacrifice. Zephaniah singled out another sin, however, that was just as damaging: complacency. They weren't formal atheists, but they acted like it.

The Great Day of the LORD

14 The great day of the LORD is near,
near and hastening fast;
the sound of the day of the LORD is bitter,
the warrior cries aloud there.
15 That day will be a day of wrath,
a day of distress and anguish,
a day of ruin and devastation,
a day of darkness and gloom,
a day of clouds and thick darkness,
16 a day of trumpet blast and battle cry
against the fortified cities
and against the lofty battlements.

17 I will bring such distress upon people
that they shall walk like the blind;
because they have sinned against the LORD,
their blood shall be poured out like dust,
and their flesh like dung.
18 Neither their silver nor their gold
will be able to save them
on the day of the LORD's wrath;
in the fire of his passion
the whole earth shall be consumed;
for a full, a terrible end
he will make of all the inhabitants of
the earth.

Judgment on Israel's Enemies

2 Gather together, gather,
O shameless nation,
2 before you are driven away
like the drifting chaff,[e]
before there comes upon you
the fierce anger of the LORD,
before there comes upon you
the day of the LORD's wrath.
3 Seek the LORD, all you humble of the
land,
who do his commands;
seek righteousness, seek humility;
perhaps you may be hidden

on the day of the LORD's wrath.
4 For Gaza shall be deserted,
and Ashkelon shall become a
desolation;
Ashdod's people shall be driven out at
noon,
and Ekron shall be uprooted.

5 Ah, inhabitants of the seacoast,
you nation of the Cherethites!
The word of the LORD is against you,
O Canaan, land of the Philistines;
and I will destroy you until no
inhabitant is left.
6 And you, O seacoast, shall be pastures,
meadows for shepherds
and folds for flocks.
7 The seacoast shall become the possession
of the remnant of the house of Judah,
on which they shall pasture,
and in the houses of Ashkelon
they shall lie down at evening.
For the LORD their God will be mindful of
them
and restore their fortunes.

8 I have heard the taunts of Moab
and the revilings of the Ammonites,
how they have taunted my people
and made boasts against their territory.
9 Therefore, as I live, says the LORD of
hosts,
the God of Israel,
Moab shall become like Sodom
and the Ammonites like Gomorrah,
a land possessed by nettles and salt pits,
and a waste forever.
The remnant of my people shall plunder
them,
and the survivors of my nation shall
possess them.
10 This shall be their lot in return for their
pride,
because they scoffed and boasted
against the people of the LORD of hosts.
11 The LORD will be terrible against them;
he will shrivel all the gods of the earth,
and to him shall bow down,
each in its place,
all the coasts and islands of
the nations.

12 You also, O Ethiopians,[f]
shall be killed by my sword.

13 And he will stretch out his hand against
the north,
and destroy Assyria;
and he will make Nineveh a desolation,

---

e Cn Compare Gk Syr: Heb *before a decree is born; like chaff a day has passed away*   f Or *Nubians*; Heb *Cushites* a dry waste like the desert.

14 Herds shall lie down in it,
 every wild animal;*g*
the desert owl*h* and the screech owl*h*
 shall lodge on its capitals;
the owl*i* shall hoot at the window,
 the raven*j* croak on the threshold;
 for its cedar work will be laid bare.

15 Is this the exultant city
 that lived secure,
that said to itself,
 "I am, and there is no one else"?
What a desolation it has become,
 a lair for wild animals!
Everyone who passes by it
 hisses and shakes the fist.

The Wickedness of Jerusalem

3 Ah, soiled, defiled,
 oppressing city!
2 It has listened to no voice;
 it has accepted no correction.
It has not trusted in the LORD;
 it has not drawn near to its God.

3 The officials within it
 are roaring lions;
its judges are evening wolves
 that leave nothing until the morning.
4 Its prophets are reckless,
 faithless persons;
its priests have profaned what is sacred,
 they have done violence to the law.
5 The LORD within it is righteous;
 he does no wrong.
Every morning he renders his judgment,
 each dawn without fail;
 but the unjust knows no shame.

6 I have cut off nations;
 their battlements are in ruins;
I have laid waste their streets
 so that no one walks in them;
their cities have been made desolate,
 without people, without inhabitants.
7 I said, "Surely the city*k* will fear me,
 it will accept correction;
it will not lose sight*l*
 of all that I have brought upon it."
But they were the more eager
 to make all their deeds corrupt.

Punishment and Conversion of the Nations

8 Therefore wait for me, says the LORD,
 for the day when I arise as a witness.
For my decision is to gather nations,
 to assemble kingdoms,
to pour out upon them my indignation,
 all the heat of my anger;
for in the fire of my passion
 all the earth shall be consumed.

9 At that time I will change the speech of
  the peoples
 to a pure speech,
that all of them may call on the name of
  the LORD
 and serve him with one accord.
10 From beyond the rivers of Ethiopia*m*
 my suppliants, my scattered ones,
 shall bring my offering.

11 On that day you shall not be put
  to shame
because of all the deeds by which you
  have rebelled against me;
for then I will remove from your midst
 your proudly exultant ones,
and you shall no longer be haughty
 in my holy mountain.
12 For I will leave in the midst of you
 a people humble and lowly.
They shall seek refuge in the name of the
  LORD —

3.12 Meek Will Inherit

As on Wall Street, as in the streets of many cities, "survival of the fittest" might have been Jerusalem's motto. Its officials were like wolves, devouring everything in sight (verse 3). Could only the ruthless survive? Zephaniah said no. In fact, he claimed, only the meek and the humble, those who trust God and simply tell the truth, would live in security. Jesus said something similar: "Blessed are the meek, for they will inherit the earth" (Matthew 5.5).

13 the remnant of Israel;
they shall do no wrong
 and utter no lies,
nor shall a deceitful tongue
 be found in their mouths.
Then they will pasture and lie down,
 and no one shall make them afraid.

A Song of Joy

14 Sing aloud, O daughter Zion;
 shout, O Israel!
Rejoice and exult with all your heart,
 O daughter Jerusalem!
15 The LORD has taken away the judgments
 against you,

g Tg Compare Gk: Heb *nation*   *h* Meaning of Heb uncertain   *i* Cn: Heb *a voice*   *j* Gk Vg: Heb *desolation*
k Heb *it*   *l* Gk Syr: Heb *its dwelling will not be cut off*   *m* Or *Nubia*; Heb *Cush*

he has turned away your enemies.
The king of Israel, the LORD, is in your
  midst;
  you shall fear disaster no more.
16 On that day it shall be said to Jerusalem:
Do not fear, O Zion;
  do not let your hands grow weak.
17 The LORD, your God, is in your midst,
  a warrior who gives victory;
he will rejoice over you with gladness,
  he will renew you[n] in his love;
he will exult over you with loud singing
18   as on a day of festival.[o]
I will remove disaster from you,[p]

so that you will not bear reproach for
  it.
19 I will deal with all your oppressors
  at that time.
And I will save the lame
  and gather the outcast,
and I will change their shame into praise
  and renown in all the earth.
20 At that time I will bring you home,
  at the time when I gather you;
for I will make you renowned and praised
  among all the peoples of the earth,
when I restore your fortunes
  before your eyes, says the LORD.

---

n Gk Syr: Heb he will be silent   o Gk Syr: Meaning of Heb uncertain   p Cn: Heb I will remove from you; they were

HAGGAI

The Prophet Who Got Results
For once, God's people listened

> All the remnant of the people ... obeyed the voice of the LORD their God, and the words of the prophet Haggai, as the LORD their God had sent him. 1.12

SOMETIMES, AT CRUCIAL MOMENTS, A single voice can stir a directionless mass of people to action. Prime minister Winston Churchill's inspiring oratory may have saved Britain in World War II. American clergyman and civil rights leader Martin Luther King's sermons and speeches captured America's conscience in the 1950s and 60s.

Haggai's words, similarly, rang clear in a time of confusion. The Jews had come back from their exile in Babylon nearly 20 years before. But they seemed to have forgotten the point of returning. After one false start on the temple, the returned exiles had devoted their energy to building their own houses. The ruins of Solomon's temple stood as a nagging reminder that they had neglected God.

Now Haggai urged these pioneers to "consider" their situation. He did not rage like Jeremiah or build eloquent poems like Isaiah. He put it simply and logically. They had worked hard, but what had it earned them? Their crops were unsuccessful. Their money disappeared as soon as they earned it. Why? Haggai asked. Because they had mistaken their priorities. They needed to put God first. They needed to rebuild his temple.

A Response from the Heart

People responded to Haggai immediately. Prophets before him, such as Amos, Isaiah, and Jeremiah, had spoken for decades without seeing such a heartfelt reaction. Haggai's messages span a mere four months, but he accomplished everything he set out to do. In four years the temple was complete.

What made the temple so important? After all, the proper sacrifices and rituals could be carried out on a makeshift altar. But God's reputation was at stake. He could not be properly honored so long as the house he called home lay in ruins. The temple symbolized God's presence, and Israel's priorities.

Would rebuilding the temple change Israel's financial situation? Haggai's first words promised nothing. He simply said, "Consider how you have fared," and pointed out that Israel's lack of prosperity was God's doing. They had worked hard, but God had withheld the rain their crops needed. A month later (2.1–9) Haggai said that God had glorious plans for Israel, plans that would shake the whole earth. But he referred to God's presence with them, not to good crops.

Only on the last day accounted for in this brief book did Haggai get back to the subject of harvests. He said that God wanted his people to "consider" again—this time to the dramatic difference they would see in their harvests now that they had put God first. "From this day on I will bless you," God said through Haggai (2.18–19).

How to Read Haggai

One of the shortest books in the Bible, Haggai can easily be read at one sitting. Haggai's words came at a critical time in the life of the nation of Israel. They mark one of the few times in all history when God spoke and his people quickly and unquestioningly obeyed. For the historical background, read Ezra 1—6. Haggai's crucial message is mentioned in Ezra 5.1–2. "A Lineup of Rulers," pages 1349-1357, can help you place Haggai in Israelite history.

There is a progression to God's warnings and his promises through Haggai. Study each of Haggai's messages, and note what *encouragement*, what *warning*, and what *hope* God offered Israel. How did God motivate them to obey him?

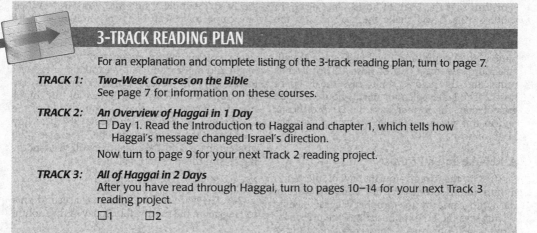

3-TRACK READING PLAN

For an explanation and complete listing of the 3-track reading plan, turn to page 7.

TRACK 1: *Two-Week Courses on the Bible*
See page 7 for information on these courses.

TRACK 2: *An Overview of Haggai in 1 Day*
☐ Day 1. Read the Introduction to Haggai and chapter 1, which tells how Haggai's message changed Israel's direction.

Now turn to page 9 for your next Track 2 reading project.

TRACK 3: *All of Haggai in 2 Days*
After you have read through Haggai, turn to pages 10–14 for your next Track 3 reading project.
☐ 1   ☐ 2

The Command to Rebuild the Temple

1 In the second year of King Darius, in the sixth month, on the first day of the month, the word of the LORD came by the prophet Haggai to Zerubbabel son of Shealtiel, governor of Judah, and to Joshua son of Jehozadak, the high priest: ²Thus says the LORD of hosts: These people say the time has not yet come to rebuild the LORD's

1.2–13 Change of Tone

For two decades the Israelites had ignored God's strong desire for them to rebuild the temple. When they finally responded and got to work, however, God's sternness melted immediately. "I am with you," he told them. And though the new temple going up seemed a sad imitation of Solomon's masterpiece, God still spoke with gentleness and kindness (2.2–5). Haggai, one of the last prophets, indicates God's eagerness to respond with mercy.

house. ³Then the word of the LORD came by the prophet Haggai, saying: ⁴Is it a time for you yourselves to live in your paneled houses, while this house lies in ruins? ⁵Now therefore thus says the LORD of hosts: Consider how you have fared. ⁶You have sown much, and harvested little; you eat, but you never have enough; you drink, but you never have your fill; you clothe yourselves, but no one is warm; and you that earn wages earn wages to put them into a bag with holes.

7 Thus says the LORD of hosts: Consider how you have fared. ⁸Go up to the hills and bring wood and build the house, so that I may take pleasure in it and be honored, says the LORD. ⁹You have looked for much, and, lo, it came to little; and when you brought it home, I blew it away. Why? says the LORD of hosts. Because my

house lies in ruins, while all of you hurry off to your own houses. ¹⁰Therefore the heavens above you have withheld the dew, and the earth has withheld its produce. ¹¹And I have called for a drought on the land and the hills, on the grain, the new wine, the oil, on what the soil produces, on human beings and animals, and on all their labors.

12 Then Zerubbabel son of Shealtiel, and Joshua son of Jehozadak, the high priest, with all the remnant of the people, obeyed the voice of the LORD their God, and the words of the prophet Haggai, as the LORD their God had sent him; and the people feared the LORD. ¹³Then Haggai, the messenger of the LORD, spoke to the people with the LORD's message, saying, I am with you, says the LORD. ¹⁴And the LORD stirred up the spirit of Zerubbabel son of Shealtiel, governor of Judah, and the spirit of Joshua son of Jehozadak, the high priest, and the spirit of all the remnant of the people; and they came and worked on the house of the LORD of hosts, their God, ¹⁵on the twenty-fourth day of the month, in the sixth month.

The Future Glory of the Temple

2 In the second year of King Darius, ¹in the seventh month, on the twenty-first day of the month, the word of the LORD came by the prophet Haggai, saying: ²Speak now to Zerubbabel son of Shealtiel, governor of Judah, and to Joshua son of Jehozadak, the high priest, and to the remnant of the people, and say, ³Who is left among you that saw this house in its former glory? How does it look to you now? Is it not in your sight as nothing? ⁴Yet now take courage, O Zerubbabel, says the LORD; take courage, O Joshua, son of Jehozadak, the high priest; take courage, all you people of the land, says the LORD; work, for I am with you, says the LORD of hosts, ⁵according to the promise that I made you when you came out of Egypt. My spirit abides among you; do not fear.

6For thus says the LORD of hosts: Once again, in a little while, I will shake the heavens and the earth and the sea and the dry land; 7and I will shake all the nations, so that the treasure of all nations shall come, and I will fill this house with splendor, says the LORD of hosts. 8The silver is mine, and the gold is mine, says the LORD of hosts. 9The latter splendor of this house shall be greater than the former, says the LORD of hosts; and in this place I will give prosperity, says the LORD of hosts.

A Rebuke and a Promise

10 On the twenty-fourth day of the ninth month, in the second year of Darius, the word of the LORD came by the prophet Haggai, saying: 11Thus says the LORD of hosts: Ask the priests for a ruling: 12If one carries consecrated meat in the fold of one's garment, and with the fold touches bread, or stew, or wine, or oil, or any kind of food, does it become holy? The priests answered, "No." 13Then Haggai said, "If one who is unclean by contact with a dead body touches any of these, does it become unclean?" The priests answered, "Yes, it becomes unclean." 14Haggai then said, So is it with this people, and with this nation before me, says the LORD; and so with every work of their hands; and what they offer there is unclean. 15But now, consider what will come to pass from this day on. Before a stone was placed upon a stone in

2.12 One-way Contamination

"One bad apple spoils the barrel," the saying goes; but one good apple doesn't clean up the rotten ones. In a similar vein, Haggai asked, "Which is contagious, good or evil?" In the Old Testament law, he found that consecrated meat—set aside to be used in sacrificial worship—did not "spread" its holiness. But a person who became "unclean" did spread his or her defilement. Under the Old Testament law, evil spread, but goodness did not. The Israelites' failure to rebuild the temple had defiled everything they touched—even their good deeds.

the LORD's temple, 16how did you fare?a When one came to a heap of twenty measures, there were but ten; when one came to the wine vat to draw fifty measures, there were but twenty. 17I struck you and all the products of your toil with blight and mildew and hail; yet you did not return to me, says the LORD. 18Consider from this day on, from the twenty-fourth day of the ninth month. Since the day that the foundation of the LORD's temple was laid, consider: 19Is there any seed left in the barn? Do the vine, the fig tree, the pomegranate, and the olive tree still yield nothing? From this day on I will bless you.

God's Promise to Zerubbabel

20 The word of the LORD came a second time to Haggai on the twenty-fourth day of the month:

2.23 The Imprint of the Master

Some 78 years before, King Jehoiachin had been captured and taken to Babylon. God had rejected him: "Even if King Coniah . . . were the signet ring on my right hand, even from there I would tear you off" (Jeremiah 22.24).

But now his grandson Zerubbabel had come back to Jerusalem, chosen again as the Lord's "signet ring." Such a ring was used in place of a signature, to impress the king's seal on important documents. God had accepted men from the royal line of David as his chosen leaders again. The complete fulfillment of this prophecy would have to wait for Zerubbabel's descendant Jesus, a son of David who fully printed God's image on humanity.

21Speak to Zerubbabel, governor of Judah, saying, I am about to shake the heavens and the earth, 22and to overthrow the throne of kingdoms; I am about to destroy the strength of the kingdoms of the nations, and overthrow the chariots and their riders; and the horses and their riders shall fall, every one by the sword of a comrade. 23On that day, says the LORD of hosts, I will take you, O Zerubbabel my servant, son of Shealtiel, says the LORD, and make you like a signet ring; for I have chosen you, says the LORD of hosts.

---

a Gk: Heb *since they were*

ZECHARIAH

Starting Over
How could they rebuild with broken pieces?

W HEN THE JEWS REVIEWED THEIR history, it looked like a long slide
downhill. Consistently, they had responded to God's love by grumbling
against him, by disobeying his law, by worshiping idols. Finally, after centuries of warning, punishment had come. Jerusalem was flattened. The survivors marched off in chains toward the other end of the world.

> Says the LORD, I
> have returned to
> Jerusalem with com-
> passion; my house
> shall be built in it.
> 1.16

They had not merely lost a battle. They had lost, seemingly, their place in
God's heart and their future as his special people.

But hope for a new start came in exile. When Persian emperor Cyrus took power, he offered Jews a
chance to return to their land and rebuild their temple. Some jumped at the chance. They took the
long journey to a homeland most of them had never seen (you can read about the trip in the first
chapters of Ezra). They wanted not merely to rebuild; they hoped somehow to escape the downward,
anti-God trend that had plagued their nation from its beginnings.

Hope Begins to Fade

They found a disheartening scene. Their once-beautiful city was a ghost town. Everything of value
had been destroyed. Fertile fields were overgrown. The region was almost empty of people.

The small band of returned exiles built an altar on the grounds of the ruined temple. But soon they
grew discouraged about actual rebuilding. They had enough trouble finding shelter and scratching out
a living from the land. When their non-Jewish neighbors fought against rebuilding the temple, the former exiles gave up. Their hopes of a glorious "new beginning" began to fade.

The temple stayed in a state of disrepair for nearly 20 years, until the prophets Haggai and
Zechariah stirred up renewed interest. These prophets saw that as long as the temple lay in ruins,
Israel's distinctive character as a people of God was ruined, too. At their urging, the Jews organized to
build again.

The book of Zechariah is a record from that critical period of rebuilding. Its first recorded message
dates from approximately two months after the temple foundation was laid. The temple was completed four years later, at least partly due to Zechariah's encouraging words.

Needed: A Change of Heart

Zechariah wasn't mainly interested in a building, however. More important was the relationship
with God that the temple symbolized. In his first recorded words Zechariah warned his people not to
be like their ancestors. What good had a temple done them? A really new beginning required a
change of heart. "Return to me, says the LORD of hosts, and I will return to you"(1.3).

The last half of Zechariah widens its view to the whole world. The small refugee community of
Jews, Zechariah says, holds the world's future. Their new beginning would become the hope of the
world.

How to Read Zechariah

M ost people find Zechariah difficult to understand. Throughout the book you will find
references to people and events that are hard to interpret. A commentary can be a great
help, clarifying the meaning of these details. For historical background on Zechariah's
times, read Ezra 1—6. Zechariah is mentioned by name in Ezra 5.1.

The book of Zechariah breaks into three parts. The first six chapters offer eight symbolic visions, which were meant to encourage the builders of the temple. They are not too difficult to understand if you take them one at a time and don't rush through them. Their main emphasis: God is at work again. He plans to live with his people in Jerusalem. He will protect them from their enemies, cleanse them from their sins, banish evil. He is making a new beginning for them.

Chapters 7–8 address the quality of life God wants his renewed people to enjoy. These words contain many encouraging promises to Israel.

The last six chapters are packed with puzzling references to the struggles Israel must endure in becoming what God wants. You will find predictions of terrible suffering and absolute victory. These chapters, as complex as they are, helped the Gospel writers understand Jesus' suffering, death, and resurrection. The writers quoted these chapters as they wrote of Jesus' final days. The book of Revelation, telling of the final goal of history, also drew on Zechariah's predictions.

3-TRACK READING PLAN

For an explanation and complete listing of the 3-track reading plan, turn to page 7.

TRACK 1: *Two-Week Courses on the Bible*
See page 7 for information on these courses.

TRACK 2: *An Overview of Zechariah in 1 Day*
☐ Day 1. Read the Introduction to Zechariah and chapter 8, which describes the future God has in mind for his people.

Now turn to page 9 for your next Track 2 reading project.

TRACK 3: *All of Zechariah in 11 Days*
After you have read through Zechariah, turn to pages 10–14 for your next Track 3 reading project.

☐1   ☐2–3   ☐4–5   ☐6   ☐7   ☐8   ☐9   ☐10
☐11   ☐12–13 ☐14

Israel Urged to Repent

1 In the eighth month, in the second year of Darius, the word of the LORD came to the prophet Zechariah son of Berechiah son of Iddo, saying: ²The LORD was very angry with your ancestors. ³Therefore say to them, Thus says the LORD of hosts: Return to me, says the LORD of hosts, and I will return to you, says the LORD of hosts. ⁴Do not be like your ancestors, to whom the former prophets proclaimed, "Thus says the LORD of hosts, Return from your evil ways and from your evil deeds." But they did not hear or heed me, says the LORD. ⁵Your ancestors, where are they? And the prophets, do they live forever? ⁶But my words and my statutes, which I commanded my servants the prophets, did they not overtake your ancestors? So they repented and said, "The LORD of hosts has dealt with us according to our ways and deeds, just as he planned to do."

First Vision: The Horsemen

7 On the twenty-fourth day of the eleventh month, the month of Shebat, in the second year of Darius, the word of the LORD came to the prophet Zechariah son of Berechiah son of Iddo; and Zechariah*a* said, ⁸In the night I saw a man riding on a red horse! He was standing among the myrtle trees in the glen; and behind him were red, sorrel, and white horses. ⁹Then I said, "What are these, my lord?" The angel who talked with me said to me, "I will show you what they are." ¹⁰So the man who was standing among the myrtle trees answered, "They are those whom the LORD has sent to patrol the earth." ¹¹Then they spoke to the angel of the LORD who was standing among the myrtle trees, "We have patrolled the earth, and lo, the whole earth remains at peace." ¹²Then the angel of the LORD said, "O LORD of hosts, how long will you withhold mercy from Jerusalem and the cities of Judah, with which you have been angry these seventy years?" ¹³Then the LORD replied with gracious and comforting words to the angel who talked with me. ¹⁴So the angel who talked with me said to me, Proclaim this message: Thus says the LORD of hosts; I am very jealous for

a Heb *and he*

Jerusalem and for Zion. [15]And I am extremely angry with the nations that are at ease; for while I was only a little angry, they made the disaster worse. [16]Therefore, thus says the LORD, I have returned to Jerusalem with compassion; my house shall be built in it, says the LORD of hosts, and the measuring line shall be stretched out over Jerusalem. [17]Proclaim further: Thus says the LORD of hosts: My cities shall again overflow with prosperity; the LORD will again comfort Zion and again choose Jerusalem.

Second Vision: The Horns and the Smiths

[18][b] And I looked up and saw four horns. [19]I

1.18 Brute Power

In an agricultural society that does its plowing with oxen, nothing is stronger than a bull. Probably because of this, horns are frequently used as symbols of power in the Old Testament. In our day we might say "bulldozer."

asked the angel who talked with me, "What are these?" And he answered me, "These are the horns that have scattered Judah, Israel, and Jerusalem." [20]Then the LORD showed me four blacksmiths. [21]And I asked, "What are they coming to do?" He answered, "These are the horns that scattered Judah, so that no head could be raised; but these have come to terrify them, to strike down the horns of the nations that lifted up their horns against the land of Judah to scatter its people."[c]

Third Vision: The Man with a Measuring Line

2 [d] I looked up and saw a man with a measuring line in his hand. [2]Then I asked, "Where are you going?" He answered me, "To measure Jerusalem, to see what is its width and what is its length." [3]Then the angel who talked with me came forward, and another angel came forward to meet him, [4]and said to him, "Run, say to that young man: Jerusalem shall be inhabited like villages without walls, because of the multitude of people and animals in it. [5]For I will be a wall of fire all around it, says the LORD, and I will be the glory within it."

Interlude: An Appeal to the Exiles

[6] Up, up! Flee from the land of the north, says the LORD; for I have spread you abroad like the four winds of heaven, says the LORD. [7]Up! Escape to Zion, you that live with daughter Babylon. [8]For thus said the LORD of hosts (after his glory[e] sent me) regarding the nations that plundered you:

Truly, one who touches you touches the apple of my eye.[f] [9]See now, I am going to raise[g] my hand against them, and they shall become plunder for their own slaves. Then you will know that the LORD of hosts has sent me. [10]Sing and rejoice, O daughter Zion! For lo, I will come and dwell in your midst, says the LORD. [11]Many nations shall join themselves to the LORD on that day, and shall be my people; and I will dwell in your midst. And you shall know that the LORD of hosts has sent me to you. [12]The LORD will inherit Judah as his portion in the holy land, and will again choose Jerusalem.

[13] Be silent, all people, before the LORD; for he has roused himself from his holy dwelling.

Fourth Vision: Joshua and Satan

3 Then he showed me the high priest Joshua standing before the angel of the LORD, and Satan[h] standing at his right hand to accuse him.

3.1–4 Bad News, Good News

References to the high priest Joshua also appear throughout Haggai. Whereas Zechariah uses him as a symbol of the rebellious nation, Haggai tells of Joshua's later transformation and obedience to God. Although Haggai and Zechariah cover the same time period, they show radically different styles. Haggai emphasizes the positive and gives a very straightforward message; Zechariah warns of danger and conveys his message in visions and symbols.

[2]And the LORD said to Satan,[h] "The LORD rebuke you, O Satan![h] The LORD who has chosen Jerusalem rebuke you! Is not this man a brand plucked from the fire?" [3]Now Joshua was dressed with filthy clothes as he stood before the angel. [4]The angel said to those who were standing before him, "Take off his filthy clothes." And to him he said, "See, I have taken your guilt away from you, and I will clothe you with festal apparel." [5]And I said, "Let them put a clean turban on his head." So they put a clean turban on his head and clothed him with the apparel; and the angel of the LORD was standing by.

[6] Then the angel of the LORD assured Joshua, saying [7]"Thus says the LORD of hosts: If you will walk in my ways and keep my requirements, then you shall rule my house and have charge of my courts, and I will give you the right of access among those who are standing here. [8]Now listen, Joshua, high priest, you and your colleagues who sit before you! For they are an omen of things to come: I am going to bring my servant the Branch.

---

[b] Ch 2.1 in Heb   [c] Heb *it*   [d] Ch 2.5 in Heb   [e] Cn: Heb *after glory he*   [f] Heb *his eye*   [g] Or *wave*
[h] Or *the Accuser*; Heb *the Adversary*

[9]For on the stone that I have set before Joshua, on a single stone with seven facets, I will engrave its inscription, says the LORD of hosts, and I will remove the guilt of this land in a single day. [10]On that day, says the LORD of hosts, you shall invite each other to come under your vine and fig tree."

Fifth Vision: The Lampstand and Olive Trees

4 The angel who talked with me came again, and wakened me, as one is wakened from sleep. [2]He said to me, "What do you see?" And I said, "I see a lampstand all of gold, with a bowl on the top of it; there are seven lamps on it, with seven lips on each of the lamps that are on the top of it. [3]And by it there are two olive trees, one on the right of the bowl and the other on its left." [4]I said to the angel who talked with me, "What are these, my lord?" [5]Then the angel who talked with me answered me, "Do you not know what these are?" I said, "No, my lord." [6]He said to me, "This is the word of the LORD to Zerubbabel: Not by might, nor by power, but by my spirit, says the LORD of hosts. [7]What are you, O great mountain? Before Zerubbabel you shall become a plain; and he shall bring out the top stone amid shouts of 'Grace, grace to it!'"

[8] Moreover the word of the LORD came to me, saying, [9]"The hands of Zerubbabel have laid the foundation of this house; his hands shall also complete it. Then you will know that the LORD of hosts has sent me to you. [10]For whoever has despised the day of small things shall rejoice, and shall see the plummet in the hand of Zerubbabel.

"These seven are the eyes of the LORD, which range through the whole earth." [11]Then I said to him, "What are these two olive trees on the right and the left of the lampstand?" [12]And a second time I said to him, "What are these two branches of the olive trees, which pour out the oil[i] through the two golden pipes?" [13]He said to me, "Do you not know what these are?" I said, "No, my lord." [14]Then he said, "These are the two anointed ones who stand by the Lord of the whole earth."

Sixth Vision: The Flying Scroll

5 Again I looked up and saw a flying scroll. [2]And he said to me, "What do you see?" I answered, "I see a flying scroll; its length is twenty cubits, and its width ten cubits." [3]Then he said to me, "This is the curse that goes out over the face of the whole land; for everyone who steals shall be cut off according to the writing on one side, and everyone who swears falsely[j] shall be cut off according to the writing on the other side. [4]I have sent it out, says the LORD of hosts, and it shall enter the house of the thief, and the house of

anyone who swears falsely by my name; and it shall abide in that house and consume it, both timber and stones."

Seventh Vision: The Woman in a Basket

[5] Then the angel who talked with me came forward and said to me, "Look up and see what this is that is coming out." [6]I said, "What is it?"

5.1 A Message for Everyone

The flying scroll probably symbolizes God's law, which condemns sin. It is unrolled and flying like a banner for all to read—not rolled up for only priests to read.

He said, "This is a basket[k] coming out." And he said, "This is their iniquity[l] in all the land." [7]Then a leaden cover was lifted, and there was a woman sitting in the basket! [k] [8]And he said, "This is Wickedness." So he thrust her back into the basket,[k] and pressed the leaden weight down on its mouth. [9]Then I looked up and saw two women coming forward. The wind was in their wings; they had wings like the wings of a stork, and they lifted up the basket[k] between earth and sky. [10]Then I said to the angel who talked with me, "Where are they taking the basket?"[k] [11]He said to me, "To the land of Shinar, to build a house for it; and when this is prepared, they will set the basket[k] down there on its base."

Eighth Vision: Four Chariots

6 And again I looked up and saw four chariots coming out from between two mountains— mountains of bronze. [2]The first chariot had red horses, the second chariot black horses, [3]the third chariot white horses, and the fourth chariot dappled gray[m] horses. [4]Then I said to the angel who talked with me, "What are these, my lord?" [5]The angel answered me, "These are the four winds[n] of heaven going out, after presenting themselves before the Lord of all the earth. [6]The chariot with the black horses goes toward the north country, the white ones go toward the west country,[o] and the dappled ones go toward the south country." [7]When the steeds came out, they were impatient to get off and patrol the earth. And he said, "Go, patrol the earth." So they patrolled the earth. [8]Then he cried out to me, "Lo, those who go toward the north country have set my spirit at rest in the north country."

The Coronation of the Branch

[9] The word of the LORD came to me: [10]Collect silver and gold[p] from the exiles—from Heldai,

---

[i] Cn: Heb gold   [j] The word *falsely* added from verse 4
[m] Compare Gk: Meaning of Heb uncertain   [n] Or *spirits*
lacks *silver and gold*

[k] Heb *ephah*   [l] Gk Compare Syr: Heb *their eye*
[o] Cn: Heb *go after them*   [p] Cn Compare verse 11: Heb

Tobijah, and Jedaiah—who have arrived from Babylon; and go the same day to the house of Josiah son of Zephaniah. 11Take the silver and gold and make a crown,[q] and set it on the head of the high priest Joshua son of Jehozadak; 12say to him: Thus says the LORD of hosts: Here is a man whose name is Branch: for he shall branch out in his place, and he shall build the temple of the LORD. 13It is he that shall build the temple of the LORD; he shall bear royal honor, and shall sit upon his throne and rule. There shall be a priest by his throne, with peaceful understanding between the two of them. 14And the crown[r] shall be in the care of Heldai,[s] Tobijah, Jedaiah, and Josiah[t] son of Zephaniah, as a memorial in the temple of the LORD.

15 Those who are far off shall come and help to build the temple of the LORD; and you shall know that the LORD of hosts has sent me to you. This will happen if you diligently obey the voice of the LORD your God.

Hypocritical Fasting Condemned

7 In the fourth year of King Darius, the word of the LORD came to Zechariah on the fourth day of the ninth month, which is Chislev. 2Now the people of Bethel had sent Sharezer and Regem-melech and their men, to entreat the favor of the LORD, 3and to ask the priests of the house of the LORD of hosts and the prophets, "Should I mourn and practice abstinence in the fifth month, as I have done for so many years?" 4Then the word of the LORD of hosts came to me: 5Say to all the people of the land and the priests: When you fasted and lamented in the fifth month and in the seventh, for these seventy years, was it for me that you fasted? 6And when you eat and when you drink, do you not eat and drink only for yourselves? 7Were not these the words that the LORD proclaimed by the former prophets, when Jerusalem was inhabited and in prosperity, along with the towns around it, and when the Negeb and the Shephelah were inhabited?

7.3 Repent for How Long?

While in exile, Jews had fasted and mourned on certain days in memory of the siege and overthrow of Jerusalem. Now that they had returned to Jerusalem they wanted to know: Should we keep fasting? Zechariah's answer came in 8.19: Fasting should now be replaced with feasting. But Zechariah warned that all religious ceremonies, however proper, were meaningless unless people's lives were controlled by God.

Punishment for Rejecting God's Demands

8 The word of the LORD came to Zechariah, saying: 9Thus says the LORD of hosts: Render true judgments, show kindness and mercy to one another; 10do not oppress the widow, the orphan, the alien, or the poor; and do not devise evil in your hearts against one another. 11But they refused to listen, and turned a stubborn shoulder, and stopped their ears in order not to hear. 12They made their hearts adamant in order not to hear the law and the words that the LORD of hosts had sent by his spirit through the former prophets. Therefore great wrath came from the LORD of hosts. 13Just as, when I[u] called, they would not hear, so, when they called, I would not hear, says the LORD of hosts, 14and I scattered them with a whirlwind among all the nations that they had not known. Thus the land they left was desolate, so that no one went to and fro, and a pleasant land was made desolate.

God's Promises to Zion

8 The word of the LORD of hosts came to me, saying: 2Thus says the LORD of hosts: I am jealous for Zion with great jealousy, and I am jealous for her with great wrath. 3Thus says the LORD: I will return to Zion, and will dwell in the midst of Jerusalem; Jerusalem shall be called the faithful city, and the mountain of the LORD of hosts shall be called the holy mountain. 4Thus says the LORD of hosts: Old men and old women shall again sit in the streets of Jerusalem, each with staff in hand because of their great age. 5And the streets of the city shall be full of boys and girls playing in its streets. 6Thus says the LORD of hosts: Even though it seems impossible to the remnant of this people in these days, should it also seem impossible to me, says the LORD of hosts? 7Thus says the LORD of hosts: I will save my people from the east country and from the west country; 8and I will bring them to live in Jerusalem. They shall be my people and I will be their God, in faithfulness and in righteousness.

8.4 Safe Streets

To refugees inhabiting a city overrun by conquerors, the promise of streets safe for senior citizens and playful children seemed almost too much to ask. But God assured them Jerusalem would once again become stable and secure. "Should it also seem impossible to me?" he asks, with a touch of irony (verse 6).

9 Thus says the LORD of hosts: Let your hands be strong—you that have recently been hearing

[q] Gk Mss Syr Tg: Heb *crowns* [r] Gk Syr: Heb *crowns* [s] Syr Compare verse 10: Heb *Helem* [t] Syr Compare verse 10: Heb *Hen* [u] Heb *he*

these words from the mouths of the prophets who were present when the foundation was laid for the rebuilding of the temple, the house of the LORD of hosts. [10]For before those days there were no wages for people or for animals, nor was there any safety from the foe for those who went out or came in, and I set them all against one other. [11]But now I will not deal with the remnant of this people as in the former days, says the LORD of hosts. [12]For there shall be a sowing of peace; the vine shall yield its fruit, the ground shall give its produce, and the skies shall give their dew; and I will cause the remnant of this people to possess all these things. [13]Just as you have been a cursing among the nations, O house of Judah and house of Israel, so I will save you and you shall be a blessing. Do not be afraid, but let your hands be strong.

14 For thus says the LORD of hosts: Just as I purposed to bring disaster upon you, when your ancestors provoked me to wrath, and I did not relent, says the LORD of hosts, [15]so again I have purposed in these days to do good to Jerusalem and to the house of Judah; do not be afraid. [16]These are the things that you shall do: Speak the truth to one another, render in your gates judgments that are true and make for peace, [17]do not devise evil in your hearts against one another, and love no false oath; for all these are things that I hate, says the LORD.

Joyful Fasting

18 The word of the LORD of hosts came to me, saying: [19]Thus says the LORD of hosts: The fast of the fourth month, and the fast of the fifth, and the fast of the seventh, and the fast of the tenth, shall be seasons of joy and gladness, and cheerful festivals for the house of Judah: therefore love truth and peace.

Many Peoples Drawn to Jerusalem

20 Thus says the LORD of hosts: Peoples shall yet come, the inhabitants of many cities; [21]the inhabitants of one city shall go to another, saying, "Come, let us go to entreat the favor of the LORD, and to seek the LORD of hosts; I myself am going." [22]Many peoples and strong nations shall come to seek the LORD of hosts in Jerusalem, and to entreat the favor of the LORD. [23]Thus says the LORD of hosts: In those days ten men from nations of every language shall take hold of a Jew, grasping his garment and saying, "Let us go with you, for we have heard that God is with you."

Judgment on Israel's Enemies

9

An Oracle.
The word of the LORD is against the land
of Hadrach

and will rest upon Damascus.
For to the LORD belongs the capital[v] of
Aram,[w]
as do all the tribes of Israel;
2 Hamath also, which borders on it,
Tyre and Sidon, though they are very
wise.
3 Tyre has built itself a rampart,
and heaped up silver like dust,
and gold like the dirt of the streets.
4 But now, the Lord will strip it of its
possessions
and hurl its wealth into the sea,
and it shall be devoured by fire.

5 Ashkelon shall see it and be afraid;
Gaza too, and shall writhe in anguish;
Ekron also, because its hopes
are withered.
The king shall perish from Gaza;
Ashkelon shall be uninhabited;
6 a mongrel people shall settle in Ashdod,
and I will make an end of the pride of
Philistia.
7 I will take away its blood from its mouth,
and its abominations from between its
teeth;
it too shall be a remnant for our God;
it shall be like a clan in Judah,
and Ekron shall be like the Jebusites.
8 Then I will encamp at my house as a
guard,
so that no one shall march to and fro;
no oppressor shall again overrun them,
for now I have seen with my own eyes.

The Coming Ruler of God's People

9 Rejoice greatly, O daughter Zion!
Shout aloud, O daughter Jerusalem!
Lo, your king comes to you;
triumphant and victorious is he,
humble and riding on a donkey,
on a colt, the foal of a donkey.

9.9 Donkey of Peace

The Gospel writers refer back to this verse in connection with Jesus' triumphal entry into Jerusalem (Matthew 21.5; John 12.15). More warlike leaders normally rode on stallions, but Zechariah pointedly notes that the coming king will ban chariots and war-horses (verse 10). Jesus scrupulously followed the pattern of a king described here—often disappointing his followers, who sought a more militaristic leader.

---

v Heb *eye* w Cn: Heb *of Adam* (or *of humankind*)

10 He[x] will cut off the chariot
    from Ephraim
  and the war-horse from Jerusalem;
  and the battle bow shall be cut off,
    and he shall command peace to the
    nations;
his dominion shall be from sea to sea,
  and from the River to the ends of the
  earth.

11 As for you also, because of the blood of
    my covenant with you,
  I will set your prisoners free from the
  waterless pit.
12 Return to your stronghold, O prisoners of
  hope;
  today I declare that I will restore to
  you double.
13 For I have bent Judah as my bow;
  I have made Ephraim its arrow.
I will arouse your sons, O Zion,
  against your sons, O Greece,
  and wield you like a warrior's sword.

14 Then the LORD will appear over them,
  and his arrow go forth like lightning;

x Gk: Heb I   y Cn: Heb the slingstones   z Gk: Heb shall drink

the Lord GOD will sound the trumpet
  and march forth in the whirlwinds of
  the south.
15 The LORD of hosts will protect them,
  and they shall devour and tread down
    the slingers;[y]
they shall drink their blood[z] like wine,
  and be full like a bowl,
  drenched like the corners of the altar.

16 On that day the LORD their God will save
  them
  for they are the flock of his people;
for like the jewels of a crown
  they shall shine on his land.
17 For what goodness and beauty are his!
  Grain shall make the young
  men flourish,
  and new wine the young women.

Restoration of Judah and Israel

10 Ask rain from the LORD
  in the season of the spring rain,
from the LORD who makes the storm
  clouds,
  who gives showers of rain to you,[a]

a Heb them

New King, New Kingdom
The paradox of leadership that triumphs through suffering

THE BOOK OF ZECHARIAH TAKES a radical turn at chapter 9. A series of messages from God, expressed in fragmented images, tells the future of the world—and the role of God's people in it.

These chapters are difficult to understand, even in our day. The ultimate future is clearly good, however: Instead of remaining a small, subject nation, God's people will shake the world. The nations will worship at Jerusalem. "The LORD will become king over all the earth" (14.9).

How could it be? Even for the Israelites this dream sounded farfetched. In Zechariah's day they needed clearance from the far-off Persian government just to rebuild their temple. Persia was the center of their world. Jerusalem hardly mattered. How could Israel become a great nation?

> Your king comes to you; triumphant and victorious is he, humble and riding on a donkey. 9.9

A Rejected Leader

These chapters of Zechariah show Israel's greatness emerging through struggle and suffering. No one who reads these words could have a glib idea that God makes things easy. Evil and misery virtually triumph before God's final intervention.

The key to Israel's future is a coming leader—a very unusual leader. People naturally expected the Messiah to be a triumphant warrior, especially since many Old Testament prophecies spoke of him that way. But this king would come on a donkey instead of a war-horse (9.9). Zechariah speaks of a shepherd—a term for "leader"—who would be rejected by the nation (11.4–17). It describes a nation in mourning for "the one whom they have pierced" (12.10).

All these predictions of a coming leader were quoted in the New Testament as applying to Jesus: a king without an army, whose crown was made of thorns. In all the Old Testament, only Isaiah (especially in chapter 53) captures so fully the paradox of Jesus' life: gentle leadership that triumphs through suffering.

Life Questions: Who is the "greatest" person you've known up close? Did some kind of suffering contribute to his or her greatness?

the vegetation in the field to everyone.
2 For the teraphim[b] utter nonsense,
    and the diviners see lies;
the dreamers tell false dreams,
    and give empty consolation.
Therefore the people wander like sheep;
    they suffer for lack of a shepherd.

3 My anger is hot against the shepherds,
    and I will punish the leaders;[c]
for the LORD of hosts cares for his flock,
    the house of Judah,
    and will make them like his proud
        war-horse.
4 Out of them shall come the cornerstone,
    out of them the tent peg,
    out of them the battle bow,
    out of them every commander.
5 Together they shall be like warriors in
        battle,
    trampling the foe in the mud of the
        streets;
they shall fight, for the LORD is with them,
    and they shall put to shame the riders
        on horses.

6 I will strengthen the house of Judah,
    and I will save the house of Joseph.
I will bring them back because I have
        compassion on them,
    and they shall be as though I had not
        rejected them;
for I am the LORD their God and I will
        answer them.
7 Then the people of Ephraim shall become
        like warriors,
    and their hearts shall be glad as with
        wine.
Their children shall see it and rejoice,
    their hearts shall exult in the LORD.

8 I will signal for them and gather them in,
    for I have redeemed them,
    and they shall be as numerous as they
        were before.
9 Though I scattered them among
        the nations,
    yet in far countries they shall
        remember me,
    and they shall rear their children and
        return.
10 I will bring them home from the land of
        Egypt,
    and gather them from Assyria;
I will bring them to the land of Gilead
        and to Lebanon,
    until there is no room for them.
11 They[d] shall pass through the sea of
        distress,

    and the waves of the sea shall be struck
        down,
    and all the depths of the Nile dried up.
The pride of Assyria shall be laid low,
    and the scepter of Egypt shall depart.
12 I will make them strong in the LORD,
    and they shall walk in his name,
        says the LORD.

11 Open your doors, O Lebanon,
    so that fire may devour your cedars!
2 Wail, O cypress, for the cedar has fallen,
    for the glorious trees are ruined!
Wail, oaks of Bashan,
    for the thick forest has been felled!
3 Listen, the wail of the shepherds,
    for their glory is despoiled!
Listen, the roar of the lions,
    for the thickets of the Jordan
        are destroyed!

Two Kinds of Shepherds

4 Thus said the LORD my God: Be a shepherd of the flock doomed to slaughter. 5Those who buy them kill them and go unpunished; and those who sell them say, "Blessed be the LORD, for I have become rich"; and their own shepherds have no pity on them. 6For I will no longer have pity on the inhabitants of the earth, says the LORD. I will cause them, every one, to fall each into the hand of a neighbor, and each into the hand of the king; and they shall devastate the earth, and I will deliver no one from their hand.

7 So, on behalf of the sheep merchants, I became the shepherd of the flock doomed to slaughter. I took two staffs; one I named Favor, the

11.7 Who Are the Shepherds?

The prophets' messages often had a double meaning: one for the people who first heard them, and another, deeper meaning for future times. In this passage, Zechariah plays the role of the good shepherd who is rejected, an image that Jesus later applied to himself. Similarly, the Jews in Zechariah's day had many "worthless shepherd" leaders, but this description (verses 15–17) may also foreshadow the New Testament's "antichrist."

other I named Unity, and I tended the sheep. 8In one month I disposed of the three shepherds, for I had become impatient with them, and they also detested me. 9So I said, "I will not be your shepherd. What is to die, let it die; what is to be destroyed, let it be destroyed; and let those that are left devour the flesh of one another!" 10I took my staff Favor and broke it, annulling the cove-

---

[b] Or *household gods*   [c] Or *male goats*   [d] Gk: Heb *He*

nant that I had made with all the peoples. ¹¹So it was annulled on that day, and the sheep merchants, who were watching me, knew that it was the word of the LORD. ¹²I then said to them, "If it seems right to you, give me my wages; but if not, keep them." So they weighed out as my wages thirty shekels of silver. ¹³Then the LORD said to me, "Throw it into the treasury"ᵉ—this lordly price at which I was valued by them. So I took the thirty shekels of silver and threw them into the treasuryᵉ in the house of the LORD. ¹⁴Then I broke my second staff Unity, annulling the family ties between Judah and Israel.

15 Then the LORD said to me: Take once more the implements of a worthless shepherd. ¹⁶For I am now raising up in the land a shepherd who does not care for the perishing, or seek the wandering,ᶠ or heal the maimed, or nourish the healthy,ᵍ but devours the flesh of the fat ones, tearing off even their hoofs.
¹⁷ Oh, my worthless shepherd,
    who deserts the flock!
  May the sword strike his arm
    and his right eye!
  Let his arm be completely withered,
    his right eye utterly blinded!

Jerusalem's Victory

12
          An Oracle.

The word of the LORD concerning Israel: Thus says the LORD, who stretched out the heavens and founded the earth and formed the human spirit within: ²See, I am about to make Jerusalem a cup of reeling for all the surrounding peoples; it will be against Judah also in the siege against Jerusalem. ³On that day I will make Jerusalem a heavy stone for all the peoples; all who lift it shall grievously hurt themselves. And all the nations of the earth shall come together against it. ⁴On that day, says the LORD, I will strike every horse with panic, and its rider with madness. But on the house of Judah I will keep a watchful eye, when I strike every horse of the peoples with blindness. ⁵Then the clans of Judah shall say to themselves, "The inhabitants of Jerusalem have strength through the LORD of hosts, their God."

6 On that day I will make the clans of Judah like a blazing pot on a pile of wood, like a flaming torch among sheaves; and they shall devour to the right and to the left all the surrounding peoples, while Jerusalem shall again be inhabited in its place, in Jerusalem.

7 And the LORD will give victory to the tents of Judah first, that the glory of the house of David and the glory of the inhabitants of Jerusalem may not be exalted over that of Judah. ⁸On that day the LORD will shield the inhabitants of Jerusalem so that the feeblest among them on that day shall be like David, and the house of David shall be like God, like the angel of the LORD, at their head. ⁹And on that day I will seek to destroy all the nations that come against Jerusalem.

Mourning for the Pierced One

10 And I will pour out a spirit of compassion and supplication on the house of David and the inhabitants of Jerusalem, so that, when they look on the oneʰ whom they have pierced, they shall mourn for him, as one mourns for an only child, and weep bitterly over him, as one weeps over a firstborn. ¹¹On that day the mourning in Jerusalem will be as great as the mourning for Hadadrimmon in the plain of Megiddo. ¹²The land shall mourn, each family by itself; the family of the house of David by itself, and their wives by themselves; the family of the house of Nathan by itself, and their wives by themselves; ¹³the family of the house of Levi by itself, and their wives by themselves; the family of the Shimeites by itself, and their wives by themselves; ¹⁴and all the families that are left, each by itself, and their wives by themselves.

13
On that day a fountain shall be opened for the house of David and the inhabitants of Jerusalem, to cleanse them from sin and impurity.

Idolatry Cut Off

2 On that day, says the LORD of hosts, I will cut off the names of the idols from the land, so that they shall be remembered no more; and also I will remove from the land the prophets and the unclean spirit. ³And if any prophets appear again, their fathers and mothers who bore them will say to them, "You shall not live, for you speak lies in the name of the LORD"; and their fathers and their mothers who bore them shall pierce them through when they prophesy. ⁴On that day the prophets will be ashamed, every one, of their visions when they prophesy; they will not put on a hairy mantle in order to deceive, ⁵but each of them will say, "I am no prophet, I am a tiller of

13.7 A Prophecy of Jesus

Jesus applied this verse to himself just before he died (Matthew 26.31). Some commentators believe that his words about the shepherd who "lays down his life for the sheep" (John 10.11) also drew on this passage. Zechariah's prophecies were on the minds of the Gospel writers: 9.9 is quoted in Matthew 21.5; 12.10 in John 19.37; and 11.12–13 in Matthew 27.9.

ᵉ Syr: Heb *it to the potter*   ᶠ Syr Compare Gk Vg: Heb *the youth*   ᵍ Meaning of Heb uncertain   ʰ Heb *on me*

the soil; for the land has been my possession[i] since my youth." [6]And if anyone asks them, "What are these wounds on your chest?"[j] the answer will be "The wounds I received in the house of my friends."

The Shepherd Struck, the Flock Scattered

[7] "Awake, O sword, against my shepherd,
    against the man who is my associate,"
                  says the LORD of hosts.
Strike the shepherd, that the sheep may
    be scattered;
    I will turn my hand against
        the little ones.
[8] In the whole land, says the LORD,
    two-thirds shall be cut off and perish,
    and one-third shall be left alive.
[9] And I will put this third into the fire,
    refine them as one refines silver,
    and test them as gold is tested.
They will call on my name,
    and I will answer them.
I will say, "They are my people";
    and they will say, "The LORD is our God."

Future Warfare and Final Victory

14 See, a day is coming for the LORD, when the plunder taken from you will be divided in your midst. [2]For I will gather all the nations against Jerusalem to battle, and the city shall be taken and the houses looted and the women raped; half the city shall go into exile, but the rest of the people shall not be cut off from the city. [3]Then the LORD will go forth and fight against those nations as when he fights on a day of battle. [4]On that day his feet shall stand on the Mount of Olives, which lies before Jerusalem on the east; and the Mount of Olives shall be split in two from east to west by a very wide valley; so that one half of the Mount shall withdraw northward, and the other half southward. [5]And you shall flee by the valley of the LORD's mountain,[k] for the valley between the mountains shall reach to Azal;[l] and you shall flee as you fled from the earthquake in the days of King Uzziah of Judah. Then the LORD my God will come, and all the holy ones with him.

[6] On that day there shall not be[m] either cold or frost.[n] [7]And there shall be continuous day (it is known to the LORD), not day and not night, for at evening time there shall be light.

[8] On that day living waters shall flow out from Jerusalem, half of them to the eastern sea and half of them to the western sea; it shall continue in summer as in winter.

[9] And the LORD will become king over all the earth; on that day the LORD will be one and his name one.

[10] The whole land shall be turned into a plain from Geba to Rimmon south of Jerusalem. But Jerusalem shall remain aloft on its site from the Gate of Benjamin to the place of the former gate, to the Corner Gate, and from the Tower of Hananel to the king's wine presses. [11]And it shall be

14.9 Catastrophes to Come?

Biblical scholars disagree on how to understand the images in this chapter. To some, the catastrophes portrayed—a mountain splitting in two, a day without light or cold, people rotting on their feet (verses 4,6,12)—take on added significance in an era of nuclear weapons and a possible greenhouse effect. Others interpret these images in more symbolic ways. Regardless, Zechariah makes clear that the end result of the earth's turmoil will be good news for all followers of God.

inhabited, for never again shall it be doomed to destruction; Jerusalem shall abide in security.

[12] This shall be the plague with which the LORD will strike all the peoples that wage war against Jerusalem: their flesh shall rot while they are still on their feet; their eyes shall rot in their sockets, and their tongues shall rot in their mouths. [13]On that day a great panic from the LORD shall fall on them, so that each will seize the hand of a neighbor, and the hand of the one will be raised against the hand of the other; [14]even Judah will fight at Jerusalem. And the wealth of all the surrounding nations shall be collected—gold, silver, and garments in great abundance. [15]And a plague like this plague shall fall on the horses, the mules, the camels, the donkeys, and whatever animals may be in those camps.

14.21 No More Separation

The priests and the temple had always been separate and more holy than the rest of Israel. "Holy to the LORD" had been inscribed on the priests' turbans (Exodus 28.36) as a symbol of this. But, Zechariah predicted, in the future such words would decorate even horses. Ordinary kitchen pots would become as sacred as the holy sacramental vessels. There would no longer be a distinction between the sacred and secular, for everything would be sacred.

[16] Then all who survive of the nations that have come against Jerusalem shall go up year after year to worship the King, the LORD of hosts, and to keep the festival of booths.[o] [17]If any of the

---

[i] Cn: Heb *for humankind has caused me to possess*   [j] Heb *wounds between your hands*   [k] Heb *my mountains*
[l] Meaning of Heb uncertain   [m] Cn: Heb *there shall not be light*   [n] Compare Gk Syr Vg Tg: Meaning of Heb uncertain
[o] Or *tabernacles*; Heb *succoth*

families of the earth do not go up to Jerusalem to worship the King, the LORD of hosts, there will be no rain upon them. [18]And if the family of Egypt do not go up and present themselves, then on them shall[p] come the plague that the LORD inflicts on the nations that do not go up to keep the festival of booths.[q] [19]Such shall be the punishment of Egypt and the punishment of all the nations that do not go up to keep the festival of booths.[q]

20 On that day there shall be inscribed on the bells of the horses, "Holy to the LORD." And the cooking pots in the house of the LORD shall be as holy as[r] the bowls in front of the altar; [21]and every cooking pot in Jerusalem and Judah shall be sacred to the LORD of hosts, so that all who sacrifice may come and use them to boil the flesh of the sacrifice. And there shall no longer be traders[s] in the house of the LORD of hosts on that day.

MALACHI

When Faith Grows Weary
Malachi spoke to people "going through the motions"

> *A son honors his father, and servants their master. If then I am a father, where is the honor due me?*
> 1.6

SUCCESS HAS DANGERS OF ITS own. When you reach the top, you may tend to slack off. Spiritual life can gradually deteriorate too.

Malachi, in this short book, tried to awaken Israel from slackness in relating to God. Years before, they had optimistically returned to Jerusalem after a long exile. Their faith had grown deeper through difficulties. Despite fierce opposition they had rebuilt the temple, the symbol of their hope in God. They had expected God to supernaturally fill it with his glory and make their nation the center of the world.

By Malachi's time Israel's hope had faded. In fact, life seemed to have passed the Israelites by. They could not see that God loved them (1.2), and they felt that serving God brought no reward (2.17; 3.14).

No Big Sinners

The people of Jerusalem had become lukewarm. Their complaints showed it, and so did their actions. They were not "big" sinners like the people before the exile, who had practiced child sacrifice and brought idols into the temple. Malachi's people had kept their religion, but they had lost contact with the God whom the religion was all about.

While Malachi mentioned the same injustices and evils earlier prophets had blasted (3.5), he concentrated most of his energy on problems that may seem petty in comparison: mixed marriages, divorce, and apathetic worship (shown in their second-rate offerings). Through Malachi's eyes, we see the Israelites going through the motions of their faith, doing the bare minimum.

How do you heat up a lukewarm faith? Malachi used several tactics. He began with God's love. To his audience, it was not apparent. But if they would compare their situation with neighboring Edom's, they would see that God had been caring for them all along.

Curing a Careless Attitude

Malachi then challenged the Jews to take obedience seriously. They were bringing injured or sick animals to God for offerings. "Try presenting that to your governor," Malachi said. "Will he be pleased with you or show you favor?" (1.8). Malachi urged them to bring the perfect animals God's law demands and his honor requires. Malachi further demanded that they stop marrying women of other religions, a practice that inevitably introduced religious compromise. They must also put an end to divorce. And finally, they must bring a full tenth—the "tithe"—of their income to God at the temple. Their skimping amounted to robbery—robbery from God.

Malachi didn't demand these changes just because they were in the rulebook. They were actions meant to symbolize an inner attitude. The people must practice their faith seriously. "Put me to the test, says the LORD of hosts; see if I will not open the windows of heaven for you and pour down for you an overflowing blessing" (3.10).

The Last Voice

Malachi's was the last Old Testament voice. It reverberated through 400 or more years of biblical silence. During those years at least some of Malachi's message took hold. Led by the Pharisees, Jews became increasingly devoted to keeping the Old Testament law. Unfortunately, many of them lost Malachi's main point. They forgot that the law was not an end in itself. It was a means by which to give God the honor he deserves.

How to Read Malachi

God's voice dominates Malachi, the voice of a loving father pleading with his children. The people's response is given in the form of seven questions or complaints. The result is a kind of dialogue—almost an argument—which lets you see into the personal attitudes of God and the people he is speaking to.

As in most arguments, a variety of issues are raised, but they are all rooted in a few basic attitudes. As you read through Malachi, try to see what attitudes lay behind the questions, complaints, and problems of God's people. Also note what attitudes lay behind God's words and promises to them.

You can place Malachi's message in the context of Israelite history by looking up "A Lineup of Rulers," pages 1349–1357.

3-TRACK READING PLAN

For an explanation and complete listing of the 3-track reading plan, turn to page 7.

TRACK 1: *Two-Week Courses on the Bible*
See page 7 for information on these courses.

TRACK 2: *An Overview of Malachi in 1 Day*
☐ Day 1. Read the Introduction to Malachi and chapter 3, which lays out some of God's promises and expectations for his people.

Now turn to page 9 for your next Track 2 reading project.

TRACK 3: *All of Malachi in 3 Days*
After you have read through Malachi, turn to pages 10–14 for your next Track 3 reading project.

☐1   ☐2   ☐3–4

1 An oracle. The word of the LORD to Israel by Malachi.[a]

Israel Preferred to Edom

2 I have loved you, says the LORD. But you say, "How have you loved us?" Is not Esau Jacob's brother? says the LORD. Yet I have loved Jacob 3but I have hated Esau; I have made his hill country a desolation and his heritage a desert for jackals. 4If Edom says, "We are shattered but we will rebuild the ruins," the LORD of hosts says: They may build, but I will tear down, until they are called the wicked country, the people with whom the LORD is angry forever. 5Your own eyes shall see this, and you shall say, "Great is the LORD beyond the borders of Israel!"

Corruption of the Priesthood

6 A son honors his father, and servants their master. If then I am a father, where is the honor due me? And if I am a master, where is the respect due me? says the LORD of hosts to you, O priests, who despise my name. You say, "How have we despised your name?" 7By offering polluted food on my altar. And you say, "How have we polluted it?"[b] By thinking that the LORD's table may be despised. 8When you offer blind animals in sacrifice, is that not wrong? And when you offer those that are lame or sick, is that not wrong? Try presenting that to your governor; will he be pleased

1.2 Spurned

Lovers remember when they first fell for someone. They also remember how that person responded, especially if their love met rejection.

In Malachi, God starts the conversation: "I have loved you." Then he traces all of Israel's sins back to their underlying contempt for that love. They have not honored him as a father (verse 6) or worshiped him as the great King he is (verse 11). Instead, they have shown contempt, bringing second-rate offerings (verse 8), saying, "What a weariness this is" and sniffing contemptuously at his table (verse 13).

with you or show you favor? says the LORD of hosts. 9And now implore the favor of God, that he may be gracious to us. The fault is yours. Will he show favor to any of you? says the LORD of hosts.

a Or *by my messenger*   *b* Gk: Heb *you*

[10]Oh, that someone among you would shut the temple[c] doors, so that you would not kindle fire on my altar in vain! I have no pleasure in you, says the LORD of hosts, and I will not accept an offering from your hands. [11]For from the rising of the sun to its setting my name is great among the nations, and in every place incense is offered to my name, and a pure offering; for my name is great among the nations, says the LORD of hosts. [12]But you profane it when you say that the Lord's table is polluted, and the food for it[d] may be despised. [13]"What a weariness this is," you say, and you sniff at me,[e] says the LORD of hosts. You bring what has been taken by violence or is lame or sick, and this you bring as your offering! Shall I accept that from your hand? says the LORD. [14]Cursed be the cheat who has a male in the flock and vows to give it, and yet sacrifices to the Lord what is blemished; for I am a great King, says the LORD of hosts, and my name is reverenced among the nations.

2 And now, O priests, this command is for you. [2]If you will not listen, if you will not lay it to heart to give glory to my name, says the LORD of hosts, then I will send the curse on you and I will curse your blessings; indeed I have already cursed them,[f] because you do not lay it to heart. [3]I will rebuke your offspring, and spread dung on your faces, the dung of your offerings, and I will put you out of my presence.[g]

4 Know, then, that I have sent this command to you, that my covenant with Levi may hold, says the LORD of hosts. [5]My covenant with him was a covenant of life and well-being, which I gave him; this called for reverence, and he revered me and stood in awe of my name. [6]True instruction was in his mouth, and no wrong was found on his lips. He walked with me in integrity and uprightness, and he turned many from iniquity. [7]For the lips of a priest should guard knowledge, and people should seek instruction from his mouth, for he is the messenger of the LORD of hosts. [8]But you have turned aside from the way; you have caused many to stumble by your instruction; you have corrupted the covenant of Levi, says the LORD of hosts, [9]and so I make you despised and abased before all the people, inasmuch as you have not kept my ways but have shown partiality in your instruction.

The Covenant Profaned by Judah

10 Have we not all one father? Has not one God created us? Why then are we faithless to one another, profaning the covenant of our ancestors? [11]Judah has been faithless, and abomination has been committed in Israel and in Jerusalem; for Judah has profaned the sanctuary of the LORD, which he loves, and has married the daughter of a foreign god. [12]May the LORD cut off from the tents of Jacob anyone who does this—any to witness[h] or answer, or to bring an offering to the LORD of hosts.

13 And this you do as well: You cover the LORD's altar with tears, with weeping and groaning because he no longer regards the offering or accepts it with favor at your hand. [14]You ask, "Why does he not?" Because the LORD was a witness between you and the wife of your youth, to whom you have been faithless, though she is your companion and your wife by covenant. [15]Did not one God make her?[i] Both flesh and spirit are his.[j] And what does the one God[k] desire? Godly offspring. So look to yourselves, and do not let anyone be faithless to the wife of his youth. [16]For I hate[l] divorce, says the LORD, the God of Israel, and covering one's garment with violence, says the LORD of hosts. So take heed to yourselves and do not be faithless.

2.16 I Hate Divorce

Divorce was legal in Israel (see Deuteronomy 24.1–4), so perhaps people made no connection between their troubles and the divorce statistics. Malachi straightens them out. God hates divorce, legal or not. The marriage covenant between a man and woman should be kept faithfully. Jesus said much the same thing in Matthew 19.1–9.

17 You have wearied the LORD with your words. Yet you say, "How have we wearied him?" By saying, "All who do evil are good in the sight of the LORD, and he delights in them." Or by asking, "Where is the God of justice?"

The Coming Messenger

3 See, I am sending my messenger to prepare the way before me, and the Lord whom you seek will suddenly come to his temple. The messenger of the covenant in whom you delight—indeed, he is coming, says the LORD of hosts. [2]But who can endure the day of his coming, and who can stand when he appears?

For he is like a refiner's fire and like fullers' soap; [3]he will sit as a refiner and purifier of silver, and he will purify the descendants of Levi and refine them like gold and silver, until they present offerings to the LORD in righteousness.[m] [4]Then the offering of Judah and Jerusalem will be pleasing to the LORD as in the days of old and as in former years.

5 Then I will draw near to you for judgment;

---

[c] Heb lacks *temple* [d] Compare Syr Tg: Heb *its fruit, its food* [e] Another reading is *at it* [f] Heb *it*
[g] Cn Compare Gk Syr: Heb *and he shall bear you to it* [h] Cn Compare Gk: Heb *arouse* [i] Or *Has he not made one?*
[j] Cn: Heb *and a remnant of spirit was his* [k] Heb *he* [l] Cn: Heb *he hates* [m] Or *right offerings to the LORD*

I will be swift to bear witness against the sorcerers, against the adulterers, against those who swear falsely, against those who oppress the hired workers in their wages, the widow and the orphan,

---

2.17 Why Serve God?

Here and in 3.14 people harshly complained they could see no point in serving God, when you got no special reward. In responding, God did not try to convince them that the righteous were, in fact, better off. He told them that he keeps a "book of remembrance" (3.16), on which he records those who fear him, and that sometime in the future he will come as judge, destroying the wicked and preserving those who fear him. The value of serving him will be obvious someday, even if it is not today.

---

against those who thrust aside the alien, and do not fear me, says the LORD of hosts.

6 For I the LORD do not change; therefore you, O children of Jacob, have not perished. [7]Ever since the days of your ancestors you have turned aside from my statutes and have not kept them. Return to me, and I will return to you, says the LORD of hosts. But you say, "How shall we return?"

Do Not Rob God

8 Will anyone rob God? Yet you are robbing me! But you say, "How are we robbing you?" In your tithes and offerings! [9]You are cursed with a curse, for you are robbing me—the whole nation of you! [10]Bring the full tithe into the storehouse, so that there may be food in my house, and thus put me to the test, says the LORD of hosts; see if I will not open the windows of heaven for you and pour down for you an overflowing blessing. [11]I will rebuke the locust[n] for you, so that it will not destroy the produce of your soil; and your vine in the field shall not be barren, says the LORD of

---

3.10 Testing the Tithe

Like a salesman offering a free sample, God urges the Israelites to test him out. If they bring their tithes to the temple, they will see how God blesses them, opening the "windows of heaven" to pour out an abundance. The "tithe" was at least a tenth of their income, used to feed the priests, pay temple expenses, and help the poor.

---

hosts. [12]Then all nations will count you happy, for you will be a land of delight, says the LORD of hosts.

13 You have spoken harsh words against me, says the LORD. Yet you say, "How have we spoken against you?" [14]You have said, "It is vain to serve God. What do we profit by keeping his command or by going about as mourners before the LORD of hosts? [15]Now we count the arrogant happy; evildoers not only prosper, but when they put God to the test they escape."

The Reward of the Faithful

16 Then those who revered the LORD spoke with one another. The LORD took note and listened, and a book of remembrance was written before him of those who revered the LORD and thought on his name. [17]They shall be mine, says the LORD of hosts, my special possession on the day when I act, and I will spare them as parents spare their children who serve them. [18]Then once more you shall see the difference between the righteous and the wicked, between one who serves God and one who does not serve him.

The Great Day of the LORD

4[o] See, the day is coming, burning like an oven, when all the arrogant and all evildoers will be stubble; the day that comes shall burn them up, says the LORD of hosts, so that it will leave them neither root nor branch. [2]But for you who revere my name the sun of righteousness shall rise, with healing in its wings. You shall go out leaping like calves from the stall. [3]And you shall tread down the wicked, for they will be ashes under the soles of your feet, on the day when I act, says the LORD of hosts.

4 Remember the teaching of my servant Moses, the statutes and ordinances that I commanded him at Horeb for all Israel.

5 Lo, I will send you the prophet Elijah before

4.5 The Second Elijah

The prophet Elijah, Malachi predicted, would precede the Lord. This prophecy was carefully noted in the New Testament. Jesus identified John the Baptist as the one predicted (Matthew 11.14; 17.9–13).

---

the great and terrible day of the LORD comes. [6]He will turn the hearts of parents to their children and the hearts of children to their parents, so that I will not come and strike the land with a curse.[p]

---

[n] Heb *devourer*   [o] Ch 4.1-6 are Ch 3.19-24 in Heb   [p] Or *a ban of utter destruction*

Outline of Old Testament History

This outline emphasizes broad historical periods rather than specific events. Dates, which often depend on scholarly interpretation, are approximate.

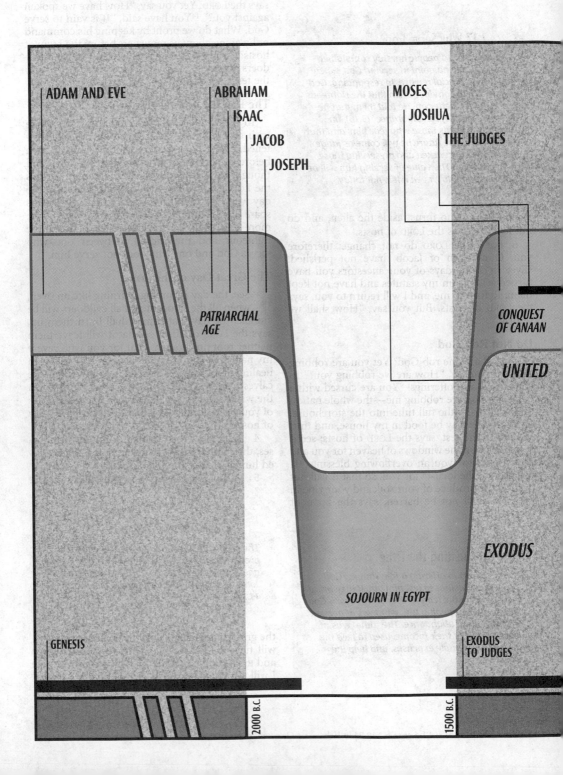

ADAM AND EVE

ABRAHAM

ISAAC

JACOB

JOSEPH

MOSES

JOSHUA

THE JUDGES

PATRIARCHAL
AGE

CONQUEST
OF CANAAN

UNITED

EXODUS

SOJOURN IN EGYPT

GENESIS

EXODUS
TO JUDGES

2000 B.C.

1500 B.C.

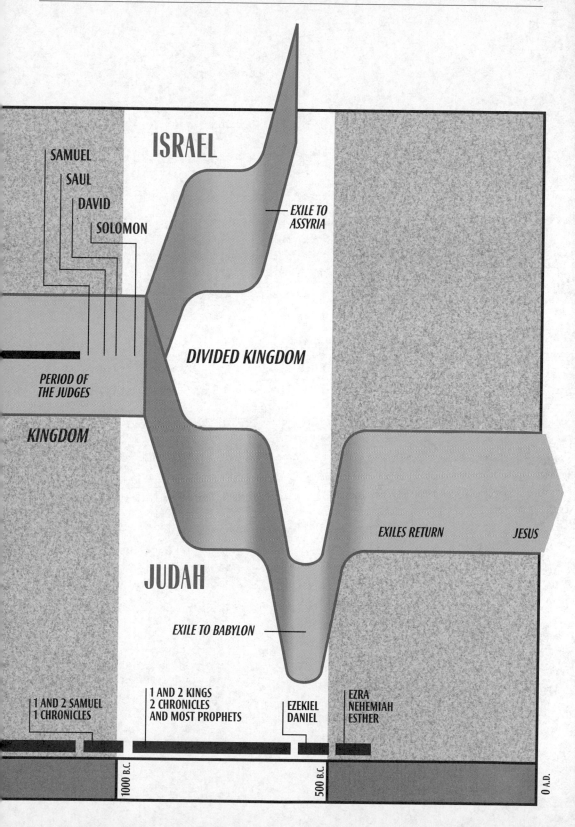

ISRAEL

SAMUEL
SAUL
DAVID
SOLOMON

EXILE TO
ASSYRIA

DIVIDED KINGDOM

PERIOD OF
THE JUDGES

KINGDOM

EXILES RETURN   JESUS

JUDAH

EXILE TO BABYLON

1 AND 2 SAMUEL
1 CHRONICLES

1 AND 2 KINGS
2 CHRONICLES
AND MOST PROPHETS

EZEKIEL
DANIEL

EZRA
NEHEMIAH
ESTHER

1000 B.C.

500 B.C.

0 A.D.

THE
NEW
TESTAMENT

MATTHEW

A Bridge from Old to New
Why start with a list of names?

FOR FOUR HUNDRED YEARS, NOTHING new was added to the Bible. The prophets fell silent. During this time, Middle Eastern empires rose and fell, and the tiny nation of Israel suffered under the domination of greater powers like Greece and Rome.

And then something momentous happened. A baby was born—a baby unlike any who had ever come before. By introducing this baby who grew into the man Jesus, the book of Matthew opens a whole new section of the Bible—the New Testament.

Matthew makes his intentions clear from the very first sentence: He connects Jesus' arrival with the Old Testament story line. Jesus was a Jew, he says, the son of Abraham. And also a king, the son of David. Matthew then sets out to prove an audacious claim: This Jesus, from the humble town of Nazareth, is the very "Messiah," the deliverer promised back in the Old Testament. (*Christ* is a Greek translation of the word *Messiah*.)

Jesus' Family Tree

People all over the world, especially Jews, had been eagerly awaiting the Messiah. His coming would change the entire history of the world, they believed. Could this carpenter's son be the long-expected king? To answer that question, Matthew starts with a genealogy.

Genealogies—long lists of names—rarely prove interesting to anyone but the people directly involved. To those people, however, the lists are anything but boring.

Listen to one modern author describe what it was like to hear an ancient genealogy: "There is an expression, 'the peak experience,' a moment which emotionally can never again be equaled in your life. I had mine, that first day in the village of Juffure, in black west Africa ... Goose bumps came out on me the size of marbles." With those words, Alex Haley, author of *Roots*, recalls the day he first heard, from the lips of an aged storyteller, the account of young Kunta Kinte being taken captive by slave traders in 1752.

The Importance of Roots

Haley's ancestors in Tennessee and Virginia had descended directly from a native African captured in a tiny village in Gambia. The day he listened to the gentle African elder recite, "And so-and-so took as a wife so-and-so, and begat so-and-so," the final link in Haley's family chain snapped into place. *Roots* tells the story of this connection.

In a similar way, the book of Matthew doesn't begin with Jesus' birth, but reaches back further to establish his roots. If indeed Jesus is the Messiah, his ancestors must match up to that claim. As any student of history knows, kings don't merely declare themselves; they must belong to a royal line. Matthew traces Jesus' lineage to the father of the Jewish race, Abraham—who first received the promise of the Messiah—then to the great Jewish king David.

Links to the Old Testament

After recording Jesus' bloodline, Matthew narrates the story of Jesus' life on earth. He relies heavily on the Old Testament, quoting it more frequently than does any other New Testament author. (Note such phrases as "So that what had been spoken through the prophets might be fulfilled.")

The first book in the New Testament, then, stands as the Gospel that pulls things together, the link between the old and the new. Matthew starts with Jesus' roots, but he also contrasts Jesus with the traditional Jewish picture of the Messiah. Jesus, a king, ended thousands of years of eager waiting. But he came to establish a wholly new kind of kingdom—a kingdom different from what anyone expected.

How to Read Matthew

Anybody who has looked over an Internal Revenue Service (IRS) form knows what tax collectors like: neat, orderly rows of figures, with all expenses and income classified by type and source. Fittingly, the Gospel attributed to former tax collector Matthew reflects systematic, ledger-sheet thinking. He doesn't tell Jesus' story chronologically; he groups facts topically.

Matthew collects Jesus' sayings in five main places. First comes the famous Sermon on the Mount in chapters 5–7. Chapter 10 records Jesus' instructions to his disciples about their mission; chapter 13, a series of parables on the kingdom; chapter 18, Christ's words on the church as a community; and chapters 23–25, Jesus' thoughts on religious hypocrisy and his predictions of the future. Sandwiched in among these five great discourses you'll find connected scenes of Jesus in action.

The skillful blending of Jesus' action and teaching has helped earn this Gospel an esteemed place in literature. Artists are often drawn to it as a capsule summary of Jesus' ministry: witness J.S. Bach's greatest choral work, *Saint Matthew's Passion*, the joyous play *Godspell*, and Italian film maker Pasolini's film *The Gospel according to Saint Matthew*. The French skeptic Renan praised Matthew as "the most important book of Christendom—the most important book that has ever been written."

Two approaches will help in a detailed study of Matthew. First, consider how it differs from the other three Gospels; this will give you some idea of Matthew's distinctive purpose. Then, you will find it enlightening to look up many of Matthew's references to the Old Testament.

PEOPLE YOU'LL MEET IN MATTHEW

JOSEPH *(p. 990)*
JOHN THE BAPTIST *(p. 1000)*
THE HERODS *(p. 1005)*

3-TRACK READING PLAN

For an explanation and complete listing of the 3-track reading plan, turn to page 7.

TRACK 1: *Two-Week Courses on the Bible*
The Track 1 reading program on the Life and Teachings of Jesus includes four chapters from Matthew. See page 7 for a complete listing of this course.

TRACK 2: *An Overview of Matthew in 7 Days*
☐ Day 1. Read the Introduction to Matthew. Then turn to Matthew 5 and begin the Sermon on the Mount.
☐ Day 2. Read chapter 6, a continuation of Jesus' longest single speech, perhaps the most familiar passage in the entire Bible.
☐ Day 3. Matthew 13 records some of Jesus' parables—concise stories with a powerful meaning behind them. Read these parables about the "kingdom of heaven," referring to "What Should a Leader Look Like?" page 1003, for help in understanding.
☐ Day 4. As a former tax collector, Matthew was especially sensitive to what Jesus had to say about money. Read his comments on this and other topics in chapter 19.
☐ Day 5. The last three chapters of Matthew give a complete, factual account of Jesus' death. Read chapter 26, the story of the arrest and trial.
☐ Day 6. Continue the crucifixion story with chapter 27.
☐ Day 7. Read chapter 28, which tells of Jesus' resurrection.

Now turn to page 9 for your next Track 2 reading project.

TRACK 3: **All of Matthew in 28 Days**
After you have read through Matthew a chapter a day, turn to pages 10–14 for your next Track 3 reading project.

☐1 ☐2 ☐3 ☐4 ☐5 ☐6 ☐7 ☐8
☐9 ☐10 ☐11 ☐12 ☐13 ☐14 ☐15 ☐16
☐17 ☐18 ☐19 ☐20 ☐21 ☐22 ☐23 ☐24
☐25 ☐26 ☐27 ☐28

The Genealogy of Jesus the Messiah

▶ See Ruth 4.18–22; 1 Chronicles 3.10–17; Luke 3.23–38

1 An account of the genealogy[a] of Jesus the Messiah,[b] the son of David, the son of Abraham.

2 Abraham was the father of Isaac, and Isaac the father of Jacob, and Jacob the father of Judah and his brothers, [3]and Judah the father of Perez and Zerah by Tamar, and Perez the father of Hezron, and Hezron the father of Aram, [4]and Aram the father of Aminadab, and Aminadab the father of Nahshon, and Nahshon the father of Salmon, [5]and Salmon the father of Boaz by Rahab, and Boaz the father of Obed by Ruth, and Obed the father of Jesse, [6]and Jesse the father of King David.

1.6 Shady Ancestors

Matthew's list differs from many Jewish genealogies by including women, and a surprising selection of women at that. Tamar, a Gentile, tricked and seduced her father-in-law, then bore illegitimate twins (Genesis 38); Rahab, another Gentile, once worked as a prostitute (Joshua 2; 6); Ruth also grew up as a pagan Gentile (Ruth 1–4); and Uriah's wife Bathsheba committed adultery with King David (2 Samuel 11–12). Many of the men listed had unsavory pasts as well; taken together, these ancestors of Jesus vividly demonstrate God's ability to work with all sorts of people.

And David was the father of Solomon by the wife of Uriah, [7]and Solomon the father of Rehoboam, and Rehoboam the father of Abijah, and Abijah the father of Asaph,[c] [8]and Asaph[c] the father of Jehoshaphat, and Jehoshaphat the father of Joram, and Joram the father of Uzziah, [9]and Uzziah the father of Jotham, and Jotham the father of Ahaz, and Ahaz the father of Hezekiah, [10]and Hezekiah the father of Manasseh, and Manasseh the father of Amos,[d] and Amos[d] the father of Josiah, [11]and Josiah the father of Jechoniah

and his brothers, at the time of the deportation to Babylon.

12 And after the deportation to Babylon: Jechoniah was the father of Salathiel, and Salathiel the father of Zerubbabel, [13]and Zerubbabel the father of Abiud, and Abiud the father of Eliakim, and Eliakim the father of Azor, [14]and Azor the father of Zadok, and Zadok the father of Achim, and Achim the father of Eliud, [15]and Eliud the father of Eleazar, and Eleazar the father of Matthan, and Matthan the father of Jacob, [16]and Jacob the father of Joseph the husband of Mary, of whom Jesus was born, who is called the Messiah.[e]

17 So all the generations from Abraham to David are fourteen generations; and from David to the deportation to Babylon, fourteen generations; and from the deportation to Babylon to the Messiah,[e] fourteen generations.

The Birth of Jesus the Messiah

18 Now the birth of Jesus the Messiah[b] took place in this way. When his mother Mary had been engaged to Joseph, but before they lived together, she was found to be with child from the Holy Spirit. [19]Her husband Joseph, being a righteous man and unwilling to expose her to public disgrace, planned to dismiss her quietly. [20]But just when he had resolved to do this, an angel of the Lord appeared to him in a dream and said, "Joseph, son of David, do not be afraid to take Mary as your wife, for the child conceived in her is from the Holy Spirit. [21]She will bear a son, and you are to name him Jesus, for he will save his people

1.18–20 More Than Engaged

Jewish custom in Joseph and Mary's day recognized a state called "betrothal" that fell somewhere between our modern commitments of engagement and marriage. A betrothal was more binding than an engagement: It could only be broken with an act of divorce. And if a betrothed woman became pregnant, she was regarded as an adulteress.

---

[a] Or *birth*   [b] Or *Jesus Christ*   [c] Other ancient authorities read *Asa*   [d] Other ancient authorities read *Amon*
[e] Or *the Christ*

from their sins." [22]All this took place to fulfill what had been spoken by the Lord through the prophet:

[23] "Look, the virgin shall conceive and bear
a son,
and they shall name him Emmanuel,"

which means, "God is with us." [24]When Joseph awoke from sleep, he did as the angel of the Lord commanded him; he took her as his wife, [25]but had no marital relations with her until she had borne a son;[f] and he named him Jesus.

The Visit of the Wise Men

2 In the time of King Herod, after Jesus was born in Bethlehem of Judea, wise men[g] from the East came to Jerusalem, [2]asking, "Where is the child who has been born king of the Jews? For we observed his star at its rising,[h] and have come to pay him homage." [3]When King Herod heard this, he was frightened, and all Jerusalem with him; [4]and calling together all the chief priests and scribes of the people, he inquired of them where the Messiah[i] was to be born. [5]They told him, "In Bethlehem of Judea; for so it has been written by the prophet:

[6] 'And you, Bethlehem, in the land
of Judah,
are by no means least among the rulers
of Judah;
for from you shall come a ruler
who is to shepherd[j] my
people Israel.'"

[7] Then Herod secretly called for the wise men[g] and learned from them the exact time when the star had appeared. [8]Then he sent them to Bethlehem, saying, "Go and search diligently for the child; and when you have found him, bring me word so that I may also go and pay him homage." [9]When they had heard the king, they set out; and there, ahead of them, went the star that they had seen at its rising,[h] until it stopped over the place where the child was. [10]When they saw that the star had stopped,[k] they were overwhelmed with joy. [11]On entering the house, they saw the child with Mary his mother; and they knelt down and paid him homage. Then, opening their treasure chests, they offered him gifts of gold, frankincense, and myrrh. [12]And having been warned in a dream not to return to Herod, they left for their own country by another road.

The Escape to Egypt

[13] Now after they had left, an angel of the Lord appeared to Joseph in a dream and said, "Get up, take the child and his mother, and flee to Egypt, and remain there until I tell you; for Herod is about to search for the child, to destroy him." [14]Then Joseph[l] got up, took the child and his mother by night, and went to Egypt, [15]and remained there until the death of Herod. This was to fulfill what had been spoken by the Lord through the prophet, "Out of Egypt I have called my son."

The Massacre of the Infants

[16] When Herod saw that he had been tricked by the wise men,[g] he was infuriated, and he sent and killed all the children in and around Bethle-

---

f Other ancient authorities read *her firstborn son*   g Or *astrologers*; Gk *magi*   h Or *in the East*   i Or *the Christ*
j Or *rule*   k Gk *saw the star*   l Gk *he*

JOSEPH *Stepfather*

STEPPARENTS TAKE ON ONE OF the hardest tasks in life—raising a child who isn't biologically theirs. When Joseph first learned that his fiancée Mary was bearing someone else's child, he must have felt deep heartache. By law, he had the right to accuse Mary of adultery and have her executed. Then an angel brought instructions in a dream: Joseph was to stay with Mary, for her child was from God.

Three times Joseph received angelic messages in dreams, and each time they called for moves he had not planned and could hardly wish. First he was called to care for a wife he had never slept with and a child who was not his. Then he was ordered to flee as a refugee to far-off Egypt. Finally an angel told him to return home, where skeptical neighbors probably remembered that Mary had been pregnant before her marriage.

We know one thing about Joseph: He obeyed, following the angel's orders in each difficult case. A dutiful stepfather, he treated his son as his own, raising him according to the Jewish law. As a carpenter, he taught Jesus to hammer and saw. As a righteous man, he modeled for him an obedient life.

We last hear of Joseph when Jesus was 12. After that, the Bible only mentions Jesus' mother, Mary, and Jesus' brothers. (Joseph probably died before Jesus began his ministry. From the cross, Jesus committed the care of his mother to one of his disciples [John 19.25–27].) Through his faithfulness as a stepfather, however, Joseph made a lasting contribution to the world.

Life Questions: Has God asked you to do any thankless tasks? What were they, and how did they turn out?

hem who were two years old or under, according to the time that he had learned from the wise men.*m* 17Then was fulfilled what had been spoken through the prophet Jeremiah:

2.11 The Wise Men

Of the four Gospels, Matthew alone tells of the visit of the magi, or wise men. This incident shows that people from other parts of the world, not just from Israel, were anticipating the Messiah. The magi's visit underscores that Jesus came for all people, not just the Jews. The last words of this Gospel spell out that mission very clearly.

18 "A voice was heard in Ramah,
    wailing and loud lamentation,
Rachel weeping for her children;
    she refused to be consoled, because
        they are no more."

The Return from Egypt

19 When Herod died, an angel of the Lord suddenly appeared in a dream to Joseph in Egypt and said, 20"Get up, take the child and his mother, and go to the land of Israel, for those who were seeking the child's life are dead." 21Then Joseph*n* got up, took the child and his mother, and went to the land of Israel. 22But when he heard that Archelaus was ruling over Judea in place of his father Herod, he was afraid to go there. And after being warned in a dream, he went away to the district of Galilee. 23There he made his home in a town called Nazareth, so that what had been spoken through the prophets might be fulfilled, "He will be called a Nazorean."

The Proclamation of John the Baptist

▶ *See Mark 1.3–8; Luke 3.2–17*

3 In those days John the Baptist appeared in the wilderness of Judea, proclaiming, 2"Repent, for the kingdom of heaven has come near."*o* 3This is the one of whom the prophet Isaiah spoke when he said,
    "The voice of one crying out in
        the wilderness:
    'Prepare the way of the Lord,
        make his paths straight.'"
4Now John wore clothing of camel's hair with a leather belt around his waist, and his food was locusts and wild honey. 5Then the people of Jerusalem and all Judea were going out to him, and all the region along the Jordan, 6and they were baptized by him in the river Jordan, confessing their sins.

7 But when he saw many Pharisees and Sad-

ducees coming for baptism, he said to them, "You brood of vipers! Who warned you to flee from the wrath to come? 8Bear fruit worthy of repentance. 9Do not presume to say to yourselves, 'We have Abraham as our ancestor'; for I tell you, God is able from these stones to raise up children to Abraham. 10Even now the ax is lying at the root of the trees; every tree therefore that does not bear good fruit is cut down and thrown into the fire.

11 "I baptize you with*p* water for repentance, but one who is more powerful than I is coming after me; I am not worthy to carry his sandals. He will baptize you with*p* the Holy Spirit and fire. 12His winnowing fork is in his hand, and he will clear his threshing floor and will gather his wheat into the granary; but the chaff he will burn with unquenchable fire."

The Baptism of Jesus

▶ *See Mark 1.9–11; Luke 3.21–22; John 1.31–34*

13 Then Jesus came from Galilee to John at the Jordan, to be baptized by him. 14John would have prevented him, saying, "I need to be baptized by you, and do you come to me?" 15But Jesus answered him, "Let it be so now; for it is proper for us in this way to fulfill all righteousness." Then he consented. 16And when Jesus had been baptized, just as he came up from the water, suddenly the heavens were opened to him and he saw the Spirit of God descending like a dove and alighting on him. 17And a voice from heaven said, "This is my Son, the Beloved,*q* with whom I am well pleased."

The Temptation of Jesus

▶ *See Mark 1.12–13; Luke 4.1–13*

4 Then Jesus was led up by the Spirit into the wilderness to be tempted by the devil. 2He fasted forty days and forty nights, and afterwards he was famished. 3The tempter came and said to him, "If you are the Son of God, command these stones to become loaves of bread." 4But he answered, "It is written,
    'One does not live by bread alone,
        but by every word that comes from the
            mouth of God.'"
5 Then the devil took him to the holy city and placed him on the pinnacle of the temple, 6saying to him, "If you are the Son of God, throw yourself down; for it is written,
    'He will command his angels concerning
        you,'
    and 'On their hands they will bear you
        up,
    so that you will not dash your foot
        against a stone.'"
7Jesus said to him, "Again it is written, 'Do not put the Lord your God to the test.'"
8 Again, the devil took him to a very high

mountain and showed him all the kingdoms of the world and their splendor; [9]and he said to him, "All these I will give you, if you will fall down and worship me." [10]Jesus said to him, "Away with you, Satan! for it is written,

'Worship the Lord your God,
and serve only him.'"

[11]Then the devil left him, and suddenly angels came and waited on him.

Jesus Begins His Ministry in Galilee

12 Now when Jesus[r] heard that John had been arrested, he withdrew to Galilee. [13]He left Nazareth and made his home in Capernaum by the sea, in the territory of Zebulun and Naphtali, [14]so that what had been spoken through the prophet Isaiah might be fulfilled:

[15] "Land of Zebulun, land of Naphtali,
on the road by the sea, across the
Jordan, Galilee of the Gentiles—
[16] the people who sat in darkness
have seen a great light,
and for those who sat in the region and
shadow of death
light has dawned."

[17]From that time Jesus began to proclaim, "Repent, for the kingdom of heaven has come near."[s]

4.17 Words for Jewish Readers

Matthew wrote for a primarily Jewish audience. Starting with his opening chapter, he affirms that Jesus is the Messiah, backing up that claim by constant reference to the Old Testament. Often Matthew leaves Jewish phrases and customs unexplained, assuming that his readers are familiar with them. And, where other Gospel writers say, "kingdom of God," he uses the phrase "kingdom of heaven," out of respect for Jews, who never wrote out the word God.

Jesus Calls the First Disciples

▶ *See Mark 1.16–20; Luke 5.2–11; John 1.35–42*

18 As he walked by the Sea of Galilee, he saw two brothers, Simon, who is called Peter, and Andrew his brother, casting a net into the sea—for they were fishermen. [19]And he said to them, "Follow me, and I will make you fish for people." [20]Immediately they left their nets and followed him. [21]As he went from there, he saw two other brothers, James son of Zebedee and his brother John, in the boat with their father Zebedee, mending their nets, and he called them. [22]Immediately they left the boat and their father, and followed him.

Jesus Ministers to Crowds of People

23 Jesus[t] went throughout Galilee, teaching in their synagogues and proclaiming the good news[u] of the kingdom and curing every disease and every sickness among the people. [24]So his fame spread throughout all Syria, and they brought to him all the sick, those who were afflicted with various diseases and pains, demoniacs, epileptics, and paralytics, and he cured them. [25]And great crowds followed him from Galilee, the Decapolis, Jerusalem, Judea, and from beyond the Jordan.

The Beatitudes

▶ *See Luke 6.20–23*

5 When Jesus[r] saw the crowds, he went up the mountain; and after he sat down, his disciples came to him. [2]Then he began to speak, and taught them, saying:

3 "Blessed are the poor in spirit, for theirs is the kingdom of heaven.

4 "Blessed are those who mourn, for they will be comforted.

5 "Blessed are the meek, for they will inherit the earth.

6 "Blessed are those who hunger and thirst for righteousness, for they will be filled.

7 "Blessed are the merciful, for they will receive mercy.

8 "Blessed are the pure in heart, for they will see God.

9 "Blessed are the peacemakers, for they will be called children of God.

10 "Blessed are those who are persecuted for righteousness' sake, for theirs is the kingdom of heaven.

11 "Blessed are you when people revile you and persecute you and utter all kinds of evil against you falsely[v] on my account. [12]Rejoice and be glad, for your reward is great in heaven, for in the same way they persecuted the prophets who were before you.

Salt and Light

13 "You are the salt of the earth; but if salt has lost its taste, how can its saltiness be restored? It is no longer good for anything, but is thrown out and trampled under foot.

14 "You are the light of the world. A city built on a hill cannot be hid. [15]No one after lighting a lamp puts it under the bushel basket, but on the lampstand, and it gives light to all in the house. [16]In the same way, let your light shine before others, so that they may see your good works and give glory to your Father in heaven.

The Law and the Prophets

17 "Do not think that I have come to abolish

---

[r] Gk *he*　　[s] Or *is at hand*　　[t] Gk *He*　　[u] Gk *gospel*　　[v] Other ancient authorities lack *falsely*

the law or the prophets; I have come not to abolish but to fulfill. ¹⁸For truly I tell you, until heaven and earth pass away, not one letter,ʷ not one stroke of a letter, will pass from the law until all

---

5.17 Jesus and Moses' Law

In this statement, Jesus clarifies his relationship to the law of Moses. The next verses get more specific, contrasting Jesus' teaching with many common interpretations of that law. "You have heard that it was said . . . ," he begins, and then concludes, "But I say to you . . ." Jesus revealed the true intent of the Old Testament law, rather than its legalistic interpretations.

---

is accomplished. ¹⁹Therefore, whoever breaksˣ one of the least of these commandments, and teaches others to do the same, will be called least in the kingdom of heaven; but whoever does them and teaches them will be called great in the kingdom of heaven. ²⁰For I tell you, unless your righteousness exceeds that of the scribes and Pharisees, you will never enter the kingdom of heaven.

Concerning Anger

21 "You have heard that it was said to those of ancient times, 'You shall not murder'; and 'whoever murders shall be liable to judgment.' ²²But I say to you that if you are angry with a brother or sister,ʸ you will be liable to judgment; and if you insultᶻ a brother or sister,ᵃ you will be liable to the council; and if you say, 'You fool,' you will be liable to the hellʰ of fire. ²³So when you are offering your gift at the altar, if you remember that your brother or sisterᶜ has something against you, ²⁴leave your gift there before the altar and go; first be reconciled to your brother or sister,ᶜ and then come and offer your gift. ²⁵Come to terms quickly with your accuser while you are on the way to courtᵈ with him, or your accuser may hand you over to the judge, and the judge to the guard, and you will be thrown into prison. ²⁶Truly I tell you, you will never get out until you have paid the last penny.

Concerning Adultery

27 "You have heard that it was said, 'You shall not commit adultery.' ²⁸But I say to you that everyone who looks at a woman with lust has already committed adultery with her in his heart. ²⁹If your right eye causes you to sin, tear it out and throw it away; it is better for you to lose one of your members than for your whole body to be thrown into hell.ᵇ ³⁰And if your right hand

causes you to sin, cut it off and throw it away; it is better for you to lose one of your members than for your whole body to go into hell.ᵇ

Concerning Divorce

31 "It was also said, 'Whoever divorces his wife, let him give her a certificate of divorce.' ³²But I say to you that anyone who divorces his wife, except on the ground of unchastity, causes her to commit adultery; and whoever marries a divorced woman commits adultery.

Concerning Oaths

33 "Again, you have heard that it was said to those of ancient times, 'You shall not swear falsely, but carry out the vows you have made to the Lord.' ³⁴But I say to you, Do not swear at all, either by heaven, for it is the throne of God, ³⁵or by the earth, for it is his footstool, or by Jerusalem, for it is the city of the great King. ³⁶And do not swear by your head, for you cannot make one hair white or black. ³⁷Let your word be 'Yes, Yes' or 'No, No'; anything more than this comes from the evil one.ᵉ

Concerning Retaliation

38 "You have heard that it was said, 'An eye for an eye and a tooth for a tooth.' ³⁹But I say to you, Do not resist an evildoer. But if anyone strikes you on the right cheek, turn the other also; ⁴⁰and if anyone wants to sue you and take your coat, give your cloak as well; ⁴¹and if anyone forces you to go one mile, go also the second mile. ⁴²Give to everyone who begs from you, and do not refuse anyone who wants to borrow from you.

Love for Enemies

43 "You have heard that it was said, 'You shall love your neighbor and hate your enemy.' ⁴⁴But I say to you, Love your enemies and pray

---

5.44 Praying for Persecutors

Jesus got a chance to live out these words when, nailed to a cross, he prayed for his persecutors (Luke 23.34). The example of Stephen, the first Christian martyr (Acts 7.60), shows that some followers also put Jesus' command into practice—a fact that surely impressed one persecutor named Saul.

---

for those who persecute you, ⁴⁵so that you may be children of your Father in heaven; for he makes his sun rise on the evil and on the good, and sends rain on the righteous and on the unrighteous. ⁴⁶For if you love those who love you, what reward

---

ʷ Gk *one iota*   ˣ Or *annuls*   ʸ Gk *a brother*; other ancient authorities add *without cause*   ᶻ Gk *say Raca to* (an obscure term of abuse)   ᵃ Gk *a brother*   ᵇ Gk *Gehenna*   ᶜ Gk *your brother*   ᵈ Gk lacks *to court*   ᵉ Or *evil*

do you have? Do not even the tax collectors do the same? [47]And if you greet only your brothers and sisters,*f* what more are you doing than others? Do not even the Gentiles do the same? [48]Be perfect, therefore, as your heavenly Father is perfect.

Concerning Almsgiving

6 "Beware of practicing your piety before others in order to be seen by them; for then you have no reward from your Father in heaven.

2 "So whenever you give alms, do not sound a trumpet before you, as the hypocrites do in the synagogues and in the streets, so that they may be praised by others. Truly I tell you, they have received their reward. [3]But when you give alms, do not let your left hand know what your right hand is doing, [4]so that your alms may be done in secret; and your Father who sees in secret will reward you.*g*

f Gk *your brothers*   *g* Other ancient authorities add *openly*

Concerning Prayer

▶ *See Luke 11.2–4*

5 "And whenever you pray, do not be like the hypocrites; for they love to stand and pray in the synagogues and at the street corners, so that they may be seen by others. Truly I tell you, they have received their reward. [6]But whenever you pray, go into your room and shut the door and pray to your Father who is in secret; and your Father who sees in secret will reward you.*g*

7 "When you are praying, do not heap up empty phrases as the Gentiles do; for they think that they will be heard because of their many words. [8]Do not be like them, for your Father knows what you need before you ask him.

9 "Pray then in this way:
    Our Father in heaven,
        hallowed be your name.
10   Your kingdom come.

Letting the Inside Match the Outside

Is everyone a hypocrite?

> "Your Father who sees in secret will reward you." 6.4

ALMOST ALL OF US LIVE two lives: what people see outside and what is really going on inside. In school we learn what outward signs of attention will please the teacher. At a job we learn to "put up a good front" whenever the boss happens to stroll by. As if putting on masks, we style our hair, choose our clothes, and use body language to impress those around us. Over time, we learn to excel at hiding truly serious problems.

People tend to judge by outward appearances and so can easily be fooled. Acquaintances are often shocked when a mass-murderer is arrested. "He seemed like such a nice man!" they insist. The outside appearance did not match the inside reality.

A Blast at Hypocrites

Chapters 5–7 announce that the time has come for us to change not just the outside, but also the inside. In Jesus' day, religious people tried to impress each other with showy outward behavior. They wore gaunt and hungry looks during a brief fast, prayed grandiosely if people were watching, and went so far as to wear Bible verses strapped to their foreheads and left arms.

In his famous Sermon on the Mount, Jesus blasts the hypocrisy behind such seemingly harmless practices. God is not fooled by appearances. We cannot fake behavior to impress him. He knows that inside the best of us lurk dark thoughts of hatred, pride, and lust—internal problems only he can deal with. Jesus goes on to present a truly radical way of life, free of pretense.

Familiar Yet Startling Words

These three chapters, among the most analyzed in the entire Bible, present a fresh view of the world. You will likely recognize many familiar sections, including the Golden Rule and the Lord's Prayer.

In one sense, Jesus says, the truths presented here are not new: they fulfill, rather than abolish the Old Testament law. In another sense the way of life described is more radical than anything before or since. Jesus' words turn many normal assumptions upside down. With statements like, "Blessed are the poor in spirit . . . those who mourn . . . the meek . . . the peacemakers . . . those who are persecuted," Jesus attacks those who strive to build a good image by appearing powerful, successful, and assertive.

Perhaps most radical of all, The Sermon on the Mount introduces the possibility of living solely for God and not for appearances. At last we can bring our inner and outer lives together.

Life Questions: Do other people see what you're really like inside? How do your friends try to impress each other?

Your will be done,
　　on earth as it is in heaven.
11　Give us this day our daily bread.*h*
12　And forgive us our debts,
　　as we also have forgiven
　　　our debtors.
13　And do not bring us to the time of
　　　trial,*i*
　　but rescue us from the evil one.*j*

14For if you forgive others their trespasses, your heavenly Father will also forgive you; 15but if you do not forgive others, neither will your Father forgive your trespasses.

Concerning Fasting

16 "And whenever you fast, do not look dismal, like the hypocrites, for they disfigure their faces so as to show others that they are fasting. Truly I tell you, they have received their reward. 17But when you fast, put oil on your head and wash your face, 18so that your fasting may be seen not by others but by your Father who is in secret; and your Father who sees in secret will reward you.*k*

Concerning Treasures

19 "Do not store up for yourselves treasures on earth, where moth and rust*l* consume and where thieves break in and steal; 20but store up for yourselves treasures in heaven, where neither moth nor rust*l* consumes and where thieves do not break in and steal. 21For where your treasure is, there your heart will be also.

The Sound Eye

22 "The eye is the lamp of the body. So, if your eye is healthy, your whole body will be full of light; 23but if your eye is unhealthy, your whole body will be full of darkness. If then the light in you is darkness, how great is the darkness!

Serving Two Masters

24 "No one can serve two masters; for a slave will either hate the one and love the other, or be devoted to the one and despise the other. You cannot serve God and wealth.*m*

Do Not Worry

▶ *See Luke 12.22-31*

25 "Therefore I tell you, do not worry about your life, what you will eat or what you will drink,*n* or about your body, what you will wear. Is not life more than food, and the body more than clothing? 26Look at the birds of the air; they neither sow nor reap nor gather into barns, and yet your heavenly Father feeds them. Are you not of more value than they? 27And can any of you by worrying add a single hour to your span of life?*o* 28And why do you worry about clothing? Consider the lilies of the field, how they grow; they neither toil nor spin, 29yet I tell you, even Solomon in all his glory was not clothed like one of these. 30But if God so clothes the grass of the field, which is alive today and tomorrow is thrown into the oven, will he not much more clothe you—you of little faith? 31Therefore do not worry, saying, 'What will we eat?' or 'What will we drink?' or 'What will we wear?' 32For it is the Gentiles who strive for all these things; and indeed your heavenly Father knows that you need all these things. 33But strive first for the kingdom of God*p* and his*q* righteousness, and all these things will be given to you as well.

34 "So do not worry about tomorrow, for tomorrow will bring worries of its own. Today's trouble is enough for today.

Judging Others

▶ *See Luke 6.41-42*

7 "Do not judge, so that you may not be judged. 2For with the judgment you make you will be judged, and the measure you give will be the measure you get. 3Why do you see the speck in your neighbor's*r* eye, but do not notice the log in your own eye? 4Or how can you say to your neighbor,*s* 'Let me take the speck out of your eye,' while the log is in your own eye? 5You hypocrite, first take the log out of your own eye, and then you will see clearly to take the speck out of your neighbor's*r* eye.

Profaning the Holy

6 "Do not give what is holy to dogs; and do not throw your pearls before swine, or they will trample them under foot and turn and maul you.

Ask, Search, Knock

▶ *See Luke 11.9-13*

7 "Ask, and it will be given you; search, and you will find; knock, and the door will be opened for you. 8For everyone who asks receives, and everyone who searches finds, and for everyone who knocks, the door will be opened. 9Is there anyone among you who, if your child asks for bread, will give a stone? 10Or if the child asks for a fish, will give a snake? 11If you then, who are evil, know how to give good gifts to your children, how much more will your Father in heaven give good things to those who ask him!

The Golden Rule

12 "In everything do to others as you would

---

h Or *our bread for tomorrow*　　*i* Or *us into temptation*　　*j* Or *from evil.* Other ancient authorities add, in some form, *For the kingdom and the power and the glory are yours forever. Amen.*　　*k* Other ancient authorities add *openly*　　*l* Gk *eating*　　*m* Gk *mammon*　　*n* Other ancient authorities lack *or what you will drink*　　*o* Or *add one cubit to your height*　　*p* Other ancient authorities lack *of God*　　*q* Or *its*　　*r* Gk *brother's*　　*s* Gk *brother*

have them do to you; for this is the law and the prophets.

The Narrow Gate

13 "Enter through the narrow gate; for the gate is wide and the road is easy[t] that leads to destruction, and there are many who take it. 14For the gate is narrow and the road is hard that leads to life, and there are few who find it.

7.12 Golden Rule

Other religions (Judaism, Hinduism, Buddhism, Confucianism) had some form of this saying, but most were stated negatively: "Don't do to others what you wouldn't want them to do to you." Jesus' version is far more open-ended and challenging.

A Tree and Its Fruit

15 "Beware of false prophets, who come to you in sheep's clothing but inwardly are ravenous wolves. 16You will know them by their fruits. Are grapes gathered from thorns, or figs from thistles? 17In the same way, every good tree bears good fruit, but the bad tree bears bad fruit. 18A good tree cannot bear bad fruit, nor can a bad tree bear good fruit. 19Every tree that does not bear good fruit is cut down and thrown into the fire. 20Thus you will know them by their fruits.

Concerning Self-Deception

21 "Not everyone who says to me, 'Lord, Lord,' will enter the kingdom of heaven, but only the one who does the will of my Father in heaven. 22On that day many will say to me, 'Lord, Lord, did we not prophesy in your name, and cast out demons in your name, and do many deeds of power in your name?' 23Then I will declare to them, 'I never knew you; go away from me, you evildoers.'

Hearers and Doers

▶ See Luke 6.47–49

24 "Everyone then who hears these words of mine and acts on them will be like a wise man who built his house on rock. 25The rain fell, the floods came, and the winds blew and beat on that house, but it did not fall, because it had been founded on rock. 26And everyone who hears these words of mine and does not act on them will be like a foolish man who built his house on sand. 27The rain fell, and the floods came, and the winds blew and beat against that house, and it fell—and great was its fall!"

28 Now when Jesus had finished saying these things, the crowds were astounded at his teaching, 29for he taught them as one having authority, and not as their scribes.

Jesus Cleanses a Leper

▶ See Mark 1.40–44; Luke 5.12–14

8 When Jesus[u] had come down from the mountain, great crowds followed him; 2and there was a leper[v] who came to him and knelt before him, saying, "Lord, if you choose, you can make me clean." 3He stretched out his hand and touched him, saying, "I do choose. Be made clean!" Immediately his leprosy[v] was cleansed. 4Then Jesus said to him, "See that you say nothing to anyone; but go, show yourself to the priest, and offer the gift that Moses commanded, as a testimony to them."

Jesus Heals a Centurion's Servant

▶ See Luke 7.1–10

5 When he entered Capernaum, a centurion came to him, appealing to him 6and saying, "Lord, my servant is lying at home paralyzed, in terrible distress." 7And he said to him, "I will come and cure him." 8The centurion answered, "Lord, I am not worthy to have you come under my roof; but only speak the word, and my servant will be healed. 9For I also am a man under authority, with soldiers under me; and I say to one, 'Go,' and he goes, and to another, 'Come,' and he comes, and to my slave, 'Do this,' and the slave does it." 10When Jesus heard him, he was amazed and said to those who followed him, "Truly I tell you, in no one[w] in Israel have I found such faith. 11I tell you, many will come from east and west and will eat with Abraham and Isaac and Jacob in the kingdom of heaven, 12while the heirs of the kingdom will be thrown into the outer darkness, where there will be weeping and gnashing of teeth." 13And to the centurion Jesus said, "Go; let it be done for you according to your faith." And the servant was healed in that hour.

Jesus Heals Many at Peter's House

▶ See Mark 1.29–34; Luke 4.38–41

14 When Jesus entered Peter's house, he saw his mother-in-law lying in bed with a fever; 15he touched her hand, and the fever left her, and she got up and began to serve him. 16That evening they brought to him many who were possessed with demons; and he cast out the spirits with a word, and cured all who were sick. 17This was to fulfill what had been spoken through the prophet Isaiah, "He took our infirmities and bore our diseases."

---

[t] Other ancient authorities read *for the road is wide and easy* several diseases   [w] Other ancient authorities read *Truly I tell you, not even*   [u] Gk *he*   [v] The terms *leper* and *leprosy* can refer to

Would-Be Followers of Jesus

▶ *See Luke 9.57–60*

18 Now when Jesus saw great crowds around him, he gave orders to go over to the other side.

8.14 Actions Follow Words

Typically, Matthew blends together Jesus' words and actions. Chapters 5–7 contain Jesus' longest recorded speech, the Sermon on the Mount—a speech that greatly impressed the audience. The next few chapters mention ten miracles performed by Jesus, which further established his authority. Those who benefited—a despised leprosy victim, a Roman officer, a housewife, two violent demoniacs, a quadriplegic, a synagogue ruler—demonstrate the "wideness in God's mercy" Jesus had just described.

19A scribe then approached and said, "Teacher, I will follow you wherever you go." 20And Jesus said to him, "Foxes have holes, and birds of the air have nests; but the Son of Man has nowhere to lay his head." 21Another of his disciples said to him, "Lord, first let me go and bury my father." 22But Jesus said to him, "Follow me, and let the dead bury their own dead."

Jesus Stills the Storm

▶ *See Mark 4.36–41; Luke 8.22–25*

23 And when he got into the boat, his disciples followed him. 24A windstorm arose on the sea, so great that the boat was being swamped by the waves; but he was asleep. 25And they went and woke him up, saying, "Lord, save us! We are perishing!" 26And he said to them, "Why are you afraid, you of little faith?" Then he got up and rebuked the winds and the sea; and there was a dead calm. 27They were amazed, saying, "What sort of man is this, that even the winds and the sea obey him?"

Jesus Heals the Gadarene Demoniacs

▶ *See Mark 5.1–17; Luke 8.26–37*

28 When he came to the other side, to the country of the Gadarenes,x two demoniacs coming out of the tombs met him. They were so fierce that no one could pass that way. 29Suddenly they shouted, "What have you to do with us, Son of God? Have you come here to torment us before the time?" 30Now a large herd of swine was feeding at some distance from them. 31The demons begged him, "If you cast us out, send us into the herd of swine." 32And he said to them, "Go!" So they came out and entered the swine; and suddenly, the whole herd rushed down the steep bank into the sea and perished in the water. 33The swineherds ran off, and on going into the town, they told the whole story about what had happened to the demoniacs. 34Then the whole town came out to meet Jesus; and when they saw him, they begged him to leave their neighborhood.

9 1And after getting into a boat he crossed the sea and came to his own town.

Jesus Heals a Paralytic

▶ *See Mark 2.3–12; Luke 5.18–26*

2 And just then some people were carrying a paralyzed man lying on a bed. When Jesus saw their faith, he said to the paralytic, "Take heart, son; your sins are forgiven." 3Then some of the scribes said to themselves, "This man is blaspheming." 4But Jesus, perceiving their thoughts, said, "Why do you think evil in your hearts? 5For which is easier, to say, 'Your sins are forgiven,' or to say, 'Stand up and walk'? 6But so that you may know that the Son of Man has authority on earth to forgive sins"—he then said to the paralytic— "Stand up, take your bed and go to your home." 7And he stood up and went to his home. 8When the crowds saw it, they were filled with awe, and they glorified God, who had given such authority to human beings.

The Call of Matthew

▶ *See Mark 2.14–17; Luke 5.27–32*

9 As Jesus was walking along, he saw a man called Matthew sitting at the tax booth; and he said to him, "Follow me." And he got up and followed him.

9.9 Unpopular Profession

Tax collectors like Matthew were even less popular in Jesus' day than now. Many Jews viewed them as traitors serving the hated Roman empire. To make things worse, they worked on a commission basis, allowing them to set their own rates, which often led to extortion.

In this poignant scene, the Gospel tells how Jesus first called Matthew and then came to his house to mingle freely with "tax collectors and sinners." By following Jesus, Matthew turned his back on a lucrative government job. He was gradually transformed into a loyal disciple who applied his orderly mind to organize this account of Jesus' life.

10 And as he sat at dinnery in the house, many tax collectors and sinners came and were sittingz with him and his disciples. 11When the Pharisees saw this, they said to his disciples, "Why does your teacher eat with tax collectors

---

x Other ancient authorities read *Gergesenes*; others, *Gerasenes* y Gk *reclined* z Gk *were reclining*

and sinners?" [12]But when he heard this, he said, "Those who are well have no need of a physician, but those who are sick. [13]Go and learn what this means, 'I desire mercy, not sacrifice.' For I have come to call not the righteous but sinners."

The Question about Fasting

▶ *See Mark 2.18–22; Luke 5.33–39*

14   Then the disciples of John came to him, saying, "Why do we and the Pharisees fast often,[a] but your disciples do not fast?" [15]And Jesus said to them, "The wedding guests cannot mourn as long as the bridegroom is with them, can they? The days will come when the bridegroom is taken away from them, and then they will fast. [16]No one sews a piece of unshrunk cloth on an old cloak, for the patch pulls away from the cloak, and a worse tear is made. [17]Neither is new wine put into old wineskins; otherwise, the skins burst, and the wine is spilled, and the skins are destroyed; but new wine is put into fresh wineskins, and so both are preserved."

A Girl Restored to Life
and a Woman Healed

▶ *See Mark 5.22–43; Luke 8.41–56*

18   While he was saying these things to them, suddenly a leader of the synagogue[b] came in and knelt before him, saying, "My daughter has just died; but come and lay your hand on her, and she will live." [19]And Jesus got up and followed him, with his disciples. [20]Then suddenly a woman who had been suffering from hemorrhages for twelve years came up behind him and touched the fringe of his cloak, [21]for she said to herself, "If I only touch his cloak, I will be made well." [22]Jesus turned, and seeing her he said, "Take heart, daughter; your faith has made you well." And instantly the woman was made well. [23]When Jesus came to the leader's house and saw the flute players and the crowd making a commotion, [24]he said, "Go away; for the girl is not dead but sleeping." And they laughed at him. [25]But when the crowd had been put outside, he went in and took her by the hand, and the girl got up. [26]And the report of this spread throughout that district.

Jesus Heals Two Blind Men

27   As Jesus went on from there, two blind men followed him, crying loudly, "Have mercy on us, Son of David!" [28]When he entered the house, the blind men came to him; and Jesus said to them, "Do you believe that I am able to do this?" They said to him, "Yes, Lord." [29]Then he touched their eyes and said, "According to your faith let it be done to you." [30]And their eyes were opened. Then Jesus sternly ordered them, "See

that no one knows of this." [31]But they went away and spread the news about him throughout that district.

Jesus Heals One Who Was Mute

32   After they had gone away, a demoniac who was mute was brought to him. [33]And when the demon had been cast out, the one who had been mute spoke; and the crowds were amazed and said, "Never has anything like this been seen in Israel." [34]But the Pharisees said, "By the ruler of the demons he casts out the demons."[c]

The Harvest Is Great, the Laborers Few

35   Then Jesus went about all the cities and villages, teaching in their synagogues, and proclaiming the good news of the kingdom, and curing every disease and every sickness. [36]When he saw the crowds, he had compassion for them, because they were harassed and helpless, like sheep without a shepherd. [37]Then he said to his disciples, "The harvest is plentiful, but the laborers are few; [38]therefore ask the Lord of the harvest to send out laborers into his harvest."

The Twelve Apostles

▶ *See Mark 6.8–11; Luke 9.3–5; 10.4–12*

10   Then Jesus[d] summoned his twelve disciples and gave them authority over unclean spirits, to cast them out, and to cure every disease and every sickness. [2]These are the names of the twelve apostles: first, Simon, also known as Peter, and his brother Andrew; James son of Zebedee, and his brother John; [3]Philip and Bartholomew; Thomas and Matthew the tax collector; James son of Alphaeus, and Thaddaeus;[e] [4]Simon the Cananaean, and Judas Iscariot, the one who betrayed him.

The Mission of the Twelve

5   These twelve Jesus sent out with the following instructions: "Go nowhere among the Gentiles, and enter no town of the Samaritans, [6]but go rather to the lost sheep of the house of Israel. [7]As you go, proclaim the good news, 'The kingdom of heaven has come near.'[f] [8]Cure the sick, raise the dead, cleanse the lepers,[g] cast out demons. You received without payment; give without payment. [9]Take no gold, or silver, or copper in your belts, [10]no bag for your journey, or two tunics, or sandals, or a staff; for laborers deserve their food. [11]Whatever town or village you enter, find out who in it is worthy, and stay there until you leave. [12]As you enter the house, greet it. [13]If the house is worthy, let your peace come upon it; but if it is not worthy, let your peace return to you. [14]If anyone will not welcome you or listen to your words,

---

[a] Other ancient authorities lack *often*   [b] Gk lacks *of the synagogue*   [c] Other ancient authorities lack this verse
[d] Gk *he*   [e] Other ancient authorities read *Lebbaeus*, or *Lebbaeus called Thaddaeus*   [f] Or *is at hand*   [g] The terms *leper* and *leprosy* can refer to several diseases

shake off the dust from your feet as you leave that house or town. [15]Truly I tell you, it will be more tolerable for the land of Sodom and Gomorrah on the day of judgment than for that town.

Coming Persecutions

16 "See, I am sending you out like sheep into the midst of wolves; so be wise as serpents and innocent as doves. [17]Beware of them, for they will hand you over to councils and flog you in their synagogues; [18]and you will be dragged before governors and kings because of me, as a testimony to them and the Gentiles. [19]When they hand you over, do not worry about how you are to speak or what you are to say; for what you are to say will be given to you at that time; [20]for it is not you who speak, but the Spirit of your Father speaking through you. [21]Brother will betray brother to death, and a father his child, and children will rise against parents and have them put to death; [22]and you will be hated by all because of my name. But the one who endures to the end will be saved. [23]When they persecute you in one town, flee to the next; for truly I tell you, you will not have gone through all the towns of Israel before the Son of Man comes.

24 "A disciple is not above the teacher, nor a slave above the master; [25]it is enough for the disciple to be like the teacher, and the slave like the master. If they have called the master of the house Beelzebul, how much more will they malign those of his household!

Whom to Fear

26 "So have no fear of them; for nothing is covered up that will not be uncovered, and nothing secret that will not become known. [27]What I say to you in the dark, tell in the light; and what you hear whispered, proclaim from the housetops. [28]Do not fear those who kill the body but cannot kill the soul; rather fear him who can destroy both soul and body in hell.[h] [29]Are not two sparrows sold for a penny? Yet not one of them will fall to the ground apart from your Father. [30]And even the hairs of your head are all counted. [31]So do not be afraid; you are of more value than many sparrows.

32 "Everyone therefore who acknowledges me before others, I also will acknowledge before my Father in heaven; [33]but whoever denies me before others, I also will deny before my Father in heaven.

Not Peace, but a Sword

34 "Do not think that I have come to bring peace to the earth; I have not come to bring peace, but a sword.

35 For I have come to set a man against his
        father,
    and a daughter against her mother,
    and a daughter-in-law against her
        mother-in-law;
[36] and one's foes will be members of one's
        own household.

[37]Whoever loves father or mother more than me is not worthy of me; and whoever loves son or daughter more than me is not worthy of me; [38]and whoever does not take up the cross and follow me is not worthy of me. [39]Those who find their life will lose it, and those who lose their life for my sake will find it.

Rewards

40 "Whoever welcomes you welcomes me, and whoever welcomes me welcomes the one who sent me. [41]Whoever welcomes a prophet in the name of a prophet will receive a prophet's reward; and whoever welcomes a righteous person in the name of a righteous person will receive the reward of the righteous; [42]and whoever gives even a cup of cold water to one of these little ones in the name of a disciple—truly I tell you, none of these will lose their reward."

11 Now when Jesus had finished instructing his twelve disciples, he went on from there to teach and proclaim his message in their cities.

Messengers from John the Baptist

▶ See Luke 7.18–35

2 When John heard in prison what the Messiah[i] was doing, he sent word by his[j] disciples

11.2 The One to Come?

John's question here may reflect confusion over the Messiah's role. If, like many Jews, John was expecting a political Messiah who would overthrow the Romans, his imprisonment may have caused him to wonder why Jesus wasn't taking action. Jesus responded by clarifying the kind of kingdom he came to establish: a kingdom that brought healing, liberation, and good news—but not necessarily political power.

[3]and said to him, "Are you the one who is to come, or are we to wait for another?" [4]Jesus answered them, "Go and tell John what you hear and see: [5]the blind receive their sight, the lame walk, the lepers[k] are cleansed, the deaf hear, the dead are raised, and the poor have good news brought to them. [6]And blessed is anyone who takes no offense at me."

---

[h] Gk *Gehenna* [i] Or *the Christ* [j] Other ancient authorities read *two of his* [k] The terms *leper* and *leprosy* can refer to several diseases

Jesus Praises John the Baptist

7 As they went away, Jesus began to speak to the crowds about John: "What did you go out into the wilderness to look at? A reed shaken by the wind? [8]What then did you go out to see? Someone[l] dressed in soft robes? Look, those who wear soft robes are in royal palaces. [9]What then did you go out to see? A prophet?[m] Yes, I tell you, and more than a prophet. [10]This is the one about whom it is written,

'See, I am sending my messenger ahead of you,
who will prepare your way before you.'

[11]Truly I tell you, among those born of women no one has arisen greater than John the Baptist; yet the least in the kingdom of heaven is greater than he. [12]From the days of John the Baptist until now the kingdom of heaven has suffered violence,[n] and the violent take it by force. [13]For all the prophets and the law prophesied until John came; [14]and if you are willing to accept it, he is Elijah who is to come. [15]Let anyone with ears[o] listen!

16 "But to what will I compare this generation? It is like children sitting in the marketplaces and calling to one another,

[17] 'We played the flute for you, and you did not dance;
we wailed, and you did not mourn.'

[18]For John came neither eating nor drinking, and they say, 'He has a demon'; [19]the Son of Man came eating and drinking, and they say, 'Look, a glutton and a drunkard, a friend of tax collectors and sinners!' Yet wisdom is vindicated by her deeds."[p]

Woes to Unrepentant Cities

▶ See Luke 10.13–15

20 Then he began to reproach the cities in which most of his deeds of power had been done,

11.20 Miracles Aren't Enough

Surprisingly, seeing supernatural miracles didn't lead people to repent and follow Jesus' teaching. Throughout his ministry, Jesus showed annoyance with crowds who flocked to see a popular leader do something supernatural. He wanted from them not applause, but commitment. Gradually, he relied more and more on parables, which, in private, he would explain to his disciples (see 13.11–17).

because they did not repent. [21]"Woe to you, Chorazin! Woe to you, Bethsaida! For if the deeds of power done in you had been done in Tyre and

[l] Or *Why then did you go out? To see someone prophet?* [n] Or *has been coming violently* read *children*   [m] Other ancient authorities read *Why then did you go out? To see a prophet?*   [o] Other ancient authorities add *to hear*   [p] Other ancient authorities

JOHN THE BAPTIST *Something New*

FASHION STARTS WITH A SINGLE purpose: to turn people's heads. At first the new look is a shock. Many say, "Wow"; some say, "Ugh!" Whether it's short skirts or long, nose rings or earrings, paisleys or pastels, the new must stand out to gain attention.

John the Baptist was something new, and he certainly stood out from his surroundings. Though he could have been a priest like his father, he exchanged those linen robes for a garment of coarse camel's hair. He took to the wilderness, scavenging grasshoppers and wild honey rather than settling in Jerusalem where he could have savored a portion of the offerings people presented to God.

John's unusual style helped direct attention to his burning message: The Messiah was about to arrive, and people must change their ways. Crowds flocked to hear John, and he baptized them in the Jordan River as a sign of their repentance, thus earning himself the nickname "the Baptist."

No less an authority than Jesus said that John was as great as any man who had ever lived (11.11). In the same breath Jesus added that the lowest-ranking person in the kingdom of God, now drawing near, was even greater than John. Although John represented the best of the old order, the new order of God's kingdom would outshine his greatness by far.

John had no difficulty accepting this comparison. When he saw Jesus he recognized "the Lamb of God who takes away the sin of the world" (John 1.29). He considered himself unworthy even to untie Jesus' sandals. John the Baptist did not intend to attract attention to himself; rather, he pointed to Jesus.

When Herod Antipas arrested and executed John (14.1–12), most of John's disciples followed Jesus. It took a long time, however, for some who lived in far-off parts of the world to get the full message about Jesus (see Acts 18.24–26, 19.1–7). They, too, quickly adopted the Christian way. Despite John's great influence, it was a mark of his success that he left no distinctive "church" of his own. His followers were ready for Jesus.

Life Questions: How can your lifestyle help prepare people for Jesus?

Sidon, they would have repented long ago in sackcloth and ashes. ²²But I tell you, on the day of judgment it will be more tolerable for Tyre and Sidon than for you. ²³And you, Capernaum,

will you be exalted to heaven?
No, you will be brought down
to Hades.

For if the deeds of power done in you had been done in Sodom, it would have remained until this day. ²⁴But I tell you that on the day of judgment it will be more tolerable for the land of Sodom than for you."

Jesus Thanks His Father

▶ See Luke 10.21–22

25 At that time Jesus said, "I thank*q* you, Father, Lord of heaven and earth, because you have hidden these things from the wise and the intelligent and have revealed them to infants; ²⁶yes, Father, for such was your gracious will.*r* ²⁷All things have been handed over to me by my Father; and no one knows the Son except the Father, and no one knows the Father except the Son and anyone to whom the Son chooses to reveal him.

28 "Come to me, all you that are weary and are carrying heavy burdens, and I will give you rest. ²⁹Take my yoke upon you, and learn from me; for I am gentle and humble in heart, and you will find rest for your souls. ³⁰For my yoke is easy, and my burden is light."

Plucking Grain on the Sabbath

▶ See Mark 2.23—3.6; Luke 6.1–11

12 At that time Jesus went through the grainfields on the sabbath; his disciples were hungry, and they began to pluck heads of grain and to eat. ²When the Pharisees saw it, they said to him, "Look, your disciples are doing what is not lawful to do on the sabbath." ³He said to them, "Have you not read what David did when he and his companions were hungry? ⁴He entered the house of God and ate the bread of the Presence, which it was not lawful for him or his companions to eat, but only for the priests? ⁵Or have you not read in the law that on the sabbath the priests in the temple break the sabbath and yet are guiltless? ⁶I tell you, something greater than the temple is here. ⁷But if you had known what this means, 'I desire mercy and not sacrifice,' you would not have condemned the guiltless. ⁸For the Son of Man is lord of the sabbath."

The Man with a Withered Hand

9 He left that place and entered their synagogue; ¹⁰a man was there with a withered hand, and they asked him, "Is it lawful to cure on the sabbath?" so that they might accuse him. ¹¹He said to them, "Suppose one of you has only one

sheep and it falls into a pit on the sabbath; will you not lay hold of it and lift it out? ¹²How much more valuable is a human being than a sheep! So it is lawful to do good on the sabbath." ¹³Then he

12.12 Pharisees Take Offense

Chapter 12 gives insight into why the Pharisees were offended by Jesus. First, his disciples picked grain on the sabbath (verses 1–7), something forbidden by the Pharisees. A provocative healing on the sabbath followed. Jesus accused the Pharisees of caring more for the letter of the law than the spirit, so much so that they showed more concern for animal life than human.

said to the man, "Stretch out your hand." He stretched it out, and it was restored, as sound as the other. ¹⁴But the Pharisees went out and conspired against him, how to destroy him.

God's Chosen Servant

15 When Jesus became aware of this, he departed. Many crowds*s* followed him, and he cured all of them, ¹⁶and he ordered them not to make him known. ¹⁷This was to fulfill what had been spoken through the prophet Isaiah:

18 "Here is my servant, whom I
have chosen,
my beloved, with whom my soul is
well pleased.
I will put my Spirit upon him,
and he will proclaim justice to the
Gentiles.
19 He will not wrangle or cry aloud,
nor will anyone hear his voice in the
streets.
20 He will not break a bruised reed
or quench a smoldering wick
until he brings justice to victory.
21 And in his name the Gentiles will
hope."

Jesus and Beelzebul

▶ See Mark 3.23–27; Luke 11.17–22

22 Then they brought to him a demoniac who was blind and mute; and he cured him, so that the one who had been mute could speak and see. ²³All the crowds were amazed and said, "Can this be the Son of David?" ²⁴But when the Pharisees heard it, they said, "It is only by Beelzebul, the ruler of the demons, that this fellow casts out the demons." ²⁵He knew what they were thinking and said to them, "Every kingdom divided against itself is laid waste, and no city or house divided against itself will stand. ²⁶If Satan casts out Satan,

---

q Or *praise*   *r* Or *for so it was well-pleasing in your sight*   *s* Other ancient authorities lack *crowds*

he is divided against himself; how then will his kingdom stand? ²⁷If I cast out demons by Beelzebul, by whom do your own exorcists*t* cast them out? Therefore they will be your judges. ²⁸But if it is by the Spirit of God that I cast out demons, then the kingdom of God has come to you. ²⁹Or how can one enter a strong man's house and plunder his property, without first tying up the strong man? Then indeed the house can be plundered. ³⁰Whoever is not with me is against me, and whoever does not gather with me scatters. ³¹Therefore I tell you, people will be forgiven for every sin and blasphemy, but blasphemy against the Spirit will not be forgiven. ³²Whoever speaks a word against the Son of Man will be forgiven, but whoever speaks against the Holy Spirit will not be forgiven, either in this age or in the age to come.

A Tree and Its Fruit

33 "Either make the tree good, and its fruit good; or make the tree bad, and its fruit bad; for the tree is known by its fruit. ³⁴You brood of vipers! How can you speak good things, when you are evil? For out of the abundance of the heart the mouth speaks. ³⁵The good person brings good things out of a good treasure, and the evil person brings evil things out of an evil treasure. ³⁶I tell you, on the day of judgment you will have to give an account for every careless word you utter; ³⁷for by your words you will be justified, and by your words you will be condemned."

The Sign of Jonah

▶ *See Luke 11.29–32*

38 Then some of the scribes and Pharisees said to him, "Teacher, we wish to see a sign from you." ³⁹But he answered them, "An evil and adulterous generation asks for a sign, but no sign will be given to it except the sign of the prophet Jonah. ⁴⁰For just as Jonah was three days and three nights in the belly of the sea monster, so for three days and three nights the Son of Man will be in the heart of the earth. ⁴¹The people of Nineveh will rise up at the judgment with this generation and condemn it, because they repented at the proclamation of Jonah, and see, something greater than Jonah is here! ⁴²The queen of the South will rise up at the judgment with this generation and condemn it, because she came from the ends of the earth to listen to the wisdom of Solomon, and see, something greater than Solomon is here!

The Return of the Unclean Spirit

43 "When the unclean spirit has gone out of a person, it wanders through waterless regions looking for a resting place, but it finds none. ⁴⁴Then it says, 'I will return to my house from

which I came.' When it comes, it finds it empty, swept, and put in order. ⁴⁵Then it goes and brings along seven other spirits more evil than itself, and they enter and live there; and the last state of that person is worse than the first. So will it be also with this evil generation."

The True Kindred of Jesus

▶ *See Mark 3.31–35; Luke 8.19–21*

46 While he was still speaking to the crowds, his mother and his brothers were standing outside, wanting to speak to him. ⁴⁷Someone told him, "Look, your mother and your brothers are standing outside, wanting to speak to you."*u* ⁴⁸But to the one who had told him this, Jesus*v* replied, "Who is my mother, and who are my brothers?" ⁴⁹And pointing to his disciples, he said, "Here are my mother and my brothers! ⁵⁰For whoever does the will of my Father in heaven is my brother and sister and mother."

The Parable of the Sower

▶ *See Mark 4.1–20; Luke 8.4–15*

13 That same day Jesus went out of the house and sat beside the sea. ²Such great crowds gathered around him that he got into a boat and sat there, while the whole crowd stood on the beach. ³And he told them many things in parables, saying: "Listen! A sower went out to sow. ⁴And as he sowed, some seeds fell on the path, and the birds came and ate them up. ⁵Other seeds fell on rocky ground, where they did not have much soil, and they sprang up quickly, since they had no depth of soil. ⁶But when the sun rose, they were scorched; and since they had no root, they withered away. ⁷Other seeds fell among thorns, and the thorns grew up and choked them. ⁸Other seeds fell on good soil and brought forth grain, some a hundredfold, some sixty, some thirty. ⁹Let anyone with ears*w* listen!"

The Purpose of the Parables

10 Then the disciples came and asked him, "Why do you speak to them in parables?" ¹¹He

13.10 Stories to Remember

An illiterate society (like much of Palestine in Jesus' day) passes down wisdom in the form of proverbs and stories. Everybody likes a story, and stories are easier to remember than concepts or logical outlines. Jesus spoke in terms that would hold the interest of a society of farmers and fishermen, and about 30 of his masterful parables—stories with a point—have survived in the Gospels.

---

t Gk *sons*   *u* Other ancient authorities lack verse 47   *v* Gk *he*   *w* Other ancient authorities add *to hear*

answered, "To you it has been given to know the secrets[x] of the kingdom of heaven, but to them it has not been given. 12For to those who have, more will be given, and they will have an abundance; but from those who have nothing, even what they have will be taken away. 13The reason I speak to them in parables is that 'seeing they do not perceive, and hearing they do not listen, nor do they understand.' 14With them indeed is fulfilled the prophecy of Isaiah that says:

> 'You will indeed listen, but never
>   understand,
> and you will indeed look, but never
>   perceive.
> 15 For this people's heart has grown dull,
>   and their ears are hard of hearing,

[x] Or *mysteries*

What Should a Leader Look Like?
Not everyone wanted Jesus' kind of kingdom

IMPORTANT LEADERS, SUCH AS PRESIDENTS and prime ministers, work hard to convey an impression of confidence and power. A leader, they assume, should look like a leader, and many of them hire an "image specialist" to learn how. Wherever they go, press agents, bodyguards, loyal assistants, and throngs of eager admirers follow in their wake.

Matthew depicts Jesus as a true leader—a king, in fact—but one who broke stereotypes. Jesus had undeniable power. He could quiet an angry storm and even walk on the surface of a lake. Yet he used that power compassionately, for the sake of others: to feed the hungry and heal the sick. He wasn't concerned about a powerful image.

> *"Where did this man get this wisdom and these deeds of power? Is not this the carpenter's son?"*
> 13.54–55

A New Kind of Kingdom

First-century Jews, who hated the Roman empire, would have rallied eagerly around a militant Jewish king. They rebelled often until a vengeful Roman general flattened Jerusalem in A.D. 70. The kingdom Jesus presented, however, didn't meet their expectations.

At the beginning of his ministry, Jesus turned down a tempting offer of glory and territory (4.8–11), and he consistently bucked the pressures of the crowd. Although he was the most powerful leader ever, he spent his time telling stories, not raising an army. As a true Messiah, he sought not to satisfy people's false image of him, but to please God.

In chapter 13, Matthew collects several of the stories Jesus told to describe his "kingdom of heaven"—a phrase used 32 times in Matthew. Although Jesus never concisely defined the phrase, he gave many clues about the nature of his kingdom. The kingdom is so important, he said, that belonging to it is worth selling everything a person owns.

Jesus said his kingdom doesn't have geographical boundaries. Unlike, say, Greece or China or Spain, it can't be charted on a map. Its followers live right among their enemies, not separated from them by a moat or a wall. Yet Jesus predicted that his kingdom would show remarkable growth even in an evil environment bent on its destruction.

The Disciples Fail to Understand

The "kingdom of heaven" consists of the rule of God in the world. It's made up of people of all races and from all nations who loyally follow God's will on earth. Jesus stressed that this new kingdom was a major advance in God's plan: its least member, he said, is even greater than John the Baptist (11.11).

The disciples, accustomed to more traditional images of power and leadership, couldn't quite grasp Jesus' concept of the kingdom. They kept asking him to explain his parables even as they jockeyed vainly for status.

As the days passed, the disciples became convinced that Jesus was "the Messiah, the Son of the living God!" — Peter won warm praise for that assertion (16.17). But he received Jesus' strongest rebuke in the next scene when he recoiled from the idea that his leader might soon suffer and die.

The paradoxes of Jesus' style of leadership deepened as he neared Jerusalem, the capital city. He allowed one moment of public triumph, on the day we call Palm Sunday. Yet, even then he rode not a chariot or a stallion, but a donkey colt. And a few days later he left his followers an enduring emblem: not a royal banner or a scepter, but an executioner's cross.

Life Questions: Could Jesus run for political office in the United States? What kind of leader do people want today?

and they have shut their eyes;
    so that they might not look with
        their eyes,
    and listen with their ears,
and understand with their heart and
        turn—
    and I would heal them.'

16But blessed are your eyes, for they see, and your ears, for they hear. 17Truly I tell you, many prophets and righteous people longed to see what you see, but did not see it, and to hear what you hear, but did not hear it.

The Parable of the Sower Explained

18 "Hear then the parable of the sower. 19When anyone hears the word of the kingdom and does not understand it, the evil one comes and snatches away what is sown in the heart; this is what was sown on the path. 20As for what was sown on rocky ground, this is the one who hears the word and immediately receives it with joy; 21yet such a person has no root, but endures only for a while, and when trouble or persecution arises on account of the word, that person immediately falls away.y 22As for what was sown among thorns, this is the one who hears the word, but the cares of the world and the lure of wealth choke the word, and it yields nothing. 23But as for what was sown on good soil, this is the one who hears the word and understands it, who indeed bears fruit and yields, in one case a hundredfold, in another sixty, and in another thirty."

The Parable of Weeds among the Wheat

24 He put before them another parable: "The kingdom of heaven may be compared to someone who sowed good seed in his field; 25but while everybody was asleep, an enemy came and sowed weeds among the wheat, and then went away. 26So when the plants came up and bore grain, then the weeds appeared as well. 27And the slaves of the householder came and said to him, 'Master, did you not sow good seed in your field? Where, then, did these weeds come from?' 28He answered, 'An enemy has done this.' The slaves said to him, 'Then do you want us to go and gather them?' 29But he replied, 'No; for in gathering the weeds you would uproot the wheat along with them. 30Let both of them grow together until the harvest; and at harvest time I will tell the reapers, Collect the weeds first and bind them in bundles to be burned, but gather the wheat into my barn.'"

The Parable of the Mustard Seed

▶ See Mark 4.30–32; Luke 13.18–21

31 He put before them another parable: "The kingdom of heaven is like a mustard seed that someone took and sowed in his field; 32it is the smallest of all the seeds, but when it has grown it is the greatest of shrubs and becomes a tree, so that the birds of the air come and make nests in its branches."

The Parable of the Yeast

33 He told them another parable: "The kingdom of heaven is like yeast that a woman took and mixed in withz three measures of flour until all of it was leavened."

The Use of Parables

34 Jesus told the crowds all these things in parables; without a parable he told them nothing. 35This was to fulfill what had been spoken through the prophet:a
    "I will open my mouth to speak
        in parables;
    I will proclaim what has been hidden
        from the foundation of the
        world."b

Jesus Explains the Parable of the Weeds

36 Then he left the crowds and went into the house. And his disciples approached him, saying, "Explain to us the parable of the weeds of the field." 37He answered, "The one who sows the good seed is the Son of Man; 38the field is the world, and the good seed are the children of the kingdom; the weeds are the children of the evil one, 39and the enemy who sowed them is the devil; the harvest is the end of the age, and the reapers are angels. 40Just as the weeds are collected and burned up with fire, so will it be at the end of the age. 41The Son of Man will send his angels, and they will collect out of his kingdom all causes of sin and all evildoers, 42and they will throw them into the furnace of fire, where there will be weeping and gnashing of teeth. 43Then the righteous will shine like the sun in the kingdom of their Father. Let anyone with earsc listen!

Three Parables

44 "The kingdom of heaven is like treasure hidden in a field, which someone found and hid; then in his joy he goes and sells all that he has and buys that field.

45 "Again, the kingdom of heaven is like a merchant in search of fine pearls; 46on finding one pearl of great value, he went and sold all that he had and bought it.

47 "Again, the kingdom of heaven is like a net that was thrown into the sea and caught fish of every kind; 48when it was full, they drew it ashore, sat down, and put the good into baskets but threw out the bad. 49So it will be at the end of the age. The angels will come out and separate the evil

---

y Gk *stumbles*   z Gk *hid in*   a Other ancient authorities read *the prophet Isaiah*   b Other ancient authorities lack
of the world   c Other ancient authorities add *to hear*

from the righteous [50]and throw them into the furnace of fire, where there will be weeping and gnashing of teeth.

Treasures New and Old

51 "Have you understood all this?" They answered, "Yes." [52]And he said to them, "Therefore every scribe who has been trained for the kingdom of heaven is like the master of a household who brings out of his treasure what is new and what is old." [53]When Jesus had finished these parables, he left that place.

The Rejection of Jesus at Nazareth

▶ See Mark 6.1–6

54 He came to his hometown and began to teach the people[d] in their synagogue, so that they were astounded and said, "Where did this man get this wisdom and these deeds of power? [55]Is not this the carpenter's son? Is not his mother called Mary? And are not his brothers James and Joseph and Simon and Judas? [56]And are not all his sisters with us? Where then did this man get all this?" [57]And they took offense at him. But Jesus

[d] Gk them   [e] Gk tetrarch

said to them, "Prophets are not without honor except in their own country and in their own house." [58]And he did not do many deeds of power there, because of their unbelief.

13.57 No Respect at Home

Jesus had opened his ministry at home in a synagogue, an occasion marked by a near-riot. When he returned later, he aroused great curiosity but little belief. The townsfolk couldn't fathom that one who'd been raised in their midst by a carpenter was now teaching like a rabbi and performing miracles. Jesus declined to display his supernatural power for them, and quietly withdrew.

The Death of John the Baptist

▶ See Mark 6.14–29

14 At that time Herod the ruler[e] heard reports about Jesus; [2]and he said to his servants, "This is John the Baptist; he has been raised

THE HERODS *Lower Authority*

THE HEROD FAMILY WEAVES ITS way through the background of the New Testament, like minor supporting characters in a play. Oddly enough, in their own minds—and in the minds of most people then—they were major players.

Like the Kennedys in modern America, or the many royal families in European history, the Herods were a family dynasty. They ruled on behalf of the Romans with nearly absolute power. Such power did not impress the early Christians, however. They worshiped a higher authority, one whom the Herods were too spiritually dense to recognize.

Three different rulers go by the name of Herod in the New Testament. (A fourth, Agrippa, descended from the same family [see Agrippa, page 1157].) All three clashed with Jesus or his followers.

Herod the Great reigned as king when Jesus was born. He met the Magi, pointed them toward Bethlehem and then, when they disappeared without identifying the baby king, had all the infants in the area slaughtered (Matthew 2). Other historical sources suggest that such behavior was all too typical of this Herod—he even had his own sons murdered when he thought they threatened his power.

Herod the tetrarch, also known as Herod Antipas, was among Herod the Great's sons who survived the violence. At his father's death, he took command over Jesus' home area of Galilee. When John the Baptist offended Herod and his mistress by criticizing their morals, Herod imprisoned John and later had him beheaded. Jesus himself fell into this Herod's hands during his trial. Herod had heard of Jesus and hoped to see him do a miracle; when Jesus wouldn't cooperate, Herod ridiculed him and sent him back to Pilate (Luke 23.6–12).

Herod Agrippa I, grandson of Herod the Great, continued the pattern into the next generation. He ruled Jerusalem when the church first began growing there. He clamped down on the early Christians, executing James and arresting a number of others, including Peter. When Peter "escaped" with God's help, Herod had the guards executed (Acts 12). Acts tells us that Herod Agrippa died a sudden death, because he "had not given the glory to God" when a crowd of admirers hailed him as divine (Acts 12.23).

As modern people we tend to focus on the Herods' brutal behavior, but most rulers behaved brutally in those days. Even more importantly, in the Bible's eyes, the Herods failed to recognize the real power on earth—that belonging to God.

Life Questions: What dangers do Christians in the modern world face from the "lower authority" of politicians and rulers?

from the dead, and for this reason these powers are at work in him." ³For Herod had arrested John, bound him, and put him in prison on account of Herodias, his brother Philip's wife,ᶠ ⁴because John had been telling him, "It is not lawful for you to have her." ⁵Though Herodᵍ wanted to put him to death, he feared the crowd,

14.5 A Wife's Revenge

John the Baptist offended King Herod with his blunt accusations, but Mark 6 points out that most of the venom came from Herod's wife (whom the king had stolen from his brother Philip). Herod had mixed feelings about John. He liked to listen to the prophet and had a respectful fear of him and his stern message. After falling into a trap set by his wife and stepdaughter, however, he succumbed to peer pressure and ordered John's execution.

because they regarded him as a prophet. ⁶But when Herod's birthday came, the daughter of Herodias danced before the company, and she pleased Herod ⁷so much that he promised on oath to grant her whatever she might ask. ⁸Prompted by her mother, she said, "Give me the head of John the Baptist here on a platter." ⁹The king was grieved, yet out of regard for his oaths and for the guests, he commanded it to be given; ¹⁰he sent and had John beheaded in the prison. ¹¹The head was brought on a platter and given to the girl, who brought it to her mother. ¹²His disciples came and took the body and buried it; then they went and told Jesus.

Feeding the Five Thousand

▶ *See Mark 6.32–44; Luke 9.10–17; John 6.1–13*

13 Now when Jesus heard this, he withdrew from there in a boat to a deserted place by himself. But when the crowds heard it, they followed him on foot from the towns. ¹⁴When he went ashore, he saw a great crowd; and he had compassion for them and cured their sick. ¹⁵When it was evening, the disciples came to him and said, "This is a deserted place, and the hour is now late; send the crowds away so that they may go into the villages and buy food for themselves." ¹⁶Jesus said to them, "They need not go away; you give them something to eat." ¹⁷They replied, "We have nothing here but five loaves and two fish." ¹⁸And he said, "Bring them here to me." ¹⁹Then he ordered the crowds to sit down on the grass. Taking the five loaves and the two fish, he looked up to heaven, and blessed and broke the loaves, and gave them to the disciples, and the disciples gave them to the crowds. ²⁰And all ate and were filled;

and they took up what was left over of the broken pieces, twelve baskets full. ²¹And those who ate were about five thousand men, besides women and children.

Jesus Walks on the Water

▶ *See Mark 6.45–51; John 6.15–21*

22 Immediately he made the disciples get into the boat and go on ahead to the other side, while he dismissed the crowds. ²³And after he had dismissed the crowds, he went up the mountain by himself to pray. When evening came, he was there alone, ²⁴but by this time the boat, battered by the waves, was far from the land,ʰ for the wind was against them. ²⁵And early in the morning he came walking toward them on the sea. ²⁶But when the disciples saw him walking on the sea, they were terrified, saying, "It is a ghost!" And they cried out in fear. ²⁷But immediately Jesus spoke to them and said, "Take heart, it is I; do not be afraid."

28 Peter answered him, "Lord, if it is you, command me to come to you on the water." ²⁹He said, "Come." So Peter got out of the boat, started walking on the water, and came toward Jesus. ³⁰But when he noticed the strong wind,ⁱ he became frightened, and beginning to sink, he cried out, "Lord, save me!" ³¹Jesus immediately reached out his hand and caught him, saying to him, "You of little faith, why did you doubt?" ³²When they got into the boat, the wind ceased. ³³And those in the boat worshiped him, saying, "Truly you are the Son of God."

Jesus Heals the Sick in Gennesaret

34 When they had crossed over, they came to land at Gennesaret. ³⁵After the people of that place recognized him, they sent word throughout the region and brought all who were sick to him, ³⁶and begged him that they might touch even the fringe of his cloak; and all who touched it were healed.

The Tradition of the Elders

▶ *See Mark 7.1–23*

15 Then Pharisees and scribes came to Jesus from Jerusalem and said, ²"Why do your

15.1 Attacking Legalism

The Pharisees and teachers of the law considered their own strict traditions as binding as Old Testament law. In this passage, Jesus points out glaring inconsistencies in those traditions.

ᶠ Other ancient authorities read *his brother's wife*   ᵍ Gk *he*
ⁱ Other ancient authorities read *the wind*

ʰ Other ancient authorities read *was out on the sea*

disciples break the tradition of the elders? For they do not wash their hands before they eat." ³He answered them, "And why do you break the commandment of God for the sake of your tradition? ⁴For God said,ʲ 'Honor your father and your mother,' and, 'Whoever speaks evil of father or mother must surely die.' ⁵But you say that whoever tells father or mother, 'Whatever support you might have had from me is given to God,'ᵏ then that person need not honor the father.ˡ ⁶So, for the sake of your tradition, you make void the wordᵐ of God. ⁷You hypocrites! Isaiah prophesied rightly about you when he said:

⁸ 'This people honors me with their lips,
     but their hearts are far from me;
⁹ in vain do they worship me,
     teaching human precepts as
          doctrines.'"

Things That Defile

10 Then he called the crowd to him and said to them, "Listen and understand: ¹¹it is not what goes into the mouth that defiles a person, but it is what comes out of the mouth that defiles." ¹²Then the disciples approached and said to him, "Do you know that the Pharisees took offense when they heard what you said?" ¹³He answered, "Every plant that my heavenly Father has not planted will be uprooted. ¹⁴Let them alone; they are blind guides of the blind.ⁿ And if one blind person guides another, both will fall into a pit." ¹⁵But Peter said to him, "Explain this parable to us." ¹⁶Then he said, "Are you also still without understanding? ¹⁷Do you not see that whatever goes into the mouth enters the stomach, and goes out into the sewer? ¹⁸But what comes out of the mouth proceeds from the heart, and this is what defiles. ¹⁹For out of the heart come evil intentions, murder, adultery, fornication, theft, false witness, slander. ²⁰These are what defile a person, but to eat with unwashed hands does not defile."

The Canaanite Woman's Faith

▶ *See Mark 7.24–30*

21 Jesus left that place and went away to the district of Tyre and Sidon. ²²Just then a Canaanite woman from that region came out and started shouting, "Have mercy on me, Lord, Son of David; my daughter is tormented by a demon." ²³But he did not answer her at all. And his disciples came and urged him, saying, "Send her away, for she keeps shouting after us." ²⁴He answered, "I was sent only to the lost sheep of the house of Israel." ²⁵But she came and knelt before him, saying, "Lord, help me." ²⁶He answered, "It is not fair to take the children's food and throw it to the dogs." ²⁷She said, "Yes, Lord, yet even the dogs

eat the crumbs that fall from their masters' table." ²⁸Then Jesus answered her, "Woman, great is your faith! Let it be done for you as you wish." And her daughter was healed instantly.

Jesus Cures Many People

▶ *See Mark 8.1–10*

29 After Jesus had left that place, he passed along the Sea of Galilee, and he went up the

15.29–39 Two Feedings

In back-to-back chapters, Matthew reports on two incidents that can be easily confused. The feeding of the 5,000 (chapter 14) came at the height of Jesus' popularity and made a huge impression: all four Gospels report on it. Only Matthew and Mark, however, record this separate miracle performed for a slightly smaller crowd. In Mark's account (Mark 8.1–10), Jesus seems amazed that his disciples, having seen the first miracle, doubt his ability to supply a crowd's needs this second time.

mountain, where he sat down. ³⁰Great crowds came to him, bringing with them the lame, the maimed, the blind, the mute, and many others. They put them at his feet, and he cured them, ³¹so that the crowd was amazed when they saw the mute speaking, the maimed whole, the lame walking, and the blind seeing. And they praised the God of Israel.

Feeding the Four Thousand

32 Then Jesus called his disciples to him and said, "I have compassion for the crowd, because they have been with me now for three days and have nothing to eat; and I do not want to send them away hungry, for they might faint on the way." ³³The disciples said to him, "Where are we to get enough bread in the desert to feed so great a crowd?" ³⁴Jesus asked them, "How many loaves have you?" They said, "Seven, and a few small fish." ³⁵Then ordering the crowd to sit down on the ground, ³⁶he took the seven loaves and the fish; and after giving thanks he broke them and gave them to the disciples, and the disciples gave them to the crowds. ³⁷And all of them ate and were filled; and they took up the broken pieces left over, seven baskets full. ³⁸Those who had eaten were four thousand men, besides women and children. ³⁹After sending away the crowds, he got into the boat and went to the region of Magadan.ᵒ

ʲ Other ancient authorities read *commanded, saying*   ᵏ Or *is an offering*   ˡ Other ancient authorities add *or the mother*   ᵐ Other ancient authorities read *law*; others, *commandment*   ⁿ Other ancient authorities lack *of the blind*
ᵒ Other ancient authorities read *Magdala* or *Magdalan*

The Demand for a Sign

▶ *See Mark 8.11–21*

16 The Pharisees and Sadducees came, and to test Jesus[p] they asked him to show them a sign from heaven. ²He answered them, "When it is evening, you say, 'It will be fair weather, for the sky is red.' ³And in the morning, 'It will be stormy today, for the sky is red and threatening.' You know how to interpret the appearance of the sky, but you cannot interpret the signs of the times.[q] ⁴An evil and adulterous generation asks for a sign, but no sign will be given to it except the sign of Jonah." Then he left them and went away.

The Yeast of the Pharisees and Sadducees

5 When the disciples reached the other side, they had forgotten to bring any bread. ⁶Jesus said to them, "Watch out, and beware of the yeast of the Pharisees and Sadducees." ⁷They said to one another, "It is because we have brought no bread." ⁸And becoming aware of it, Jesus said, "You of little faith, why are you talking about having no bread? ⁹Do you still not perceive? Do you not remember the five loaves for the five thousand, and how many baskets you gathered? ¹⁰Or the seven loaves for the four thousand, and how many baskets you gathered? ¹¹How could you fail to perceive that I was not speaking about bread? Beware of the yeast of the Pharisees and Sadducees!" ¹²Then they understood that he had not told them to beware of the yeast of bread, but of the teaching of the Pharisees and Sadducees.

Peter's Declaration about Jesus

▶ *See Mark 8.27–29; Luke 9.18–20*

13 Now when Jesus came into the district of Caesarea Philippi, he asked his disciples, "Who

16.13 Peter's Highs and Lows

The disciple Peter earned a reputation for impulsiveness, and this chapter shows him at his very best and very worst. He won highest praise for discerning Jesus' true identity, but in the very next paragraph he made one of his biggest blunders. He wanted Jesus to avoid pain, not understanding that the pain of the cross would bring salvation to the whole world.

do people say that the Son of Man is?" ¹⁴And they said, "Some say John the Baptist, but others Elijah, and still others Jeremiah or one of the prophets." ¹⁵He said to them, "But who do you say that I am?" ¹⁶Simon Peter answered, "You are the Messiah,[r] the Son of the living God." ¹⁷And Jesus

answered him, "Blessed are you, Simon son of Jonah! For flesh and blood has not revealed this to you, but my Father in heaven. ¹⁸And I tell you, you are Peter,[s] and on this rock[t] I will build my church, and the gates of Hades will not prevail against it. ¹⁹I will give you the keys of the kingdom of heaven, and whatever you bind on earth will be bound in heaven, and whatever you loose on earth will be loosed in heaven." ²⁰Then he sternly ordered the disciples not to tell anyone that he was[u] the Messiah.[r]

Jesus Foretells His Death and Resurrection

▶ *See Mark 8.31—9.1; Luke 9.22–27*

21 From that time on, Jesus began to show his disciples that he must go to Jerusalem and undergo great suffering at the hands of the elders and chief priests and scribes, and be killed, and on the third day be raised. ²²And Peter took him aside and began to rebuke him, saying, "God forbid it, Lord! This must never happen to you." ²³But he turned and said to Peter, "Get behind me, Satan! You are a stumbling block to me; for you are setting your mind not on divine things but on human things."

The Cross and Self-Denial

24 Then Jesus told his disciples, "If any want to become my followers, let them deny themselves and take up their cross and follow me. ²⁵For those who want to save their life will lose it, and those who lose their life for my sake will find it. ²⁶For what will it profit them if they gain the whole world but forfeit their life? Or what will they give in return for their life?

27 "For the Son of Man is to come with his angels in the glory of his Father, and then he will repay everyone for what has been done. ²⁸Truly I tell you, there are some standing here who will not taste death before they see the Son of Man coming in his kingdom."

The Transfiguration

▶ *See Mark 9.2–13; Luke 9.28–36*

17 Six days later, Jesus took with him Peter and James and his brother John and led them up a high mountain, by themselves. ²And he was transfigured before them, and his face shone like the sun, and his clothes became dazzling white. ³Suddenly there appeared to them Moses and Elijah, talking with him. ⁴Then Peter said to Jesus, "Lord, it is good for us to be here; if you wish, I[v] will make three dwellings[w] here, one for you, one for Moses, and one for Elijah." ⁵While he was still speaking, suddenly a bright cloud overshadowed them, and from the cloud a voice said, "This is my Son, the Beloved;[x] with him I

---

[p] Gk *him* [q] Other ancient authorities lack ²*When it is . . . of the times* [r] Or *the Christ* [s] Gk *Petros*
[t] Gk *petra* [u] Other ancient authorities add *Jesus* [v] Other ancient authorities read *we* [w] Or *tents*
[x] Or *my beloved Son*

am well pleased; listen to him!" ⁶When the disciples heard this, they fell to the ground and were overcome by fear. ⁷But Jesus came and touched them, saying, "Get up and do not be afraid." ⁸And

17.5 Unforgettable Moment

Three of Jesus' disciples had the opportunity to observe this dramatic scene of God's approving of his Son Jesus. Moses, the first great lawgiver, and Elijah, the first great prophet, appeared with Jesus, and God spoke from heaven. The apostle Peter described the impact of this experience in 2 Peter 1.16–18.

when they looked up, they saw no one except Jesus himself alone.

9 As they were coming down the mountain, Jesus ordered them, "Tell no one about the vision until after the Son of Man has been raised from the dead." ¹⁰And the disciples asked him, "Why, then, do the scribes say that Elijah must come first?" ¹¹He replied, "Elijah is indeed coming and will restore all things; ¹²but I tell you that Elijah has already come, and they did not recognize him, but they did to him whatever they pleased. So also the Son of Man is about to suffer at their hands." ¹³Then the disciples understood that he was speaking to them about John the Baptist.

Jesus Cures a Boy with a Demon

▶ *See Mark 9.14–28; Luke 9.37–42*

14 When they came to the crowd, a man came to him, knelt before him, ¹⁵and said, "Lord, have mercy on my son, for he is an epileptic and he suffers terribly; he often falls into the fire and often into the water. ¹⁶And I brought him to your disciples, but they could not cure him." ¹⁷Jesus answered, "You faithless and perverse generation, how much longer must I be with you? How much longer must I put up with you? Bring him here to me." ¹⁸And Jesus rebuked the demon,ʸ and itᶻ came out of him, and the boy was cured instantly. ¹⁹Then the disciples came to Jesus privately and said, "Why could we not cast it out?" ²⁰He said to them, "Because of your little faith. For truly I tell you, if you have faith the size of aᵃ mustard seed, you will say to this mountain, 'Move from here to there,' and it will move; and nothing will be impossible for you."ᵇ

Jesus Again Foretells His Death and Resurrection

22 As they were gatheringᶜ in Galilee, Jesus said to them, "The Son of Man is going to be betrayed into human hands, ²³and they will kill him, and on the third day he will be raised." And they were greatly distressed.

Jesus and the Temple Tax

24 When they reached Capernaum, the collectors of the temple taxᵈ came to Peter and said, "Does your teacher not pay the temple tax?"ᵈ ²⁵He said, "Yes, he does." And when he came home, Jesus spoke of it first, asking, "What do you think, Simon? From whom do kings of the earth take toll or tribute? From their children or from others?" ²⁶When Peterᵉ said, "From others," Jesus said to him, "Then the children are free. ²⁷However, so that we do not give offense to them, go to the sea and cast a hook; take the first fish that comes up; and when you open its mouth, you will find a coin;ᶠ take that and give it to them for you and me."

True Greatness

▶ *See Mark 9.33–37; Luke 9.46–48*

18 At that time the disciples came to Jesus and asked, "Who is the greatest in the kingdom of heaven?" ²He called a child, whom he put among them, ³and said, "Truly I tell you, unless you change and become like children, you will never enter the kingdom of heaven. ⁴Whoever becomes humble like this child is the greatest in the kingdom of heaven. ⁵Whoever welcomes one such child in my name welcomes me.

Temptations to Sin

6 "If any of you put a stumbling block before one of these little ones who believe in me, it would be better for you if a great millstone were fastened around your neck and you were drowned in the depth of the sea. ⁷Woe to the world because of stumbling blocks! Occasions for stumbling are bound to come, but woe to the one by whom the stumbling block comes!

8 "If your hand or your foot causes you to stumble, cut it off and throw it away; it is better for you to enter life maimed or lame than to have two hands or two feet and to be thrown into the eternal fire. ⁹And if your eye causes you to stumble, tear it out and throw it away; it is better for you to enter life with one eye than to have two eyes and to be thrown into the hellᵍ of fire.

The Parable of the Lost Sheep

▶ *See Luke 15.4–7*

10 "Take care that you do not despise one of these little ones; for, I tell you, in heaven their angels continually see the face of my Father in heaven.ʰ ¹²What do you think? If a shepherd has

---

ʸ Gk *it or him*   ᶻ Gk *the demon*   ᵃ Gk *faith as a grain of does not come out except by prayer and fasting*   ᶜ Other ancient authorities read *living*   ᵉ Gk *he*   ᶠ Gk *stater*; the stater was worth two didrachmas   verse 11, *For the Son of Man came to save the lost*   ᵇ Other ancient authorities add verse 21, *But this kind*   ᵈ Gk *didrachma*   ᵍ Gk *Gehenna*   ʰ Other ancient authorities add

a hundred sheep, and one of them has gone astray, does he not leave the ninety-nine on the mountains and go in search of the one that went astray? 13And if he finds it, truly I tell you, he rejoices over it more than over the ninety-nine that never went astray. 14So it is not the will of your[i] Father in heaven that one of these little ones should be lost.

Reproving Another Who Sins

15 "If another member of the church[j] sins against you,[k] go and point out the fault when the two of you are alone. If the member listens to you, you have regained that one.[l] 16But if you are not listened to, take one or two others along with you, so that every word may be confirmed by the evidence of two or three witnesses. 17If the member refuses to listen to them, tell it to the church; and if the offender refuses to listen even to the church, let such a one be to you as a Gentile and a tax collector. 18Truly I tell you, whatever you bind on earth will be bound in heaven, and whatever you loose on earth will be loosed in heaven. 19Again, truly I tell you, if two of you agree on earth about anything you ask, it will be done for you by my Father in heaven. 20For where two or three are gathered in my name, I am there among them."

Forgiveness

21 Then Peter came and said to him, "Lord, if another member of the church[m] sins against me, how often should I forgive? As many as seven times?" 22Jesus said to him, "Not seven times, but, I tell you, seventy-seven[n] times.

The Parable of the Unforgiving Servant

23 "For this reason the kingdom of heaven may be compared to a king who wished to settle

18.23 Matthew and Money

Just as Luke, a doctor, gives more descriptive accounts of physical healings, Matthew, a former tax collector, highlights stories about money. This story in chapter 18, as well as others in chapters 20 and 25, appears only in Matthew's Gospel. Significantly, the former tax collector records Jesus' strongest words on treatment of the poor and needy.

accounts with his slaves. 24When he began the reckoning, one who owed him ten thousand talents[o] was brought to him; 25and, as he could not pay, his lord ordered him to be sold, together

with his wife and children and all his possessions, and payment to be made. 26So the slave fell on his knees before him, saying, 'Have patience with me, and I will pay you everything.' 27And out of pity for him, the lord of that slave released him and forgave him the debt. 28But that same slave, as he went out, came upon one of his fellow slaves who owed him a hundred denarii;[p] and seizing him by the throat, he said, 'Pay what you owe.' 29Then his fellow slave fell down and pleaded with him, 'Have patience with me, and I will pay you.' 30But he refused; then he went and threw him into prison until he would pay the debt. 31When his fellow slaves saw what had happened, they were greatly distressed, and they went and reported to their lord all that had taken place. 32Then his lord summoned him and said to him, 'You wicked slave! I forgave you all that debt because you pleaded with me. 33Should you not have had mercy on your fellow slave, as I had mercy on you?' 34And in anger his lord handed him over to be tortured until he would pay his entire debt. 35So my heavenly Father will also do to every one of you, if you do not forgive your brother or sister[q] from your heart."

Teaching about Divorce

▶ *See Mark 10.1–12*

19 When Jesus had finished saying these things, he left Galilee and went to the region of Judea beyond the Jordan. 2Large crowds followed him, and he cured them there.

3 Some Pharisees came to him, and to test him they asked, "Is it lawful for a man to divorce his wife for any cause?" 4He answered, "Have you not read that the one who made them at the beginning 'made them male and female,' 5and said, 'For this reason a man shall leave his father and mother and be joined to his wife, and the two shall become one flesh'? 6So they are no longer two, but one flesh. Therefore what God has joined together, let no one separate." 7They said to him, "Why then did Moses command us to give a certificate of dismissal and to divorce her?" 8He said to them, "It was because you were so hardhearted that Moses allowed you to divorce your wives, but from the beginning it was not so. 9And I say to you, whoever divorces his wife, except for unchastity, and marries another commits adultery."[r]

10 His disciples said to him, "If such is the case of a man with his wife, it is better not to marry." 11But he said to them, "Not everyone can accept this teaching, but only those to whom it is given. 12For there are eunuchs who have been so

---

i Other ancient authorities read *my brother* j Gk *If your brother* k Other ancient authorities lack *against you* l Gk *the* m Gk *if my brother* n Or *seventy times seven* o A talent was worth more than fifteen years' wages of a laborer p The denarius was the usual day's wage for a laborer q Gk *brother* r Other ancient authorities read *except on the ground of unchastity, causes her to commit adultery*; others add at the end of the verse *and he who marries a divorced woman commits adultery*

from birth, and there are eunuchs who have been made eunuchs by others, and there are eunuchs who have made themselves eunuchs for the sake of the kingdom of heaven. Let anyone accept this who can."

19.9 No-Fault Divorce?

In Jesus' day Pharisees debated how to interpret Old Testament rules concerning divorce. As usual, they tried to pull Jesus into the dispute. A famous rabbi named Hillel taught that a man could divorce his wife if she did anything at all to displease him, such as burning his food. A stricter school headed by Shammai limited grounds for divorce to marital infidelity. Jesus clearly sided with Shammai but pointed much deeper, beyond the technicalities of divorce to God's original design for marriage.

Jesus Blesses Little Children

▶ *See Mark 10.13–16; Luke 18.15–17*

13 Then little children were being brought to him in order that he might lay his hands on them and pray. The disciples spoke sternly to those who brought them; ¹⁴but Jesus said, "Let the little children come to me, and do not stop them; for it is to such as these that the kingdom of heaven belongs." ¹⁵And he laid his hands on them and went on his way.

The Rich Young Man

▶ *See Mark 10.17–30; Luke 18.18–30*

16 Then someone came to him and said, "Teacher, what good deed must I do to have eternal life?" ¹⁷And he said to him, "Why do you ask me about what is good? There is only one who is good. If you wish to enter into life, keep the commandments." ¹⁸He said to him, "Which ones?" And Jesus said, "You shall not murder; You shall not commit adultery; You shall not steal; You shall not bear false witness; ¹⁹Honor your father and mother; also, You shall love your neighbor as yourself." ²⁰The young man said to him, "I have kept all these;ˢ what do I still lack?" ²¹Jesus said to him, "If you wish to be perfect, go, sell your possessions, and give the moneyᵗ to the poor, and you will have treasure in heaven; then come, follow me." ²²When the young man heard this word, he went away grieving, for he had many possessions.

23 Then Jesus said to his disciples, "Truly I tell you, it will be hard for a rich person to enter the kingdom of heaven. ²⁴Again I tell you, it is easier for a camel to go through the eye of a needle than for someone who is rich to enter the kingdom of God." ²⁵When the disciples heard this, they were greatly astounded and said, "Then who can be saved?" ²⁶But Jesus looked at them and said, "For mortals it is impossible, but for God all things are possible."

27 Then Peter said in reply, "Look, we have left everything and followed you. What then will we have?" ²⁸Jesus said to them, "Truly I tell you, at the renewal of all things, when the Son of Man is seated on the throne of his glory, you who have followed me will also sit on twelve thrones, judging the twelve tribes of Israel. ²⁹And everyone who has left houses or brothers or sisters or father or mother or children or fields, for my name's sake, will receive a hundredfold,ᵘ and will inherit eternal life. ³⁰But many who are first will be last, and the last will be first.

The Laborers in the Vineyard

20 "For the kingdom of heaven is like a landowner who went out early in the morning

20.1 Unfair Pay

Jesus' story makes little economic sense, which was his point exactly. He is giving a parable about grace, and you can't calculate the grace of God like you can a day's wages. We receive it as a gift from God, not as something we work hard to earn. The person who comes to God at the end of life—like the robber on the cross— enjoys the same ultimate benefits as someone who follows God from early childhood. Jealousy of another's "unfair" rewards can take the joy from your own.

to hire laborers for his vineyard. ²After agreeing with the laborers for the usual daily wage,ᵛ he sent them into his vineyard. ³When he went out about nine o'clock, he saw others standing idle in the marketplace; ⁴and he said to them, 'You also go into the vineyard, and I will pay you whatever is right.' So they went. ⁵When he went out again about noon and about three o'clock, he did the same. ⁶And about five o'clock he went out and found others standing around; and he said to them, 'Why are you standing here idle all day?' ⁷They said to him, 'Because no one has hired us.' He said to them, 'You also go into the vineyard.' ⁸When evening came, the owner of the vineyard said to his manager, 'Call the laborers and give them their pay, beginning with the last and then going to the first.' ⁹When those hired about five o'clock came, each of them received the usual daily wage.ᵛ ¹⁰Now when the first came, they thought they would receive more; but each of

---

ˢ Other ancient authorities add *from my youth*   ᵗ Gk lacks *the money*   ᵘ Other ancient authorities read *manifold*
ᵛ Gk *a denarius*

them also received the usual daily wage.[w] [11]And when they received it, they grumbled against the landowner, [12]saying, 'These last worked only one hour, and you have made them equal to us who have borne the burden of the day and the scorching heat.' [13]But he replied to one of them, 'Friend, I am doing you no wrong; did you not agree with me for the usual daily wage?[w] [14]Take what belongs to you and go; I choose to give to this last the same as I give to you. [15]Am I not allowed to do what I choose with what belongs to me? Or are you envious because I am generous?'[x] [16]So the last will be first, and the first will be last."[y]

A Third Time Jesus Foretells His Death and Resurrection

▶ *See Mark 10.32–34; Luke 18.31–33*

17 While Jesus was going up to Jerusalem, he took the twelve disciples aside by themselves, and said to them on the way, [18]"See, we are going up to Jerusalem, and the Son of Man will be handed over to the chief priests and scribes, and they will condemn him to death; [19]then they will hand him over to the Gentiles to be mocked and flogged and crucified; and on the third day he will be raised."

The Request of the Mother of James and John

▶ *See Mark 10.35–45*

20 Then the mother of the sons of Zebedee came to him with her sons, and kneeling before him, she asked a favor of him. [21]And he said to her, "What do you want?" She said to him, "Declare that these two sons of mine will sit, one at your right hand and one at your left, in your kingdom." [22]But Jesus answered, "You do not know what you are asking. Are you able to drink the cup that I am about to drink?"[z] They said to him, "We are able." [23]He said to them, "You will indeed drink my cup, but to sit at my right hand and at my left, this is not mine to grant, but it is for those for whom it has been prepared by my Father."

24 When the ten heard it, they were angry with the two brothers. [25]But Jesus called them to him and said, "You know that the rulers of the Gentiles lord it over them, and their great ones are tyrants over them. [26]It will not be so among you; but whoever wishes to be great among you must be your servant, [27]and whoever wishes to be first among you must be your slave; [28]just as the Son of Man came not to be served but to serve, and to give his life a ransom for many."

Jesus Heals Two Blind Men

▶ *See Mark 10.46–52; Luke 18.35–43*

29 As they were leaving Jericho, a large crowd followed him. [30]There were two blind men sitting by the roadside. When they heard that Jesus was passing by, they shouted, "Lord,[a] have mercy on us, Son of David!" [31]The crowd sternly ordered them to be quiet; but they shouted even more loudly, "Have mercy on us, Lord, Son of David!" [32]Jesus stood still and called them, saying, "What do you want me to do for you?" [33]They said to him, "Lord, let our eyes be opened." [34]Moved with compassion, Jesus touched their eyes. Immediately they regained their sight and followed him.

Jesus' Triumphal Entry into Jerusalem

▶ *See Mark 11.1–10; Luke 19.29–38; John 12.12–15*

21 When they had come near Jerusalem and had reached Bethphage, at the Mount of Olives, Jesus sent two disciples, [2]saying to them, "Go into the village ahead of you, and immediately you will find a donkey tied, and a colt with her; untie them and bring them to me. [3]If anyone says anything to you, just say this, 'The Lord needs them.' And he will send them immediately.[b]" [4]This took place to fulfill what had been spoken through the prophet, saying,

5 "Tell the daughter of Zion,
    Look, your king is coming to you,
        humble, and mounted on a donkey,
            and on a colt, the foal of a donkey."

[6]The disciples went and did as Jesus had directed them; [7]they brought the donkey and the colt, and put their cloaks on them, and he sat on them. [8]A very large crowd[c] spread their cloaks on the road, and others cut branches from the trees and spread them on the road. [9]The crowds that

21.12 Drastic Action

In Jesus' day, activities at the temple, supposedly the center for worship of God, had taken on a commercial cast. Merchants sold sacrificial animals to pilgrims and foreigners at inflated prices. The system was designed more for profit than for true worship. Jesus responded first by aggressively turning out these "robbers," and then by turning his attention to the people with real needs, the blind and the lame.

---

[w] Gk *a denarius*   [x] Gk *is your eye evil because I am good?*   [y] Other ancient authorities add *for many are called but few are chosen*   [z] Other ancient authorities add *or to be baptized with the baptism that I am baptized with?*   [a] Other ancient authorities lack *Lord*   [b] Or *'The Lord needs them and will send them back immediately.'*   [c] Or *Most of the crowd*

went ahead of him and that followed were shouting,

> "Hosanna to the Son of David!
> Blessed is the one who comes in the
>   name of the Lord!
> Hosanna in the highest heaven!"

[10]When he entered Jerusalem, the whole city was in turmoil, asking, "Who is this?" [11]The crowds were saying, "This is the prophet Jesus from Nazareth in Galilee."

[d] Other ancient authorities add *of God*

Jesus Cleanses the Temple

▶ *See Mark 11.15–18; Luke 19.45–47*

12 Then Jesus entered the temple[d] and drove out all who were selling and buying in the temple, and he overturned the tables of the money changers and the seats of those who sold doves. [13]He said to them, "It is written,

> 'My house shall be called a house
>   of prayer';

Out to Get Jesus
Jesus confronts his enemies

THE MERE BIRTH OF JESUS had threatened King Herod so much that he had ordered a bloody slaughter of boy babies. The pattern of opposition continued. Early on, Jesus openly predicted his own death.

Beginning in chapter 19, Matthew explains some of the escalating tensions between Jesus and the groups who resisted him. Enemies followed him from town to town, setting traps. Even so, Jesus neither tempered his words nor tried to hide. Instead, he used the occasions of conflict to warn his disciples and the watching crowds against those enemies, whose fury only increased.

Chapter 22 shows Jesus confronting three different groups of enemies on the same day: two religious sects, the Pharisees and the Sadducees, as well as the political Herodians. Jesus easily avoided their carefully devised verbal traps. In fact, he succeeded so brilliantly that Matthew concludes, "Nor from that day did anyone dare to ask him any more questions" (22.46).

> *When the chief priests and the Pharisees heard his parables, they realized that he was speaking about them. They wanted to arrest him, but they feared the crowds. 21.45–46*

What Did Jesus Have Against the Pharisees?

Students of history have often puzzled over why Jesus lashed out so strongly at one Jewish sect, the Pharisees—a group the New Testament mentions 100 times. At first glance, they seem like people Jesus should have liked. They were the most religious people of the day. More than any other group, they strove to follow the letter of the Old Testament law. Their very name, meaning "separatists," hinted at their desire to rise above normal behavior.

Pharisees were legalists. Besides unduly focusing on minute details of the law, they embellished it with their own strict traditions. For example, a person could ride a donkey without breaking the Sabbath rules, but if he carried a switch to speed up the animal, he would be guilty of laying a burden on it.

A Pharisee could give to a beggar on the sabbath only if the beggar stuck his hand inside the home of the Pharisee so that the Pharisee needn't reach outside. A woman couldn't look in the mirror on the sabbath—she might see a gray hair and be tempted to pull it out.

Matthew 23 records Jesus' eloquent verdict on the Pharisees. He chastised them for being proud and cliquish and petty, and for refusing to admit their wrongs. External, showy forms of legalism, he said, tend to divert attention away from a person's inner attitude toward God and other people.

Are There Pharisees Now?

As he entered into the last weeks of his life on earth, Jesus polarized people. He boldly contrasted his own teaching with that of his opponents. In addition, he warned his followers about what to expect after his death. Opposition from enemies like the Pharisees wouldn't fade away when he departed. Rather, it would crescendo until the day of final judgment.

Jesus singled out the Pharisees as an example of legalism carried to an extreme. But he wasn't talking merely against an ancient Jewish sect. His words describe persistent tendencies of human beings, then and now. The errors he mentioned have characterized the church throughout its history. Christians still battle against pride and intolerance and a religion based on deeds.

Life Questions: Jesus describes characteristics of Pharisees in the first century. But what about our own time? What Pharisee-like qualities exist in your church? In you?

but you are making it a den
of robbers."

14 The blind and the lame came to him in the temple, and he cured them. ¹⁵But when the chief priests and the scribes saw the amazing things that he did, and heard*ᵉ* the children crying out in the temple, "Hosanna to the Son of David," they became angry ¹⁶and said to him, "Do you hear what these are saying?" Jesus said to them, "Yes; have you never read,

'Out of the mouths of infants and nursing babies
you have prepared praise for yourself'?"

¹⁷He left them, went out of the city to Bethany, and spent the night there.

Jesus Curses the Fig Tree

▶ *See Mark 11.12–14,20–24*

18 In the morning, when he returned to the city, he was hungry. ¹⁹And seeing a fig tree by the side of the road, he went to it and found nothing at all on it but leaves. Then he said to it, "May no fruit ever come from you again!" And the fig tree withered at once. ²⁰When the disciples saw it, they were amazed, saying, "How did the fig tree wither at once?" ²¹Jesus answered them, "Truly I tell you, if you have faith and do not doubt, not only will you do what has been done to the fig tree, but even if you say to this mountain, 'Be lifted up and thrown into the sea,' it will be done. ²²Whatever you ask for in prayer with faith, you will receive."

The Authority of Jesus Questioned

▶ *See Mark 11.27–33; Luke 20.1–8*

23 When he entered the temple, the chief priests and the elders of the people came to him as he was teaching, and said, "By what authority are you doing these things, and who gave you this authority?" ²⁴Jesus said to them, "I will also ask you one question; if you tell me the answer, then I will also tell you by what authority I do these things. ²⁵Did the baptism of John come from heaven, or was it of human origin?" And they argued with one another, "If we say, 'From heaven,' he will say to us, 'Why then did you not believe him?' ²⁶But if we say, 'Of human origin,' we are afraid of the crowd; for all regard John as a prophet." ²⁷So they answered Jesus, "We do not know." And he said to them, "Neither will I tell you by what authority I am doing these things.

The Parable of the Two Sons

28 "What do you think? A man had two sons; he went to the first and said, 'Son, go and work in the vineyard today.' ²⁹He answered, 'I will not'; but later he changed his mind and went. ³⁰The father*ᶠ* went to the second and said the same; and he answered, 'I go, sir'; but he did not go. ³¹Which of the two did the will of his father?"

They said, "The first." Jesus said to them, "Truly I tell you, the tax collectors and the prostitutes are going into the kingdom of God ahead of you. ³²For John came to you in the way of righteousness and you did not believe him, but the tax collectors and the prostitutes believed him; and even after you saw it, you did not change your minds and believe him.

The Parable of the Wicked Tenants

▶ *See Mark 12.1–12; Luke 20.9–19*

33 "Listen to another parable. There was a landowner who planted a vineyard, put a fence around it, dug a wine press in it, and built a watchtower. Then he leased it to tenants and went to another country. ³⁴When the harvest time had come, he sent his slaves to the tenants to collect his produce. ³⁵But the tenants seized his slaves and beat one, killed another, and stoned another. ³⁶Again he sent other slaves, more than the first; and they treated them in the same way. ³⁷Finally he sent his son to them, saying, 'They will respect my son.' ³⁸But when the tenants saw the son, they said to themselves, 'This is the heir; come, let us kill him and get his inheritance.' ³⁹So they seized him, threw him out of the vineyard, and killed him. ⁴⁰Now when the owner of the vineyard comes, what will he do to those tenants?" ⁴¹They said to him, "He will put those wretches to a miserable death, and lease the vineyard to other tenants who will give him the produce at the harvest time."

42 Jesus said to them, "Have you never read in the scriptures:

'The stone that the builders rejected
has become the cornerstone;*ᵍ*
this was the Lord's doing,
and it is amazing in our eyes'?

⁴³Therefore I tell you, the kingdom of God will be taken away from you and given to a people that produces the fruits of the kingdom.*ʰ* ⁴⁴The one who falls on this stone will be broken to pieces; and it will crush anyone on whom it falls."*ⁱ*

45 When the chief priests and the Pharisees heard his parables, they realized that he was speaking about them. ⁴⁶They wanted to arrest him, but they feared the crowds, because they regarded him as a prophet.

The Parable of the Wedding Banquet

22 Once more Jesus spoke to them in parables, saying: ²"The kingdom of heaven may be compared to a king who gave a wedding banquet for his son. ³He sent his slaves to call those who had been invited to the wedding banquet, but they would not come. ⁴Again he sent other slaves, saying, 'Tell those who have been invited: Look, I have prepared my dinner, my oxen and my fat calves have been slaughtered,

---

ᵉ Gk lacks *heard*   *ᶠ* Gk *He*   *ᵍ* Or *keystone*   *ʰ* Gk *the fruits of it*   *ⁱ* Other ancient authorities lack verse 44

and everything is ready; come to the wedding banquet.' ⁵But they made light of it and went away, one to his farm, another to his business, ⁶while the rest seized his slaves, mistreated them, and killed them. ⁷The king was enraged. He sent his troops, destroyed those murderers, and burned their city. ⁸Then he said to his slaves, 'The wedding is ready, but those invited were not worthy. ⁹Go therefore into the main streets, and invite everyone you find to the wedding banquet.' ¹⁰Those slaves went out into the streets and gathered all whom they found, both good and bad; so the wedding hall was filled with guests.

11 "But when the king came in to see the guests, he noticed a man there who was not wearing a wedding robe, ¹²and he said to him, 'Friend, how did you get in here without a wedding robe?' And he was speechless. ¹³Then the king said to the attendants, 'Bind him hand and foot, and throw him into the outer darkness, where there will be weeping and gnashing of teeth.' ¹⁴For many are called, but few are chosen."

The Question about Paying Taxes

▶ *See Mark 12.13–17; Luke 20.20–26*

15 Then the Pharisees went and plotted to entrap him in what he said. ¹⁶So they sent their disciples to him, along with the Herodians, saying, "Teacher, we know that you are sincere, and teach the way of God in accordance with truth, and show deference to no one; for you do not regard people with partiality. ¹⁷Tell us, then, what you think. Is it lawful to pay taxes to the emperor,

22.17 A Double Bind

The Pharisees, allied with a party following King Herod, posed a question designed to trap Jesus regardless of his answer. If Jesus said, Pay the taxes, he would lose the support of the independence-minded Jews; if he said, Don't pay, he could be turned in to Rome for breaking the law.

or not?" ¹⁸But Jesus, aware of their malice, said, "Why are you putting me to the test, you hypocrites? ¹⁹Show me the coin used for the tax." And they brought him a denarius. ²⁰Then he said to them, "Whose head is this, and whose title?" ²¹They answered, "The emperor's." Then he said to them, "Give therefore to the emperor the things that are the emperor's, and to God the things that are God's." ²²When they heard this, they were amazed; and they left him and went away.

The Question about the Resurrection

▶ *See Mark 12.18–27; Luke 20.27–40*

23 The same day some Sadducees came to him, saying there is no resurrection;ʲ and they asked him a question, saying, ²⁴"Teacher, Moses said, 'If a man dies childless, his brother shall marry the widow, and raise up children for his brother.' ²⁵Now there were seven brothers among us; the first married, and died childless, leaving the widow to his brother. ²⁶The second did the same, so also the third, down to the seventh. ²⁷Last of all, the woman herself died. ²⁸In the resurrection, then, whose wife of the seven will she be? For all of them had married her."

29 Jesus answered them, "You are wrong, because you know neither the scriptures nor the power of God. ³⁰For in the resurrection they neither marry nor are given in marriage, but are like angelsᵏ in heaven. ³¹And as for the resurrection of the dead, have you not read what was said to you by God, ³²'I am the God of Abraham, the God of Isaac, and the God of Jacob'? He is God not of the dead, but of the living." ³³And when the crowd heard it, they were astounded at his teaching.

The Greatest Commandment

▶ *See Mark 12.28–31*

34 When the Pharisees heard that he had silenced the Sadducees, they gathered together, ³⁵and one of them, a lawyer, asked him a question to test him. ³⁶"Teacher, which commandment in the law is the greatest?" ³⁷He said to him, "'You shall love the Lord your God with all your heart, and with all your soul, and with all your mind.' ³⁸This is the greatest and first commandment. ³⁹And a second is like it: 'You shall love your neighbor as yourself.' ⁴⁰On these two commandments hang all the law and the prophets."

The Question about David's Son

▶ *See Mark 12.35–37; Luke 20.41–44*

41 Now while the Pharisees were gathered together, Jesus asked them this question: ⁴²"What do you think of the Messiah?ˡ Whose son is he?" They said to him, "The son of David." ⁴³He said to them, "How is it then that David by the Spiritᵐ calls him Lord, saying,

⁴⁴ 'The Lord said to my Lord,
   "Sit at my right hand,
      until I put your enemies under your
         feet" '?

⁴⁵If David thus calls him Lord, how can he be his son?" ⁴⁶No one was able to give him an answer, nor from that day did anyone dare to ask him any more questions.

ʲ Other ancient authorities read *who say that there is no resurrection*   ᵏ Other ancient authorities add *of God*
ˡ Or *Christ*   ᵐ Gk *in spirit*

Jesus Denounces Scribes and Pharisees

▶ *See Mark 12.38–39; Luke 20.45–46*

23 Then Jesus said to the crowds and to his disciples, [2]"The scribes and the Pharisees sit on Moses' seat; [3]therefore, do whatever they teach you and follow it; but do not do as they do, for they do not practice what they teach. [4]They tie up heavy burdens, hard to bear, [n] and lay them on the shoulders of others; but they themselves are unwilling to lift a finger to move them. [5]They do all their deeds to be seen by others; for they make their phylacteries broad and their fringes long. [6]They love to have the place of honor at banquets and the best seats in the synagogues, [7]and to be greeted with respect in the marketplaces, and to have people call them rabbi. [8]But you are not to be called rabbi, for you have one teacher, and you are all students. [o] [9]And call no one your father on earth, for you have one Father—the one in heaven. [10]Nor are you to be called instructors, for you have one instructor, the Messiah. [p] [11]The greatest among you will be your servant. [12]All who exalt themselves will be humbled, and all who humble themselves will be exalted.

13 "But woe to you, scribes and Pharisees, hypocrites! For you lock people out of the kingdom of heaven. For you do not go in yourselves, and when others are going in, you stop them. [q] [15]Woe to you, scribes and Pharisees, hypocrites! For you cross sea and land to make a single convert, and you make the new convert twice as much a child of hell [r] as yourselves.

16 "Woe to you, blind guides, who say, 'Whoever swears by the sanctuary is bound by nothing, but whoever swears by the gold of the sanctuary is bound by the oath.' [17]You blind fools! For which is greater, the gold or the sanctuary that has made the gold sacred? [18]And you say, 'Whoever swears by the altar is bound by nothing, but whoever swears by the gift that is on the altar is bound by the oath.' [19]How blind you are! For which is greater, the gift or the altar that makes the gift sacred? [20]So whoever swears by the altar, swears by it and by everything on it; [21]and whoever swears by the sanctuary, swears by it and by the one who dwells in it; [22]and whoever swears by heaven, swears by the throne of God and by the one who is seated upon it.

23 "Woe to you, scribes and Pharisees, hypocrites! For you tithe mint, dill, and cummin, and have neglected the weightier matters of the law: justice and mercy and faith. It is these you ought to have practiced without neglecting the others. [24]You blind guides! You strain out a gnat but swallow a camel!

25 "Woe to you, scribes and Pharisees, hypocrites! For you clean the outside of the cup and of the plate, but inside they are full of greed and self-indulgence. [26]You blind Pharisee! First clean the inside of the cup, [s] so that the outside also may become clean.

23.24–28 Straining at Gnats

The Pharisees, who literally strained water through a cloth to filter out unclean gnats, could hardly miss the point of Jesus' biting humor. Jesus was not attacking them for being strict per se, but rather for fixating on trivial matters while ignoring more important issues: justice, mercy, faithfulness. He blasted their smug, hypocritical sense of superiority.

27 "Woe to you, scribes and Pharisees, hypocrites! For you are like whitewashed tombs, which on the outside look beautiful, but inside they are full of the bones of the dead and of all kinds of filth. [28]So you also on the outside look righteous to others, but inside you are full of hypocrisy and lawlessness.

29 "Woe to you, scribes and Pharisees, hypocrites! For you build the tombs of the prophets and decorate the graves of the righteous, [30]and you say, 'If we had lived in the days of our ancestors, we would not have taken part with them in shedding the blood of the prophets.' [31]Thus you testify against yourselves that you are descendants of those who murdered the prophets. [32]Fill up, then, the measure of your ancestors. [33]You snakes, you brood of vipers! How can you escape being sentenced to hell? [r] [34]Therefore I send you prophets, sages, and scribes, some of whom you will kill and crucify, and some you will flog in your synagogues and pursue from town to town, [35]so that upon you may come all the righteous blood shed on earth, from the blood of righteous Abel to the blood of Zechariah son of Barachiah, whom you murdered between the sanctuary and the altar. [36]Truly I tell you, all this will come upon this generation.

The Lament over Jerusalem

37 "Jerusalem, Jerusalem, the city that kills the prophets and stones those who are sent to it! How often have I desired to gather your children together as a hen gathers her brood under her wings, and you were not willing! [38]See, your house is left to you, desolate. [t] [39]For I tell you, you will not see me again until you say, 'Blessed is the one who comes in the name of the Lord.'"

[n] Other ancient authorities lack *hard to bear*   [o] Gk *brothers*   [p] Or *the Christ*   [q] Other authorities add here (or after verse 12) verse 14, *Woe to you, scribes and Pharisees, hypocrites! For you devour widows' houses and for the sake of appearance you make long prayers; therefore you will receive the greater condemnation*   [r] Gk *Gehenna*   [s] Other ancient authorities add *and of the plate*   [t] Other ancient authorities lack *desolate*

The Destruction of the Temple Foretold

▶ *See Mark 13.1–37; Luke 21.5–36*

24 As Jesus came out of the temple and was going away, his disciples came to point out to him the buildings of the temple. ²Then he asked them, "You see all these, do you not? Truly I tell you, not one stone will be left here upon another; all will be thrown down."

24.2 Stones Overturned

Jesus' prediction came true four decades after his death, in A.D. 70, when the Roman army crushed a Jewish rebellion in Jerusalem. Soldiers knocked down the massive stones of the temple in search of the melted gold that had run down between the stones as the temple burned. The largest stones weighed over 400 tons, but General Titus's soldiers leveled them all.

Signs of the End of the Age

3 When he was sitting on the Mount of Olives, the disciples came to him privately, saying, "Tell us, when will this be, and what will be the sign of your coming and of the end of the age?" ⁴Jesus answered them, "Beware that no one leads you astray. ⁵For many will come in my name, saying, 'I am the Messiah!'ᵘ and they will lead many astray. ⁶And you will hear of wars and rumors of wars; see that you are not alarmed; for this must take place, but the end is not yet. ⁷For nation will rise against nation, and kingdom against kingdom, and there will be faminesᵛ and earthquakes in various places: ⁸all this is but the beginning of the birth pangs.

Persecutions Foretold

9 "Then they will hand you over to be tortured and will put you to death, and you will be hated by all nations because of my name. ¹⁰Then many will fall away,ʷ and they will betray one another and hate one another. ¹¹And many false prophets will arise and lead many astray. ¹²And because of the increase of lawlessness, the love of many will grow cold. ¹³But the one who endures to the end will be saved. ¹⁴And this good newsˣ of the kingdom will be proclaimed throughout the world, as a testimony to all the nations; and then the end will come.

The Desolating Sacrilege

15 "So when you see the desolating sacrilege standing in the holy place, as was spoken of by the prophet Daniel (let the reader understand), ¹⁶then those in Judea must flee to the mountains; ¹⁷the one on the housetop must not go down to take what is in the house; ¹⁸the one in the field must not turn back to get a coat. ¹⁹Woe to those who are pregnant and to those who are nursing infants in those days! ²⁰Pray that your flight may not be in winter or on a sabbath. ²¹For at that time there will be great suffering, such as has not been from the beginning of the world until now, no, and never will be. ²²And if those days had not been cut short, no one would be saved; but for the sake of the elect those days will be cut short. ²³Then if anyone says to you, 'Look! Here is the Messiah!'ᵘ or 'There he is!'—do not believe it. ²⁴For false messiahsʸ and false prophets will appear and produce great signs and omens, to lead astray, if possible, even the elect. ²⁵Take note, I have told you beforehand. ²⁶So, if they say to you, 'Look! He is in the wilderness,' do not go out. If they say, 'Look! He is in the inner rooms,' do not believe it. ²⁷For as the lightning comes from the east and flashes as far as the west, so will be the coming of the Son of Man. ²⁸Wherever the corpse is, there the vultures will gather.

The Coming of the Son of Man

29 "Immediately after the suffering of those days

the sun will be darkened,
and the moon will not give its light;
the stars will fall from heaven,
and the powers of heaven will
be shaken.

³⁰Then the sign of the Son of Man will appear in heaven, and then all the tribes of the earth will mourn, and they will see 'the Son of Man coming on the clouds of heaven' with power and great glory. ³¹And he will send out his angels with a loud trumpet call, and they will gather his elect from the four winds, from one end of heaven to the other.

The Lesson of the Fig Tree

32 "From the fig tree learn its lesson: as soon as its branch becomes tender and puts forth its leaves, you know that summer is near. ³³So also, when you see all these things, you know that heᶻ is near, at the very gates. ³⁴Truly I tell you, this generation will not pass away until all these things have taken place. ³⁵Heaven and earth will pass away, but my words will not pass away.

The Necessity for Watchfulness

▶ *See Luke 12.42–46; 17.26–27*

36 "But about that day and hour no one knows, neither the angels of heaven, nor the Son,ᵃ but only the Father. ³⁷For as the days of Noah were, so will be the coming of the Son of Man. ³⁸For as in those days before the flood they

---

ᵘ Or *the Christ*   ᵛ Other ancient authorities add *and pestilences*   ʷ Or *stumble*   ˣ Or *gospel*   ʸ Or *christs*
ᶻ Or *it*   ᵃ Other ancient authorities lack *nor the Son*

were eating and drinking, marrying and giving in marriage, until the day Noah entered the ark, [39]and they knew nothing until the flood came and swept them all away, so too will be the coming of

---

24.36 When Will Jesus Return?

Matthew 24 records one of Jesus' longest statements about the future. Jesus gives direct clues to events that will precede his second coming. But, notably, almost half the chapter consists of warnings that no one can predict the precise time of his coming.

---

the Son of Man. [40]Then two will be in the field; one will be taken and one will be left. [41]Two women will be grinding meal together; one will be taken and one will be left. [42]Keep awake therefore, for you do not know on what day[b] your Lord is coming. [43]But understand this: if the owner of the house had known in what part of the night the thief was coming, he would have stayed awake and would not have let his house be broken into. [44]Therefore you also must be ready, for the Son of Man is coming at an unexpected hour.

The Faithful or the Unfaithful Slave

45 "Who then is the faithful and wise slave, whom his master has put in charge of his household, to give the other slaves[c] their allowance of food at the proper time? [46]Blessed is that slave whom his master will find at work when he arrives. [47]Truly I tell you, he will put that one in charge of all his possessions. [48]But if that wicked slave says to himself, 'My master is delayed,' [49]and he begins to beat his fellow slaves, and eats and drinks with drunkards, [50]the master of that slave will come on a day when he does not expect him and at an hour that he does not know. [51]He will cut him in pieces[d] and put him with the hypocrites, where there will be weeping and gnashing of teeth.

The Parable of the Ten Bridesmaids

25 "Then the kingdom of heaven will be like this. Ten bridesmaids[e] took their lamps and went to meet the bridegroom.[f] [2]Five of them were foolish, and five were wise. [3]When the foolish took their lamps, they took no oil with them; [4]but the wise took flasks of oil with their lamps. [5]As the bridegroom was delayed, all of them became drowsy and slept. [6]But at midnight there was a shout, 'Look! Here is the bridegroom! Come out to meet him.' [7]Then all those bridesmaids[e] got up and trimmed their lamps. [8]The

foolish said to the wise, 'Give us some of your oil, for our lamps are going out.' [9]But the wise replied, 'No! there will not be enough for you and for us; you had better go to the dealers and buy some for yourselves.' [10]And while they went to buy it, the bridegroom came, and those who were ready went with him into the wedding banquet; and the door was shut. [11]Later the other bridesmaids[e] came also, saying, 'Lord, lord, open to us.' [12]But he replied, 'Truly I tell you, I do not know you.' [13]Keep awake therefore, for you know neither the day nor the hour.[g]

The Parable of the Talents

14 "For it is as if a man, going on a journey, summoned his slaves and entrusted his property to them; [15]to one he gave five talents,[h] to another two, to another one, to each according to his

---

25.15–30 Original Talent

Today when we speak of a "talented" musician or athlete, we are actually harking back to this parable. A talent in Jesus' time was a valuable sum of money worth about two years' wages. Because of this parable, the word acquired a different meaning. Each person in the kingdom of heaven is given a certain number of gifts and opportunities ("talents") to serve God. We can either waste those opportunities or invest them in a way that furthers the kingdom.

---

ability. Then he went away. [16]The one who had received the five talents went off at once and traded with them, and made five more talents. [17]In the same way, the one who had the two talents made two more talents. [18]But the one who had received the one talent went off and dug a hole in the ground and hid his master's money. [19]After a long time the master of those slaves came and settled accounts with them. [20]Then the one who had received the five talents came forward, bringing five more talents, saying, 'Master, you handed over to me five talents; see, I have made five more talents.' [21]His master said to him, 'Well done, good and trustworthy slave; you have been trustworthy in a few things, I will put you in charge of many things; enter into the joy of your master.' [22]And the one with the two talents also came forward, saying, 'Master, you handed over to me two talents; see, I have made two more talents.' [23]His master said to him, 'Well done, good and trustworthy slave; you have been trustworthy in a few things, I will put you in charge of many things; enter into the joy of your master.' [24]Then the one who had received the one talent also came

---

[b] Other ancient authorities read *at what hour*   [c] Gk *to give them*   [d] Or *cut him off*   [e] Gk *virgins*
[f] Other ancient authorities add *and the bride*   [g] Other ancient authorities add *in which the Son of Man is coming*
[h] A talent was worth more than fifteen years' wages of a laborer

forward, saying, 'Master, I knew that you were a harsh man, reaping where you did not sow, and gathering where you did not scatter seed; ²⁵so I was afraid, and I went and hid your talent in the ground. Here you have what is yours.' ²⁶But his master replied, 'You wicked and lazy slave! You knew, did you, that I reap where I did not sow, and gather where I did not scatter? ²⁷Then you ought to have invested my money with the bankers, and on my return I would have received what was my own with interest. ²⁸So take the talent from him, and give it to the one with the ten talents. ²⁹For to all those who have, more will be given, and they will have an abundance; but from those who have nothing, even what they have will be taken away. ³⁰As for this worthless slave, throw him into the outer darkness, where there will be weeping and gnashing of teeth.'

The Judgment of the Nations

31 "When the Son of Man comes in his glory, and all the angels with him, then he will sit on the throne of his glory. ³²All the nations will be gathered before him, and he will separate people one from another as a shepherd separates the sheep from the goats, ³³and he will put the sheep at his right hand and the goats at the left. ³⁴Then the king will say to those at his right hand, 'Come, you that are blessed by my Father, inherit the kingdom prepared for you from the foundation of the world; ³⁵for I was hungry and you gave me food, I was thirsty and you gave me something to drink, I was a stranger and you welcomed me, ³⁶I was naked and you gave me clothing, I was sick and you took care of me, I was in prison and you visited me.' ³⁷Then the righteous will answer him, 'Lord, when was it that we saw you hungry and gave you food, or thirsty and gave you something to drink? ³⁸And when was it that we saw you a stranger and welcomed you, or naked and gave you clothing? ³⁹And when was it that we saw you sick or in prison and visited you?' ⁴⁰And the king will answer them, 'Truly I tell you, just as you did it to one of the least of these who are members of my family,ⁱ you did it to me.' ⁴¹Then he will say to those at his left hand, 'You that are accursed, depart from me into the eternal fire prepared for the devil and his angels; ⁴²for I was hungry and you gave me no food, I was thirsty and you gave me nothing to drink, ⁴³I was a stranger and you did not welcome me, naked and you did not give me clothing, sick and in prison and you did not visit me.' ⁴⁴Then they also will answer, 'Lord, when was it that we saw you hungry or thirsty or a stranger or naked or sick or in prison, and did not take care of you?' ⁴⁵Then he will answer them, 'Truly I tell you, just as you did not do it to one of the least of these, you did not do it to me.'

⁴⁶And these will go away into eternal punishment, but the righteous into eternal life."

The Plot to Kill Jesus

▶ See Mark 14.1–2; Luke 22.1–2

26 When Jesus had finished saying all these things, he said to his disciples, ²"You know that after two days the Passover is coming, and the Son of Man will be handed over to be crucified."

3 Then the chief priests and the elders of the people gathered in the palace of the high priest, who was called Caiaphas, ⁴and they conspired to

26.4 "By Stealth"

The religious leaders failed in their plan to dispose of Jesus quietly. He was killed during a national holiday while Jerusalem swarmed with pilgrims. Yet his death sparked no riots, and in the end even his devoted followers abandoned him. The chief priests and elders might have congratulated themselves on a successful mission—except for what happened on Easter Sunday.

arrest Jesus by stealth and kill him. ⁵But they said, "Not during the festival, or there may be a riot among the people."

The Anointing at Bethany

▶ See Mark 14.3–9

6 Now while Jesus was at Bethany in the house of Simon the leper,ʲ ⁷a woman came to him with an alabaster jar of very costly ointment, and she poured it on his head as he sat at the table. ⁸But when the disciples saw it, they were angry and said, "Why this waste? ⁹For this ointment could have been sold for a large sum, and the money given to the poor." ¹⁰But Jesus, aware of this, said to them, "Why do you trouble the woman? She has performed a good service for me. ¹¹For you always have the poor with you, but you will not always have me. ¹²By pouring this ointment on my body she has prepared me for burial. ¹³Truly I tell you, wherever this good newsᵏ is proclaimed in the whole world, what she has done will be told in remembrance of her."

Judas Agrees to Betray Jesus

▶ See Mark 14.10–11; Luke 22.3–6

14 Then one of the twelve, who was called Judas Iscariot, went to the chief priests ¹⁵and said, "What will you give me if I betray him to you?" They paid him thirty pieces of silver. ¹⁶And from

---

ⁱ Gk *these my brothers*   ʲ The terms *leper* and *leprosy* can refer to several diseases   ᵏ Or *gospel*

that moment he began to look for an opportunity to betray him.

The Passover with the Disciples

▶ *See Mark 14.12–25; Luke 22.7–13*

17 On the first day of Unleavened Bread the disciples came to Jesus, saying, "Where do you want us to make the preparations for you to eat the Passover?" [18]He said, "Go into the city to a certain man, and say to him, 'The Teacher says, My time is near; I will keep the Passover at your house with my disciples.'" [19]So the disciples did as Jesus had directed them, and they prepared the Passover meal.

20 When it was evening, he took his place with the twelve;[l] [21]and while they were eating, he said, "Truly I tell you, one of you will betray me." [22]And they became greatly distressed and began to say to him one after another, "Surely not I, Lord?" [23]He answered, "The one who has dipped his hand into the bowl with me will betray me. [24]The Son of Man goes as it is written of him, but woe to that one by whom the Son of Man is betrayed! It would have been better for that one not to have been born." [25]Judas, who betrayed him, said, "Surely not I, Rabbi?" He replied, "You have said so."

The Institution of the Lord's Supper

26 While they were eating, Jesus took a loaf of bread, and after blessing it he broke it, gave it to the disciples, and said, "Take, eat; this is my body." [27]Then he took a cup, and after giving thanks he gave it to them, saying, "Drink from it, all of you; [28]for this is my blood of the[m] covenant, which is poured out for many for the forgiveness of sins. [29]I tell you, I will never again drink of this fruit of the vine until that day when I drink it new with you in my Father's kingdom."

30 When they had sung the hymn, they went out to the Mount of Olives.

Peter's Denial Foretold

▶ *See Mark 14.27–31; Luke 22.31–34*

31 Then Jesus said to them, "You will all become deserters because of me this night; for it is written,
　　'I will strike the shepherd,
　　　　and the sheep of the flock will
　　　　　　be scattered.'
[32]But after I am raised up, I will go ahead of you to Galilee." [33]Peter said to him, "Though all become deserters because of you, I will never desert you." [34]Jesus said to him, "Truly I tell you, this very night, before the cock crows, you will deny me three times." [35]Peter said to him, "Even though I must die with you, I will not deny you." And so said all the disciples.

Jesus Prays in Gethsemane

▶ *See Mark 14.32–42; Luke 22.40–46*

36 Then Jesus went with them to a place called Gethsemane; and he said to his disciples, "Sit here while I go over there and pray." [37]He took with him Peter and the two sons of Zebedee, and began to be grieved and agitated. [38]Then he said to them, "I am deeply grieved, even to death; remain here, and stay awake with me." [39]And going a little farther, he threw himself on the ground and prayed, "My Father, if it is possible, let this cup pass from me; yet not what I want but what you want." [40]Then he came to the disciples and found them sleeping; and he said to Peter, "So, could you not stay awake with me one hour? [41]Stay awake and pray that you may not come into the time of trial;[n] the spirit indeed is willing, but the flesh is weak." [42]Again he went away for the second time and prayed, "My Father, if this cannot pass unless I drink it, your will be done." [43]Again he came and found them sleeping, for their eyes were heavy. [44]So leaving them again, he went away and prayed for the third time, saying the same words. [45]Then he came to the disciples and said to them, "Are you still sleeping and taking your rest? See, the hour is at hand, and the Son of Man is betrayed into the hands of sinners. [46]Get up, let us be going. See, my betrayer is at hand."

The Betrayal and Arrest of Jesus

▶ *See Mark 14.43–50; Luke 22.47–53*

47 While he was still speaking, Judas, one of the twelve, arrived; with him was a large crowd with swords and clubs, from the chief priests and

26.47 A Name Disgraced

Judas (like Jesus) was a common name for Jewish men in those days; it is the Greek form of Judah. He came from a region called Judea, whereas all the other disciples came from Galilee. Yet he gained enough trust to be named the disciples' treasurer. The Bible gives few details on Judas's motive for betraying Jesus. He may have become disillusioned when Jesus didn't fulfill his expectations of a powerful king and Messiah.

the elders of the people. [48]Now the betrayer had given them a sign, saying, "The one I will kiss is the man; arrest him." [49]At once he came up to Jesus and said, "Greetings, Rabbi!" and kissed him. [50]Jesus said to him, "Friend, do what you are here to do." Then they came and laid hands on Jesus and arrested him. [51]Suddenly, one of those with Jesus put his hand on his sword, drew it, and

---

[l] Other ancient authorities add *disciples*　　[m] Other ancient authorities add *new*　　[n] Or *into temptation*

struck the slave of the high priest, cutting off his ear. 52Then Jesus said to him, "Put your sword back into its place; for all who take the sword will perish by the sword. 53Do you think that I cannot appeal to my Father, and he will at once send me more than twelve legions of angels? 54But how then would the scriptures be fulfilled, which say it must happen in this way?" 55At that hour Jesus said to the crowds, "Have you come out with swords and clubs to arrest me as though I were a bandit? Day after day I sat in the temple teaching, and you did not arrest me. 56But all this has taken place, so that the scriptures of the prophets may be fulfilled." Then all the disciples deserted him and fled.

Jesus before the High Priest

▶ *See Mark 14.53–65; John 18.12–13,19–24*

57 Those who had arrested Jesus took him to Caiaphas the high priest, in whose house the scribes and the elders had gathered. 58But Peter was following him at a distance, as far as the courtyard of the high priest; and going inside, he sat with the guards in order to see how this would end. 59Now the chief priests and the whole council were looking for false testimony against Jesus so that they might put him to death, 60but they found none, though many false witnesses came forward. At last two came forward 61and said, "This fellow said, 'I am able to destroy the temple of God and to build it in three days.'" 62The high priest stood up and said, "Have you no answer? What is it that they testify against you?" 63But Jesus was silent. Then the high priest said to him, "I put you under oath before the living God, tell us if you are the Messiah,[o] the Son of God." 64Jesus said to him, "You have said so. But I tell you,

From now on you will see the
Son of Man
seated at the right hand of Power
and coming on the clouds of heaven."

65Then the high priest tore his clothes and said, "He has blasphemed! Why do we still need witnesses? You have now heard his blasphemy. 66What is your verdict?" They answered, "He deserves death." 67Then they spat in his face and struck him; and some slapped him, 68saying, "Prophesy to us, you Messiah![o] Who is it that struck you?"

Peter's Denial of Jesus

▶ *See Mark 14.66–72; Luke 22.52–62; John 18.16–18,25–27*

69 Now Peter was sitting outside in the courtyard. A servant-girl came to him and said, "You also were with Jesus the Galilean." 70But he denied it before all of them, saying, "I do not know what you are talking about." 71When he went out to the porch, another servant-girl saw him, and she said to the bystanders, "This man was with Jesus of Nazareth."[p] 72Again he denied it with an oath, "I do not know the man." 73After a little while the bystanders came up and said to Peter, "Certainly you are also one of them, for your accent betrays you." 74Then he began to curse, and he swore an oath, "I do not know the man!" At that moment the cock crowed. 75Then Peter remembered what Jesus had said: "Before the cock crows, you will deny me three times." And he went out and wept bitterly.

26.73 Telltale Accent

Revolutionaries and troublemakers in Palestine usually operated in the rugged countryside. In Jerusalem, a city abuzz with rumors, Peter's Galilean accent made him suspect, for it marked him as a non-local. Jesus, also from Galilee, had already been arrested.

Jesus Brought before Pilate

27 When morning came, all the chief priests and the elders of the people conferred together against Jesus in order to bring about his death. 2They bound him, led him away, and handed him over to Pilate the governor.

The Suicide of Judas

3 When Judas, his betrayer, saw that Jesus[q] was condemned, he repented and brought back the thirty pieces of silver to the chief priests and the elders. 4He said, "I have sinned by betraying innocent[r] blood." But they said, "What is that to us? See to it yourself." 5Throwing down the pieces of silver in the temple, he departed; and he went and hanged himself. 6But the chief priests, taking the pieces of silver, said, "It is not lawful to put them into the treasury, since they are blood money." 7After conferring together, they used them to buy the potter's field as a place to bury foreigners. 8For this reason that field has been called the Field of Blood to this day. 9Then was fulfilled what had been spoken through the prophet Jeremiah,[s] "And they took[t] the thirty pieces of silver, the price of the one on whom a price had been set,[u] on whom some of the people of Israel had set a price, 10and they gave[v] them for the potter's field, as the Lord commanded me."

[o] Or *Christ* [p] Gk *the Nazorean* [q] Gk *he* [r] Other ancient authorities read *righteous* [s] Other ancient authorities read *Zechariah* or *Isaiah* [t] Or *I took* [u] Or *the price of the precious One* [v] Other ancient authorities read *I gave*

Pilate Questions Jesus

▶ *See Mark 15.2–15; Luke 23.2–3,18–25; John 18.29—19.16*

11 Now Jesus stood before the governor; and the governor asked him, "Are you the King of the Jews?" Jesus said, "You say so." [12]But when he was accused by the chief priests and elders, he did not answer. [13]Then Pilate said to him, "Do you not hear how many accusations they make against you?" [14]But he gave him no answer, not even to a single charge, so that the governor was greatly amazed.

Barabbas or Jesus?

15 Now at the festival the governor was accustomed to release a prisoner for the crowd, anyone whom they wanted. [16]At that time they had a notorious prisoner, called Jesus[w] Barabbas. [17]So after they had gathered, Pilate said to them, "Whom do you want me to release for you, Jesus[w] Barabbas or Jesus who is called the Messiah?"[x] [18]For he realized that it was out of jealousy that they had handed him over. [19]While he was sitting on the judgment seat, his wife sent word to him, "Have nothing to do with that innocent man, for today I have suffered a great deal be-

cause of a dream about him." [20]Now the chief priests and the elders persuaded the crowds to ask for Barabbas and to have Jesus killed. [21]The governor again said to them, "Which of the two do you want me to release for you?" And they said, "Barabbas." [22]Pilate said to them, "Then what should I do with Jesus who is called the Messiah?"[x] All of them said, "Let him be crucified!" [23]Then he asked, "Why, what evil has he done?" But they shouted all the more, "Let him be crucified!"

Pilate Hands Jesus over to Be Crucified

24 So when Pilate saw that he could do nothing, but rather that a riot was beginning, he took some water and washed his hands before the crowd, saying, "I am innocent of this man's blood;[y] see to it yourselves." [25]Then the people as a whole answered, "His blood be on us and on our children!" [26]So he released Barabbas for them; and after flogging Jesus, he handed him over to be crucified.

The Soldiers Mock Jesus

▶ *See Mark 15.16–20*

27 Then the soldiers of the governor took

---

[w] Other ancient authorities lack *Jesus*   [x] Or *the Christ*   [y] Other ancient authorities read *this righteous blood*, or *this righteous man's blood*

The Killing of a King
Arrest, trial, and execution

IN SPARE, UNADORNED LANGUAGE THE last three chapters of Matthew draw together the deep ironies of Jesus' life. From the first sentence, Matthew has stressed that Jesus is the Messiah, a true king. This Gospel is sometimes called the "royal" Gospel because it refers so many times to kingship.

But at the end of his life, the man whom wise men had crossed a continent to worship was sold, like a slave, for thirty pieces of silver. Jesus got a royal robe and crown at last—but as a cruel, mocking joke. Blood from the wounds on his back clotted on the robe, and the crown of thorns streaked his face with more blood.

A short time before, he had blistered the religious leaders with accusations. But when they put him on the stand and accused him, his strong voice stayed mostly silent.

> *Pilate said to them, "Then what should I do with Jesus who is called the Messiah?" All of them said, "Let him be crucified!"*
> 27.22

Jesus' Self-Defense

Jesus' enemies asked him two chief questions: "Are you the King of the Jews?" and "Are you the Messiah?" He answered with a simple "You say so" (27.11), confirming the major themes woven throughout Matthew's book. Finally he was executed, with his "crime"—being a king—posted above his sagging body.

Jesus was indeed a king, but not the kind of king people expected. Even his disciples, who had known Jesus intimately for three years, slipped away in doubt.

The story, however, doesn't end with the death scene in chapter 27. Good Friday would never have been called "good" without the miracle described next. The king came back! And the writer who opened his book by tracing Jesus' Jewish roots ends it with Jesus' stirring call to take the good news to all nations.

Life Questions: The people who crucified Jesus—what did they hate in him? Is it the same today?

Jesus into the governor's headquarters,[z] and they gathered the whole cohort around him. [28]They stripped him and put a scarlet robe on him, [29]and after twisting some thorns into a crown, they put it on his head. They put a reed in his right hand and knelt before him and mocked him, saying, "Hail, King of the Jews!" [30]They spat on him, and took the reed and struck him on the head. [31]After mocking him, they stripped him of the robe and put his own clothes on him. Then they led him away to crucify him.

The Crucifixion of Jesus

▶ See Mark 15.22–32; Luke 23.33–43; John 19.17–24

32 As they went out, they came upon a man from Cyrene named Simon; they compelled this man to carry his cross. [33]And when they came to a place called Golgotha (which means Place of a Skull), [34]they offered him wine to drink, mixed with gall; but when he tasted it, he would not drink it. [35]And when they had crucified him, they divided his clothes among themselves by casting lots;[a] [36]then they sat down there and kept watch over him. [37]Over his head they put the charge against him, which read, "This is Jesus, the King of the Jews."

38 Then two bandits were crucified with him, one on his right and one on his left. [39]Those who passed by derided[b] him, shaking their heads [40]and saying, "You who would destroy the temple and build it in three days, save yourself! If you are the Son of God, come down from the cross." [41]In the same way the chief priests also, along with the scribes and elders, were mocking him, saying, [42]"He saved others; he cannot save himself.[c] He is the King of Israel; let him come down from the cross now, and we will believe in him. [43]He trusts in God; let God deliver him now, if he wants to; for he said, 'I am God's Son.'" [44]The bandits who were crucified with him also taunted him in the same way.

The Death of Jesus

▶ See Mark 15.33–41; Luke 23.44–49

45 From noon on, darkness came over the whole land[d] until three in the afternoon. [46]And about three o'clock Jesus cried with a loud voice, "Eli, Eli, lema sabachthani?" that is, "My God, my God, why have you forsaken me?" [47]When some of the bystanders heard it, they said, "This man is calling for Elijah." [48]At once one of them ran and got a sponge, filled it with sour wine, put it on a stick, and gave it to him to drink. [49]But the others said, "Wait, let us see whether Elijah will come to save him."[e] [50]Then Jesus cried again with a loud voice and breathed his last.[f] [51]At that moment

the curtain of the temple was torn in two, from top to bottom. The earth shook, and the rocks were split. [52]The tombs also were opened, and many bodies of the saints who had fallen asleep

27.51 A Curtain Is Torn

At Jesus' death, the massive, thick curtain in the temple in Jerusalem ripped in two. This curtain sealed off the most holy place. No one except the high priest was allowed into the presence of God in that most holy place. And the high priest was permitted in only once a year, on a special day. The author of Hebrews looked on the miraculously torn curtain as symbolic: it signified the immediate access to God made possible by Jesus' death (Hebrews 10.19–20).

were raised. [53]After his resurrection they came out of the tombs and entered the holy city and appeared to many. [54]Now when the centurion and those with him, who were keeping watch over Jesus, saw the earthquake and what took place, they were terrified and said, "Truly this man was God's Son!"[g]

55 Many women were also there, looking on from a distance; they had followed Jesus from Galilee and had provided for him. [56]Among them were Mary Magdalene, and Mary the mother of James and Joseph, and the mother of the sons of Zebedee.

The Burial of Jesus

▶ See Mark 15.42–47; Luke 23.50–56; John 19.38–42

57 When it was evening, there came a rich man from Arimathea, named Joseph, who was also a disciple of Jesus. [58]He went to Pilate and asked for the body of Jesus; then Pilate ordered it to be given to him. [59]So Joseph took the body and wrapped it in a clean linen cloth [60]and laid it in his own new tomb, which he had hewn in the rock. He then rolled a great stone to the door of the tomb and went away. [61]Mary Magdalene and the other Mary were there, sitting opposite the tomb.

The Guard at the Tomb

62 The next day, that is, after the day of Preparation, the chief priests and the Pharisees gathered before Pilate [63]and said, "Sir, we remember what that impostor said while he was still alive, 'After three days I will rise again.' [64]Therefore command the tomb to be made secure until the third day; otherwise his disciples may go and steal him away, and tell the people, 'He has been raised

---

[z] Gk the praetorium   [a] Other ancient authorities add in order that what had been spoken through the prophet might be fulfilled, "They divided my clothes among themselves, and for my clothing they cast lots."   [b] Or blasphemed   [c] Or is he unable to save himself?   [d] Or earth   [e] Other ancient authorities add And another took a spear and pierced his side, and out came water and blood   [f] Or gave up his spirit   [g] Or a son of God

from the dead,' and the last deception would be worse than the first." 65Pilate said to them, "You have a guard[h] of soldiers; go, make it as secure as you can."[i] 66So they went with the guard and made the tomb secure by sealing the stone.

The Resurrection of Jesus

▶ *See Mark 16.1–8; Luke 24.1–10*

28 After the sabbath, as the first day of the week was dawning, Mary Magdalene and the other Mary went to see the tomb. 2And suddenly there was a great earthquake; for an angel of the Lord, descending from heaven, came and rolled back the stone and sat on it. 3His appearance was like lightning, and his clothing white as snow. 4For fear of him the guards shook and became like dead men. 5But the angel said to the

28.4 Coverup

Throughout Jesus' extraordinary life, people found all sorts of reasons to doubt him, even in the face of unexplainable events. These guards, for instance, were virtual eyewitnesses of the greatest miracle of all time, Jesus' resurrection. Yet a few hours later they made a deal with the chief priests to cover up the story (verses 11–15). Then, as now, people who choose not to believe can always find a rationale.

women, "Do not be afraid; I know that you are looking for Jesus who was crucified. 6He is not here; for he has been raised, as he said. Come, see the place where he[j] lay. 7Then go quickly and tell

his disciples, 'He has been raised from the dead,[k] and indeed he is going ahead of you to Galilee; there you will see him.' This is my message for you." 8So they left the tomb quickly with fear and great joy, and ran to tell his disciples. 9Suddenly Jesus met them and said, "Greetings!" And they came to him, took hold of his feet, and worshiped him. 10Then Jesus said to them, "Do not be afraid; go and tell my brothers to go to Galilee; there they will see me."

The Report of the Guard

11 While they were going, some of the guard went into the city and told the chief priests everything that had happened. 12After the priests[l] had assembled with the elders, they devised a plan to give a large sum of money to the soldiers, 13telling them, "You must say, 'His disciples came by night and stole him away while we were asleep.' 14If this comes to the governor's ears, we will satisfy him and keep you out of trouble." 15So they took the money and did as they were directed. And this story is still told among the Jews to this day.

The Commissioning of the Disciples

16 Now the eleven disciples went to Galilee, to the mountain to which Jesus had directed them. 17When they saw him, they worshiped him; but some doubted. 18And Jesus came and said to them, "All authority in heaven and on earth has been given to me. 19Go therefore and make disciples of all nations, baptizing them in the name of the Father and of the Son and of the Holy Spirit, 20and teaching them to obey everything that I have commanded you. And remember, I am with you always, to the end of the age."[m]

---

[h] Or *Take a guard*   [i] Gk *you know how*   [j] Other ancient authorities read *the Lord*   [k] Other ancient authorities lack *from the dead*   [l] Gk *they*   [m] Other ancient authorities add *Amen*

MARK

The Fast-paced Gospel
Mark reads like the script for an action movie

BRIEF INTRODUCTORY CREDITS FLASH ON the screen. Then the camera pans across an expanse of bleached sand, inhabited mostly by scorpions, lizards, and tarantulas. At last, through the shimmering heat, a lone figure appears: an eccentric wearing camel's hair and crying something in the thin desert air. So begins Mark.

At once his fame began to spread throughout the surrounding region of Galilee. 1.28

It helps to imagine the book of Mark as a concisely edited documentary film. Unlike the other Gospels, this one has little tolerance for dialogue and personal reflection. The author is writing to a restless, impatient audience—people more like moviegoers than readers.

Mark deftly controls camera angles, alternately panning across large crowds and zooming in on individual people. He leaves no doubt about the main character. After the opening shot of John the Baptist, he moves Jesus to center stage and the camera follows him everywhere.

An Emphasis on Action

Those who look for an outline in Mark come away baffled: all the spliced-together scenes defy structure. One author observed that Mark shows Jesus "scattering miracles like rice at a wedding." Matthew and Luke each give four chapters of historical warm-up before recording a miracle by Jesus; Mark covers three miracles and a group event in the first chapter alone.

In contrast to all its action scenes, the book includes only a sampling of Jesus' parables. It focuses on events, not speeches or editorial comments. Mark shows gymnasium-size crowds pressing around Jesus so tightly that he launches a boat to escape them. Wherever he goes, the crowds follow, buzzing about his remarkable life. "Is he the Holy One of God?" "Is he mad?" "Isn't this the carpenter's boy?"

A Breathless Pace

By dispensing with all but bare-bones action, Mark manages to achieve more drama than perhaps any other biblical writer. Action guarantees an attentive audience, and Mark jams sequences together breathlessly. *At once* the Spirit sends Jesus into the desert; *at once* the disciples respond to Jesus' call to follow him; Jesus' touch *immediately* heals a man with leprosy—42 times this book uses the Greek hurry-up adverb translated several different ways into English.

Characters rush from place to place, jostle among crowds, are astonished at mighty works. Mark is a Gospel of exclamation points, full of words like *amazed, astounded, terrified.* A phenomenon is loose on the earth, and the author is determined to capture its impact for future generations.

How to Read Mark

About 90 percent of Mark's content appears in the other three Gospels, but the book makes an ideal starting place for someone who knows little about Jesus. Its style—simple sentences, without complicated transitions or long speeches—makes understanding easier. In fact, Mark was probably written as a missionary book to people who knew next to nothing about the new Christian faith.

Except where he cites Jesus' own quotations, Mark quotes the Old Testament directly in only one place (1.2–3). In addition, Mark doesn't refer to the Old Testament Law, a striking difference from the other Gospels. Such facts indicate his book was written to a non-Jewish audience, probably the Romans.

You'll need no special instructions on reading Mark. This book's breezy style makes it as understandable as a newspaper. Because it loosely follows the chronology of Jesus' life, Mark offers an excellent introduction to the life of Jesus. As you read, stop and ponder the events Mark records. Why did the author select these facts? What meaning did they have for the people in Jesus' day? What about for you?

PEOPLE YOU'LL MEET IN MARK

JAMES (p. 1041)

3-TRACK READING PLAN

For an explanation and complete listing of the 3-track reading plan, turn to page 7.

TRACK 1: **Two-Week Courses on the Bible**
The Track 1 reading program on the Life and Teachings of Jesus includes two chapters from Mark. See page 7 for a complete listing of this course.

TRACK 2: **An Overview of Mark in 15 Days**
Reading Mark will give you a quick summary of Jesus' acts on this earth. For this reason, plan to spend two weeks reading all 16 chapters of Mark.

- ☐ Day 1. Read the Introduction to Mark, then chapter 1.
- ☐ Day 2. Read chapter 2's record of scenes from Jesus' life during a period of popular acclaim.
- ☐ Day 3. Read chapter 3, which shows Jesus calling his 12 disciples.
- ☐ Day 4. Read the brief parables and the account of the calming of a storm in chapter 4.
- ☐ Day 5. Mark 5 tells of three miracles of healing; note the different crowd reaction to each one.
- ☐ Day 6. Read chapter 6, which includes several famous miracles and also the story of John the Baptist's beheading.
- ☐ Day 7. Read chapter 7, which shows the Pharisees' opposition to Jesus beginning to mount.
- ☐ Day 8. As you read chapter 8, notice, on the one hand, Jesus' increasing popularity and, on the other, the growing tension that will eventually culminate in his death.
- ☐ Day 9. Read the account of Jesus' transfiguration and the other events recorded in chapter 9.
- ☐ Day 10. Mark 10 records Jesus' teaching on divorce, humility, and wealth.
- ☐ Day 11. Read chapter 11's account of Jesus' entry into Jerusalem for the last week of his life.
- ☐ Day 12. Read chapter 12, which includes Jesus' teaching on a variety of topics.
- ☐ Day 13. Read chapter 13 for Jesus' predictions of the end of the world.
- ☐ Day 14. Mark 14 records the events leading up to Jesus' arrest, as well as his trial before a Jewish court.
- ☐ Day 15. Read chapters 15 and 16, which report the last events in Jesus' life on earth.

Now turn to page 9 for your next Track 2 reading project.

TRACK 3: **All of Mark in 15 Days**
After you have read through Mark, turn to pages 10–14 for your next Track 3 reading project.

☐1 ☐2 ☐3 ☐4 ☐5 ☐6 ☐7 ☐8
☐9 ☐10 ☐11 ☐12 ☐13 ☐14 ☐15–16

The Proclamation of John the Baptist

▶ *See Matthew 3.1–11; Luke 3.2–16*

1 The beginning of the good news*a* of Jesus Christ, the Son of God.*b*

2 As it is written in the prophet Isaiah,*c*

"See, I am sending my messenger ahead of you,*d*
who will prepare your way;

3 the voice of one crying out in the wilderness:
'Prepare the way of the Lord,
make his paths straight,'"

4John the baptizer appeared*e* in the wilderness, proclaiming a baptism of repentance for the forgiveness of sins. 5And people from the whole Judean countryside and all the people of Jerusalem were going out to him, and were baptized by him in the river Jordan, confessing their sins. 6Now John was clothed with camel's hair, with a leather belt around his waist, and he ate locusts and wild honey. 7He proclaimed, "The one who is more powerful than I is coming after me; I am not worthy to stoop down and untie the thong of his sandals. 8I have baptized you with*f* water; but he will baptize you with*f* the Holy Spirit."

The Baptism of Jesus

▶ *See Matthew 3.13–17; 4.1–11; Luke 3.21–22; 4.1–13*

9 In those days Jesus came from Nazareth of Galilee and was baptized by John in the Jordan. 10And just as he was coming up out of the water, he saw the heavens torn apart and the Spirit descending like a dove on him. 11And a voice came from heaven, "You are my Son, the Beloved;*g* with you I am well pleased."

The Temptation of Jesus

12 And the Spirit immediately drove him out into the wilderness. 13He was in the wilderness forty days, tempted by Satan; and he was with the wild beasts; and the angels waited on him.

The Beginning of the Galilean Ministry

▶ *See Matthew 4.18–22; Luke 5.2–11; John 1.35–42*

14 Now after John was arrested, Jesus came to Galilee, proclaiming the good news*a* of God,*h* 15and saying, "The time is fulfilled, and the kingdom of God has come near;*i* repent, and believe in the good news."*a*

Jesus Calls the First Disciples

16 As Jesus passed along the Sea of Galilee, he saw Simon and his brother Andrew casting a net into the sea—for they were fishermen. 17And Jesus said to them, "Follow me and I will make you fish for people." 18And immediately they left their nets and followed him. 19As he went a little farther, he saw James son of Zebedee and his brother John, who were in their boat mending the

1.14 Into the Countryside

Possibly, Jesus withdrew to Galilee in order to escape the political turmoil spawned by John's arrest. He went on to spend almost two-thirds of his working life in this rather remote northern region, the lushest and most picturesque portion of Palestine. Except for festival times when he traveled to Jerusalem, Jesus showed a marked preference for rural and small-town areas.

nets. 20Immediately he called them; and they left their father Zebedee in the boat with the hired men, and followed him.

The Man with an Unclean Spirit

▶ *See Luke 4.31–37*

21 They went to Capernaum; and when the sabbath came, he entered the synagogue and taught. 22They were astounded at his teaching, for he taught them as one having authority, and not as the scribes. 23Just then there was in their synagogue a man with an unclean spirit, 24and he cried out, "What have you to do with us, Jesus of Nazareth? Have you come to destroy us? I know who you are, the Holy One of God." 25But Jesus rebuked him, saying, "Be silent, and come out of him!" 26And the unclean spirit, convulsing him and crying with a loud voice, came out of him. 27They were all amazed, and they kept on asking one another, "What is this? A new teaching—with authority! He*j* commands even the unclean spirits, and they obey him." 28At once his fame began to spread throughout the surrounding region of Galilee.

Jesus Heals Many at Simon's House

▶ *See Matthew 8.14–17; Luke 4.38–41*

29 As soon as they*k* left the synagogue, they entered the house of Simon and Andrew, with James and John. 30Now Simon's mother-in-law was in bed with a fever, and they told him about her at once. 31He came and took her by the hand and lifted her up. Then the fever left her, and she began to serve them.

32 That evening, at sundown, they brought to him all who were sick or possessed with demons. 33And the whole city was gathered around the door. 34And he cured many who were sick with

---

a Or *gospel*   *b* Other ancient authorities lack *the Son of God*   *c* Other ancient authorities read *in the prophets*
d Gk *before your face*   *e* Other ancient authorities read *John was baptizing*   *f* Or *in*   *g* Or *my beloved Son*
h Other ancient authorities read *of the kingdom*   *i* Or *is at hand*   *j* Or *A new teaching! With authority he*
k Other ancient authorities read *he*

various diseases, and cast out many demons; and he would not permit the demons to speak, because they knew him.

A Preaching Tour in Galilee

▶ See Luke 4.42–43

35 In the morning, while it was still very dark, he got up and went out to a deserted place, and there he prayed. [36]And Simon and his companions hunted for him. [37]When they found him, they said to him, "Everyone is searching for you." [38]He answered, "Let us go on to the neighboring towns, so that I may proclaim the message there also; for that is what I came out to do." [39]And he went throughout Galilee, proclaiming the message in their synagogues and casting out demons.

Jesus Cleanses a Leper

▶ See Matthew 8.2–4; Luke 5.12–14

40 A leper[l] came to him begging him, and kneeling[m] he said to him, "If you choose, you can make me clean." [41]Moved with pity,[n] Jesus[o] stretched out his hand and touched him, and said to him, "I do choose. Be made clean!" [42]Immediately the leprosy[l] left him, and he was made clean. [43]After sternly warning him he sent him away at once, [44]saying to him, "See that you say nothing to anyone; but go, show yourself to the priest, and offer for your cleansing what Moses commanded, as a testimony to them." [45]But he went out and began to proclaim it freely, and to spread the word, so that Jesus[o] could no longer go into a town openly, but stayed out in the country; and people came to him from every quarter.

Jesus Heals a Paralytic

▶ See Matthew 9.2–8; Luke 5.18–26

2 When he returned to Capernaum after some days, it was reported that he was at home. [2]So many gathered around that there was no longer room for them, not even in front of the door; and he was speaking the word to them. [3]Then some people[p] came, bringing to him a paralyzed man, carried by four of them. [4]And when they could not bring him to Jesus because of the crowd, they removed the roof above him; and after having dug through it, they let down the mat on which the paralytic lay. [5]When Jesus saw their faith, he said to the paralytic, "Son, your sins are forgiven." [6]Now some of the scribes were sitting there, questioning in their hearts, [7]"Why does this fellow speak in this way? It is blasphemy! Who can forgive sins but God alone?" [8]At once Jesus perceived in his spirit that they were discussing these questions among themselves; and he said to them, "Why do you raise such questions in your hearts?

[9]Which is easier, to say to the paralytic, 'Your sins are forgiven,' or to say, 'Stand up and take your mat and walk'? [10]But so that you may know that the Son of Man has authority on earth to forgive sins"—he said to the paralytic— [11]"I say to you, stand up, take your mat and go to your home."

2.4 Barriers to the Disabled

One disabled person has pointed out this story's relevance to the modern controversy over accessibility. "Any disabled person can supply lots of stories like this one—entering a church through the sacristy (or, worse, having to be carried up the front steps like a child), coming into a lecture hall by means of a freight elevator and then through the kitchen or utility room before being able to join the 'normal' people who come in the front door." The paralytic's friends found a rather drastic solution to the problem, and Jesus, impressed, honored their (plural) faith.

[12]And he stood up, and immediately took the mat and went out before all of them; so that they were all amazed and glorified God, saying, "We have never seen anything like this!"

Jesus Calls Levi

▶ See Matthew 9.9–13; Luke 5.27–32

13 Jesus[q] went out again beside the sea; the whole crowd gathered around him, and he taught them. [14]As he was walking along, he saw Levi son of Alphaeus sitting at the tax booth, and he said to him, "Follow me." And he got up and followed him.

15 And as he sat at dinner[r] in Levi's[s] house, many tax collectors and sinners were also sitting[t] with Jesus and his disciples—for there were many who followed him. [16]When the scribes of[u] the Pharisees saw that he was eating with sinners and tax collectors, they said to his disciples, "Why does he eat[v] with tax collectors and sinners?" [17]When Jesus heard this, he said to them, "Those who are well have no need of a physician, but those who are sick; I have come to call not the righteous but sinners."

The Question about Fasting

▶ See Matthew 9.14–17; Luke 5.33–38

18 Now John's disciples and the Pharisees were fasting; and people[p] came and said to him, "Why do John's disciples and the disciples of the Pharisees fast, but your disciples do not fast?"

---

[l] The terms *leper* and *leprosy* can refer to several diseases   [m] Other ancient authorities lack *kneeling*   [n] Other ancient authorities read *anger*   [o] Gk *he*   [p] Gk *they*   [q] Gk *He*   [r] Gk *reclined*   [s] Gk *his*   [t] Gk *reclining*   [u] Other ancient authorities read *and*   [v] Other ancient authorities add *and drink*

[19]Jesus said to them, "The wedding guests cannot fast while the bridegroom is with them, can they? As long as they have the bridegroom with them, they cannot fast. [20]The days will come when the bridegroom is taken away from them, and then they will fast on that day.

[21] "No one sews a piece of unshrunk cloth on an old cloak; otherwise, the patch pulls away from it, the new from the old, and a worse tear is made. [22]And no one puts new wine into old wineskins; otherwise, the wine will burst the skins, and the wine is lost, and so are the skins; but one puts new wine into fresh wineskins."[w]

Pronouncement about the Sabbath

▶ See Matthew 12.1–14; Luke 6.1–11

23 One sabbath he was going through the grainfields; and as they made their way his disciples began to pluck heads of grain. [24]The Pharisees said to him, "Look, why are they doing what is not lawful on the sabbath?" [25]And he said to them, "Have you never read what David did when he and his companions were hungry and in need of food? [26]He entered the house of God, when Abiathar was high priest, and ate the bread of the Presence, which it is not lawful for any but the priests to eat, and he gave some to his companions." [27]Then he said to them, "The sabbath was made for humankind, and not humankind for the sabbath; [28]so the Son of Man is lord even of the sabbath."

The Man with a Withered Hand

3 Again he entered the synagogue, and a man was there who had a withered hand. [2]They watched him to see whether he would cure him on the sabbath, so that they might accuse him. [3]And he said to the man who had the withered hand, "Come forward." [4]Then he said to them, "Is it lawful to do good or to do harm on the sabbath, to save life or to kill?" But they were silent. [5]He looked around at them with anger; he was grieved at their hardness of heart and said to the man, "Stretch out your hand." He stretched it out, and his hand was restored. [6]The Pharisees went out and immediately conspired with the Herodians against him, how to destroy him.

A Multitude at the Seaside

▶ See Matthew 12.15–16; Luke 6.17–19

7 Jesus departed with his disciples to the sea, and a great multitude from Galilee followed him; [8]hearing all that he was doing, they came to him in great numbers from Judea, Jerusalem, Idumea, beyond the Jordan, and the region around Tyre and Sidon. [9]He told his disciples to have a boat ready for him because of the crowd, so that they would not crush him; [10]for he had cured many, so that all who had diseases pressed upon him to touch him. [11]Whenever the unclean spirits saw him, they fell down before him and shouted, "You are the Son of God!" [12]But he sternly ordered them not to make him known.

Jesus Appoints the Twelve

13 He went up the mountain and called to him those whom he wanted, and they came to him. [14]And he appointed twelve, whom he also named apostles,[x] to be with him, and to be sent out to proclaim the message, [15]and to have authority to cast out demons. [16]So he appointed the twelve:[y] Simon (to whom he gave the name Peter); [17]James son of Zebedee and John the brother of James (to whom he gave the name Boanerges, that is, Sons of Thunder); [18]and Andrew, and Philip, and Bartholomew, and Matthew, and Thomas, and James son of Alphaeus, and Thaddaeus, and Simon the Cananaean, [19]and Judas Iscariot, who betrayed him.

Jesus and Beelzebul

▶ See Matthew 12.25–29; Luke 11.17–22

Then he went home; [20]and the crowd came together again, so that they could not even eat. [21]When his family heard it, they went out to restrain him, for people were saying, "He has gone out of his mind." [22]And the scribes who came down from Jerusalem said, "He has Beelzebul, and by the ruler of the demons he casts out demons." [23] And he called them to him, and spoke to them in parables, "How can Satan cast out Satan? [24]If a kingdom is divided against itself, that kingdom cannot stand. [25]And if a house is divided against itself, that house will not be able to stand. [26]And if Satan has risen up against himself and is divided, he cannot stand, but his end has come. [27]But no one can enter a strong man's house and plunder his property without first tying up the strong man; then indeed the house can be plundered.

28 "Truly I tell you, people will be forgiven for their sins and whatever blasphemies they utter; [29]but whoever blasphemes against the Holy Spirit can never have forgiveness, but is guilty of an eternal sin"— [30]for they had said, "He has an unclean spirit."

The True Kindred of Jesus

▶ See Matthew 12.46–50; Luke 8.19–21

31 Then his mother and his brothers came; and standing outside, they sent to him and called him. [32]A crowd was sitting around him; and they

---

[w] Other ancient authorities lack *but one puts new wine into fresh wineskins* [x] Other ancient authorities lack *whom he also named apostles* [y] Other ancient authorities lack *So he appointed the twelve*

said to him, "Your mother and your brothers and sisters[z] are outside, asking for you." 33And he replied, "Who are my mother and my brothers?" 34And looking at those who sat around him, he said, "Here are my mother and my brothers! 35Whoever does the will of God is my brother and sister and mother."

[z] Other ancient authorities lack and sisters

The Parable of the Sower

▶ See Matthew 13.1–15,18–23; Luke 8.4–15

4 Again he began to teach beside the sea. Such a very large crowd gathered around him that he got into a boat on the sea and sat there, while the whole crowd was beside the sea on the land.

Why Come to Earth?
The only way God could get through

> They were filled with great awe and said to one another, "Who then is this, that even the wind and the sea obey him?" 4.41

AMERICAN RADIO BROADCASTER PAUL HARVEY once told a modern parable about a religious skeptic who worked as a farmer. One raw winter night the man heard an irregular thumping sound against the kitchen storm door. He went to a window and watched as tiny, shivering sparrows, attracted to the evident warmth inside, beat in vain against the glass.

Touched, the farmer bundled up and trudged through fresh snow to open the barn door for the struggling birds. He turned on the lights and tossed some hay in a corner. But the sparrows, which had scattered in all directions when he emerged from the house, hid in the darkness, afraid.

The man tried various tactics to get them into the barn. He laid down a trail of Saltine cracker crumbs to direct them. He tried circling behind the birds to drive them toward the barn. Nothing worked. He, a huge, alien creature, had terrified them; the birds couldn't comprehend that he actually desired to help.

The farmer withdrew to his house and watched the doomed sparrows through a window. As he stared, a thought hit him like lightning from a clear blue sky: *If only I could become a bird—one of them—just for a moment. Then I wouldn't frighten them so. I could show them the way to warmth and safety.*

At the same moment, another thought dawned on him. He had grasped the reason Jesus was born.

When God Came to Earth

A man becoming a bird is nothing compared to God becoming a man. The concept of a sovereign eternal being who created the universe, confining himself to a human body was—and is—too much for some people to believe. But how else could God truly communicate with us?

We don't know what God looked like as a man; no Gospel writer described the physical appearance of Jesus. But, in other ways, Mark painted a full picture of his humanity. Jesus, who claimed to be God, didn't have a supernatural "glow" about him. His own neighbors and family marveled that he seemed so, well, normal.

Mark does not diminish Jesus. He shows the power of a man who healed the blind with a simple touch (8.25), and the authority of a teacher so captivating that people sat three days straight, with empty stomachs, just to hear him (8.2). Even after Jesus hushed them, people wouldn't stop talking about his miracles.

But Mark also reveals the full range of Jesus' emotions: a surge of compassion for a person with leprosy (1.41), a deep sigh in response to nagging Pharisees (8.12), a look of anger and distress at cold-hearted legalists (3.5), and then an awful cry on the cross, "My God, my God, why have you forsaken me?" (15.34). Jesus was sometimes witty, and he sometimes cried. He got tired: Five times, Mark records, he sought a quiet place for rest away from the crowds.

Like No One Else

Jesus was like no other person who ever lived. Twelve men left their jobs and families at a single command to follow him. Yet Jesus was also fully "one of us." He needed food and friends. He got lonely and tired. He showed anger and disappointment. Because Jesus experienced all we experience as human beings, he can understand us completely, and share in our joys and sorrows.

Mark portrays both sides of Jesus—the divine and the human. The disciples needed to see both dimensions to give their lives to him.

Life Questions: Suppose that Jesus had never come, that God had merely sent an elaborate love note. What difference would that make?

[2]He began to teach them many things in parables, and in his teaching he said to them: [3]"Listen! A sower went out to sow. [4]And as he sowed, some seed fell on the path, and the birds came and ate

3.30 Out of His Mind?

Jesus provoked a strong reaction in just about everyone. In this instance, Jesus' own family members questioned his sanity, and teachers of the law wondered about demon-possession. He aroused the fiercest opposition among his own neighbors and among the religious "professionals" of his day. But, as Mark shows, throngs of other people were amazed by his authoritative teaching and his miraculous powers. Personal contact with Jesus left virtually no one unmoved.

it up. [5]Other seed fell on rocky ground, where it did not have much soil, and it sprang up quickly, since it had no depth of soil. [6]And when the sun rose, it was scorched; and since it had no root, it withered away. [7]Other seed fell among thorns, and the thorns grew up and choked it, and it yielded no grain. [8]Other seed fell into good soil and brought forth grain, growing up and increasing and yielding thirty and sixty and a hundredfold." [9]And he said, "Let anyone with ears to hear listen!"

The Purpose of the Parables

[10]When he was alone, those who were around him along with the twelve asked him about the parables. [11]And he said to them, "To you has been given the secret[a] of the kingdom of God, but for those outside, everything comes in parables; [12]in order that

'they may indeed look, but not perceive,
and may indeed listen, but not
understand;
so that they may not turn again and be
forgiven.'"

[13]And he said to them, "Do you not understand this parable? Then how will you understand all the parables? [14]The sower sows the word. [15]These are the ones on the path where the word is sown: when they hear, Satan immediately comes and takes away the word that is sown in them. [16]And these are the ones sown on rocky ground: when they hear the word, they immediately receive it with joy. [17]But they have no root, and endure only for a while; then, when trouble or persecution arises on account of the word, immediately they fall away.[b] [18]And others are those sown among the thorns: these are the ones who hear the word, [19]but the cares of the world, and the lure of wealth, and the desire for other things

come in and choke the word, and it yields nothing. [20]And these are the ones sown on the good soil: they hear the word and accept it and bear fruit, thirty and sixty and a hundredfold."

A Lamp under a Bushel Basket

[21]He said to them, "Is a lamp brought in to be put under the bushel basket, or under the bed, and not on the lampstand? [22]For there is nothing hidden, except to be disclosed; nor is anything secret, except to come to light. [23]Let anyone with ears to hear listen!" [24]And he said to them, "Pay attention to what you hear; the measure you give will be the measure you get, and still more will be given you. [25]For to those who have, more will be given; and from those who have nothing, even what they have will be taken away."

The Parable of the Growing Seed

[26]He also said, "The kingdom of God is as if someone would scatter seed on the ground, [27]and would sleep and rise night and day, and the seed would sprout and grow, he does not know how. [28]The earth produces of itself, first the stalk, then the head, then the full grain in the head. [29]But when the grain is ripe, at once he goes in with his sickle, because the harvest has come."

The Parable of the Mustard Seed

▶ *See Matthew 13.31–32; Luke 13.18–19*

[30]He also said, "With what can we compare the kingdom of God, or what parable will we use

4.30 Scarce Parables

Unlike Matthew and Luke, Mark devotes little space to parables, the unique form of teaching Jesus often relied on. Yet Mark includes as many miracles as does any Gospel. Clearly, this book emphasizes action over words.

for it? [31]It is like a mustard seed, which, when sown upon the ground, is the smallest of all the seeds on earth; [32]yet when it is sown it grows up and becomes the greatest of all shrubs, and puts forth large branches, so that the birds of the air can make nests in its shade."

The Use of Parables

[33]With many such parables he spoke the word to them, as they were able to hear it; [34]he did not speak to them except in parables, but he explained everything in private to his disciples.

Jesus Stills a Storm

▶ *See Matthew 8.18,23–27; Luke 8.22–25*

[35]On that day, when evening had come, he said to them, "Let us go across to the other side."

---

[a] Or *mystery*   [b] Or *stumble*

³⁶And leaving the crowd behind, they took him with them in the boat, just as he was. Other boats were with him. ³⁷A great windstorm arose, and the waves beat into the boat, so that the boat was already being swamped. ³⁸But he was in the stern, asleep on the cushion; and they woke him up and said to him, "Teacher, do you not care that we are perishing?" ³⁹He woke up and rebuked the wind, and said to the sea, "Peace! Be still!" Then the wind ceased, and there was a dead calm. ⁴⁰He said to them, "Why are you afraid? Have you still no faith?" ⁴¹And they were filled with great awe and said to one another, "Who then is this, that even the wind and the sea obey him?"

Jesus Heals the Gerasene Demoniac

▶ See Matthew 8.28–34; Luke 8.26–39

5 They came to the other side of the sea, to the country of the Gerasenes.ᶜ ²And when he had stepped out of the boat, immediately a man out of the tombs with an unclean spirit met him. ³He lived among the tombs; and no one could restrain him any more, even with a chain; ⁴for he had often been restrained with shackles and chains, but the chains he wrenched apart, and the shackles he broke in pieces; and no one had the strength to subdue him. ⁵Night and day among the tombs and on the mountains he was always howling and bruising himself with stones. ⁶When he saw Jesus from a distance, he ran and bowed down before him; ⁷and he shouted at the top of his voice, "What have you to do with me, Jesus, Son of the Most High God? I adjure you by God, do not torment me." ⁸For he had said to him, "Come out of the man, you unclean spirit!" ⁹Then Jesusᵈ asked him, "What is your name?" He replied, "My name is Legion; for we are many." ¹⁰He begged him earnestly not to send them out of the country. ¹¹Now there on the hillside a great herd of swine was feeding; ¹²and the unclean spiritsᵉ begged him, "Send us into the swine; let us enter them." ¹³So he gave them permission. And the unclean spirits came out and entered the swine; and the herd, numbering about two thousand, rushed down the steep bank into the sea, and were drowned in the sea.

14 The swineherds ran off and told it in the city and in the country. Then people came to see what it was that had happened. ¹⁵They came to Jesus and saw the demoniac sitting there, clothed and in his right mind, the very man who had had the legion; and they were afraid. ¹⁶Those who had seen what had happened to the demoniac and to the swine reported it. ¹⁷Then they began to beg Jesusᶠ to leave their neighborhood. ¹⁸As he was getting into the boat, the man who had been possessed by demons begged him that he might be with him. ¹⁹But Jesusᵈ refused, and said to him,

"Go home to your friends, and tell them how much the Lord has done for you, and what mercy he has shown you." ²⁰And he went away and began to proclaim in the Decapolis how much Jesus had done for him; and everyone was amazed.

A Girl Restored to Life and a Woman Healed

▶ See Matthew 9.18–26; Luke 8.41–56

21 When Jesus had crossed again in the boatᵍ to the other side, a great crowd gathered around him; and he was by the sea. ²²Then one of the leaders of the synagogue named Jairus came and, when he saw him, fell at his feet ²³and begged him repeatedly, "My little daughter is at the point of death. Come and lay your hands on her, so that she may be made well, and live." ²⁴So he went with him.

And a large crowd followed him and pressed in on him. ²⁵Now there was a woman who had been suffering from hemorrhages for twelve years. ²⁶She had endured much under many physicians, and had spent all that she had; and she was no better, but rather grew worse. ²⁷She had heard about Jesus, and came up behind him in the crowd and touched his cloak, ²⁸for she said, "If I but touch his clothes, I will be made well." ²⁹Immediately her hemorrhage stopped; and she felt in her body that she was healed of her disease. ³⁰Immediately aware that power had gone forth from him, Jesus turned about in the crowd and said, "Who touched my clothes?" ³¹And his disciples said to him, "You see the crowd pressing in on you; how can you say, 'Who touched me?'" ³²He looked all around to see who had done it. ³³But the woman, knowing what had happened to her, came in fear and trembling, fell down before him, and told him the whole truth. ³⁴He said to her, "Daughter, your faith has made you well; go in peace, and be healed of your disease."

35 While he was still speaking, some people came from the leader's house to say, "Your daughter is dead. Why trouble the teacher any further?" ³⁶But overhearingʰ what they said,

5.43 Don't Tell

Seven times in Mark, Jesus asked people who had seen a miracle not to tell anyone. He was protecting himself from the crush of crowds that flocked to him when word of his miracles spread—as it usually did, despite his orders— and from the opposition forces who were already tailing him. Jesus recognized early on that the kind of excitement generated by miracles did not automatically convert into the life-changing faith he sought to arouse.

ᶜ Other ancient authorities read *Gergesenes*; others, *Gadarenes* ancient authorities lack *in the boat* ᵈ Gk *he* ᵉ Gk *they* ᶠ Gk *him* ᵍ Other
ʰ Or *ignoring*; other ancient authorities read *hearing*

Jesus said to the leader of the synagogue, "Do not fear, only believe." 37He allowed no one to follow him except Peter, James, and John, the brother of James. 38When they came to the house of the leader of the synagogue, he saw a commotion, people weeping and wailing loudly. 39When he had entered, he said to them, "Why do you make a commotion and weep? The child is not dead but sleeping." 40And they laughed at him. Then he put them all outside, and took the child's father and mother and those who were with him, and went in where the child was. 41He took her by the hand and said to her, "Talitha cum," which means, "Little girl, get up!" 42And immediately the girl got up and began to walk about (she was twelve years of age). At this they were overcome with amazement. 43He strictly ordered them that no one should know this, and told them to give her something to eat.

i Other ancient authorities read *son of the carpenter and of Mary*

The Rejection of Jesus at Nazareth

▶ See Matthew 13.54–58

6 He left that place and came to his hometown, and his disciples followed him. 2On the sabbath he began to teach in the synagogue, and many who heard him were astounded. They said, "Where did this man get all this? What is this wisdom that has been given to him? What deeds of power are being done by his hands! 3Is not this the carpenter, the son of Mary*i* and brother of James and Joses and Judas and Simon, and are not his sisters here with us?" And they took offense*j* at him. 4Then Jesus said to them, "Prophets are not without honor, except in their hometown, and among their own kin, and in their own house." 5And he could do no deed of power there, except that he laid his hands on a few sick people and cured them. 6And he was amazed at their unbelief.

j Or *stumbled*

Eyewitness Reports
Where did Mark get his facts?

> He allowed no one to follow him except Peter, James, and John, the brother of James. 5.37

WHEN PEOPLE TRANSLATE THE BIBLE into a new language, they have a lot of explaining to do. How do you convey Christianity to someone who has never heard of Abraham or Moses or the apostles Peter and Paul? Where do you start?

More often than not, translators begin with the book of Mark. Its simple sentences and brief, action-filled scenes allow for easier translation. It reads like a newspaper. And the book seems written for a foreign culture (perhaps the Romans) in the first place: Common Jewish customs are explained in parentheses.

The Peter Connection

Perhaps the most compelling feature of Mark to an unfamiliar reader, though, is its vividness. It has the feel of an eyewitness account. Those who study such things have concluded that Mark probably got his facts from Peter, one of Jesus' intimate disciples. Peter, or someone like him, provided believable, close-up details.

Jesus spent his time in the desert "with the wild beasts" (1.13). When he went to pray, he got up "in the morning, while it was still very dark" (1.35)—a memorable detail to Jesus' disciples, sometimes known for their untimely sleeping habits. In the midst of a furious squall Jesus lay in a boat "asleep on the cushion" (4.38).

Whoever told Mark about the scene on the Mount of Transfiguration described Jesus' clothes as "dazzling white, such as no one on earth could bleach them" (9.3). And only Mark tells us that Peter sat with the guards during Jesus' trial, warming himself by the fire.

Why Details Matter

You can say these details don't matter, and it's true that Matthew and Luke recounted the same events without them. But as any good writer knows, details like these make a story come alive. Vivid images that stuck in the eyewitness's memory will likely stick with the reader as well.

For example, Mark could have matter-of-factly told of people being healed, but it just didn't happen that way. A blind man, "throwing off his cloak, he sprang up and came to Jesus" (10.50). And after the paralytic stood up, "This amazed everyone and they praised God, saying, 'We have never seen anything like this!'" (2.12).

Life Questions: As you read Mark, what "eyewitness details" stand out to you?

The Mission of the Twelve

▶ *See Matthew 10.1,9–14; Luke 9.1,3–5*

Then he went about among the villages teaching. [7]He called the twelve and began to send them out two by two, and gave them authority over the unclean spirits. [8]He ordered them to take nothing for their journey except a staff; no bread, no bag, no money in their belts; [9]but to wear sandals and not to put on two tunics. [10]He said to them, "Wherever you enter a house, stay there until you leave the place. [11]If any place will not welcome you and they refuse to hear you, as you leave, shake off the dust that is on your feet as a testimony against them." [12]So they went out and proclaimed that all should repent. [13]They cast out many demons, and anointed with oil many who were sick and cured them.

The Death of John the Baptist

▶ *See Matthew 14.1–12*

14 King Herod heard of it, for Jesus'[k] name had become known. Some were[l] saying, "John the baptizer has been raised from the dead; and for this reason these powers are at work in him." [15]But others said, "It is Elijah." And others said, "It is a prophet, like one of the prophets of old." [16]But when Herod heard of it, he said, "John, whom I beheaded, has been raised."

17 For Herod himself had sent men who arrested John, bound him, and put him in prison on account of Herodias, his brother Philip's wife, because Herod[m] had married her. [18]For John had been telling Herod, "It is not lawful for you to have your brother's wife." [19]And Herodias had a grudge against him, and wanted to kill him. But she could not, [20]for Herod feared John, knowing that he was a righteous and holy man, and he protected him. When he heard him, he was greatly perplexed;[n] and yet he liked to listen to him. [21]But an opportunity came when Herod on his birthday gave a banquet for his courtiers and officers and for the leaders of Galilee. [22]When his daughter Herodias[o] came in and danced, she pleased Herod and his guests; and the king said to the girl, "Ask me for whatever you wish, and I will give it." [23]And he solemnly swore to her, "Whatever you ask me, I will give you, even half of my kingdom." [24]She went out and said to her mother, "What should I ask for?" She replied, "The head of John the baptizer." [25]Immediately she rushed back to the king and requested, "I want you to give me at once the head of John the Baptist on a platter." [26]The king was deeply grieved; yet out of regard for his oaths and for the guests, he did not want to refuse her. [27]Immediately the king sent a soldier of the guard with orders to bring John's[k] head. He went and beheaded him in the prison, [28]brought his head on a platter, and gave it to the girl. Then the girl gave it to her mother. [29]When his disciples heard about it, they came and took his body, and laid it in a tomb.

6.29 New Recruits

Jesus got some of his original disciples from John the Baptist (see John 1.35,40), and after John's execution even more of them joined up with Jesus. But as Acts 19.1–5 makes clear, some of John's disciples never got the word about Jesus. Two decades after John's death, Paul stumbled across a group of loyal followers in Ephesus, hundreds of miles away.

Feeding the Five Thousand

▶ *See Matthew 14.13–21; Luke 9.10–17; John 6.5–13*

30 The apostles gathered around Jesus, and told him all that they had done and taught. [31]He said to them, "Come away to a deserted place all by yourselves and rest a while." For many were coming and going, and they had no leisure even

6.31 The Need to Get Away

Mark graphically shows the press of the crowds around Jesus. Wherever he went, people followed, bringing him the sick to heal and challenging him with questions. In five separate places (3.7–9; 6.31; 6.45; 7.24; 9.30) Mark records that Jesus took his disciples aside to some quiet place to escape the crush of the crowd.

to eat. [32]And they went away in the boat to a deserted place by themselves. [33]Now many saw them going and recognized them, and they hurried there on foot from all the towns and arrived ahead of them. [34]As he went ashore, he saw a great crowd; and he had compassion for them, because they were like sheep without a shepherd; and he began to teach them many things. [35]When it grew late, his disciples came to him and said, "This is a deserted place, and the hour is now very late; [36]send them away so that they may go into the surrounding country and villages and buy something for themselves to eat." [37]But he answered them, "You give them something to eat." They said to him, "Are we to go and buy two hundred denarii[p] worth of bread, and give it to them to eat?" [38]And he said to them, "How many loaves have you? Go and see." When they had found out, they said, "Five, and two fish." [39]Then he ordered them to get all the people to sit down in groups on the green grass. [40]So they sat down

---

k Gk *his*   *l* Other ancient authorities read *He was*   *m* Gk *he*   *n* Other ancient authorities read *he did many things*
o Other ancient authorities read *the daughter of Herodias herself*   *p* The denarius was the usual day's wage for a laborer

in groups of hundreds and of fifties. 41Taking the
five loaves and the two fish, he looked up to heav-
en, and blessed and broke the loaves, and gave
them to his disciples to set before the people; and
he divided the two fish among them all. 42And all
ate and were filled; 43and they took up twelve
baskets full of broken pieces and of the fish.
44Those who had eaten the loaves numbered five
thousand men.

Jesus Walks on the Water

▶ *See Matthew 14.22–32; John 6.15–21*

45 Immediately he made his disciples get into
the boat and go on ahead to the other side, to
Bethsaida, while he dismissed the crowd. 46After
saying farewell to them, he went up on the mountain to pray.
47 When evening came, the boat was out on
the sea, and he was alone on the land. 48When he
saw that they were straining at the oars against an
adverse wind, he came towards them early in the
morning, walking on the sea. He intended to pass
them by. 49But when they saw him walking on the
sea, they thought it was a ghost and cried out;
50for they all saw him and were terrified. But immediately he spoke to them and said, "Take heart,
it is I; do not be afraid." 51Then he got into the
boat with them and the wind ceased. And they
were utterly astounded, 52for they did not understand about the loaves, but their hearts were
hardened.

Healing the Sick in Gennesaret

53 When they had crossed over, they came to
land at Gennesaret and moored the boat. 54When
they got out of the boat, people at once recognized him, 55and rushed about that whole region
and began to bring the sick on mats to wherever
they heard he was. 56And wherever he went, into
villages or cities or farms, they laid the sick in the
marketplaces, and begged him that they might
touch even the fringe of his cloak; and all who
touched it were healed.

The Tradition of the Elders

▶ *See Matthew 15.1–20*

7 Now when the Pharisees and some of the
scribes who had come from Jerusalem gathered around him, 2they noticed that some of his
disciples were eating with defiled hands, that is,
without washing them. 3(For the Pharisees, and
all the Jews, do not eat unless they thoroughly
wash their hands,[q] thus observing the tradition
of the elders; 4and they do not eat anything from
the market unless they wash it;[r] and there are
also many other traditions that they observe, the
washing of cups, pots, and bronze kettles.[s]) 5So
the Pharisees and the scribes asked him, "Why do
your disciples not live[t] according to the tradition
of the elders, but eat with defiled hands?" 6He said
to them, "Isaiah prophesied rightly about you
hypocrites, as it is written,

> **7.3 Explaining Jewish Customs**
>
> ***The parenthetical remark in verses 3–4 explains a common Jewish custom of ceremonial hand-washing. Such remarks as these indicate Mark was writing to a non-Jewish audience who needed background explanations.***

'This people honors me with their lips,
but their hearts are far from me;
7 in vain do they worship me,
teaching human precepts as doctrines.'
8You abandon the commandment of God and
hold to human tradition."
9 Then he said to them, "You have a fine way
of rejecting the commandment of God in order to
keep your tradition! 10For Moses said, 'Honor
your father and your mother'; and, 'Whoever
speaks evil of father or mother must surely die.'
11But you say that if anyone tells father or mother,
'Whatever support you might have had from me
is Corban' (that is, an offering to God[u])— 12then
you no longer permit doing anything for a father
or mother, 13thus making void the word of God
through your tradition that you have handed on.
And you do many things like this."
14 Then he called the crowd again and said to
them, "Listen to me, all of you, and understand:
15there is nothing outside a person that by going
in can defile, but the things that come out are
what defile."[v]
17 When he had left the crowd and entered
the house, his disciples asked him about the parable. 18He said to them, "Then do you also fail to
understand? Do you not see that whatever goes
into a person from outside cannot defile, 19since
it enters, not the heart but the stomach, and goes
out into the sewer?" (Thus he declared all foods
clean.) 20And he said, "It is what comes out of a
person that defiles. 21For it is from within, from
the human heart, that evil intentions come: fornication, theft, murder, 22adultery, avarice, wickedness, deceit, licentiousness, envy, slander, pride,
folly. 23All these evil things come from within, and
they defile a person."

The Syrophoenician Woman's Faith

▶ *See Matthew 15.21–28*

24 From there he set out and went away to the

[q] Meaning of Gk uncertain [r] Other ancient authorities read *and when they come from the marketplace, they do not eat unless they purify themselves* [s] Other ancient authorities add *and beds* [t] Gk *walk* [u] Gk lacks *to God*
[v] Other ancient authorities add verse 16, *"Let anyone with ears to hear listen"*

region of Tyre.ʷ He entered a house and did not want anyone to know he was there. Yet he could not escape notice, ²⁵but a woman whose little daughter had an unclean spirit immediately heard about him, and she came and bowed down at his feet. ²⁶Now the woman was a Gentile, of Syrophoenician origin. She begged him to cast the demon out of her daughter. ²⁷He said to her, "Let the children be fed first, for it is not fair to take the children's food and throw it to the dogs." ²⁸But she answered him, "Sir,ˣ even the dogs under the table eat the children's crumbs." ²⁹Then he said to her, "For saying that, you may go—the demon has left your daughter." ³⁰So she went home, found the child lying on the bed, and the demon gone.

Jesus Cures a Deaf Man

▶ See Matthew 15.29–31

31   Then he returned from the region of Tyre, and went by way of Sidon towards the Sea of Galilee, in the region of the Decapolis. ³²They brought to him a deaf man who had an impediment in his speech; and they begged him to lay his hand on him. ³³He took him aside in private, away from the crowd, and put his fingers into his ears, and he spat and touched his tongue. ³⁴Then looking up to heaven, he sighed and said to him, "Ephphatha," that is, "Be opened." ³⁵And immediately his ears were opened, his tongue was released, and he spoke plainly. ³⁶Then Jesusʸ ordered them to tell no one; but the more he ordered them, the more zealously they proclaimed it. ³⁷They were astounded beyond measure, saying, "He has done everything well; he even makes the deaf to hear and the mute to speak."

Feeding the Four Thousand

▶ See Matthew 15.32–39

8 In those days when there was again a great crowd without anything to eat, he called his disciples and said to them, ²"I have compassion for the crowd, because they have been with me now for three days and have nothing to eat. ³If I send them away hungry to their homes, they will faint on the way—and some of them have come from a great distance." ⁴His disciples replied, "How can one feed these people with bread here in the desert?" ⁵He asked them, "How many loaves do you have?" They said, "Seven." ⁶Then he ordered the crowd to sit down on the ground; and he took the seven loaves, and after giving thanks he broke them and gave them to his disciples to distribute; and they distributed them to the crowd. ⁷They had also a few small fish; and after blessing them, he ordered that these too

should be distributed. ⁸They ate and were filled; and they took up the broken pieces left over, seven baskets full. ⁹Now there were about four thousand people. And he sent them away. ¹⁰And immediately he got into the boat with his disciples and went to the district of Dalmanutha.ᶻ

8.8 Lost in Translation

Often details get lost when a book is translated from one language to another. For example, the Greek word for the "baskets" used in the feeding of the 5,000 (6.43) is used for small, lunchbox-size baskets. In the feeding of the 4,000, leftovers filled seven large baskets; the same word describes the basket the apostle Paul would hide in to escape from Damascus (Acts 9.25).

The Demand for a Sign

11   The Pharisees came and began to argue with him, asking him for a sign from heaven, to test him. ¹²And he sighed deeply in his spirit and said, "Why does this generation ask for a sign? Truly I tell you, no sign will be given to this generation." ¹³And he left them, and getting into the boat again, he went across to the other side.

The Yeast of the Pharisees and of Herod

14   Now the disciplesᵃ had forgotten to bring any bread; and they had only one loaf with them in the boat. ¹⁵And he cautioned them, saying, "Watch out—beware of the yeast of the Pharisees and the yeast of Herod."ᵇ ¹⁶They said to one another, "It is because we have no bread." ¹⁷And becoming aware of it, Jesus said to them, "Why are you talking about having no bread? Do you still not perceive or understand? Are your hearts hardened? ¹⁸Do you have eyes, and fail to see? Do you have ears, and fail to hear? And do you not remember? ¹⁹When I broke the five loaves for the five thousand, how many baskets full of broken pieces did you collect?" They said to him, "Twelve." ²⁰"And the seven for the four thousand, how many baskets full of broken pieces did you collect?" And they said to him, "Seven." ²¹Then he said to them, "Do you not yet understand?"

Jesus Cures a Blind Man at Bethsaida

22   They came to Bethsaida. Some peopleᶜ brought a blind man to him and begged him to touch him. ²³He took the blind man by the hand and led him out of the village; and when he had put saliva on his eyes and laid his hands on him, he asked him, "Can you see anything?" ²⁴And the manʸ looked up and said, "I can see people, but

---

ʷ Other ancient authorities add *and Sidon*   ˣ Or *Lord*; other ancient authorities prefix *Yes*   ʸ Gk *he*   ᶻ Other ancient authorities read *Mageda* or *Magdala*   ᵃ Gk *they*   ᵇ Other ancient authorities read *the Herodians* ᶜ Gk *They*

they look like trees, walking." 25Then Jesus[d] laid his hands on his eyes again; and he looked intently and his sight was restored, and he saw everything clearly. 26Then he sent him away to his home, saying, "Do not even go into the village."[e]

Peter's Declaration about Jesus

▶ See Matthew 16.13–16; Luke 9.18–20

27 Jesus went on with his disciples to the villages of Caesarea Philippi; and on the way he asked his disciples, "Who do people say that I am?" 28And they answered him, "John the Baptist; and others, Elijah; and still others, one of the prophets." 29He asked them, "But who do you say that I am?" Peter answered him, "You are the

8.29 Peter Learns Humility

Most scholars believe that Mark got his eyewitness details from the disciple Peter. If so, the book reveals something about how Peter changed. Mark tells of three separate instances when Jesus rebuked Peter (see, for example, verse 33), but omits several compliments paid him. For example, compare this passage to a parallel account in Matthew 16.13–20, where Jesus commended Peter highly. Evidently, brash Peter learned a few lessons about humility along the way.

Messiah."[f] 30And he sternly ordered them not to tell anyone about him.

Jesus Foretells His Death and Resurrection

▶ See Matthew 16.21–28; Luke 9.22–27

31 Then he began to teach them that the Son of Man must undergo great suffering, and be rejected by the elders, the chief priests, and the scribes, and be killed, and after three days rise again. 32He said all this quite openly. And Peter took him aside and began to rebuke him. 33But turning and looking at his disciples, he rebuked Peter and said, "Get behind me, Satan! For you are setting your mind not on divine things but on human things."

34 He called the crowd with his disciples, and said to them, "If any want to become my followers, let them deny themselves and take up their cross and follow me. 35For those who want to save their life will lose it, and those who lose their life for my sake, and for the sake of the gospel,[g] will save it. 36For what will it profit them to gain the whole world and forfeit their life? 37Indeed, what can they give in return for their life? 38Those who are ashamed of me and of my words[h] in this adulterous and sinful generation, of them the Son of Man will also be ashamed when he comes in the glory of his Father with the holy angels." 9 1And he said to them, "Truly I tell you, there are some standing here who will not taste death until they see that the kingdom of God has come with[i] power."

The Transfiguration

▶ See Matthew 17.1–13; Luke 9.28–36

2 Six days later, Jesus took with him Peter and James and John, and led them up a high mountain apart, by themselves. And he was transfigured before them, 3and his clothes became dazzling white, such as no one[j] on earth could bleach them. 4And there appeared to them Elijah with Moses, who were talking with Jesus. 5Then Peter said to Jesus, "Rabbi, it is good for us to be here; let us make three dwellings,[k] one for you, one for Moses, and one for Elijah." 6He did not know what to say, for they were terrified. 7Then a cloud overshadowed them, and from the cloud there came a voice, "This is my Son, the Beloved;[l] listen to him!" 8Suddenly when they looked around, they saw no one with them any more, but only Jesus.

The Coming of Elijah

9 As they were coming down the mountain, he ordered them to tell no one about what they had seen, until after the Son of Man had risen from the dead. 10So they kept the matter to themselves, questioning what this rising from the dead could mean. 11Then they asked him, "Why do the scribes say that Elijah must come first?" 12He said to them, "Elijah is indeed coming first to restore all things. How then is it written about the Son of Man, that he is to go through many sufferings and be treated with contempt? 13But I tell you that Elijah has come, and they did to him whatever they pleased, as it is written about him."

The Healing of a Boy with a Spirit

▶ See Matthew 17.14–19,22–23; Luke 9.37–45

14 When they came to the disciples, they saw a great crowd around them, and some scribes arguing with them. 15When the whole crowd saw him, they were immediately overcome with awe, and they ran forward to greet him. 16He asked them, "What are you arguing about with them?" 17Someone from the crowd answered him, "Teacher, I brought you my son; he has a spirit that makes him unable to speak; 18and whenever it seizes him, it dashes him down; and he foams and grinds his teeth and becomes rigid; and I asked your disciples to cast it out, but they could not do so." 19He answered them, "You faithless generation, how much longer must I be among

---

[d] Gk he [e] Other ancient authorities add *or tell anyone in the village* [f] Or *the Christ* [g] Other ancient authorities read *lose their life for the sake of the gospel* [h] Other ancient authorities read *and of mine* [i] Or *in* [j] Gk *no* fuller [k] Or *tents* [l] Or *my beloved Son*

you? How much longer must I put up with you? Bring him to me." 20And they brought the boy[m] to him. When the spirit saw him, immediately it convulsed the boy,[m] and he fell on the ground and rolled about, foaming at the mouth. 21Jesus[n] asked the father, "How long has this been happening to him?" And he said, "From childhood. 22It has often cast him into the fire and into the water, to destroy him; but if you are able to do anything, have pity on us and help us." 23Jesus said to him, "If you are able!—All things can be done for the one who believes." 24Immediately the father of the child cried out,[o] "I believe; help my unbelief!" 25When Jesus saw that a crowd came running together, he rebuked the unclean spirit, saying to it, "You spirit that keeps this boy from speaking and hearing, I command you, come out of him, and never enter him again!" 26After crying out and convulsing him terribly, it came out, and the boy was like a corpse, so that most of them said, "He is dead." 27But Jesus took him by the hand and lifted him up, and he was able to stand. 28When he had entered the house, his disciples asked him privately, "Why could we not cast it out?" 29He said to them, "This kind can come out only through prayer."[p]

Jesus Again Foretells His Death and Resurrection

30 They went on from there and passed through Galilee. He did not want anyone to know it; 31for he was teaching his disciples, saying to them, "The Son of Man is to be betrayed into human hands, and they will kill him, and three days after being killed, he will rise again." 32But they did not understand what he was saying and were afraid to ask him.

---

[m] Gk him   [n] Gk He   [o] Other ancient authorities add with tears   [p] Other ancient authorities add and fasting

---

Training the 12 Disciples
A most unpromising group of recruits

A SKILLED DRAMATIST, MARK DESCRIBES THE crowd reactions to Jesus all through his account. He shows people astonished, confused, and upset by Jesus' actions. Always, twelve people, the disciples, linger in the background, working out the logistics of Jesus' ministry.

> "Do you have eyes, and fail to see? Do you have ears, and fail to hear?" 8.18

At first, the disciples did not distinguish themselves—to put it mildly. Their most obvious trait was denseness: "Do you also fail to understand?" Jesus asked (7.18), and again, "How much longer must I put up with you?" (9.19).

Dense Disciples

About halfway through the book of Mark (chapter 8), the focus shifts away from the crowds and onto the disciples. In spite of their erratic performance, Jesus devoted much of his time to them. Outsiders still gathered to watch and listen, but Jesus concentrated on training the Twelve, preparing them to carry on his work after his departure.

How did the disciples handle the increased attention? If anything, they proved even more inept. When Jesus referred to his coming death, they either missed the point or foolishly protested his plans. Sometimes they squabbled about who deserved the most favored position. They obviously didn't understand the dazzling events going on around them. In short, the disciples amply demonstrated the mixture of good and bad present in all of us.

Near the end of Mark, as events conspired toward Jesus' death, the disciples grew more anxious and assertive. Jesus singled out two followers in particular, John and Peter, for his strongest reprimands. Ultimately, despite vigorous pronouncements of loyalty, each one of the Twelve sneaked quietly and ashamedly away from Jesus in his moment of deepest need.

A Decisive Change

One event, however, dramatically altered them. Something passed through their lives like a flame: Jesus' resurrection from death. After that, Jesus' patient hours of training seemed to bear fruit at last.

The disciples' change in behavior is astonishing. Of the proofs for the resurrection of Jesus, one of the most compelling is simply to compare these cowering disciples as portrayed in a Gospel like Mark with the bold, confident figures in the book of Acts. There, in a remarkable irony, we see the incredible advance of the early church being led by the two disciples with the thickest heads of all: Peter and John.

Life Questions: Sometimes we think of the disciples as saints or heroes, but Mark shows their weak spots. What weak spots keep you from following Jesus as you might?

Who Is the Greatest?

▶ *See Matthew 18.1–5; Luke 9.46–48*

33 Then they came to Capernaum; and when he was in the house he asked them, "What were

9.31 Baffling Thoughts

At the height of his popularity, as throngs of people were following him, Jesus began to talk about his suffering and death. Such talk baffled his disciples, whose image of a Messiah included no such dark notions. (When reality finally hit, they would all desert him and flee 14.50.) Although Jesus made a point of mentioning his resurrection whenever he talked about his death, the disciples grasped neither concept—until he had died and then come back.

you arguing about on the way?" [34]But they were silent, for on the way they had argued with one another who was the greatest. [35]He sat down, called the twelve, and said to them, "Whoever wants to be first must be last of all and servant of all." [36]Then he took a little child and put it among them; and taking it in his arms, he said to them, [37]"Whoever welcomes one such child in my name welcomes me, and whoever welcomes me welcomes not me but the one who sent me."

Another Exorcist

▶ *See Luke 9.49–50*

38 John said to him, "Teacher, we saw someone[q] casting out demons in your name, and we tried to stop him, because he was not following us." [39]But Jesus said, "Do not stop him; for no one who does a deed of power in my name will be able soon afterward to speak evil of me. [40]Whoever is not against us is for us. [41]For truly I tell you, whoever gives you a cup of water to drink because you bear the name of Christ will by no means lose the reward.

Temptations to Sin

42 "If any of you put a stumbling block before one of these little ones who believe in me,[r] it would be better for you if a great millstone were hung around your neck and you were thrown into the sea. [43]If your hand causes you to stumble, cut it off; it is better for you to enter life maimed than to have two hands and to go to hell,[s] to the unquenchable fire.[t] [45]And if your foot causes you to stumble, cut it off; it is better for you to enter life lame than to have two feet and to be

thrown into hell.[s,t] [47]And if your eye causes you to stumble, tear it out; it is better for you to enter the kingdom of God with one eye than to have two eyes and to be thrown into hell,[s] [48]where their worm never dies, and the fire is never quenched.

49 "For everyone will be salted with fire.[u] [50]Salt is good; but if salt has lost its saltiness, how can you season it?[v] Have salt in yourselves, and be at peace with one another."

Teaching about Divorce

▶ *See Matthew 19.1–9*

10 He left that place and went to the region of Judea and[w] beyond the Jordan. And crowds again gathered around him; and, as was his custom, he again taught them.

2 Some Pharisees came, and to test him they asked, "Is it lawful for a man to divorce his wife?"

10.2–12 Teaching on Divorce

The Pharisees tested Jesus with questions about common practices of divorce and remarriage. Jesus responded by pointing back to the origin of marriage at creation. His disciples were surprised by his strict views on divorce, and questioned him further in private. For other passages on this topic, see Matthew 19.1–12 and 1 Corinthians 7.1–16.

[3]He answered them, "What did Moses command you?" [4]They said, "Moses allowed a man to write a certificate of dismissal and to divorce her." [5]But Jesus said to them, "Because of your hardness of heart he wrote this commandment for you. [6]But from the beginning of creation, 'God made them male and female.' [7]For this reason a man shall leave his father and mother and be joined to his wife,[x] [8]and the two shall become one flesh.' So they are no longer two, but one flesh. [9]Therefore what God has joined together, let no one separate."

10 Then in the house the disciples asked him again about this matter. [11]He said to them, "Whoever divorces his wife and marries another commits adultery against her; [12]and if she divorces her husband and marries another, she commits adultery."

Jesus Blesses Little Children

▶ *See Matthew 19.13–15; Luke 18.15–17*

13 People were bringing little children to him in order that he might touch them; and the disciples spoke sternly to them. [14]But when Jesus saw

[q] Other ancient authorities add *who does not follow us*   [r] Other ancient authorities lack *in me*   [s] Gk *Gehenna*
[t] Verses 44 and 46 (which are identical with verse 48) are lacking in the best ancient authorities   [u] Other ancient authorities either add or substitute *and every sacrifice will be salted with salt*   [v] Or *how can you restore its saltiness?*
[w] Other ancient authorities lack *and*   [x] Other ancient authorities lack *and be joined to his wife*

this, he was indignant and said to them, "Let the little children come to me; do not stop them; for it is to such as these that the kingdom of God belongs. 15Truly I tell you, whoever does not receive the kingdom of God as a little child will never enter it." 16And he took them up in his arms, laid his hands on them, and blessed them.

The Rich Man

▶ See Matthew 19.16–30; Luke 18.18–30

17 As he was setting out on a journey, a man ran up and knelt before him, and asked him, "Good Teacher, what must I do to inherit eternal life?" 18Jesus said to him, "Why do you call me good? No one is good but God alone. 19You know the commandments: 'You shall not murder; You shall not commit adultery; You shall not steal; You shall not bear false witness; You shall not defraud; Honor your father and mother.'" 20He said to him, "Teacher, I have kept all these since my youth." 21Jesus, looking at him, loved him and said, "You lack one thing; go, sell what you own, and give the money*y* to the poor, and you will have treasure in heaven; then come, follow me." 22When he heard this, he was shocked and went away grieving, for he had many possessions.

23 Then Jesus looked around and said to his disciples, "How hard it will be for those who have wealth to enter the kingdom of God!" 24And the disciples were perplexed at these words. But Jesus said to them again, "Children, how hard it is*z* to enter the kingdom of God! 25It is easier for a camel to go through the eye of a needle than for someone who is rich to enter the kingdom of God." 26They were greatly astounded and said to

10.26 The Wealth Barrier

Religious teachers of that time saw wealth as a positive sign of God's approval, which explains the disciples' bewilderment. Jesus contradicted such ideas by teaching that wealth can actually be a barrier keeping people out of the kingdom of God.

one another,*a* "Then who can be saved?" 27Jesus looked at them and said, "For mortals it is impossible, but not for God; for God all things are possible."

28 Peter began to say to him, "Look, we have left everything and followed you." 29Jesus said, "Truly I tell you, there is no one who has left house or brothers or sisters or mother or father or children or fields, for my sake and for the sake of the good news,*b* 30who will not receive a hundredfold now in this age—houses, brothers and

sisters, mothers and children, and fields, with persecutions—and in the age to come eternal life. 31But many who are first will be last, and the last will be first."

A Third Time Jesus Foretells His Death and Resurrection

▶ See Matthew 20.17–19; Luke 18.31–33

32 They were on the road, going up to Jerusalem, and Jesus was walking ahead of them; they were amazed, and those who followed were afraid. He took the twelve aside again and began to tell them what was to happen to him, 33saying, "See, we are going up to Jerusalem, and the Son of Man will be handed over to the chief priests and the scribes, and they will condemn him to death; then they will hand him over to the Gentiles; 34they will mock him, and spit upon him, and flog him, and kill him; and after three days he will rise again."

The Request of James and John

▶ See Matthew 20.20–28

35 James and John, the sons of Zebedee, came forward to him and said to him, "Teacher, we want you to do for us whatever we ask of you." 36And he said to them, "What is it you want me to do for you?" 37And they said to him, "Grant us to sit, one at your right hand and one at your left, in your glory." 38But Jesus said to them, "You do not know what you are asking. Are you able to drink the cup that I drink, or be baptized with the baptism that I am baptized with?" 39They replied, "We are able." Then Jesus said to them, "The cup that I drink you will drink; and with the baptism with which I am baptized, you will be baptized; 40but to sit at my right hand or at my left is not mine to grant, but it is for those for whom it has been prepared."

41 When the ten heard this, they began to be angry with James and John. 42So Jesus called them and said to them, "You know that among the Gentiles those whom they recognize as their rulers lord it over them, and their great ones are tyrants over them. 43But it is not so among you; but whoever wishes to become great among you must be your servant, 44and whoever wishes to be first among you must be slave of all. 45For the Son of Man came not to be served but to serve, and to give his life a ransom for many."

The Healing of Blind Bartimaeus

▶ See Matthew 20.29–34; Luke 18.35–43

46 They came to Jericho. As he and his disciples and a large crowd were leaving Jericho, Bartimaeus son of Timaeus, a blind beggar, was sitting by the roadside. 47When he heard that it was Jesus

---

y Gk lacks *the money to him*   *z* Other ancient authorities add *for those who trust in riches*   *a* Other ancient authorities read
b Or *gospel*

of Nazareth, he began to shout out and say, "Jesus, Son of David, have mercy on me!" [48]Many sternly ordered him to be quiet, but he cried out even more loudly, "Son of David, have mercy on me!" [49]Jesus stood still and said, "Call him here." And they called the blind man, saying to him, "Take heart; get up, he is calling you." [50]So throwing off his cloak, he sprang up and came to Jesus. [51]Then Jesus said to him, "What do you want me to do for you?" The blind man said to him, "My teacher,[c] let me see again." [52]Jesus said to him, "Go; your faith has made you well." Immediately he regained his sight and followed him on the way.

Jesus' Triumphal Entry into Jerusalem

▶ See Matthew 21.1–9; Luke 19.29–38; John 12.12–15

11 When they were approaching Jerusalem, at Bethphage and Bethany, near the Mount of Olives, he sent two of his disciples [2]and said to them, "Go into the village ahead of you, and immediately as you enter it, you will find tied there a colt that has never been ridden; untie it and bring it. [3]If anyone says to you, 'Why are you doing this?' just say this, 'The Lord needs it and will send it back here immediately.'" [4]They went away and found a colt tied near a door, outside in the street. As they were untying it, [5]some of the bystanders said to them, "What are you doing, untying the colt?" [6]They told them what Jesus had

[c] Aramaic *Rabbouni*

said; and they allowed them to take it. [7]Then they brought the colt to Jesus and threw their cloaks on it; and he sat on it. [8]Many people spread their cloaks on the road, and others spread leafy branches that they had cut in the fields. [9]Then those who went ahead and those who followed were shouting,

"Hosanna!
Blessed is the one who comes in the
name of the Lord!

11.9 Short-lived Acceptance

During much of his ministry, Jesus hushed up news about his miraculous power and his identity as the true Messiah. But in this rare scene, large crowds clearly recognized him as the Messiah and honored him as such. The next few chapters, however, demonstrate how tragically short-lived public acceptance proved to be.

---

[10] Blessed is the coming kingdom of our
ancestor David!
Hosanna in the highest heaven!"

[11] Then he entered Jerusalem and went into the temple; and when he had looked around at everything, as it was already late, he went out to Bethany with the twelve.

JAMES *Inner Circle*

THINK OF YOUR FRIENDS AS a series of concentric circles. The outer circle holds casual acquaintances: the drug store clerk, the neighbor who waves when she drives past. Closer in are real friends, people you trust and care about—perhaps classmates or friends from work. The innermost circle—the bullseye—includes only a handful: those people whose company you seek for the most important events of your life.

Jesus had a wide outer circle. He ministered to thousands of people who crowded around him wherever he went. Closer in were his disciples, the group of people who seriously followed him. The twelve apostles formed a smaller, more committed group. And near the center was an inner core: Peter, James and John.

James and his brother John worked alongside their father and another pair of brothers, Peter and Andrew, in a modest fishing fleet on the Sea of Galilee. These were the first disciples whom Jesus called, and from them Jesus chose his inner circle. During the critical times of his life, Jesus sought the company of his inner circle. At Jairus's house, only James, Peter and John accompanied him to see the dead child (5.37). At the transfiguration, the same three were chosen to climb the mountain (Matthew 17.1). In Gethsemane, Jesus sought their company and their prayers during his time of agony (14.33).

Belonging to Jesus' inner circle brought privileges but also temptations. Jesus' closest companions were susceptible to pride, a trap that caught James and his brother John at least twice. Once, when people failed to give Jesus the reception they thought appropriate, James and John were ready to call down fire from heaven (Luke 9.51–56).

In another incident reported in this chapter, the two brothers asked for special treatment when Jesus came to power. Gently, Jesus told them they did not know what they were asking. To be in the inner circle, Jesus said, meant living as a servant, not as a king.

Life Questions: Who is in your inner circle? How does your inner circle treat those who are outside?

Jesus Curses the Fig Tree

▶ *See Matthew 21.12–16; Luke 19.45–47; John 2.13–16*

12 On the following day, when they came from Bethany, he was hungry. ¹³Seeing in the distance a fig tree in leaf, he went to see whether perhaps he would find anything on it. When he came to it, he found nothing but leaves, for it was not the season for figs. ¹⁴He said to it, "May no one ever eat fruit from you again." And his disciples heard it.

Jesus Cleanses the Temple

15 Then they came to Jerusalem. And he entered the temple and began to drive out those who were selling and those who were buying in the temple, and he overturned the tables of the money changers and the seats of those who sold doves; ¹⁶and he would not allow anyone to carry

11.16 Big Business

The outer court of the temple, accessible to non-Jews, encompassed a huge area the size of ten football fields. Some business there was legitimate: Out-of-town pilgrims needed a way to obtain sacrificial animals and to change money into local currency. Apparently, though, the business had fallen into the hands of people more interested in profit than in worship.

anything through the temple. ¹⁷He was teaching and saying, "Is it not written,

'My house shall be called a house of
     prayer for all the nations'?
But you have made it a den
     of robbers.'"

¹⁸And when the chief priests and the scribes heard it, they kept looking for a way to kill him; for they were afraid of him, because the whole crowd was spellbound by his teaching. ¹⁹And when evening came, Jesus and his disciples*d* went out of the city.

The Lesson from the Withered Fig Tree

▶ *See Matthew 21.19–22*

20 In the morning as they passed by, they saw the fig tree withered away to its roots. ²¹Then Peter remembered and said to him, "Rabbi, look! The fig tree that you cursed has withered." ²²Jesus answered them, "Have*e* faith in God. ²³Truly I tell you, if you say to this mountain, 'Be taken up and thrown into the sea,' and if you do not doubt in your heart, but believe that what you say will

come to pass, it will be done for you. ²⁴So I tell you, whatever you ask for in prayer, believe that you have received*f* it, and it will be yours.

25 "Whenever you stand praying, forgive, if you have anything against anyone; so that your Father in heaven may also forgive you your trespasses."*g*

Jesus' Authority Is Questioned

▶ *See Matthew 21.23–27; Luke 20.1–8*

27 Again they came to Jerusalem. As he was walking in the temple, the chief priests, the scribes, and the elders came to him ²⁸and said, "By what authority are you doing these things? Who gave you this authority to do them?" ²⁹Jesus said to them, "I will ask you one question; answer me, and I will tell you by what authority I do these things. ³⁰Did the baptism of John come from heaven, or was it of human origin? Answer me." ³¹They argued with one another, "If we say, 'From heaven,' he will say, 'Why then did you not believe him?' ³²But shall we say, 'Of human origin'?"—they were afraid of the crowd, for all regarded John as truly a prophet. ³³So they answered Jesus, "We do not know." And Jesus said to them, "Neither will I tell you by what authority I am doing these things."

The Parable of the Wicked Tenants

▶ *See Matthew 21.33–46; Luke 20.9–19*

12 Then he began to speak to them in parables. "A man planted a vineyard, put a fence around it, dug a pit for the wine press, and built a watchtower; then he leased it to tenants and went to another country. ²When the season came, he sent a slave to the tenants to collect from them his share of the produce of the vineyard. ³But they seized him, and beat him, and sent him away empty-handed. ⁴And again he sent another slave to them; this one they beat over the head and insulted. ⁵Then he sent another, and that one they killed. And so it was with many others; some they beat, and others they killed. ⁶He had still one other, a beloved son. Finally he sent him to them, saying, 'They will respect my son.' ⁷But those tenants said to one another, 'This is the heir; come, let us kill him, and the inheritance will be ours.' ⁸So they seized him, killed him, and threw him out of the vineyard. ⁹What then will the owner of the vineyard do? He will come and destroy the tenants and give the vineyard to others. ¹⁰Have you not read this scripture:

'The stone that the builders rejected
     has become the cornerstone;*h*
¹¹ this was the Lord's doing,
     and it is amazing in our eyes'?"

12 When they realized that he had told this

---

d Gk *they*: other ancient authorities read *he*   *e* Other ancient authorities read *"If you have*   *f* Other ancient authorities read *are receiving*   *g* Other ancient authorities add verse 26, *"But if you do not forgive, neither will your Father in heaven forgive your trespasses."*   *h* Or *keystone*

parable against them, they wanted to arrest him, but they feared the crowd. So they left him and went away.

The Question about Paying Taxes

▶ *See Matthew 22.15–22; Luke 20.20–26*

13 Then they sent to him some Pharisees and some Herodians to trap him in what he said.

12.13 Opposition Heats Up

While in Jerusalem, Jesus was surrounded by hostile groups. Mark 12 records a series of attempts to bait him: by the Pharisees and Sadducees, by the political Herodians, and by the scribes. Each group challenged Jesus with a situation designed to trap him and anger the crowd.

14And they came and said to him, "Teacher, we know that you are sincere, and show deference to no one; for you do not regard people with partiality, but teach the way of God in accordance with truth. Is it lawful to pay taxes to the emperor, or not? 15Should we pay them, or should we not?" But knowing their hypocrisy, he said to them, "Why are you putting me to the test? Bring me a denarius and let me see it." 16And they brought one. Then he said to them, "Whose head is this, and whose title?" They answered, "The emperor's." 17Jesus said to them, "Give to the emperor the things that are the emperor's, and to God the things that are God's." And they were utterly amazed at him.

The Question about the Resurrection

▶ *See Matthew 22.23–33; Luke 20.27–38*

18 Some Sadducees, who say there is no resurrection, came to him and asked him a question, saying, 19"Teacher, Moses wrote for us that if a man's brother dies, leaving a wife but no child, the man*i* shall marry the widow and raise up children for his brother. 20There were seven brothers; the first married and, when he died, left no children; 21and the second married the widow*j* and died, leaving no children; and the third likewise; 22none of the seven left children. Last of all the woman herself died. 23In the resurrection*k* whose wife will she be? For the seven had married her."

24 Jesus said to them, "Is not this the reason you are wrong, that you know neither the scriptures nor the power of God? 25For when they rise from the dead, they neither marry nor are given in marriage, but are like angels in heaven. 26And as for the dead being raised, have you not read in the book of Moses, in the story about the bush, how God said to him, 'I am the God of Abraham, the God of Isaac, and the God of Jacob'? 27He is God not of the dead, but of the living; you are quite wrong."

The First Commandment

▶ *See Matthew 22.34–40*

28 One of the scribes came near and heard them disputing with one another, and seeing that he answered them well, he asked him, "Which commandment is the first of all?" 29Jesus answered, "The first is, 'Hear, O Israel: the Lord our God, the Lord is one; 30you shall love the Lord your God with all your heart, and with all your soul, and with all your mind, and with all your strength.' 31The second is this, 'You shall love your neighbor as yourself.' There is no other commandment greater than these." 32Then the scribe said to him, "You are right, Teacher; you have truly said that 'he is one, and besides him there is no other'; 33and 'to love him with all the heart, and with all the understanding, and with all the strength,' and 'to love one's neighbor as oneself,'—this is much more important than all whole burnt offerings and sacrifices." 34When Jesus saw that he answered wisely, he said to him, "You are not far from the kingdom of God." After that no one dared to ask him any question.

The Question about David's Son

▶ *See Matthew 22.41–46; Luke 20.41–47*

35 While Jesus was teaching in the temple, he said, "How can the scribes say that the Messiah*l* is the son of David? 36David himself, by the Holy Spirit, declared,

'The Lord said to my Lord,
  "Sit at my right hand,
    until I put your enemies under your
      feet."'

37David himself calls him Lord; so how can he be his son?" And the large crowd was listening to him with delight.

Jesus Denounces the Scribes

38 As he taught, he said, "Beware of the scribes, who like to walk around in long robes, and to be greeted with respect in the marketplaces, 39and to have the best seats in the synagogues and places of honor at banquets! 40They devour widows' houses and for the sake of appearance say long prayers. They will receive the greater condemnation."

The Widow's Offering

▶ *See Luke 21.1–4*

41 He sat down opposite the treasury, and watched the crowd putting money into the treasury. Many rich people put in large sums. 42A

---

i Gk *his brother*   *j* Gk *her*   *k* Other ancient authorities add *when they rise*   *l* Or *the Christ*

poor widow came and put in two small copper coins, which are worth a penny. ⁴³Then he called his disciples and said to them, "Truly I tell you, this poor widow has put in more than all those who are contributing to the treasury. ⁴⁴For all of them have contributed out of their abundance; but she out of her poverty has put in everything she had, all she had to live on."

12.42 Exploiting Widows

The simple act of faithfulness by an impoverished widow made a stark contrast to others' pompous public displays. Some scribes "devour widows' houses," Jesus had said (verse 40). Scribes lived off the gifts of supporters, and, then as now, the gullible poor made a tempting target.

The Destruction of the Temple Foretold

▶ *See Matthew 24.1–51; Luke 21.5–36*

13 As he came out of the temple, one of his disciples said to him, "Look, Teacher, what large stones and what large buildings!" ²Then Jesus asked him, "Do you see these great buildings? Not one stone will be left here upon another; all will be thrown down."

3 When he was sitting on the Mount of Olives opposite the temple, Peter, James, John, and Andrew asked him privately, ⁴"Tell us, when will this be, and what will be the sign that all these things are about to be accomplished?" ⁵Then Jesus began to say to them, "Beware that no one leads you astray. ⁶Many will come in my name and say, 'I am he!'ᵐ and they will lead many astray. ⁷When you hear of wars and rumors of wars, do not be alarmed; this must take place, but the end is still to come. ⁸For nation will rise against nation, and kingdom against kingdom; there will be earthquakes in various places; there will be famines. This is but the beginning of the birth pangs.

Persecution Foretold

9 "As for yourselves, beware; for they will hand you over to councils; and you will be beaten in synagogues; and you will stand before gover-

13.10 To All Nations

Preaching the gospel to all nations was probably a new thought to the disciples, who still thought in terms of a Messiah for the Jews. But some of them would spend the remainder of their lives making this prophecy come true.

nors and kings because of me, as a testimony to them. ¹⁰And the good newsⁿ must first be proclaimed to all nations. ¹¹When they bring you to trial and hand you over, do not worry beforehand about what you are to say; but say whatever is given you at that time, for it is not you who speak, but the Holy Spirit. ¹²Brother will betray brother to death, and a father his child, and children will rise against parents and have them put to death; ¹³and you will be hated by all because of my name. But the one who endures to the end will be saved.

The Desolating Sacrilege

14 "But when you see the desolating sacrilege set up where it ought not to be (let the reader understand), then those in Judea must flee to the mountains; ¹⁵the one on the housetop must not go down or enter the house to take anything away; ¹⁶the one in the field must not turn back to get a coat. ¹⁷Woe to those who are pregnant and to those who are nursing infants in those days! ¹⁸Pray that it may not be in winter. ¹⁹For in those days there will be suffering, such as has not been from the beginning of the creation that God created until now, no, and never will be. ²⁰And if the Lord had not cut short those days, no one would be saved; but for the sake of the elect, whom he chose, he has cut short those days. ²¹And if anyone says to you at that time, 'Look! Here is the Messiah!'ᵒ or 'Look! There he is!'—do not believe it. ²²False messiahsᵖ and false prophets will appear and produce signs and omens, to lead astray, if possible, the elect. ²³But be alert; I have already told you everything.

The Coming of the Son of Man

24 "But in those days, after that suffering,
  the sun will be darkened,
    and the moon will not give its light,
25 and the stars will be falling from heaven,
    and the powers in the heavens will be
      shaken.

²⁶Then they will see 'the Son of Man coming in clouds' with great power and glory. ²⁷Then he will send out the angels, and gather his elect from the four winds, from the ends of the earth to the ends of heaven.

The Lesson of the Fig Tree

28 "From the fig tree learn its lesson: as soon as its branch becomes tender and puts forth its leaves, you know that summer is near. ²⁹So also, when you see these things taking place, you know that heᑫ is near, at the very gates. ³⁰Truly I tell you, this generation will not pass away until all these things have taken place. ³¹Heaven and earth will pass away, but my words will not pass away.

ᵐ Gk I am   ⁿ Gk gospel   ᵒ Or the Christ   ᵖ Or christs   ᑫ Or it

The Necessity for Watchfulness

32 "But about that day or hour no one knows, neither the angels in heaven, nor the Son, but only the Father. [33]Beware, keep alert;[r] for you do not know when the time will come. [34]It is like a man going on a journey, when he leaves home and puts his slaves in charge, each with his work, and commands the doorkeeper to be on the watch. [35]Therefore, keep awake—for you do not know when the master of the house will come, in the evening, or at midnight, or at cockcrow, or at dawn, [36]or else he may find you asleep when he comes suddenly. [37]And what I say to you I say to all: Keep awake."

The Plot to Kill Jesus

▶ See Matthew 26.2–16; Luke 22.1–6

14 It was two days before the Passover and the festival of Unleavened Bread. The chief priests and the scribes were looking for a way to

---

14.1 Festival Time in Jerusalem

The Passover, celebrating the Jews' deliverance from Egypt, was one of the high points of the Jewish calendar. All males older than age 12 went to Jerusalem for the holiday. Thus the city was filled with hundreds of thousands of pilgrims at the time of Jesus' death.

---

arrest Jesus[s] by stealth and kill him; [2]for they said, "Not during the festival, or there may be a riot among the people."

The Anointing at Bethany

3 While he was at Bethany in the house of Simon the leper,[t] as he sat at the table, a woman came with an alabaster jar of very costly ointment of nard, and she broke open the jar and poured the ointment on his head. [4]But some were there who said to one another in anger, "Why was the ointment wasted in this way? [5]For this ointment could have been sold for more than three hundred denarii,[u] and the money given to the poor." And they scolded her. [6]But Jesus said, "Let her alone; why do you trouble her? She has performed a good service for me. [7]For you always have the poor with you, and you can show kindness to them whenever you wish; but you will not always have me. [8]She has done what she could; she has anointed my body beforehand for its burial. [9]Truly I tell you, wherever the good news[v] is proclaimed in the whole world, what she has done will be told in remembrance of her."

Judas Agrees to Betray Jesus

10 Then Judas Iscariot, who was one of the twelve, went to the chief priests in order to betray him to them. [11]When they heard it, they were greatly pleased, and promised to give him money. So he began to look for an opportunity to betray him.

The Passover with the Disciples

▶ See Matthew 26.17–30; Luke 22.7–23

12 On the first day of Unleavened Bread, when the Passover lamb is sacrificed, his disciples said to him, "Where do you want us to go and make the preparations for you to eat the Passover?" [13]So he sent two of his disciples, saying to them, "Go into the city, and a man carrying a jar of water will meet you; follow him, [14]and wherever he enters, say to the owner of the house, 'The Teacher asks, Where is my guest room where I may eat the Passover with my disciples?' [15]He will show you a large room upstairs, furnished and ready. Make preparations for us there." [16]So the disciples set out and went to the city, and found everything as he had told them; and they prepared the Passover meal.

17 When it was evening, he came with the twelve. [18]And when they had taken their places and were eating, Jesus said, "Truly I tell you, one of you will betray me, one who is eating with me." [19]They began to be distressed and to say to him one after another, "Surely, not I?" [20]He said to them, "It is one of the twelve, one who is dipping bread[w] into the bowl[x] with me. [21]For the Son of Man goes as it is written of him, but woe to that one by whom the Son of Man is betrayed! It would have been better for that one not to have been born."

The Institution of the Lord's Supper

22 While they were eating, he took a loaf of bread, and after blessing it he broke it, gave it to

---

14.22–26 Original Lord's Supper

Virtually all Christian churches celebrate the practice of Communion (Mass, Eucharist, or Lord's Supper) in some form. Matthew, Mark, and Luke each record the original Passover meal when Jesus instituted the practice.

---

them, and said, "Take; this is my body." [23]Then he took a cup, and after giving thanks he gave it to them, and all of them drank from it. [24]He said to them, "This is my blood of the[y] covenant, which is poured out for many. [25]Truly I tell you,

---

[r] Other ancient authorities add *and pray*   [s] Gk *him*   [t] The terms *leper* and *leprosy* can refer to several diseases   [u] The denarius was the usual day's wage for a laborer   [v] Or *gospel*   [w] Gk lacks *bread*   [x] Other ancient authorities read *same bowl*   [y] Other ancient authorities add *new*

I will never again drink of the fruit of the vine until that day when I drink it new in the kingdom of God."

Peter's Denial Foretold

▶ *See Matthew 26.31–35*

26 When they had sung the hymn, they went out to the Mount of Olives. 27And Jesus said to them, "You will all become deserters; for it is written,

'I will strike the shepherd,
and the sheep will be scattered.'

28But after I am raised up, I will go before you to Galilee." 29Peter said to him, "Even though all become deserters, I will not." 30Jesus said to him, "Truly I tell you, this day, this very night, before the cock crows twice, you will deny me three times." 31But he said vehemently, "Even though I must die with you, I will not deny you." And all of them said the same.

Jesus Prays in Gethsemane

▶ *See Matthew 26.36–46; Luke 22.40–46*

32 They went to a place called Gethsemane; and he said to his disciples, "Sit here while I

14.32 Seeking Privacy

Where to pray? The temple was crowded, and synagogues were reserved for public meetings. In order to find some privacy, Jesus would often rise early in the morning or spend all night in prayer. Luke reports that this garden was one of Jesus' favorite places (Luke 22.39).

pray." 33He took with him Peter and James and John, and began to be distressed and agitated. 34And he said to them, "I am deeply grieved, even to death; remain here, and keep awake." 35And going a little farther, he threw himself on the ground and prayed that, if it were possible, the hour might pass from him. 36He said, "Abba,z Father, for you all things are possible; remove this cup from me; yet, not what I want, but what you want." 37He came and found them sleeping; and he said to Peter, "Simon, are you asleep? Could you not keep awake one hour? 38Keep awake and pray that you may not come into the time of trial;a the spirit indeed is willing, but the flesh is weak." 39And again he went away and prayed, saying the same words. 40And once more he came and found them sleeping, for their eyes were very heavy; and they did not know what to say to him. 41He came a third time and said to them, "Are you still sleeping and taking your rest? Enough! The hour has come; the Son of Man is betrayed

into the hands of sinners. 42Get up, let us be going. See, my betrayer is at hand."

The Betrayal and Arrest of Jesus

▶ *See Matthew 26.47–56; Luke 22.47–50; John 18.3–11*

43 Immediately, while he was still speaking, Judas, one of the twelve, arrived; and with him there was a crowd with swords and clubs, from the chief priests, the scribes, and the elders. 44Now the betrayer had given them a sign, saying, "The one I will kiss is the man; arrest him and lead him away under guard." 45So when he came, he went up to him at once and said, "Rabbi!" and kissed him. 46Then they laid hands on him and arrested him. 47But one of those who stood near drew his sword and struck the slave of the high priest, cutting off his ear. 48Then Jesus said to them, "Have you come out with swords and clubs to arrest me as though I were a bandit? 49Day after day I was with you in the temple teaching, and you did not arrest me. But let the scriptures be fulfilled." 50All of them deserted him and fled.

51 A certain young man was following him, wearing nothing but a linen cloth. They caught

14.51 The Anonymous Author?

Many scholars believe the young man in this verse was none other than Mark himself, author of this Gospel. Often, in ancient days, an author wouldn't use his name, but would plant a clue such as this (see John 21.24).

hold of him, 52but he left the linen cloth and ran off naked.

Jesus before the Council

▶ *See Matthew 26.57–68; John 18.12–13,19–24*

53 They took Jesus to the high priest; and all the chief priests, the elders, and the scribes were assembled. 54Peter had followed him at a distance, right into the courtyard of the high priest; and he was sitting with the guards, warming himself at the fire. 55Now the chief priests and the whole council were looking for testimony against Jesus to put him to death; but they found none. 56For many gave false testimony against him, and their testimony did not agree. 57Some stood up and gave false testimony against him, saying, 58"We heard him say, 'I will destroy this temple that is made with hands, and in three days I will build another, not made with hands.'" 59But even on this point their testimony did not agree. 60Then the high priest stood up before them and asked Jesus, "Have you no answer? What is it that they

z Aramaic for *Father*   a Or *into temptation*

testify against you?" 61But he was silent and did not answer. Again the high priest asked him, "Are you the Messiah,*b* the Son of the Blessed One?" 62Jesus said, "I am; and

'you will see the Son of Man
seated at the right hand of the Power,'
and 'coming with the clouds of heaven.'"

63Then the high priest tore his clothes and said, "Why do we still need witnesses? 64You have heard his blasphemy! What is your decision?" All of them condemned him as deserving death. 65Some began to spit on him, to blindfold him, and to strike him, saying to him, "Prophesy!" The guards also took him over and beat him.

Peter Denies Jesus

▶ *See Matthew 26.69–75; Luke 22.56–62; John 18.16–18,25–27*

66 While Peter was below in the courtyard, one of the servant-girls of the high priest came by. 67When she saw Peter warming himself, she stared at him and said, "You also were with Jesus, the man from Nazareth." 68But he denied it, saying, "I do not know or understand what you are talking about." And he went out into the fore-court.*c* Then the cock crowed.*d* 69And the servant-girl, on seeing him, began again to say to the bystanders, "This man is one of them." 70But again he denied it. Then after a little while the bystanders again said to Peter, "Certainly you are one of them; for you are a Galilean." 71But he began to curse, and he swore an oath, "I do not know this man you are talking about." 72At that moment the cock crowed for the second time. Then Peter remembered that Jesus had said to him, "Before the cock crows twice, you will deny me three times." And he broke down and wept.

Jesus before Pilate

▶ *See Matthew 27.11–26; Luke 23.2–3,18–25; John 18.29—19.16*

15 As soon as it was morning, the chief priests held a consultation with the elders and scribes and the whole council. They bound Jesus,

led him away, and handed him over to Pilate. 2Pilate asked him, "Are you the King of the Jews?" He answered him, "You say so." 3Then the chief priests accused him of many things. 4Pilate asked him again, "Have you no answer? See how many charges they bring against you." 5But Jesus made no further reply, so that Pilate was amazed.

Pilate Hands Jesus over to Be Crucified

6 Now at the festival he used to release a prisoner for them, anyone for whom they asked. 7Now a man called Barabbas was in prison with the rebels who had committed murder during the insurrection. 8So the crowd came and began to ask Pilate to do for them according to his custom. 9Then he answered them, "Do you want me to release for you the King of the Jews?" 10For he realized that it was out of jealousy that the chief priests had handed him over. 11But the chief priests stirred up the crowd to have him release Barabbas for them instead. 12Pilate spoke to them again, "Then what do you wish me to do*e* with the man you call*f* the King of the Jews?" 13They shouted back, "Crucify him!" 14Pilate asked them, "Why, what evil has he done?" But they shouted all the more, "Crucify him!" 15So Pilate, wishing to satisfy the crowd, released Barabbas for them; and after flogging Jesus, he handed him over to be crucified.

The Soldiers Mock Jesus

▶ *See Matthew 27.27–31*

16 Then the soldiers led him into the courtyard of the palace (that is, the governor's headquarters*g*); and they called together the whole cohort. 17And they clothed him in a purple cloak; and after twisting some thorns into a crown, they put it on him. 18And they began saluting him, "Hail, King of the Jews!" 19They struck his head with a reed, spat upon him, and knelt down in homage to him. 20After mocking him, they stripped him of the purple cloak and put his own clothes on him. Then they led him out to crucify him.

The Crucifixion of Jesus

▶ *See Matthew 27.33–44; Luke 23.33–43; John 19.17–24*

21 They compelled a passer-by, who was coming in from the country, to carry his cross; it was Simon of Cyrene, the father of Alexander and Rufus. 22Then they brought Jesus*h* to the place called Golgotha (which means the place of a skull). 23And they offered him wine mixed with myrrh; but he did not take it. 24And they crucified

15.1 Appeal for a Death Penalty

Roman law granted the Jews many freedoms, including the right to their Jewish court system, a council called the Sanhedrin. However, the Sanhedrin had no authority to order the death penalty. Seeking that sentence, Jesus' opponents sent him to Pilate, the Roman governor.

b Or the Christ   *c Or gateway*   *d Other ancient authorities lack Then the cock crowed*   *e Other ancient* authorities read *what should I do*   *f Other ancient authorities lack the man you call*   *g Gk the praetorium* *h Gk him*

him, and divided his clothes among them, casting lots to decide what each should take.

25 It was nine o'clock in the morning when they crucified him. [26]The inscription of the charge against him read, "The King of the Jews." [27]And with him they crucified two bandits, one on his right and one on his left.[i] [29]Those who passed by derided[j] him, shaking their heads and saying, "Aha! You who would destroy the temple and build it in three days, [30]save yourself, and come down from the cross!" [31]In the same way the chief priests, along with the scribes, were also mocking him among themselves and saying, "He saved others; he cannot save himself. [32]Let the Messiah,[k] the King of Israel, come down from the cross now, so that we may see and believe." Those who were crucified with him also taunted him.

The Death of Jesus

▶ See Matthew 27.45–56; Luke 23.44–49

33 When it was noon, darkness came over the

---

[i] Other ancient authorities add verse 28, *And the scripture was fulfilled that says, "And he was counted among the lawless."*
[j] Or *blasphemed*   [k] Or *the Christ*

The Day of Execution
The disciples were totally unprepared

EVENTS IN JESUS' LIFE—THE BIRTH in a manger, the death on a cross—can become so familiar that we miss the point. They're too close to us. In thinking about them, it sometimes helps to let the mind wander and search out whole new images.

A Bible study group was asked to suggest word images that might apply to Jesus. Common ones surfaced first: a shepherd, a lamb, a door. Then out of nowhere came a wildly different metaphor: "fireworks in reverse." Everyone turned, puzzled, to the middle-aged woman who had spoken.

"Think about it," she said. "Fireworks explode with brilliant, dazzling colors and loud noises ... yet they start out in an ordinary-looking paper package. When God became a man, the opposite happened. The Creator of everything in the universe confined himself to an unimpressive human package."

> Now when the centurion, who stood facing them, saw that in this way he breathed his last, he said, "Truly this man was God's Son!" 15.39

When the Impossible Happened

No event in the life of Jesus fits the woman's metaphor better than his execution in Jerusalem. The idea was inconceivable, even to Jesus' closest followers. The Son of God die? How could this be?

Could the Creator of all things succumb to his creation? Disciples who had slogged through every other confrontation by his side now forsook him. It made no sense for Jesus, the Messiah, to die.

Not until later would other thoughts click into place: memories of Old Testament customs that hauntingly pointed to a cross, prophecies of a Messiah who was King but also a Suffering Servant (see Isaiah 53). To die was, after all, the central reason Jesus came to earth; he had insisted on that from the beginning.

The Most Important Week

Jesus' last week so impressed the disciples that the four chroniclers of his life, including Mark, devoted one-third of their space to that final week in Jerusalem. By the time they wrote it down, of course, they could see his death in a new light: as a mournful prelude to the greatest miracle of all, his resurrection.

Even so, nothing could erase the impact of those fear-filled, final days. When the eerie darkness had lifted and Jesus had breathed his last, the disciples had learned something profound about God, and about love.

Dorothy Sayers put it this way: "Whatever game He is playing with His creation, He has kept His own rules and played fair. He can exact nothing from man that He has not exacted from Himself. He has Himself gone through the whole of human experience, from the trivial irritations of family life and the cramping restriction of hard work and lack of money to the worst horrors of pain and humiliation, defeat, despair, and death. When He was a man, He played the man. He was born in poverty and died in disgrace and thought it well worthwhile" (from *Christian Letters to a Post-Christian World*).

At no other point in history did the fireworks appear so powerless as the day Jesus died. They had not yet been lit.

Life Questions: Put yourself in the disciples' place. How would you have responded to news of Jesus' death? Would you have believed in him still?

whole land[l] until three in the afternoon. [34]At three o'clock Jesus cried out with a loud voice, "Eloi, Eloi, lema sabachthani?" which means, "My God, my God, why have you forsaken me?"[m] [35]When some of the bystanders heard it, they said, "Listen, he is calling for Elijah." [36]And someone ran, filled a sponge with sour wine, put it on a stick, and gave it to him to drink, saying, "Wait, let us see whether Elijah will come to take him down." [37]Then Jesus gave a loud cry and breathed his last. [38]And the curtain of the temple was torn in two, from top to bottom. [39]Now when the centurion, who stood facing him, saw that in this way he[n] breathed his last, he said, "Truly this man was God's Son!"[o]

15.39 Death Without Dignity

Romans reserved their cruelest form of execution—crucifixion—for slaves and the worst criminals. Skeletons of crucifixion victims show that thick nails were pounded through the wrist and heel bones. Death (from asphyxiation) usually took many hours or even several days.

40 There were also women looking on from a distance; among them were Mary Magdalene, and Mary the mother of James the younger and of Joses, and Salome. [41]These used to follow him and provided for him when he was in Galilee; and there were many other women who had come up with him to Jerusalem.

The Burial of Jesus

▶ *See Matthew 27.57–61; Luke 23.50–56; John 19.38–42*

42 When evening had come, and since it was the day of Preparation, that is, the day before the sabbath, [43]Joseph of Arimathea, a respected member of the council, who was also himself waiting expectantly for the kingdom of God, went boldly to Pilate and asked for the body of Jesus. [44]Then Pilate wondered if he were already dead; and summoning the centurion, he asked him whether he had been dead for some time. [45]When he learned from the centurion that he was dead, he granted the body to Joseph. [46]Then Joseph[p] bought a linen cloth, and taking down the body,[q] wrapped it in the linen cloth, and laid it in a tomb that had been hewn out of the rock. He then rolled a stone against the door of the tomb.

[47]Mary Magdalene and Mary the mother of Joses saw where the body[q] was laid.

The Resurrection of Jesus

▶ *See Matthew 28.1–8; Luke 24.1–10*

16 When the sabbath was over, Mary Magdalene, and Mary the mother of James, and Salome bought spices, so that they might go and

16.1 A Late Anointing

Jewish rules forbade handling dead bodies during the sabbath. Because Jesus died during the sabbath celebration, his friends and relatives couldn't properly embalm and prepare his body. They returned to the tomb later for this purpose, only to find the greatest surprise of their lives.

anoint him. [2]And very early on the first day of the week, when the sun had risen, they went to the tomb. [3]They had been saying to one another, "Who will roll away the stone for us from the entrance to the tomb?" [4]When they looked up, they saw that the stone, which was very large, had already been rolled back. [5]As they entered the tomb, they saw a young man, dressed in a white robe, sitting on the right side; and they were alarmed. [6]But he said to them, "Do not be alarmed; you are looking for Jesus of Nazareth, who was crucified. He has been raised; he is not here. Look, there is the place they laid him. [7]But go, tell his disciples and Peter that he is going ahead of you to Galilee; there you will see him,

16.7 . . . and Peter

The messenger who informed the women about Jesus' resurrection pointedly asked them to tell "his disciples and Peter," singling out the disciple who had vehemently denied Jesus. John 21 records a further, moving scene in which Jesus specifically reinstated Peter.

just as he told you." [8]So they went out and fled from the tomb, for terror and amazement had seized them; and they said nothing to anyone, for they were afraid.[r]

THE SHORTER ENDING OF MARK

⟦And all that had been commanded them they told briefly to those around Peter. And afterward Jesus himself sent out through them, from east to

---

[l] Or *earth* [m] Other ancient authorities read *made me a reproach* [n] Other ancient authorities add *cried out and* [o] Or *a son of God* [p] Gk *he* [q] Gk *it* [r] Some of the most ancient authorities bring the book to a close at the end of verse 8. One authority concludes the book with the shorter ending; others include the shorter ending and then continue with verses 9-20. In most authorities verses 9-20 follow immediately after verse 8, though in some of these authorities the passage is marked as being doubtful.

west, the sacred and imperishable proclamation of eternal salvation.[s]]

The Longer Ending of Mark

Jesus Appears to Mary Magdalene

9 [Now after he rose early on the first day of the week, he appeared first to Mary Magdalene, from whom he had cast out seven demons. [10]She went out and told those who had been with him, while they were mourning and weeping. [11]But when they heard that he was alive and had been seen by her, they would not believe it.

Jesus Appears to Two Disciples

12 After this he appeared in another form to two of them, as they were walking into the country. [13]And they went back and told the rest, but they did not believe them.

Jesus Commissions the Disciples

14 Later he appeared to the eleven themselves as they were sitting at the table; and he upbraided them for their lack of faith and stubbornness, because they had not believed those who saw him after he had risen.[t] [15]And he said to them, "Go into all the world and proclaim the good news[u] to the whole creation. [16]The one who believes and is baptized will be saved; but the one who does not believe will be condemned. [17]And these signs will accompany those who believe: by using my name they will cast out demons; they will speak in new tongues; [18]they will pick up snakes in their hands,[v] and if they drink any deadly thing, it will not hurt them; they will lay their hands on the sick, and they will recover."

The Ascension of Jesus

19 So then the Lord Jesus, after he had spoken to them, was taken up into heaven and sat down at the right hand of God. [20]And they went out and proclaimed the good news everywhere, while the Lord worked with them and confirmed the message by the signs that accompanied it.[s]]

---

[s] Other ancient authorities add *Amen*   [t] Other ancient authorities add, in whole or in part, *And they excused themselves, saying, "This age of lawlessness and unbelief is under Satan, who does not allow the truth and power of God to prevail over the unclean things of the spirits. Therefore reveal your righteousness now"—thus they spoke to Christ. And Christ replied to them, "The term of years of Satan's power has been fulfilled, but other terrible things draw near. And for those who have sinned I was handed over to death, that they may return to the truth and sin no more, that they may inherit the spiritual and imperishable glory of righteousness that is in heaven."*   [u] Or *gospel*   [v] Other ancient authorities lack *in their hands*

LUKE

Like a Joy-filled Musical
Something was brewing on planet Earth

> But the angel said to them, "Do not be afraid; for see—I am bringing you good news of great joy for all the people." 2.10

ALTHOUGH LUKE COVERS THE SAME basic territory as Matthew and Mark, he gives away his own slant in the very first chapters. Matthew begins with a formal family genealogy; Mark opens with a bleached desert scene. In contrast, Luke describes a hearty celebration.

The way Luke tells it, events surrounding Jesus' birth resembled a joy-filled musical. Characters crowded into the scene: a white-haired great-uncle, an astonished virgin, a tottery old prophetess. They all smiled broadly and, as likely as not, burst into song.

Once Mary had recovered from the shock of seeing an angel, she let loose with a beautiful hymn. The old priest Zechariah broke nine months of muteness with a rousing poem, and even the unborn John the Baptist kicked for joy inside his mother's womb (1.44). When Jesus finally made an entrance, in an inconspicuous stable, the sky filled with singing angels. Clearly, something was brewing on planet Earth.

History Split in Two

You get the feeling when you read his account that Luke wanted to capture in words the spirit of "great joy" that the angel predicted (2.10). Among dreary, defeated villagers in a remote corner of the Roman empire, something climactically good was bursting out.

The author tells us (1.1–4) that he researched many accounts of Jesus' life. Intimate details in these first two chapters show he relied heavily on eyewitnesses, for no other Gospel writer picked up so many facts. Careful attention to detail and an undergirding tone of joy characterize Luke's book.

Jesus' birth literally split history into two parts; we memorialize the event whenever we write a date. The book of Luke takes us back to the world before there was an A.D. or B.C., when Jesus' life was just beginning.

Even now, almost 2,000 years later, the commemoration of Jesus' birth still gives cause for joy. We eat better during the Christmas season, buy gifts for others, donate to charity, and sing more often. Our feelings of celebration are gentle aftershocks, reminders of the remarkable moment when God became a man and lived on earth.

How to Read Luke

Luke probably did not know Jesus personally. But as a dedicated convert in the early church, he accompanied the apostle Paul on missionary trips. In three of his letters, Paul refers to Luke with great affection.

As he mentions in his introduction, Luke eventually saw the need to draw up a carefully researched account of the life of Christ. Many accounts of varying quality existed then, but Luke set out to interview eyewitnesses and compose a thoughtful summary. His book shows thoroughness and detail. It starts before Jesus' birth, and ends with his ascension into heaven.

You should find Luke a very appealing book to read. Luke was a gifted writer, and the stories he recorded have won their place among the classics of literature: the Good Samaritan, the Prodigal and His Brother, the Rich Man and Lazarus. If Mark is a Gospel of action, Luke is a Gospel of relationships. It contains very good character descriptions.

Look for the many different ethnic, religious, economic, and social groups in Luke. Think of the diverse groups in a country like the United States today. How do you think each of them would respond to Jesus in the flesh?

Note especially two large sections of Luke that present material found nowhere else: chapters 1–2 and chapters 10–19.

PEOPLE YOU'LL MEET IN LUKE

ELIZABETH AND ZECHARIAH *(p. 1053)*
MARY, MOTHER OF JESUS *(p. 1055)*
MARTHA AND MARY OF BETHANY *(p. 1070)*

3-TRACK READING PLAN

For an explanation and complete listing of the 3-track reading plan, turn to page 7.

TRACK 1: *Two-Week Courses on the Bible*
The Track 1 reading program on the Life and Teachings of Jesus includes four chapters from Luke. See page 7 for a complete listing of this course.

TRACK 2: *An Overview of Luke in 8 Days*
Over the next eight days, read from the material that's found in no other Gospel but Luke's.

☐ Day 1. Read the Introduction to Luke and then Luke's account in chapter 1 of the events preceding Jesus' birth.
☐ Day 2. Read the familiar Christmas passage, chapter 2.
☐ Day 3. Read chapter 10, which includes the parable of the Good Samaritan.
☐ Day 4. Read chapter 12, in which Jesus draws a strong contrast between those who trust him, no matter how poor, and haughty rich people.
☐ Day 5. Read the famous parables, or short stories, that Jesus tells in chapter 15.
☐ Day 6. Read chapter 16's two familiar stories: the shrewd manager and the rich man and Lazarus.
☐ Day 7. Read chapter 18.
☐ Day 8. How did Jesus' disciples react to his resurrection? Read a good description in chapter 24.

Now turn to page 9 for your next Track 2 reading project.

TRACK 3: *All of Luke in 24 Days*
After you have read through Luke, turn to pages 10–14 for your next Track 3 reading project.

☐1	☐2	☐3	☐4	☐5	☐6	☐7	☐8
☐9	☐10	☐11	☐12	☐13	☐14	☐15	☐16
☐17	☐18	☐19	☐20	☐21	☐22	☐23	☐24

Dedication to Theophilus

1 Since many have undertaken to set down an orderly account of the events that have been fulfilled among us, [2]just as they were handed on to us by those who from the beginning were eyewitnesses and servants of the word, [3]I too decided, after investigating everything carefully from the very first,[a] to write an orderly account for you, most excellent Theophilus, [4]so that you may know the truth concerning the things about which you have been instructed.

The Birth of John the Baptist Foretold

5 In the days of King Herod of Judea, there was a priest named Zechariah, who belonged to the priestly order of Abijah. His wife was a descendant of Aaron, and her name was Elizabeth. [6]Both of them were righteous before God, living

a Or for a long time

blamelessly according to all the commandments and regulations of the Lord. [7]But they had no children, because Elizabeth was barren, and both were getting on in years.

1.3 Luke the Historian

A historian looks for original sources of information—people who were personally involved in the events being described. Luke doesn't claim to be an eyewitness himself, but he had carefully interviewed many who were. As the apostle Paul's traveling companion, Luke must have met many such sources. The Gospel of Luke is the first of a two-part work; the book of Acts continues the story.

8 Once when he was serving as priest before God and his section was on duty, [9]he was chosen by lot, according to the custom of the priesthood, to enter the sanctuary of the Lord and offer incense. [10]Now at the time of the incense offering, the whole assembly of the people was praying outside. [11]Then there appeared to him an angel of the Lord, standing at the right side of the altar of incense. [12]When Zechariah saw him, he was terrified; and fear overwhelmed him. [13]But the angel said to him, "Do not be afraid, Zechariah, for your prayer has been heard. Your wife Elizabeth will bear you a son, and you will name him John. [14]You will have joy and gladness, and many will rejoice at his birth, [15]for he will be great in the sight of the Lord. He must never drink wine or strong drink; even before his birth he will be filled with the Holy Spirit. [16]He will turn many of the people of Israel to the Lord their God. [17]With the spirit and power of Elijah he will go before him, to turn the hearts of parents to their children, and the disobedient to the wisdom of the righteous, to make ready a people prepared for the Lord." [18]Zechariah said to the angel, "How will I know that this is so? For I am an old man, and my wife is getting on in years." [19]The angel replied, "I am Gabriel. I stand in the presence of God, and I have been sent to speak to you and to bring you this good news. [20]But now, because you did not believe my words, which will be fulfilled in their time, you will become mute, unable to speak, until the day these things occur."

21 Meanwhile the people were waiting for Zechariah, and wondered at his delay in the sanctuary. [22]When he did come out, he could not speak to them, and they realized that he had seen a vision in the sanctuary. He kept motioning to them and remained unable to speak. [23]When his time of service was ended, he went to his home.

24 After those days his wife Elizabeth conceived, and for five months she remained in seclusion. She said, [25]"This is what the Lord has done for me when he looked favorably on me and took away the disgrace I have endured among my people."

The Birth of Jesus Foretold

26 In the sixth month the angel Gabriel was sent by God to a town in Galilee called Nazareth, [27]to a virgin engaged to a man whose name was Joseph, of the house of David. The virgin's name was Mary. [28]And he came to her and said, "Greet-

ELIZABETH AND ZECHARIAH *End of an Era*

"THE END OF AN ERA," people say when a retiring coach hands over his clipboard to a young assistant. Similarly, when a new president, a new pastor or a new principal moves in, one era ends and another begins. As fresh faces take over, new ways surely follow.

Elizabeth and Zechariah were among the very first to sense the change that came with Jesus. Devout believers from priestly families, they represented the best of the old order. They had devoted many years to serving God under the Old Testament law. Yet a cloud of sadness hung over their lives, for they were growing old and the greatest blessing they could imagine had been denied them. Childless, they knew their line would die out when they passed away.

Then the new era abruptly broke in. One day as Zechariah was performing his duties in the temple, an angel brought some astounding news: He would have a son! Zechariah, long past the age of parenthood, asked for proof and got perhaps more than he bargained for (1.20).

A short while later a relative of Elizabeth's named Mary brought even greater news. The Messiah, the Savior the Jews had been longing for, was on the way! Not only had God answered Elizabeth's and Zechariah's personal prayers, their nation's long waiting would soon come to an end as well.

Soon the old priest Zechariah and his elderly wife Elizabeth were bringing up the young and vigorous John the Baptist, a true original who would prepare the way for Jesus. With unusual foresight, the old couple greeted the new era with joy. In it they saw not the loss of their old order, but the fulfillment of their dreams.

Life Questions: Think of a time in your life when an "old era" ended and something quite new began: a move, a marriage, a new job or perhaps an experience with God. What made the change difficult? What made it joyful? How was God involved?

ings, favored one! The Lord is with you."[b] 29But she was much perplexed by his words and pondered what sort of greeting this might be. 30The angel said to her, "Do not be afraid, Mary, for you have found favor with God. 31And now, you will conceive in your womb and bear a son, and you will name him Jesus. 32He will be great, and will be called the Son of the Most High, and the Lord God will give to him the throne of his ancestor David. 33He will reign over the house of Jacob forever, and of his kingdom there will be no end." 34Mary said to the angel, "How can this be, since I am a virgin?"[c] 35The angel said to her, "The Holy Spirit will come upon you, and the power of the Most High will overshadow you; therefore the child to be born[d] will be holy; he will be called Son of God. 36And now, your relative Elizabeth in her old age has also conceived a son; and this is the sixth month for her who was said to be barren. 37For nothing will be impossible with God." 38Then Mary said, "Here am I, the servant of the Lord; let it be with me according to your word." Then the angel departed from her.

Mary Visits Elizabeth

39 In those days Mary set out and went with haste to a Judean town in the hill country, 40where she entered the house of Zechariah and greeted Elizabeth. 41When Elizabeth heard Mary's greeting, the child leaped in her womb. And Elizabeth was filled with the Holy Spirit 42and exclaimed with a loud cry, "Blessed are you among women, and blessed is the fruit of your womb. 43And why has this happened to me, that the mother of my Lord comes to me? 44For as soon as I heard the sound of your greeting, the child in my womb leaped for joy. 45And blessed is she who believed that there would be[e] a fulfillment of what was spoken to her by the Lord."

Mary's Song of Praise

▶ See 1 Samuel 2.1–10

46 And Mary[f] said,
"My soul magnifies the Lord,
47   and my spirit rejoices in God
          my Savior,
48   for he has looked with favor on the
          lowliness of his servant.
       Surely, from now on all generations
          will call me blessed;
49   for the Mighty One has done great things
          for me,
       and holy is his name.
50 His mercy is for those who fear him
          from generation to generation.
51 He has shown strength with his arm;

he has scattered the proud in the
          thoughts of their hearts.
52 He has brought down the powerful from
          their thrones,
       and lifted up the lowly;
53 he has filled the hungry with good things,
       and sent the rich away empty.
54 He has helped his servant Israel,
       in remembrance of his mercy,
55 according to the promise he made to our
          ancestors,
       to Abraham and to his descendants
          forever."

56 And Mary remained with her about three months and then returned to her home.

The Birth of John the Baptist

57 Now the time came for Elizabeth to give birth, and she bore a son. 58Her neighbors and relatives heard that the Lord had shown his great mercy to her, and they rejoiced with her.

59 On the eighth day they came to circumcise the child, and they were going to name him Zechariah after his father. 60But his mother said, "No; he is to be called John." 61They said to her, "None of your relatives has this name." 62Then they began motioning to his father to find out what name he wanted to give him. 63He asked for a writing tablet and wrote, "His name is John." And all of them were amazed. 64Immediately his mouth was opened and his tongue freed, and he began to speak, praising God. 65Fear came over all their neighbors, and all these things were talked about throughout the entire hill country of Judea. 66All who heard them pondered them and said, "What then will this child become?" For, indeed, the hand of the Lord was with him.

Zechariah's Prophecy

67 Then his father Zechariah was filled with the Holy Spirit and spoke this prophecy:
68 "Blessed be the Lord God of Israel,
       for he has looked favorably on his
          people and redeemed them.
69 He has raised up a mighty savior[g] for us
       in the house of his servant David,
70 as he spoke through the mouth of his
          holy prophets from of old,
71   that we would be saved from our
          enemies and from the hand of all
          who hate us.
72 Thus he has shown the mercy promised
          to our ancestors,
       and has remembered his
          holy covenant,
73   the oath that he swore to our ancestor
          Abraham,

---

[b] Other ancient authorities add Blessed are you among women authorities add of you   [e] Or believed, for there will be salvation   [c] Gk I do not know a man   [d] Other ancient   [f] Other ancient authorities read Elizabeth   [g] Gk a horn of

to grant us [74]that we, being rescued
    from the hands of our enemies,
might serve him without fear, [75]in
    holiness and righteousness
    before him all our days.
[76] And you, child, will be called the prophet
    of the Most High;
    for you will go before the Lord to
    prepare his ways,
[77] to give knowledge of salvation to his
    people
    by the forgiveness of their sins.
[78] By the tender mercy of our God,
    the dawn from on high will break
    upon[h] us,
[79] to give light to those who sit in darkness
    and in the shadow of death,
    to guide our feet into the way
    of peace."

80 The child grew and became strong in spirit, and he was in the wilderness until the day he appeared publicly to Israel.

The Birth of Jesus

2 In those days a decree went out from Emperor Augustus that all the world should be registered. [2]This was the first registration and was taken while Quirinius was governor of Syria. [3]All went to their own towns to be registered. [4]Joseph also went from the town of Nazareth in Galilee to Judea, to the city of David called Bethlehem, because he was descended from the house and family of David. [5]He went to be registered with Mary, to whom he was engaged and who was expecting a child. [6]While they were there, the time came for her to deliver her child. [7]And she gave birth to her firstborn son and wrapped him in bands of cloth,

and laid him in a manger, because there was no place for them in the inn.

The Shepherds and the Angels

8 In that region there were shepherds living in the fields, keeping watch over their flock by night. [9]Then an angel of the Lord stood before them,

2.1 Dating by Emperors

Among biblical writers, only Luke dated the events he wrote about by referring to Roman emperors. He had determined (1.1–4) to write a thorough, factual account of Jesus' life, which included setting the events in historical context. Because of the Roman census mentioned here, Mary had to travel from her hometown in a very advanced state of pregnancy. As a result, the Messiah was born in Bethlehem, fulfilling an ancient prophecy.

and the glory of the Lord shone around them, and they were terrified. [10]But the angel said to them, "Do not be afraid; for see—I am bringing you good news of great joy for all the people: [11]to you is born this day in the city of David a Savior, who is the Messiah,[i] the Lord. [12]This will be a sign for you: you will find a child wrapped in bands of cloth and lying in a manger." [13]And suddenly there was with the angel a multitude of the heavenly host,[j] praising God and saying,

[14]   "Glory to God in the highest heaven,
    and on earth peace among those whom
    he favors!"[k]

15 When the angels had left them and gone into heaven, the shepherds said to one another,

[h] Other ancient authorities read *has broken upon*   [i] Or *the Christ*   [j] Gk *army*   [k] Other ancient authorities read
peace, goodwill among people

MARY, MOTHER OF JESUS *Saying Yes to God*

MARY RECEIVED THE GREATEST HONOR God can pay: He chose her to mother his son.
    Probably a teenager at the time, Mary had done nothing to deserve such favor. Yet her simple response spoke deeply of her humble faith. "Here am I, the servant of the Lord; let it be with me according to your word" (Luke 1.38). Without hesitation, Mary said yes to God's plan to take over her life.
    Saying yes to God usually involves sacrifice. It did for Mary, who endured the doubts of her fiancé and the scorn of neighbors who saw her pregnant before marriage. Saying yes meant bearing the pain of childbirth. It meant fleeing to far-off Egypt to protect her baby from Herod's soldiers. It meant raising a child she did not completely understand. (Once during his ministry she came to take charge of Jesus, thinking him out of his mind [Mark 3.21].) Most of all, it meant watching her son die on the cross.
    Our last glimpse of Mary, though, shows her among the disciples after the resurrection, praying for the Holy Spirit Jesus had promised (Acts 1.14). Mary had begun her relationship with Jesus by holding his tiny form in her arms. In the end she realized she must let Jesus hold her. He was not only her child, he was her Lord. To that, too, Mary said yes.

Life Questions: To what is God asking you to say yes? What sacrifice may be involved?

"Let us go now to Bethlehem and see this thing that has taken place, which the Lord has made known to us." [16]So they went with haste and found Mary and Joseph, and the child lying in the manger. [17]When they saw this, they made known what had been told them about this child; [18]and all who heard it were amazed at what the shepherds told them. [19]But Mary treasured all these words and pondered them in her heart. [20]The shepherds returned, glorifying and praising God for all they had heard and seen, as it had been told them.

2.20 Cast of Characters

If a public relations firm planned the introduction of God's Son on earth, whom would they invite? Certainly not the group Luke introduces. No Roman emperor or Greek philosopher attended. Instead, Luke tells of an obscure priest and his wife, a carpenter and his young fiancée, a group of shepherds, and two elderly people. Jesus never had much to do with the high and mighty, except during his trial and execution. He would change the world through the lives of ordinary people.

Jesus Is Named

21 After eight days had passed, it was time to circumcise the child; and he was called Jesus, the name given by the angel before he was conceived in the womb.

Jesus Is Presented in the Temple

22 When the time came for their purification according to the law of Moses, they brought him up to Jerusalem to present him to the Lord [23](as it is written in the law of the Lord, "Every firstborn male shall be designated as holy to the Lord"), [24]and they offered a sacrifice according to what is stated in the law of the Lord, "a pair of turtledoves or two young pigeons."

25 Now there was a man in Jerusalem whose name was Simeon;[l] this man was righteous and devout, looking forward to the consolation of Israel, and the Holy Spirit rested on him. [26]It had been revealed to him by the Holy Spirit that he would not see death before he had seen the Lord's Messiah.[m] [27]Guided by the Spirit, Simeon[n] came into the temple; and when the parents brought in the child Jesus, to do for him what was customary under the law, [28]Simeon[o] took him in his arms and praised God, saying,

29 "Master, now you are dismissing your
      servant[p] in peace,
    according to your word;
30 for my eyes have seen your salvation,

31   which you have prepared in the
      presence of all peoples,
32 a light for revelation to the Gentiles
    and for glory to your people Israel."

33 And the child's father and mother were amazed at what was being said about him. [34]Then Simeon[l] blessed them and said to his mother Mary, "This child is destined for the falling and the rising of many in Israel, and to be a sign that will be opposed [35]so that the inner thoughts of many will be revealed—and a sword will pierce your own soul too."

36 There was also a prophet, Anna[q] the daughter of Phanuel, of the tribe of Asher. She was of a great age, having lived with her husband seven years after her marriage, [37]then as a widow to the age of eighty-four. She never left the temple but worshiped there with fasting and prayer night and day. [38]At that moment she came, and began to praise God and to speak about the child[r] to all who were looking for the redemption of Jerusalem.

The Return to Nazareth

39 When they had finished everything required by the law of the Lord, they returned to Galilee, to their own town of Nazareth. [40]The child grew and became strong, filled with wisdom; and the favor of God was upon him.

The Boy Jesus in the Temple

41 Now every year his parents went to Jerusalem for the festival of the Passover. [42]And when

2.41 Jesus' Childhood

Most Christmas pageants rely heavily on Luke because of his thoroughness in reporting the facts of Jesus' birth. And only Luke recorded the brief glimpses of Jesus' early years given in this chapter. For this reason, many scholars believe Luke must have interviewed Mary, mother of Jesus, during his investigations into Jesus' life.

he was twelve years old, they went up as usual for the festival. [43]When the festival was ended and they started to return, the boy Jesus stayed behind in Jerusalem, but his parents did not know it. [44]Assuming that he was in the group of travelers, they went a day's journey. Then they started to look for him among their relatives and friends. [45]When they did not find him, they returned to Jerusalem to search for him. [46]After three days they found him in the temple, sitting among the teachers, listening to them and asking them questions. [47]And all who heard him were amazed at his understanding and his answers. [48]When his

[l] Gk Symeon   [m] Or the Lord's Christ   [n] Gk In the Spirit, he   [o] Gk he   [p] Gk slave   [q] Gk Hanna
[r] Gk him

parents[s] saw him they were astonished; and his mother said to him, "Child, why have you treated us like this? Look, your father and I have been searching for you in great anxiety." [49]He said to them, "Why were you searching for me? Did you not know that I must be in my Father's house?"[t] [50]But they did not understand what he said to them. [51]Then he went down with them and came to Nazareth, and was obedient to them. His mother treasured all these things in her heart.

52 And Jesus increased in wisdom and in years,[u] and in divine and human favor.

The Proclamation of John the Baptist

▶ See Matthew 3.1–10; Mark 1.3–5

3 In the fifteenth year of the reign of Emperor Tiberius, when Pontius Pilate was governor of Judea, and Herod was ruler[v] of Galilee, and his brother Philip ruler[v] of the region of Ituraea and Trachonitis, and Lysanias ruler[v] of Abilene, [2]during the high priesthood of Annas and Caiaphas, the word of God came to John son of Zechariah in the wilderness. [3]He went into all the region around the Jordan, proclaiming a baptism of repentance for the forgiveness of sins, [4]as it is written in the book of the words of the prophet Isaiah,

"The voice of one crying out in
      the wilderness:
'Prepare the way of the Lord,
   make his paths straight.
[5] Every valley shall be filled,
      and every mountain and hill shall be
         made low,
   and the crooked shall be made straight,
      and the rough ways made smooth;
[6] and all flesh shall see the salvation of
         God.'"

7 John said to the crowds that came out to be baptized by him, "You brood of vipers! Who warned you to flee from the wrath to come? [8]Bear fruits worthy of repentance. Do not begin to say to yourselves, 'We have Abraham as our ancestor'; for I tell you, God is able from these stones to raise up children to Abraham. [9]Even now the ax is lying at the root of the trees; every tree therefore that does not bear good fruit is cut down and thrown into the fire."

10 And the crowds asked him, "What then should we do?" [11]In reply he said to them, "Whoever has two coats must share with anyone who has none; and whoever has food must do likewise." [12]Even tax collectors came to be baptized, and they asked him, "Teacher, what should we do?" [13]He said to them, "Collect no more than the amount prescribed for you." [14]Soldiers also asked him, "And we, what should we do?" He said to them, "Do not extort money from anyone by threats or false accusation, and be satisfied with your wages."

15 As the people were filled with expectation, and all were questioning in their hearts concerning John, whether he might be the Messiah,[w] [16]John answered all of them by saying, "I baptize you with water; but one who is more powerful than I is coming; I am not worthy to untie the thong of his sandals. He will baptize you with[x] the Holy Spirit and fire. [17]His winnowing fork is in his hand, to clear his threshing floor and to gather the wheat into his granary; but the chaff he will burn with unquenchable fire."

18 So, with many other exhortations, he proclaimed the good news to the people. [19]But Herod the ruler,[v] who had been rebuked by him because of Herodias, his brother's wife, and because of all the evil things that Herod had done, [20]added to them all by shutting up John in prison.

The Baptism of Jesus

▶ See Matthew 1.1–17; 3.13–17; Mark 1.9–11

21 Now when all the people were baptized, and when Jesus also had been baptized and was praying, the heaven was opened, [22]and the Holy Spirit descended upon him in bodily form like a dove. And a voice came from heaven, "You are my Son, the Beloved;[y] with you I am well pleased."[z]

The Ancestors of Jesus

23 Jesus was about thirty years old when he began his work. He was the son (as was thought) of Joseph son of Heli, [24]son of Matthat, son of Levi, son of Melchi, son of Jannai, son of Joseph, [25]son of Mattathias, son of Amos, son of Nahum, son of Esli, son of Naggai, [26]son of Maath, son of Mattathias, son of Semein, son of Josech, son of Joda, [27]son of Joanan, son of Rhesa, son of Zerubbabel, son of Shealtiel,[a] son of Neri, [28]son of Melchi, son of Addi, son of Cosam, son of Elmadam, son of Er, [29]son of Joshua, son of Eliezer, son of Jorim, son of Matthat, son of Levi, [30]son of Simeon, son of Judah, son of Joseph, son of Jonam, son of Eliakim, [31]son of Melea, son of Menna, son of Mattatha, son of Nathan, son of David, [32]son of Jesse, son of Obed, son of Boaz, son of Sala,[b] son of Nahshon, [33]son of Amminadab, son of Admin, son of Arni,[c] son of Hezron, son of Perez, son of Judah, [34]son of Jacob, son of Isaac, son of Abraham, son of Terah, son of Nahor, [35]son of Serug, son of Reu, son of Peleg, son of Eber, son of Shelah, [36]son of Cainan, son of Arphaxad, son of Shem, son of Noah, son of Lamech, [37]son of Methuselah, son of Enoch, son of

---

[s] Gk they   [t] Or be about my Father's interests?   [u] Or in stature   [v] Gk tetrarch   [w] Or the Christ   [x] Or in
[y] Or my beloved Son   [z] Other ancient authorities read You are my Son, today I have begotten you   [a] Gk Salathiel
[b] Other ancient authorities read Salmon   [c] Other ancient authorities read Amminadab, son of Aram; others vary widely

Jared, son of Mahalaleel, son of Cainan, ³⁸son of Enos, son of Seth, son of Adam, son of God.

The Temptation of Jesus

▶ See Matthew 4.1–11; Mark 1.12–13

4 Jesus, full of the Holy Spirit, returned from the Jordan and was led by the Spirit in the

---

3.38 A Gospel for the Gentiles

Matthew's Gospel traced Jesus' roots back to Abraham, father of the Jewish race. But Luke, probably the only Gentile writer of the New Testament, emphasized that Jesus' good news was for all people, not just the Jews. In keeping with that purpose, he carried Jesus' lineage all the way back to the first man, Adam.

---

wilderness, ²where for forty days he was tempted by the devil. He ate nothing at all during those days, and when they were over, he was famished. ³The devil said to him, "If you are the Son of God, command this stone to become a loaf of bread." ⁴Jesus answered him, "It is written, 'One does not live by bread alone.'"

5 Then the devil*ᵈ* led him up and showed him in an instant all the kingdoms of the world. ⁶And the devil*ᵈ* said to him, "To you I will give their glory and all this authority; for it has been given over to me, and I give it to anyone I please. ⁷If you, then, will worship me, it will all be yours." ⁸Jesus answered him, "It is written,

'Worship the Lord your God,
     and serve only him.'"

9 Then the devil*ᵈ* took him to Jerusalem, and placed him on the pinnacle of the temple, saying to him, "If you are the Son of God, throw yourself down from here, ¹⁰for it is written,

'He will command his angels concerning
          you,
     to protect you,'
¹¹and
'On their hands they will bear you up,
     so that you will not dash your foot
          against a stone.'"
¹²Jesus answered him, "It is said, 'Do not put the Lord your God to the test.'" ¹³When the devil had finished every test, he departed from him until an opportune time.

The Beginning of the Galilean Ministry

14 Then Jesus, filled with the power of the Spirit, returned to Galilee, and a report about him spread through all the surrounding country. ¹⁵He began to teach in their synagogues and was praised by everyone.

The Rejection of Jesus at Nazareth

16 When he came to Nazareth, where he had been brought up, he went to the synagogue on the sabbath day, as was his custom. He stood up to read, ¹⁷and the scroll of the prophet Isaiah was given to him. He unrolled the scroll and found the place where it was written:
¹⁸ "The Spirit of the Lord is upon me,
     because he has anointed me
          to bring good news to the poor.
He has sent me to proclaim release to the
          captives
     and recovery of sight to the blind,
          to let the oppressed go free,
¹⁹ to proclaim the year of the Lord's favor."
²⁰And he rolled up the scroll, gave it back to the attendant, and sat down. The eyes of all in the synagogue were fixed on him. ²¹Then he began to say to them, "Today this scripture has been fulfilled in your hearing." ²²All spoke well of him and were amazed at the gracious words that came from his mouth. They said, "Is not this Joseph's son?" ²³He said to them, "Doubtless you will quote to me this proverb, 'Doctor, cure yourself!' And you will say, 'Do here also in your hometown the things that we have heard you did at Capernaum.'" ²⁴And he said, "Truly I tell you, no prophet is accepted in the prophet's hometown. ²⁵But the truth is, there were many widows in Israel in the time of Elijah, when the heaven was shut up three years and six months, and there was a severe famine over all the land; ²⁶yet Elijah was sent to none of them except to a widow at Zarephath in Sidon.

4.26 Hard Words for the Jews

Luke's book stresses the universal appeal of the gospel. In both of these Old Testament stories (the Zarephath widow and Naaman), God sent a prophet to perform a miracle for foreigners (non-Jews). Such an emphasis scandalized the Jews, who saw themselves as God's uniquely chosen people. Jesus' words proved so inflammatory that a mob attempted to kill him. As far as is known, Jesus never returned to his home territory of Nazareth.

---

²⁷There were also many lepers*ᵉ* in Israel in the time of the prophet Elisha, and none of them was cleansed except Naaman the Syrian." ²⁸When they heard this, all in the synagogue were filled with rage. ²⁹They got up, drove him out of the town, and led him to the brow of the hill on which their town was built, so that they might hurl him off the cliff. ³⁰But he passed through the midst of them and went on his way.

ᵈ Gk *he*   *ᵉ* The terms *leper* and *leprosy* can refer to several diseases

The Man with an Unclean Spirit

31 He went down to Capernaum, a city in Galilee, and was teaching them on the sabbath. 32They were astounded at his teaching, because he spoke with authority. 33In the synagogue there was a man who had the spirit of an unclean demon, and he cried out with a loud voice, 34"Let us alone! What have you to do with us, Jesus of Nazareth? Have you come to destroy us? I know who you are, the Holy One of God." 35But Jesus rebuked him, saying, "Be silent, and come out of him!" When the demon had thrown him down before them, he came out of him without having done him any harm. 36They were all amazed and kept saying to one another, "What kind of utterance is this? For with authority and power he commands the unclean spirits, and out they come!" 37And a report about him began to reach every place in the region.

Healings at Simon's House

▶ See Matthew 8.14–17; Mark 1.29–38

38 After leaving the synagogue he entered Simon's house. Now Simon's mother-in-law was suffering from a high fever, and they asked him about her. 39Then he stood over her and rebuked the fever, and it left her. Immediately she got up and began to serve them.

40 As the sun was setting, all those who had any who were sick with various kinds of diseases brought them to him; and he laid his hands on each of them and cured them. 41Demons also came out of many, shouting, "You are the Son of God!" But he rebuked them and would not allow them to speak, because they knew that he was the Messiah.f

Jesus Preaches in the Synagogues

42 At daybreak he departed and went into a deserted place. And the crowds were looking for him; and when they reached him, they wanted to prevent him from leaving them. 43But he said to them, "I must proclaim the good news of the kingdom of God to the other cities also; for I was sent for this purpose." 44So he continued proclaiming the message in the synagogues of Judea.g

Jesus Calls the First Disciples

▶ See Matthew 4.18–22; Mark 1.16–20; John 1.40–42

5 Once while Jesush was standing beside the lake of Gennesaret, and the crowd was pressing in on him to hear the word of God, 2he saw two boats there at the shore of the lake; the fishermen had gone out of them and were washing their nets. 3He got into one of the boats, the one belonging to Simon, and asked him to put out a little way from the shore. Then he sat down and taught the crowds from the boat. 4When he had finished speaking, he said to Simon, "Put out into the deep water and let down your nets for a catch." 5Simon answered, "Master, we have worked all night long but have caught nothing. Yet if you say so, I will let down the nets." 6When they had done this, they caught so many fish that their nets were beginning to break. 7So they signaled their partners in the other boat to come and help them. And they came and filled both boats, so that they began to sink. 8But when Simon Peter saw it, he fell down at Jesus' knees, saying, "Go away from me, Lord, for I am a sinful man!" 9For he and all who were with him were amazed at the catch of fish that they had taken; 10and so also were James and John, sons of Zebedee, who were partners with Simon. Then Jesus said to Simon, "Do not be afraid; from now on you will be catching people." 11When they had brought their boats to shore, they left everything and followed him.

Jesus Cleanses a Leper

▶ See Matthew 8.2–4; Mark 1.40–44

12 Once, when he was in one of the cities, there was a man covered with leprosy.i When he saw Jesus, he bowed with his face to the ground and begged him, "Lord, if you choose, you can make me clean." 13Then Jesush stretched out his hand, touched him, and said, "I do choose. Be made clean." Immediately the leprosyi left him. 14And he ordered him to tell no one. "Go," he said, "and show yourself to the priest, and, as Moses commanded, make an offering for your cleansing, for a testimony to them." 15But now more than ever the word about Jesusj spread abroad; many crowds would gather to hear him and to be cured of their diseases. 16But he would withdraw to deserted places and pray.

Jesus Heals a Paralytic

▶ See Matthew 9.2–8; Mark 2.3–12

17 One day, while he was teaching, Pharisees and teachers of the law were sitting near by (they had come from every village of Galilee and Judea and from Jerusalem); and the power of the Lord was with him to heal.k 18Just then some men came, carrying a paralyzed man on a bed. They were trying to bring him in and lay him before Jesus;j 19but finding no way to bring him in because of the crowd, they went up on the roof and let him down with his bed through the tiles into the middle of the crowdl in front of Jesus. 20When he saw their faith, he said, "Friend,m your

---

f Or the Christ　g Other ancient authorities read Galilee　h Gk he　i The terms leper and leprosy can refer to several diseases　j Gk him　k Other ancient authorities read was present to heal them　l Gk into the midst　m Gk Man

sins are forgiven you." [21]Then the scribes and the Pharisees began to question, "Who is this who is speaking blasphemies? Who can forgive sins but God alone?" [22]When Jesus perceived their questionings, he answered them, "Why do you raise such questions in your hearts? [23]Which is easier, to say, 'Your sins are forgiven you,' or to say, 'Stand up and walk'? [24]But so that you may know that the Son of Man has authority on earth to forgive sins"—he said to the one who was paralyzed—"I say to you, stand up and take your bed and go to your home." [25]Immediately he stood up before them, took what he had been lying on, and went to his home, glorifying God. [26]Amazement seized all of them, and they glorified God and were filled with awe, saying, "We have seen strange things today."

5.20 Group Faith

The paralytic's friends showed remarkable determination to get him to Jesus. Luke writes that their faith—the man's and his friends'—moved Jesus to forgive and to heal. Jesus recognized that a helpless man needed help to come to him. Often an individual comes to Christ only with the persistent encouragement of friends and family.

Jesus Calls Levi

▶ *See Matthew 9.9–13; Mark 2.14–17*

27 After this he went out and saw a tax collector named Levi, sitting at the tax booth; and he

A Physician Looks at the Poor

The surprising emphasis of an upper-class writer

A GREAT DOCTOR ONCE COMPARED HIS professional duties to working at the complaint desk of a large department store. "All through medical school I studied the body's wonderful engineering. A healthy body is perfect—absolutely beautiful to observe. But in practice I spend my time treating people whose bodies don't work right. I hear only complaints. After a while, it's easy to lose perspective."

> "Those who are well have no need of a physician, but those who are sick." 5.31

Luke, a physician, knew firsthand about sick and suffering people; he, too, heard their daily complaints. Yet somehow he never became callous. In fact, his Gospel focuses on Jesus' ministry to society's "complaint desk": the poor, the sick, and the neglected.

Jesus Announces His Mission

In Luke, even Mary's opening song strikes a chord for the poor and hungry (1.46–55). Using his favorite title for Jesus ("Son of Man") 25 times, Luke reveals him as a true servant of all humanity.

Luke 4 shows Jesus boldly declaring why he came to earth. He had just resisted temptations of wealth and power, and returned from the desert to his hometown. There Jesus, a local village boy, announced his unique mission from God: to preach good news to the poor, to free prisoners, heal the blind, and release the oppressed (4.18–19).

With little editorial comment, Luke follows Jesus from town to town. Jesus avoided such fashionable places as the resort town of Tiberias. He stayed near the farming communities and fishing villages clustered around the Sea of Galilee, serving the needs of humble people.

Reaction to Jesus varied. Naturally, the sick clamored for his attention, begging for healing. Even a few powerful people believed in him, including a respected Roman centurion and a synagogue ruler. But the religious leaders constantly challenged his actions, and his own neighbors angrily chased him out of town.

An Unlikely Friend of the Poor

Luke skillfully brings his characters to life in vignettes. Learned and sophisticated, he uses the finest Greek of any Gospel writer; but, ironically, he focuses mainly on the poor and the outcast. Women, largely ignored by ancient historians, play a large role: Luke introduces 13 women mentioned in no other Gospel. He also shows a delight and appreciation for children.

It may seem strange that Luke, by education and profession a member of the upper class, emerged as a champion of the poor and the oppressed. Evidently Jesus' message had affected him deeply. As Jesus said, "Those who are well have no need of a physician, but those who are sick; I have come to call not the righteous but sinners to repentance" (5.31–32).

Life Questions: As Luke tells it, Jesus threatened the rich and powerful, but appealed to the poor and outcast. If Jesus came today, how would those two groups in our society respond to him?

said to him, "Follow me." [28]And he got up, left everything, and followed him.

29 Then Levi gave a great banquet for him in his house; and there was a large crowd of tax collectors and others sitting at the table[n] with them. [30]The Pharisees and their scribes were complaining to his disciples, saying, "Why do you eat and drink with tax collectors and sinners?" [31]Jesus answered, "Those who are well have no need of a physician, but those who are sick; [32]I have come to call not the righteous but sinners to repentance."

The Question about Fasting

▶ *See Matthew 9.14–17; Mark 2.18–22*

33 Then they said to him, "John's disciples, like the disciples of the Pharisees, frequently fast and pray, but your disciples eat and drink." [34]Jesus said to them, "You cannot make wedding guests fast while the bridegroom is with them, can you? [35]The days will come when the bridegroom will be taken away from them, and then they will fast in those days." [36]He also told them a parable: "No one tears a piece from a new garment and sews it on an old garment; otherwise the new will be torn, and the piece from the new will not match the old. [37]And no one puts new wine into old wineskins; otherwise the new wine will burst the skins and will be spilled, and the skins will be destroyed. [38]But new wine must be put into fresh wineskins. [39]And no one after drinking old wine desires new wine, but says, 'The old is good.'"[o]

The Question about the Sabbath

▶ *See Matthew 12.1–14; Mark 2.23—3.6*

6 One sabbath[p] while Jesus[q] was going through the grainfields, his disciples plucked some heads of grain, rubbed them in their hands, and ate them. [2]But some of the Pharisees said, "Why are you doing what is not lawful[r] on the sabbath?" [3]Jesus answered, "Have you not read what David did when he and his companions were hungry? [4]He entered the house of God and took and ate the bread of the Presence, which it is not lawful for any but the priests to eat, and gave some to his companions?" [5]Then he said to them, "The Son of Man is lord of the sabbath."

The Man with a Withered Hand

6 On another sabbath he entered the synagogue and taught, and there was a man there whose right hand was withered. [7]The scribes and the Pharisees watched him to see whether he would cure on the sabbath, so that they might find an accusation against him. [8]Even though he knew what they were thinking, he said to the man who had the withered hand, "Come and stand here." He got up and stood there. [9]Then Jesus said to them, "I ask you, is it lawful to do good or to do harm on the sabbath, to save life or to destroy it?" [10]After looking around at all of them, he said to him, "Stretch out your hand." He did

6.9 Rules Without Love

Luke's vignettes on Jesus and the sabbath (see also 13.10–17) demonstrate the legalism Jesus opposed. Jews of his day observed very strict rules governing what could be done on the sabbath. Religious leaders became furious at Jesus for "breaking" the traditions. His crime? Healing people on the sabbath. Jesus refused to let traditions interfere with compassion for needy people.

so, and his hand was restored. [11]But they were filled with fury and discussed with one another what they might do to Jesus.

Jesus Chooses the Twelve Apostles

▶ *See Matthew 10.2–4; Mark 3.16–19; Acts 1.13*

12 Now during those days he went out to the mountain to pray; and he spent the night in prayer to God. [13]And when day came, he called his disciples and chose twelve of them, whom he also named apostles: [14]Simon, whom he named Peter, and his brother Andrew, and James, and John, and Philip, and Bartholomew, [15]and Matthew, and Thomas, and James son of Alphaeus, and Simon, who was called the Zealot, [16]and Judas son of James, and Judas Iscariot, who became a traitor.

Jesus Teaches and Heals

▶ *See Matthew 5.3–12*

17 He came down with them and stood on a level place, with a great crowd of his disciples and a great multitude of people from all Judea, Jerusalem, and the coast of Tyre and Sidon. [18]They had come to hear him and to be healed of their diseases; and those who were troubled with unclean spirits were cured. [19]And all in the crowd were trying to touch him, for power came out from him and healed all of them.

Blessings and Woes

20 Then he looked up at his disciples and said:

"Blessed are you who are poor,
  for yours is the kingdom of God.
21 "Blessed are you who are hungry now,
  for you will be filled.
"Blessed are you who weep now,
  for you will laugh.

[n] Gk *reclining* [o] Other ancient authorities read *better*; others lack verse 39 [p] Other ancient authorities read *On the second first sabbath* [q] Gk *he* [r] Other ancient authorities add *to do*

22 "Blessed are you when people hate you, and when they exclude you, revile you, and defame you[s] on account of the Son of Man. 23Rejoice in that day and leap for joy, for surely your reward is great in heaven; for that is what their ancestors did to the prophets.

24 "But woe to you who are rich,
  for you have received your consolation.
25 "Woe to you who are full now,
  for you will be hungry.
"Woe to you who are laughing now,
  for you will mourn and weep.

26 "Woe to you when all speak well of you, for that is what their ancestors did to the false prophets.

Love for Enemies

27 "But I say to you that listen, Love your enemies, do good to those who hate you, 28bless those who curse you, pray for those who abuse you. 29If anyone strikes you on the cheek, offer the other also; and from anyone who takes away your coat do not withhold even your shirt. 30Give to everyone who begs from you; and if anyone takes away your goods, do not ask for them again. 31Do to others as you would have them do to you.

32 "If you love those who love you, what credit is that to you? For even sinners love those who love them. 33If you do good to those who do good to you, what credit is that to you? For even sinners do the same. 34If you lend to those from whom you hope to receive, what credit is that to you? Even sinners lend to sinners, to receive as much again. 35But love your enemies, do good, and lend, expecting nothing in return.[t] Your reward will be great, and you will be children of the Most High; for he is kind to the ungrateful and the wicked. 36Be merciful, just as your Father is merciful.

Judging Others

▶ See Matthew 7.1–5

37 "Do not judge, and you will not be judged; do not condemn, and you will not be condemned. Forgive, and you will be forgiven; 38give, and it will be given to you. A good measure, pressed down, shaken together, running over, will be put into your lap; for the measure you give will be the measure you get back."

39 He also told them a parable: "Can a blind person guide a blind person? Will not both fall into a pit? 40A disciple is not above the teacher, but everyone who is fully qualified will be like the teacher. 41Why do you see the speck in your neighbor's[u] eye, but do not notice the log in your own eye? 42Or how can you say to your neighbor,[v] 'Friend,[v] let me take out the speck in your eye,' when you yourself do not see the log in your own eye? You hypocrite, first take the log out of your own eye, and then you will see clearly to take the speck out of your neighbor's[u] eye.

A Tree and Its Fruit

▶ See Matthew 7.16,18,20

43 "No good tree bears bad fruit, nor again does a bad tree bear good fruit; 44for each tree is known by its own fruit. Figs are not gathered from thorns, nor are grapes picked from a bramble bush. 45The good person out of the good treasure of the heart produces good, and the evil person out of evil treasure produces evil; for it is out of the abundance of the heart that the mouth speaks.

The Two Foundations

▶ See Matthew 7.24–27

46 "Why do you call me 'Lord, Lord,' and do not do what I tell you? 47I will show you what someone is like who comes to me, hears my words, and acts on them. 48That one is like a man building a house, who dug deeply and laid the foundation on rock; when a flood arose, the river burst against that house but could not shake it, because it had been well built.[w] 49But the one who hears and does not act is like a man who built a house on the ground without a foundation. When the river burst against it, immediately it fell, and great was the ruin of that house."

Jesus Heals a Centurion's Servant

▶ See Matthew 8.5–13

7 After Jesus[x] had finished all his sayings in the hearing of the people, he entered Capernaum. 2A centurion there had a slave whom he valued highly, and who was ill and close to death. 3When he heard about Jesus, he sent some Jewish elders to him, asking him to come and heal his slave. 4When they came to Jesus, they appealed to him earnestly, saying, "He is worthy of having you do this for him, 5for he loves our people, and it is he who built our synagogue for us." 6And Jesus went with them, but when he was not far from the house, the centurion sent friends to say to him, "Lord, do not trouble yourself, for I am not worthy to have you come under my roof; 7therefore I did not presume to come to you. But only speak the word, and let my servant be healed. 8For I also am a man set under authority, with soldiers under me; and I say to one, 'Go,' and he goes, and to another, 'Come,' and he comes, and to my slave, 'Do this,' and the slave does it." 9When Jesus heard this he was amazed at him, and turning to the crowd that followed him, he said, "I tell you, not even in Israel have I found such faith." 10When those who had been

---

s Gk cast out your name as evil   t Other ancient authorities read despairing of no one   u Gk brother's
v Gk brother   w Other ancient authorities read founded upon the rock   x Gk he

sent returned to the house, they found the slave in good health.

Jesus Raises the Widow's Son at Nain

11 Soon afterwards[y] he went to a town called Nain, and his disciples and a large crowd went with him. [12]As he approached the gate of the town, a man who had died was being carried out. He was his mother's only son, and she was a widow; and with her was a large crowd from the town. [13]When the Lord saw her, he had compassion for her and said to her, "Do not weep." [14]Then he came forward and touched the bier, and the bearers stood still. And he said, "Young man, I say to you, rise!" [15]The dead man sat up and began to speak, and Jesus[z] gave him to his mother. [16]Fear seized all of them; and they glorified God, saying, "A great prophet has risen among us!" and "God has looked favorably on his people!" [17]This word about him spread throughout Judea and all the surrounding country.

Messengers from John the Baptist

▶ *See Matthew 11.2–19*

18 The disciples of John reported all these things to him. So John summoned two of his disciples [19]and sent them to the Lord to ask, "Are you the one who is to come, or are we to wait for

---

7.19 Even John Questioned

The crowds Jesus attracted wavered between enthusiastic support and outright rejection of him. Evidently, some of the controversy even affected John the Baptist, who had baptized Jesus and pronounced him the Son of God (see John 1.34). John, then in prison, sent his disciples to confirm whether Jesus was the true Messiah. Jesus reassured him with a direct reference to the prophecies of Isaiah 61 (see also Luke 4.18–21).

---

another?" [20]When the men had come to him, they said, "John the Baptist has sent us to you to ask, 'Are you the one who is to come, or are we to wait for another?'" [21]Jesus[a] had just then cured many people of diseases, plagues, and evil spirits, and had given sight to many who were blind. [22]And he answered them, "Go and tell John what you have seen and heard: the blind receive their sight, the lame walk, the lepers[b] are cleansed, the deaf hear, the dead are raised, the poor have good news brought to them. [23]And blessed is anyone who takes no offense at me."

24 When John's messengers had gone, Jesus[z] began to speak to the crowds about John:[c]

"What did you go out into the wilderness to look at? A reed shaken by the wind? [25]What then did you go out to see? Someone[d] dressed in soft robes? Look, those who put on fine clothing and live in luxury are in royal palaces. [26]What then did you go out to see? A prophet? Yes, I tell you, and more than a prophet. [27]This is the one about whom it is written,

'See, I am sending my messenger ahead of
  you,
  who will prepare your way before you.'

[28]I tell you, among those born of women no one is greater than John; yet the least in the kingdom of God is greater than he." [29](And all the people who heard this, including the tax collectors, acknowledged the justice of God,[e] because they had been baptized with John's baptism. [30]But by refusing to be baptized by him, the Pharisees and the lawyers rejected God's purpose for themselves.)

31 "To what then will I compare the people of this generation, and what are they like? [32]They are like children sitting in the marketplace and calling to one another,

'We played the flute for you, and you did
  not dance;
  we wailed, and you did not weep.'

[33]For John the Baptist has come eating no bread and drinking no wine, and you say, 'He has a demon'; [34]the Son of Man has come eating and drinking, and you say, 'Look, a glutton and a drunkard, a friend of tax collectors and sinners!' [35]Nevertheless, wisdom is vindicated by all her children."

A Sinful Woman Forgiven

36 One of the Pharisees asked Jesus[c] to eat with him, and he went into the Pharisee's house and took his place at the table. [37]And a woman in the city, who was a sinner, having learned that he was eating in the Pharisee's house, brought an alabaster jar of ointment. [38]She stood behind him at his feet, weeping, and began to bathe his feet with her tears and to dry them with her hair. Then she continued kissing his feet and anointing them with the ointment. [39]Now when the Pharisee who had invited him saw it, he said to himself, "If this man were a prophet, he would have known who and what kind of woman this is who is touching him—that she is a sinner." [40]Jesus spoke up and said to him, "Simon, I have something to say to you." "Teacher," he replied, "speak." [41]"A certain creditor had two debtors; one owed five hundred denarii,[f] and the other fifty. [42]When they could not pay, he canceled the debts for both of them. Now which of them will love him more?" [43]Simon answered, "I suppose the one for whom he can-

---

[y] Other ancient authorities read *Next day*   [z] Gk *he*   [a] Gk *He*   [b] The terms *leper* and *leprosy* can refer to several diseases   [c] Gk *him*   [d] Or *Why then did you go out? To see someone*   [e] Or *praised God*   [f] The denarius was the usual day's wage for a laborer

celed the greater debt." And Jesus[g] said to him, "You have judged rightly." 44Then turning toward the woman, he said to Simon, "Do you see this woman? I entered your house; you gave me no water for my feet, but she has bathed my feet with her tears and dried them with her hair. 45You gave me no kiss, but from the time I came in she has not stopped kissing my feet. 46You did not anoint my head with oil, but she has anointed my feet with ointment. 47Therefore, I tell you, her sins, which were many, have been forgiven; hence she has shown great love. But the one to whom little is forgiven, loves little." 48Then he said to her, "Your sins are forgiven." 49But those who were at the table with him began to say among themselves, "Who is this who even forgives sins?" 50And he said to the woman, "Your faith has saved you; go in peace."

Some Women Accompany Jesus

▶ See Matthew 13.2–23; Mark 4.1–20

8 Soon afterwards he went on through cities and villages, proclaiming and bringing the good news of the kingdom of God. The twelve were with him, 2as well as some women who had been cured of evil spirits and infirmities: Mary, called Magdalene, from whom seven demons had gone out, 3and Joanna, the wife of Herod's steward Chuza, and Susanna, and many others, who provided for them[h] out of their resources.

8.3 Jesus' Support

In the Middle East of that day, teachers traveled from town to town, accepting the gifts of appreciative listeners. Luke points out that certain women who had been healed by Jesus helped provide for him. In all, Luke introduces 13 women who do not appear in the other Gospels.

The Parable of the Sower

4 When a great crowd gathered and people from town after town came to him, he said in a parable: 5"A sower went out to sow his seed; and as he sowed, some fell on the path and was trampled on, and the birds of the air ate it up. 6Some fell on the rock; and as it grew up, it withered for lack of moisture. 7Some fell among thorns, and the thorns grew with it and choked it. 8Some fell into good soil, and when it grew, it produced a hundredfold." As he said this, he called out, "Let anyone with ears to hear listen!"

The Purpose of the Parables

9 Then his disciples asked him what this parable meant. 10He said, "To you it has been given to know the secrets[i] of the kingdom of God; but to others I speak[j] in parables, so that

'looking they may not perceive,
and listening they may not
understand.'

The Parable of the Sower Explained

11 "Now the parable is this: The seed is the word of God. 12The ones on the path are those who have heard; then the devil comes and takes away the word from their hearts, so that they may not believe and be saved. 13The ones on the rock are those who, when they hear the word, receive it with joy. But these have no root; they believe only for a while and in a time of testing fall away. 14As for what fell among the thorns, these are the ones who hear; but as they go on their way, they are choked by the cares and riches and pleasures of life, and their fruit does not mature. 15But as for that in the good soil, these are the ones who, when they hear the word, hold it fast in an honest and good heart, and bear fruit with patient endurance.

A Lamp under a Jar

16 "No one after lighting a lamp hides it under a jar, or puts it under a bed, but puts it on a lampstand, so that those who enter may see the light. 17For nothing is hidden that will not be disclosed, nor is anything secret that will not become known and come to light. 18Then pay attention to how you listen; for to those who have, more will be given; and from those who do not have, even what they seem to have will be taken away."

The True Kindred of Jesus

▶ See Matthew 12.46–50; Mark 3.31–35

19 Then his mother and his brothers came to him, but they could not reach him because of the crowd. 20And he was told, "Your mother and your brothers are standing outside, wanting to see you." 21But he said to them, "My mother and my brothers are those who hear the word of God and do it."

Jesus Calms a Storm

▶ See Matthew 8.23–27; Mark 4.36–41

22 One day he got into a boat with his disciples, and he said to them, "Let us go across to the other side of the lake." So they put out, 23and while they were sailing he fell asleep. A windstorm swept down on the lake, and the boat was filling with water, and they were in danger. 24They went to him and woke him up, shouting, "Master, Master, we are perishing!" And he woke up and rebuked the wind and the raging waves; they

---

g Gk *he*   h Other ancient authorities read *him*   i Or *mysteries*   j Gk lacks *I speak*

ceased, and there was a calm. 25He said to them, "Where is your faith?" They were afraid and amazed, and said to one another, "Who then is this, that he commands even the winds and the water, and they obey him?"

Jesus Heals the Gerasene Demoniac

▶ *See Matthew 8.28–34; Mark 5.1–20*

26 Then they arrived at the country of the Gerasenes,[k] which is opposite Galilee. 27As he stepped out on land, a man of the city who had demons met him. For a long time he had worn[l] no clothes, and he did not live in a house but in

8.27 Homeless

Much as some mentally troubled people live under bridges today, this disturbed man had fled society to live in the tombs. Cemeteries in the ancient world were located far from town, because people feared the spirits of the dead. The man was violent and uncontrollable, and he greeted Jesus with bizarre behavior. Jesus, rather than avoiding him, went straight to the heart of his problem.

the tombs. 28When he saw Jesus, he fell down before him and shouted at the top of his voice, "What have you to do with me, Jesus, Son of the Most High God? I beg you, do not torment me"— 29for Jesus[m] had commanded the unclean spirit to come out of the man. (For many times it had seized him; he was kept under guard and bound with chains and shackles, but he would break the bonds and be driven by the demon into the wilds.) 30Jesus then asked him, "What is your name?" He said, "Legion"; for many demons had entered him. 31They begged him not to order them to go back into the abyss.

32 Now there on the hillside a large herd of swine was feeding; and the demons[n] begged Jesus[o] to let them enter these. So he gave them permission. 33Then the demons came out of the man and entered the swine, and the herd rushed down the steep bank into the lake and was drowned.

34 When the swineherds saw what had happened, they ran off and told it in the city and in the country. 35Then people came out to see what had happened, and when they came to Jesus, they found the man from whom the demons had gone sitting at the feet of Jesus, clothed and in his right mind. And they were afraid. 36Those who had seen it told them how the one who had been

possessed by demons had been healed. 37Then all the people of the surrounding country of the Gerasenes[k] asked Jesus[o] to leave them; for they were seized with great fear. So he got into the boat and returned. 38The man from whom the demons had gone begged that he might be with him; but Jesus[m] sent him away, saying, 39"Return to your home, and declare how much God has done for you." So he went away, proclaiming throughout the city how much Jesus had done for him.

A Girl Restored to Life and a Woman Healed

▶ *See Matthew 9.18–26; Mark 5.22–43*

40 Now when Jesus returned, the crowd welcomed him, for they were all waiting for him. 41Just then there came a man named Jairus, a leader of the synagogue. He fell at Jesus' feet and begged him to come to his house, 42for he had an only daughter, about twelve years old, who was dying.

As he went, the crowds pressed in on him. 43Now there was a woman who had been suffering from hemorrhages for twelve years; and though she had spent all she had on physicians,[p] no one could cure her. 44She came up behind him and touched the fringe of his clothes, and immediately her hemorrhage stopped. 45Then Jesus asked, "Who touched me?" When all denied it, Peter[q] said, "Master, the crowds surround you and press in on you." 46But Jesus said, "Someone touched me; for I noticed that power had gone out from me." 47When the woman saw that she could not remain hidden, she came trembling; and falling down before him, she declared in the presence of all the people why she had touched him, and how she had been immediately healed. 48He said to her, "Daughter, your faith has made you well; go in peace."

49 While he was still speaking, someone came from the leader's house to say, "Your daughter is dead; do not trouble the teacher any longer." 50When Jesus heard this, he replied, "Do not fear. Only believe, and she will be saved." 51When he came to the house, he did not allow anyone to enter with him, except Peter, John, and James, and the child's father and mother. 52They were all weeping and wailing for her; but he said, "Do not weep; for she is not dead but sleeping." 53And they laughed at him, knowing that she was dead. 54But he took her by the hand and called out, "Child, get up!" 55Her spirit returned, and she got up at once. Then he directed them to give her something to eat. 56Her parents were astounded; but he ordered them to tell no one what had happened.

---

[k] Other ancient authorities read *Gadarenes*; others, *Gergesenes*   [l] Other ancient authorities read *a man of the city who*
had had demons for a long time met him. He wore   [m] Gk *he*   [n] Gk *they*   [o] Gk *him*   [p] Other ancient
authorities lack *and though she had spent all she had on physicians*   [q] Other ancient authorities add *and those who were*
with him

The Mission of the Twelve

▶ *See Matthew 10.9–15; Mark 6.8–11*

9 Then Jesus[r] called the twelve together and gave them power and authority over all demons and to cure diseases, [2]and he sent them out to proclaim the kingdom of God and to heal. [3]He said to them, "Take nothing for your journey, no staff, nor bag, nor bread, nor money—not even an extra tunic. [4]Whatever house you enter, stay there, and leave from there. [5]Wherever they do not welcome you, as you are leaving that town shake the dust off your feet as a testimony against them." [6]They departed and went through the villages, bringing the good news and curing diseases everywhere.

Herod's Perplexity

[7] Now Herod the ruler[s] heard about all that had taken place, and he was perplexed, because it was said by some that John had been raised from the dead, [8]by some that Elijah had appeared, and by others that one of the ancient prophets had arisen. [9]Herod said, "John I beheaded; but who is this about whom I hear such things?" And he tried to see him.

Feeding the Five Thousand

▶ *See Matthew 14.13–21; Mark 6.32–44; John 6.5–13*

[10] On their return the apostles told Jesus[t] all they had done. He took them with him and withdrew privately to a city called Bethsaida. [11]When the crowds found out about it, they followed him; and he welcomed them, and spoke to them about the kingdom of God, and healed those who needed to be cured.

[12] The day was drawing to a close, and the twelve came to him and said, "Send the crowd away, so that they may go into the surrounding villages and countryside, to lodge and get provisions; for we are here in a deserted place." [13]But he said to them, "You give them something to eat." They said, "We have no more than five loaves and two fish—unless we are to go and buy food for all these people." [14]For there were about five thousand men. And he said to his disciples, "Make them sit down in groups of about fifty each." [15]They did so and made them all sit down. [16]And taking the five loaves and the two fish, he looked up to heaven, and blessed and broke them, and gave them to the disciples to set before the crowd. [17]And all ate and were filled. What was left over was gathered up, twelve baskets of broken pieces.

Peter's Declaration about Jesus

▶ *See Matthew 16.13–16; Mark 8.27–29*

[18] Once when Jesus[r] was praying alone, with only the disciples near him, he asked them, "Who do the crowds say that I am?" [19]They answered, "John the Baptist; but others, Elijah; and still others, that one of the ancient prophets has arisen." [20]He said to them, "But who do you say that I am?" Peter answered, "The Messiah[u] of God."

Jesus Foretells His Death and Resurrection

[21] He sternly ordered and commanded them not to tell anyone, [22]saying, "The Son of Man must undergo great suffering, and be rejected by the elders, chief priests, and scribes, and be killed, and on the third day be raised."

[23] Then he said to them all, "If any want to become my followers, let them deny themselves and take up their cross daily and follow me. [24]For those who want to save their life will lose it, and those who lose their life for my sake will save it. [25]What does it profit them if they gain the whole world, but lose or forfeit themselves? [26]Those who are ashamed of me and of my words, of them the Son of Man will be ashamed when he comes in his glory and the glory of the Father and of the holy angels. [27]But truly I tell you, there are some standing here who will not taste death before they see the kingdom of God."

The Transfiguration

▶ *See Matthew 17.1–8; Mark 9.2–8*

[28] Now about eight days after these sayings Jesus[r] took with him Peter and John and James,

9.28–33 Seeing the Kingdom

Jesus predicted that some of his disciples would "see the kingdom of God" (verse 27) before tasting death. Eight days later, three of them witnessed Jesus gleaming like a flash of lightning and talking with the long-dead Moses and Elijah (verses 29–30). Many scholars think the Transfiguration fulfilled Jesus' "seeing the kingdom" prediction. Apart from this moment, Jesus looked like any other man during his years on earth. He had none of the brilliant glory associated with God in the Old Testament (see Exodus 40.34).

and went up on the mountain to pray. [29]And while he was praying, the appearance of his face changed, and his clothes became dazzling white. [30]Suddenly they saw two men, Moses and Elijah, talking to him. [31]They appeared in glory and were speaking of his departure, which he was about to accomplish at Jerusalem. [32]Now Peter and his companions were weighed down with sleep; but since they had stayed awake,[v] they saw his glory and the two men who stood with him. [33]Just as they were leaving him, Peter said to Jesus, "Mas-

---

[r] Gk *he*   [s] Gk *tetrarch*   [t] Gk *him*   [u] Or *The Christ*   [v] Or *but when they were fully awake*

ter, it is good for us to be here; let us make three dwellings,[w] one for you, one for Moses, and one for Elijah"—not knowing what he said. [34]While he was saying this, a cloud came and overshadowed them; and they were terrified as they entered the cloud. [35]Then from the cloud came a voice that said, "This is my Son, my Chosen;[x] listen to him!" [36]When the voice had spoken, Jesus was found alone. And they kept silent and in those days told no one any of the things they had seen.

Jesus Heals a Boy with a Demon

▶ See Matthew 17.14–18,22–23; Mark 9.14–27,30–32

[37] On the next day, when they had come down from the mountain, a great crowd met him. [38]Just then a man from the crowd shouted, "Teacher, I beg you to look at my son; he is my only child. [39]Suddenly a spirit seizes him, and all at once he[y] shrieks. It convulses him until he foams at the mouth; it mauls him and will scarcely leave him. [40]I begged your disciples to cast it out, but they could not." [41]Jesus answered, "You faithless and perverse generation, how much longer must I be with you and bear with you? Bring your son here." [42]While he was coming, the demon dashed him to the ground in convulsions. But Jesus rebuked the unclean spirit, healed the boy, and gave him back to his father. [43]And all were astounded at the greatness of God.

Jesus Again Foretells His Death

While everyone was amazed at all that he was doing, he said to his disciples, [44]"Let these words sink into your ears: The Son of Man is going to be betrayed into human hands." [45]But they did not understand this saying; its meaning was concealed from them, so that they could not perceive it. And they were afraid to ask him about this saying.

True Greatness

▶ See Matthew 18.1–5; Mark 9.33–40

[46] An argument arose among them as to which one of them was the greatest. [47]But Jesus, aware of their inner thoughts, took a little child and put it by his side, [48]and said to them, "Whoever welcomes this child in my name welcomes me, and whoever welcomes me welcomes the one who sent me; for the least among all of you is the greatest."

Another Exorcist

[49] John answered, "Master, we saw someone casting out demons in your name, and we tried to stop him, because he does not follow with us." [50]But Jesus said to him, "Do not stop him; for whoever is not against you is for you."

A Samaritan Village Refuses to Receive Jesus

[51] When the days drew near for him to be taken up, he set his face to go to Jerusalem. [52]And he sent messengers ahead of him. On their way they entered a village of the Samaritans to make ready for him; [53]but they did not receive him, because his face was set toward Jerusalem. [54]When his disciples James and John saw it, they said, "Lord, do you want us to command fire to come down from heaven and consume them?"[z] [55]But he turned and rebuked them. [56]Then[a] they went on to another village.

Would-Be Followers of Jesus

▶ See Matthew 8.19–22

[57] As they were going along the road, someone said to him, "I will follow you wherever you go." [58]And Jesus said to him, "Foxes have holes, and birds of the air have nests; but the Son of Man has nowhere to lay his head." [59]To another he said, "Follow me." But he said, "Lord, first let

9.59 Burying His Father

The man's request to "let me go and bury my father" didn't necessarily mean that the man's father had just died. Possibly the expression was a figure of speech, a way of saying, "Let me wait until my father has died." Jesus instead stressed the urgency of his mission.

me go and bury my father." [60]But Jesus[b] said to him, "Let the dead bury their own dead; but as for you, go and proclaim the kingdom of God." [61]Another said, "I will follow you, Lord; but let me first say farewell to those at my home." [62]Jesus said to him, "No one who puts a hand to the plow and looks back is fit for the kingdom of God."

The Mission of the Seventy

▶ See Luke 9.3–5

10 After this the Lord appointed seventy[c] others and sent them on ahead of him in pairs to every town and place where he himself intended to go. [2]He said to them, "The harvest is plentiful, but the laborers are few; therefore ask the Lord of the harvest to send out laborers into his harvest. [3]Go on your way. See, I am sending you out like lambs into the midst of wolves. [4]Car-

---

[w] Or *tents*   [x] Other ancient authorities read *my Beloved*   [y] Or *it*   [z] Other ancient authorities add *as Elijah did*
[a] Other ancient authorities read *rebuked them, and said, "You do not know what spirit you are of, [56]for the Son of Man has not come to destroy the lives of human beings but to save them." Then*   [b] Gk *he*   [c] Other ancient authorities read *seventy-two*

ry no purse, no bag, no sandals; and greet no one on the road. ⁵Whatever house you enter, first say, 'Peace to this house!' ⁶And if anyone is there who shares in peace, your peace will rest on that person; but if not, it will return to you. ⁷Remain in the same house, eating and drinking whatever they provide, for the laborer deserves to be paid. Do not move about from house to house. ⁸Whenever you enter a town and its people welcome you, eat what is set before you; ⁹cure the sick who are there, and say to them, 'The kingdom of God has come near to you.'ᵈ ¹⁰But whenever you enter a town and they do not welcome you, go out into its streets and say, ¹¹'Even the dust of your town that clings to our feet, we wipe off in protest against you. Yet know this: the kingdom of God has come near.'ᵉ ¹²I tell you, on that day it will be more tolerable for Sodom than for that town.

Woes to Unrepentant Cities

13 "Woe to you, Chorazin! Woe to you, Bethsaida! For if the deeds of power done in you had

ᵈ Or is at hand for you   ᵉ Or is at hand

The Power of a Name
Jesus' time on earth was running out

CHRISTIANS SPEAK "IN THE NAME of Jesus." But that familiar phrase may have lost meaning for some of us. Consider:

College sophomore Tom Bowers took a summer job as an intern on the governor of Michigan's staff. He spent the first few weeks cranking out memos, returning mundane phone calls, and straightening files. But one day a harried manager asked Tom to write a public statement on the state's new law enforcement program. Tom composed a brief announcement and took it to the governor.

The next day, as he rounded the corner of a newsstand, his eyes snapped wide open. Headlined across the front page of the *Detroit News* was the announcement he had composed. It dawned on him that, all over the city, people would be reading his very own words as the governor's.

Throughout that summer, Tom discovered the power of the governor's name. If he sent a letter to a mayor under his own signature, it would likely be filed under "Ignore." Who was Tom Bowers, sophomore summer intern? If, however, the governor put his name at the bottom, the letter got instant attention anywhere in the state. That summer Tom worked "in the name of the governor"—he represented the governor.

> "Whoever listens to you listens to me, and whoever rejects you rejects me."
> 10.16

Jesus' Crash Training Course

It is one thing to represent the governor of Michigan; it is quite another to represent God and use his name. Yet Jesus had exactly that plan in mind for his followers. He hand-selected simple folk like James and Andrew to bear his name and represent him to the world. In the same way that a governor or president delegates authority to people acting on his behalf, Jesus gave his followers his own authority and power.

Jesus' time on earth was running out. Luke 9.51 records that he "set his face to go to Jerusalem," on his way to die. Only a few weeks remained for him to train those people who would be left behind to carry his name: "Christ-ians." Jesus used the time as a crash training course for his followers.

Chapters 9—19 contain many of Jesus' events and sayings found nowhere else in the Bible. First he sent out the Twelve, then 72 others, to announce his message to all who would listen. These chapters convey Jesus' last detailed instructions to his loyal followers.

Final Instructions

Everything about Jesus' life increased in intensity along the treacherous road to Jerusalem. As he taught his small group of disciples, gawking crowds shoved in from all sides, sometimes even trampling each other. From those crowds, Pharisees tossed out loaded questions, seeking to trap Jesus.

Jesus did not soften his words in the face of danger. Instead, he emphasized the severe cost of following him. Frequently he talked about prayer, the church's life-giving connection to the Father.

Later, the apostle Paul would say that we, the church, actually form Christ's body in the world. By coming to earth and then leaving, Jesus ushered in a completely new chapter in history. And, as he prepared for departure, he called on his people—the disciples and us—to represent him. In every sense, we bear his name.

Life Questions: What does it mean to pray "in Jesus' name"? How can your life have the power and authority of Jesus behind it?

been done in Tyre and Sidon, they would have repented long ago, sitting in sackcloth and ashes. 14But at the judgment it will be more tolerable for Tyre and Sidon than for you. 15And you, Capernaum,

will you be exalted to heaven?

No, you will be brought down
to Hades.

16 "Whoever listens to you listens to me, and whoever rejects you rejects me, and whoever rejects me rejects the one who sent me."

The Return of the Seventy

17 The seventy*f* returned with joy, saying, "Lord, in your name even the demons submit to us!" 18He said to them, "I watched Satan fall from heaven like a flash of lightning. 19See, I have given you authority to tread on snakes and scorpions, and over all the power of the enemy; and nothing will hurt you. 20Nevertheless, do not rejoice at this, that the spirits submit to you, but rejoice that your names are written in heaven."

10.20 Taste of Power

Power can go to your head, especially if you've never had any. The disciples—mainly farmers and fishermen—were overwhelmed to discover their spiritual authority. Jesus urged them to keep it in perspective. Their salvation, he said—their names written in heaven—mattered more than their power. The Bible often speaks of God's people having their names recorded in a heavenly book (Daniel 12.1; Revelation 3.5).

Jesus Rejoices

21 At that same hour Jesus*g* rejoiced in the Holy Spirit*h* and said, "I thank*i* you, Father, Lord of heaven and earth, because you have hidden these things from the wise and the intelligent and have revealed them to infants; yes, Father, for such was your gracious will.*j* 22All things have been handed over to me by my Father; and no one knows who the Son is except the Father, or who the Father is except the Son and anyone to whom the Son chooses to reveal him."

23 Then turning to the disciples, Jesus*g* said to them privately, "Blessed are the eyes that see what you see! 24For I tell you that many prophets and kings desired to see what you see, but did not see it, and to hear what you hear, but did not hear it."

The Parable of the Good Samaritan

▶ See Matthew 22.34–40; Mark 12.28–31

25 Just then a lawyer stood up to test Jesus.*k*

"Teacher," he said, "what must I do to inherit eternal life?" 26He said to him, "What is written in the law? What do you read there?" 27He answered, "You shall love the Lord your God with all your heart, and with all your soul, and with all your strength, and with all your mind; and your neighbor as yourself." 28And he said to him, "You have given the right answer; do this, and you will live."

29 But wanting to justify himself, he asked Jesus, "And who is my neighbor?" 30Jesus replied, "A man was going down from Jerusalem to Jericho, and fell into the hands of robbers, who stripped him, beat him, and went away, leaving him half dead. 31Now by chance a priest was going down that road; and when he saw him, he

10.31 Which One Showed Love?

The priest saw the robbery victim in a half-dead state. According to Old Testament law, a priest who touched a dead body made himself ceremonially impure (Leviticus 21.1–4). The priest and religious Levite decided not to get involved. Jesus' audience might have been expecting the third character to be a Jewish layperson. But Jesus added a twist by making the one who showed love a Samaritan—a racial minority despised in Israel. In this way, Jesus contrasted mere religious beliefs with true love.

passed by on the other side. 32So likewise a Levite, when he came to the place and saw him, passed by on the other side. 33But a Samaritan while traveling came near him; and when he saw him, he was moved with pity. 34He went to him and bandaged his wounds, having poured oil and wine on them. Then he put him on his own animal, brought him to an inn, and took care of him. 35The next day he took out two denarii,*l* gave them to the innkeeper, and said, 'Take care of him; and when I come back, I will repay you whatever more you spend.' 36Which of these three, do you think, was a neighbor to the man who fell into the hands of the robbers?" 37He said, "The one who showed him mercy." Jesus said to him, "Go and do likewise."

Jesus Visits Martha and Mary

38 Now as they went on their way, he entered a certain village, where a woman named Martha welcomed him into her home. 39She had a sister named Mary, who sat at the Lord's feet and listened to what he was saying. 40But Martha was distracted by her many tasks; so she came to him and asked, "Lord, do you not care that my sister has left me to do all the work by myself? Tell her then to help me." 41But the Lord answered her,

---

f Other ancient authorities read *seventy-two*   *g* Gk *he*   *h* Other authorities read *in the spirit*   *i* Or *praise*
j Or *for so it was well-pleasing in your sight*   *k* Gk *him*   *l* The denarius was the usual day's wage for a laborer

"Martha, Martha, you are worried and distracted by many things; [42]there is need of only one thing.[m] Mary has chosen the better part, which will not be taken away from her."

The Lord's Prayer

▶ *See Matthew 6.9–13; 7.7–11*

11 He was praying in a certain place, and after he had finished, one of his disciples said to him, "Lord, teach us to pray, as John taught his disciples." [2]He said to them, "When you pray, say:

Father,[n] hallowed be your name.
    Your kingdom come.[o]
3   Give us each day our daily bread.[p]
4   And forgive us our sins,
        for we ourselves forgive everyone
        indebted to us.
    And do not bring us to the time of
        trial."[q]

Perseverance in Prayer

5 And he said to them, "Suppose one of you has a friend, and you go to him at midnight and say to him, 'Friend, lend me three loaves of bread; [6]for a friend of mine has arrived, and I have nothing to set before him.' [7]And he answers from within, 'Do not bother me; the door has already been locked, and my children are with me in bed; I cannot get up and give you anything.' [8]I tell you, even though he will not get up and give him anything because he is his friend, at least because of his persistence he will get up and give him whatever he needs.

9 "So I say to you, Ask, and it will be given you; search, and you will find; knock, and the door will be opened for you. [10]For everyone who asks receives, and everyone who searches finds, and for everyone who knocks, the door will be opened. [11]Is there anyone among you who, if your child asks for[r] a fish, will give a snake instead of a fish? [12]Or if the child asks for an egg, will give a scorpion? [13]If you then, who are evil, know how to give good gifts to your children, how much more will the heavenly Father give the Holy Spirit[s] to those who ask him!"

Jesus and Beelzebul

▶ *See Matthew 12.22,24–29,43–45; Mark 3.23–27*

14 Now he was casting out a demon that was mute; when the demon had gone out, the one who had been mute spoke, and the crowds were amazed. [15]But some of them said, "He casts out demons by Beelzebul, the ruler of the demons." [16]Others, to test him, kept demanding from him a sign from heaven. [17]But he knew what they were thinking and said to them, "Every kingdom divided against itself becomes a desert, and house falls on house. [18]If Satan also is divided against himself, how will his kingdom stand? —for you say that I cast out the demons by Beelzebul. [19]Now if I cast out the demons by Beelzebul, by whom do your exorcists[t] cast them out? Therefore they will be your judges. [20]But if it is by the finger of God that I cast out the demons, then the kingdom of God has come to you. [21]When a strong man, fully armed, guards his castle, his property is safe. [22]But when one stronger than he attacks him and overpowers him, he takes away his armor in which he trusted and divides his

---

[m] Other ancient authorities read *few things are necessary, or only one*   [n] Other ancient authorities read *Our Father in heaven*   [o] A few ancient authorities read *Your Holy Spirit come upon us and cleanse us.* Other ancient authorities add *Your will be done, on earth as in heaven*   [p] Or *our bread for tomorrow*   [q] Or *us into temptation.* Other ancient authorities add *but rescue us from the evil one* (or *from evil*)   [r] Other ancient authorities add *bread, will give a stone; or if your child asks for*   [s] Other ancient authorities read *the Father give the Holy Spirit from heaven*   [t] Gk *sons*

MARTHA AND MARY OF BETHANY *Doer and Seeker*

MARY AND MARTHA BOTH HAD a close relationship with Jesus, who loved them deeply. He visited the sisters' home three times that we know of, and probably many more. They lived with their brother Lazarus in Bethany, a village just outside Jerusalem. Like many sisters, Mary and Martha had quite different personalities, and we can see the difference clearly in how they related to Jesus.

Mary could drop everything and listen to Jesus. When he called, she answered instantly. She showed her love for him in extravagant ways, once lavishing a huge amount of expensive perfume on his feet (John 12.3). For Mary, everything stopped when Jesus was present.

Mary's ways sometimes annoyed her sister Martha, who showed more obsessive concern about getting things done. "Duty first" was Martha's motto. She served Jesus by preparing meals and doing the work of hosting.

Which way was better? Martha preferred her own hard-working style, and she asked Jesus to set Mary straight. Jesus gently disagreed. Mary, who simply sat at his feet and listened, did the one really necessary thing in life, he said, and he would not reprove her (10.41).

Life Questions: Are you more like Mary or like Martha? Why do you think Jesus preferred Mary's way?

plunder. 23Whoever is not with me is against me, and whoever does not gather with me scatters.

The Return of the Unclean Spirit

24 "When the unclean spirit has gone out of a person, it wanders through waterless regions looking for a resting place, but not finding any, it says, 'I will return to my house from which I came.' 25When it comes, it finds it swept and put in order. 26Then it goes and brings seven other spirits more evil than itself, and they enter and live there; and the last state of that person is worse than the first."

11.17 Jesus or Lincoln?

Abraham Lincoln is often credited with saying, "A house divided against itself cannot stand." Actually, Lincoln quoted Jesus, who was refuting a frivolous accusation that his power came from Satan (Beelzebul). Jesus suggested that if Satan used his power against his own cause, Satan's kingdom would soon fall. Lincoln applied this principle to the not-so-United States just before the Civil War: A nation divided over such a fundamental issue as slavery could not endure.

True Blessedness

27 While he was saying this, a woman in the crowd raised her voice and said to him, "Blessed is the womb that bore you and the breasts that nursed you!" 28But he said, "Blessed rather are those who hear the word of God and obey it!"

The Sign of Jonah

▶ *See Matthew 12.39–42*

29 When the crowds were increasing, he began to say, "This generation is an evil generation; it asks for a sign, but no sign will be given to it except the sign of Jonah. 30For just as Jonah became a sign to the people of Nineveh, so the Son of Man will be to this generation. 31The queen of the South will rise at the judgment with the people

11.29 Sensation-Seekers

Jesus had no tolerance for people who begged for miraculous signs. Here and elsewhere he declared that no amount of proof would convince those who stubbornly refused to believe in him. In contrast, certain Old Testament Gentiles believed even though they had far less evidence.

of this generation and condemn them, because she came from the ends of the earth to listen to the wisdom of Solomon, and see, something greater than Solomon is here! 32The people of Nineveh will rise up at the judgment with this generation and condemn it, because they repented at the proclamation of Jonah, and see, something greater than Jonah is here!

The Light of the Body

▶ *See Matthew 6.22–23*

33 "No one after lighting a lamp puts it in a cellar,*u* but on the lampstand so that those who enter may see the light. 34Your eye is the lamp of your body. If your eye is healthy, your whole body is full of light; but if it is not healthy, your body is full of darkness. 35Therefore consider whether the light in you is not darkness. 36If then your whole body is full of light, with no part of it in darkness, it will be as full of light as when a lamp gives you light with its rays."

Jesus Denounces Pharisees and Lawyers

37 While he was speaking, a Pharisee invited him to dine with him; so he went in and took his place at the table. 38The Pharisee was amazed to see that he did not first wash before dinner. 39Then the Lord said to him, "Now you Pharisees clean the outside of the cup and of the dish, but inside you are full of greed and wickedness. 40You fools! Did not the one who made the outside make the inside also? 41So give for alms those things that are within; and see, everything will be clean for you.

42 "But woe to you Pharisees! For you tithe mint and rue and herbs of all kinds, and neglect justice and the love of God; it is these you ought to have practiced, without neglecting the others. 43Woe to you Pharisees! For you love to have the seat of honor in the synagogues and to be greeted with respect in the marketplaces. 44Woe to you! For you are like unmarked graves, and people walk over them without realizing it."

45 One of the lawyers answered him, "Teacher, when you say these things, you insult us too." 46And he said, "Woe also to you lawyers! For you load people with burdens hard to bear, and you yourselves do not lift a finger to ease them. 47Woe to you! For you build the tombs of the prophets whom your ancestors killed. 48So you are witnesses and approve of the deeds of your ancestors; for they killed them, and you build their tombs. 49Therefore also the Wisdom of God said, 'I will send them prophets and apostles, some of whom they will kill and persecute,' 50so that this generation may be charged with the blood of all the prophets shed since the foundation of the world, 51from the blood of Abel to the blood of Zechariah, who perished between the altar and

---

u Other ancient authorities add *or under the bushel basket*

the sanctuary. Yes, I tell you, it will be charged against this generation. 52Woe to you lawyers! For you have taken away the key of knowledge; you did not enter yourselves, and you hindered those who were entering."

53 When he went outside, the scribes and the Pharisees began to be very hostile toward him and to cross-examine him about many things, 54lying in wait for him, to catch him in something he might say.

A Warning against Hypocrisy

▶ See Matthew 10.26–33

12 Meanwhile, when the crowd gathered by the thousands, so that they trampled on one another, he began to speak first to his disciples, "Beware of the yeast of the Pharisees, that is, their hypocrisy. 2Nothing is covered up that will not be uncovered, and nothing secret that will not become known. 3Therefore whatever you have said in the dark will be heard in the light, and what you have whispered behind closed doors will be proclaimed from the housetops.

Exhortation to Fearless Confession

4 "I tell you, my friends, do not fear those who kill the body, and after that can do nothing more. 5But I will warn you whom to fear: fear him who, after he has killed, has authority[v] to cast into hell.[w] Yes, I tell you, fear him! 6Are not five sparrows sold for two pennies? Yet not one of them is forgotten in God's sight. 7But even the hairs of your head are all counted. Do not be afraid; you are of more value than many sparrows.

8 "And I tell you, everyone who acknowledges me before others, the Son of Man also will acknowledge before the angels of God; 9but whoever denies me before others will be denied before the angels of God. 10And everyone who speaks a word against the Son of Man will be forgiven; but whoever blasphemes against the Holy Spirit will not be forgiven. 11When they bring you before the synagogues, the rulers, and the authorities, do not worry about how[x] you are to defend yourselves or what you are to say; 12for the Holy Spirit will teach you at that very hour what you ought to say."

The Parable of the Rich Fool

13 Someone in the crowd said to him, "Teacher, tell my brother to divide the family inheritance with me." 14But he said to him, "Friend, who set me to be a judge or arbitrator over you?" 15And he said to them, "Take care! Be on your guard against all kinds of greed; for one's life does not consist in the abundance of possessions." 16Then he told them a parable: "The land

of a rich man produced abundantly. 17And he thought to himself, 'What should I do, for I have no place to store my crops?' 18Then he said, 'I will do this: I will pull down my barns and build larger ones, and there I will store all my grain and my

12.15 When Money Is Useless

Jesus refused to get involved in a family dispute about money. In this statement, he neatly summarized his usual approach to money. He did not condemn the possession of it. But he did warn against putting faith in money to secure the future. The rich man's money did him absolutely no good the night of his death. To emphasize his point, Jesus referred back to King Solomon, the richest man in the Old Testament (verse 27). The lesson: Trust in God and his kingdom, and free yourself of worry about money and possessions.

goods. 19And I will say to my soul, Soul, you have ample goods laid up for many years; relax, eat, drink, be merry.' 20But God said to him, 'You fool! This very night your life is being demanded of you. And the things you have prepared, whose will they be?' 21So it is with those who store up treasures for themselves but are not rich toward God."

Do Not Worry

▶ See Matthew 6.25–33

22 He said to his disciples, "Therefore I tell you, do not worry about your life, what you will eat, or about your body, what you will wear. 23For life is more than food, and the body more than clothing. 24Consider the ravens: they neither sow nor reap, they have neither storehouse nor barn, and yet God feeds them. Of how much more value are you than the birds! 25And can any of you by worrying add a single hour to your span of life?[y] 26If then you are not able to do so small a thing as that, why do you worry about the rest? 27Consider the lilies, how they grow: they neither toil nor spin;[z] yet I tell you, even Solomon in all his glory was not clothed like one of these. 28But if God so clothes the grass of the field, which is alive today and tomorrow is thrown into the oven, how much more will he clothe you—you of little faith! 29And do not keep striving for what you are to eat and what you are to drink, and do not keep worrying. 30For it is the nations of the world that strive after all these things, and your Father knows that you need them. 31Instead, strive for his[a] kingdom, and these things will be given to you as well.

32 "Do not be afraid, little flock, for it is your

---

v Or *power*   w Gk *Gehenna*   x Other ancient authorities add *or what*   y Or *add a cubit to your stature*
z Other ancient authorities read *Consider the lilies; they neither spin nor weave*   a Other ancient authorities read *God's*

Father's good pleasure to give you the kingdom. [33]Sell your possessions, and give alms. Make purses for yourselves that do not wear out, an unfailing treasure in heaven, where no thief comes near and no moth destroys. [34]For where your treasure is, there your heart will be also.

Watchful Slaves

▶ *See Matthew 24.43–51; Mark 13.33–37*

35 "Be dressed for action and have your lamps lit; [36]be like those who are waiting for their master to return from the wedding banquet, so that they may open the door for him as soon as he comes and knocks. [37]Blessed are those slaves whom the master finds alert when he comes; truly I tell you, he will fasten his belt and have them sit down to eat, and he will come and serve them. [38]If he comes during the middle of the night, or near dawn, and finds them so, blessed are those slaves.

39 "But know this: if the owner of the house had known at what hour the thief was coming, he[b] would not have let his house be broken into. [40]You also must be ready, for the Son of Man is coming at an unexpected hour."

The Faithful or the Unfaithful Slave

41 Peter said, "Lord, are you telling this parable for us or for everyone?" [42]And the Lord said, "Who then is the faithful and prudent manager whom his master will put in charge of his slaves, to give them their allowance of food at the proper time? [43]Blessed is that slave whom his master will find at work when he arrives. [44]Truly I tell you, he will put that one in charge of all his possessions. [45]But if that slave says to himself, 'My master is delayed in coming,' and if he begins to beat the other slaves, men and women, and to eat and drink and get drunk, [46]the master of that slave will come on a day when he does not expect him and at an hour that he does not know, and will cut him in pieces,[c] and put him with the unfaithful. [47]That slave who knew what his master wanted, but did not prepare himself or do what was wanted, will receive a severe beating. [48]But the one who did not know and did what deserved a beating will receive a light beating. From everyone to whom much has been given, much will be required; and from the one to whom much has been entrusted, even more will be demanded.

Jesus the Cause of Division

▶ *See Matthew 10.34–36*

49 "I came to bring fire to the earth, and how I wish it were already kindled! [50]I have a baptism with which to be baptized, and what stress I am under until it is completed! [51]Do you think that I have come to bring peace to the earth? No, I tell you, but rather division! [52]From now on five in

one household will be divided, three against two and two against three; [53]they will be divided:

father against son
    and son against father,
mother against daughter
    and daughter against mother,
mother-in-law against her
        daughter-in-law
    and daughter-in-law against
        mother-in-law."

Interpreting the Time

54 He also said to the crowds, "When you see a cloud rising in the west, you immediately say, 'It is going to rain'; and so it happens. [55]And when you see the south wind blowing, you say, 'There will be scorching heat'; and it happens. [56]You hypocrites! You know how to interpret the appearance of earth and sky, but why do you not know how to interpret the present time?

Settling with Your Opponent

57 "And why do you not judge for yourselves what is right? [58]Thus, when you go with your accuser before a magistrate, on the way make an effort to settle the case,[d] or you may be dragged before the judge, and the judge hand you over to the officer, and the officer throw you in prison. [59]I tell you, you will never get out until you have paid the very last penny."

Repent or Perish

13 At that very time there were some present who told him about the Galileans whose blood Pilate had mingled with their sacrifices. [2]He asked them, "Do you think that because these Galileans suffered in this way they were worse sinners than all other Galileans? [3]No, I tell you; but unless you repent, you will all perish as they did. [4]Or those eighteen who were killed when the tower of Siloam fell on them—do you think that they were worse offenders than all the others living in Jerusalem? [5]No, I tell you; but unless you repent, you will all perish just as they did."

The Parable of the Barren Fig Tree

6 Then he told this parable: "A man had a fig tree planted in his vineyard; and he came looking for fruit on it and found none. [7]So he said to the gardener, 'See here! For three years I have come looking for fruit on this fig tree, and still I find none. Cut it down! Why should it be wasting the soil?' [8]He replied, 'Sir, let it alone for one more year, until I dig around it and put manure on it. [9]If it bears fruit next year, well and good; but if not, you can cut it down.'"

Jesus Heals a Crippled Woman

10 Now he was teaching in one of the syna-

---

[b] Other ancient authorities add *would have watched and*   [c] Or *cut him off*   [d] Gk *settle with him*

gogues on the sabbath. ¹¹And just then there appeared a woman with a spirit that had crippled her for eighteen years. She was bent over and was quite unable to stand up straight. ¹²When Jesus saw her, he called her over and said, "Woman, you are set free from your ailment." ¹³When he laid his hands on her, immediately she stood up straight and began praising God. ¹⁴But the leader of the synagogue, indignant because Jesus had cured on the sabbath, kept saying to the crowd, "There are six days on which work ought to be done; come on those days and be cured, and not on the sabbath day." ¹⁵But the Lord answered him and said, "You hypocrites! Does not each of you on the sabbath untie his ox or his donkey from the manger, and lead it away to give it water? ¹⁶And ought not this woman, a daughter of Abraham whom Satan bound for eighteen long years, be set free from this bondage on the sabbath day?" ¹⁷When he said this, all his opponents were put to shame; and the entire crowd was rejoicing at all the wonderful things that he was doing.

The Parable of the Mustard Seed

▶ See Matthew 13.31–33; Mark 4.30–32

18 He said therefore, "What is the kingdom of God like? And to what should I compare it? ¹⁹It is like a mustard seed that someone took and sowed in the garden; it grew and became a tree, and the birds of the air made nests in its branches."

The Parable of the Yeast

20 And again he said, "To what should I compare the kingdom of God? ²¹It is like yeast that a woman took and mixed in with*e* three measures of flour until all of it was leavened."

The Narrow Door

22 Jesus*f* went through one town and village after another, teaching as he made his way to Jerusalem. ²³Someone asked him, "Lord, will only a few be saved?" He said to them, ²⁴"Strive to enter through the narrow door; for many, I tell you, will try to enter and will not be able. ²⁵When once the owner of the house has got up and shut the door, and you begin to stand outside and to knock at the door, saying, 'Lord, open to us,' then in reply he will say to you, 'I do not know where you come from.' ²⁶Then you will begin to say, 'We ate and drank with you, and you taught in our streets.' ²⁷But he will say, 'I do not know where you come from; go away from me, all you evildoers!' ²⁸There will be weeping and gnashing of teeth when you see Abraham and Isaac and Jacob and all the prophets in the kingdom of God, and you yourselves thrown out. ²⁹Then people

will come from east and west, from north and south, and will eat in the kingdom of God. ³⁰Indeed, some are last who will be first, and some are first who will be last."

The Lament over Jerusalem

▶ See Matthew 23.37–39

31 At that very hour some Pharisees came and said to him, "Get away from here, for Herod wants to kill you." ³²He said to them, "Go and tell that fox for me,*g* 'Listen, I am casting out demons and performing cures today and tomorrow, and on the third day I finish my work. ³³Yet

13.32 Who Had Real Power?

Jesus was executed by powerful political authorities, among them the Roman official Herod. But this statement, spoken before his arrest, reveals who had the real power. Jesus dismissed Herod as "that fox," a Jewish expression for a worthless or insignificant person. Jesus' death on a cross came as no surprise to him; in fact, here Jesus calls it his "work."

today, tomorrow, and the next day I must be on my way, because it is impossible for a prophet to be killed outside of Jerusalem.' ³⁴Jerusalem, Jerusalem, the city that kills the prophets and stones those who are sent to it! How often have I desired to gather your children together as a hen gathers her brood under her wings, and you were not willing! ³⁵See, your house is left to you. And I tell you, you will not see me until the time comes when*h* you say, 'Blessed is the one who comes in the name of the Lord.'"

Jesus Heals the Man with Dropsy

14 On one occasion when Jesus*i* was going to the house of a leader of the Pharisees to eat a meal on the sabbath, they were watching him closely. ²Just then, in front of him, there was a man who had dropsy. ³And Jesus asked the lawyers and Pharisees, "Is it lawful to cure people on the sabbath, or not?" ⁴But they were silent. So Jesus*i* took him and healed him, and sent him away. ⁵Then he said to them, "If one of you has a child*j* or an ox that has fallen into a well, will you not immediately pull it out on a sabbath day?" ⁶And they could not reply to this.

Humility and Hospitality

7 When he noticed how the guests chose the places of honor, he told them a parable. ⁸"When you are invited by someone to a wedding banquet, do not sit down at the place of honor, in

e Gk hid in   *f* Gk He   *g* Gk lacks for me   *h* Other ancient authorities lack the time comes when
i Gk he   *j* Other ancient authorities read a donkey

case someone more distinguished than you has been invited by your host; [9]and the host who invited both of you may come and say to you, 'Give this person your place,' and then in disgrace you would start to take the lowest place. [10]But when you are invited, go and sit down at the lowest place, so that when your host comes, he may say to you, 'Friend, move up higher'; then you will be honored in the presence of all who sit at the table with you. [11]For all who exalt themselves will be humbled, and those who humble themselves will be exalted."

12 He said also to the one who had invited him, "When you give a luncheon or a dinner, do not invite your friends or your brothers or your relatives or rich neighbors, in case they may invite you in return, and you would be repaid. [13]But when you give a banquet, invite the poor, the crippled, the lame, and the blind. [14]And you will be blessed, because they cannot repay you, for you will be repaid at the resurrection of the righteous."

The Parable of the Great Dinner

15 One of the dinner guests, on hearing this, said to him, "Blessed is anyone who will eat bread in the kingdom of God!" [16]Then Jesus[k] said to him, "Someone gave a great dinner and invited many. [17]At the time for the dinner he sent his slave to say to those who had been invited, 'Come; for everything is ready now.' [18]But they all alike began to make excuses. The first said to him, 'I have bought a piece of land, and I must go out and see it; please accept my regrets.' [19]Another said, 'I have bought five yoke of oxen, and I am going to try them out; please accept my regrets.' [20]Another said, 'I have just been married, and therefore I cannot come.' [21]So the slave returned and reported this to his master. Then the owner of the house became angry and said to his slave, 'Go out at once into the streets and lanes of the town and bring in the poor, the crippled, the blind, and the lame.' [22]And the slave said, 'Sir, what you ordered has been done, and there is still room.' [23]Then the master said to the slave, 'Go out into the roads and lanes, and compel people to come in, so that my house may be filled. [24]For I tell you,[l] none of those who were invited will taste my dinner.'"

The Cost of Discipleship

25 Now large crowds were traveling with him; and he turned and said to them, [26]"Whoever comes to me and does not hate father and mother, wife and children, brothers and sisters, yes, and even life itself, cannot be my disciple. [27]Whoever does not carry the cross and follow me cannot be my disciple. [28]For which of you, intending to build a tower, does not first sit down and estimate the cost, to see whether he has enough to complete it? [29]Otherwise, when he has laid a foundation and is not able to finish, all who see it will begin to ridicule him, [30]saying, 'This fellow began to build and was not able to finish.' [31]Or what king, going out to wage war against another king, will not sit down first and consider whether he is able with ten thousand to oppose the one who comes against him with twenty thousand? [32]If he cannot, then, while the other is still far away, he sends a delegation and asks for the terms of peace. [33]So therefore, none of you can become my disciple if you do not give up all your possessions.

About Salt

34 "Salt is good; but if salt has lost its taste, how can its saltiness be restored?[m] [35]It is fit neither for the soil nor for the manure pile; they throw it away. Let anyone with ears to hear listen!"

The Parable of the Lost Sheep

▶ See Matthew 18.12–14

15 Now all the tax collectors and sinners were coming near to listen to him. [2]And the Pharisees and the scribes were grumbling and saying, "This fellow welcomes sinners and eats with them."

15.3 Severe and Gentle Stories

The collection of stories in chapters 14 and 15, found only in Luke's Gospel, shows the two-edged thrust of Jesus' message. The stern warnings in chapter 14 are directed to the proud, who either see no need for God or refuse to pay the cost of following him. The three stories in the next chapter progressively show the limitless love of God for those in real need. He stands ready to forgive all who turn to him.

3 So he told them this parable: [4]"Which one of you, having a hundred sheep and losing one of them, does not leave the ninety-nine in the wilderness and go after the one that is lost until he finds it? [5]When he has found it, he lays it on his shoulders and rejoices. [6]And when he comes home, he calls together his friends and neighbors, saying to them, 'Rejoice with me, for I have found my sheep that was lost.' [7]Just so, I tell you, there will be more joy in heaven over one sinner who repents than over ninety-nine righteous persons who need no repentance.

The Parable of the Lost Coin

8 "Or what woman having ten silver coins,[n]

[k] Gk he　　[l] The Greek word for *you* here is plural　　[m] Or *how can it be used for seasoning?*　　[n] Gk *drachmas*, each worth about a day's wage for a laborer

if she loses one of them, does not light a lamp, sweep the house, and search carefully until she finds it? [9]When she has found it, she calls together her friends and neighbors, saying, 'Rejoice with me, for I have found the coin that I had lost.' [10]Just so, I tell you, there is joy in the presence of the angels of God over one sinner who repents."

The Parable of the Prodigal and His Brother

11 Then Jesus[o] said, "There was a man who had two sons. [12]The younger of them said to his father, 'Father, give me the share of the property that will belong to me.' So he divided his property between them. [13]A few days later the younger son gathered all he had and traveled to a distant country, and there he squandered his property in dissolute living. [14]When he had spent everything, a severe famine took place throughout that country, and he began to be in need. [15]So he went and hired himself out to one of the citizens of that country, who sent him to his fields to feed the pigs. [16]He would gladly have filled himself with[p] the pods that the pigs were eating; and no one gave him anything. [17]But when he came to himself he said, 'How many of my father's hired hands have bread enough and to spare, but here I am dying of hunger! [18]I will get up and go to my father, and I will say to him, "Father, I have sinned against heaven and before you; [19]I am no longer worthy to be called your son; treat me like one of your hired hands."' [20]So he set off and went to his father. But while he was still far off, his father saw him and was filled with compassion; he ran and put his arms around him and kissed him. [21]Then the son said to him, 'Father, I have sinned against heaven and before you; I am no longer worthy to be called your son.'[q] [22]But the father said to his slaves, 'Quickly, bring out a robe—the best one—and put it on him; put a ring on his finger and sandals on his feet. [23]And get the fatted calf and kill it, and let us eat and celebrate; [24]for this son of mine was dead and is alive again; he was lost and is found!' And they began to celebrate.

25 "Now his elder son was in the field; and when he came and approached the house, he heard music and dancing. [26]He called one of the slaves and asked what was going on. [27]He replied, 'Your brother has come, and your father has killed the fatted calf, because he has got him back safe and sound.' [28]Then he became angry and refused to go in. His father came out and began to plead with him. [29]But he answered his father, 'Listen! For all these years I have been working like a slave for you, and I have never disobeyed your command; yet you have never given me even a young goat so that I might celebrate with

my friends. [30]But when this son of yours came back, who has devoured your property with prostitutes, you killed the fatted calf for him!' [31]Then the father[o] said to him, 'Son, you are always with

15.28 Two Lost Brothers?

The parable of the Prodigal and His Brother tells of two sons, one irresponsible, the other hardworking. One wastes his life and comes home humbled; the other proudly refuses to celebrate his brother's homecoming. The story ends with one son in a joyful family celebration, and his brother outside, bitterly unwilling to forgive. Which son is really lost?

me, and all that is mine is yours. [32]But we had to celebrate and rejoice, because this brother of yours was dead and has come to life; he was lost and has been found.'"

The Parable of the Dishonest Manager

16 Then Jesus[o] said to the disciples, "There was a rich man who had a manager, and charges were brought to him that this man was squandering his property. [2]So he summoned him and said to him, 'What is this that I hear about you? Give me an accounting of your management, because you cannot be my manager any longer.' [3]Then the manager said to himself, 'What will I do, now that my master is taking the position away from me? I am not strong enough to dig, and I am ashamed to beg. [4]I have decided what to do so that, when I am dismissed as manager, people may welcome me into their homes.' [5]So, summoning his master's debtors one by one, he asked the first, 'How much do you owe my master?' [6]He answered, 'A hundred jugs of olive oil.' He said to him, 'Take your bill, sit down quickly, and make it fifty.' [7]Then he asked another, 'And how much do you owe?' He replied, 'A hundred containers of wheat.' He said to him, 'Take your bill and make it eighty.' [8]And his master commended the dishonest manager because he had acted shrewdly; for the children of this age are more shrewd in dealing with their own generation than are the children of light. [9]And I tell you, make friends for yourselves by means of dishonest wealth[r] so that when it is gone, they may welcome you into the eternal homes.[s]

10 "Whoever is faithful in a very little is faithful also in much; and whoever is dishonest in a very little is dishonest also in much. [11]If then you have not been faithful with the dishonest wealth,[r] who will entrust to you the true riches? [12]And if you have not been faithful with what belongs to another, who will give you what is your own?

[o] Gk *he*   [p] Other ancient authorities read *filled his stomach with* of your hired servants   [r] Gk *mammon*   [s] Gk *tents*   [q] Other ancient authorities add *Treat me like one*

[13]No slave can serve two masters; for a slave will either hate the one and love the other, or be devoted to the one and despise the other. You cannot serve God and wealth."[t]

The Law and the Kingdom of God

14 The Pharisees, who were lovers of money, heard all this, and they ridiculed him. [15]So he said to them, "You are those who justify yourselves in the sight of others; but God knows your hearts; for what is prized by human beings is an abomination in the sight of God.

16 "The law and the prophets were in effect until John came; since then the good news of the kingdom of God is proclaimed, and everyone tries to enter it by force.[u] [17]But it is easier for heaven and earth to pass away, than for one stroke of a letter in the law to be dropped.

18 "Anyone who divorces his wife and marries another commits adultery, and whoever marries a woman divorced from her husband commits adultery.

The Rich Man and Lazarus

19 "There was a rich man who was dressed in purple and fine linen and who feasted sumptuously every day. [20]And at his gate lay a poor man named Lazarus, covered with sores, [21]who longed to satisfy his hunger with what fell from the rich man's table; even the dogs would come and lick his sores. [22]The poor man died and was carried away by the angels to be with Abraham.[v] The rich man also died and was buried. [23]In Hades, where he was being tormented, he looked up and saw Abraham far away with Lazarus by his side.[w] [24]He called out, 'Father Abraham, have mercy on me, and send Lazarus to dip the tip of his finger in water and cool my tongue; for I am in agony in these flames.' [25]But Abraham said, 'Child, remember that during your lifetime you received your good things, and Lazarus in like manner evil things; but now he is comforted here, and you are in agony. [26]Besides all this, between you and us a great chasm has been fixed, so that those who might want to pass from here to you cannot do so, and no one can cross from there to us.' [27]He said, 'Then, father, I beg you to send him to my father's house— [28]for I have five brothers—that he may warn them, so that they will not also come into this place of torment.' [29]Abraham replied, 'They have Moses and the prophets; they should listen to them.' [30]He said, 'No, father Abraham; but if someone goes to them from the dead, they will repent.' [31]He said to him, 'If they do not listen to Moses and the prophets, neither will they be convinced even if someone rises from the dead.'"

Some Sayings of Jesus

17 Jesus[x] said to his disciples, "Occasions for stumbling are bound to come, but woe to anyone by whom they come! [2]It would be better

> ### 16.31 Stubbornly Unconvinced
> *With the concluding statement in this famous story of Lazarus, Jesus made a poignant prophecy, although his listeners at the time probably missed the point. Many of them, especially the Pharisees, refused to believe him even after he rose from the dead.*

for you if a millstone were hung around your neck and you were thrown into the sea than for you to cause one of these little ones to stumble. [3]Be on your guard! If another disciple[y] sins, you must rebuke the offender, and if there is repentance, you must forgive. [4]And if the same person sins against you seven times a day, and turns back to you seven times and says, 'I repent,' you must forgive."

5 The apostles said to the Lord, "Increase our faith!" [6]The Lord replied, "If you had faith the size of a[z] mustard seed, you could say to this mulberry tree, 'Be uprooted and planted in the sea,' and it would obey you.

7 "Who among you would say to your slave who has just come in from plowing or tending sheep in the field, 'Come here at once and take your place at the table'? [8]Would you not rather say to him, 'Prepare supper for me, put on your apron and serve me while I eat and drink; later you may eat and drink'? [9]Do you thank the slave for doing what was commanded? [10]So you also, when you have done all that you were ordered to do, say, 'We are worthless slaves; we have done only what we ought to have done!'"

Jesus Cleanses Ten Lepers

11 On the way to Jerusalem Jesus[a] was going through the region between Samaria and Galilee. [12]As he entered a village, ten lepers[b] approached him. Keeping their distance, [13]they called out, saying, "Jesus, Master, have mercy on us!" [14]When he saw them, he said to them, "Go and show yourselves to the priests." And as they went, they were made clean. [15]Then one of them, when he saw that he was healed, turned back, praising God with a loud voice. [16]He prostrated himself at Jesus'[c] feet and thanked him. And he was a Samaritan. [17]Then Jesus asked, "Were not ten made clean? But the other nine, where are they? [18]Was none of them found to return and give praise to

---

[t] Gk *mammon*   [u] Or *everyone is strongly urged to enter it*
[x] Gk *He*   [y] Gk *your brother*   [z] Gk *faith as a grain of several diseases*   [c] Gk *his*

[v] Gk *to Abraham's bosom*   [w] Gk *in his bosom*
[a] Gk *he*   [b] The terms *leper* and *leprosy* can refer to

God except this foreigner?" ¹⁹Then he said to him, "Get up and go on your way; your faith has made you well."

The Coming of the Kingdom

20 Once Jesus*d* was asked by the Pharisees when the kingdom of God was coming, and he answered, "The kingdom of God is not coming with things that can be observed; ²¹nor will they say, 'Look, here it is!' or 'There it is!' For, in fact, the kingdom of God is among*e* you."

22 Then he said to the disciples, "The days are coming when you will long to see one of the days of the Son of Man, and you will not see it. ²³They will say to you, 'Look there!' or 'Look here!' Do not go, do not set off in pursuit. ²⁴For as the lightning flashes and lights up the sky from one side to the other, so will the Son of Man be in his day.*f* ²⁵But first he must endure much suffering and be rejected by this generation. ²⁶Just as it was in the days of Noah, so too it will be in the days of the Son of Man. ²⁷They were eating and drinking, and marrying and being given in marriage, until the day Noah entered the ark, and the flood came and destroyed all of them. ²⁸Likewise, just as it was in the days of Lot: they were eating and drinking, buying and selling, planting and building, ²⁹but on the day that Lot left Sodom, it rained fire and sulfur from heaven and destroyed all of them ³⁰—it will be like that on the day that the Son of Man is revealed. ³¹On that day, anyone on the housetop who has belongings in the house must not come down to take them away; and likewise anyone in the field must not turn back. ³²Remember Lot's wife. ³³Those who try to make their life secure will lose it, but those who lose their life will keep it. ³⁴I tell you, on that night there will be two in one bed; one will be taken and the other left. ³⁵There will be two women grinding meal together; one will be taken and the other left."*g* ³⁷Then they asked him, "Where, Lord?" He said to them, "Where the corpse is, there the vultures will gather."

The Parable of the Widow and the Unjust Judge

18 Then Jesus*d* told them a parable about their need to pray always and not to lose heart. ²He said, "In a certain city there was a judge who neither feared God nor had respect for people. ³In that city there was a widow who kept coming to him and saying, 'Grant me justice against my opponent.' ⁴For a while he refused; but later he said to himself, 'Though I have no fear of God and no respect for anyone, ⁵yet because this widow keeps bothering me, I will grant her justice, so that she may not wear me out by continually coming.'"*h* ⁶And the Lord said, "Lis-

ten to what the unjust judge says. ⁷And will not God grant justice to his chosen ones who cry to him day and night? Will he delay long in helping them? ⁸I tell you, he will quickly grant justice to them. And yet, when the Son of Man comes, will he find faith on earth?"

The Parable of the Pharisee and the Tax Collector

9 He also told this parable to some who trusted in themselves that they were righteous and

18.9 Luke and the Underdog

Luke's concern for the humble comes through clearly in the stories he selected, especially in chapters 18 and 19. The parable of the Pharisee and the tax collector, for example, draws a sharp contrast between the proud and the humble. Stories that follow also feature the humble: little children, a blind beggar, another tax collector.

regarded others with contempt: ¹⁰"Two men went up to the temple to pray, one a Pharisee and the other a tax collector. ¹¹The Pharisee, standing by himself, was praying thus, 'God, I thank you that I am not like other people: thieves, rogues, adulterers, or even like this tax collector. ¹²I fast twice a week; I give a tenth of all my income.' ¹³But the tax collector, standing far off, would not even look up to heaven, but was beating his breast and saying, 'God, be merciful to me, a sinner!' ¹⁴I tell you, this man went down to his home justified rather than the other; for all who exalt themselves will be humbled, but all who humble themselves will be exalted."

Jesus Blesses Little Children

▶ *See Matthew 19.13–15; Mark 10.13–16*

15 People were bringing even infants to him that he might touch them; and when the disciples saw it, they sternly ordered them not to do it. ¹⁶But Jesus called for them and said, "Let the little children come to me, and do not stop them; for it is to such as these that the kingdom of God belongs. ¹⁷Truly I tell you, whoever does not receive the kingdom of God as a little child will never enter it."

The Rich Ruler

▶ *See Matthew 19.16–29; Mark 10.17–30*

18 A certain ruler asked him, "Good Teacher, what must I do to inherit eternal life?" ¹⁹Jesus said to him, "Why do you call me good? No one is good but God alone. ²⁰You know the command-

---

d Gk he *e* Or within *f* Other ancient authorities lack *in his day* *g* Other ancient authorities add verse 36, *"Two will be in the field; one will be taken and the other left."* *h* Or *so that she may not finally come and slap me in the face*

ments: 'You shall not commit adultery; You shall not murder; You shall not steal; You shall not bear false witness; Honor your father and mother.' " 21He replied, "I have kept all these since my youth." 22When Jesus heard this, he said to him, "There is still one thing lacking. Sell all that you own and distribute the money[i] to the poor, and you will have treasure in heaven; then come, follow me." 23But when he heard this, he became sad; for he was very rich. 24Jesus looked at him and said, "How hard it is for those who have wealth to enter the kingdom of God! 25Indeed, it is easier for a camel to go through the eye of a needle than for someone who is rich to enter the kingdom of God."

26 Those who heard it said, "Then who can be saved?" 27He replied, "What is impossible for mortals is possible for God."

28 Then Peter said, "Look, we have left our homes and followed you." 29And he said to them, "Truly I tell you, there is no one who has left house or wife or brothers or parents or children, for the sake of the kingdom of God, 30who will not get back very much more in this age, and in the age to come eternal life."

A Third Time Jesus Foretells His Death and Resurrection

▶ See Matthew 20.17–19; Mark 10.32–34

31 Then he took the twelve aside and said to them, "See, we are going up to Jerusalem, and everything that is written about the Son of Man by the prophets will be accomplished. 32For he will be handed over to the Gentiles; and he will be mocked and insulted and spat upon. 33After they have flogged him, they will kill him, and on the third day he will rise again." 34But they understood nothing about all these things; in fact, what he said was hidden from them, and they did not grasp what was said.

Jesus Heals a Blind Beggar Near Jericho

▶ See Matthew 20.29–34; Mark 10.46–52

35 As he approached Jericho, a blind man was sitting by the roadside begging. 36When he heard a crowd going by, he asked what was happening. 37They told him, "Jesus of Nazareth[j] is passing by." 38Then he shouted, "Jesus, Son of David, have mercy on me!" 39Those who were in front sternly ordered him to be quiet; but he shouted even more loudly, "Son of David, have mercy on me!" 40Jesus stood still and ordered the man to be brought to him; and when he came near, he asked him, 41"What do you want me to do for you?" He said, "Lord, let me see again." 42Jesus said to him, "Receive your sight; your faith has saved you." 43Immediately he regained his

sight and followed him, glorifying God; and all the people, when they saw it, praised God.

Jesus and Zacchaeus

19 He entered Jericho and was passing through it. 2A man was there named Zacchaeus; he was a chief tax collector and was rich. 3He was trying to see who Jesus was, but on account of the crowd he could not, because he was short in stature. 4So he ran ahead and climbed a sycamore tree to see him, because he was going to pass that way. 5When Jesus came to the place, he looked up and said to him, "Zacchaeus, hurry and come down; for I must stay at your house today." 6So he hurried down and was happy to welcome him. 7All who saw it began to grumble and said, "He has gone to be the guest of one who is a sinner." 8Zacchaeus stood there and said to the Lord, "Look, half of my possessions, Lord, I will give to the poor; and if I have defrauded anyone of anything, I will pay back four times as much." 9Then Jesus said to him, "Today salvation has come to this house, because he too is a son of Abraham. 10For the Son of Man came to seek out and to save the lost."

19.10 Seek and Save

A Jew who had sided with the hated Roman oppressors, Zacchaeus still had enough religious sensitivity to be curious about Jesus. Seeing his interest, Jesus took the initiative. He stopped the procession and called out to Zacchaeus, inviting himself to a meal at Zacchaeus's home. Though befriending this tax collector upset the crowd, Jesus proclaimed it as typical of his ministry: to seek and to save the lost.

The Parable of the Ten Pounds

11 As they were listening to this, he went on to tell a parable, because he was near Jerusalem, and because they supposed that the kingdom of God was to appear immediately. 12So he said, "A nobleman went to a distant country to get royal power for himself and then return. 13He summoned ten of his slaves, and gave them ten pounds,[k] and said to them, 'Do business with these until I come back.' 14But the citizens of his country hated him and sent a delegation after him, saying, 'We do not want this man to rule over us.' 15When he returned, having received royal power, he ordered these slaves, to whom he had given the money, to be summoned so that he might find out what they had gained by trading. 16The first came forward and said, 'Lord, your

---

[i] Gk lacks *the money*   [j] Gk *the Nazorean*   [k] The mina, rendered here by *pound*, was about three months' wages for a laborer

pound has made ten more pounds.' ¹⁷He said to him, 'Well done, good slave! Because you have been trustworthy in a very small thing, take charge of ten cities.' ¹⁸Then the second came, saying, 'Lord, your pound has made five pounds.' ¹⁹He said to him, 'And you, rule over five cities.' ²⁰Then the other came, saying, 'Lord, here is your pound. I wrapped it up in a piece of cloth, ²¹for I was afraid of you, because you are a harsh man; you take what you did not deposit, and reap what you did not sow.' ²²He said to him, 'I will judge you by your own words, you wicked slave! You

knew, did you, that I was a harsh man, taking what I did not deposit and reaping what I did not sow? ²³Why then did you not put my money into the bank? Then when I returned, I could have collected it with interest.' ²⁴He said to the bystanders, 'Take the pound from him and give it to the one who has ten pounds.' ²⁵(And they said to him, 'Lord, he has ten pounds!') ²⁶'I tell you, to all those who have, more will be given; but from those who have nothing, even what they have will be taken away. ²⁷But as for these enemies of mine who did not want me to be king over them—

Handling Tough Questions
Why so many stories?

SUFFERING STRIKES LIKE AN EARTHQUAKE, without warning, causing sudden devastation. Twenty-nine teenagers die when a school bus plunges off a bridge. A hurricane smashes into Mexico. An epidemic of cholera breaks out in South America.

Psychological tremors follow, often in the form of questions. "Why did God let this happen? Did we do something wrong? Why does God permit such suffering?"

In Jesus' day, rumors buzzed about two catastrophes: Pontius Pilate's slaughter of Galileans and the collapse of a tower (13.1–4). Naturally, people around Jesus questioned him about these events, but his answers puzzled them. He refused to be drawn into a discussion of the age-old problem of pain. He merely dismissed the common opinion that tragedies happen to people who deserve them and deflected the issue back to the questioners as a general warning (13.4–5; see also "What Job Teaches about Suffering," page 544).

> The chief priests, the scribes, and the leaders of the people kept looking for a way to kill him; but they did not find anything they could do, for all the people were spellbound by what they heard. 19.47–48

The Heart of the Question

Jesus' response to the questions on suffering illustrate how he dealt with difficult issues. Religious leaders and philosophical types were constantly trying to stop him with an arsenal of tough questions. Usually their tactics backfired as Jesus expertly turned their questions back on them.

Conscious of the listening crowds, Jesus avoided long arguments, instead emphasizing the need for people to change behavior. His answers cut to the heart of the question, and to the hearts of his listeners.

When teaching, Jesus often relied on a parable—a compact short story with a moral. Speaking in parables allowed him to continue training his disciples "privately," despite the throngs of onlookers (8.10). He could explain the meaning to the disciples later on when they were alone together. Parables also helped preserve his message: Years later, as people reflected on what Jesus taught, his parables came to mind in vivid detail.

Simple Stories with a Profound Point

Luke, a master storyteller, collected 18 parables that appear nowhere else, and he also retold some of the most familiar. While Matthew emphasizes parables of the kingdom, Luke adds those that focus on people: the good Samaritan, a persistent widow, the lost son. His parables speak to heavy subjects, but in an unexpectedly disarming way.

Jesus' style of handling tough questions contrasts sharply with Paul's. The apostle Paul wrapped concepts in theological words and gave formal explanations. In careful prose he patiently probed such complex words as *forgiveness* and *justification.*

Jesus, speaking to a restless crowd of thousands, communicated the same message in three progressive stories—the Lost Sheep, the Lost Coin, and the Prodigal and His Brother (15.1–32). Scottish Christians like to call that last story "The Wonderful Father." It expresses the heart of Jesus' message about as well as any ten-volume theological work.

Life Questions: What one question would you most like to ask Jesus in person? Given how he handled tough questions in Luke, can you imagine how he might respond to yours?

bring them here and slaughter them in my presence.'"

Jesus' Triumphal Entry into Jerusalem

▶ *See Matthew 21.1–9; Mark 11.1–10; John 12.12–15*

28 After he had said this, he went on ahead, going up to Jerusalem. 29 When he had come near Bethphage and Bethany, at the place called the Mount of Olives, he sent two of the disciples, 30saying, "Go into the village ahead of you, and as you enter it you will find tied there a colt that has never been ridden. Untie it and bring it here. 31If anyone asks you, 'Why are you untying it?' just say this, 'The Lord needs it.'" 32So those who were sent departed and found it as he had told them. 33As they were untying the colt, its owners asked them, "Why are you untying the colt?" 34They said, "The Lord needs it." 35Then they brought it to Jesus; and after throwing their cloaks on the colt, they set Jesus on it. 36As he rode along, people kept spreading their cloaks on the road. 37As he was now approaching the path down from the Mount of Olives, the whole multitude of the disciples began to praise God joyfully with a loud voice for all the deeds of power that they had seen, 38saying,

"Blessed is the king
   who comes in the name of the Lord!
Peace in heaven,
   and glory in the highest heaven!"

39Some of the Pharisees in the crowd said to him, "Teacher, order your disciples to stop." 40He answered, "I tell you, if these were silent, the stones would shout out."

Jesus Weeps over Jerusalem

41 As he came near and saw the city, he wept over it, 42saying, "If you, even you, had only recognized on this day the things that make for peace! But now they are hidden from your eyes. 43Indeed, the days will come upon you, when your enemies will set up ramparts around you and surround you, and hem you in on every side. 44They will crush you to the ground, you and your children within you, and they will not leave within you one stone upon another; because you did not recognize the time of your visitation from God."[1]

Jesus Cleanses the Temple

▶ *See Matthew 21.12–16; Mark 11.15–18; John 2.13–16*

45 Then he entered the temple and began to drive out those who were selling things there; 46and he said, "It is written,

'My house shall be a house of prayer';
   but you have made it a den
      of robbers."

47 Every day he was teaching in the temple. The chief priests, the scribes, and the leaders of the people kept looking for a way to kill him; 48but they did not find anything they could do, for all the people were spellbound by what they heard.

The Authority of Jesus Questioned

▶ *See Matthew 21.23–27; Mark 11.27–33*

20 One day, as he was teaching the people in the temple and telling the good news, the chief priests and the scribes came with the elders 2and said to him, "Tell us, by what authority are you doing these things? Who is it who gave you this authority?" 3He answered them, "I will also ask you a question, and you tell me: 4Did the baptism of John come from heaven, or was it of human origin?" 5They discussed it with one another, saying, "If we say, 'From heaven,' he will say, 'Why did you not believe him?' 6But if we say, 'Of human origin,' all the people will stone us; for they are convinced that John was a prophet." 7So they answered that they did not know where it came from. 8Then Jesus said to them, "Neither will I tell you by what authority I am doing these things."

The Parable of the Wicked Tenants

▶ *See Matthew 21.33–46; Mark 12.1–12*

9 He began to tell the people this parable: "A man planted a vineyard, and leased it to tenants, and went to another country for a long time. 10When the season came, he sent a slave to the tenants in order that they might give him his share of the produce of the vineyard; but the tenants beat him and sent him away empty-handed. 11Next he sent another slave; that one also they beat and insulted and sent away empty-handed. 12And he sent still a third; this one also they wounded and threw out. 13Then the owner of the vineyard said, 'What shall I do? I will send my beloved son; perhaps they will respect him.' 14But when the tenants saw him, they discussed it among themselves and said, 'This is the heir; let us kill him so that the inheritance may be ours.' 15So they threw him out of the vineyard and killed him. What then will the owner of the vineyard do

19.44 Wailing Wall

Jesus' tearful prediction of total destruction was fulfilled in A.D. 70, when the Romans crushed a Jewish revolt by razing the city. In modern Jerusalem, the Wailing Wall is one of the few places where some of the original stonework of Jerusalem can still be seen.

[1] Gk lacks *from God*

to them? [16]He will come and destroy those tenants and give the vineyard to others." When they heard this, they said, "Heaven forbid!" [17]But he looked at them and said, "What then does this text mean:

'The stone that the builders rejected
    has become the cornerstone'?[m]
[18]Everyone who falls on that stone will be broken to pieces; and it will crush anyone on whom it falls." [19]When the scribes and chief priests realized that he had told this parable against them, they wanted to lay hands on him at that very hour, but they feared the people.

The Question about Paying Taxes

▶ See Matthew 22.15–22; Mark 12.13–17

20 So they watched him and sent spies who pretended to be honest, in order to trap him by what he said, so as to hand him over to the jurisdiction and authority of the governor. [21]So they asked him, "Teacher, we know that you are right in what you say and teach, and you show deference to no one, but teach the way of God in accordance with truth. [22]Is it lawful for us to pay taxes to the emperor, or not?" [23]But he perceived their craftiness and said to them, [24]"Show me a denarius. Whose head and whose title does it bear?" They said, "The emperor's." [25]He said to them, "Then give to the emperor the things that are the emperor's, and to God the things that are God's." [26]And they were not able in the presence of the people to trap him by what he said; and being amazed by his answer, they became silent.

The Question about the Resurrection

▶ See Matthew 22.23–33; Mark 12.18–27

27 Some Sadducees, those who say there is no resurrection, came to him [28]and asked him a question, "Teacher, Moses wrote for us that if a man's brother dies, leaving a wife but no children, the man[n] shall marry the widow and raise up children for his brother. [29]Now there were seven brothers; the first married, and died childless; [30]then the second [31]and the third married her, and so in the same way all seven died childless. [32]Finally the woman also died. [33]In the resurrection, therefore, whose wife will the woman be? For the seven had married her."

34 Jesus said to them, "Those who belong to this age marry and are given in marriage; [35]but those who are considered worthy of a place in that age and in the resurrection from the dead neither marry nor are given in marriage. [36]Indeed they cannot die anymore, because they are like angels and are children of God, being children of the resurrection. [37]And the fact that the dead are raised Moses himself showed, in the story about the bush, where he speaks of the Lord as the God of Abraham, the God of Isaac, and the God of

Jacob. [38]Now he is God not of the dead, but of the living; for to him all of them are alive." [39]Then some of the scribes answered, "Teacher, you have spoken well." [40]For they no longer dared to ask him another question.

The Question about David's Son

▶ See Matthew 22.41–23.7; Mark 12.35–40

41 Then he said to them, "How can they say that the Messiah[o] is David's son? [42]For David himself says in the book of Psalms,

'The Lord said to my Lord,
    "Sit at my right hand,
[43]   until I make your enemies your
        footstool." '
[44]David thus calls him Lord; so how can he be his son?"

20.41–44 Jesus Asks a Question

In the midst of many questions thrown at him, Jesus offers one back. The passage, quoting Psalm 110.1, is difficult to understand, but Jesus may have been trying to clear up a misunderstanding about the Messiah. Nationalistic Jews of that day were expecting a Messiah, or "David's son," out of the same mold as the great Jewish king who defeated Israel's enemies. But Jesus shows that David himself acknowledged the Messiah to come as "Lord," or One far greater than a mere earthly king.

Jesus Denounces the Scribes

45 In the hearing of all the people he said to the[p] disciples, [46]"Beware of the scribes, who like to walk around in long robes, and love to be greeted with respect in the marketplaces, and to have the best seats in the synagogues and places of honor at banquets. [47]They devour widows' houses and for the sake of appearance say long prayers. They will receive the greater condemnation."

The Widow's Offering

▶ See Mark 12.41–44

21 He looked up and saw rich people putting their gifts into the treasury; [2]he also saw a poor widow put in two small copper coins. [3]He said, "Truly I tell you, this poor widow has put in more than all of them; [4]for all of them have contributed out of their abundance, but she out of her poverty has put in all she had to live on."

The Destruction of the Temple Foretold

▶ See Matthew 24; Mark 13

5 When some were speaking about the tem-

---

[m] Or keystone   [n] Gk his brother   [o] Or the Christ   [p] Other ancient authorities read his

ple, how it was adorned with beautiful stones and gifts dedicated to God, he said, 6"As for these things that you see, the days will come when not one stone will be left upon another; all will be thrown down."

Signs and Persecutions

7 They asked him, "Teacher, when will this be, and what will be the sign that this is about to take place?" 8And he said, "Beware that you are not led astray; for many will come in my name and say, 'I am he!'*q* and, 'The time is near!'*r* Do not go after them.

9 "When you hear of wars and insurrections, do not be terrified; for these things must take place first, but the end will not follow immediately." 10Then he said to them, "Nation will rise against nation, and kingdom against kingdom; 11there will be great earthquakes, and in various places famines and plagues; and there will be dreadful portents and great signs from heaven.

12 "But before all this occurs, they will arrest you and persecute you; they will hand you over to synagogues and prisons, and you will be brought before kings and governors because of my name. 13This will give you an opportunity to testify. 14So make up your minds not to prepare your defense in advance; 15for I will give you words*s* and a wisdom that none of your opponents will be able to withstand or contradict. 16You will be betrayed even by parents and brothers, by relatives and friends; and they will put some of you to death. 17You will be hated by all because of my name. 18But not a hair of your head will perish. 19By your endurance you will gain your souls.

The Destruction of Jerusalem Foretold

20 "When you see Jerusalem surrounded by armies, then know that its desolation has come near.*t* 21Then those in Judea must flee to the mountains, and those inside the city must leave it, and those out in the country must not enter it; 22for these are days of vengeance, as a fulfillment of all that is written. 23Woe to those who are pregnant and to those who are nursing infants in those days! For there will be great distress on the earth and wrath against this people; 24they will fall by the edge of the sword and be taken away as captives among all nations; and Jerusalem will be trampled on by the Gentiles, until the times of the Gentiles are fulfilled.

The Coming of the Son of Man

25 "There will be signs in the sun, the moon, and the stars, and on the earth distress among nations confused by the roaring of the sea and the waves. 26People will faint from fear and foreboding of what is coming upon the world, for the powers of the heavens will be shaken. 27Then they

will see 'the Son of Man coming in a cloud' with power and great glory. 28Now when these things begin to take place, stand up and raise your heads, because your redemption is drawing near."

The Lesson of the Fig Tree

29 Then he told them a parable: "Look at the fig tree and all the trees; 30as soon as they sprout leaves you can see for yourselves and know that summer is already near. 31So also, when you see these things taking place, you know that the kingdom of God is near. 32Truly I tell you, this generation will not pass away until all things have taken place. 33Heaven and earth will pass away, but my words will not pass away.

Exhortation to Watch

34 "Be on guard so that your hearts are not weighed down with dissipation and drunkenness and the worries of this life, and that day does not catch you unexpectedly, 35like a trap. For it will come upon all who live on the face of the whole earth. 36Be alert at all times, praying that you may have the strength to escape all these things that will take place, and to stand before the Son of Man."

37 Every day he was teaching in the temple, and at night he would go out and spend the night on the Mount of Olives, as it was called. 38And all the people would get up early in the morning to listen to him in the temple.

The Plot to Kill Jesus

▶ *See Matthew 26.2–5; Mark 14.1–2,10–11*

22 Now the festival of Unleavened Bread, which is called the Passover, was near. 2The chief priests and the scribes were looking for a way to put Jesus*u* to death, for they were afraid of the people.

3 Then Satan entered into Judas called Iscariot, who was one of the twelve; 4he went away and conferred with the chief priests and officers of the temple police about how he might betray him to them. 5They were greatly pleased and agreed to give him money. 6So he consented and began to look for an opportunity to betray him to them when no crowd was present.

The Preparation of the Passover

▶ *See Matthew 26.17–19,26–29; Mark 14.12–16,22–25*

7 Then came the day of Unleavened Bread, on which the Passover lamb had to be sacrificed. 8So Jesus*v* sent Peter and John, saying, "Go and prepare the Passover meal for us that we may eat it." 9They asked him, "Where do you want us to make preparations for it?" 10"Listen," he said to them, "when you have entered the city, a man carrying a jar of water will meet you; follow him

---

q Gk *I am*   *r* Or *at hand*   *s* Gk *a mouth*   *t* Or *is at hand*   *u* Gk *him*   *v* Gk *he*

into the house he enters 11and say to the owner of the house, 'The teacher asks you, "Where is the guest room, where I may eat the Passover with my disciples?" ' 12He will show you a large room upstairs, already furnished. Make preparations for us there." 13So they went and found everything as he had told them; and they prepared the Passover meal.

The Institution of the Lord's Supper

14 When the hour came, he took his place at the table, and the apostles with him. 15He said to them, "I have eagerly desired to eat this Passover with you before I suffer; 16for I tell you, I will not eat it*w* until it is fulfilled in the kingdom of God." 17Then he took a cup, and after giving thanks he said, "Take this and divide it among yourselves; 18for I tell you that from now on I will not drink of the fruit of the vine until the kingdom of God comes." 19Then he took a loaf of bread, and when he had given thanks, he broke it and gave it to them, saying, "This is my body, which is given for you. Do this in remembrance of me." 20And he did the same with the cup after supper, saying, "This cup that is poured out for you is the new covenant in my blood.*x* 21But see, the one who betrays me is with me, and his hand is on the table. 22For the Son of Man is going as it has been determined, but woe to that one by whom he is betrayed!" 23Then they began to ask one another which one of them it could be who would do this.

The Dispute about Greatness

24 A dispute also arose among them as to which one of them was to be regarded as the

22.24 Status-conscious Disciples

Even at the emotional Last Supper scene described here, the disciples fell into their habit of worrying about rank and status. Not until after Jesus had died and returned did they understand the true nature of the kingdom he was setting into motion. It is a kingdom primarily of spiritual, not political, power. And in it, the greatest is the one who serves others.

greatest. 25But he said to them, "The kings of the Gentiles lord it over them; and those in authority over them are called benefactors. 26But not so with you; rather the greatest among you must become like the youngest, and the leader like one who serves. 27For who is greater, the one who is at the table or the one who serves? Is it not the one at the table? But I am among you as one who serves.

28 "You are those who have stood by me in my trials; 29and I confer on you, just as my Father has conferred on me, a kingdom, 30so that you may eat and drink at my table in my kingdom, and you will sit on thrones judging the twelve tribes of Israel.

Jesus Predicts Peter's Denial

31 "Simon, Simon, listen! Satan has demanded*y* to sift all of you like wheat, 32but I have prayed for you that your own faith may not fail; and you, when once you have turned back, strengthen your brothers." 33And he said to him, "Lord, I am ready to go with you to prison and to death!" 34Jesus*z* said, "I tell you, Peter, the cock will not crow this day, until you have denied three times that you know me."

Purse, Bag, and Sword

35 He said to them, "When I sent you out without a purse, bag, or sandals, did you lack anything?" They said, "No, not a thing." 36He said to them, "But now, the one who has a purse must take it, and likewise a bag. And the one who has no sword must sell his cloak and buy one. 37For I tell you, this scripture must be fulfilled in me, 'And he was counted among the lawless'; and indeed what is written about me is being fulfilled." 38They said, "Lord, look, here are two swords." He replied, "It is enough."

Jesus Prays on the Mount of Olives

▶ *See Matthew 26.36–46; Mark 14.32–42*

39 He came out and went, as was his custom, to the Mount of Olives; and the disciples followed him. 40When he reached the place, he said to them, "Pray that you may not come into the time of trial."*a* 41Then he withdrew from them about a stone's throw, knelt down, and prayed, 42"Father, if you are willing, remove this cup from me; yet, not my will but yours be done." ⟦43Then an angel from heaven appeared to him and gave him strength. 44In his anguish he prayed more earnestly, and his sweat became like great drops of blood falling down on the ground.⟧*b* 45When he got up from prayer, he came to the disciples and found them sleeping because of grief, 46and he said to them, "Why are you sleeping? Get up and pray that you may not come into the time of trial."*a*

The Betrayal and Arrest of Jesus

▶ *See Matthew 26.47–56; Mark 14.43–50; John 18.3–11*

47 While he was still speaking, suddenly a crowd came, and the one called Judas, one of the twelve, was leading them. He approached Jesus to

---

w Other ancient authorities read *never eat it again* (*which is given . . . in my blood*) *y* Or *has obtained permission* *x* Other ancient authorities lack, in whole or in part, verses 19b-20 *z* Gk He *a* Or *into temptation* *b* Other ancient authorities lack verses 43 and 44

kiss him; [48]but Jesus said to him, "Judas, is it with a kiss that you are betraying the Son of Man?" [49]When those who were around him saw what was coming, they asked, "Lord, should we strike with the sword?" [50]Then one of them struck the slave of the high priest and cut off his right ear. [51]But Jesus said, "No more of this!" And he touched his ear and healed him. [52]Then Jesus said to the chief priests, the officers of the temple police, and the elders who had come for him, "Have you come out with swords and clubs as if I were a bandit? [53]When I was with you day after day in the temple, you did not lay hands on me. But this is your hour, and the power of darkness!"

Peter Denies Jesus

▶ See Matthew 26.69–75; Mark 14.66–72; John 18.16–18,25–27

54 Then they seized him and led him away, bringing him into the high priest's house. But Peter was following at a distance. [55]When they had kindled a fire in the middle of the courtyard and sat down together, Peter sat among them. [56]Then a servant-girl, seeing him in the firelight, stared at him and said, "This man also was with him." [57]But he denied it, saying, "Woman, I do not know him." [58]A little later someone else, on seeing him, said, "You also are one of them." But

22.58 Deserted by His Friends

Peter showed courage by following Jesus, rather than going into hiding. Perhaps trying to gain information, he even went into the high priest's courtyard. But there he was recognized, partly because of his Galilean accent (see Matthew 26.73). After denying that he knew Jesus, Peter remembered with pain his boast that he would be willing to die with Jesus (verse 33). Jesus had accurately predicted even Peter would desert him.

Peter said, "Man, I am not!" [59]Then about an hour later still another kept insisting, "Surely this man also was with him; for he is a Galilean." [60]But Peter said, "Man, I do not know what you are talking about!" At that moment, while he was still speaking, the cock crowed. [61]The Lord turned and looked at Peter. Then Peter remembered the word of the Lord, how he had said to him, "Before the cock crows today, you will deny me three times." [62]And he went out and wept bitterly.

The Mocking and Beating of Jesus

▶ See Matthew 26.67–68; Mark 14.65; John 18.22–23

63 Now the men who were holding Jesus began to mock him and beat him; [64]they also blind-folded him and kept asking him, "Prophesy! Who is it that struck you?" [65]They kept heaping many other insults on him.

Jesus before the Council

▶ See Matthew 26.63–66; Mark 14.61–63; John 18.19–21

66 When day came, the assembly of the elders of the people, both chief priests and scribes, gathered together, and they brought him to their council. [67]They said, "If you are the Messiah,[c] tell us." He replied, "If I tell you, you will not believe; [68]and if I question you, you will not answer. [69]But from now on the Son of Man will be seated at the right hand of the power of God." [70]All of them asked, "Are you, then, the Son of God?" He said to them, "You say that I am." [71]Then they said, "What further testimony do we need? We have heard it ourselves from his own lips!"

Jesus before Pilate

23 Then the assembly rose as a body and brought Jesus[d] before Pilate. [2]They began to accuse him, saying, "We found this man perverting our nation, forbidding us to pay taxes to the emperor, and saying that he himself is the Messiah, a king."[e] [3]Then Pilate asked him, "Are you the king of the Jews?" He answered, "You say so." [4]Then Pilate said to the chief priests and the crowds, "I find no basis for an accusation against this man." [5]But they were insistent and said, "He stirs up the people by teaching throughout all Judea, from Galilee where he began even to this place."

Jesus before Herod

6 When Pilate heard this, he asked whether the man was a Galilean. [7]And when he learned that he was under Herod's jurisdiction, he sent him off to Herod, who was himself in Jerusalem at that time. [8]When Herod saw Jesus, he was very glad, for he had been wanting to see him for a long time, because he had heard about him and was hoping to see him perform some sign. [9]He questioned him at some length, but Jesus[f] gave him no answer. [10]The chief priests and the scribes stood by, vehemently accusing him. [11]Even Herod with his soldiers treated him with contempt and mocked him; then he put an elegant robe on him, and sent him back to Pilate. [12]That same day Herod and Pilate became friends with each other; before this they had been enemies.

Jesus Sentenced to Death

13 Pilate then called together the chief priests, the leaders, and the people, [14]and said to them, "You brought me this man as one who was perverting the people; and here I have examined him in your presence and have not found this man

c Or the Christ   d Gk him   e Or is an anointed king   f Gk he

guilty of any of your charges against him. [15]Neither has Herod, for he sent him back to us. Indeed, he has done nothing to deserve death. [16]I will therefore have him flogged and release him."[g]

18 Then they all shouted out together, "Away with this fellow! Release Barabbas for us!" [19](This was a man who had been put in prison for an insurrection that had taken place in the city, and for murder.) [20]Pilate, wanting to release Jesus, addressed them again; [21]but they kept shouting, "Crucify, crucify him!" [22]A third time he said to them, "Why, what evil has he done? I have found in him no ground for the sentence of death; I will therefore have him flogged and then release him." [23]But they kept urgently demanding with loud shouts that he should be crucified; and their voices prevailed. [24]So Pilate gave his verdict that their demand should be granted. [25]He released the man they asked for, the one who had been put

[g] Here, or after verse 19, other ancient authorities add verse 17, *Now he was obliged to release someone for them at the festival*

Final Glimpses of Jesus
The most important week in history

> They kept urgently demanding with loud shouts that he should be crucified; and their voices prevailed. 23.23

EVERYTHING ABOUT JESUS SEEMED TO come together during his last few days on earth, and surely those days offer a key to understanding him. As if on a roller coaster, people's reactions to him plunged from heady exhilaration to murderous rejection overnight.

Those last days included one scene of triumph, a grand entry into Jerusalem. Pilgrims were filling the streets in holiday celebration. In a gallant gesture for Jesus, they laid their coats before him, and they roared their approval as he approached. But against that tumultuous background, Jesus sat weeping, painfully aware that their praise was hollow.

Even as Jesus' popularity with the masses was soaring, spies joined the ranks of onlookers, assailing him with questions and verbal traps. Jesus knew he wasn't safe anywhere, even in an intimate gathering with his disciples. During his and his disciples' last meal together, one of the Twelve rose and left the room to bargain for Jesus' life.

The Darkest Day and the Brightest

At Jesus' arrest, the religious and political power brokers had a look at him at last. They had heard many intriguing rumors, and hoped he would perform for them like a magician (23.8). Jesus declined. He had never sought their kind of power, and would not then, even with his life at stake.

Outside, the crowd that previously had shouted, "Blessed is the king!" took up a very different chant: "Crucify him!" Jesus' life was doomed. The one who had come to save the world was about to be destroyed by it.

In two back-to-back closing chapters Luke records the darkest day in history . . . and the brightest. No one was more surprised than Jesus' disciples to hear reports that the man they had seen die on Friday was walking around on Sunday. It seemed like hysterical nonsense at first—until he did appear, and they could deny it no longer.

Ordinary People, an Extraordinary Discovery

Luke adds one scene that captures the terrible confusion of those final days. Two of Jesus' disciples were walking away from Jerusalem, downhearted. Their dream was over; all the mounting hopes of the last few years had died with Jesus on the cross.

A strange man appeared beside the two forlorn disciples. Bizarrely, he seemed the only man alive who hadn't heard about the incredible week in Jerusalem. He talked with them, tracing the whole story of the gospel, beginning with Moses and the prophets.

The stranger intrigued them, and they asked him to stay longer. At mealtime the last link snapped into place. It was Jesus! No one else. Without a doubt, he was alive.

Ordinary people, with more than a touch of cowardice, had followed Jesus, listened to him, and watched him die (from a distance, to keep themselves safe). But seeing Jesus alive changed all that. Luke's story began with joy, and it ends that way: "And they worshiped him, and returned to Jerusalem with great joy" (24.52). Before long they were out telling the world about it.

Life Questions: Suppose you had been in the room to hear the first news of Jesus' resurrection. Would you have believed it? What makes you believe it now?

in prison for insurrection and murder, and he handed Jesus over as they wished.

The Crucifixion of Jesus

▶ *See Matthew 27.33–44; Mark 15.22–32; John 19.17–24*

26 As they led him away, they seized a man, Simon of Cyrene, who was coming from the country, and they laid the cross on him, and made him carry it behind Jesus. 27A great number

23.25 Who Should Try Jesus?

The Gospels record a "pass-the-buck" sequence in Jesus' encounter with Roman justice. The Jewish court, or Sanhedrin, judged Jesus guilty of blasphemy, but it had no authority to carry out a death sentence. Therefore, the religious leaders took Jesus to Pilate, the Roman governor of Judea. Along the way, they changed the religious charge against Jesus to a political one, which alone would call for Roman punishment.

Pilate showed cowardice. First, he deferred the case to Herod, who had jurisdiction over Jesus' home region. Herod taunted and mocked Jesus, and then sent him back. Three times Pilate tried to get the Jewish leaders to release Jesus, but finally he yielded to the demands for capital punishment.

of the people followed him, and among them were women who were beating their breasts and wailing for him. 28But Jesus turned to them and said, "Daughters of Jerusalem, do not weep for me, but weep for yourselves and for your children. 29For the days are surely coming when they will say, 'Blessed are the barren, and the wombs that never bore, and the breasts that never nursed.' 30Then they will begin to say to the mountains, 'Fall on us'; and to the hills, 'Cover us.' 31For if they do this when the wood is green, what will happen when it is dry?"

32 Two others also, who were criminals, were led away to be put to death with him. 33When they came to the place that is called The Skull, they crucified Jesus*h* there with the criminals, one on his right and one on his left. [[34Then Jesus said, "Father, forgive them; for they do not know what they are doing."]]*i* And they cast lots to divide his clothing. 35And the people stood by, watching; but the leaders scoffed at him, saying, "He saved others; let him save himself if he is the Messiah*j* of God, his chosen one!" 36The soldiers also mocked him, coming up and offering him

sour wine, 37and saying, "If you are the King of the Jews, save yourself!" 38There was also an inscription over him,*k* "This is the King of the Jews."

39 One of the criminals who were hanged there kept deriding*l* him and saying, "Are you not the Messiah?*j* Save yourself and us!" 40But the other rebuked him, saying, "Do you not fear God, since you are under the same sentence of condemnation? 41And we indeed have been condemned justly, for we are getting what we deserve for our deeds, but this man has done nothing wrong." 42Then he said, "Jesus, remember me when you come into*m* your kingdom." 43He replied, "Truly I tell you, today you will be with me in Paradise."

The Death of Jesus

▶ *See Matthew 27.45–56; Mark 15.33–41*

44 It was now about noon, and darkness came over the whole land*n* until three in the afternoon, 45while the sun's light failed;*o* and the curtain of the temple was torn in two. 46Then Jesus, crying with a loud voice, said, "Father, into your hands I commend my spirit." Having said this, he breathed his last. 47When the centurion saw what had taken place, he praised God and said, "Certainly this man was innocent."*p* 48And when all the crowds who had gathered there for this spectacle saw what had taken place, they returned home, beating their breasts. 49But all his acquaintances, including the women who had followed him from Galilee, stood at a distance, watching these things.

The Burial of Jesus

▶ *See Matthew 27.57–61; Mark 15.42–47; John 19.38–42*

50 Now there was a good and righteous man named Joseph, who, though a member of the council, 51had not agreed to their plan and action. He came from the Jewish town of Arimathea, and he was waiting expectantly for the kingdom of God. 52This man went to Pilate and asked for the body of Jesus. 53Then he took it down, wrapped it in a linen cloth, and laid it in a rock-hewn tomb where no one had ever been laid. 54It was the day of Preparation, and the sabbath was beginning.*q* 55The women who had come with him from Galilee followed, and they saw the tomb and how his body was laid. 56Then they returned, and prepared spices and ointments.

On the sabbath they rested according to the commandment.

---

h Gk *him*   *i* Other ancient authorities lack the sentence *Then Jesus . . . what they are doing*   *j* Or *the Christ*
k Other ancient authorities add *written in Greek and Latin and Hebrew* (that is, *Aramaic*)   *l* Or *blaspheming*
m Other ancient authorities read *in*   *n* Or *earth*   *o* Or *the sun was eclipsed.* Other ancient authorities read *the sun was darkened*   *p* Or *righteous*   *q* Gk *was dawning*

The Resurrection of Jesus

▶ See Matthew 28.1–8; Mark 16.1–8; John 20.1–8

24 But on the first day of the week, at early dawn, they came to the tomb, taking the spices that they had prepared. 2They found the stone rolled away from the tomb, 3but when they went in, they did not find the body.[r] 4While they were perplexed about this, suddenly two men in dazzling clothes stood beside them. 5The women[s] were terrified and bowed their faces to the ground, but the men[t] said to them, "Why do you look for the living among the dead? He is not here, but has risen.[u] 6Remember how he told you, while he was still in Galilee, 7that the Son of Man must be handed over to sinners, and be crucified, and on the third day rise again." 8Then they remembered his words, 9and returning from the tomb, they told all this to the eleven and to all the rest. 10Now it was Mary Magdalene, Joanna, Mary the mother of James, and the other women with them who told this to the apostles. 11But these words seemed to them an idle tale, and they did not believe them. 12But Peter got up and ran to the tomb; stooping and looking in, he saw the linen cloths by themselves; then he went home, amazed at what had happened.[v]

The Walk to Emmaus

13 Now on that same day two of them were going to a village called Emmaus, about seven miles[w] from Jerusalem, 14and talking with each other about all these things that had happened. 15While they were talking and discussing, Jesus himself came near and went with them, 16but their eyes were kept from recognizing him. 17And he said to them, "What are you discussing with each other while you walk along?" They stood still, looking sad.[x] 18Then one of them, whose name was Cleopas, answered him, "Are you the only stranger in Jerusalem who does not know the things that have taken place there in these days?" 19He asked them, "What things?" They replied, "The things about Jesus of Nazareth,[y] who was a prophet mighty in deed and word before God and all the people, 20and how our chief priests and leaders handed him over to be condemned to death and crucified him. 21But we had hoped that he was the one to redeem Israel.[z] Yes, and besides all this, it is now the third day since these things took place. 22Moreover, some women of our group astounded us. They were at the tomb early this morning, 23and when they did not find his body there, they came back and told us that they had indeed seen a vision of angels who said that he was alive. 24Some of those who were with

us went to the tomb and found it just as the women had said; but they did not see him." 25Then he said to them, "Oh, how foolish you are, and how slow of heart to believe all that the prophets have declared! 26Was it not necessary that the Messiah[a] should suffer these things and then enter into his glory?" 27Then beginning with Moses and all the prophets, he interpreted to them the things about himself in all the scriptures.

24.27 Old Testament 101

When the disciples first began to tell about Jesus' resurrection, they quoted Old Testament Scriptures and explained how Jesus fulfilled their predictions. (See, for example, Peter's sermons in Acts 2 and 3.) They were probably following what Jesus had taught on the road to Emmaus. Jesus went through the entire Old Testament, explaining how his life crowned centuries of God's work.

28 As they came near the village to which they were going, he walked ahead as if he were going on. 29But they urged him strongly, saying, "Stay with us, because it is almost evening and the day is now nearly over." So he went in to stay with them. 30When he was at the table with them, he took bread, blessed and broke it, and gave it to them. 31Then their eyes were opened, and they recognized him; and he vanished from their sight. 32They said to each other, "Were not our hearts burning within us[b] while he was talking to us on the road, while he was opening the scriptures to us?" 33That same hour they got up and returned to Jerusalem; and they found the eleven and their companions gathered together. 34They were saying, "The Lord has risen indeed, and he has appeared to Simon!" 35Then they told what had happened on the road, and how he had been made known to them in the breaking of the bread.

Jesus Appears to His Disciples

36 While they were talking about this, Jesus himself stood among them and said to them, "Peace be with you."[c] 37They were startled and terrified, and thought that they were seeing a ghost. 38He said to them, "Why are you frightened, and why do doubts arise in your hearts? 39Look at my hands and my feet; see that it is I myself. Touch me and see; for a ghost does not have flesh and bones as you see that I have." 40And when he had said this, he showed them his

---

[r] Other ancient authorities add *of the Lord Jesus*   [s] Gk *They*   [t] Gk *but they*   [u] Other ancient authorities lack *He is not here, but has risen*   [v] Other ancient authorities lack verse 12   [w] Gk *sixty stadia;* other ancient authorities read *a hundred sixty stadia*   [x] Other ancient authorities read *walk along, looking sad?"*   [y] Other ancient authorities read *Jesus the Nazorean*   [z] Or *to set Israel free*   [a] Or *the Christ*   [b] Other ancient authorities lack *within us*   [c] Other ancient authorities lack *and said to them, "Peace be with you."*

hands and his feet.*d* *41*While in their joy they were disbelieving and still wondering, he said to them, "Have you anything here to eat?" *42*They gave him a piece of broiled fish, *43*and he took it and ate in their presence.

44 Then he said to them, "These are my words that I spoke to you while I was still with you—that everything written about me in the law of Moses, the prophets, and the psalms must be fulfilled." *45*Then he opened their minds to understand the scriptures, *46*and he said to them, "Thus it is written, that the Messiah*e* is to suffer and to rise from the dead on the third day, *47*and that repentance and forgiveness of sins is to be proclaimed in his name to all nations, beginning from Jerusalem. *48*You are witnesses*f* of these things. *49*And see, I am sending upon you what my Father promised; so stay here in the city until you have been clothed with power from on high."

The Ascension of Jesus

50 Then he led them out as far as Bethany, and, lifting up his hands, he blessed them. *51*While he was blessing them, he withdrew from them and was carried up into heaven.*g* *52*And they worshiped him, and*h* returned to Jerusalem with great joy; *53*and they were continually in the temple blessing God.*i*

---

d Other ancient authorities lack verse 40   *e* Or *the Christ*
g Other ancient authorities lack *and was carried up into heaven*
i Other ancient authorities add *Amen*
f Or *nations. Beginning from Jerusalem* *48you are witnesses*
h Other ancient authorities lack *worshiped him, and*

JOHN

God Breaks the Silence
He spoke in the only way we could truly understand

U NLESS A PERSON COMMUNICATES TO you, in speech or gestures or even facial expressions, you can't get to know him or her. What goes on behind the mask of skin will always remain a mystery.

> And the Word became flesh and lived among us.
> 1.14

God, too, was a mystery until he broke his silence. He spoke once, and all creation sprang to life—quasars, oceans, whales, giraffes, orchids, and beetles. He spoke again, says John, and this time the Word took the form of a man, Jesus Christ. John's book tells the story of that Word who became flesh.

Different from Other Gospels

It's clear from the first few paragraphs that John broke sharply from the style of Matthew, Mark, and Luke. The other Gospel writers focused on events, following Jesus through the bustling marketplaces and villages.

Unlike them, John assumed readers knew the basic facts about Jesus. Instead of focusing on facts, he mulled over the profound meaning of what Jesus had said and done. The book of John reads as if it were written under a great, shady tree by an author who had lots of time for reflection.

In his first sentence, John highlights Christ's nature. There are no Christmas scenes here: no stables, shepherds, or wise men. John tells nothing of Jesus' birth and youth. He introduces him as the adult Son of God. After an eloquent prologue, the book shows John the Baptist humbly pointing to Jesus, the thong of whose sandal "I am not worthy to untie" (1.27).

Jesus Sent with a Mission

John selected vignettes from no more than 20 days in Jesus' life, and arranged them so that they present a Messiah who knows "where I have come from and where I am going" (8.14). Jesus was not simply a "man who fell to earth," but God's Son, sent to do the work of the Father. His repeated references to the One "who sent me" give a cadence to the book.

According to John, Christ participated in the original creation act. But later he was sent to earth as the Word, the sum of all that God wanted to say. God spoke in the only way we could truly understand: by becoming one of us.

How to Read John

N ew Christians often turn to the book of John because it spells out so clearly the basics of the faith. Jesus proves who he is, diagnoses humanity's problems, and bluntly describes what is necessary for conversion. You will likely recognize familiar verses and phrases in this remarkable book (such as Jesus' "I am" sayings).

John selected seven "signs" or miracles (five of which aren't reported elsewhere) and built a story around them. As you read John, note how the author weaves together his story and its meaning.

It's best to read John in units. Don't just read a paragraph or a chapter. Follow the boldface sectional headings and read a complete section, both the action and the commentary on it. John does not primarily relate events; he interprets those events.

Look carefully for the audiences Jesus addresses. Is he talking to his disciples? To his opponents? To the large crowds? He treats each audience differently.

PEOPLE YOU'LL MEET IN JOHN

NICODEMUS *(p. 1094)*
ANDREW *(p. 1098)*
JUDAS *(p. 1100)*
ANNAS AND CAIAPHAS *(p. 1107)*

THOMAS *(p. 1111)*
PONTIUS PILATE *(p. 1117)*
MARY MAGDALENE *(p. 1118)*
JOHN *(p. 1119)*

3-TRACK READING PLAN

For an explanation and complete listing of the 3-track reading plan, turn to page 7.

TRACK 1: *Two-Week Courses on the Bible*
The Track 1 reading program on the Life and Teachings of Jesus includes four chapters from John. See page 7 for a complete listing of this course.

TRACK 2: *An Overview of John in 8 Days*
☐ Day 1. Read the Introduction to John and then turn to John 3, which contains perhaps the best-known verse in the entire Bible (verse 16). Read Jesus' conversation with Nicodemus.
☐ Day 2. John 5 and 6 contain Jesus' blunt teaching about who he was and why he came to earth. Read chapter 6, noting how John weaves together a miracle, the crowd's reaction to it, then Jesus' comments on it.
☐ Day 3. Read chapter 10, another familiar passage.
☐ Day 4. The next four readings are taken from John's report of the Last Supper. Begin with chapter 14.
☐ Day 5. Read chapter 15, where Jesus explains the image of a vine and its branches.
☐ Day 6. Read chapter 16, noting especially what Jesus says about the Holy Spirit. John contains more teaching about the Holy Spirit than any other Gospel.
☐ Day 7. Read chapter 17, a farewell prayer Jesus prayed for his disciples.
☐ Day 8. Read John's account of Jesus' resurrection, chapter 20.

Now turn to page 9 for your next Track 2 reading project.

TRACK 3: *All of John in 21 Days*
After you have read through John, turn to pages 10–14 for your next Track 3 reading project.

☐1 ☐2 ☐3 ☐4 ☐5 ☐6 ☐7 ☐8
☐9 ☐10 ☐11 ☐12 ☐13 ☐14 ☐15 ☐16
☐17 ☐18 ☐19 ☐20 ☐21

The Word Became Flesh

1 In the beginning was the Word, and the Word was with God, and the Word was God. [2]He was in the beginning with God. [3]All things came into being through him, and without him not one thing came into being. What has come into being [4]in him was life,[a] and the life was the light of all people. [5]The light shines in the darkness, and the darkness did not overcome it.

6 There was a man sent from God, whose name was John. [7]He came as a witness to testify to the light, so that all might believe through him. [8]He himself was not the light, but he came to testify to the light. [9]The true light, which enlightens everyone, was coming into the world.[b]

10 He was in the world, and the world came into being through him; yet the world did not know him. [11]He came to what was his own,[c] and his own people did not accept him. [12]But to all who received him, who believed in his name, he gave power to become children of God, [13]who were born, not of blood or of the will of the flesh or of the will of man, but of God.

14 And the Word became flesh and lived among us, and we have seen his glory, the glory as of a father's only son,[d] full of grace and truth.

---

[a] Or [3]through him. And without him not one thing came into being that has come into being. [4]In him was life   [b] Or He was the true light that enlightens everyone coming into the world   [c] Or to his own home   [d] Or the Father's only Son

15(John testified to him and cried out, "This was he of whom I said, 'He who comes after me ranks ahead of me because he was before me.'") 16From his fullness we have all received, grace upon grace. 17The law indeed was given through Moses; grace and truth came through Jesus Christ. 18No one has ever seen God. It is God the only Son,e who is close to the Father's heart,f who has made him known.

1.14 Jesus the Word

John used language with special meaning for both Greek and Jewish readers. In Greek philosophy, "word" (logos) was a key term, often referring to the power of reason undergirding all creation. For Jews, too, "word" had great significance, for God spoke his word to create the world and to transform his people. Yet John's meaning passed beyond the Greek and Jewish ideas. An eight-year-old girl expressed it well. When asked why Jesus was called the Word, she said, "Because Jesus is all God wanted to say to us."

The Testimony of John the Baptist

19 This is the testimony given by John when the Jews sent priests and Levites from Jerusalem to ask him, "Who are you?" 20He confessed and did not deny it, but confessed, "I am not the Messiah."g 21And they asked him, "What then? Are you Elijah?" He said, "I am not." "Are you the prophet?" He answered, "No." 22Then they said to him, "Who are you? Let us have an answer for those who sent us. What do you say about yourself?" 23He said,

"I am the voice of one crying out in the
wilderness,
'Make straight the way of the Lord,'"
as the prophet Isaiah said.
24 Now they had been sent from the Pharisees. 25They asked him, "Why then are you baptizing if you are neither the Messiah,g nor Elijah, nor the prophet?" 26John answered them, "I baptize with water. Among you stands one whom you do not know, 27the one who is coming after me; I am not worthy to untie the thong of his sandal." 28This took place in Bethany across the Jordan where John was baptizing.

The Lamb of God

29 The next day he saw Jesus coming toward him and declared, "Here is the Lamb of God who takes away the sin of the world! 30This is he of whom I said, 'After me comes a man who ranks ahead of me because he was before me.' 31I myself

did not know him; but I came baptizing with water for this reason, that he might be revealed to Israel." 32And John testified, "I saw the Spirit descending from heaven like a dove, and it remained on him. 33I myself did not know him, but the one who sent me to baptize with water said to me, 'He on whom you see the Spirit descend and remain is the one who baptizes with the Holy Spirit.' 34And I myself have seen and have testified that this is the Son of God."h

The First Disciples of Jesus

35 The next day John again was standing with two of his disciples, 36and as he watched Jesus walk by, he exclaimed, "Look, here is the Lamb of God!" 37The two disciples heard him say this, and they followed Jesus. 38When Jesus turned and saw them following, he said to them, "What are you looking for?" They said to him, "Rabbi" (which translated means Teacher), "where are you staying?" 39He said to them, "Come and see." They came and saw where he was staying, and they remained with him that day. It was about four

1.39 Gradual Disciples

Other Gospels show the disciples dropping their nets and following Jesus instantly. John describes a more gradual process. When two of John the Baptist's disciples grew curious, Jesus invited them to come and spend a day with him. Soon, they were ready to tell others what they had seen and heard.

o'clock in the afternoon. 40One of the two who heard John speak and followed him was Andrew, Simon Peter's brother. 41He first found his brother Simon and said to him, "We have found the Messiah" (which is translated Anointedi). 42He brought Simonj to Jesus, who looked at him and said, "You are Simon son of John. You are to be called Cephas" (which is translated Peterk).

Jesus Calls Philip and Nathanael

43 The next day Jesus decided to go to Galilee. He found Philip and said to him, "Follow me." 44Now Philip was from Bethsaida, the city of Andrew and Peter. 45Philip found Nathanael and said to him, "We have found him about whom Moses in the law and also the prophets wrote, Jesus son of Joseph from Nazareth." 46Nathanael said to him, "Can anything good come out of Nazareth?" Philip said to him, "Come and see." 47When Jesus saw Nathanael coming toward him, he said of him, "Here is truly an Israelite in whom there is no deceit!" 48Nathanael asked him,

---

e Other ancient authorities read *It is an only Son, God,* or *It is the only Son*   f Gk *bosom*   g Or *the Christ*
h Other ancient authorities read *is God's chosen one*   i Or *Christ*   j Gk *him*   k From the word for *rock* in
Aramaic (*kepha*) and Greek (*petra*), respectively

"Where did you get to know me?" Jesus answered, "I saw you under the fig tree before Philip called you." ⁴⁹Nathanael replied, "Rabbi, you are the Son of God! You are the King of Israel!" ⁵⁰Jesus answered, "Do you believe because I told you that I saw you under the fig tree? You will see greater things than these." ⁵¹And he said to him, "Very truly, I tell you,[l] you will see heaven opened and the angels of God ascending and descending upon the Son of Man."

The Wedding at Cana

2 On the third day there was a wedding in Cana of Galilee, and the mother of Jesus was there. ²Jesus and his disciples had also been invited to the wedding. ³When the wine gave out, the mother of Jesus said to him, "They have no wine." ⁴And Jesus said to her, "Woman, what concern is that to you and to me? My hour has not yet come." ⁵His mother said to the servants, "Do whatever he tells you." ⁶Now standing there were six stone water jars for the Jewish rites of purification, each holding twenty or thirty gallons. ⁷Jesus

2.6 Eyewitness Details

Numerous specific details show that an eyewitness wrote the book of John. Here, the author describes stone water jars; elsewhere, he records the exact number of fish caught (21.11).

said to them, "Fill the jars with water." And they filled them up to the brim. ⁸He said to them, "Now draw some out, and take it to the chief steward." So they took it. ⁹When the steward tasted the water that had become wine, and did not know where it came from (though the servants who had drawn the water knew), the steward called the bridegroom ¹⁰and said to him, "Everyone serves the good wine first, and then the inferior wine after the guests have become drunk. But you have kept the good wine until now." ¹¹Jesus did this, the first of his signs, in Cana of Galilee, and revealed his glory; and his disciples believed in him.

12 After this he went down to Capernaum with his mother, his brothers, and his disciples; and they remained there a few days.

Jesus Cleanses the Temple

▶ *See Matthew 21.12–13; Mark 11.15–17; Luke 19.45–46*

13 The Passover of the Jews was near, and Jesus went up to Jerusalem. ¹⁴In the temple he found people selling cattle, sheep, and doves, and the money changers seated at their tables. ¹⁵Making a whip of cords, he drove all of them out of the temple, both the sheep and the cattle. He also poured out the coins of the money changers and overturned their tables. ¹⁶He told those who were selling the doves, "Take these things out of here! Stop making my Father's house a marketplace!" ¹⁷His disciples remembered that it was written, "Zeal for your house will consume me." ¹⁸The Jews then said to him, "What sign can you show us for doing this?" ¹⁹Jesus answered them, "Destroy this temple, and in three days I will raise it up." ²⁰The Jews then said, "This temple has been under construction for forty-six years, and will you raise it up in three days?" ²¹But he was speaking of the temple of his body. ²²After he was raised from the dead, his disciples remembered that he had said this; and they believed the scripture and the word that Jesus had spoken.

23 When he was in Jerusalem during the Passover festival, many believed in his name because they saw the signs that he was doing. ²⁴But Jesus on his part would not entrust himself to them, because he knew all people ²⁵and needed no one to testify about anyone; for he himself knew what was in everyone.

Nicodemus Visits Jesus

3 Now there was a Pharisee named Nicodemus, a leader of the Jews. ²He came to Jesus[m] by night and said to him, "Rabbi, we know that you are a teacher who has come from God; for no one can do these signs that you do apart from the presence of God." ³Jesus answered him, "Very truly, I tell you, no one can see the kingdom of God without being born from above."[n] ⁴Nicodemus said to him, "How can anyone be born after having grown old? Can one enter a second time into the mother's womb and be born?" ⁵Jesus answered, "Very truly, I tell you, no one can enter the kingdom of God without being born of water and Spirit. ⁶What is born of the flesh is flesh, and what is born of the Spirit is spirit.[o] ⁷Do not be astonished that I said to you, 'You[p] must be born from above.'[q] ⁸The wind[o] blows where it chooses, and you hear the sound of it, but you do not know where it comes from or where it goes. So it is with everyone who is born of the Spirit." ⁹Nicodemus said to him, "How can these things be?" ¹⁰Jesus answered, "Are you a teacher of Israel, and yet you do not understand these things?

11 "Very truly, I tell you, we speak of what we know and testify to what we have seen; yet you[r] do not receive our testimony. ¹²If I have told you about earthly things and you do not believe, how can you believe if I tell you about heavenly things?

---

[l] Both instances of the Greek word for *you* in this verse are plural   [m] Gk *him*   [n] Or *born anew*   [o] The same
Greek word means both *wind* and *spirit*   [p] The Greek word for *you* here is plural   [q] Or *anew*   [r] The Greek
word for *you* here and in verse 12 is plural

[13]No one has ascended into heaven except the one who descended from heaven, the Son of Man.[s] [14]And just as Moses lifted up the serpent in the wilderness, so must the Son of Man be lifted up, [15]that whoever believes in him may have eternal life.[t]

16 "For God so loved the world that he gave his only Son, so that everyone who believes in him may not perish but may have eternal life.

3.16 The Gospel in a Nutshell

This verse has probably been memorized more than any other in the Bible. In a few words it tells the story of salvation: God's love for the world, God's gift of his Son, and the opportunity for anyone who believes to be saved.

17 "Indeed, God did not send the Son into the world to condemn the world, but in order that the world might be saved through him. [18]Those who believe in him are not condemned; but those who do not believe are condemned already, because they have not believed in the name of the only Son of God. [19]And this is the judgment, that the light has come into the world, and people loved darkness rather than light because their deeds were evil. [20]For all who do evil hate the light and do not come to the light, so that their deeds may not be exposed. [21]But those who do what is true come to the light, so that it may be clearly seen that their deeds have been done in God."[t]

Jesus and John the Baptist

22 After this Jesus and his disciples went into the Judean countryside, and he spent some time there with them and baptized. [23]John also was baptizing at Aenon near Salim because water was abundant there; and people kept coming and were being baptized [24]—John, of course, had not yet been thrown into prison.

25 Now a discussion about purification arose between John's disciples and a Jew.[u] [26]They came to John and said to him, "Rabbi, the one who was with you across the Jordan, to whom you testified, here he is baptizing, and all are going to him." [27]John answered, "No one can receive anything except what has been given from heaven. [28]You yourselves are my witnesses that I said, 'I am not the Messiah,[v] but I have been sent ahead of him.' [29]He who has the bride is the bridegroom. The friend of the bridegroom, who stands and hears him, rejoices greatly at the bridegroom's voice. For this reason my joy has been fulfilled. [30]He must increase, but I must decrease."[w]

The One Who Comes from Heaven

31 The one who comes from above is above all; the one who is of the earth belongs to the earth and speaks about earthly things. The one who comes from heaven is above all. [32]He testifies to what he has seen and heard, yet no one accepts his testimony. [33]Whoever has accepted his testi-

[s] Other ancient authorities add *who is in heaven*   [t] Some interpreters hold that the quotation concludes with verse 15   [u] Other ancient authorities read *the Jews*   [v] Or *the Christ*   [w] Some interpreters hold that the quotation continues through verse 36

NICODEMUS *A Reputation at Stake*

MOST OF JESUS' DISCIPLES WERE ordinary people with no status to worry about losing. A fisherman or tax collector would not forfeit much standing if he followed an unorthodox teacher. In contrast, Nicodemus had quite a reputation at stake. As a member of the Jewish Sanhedrin, he held an important ruling post. As a Pharisee, he was committed to a certain set of beliefs. And as a prominent religious teacher, he was a respected interpreter of God's law.

No doubt that is why Nicodemus first asked Jesus to meet him at night. As time went on, however, Nicodemus grew more bold. When the Sanhedrin discussed Jesus, he spoke out against their willingness to condemn the man without talking to him. For that, Nicodemus received scalding criticism (7.50–52).

After Jesus' death, Nicodemus let his sentiments become more public. Along with Joseph of Arimathea, he took Jesus' body from Calvary and prepared it for burial.

The Bible tells us no more about Nicodemus, so we can't be sure whether he ever openly confessed faith in Jesus. It seems likely, however, that John mentions these incidents because Nicodemus was willing to talk about what he had seen and heard and believed. How else would John have learned the intimate details of Nicodemus's actions? This Gospel gives reason to hope that Nicodemus sacrificed his reputation—and gained a new birth—in the end.

Life Questions: Are there questions about God you feel you cannot ask in public? What are they, and who could you ask in private?

mony has certified[x] this, that God is true. [34]He whom God has sent speaks the words of God, for he gives the Spirit without measure. [35]The Father loves the Son and has placed all things in his hands. [36]Whoever believes in the Son has eternal life; whoever disobeys the Son will not see life, but must endure God's wrath.

Jesus and the Woman of Samaria

4 Now when Jesus[y] learned that the Pharisees had heard, "Jesus is making and baptizing more disciples than John" [2]— although it was not Jesus himself but his disciples who baptized— [3]he left Judea and started back to Galilee. [4]But he had to go through Samaria. [5]So he came to a Samaritan city called Sychar, near the plot of ground that Jacob had given to his son Joseph. [6]Jacob's well was there, and Jesus, tired out by his journey, was sitting by the well. It was about noon.

7 A Samaritan woman came to draw water, and Jesus said to her, "Give me a drink." [8](His disciples had gone to the city to buy food.) [9]The Samaritan woman said to him, "How is it that you, a Jew, ask a drink of me, a woman of Samaria?" (Jews do not share things in common with

---

4.9 Bridging Differences

When one church brands another a cult, it usually creates long-standing bitterness. The Samaritans and the Jews felt that way about each other. Samaritan religion closely resembled Judaism, but on key issues its followers had gone their own way. They accepted only the first five books of the Old Testament, and insisted that Mount Gerizim, not Jerusalem, was the proper place to worship God. Though Jews and Samaritans usually avoided each other, Jesus reached across these barriers.

Samaritans.)[z] [10]Jesus answered her, "If you knew the gift of God, and who it is that is saying to you, 'Give me a drink,' you would have asked him, and he would have given you living water." [11]The woman said to him, "Sir, you have no bucket, and the well is deep. Where do you get that living water? [12]Are you greater than our ancestor Jacob, who gave us the well, and with his sons and his flocks drank from it?" [13]Jesus said to her, "Everyone who drinks of this water will be thirsty again, [14]but those who drink of the water that I will give them will never be thirsty. The water that I will

give will become in them a spring of water gushing up to eternal life." [15]The woman said to him, "Sir, give me this water, so that I may never be thirsty or have to keep coming here to draw water."

16 Jesus said to her, "Go, call your husband, and come back." [17]The woman answered him, "I have no husband." Jesus said to her, "You are right in saying, 'I have no husband'; [18]for you have had five husbands, and the one you have now is not your husband. What you have said is true!" [19]The woman said to him, "Sir, I see that you are a prophet. [20]Our ancestors worshiped on this mountain, but you[a] say that the place where people must worship is in Jerusalem." [21]Jesus said to her, "Woman, believe me, the hour is coming when you will worship the Father neither on this mountain nor in Jerusalem. [22]You worship what you do not know; we worship what we know, for salvation is from the Jews. [23]But the hour is coming, and is now here, when the true worshipers will worship the Father in spirit and truth, for the Father seeks such as these to worship him. [24]God is spirit, and those who worship him must worship in spirit and truth." [25]The woman said to him, "I know that Messiah is coming" (who is called Christ). "When he comes, he will proclaim all things to us." [26]Jesus said to her, "I am he,[b] the one who is speaking to you."

27 Just then his disciples came. They were astonished that he was speaking with a woman, but no one said, "What do you want?" or, "Why are you speaking with her?" [28]Then the woman left her water jar and went back to the city. She said to the people, [29]"Come and see a man who told me everything I have ever done! He cannot be the Messiah,[c] can he?" [30]They left the city and were on their way to him.

31 Meanwhile the disciples were urging him, "Rabbi, eat something." [32]But he said to them, "I have food to eat that you do not know about." [33]So the disciples said to one another, "Surely no one has brought him something to eat?" [34]Jesus said to them, "My food is to do the will of him who sent me and to complete his work. [35]Do you not say, 'Four months more, then comes the harvest'? But I tell you, look around you, and see how the fields are ripe for harvesting. [36]The reaper is already receiving[d] wages and is gathering fruit for eternal life, so that sower and reaper may rejoice together. [37]For here the saying holds true, 'One sows and another reaps.' [38]I sent you to reap that for which you did not labor. Others have labored, and you have entered into their labor."

39 Many Samaritans from that city believed in him because of the woman's testimony, "He

---

[x] Gk *set a seal to*   [y] Other ancient authorities read *the Lord*   [z] Other ancient authorities lack this sentence
[a] The Greek word for *you* here and in verses 21 and 22 is plural   [b] Gk *I am*   [c] Or *the Christ*   [d] Or [35] ... the
fields are already ripe for harvesting. [36]*The reaper is receiving*

told me everything I have ever done." ⁴⁰So when the Samaritans came to him, they asked him to stay with them; and he stayed there two days. ⁴¹And many more believed because of his word. ⁴²They said to the woman, "It is no longer because of what you said that we believe, for we have heard for ourselves, and we know that this is truly the Savior of the world."

Jesus Returns to Galilee

43 When the two days were over, he went from that place to Galilee ⁴⁴(for Jesus himself had testified that a prophet has no honor in the prophet's own country). ⁴⁵When he came to Galilee, the Galileans welcomed him, since they had seen all that he had done in Jerusalem at the festival; for they too had gone to the festival.

ᵉ Both instances of the Greek word for *you* in this verse are plural

Jesus Heals an Official's Son

46 Then he came again to Cana in Galilee where he had changed the water into wine. Now there was a royal official whose son lay ill in Capernaum. ⁴⁷When he heard that Jesus had come from Judea to Galilee, he went and begged him to come down and heal his son, for he was at the point of death. ⁴⁸Then Jesus said to him, "Unless youᵉ see signs and wonders you will not believe." ⁴⁹The official said to him, "Sir, come down before my little boy dies." ⁵⁰Jesus said to him, "Go; your son will live." The man believed the word that Jesus spoke to him and started on his way. ⁵¹As he was going down, his slaves met him and told him that his child was alive. ⁵²So he asked them the hour when he began to recover, and they said to him, "Yesterday at one in the afternoon the fever

Conversations with Jesus
How did Jesus talk to ordinary people?

WATER. WHERE IT'S PLENTIFUL, WE tend to take it for granted, like air. We linger in the shower, hose down a dusty driveway, let a sprinkler spurt for hours to keep the lawn green.

Not so in the desert, where even plants hoard water with bristly defenses. There, water takes on a mythical aura. Taunting visions of pools and streams dance in the heat waves. A craving for water crowds out all other thoughts, and one spoonful, on a parched tongue, is worth gold.

To a woman in a dry land who spent part of each day hauling clay jugs to and from a well, water was the most powerful symbol imaginable. Little wonder that when Jesus offered "living water" that would never run dry (4.10,14), the Samaritan woman paid attention.

> The woman said to him, "I know that Messiah is coming" (who is called Christ). "When he comes, he will proclaim all things to us." Jesus said to her, "I am he, the one who is speaking to you." 4.25–26

Profoundly Simple Words

A simple word or phrase with a profound meaning: that is the style of Jesus' teaching as presented in John. No biblical author used simpler, more commonplace words: *water, world, light, life, birth, love, truth.* Yet John used them with such depth that hundreds of authors since have tried to plumb their meaning.

Reading John is like sitting in a canoe in the middle of a deep, pristine lake. The clarity of the water reveals everything under the surface—you think. Yet, as you gaze deeper, you can never see the bottom. Something always remains hidden.

Those who look for a neat scheme of organization in John usually fail. John's Gospel omits many of the events recorded in Mark, most of the long public speeches of Matthew, and all of the parables of Luke. Its teaching emerges mainly through Jesus' intimate encounters with diverse people.

Listening in on Private Conversations

Jesus uttered some of his most memorable sayings in the midst of very ordinary conversations. The book of John rarely shows him speaking to large crowds. Instead, we see Jesus meeting secretly with a nervous religious leader (3.1–21), or talking with a promiscuous woman (4.5–26) beside a well. Both visitors carried away simple-yet-profound images (a second birth, living water), and today we recall those words as among the most familiar in all the Bible.

John paints close-ups of individuals who responded to Jesus on earth. Some followed him courageously, others remained skeptical, and still others reacted with hostility. Often, John reports, people simply "did not understand," despite Jesus' use of visual images. In short, response to the Son of God on earth nearly 2,000 years ago bears a striking resemblance to the world's response to him now.

Life Questions: Imagine yourself in a private conversation with Jesus, much like the Samaritan woman's. What would you want to talk about?

left him." ⁵³The father realized that this was the hour when Jesus had said to him, "Your son will live." So he himself believed, along with his whole household. ⁵⁴Now this was the second sign that Jesus did after coming from Judea to Galilee.

4.50 A Long-distance Miracle

This miracle has certain similarities to another performed at the request of a Roman centurion (Luke 7.2–10; Matthew 8.5–13). Of Jesus' two dozen recorded miracles of healing, only these occurred over a distance.

Jesus Heals on the Sabbath

5 After this there was a festival of the Jews, and Jesus went up to Jerusalem.

2 Now in Jerusalem by the Sheep Gate there is a pool, called in Hebrewᶠ Beth-zatha,ᵍ which has five porticoes. ³In these lay many invalids— blind, lame, and paralyzed.ʰ ⁵One man was there who had been ill for thirty-eight years. ⁶When Jesus saw him lying there and knew that he had been there a long time, he said to him, "Do you want to be made well?" ⁷The sick man answered him, "Sir, I have no one to put me into the pool when the water is stirred up; and while I am making my way, someone else steps down ahead of me." ⁸Jesus said to him, "Stand up, take your mat and walk." ⁹At once the man was made well, and he took up his mat and began to walk.

Now that day was a sabbath. ¹⁰So the Jews said to the man who had been cured, "It is the sabbath; it is not lawful for you to carry your mat." ¹¹But he answered them, "The man who made me well said to me, 'Take up your mat and walk.'" ¹²They asked him, "Who is the man who said to you, 'Take it up and walk'?" ¹³Now the man who had been healed did not know who it was, for Jesus had disappeared inⁱ the crowd that was there. ¹⁴Later Jesus found him in the temple and said to him, "See, you have been made well! Do not sin any more, so that nothing worse happens to you." ¹⁵The man went away and told the Jews that it was Jesus who had made him well. ¹⁶Therefore the Jews started persecuting Jesus, because he was doing such things on the sabbath. ¹⁷But Jesus answered them, "My Father is still working, and I also am working." ¹⁸For this reason the Jews were seeking all the more to kill him, because he was not only breaking the sabbath, but was also calling God his own Father, thereby making himself equal to God.

The Authority of the Son

19 Jesus said to them, "Very truly, I tell you, the Son can do nothing on his own, but only what he sees the Father doing; for whatever the Fatherʲ does, the Son does likewise. ²⁰The Father loves the Son and shows him all that he himself is doing; and he will show him greater works than these, so that you will be astonished. ²¹Indeed, just as the Father raises the dead and gives them life, so also the Son gives life to whomever he wishes. ²²The Father judges no one but has given all judgment to the Son, ²³so that all may honor the Son just as they honor the Father. Anyone who does not honor the Son does not honor the Father who sent him. ²⁴Very truly, I tell you, anyone who hears my word and believes him who sent me has eternal life, and does not come under judgment, but has passed from death to life.

25 "Very truly, I tell you, the hour is coming, and is now here, when the dead will hear the voice of the Son of God, and those who hear will live. ²⁶For just as the Father has life in himself, so he has granted the Son also to have life in himself; ²⁷and he has given him authority to execute judgment, because he is the Son of Man. ²⁸Do not be astonished at this; for the hour is coming when all who are in their graves will hear his voice ²⁹and will come out—those who have done good, to the resurrection of life, and those who have done evil, to the resurrection of condemnation.

Witnesses to Jesus

30 "I can do nothing on my own. As I hear, I judge; and my judgment is just, because I seek to do not my own will but the will of him who sent me.

31 "If I testify about myself, my testimony is not true. ³²There is another who testifies on my behalf, and I know that his testimony to me is true. ³³You sent messengers to John, and he testified to the truth. ³⁴Not that I accept such human testimony, but I say these things so that you may be saved. ³⁵He was a burning and shining lamp, and you were willing to rejoice for a while in his light. ³⁶But I have a testimony greater than John's. The works that the Father has given me to complete, the very works that I am doing, testify on my behalf that the Father has sent me. ³⁷And the Father who sent me has himself testified on my behalf. You have never heard his voice or seen his form, ³⁸and you do not have his word abiding in you, because you do not believe him whom he has sent.

39 "You search the scriptures because you think that in them you have eternal life; and it is they that testify on my behalf. ⁴⁰Yet you refuse to

---

ᶠ That is, *Aramaic*   ᵍ Other ancient authorities read *Bethesda*, others *Bethsaida*   ʰ Other ancient authorities add, wholly or in part, *waiting for the stirring of the water;* ⁴*for an angel of the Lord went down at certain seasons into the pool, and stirred up the water; whoever stepped in first after the stirring of the water was made well from whatever disease that person had.*   ⁱ Or *had left because of*   ʲ Gk *that one*

come to me to have life. [41]I do not accept glory from human beings. [42]But I know that you do not have the love of God in[k] you. [43]I have come in my Father's name, and you do not accept me; if another comes in his own name, you will accept him. [44]How can you believe when you accept glory from one another and do not seek the glory that comes from the one who alone is God? [45]Do not think that I will accuse you before the Father; your accuser is Moses, on whom you have set your hope. [46]If you believed Moses, you would believe me, for he wrote about me. [47]But if you do not believe what he wrote, how will you believe what I say?"

Feeding the Five Thousand

▶ *See Matthew 14.13–21; Mark 6.32–44; Luke 9.10–17*

6 After this Jesus went to the other side of the Sea of Galilee, also called the Sea of Tiberias.[l] [2]A large crowd kept following him, because they saw the signs that he was doing for the sick. [3]Jesus went up the mountain and sat down there with his disciples. [4]Now the Passover, the festival of the Jews, was near. [5]When he looked up and saw a large crowd coming toward him, Jesus said to Philip, "Where are we to buy bread for these people to eat?" [6]He said this to test him, for he himself knew what he was going to do. [7]Philip answered him, "Six months' wages[m] would not buy enough bread for each of them to get a little." [8]One of his disciples, Andrew, Simon Peter's brother, said to him, [9]"There is a boy here who has five barley loaves and two fish. But what are they among so many people?" [10]Jesus said, "Make the people sit down." Now there was a great deal of grass in the place; so they[n] sat down, about five thousand in all. [11]Then Jesus took the loaves, and when he had given thanks, he distributed them to those who were seated; so also the fish, as much as they wanted. [12]When they were satisfied,

he told his disciples, "Gather up the fragments left over, so that nothing may be lost." [13]So they gathered them up, and from the fragments of the five barley loaves, left by those who had eaten, they

6.9 Better Bread

The feeding of the five thousand is the only miracle (except Jesus' resurrection) that all four Gospels record. It shows Jesus meeting the most basic human need, using barley loaves, the least expensive kind of bread. Many Jews believed that the Messiah would renew the miraculous manna that their ancestors had eaten under Moses. Jesus pointed to a better, life-changing meal—himself. As the bread of life (verse 35), he would nourish his people far better than any miraculous meal.

filled twelve baskets. [14]When the people saw the sign that he had done, they began to say, "This is indeed the prophet who is to come into the world."

15 When Jesus realized that they were about to come and take him by force to make him king, he withdrew again to the mountain by himself.

Jesus Walks on the Water

▶ *See Matthew 14.22–33; Mark 6.47–51*

16 When evening came, his disciples went down to the sea, [17]got into a boat, and started across the sea to Capernaum. It was now dark, and Jesus had not yet come to them. [18]The sea became rough because a strong wind was blowing. [19]When they had rowed about three or four miles,[o] they saw Jesus walking on the sea and coming near the boat, and they were terrified. [20]But he said to them, "It is I;[p] do not be afraid." [21]Then they wanted to take him into the boat, and

---

[k] Or *among*　　[l] Gk *of Galilee of Tiberias*　　[m] Gk *Two hundred denarii*; the denarius was the usual day's wage for a laborer　　[n] Gk *the men*　　[o] Gk *about twenty-five or thirty stadia*　　[p] Gk *I am*

ANDREW　*Out of the Spotlight*

ANDREW OPERATED MOSTLY BEHIND THE scenes. As Simon Peter's brother and one of Jesus' first followers, he got involved in many important happenings. Yet all of Andrew's appearances in the Gospels show him bringing attention to someone else, not himself.

His greatest recorded achievement was making an introduction. When Andrew heard John the Baptist commend Jesus as "the Lamb of God," he dropped everything to follow Jesus. (He was one of the first to recognize Jesus as the "Messiah.") Then, after spending the day with Jesus, he went to fetch Peter, his brother and fishing partner. Andrew introduced the two, and the rest is history.

The Gospels show two other occasions on which Andrew served as a facilitator: He drew Jesus' attention to a boy carrying a lunch (6.8–9) and helped introduce Jesus to some Greek visitors (12.20). Both incidents led to impressive miracles.

Life Questions: How can a behind-the-scenes person today have a role in introducing others to Jesus?

immediately the boat reached the land toward which they were going.

The Bread from Heaven

22 The next day the crowd that had stayed on the other side of the sea saw that there had been only one boat there. They also saw that Jesus had not got into the boat with his disciples, but that his disciples had gone away alone. 23Then some boats from Tiberias came near the place where they had eaten the bread after the Lord had given thanks.q 24So when the crowd saw that neither Jesus nor his disciples were there, they themselves got into the boats and went to Capernaum looking for Jesus.

25 When they found him on the other side of the sea, they said to him, "Rabbi, when did you come here?" 26Jesus answered them, "Very truly, I tell you, you are looking for me, not because you saw signs, but because you ate your fill of the loaves. 27Do not work for the food that perishes, but for the food that endures for eternal life, which the Son of Man will give you. For it is on him that God the Father has set his seal." 28Then they said to him, "What must we do to perform the works of God?" 29Jesus answered them, "This is the work of God, that you believe in him whom he has sent." 30So they said to him, "What sign are you going to give us then, so that we may see it and believe you? What work are you performing? 31Our ancestors ate the manna in the wilderness; as it is written, 'He gave them bread from heaven to eat.'" 32Then Jesus said to them, "Very truly, I tell you, it was not Moses who gave you the bread from heaven, but it is my Father who gives you the true bread from heaven. 33For the bread of God is that whichr comes down from heaven and gives life to the world." 34They said to him, "Sir, give us this bread always."

35 Jesus said to them, "I am the bread of life. Whoever comes to me will never be hungry, and whoever believes in me will never be thirsty. 36But I said to you that you have seen me and yet do not believe. 37Everything that the Father gives me will come to me, and anyone who comes to me I will never drive away; 38for I have come down from heaven, not to do my own will, but the will of him who sent me. 39And this is the will of him who sent me, that I should lose nothing of all that he has given me, but raise it up on the last day. 40This is indeed the will of my Father, that all who see the Son and believe in him may have eternal life; and I will raise them up on the last day."

41 Then the Jews began to complain about him because he said, "I am the bread that came down from heaven." 42They were saying, "Is not this Jesus, the son of Joseph, whose father and mother we know? How can he now say, 'I have come down from heaven'?" 43Jesus answered

them, "Do not complain among yourselves. 44No one can come to me unless drawn by the Father who sent me; and I will raise that person up on the last day. 45It is written in the prophets, 'And they shall all be taught by God.' Everyone who has heard and learned from the Father comes to me. 46Not that anyone has seen the Father except the one who is from God; he has seen the Father. 47Very truly, I tell you, whoever believes has eternal life. 48I am the bread of life. 49Your ancestors ate the manna in the wilderness, and they died. 50This is the bread that comes down from heaven, so that one may eat of it and not die. 51I am the living bread that came down from heaven. Whoever eats of this bread will live forever; and the bread that I will give for the life of the world is my flesh."

52 The Jews then disputed among themselves, saying, "How can this man give us his flesh to eat?" 53So Jesus said to them, "Very truly, I tell you, unless you eat the flesh of the Son of Man and drink his blood, you have no life in you. 54Those who eat my flesh and drink my blood have eternal life, and I will raise them up on the last day; 55for my flesh is true food and my blood is true drink. 56Those who eat my flesh and drink my blood abide in me, and I in them. 57Just as the living Father sent me, and I live because of the Father, so whoever eats me will live because of me. 58This is the bread that came down from heaven, not like that which your ancestors ate, and they died. But the one who eats this bread will live forever." 59He said these things while he was teaching in the synagogue at Capernaum.

The Words of Eternal Life

60 When many of his disciples heard it, they said, "This teaching is difficult; who can accept

6.60 Too Hard to Swallow

Chapter 6 shows the full cycle of people's response to Jesus. At first, excited by his miracle of feeding the 5,000, people tried to make him king. But Jesus escaped. The next day he rebuked them for having an interest only in physical concerns, not in spiritual truth (verse 26). He used the miracle of the feeding to give an important lesson on the bread of life, using words that were later applied to the Lord's Supper, or the Eucharist. These words, however, so disappointed the sensation-seeking crowd that many turned away from him.

it?" 61But Jesus, being aware that his disciples were complaining about it, said to them, "Does this offend you? 62Then what if you were to see

q Other ancient authorities lack *after the Lord had given thanks*   r Or *he who*

the Son of Man ascending to where he was before? [63]It is the spirit that gives life; the flesh is useless. The words that I have spoken to you are spirit and life. [64]But among you there are some who do not believe." For Jesus knew from the first who were the ones that did not believe, and who was the one that would betray him. [65]And he said, "For this reason I have told you that no one can come to me unless it is granted by the Father."

66 Because of this many of his disciples turned back and no longer went about with him. [67]So Jesus asked the twelve, "Do you also wish to go away?" [68]Simon Peter answered him, "Lord, to whom can we go? You have the words of eternal life. [69]We have come to believe and know that you are the Holy One of God."[s] [70]Jesus answered them, "Did I not choose you, the twelve? Yet one of you is a devil." [71]He was speaking of Judas son of Simon Iscariot,[t] for he, though one of the twelve, was going to betray him.

The Unbelief of Jesus' Brothers

7 After this Jesus went about in Galilee. He did not wish[u] to go about in Judea because the Jews were looking for an opportunity to kill him. [2]Now the Jewish festival of Booths[v] was near. [3]So his brothers said to him, "Leave here and go to Judea so that your disciples also may see the works you are doing; [4]for no one who wants[w] to be widely known acts in secret. If you do these things, show yourself to the world." [5](For not even his brothers believed in him.) [6]Jesus said to them, "My time has not yet come, but your time is always here. [7]The world cannot hate you, but it hates me because I testify against it that its works are evil. [8]Go to the festival yourselves. I am not[x] going to this festival, for my time has not yet fully come." [9]After saying this, he remained in Galilee.

Jesus at the Festival of Booths

10 But after his brothers had gone to the festival, then he also went, not publicly but as it were[y] in secret. [11]The Jews were looking for him at the festival and saying, "Where is he?" [12]And there was considerable complaining about him among the crowds. While some were saying, "He is a good man," others were saying, "No, he is deceiving the crowd." [13]Yet no one would speak openly about him for fear of the Jews.

14 About the middle of the festival Jesus went up into the temple and began to teach. [15]The Jews were astonished at it, saying, "How does this man have such learning,[z] when he has never been taught?" [16]Then Jesus answered them, "My teaching is not mine but his who sent me. [17]Anyone who resolves to do the will of God will know

[s] Other ancient authorities read *the Christ, the Son of the living God of Simon*; others, *Judas son of Simon from Karyot* (Kerioth) [t] Other ancient authorities read *Judas Iscariot son of Simon* [u] Other ancient authorities read *was not at liberty* [v] Or *Tabernacles* [w] Other ancient authorities read *wants it* [x] Other ancient authorities add *yet* [y] Other ancient authorities lack *as it were* [z] Or *this man know his letters*

JUDAS *Devil Man*

HUMAN BEINGS ARE BOTH "THE scum and glory of the universe," said Blaise Pascal. The Bible, too, paints a realistic picture of people as definite mixtures of good and bad. Apart from Jesus, no one is so good as to be flawless, but rarely is anyone portrayed as all bad.

Judas Iscariot is a major exception. No doubt he had some good qualities, or else why would Jesus have picked him as a disciple? Yet these good qualities were swallowed up by characteristics the Bible clearly labels satanic. In fact, Jesus himself described Judas as a devil (6.70).

How does a human being fall so low? From the evidence of the New Testament, it seems that Judas let greed get the better of him. While handling the cash as the disciples' treasurer, he began to take money for himself (12.6).

Possibly, too, Judas became frustrated over Jesus' unwillingness to be crowned king and lead a revolt against the Romans. Although other disciples struggled with that same issue, only Judas left himself so open to evil that Satan took control. Both John and Luke say that Satan entered into Judas (Luke 22.3; John 13.27). In a final, terrible act, he betrayed his Master, identifying him with a kiss in a crowd on a dark night.

Afterward, Judas felt shame and remorse. But so did the other disciples, who had also abandoned and denied Jesus. Judas should have gone to Jesus for forgiveness—after all, Jesus mercifully forgave Peter's brazen denial. Instead Judas went to the wrong people, attempting to undo his betrayal by meeting with the very ones who had financed it.

Rebuffed by his co-conspirators, Judas killed himself (Matthew 27.5). He went down in history as perhaps the most famous of all of Jesus' disciples—famous as an object lesson of what can happen, even among Jesus' followers, if they let evil have its way.

Life Questions: In Judas's life, one sin led to other, bigger ones. Have you ever seen this process in action? Where and how? What steps can you take to counteract this process?

whether the teaching is from God or whether I am speaking on my own. [18]Those who speak on their own seek their own glory; but the one who seeks the glory of him who sent him is true, and there is nothing false in him.

[19] "Did not Moses give you the law? Yet none of you keeps the law. Why are you looking for an opportunity to kill me?" [20]The crowd answered, "You have a demon! Who is trying to kill you?" [21]Jesus answered them, "I performed one work, and all of you are astonished. [22]Moses gave you circumcision (it is, of course, not from Moses, but from the patriarchs), and you circumcise a man on the sabbath. [23]If a man receives circumcision on the sabbath in order that the law of Moses may not be broken, are you angry with me because I healed a man's whole body on the sabbath? [24]Do not judge by appearances, but judge with right judgment."

Is This the Christ?

[25] Now some of the people of Jerusalem were saying, "Is not this the man whom they are trying to kill? [26]And here he is, speaking openly, but they say nothing to him! Can it be that the authorities really know that this is the Messiah?[a] [27]Yet we know where this man is from; but when the Messiah[a] comes, no one will know where he is from." [28]Then Jesus cried out as he was teaching in the temple, "You know me, and you know where I am from. I have not come on my own. But the one who sent me is true, and you do not know him. [29]I know him, because I am from him, and he sent me." [30]Then they tried to arrest him, but no one laid hands on him, because his hour had not yet come. [31]Yet many in the crowd believed in him and were saying, "When the Messiah[a]

comes, will he do more signs than this man has done?"[b]

Officers Are Sent to Arrest Jesus

[32] The Pharisees heard the crowd muttering such things about him, and the chief priests and Pharisees sent temple police to arrest him. [33]Jesus then said, "I will be with you a little while longer, and then I am going to him who sent me. [34]You will search for me, but you will not find me; and where I am, you cannot come." [35]The Jews said to one another, "Where does this man intend to go that we will not find him? Does he intend to go to the Dispersion among the Greeks and teach the Greeks? [36]What does he mean by saying, 'You will search for me and you will not find me' and 'Where I am, you cannot come'?"

Rivers of Living Water

[37] On the last day of the festival, the great day, while Jesus was standing there, he cried out, "Let anyone who is thirsty come to me, [38]and let the one who believes in me drink. As[c] the scripture has said, 'Out of the believer's heart[d] shall flow rivers of living water.'" [39]Now he said this about the Spirit, which believers in him were to receive; for as yet there was no Spirit,[e] because Jesus was not yet glorified.

Division among the People

[40] When they heard these words, some in the crowd said, "This is really the prophet." [41]Others said, "This is the Messiah."[a] But some asked, "Surely the Messiah[a] does not come from Galilee, does he? [42]Has not the scripture said that the Messiah[a] is descended from David and comes from Bethlehem, the village where David lived?" [43]So there was a division in the crowd because of him. [44]Some of them wanted to arrest him, but no one laid hands on him.

The Unbelief of Those in Authority

[45] Then the temple police went back to the chief priests and Pharisees, who asked them, "Why did you not arrest him?" [46]The police answered, "Never has anyone spoken like this!" [47]Then the Pharisees replied, "Surely you have not been deceived too, have you? [48]Has any one of the authorities or of the Pharisees believed in him? [49]But this crowd, which does not know the law—they are accursed." [50]Nicodemus, who had gone to Jesus[f] before, and who was one of them, asked, [51]"Our law does not judge people without first giving them a hearing to find out what they are doing, does it?" [52]They replied, "Surely you are not also from Galilee, are you? Search and you will see that no prophet is to arise from Galilee."

---

[a] Or *the Christ*   [b] Other ancient authorities read *is doing*   [c] Or *come to me and drink.* [38]*The one who believes in me, as*   [d] Gk *out of his belly*   [e] Other ancient authorities read *for as yet the Spirit* (others, *Holy Spirit*) *had not been given*   [f] Gk *him*

The Woman Caught in Adultery

8 ⟦[53]Then each of them went home, [1]while Jesus went to the Mount of Olives. [2]Early in the morning he came again to the temple. All the people came to him and he sat down and began to teach them. [3]The scribes and the Pharisees brought a woman who had been caught in adultery; and making her stand before all of them, [4]they said to him, "Teacher, this woman was caught in the very act of committing adultery. [5]Now in the law Moses commanded us to stone such women. Now what do you say?" [6]They said this to test him, so that they might have some charge to bring against him. Jesus bent down and

8.6 Belong in the Bible?

Because most ancient manuscripts don't include this story about the woman caught in adultery, many scholars question whether it was added later or perhaps originally fell at a different place in the Gospel. According to the story, the Pharisees weren't following Moses' law, which required the woman's partner in crime to appear also. Interestingly, verse 6 records the only scene of Jesus writing.

wrote with his finger on the ground. [7]When they kept on questioning him, he straightened up and said to them, "Let anyone among you who is without sin be the first to throw a stone at her." [8]And once again he bent down and wrote on the ground.[g] [9]When they heard it, they went away, one by one, beginning with the elders; and Jesus was left alone with the woman standing before him. [10]Jesus straightened up and said to her, "Woman, where are they? Has no one condemned you?" [11]She said, "No one, sir."[h] And Jesus said, "Neither do I condemn you. Go your way, and from now on do not sin again."⟧[i]

Jesus the Light of the World

12 Again Jesus spoke to them, saying, "I am the light of the world. Whoever follows me will never walk in darkness but will have the light of life." [13]Then the Pharisees said to him, "You are testifying on your own behalf; your testimony is not valid." [14]Jesus answered, "Even if I testify on my own behalf, my testimony is valid because I know where I have come from and where I am going, but you do not know where I come from or where I am going. [15]You judge by human standards;[j] I judge no one. [16]Yet even if I do

judge, my judgment is valid; for it is not I alone who judge, but I and the Father[k] who sent me. [17]In your law it is written that the testimony of two witnesses is valid. [18]I testify on my own behalf, and the Father who sent me testifies on my behalf." [19]Then they said to him, "Where is your Father?" Jesus answered, "You know neither me nor my Father. If you knew me, you would know my Father also." [20]He spoke these words while he was teaching in the treasury of the temple, but no one arrested him, because his hour had not yet come.

Jesus Foretells His Death

21 Again he said to them, "I am going away, and you will search for me, but you will die in your sin. Where I am going, you cannot come." [22]Then the Jews said, "Is he going to kill himself? Is that what he means by saying, 'Where I am going, you cannot come'?" [23]He said to them, "You are from below, I am from above; you are of this world, I am not of this world. [24]I told you that you would die in your sins, for you will die in your sins unless you believe that I am he."[l] [25]They said to him, "Who are you?" Jesus said to them, "Why do I speak to you at all?[m] [26]I have much to say about you and much to condemn; but the one who sent me is true, and I declare to the world what I have heard from him." [27]They did not understand that he was speaking to them about the Father. [28]So Jesus said, "When you have lifted up the Son of Man, then you will realize that I am he,[l] and that I do nothing on my own, but I speak these things as the Father instructed me. [29]And the one who sent me is with me; he has not left me alone, for I always do what is pleasing to him." [30]As he was saying these things, many believed in him.

True Disciples

31 Then Jesus said to the Jews who had believed in him, "If you continue in my word, you are truly my disciples; [32]and you will know the truth, and the truth will make you free." [33]They answered him, "We are descendants of Abraham and have never been slaves to anyone. What do you mean by saying, 'You will be made free'?"

34 Jesus answered them, "Very truly, I tell you, everyone who commits sin is a slave to sin. [35]The slave does not have a permanent place in the household; the son has a place there forever. [36]So if the Son makes you free, you will be free indeed. [37]I know that you are descendants of Abraham; yet you look for an opportunity to kill

---

g Other ancient authorities add *the sins of each of them*   h Or *Lord*   i The most ancient authorities lack 7.53—8.11; other authorities add the passage here or after 7.36 or after 21.25 or after Luke 21.38, with variations of text; some mark the passage as doubtful.   j Gk *according to the flesh*   k Other ancient authorities read *he*   l Gk *I am*
m Or *What I have told you from the beginning*

me, because there is no place in you for my word. [38]I declare what I have seen in the Father's presence; as for you, you should do what you have heard from the Father." [n]

Jesus and Abraham

39 They answered him, "Abraham is our father." Jesus said to them, "If you were Abraham's children, you would be doing [o] what Abraham did, [40]but now you are trying to kill me, a man who has told you the truth that I heard from God. This is not what Abraham did. [41]You are indeed doing what your father does." They said to him, "We are not illegitimate children; we have one father, God himself." [42]Jesus said to them, "If God were your Father, you would love me, for I came from God and now I am here. I did not come on my own, but he sent me. [43]Why do you not understand what I say? It is because you cannot accept my word. [44]You are from your father the devil, and you choose to do your father's desires. He was a murderer from the beginning and does not stand in the truth, because there is no truth in him. When he lies, he speaks according to his own nature, for he is a liar and the father of lies. [45]But because I tell the truth, you do not believe me. [46]Which of you convicts me of sin? If I tell the truth, why do you not believe me? [47]Whoever is from God hears the words of God. The reason you do not hear them is that you are not from God."

48 The Jews answered him, "Are we not right in saying that you are a Samaritan and have a demon?" [49]Jesus answered, "I do not have a demon; but I honor my Father, and you dishonor me. [50]Yet I do not seek my own glory; there is one who seeks it and he is the judge. [51]Very truly, I tell you, whoever keeps my word will never see death." [52]The Jews said to him, "Now we know that you have a demon. Abraham died, and so did the prophets; yet you say, 'Whoever keeps my word will never taste death.' [53]Are you greater than our father Abraham, who died? The prophets also died. Who do you claim to be?" [54]Jesus answered, "If I glorify myself, my glory is nothing. It is my Father who glorifies me, he of whom you say, 'He is our God,' [55]though you do not know him. But I know him; if I would say that I do not know him, I would be a liar like you. But I do know him and I keep his word. [56]Your ancestor Abraham rejoiced that he would see my day; he saw it and was glad." [57]Then the Jews said to him, "You are not yet fifty years old, and have you seen Abraham?" [p] [58]Jesus said to them, "Very truly, I tell you, before Abraham was, I am." [59]So they picked up stones to throw at him, but Jesus hid himself and went out of the temple.

A Man Born Blind Receives Sight

9 As he walked along, he saw a man blind from birth. [2]His disciples asked him, "Rabbi, who sinned, this man or his parents, that he was born

9.2 Suffering and Sin

In this story, Jesus corrects a commonly held notion that suffering comes because of sin. The healed man became a loyal spokesman for Jesus. His testimony, however, failed to convince the Pharisees, who also rejected Jesus' teaching about why the man had been born blind (verse 34). In typical style, John wove together the incident with Jesus' comments on a different kind of blindness.

blind?" [3]Jesus answered, "Neither this man nor his parents sinned; he was born blind so that God's works might be revealed in him. [4]We [q] must work the works of him who sent me [r] while it is day; night is coming when no one can work. [5]As long as I am in the world, I am the light of the world." [6]When he had said this, he spat on the ground and made mud with the saliva and spread the mud on the man's eyes, [7]saying to him, "Go, wash in the pool of Siloam" (which means Sent). Then he went and washed and came back able to see. [8]The neighbors and those who had seen him before as a beggar began to ask, "Is this not the man who used to sit and beg?" [9]Some were saying, "It is he." Others were saying, "No, but it is someone like him." He kept saying, "I am the man." [10]But they kept asking him, "Then how were your eyes opened?" [11]He answered, "The man called Jesus made mud, spread it on my eyes, and said to me, 'Go to Siloam and wash.' Then I went and washed and received my sight." [12]They said to him, "Where is he?" He said, "I do not know."

The Pharisees Investigate the Healing

13 They brought to the Pharisees the man who had formerly been blind. [14]Now it was a sabbath day when Jesus made the mud and opened his eyes. [15]Then the Pharisees also began to ask him how he had received his sight. He said to them, "He put mud on my eyes. Then I washed, and now I see." [16]Some of the Pharisees said, "This man is not from God, for he does not observe the sabbath." But others said, "How can a man who is a sinner perform such signs?" And they were divided. [17]So they said again to the blind man, "What do you say about him? It was

---

[n] Other ancient authorities read *you do what you have heard from your father*   [o] Other ancient authorities read *If you are Abraham's children, then do*   [p] Other ancient authorities read *has Abraham seen you?*   [q] Other ancient authorities read *I*   [r] Other ancient authorities read *us*

your eyes he opened." He said, "He is a prophet."

18 The Jews did not believe that he had been blind and had received his sight until they called the parents of the man who had received his sight [19]and asked them, "Is this your son, who you say was born blind? How then does he now see?" [20]His parents answered, "We know that this is our son, and that he was born blind; [21]but we do not know how it is that now he sees, nor do we know who opened his eyes. Ask him; he is of age. He will speak for himself." [22]His parents said this because they were afraid of the Jews; for the Jews had already agreed that anyone who confessed Jesus[s] to be the Messiah[t] would be put out of the synagogue. [23]Therefore his parents said, "He is of age; ask him."

24 So for the second time they called the man who had been blind, and they said to him, "Give glory to God! We know that this man is a sinner." [25]He answered, "I do not know whether he is a sinner. One thing I do know, that though I was blind, now I see." [26]They said to him, "What did he do to you? How did he open your eyes?" [27]He answered them, "I have told you already, and you would not listen. Why do you want to hear it again? Do you also want to become his disciples?" [28]Then they reviled him, saying, "You are his disciple, but we are disciples of Moses. [29]We know that God has spoken to Moses, but as for this man, we do not know where he comes from." [30]The man answered, "Here is an astonishing thing! You do not know where he comes from, and yet he opened my eyes. [31]We know that God does not listen to sinners, but he does listen to one who worships him and obeys his will. [32]Never since the world began has it been heard that anyone opened the eyes of a person born blind. [33]If this man were not from God, he could do nothing." [34]They answered him, "You were born entirely in sins, and are you trying to teach us?" And they drove him out.

Spiritual Blindness

35 Jesus heard that they had driven him out, and when he found him, he said, "Do you believe in the Son of Man?"[u] [36]He answered, "And who is he, sir?[v] Tell me, so that I may believe in him." [37]Jesus said to him, "You have seen him, and the one speaking with you is he." [38]He said, "Lord,[v] I believe." And he worshiped him. [39]Jesus said, "I came into this world for judgment so that those who do not see may see, and those who do see may become blind." [40]Some of the Pharisees near him heard this and said to him, "Surely we are not blind, are we?" [41]Jesus said to them, "If you were blind, you would not have sin. But now that you say, 'We see,' your sin remains.

Jesus the Good Shepherd

10 "Very truly, I tell you, anyone who does not enter the sheepfold by the gate but climbs in by another way is a thief and a bandit. [2]The one who enters by the gate is the shepherd of the sheep. [3]The gatekeeper opens the gate for him, and the sheep hear his voice. He calls his own sheep by name and leads them out. [4]When he has brought out all his own, he goes ahead of them, and the sheep follow him because they know his voice. [5]They will not follow

10.4 Good Shepherd

Unlike modern-day shepherds, who use dogs to drive their flocks, Palestinian shepherds walked ahead, calling the sheep to follow. Only a familiar voice would make them come. In the Old Testament, God was called the "Shepherd of Israel" (Psalm 80.1), and God's appointed leaders were often referred to as shepherds. In claiming to be the good shepherd, Jesus was asserting his leadership over a flock he was willing to die for.

a stranger, but they will run from him because they do not know the voice of strangers." [6]Jesus used this figure of speech with them, but they did not understand what he was saying to them.

7 So again Jesus said to them, "Very truly, I tell you, I am the gate for the sheep. [8]All who came before me are thieves and bandits; but the sheep did not listen to them. [9]I am the gate. Whoever enters by me will be saved, and will come in and go out and find pasture. [10]The thief comes only to steal and kill and destroy. I came that they may have life, and have it abundantly.

11 "I am the good shepherd. The good shepherd lays down his life for the sheep. [12]The hired hand, who is not the shepherd and does not own the sheep, sees the wolf coming and leaves the sheep and runs away—and the wolf snatches them and scatters them. [13]The hired hand runs away because a hired hand does not care for the sheep. [14]I am the good shepherd. I know my own and my own know me, [15]just as the Father knows me and I know the Father. And I lay down my life for the sheep. [16]I have other sheep that do not belong to this fold. I must bring them also, and they will listen to my voice. So there will be one flock, one shepherd. [17]For this reason the Father loves me, because I lay down my life in order to take it up again. [18]No one takes[w] it from me, but I lay it down of my own accord. I have power to

---

[s] Gk *him*   [t] Or *the Christ*   [u] Other ancient authorities read *the Son of God*   [v] *Sir* and *Lord* translate the same Greek word   [w] Other ancient authorities read *has taken*

lay it down, and I have power to take it up again. I have received this command from my Father."

19 Again the Jews were divided because of these words. ²⁰Many of them were saying, "He has a demon and is out of his mind. Why listen to him?" ²¹Others were saying, "These are not the words of one who has a demon. Can a demon open the eyes of the blind?"

x Or the Christ

Jesus Is Rejected by the Jews

22 At that time the festival of the Dedication took place in Jerusalem. It was winter, ²³and Jesus was walking in the temple, in the portico of Solomon. ²⁴So the Jews gathered around him and said to him, "How long will you keep us in suspense? If you are the Messiah,ˣ tell us plainly." ²⁵Jesus answered, "I have told you, and you do not be-

A Modern Shepherd
What a "good shepherd" would look like today

"I came that they may have life, and have it abundantly." 10.10

SOME OF THE BIBLE'S RURAL illustrations simply do not transfer easily into modern life. What is a "good shepherd" like? What did Jesus mean by the term?

A small drama that took place on the slopes of Washington's Mount Rainier may shed light on the meaning of the "good shepherd." One Memorial Day weekend a Christian dentist named James Reddick was teaching his 12-year-old daughter and 11-year-old son the joy of mountain hiking. A sudden storm came up, battering them with hurricane-force winds and thick, wet sheets of snow. A blinding "whiteout" made it impossible to see or move on the steep slopes.

Willing to Die

Reddick laboriously dug an oblong trench with an aluminum mess kit, then tucked his children into sleeping bags away from the entrance. He covered the opening with a tarp, but it kept blowing away, exposing the trench to the swirling snow outside. Reddick found he had to lie directly across the opening, using his own weight to hold down the edges of the tarp. His body protected his son and daughter from the howling wind.

Two days passed before searchers finally noticed the corner of a backpack protruding from deep snow. They rushed to the site, hoping the snow-covered mound would contain the three missing hikers. Inside, they found Sharon and David Reddick, very much alive. But the stiff body of their father lay against one wall of the snow cave. He had "taken the cold spot," in one searcher's words, by using his own back as the outer wall.

An image something like that must have filled the minds of Jesus' listeners as he described a good shepherd who "lays down his life" for his sheep (10.11). Nothing—not ravaging cold, thieves, or wolves—would come between the good shepherd and his sheep. He would die for their protection.

Popularity, for a While

As Jesus headed toward final tragedy in Jerusalem, the theme of death, *his* death, kept surfacing in his parables and direct statements. Ironically, his followers were growing in numbers. His popularity had reached a peak with the feeding of 5,000 people on a handful of morsels, a miracle mentioned by all four Gospel writers.

The ground swell of support to make Jesus king deeply impressed his followers; Jesus, however, escaped into the hills (6.15). He would not be a king on the crowd's terms. He continued on his lonely mission, stirring up controversy and hatred by healing people on the sabbath and by proclaiming himself equal with God.

Ignoring an Impressive Miracle

Many Jews came over to Jesus after one of his most impressive signs: bringing Lazarus back to life. But, simultaneously, religious leaders concluded callously that it was best for one man (Jesus) to die rather than upset the whole world (11.50). Four separate times they tried to seize him.

Jesus came to offer "life"—one of those one-syllable words, swollen with meaning, that John threaded through his narrative. Lazarus received that life in an astonishingly literal way, providing yet another sign of Jesus' ultimate power. Jesus, though, made preparations to give up his own life, making the ultimate sacrifice of the good shepherd.

Life Questions: What have you sacrificed for the sake of another person?

lieve. The works that I do in my Father's name testify to me; [26]but you do not believe, because you do not belong to my sheep. [27]My sheep hear my voice. I know them, and they follow me. [28]I give them eternal life, and they will never perish. No one will snatch them out of my hand. [29]What my Father has given me is greater than all else, and no one can snatch it out of the Father's hand.[y] [30]The Father and I are one."

31 The Jews took up stones again to stone him. [32]Jesus replied, "I have shown you many good works from the Father. For which of these are you going to stone me?" [33]The Jews answered, "It is not for a good work that we are going to stone you, but for blasphemy, because you, though only a human being, are making yourself God." [34]Jesus answered, "Is it not written in your law,[z] 'I said, you are gods'? [35]If those to whom the word of God came were called 'gods'—and the scripture cannot be annulled— [36]can you say that the one whom the Father has sanctified and sent into the world is blaspheming because I said, 'I am God's Son'? [37]If I am not doing the works of my Father, then do not believe me. [38]But if I do them, even though you do not believe me, believe the works, so that you may know and understand[a] that the Father is in me and I am in the Father." [39]Then they tried to arrest him again, but he escaped from their hands.

40 He went away again across the Jordan to the place where John had been baptizing earlier, and he remained there. [41]Many came to him, and they were saying, "John performed no sign, but everything that John said about this man was true." [42]And many believed in him there.

The Death of Lazarus

11 Now a certain man was ill, Lazarus of Bethany, the village of Mary and her sister Martha. [2]Mary was the one who anointed the Lord with perfume and wiped his feet with her hair; her brother Lazarus was ill. [3]So the sisters sent a message to Jesus,[b] "Lord, he whom you love is ill." [4]But when Jesus heard it, he said, "This illness does not lead to death; rather it is for God's glory, so that the Son of God may be glorified through it." [5]Accordingly, though Jesus loved Martha and her sister and Lazarus, [6]after having heard that Lazarus[c] was ill, he stayed two days longer in the place where he was.

7 Then after this he said to the disciples, "Let us go to Judea again." [8]The disciples said to him, "Rabbi, the Jews were just now trying to stone you, and are you going there again?" [9]Jesus answered, "Are there not twelve hours of daylight? Those who walk during the day do not stumble,

because they see the light of this world. [10]But those who walk at night stumble, because the light is not in them." [11]After saying this, he told them, "Our friend Lazarus has fallen asleep, but I am going there to awaken him." [12]The disciples said to him, "Lord, if he has fallen asleep, he will be all right." [13]Jesus, however, had been speaking about his death, but they thought that he was referring merely to sleep. [14]Then Jesus told them plainly, "Lazarus is dead. [15]For your sake I am glad I was not there, so that you may believe. But let us go to him." [16]Thomas, who was called the Twin,[d] said to his fellow disciples, "Let us also go, that we may die with him."

Jesus the Resurrection and the Life

17 When Jesus arrived, he found that Lazarus[c] had already been in the tomb four days. [18]Now Bethany was near Jerusalem, some two miles[e] away, [19]and many of the Jews had come to Martha and Mary to console them about their brother. [20]When Martha heard that Jesus was coming, she went and met him, while Mary stayed at home. [21]Martha said to Jesus, "Lord, if you had been here, my brother would not have

11.21 If Only . . .

Mary and Martha had very different personalities, but the same response to pain. Both sisters, meeting Jesus, said the same thing: "If you had been here, my brother would not have died" (verses 21,32). They had asked Jesus to come, and for reasons they could not understand, he had delayed. The healing they longed for had not occurred. Jesus gave the sisters no explanation of his timing, but showed he had a reason: to demonstrate his power over death.

died. [22]But even now I know that God will give you whatever you ask of him." [23]Jesus said to her, "Your brother will rise again." [24]Martha said to him, "I know that he will rise again in the resurrection on the last day." [25]Jesus said to her, "I am the resurrection and the life.[f] Those who believe in me, even though they die, will live, [26]and everyone who lives and believes in me will never die. Do you believe this?" [27]She said to him, "Yes, Lord, I believe that you are the Messiah,[g] the Son of God, the one coming into the world."

Jesus Weeps

28 When she had said this, she went back and

y Other ancient authorities read *My Father who has given them to me is greater than all, and no one can snatch them out of the Father's hand*　z Other ancient authorities read *in the law*　a Other ancient authorities lack *and understand;* others read *and believe*　b Gk *him*　c Gk *he*　d Gk *Didymus*　e Gk *fifteen stadia*　f Other ancient authorities lack *and the life*　g Or *the Christ*

called her sister Mary, and told her privately, "The Teacher is here and is calling for you." ²⁹And when she heard it, she got up quickly and went to him. ³⁰Now Jesus had not yet come to the village, but was still at the place where Martha had met him. ³¹The Jews who were with her in the house, consoling her, saw Mary get up quickly and go out. They followed her because they thought that she was going to the tomb to weep there. ³²When Mary came where Jesus was and saw him, she knelt at his feet and said to him, "Lord, if you had been here, my brother would not have died." ³³When Jesus saw her weeping, and the Jews who came with her also weeping, he was greatly disturbed in spirit and deeply moved. ³⁴He said, "Where have you laid him?" They said to him, "Lord, come and see." ³⁵Jesus began to weep. ³⁶So the Jews said, "See how he loved him!" ³⁷But some of them said, "Could not he who opened the eyes of the blind man have kept this man from dying?"

Jesus Raises Lazarus to Life

38　Then Jesus, again greatly disturbed, came to the tomb. It was a cave, and a stone was lying against it. ³⁹Jesus said, "Take away the stone." Martha, the sister of the dead man, said to him, "Lord, already there is a stench because he has been dead four days." ⁴⁰Jesus said to her, "Did I not tell you that if you believed, you would see the glory of God?" ⁴¹So they took away the stone. And Jesus looked upward and said, "Father, I thank you for having heard me. ⁴²I knew that you

h Or *our temple*; Greek *our place*

always hear me, but I have said this for the sake of the crowd standing here, so that they may believe that you sent me." ⁴³When he had said this, he cried with a loud voice, "Lazarus, come out!" ⁴⁴The dead man came out, his hands and feet bound with strips of cloth, and his face wrapped in a cloth. Jesus said to them, "Unbind him, and let him go."

The Plot to Kill Jesus

45　Many of the Jews therefore, who had come with Mary and had seen what Jesus did, believed in him. ⁴⁶But some of them went to the Pharisees and told them what he had done. ⁴⁷So the chief priests and the Pharisees called a meeting of the council, and said, "What are we to do? This man is performing many signs. ⁴⁸If we let him go on like this, everyone will believe in him, and the Romans will come and destroy both our holy place^h and our nation." ⁴⁹But one of them, Caiaphas, who was high priest that year, said to them, "You know nothing at all! ⁵⁰You do not understand that it is better for you to have one man die for the people than to have the whole nation destroyed." ⁵¹He did not say this on his own, but being high priest that year he prophesied that Jesus was about to die for the nation, ⁵²and not for the nation only, but to gather into one the dispersed children of God. ⁵³So from that day on they planned to put him to death.

54　Jesus therefore no longer walked about openly among the Jews, but went from there to a town called Ephraim in the region near the

ANNAS AND CAIAPHAS *Collaborators*

THE ANCIENT ROMANS KNEW HOW the Jews valued their faith, which is why they insisted on appointing Israel's high priest. Much like the Soviet Communists and German Nazis in our own century, first-century Romans sought to keep the religious dimension of life under their control.

Annas and Caiaphas fit the Romans' plans perfectly. Caiaphas held office during Jesus' ministry, but Annas, his father-in-law and a former high priest, retained so much influence that he was sometimes called by the title. Both were Sadducees, an aristocratic group who had a very this-worldly understanding of Judaism. Sadducees bent over backward to cooperate with whatever group held political power, and as a result they prospered.

When Jesus started making waves in Israel, Annas and Caiaphas viewed him as a political threat. As John explains it, they feared Jesus would attract so many followers that the Romans would grow alarmed and step in. In classic "Don't rock the boat" thinking, Caiaphas concluded it was better to do away with Jesus than jeopardize the future of Israel. Jesus' miracles, his teachings and his character made no difference to Caiaphas. Political survival mattered above all (11.45–53).

With that in mind, religious leaders secretly kidnapped Jesus, put him on trial, and brought him to the Romans for execution. They later persecuted the church that sprang up after Jesus' resurrection.

The nation of Israel did survive, though not for long. In AD 70 the Romans wiped Israel out of existence, in the process destroying the temple where the high priest officiated. Not until 1948 would the Jews again control Jerusalem.

Life Questions: Is it possible to be so concerned with keeping the peace that you end up opposing what God is doing? What examples can you think of today?

wilderness; and he remained there with the disciples.

55 Now the Passover of the Jews was near, and many went up from the country to Jerusalem before the Passover to purify themselves. 56They were looking for Jesus and were asking one another as they stood in the temple, "What do you think? Surely he will not come to the festival, will

11.53 Climax of the Drama

John wrote his book with a great sense of drama. The first six chapters reveal the identity of Jesus. The next six chapters (7–12) show the increasingly divided opinions about Jesus. On the one hand, his disciples were won over, and Jesus gained a loyal following among the people. On the other hand, his enemies rejected all the evidence about him. Their opposition culminated in this plot, which finally brought about Jesus' death.

he?" 57Now the chief priests and the Pharisees had given orders that anyone who knew where Jesus*i* was should let them know, so that they might arrest him.

Mary Anoints Jesus

12 Six days before the Passover Jesus came to Bethany, the home of Lazarus, whom he had raised from the dead. 2There they gave a dinner for him. Martha served, and Lazarus was one of those at the table with him. 3Mary took a pound of costly perfume made of pure nard, anointed Jesus' feet, and wiped them*j* with her hair. The house was filled with the fragrance of the perfume. 4But Judas Iscariot, one of his disciples (the one who was about to betray him), said, 5"Why was this perfume not sold for three hundred denarii*k* and the money given to the poor?" 6(He said this not because he cared about the poor, but because he was a thief; he kept the common purse and used to steal what was put into it.) 7Jesus said, "Leave her alone. She bought it*l* so that she might keep it for the day of my burial. 8You always have the poor with you, but you do not always have me."

The Plot to Kill Lazarus

9 When the great crowd of the Jews learned that he was there, they came not only because of Jesus but also to see Lazarus, whom he had raised ʿm the dead. 10So the chief priests planned to azarus to death as well, 11since it was on ʿ him that many of the Jews were deserting believing in Jesus.

Jesus' Triumphal Entry into Jerusalem

▶ *See Matthew 21.4–9; Mark 11.7–10; Luke 19.35–38*

12 The next day the great crowd that had come to the festival heard that Jesus was coming to Jerusalem. 13So they took branches of palm trees and went out to meet him, shouting,

"Hosanna!
Blessed is the one who comes in
the name of the Lord—
the King of Israel!"

14Jesus found a young donkey and sat on it; as it is written:
15 "Do not be afraid, daughter of Zion.
Look, your king is coming,
sitting on a donkey's colt!"

16His disciples did not understand these things at first; but when Jesus was glorified, then they remembered that these things had been written of him and had been done to him. 17So the crowd that had been with him when he called Lazarus out of the tomb and raised him from the dead continued to testify.*m* 18It was also because they heard that he had performed this sign that the crowd went to meet him. 19The Pharisees then said to one another, "You see, you can do nothing. Look, the world has gone after him!"

Some Greeks Wish to See Jesus

20 Now among those who went up to worship at the festival were some Greeks. 21They came to Philip, who was from Bethsaida in Galilee, and said to him, "Sir, we wish to see Jesus." 22Philip went and told Andrew; then Andrew and Philip went and told Jesus. 23Jesus answered them, "The hour has come for the Son of Man to be glorified. 24Very truly, I tell you, unless a grain of wheat falls into the earth and dies, it remains just a single grain; but if it dies, it bears much fruit. 25Those who love their life lose it, and those who hate their life in this world will keep it for eternal life. 26Whoever serves me must follow me, and where I am, there will my servant be also. Whoever serves me, the Father will honor.

Jesus Speaks about His Death

27 "Now my soul is troubled. And what should I say—'Father, save me from this hour'? No, it is for this reason that I have come to this hour. 28Father, glorify your name." Then a voice came from heaven, "I have glorified it, and I will glorify it again." 29The crowd standing there heard it and said that it was thunder. Others said, "An angel has spoken to him." 30Jesus answered, "This voice has come for your sake, not for mine. 31Now is the judgment of this world; now the ruler of this world will be driven out. 32And I, when I am lifted up from the earth, will draw all

k Three hundred denarii would be nearly a year's wages for a laborer   *l* Gk lacks *She*
* authorities read *with him began to testify that he had called . . . from the dead*

people*n* to myself." ³³He said this to indicate the kind of death he was to die. ³⁴The crowd answered him, "We have heard from the law that the Messiah*o* remains forever. How can you say that the Son of Man must be lifted up? Who is this Son of Man?" ³⁵Jesus said to them, "The light is with you for a little longer. Walk while you have the light, so that the darkness may not overtake you. If you walk in the darkness, you do not know where you are going. ³⁶While you have the light,

believe in the light, so that you may become children of light."

The Unbelief of the People

After Jesus had said this, he departed and hid from them. ³⁷Although he had performed so many signs in their presence, they did not believe in him. ³⁸This was to fulfill the word spoken by the prophet Isaiah:

"Lord, who has believed our message,

---

n Other ancient authorities read *all things*   *o* Or *the Christ*

John's Reason for Writing
Handpicked incidents that prove a point

PRESIDENT ABRAHAM LINCOLN ATTRACTS BIOGRAPHERS like candy attracts ants; books about his life would easily fill a large room. Some explore his religious beliefs, some his military strategy, some his eloquence, and others his character. Imagine, though, a biography written about only one aspect of the man: Lincoln the lawyer.

Stories from the childhood of Abe—his reading by light filtered through chinks in the wall or his traipsing across town to return a customer's change—would likely never make it into such a book. Yet the precise wording of the Emancipation Proclamation might merit an entire chapter. Long chapters would dwell on an obscure period in Springfield, Illinois, when Lincoln practiced law. But his political campaigns would get scarce mention.

Such an incomplete biography would serve one purpose: to establish Lincoln's ability in law. All other details would fade into the background.

> "Believe me that I am in the Father and the Father is in me; but if you do not, then believe me because of the works themselves."
> 14.11

Everything for a Purpose

Like such a biographer, John wrote his book about Jesus for a similarly limited purpose, which he states very clearly: "These are written so that you may come to believe that Jesus is the Messiah, the Son of God, and that through believing you may have life in his name" (20:31). The book is not so much a biography as an argument. Its author has handpicked incidents to demonstrate that Jesus is unlike any man who has ever lived; he is the Son of God.

This purpose shows up, for example, in how John treats Jesus' miracles. Although Matthew, Mark, and Luke all record miracles, John goes one step further and calls them "signs." A sign points to something. In John, supernatural acts are one more proof of Jesus' unique nature. Jesus refused to perform miracles as magic to dazzle the crowds but used them instead as object lessons to teach about himself.

After feeding 5,000 people from one sack lunch, Jesus described himself as the bread of life (6.1–59). Just before restoring sight to a blind man, he called himself the light of the world (9.1–7). Nothing "just happens" in John; everything underscores the author's overall theme.

Merely a Great Man?

Because Jesus is so clear in describing his own nature, a statement like "I'm ready to accept Jesus as a great moral teacher, but I don't accept his claim to be God" doesn't hold up. As C.S. Lewis has said, "That is the one thing we must not say. A man who was merely a man and said the sort of things Jesus said would not be a great moral teacher. He would either be a lunatic—on a level with the man who says he is a poached egg—or else he would be the Devil of Hell. You must make your choice. Either this man was, and is, the Son of God: or else a madman or something worse."

According to John, not everyone believed Jesus was divine: "Who do you claim to be?" some indignantly demanded (8.53). Doubters had him killed for making such an audacious claim. But it is hardly possible to read John without being convinced that Jesus himself claimed to be God.

Life Questions: Despite what C.S. Lewis says, many people do think of Jesus as "merely a great man." How do they rationalize it?

and to whom has the arm of the Lord
been revealed?"

³⁹And so they could not believe, because Isaiah also said,

⁴⁰ "He has blinded their eyes
and hardened their heart,
so that they might not look with their eyes,
and understand with their heart and
turn—
and I would heal them."

⁴¹Isaiah said this because^p he saw his glory and spoke about him. ⁴²Nevertheless many, even of the authorities, believed in him. But because of the Pharisees they did not confess it, for fear that they would be put out of the synagogue; ⁴³for they loved human glory more than the glory that comes from God.

Summary of Jesus' Teaching

44 Then Jesus cried aloud: "Whoever believes in me believes not in me but in him who sent me. ⁴⁵And whoever sees me sees him who sent me. ⁴⁶I have come as light into the world, so that everyone who believes in me should not remain in the darkness. ⁴⁷I do not judge anyone who hears my words and does not keep them, for I came not to judge the world, but to save the world. ⁴⁸The one who rejects me and does not receive my word has a judge; on the last day the word that I have spoken will serve as judge, ⁴⁹for I have not spoken on my own, but the Father who sent me has himself given me a commandment about what to say and what to speak. ⁵⁰And I know that his commandment is eternal life. What I speak, therefore, I speak just as the Father has told me."

Jesus Washes the Disciples' Feet

13 Now before the festival of the Passover, Jesus knew that his hour had come to depart from this world and go to the Father. Having loved his own who were in the world, he loved them to the end. ²The devil had already put it into the heart of Judas son of Simon Iscariot to betray him. And during supper ³Jesus, knowing that the Father had given all things into his hands, and that he had come from God and was going to God, ⁴got up from the table,^q took off his outer robe, and tied a towel around himself. ⁵Then he poured water into a basin and began to wash the disciples' feet and to wipe them with the towel that was tied around him. ⁶He came to Simon Peter, who said to him, "Lord, are you going to wash my feet?" ⁷Jesus answered, "You do not know now what I am doing, but later you will understand." ⁸Peter said to him, "You will never wash my feet." Jesus answered, "Unless I wash you, you have no share with me." ⁹Simon Peter said to him, "Lord, not my feet only but also my

hands and my head!" ¹⁰Jesus said to him, "One who has bathed does not need to wash, except for the feet,^r but is entirely clean. And you^s are clean, though not all of you." ¹¹For he knew who was to betray him; for this reason he said, "Not all of you are clean."

> ### 13.4 The Role of a Servant
>
> *Before beginning an intimate meal with his disciples, Jesus gave them a lesson about humility. Normally, slaves performed the act of washing the feet of dinner guests. Here Jesus, the guest of honor, dressed himself like a slave, with a towel around his waist, and insisted on washing the feet of his disciples. Paul comments on Jesus' servanthood in Philippians 2.5–11.*

12 After he had washed their feet, had put on his robe, and had returned to the table, he said to them, "Do you know what I have done to you? ¹³You call me Teacher and Lord—and you are right, for that is what I am. ¹⁴So if I, your Lord and Teacher, have washed your feet, you also ought to wash one another's feet. ¹⁵For I have set you an example, that you also should do as I have done to you. ¹⁶Very truly, I tell you, servants^t are not greater than their master, nor are messengers greater than the one who sent them. ¹⁷If you know these things, you are blessed if you do them. ¹⁸I am not speaking of all of you; I know whom I have chosen. But it is to fulfill the scripture, 'The one who ate my bread^u has lifted his heel against me.' ¹⁹I tell you this now, before it occurs, so that when it does occur, you may believe that I am he.^v ²⁰Very truly, I tell you, whoever receives one whom I send receives me; and whoever receives me receives him who sent me."

Jesus Foretells His Betrayal

21 After saying this Jesus was troubled in spirit, and declared, "Very truly, I tell you, one of you will betray me." ²²The disciples looked at one another, uncertain of whom he was speaking. ²³One of his disciples—the one whom Jesus loved—was reclining next to him; ²⁴Simon Peter therefore motioned to him to ask Jesus of whom he was speaking. ²⁵So while reclining next to Jesus, he asked him, "Lord, who is it?" ²⁶Jesus answered, "It is the one to whom I give this piece of bread when I have dipped it in the dish."^w So when he had dipped the piece of bread, he gave it to Judas son of Simon Iscariot.^x ²⁷After he received the piece of bread,^y Satan entered into him. Jesus said to him, "Do quickly what you are

---

^p Other ancient witnesses read *when*   ^q Gk *from supper*   ^r Other ancient authorities lack *except for the feet*   ^s The Greek word for *you* here is plural   ^t Gk *slaves*   ^u Other ancient authorities read *ate bread with me*   ^v Gk *I am*   ^w Gk *dipped it*   ^x Other ancient authorities read *Judas Iscariot son of Simon*; others, *Judas son of Simon from Karyot* (Kerioth)   ^y Gk *After the piece of bread*

going to do." ²⁸Now no one at the table knew why he said this to him. ²⁹Some thought that, because Judas had the common purse, Jesus was telling him, "Buy what we need for the festival"; or, that he should give something to the poor. ³⁰So, after receiving the piece of bread, he immediately went out. And it was night.

The New Commandment

▶ See Matthew 26.33–35; Mark 14.29–31; Luke 22.33–34

31 When he had gone out, Jesus said, "Now the Son of Man has been glorified, and God has been glorified in him. ³²If God has been glorified in him,ᶻ God will also glorify him in himself and will glorify him at once. ³³Little children, I am with you only a little longer. You will look for me; and as I said to the Jews so now I say to you, 'Where I am going, you cannot come.' ³⁴I give you a new commandment, that you love one another. Just as I have loved you, you also should love one another. ³⁵By this everyone will know that you are my disciples, if you have love for one another."

Jesus Foretells Peter's Denial

36 Simon Peter said to him, "Lord, where are you going?" Jesus answered, "Where I am going, you cannot follow me now; but you will follow afterward." ³⁷Peter said to him, "Lord, why can I not follow you now? I will lay down my life for you." ³⁸Jesus answered, "Will you lay down your life for me? Very truly, I tell you, before the cock crows, you will have denied me three times.

Jesus the Way to the Father

14 "Do not let your hearts be troubled. Believeᵃ in God, believe also in me. ²In my Father's house there are many dwelling places. If it were not so, would I have told you that I go to prepare a place for you?ᵇ ³And if I go and prepare a place for you, I will come again and will take you to myself, so that where I am, there you may be also. ⁴And you know the way to the place where I am going."ᶜ ⁵Thomas said to him, "Lord, we do not know where you are going. How can we know the way?" ⁶Jesus said to him, "I am the way, and the truth, and the life. No one comes to the Father except through me. ⁷If you know me, you will knowᵈ my Father also. From now on you do know him and have seen him."

8 Philip said to him, "Lord, show us the Father, and we will be satisfied." ⁹Jesus said to him, "Have I been with you all this time, Philip, and you still do not know me? Whoever has seen me has seen the Father. How can you say, 'Show us the Father'? ¹⁰Do you not believe that I am in the Father and the Father is in me? The words that I say to you I do not speak on my own; but the Father who dwells in me does his works. ¹¹Believe me that I am in the Father and the Father is in me; but if you do not, then believe me because of the works themselves. ¹²Very truly, I tell you, the one who believes in me will also do the works that I do and, in fact, will do greater works than these, because I am going to the Father. ¹³I will do whatever you ask in my name, so that the Father may be glorified in the Son. ¹⁴If in my name you ask meᵉ for anything, I will do it.

ᶻ Other ancient authorities lack If God has been glorified in him have told you; for I go to prepare a place for you ᶜ Other ancient authorities read Where I am going you know, and the way you know ᵈ Other ancient authorities read If you had known me, you would have known ᵃ Or You believe ᵇ Or If it were not so, I would ᵉ Other ancient authorities lack me

THOMAS Honest Questions

BETWEEN STUBBORN SKEPTICISM AND HONEST questioning there is a huge gap, and the disciple named Thomas illustrates the difference. Popularly known as "Doubting Thomas," this disciple stands out for his practical honesty, not for his unbelief.

When Jesus' friend Lazarus died, Thomas frankly showed his despondency along with his intense loyalty to Jesus: "Let us also go [to Lazarus' grave], that we may die with him" (11.16). At Jesus' last meal with his disciples, he expressed the confusion that was surely on all the disciples' minds (14.5). Thomas never pretended. If he didn't understand something, he said so; if he felt discouraged, he acted like it.

Thomas got his reputation as a doubter primarily because of his reaction when told of Jesus' resurrection. He simply insisted, "I need to see it for myself." The implications of a risen Jesus were too great, he believed, to take someone else's word for it. Jesus honored this honest doubt, and when he visited Thomas in person to offer proof, Thomas responded with the ultimate statement of faith: "My Lord and my God" (20.28). He was, in fact, the only disciple who specifically addressed Jesus as God.

Thomas's questions led to faith because he expressed them sincerely and looked for answers. The last mention of him in the Bible shows Thomas not questioning but praying, waiting with the other disciples for the Holy Spirit to come (Acts 1.12–14).

Life Questions: What honest questions do you need to bring before God?

The Promise of the Holy Spirit

15 "If you love me, you will keep[f] my commandments. 16And I will ask the Father, and he will give you another Advocate,[g] to be with you forever. 17This is the Spirit of truth, whom the world cannot receive, because it neither sees him nor knows him. You know him, because he abides with you, and he will be in[h] you.

18 "I will not leave you orphaned; I am coming to you. 19In a little while the world will no longer see me, but you will see me; because I live, you also will live. 20On that day you will know that I am in my Father, and you in me, and I in you. 21They who have my commandments and keep them are those who love me; and those who love me will be loved by my Father, and I will love them and reveal myself to them." 22Judas (not Iscariot) said to him, "Lord, how is it that you will reveal yourself to us, and not to the world?" 23Jesus answered him, "Those who love me will keep my word, and my Father will love them, and we will come to them and make our home with them. 24Whoever does not love me does not keep my words; and the word that you hear is not mine, but is from the Father who sent me.

25 "I have said these things to you while I am still with you. 26But the Advocate,[g] the Holy Spirit, whom the Father will send in my name, will teach you everything, and remind you of all that I have said to you. 27Peace I leave with you; my peace I give to you. I do not give to you as the world gives. Do not let your hearts be troubled, and do not let them be afraid. 28You heard me say to you, 'I am going away, and I am coming to you.' If you loved me, you would rejoice that I am going to the Father, because the Father is greater than I. 29And now I have told you this before it occurs, so that when it does occur, you may believe. 30I will no longer talk much with you, for the ruler of this world is coming. He has no power over me; 31but I do as the Father has commanded me, so that the world may know that I love the Father. Rise, let us be on our way.

Jesus the True Vine

15 "I am the true vine, and my Father is the vinegrower. 2He removes every branch in me that bears no fruit. Every branch that bears fruit he prunes[i] to make it bear more fruit. 3You have already been cleansed[i] by the word that I have spoken to you. 4Abide in me as I abide in you. Just as the branch cannot bear fruit by itself unless it abides in the vine, neither can you unless you abide in me. 5I am the vine, you are the branches. Those who abide in me and I in them bear much fruit, because apart from me you can do nothing. 6Whoever does not abide in me is thrown away like a branch and withers; such branches are gathered, thrown into the fire, and burned. 7If you abide in me, and my words abide in you, ask for whatever you wish, and it will be done for you. 8My Father is glorified by this, that

15.1 Jesus as the Vine

Old Testament prophets referred to the Israelites as God's "vine," or "vineyard." But as Jesus often pointed out, the Jews had failed to bear fruit. Here he claims the image for himself, "I am the true vine."

John frequently records Jesus' use of the words I am: "I am the bread of life," "I am the way, and the truth, and the life." The phrase stood out sharply to Jewish leaders, because God had been known as the great I AM to the Jews (Exodus 3.14). Jewish unbelievers, recognizing that Jesus was claiming to be God, reacted with shock and outrage.

you bear much fruit and become[j] my disciples. 9As the Father has loved me, so I have loved you; abide in my love. 10If you keep my commandments, you will abide in my love, just as I have kept my Father's commandments and abide in his love. 11I have said these things to you so that my joy may be in you, and that your joy may be complete.

12 "This is my commandment, that you love one another as I have loved you. 13No one has greater love than this, to lay down one's life for one's friends. 14You are my friends if you do what I command you. 15I do not call you servants[k] any longer, because the servant[l] does not know what the master is doing; but I have called you friends, because I have made known to you everything that I have heard from my Father. 16You did not choose me but I chose you. And I appointed you to go and bear fruit, fruit that will last, so that the Father will give you whatever you ask him in my name. 17I am giving you these commands so that you may love one another.

The World's Hatred

18 "If the world hates you, be aware that it hated me before it hated you. 19If you belonged to the world,[m] the world would love you as its own. Because you do not belong to the world, but I have chosen you out of the world—therefore the world hates you. 20Remember the word that I said to you, 'Servants[n] are not greater than their master.' If they persecuted me, they will persecute you; if they kept my word, they will keep yours also. 21But they will do all these things to you on account of my name, because they do not know

---

f Other ancient authorities read *me, keep* and cleansing   j Or *be*   g Or *Helper*   k Gk *slaves*   l Gk *slave*   h Or *among*   m Gk *were of the world*   i The same Greek root refers to pruning   n Gk *Slaves*

him who sent me. 22If I had not come and spoken to them, they would not have sin; but now they have no excuse for their sin. 23Whoever hates me hates my Father also. 24If I had not done among them the works that no one else did, they would not have sin. But now they have seen and hated both me and my Father. 25It was to fulfill the word that is written in their law, 'They hated me without a cause.'

26 "When the Advocate*o* comes, whom I will send to you from the Father, the Spirit of truth who comes from the Father, he will testify on my behalf. 27You also are to testify because you have been with me from the beginning.

16 "I have said these things to you to keep you from stumbling. 2They will put you out of the synagogues. Indeed, an hour is coming when

those who kill you will think that by doing so they are offering worship to God. 3And they will do this because they have not known the Father or me. 4But I have said these things to you so that when their hour comes you may remember that I told you about them.

The Work of the Spirit

"I did not say these things to you from the beginning, because I was with you. 5But now I am going to him who sent me; yet none of you asks me, 'Where are you going?' 6But because I have said these things to you, sorrow has filled your hearts. 7Nevertheless I tell you the truth: it is to your advantage that I go away, for if I do not go away, the Advocate*o* will not come to you; but if I go, I will send him to you. 8And when he comes,

o Or *Helper*

The Last Meal Together
The longest, most emotional night of Jesus' life

JOHN DEVOTED ONE-THIRD OF HIS book to the last 24-hour period Jesus spent on earth. The next five chapters (13–17) describe one of the scenes from that period, and nothing like these chapters exists elsewhere in the Bible. In their slow-motion, realistic detail, they provide an intimate memoir of Jesus' most anguished evening.

> *"You will have pain, but your pain will turn into joy."*
> 16.20

Leonardo da Vinci immortalized the setting in his famous painting *The Last Supper*, with the participants arranged on one side of the table as if posing for the artist. But John gives few physical details; instead, he focuses on a whirlpool of emotional currents.

John holds a light to the disciples' faces, and you can almost see the awareness flickering in their eyes. All that Jesus had told them was slowly settling in. As for Jesus, "having loved his own who were in the world, he loved them to the end" (13.1).

Jesus Prepares to Leave

Never before had Jesus been so direct with them. Around the table he avoided parables and painstakingly answered the disciples' redundant questions. Never was he more "theological." He alone fully recognized the significance of this last evening before his death. The world was about to undergo a convulsive trauma, and the 11 fearful men with him were his hope for that world.

"It is to your advantage that I go away," Jesus said (16.7), but the disciples were too busy discussing the meaning of "going away" to comprehend the good that would follow.

Nevertheless, Jesus kept explaining until at last the disciples showed signs of understanding. God's Son had entered the world to reside in one body. He was leaving earth to return to the Father. But the Spirit would come and reside in many bodies. Jesus seemed aware that much of what they nodded their heads at now would not sink in until later.

Pain before Joy

Jesus concluded his words with a ringing declaration, "Take courage; I have conquered the world!" (16.33). How hollow this statement would seem the next evening, when his pale, abused body hung on an executioner's cross. The disciples' emotions—and faith—would rise and plummet in one unforgettable day. Jesus predicted this, too, likening the pain to the spasms of childbirth before great joy breaks through (16.21–22).

In his longest recorded prayer, Jesus summed up his feelings and his plans for the tight circle of friends gathered around him. He prayed, too, for the others who would follow them, stretching in an unbroken chain throughout history. And then he led the little band to his appointment with death.

Life Questions: Have you ever been around someone facing death? How did he or she act? What does Jesus' response to impending death reveal about why he came to earth?

he will prove the world wrong about[p] sin and righteousness and judgment: [9]about sin, because they do not believe in me; [10]about righteousness, because I am going to the Father and you will see me no longer; [11]about judgment, because the ruler of this world has been condemned.

[12] "I still have many things to say to you, but you cannot bear them now. [13]When the Spirit of truth comes, he will guide you into all the truth; for he will not speak on his own, but will speak whatever he hears, and he will declare to you the things that are to come. [14]He will glorify me, because he will take what is mine and declare it to you. [15]All that the Father has is mine. For this reason I said that he will take what is mine and declare it to you.

Sorrow Will Turn into Joy

[16] "A little while, and you will no longer see me, and again a little while, and you will see me." [17]Then some of his disciples said to one another, "What does he mean by saying to us, 'A little while, and you will no longer see me, and again a little while, and you will see me'; and 'Because I am going to the Father'?" [18]They said, "What does he mean by this 'a little while'? We do not know what he is talking about." [19]Jesus knew that they wanted to ask him, so he said to them, "Are you discussing among yourselves what I meant when I said, 'A little while, and you will no longer see me, and again a little while, and you will see me'? [20]Very truly, I tell you, you will weep and mourn, but the world will rejoice; you will have

16.20 Filled with Grief

Good-byes are always sad, and for the disciples this farewell speech was especially so. They had staked their lives on Jesus, and without him they could see no future. Jesus, however, promised that he was leaving for their own good. He would send the Holy Spirit to guide them into "all the truth" (verse 13). In fact, as Acts shows, only after Jesus' departure did these confused disciples fully grasp the meaning of his death and resurrection and begin to proclaim it joyfully to everyone around them.

pain, but your pain will turn into joy. [21]When a woman is in labor, she has pain, because her hour has come. But when her child is born, she no longer remembers the anguish because of the joy of having brought a human being into the world. [22]So you have pain now; but I will see you again,

and your hearts will rejoice, and no one will take your joy from you. [23]On that day you will ask nothing of me.[q] Very truly, I tell you, if you ask anything of the Father in my name, he will give it to you.[r] [24]Until now you have not asked for anything in my name. Ask and you will receive, so that your joy may be complete.

Peace for the Disciples

[25] "I have said these things to you in figures of speech. The hour is coming when I will no longer speak to you in figures, but will tell you plainly of the Father. [26]On that day you will ask in my name. I do not say to you that I will ask the Father on your behalf; [27]for the Father himself loves you, because you have loved me and have believed that I came from God.[s] [28]I came from the Father and have come into the world; again, I am leaving the world and am going to the Father."

[29] His disciples said, "Yes, now you are speaking plainly, not in any figure of speech! [30]Now we know that you know all things, and do not need to have anyone question you; by this we believe that you came from God." [31]Jesus answered them, "Do you now believe? [32]The hour is coming, indeed it has come, when you will be scattered, each one to his home, and you will leave me alone. Yet I am not alone because the Father is with me. [33]I have said this to you, so that in me you may have peace. In the world you face persecution. But take courage; I have conquered the world!"

Jesus Prays for His Disciples

17 After Jesus had spoken these words, he looked up to heaven and said, "Father, the hour has come; glorify your Son so that the Son may glorify you, [2]since you have given him authority over all people,[t] to give eternal life to all whom you have given him. [3]And this is eternal life, that they may know you, the only true God, and Jesus Christ whom you have sent. [4]I glorified you on earth by finishing the work that you gave me to do. [5]So now, Father, glorify me in your own presence with the glory that I had in your presence before the world existed.

[6] "I have made your name known to those whom you gave me from the world. They were yours, and you gave them to me, and they have kept your word. [7]Now they know that everything you have given me is from you; [8]for the words that you gave to me I have given to them, and they have received them and know in truth that I came from you; and they have believed that you sent me. [9]I am asking on their behalf; I am not asking on behalf of the world, but on behalf of

---

p Or *convict the world of*   q Or *will ask me no question in my name*   s Other ancient authorities read *the Father*   r Other ancient authorities read *Father, he will give it to you*   t Gk *flesh*

those whom you gave me, because they are yours. [10]All mine are yours, and yours are mine; and I have been glorified in them. [11]And now I am no longer in the world, but they are in the world, and I am coming to you. Holy Father, protect them in your name that you have given me, so that they may be one, as we are one. [12]While I was with them, I protected them in your name that[u] you have given me. I guarded them, and not one of them was lost except the one destined to be lost,[v] so that the scripture might be fulfilled. [13]But now I am coming to you, and I speak these things in the world so that they may have my joy made complete in themselves.[w] [14]I have given them your word, and the world has hated them because they do not belong to the world, just as I do not belong to the world. [15]I am not asking you to take them out of the world, but I ask you to protect them from the evil one.[x] [16]They do not belong to the world, just as I do not belong to the world. [17]Sanctify them in the truth; your word is truth. [18]As you have sent me into the world, so I have sent them into the world. [19]And for their sakes I sanctify myself, so that they also may be sanctified in truth.

20 "I ask not only on behalf of these, but also on behalf of those who will believe in me through their word, [21]that they may all be one. As you, Father, are in me and I am in you, may they also be in us,[y] so that the world may believe that you

17.21 Jesus' Longest Prayer

The famous prayer recorded here concludes a kind of commissioning or graduation. In it, Jesus turns over his mission to the disciples and, by extension, to all believers who would follow.

have sent me. [22]The glory that you have given me I have given them, so that they may be one, as we are one, [23]I in them and you in me, that they may become completely one, so that the world may know that you have sent me and have loved them even as you have loved me. [24]Father, I desire that those also, whom you have given me, may be with me where I am, to see my glory, which you have given me because you loved me before the foundation of the world.

25 "Righteous Father, the world does not know you, but I know you; and these know that you have sent me. [26]I made your name known to them, and I will make it known, so that the love with which you have loved me may be in them, and I in them."

The Betrayal and Arrest of Jesus

▶ *See Matthew 26.47–56; Mark 14.43–50; Luke 22.47–53*

18 After Jesus had spoken these words, he went out with his disciples across the Kidron valley to a place where there was a garden, which he and his disciples entered. [2]Now Judas, who betrayed him, also knew the place, because Jesus often met there with his disciples. [3]So Judas brought a detachment of soldiers together with police from the chief priests and the Pharisees, and they came there with lanterns and torches and weapons. [4]Then Jesus, knowing all that was to happen to him, came forward and asked them, "Whom are you looking for?" [5]They answered, "Jesus of Nazareth."[z] Jesus replied, "I am he."[a] Judas, who betrayed him, was standing with them. [6]When Jesus[b] said to them, "I am he,"[a] they stepped back and fell to the ground. [7]Again he asked them, "Whom are you looking for?" And they said, "Jesus of Nazareth."[z] [8]Jesus answered, "I told you that I am he.[a] So if you are looking for me, let these men go." [9]This was to fulfill the word that he had spoken, "I did not lose a single one of those whom you gave me." [10]Then Simon Peter, who had a sword, drew it, struck the high priest's slave, and cut off his right ear. The slave's name was Malchus. [11]Jesus said to Peter, "Put your sword back into its sheath. Am I not to drink the cup that the Father has given me?"

Jesus before the High Priest

▶ *See Matthew 26.57*

12 So the soldiers, their officer, and the Jewish police arrested Jesus and bound him. [13]First they took him to Annas, who was the father-in-law of Caiaphas, the high priest that year. [14]Caiaphas was the one who had advised the Jews that it was better to have one person die for the people.

Peter Denies Jesus

▶ *See Matthew 26.69–70; Mark 14.66–68; Luke 22.55–57*

15 Simon Peter and another disciple followed Jesus. Since that disciple was known to the high priest, he went with Jesus into the courtyard of the high priest, [16]but Peter was standing outside at the gate. So the other disciple, who was known to the high priest, went out, spoke to the woman who guarded the gate, and brought Peter in. [17]The woman said to Peter, "You are not also one of this man's disciples, are you?" He said, "I am not." [18]Now the slaves and the police had made a charcoal fire because it was cold, and they were standing around it and warming themselves. Pe-

---

[u] Other ancient authorities read *protected in your name those whom*   [v] Gk *except the son of destruction*
[w] Or *among themselves*   [x] Or *from evil*   [y] Other ancient authorities read *be one in us*   [z] Gk *the Nazorean*
[a] Gk *I am*   [b] Gk *he*

ter also was standing with them and warming himself.

The High Priest Questions Jesus

▶ *See Matthew 26.59–68; Mark 14.55–65; Luke 22.63–71*

19 Then the high priest questioned Jesus about his disciples and about his teaching. 20Jesus answered, "I have spoken openly to the world; I have always taught in synagogues and in the temple, where all the Jews come together. I have said nothing in secret. 21Why do you ask me? Ask those who heard what I said to them; they know what I said." 22When he had said this, one of the police standing nearby struck Jesus on the face, saying, "Is that how you answer the high priest?" 23Jesus answered, "If I have spoken wrongly, testify to the wrong. But if I have spoken rightly, why do you strike me?" 24Then Annas sent him bound to Caiaphas the high priest.

Peter Denies Jesus Again

▶ *See Matthew 26.71–75; Mark 14.69–72; Luke 22.58–62*

25 Now Simon Peter was standing and warming himself. They asked him, "You are not also one of his disciples, are you?" He denied it and said, "I am not." 26One of the slaves of the high priest, a relative of the man whose ear Peter had cut off, asked, "Did I not see you in the garden with him?" 27Again Peter denied it, and at that moment the cock crowed.

Jesus before Pilate

▶ *See Matthew 27.11–18,20–23; Mark 15.2–15; Luke 23.2–3,18–25*

28 Then they took Jesus from Caiaphas to Pilate's headquarters.*c* It was early in the morning. They themselves did not enter the headquarters,*c* so as to avoid ritual defilement and to be able to eat the Passover. 29So Pilate went out to them and said, "What accusation do you bring against this man?" 30They answered, "If this man were not a criminal, we would not have handed him over to you." 31Pilate said to them, "Take him yourselves and judge him according to your law." The Jews replied, "We are not permitted to put anyone to death." 32(This was to fulfill what Jesus had said when he indicated the kind of death he was to die.)

33 Then Pilate entered the headquarters*c* again, summoned Jesus, and asked him, "Are you the King of the Jews?" 34Jesus answered, "Do you ask this on your own, or did others tell you about me?" 35Pilate replied, "I am not a Jew, am I? Your own nation and the chief priests have handed you over to me. What have you done?" 36Jesus an-swered, "My kingdom is not from this world. If my kingdom were from this world, my followers would be fighting to keep me from being handed over to the Jews. But as it is, my kingdom is not from here." 37Pilate asked him, "So you are a king?" Jesus answered, "You say that I am a king. For this I was born, and for this I came into the world, to testify to the truth. Everyone who belongs to the truth listens to my voice." 38Pilate asked him, "What is truth?"

Jesus Sentenced to Death

▶ *See Matthew 27.27–31; Mark 15.16–20*

After he had said this, he went out to the Jews again and told them, "I find no case against him. 39But you have a custom that I release someone for you at the Passover. Do you want me to release for you the King of the Jews?" 40They shouted in reply, "Not this man, but Barabbas!" Now Barabbas was a bandit.

19 Then Pilate took Jesus and had him flogged. 2And the soldiers wove a crown of thorns and put it on his head, and they dressed him in a purple robe. 3They kept coming up to him, saying, "Hail, King of the Jews!" and striking him on the face. 4Pilate went out again and said to them, "Look, I am bringing him out to you to let you know that I find no case against him." 5So Jesus came out, wearing the crown of thorns and the purple robe. Pilate said to them, "Here is the man!" 6When the chief priests and the police saw him, they shouted, "Crucify him! Crucify him!" Pilate said to them, "Take him yourselves and crucify him; I find no case against him." 7The Jews answered him, "We have a law, and according to that law he ought to die because he has claimed to be the Son of God."

8 Now when Pilate heard this, he was more afraid than ever. 9He entered his headquarters*c* again and asked Jesus, "Where are you from?" But Jesus gave him no answer. 10Pilate therefore said to him, "Do you refuse to speak to me? Do you not know that I have power to release you, and power to crucify you?" 11Jesus answered him, "You would have no power over me unless it had been given you from above; therefore the one who handed me over to you is guilty of a greater sin." 12From then on Pilate tried to release him, but the Jews cried out, "If you release this man, you are no friend of the emperor. Everyone who claims to be a king sets himself against the emperor."

13 When Pilate heard these words, he brought Jesus outside and sat*d* on the judge's bench at a place called The Stone Pavement, or in Hebrew*e* Gabbatha. 14Now it was the day of Preparation for the Passover; and it was about noon. He said to the Jews, "Here is your King!"

---

c Gk *the praetorium*   *d* Or *seated him*   *e* That is, *Aramaic*

¹⁵They cried out, "Away with him! Away with him! Crucify him!" Pilate asked them, "Shall I crucify your King?" The chief priests answered, "We have no king but the emperor." ¹⁶Then he handed him over to them to be crucified.

The Crucifixion of Jesus

▶ See Matthew 27.33–44; Mark 15.22–32; Luke 23.33–43

So they took Jesus; ¹⁷and carrying the cross by himself, he went out to what is called The Place of the Skull, which in Hebrewᶠ is called Golgotha. ¹⁸There they crucified him, and with him two others, one on either side, with Jesus between them. ¹⁹Pilate also had an inscription written and put on the cross. It read, "Jesus of Nazareth,ᵍ the King of the Jews." ²⁰Many of the Jews read this inscription, because the place where Jesus was crucified was near the city; and it was written in Hebrew,ᶠ in Latin, and in Greek. ²¹Then the chief priests of the Jews said to Pilate, "Do not write, 'The King of the Jews,' but, 'This man said, I am King of the Jews.'" ²²Pilate answered, "What I have written I have written." ²³When the soldiers had crucified Jesus, they took his clothes and divided them into four parts, one for each soldier. They also took his tunic; now the tunic was seamless, woven in one piece from the top. ²⁴So they said to one another, "Let us not tear it, but cast lots for it to see who will get it." This was to fulfill what the scripture says,

"They divided my clothes among themselves,
  and for my clothing they cast lots."

²⁵And that is what the soldiers did.

Meanwhile, standing near the cross of Jesus were his mother, and his mother's sister, Mary the wife of Clopas, and Mary Magdalene. ²⁶When Jesus saw his mother and the disciple whom he loved standing beside her, he said to his mother, "Woman, here is your son." ²⁷Then he said to the disciple, "Here is your mother." And from that hour the disciple took her into his own home.

28 After this, when Jesus knew that all was now finished, he said (in order to fulfill the scripture), "I am thirsty." ²⁹A jar full of sour wine was standing there. So they put a sponge full of the wine on a branch of hyssop and held it to his mouth. ³⁰When Jesus had received the wine, he said, "It is finished." Then he bowed his head and gave up his spirit.

Jesus' Side Is Pierced

31 Since it was the day of Preparation, the Jews did not want the bodies left on the cross during the sabbath, especially because that sabbath was a day of great solemnity. So they asked Pilate to have the legs of the crucified men broken and the bodies removed. ³²Then the soldiers came and broke the legs of the first and of the other who had been crucified with him. ³³But when they came to Jesus and saw that he was already dead, they did not break his legs. ³⁴Instead, one of

---

ᶠ That is, Aramaic   ᵍ Gk the Nazorean

PONTIUS PILATE *Governor Cynic*

WHENEVER LOCAL RULERS FAILED TO keep the colonies in line, Rome appointed its own strongmen, called "procurators" or "governors." Pilate served as Roman procurator of Judea, a regional ruler for the most powerful empire in the history of the planet up to that time. Yet, as Pilate discovered, having absolute power does not guarantee peace. The Jews hated Roman rule, and religious and nationalist emotions constantly flared up in Judea.

According to the first-century historian Josephus, Pilate marched Roman soldiers into Jerusalem, learning too late that Jews would die to keep Rome's military emblems out. (They considered images of the emperor blasphemous.) When Pilate set out to build an aqueduct for Jerusalem, he caused a bloody riot by appropriating temple offerings to pay the bill. Pilate's soldiers brutally put down many such disturbances.

When Pilate met Jesus, he mainly saw one more source of trouble. Pilate tried to pass the buck (to Herod). He even offered to set the prisoner free. But in the end Pilate was willing to sacrifice Jesus if that would buy order. Pilate's most famous words were a cynical question, "What is truth?" (18.38). The answer was standing right in front of him, but Pilate didn't really want to know.

Pilate must have considered Jesus' execution a success (it didn't start any riots), but his balancing act was upturned just a few years later. Some Samaritans—the mixed-race group whom Jews despised—heard a crazy report that Moses had buried treasures on Mt. Gerizim. A crowd gathered to climb the mountain. Pilate, thinking these pilgrims might be dangerous, sent in troops. Soon he had a massacre on his hands. For his overreaction he was relieved from command and sent back to Rome to stand trial.

Life Questions: Are there situations in your life where you would buy peace at any cost? What happens to the truth when you do so?

the soldiers pierced his side with a spear, and at once blood and water came out. ³⁵(He who saw this has testified so that you also may believe. His testimony is true, and he knows[h] that he tells the truth.) ³⁶These things occurred so that the scripture might be fulfilled, "None of his bones shall be broken." ³⁷And again another passage of scripture says, "They will look on the one whom they have pierced."

19.31 Speeding up Death

Soldiers broke the bones of crucified men to speed up their dying, here so the bodies could be removed before the holy day that followed. Jesus had already died, so his bones were left intact. This fulfilled Old Testament promises that the Messiah's bones would not be broken and that his side would be pierced with a spear (Exodus 12.46; Zechariah 12.10).

The Burial of Jesus

▶ *See Matthew 27.57–61; Mark 15.42–47; Luke 23.50–56*

38 After these things, Joseph of Arimathea, who was a disciple of Jesus, though a secret one because of his fear of the Jews, asked Pilate to let him take away the body of Jesus. Pilate gave him permission; so he came and removed his body. ³⁹Nicodemus, who had at first come to Jesus by night, also came, bringing a mixture of myrrh and aloes, weighing about a hundred pounds. ⁴⁰They took the body of Jesus and wrapped it with the spices in linen cloths, according to the burial custom of the Jews. ⁴¹Now there was a garden in the place where he was crucified, and in the garden there was a new tomb in which no one had ever been laid. ⁴²And so, because it was the Jewish day of Preparation, and the tomb was nearby, they laid Jesus there.

The Resurrection of Jesus

▶ *See Matthew 28.1–8; Mark 16.1–8; Luke 24.1–10*

20 Early on the first day of the week, while it was still dark, Mary Magdalene came to the tomb and saw that the stone had been removed from the tomb. ²So she ran and went to Simon Peter and the other disciple, the one whom Jesus loved, and said to them, "They have taken the Lord out of the tomb, and we do not know where they have laid him." ³Then Peter and the other disciple set out and went toward the tomb. ⁴The two were running together, but the other disciple outran Peter and reached the tomb first. ⁵He bent down to look in and saw the linen wrappings lying there, but he did not go in. ⁶Then Simon Peter came, following him, and went into the tomb. He saw the linen wrappings lying there, ⁷and the cloth that had been on Jesus' head, not lying with the linen wrappings but rolled up in a place by itself. ⁸Then the other disciple, who reached the tomb first, also went in, and he saw and believed; ⁹for as yet they did not understand the scripture, that he must rise from the dead. ¹⁰Then the disciples returned to their homes.

Jesus Appears to Mary Magdalene

11 But Mary stood weeping outside the tomb. As she wept, she bent over to look[i] into the tomb; ¹²and she saw two angels in white, sitting where the body of Jesus had been lying, one at the head and the other at the feet. ¹³They said to her,

---

[h] Or *there is one who knows*   [i] Gk lacks *to look*

MARY MAGDALENE *First to See*

MARY MAGDALENE HAS BECOME FAMOUS. *Jesus Christ Superstar* and other plays and movies have portrayed her as a sensuous woman, sometimes as a reformed prostitute. In reality, the Bible gives no indication of anything tawdry about her. All we know is that she came from Magdala, a city on the Sea of Galilee, and that Jesus drove seven demons from her. Having been healed by him, she dedicated her life to Jesus.

The Gospels, which focus on Jesus' twelve disciples, also mention that a good-sized crowd of women left their homes and families to follow Jesus (Matthew 27.55–56). Mary Magdalene heads the list of the women who helped finance his ministry.

When Jesus was crucified in Jerusalem, far from his home in Galilee, Mary Magdalene stayed near him. She carefully observed where he was buried and faithfully went there at the earliest opportunity to care for his body. As a result, she was the very first person to see Jesus risen from the dead and the first to spread the word (20.18).

Women in that time were usually given second place, if any place at all. Jewish courts did not even accept their testimony. At the great miracle of Jesus' resurrection, however, Mary Magdalene had the honor of being the first witness on the scene.

Life Questions: Have you been able to witness God's work? Where and how?

"Woman, why are you weeping?" She said to them, "They have taken away my Lord, and I do not know where they have laid him." [14]When she had said this, she turned around and saw Jesus standing there, but she did not know that it was Jesus. [15]Jesus said to her, "Woman, why are you weeping? Whom are you looking for?" Supposing him to be the gardener, she said to him, "Sir, if you have carried him away, tell me where you have laid him, and I will take him away." [16]Jesus said to her, "Mary!" She turned and said to him in Hebrew,[j] "Rabbouni!" (which means Teacher). [17]Jesus said to her, "Do not hold on to me, because I have not yet ascended to the Father. But go to my brothers and say to them, 'I am ascending to my Father and your Father, to my God and your God.'" [18]Mary Magdalene went and announced to the disciples, "I have seen the Lord"; and she told them that he had said these things to her.

Jesus Appears to the Disciples

19 When it was evening on that day, the first day of the week, and the doors of the house where the disciples had met were locked for fear of the Jews, Jesus came and stood among them and said, "Peace be with you." [20]After he said this, he showed them his hands and his side. Then the disciples rejoiced when they saw the Lord [21]Jesus said to them again, "Peace be with you. As the Father has sent me, so I send you." [22]When he had said this, he breathed on them and said to them, "Receive the Holy Spirit. [23]If you forgive the sins of any, they are forgiven them; if you retain the sins of any, they are retained."

Jesus and Thomas

24 But Thomas (who was called the Twin[k]), one of the twelve, was not with them when Jesus came. [25]So the other disciples told him, "We have seen the Lord." But he said to them, "Unless I see the mark of the nails in his hands, and put my finger in the mark of the nails and my hand in his side, I will not believe."

26 A week later his disciples were again in the house, and Thomas was with them. Although the doors were shut, Jesus came and stood among them and said, "Peace be with you." [27]Then he said to Thomas, "Put your finger here and see my hands. Reach out your hand and put it in my side. Do not doubt but believe." [28]Thomas answered him, "My Lord and my God!" [29]Jesus said to him, "Have you believed because you have seen me? Blessed are those who have not seen and yet have come to believe."

The Purpose of This Book

30 Now Jesus did many other signs in the presence of his disciples, which are not written in this book. [31]But these are written so that you may

---

[j] That is, *Aramaic*   [k] Gk *Didymus*

A Change of Heart and Mind
Whatever happened to the "Son of Thunder"?

> This is the disciple who is testifying to these things and has written them, and we know that his testimony is true. 21.24

THE DISCIPLE JOHN HAD BEEN favored to share private moments with Jesus. As part of an inner circle of three, he saw Jesus transfigured, watched him bring Jairus's daughter back to life, and waited for him in the Garden of Gethsemane.

After Jesus was arrested, John witnessed the sequence of his trials. He was the only disciple mentioned as being near the cross at Jesus' death and one of the very first to learn of Christ's resurrection. Somehow, this process changed John.

From Thunder to Love

John wore an amusing nickname, "Son of Thunder" (Mark 3.17), and several incidents in the Gospels hint that this name reflected his stormy personality. John jealously resented competition from rival miracle workers (Mark 9.38), and he insisted on the best seat in the kingdom of heaven for himself. Once, he wanted to call fire down from heaven to destroy a hostile town (Luke 9.54).

Somewhere in his life, the thunderclouds broke apart. Eventually he got a new nickname: "the apostle of love." John's books—this Gospel and the letters John wrote later—are marked by a recurring emphasis on love.

Naturally, John's spiritual pilgrimage influenced his written record of Jesus' life. His changed personality may provide a clue to his unique style of telling Jesus' story through a handful of poignant episodes. Perhaps these few scenes are the memories of Jesus that finally convinced John himself that Jesus was, indeed, the Son of God.

Life Questions: Getting to know Jesus changes a person. How have you been changed?

come to believe[l] that Jesus is the Messiah,[m] the Son of God, and that through believing you may have life in his name.

20.25 Doubting Thomas

The skeptical Thomas is sometimes singled out, as though he had unusual doubts. In reality, none of the disciples believed in Jesus' resurrection until they saw him for themselves. Thomas had been absent, though, when Jesus first appeared to the others. He stayed skeptical until Jesus appeared again, and summoned Thomas to touch him. Seeing was believing for all the disciples, but Jesus specially commended those who believed without such firsthand evidence.

Jesus Appears to Seven Disciples

21 After these things Jesus showed himself again to the disciples by the Sea of Tiberias; and he showed himself in this way. 2Gathered there together were Simon Peter, Thomas called the Twin,[n] Nathanael of Cana in Galilee, the sons of Zebedee, and two others of his disciples. 3Simon Peter said to them, "I am going fishing." They said to him, "We will go with you." They went out and got into the boat, but that night they caught nothing.

4 Just after daybreak, Jesus stood on the beach; but the disciples did not know that it was Jesus. 5Jesus said to them, "Children, you have no fish, have you?" They answered him, "No." 6He said to them, "Cast the net to the right side of the boat, and you will find some." So they cast it, and now they were not able to haul it in because there were so many fish. 7That disciple whom Jesus loved said to Peter, "It is the Lord!" When Simon Peter heard that it was the Lord, he put on some clothes, for he was naked, and jumped into the sea. 8But the other disciples came in the boat, dragging the net full of fish, for they were not far from the land, only about a hundred yards[o] off.

9 When they had gone ashore, they saw a charcoal fire there, with fish on it, and bread. 10Jesus said to them, "Bring some of the fish that you have just caught." 11So Simon Peter went aboard and hauled the net ashore, full of large fish, a hundred fifty-three of them; and though there were so many, the net was not torn. 12Jesus said to them, "Come and have breakfast." Now none of the disciples dared to ask him, "Who are you?" because they knew it was the Lord. 13Jesus came and took the bread and gave it to them, and did the same with the fish. 14This was now the third time that Jesus appeared to the disciples after he was raised from the dead.

Jesus and Peter

15 When they had finished breakfast, Jesus said to Simon Peter, "Simon son of John, do you love me more than these?" He said to him, "Yes, Lord; you know that I love you." Jesus said to him, "Feed my lambs." 16A second time he said to him, "Simon son of John, do you love me?" He said to him, "Yes, Lord; you know that I love you." Jesus said to him, "Tend my sheep." 17He said to him the third time, "Simon son of John, do you love me?" Peter felt hurt because he said to him the third time, "Do you love me?" And he said to him, "Lord, you know everything; you know that I love you." Jesus said to him, "Feed my sheep. 18Very truly, I tell you, when you were younger, you used to fasten your own belt and to go wherever you wished. But when you grow old, you will stretch out your hands, and someone else will fasten a belt around you and take you where you do not wish to go." 19(He said this to indicate the kind of death by which he would glorify God.) After this he said to him, "Follow me."

21.15 Do You Love Me?

John ends his book with a moving scene in which Jesus spoke to Peter and "the disciple whom Jesus loved," presumably John himself. Jesus asked Peter the same question three times, a painful reminder of Peter's three denials of him. But this reinstatement helped embolden Peter to become one of the early church's most fearless spokesmen.

Jesus and the Beloved Disciple

20 Peter turned and saw the disciple whom Jesus loved following them; he was the one who had reclined next to Jesus at the supper and had said, "Lord, who is it that is going to betray you?" 21When Peter saw him, he said to Jesus, "Lord, what about him?" 22Jesus said to him, "If it is my will that he remain until I come, what is that to you? Follow me!" 23So the rumor spread in the community[p] that this disciple would not die. Yet Jesus did not say to him that he would not die, but, "If it is my will that he remain until I come, what is that to you?"[q]

24 This is the disciple who is testifying to these things and has written them, and we know that his testimony is true. 25But there are also many other things that Jesus did; if every one of them were written down, I suppose that the world itself could not contain the books that would be written.

---

[l] Other ancient authorities read *may continue to believe*   [m] Or *the Christ*   [n] Gk *Didymus*   [o] Gk *two hundred cubits*   [p] Gk *among the brothers*   [q] Other ancient authorities lack *what is that to you*

ACTS

The Linking Book
Imagine a Bible without the book of Acts

> "You will receive power when the Holy Spirit has come upon you; and you will be my witnesses." 1.8

THE NEW TESTAMENT DIVIDES NEATLY into two nearly equal sections. The first consists of four Gospels that tell about Jesus' life on earth. The second section, beginning with Romans, concerns churches that sprang up after Jesus left. In between stands the book of Acts.

The best way to appreciate Acts is to imagine a Bible without it. You have just read the life of Jesus, underscored by four different authors, and you turn to Romans: "Paul, a servant of Jesus Christ, . . . to all God's beloved in Rome, who are called to be saints." Rome? How did the story get there from Jerusalem?

Next you'd find two books, also from Paul (who's he?), addressed to "the church of God that is in Corinth." Another book follows, written to the church in Galatia, then one to Ephesus, and so on with more letters to other exotic locales. Obviously, something is missing. Without Acts, the New Testament leaps from an orderly history of one man, Jesus, to a collection of unexplained personal correspondence.

A Plan Revealed by Jesus

With Acts, everything fits into place. This book gives a transition from the life of Christ to the new church. It introduces Paul and explains how a minority religion crossed the sea to Rome, the capital of the empire. A reader of Acts visits key cities sprinkled around the Mediterranean, meets the principal leaders of the new movement, and gets a strong scent of the problems that will occupy Paul's letters.

Luke, a physician, had written the third Gospel as an account of "all that Jesus did and taught" (Acts 1.1). The book of Acts resumes the story, hinting that this history, too, will show Jesus at work, but in a quite different form. "I will build my church," Jesus had promised (Matthew 16.18), and Acts graphically shows how that process began.

Jesus himself had laid out the plot in his last recorded words on earth: "You will be my witnesses in Jerusalem, in all Judea and Samaria, and to the ends of the earth" (1.8). Acts faithfully follows that outline: The first seven chapters show the church in Jerusalem, the next five focus on Judea and Samaria, and the rest of the book follows the spread of the gospel to the outposts of Roman civilization.

Boisterous Beginnings

The book opens in Jerusalem, during the Pentecost holiday. Over a million pilgrims were milling about the city when suddenly a group of 120 believers came alive. Jesus' followers hit the streets with a bold new style, and 3,000 joined up on the first day alone. Starting with that boisterous scene, Luke spins a historical adventure tale.

Due to Luke's writing skill, Acts reads like a novel, skipping from one exhilarating scene to the next. Wherever the apostles went, action swirled, riots erupted, and a small church took root. In an era when new religions were a dime a dozen, the Christian faith became a worldwide phenomenon. Acts tells how.

How to Read Acts

Acts reads like well-written history. It follows a logical plan, includes fascinating details, and focuses on the most dramatic events. In that sense, it is self-explanatory.

The first twelve chapters concentrate mainly on the apostle Peter. The rest of Acts features Paul (also called Saul), and the book explains how he became accepted as the first and foremost Christian missionary. Paul made three extensive trips in Acts, then a final voyage in chains to Rome (see map, "Paul's Missionary Journeys," at the back of this Bible).

Acts records the early history of relations between the church and the Roman empire. It also gives important background information on such cities as Corinth, Ephesus, and Philippi—cities Paul later wrote letters to. The material in Acts will help you understand what Paul is writing about in 1 and 2 Corinthians, Ephesians, Philippians, and the other letters.

Acts also summarizes 18 different speeches by Paul, Peter, and a few others. These speeches make a fascinating study in themselves: The apostles were beginning to interpret the facts of Jesus' life in light of their spiritual significance. As you read them, note how the speakers chose their words and content with the audience in mind, and then note audience reaction.

PEOPLE YOU'LL MEET IN ACTS

STEPHEN (p. 1130)
PHILIP (p. 1134)
CORNELIUS (p. 1138)
BARNABAS (p. 1140)

MARK (JOHN MARK) (p. 1144)
SILAS (p. 1146)
PRISCILLA AND AQUILA (p.1149)
AGRIPPA (p. 1157)

3-TRACK READING PLAN

For an explanation and complete listing of the 3-track reading plan, turn to page 7.

TRACK 1: *Two-Week Courses on the Bible*
The Track 1 reading program on the Life and Teachings of Paul includes six chapters from Acts. See page 7 for a complete listing of this course.

TRACK 2: *An Overview of Acts in 9 Days*
☐ Day 1. Read the Introduction to Acts and then Acts 1, which describes Jesus' last appearance to the disciples.
☐ Day 2. Read about the remarkable events of Pentecost in chapter 2.
☐ Day 3. Chapter 5 gives a glimpse of life in the early Christian church—some good parts and also a tragic scene of failure.
☐ Day 4. Read Acts 9 to learn the details of Saul's conversion.
☐ Day 5. Chapter 16 tells of Paul's dramatic experiences in Philippi, a city that produced one of Paul's favorite churches.
☐ Day 6. Chapter 17 shows Paul on some of the most difficult assignments of his missionary journeys.
☐ Day 7. Read chapter 26, Paul's recounting of his personal story to a king.
☐ Day 8. Read chapter 27, which tells of Paul's shipwreck on the way to Rome.
☐ Day 9. Read chapter 28, which describes Paul's last setting, under house arrest in Rome, where he probably wrote some of his New Testament letters.

Now turn to page 9 for your next Track 2 reading project.

TRACK 3: *All of Acts in 28 Days*
After you have read through Acts, turn to pages 10–14 for your next Track 3 reading project.

☐1 ☐2 ☐3 ☐4 ☐5 ☐6 ☐7 ☐8
☐9 ☐10 ☐11 ☐12 ☐13 ☐14 ☐15 ☐16
☐17 ☐18 ☐19 ☐20 ☐21 ☐22 ☐23 ☐24
☐25 ☐26 ☐27 ☐28

The Promise of the Holy Spirit

1 In the first book, Theophilus, I wrote about all that Jesus did and taught from the beginning ²until the day when he was taken up to heaven, after giving instructions through the Holy Spirit to the apostles whom he had chosen. ³After his suffering he presented himself alive to them by many convincing proofs, appearing to them during forty days and speaking about the kingdom of God. ⁴While staying*a* with them, he ordered them not to leave Jerusalem, but to wait there for the promise of the Father. "This," he said, "is what you have heard from me; ⁵for John baptized with water, but you will be baptized with*b* the Holy Spirit not many days from now."

The Ascension of Jesus

6 So when they had come together, they asked him, "Lord, is this the time when you will restore the kingdom to Israel?" ⁷He replied, "It is not for you to know the times or periods that the Father has set by his own authority. ⁸But you will receive power when the Holy Spirit has come upon you; and you will be my witnesses in Jerusalem, in all Judea and Samaria, and to the ends of the earth." ⁹When he had said this, as they were watching, he was lifted up, and a cloud took him out of their sight. ¹⁰While he was going and they were gazing up toward heaven, suddenly two men in white robes stood by them. ¹¹They said, "Men of Galilee, why do you stand looking up toward heaven? This Jesus, who has been taken up from you into heaven, will come in the same way as you saw him go into heaven."

Matthias Chosen to Replace Judas

12 Then they returned to Jerusalem from the mount called Olivet, which is near Jerusalem, a sabbath day's journey away. ¹³When they had entered the city, they went to the room upstairs where they were staying, Peter, and John, and James, and Andrew, Philip and Thomas, Bartholomew and Matthew, James son of Alphaeus, and Simon the Zealot, and Judas son of*c* James. ¹⁴All these were constantly devoting themselves to prayer, together with certain women, including Mary the mother of Jesus, as well as his brothers.

15 In those days Peter stood up among the believers*d* (together the crowd numbered about one hundred twenty persons) and said, ¹⁶"Friends,*e* the scripture had to be fulfilled, which the Holy Spirit through David foretold concerning Judas, who became a guide for those who arrested Jesus— ¹⁷for he was numbered among us and was allotted his share in this ministry." ¹⁸(Now this man acquired a field with the reward of his wickedness; and falling headlong,*f* he burst open in the middle and all his bowels gushed out. ¹⁹This became known to all the residents of Jerusalem, so that the field was called in their language Hakeldama, that is, Field of Blood.) ²⁰"For it is written in the book of Psalms,

'Let his homestead become desolate,
     and let there be no one to live in it';

and

'Let another take his position of overseer.'

²¹So one of the men who have accompanied us during all the time that the Lord Jesus went in and

1.21 Inner Circle

The group of Jesus' closest disciples known as the twelve became "the eleven" after Judas's death. In choosing a replacement for the betrayer, the disciples favored an old-timer who had been with Jesus from the very beginning. Evidently several people qualified, and the group cast lots between two to make the final choice. This is the Bible's last mention of casting lots, a method used in the Old Testament to discern God's will; after Pentecost the disciples relied directly on the Holy Spirit for guidance.

out among us, ²²beginning from the baptism of John until the day when he was taken up from us—one of these must become a witness with us to his resurrection." ²³So they proposed two, Joseph called Barsabbas, who was also known as Justus, and Matthias. ²⁴Then they prayed and said, "Lord, you know everyone's heart. Show us which one of these two you have chosen ²⁵to take the place*g* in this ministry and apostleship from which Judas turned aside to go to his own place." ²⁶And they cast lots for them, and the lot fell on Matthias; and he was added to the eleven apostles.

The Coming of the Holy Spirit

2 When the day of Pentecost had come, they were all together in one place. ²And suddenly from heaven there came a sound like the rush of a violent wind, and it filled the entire house where they were sitting. ³Divided tongues, as of fire, appeared among them, and a tongue rested on each of them. ⁴All of them were filled with the Holy Spirit and began to speak in other languages, as the Spirit gave them ability.

5 Now there were devout Jews from every nation under heaven living in Jerusalem. ⁶And at this sound the crowd gathered and was bewildered, because each one heard them speaking in the native language of each. ⁷Amazed and astonished, they asked, "Are not all these who are speaking Galileans? ⁸And how is it that we hear, each of us, in our own native language? ⁹Parthi-

---

a Or *eating*   *b* Or *by*   *c* Or *the brother of*   *d* Gk *brothers*   *e* Gk *Men, brothers*   *f* Or *swelling up*
g Other ancient authorities read *the share*

ans, Medes, Elamites, and residents of Mesopotamia, Judea and Cappadocia, Pontus and Asia, [10]Phrygia and Pamphylia, Egypt and the parts of Libya belonging to Cyrene, and visitors from Rome, both Jews and proselytes, [11]Cretans and Arabs—in our own languages we hear them speaking about God's deeds of power." [12]All were amazed and perplexed, saying to one another, "What does this mean?" [13]But others sneered and said, "They are filled with new wine."

Peter Addresses the Crowd

14 But Peter, standing with the eleven, raised his voice and addressed them, "Men of Judea and all who live in Jerusalem, let this be known to you, and listen to what I say. [15]Indeed, these are not drunk, as you suppose, for it is only nine o'clock in the morning. [16]No, this is what was spoken through the prophet Joel:

[17] 'In the last days it will be, God declares,
    that I will pour out my Spirit upon all
      flesh,
    and your sons and your daughters shall
      prophesy,
    and your young men shall see visions,
    and your old men shall dream dreams.
[18] Even upon my slaves, both men and
      women,
    in those days I will pour out my Spirit;
      and they shall prophesy.
[19] And I will show portents in the heaven
      above
    and signs on the earth below,
      blood, and fire, and smoky mist.
[20] The sun shall be turned to darkness
    and the moon to blood,
      before the coming of the Lord's
      great and glorious day.
[21] Then everyone who calls on the name of
      the Lord shall be saved.'

22 "You that are Israelites,[h] listen to what I have to say: Jesus of Nazareth,[i] a man attested to you by God with deeds of power, wonders, and signs that God did through him among you, as you yourselves know— [23]this man, handed over to you according to the definite plan and foreknowledge of God, you crucified and killed by the hands of those outside the law. [24]But God raised him up, having freed him from death,[j] because it was impossible for him to be held in its power. [25]For David says concerning him,

'I saw the Lord always before me,
    for he is at my right hand so that I will
      not be shaken;
[26] therefore my heart was glad, and my
      tongue rejoiced;
    moreover my flesh will live in hope.

[27] For you will not abandon my soul to
      Hades,
    or let your Holy One experience
      corruption.
[28] You have made known to me the ways of
      life;
    you will make me full of gladness with
      your presence.'

29 "Fellow Israelites,[k] I may say to you confidently of our ancestor David that he both died and was buried, and his tomb is with us to this day. [30]Since he was a prophet, he knew that God had sworn with an oath to him that he would put one of his descendants on his throne. [31]Foreseeing this, David[l] spoke of the resurrection of the Messiah,[m] saying,

'He was not abandoned to Hades,
    nor did his flesh experience
      corruption.'

[32]This Jesus God raised up, and of that all of us are witnesses. [33]Being therefore exalted at[n] the right hand of God, and having received from the Father the promise of the Holy Spirit, he has poured out this that you both see and hear. [34]For David did not ascend into the heavens, but he himself says,

'The Lord said to my Lord,
    "Sit at my right hand,
[35]   until I make your enemies your
      footstool." '

[36]Therefore let the entire house of Israel know with certainty that God has made him both Lord and Messiah,[o] this Jesus whom you crucified."

The First Converts

37 Now when they heard this, they were cut to the heart and said to Peter and to the other apostles, "Brothers,[k] what should we do?" [38]Peter said to them, "Repent, and be baptized every one of you in the name of Jesus Christ so that your sins may be forgiven; and you will receive the gift of the Holy Spirit. [39]For the promise is for you, for your children, and for all who are far away, everyone whom the Lord our God calls to him." [40]And he testified with many other arguments

2.42 Infant Church

Acts records a series of stages through which the Christian church became a separate movement. At this point, the followers of Jesus were still keeping the pattern of traditional Jewish worship: prayers in the temple at 9 A.M., 3 P.M., and sunset (3.1). Yet this paragraph shows them also developing a new form of "house churches" based on communal sharing and fellowship.

---

[h] Gk *Men, Israelites*   [i] Gk *the Nazorean*   [j] Gk *the pains of death*   [k] Gk *Men, brothers*   [l] Gk *he*   [m] Or *the*
Christ   [n] Or *by*   [o] Or *Christ*

and exhorted them, saying, "Save yourselves from
this corrupt generation." 41 So those who welcomed
his message were baptized, and that day about
three thousand persons were added. 42 They devoted
themselves to the apostles' teaching and fellowship,
to the breaking of bread and the prayers.

Life among the Believers

43 Awe came upon everyone, because many
wonders and signs were being done by the apostles. 44 All who believed were together and had all
things in common; 45 they would sell their possessions and goods and distribute the proceeds[p] to
all, as any had need. 46 Day by day, as they spent
much time together in the temple, they broke
bread at home[q] and ate their food with glad and
generous[r] hearts, 47 praising God and having the
goodwill of all the people. And day by day the
Lord added to their number those who were being saved.

Peter Heals a Crippled Beggar

3 One day Peter and John were going up to the
temple at the hour of prayer, at three o'clock

[p] Gk *them* [q] Or *from house to house* [r] Or *sincere*

More than a Ghost

The best proof that Jesus is alive

> ***"You killed the Author of life, whom God raised from the dead. To this we are witnesses." 3.15***

"HE LOOKS AS IF HE'S seen a ghost!" What image comes to mind when you hear that? A face drained of blood, a trembling jaw, pasty skin and thin lips, a look of terror.

Seeing a ghost doesn't make a person stronger and more confident. The witness is usually reluctant to talk about the experience. Self-doubt attacks in waves: *Was it real? Maybe I was hallucinating . . . it was so dark and eerie.*

A Convincing Change

When Jesus showed up after his death, his disciples went through a did-we-see-a-ghost? phase, complete with terror, disbelief, and wild rumors. But it didn't last long. In 40 days Jesus made enough undeniable appearances to convince each of his disciples—even skeptical Thomas—that he had indeed overthrown death.

As Acts shows, the disciples began acting the opposite of people who think they've seen a ghost. Rather, they acted like people who had just witnessed the most astounding event in all history. They couldn't wait to tell the world about it.

Exuberance, not fear, lit up the disciples' faces. In the streets of Jerusalem and in the temple, to anyone who would listen, they cried out the news that couldn't be true, but was. "Jesus is alive! The man who died has come back—he's the Messiah we've been waiting for!"

If you're ever tempted to doubt Jesus' resurrection, take a sober look at his changed followers in Acts. Consider Peter, for instance. He had cowered in the shadows at the trial scene, trying to look inconspicuous. Out of fear of arrest, he had even cursed and denied knowing Jesus. Could this be the same man, standing before the most distinguished religious leaders in the land, blasting them as murderers (chapter 3)? Something ignited Peter that would not easily be snuffed out.

Response to a New Message

When Jesus was on earth he mostly preached "the kingdom," sometimes even warning his followers not to mention he was the Messiah. In Acts, the word is out. Jesus is the theme of every speech, whether delivered in the temple square or in the luxurious setting of a royal palace, to working-class pagans or cultured Greek philosophers. Reports of his resurrection resound throughout Acts.

To those who heard, the message sounded like the first note of music to people born deaf. Five thousand men believed (4.4), as did many priests (6.7) and many thousands of Jews (21.20). The scanty band of followers Jesus had left behind was soon organizing and electing officers to handle the needs of a growing church.

Acts follows the core of leaders from place to place, as a remarkable drama unfolds. A few men, mostly unlearned, were setting into motion a worldwide outreach that would ultimately reshape civilization. A revolution was underway, but not one with weapons. This one was powered by the work of God in simple men who had seen a miracle. As Peter said, "We cannot keep from speaking about what we have seen and heard" (4.20).

Life Questions: The disciples led mass conversions to Christ. What made them such effective spokesmen?

in the afternoon. ²And a man lame from birth was being carried in. People would lay him daily at the gate of the temple called the Beautiful Gate so that he could ask for alms from those entering the temple. ³When he saw Peter and John about to go into the temple, he asked them for alms. ⁴Peter looked intently at him, as did John, and said, "Look at us." ⁵And he fixed his attention on them, expecting to receive something from them. ⁶But Peter said, "I have no silver or gold, but what I have I give you; in the name of Jesus Christ of Nazareth,ˢ stand up and walk." ⁷And he took him by the right hand and raised him up; and immediately his feet and ankles were made strong. ⁸Jumping up, he stood and began to walk, and he entered the temple with them, walking and leaping and praising God. ⁹All the people saw him walking and praising God, ¹⁰and they recognized him as the one who used to sit and ask for alms at the Beautiful Gate of the temple; and they were filled with wonder and amazement at what had happened to him.

Peter Speaks in Solomon's Portico

11 While he clung to Peter and John, all the people ran together to them in the portico called Solomon's Portico, utterly astonished. ¹²When Peter saw it, he addressed the people, "You Israel-ites,ᵗ why do you wonder at this, or why do you stare at us, as though by our own power or piety we had made him walk? ¹³The God of Abraham, the God of Isaac, and the God of Jacob, the God of our ancestors has glorified his servantᵘ Jesus, whom you handed over and rejected in the presence of Pilate, though he had decided to release him. ¹⁴But you rejected the Holy and Righteous One and asked to have a murderer given to you, ¹⁵and you killed the Author of life, whom God raised from the dead. To this we are witnesses. ¹⁶And by faith in his name, his name itself has made this man strong, whom you see and know; and the faith that is through Jesusᵛ has given him

this perfect health in the presence of all of you. 17 "And now, friends,ʷ I know that you acted in ignorance, as did also your rulers. ¹⁸In this way God fulfilled what he had foretold through all the prophets, that his Messiahˣ would suffer. ¹⁹Repent therefore, and turn to God so that your sins may be wiped out, ²⁰so that times of refreshing may come from the presence of the Lord, and that he may send the Messiahʸ appointed for you, that is, Jesus, ²¹who must remain in heaven until the time of universal restoration that God announced long ago through his holy prophets. ²²Moses said, 'The Lord your God will raise up for you from your own peopleʷ a prophet like me. You must listen to whatever he tells you. ²³And it will be that everyone who does not listen to that prophet will be utterly rooted out of the people.' ²⁴And all the prophets, as many as have spoken, from Samuel and those after him, also predicted these days. ²⁵You are the descendants of the prophets and of the covenant that God gave to your ancestors, saying to Abraham, 'And in your descendants all the families of the earth shall be blessed.' ²⁶When God raised up his servant,ᵘ he sent him first to you, to bless you by turning each of you from your wicked ways."

Peter and John before the Council

4 While Peter and Johnᶻ were speaking to the people, the priests, the captain of the temple,

4.1 Alarmed Sadducees

The coalition arrayed against the disciples resembled the group that had arrested Jesus in Gethsemane. The priests were working hand in hand with Roman rulers, who allowed them to maintain a police force to keep order in the temple. Reports of Jesus' resurrection from the dead especially alarmed the Sadducees, a party of priests who denied there would ever be a resurrection from the dead (see also 5.17 and 23.6–8).

and the Sadducees came to them, ²much annoyed because they were teaching the people and proclaiming that in Jesus there is the resurrection of the dead. ³So they arrested them and put them in custody until the next day, for it was already evening. ⁴But many of those who heard the word believed; and they numbered about five thousand.

5 The next day their rulers, elders, and scribes assembled in Jerusalem, ⁶with Annas the high priest, Caiaphas, John,ᵃ and Alexander, and all who were of the high-priestly family. ⁷When they had made the prisonersᵇ stand in their midst,

3.12 Knowing the Audience

Peter's speeches in chapters 2 and 3 offer excellent examples of adapting the gospel message to a particular audience. Preaching to Jews gathered in Jerusalem to celebrate Pentecost, he relied heavily on quotations from the Old Testament. Although his main intent was to tell them about Jesus, he referred to Joel, David, Abraham, Isaac, Jacob, Moses, and Samuel. His words proved so effective that 3,000 people were converted the first day. Jewish leaders soon arrested Peter and John.

ˢ Gk the Nazorean   ᵗ Gk Men, Israelites   ᵘ Or child   ᵛ Gk him   ʷ Gk brothers   ˣ Or his Christ
ʸ Or the Christ   ᶻ Gk While they   ᵃ Other ancient authorities read Jonathan   ᵇ Gk them

they inquired, "By what power or by what name did you do this?" [8]Then Peter, filled with the Holy Spirit, said to them, "Rulers of the people and elders, [9]if we are questioned today because of a good deed done to someone who was sick and was asked how this man has been healed, [10]let it be known to all of you, and to all the people of Israel, that this man is standing before you in good health by the name of Jesus Christ of Nazareth,[c] whom you crucified, whom God raised from the dead. [11]This Jesus[d] is

'the stone that was rejected by you, the builders;
　　　it has become the cornerstone.'[e]

[12]There is salvation in no one else, for there is no other name under heaven given among mortals by which we must be saved."

13　Now when they saw the boldness of Peter and John and realized that they were uneducated and ordinary men, they were amazed and recognized them as companions of Jesus. [14]When they saw the man who had been cured standing beside them, they had nothing to say in opposition. [15]So they ordered them to leave the council while they discussed the matter with one another. [16]They said, "What will we do with them? For it is obvious to all who live in Jerusalem that a notable sign has been done through them; we cannot deny it. [17]But to keep it from spreading further among the people, let us warn them to speak no more to anyone in this name." [18]So they called them and ordered them not to speak or teach at all in the name of Jesus. [19]But Peter and John answered them, "Whether it is right in God's sight to listen to you rather than to God, you must judge; [20]for we cannot keep from speaking about what we have seen and heard." [21]After threatening them again, they let them go, finding no way to punish them because of the people, for all of them praised God for what had happened. [22]For the man on whom this sign of healing had been performed was more than forty years old.

The Believers Pray for Boldness

23　After they were released, they went to their friends[f] and reported what the chief priests and the elders had said to them. [24]When they heard it, they raised their voices together to God and said, "Sovereign Lord, who made the heaven and the earth, the sea, and everything in them, [25]it is you who said by the Holy Spirit through our ancestor David, your servant:[g]

'Why did the Gentiles rage,
　　　and the peoples imagine vain things?
26　The kings of the earth took their stand,
　　　and the rulers have gathered together
　　　　　against the Lord and against his
　　　　　　　　Messiah.'[h]

[27]For in this city, in fact, both Herod and Pontius Pilate, with the Gentiles and the peoples of Israel, gathered together against your holy servant[g] Jesus, whom you anointed, [28]to do whatever your hand and your plan had predestined to take place. [29]And now, Lord, look at their threats, and grant to your servants[i] to speak your word with all boldness, [30]while you stretch out your hand to heal, and signs and wonders are performed through the name of your holy servant[g] Jesus." [31]When they had prayed, the place in which they were gathered together was shaken; and they were all filled with the Holy Spirit and spoke the word of God with boldness.

The Believers Share Their Possessions

32　Now the whole group of those who believed were of one heart and soul, and no one claimed private ownership of any possessions, but everything they owned was held in common. [33]With great power the apostles gave their testimony to the resurrection of the Lord Jesus, and great grace was upon them all. [34]There was not a needy person among them, for as many as owned lands or houses sold them and brought the proceeds of what was sold. [35]They laid it at the apostles' feet, and it was distributed to each as any had need. [36]There was a Levite, a native of Cyprus, Joseph, to whom the apostles gave the name Barnabas (which means "son of encouragement"). [37]He sold a field that belonged to him, then brought the money, and laid it at the apostles' feet.

Ananias and Sapphira

5　But a man named Ananias, with the consent of his wife Sapphira, sold a piece of property; [2]with his wife's knowledge, he kept back some of the proceeds, and brought only a part and laid it at the apostles' feet. [3]"Ananias," Peter asked, "why has Satan filled your heart to lie to the Holy Spirit and to keep back part of the proceeds of the land? [4]While it remained unsold, did it not remain your own? And after it was sold, were not the proceeds at your disposal? How is it that you have contrived this deed in your heart? You did

5.4 Deadly Deceit

As Peter makes clear, Ananias and Sapphira were punished not for holding back money but for lying about it. They were misrepresenting themselves spiritually, trying to appear especially pious and generous. At the very beginning of the church (the word first appears in Acts in verse 11), God set a stern standard of absolute honesty and integrity.

---

[c] Gk *the Nazorean*　　[d] Gk *This*　　[e] Or *keystone*　　[f] Gk *their own*　　[g] Or *child*　　[h] Or *his Christ*　　[i] Gk *slaves*

not lie to us,ʲ but to God!" ⁵Now when Ananias heard these words, he fell down and died. And great fear seized all who heard of it. ⁶The young men came and wrapped up his body,ᵏ then carried him out and buried him.

7 After an interval of about three hours his wife came in, not knowing what had happened. ⁸Peter said to her, "Tell me whether you and your husband sold the land for such and such a price." And she said, "Yes, that was the price." ⁹Then Peter said to her, "How is it that you have agreed together to put the Spirit of the Lord to the test? Look, the feet of those who have buried your husband are at the door, and they will carry you out." ¹⁰Immediately she fell down at his feet and died. When the young men came in they found her dead, so they carried her out and buried her beside her husband. ¹¹And great fear seized the whole church and all who heard of these things.

The Apostles Heal Many

12 Now many signs and wonders were done among the people through the apostles. And they were all together in Solomon's Portico. ¹³None of the rest dared to join them, but the people held them in high esteem. ¹⁴Yet more than ever believers were added to the Lord, great numbers of both men and women, ¹⁵so that they even carried out the sick into the streets, and laid them on cots and mats, in order that Peter's shadow might fall on some of them as he came by. ¹⁶A great number of people would also gather from the towns around Jerusalem, bringing the sick and those tormented by unclean spirits, and they were all cured.

The Apostles Are Persecuted

17 Then the high priest took action; he and all who were with him (that is, the sect of the Sadducees), being filled with jealousy, ¹⁸arrested the apostles and put them in the public prison. ¹⁹But during the night an angel of the Lord opened the prison doors, brought them out, and said, ²⁰"Go, stand in the temple and tell the people the whole

ʲ Gk to men   ᵏ Meaning of Gk uncertain

The Secret to the Early Church
The real power at work in Acts

AUTHOR J.B. PHILLIPS, AFTER SPENDING 14 years translating the New Testament, sat back and reflected on his most lasting impressions. He kept returning to the book of Acts and its portrait of an infant church. "The sick are not merely prayed about," said Phillips, "they are healed, often suddenly and dramatically.... Human nature is changed. The fresh air of Heaven blows gustily through these pages.

"The early church lived dangerously, but never before has such a handful of people exerted such widespread influence.... To put it shortly, the lasting excitement which follows the reading of the book is this: *the thing works!*"

Who Was behind the Success?

Why did it work? Acts points decisively to the power of God, through his Holy Spirit. Luke carefully notes that every major decision of the young church was made under the Spirit's guidance. Indeed, some have suggested Acts should really be titled *Acts of the Holy Spirit* because of his dominant role. Luke mentions the Holy Spirit 57 times in Acts.

The disciples waited on the Spirit in Jerusalem before beginning to preach (2.4). According to Luke, the Holy Spirit fell on each new group of believers: on Jews (4.31), then on Samaritans (8.17), then on Gentiles (10.44), and finally on John the Baptist's disciples (19.6).

For Their Good

As the church grew, the disciples gradually began to understand what Jesus had meant when he said, "It is to your advantage that I go away, for if I do not go away, the Advocate will not come to you; but if I go, I will send him to you" (John 16.7). Although Jesus himself departed, God became present in each one of them, making his activity in the world more widespread than ever before.

The Spirit personally directed each major advance of the church. He sent Philip into the desert to meet an Ethiopian (8.29), set apart missionaries in Antioch (13.2), guided the first big church council (15.1–28), and helped plan Paul's itinerary (13.4; 16.6). As presented in Acts, the Spirit was no vague mist but a living person who spoke, guided in decisions, and fueled the church with the energy of faith.

Life Questions: How is the Holy Spirit active in your life?

> "Keep away from these men and let them alone; because if this plan or this undertaking is of human origin, it will fail; but if it is of God, you will not be able to overthrow them—in that case you may even be found fighting against God!"
> 5.38–39

message about this life." [21]When they heard this, they entered the temple at daybreak and went on with their teaching.

When the high priest and those with him arrived, they called together the council and the whole body of the elders of Israel, and sent to the prison to have them brought. [22]But when the temple police went there, they did not find them in the prison; so they returned and reported, [23]"We found the prison securely locked and the guards standing at the doors, but when we opened them, we found no one inside." [24]Now when the captain of the temple and the chief priests heard these words, they were perplexed about them, wondering what might be going on. [25]Then someone arrived and announced, "Look, the men whom you put in prison are standing in the temple and teaching the people!" [26]Then the captain went with the temple police and brought them, but without violence, for they were afraid of being stoned by the people.

27 When they had brought them, they had them stand before the council. The high priest questioned them, [28]saying, "We gave you strict orders not to teach in this name,[l] yet here you have filled Jerusalem with your teaching and you are determined to bring this man's blood on us." [29]But Peter and the apostles answered, "We must obey God rather than any human authority.[m] [30]The God of our ancestors raised up Jesus, whom you had killed by hanging him on a tree. [31]God exalted him at his right hand as Leader and Savior that he might give repentance to Israel and forgiveness of sins. [32]And we are witnesses to these things, and so is the Holy Spirit whom God has given to those who obey him."

33 When they heard this, they were enraged and wanted to kill them. [34]But a Pharisee in the council named Gamaliel, a teacher of the law, respected by all the people, stood up and ordered

the men to be put outside for a short time. [35]Then he said to them, "Fellow Israelites,[n] consider carefully what you propose to do to these men. [36]For some time ago Theudas rose up, claiming to be somebody, and a number of men, about four hundred, joined him; but he was killed, and all who followed him were dispersed and disappeared. [37]After him Judas the Galilean rose up at the time of the census and got people to follow him; he also perished, and all who followed him were scattered. [38]So in the present case, I tell you, keep away from these men and let them alone; because if this plan or this undertaking is of human origin, it will fail; [39]but if it is of God, you will not be able to overthrow them—in that case you may even be found fighting against God!"

They were convinced by him, [40]and when they had called in the apostles, they had them flogged. Then they ordered them not to speak in the name of Jesus, and let them go. [41]As they left the council, they rejoiced that they were considered worthy to suffer dishonor for the sake of the name. [42]And every day in the temple and at home[o] they did not cease to teach and proclaim Jesus as the Messiah.[p]

Seven Chosen to Serve

6 Now during those days, when the disciples were increasing in number, the Hellenists complained against the Hebrews because their widows were being neglected in the daily distribution of food. [2]And the twelve called together the whole community of the disciples and said, "It is not right that we should neglect the word of God in order to wait on tables.[q] [3]Therefore, friends,[r] select from among yourselves seven men of good standing, full of the Spirit and of wisdom, whom we may appoint to this task, [4]while we, for our part, will devote ourselves to prayer and to serving the word." [5]What they said pleased the whole community, and they chose Stephen, a man full of faith and the Holy Spirit, together with Philip, Prochorus, Nicanor, Timon, Parmenas, and Nicolaus, a proselyte of Antioch. [6]They had these men stand before the apostles, who prayed and laid their hands on them.

7 The word of God continued to spread; the number of the disciples increased greatly in Jerusalem, and a great many of the priests became obedient to the faith.

The Arrest of Stephen

8 Stephen, full of grace and power, did great wonders and signs among the people. [9]Then some of those who belonged to the synagogue of the Freedmen (as it was called), Cyrenians, Alexandrians, and others of those from Cilicia and

5.34 Ancient Terrorism

Terrorist acts have had a long history in the Middle East, as Gamaliel's speech shows. During the years surrounding Jesus' life, several revolutionaries had led armed uprisings, two of whom Gamaliel refers to here. Several decades later, the apostle Paul was mistaken for an Egyptian who had staged a terrorist revolt in the desert (21.38).

Gamaliel, who urged a cautious approach on the issue, was a revered and wise rabbi in his day. He followed the progressive branch of Judaism that originated with the rabbi Hillel, and Saul (who became the apostle Paul) was one of his pupils (22.3).

---

[l] Other ancient authorities read *Did we not give you strict orders not to teach in this name?*   [m] Gk *than men*
[n] Gk *Men, Israelites*   [o] Or *from house to house*   [p] Or *the Christ*   [q] Or *keep accounts*   [r] Gk *brothers*

Asia, stood up and argued with Stephen. [10]But they could not withstand the wisdom and the Spirit[s] with which he spoke. [11]Then they secretly instigated some men to say, "We have heard him speak blasphemous words against Moses and God." [12]They stirred up the people as well as the elders and the scribes; then they suddenly confronted him, seized him, and brought him before the council. [13]They set up false witnesses who said, "This man never stops saying things against this holy place and the law; [14]for we have heard him say that this Jesus of Nazareth[t] will destroy this place and will change the customs that Moses handed on to us." [15]And all who sat in the council looked intently at him, and they saw that his face was like the face of an angel.

Stephen's Speech to the Council

7 Then the high priest asked him, "Are these things so?" [2]And Stephen replied:
"Brothers[u] and fathers, listen to me. The God of glory appeared to our ancestor Abraham when he was in Mesopotamia, before he lived in Haran, [3]and said to him, 'Leave your country and your relatives and go to the land that I will show you.' [4]Then he left the country of the Chaldeans and settled in Haran. After his father died, God had him move from there to this country in which you are now living. [5]He did not give him any of it as a heritage, not even a foot's length, but promised to give it to him as his possession and to his descendants after him, even though he had no child. [6]And God spoke in these terms, that his descendants would be resident aliens in a country belonging to others, who would enslave them and mistreat them during four hundred years. [7]'But I will judge the nation that they serve,' said God, 'and after that they shall come out and worship me in this place.' [8]Then he gave him the covenant of circumcision. And so Abraham[v] became the father of Isaac and circumcised him on the eighth day; and Isaac became the father of Jacob, and Jacob of the twelve patriarchs.

9 "The patriarchs, jealous of Joseph, sold him into Egypt; but God was with him, [10]and rescued

> ## 6.5 A Cure for Discrimination
>
> *Early on, the church ran into complaints from a neglected minority, the Grecian Jews, or Hellenists. This branch of Jews retained many Greek customs and chose to speak Greek rather than Hebrew. The disciples' response in creating a new church office shows considerable diplomacy. The names of the seven appointees indicate they were all Grecian Jews. In other words, the disciples entrusted the minority with full authority to solve their own problems. The first Christian martyr, Stephen, came out of that group of seven.*

[s] Or *spirit*   [t] Gk *the Nazorean*   [u] Gk *Men, brothers*   [v] Gk *he*

STEPHEN *Dying to Live*

THOUSANDS OF CHRISTIANS HAVE DIED for their faith over the centuries. Even today Christians are persecuted in countries like Algeria, Iran, Sudan and China. Stephen was the first martyr, setting the standard for all Christians who have come under fire for their faith.

While on trial, Stephen spoke so courageously and clearly that members of the sophisticated Sanhedrin lost all control. They gnashed their teeth, covered their ears and, yelling at the top of their voices, rushed at Stephen in their fury. Then, in a mob action, they stoned him to death.

Stephen had begun his public service for Christ when the apostles chose him, with six others, to make sure that Greek-speaking widows got their fair share of food. As it turned out, he did far more than administrate charity. God gave him the power to do miracles and to speak convincingly to other Greek-speaking Jews.

Stephen angered the religious establishment for some of the same reasons Jesus did. The Jews claimed that he had dishonored their revered temple and the Old Testament Law. There was a shred of truth in the charges. For Stephen, God's grace was greater than any building or any rule book.

At his trial, Stephen presented his case loud and clear. He recast the history of Israel as the story of God saving his people *in spite of* their stubborn resistance. Had anything changed? The very people who most honored the temple and the Law—weren't these the same ones who "betrayed and murdered" Jesus?

Like Jesus, Stephen was tried and executed because he upset the establishment. Like Jesus, he died breathing forgiveness, not condemnation. Even while dying, he prayed for those who stoned him. Stephen's final prayer was answered spectacularly, for a man named Saul stood among the persecutors. As Augustine said, "If Stephen had not prayed, the church would not have had Paul."

Life Questions: How would you react if you were put on trial and asked to justify your faith in Christ? What would you say?

him from all his afflictions, and enabled him to win favor and to show wisdom when he stood before Pharaoh, king of Egypt, who appointed him ruler over Egypt and over all his household. ¹¹Now there came a famine throughout Egypt and Canaan, and great suffering, and our ancestors could find no food. ¹²But when Jacob heard that there was grain in Egypt, he sent our ancestors there on their first visit. ¹³On the second visit Joseph made himself known to his brothers, and Joseph's family became known to Pharaoh. ¹⁴Then Joseph sent and invited his father Jacob and all his relatives to come to him, seventy-five in all; ¹⁵so Jacob went down to Egypt. He himself died there as well as our ancestors, ¹⁶and their bodies*w* were brought back to Shechem and laid in the tomb that Abraham had bought for a sum of silver from the sons of Hamor in Shechem.

17 "But as the time drew near for the fulfillment of the promise that God had made to Abraham, our people in Egypt increased and multiplied ¹⁸until another king who had not known Joseph ruled over Egypt. ¹⁹He dealt craftily with our race and forced our ancestors to abandon their infants so that they would die. ²⁰At this time Moses was born, and he was beautiful before God. For three months he was brought up in his father's house; ²¹and when he was abandoned, Pharaoh's daughter adopted him and brought him up as her own son. ²²So Moses was instructed in all the wisdom of the Egyptians and was powerful in his words and deeds.

23 "When he was forty years old, it came into his heart to visit his relatives, the Israelites.*x* ²⁴When he saw one of them being wronged, he defended the oppressed man and avenged him by striking down the Egyptian. ²⁵He supposed that his kinsfolk would understand that God through him was rescuing them, but they did not understand. ²⁶The next day he came to some of them as they were quarreling and tried to reconcile them, saying, 'Men, you are brothers; why do you wrong each other?' ²⁷But the man who was wronging his neighbor pushed Moses*y* aside, saying, 'Who made you a ruler and a judge over us? ²⁸Do you want to kill me as you killed the Egyptian yesterday?' ²⁹When he heard this, Moses fled and became a resident alien in the land of Midian. There he became the father of two sons.

30 "Now when forty years had passed, an angel appeared to him in the wilderness of Mount Sinai, in the flame of a burning bush. ³¹When Moses saw it, he was amazed at the sight; and as he approached to look, there came the voice of the Lord: ³²'I am the God of your ancestors, the God of Abraham, Isaac, and Jacob.' Moses began to tremble and did not dare to look. ³³Then the Lord said to him, 'Take off the sandals from your feet, for the place where you are standing is holy ground. ³⁴I have surely seen the mistreatment of my people who are in Egypt and have heard their groaning, and I have come down to rescue them. Come now, I will send you to Egypt.'

35 "It was this Moses whom they rejected when they said, 'Who made you a ruler and a judge?' and whom God now sent as both ruler and liberator through the angel who appeared to

7.35 Provocative Words

The early part of Stephen's speech must have pleased his Jewish audience. He was, in effect, giving a capsule view of history from the Jewish point of view, featuring such famous ancestors as Abraham, Joseph, Moses, and David. But then Stephen turned the tables, directly attacking the Jewish establishment.

He compared their treatment of Jesus with earlier Jewish rejection of God's messengers. He also called into question Jewish temple worship, claiming that "the Most High does not dwell in houses made with human hands" (verse 48). He ended the speech by calling them traitors and murderers. Stephen's death and the resulting persecution in Jerusalem scattered the disciples, helping to fulfill what Jesus had predicted just before leaving the earth (1.8).

him in the bush. ³⁶He led them out, having performed wonders and signs in Egypt, at the Red Sea, and in the wilderness for forty years. ³⁷This is the Moses who said to the Israelites, 'God will raise up a prophet for you from your own people*z* as he raised me up.' ³⁸He is the one who was in the congregation in the wilderness with the angel who spoke to him at Mount Sinai, and with our ancestors; and he received living oracles to give to us. ³⁹Our ancestors were unwilling to obey him; instead, they pushed him aside, and in their hearts they turned back to Egypt, ⁴⁰saying to Aaron, 'Make gods for us who will lead the way for us; as for this Moses who led us out from the land of Egypt, we do not know what has happened to him.' ⁴¹At that time they made a calf, offered a sacrifice to the idol, and reveled in the works of their hands. ⁴²But God turned away from them and handed them over to worship the host of heaven, as it is written in the book of the prophets:

'Did you offer to me slain victims and
        sacrifices
    forty years in the wilderness, O house
        of Israel?
⁴³ No; you took along the tent of Moloch,
    and the star of your god Rephan,

---

w Gk *they*   *x* Gk *his brothers, the sons of Israel*   *y* Gk *him*   *z* Gk *your brothers*

the images that you made
to worship;
so I will remove you beyond Babylon.'

44 "Our ancestors had the tent of testimony in the wilderness, as God[a] directed when he spoke to Moses, ordering him to make it according to the pattern he had seen. 45Our ancestors in turn brought it in with Joshua when they dispossessed the nations that God drove out before our ancestors. And it was there until the time of David, 46who found favor with God and asked that he might find a dwelling place for the house of Jacob.[b] 47But it was Solomon who built a house for him. 48Yet the Most High does not dwell in houses made with human hands;[c] as the prophet says,

49 'Heaven is my throne,
and the earth is my footstool.
What kind of house will you build for
me, says the Lord,
or what is the place of my rest?
50 Did not my hand make all these things?'

51 "You stiff-necked people, uncircumcised in heart and ears, you are forever opposing the Holy Spirit, just as your ancestors used to do. 52Which of the prophets did your ancestors not persecute? They killed those who foretold the coming of the Righteous One, and now you have become his betrayers and murderers. 53You are the ones that received the law as ordained by angels, and yet you have not kept it."

The Stoning of Stephen

54 When they heard these things, they became enraged and ground their teeth at Stephen.[d] 55But filled with the Holy Spirit, he gazed into heaven and saw the glory of God and Jesus standing at the right hand of God. 56"Look," he said, "I see the heavens opened and the Son of Man standing at the right hand of God!" 57But they covered their ears, and with a loud shout all rushed together against him. 58Then they dragged him out of the city and began to stone him; and the witnesses laid their coats at the feet of a young man named Saul. 59While they were stoning Stephen, he prayed, "Lord Jesus, receive my spirit." 60Then he knelt down and cried out in a loud voice, "Lord, do not hold this sin against them." 8 When he had said this, he died.[e] 1And Saul approved of their killing him.

Saul Persecutes the Church

That day a severe persecution began against the church in Jerusalem, and all except the apostles were scattered throughout the countryside of Judea and Samaria. 2Devout men buried Stephen and made loud lamentation over him. 3But Saul was ravaging the church by entering house after house; dragging off both men and women, he committed them to prison.

Philip Preaches in Samaria

4 Now those who were scattered went from place to place, proclaiming the word. 5Philip went down to the city[f] of Samaria and proclaimed the

8.5 Crossing Racial Barriers

Philip's visit to Samaria was quite remarkable in its day. Jewish people had little to do with the Samaritans, whom they looked down on for racial and religious reasons. Later, Philip met with an Ethiopian official on a mission that crossed racial barriers. The modern Christian church in Ethiopia claims an uninterrupted descent from the conversion described in chapter 8.

Messiah[g] to them. 6The crowds with one accord listened eagerly to what was said by Philip, hearing and seeing the signs that he did, 7for unclean spirits, crying with loud shrieks, came out of many who were possessed; and many others who were paralyzed or lame were cured. 8So there was great joy in that city.

9 Now a certain man named Simon had previously practiced magic in the city and amazed the people of Samaria, saying that he was someone great. 10All of them, from the least to the greatest, listened to him eagerly, saying, "This man is the power of God that is called Great." 11And they listened eagerly to him because for a long time he had amazed them with his magic. 12But when they believed Philip, who was proclaiming the good news about the kingdom of God and the name of Jesus Christ, they were baptized, both men and women. 13Even Simon himself believed. After being baptized, he stayed constantly with Philip and was amazed when he saw the signs and great miracles that took place.

14 Now when the apostles at Jerusalem heard that Samaria had accepted the word of God, they sent Peter and John to them. 15The two went

8.20 Gospel Greed

The tendency to exploit spiritual power for material profit did not originate with the television age. Simon, a local magician, saw the gospel as a way to increase his own fame. The disciples had no more tolerance for his attitude than they had for the lies of Ananias and Sapphira (Acts 5).

down and prayed for them that they might receive the Holy Spirit [16](for as yet the Spirit had not come[h] upon any of them; they had only been baptized in the name of the Lord Jesus). [17]Then Peter and John[i] laid their hands on them, and they received the Holy Spirit. [18]Now when Simon saw that the Spirit was given through the laying on of the apostles' hands, he offered them money, [19]saying, "Give me also this power so that anyone on whom I lay my hands may receive the Holy Spirit." [20]But Peter said to him, "May your silver perish with you, because you thought you could obtain God's gift with money! [21]You have no part or share in this, for your heart is not right before God. [22]Repent therefore of this wickedness of yours, and pray to the Lord that, if possible, the intent of your heart may be forgiven you. [23]For I

see that you are in the gall of bitterness and the chains of wickedness." [24]Simon answered, "Pray for me to the Lord, that nothing of what you[j] have said may happen to me."

25 Now after Peter and John[k] had testified and spoken the word of the Lord, they returned to Jerusalem, proclaiming the good news to many villages of the Samaritans.

Philip and the Ethiopian Eunuch

26 Then an angel of the Lord said to Philip, "Get up and go toward the south[l] to the road that goes down from Jerusalem to Gaza." (This is a wilderness road.) [27]So he got up and went. Now there was an Ethiopian eunuch, a court official of the Candace, queen of the Ethiopians, in charge of her entire treasury. He had come to Jerusalem

[h] Gk *fallen*   [i] Gk *they*   [j] The Greek word for *you* and the verb *pray* are plural   [k] Gk *after they*
[l] Or *go at noon*

The Danger in Being a Christian
It began as a Jewish sect; fierce persecution only helped it spread

IN SOME COUNTRIES, A PERSON who becomes a Christian forfeits a good education and job. And in a few countries, a person who converts risks his or her life. One church historian estimates more Christians have been martyred in this century than in all preceding centuries put together.

Yet, strangely, more often than not, intense persecution of Christians leads to a spurt of growth in the church. An ancient saying expresses this phenomenon, "The blood of martyrs is the seed of the church."

> *That day a severe persecution began against the church in Jerusalem, and all except the apostles were scattered throughout the countryside of Judea and Samaria. 8.1*

The First Big Advance

For a while, the new faith enjoyed popular favor. But very soon it involved grave risk. In the book of Acts, the persecution that produced the first Christian martyr, Stephen, ironically brought about the advance of Christianity outside its Jewish base. Forced out of stormy Jerusalem, the scattering Jewish Christians turned to other races and ethnic groups. Philip preached first to the despised Samaritans, and then crossed racial barriers by helping to convert an official from Ethiopia.

Acts documents a dramatic change in the faith. What had been viewed as an offshoot of the Jewish religion, a "sect of the Nazarenes," began to encompass people from other religions, races, and cultures. Before long, the center of church activity moved from Jerusalem to the city of Antioch. There, people coined the word *Christian*, indicating how separate the new faith had become. Never again would it be considered "just a Jewish thing."

Breaking the Jewish Mold

As Luke tells it, the transition to other ethnic groups required some adjustments. Jewish disciples balked at letting go of their centuries-old traditions and allowing the church to be flooded with non-Jews.

Peter, one of the most loyal Jews, explained his dilemma this way, "Who was I that I could hinder God?" (11.17). A direct, unmistakable vision from God (10.9–23) overcame Peter's resistance to accepting non-Jews, and later a decisive church council settled on a policy toward them (15.1–21).

As the pages of Acts turn, whole provinces and cultures open up to the gospel. The faith that had been guarded by a small knot of intimates, all Jews who knew Jesus personally, broke out into a rough world of soldiers, sorcerers, merchants, and antagonists from other religions. This process was not without its bloody and frightening moments.

Life Questions: If severe persecution came to the church in your region today, what would happen to your faith?

to worship [28]and was returning home; seated in his chariot, he was reading the prophet Isaiah. [29]Then the Spirit said to Philip, "Go over to this chariot and join it." [30]So Philip ran up to it and heard him reading the prophet Isaiah. He asked, "Do you understand what you are reading?" [31]He replied, "How can I, unless someone guides me?" And he invited Philip to get in and sit beside him. [32]Now the passage of the scripture that he was reading was this:

"Like a sheep he was led to the slaughter,
　　and like a lamb silent before
　　　　its shearer,
　　　so he does not open his mouth.
[33] 　In his humiliation justice was denied him.
　　Who can describe his generation?
　　For his life is taken away from the
　　　　earth."

[34]The eunuch asked Philip, "About whom, may I ask you, does the prophet say this, about himself or about someone else?" [35]Then Philip began to speak, and starting with this scripture, he proclaimed to him the good news about Jesus. [36]As they were going along the road, they came to some water; and the eunuch said, "Look, here is water! What is to prevent me from being baptized?"[m] [38]He commanded the chariot to stop, and both of them, Philip and the eunuch, went down into the water, and Philip[n] baptized him. [39]When they came up out of the water, the Spirit of the Lord snatched Philip away; the eunuch saw him no more, and went on his way rejoicing. [40]But Philip found himself at Azotus, and as he was passing through the region, he proclaimed the good news to all the towns until he came to Caesarea.

The Conversion of Saul

9 Meanwhile Saul, still breathing threats and murder against the disciples of the Lord, went to the high priest [2]and asked him for letters to the synagogues at Damascus, so that if he found any who belonged to the Way, men or women, he might bring them bound to Jerusalem. [3]Now as he was going along and approaching Damascus, suddenly a light from heaven flashed around him. [4]He fell to the ground and heard a voice saying to him, "Saul, Saul, why do you persecute me?" [5]He asked, "Who are you, Lord?" The reply came, "I am Jesus, whom you are persecuting. [6]But get up and enter the city, and you will be told what you are to do." [7]The men who were traveling with him stood speechless because they heard the voice but saw no one. [8]Saul got up from the ground, and though his eyes were open, he could see nothing; so they led him by the hand

[m] Other ancient authorities add all or most of verse 37, *And Philip said, "If you believe with all your heart, you may." And he replied, "I believe that Jesus Christ is the Son of God."*　　[n] Gk *he*

PHILIP *Breakthrough Man*

RELIGION EASILY GETS ASSOCIATED WITH ethnic groups. Arabs are stereotypically Muslim, Indians are Hindu, Japanese are Shinto or Buddhist. Initially, that same pattern held true for early Christians as well. All the original disciples were Jews, and although Jesus had told them to spread the good news to all ethnic groups they found such a prospect hard to imagine.

Philip (not to be confused with the apostle Philip, one of Jesus' original Twelve) was one of the very first to put the Great Commission into practice. He was a pioneer in carrying Jesus' love across racial lines.

Philip originally came to prominence as one of seven men named by the early church to care for poor widows (6.1–7). Greek-speaking Jews had complained about being overlooked, and the apostles wanted someone to take on the problems of providing food and care for these and other individuals. By appointing Philip and six of his colleagues (all Greek-speaking themselves, to judge from their Greek names), the apostles showed their concern for Christians who were not traditional Hebrews.

Still, no one thought of inviting Samaritans—people who had some Jewish blood but were disdained by Jews as heretics and half-breeds—into the fellowship. Then Philip, pushed out of Jerusalem by persecution, began preaching to Samaritans, with amazing results. For the first time, non-Jews joined in following Jesus.

And Philip was just beginning. Next he brought the word about Jesus to a traveling Ethiopian official. Thus Philip was responsible for the first African Christian (8.26–40), and legend has it that the strong North African church of the first few centuries could be traced back to this convert.

Years later the apostle Paul visited Philip, staying with him on his way to Jerusalem (21.7–16). Acts mentions that Philip "the evangelist" had four daughters who prophesied. Since women rarely had a public role in those days, this may indicate that Philip was involved in one more breakthrough—this time involving his own family.

Life Questions: Think of some barriers that you would like to see the gospel "break through." What kind of men or women of God will be needed for that to happen? Are you one of those individuals?

and brought him into Damascus. [9]For three days he was without sight, and neither ate nor drank.

10 Now there was a disciple in Damascus named Ananias. The Lord said to him in a vision,

9.2 Naming the New Religion

In the early days of the church, its believers were given a variety of labels. Here, they are called members of "the Way"; elsewhere, "the believers" (9.30), and "the sect of the Nazarenes" (24.5). Luke reports (11.26) that in the city of Antioch they were first called "Christians," a name that stuck. Roman writers often used the word Christian in a derisive sense, reflecting the hostility that greeted the first believers.

"Ananias." He answered, "Here I am, Lord." [11]The Lord said to him, "Get up and go to the street called Straight, and at the house of Judas look for a man of Tarsus named Saul. At this moment he is praying, [12]and he has seen in a vision[o] a man named Ananias come in and lay his hands on him so that he might regain his sight." [13]But Ananias answered, "Lord, I have heard from many about this man, how much evil he has done to your saints in Jerusalem; [14]and here he has authority from the chief priests to bind all who invoke your name." [15]But the Lord said to him, "Go, for he is an instrument whom I have chosen to bring my name before Gentiles and kings and before the people of Israel; [16]I myself will show him how much he must suffer for the sake of my name." [17]So Ananias went and entered the house. He laid his hands on Saul[p] and said, "Brother Saul, the Lord Jesus, who appeared to you on your way here, has sent me so that you may regain your sight and be filled with the Holy Spirit." [18]And immediately something like scales fell from his eyes, and his sight was restored. Then he got up and was baptized, [19]and after taking some food, he regained his strength.

Saul Preaches in Damascus

For several days he was with the disciples in Damascus, [20]and immediately he began to proclaim Jesus in the synagogues, saying, "He is the Son of God." [21]All who heard him were amazed and said, "Is not this the man who made havoc in Jerusalem among those who invoked this name? And has he not come here for the purpose of bringing them bound before the chief priests?" [22]Saul became increasingly more powerful and confounded the Jews who lived in Damascus by proving that Jesus[q] was the Messiah.[r]

Saul Escapes from the Jews

23 After some time had passed, the Jews plotted to kill him, [24]but their plot became known to Saul. They were watching the gates day and night so that they might kill him; [25]but his disciples took him by night and let him down through an opening in the wall,[s] lowering him in a basket.

9.21 Altered Mission

Damascus, said to be the oldest continually occupied city in the world, is now capital of present-day Syria. Saul undertook the 150-mile journey from Jerusalem in order to persecute Christians there, but on the "Damascus Road" he had an encounter that changed his life forever. In the end, Paul had to flee the Jewish zealots he had originally come to aid.

Although Luke does not mention it, sometime during this period Paul withdrew to Arabia, where he had an extended time to think through his new faith and mission (Galatians 1.17).

Saul in Jerusalem

26 When he had come to Jerusalem, he attempted to join the disciples; and they were all afraid of him, for they did not believe that he was a disciple. [27]But Barnabas took him, brought him to the apostles, and described for them how on the road he had seen the Lord, who had spoken to him, and how in Damascus he had spoken boldly in the name of Jesus. [28]So he went in and out among them in Jerusalem, speaking boldly in the name of the Lord. [29]He spoke and argued with the Hellenists; but they were attempting to kill him. [30]When the believers[t] learned of it, they brought him down to Caesarea and sent him off to Tarsus.

31 Meanwhile the church throughout Judea, Galilee, and Samaria had peace and was built up. Living in the fear of the Lord and in the comfort of the Holy Spirit, it increased in numbers.

The Healing of Aeneas

32 Now as Peter went here and there among all the believers,[u] he came down also to the saints living in Lydda. [33]There he found a man named Aeneas, who had been bedridden for eight years, for he was paralyzed. [34]Peter said to him, "Aeneas, Jesus Christ heals you; get up and make your bed!" And immediately he got up. [35]And all the residents of Lydda and Sharon saw him and turned to the Lord.

[o] Other ancient authorities lack *in a vision*   [p] Gk *him*   [q] Gk *that this*   [r] Or *the Christ*   [s] Gk *through the wall*
[t] Gk *brothers*   [u] Gk *all of them*

Peter in Lydda and Joppa

36 Now in Joppa there was a disciple whose name was Tabitha, which in Greek is Dorcas.ᵛ She was devoted to good works and acts of charity. ³⁷At that time she became ill and died. When they had washed her, they laid her in a room upstairs. ³⁸Since Lydda was near Joppa, the disciples, who heard that Peter was there, sent two men to him with the request, "Please come to us without delay." ³⁹So Peter got up and went with them; and when he arrived, they took him to the room upstairs. All the widows stood beside him, weeping and showing tunics and other clothing that Dorcas had made while she was with them. ⁴⁰Peter put all of them outside, and then he knelt down and prayed. He turned to the body and said, "Tabitha, get up." Then she opened her eyes, and seeing Peter, she sat up. ⁴¹He gave her his hand and helped her up. Then calling the saints and widows, he showed her to be alive. ⁴²This became known throughout Joppa, and many believed in the Lord. ⁴³Meanwhile he stayed in Joppa for some time with a certain Simon, a tanner.

Peter and Cornelius

10 In Caesarea there was a man named Cornelius, a centurion of the Italian Cohort, as it was called. ²He was a devout man who feared God with all his household; he gave alms generously to the people and prayed constantly to God. ³One afternoon at about three o'clock he had a vision in which he clearly saw an angel of God coming in and saying to him, "Cornelius." ⁴He stared at him in terror and said, "What is it, Lord?" He answered, "Your prayers and your alms have ascended as a memorial before God. ⁵Now send men to Joppa for a certain Simon who is called Peter; ⁶he is lodging with Simon, a tanner, whose house is by the seaside." ⁷When the angel who spoke to him had left, he called two of his slaves and a devout soldier from the ranks of those who served him, ⁸and after telling them everything, he sent them to Joppa.

9 About noon the next day, as they were on their journey and approaching the city, Peter went up on the roof to pray. ¹⁰He became hungry and wanted something to eat; and while it was being prepared, he fell into a trance. ¹¹He saw the heaven opened and something like a large sheet coming down, being lowered to the ground by its four corners. ¹²In it were all kinds of four-footed creatures and reptiles and birds of the air. ¹³Then he heard a voice saying, "Get up, Peter; kill and eat." ¹⁴But Peter said, "By no means, Lord; for I have never eaten anything that is profane or unclean." ¹⁵The voice said to him again, a second time, "What God has made clean, you must not

call profane." ¹⁶This happened three times, and the thing was suddenly taken up to heaven.

17 Now while Peter was greatly puzzled about what to make of the vision that he had seen, suddenly the men sent by Cornelius appeared. They were asking for Simon's house and were standing

10.9 A Shift from Peter to Paul

The first part of Acts, especially chapters 9–12, concentrates on the life of Peter. He represented the conservative Jewish contingent, and Acts reports that God gave him direct revelation to understand his plan of outreach to the Gentiles. But a man named Saul had been converted, and beginning with chapter 13, Acts follows his story almost exclusively.

by the gate. ¹⁸They called out to ask whether Simon, who was called Peter, was staying there. ¹⁹While Peter was still thinking about the vision, the Spirit said to him, "Look, threeʷ men are searching for you. ²⁰Now get up, go down, and go with them without hesitation; for I have sent them." ²¹So Peter went down to the men and said, "I am the one you are looking for; what is the reason for your coming?" ²²They answered, "Cornelius, a centurion, an upright and God-fearing man, who is well spoken of by the whole Jewish nation, was directed by a holy angel to send for you to come to his house and to hear what you have to say." ²³So Peterˣ invited them in and gave them lodging.

The next day he got up and went with them, and some of the believersʸ from Joppa accompanied him. ²⁴The following day they came to Caesarea. Cornelius was expecting them and had called together his relatives and close friends. ²⁵On Peter's arrival Cornelius met him, and falling at his feet, worshiped him. ²⁶But Peter made him get up, saying, "Stand up; I am only a mortal." ²⁷And as he talked with him, he went in and found that many had assembled; ²⁸and he said to them, "You yourselves know that it is unlawful for a Jew to associate with or to visit a Gentile; but God has shown me that I should not call anyone profane or unclean. ²⁹So when I was sent for, I came without objection. Now may I ask why you sent for me?"

30 Cornelius replied, "Four days ago at this very hour, at three o'clock, I was praying in my house when suddenly a man in dazzling clothes stood before me. ³¹He said, 'Cornelius, your prayer has been heard and your alms have been remembered before God. ³²Send therefore to Joppa and ask for Simon, who is called Peter; he is staying in the home of Simon, a tanner, by the

---

ᵛ The name Tabitha in Aramaic and the name Dorcas in Greek mean *a gazelle*   ʷ One ancient authority reads *two;*
others lack the word   ˣ Gk *he*   ʸ Gk *brothers*

Recruiting from the Opposition
A former bounty hunter breaks through to the Gentiles

> All who heard him were amazed and said, "Is not this the man who made havoc in Jerusalem among those who invoked this name?"
> 9:21

WITH A TOUCH OF THEATRICS, the Indianapolis judge shook his head very slowly back and forth as his clerk read off John Erwin's offenses from a red record book. He had skipped school too many times to count. He had stolen petty items, like flashlight batteries, only to discard them. He had stolen bicycles, ridden them to the junkyard, and destroyed them.

Most recently, twelve-year-old John had joined a gang of young toughs and threatened his foster parents with a .22 rifle. The judge leaned forward and announced, "Young man, I don't know how any one boy can be as mean as they say you are. But I'm convinced you'll never change. I'm going to send you to a Manual Labor Institute for correction, and I predict you'll spend most of your life in institutions."

Voluntary Life Imprisonment

Three decades later the judge's prophecy has been partially fulfilled: In all, John Erwin has spent over 25 years in a large, notorious institution—Chicago's Cook County jail. But not as an inmate. The judge was mostly wrong: John did change. Remarkably.

During a stint in the army, Erwin met a family who adopted him, determined to show him the same love they had shown their own children. The defenses he had built up in a childhood of violence and sexual abuse slowly melted. He experienced God's love and forgiveness, and he became a new person.

As a free man determined to help set others free, he founded and led the PACE Institute, one of America's most successful prison rehabilitation programs. Then he went on to join the staff of Charles Colson's Prison Fellowship.

When asked why he has been so effective in the failure-littered field of prison work, Erwin replies, "Maybe it's because I've been behind bars, like these prisoners. Most of them came from miserable homes also, and were abused by their parents. I understand what makes life so hard for them—and my story gives them hope. I don't give up on people. If God can change me, he can change them too."

A Complete Turnaround

Converts like John Erwin often make the best crusaders. Former alcoholics can convince others of drinking's dangers. Exiles from Communist countries, such as Alexander Solzhenitsyn, often become the most vehement anti-Communists. And when the book of Acts introduces the most effective Christian missionary of all time, he turns out to be a former bounty hunter of Christians.

How did a Jewish sect become the largest Gentile religion? How did an Asian faith become associated with European civilization? The answers trace back to the remarkable career of Paul, apostle to the Gentiles.

Paul (formerly called Saul) made his first appearance in Acts (8.1), assisting at the brutal stoning of Stephen. Later, he led a gang of persecutors on a violent campaign against Christian believers. But then came a miraculous turnabout on the road to Damascus (9.1–19).

A Courageous Career

Acts is constructed like a drama that delays introducing the hero until the stage is finally set. Beginning in chapter 13, the spotlight in Acts moves from Peter to Paul and follows him throughout the rest of the book. Other Christians, knowing Paul's old reputation, were initially skeptical about his conversion. But he soon proved to be as fiery and intense in preaching Christ as he had been in working against him.

Paul spearheaded the campaign to grant Gentiles full acceptance without subjecting them to Jewish law. He had himself been liberated from bondage to confining laws, and he insisted on a life based on God's free forgiveness, not legalism.

During his journeys, Paul wrote half the New Testament books, and in them he laid the groundwork for much of Christian theology. All the while he carried on a courageous career despite jailings, beatings and riots. He was perhaps the most thoroughly converted man who ever lived.

Life Questions: Has your life changed quickly and dramatically, as Paul's did, or slowly and gradually?

sea.' ³³Therefore I sent for you immediately, and you have been kind enough to come. So now all of us are here in the presence of God to listen to all that the Lord has commanded you to say."

Gentiles Hear the Good News

34 Then Peter began to speak to them: "I truly understand that God shows no partiality, ³⁵but in every nation anyone who fears him and does what is right is acceptable to him. ³⁶You know the message he sent to the people of Israel, preaching peace by Jesus Christ—he is Lord of all. ³⁷That message spread throughout Judea, beginning in Galilee after the baptism that John announced: ³⁸how God anointed Jesus of Nazareth with the Holy Spirit and with power; how he went about doing good and healing all who were oppressed by the devil, for God was with him. ³⁹We are witnesses to all that he did both in Judea and in Jerusalem. They put him to death by hanging him on a tree; ⁴⁰but God raised him on the third day and allowed him to appear, ⁴¹not to all the people but to us who were chosen by God as witnesses, and who ate and drank with him after he rose from the dead. ⁴²He commanded us to preach to the people and to testify that he is the one ordained by God as judge of the living and the dead. ⁴³All the prophets testify about him that everyone who believes in him receives forgiveness of sins through his name."

Gentiles Receive the Holy Spirit

44 While Peter was still speaking, the Holy Spirit fell upon all who heard the word. ⁴⁵The circumcised believers who had come with Peter were astounded that the gift of the Holy Spirit had been poured out even on the Gentiles, ⁴⁶for they heard them speaking in tongues and extolling God. Then Peter said, ⁴⁷"Can anyone withhold the water for baptizing these people who have received the Holy Spirit just as we have?" ⁴⁸So he ordered them to be baptized in the name of Jesus Christ. Then they invited him to stay for several days.

Peter's Report to the Church at Jerusalem

11 Now the apostles and the believers*z* who were in Judea heard that the Gentiles had also accepted the word of God. ²So when Peter went up to Jerusalem, the circumcised believers*a* criticized him, ³saying, "Why did you go to uncircumcised men and eat with them?" ⁴Then Peter began to explain it to them, step by step, saying, ⁵"I was in the city of Joppa praying, and in a trance I saw a vision. There was something like a large sheet coming down from heaven, being lowered by its four corners; and it came close to me. ⁶As I looked at it closely I saw four-footed animals, beasts of prey, reptiles, and birds of the air. ⁷I also heard a voice saying to me, 'Get up, Peter; kill and eat.' ⁸But I replied, 'By no means, Lord; for nothing profane or unclean has ever entered my mouth.' ⁹But a second time the voice answered from heaven, 'What God has made clean, you must not call profane.' ¹⁰This happened three times; then everything was pulled up again to

---

z Gk *brothers*   *a* Gk lacks *believers*

CORNELIUS *Least Likely Convert*

WHO WOULD YOU NOMINATE AS 'least likely to become a Christian?' A fundamentalist Muslim from Iran? A drug dealer? A hardened, hate-filled criminal? Most of us have a stereotype of who is—and is not—a candidate for Christianity.

To Jesus' first disciples, Cornelius certainly fit the "least likely" description. He was a Roman, which meant that he represented the absolute opposite of Jewish culture and religion. A good Jew could never even enter the home of a Roman, let alone share a meal with him.

Furthermore, Cornelius held the position of centurion, an officer in the brutal occupying army that all good Jews resented and despised. A Jewish fisherman like Simon Peter would never have expected such a man to become a Christian. And Cornelius never would have, had not God used supernatural means to bring Cornelius and Peter together. (The vision Peter received helps explain why Christians today eat such foods as pork and shrimp rather than following Jewish dietary laws.)

While Cornelius the Roman soldier made an unlikely candidate for conversion, Cornelius the *man* was far more ready than most. Acts tells us he gave generously to the poor, prayed often and actively sought God. In short, he had a sterling character. When an angel told him where to seek help, Cornelius responded immediately. Not only did he send for Peter, but he had enough faith to assemble friends and relatives in his home in expectation of Peter's arrival.

Peter, who probably had never stepped inside a non-Jewish house before, was stunned when he heard Cornelius's story. He quickly grasped the point: "I truly understand that God shows no partiality, but in every nation anyone who fears him and does what is right is acceptable to him" (10.34–35).

Life Questions: Who in your circle do you feel is "least likely" to become a Christian? Do you really know what goes on underneath the surface, or are you making assumptions?

heaven. ¹¹At that very moment three men, sent to me from Caesarea, arrived at the house where we were. ¹²The Spirit told me to go with them and not to make a distinction between them and us.ᵇ

These six brothers also accompanied me, and we entered the man's house. ¹³He told us how he had seen the angel standing in his house and saying, 'Send to Joppa and bring Simon, who is called Peter; ¹⁴he will give you a message by which you and your entire household will be saved.' ¹⁵And as I began to speak, the Holy Spirit fell upon them just as it had upon us at the beginning. ¹⁶And I remembered the word of the Lord, how he had said, 'John baptized with water, but you will be baptized with the Holy Spirit.' ¹⁷If then God gave them the same gift that he gave us when we believed in the Lord Jesus Christ, who was I that I could hinder God?" ¹⁸When they heard this, they were silenced. And they praised God, saying, "Then God has given even to the Gentiles the repentance that leads to life."

The Church in Antioch

19 Now those who were scattered because of the persecution that took place over Stephen traveled as far as Phoenicia, Cyprus, and Antioch, and they spoke the word to no one except Jews. ²⁰But among them were some men of Cyprus and Cyrene who, on coming to Antioch, spoke to the Hellenistsᶜ also, proclaiming the Lord Jesus. ²¹The hand of the Lord was with them, and a great number became believers and turned to the Lord. ²²News of this came to the ears of the church in Jerusalem, and they sent Barnabas to Antioch. ²³When he came and saw the grace of God, he rejoiced, and he exhorted them all to remain faithful to the Lord with steadfast devotion; ²⁴for he was a good man, full of the Holy Spirit and of faith. And a great many people were brought to the Lord. ²⁵Then Barnabas went to Tarsus to look for Saul, ²⁶and when he had found him, he brought him to Antioch. So it was that for an entire year they met withᵈ the church and taught a great many people, and it was in Antioch that the disciples were first called "Christians."

27 At that time prophets came down from Jerusalem to Antioch. ²⁸One of them named Agabus stood up and predicted by the Spirit that there would be a severe famine over all the world; and this took place during the reign of Claudius.

²⁹The disciples determined that according to their ability, each would send relief to the believersᵉ living in Judea; ³⁰this they did, sending it to the elders by Barnabas and Saul.

James Killed and Peter Imprisoned

12 About that time King Herod laid violent hands upon some who belonged to the church. ²He had James, the brother of John, killed with the sword. ³After he saw that it pleased the Jews, he proceeded to arrest Peter also. (This was during the festival of Unleavened Bread.) ⁴When he had seized him, he put him in prison and handed him over to four squads of soldiers to guard him, intending to bring him out to the people after the Passover. ⁵While Peter was kept in prison, the church prayed fervently to God for him.

Peter Delivered from Prison

6 The very night before Herod was going to bring him out, Peter, bound with two chains, was sleeping between two soldiers, while guards in front of the door were keeping watch over the prison. ⁷Suddenly an angel of the Lord appeared and a light shone in the cell. He tapped Peter on the side and woke him, saying, "Get up quickly." And the chains fell off his wrists. ⁸The angel said to him, "Fasten your belt and put on your sandals." He did so. Then he said to him, "Wrap your cloak around you and follow me." ⁹Peterᶠ went out and followed him; he did not realize that what was happening with the angel's help was real; he thought he was seeing a vision. ¹⁰After they had passed the first and the second guard, they came before the iron gate leading into the city. It opened for them of its own accord, and they went outside and walked along a lane, when suddenly the angel left him. ¹¹Then Peter came to

ᵇ Or *not to hesitate*   ᶜ Other ancient authorities read *Greeks*   ᵈ Or *were guests of*   ᵉ Gk *brothers*
ᶠ Gk *He*

himself and said, "Now I am sure that the Lord has sent his angel and rescued me from the hands of Herod and from all that the Jewish people were expecting."

12 As soon as he realized this, he went to the house of Mary, the mother of John whose other name was Mark, where many had gathered and were praying. ¹³When he knocked at the outer gate, a maid named Rhoda came to answer. ¹⁴On recognizing Peter's voice, she was so overjoyed that, instead of opening the gate, she ran in and announced that Peter was standing at the gate. ¹⁵They said to her, "You are out of your mind!" But she insisted that it was so. They said, "It is his angel." ¹⁶Meanwhile Peter continued knocking; and when they opened the gate, they saw him and were amazed. ¹⁷He motioned to them with his hand to be silent, and described for them how the Lord had brought him out of the prison. And he added, "Tell this to James and to the believers."ᵍ Then he left and went to another place.

18 When morning came, there was no small commotion among the soldiers over what had become of Peter. ¹⁹When Herod had searched for him and could not find him, he examined the guards and ordered them to be put to death. Then he went down from Judea to Caesarea and stayed there.

The Death of Herod

20 Now Herodʰ was angry with the people of Tyre and Sidon. So they came to him in a body; and after winning over Blastus, the king's chamberlain, they asked for a reconciliation, because their country depended on the king's country for food. ²¹On an appointed day Herod put on his royal robes, took his seat on the platform, and delivered a public address to them. ²²The people kept shouting, "The voice of a god, and not of a mortal!" ²³And immediately, because he had not given the glory to God, an angel of the Lord struck him down, and he was eaten by worms and died.

24 But the word of God continued to advance and gain adherents. ²⁵Then after completing their mission Barnabas and Saul returned toⁱ Jerusalem and brought with them John, whose other name was Mark.

12.19 Guards Without Allies

The soldiers who had unsuccessfully guarded Jesus' tomb were protected by a conspiracy hatched by the Jewish establishment (Matthew 28.12–15). This passage sheds light on their eagerness to agree to a cover-up plan: Rome dealt harshly with guards who did not perform their duty. In contrast, the guards who had been on duty when Peter "escaped" (he was set free by an angel) had no one to plead for them. Herod ordered their execution.

Barnabas and Saul Commissioned

13 Now in the church at Antioch there were prophets and teachers: Barnabas, Simeon who was called Niger, Lucius of Cyrene, Manaen a member of the court of Herod the ruler,ʲ and Saul. ²While they were worshiping the Lord and fasting, the Holy Spirit said, "Set apart for me

g Gk *brothers*   h Gk *he*   i Other ancient authorities read *from*   j Gk *tetrarch*

BARNABAS *The Encourager*

THOUGH HIS REAL NAME WAS Joseph, he became known as "Barnabas," an apt nickname meaning "Son of Encouragement." Barnabas had a knack for recognizing and encouraging others' potential. His most notable beneficiary? None other than the apostle Paul.

Even after his dramatic conversion, Paul frightened Jewish Christians—so much so that when he reached Jerusalem they all kept their distance. Wasn't this the fire-breather who had hurt so many believers? But Barnabas took his life in his hands and went to see Paul. Convinced that his conversion was genuine, Barnabas led Paul to the apostles and introduced them (9.26–27).

Later, when the first Gentile church sprang to life in Antioch, Barnabas encouraged these new Christians and then thought of a role for Paul (11.25–26). Barnabas helped Paul find his real calling: to nurture churches that crossed Jewish-Gentile lines. (Paul would eventually become known as the "Apostle to the Gentiles.") Soon God would hand-pick the two of them to leave Antioch on the first missionary journey (13.1–3).

Ironically, Barnabas's encouraging outlook put him at odds with Paul. On that first trip they took along Barnabas's young cousin John Mark, who quit in mid-journey. When they were planning a second trip, Barnabas wanted to give Mark another chance, but Paul refused. Consequently they split and went their separate ways (15.36–40). Barnabas proved right on this point, for Mark proved trustworthy and Paul ultimately came to depend on him (2 Timothy 4.11).

Life Questions: Whom do you encourage, and how do you do it? Who encourages you?

Barnabas and Saul for the work to which I have called them." ³Then after fasting and praying they laid their hands on them and sent them off.

The Apostles Preach in Cyprus

4 So, being sent out by the Holy Spirit, they went down to Seleucia; and from there they sailed to Cyprus. ⁵When they arrived at Salamis, they proclaimed the word of God in the synagogues of the Jews. And they had John also to assist them. ⁶When they had gone through the whole island as far as Paphos, they met a certain magician, a Jewish false prophet, named Bar-Jesus. ⁷He was with the proconsul, Sergius Paulus, an intelligent man, who summoned Barnabas and Saul and wanted to hear the word of God. ⁸But the magician Elymas (for that is the translation of his name) opposed them and tried to turn the proconsul away from the faith. ⁹But Saul, also known as Paul, filled with the Holy Spirit, looked intently at him ¹⁰and said, "You son of the devil, you enemy of all righteousness, full of all deceit and villainy, will you not stop making crooked the straight paths of the Lord? ¹¹And now listen—the hand of the Lord is against you, and you will be blind for a while, unable to see the sun." Immediately mist and darkness came over him, and he went about groping for someone to lead him by the hand. ¹²When the proconsul saw what had happened, he believed, for he was astonished at the teaching about the Lord.

Paul and Barnabas in Antioch of Pisidia

13 Then Paul and his companions set sail from Paphos and came to Perga in Pamphylia. John, however, left them and returned to Jerusalem; ¹⁴but they went on from Perga and came to Antioch in Pisidia. And on the sabbath day they went into the synagogue and sat down. ¹⁵After the reading of the law and the prophets, the officials of the synagogue sent them a message, saying, "Brothers, if you have any word of exhortation for the people, give it." ¹⁶So Paul stood up and with a gesture began to speak:

"You Israelites,ᵏ and others who fear God,

listen. ¹⁷The God of this people Israel chose our ancestors and made the people great during their stay in the land of Egypt, and with uplifted arm he led them out of it. ¹⁸For about forty years he put up withˡ them in the wilderness. ¹⁹After he had destroyed seven nations in the land of Canaan, he gave them their land as an inheritance ²⁰for about four hundred fifty years. After that he gave them judges until the time of the prophet Samuel. ²¹Then they asked for a king; and God gave them Saul son of Kish, a man of the tribe of Benjamin, who reigned for forty years. ²²When he had removed him, he made David their king. In his testimony about him he said, 'I have found David, son of Jesse, to be a man after my heart, who will carry out all my wishes.' ²³Of this man's posterity God has brought to Israel a Savior, Jesus, as he promised; ²⁴before his coming John had already proclaimed a baptism of repentance to all the people of Israel. ²⁵And as John was finishing his work, he said, 'What do you suppose that I am? I am not he. No, but one is coming after me; I am not worthy to untie the thong of the sandalsᵐ on his feet.'

26 "My brothers, you descendants of Abraham's family, and others who fear God, to usⁿ the message of this salvation has been sent. ²⁷Because the residents of Jerusalem and their leaders did not recognize him or understand the words of the prophets that are read every sabbath, they fulfilled those words by condemning him. ²⁸Even though they found no cause for a sentence of death, they asked Pilate to have him killed. ²⁹When they had carried out everything that was written about him, they took him down from the tree and laid him in a tomb. ³⁰But God raised him from the dead; ³¹and for many days he appeared to those who came up with him from Galilee to Jerusalem, and they are now his witnesses to the people. ³²And we bring you the good news that what God promised to our ancestors ³³he has fulfilled for us, their children, by raising Jesus; as also it is written in the second psalm,

'You are my Son;
today I have begotten you.'

³⁴As to his raising him from the dead, no more to return to corruption, he has spoken in this way,

'I will give you the holy promises made to David.'

³⁵Therefore he has also said in another psalm,

'You will not let your Holy One experience corruption.'

³⁶For David, after he had served the purpose of God in his own generation, died,ᵒ was laid beside his ancestors, and experienced corruption; ³⁷but he whom God raised up experienced no corruption. ³⁸Let it be known to you therefore, my

13.15 Visiting Speaker

Synagogue rulers customarily invited a visiting rabbi to address the congregation, and in this case the apostle Paul responded by delivering his longest-recorded sermon. The rulers got more than they bargained for: The next week virtually the whole city turned out to hear him, resulting in a near-riot (verses 44–45).

ᵏ Gk *Men, Israelites*   ˡ Other ancient authorities read *cared for*   ᵐ Gk *untie the sandals*   ⁿ Other ancient
authorities read *you*   ᵒ Gk *fell asleep*

brothers, that through this man forgiveness of sins is proclaimed to you; [39]by this Jesus[p] everyone who believes is set free from all those sins[q] from which you could not be freed by the law of Moses. [40]Beware, therefore, that what the prophets said does not happen to you:

[41] 'Look, you scoffers!
Be amazed and perish,
for in your days I am doing a work,
    a work that you will never believe, even
        if someone tells you.' "

42 As Paul and Barnabas[r] were going out, the people urged them to speak about these things again the next sabbath. [43]When the meeting of the synagogue broke up, many Jews and devout converts to Judaism followed Paul and Barnabas, who spoke to them and urged them to continue in the grace of God.

44 The next sabbath almost the whole city gathered to hear the word of the Lord.[s] [45]But when the Jews saw the crowds, they were filled with jealousy; and blaspheming, they contradicted what was spoken by Paul. [46]Then both Paul and Barnabas spoke out boldly, saying, "It was necessary that the word of God should be spoken first to you. Since you reject it and judge yourselves to be unworthy of eternal life, we are now

13.46 Apostle to the Gentiles

This incident is the first of several occasions in Acts showing Paul turning away from the Jews (see 18.6; 19.9). When the Jews rejected his message, he went to the Gentiles. Eventually he became known as the "apostle to the Gentiles," even though he maintained a deep love for his own people (see Romans 9.1–5).

turning to the Gentiles. [47]For so the Lord has commanded us, saying,

'I have set you to be a light for
    the Gentiles,
so that you may bring salvation to the
    ends of the earth.' "

48 When the Gentiles heard this, they were glad and praised the word of the Lord; and as many as had been destined for eternal life became believers. [49]Thus the word of the Lord spread throughout the region. [50]But the Jews incited the devout women of high standing and the leading men of the city, and stirred up persecution against Paul and Barnabas, and drove them out of their region. [51]So they shook the dust off their feet in protest against them, and went to Iconium. [52]And the disciples were filled with joy and with the Holy Spirit.

Paul and Barnabas in Iconium

14 The same thing occurred in Iconium, where Paul and Barnabas[r] went into the Jewish synagogue and spoke in such a way that a great number of both Jews and Greeks became believers. [2]But the unbelieving Jews stirred up the Gentiles and poisoned their minds against the brothers. [3]So they remained for a long time, speaking boldly for the Lord, who testified to the word of his grace by granting signs and wonders to be done through them. [4]But the residents of the city were divided; some sided with the Jews, and some with the apostles. [5]And when an attempt was made by both Gentiles and Jews, with their rulers, to mistreat them and to stone them, [6]the apostles[r] learned of it and fled to Lystra and Derbe, cities of Lycaonia, and to the surrounding country; [7]and there they continued proclaiming the good news.

Paul and Barnabas in Lystra and Derbe

8 In Lystra there was a man sitting who could not use his feet and had never walked, for he had been crippled from birth. [9]He listened to Paul as he was speaking. And Paul, looking at him intently and seeing that he had faith to be healed, [10]said in a loud voice, "Stand upright on your feet." And the man[t] sprang up and began to walk. [11]When the crowds saw what Paul had done, they shouted in the Lycaonian language, "The gods have come down to us in human form!" [12]Barnabas they called Zeus, and Paul they called Hermes, because he was the chief speaker. [13]The priest of Zeus, whose temple was just outside the city,[u] brought oxen and garlands to the gates; he and the crowds wanted to offer sacrifice. [14]When the apostles Barnabas and Paul heard of it, they tore their clothes and rushed out into the crowd, shouting, [15]"Friends,[v] why are you doing this? We are mortals just like you, and we bring you good news, that you should turn from these worthless things to the living God, who made the heaven and the earth and the sea and all that is in them. [16]In past generations he allowed all the nations to follow their own ways; [17]yet he has not left himself without a witness in doing good—giving you rains from heaven and fruitful seasons, and filling you with food and your hearts with joy." [18]Even with these words, they scarcely restrained the crowds from offering sacrifice to them.

19 But Jews came there from Antioch and Iconium and won over the crowds. Then they stoned Paul and dragged him out of the city, supposing that he was dead. [20]But when the disciples surrounded him, he got up and went into the city. The next day he went on with Barnabas to Derbe.

p Gk *this*   q Gk *all*   r Gk *they*   s Other ancient authorities read *God*   t Gk *he*   u Or *The priest of Zeus-Outside-the-City*   v Gk *Men*

The Return to Antioch in Syria

21 After they had proclaimed the good news to that city and had made many disciples, they returned to Lystra, then on to Iconium and Antioch. ²²There they strengthened the souls of the disciples and encouraged them to continue in the faith, saying, "It is through many persecutions that we must enter the kingdom of God." ²³And after they had appointed elders for them in each church, with prayer and fasting they entrusted them to the Lord in whom they had come to believe.

24 Then they passed through Pisidia and came to Pamphylia. ²⁵When they had spoken the word in Perga, they went down to Attalia. ²⁶From there they sailed back to Antioch, where they had been commended to the grace of God for the work[w] that they had completed. ²⁷When they arrived, they called the church together and related all that God had done with them, and how he had opened a door of faith for the Gentiles. ²⁸And they stayed there with the disciples for some time.

The Council at Jerusalem

15 Then certain individuals came down from Judea and were teaching the brothers, "Unless you are circumcised according to the custom of Moses, you cannot be saved." ²And after Paul and Barnabas had no small dissension and debate with them, Paul and Barnabas and some of the others were appointed to go up to Jerusalem to discuss this question with the apostles and the elders. ³So they were sent on their way by the church, and as they passed through both Phoenicia and Samaria, they reported the conversion of the Gentiles, and brought great joy to all the believers.[x] ⁴When they came to Jerusalem, they were welcomed by the church and the apostles and the elders, and they reported all that God had done with them. ⁵But some believers who belonged to the sect of the Pharisees stood up and said, "It is necessary for them to be circumcised and ordered to keep the law of Moses."

6 The apostles and the elders met together to consider this matter. ⁷After there had been much debate, Peter stood up and said to them, "My brothers,[y] you know that in the early days God made a choice among you, that I should be the one through whom the Gentiles would hear the message of the good news and become believers. ⁸And God, who knows the human heart, testified to them by giving them the Holy Spirit, just as he did to us; ⁹and in cleansing their hearts by faith he has made no distinction between them and us. ¹⁰Now therefore why are you putting God to the test by placing on the neck of the disciples a yoke that neither our ancestors nor we have been able

to bear? ¹¹On the contrary, we believe that we will be saved through the grace of the Lord Jesus, just as they will."

12 The whole assembly kept silence, and listened to Barnabas and Paul as they told of all the

15.7 The First Church Council

Chapter 15 gives a fascinating glimpse into Jewish/Gentile politics in the early church, recounting a debate between such leaders as Peter, Paul, and James. "In the early days," Peter began his speech—about ten years had passed since his startling experience with Gentiles recorded in Acts 10. By now Gentiles probably outnumbered Jewish believers worldwide.

The leaders agreed on a compromise position that removed some of the barriers between the two groups. They issued a formal position paper, reproduced here, in which Jewish Christians asked the Gentiles to honor four of their practices, two moral issues and two cultural. The two on food relate to a "kosher" method of food preparation designed to keep people from ingesting any animal blood.

signs and wonders that God had done through them among the Gentiles. ¹³After they finished speaking, James replied, "My brothers,[y] listen to me. ¹⁴Simeon has related how God first looked favorably on the Gentiles, to take from among them a people for his name. ¹⁵This agrees with the words of the prophets, as it is written,

¹⁶ 'After this I will return,
　and I will rebuild the dwelling of David,
　　which has fallen;
　from its ruins I will rebuild it,
　　and I will set it up,
¹⁷ so that all other peoples may seek the
　　Lord—
　even all the Gentiles over whom my
　　name has been called.
　Thus says the Lord, who has been
　　making these things ¹⁸known
　　from long ago.'[z]

¹⁹Therefore I have reached the decision that we should not trouble those Gentiles who are turning to God, ²⁰but we should write to them to abstain only from things polluted by idols and from fornication and from whatever has been strangled[a] and from blood. ²¹For in every city, for generations past, Moses has had those who proclaim him, for he has been read aloud every sabbath in the synagogues."

---

w Or committed in the grace of God to the work　　*x Gk brothers*　　*y Gk Men, brothers*　　*z Other ancient authorities read things. 18Known to God from of old are all his works.'*　　*a Other ancient authorities lack and from whatever has been strangled*

The Council's Letter to Gentile Believers

22 Then the apostles and the elders, with the consent of the whole church, decided to choose men from among their members[b] and to send them to Antioch with Paul and Barnabas. They sent Judas called Barsabbas, and Silas, leaders among the brothers, [23]with the following letter: "The brothers, both the apostles and the elders, to the believers[c] of Gentile origin in Antioch and Syria and Cilicia, greetings. [24]Since we have heard that certain persons who have gone out from us, though with no instructions from us, have said things to disturb you and have unsettled your minds,[d] [25]we have decided unanimously to choose representatives[e] and send them to you, along with our beloved Barnabas and Paul, [26]who have risked their lives for the sake of our Lord Jesus Christ. [27]We have therefore sent Judas and Silas, who themselves will tell you the same things by word of mouth. [28]For it has seemed good to the Holy Spirit and to us to impose on you no further burden than these essentials: [29]that you abstain from what has been sacrificed to idols and from blood and from what is strangled[f] and from fornication. If you keep yourselves from these, you will do well. Farewell."

30 So they were sent off and went down to Antioch. When they gathered the congregation together, they delivered the letter. [31]When its members[g] read it, they rejoiced at the exhortation. [32]Judas and Silas, who were themselves prophets, said much to encourage and strengthen the believers.[c] [33]After they had been there for some time, they were sent off in peace by the believers[c] to those who had sent them.[h] [35]But Paul and Barnabas remained in Antioch, and there, with many others, they taught and proclaimed the word of the Lord.

Paul and Barnabas Separate

36 After some days Paul said to Barnabas, "Come, let us return and visit the believers[c] in every city where we proclaimed the word of the Lord and see how they are doing." [37]Barnabas wanted to take with them John called Mark. [38]But Paul decided not to take with them one who had deserted them in Pamphylia and had not accompanied them in the work. [39]The disagreement became so sharp that they parted company; Barnabas took Mark with him and sailed away to Cyprus. [40]But Paul chose Silas and set out, the believers[c] commending him to the grace of the Lord. [41]He went through Syria and Cilicia, strengthening the churches.

Timothy Joins Paul and Silas

16 Paul[i] went on also to Derbe and to Lystra, where there was a disciple named Timothy, the son of a Jewish woman who was a believer; but his father was a Greek. [2]He was well spoken of by the believers[c] in Lystra and Iconium. [3]Paul wanted Timothy to accompany him; and he took

[b] Gk from among them   [c] Gk brothers   [d] Other ancient authorities add saying, 'You must be circumcised and keep the law,'   [e] Gk men   [f] Other ancient authorities lack and from what is strangled   [g] Gk When they   [h] Other ancient authorities add verse 34, But it seemed good to Silas to remain there   [i] Gk He

MARK (JOHN MARK) Slow Starter

FOR MORE THAN 75 YEARS, England has chosen an All-England soccer team for players under the age of 15. Selections each year represent the very best young players, England's future. Yet a long-term study of these players unearthed a disturbing fact. Of more than 1,200 young players, only 29 went on to play for the All-England adult team. In other words, only two percent of the best remained the best as adults.

It's risky to size someone up too early. Why? Because people change. That was the case with John Mark. As a young man living in Jerusalem, he had a ringside seat for the coming of Christ and the early days of the church. His mother Mary, apparently a widow, opened her home to the early Christians. His cousin Barnabas served as one of the early deacons. Surely Mark would become an outstanding Christian leader!

Paul and Barnabas certainly must have thought so when they took Mark along on their first missionary journey. But the young man failed, deserting them in the middle of the trip. Terribly disappointed, Paul refused to allow Mark on the next journey. This refusal led to a rift with Barnabas (15.39).

Although Paul may have sized up the young man as hopeless, he later changed his opinion. Mark eventually became a valued assistant to Paul, and three of the apostle's letters mention him with gratitude.

Another apostle, Peter, refers warmly to Mark as "my son" (1 Peter 5.13). Tradition has it that Mark accompanied Peter to Rome, where Peter helped him write the Gospel account that bears Mark's name.

Life Questions: If someone were to evaluate you now, as against five years ago, would you show improvement?

him and had him circumcised because of the Jews who were in those places, for they all knew that his father was a Greek. ⁴As they went from town to town, they delivered to them for observance the decisions that had been reached by the apostles and elders who were in Jerusalem. ⁵So the churches were strengthened in the faith and increased in numbers daily.

Paul's Vision of the Man of Macedonia

6 They went through the region of Phrygia and Galatia, having been forbidden by the Holy Spirit to speak the word in Asia. ⁷When they had come opposite Mysia, they attempted to go into Bithynia, but the Spirit of Jesus did not allow them; ⁸so, passing by Mysia, they went down to Troas. ⁹During the night Paul had a vision: there stood a man of Macedonia pleading with him and saying, "Come over to Macedonia and help us." ¹⁰When he had seen the vision, we immediately tried to cross over to Macedonia, being convinced that God had called us to proclaim the good news to them.

16.10 Firsthand Report

In Acts 16, 21, and 28, Luke uses "we" in writing, for he accompanied the apostle Paul on some of his trips. His close association with Paul meant he had immediate access to the central character in Acts 13–28.

The Conversion of Lydia

11 We set sail from Troas and took a straight course to Samothrace, the following day to Neapolis, ¹²and from there to Philippi, which is a leading city of the district ʲ of Macedonia and a Roman colony. We remained in this city for some days. ¹³On the sabbath day we went outside the gate by the river, where we supposed there was a place of prayer; and we sat down and spoke to the women who had gathered there. ¹⁴A certain woman named Lydia, a worshiper of God, was listening to us; she was from the city of Thyatira and a dealer in purple cloth. The Lord opened her heart to listen eagerly to what was said by Paul. ¹⁵When she and her household were baptized, she urged us, saying, "If you have judged me to be faithful to the Lord, come and stay at my home." And she prevailed upon us.

Paul and Silas in Prison

16 One day, as we were going to the place of prayer, we met a slave-girl who had a spirit of divination and brought her owners a great deal of money by fortune-telling. ¹⁷While she followed Paul and us, she would cry out, "These men are slaves of the Most High God, who proclaim to youᵏ a way of salvation." ¹⁸She kept doing this for many days. But Paul, very much annoyed, turned and said to the spirit, "I order you in the name of Jesus Christ to come out of her." And it came out that very hour.

19 But when her owners saw that their hope of making money was gone, they seized Paul and Silas and dragged them into the marketplace before the authorities. ²⁰When they had brought them before the magistrates, they said, "These men are disturbing our city; they are Jews ²¹and are advocating customs that are not lawful for us as Romans to adopt or observe." ²²The crowd joined in attacking them, and the magistrates had them stripped of their clothing and ordered them to be beaten with rods. ²³After they had given them a severe flogging, they threw them into prison and ordered the jailer to keep them securely. ²⁴Following these instructions, he put them in the innermost cell and fastened their feet in the stocks.

25 About midnight Paul and Silas were praying and singing hymns to God, and the prisoners were listening to them. ²⁶Suddenly there was an earthquake, so violent that the foundations of the prison were shaken; and immediately all the doors were opened and everyone's chains were unfastened. ²⁷When the jailer woke up and saw the prison doors wide open, he drew his sword and was about to kill himself, since he supposed that the prisoners had escaped. ²⁸But Paul shouted in a loud voice, "Do not harm yourself, for we are all here." ²⁹The jailerˡ called for lights, and rushing in, he fell down trembling before Paul and Silas. ³⁰Then he brought them outside and said, "Sirs, what must I do to be saved?" ³¹They answered, "Believe on the Lord Jesus, and you will be saved, you and your household." ³²They spoke the word of the Lordᵐ to him and to all who were in his house. ³³At the same hour of the night he took them and washed their wounds; then he and his entire family were baptized without delay. ³⁴He brought them up into the house and set food before them; and he and his entire household rejoiced that he had become a believer in God.

35 When morning came, the magistrates sent the police, saying, "Let those men go." ³⁶And the jailer reported the message to Paul, saying, "The magistrates sent word to let you go; therefore come out now and go in peace." ³⁷But Paul replied, "They have beaten us in public, uncondemned, men who are Roman citizens, and have thrown us into prison; and now are they going to discharge us in secret? Certainly not! Let them come and take us out themselves." ³⁸The police

---

ʲ Other authorities read *a city of the first district*   ᵏ Other ancient authorities read *to us*   ˡ Gk *He*
ᵐ Other ancient authorities read *word of God*

reported these words to the magistrates, and they were afraid when they heard that they were Roman citizens; [39]so they came and apologized to them. And they took them out and asked them to leave the city. [40]After leaving the prison they went to Lydia's home; and when they had seen and encouraged the brothers and sisters[n] there, they departed.

The Uproar in Thessalonica

17 After Paul and Silas[o] had passed through Amphipolis and Apollonia, they came to Thessalonica, where there was a synagogue of the Jews. [2]And Paul went in, as was his custom, and on three sabbath days argued with them from the scriptures, [3]explaining and proving that it was necessary for the Messiah[p] to suffer and to rise from the dead, and saying, "This is the Messiah,[p] Jesus whom I am proclaiming to you." [4]Some of them were persuaded and joined Paul and Silas, as did a great many of the devout Greeks and not a few of the leading women. [5]But the Jews became jealous, and with the help of some ruffians in the marketplaces they formed a mob and set the city in an uproar. While they were searching for Paul and Silas to bring them out to the assembly, they attacked Jason's house. [6]When they could not find them, they dragged Jason and some believers[n] before the city authorities,[q] shouting, "These people who have been turning the world upside down have come here also, [7]and Jason has entertained them as guests. They are all acting contrary to the decrees of the emperor, saying that there is another king named Jesus." [8]The people and the city officials were disturbed when they heard this, [9]and after they had taken bail from Jason and the others, they let them go.

Paul and Silas in Beroea

10 That very night the believers[n] sent Paul and Silas off to Beroea; and when they arrived, they went to the Jewish synagogue. [11]These Jews were more receptive than those in Thessalonica, for they welcomed the message very eagerly and examined the scriptures every day to see whether these things were so. [12]Many of them therefore believed, including not a few Greek women and men of high standing. [13]But when the Jews of Thessalonica learned that the word of God had been proclaimed by Paul in Beroea as well, they came there too, to stir up and incite the crowds. [14]Then the believers[n] immediately sent Paul away to the coast, but Silas and Timothy remained behind. [15]Those who conducted Paul brought him as far as Athens; and after receiving instructions to have Silas and Timothy join him as soon as possible, they left him.

Paul in Athens

16 While Paul was waiting for them in Athens, he was deeply distressed to see that the city was full of idols. [17]So he argued in the synagogue with the Jews and the devout persons, and also in the marketplace[r] every day with those who happened to be there. [18]Also some Epicurean and Stoic philosophers debated with him. Some said, "What does this babbler want to say?" Others said, "He seems to be a proclaimer of foreign divinities." (This was because he was telling the good news about Jesus and the resurrection.) [19]So

---

[n] Gk brothers   [o] Gk they   [p] Or the Christ   [q] Gk politarchs   [r] Or civic center; Gk agora

---

SILAS *Singing in Prison*

THE NEW CHURCH EXPLODED OUTWARD, persecution pounded inward and change hung everywhere in the air. Boredom never troubled the early Christians—especially the small band who, with the apostle Paul, boldly carried the good news into uncharted territory.

Silas was one of that elite, brave group. A leader in the Jerusalem church, he journeyed to Antioch with an official church message. Something about that city's multicultural church apparently got under his skin, because he volunteered to accompany the apostle Paul on a lengthy missionary trip. Any trip with the fearless Paul guaranteed excitement.

Even today, in some parts of the world, missionary work can be risky business. In those early days of the church, Paul and Silas found trouble ready at hand. In Philippi, the authorities beat up the two missionaries and threw them in jail. While they were singing hymns at midnight behind bars, an earthquake freed them, yet the two stayed around to lead the jailer to faith in Christ. At the next stop, Thessalonica, the pair inadvertently started a riot. Narrowly escaping injury, they went on to Berea, where more trouble ensued.

Such excitement came with the job. The message about Jesus proved challenging and sometimes offensive to those who heard. Silas dedicated his life to spreading the word. Besides preaching the good news, he evidently helped in the writing of 1 and 2 Thessalonians and 1 Peter (1 Thessalonians 1.1; 2 Thessalonians 1.1; 1 Peter 5.12).

Life Questions: Can you imagine serving God as exciting? What would make it so for you?

they took him and brought him to the Areopagus and asked him, "May we know what this new teaching is that you are presenting? [20]It sounds rather strange to us, so we would like to know

17.16 Flexible Approach

In places like Thessalonica and Beroea, Paul went first to the synagogues, where he tried to convince fellow Jews that Jesus Christ was the Messiah promised in the Old Testament. In Athens he initially took that same approach, but few Athenians had the Old Testament background to understand his argument. Paul soon began comparing his God to the many gods they worshiped. The ancients used to say, "It is easier to find a god than a man in Athens."

what it means." [21]Now all the Athenians and the foreigners living there would spend their time in nothing but telling or hearing something new.

22 Then Paul stood in front of the Areopagus and said, "Athenians, I see how extremely religious you are in every way. [23]For as I went through the city and looked carefully at the objects of your worship, I found among them an altar with the inscription, 'To an unknown god.' What therefore you worship as unknown, this I proclaim to you. [24]The God who made the world and everything in it, he who is Lord of heaven and earth, does not live in shrines made by human hands, [25]nor is he served by human hands, as though he needed anything, since he himself gives to all mortals life and breath and all things. [26]From one ancestor[s] he made all nations to inhabit the whole earth, and he allotted the times of their existence and the boundaries of the places where they would live, [27]so that they would search for God[t] and perhaps grope for him and find him—though indeed he is not far from each one of us. [28]For 'In him we live and move and have our being'; as even some of your own poets have said,

'For we too are his offspring.'

[29]Since we are God's offspring, we ought not to think that the deity is like gold, or silver, or stone, an image formed by the art and imagination of mortals. [30]While God has overlooked the times of human ignorance, now he commands all people everywhere to repent, [31]because he has fixed a day on which he will have the world judged in righteousness by a man whom he has appointed, and of this he has given assurance to all by raising him from the dead."

32 When they heard of the resurrection of the dead, some scoffed; but others said, "We will hear you again about this." [33]At that point Paul left them. [34]But some of them joined him and became believers, including Dionysius the Areopagite and a woman named Damaris, and others with them.

17.32 A Tough Audience

Paul gave a remarkable speech to a gathering of philosophers and thinkers in the sophisticated university city of Athens. It appears he met with little success, and the results may have troubled him greatly. Acts 18.5 hints at a shift in his approach. Some scholars believe that the first four chapters of 1 Corinthians, reflecting on this period of time, may describe the strong impact of his experience in Athens.

Paul in Corinth

18 After this Paul[u] left Athens and went to Corinth. [2]There he found a Jew named Aquila, a native of Pontus, who had recently come from Italy with his wife Priscilla, because Claudius had ordered all Jews to leave Rome. Paul[v] went to see them, [3]and, because he was of the same trade, he stayed with them, and they worked together—by trade they were tentmakers. [4]Every sabbath he would argue in the synagogue and would try to convince Jews and Greeks.

5 When Silas and Timothy arrived from Macedonia, Paul was occupied with proclaiming the word,[w] testifying to the Jews that the Messiah[x] was Jesus. [6]When they opposed and reviled him, in protest he shook the dust from his clothes[y] and said to them, "Your blood be on your own heads! I am innocent. From now on I will go to the Gentiles." [7]Then he left the synagogue[z] and went to the house of a man named Titius[a] Justus, a worshiper of God; his house was next door to the synagogue. [8]Crispus, the official of the synagogue, became a believer in the Lord, together with all his household; and many of the Corinthians who heard Paul became believers and were baptized. [9]One night the Lord said to Paul in a vision, "Do not be afraid, but speak and do not be silent; [10]for I am with you, and no one will lay a hand on you to harm you, for there are many in this city who are my people." [11]He stayed there a year and six months, teaching the word of God among them.

12 But when Gallio was proconsul of Achaia, the Jews made a united attack on Paul and

---

[s] Gk *From one*; other ancient authorities read *From one blood*   [t] Other ancient authorities read *the Lord*   [u] Gk *he*
[v] Gk *He*   [w] Gk *with the word*   [x] Or *the Christ*   [y] Gk *reviled him, he shook out his clothes*   [z] Gk *left there*
[a] Other ancient authorities read *Titus*

brought him before the tribunal. [13]They said, "This man is persuading people to worship God in ways that are contrary to the law." [14]Just as Paul was about to speak, Gallio said to the Jews, "If it were a matter of crime or serious villainy, I would be justified in accepting the complaint of you Jews; [15]but since it is a matter of questions about words and names and your own law, see to it yourselves; I do not wish to be a judge of these matters." [16]And he dismissed them from the tribunal. [17]Then all of them[b] seized Sosthenes, the official of the synagogue, and beat him in front of the tribunal. But Gallio paid no attention to any of these things.

Paul's Return to Antioch

18 After staying there for a considerable time, Paul said farewell to the believers[c] and sailed for Syria, accompanied by Priscilla and Aquila. At Cenchreae he had his hair cut, for he was under a vow. [19]When they reached Ephesus, he left them there, but first he himself went into the synagogue and had a discussion with the Jews. [20]When they asked him to stay longer, he declined; [21]but on taking leave of them, he said, "I[d] will return to you, if God wills." Then he set sail from Ephesus.

22 When he had landed at Caesarea, he went up to Jerusalem[e] and greeted the church, and then went down to Antioch. [23]After spending

[b] Other ancient authorities read *all the Greeks keep the approaching festival in Jerusalem, but I*   [c] Gk *brothers*   [e] Gk *went up*   [d] Other ancient authorities read *I must at all costs*

On the Road with the Apostle Paul
Paul, both Jewish and Roman, took the gospel into the melting pot

THE BOOK OF ACTS FOLLOWS Paul on three distinct missionary journeys along the northeastern shores of the Mediterranean Sea. Normally in the ancient world, travel posed great hazards, with pirates, barbarian armies, and hostile border guards clogging up the roads. But by Paul's lifetime, Rome had established absolute mastery over a vast territory. Empire-wide peace, the famous *Pax Romana*—a condition that existed only twice in 700 years—prevailed.

Roman engineers had crisscrossed the empire with a network of roads (built so well that many still survive), and as a Roman citizen Paul had a passport to any destination. Language, too, was unified. The Greek tongue, as well as the Greek style of thinking, crossed ethnic barriers.

> When they opposed and reviled him, in protest he shook the dust from his clothes and said to them, "Your blood be on your own heads! I am innocent. From now on I will go to the Gentiles." 18.6

Paul's Strategy

In his missionary ventures, Paul focused primarily on chief trade towns, capital cities, and Roman colonies. Like modern cities today, these comprised a melting pot of diverse cultures. From these places, the gospel message would be carried across the globe.

Usually, Paul began with a visit to a local synagogue, establishing contact with fellow Jews. If they rejected his message, as often happened, he quickly turned to a non-Jewish audience.

When a promising church was established, Paul stayed on—sometimes as long as three years—to teach and to direct its spiritual growth. His letters glow with affection for the friends he developed in this way. (Acts 20 gives a glimpse of the intimacy he shared with one such group.) On his second and third journeys Paul revisited many of the churches he had founded.

Unusual Qualifications, Impressive Results

Paul's background uniquely qualified him for his adventures. A Pharisee who had studied with the famous teacher Gamaliel, he fully understood the Jewish mind. Roman citizenship gave him the status and respect he needed to gain official recognition and to survive threatening legal scrapes.

Paul's mastery of languages helped him also. He used Aramaic to relate to the early church leaders in Jerusalem, and fluency in Greek made possible a speech before philosophers in Athens.

Sometimes Paul was used by God to work miracles. In one tragicomic episode, a sleepy listener succumbed to Paul's all-night sermon and fell out of a third-story window (20.7–12); Paul raised him from the dead.

By the end of his eventful life, Paul had left a ring of burgeoning churches around the eastern Mediterranean. To make sure his work would go on, he trained such leaders as Silas, Titus, Timothy, and the man who recorded much of what we know about Paul's life—Luke himself.

Life Questions: Why did God choose Paul to lead the early church? What special qualifications do you have that God could use?

some time there he departed and went from place to place through the region of Galatia[f] and Phrygia, strengthening all the disciples.

Ministry of Apollos

24 Now there came to Ephesus a Jew named

Apollos, a native of Alexandria. He was an eloquent man, well-versed in the scriptures. [25]He had been instructed in the Way of the Lord; and he spoke with burning enthusiasm and taught accurately the things concerning Jesus, though he knew only the baptism of John. [26]He began to speak boldly in the synagogue; but when Priscilla and Aquila heard him, they took him aside and

[f] Gk *the Galatian region*   [g] Gk *brothers*   [h] Or *the Christ*

explained the Way of God to him more accurately. [27]And when he wished to cross over to Achaia, the believers[g] encouraged him and wrote to the disciples to welcome him. On his arrival he greatly helped those who through grace had become believers, [28]for he powerfully refuted the Jews in public, showing by the scriptures that the Messiah[h] is Jesus.

Paul in Ephesus

19 While Apollos was in Corinth, Paul passed through the interior regions and came to Ephesus, where he found some disciples. [2]He said to them, "Did you receive the Holy Spirit when you became believers?" They replied, "No, we have not even heard that there is a Holy Spirit." [3]Then he said, "Into what then were you baptized?" They answered, "Into John's baptism." [4]Paul said, "John baptized with the baptism of repentance, telling the people to believe in the one who was to come after him, that is, in Jesus." [5]On hearing this, they were baptized in the name of the Lord Jesus. [6]When Paul had laid his hands on them, the Holy Spirit came upon them, and they spoke in tongues and prophesied— [7]altogether there were about twelve of them.

8 He entered the synagogue and for three months spoke out boldly, and argued persuasively about the kingdom of God. [9]When some stubbornly refused to believe and spoke evil of the Way before the congregation, he left them, taking the disciples with him, and argued daily in the lecture hall of Tyrannus.[i] [10]This continued for

[i] Other ancient authorities read *of a certain Tyrannus,*

two years, so that all the residents of Asia, both Jews and Greeks, heard the word of the Lord.

The Sons of Sceva

11 God did extraordinary miracles through Paul, [12]so that when the handkerchiefs or aprons that had touched his skin were brought to the sick, their diseases left them, and the evil spirits came out of them. [13]Then some itinerant Jewish exorcists tried to use the name of the Lord Jesus over those who had evil spirits, saying, "I adjure you by the Jesus whom Paul proclaims." [14]Seven

19.9 Sports and Education

Greek lecture halls or gymnasiums, such as this one at Tyrannus, often were built as training rooms for Olympic athletes and later converted to educational purposes. (The word "gymnasium" comes from a Greek word that means, literally, "to train in the nude.") Modern Americans use this ancient word for athletic facilities; Europeans, especially Germans, use it in referring to college-prep schools.

sons of a Jewish high priest named Sceva were doing this. [15]But the evil spirit said to them in reply, "Jesus I know, and Paul I know; but who are you?" [16]Then the man with the evil spirit leaped on them, mastered them all, and so overpowered them that they fled out of the house naked and wounded. [17]When this became known to all residents of Ephesus, both Jews and Greeks, everyone was awestruck; and the name of the Lord Jesus was praised. [18]Also many of those who became believers confessed and disclosed their practices. [19]A number of those who practiced magic collected their books and burned them publicly; when the value of these books[j] was calculated, it was found to come to fifty thousand silver coins. [20]So the word of the Lord grew mightily and prevailed.

The Riot in Ephesus

21 Now after these things had been accomplished, Paul resolved in the Spirit to go through Macedonia and Achaia, and then to go on to Jerusalem. He said, "After I have gone there, I must also see Rome." [22]So he sent two of his helpers, Timothy and Erastus, to Macedonia, while he himself stayed for some time longer in Asia.

23 About that time no little disturbance broke out concerning the Way. [24]A man named Demetrius, a silversmith who made silver shrines of Artemis, brought no little business to the artisans. [25]These he gathered together, with the workers of the same trade, and said, "Men, you know that we get our wealth from this business. [26]You also see and hear that not only in Ephesus but in almost the whole of Asia this Paul has persuaded and drawn away a considerable number of people by

19.24 Commercialized Religion

Ephesus was devoted to idolatry and to profit, and Paul's message threatened both. The citizens took great pride in their temple, one of the seven wonders of the ancient world, and were outraged at anyone who might interfere with their profitable businesses dependent on religious pilgrims. The story presents a clear case of mob psychology. Paul started a riot, but he also founded one of his strongest churches, a community that later inspired the book of Ephesians.

saying that gods made with hands are not gods. [27]And there is danger not only that this trade of ours may come into disrepute but also that the temple of the great goddess Artemis will be scorned, and she will be deprived of her majesty that brought all Asia and the world to worship her."

28 When they heard this, they were enraged and shouted, "Great is Artemis of the Ephesians!" [29]The city was filled with the confusion; and people[k] rushed together to the theater, dragging with them Gaius and Aristarchus, Macedonians who were Paul's travel companions. [30]Paul wished to go into the crowd, but the disciples would not let him; [31]even some officials of the province of Asia,[l] who were friendly to him, sent him a message urging him not to venture into the theater. [32]Meanwhile, some were shouting one thing, some another; for the assembly was in confusion, and most of them did not know why they had come together. [33]Some of the crowd gave instructions to Alexander, whom the Jews had pushed forward. And Alexander motioned for silence and tried to make a defense before the people. [34]But when they recognized that he was a Jew, for about two hours all of them shouted in unison, "Great is Artemis of the Ephesians!" [35]But when the town clerk had quieted the crowd, he said, "Citizens of Ephesus, who is there that does not know that the city of the Ephesians is the temple keeper of the great Artemis and of the statue that fell from heaven?[m] [36]Since these things cannot be denied, you ought to be quiet and do nothing rash. [37]You have brought these men here who are neither temple robbers nor blasphemers of our[n] goddess. [38]If therefore Demetrius and the artisans with him have a complaint against anyone, the

j Gk *them*   k Gk *they*   l Gk *some of the Asiarchs*   m Meaning of Gk uncertain   n Other ancient authorities read *your* courts are open, and there are proconsuls; let them bring charges there against one another. 39If there is anything further*o* you want to know, it must be settled in the regular assembly. 40For we are in danger of being charged with rioting today, since there is no cause that we can give to justify this commotion." 41When he had said this, he dismissed the assembly.

Paul Goes to Macedonia and Greece

20 After the uproar had ceased, Paul sent for the disciples; and after encouraging them and saying farewell, he left for Macedonia. 2When he had gone through those regions and had given the believers*p* much encouragement, he came to Greece, 3where he stayed for three months. He

was about to set sail for Syria when a plot was made against him by the Jews, and so he decided to return through Macedonia. 4He was accompanied by Sopater son of Pyrrhus from Beroea, by Aristarchus and Secundus from Thessalonica, by Gaius from Derbe, and by Timothy, as well as by Tychicus and Trophimus from Asia. 5They went ahead and were waiting for us in Troas; 6but we sailed from Philippi after the days of Unleavened Bread, and in five days we joined them in Troas, where we stayed for seven days.

Paul's Farewell Visit to Troas

7 On the first day of the week, when we met to break bread, Paul was holding a discussion with them; since he intended to leave the next

---

o Other ancient authorities read *about other matters*   *p* Gk *given them*

Paul's Legal Battles
470 Roman soldiers protected him from a lynch mob

THE DRUMBEAT STARTS WITH THE last verse in chapter 20: "There was much . . . grieving especially because of what he had said, that they would not see him again." After this, wherever he went, Paul's friends begged him not to go to Jerusalem. One of them bound his own hands and feet with Paul's belt, publicly role-playing what was in store for Paul (21.10–11).

But Paul had survived shipwrecks, a stoning, beatings, and long nights in jail, and fear had never stopped him. Besides, he knew that God wanted him to take his word to Rome, and no disaster in Jerusalem could prevent that.

A Dangerous Revolutionary?

Thus, against all advice Paul went to Jerusalem. His reputation as a Christian missionary had spread, to such an extent that it took a brigade of 470 Roman soldiers to protect him from a Jewish lynch mob.

Luke details the process of Roman justice so thoroughly that some have speculated he wrote Acts as a legal brief for Paul's defense. Was Paul a violent terrorist intent on inciting revolt? Luke meticulously records that, no, Paul had no political ambitions and consistently worked within Roman law.

Most of the time, Roman law found Paul innocent. An official in Corinth dismissed charges against him (18.15), as did the town clerk at Ephesus (19.35–41). In Judea Governor Festus and King Agrippa both concluded Paul might have been freed outright had he not appealed to Caesar (26.32).

The Beginning of the End

Paul's last days of freedom summarize his turbulent life. His friends' fears regarding Jerusalem proved well-founded. A murderous mob there assailed him with trumped-up charges, and he had to be rescued bodily by soldiers.

In typical brazen style, Paul asked to address the unruly crowd, using the chance to confront them with his life's testimony. The crowd listened until he got to the part about a mission to the Gentiles; then it erupted.

In his speech (22.3–21), Paul referred back to the day he stood on the sidelines cheering as Stephen, the first Christian martyr, was killed. That violent scene was forever etched in Paul's mind as a reminder of his former life. But another memory was even more powerful: the blinding light on the road to Damascus. Ever after that event in Damascus, Paul seemed determined to stun the human race as he had been stunned on that desert road. No matter how many nights in jail it cost him.

Life Questions: Acts 20 shows Paul's closeness to other Christians. What produced such intense feelings? What could increase your closeness with others?

> "And now, as a captive to the Spirit, I am on my way to Jerusalem, not knowing what will happen to me there, except that the Holy Spirit testifies to me in every city that imprisonment and persecutions are waiting for me."
> 20.22–23

day, he continued speaking until midnight. [8]There were many lamps in the room upstairs where we were meeting. [9]A young man named Eutychus, who was sitting in the window, began

20.4 No Cheating

In the days before electronic banking, money had to be carried in person. Thus Paul's plan to transfer the famine relief funds collected in Greece and Asia to the churches in Judea (see 24.17) posed some problems. Eager to avoid suspicion, Paul invited representatives from the donating churches to accompany him. That way he could assure everyone the money was used as promised, and not for personal gain. Second Corinthians 8 gives more details about this offering.

to sink off into a deep sleep while Paul talked still longer. Overcome by sleep, he fell to the ground three floors below and was picked up dead. [10]But Paul went down, and bending over him took him in his arms, and said, "Do not be alarmed, for his life is in him." [11]Then Paul went upstairs, and after he had broken bread and eaten, he continued to converse with them until dawn; then he left. [12]Meanwhile they had taken the boy away alive and were not a little comforted.

The Voyage from Troas to Miletus

13 We went ahead to the ship and set sail for Assos, intending to take Paul on board there; for he had made this arrangement, intending to go by land himself. [14]When he met us in Assos, we took him on board and went to Mitylene. [15]We sailed from there, and on the following day we arrived opposite Chios. The next day we touched at Samos, and[q] the day after that we came to Miletus. [16]For Paul had decided to sail past Ephesus, so that he might not have to spend time in Asia; he was eager to be in Jerusalem, if possible, on the day of Pentecost.

Paul Speaks to the Ephesian Elders

17 From Miletus he sent a message to Ephesus, asking the elders of the church to meet him. [18]When they came to him, he said to them:

"You yourselves know how I lived among you the entire time from the first day that I set foot in Asia, [19]serving the Lord with all humility and with tears, enduring the trials that came to me through the plots of the Jews. [20]I did not shrink from doing anything helpful, proclaiming the message to you and teaching you publicly and from house to house, [21]as I testified to both Jews and Greeks about repentance toward God and faith toward

our Lord Jesus. [22]And now, as a captive to the Spirit,[r] I am on my way to Jerusalem, not knowing what will happen to me there, [23]except that the Holy Spirit testifies to me in every city that imprisonment and persecutions are waiting for me. [24]But I do not count my life of any value to myself, if only I may finish my course and the ministry that I received from the Lord Jesus, to testify to the good news of God's grace.

25 "And now I know that none of you, among whom I have gone about proclaiming the kingdom, will ever see my face again. [26]Therefore I declare to you this day that I am not responsible for the blood of any of you, [27]for I did not shrink from declaring to you the whole purpose of God. [28]Keep watch over yourselves and over all the flock, of which the Holy Spirit has made you overseers, to shepherd the church of God[s] that he obtained with the blood of his own Son.[t] [29]I know that after I have gone, savage wolves will come in among you, not sparing the flock. [30]Some even from your own group will come distorting the truth in order to entice the disciples to follow them. [31]Therefore be alert, remembering that for three years I did not cease night or day to warn everyone with tears. [32]And now I commend you to God and to the message of his grace, a message that is able to build you up and to give you the inheritance among all who are sanctified. [33]I coveted no one's silver or gold or clothing. [34]You know for yourselves that I worked with my own hands to support myself and my companions. [35]In all this I have given you an example that by such work we must support the weak, remembering the words of the Lord Jesus, for he himself said, 'It is more blessed to give than to receive.'"

20.35 Emotional Farewell

Paul had worked in Ephesus longer than any other city. Before leaving on his fateful trip to Jerusalem, he called the elders to Miletus for a final farewell (verse 17). In his speech, he quotes a saying from Jesus—the only New Testament quotation from Jesus not found in the Gospels.

36 When he had finished speaking, he knelt down with them all and prayed. [37]There was much weeping among them all; they embraced Paul and kissed him, [38]grieving especially because of what he had said, that they would not see him again. Then they brought him to the ship.

Paul's Journey to Jerusalem

21 When we had parted from them and set sail, we came by a straight course to Cos,

---

[q] Other ancient authorities add *after remaining at Trogyllium*   [r] Or *And now, bound in the spirit*   [s] Other ancient authorities read *of the Lord*   [t] Or *with his own blood*; Gk *with the blood of his Own*

and the next day to Rhodes, and from there to Patara.ᵘ ²When we found a ship bound for Phoenicia, we went on board and set sail. ³We came in sight of Cyprus; and leaving it on our left, we sailed to Syria and landed at Tyre, because the ship was to unload its cargo there. ⁴We looked up the disciples and stayed there for seven days. Through the Spirit they told Paul not to go on to Jerusalem. ⁵When our days there were ended, we left and proceeded on our journey; and all of them, with wives and children, escorted us outside the city. There we knelt down on the beach and prayed ⁶and said farewell to one another. Then we went on board the ship, and they returned home.

7 When we had finishedᵛ the voyage from Tyre, we arrived at Ptolemais; and we greeted the believersʷ and stayed with them for one day. ⁸The next day we left and came to Caesarea; and we went into the house of Philip the evangelist, one of the seven, and stayed with him. ⁹He had four unmarried daughtersˣ who had the gift of prophecy. ¹⁰While we were staying there for several days, a prophet named Agabus came down from Judea. ¹¹He came to us and took Paul's belt, bound his own feet and hands with it, and said, "Thus says the Holy Spirit, 'This is the way the Jews in Jerusalem will bind the man who owns this belt and will hand him over to the Gentiles.'" ¹²When we heard this, we and the people there urged him not to go up to Jerusalem. ¹³Then Paul answered, "What are you doing, weeping and breaking my heart? For I am ready not only to be bound but even to die in Jerusalem for the name of the Lord Jesus." ¹⁴Since he would not be persuaded, we remained silent except to say, "The Lord's will be done."

15 After these days we got ready and started to go up to Jerusalem. ¹⁶Some of the disciples from Caesarea also came along and brought us to the house of Mnason of Cyprus, an early disciple, with whom we were to stay.

Paul Visits James at Jerusalem

17 When we arrived in Jerusalem, the brothers welcomed us warmly. ¹⁸The next day Paul went with us to visit James; and all the elders were present. ¹⁹After greeting them, he related one by one the things that God had done among the Gentiles through his ministry. ²⁰When they heard it, they praised God. Then they said to him, "You see, brother, how many thousands of believers there are among the Jews, and they are all zealous for the law. ²¹They have been told about you that you teach all the Jews living among the Gentiles to forsake Moses, and that you tell them not to circumcise their children or observe the customs. ²²What then is to be done? They will certainly

hear that you have come. ²³So do what we tell you. We have four men who are under a vow. ²⁴Join these men, go through the rite of purification with them, and pay for the shaving of their heads. Thus all will know that there is nothing in what they have been told about you, but that you yourself observe and guard the law. ²⁵But as for the Gentiles who have become believers, we have sent a letter with our judgment that they should abstain from what has been sacrificed to idols and from blood and from what is strangledʸ and from fornication." ²⁶Then Paul took the men, and the next day, having purified himself, he entered the temple with them, making public the completion of the days of purification when the sacrifice would be made for each of them.

Paul Arrested in the Temple

27 When the seven days were almost completed, the Jews from Asia, who had seen him in the temple, stirred up the whole crowd. They seized him, ²⁸shouting, "Fellow Israelites, help! This is the man who is teaching everyone everywhere against our people, our law, and this place; more than that, he has actually brought Greeks into the temple and has defiled this holy place."

21.28 A Trumped-up Charge

Ironically, the arrest that led to Paul's final imprisonment came about because of a misunderstanding. He was actually trying to reassure the Jerusalem church of his loyalty by agreeing to take Jewish vows. But a rumor spread that Paul had illegally taken an "unclean" Gentile into a forbidden part of the temple, and a mob scene ensued. The remainder of Acts reports on various stages of Paul's legal appeals.

²⁹For they had previously seen Trophimus the Ephesian with him in the city, and they supposed that Paul had brought him into the temple. ³⁰Then all the city was aroused, and the people rushed together. They seized Paul and dragged him out of the temple, and immediately the doors were shut. ³¹While they were trying to kill him, word came to the tribune of the cohort that all Jerusalem was in an uproar. ³²Immediately he took soldiers and centurions and ran down to them. When they saw the tribune and the soldiers, they stopped beating Paul. ³³Then the tribune came, arrested him, and ordered him to be bound with two chains; he inquired who he was and what he had done. ³⁴Some in the crowd shouted one thing, some another; and as he could not learn the facts because of the uproar, he or-

ᵘ Other ancient authorities add *and Myra*   ᵛ Or *continued*   ʷ Gk *brothers*   ˣ Gk *four daughters, virgins,*
ʸ Other ancient authorities lack *and from what is strangled*

dered him to be brought into the barracks. [35]When Paul[z] came to the steps, the violence of the mob was so great that he had to be carried by the soldiers. [36]The crowd that followed kept shouting, "Away with him!"

Paul Defends Himself

37 Just as Paul was about to be brought into the barracks, he said to the tribune, "May I say something to you?" The tribune[a] replied, "Do you know Greek? [38]Then you are not the Egyptian who recently stirred up a revolt and led the four thousand assassins out into the wilderness?" [39]Paul replied, "I am a Jew, from Tarsus in Cilicia, a citizen of an important city; I beg you, let me speak to the people." [40]When he had given him permission, Paul stood on the steps and motioned to the people for silence; and when there was a great hush, he addressed them in the Hebrew[b] language, saying:

22 "Brothers and fathers, listen to the defense that I now make before you."

2 When they heard him addressing them in Hebrew,[b] they became even more quiet. Then he said:

3 "I am a Jew, born in Tarsus in Cilicia, but brought up in this city at the feet of Gamaliel, educated strictly according to our ancestral law, being zealous for God, just as all of you are today. [4]I persecuted this Way up to the point of death by binding both men and women and putting them in prison, [5]as the high priest and the whole council of elders can testify about me. From them I also received letters to the brothers in Damascus, and I went there in order to bind those who were there and to bring them back to Jerusalem for punishment.

Paul Tells of His Conversion

6 "While I was on my way and approaching Damascus, about noon a great light from heaven suddenly shone about me. [7]I fell to the ground and heard a voice saying to me, 'Saul, Saul, why are you persecuting me?' [8]I answered, 'Who are

you, Lord?' Then he said to me, 'I am Jesus of Nazareth[c] whom you are persecuting.' [9]Now those who were with me saw the light but did not hear the voice of the one who was speaking to me. [10]I asked, 'What am I to do, Lord?' The Lord said to me, 'Get up and go to Damascus; there you will be told everything that has been assigned to you to do.' [11]Since I could not see because of the brightness of that light, those who were with me took my hand and led me to Damascus.

12 "A certain Ananias, who was a devout man according to the law and well spoken of by all the Jews living there, [13]came to me; and standing beside me, he said, 'Brother Saul, regain your sight!' In that very hour I regained my sight and saw him. [14]Then he said, 'The God of our ancestors has chosen you to know his will, to see the Righteous One and to hear his own voice; [15]for you will be his witness to all the world of what you have seen and heard. [16]And now why do you delay? Get up, be baptized, and have your sins washed away, calling on his name.'

Paul Sent to the Gentiles

17 "After I had returned to Jerusalem and while I was praying in the temple, I fell into a trance [18]and saw Jesus[d] saying to me, 'Hurry and get out of Jerusalem quickly, because they will not accept your testimony about me.' [19]And I said, 'Lord, they themselves know that in every synagogue I imprisoned and beat those who believed in you. [20]And while the blood of your witness Stephen was shed, I myself was standing by, approving and keeping the coats of those who killed him.' [21]Then he said to me, 'Go, for I will send you far away to the Gentiles.'"

Paul and the Roman Tribune

22 Up to this point they listened to him, but then they shouted, "Away with such a fellow from the earth! For he should not be allowed to live." [23]And while they were shouting, throwing off their cloaks, and tossing dust into the air, [24]the tribune directed that he was to be brought into the barracks, and ordered him to be examined by flogging, to find out the reason for this outcry against him. [25]But when they had tied him up with thongs,[e] Paul said to the centurion who was standing by, "Is it legal for you to flog a Roman citizen who is uncondemned?" [26]When the centurion heard that, he went to the tribune and said to him, "What are you about to do? This man is a Roman citizen." [27]The tribune came and asked Paul,[d] "Tell me, are you a Roman citizen?" And he said, "Yes." [28]The tribune answered, "It cost me a large sum of money to get my citizenship." Paul said, "But I was born a citizen." [29]Immediately those who were about to examine him drew back from him; and the tribune also was afraid,

22.6 Three Versions

Paul's change from persecutor to Christian missionary makes for one of the most dramatic conversion stories in the New Testament. Acts gives three versions: Luke's historical report in chapter 9; Paul's self-defense here before a Jewish mob; and his formal testimony before Agrippa (chapter 26), a descendant of the ruler who tried to kill the infant Jesus in Bethlehem. Each version adds new details custom-tailored to the specific audience.

[z] Gk he   [a] Gk He   [b] That is, *Aramaic*   [c] Gk *the Nazorean*   [d] Gk *him*   [e] Or *up for the lashes*

for he realized that Paul was a Roman citizen and that he had bound him.

Paul before the Council

30 Since he wanted to find out what Paul*f* was being accused of by the Jews, the next day he released him and ordered the chief priests and the entire council to meet. He brought Paul down and had him stand before them.

23 While Paul was looking intently at the council he said, "Brothers,*g* up to this day I have lived my life with a clear conscience before God." ²Then the high priest Ananias ordered those standing near him to strike him on the mouth. ³At this Paul said to him, "God will strike you, you whitewashed wall! Are you sitting there to judge me according to the law, and yet in violation of the law you order me to be struck?" ⁴Those standing nearby said, "Do you dare to insult God's high priest?" ⁵And Paul said, "I did not realize, brothers, that he was high priest; for it is written, 'You shall not speak evil of a leader of your people.'"

6 When Paul noticed that some were Sadducees and others were Pharisees, he called out in the council, "Brothers, I am a Pharisee, a son of Pharisees. I am on trial concerning the hope of

23.6 Paul under Attack

Under pressure, Paul proved to be a formidable opponent. In this scene, he spoke back to a priest who struck him on the mouth. Using great skill, Paul divided his accusers by exploiting the differences between two Jewish sects, the Pharisees and Sadducees (see note on 4.1). Paul managed to arouse such intense opposition that a group of 40 conspirators vowed not to eat or drink until they had killed him.

the resurrection*h* of the dead." ⁷When he said this, a dissension began between the Pharisees and the Sadducees, and the assembly was divided. ⁸(The Sadducees say that there is no resurrection, or angel, or spirit; but the Pharisees acknowledge all three.) ⁹Then a great clamor arose, and certain scribes of the Pharisees' group stood up and contended, "We find nothing wrong with this man. What if a spirit or an angel has spoken to him?" ¹⁰When the dissension became violent, the tribune, fearing that they would tear Paul to pieces, ordered the soldiers to go down, take him by force, and bring him into the barracks.

11 That night the Lord stood near him and said, "Keep up your courage! For just as you have testified for me in Jerusalem, so you must bear witness also in Rome."

The Plot to Kill Paul

12 In the morning the Jews joined in a conspiracy and bound themselves by an oath neither to eat nor drink until they had killed Paul. ¹³There were more than forty who joined in this conspiracy. ¹⁴They went to the chief priests and elders and said, "We have strictly bound ourselves by an oath to taste no food until we have killed Paul. ¹⁵Now then, you and the council must notify the tribune to bring him down to you, on the pretext that you want to make a more thorough examination of his case. And we are ready to do away with him before he arrives."

16 Now the son of Paul's sister heard about the ambush; so he went and gained entrance to

23.16 Paul's Family

This mention of Paul's nephew is the only reference to Paul's family. Born a Roman citizen in Tarsus (22.28), Paul likely came from a rather prominent family. Only a minority of people in the Roman empire held citizenship, especially in occupied lands. Citizenship could be purchased at a great price or awarded by Roman authorities, but Paul specifies his came through inheritance.

the barracks and told Paul. ¹⁷Paul called one of the centurions and said, "Take this young man to the tribune, for he has something to report to him." ¹⁸So he took him, brought him to the tribune, and said, "The prisoner Paul called me and asked me to bring this young man to you; he has something to tell you." ¹⁹The tribune took him by the hand, drew him aside privately, and asked, "What is it that you have to report to me?" ²⁰He answered, "The Jews have agreed to ask you to bring Paul down to the council tomorrow, as though they were going to inquire more thoroughly into his case. ²¹But do not be persuaded by them, for more than forty of their men are lying in ambush for him. They have bound themselves by an oath neither to eat nor drink until they kill him. They are ready now and are waiting for your consent." ²²So the tribune dismissed the young man, ordering him, "Tell no one that you have informed me of this."

Paul Sent to Felix the Governor

23 Then he summoned two of the centurions and said, "Get ready to leave by nine o'clock tonight for Caesarea with two hundred soldiers, seventy horsemen, and two hundred spearmen. ²⁴Also provide mounts for Paul to ride, and take him safely to Felix the governor." ²⁵He wrote a letter to this effect:

f Gk *he*   *g* Gk *Men, brothers*   *h* Gk *concerning hope and resurrection*

26 "Claudius Lysias to his Excellency the governor Felix, greetings. 27This man was seized by the Jews and was about to be killed by them, but when I had learned that he was a Roman citizen, I came with the guard and rescued him. 28Since I wanted to know the charge for which they accused him, I had him brought to their council. 29I found that he was accused concerning questions of their law, but was charged with nothing deserving death or imprisonment. 30When I was informed that there would be a plot against the man, I sent him to you at once, ordering his accusers also to state before you what they have against him.*"

31 So the soldiers, according to their instructions, took Paul and brought him during the night to Antipatris. 32The next day they let the horsemen go on with him, while they returned to the barracks. 33When they came to Caesarea and delivered the letter to the governor, they presented Paul also before him. 34On reading the letter, he asked what province he belonged to, and when he learned that he was from Cilicia, 35he said, "I will give you a hearing when your accusers arrive." Then he ordered that he be kept under guard in Herod's headquarters.*

Paul before Felix at Caesarea

24 Five days later the high priest Ananias came down with some elders and an attorney, a certain Tertullus, and they reported their case against Paul to the governor. 2When Paul* had been summoned, Tertullus began to accuse him, saying:

"Your Excellency,* because of you we have long enjoyed peace, and reforms have been made for this people because of your foresight. 3We welcome this in every way and everywhere with utmost gratitude. 4But, to detain you no further, I beg you to hear us briefly with your customary graciousness. 5We have, in fact, found this man a pestilent fellow, an agitator among all the Jews throughout the world, and a ringleader of the sect of the Nazarenes.* 6He even tried to profane the temple, and so we seized him.* 8By examining him yourself you will be able to learn from him concerning everything of which we accuse him."

9 The Jews also joined in the charge by asserting that all this was true.

Paul's Defense before Felix

10 When the governor motioned to him to speak, Paul replied:

"I cheerfully make my defense, knowing that for many years you have been a judge over this nation. 11As you can find out, it is not more than twelve days since I went up to worship in Jerusalem. 12They did not find me disputing with anyone in the temple or stirring up a crowd either in the synagogues or throughout the city. 13Neither can they prove to you the charge that they now bring against me. 14But this I admit to you, that according to the Way, which they call a sect, I worship the God of our ancestors, believing everything laid down according to the law or written in the prophets. 15I have a hope in God—a hope that they themselves also accept—that there will be a resurrection of both* the righteous and the unrighteous. 16Therefore I do my best always to have a clear conscience toward God and all people. 17Now after some years I came to bring alms to my nation and to offer sacrifices. 18While I was doing this, they found me in the temple, completing the rite of purification, without any crowd or disturbance. 19But there were some Jews from Asia—they ought to be here before you to make an accusation, if they have anything against me. 20Or let these men here tell what crime they had found when I stood before the council, 21unless it was this one sentence that I called out while standing before them, 'It is about the resurrection of the dead that I am on trial before you today.'"

22 But Felix, who was rather well informed about the Way, adjourned the hearing with the comment, "When Lysias the tribune comes down, I will decide your case." 23Then he ordered the centurion to keep him in custody, but to let him have some liberty and not to prevent any of his friends from taking care of his needs.

Paul Held in Custody

24 Some days later when Felix came with his wife Drusilla, who was Jewish, he sent for Paul and heard him speak concerning faith in Christ Jesus. 25And as he discussed justice, self-control, and the coming judgment, Felix became frightened and said, "Go away for the present; when I have an opportunity, I will send for you." 26At the same time he hoped that money would be given

24.27 Left in Chains

Felix was unpopular with the Jews of Palestine. The brief report in Acts shows him to be shrewd and even corrupt (verse 26). Recalled by Rome because of his troubles with the Jews, Felix left Paul in chains for a period of two years. When the new Roman ruler arrived, the controversy over Paul hadn't died down. Jewish leaders immediately confronted Festus with their charges against Paul.

---

i Other ancient authorities add *Farewell* *j* Gk *praetorium* *k* Gk *he* *l* Gk lacks *Your Excellency* *m* Gk *Nazoreans* *n* Other ancient authorities add *and we would have judged him according to our law.* 7*But the chief captain Lysias came and with great violence took him out of our hands,* 8*commanding his accusers to come before you.* *o* Other ancient authorities read *of the dead, both of*

him by Paul, and for that reason he used to send for him very often and converse with him.

27 After two years had passed, Felix was succeeded by Porcius Festus; and since he wanted to grant the Jews a favor, Felix left Paul in prison.

Paul Appeals to the Emperor

25 Three days after Festus had arrived in the province, he went up from Caesarea to Jerusalem ²where the chief priests and the leaders of the Jews gave him a report against Paul. They appealed to him ³and requested, as a favor to them against Paul,ᵖ to have him transferred to Jerusalem. They were, in fact, planning an ambush to kill him along the way. ⁴Festus replied that Paul was being kept at Caesarea, and that he himself intended to go there shortly. ⁵"So," he said, "let those of you who have the authority come down with me, and if there is anything wrong about the man, let them accuse him."

6 After he had stayed among them not more than eight or ten days, he went down to Caesarea; the next day he took his seat on the tribunal and ordered Paul to be brought. ⁷When he arrived, the Jews who had gone down from Jerusalem surrounded him, bringing many serious charges against him, which they could not prove. ⁸Paul said in his defense, "I have in no way committed an offense against the law of the Jews, or against the temple, or against the emperor." ⁹But Festus, wishing to do the Jews a favor, asked Paul, "Do you wish to go up to Jerusalem and be tried there before me on these charges?" ¹⁰Paul said, "I am appealing to the emperor's tribunal; this is where I should be tried. I have done no wrong to the

ᵖ Gk *him*

Jews, as you very well know. ¹¹Now if I am in the wrong and have committed something for which I deserve to die, I am not trying to escape death; but if there is nothing to their charges against me, no one can turn me over to them. I appeal to the emperor." ¹²Then Festus, after he had conferred with his council, replied, "You have appealed to the emperor; to the emperor you will go."

Festus Consults King Agrippa

13 After several days had passed, King Agrippa and Bernice arrived at Caesarea to welcome

25.13 Two Rulers

In Jesus' day Rome ruled Palestine through local rulers (the Herods) and their overseer Pilate, a governor who reported directly to Rome. Now, around A.D. 59 or 60, their counterparts were the Roman governor Festus and the last of the Herods, Agrippa II. Festus, a responsible leader, dealt with Paul's case promptly, whereas his predecessor Felix had stalled for two years, leaving Paul in prison. Festus used the visit of Herod Agrippa to schedule this special inquiry into Paul's case.

Festus. ¹⁴Since they were staying there several days, Festus laid Paul's case before the king, saying, "There is a man here who was left in prison by Felix. ¹⁵When I was in Jerusalem, the chief priests and the elders of the Jews informed me about him and asked for a sentence against him.

AGRIPPA *Roman Heart*

MEMBERS OF THE HEROD FAMILY were native to Palestine, but their loyalties lay elsewhere—in Rome, where their bread was buttered. The Herods play a leading role in New Testament history, but mostly a negative one.

Agrippa, known to historians as Herod Agrippa II, was the last of a series of Herods who ruled Palestine on Rome's behalf. His great uncle had beheaded John the Baptist and presided over one of Jesus' trials; that man's father had ordered the massacre of babies after Jesus' birth. Now, Agrippa had to pass judgment on the apostle Paul, fiery missionary of the new cause.

Educated in Rome, Agrippa came to power at the age of 17 when his father died. Apparently Agrippa picked up some loose morals in Rome as well; his sister Bernice, who accompanied him to hear Paul's trial, was also his mistress. She tried marriage a number of times, and was mistress to other powerful men, but always she returned to her brother. Their incest fueled Roman gossip.

Nonetheless Paul assumed that Agrippa had some background knowledge of the gospel. As overseer of the Jewish temple, he knew about the increasing number of Jesus-followers and their claims that the prophets' predictions of a Messiah had been fulfilled. Agrippa, however, brushed off Paul's appeal. He was not about to get into a Biblical discussion in front of a Roman governor.

As far as we know, Agrippa stayed loyal to Rome until the end. When Jerusalem revolted against Nero in the year 66, Agrippa backed Rome completely. He was involved in Rome's complete destruction of Jerusalem and its temple in AD 70. His death marked the end of the Herods.

Life Questions: Agrippa put his loyalty to Rome above God's claims. Do you feel any conflict between competing loyalties? Where and why?

[16]I told them that it was not the custom of the Romans to hand over anyone before the accused had met the accusers face to face and had been given an opportunity to make a defense against the charge. [17]So when they met here, I lost no time, but on the next day took my seat on the tribunal and ordered the man to be brought. [18]When the accusers stood up, they did not charge him with any of the crimes[q] that I was expecting. [19]Instead they had certain points of disagreement with him about their own religion and about a certain Jesus, who had died, but whom Paul asserted to be alive. [20]Since I was at a loss how to investigate these questions, I asked whether he wished to go to Jerusalem and be tried there on these charges.[r] [21]But when Paul had appealed to be kept in custody for the decision of his Imperial Majesty, I ordered him to be held until I could send him to the emperor." [22]Agrippa said to Festus, "I would like to hear the man myself." "Tomorrow," he said, "you will hear him."

Paul Brought before Agrippa

23 So on the next day Agrippa and Bernice came with great pomp, and they entered the audience hall with the military tribunes and the prominent men of the city. Then Festus gave the order and Paul was brought in. [24]And Festus said, "King Agrippa and all here present with us, you see this man about whom the whole Jewish community petitioned me, both in Jerusalem and here, shouting that he ought not to live any longer. [25]But I found that he had done nothing deserving death; and when he appealed to his Imperial Majesty, I decided to send him. [26]But I have nothing definite to write to our sovereign about him. Therefore I have brought him before all of you, and especially before you, King Agrippa, so that, after we have examined him, I may have something to write— [27]for it seems to me unreasonable to send a prisoner without indicating the charges against him."

Paul Defends Himself before Agrippa

26 Agrippa said to Paul, "You have permission to speak for yourself." Then Paul stretched out his hand and began to defend himself:

2 "I consider myself fortunate that it is before you, King Agrippa, I am to make my defense today against all the accusations of the Jews, [3]because you are especially familiar with all the customs and controversies of the Jews; therefore I beg of you to listen to me patiently.

4 "All the Jews know my way of life from my youth, a life spent from the beginning among my own people and in Jerusalem. [5]They have known for a long time, if they are willing to testify, that I have belonged to the strictest sect of our religion and lived as a Pharisee. [6]And now I stand here on trial on account of my hope in the promise made by God to our ancestors, [7]a promise that our twelve tribes hope to attain, as they earnestly worship day and night. It is for this hope, your Excellency,[s] that I am accused by Jews! [8]Why is it thought incredible by any of you that God raises the dead?

9 "Indeed, I myself was convinced that I ought to do many things against the name of Jesus of Nazareth.[t] [10]And that is what I did in Jerusalem; with authority received from the chief priests, I not only locked up many of the saints in prison, but I also cast my vote against them when they were being condemned to death. [11]By punishing them often in all the synagogues I tried to force them to blaspheme; and since I was so furiously enraged at them, I pursued them even to foreign cities.

Paul Tells of His Conversion

12 "With this in mind, I was traveling to Damascus with the authority and commission of the chief priests, [13]when at midday along the road, your Excellency,[s] I saw a light from heaven, brighter than the sun, shining around me and my companions. [14]When we had all fallen to the ground, I heard a voice saying to me in the Hebrew[u] language, 'Saul, Saul, why are you persecuting me? It hurts you to kick against the goads.'

26.14 Kicking the Goads

The proverb comes from a sharp "goad" farmers used to control their oxen hitched to a plow. It means something like, "You are only hurting yourself."

[15]I asked, 'Who are you, Lord?' The Lord answered, 'I am Jesus whom you are persecuting. [16]But get up and stand on your feet; for I have appeared to you for this purpose, to appoint you to serve and testify to the things in which you have seen me[v] and to those in which I will appear to you. [17]I will rescue you from your people and from the Gentiles—to whom I am sending you [18]to open their eyes so that they may turn from darkness to light and from the power of Satan to God, so that they may receive forgiveness of sins and a place among those who are sanctified by faith in me.'

Paul Tells of His Preaching

19 "After that, King Agrippa, I was not disobedient to the heavenly vision, [20]but declared

q Other ancient authorities read *with anything*   r Gk *on them*   s Gk O *king*   t Gk *the Nazorean*   u That is, *Aramaic*   v Other ancient authorities read *the things that you have seen*

first to those in Damascus, then in Jerusalem and throughout the countryside of Judea, and also to the Gentiles, that they should repent and turn to God and do deeds consistent with repentance. ²¹For this reason the Jews seized me in the temple and tried to kill me. ²²To this day I have had help from God, and so I stand here, testifying to both small and great, saying nothing but what the prophets and Moses said would take place: ²³that the Messiah^w must suffer, and that, by being the first to rise from the dead, he would proclaim light both to our people and to the Gentiles."

Paul Appeals to Agrippa to Believe

24 While he was making this defense, Festus exclaimed, "You are out of your mind, Paul! Too much learning is driving you insane!" ²⁵But Paul said, "I am not out of my mind, most excellent Festus, but I am speaking the sober truth. ²⁶Indeed the king knows about these things, and to him I speak freely; for I am certain that none of these things has escaped his notice, for this was not done in a corner. ²⁷King Agrippa, do you believe the prophets? I know that you believe." ²⁸Agrippa said to Paul, "Are you so quickly persuading me to become a Christian?"^x ²⁹Paul replied, "Whether quickly or not, I pray to God that

not only you but also all who are listening to me today might become such as I am—except for these chains."

30 Then the king got up, and with him the governor and Bernice and those who had been seated with them; ³¹and as they were leaving, they said to one another, "This man is doing nothing to deserve death or imprisonment." ³²Agrippa said to Festus, "This man could have been set free if he had not appealed to the emperor."

Paul Sails for Rome

27 When it was decided that we were to sail for Italy, they transferred Paul and some other prisoners to a centurion of the Augustan Cohort, named Julius. ²Embarking on a ship of Adramyttium that was about to set sail to the ports along the coast of Asia, we put to sea, accompanied by Aristarchus, a Macedonian from Thessalonica. ³The next day we put in at Sidon; and Julius treated Paul kindly, and allowed him to go to his friends to be cared for. ⁴Putting out to sea from there, we sailed under the lee of Cyprus, because the winds were against us. ⁵After we had sailed across the sea that is off Cilicia and Pamphylia, we came to Myra in Lycia. ⁶There the centurion found an Alexandrian ship bound for

---

^w Or the Christ   ^x Or Quickly you will persuade me to play the Christian

---

Rome at Last
Paul finally made it to the capital—in chains

ACTS RECORDS 18 SPEECHES IN all, the last three of which were delivered before a very select audience. Roman officials, intrigued by the most talked-about prisoner in their corner of the empire, brought Paul out and asked him to perform, like a trained bear. As a result of their inquisition, he got his long-awaited trip to Rome.

It is hard for us today to realize how completely the city of Rome then dominated the world. "All roads lead to Rome" was more than a figure of speech. Like a center of gravity, the city attracted all the roads and commerce, all the leaders and thinkers and fortune-seekers of the empire. Political and military power fanned out from Rome. It was the indisputable capital of the world. If Christianity was to gain a foothold anywhere, it had to be in Rome.

> From morning until evening he explained the matter to them, testifying to the kingdom of God and trying to convince them about Jesus both from the law of Moses and from the prophets. 28.23

A Missionary in Chains

Ironically, Paul, the greatest spokesman for the Christian faith, arrived in Rome as a prisoner. He was exhausted, having just survived a harrowing shipwreck. In Rome, Paul got hours of quiet solitude to work on fond letters to the churches he had left behind.

In one sense, Acts ends anticlimactically, for Luke leaves Paul's life dangling. Most scholars believe Paul was released from this imprisonment and expanded his ministry into new frontiers. Luke records nothing of this period, and nothing about the trial of Paul or his eventual fate. He ends with a single memory, frozen in time: Paul, confined to his house, welcoming and preaching to all who come.

Paul could no longer choose his audience; they had to seek him. But boldly, in the heart of mighty Rome, he talked of a new kingdom and a new king. Christianity had made the journey, and the transition, from Jerusalem to Rome.

Life Questions: Is it better for Christianity to be popular or unpopular?

Italy and put us on board. [7]We sailed slowly for a number of days and arrived with difficulty off Cnidus, and as the wind was against us, we sailed under the lee of Crete off Salmone. [8]Sailing past it with difficulty, we came to a place called Fair Havens, near the city of Lasea.

[9] Since much time had been lost and sailing was now dangerous, because even the Fast had already gone by, Paul advised them, [10]saying, "Sirs, I can see that the voyage will be with danger and much heavy loss, not only of the cargo and the ship, but also of our lives." [11]But the centurion paid more attention to the pilot and to the owner of the ship than to what Paul said. [12]Since the harbor was not suitable for spending the winter, the majority was in favor of putting to sea from there, on the chance that somehow they could reach Phoenix, where they could spend the winter. It was a harbor of Crete, facing southwest and northwest.

The Storm at Sea

[13] When a moderate south wind began to blow, they thought they could achieve their purpose; so they weighed anchor and began to sail

27.13–41 Sailing Log

Luke was no sailor, but he portrays an authentically detailed account of the trip and storm. For example, sailors can sense they are "approaching land" (verse 27) long before they see it, both by an acutely developed sense of smell and also by the sound of breaking waves, which carries far out to sea. In the eastern Mediterranean, autumn winds blow from the west, which made westward sailing difficult for ships of that day.

past Crete, close to the shore. [14]But soon a violent wind, called the northeaster, rushed down from Crete.[y] [15]Since the ship was caught and could not be turned head-on into the wind, we gave way to it and were driven. [16]By running under the lee of a small island called Cauda[z] we were scarcely able to get the ship's boat under control. [17]After hoisting it up they took measures[a] to undergird the ship; then, fearing that they would run on the Syrtis, they lowered the sea anchor and so were driven. [18]We were being pounded by the storm so violently that on the next day they began to throw the cargo overboard, [19]and on the third day with their own hands they threw the ship's tackle overboard. [20]When neither sun nor stars appeared for many days, and no small tempest raged, all hope of our being saved was at last abandoned.

[21] Since they had been without food for a long time, Paul then stood up among them and said, "Men, you should have listened to me and not have set sail from Crete and thereby avoided this damage and loss. [22]I urge you now to keep up your courage, for there will be no loss of life among you, but only of the ship. [23]For last night there stood by me an angel of the God to whom I belong and whom I worship, [24]and he said, 'Do not be afraid, Paul; you must stand before the emperor; and indeed, God has granted safety to all those who are sailing with you.' [25]So keep up your courage, men, for I have faith in God that it will be exactly as I have been told. [26]But we will have to run aground on some island."

[27] When the fourteenth night had come, as we were drifting across the sea of Adria, about midnight the sailors suspected that they were nearing land. [28]So they took soundings and found twenty fathoms; a little farther on they took soundings again and found fifteen fathoms. [29]Fearing that we might run on the rocks, they let down four anchors from the stern and prayed for day to come. [30]But when the sailors tried to escape from the ship and had lowered the boat into the sea, on the pretext of putting out anchors from the bow, [31]Paul said to the centurion and the soldiers, "Unless these men stay in the ship, you cannot be saved." [32]Then the soldiers cut away the ropes of the boat and set it adrift.

[33] Just before daybreak, Paul urged all of them to take some food, saying, "Today is the fourteenth day that you have been in suspense and remaining without food, having eaten nothing. [34]Therefore I urge you to take some food, for it will help you survive; for none of you will lose a hair from your heads." [35]After he had said this, he took bread; and giving thanks to God in the presence of all, he broke it and began to eat. [36]Then all of them were encouraged and took food for themselves. [37](We were in all two hundred seventy-six[b] persons in the ship.) [38]After they had satisfied their hunger, they lightened the ship by throwing the wheat into the sea.

The Shipwreck

[39] In the morning they did not recognize the land, but they noticed a bay with a beach, on which they planned to run the ship ashore, if they could. [40]So they cast off the anchors and left them in the sea. At the same time they loosened the ropes that tied the steering-oars; then hoisting the foresail to the wind, they made for the beach. [41]But striking a reef,[c] they ran the ship aground; the bow stuck and remained immovable, but the stern was being broken up by the force of the waves. [42]The soldiers' plan was to kill the prisoners, so that none might swim away and escape; [43]but the centurion, wishing to save Paul, kept

y Gk *it*   z Other ancient authorities read *Clauda*   a Gk *helps*   b Other ancient authorities read *seventy-six*; others, about seventy-six   c Gk *place of two seas*

them from carrying out their plan. He ordered those who could swim to jump overboard first and make for the land, 44and the rest to follow, some on planks and others on pieces of the ship. And so it was that all were brought safely to land.

Paul on the Island of Malta

28 After we had reached safety, we then learned that the island was called Malta. 2The natives showed us unusual kindness. Since it had begun to rain and was cold, they kindled a fire and welcomed all of us around it. 3Paul had gathered a bundle of brushwood and was putting it on the fire, when a viper, driven out by the heat, fastened itself on his hand. 4When the natives saw the creature hanging from his hand, they said to one another, "This man must be a murderer; though he has escaped from the sea, justice has not allowed him to live." 5He, however, shook off the creature into the fire and suffered no harm. 6They were expecting him to swell up or drop dead, but after they had waited a long time and saw that nothing unusual had happened to him, they changed their minds and began to say that he was a god.

7 Now in the neighborhood of that place were lands belonging to the leading man of the island, named Publius, who received us and entertained us hospitably for three days. 8It so happened that the father of Publius lay sick in bed with fever and dysentery. Paul visited him and cured him by praying and putting his hands on him. 9After this happened, the rest of the people on the island who had diseases also came and were cured. 10They bestowed many honors on us, and when we were about to sail, they put on board all the provisions we needed.

Paul Arrives at Rome

11 Three months later we set sail on a ship that had wintered at the island, an Alexandrian ship with the Twin Brothers as its figurehead. 12We put in at Syracuse and stayed there for three days; 13then we weighed anchor and came to Rhegium. After one day there a south wind sprang up, and on the second day we came to Puteoli. 14There we found believers*d* and were invited to stay with them for seven days. And so we came to Rome. 15The believers*d* from there, when they heard of us, came as far as the Forum of Appius and Three Taverns to meet us. On seeing them, Paul thanked God and took courage.

16 When we came into Rome, Paul was allowed to live by himself, with the soldier who was guarding him.

Paul and Jewish Leaders in Rome

17 Three days later he called together the local leaders of the Jews. When they had assembled, he said to them, "Brothers, though I had done nothing against our people or the customs of our ancestors, yet I was arrested in Jerusalem and handed over to the Romans. 18When they had

28.16 Time on His Hands

Luke reports that controversy about the Christian "sect" had preceded Paul to Rome (verse 22). The apostle put his time of house arrest to good use, evangelizing all who came to see him and writing to the churches he had founded along the way. Such New Testament books as Philippians, Colossians, Ephesians, and Philemon came out of this period of protective custody, which may have lasted four years.

examined me, the Romans*e* wanted to release me, because there was no reason for the death penalty in my case. 19But when the Jews objected, I was compelled to appeal to the emperor—even though I had no charge to bring against my nation. 20For this reason therefore I have asked to see you and speak with you,*f* since it is for the sake of the hope of Israel that I am bound with this chain." 21They replied, "We have received no letters from Judea about you, and none of the brothers coming here has reported or spoken anything evil about you. 22But we would like to hear from you what you think, for with regard to this sect we know that everywhere it is spoken against."

Paul Preaches in Rome

23 After they had set a day to meet with him, they came to him at his lodgings in great numbers. From morning until evening he explained the matter to them, testifying to the kingdom of God and trying to convince them about Jesus both from the law of Moses and from the prophets. 24Some were convinced by what he had said, while others refused to believe. 25So they disagreed with each other; and as they were leaving, Paul made one further statement: "The Holy Spirit was right in saying to your ancestors through the prophet Isaiah,

26 'Go to this people and say,
    You will indeed listen, but never
        understand,
    and you will indeed look, but never
        perceive.
27 For this people's heart has grown dull,
    and their ears are hard of hearing,
        and they have shut their eyes;
    so that they might not look with
        their eyes,
    and listen with their ears,

---

d Gk brothers   *e* Gk they   *f* Or I have asked you to see me and speak with me

and understand with their heart and turn—
and I would heal them.'
28Let it be known to you then that this salvation of God has been sent to the Gentiles; they will listen." g

30 He lived there two whole years at his own expenseh and welcomed all who came to him, 31proclaiming the kingdom of God and teaching about the Lord Jesus Christ with all boldness and without hindrance.

g Other ancient authorities add verse 29, *And when he had said these words, the Jews departed, arguing vigorously among themselves*   h Or *in his own hired dwelling*

ROMANS

A Most Demanding Audience

If you were stranded on a deserted island, what book would you want along?

I MAGINE YOURSELF IN A COLLEGE speech course. Your assignment: a brief speech on "the meaning of life." Over late-night cups of coffee, you outline the Christian faith and what it means to you. You devote a lot of time to this assignment—after all, this speech may be the only clear expression of faith your classmates will ever hear.

But what if you were asked to write up the speech for your local paper? Instead of a few dozen listeners, you would have thousands of readers. Undoubtedly, you would devote even more time and care to preparation.

> *I thank my God through Jesus Christ for all of you, because your faith is proclaimed throughout the world. 1.8*

Letter to the Center of the World

Let your imagination run even further. How would you react if you were asked to adapt this same speech for a front-page story in the *New York Times*? This newspaper has sophisticated, demanding readers. In writing for them, you would meticulously pore over every word, polishing phrases and making sure your thoughts were complete and well-expressed.

You can see a similar process at work in the apostle Paul's various letters. Some of his letters were, like a college speech, addressed to a small cluster of people he knew by name. Often they consisted of warm, personal words of advice or even fatherly scolding.

But, *Romans* . . . the very title of this book conjures up images of the powerful empire that ruled the western world. To people of Paul's day, Rome was the center of the world in every way: law, culture, power, and learning. A letter to this sophisticated audience had to be impressive indeed.

In Romans, Paul brilliantly set down the whole scope of Christian doctrine, which, at that time, was still being passed along orally from town to town. Paul wanted to convince those demanding readers that Christ held the answers to all of life's important questions.

One-Volume Summary

Literary types are often asked questions like this: "What one book would you most want along if you were stranded on a deserted island?" (Victorian author G.K. Chesterton gave a classic reply: *"Thomas's Guide to Practical Shipbuilding"*!) If asked the same question about a single book of the Bible, many Christians would choose Romans. Compact enough to fit on one spread of a modern newspaper, Romans yet manages to encompass all essentials of the Christian faith.

Despite its thoroughness, however, Romans does not read like a dry book of theology. Great revivals in church history have been spawned by a study of this book. Augustine, Martin Luther, and John Wesley all trace their spiritual renewals to a reading of Romans. It gives the apostle Paul's final answer to questions about the "meaning of life."

How to Read Romans

R omans is a book to savor, slowly and carefully. Paul is developing an argument, and his logic unfolds thought by thought from the very first chapter. You may recognize many well-known verses in Romans; note these in their context as a part of Paul's overall presentation.

Romans divides into a clear outline. Chapters 1–3 introduce the book and give the need for the good news of the gospel. The end of chapter 3, called the "central theological passage in the Bible," compresses the core message in a brief paragraph. Chapters 4 and 5 expand on that message.

Romans 6–8 discuss the working out of the gospel in a Christian's life. Paul then pauses for three chapters (9–11) to link his argument to the Old Testament history of the Jews. From there, he proceeds to give practical advice on specific problems (12–16).

It will require time and concentration to grasp fully the teachings of Romans; few people would claim to have 'mastered' this book. But it has no equal as a concise, reasonable statement of the Christian faith.

PEOPLE YOU'LL MEET IN ROMANS

PAUL *(p. 1166)*

3-TRACK READING PLAN

For an explanation and complete listing of the 3-track reading plan, turn to page 7.

TRACK 1: *Two-Week Courses on the Bible*
The Track 1 reading program on the Life and Teachings of Paul includes three chapters from Romans. See page 7 for a complete listing of this course.

TRACK 2: *An Overview of Romans in 4 Days*
☐ Day 1. Read the Introduction to Romans and then read chapter 3 as a summary of the whole book. Take your time as you read the end, verses 21–31.
☐ Day 2. Read of Paul's struggles against sin in chapter 7.
☐ Day 3. Paul concludes this great section on the Christian life with the triumphant message of chapter 8.
☐ Day 4. Paul gets practical toward the end of the book. Read his direct instructions on how to live in chapter 12.

Now turn to page 9 for your next Track 2 reading project.

TRACK 3: *All of Romans in 14 Days*
After you have read through Romans, turn to pages 10–14 for your next Track 3 reading project.

☐1   ☐2   ☐3   ☐4   ☐5   ☐6   ☐7   ☐8
☐9   ☐10   ☐11   ☐12–13 ☐14   ☐15–16

Salutation

1 Paul, a servant[a] of Jesus Christ, called to be an apostle, set apart for the gospel of God, [2]which he promised beforehand through his prophets in the holy scriptures, [3]the gospel concerning his Son, who was descended from David according to the flesh [4]and was declared to be Son of God with power according to the spirit[b] of holiness by resurrection from the dead, Jesus Christ our Lord, [5]through whom we have received grace and apostleship to bring about the obedience of faith among all the Gentiles for the sake of his name, [6]including yourselves who are called to belong to Jesus Christ,

7 To all God's beloved in Rome, who are called to be saints:

Grace to you and peace from God our Father and the Lord Jesus Christ.

Prayer of Thanksgiving

8 First, I thank my God through Jesus Christ for all of you, because your faith is proclaimed throughout the world. [9]For God, whom I serve with my spirit by announcing the gospel[c] of his Son, is my witness that without ceasing I remember you always in my prayers, [10]asking that by God's will I may somehow at last succeed in coming to you. [11]For I am longing to see you so that I may share with you some spiritual gift to strengthen you— [12]or rather so that we may be mutually encouraged by each other's faith, both

---

a Gk *slave*   *b* Or *Spirit*   *c* Gk *my spirit in the gospel*

yours and mine. [13]I want you to know, brothers and sisters,[d] that I have often intended to come to you (but thus far have been prevented), in order that I may reap some harvest among you as I have among the rest of the Gentiles. [14]I am a debtor both to Greeks and to barbarians, both to the wise and to the foolish [15]— hence my eagerness to proclaim the gospel to you also who are in Rome.

The Power of the Gospel

16 For I am not ashamed of the gospel; it is the power of God for salvation to everyone who has faith, to the Jew first and also to the Greek. [17]For in it the righteousness of God is revealed through faith for faith; as it is written, "The one who is righteous will live by faith."[e]

1.17 Luther's Gateway

Verses 16–17, a capsule summary of Paul's message to the Romans, changed Martin Luther forever. After he finally understood the phrase "righteousness of God," Luther said, "I felt myself to be reborn and to have gone through open doors into paradise. The whole of scripture took on a new meaning . . . . This passage of Paul became to me a gateway to heaven."

The Guilt of Humankind

18 For the wrath of God is revealed from heaven against all ungodliness and wickedness of those who by their wickedness suppress the truth. [19]For what can be known about God is plain to them, because God has shown it to them. [20]Ever since the creation of the world his eternal power and divine nature, invisible though they are, have been understood and seen through the things he

1.20 No Excuses

From Adam and Eve onward, people have tended to blame others, not themselves, for what goes wrong. Romans 1–3 sets forth an important principle that has been widely recognized by recovery groups such as Alcoholics Anonymous: Unless you first accept responsibility for wrong behavior and stop blaming others, you'll never get well.

has made. So they are without excuse; [21]for though they knew God, they did not honor him as God or give thanks to him, but they became futile in their thinking, and their senseless minds were darkened. [22]Claiming to be wise, they be-

came fools; [23]and they exchanged the glory of the immortal God for images resembling a mortal human being or birds or four-footed animals or reptiles.

24 Therefore God gave them up in the lusts of their hearts to impurity, to the degrading of their bodies among themselves, [25]because they exchanged the truth about God for a lie and worshiped and served the creature rather than the Creator, who is blessed forever! Amen.

26 For this reason God gave them up to degrading passions. Their women exchanged natural intercourse for unnatural, [27]and in the same way also the men, giving up natural intercourse with women, were consumed with passion for one another. Men committed shameless acts with men and received in their own persons the due penalty for their error.

28 And since they did not see fit to acknowledge God, God gave them up to a debased mind and to things that should not be done. [29]They were filled with every kind of wickedness, evil, covetousness, malice. Full of envy, murder, strife, deceit, craftiness, they are gossips, [30]slanderers, God-haters,[f] insolent, haughty, boastful, inventors of evil, rebellious toward parents, [31]foolish, faithless, heartless, ruthless. [32]They know God's decree, that those who practice such things deserve to die—yet they not only do them but even applaud others who practice them.

The Righteous Judgment of God

2 Therefore you have no excuse, whoever you are, when you judge others; for in passing judgment on another you condemn yourself, because you, the judge, are doing the very same

2.1 Unsettling Proverbs

"It takes one to know one." "The pot calls the kettle black." Or, as the Spanish say, "The donkey calls the pig 'long ears.' " All these proverbs echo Paul's point: We often criticize in others the very thing we ourselves say or do.

things. [2]You say,[g] "We know that God's judgment on those who do such things is in accordance with truth." [3]Do you imagine, whoever you are, that when you judge those who do such things and yet do them yourself, you will escape the judgment of God? [4]Or do you despise the riches of his kindness and forbearance and patience? Do you not realize that God's kindness is meant to lead you to repentance? [5]But by your hard and impenitent heart you are storing up wrath for yourself on the day of wrath, when God's righteous judgment will be revealed. [6]For he will repay according to each one's deeds: [7]to those who by patiently doing good seek for glory and honor and immortality, he will give eternal life; [8]while for those who are self-seeking and who obey not the truth but wickedness, there will be wrath and fury. [9]There will be anguish and distress for everyone who does evil, the Jew first and also the Greek, [10]but glory and honor and peace for everyone who does good, the Jew first and also the Greek. [11]For God shows no partiality.

12 All who have sinned apart from the law will also perish apart from the law, and all who have sinned under the law will be judged by the law. [13]For it is not the hearers of the law who are righteous in God's sight, but the doers of the law who will be justified. [14]When Gentiles, who do not possess the law, do instinctively what the law requires, these, though not having the law, are a law to themselves. [15]They show that what the law requires is written on their hearts, to which their own conscience also bears witness; and their conflicting thoughts will accuse or perhaps excuse them [16]on the day when, according to my gospel, God, through Jesus Christ, will judge the secret thoughts of all.

The Jews and the Law

17 But if you call yourself a Jew and rely on the law and boast of your relation to God [18]and know his will and determine what is best because you are instructed in the law, [19]and if you are sure that you are a guide to the blind, a light to those who are in darkness, [20]a corrector of the foolish, a teacher of children, having in the law the embodiment of knowledge and truth, [21]you, then, that teach others, will you not teach yourself? While you preach against stealing, do you steal? [22]You that forbid adultery, do you commit adultery? You that abhor idols, do you rob temples? [23]You that boast in the law, do you dishonor God by breaking the law? [24]For, as it is written, "The name of God is blasphemed among the Gentiles because of you."

25 Circumcision indeed is of value if you obey the law; but if you break the law, your circumcision has become uncircumcision. [26]So, if those who are uncircumcised keep the requirements of the law, will not their uncircumcision be regarded as circumcision? [27]Then those who are physically uncircumcised but keep the law will condemn you that have the written code and cir-

PAUL *Turnaround*

THOUGH PAUL BEGAN HIS CAREER as a fanatical enemy of Christianity, he became its greatest leader. After Jesus, he is unquestionably the most important person in the New Testament. Paul was not just an activist committed to the cause, and not just a theologian thinking deep thoughts about God. He was *both*—and his passionate, committed life still serves as a model.

Unlike the twelve apostles, Paul started out with status and education. He was born a Roman citizen, a rare and precious privilege for any Jew. Paul's fluent Greek writings show him to be a man of the world, well versed in secular literature.

Fundamentally, though, Paul saw himself as a devout Jew. He had studied theology in Jerusalem under the famous rabbi Gamaliel. He joined the campaign to arrest, imprison and even execute Christians because he believed they were blaspheming God by worshiping a man, and he was determined to stamp out such heresy.

Jesus' searing appearance on the road to Damascus turned Paul's life upside down (Acts 9.1–19). In one of the most dramatic conversions ever, Paul became the very thing he had so hated—a Christian. Paul later wrote to the Philippian believers, "For to me, to live is Christ" (Philippians 1.21). Nobody could doubt it. A passionate focus on Jesus shines through every line he wrote and was the reason for every mile he traveled. He remains what every Christian means by "Christ-centered."

Some years passed, though, before Paul found his role. He discovered it in Antioch, an important Roman city in modern-day Turkey, where the first sizable congregation of non-Jewish Christians sprang up. From then on Paul was every inch a missionary, taking the Good News about Jesus to the whole world. He traveled almost incessantly, moving from city to city around the Mediterranean Sea, preaching to both Jews and Gentiles.

Paul's life was marked with excitement: a shipwreck, a snakebite, beatings, narrow escapes. He started many churches, and thirteen letters of the New Testament have his name on them—all of them addressing problems in those first churches.

Though Paul never stopped thinking of himself as a devout Jew, he spent much of his life explaining that Jews and Gentiles were equally loved by God. Many people talk about racial reconciliation. Paul was one of the first to fight for it. He struggled hard against those who wanted Gentiles to submit to the whole Jewish law. Non-Jewish Christians, he was determined, should be considered first-class citizens of the kingdom of God. Faith in Jesus was all that God required.

Life Questions: To what role does God call you? How does your pursuit of that compare with the apostle Paul's?

cumcision but break the law. [28]For a person is not a Jew who is one outwardly, nor is true circumcision something external and physical. [29]Rather, a person is a Jew who is one inwardly, and real circumcision is a matter of the heart—it is spiritual and not literal. Such a person receives praise not from others but from God.

3 Then what advantage has the Jew? Or what is the value of circumcision? [2]Much, in every way. For in the first place the Jews[h] were entrusted with the oracles of God. [3]What if some were unfaithful? Will their faithlessness nullify the faithfulness of God? [4]By no means! Although everyone is a liar, let God be proved true, as it is written,

"So that you may be justified in your words,
    and prevail in your judging."[i]

[5]But if our injustice serves to confirm the justice of God, what should we say? That God is unjust to inflict wrath on us? (I speak in a human way.) [6]By no means! For then how could God judge the world? [7]But if through my falsehood God's truthfulness abounds to his glory, why am I still being condemned as a sinner? [8]And why not say (as some people slander us by saying that we say), "Let us do evil so that good may come"? Their condemnation is deserved!

None Is Righteous

[9] What then? Are we any better off?[j] No, not at all; for we have already charged that all, both Jews and Greeks, are under the power of sin, [10]as it is written:

"There is no one who is righteous, not even one;
[11]   there is no one who has understanding,
    there is no one who seeks God.

3.10–18 Need for a Cure

If a doctor suddenly appeared on a television news program announcing, in an excited voice, a cure for the Paraguayan flu, who would notice? For his discovery to impress us so deeply that we would seek vaccination, he would first need to prove the terrible danger of the unknown virus.

Paul's message in Romans is the great news about God's amazing grace: A complete cure is available to all. But people won't seek a cure until they know they are ill. Thus, Romans begins with one of the darkest descriptions in the Bible. Paul concludes, "There is no one who is righteous, not even one." The entire world is doomed to spiritual death unless a cure can be found.

[12]   All have turned aside, together they have become worthless;
    there is no one who shows kindness,
        there is not even one."
[13]   "Their throats are opened graves;
        they use their tongues to deceive."
    "The venom of vipers is under their lips."
[14]   "Their mouths are full of cursing and bitterness."
[15]   "Their feet are swift to shed blood;
[16]   ruin and misery are in their paths,
[17]   and the way of peace they have not known."
[18]   "There is no fear of God before their eyes."

[19] Now we know that whatever the law says, it speaks to those who are under the law, so that every mouth may be silenced, and the whole world may be held accountable to God. [20]For "no human being will be justified in his sight" by deeds prescribed by the law, for through the law comes the knowledge of sin.

Righteousness through Faith

[21] But now, apart from law, the righteousness of God has been disclosed, and is attested by the law and the prophets, [22]the righteousness of God through faith in Jesus Christ[k] for all who believe. For there is no distinction, [23]since all have sinned and fall short of the glory of God; [24]they are now justified by his grace as a gift, through the redemption that is in Christ Jesus, [25]whom God put forward as a sacrifice of atonement[l] by his blood, effective through faith. He did this to show his righteousness, because in his divine forbearance he had passed over the sins previously committed; [26]it was to prove at the present time that he himself is righteous and that he justifies the one who has faith in Jesus.[m]

[27] Then what becomes of boasting? It is excluded. By what law? By that of works? No, but by the law of faith. [28]For we hold that a person is justified by faith apart from works prescribed by the law. [29]Or is God the God of Jews only? Is he not the God of Gentiles also? Yes, of Gentiles also, [30]since God is one; and he will justify the circumcised on the ground of faith and the uncircumcised through that same faith. [31]Do we then overthrow the law by this faith? By no means! On the contrary, we uphold the law.

The Example of Abraham

4 What then are we to say was gained by[n] Abraham, our ancestor according to the flesh? [2]For if Abraham was justified by works, he has something to boast about, but not before God. [3]For what does the scripture say? "Abraham

h Gk they   i Gk when you are being judged   j Or at any disadvantage?   k Or through the faith of Jesus Christ
l Or a place of atonement   m Or who has the faith of Jesus   n Other ancient authorities read say about

believed God, and it was reckoned to him as righteousness." [4]Now to one who works, wages are not reckoned as a gift but as something due. [5]But to one who without works trusts him who justifies the ungodly, such faith is reckoned as righteousness. [6]So also David speaks of the blessedness of those to whom God reckons righteousness apart from works:

[7] "Blessed are those whose iniquities are
    forgiven,
    and whose sins are covered;
[8] blessed is the one against whom the Lord
    will not reckon sin."

[9] Is this blessedness, then, pronounced only on the circumcised, or also on the uncircumcised? We say, "Faith was reckoned to Abraham as righteousness." [10]How then was it reckoned to him? Was it before or after he had been circumcised? It was not after, but before he was circumcised. [11]He received the sign of circumcision as a seal of the righteousness that he had by faith while he was still uncircumcised. The purpose was to make him the ancestor of all who believe without being circumcised and who thus have righteousness reckoned to them, [12]and likewise the ancestor of the circumcised who are not only circumcised but who also follow the example of the faith that our ancestor Abraham had before he was circumcised.

God's Promise Realized through Faith

[13] For the promise that he would inherit the world did not come to Abraham or to his descendants through the law but through the righteous-

4.13 How to Please God

Paul goes to great lengths in chapter 4 to make a theological point. He traces the Jewish heritage back to Abraham, who lived hundreds of years before Moses and the Old Testament law. Abraham, says Paul, pleased God exactly as we do: through faith. The Old Testament law was never meant to bridge the gap between God and people. Only Jesus Christ could do that. Paul stresses that the law was given not to bring about redemption, but to point up the need for it (5.20).

ness of faith. [14]If it is the adherents of the law who are to be the heirs, faith is null and the promise is void. [15]For the law brings wrath; but where there is no law, neither is there violation.

[16] For this reason it depends on faith, in order that the promise may rest on grace and be guaranteed to all his descendants, not only to the adherents of the law but also to those who share

the faith of Abraham (for he is the father of all of us, [17]as it is written, "I have made you the father of many nations")—in the presence of the God in whom he believed, who gives life to the dead and calls into existence the things that do not exist. [18]Hoping against hope, he believed that he would become "the father of many nations," according to what was said, "So numerous shall your descendants be." [19]He did not weaken in faith when he considered his own body, which was already[o] as good as dead (for he was about a hundred years old), or when he considered the barrenness of Sarah's womb. [20]No distrust made him waver concerning the promise of God, but he grew strong in his faith as he gave glory to God, [21]being fully convinced that God was able to do what he had promised. [22]Therefore his faith[p] "was reckoned to him as righteousness." [23]Now the words, "it was reckoned to him," were written not for his sake alone, [24]but for ours also. It will be reckoned to us who believe in him who raised Jesus our Lord from the dead, [25]who was handed over to death for our trespasses and was raised for our justification.

Results of Justification

5 Therefore, since we are justified by faith, we[q] have peace with God through our Lord Jesus

5.1 What It's There For

In Romans, Paul constructs a step-by-step argument much like a legal brief, as shown by his frequent use of the legalese word "therefore" (20 times in all). Step one: No one is righteous and we all need help (3.20); Step two: God has provided that help in the form of his Son, making peace with us (5.11); Step three: Therefore God no longer condemns those who are in Christ (8.1).

Christ, [2]through whom we have obtained access[r] to this grace in which we stand; and we[s] boast in our hope of sharing the glory of God. [3]And not only that, but we[s] also boast in our sufferings, knowing that suffering produces endurance, [4]and endurance produces character, and character produces hope, [5]and hope does not disappoint us, because God's love has been poured into our hearts through the Holy Spirit that has been given to us.

[6] For while we were still weak, at the right time Christ died for the ungodly. [7]Indeed, rarely will anyone die for a righteous person—though perhaps for a good person someone might actually dare to die. [8]But God proves his love for us in that while we still were sinners Christ died for us.

---

[o] Other ancient authorities lack *already*   [p] Gk *Therefore it*   [q] Other ancient authorities read *let us*   [r] Other
ancient authorities add *by faith*   [s] Or *let us*

A Modern Peace Child

God spans the gulf

DON RICHARDSON SPENT SEVERAL FRUSTRATING years among the Sawi tribe in New Guinea. He had come from America as an anthropologist/missionary, hoping to bring the Christian message to a nearly stone-age tribe. But his message kept colliding with the tribe's unusual beliefs.

Christian values of love and forgiveness had no appeal to the Sawi, for they held up deceit as the highest virtue. They saw no reason to change their patterns of cruelty and cannibalism. In fact, when Richardson told them the story of Jesus, only one incident sparked their interest: the story of Judas's betrayal! To the Sawi, Judas was a genuine hero; he had shrewdly penetrated the trusted inner circle of disciples before turning against Jesus.

A Mysterious Ceremony

Every time Richardson tried to share Christ with the Sawi, the attempt miscarried. Finally, after watching the fourteenth bloody battle fought outside his home, Richardson reached the end of his patience. How could he ever break through to such violent people? He decided to leave New Guinea, despite the Sawi's pleas that he stay.

Just before Richardson left, the Sawi and their deadly enemies, the Haenam tribe, staged an elaborate ceremony in front of his home. It was their final effort to convince the missionary to stay.

The entire village gathered to watch the event. All were silent except the Sawi chief's wife. She screamed loudly as the chief seized their six-month-old baby from her arms and held him high in the air. The chief then carried his son to the enemy chief and gave him to his enemies. A member of the tribe explained to Richardson that the Haenam tribe would rename the baby and rear him as one of its own.

Breakthrough

Richardson knew that no Sawi could be fully trusted, since any action might be part of an elaborate deception. But that memorable day he learned of the one great exception: the peace child. A chief's giving his own son to his enemies—that profound, painful act would overcome all suspicion. By mutual agreement, as long as the peace child lived, no wars could be fought between the two tribes.

Something clicked in Don Richardson's mind as he watched the spectacle. At last he had found an analogy—a parallel story—built into the Sawi's culture that could convey the message of a forgiving God. He gathered members of the tribe around him and, with a pounding heart and dry throat, told them of God's peace child. God had sent his own Son, Jesus, to live among enemies, to make peace with humankind.

A Key Passage

Perhaps Paul felt that same pounding heart and dry throat as he presented in 11 concise verses, Romans 3.21–31, the meaning of God's offering of his peace child Jesus. The first part of Romans spelled out the vast gulf between God and people. Now Paul describes how God spanned this gulf. Some have called this section "the central theological passage in the Bible."

After stating the facts, Paul backs them up with historical proofs in chapters 4 and 5. American politicians often defend their positions by appealing to founding fathers, men like George Washington and Abraham Lincoln. Similarly, Paul keeps his Jewish audience in mind. He supports his concepts by citing Abraham, Moses, and even Adam.

Christ's death, says Paul, was not a new idea, an addition to the Old Testament law. Rather, it was the completion of the law, what the Old Testament implied and foreshadowed. Like the Sawi, the Jewish culture had its own "redemptive analogies"; and they all found true fulfillment in Jesus Christ.

Life Questions: Have you ever felt far from God? Does Romans 3–5 say anything that might help during those times?

⁹Much more surely then, now that we have been justified by his blood, will we be saved through him from the wrath of God.ᵗ ¹⁰For if while we were enemies, we were reconciled to God through the death of his Son, much more surely, having been reconciled, will we be saved by his life. ¹¹But more than that, we even boast in God through our Lord Jesus Christ, through whom we have now received reconciliation.

Adam and Christ

12 Therefore, just as sin came into the world through one man, and death came through sin, and so death spread to all because all have sinned— ¹³sin was indeed in the world before the law, but sin is not reckoned when there is no law. ¹⁴Yet death exercised dominion from Adam to Moses, even over those whose sins were not like the transgression of Adam, who is a type of the one who was to come.

15 But the free gift is not like the trespass. For if the many died through the one man's trespass, much more surely have the grace of God and the free gift in the grace of the one man, Jesus Christ, abounded for the many. ¹⁶And the free gift is not like the effect of the one man's sin. For the judgment following one trespass brought condemnation, but the free gift following many trespasses brings justification. ¹⁷If, because of the one man's trespass, death exercised dominion through that one, much more surely will those who receive the abundance of grace and the free gift of righteousness exercise dominion in life through the one man, Jesus Christ.

18 Therefore just as one man's trespass led to condemnation for all, so one man's act of righteousness leads to justification and life for all. ¹⁹For just as by the one man's disobedience the many were made sinners, so by the one man's obedience the many will be made righteous. ²⁰But law came in, with the result that the trespass multiplied; but where sin increased, grace abounded all the more, ²¹so that, just as sin exercised dominion in death, so grace might also exercise dominion through justificationᵘ leading to eternal life through Jesus Christ our Lord.

Dying and Rising with Christ

6 What then are we to say? Should we continue in sin in order that grace may abound? ²By no means! How can we who died to sin go on living in it? ³Do you not know that all of us who have been baptized into Christ Jesus were baptized into his death? ⁴Therefore we have been buried with him by baptism into death, so that, just as Christ was raised from the dead by the glory of the Father, so we too might walk in newness of life.

5 For if we have been united with him in a death like his, we will certainly be united with him in a resurrection like his. ⁶We know that our old self was crucified with him so that the body of sin might be destroyed, and we might no longer be

6.1 More Sin, More Forgiveness?

Paul often uses this writing technique: He pauses in the middle of an argument to answer objections or questions that may be occurring to the reader. Some people have actually reached the conclusion that horrifies Paul in this passage. The Russian monk Rasputin, for example, concluded, "I'll sin more to earn more forgiveness." He lived a bizarre life of immorality.

enslaved to sin. ⁷For whoever has died is freed from sin. ⁸But if we have died with Christ, we believe that we will also live with him. ⁹We know that Christ, being raised from the dead, will never die again; death no longer has dominion over him. ¹⁰The death he died, he died to sin, once for all; but the life he lives, he lives to God. ¹¹So you also must consider yourselves dead to sin and alive to God in Christ Jesus.

12 Therefore, do not let sin exercise dominion in your mortal bodies, to make you obey their passions. ¹³No longer present your members to sin as instrumentsᵛ of wickedness, but present yourselves to God as those who have been brought from death to life, and present your members to God as instrumentsᵛ of righteousness. ¹⁴For sin will have no dominion over you, since you are not under law but under grace.

Slaves of Righteousness

15 What then? Should we sin because we are not under law but under grace? By no means! ¹⁶Do you not know that if you present yourselves to anyone as obedient slaves, you are slaves of the one whom you obey, either of sin, which leads to death, or of obedience, which leads to righteousness? ¹⁷But thanks be to God that you, having once been slaves of sin, have become obedient from the heart to the form of teaching to which you were entrusted, ¹⁸and that you, having been set free from sin, have become slaves of righteousness. ¹⁹I am speaking in human terms because of your natural limitations.ʷ For just as you once presented your members as slaves to impurity and to greater and greater iniquity, so now present your members as slaves to righteousness for sanctification.

20 When you were slaves of sin, you were free in regard to righteousness. ²¹So what advantage did you then get from the things of which you now are ashamed? The end of those things is

death. ²²But now that you have been freed from sin and enslaved to God, the advantage you get is sanctification. The end is eternal life. ²³For the wages of sin is death, but the free gift of God is eternal life in Christ Jesus our Lord.

An Analogy from Marriage

7 Do you not know, brothers and sisters*— for I am speaking to those who know the law—that the law is binding on a person only during that person's lifetime? ²Thus a married woman is bound by the law to her husband as long as he lives; but if her husband dies, she is discharged from the law concerning the husband. ³Accordingly, she will be called an adulteress if she lives with another man while her husband is alive. But if her husband dies, she is free from that law, and if she marries another man, she is not an adulteress.

4 In the same way, my friends,* you have

x Gk *brothers*

died to the law through the body of Christ, so that you may belong to another, to him who has been raised from the dead in order that we may bear fruit for God. ⁵While we were living in the flesh, our sinful passions, aroused by the law, were at work in our members to bear fruit for death. ⁶But now we are discharged from the law, dead to that which held us captive, so that we are slaves not under the old written code but in the new life of the Spirit.

The Law and Sin

7 What then should we say? That the law is sin? By no means! Yet, if it had not been for the law, I would not have known sin. I would not have known what it is to covet if the law had not said, "You shall not covet." ⁸But sin, seizing an opportunity in the commandment, produced in me all kinds of covetousness. Apart from the law sin lies dead. ⁹I was once alive apart from the law,

Inner Struggles
A battle, and a victory

THE FIRST PART OF ROMANS paints a grand picture of God's grace and forgiveness, so grand that Paul opens himself up to some tricky questions. "I think I like what I'm hearing," a devious person may exclaim as he or she finishes the first part of Romans. "The more I sin, the more opportunity God has to forgive me, right? Then I can live any way I want!"

> So I find it to be a law that when I want to do good, evil lies close at hand. 7.21

In chapter 6, Paul reacts to the "Now I have an excuse to sin" line of thinking with shock and outrage. And then he turns to practical issues in the Christian life. Why is it that sin is so hard to overcome? Does God forgive every sin, no matter how bad? What really happens when we become Christians? Do we change or don't we?

Illustrations from Life

When Paul was trying to be a good person (by keeping all the law) in his own strength, he was ultimately defeated by the sin problem. Although his intentions were good, he was attempting to win the battle over sin by his own plan and ability. There is only one solution to that kind of struggle. Paul concludes at the end, "Wretched man that I am! Who will rescue me from this body of death? Thanks be to God through Jesus Christ our Lord!" (7.24–25a).

The very best proof of the Christian faith is a believer with a changed life. Paul calls Christians to "consider yourselves dead to sin and alive to God in Christ Jesus" (6.11), and he wrote as if this were really possible!

A Final Answer

Then, like a gust of fresh air, chapter 8 follows with one of the most hopeful passages in the Bible. The Holy Spirit is its theme, and Paul defines the Spirit's role in our lives. The Spirit works alongside us as we relate to God, even praying for us when we don't know what to ask (8.26). Mainly, the Spirit teaches us the benefits of being a child of God.

Conflict won't disappear completely yet, says Paul, for we are part of a "groaning," imperfect creation (8.18–25). But with God working for us, we can be more than conquerors, and one day God will make all of creation perfect again. That promise should assure us that nothing can separate us from God's love (8.38–39).

Life Questions: Which person do you identify with—the one who is struggling to please God on personal strength alone, or the one who is trusting in Christ for victory over sin?

but when the commandment came, sin revived [10]and I died, and the very commandment that promised life proved to be death to me. [11]For sin, seizing an opportunity in the commandment, deceived me and through it killed me. [12]So the law

7.7 Hidden Dangers

A strict disciplinarian like Paul had little trouble keeping most of the Ten Commandments. Outward actions such as swearing, murder, adultery, stealing, and lying could be measured and controlled. But the internal, invisible sin of coveting proved far more bedeviling. As Jesus made clear in the Sermon on the Mount, invisible sins like coveting, lust, and anger can have the same toxic effects as the more outward manifestations of stealing, adultery, and murder.

is holy, and the commandment is holy and just and good.

13 Did what is good, then, bring death to me? By no means! It was sin, working death in me through what is good, in order that sin might be shown to be sin, and through the commandment might become sinful beyond measure.

The Inner Conflict

14 For we know that the law is spiritual; but I am of the flesh, sold into slavery under sin.[y] [15]I do not understand my own actions. For I do not do what I want, but I do the very thing I hate. [16]Now if I do what I do not want, I agree that the law is good. [17]But in fact it is no longer I that do it, but sin that dwells within me. [18]For I know that nothing good dwells within me, that is, in my flesh. I can will what is right, but I cannot do it. [19]For I do not do the good I want, but the evil I do not want is what I do. [20]Now if I do what I do not want, it is no longer I that do it, but sin that dwells within me.

21 So I find it to be a law that when I want to do what is good, evil lies close at hand. [22]For I delight in the law of God in my inmost self, [23]but I see in my members another law at war with the law of my mind, making me captive to the law of sin that dwells in my members. [24]Wretched man that I am! Who will rescue me from this body of death? [25]Thanks be to God through Jesus Christ our Lord!

So then, with my mind I am a slave to the law of God, but with my flesh I am a slave to the law of sin.

Life in the Spirit

8 There is therefore now no condemnation for those who are in Christ Jesus. [2]For the law of the Spirit[z] of life in Christ Jesus has set you[a] free from the law of sin and of death. [3]For God has done what the law, weakened by the flesh, could not do: by sending his own Son in the likeness of sinful flesh, and to deal with sin,[b] he condemned sin in the flesh, [4]so that the just requirement of the law might be fulfilled in us, who walk not according to the flesh but according to the Spirit.[z] [5]For those who live according to the flesh set their minds on the things of the flesh, but those who live according to the Spirit[z] set their minds on the things of the Spirit.[z] [6]To set the mind on the flesh is death, but to set the mind on the Spirit[z] is life and peace. [7]For this reason the mind that is set on the flesh is hostile to God; it does not submit to God's law—indeed it cannot, [8]and those who are in the flesh cannot please God.

9 But you are not in the flesh; you are in the Spirit,[z] since the Spirit of God dwells in you. Anyone who does not have the Spirit of Christ does not belong to him. [10]But if Christ is in you, though the body is dead because of sin, the Spirit[z] is life because of righteousness. [11]If the Spirit of him who raised Jesus from the dead dwells in you, he who raised Christ[c] from the dead will give life to your mortal bodies also through[d] his Spirit that dwells in you.

12 So then, brothers and sisters,[e] we are debtors, not to the flesh, to live according to the flesh— [13]for if you live according to the flesh, you will die; but if by the Spirit you put to death the deeds of the body, you will live. [14]For all who are led by the Spirit of God are children of God. [15]For you did not receive a spirit of slavery to fall back into fear, but you have received a spirit of adoption. When we cry, "Abba![f] Father!" [16]it is that very Spirit bearing witness[g] with our spirit that we are children of God, [17]and if children, then heirs, heirs of God and joint heirs with Christ— if, in fact, we suffer with him so that we may also be glorified with him.

Future Glory

18 I consider that the sufferings of this present time are not worth comparing with the glory about to be revealed to us. [19]For the creation waits with eager longing for the revealing of the children of God; [20]for the creation was subjected to futility, not of its own will but by the will of the one who subjected it, in hope [21]that the creation itself will be set free from its bondage to decay and will obtain the freedom of the glory of the

---

[y] Gk *sold under sin* [z] Or *spirit* or *us* [b] Or *and as a sin offering* [a] Here the Greek word *you* is singular number; other ancient authorities read *me* [c] Other ancient authorities read *the Christ* or *Christ Jesus* or *Jesus Christ* [d] Other ancient authorities read *on account of* [e] Gk *brothers* [f] Aramaic for *Father* [g] Or [15]*a spirit of adoption, by which we cry,* "Abba! Father!" [16]*The Spirit itself bears witness*

children of God. [22]We know that the whole creation has been groaning in labor pains until now; [23]and not only the creation, but we ourselves, who have the first fruits of the Spirit, groan inwardly

8.18 Worth the Struggle

Paul never minimizes suffering; after all, his own life included beatings, imprisonment, shipwrecks, assassination attempts, and chronic illness. But he insists with absolute conviction that future rewards will outweigh all present sufferings.

Olympic athletes endure years of eight-hour practice sessions and much discipline and pain for the goal of winning a gold medal. Similarly, the Christian's life on earth may involve many difficulties (verses 22–23), but the end result will make them seem worthwhile.

while we wait for adoption, the redemption of our bodies. [24]For in[h] hope we were saved. Now hope that is seen is not hope. For who hopes[i] for what is seen? [25]But if we hope for what we do not see, we wait for it with patience.

26 Likewise the Spirit helps us in our weakness; for we do not know how to pray as we ought, but that very Spirit intercedes[j] with sighs too deep for words. [27]And God,[k] who searches the heart, knows what is the mind of the Spirit, because the Spirit[l] intercedes for the saints according to the will of God.[m]

28 We know that all things work together for good[n] for those who love God, who are called

8.28 Only Good Things?

This famous verse is often misquoted or stretched to mean more than it says. It should be read along with the next two paragraphs. Paul doesn't promise that only good, or pleasurable, things will come to the Christian. What he does say is that even the difficult experiences described in verses 35–39 can be used in God's overall plan for good. And nothing can separate us from the love of God.

according to his purpose. [29]For those whom he foreknew he also predestined to be conformed to the image of his Son, in order that he might be the firstborn within a large family.[o] [30]And those whom he predestined he also called; and those whom he called he also justified; and those whom he justified he also glorified.

God's Love in Christ Jesus

31 What then are we to say about these things? If God is for us, who is against us? [32]He who did not withhold his own Son, but gave him up for all of us, will he not with him also give us everything else? [33]Who will bring any charge against God's elect? It is God who justifies. [34]Who is to condemn? It is Christ Jesus, who died, yes, who was raised, who is at the right hand of God, who indeed intercedes for us.[p] [35]Who will separate us from the love of Christ? Will hardship, or distress, or persecution, or famine, or nakedness, or peril, or sword? [36]As it is written,

"For your sake we are being killed all day
　　　long;
we are accounted as sheep to be
　　　slaughtered."

[37]No, in all these things we are more than conquerors through him who loved us. [38]For I am convinced that neither death, nor life, nor angels, nor rulers, nor things present, nor things to come, nor powers, [39]nor height, nor depth, nor anything else in all creation, will be able to separate us from the love of God in Christ Jesus our Lord.

God's Election of Israel

9 I am speaking the truth in Christ—I am not lying; my conscience confirms it by the Holy Spirit— [2]I have great sorrow and unceasing anguish in my heart. [3]For I could wish that I myself were accursed and cut off from Christ for the sake of my own people,[q] my kindred according to the flesh. [4]They are Israelites, and to them belong the adoption, the glory, the covenants, the giving of the law, the worship, and the promises; [5]to them belong the patriarchs, and from them, according to the flesh, comes the Messiah,[r] who is over all, God blessed forever.[s] Amen.

6 It is not as though the word of God had failed. For not all Israelites truly belong to Israel, [7]and not all of Abraham's children are his true descendants; but "It is through Isaac that descendants shall be named for you." [8]This means that it is not the children of the flesh who are the children of God, but the children of the promise are counted as descendants. [9]For this is what the promise said, "About this time I will return and Sarah shall have a son." [10]Nor is that all; something similar happened to Rebecca when she had conceived children by one husband, our ancestor Isaac. [11]Even before they had been born or had done anything good or bad (so that God's purpose of election might continue, [12]not by works

---

[h] Or by　　[i] Other ancient authorities read *awaits*　　[j] Other ancient authorities add *for us*　　[k] Gk *the one*
[l] Gk *he* or *it*　　[m] Gk *according to God*　　[n] Other ancient authorities read *God makes all things work together for good,* or *in all things God works for good*　　[o] Gk *among many brothers*　　[p] Or *Is it Christ Jesus . . . for us?*　　[q] Gk *my brothers*　　[r] Or *the Christ*　　[s] Or *Messiah, who is God over all, blessed forever;* or *Messiah. May he who is God over all be blessed forever*

but by his call) she was told, "The elder shall serve the younger." 13As it is written,

"I have loved Jacob,
    but I have hated Esau."

14 What then are we to say? Is there injustice on God's part? By no means! 15For he says to Moses,

"I will have mercy on whom I
        have mercy,
    and I will have compassion on whom I
        have compassion."

16So it depends not on human will or exertion, but on God who shows mercy. 17For the scripture says to Pharaoh, "I have raised you up for the very purpose of showing my power in you, so that my name may be proclaimed in all the earth." 18So then he has mercy on whomever he chooses, and he hardens the heart of whomever he chooses.

God's Wrath and Mercy

19 You will say to me then, "Why then does he still find fault? For who can resist his will?" 20But who indeed are you, a human being, to argue with God? Will what is molded say to the one who molds it, "Why have you made me like this?" 21Has the potter no right over the clay, to make out of the same lump one object for special use and another for ordinary use? 22What if God, desiring to show his wrath and to make known his power, has endured with much patience the objects of wrath that are made for destruction; 23and what if he has done so in order to make known the riches of his glory for the objects of

9.19 Questions, Anyone?

Frequently Paul interrupts his writing with a question or series of questions. In doing so, he is imitating the style he learned from rabbis in his earlier training. The story is told of one student who asked, "Why do you rabbis so often put your teaching in the form of a question?" The reply: "So what's wrong with a question?"

mercy, which he has prepared beforehand for glory— 24including us whom he has called, not from the Jews only but also from the Gentiles? 25As indeed he says in Hosea,

"Those who were not my people I will
        call 'my people,'
    and her who was not beloved I will call
        'beloved.'"
26 "And in the very place where it was said
        to them, 'You are not my people,'
    there they shall be called children of
        the living God."

27 And Isaiah cries out concerning Israel,

A Crushing Blow to Paul
Does God break his promises?

I have great sorrow and unceasing anguish in my heart. 9.2

DOES ANYTHING BRING MORE PAIN to a new Christian than family rejection? A teenager converts to Christianity. Her parents overreact, assuming their daughter has fallen for some weird cult. They slap away all her attempts to present the appealing facts of the gospel. What is good news for her is seen as bad news by the family.

Some new Christians can melt down the walls of suspicion and hostility. But others are treated like diseased persons by other family members and forced to live in a state of emotional quarantine.

Anyone who has lived through such an experience can understand the agonizing dilemma Paul faced. Members of his own race, the Jews, were rejecting the gospel he had committed his life to.

Can God Be Trusted?

Rejection by the Jews was a crushing blow to Paul, and he interrupted his letter to the Romans to consider the dilemma. These three chapters (9–11) contain some of his strongest words ever, including an offer to forfeit his own relationship with Christ for the sake of his race (9.3).

The issues discussed here apply to non-Jews as well, for they raise basic questions about God. Had he given up on the Jewish people, ignoring the promises he made to them in Old Testament times? If so, couldn't he also break promises made to us today?

For Paul, a Jew who called himself an apostle to the Gentiles, no other issue was so important to resolve. He couldn't rest until he linked the brilliant theology set forth in Romans to God's past, present and future activity among the Jews.

Life Questions: Romans 9–11 explains how God worked with people disappointed in him: the Jews. Have you ever been deeply disappointed in God? What does Paul say that might help answer your questions?

"Though the number of the children of Israel were like the sand of the sea, only a remnant of them will be saved; [28]for the Lord will execute his sentence on the earth quickly and decisively."[t] [29]And as Isaiah predicted,

"If the Lord of hosts had not left
survivors[u] to us,
we would have fared like Sodom
and been made like Gomorrah."

Israel's Unbelief

30 What then are we to say? Gentiles, who did not strive for righteousness, have attained it, that is, righteousness through faith; [31]but Israel, who did strive for the righteousness that is based on the law, did not succeed in fulfilling that law. [32]Why not? Because they did not strive for it on the basis of faith, but as if it were based on works. They have stumbled over the stumbling stone, [33]as it is written,

"See, I am laying in Zion a stone that will
make people stumble, a rock that
will make them fall,
and whoever believes in him[v] will not
be put to shame."

10 Brothers and sisters,[w] my heart's desire and prayer to God for them is that they may be saved. [2]I can testify that they have a zeal for God, but it is not enlightened. [3]For, being ignorant of the righteousness that comes from God, and seeking to establish their own, they have not submitted to God's righteousness. [4]For Christ is the end of the law so that there may be righteousness for everyone who believes.

Salvation Is for All

5 Moses writes concerning the righteousness that comes from the law, that "the person who does these things will live by them." [6]But the righteousness that comes from faith says, "Do not say in your heart, 'Who will ascend into heaven?'" (that is, to bring Christ down) [7]"or 'Who will descend into the abyss?'" (that is, to bring Christ up from the dead). [8]But what does it say?

"The word is near you,
on your lips and in your heart"

(that is, the word of faith that we proclaim); [9]because[x] if you confess with your lips that Jesus is Lord and believe in your heart that God raised him from the dead, you will be saved. [10]For one believes with the heart and so is justified, and one confesses with the mouth and so is saved. [11]The scripture says, "No one who believes in him will be put to shame." [12]For there is no distinction between Jew and Greek; the same Lord is Lord of all and is generous to all who call on him. [13]For,

"Everyone who calls on the name of the Lord shall be saved."

14 But how are they to call on one in whom they have not believed? And how are they to believe in one of whom they have never heard? And how are they to hear without someone to proclaim him? [15]And how are they to proclaim him unless they are sent? As it is written, "How beautiful are the feet of those who bring good news!" [16]But not all have obeyed the good news;[y] for Isaiah says, "Lord, who has believed our message?" [17]So faith comes from what is heard, and what is heard comes through the word of Christ.[z]

18 But I ask, have they not heard? Indeed they have; for

"Their voice has gone out to all the earth,
and their words to the ends of the
world."

[19]Again I ask, did Israel not understand? First Moses says,

"I will make you jealous of those who are
not a nation;
with a foolish nation I will make you
angry."

[20]Then Isaiah is so bold as to say,

"I have been found by those who did not
seek me;
I have shown myself to those who did
not ask for me."

[21]But of Israel he says, "All day long I have held out my hands to a disobedient and contrary people."

Israel's Rejection Is Not Final

11 I ask, then, has God rejected his people? By no means! I myself am an Israelite, a descendant of Abraham, a member of the tribe of Benjamin. [2]God has not rejected his people whom he foreknew. Do you not know what the scripture says of Elijah, how he pleads with God against Israel? [3]"Lord, they have killed your prophets, they have demolished your altars; I alone am left, and they are seeking my life." [4]But what is the divine reply to him? "I have kept for myself seven thousand who have not bowed the knee to Baal." [5]So too at the present time there is a remnant, chosen by grace. [6]But if it is by grace, it is no longer on the basis of works, otherwise grace would no longer be grace.[a]

7 What then? Israel failed to obtain what it was seeking. The elect obtained it, but the rest were hardened, [8]as it is written,

"God gave them a sluggish spirit,
eyes that would not see
and ears that would not hear,
down to this very day."

---

[t] Other ancient authorities read *for he will finish his work and cut it short in righteousness, because the Lord will make the sentence shortened on the earth*   [u] Or *descendants*; Gk *seed*   [v] Or *trusts in it*   [w] Gk *Brothers*   [x] Or *namely, that*   [y] Or *gospel*   [z] Or *about Christ*; other ancient authorities read *of God*   [a] Other ancient authorities add *But if it is by works, it is no longer on the basis of grace, otherwise work would no longer be work*

9And David says,
"Let their table become a snare
and a trap,
a stumbling block and a retribution for
them;
10 let their eyes be darkened so that they
cannot see,
and keep their backs forever bent."

The Salvation of the Gentiles

11 So I ask, have they stumbled so as to fall? By no means! But through their stumbling*b* salvation has come to the Gentiles, so as to make

---

11.11 The Future of the Jews

In chapters 9 and 10, Paul painfully admits that, on the whole, the Jews did not believe in Christ. Despite all the advantages of Old Testament history, they "stumbled over the stumbling stone" (9.32). In chapter 11, Paul goes back over that history and asks whether it was futile. Will the Jews come to believe in Christ some day? Did their tragic experience produce any advantage for the rest of the world? This chapter clearly shows God's eternal love for his chosen people. Paul concludes with a poetic outburst, celebrating God's mysterious ways of working on earth.

Israel*c* jealous. 12Now if their stumbling*b* means riches for the world, and if their defeat means riches for Gentiles, how much more will their full inclusion mean!

13 Now I am speaking to you Gentiles. Inasmuch then as I am an apostle to the Gentiles, I glorify my ministry 14in order to make my own people*d* jealous, and thus save some of them. 15For if their rejection is the reconciliation of the world, what will their acceptance be but life from the dead! 16If the part of the dough offered as first fruits is holy, then the whole batch is holy; and if the root is holy, then the branches also are holy.

17 But if some of the branches were broken off, and you, a wild olive shoot, were grafted in their place to share the rich root*e* of the olive tree, 18do not boast over the branches. If you do boast, remember that it is not you that support the root, but the root that supports you. 19You will say, "Branches were broken off so that I might be grafted in." 20That is true. They were broken off because of their unbelief, but you stand only through faith. So do not become proud, but stand in awe. 21For if God did not spare the natural branches, perhaps he will not spare you.*f* 22Note then the kindness and the

severity of God: severity toward those who have fallen, but God's kindness toward you, provided you continue in his kindness; otherwise you also will be cut off. 23And even those of Israel,*g* if they do not persist in unbelief, will be grafted in, for God has the power to graft them in again. 24For if you have been cut from what is by nature a wild olive tree and grafted, contrary to nature, into a cultivated olive tree, how much more will these natural branches be grafted back into their own olive tree.

11.24 Unnatural Botany

Botanists and orchard growers commonly use grafting to improve their stock of flowers and fruit. Usually they graft a weaker, cultivated branch onto a wild but sturdy root stock. Paul admits that "contrary to nature" God has grafted the wild branches (Gentiles) onto the cultivated roots (Jews)—a reverse technique sometimes used to reinvigorate an olive tree.

All Israel Will Be Saved

25 So that you may not claim to be wiser than you are, brothers and sisters,*h* I want you to understand this mystery: a hardening has come upon part of Israel, until the full number of the Gentiles has come in. 26And so all Israel will be saved; as it is written,
"Out of Zion will come the Deliverer;
he will banish ungodliness from Jacob."
27 "And this is my covenant with them,
when I take away their sins."
28As regards the gospel they are enemies of God*i* for your sake; but as regards election they are beloved, for the sake of their ancestors; 29for the gifts and the calling of God are irrevocable. 30Just as you were once disobedient to God but have now received mercy because of their disobedience, 31so they have now been disobedient in order that, by the mercy shown to you, they too may now*j* receive mercy. 32For God has imprisoned all in disobedience so that he may be merciful to all.

33 O the depth of the riches and wisdom and knowledge of God! How unsearchable are his judgments and how inscrutable his ways!
34 "For who has known the mind of the Lord?
Or who has been his counselor?"
35 "Or who has given a gift to him,
to receive a gift in return?"
36For from him and through him and to him are all things. To him be the glory forever. Amen.

---

b Gk *transgression*   *c* Gk *them*   *d* Gk *my flesh*   *e* Other ancient authorities read *the richness*   *f* Other ancient authorities read *neither will he spare you*   *g* Gk lacks *of Israel*   *h* Gk *brothers*   *i* Gk lacks *of God*   *j* Other ancient authorities lack *now*

The New Life in Christ

12 I appeal to you therefore, brothers and sisters,[k] by the mercies of God, to present your bodies as a living sacrifice, holy and acceptable to God, which is your spiritual[l] worship. ²Do not be conformed to this world,[m] but be transformed by the renewing of your minds, so that you may discern what is the will of God— what is good and acceptable and perfect.[n]

3 For by the grace given to me I say to everyone among you not to think of yourself more highly than you ought to think, but to think with sober judgment, each according to the measure of faith that God has assigned. ⁴For as in one body we have many members, and not all the members have the same function, ⁵so we, who are many, are one body in Christ, and individually we are members one of another. ⁶We have gifts that differ according to the grace given to us: prophecy, in proportion to faith; ⁷ministry, in ministering; the teacher, in teaching; ⁸the exhorter, in exhortation; the giver, in generosity; the leader, in diligence; the compassionate, in cheerfulness.

Marks of the True Christian

9 Let love be genuine; hate what is evil, hold fast to what is good; ¹⁰love one another with mutual affection; outdo one another in showing honor. ¹¹Do not lag in zeal, be ardent in spirit, serve the Lord.[o] ¹²Rejoice in hope, be patient in suffering, persevere in prayer. ¹³Contribute to the needs of the saints; extend hospitality to strangers.

14 Bless those who persecute you; bless and do not curse them. ¹⁵Rejoice with those who rejoice, weep with those who weep. ¹⁶Live in harmony with one another; do not be haughty, but associate with the lowly;[p] do not claim to be wiser than you are. ¹⁷Do not repay anyone evil for evil, but take thought for what is noble in the sight of all. ¹⁸If it is possible, so far as it depends on you, live peaceably with all. ¹⁹Beloved, never avenge yourselves, but leave room for the wrath of God;[q] for it is written, "Vengeance is mine, I will repay, says the Lord." ²⁰No, "if your enemies are hungry, feed them; if they are thirsty, give them something to drink; for by doing this you will heap burning coals on their heads." ²¹Do not be overcome by evil, but overcome evil with good.

Being Subject to Authorities

13 Let every person be subject to the governing authorities; for there is no authority except from God, and those authorities that exist have been instituted by God. ²Therefore whoever resists authority resists what God has appointed, and those who resist will incur judgment. ³For rulers are not a terror to good conduct, but to

k Gk brothers   l Or reasonable   m Gk age   n Or what is the good and acceptable and perfect will of God
o Other ancient authorities read serve the opportune time   p Or give yourselves to humble tasks   q Gk the wrath

Down-To-Earth Problems
When Christians disagree about what's right and wrong

> Hate what is evil, hold fast to what is good. 12.9

TOO OFTEN THEOLOGY IS VIEWED as stuff for hermits and marooned shipwreck victims. When there's nothing else to do, *then* is the time to ask abstract questions about God.

Such a notion would surely have exasperated the apostle Paul. To him, theology *was* worthless unless it made a difference in how people lived. Therefore, he concluded the most concise theological book in the Bible with a down-to-earth discussion of contemporary problems.

Revolutionaries and Weaker Brothers

The issue of politics surfaces in Romans (13.1–7). How should a Christian relate to government? In Paul's day, when Christians were living under Nero's tyrannical regime, that question was hotly debated, as it still is in our revolution-oriented era.

Christians in Rome were also disagreeing on what was proper behavior for a Christian (14.1–15.4). One person was sure another was sinning; but that "offender" was convinced his accuser was hopelessly narrow-minded. Who was right? The specific issues change with each culture, but Paul's guidelines on the proper attitudes apply to all.

Paul did not live as an intellectual recluse. He applied his theology to life, practicing what he preached. In fact, the lofty book of Romans was written while he was out raising money for famine victims in Jerusalem (15.25–27).

Life Questions: Christians in Paul's day hotly debated such issues as eating meat, celebrating holidays, and drinking wine. What issues do Christians debate today? What attitude should we have toward Christians we differ with?

bad. Do you wish to have no fear of the authority? Then do what is good, and you will receive its approval; 4for it is God's servant for your good. But if you do what is wrong, you should be afraid,

13.1 Christians and the Empire

For most of his ministry, Paul benefited from the legal protection of the Roman empire. The first generation of Christians received the same freedom of worship and legal protection as did the Jews. But soon emperors such as Nero vengefully turned on Christians, torturing and murdering thousands of them, probably including Paul himself. History shows that most of them followed Paul's difficult advice in this passage, refusing to revolt against the government no matter how hostile it became.

for the authority*r* does not bear the sword in vain! It is the servant of God to execute wrath on the wrongdoer. 5Therefore one must be subject, not only because of wrath but also because of conscience. 6For the same reason you also pay taxes, for the authorities are God's servants, busy with this very thing. 7Pay to all what is due them—taxes to whom taxes are due, revenue to whom revenue is due, respect to whom respect is due, honor to whom honor is due.

Love for One Another

8 Owe no one anything, except to love one another; for the one who loves another has fulfilled the law. 9The commandments, "You shall not commit adultery; You shall not murder; You shall not steal; You shall not covet"; and any other commandment, are summed up in this word, "Love your neighbor as yourself." 10Love does no wrong to a neighbor; therefore, love is the fulfilling of the law.

An Urgent Appeal

11 Besides this, you know what time it is, how it is now the moment for you to wake from sleep. For salvation is nearer to us now than when we became believers; 12the night is far gone, the day is near. Let us then lay aside the works of darkness and put on the armor of light; 13let us live honorably as in the day, not in reveling and drunkenness, not in debauchery and licentiousness, not in quarreling and jealousy. 14Instead, put on the Lord Jesus Christ, and make no provision for the flesh, to gratify its desires.

Do Not Judge Another

14 Welcome those who are weak in faith,*s* but not for the purpose of quarreling over opinions. 2Some believe in eating anything, while the weak eat only vegetables. 3Those who eat must not despise those who abstain, and those who abstain must not pass judgment on those who eat; for God has welcomed them. 4Who are you to pass judgment on servants of another? It is before their own lord that they stand or fall. And they will be upheld, for the Lord*t* is able to make them stand.

14.2 Weak or Strong?

According to Paul, a weaker brother is a new believer who needs many rules and regulations. Christians in Paul's day debated such issues as vegetarianism, eating meat sacrificed to idols, and celebrating pagan festival days. Paul's advice to both weak and strong Christians of his day applies to people in all cultures who debate questionable issues. Elsewhere, Paul speaks to legalists: "strong" Christians who nevertheless insist on many rules and regulations (see Colossians 2.16–23).

5 Some judge one day to be better than another, while others judge all days to be alike. Let all be fully convinced in their own minds. 6Those who observe the day, observe it in honor of the Lord. Also those who eat, eat in honor of the Lord, since they give thanks to God; while those who abstain, abstain in honor of the Lord and give thanks to God.

7 We do not live to ourselves, and we do not die to ourselves. 8If we live, we live to the Lord, and if we die, we die to the Lord; so then, whether we live or whether we die, we are the Lord's. 9For to this end Christ died and lived again, so that he might be Lord of both the dead and the living.

10 Why do you pass judgment on your brother or sister?*u* Or you, why do you despise your brother or sister?*u* For we will all stand before the judgment seat of God.*v* 11For it is written,

> "As I live, says the Lord, every knee shall
> bow to me,
> and every tongue shall give praise to*w*
> God."

12So then, each of us will be accountable to God.*x*

Do Not Make Another Stumble

13 Let us therefore no longer pass judgment on one another, but resolve instead never to put a stumbling block or hindrance in the way of another.*y* 14I know and am persuaded in the Lord Jesus that nothing is unclean in itself; but it is unclean for anyone who thinks it unclean. 15If

---

r Gk *it*   *s* Or *conviction*   *t* Other ancient authorities read *for God*   *u* Gk *brother*   *v* Other ancient authorities read *of Christ*   *w* Or *confess*   *x* Other ancient authorities lack *to God*   *y* Gk *of a brother*

your brother or sister[z] is being injured by what you eat, you are no longer walking in love. Do not let what you eat cause the ruin of one for whom Christ died. [16]So do not let your good be spoken of as evil. [17]For the kingdom of God is not food and drink but righteousness and peace and joy in the Holy Spirit. [18]The one who thus serves Christ is acceptable to God and has human approval. [19]Let us then pursue what makes for peace and for mutual upbuilding. [20]Do not, for the sake of food, destroy the work of God. Everything is indeed clean, but it is wrong for you to make others fall by what you eat; [21]it is good not to eat meat or drink wine or do anything that makes your brother or sister[z] stumble.[a] [22]The faith that you have, have as your own conviction before God. Blessed are those who have no reason to condemn themselves because of what they approve. [23]But those who have doubts are condemned if they eat, because they do not act from faith;[b] for whatever does not proceed from faith[b] is sin.[c]

Please Others, Not Yourselves

15 We who are strong ought to put up with the failings of the weak, and not to please ourselves. [2]Each of us must please our neighbor for the good purpose of building up the neighbor. [3]For Christ did not please himself; but, as it is written, "The insults of those who insult you have fallen on me." [4]For whatever was written in former days was written for our instruction, so that by steadfastness and by the encouragement of the scriptures we might have hope. [5]May the God of steadfastness and encouragement grant you to live in harmony with one another, in accordance with Christ Jesus, [6]so that together you may with one voice glorify the God and Father of our Lord Jesus Christ.

The Gospel for Jews and Gentiles Alike

[7] Welcome one another, therefore, just as Christ has welcomed you, for the glory of God. [8]For I tell you that Christ has become a servant of the circumcised on behalf of the truth of God in order that he might confirm the promises given to the patriarchs, [9]and in order that the Gentiles might glorify God for his mercy. As it is written,

"Therefore I will confess[d] you among the
Gentiles,
and sing praises to your name";

[10]and again he says,

"Rejoice, O Gentiles, with his people";

[11]and again,

"Praise the Lord, all you Gentiles,
and let all the peoples praise him";

[12]and again Isaiah says,

"The root of Jesse shall come,
the one who rises to rule the Gentiles;
in him the Gentiles shall hope."

[13]May the God of hope fill you with all joy and peace in believing, so that you may abound in hope by the power of the Holy Spirit.

Paul's Reason for Writing So Boldly

14 I myself feel confident about you, my brothers and sisters,[e] that you yourselves are full of goodness, filled with all knowledge, and able to instruct one another. [15]Nevertheless on some points I have written to you rather boldly by way of reminder, because of the grace given me by God [16]to be a minister of Christ Jesus to the Gentiles in the priestly service of the gospel of God, so that the offering of the Gentiles may be acceptable, sanctified by the Holy Spirit. [17]In Christ Jesus, then, I have reason to boast of my work for God. [18]For I will not venture to speak of anything except what Christ has accomplished[f] through me to win obedience from the Gentiles, by word and deed, [19]by the power of signs and wonders, by the power of the Spirit of God,[g] so that from Jerusalem and as far around as Illyricum I have fully proclaimed the good news[h] of Christ. [20]Thus I make it my ambition to proclaim the good news,[h] not where Christ has already been named, so that I do not build on someone else's foundation, [21]but as it is written,

"Those who have never been told of him
shall see,
and those who have never heard of
him shall understand."

Paul's Plan to Visit Rome

22 This is the reason that I have so often been hindered from coming to you. [23]But now, with no further place for me in these regions, I desire, as I have for many years, to come to you [24]when I go to Spain. For I do hope to see you on my journey and to be sent on by you, once I have enjoyed your company for a little while. [25]At present, however, I am going to Jerusalem in a ministry to the saints; [26]for Macedonia and Achaia have been pleased to share their resources with the poor among the saints at Jerusalem. [27]They were pleased to do this, and indeed they owe it to them; for if the Gentiles have come to share in their spiritual blessings, they ought also to be of service to them in material things. [28]So, when I have completed this, and have delivered to them what has been collected,[i] I will set out by way of you to Spain; [29]and I know that when I come to you,

---

[z] Gk *brother*   [a] Other ancient authorities add *or be upset or be weakened*   [b] Or *conviction*   [c] Other authorities, some ancient, add here 16.25-27   [d] Or *thank*   [e] Gk *brothers*   [f] Gk *speak of those things that Christ has not accomplished*   [g] Other ancient authorities read *of the Spirit* or *of the Holy Spirit*   [h] Or *gospel*   [i] Gk *have sealed to them this fruit*

I will come in the fullness of the blessing*j* of Christ.

30 I appeal to you, brothers and sisters,*k* by our Lord Jesus Christ and by the love of the Spirit, to join me in earnest prayer to God on my behalf, 31that I may be rescued from the unbelievers in Judea, and that my ministry*l* to Jerusalem may be acceptable to the saints, 32so that by God's will I may come to you with joy and be refreshed in your company. 33The God of peace be with all of you.*m* Amen.

15.26 Paul the Fund-raiser

Paul wrote Romans while traveling to raise funds for famine relief. Another letter (2 Corinthians 8) gives more details on this mercy mission on behalf of the Jews in Jerusalem. Paul's actions set an example of unity for a church composed of both Jews and Gentiles—unity sorely needed by groups racked by the divisions described in chapter 14.

Personal Greetings

16 I commend to you our sister Phoebe, a deacon*n* of the church at Cenchreae, 2so that you may welcome her in the Lord as is fitting for the saints, and help her in whatever she may require from you, for she has been a benefactor of many and of myself as well.

3 Greet Prisca and Aquila, who work with me in Christ Jesus, 4and who risked their necks for my life, to whom not only I give thanks, but also all the churches of the Gentiles. 5Greet also the church in their house. Greet my beloved Epaenetus, who was the first convert*o* in Asia for Christ. 6Greet Mary, who has worked very hard among you. 7Greet Andronicus and Junia,*p* my relatives*q* who were in prison with me; they are prominent among the apostles, and they were in Christ before I was. 8Greet Ampliatus, my beloved in the Lord. 9Greet Urbanus, our co-worker in Christ, and my beloved Stachys. 10Greet Apelles, who is approved in Christ. Greet those who belong to the family of Aristobulus. 11Greet my relative*r* Herodion. Greet those in the Lord who belong to the family of Narcissus. 12Greet those workers in the Lord, Tryphaena and Tryphosa. Greet the beloved Persis, who has worked hard in the Lord. 13Greet Rufus, chosen in the Lord; and greet his mother—a mother to me also. 14Greet

Asyncritus, Phlegon, Hermes, Patrobas, Hermas, and the brothers and sisters*k* who are with them. 15Greet Philologus, Julia, Nereus and his sister, and Olympas, and all the saints who are with them. 16Greet one another with a holy kiss. All the churches of Christ greet you.

Final Instructions

17 I urge you, brothers and sisters,*k* to keep an eye on those who cause dissensions and offenses, in opposition to the teaching that you have learned; avoid them. 18For such people do not serve our Lord Christ, but their own appetites,*s* and by smooth talk and flattery they deceive the hearts of the simple-minded. 19For while your obedience is known to all, so that I rejoice over you, I want you to be wise in what is good and guileless in what is evil. 20The God of peace will shortly crush Satan under your feet. The grace of our Lord Jesus Christ be with you.*t*

21 Timothy, my co-worker, greets you; so do Lucius and Jason and Sosipater, my relatives.*q*

22 I Tertius, the writer of this letter, greet you in the Lord.*u*

23 Gaius, who is host to me and to the whole church, greets you. Erastus, the city treasurer, and our brother Quartus, greet you.*v*

Final Doxology

25 Now to God*w* who is able to strengthen you according to my gospel and the proclamation

16.23 Paul's Friends

This chapter contains a fascinating list of Paul's friends and co-workers, many of whom would be unknown apart from their mention here. Although Paul himself had not yet visited Rome, a Christian community had taken root in the imperial capital. The list includes prominent women in the church (Phoebe, Priscilla, Junia, Tryphaena, Tryphosa, Persis), common slave names (Ampliatus, Urbanus, Stachys, Apelles), and possible royalty (the household of Aristobulus—probably the grandson of Herod the Great).

Paul was writing from Corinth, where his friends included the city's director of public works. At Corinth archaeologists have dug up a block of stone that may refer to this man: It bears the Latin inscription "Erastus, commissioner of public works, bore the expense of this pavement."

---

j Other ancient authorities add *of the gospel*   *k* Gk *brothers*   *l* Other ancient authorities read *my bringing of a gift*   *m* One ancient authority adds 16.25-27 here   *n* Or *minister*   *o* Gk *first fruits*   *p* Or *Junias*; other ancient authorities read *Julia*   *q* Or *compatriots*   *r* Or *compatriot*   *s* Gk *their own belly*   *t* Other ancient authorities lack this sentence   *u* Or *I Tertius, writing this letter in the Lord, greet you our Lord Jesus Christ be with all of you. Amen.*   *w* Gk *the one*   *v* Other ancient authorities add verse 24, *The grace of*

of Jesus Christ, according to the revelation of the mystery that was kept secret for long ages [26]but is now disclosed, and through the prophetic writings is made known to all the Gentiles, according to the command of the eternal God, to bring about the obedience of faith— [27]to the only wise God, through Jesus Christ, to whom[x] be the glory forever! Amen.[y]

1 CORINTHIANS

The Last Place to Start a Church
No one expected much from crazy Corinth

E VERY LARGE CITY HAS ONE pocket where prostitutes, strippers, gamblers, and drug dealers hang out. Tourists stroll by to gawk at the sights. In New York, it's Times Square; in San Francisco, the North Beach district; in New Orleans, Bourbon Street; and in Las Vegas, it's virtually anywhere.

In the ancient world, the whole city of Corinth was known for that kind of lifestyle. Romans made the Corinthians the butt of dirty jokes, and playwrights consistently portrayed them as drunken brawlers. The Greek verb "to Corinthianize" meant to live shamelessly and immorally.

A Wide-Open City

Everyone knew what the Corinthians worshiped: money and the kinky things it could buy. Money flowed freely, for Corinth straddled one of the Roman empire's most vital trade routes. When a ship wrecked nearby, salvage companies housed the hapless sailors at inflated prices while they scrambled to auction off the ship's cargo. The city was a sprawling open-air market, filled with slaves, Orientals, Jews, Greeks, Egyptians, sailors, athletes, gamblers, and charioteers.

Yet Corinth was no blue-collar town. It had a population of 700,000, second only to Rome's, and as the capital of a large province, the city hosted a parade of Roman diplomats and dignitaries. Its clever citizens showcased new "Corinthian" architecture and prided themselves on having a cosmopolitan outlook.

For their religious ideal, the fun-loving Corinthians adopted Venus, the goddess of love. A temple built in her honor employed more than 1,000 prostitutes.

Paul Takes on the Corinthians

Due to all these influences, Corinth loomed as the one city "least likely to convert" to the Christian faith. What crazy cults and new religions did spring up there quickly gave in to the prevailing good-time atmosphere.

The mighty Paul, reeling from one of his most difficult missionary assignments in Athens, came to Corinth "in weakness and in fear and in much trembling" (2.3). He knew its strategic importance: If the gospel could take root there, it could transplant anywhere—and probably would, considering Corinth's crossroads location.

Paul worked in Corinth for 18 months. To everyone's surprise , the church he founded became one of the largest in the first century. But several years later he heard reports that the church, true to its city's heritage, had broken out in a series of spiritual ills. The distressing news prompted the letter known as 1 Corinthians.

The tone of this letter differs drastically from the one that precedes it. If Romans was stylistically carved in stone, 1 Corinthians was dashed off in tears and anger. One of Paul's longest letters, it covers the greatest variety of topics, partly because the Corinthians added bizarre new twists to ethical issues. In it, Paul gives practical advice on a series of church problems as well as a fascinating glimpse into the personal lives of early Christians.

> Consider your own call, brothers and sisters: not many of you were wise by human standards, not many were powerful, not many were of noble birth. But God chose what is foolish in the world to shame the wise; God chose what is weak in the world to shame the strong. 1.26–27

How to Read 1 Corinthians

To fully appreciate Paul's letters, keep in mind that they are personal correspondence. We are actually reading someone else's mail.

In 1 Corinthians a riled-up apostle gives direct, forthright advice to a troubled local church. Paul saw alarming trends at work, and he used his full literary powers to set its members on the right course. He tried sarcasm, emotional pleas, autobiography, poetry, and lengthy arguments.

First, you will encounter the problems that had been reported to Paul: divisions in the church, a case of incest, court cases, the abuse of Christian freedom, chaos in the worship services. Paul lunges into these problems early in the book. Then, beginning with chapter 7, he takes up some other problems the Corinthians had written him about: marriage and the single life, pagan festivals, behavior of women, spiritual gifts, and the resurrection of the dead.

This first letter to the Corinthians presents a foundation for practical Christian ethics. Use the boldface sectional headings throughout the book to locate those issues that especially trouble you. Not all the problems discussed will apply directly to modern situations. But the general principles underlying Paul's advice do apply. As you read, look for those principles behind Paul's arguments.

PEOPLE YOU'LL MEET IN 1 CORINTHIANS

APOLLOS *(p. 1186)*

3-TRACK READING PLAN

For an explanation and complete listing of the 3-track reading plan, turn to page 7.

TRACK 1: *Two-Week Courses on the Bible*
The Track 1 reading program on the Life and Teachings of Paul includes two chapters from 1 Corinthians. See page 7 for a complete listing of this course.

TRACK 2: *An Overview of 1 Corinthians in 2 Days*
The emotional tone of 1 Corinthians makes for exciting reading throughout, but two chapters especially can't be missed.
☐ Day 1. Read the Introduction to 1 Corinthians, then chapter 13. Paul is at the top of his literary form as he defines love in one of the most famous passages in all of literature.
☐ Day 2. Read chapter 15, a crucial passage on life after death and resurrection from the dead.
Now turn to page 9 for your next Track 2 reading project.

TRACK 3: *All of 1 Corinthians in 14 Days*
After you have read through 1 Corinthians, turn to pages 10–14 for your next Track 3 reading project.
☐1 ☐2 ☐3 ☐4–5 ☐6 ☐7 ☐8–9 ☐10
☐11 ☐12 ☐13 ☐14 ☐15 ☐16

Salutation

1 Paul, called to be an apostle of Christ Jesus by the will of God, and our brother Sosthenes,

2 To the church of God that is in Corinth, to those who are sanctified in Christ Jesus, called to be saints, together with all those who in every place call on the name of our Lord Jesus Christ, both their Lord[a] and ours:

3 Grace to you and peace from God our Father and the Lord Jesus Christ.

4 I give thanks to my[b] God always for you because of the grace of God that has been given you in Christ Jesus, [5]for in every way you have been enriched in him, in speech and knowledge of every kind— [6]just as the testimony of[c] Christ has been strengthened among you— [7]so that you are not lacking in any spiritual gift as you wait for the revealing of our Lord Jesus Christ. [8]He will also strengthen you to the end, so that you may be blameless on the day of our Lord Jesus Christ. [9]God is faithful; by him you were called into the fellowship of his Son, Jesus Christ our Lord.

Divisions in the Church

10 Now I appeal to you, brothers and sisters,[d] by the name of our Lord Jesus Christ, that all of you be in agreement and that there be no divisions among you, but that you be united in the same mind and the same purpose. [11]For it has been reported to me by Chloe's people that there are quarrels among you, my brothers and sisters.[e] [12]What I mean is that each of you says, "I belong to Paul," or "I belong to Apollos," or "I belong to Cephas," or "I belong to Christ." [13]Has Christ been divided? Was Paul crucified for you? Or were you baptized in the name of Paul? [14]I thank God[f] that I baptized none of you except Crispus and Gaius, [15]so that no one can say that you were baptized in my name. [16](I did baptize also the household of Stephanas; beyond that, I do not know whether I baptized anyone else.) [17]For Christ did not send me to baptize but to proclaim the gospel, and not with eloquent wisdom, so that the cross of Christ might not be emptied of its power.

Christ the Power and Wisdom of God

18 For the message about the cross is foolishness to those who are perishing, but to us who are being saved it is the power of God. [19]For it is written,

> "I will destroy the wisdom of the wise,
>   and the discernment of the discerning I
>   will thwart."

[20]Where is the one who is wise? Where is the scribe? Where is the debater of this age? Has not God made foolish the wisdom of the world? [21]For since, in the wisdom of God, the world did not know God through wisdom, God decided, through the foolishness of our proclamation, to save those who believe. [22]For Jews demand signs and Greeks desire wisdom, [23]but we proclaim Christ crucified, a stumbling block to Jews and foolishness to Gentiles, [24]but to those who are the called, both Jews and Greeks, Christ the power of God and the wisdom of God. [25]For God's foolishness is wiser than human wisdom, and God's weakness is stronger than human strength.

26 Consider your own call, brothers and sisters:[d] not many of you were wise by human standards,[g] not many were powerful, not many were of noble birth. [27]But God chose what is foolish in the world to shame the wise; God chose what is weak in the world to shame the strong; [28]God chose what is low and despised in the world, things that are not, to reduce to nothing things that are, [29]so that no one[h] might boast in the presence of God. [30]He is the source of your life in Christ Jesus, who became for us wisdom from God, and righteousness and sanctification and redemption, [31]in order that, as it is written, "Let the one who boasts, boast in[i] the Lord."

Proclaiming Christ Crucified

2 When I came to you, brothers and sisters,[d] I did not come proclaiming the mystery[j] of God to you in lofty words or wisdom. [2]For I decided to know nothing among you except Jesus Christ, and him crucified. [3]And I came to you in

2.3 Paul at a Crossroads

This brief paragraph hints at a grave personal crisis in the apostle Paul's ministry, and Acts 16–18 gives important background. In three cities Paul saw a promising beginning crushed by fanatical Jews. Then in Athens he met little success in communicating to the intelligentsia. Many scholars believe that he reached Corinth shaken and discouraged and that he resolved to make Christ the sole subject of his teaching and preaching while there.

weakness and in fear and in much trembling. [4]My speech and my proclamation were not with plausible words of wisdom,[k] but with a demonstration of the Spirit and of power, [5]so that your faith might rest not on human wisdom but on the power of God.

The True Wisdom of God

6 Yet among the mature we do speak wisdom,

---

a Gk *theirs*   *b* Other ancient authorities lack *my*   *c* Or *to*   *d* Gk *brothers*   *e* Gk *my brothers*   *f* Other ancient authorities read *I am thankful*   *g* Gk *according to the flesh*   *h* Gk *no flesh*   *i* Or *of*   *j* Other ancient authorities read *testimony*   *k* Other ancient authorities read *the persuasiveness of wisdom*

though it is not a wisdom of this age or of the rulers of this age, who are doomed to perish. [7]But we speak God's wisdom, secret and hidden, which God decreed before the ages for our glory. [8]None of the rulers of this age understood this; for if they had, they would not have crucified the Lord of glory. [9]But, as it is written,

"What no eye has seen, nor ear heard,
   nor the human heart conceived,
what God has prepared for those who
   love him"—

[10]these things God has revealed to us through the Spirit; for the Spirit searches everything, even the depths of God. [11]For what human being knows what is truly human except the human spirit that is within? So also no one comprehends what is truly God's except the Spirit of God. [12]Now we have received not the spirit of the world, but the Spirit that is from God, so that we may understand the gifts bestowed on us by God. [13]And we speak of these things in words not taught by human wisdom but taught by the Spirit, interpreting spiritual things to those who are spiritual.[l]

14 Those who are unspiritual[m] do not receive the gifts of God's Spirit, for they are foolishness to them, and they are unable to understand them because they are spiritually discerned. [15]Those who are spiritual discern all things, and they are themselves subject to no one else's scrutiny.

[16] "For who has known the mind
         of the Lord
      so as to instruct him?"

But we have the mind of Christ.

On Divisions in the Corinthian Church

3 And so, brothers and sisters,[n] I could not speak to you as spiritual people, but rather as people of the flesh, as infants in Christ. [2]I fed you with milk, not solid food, for you were not ready for solid food. Even now you are still not ready, [3]for you are still of the flesh. For as long as there is jealousy and quarreling among you, are you not of the flesh, and behaving according to human

---

[l] Or *interpreting spiritual things in spiritual language,* or *comparing spiritual things with spiritual*   [m] Or *natural*
[n] Gk *brothers*

Like an Angry Letter from Home
A well-deserved scolding from a grieving "parent"

IMAGINE A COLLEGE FRESHMAN, STANDING in a corridor amid a swirl of chattering students. In two minutes the next class will begin. But, for her, time has stopped. She has just opened a tearstained, 12-page letter from her parents.

I am not writing this to make you ashamed, but to admonish you as my beloved children. 4.14

The tone of the letter takes her by surprise. Her parents are normally reserved, not given to emotional outbursts. Their letters are warm and friendly. Not this time. Somehow they have heard about her recent behavior on campus, and they are very hurt. In a torrent of words, they pour out their feelings for her and their equally deep disappointment.

First Corinthians reflects the same tone: it is an intimate, well-deserved scolding from a grieved parent. "I am not writing this to make you ashamed," says Paul, "but to admonish you as my beloved children" (4.14).

Paul's Shifting Moods

No other letter in the New Testament reveals such a wide range of Paul's emotions. At his own financial expense, he had invested 18 risk-filled months in Corinth. But afterwards his rebellious "children" had launched personal attacks against him. Paul reacted like any parent first informed of his child's shocking behavior. His moods in 1 Corinthians bounce from anger to shame, from sorrow to indignation.

Chapter 3, for example, begins with a stern lecture to "infants in Christ." This leads to biting sarcasm (4.8), which melts into the tender pleas of a spiritual father. Six times in chapter 6 Paul asks, "Do you not know ... ?" Finally, in chapter 7, he gets to the practical questions that had prompted his letter in the first place.

The apostle Paul was a superbly educated logician who could skillfully weave together history and philosophy. But he also brooded over his missionary churches like a parent. He asked the Corinthians pointedly, "Am I to come to you with a stick, or with love in a spirit of gentleness?" (4.21). In this letter, we see a little of both.

Life Questions: How do you react when someone—a parent, teacher, boss, pastor—tries to straighten you out?

inclinations? ⁴For when one says, "I belong to Paul," and another, "I belong to Apollos," are you not merely human?

5 What then is Apollos? What is Paul? Servants through whom you came to believe, as the

3.5–9 Personality Cults

In this chapter, Paul expands on a theme first introduced in 1.12. Converts were lining up behind various church leaders: Peter, who had walked and talked with Christ on earth; Apollos, with his sophisticated, cultivated style; Paul, the famous missionary; and Christ himself. Paul had no tolerance for that kind of hero worship. He stressed vigorously that the Corinthians belonged only to God, not to any human worker.

Lord assigned to each. ⁶I planted, Apollos watered, but God gave the growth. ⁷So neither the one who plants nor the one who waters is anything, but only God who gives the growth. ⁸The one who plants and the one who waters have a common purpose, and each will receive wages according to the labor of each. ⁹For we are God's servants, working together; you are God's field, God's building.

10 According to the grace of God given to me, like a skilled master builder I laid a foundation, and someone else is building on it. Each builder must choose with care how to build on it. ¹¹For no one can lay any foundation other than the one that has been laid; that foundation is Jesus Christ. ¹²Now if anyone builds on the foundation with gold, silver, precious stones, wood, hay, straw—

¹³the work of each builder will become visible, for the Day will disclose it, because it will be revealed with fire, and the fire will test what sort of work each has done. ¹⁴If what has been built on the foundation survives, the builder will receive a reward. ¹⁵If the work is burned up, the builder will suffer loss; the builder will be saved, but only as through fire.

16 Do you not know that you are God's temple and that God's Spirit dwells in you?ᵒ ¹⁷If anyone destroys God's temple, God will destroy that person. For God's temple is holy, and you are that temple.

18 Do not deceive yourselves. If you think that you are wise in this age, you should become fools so that you may become wise. ¹⁹For the wisdom of this world is foolishness with God. For it is written,

"He catches the wise in their craftiness,"

²⁰and again,

"The Lord knows the thoughts of the
        wise,
    that they are futile."

²¹So let no one boast about human leaders. For all things are yours, ²²whether Paul or Apollos or Cephas or the world or life or death or the present or the future—all belong to you, ²³and you belong to Christ, and Christ belongs to God.

The Ministry of the Apostles

4 Think of us in this way, as servants of Christ and stewards of God's mysteries. ²Moreover, it is required of stewards that they be found trustworthy. ³But with me it is a very small thing that I should be judged by you or by any human court. I do not even judge myself. ⁴I am not aware of anything against myself, but I am not thereby

---

ᵒ In verses 16 and 17 the Greek word for *you* is plural

APOLLOS *Brimming with Confidence*

APOLLOS CAME ON THE SCENE at Ephesus like a whirlwind (Acts 18.24–26). He knew the Scriptures inside out and went immediately to the Jewish synagogue to present Jesus as their long-awaited Messiah. Apollos had a few things to learn (Priscilla and Aquila found it necessary to update his information privately), but he was fearless in telling what he knew.

Brimming with confidence, Apollos hailed from one of the largest, most cultured cities in the world. Alexandria in Egypt boasted a centuries-old university and library, and had a thriving, scholarly Jewish sector. It was in Alexandria that the Old Testament had been translated into Greek.

Apollos later traveled to Corinth, where he became an extremely effective leader in the church. Indeed, he made such an impact that a "pro-Apollos" faction gathered around him, threatening to split the church in two. The apostle Paul had to warn the Corinthians to stay together, rather than taking sides.

When Paul wrote this letter, Apollos apparently was with him (16.12). Paul urged Apollos to return to Corinth, but he declined. Divisions in the church were no doubt as troubling to Apollos as they were to Paul.

Life Questions: How can charismatic leaders avoid attracting attention to themselves rather than their message?

acquitted. It is the Lord who judges me. 5Therefore do not pronounce judgment before the time, before the Lord comes, who will bring to light the things now hidden in darkness and will disclose the purposes of the heart. Then each one will receive commendation from God.

6 I have applied all this to Apollos and myself for your benefit, brothers and sisters,p so that you may learn through us the meaning of the saying, "Nothing beyond what is written," so that none of you will be puffed up in favor of one against another. 7For who sees anything different in you?q What do you have that you did not receive? And if you received it, why do you boast as if it were not a gift?

8 Already you have all you want! Already you have become rich! Quite apart from us you have become kings! Indeed, I wish that you had become kings, so that we might be kings with you!

4.8–13 A Hint of Trials to Come

Paul's intense feelings come to the surface in this paragraph, as sharply worded as any in the New Testament. He alludes (verse 9) to the Roman practice of parading the gladiators condemned to death—a poignant reference in light of the martyr's fate that awaited him and other apostles.

9For I think that God has exhibited us apostles as last of all, as though sentenced to death, because we have become a spectacle to the world, to angels and to mortals. 10We are fools for the sake of Christ, but you are wise in Christ. We are weak, but you are strong. You are held in honor, but we in disrepute. 11To the present hour we are hungry and thirsty, we are poorly clothed and beaten and homeless, 12and we grow weary from the work of our own hands. When reviled, we bless; when persecuted, we endure; 13when slandered, we speak kindly. We have become like the rubbish of the world, the dregs of all things, to this very day.

Fatherly Admonition

14 I am not writing this to make you ashamed, but to admonish you as my beloved children. 15For though you might have ten thousand guardians in Christ, you do not have many fathers. Indeed, in Christ Jesus I became your father through the gospel. 16I appeal to you, then, be imitators of me. 17For this reason I sentr you Timothy, who is my beloved and faithful child in the Lord, to remind you of my ways in Christ Jesus, as I teach them everywhere in every church. 18But some of you, thinking that I am not coming to you, have become arrogant. 19But I will come

to you soon, if the Lord wills, and I will find out not the talk of these arrogant people but their power. 20For the kingdom of God depends not on talk but on power. 21What would you prefer? Am I to come to you with a stick, or with love in a spirit of gentleness?

Sexual Immorality Defiles the Church

5 It is actually reported that there is sexual immorality among you, and of a kind that is not found even among pagans; for a man is living with his father's wife. 2And you are arrogant! Should you not rather have mourned, so that he who has done this would have been removed from among you?

3 For though absent in body, I am present in spirit; and as if present I have already pronounced judgment 4in the name of the Lord Jesus on the man who has done such a thing.s When you are assembled, and my spirit is present with the power of our Lord Jesus, 5you are to hand this man over to Satan for the destruction of the flesh, so that his spirit may be saved in the day of the Lord.t

5.5 Handed Over to Satan

The strong phrase used in this verse has a Biblical parallel in 1 Timothy 1.20. To Paul, expelling someone from the church and Christian privileges meant pushing them out into the world ruled by Satan. In both references, however, Paul stresses that the action was designed to teach the offender a lesson.

6 Your boasting is not a good thing. Do you not know that a little yeast leavens the whole batch of dough? 7Clean out the old yeast so that you may be a new batch, as you really are unleavened. For our paschal lamb, Christ, has been sacrificed. 8Therefore, let us celebrate the festival, not with the old yeast, the yeast of malice and evil, but with the unleavened bread of sincerity and truth.

Sexual Immorality Must Be Judged

9 I wrote to you in my letter not to associate with sexually immoral persons— 10not at all meaning the immoral of this world, or the greedy and robbers, or idolaters, since you would then need to go out of the world. 11But now I am writing to you not to associate with anyone who bears the name of brother or sisteru who is sexually immoral or greedy, or is an idolater, reviler, drunkard, or robber. Do not even eat with such a one. 12For what have I to do with judging those outside? Is it not those who are inside that you are

p Gk brothers   q Or Who makes you different from another?   r Or am sending   s Or on the man who has done such a thing in the name of the Lord Jesus   t Other ancient authorities add Jesus   u Gk brother

to judge? [13]God will judge those outside. "Drive out the wicked person from among you."

Lawsuits among Believers

6 When any of you has a grievance against another, do you dare to take it to court before the unrighteous, instead of taking it before the saints? [2]Do you not know that the saints will judge the world? And if the world is to be judged by you, are you incompetent to try trivial cases? [3]Do you not know that we are to judge angels—to say nothing of ordinary matters? [4]If you have ordinary cases, then, do you appoint as judges those who have no standing in the church? [5]I say this to your shame. Can it be that there is no one among you wise enough to decide between one believer[v] and another, [6]but a believer[v] goes to court against a believer[v]—and before unbelievers at that?

7 In fact, to have lawsuits at all with one another is already a defeat for you. Why not rather be wronged? Why not rather be defrauded? [8]But you yourselves wrong and defraud—and believers[w] at that.

9 Do you not know that wrongdoers will not inherit the kingdom of God? Do not be deceived! Fornicators, idolaters, adulterers, male prostitutes, sodomites, [10]thieves, the greedy, drunkards, revilers, robbers—none of these will inherit the kingdom of God. [11]And this is what some of you used to be. But you were washed, you were sanctified, you were justified in the name of the Lord Jesus Christ and in the Spirit of our God.

Glorify God in Body and Spirit

12 "All things are lawful for me," but not all things are beneficial. "All things are lawful for me," but I will not be dominated by anything.

6.12 Corinthian Slogans

The phrases given here in quotes ("All things are lawful for me"; "Food is meant for the stomach and the stomach for food") appear to be slogans the Corinthians had used in justifying their loose behavior. Paul doesn't refute their ideas outright, but rather points to the ultimate effect of their excesses.

[13]"Food is meant for the stomach and the stomach for food,"[x] and God will destroy both one and the other. The body is meant not for fornication but for the Lord, and the Lord for the body. [14]And God raised the Lord and will also raise us by his power. [15]Do you not know that your bodies are members of Christ? Should I therefore take the members of Christ and make them members of a prostitute? Never! [16]Do you not know that whoever is united to a prostitute becomes one body with her? For it is said, "The two shall be one flesh." [17]But anyone united to the Lord becomes one spirit with him. [18]Shun fornication! Every sin that a person commits is outside the body; but the fornicator sins against the body itself. [19]Or do you not know that your body is a temple[y] of the Holy Spirit within you, which you have from God, and that you are not your own? [20]For you were bought with a price; therefore glorify God in your body.

Directions concerning Marriage

7 Now concerning the matters about which you wrote: "It is well for a man not to touch a woman." [2]But because of cases of sexual immorality, each man should have his own wife and each woman her own husband. [3]The husband should give to his wife her conjugal rights, and likewise the wife to her husband. [4]For the wife does not have authority over her own body, but the husband does; likewise the husband does not have authority over his own body, but the wife does. [5]Do not deprive one another except perhaps by agreement for a set time, to devote yourselves to prayer, and then come together again, so that Satan may not tempt you because of your lack of self-control. [6]This I say by way of concession, not of command. [7]I wish that all were as I myself am. But each has a particular gift from God, one having one kind and another a different kind.

8 To the unmarried and the widows I say that it is well for them to remain unmarried as I am. [9]But if they are not practicing self-control, they should marry. For it is better to marry than to be aflame with passion.

10 To the married I give this command—not I but the Lord—that the wife should not separate from her husband [11](but if she does separate, let her remain unmarried or else be reconciled to her husband), and that the husband should not divorce his wife.

12 To the rest I say—I and not the Lord—that if any believer[v] has a wife who is an unbeliever, and she consents to live with him, he should not divorce her. [13]And if any woman has a husband who is an unbeliever, and he consents to live with her, she should not divorce him. [14]For the unbelieving husband is made holy through his wife, and the unbelieving wife is made holy through her husband. Otherwise, your children would be unclean, but as it is, they are holy. [15]But if the unbelieving partner separates, let it be so; in such a case the brother or sister is not bound. It is to peace that God has called you.[z] [16]Wife, for all you know, you might save your husband. Husband, for all you know, you might save your wife.

[v] Gk *brother*   [w] Gk *brothers*   [x] The quotation may extend to the word *other*   [y] Or *sanctuary*   [z] Other ancient authorities read *us*

The Life That the Lord Has Assigned

17 However that may be, let each of you lead the life that the Lord has assigned, to which God called you. This is my rule in all the churches. [18]Was anyone at the time of his call already circumcised? Let him not seek to remove the marks of circumcision. Was anyone at the time of his call uncircumcised? Let him not seek circumcision. [19]Circumcision is nothing, and uncircumcision is nothing; but obeying the commandments of God is everything. [20]Let each of you remain in the condition in which you were called.

21 Were you a slave when called? Do not be concerned about it. Even if you can gain your freedom, make use of your present condition now more than ever.[a] [22]For whoever was called in the Lord as a slave is a freed person belonging to the Lord, just as whoever was free when called is a slave of Christ. [23]You were bought with a price; do not become slaves of human masters. [24]In whatever condition you were called, brothers and sisters,[b] there remain with God.

The Unmarried and the Widows

25 Now concerning virgins, I have no command of the Lord, but I give my opinion as one

7.25 Paul's Personal Opinions

In discussing the thorny issue of singleness and marriage, Paul carefully distinguishes what is his personal opinion and what is a clear revelation from God. He explains in verse 29 why he reached these conclusions.

who by the Lord's mercy is trustworthy. [26]I think that, in view of the impending[c] crisis, it is well for you to remain as you are. [27]Are you bound to a wife? Do not seek to be free. Are you free from a wife? Do not seek a wife. [28]But if you marry, you do not sin, and if a virgin marries, she does not sin. Yet those who marry will experience distress in this life,[d] and I would spare you that. [29]I mean, brothers and sisters,[b] the appointed time has grown short; from now on, let even those who have wives be as though they had none, [30]and those who mourn as though they were not mourning, and those who rejoice as though they were not rejoicing, and those who buy as though they had no possessions, [31]and those who deal with the world as though they had no dealings with it. For the present form of this world is passing away.

32 I want you to be free from anxieties. The unmarried man is anxious about the affairs of the Lord, how to please the Lord; [33]but the married

man is anxious about the affairs of the world, how to please his wife, [34]and his interests are divided. And the unmarried woman and the virgin are anxious about the affairs of the Lord, so that they may be holy in body and spirit; but the married woman is anxious about the affairs of the world, how to please her husband. [35]I say this for your own benefit, not to put any restraint upon you, but to promote good order and unhindered devotion to the Lord.

36 If anyone thinks that he is not behaving properly toward his fiancée,[e] if his passions are strong, and so it has to be, let him marry as he wishes; it is no sin. Let them marry. [37]But if someone stands firm in his resolve, being under no necessity but having his own desire under control, and has determined in his own mind to keep her as his fiancée,[e] he will do well. [38]So then, he who marries his fiancée[e] does well; and he who refrains from marriage will do better.

39 A wife is bound as long as her husband lives. But if the husband dies,[f] she is free to marry anyone she wishes, only in the Lord. [40]But in my judgment she is more blessed if she remains as she is. And I think that I too have the Spirit of God.

Food Offered to Idols

8 Now concerning food sacrificed to idols: we know that "all of us possess knowledge." Knowledge puffs up, but love builds up. [2]Anyone who claims to know something does not yet have the necessary knowledge; [3]but anyone who loves God is known by him.

4 Hence, as to the eating of food offered to idols, we know that "no idol in the world really exists," and that "there is no God but one." [5]Indeed, even though there may be so-called gods in heaven or on earth—as in fact there are many gods and many lords— [6]yet for us there is one God, the Father, from whom are all things and for whom we exist, and one Lord, Jesus Christ, through whom are all things and through whom we exist.

7 It is not everyone, however, who has this knowledge. Since some have become so accustomed to idols until now, they still think of the food they eat as food offered to an idol; and their conscience, being weak, is defiled. [8]"Food will not bring us close to God."[g] We are no worse off if we do not eat, and no better off if we do. [9]But take care that this liberty of yours does not somehow become a stumbling block to the weak. [10]For if others see you, who possess knowledge, eating in the temple of an idol, might they not, since their conscience is weak, be encouraged to the point of eating food sacrificed to idols? [11]So by your knowledge those weak believers for whom Christ

---

[a] Or *avail yourself of the opportunity*   [b] Gk *brothers*   [c] Or *present*   [d] Gk *in the flesh*   [e] Gk *virgin*
[f] Gk *falls asleep*   [g] The quotation may extend to the end of the verse

died are destroyed.[h] 12But when you thus sin against members of your family,[i] and wound their conscience when it is weak, you sin against Christ. 13Therefore, if food is a cause of their falling,[j] I will never eat meat, so that I may not cause one of them[k] to fall.

The Rights of an Apostle

9 Am I not free? Am I not an apostle? Have I not seen Jesus our Lord? Are you not my work in the Lord? 2If I am not an apostle to others, at least I am to you; for you are the seal of my apostleship in the Lord.

3 This is my defense to those who would examine me. 4Do we not have the right to our food and drink? 5Do we not have the right to be accompanied by a believing wife,[l] as do the other apostles and the brothers of the Lord and Cephas? 6Or is it only Barnabas and I who have no right to refrain from working for a living? 7Who at any time pays the expenses for doing military service? Who plants a vineyard and does not eat any of its fruit? Or who tends a flock and does not get any of its milk?

8 Do I say this on human authority? Does not the law also say the same? 9For it is written in the law of Moses, "You shall not muzzle an ox while it is treading out the grain." Is it for oxen that God is concerned? 10Or does he not speak entirely for our sake? It was indeed written for our sake, for whoever plows should plow in hope and whoever threshes should thresh in hope of a share in the crop. 11If we have sown spiritual good among you, is it too much if we reap your material benefits? 12If others share this rightful claim on you, do not we still more?

Nevertheless, we have not made use of this right, but we endure anything rather than put an obstacle in the way of the gospel of Christ. 13Do you not know that those who are employed in the temple service get their food from the temple, and those who serve at the altar share in what is sacrificed on the altar? 14In the same way, the Lord commanded that those who proclaim the gospel should get their living by the gospel.

15 But I have made no use of any of these rights, nor am I writing this so that they may be applied in my case. Indeed, I would rather die than that—no one will deprive me of my ground for boasting! 16If I proclaim the gospel, this gives me no ground for boasting, for an obligation is laid on me, and woe to me if I do not proclaim the gospel! 17For if I do this of my own will, I have a reward; but if not of my own will, I am entrusted with a commission. 18What then is my reward? Just this: that in my proclamation I may make the gospel free of charge, so as not to make full use of my rights in the gospel.

---

[h] Gk the weak brother . . . is destroyed   [i] Gk against the brothers   [j] Gk my brother's falling   [k] Gk cause my brother   [l] Gk a sister as wife

---

When Everything Goes Wrong
A church of former idolaters, adulterers, thieves, and drunkards

Now concerning the matters about which you wrote . . .
7.1

"IF ANYTHING CAN GO WRONG, it will." This tongue-in-cheek principle, known as Murphy's Law, is cited by economists, sports team owners, and big-city mayors. Human nature somehow guarantees that nothing turns out quite the way it's supposed to. And the church at Corinth provides a darkly shining example of Murphy's Law.

To be sure, Corinthian Christians started out with the odds stacked against them. Imagine a church composed of converted idolaters, adulterers, male prostitutes, thieves, drunkards, and swindlers (6.9–11). The church made up of people from such backgrounds soon encountered a thicket of problems. Paul faced a huge challenge: For one thing, he had to convince these people of the immorality of sexual activities that had been a part of everyday worship under their old religion.

Local and Universal Issues

First Corinthians is Paul's careful response to that thicket of problems, some of which had been posed to him as questions in a letter (7.1). Many of his answers relate directly to Corinth's local situation. In that culture, as in Muslim countries today, whether or not to wear a veil was a major issue for women (11.3–10). Eating meat sacrificed to pagan idols also disturbed some new Christians (10.18–33).

But other problems discussed here turn up in every culture: divisions in the church, lawsuits, immorality, the single life, the extent of Christian freedoms, differing views of worship and the place of tongue-speaking and other spiritual gifts. Not every breakdown in Corinth will recur in churches today, but Paul's principles apply to our own unpredictable experiences with Murphy's Law.

Life Questions: Think of the most "Corinthian" television show you know. Then imagine: If the lead characters became Christians, what problems would they encounter?

19 For though I am free with respect to all, I have made myself a slave to all, so that I might win more of them. 20To the Jews I became as a Jew, in order to win Jews. To those under the law I became as one under the law (though I myself am not under the law) so that I might win those under the law. 21To those outside the law I became as one outside the law (though I am not free from God's law but am under Christ's law) so that I might win those outside the law. 22To the weak I became weak, so that I might win the weak. I have become all things to all people, that I might

---

9.22 A Positive and a Negative

After discussing the specific questions that had surfaced in the church at Corinth, Paul gives two examples from life. The first, a positive one, points to the actions of the apostles. Although they had certain "rights" and freedoms, they didn't insist on them. Rather, they adapted to the practices of people around them to win them over. In contrast, the ancient Israelites (chapter 10) had consistently given in to their own weaknesses. Paul urges the Corinthians to follow his example, not that of the Israelites (11.1).

---

by all means save some. 23I do it all for the sake of the gospel, so that I may share in its blessings.

24 Do you not know that in a race the runners all compete, but only one receives the prize? Run in such a way that you may win it. 25Athletes exercise self-control in all things; they do it to receive a perishable wreath, but we an imperishable one. 26So I do not run aimlessly, nor do I box as though beating the air; 27but I punish my body and enslave it, so that after proclaiming to others I myself should not be disqualified.

Warnings from Israel's History

10 I do not want you to be unaware, brothers and sisters,*m* that our ancestors were all under the cloud, and all passed through the sea, 2and all were baptized into Moses in the cloud and in the sea, 3and all ate the same spiritual food, 4and all drank the same spiritual drink. For they drank from the spiritual rock that followed them, and the rock was Christ. 5Nevertheless, God was not pleased with most of them, and they were struck down in the wilderness.

6 Now these things occurred as examples for us, so that we might not desire evil as they did. 7Do not become idolaters as some of them did; as it is written, "The people sat down to eat and drink, and they rose up to play." 8We must not indulge in sexual immorality as some of them did, and twenty-three thousand fell in a single day.

9We must not put Christ*n* to the test, as some of them did, and were destroyed by serpents. 10And do not complain as some of them did, and were destroyed by the destroyer. 11These things happened to them to serve as an example, and they were written down to instruct us, on whom the ends of the ages have come. 12So if you think you are standing, watch out that you do not fall. 13No testing has overtaken you that is not common to everyone. God is faithful, and he will not let you be tested beyond your strength, but with the testing he will also provide the way out so that you may be able to endure it.

14 Therefore, my dear friends,*o* flee from the worship of idols. 15I speak as to sensible people; judge for yourselves what I say. 16The cup of blessing that we bless, is it not a sharing in the blood of Christ? The bread that we break, is it not a sharing in the body of Christ? 17Because there is one bread, we who are many are one body, for we all partake of the one bread. 18Consider the people of Israel;*p* are not those who eat the sacrifices partners in the altar? 19What do I imply then? That food sacrificed to idols is anything, or that an idol is anything? 20No, I imply that what pagans sacrifice, they sacrifice to demons and not to God. I do not want you to be partners with demons. 21You cannot drink the cup of the Lord and the cup of demons. You cannot partake of the table of the Lord and the table of demons. 22Or are we provoking the Lord to jealousy? Are we stronger than he?

Do All to the Glory of God

23 "All things are lawful," but not all things are beneficial. "All things are lawful," but not all things build up. 24Do not seek your own advantage, but that of the other. 25Eat whatever is sold in the meat market without raising any question on the ground of conscience, 26for "the earth and its fullness are the Lord's." 27If an unbeliever invites you to a meal and you are disposed to go, eat whatever is set before you without raising any question on the ground of conscience. 28But if someone says to you, "This has been offered in sacrifice," then do not eat it, out of consideration for the one who informed you, and for the sake of conscience— 29I mean the other's conscience, not your own. For why should my liberty be subject to the judgment of someone else's conscience? 30If I partake with thankfulness, why should I be denounced because of that for which I give thanks?

31 So, whether you eat or drink, or whatever you do, do everything for the glory of God. 32Give no offense to Jews or to Greeks or to the church of God, 33just as I try to please everyone in everything I do, not seeking my own advantage, but

---

m Gk *brothers*   *n* Other ancient authorities read *the Lord*   *o* Gk *my beloved*   *p* Gk *Israel according to the flesh*

11

that of many, so that they may be saved. ¹Be imitators of me, as I am of Christ.

Head Coverings

2 I commend you because you remember me in everything and maintain the traditions just as I handed them on to you. ³But I want you to understand that Christ is the head of every man, and the husband^q is the head of his wife,^r and God is the head of Christ. ⁴Any man who prays or prophesies with something on his head disgraces his head, ⁵but any woman who prays or prophesies with her head unveiled disgraces her head— it is one and the same thing as having her head

11.5 Women in Corinth

In the Middle East, a woman who appeared in public barefaced, without a veil, showed loose morals. Some Muslim countries today still retain that custom. Paul's advice applied directly to the cultural situation in Corinth, where unruly women were disrupting the worship services.

shaved. ⁶For if a woman will not veil herself, then she should cut off her hair; but if it is disgraceful for a woman to have her hair cut off or to be shaved, she should wear a veil. ⁷For a man ought not to have his head veiled, since he is the image and reflection^s of God; but woman is the reflection^s of man. ⁸Indeed, man was not made from woman, but woman from man. ⁹Neither was man created for the sake of woman, but woman for the sake of man. ¹⁰For this reason a woman ought to have a symbol of^t authority on her head,^u because of the angels. ¹¹Nevertheless, in the Lord woman is not independent of man or man independent of woman. ¹²For just as woman came from man, so man comes through woman; but all things come from God. ¹³Judge for yourselves: is it proper for a woman to pray to God with her head unveiled? ¹⁴Does not nature itself teach you that if a man wears long hair, it is degrading to him, ¹⁵but if a woman has long hair, it is her glory? For her hair is given to her for a covering. ¹⁶But if anyone is disposed to be contentious— we have no such custom, nor do the churches of God.

Abuses at the Lord's Supper

17 Now in the following instructions I do not commend you, because when you come together it is not for the better but for the worse. ¹⁸For, to begin with, when you come together as a church,

I hear that there are divisions among you; and to some extent I believe it. ¹⁹Indeed, there have to be factions among you, for only so will it become clear who among you are genuine. ²⁰When you come together, it is not really to eat the Lord's supper. ²¹For when the time comes to eat, each of you goes ahead with your own supper, and one goes hungry and another becomes drunk. ²²What! Do you not have homes to eat and drink in? Or do you show contempt for the church of God and humiliate those who have nothing? What should I say to you? Should I commend you? In this matter I do not commend you!

The Institution of the Lord's Supper

23 For I received from the Lord what I also handed on to you, that the Lord Jesus on the night when he was betrayed took a loaf of bread, ²⁴and when he had given thanks, he broke it and said, "This is my body that is for^v you. Do this in remembrance of me." ²⁵In the same way he took the cup also, after supper, saying, "This cup is the new covenant in my blood. Do this, as often as you drink it, in remembrance of me." ²⁶For as often as you eat this bread and drink the cup, you proclaim the Lord's death until he comes.

Partaking of the Supper Unworthily

27 Whoever, therefore, eats the bread or drinks the cup of the Lord in an unworthy manner will be answerable for the body and blood of the Lord. ²⁸Examine yourselves, and only then eat of the bread and drink of the cup. ²⁹For all who eat and drink^w without discerning the body,^x eat and drink judgment against themselves. ³⁰For this reason many of you are weak and ill, and some have died.^y ³¹But if we judged ourselves, we would not be judged. ³²But when we are judged by the Lord, we are disciplined^z so that we may not be condemned along with the world.

33 So then, my brothers and sisters,^a when you come together to eat, wait for one another. ³⁴If you are hungry, eat at home, so that when you come together, it will not be for your condemnation. About the other things I will give instructions when I come.

Spiritual Gifts

12

Now concerning spiritual gifts,^b brothers and sisters,^a I do not want you to be uninformed. ²You know that when you were pagans, you were enticed and led astray to idols that could not speak. ³Therefore I want you to understand that no one speaking by the Spirit of God ever says "Let Jesus be cursed!" and no one can say "Jesus is Lord" except by the Holy Spirit.

4 Now there are varieties of gifts, but the same

---

q The same Greek word means *man* or *husband*   r Or *head of the woman*   s Or *glory*   t Gk lacks *a symbol of*
u Or *have freedom of choice regarding her head*   v Other ancient authorities read *is broken for*   w Other ancient
authorities add *in an unworthy manner,*   x Other ancient authorities read *the Lord's body*   y Gk *fallen asleep*
z Or *When we are judged, we are being disciplined by the Lord*   a Gk *brothers*   b Or *spiritual persons*

Spirit; [5]and there are varieties of services, but the same Lord; [6]and there are varieties of activities, but it is the same God who activates all of them in everyone. [7]To each is given the manifestation of the Spirit for the common good. [8]To one is given through the Spirit the utterance of wisdom, and to another the utterance of knowledge according to the same Spirit, [9]to another faith by the same Spirit, to another gifts of healing by the one Spirit, [10]to another the working of miracles, to another prophecy, to another the discernment of spirits, to another various kinds of tongues, to another the interpretation of tongues. [11]All these are activated by one and the same Spirit, who allots to each one individually just as the Spirit chooses.

One Body with Many Members

12 For just as the body is one and has many members, and all the members of the body, though many, are one body, so it is with Christ. [13]For in the one Spirit we were all baptized into one body—Jews or Greeks, slaves or free—and we were all made to drink of one Spirit.

14 Indeed, the body does not consist of one member but of many. [15]If the foot would say, "Because I am not a hand, I do not belong to the body," that would not make it any less a part of the body. [16]And if the ear would say, "Because I am not an eye, I do not belong to the body," that would not make it any less a part of the body. [17]If the whole body were an eye, where would the hearing be? If the whole body were hearing, where would the sense of smell be? [18]But as it is, God arranged the members in the body, each one of them, as he chose. [19]If all were a single member, where would the body be? [20]As it is, there are many members, yet one body. [21]The eye cannot say to the hand, "I have no need of you," nor again the head to the feet, "I have no need of you." [22]On the contrary, the members of the body that seem to be weaker are indispensable, [23]and those members of the body that we think less honorable we clothe with greater honor, and our

Lessons from the Human Body
The body needs an eye, and the eye needs a body

CAN YOU GET ALONG IN life without eyes? Of course, but you must make adjustments. You must rely more on other senses and depend on friends, or perhaps a seeing-eye dog, for extra help. Regardless of what adjustments you make, however, your body will remain incomplete without eyes. You will miss out on color and design and all the visual delights this world offers.

An eyeless body can cope, but a bodyless eye is unimaginable. The most beautiful eyes in the world, when detached from a body, are lifeless and worthless. Eyes need a body that will bring them blood and receive their nerve impulses.

> Just as the body is one and has many members, and all the members of the body, though many, are one body, so it is with Christ. 12.12

Many Parts, All Working Together

In chapter 12 Paul gives a clever anatomy lesson, with a purpose. By comparing members of the church of Christ to parts of a human body, he neatly explains two complementary truths the Corinthians had failed to comprehend. Any part of a body, he says—such as an eye or a foot—makes a valuable contribution to the whole body. Whenever a single member is missing, the entire body suffers.

And, he continues, no member can survive if isolated from the rest. Alone, an eye is useless. All parts must cooperate to form a single, unified body.

Paul relied on body images to explain both the diversity and unity of God's followers. The body analogy fit so well that he referred to it two dozen times in his various letters. It became his favorite way of portraying the church.

An Emphasis on Unity

A church as diverse as Corinth knew about the differences among various members, so Paul's letter to them stressed the unity part of the analogy. How can diverse people work together in a spiritual body? He answered that question with the famous lyrical description of love in chapter 13. After that eloquent statement, he went on to discuss the Corinthians' various spiritual gifts.

Chapters 12–14 address issues that troubled the patchwork Corinthian church and that still disturb the church today. The solution, in our time as well as Paul's, is for each person to respect other members of the body and to take direction from Jesus Christ, the head.

Life Questions: Of Paul's list of spiritual gifts, which are prominent in your church? Are any overlooked? How do you fit in?

less respectable members are treated with greater respect; 24whereas our more respectable members do not need this. But God has so arranged the body, giving the greater honor to the inferior member, 25that there may be no dissension within the body, but the members may have the same care for one another. 26If one member suffers, all suffer together with it; if one member is honored, all rejoice together with it.

27 Now you are the body of Christ and individually members of it. 28And God has appointed in the church first apostles, second prophets, third teachers; then deeds of power, then gifts of healing, forms of assistance, forms of leadership, various kinds of tongues. 29Are all apostles? Are all prophets? Are all teachers? Do all work miracles? 30Do all possess gifts of healing? Do all speak in tongues? Do all interpret? 31But strive for the greater gifts. And I will show you a still more excellent way.

The Gift of Love

13 If I speak in the tongues of mortals and of angels, but do not have love, I am a noisy gong or a clanging cymbal. 2And if I have prophetic powers, and understand all mysteries and all knowledge, and if I have all faith, so as to remove mountains, but do not have love, I am nothing. 3If I give away all my possessions, and if I hand over my body so that I may boast,c but do not have love, I gain nothing.

4 Love is patient; love is kind; love is not envious or boastful or arrogant 5or rude. It does not insist on its own way; it is not irritable or resentful; 6it does not rejoice in wrongdoing, but rejoices in the truth. 7It bears all things, believes all things, hopes all things, endures all things.

8 Love never ends. But as for prophecies, they will come to an end; as for tongues, they will cease; as for knowledge, it will come to an end. 9For we know only in part, and we prophesy only in part; 10but when the complete comes, the partial will come to an end. 11When I was a child, I spoke like a child, I thought like a child, I reasoned like a child; when I became an adult, I put an end to childish ways. 12For now we see in a mirror, dimly,d but then we will see face to face. Now I know only in part; then I will know fully, even as I have been fully known. 13And now faith, hope, and love abide, these three; and the greatest of these is love.

Gifts of Prophecy and Tongues

14 Pursue love and strive for the spiritual gifts, and especially that you may prophesy. 2For those who speak in a tongue do not speak to other people but to God; for nobody understands them, since they are speaking mysteries in the Spirit. 3On the other hand, those who prophesy speak to other people for their upbuilding and encouragement and consolation. 4Those who speak in a tongue build up themselves, but those who prophesy build up the church. 5Now I would like

14.2 Speaking in Tongues

1 Corinthians 12–14 gives the New Testament's most complete teaching on supernatural gifts such as healing and speaking in tongues. Paul stresses two concerns: (1) "Sensational" gifts must not be given higher rank than they deserve (chapter 13 stresses the superiority of simple love). (2) These gifts should contribute to orderly and proper worship, not confusion. The Corinthians seemed to take everything to excess—whether practicing immorality, celebrating the Lord's Supper, or exercising spiritual gifts.

all of you to speak in tongues, but even more to prophesy. One who prophesies is greater than one who speaks in tongues, unless someone interprets, so that the church may be built up.

6 Now, brothers and sisters,e if I come to you speaking in tongues, how will I benefit you unless I speak to you in some revelation or knowledge or prophecy or teaching? 7It is the same way with lifeless instruments that produce sound, such as the flute or the harp. If they do not give distinct notes, how will anyone know what is being played? 8And if the bugle gives an indistinct sound, who will get ready for battle? 9So with yourselves; if in a tongue you utter speech that is not intelligible, how will anyone know what is being said? For you will be speaking into the air. 10There are doubtless many different kinds of sounds in the world, and nothing is without sound. 11If then I do not know the meaning of a sound, I will be a foreigner to the speaker and the speaker a foreigner to me. 12So with yourselves; since you are eager for spiritual gifts, strive to excel in them for building up the church.

13 Therefore, one who speaks in a tongue should pray for the power to interpret. 14For if I pray in a tongue, my spirit prays but my mind is unproductive. 15What should I do then? I will pray with the spirit, but I will pray with the mind also; I will sing praise with the spirit, but I will sing praise with the mind also. 16Otherwise, if you say a blessing with the spirit, how can anyone in the position of an outsider say the "Amen" to your thanksgiving, since the outsider does not know what you are saying? 17For you may give thanks well enough, but the other person is not built up. 18I thank God that I speak in tongues more than all of you; 19nevertheless, in church I would rather speak five words with my mind, in

---

c Other ancient authorities read *body to be burned*   d Gk *in a riddle*   e Gk *brothers*

order to instruct others also, than ten thousand words in a tongue.

20 Brothers and sisters,[f] do not be children in your thinking; rather, be infants in evil, but in thinking be adults. 21In the law it is written,

"By people of strange tongues
　and by the lips of foreigners
I will speak to this people;
　yet even then they will not listen to
　　me,"

says the Lord. 22Tongues, then, are a sign not for believers but for unbelievers, while prophecy is not for unbelievers but for believers. 23If, therefore, the whole church comes together and all speak in tongues, and outsiders or unbelievers enter, will they not say that you are out of your mind? 24But if all prophesy, an unbeliever or outsider who enters is reproved by all and called to account by all. 25After the secrets of the unbeliever's heart are disclosed, that person will bow down before God and worship him, declaring, "God is really among you."

Orderly Worship

26 What should be done then, my friends?[f] When you come together, each one has a hymn, a lesson, a revelation, a tongue, or an interpretation. Let all things be done for building up. 27If anyone speaks in a tongue, let there be only two or at most three, and each in turn; and let one interpret. 28But if there is no one to interpret, let them be silent in church and speak to themselves and to God. 29Let two or three prophets speak, and let the others weigh what is said. 30If a revelation is made to someone else sitting nearby, let the first person be silent. 31For you can all prophesy one by one, so that all may learn and all be encouraged. 32And the spirits of prophets are subject to the prophets, 33for God is a God not of disorder but of peace.

(As in all the churches of the saints, 34women should be silent in the churches. For they are not permitted to speak, but should be subordinate, as the law also says. 35If there is anything they desire to know, let them ask their husbands at home. For it is shameful for a woman to speak in church.[g] 36Or did the word of God originate with you? Or are you the only ones it has reached?)

37 Anyone who claims to be a prophet, or to have spiritual powers, must acknowledge that what I am writing to you is a command of the Lord. 38Anyone who does not recognize this is not to be recognized. 39So, my friends,[h] be eager to prophesy, and do not forbid speaking in tongues; 40but all things should be done decently and in order.

The Resurrection of Christ

15 Now I would remind you, brothers and sisters,[f] of the good news[i] that I proclaimed to you, which you in turn received, in which also you stand, 2through which also you are being

---

[f] Gk brothers　　[g] Other ancient authorities put verses 34-35 after verse 40　　[h] Gk my brothers　　[i] Or gospel

---

The Worst Danger of All
Why believe in life after death?

> If there is no resurrection of the dead, then Christ has not been raised; and if Christ has not been raised, then our proclamation has been in vain and your faith has been in vain.　15.13–14

MOST OF THE PROBLEMS RAISED by the church at Corinth concerned personal behavior. After tackling each of those problems, Paul turned to one last question, a matter of doctrine. Some people in the church were challenging the Christian belief in an afterlife. Death, they said, is the end.

Many people have questioned the afterlife. In Jesus' day, a Jewish sect called Sadducees denied the resurrection from the dead. Doubters persist today (among them: many Black Muslims, Buddhists, and Marxists and most atheists). But Paul saw the matter of life after death as the most explosive issue in the Corinthian church.

Pitiable Christians

If there's no future life, he thundered, the entire Christian message would be a lie. He, Paul, would have no reason to continue as a minister; Christ's death would have merely wasted blood; and Christians would be the most pitiable of all people.

Chapter 15 weaves together the threads of Christian belief about death. It shows how death is finally conquered and becomes, not an end, but a beginning. Cheered by such a triumphant note, the apostle Paul sums up his counsel to the Corinthians with a ringing challenge to "stand firm."

Life Questions: Which of Paul's arguments in chapter 15 do you find most convincing? How does belief in an afterlife affect you?

saved, if you hold firmly to the message that I proclaimed to you—unless you have come to believe in vain.

3 For I handed on to you as of first importance what I in turn had received: that Christ died for our sins in accordance with the scriptures, [4]and that he was buried, and that he was raised on the third day in accordance with the scriptures, [5]and that he appeared to Cephas, then to the twelve. [6]Then he appeared to more than five hundred brothers and sisters[j] at one time, most of whom are still alive, though some have died.[k] [7]Then he appeared to James, then to all the apostles. [8]Last of all, as to one untimely born, he appeared also to me. [9]For I am the least of the

15.8 Basic Christianity

Paul stresses the basics every Christian must believe: that Christ died for our sins, that he was buried (really dead), and that he rose again. Listing some of the many people who saw Jesus after his resurrection, Paul includes himself last of all. He is referring to his encounter with Christ on the road to Damascus (see Acts 9).

apostles, unfit to be called an apostle, because I persecuted the church of God. [10]But by the grace of God I am what I am, and his grace toward me has not been in vain. On the contrary, I worked harder than any of them—though it was not I, but the grace of God that is with me. [11]Whether then it was I or they, so we proclaim and so you have come to believe.

The Resurrection of the Dead

12 Now if Christ is proclaimed as raised from the dead, how can some of you say there is no resurrection of the dead? [13]If there is no resurrection of the dead, then Christ has not been raised; [14]and if Christ has not been raised, then our proclamation has been in vain and your faith has been in vain. [15]We are even found to be misrepresenting God, because we testified of God that he raised Christ—whom he did not raise if it is true that the dead are not raised. [16]For if the dead are not raised, then Christ has not been raised. [17]If Christ has not been raised, your faith is futile and you are still in your sins. [18]Then those also who have died[k] in Christ have perished. [19]If for this life only we have hoped in Christ, we are of all people most to be pitied.

20 But in fact Christ has been raised from the dead, the first fruits of those who have died.[k] [21]For since death came through a human being, the resurrection of the dead has also come through a human being; [22]for as all die in Adam, so all will be made alive in Christ. [23]But each in his own order: Christ the first fruits, then at his coming those who belong to Christ. [24]Then comes the end,[l] when he hands over the kingdom to God the Father, after he has destroyed every ruler and every authority and power. [25]For he must reign until he has put all his enemies under his feet. [26]The last enemy to be destroyed is death. [27]For "God[m] has put all things in subjection under his feet." But when it says, "All things are put in subjection," it is plain that this does not include the one who put all things in subjection under him. [28]When all things are subjected to him, then the Son himself will also be subjected to the one who put all things in subjection under him, so that God may be all in all.

29 Otherwise, what will those people do who receive baptism on behalf of the dead? If the dead are not raised at all, why are people baptized on their behalf?

30 And why are we putting ourselves in danger every hour? [31]I die every day! That is as certain, brothers and sisters,[j] as my boasting of you—a boast that I make in Christ Jesus our Lord. [32]If with merely human hopes I fought with wild animals at Ephesus, what would I have gained by it? If the dead are not raised,

"Let us eat and drink,
    for tomorrow we die."
[33]Do not be deceived:
    "Bad company ruins good morals."
[34]Come to a sober and right mind, and sin no more; for some people have no knowledge of God. I say this to your shame.

The Resurrection Body

35 But someone will ask, "How are the dead raised? With what kind of body do they come?" [36]Fool! What you sow does not come to life unless it dies. [37]And as for what you sow, you do not sow the body that is to be, but a bare seed, perhaps of wheat or of some other grain. [38]But God gives it a body as he has chosen, and to each kind of seed its own body. [39]Not all flesh is alike, but there is one flesh for human beings, another for animals, another for birds, and another for fish. [40]There are both heavenly bodies and earthly bodies, but the glory of the heavenly is one thing, and that of the earthly is another. [41]There is one glory of the sun, and another glory of the moon, and another glory of the stars; indeed, star differs from star in glory.

42 So it is with the resurrection of the dead. What is sown is perishable, what is raised is imperishable. [43]It is sown in dishonor, it is raised in glory. It is sown in weakness, it is raised in power. [44]It is sown a physical body, it is raised a spiritual body. If there is a physical body, there is also a spiritual body. [45]Thus it is written, "The first man,

---

[j] Gk brothers   [k] Gk fallen asleep   [l] Or Then come the rest   [m] Gk he

Adam, became a living being"; the last Adam became a life-giving spirit. [46]But it is not the spiritual that is first, but the physical, and then the spiritual. [47]The first man was from the earth, a man of dust; the second man is[n] from heaven. [48]As was the man of dust, so are those who are of the dust; and as is the man of heaven, so are those who are of heaven. [49]Just as we have borne the image of the man of dust, we will[o] also bear the image of the man of heaven.

50 What I am saying, brothers and sisters,[p] is this: flesh and blood cannot inherit the kingdom of God, nor does the perishable inherit the imperishable. [51]Listen, I will tell you a mystery! We will not all die,[q] but we will all be changed, [52]in a moment, in the twinkling of an eye, at the last trumpet. For the trumpet will sound, and the dead will be raised imperishable, and we will be changed. [53]For this perishable body must put on imperishability, and this mortal body must put on immortality. [54]When this perishable body puts on imperishability, and this mortal body puts on immortality, then the saying that is written will be fulfilled:

"Death has been swallowed up
        in victory."
55 "Where, O death, is your victory?
        Where, O death, is your sting?"
[56]The sting of death is sin, and the power of sin is the law. [57]But thanks be to God, who gives us the victory through our Lord Jesus Christ.

58 Therefore, my beloved,[r] be steadfast, immovable, always excelling in the work of the Lord, because you know that in the Lord your labor is not in vain.

The Collection for the Saints

16 Now concerning the collection for the saints: you should follow the directions I gave to the churches of Galatia. [2]On the first day of every week, each of you is to put aside and save whatever extra you earn, so that collections need

16.1 Remembering the Poor

Paul's deep concern for the poor in Jerusalem comes up often in the New Testament. He mentions taking a collection here, as well as in Romans and 2 Corinthians. He knew that widespread concern for the mother church in Jerusalem would do much to further unity between Jewish and Gentile Christians.

not be taken when I come. [3]And when I arrive, I will send any whom you approve with letters to take your gift to Jerusalem. [4]If it seems advisable that I should go also, they will accompany me.

Plans for Travel

5 I will visit you after passing through Macedonia—for I intend to pass through Macedonia— [6]and perhaps I will stay with you or even spend the winter, so that you may send me on my way, wherever I go. [7]I do not want to see you now just in passing, for I hope to spend some time with you, if the Lord permits. [8]But I will stay in Ephesus until Pentecost, [9]for a wide door for effective work has opened to me, and there are many adversaries.

10 If Timothy comes, see that he has nothing to fear among you, for he is doing the work of the Lord just as I am; [11]therefore let no one despise him. Send him on his way in peace, so that he may come to me; for I am expecting him with the brothers.

12 Now concerning our brother Apollos, I strongly urged him to visit you with the other brothers, but he was not at all willing[s] to come now. He will come when he has the opportunity.

Final Messages and Greetings

13 Keep alert, stand firm in your faith, be courageous, be strong. [14]Let all that you do be done in love.

15 Now, brothers and sisters,[p] you know that members of the household of Stephanas were the first converts in Achaia, and they have devoted themselves to the service of the saints; [16]I urge you to put yourselves at the service of such people, and of everyone who works and toils with them. [17]I rejoice at the coming of Stephanas and Fortunatus and Achaicus, because they have made up for your absence; [18]for they refreshed my spirit as well as yours. So give recognition to such persons.

19 The churches of Asia send greetings. Aquila and Prisca, together with the church in their house, greet you warmly in the Lord. [20]All the brothers and sisters[p] send greetings. Greet one another with a holy kiss.

21 I, Paul, write this greeting with my own hand. [22]Let anyone be accursed who has no love for the Lord. Our Lord, come![t] [23]The grace of the Lord Jesus be with you. [24]My love be with all of you in Christ Jesus.[u]

---

[n] Other ancient authorities add *the Lord*   [o] Other ancient authorities read *let us*   [p] Gk *brothers*   [q] Gk *fall asleep*
[r] Gk *beloved brothers*   [s] Or *it was not at all God's will for him*   [t] Gk *Marana tha*. These Aramaic words can also be read *Maran atha*, meaning *Our Lord has come*   [u] Other ancient authorities add *Amen*

2 CORINTHIANS

A Book of Joy and Sadness
Why isn't Paul celebrating his victory?

ATHLETES SOMETIMES HAVE A STRANGE reaction to a great victory. Some call it "morning-after sickness." An Olympic gymnast who has trained for 15 years wakes up the day after her gold medal performance feeling oddly depressed. Paradoxically, the sweet taste of victory can take on a bitter edge.

An even more pungent feeling may hit those who prevail in personal disputes. The man who wins a crucial court case is stabbed by sympathy for those he defeated. The politician who waves jubilantly to a cheering crowd on primary night winces inwardly at the bruises she suffered—and inflicted—during the campaign. The husband who insisted on a divorce leaves the final settlement feeling sad and burdened.

> *Indeed, we felt that we had received the sentence of death so that we would rely not on ourselves but on God who raises the dead. 1.9*

Lingering Pain

Something like that bittersweet state must have plagued the apostle Paul when he wrote 2 Corinthians. He had just won a great victory in convincing the Corinthians to come over to his side. His spirit had surged upon hearing Titus's news of their wave of support for him (7.6–16). His previous letter, a personal risk, had paid off. Reflecting Paul's triumph, this letter spontaneously breaks out in jubilant praise and thanksgiving.

And yet, in no other letter does Paul so openly admit his frustrations. Immediately after a spare greeting he mentions hardships so severe that "we despaired of life itself" (1.8). Numerous references crop up regarding the tense relations he and the Corinthians have had. Paul wonders aloud if he has been too hard on them; he acknowledges his own lingering pain.

A Diary for Two Audiences

Second Corinthians, full of allusions and personal references, reads more like a diary than a public document. If 1 Corinthians analyzes the problems of the Corinthian church, this sequel reveals the problems Paul himself experienced.

He doesn't gloat over his victory in getting the Corinthians' support. Rather, he makes himself vulnerable and opens a window into his inner self. He summarizes his state as "afflicted in every way, but not crushed; perplexed, but not driven to despair; persecuted, but not forsaken; struck down, but not destroyed" (4.8–9).

Although random selections from 2 Corinthians demonstrate the author's seesawing moods, the book as a whole reveals a tenacious man on the rebound. Paul expresses relief that the Corinthians' problems are being resolved, even as he points out new danger signs in the church. Always he keeps in mind a dual readership: the majority who support him, for whom he has warm, loving words, and the minority of dissenters who pose a grave threat to church unity.

How to Read 2 Corinthians

Of all Paul's letters, 2 Corinthians reads most like a personal letter and least like a public document. He wrote it when an intense struggle with the Corinthian church was coming to a head. As a result, it reveals much about Paul's troubled state. He half-apologized for speaking so freely, for appearing to be boasting, and for spending time on "foolishness."

Read 2 Corinthians like you would read any personal letter. Try to visualize the mood of the apostle Paul as he was writing, and look between the lines for clues that would help explain his relationship with the church at Corinth. What were his enemies accusing him of? Watch especially for Paul's spirited reply to criticism, especially in the last four chapters. He tells about certain events in his life that are recorded nowhere else.

You will likely notice that Paul is tying up loose ends in this letter: for example, he is preparing for a third visit to Corinth and asking them to get a collection ready. Yet amid these practical matters he pauses to write profound words on such topics as suffering, giving, and personal ministry.

3-TRACK READING PLAN

For an explanation and complete listing of the 3-track reading plan, turn to page 7.

TRACK 1: **Two-Week Courses on the Bible**
See page 7 for information on these courses.

TRACK 2: **An Overview of 2 Corinthians in 2 Days**
☐ Read the Introduction to 2 Corinthians, then chapter 4. It helps explain how Paul kept going despite all his hardships.
☐ Day 2. Read chapter 12, which includes a brief description of Paul's "out-of-the-body" experience and his mysterious "thorn in the flesh."

Now turn to page 9 for your next Track 2 reading project.

TRACK 3: **All of 2 Corinthians in 10 Days**
After you have read through 2 Corinthians, turn to pages 10–14 for your next Track 3 reading project.

☐1 ☐2–3 ☐4 ☐5 ☐6 ☐7 ☐8–9 ☐10
☐11 ☐12–13

Salutation

1 Paul, an apostle of Christ Jesus by the will of God, and Timothy our brother,

To the church of God that is in Corinth, including all the saints throughout Achaia:

2 Grace to you and peace from God our Father and the Lord Jesus Christ.

Paul's Thanksgiving after Affliction

3 Blessed be the God and Father of our Lord Jesus Christ, the Father of mercies and the God of all consolation, 4who consoles us in all our affliction, so that we may be able to console those who are in any affliction with the consolation with which we ourselves are consoled by God. 5For just as the sufferings of Christ are abundant for us, so also our consolation is abundant through Christ. 6If we are being afflicted, it is for your consolation and salvation; if we are being consoled, it is for your consolation, which you experience when you patiently endure the same sufferings that we are also suffering. 7Our hope for you is unshaken; for we know that as you share in our sufferings, so also you share in our consolation.

8 We do not want you to be unaware, brothers and sisters,[a] of the affliction we experienced in Asia; for we were so utterly, unbearably crushed that we despaired of life itself. 9Indeed, we felt that we had received the sentence of death so that we would rely not on ourselves but on God who raises the dead. 10He who rescued us

1.8 On the Rebound

Paul does not tell what specific hardships he had faced in Asia; they were probably known to the original audience. But four separate places in this letter (chapters 4,6,11,12) he spells out an accumulation of hardships that plagued his ministry. Such life-threatening trials had recently driven him into a deep state of despair. He survived, though, and was now using his newfound vitality to comfort and reassure concerned friends in Corinth.

from so deadly a peril will continue to rescue us; on him we have set our hope that he will rescue us again, 11as you also join in helping us by your prayers, so that many will give thanks on our[b] behalf for the blessing granted us through the prayers of many.

a Gk *brothers*   b Other ancient authorities read *your*

The Postponement of Paul's Visit

12 Indeed, this is our boast, the testimony of our conscience: we have behaved in the world with frankness[c] and godly sincerity, not by earthly wisdom but by the grace of God—and all the more toward you. [13]For we write you nothing other than what you can read and also understand; I hope you will understand until the end— [14]as you have already understood us in part— that on the day of the Lord Jesus we are your boast even as you are our boast.

15 Since I was sure of this, I wanted to come to you first, so that you might have a double favor;[d] [16]I wanted to visit you on my way to Macedonia, and to come back to you from Macedonia and have you send me on to Judea. [17]Was I vacillating when I wanted to do this? Do I make my plans according to ordinary human standards,[e] ready to say "Yes, yes" and "No, no" at the same time? [18]As surely as God is faithful, our word to you has not been "Yes and No." [19]For the Son of God, Jesus Christ, whom we proclaimed among you, Silvanus and Timothy and I, was not "Yes and No"; but in him it is always "Yes." [20]For in him every one of God's promises is a "Yes." For this reason it is through him that we say the "Amen," to the glory of God. [21]But it is God who establishes us with you in Christ and has anointed us, [22]by putting his seal on us and giving us his Spirit in our hearts as a first installment.

23 But I call on God as witness against me: it was to spare you that I did not come again to Corinth. [24]I do not mean to imply that we lord it over your faith; rather, we are workers with you for your joy, because you stand firm in the faith.

2 [1]So I made up my mind not to make you another painful visit. [2]For if I cause you pain, who is there to make me glad but the one whom I have pained? [3]And I wrote as I did, so that when I came, I might not suffer pain from those who should have made me rejoice; for I am confident about all of you, that my joy would be the joy of all of you. [4]For I wrote you out of much distress and anguish of heart and with many tears, not to cause you pain, but to let you know the abundant love that I have for you.

Forgiveness for the Offender

5 But if anyone has caused pain, he has caused it not to me, but to some extent—not to exaggerate it—to all of you. [6]This punishment by the majority is enough for such a person; [7]so now instead you should forgive and console him, so that he may not be overwhelmed by excessive sorrow. [8]So I urge you to reaffirm your love for him. [9]I wrote for this reason: to test you and to know whether you are obedient in everything. [10]Anyone whom you forgive, I also forgive. What

I have forgiven, if I have forgiven anything, has been for your sake in the presence of Christ. [11]And we do this so that we may not be outwitted by Satan; for we are not ignorant of his designs.

Paul's Anxiety in Troas

12 When I came to Troas to proclaim the good news of Christ, a door was opened for me in the Lord; [13]but my mind could not rest because I did not find my brother Titus there. So I said farewell to them and went on to Macedonia.

14 But thanks be to God, who in Christ always leads us in triumphal procession, and through us spreads in every place the fragrance

2.14 Victory Party

On their return from battle, Roman generals were honored with a triumphal procession, much like the ticker-tape parades given modern heroes. As the victorious army paraded their loot and conquered captives, the streets would be filled with fragrance from burning incense and the smells of the victory feast being prepared.

that comes from knowing him. [15]For we are the aroma of Christ to God among those who are being saved and among those who are perishing; [16]to the one a fragrance from death to death, to the other a fragrance from life to life. Who is sufficient for these things? [17]For we are not peddlers of God's word like so many;[f] but in Christ we speak as persons of sincerity, as persons sent from God and standing in his presence.

Ministers of the New Covenant

3 Are we beginning to commend ourselves again? Surely we do not need, as some do, letters of recommendation to you or from you, do we? [2]You yourselves are our letter, written on

3.2 A Human Letter

Chapters 3–5 form one of the Bible's great passages on professional ministry: what is involved in representing Christ on earth. Responding to attacks, Paul defends his "style" of ministry. He discusses the ultimate goal of ministry and the grace of God in using mere "clay jars" (4.7) to accomplish his work. But the final proof of effectiveness, he says, is people's lives. In this way, the Corinthians themselves are his best letter of recommendation, for he brought them the gospel in the first place.

---

c Other ancient authorities read holiness   d Other ancient authorities read pleasure   e Gk according to the flesh
f Other ancient authorities read like the others

our[g] hearts, to be known and read by all; [3]and you show that you are a letter of Christ, prepared by us, written not with ink but with the Spirit of the living God, not on tablets of stone but on tablets of human hearts.

4 Such is the confidence that we have through Christ toward God. [5]Not that we are competent of ourselves to claim anything as coming from us; our competence is from God, [6]who has made us competent to be ministers of a new covenant, not of letter but of spirit; for the letter kills, but the Spirit gives life.

7 Now if the ministry of death, chiseled in letters on stone tablets,[h] came in glory so that the people of Israel could not gaze at Moses' face because of the glory of his face, a glory now set aside, [8]how much more will the ministry of the Spirit come in glory? [9]For if there was glory in the ministry of condemnation, much more does the ministry of justification abound in glory! [10]Indeed, what once had glory has lost its glory because of the greater glory; [11]for if what was set aside came through glory, much more has the permanent come in glory!

12 Since, then, we have such a hope, we act with great boldness, [13]not like Moses, who put a veil over his face to keep the people of Israel from gazing at the end of the glory that[i] was being set aside. [14]But their minds were hardened. Indeed, to this very day, when they hear the reading of the old covenant, that same veil is still there, since only in Christ is it set aside. [15]Indeed, to this very day whenever Moses is read, a veil lies over their minds; [16]but when one turns to the Lord, the veil is removed. [17]Now the Lord is the Spirit, and where the Spirit of the Lord is, there is freedom.

---

[g] Other ancient authorities read *your*   [h] Gk *on stones*   [i] Gk *of what*

A Mysterious Visit
Paul's break with the Corinthians

> So I made up my mind not to make you another painful visit. 2.1

THOSE WHO TRY TO PIECE together Paul's life story from fragments in the two Corinthian letters and the book of Acts usually come away puzzled. Paul, addressing friends who knew that history intimately, saw no need to review every stage of their relationship. Yet for us, reading centuries later, some chronology would help explain his allusions and his emotional state.

Many scholars believe two events occurred to which Paul refers only in passing: the "painful visit" and the letter written "out of much distress."

A Change in Plans

In the first two chapters Paul explains a change of plans whereby he decided not to visit Corinth because he didn't want to make "another painful visit" (2.1). What visit was he referring to?

During his first visit to Corinth, spanning 18 months, the church took shape (Acts 18.11). Paul probably would not have described that time as a "painful visit," for his relationship with them at that time was basically positive. Evidently he made a second visit to Corinth, not recorded in Acts, that included a painful confrontation.

Paul planned a third visit to Corinth, but postponed it because he didn't want to stir up the conflict. Later, he wondered about rescheduling that third visit (12.14; 13.1).

The Longed-for Reconciliation

Second Corinthians also mentions a letter written out of great distress and with many tears (2.4; 7.8). This letter, coming after Paul's unsettling second visit, contained such strong wording that he feared the Corinthians' response. He fleetingly regretted having written the letter. Had it ruptured their relationship? While he preached in the seaport town of Troas, Paul anxiously awaited some report of their reaction, through Titus.

One can imagine Paul rushing to the dock as ships from Macedonia came to unload, fervently scanning the vessels for some sign of Titus. Finally, unable to find peace of mind, he left his ministry in Troas to seek out Titus in Macedonia.

News from Titus at last calmed Paul. The Corinthians had indeed repented (7.7–9) and now wanted to restore ties with him. Feeling encouraged, Paul contemplated a third visit as he wrote 2 Corinthians. He used the letter to rebuild his relationship with them and to spell out his reasons for coming.

Life Questions: Have you ever experienced a tear in a relationship like the one described here? How have you found healing?

18And all of us, with unveiled faces, seeing the glory of the Lord as though reflected in a mirror, are being transformed into the same image from one degree of glory to another; for this comes from the Lord, the Spirit.

Treasure in Clay Jars

4 Therefore, since it is by God's mercy that we are engaged in this ministry, we do not lose heart. 2We have renounced the shameful things that one hides; we refuse to practice cunning or to falsify God's word; but by the open statement of the truth we commend ourselves to the conscience of everyone in the sight of God. 3And even if our gospel is veiled, it is veiled to those who are perishing. 4In their case the god of this world has blinded the minds of the unbelievers, to keep them from seeing the light of the gospel of the glory of Christ, who is the image of God. 5For we do not proclaim ourselves; we proclaim Jesus Christ as Lord and ourselves as your slaves for Jesus' sake. 6For it is the God who said, "Let light shine out of darkness," who has shone in our hearts to give the light of the knowledge of the glory of God in the face of Jesus Christ.

7 But we have this treasure in clay jars, so that it may be made clear that this extraordinary power belongs to God and does not come from us.

4.7 A Picture of Weakness

Where would you keep expensive jewelry? You would want a safe, secure place. You wouldn't stash valuables in, say, a tattered cardboard box. Yet this image comes close to the one Paul used to describe his ministry: "clay jars." In his day jars were about as common—and as safe— as cardboard boxes are today.

The treasure Paul refers to is the incredible message of the gospel: God's good news of forgiveness and the promise of life forever. Yet, amazingly, God chose to enclose that treasure in people who are like "clay jars." Clay jars are ordinary and highly breakable, and Paul tells us he is both. An immortal God chooses mere humans as his personal representatives. "Who is sufficient for these things?" Paul asks (2.16). He determines to draw attention to the treasure inside him, not to himself.

8We are afflicted in every way, but not crushed; perplexed, but not driven to despair; 9persecuted, but not forsaken; struck down, but not destroyed; 10always carrying in the body the death of Jesus, so that the life of Jesus may also be made visible in our bodies. 11For while we live, we are always being given up to death for Jesus' sake, so that the life of Jesus may be made visible in our mortal flesh. 12So death is at work in us, but life in you.

13 But just as we have the same spirit of faith that is in accordance with scripture—"I believed, and so I spoke"—we also believe, and so we speak, 14because we know that the one who raised the Lord Jesus will raise us also with Jesus, and will bring us with you into his presence. 15Yes, everything is for your sake, so that grace, as it extends to more and more people, may increase thanksgiving, to the glory of God.

Living by Faith

16 So we do not lose heart. Even though our outer nature is wasting away, our inner nature is being renewed day by day. 17For this slight momentary affliction is preparing us for an eternal weight of glory beyond all measure, 18because we look not at what can be seen but at what cannot be seen; for what can be seen is temporary, but what cannot be seen is eternal.

5 For we know that if the earthly tent we live in is destroyed, we have a building from God, a house not made with hands, eternal in the heavens. 2For in this tent we groan, longing to be

5.1 The Body as a Tent

Paul often refers to his frail and abused body in this letter. But in this passage he looks past life on earth to a future life when, he says, we will have new bodies "not made with hands." The contrast between tent and house shows the temporary nature of a body in this life compared to what is to come.

clothed with our heavenly dwelling— 3if indeed, when we have taken it offj we will not be found naked. 4For while we are still in this tent, we groan under our burden, because we wish not to be unclothed but to be further clothed, so that what is mortal may be swallowed up by life. 5He who has prepared us for this very thing is God, who has given us the Spirit as a guarantee.

6 So we are always confident; even though we know that while we are at home in the body we are away from the Lord— 7for we walk by faith, not by sight. 8Yes, we do have confidence, and we would rather be away from the body and at home with the Lord. 9So whether we are at home or away, we make it our aim to please him. 10For all of us must appear before the judgment seat of Christ, so that each may receive recompense for what has been done in the body, whether good or evil.

The Ministry of Reconciliation

11 Therefore, knowing the fear of the Lord,

---

j Other ancient authorities read *put it on*

we try to persuade others; but we ourselves are well known to God, and I hope that we are also well known to your consciences. ¹²We are not commending ourselves to you again, but giving you an opportunity to boast about us, so that you may be able to answer those who boast in outward appearance and not in the heart. ¹³For if we are beside ourselves, it is for God; if we are in our right mind, it is for you. ¹⁴For the love of Christ urges us on, because we are convinced that one has died for all; therefore all have died. ¹⁵And he died for all, so that those who live might live no longer for themselves, but for him who died and was raised for them.

16 From now on, therefore, we regard no one from a human point of view;ᵏ even though we once knew Christ from a human point of view,ᵏ we know him no longer in that way. ¹⁷So if anyone is in Christ, there is a new creation: everything old has passed away; see, everything has become new! ¹⁸All this is from God, who reconciled us to himself through Christ, and has given us the ministry of reconciliation; ¹⁹that is, in Christ God was reconciling the world to himself,ˡ not counting their trespasses against them, and entrusting the message of reconciliation to us. ²⁰So we are ambassadors for Christ, since God is making his appeal through us; we entreat you on behalf of Christ, be reconciled to God. ²¹For our sake he made him to be sin who knew no sin, so that in him we might become the righteousness of God.

6 As we work together with him,ᵐ we urge you also not to accept the grace of God in vain. ²For he says,

"At an acceptable time I have listened to
   you,
   and on a day of salvation I have helped
      you."

See, now is the acceptable time; see, now is the day of salvation! ³We are putting no obstacle in anyone's way, so that no fault may be found with our ministry, ⁴but as servants of God we have commended ourselves in every way: through great endurance, in afflictions, hardships, calamities, ⁵beatings, imprisonments, riots, labors, sleepless nights, hunger; ⁶by purity, knowledge, patience, kindness, holiness of spirit, genuine love, ⁷truthful speech, and the power of God; with the weapons of righteousness for the right hand and for the left; ⁸in honor and dishonor, in ill repute and good repute. We are treated as impostors, and yet are true; ⁹as unknown, and yet are well known; as dying, and see—we are alive; as punished, and yet not killed; ¹⁰as sorrowful, yet always rejoicing; as poor, yet making many rich; as having nothing, and yet possessing everything.

11 We have spoken frankly to you Corinthi-

ans; our heart is wide open to you. ¹²There is no restriction in our affections, but only in yours. ¹³In return—I speak as to children—open wide your hearts also.

The Temple of the Living God

14 Do not be mismatched with unbelievers. For what partnership is there between righteousness and lawlessness? Or what fellowship is there

6.14 Unequal Yokes

A yoke is a curved wooden bar that fits across the necks of two animals used to pull a plow or wagon. Yoke together a short, speedy calf with a tall, sluggish ox, and you're asking for trouble. Paul probably had in mind the false teachers who so often bedeviled the Corinthians, but his wise principle applies to many other alliances between believers and unbelievers.

between light and darkness? ¹⁵What agreement does Christ have with Beliar? Or what does a believer share with an unbeliever? ¹⁶What agreement has the temple of God with idols? For weⁿ are the temple of the living God; as God said,

"I will live in them and walk among
      them,
   and I will be their God,
   and they shall be my people.
¹⁷ Therefore come out from them,
   and be separate from them, says the
      Lord,
   and touch nothing unclean;
   then I will welcome you,
¹⁸ and I will be your father,
   and you shall be my sons and
      daughters,
   says the Lord Almighty."

7 Since we have these promises, beloved, let us cleanse ourselves from every defilement of body and of spirit, making holiness perfect in the fear of God.

Paul's Joy at the Church's Repentance

2 Make room in your heartsᵒ for us; we have wronged no one, we have corrupted no one, we have taken advantage of no one. ³I do not say this to condemn you, for I said before that you are in our hearts, to die together and to live together. ⁴I often boast about you; I have great pride in you; I am filled with consolation; I am overjoyed in all our affliction.

5 For even when we came into Macedonia, our bodies had no rest, but we were afflicted in every way—disputes without and fears within.

ᵏ Gk *according to the flesh*   ˡ Or *God was in Christ reconciling the world to himself*   ᵐ Gk *As we work together*
ⁿ Other ancient authorities read *you*   ᵒ Gk lacks *in your hearts*

⁶But God, who consoles the downcast, consoled us by the arrival of Titus, ⁷and not only by his coming, but also by the consolation with which he was consoled about you, as he told us of your longing, your mourning, your zeal for me, so that I rejoiced still more. ⁸For even if I made you sorry with my letter, I do not regret it (though I did regret it, for I see that I grieved you with that letter, though only briefly). ⁹Now I rejoice, not because you were grieved, but because your grief led to repentance; for you felt a godly grief, so that you were not harmed in any way by us. ¹⁰For godly grief produces a repentance that leads to salvation and brings no regret, but worldly grief produces death. ¹¹For see what earnestness this godly grief has produced in you, what eagerness to clear yourselves, what indignation, what alarm, what longing, what zeal, what punishment! At every point you have proved yourselves guiltless in the matter. ¹²So although I wrote to you, it was not on account of the one who did the wrong, nor on account of the one who was wronged, but in order that your zeal for us might be made known to you before God. ¹³In this we find comfort.

In addition to our own consolation, we rejoiced still more at the joy of Titus, because his mind has been set at rest by all of you. ¹⁴For if I have been somewhat boastful about you to him, I was not disgraced; but just as everything we said

_p_ Gk _brothers_

to you was true, so our boasting to Titus has proved true as well. ¹⁵And his heart goes out all the more to you, as he remembers the obedience of all of you, and how you welcomed him with fear and trembling. ¹⁶I rejoice, because I have complete confidence in you.

7.11 What Suffering Produces

When he wrote about suffering, Paul concentrated not merely on the pain itself, but on what qualities it produced in those who had faith. In this case, he cites the emotional suffering the Corinthians had experienced because of his letter. Although the suffering was unpleasant, it produced something of great value: an abrupt change in their attitudes.

Encouragement to Be Generous

8 We want you to know, brothers and sisters,_p_ about the grace of God that has been granted to the churches of Macedonia; ²for during a severe ordeal of affliction, their abundant joy and their extreme poverty have overflowed in a wealth of generosity on their part. ³For, as I can testify,

Don't Forget the Poor
A fund-raising letter from Paul himself

EVERY DAY IN MILLIONS OF mailboxes across the United States, letters with special "non-profit" postage stamps appear, stuffed among catalogs, magazines, and flyers from retail stores. Fund-raising through the mail is big business for Jews, Catholics, Protestants and a passel of charitable organizations.

The apostle Paul assuredly never engineered a million-piece charity appeal—the empire's postal service and the cost of papyrus made such an idea unthinkable. But 2 Corinthians does present a direct appeal for funds (chapters 8–9). Jewish Christians near Jerusalem were reportedly on the edge of starvation. Paul seized on the crisis as a perfect chance for Gentile Christians to reach out in compassion and demonstrate their spiritual unity with Jewish Christians.

> Each of you must give as you have made up your mind, not reluctantly or under compulsion, for God loves a cheerful giver. 9.7

Practicing What He Preached

In these two chapters, Paul outlines a philosophy of Christian giving, holding up Jesus Christ as a model. He explains the goal of such giving and the proper attitude of the givers. He even applies a little pressure by citing examples of Christians less well-heeled than the Corinthians (8.1–6; 9.1–5).

This brief passage on giving shows Paul's holistic concerns. While still recuperating from personal trauma, he had agreed to head up a major fund-raising drive on behalf of the needy in Jerusalem. Later, working on that very project, he paused to write the profoundly theological book of Romans (Romans 15.25–26). His scholarship didn't dampen a zeal for practical Christian love; his concern for souls didn't crowd out concern for their hungry bodies.

Life Questions: Compare Paul's appeal for funds with those you see in the mail and in the media. Is there a different emphasis?

they voluntarily gave according to their means, and even beyond their means, [4]begging us earnestly for the privilege[q] of sharing in this ministry to the saints— [5]and this, not merely as we expected; they gave themselves first to the Lord and, by the will of God, to us, [6]so that we might urge Titus that, as he had already made a beginning, so he should also complete this generous undertaking[r] among you. [7]Now as you excel in everything—in faith, in speech, in knowledge, in utmost eagerness, and in our love for you[s]—so we want you to excel also in this generous undertaking.[r]

8 I do not say this as a command, but I am testing the genuineness of your love against the earnestness of others. [9]For you know the generous act[t] of our Lord Jesus Christ, that though he was rich, yet for your sakes he became poor, so that by his poverty you might become rich. [10]And in this matter I am giving my advice: it is appropriate for you who began last year not only to do something but even to desire to do something— [11]now finish doing it, so that your eagerness may be matched by completing it according to your means. [12]For if the eagerness is there, the gift is acceptable according to what one has—not according to what one does not have. [13]I do not mean that there should be relief for others and pressure on you, but it is a question of a fair balance between [14]your present abundance and their need, so that their abundance may be for your need, in order that there may be a fair balance. [15]As it is written,

"The one who had much did not have
         too much,
and the one who had little did not
         have too little."

Commendation of Titus

16 But thanks be to God who put in the heart of Titus the same eagerness for you that I myself have. [17]For he not only accepted our appeal, but since he is more eager than ever, he is going to you of his own accord. [18]With him we are sending the brother who is famous among all the churches for his proclaiming the good news;[u] [19]and not only that, but he has also been appointed by the churches to travel with us while we are administering this generous undertaking[r] for the glory of the Lord himself[v] and to show our goodwill. [20]We intend that no one should blame us about this generous gift that we are administering, [21]for we intend to do what is right not only in the Lord's sight but also in the sight of others. [22]And with them we are sending our brother whom we have often tested and found eager in many matters, but who is now more eager than ever because

of his great confidence in you. [23]As for Titus, he is my partner and co-worker in your service; as for our brothers, they are messengers[w] of the churches, the glory of Christ. [24]Therefore openly before the churches, show them the proof of your love and of our reason for boasting about you.

The Collection for Christians at Jerusalem

9 Now it is not necessary for me to write you about the ministry to the saints, [2]for I know your eagerness, which is the subject of my boasting about you to the people of Macedonia, saying that Achaia has been ready since last year; and your zeal has stirred up most of them. [3]But I am sending the brothers in order that our boasting about you may not prove to have been empty in this case, so that you may be ready, as I said you would be; [4]otherwise, if some Macedonians come with me and find that you are not ready, we would be humiliated—to say nothing of you—in this undertaking.[x] [5]So I thought it necessary to urge the brothers to go on ahead to you, and arrange in advance for this bountiful gift that you have promised, so that it may be ready as a voluntary gift and not as an extortion.

6 The point is this: the one who sows sparingly will also reap sparingly, and the one who sows

9.6 Bonuses of Giving

In taking his collection for poor people, Paul mainly appealed to the Christian responsibility to help those in need. But in this passage he details generosity's side effects. Giving actually enriches and benefits the giver, he says. Also, a gift can serve as an act of worship to God and can inspire other people's faith and thanksgiving.

bountifully will also reap bountifully. [7]Each of you must give as you have made up your mind, not reluctantly or under compulsion, for God loves a cheerful giver. [8]And God is able to provide you with every blessing in abundance, so that by always having enough of everything, you may share abundantly in every good work. [9]As it is written,

"He scatters abroad, he gives to the poor;
         his righteousness[y] endures forever."
[10]He who supplies seed to the sower and bread for food will supply and multiply your seed for sowing and increase the harvest of your righteousness.[y] [11]You will be enriched in every way for your great generosity, which will produce thanksgiving to God through us; [12]for the rendering of this ministry not only supplies the needs of the

---

q Gk *grace*   *r* Gk *this grace*   *s* Other ancient authorities read *your love for us*   *t* Gk *the grace*   *u* Or *the gospel*
v Other ancient authorities lack *himself*   *w* Gk *apostles*   *x* Other ancient authorities add *of boasting*
y Or *benevolence*

saints but also overflows with many thanksgivings to God. [13]Through the testing of this ministry you glorify God by your obedience to the confession of the gospel of Christ and by the generosity of your sharing with them and with all others, [14]while they long for you and pray for you because of the surpassing grace of God that he has given you. [15]Thanks be to God for his indescribable gift!

Paul Defends His Ministry

10 I myself, Paul, appeal to you by the meekness and gentleness of Christ—I who am humble when face to face with you, but bold toward you when I am away!— [2]I ask that when I am present I need not show boldness by daring to oppose those who think we are acting according to human standards.[z] [3]Indeed, we live as human beings,[a] but we do not wage war according to human standards;[z] [4]for the weapons of our warfare are not merely human,[b] but they have divine power to destroy strongholds. We destroy arguments [5]and every proud obstacle raised up against the knowledge of God, and we take every

thought captive to obey Christ. [6]We are ready to punish every disobedience when your obedience is complete.

7 Look at what is before your eyes. If you are confident that you belong to Christ, remind yourself of this, that just as you belong to Christ, so also do we. [8]Now, even if I boast a little too much of our authority, which the Lord gave for building you up and not for tearing you down, I will not be ashamed of it. [9]I do not want to seem as though I am trying to frighten you with my letters. [10]For they say, "His letters are weighty and strong, but his bodily presence is weak, and his speech contemptible." [11]Let such people understand that what we say by letter when absent, we will also do when present.

12 We do not dare to classify or compare ourselves with some of those who commend themselves. But when they measure themselves by one another, and compare themselves with one another, they do not show good sense. [13]We, however, will not boast beyond limits, but will keep within the field that God has assigned to us, to reach out even as far as you. [14]For we were not

[z] Gk according to the flesh   [a] Gk in the flesh   [b] Gk fleshly

Paul Has Had Enough
Answering his critics

> I repeat, let no one think that I am a fool. 11.16

VERSE 1 OF CHAPTER 10 introduces a dramatic shift in tone. The first nine chapters mainly show Paul's relief at seeing encouraging signs in Corinth. But these last four chapters make clear that hostility was still raging. In fact, some have guessed this section was taken from the painful letter Paul referred to earlier (2.4). Here at the end of 2 Corinthians, Paul boldly confronts his critics.

Who were his antagonists? A picture of them emerges if you compile all the accusations Paul answers throughout the letter. Basically, they were carping troublemakers. In their eyes, Paul could do nothing right.

Paul's enemies in Corinth had blasted him for not visiting them as promised; yet when he did visit they gossiped, "His bodily presence is weak, and his speech contemptible" (10.10). They had criticized him for not taking a salary and then hinted he was misusing funds (8.20; 11.7–9). To these "super-apostles" (11.5), Paul somehow appeared simultaneously unimpressive and yet crafty; overly strict and yet worldly. Some even hinted he was out of his mind (5.13).

A Ringing Self-Defense

You can almost sense Paul declaring "I've had it!" and then rolling up his sleeves to refute the charges. He insists that the future of the Corinthian church, not just his own reputation, is at stake. What does he feel? Something like the burning jealousy of a father who watches his virgin daughter being seduced away from her true lover (11.2–3).

These four remarkable chapters show Paul's passionate nature. Frustrated by having to defend himself, he almost stammers in print. He is determined to convince the Corinthians that he is motivated by a desire to serve God, not by any schemes of profit or power. Along the way, he lists an amazing catalog of his physical sufferings and reveals intimate details of his spiritual life, including one incident still shrouded in mystery (12.1–6).

Judge for yourself, Paul seems to say, to the Corinthians and to all of us. Look at my life and decide, Whose fool am I?

Life Questions: Have you ever been wrongly accused of something? How did you react to your accusers?

overstepping our limits when we reached you; we were the first to come all the way to you with the good news[c] of Christ. [15]We do not boast beyond limits, that is, in the labors of others; but our hope

10.7–18 Style or Substance?

Paul had an image problem, and his enemies were taking advantage of it by ridiculing his unimpressive personal style. Though a powerful, direct, and engaging speaker, Paul was spurned by those who preferred a more golden-tongued style, with lots of rhetorical flourish (verse 10). Such orators may have attracted applause and money, but Paul was looking for results in the form of changed lives, not profit or fame.

In the next two chapters, Paul reviews his qualifications, but he also ironically "boasts" of his weaknesses. Judge a messenger by the substance of the gospel he or she preaches, Paul seems to say—not by fancy words or a flashy style.

is that, as your faith increases, our sphere of action among you may be greatly enlarged, [16]so that we may proclaim the good news[c] in lands beyond you, without boasting of work already done in someone else's sphere of action. [17]"Let the one who boasts, boast in the Lord." [18]For it is not those who commend themselves that are approved, but those whom the Lord commends.

Paul and the False Apostles

11 I wish you would bear with me in a little foolishness. Do bear with me! [2]I feel a divine jealousy for you, for I promised you in marriage to one husband, to present you as a chaste virgin to Christ. [3]But I am afraid that as the serpent deceived Eve by its cunning, your thoughts will be led astray from a sincere and pure[d] devotion to Christ. [4]For if someone comes and proclaims another Jesus than the one we proclaimed, or if you receive a different spirit from the one you received, or a different gospel from the one you accepted, you submit to it readily enough. [5]I think that I am not in the least inferior to these super-apostles. [6]I may be untrained in speech, but not in knowledge; certainly in every way and in all things we have made this evident to you.

7 Did I commit a sin by humbling myself so that you might be exalted, because I proclaimed God's good news[e] to you free of charge? [8]I robbed other churches by accepting support from them in order to serve you. [9]And when I was with you and was in need, I did not burden anyone, for my needs were supplied by the friends[f] who

came from Macedonia. So I refrained and will continue to refrain from burdening you in any way. [10]As the truth of Christ is in me, this boast of mine will not be silenced in the regions of Achaia. [11]And why? Because I do not love you? God knows I do!

12 And what I do I will also continue to do, in order to deny an opportunity to those who want an opportunity to be recognized as our equals in what they boast about. [13]For such boasters are false apostles, deceitful workers, disguising themselves as apostles of Christ. [14]And no wonder! Even Satan disguises himself as an angel of light. [15]So it is not strange if his ministers also disguise themselves as ministers of righteousness. Their end will match their deeds.

Paul's Sufferings as an Apostle

16 I repeat, let no one think that I am a fool; but if you do, then accept me as a fool, so that I too may boast a little. [17]What I am saying in regard to this boastful confidence, I am saying not with the Lord's authority, but as a fool; [18]since many boast according to human standards,[g] I will also boast. [19]For you gladly put up with fools, being wise yourselves! [20]For you put up with it when someone makes slaves of you, or preys upon you, or takes advantage of you, or puts on airs, or gives you a slap in the face. [21]To my shame, I must say, we were too weak for that!

But whatever anyone dares to boast of—I am speaking as a fool—I also dare to boast of that. [22]Are they Hebrews? So am I. Are they Israelites? So am I. Are they descendants of Abraham? So am I. [23]Are they ministers of Christ? I am talking like a madman—I am a better one: with far greater labors, far more imprisonments, with countless floggings, and often near death. [24]Five times I have received from the Jews the forty lashes minus one. [25]Three times I was beaten with rods. Once I received a stoning. Three times I was shipwrecked; for a night and a day I was adrift at sea;

11.24 Paul's Many Trials

Acts records many of the apostle Paul's adventures and trials, but this passage shows that other disasters occurred as well. "Forty lashes minus one" was the maximum punishment allowed under Jewish law—five times Paul had been judged and sentenced by the Jews for his activities as a Christian. In addition, he was often imprisoned under Roman law and sometimes beaten with rods (an illegal punishment for a Roman citizen such as Paul).

[c] Or *the gospel*   [d] Other ancient authorities lack *and pure*   [e] Gk *the gospel of God*   [f] Gk *brothers*
[g] Gk *according to the flesh*

[26]on frequent journeys, in danger from rivers, danger from bandits, danger from my own people, danger from Gentiles, danger in the city, danger in the wilderness, danger at sea, danger from false brothers and sisters;[h] [27]in toil and hardship, through many a sleepless night, hungry and thirsty, often without food, cold and naked. [28]And, besides other things, I am under daily pressure because of my anxiety for all the churches. [29]Who is weak, and I am not weak? Who is made to stumble, and I am not indignant? 30 If I must boast, I will boast of the things that show my weakness. [31]The God and Father of the Lord Jesus (blessed be he forever!) knows that I do not lie. [32]In Damascus, the governor[i] under King Aretas guarded the city of Damascus in order to[j] seize me, [33]but I was let down in a basket through a window in the wall,[k] and escaped from his hands.

Paul's Visions and Revelations

12 It is necessary to boast; nothing is to be gained by it, but I will go on to visions and revelations of the Lord. [2]I know a person in Christ who fourteen years ago was caught up to the third heaven—whether in the body or out of the body I do not know; God knows. [3]And I know that such a person—whether in the body or out of the body I do not know; God knows— [4]was caught up into Paradise and heard things that are not to be told, that no mortal is permitted to repeat. [5]On behalf of such a one I will boast, but on my own behalf I will not boast, except of my weaknesses. [6]But if I wish to boast, I will not be a fool, for I will be speaking the truth. But I refrain from it, so that no one may think better of me than what is seen in me or heard from me, [7]even considering the exceptional character of the revelations. Therefore, to keep[l] me from being too elated, a

12.7 The Thorn in Paul's Flesh

Bible scholars don't agree on the precise nature of Paul's "thorn." Some suggest a physical ailment, such as an eye disease, malaria, or epilepsy. Others interpret it as a spiritual temptation, or a sequence of failures in his ministry. The Bible gives no clear evidence on the precise nature of this affliction. Regardless, Paul stresses that God permitted the thorn to continue, despite his prayers for relief, to teach him an important lesson about grace and dependence. This conclusion echoes Paul's thoughts on the Corinthians' suffering in chapter 7.

thorn was given me in the flesh, a messenger of Satan to torment me, to keep me from being too elated.[m] [8]Three times I appealed to the Lord about this, that it would leave me, [9]but he said to me, "My grace is sufficient for you, for power[n] is made perfect in weakness." So, I will boast all the more gladly of my weaknesses, so that the power of Christ may dwell in me. [10]Therefore I am content with weaknesses, insults, hardships, persecutions, and calamities for the sake of Christ; for whenever I am weak, then I am strong.

Paul's Concern for the Corinthian Church

11 I have been a fool! You forced me to it. Indeed you should have been the ones commending me, for I am not at all inferior to these super-apostles, even though I am nothing. [12]The signs of a true apostle were performed among you with utmost patience, signs and wonders and mighty works. [13]How have you been worse off than the other churches, except that I myself did not burden you? Forgive me this wrong!

14 Here I am, ready to come to you this third time. And I will not be a burden, because I do not want what is yours but you; for children ought not to lay up for their parents, but parents for their children. [15]I will most gladly spend and be spent for you. If I love you more, am I to be loved less? [16]Let it be assumed that I did not burden you. Nevertheless (you say) since I was crafty, I took you in by deceit. [17]Did I take advantage of you through any of those whom I sent to you? [18]I urged Titus to go, and sent the brother with him. Titus did not take advantage of you, did he? Did we not conduct ourselves with the same spirit? Did we not take the same steps?

19 Have you been thinking all along that we have been defending ourselves before you? We are speaking in Christ before God. Everything we do, beloved, is for the sake of building you up. [20]For I fear that when I come, I may find you not as I wish, and that you may find me not as you wish; I fear that there may perhaps be quarreling, jealousy, anger, selfishness, slander, gossip, conceit, and disorder. [21]I fear that when I come again, my God may humble me before you, and that I may have to mourn over many who previously sinned and have not repented of the impurity, sexual immorality, and licentiousness that they have practiced.

Further Warning

13 This is the third time I am coming to you. "Any charge must be sustained by the evidence of two or three witnesses." [2]I warned those who sinned previously and all the others, and I warn them now while absent, as I did when

---

[h] Gk *brothers*   [i] Gk *ethnarch*   [j] Other ancient authorities read *and wanted to*   [k] Gk *through the wall*
[l] Other ancient authorities read *To keep*   [m] Other ancient authorities lack *to keep me from being too elated*
[n] Other ancient authorities read *my power*

present on my second visit, that if I come again, I will not be lenient— ³since you desire proof that Christ is speaking in me. He is not weak in dealing with you, but is powerful in you. ⁴For he was crucified in weakness, but lives by the power of God. For we are weak in him,ᵒ but in dealing with you we will live with him by the power of God.

5 Examine yourselves to see whether you are living in the faith. Test yourselves. Do you not realize that Jesus Christ is in you?—unless, indeed, you fail to meet the test! ⁶I hope you will find out that we have not failed. ⁷But we pray to God that you may not do anything wrong—not that we may appear to have met the test, but that you may do what is right, though we may seem to have failed. ⁸For we cannot do anything against the truth, but only for the truth. ⁹For we rejoice when we are weak and you are strong. This is what we pray for, that you may become perfect. ¹⁰So I write these things while I am away from you, so that when I come, I may not have to be severe in using the authority that the Lord has given me for building up and not for tearing down.

Final Greetings and Benediction

11 Finally, brothers and sisters,ᵖ farewell.�q Put things in order, listen to my appeal,ʳ agree with one another, live in peace; and the God of love and peace will be with you. ¹²Greet one another with a holy kiss. All the saints greet you.

13 The grace of the Lord Jesus Christ, the love of God, and the communion ofˢ the Holy Spirit be with all of you.

ᵒ Other ancient authorities read *with him*   ᵖ Gk *brothers*   q Or *rejoice*   ʳ Or *encourage one another*   ˢ Or *and the sharing in*

GALATIANS

No Second-Class Christians
A protest against treason

> But even if we or an angel from heaven should proclaim to you a gospel contrary to what we proclaimed to you, let that one be accursed! 1.8

PAUL IS ANGRY. YOU CAN almost see his face: flushed red, with lines of tension working in his jaw. Typically, he greets his readers briefly and then launches into warm praise of them. But in this letter shock and dismay replace the usual warmth. A crisis threatens the Galatians, and Paul opens with a withering blast against the people responsible.

What's the Problem?

Yet, when you read a few chapters, you may wonder why the apostle is so upset. Galatia seems innocent of the kinkiness of Corinth; Paul describes no incest or idolatry here. Instead, he brings up common, everyday Jewish affairs such as the observance of festival days and the practice of ancient traditions, especially circumcision. Where is the big crisis?

Paul could foresee the outcome of the Galatians' thinking: By unduly stressing their Jewish heritage, the Galatians would soon devalue what Christ had done. They would start trusting in their own human effort (their keeping of "the law") to gain acceptance by God (3.1–5).

If the Galatians continued their policies, the bedrock of the gospel would crumble. Faith in Christ would become just one of many steps in salvation, not the only one. The gospel itself would be perverted (1.6–9).

A Dangerous Class Structure

Paul saw other ominous dangers ahead for the fledgling Christian church. As a Jewish Roman citizen who spoke Greek, he knew well the innate human tendency to look down on people. Roman citizens snubbed non-Romans; Greeks looked down their noses at Romans; and Jews, with their exalted history and highly developed religion, felt superior to other cultures.

The Galatians' insistence on strict Jewish rules would bring side effects. Subtle distinctions between Christians would inevitably creep in: *Faith in Christ is fine, but a circumcised person who keeps the Jewish law . . . that's far better.* Already, such thoughts had infected two esteemed apostles, Peter and Barnabas. Circumcised Christians were snubbing uncircumcised ones as second-class citizens.

The letter to the Galatians, then, is protesting against treason. It lashes out against subtle dangers that can ultimately pervert the gospel and divide the church. Paul insists that Jesus Christ came to tear down walls between people, not to build them up. In him there is neither Jew nor Greek, slave nor free, male nor female (3.28). Faith in him, not anyone's set of laws (2.16), opens the door to acceptance by God.

How to Read Galatians

Galatians reads like a dramatic court trial. On one side of the courtroom stand Paul's accusers. Persuasive and powerful, these "Judaizers" have followed Paul from town to town, spreading rumors and contradicting his version of the Christian faith.

On the other side sits the jury, the Galatian Christians. They have enjoyed warm friendship with Paul in the past, but some of the charges against him are serious. Did he invent parts of the gospel he preached to them? Has God really given him a special insight? Is it true that his message of "freedom" will lead to a weak, immoral church? Should they turn their backs on their Jewish heritage?

Paul, acting in his own self-defense, paces the courtroom. He uses a variety of debating styles: tight logic, historical reviews, and personal outrage. His integrity, and ultimately Jesus Christ's integrity, is at stake.

In topical content, Galatians covers much the same ground as Romans. But in style, it crackles with a fighting spirit. As you read it, try to visualize that courtroom scene, and judge for yourself Paul's effectiveness as a defendant.

3-TRACK READING PLAN

For an explanation and complete listing of the 3-track reading plan, turn to page 7.

TRACK 1: ***Two-Week Courses on the Bible***
The Track 1 reading program on the Life and Teachings of Paul includes one chapter from Galatians. See page 7 for a complete listing of this course.

TRACK 2: ***An Overview of Galatians in 1 Day***
☐ Day 1. Read the Introduction to Galatians, then chapter 3. You'll have to concentrate to follow all the arguments. But this chapter gives an essential interpretation of the Old Testament. Study it as a sample of Paul's defense in Galatians.

Now turn to page 9 for your next Track 2 reading project.

TRACK 3: ***All of Galatians in 5 Days***
After you have read through Galatians, turn to pages 10–14 for your next Track 3 reading project.
☐1   ☐2   ☐3   ☐4   ☐5–6

Salutation

1 Paul an apostle—sent neither by human commission nor from human authorities, but through Jesus Christ and God the Father, who raised him from the dead— ²and all the members of God's family*a* who are with me,

To the churches of Galatia:

3 Grace to you and peace from God our Father and the Lord Jesus Christ, ⁴who gave himself for our sins to set us free from the present evil age, according to the will of our God and Father, ⁵to whom be the glory forever and ever. Amen.

There Is No Other Gospel

6 I am astonished that you are so quickly deserting the one who called you in the grace of Christ and are turning to a different gospel— ⁷not that there is another gospel, but there are some who are confusing you and want to pervert the gospel of Christ. ⁸But even if we or an angel*b* from heaven should proclaim to you a gospel contrary to what we proclaimed to you, let that one be accursed! ⁹As we have said before, so now I repeat, if anyone proclaims to you a gospel contrary to what you received, let that one be accursed!

10 Am I now seeking human approval, or God's approval? Or am I trying to please people?

If I were still pleasing people, I would not be a servant*c* of Christ.

Paul's Vindication of His Apostleship

11 For I want you to know, brothers and sisters,*d* that the gospel that was proclaimed by me is not of human origin; ¹²for I did not receive it from a human source, nor was I taught it, but I received it through a revelation of Jesus Christ.

13 You have heard, no doubt, of my earlier life in Judaism. I was violently persecuting the church of God and was trying to destroy it. ¹⁴I advanced in Judaism beyond many among my people of the same age, for I was far more zealous for the traditions of my ancestors. ¹⁵But when God, who had set me apart before I was born and called me through his grace, was pleased ¹⁶to reveal his Son to me,*e* so that I might proclaim him among the Gentiles, I did not confer with any human being, ¹⁷nor did I go up to Jerusalem to those who were already apostles before me, but I went away at once into Arabia, and afterwards I returned to Damascus.

18 Then after three years I did go up to Jerusalem to visit Cephas and stayed with him fifteen days; ¹⁹but I did not see any other apostle except James the Lord's brother. ²⁰In what I am writing to you, before God, I do not lie! ²¹Then I went into the regions of Syria and Cilicia, ²²and I was

---

a Gk *all the brothers*   *b* Or *a messenger*   *c* Gk *slave*   *d* Gk *brothers*   *e* Gk *in me*

still unknown by sight to the churches of Judea that are in Christ; [23]they only heard it said, "The one who formerly was persecuting us is now proclaiming the faith he once tried to destroy." [24]And they glorified God because of me.

Paul and the Other Apostles

2 Then after fourteen years I went up again to Jerusalem with Barnabas, taking Titus along with me. [2]I went up in response to a revelation. Then I laid before them (though only in a private meeting with the acknowledged leaders) the gospel that I proclaim among the Gentiles, in order to make sure that I was not running, or had not run, in vain. [3]But even Titus, who was with me, was not compelled to be circumcised, though he was a Greek. [4]But because of false believers[f] secretly brought in, who slipped in to spy on the freedom we have in Christ Jesus, so that they might enslave us— [5]we did not submit to them even for a moment, so that the truth of the gospel might always remain with you. [6]And from those who were supposed to be acknowledged leaders (what they actually were makes no difference to me; God shows no partiality)—those leaders contributed nothing to me. [7]On the contrary, when they saw that I had been entrusted with the gospel for the uncircumcised, just as Peter had been entrusted with the gospel for the circumcised [8](for he who worked through Peter making him an apostle to the circumcised also worked through me in sending me to the Gentiles), [9]and when James and Cephas and John, who were acknowledged pillars, recognized the grace that had been given to me, they gave to Barnabas and me the right hand of fellowship, agreeing that we should go to the Gentiles and they to the circumcised. [10]They asked only one thing, that we remember the poor, which was actually what I was[g] eager to do.

Paul Rebukes Peter at Antioch

11 But when Cephas came to Antioch, I opposed him to his face, because he stood self-condemned; [12]for until certain people came from James, he used to eat with the Gentiles. But after they came, he drew back and kept himself separate for fear of the circumcision faction. [13]And the other Jews joined him in this hypocrisy, so that even Barnabas was led astray by their hypocrisy. [14]But when I saw that they were not acting consistently with the truth of the gospel, I said to Cephas before them all, "If you, though a Jew, live like a Gentile and not like a Jew, how can you compel the Gentiles to live like Jews?"[h]

Jews and Gentiles Are Saved by Faith

15 We ourselves are Jews by birth and not Gentile sinners; [16]yet we know that a person is justified[i] not by the works of the law but through

2.11 Forcing a Confrontation

Galatians 2 gives a fascinating behind-the-scenes account of how the Jewish/Gentile question was splitting the early church. Peter and James, sympathetic to Jewish Christians, acted hypocritically in their treatment of Gentiles until Paul confronted them publicly. Acts 15 gives a more detailed account of the official disagreements and how they were finally resolved.

faith in Jesus Christ.[j] And we have come to believe in Christ Jesus, so that we might be justified by faith in Christ,[k] and not by doing the works of the law, because no one will be justified by the works of the law. [17]But if, in our effort to be justified in Christ, we ourselves have been found to be sinners, is Christ then a servant of sin? Certainly not! [18]But if I build up again the very things that I once tore down, then I demonstrate that I am a transgressor. [19]For through the law I died to the law, so that I might live to God. I have been crucified with Christ; [20]and it is no longer I who live, but it is Christ who lives in me. And the life I now live in the flesh I live by faith in the Son of God,[l] who loved me and gave himself for me. [21]I do not nullify the grace of God; for if justification[m] comes through the law, then Christ died for nothing.

Law or Faith

3 You foolish Galatians! Who has bewitched you? It was before your eyes that Jesus Christ was publicly exhibited as crucified! [2]The only thing I want to learn from you is this: Did you receive the Spirit by doing the works of the law or by believing what you heard? [3]Are you so foolish? Having started with the Spirit, are you now ending with the flesh? [4]Did you experience so much for nothing?—if it really was for nothing. [5]Well then, does God[n] supply you with the Spirit and work miracles among you by your doing the works of the law, or by your believing what you heard?

6 Just as Abraham "believed God, and it was reckoned to him as righteousness," [7]so, you see, those who believe are the descendants of Abraham. [8]And the scripture, foreseeing that God would justify the Gentiles by faith, declared the gospel beforehand to Abraham, saying, "All the

---

f Gk *false brothers*   g Or *had been*   h Some interpreters hold that the quotation extends into the following paragraph
i Or *reckoned as righteous;* and so elsewhere   j Or *the faith of Jesus Christ*   k Or *the faith of Christ*   l Or *by the faith of the Son of God*   m Or *righteousness*   n Gk *he*

Gentiles shall be blessed in you." [9]For this reason, those who believe are blessed with Abraham who believed.

10 For all who rely on the works of the law are under a curse; for it is written, "Cursed is everyone who does not observe and obey all the things written in the book of the law." [11]Now it is evident that no one is justified before God by the law; for "The one who is righteous will live by faith."[o] [12]But the law does not rest on faith; on the contrary, "Whoever does the works of the law[p] will live by them." [13]Christ redeemed us from the curse of the law by becoming a curse for us—for it is written, "Cursed is everyone who hangs on a tree"— [14]in order that in Christ Jesus the blessing of Abraham might come to the Gentiles, so that we might receive the promise of the Spirit through faith.

The Promise to Abraham

15 Brothers and sisters,[q] I give an example from daily life: once a person's will[r] has been ratified, no one adds to it or annuls it. [16]Now the promises were made to Abraham and to his offspring;[s] it does not say, "And to offsprings,"[t] as of many; but it says, "And to your offspring,"[s] that is, to one person, who is Christ. [17]My point is this: the law, which came four hundred thirty years later, does not annul a covenant previously ratified by God, so as to nullify the promise. [18]For if the inheritance comes from the law, it no longer comes from the promise; but God granted it to Abraham through the promise.

3.17 The 430-Year Gap

In chapter 3, Paul uses clever arguments to put the entire Old Testament law in a new perspective. The law was never intended to make possible a way to God, he says (verses 11,21). Rather, the law was given as a "disciplinarian until Christ came" (verse 24) to convince us of the impossibility of gaining God's acceptance on our own. To prove his point, Paul mentions a 430-year gap between Abraham and Moses. God gave his promises to Abraham, who lived long before Moses ever received the law; therefore, Abraham couldn't possibly have depended on the law. God's promise reached final fulfillment in Jesus, whom Paul calls Abraham's "offspring" (verse 16).

The Purpose of the Law

19 Why then the law? It was added because of transgressions, until the offspring[s] would come

---

[o] Or *The one who is righteous through faith will live* (as in verse 17)   [p] Gk *does them*   [q] Gk *Brothers*   [r] Or *covenant* (as in verse 17)   [s] Gk *seed*   [t] Gk *seeds*

Legalism
Can we do anything to make God love us more?

BEFORE HIS CONVERSION, PAUL WAS one of the best legalists who ever lived. A loyal Jew, he tortured Christians who stepped outside Jewish tradition to follow Christ. If a person could reach God by obeying the law, then he, the strict Pharisee, would have done it.

But in Galatians, he blasts the idea that God's love is conditioned by how many rules we obey. Legalism is like a cage: It can only condemn people and lock them behind bars. As Paul points out, no one has kept all of God's laws perfectly, and all who try ultimately fail (3.10–11).

Now, however, that you have come to know God . . . how can you turn your back again to the weak and beggarly elemental spirits? 4.9

No Strings Attached

Chapters 3—4 draw sharp contrasts: a prisoner and a free man, a sheltered child and an adult. Don't act like a slave or a child, Paul says. Act like a privileged son, an heir to a great fortune!

Galatians has been called the "Magna Charta of Christian liberty." "For freedom Christ has set us free," Paul declares (5.1). Galatians teaches that there is nothing we can do to make God love us more—or love us less. We don't have to "earn" God's love by slavishly following rules.

Martin Luther said Galatians was "my own little epistle. I have betrothed myself to it; it is my Katie von Bora [Luther's wife]." This slim book proclaims that God has given his love freely, with no strings attached. We should never get over the awesome implications of that truth, Galatians says. Evidently, Paul didn't.

Life Questions: The early Christians went in two directions. Some, like the people in Galatia, became obsessed with legalism. Others took their Christian freedom too far: They refused to follow anyone's rules. Which is the greater danger in your circle?

to whom the promise had been made; and it was ordained through angels by a mediator. 20Now a mediator involves more than one party; but God is one.

21 Is the law then opposed to the promises of God? Certainly not! For if a law had been given that could make alive, then righteousness would indeed come through the law. 22But the scripture has imprisoned all things under the power of sin, so that what was promised through faith in Jesus Christ[u] might be given to those who believe.

23 Now before faith came, we were imprisoned and guarded under the law until faith would be revealed. 24Therefore the law was our disciplinarian until Christ came, so that we might be justified by faith. 25But now that faith has come, we are no longer subject to a disciplinarian, 26for in Christ Jesus you are all children of God through faith. 27As many of you as were baptized into Christ have clothed yourselves with Christ. 28There is no longer Jew or Greek, there is no longer slave or free, there is no longer male and female; for all of you are one in Christ Jesus. 29And if you belong to Christ, then you are Abraham's offspring,[v] heirs according to the promise.

4 My point is this: heirs, as long as they are minors, are no better than slaves, though they are the owners of all the property; 2but they remain under guardians and trustees until the date set by the father. 3So with us; while we were minors, we were enslaved to the elemental spirits[w] of the world. 4But when the fullness of time had come, God sent his Son, born of a woman, born under the law, 5in order to redeem those who were under the law, so that we might receive adoption as children. 6And because you are children, God has sent the Spirit of his Son into our[x] hearts, crying, "Abba![y] Father!" 7So you are no longer a slave but a child, and if a child then also an heir, through God.[z]

Paul Reproves the Galatians

8 Formerly, when you did not know God, you were enslaved to beings that by nature are not gods. 9Now, however, that you have come to know God, or rather to be known by God, how can you turn back again to the weak and beggarly elemental spirits?[a] How can you want to be enslaved to them again? 10You are observing special days, and months, and seasons, and years. 11I am afraid that my work for you may have been wasted.

12 Friends,[b] I beg you, become as I am, for I also have become as you are. You have done me no wrong. 13You know that it was because of a physical infirmity that I first announced the gospel to you; 14though my condition put you to the test, you did not scorn or despise me, but welcomed me as an angel of God, as Christ Jesus. 15What has become of the goodwill you felt? For I testify that, had it been possible, you would have torn out your eyes and given them to me. 16Have I now become your enemy by telling you the

4.16 Paul's Anguish

Paul's letter wavers between abstract reasoning and intensely emotional pleading. As this paragraph shows, Paul had once enjoyed intimate closeness with the people of Galatia. He feels anguish and personal rejection because they now seem to be turning their backs on the faith he had carefully taught them. He is in the pains of childbirth, he says, waiting anxiously for them to grow out of their false ideas (verse 19).

truth? 17They make much of you, but for no good purpose; they want to exclude you, so that you may make much of them. 18It is good to be made much of for a good purpose at all times, and not only when I am present with you. 19My little children, for whom I am again in the pain of childbirth until Christ is formed in you, 20I wish I were present with you now and could change my tone, for I am perplexed about you.

The Allegory of Hagar and Sarah

21 Tell me, you who desire to be subject to the law, will you not listen to the law? 22For it is written that Abraham had two sons, one by a slave woman and the other by a free woman. 23One, the child of the slave, was born according to the flesh; the other, the child of the free woman, was born through the promise. 24Now this is an allegory: these women are two covenants. One woman, in fact, is Hagar, from Mount Sinai, bearing children for slavery. 25Now Hagar is Mount Sinai in Arabia[c] and corresponds to the present Jerusalem, for she is in slavery with her children. 26But the other woman corresponds to the Jerusalem above; she is free, and she is our mother. 27For it is written,

> "Rejoice, you childless one, you who bear
> no children,
> burst into song and shout, you who
> endure no birth pangs;
> for the children of the desolate woman
> are more numerous
> than the children of the one who is
> married."

---

[u] Or *through the faith of Jesus Christ*   [v] Gk *seed*   [w] Or *the rudiments*   [x] Other ancient authorities read *your*
[y] Aramaic for *Father*   [z] Other ancient authorities read *an heir of God through Christ*   [a] Or *beggarly rudiments*
[b] Gk *Brothers*   [c] Other ancient authorities read *For Sinai is a mountain in Arabia*

28Now you,[d] my friends,[e] are children of the promise, like Isaac. 29But just as at that time the child who was born according to the flesh persecuted the child who was born according to the Spirit, so it is now also. 30But what does the scripture say? "Drive out the slave and her child; for the child of the slave will not share the inheritance with the child of the free woman." 31So then, friends,[e] we are children, not of the slave but of 5 the free woman. 1For freedom Christ has set us free. Stand firm, therefore, and do not submit again to a yoke of slavery.

The Nature of Christian Freedom

2 Listen! I, Paul, am telling you that if you let yourselves be circumcised, Christ will be of no benefit to you. 3Once again I testify to every man who lets himself be circumcised that he is obliged to obey the entire law. 4You who want to be justified by the law have cut yourselves off from Christ; you have fallen away from grace. 5For through the Spirit, by faith, we eagerly wait for the hope of righteousness. 6For in Christ Jesus neither circumcision nor uncircumcision counts for anything; the only thing that counts is faith working[f] through love.

7 You were running well; who prevented you from obeying the truth? 8Such persuasion does not come from the one who calls you. 9A little yeast leavens the whole batch of dough. 10I am confident about you in the Lord that you will not think otherwise. But whoever it is that is confusing you will pay the penalty. 11But my friends,[e] why am I still being persecuted if I am still preaching circumcision? In that case the offense of the cross has been removed. 12I wish those who unsettle you would castrate themselves!

13 For you were called to freedom, brothers and sisters;[e] only do not use your freedom as an opportunity for self-indulgence,[g] but through love become slaves to one another. 14For the whole law is summed up in a single commandment, "You shall love your neighbor as yourself." 15If, however, you bite and devour one another, take care that you are not consumed by one another.

The Works of the Flesh

16 Live by the Spirit, I say, and do not gratify the desires of the flesh. 17For what the flesh desires is opposed to the Spirit, and what the Spirit desires is opposed to the flesh; for these are opposed to each other, to prevent you from doing what you want. 18But if you are led by the Spirit, you are not subject to the law. 19Now the works of the flesh are obvious: fornication, impurity, licen-

[d] Other ancient authorities read we   [e] Gk brothers   [f] Or made effective   [g] Gk the flesh

Paul Fights Back
When freedom gets dangerous

OVER THE YEARS PAUL CAUGHT on to his opponents' crafty ways of undermining him. Galatians provides a textbook case of his response to critics.

First, Paul answered their personal attacks. Some had questioned his right to be called an apostle. In chapters 1 and 2, Paul insists that he received the gospel directly from God. In addition, he has met every criterion of an apostle.

Chapters 3 and 4 deal with Paul's ideas. Had he strayed too far from Old Testament law and customs? Some hinted that Paul was preaching an incomplete gospel. He answered those objections with a carefully reasoned look at the Old Testament, focusing on Abraham, the father of the Jewish race.

> The only thing that counts is faith working through love. 5.6

What to Do with Freedom

Then Paul turned to more practical matters. Stressing freedom, not rules, left him open to criticism. Did his strong emphasis on freedom lead to loose morals? To answer this question, he ended Galatians, a letter devoted to Christian liberty, with a warning.

"Why did Christ set us free?" Paul asks. To make possible a life of orgies, drunkenness, and witchcraft? Obviously no. Christ freed us from worrying about whether we are "doing enough" to please God and from uselessly following external forms. But we should use that freedom to serve one another in love and to live a Spirit-filled life.

His arguments and emotions exhausted, Paul concludes, "Neither circumcision nor uncircumcision is anything; but a new creation is everything!" (6.15). A released prisoner, a freed slave, the bountiful fruit of a living tree—all the images in Galatians convey *life*, an abundant life in the Spirit of God, readily available to every Christian.

Life Questions: Read over the qualities of life in the Spirit listed in 5.22–23. Do these characterize your life?

tiousness, 20idolatry, sorcery, enmities, strife, jealousy, anger, quarrels, dissensions, factions, 21envy,*h* drunkenness, carousing, and things like these. I am warning you, as I warned you before: those who do such things will not inherit the kingdom of God.

The Fruit of the Spirit

22 By contrast, the fruit of the Spirit is love, joy, peace, patience, kindness, generosity, faithfulness, 23gentleness, and self-control. There is no law against such things. 24And those who belong to Christ Jesus have crucified the flesh with its passions and desires. 25If we live by the Spirit, let us also be guided by the Spirit. 26Let us not become conceited, competing against one another, envying one another.

Bear One Another's Burdens

6 My friends,*i* if anyone is detected in a transgression, you who have received the Spirit should restore such a one in a spirit of gentleness. Take care that you yourselves are not tempted. 2Bear one another's burdens, and in this way you

6.2 Mixing Gentleness with Harshness

Galatians contains some of Paul's harshest language, for he sensed a danger that could destroy the church's faith. But the book also includes some of Paul's most familiar and comforting words. Chapter 6 describes a spirit of tolerance and forgiveness toward those who fail. It also offers encouragement for people who grow tired of doing good when it appears justice is not working out.

will fulfill*j* the law of Christ. 3For if those who are nothing think they are something, they deceive themselves. 4All must test their own work; then that work, rather than their neighbor's work, will become a cause for pride. 5For all must carry their own loads.

6 Those who are taught the word must share in all good things with their teacher.

7 Do not be deceived; God is not mocked, for you reap whatever you sow. 8If you sow to your own flesh, you will reap corruption from the flesh; but if you sow to the Spirit, you will reap eternal life from the Spirit. 9So let us not grow weary in doing what is right, for we will reap at harvest time, if we do not give up. 10So then, whenever we have an opportunity, let us work for the good of all, and especially for those of the family of faith.

Final Admonitions and Benediction

11 See what large letters I make when I am writing in my own hand! 12It is those who want to make a good showing in the flesh that try to compel you to be circumcised—only that they may not be persecuted for the cross of Christ. 13Even the circumcised do not themselves obey the law, but they want you to be circumcised so that they may boast about your flesh. 14May I never boast of anything except the cross of our Lord Jesus Christ, by which*k* the world has been crucified to me, and I to the world. 15For*l* neither circumcision nor uncircumcision is anything; but a new creation is everything! 16As for those who will follow this rule—peace be upon them, and mercy, and upon the Israel of God.

17 From now on, let no one make trouble for me; for I carry the marks of Jesus branded on my body.

18 May the grace of our Lord Jesus Christ be with your spirit, brothers and sisters.*m* Amen.

---

h Other ancient authorities add *murder*   *i* Gk *Brothers*   *j* Other ancient authorities read *in this way fulfill*
k Or *through whom*   *l* Other ancient authorities add *in Christ Jesus*   *m* Gk *brothers*

EPHESIANS

For the Discouraged
Good news for those who feel abandoned and unloved

IMAGINE YOURSELF A CHILD, ABANDONED on the streets of New York. Your immigrant parents died on the ship on the way to America. You have no money and no relatives. You can't speak English. And you are left to fend for yourself.

As many as 30,000 orphans found themselves in exactly that predicament in 1850. They slept in alleys, huddling for warmth in boxes or metal drums. To survive, the boys mostly stole, caught rats to eat, or rummaged in garbage cans. Girls sometimes worked as "panel thieves" for prostitutes, slipping their tiny hands through camouflaged openings in the walls to lift a watch or wallet from a preoccupied customer.

Immigrants were flooding New York City then, and no one had the time or money to look after the orphans—no one, that is, except Charles Loring Brace, a 26-year-old minister. Horrified by their plight, he organized a unique solution, the Orphan Train. The idea was simple: Pack hundreds of orphans on a train heading west and announce to towns along the way that anyone could claim a new son or daughter when the Orphan Train chugged through.

> *You are no longer strangers and aliens, but you are citizens with the saints and also members of the household of God.*
> *2.19*

Adopted into a New Life

By the time the last Orphan Train steamed west in 1929, 100,000 children had found new homes and new lives. Two orphans from such trains became governors, one served as a United States congressman, and still another was a U.S. Supreme Court justice.

The Orphan Train provides a vivid parable of the message of Ephesians. To capture Paul's enthusiasm in this book, imagine one more stage in your life as a street urchin in New York.

You have learned to survive and fight off starvation. But one day, someone takes you and puts you on a smoke-belching train jammed with hundreds of other foreign-speaking youngsters. Three days later you are selected by a kindly middle-aged couple in Michigan who introduce themselves as Mr. and Mrs. Henry Ford. You are driven (in an automobile!) to the largest house you have ever seen, and they quietly explain that you are now part of their family. Everything they have is yours to use and enjoy. At long last, by some miracle, you have a family and a home—and what a home!

Welcome to the Family

Paul conveys a feeling something like that in Ephesians, a rich book that expands the message of Jesus' parable of the Prodigal and His Brother (Luke 15). A big "Welcome Home!" banner is stretched across the lawn, confetti swirls in the air, balloons lunge skyward, and a band plays. Christians have been adopted directly into the family of God. This is a good news book, to put it mildly.

If you feel discouraged or wonder if God really cares or question whether the Christian life is worth the effort, read Ephesians. You will no longer feel like an orphan. Paul describes the "riches of Christ" available to all and points to us, God's adopted children, as his sparkling "Exhibit A" in all the universe (3.10).

Ephesians contains staggering thoughts. Paul wants his readers to grasp "the breadth and length and height and depth" of the love of Christ (3.18). He cranks up the volume to express that love, and not one low, mournful note sneaks in.

How to Read Ephesians

In many ways, Ephesians is Paul's "summing-up" book. The same subjects appear in greater detail in books like Romans, 1 Corinthians and 1 Thessalonians. But in Ephesians, Paul gives an overall view of the grand scheme of the gospel. Only now, Paul says, has God's hidden plan for all of history come to light.

Because it compresses such large thoughts into such a short space, Ephesians deserves very careful study. Read the first three chapters slowly, digesting one paragraph at a time. Such study will prove rewarding: Ephesians gives exuberant good news about the nature of the universe and God's plan for believers.

Like other letters from Paul, Ephesians divides fairly neatly between doctrine (chapters 1–3) and practical advice (4–6). The last half details how our lives should change as a result of the great things described in the first part.

3-TRACK READING PLAN

For an explanation and complete listing of the 3-track reading plan, turn to page 7.

TRACK 1: *Two-Week Courses on the Bible*
The Track 1 reading program on the Life and Teachings of Paul includes one chapter from Ephesians. See page 7 for a complete listing of this course.

TRACK 2: *An Overview of Ephesians in 2 Days*
☐ Day 1. Read the Introduction to Ephesians, then chapter 2.
☐ Day 2. Read chapter 3. You may also want to look at the famous "armor" passage (6.10–18).
Now turn to page 9 for your next Track 2 reading project.

TRACK 3: *All of Ephesians in 6 Days*
After you have read through Ephesians, turn to pages 10–14 for your next Track 3 reading project.
☐1   ☐2   ☐3   ☐4   ☐5   ☐6

Salutation

1 Paul, an apostle of Christ Jesus by the will of God,
To the saints who are in Ephesus and are faithful[a] in Christ Jesus:

2 Grace to you and peace from God our Father and the Lord Jesus Christ.

Spiritual Blessings in Christ

3 Blessed be the God and Father of our Lord Jesus Christ, who has blessed us in Christ with every spiritual blessing in the heavenly places, [4]just as he chose us in Christ[b] before the foundation of the world to be holy and blameless before him in love. [5]He destined us for adoption as his children through Jesus Christ, according to the good pleasure of his will, [6]to the praise of his glorious grace that he freely bestowed on us in the Beloved. [7]In him we have redemption through his blood, the forgiveness of our trespasses, according to the riches of his grace [8]that he lavished on us. With all wisdom and insight [9]he has made known to us the mystery of his will, according to his good pleasure that he set forth in Christ, [10]as a plan for the fullness of time, to gather up all things in him, things in heaven and things on earth. [11]In Christ we have also obtained an inheritance,[c] having been destined according to the purpose of him who accomplishes all things according to his counsel and will, [12]so that we, who were the first to set our hope on Christ, might live for the praise of his glory. [13]In him you also, when you had heard the word of truth, the gospel of

1.13 Branded

Cattle ranchers brand their cattle, loggers carve a symbol on a tree, dignitaries seal their important papers with wax—all these are marks of ownership. According to Paul, the Holy Spirit is God's proof of ownership for Christians. More, he is a "deposit" guaranteeing a great inheritance.

---

[a] Other ancient authorities lack *in Ephesus*, reading *saints who are also faithful*   [b] Gk *in him*   [c] Or *been made a heritage*

your salvation, and had believed in him, were marked with the seal of the promised Holy Spirit; [14]this[d] is the pledge of our inheritance toward redemption as God's own people, to the praise of his glory.

Paul's Prayer

15 I have heard of your faith in the Lord Jesus and your love[e] toward all the saints, and for this reason [16]I do not cease to give thanks for you as I remember you in my prayers. [17]I pray that the God of our Lord Jesus Christ, the Father of glory, may give you a spirit of wisdom and revelation as you come to know him, [18]so that, with the eyes of your heart enlightened, you may know what is the hope to which he has called you, what are the riches of his glorious inheritance among the saints, [19]and what is the immeasurable greatness of his power for us who believe, according to

1.19 Proven Power

Throughout the Old Testament, God cites the liberation of slaves from Egypt as evidence of his power (over the most powerful nation of the time). "I am the God who brought you out of Egypt," he says. The New Testament holds up an even greater proof: God's ability to give life to the dead. That same life-giving power is available to the individual believer, Paul proclaims.

the working of his great power. [20]God[f] put this power to work in Christ when he raised him from the dead and seated him at his right hand in the heavenly places, [21]far above all rule and authority and power and dominion, and above every name that is named, not only in this age but also in the age to come. [22]And he has put all things under his feet and has made him the head over all things for the church, [23]which is his body, the fullness of him who fills all in all.

From Death to Life

2 You were dead through the trespasses and sins [2]in which you once lived, following the course of this world, following the ruler of the power of the air, the spirit that is now at work among those who are disobedient. [3]All of us once lived among them in the passions of our flesh, following the desires of flesh and senses, and we were by nature children of wrath, like everyone else. [4]But God, who is rich in mercy, out of the great love with which he loved us [5]even when we were dead through our trespasses, made us alive together with Christ[g]—by grace you have been saved— [6]and raised us up with him and seated us

with him in the heavenly places in Christ Jesus, [7]so that in the ages to come he might show the immeasurable riches of his grace in kindness toward us in Christ Jesus. [8]For by grace you have been saved through faith, and this is not your

2.8 Given, Not Earned

As a converted legalist, Paul insisted on one fact of the gospel: Eternal life comes not by any ritual of rule-keeping (which he calls "works"), but by the grace of God. Yet in this paragraph he notes that God intends for us to "do good works." Paul makes a clear distinction: Good works do nothing to help us obtain God's favor, but they follow naturally as we experience the love of Christ.

own doing; it is the gift of God— [9]not the result of works, so that no one may boast. [10]For we are what he has made us, created in Christ Jesus for good works, which God prepared beforehand to be our way of life.

One in Christ

11 So then, remember that at one time you Gentiles by birth,[h] called "the uncircumcision" by those who are called "the circumcision"—a physical circumcision made in the flesh by human hands— [12]remember that you were at that time without Christ, being aliens from the commonwealth of Israel, and strangers to the covenants of promise, having no hope and without God in the world. [13]But now in Christ Jesus you who once were far off have been brought near by the blood of Christ. [14]For he is our peace; in his flesh he has made both groups into one and has broken down the dividing wall, that is, the hostility between us. [15]He has abolished the law with its commandments and ordinances, that he might create in

2.14 Destroying the Barriers

A Jewish missionary to the Gentiles, Paul wrote and talked constantly about tearing down the barriers between Jews and Gentiles. Jews kept themselves separate from Gentiles by many cultural and religious barriers. Perhaps the most vivid symbol of separation was an actual wall in the temple. Non-Jews could never enter the temple courts beyond that wall, and a further wall separated Jewish men from Jewish women. Here Paul describes how Christ utterly destroyed the "dividing wall . . . the hostility between us." (See also Galatians 3.28.)

---

[d] Other ancient authorities read *who*   [e] Other ancient authorities lack *and your love*   [f] Gk *He*   [g] Other ancient
authorities read *in Christ*   [h] Gk *in the flesh*

himself one new humanity in place of the two, thus making peace, [16]and might reconcile both groups to God in one body[i] through the cross, thus putting to death that hostility through it.[j] [17]So he came and proclaimed peace to you who were far off and peace to those who were near; [18]for through him both of us have access in one Spirit to the Father. [19]So then you are no longer strangers and aliens, but you are citizens with the saints and also members of the household of God, [20]built upon the foundation of the apostles and prophets, with Christ Jesus himself as the cornerstone.[k] [21]In him the whole structure is joined together and grows into a holy temple in the Lord; [22]in whom you also are built together spiritually[l] into a dwelling place for God.

Paul's Ministry to the Gentiles

3 This is the reason that I Paul am a prisoner for[m] Christ Jesus for the sake of you Gentiles— [2]for surely you have already heard of the commission of God's grace that was given me for you, [3]and how the mystery was made known to me by revelation, as I wrote above in a few words, [4]a reading of which will enable you to perceive my understanding of the mystery of Christ. [5]In former generations this mystery[n] was not made known to humankind, as it has now been revealed to his holy apostles and prophets by the Spirit: [6]that is, the Gentiles have become fellow heirs, members of the same body, and sharers in the promise in Christ Jesus through the gospel.

7 Of this gospel I have become a servant according to the gift of God's grace that was given me by the working of his power. [8]Although I am the very least of all the saints, this grace was given to me to bring to the Gentiles the news of the boundless riches of Christ, [9]and to make everyone see[o] what is the plan of the mystery hidden for ages in[p] God who created all things; [10]so that through the church the wisdom of God in its rich variety might now be made known to the rulers and authorities in the heavenly places. [11]This was in accordance with the eternal purpose that he has carried out in Christ Jesus our Lord, [12]in whom we have access to God in boldness and confidence through faith in him.[q] [13]I pray therefore that you[r] may not lose heart over my sufferings for you; they are your glory.

Prayer for the Readers

14 For this reason I bow my knees before the Father,[s] [15]from whom every family[t] in heaven and on earth takes its name. [16]I pray that, according to the riches of his glory, he may grant that you may be strengthened in your inner being with power through his Spirit, [17]and that Christ may dwell in your hearts through faith, as you are being rooted and grounded in love. [18]I pray that you may have the power to comprehend, with all the saints, what is the breadth and length and

3.16 Reading Between Lines

Paul's prayers often give some of the best insights into the local situation. This prayer (verses 14–21) and the one in chapter 1 (verses 15–23) indicate the church at Ephesus was well-grounded. In Ephesians Paul does not dwell on any urgent problems; instead, he tries to raise the sights of young Christians who have not fully grasped the extent of God's love and grace.

height and depth, [19]and to know the love of Christ that surpasses knowledge, so that you may be filled with all the fullness of God.

20 Now to him who by the power at work within us is able to accomplish abundantly far more than all we can ask or imagine, [21]to him be glory in the church and in Christ Jesus to all generations, forever and ever. Amen.

Unity in the Body of Christ

4 I therefore, the prisoner in the Lord, beg you to lead a life worthy of the calling to which you have been called, [2]with all humility and gentleness, with patience, bearing with one another in love, [3]making every effort to maintain the unity of the Spirit in the bond of peace. [4]There is one body and one Spirit, just as you were called to the one hope of your calling, [5]one Lord, one faith, one baptism, [6]one God and Father of all, who is above all and through all and in all.

7 But each of us was given grace according to the measure of Christ's gift. [8]Therefore it is said,
"When he ascended on high he made
captivity itself a captive;
he gave gifts to his people."
[9](When it says, "He ascended," what does it mean but that he had also descended[u] into the lower parts of the earth? [10]He who descended is the same one who ascended far above all the heavens, so that he might fill all things.) [11]The gifts he gave were that some would be apostles, some prophets, some evangelists, some pastors and teachers, [12]to equip the saints for the work of ministry, for building up the body of Christ, [13]until all of us come to the unity of the faith and of the knowledge of the Son of God, to maturity, to the measure of the full stature of Christ. [14]We must no longer be children, tossed to and fro and blown about by every wind of doctrine, by people's

---

[i] Or *reconcile both of us in one body for God*   [j] Or *in him,* or *in himself*   [k] Or *keystone*   [l] Gk *in the Spirit*
[m] Or *of*   [n] Gk *it*   [o] Other ancient authorities read *to bring to light*   [p] Or *by*   [q] Or *the faith of him*   [r] Or *I*
[s] Other ancient authorities add *of our Lord Jesus Christ*   [t] Gk *fatherhood*   [u] Other ancient authorities add *first*

trickery, by their craftiness in deceitful scheming. [15]But speaking the truth in love, we must grow up in every way into him who is the head, into Christ, [16]from whom the whole body, joined and knit together by every ligament with which it is equipped, as each part is working properly, promotes the body's growth in building itself up in love.

The Old Life and the New

17 Now this I affirm and insist on in the Lord: you must no longer live as the Gentiles live, in the futility of their minds. [18]They are darkened in their understanding, alienated from the life of God because of their ignorance and hardness of heart. [19]They have lost all sensitivity and have abandoned themselves to licentiousness, greedy to practice every kind of impurity. [20]That is not the way you learned Christ! [21]For surely you have heard about him and were taught in him, as truth is in Jesus. [22]You were taught to put away your former way of life, your old self, corrupt and deluded by its lusts, [23]and to be renewed in the spirit of your minds, [24]and to clothe yourselves with the new self, created according to the likeness of God in true righteousness and holiness.

4.19 Loss of Sensitivity

Medical conditions that destroy nerves— leprosy, spinal cord injury, diabetes—are among the most difficult to treat. Without a sense of touch or pain, the patient can get a bedsore by lying in the same position too long, or a footsore by wearing too-tight shoes. The body no longer warns of danger. According to Paul, people can also develop a kind of moral insensitivity, silencing their consciences and hardening their hearts. That condition can prove fatal.

Letters from Prison
Time at last to tackle the grandest question of all

TO STIMULATE CREATIVITY, MANY AUTHORS seek out a scenic setting. Yet some of the world's most famous literature originated in, of all places, a prison cell. John Bunyan wrote his *Pilgrim's Progress* there. Russian novelist Alexander Solzhenitsyn's vast output had its conception behind barbed wire, as did his compatriot Dostoevski's.

Parts of the Bible were written in prison as well. Ephesians represents one of Paul's "prison letters" (along with Philippians, Colossians, and Philemon).

I am an ambassador in chains. Pray that I may declare it [the gospel] boldly, as I must speak. 6.20

Time on His Hands

Prison offers authors one precious commodity: time to think and reflect. When Paul wrote his prison letters, he was no longer journeying from town to town, stamping out fires set by his enemies. Settled into passably comfortable surroundings (probably confined to a house), he could slip off his sandals and devote attention to lofty concepts.

Unlike Paul's other letters, Ephesians does not address any urgent problems. With a sigh of relief, the apostle turned to the grandest question of all: "What is God's overall purpose for this world?" Paul answers the question this way: "To gather up all things in him, things in heaven and things on earth" (1.10).

A Positive Approach

The apostle Paul often borrowed from the language of athletics to press home a crucial point, and Ephesians ends with a well-composed pep talk. In keeping with this letter's uplifting style, Paul does not scold or warn; rather, he begins, "I . . . beg you to live a life worthy of the calling to which you have been called" (4.1).

Already Paul has taught that Christ lives in each Christian—we are his body. Now he exhorts his readers to think through what it means to represent Christ in the world. When people look at Christians, do they see the qualities of Christ on display?

The last half of Ephesians spells out practical steps toward Christian maturity. Paul blends each new thought into his overall theme, urging us to love *as Christ loved*, to forgive *as Christ forgave*, to submit *as you would to Christ* (5.2; 4.32; 5.21).

Ironically, it took a stint in prison to free up Paul for this endeavor. The book of Ephesians can hardly introduce a new thought without bursting into a song or a prayer. It is no wonder the English poet Samuel Taylor Coleridge called the book "the divinest composition of man."

Life Questions: Suppose you were put in prison. What kind of letters would you write?

Rules for the New Life

25 So then, putting away falsehood, let all of us speak the truth to our neighbors, for we are members of one another. [26]Be angry but do not sin; do not let the sun go down on your anger, [27]and do not make room for the devil. [28]Thieves must give up stealing; rather let them labor and work honestly with their own hands, so as to have something to share with the needy. [29]Let no evil talk come out of your mouths, but only what is useful for building up,[v] as there is need, so that your words may give grace to those who hear. [30]And do not grieve the Holy Spirit of God, with which you were marked with a seal for the day of redemption. [31]Put away from you all bitterness and wrath and anger and wrangling and slander, together with all malice, [32]and be kind to one another, tenderhearted, forgiving one another, as God in Christ has forgiven you.[w] [1]Therefore be imitators of God, as beloved children, [2]and live in love, as Christ loved us[x] and gave himself up for us, a fragrant offering and sacrifice to God.

Renounce Pagan Ways

3 But fornication and impurity of any kind, or greed, must not even be mentioned among you, as is proper among saints. [4]Entirely out of place is obscene, silly, and vulgar talk; but instead, let there be thanksgiving. [5]Be sure of this, that no fornicator or impure person, or one who is greedy (that is, an idolater), has any inheritance in the kingdom of Christ and of God.

6 Let no one deceive you with empty words, for because of these things the wrath of God comes on those who are disobedient. [7]Therefore do not be associated with them. [8]For once you were darkness, but now in the Lord you are light. Live as children of light— [9]for the fruit of the light is found in all that is good and right and true. [10]Try to find out what is pleasing to the Lord. [11]Take no part in the unfruitful works of darkness, but instead expose them. [12]For it is shameful even to mention what such people do secretly; [13]but everything exposed by the light becomes visible, [14]for everything that becomes visible is light. Therefore it says,

"Sleeper, awake!
Rise from the dead,
and Christ will shine on you."

15 Be careful then how you live, not as unwise people but as wise, [16]making the most of the time, because the days are evil. [17]So do not be foolish, but understand what the will of the Lord is. [18]Do not get drunk with wine, for that is debauchery; but be filled with the Spirit, [19]as you sing psalms and hymns and spiritual songs among yourselves, singing and making melody to the Lord in your hearts, [20]giving thanks to God the Father at all times and for everything in the name of our Lord Jesus Christ.

The Christian Household

21 Be subject to one another out of reverence for Christ.

5.21 The Key to Submission

Many readers have struggled with the advice Paul gives in the next few paragraphs. This simple sentence sets the tone for all that follows: We are to submit to others because of our reverence for Christ. In other words, in any human relationship—husband and wife, child and parent, slave and master—a third party is involved, Christ himself. Paul urges us to conduct those relationships in light of Christ's own spirit.

22 Wives, be subject to your husbands as you are to the Lord. [23]For the husband is the head of the wife just as Christ is the head of the church, the body of which he is the Savior. [24]Just as the church is subject to Christ, so also wives ought to be, in everything, to their husbands.

25 Husbands, love your wives, just as Christ loved the church and gave himself up for her, [26]in order to make her holy by cleansing her with the washing of water by the word, [27]so as to present the church to himself in splendor, without a spot or wrinkle or anything of the kind—yes, so that she may be holy and without blemish. [28]In the same way, husbands should love their wives as they do their own bodies. He who loves his wife loves himself. [29]For no one ever hates his own body, but he nourishes and tenderly cares for it, just as Christ does for the church, [30]because we are members of his body.[y] [31]"For this reason a man will leave his father and mother and be joined to his wife, and the two will become one flesh." [32]This is a great mystery, and I am applying it to Christ and the church. [33]Each of you, however, should love his wife as himself, and a wife should respect her husband.

Children and Parents

6 Children, obey your parents in the Lord,[z] for this is right. [2]"Honor your father and mother"—this is the first commandment with a promise: [3]"so that it may be well with you and you may live long on the earth."

4 And, fathers, do not provoke your children to anger, but bring them up in the discipline and instruction of the Lord.

---

v Other ancient authorities read *building up faith*   w Other ancient authorities read *us*   x Other ancient authorities read *you*   y Other ancient authorities add *of his flesh and of his bones*   z Other ancient authorities lack *in the Lord*

Slaves and Masters

5 Slaves, obey your earthly masters with fear and trembling, in singleness of heart, as you obey Christ; [6]not only while being watched, and in order to please them, but as slaves of Christ, doing the will of God from the heart. [7]Render service with enthusiasm, as to the Lord and not to men and women, [8]knowing that whatever good we do, we will receive the same again from the Lord, whether we are slaves or free.

9 And, masters, do the same to them. Stop threatening them, for you know that both of you have the same Master in heaven, and with him there is no partiality.

The Whole Armor of God

10 Finally, be strong in the Lord and in the strength of his power. [11]Put on the whole armor of God, so that you may be able to stand against the wiles of the devil. [12]For our[a] struggle is not against enemies of blood and flesh, but against the rulers, against the authorities, against the cosmic powers of this present darkness, against the spiritual forces of evil in the heavenly places. [13]Therefore take up the whole armor of God, so that you may be able to withstand on that evil day, and having done everything, to stand firm. [14]Stand therefore, and fasten the belt of truth around your waist, and put on the breastplate of righteousness. [15]As shoes for your feet put on whatever will make you ready to proclaim the gospel of peace. [16]With all of these,[b] take the shield of faith, with which you will be able to quench all the flaming arrows of the evil one. [17]Take the helmet of salvation, and the sword of the Spirit, which is the word of God.

18 Pray in the Spirit at all times in every prayer and supplication. To that end keep alert and always persevere in supplication for all the saints. [19]Pray also for me, so that when I speak, a message may be given to me to make known with boldness the mystery of the gospel,[c] [20]for which I am an ambassador in chains. Pray that I may declare it boldly, as I must speak.

Personal Matters and Benediction

21 So that you also may know how I am and what I am doing, Tychicus will tell you everything. He is a dear brother and a faithful minister in the Lord. [22]I am sending him to you for this very purpose, to let you know how we are, and to encourage your hearts.

23 Peace be to the whole community,[d] and love with faith, from God the Father and the Lord Jesus Christ. [24]Grace be with all who have an undying love for our Lord Jesus Christ.[e]

6.11 The Armor of God

Ephesians concludes with a concise analogy, perhaps inspired by a glimpse of a Roman soldier, outfitted in armor, patrolling the grounds of Paul's prison. Paul viewed the Christian life as a kind of warfare, and he wanted his readers to prepare for combat with a dangerous opponent. Bible scholars often note two details: (1) Only the "sword of the Spirit" is an offensive weapon; all the rest were used for defense. (2) No armor protects the back and rear; Paul made no provision for running away from a spiritual battle.

---

[a] Other ancient authorities read *your*   [b] Or *In all circumstances*   [c] Other ancient authorities lack *of the gospel*
[d] Gk *to the brothers*   [e] Other ancient authorities add *Amen*

PHILIPPIANS

Cheerful Sounds from a Jail Cell
Joy when it's least expected

> Finally, my brothers and sisters, rejoice in the Lord. 3.1

JOY. THE WORD HAS A quick, poignant ring to it. Yet it, like other words, has been drained of meaning over the years, even tapped as a name for a dishwashing detergent. Nowadays *joy* is used most commonly for a sensation like *thrill*.

We think of joy as something you save up for months to experience and then splurge on in a moment of exhilaration: a trip to Disney World, a free-fall dive, a heart-stopping ride on the world's meanest roller coaster, a hot-air balloon trip. Paul had a different understanding of the word, as this letter reveals.

When You Feel Like Despairing

Philippians uses the word *joy* or *rejoice* every few paragraphs, but the joy it describes doesn't vanish after your heart starts beating normally again. Rejoice, says Paul, when someone selfishly tries to steal the limelight from you. And when you meet persecution for your faith. And when you are facing death.

In fact, the most joyous book in the Bible comes from the pen of an author chained to a Roman guard. Many scholars believe Paul wrote Philippians in Rome just about the time Nero began tossing Christians to ravenous lions and burning them as torches to illuminate his banquets. How could a rational man devote a letter to the topic of joy while his survival was in serious jeopardy? In such an environment, how could joy possibly thrive?

Turning Evil into Good

Paul hints at an answer in a burst of eloquence in chapter 2 (verses 5–11). This pithy, metrical paragraph may have been a hymn familiar to the early church. In it, Paul discusses Christ's perspective in coming to earth.

During the Christmas season we celebrate the grand night God visited earth as a baby. But to the rest of the universe the event looked like an astounding humiliation. God, the Creator of all, took on the unimpressive body of a human being to endure a confining life and grisly death on planet Earth.

Paul points to this death to show that God can take even the darkest moment in history and turn it into good. The cross, and Jesus' not staying dead, proves that nothing is powerful enough to stamp out a reason for joy—joy "in the Lord," as Paul says.

Victory in Jail

Thus even the normally depressing state of imprisonment didn't bother Paul. As he wrote Philippians, he must have recalled his first visit to Philippi. Then, a most unusual jailbreak occurred: The jail broke, but the prisoners didn't (Acts 16.22–28).

Even when Paul stayed in jail for long periods, God used the experience to advance the gospel. As he wrote Philippians, conversions were occurring among the Roman palace soldiers, forced by guard duty to overhear Paul's daily ministry.

Paul summarized his life philosophy in a famous "to be or not to be" soliloquy, concluding that "living is Christ and dying is gain" (1.21). God is even stronger than death, and that makes a Christian's joy indestructible.

How to Read Philippians

Philippians is simple and straightforward. It's not a formal treatise, but a warm letter to friends. Read it like you would read any personal letter. From the clues Paul gives, try to imagine the relationship between him and the Philippians. What did he like about them? Why were they so important to him?

The Introduction refers to the common use of the words *joy* and *rejoice*. Check out each of these, noticing how Paul can find joy in any circumstances. Use Philippians like a devotional book, first reflecting on what it says, then applying it to your own life.

3-TRACK READING PLAN

For an explanation and complete listing of the 3-track reading plan, turn to page 7.

TRACK 1: **Two-Week Courses on the Bible**
The Track 1 reading program on the Life and Teachings of Paul includes one chapter from Philippians. See page 7 for a complete listing of this course.

TRACK 2: **An Overview of Philippians in 1 Day**
☐ Day 1. Read the Introduction to Philippians, then chapter 2, noticing especially the central passage set off in poetic form (verses 5–11).

Now turn to page 9 for your next Track 2 reading project.

TRACK 3: **All of Philippians in 4 Days**
After you have read through Philippians, turn to pages 10–14 for your next Track 3 reading project.
☐1 ☐2 ☐3 ☐4

Salutation

1 Paul and Timothy, servants[a] of Christ Jesus,
To all the saints in Christ Jesus who are in Philippi, with the bishops[b] and deacons:[c]

2 Grace to you and peace from God our Father and the Lord Jesus Christ.

Paul's Prayer for the Philippians

3 I thank my God every time I remember you, [4]constantly praying with joy in every one of my prayers for all of you, [5]because of your sharing in the gospel from the first day until now. [6]I am confident of this, that the one who began a good work among you will bring it to completion by the day of Jesus Christ. [7]It is right for me to think this way about all of you, because you hold me in your heart,[d] for all of you share in God's grace[e] with me, both in my imprisonment and in the defense and confirmation of the gospel. [8]For God is my witness, how I long for all of you with the compassion of Christ Jesus. [9]And this is my prayer, that your love may overflow more and more with knowledge and full insight [10]to help you to determine what is best, so that in the day of Christ you may be pure and blameless, [11]having produced the harvest of righteousness that comes through Jesus Christ for the glory and praise of God.

Paul's Present Circumstances

12 I want you to know, beloved,[f] that what has happened to me has actually helped to spread the gospel, [13]so that it has become known

1.7 Paul's Partners

Strong-minded though he was, Paul never worked alone. The warmth in this book comes partly from his confidence that the Philippian Christians were his partners (verse 5), sharing in God's grace. He counted on their prayers (verse 19). At the end of this letter, Paul returns to this theme of partnership, rejoicing in the Philippians' love and thoughtfulness (4.10–19).

throughout the whole imperial guard[g] and to everyone else that my imprisonment is for Christ; [14]and most of the brothers and sisters,[f] having been made confident in the Lord by my imprisonment, dare to speak the word[h] with greater boldness and without fear.

---

[a] Gk *slaves*   [b] Or *overseers*   [c] Or *overseers and helpers*   [d] Or *because I hold you in my heart*   [e] Gk *in grace*
[f] Gk *brothers*   [g] Gk *whole praetorium*   [h] Other ancient authorities read *word of God*

15 Some proclaim Christ from envy and rivalry, but others from goodwill. [16]These proclaim Christ out of love, knowing that I have been put here for the defense of the gospel; [17]the others proclaim Christ out of selfish ambition, not sincerely but intending to increase my suffering in my imprisonment. [18]What does it matter? Just this, that Christ is proclaimed in every way, whether out of false motives or true; and in that I rejoice.

Yes, and I will continue to rejoice, [19]for I know that through your prayers and the help of the Spirit of Jesus Christ this will turn out for my deliverance. [20]It is my eager expectation and hope that I will not be put to shame in any way, but that by my speaking with all boldness, Christ will be exalted now as always in my body, whether by life or by death. [21]For to me, living is Christ and dying is gain. [22]If I am to live in the flesh, that means fruitful labor for me; and I do not know which I prefer. [23]I am hard pressed between the two: my desire is to depart and be with Christ, for that is far better; [24]but to remain in the flesh is more necessary for you. [25]Since I am convinced of this, I know that I will remain and continue with all of you for your progress and joy in faith, [26]so that I may share abundantly in your boasting in Christ Jesus when I come to you again.

27 Only, live your life in a manner worthy of the gospel of Christ, so that, whether I come and see you or am absent and hear about you, I will know that you are standing firm in one spirit, striving side by side with one mind for the faith of the gospel, [28]and are in no way intimidated by your opponents. For them this is evidence of their destruction, but of your salvation. And this is God's doing. [29]For he has graciously granted you the privilege not only of believing in Christ, but of suffering for him as well— [30]since you are having the same struggle that you saw I had and now hear that I still have.

Imitating Christ's Humility

2 If then there is any encouragement in Christ, any consolation from love, any sharing in the Spirit, any compassion and sympathy, [2]make my joy complete: be of the same mind, having the same love, being in full accord and of one mind. [3]Do nothing from selfish ambition or conceit, but in humility regard others as better than yourselves. [4]Let each of you look not to your own interests, but to the interests of others. [5]Let the

Paul's Favorite Church
When others failed, these friends didn't

THE CHRISTIAN CHURCH HASN'T HAD a perfect record throughout history. If you take a random sample of adjectives people use to describe the church, the list will likely include such labels as *racist, judgmental, narrow, divided, pompous.*

The church of Jesus Christ has fallen far short of the ideals he entrusted to it—so far short that we may sometimes forget what the church is supposed to look like. Problems existed from the beginning: Paul's letters to Galatia, Corinth, and Colosse flame with indignation against defects in the early church.

Occasionally, however, a church came along that worked, against all odds. Philippi was one of those rare congregations.

I thank my God every time I remember you. 1.3

Loyal Friends

From its birth, the church in Philippi had two strikes against it. Its first recorded converts were an Asiatic Jewish merchant, a Greek slave girl employed as a sideshow fortune-teller, and a gruff Roman jailer (Acts 16). Yet more than a decade later, when Paul wrote the church, he could hardly find words warm enough to express his pride and affection.

Paul turned down money gifts from other churches, out of fear that his enemies might twist the facts and accuse him of being a crook. But he trusted the Philippians. At least four separate times they sacrificed to meet his needs. And they also sent Epaphroditus on an arduous journey to care for Paul in prison.

Paul wrote Philippians, in fact, mainly as a thank-you for all that his friends had done. Its bright, happy tone reflects the fondness he felt for his favorite church.

Nevertheless, Paul couldn't resist an opportunity to give some fatherly advice. In a fireside-chat tone, he warned of encroaching dangers: divisions, a strain of perfectionism, and inroads by those who wished to turn Christians back to the Jewish faith. Always, though, he returned to his underlying theme of joy, an emotion that seemed to come easily when Paul remembered the Philippians.

Life Questions: What does Paul single out for praise in the Philippian church? How are those qualities present in your church?

same mind be in you that was[i] in Christ Jesus,
6 who, though he was in the form of God,
did not regard equality with God
as something to be exploited,
7 but emptied himself,
taking the form of a slave,
being born in human likeness.
And being found in human form,
8 he humbled himself
and became obedient to the point of
death—
even death on a cross.

9 Therefore God also highly exalted him
and gave him the name
that is above every name,
10 so that at the name of Jesus
every knee should bend,
in heaven and on earth and under the
earth,
11 and every tongue should confess
that Jesus Christ is Lord,
to the glory of God the Father.

Shining as Lights in the World

12 Therefore, my beloved, just as you have always obeyed me, not only in my presence, but much more now in my absence, work out your own salvation with fear and trembling; 13for it is God who is at work in you, enabling you both to will and to work for his good pleasure.

2.12–13 Working with God

Philippians, a practical book, presents theology simply and without elaboration. These verses describe both the human and divine element in our faith: We "work out" our salvation, and yet God "works" in us to accomplish it. Philippians 3.16 expresses a similar paradox: Paul urges that we "hold fast to what we have attained."

14 Do all things without murmuring and arguing, 15so that you may be blameless and innocent, children of God without blemish in the midst of a crooked and perverse generation, in which you shine like stars in the world. 16It is by your holding fast to the word of life that I can boast on the day of Christ that I did not run in vain or labor in vain. 17But even if I am being poured out as a libation over the sacrifice and the offering of your faith, I am glad and rejoice with all of you— 18and in the same way you also must be glad and rejoice with me.

Timothy and Epaphroditus

19 I hope in the Lord Jesus to send Timothy to you soon, so that I may be cheered by news of you. 20I have no one like him who will be genuinely concerned for your welfare. 21All of them are seeking their own interests, not those of Jesus Christ. 22But Timothy's[j] worth you know, how like a son with a father he has served with me in the work of the gospel. 23I hope therefore to send him as soon as I see how things go with me; 24and I trust in the Lord that I will also come soon.

25 Still, I think it necessary to send to you Epaphroditus—my brother and co-worker and fellow soldier, your messenger[k] and minister to

2.25 A Helper for Paul

The paragraph on Epaphroditus reveals the warm feelings between Paul and the church at Philippi. If Paul was imprisoned at Rome, as many scholars believe, then Epaphroditus traveled more than 700 miles to be with him. He fell sick while visiting Paul and was now returning to Philippi, probably carrying this letter to hand-deliver.

my need; 26for he has been longing for[l] all of you, and has been distressed because you heard that he was ill. 27He was indeed so ill that he nearly died. But God had mercy on him, and not only on him but on me also, so that I would not have one sorrow after another. 28I am the more eager to send him, therefore, in order that you may rejoice at seeing him again, and that I may be less anxious. 29Welcome him then in the Lord with all joy, and honor such people, 30because he came close to death for the work of Christ,[m] risking his life to make up for those services that you could not give me.

3 Finally, my brothers and sisters,[n] rejoice[o] in the Lord.

Breaking with the Past

To write the same things to you is not troublesome to me, and for you it is a safeguard.

2 Beware of the dogs, beware of the evil workers, beware of those who mutilate the flesh![p] 3For it is we who are the circumcision, who worship in the Spirit of God[q] and boast in Christ Jesus and have no confidence in the flesh— 4even though I, too, have reason for confidence in the flesh.

If anyone else has reason to be confident in the flesh, I have more: 5circumcised on the eighth day, a member of the people of Israel, of the tribe of Benjamin, a Hebrew born of Hebrews; as to the

---

[i] Or *that you have*   [j] Gk *his*   [k] Gk *apostle*   [l] Other ancient authorities read *longing to see*   [m] Other ancient authorities read *of the Lord*   [n] Gk *my brothers*   [o] Or *farewell*   [p] Gk *the mutilation*   [q] Other ancient authorities read *worship God in spirit*

law, a Pharisee; [6]as to zeal, a persecutor of the church; as to righteousness under the law, blameless.

7 Yet whatever gains I had, these I have come to regard as loss because of Christ. [8]More than that, I regard everything as loss because of the surpassing value of knowing Christ Jesus my Lord. For his sake I have suffered the loss of all things, and I regard them as rubbish, in order that I may gain Christ [9]and be found in him, not having a righteousness of my own that comes from the law, but one that comes through faith in Christ,[r] the righteousness from God based on faith. [10]I want to know Christ[s] and the power of his resurrection and the sharing of his sufferings by becoming like him in his death, [11]if somehow I may attain the resurrection from the dead.

Pressing toward the Goal

12 Not that I have already obtained this or have already reached the goal;[t] but I press on to make it my own, because Christ Jesus has made me his own. [13]Beloved,[u] I do not consider that I have made it my own;[v] but this one thing I do: forgetting what lies behind and straining forward to what lies ahead, [14]I press on toward the goal for the prize of the heavenly[w] call of God in Christ Jesus. [15]Let those of us then who are mature be of the same mind; and if you think differently about anything, this too God will reveal to you. [16]Only let us hold fast to what we have attained.

17 Brothers and sisters,[u] join in imitating me, and observe those who live according to the example you have in us. [18]For many live as enemies of the cross of Christ; I have often told you of them, and now I tell you even with tears. [19]Their end is destruction; their god is the belly; and their glory is in their shame; their minds are set on earthly things. [20]But our citizenship[x] is in heaven, and it is from there that we are expecting a Savior, the Lord Jesus Christ. [21]He will transform the body of our humiliation[y] that it may be conformed to the body of his glory,[z] by the power that also enables him to make all things subject

4 to himself. [1]Therefore, my brothers and sisters,[a] whom I love and long for, my joy and crown, stand firm in the Lord in this way, my beloved.

Exhortations

2 I urge Euodia and I urge Syntyche to be of the same mind in the Lord. [3]Yes, and I ask you also, my loyal companion,[b] help these women, for they have struggled beside me in the work of

the gospel, together with Clement and the rest of my co-workers, whose names are in the book of life.

4 Rejoice[c] in the Lord always; again I will say, Rejoice.[c] [5]Let your gentleness be known to everyone. The Lord is near. [6]Do not worry about anything, but in everything by prayer and supplication with thanksgiving let your requests be

---

4.2 Women in the Church

Although these two women were stirring up trouble in Philippi, women played a positive role in that church. In fact, Paul's first convert in Europe was Lydia, a businesswoman. Paul met with her and a group of women by a river, and later stayed in her house (see Acts 16).

---

made known to God. [7]And the peace of God, which surpasses all understanding, will guard your hearts and your minds in Christ Jesus.

8 Finally, beloved,[d] whatever is true, whatever is honorable, whatever is just, whatever is pure, whatever is pleasing, whatever is commendable, if there is any excellence and if there is anything worthy of praise, think about[e] these things. [9]Keep on doing the things that you have learned and received and heard and seen in me, and the God of peace will be with you.

Acknowledgment of the Philippians' Gift

10 I rejoice[f] in the Lord greatly that now at last you have revived your concern for me; indeed, you were concerned for me, but had no opportunity to show it.[g] [11]Not that I am referring to being in need; for I have learned to be content with whatever I have. [12]I know what it is to have little, and I know what it is to have plenty. In any and all circumstances I have learned the secret of being well-fed and of going hungry, of having

---

4.13 Paul's Secret

Shipwrecked, beaten, imprisoned, Paul had seen the down side of life. He had also known prosperity. Both, he suggests, offer temptations. But Paul had discovered a secret for contentment in all situations: his deeply personal sense of living in Christ. In this he found strength to handle anything.

---

[r] Or *through the faith of Christ* [s] Gk *him* [t] Or *have already been made perfect* [u] Gk *Brothers* [v] Other ancient authorities read *my own yet* [w] Gk *upward* [x] Or *commonwealth* [y] Or *our humble bodies* [z] Or *his glorious body* [a] Gk *my brothers* [b] Or *loyal Syzygus* [c] Or *Farewell* [d] Gk *brothers* [e] Gk *take account of* [f] Gk *I rejoiced* [g] Gk lacks *to show it*

plenty and of being in need. [13]I can do all things through him who strengthens me. [14]In any case, it was kind of you to share my distress.

15 You Philippians indeed know that in the early days of the gospel, when I left Macedonia, no church shared with me in the matter of giving and receiving, except you alone. [16]For even when I was in Thessalonica, you sent me help for my needs more than once. [17]Not that I seek the gift, but I seek the profit that accumulates to your account. [18]I have been paid in full and have more than enough; I am fully satisfied, now that I have received from Epaphroditus the gifts you sent, a fragrant offering, a sacrifice acceptable and pleasing to God. [19]And my God will fully satisfy every need of yours according to his riches in glory in Christ Jesus. [20]To our God and Father be glory forever and ever. Amen.

Final Greetings and Benediction

21 Greet every saint in Christ Jesus. The friends[h] who are with me greet you. [22]All the saints greet you, especially those of the emperor's household.

23 The grace of the Lord Jesus Christ be with your spirit.[i]

---

[h] Gk brothers   [i] Other ancient authorities add Amen

COLOSSIANS

Battling the Cults
For everything worthwhile, there exists a counterfeit

> See to it that no one takes you captive through philosophy and empty deceit.
> 2.8

YOU SEE THEM IN STRANGE outfits on street corners, chanting phrases with too many vowels and punctuating the chants with a noisy tambourine. Or in airports, thrusting books or flowers into your face. Or in California, all over California. You think of them as crazy cults, populated by misfits. Then one day you hear about a friend of yours.

She seemed normal until suddenly, without warning, she snapped. Her parents searched desperately, even hiring private detectives to help get her back. They found her surrounded by allies, with a new name, a new hairstyle, and, so it seemed, a new brain. She stared at them with clear eyes and told them they were missing out on the most wonderful experience of life. She had joined a cult.

A Breeding Ground

Cults come in all varieties, some recent spin-offs from the New Age movement, others sporting exotic names like Hare Krishna or the Church of Scientology. They demand much from their members: a lifetime of discipline and absolute loyalty. And they also promise much in return: the pathway to a secret, hidden knowledge available only to those who follow them.

The first-century town of Colosse was a perfect breeding ground for cults. Situated on a major trade route from the East, Colosse entertained a steady stream of Oriental traders with mysterious religious ideas. Even Jews in that area worshiped angels and river spirits.

Early Christian converts soon confronted new variations of the gospel. Then, as now, many cults didn't reject Jesus Christ outright; they merely worked him into a more elaborate scheme. Christ and simple forms of worship, they taught, were fine for beginners, but for the "depths of God," well, some further steps would be required.

The Best Defense

Paul doesn't give a complete glossary of the "philosophy and empty deceit" the Colossians were sorting through. From his arguments, we can gather that the philosophy must have included strains of Jewish legalism mixed in with angel worship, Greek philosophy, and strict self-denial.

The best defense is a good offense. Rather than attacking each peculiar belief point by point, Paul countered with a positive theology. The principles he outlines in this book can be used today to judge new cults.

"Christ is enough," Paul declares. He is God, the fullness of God, the One who made the world, the reason that everything exists. All the mystery and treasure and wisdom you could ask for are found in the person of Jesus Christ; there is no need to look elsewhere.

Approach God Directly

Because Jesus bridged the chasm between God and us, we don't have to approach God indirectly, through a ladder of angels or other gods. We have no need to prove our worth through superior behavior. We can come to God directly and boldly because of Christ.

As for Jewish practices, they were mere shadows, made obsolete by Christ's coming. Why not concentrate on the actual image that God sent to earth?

Before Christ, Paul grants, a mystery was kept hidden for many centuries (1.26). But with Christ, everything broke out into the open. The fullness of God lived, died, and came back from death in broad daylight. Why settle for counterfeits?

How to Read Colossians

Although this letter was written to counter specific problems in the church at Colosse, it includes some of Paul's most eloquent writing about Jesus Christ. Chapter 1 contains a soaring paragraph (1.15–20) that may have been used as a hymn by the early church. Note in this book how Paul concludes all his arguments by referring to Christ.

Chapters 2 and 3 deal with dangerous tendencies in Colosse. Paul argues against a "mystery" religion by firmly asserting that Christ is the complete expression of the mystery of God. As you read these two chapters, try to imagine what kind of behavior at Colosse troubled Paul.

3-TRACK READING PLAN

For an explanation and complete listing of the 3-track reading plan, turn to page 7.

TRACK 1: **Two-Week Courses on the Bible**
See page 7 for information on these courses.

TRACK 2: **An Overview of Colossians in 1 Day**
☐ Day 1. Read the Introduction to Colossians, then chapter 1, noting especially Paul's prayer, which precedes the hymnlike paragraph (verses 15–20).

Now turn to page 9 for your next Track 2 reading project.

TRACK 3: **All of Colossians in 4 Days**
After you have read through Colossians, turn to pages 10–14 for your next Track 3 reading project.
☐1   ☐2   ☐3   ☐4

Salutation

1 Paul, an apostle of Christ Jesus by the will of God, and Timothy our brother,

2 To the saints and faithful brothers and sisters*a* in Christ in Colossae:

Grace to you and peace from God our Father.

Paul Thanks God for the Colossians

3 In our prayers for you we always thank God, the Father of our Lord Jesus Christ, 4for we have heard of your faith in Christ Jesus and of the love that you have for all the saints, 5because of the hope laid up for you in heaven. You have heard of this hope before in the word of the truth, the gospel 6that has come to you. Just as it is bearing fruit and growing in the whole world, so it has been bearing fruit among yourselves from the day you heard it and truly comprehended the grace of God. 7This you learned from Epaphras, our beloved fellow servant.*b* He is a faithful minister of Christ on your*c* behalf, 8and he has made known to us your love in the Spirit.

9 For this reason, since the day we heard it, we have not ceased praying for you and asking that you may be filled with the knowledge of God's*d* will in all spiritual wisdom and understanding, 10so that you may lead lives worthy of the Lord, fully pleasing to him, as you bear fruit in every good work and as you grow in the knowledge of God. 11May you be made strong with all the strength that comes from his glorious power, and may you be prepared to endure everything with patience, while joyfully 12giving thanks to the Father, who has enabled*e* you*f* to share in the inheritance of the saints in the light. 13He has rescued us from the power of darkness and transferred us into the kingdom of his beloved Son, 14in whom we have redemption, the forgiveness of sins.*g*

The Supremacy of Christ

15 He is the image of the invisible God, the firstborn of all creation; 16for in*h* him all things in heaven and on earth were created, things visible and invisible, whether thrones or dominions or rulers or powers—all things have been created through him and for him. 17He himself is before all things, and in*h* him all things hold together. 18He is the head of the body, the church; he is the beginning, the firstborn from the dead, so that he might come to have first place in everything. 19For in him all the fullness of God was pleased to dwell, 20and through him God was pleased to reconcile to himself all things, whether on earth or in

---

a Gk *brothers*   *b* Gk *slave*   *c* Other ancient authorities read *our*   *d* Gk *his*   *e* Other ancient authorities read
called   *f* Other ancient authorities read *us*   *g* Other ancient authorities add *through his blood*   *h* Or *by*

heaven, by making peace through the blood of his cross.

21 And you who were once estranged and hostile in mind, doing evil deeds, [22]he has now

---

1.21 Getting Practical

Although Paul's letters often launch out into theological deep water, they always lead back to practical issues: What difference does theology make to daily life? The preceding paragraph (verses 15–20) contains a compressed summary of the absolute supremacy of Christ. Now Paul turns to the practical: Christ's supreme power does not distance us from but rather brings us closer to God. He alone has the ability to span the vast gap between God and humanity.

---

reconciled[i] in his fleshly body[j] through death, so as to present you holy and blameless and irreproachable before him— [23]provided that you continue securely established and steadfast in the faith, without shifting from the hope promised by the gospel that you heard, which has been proclaimed to every creature under heaven. I, Paul, became a servant of this gospel.

Paul's Interest in the Colossians

24 I am now rejoicing in my sufferings for your sake, and in my flesh I am completing what is lacking in Christ's afflictions for the sake of his body, that is, the church. [25]I became its servant according to God's commission that was given to me for you, to make the word of God fully known, [26]the mystery that has been hidden throughout the ages and generations but has now been revealed to his saints. [27]To them God chose to make known how great among the Gentiles are the riches of the glory of this mystery, which is Christ in you, the hope of glory. [28]It is he whom we proclaim, warning everyone and teaching everyone in all wisdom, so that we may present everyone mature in Christ. [29]For this I toil and struggle with all the energy that he powerfully inspires within me.

2 For I want you to know how much I am struggling for you, and for those in Laodicea, and for all who have not seen me face to face. [2]I want their hearts to be encouraged and united in love, so that they may have all the riches of assured understanding and have the knowledge of God's mystery, that is, Christ himself,[k] [3]in whom are hidden all the treasures of wisdom and knowledge. [4]I am saying this so that no one may deceive

you with plausible arguments. [5]For though I am absent in body, yet I am with you in spirit, and I rejoice to see your morale and the firmness of your faith in Christ.

Fullness of Life in Christ

6 As you therefore have received Christ Jesus the Lord, continue to live your lives[l] in him, [7]rooted and built up in him and established in the faith, just as you were taught, abounding in thanksgiving.

8 See to it that no one takes you captive through philosophy and empty deceit, according to human tradition, according to the elemental spirits of the universe,[m] and not according to Christ. [9]For in him the whole fullness of deity dwells bodily, [10]and you have come to fullness in him, who is the head of every ruler and authority. [11]In him also you were circumcised with a spiritual circumcision,[n] by putting off the body of the flesh in the circumcision of Christ; [12]when you were buried with him in baptism, you were also raised with him through faith in the power of God, who raised him from the dead. [13]And when you were dead in trespasses and the uncircumcision of your flesh, God[o] made you[p] alive together with him, when he forgave us all our trespasses, [14]erasing the record that stood against us with its legal demands. He set this aside, nailing it to the cross. [15]He disarmed[q] the rulers and authorities and made a public example of them, triumphing over them in it.

16 Therefore do not let anyone condemn you in matters of food and drink or of observing festivals, new moons, or sabbaths. [17]These are only a shadow of what is to come, but the substance

---

2.16 The Search for Wholeness

Legalism in Paul's day concerned such issues as diet, festival days, and religious ceremony. In these two paragraphs, Paul tells why such rules that appear "spiritual" can actually lead a person away from God. Then, in chapter 3, he details what holy living should look like.

In his letter, Paul portrays the Christian life very optimistically. The Christians in Colosse were searching for "fullness" in the same way modern people work to become "holistic" or "self-actualized." After first affirming that Jesus contains all the fullness of God, Paul asserts that true fullness is found only in Christ (verse 10).

---

[i] Other ancient authorities read *you have now been reconciled* [j] Gk *in the body of his flesh* [k] Other ancient authorities read *of the mystery of God, both of the Father and of Christ* [l] Gk *to walk* [m] Or *the rudiments* of the world [n] Gk *a circumcision made without hands* [o] Gk *he* [p] Other ancient authorities read *made us;* others, *made* [q] Or *divested himself of*

belongs to Christ. [18]Do not let anyone disqualify you, insisting on self-abasement and worship of angels, dwelling[r] on visions,[s] puffed up without cause by a human way of thinking,[t] [19]and not holding fast to the head, from whom the whole body, nourished and held together by its ligaments and sinews, grows with a growth that is from God.

Warnings against False Teachers

20 If with Christ you died to the elemental spirits of the universe,[u] why do you live as if you still belonged to the world? Why do you submit to regulations, [21]"Do not handle, Do not taste, Do not touch"? [22]All these regulations refer to things that perish with use; they are simply human commands and teachings. [23]These have indeed an appearance of wisdom in promoting self-imposed piety, humility, and severe treatment of the body, but they are of no value in checking self-indulgence.[v]

The New Life in Christ

3 So if you have been raised with Christ, seek the things that are above, where Christ is,

3.1 Familiar Words

If Colossians strikes you as vaguely familiar, don't be surprised. Paul's letters tend to follow a pattern: a greeting, a prayer, some doctrine, and a practical application of how we should live. Colossians sounds especially familiar because many of its verses have close parallels in Ephesians. In fact, of Ephesians's 155 verses, 78 appear in some form in Colossians.

seated at the right hand of God. [2]Set your minds on things that are above, not on things that are on earth, [3]for you have died, and your life is hidden with Christ in God. [4]When Christ who is your[w] life is revealed, then you also will be revealed with him in glory.

5 Put to death, therefore, whatever in you is earthly: fornication, impurity, passion, evil desire, and greed (which is idolatry). [6]On account of these the wrath of God is coming on those who are disobedient.[x] [7]These are the ways you also once followed, when you were living that life.[y] [8]But now you must get rid of all such things— anger, wrath, malice, slander, and abusive[z] language from your mouth. [9]Do not lie to one another, seeing that you have stripped off the old

self with its practices [10]and have clothed yourselves with the new self, which is being renewed in knowledge according to the image of its creator. [11]In that renewal[a] there is no longer Greek and Jew, circumcised and uncircumcised, barbarian, Scythian, slave and free; but Christ is all and in all!

3.11 The Original Barbarians

The word "barbarians" meant those who did not speak Greek. To civilized people of that day, their languages sounded like a stammering repetition of the same syllables— barbarbarbar—hence the word barbarian. Scythians were likewise considered uncivilized and brutish. By mentioning such people, Paul was underscoring the all-encompassing breadth of God's grace.

12 As God's chosen ones, holy and beloved, clothe yourselves with compassion, kindness, humility, meekness, and patience. [13]Bear with one another and, if anyone has a complaint against another, forgive each other; just as the Lord[b] has forgiven you, so you also must forgive. [14]Above all, clothe yourselves with love, which binds everything together in perfect harmony. [15]And let the peace of Christ rule in your hearts, to which indeed you were called in the one body. And be thankful. [16]Let the word of Christ[c] dwell in you richly; teach and admonish one another in all wisdom; and with gratitude in your hearts sing psalms, hymns, and spiritual songs to God.[d] [17]And whatever you do, in word or deed, do everything in the name of the Lord Jesus, giving thanks to God the Father through him.

Rules for Christian Households

18 Wives, be subject to your husbands, as is fitting in the Lord. [19]Husbands, love your wives and never treat them harshly.

20 Children, obey your parents in everything, for this is your acceptable duty in the Lord. [21]Fathers, do not provoke your children, or they may lose heart. [22]Slaves, obey your earthly masters[e] in everything, not only while being watched and in order to please them, but wholeheartedly, fearing the Lord.[e] [23]Whatever your task, put yourselves into it, as done for the Lord and not for your masters,[f] [24]since you know that from the Lord you will receive the inheritance as your reward; you serve[g] the Lord Christ. [25]For the wrongdoer will be paid back for whatever wrong has been

r Other ancient authorities read *not dwelling*   s Meaning of Gk uncertain   t Gk *by the mind of his flesh*
u Or *the rudiments of the world*   v Or *are of no value, serving only to indulge the flesh*   w Other authorities read *our*
x Other ancient authorities lack *on those who are disobedient* (Gk *the children of disobedience*)   y Or *living among such people*   z Or *filthy*   a Gk *its creator,* [11]*where*   b Other ancient authorities read *just as Christ*   c Other ancient authorities read *of God,* or *of the Lord*   d Other ancient authorities read *to the Lord*   e In Greek the same word is used for *master* and *Lord*   f Gk *not for men*   g Or *you are slaves of,* or *be slaves of*

4 done, and there is no partiality. [1]Masters, treat your slaves justly and fairly, for you know that you also have a Master in heaven.

Further Instructions

2 Devote yourselves to prayer, keeping alert in it with thanksgiving. [3]At the same time pray for us as well that God will open to us a door for the word, that we may declare the mystery of Christ, for which I am in prison, [4]so that I may reveal it clearly, as I should.

5 Conduct yourselves wisely toward outsiders, making the most of the time.[h] [6]Let your speech always be gracious, seasoned with salt, so that you may know how you ought to answer everyone.

Final Greetings and Benediction

7 Tychicus will tell you all the news about me; he is a beloved brother, a faithful minister, and a fellow servant[i] in the Lord. [8]I have sent him to you for this very purpose, so that you may know how we are[j] and that he may encourage your hearts; [9]he is coming with Onesimus, the faithful and beloved brother, who is one of you. They will tell you about everything here.

10 Aristarchus my fellow prisoner greets you, as does Mark the cousin of Barnabas, concerning whom you have received instructions—if he comes to you, welcome him. [11]And Jesus who is called Justus greets you. These are the only ones of the circumcision among my co-workers for the kingdom of God, and they have been a comfort to me. [12]Epaphras, who is one of you, a servant[i] of Christ Jesus, greets you. He is always wrestling in his prayers on your behalf, so that you may stand mature and fully assured in everything that God wills. [13]For I testify for him that he has worked

4.12 Prominent Names

Characteristically, Paul ended his letters with personal messages. Epaphras, who is mentioned twice in Colossians (1.7; 4.12), served with Paul and may have founded the church there. The short book of Philemon (verse 23) mentions him as a fellow prisoner with Paul. The main characters in that book, Philemon and his slave Onesimus, also came from Colosse, and Paul refers to a hoped-for visit to Colosse in his letter to Philemon (verse 22).

hard for you and for those in Laodicea and in Hierapolis. [14]Luke, the beloved physician, and Demas greet you. [15]Give my greetings to the brothers and sisters[k] in Laodicea, and to Nympha and the church in her house. [16]And when this letter has been read among you, have it read also in the church of the Laodiceans; and see that you read also the letter from Laodicea. [17]And say to Archippus, "See that you complete the task that you have received in the Lord."

18 I, Paul, write this greeting with my own hand. Remember my chains. Grace be with you.[l]

---

1 THESSALONIANS

What Made Paul Successful?
The apostle fusses over the city that once chased him away

A MODERN-DAY EVANGELIST LAMENTED, "WHENEVER THE apostle Paul visited a city, the residents started a riot; when I visit one, they serve tea." The church in Thessalonica, like many of Paul's churches, was born amid violent upheaval. An angry mob took offense at Paul's work and chased him out of town, accusing him of "turning the world upside down" (Acts 17.6).

Generally, people do not start riots without a good reason, and in Paul's case they had one. Almost everywhere he visited, an enthusiastic church came to life, provoking the jealousy of the Jewish and Roman establishments.

> How can we thank God enough for you in return for all the joy that we feel before our God because of you? 3.9

A Concerned Parent

This letter, 1 Thessalonians, gives important clues into what made Paul so effective at founding churches. Accepted as one of the earliest of Paul's letters, it probably dates from A.D. 50 or 51 and provides a firsthand account of Paul's relationship with a missionary church barely 20 years after Jesus' departure.

Someone once asked John and Charles Wesley's mother which of her ten surviving children she loved the most. She replied, "The one who is sick until he's well, and the one who's away from home until he's back." If someone had asked Paul which church concerned him most, he probably would have answered, "The one with the most problems until it's healthy, the one I've been separated from longest until I return."

When Paul lived with the Thessalonians, he was gentle and loving, "like a nurse tenderly caring for her own children" (2.7). Later, absent from them, he wrote as if he had only them on his mind all day. In 1 Thessalonians, he praised their strengths, fussed over reports of their weaknesses, and continually thanked God for their spiritual progress.

Questioning Paul's Motives

Some people in the church had questioned Paul's motives, so he opened the letter with a careful review of his work among them. In those days free-lance teachers of religion and philosophy sought a profit; Paul reminded the Thessalonians that he had worked night and day to avoid becoming a financial burden. He also painstakingly explained his unavoidable absence from them.

First Thessalonians stands out from the four books that precede it because, unlike them, this letter doesn't major in theology. Rather, it reveals the gratitude, disappointment, and joy of a beloved missionary who can't stop thinking about the church he left behind. Surely one reason for Paul's success centers on his churches' having made as big an impression on Paul as he made on them.

How to Read 1 Thessalonians

This book provides a touching glimpse of Paul as a pastor. Paul visited Thessalonica at a troubled time in his ministry, while enemies were tailing him from town to town (see Acts 16–17). After he left, the church continued to meet hostility.

First Thessalonians is our earliest record of the life of a Christian community. Paul wrote this letter after receiving a mostly positive report (from Timothy) on the Thessalonians' spiritual health. He rejoiced at the good news, but also showed concern over the church's problems.

As you read 1 Thessalonians, notice the issues that Paul addresses: Christians were raising questions about Jesus' return to earth and were disagreeing on matters of morality. But mainly, look for signs of Paul's relationship to the church at Thessalonica.

3-TRACK READING PLAN

For an explanation and complete listing of the 3-track reading plan, turn to page 7.

TRACK 1: *Two-Week Courses on the Bible*
See page 7 for information on these courses.

TRACK 2: *An Overview of 1 Thessalonians in 1 Day*
☐ Day 1. Read the Introduction to 1 Thessalonians, then chapters 3 and 4. The chapters are very short, so you can easily read two together.

Now turn to page 9 for your next Track 2 reading project.

TRACK 3: *All of 1 Thessalonians in 3 Days*
After you have read through 1 Thessalonians, turn to pages 10–14 for your next Track 3 reading project.
☐1–2   ☐3–4   ☐5

Salutation

1 Paul, Silvanus, and Timothy,
To the church of the Thessalonians in God the Father and the Lord Jesus Christ:
Grace to you and peace.

The Thessalonians' Faith and Example

2 We always give thanks to God for all of you and mention you in our prayers, constantly [3]remembering before our God and Father your work of faith and labor of love and steadfastness of hope in our Lord Jesus Christ. [4]For we know, brothers and sisters[a] beloved by God, that he has chosen you, [5]because our message of the gospel came to you not in word only, but also in power and in the Holy Spirit and with full conviction; just as you know what kind of persons we proved to be among you for your sake. [6]And you became imitators of us and of the Lord, for in spite of persecution you received the word with joy inspired by the Holy Spirit, [7]so that you became an example to all the believers in Macedonia and in Achaia. [8]For the word of the Lord has sounded forth from you not only in Macedonia and Achaia, but in every place your faith in God has become known, so that we have no need to speak about it. [9]For the people of those regions[b] report about us what kind of welcome we had among you, and how you turned to God from idols, to serve a living and true God, [10]and to wait for his Son from heaven, whom he raised from the dead—Jesus, who rescues us from the wrath that is coming.

Paul's Ministry in Thessalonica

2 You yourselves know, brothers and sisters,[a] that our coming to you was not in vain, [2]but though we had already suffered and been shamefully mistreated at Philippi, as you know, we had courage in our God to declare to you the gospel of God in spite of great opposition. [3]For our appeal does not spring from deceit or impure motives or trickery, [4]but just as we have been approved by God to be entrusted with the message of the gospel, even so we speak, not to please mortals, but to please God who tests our hearts. [5]As you know and as God is our witness, we never came with words of flattery or with a pretext for greed; [6]nor did we seek praise from mortals, whether from you or from others, [7]though we might have made demands as apostles of Christ. But we were gentle[c] among you, like a nurse tenderly caring for her own children. [8]So deeply do we care for you that we are determined to share with you not only the gospel of God but also our own selves, because you have become very dear to us.

9 You remember our labor and toil, brothers and sisters;[a] we worked night and day, so that we might not burden any of you while we proclaimed to you the gospel of God. [10]You are witnesses, and God also, how pure, upright, and blameless our conduct was toward you believers. [11]As you know, we dealt with each one of you like a father with his children, [12]urging and encouraging you and pleading that you lead a life worthy of God, who calls you into his own kingdom and glory.

a Gk *brothers*   *b* Gk *For they*   *c* Other ancient authorities read *infants*

13 We also constantly give thanks to God for this, that when you received the word of God that you heard from us, you accepted it not as a human word but as what it really is, God's word, which is also at work in you believers. ¹⁴For you,

2.9 Working for a Living

Paul supported his own ministry with a trade (tentmaking) rather than take funds from others. He did this to avoid suspicion that he was profiting financially from his spiritual work. With the Thessalonians, his hard work gave another advantage: It set a good example for those who were quitting their jobs in anticipation of Christ's return to earth.

brothers and sisters,ᵈ became imitators of the churches of God in Christ Jesus that are in Judea, for you suffered the same things from your own compatriots as they did from the Jews, ¹⁵who killed both the Lord Jesus and the prophets,ᵉ and drove us out; they displease God and oppose everyone ¹⁶by hindering us from speaking to the Gentiles so that they may be saved. Thus they have constantly been filling up the measure of their sins; but God's wrath has overtaken them at last.ᶠ

Paul's Desire to Visit the Thessalonians Again

17 As for us, brothers and sisters,ᵈ when, for a short time, we were made orphans by being separated from you—in person, not in heart—we longed with great eagerness to see you face to face. ¹⁸For we wanted to come to you—certainly I, Paul, wanted to again and again—but Satan blocked our way. ¹⁹For what is our hope or joy or crown of boasting before our Lord Jesus at his coming? Is it not you? ²⁰Yes, you are our glory and joy!

3 Therefore when we could bear it no longer, we decided to be left alone in Athens; ²and we sent Timothy, our brother and co-worker for God in proclaimingᵍ the gospel of Christ, to

3.4 Paul Defends His Actions

First Thessalonians indicates some people had questioned Paul's true motives regarding their church. Throughout his ministry, Paul endured constant criticism and personal attacks. Here he replies by reviewing his history with the church. This section (2.17–3.10) details Paul's foiled attempts at a personal visit and then his sending Timothy as a messenger.

strengthen and encourage you for the sake of your faith, ³so that no one would be shaken by these persecutions. Indeed, you yourselves know that this is what we are destined for. ⁴In fact, when we were with you, we told you beforehand that we were to suffer persecution; so it turned out, as you know. ⁵For this reason, when I could bear it no longer, I sent to find out about your faith; I was afraid that somehow the tempter had tempted you and that our labor had been in vain.

Timothy's Encouraging Report

6 But Timothy has just now come to us from you, and has brought us the good news of your faith and love. He has told us also that you always remember us kindly and long to see us—just as we long to see you. ⁷For this reason, brothers and sisters,ᵈ during all our distress and persecution we have been encouraged about you through your faith. ⁸For we now live, if you continue to stand firm in the Lord. ⁹How can we thank God enough for you in return for all the joy that we feel before our God because of you? ¹⁰Night and day we pray most earnestly that we may see you face to face and restore whatever is lacking in your faith.

11 Now may our God and Father himself and our Lord Jesus direct our way to you. ¹²And may the Lord make you increase and abound in love for one another and for all, just as we abound in love for you. ¹³And may he so strengthen your hearts in holiness that you may be blameless before our God and Father at the coming of our Lord Jesus with all his saints.

A Life Pleasing to God

4 Finally, brothers and sisters,ᵈ we ask and urge you in the Lord Jesus that, as you learned from us how you ought to live and to please God (as, in fact, you are doing), you should do so more and more. ²For you know what instructions we gave you through the Lord Jesus. ³For this is the will of God, your sanctification: that you abstain from fornication; ⁴that each one of you know how to control your own bodyʰ in holiness and honor, ⁵not with lustful passion, like the Gentiles who do not know God; ⁶that no one wrong or exploit a brother or sisterⁱ in this matter, because the Lord is an avenger in all these things, just as we have already told you beforehand and solemnly warned you. ⁷For God did not call us to impurity but in holiness. ⁸Therefore whoever rejects this rejects not human authority but God, who also gives his Holy Spirit to you.

9 Now concerning love of the brothers and sisters,ᵈ you do not need to have anyone write to you, for you yourselves have been taught by God to love one another; ¹⁰and indeed you do love all

---

ᵈ Gk *brothers*   ᵉ Other ancient authorities read *their own prophets*   ᶠ Or *completely* or *forever*
ᵍ Gk lacks *proclaiming*   ʰ Or *how to take a wife for himself*   ⁱ Gk *brother*

the brothers and sisters[j] throughout Macedonia. But we urge you, beloved,[j] to do so more and more, [11]to aspire to live quietly, to mind your own affairs, and to work with your hands, as we directed you, [12]so that you may behave properly toward outsiders and be dependent on no one.

The Coming of the Lord

13 But we do not want you to be uninformed, brothers and sisters,[j] about those who have died,[k] so that you may not grieve as others do who have no hope. [14]For since we believe that Jesus died and rose again, even so, through Jesus, God will bring with him those who have died.[k] [15]For this we declare to you by the word of the Lord, that we who are alive, who are left until the coming of the Lord, will by no means precede those who have died.[k] [16]For the Lord himself, with a cry of command, with the archangel's call and with the sound of God's trumpet, will descend from heaven, and the dead in Christ will rise first. [17]Then we who are alive, who are left, will be caught up in the clouds together with them to meet the Lord in the air; and so we will be with the Lord forever. [18]Therefore encourage one another with these words.

5 Now concerning the times and the seasons, brothers and sisters,[j] you do not need to have anything written to you. [2]For you yourselves know very well that the day of the Lord will come like a thief in the night. [3]When they say, "There is peace and security," then sudden destruction

---

[j] Gk brothers   [k] Gk fallen asleep

Preparing for the End
Obsessed with Jesus' second coming

YOU SEE THEM OCCASIONALLY ON the street corners of modern cities: strange–looking people with hand-lettered wooden signs draped over their bodies. "Jesus is coming again!" they proclaim. "Prepare to meet thy doom!" Similar messages are scrawled on rocks or on highway overpasses. And every few years a new prophet comes along suggesting a new, revised date for Jesus' return.

> Now concerning the times and the seasons, brothers and sisters, you do not need to have anything written to you. 5.1

Archaeologists have yet to unearth Thessalonican graffiti, but this letter makes clear that 19 centuries ago people were already awaiting Jesus' promised return to earth. In fact, they were worried. What about people who died before Jesus returned? they wondered. Would they somehow miss out on life after death? Paul gives a direct and encouraging answer.

A Mixture of Fear and Hope

The Thessalonians had good reason to concern themselves with the future: They lived in constant danger of persecution by the authorities. On any night a knock on the door or the scrape of footsteps outside could mean imprisonment or death. Understandably, the young church looked to Jesus' second coming with longing and hope.

Paul assured them that hope in the future was well-founded, whether or not they lived to see Jesus' return. But he warned against an undue fixation on the future. He urged the Thessalonians to get back to work, indicating that some enthusiasts had quit their jobs to prepare for Jesus' return. Lead a quiet life and mind your own business, Paul advised (4.11).

Waiting for Jesus' Return

The Thessalonians were merely the first in a long line of Christians obsessed with future events. Whole generations since have been caught up in frenzied speculations on the exact time and place of the second coming, only to watch their predictions misfire. Paul shrugs off such speculation (5.1–2). He presents the right way and the wrong way to prepare for Jesus' return.

Paul does not show undue alarm. The mild tone of his rebukes indicates his confidence in the Thessalonians. He asks that they follow God "more and more," as in fact they are already doing (4.1,10; 5.11).

History records that the first readers of this letter responded well. Despite lurking problems (4.3–12), the church in Thessalonica continued to show vigor and health for many years. Christians there stayed so faithful throughout persecutions that their city became known as "The City of Orthodoxy."

Life Questions: How should Jesus' second coming affect us and how can we prepare for it? What extremes does Paul warn against?

will come upon them, as labor pains come upon a pregnant woman, and there will be no escape! [4]But you, beloved,[l] are not in darkness, for that day to surprise you like a thief; [5]for you are all

4.13 The Sleep of Death

The Bible sometimes uses the word asleep to describe people who have died. In this context, Paul was answering a question the Thessalonians had asked. What of people who died before Christ's second coming—would they be left behind? Paul assures them that all people in Christ would have an afterlife with him—not just those still alive when he returned.

children of light and children of the day; we are not of the night or of darkness. [6]So then let us not fall asleep as others do, but let us keep awake and be sober; [7]for those who sleep sleep at night, and those who are drunk get drunk at night. [8]But since we belong to the day, let us be sober, and put on the breastplate of faith and love, and for a helmet the hope of salvation. [9]For God has destined us not for wrath but for obtaining salvation through our Lord Jesus Christ, [10]who died for us, so that whether we are awake or asleep we may live with him. [11]Therefore encourage one another and build up each other, as indeed you are doing.

Final Exhortations, Greetings, and Benediction

[12] But we appeal to you, brothers and sisters,[l] to respect those who labor among you, and have charge of you in the Lord and admonish you; [13]esteem them very highly in love because of their work. Be at peace among yourselves. [14]And we urge you, beloved,[l] to admonish the idlers, encourage the fainthearted, help the weak, be patient with all of them. [15]See that none of you repays evil for evil, but always seek to do good to one another and to all. [16]Rejoice always, [17]pray without ceasing, [18]give thanks in all circumstances; for this is the will of God in Christ Jesus for you. [19]Do not quench the Spirit. [20]Do not despise the words of prophets,[m] [21]but test everything; hold fast to what is good; [22]abstain from every form of evil.

[23] May the God of peace himself sanctify you entirely; and may your spirit and soul and body be kept sound[n] and blameless at the coming of our Lord Jesus Christ. [24]The one who calls you is faithful, and he will do this.

[25] Beloved,[o] pray for us.

[26] Greet all the brothers and sisters[l] with a holy kiss. [27]I solemnly command you by the Lord that this letter be read to all of them.[p]

[28] The grace of our Lord Jesus Christ be with you.[q]

---

[l] Gk *brothers*   [m] Gk *despise prophecies*   [n] Or *complete*   [o] Gk *Brothers*   [p] Gk *to all the brothers*
[q] Other ancient authorities add *Amen*

2 THESSALONIANS

A Patient Who Didn't Follow Orders
When good advice goes ignored

> Brothers and sisters, do not be weary in doing what is right.
> 3.13

H IS LIGHT HUMOR AND CASUAL manner are gone now. When he was setting the bone, the doctor joked about the benefits of your wearing your arm in a sling every day: instant sympathy from your friends, an opportunity for wild stories on how you got hurt, an easy alibi to avoid heavy work.

But now, three weeks later, lines of concern crease his forehead as he studies the X-rays and notes the slow progress of healing. "I told you to take it easy! Are you giving that arm any rest at all? You can't expect new bone to grow overnight, you know."

When you describe the throbbing pain of the last few days, he grimaces, shakes his head, and scribbles something on a prescription pad. "You shouldn't be feeling pain at this stage," he grumbles. "If you had followed my advice from the beginning you wouldn't need these pills." He then repeats all the instructions he gave you on the first visit, using stronger, less friendly words.

Same Advice, Sterner Words

The book of 2 Thessalonians resembles such a follow-up visit to a family doctor. If you list the topics Paul covers, you will find an uncanny similarity to the subjects of his first letter: Jesus' second coming, spiritual growth, idleness among certain nonworkers . However, a sterner, more formal approach replaces the warm tenderness of the first letter.

Obviously, the Thessalonians failed to listen well the first time. Paul wrote this second letter just a few months later, summarizing his message this way: "So then, brothers and sisters, stand firm and hold fast to the traditions that you were taught by us, either by word of mouth or by our letter" (2.15). Instead of coaxing, Paul now commands.

Squelching a Rumor

One topic, Jesus' return, dominates 2 Thessalonians more than any other. Church members were stirred up by a false report, allegedly from Paul, claiming the last days had already arrived (2.2). Paul denies the report and outlines several events that must occur before the day of the Lord arrives.

Here, as elsewhere, the Bible does not focus on the last days in an abstract, theoretical way. Rather, it draws a practical application to how we should live. Paul cautions his readers to be patient and steady. He asks them to trust that Jesus' return will finally bring justice to the earth, urges them to live worthily for that day, and commands them not to tolerate idleness—a prescription for health that has equal potency today.

How to Read 2 Thessalonians

S econd Thessalonians has many parallels to its companion letter. The Christians in Thessalonica were still struggling with major problems, and each of the three chapters of this book concerns one of them.

Chapter 1 gives encouragement to Christians who were undergoing persecution for their faith. Chapter 2 attacks head-on the false teaching about the day of the Lord. Rumors about the day of the Lord had caused great excitement and speculation, leading to the practical errors Paul addresses in chapter 3.

Paul's specific words about what must happen before the day of the Lord make this letter a key part of New Testament prophecy. The prophecy passages aren't self-explanatory, and may require a Bible reference book for understanding.

Although 2 Thessalonians is Paul's shortest letter to a church, it contains four of his prayers. Note especially his concern for the Thessalonians as expressed in the prayers.

3-TRACK READING PLAN

For an explanation and complete listing of the 3-track reading plan, turn to page 7.

TRACK 1: **Two-Week Courses on the Bible**
See page 7 for information on these courses.

TRACK 2: **An Overview of 2 Thessalonians in 1 Day**
☐ Day 1. Read the Introduction to 2 Thessalonians, then chapter 2, the key chapter predicting what events will precede Jesus' return.

Now turn to page 9 for your next Track 2 reading project.

TRACK 3: **All of 2 Thessalonians in 2 Days**
After you have read through 2 Thessalonians, turn to pages 10–14 for your next Track 3 reading project.
☐1–2   ☐3

Salutation

1 Paul, Silvanus, and Timothy,
To the church of the Thessalonians in God our Father and the Lord Jesus Christ:
2 Grace to you and peace from God our[a] Father and the Lord Jesus Christ.

Thanksgiving

3 We must always give thanks to God for you, brothers and sisters,[b] as is right, because your faith is growing abundantly, and the love of everyone of you for one another is increasing. [4]Therefore we ourselves boast of you among the churches of God for your steadfastness and faith during all your persecutions and the afflictions that you are enduring.

The Judgment at Christ's Coming

5 This is evidence of the righteous judgment of God, and is intended to make you worthy of the kingdom of God, for which you are also suffering. [6]For it is indeed just of God to repay with affliction those who afflict you, [7]and to give relief to the afflicted as well as to us, when the Lord Jesus is revealed from heaven with his mighty angels [8]in flaming fire, inflicting vengeance on those who do not know God and on those who do not obey the gospel of our Lord Jesus. [9]These will suffer the punishment of eternal destruction, separated from the presence of the Lord and from the glory of his might, [10]when he comes to be glorified by his saints and to be marveled at on that day among all who have believed, because our testimony to you was believed. [11]To this end we always pray for you, asking that our God will make you worthy of his call and will fulfill by his power every good resolve and work of faith, [12]so that the name of our Lord Jesus may be glorified in you, and you in him, according to the grace of our God and the Lord Jesus Christ.

The Man of Lawlessness

2 As to the coming of our Lord Jesus Christ and our being gathered together to him, we beg you, brothers and sisters,[b] [2]not to be quickly shaken in mind or alarmed, either by spirit or by word or by letter, as though from us, to the effect that the day of the Lord is already here. [3]Let no one deceive you in any way; for that day will not come unless the rebellion comes first and the lawless one[c] is revealed, the one destined for destruction.[d] [4]He opposes and exalts himself above every so-called god or object of worship, so that

1.6 Is Life Unfair?

This question bothers nearly everyone who gets persecuted or who sees someone profit from wrongdoing. Paul's answer would likely be, "Yes, but only temporarily." He had the firm conviction that one day God would indeed turn the tables on the unfairness of life.

---

a Other ancient authorities read *the man of sin*   b Gk *brothers*   c Gk *the man of lawlessness*; other ancient authorities read *the*   d Gk *the son of destruction*

he takes his seat in the temple of God, declaring himself to be God. [5]Do you not remember that I told you these things when I was still with you? [6]And you know what is now restraining him, so that he may be revealed when his time comes. [7]For the mystery of lawlessness is already at work, but only until the one who now restrains it is

2.7 Exactly What Will Happen?

Nearly every age has come up with a different interpretation of this passage. No one is certain about the "mystery of lawlessness" or "the one who now restrains it." A British writer, Tom Davies, quite sincerely, proposes television as the lawless one, since it has made violence so popular. This passage is obscure because Paul refers to further information he had taught the Thessalonians in person. (Even another New Testament author admitted that Paul's letters contain some things that are "hard to understand" [2 Peter 3.16].)

removed. [8]And then the lawless one will be revealed, whom the Lord Jesus[e] will destroy[f] with the breath of his mouth, annihilating him by the manifestation of his coming. [9]The coming of the lawless one is apparent in the working of Satan, who uses all power, signs, lying wonders, [10]and every kind of wicked deception for those who are perishing, because they refused to love the truth and so be saved. [11]For this reason God sends them a powerful delusion, leading them to believe what is false, [12]so that all who have not believed the truth but took pleasure in unrighteousness will be condemned.

Chosen for Salvation

13 But we must always give thanks to God for you, brothers and sisters[g] beloved by the Lord, because God chose you as the first fruits[h] for salvation through sanctification by the Spirit and through belief in the truth. [14]For this purpose he called you through our proclamation of the good news,[i] so that you may obtain the glory of our Lord Jesus Christ. [15]So then, brothers and sisters,[g] stand firm and hold fast to the traditions that you were taught by us, either by word of mouth or by our letter.

16 Now may our Lord Jesus Christ himself and God our Father, who loved us and through grace gave us eternal comfort and good hope, [17]comfort your hearts and strengthen them in every good work and word.

Request for Prayer

3 Finally, brothers and sisters,[g] pray for us, so that the word of the Lord may spread rapidly and be glorified everywhere, just as it is among you, [2]and that we may be rescued from wicked and evil people; for not all have faith. [3]But the Lord is faithful; he will strengthen you and guard you from the evil one.[j] [4]And we have confidence in the Lord concerning you, that you are doing and will go on doing the things that we command. [5]May the Lord direct your hearts to the love of God and to the steadfastness of Christ.

Warning against Idleness

6 Now we command you, beloved,[g] in the name of our Lord Jesus Christ, to keep away from believers who are[k] living in idleness and not according to the tradition that they[l] received from us. [7]For you yourselves know how you ought to imitate us; we were not idle when we were with you, [8]and we did not eat anyone's bread without paying for it; but with toil and labor we worked night and day, so that we might not burden any of you. [9]This was not because we do not have that right, but in order to give you an example to imitate. [10]For even when we were with you, we gave you this command: Anyone unwilling to

3.10 No Work, No Eat

Paul's first letter to the Thessalonians had affirmed that Jesus could return at any time, unexpectedly. Evidently, this anticipation had prompted some to quit their jobs and do nothing but wait for the second coming. (Dozens of times religious sects have followed the same pattern in the United States by heading for remote areas to await Christ's return.) To correct the imbalance, in this second letter Paul stresses that certain events must happen before Christ's return. He also strongly warns against idleness.

work should not eat. [11]For we hear that some of you are living in idleness, mere busybodies, not doing any work. [12]Now such persons we command and exhort in the Lord Jesus Christ to do their work quietly and to earn their own living. [13]Brothers and sisters,[m] do not be weary in doing what is right.

14 Take note of those who do not obey what we say in this letter; have nothing to do with

---

e Other ancient authorities lack *Jesus*
authorities read *from the beginning*
l Other ancient authorities read *you*

f Other ancient authorities read *consume*
i Or *through our gospel*
m Gk *Brothers*

j Or *from evil*

g Gk *brothers*
k Gk *from every brother who is*

h Other ancient

them, so that they may be ashamed. [15]Do not regard them as enemies, but warn them as believers.[n]

Final Greetings and Benediction

16 Now may the Lord of peace himself give you peace at all times in all ways. The Lord be with all of you.

17 I, Paul, write this greeting with my own hand. This is the mark in every letter of mine; it is the way I write. [18]The grace of our Lord Jesus Christ be with all of you.[o]

[n] Gk a brother   [o] Other ancient authorities add Amen

1 TIMOTHY

The Hardest Job
Timothy steps into a hornet's nest

> *Let no one despise your youth, but set the believers an example. 4.12*

WHO HAS THE MOST DIFFICULT job? A brain surgeon? A trapeze artist who risks death with every leap? A nuclear engineer? Or perhaps an air traffic controller, who determines the safety of thousands of passengers. A number of professions might be nominated as the most difficult of all.

But if the apostle Paul were alive today, to that question he would very likely reply, "Without doubt—a pastor's job is hardest." In contrast to professionals who specialize, a pastor must call upon wide-ranging skills. In a given week a pastor may act as a psychologist, priest, social worker, hospital chaplain, administrator, personnel supervisor, philosopher, and communicator.

Paul was acutely aware of the vital nature of such a job. Churches sprouted up wherever he visited, but whether they survived or failed depended largely on what kind of local leadership developed.

Final Words to a Young Friend

To assure that his work would continue, Paul turned more and more to a few loyal friends, especially Timothy and Titus. He wrote them explicit instructions in the three letters that follow, known collectively as "The Pastoral Letters."

Paul wrote 1 Timothy near the end of his life. Rugged years of ministry had passed, years marked by stonings, beatings, jailings, and riots. Paul knew that his age, his enemies, or the increasingly brutal Roman empire would soon catch up with him.

Timothy, a young man, ranked high in Paul's esteem. Converted during Paul's first missionary journey, he had over the years gained the apostle's complete trust. When a volcano of discontent rumbled in some distant church like Corinth or Thessalonica, Paul quickly dispatched Timothy to try and prevent an eruption.

"I have no one like him," Paul once wrote of Timothy. "Like a son with a father he has served with me in the work of the gospel" (Philippians 2.20,22). Through a swarm of controversies, into prison, on the road—wherever Paul went—Timothy loyally followed. Six of Paul's letters begin with the news that Timothy is at his side.

Timothy Becomes a Pastor

Timothy took on, at Paul's request, that difficult job of heading a local church. The congregation at Ephesus, loose and informal, needed order and a more defined structure. To muddle the scene further, certain members of the church had embraced false doctrines. In this letter, Paul advises his understudy on such matters as worship procedures, the control of unruly women, leadership standards, and policies regarding widows, slaves, and rich people.

Although this book addresses a historical situation from the first century, many problems in the early church—underpaid staff members, a generation gap, an integrity shortage, abuse of social aid, love of money—persist today. A pastor's job description hasn't changed much, or grown any easier, over the centuries.

How to Read 1 Timothy

Despite a weak stomach and timid disposition, Timothy had proved his mettle to Paul in many ways, and Paul wrote this letter to challenge him to a difficult task.

Paul doesn't give many details on the false doctrines Timothy had to combat. These letters, however, include vague hints about super-spiritual living, Jewish genealogies, myths, and fables. Look for the problems Paul alludes to and ask yourself whether they have any modern equivalents.

In his instructions, Paul counseled Timothy to combat heresy not by being forceful and argumentative, but by living an exemplary life and by bringing order to the church. Paul's challenge to live a model life applies directly to us; it remains a powerful prescription for the Christian life.

PEOPLE YOU'LL MEET IN 1 TIMOTHY

TIMOTHY *(p. 1244)*

3-TRACK READING PLAN

For an explanation and complete listing of the 3-track reading plan, turn to page 7.

TRACK 1: **Two-Week Courses on the Bible**
See page 7 for information on these courses.

TRACK 2: **An Overview of 1 Timothy in 1 Day**
☐ Day 1. Read the Introduction to 1 Timothy, then chapter 1, which serves as a good introduction to Paul's "Pastoral Letters."
Now turn to page 9 for your next Track 2 reading project.

TRACK 3: **All of 1 Timothy in 4 Days**
After you have read through 1 Timothy, turn to pages 10–14 for your next Track 3 reading project.
☐ 1–2   ☐ 3–4   ☐ 5   ☐ 6

Salutation

1 Paul, an apostle of Christ Jesus by the command of God our Savior and of Christ Jesus our hope,

2 To Timothy, my loyal child in the faith:
Grace, mercy, and peace from God the Father and Christ Jesus our Lord.

Warning against False Teachers

3 I urge you, as I did when I was on my way to Macedonia, to remain in Ephesus so that you may instruct certain people not to teach any different doctrine, 4and not to occupy themselves with myths and endless genealogies that promote speculations rather than the divine training[a] that is known by faith. 5But the aim of such instruction is love that comes from a pure heart, a good conscience, and sincere faith. 6Some people have deviated from these and turned to meaningless

talk, 7desiring to be teachers of the law, without understanding either what they are saying or the things about which they make assertions.

8 Now we know that the law is good, if one

1.3 Strategic Place

The city of Ephesus crops up throughout the New Testament, which indicates its strategic importance as gateway to Asia. Paul's first visit there resulted in a major riot (Acts 19). He nevertheless stayed on three years, instructing believers and establishing a powerful church. As this letter was written, Paul's trusted associate Timothy was serving as pastor in Ephesus. Revelation 2 indicates that Timothy had mixed success in combating the problems identified in this letter.

a Or plan

uses it legitimately. [9]This means understanding that the law is laid down not for the innocent but for the lawless and disobedient, for the godless and sinful, for the unholy and profane, for those who kill their father or mother, for murderers, [10]fornicators, sodomites, slave traders, liars, perjurers, and whatever else is contrary to the sound teaching [11]that conforms to the glorious gospel of the blessed God, which he entrusted to me.

Gratitude for Mercy

12 I am grateful to Christ Jesus our Lord, who has strengthened me, because he judged me faithful and appointed me to his service, [13]even though I was formerly a blasphemer, a persecutor, and a man of violence. But I received mercy because I had acted ignorantly in unbelief, [14]and the grace of our Lord overflowed for me with the faith and love that are in Christ Jesus. [15]The saying is sure and worthy of full acceptance, that Christ Jesus came into the world to save sinners—of whom I am the foremost. [16]But for that very reason I received mercy, so that in me, as the foremost, Jesus Christ might display the utmost patience, making me an example to those who would come to believe in him for eternal life. [17]To the King of the ages, immortal, invisible, the only God, be honor and glory forever and ever.[b] Amen.

18 I am giving you these instructions, Timothy, my child, in accordance with the prophecies made earlier about you, so that by following them

1.18 Timothy's Calling

In three separate places in his letters to Timothy, Paul refers to his associate's special calling to the ministry. This passage alludes to prophecies made about him. 1 Timothy 4.14 mentions a special ceremony when the church elders laid their hands on him. And in 2 Timothy (1.6) Paul specifies that he, too, had been part of such a ceremony. Timothy came from a Christian household; both his grandmother and mother were believers (2 Timothy 1.5).

you may fight the good fight, [19]having faith and a good conscience. By rejecting conscience, certain persons have suffered shipwreck in the faith; [20]among them are Hymenaeus and Alexander, whom I have turned over to Satan, so that they may learn not to blaspheme.

Instructions concerning Prayer

2 First of all, then, I urge that supplications, prayers, intercessions, and thanksgivings be made for everyone, [2]for kings and all who are in high positions, so that we may lead a quiet and peaceable life in all godliness and dignity. [3]This is right and is acceptable in the sight of God our

2.1 Time to Get Organized

Chapters 2 and 3 give detailed instructions concerning worship and church organization. When Paul wrote this letter, near the end of his life, churches such as Ephesus had been established for many years. The time had come for a more formal organization and for instructions governing appropriate and inappropriate behavior in church.

Savior, [4]who desires everyone to be saved and to come to the knowledge of the truth. [5]For

there is one God;
there is also one mediator between
God and humankind,
Christ Jesus, himself human,
6 who gave himself a ransom for all

—this was attested at the right time. [7]For this I was appointed a herald and an apostle (I am telling the truth,[c] I am not lying), a teacher of the Gentiles in faith and truth.

8 I desire, then, that in every place the men should pray, lifting up holy hands without anger or argument; [9]also that the women should dress themselves modestly and decently in suitable clothing, not with their hair braided, or with gold, pearls, or expensive clothes, [10]but with good works, as is proper for women who profess reverence for God. [11]Let a woman[d] learn in silence with full submission. [12]I permit no woman[d] to teach or to have authority over a man;[e] she is to keep silent. [13]For Adam was formed first, then Eve; [14]and Adam was not deceived, but the woman was deceived and became a transgressor. [15]Yet she will be saved through childbearing, provided they continue in faith and love and holiness, with modesty.

Qualifications of Bishops

3 The saying is sure:[f] whoever aspires to the office of bishop[g] desires a noble task. [2]Now a bishop[h] must be above reproach, married only once,[i] temperate, sensible, respectable, hospitable, an apt teacher, [3]not a drunkard, not violent but gentle, not quarrelsome, and not a lover of money. [4]He must manage his own household well, keeping his children submissive and respectful in every way— [5]for if someone does not know

how to manage his own household, how can he
take care of God's church? 6He must not be a
recent convert, or he may be puffed up with conceit and fall into the condemnation of the devil.
7Moreover, he must be well thought of by outsiders, so that he may not fall into disgrace and the
snare of the devil.

Qualifications of Deacons

8 Deacons likewise must be serious, not
double-tongued, not indulging in much wine, not
greedy for money; 9they must hold fast to the
mystery of the faith with a clear conscience. 10And
let them first be tested; then, if they prove themselves blameless, let them serve as deacons.

> **3.10 Too Young for the Job?**
>
> ***Few people succeed in athletics or professional careers without practice, time, and effort. Paul looked for some of those same qualities in choosing experienced leaders for churches. Ironically, however, Timothy himself was only in his thirties. His upbringing had prepared him early for spiritual leadership, and in his case Paul urged boldness and confidence (4.12).***

11Women[j] likewise must be serious, not slanderers, but temperate, faithful in all things. 12Let deacons be married only once,[k] and let them manage their children and their households well; 13for
those who serve well as deacons gain a good
standing for themselves and great boldness in the
faith that is in Christ Jesus.

The Mystery of Our Religion

14 I hope to come to you soon, but I am
writing these instructions to you so that, 15if I am
delayed, you may know how one ought to behave
in the household of God, which is the church of
the living God, the pillar and bulwark of the truth.
16Without any doubt, the mystery of our religion
is great:

He[l] was revealed in flesh,
  vindicated[m] in spirit,[n]
    seen by angels,
proclaimed among Gentiles,
  believed in throughout the world,
    taken up in glory.

False Asceticism

4 Now the Spirit expressly says that in later[o]
times some will renounce the faith by paying
attention to deceitful spirits and teachings of demons, 2through the hypocrisy of liars whose consciences are seared with a hot iron. 3They forbid
marriage and demand abstinence from foods,
which God created to be received with thanksgiving by those who believe and know the truth. 4For
everything created by God is good, and nothing is
to be rejected, provided it is received with thanksgiving; 5for it is sanctified by God's word and by
prayer.

A Good Minister of Jesus Christ

6 If you put these instructions before the
brothers and sisters,[p] you will be a good servant[q] of Christ Jesus, nourished on the words of
the faith and of the sound teaching that you have
followed. 7Have nothing to do with profane
myths and old wives' tales. Train yourself in godliness, 8for, while physical training is of some value, godliness is valuable in every way, holding
promise for both the present life and the life to
come. 9The saying is sure and worthy of full acceptance. 10For to this end we toil and struggle,[r]
because we have our hope set on the living God,
who is the Savior of all people, especially of those
who believe.

11 These are the things you must insist on
and teach. 12Let no one despise your youth, but
set the believers an example in speech and conduct, in love, in faith, in purity. 13Until I arrive,
give attention to the public reading of scripture,[s]
to exhorting, to teaching. 14Do not neglect the gift
that is in you, which was given to you through
prophecy with the laying on of hands by the
council of elders.[t] 15Put these things into practice, devote yourself to them, so that all may see
your progress. 16Pay close attention to yourself
and to your teaching; continue in these things, for
in doing this you will save both yourself and your
hearers.

Duties toward Believers

5 Do not speak harshly to an older man,[u] but
speak to him as to a father, to younger men
as brothers, 2to older women as mothers, to
younger women as sisters—with absolute purity.
3 Honor widows who are really widows. 4If a
widow has children or grandchildren, they should
first learn their religious duty to their own family
and make some repayment to their parents; for
this is pleasing in God's sight. 5The real widow,
left alone, has set her hope on God and continues
in supplications and prayers night and day; 6but
the widow[v] who lives for pleasure is dead even
while she lives. 7Give these commands as well, so
that they may be above reproach. 8And whoever

[j] Or *Their wives,* or *Women deacons* [k] Gk *be husbands of one wife* [l] Gk *Who;* other ancient authorities read *God;* others, *Which* [m] Or *justified* [n] Or *by the Spirit* [o] Or *the last* [p] Gk *brothers* [q] Or *deacon* [r] Other ancient authorities read *suffer reproach* [s] Gk *to the reading* [t] Gk *by the presbytery* [u] Or *an elder,* or *a presbyter* [v] Gk *she*

does not provide for relatives, and especially for family members, has denied the faith and is worse than an unbeliever.

9 Let a widow be put on the list if she is not less than sixty years old and has been married only once;[w] 10she must be well attested for her good works, as one who has brought up children,

shown hospitality, washed the saints' feet, helped the afflicted, and devoted herself to doing good in every way. 11But refuse to put younger widows on the list; for when their sensual desires alienate them from Christ, they want to marry, 12and so they incur condemnation for having violated their first pledge. 13Besides that, they learn to be

[w] Gk *the wife of one husband*

Athlete in Training
Overcoming personal disabilities

> *Train yourself in godliness, for, while physical training is of some value, godliness is valuable in every way, holding promise for both the present life and the life to come.*
> 4.7–8

BRAD LAUWERS WAS IN THE locker room, showering after a grueling football workout, when he first noticed the lump. He bent down and rubbed his ankle gently, cupping his hand around the swelling. He felt no pain or stiffness. *Probably just some fluid*, he thought. *It will disappear in a few days.*

But the swelling didn't disappear, and a month later Brad lay in a hospital bed awaiting amputation of his left leg. The lump turned out to be a malignant tumor that was sending runners out in several directions in Brad's foot. The next day a surgeon removed Brad's leg just inches below the knee.

Of all the adjustments to his new life—including "one-legged" jokes, the awkward reactions of friends, and learning to walk on an artificial leg—Brad most feared the loss of athletics, his main love in life. He had been a standout on his high school basketball and football teams in Alaska, a sports-crazy state. His doctor, also an amputee (from a war injury), tried to be encouraging: "Remember, Brad, there's *nothing* you cannot do."

Against All Odds

Four months later, Brad visited the campus of UCLA for a prosthetic leg fitting. Even before fully learning to walk on his artificial leg, he sought out a basketball backboard and began tossing up reverse lay-ups. The designers had warned him against subjecting the leg to the jarring stops and turns of basketball and had vetoed football outright, suggesting he take up swimming or water-skiing instead. But Brad never gave up his dream of returning to his two favorite sports.

As he trained, his artificial limb rubbed his leg stump raw and covered it with blisters. Undaunted, he ran until the blisters hardened into calluses. Then he began working on jumps and pivots.

Incredibly, in August, less than one year after the amputation, Brad played his first game as a one-legged quarterback for Dimond High School. Some thought his appearance was a mere sentimental gesture. They were wrong: Brad ended the year leading the state in passing! He completed 58 percent of his passes and racked up 662 yards in seven games as a part-time quarterback on the state championship squad. After football season, he started on Dimond's basketball team. From there, he went on to major in physical education at Washington State University.

When asked about his exploits, Brad shrugs and mentions two factors in his extraordinary achievement: gritty determination and long hours of often painful training.

A Lesson from Athletics

Paul uses the analogy of physical training in his letter to Timothy, urging him to train himself for godliness the same way disciplined athletes train for competition. Brad Lauwers had to overcome physical barriers; Timothy faced personality barriers. Several times Paul refers to Timothy's reserved, timid disposition, which probably contributed to his chronic stomach trouble.

Given his shyness and his half-Jewish, half-Gentile ancestry, Timothy did not seem the ideal choice for a heresy fighter in a turbulent church. But Paul was convinced he could do the job. He encouraged Timothy with such motivational phrases as "I charge you" and "I urge you." He also reminded Timothy of his ordination, a commitment he had made long before.

Harassed Christians need a model, an example of how they should live, perhaps even more than they need words of wisdom. In 1 Timothy, Paul urges his loyal friend to become that model by accepting the discipline and hard work required.

Life Questions: Do you have any personality traits that make Christian service seem difficult? What specific "training instructions" did Paul give Timothy that might also apply to you?

idle, gadding about from house to house; and they are not merely idle, but also gossips and busybodies, saying what they should not say. [14]So I would have younger widows marry, bear children, and manage their households, so as to give

those who benefit by their service are believers and beloved.[b]

False Teaching and True Riches

Teach and urge these duties. [3]Whoever teaches otherwise and does not agree with the sound words of our Lord Jesus Christ and the teaching that is in accordance with godliness, [4]is conceited, understanding nothing, and has a morbid craving for controversy and for disputes about words. From these come envy, dissension, slander, base suspicions, [5]and wrangling among those who are depraved in mind and bereft of the truth, imagining that godliness is a means of gain.[c] [6]Of course, there is great gain in godliness combined with contentment; [7]for we brought nothing into the

---

5.9 Welfare Mentality

Chapter 5 gives fascinating insight into early church problems that have parallels in today's social programs. Evidently, some members of the Ephesus congregation had been taking advantage of others' charity. Young widows were using the church's resources when they should have been looking for other means of support. Paul outlines a form of "enrollment" to establish who was truly needy.

6.7 Two Familiar Quotes

Paul's parting advice to Timothy includes two sayings that have become familiar quotations. Verse 7 is usually quoted accurately. But verse 10, also familiar, is often misquoted as "money is the root of all evil." An established church had already developed a professional class of Christian workers, and Paul warned against the motive of profit-seeking.

---

the adversary no occasion to revile us. [15]For some have already turned away to follow Satan. [16]If any believing woman[x] has relatives who are really widows, let her assist them; let the church not be burdened, so that it can assist those who are real widows.

17 Let the elders who rule well be considered worthy of double honor,[y] especially those who labor in preaching and teaching; [18]for the scripture says, "You shall not muzzle an ox while it is treading out the grain," and, "The laborer deserves to be paid." [19]Never accept any accusation against an elder except on the evidence of two or three witnesses. [20]As for those who persist in sin, rebuke them in the presence of all, so that the rest also may stand in fear. [21]In the presence of God and of Christ Jesus and of the elect angels, I warn you to keep these instructions without prejudice, doing nothing on the basis of partiality. [22]Do not ordain[z] anyone hastily, and do not participate in the sins of others; keep yourself pure.

23 No longer drink only water, but take a little wine for the sake of your stomach and your frequent ailments.

24 The sins of some people are conspicuous and precede them to judgment, while the sins of others follow them there. [25]So also good works are conspicuous; and even when they are not, they cannot remain hidden.

6 Let all who are under the yoke of slavery regard their masters as worthy of all honor, so that the name of God and the teaching may not be blasphemed. [2]Those who have believing masters must not be disrespectful to them on the ground that they are members of the church;[a] rather they must serve them all the more, since

world, so that[d] we can take nothing out of it; [8]but if we have food and clothing, we will be content with these. [9]But those who want to be rich fall into temptation and are trapped by many senseless and harmful desires that plunge people into ruin and destruction. [10]For the love of money is a root of all kinds of evil, and in their eagerness to be rich some have wandered away from the faith and pierced themselves with many pains.

The Good Fight of Faith

11 But as for you, man of God, shun all this; pursue righteousness, godliness, faith, love, endurance, gentleness. [12]Fight the good fight of the faith; take hold of the eternal life, to which you were called and for which you made[e] the good confession in the presence of many witnesses. [13]In the presence of God, who gives life to all things, and of Christ Jesus, who in his testimony before Pontius Pilate made the good confession, I charge you [14]to keep the commandment without spot or blame until the manifestation of our Lord Jesus Christ, [15]which he will bring about at the right time—he who is the blessed and only Sovereign, the King of kings and Lord of lords. [16]It is he alone who has immortality and dwells in unap-

---

x Other ancient authorities read *believing man or woman*; others, *believing man*   y Or *compensation*   z Gk *Do not lay hands on*   a Gk *are brothers*   b Or *since they are believers and beloved, who devote themselves to good deeds* c Other ancient authorities add *Withdraw yourself from such people*   d Other ancient authorities read *world—it is certain that*   e Gk *confessed*

proachable light, whom no one has ever seen or can see; to him be honor and eternal dominion. Amen.

17 As for those who in the present age are rich, command them not to be haughty, or to set their hopes on the uncertainty of riches, but rather on God who richly provides us with everything for our enjoyment. [18]They are to do good, to be rich in good works, generous, and ready to share, [19]thus storing up for themselves the treasure of a good foundation for the future, so that they may take hold of the life that really is life.

Personal Instructions and Benediction

20 Timothy, guard what has been entrusted to you. Avoid the profane chatter and contradictions of what is falsely called knowledge; [21]by professing it some have missed the mark as regards the faith.

Grace be with you.[f]

2 TIMOTHY

Passing the Torch
The apostle Paul's last known words

> And what you have heard from me through many witnesses entrust to faithful people who will be able to teach others as well. 2.2

EVERY FOUR YEARS THE WORLD watches an ancient ritual unfold: the passing of the Olympic torch. The spectacular pageantry of the opening ceremonies cannot begin until the final carrier of the torch arrives in the stadium. The torch symbolically links the modern Olympic Games to their 2,700-year history.

"Passing the torch" has become a familiar phrase, used when the president of a corporation such as General Motors introduces his successor to the public, or when an esteemed orchestra conductor hands over his baton, or a great sports figure tutors her replacement. Often the retiring person delivers an emotional farewell speech. He or she has finished the work; the time has come to pass the torch to another.

Choosing Timothy

As the weary apostle Paul neared certain death, with imprisonment preventing him from traveling, he, too, began to think of a successor. It was time to pass the torch, and he decided on the young man Timothy.

At first glance, shy Timothy hardly seemed an adequate replacement, but Paul had few options. "All who are in Asia have turned away from me," he lamented (1.15). This letter, 2 Timothy, reveals his deep reliance on Timothy's loyal friendship. Life was closing in on the apostle, and he felt a somber sense of abandonment.

At times in this letter, Paul lectures Timothy like a master sergeant, calling on him to stand firm, overcome shame, and hold to the faith. Elsewhere, his tone softens into the fond affirmation of a grateful father. Throughout, the bonds of deep friendship are evident: from Paul recalling Timothy's family heritage (1.5) to his urging Timothy to bring him a heavy coat before winter (4.13,21).

An Emotional Moment

Paul's moods alternate between sadness and confidence, nostalgia and grave concern. As he wrote this letter, he contemplated the disquieting months ahead and the prospect of young, divided churches left without his guidance. In these, his last known written words, he sought to prepare Timothy for the inevitable day when the message of God would depend on him and other reliable workers (2.2).

Despite his circumstances, Paul's farewell message from behind bars is gracious, even triumphant. The spreading of the gospel is far too big a task to be limited to any one man. "I am . . . chained like a criminal," Paul declares, "but the word of God is not chained" (2.9).

How to Read 2 Timothy

Second Timothy has proved encouraging to Christian workers throughout history. Paul, facing death, did not wallow in self-pity, but instead used this last communication to inspire and challenge his associate Timothy.

This letter reveals much about Paul's emotional state and physical circumstances. As you read it, look for glimpses into Paul's loneliness and suffering. The apostle tells where he turned for strength when he faced personal trials.

In addition, 2 Timothy gives much valuable counsel to those of us who, like Timothy, have inherited the task of representing Christ on earth. Paul stresses the importance of relying on Scripture and of living a life of discipline. As you read this letter, put yourself in Timothy's place; imagine receiving one last personal letter from your great mentor. What final words of advice does he give?

3-TRACK READING PLAN

For an explanation and complete listing of the 3-track reading plan, turn to page 7.

TRACK 1: *Two-Week Courses on the Bible*
See page 7 for information on these courses.

TRACK 2: *An Overview of 2 Timothy in 1 Day*
☐ Day 1. Read the Introduction to 2 Timothy and then chapter 2, which contains a summary of Paul's challenge to Timothy.

Now turn to page 9 for your next Track 2 reading project.

TRACK 3: *All of 2 Timothy in 4 Days*
After you have read through 2 Timothy, turn to pages 10–14 for your next Track 3 reading project.
☐1   ☐2   ☐3   ☐4

Salutation

1 Paul, an apostle of Christ Jesus by the will of God, for the sake of the promise of life that is in Christ Jesus,

2 To Timothy, my beloved child:

Grace, mercy, and peace from God the Father and Christ Jesus our Lord.

Thanksgiving and Encouragement

3 I am grateful to God—whom I worship with a clear conscience, as my ancestors did—when I remember you constantly in my prayers night and day. [4]Recalling your tears, I long to see you so that I may be filled with joy. [5]I am reminded of your sincere faith, a faith that lived first in your grandmother Lois and your mother Eunice and now, I am sure, lives in you. [6]For this reason I remind you to rekindle the gift of God that is within you through the laying on of my hands; [7]for God did not give us a spirit of cowardice, but rather a spirit of power and of love and of self-discipline.

8 Do not be ashamed, then, of the testimony about our Lord or of me his prisoner, but join with me in suffering for the gospel, relying on the power of God, [9]who saved us and called us with a holy calling, not according to our works but according to his own purpose and grace. This grace was given to us in Christ Jesus before the ages began, [10]but it has now been revealed through the appearing of our Savior Christ Jesus, who abolished death and brought life and immortality to light through the gospel. [11]For this gospel

I was appointed a herald and an apostle and a teacher,[a] [12]and for this reason I suffer as I do. But I am not ashamed, for I know the one in whom I have put my trust, and I am sure that he is able to guard until that day what I have entrusted to him.[b] [13]Hold to the standard of sound teaching that you have heard from me, in the faith and love that are in Christ Jesus. [14]Guard the good treasure entrusted to you, with the help of the Holy Spirit living in us.

15 You are aware that all who are in Asia have turned away from me, including Phygelus and Hermogenes. [16]May the Lord grant mercy to the household of Onesiphorus, because he often refreshed me and was not ashamed of my chain; [17]when he arrived in Rome, he eagerly[c] searched for me and found me [18]—may the Lord grant that he will find mercy from the Lord on that day! And you know very well how much service he rendered in Ephesus.

A Good Soldier of Christ Jesus

2 You then, my child, be strong in the grace that is in Christ Jesus; [2]and what you have heard from me through many witnesses entrust to faithful people who will be able to teach others as well. [3]Share in suffering like a good soldier of Christ Jesus. [4]No one serving in the army gets entangled in everyday affairs; the soldier's aim is to please the enlisting officer. [5]And in the case of an athlete, no one is crowned without competing according to the rules. [6]It is the farmer who does the work who ought to have the first share of the

---

[a] Other ancient authorities add *of the Gentiles*   [b] Or *what has been entrusted to me*   [c] Or *promptly*

crops. 7Think over what I say, for the Lord will give you understanding in all things.

8 Remember Jesus Christ, raised from the dead, a descendant of David—that is my gospel,

2.4 Soldier, Athlete, Farmer

Writing to a friend who knew him well, Paul saw no need to expand on the three analogies in this paragraph; he simply mentions them and tells Timothy to reflect on them. Paul was fully conscious of the threats and dangers facing his own life, and he wanted Timothy to train himself in preparation for any hardships that he might have to face.

9for which I suffer hardship, even to the point of being chained like a criminal. But the word of God is not chained. 10Therefore I endure everything for the sake of the elect, so that they may also obtain the salvation that is in Christ Jesus, with eternal glory. 11The saying is sure:

If we have died with him, we will also live
    with him;
12 if we endure, we will also reign with him;
    if we deny him, he will also deny us;
13 if we are faithless, he remains faithful—
    for he cannot deny himself.

A Worker Approved by God

14 Remind them of this, and warn them before God*d* that they are to avoid wrangling over words, which does no good but only ruins those who are listening. 15Do your best to present yourself to God as one approved by him, a worker who has no need to be ashamed, rightly explaining the word of truth. 16Avoid profane chatter, for it will lead people into more and more impiety, 17and their talk will spread like gangrene. Among them are Hymenaeus and Philetus, 18who have swerved from the truth by claiming that the resurrection has already taken place. They are upsetting the faith of some. 19But God's firm foundation stands, bearing this inscription: "The Lord knows those who are his," and, "Let everyone who calls on the name of the Lord turn away from wickedness."

20 In a large house there are utensils not only of gold and silver but also of wood and clay, some for special use, some for ordinary. 21All who cleanse themselves of the things I have mentioned*e* will become special utensils, dedicated and useful to the owner of the house, ready for every good work. 22Shun youthful passions and pursue righteousness, faith, love, and peace, along with those who call on the Lord from a pure heart. 23Have nothing to do with stupid and senseless controversies; you know that they breed quarrels. 24And the Lord's servant*f* must not be quarrelsome but kindly to everyone, an apt teacher, patient, 25correcting opponents with gentleness. God may perhaps grant that they will repent and come to know the truth, 26and that they may escape from the snare of the devil, having been held captive by him to do his will.*g*

Godlessness in the Last Days

3 You must understand this, that in the last days distressing times will come. 2For people will be lovers of themselves, lovers of money, boasters, arrogant, abusive, disobedient to their parents, ungrateful, unholy, 3inhuman, implacable, slanderers, profligates, brutes, haters of good, 4treacherous, reckless, swollen with conceit, lovers of pleasure rather than lovers of God, 5holding to the outward form of godliness but denying its power. Avoid them! 6For among them are those who make their way into households and captivate silly women, overwhelmed by their sins and swayed by all kinds of desires, 7who are always being instructed and can never arrive at a knowledge of the truth. 8As Jannes and Jambres opposed Moses, so these people, of corrupt mind

3.8 Who Were Jannes and Jambres?

These names, not mentioned in the Old Testament, were handed down in Jewish tradition as the names of the Egyptian magicians who opposed Moses during the ten plagues against Egypt (Exodus 7.11; 9.11).

and counterfeit faith, also oppose the truth. 9But they will not make much progress, because, as in the case of those two men,*h* their folly will become plain to everyone.

Paul's Charge to Timothy

10 Now you have observed my teaching, my conduct, my aim in life, my faith, my patience, my love, my steadfastness, 11my persecutions, and my suffering the things that happened to me in Antioch, Iconium, and Lystra. What persecutions I endured! Yet the Lord rescued me from all of them. 12Indeed, all who want to live a godly life in Christ Jesus will be persecuted. 13But wicked people and impostors will go from bad to worse, deceiving others and being deceived. 14But as for you, continue in what you have learned and firmly believed, knowing from whom you learned it, 15and how from childhood you have known the sacred writings that are able to instruct you for salvation through faith in Christ Jesus. 16All scripture is inspired by God and is*i* useful for teach-

d Other ancient authorities read *the Lord*   *e* Gk *of these things*   *f* Gk *slave*   *g* Or *by him, to do his* (that is, God's) *will*
h Gk lacks *two men*   *i* Or *Every scripture inspired by God is also*

ing, for reproof, for correction, and for training in righteousness, [17]so that everyone who belongs to God may be proficient, equipped for every good work.

3.16 Scripture Is God-breathed

This important verse gives the origin of the term inspiration, which literally means "God-breathed." Although the Bible doesn't spell out the mechanics of how God inspired the writers, it makes clear the ultimate source was God himself.

4 In the presence of God and of Christ Jesus, who is to judge the living and the dead, and in view of his appearing and his kingdom, I solemnly urge you: [2]proclaim the message; be persistent whether the time is favorable or unfavorable; convince, rebuke, and encourage, with the utmost patience in teaching. [3]For the time is coming when people will not put up with sound doctrine,

[j] Other ancient authorities read *Gaul*

but having itching ears, they will accumulate for themselves teachers to suit their own desires, [4]and will turn away from listening to the truth and wander away to myths. [5]As for you, always be sober, endure suffering, do the work of an evangelist, carry out your ministry fully.

6 As for me, I am already being poured out as a libation, and the time of my departure has come. [7]I have fought the good fight, I have finished the race, I have kept the faith. [8]From now on there is reserved for me the crown of righteousness, which the Lord, the righteous judge, will give me on that day, and not only to me but also to all who have longed for his appearing.

Personal Instructions

9 Do your best to come to me soon, [10]for Demas, in love with this present world, has deserted me and gone to Thessalonica; Crescens has gone to Galatia,[j] Titus to Dalmatia. [11]Only Luke is with me. Get Mark and bring him with you, for he is useful in my ministry. [12]I have sent Tychicus to Ephesus. [13]When you come, bring the cloak that I left with Carpus at Troas, also the books,

A Letter from Death Row
Paul sees the end

OCCASIONALLY, WRITINGS SURFACE FROM DEATH row, the earnest scratchings of prisoners who know each word may be their last. Whole books, for example, were discovered amid the ruins of Nazi death camps. Understandably, these writings don't usually dwell on abstract, philosophical themes. They chronicle the day-to-day reality of the struggle to survive.

> *I am already being poured out as a libation, and the time of my departure has come.* 4.6

Quite naturally, Paul did not devote much space to doctrine in his death row letter. He stuck to personal advice on vital issues such as courage and personal integrity.

Paul's Grim Future

Although Paul does not elaborate on his present circumstances in 2 Timothy, he mentions that at his first trial not a single witness came forward to defend him (4.16). Through supernatural strength he successfully defended himself, but his prospects in a new trial appeared grim (4.6).

Paul's arrest probably occurred in the wave of anti-Christian persecutions begun by Nero in A.D. 64. That crazed emperor tortured Christians by crucifying them, by wrapping them in animal skins and turning his hunting dogs loose on them, and by burning them alive, as human torches, to illuminate the games in his garden. Is it any wonder that Paul, imprisoned in that era, exhorted Timothy on the need for boldness and the likelihood of suffering for Christ?

The Coming Conflict

Toward the end of his life, Paul viewed the future as a growing struggle. Immorality and false teaching would "spread like gangrene" (2.17); he urged Christians to counteract those forces with personal purity. The battle between good and evil would only intensify, he said.

After making some predictions about "the last days," Paul composed a formal charge to Timothy—a last will and testament to his spiritual son (4.1–8). He concluded, "I have fought the good fight, I have finished the race, I have kept the faith" (4.7). Tradition teaches that Paul was killed by Rome for his faith. But because of his life and the legacy he passed on, the world would never be the same.

Life Questions: If you drafted a spiritual "last will and testament" for your friends, what would you say?

and above all the parchments. [14]Alexander the coppersmith did me great harm; the Lord will pay him back for his deeds. [15]You also must beware of him, for he strongly opposed our message.

16 At my first defense no one came to my

4.17 Second Imprisonment in Rome

Acts 28 describes a period when Paul was held under house arrest in Rome, but the conditions hinted at in this letter are quite different. Paul wrote 2 Timothy much later, after the Roman empire had turned against Christians, and the tone of this letter (verses 6–9) implies that he had little hope of freedom. His request for a cloak and parchments (verse 13) indicates he was arrested suddenly, without warning.

support, but all deserted me. May it not be counted against them! [17]But the Lord stood by me and gave me strength, so that through me the message might be fully proclaimed and all the Gentiles might hear it. So I was rescued from the lion's mouth. [18]The Lord will rescue me from every evil attack and save me for his heavenly kingdom. To him be the glory forever and ever. Amen.

Final Greetings and Benediction

19 Greet Prisca and Aquila, and the household of Onesiphorus. [20]Erastus remained in Corinth; Trophimus I left ill in Miletus. [21]Do your best to come before winter. Eubulus sends greetings to you, as do Pudens and Linus and Claudia and all the brothers and sisters.[k]

22 The Lord be with your spirit. Grace be with you.[l]

---

[k] Gk *all the brothers*   [l] The Greek word for *you* here is plural. Other ancient authorities add *Amen*

TITUS

Diverse People, Diverse Problems
An island of liars, brutes, and gluttons

> Declare these things.
> 2.15

MODERN PEOPLE READING ABOUT THE past can blur people together into a uniform, faceless crowd of strangers. It's hard to visualize individual people you read about.

Actually, the people Paul addressed were as diverse as those you might meet on the streets of Los Angeles or New York City today. Consider Crete, an island populated by five fiercely independent ethnic groups. Its main knowledge of the outside world came through pirates and coarse sailors. Add to that mix a large community of straight-laced Jews, and you can see why the Cretan church was born amid conflict.

Titus the Troubleshooter

When problems erupted in this stormy congregation, Paul dispatched Titus, his trusted associate of 15 years. The book of Galatians (2.1–5) introduced Titus as proof that a non-Jew could become a fully acceptable Christian.

When Titus's name occurs in the New Testament, he is usually seen serving as Paul's troubleshooter, the one called on to deal with local crises. Twice he was sent on a diplomatic mission to the rowdy church at Corinth. This letter indicates he faced an equally challenging task on Crete. Paul wrote the book of Titus as a set of personal instructions on how to handle a difficult assignment.

Because he was writing to people who knew the local circumstances well, Paul rarely bothered to give background for us years-later "over-the-shoulder" readers. But we can gain insights into the conditions by reading between the lines. For example, when Paul tells Titus to search for a leader not "quick-tempered or addicted to wine or violent or greedy for gain" (1.7), that description implies something about the average Cretan. One of the island's own poets described Cretans as "always liars, vicious brutes, lazy gluttons" (1.12), and the Greeks had even coined a special verb for lying: "to Cretize."

Practical Theology

Titus 2 lists some of the diverse groups in the church: older men, older women, younger women, young men, slaves. Each presented a set of problems that needed attention, and Paul gave Titus specific counsel on each group. Although he was mainly emphasizing the need for good living, Paul also dropped in a few concise restatements of the gospel message. His theology was never distantly theoretical; he applied it to real-life human problems.

Taken as a group, the three pastoral letters (1 and 2 Timothy plus Titus) show Paul, an old man now, learning to rely more and more on capable assistants to carry on his work. The Cretans needed a hard-hitting, practical reminder of "sound doctrine" based on a God "who never lies" (1.2). The instructions in Titus give the man for whom the book was named—and us—the needed jolt.

How to Read Titus

Like 1 and 2 Timothy, Titus was written to an individual, not a church. This letter has similarities to 1 Timothy, but is less personal and more official. The book of Acts doesn't mention Titus, but 14 references to him in Paul's letters indicate that he was one of Paul's most trusted helpers.

In some letters, such as Galatians, Paul fought valiantly against legalism. But the church on Crete, full of immature Christians, needed basic lessons in morality, and Paul spelled them out for Titus. Using a very straightforward style, he told his associate what he would prescribe in such circumstances.

Because it is written in such a direct style—almost like a training manual—Titus needs little explanation. Paul's meaning comes through clearly. Note particularly how Paul adapts his overall principles to specific groups in chapter 2. And give careful study to the 'nuggets' of theology in these passages: 1.1–4, 2.11–14, and 3.4–7.

PEOPLE YOU'LL MEET IN TITUS

TITUS *(p. 1256)*

3-TRACK READING PLAN

For an explanation and complete listing of the 3-track reading plan, turn to page 7.

TRACK 1: **_Two-Week Courses on the Bible_**
See page 7 for information on these courses.

TRACK 2: **_An Overview of Titus in 1 Day_**
☐ Day 1. Read the Introduction to Titus, then chapter 2, which contains Paul's practical advice for the diverse groups in the Cretan church.

Now turn to page 9 for your next Track 2 reading project.

TRACK 3: **_All of Titus in 2 Days_**
After you have read through Titus, turn to pages 10–14 for your next Track 3 reading project.
☐1   ☐2–3

Salutation

1 Paul, a servant[a] of God and an apostle of Jesus Christ, for the sake of the faith of God's elect and the knowledge of the truth that is in accordance with godliness, [2]in the hope of eternal life that God, who never lies, promised before the

1.2 No Lies

Right away Paul characterizes God as the One who does not lie. God's truthfulness made a sharp contrast to the Cretans themselves (verse 12) as well as to many gods of that era. The Romans exalted their emperors, worshiping them as divine despite the flaws and weaknesses that everyone knew about. Paul contrasts the message about Jesus as the eternal "word" of truth.

ages began— [3]in due time he revealed his word through the proclamation with which I have been entrusted by the command of God our Savior,

4 To Titus, my loyal child in the faith we share:

Grace[b] and peace from God the Father and Christ Jesus our Savior.

Titus in Crete

5 I left you behind in Crete for this reason, so that you should put in order what remained to be done, and should appoint elders in every town, as I directed you: [6]someone who is blameless, married only once,[c] whose children are believers, not accused of debauchery and not rebellious. [7]For a bishop,[d] as God's steward, must be blameless; he must not be arrogant or quick-tempered or addicted to wine or violent or greedy for gain; [8]but he must be hospitable, a lover of goodness, prudent, upright, devout, and self-controlled. [9]He must have a firm grasp of the word that is trustworthy in accordance with the teaching, so that he may be able both to preach with sound doctrine and to refute those who contradict it.

10 There are also many rebellious people, idle talkers and deceivers, especially those of the circumcision; [11]they must be silenced, since they are

---

a Gk *slave*   *b* Other ancient authorities read *Grace, mercy,*   *c* Gk *husband of one wife*   *d* Or *an overseer*

upsetting whole families by teaching for sordid gain what it is not right to teach. ¹²It was one of them, their very own prophet, who said,

"Cretans are always liars, vicious brutes, lazy gluttons."

¹³That testimony is true. For this reason rebuke them sharply, so that they may become sound in the faith, ¹⁴not paying attention to Jewish myths or to commandments of those who reject the truth. ¹⁵To the pure all things are pure, but to the corrupt and unbelieving nothing is pure. Their very minds and consciences are corrupted. ¹⁶They profess to know God, but they deny him by their actions. They are detestable, disobedient, unfit for any good work.

Teach Sound Doctrine

2 But as for you, teach what is consistent with sound doctrine. ²Tell the older men to be temperate, serious, prudent, and sound in faith, in love, and in endurance.

3 Likewise, tell the older women to be reverent in behavior, not to be slanderers or slaves to drink; they are to teach what is good, ⁴so that they may encourage the young women to love their husbands, to love their children, ⁵to be self-controlled, chaste, good managers of the household, kind, being submissive to their husbands, so that the word of God may not be discredited.

6 Likewise, urge the younger men to be self-controlled. ⁷Show yourself in all respects a model of good works, and in your teaching show integrity, gravity, ⁸and sound speech that cannot be censured; then any opponent will be put to shame, having nothing evil to say of us.

9 Tell slaves to be submissive to their masters and to give satisfaction in every respect; they are not to talk back, ¹⁰not to pilfer, but to show complete and perfect fidelity, so that in everything they may be an ornament to the doctrine of God our Savior.

11 For the grace of God has appeared, bringing salvation to all,ᵉ ¹²training us to renounce impiety and worldly passions, and in the present age to live lives that are self-controlled, upright, and godly, ¹³while we wait for the blessed hope and the manifestation of the glory of our great God and Savior,ᶠ Jesus Christ. ¹⁴He it is who gave himself for us that he might redeem us from all iniquity and purify for himself a people of his own who are zealous for good deeds.

15 Declare these things; exhort and reprove with all authority.ᵍ Let no one look down on you.

Maintain Good Deeds

3 Remind them to be subject to rulers and authorities, to be obedient, to be ready for every good work, ²to speak evil of no one, to avoid

quarreling, to be gentle, and to show every courtesy to everyone. ³For we ourselves were once foolish, disobedient, led astray, slaves to various passions and pleasures, passing our days in malice and envy, despicable, hating one another. ⁴But

2.15 Foolish Questions

In addition to the problems hinted at in chapter 2, the Cretan church struggled with issues its Jewish members introduced. These trends toward myths and "stupid controversies, genealogies, dissensions, and quarrels about the law" (3.9) resemble the heresies Paul had warned against in the book of Colossians. Titus had to be prepared to deal with problems both of doctrine and of righteous living.

when the goodness and loving kindness of God our Savior appeared, ⁵he saved us, not because of any works of righteousness that we had done, but according to his mercy, through the waterʰ of rebirth and renewal by the Holy Spirit. ⁶This Spirit he poured out on us richly through Jesus Christ our Savior, ⁷so that, having been justified by his grace, we might become heirs according to the hope of eternal life. ⁸The saying is sure.

3.5 Nuggets of Theology

Despite its practical, instructive tone, Titus contains three outstanding passages of Paul's theology. They appear in 1.1–4, 2.11–14, and 3.4–7. This last passage balances off Paul's stress on clean living in Titus. Verse 5 makes clear that "works of righteousness" do not earn us acceptance by God. Rather, they are a natural response from people who have experienced God's forgiveness and love.

I desire that you insist on these things, so that those who have come to believe in God may be careful to devote themselves to good works; these things are excellent and profitable to everyone. ⁹But avoid stupid controversies, genealogies, dissensions, and quarrels about the law, for they are unprofitable and worthless. ¹⁰After a first and second admonition, have nothing more to do with anyone who causes divisions, ¹¹since you know that such a person is perverted and sinful, being self-condemned.

Final Messages and Benediction

12 When I send Artemas to you, or Tychicus,

ᵉ Or *has appeared to all, bringing salvation*   ᶠ Or *of the great God and our Savior*   ᵍ Gk *commandment*
ʰ Gk *washing*

3.12 Mail Carriers

In Roman times, the most reliable postal system was to give a letter to a trusted friend. Paul used Tychicus to carry letters both to Ephesus and to Colosse. Tychicus also accompanied Paul on his trip to distribute gifts to the poor of Jerusalem (Acts 20.4).

do your best to come to me at Nicopolis, for I have decided to spend the winter there. [13]Make every effort to send Zenas the lawyer and Apollos on their way, and see that they lack nothing. [14]And let people learn to devote themselves to good works in order to meet urgent needs, so that they may not be unproductive.

15 All who are with me send greetings to you. Greet those who love us in the faith.

Grace be with all of you.[i]

PHILEMON

Letter to a Slave Owner
A slave's life hangs in the balance

> Though I am bold enough in Christ to command you to do your duty, yet I would rather appeal to you on the basis of love. 8–9

ONESIMUS WAS A RUNAWAY SLAVE, a hunted fugitive whose life was in constant danger. He had two options. He could spend his days hiding in the dark, grimy alleys of a Roman city, dodging soldiers and bounty hunters. Or, he could do the unthinkable and return to his master.

The laws of the empire were harsh. If Onesimus did return, his master Philemon had the legal power to sentence him to immediate execution. If Philemon mercifully decided to let him live, Onesimus would have the letter *F* (for *Fugitivus*) seared on his forehead with a branding iron, marking him for life.

Paul Defends a Runaway

His conversion to Christ through Paul's ministry greatly complicated the decision of the runaway slave. Onesimus knew he couldn't keep running all his life. He had wronged his legal owner, and, painful as it seemed, he needed to make amends.

The apostle Paul, sympathetic to the slave's cause, agreed to use his full influence on Philemon. Onesimus's life hung in the balance. This 468-word letter to the slave owner masterfully brings together Paul's skills of persuasion and diplomacy.

Every phrase in Philemon is crafted to produce the best possible effect. Paul appeals to Philemon's friendship, his status as a Christian leader, his sense of love and compassion. He doesn't outright order Philemon to consent, yet he applies blatant pressure, reminding Philemon about "your owing me even your own self" (verse 19). Addressing the letter to Philemon's church (verse 2) increases the pressure, as does Paul's promise of a personal visit (verse 22).

Christianity and Slavery

Slavery existed for 1,800 years after this letter was written, and it took the full moral force of Christianity to ban it from the globe. But the tiny book of Philemon shows that the faith had a profound impact on slavery long before abolition.

Christ can revolutionize any social relationship. Onesimus, a runaway, decided to turn himself in. In Philemon, Paul asks for a second miracle. He pleads with the owner to "welcome him as you would welcome me" (verse 17). Such an attitude, in that culture, was social dynamite.

How to Read Philemon

Obviously, Paul had a close relationship with both the slave Onesimus and his owner Philemon. Some scholars believe that Onesimus first heard about Christ when he shared a jail cell with the apostle (see verses 9–10). As you read Philemon, look for clues into Paul's relationship with each person.

Philemon gives us a model of Christian diplomacy. As you read it, think of awkward social situations you know about: two estranged friends or a parent-child conflict, for example. Notice the kind of persuasion used by Paul, and try to apply it to your own circumstances.

3-TRACK READING PLAN

For an explanation and complete listing of the 3-track reading plan, turn to page 7.

TRACK 1: *Two-Week Courses on the Bible*
See page 7 for information on these courses.

TRACK 2: *Philemon in 1 Day*
☐ Day 1. Just one chapter long, Philemon will take only a few minutes to read.
Now turn to page 9 for your next Track 2 reading project.

TRACK 3: *All of Philemon in 1 Day*
After you have read through Philemon, turn to pages 10–14 for your next Track 3 reading project.
☐Philemon

Salutation

1 Paul, a prisoner of Christ Jesus, and Timothy our brother,[a]

To Philemon our dear friend and co-worker, [2]to Apphia our sister,[b] to Archippus our fellow soldier, and to the church in your house: [3] Grace to you and peace from God our Father and the Lord Jesus Christ.

Philemon's Love and Faith

4 When I remember you[c] in my prayers, I always thank my God [5]because I hear of your love for all the saints and your faith toward the Lord Jesus. [6]I pray that the sharing of your faith may become effective when you perceive all the good that we[d] may do for Christ. [7]I have indeed received much joy and encouragement from your love, because the hearts of the saints have been refreshed through you, my brother.

Paul's Plea for Onesimus

8 For this reason, though I am bold enough in Christ to command you to do your duty, [9]yet I would rather appeal to you on the basis of love—and I, Paul, do this as an old man, and now also as a prisoner of Christ Jesus.[e] [10]I am appealing to you for my child, Onesimus, whose father I have become during my imprisonment. [11]Formerly he was useless to you, but now he is indeed useful[f] both to you and to me. [12]I am sending him, that is, my own heart, back to you. [13]I wanted to keep him with me, so that he might be of service to me in your place during my imprisonment for the gospel; [14]but I preferred to do nothing without your consent, in order that your good deed might be voluntary and not something forced. [15]Perhaps this is the reason he was separated from you for a while, so that you might have him back forever, [16]no longer as a slave but more than a slave, a beloved brother—especially to me but how much more to you, both in the flesh and in the Lord.

11 No Longer Useless

Onesimus in Greek means "useful," and Paul playfully makes a pun from the name. A runaway slave was useless; a converted former slave can prove very useful—provided Philemon receives him in the right spirit. Accept him back, urges Paul, "no longer as a slave but . . . a beloved brother" (verse 16).

17 So if you consider me your partner, welcome him as you would welcome me. [18]If he has wronged you in any way, or owes you anything, charge that to my account. [19]I, Paul, am writing this with my own hand: I will repay it. I say nothing about your owing me even your own self. [20]Yes, brother, let me have this benefit from you in the Lord! Refresh my heart in Christ. [21]Confident of your obedience, I am writing to you, knowing that you will do even more than I say. [22]One thing more—prepare a guest room for me, for I am hoping through your prayers to be restored to you.

Final Greetings and Benediction

23 Epaphras, my fellow prisoner in Christ Jesus, sends greetings to you,[g] [24]and so do Mark, Aristarchus, Demas, and Luke, my fellow workers.

25 The grace of the Lord Jesus Christ be with your spirit.[h]

---

[a] Gk *the brother*   [b] Gk *the sister*   [c] From verse 4 through verse 21, *you* is singular   [d] Other ancient authorities read *you* (plural)   [e] Or *as an ambassador of Christ Jesus, and now also his prisoner*   [f] The name Onesimus means *useful* or (compare verse 20) *beneficial*   [g] Here *you* is singular   [h] Other ancient authorities add *Amen*

HEBREWS

Time to Decide
Does it matter what you believe as long as you're sincere?

> How can we escape if we neglect so great a salvation?
> 2.3

YOU CAN GO THROUGH MUCH of life deliberately avoiding hard decisions. But sometimes you have no choice; the situation forces you to make a decision. Consider an example from the sport of rock-climbing.

Sooner or later, every rock-climber faces a dreaded section of slick granite that offers no ledges or cracks to grasp. When you come to such a wall, you can abandon the climb. Or, you can risk a move like "the pendulum."

The Pendulum

The pendulum works the way it sounds: as high above you as you can reach, you fasten a loop with a metal nut and slide the rope through the loop. Then you climb down a few feet, dangle on the end of the rope, and try to swing across the sheer section. It takes nerve. You must lean out against the rope into empty space and, with a well-timed push, vault across the face of the cliff. If your lunge toward a safer spot fails, you swing helplessly back and try again.

After your entire party has swung the pendulum, you pull the rope all the way through the loop. From then on, there's no turning back. You have crossed a section of cliff that requires a rope to swing on and a loop to attach it to. The loop is now out of your reach, and the rope coiled at your feet. There is only one way to go: up.

Worth the Risk?

The author of Hebrews wrote to people who faced just such a climactic, can't-turn-back decision. It involved not a rock climb, but their entire future. Should they stick with the familiar routine of the Jewish religion? After all, it enjoyed Rome's official protection and had traditions going back thousands of years. Or should they take a risk and join the growing body of people who called themselves Christians? Those readers needed some compelling reasons to choose Christianity. At that time new converts were being thrown out of Jewish temples, tossed into jail, and even tortured. Was faith in Christ worth the risk?

The tug of the old and the fear of the new kept many interested people, especially Jews, teetering on the edge of Christianity. And the book of Hebrews seems designed to push such people toward a decisive commitment, in one direction or the other. Point by point, the author shows how Christ improved on the Jewish way. Hebrews is a no-holds-barred argument on why Christianity is *better* (a key word in Hebrews) than Judaism. The new faith is worth any risk.

Drawing on the Old Testament

For the sake of Jewish readers, the author painstakingly cites Old Testament passages, more than 80 times in all. He develops the case for Christ like a lawyer, but with the charged emotions befitting the life-and-death issues involved.

Although Hebrews mainly focuses on the Jewish religion, comparing it to Christianity, the book also speaks to our time. Today people ask, "Are religions all that different? Isn't the most important thing to be sincere?" Hebrews insists there are decisive reasons to choose Christ. The author urges his readers to leap forward to a new experience with God through Jesus.

How to Read Hebrews

Who wrote Hebrews? Did the author have a particular group of readers in mind? Scholars have debated these questions for centuries without reaching agreement. The truth is, no one knows for certain either the author or the intended audience of Hebrews.

Nevertheless, the book does give some information about its first readers. They had heard the gospel through contemporaries of Jesus (2.3), and their conversion had brought on physical persecution (10.32–34). One fact leaps out: Their spiritual state greatly distressed the unidentified author. Five times in the book of Hebrews he interrupts a careful line of reasoning to fire off a warning (2.1; 3.7; 5.11; 10.26; 12.25).

Hebrews is actually a commentary on the Old Testament. It examines many Jewish customs and shows how Jesus brought about a "better covenant" to replace many of those laws. (*Covenant* means the same thing as *Testament*: a firm agreement between God and humanity.) Therefore, to fully appreciate Hebrews, you should have some familiarity with such books as Exodus, Leviticus, and Numbers.

As you read, look at the bottom of each page for NRSV footnotes referring to the Old Testament. If you can't figure out what a text in Hebrews means, try looking back to the original passage.

To follow the logic in Hebrews, note each use of the word *better* and *superior*. The author compares Jesus Christ to the angels, to Moses, to the priests Aaron and Melchizedek, and to Abraham.

3-TRACK READING PLAN

For an explanation and complete listing of the 3-track reading plan, turn to page 7.

TRACK 1: **Two-Week Courses on the Bible**
See page 7 for information on these courses.

TRACK 2: **An Overview of Hebrews in 3 Days**
☐ Day 1. Read the Introduction to Hebrews, then chapter 2. There you will learn about God's decision to send his Son to earth and why it was so important that Jesus come as a fully *human* being, not as some kind of alien.
☐ Day 2. Hebrews 11 lists many Old Testament heroes, with a capsule description of how each one demonstrated faith. Read this famous chapter.
☐ Day 3. Read Hebrews 12, which combines a pep talk with a brief summary of the entire book.

Now turn to page 9 for your next Track 2 reading project.

TRACK 3: **All of Hebrews in 11 Days**
After you have read through Hebrews, turn to pages 10–14 for your next Track 3 reading project.

☐1   ☐2   ☐3–4   ☐5–6   ☐7   ☐8   ☐9   ☐10
☐11   ☐12   ☐13

God Has Spoken by His Son

1 Long ago God spoke to our ancestors in many and various ways by the prophets, ²but in these last days he has spoken to us by a Son,ᵃ whom he appointed heir of all things, through whom he also created the worlds. ³He is the reflection of God's glory and the exact imprint of God's very being, and he sustainsᵇ all things by his powerful word. When he had made purification for sins, he sat down at the right hand of the Majesty on high, ⁴having become as much superi-

or to angels as the name he has inherited is more excellent than theirs.

The Son Is Superior to Angels

5 For to which of the angels did God ever say,

"You are my Son;
    today I have begotten you"?
Or again,
"I will be his Father,
    and he will be my Son"?

ᵃ Or *the Son*   ᵇ Or *bears along*

6And again, when he brings the firstborn into the world, he says,

"Let all God's angels worship him."

7Of the angels he says,

"He makes his angels winds,
and his servants flames of fire."

8But of the Son he says,

"Your throne, O God, is[c] forever and
ever,
and the righteous scepter is the scepter
of your[d] kingdom.

9 You have loved righteousness and hated
wickedness;
therefore God, your God, has anointed
you
with the oil of gladness beyond your
companions."

10And,

"In the beginning, Lord, you founded the
earth,
and the heavens are the work of your
hands;

1.10 Not by Chance

Quotations from the Old Testament fill the book of Hebrews from the second paragraph onwards. The author is making the point that God's plan, unfolding from the beginning of time, has now culminated in the visit of the Son to earth.

11 they will perish, but you remain;
they will all wear out like clothing;

12 like a cloak you will roll them up,
and like clothing[e] they will be
changed.
But you are the same,
and your years will never end."

13But to which of the angels has he ever said,

"Sit at my right hand
until I make your enemies a footstool
for your feet"?

14Are not all angels[f] spirits in the divine service, sent to serve for the sake of those who are to inherit salvation?

Warning to Pay Attention

2 Therefore we must pay greater attention to what we have heard, so that we do not drift away from it. 2For if the message declared through angels was valid, and every transgression or disobedience received a just penalty, 3how can we escape if we neglect so great a salvation? It was declared at first through the Lord, and it was attested to us by those who heard him, 4while God added his testimony by signs and wonders and various miracles, and by gifts of the Holy Spirit, distributed according to his will.

1.14 Respect for Angels

In earlier times, people freely accepted the existence of angels and accorded them honor and respect. Jewish people retold stories of how angels had assisted Abraham, Moses, Elijah, Balaam, and Daniel. (In fact, several New Testament letters warn Jewish Christians against the common practice of worshiping angels.) To prove its argument about Christ being superior, Hebrews must show that angels served his purposes, not vice versa.

Exaltation through Abasement

5 Now God[g] did not subject the coming world, about which we are speaking, to angels. 6But someone has testified somewhere,

"What are human beings that you are
mindful of them,[h]
or mortals, that you care for them?[i]

7 You have made them for a little while
lower[j] than the angels;
you have crowned them with glory and
honor,[k]

8 subjecting all things under their feet."

Now in subjecting all things to them, God[g] left nothing outside their control. As it is, we do not yet see everything in subjection to them, 9but we do see Jesus, who for a little while was made lower[l] than the angels, now crowned with glory and honor because of the suffering of death, so that by the grace of God[m] he might taste death for everyone.

10 It was fitting that God,[g] for whom and through whom all things exist, in bringing many children to glory, should make the pioneer of their salvation perfect through sufferings. 11For the one who sanctifies and those who are sanctified all have one Father.[n] For this reason Jesus[g] is not ashamed to call them brothers and sisters,[o] 12saying,

"I will proclaim your name to my
brothers and sisters,[o]
in the midst of the congregation I will
praise you."

13And again,

"I will put my trust in him."

---

[c] Or *God is your throne* [d] Other ancient authorities read *his*
[f] Gk *all of them* [g] Gk *he* [h] Gk *What is man that you are mindful of him?* [i] Gk *or the son of man that you care for him?* In the Hebrew of Psalm 8.4-6 both *man* and *son of man* refer to all humankind [j] Or *them only a little lower*
[k] Other ancient authorities add *and set them over the works of your hands* [l] Or *who was made a little lower*
[m] Other ancient authorities read *apart from God* [n] Gk *are all of one* [o] Gk *brothers* [e] Other ancient authorities lack *like clothing*

And again,

> "Here am I and the children whom God
>   has given me."

14 Since, therefore, the children share flesh and blood, he himself likewise shared the same things, so that through death he might destroy the one who has the power of death, that is, the devil, 15and free those who all their lives were held in slavery by the fear of death. 16For it is clear that he did not come to help angels, but the descendants of Abraham. 17Therefore he had to become like his brothers and sisters*p* in every respect, so that he might be a merciful and faithful high priest in the service of God, to make a sacrifice of atonement for the sins of the people. 18Because he himself was tested by what he suffered, he is able to help those who are being tested.

Moses a Servant, Christ a Son

3 Therefore, brothers and sisters,*p* holy partners in a heavenly calling, consider that Jesus,

the apostle and high priest of our confession, 2was faithful to the one who appointed him, just as Moses also "was faithful in all*q* God's*r* house." 3Yet Jesus*s* is worthy of more glory than Moses, just as the builder of a house has more honor than the house itself. 4(For every house is built by

---

2.17 Like Us in Every Way

Hebrews goes further than any other New Testament book in explaining Jesus' human nature. Why was it so important that Jesus share our humanity? Hebrews stresses three reasons: (1) so that, in dying, he could free us from the power of death (verses 14–15); (2) so that, by becoming the final sacrifice for sin, he could reconcile us to God (5.8–9); and (3) so that, in experiencing temptation, he can better help us with our own temptations (verse 18).

---

p Gk brothers   *q* Other ancient authorities lack all   *r* Gk his   *s* Gk this one

---

Is Christ Better?
The uniqueness of Jesus

IN TIME, A WORK OF art by a great artist gains enormous value because of its creator's reputation. Even a musty notebook full of scratchings, if found to be Leonardo da Vinci's, would suddenly be worth millions of dollars. Similarly, every house designed by American architect Frank Lloyd Wright retains high value simply because of his name.

To dramatize his argument that Christ is superior to any religious system, the author of Hebrews uses an analogy: Which has greater honor, the builder of a house or the house itself? Obviously, the builder has more honor; the house is just one expression of his genius.

> *Jesus is worthy of more glory than Moses, just as the builder of a house has more honor than the house itself. 3.3*

In a Category by Himself

Likewise, Hebrews says, Christ has more honor than anyone else on earth. As Creator of the universe, he actually designed and made all people (1.2). That puts him in a different category of greatness, far above Moses, Aaron, and other Jewish heroes.

"Therefore," Hebrews urges, "consider . . . Jesus" (3.1). He deserves all respect and allegiance. By becoming human, Jesus learned firsthand the temptations and sufferings that people undergo, so that he can now represent us sympathetically to God (4.14–15). The author goes on to prove that Jesus fulfilled all the Old Testament requirements. He was the one priest who could permanently bring together God and the human race (7.23–27). And, as God, he had the power through his death to remove the final barrier of sin between God and humankind (9.11–15).

Free Access to God

Over time, the author argues, God chose various ways to reveal himself: creation, the prophets, and the Old Testament scriptures. But the final, complete self-expression culminated in his Son. Jesus is the one worthy of honor.

Because of Jesus, we no longer have to approach God through a priest, as the Israelites did. Christ's work makes God available to all who have faith in him. And God no longer dwells in an elaborately designed temple; *we* have become his house (3.6), his work of art.

Life Questions: People sometimes say about Jesus, "I don't believe he was God, but he was a very fine man—like Gandhi or Buddha." What arguments does the author of Hebrews use to contradict this?

someone, but the builder of all things is God.)
[5]Now Moses was faithful in all God's[t] house as a servant, to testify to the things that would be spoken later. [6]Christ, however, was faithful over God's[t] house as a son, and we are his house if we hold firm[u] the confidence and the pride that belong to hope.

Warning against Unbelief

[7] Therefore, as the Holy Spirit says,
"Today, if you hear his voice,
[8] do not harden your hearts as in
      the rebellion,
      as on the day of testing in the wilderness,
[9] where your ancestors put me to the test,
      though they had seen my works [10]for
      forty years.
Therefore I was angry with that generation,
and I said, 'They always go astray in their
      hearts,
and they have not known my ways.'
[11] As in my anger I swore,
'They will not enter my rest.'"
[12]Take care, brothers and sisters,[v] that none of you may have an evil, unbelieving heart that turns away from the living God. [13]But exhort one another every day, as long as it is called "today," so that none of you may be hardened by the deceitfulness of sin. [14]For we have become partners of Christ, if only we hold our first confidence firm to the end. [15]As it is said,
"Today, if you hear his voice,
do not harden your hearts as in
      the rebellion."
[16]Now who were they who heard and yet were rebellious? Was it not all those who left Egypt under the leadership of Moses? [17]But with whom was he angry forty years? Was it not those who sinned, whose bodies fell in the wilderness? [18]And to whom did he swear that they would not enter his rest, if not to those who were disobedient? [19]So we see that they were unable to enter because of unbelief.

The Rest That God Promised

4 Therefore, while the promise of entering his rest is still open, let us take care that none of you should seem to have failed to reach it. [2]For indeed the good news came to us just as to them; but the message they heard did not benefit them, because they were not united by faith with those who listened.[w] [3]For we who have believed enter that rest, just as God[x] has said,
"As in my anger I swore,
'They shall not enter my rest,'"
though his works were finished at the foundation of the world. [4]For in one place it speaks about the seventh day as follows, "And God rested on the

seventh day from all his works." [5]And again in this place it says, "They shall not enter my rest." [6]Since therefore it remains open for some to enter it, and those who formerly received the good news failed to enter because of disobedience, [7]again he sets a certain day—"today"—saying through David much later, in the words already quoted,
"Today, if you hear his voice,
do not harden your hearts."
[8]For if Joshua had given them rest, God[x] would not speak later about another day. [9]So then, a sabbath rest still remains for the people of God; [10]for those who enter God's rest also cease from their labors as God did from his. [11]Let us therefore make every effort to enter that rest, so that no one may fall through such disobedience as theirs.

[12] Indeed, the word of God is living and active, sharper than any two-edged sword, piercing until it divides soul from spirit, joints from marrow; it is able to judge the thoughts and intentions of the heart. [13]And before him no creature is hidden, but all are naked and laid bare to the eyes of the one to whom we must render an account.

4.13 Mind Reader

Advances in technology—MRI tests, x-ray machines, CAT scans—make it possible for doctors to peer inside the human body and judge what goes on there. But no one has yet devised a machine that can peer inside the brain to detect thoughts and attitudes. God has such ability; why try to hide?

Jesus the Great High Priest

[14] Since, then, we have a great high priest who has passed through the heavens, Jesus, the Son of God, let us hold fast to our confession. [15]For we do not have a high priest who is unable to sympathize with our weaknesses, but we have one who in every respect has been tested[y] as we are, yet without sin. [16]Let us therefore approach the throne of grace with boldness, so that we may receive mercy and find grace to help in time of need.

5 Every high priest chosen from among mortals is put in charge of things pertaining to God on their behalf, to offer gifts and sacrifices for sins. [2]He is able to deal gently with the ignorant and wayward, since he himself is subject to weakness; [3]and because of this he must offer sacrifice for his own sins as well as for those of the people. [4]And one does not presume to take this honor, but takes it only when called by God, just as Aaron was.

---

[t] Gk his   [u] Other ancient authorities add to the end   [v] Gk brothers   [w] Other ancient authorities read it did not meet with faith in those who listened   [x] Gk he   [y] Or tempted

5 So also Christ did not glorify himself in becoming a high priest, but was appointed by the one who said to him,

"You are my Son,
today I have begotten you";

[6]as he says also in another place,

"You are a priest forever,
according to the order of
Melchizedek."

7 In the days of his flesh, Jesus[z] offered up prayers and supplications, with loud cries and tears, to the one who was able to save him from death, and he was heard because of his reverent submission. [8]Although he was a Son, he learned obedience through what he suffered; [9]and having been made perfect, he became the source of eternal salvation for all who obey him, [10]having been designated by God a high priest according to the order of Melchizedek.

Warning against Falling Away

11 About this[a] we have much to say that is hard to explain, since you have become dull in understanding. [12]For though by this time you ought to be teachers, you need someone to teach you again the basic elements of the oracles of God. You need milk, not solid food; [13]for everyone who lives on milk, being still an infant, is unskilled in the word of righteousness. [14]But solid food is for the mature, for those whose faculties have been trained by practice to distinguish good from evil.

The Peril of Falling Away

6 Therefore let us go on toward perfection,[b] leaving behind the basic teaching about Christ, and not laying again the foundation: repentance from dead works and faith toward God, [2]instruction about baptisms, laying on of hands, resurrection of the dead, and eternal judgment. [3]And we will do[c] this, if God permits. [4]For it is impossible to restore again to repentance those who have once been enlightened, and have tasted the heavenly gift, and have shared in the Holy Spirit, [5]and have tasted the goodness of the word of God and the powers of the age to come, [6]and then have fallen away, since on their own they are crucifying again the Son of God and are holding him up to contempt. [7]Ground that drinks up the rain falling on it repeatedly, and that produces a crop useful to those for whom it is cultivated, receives a blessing from God. [8]But if it produces thorns and thistles, it is worthless and on the verge of being cursed; its end is to be burned over.

9 Even though we speak in this way, beloved, we are confident of better things in your case, things that belong to salvation. [10]For God is not unjust; he will not overlook your work and the love that you showed for his sake[d] in serving the saints, as you still do. [11]And we want each one of you to show the same diligence so as to realize the full assurance of hope to the very end, [12]so that you may not become sluggish, but imitators of those who through faith and patience inherit the promises.

6.4 Can a Believer Fall Away?

This passage has caused interpreters great difficulty. People who don't believe in "eternal security" think the passage refers to Christians who fall away from the faith. Others, such as John Calvin, insist that the author of Hebrews must be referring to people who never fully became Christians, because other verses seem to teach the eternal security of those in Christ (see John 5.24; 6.37; Romans 8.1; Hebrews 8.12). Regardless, the author is writing about a hypothetical situation. He is not describing what happened, but only what could happen: If such a falling away ever did occur, it would be impossible to rescue such people again. A somewhat similar argument appears at the end of chapter 10.

The Certainty of God's Promise

13 When God made a promise to Abraham, because he had no one greater by whom to swear, he swore by himself, [14]saying, "I will surely bless you and multiply you." [15]And thus Abraham,[z] having patiently endured, obtained the promise. [16]Human beings, of course, swear by someone greater than themselves, and an oath given as confirmation puts an end to all dispute. [17]In the same way, when God desired to show even more clearly to the heirs of the promise the unchangeable character of his purpose, he guaranteed it by an oath, [18]so that through two unchangeable things, in which it is impossible that God would prove false, we who have taken refuge might be strongly encouraged to seize the hope set before us. [19]We have this hope, a sure and steadfast anchor of the soul, a hope that enters the inner shrine behind the curtain, [20]where Jesus, a forerunner on our behalf, has entered, having become a high priest forever according to the order of Melchizedek.

The Priestly Order of Melchizedek

7 This "King Melchizedek of Salem, priest of the Most High God, met Abraham as he was returning from defeating the kings and blessed him"; [2]and to him Abraham apportioned "one-tenth of everything." His name, in the first place, means "king of righteousness"; next he is also king of Salem, that is, "king of peace." [3]Without

---

[z] Gk *he*   [a] Or *him*   [b] Or *toward maturity*   [c] Other ancient authorities read *let us do*   [d] Gk *for his name*

father, without mother, without genealogy, having neither beginning of days nor end of life, but resembling the Son of God, he remains a priest forever.

7.1 Who Is Melchizedek?

This mysterious person appears in only two places in the Old Testament: Genesis 14 and Psalm 110. Although a Gentile, Melchizedek worshiped the true God. In addition to being a priest, he was also a king. (The Jews would never have permitted such dual office-holding.) Hebrews demonstrates that the priesthood of Melchizedek was superior to that of Aaron; but both of them were exceeded by the great high priest, Jesus himself. Because he is both priest and king, Jesus is "according to the order of" Melchizedek. (See "The Twelfth Man," page 625, for more details.)

4 See how great he is! Even[e] Abraham the patriarch gave him a tenth of the spoils. 5And those descendants of Levi who receive the priestly office have a commandment in the law to collect tithes[f] from the people, that is, from their kindred,[g] though these also are descended from Abraham. 6But this man, who does not belong to their ancestry, collected tithes[f] from Abraham and blessed him who had received the promises. 7It is beyond dispute that the inferior is blessed by the superior. 8In the one case, tithes are received by those who are mortal; in the other, by one of whom it is testified that he lives. 9One might even say that Levi himself, who receives tithes, paid tithes through Abraham, 10for he was still in the loins of his ancestor when Melchizedek met him.

Another Priest, Like Melchizedek

11 Now if perfection had been attainable through the levitical priesthood—for the people received the law under this priesthood—what further need would there have been to speak of another priest arising according to the order of Melchizedek, rather than one according to the order of Aaron? 12For when there is a change in the priesthood, there is necessarily a change in the law as well. 13Now the one of whom these things are spoken belonged to another tribe, from which no one has ever served at the altar. 14For it is evident that our Lord was descended from Judah, and in connection with that tribe Moses said nothing about priests.

15 It is even more obvious when another priest arises, resembling Melchizedek, 16one who has become a priest, not through a legal requirement concerning physical descent, but through

the power of an indestructible life. 17For it is attested of him,

"You are a priest forever,
    according to the order of
        Melchizedek."

18There is, on the one hand, the abrogation of an earlier commandment because it was weak and ineffectual 19(for the law made nothing perfect); there is, on the other hand, the introduction of a better hope, through which we approach God.

7.19 Drawing Near

The original Jewish readers of Hebrews were still following the "old covenant" law, and this book was written to show them how things had changed to their benefit. In Old Testament times only the high priest could approach God, and that only once a year when he entered the curtained-off most holy place. As Hebrews points out, Jesus entered that inner room on our behalf (6.20). When he died, the curtain ripped in two; now any of us can draw near without fear.

20 This was confirmed with an oath; for others who became priests took their office without an oath, 21but this one became a priest with an oath, because of the one who said to him,

"The Lord has sworn
    and will not change his mind,
'You are a priest forever'"—

22accordingly Jesus has also become the guarantee of a better covenant.

23 Furthermore, the former priests were many in number, because they were prevented by death from continuing in office; 24but he holds his priesthood permanently, because he continues forever. 25Consequently he is able for all time to save[h] those who approach God through him, since he always lives to make intercession for them.

26 For it was fitting that we should have such a high priest, holy, blameless, undefiled, separated from sinners, and exalted above the heavens. 27Unlike the other[i] high priests, he has no need to offer sacrifices day after day, first for his own sins, and then for those of the people; this he did once for all when he offered himself. 28For the law appoints as high priests those who are subject to weakness, but the word of the oath, which came later than the law, appoints a Son who has been made perfect forever.

Mediator of a Better Covenant

8 Now the main point in what we are saying is this: we have such a high priest, one who is

---

e Other ancient authorities lack *Even*   f Or *a tenth*   g Gk *brothers*   h Or *able to save completely*
i Gk lacks *other*

seated at the right hand of the throne of the Majesty in the heavens, ²a minister in the sanctuary and the true tent*j* that the Lord, and not any mortal, has set up. ³For every high priest is appointed to offer gifts and sacrifices; hence it is necessary for this priest also to have something to offer. ⁴Now if he were on earth, he would not be a priest at all, since there are priests who offer gifts according to the law. ⁵They offer worship in a sanctuary that is a sketch and shadow of the heavenly one; for Moses, when he was about to erect the tent,*j* was warned, "See that you make everything according to the pattern that was shown you on the mountain." ⁶But Jesus*k* has now obtained a more excellent ministry, and to that degree he is the mediator of a better covenant, which has been enacted through better promises. ⁷For if that first covenant had been faultless, there would have been no need to look for a second one.

8 God*l* finds fault with them when he says:
"The days are surely coming, says the
    Lord,
when I will establish a new covenant
    with the house of Israel
    and with the house of Judah;

j Or *tabernacle*   *k* Gk *he*   *l* Gk *He*

New Light on the Old Testament
The advantages of living now

TO UNDERSTAND THE DIFFERENCE BETWEEN an original and a copy, consider trying to photograph the largest animal, a whale. Roy Chapman Andrews describes it:

"Once in Alaska we raised a humpback's spout and ran up close before the animal submerged. Ten minutes later, without warning, the floor of the ocean seemed to rise and a mountainous black body, dripping with foam, heaved upward, almost over our heads. It paused an instant, then fell sidewise to be swallowed up by a vortex of green water. With the camera ready in my hands I stared at the thing. The whale had dropped back scarcely twenty feet away; if it had fallen the other way, the vessel would have been crushed beneath its forty tons."

> For if that first covenant had been faultless, there would have been no need to look for a second one. 8.7

How can you adequately communicate the impact of something that immense? Photographers have recorded humpback whales bursting from the water, or "lobtailing" (standing on their heads and waving their mighty flukes high in the air). But no photograph can capture the sheer bigness of such an animal. A baby blue whale gains a ton of weight a month. An adult blue whale's heart weighs 1,000 pounds. How can any two-dimensional photograph convey such gargantuan size?

Comparing the Copy to the Original

Even the best photograph is just a copy, a representation of its subject's reality. No 8x10 rectangle can contain a whale. No photo sequence of the Grand Canyon is as grand as the canyon itself. The photograph preserves a mere two-dimensional copy of reality.

Hebrews uses that word *copy* to describe the images and rituals of the Old Testament: passover feasts, sacrifices, and other priestly duties. They were mere shadows, expressing the reality to come in Jesus Christ. No ceremony alone, however elaborate, can adequately express the experience of God himself, any more than a photograph of a whale or a mountain can adequately represent a whale or a mountain.

According to Hebrews, the Old Testament rituals were a copy, but Christ is the original. The author pulls up time-hallowed images from the Jewish tradition—sacrifices, laws, blood, the tabernacle, the priest, the day of atonement—and explains how Christ revealed once and for all the meaning these images only hinted at. The incomplete, shadowy copy contrasts with the perfect, genuine reality.

Which Is Better?

As always, Hebrews stresses the advantages of living now, rather than in the Old Testament ("the first covenant"). Because of Christ, sacrifices are no longer necessary (10.11–12), and God's laws are now written in our minds and on our hearts, not in a formal code (8.10). "It is finished," Christ cried out from the cross (John 19.30); the author of Hebrews describes how.

Copies have some value. A photograph of a whale, for example, conveys much to those who will never encounter one. But, as the author of Hebrews asks, who would prefer a copy to the real thing?

Life Questions: What practical help does Hebrews give on how to read the Old Testament? Of what value are the Old Testament laws and religious rituals?

9 not like the covenant that I made with
   their ancestors,
on the day when I took them by the
   hand to lead them out of the land
   of Egypt;
for they did not continue in my covenant,
   and so I had no concern for them, says
   the Lord.
10 This is the covenant that I will make with
   the house of Israel
after those days, says the Lord:
I will put my laws in their minds,
   and write them on their hearts,
and I will be their God,
   and they shall be my people.
11 And they shall not teach one another
   or say to each other, 'Know the Lord,'
for they shall all know me,
   from the least of them to the greatest.
12 For I will be merciful toward their
   iniquities,
and I will remember their sins
   no more."

13In speaking of "a new covenant," he has made
the first one obsolete. And what is obsolete and
growing old will soon disappear.

The Earthly and the Heavenly Sanctuaries

9 Now even the first covenant had regulations
for worship and an earthly sanctuary. 2For a
tent*m* was constructed, the first one, in which
were the lampstand, the table, and the bread of
the Presence;*n* this is called the Holy Place. 3Be-
hind the second curtain was a tent*m* called the
Holy of Holies. 4In it stood the golden altar of
incense and the ark of the covenant overlaid on
all sides with gold, in which there were a golden
urn holding the manna, and Aaron's rod that
budded, and the tablets of the covenant; 5above it
were the cherubim of glory overshadowing the
mercy seat.*o* Of these things we cannot speak
now in detail.

6 Such preparations having been made, the
priests go continually into the first tent*m* to carry
out their ritual duties; 7but only the high priest
goes into the second, and he but once a year, and
not without taking the blood that he offers for
himself and for the sins committed unintentionally by the people. 8By this the Holy Spirit indicates
that the way into the sanctuary has not yet been
disclosed as long as the first tent*m* is still standing.
9This is a symbol*p* of the present time, during
which gifts and sacrifices are offered that cannot
perfect the conscience of the worshiper, 10but deal
only with food and drink and various baptisms,

regulations for the body imposed until the time
comes to set things right.

11 But when Christ came as a high priest of
the good things that have come,*q* then through
the greater and perfect*r* tent*m* (not made with
hands, that is, not of this creation), 12he entered
once for all into the Holy Place, not with the

> ### 9.11 More Perfect
>
> *Descriptions of the tabernacle and offerings
> take up much of Exodus, Leviticus, Numbers,
> and Deuteronomy, leading some scholars to
> judge it the largest single subject covered in the
> Bible. Yet Hebrews, concerned to prove the
> superiority of a new covenant, devotes a mere
> 10 verses to the tabernacle (verses 1–10). The
> great high priest, Christ himself, has made the
> old system obsolete.*

blood of goats and calves, but with his own blood,
thus obtaining eternal redemption. 13For if the
blood of goats and bulls, with the sprinkling of
the ashes of a heifer, sanctifies those who have
been defiled so that their flesh is purified, 14how
much more will the blood of Christ, who through
the eternal Spirit*s* offered himself without blemish to God, purify our*t* conscience from dead
works to worship the living God!

15 For this reason he is the mediator of a new
covenant, so that those who are called may receive the promised eternal inheritance, because a
death has occurred that redeems them from the
transgressions under the first covenant.*u*
16Where a will*u* is involved, the death of the one
who made it must be established. 17For a will*u*
takes effect only at death, since it is not in force
as long as the one who made it is alive. 18Hence
not even the first covenant was inaugurated without blood. 19For when every commandment had
been told to all the people by Moses in accordance with the law, he took the blood of calves
and goats,*v* with water and scarlet wool and hyssop, and sprinkled both the scroll itself and all the
people, 20saying, "This is the blood of the covenant that God has ordained for you." 21And in the
same way he sprinkled with the blood both the
tent*m* and all the vessels used in worship. 22In-
deed, under the law almost everything is purified
with blood, and without the shedding of blood
there is no forgiveness of sins.

Christ's Sacrifice Takes Away Sin

23 Thus it was necessary for the sketches of
the heavenly things to be purified with these rites,

---

m Or *tabernacle*   *n* Gk *the presentation of the loaves*   *o* Or *the place of atonement*   *p* Gk *parable*   *q* Other
ancient authorities read *good things to come*   *r* Gk *more perfect*   *s* Other ancient authorities read *Holy Spirit*
t Other ancient authorities read *your*   *u* The Greek word used here means both *covenant* and *will*   *v* Other ancient
authorities lack *and goats*

but the heavenly things themselves need better sacrifices than these. 24For Christ did not enter a sanctuary made by human hands, a mere copy of the true one, but he entered into heaven itself, now to appear in the presence of God on our behalf. 25Nor was it to offer himself again and again, as the high priest enters the Holy Place year after year with blood that is not his own; 26for then he would have had to suffer again and again since the foundation of the world. But as it is, he has appeared once for all at the end of the age to

9.26 A Once-for-all Sacrifice

Jewish readers of Hebrews were very familiar with the religious rituals described in this chapter (see Leviticus 9 and 16 for the original instructions). Step by step, the author shows how Christ's new covenant improves on the old one. Instead of many sacrifices, he made only one, himself, thus gaining free and complete forgiveness for us. The chapter uses an analogy to explain why Christ's death was necessary (verse 17). It compares God's grace to a will. Wealth is only passed down when a death occurs; Christ's death freed the inheritance for us.

remove sin by the sacrifice of himself. 27And just as it is appointed for mortals to die once, and after that the judgment, 28so Christ, having been offered once to bear the sins of many, will appear a second time, not to deal with sin, but to save those who are eagerly waiting for him.

Christ's Sacrifice Once for All

10 Since the law has only a shadow of the good things to come and not the true form of these realities, it*w* can never, by the same sacrifices that are continually offered year after year, make perfect those who approach. 2Otherwise, would they not have ceased being offered, since the worshipers, cleansed once for all, would no longer have any consciousness of sin? 3But in these sacrifices there is a reminder of sin year after year. 4For it is impossible for the blood of bulls and goats to take away sins. 5Consequently, when Christ*x* came into the world, he said,

"Sacrifices and offerings you have not
    desired,
    but a body you have prepared for me;
6 in burnt offerings and sin offerings
    you have taken no pleasure.
7 Then I said, 'See, God, I have come to do
        your will, O God'
    (in the scroll of the book*y* it is written
        of me)."

8When he said above, "You have neither desired nor taken pleasure in sacrifices and offerings and burnt offerings and sin offerings" (these are offered according to the law), 9then he added, "See, I have come to do your will." He abolishes the first in order to establish the second. 10And it is by God's will*z* that we have been sanctified through the offering of the body of Jesus Christ once for all.

11 And every priest stands day after day at his service, offering again and again the same sacrifices that can never take away sins. 12But when Christ*a* had offered for all time a single sacrifice for sins, "he sat down at the right hand of God,"

10.12 Why Christ Sat Down

Hebrews makes special mention that Christ "sat down" after finishing his priestly duties. Jewish priests never sat down; the tabernacle and the temple did not have seats. They did their work standing up as a symbol that it was never finished. Having finished the work of a priest once for all, Christ "sat down."

13and since then has been waiting "until his enemies would be made a footstool for his feet." 14For by a single offering he has perfected for all time those who are sanctified. 15And the Holy Spirit also testifies to us, for after saying,
16 "This is the covenant that I will make
        with them
    after those days, says the Lord:
I will put my laws in their hearts,
    and I will write them on their minds,"
17he also adds,
    "I will remember*b* their sins and their
        lawless deeds no more."
18Where there is forgiveness of these, there is no longer any offering for sin.

A Call to Persevere

19 Therefore, my friends,*c* since we have confidence to enter the sanctuary by the blood of Jesus, 20by the new and living way that he opened for us through the curtain (that is, through his flesh), 21and since we have a great priest over the house of God, 22let us approach with a true heart in full assurance of faith, with our hearts sprinkled clean from an evil conscience and our bodies washed with pure water. 23Let us hold fast to the confession of our hope without wavering, for he who has promised is faithful. 24And let us consider how to provoke one another to love and good deeds, 25not neglecting to meet together, as is the habit of some, but encouraging one another, and all the more as you see the Day approaching.

w Other ancient authorities read *they*   *x* Gk *he*   *y* Meaning of Gk uncertain   *z* Gk *by that will*   *a* Gk *this one*
b Gk *on their minds and I will remember*   *c* Gk *Therefore, brothers*

26 For if we willfully persist in sin after having received the knowledge of the truth, there no longer remains a sacrifice for sins, 27but a fearful prospect of judgment, and a fury of fire that will consume the adversaries. 28Anyone who has violated the law of Moses dies without mercy "on the testimony of two or three witnesses." 29How much worse punishment do you think will be deserved by those who have spurned the Son of God, profaned the blood of the covenant by which they were sanctified, and outraged the Spirit of grace? 30For we know the one who said, "Vengeance is mine, I will repay." And again, "The Lord will judge his people." 31It is a fearful thing to fall into the hands of the living God.

32 But recall those earlier days when, after you had been enlightened, you endured a hard struggle with sufferings, 33sometimes being publicly exposed to abuse and persecution, and sometimes being partners with those so treated. 34For you had compassion for those who were in prison, and you cheerfully accepted the plundering of your possessions, knowing that you yourselves possessed something better and more lasting. 35Do not, therefore, abandon that confidence of yours; it brings a great reward. 36For you need endurance, so that when you have done the will of God, you may receive what was promised. 37For yet

"in a very little while,
    the one who is coming will come and
        will not delay;
38 but my righteous one will live by faith.
    My soul takes no pleasure in anyone
        who shrinks back."

39But we are not among those who shrink back and so are lost, but among those who have faith and so are saved.

The Meaning of Faith

11 Now faith is the assurance of things hoped for, the conviction of things not seen. 2Indeed, by faith[d] our ancestors received approval. 3By faith we understand that the worlds were pre-

d Gk by this

What Is True Faith?

Not even giants of faith get exactly what they want

WHAT IS FAITH? AND HOW can you be sure you've got it? Some Christians think of faith as an almost magical force: If you muster up enough of it, you'll get rich, stay healthy, and live a contented life, they say. Yet how does one "muster up" faith? What are signs of true faith?

The author of Hebrews launches into a detailed description of faith, complete with references to several dozen biographical models. (Some have dubbed Hebrews 11 the "Faith Hall of Fame.") "Without faith," Hebrews says bluntly, "it is impossible to please God" (11.6).

All these, though they were commended for their faith, did not receive what was promised. 11.39

Not What You'd Expect

But the picture of faith emerging from these chapters contains some surprises. The author uses words and phrases like "perseverance," "endurance," "do not lose heart." In many instances, the heroes cited did not receive the promise they hoped for; some ended up flogged and destitute, hiding out in goatskins (11.36–38). Many died horrible deaths.

Faith, concludes the author, most resembles a difficult race. The runner has his or her eyes on the winner's prize, and, despite nagging temptations to slacken the pace, refuses to let up until he or she crosses the finish line. "Lay aside every weight," Hebrews coaches (12.1). "Lift your drooping hands and strengthen your weak knees" (12.12).

Is It Worth the Struggle?

Why do people punish their bodies to run a grueling marathon race? Most runners name two reasons: the sense of personal reward they get and the physical benefits of the exercise. The same two rewards apply in the spiritual realm: Great prizes await those who persevere, and the very process of living by faith builds strong character. In this race, no one loses. If you finish, you get the reward.

Here, as elsewhere, Hebrews holds up Jesus, who endured great suffering for our sakes (12.2–3), as the ultimate example. The faith described in Hebrews is not sugarcoated; God does not guarantee a life of luxury and ease. It is tough faith: a constant commitment to hang on and believe God against all odds, no matter what.

Life Questions: Hebrews 11 mentions some people who prospered and some who suffered, yet all had faith. Taking into account what this passage says, try to come up with your own definition of faith.

pared by the word of God, so that what is seen was made from things that are not visible.*e*

The Examples of Abel, Enoch, and Noah

4 By faith Abel offered to God a more accept-able*f* sacrifice than Cain's. Through this he received approval as righteous, God himself giving approval to his gifts; he died, but through his faith*g* he still speaks. 5By faith Enoch was taken so that he did not experience death; and "he was not found, because God had taken him." For it was attested before he was taken away that "he had pleased God." 6And without faith it is impossible to please God, for whoever would approach him must believe that he exists and that he rewards those who seek him. 7By faith Noah, warned by God about events as yet unseen, respected the warning and built an ark to save his household; by this he condemned the world and became an heir to the righteousness that is in accordance with faith.

The Faith of Abraham

8 By faith Abraham obeyed when he was called to set out for a place that he was to receive as an inheritance; and he set out, not knowing where he was going. 9By faith he stayed for a time in the land he had been promised, as in a foreign land, living in tents, as did Isaac and Jacob, who were heirs with him of the same promise. 10For he looked forward to the city that has foundations, whose architect and builder is God. 11By faith he received power of procreation, even though he was too old—and Sarah herself was barren—because he considered him faithful who had promised.*h* 12Therefore from one person, and this one as good as dead, descendants were born, "as many as the stars of heaven and as the innumerable grains of sand by the seashore."

13 All of these died in faith without having received the promises, but from a distance they saw and greeted them. They confessed that they were strangers and foreigners on the earth, 14for people who speak in this way make it clear that they are seeking a homeland. 15If they had been thinking of the land that they had left behind, they would have had opportunity to return. 16But as it is, they desire a better country, that is, a heavenly one. Therefore God is not ashamed to be called their God; indeed, he has prepared a city for them.

17 By faith Abraham, when put to the test, offered up Isaac. He who had received the promises was ready to offer up his only son, 18of whom he had been told, "It is through Isaac that descendants shall be named for you." 19He considered

the fact that God is able even to raise someone from the dead—and figuratively speaking, he did receive him back. 20By faith Isaac invoked blessings for the future on Jacob and Esau. 21By faith Jacob, when dying, blessed each of the sons of Joseph, "bowing in worship over the top of his

11.16 Not Ashamed

The list of God's favorites in Hebrews 11 includes blemished characters such as Samson and Rahab, triumphant winners such as David and Barak, and then a whole list of anonymous "failures" who faced torture and persecution. Yet at some point all of these displayed the kind of faith that pleases God.

staff." 22By faith Joseph, at the end of his life, made mention of the exodus of the Israelites and gave instructions about his burial.*i*

The Faith of Moses

23 By faith Moses was hidden by his parents for three months after his birth, because they saw that the child was beautiful; and they were not afraid of the king's edict.*j* 24By faith Moses, when he was grown up, refused to be called a son of Pharaoh's daughter, 25choosing rather to share ill-treatment with the people of God than to enjoy the fleeting pleasures of sin. 26He considered abuse suffered for the Christ*k* to be greater wealth than the treasures of Egypt, for he was looking ahead to the reward. 27By faith he left Egypt, unafraid of the king's anger; for he persevered as though*l* he saw him who is invisible. 28By faith he kept the Passover and the sprinkling of blood, so that the destroyer of the firstborn would not touch the firstborn of Israel.*m*

The Faith of Other Israelite Heroes

29 By faith the people passed through the Red Sea as if it were dry land, but when the Egyptians attempted to do so they were drowned. 30By faith the walls of Jericho fell after they had been encircled for seven days. 31By faith Rahab the prostitute did not perish with those who were disobedient,*n* because she had received the spies in peace.

32 And what more should I say? For time would fail me to tell of Gideon, Barak, Samson, Jephthah, of David and Samuel and the prophets— 33who through faith conquered kingdoms, administered justice, obtained promises, shut the mouths of lions, 34quenched raging fire, escaped the edge of the sword, won strength out

---

e Or was not made out of visible things   *f Gk greater*   *g Gk through it*   *h Or By faith Sarah herself, though barren, received power to conceive, even when she was too old, because she considered him faithful who had promised.*   *i Gk his bones*   *j Other ancient authorities add By faith Moses, when he was grown up, killed the Egyptian, because he observed the humiliation of his people (Gk brothers)*   *k Or the Messiah*   *l Or because*   *m Gk would not touch them*   *n Or unbelieving*

of weakness, became mighty in war, put foreign
armies to flight. 35Women received their dead by
resurrection. Others were tortured, refusing to accept release, in order to obtain a better resurrection. 36Others suffered mocking and flogging, and
even chains and imprisonment. 37They were
stoned to death, they were sawn in two,[o] they
were killed by the sword; they went about in skins
of sheep and goats, destitute, persecuted, tormented— 38of whom the world was not worthy. They wandered in deserts and mountains,
and in caves and holes in the ground.

39 Yet all these, though they were commended for their faith, did not receive what was promised, 40since God had provided something better
so that they would not, apart from us, be made
perfect.

The Example of Jesus

12 Therefore, since we are surrounded by so
great a cloud of witnesses, let us also lay
aside every weight and the sin that clings so closely,[p] and let us run with perseverance the race that
is set before us, 2looking to Jesus the pioneer and
perfecter of our faith, who for the sake of[q] the joy
that was set before him endured the cross, disre-
garding its shame, and has taken his seat at the
right hand of the throne of God.

3 Consider him who endured such hostility
against himself from sinners,[r] so that you may
not grow weary or lose heart. 4In your struggle
against sin you have not yet resisted to the point
of shedding your blood. 5And you have forgotten
the exhortation that addresses you as children—

"My child, do not regard lightly the
discipline of the Lord,
or lose heart when you are punished
by him;
6 for the Lord disciplines those whom he
loves,
and chastises every child whom he
accepts."

7Endure trials for the sake of discipline. God is
treating you as children; for what child is there
whom a parent does not discipline? 8If you do not
have that discipline in which all children share,
then you are illegitimate and not his children.
9Moreover, we had human parents to discipline
us, and we respected them. Should we not be even
more willing to be subject to the Father of spirits
and live? 10For they disciplined us for a short time
as seemed best to them, but he disciplines us for
our good, in order that we may share his holiness.
11Now, discipline always seems painful rather
than pleasant at the time, but later it yields the
peaceful fruit of righteousness to those who have
been trained by it.

12 Therefore lift your drooping hands and
strengthen your weak knees, 13and make straight
paths for your feet, so that what is lame may not
be put out of joint, but rather be healed.

12.1 Pep Talk

Chapter 12 makes clear why Hebrews 11 devoted such attention to martyrs from the past. The early Christians who first read this book were facing persecution, and their faith was bending under the pressure. Think of the "great cloud of witnesses" who have gone before, Hebrews urges, and fix your eyes on Jesus, who volunteered to die on your behalf. With its imagery borrowed from athletics, this portion of Hebrews sounds like a coach's halftime speech delivered to competitors in danger of giving up.

Warnings against Rejecting God's Grace

14 Pursue peace with everyone, and the holiness without which no one will see the Lord. 15See
to it that no one fails to obtain the grace of God;
that no root of bitterness springs up and causes
trouble, and through it many become defiled.
16See to it that no one becomes like Esau, an
immoral and godless person, who sold his birthright for a single meal. 17You know that later,
when he wanted to inherit the blessing, he was
rejected, for he found no chance to repent,[s] even
though he sought the blessing[t] with tears.

18 You have not come to something[u] that
can be touched, a blazing fire, and darkness, and
gloom, and a tempest, 19and the sound of a trumpet, and a voice whose words made the hearers
beg that not another word be spoken to them.
20(For they could not endure the order that was
given, "If even an animal touches the mountain,
it shall be stoned to death." 21Indeed, so terrifying
was the sight that Moses said, "I tremble with

12.18 A Vivid Contrast

The author of Hebrews has been arguing that Christ's new covenant is far better than the old one between God and the Jews. This one section (verses 18–28) uses powerful images to summarize the great difference between encountering God in the way Moses did in the Old Testament and encountering him through Jesus. It also predicts that even greater things are in store: a new kingdom and new creation.

[o] Other ancient authorities add *they were tempted* [p] Other ancient authorities read *sin that easily distracts*
[q] Or *who instead of* [r] Other ancient authorities read *such hostility from sinners against themselves* [s] Or *no chance to change his father's mind* [t] Gk *it* [u] Other ancient authorities read *a mountain*

fear.") [22]But you have come to Mount Zion and to the city of the living God, the heavenly Jerusalem, and to innumerable angels in festal gathering, [23]and to the assembly[v] of the firstborn who are enrolled in heaven, and to God the judge of all, and to the spirits of the righteous made perfect, [24]and to Jesus, the mediator of a new covenant, and to the sprinkled blood that speaks a better word than the blood of Abel.

25 See that you do not refuse the one who is speaking; for if they did not escape when they refused the one who warned them on earth, how much less will we escape if we reject the one who warns from heaven! [26]At that time his voice shook the earth; but now he has promised, "Yet once more I will shake not only the earth but also the heaven." [27]This phrase, "Yet once more," indicates the removal of what is shaken—that is, created things—so that what cannot be shaken may remain. [28]Therefore, since we are receiving a kingdom that cannot be shaken, let us give thanks, by which we offer to God an acceptable worship with reverence and awe; [29]for indeed our God is a consuming fire.

Service Well-Pleasing to God

13 Let mutual love continue. [2]Do not neglect to show hospitality to strangers, for by doing that some have entertained angels without knowing it. [3]Remember those who are in prison, as though you were in prison with them; those who are being tortured, as though you yourselves were being tortured.[w] [4]Let marriage be held in honor by all, and let the marriage bed be kept undefiled; for God will judge fornicators and adulterers. [5]Keep your lives free from the love of money, and be content with what you have; for he has said, "I will never leave you or forsake you." [6]So we can say with confidence,

"The Lord is my helper;
I will not be afraid.
What can anyone do to me?"

7 Remember your leaders, those who spoke the word of God to you; consider the outcome of their way of life, and imitate their faith. [8]Jesus Christ is the same yesterday and today and forever. [9]Do not be carried away by all kinds of strange teachings; for it is well for the heart to be strengthened by grace, not by regulations about food,[x] which have not benefited those who observe them. [10]We have an altar from which those who officiate in the tent[y] have no right to eat. [11]For the bodies of those animals whose blood is brought into the sanctuary by the high priest as a sacrifice for sin are burned outside the camp. [12]Therefore Jesus also suffered outside the city gate in order to sanctify the people by his own blood. [13]Let us then go to him outside the camp and bear the abuse he endured. [14]For here we have no lasting city, but we are looking for the city that is to come. [15]Through him, then, let us continually offer a sacrifice of praise to God, that

13.15 Sacrifice of Praise

In form, Hebrews is more theological than practical. But in the last chapter the author adds a list of specific commands and suggestions. Even here, however, he makes one last reference to sacrifice. Now, we have only a "sacrifice of praise" to offer, because Christ accomplished all that was needed.

is, the fruit of lips that confess his name. [16]Do not neglect to do good and to share what you have, for such sacrifices are pleasing to God.

17 Obey your leaders and submit to them, for they are keeping watch over your souls and will give an account. Let them do this with joy and not with sighing—for that would be harmful to you.

18 Pray for us; we are sure that we have a clear conscience, desiring to act honorably in all things. [19]I urge you all the more to do this, so that I may be restored to you very soon.

Benediction

20 Now may the God of peace, who brought back from the dead our Lord Jesus, the great shepherd of the sheep, by the blood of the eternal covenant, [21]make you complete in everything good so that you may do his will, working among us[z] that which is pleasing in his sight, through Jesus Christ, to whom be the glory forever and ever. Amen.

Final Exhortation and Greetings

22 I appeal to you, brothers and sisters,[a] bear with my word of exhortation, for I have written to you briefly. [23]I want you to know that our brother Timothy has been set free; and if he comes in time, he will be with me when I see you. [24]Greet all your leaders and all the saints. Those from Italy send you greetings. [25]Grace be with all of you.[b]

---

[v] Or *angels, and to the festal gathering* [23]*and assembly* [w] Gk *were in the body* [x] Gk *not by foods*
[y] Or *tabernacle* [z] Other ancient authorities read *you* [a] Gk *brothers* [b] Other ancient authorities add *Amen*

JAMES

Words Are Not Enough
You can believe all the right things, yet still be dead wrong

> But be doers of the word, and not merely hearers who deceive themselves.
> 1.22

WHERE THERE IS LIFE, THERE is motion. Some antelopes, as well as the cheetah, can sprint faster than some cars on the highway. Bighorn sheep, charging one another headfirst, collide with such force that the sound echoes like a gunshot through mountain ranges. Canada geese, fanned out across the sky in an orderly *V*, battle winds for 1,000 miles, nonstop, before dropping back to earth.

Sometimes we keep relics of life: an elkhead hanging above a fireplace, a fragile, perfect seashell, an exotic butterfly mounted on a pin. But these are mere mementos: life has gone from them, and with it motion.

A Sure Sign of Life

Authors of the Bible often look to nature for analogies to express spiritual truth. And the book of James, controversial because of its emphasis on "good works," is perhaps best understood through the analogy of motion. In the spiritual realm also, where there's life there will be motion.

When a person becomes a Christian, new life begins, and inevitably that life must express itself through "spiritual motion," or good deeds. In James's words, "What good is it . . . if you say you have faith but do not have works?" (2.14).

Movement does not cause life, but it does invariably follow life. It's a sure sign that life is present. Similarly, genuine faith in Christ should always result in actions that demonstrate faith.

Does James Contradict Paul?

James is not writing about how to become a Christian, but rather how to act like one. Having all the correct beliefs about God will hardly suffice: Even demons believe in God. Real, life-giving faith should produce motion, and James minces no words in describing the specific spiritual actions expected of Christians.

Christian thinkers, notably Martin Luther, have struggled to reconcile the message of James with that of Paul, who so firmly warned against slavish legalism. But Paul never belittled holy living. When he wrote to carousers, such as in his letters to the Corinthians, he railed against immorality as strongly as James.

Evidently, James's readers were not even flirting with legalism. They lived at the other extreme, ignoring those laws God had clearly revealed. James had a simple remedy: "Be doers of the word, and not merely hearers" (1.22).

Straight to the Point

Unlike the apostle Paul, James was no urbane man of letters. He was a simple, homespun preacher, perturbed at people who were not living right. His letter covers a wide range of topics, applying the Christian faith to specific problems and commanding readers to live out their beliefs.

Be humble! James orders. *Submit to God! Stop sinning!* James is as forthright as an Old Testament prophet; it's hard to miss his point.

Modern readers of James face the same dilemma as the first recipients of this unsettling letter. His words are easy enough to understand, but are we doing what he says? What kind of motion characterizes our spiritual lives? As Luther himself said, "You are saved by faith alone, but if faith is alone it is not faith."

How to Read James

Few New Testament writers achieve the clarity or the "punch" of James. He doesn't spend time expanding subpoints or worrying about literary structure. As a result, the book of James reads like a collection of pithy proverbs. (It's sometimes called the "Proverbs of the New Testament.") In your study, it may help to group the material by subject; James tends to return to themes repeatedly.

As leader of the headquarters church in Jerusalem, James knew how to speak with authority. You don't have to look for hidden meanings in this book. James tells you clearly how you should act, in 54 direct commands. Note that many of these have parallels to Jesus' Sermon on the Mount. As you read, keep in mind the diverse audience he was addressing, which included the rich and the poor. Note his "asides" to specific groups.

3-TRACK READING PLAN

For an explanation and complete listing of the 3-track reading plan, turn to page 7.

TRACK 1: *Two-Week Courses on the Bible*
See page 7 for information on these courses.

TRACK 2: *An Overview of James in 1 Day*
☐ Day 1. Read the Introduction to James, then chapter 1, on how the Christian should respond to tough times, or "trials."
Now turn to page 9 for your next Track 2 reading project.

TRACK 3: *All of James in 4 Days*
After you have read through James, turn to pages 10–14 for your next Track 3 reading project.
☐1   ☐2   ☐3–4   ☐5

Salutation

1 James, a servant[a] of God and of the Lord Jesus Christ,
To the twelve tribes in the Dispersion:
Greetings.

Faith and Wisdom

2 My brothers and sisters,[b] whenever you face trials of any kind, consider it nothing but joy, ³because you know that the testing of your faith produces endurance; ⁴and let endurance have its full effect, so that you may be mature and complete, lacking in nothing.

1.3 Productive Pain

James's call for joy in the face of trials may seem shocking or even insensitive at first. A close reading, though, makes clear that James finds joy in the results of the trials, not in the trials themselves. Even difficult times can produce good qualities, such as perseverance. This positive, or "redemptive," approach to suffering surfaces throughout the New Testament (see Romans 5.1–5; 1 Peter 1.3–9).

5 If any of you is lacking in wisdom, ask God, who gives to all generously and ungrudgingly, and it will be given you. ⁶But ask in faith, never doubting, for the one who doubts is like a wave of the sea, driven and tossed by the wind; ⁷, ⁸for the doubter, being double-minded and unstable in every way, must not expect to receive anything from the Lord.

Poverty and Riches

9 Let the believer[c] who is lowly boast in being raised up, ¹⁰and the rich in being brought low, because the rich will disappear like a flower in the field. ¹¹For the sun rises with its scorching heat and withers the field; its flower falls, and its beauty perishes. It is the same way with the rich; in the midst of a busy life, they will wither away.

Trial and Temptation

12 Blessed is anyone who endures temptation. Such a one has stood the test and will receive the crown of life that the Lord[d] has promised to those who love him. ¹³No one, when tempted, should say, "I am being tempted by God"; for God cannot be tempted by evil and he himself

---

[a] Gk *slave*   [b] Gk *brothers*   [c] Gk *brother*   [d] Gk *he*; other ancient authorities read *God*

tempts no one. ¹⁴But one is tempted by one's own desire, being lured and enticed by it; ¹⁵then, when that desire has conceived, it gives birth to sin, and that sin, when it is fully grown, gives birth to death. ¹⁶Do not be deceived, my beloved.ᵉ

17 Every generous act of giving, with every perfect gift, is from above, coming down from the Father of lights, with whom there is no variation or shadow due to change.ᶠ ¹⁸In fulfillment of his own purpose he gave us birth by the word of truth, so that we would become a kind of first fruits of his creatures.

Hearing and Doing the Word

19 You must understand this, my beloved:ᵉ let everyone be quick to listen, slow to speak, slow to anger; ²⁰for your anger does not produce God's righteousness. ²¹Therefore rid yourselves of all sordidness and rank growth of wickedness, and welcome with meekness the implanted word that has the power to save your souls.

22 But be doers of the word, and not merely hearers who deceive themselves. ²³For if any are hearers of the word and not doers, they are like those who look at themselvesᵍ in a mirror; ²⁴for they look at themselves and, on going away, immediately forget what they were like. ²⁵But those who look into the perfect law, the law of liberty, and persevere, being not hearers who forget but doers who act—they will be blessed in their doing.

26 If any think they are religious, and do not bridle their tongues but deceive their hearts, their religion is worthless. ²⁷Religion that is pure and undefiled before God, the Father, is this: to care for orphans and widows in their distress, and to keep oneself unstained by the world.

Warning against Partiality

2 My brothers and sisters,ʰ do you with your acts of favoritism really believe in our glorious Lord Jesus Christ?ⁱ ²For if a person with gold

2.1 Play No Favorites

James 1 tells Christians to act out their faith. James 2 gives a very pointed example of church members deferring to the wealthy and powerful. This direct application, hitting close to home, characterizes James. He leaves no room for ambiguity.

rings and in fine clothes comes into your assembly, and if a poor person in dirty clothes also comes in, ³and if you take notice of the one wearing the fine clothes and say, "Have a seat here,

please," while to the one who is poor you say, "Stand there," or, "Sit at my feet,"ʲ ⁴have you not made distinctions among yourselves, and become judges with evil thoughts? ⁵Listen, my beloved brothers and sisters.ᵏ Has not God chosen the poor in the world to be rich in faith and to be heirs of the kingdom that he has promised to those who love him? ⁶But you have dishonored the poor. Is it not the rich who oppress you? Is it not they who drag you into court? ⁷Is it not they who blaspheme the excellent name that was invoked over you?

8 You do well if you really fulfill the royal law according to the scripture, "You shall love your neighbor as yourself." ⁹But if you show partiality, you commit sin and are convicted by the law as transgressors. ¹⁰For whoever keeps the whole law but fails in one point has become accountable for all of it. ¹¹For the one who said, "You shall not commit adultery," also said, "You shall not murder." Now if you do not commit adultery but if you murder, you have become a transgressor of the law. ¹²So speak and so act as those who are to be judged by the law of liberty. ¹³For judgment will be without mercy to anyone who has shown no mercy; mercy triumphs over judgment.

Faith without Works Is Dead

14 What good is it, my brothers and sisters,ᵏ if you say you have faith but do not have works? Can faith save you? ¹⁵If a brother or sister is naked and lacks daily food, ¹⁶and one of you says to them, "Go in peace; keep warm and eat your fill," and yet you do not supply their bodily needs, what is the good of that? ¹⁷So faith by itself, if it has no works, is dead.

18 But someone will say, "You have faith and I have works." Show me your faith apart from your works, and I by my works will show you my faith. ¹⁹You believe that God is one; you do well. Even the demons believe—and shudder. ²⁰Do you want to be shown, you senseless person, that faith apart from works is barren? ²¹Was not our ancestor Abraham justified by works when he offered his son Isaac on the altar? ²²You see that faith was active along with his works, and faith was brought to completion by the works. ²³Thus the scripture was fulfilled that says, "Abraham believed God, and it was reckoned to him as righteousness," and he was called the friend of God. ²⁴You see that a person is justified by works and not by faith alone. ²⁵Likewise, was not Rahab the prostitute also justified by works when she welcomed the messengers and sent them out by another road? ²⁶For just as the body without the spirit is dead, so faith without works is also dead.

ᵉ Gk *my beloved brothers*   ᶠ Other ancient authorities read *variation due to a shadow of turning*   ᵍ Gk *at the face of his birth*   ʰ Gk *My brothers*   ⁱ Or *hold the faith of our glorious Lord Jesus Christ without acts of favoritism*   ʲ Gk *Sit under my footstool*   ᵏ Gk *brothers*

Taming the Tongue

3 Not many of you should become teachers, my brothers and sisters,[l] for you know that we who teach will be judged with greater strictness. [2]For all of us make many mistakes. Anyone who makes no mistakes in speaking is perfect, able to keep the whole body in check with a bridle. [3]If we put bits into the mouths of horses to make them obey us, we guide their whole bodies. [4]Or look at ships: though they are so large that it takes strong winds to drive them, yet they are guided by a very small rudder wherever the will of the pilot directs. [5]So also the tongue is a small member, yet it boasts of great exploits.

3.3 Colorful Language

Vivid, homey pictures from nature give a visual character to James's words, almost as if each thought were a photograph. He refers to sea froth, wilted flowers, a forest fire, a horse's bit, the morning mist, a hungry moth, the farmer's spring rains, a giant ship, and a saltwater spring. Paul, a more educated writer, alluded to culture and athletics and human relationships. But James felt most comfortable borrowing simple images from nature.

How great a forest is set ablaze by a small fire! [6]And the tongue is a fire. The tongue is placed among our members as a world of iniquity; it stains the whole body, sets on fire the cycle of nature,[m] and is itself set on fire by hell.[n] [7]For every species of beast and bird, of reptile and sea creature, can be tamed and has been tamed by the human species, [8]but no one can tame the tongue—a restless evil, full of deadly poison. [9]With it we bless the Lord and Father, and with it we curse those who are made in the likeness of God. [10]From the same mouth come blessing and cursing. My brothers and sisters,[o] this ought not to be so. [11]Does a spring pour forth from the same opening both fresh and brackish water? [12]Can a fig tree, my brothers and sisters,[p] yield olives, or a grapevine figs? No more can salt water yield fresh.

Two Kinds of Wisdom

13 Who is wise and understanding among you? Show by your good life that your works are done with gentleness born of wisdom. [14]But if you have bitter envy and selfish ambition in your hearts, do not be boastful and false to the truth. [15]Such wisdom does not come down from above, but is earthly, unspiritual, devilish. [16]For where there is envy and selfish ambition, there will also be disorder and wickedness of every kind. [17]But the wisdom from above is first pure, then peaceable, gentle, willing to yield, full of mercy and good fruits, without a trace of partiality or hypocrisy. [18]And a harvest of righteousness is sown in peace for[q] those who make peace.

Friendship with the World

4 Those conflicts and disputes among you, where do they come from? Do they not come from your cravings that are at war within you?

4.1 The Need for Self-Control

If you had to distill the message of James into one word, it might be self-control. Chapters 4 and 5, which contain some of James's most striking imagery, show how simple greed and desire can corrode the church and destroy unity. And, indeed, many of the Jewish Christians he was writing to soon experienced an abrupt turn of fortune. They lost their wealth and suffered severe persecution.

[2]You want something and do not have it; so you commit murder. And you covet[r] something and cannot obtain it; so you engage in disputes and conflicts. You do not have, because you do not ask. [3]You ask and do not receive, because you ask wrongly, in order to spend what you get on your pleasures. [4]Adulterers! Do you not know that friendship with the world is enmity with God? Therefore whoever wishes to be a friend of the world becomes an enemy of God. [5]Or do you suppose that it is for nothing that the scripture says, "God[s] yearns jealously for the spirit that he has made to dwell in us"? [6]But he gives all the more grace; therefore it says,

"God opposes the proud,
　　but gives grace to the humble."
[7]Submit yourselves therefore to God. Resist the devil, and he will flee from you. [8]Draw near to God, and he will draw near to you. Cleanse your hands, you sinners, and purify your hearts, you double-minded. [9]Lament and mourn and weep. Let your laughter be turned into mourning and your joy into dejection. [10]Humble yourselves before the Lord, and he will exalt you.

Warning against Judging Another

11 Do not speak evil against one another, brothers and sisters.[l] Whoever speaks evil against another or judges another, speaks evil against the law and judges the law; but if you judge the law, you are not a doer of the law but a judge. [12]There is one lawgiver and judge who is

---

[l] Gk brothers　　[m] Or wheel of birth　　[n] Gk Gehenna　　[o] Gk My brothers　　[p] Gk my brothers　　[q] Or by
[r] Or you murder and you covet　　[s] Gk He

able to save and to destroy. So who, then, are you to judge your neighbor?

Boasting about Tomorrow

13 Come now, you who say, "Today or tomorrow we will go to such and such a town and spend a year there, doing business and making money." [14]Yet you do not even know what tomorrow will bring. What is your life? For you are a mist that appears for a little while and then vanishes. [15]Instead you ought to say, "If the Lord wishes, we will live and do this or that." [16]As it is, you boast in your arrogance; all such boasting is evil. [17]Anyone, then, who knows the right thing to do and fails to do it, commits sin.

Warning to Rich Oppressors

5 Come now, you rich people, weep and wail for the miseries that are coming to you. [2]Your riches have rotted, and your clothes are moth-eaten. [3]Your gold and silver have rusted, and their rust will be evidence against you, and it will eat your flesh like fire. You have laid up treasure[t] for the last days. [4]Listen! The wages of the laborers who mowed your fields, which you kept back by fraud, cry out, and the cries of the harvesters have reached the ears of the Lord of hosts. [5]You have lived on the earth in luxury and in pleasure; you have fattened your hearts in a day of slaughter. [6]You have condemned and murdered the righteous one, who does not resist you.

Patience in Suffering

7 Be patient, therefore, beloved,[u] until the coming of the Lord. The farmer waits for the precious crop from the earth, being patient with it until it receives the early and the late rains. [8]You also must be patient. Strengthen your hearts, for the coming of the Lord is near.[v] [9]Beloved,[w] do not grumble against one another, so that you may not be judged. See, the Judge is standing at the doors! [10]As an example of suffering and patience, beloved,[u] take the prophets who spoke in the name of the Lord. [11]Indeed we call blessed those who showed endurance. You have heard of the endurance of Job, and you have seen the purpose of the Lord, how the Lord is compassionate and merciful.

[t] Or will eat your flesh, since you have stored up fire   [u] Gk brothers   [v] Or is at hand   [w] Gk Brothers

Conflicts of Rich and Poor
A different kind of class struggle

OUR SOCIETY TENDS TO DIVIDE the rich and the poor. The two groups have little daily contact, and you would have a very hard time communicating a unified message to both the very rich and the very poor.

"God opposes the proud, but gives grace to the humble." 4.6

Yet it seems James's original readers included both those groups. In one paragraph James addresses the haughty, privileged people of wealth, and in the next paragraph he turns to poor people undergoing severe trials. (Note the shift between 5.1 and 5.7.)

The two groups had different problems. The wealthy were selfish. They showed insensitivity and snobbishness to the poor. For their part, the poor responded with envy and grumbling. They blamed God for their poverty.

Who Is Double-minded?

James gave advice on the specific problems of each group, but he also implied they have much in common. For both rich and poor the most important struggle is not outside—the conditions we live in—but rather inside. All of us experience the inner conflict of being pulled by powerful, contrary forces. Will we move toward Christ and the life he taught, or in the opposite direction? Will we trust God or reject him?

James coined a new word to describe this inner conflict: he called it being "double-minded" (4.8). For rich and poor, this conflict may express itself in different ways, as James went on to explain. But double-mindedness is a tug-of-war between divided loyalties. The essential struggle to obey God is no different for either group.

As he discussed the rich and the poor, James relied on many of the actual phrases Jesus had used, especially in the Sermon on the Mount. (This is quite understandable if the author was James the brother of Jesus, as many scholars believe.) He applied what Jesus taught in a fresh, new way, calling on all of us—rich and poor—to be single-minded in our commitment to follow that way.

Life Questions: James 2 warns against favoritism based on social class. Does such favoritism happen among Christians today? Is there any difference between the way rich and poor people think about following Jesus?

12 Above all, my beloved,ˣ do not swear, either by heaven or by earth or by any other oath, but let your "Yes" be yes and your "No" be no, so that you may not fall under condemnation.

The Prayer of Faith

13 Are any among you suffering? They should pray. Are any cheerful? They should sing songs of praise. ¹⁴Are any among you sick? They should call for the elders of the church and have them pray over them, anointing them with oil in the name of the Lord. ¹⁵The prayer of faith will save the sick, and the Lord will raise them up; and anyone who has committed sins will be forgiven. ¹⁶Therefore confess your sins to one another, and pray for one another, so that you may be healed. The prayer of the righteous is powerful and effective. ¹⁷Elijah was a human being like us, and he prayed fervently that it might not rain, and for three years and six months it did not rain on the earth. ¹⁸Then he prayed again, and the heaven gave rain and the earth yielded its harvest.

19 My brothers and sisters,ʸ if anyone among you wanders from the truth and is brought back by another, ²⁰you should know that whoever brings back a sinner from wandering will save the sinner'sᶻ soul from death and will cover a multitude of sins.

5.10 Waiting It Out

In this section, James expands on the idea (1.2–4) that God can use suffering for our benefit. He realistically concedes that rejoicing in the face of trials may not come right away. To develop such an attitude will take patience and perseverance. James mentions two sources of support for someone trying to cope with suffering: (1) the past example of people like the prophets and Job; (2) the church's ministry of healing and prayer.

ˣ Gk brothers   ʸ Gk My brothers   ᶻ Gk his

1 PETER

A Word to the Suffering
What to do when trouble comes

> *Beloved, do not be surprised at the fiery ordeal that is taking place among you to test you, as though something strange were happening to you. 4.12*

A DISTANT, SWIRLING CLOUD OF DUST signaled the approach of Turkish death squads. But who could escape? The villages of Armenia sat exposed and defenseless on a rocky plain. Doomed Christians clung together on the floors of their homes, praying, singing, and shivering with fear.

This scene was repeated often during World War I, and it usually ended in a massacre. The Turkish assault against Armenian Christians was one of history's worst religion-inspired bloodbaths: Over one million people died. But, sadly, the Armenian tragedy was but one of many attacks against 20th-century Christians.

More people have died for their religious faith in this century than in all the rest of history combined. Thousands of Christians died in East Africa, first in the Mau Mau uprising and then during Ugandan dictator Idi Amin's reign of terror. Millions more suffered under Soviet and Chinese governments. And the oppression goes on: Even today some countries imprison and torture converts to Christianity. This fact alone makes the book of 1 Peter starkly relevant for modern readers.

How to Respond to Persecution

What advice would you give Christians about to undergo persecution? The apostle Peter took up that challenge just as ominous rumblings from Rome were striking fear in every Christian community. Half-crazed Nero had seized on believers as scapegoats for the ills of his empire.

Should the persecuted Christians flee or resist? Should they tone down their outward signs of faith? Give up? Peter's readers, their lives in danger, needed clear advice on suffering.

They also wanted explanations of the meaning of suffering. Why does God allow it? Can good result? Does God care? In short, they were asking the questions that occur to any Christian who goes through great trial.

According to Peter, suffering should not catch a Christian off guard. We are "exiles" (1.17) in a hostile world, and where Christians thrive, storm clouds may gather. Suffering is an expected part of a life of sincere faith.

Peter's Own Experience

On the subject of suffering, Peter makes an ideal counselor for readers then and now. He had been flogged and imprisoned for his own faith, once even expecting execution (Acts 12). Also, Peter had personally watched Jesus endure suffering, and in this letter he points to him as an example of how to respond.

Peter encourages his readers to "conduct yourselves honorably among the Gentiles, so that, though they malign you as evildoers, they may see your honorable deeds and glorify God" (2.12). Suffering can refine believers and give us an opportunity to prove our faith, the result thus working out for our benefit.

This book emphasizes a further point also: Suffering is temporary, to be endured only for "a little while" (1.6; 5.10). Those who suffer with Christ will also glory with him in a life forever free of pain. Skeptics have criticized the church for stressing a future life rather than working to improve this one. "You promise pie in the sky by and by," they taunt. But to Peter's readers—wary of enemies on the prowl, unsure of surviving another day—that message was as tangible and nourishing as food.

According to 1 Peter, our hope that suffering will one day cease is not a mirage but a "living hope" (1.3) in the One who has conquered death.

How to Read 1 Peter

At first Christianity enjoyed official toleration by the Roman empire, but gradually the government turned against it. Rome resented the Christians' talk about another kingdom and their objections to idolatry and decadence.

Although 1 Peter was originally written to people in severe danger, its lessons apply to all of us, for we all experience pain of some kind. Why don't things work out the way we want? Is God trying to tell us something? Peter gives authoritative answers. As you read, try to apply what he says to your own situation.

Peter's writing style reveals his simple fisherman background: He uses pithy peasant expressions and awkwardly shifts back and forth between doctrine and advice. Chapter 2 (verses 18–25) shows an excellent example. Peter gives a deep insight into what it meant for Christ to suffer on our behalf, but he includes it in a practical section on slaves and governments. Thus, he blends doctrine (what to believe) with practice (how to behave).

More a preacher than a writer, Peter structured his book like a rambling sermon. Look for the 34 direct commands included. Peter's reliance on common figures of speech—a cornerstone, a lamb, a shepherd—makes the book very quotable.

But Peter was not simply giving homespun advice; he was well-grounded in the teachings of Jesus and the prophets. Proportionately, he quotes from the Old Testament more than any other New Testament author.

PEOPLE YOU'LL MEET IN 1 PETER

PETER *(p. 1286)*

3-TRACK READING PLAN

For an explanation and complete listing of the 3-track reading plan, turn to page 7.

TRACK 1:   ***Two-Week Courses on the Bible***
See page 7 for information on these courses.

TRACK 2:   ***An Overview of 1 Peter in 1 Day***
☐ Day 1. Read the Introduction to 1 Peter, then chapter 1 for a capsule summary of the letter's style and message.

Now turn to page 9 for your next Track 2 reading project.

TRACK 3:   ***All of 1 Peter in 4 Days***
After you have read through 1 Peter, turn to pages 10–14 for your next Track 3 reading project.

☐1   ☐2   ☐3   ☐4–5

Salutation

1 Peter, an apostle of Jesus Christ,
To the exiles of the Dispersion in Pontus, Galatia, Cappadocia, Asia, and Bithynia, ²who have been chosen and destined by God the Father and sanctified by the Spirit to be obedient to Jesus Christ and to be sprinkled with his blood:

May grace and peace be yours in abundance.

A Living Hope

3 Blessed be the God and Father of our Lord Jesus Christ! By his great mercy he has given us a new birth into a living hope through the resurrection of Jesus Christ from the dead, ⁴and into an inheritance that is imperishable, undefiled, and unfading, kept in heaven for you, ⁵who are being protected by the power of God through faith for a salvation ready to be revealed in the last time. ⁶In this you rejoice,ᵃ even if now for a little while you have had to suffer various trials, ⁷so that the genuineness of your faith—being more precious than gold that, though perishable, is tested by fire—may be found to result in praise and glory and honor when Jesus Christ is revealed. ⁸Al-

---

a Or Rejoice in this

though you have not seen[b] him, you love him; and even though you do not see him now, you believe in him and rejoice with an indescribable and glorious joy, [9]for you are receiving the outcome of your faith, the salvation of your souls.

1.7 Refiner's Fire

A prospector who discovers gold-bearing rock sends it to an assayer for evaluation. Testing by fire will melt off most impurities, and the true gold will emerge purified. Suffering acts in much the same way, says Peter: It exposes and refines true faith. In addition, faith in the midst of such trials will earn future rewards.

10 Concerning this salvation, the prophets who prophesied of the grace that was to be yours made careful search and inquiry, [11]inquiring about the person or time that the Spirit of Christ within them indicated when it testified in advance to the sufferings destined for Christ and the subsequent glory. [12]It was revealed to them that they were serving not themselves but you, in regard to the things that have now been announced to you through those who brought you good news by the Holy Spirit sent from heaven—things into which angels long to look!

A Call to Holy Living

13 Therefore prepare your minds for action;[c] discipline yourselves; set all your hope on the grace that Jesus Christ will bring you when he is revealed. [14]Like obedient children, do not be conformed to the desires that you formerly had in ignorance. [15]Instead, as he who called you is holy, be holy yourselves in all your conduct; [16]for it is written, "You shall be holy, for I am holy."

17 If you invoke as Father the one who judges all people impartially according to their deeds, live in reverent fear during the time of your exile. [18]You know that you were ransomed from the futile ways inherited from your ancestors, not with perishable things like silver or gold, [19]but with the precious blood of Christ, like that of a lamb without defect or blemish. [20]He was destined before the foundation of the world, but was revealed at the end of the ages for your sake. [21]Through him you have come to trust in God, who raised him from the dead and gave him glory, so that your faith and hope are set on God.

22 Now that you have purified your souls by your obedience to the truth[d] so that you have genuine mutual love, love one another deeply[e] from the heart.[f] [23]You have been born anew, not

of perishable but of imperishable seed, through the living and enduring word of God.[g] [24]For

"All flesh is like grass
     and all its glory like the flower of grass.
The grass withers,
     and the flower falls,
25   but the word of the Lord endures
          forever."

That word is the good news that was announced to you.

The Living Stone and a Chosen People

2 Rid yourselves, therefore, of all malice, and all guile, insincerity, envy, and all slander. [2]Like newborn infants, long for the pure, spiritual milk, so that by it you may grow into salvation— [3]if indeed you have tasted that the Lord is good.

4 Come to him, a living stone, though rejected by mortals yet chosen and precious in God's

2.4 A Play on Words

In verses 4–9, Peter constructs a detailed metaphor out of a very common object: a stone. He refers to Christ as a stone rejected by builders, the kind of useless rock someone trips over. Yet this stone, Jesus, becomes the cornerstone of a new building composed of Christians ("living stones"). This metaphor has much in common with Paul's references to the "body of Christ," but Peter (nicknamed the "rock") uses architectural rather than biological terms.

sight, and [5]like living stones, let yourselves be built[h] into a spiritual house, to be a holy priesthood, to offer spiritual sacrifices acceptable to God through Jesus Christ. [6]For it stands in scripture:

"See, I am laying in Zion a stone,
     a cornerstone chosen and precious;
and whoever believes in him[i] will not be
          put to shame."

[7]To you then who believe, he is precious; but for those who do not believe,

"The stone that the builders rejected
     has become the very head of
          the corner,"

[8]and

"A stone that makes them stumble,
     and a rock that makes them fall."

They stumble because they disobey the word, as they were destined to do.

9 But you are a chosen race, a royal priesthood, a holy nation, God's own people,[j] in order that you may proclaim the mighty acts of him

---

[b] Other ancient authorities read *known through the Spirit*   [c] Gk *gird up the loins of your mind*   [d] Other ancient authorities add *through the Spirit*   [e] Or *constantly*   [f] Other ancient authorities read *a pure heart*   [g] Or *through the word of the living and enduring God*   [h] Or *you yourselves are being built*   [i] Or *it*   [j] Gk *a people for his possession*

who called you out of darkness into his marvelous light. [10] Once you were not a people,
but now you are God's people;
once you had not received mercy,
but now you have received mercy.

Live as Servants of God

11 Beloved, I urge you as aliens and exiles to abstain from the desires of the flesh that wage war

2.11 Endangered Exiles

At first Christians had enjoyed the official protection of the Roman empire. Under Nero (A.D. 54–68) all that changed, and the apostles Peter and Paul were probably martyred during Nero's regime. Peter addressed this letter to "the exiles" (1.1), an indication that Christians were now viewed as a separate, persecuted minority without legal rights.

against the soul. [12]Conduct yourselves honorably among the Gentiles, so that, though they malign you as evildoers, they may see your honorable deeds and glorify God when he comes to judge.[k] 13 For the Lord's sake accept the authority of every human institution,[l] whether of the emperor as supreme, [14]or of governors, as sent by him to punish those who do wrong and to praise those who do right. [15]For it is God's will that by doing right you should silence the ignorance of the foolish. [16]As servants[m] of God, live as free people, yet do not use your freedom as a pretext for evil. [17]Honor everyone. Love the family of believers.[n] Fear God. Honor the emperor.

The Example of Christ's Suffering

18 Slaves, accept the authority of your masters with all deference, not only those who are kind and gentle but also those who are harsh. [19]For it is a credit to you if, being aware of God, you endure pain while suffering unjustly. [20]If you endure when you are beaten for doing wrong, what credit is that? But if you endure when you do right and suffer for it, you have God's approval. [21]For to this you have been called, because Christ also suffered for you, leaving you an example, so that you should follow in his steps.
22 "He committed no sin,
and no deceit was found in
his mouth."
[23]When he was abused, he did not return abuse; when he suffered, he did not threaten; but he entrusted himself to the one who judges justly. [24]He himself bore our sins in his body on the cross,[o] so that, free from sins, we might live for

righteousness; by his wounds[p] you have been healed. [25]For you were going astray like sheep, but now you have returned to the shepherd and guardian of your souls.

Wives and Husbands

3 Wives, in the same way, accept the authority of your husbands, so that, even if some of them do not obey the word, they may be won over without a word by their wives' conduct, [2]when they see the purity and reverence of your lives. [3]Do not adorn yourselves outwardly by braiding your hair, and by wearing gold ornaments or fine clothing; [4]rather, let your adornment be the inner self with the lasting beauty of a gentle and quiet spirit, which is very precious in God's sight. [5]It was in this way long ago that the holy women who hoped in God used to adorn themselves by accepting the authority of their husbands. [6]Thus Sarah obeyed Abraham and called him lord. You have become her daughters as long as you do what is good and never let fears alarm you.
7 Husbands, in the same way, show consideration for your wives in your life together, paying honor to the woman as the weaker sex,[q] since they too are also heirs of the gracious gift of life— so that nothing may hinder your prayers.

Suffering for Doing Right

8 Finally, all of you, have unity of spirit, sympathy, love for one another, a tender heart, and a humble mind. [9]Do not repay evil for evil or abuse for abuse; but, on the contrary, repay with a blessing. It is for this that you were called—that you might inherit a blessing. [10]For
"Those who desire life
and desire to see good days,
let them keep their tongues from evil
and their lips from speaking deceit;
[11] let them turn away from evil and do
good;
let them seek peace and pursue it.
[12] For the eyes of the Lord are on
the righteous,
and his ears are open to their prayer.
But the face of the Lord is against those
who do evil."
13 Now who will harm you if you are eager to do what is good? [14]But even if you do suffer for doing what is right, you are blessed. Do not fear what they fear,[r] and do not be intimidated, [15]but in your hearts sanctify Christ as Lord. Always be ready to make your defense to anyone who demands from you an accounting for the hope that is in you; [16]yet do it with gentleness and rever-

---

[k] Gk *God on the day of visitation*   [l] Or *every institution ordained for human beings*   [m] Gk *slaves*   [n] Gk *Love the brotherhood*   [o] Or *carried up our sins in his body to the tree*   [p] Gk *bruise*   [q] Gk *vessel*   [r] Gk *their fear*

ence.[s] Keep your conscience clear, so that, when you are maligned, those who abuse you for your good conduct in Christ may be put to shame. [17]For it is better to suffer for doing good, if suffering should be God's will, than to suffer for doing evil. [18]For Christ also suffered[t] for sins once for all, the righteous for the unrighteous, in order to bring you[u] to God. He was put to death in the flesh, but made alive in the spirit, [19]in which also he went and made a proclamation to the spirits in prison, [20]who in former times did not obey, when God waited patiently in the days of Noah, during the building of the ark, in which a few, that is,

eight persons, were saved through water. [21]And baptism, which this prefigured, now saves you— not as a removal of dirt from the body, but as an appeal to God for[v] a good conscience, through the resurrection of Jesus Christ, [22]who has gone into heaven and is at the right hand of God, with angels, authorities, and powers made subject to him.

Good Stewards of God's Grace

4 Since therefore Christ suffered in the flesh,[w] arm yourselves also with the same intention (for whoever has suffered in the flesh has finished

---

[s] Or respect   [t] Other ancient authorities read died   [u] Other ancient authorities read us   [v] Or a pledge to God
from   [w] Other ancient authorities add for us; others, for you

---

A Man Named "The Rock"
Peter slowly learned how to live up to his nickname

> Humble yourselves therefore under the mighty hand of God, so that he may exalt you in due time. 5.6

YOU CAN'T MISS PETER IN the four Gospels. He stands out like a bumpkin, pushing to the head of the line and coming out with loud, outrageous assertions. Every list of the disciples names him first, and Peter is often seen elbowing his way to center stage.

He was likable enough, with a big heart and unlimited enthusiasm. He just had too many rough edges. He swung like a pendulum, bold and courageous at one moment, yet cowardly when it really counted.

Signs of Mellowing

But by the time Peter sat down to write this letter, late in his life, a lot had changed. You can sense the change in the very words he chooses: words like humble and submit. This book contains nothing of the brash, aggressive style evident in the Gospels. He is heeding Jesus' last command to him: "Feed my sheep" (John 21.17). Gruff Peter has become a tender shepherd.

To get the full impact of Peter's transformation, you must read about him in the Gospels (especially in Mark), and then turn directly to this letter. Blustery, loudmouthed Peter now counsels wives to have "the lasting beauty of a gentle and quiet spirit" (3.4) and husbands to treat their wives with consideration and respect (3.7). The man who sliced off an ear in Jesus' defense (John 18.10) now advises submission to every government authority (2.13). Peter once vigorously protested Jesus' prediction of death (Mark 8.32); now he solemnly commends Christ's suffering as an ideal (2.21–24).

It's easy to believe Peter is describing himself when he writes such statements as "Once you were not a people, but now you are God's people" (2.10) and "You were going astray like sheep, but now you have returned to the shepherd and guardian of your souls" (2.25). Over time the shifting sand of Peter's personality solidified into granite.

Never Too Late

Peter finally earned the nickname that Jesus gave him long before: the "rock" (Matthew 16.18). And when he instructs his readers to stand fast in the true grace of God (5.12), you get the feeling Peter has learned through hard experience the lessons he is now passing on to others.

If Paul is the apostle of faith, Peter is the apostle of hope. God does not give up on people, as Peter's life amply demonstrates. We have reason to hope, whatever our circumstances—even when facing suffering or death.

Tradition reports that Peter was crucified head downward on a Roman cross; he thought himself unworthy to die right side up like Jesus. Peter died still believing his promise of a happy ending: "And after you have suffered for a little while, the God of all grace, who has called you to his eternal glory in Christ, will himself restore, support, strengthen, and establish you" (5.10). He wrote like a man who knew.

Life Questions: If Jesus were to give you a nickname, what would it be? Has your personality undergone major changes? What still needs work?

with sin), ²so as to live for the rest of your earthly life[x] no longer by human desires but by the will of God. ³You have already spent enough time in doing what the Gentiles like to do, living in licentiousness, passions, drunkenness, revels, carousing, and lawless idolatry. ⁴They are surprised that

3.19 The Spirits in Prison

At least 18 major theories have been proposed to explain Peter's meaning in verses 18–22. Primarily, scholars differ over what the phrase "spirits in prison" refers to. Were "the spirits" people in some intermediate state of death, or the fallen angels alluded to in Genesis 6.1–4? No one knows for sure. Peter uses the obscure reference to make a point about the ultimate good that came from the suffering Jesus endured.

you no longer join them in the same excesses of dissipation, and so they blaspheme.[y] ⁵But they will have to give an accounting to him who stands ready to judge the living and the dead. ⁶For this is the reason the gospel was proclaimed even to the dead, so that, though they had been judged in the flesh as everyone is judged, they might live in the spirit as God does.

7 The end of all things is near;[z] therefore be serious and discipline yourselves for the sake of your prayers. ⁸Above all, maintain constant love for one another, for love covers a multitude of sins. ⁹Be hospitable to one another without complaining. ¹⁰Like good stewards of the manifold grace of God, serve one another with whatever gift each of you has received. ¹¹Whoever speaks must do so as one speaking the very words of God; whoever serves must do so with the strength that God supplies, so that God may be glorified in all things through Jesus Christ. To him belong the glory and the power forever and ever. Amen.

Suffering as a Christian

12 Beloved, do not be surprised at the fiery ordeal that is taking place among you to test you, as though something strange were happening to you. ¹³But rejoice insofar as you are sharing Christ's sufferings, so that you may also be glad and shout for joy when his glory is revealed. ¹⁴If you are reviled for the name of Christ, you are blessed, because the spirit of glory,[a] which is the Spirit of God, is resting on you.[b] ¹⁵But let none of you suffer as a murderer, a thief, a criminal, or even as a mischief maker. ¹⁶Yet if any of you

suffers as a Christian, do not consider it a disgrace, but glorify God because you bear this name. ¹⁷For the time has come for judgment to begin with the household of God; if it begins with us, what will be the end for those who do not obey the gospel of God? ¹⁸And

"If it is hard for the righteous
to be saved,
what will become of the ungodly and
the sinners?"

¹⁹Therefore, let those suffering in accordance with God's will entrust themselves to a faithful Creator, while continuing to do good.

4.13 Radical Shift

This one verse, above all others, shows how much Peter had changed. He received Jesus' strongest rebuke (Mark 8.33) for objecting to the suggestion that Jesus would suffer. But now he presents suffering for Christ as a privilege, a way to participate in Christ's glory.

Tending the Flock of God

5 Now as an elder myself and a witness of the sufferings of Christ, as well as one who shares in the glory to be revealed, I exhort the elders among you ²to tend the flock of God that is in your charge, exercising the oversight,[c] not under compulsion but willingly, as God would have you do it[d]—not for sordid gain but eagerly. ³Do not lord it over those in your charge, but be examples to the flock. ⁴And when the chief shepherd appears, you will win the crown of glory that never fades away. ⁵In the same way, you who are younger must accept the authority of the elders.[e] And all of you must clothe yourselves with humility in your dealings with one another, for

"God opposes the proud,
but gives grace to the humble."

6 Humble yourselves therefore under the mighty hand of God, so that he may exalt you in due time. ⁷Cast all your anxiety on him, because he cares for you. ⁸Discipline yourselves, keep alert.[f] Like a roaring lion your adversary the devil prowls around, looking for someone to devour. ⁹Resist him, steadfast in your faith, for you know that your brothers and sisters[g] in all the world are undergoing the same kinds of suffering. ¹⁰And after you have suffered for a little while, the God of all grace, who has called you to his eternal glory in Christ, will himself restore, support,

---

[x] Gk *rest of the time in the flesh*   [y] Or *they malign you*   [z] Or *is at hand*   [a] Other ancient authorities add *and of power*   [b] Other ancient authorities add *On their part he is blasphemed, but on your part he is glorified*   [c] Other ancient authorities lack *exercising the oversight*   [d] Other ancient authorities lack *as God would have you do it*   [e] Or *of those who are older*   [f] Or *be vigilant*   [g] Gk *your brotherhood*

strengthen, and establish you. [11]To him be the power forever and ever. Amen.

Final Greetings and Benediction

12 Through Silvanus, whom I consider a faithful brother, I have written this short letter to encourage you and to testify that this is the true grace of God. Stand fast in it. [13]Your sister church[h] in Babylon, chosen together with you, sends you greetings; and so does my son Mark. [14]Greet one another with a kiss of love.

Peace to all of you who are in Christ.[i]

2 PETER

A Threat from Within
The worst dangers aren't always well marked

FIRST-CENTURY APOSTLES MUST HAVE FELT like pioneers in a mosquito-infested swamp. A pest attacked them. *Slap!* They'd kill it, and instantly another would land. Wherever they went new dangers swarmed up.

One group denied Jesus was God; then another declared him God but not fully man. The apostles denounced legalism, only to encounter free-swingers who assumed "anything goes." Members of one church quit work and huddled together to await Jesus' return; those of another gave up on his returning at all.

> This is now, beloved, the second letter I am writing to you; in them I am trying to arouse your sincere attention. 3.1

Second Peter was written in response to a young church's jumpy tendencies. Whereas 1 Peter centered on fearsome dangers from outside, this letter speaks to dangers from within. False teachers were stirring up dissent, questioning basic doctrines, and leading Christians into immorality.

Warning Signs

In its advice to the various squabbling groups, 2 Peter calls for a return to the true gospel. "I intend to keep on reminding you of these things," the author says (1.12) and proceeds to go over some basic facts of how Christians should believe and behave. The book doesn't introduce many new insights; rather, it erects a giant warning sign against common pitfalls that endanger the church.

A key word, *knowledge*, echoes throughout this letter: 2 Peter refreshes readers' memories regarding the proper knowledge that makes possible "everything needed for life and godliness" (1.3). The author carefully grounds his knowledge in Old Testament prophets and eyewitness accounts of Jesus' life, not in "cleverly devised myths" (1.16). And he urges his readers to resist dangers by living blamelessly.

The answer to false knowledge, the author bluntly insists, is true knowledge; the answer to immoral living is moral living. As he prepares to die (1.14), the author of 2 Peter gets in one last appeal for truth.

How to Read 2 Peter

Although 1 and 2 Peter claim the same author, they have large differences in style and approach. Second Peter is unrefined in writing style, more shrill and less gentle than the first letter. (Many scholars question whether the apostle Peter actually wrote the whole letter, but the letter does claim his authorship and shows some signs of his influence.)

Perhaps the difference in audiences explains the two approaches. The Bible views suffering—persecution from outside—as a purifying influence that often results in an even stronger church. Thus 1 Peter has an encouraging and devotional tone. But the real danger to a church comes from the inside, from immoral behavior and false teaching. Second Peter, in strong words, addresses those "inside" dangers.

As you read it, try to put yourself in the place of the original audience. What dangers does the author warn against? Are there parallels today? Chapters 1 and 3 can be universally applied. Chapter 2 concerns itself more directly with the particular false teachers plaguing the first-century church.

In tone and actual content, 2 Peter resembles the tiny book of Jude. Both deal with the same problems and propose the same solutions.

When reading 2 Peter, look for the key word *knowledge,* and related words like *think,* *reminding,* and *remember.* The author appeals to true knowledge that can correct many of the young church's errors.

3-TRACK READING PLAN

For an explanation and complete listing of the 3-track reading plan, turn to page 7.

TRACK 1: *Two-Week Courses on the Bible*
See page 7 for information on these courses.

TRACK 2: *An Overview of 2 Peter in 1 Day*
☐ Day 1. Read the Introduction to 2 Peter, then chapter 1.

Now turn to page 9 for your next Track 2 reading project.

TRACK 3: *All of 2 Peter in 3 Days*
After you have read through 2 Peter, turn to pages 10–14 for your next Track 3 reading project.
☐1   ☐2   ☐3

Salutation

1 Simeon[a] Peter, a servant[b] and apostle of Jesus Christ,
To those who have received a faith as precious as ours through the righteousness of our God and Savior Jesus Christ:[c]
2 May grace and peace be yours in abundance in the knowledge of God and of Jesus our Lord.

The Christian's Call and Election

3 His divine power has given us everything needed for life and godliness, through the knowledge of him who called us by[d] his own glory and goodness. [4]Thus he has given us, through these things, his precious and very great promises, so that through them you may escape from the corruption that is in the world because of lust, and may become participants of the divine nature. [5]For this very reason, you must make every effort to support your faith with goodness, and goodness with knowledge, [6]and knowledge with self-control, and self-control with endurance, and endurance with godliness, [7]and godliness with mutual[e] affection, and mutual[e] affection with love. [8]For if these things are yours and are increasing among you, they keep you from being ineffective and unfruitful in the knowledge of our Lord Jesus Christ. [9]For anyone who lacks these things is nearsighted and blind, and is forgetful of the cleansing of past sins. [10]Therefore, brothers and sisters,[f] be all the more eager to confirm your call and election, for if you do this, you will never stumble. [11]For in this way, entry into the

eternal kingdom of our Lord and Savior Jesus Christ will be richly provided for you.
12 Therefore I intend to keep on reminding you of these things, though you know them already and are established in the truth that has come to you. [13]I think it right, as long as I am in this body,[g] to refresh your memory, [14]since I know that my death[h] will come soon, as indeed our Lord Jesus Christ has made clear to me.

1.14 Approaching Death

The person writing these words was nearing death, a fact that may partially explain the book's forceful tone. An eyewitness (verse 16) of Jesus on earth was watching a young church stray from Christ's clear teaching. This letter may offer the last chance to oppose the deterioration.

[15]And I will make every effort so that after my departure you may be able at any time to recall these things.

Eyewitnesses of Christ's Glory

16 For we did not follow cleverly devised myths when we made known to you the power and coming of our Lord Jesus Christ, but we had been eyewitnesses of his majesty. [17]For he received honor and glory from God the Father when that voice was conveyed to him by the Majestic Glory, saying, "This is my Son, my Beloved,[i] with whom I am well pleased." [18]We our-

---

a Other ancient authorities read *Simon*   *b* Gk *slave*   *c* Or *of our God and the Savior Jesus Christ*   *d* Other ancient authorities read *through*   *e* Gk *brotherly*   *f* Gk *brothers*   *g* Gk *tent*   *h* Gk *the putting off of my tent*
i Other ancient authorities read *my beloved Son*

selves heard this voice come from heaven, while we were with him on the holy mountain.

19 So we have the prophetic message more fully confirmed. You will do well to be attentive to this as to a lamp shining in a dark place, until the day dawns and the morning star rises in your hearts. 20First of all you must understand this, that no prophecy of scripture is a matter of one's own interpretation, 21because no prophecy ever came by human will, but men and women moved by the Holy Spirit spoke from God.*j*

False Prophets and Their Punishment

2 But false prophets also arose among the people, just as there will be false teachers among you, who will secretly bring in destructive opinions. They will even deny the Master who bought them—bringing swift destruction on themselves. 2Even so, many will follow their licentious ways, and because of these teachers*k* the way of truth will be maligned. 3And in their greed they will exploit you with deceptive words. Their condemnation, pronounced against them long ago, has not been idle, and their destruction is not asleep.

4 For if God did not spare the angels when they sinned, but cast them into hell*l* and committed them to chains*m* of deepest darkness to be kept until the judgment; 5and if he did not spare the ancient world, even though he saved Noah, a herald of righteousness, with seven others, when he brought a flood on a world of the ungodly;

2.5 Three Worlds

Second Peter refers to three great ages of the earth. The first, the ancient world, was destroyed by the flood in Noah's day. The present time, in which we are now living, will be destroyed by fire (3.10). But the author points with hope to an age that has not yet come: a new heaven and a new earth (3.13).

6and if by turning the cities of Sodom and Gomorrah to ashes he condemned them to extinction*n* and made them an example of what is coming to the ungodly;*o* 7and if he rescued Lot, a righteous man greatly distressed by the licentiousness of the lawless 8(for that righteous man, living among them day after day, was tormented in his righteous soul by their lawless deeds that he saw and heard), 9then the Lord knows how to rescue the godly from trial, and to keep the unrighteous under punishment until the day of judgment 10—especially those who indulge their flesh in depraved lust, and who despise authority.

Bold and willful, they are not afraid to slander the glorious ones,*p* 11whereas angels, though greater in might and power, do not bring against them a slanderous judgment from the Lord.*q* 12These people, however, are like irrational animals, mere creatures of instinct, born to be caught and killed. They slander what they do not understand, and when those creatures are destroyed,*r* they also will be destroyed, 13suffering*s* the penalty for doing wrong. They count it a pleasure to revel in the daytime. They are blots and blemishes, reveling in their dissipation*t* while they feast with you. 14They have eyes full of adultery, insatiable for sin. They entice unsteady souls. They have hearts trained in greed. Accursed children! 15They have left the straight road and have gone astray, following the road of Balaam son of Bosor,*u* who loved the wages of doing wrong, 16but was rebuked for his own transgression; a speechless donkey spoke with a human voice and restrained the prophet's madness.

17 These are waterless springs and mists driven by a storm; for them the deepest darkness has been reserved. 18For they speak bombastic nonsense, and with licentious desires of the flesh they entice people who have just*v* escaped from those who live in error. 19They promise them freedom, but they themselves are slaves of corruption; for people are slaves to whatever masters them. 20For if, after they have escaped the defilements of the world through the knowledge of our Lord and Savior Jesus Christ, they are again entangled in them and overpowered, the last state has become worse for them than the first. 21For it would have been better for them never to have known the way of righteousness than, after knowing it, to turn back from the holy commandment that was passed on to them. 22It has happened to them according to the true proverb,
   "The dog turns back to its own vomit,"
and,
   "The sow is washed only to wallow in the mud."

The Promise of the Lord's Coming

3 This is now, beloved, the second letter I am writing to you; in them I am trying to arouse your sincere intention by reminding you 2that you should remember the words spoken in the past by the holy prophets, and the commandment of the Lord and Savior spoken through your apostles. 3First of all you must understand this, that in the last days scoffers will come, scof-

j Other ancient authorities read *but moved by the Holy Spirit saints of God spoke*   *k* Gk *because of them*   *l* Gk *Tartaros*   *m* Other ancient authorities read *pits*   *n* Other ancient authorities lack *to extinction*   *o* Other ancient authorities read *an example to those who were to be ungodly*   *p* Or *angels*; Gk *glories*   *q* Other ancient authorities read *before the Lord*; others lack the phrase   *r* Gk *in their destruction*   *s* Other ancient authorities read *receiving*   *t* Other ancient authorities read *love-feasts*   *u* Other ancient authorities read *Beor*   *v* Other ancient authorities read *actually*

fing and indulging their own lusts [4]and saying, "Where is the promise of his coming? For ever since our ancestors died,[w] all things continue as they were from the beginning of creation!" [5]They deliberately ignore this fact, that by the word of God heavens existed long ago and an earth was formed out of water and by means of water, [6]through which the world of that time was deluged with water and perished. [7]But by the same word the present heavens and earth have been reserved for fire, being kept until the day of judgment and destruction of the godless.

8 But do not ignore this one fact, beloved, that with the Lord one day is like a thousand years, and a thousand years are like one day. [9]The Lord is not slow about his promise, as some think of slowness, but is patient with you,[x] not wanting any to perish, but all to come to repentance. [10]But the day of the Lord will come like a thief, and then the heavens will pass away with a loud noise, and the elements will be dissolved with fire, and the earth and everything that is done on it will be disclosed.[y]

11 Since all these things are to be dissolved in

3.10 The Fate of the Earth

The time of global destruction described here was a common theme in letters to the early churches. Talk of a coming judgment and the overthrow of the existing world threatened and alarmed Rome, the chief power in the existing world then. Such doomsday prophecies aroused Roman hostility against Christians.

this way, what sort of persons ought you to be in leading lives of holiness and godliness, [12]waiting for and hastening[z] the coming of the day of God, because of which the heavens will be set ablaze and dissolved, and the elements will melt with fire? [13]But, in accordance with his promise, we wait for new heavens and a new earth, where righteousness is at home.

Final Exhortation and Doxology

14 Therefore, beloved, while you are waiting for these things, strive to be found by him at peace, without spot or blemish; [15]and regard the patience of our Lord as salvation. So also our beloved brother Paul wrote to you according to

3.15 A Fellow Author

This comment is one of the rare instances in which a New Testament author refers directly to another New Testament book. Evidently, 2 Peter was written late enough that a group of Paul's letters already existed. Scholars use clues like this one to date books of the Bible.

the wisdom given him, [16]speaking of this as he does in all his letters. There are some things in them hard to understand, which the ignorant and unstable twist to their own destruction, as they do the other scriptures. [17]You therefore, beloved, since you are forewarned, beware that you are not carried away with the error of the lawless and lose your own stability. [18]But grow in the grace and knowledge of our Lord and Savior Jesus Christ. To him be the glory both now and to the day of eternity. Amen.[a]

---

[w] Gk *our fathers fell asleep*   [x] Other ancient authorities read *on your account*   [y] Other ancient authorities read *will be burned up*   [z] Or *earnestly desiring*   [a] Other ancient authorities lack *Amen*

1 JOHN

Words That Get Polluted
A problem with the new generation

> Let us love, not in word or speech, but in truth and action.
> 3.18

OVER TIME, COMMON PHRASES CAN be stripped of meaning and applied to something else entirely. Take "born again," for example. First coined by Jesus, this phrase was resurrected in the sixties during the Jesus Movement. Soon it was snatched up as an advertising slogan to describe such things as a used car and even a comeback football player.

Christianity has been around so long that people borrow its words for quite different meanings. *Jesus,* the center of our faith, is also a common curse word.

Same Words, Different Meanings

This tendency to pollute language is not new. Even at the close of the first century, words were being twisted and drained of their original meanings. When the apostle John wrote his letters, the Christian faith was perhaps 50 or 60 years old. A generation had grown up in Christian homes, and a distinct subculture was already developing.

Some people were using familiar phrases such as "knowing God," "walk in the light," and "born of God," but with new, distorted meanings. The apostle responded with fire. He knew that a confused, subtle distortion of truth is harder to resist than an outright denial.

In this book, John chooses key words (*light, sin, Christ, love, faith,* etc.), "disinfects" them, and then restores their original meanings. He points back to the truths behind the words. Repeatedly, he begins with the phrase "If we say . . . " and proceeds to show what actions must result if we claim to live in the true light and to know God.

A Step Further

John wrote his Gospel account of Jesus' life in order to bring readers to a belief in Christ (John 20.31). He directed this letter to people who were already Christians, outlining how that faith should affect a person's life. God is light, he says; so walk in the light. He is spirit; so worship him in the proper spirit. He is love; so demonstrate that love to others.

At times John shows the tender concern of a pastor, calling his readers "my little children" (2.1) and urging them to "love one another" (3.11). But in other places his stern language hints at why he once wore the nickname "Son of Thunder."

John was probably the last surviving apostle when he wrote this book. He lived almost to the end of the first century. But he was not too old to fight vigorously against whatever might corrupt the faith that had inspired him for so many years.

How to Read 1 John

First John is constructed like a piece of music. Its author states a few simple themes—light, truth, life, love—then builds variations on them. Relying on simple words and a rhythmic style, John writes in universal terms that apply to any time period.

Yet the book is understood far better if you know something about the environment in which John was writing. Therefore, begin your reading with "Who Were the Gnostics?" on page 1297.

As you read John, note the pattern. He defines a word, such as *light,* discusses its opposite, *darkness,* and then describes what a life in the light should look like. In every case, he shows God as the source of power in the Christian life.

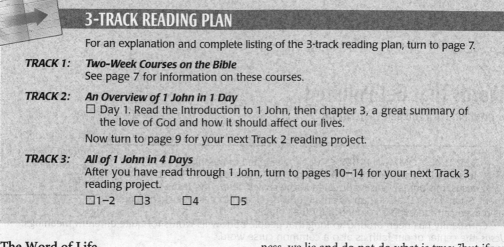

3-TRACK READING PLAN

For an explanation and complete listing of the 3-track reading plan, turn to page 7.

TRACK 1: ***Two-Week Courses on the Bible***
See page 7 for information on these courses.

TRACK 2: ***An Overview of 1 John in 1 Day***
☐ Day 1. Read the Introduction to 1 John, then chapter 3, a great summary of the love of God and how it should affect our lives.

Now turn to page 9 for your next Track 2 reading project.

TRACK 3: ***All of 1 John in 4 Days***
After you have read through 1 John, turn to pages 10–14 for your next Track 3 reading project.
☐1–2   ☐3   ☐4   ☐5

The Word of Life

1 We declare to you what was from the beginning, what we have heard, what we have seen with our eyes, what we have looked at and touched with our hands, concerning the word of life— ² this life was revealed, and we have seen it and testify to it, and declare to you the eternal life that was with the Father and was revealed to us— ³we declare to you what we have seen and heard so that you also may have fellowship with us; and truly our fellowship is with the Father and with his Son Jesus Christ. ⁴We are writing these things so that our*a* joy may be complete.

1.3–4 Eyewitness

In contrast to most New Testament letters, this one does not identify its author. Certain hints and distinctive patterns of style, though, make it very likely that the apostle John wrote it in advanced age. Simply compare the first paragraph of this letter with the first few paragraphs of the Gospel of John to see the similarities. The author also emphasizes that he was a close eyewitness of Jesus' life, a fact consistent with the "disciple whom Jesus loved."

God Is Light

5 This is the message we have heard from him and proclaim to you, that God is light and in him there is no darkness at all. ⁶If we say that we have fellowship with him while we are walking in dark-

ness, we lie and do not do what is true; ⁷but if we walk in the light as he himself is in the light, we have fellowship with one another, and the blood of Jesus his Son cleanses us from all sin. ⁸If we say that we have no sin, we deceive ourselves, and the truth is not in us. ⁹If we confess our sins, he who is faithful and just will forgive us our sins and cleanse us from all unrighteousness. ¹⁰If we say that we have not sinned, we make him a liar, and his word is not in us.

Christ Our Advocate

2 My little children, I am writing these things to you so that you may not sin. But if anyone does sin, we have an advocate with the Father, Jesus Christ the righteous; ²and he is the atoning sacrifice for our sins, and not for ours only but also for the sins of the whole world.

3 Now by this we may be sure that we know him, if we obey his commandments. ⁴Whoever says, "I have come to know him," but does not obey his commandments, is a liar, and in such a person the truth does not exist; ⁵but whoever obeys his word, truly in this person the love of God has reached perfection. By this we may be sure that we are in him: ⁶whoever says, "I abide in him," ought to walk just as he walked.

A New Commandment

7 Beloved, I am writing you no new commandment, but an old commandment that you have had from the beginning; the old commandment is the word that you have heard. ⁸Yet I am writing you a new commandment that is true in him and in you, because*b* the darkness is passing away and the true light is already shining. ⁹Who-

---

a Other ancient authorities read *your*   *b* Or *that*

ever says, "I am in the light," while hating a brother or sister,[c] is still in the darkness. [10]Whoever loves a brother or sister[d] lives in the light, and in such a person[e] there is no cause for stumbling. [11]But whoever hates another believer[f] is in the darkness, walks in the darkness, and does not know the way to go, because the darkness has brought on blindness.

[12] I am writing to you, little children,
because your sins are forgiven on
account of his name.

2.12 A Friendly Interruption

John begins his book with a stern warning against false ideas. But this lyrical section interrupts the flow with a warm greeting to true believers in the church. Many commentators believe that John intended the three categories (dear children, young men, fathers) to represent three different stages in his readers' spiritual lives.

[13] I am writing to you, fathers,
because you know him who is from
the beginning.
I am writing to you, young people,
because you have conquered
the evil one.
[14] I write to you, children,
because you know the Father.
I write to you, fathers,
because you know him who is from
the beginning.
I write to you, young people,
because you are strong
and the word of God abides in you,
and you have overcome the evil one.

[15] Do not love the world or the things in the world. The love of the Father is not in those who love the world; [16]for all that is in the world—the desire of the flesh, the desire of the eyes, the pride in riches—comes not from the Father but from the world. [17]And the world and its desire[g] are passing away, but those who do the will of God live forever.

Warning against Antichrists

[18] Children, it is the last hour! As you have heard that antichrist is coming, so now many antichrists have come. From this we know that it is the last hour. [19]They went out from us, but they did not belong to us; for if they had belonged to us, they would have remained with us. But by going out they made it plain that none of them belongs to us. [20]But you have been anointed by the Holy One, and all of you have knowledge.[h] [21]I write to you, not because you do not know the truth, but because you know it, and you know that no lie comes from the truth. [22]Who is the liar but the one who denies that Jesus is the Christ?[i]

2.22 Tough Love

John had two nicknames. "The apostle of love" uses the word love 35 times in this brief letter alone. But the letter also hints why he earned his original nickname, "Son of Thunder" (Mark 3.17). As one of Jesus' disciples, John had wanted to call fire down from heaven on unresponsive villages (Luke 9.54). Jesus rebuked such a notion, and John mellowed considerably over the years. Still, he reserves some choice words for enemies of the gospel: He brands them antichrists (2.18), liars (2.22), and children of the devil (3.10).

This is the antichrist, the one who denies the Father and the Son. [23]No one who denies the Son has the Father; everyone who confesses the Son has the Father also. [24]Let what you heard from the beginning abide in you. If what you heard from the beginning abides in you, then you will abide in the Son and in the Father. [25]And this is what he has promised us,[j] eternal life.

[26] I write these things to you concerning those who would deceive you. [27]As for you, the anointing that you received from him abides in you, and so you do not need anyone to teach you. But as his anointing teaches you about all things, and is true and is not a lie, and just as it has taught you, abide in him.[k]

[28] And now, little children, abide in him, so that when he is revealed we may have confidence and not be put to shame before him at his coming.

Children of God

[29] If you know that he is righteous, you may be sure that everyone who does right has been born of him. [1]See what love the Father has given us, that we should be called children of God; and that is what we are. The reason the world does not know us is that it did not know him. [2]Beloved, we are God's children now; what we will be has not yet been revealed. What we do know is this: when he[k] is revealed, we will be like him, for we will see him as he is. [3]And all who have this hope in him purify themselves, just as he is pure.

[4] Everyone who commits sin is guilty of lawlessness; sin is lawlessness. [5]You know that he was

revealed to take away sins, and in him there is no sin. [6]No one who abides in him sins; no one who sins has either seen him or known him. [7]Little children, let no one deceive you. Everyone who does what is right is righteous, just as he is righteous. [8]Everyone who commits sin is a child of the devil; for the devil has been sinning from the beginning. The Son of God was revealed for this purpose, to destroy the works of the devil. [9]Those who have been born of God do not sin, because God's seed abides in them;[l] they cannot sin, because they have been born of God. [10]The children of God and the children of the devil are revealed in this way: all who do not do what is right are not from God, nor are those who do not love their brothers and sisters.[m]

Love One Another

11 For this is the message you have heard from the beginning, that we should love one another. [12]We must not be like Cain who was from

> ### 3.11 Love Versus Hate
>
> *Very often John defines words in relation to their opposites: light versus darkness, truth versus falsehood, life versus death. In this paragraph, he begins with a command to "love one another," then goes on to illustrate the life of hate before coming back to define love. Many of 1 John's themes are developed in this "circular" method.*

the evil one and murdered his brother. And why did he murder him? Because his own deeds were evil and his brother's righteous. [13]Do not be astonished, brothers and sisters,[n] that the world hates you. [14]We know that we have passed from death to life because we love one another. Whoever does not love abides in death. [15]All who hate a brother or sister[m] are murderers, and you know that murderers do not have eternal life abiding in them. [16]We know love by this, that he laid down his life for us—and we ought to lay down our lives for one another. [17]How does God's love abide in anyone who has the world's goods and sees a brother or sister[o] in need and yet refuses help?

18 Little children, let us love, not in word or speech, but in truth and action. [19]And by this we will know that we are from the truth and will reassure our hearts before him [20]whenever our hearts condemn us; for God is greater than our hearts, and he knows everything. [21]Beloved, if our hearts do not condemn us, we have boldness before God; [22]and we receive from him whatever

we ask, because we obey his commandments and do what pleases him.

23 And this is his commandment, that we should believe in the name of his Son Jesus Christ and love one another, just as he has commanded us. [24]All who obey his commandments abide in him, and he abides in them. And by this we know that he abides in us, by the Spirit that he has given us.

Testing the Spirits

4 Beloved, do not believe every spirit, but test the spirits to see whether they are from God; for many false prophets have gone out into the world. [2]By this you know the Spirit of God: every spirit that confesses that Jesus Christ has come in the flesh is from God, [3]and every spirit that does not confess Jesus[p] is not from God. And this is the spirit of the antichrist, of which you have heard that it is coming; and now it is already in the world. [4]Little children, you are from God, and have conquered them; for the one who is in you is greater than the one who is in the world. [5]They are from the world; therefore what they say is from the world, and the world listens to them. [6]We are from God. Whoever knows God listens to us, and whoever is not from God does not listen to us. From this we know the spirit of truth and the spirit of error.

God Is Love

7 Beloved, let us love one another, because love is from God; everyone who loves is born of God and knows God. [8]Whoever does not love does not know God, for God is love. [9]God's love was revealed among us in this way: God sent his only Son into the world so that we might live through him. [10]In this is love, not that we loved God but that he loved us and sent his Son to be the atoning sacrifice for our sins. [11]Beloved, since God loved us so much, we also ought to love one another. [12]No one has ever seen God; if we love one another, God lives in us, and his love is perfected in us.

13 By this we know that we abide in him and he in us, because he has given us of his Spirit. [14]And we have seen and do testify that the Father has sent his Son as the Savior of the world. [15]God abides in those who confess that Jesus is the Son of God, and they abide in God. [16]So we have known and believe the love that God has for us.

God is love, and those who abide in love abide in God, and God abides in them. [17]Love has been perfected among us in this: that we may have boldness on the day of judgment, because as he is, so are we in this world. [18]There is no fear in love, but perfect love casts out fear; for fear has to

---

[l] Or *because the children of God abide in him*   [m] Gk *his brother*   [n] Gk *brothers*   [o] Gk *brother*   [p] Other ancient authorities read *does away with Jesus* (Gk *dissolves Jesus*)

do with punishment, and whoever fears has not reached perfection in love. [19]We love[q] because he first loved us. [20]Those who say, "I love God," and hate their brothers or sisters,[r] are liars; for those who do not love a brother or sister[s] whom they have seen, cannot love God whom they have not seen. [21]The commandment we have from him is this: those who love God must love their brothers and sisters[r] also.

Faith Conquers the World

5 Everyone who believes that Jesus is the Christ[t] has been born of God, and everyone who loves the parent loves the child. [2]By this we know that we love the children of God, when we love God and obey his commandments. [3]For the love of God is this, that we obey his commandments. And his commandments are not burdensome, [4]for whatever is born of God conquers the world. And this is the victory that conquers the world, our faith. [5]Who is it that conquers the world but the one who believes that Jesus is the Son of God?

Testimony concerning the Son of God

6 This is the one who came by water and blood, Jesus Christ, not with the water only but with the water and the blood. And the Spirit is the one that testifies, for the Spirit is the truth. [7]There are three that testify:[u] [8]the Spirit and the water

[q] Other ancient authorities add *him*; others add *God*   [r] Gk *brothers*   [s] Gk *brother*   [t] Or *the Messiah*   [u] A few other authorities read (with variations) [7]*There are three that testify in heaven, the Father, the Word, and the Holy Spirit, and these three are one.* [8]*And there are three that testify on earth:*

Who Were the Gnostics?

A dangerous cult that proved fatally attractive

> By this you know the Spirit of God: every spirit that confesses that Jesus Christ has come in the flesh is from God. 4.2

AS CHRISTIANITY SPREAD ACROSS THE Mediterranean, it came into contact with other religions. Greeks and Romans tried to absorb the faith into their own philosophies, just as some Jews had initially.

Intellectual centers of the Mediterranean raised questions about Jesus: Who was he? If he was God, how could he die? And a popular new cult called Gnosticism (from the Greek word for knowledge, *gnosis*) gained ground in an attempt to explain these things. The cult thrived, especially among the intellectual elite.

Could God Have a Body?

Gnostics balked at the Christian concept of God's becoming human. Because they believed a physical body was intrinsically evil, they denied that a pure God could take on a body. Some dealt with the problem by claiming that Jesus was never a real human being, but a phantom, a temporary appearance of God who only looked human. Others proposed that God had "descended" on Jesus at his baptism, but left him before his death.

The apostle John debated in person with Gnostics of his day, and he had Gnostic thinking in mind when he wrote this letter. The very first sentence expressly states that the author has seen, heard, and touched Jesus—implying he could not have been a phantom, or pure spirit. Throughout the letter, and especially in 4.2–3, the author lambastes those who deny that Jesus came in the flesh.

Live As You Please

To Gnostics, all matter was evil. Only the spirit was pure, and Gnostics sought to rise to a higher, more spiritual plane. This teaching often produced a side effect: People who strove to rise above matter didn't care about personal ethics. Their pure spirits could not be tainted by "earthly" sin. Thus, they could act any way they wanted.

Aging John roared out against the twin dangers of Gnosticism: immoral living and doubts that Christ became a man. Beliefs must be judged by the actions they produce, and John stresses the theme of brotherly love. He primarily refutes errors by presenting a wholesome picture of the Christian life as it is supposed to be lived.

True fellowship is not a secret initiation into a New Age-type elite, but a relationship with the Father through Christ. And that also entails responsibilities to others in God's family.

Life Questions: Gnosticism showed itself in several ways: the belief that matter was evil, a desire for "super-spirituality," a tendency toward loose morals. How can we counter those same trends among Christians today?

and the blood, and these three agree. [9]If we receive human testimony, the testimony of God is greater; for this is the testimony of God that he has testified to his Son. [10]Those who believe in the

5.8 Water, Blood, and Spirit

The apostle John relied heavily on symbolic language in his Gospel account of Jesus' life. Here, too, he uses symbols in giving proofs of Jesus. Water may refer to Jesus' baptism, blood to his death on the cross, and the Spirit to the Holy Spirit who descended on Jesus. John refers to these three as a "testimony" from God about his Son.

Son of God have the testimony in their hearts. Those who do not believe in God[v] have made him a liar by not believing in the testimony that God has given concerning his Son. [11]And this is the testimony: God gave us eternal life, and this life is in his Son. [12]Whoever has the Son has life; whoever does not have the Son of God does not have life.

Epilogue

[13] I write these things to you who believe in the name of the Son of God, so that you may know that you have eternal life.

[14] And this is the boldness we have in him, that if we ask anything according to his will, he hears us. [15]And if we know that he hears us in whatever we ask, we know that we have obtained the requests made of him. [16]If you see your brother or sister[w] committing what is not a mortal sin, you will ask, and God[x] will give life to such a one—to those whose sin is not mortal. There is sin that is mortal; I do not say that you should pray about that. [17]All wrongdoing is sin, but there is sin that is not mortal.

[18] We know that those who are born of God do not sin, but the one who was born of God protects them, and the evil one does not touch them. [19]We know that we are God's children, and that the whole world lies under the power of the evil one. [20]And we know that the Son of God has come and has given us understanding so that we may know him who is true;[y] and we are in him who is true, in his Son Jesus Christ. He is the true God and eternal life.

[21] Little children, keep yourselves from idols.[z]

---

v Other ancient authorities read *in the Son the true God*   *w* Gk *your brother*   *x* Gk *he*   *y* Other ancient authorities read *know*   *z* Other ancient authorities add *Amen*

2 JOHN

Undesirable Guests
When a "Welcome" sign is inappropriate

Be on your guard, so that you do not lose what we have worked for. 8

ROMAN ROADS MADE FIRST-CENTURY TRAVEL safer and easier than ever before, but Holiday Inns were still centuries away. Therefore, when teachers of the Christian faith traveled the empire, they relied on local Christians for food and lodging.

Before long, false teachers (such as Gnostics) also hit the circuit, joined by religious racketeers attracted primarily to the free food and lodging. The two letters, 2 John and 3 John, the shortest books in the entire Bible, concern themselves with the mounting problems of hospitality for the "circuit-rider" teachers.

Show Discretion, But Also Love

Heresies had already sprung up in many local churches, and 2 John urges true Christians to use discretion in testing a visitor's message and motive. The author cautions against entertaining visitors who do not teach the truth about Christ.

True to his nickname, the apostle of love repeats his motto, "Love one another," even in this letter of warning. The ancient writer Jerome (A.D. 374–419) tells of the frail apostle John, in extreme old age, being carried into his congregation mumbling only, "Love one another." When asked why he talked of nothing else, John replied, "Because it is the Lord's command, and if this only is done, it is enough."

How to Read 2 and 3 John

These two books are best read together, since each gives one side of a problem facing a young church. Try to imagine the setting back then, when Christianity was still new and many teachers came along claiming special insights. Do you see any parallels among Christians today? Look for the specific advice John gave in those circumstances.

3-TRACK READING PLAN

For an explanation and complete listing of the 3-track reading plan, turn to page 7.

TRACK 1: **Two-Week Courses on the Bible**
See page 7 for information on these courses.

TRACK 2: **Read 2 and 3 John Together in 1 Day**
☐ Day 1. These books are only one short chapter each, so you can easily read the two together.

Now turn to page 9 for your next Track 2 reading project.

TRACK 3: **All of 2 and 3 John in 1 Day**
Read both books in one day. After you have finished, turn to pages 10–14 for your next Track 3 reading project.
☐2 John, 3 John

Salutation

1 The elder to the elect lady and her children, whom I love in the truth, and not only I but also all who know the truth, [2]because of the truth that abides in us and will be with us forever:

3 Grace, mercy, and peace will be with us from God the Father and from[a] Jesus Christ, the Father's Son, in truth and love.

Truth and Love

4 I was overjoyed to find some of your children walking in the truth, just as we have been commanded by the Father. [5]But now, dear lady, I ask you, not as though I were writing you a new commandment, but one we have had from the beginning, let us love one another. [6]And this is love, that we walk according to his commandments; this is the commandment just as you have heard it from the beginning—you must walk in it.

7 Many deceivers have gone out into the world, those who do not confess that Jesus Christ has come in the flesh; any such person is the deceiver and the antichrist! [8]Be on your guard, so that you do not lose what we[b] have worked for, but may receive a full reward. [9]Everyone who does not abide in the teaching of Christ, but goes beyond it, does not have God; whoever abides in the teaching has both the Father and the Son. [10]Do not receive into the house or welcome anyone who comes to you and does not bring this teaching; [11]for to welcome is to participate in the evil deeds of such a person.

7 Pesky Deceivers

This paragraph shows that the enemies warned about in 1 John were still roaming about, stirring up trouble in the churches. The description of their beliefs—"who do not confess that Jesus Christ has come in the flesh"—brings to mind the teaching of the Gnostics (see "Who Were the Gnostics?" page 1297), one of the main targets of that first letter.

Final Greetings

12 Although I have much to write to you, I would rather not use paper and ink; instead I hope to come to you and talk with you face to face, so that our joy may be complete.

13 The children of your elect sister send you their greetings.[c]

---

[a] Other ancient authorities add *the Lord*   [b] Other ancient authorities read *you*   [c] Other ancient authorities add *Amen*

3 JOHN

Guidelines for Hospitality
The same questions crop up in every age, in every place

T AKEN TOGETHER, THIS LETTER AND its companion give a balanced view of proper Christian hospitality. Second John warned against entertaining false teachers. But 3 John praises a man named Gaius for warmly welcoming genuine Christian teachers. His actions had been opposed by Diotrephes, a cantankerous church dictator, who was also gossiping against John.

> *I have no greater joy than this, to hear that my children are walking in the truth. 4*

In a very condensed form, John's two letters deal with heresy and church splits, two problems that have plagued the church in every age, in every place. To defend against those dangers, John urges love and discernment. Believers must know whom to accept and support, and whom to resist.

How to Read 3 John

See How to Read 2 and 3 John, page 1299.

Salutation

1 The elder to the beloved Gaius, whom I love in truth.

Gaius Commended for His Hospitality

2 Beloved, I pray that all may go well with you and that you may be in good health, just as it is well with your soul. ³I was overjoyed when some of the friends*ᵃ* arrived and testified to your faithfulness to the truth, namely how you walk in the truth. ⁴I have no greater joy than this, to hear that my children are walking in the truth.

5 Beloved, you do faithfully whatever you do for the friends,*ᵃ* even though they are strangers to you; ⁶they have testified to your love before the church. You will do well to send them on in a manner worthy of God; ⁷for they began their journey for the sake of Christ,*ᵇ* accepting no support from non-believers.*ᶜ* ⁸Therefore we ought to support such people, so that we may become co-workers with the truth.

Diotrephes and Demetrius

9 I have written something to the church; but Diotrephes, who likes to put himself first, does not acknowledge our authority. ¹⁰So if I come, I will call attention to what he is doing in spreading false charges against us. And not content with those charges, he refuses to welcome the friends,*ᵃ*

4 No Greater Joy

Scholars estimate that the apostle John was between 80 and 90 years old when he wrote the letters bearing his name. He identifies himself as "the elder" (which may also refer to his office in a local church) and writes fondly of "my children." The letters carry the tone of an old man dispensing his last words of advice and taking grandfatherly pride in the progress of his spiritual heirs.

and even prevents those who want to do so and expels them from the church.

11 Beloved, do not imitate what is evil but imitate what is good. Whoever does good is from God; whoever does evil has not seen God. ¹²Everyone has testified favorably about Demetrius,

---

ᵃ Gk *brothers*   *ᵇ* Gk *for the sake of the name*   *ᶜ* Gk *the Gentiles*

and so has the truth itself. We also testify for him,[d] and you know that our testimony is true.

Final Greetings

13 I have much to write to you, but I would rather not write with pen and ink; [14]instead I hope to see you soon, and we will talk together face to face.

15 Peace to you. The friends send you their greetings. Greet the friends there, each by name.

JUDE

Watch Out!
Sounding an alarm

> I find it necessary to write and appeal to you to contend for the faith. 3

IF YOU SIGN UP FOR a driver's training course, you'll begin with several hours of classroom lectures on "Rules of the Road." The instructor will drill you on the shapes and colors of warning signs—signs that announce danger on the highways.

Driving seems all very academic, until you slide behind the wheel. There, a missed stop sign won't just lower a test score; it could cost you your life. Your instructor, rather than calmly correcting you, will shout, "Look out!"

Jude writes in the style of a teacher who is watching a freight train bear down on his student driver. Bells ring out, crossing gates go down, red lights flash. He admits this kind of letter isn't his preference; he intended a more high-minded treatise on salvation (verse 3). But the church was facing mortal dangers, and so Jude dashed off a vehement warning.

Who Were the Troublemakers?

Jude doesn't elaborate on what the troublemakers (verse 4) were teaching—perhaps he didn't want to honor their ideas by discussing them. Their behavior, however, is fair game: he fires away at their hypocrisy, divisiveness, and loose morals. He calls them spies and urges believers to fight for the true faith. At his poetic best, he borrows vivid images from nature to describe these people (12–13).

Short and vigorous, the book of Jude brings to mind a message from one of the fiery Old Testament prophets. Yet Jude holds out hope for his readers. Sincere believers can keep themselves in God's love, and some wavering souls can still be snatched "out of the fire" (21–23). (Even when battling heretics, Jude does not hint at persecuting the offenders—no burnings at the stake here.)

Jude closes with a familiar and joy-filled doxology, the one part of his letter still quoted widely in modern churches.

How to Read Jude

In tone, Jude reads a lot like James and 2 Peter: It is simple, hard-hitting, and stern. In fact, it seems to copy entire sections of 2 Peter.

You can read through Jude in a few minutes, to get the force of his argument. But to truly appreciate his letter, you should reflect on (and look up) his various Old Testament references. Jude supports his arguments with extensive illustrations from history, and he even quotes from two Jewish books not accepted as part of the Bible, *The Assumption of Moses* (verse 9) and the book of *Enoch* (verse 14).

All these citations support Jude's main thrust, which he summarizes eloquently in the last few paragraphs.

3-TRACK READING PLAN

For an explanation and complete listing of the 3-track reading plan, turn to page 7.

TRACK 1: **Two-Week Courses on the Bible**
See page 7 for information on these courses.

TRACK 2: **Read Jude in 1 Day**
☐ Day 1. Just one chapter long, Jude will take only a few minutes to read.
Now turn to page 9 for your next Track 2 reading project.

TRACK 3: **All of Jude in 1 Day**
After you have read Jude, turn to pages 10–14 for your next Track 3 reading project.
☐ Jude

Salutation

1 Jude,[a] a servant[b] of Jesus Christ and brother of James,

To those who are called, who are beloved[c] in[d] God the Father and kept safe for[d] Jesus Christ:

2 May mercy, peace, and love be yours in abundance.

Occasion of the Letter

3 Beloved, while eagerly preparing to write to you about the salvation we share, I find it necessary to write and appeal to you to contend for the faith that was once for all entrusted to the saints. [4]For certain intruders have stolen in among you, people who long ago were designated for this condemnation as ungodly, who pervert the grace of our God into licentiousness and deny our only Master and Lord, Jesus Christ.[e]

Judgment on False Teachers

5 Now I desire to remind you, though you are fully informed, that the Lord, who once for all saved[f] a people out of the land of Egypt, afterward destroyed those who did not believe. [6]And the angels who did not keep their own position, but left their proper dwelling, he has kept in eternal chains in deepest darkness for the judgment of the great day. [7]Likewise, Sodom and Gomorrah and the surrounding cities, which, in the same manner as they, indulged in sexual immorality and pursued unnatural lust,[g] serve as an example by undergoing a punishment of eternal fire.

8 Yet in the same way these dreamers also defile the flesh, reject authority, and slander the glorious ones.[h] [9]But when the archangel Michael contended with the devil and disputed about the body of Moses, he did not dare to bring a condemnation of slander[i] against him, but said, "The Lord rebuke you!" [10]But these people slander whatever they do not understand, and they are destroyed by those things that, like irrational animals, they know by instinct. [11]Woe to them! For they go the way of Cain, and abandon themselves to Balaam's error for the sake of gain, and perish in Korah's rebellion. [12]These are blemishes[j] on your love-feasts, while they feast with you without fear, feeding themselves.[k] They are waterless clouds carried along by the winds; autumn trees without fruit, twice dead, uprooted; [13]wild waves of the sea, casting up the foam of their own shame; wandering stars, for whom the deepest darkness has been reserved forever.

11 Bad Models

Jude mentions three Old Testament characters as powerful illustrations of qualities to avoid: the selfishness of Cain, the greed of Balaam, the rebelliousness of Korah. (Their stories can be found in Genesis 4, Numbers 22, and Numbers 16.) After filling his letter with such negative examples, however, Jude concludes triumphantly that God "is able to keep you from falling" (verse 24).

14 It was also about these that Enoch, in the seventh generation from Adam, prophesied, saying, "See, the Lord is coming[l] with ten thousands of his holy ones, [15]to execute judgment on all, and to convict everyone of all the deeds of ungodliness that they have committed in such an ungodly way, and of all the harsh things that ungodly sinners have spoken against him." [16]These are grumblers and malcontents; they indulge their own lusts; they are bombastic in speech, flattering people to their own advantage.

Warnings and Exhortations

17 But you, beloved, must remember the predictions of the apostles of our Lord Jesus Christ;

---

a Gk *Judas*   *b* Gk *slave*   *c* Other ancient authorities read *sanctified*   *d* Or *by*   *e* Or *the only Master and our Lord Jesus Christ*   *f* Other ancient authorities read *though you were once for all fully informed, that Jesus* (or *Joshua*) *who saved*   *g* Gk *went after other flesh*   *h* Or *angels*; Gk *glories*   *i* Or *condemnation for blasphemy*   *j* Or *reefs*   *k* Or *without fear. They are shepherds who care only for themselves*   *l* Gk *came*

[18]for they said to you, "In the last time there will be scoffers, indulging their own ungodly lusts." [19]It is these worldly people, devoid of the Spirit, who are causing divisions. [20]But you, beloved, build yourselves up on your most holy faith; pray in the Holy Spirit; [21]keep yourselves in the love of God; look forward to the mercy of our Lord Jesus Christ that leads to[m] eternal life. [22]And have mercy on some who are wavering; [23]save others by snatching them out of the fire; and have mercy on still others with fear, hating even the tunic defiled by their bodies.[n]

Benediction

24 Now to him who is able to keep you from falling, and to make you stand without blemish in the presence of his glory with rejoicing, [25]to the only God our Savior, through Jesus Christ our Lord, be glory, majesty, power, and authority, before all time and now and forever. Amen.

---

[m] Gk Christ to   [n] Gk by the flesh. The Greek text of verses 22-23 is uncertain at several points

REVELATION

A Book Full of Mysteries
Why Revelation is hard to understand

THE ROMAN EMPIRE HAD ITS own version of Alcatraz: a rocky island called Patmos. Prisoners banished to that hard-labor colony usually wasted away and died. In that desolate setting a man named John had a series of visions he wrote down as Revelation, the strangest book in the New Testament.

John probably wrote this book about 60 years after Jesus left the earth. Questions were troubling the church. Was Jesus coming back as he had promised? Where did he go? To do what? Why didn't he return immediately? Revelation addresses those issues.

> *Blessed is the one who reads aloud the words of the prophecy, and blessed are those who hear and who keep what is written in it; for the time is near. 1.3*

Writing in Code

No other New Testament book resembles Revelation in style. Yet during its time similar Jewish "apocalyptic" books (books that symbolically picture the ultimate destruction of evil and the triumph of good) flourished. Authors, writing to persecuted Christians anxious about their future, predicted what would take place. Often, they used coded language to protect theselves; for example, they substituted a word like *Babylon* when criticizing Rome, just in case their writings fell into the wrong hands.

The codes in Revelation are effective—so effective that few people today agree on exactly what they mean. Some people think many of the predictions in Revelation have not yet been fulfilled; perhaps John was writing about events that will come to pass in our own generation, they say. A best-selling book, Hal Lindsey's *The Late Great Planet Earth,* interprets Revelation that way.

Others explain Revelation in terms of the first century, concluding that many of the events prophesied in code took place during the Roman empire. Still others find clues to John's meaning spread out over 2,000 years of church history, or surmise that he employed symbols merely to describe an idealized battle of good and evil.

Two Dangers

Because of all the conflicting theories about Revelation, readers are tempted to respond in one of two ways. Some judge the book so perplexingly weird that they can find no reason to read it at all. How can anyone be sure of its meaning?

Others fall prey to the opposite danger. They pore over Revelation and conclude they have discovered the secret explanation of each obscure detail. To the latter group, it may be humbling to learn that every generation since the first century has come up with different interpretations of the prophecies.

Why Read Revelation?

Why read this strange book? John gives a good clue in the first phrase, which introduces this book as "the revelation of Jesus Christ." Revelation gives a unique picture of Jesus Christ, and the New Testament would be incomplete without it. The Gospels describe Jesus' life on earth from four different viewpoints. The letters discuss the deep significance of the resurrected Christ and what he accomplished. But Revelation shows Jesus Christ from a new perspective: as the mighty ruler of the cosmic forces of good. When John saw him in this exalted state, he fell at Jesus' feet as though dead (1.17).

Although Revelation does not remove the mystery surrounding Jesus' return and the end of the world, it does throw light on those events. It cannot be reduced to a mere timetable of events; it speaks lasting truths to every generation of readers. Revelation tells of Christ's future triumph over all the evil in the universe. This crucial message of final hope was needed by its original readers in the first century and is still needed by us today.

How to Read Revelation

Revelation is probably the most intimidating book in the Bible. It packs in so many symbols and obscure details that most readers find themselves plagued by the sensation that they are missing something.

All new forms of writing seem intimidating at first: for example, consider your very first science fiction book, filled with weird names and unearthly creatures, and governed by its own rules of writing. Science fiction seems very strange until you learn the techniques used by virtually all science fiction writers. Once you understand the form, it makes more sense. The same applies to Revelation. It will likely seem strange at first, because it uses techniques of symbolism and visions not commonly used elsewhere in the New Testament.

It is best to read Revelation one vision at a time, rather than all at once. The seven main visions give a view of similar events from different angles.

1. The church on earth (1–3)
2. The Lamb and the seven seals (4–7)
3. Seven angels with trumpets (8–11)
4. The church persecuted by Satan and the beast (12–14)
5. The seven bowls of God's wrath (15–16)
6. Judgment of Babylon (17–19.10).
7. Final judgment and final victory (19.11 to end).

Try to read completely through a vision, following the boldface sectional headings marked in the Bible text.

As you read, look behind the visual symbols for the meaning they point to. Ask yourself, What does this tell me about Christ, about God, about the real meaning of history? Don't try to analyze details at first; just follow the main flow of thought.

Keep in mind also the condition of the persecuted Christians who first received this book. They needed not a precise calendar of future events, but rather a word of encouragement and hope. They needed faith that, no matter how things looked, God was in charge of history and good would ultimately triumph. Revelation provides this hope, for them and for us.

Finally, a good Bible dictionary or commentary will clear up much of the confusion about Revelation.

3-TRACK READING PLAN

For an explanation and complete listing of the 3-track reading plan, turn to page 7.

TRACK 1: *Two-Week Courses on the Bible*
See page 7 for information on these courses.

TRACK 2: *An Overview of Revelation in 3 Days*
☐ Day 1. Read the Introduction to Revelation, then chapter 1, to see how John introduces this book.
☐ Day 2. Read chapter 12 as a sample of the writing contained in this book of visions.
☐ Day 3. Read chapter 21 for a glimpse of the final end of the universe.

Now turn to page 9 for your next Track 2 reading project.

TRACK 3: *All of Revelation in 19 Days*
After you have read through Revelation, turn to pages 10–14 for your next Track 3 reading project.

☐1　　☐2　　☐3　　☐4–5　☐6　　☐7　　☐8　　☐9
☐10–11 ☐12　　☐13　　☐14　☐15–16 ☐17　☐18　☐19
☐20　　☐21　　☐22

Introduction and Salutation

1 The revelation of Jesus Christ, which God gave him to show his servants[a] what must soon take place; he made[b] it known by sending his angel to his servant[c] John, [2]who testified to the word of God and to the testimony of Jesus Christ, even to all that he saw.

3 Blessed is the one who reads aloud the words of the prophecy, and blessed are those who hear and who keep what is written in it; for the time is near.

4 John to the seven churches that are in Asia:

Grace to you and peace from him who is and who was and who is to come, and from the seven spirits who are before his throne, [5]and from Jesus Christ, the faithful witness, the firstborn of the dead, and the ruler of the kings of the earth.

To him who loves us and freed[d] us from our sins by his blood, [6]and made[b] us to be a kingdom, priests serving[e] his God and Father, to him be glory and dominion forever and ever. Amen.

7 Look! He is coming with the clouds;
every eye will see him,
even those who pierced him;
and on his account all the tribes of the
earth will wail.
So it is to be. Amen.

8 "I am the Alpha and the Omega," says the Lord God, who is and who was and who is to come, the Almighty.

A Vision of Christ

9 I, John, your brother who share with you in Jesus the persecution and the kingdom and the patient endurance, was on the island called Patmos because of the word of God and the testimony of Jesus.[f] [10]I was in the spirit[g] on the Lord's day, and I heard behind me a loud voice like a trumpet [11]saying, "Write in a book what you see and send it to the seven churches, to Ephesus, to Smyrna, to Pergamum, to Thyatira, to Sardis, to Philadelphia, and to Laodicea."

12 Then I turned to see whose voice it was that spoke to me, and on turning I saw seven golden lampstands, [13]and in the midst of the lampstands I saw one like the Son of Man, clothed with a long robe and with a golden sash across his chest. [14]His head and his hair were white as white

1.13 Familiar Title

Revelation's original readers would have recognized this description immediately, for Jesus used the title "Son of Man" about 90 times in the Gospels.

wool, white as snow; his eyes were like a flame of fire, [15]his feet were like burnished bronze, refined as in a furnace, and his voice was like the sound of many waters. [16]In his right hand he held seven stars, and from his mouth came a sharp, two-edged sword, and his face was like the sun shining with full force.

17 When I saw him, I fell at his feet as though dead. But he placed his right hand on me, saying, "Do not be afraid; I am the first and the last, [18]and the living one. I was dead, and see, I am alive forever and ever; and I have the keys of Death and of Hades. [19]Now write what you have seen, what is, and what is to take place after this. [20]As for the mystery of the seven stars that you saw in my right hand, and the seven golden lampstands: the seven stars are the angels of the seven churches, and the seven lampstands are the seven churches.

The Message to Ephesus

2 "To the angel of the church in Ephesus write: These are the words of him who holds the seven stars in his right hand, who walks among the seven golden lampstands:

2 "I know your works, your toil and your patient endurance. I know that you cannot tolerate evildoers; you have tested those who claim to be apostles but are not, and have found them to be false. [3]I also know that you are enduring patiently and bearing up for the sake of my name, and that you have not grown weary. [4]But I have this against you, that you have abandoned the love you had at first. [5]Remember then from what you have fallen; repent, and do the works you did at first. If not, I will come to you and remove your lampstand from its place, unless you repent. [6]Yet this is to your credit: you hate the works of the Nicolaitans, which I also hate. [7]Let anyone who has an ear listen to what the Spirit is saying to the churches. To everyone who conquers, I will give permission to eat from the tree of life that is in the paradise of God.

The Message to Smyrna

8 "And to the angel of the church in Smyrna write: These are the words of the first and the last, who was dead and came to life:

9 "I know your affliction and your poverty, even though you are rich. I know the slander on the part of those who say that they are Jews and are not, but are a synagogue of Satan. [10]Do not fear what you are about to suffer. Beware, the devil is about to throw some of you into prison so that you may be tested, and for ten days you will have affliction. Be faithful until death, and I will give you the crown of life. [11]Let anyone who has an ear listen to what the Spirit is saying to the

---

[a] Gk *slaves*   [b] Gk *and he made*   [c] Gk *slave*   [d] Other ancient authorities read *washed*   [e] Gk *priests to*
[f] Or *testimony to Jesus*   [g] Or *in the Spirit*

churches. Whoever conquers will not be harmed by the second death.

The Message to Pergamum

12 "And to the angel of the church in Pergamum write: These are the words of him who has the sharp two-edged sword:

13 "I know where you are living, where Satan's throne is. Yet you are holding fast to my name, and you did not deny your faith in me[h] even in the days of Antipas my witness, my faithful one, who was killed among you, where Satan

2.13 Satan's Throne

When John wrote Revelation, the first century was drawing to a close. Now clearly separate from Judaism, the Christian church had lost its semi-official protection, and Roman emperors such as Nero had directed bloody persecutions. Antipas, mentioned here, was the first martyr of western Asia. The city of Pergamum served as headquarters for several pagan cults, and the practice of emperor worship spread from here throughout the region—possibly the meaning behind the phrase "where Satan's throne is."

lives. [14]But I have a few things against you: you have some there who hold to the teaching of Balaam, who taught Balak to put a stumbling block before the people of Israel, so that they would eat food sacrificed to idols and practice fornication. [15]So you also have some who hold to the teaching of the Nicolaitans. [16]Repent then. If not, I will come to you soon and make war against them with the sword of my mouth. [17]Let anyone who has an ear listen to what the Spirit is saying to the churches. To everyone who conquers I will give some of the hidden manna, and I will give a white stone, and on the white stone is written a new name that no one knows except the one who receives it.

The Message to Thyatira

18 "And to the angel of the church in Thyatira write: These are the words of the Son of God, who has eyes like a flame of fire, and whose feet are like burnished bronze:

19 "I know your works—your love, faith, service, and patient endurance. I know that your last works are greater than the first. [20]But I have this against you: you tolerate that woman Jezebel, who calls herself a prophet and is teaching and beguiling my servants[i] to practice fornication and to eat food sacrificed to idols. [21]I gave her time to repent, but she refuses to repent of her fornication. [22]Beware, I am throwing her on a bed, and

those who commit adultery with her I am throwing into great distress, unless they repent of her doings; [23]and I will strike her children dead. And all the churches will know that I am the one who searches minds and hearts, and I will give to each of you as your works deserve. [24]But to the rest of you in Thyatira, who do not hold this teaching, who have not learned what some call 'the deep things of Satan,' to you I say, I do not lay on you any other burden; [25]only hold fast to what you have until I come. [26]To everyone who conquers and continues to do my works to the end,

I will give authority over the nations;
[27]   to rule[j] them with an iron rod,
      as when clay pots are shattered—
[28]even as I also received authority from my Father. To the one who conquers I will also give the morning star. [29]Let anyone who has an ear listen to what the Spirit is saying to the churches.

The Message to Sardis

3 "And to the angel of the church in Sardis write: These are the words of him who has the seven spirits of God and the seven stars:

"I know your works; you have a name of being

3.1 Cities on a Mail Route

The cities mentioned in chapters 2 and 3 were actual cities in the ancient world where a church existed. John listed them in the order in which a messenger on the road would have found them, starting with the chief city of Ephesus and then circling back clockwise. The cities lie in what is now part of modern Turkey. Religious wars took their toll: None of the churches in these cities survived.

alive, but you are dead. [2]Wake up, and strengthen what remains and is on the point of death, for I have not found your works perfect in the sight of my God. [3]Remember then what you received and heard; obey it, and repent. If you do not wake up, I will come like a thief, and you will not know at what hour I will come to you. [4]Yet you have still a few persons in Sardis who have not soiled their clothes; they will walk with me, dressed in white, for they are worthy. [5]If you conquer, you will be clothed like them in white robes, and I will not blot your name out of the book of life; I will confess your name before my Father and before his angels. [6]Let anyone who has an ear listen to what the Spirit is saying to the churches.

The Message to Philadelphia

7 "And to the angel of the church in Philadelphia write:

h Or *deny my faith*   i Gk *slaves*   j Or *to shepherd*

These are the words of the holy one, the
true one,
who has the key of David,
who opens and no one will shut,
who shuts and no one opens:

8 "I know your works. Look, I have set before
you an open door, which no one is able to shut.
I know that you have but little power, and yet you
have kept my word and have not denied my
name. [9]I will make those of the synagogue of
Satan who say that they are Jews and are not, but
are lying—I will make them come and bow down
before your feet, and they will learn that I have
loved you. [10]Because you have kept my word of
patient endurance, I will keep you from the hour
of trial that is coming on the whole world to test
the inhabitants of the earth. [11]I am coming soon;
hold fast to what you have, so that no one may
seize your crown. [12]If you conquer, I will make
you a pillar in the temple of my God; you will
never go out of it. I will write on you the name of
my God, and the name of the city of my God, the
new Jerusalem that comes down from my God
out of heaven, and my own new name. [13]Let anyone who has an ear listen to what the Spirit is
saying to the churches.

The Message to Laodicea

14 "And to the angel of the church in Laodicea write: The words of the Amen, the faithful and
true witness, the origin[k] of God's creation:

15 "I know your works; you are neither cold
nor hot. I wish that you were either cold or hot.
[16]So, because you are lukewarm, and neither cold
nor hot, I am about to spit you out of my mouth.
[17]For you say, 'I am rich, I have prospered, and I
need nothing.' You do not realize that you are
wretched, pitiable, poor, blind, and naked.
[18]Therefore I counsel you to buy from me gold
refined by fire so that you may be rich; and white
robes to clothe you and to keep the shame of your
nakedness from being seen; and salve to anoint
your eyes so that you may see. [19]I reprove and
discipline those whom I love. Be earnest, therefore, and repent. [20]Listen! I am standing at the
door, knocking; if you hear my voice and open
the door, I will come in to you and eat with you,
and you with me. [21]To the one who conquers I
will give a place with me on my throne, just as I
myself conquered and sat down with my Father
on his throne. [22]Let anyone who has an ear listen
to what the Spirit is saying to the churches."

The Heavenly Worship

4 After this I looked, and there in heaven a
door stood open! And the first voice, which
I had heard speaking to me like a trumpet, said,
"Come up here, and I will show you what must

take place after this." [2]At once I was in the spirit,[l]
and there in heaven stood a throne, with one
seated on the throne! [3]And the one seated there
looks like jasper and carnelian, and around the
throne is a rainbow that looks like an emerald.
[4]Around the throne are twenty-four thrones, and
seated on the thrones are twenty-four elders,
dressed in white robes, with golden crowns on
their heads. [5]Coming from the throne are flashes
of lightning, and rumblings and peals of thunder,
and in front of the throne burn seven flaming
torches, which are the seven spirits of God; [6]and
in front of the throne there is something like a sea
of glass, like crystal.

Around the throne, and on each side of the
throne, are four living creatures, full of eyes in
front and behind: [7]the first living creature like a
lion, the second living creature like an ox, the
third living creature with a face like a human face,
and the fourth living creature like a flying eagle.

4.7 Strange Creatures

*The Old Testament prophet Ezekiel had a
somewhat similar vision (Ezekiel 1.9–10). In his
version, however, each individual creature had
four faces: human, lion, ox, and eagle. These
symbols held special meaning for people of
that day, much as the American eagle or British
lion does today. For more information see "A
Startling Image of Jesus," page 1311.*

[8]And the four living creatures, each of them with
six wings, are full of eyes all around and inside.
Day and night without ceasing they sing,

"Holy, holy, holy,
   the Lord God the Almighty,
      who was and is and is to come."
[9]And whenever the living creatures give glory and
honor and thanks to the one who is seated on the
throne, who lives forever and ever, [10]the twenty-
four elders fall before the one who is seated on the
throne and worship the one who lives forever and
ever; they cast their crowns before the throne,
singing,
11 "You are worthy, our Lord and God,
   to receive glory and honor and power,
      for you created all things,
         and by your will they existed and were
            created."

The Scroll and the Lamb

5 Then I saw in the right hand of the one seated
on the throne a scroll written on the inside
and on the back, sealed[m] with seven seals; [2]and I
saw a mighty angel proclaiming with a loud voice,
"Who is worthy to open the scroll and break its

---

[k] Or *beginning*   [l] Or *in the Spirit*   [m] Or *written on the inside, and sealed on the back*

seals?" ³And no one in heaven or on earth or under the earth was able to open the scroll or to look into it. ⁴And I began to weep bitterly because no one was found worthy to open the scroll or to

look into it. ⁵Then one of the elders said to me, "Do not weep. See, the Lion of the tribe of Judah,

the Root of David, has conquered, so that he can open the scroll and its seven seals."

6 Then I saw between the throne and the four living creatures and among the elders a Lamb standing as if it had been slaughtered, having seven horns and seven eyes, which are the seven spirits of God sent out into all the earth. ⁷He went and took the scroll from the right hand of the one who was seated on the throne. ⁸When he had taken the scroll, the four living creatures and the twenty-four elders fell before the Lamb, each holding a harp and golden bowls full of incense, which are the prayers of the saints. ⁹They sing a new song:

"You are worthy to take the scroll
    and to open its seals,
for you were slaughtered and by your
        blood you ransomed for God
    saints from[n] every tribe and language
        and people and nation;

[n] Gk *ransomed for God from*

5.1 Seals and Scrolls

Certain words and phrases used in Revelation had a clearer meaning to ancient readers familiar with the objects. For example, important documents were sent written on a papyrus scroll sealed with several wax seals. Only the proper person, in the presence of witnesses, could open the document. Thus in this vision, only the "worthy" creature is able to break the seal.

A Startling Image of Jesus
A helpless lamb—the mightiest of all creatures

IMAGES OF JESUS ABOUND IN Revelation, and one way to study the book is to follow a single image through the entire book. After his luminous appearance in the first chapter, Jesus is presented as a king, a child, a warrior on a horse, the Lord of the whole earth, the husband of a bride. Of all the images, however, none is so startling and unlikely as the one in John's second vision. Yet it takes hold and appears repeatedly throughout the book.

And I began to weep bitterly because no one was found worthy to open the scroll or to look into it. 5.4

To set the stage for this vision, the book of Revelation uses more visual drama than a science fiction movie. Lightning flashes, the sky growls, and awesome creatures encircle a lofty throne. Four of the creatures (4.6) seem to symbolize the most impressive examples of all creation, for a common saying in those days went,

> The mightiest among the birds is the eagle.
> The mightiest among the domestic animals is the bull.
> The mightiest among the wild beasts is the lion.
> And the mightiest of all is man.

Only One Worthy

A question resounds in the heavens, "Who is worthy to open the scroll and break its seals?" (5.2). In other words, who is worthy to introduce the next phase of history? No one can answer, much to John's dismay. Not one of the four impressive creatures qualifies.

But suddenly John sees another creature, a Lamb, appearing "as if it had been slaughtered" (5.6). The image contains a great paradox. None of the majestic angels or elders or living creatures has the right to break the seals. Only a Lamb does—a helpless, slaughtered Lamb.

John records a song of celebration ("You are worthy to take the scroll and to open its seals, for you were slaughtered and by your blood you ransomed for God" [5.9]), a song later set to earthly music in Handel's *Messiah*. And elsewhere in Revelation true believers are identified as being recorded in the "Lamb's book of life" (21.27).

This powerful image resurfaces often in Revelation, a book of warfare between good and evil. Christ the King is also the Lamb, the one who died for us. His death on the cross, seemingly a great defeat, actually ushered in a decisive victory, for him and for us. Good was not destroyed; it triumphed.

Life Questions: What meaning does the image of Jesus as a slain Lamb have for you? What are your favorite "pictures" or images of Jesus?

10 you have made them to be a kingdom
     and priests serving[o] our God,
  and they will reign on earth."

11 Then I looked, and I heard the voice of many angels surrounding the throne and the living creatures and the elders; they numbered myriads of myriads and thousands of thousands, 12singing with full voice,

"Worthy is the Lamb that was slaughtered
  to receive power and wealth and wisdom
     and might
  and honor and glory and blessing!"

13Then I heard every creature in heaven and on earth and under the earth and in the sea, and all that is in them, singing,

"To the one seated on the throne and to
     the Lamb
be blessing and honor and glory and
     might
  forever and ever!"

14And the four living creatures said, "Amen!" And the elders fell down and worshiped.

The Seven Seals

6 Then I saw the Lamb open one of the seven seals, and I heard one of the four living creatures call out, as with a voice of thunder, "Come!"[p] 2I looked, and there was a white horse! Its rider had a bow; a crown was given to him, and he came out conquering and to conquer.

3 When he opened the second seal, I heard the second living creature call out, "Come!"[p] 4And out came[q] another horse, bright red; its rider was permitted to take peace from the earth, so that people would slaughter one another; and he was given a great sword.

5 When he opened the third seal, I heard the third living creature call out, "Come!"[p] I looked, and there was a black horse! Its rider held a pair of scales in his hand, 6and I heard what seemed to be a voice in the midst of the four living creatures saying, "A quart of wheat for a day's pay,[r] and three quarts of barley for a day's pay,[r] but do not damage the olive oil and the wine!"

7 When he opened the fourth seal, I heard the voice of the fourth living creature call out, "Come!"[p] 8I looked and there was a pale green horse! Its rider's name was Death, and Hades followed with him; they were given authority over a fourth of the earth, to kill with sword, famine, and pestilence, and by the wild animals of the earth.

9 When he opened the fifth seal, I saw under the altar the souls of those who had been slaughtered for the word of God and for the testimony they had given; 10they cried out with a loud voice, "Sovereign Lord, holy and true, how long will it be before you judge and avenge our blood on the inhabitants of the earth?" 11They were each given

a white robe and told to rest a little longer, until the number would be complete both of their fellow servants[s] and of their brothers and sisters,[t] who were soon to be killed as they themselves had been killed.

12 When he opened the sixth seal, I looked, and there came a great earthquake; the sun became black as sackcloth, the full moon became like blood, 13and the stars of the sky fell to the earth as the fig tree drops its winter fruit when shaken by a gale. 14The sky vanished like a scroll rolling itself up, and every mountain and island was removed from its place. 15Then the kings of the earth and the magnates and the generals and the rich and the powerful, and everyone, slave and free, hid in the caves and among the rocks of the mountains, 16calling to the mountains and rocks, "Fall on us and hide us from the face of the one seated on the throne and from the wrath of the Lamb; 17for the great day of their wrath has come, and who is able to stand?"

The 144,000 of Israel Sealed

7 After this I saw four angels standing at the four corners of the earth, holding back the four winds of the earth so that no wind could

7.1 Significant Numbers

Numbers had a great symbolic significance in the Bible, and especially to the writer of Revelation. This concept is foreign to most modern readers; a rough parallel might be the "unlucky" significance some attach to the number 13. The most obviously symbolic numbers in Revelation are 4, 7, 12, and their multiples.

The number 4 seems to stand for the created universe (four points of the compass, four winds of the earth), and thus the four living creatures (4.6) represent all creation. In the Bible, the number 7 denotes perfection or completion, probably because the Genesis creation account covers seven days. The 12 tribes of Israel in the Old Testament and 12 apostles in the New Testament indicate that the number 12 stands for the church, or God's redeemed people from both covenants.

A number multiplied by 10s, such as 144,000 (12x12x10x10x10), suggests an indefinite but very large figure. Therefore, 144,000 may stand for the entire church throughout history.

blow on earth or sea or against any tree. 2I saw another angel ascending from the rising of the sun, having the seal of the living God, and he called with a loud voice to the four angels who had been given power to damage earth and sea,

---

o Gk *priests to*   p Or *"Go!"*   q Or *went*   r Gk *a denarius*   s Gk *slaves*   t Gk *brothers*

[3]saying, "Do not damage the earth or the sea or the trees, until we have marked the servants[u] of our God with a seal on their foreheads."

4 And I heard the number of those who were sealed, one hundred forty-four thousand, sealed out of every tribe of the people of Israel:

5 From the tribe of Judah twelve thousand sealed,

from the tribe of Reuben twelve thousand, from the tribe of Gad twelve thousand,

6 from the tribe of Asher twelve thousand, from the tribe of Naphtali twelve thousand, from the tribe of Manasseh twelve thousand,

7 from the tribe of Simeon twelve thousand, from the tribe of Levi twelve thousand, from the tribe of Issachar twelve thousand,

8 from the tribe of Zebulun twelve thousand, from the tribe of Joseph twelve thousand, from the tribe of Benjamin twelve thousand sealed.

The Multitude from Every Nation

9 After this I looked, and there was a great multitude that no one could count, from every nation, from all tribes and peoples and languages, standing before the throne and before the Lamb, robed in white, with palm branches in their hands. [10]They cried out in a loud voice, saying,

"Salvation belongs to our God who is
        seated on the throne, and to the
        Lamb!"

[11]And all the angels stood around the throne and around the elders and the four living creatures, and they fell on their faces before the throne and worshiped God, [12]singing,

"Amen! Blessing and glory and wisdom
and thanksgiving and honor
and power and might
be to our God forever and ever! Amen."

13 Then one of the elders addressed me, saying, "Who are these, robed in white, and where have they come from?" [14]I said to him, "Sir, you are the one that knows." Then he said to me, "These are they who have come out of the great ordeal; they have washed their robes and made them white in the blood of the Lamb.

15 For this reason they are before the throne
        of God,
        and worship him day and night within
        his temple,
        and the one who is seated on the
        throne will shelter them.

16 They will hunger no more, and thirst no
        more;
        the sun will not strike them,
        nor any scorching heat;

17 for the Lamb at the center of the throne
        will be their shepherd,

and he will guide them to springs of
        the water of life,
and God will wipe away every tear from
        their eyes."

7.14 The Great Ordeal

Bible interpreters have proposed many theories to explain "the great ordeal" (often translated "the great tribulation"), a time of intense persecution for Christians. Some believe it will occur in the future, around the time of Christ's return. (For more detail, see "Forty-two Months of Trials," page 1318.) Others believe John was referring to persecutions against the church occurring in his own day. Regardless, John stresses the overarching promise that the time of tribulation does not last forever. One day the faithful will no longer hunger or thirst and will never again have reason to cry (verses 16–17).

The Seventh Seal and the Golden Censer

8 When the Lamb opened the seventh seal, there was silence in heaven for about half an hour. [2]And I saw the seven angels who stand before God, and seven trumpets were given to them.

8.1 Dramatic Structure

Revelation unfolds with a sense of ever-increasing drama, hinged on the symbolic number 7. Here, heaven itself pauses in silence before the opening of the seventh seal. Chapter 11 includes a long pause before the seventh trumpet sounds its judgment. Finally, in chapter 16 the seventh bowl introduces the greatest calamity of all, the battle of Harmagedon.

3 Another angel with a golden censer came and stood at the altar; he was given a great quantity of incense to offer with the prayers of all the saints on the golden altar that is before the throne. [4]And the smoke of the incense, with the prayers of the saints, rose before God from the hand of the angel. [5]Then the angel took the censer and filled it with fire from the altar and threw it on the earth; and there were peals of thunder, rumblings, flashes of lightning, and an earthquake.

The Seven Trumpets

6 Now the seven angels who had the seven trumpets made ready to blow them.

7 The first angel blew his trumpet, and there

came hail and fire, mixed with blood, and they were hurled to the earth; and a third of the earth was burned up, and a third of the trees were burned up, and all green grass was burned up.

8 The second angel blew his trumpet, and something like a great mountain, burning with fire, was thrown into the sea. 9A third of the sea became blood, a third of the living creatures in the sea died, and a third of the ships were destroyed.

· 10 The third angel blew his trumpet, and a great star fell from heaven, blazing like a torch, and it fell on a third of the rivers and on the springs of water. 11The name of the star is Wormwood. A third of the waters became wormwood, and many died from the water, because it was made bitter.

12 The fourth angel blew his trumpet, and a third of the sun was struck, and a third of the moon, and a third of the stars, so that a third of their light was darkened; a third of the day was kept from shining, and likewise the night.

13 Then I looked, and I heard an eagle crying with a loud voice as it flew in midheaven, "Woe, woe, woe to the inhabitants of the earth, at the blasts of the other trumpets that the three angels are about to blow!"

9 And the fifth angel blew his trumpet, and I saw a star that had fallen from heaven to earth, and he was given the key to the shaft of the bottomless pit; 2he opened the shaft of the bottomless pit, and from the shaft rose smoke like the smoke of a great furnace, and the sun and the air were darkened with the smoke from the shaft. 3Then from the smoke came locusts on the earth, and they were given authority like the authority of scorpions of the earth. 4They were told not to damage the grass of the earth or any green growth or any tree, but only those people who do not have the seal of God on their foreheads. 5They were allowed to torture them for five months, but not to kill them, and their torture was like the torture of a scorpion when it stings someone. 6And in those days people will seek death but will not find it; they will long to die, but death will flee from them.

7 In appearance the locusts were like horses equipped for battle. On their heads were what looked like crowns of gold; their faces were like human faces, 8their hair like women's hair, and their teeth like lions' teeth; 9they had scales like iron breastplates, and the noise of their wings was like the noise of many chariots with horses rushing into battle. 10They have tails like scorpions, with stingers, and in their tails is their power to harm people for five months. 11They have as king over them the angel of the bottomless pit; his name in Hebrew is Abaddon,v and in Greek he is called Apollyon.w

12 The first woe has passed. There are still two woes to come.

13 Then the sixth angel blew his trumpet, and I heard a voice from the fourx horns of the golden altar before God, 14saying to the sixth angel

9.12 Judgments for a Purpose

Revelation records a number of severe judgments, in chapters 6, 9, and 16. It carefully mentions the purpose of these judgments: to convince humankind that its rebellion is futile and encourage it to repent (9.20). In this way, the judgments are similar to the 10 plagues against Egypt. Like the 10 plagues, these judgments do not ultimately work. The failure of people to repent makes necessary the final judgment against the source of all evil.

who had the trumpet, "Release the four angels who are bound at the great river Euphrates." 15So the four angels were released, who had been held ready for the hour, the day, the month, and the year, to kill a third of humankind. 16The number of the troops of cavalry was two hundred million; I heard their number. 17And this was how I saw the horses in my vision: the riders wore breastplates the color of fire and of sapphirey and of sulfur; the heads of the horses were like lions' heads, and fire and smoke and sulfur came out of their mouths. 18By these three plagues a third of humankind was killed, by the fire and smoke and sulfur coming out of their mouths. 19For the power of the horses is in their mouths and in their tails; their tails are like serpents, having heads; and with them they inflict harm.

20 The rest of humankind, who were not killed by these plagues, did not repent of the works of their hands or give up worshiping demons and idols of gold and silver and bronze and stone and wood, which cannot see or hear or walk. 21And they did not repent of their murders or their sorceries or their fornication or their thefts.

The Angel with the Little Scroll

10 And I saw another mighty angel coming down from heaven, wrapped in a cloud, with a rainbow over his head; his face was like the sun, and his legs like pillars of fire. 2He held a little scroll open in his hand. Setting his right foot on the sea and his left foot on the land, 3he gave a great shout, like a lion roaring. And when he shouted, the seven thunders sounded. 4And when the seven thunders had sounded, I was about to write, but I heard a voice from heaven saying, "Seal up what the seven thunders have said, and

---

v That is, *Destruction*   w That is, *Destroyer*   x Other ancient authorities lack *four*   y Gk *hyacinth*

do not write it down." ⁵Then the angel whom I saw standing on the sea and the land
raised his right hand to heaven
⁶ and swore by him who lives forever and ever,
who created heaven and what is in it, the earth and what is in it, and the sea and what is in it:

z Gk *slaves*

"There will be no more delay, ⁷but in the days when the seventh angel is to blow his trumpet, the mystery of God will be fulfilled, as he announced to his servantsᶻ the prophets."

8 Then the voice that I had heard from heaven spoke to me again, saying, "Go, take the scroll that is open in the hand of the angel who is stand-

Revelation's Use of Symbols
Why are there so many theories explaining Revelation?

"THERE NEVER HAS BEEN A book provoking more delirium, foolishness, and irrational movements, without any relationship to Jesus Christ," concluded Jacques Ellul, author of a commentary on Revelation. Readers tend to fixate wildly on details, mainly because John relied so heavily on symbols to express his meaning in this book.

Creatures covered with eyes and sprouting horns, eagles wheeling in the sky, molten mountains hurtling into the ocean—such rich imagery excites frenzied attempts to explain every word. John interprets some symbols for us—"The seven stars are the angels of the seven churches" (1.20)—and hints broadly at the meaning of others, such as the four horsemen in chapter 6. But many questions remain unanswered. For example, do the major visions describe consecutive periods of history, or do they foretell the same events from different angles?

> The locusts were like horses equipped for battle. On their heads were what looked like crowns of gold; their faces were like human faces. 9.7

Look at the Broad Picture

Artists find that symbols communicate with special power. When Spanish artist Pablo Picasso painted his massive *Guernica*, he attempted to express what had happened in war-ravaged Spain on April 28, 1937. He created a work of art, not a photographic record. The painting does communicate the tragedy at Guernica, but artfully, symbolically.

In a similar way, John poetically renders human events so strange and climactic as to be otherwise inexpressible. If he had wanted to, God could have revealed a precise timetable of future events, but instead Jesus warned specifically against such speculation about the future. In keeping with that approach, Revelation does not so much outline future events as hint at the cosmic significance that goes on *behind* history.

Readers new to Revelation should start by viewing scenes as a whole, looking for an overall meaning. The visions are like Jesus' parables: Each has a main thrust, and some of the details may serve merely to dramatize or add literary fullness to the scene. No one can find the precise meaning behind every detail in John's visions. Those who seek to explain each symbol too quickly may easily miss the meaning of the symbol as well as the grand emotional sweep of the book.

Searching for a System

Revelation will always attract scholars who search for the meaning behind each symbol. It is no easy undertaking: Over 300 allusions to the Old Testament and an elaborate system of symbolic numbers must be factored into any explanation. History has proved thousands of explainers wrong. People from every generation—especially in the hectic days around A.D. 1000 and in the 14th and 19th centuries, as well as in contemporary times dominated by Middle East tensions—have insisted the end of the world was just around the corner.

Today, some believe that Revelation's symbols—statues that talk, fire coming from heaven, totalitarian economic control, massive changes in the earth and sea—come hauntingly close to 20th-century phenomena. The wholesale devastation of earth prophesied in the middle chapters seems eerily up-to-date.

Yet, calamities merely provide a backdrop to John's main thrust: Followers of Christ will be made safe at last. "God will wipe away every tear from their eyes," he says (7.17). Much of Revelation remains shrouded in mystery, but the final results shine out clearly.

Life Questions: Two potential dangers in reading Revelation (see Introduction) are avoiding it entirely or getting obsessed with its details. Which danger are you most familiar with? Why do we need the message of Revelation today?

ing on the sea and on the land." ⁹So I went to the angel and told him to give me the little scroll; and he said to me, "Take it, and eat; it will be bitter to your stomach, but sweet as honey in your mouth." ¹⁰So I took the little scroll from the hand of the angel and ate it; it was sweet as honey in my mouth, but when I had eaten it, my stomach was made bitter.

11 Then they said to me, "You must prophesy again about many peoples and nations and languages and kings."

The Two Witnesses

11 Then I was given a measuring rod like a staff, and I was told, "Come and measure the temple of God and the altar and those who

> ### 11.1 Old Testament Echoes
>
> *A full understanding of Revelation requires detailed study of such Old Testament prophets as Ezekiel and Daniel. John frequently borrows images from those books. For example, the passage here on the temple of God parallels Ezekiel 40. Similarly, many passages referring to kings and political empires are reminiscent of Daniel's visions.*

worship there, ²but do not measure the court outside the temple; leave that out, for it is given over to the nations, and they will trample over the holy city for forty-two months. ³And I will grant my two witnesses authority to prophesy for one thousand two hundred sixty days, wearing sackcloth."

4 These are the two olive trees and the two lampstands that stand before the Lord of the earth. ⁵And if anyone wants to harm them, fire pours from their mouth and consumes their foes; anyone who wants to harm them must be killed in this manner. ⁶They have authority to shut the sky, so that no rain may fall during the days of their prophesying, and they have authority over the waters to turn them into blood, and to strike the earth with every kind of plague, as often as they desire.

7 When they have finished their testimony, the beast that comes up from the bottomless pit will make war on them and conquer them and kill them, ⁸and their dead bodies will lie in the street of the great city that is prophetically*ᵃ* called Sodom and Egypt, where also their Lord was crucified. ⁹For three and a half days members of the peoples and tribes and languages and nations will gaze at their dead bodies and refuse to let them be placed in a tomb; ¹⁰and the inhabitants of the earth will gloat over them and celebrate and exchange presents, because these two prophets had been a torment to the inhabitants of the earth.

11 But after the three and a half days, the breath*ᵇ* of life from God entered them, and they stood on their feet, and those who saw them were terrified. ¹²Then they*ᶜ* heard a loud voice from heaven saying to them, "Come up here!" And they went up to heaven in a cloud while their enemies watched them. ¹³At that moment there was a great earthquake, and a tenth of the city fell; seven thousand people were killed in the earthquake, and the rest were terrified and gave glory to the God of heaven.

14 The second woe has passed. The third woe is coming very soon.

The Seventh Trumpet

15 Then the seventh angel blew his trumpet, and there were loud voices in heaven, saying,
"The kingdom of the world has become
　　the kingdom of our Lord
　and of his Messiah,*ᵈ*
and he will reign forever and ever."
16 Then the twenty-four elders who sit on their thrones before God fell on their faces and worshiped God, ¹⁷singing,
"We give you thanks, Lord
　　God Almighty,
　who are and who were,
for you have taken your great power
　and begun to reign.
18 The nations raged,
　but your wrath has come,
　and the time for judging the dead,
for rewarding your servants,*ᵉ*
　　the prophets
　and saints and all who fear your name,
　both small and great,
and for destroying those who destroy the
　　earth."
19 Then God's temple in heaven was opened, and the ark of his covenant was seen within his temple; and there were flashes of lightning, rumblings, peals of thunder, an earthquake, and heavy hail.

The Woman and the Dragon

12 A great portent appeared in heaven: a woman clothed with the sun, with the moon under her feet, and on her head a crown of twelve stars. ²She was pregnant and was crying out in birth pangs, in the agony of giving birth. ³Then another portent appeared in heaven: a great red dragon, with seven heads and ten horns, and seven diadems on his heads. ⁴His tail swept down a third of the stars of heaven and threw them to the earth. Then the dragon stood before the woman who was to bear a child, so that he might devour her child as soon as it was born. ⁵And she gave birth to a son, a male child, who is

---

ᵃ Or *allegorically*; Gk *spiritually*　　*ᵇ* Or *the spirit*　　*ᶜ* Other ancient authorities read *I*　　*ᵈ* Gk *Christ*　　*ᵉ* Gk *slaves*

to rule*f* all the nations with a rod of iron. But her child was snatched away and taken to God and to his throne; 6and the woman fled into the wilderness, where she has a place prepared by God, so that there she can be nourished for one thousand two hundred sixty days.

Michael Defeats the Dragon

7 And war broke out in heaven; Michael and his angels fought against the dragon. The dragon and his angels fought back, 8but they were defeated, and there was no longer any place for them in heaven. 9The great dragon was thrown down, that ancient serpent, who is called the Devil and Satan, the deceiver of the whole world—he was thrown down to the earth, and his angels were thrown down with him.

f Or *to shepherd*　　*g* Gk *Christ*　　*h* Gk *brothers*

10 Then I heard a loud voice in heaven, proclaiming,

"Now have come the salvation and the
　　　　power
　and the kingdom of our God
　and the authority of his Messiah,*g*
for the accuser of our comrades*h* has
　　　　been thrown down,
　who accuses them day and night before
　　　　our God.
11 But they have conquered him by the
　　　　blood of the Lamb
　and by the word of their testimony,
　for they did not cling to life even in the
　　　　face of death.
12 Rejoice then, you heavens
　　　　and those who dwell in them!

A Look Behind the Scenes
Christmas from heaven's perspective

CHRISTMAS DAY. WE CELEBRATE IT with a sudden splurge of money and gifts and an attempt to rediscover the joy of the first Christmas. Manger displays in town squares recreate the scene in Bethlehem on that day long ago.

As many interpret it, chapter 12 describes Christmas day also, but its point of view differs radically from that of the Gospels. Revelation does not tell of shepherds, a crazed king bent on infanticide, and a stable; rather, it pictures a murderous dragon leading a ferocious struggle in heaven. His attack when Christ was born launches a series of bloody rebellions against the forces of good.

> The dragon stood before the woman who was about to bear a child, so that he might devour her child as soon as it was born. 12.4

Two Histories at Once

The view of Christ's birth in Revelation 12 gives a glimpse into the pattern of the entire book. John is fusing things seen with things normally not seen. In daily life, two parallel histories occur simultaneously: one on earth and one in heaven. Revelation, however, views them together. It parts the curtain, allowing a quick look behind the scenes at the cosmic impact of what happens on earth.

Every inch of this planet is claimed by God and counterclaimed by Satan. We normally experience only the visible, everyday effects of this struggle. We feel it, for example, when we make a choice between what we know is wrong and what is right. But, as we are living out our lives on earth, the supernatural universe is simultaneously at war. Revelation draws the contrasts sharply: good versus evil, the Lamb versus the dragon, Jerusalem versus Babylon, the bride versus the prostitute.

Is God in Control of History?

Sometimes the "war in heaven" can break out into actual violence on earth, as it did when Jesus came. Revelation was originally written to people who were facing extreme persecution from the Roman empire. Revelation establishes that a war is being waged on this planet between good and evil, a war that reflects a larger struggle in the whole universe. But, no matter how it looks, God is in firm control of history. To first-century Christians, Rome was the arch-villain, and allusions to that empire crop up in these chapters. John asserts that Jesus Christ, and not an emperor, determines the flow of history.

Events are marching onward to a definite climax; history has meaning. Ultimately, even the despots of history will end up fulfilling the plan mapped out for them by God. Pontius Pilate and his Roman soldiers demonstrated that truth starkly. They thought they were getting rid of Jesus by crucifying him. Instead, they made possible the salvation of the world.

Life Questions: As Revelation tells it, events that appear tragic can work great good. Have you ever experienced that in your life?

But woe to the earth and the sea,
for the devil has come down to you
with great wrath,
because he knows that his time
is short!"

The Dragon Fights Again on Earth

13 So when the dragon saw that he had been thrown down to the earth, he pursued[i] the woman who had given birth to the male child. [14]But the woman was given the two wings of the great eagle, so that she could fly from the serpent into the wilderness, to her place where she is nourished for a time, and times, and half a time. [15]Then from his mouth the serpent poured water like a river after the woman, to sweep her away with the flood. [16]But the earth came to the help of the woman; it opened its mouth and swallowed the river that the dragon had poured from his mouth. [17]Then the dragon was angry with the woman, and went off to make war on the rest of her children, those who keep the commandments of God and hold the testimony of Jesus.

The First Beast

18 Then the dragon[j] took his stand on the sand of the seashore. [1]And I saw a beast rising out of the sea, having ten horns and seven heads; and on its horns were ten diadems, and on its heads were blasphemous names. [2]And the beast that I saw was like a leopard, its feet were like a bear's, and its mouth was like a lion's mouth. And the dragon gave it his power and his throne and great authority. [3]One of its heads seemed to have received a death-blow, but its mortal wound[k] had been healed. In amazement the whole earth followed the beast. [4]They worshiped the dragon, for he had given his authority to the beast, and they worshiped the beast, saying, "Who is like the beast, and who can fight against it?"

5 The beast was given a mouth uttering haughty and blasphemous words, and it was allowed to exercise authority for forty-two months. [6]It opened its mouth to utter blasphemies against God, blaspheming his name and his dwelling, that is, those who dwell in heaven. [7]Also it was allowed to make war on the saints and to conquer them.[l] It was given authority over every tribe and people and language and nation, [8]and all the inhabitants of the earth will worship it, everyone whose name has not been written from the foundation of the world in the book of life of the Lamb that was slaughtered.[m]

9 Let anyone who has an ear listen:

[10] If you are to be taken captive,
into captivity you go;
if you kill with the sword,
with the sword you must be killed.
Here is a call for the endurance and faith of the saints.

13.5 Forty-two Months of Trials

This mysterious number has prompted much speculation. Literally it means "a time, and times, and half a time" (see 12.14), that is, one year plus two years plus half a year, or three and a half years. It occurs several places in Revelation. Could it simply be half the perfect number 7, thus representing the age of the new covenant (the time between the first and second coming of Christ)? Or does it refer to literal months: a brief but intense three-and-one-half year period of great persecution against the church? If so, did these 42 months already take place during the Roman persecutions of Christians? Or are they still in the future?

Those who believe the 42 months are in the future frequently speak of the period as "the great tribulation" and call the beast the antichrist, a name used elsewhere in the Bible. Several schools of thought have developed around the tribulation. Pre-tribulationists believe that Jesus will come to remove the church from earth just before the great tribulation. Post-tribulationists believe the church will go through a time of trials before Jesus returns. Mid-tribulationists believe the church will be taken away during the tribulation.

The Second Beast

11 Then I saw another beast that rose out of the earth; it had two horns like a lamb and it spoke like a dragon. [12]It exercises all the authority of the first beast on its behalf, and it makes the earth and its inhabitants worship the first beast, whose mortal wound[n] had been healed. [13]It performs great signs, even making fire come down from heaven to earth in the sight of all; [14]and by the signs that it is allowed to perform on behalf of the beast, it deceives the inhabitants of earth, telling them to make an image for the beast that had been wounded by the sword[o] and yet lived; [15]and it was allowed to give breath[p] to the image of the beast so that the image of the beast could even speak and cause those who would not worship the image of the beast to be killed. [16]Also it causes all, both small and great, both rich and poor, both free and slave, to be marked on the right hand or

---

[i] Or *persecuted*   [j] Gk *Then he*; other ancient authorities read *Then I stood*   [k] Gk *the plague of its death*   [l] Other ancient authorities lack this sentence   [m] Or *written in the book of life of the Lamb that was slaughtered from the foundation of the world*   [n] Gk *whose plague of its death*   [o] Or *that had received the plague of the sword*
[p] Or *spirit*

the forehead, [17]so that no one can buy or sell who does not have the mark, that is, the name of the beast or the number of its name. [18]This calls for wisdom: let anyone with understanding calculate the number of the beast, for it is the number of a person. Its number is six hundred sixty-six.[q]

The Lamb and the 144,000

14 Then I looked, and there was the Lamb, standing on Mount Zion! And with him were one hundred forty-four thousand who had his name and his Father's name written on their

14.1 Good News with Bad

According to Revelation, human history will end not with a whimper but with a series of loud bangs. And yet John frequently reminds his readers that the spasms of violence will lead to a time of eternal peace, with God ruling over a restored heaven and earth. The peaceful scene of a heavenly choir in this chapter is sandwiched between two accounts of tribulation and judgment. John drops in such scenes like orchestral interludes in the midst of a tumultuous opera: They reassure us of a future in which all creation performs together in harmony.

foreheads. [2]And I heard a voice from heaven like the sound of many waters and like the sound of loud thunder; the voice I heard was like the sound of harpists playing on their harps, [3]and they sing a new song before the throne and before the four living creatures and before the elders. No one could learn that song except the one hundred forty-four thousand who have been redeemed from the earth. [4]It is these who have not defiled themselves with women, for they are virgins; these follow the Lamb wherever he goes. They have been redeemed from humankind as first fruits for God and the Lamb, [5]and in their mouth no lie was found; they are blameless.

The Messages of the Three Angels

[6] Then I saw another angel flying in midheaven, with an eternal gospel to proclaim to those who live[r] on the earth—to every nation and tribe and language and people. [7]He said in a loud voice, "Fear God and give him glory, for the hour of his judgment has come; and worship him who made heaven and earth, the sea and the springs of water."

[8] Then another angel, a second, followed, saying, "Fallen, fallen is Babylon the great! She has made all nations drink of the wine of the wrath of her fornication."

[9] Then another angel, a third, followed them, crying with a loud voice, "Those who worship the beast and its image, and receive a mark on their foreheads or on their hands, [10]they will also drink the wine of God's wrath, poured unmixed into the cup of his anger, and they will be tormented with fire and sulfur in the presence of the holy angels and in the presence of the Lamb. [11]And the smoke of their torment goes up forever and ever. There is no rest day or night for those who worship the beast and its image and for anyone who receives the mark of its name."

[12] Here is a call for the endurance of the saints, those who keep the commandments of God and hold fast to the faith of[s] Jesus.

[13] And I heard a voice from heaven saying, "Write this: Blessed are the dead who from now on die in the Lord." "Yes," says the Spirit, "they will rest from their labors, for their deeds follow them."

Reaping the Earth's Harvest

[14] Then I looked, and there was a white cloud, and seated on the cloud was one like the Son of Man, with a golden crown on his head, and a sharp sickle in his hand! [15]Another angel came out of the temple, calling with a loud voice to the one who sat on the cloud, "Use your sickle and reap, for the hour to reap has come, because the harvest of the earth is fully ripe." [16]So the one who sat on the cloud swung his sickle over the earth, and the earth was reaped.

[17] Then another angel came out of the temple in heaven, and he too had a sharp sickle. [18]Then another angel came out from the altar, the angel who has authority over fire, and he called with a loud voice to him who had the sharp sickle, "Use your sharp sickle and gather the clusters of the vine of the earth, for its grapes are ripe." [19]So the angel swung his sickle over the earth and gathered the vintage of the earth, and he threw it into the great wine press of the wrath of God. [20]And the wine press was trodden outside the city, and blood flowed from the wine press, as high as a horse's bridle, for a distance of about two hundred miles.[t]

The Angels with the Seven Last Plagues

15 Then I saw another portent in heaven, great and amazing: seven angels with seven plagues, which are the last, for with them the wrath of God is ended.

[2] And I saw what appeared to be a sea of glass mixed with fire, and those who had conquered the beast and its image and the number of its name, standing beside the sea of glass with harps of God in their hands. [3]And they sing the song of

---

[q] Other ancient authorities read *six hundred sixteen*   [r] Gk *sit*   [s] Or *to their faith in*   [t] Gk *one thousand six hundred stadia*

Moses, the servant[u] of God, and the song of the Lamb:

"Great and amazing are your deeds,
    Lord God the Almighty!
Just and true are your ways,
    King of the nations![v]
4 Lord, who will not fear
    and glorify your name?
For you alone are holy.
    All nations will come
    and worship before you,
for your judgments have been revealed."

5 After this I looked, and the temple of the tent[w] of witness in heaven was opened, 6and out of the temple came the seven angels with the seven plagues, robed in pure bright linen,[x] with golden sashes across their chests. 7Then one of the four living creatures gave the seven angels seven golden bowls full of the wrath of God, who lives forever and ever; 8and the temple was filled with smoke from the glory of God and from his power, and no one could enter the temple until the seven plagues of the seven angels were ended.

The Bowls of God's Wrath

16 Then I heard a loud voice from the temple telling the seven angels, "Go and pour out on the earth the seven bowls of the wrath of God."
2 So the first angel went and poured his bowl on the earth, and a foul and painful sore came on those who had the mark of the beast and who worshiped its image.
3 The second angel poured his bowl into the sea, and it became like the blood of a corpse, and every living thing in the sea died.
4 The third angel poured his bowl into the rivers and the springs of water, and they became blood. 5And I heard the angel of the waters say,

"You are just, O Holy One, who are and were,
    for you have judged these things;
6 because they shed the blood of saints and prophets,
    you have given them blood to drink.
    It is what they deserve!"

7And I heard the altar respond,

"Yes, O Lord God, the Almighty,
    your judgments are true and just!"

8 The fourth angel poured his bowl on the sun, and it was allowed to scorch people with fire; 9they were scorched by the fierce heat, but they cursed the name of God, who had authority over these plagues, and they did not repent and give him glory.
10 The fifth angel poured his bowl on the throne of the beast, and its kingdom was plunged into darkness; people gnawed their tongues in agony, 11and cursed the God of heaven because of their pains and sores, and they did not repent of their deeds.
12 The sixth angel poured his bowl on the great river Euphrates, and its water was dried up in order to prepare the way for the kings from the east. 13And I saw three foul spirits like frogs coming from the mouth of the dragon, from the mouth of the beast, and from the mouth of the false prophet. 14These are demonic spirits, performing signs, who go abroad to the kings of the whole world, to assemble them for battle on the great day of God the Almighty. 15("See, I am coming like a thief! Blessed is the one who stays awake and is clothed,[y] not going about naked and exposed to shame.") 16And they assembled them at the place that in Hebrew is called Harmagedon.

16.16 The Battle of Harmagedon

Harmagedon has been the site of many military struggles in Israel's history. Some historians estimate more wars have been fought here than any other location in the world. It is an appropriate setting (or symbol) for the final struggle between good and evil.

17 The seventh angel poured his bowl into the air, and a loud voice came out of the temple, from the throne, saying, "It is done!" 18And there came flashes of lightning, rumblings, peals of thunder, and a violent earthquake, such as had not occurred since people were upon the earth, so violent was that earthquake. 19The great city was split into three parts, and the cities of the nations fell. God remembered great Babylon and gave her the wine-cup of the fury of his wrath. 20And every island fled away, and no mountains were to be found; 21and huge hailstones, each weighing about a hundred pounds,[z] dropped from heaven on people, until they cursed God for the plague of the hail, so fearful was that plague.

The Great Whore and the Beast

17 Then one of the seven angels who had the seven bowls came and said to me, "Come, I will show you the judgment of the great whore who is seated on many waters, 2with whom the kings of the earth have committed fornication, and with the wine of whose fornication the inhabitants of the earth have become drunk." 3So he carried me away in the spirit[a] into a wilderness, and I saw a woman sitting on a scarlet beast that was full of blasphemous names, and it had seven heads and ten horns. 4The woman was clothed in purple and scarlet, and adorned with gold and jewels and pearls, holding in her hand a golden

---

u Gk *slave*   v Other ancient authorities read *the ages*   w Or *tabernacle*   x Other ancient authorities read *stone*
y Gk *and keeps his robes*   z Gk *weighing about a talent*   a Or *in the Spirit*

cup full of abominations and the impurities of her fornication; [5]and on her forehead was written a name, a mystery: "Babylon the great, mother of whores and of earth's abominations." [6]And I saw that the woman was drunk with the blood of the saints and the blood of the witnesses to Jesus.

When I saw her, I was greatly amazed. [7]But the angel said to me, "Why are you so amazed? I will tell you the mystery of the woman, and of the beast with seven heads and ten horns that carries her. [8]The beast that you saw was, and is not, and is about to ascend from the bottomless pit and go to destruction. And the inhabitants of the earth, whose names have not been written in the book of life from the foundation of the world, will be amazed when they see the beast, because it was and is not and is to come.

9 "This calls for a mind that has wisdom: the seven heads are seven mountains on which the woman is seated; also, they are seven kings, [10]of whom five have fallen, one is living, and the other has not yet come; and when he comes, he must remain only a little while. [11]As for the beast that was and is not, it is an eighth but it belongs to the seven, and it goes to destruction. [12]And the ten horns that you saw are ten kings who have not yet received a kingdom, but they are to receive authority as kings for one hour, together with the beast. [13]These are united in yielding their power and authority to the beast; [14]they will make war on the Lamb, and the Lamb will conquer them, for he is Lord of lords and King of kings, and those with him are called and chosen and faithful."

15 And he said to me, "The waters that you saw, where the whore is seated, are peoples and multitudes and nations and languages. [16]And the ten horns that you saw, they and the beast will hate the whore; they will make her desolate and naked; they will devour her flesh and burn her up with fire; [17]For God has put it into their hearts to carry out his purpose by agreeing to give their kingdom to the beast, until the words of God will be fulfilled. [18]The woman you saw is the great city that rules over the kings of the earth."

The Fall of Babylon

18 After this I saw another angel coming down from heaven, having great authority; and the earth was made bright with his splendor. [2]He called out with a mighty voice,
"Fallen, fallen is Babylon the great!
It has become a dwelling place
of demons,
a haunt of every foul spirit,
a haunt of every foul bird,

a haunt of every foul and
hateful beast.[b]
[3] For all the nations have drunk[c]
of the wine of the wrath of her
fornication,
and the kings of the earth have
committed fornication with her,
and the merchants of the earth have
grown rich from the power[d] of
her luxury."

18.2 What Is Babylon?

Many people believe Babylon was a coded substitute for Rome, the city set on seven hills (17.9). Revelation was almost surely written to Christians undergoing great persecution from harsh Roman emperors. Scholars who see Babylon as Rome sometimes try to identify the kings mentioned here as specific Roman rulers.

However, not all interpreters agree. Some suggest that Babylon stands for Jerusalem, and others believe we cannot clearly identify Babylon. Rather, they say, it can represent all powerful world systems that kill faithful Christians and seduce people away from God. Regardless, chapter 18 reveals that the great enemy, Babylon, will disappear forever (verse 21).

4 Then I heard another voice from heaven saying,
"Come out of her, my people,
so that you do not take part in her
sins,
and so that you do not share in her
plagues;
[5] for her sins are heaped high as heaven,
and God has remembered
her iniquities.
[6] Render to her as she herself has rendered,
and repay her double for her deeds;
mix a double draught for her in the
cup she mixed.
[7] As she glorified herself and lived
luxuriously,
so give her a like measure of torment
and grief.
Since in her heart she says,
'I rule as a queen;
I am no widow,
and I will never see grief,'
[8] therefore her plagues will come in a single
day—
pestilence and mourning and famine—
and she will be burned with fire;

b Other ancient authorities lack the words *a haunt of every foul beast* and attach the words *and hateful* to the previous line so as to read *a haunt of every foul and hateful bird*   c Other ancient authorities read *She has made all nations drink*
d Or *resources*

for mighty is the Lord God who judges
her."

9 And the kings of the earth, who committed
fornication and lived in luxury with her, will weep
and wail over her when they see the smoke of her
burning; [10]they will stand far off, in fear of her
torment, and say,

"Alas, alas, the great city,
Babylon, the mighty city!
For in one hour your judgment
has come."

11 And the merchants of the earth weep and
mourn for her, since no one buys their cargo
anymore, [12]cargo of gold, silver, jewels and pearls,
fine linen, purple, silk and scarlet, all kinds of
scented wood, all articles of ivory, all articles of
costly wood, bronze, iron, and marble, [13]cinna-
mon, spice, incense, myrrh, frankincense, wine,
olive oil, choice flour and wheat, cattle and sheep,
horses and chariots, slaves—and human lives.[e]

[14] "The fruit for which your soul longed
has gone from you,
and all your dainties and your splendor
are lost to you,
never to be found again!"

[15]The merchants of these wares, who gained
wealth from her, will stand far off, in fear of her
torment, weeping and mourning aloud,

[16] "Alas, alas, the great city,
clothed in fine linen,
in purple and scarlet,
adorned with gold,
with jewels, and with pearls!

[17] For in one hour all this wealth has been
laid waste!"

And all shipmasters and seafarers, sailors and
all whose trade is on the sea, stood far off [18]and
cried out as they saw the smoke of her burning,

"What city was like the great city?"

[19]And they threw dust on their heads, as they
wept and mourned, crying out,

"Alas, alas, the great city,
where all who had ships at sea
grew rich by her wealth!
For in one hour she has been laid waste."

20 Rejoice over her, O heaven, you saints and
apostles and prophets! For God has given judgment for you against her.

21 Then a mighty angel took up a stone like
a great millstone and threw it into the sea, saying,

"With such violence Babylon the great
city
will be thrown down,
and will be found no more;

[22] and the sound of harpists and minstrels
and of flutists and trumpeters
will be heard in you no more;
and an artisan of any trade
will be found in you no more;

and the sound of the millstone
will be heard in you no more;

[23] and the light of a lamp
will shine in you no more;

18.21 Newspaper Prophecy

*The fact that Baghdad, Iraq, sits just 50 miles
from the historical site of Babylon led some
commentators to predict that the Gulf War of
1991 would escalate into the battle of
Harmagedon. Instead, the "mother of all
battles" on the ground lasted just 100 hours.*

*Revelation has defied many such
prognosticators. A man who claimed to have
cracked the biblical code wrote the best-selling
book 88 Reasons Why the Rapture Will Be in
1988. And not long before that a well-known
television evangelist predicted the Soviet Union
would invade Israel in 1982. Revelation
contains a code intriguing enough to hold the
interest of every generation, but obscure
enough to have kept the best scholars guessing
for almost 2,000 years. That may have been
John's intent: to have each new wave of
readers grapple with its meaning in their own
historical context.*

and the voice of bridegroom and bride
will be heard in you no more;
for your merchants were the magnates of
the earth,
and all nations were deceived by your
sorcery.

24 And in you[f] was found the blood of
prophets and of saints,
and of all who have been slaughtered
on earth."

The Rejoicing in Heaven

19 After this I heard what seemed to be the
loud voice of a great multitude in heaven,
saying,

"Hallelujah!
Salvation and glory and power
to our God,

2   for his judgments are true and just;
he has judged the great whore
who corrupted the earth with her
fornication,
and he has avenged on her the blood of
his servants."[g]

[3]Once more they said,

"Hallelujah!
The smoke goes up from her forever and
ever."

[4]And the twenty-four elders and the four living

---

[e] Or *chariots, and human bodies and souls*   [f] Gk *her*   [g] Gk *slaves*

creatures fell down and worshiped God who is seated on the throne, saying,

"Amen. Hallelujah!"

5 And from the throne came a voice saying,

"Praise our God,
    all you his servants,[h]
and all who fear him,
    small and great."

[6]Then I heard what seemed to be the voice of a great multitude, like the sound of many waters and like the sound of mighty thunderpeals, crying out,

"Hallelujah!
For the Lord our God
    the Almighty reigns.
7 Let us rejoice and exult
    and give him the glory,
for the marriage of the Lamb has come,
    and his bride has made herself ready;
8 to her it has been granted to be clothed
    with fine linen, bright and pure"—
for the fine linen is the righteous deeds of the saints.

9 And the angel said[i] to me, "Write this: Blessed are those who are invited to the marriage supper of the Lamb." And he said to me, "These are true words of God." [10]Then I fell down at his feet to worship him, but he said to me, "You must not do that! I am a fellow servant[j] with you and your comrades[k] who hold the testimony of Jesus.[l] Worship God! For the testimony of Jesus[l] is the spirit of prophecy."

The Rider on the White Horse

11 Then I saw heaven opened, and there was a white horse! Its rider is called Faithful and True, and in righteousness he judges and makes war. [12]His eyes are like a flame of fire, and on his head are many diadems; and he has a name inscribed that no one knows but himself. [13]He is clothed in a robe dipped in[m] blood, and his name is called The Word of God. [14]And the armies of heaven, wearing fine linen, white and pure, were following him on white horses. [15]From his mouth comes a sharp sword with which to strike down the nations, and he will rule[n] them with a rod of iron; he will tread the wine press of the fury of the wrath of God the Almighty. [16]On his robe and on his thigh he has a name inscribed, "King of kings and Lord of lords."

The Beast and Its Armies Defeated

17 Then I saw an angel standing in the sun, and with a loud voice he called to all the birds that fly in midheaven, "Come, gather for the great supper of God, [18]to eat the flesh of kings, the flesh of captains, the flesh of the mighty, the flesh of horses and their riders—flesh of all, both free and slave, both small and great." [19]Then I saw the beast and the kings of the earth with their armies

---

[h] Gk slaves   [i] Gk he said   [j] Gk slave   [k] Gk brothers sprinkled with   [n] Or will shepherd

[l] Or to Jesus   [m] Other ancient authorities read

A Happy Ending after All
The last word is the best news of all

WE SENSE IT AT RARE moments. The first real day of spring, when the air is heavy with the scent of blooms and new life sprouts everywhere. Or even in winter, when an unexpected snowstorm clothes a gray, dingy city in pure white. Or when we watch a baby animal at play in the zoo. Or remember the first sudden twinge of romantic love.

> Then I saw a new heaven and a new earth. 21.1

This world may be full of pollution, war, crime, and hate. But inside us, all of us, linger remnants that remind us of what the world could be like—of what we could be like. The Old Testament prophets dreamed of "that day" when creation would be made new. And those sensations, following a dismal monotone of predicted catastrophes, burst out of the last few chapters of Revelation. That perfect world is not merely a dream; it will come true.

A New World at Last

There will be no more tears then, nor pain. Wild animals will frolic, not kill. Once again creation will work the way God intended. Peace will reign not only between God and individuals, but between him and all creation. The kingdom comes out into the open. The City of God flings wide its gates.

Revelation ends on a note of great triumph. Somehow, out of all the bad news augured here, good news emerges—spectacular Good News. To those who believe, Revelation becomes a book not of fear, but of hope. God will prevail. All will be made new.

The Bible began, back in Genesis, with a tragic defeat when humanity, made in the image of God, rebelled. It ends with a reunion—a marriage, Revelation calls it. There is a happy ending after all.

Life Questions: If you could design a perfect world, what would it look like?

gathered to make war against the rider on the horse and against his army. 20And the beast was captured, and with it the false prophet who had performed in its presence the signs by which he deceived those who had received the mark of the beast and those who worshiped its image. These two were thrown alive into the lake of fire that burns with sulfur. 21And the rest were killed by the sword of the rider on the horse, the sword that came from his mouth; and all the birds were gorged with their flesh.

The Thousand Years

20 Then I saw an angel coming down from heaven, holding in his hand the key to the bottomless pit and a great chain. 2He seized the dragon, that ancient serpent, who is the Devil and Satan, and bound him for a thousand years, 3and threw him into the pit, and locked and sealed it over him, so that he would deceive the nations no more, until the thousand years were ended. After that he must be let out for a little while.

4 Then I saw thrones, and those seated on them were given authority to judge. I also saw the souls of those who had been beheaded for their testimony to Jesus° and for the word of God.

20.3 The Millennium

Christians interpret the thousand-year reign referred to here in a variety of ways:

1. Postmillennialism believes that the church itself will, through its expanding influence, bring about a time of peace and prosperity in preparation for the return of Christ. This view was far more popular in the 19th century, when people were optimistic about progress and the future.

2. Premillennialism believes that Christ will return to earth and reign here in person, ushering in a period of great peace. During this period, Satan will be bound up, but will lead a final revolt at the end of the thousand years.

3. Amillennialism interprets this passage much less literally. Some amillennialists hold that the millennium has already been going on, but the reign of Christ is taking place in heaven, not on earth. Others believe the church is establishing the kingdom of Christ now, between Jesus' first and second coming.

Because so little information is given on the millennium, no one can be completely sure. The "thousand year" period itself may be symbolic, standing for a very long period of time. Regardless, all positions agree that ultimately this world will end with Jesus' establishment of an eternal kingdom.

They had not worshiped the beast or its image and had not received its mark on their foreheads or their hands. They came to life and reigned with Christ a thousand years. 5(The rest of the dead did not come to life until the thousand years were ended.) This is the first resurrection. 6Blessed and holy are those who share in the first resurrection. Over these the second death has no power, but they will be priests of God and of Christ, and they will reign with him a thousand years.

Satan's Doom

7 When the thousand years are ended, Satan will be released from his prison 8and will come out to deceive the nations at the four corners of the earth, Gog and Magog, in order to gather them for battle; they are as numerous as the sands of the sea. 9They marched up over the breadth of the earth and surrounded the camp of the saints and the beloved city. And fire came down from heaven*p* and consumed them. 10And the devil who had deceived them was thrown into the lake of fire and sulfur, where the beast and the false prophet were, and they will be tormented day and night forever and ever.

The Dead Are Judged

11 Then I saw a great white throne and the one who sat on it; the earth and the heaven fled from his presence, and no place was found for them. 12And I saw the dead, great and small, standing before the throne, and books were opened. Also another book was opened, the book of life. And the dead were judged according to their works, as recorded in the books. 13And the sea gave up the dead that were in it, Death and Hades gave up the dead that were in them, and all were judged according to what they had done. 14Then Death and Hades were thrown into the lake of fire. This is the second death, the lake of fire; 15and anyone whose name was not found written in the book of life was thrown into the lake of fire.

The New Heaven and the New Earth

21 Then I saw a new heaven and a new earth; for the first heaven and the first earth had passed away, and the sea was no more. 2And I saw the holy city, the new Jerusalem, coming down out of heaven from God, prepared as a bride adorned for her husband. 3And I heard a loud voice from the throne saying,

"See, the home*q* of God is among
        mortals.
He will dwell*r* with them;
        they will be his peoples,*s*

° Or *for the testimony of Jesus*   *p* Other ancient authorities read *from God, out of heaven,* or *out of heaven from God*
q Gk *the tabernacle*   *r* Gk *will tabernacle*   *s* Other ancient authorities read *people*

and God himself will be with them;[t]
4 he will wipe every tear from their eyes.
  Death will be no more;
  mourning and crying and pain will be no
      more,
  for the first things have passed away."

5 And the one who was seated on the throne said, "See, I am making all things new." Also he said, "Write this, for these words are trustworthy and true." [6]Then he said to me, "It is done! I am the Alpha and the Omega, the beginning and the end. To the thirsty I will give water as a gift from the spring of the water of life. [7]Those who conquer will inherit these things, and I will be their God and they will be my children. [8]But as for the cowardly, the faithless,[u] the polluted, the murderers, the fornicators, the sorcerers, the idolaters, and all liars, their place will be in the lake that burns with fire and sulfur, which is the second death."

Vision of the New Jerusalem

9 Then one of the seven angels who had the seven bowls full of the seven last plagues came and said to me, "Come, I will show you the bride, the wife of the Lamb." [10]And in the spirit[v] he carried me away to a great, high mountain and showed me the holy city Jerusalem coming down out of heaven from God. [11]It has the glory of God and a radiance like a very rare jewel, like jasper, clear as crystal. [12]It has a great, high wall with twelve gates, and at the gates twelve angels, and on the gates are inscribed the names of the twelve tribes of the Israelites; [13]on the east three gates, on the north three gates, on the south three gates, and on the west three gates. [14]And the wall of the city has twelve foundations, and on them are the twelve names of the twelve apostles of the Lamb.

15 The angel[w] who talked to me had a measuring rod of gold to measure the city and its gates and walls. [16]The city lies foursquare, its length the same as its width; and he measured the city with his rod, fifteen hundred miles;[x] its length and width and height are equal. [17]He also measured its wall, one hundred forty-four cubits[y] by human measurement, which the angel was using. [18]The wall is built of jasper, while the city is pure gold, clear as glass. [19]The foundations of the wall of the city are adorned with every jewel; the first was jasper, the second sapphire, the third agate, the fourth emerald, [20]the fifth onyx, the sixth carnelian, the seventh chrysolite, the eighth beryl, the ninth topaz, the tenth chrysoprase, the eleventh jacinth, the twelfth amethyst. [21]And the twelve gates are twelve pearls, each of the gates is a single pearl, and the street of the city is pure gold, transparent as glass.

22 I saw no temple in the city, for its temple is the Lord God the Almighty and the Lamb. [23]And the city has no need of sun or moon to shine on it, for the glory of God is its light, and its lamp is the Lamb. [24]The nations will walk by its light, and the kings of the earth will bring their glory into it. [25]Its gates will never be shut by day—and there will be no night there. [26]People will bring into it the glory and the honor of the nations. [27]But nothing unclean will enter it, nor anyone who practices abomination or falsehood, but only those who are written in the Lamb's book of life.

The River of Life

22 Then the angel[z] showed me the river of the water of life, bright as crystal, flowing

22.1 Eden Regained

The last two chapters of Revelation contain numerous parallels to the description of the Garden of Eden in the first three chapters of Genesis. Revelation describes a new creation that excludes all the things that spoiled Eden. There will be no night and no death. Satan will disappear forever, and nothing impure will enter the new city. People will walk with God again, just as they did in Eden. There will be no crying or pain. Once again humankind will rule over creation, this time with open access to the tree of life. Everything put wrong by human rebellion in Eden will be set right. In Eden, Adam and Eve were driven from the garden; in the new earth, they will see God's face.

from the throne of God and of the Lamb [2]through the middle of the street of the city. On either side of the river is the tree of life[a] with its twelve kinds of fruit, producing its fruit each month; and the leaves of the tree are for the healing of the nations. [3]Nothing accursed will be found there any more. But the throne of God and of the Lamb will be in it, and his servants[b] will worship him; [4]they will see his face, and his name will be on their foreheads. [5]And there will be no more night; they need no light of lamp or sun, for the Lord God will be their light, and they will reign forever and ever.

6 And he said to me, "These words are trustworthy and true, for the Lord, the God of the spirits of the prophets, has sent his angel to show his servants[b] what must soon take place."

7 "See, I am coming soon! Blessed is the one who keeps the words of the prophecy of this book."

---

[t] Other ancient authorities add *and be their God*   [u] Or *the unbelieving*   [v] Or *in the Spirit*   [w] Gk *He*
[x] Gk *twelve thousand stadia*   [y] That is, almost seventy-five yards   [z] Gk *he*   [a] Or *the Lamb.* [2]*In the middle of the street of the city, and on either side of the river, is the tree of life*   [b] Gk *slaves*

Epilogue and Benediction

8 I, John, am the one who heard and saw these things. And when I heard and saw them, I fell down to worship at the feet of the angel who showed them to me; [9]but he said to me, "You must not do that! I am a fellow servant[c] with you and your comrades[d] the prophets, and with those who keep the words of this book. Worship God!"

10 And he said to me, "Do not seal up the words of the prophecy of this book, for the time is near. [11]Let the evildoer still do evil, and the filthy still be filthy, and the righteous still do right, and the holy still be holy."

12 "See, I am coming soon; my reward is with me, to repay according to everyone's work. [13]I am the Alpha and the Omega, the first and the last, the beginning and the end."

14 Blessed are those who wash their robes,[e] so that they will have the right to the tree of life and may enter the city by the gates. [15]Outside are the dogs and sorcerers and fornicators and mur-derers and idolaters, and everyone who loves and practices falsehood.

16 "It is I, Jesus, who sent my angel to you with this testimony for the churches. I am the root and the descendant of David, the bright morning star."

17 The Spirit and the bride say, "Come."
And let everyone who hears say, "Come."
And let everyone who is thirsty come.
Let anyone who wishes take the water of
        life as a gift.

18 I warn everyone who hears the words of the prophecy of this book: if anyone adds to them, God will add to that person the plagues described in this book; [19]if anyone takes away from the words of the book of this prophecy, God will take away that person's share in the tree of life and in the holy city, which are described in this book.

20 The one who testifies to these things says, "Surely I am coming soon."
Amen. Come, Lord Jesus!

21 The grace of the Lord Jesus be with all the saints. Amen.[f]

---

c Gk *slave*   d Gk *brothers*   e Other ancient authorities read *do his commandments*   f Other ancient authorities lack *all*; others lack *the saints*; others lack *Amen*

Acknowledgments

Philip Yancey, General Editor of *The Student Bible,* came up with the original concept while serving as Editor of *Campus Life* magazine. He now divides his time between free-lance writing and his responsibilities as Editor at Large for *Christianity Today.* He has authored thirteen books, including *Where Is God When It Hurts?, Disappointment with God,* and *The Jesus I Never Knew.*

Tim Stafford wrote many of the notes for *The Student Bible,* especially in the Old Testament portions. He too divides his time between free-lance writing and editorial responsibilities at *Christianity Today.* His books include *That's Not What I Meant, Sexual Chaos,* and *Knowing the Face of God.*

Not long after its publication in 1986, *The Student Bible* became the best-selling edition of the Bible in the United States, and since then has attracted over three million readers. Many of these readers wrote to say that the combination of scholarship and simplicity opened up the Bible for them in a new way. Partly in response to those letters, *The Student Bible* has undergone substantial revisions.

In 1992 a new edition updated existing material and added many new features, including 400 new Highlights and a greatly expanded Subject Guide. This edition also included a "parallel passages" feature under many boldface sectional headings in Matthew, Mark, Luke and John, sending you to other places where the same event or teaching is recorded. Note also the Glossary of Nonbiblical People and Places beginning on page 1337, where you will find a brief description of names used in Introductions, Insights and Highlights. Hunter and Edith Norwood and Chase and Harriet Stafford did much of the research and initial writing of the added Highlights, and Connie Van Dyke prepared additional material for the Subject Guide.

Now, in this ten-year (1996) edition, *The Student Bible* has undergone further revision. Tim Stafford wrote the profiles of "100 People You Should Know." Sharon Wright redesigned the entire Bible, creatively combining new graphic elements and typefaces with a second color. And many changes were made to the "Where to Find It" section in the back, making it a more useful and convenient reference resource.

Any Bible publishing project relies on many people, and the following are a few of those who helped with *The Student Bible:*

Nathan Young designed the original *Student Bible* and was invaluably cheerful, flexible and skilled.

Dirk Buursma, Michael Vander Klipp, Doris Rikkers and Sandra Vander Zicht, editors at Zondervan, helped refine both words and design. In addition, they watched over the many complicated details of typesetting and production.

Virginia Vagt, through her research and common sense, turned the original concept for *The Student Bible* in new directions.

Scott Bolinder and Harold Myra helped greatly in improving, encouraging, and aiding the work.

Dr. Kenneth Kantzer made careful suggestions about questions of scholarship and theology.

Lenora Rand, Connie Van Dyke and Verlyn Verbrugge did much of the painstaking work for the Subject Guide.

In the process of developing *The Student Bible,* many helpful people and organizations contributed their insights, especially these: Association of Christian Schools International, Billy Graham Evangelistic Association, Campus Crusade for Christ, Dr. Jim Engel, Focus on the Family, Fuller Theological Seminary, the International Bible Society, InterVarsity Christian Fellowship, Josh McDowell, National Network of Youth Ministries, the Navigators, Search Institute, Student Venture, Chuck Swindoll, Dr. Mel White, Young Life, Youth for Christ and Youth Specialties.

About the N.R.S.V.

This preface is addressed to you by the Committee of translators, who wish to explain, as briefly as possible, the origin and character of our work. The publication of our revision is yet another step in the long, continual process of making the Bible available in the form of the English language that is most widely current in our day. To summarize in a single sentence: the New Revised Standard Version of the Bible is an authorized revision of the Revised Standard Version, published in 1952, which was a revision of the American Standard Version, published in 1901, which, in turn, embodied earlier revisions of the King James Version, published in 1611.

In the course of time, the King James Version came to be regarded as "the Authorized Version." With good reason it has been termed "the noblest monument of English prose," and it has entered, as no other book has, into the making of the personal character and the public institutions of the English-speaking peoples. We owe to it an incalculable debt.

Yet the King James Version has serious defects. By the middle of the nineteenth century, the development of biblical studies and the discovery of many biblical manuscripts more ancient than those on which the King James Version was based made it apparent that these defects were so many as to call for revision. The task was begun, by authority of the Church of England, in 1870. The (British) Revised Version of the Bible was published in 1881–1885; and the American Standard Version, its variant embodying the preferences of the American scholars associated with the work, was published, as was mentioned above, in 1901. In 1928 the copyright of the latter was acquired by the International Council of Religious Education and thus passed into the ownership of the churches of the United States and Canada that were associated in this Council through their boards of education and publication.

The Council appointed a committee of scholars to have charge of the text of the American Standard Version and to undertake inquiry concerning the need for further revision. After studying the questions whether or not revision should be undertaken, and if so, what its nature and extent should be, in 1937 the Council authorized a revision. The scholars who served as members of the Committee worked in two sections, one dealing with the Old Testament and one with the New Testament. In 1946 the Revised Standard Version of the New Testament was published. The publication of the Revised Standard Version of the Bible, containing the Old and New Testaments, took place on September 30, 1952. A translation of the Apocryphal/Deuterocanonical Books of the Old Testament followed in 1957. In 1977 this collection was issued in an expanded edition, containing three additional texts received by Eastern Orthodox communions (3 and 4 Maccabees and Psalm 151). Thereafter the Revised Standard Version gained the distinction of being officially authorized for use by all major Christian churches: Protestant, Anglican, Roman Catholic, and Eastern Orthodox.

The Revised Standard Version Bible Committee is a continuing body, comprising about thirty members, both men and women. Ecumenical in representation, it includes scholars affiliated with various Protestant denominations, as well as several Roman Catholic members, an Eastern Orthodox member, and a Jewish member who serves in the Old Testament section. For a period of time the Committee included several members from Canada and from England.

Because no translation of the Bible is perfect or is acceptable to all groups of readers, and because discoveries of older manuscripts and further investigation of linguistic features of the text continue to become available, renderings of the Bible have proliferated. During the years following the publication of the Revised Standard Version, twenty-six other English translations and revisions of the Bible were produced by committees and by individual scholars—not to mention twenty-five other translations and revisions of the New Testament alone. One of the latter was the second edition of the RSV New Testament, issued in 1971, twenty-five years after its initial publication.

Following the publication of the RSV Old Testament in 1952, significant advances were made in the discovery and interpretation of documents in Semitic languages related to Hebrew. In addition to the information that had become available in the late 1940s from the Dead Sea texts of Isaiah and Habakkuk, subsequent acquisitions from the same area brought to light many other early copies of all the books of the Hebrew Scriptures (except Esther), though most of these copies are fragmentary. During the same period early Greek manuscript copies of books of the New Testament also became available.

In order to take these discoveries into account, along with recent studies of documents in Semitic languages related to Hebrew, in 1974 the Policies Committee of the Revised Standard Version, which is a standing committee of the National Council of the Churches of Christ in the U.S.A., authorized the preparation of a revision of the entire RSV Bible.

For the Old Testament the Committee has made use of the *Biblia Hebraica Stuttgartensia* (1977; ed. sec. emendata, 1983). This is an edition of the Hebrew and Aramaic text as current early in the Christian era and fixed by Jewish scholars (the "Masoretes") of the sixth to the ninth centuries. The vowel signs, which were added by the Masoretes, are accepted in the main, but where a more probable and convincing reading can be obtained by assuming different vowels, this has been done. No notes are given in such cases, because the vowel points are less ancient and reliable than the consonants. When an alternative reading given by the Masoretes is translated in a footnote, this is identified by the words "Another reading is."

Departures from the consonantal text of the best manuscripts have been made only where it seems clear that errors in copying had been made before the text was standardized. Most of the corrections adopted are based on the ancient versions (translations into Greek, Aramaic, Syriac, and Latin), which were made prior to the time of the work of the Masoretes and which therefore may reflect earlier forms of the Hebrew text. In such instances a footnote specifies the version or versions from which the correction has been derived and also gives a translation of the Masoretic Text. Where it was deemed appropriate to do so, information is supplied in footnotes from subsidiary Jewish traditions concerning other textual readings (the *Tiqqune Sopherim*, "emendations of the scribes"). These are identified in the footnotes as "Ancient Heb tradition."

Occasionally it is evident that the text has suffered in transmission and that none of the versions provides a satisfactory restoration. Here we can only follow the best judgment of competent scholars as to the most probable reconstruction of the original text. Such reconstructions are indicated in footnotes by the abbreviation Cn ("Correction"), and a translation of the Masoretic Text is added.

For the New Testament the Committee has based its work on the most recent edition of *The Greek New Testament*, prepared by an interconfessional and international committee and published by the United Bible Societies (1966; 3rd ed. corrected, 1983; information concerning changes to be introduced into the critical apparatus of the forthcoming 4th edition was available to the Committee). As in that edition, double brackets are used to enclose a few passages that are generally regarded to be later additions to the text, but which we have retained because of their evident antiquity and their importance in the textual tradition. Only in very rare instances have we replaced the text or the punctuation of the Bible Societies' edition by an alternative that seemed to us to be superior. Here and there in the footnotes the phrase, "Other ancient authorities read," identifies alternative readings preserved by Greek manuscripts and early versions. In both Testaments, alternative renderings of the text are indicated by the word "Or."

As for the style of English adopted for the present revision, among the mandates given to the Committee in 1980 by the Division of Education and Ministry of the National Council of Churches of Christ (which now holds the copyright of the RSV Bible) was the directive to continue in the tradition of the King James Bible, but to introduce such changes as are warranted on the basis of accuracy, clarity, euphony, and current English usage. Within the constraints set by the original texts and by the mandates of the Division, the Committee has followed the maxim, "As literal as possible, as free as necessary." As a consequence, the New Revised Standard Version (NRSV) remains essentially a literal translation. Paraphrastic renderings have been adopted only sparingly, and then chiefly to compensate for a deficiency in the English language—the lack of a common gender third person singular pronoun.

During the almost half a century since the publication of the RSV, many in the churches have become sensitive to the danger of linguistic sexism arising from the inherent bias of the English language towards the masculine gender, a bias that in the case of the Bible has often restricted or obscured the meaning of the original text. The mandates from the Division specified that, in references to men and women, masculine-oriented language should be eliminated as far as this can be done without altering passages that reflect the historical situation of ancient patriarchal culture. As can be appreciated, more than once the Committee found that the several mandates stood in tension and even in conflict. The various concerns had to be balanced case by case in order to provide a faithful and acceptable rendering without using contrived English. Only very occasionally has the pronoun "he" or "him" been retained in passages where the reference may have been to a woman as well as to a man; for example, in several legal texts in Leviticus and Deuteronomy. In such instances of formal, legal language, the options of either putting the passage in the plural or of introducing additional nouns to avoid masculine pronouns in English seemed to the Committee to obscure the historic structure and literary character of the original. In the vast majority of cases, however, inclusiveness has been attained by simple rephrasing or by introducing plural forms when this does not distort the meaning of the passage. Of course, in narrative and in parable no attempt was made to generalize the sex of individual persons.

Another aspect of style will be detected by readers who compare the more stately English rendering of the Old Testament with the less formal rendering adopted for the New Testament. For example, the traditional distinction between *shall* and *will* in English has been retained in the Old Testament as appropriate in rendering a document that embodies what may be termed the classic form of Hebrew, while in the New Testament the abandonment of such distinctions in the usage of the future tense in English reflects the more colloquial nature of the koine Greek used by most New Testament authors except when they are quoting the Old Testament.

Careful readers will notice that here and there in the Old Testament the word LORD (or in certain cases GOD) is printed in capital letters. This represents the traditional manner in English versions of rendering the Divine Name, the "Tetragrammaton" (see the notes on Exodus 3.14, 15), following the precedent of the ancient Greek and Latin translators and the long established practice in the reading of the Hebrew Scriptures in the synagogue. While it is almost if not quite certain that the Name was originally pronounced "Yahweh," this pronunciation was not indicated when the Masoretes added vowel sounds to the consonantal Hebrew text. To the four consonants YHWH of the Name, which had come to be regarded as too sacred to be pronounced, they attached vowel signs indicating that in its place should be read the Hebrew word *Adonai* meaning "Lord" (or *Elohim* meaning "God"). Ancient Greek translators employed the word *Kyrios* ("Lord") for the Name. The Vulgate likewise used the Latin word *Dominus* ("Lord"). The form "Jehovah" is of late medieval origin; it is a combination of the consonants of the Divine Name and the vowels attached to it by the Masoretes but belonging to an entirely different word. Although the American Standard Version (1901) had used "Jehovah" to render the Tetragrammaton (the sound of Y being represented by J and the sound of W by V, as in Latin), for two reasons the Committees that produced the RSV and the NRSV returned to the more familiar usage of the King James Version. (1) The word "Jehovah" does not accurately represent any form of the Name ever used in Hebrew. (2) The use of any proper name for the one and only God, as though there were other gods from whom the true God had to be distinguished, began to be discontinued in Judaism before the Christian era and is inappropriate for the universal faith of the Christian Church.

It will be seen that in the Psalms and in other prayers addressed to God the archaic second person singular pronouns (*thee, thou, thine*) and verb forms (*art, hast, hadst*) are no longer used. Although some readers may regret this change, it should be pointed out that in the original languages neither the Old Testament nor the New makes any linguistic distinction between addressing a human being and addressing the Deity. Furthermore, in the tradition of the King James Version one will not expect to find the use of capital letters for pronouns that refer to the Deity—such capitalization is an unnecessary innovation that has only recently been introduced into a few English translations of the Bible. Finally, we have left to the discretion of the licensed publishers such matters as section headings, cross-references, and clues to the pronunciation of proper names.

This new version seeks to preserve all that is best in the English Bible as it has been known and used through the years. It is intended for use in public reading and congregational worship, as well as in private study, instruction, and meditation. We have resisted the temptation to introduce terms and phrases that merely reflect current moods, and have tried to put the message of the Scriptures in simple, enduring words and expressions that are worthy to stand in the great tradition of the King James Bible and its predecessors.

In traditional Judaism and Christianity, the Bible has been more than a historical document to be preserved or a classic of literature to be cherished and admired; it is recognized as the unique record of God's dealings with people over the ages. The Old Testament sets forth the call of a special people to enter into covenant relation with the God of justice and steadfast love and to bring God's law to the nations. The New Testament records the life and work of Jesus Christ, the one in whom "the Word became flesh," as well as describes the rise and spread of the early Christian Church. The Bible carries its full message, not to those who regard it simply as a noble literary heritage of the past or who wish to use it to enhance political purposes and advance otherwise desirable goals, but to all persons and communities who read it so that they may discern and understand what God is saying to them. That message must not be disguised in phrases that are no longer clear, or hidden under words that have changed or lost their meaning; it must be presented in language that is direct and plain and meaningful to people today. It is the hope and prayer of the translators that this version of the Bible may continue to hold a large place in congregational life and to speak to all readers, young and old alike, helping them to understand and believe and respond to its message.

For the Committee,
BRUCE M. METZGER

WHERE
TO FIND IT

100 People
YOU SHOULD KNOW

Glossary
OF NONBIBLICAL PEOPLE AND PLACES

This glossary lists the names and gives brief descriptions of most of the nonbiblical people and places cited in Introductions, Insights, and Highlights. We have made every effort to be accurate and comprehensive, while acknowledging the limitations of such a list.

Alcatraz   an island in the San Francisco Bay, former site of a famous U.S. prison (reference can be found on page 1306).

Idi Amin   (1925–) at one time the cruel dictator of the East African nation of Uganda, known for his persecution of Christians (references can be found on pages 903 and 1282).

Roy Chapman Andrews   (1884–1960) U.S. naturalist and explorer, best known for books on his central Asiatic field trips (reference can be found on page 1269).

Armenia   a region and ancient kingdom in southwestern Asia, now divided between Russia, Turkey and Iran (reference can be found on page 1282).

Augustine   (354–430) bishop of Hippo in Roman Africa who was in his day the dominant personality of the Western church (reference can be found on page 1163).

Joseph Bayly   American author, educator, and long-time columnist for *Eternity* magazine, known for books such as *The View From a Hearse* and *Psalms of My Life* (reference can be found on page 523).

Bernard of Clairvaux   (1090–1153) the abbot of Clairvaux in France, a mystic and reformer known as a writer of sermons and treatises (reference can be found on page 691).

William Booth   (1829–1912) founder of the Salvation Army, deeply committed to evangelistic and social justice activities (reference can be found on page 573).

Dietrich Bonhoeffer   (1906–1945) German theologian who resisted the Nazi regime and was executed for treason; known for such books as *The Cost of Discipleship* (reference can be found on page 679).

Charles Loring Brace   (1826–1890) U.S. reformer and pioneer social welfare worker, founder and director of the Children's Aid Society of New York City (reference can be found on page 1217).

Buddha   (563–483 B.C.) Indian philosopher, founder of Buddhism (reference can be found on page 1265).

Frederick Buechner   (1926–) ordained Presbyterian minister, called by the *New York Times* the leading clergyman/writer in the U.S., the widely read author of many novels and works of nonfiction (reference can be found on page 548).

John Bunyan   (1628–1688) English Puritan minister, considered to be the greatest literary genius to come out of the Puritan movement (reference can be found on page 1221).

John Calvin   (1509–1564) French-born Genevan theologian and reformer, a leader in the Protestant Reformation of the 16th century (reference can be found on page 1267).

Rachel Carson   (1907–1964) U.S. scientist and writer, a pioneer in the environmentalist movement, especially in her warnings about the effects of pesticides on the environment (reference can be found on page 618).

Chartres   a city in northwestern France, site of the great cathedral of Notre Dame (reference can be found on page 115).

G.K. Chesterton   (1874–1936) English journalist and author, outstanding as critic, polemicist, and rhetorical poet (reference can be found on page 1163).

Winston Churchill   (1874–1965) British statesman and orator, the great national leader during World War II (references can be found on pages 766 and 964).

Samuel Taylor Coleridge   (1772–1834) English poet, lecturer, journalist, and critic of literature, theology, philosophy, and society (reference can be found on page 1221).

Charles Colson   U.S. government official during Richard Nixon's presidency, convicted for his role in the Watergate scandal; now active as an evangelical Christian author and the founder and leader of a prison ministry (reference can be found on page 1137).

Leonardo da Vinci   (1452–1519) Florentine artist and scientist, known for such works as *The Last Supper* and the *Mona Lisa* (references can be found on pages 1163 and 1265).

Fedor Mikhailovich Dostoevski   (1821–1881) Russian novelist of international reputation, generally acknowledged as one of the profoundest creative artists of the 19th century, known for such works as *The Brothers Karamazov* (reference can be found on page 1221).

Albert Einstein (1879–1955) German-born physicist, who emigrated to the United States; creator of the theory of relativity (reference can be found on page 548).

Jacques Ellul (1912–1994) French historian and sociologist known for works such as *The Meaning of the City* and *The Technological Society* (reference can be found on page 1315).

Henry Ford (1863–1947) U.S. industrialist known as the creator of modern mass production, most notably in the assembly-line method of automobile production (reference can be found on page 1217).

Robert Frost (1874–1963) American poet who used symbols from common life to express the values of rural New England, four-time winner of the Pulitzer Prize (reference can be found on page 940).

Mohandas Karamchand Gandhi (1869–1948) architect of India's freedom through a nonviolent revolution (references can be found on pages 79 and 1265).

Grand Canyon an immense gorge cut by the Colorado River into the high plateaus of the northern part of Arizona (reference can be found on page 1269).

Alex Haley (1923–1992) African-American author best known for his book *Roots*, the basis of a made-for-television mini-series (reference can be found on page 987).

Georg Friedrich Handel (1685–1759) German-born composer who spent the majority of his life in England; the greatest English composer of the late baroque era, known best for his oratorio *The Messiah* (reference can be found on page 1311).

Hare Krishna a religious sect of Hindu character, founded by an Indian holy man; its followers are characterized by rhythmic chanting of the "Hare Krsna" (reference can be found on page 1230).

Paul Harvey (1918–) an American radio newscaster known for his unique intonation and special interest stories (reference can be found on page 1030).

Herodotus (5th century B.C.) Greek author of a history of the Persian Wars (references can be found on pages 409, 507, 509).

Hindus adherents of Hinduism, a religious system whose precepts govern a vast range of human activity outside the scope of most modern religions; the Republic of India is home to more than 95 percent of all Hindus (reference can be found on page 405).

Hiroshima a seaport city in southwestern Japan, the first city on which the U.S. air force dropped an atomic bomb in 1945 (reference can be found on page 829).

Adolf Hitler (1889–1945) Austrian-born politician, leader of the Nazi party, who became dictator of Germany in 1933 and led the nation into World War II (references can be found on pages 81, 385, 505, 903).

Homer Greek epic poet, regarded as the author of many narrative poems, and according to later tradition, author of the *Iliad* and *Odyssey* (reference can be found on page 698).

Howard Hughes (1905–1976) an eccentric American businessman who amassed a fortune but died a miserable recluse (reference can be found on page 681).

Samuel Huntington (1731–1796) signer of the Declaration of Independence, president of the continental congress (1779-81) and governor of Connecticut (reference can be found on page 300).

Saddam Hussein (1937–) the cruel president of Iraq, who led his nation into the Persian Gulf War (1991) as a result of Iraq's invasion of Kuwait (references can be found on pages 81, 903, 937).

Kali Hindu goddess, usually represented as black with bloody hands, eyes, teeth, and tongue, whose worship appears to be an extension of the widespread mother-goddess cult (reference can be found on page 405).

John F. Kennedy (1917–1963) 35th president of the U.S., the youngest man and first Roman Catholic to be elected to that office; fourth U.S. president in history to die by an assassin's bullet (reference can be found on page 460).

Ruholla Mussavi Khomeini (1900–1989) one-time religious leader of Iran, served as the leader of the Shi'ite Muslims, who comprise about 90 percent of Iran's population (reference can be found on page 903).

Derek Kidner former warden of Tyndale House, Cambridge, and author of numerous Old Testament commentaries and expositions (reference can be found on page 55).

Martin Luther King (1929–1968) U.S. African-American clergyman who received the 1964 Nobel Peace Prize for his leadership in the nonviolent struggle for racial equality in the U.S. (reference can be found on page 964).

Ku Klux Klan a secret, masked organization that, after the American Civil War, became the chief instrument of the white underground resistance movement in the south against northerners and African-Americans (reference can be found on page 937).

Ann Landers (1918–) born Esther Pauline Friedman, she is best known as "Ann Landers," syndicated advice-column writer for newspapers around the U.S. (reference can be found on page 64).

C.S. Lewis (1898–1963) Irish-born author who achieved worldwide fame for books on Christian apologetics and other subjects; known for books such as *The Screwtape Letters, Mere Christianity*, and *The Chronicles of Narnia* (reference can be found on page 1109).

Abraham Lincoln (1809–1865) 16th president of the U.S., led the nation during the Civil War; the issuer of the Emancipation Proclamation, which directly or indirectly led to freedom for hundreds of thousands of slaves (references can be found on pages 79, 586, 1071, 1109, 1169).

Martin Luther (1483–1546) German religious leader who began the Protestant Reformation (references can be found on pages 956, 1163, 1165, 1213, 1276).

Douglas MacArthur (1880–1964) American general who gained fame for his military leadership in World War II (reference can be found on page 328).

Mao Tse Tung (1893–1976) Chinese revolutionist and statesman, Communist Party leader and founder of the Chinese communist state (reference can be found on page 903).

Mau Mau a nativistic cult among the Kikuya tribe in Kenya responsible for a 1950 rebellion directed against the presence of Europeans in Kenya and their ownership of land (reference can be found on page 1282).

Michelangelo (1475–1564) a native Italian, he is considered to be the greatest painter of the Renaissance and the most famous of all sculptors since the time of the Greeks, best known for his statue of "David" and his four-year painting project in the Sistine Chapel in Rome (reference can be found on page 23).

Bill Miner (1847–1913) notorious outlaw who terrorized stagecoach runs in the western U.S. (reference can be found on page 222).

Nazis followers of the National Socialist party in Germany, a party headed by Adolf Hitler, who took control of the country in 1933 (reference can be found on page 937).

John Newton (1725–1807) one of the leaders of the Evangelical revival in England, a former seafarer who after his conversion to Christianity wrote hymns (most notably *Amazing Grace*) and devotional letters (reference can be found on page 516).

Blaise Pascal (1623–1662) French mathematician and philosopher, author of a comprehensive treatise on Christian apologetics (reference can be found on page 689).

Louis Pasteur (1822–1895) French chemist and microbiologist who developed a vaccine for rabies and the method of heat pasteurization for liquid foods and beverages (reference can be found on page 132).

J.B. Phillips British pastor who devoted much of his life to writing a fresh translation of the New Testament, publishing the entire New Testament in 1958 and revising it in 1972 (reference can be found on page 1128).

Pablo Picasso (1881–1973) Spanish painter, sculptor, and engraver, the most influential independent artist of the 20th century (reference can be found on page 1315).

Grigori Efimovich Rasputin (1872–1916) Russian peasant and mystic notorious for his phenomenal sexual appetite and his impact as the voice of the peasantry (reference can be found on page 1170).

John D. Rockefeller (1874–1960) American oil magnate and philanthropist (reference can be found on page 685).

Franklin Delano Roosevelt (1882–1945) the U.S.'s 32nd president and only president to be reelected three times, he served during the New Deal era and World War II (reference can be found on page 193).

Dorothy Sayers (1893–1957) noted English writer of mystery novels, featuring the sleuth Lord Peter Wimsey (reference can be found on page 1048).

Scientology, Church of a quasi-scientific and religious discipline founded by American Ron Hubbard, it formally became the Church of Scientology in 1955 (reference can be found on page 1230).

Ignaz Philipp Semmelweis (1818–1865) Hungarian physician who had a dramatic influence on the development of knowledge and control of infection, notably through his work in the control of puerperal (childbirth) fever (reference can be found on page 132).

William Shakespeare (1564–1616) Elizabethan Englishman generally acknowledged as not only England's, but the world's, greatest poet and playwright (references can be found on pages 631 and 698).

Sistine Chapel the pope's private chapel, built under commission from Sixtus IV; Julius II commissioned Michelangelo to paint its ceiling (reference can be found on page 23).

Aleksandr Solzhenitsyn (1918–) noted Russian author known for such works as *One Day in the Life of Ivan Denisovich* and *The Gulag Archipelago* (references can be found on pages 525, 1137, 1221).

Josef Stalin (1879–1953) leader of the Communist party of the Soviet Union, generalissimo and dictator of the USSR and one of the most powerful, complex, and controversial figures in world history (reference can be found on page 903).

J.R.R. Tolkien (1892–1973) English author best known for his imaginative works such as *Lord of the Rings* (reference can be found on page 378).

Harry Truman (1884–1972) 33rd president of the U.S., serving from 1945-1953 (reference can be found on page 328).

Abigail Van Buren (1918–) born Pauline Esther Friedman, she is best known for her work as writer of the advice column "Dear Abby" for U.S. newspapers (reference can be found on page 64).

Katie von Bora (1499–1552) a former nun, she married Protestant Reformer Martin Luther in 1525 (reference can be found on page 1213).

Lech Walesa champion of the working class in Poland who rallied the nation to independence from Russian influence (reference can be found on page 79).

George Washington (1732–1799) commander in chief, statesman, and first president of the U.S. (references can be found on pages 79, 300, 315, 444, 1169).

Charles Wesley (1707–1788) English clergyman, poet, and hymnwriter who, together with his brother John, started the Methodist movement in the Church of England (reference can be found on page 1235).

John Wesley (1703–1791) English clergyman and founder of Methodism (references can be found on pages 1163 and 1235).

Oscar Wilde (1854–1900) Irish poet and dramatist, author of such works as *The Importance of Being Earnest* and *The Picture of Dorian Gray* (reference can be found on page 681).

Thomas Wolfe (1900–1938) American novelist, known for such works as *Look Homeward, Angel* (reference can be found on page 682).

Frank Lloyd Wright (1867–1959) U.S. architect who became world famous as creator and expounder of "organic architecture," designing buildings that harmonize with users and the environment (reference can be found on page 1265).

Well-known Biblical Events

OVERVIEW OF BIBLICAL EVENTS

(in approximate order of occurrence)

Creation: *Genesis 1–2*

The first sin, or fall: *Genesis 3*

Cain kills Abel: *Genesis 4*

Noah and the ark: *Genesis 6–9*

Sodom and Gomorrah: *Genesis 18–19*

Abraham sacrifices Isaac: *Genesis 22*

Jacob's ladder: *Genesis 28:10–22*

Joseph and the coat of many colors: *Genesis 37*

Moses' birth: *Exodus 2*

Moses and the burning bush: *Exodus 3*

Plagues on Egypt: *Exodus 7–11*

The exodus: *Exodus 12–13*

The Ten Commandments: *Exodus 20*

The battle of Jericho: *Joshua 6*

Gideon and the fleece: *Judges 6–7*

Samson and Delilah: *Judges 13–16*

God calls young Samuel: *1 Samuel 1–3*

David and Goliath: *1 Samuel 17*

David and Bathsheba: *2 Samuel 11*

Elijah versus the priests of Baal: *1 Kings 18*

The miracles of Elisha: *2 Kings 4–5*

Ezekiel and the dry bones: *Ezekiel 37*

Daniel in the lions' den: *Daniel 6*

Jonah and the fish: *Jonah 1*

Hosea and his adulterous wife: *Hosea 1–3*

Jesus' birth: *Luke 1–2*

Jesus' baptism: *Mark 1:9–11*

Temptation of Jesus: *Luke 4:1–13*

Jesus clears the temple: *John 2:12–25*

The transfiguration of Jesus: *Matthew 17.1–13*

Jesus raises Lazarus from the dead: *John 11.1–46*

Jesus' triumphal entry into Jerusalem: *Mark 11.1–11*

Jesus and the widow's offering: *Mark 12.41–44*

The Last Supper: *Luke 22.7–38*

Jesus washes his disciples' feet: *John 13.1–17*

Jesus at Gethsemane: *Matthew 26.36–56*

Judas betrays Jesus: *Luke 22.1–53*

Peter denies Christ: *Luke 22.54–62*

Jesus' crucifixion: *Matthew 26.57–27.66*

Jesus' resurrection and ascension: *Luke 24*

Holy Spirit at Pentecost: *Acts 2*

Stephen martyred: *Acts 6–7*

Paul's conversion: *Acts 9:1–31*

Peter's escape from prison: *Acts 12.1–19*

Paul and Silas in prison: *Acts 16.16–40*

MINISTRY OF JESUS

(in Biblical order)

Jesus baptized: *Matthew 3.13–17; Mark 1.9–11; Luke 3.21–22; John 1.29–34*

Jesus tempted by Satan: *Matthew 4.1–11; Mark 1.12–13; Luke 4.1–13*

Jesus' first miracle: *John 2.1–11*

Jesus and Nicodemus: *John 3.1–21*

Jesus talks to a Samaritan woman: *John 4.5–42*

Jesus heals an official's son: *John 4.46–54*

People of Nazareth try to kill Jesus: *Luke 4.16–30*

Jesus calls four fishermen: *Matthew 4.18–22; Mark 1.16–20; Luke 5.1–11*

Jesus heals Peter's mother–in–law: *Matthew 8.14–15; Mark 1.29–31; Luke 4.38–39*

Jesus begins preaching in Galilee: *Matthew 4.23–25; Mark 1.35–39; Luke 4.42–44*

Matthew decides to follow Jesus: *Matthew 9.9–13; Mark 2.13–17; Luke 5.27–32*

Jesus chooses twelve disciples: *Matthew 10.2–4; Mark 3.13–19; Luke 6.12–15*

Jesus preaches the Sermon on the Mount: *Matthew 5.1–7.29; Luke 6.20–49*

A sinful woman anoints Jesus: *Luke 7.36–50*

Jesus travels again through Galilee: *Luke 8.1–3*

Jesus tells kingdom parables: *Matthew 13.1–52; Mark 4.1–34; Luke 8.4–18*

Jesus quiets the storm: *Matthew 8.23–27; Mark 4.35–41; Luke 8.22–25*

Jairus's daughter raised to life: *Matthew 9.18–26; Mark 5.21–23; Luke 8.40–56*

Jesus sends out the twelve: *Matthew 9.35–11.1; Mark 6.6–13; Luke 9.1–6*

John the Baptist killed by Herod: *Matthew 14.1–12; Mark 6.14–29; Luke 9.7–9*

Jesus feeds the 5,000: *Matthew 14.13–21; Mark 6.30–44; Luke 9.10–17; John 6.1–14*

Jesus walks on water: *Matthew 14.22–32; Mark 6.47–52; John 6.16–21*

Jesus feeds the 4,000: *Matthew 15.32–39; Mark 8.1–10*

Peter confesses Jesus as the Son of God: *Matthew 16.13–20; Mark 8.27–30; Luke 9.18–21*

Jesus predicts his death: *Matthew 16.21–26; Mark 8.31–37; Luke 9.22–25*

Jesus is transfigured: *Matthew 17.1–13; Mark 9.2–13; Luke 9.28–36*

Jesus pays his temple taxes: *Matthew 17.24–27*

Jesus attends the Feast of Tabernacles: *John 7.10–52*

Jesus heals a man born blind: *John 9.1–41*

Jesus visits Mary and Martha: *Luke 10.38–42*

Jesus raises Lazarus from the dead: *John 11.1–44*

Jesus begins his last trip to Jerusalem: *Luke 17.11*

Jesus blesses the little children: *Matthew 19.13–15; Mark 10.13–16; Luke 18.15–17*

Jesus talks to the rich young man: *Matthew 19.16–30; Mark 10.17–31; Luke 18.18–30*
Jesus again predicts his death: *Matthew 20.17–19; Mark 10.32–34; Luke 18.31–34*
Jesus heals blind Bartimaeus: *Matthew 20.29–34; Mark 10.46–52; Luke 18.35–43*
Jesus talks to Zacchaeus: *Luke 19.1–10*
Jesus visits Mary and Martha again: *John 12.1–11*

MIRACLES OF JESUS

(in Biblical order)

HEALING OF INDIVIDUALS

Man with leprosy: *Matthew 8.1–4; Mark 1.40–44; Luke 5.12–14*
Roman centurion's servant: *Matthew 8.5–13; Luke 7.1–10*
Peter's mother–in–law: *Matthew 8.14–15; Mark 1.30–31; Luke 4.38–39*
Two demon–possessed men from Gadara: *Matthew 8.28–34; Mark 5.1–15; Luke 8.27–39*
Paralyzed man: *Matthew 9.2–7; Mark 2.3–12; Luke 5.18–26*
Woman with bleeding: *Matthew 9.20–22; Mark 5.25–34; Luke 8.43–48*
Two blind men: *Matthew 9.27–31*
Mute, demon–possessed man: *Matthew 9.32–33*
Man with a shriveled hand: *Matthew 12.10–13; Mark 3.1–5; Luke 6.6–11*
Blind, mute and demon–possessed man: *Matthew 12.22–23; Luke 11.14*
Canaanite woman's daughter: *Matthew 15.21–28; Mark 7.24–30*
Boy with epilepsy: *Matthew 17.14–21; Mark 9.17–29; Luke 9.38–43*
Two blind men (including Bartimaeus): *Matthew 20.29–34; Mark 10.46–52; Luke 18.35–43*
Demon–possessed man in synagogue: *Mark 1.21–28; Luke 4.31–37*
Blind man at Bethsaida: *Mark 8.22–26*
Crippled woman: *Luke 13.10–17*
Man with dropsy: *Luke 14.1–4*
Ten men with leprosy: *Luke 17.11–19*
The high priest's servant: *Luke 22.50–51*
Official's son at Capernaum: *John 4.46–54*
Sick man at the pool of Bethesda: *John 5.1–15*
Man born blind: *John 9.1–41*

CONTROL OF NATURE

Calming the storm: *Matthew 8.23–27; Mark 4.37–41; Luke 8.22–25*
Feeding of 5,000: *Matthew 14.1–21; Mark 6.30–44; Luke 9.10–17; John 6.1–14*
Walking on water: *Matthew 14.22–32; Mark 6.47–52; John 6.16–21*
Feeding of 4,000: *Matthew 15.32–39; Mark 8.1–9*
Fish with coin: *Matthew 17.24–27*
Fig tree withers: *Matthew 21.18–22; Mark 11.12–14, 20–25*
Huge catch of fish: *Luke 5.4–11; John 21.1–11*
Water into wine: *John 2.1–11*

RAISING THE DEAD

Jairus's daughter: *Matthew 9.18–26; Mark 5.21–43; Luke 8.40–56*
Widow at Nain's son: *Luke 7.11–17*
Lazarus: *John 11.1–44*

PARABLES OF JESUS

(in alphabetical order)

Canceled debts: *Luke 7.41–43*

Cost of discipleship: *Luke 14.28–33*

Faithful servant: *Matthew 24.45–51; Luke 12.42–48*

Fig tree: *Matthew 24.32–35; Mark 13.28–31; Luke 21.29–33*

Good Samaritan: *Luke 10.30–37*

The great dinner: *Luke 14.16–24*

Growing seed: *Mark 4.26–29*

Hidden treasure and pearl: *Matthew 13.44–46*

Honor at a banquet: *Luke 14.7–14*

Laborers in the vineyard: *Matthew 20.1–16*

Light of the world: *Matthew 5.14–16; Mark 4.21–22; Luke 8.16; 11.33–36*

Lost coin: *Luke 15.8–10*

Lost sheep: *Matthew 18.12–14; Luke 15.4–7*

Mustard seed: *Matthew 13.31–32; Mark 4.30–32; Luke 13.18–19*

New cloth on an old garment: *Matthew 9.16; Mark 2.21; Luke 5.36*

New wine in old wineskins: *Matthew 9.17; Mark 2.22; Luke 5.37–39*

Net: *Matthew 13.47–50*

Obedient servants: *Luke 17.7–10*

Owner of a house: *Matthew 13.52*

Persistent friend: *Luke 11.5–8*

Persistent widow: *Luke 18.2–8*

Pharisee and the tax collector: *Luke 18.10–14*

Prodigal (lost) son: *Luke 15.11–32*

Rich fool: *Luke 12.16–21*

Rich man and Lazarus: *Luke 16.19–31*

Sheep and goats: *Matthew 25.31–46*

Shrewd manager: *Luke 16.1–8*

Sower: *Matthew 13.1–8, 18–23; Mark 4.3–8, 14–20; Luke 8.5–8, 11–15*

Talents: *Matthew 25.14–30*

Tenants: *Matthew 21.33–34; Mark 12.1–11; Luke 20.9–18*

Ten minas: *Luke 19.12–27*

Ten bridesmaids: *Matthew 25.1–13*

Two sons: *Matthew 21.28–32*

Unforgiving servant: *Matthew 18.23–35*

Unfruitful fig tree: *Luke 13.6–9*

Watchful slaves: *Mark 13.34–37; Luke 12.35–40*

Wedding banquet: *Matthew 22.2–14*

Weeds: *Matthew 13.24–30, 36–43*

Wise and foolish builders: *Matthew 7.24–27; Luke 6.47–49*

Yeast: *Matthew 13.33; Luke 13.20–21*

TEACHINGS OF JESUS

(in alphabetical order)

Beatitudes: *Matthew 5.1–12*

Bread of life: *John 6.25–59*

Born again: *John 3.1–21*

Discipleship: *Luke 14.25–35*

Give to Caesar: *Mark 12.13–17*

Good shepherd: *John 10.1–21*

Golden Rule: *Luke 6.31*

Greatest commandment: *Matthew 22.34–40*

Living water: *John 4.1–26*

Lord's prayer: *Matthew 6.5–15*

Sending out the Twelve: *Matthew 10*

Sermon on the Mount: *Matthew 5–7*

Vine and branches: *John 15.1–17*

The way and the truth and the life: *John 14.5–14*

Wealth: *Matthew 19.16–30*

Worry: *Luke 12.22–34*

JESUS' LAST WEEK

(in Biblical order)

The triumphal entry: *Matthew 21.1–11; Mark 11.1–11; Luke 19.29–44; John 12.12–19*

Jesus curses the fig tree: *Matthew 21.18–22; Mark 11.12–14*

Jesus clears the temple: *Matthew 21.12–13; Mark 11.15–18; Luke 19.45–48*

Jesus' authority questioned: *Matthew 21.23–27; Mark 11.27–33; Luke 20.1–8*

Jesus teaches in the temple: *Matthew 21.28–23.39; Mark 12.1–44; Luke 20.9–21.4*

Jesus' feet anointed: *Matthew 26.6–13; Mark 14.3–9; John 12.2–11*

The plot against Jesus: *Matthew 26.14–16; Mark 14.10–11; Luke 22.3–6*

The Last Supper: *Matthew 26.17–29; Mark 14.12–25; Luke 22.7–38; John 13.1–38*

Jesus comforts his disciples: *John 14.1–16.33*

Jesus' high priestly prayer: *John 17.1–26*

Gethsemane: *Matthew 26.36–46; Mark 14.32–42; Luke 22.40–46*

Jesus' arrest and trial: *Matthew 26.47–27.26; Mark 14.43–15.15; Luke 22.47–23.25; John 18.2–19.16*

Jesus' crucifixion and death: *Matthew 27.27–56; Mark 15.16–41; Luke 23.26–49; John 19.17–37*

Jesus' burial: *Matthew 27.57–66; Mark 15.42–47; Luke 23.50–56; John 19.38–42*

JESUS' RESURRECTION APPEARANCES

(in Biblical order)

The empty tomb : *Matthew 28.1–8; Mark 16.1–8; Luke 24.1–12; John 20.1–10*

To Mary Magdalene in the garden: *Mark 16.9–11; John 20.11–18*

To other women: *Matthew 28.9–10*

To two people going to Emmaus: *Mark 16.12–13; Luke 24.13–32*

To Peter: *Luke 24.34; 1 Corinthians 15.5*

To the ten disciples in the upper room: *Luke 24.36–43; John 20.19–25*

To the eleven disciples in the upper room: *Mark 16.14; John 20.26–31; 1 Corinthians 15.5*

To seven disciples fishing: *John 21.1–14*

To the eleven disciples on a mountain: *Matthew 28.16–20; Mark 16.15–18*

To more than 500 people: *1 Corinthians 15.6*

To James: *1 Corinthians 15.7*

To his disciples at his ascension: *Luke 24.36–51; Acts 1.3–9; 1 Corinthians 15.7*

To Paul: *Acts 9.1–19; 22.3–16; 26.9–18; 1 Corinthians 9.1*

Some Notable Psalms

A Lineup of Rulers

The two-part book of Kings can be confusing. First, there's one nation to keep track of, then two, then one again. In all, 39 rulers are profiled. Little wonder it takes a Biblical scholar to keep all the details straight.

The following list of 38 kings and one queen should help clarify the history of Israel in the North and Judah in the South. As you come across the name of a ruler in one of the history books or in a book of the prophets, simply refer to the capsule description below for a brief summary of life during the time of that ruler or prophet.

In all, the kingdoms of Israel and Judah were united for 120 years and divided for just over 200 years. Then Israel disappeared and Judah lasted alone another 135 years. After that, no independent Jewish nation existed until the 20th century.

The timeline on the bottom of pages 1351–1357 places the major prophets in the appropriate time period, along with the rulers of their era. Prophets whose names appear in gray boxes spoke to Israel; those listed against a blue background spoke to Judah. (Dating of some rulers is inexact because of overlapping reigns.)

UNITED KINGDOM

SAUL
DAVID
SOLOMON
These first three kings of Israel each ruled approximately 40 years, and so for 120 years, Israel was one nation. The books of Samuel and Chronicles, along with 1 Kings, describe their reigns in great detail. Later, Jews would look back on this time as the Golden Age of Israel.

DIVIDED KINGDOM

ISRAEL

JEROBOAM I   22 Years
He was handpicked by God to lead a reform, but this first king of the Northern Kingdom proved to be one of Israel's worst. For years afterward, evil kings were described as "walking in the ways of Jeroboam." It was he who firmly established the split-off nation of Israel, uniting 10 rebel tribes. To prevent his people from worshiping in Jerusalem (now enemy territory), he built a new capital city and set up the notorious "high places" as alternative worship sites. The high places and calf worship plagued Israel throughout its entire history. First Kings records that God decided to abandon Israel during the reign of Jeroboam, the Northern Kingdom's very first ruler. (1 Kings 11.26–15.25; 2 Chronicles 10.2–13.20)

JUDAH

REHOBOAM   17 Years
Judah's first king had a checkered career. Sometimes he obeyed God and listened to the prophets; sometimes he did not. At first, the Jewish religion gained strength when all priests and Levites came over to Judah. But, before long, idolatry found its way into Judah as well as into Israel, and Judah suffered humiliating punishment from the armies of Egypt. Thus Judah's first king set an unfortunate pattern for his successors. (1 Kings 11.43–14.31; 2 Chronicles 10–12)

ABIJAH   3 Years
War with Israel in the North dragged on throughout Abijah's three-year reign. The two splinter nations were still adjusting to each other's independence. Abijah offered no improvement on his father Rehoboam's immoral ways. (1 Kings 15.1-8; 2 Chronicles 13.1–14.1)

ISRAEL

JEROBOAM I (CONTINUED)

NADAB   2 Years

Jeroboam's son followed the errors of his father in every way, and his reign merits only eight verses. Israel's first dynasty ended abruptly when Nadab fell victim to a murder plot launched by Baasha. (1 Kings 15.25-32)

BAASHA   24 Years

After gaining the throne in a violent manner, Baasha lasted 24 years. He showed no inclination to reverse the evil practice begun by Jeroboam. The prophet Jehu predicted his death. (1 Kings 15.33—16.7; 2 Chronicles 16)

ELAH   2 years

The Bible records only one incident from Elah's reign: His chariot commander staged a military coup while Elah was off getting drunk. Elah was killed, along with all other descendants of his father, Baasha. Israel's second dynasty, therefore, only lasted 26 years, and another family took the throne. (1 Kings 16.8-14)

ZIMRI   7 Days

Evidently, mutinous chariot commander Zimri acted without his army's support. The army revolted against him, and his "reign" ended seven days after it had begun, in a suicidal fire set in his palace. (1 Kings 16.15-20)

JUDAH

ASA   41 Years

Asa and his son Jehoshaphat were the only kings mentioned in 1 Kings who did "what was right in the sight of the Lord." Second Chronicles gives a much fuller account of Asa's 41 years. He began religious reforms that turned into a kind of wildfire revival. He drove heathen cults out of the land—even removing his own grandmother as queen mother because of her idolatry. Asa also welcomed to Judah many refugees from Israel. Late in his reign he backslid and got bogged down in foreign wars, making an alliance with neighboring Aram to hold Israel at bay. (1 Kings 15.9-24; 2 Chronicles 14—16)

ISRAEL

OMRI   12 Years

Secular historians rate Omri as one of Israel's most powerful and capable political rulers. In fact, Assyrian records call Israel "the land of Omri." He outlasted a rival to the throne, expanded Israel's lands, and founded the city of Samaria, which would remain Israel's capital for 150 years. But he gets scant mention in the Bible; it dismisses him for sinning more "than all who were before him." (1 Kings 16.21-28)

AHAB   22 Years

In a competition for all-time worst king of Israel, Ahab would win hands down. He married the notorious Jezebel, a pagan priestess who promptly installed Baal worship as Israel's official religion. First Kings departs from its usually brief style to give a detailed treatment of Ahab's life and the great spiritual crisis then. During that time, Elijah appeared on the scene to represent the true God against Queen Jezebel's religion. God gave Ahab plenty of opportunities to reform. Ahab humbled himself at least once, postponing disaster, but a nasty incident over Naboth's vineyard sealed his fate. Politically, Ahab forged a successful alliance with Israel's neighbor, Judah, and the divided kingdoms lived at peace for the first time since Jeroboam. Ultimately, however, his evil practices would spread into Judah. (1 Kings 16.29–22.40; 2 Chronicles 18)

AHAZIAH   2 years

Like his father, Ahab, and mother, Jezebel, Ahaziah continued to worship Baal and to fight against Elijah. He was no match. His reign lasted only part of two years, and the descriptions of him reveal a weak, vengeful ruler. (1 Kings 22.40–2 Kings 1.18)

JORAM   12 Years

JUDAH

ASA (CONTINUED)

JEHOSHAPHAT   25 Years

Judah enjoyed the rare blessing of two good kings back to back. Jehoshaphat continued the spirit of Asa's rule, and found ways to further it. He sent out princes to teach from the Book of the Law in the cities of Judah and established courts of justice throughout the country. With a large army and well-fortified cities, he attained a level of peace and prosperity rare in Judah's history. His one serious mistake was in linking himself to Israel's wicked king Ahab through marriage and military alliance. (1 Kings 22.41-50; 2 Chronicles 17–20)

| AHAB | | AHAZIAH | JORAM |

| ELIJAH |

ASA   JEHOSHAPHAT

ISRAEL

JORAM (CONTINUED)

Although an improvement over his father and mother (Ahab and Jezebel), Joram ultimately failed to do right. He modified some of the worship of Baal, and at times had a respectful relationship with the prophet Elisha. But Joram lived in treacherous times. The nation of Aram was attacking from the east, and God had set in motion an internal plot, led by Jehu, against Ahab's heirs. Finally Joram fell victim to Jehu's arrow, ending the evil dynasty founded by Omri. (2 Kings 3.1—9.26)

JEHU   28 years

Not to be confused with the prophet of the same name, this Jehu was a fast-driving, impetuous military man. He began a holy mission to purge Ahab's influence out of Israel and Judah, but considerably overstepped his bounds. He killed Joram, had Jezebel thrown from a window, and slew 70 princes, piling their heads in two heaps by a gate. Then he slew all the priests and prophets of Baal and tricked the worshipers of Baal into a trap that led to a mass slaughter. Unfortunately, Jehu's zeal for violence did not translate into zeal for justice. His actions tore Israel apart for generations, and he did little to attend to the nation's spiritual health. Israel also began to lose political strength. (2 Kings 9—10)

JUDAH

JEHORAM   8 Years

After 60 good years under Asa and Jehoshaphat, Judah experienced a terrible regression under Jehoram. He began by killing his brothers and then marrying Athaliah, daughter of Israel's Ahab and Jezebel. She promptly led him into Baal worship. Elijah, who mostly prophesied to Israel, sent Judah's king Jehoram a letter predicting the severe bowel disease that would lead to his death. Second Chronicles reports that "he departed with no one's regret." (2 Kings 8.16-24; 2 Chronicles 21)

AHAZIAH   1 Year

In effect Ahaziah served as a mere puppet representative of the notorious queen Athaliah, daughter of Ahab and Jezebel. He fell victim to the bloody purge of Jehu. (2 Kings 8.25-29; 2 Chronicles 22.1-9)

ATHALIAH   7 Years

Queen Athaliah first corrupted her husband Jehoram and dominated her son Ahaziah. Then, after Ahaziah's death, she killed off her infant grandchildren to remove rivals to the throne. She ruled Judah for seven years, leading the kingdom into a dark time of Baal worship and evil. Providentially, however, one heir escaped her reach. The young Joash, hidden away by a relative, emerged at the age of seven. This led to a popular revolt against Athaliah. Athaliah, the only woman to rule either of the two kingdoms, was the last of Ahab's family to die. She had come within one baby of wiping out King David's royal line. (2 Kings 11; 2 Chronicles 22.10—23.21)

JOASH   40 Years

JEHU

ELISHA ▶

850 B.C.

820 B.C.

JEHORAM   AHAZIAH   ATHALIAH   JOASH

ISRAEL

JEHU (CONTINUED)

JEHOAHAZ   17 Years
After all his father Jehu had done to exterminate Baal worship, Jehoahaz immediately reinstated it. He ruled 17 years, marked by a series
of embarrassing military defeats at the hands
of neighboring Aram. He did turn to God in
desperation at least once, and Israel got some
reprieve. (2 Kings 13.1-9)

JEHOASH   16 Years
Although Jehoash did not break the evil pattern of Israel's kings, he showed some bright
spots. He honored the prophet Elisha, and God
allowed him to recover much of the territory
that Aram had taken from Israel. (Note that
Judah also had a king named Joash, the shortened version of Jehoash.) (2 Kings 13.10–
14.16)

JEROBOAM II   41 Years
It seems that God gave Israel one last chance
under King Jeroboam II. This king ruled a
strong and prosperous nation. The Bible gives
scant mention of his reign, but it lasted 41
years, during which Israel recovered nearly all
its former territory. The prophet Jonah lived
then, possibly assisting the king in his frontier
defense against Assyria. In addition, Amos and
Hosea were active, railing against the terrible
social and religious corruption of those affluent
times. In a remarkable turn of events, Israel
survived as a nation for only a few decades
after this stable period. (2 Kings 14.23-29)

ZECHARIAH   6 Months
SHALLUM   1 Month
After Jeroboam II, the nation splintered into
rival factions. The first king (Zechariah) ruled
for six months, the second (Shallum) only one
month. Both died violently. (2 Kings 15.8-16)

JUDAH

JOASH (CONTINUED)
He swept into power at the crest of a revolt
against his wicked grandmother Athaliah.
And as long as Joash followed the advice
of Jehoiada the priest, he did well. Most
notably, he organized massive projects to
repair the temple. After Jehoiada died, however, Joash allowed idolatry to prosper once
more. He strayed so far from the ideals of his
youth that he ordered the prophet Zechariah
to be stoned—the same Zechariah whose
father, Jehoiada, had saved his life. Punishment came swiftly, at the hands of a plundering army. Finally, Joash's own servants
turned against him and avenged Zechariah's
murder. (2 Kings 12; 2 Chronicles 24)

AMAZIAH   29 Years
Second Kings concludes that Amaziah "did
what was right in the sight of the LORD, yet not
like his ancestor David." Yet the author mostly
comments on Amaziah's failures. He began his
rule by executing those who had killed his
father. Then he ignored a prophet's advice
and attacked Edom, bringing back idols from
there. Flush with military success, he launched
a foolhardy campaign against Israel. The
trouncing that resulted discredited his leadership, and he spent his last 12 years in exile.
(2 Kings 14.1-22; 2 Chronicles 25)

AZARIAH   52 Years
Called Uzziah in Chronicles, this king reigned
some 50 years, the longest of Judah's kings.
As a young man, he took advice from a
prophet named Zechariah. He built up the
army of Judah and worked on its agriculture
and water supplies. Until Azariah, Judah had
been a struggling kingdom, with enemy fortifications just five miles from Jerusalem. Under
him, the nation achieved true strength. Even
so, Azariah gets a short review in the Bible
because of his spiritual failings. He did not
remove the high places, and he violated the
Law of Moses by taking on the work of priests
himself. (2 Kings 15.1-17; 2 Chronicles 26)

JEHU	JEHOAHAZ	JEHOASH		JEROBOAM II			
ELISHA (CONTINUED)				JONAH			AMOS
JOASH		AMAZIAH			AZARIAH		

820 B.C.

750 B.C.

ISRAEL

MENAHEM   10 Years

Menahem lasted for ten turbulent years. He gained the throne by murder, and his reign showed a similar ruthlessness. The first of Assyria's three invasions—Israel's "World War I" (see Introduction to 2 Kings)—occurred during Menahem's years, and he frantically tried to buy off the invaders. (2 Kings 15.14-22)

PEKAHIAH   2 Years

Israel was quickly sliding toward anarchy and extermination. Pekahiah survived only two years before a military coup overthrew him. (2 Kings 15.23-26)

PEKAH   20 Years

Pekah turned to international intrigue and conspiracy. He attempted to dethrone the king of Judah in the South. But Judah bought help from Assyria, which promptly invaded Israel for the second time. After occupying all major cities in Israel except the capital Samaria, Assyria began deporting thousands of conquered Israelites to other lands. (2 Kings 15.27-31)

HOSHEA   9 Years

The Bible judges Hoshea as less wicked than some of his predecessors. Nevertheless, Israel's death was certain. Hoshea angered Assyria by turning south to Egypt for aid. The Assyrians attacked, and after a terrible three-year siege, the last stronghold, Samaria, fell to the conquerors. Assyria deported the vast majority of Israel's population, who became the "ten lost tribes of Israel." (2 Kings 17)

JUDAH

AZARIAH (CONTINUED)

JOTHAM   16 Years

After serving as Azariah's proxy king for 15 years (while Azariah was quarantined with leprosy), Jotham took over and continued the practices of his father. He expanded Judah's economic and military strength, but did not pursue religious reforms as fully as he should have. (2 Kings 15.32-38; 2 Chronicles 27)

AHAZ   16 Years

At the very moment Ahaz was being crowned, armies from the North led by King Pekah of Israel were marching into Judah. Ahaz ignored the prophet Isaiah's advice to put his trust in God rather than military alliances. Turning to the mighty empire of Assyria, he purchased aid with treasures from the temple and the king's palace. The strategy worked temporarily: Israel's armies withdrew to defend themselves. But Ahaz opened the doors for later Assyrian invasions of Judah itself. Worse, he made copies of foreign gods and set them up in Jerusalem. Under him, religion in Judah took a precipitous drop. He went so far as to sacrifice his sons in the fire, following the detestable ways of foreign nations. (2 Kings 16; 2 Chronicles 28)

ASSYRIAN INVASION

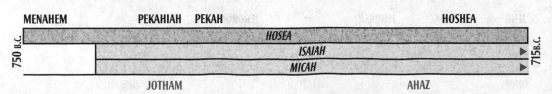

750 B.C.	MENAHEM	PEKAHIAH	PEKAH		HOSHEA	715 B.C.
			HOSEA			
		ISAIAH			▶	
		MICAH			▶	
		JOTHAM			AHAZ	

ASSYRIAN INVASION

ONLY JUDAH SURVIVES

HEZEKIAH   29 Years

King Hezekiah gets full treatment in both Kings and Chronicles. The first book stresses the political side of his reign while the second reports on his religious reforms. Both were impressive; Hezekiah was one of the best and most important kings of Judah. He immediately stopped idolatry by reopening and cleansing the temple and calling for a period of national repentance. He resurrected the Passover celebration, and worship in Israel reached a peak that had not been seen since the time of David and Solomon. In all this, he listened carefully to advice from the prophet Isaiah. Yet Hezekiah hardly lived in a peaceful era. He faced imminent danger from Assyria and barely survived an invasion and siege. God honored his faithfulness with a miraculous military intervention. In an unprecedented act, he also added 15 years to Hezekiah's life. (2 Kings 18–20; 2 Chronicles 29–32; Isaiah 36–39)

MANASSEH   55 Years

Whatever good Hezekiah had accomplished In his exemplary reign, his son Manasseh undid in 55 years of the worst rule in Judah's history. He reversed Hezekiah's reforms, bringing in all forms of idolatry, including the occult and witchcraft. He killed off prophets, erected idols in God's temple, and sacrificed his own sons on the altar of a heathen god. The Assyrian empire took Manasseh prisoner, leading him away with a hook through his nose. Later he repented, but great damage had been done. After Manasseh, God pronounced a final judgment on the future of Judah. (2 Kings 21.1-18; 2 Chronicles 33.1-20)

715 B.C.

ISAIAH (CONTINUED)

MICAH (CONTINUED)

HEZEKIAH

MANASSEH

640 B.C.

ONLY JUDAH SURVIVES

AMON   2 Years

Amon merely continued the practices of his father. He died at the hands of his servants. (2 Kings 21.19-26; 2 Chronicles 33.21-25)

JOSIAH   31 Years

Judah's slide to destruction was interrupted by the amazing rule of its all-time best king. Josiah came to the throne at age eight, but received good counsel from the high priests. In 31 years he carried out the most extensive religious reforms Judah had ever seen. He removed and destroyed the altars, idols, and symbols of ungodly worship from the temple, and destroyed pagan centers throughout the land. In a thrilling sequence of events, he oversaw the rediscovery of the Law of Moses and acted immediately on what it taught. No king equals Josiah for his sincere and devout practices. He even extended his reforms into the decimated regions of Israel in the North.

Josiah had a time of military peace, for during his reign the Assyrian empire was disintegrating. But he unwisely thrust himself into international politics by marching against Egypt. (The prophet Jeremiah had urged against the Egyptian campaign.) Judah would never recover from this fatal mistake, for Josiah died suddenly in battle. His death shocked the nation. After Josiah's death, Egypt installed a puppet king, and no one after him had the ability to rally Judah's religious or political strength. (2 Kings 22.1–23.30; 2 Chronicles 34–35)

JEHOAHAZ   3 Months

The third son of Josiah lasted only three months before being sacked by a pharaoh and carried off in chains. (2 Kings 23.30-34; 2 Chronicles 36.1-4)

640 B.C.	ZEPHANIAH		600 B.C.
	JEREMIAH	▶
	NAHUM	HABAKKUK

AMON   JEHOAHAZ

JUDAH

JEHOIAKIM   11 Years

Installed by an Egyptian pharaoh, Jehoiakim found himself trapped when Egypt was defeated by a surging Babylon. He quickly shifted allegiance to Nebuchadnezzar of Babylon. One of Judah's worst kings, he stubbornly tried to have the prophet Jeremiah put to death. (Numerous passages in Jeremiah's book make plain his scorn for Jehoiakim.) Finally, after an ill-advised revolt against Nebuchadnezzar, Jehoiakim was captured and killed. (2 Kings 23.36–24.6; 2 Chronicles 36.5-8)

JEHOIACHIN   3 Months

The struggles with Babylon were the "World War II" in Israel's history (see Introduction to 2 Kings). After holding out for three months against Nebuchadnezzar's armies, Jehoiachin surrendered, and was carried away with many other captives, including the prophet Ezekiel. He lived in a Babylonian prison for 40 years. (2 Kings 24.6-17; 25.27-30; 2 Chronicles 36.8-10)

ZEDEKIAH   11 Years

Zedekiah ruled over Judah during the last 11 years of its existence as an independent state. A weak king, he took bad advice from princes and advisers and often made unwise decisions. He ignored Jeremiah's advice to remain loyal to Babylon and joined an alliance against that empire. As a result, Nebuchadnezzar laid siege to Jerusalem for almost two years, bringing the city to the verge of starvation. At last the Babylonians made a breach in the wall and overran the city. They burned Solomon's temple, the king's palace, and other buildings, and destroyed the walls around Jerusalem. Finally, they took everything of value from the temple. The city was utterly looted. (2 Kings 24.17–25.7; 2 Chronicles 26.11-20)

BABYLONIAN INVASION

Zechariah, Haggai, and Malachi prophesied later, to the Jewish refugees who had returned from Babylon.

586 B.C. BABYLONIAN INVASION

640 B.C.				525 B.C.
		DANIEL		
JEREMIAH (CONTINUED)				
	EZEKIEL			
JEHOIAKIM	ZEDEKIAH			

Subject Guide

The Subject Guide is not a "concordance" that shows where the Bible uses a certain word. Rather, it lists major subjects that may be of interest, along with the Bible passages (not single verses, usually) that speak to these subjects. Topics of pressing interest or major significance have been highlighted within the list. Although we have tried to be comprehensive, any list of subjects must necessarily be restrictive. The italicized titles in quotes refer to Highlights, Insights, or Introductions on the subject. Page numbers are given in boldface type.

A

AARON – brother of and spokesman for Moses; became the first high priest
  character profile, *"Working Together . . . and Apart"*–**p. 170**
  with Moses, Exodus 4.10–12.50–**p. 83**
  made priest, Exodus 28–29 **p. 107**; *"The First High Priest"*–**p. 129**
  his role with golden calf, Exodus 32–**p. 111**
  budding of his staff, Numbers 17–**p. 174**
  his death, Numbers 20.23–29–**p. 177**

ABEL – Adam's second son; murdered by his brother Cain
  character profile, *"Blood Brothers"*–**p. 30**
  his life, Genesis 4.1–9–**p. 29**
  example of faith, Hebrews 11.1–4–**p. 1272**
  relationship to Christ, Hebrews 12.22–24–**p. 1275**

ABIATHAR – high priest in the days of Saul and David
  character profile, *"Outlaw Priest"*–**p. 358**

ABIGAIL – wife of Nabal, became David's wife after Nabal's death
  character profile, *"Beauty and Brains"*–**p. 317**

ABISHAI – nephew of David and one of his chief warriors
  character profile, *"Bloody Brothers"*–**p. 428**

ABNER – cousin of Saul and commander of his army
  character profile, *"On the Wrong Side"*–**p. 327**

ABORTION – death of a fetus through a medical procedure
  penalty for harming fetus, Exodus 21.22–25–**p. 101**
  unborn life important to God, Psalm 139–**p. 640**

ABRAHAM – founder of the Jewish nation
  character profile, *"Abraham"*–**p. 35**
  called by God, Genesis 11.26–12.20–**p. 35**
  his life, Genesis 11.26–25.11–**p. 35**
  and Melchizedek, Genesis 14.18–24–**p. 38**
  covenant with, Genesis 15;17–**p. 38**
  and Hagar, Genesis 16–**p. 39**
  prayed for Sodom and Gomorrah, Genesis 18.16–33–**p. 41**
  asked to sacrifice his son, Genesis 22–**p. 45**
  his death, Genesis 25.1–11–**p. 49**
  his true offspring are believers, Romans 4–**p. 1167**; Galatians 3.6–29–**p. 1212**
  faith demonstrated by deeds, James 2.20–24–**p. 1278**

ABSALOM – third son of David, by Maacah
  character profile, *"All That Glitters"*–**p. 339**
  his revenge on Amnon, 2 Samuel 13–14–**p. 336**
  in hiding, *"A Refuge with His Family"*–**p. 338**
  rebellion against David, 2 Samuel 15.1–19.8–**p. 339**; *"No Way Back"*–**p. 341**

ADAM – the first man
  character profile, *"First in Everything"*–**p. 26**
  his creation and life, Genesis 1.26–5.5–**p. 25**
  his fall into sin, Genesis 3–**p. 27**
  Jesus and the line of Adam, Luke 3.23–38–**p. 1057**
  Jesus as second Adam, Romans 5.12–21–**p. 1170**; 1 Corinthians 15.21–22,42–57–**p. 1196**

ADOPTION – becoming a child of one who is not your biological parent
  Abraham and adoption of an heir, Genesis 15.1–6–**p. 38**; Genesis 16–**p. 39**
  Israel as God's adopted son, Exodus 4.21–23–**p. 83**; Jeremiah 31.9, 16–20–**p. 95**
  Believers as God's adopted children, John 1.12–13–**p. 1091**; Romans 8.12–25–**p. 1172**; Galatians 3.26–4.7–**p. 1214**; Ephesians 1.3–8–**p. 1218**

ADULTERY – sexual unfaithfulness of a married person
  laws against, Numbers 5.12–31–**p. 160**
  David and Bathsheba, 2 Samuel 11–12–**p. 333**
  warnings against, Proverbs 5–**p. 653**; Proverbs 6.20–35–**p. 654**
  avoiding, *"A Safeguard Against Lust"*–**p. 172**
  Jesus' views on, Matthew 5.27–32–**p. 993**
  effect on the church, 1 Corinthians 5–**p. 1187**

AFTERLIFE – *see* ETERNAL LIFE, HEAVEN, HELL, RESURRECTION

AGRIPPA – descendent of Herod; king before whom Paul pled his case
  character profile, *"Roman Heart"*–**p. 1157**

AHAB – Israel's most wicked king
  character profile, *"Worst King Yet"*–**p. 383**
  ascended throne, 1 Kings 16.29–33–**p. 375**
  contest with Elijah, 1 Kings 18–**p. 378**
  and Naboth's vineyard, 1 Kings 21–**p. 381**
  his death, 1 Kings 22.34–38–**p. 386**

AHASUERUS – king of Persian empire and husband of Esther
  character of, *"Ahasuerus: A Wild Man"*–**p. 510**

ALCOHOL – *see* DRINKING ALCOHOL, WINE

Ambition – strong desire for success, honor, or power (*see also* PRIDE, SERVANTHOOD)
  competing with God, *"Human Ambition"*–**p. 34**
  at the tower of Babel, Genesis 11.1–11–**p. 34**
  results of, Matthew 16.21–27–**p. 1008**
  of disciples, Mark 9.33–37; 10.35–45–**p. 999**
  the antichrist, 2 Thessalonians 2.1–4–**p. 1241**

ANDREW — apostle; brother of Simon Peter
character profile, *"Out of the Spotlight"*—**p. 1098**

ANGELS — heavenly beings created by God
assist people, Genesis 24—**p. 47**
protect people, Psalm 91.11–13—**p. 612**
execute judgment, Matthew 13.24–50—**p. 1004**
deliver messages, *"A Message from God"*—**p. 705**; Luke
1.26–38—**p. 1053**; 2.8–15—**p. 1055**
execute judgment, Matthew 13.24–50—**p. 1004**;
Revelation 14.17–16.21—**p. 1319**
purpose of, *"Respect for Angels"*—**p. 1264**
Christ greater than, Hebrews 1.5–14—**p. 1263**
serve in heaven, Revelation 8–9—**p. 1313**
spiritual warriors, Revelation 12.7–12—**p. 1317**

ANGER
of God:
toward sin, Numbers 11.1–35—**p. 166**; *"God Is Slow to
Anger"*—**p. 951**; Romans 1.18–32—**p. 1165**
tempered with mercy, Psalm 103—**p. 617**; Hosea
11.8–11—**p. 915**
averted through Christ, Romans 5—**p. 1169**
of human beings:
Cain's, *"Improper Offerings"*—**p. 29**
Moses', Exodus 32.15–35—**p. 112**
Abigail's, *"Beauty and Brains"*—**p. 317**
Jonah's, Jonah 3–4—**p. 939**
dealing with, *"Angry Inside"*—**p. 555**
"In your anger do not sin", Ephesians 4.26—**p. 1222**
be slow to anger, James 1.19–20—**p. 1278**

ANIMALS
purpose of, *"Just for Fun"*—**p. 619**
God's love for, *"The Wildness of Animals"*—**p. 549**
showing God's power, *"Behemoth and Leviathan?"*—
p. 549

ANNAS — high priest at the time of John the Baptist;
Jesus stood trial before him in an unofficial
capacity
character profile, *"Collaborators"*—**p. 1107**

ANTICHRIST — an evil person or power; a false Christ,
expected in the end times
prophesied by Daniel, Daniel 11.36–45—**p. 904**
Jesus' teaching on, Mark 13.1–37—**p. 1044**
will be destroyed, 2 Thessalonians 2.1–12—**p. 1241**
qualities of, 1 John 2.18–23—**p. 1295**; 4.1–6—**p. 1296**
visions of, Revelation 11–13—**p. 1316**
destruction of, Revelation 19.19–21—**p. 1323**

ANXIETY
overcome by trust in God, Matthew 6.25–34—**p. 995**;
Luke 12.22–34—**p. 1072**
subdued through prayer, Philippians 4.4–9—**p. 1228**

APOLLOS — an Alexandrian Jew who preached in
Corinth
character profile, *"Brimming with Confidence"*—**p. 1186**
with Priscilla and Aquila, Acts 18.24–28—**p. 1149**
followers of, 1 Corinthians 3.1–9—**p. 1185**
partners with Paul, 1 Corinthians 4.1–7—**p. 1186**

APOSTLES — title given to the followers of Christ who
founded the early church, especially the 12
disciples and Paul
commissioned, Matthew 28.16–20—**p. 1026**
disciples called, Luke 5.1–11—**p. 1059**; 6.12–16—**p. 1061**
replacement for Judas, Acts 1.12–26—**p. 1123**
received Holy Spirit, Acts 2—**p. 1123**
Paul as, 1 Corinthians 9—**p. 1190**; Galatians 1.1–2.10—
p. 1211
foundation of the church, Ephesians 2.19–22—**p. 1220**;
Revelation 21.14—**p. 1325**

AQUILA — husband of Priscilla; co-worker with Paul
and instructor of Apollos
character profile, *"Power Couple"*—**p. 1149**

ARK OF THE COVENANT — the Israelites' sacred chest
containing the tablets of the law
description of, Exodus 25.10–22—**p. 105**
and crossing the Jordan, Joshua 3—**p. 234**
contents of, *"What's In the Ark"*—**p. 174**
represented God's power, 1 Samuel 4–5—**p. 293**
David returns it to Jerusalem, 2 Samuel 6.1–15—**p. 329**;
1 Chronicles 13.1–14—**p. 430**; 15.1–16.6—**p. 430**
reverence for, *"Why Did Uzzah Die?"*—**p. 430**
lost, *"Proof of the Covenant"*—**p. 448**

ART — creative expression such as music, dance,
painting, sculpture, writing, architecture
ordained by God, Exodus 31.1–11—**p. 111**; 35.30–36.2—
p. 116
excellence needed, Psalm 33.1–3—**p. 572**

ARTAXERXES — King of Persia; allowed Ezra to rebuild
Jerusalem temple
character profile, *"Friendly Foreigner"*—**p. 486**

ASAHEL — nephew of David and one of his warriors
character profile, *"Bloody Brothers"*—**p. 428**

ASCENSION — Christ's rising into heaven after the
resurrection
prophesied, Psalm 27—**p. 568**
described, Luke 24.36–53—**p. 1088**; Acts 1.1–11—
p. 1123
related to Pentecost, John 16.5–16—**p. 1113**; Ephesians
4.7–13—**p. 1220**

Assurance of Salvation
— certainty of God's forgiveness and love

built on trust, Psalm 37—**p. 576**
through Christ, Romans 8—**p. 1172**
produced by faith, 2 Timothy 1.8–12—**p. 1252**
achieved by obeying God, 1 John 2.28–3.24—**p. 1295**
achieved by believing God's word, 1 John 5.9–13—
p. 1298

ASTROLOGY — seeking information about human
events from the stars (*see also* WITCHCRAFT)
powerless, Isaiah 47.12–15—**p. 746**
Daniel discredits, Daniel 2—**p. 890**

ATHALIAH — after her son Ahaziah died, she made
herself queen and killed all challengers to the
throne
character profile, *"Live by the Sword . . ."*—**p. 463**

ATHENS
Paul preaching in, *"Flexible Approach"*—**p. 1147**

ATHLETICS
Christianity compared to running, 1 Corinthians
9.24–27—**p. 1191**; Hebrews 12.1–2—**p. 1274**
Christianity compared to wrestling, Ephesians 6.10–18—
p. 1224
competing according to rules, 2 Timothy 2.5—**p. 1252**
training for, *"Athlete in Training"*—**p. 1248**; *"Soldier, Athlete,
Farmer"*—**p. 1253**
in Ephesus, *"Sports and Education"*—**p. 1150**

ATONEMENT — payment for sin; associated with the
Israelites' day of atonement, when a blood
sacrifice was made for the sins of the nation (*see
also* JUSTIFICATION, SALVATION)
by sacrifice, *"The Reason for Sacrifice"*—**p. 127**
Hebrew ritual of, Leviticus 16—**p. 139**

Christ as our, Romans 3.21–26–**p. 1167**; 2 Corinthians 5.14–21–**p. 1203**; Hebrews 9–**p. 1270**; 1 Peter 2.22–25–**p. 1285**; 1 John 1.8–2.2–**p. 1294**

B

BAAL – god of the Phoenicians and Canaanites
worshiped in Israel, 1 Kings 16.29–34–**p. 375**; 2 Kings 17.7–23–**p. 405**; 21.1–9–**p. 410**
defeated by Elijah, 1 Kings 18–**p. 378**; *"Elijah Rubs It In"*– **p. 379**

BABYLON
as symbol of evil, *"An Evil Queen"*–**p. 746**; *"Apocalyptic Arrogance"*–**p. 827**; *"What Is Babylon?"*–**p. 1321**
and archaeology, *"The Throne Room"*–**p. 895**
fall of, *"Sneak Attack"*–**p. 896**
cruelty of, *"Gambling Prizes"*–**p. 922**
prophecies against, Isaiah 13.1–14.23–**p. 710**; Isaiah 21.1–10–**p. 717**; 47.1–15–**p. 745**; Jeremiah 50.1–51.58–**p. 822**

BACKSLIDING – departure from a life of faith in and obedience to God
displeases God, Psalm 78–**p. 601**
a serious sin, Hebrews 6.4–6–**p. 1267**; 10.26–31– **p. 1272**
forgiveness for, Revelation 2.4–5–**p. 1308**; Revelation 3.2–3,15–21–**p. 1309**
examples of:
Israel at Mount Sinai, Exodus 32–**p. 111**
Solomon, 1 Kings 11–**p. 367**
Hymenaeus and Alexander, 1 Timothy 1.19–20– **p. 1246**
in the end times, 2 Timothy 3.1–10–**p. 1253**

BALAAM – man employed by the Moabites to curse the Israelites
character profile, *"Whose Side is Balaam On?"*–**p. 180**
his loyalty, *"Whose Side Is Balaam On?"*–**p. 180**
stopped by God, Numbers 22–24–**p. 178**
prophecy fulfilled, *"Balaam's Prophecy"*–**p. 181**
death of, Numbers 31.1–24–**p. 187**

BAPTISM – a water ritual, used as a spiritual symbol (*see also* HOLY SPIRIT, JOHN THE BAPTIST)
Jesus' baptism, Matthew 3.13–15–**p. 991**
as sign of repentance, Matthew 3.1–12–**p. 991**
as sign of conversion, Matthew 28.16–20–**p. 1026**
in the early church, Acts 2.37–41–**p. 1124**; 8.26–39– **p. 1133**
and the believer's death and resurrection in Christ, Romans 6–**p. 1170**; Colossians 2.11–12–**p. 1232**
of the Holy Spirit, Acts 1.1–8–**p. 1123**; 1 Corinthians 12.12–13–**p. 1193**

BARABBAS – criminal released by Pilate instead of Jesus
set free, Matthew 27.11–26–**p. 1022**

BARGAINING
in the middle East, *"Let's Make a Deal"*–**p. 47**; *"Oriental Bargaining"*–**p. 87**

BARNABAS – disciple; name changed from Joseph to one that means "son of encouragement"
character profile, *"The Encourager"*–**p. 1140**

BATHSHEBA – committed adultery with David and later married him (*see also* DAVID, SOLOMON)
character profile, *"Only Following Orders"*–**p. 334**
life of, 2 Samuel 11.1–12.25–**p. 333**
helped Solomon become king, 1 Kings 1.11–31–**p. 355**

BEAUTY
inner, 1 Samuel 16.1–13–**p. 306**; *"Skin-Deep Beauty"*– **p. 659**; 1 Timothy 2.9–**p. 1246**; 1 Peter 3.1–7– **p. 1285**
of Bathsheba, 2 Samuel 11–**p. 333**
of Esther, Esther 2.1–18–**p. 507**
changing standards of, *"Tan Lines"*–**p. 693**

BEGGARS – *see* POOR

BETRAYAL
by a friend, *"Betrayed by a Friend"*–**p. 588**
of Jesus by Judas, Matthew 26.14–16,47–49–**p. 1019**

BIBLE
as history, *"Selective History"*–**p. 81**; *"Three Kinds of Bricks"*–**p. 84**; *"Unfair Credit?"*–**p. 402**; *"The Ring of Truth"*–**p. 483**; *"Off at War"*–**p. 508**; *"Is Esther Accurate?"*–**p. 513**; *"Bridge Chapters"*–**p. 732**; *"Dating by Emperors"*–**p. 1055**; *"The Linking Book"*–**p. 1120**; *"During the Reign of . . ."*–**p. 1139**; *"Sailing Log"*– **p. 1160**
compilation of, *"Out of Print"*–**p. 177**; *"Using Other Sources"*–**p. 369**; *"The Five Books"*–**p. 599** *"Belong in the Bible?"*–**p. 1102**; *"Sound Familiar?"*–**p. 587**
in praise of, Psalm 19.7–11–**p. 564**; 119.1–176–**p. 629**
used by Satan, *"Satan and the Bible"*–**p. 612**
languages, *"A Change in Language"*–**p. 890**
literary devices in, *"Well-Turned Phrase"*–**p. 820**; *"Structured Passion"*–**p. 831**; *"A Passion for Punning"*– **p. 943**
translation of, *"Lost in Translation"*–**p. 1036**
importance of, 2 Timothy 3.14–17–**p. 1253**
inspired by God, *"Scripture is God-Breathed"*–**p. 1254**; 2 Peter 1.19–21–**p. 1291**
act on, James 1.19–27–**p. 1278**
interpreting, *"A Book Full of Mysteries"*–**p. 1305**; *"Seals and Scrolls"* **p. 1311**; *"Old Testament Echoes"*–**p. 1316**

BITTERNESS – lingering resentment or anger
avoid, Ephesians 4.29–32–**p. 1222**
as sin, James 3.13–18–**p. 1279**

BLASPHEMY – bringing reproach against God and his name
a sin against God, Exodus 20.7–**p. 100**; Leviticus 24.13–23–**p. 148**
Jesus charged with, Matthew 9.1–8–**p. 997**; Matthew 26.57–67–**p. 1021**
against the Holy Spirit, Mark 3.20–30–**p. 1029**

BLESSINGS
material blessings, Deuteronomy 7.12–16–**p. 202**; Psalm 67–**p. 594**
spiritual blessings, Psalm 32–**p. 571**; John 1.14–17– **p. 1091**; Ephesians 1.3–14–**p. 1218**
showers of blessings, Ezekiel 34.26–30 **p. 874**
the Beatitudes, Matthew 5.1–11–**p. 992**; Luke 6.20–22– **p. 1061**

BLOOD – used to represent the life of a creature, often in sacrifices or rituals of cleansing
instructions to Noah about shedding, Genesis 9.1–6– **p. 33**
role in the covenant, *"Covenant Blood"*–**p. 105**
for purification of priests, Exodus 29–**p. 109**
in offerings to God, especially for sin, Leviticus 1,3,4– **p. 123**
the day of atonement, Leviticus 16–**p. 139**

BLOOD OF CHRIST – shed on the cross as Jesus died
wine as sign of, in the Lord's Supper, Matthew 26.27–29–**p. 1020**; 1 Corinthians 11.23–32–**p. 1192**
as payment for sin, Hebrews 9.11–28–**p. 1270**
redemption through, Ephesians 1.7–8–**p. 1218**; 1 Peter 1.18–19–**p. 1284**
reconciliation through, Ephesians 2.11–18–**p. 1219**
cleansing through, 1 John 1.7–10–**p. 1294**

BOASTING
   about God, *"Bragging on God"*—**p. 780**

BODY OF CHRIST
   signified by bread in the Lord's Supper, Mark 14.22–24–
      p. 1045
   as metaphor for church, Romans 12.3–8–**p. 1177**;
      1 Corinthians 12.12–31–**p. 1193**; *"Lessons from the
      Human Body"*—**p. 1193**
   Jesus as the head, Ephesians 1.22–23–**p. 1219**;
      Colossians 1.18–24–**p. 1231**
   completely human, Hebrews 2.14–18–**p. 1265**
   now a glorious body, 1 Corinthians 15.35–49–**p. 1196**;
      Philippians 3.20–21–**p. 1228**

BORN AGAIN – spiritual rebirth or conversion (*see also*
      CONVERSION, SALVATION)
   necessity of, John 3.1–21–**p. 1093**
   marked by holiness, Titus 3.4–8–**p. 1258**; 1 Peter
      1.13–23–**p. 1284**

C

CAIAPHAS – high priest at the time of Jesus' arrest
      and crucifixion
   character profile, *"Collaborators"*—**p. 1107**

CAIN – first son of Adam and Eve; murdered his
      brother Abel
   character profile, *"Blood Brothers"*—**p. 30**
   life of, Genesis 4.1–26–**p. 29**
   a warning to believers, 1 John 3.11–13–**p. 1296**

CALEB – one of 12 spies sent by Moses into promised
      land
   report of, Numbers 13.1–14.38–**p. 169**
   receives Hebron, Joshua 14.1–15–**p. 246**

CALVARY – *see* GOLGOTHA

CANAAN – land God promised to the Israelites; later
      called Palestine
   trade routes in, *"On the Road"*—**p. 36**
   promised to Abraham, Genesis 13.14–17–**p. 37**; Genesis
      15.12–21–**p. 38**
   promised to Isaac, Genesis 26.1–6–**p. 50**
   promised to Jacob, Genesis 28.10–22–**p. 53**
   Moses can't go in, Deuteronomy 34.1–12–**p. 229**
   Joshua conquers, Joshua 1–12–**p. 233**; *"Two Accounts of
      Warfare"*—**p. 244**
   inhabitants punished, *"Is a War Ever Holy?"*—**p. 243**
   inhabitants not eliminated, *"Hints of Failure"*—**p. 248**;
      "Missing an Opportunity"—**p. 249**

CELIBACY – abstaining from marriage
   calling to, Matthew 19.4–12–**p. 1010**
   advantages of, 1 Corinthians 7.32–40–**p. 1189**
   not required, 1 Timothy 4.1–5–**p. 1247**

CHARACTER
   revealed, *"Deeper Meanings"*—**p. 660**

CHEATING
   by Laban, *"Cheater"*—**p. 56**
   by Jacob, *"Misplaced Faith"*—**p. 57**
   forbidden, *"Honest Weight"*—**p. 884**

CHILDREN
   should honor parents, Exodus 20.12–**p. 100**; Ephesians
      6.1–4–**p. 1222**
   praising God, *"Children's Power"*—**p. 557**
   a gift from God, Psalm 127–**p. 636**
   formed by God in the womb, Psalm 139.13–16–**p. 640**
   should listen to instruction, Proverbs 1–**p. 650**
   suffering of, *"Pity the Children"*—**p. 833**
   punishment of, *"Rebel Son"*—**p. 915**
   used as an example of humility, Matthew 18.1–4–
      p. 1009

   blessed by Jesus, Mark 10.13–16–**p. 1039**
   of God through Christ, John 1.12–13–**p. 1091**; Romans
      8.12–17–**p. 1172**; Galatians 3.26–4.7–**p. 1214**

CHOIR
   David's, *"Bad Father, Good Kids"*—**p. 609**; *"And Now, the
      Choir . . ."*—**p. 423**
   used by Ezra and Nehemiah, *"Victory Party"*—**p. 1200**
   heavenly, *"Good News with Bad"*—**p. 1319**

CHRIST – *see* MESSIAH

Christians – name given to followers of Christ

   first called, Acts 11.26–**p. 1139**; *"Naming the New
      Religion"*—**p. 1135**
   how to become, Romans 10.9–13–**p. 1175**
   marks of, Galatians 5.22–26–**p. 1217**

CHRISTIAN LIVING
   over a lifetime, *"A View from Old Age"*—**p. 597**
   struggles, *"Inner Struggles"*—**p. 1171**; *"A Positive and a
      Negative"*—**p. 1191**
   questions about, *"Down-to-earth Problems"*—**p. 1177**;
      "Weak or Strong?"—**p. 1178**; *"When Everything Goes
      Wrong"*—**p. 1190**
   and theology, *"Getting Practical"*—**p. 1232**
   well-rounded, *"The Search for Wholeness"*—**p. 1232**;
      "Words Are Not Enough"—**p. 1275**
   not being idle, *"No Work, No Eat"*—**p. 1242**
   training for, *"Athlete in Training"*—**p. 1248**; *"Soldier, Athlete,
      Farmer"*—**p. 1253**; *"What Is True Faith?"*—**p. 1272**
   leaving, *"Can a Believer Fall Away?"*—**p. 1267**
   problems with money, *"Conflicts of Rich and Poor"*—
      p. 1280
   stages in, *"A Friendly Interruption"*—**p. 1295**

CHURCH – both the local assemblies of Christians and
      the worldwide community of believers
   promised by Christ, Matthew 16.13–20–**p. 1008**
   beginnings of, *"Infant Church"*—**p. 1124**
   growth of, *"The Linking Book"*—**p. 1120**; *"The Secret to the
      Early Church"*—**p. 1128**; *"Crossing Racial Barriers"*—
      p. 1132; *"The Danger in Being a Christian"*—**p. 1133**; *"On
      the Road with the Apostle Paul"*—**p. 1148**
   organization of, *"A Cure for Discrimination"*—**p. 1130**; *"The
      First Church Council"*—**p. 1143**; *"The Hardest Job"*—
      p. 1243; *"Time to Get Organized"*—**p. 1246**
   unity of, Romans 12.3–8–**p. 1177**; Ephesians 4.1–14–
      p. 1220
   founded on Christ and the apostles, 1 Corinthians
      3.1–15–**p. 1185**; Ephesians 2.19–22–**p. 1220**
   as body of Christ, 1 Corinthians 12.12–28–**p. 1193**
   problems in early, *"When Everything Goes Wrong"*—
      p. 1190; *"Diverse People, Diverse Problems"*—**p. 1255**
   locations of early, *"Cities on a Mail Route"*—**p. 1309**
   Christ's relationship to, Ephesians 4.7–16–**p. 1220**
   Christ's message to seven churches, Revelation 2–3–
      p. 1308

CIRCUMCISION – removal of the foreskin in males;
      established by God to signify his relationship with
      the Israelites
   sign of covenant, Genesis 17.9–14–**p. 40**
   symbolic, *"Uncircumcised Hearts"*—**p. 151**; *"Circumcised
      Hearts"*—**p. 772**
   no longer necessary, Romans 4.4–12–**p. 1168**; Galatians
      5.1–12–**p. 1215**
   linked with baptism, Colossians 2.11–12–**p. 1232**

CITIES OF REFUGE
   purpose of, *"Controlling Blood Feuds"*—**p. 191**; *"Cities of
      Refuge"*—**p. 251**

CLEANNESS
laws of clean and unclean, Leviticus 11–15–**p. 132**
cleansing from sin, Psalm 51.1–9–**p. 585**; Hebrews
10.19–22–**p. 1271**; 1 John 1.5–10–**p. 1294**

COLOSSE – city in Asia to which Paul wrote the letter
"Colossians"
Paul's friends in, *"Prominent Names"*–**p. 1234**

Comfort

through silent sharing, *"Keeping Quiet"*–**p. 517**
in grief, Job 2.11–13–**p. 517**; Psalm 23–**p. 567**
in trouble, Psalm 46–**p. 583**; Romans 8.18–39–
p. 1172
when we sin, Psalm 103–**p. 617**
when afraid, Isaiah 41.8–20–**p. 738**
from God, Isaiah 40.1–11–**p. 736**
from Holy Spirit, John 14.1–4,15–27–**p. 1111**
share with others, 2 Corinthians 1.3–7–**p. 1199**;
"Mixing Gentleness with Harshness"–**p. 1216**

COMMUNION – *see* LORD'S SUPPER

COMPASSION – to have pity for and show kindness
to another
of God, Exodus 34.4–7–**p. 113**; Psalm 103.8–12–**p. 617**;
Jonah 3–**p. 939**
commanded by God, Micah 6.6–8–**p. 947**; Galatians
6.1–10–**p. 1217**
of Jesus, Matthew 9.35–38–**p. 998**; 14.13–14–**p. 1006**;
15.29–39–**p. 1007**; John 11.17–44–**p. 1106**
sign of faith, 1 John 3.11–24–**p. 1296**

COMPLAINING
not condemned by God, *"A Shocking Lack of Piety"*–
p. 527

CONFESSION – an acknowledgment of the truth
of Christ:
Peter's, Matthew 16.13–20–**p. 1008**
Thomas's, John 20.24–31–**p. 1119**
as Lord, Romans 10.9–13–**p. 1175**; Philippians
2.9–11–**p. 1227**
as Son of God, 1 John 4.2–3,13–16–**p. 1296**
of sin:
Ezra's, Ezra 9–**p. 487**
David's, Psalm 51–**p. 585**
Isaiah's, Isaiah 6–**p. 705**
Daniel's, Daniel 9–**p. 900**
lost son's, Luke 15.11–32–**p. 1076**
tax collector's, Luke 18.9–14–**p. 1078**
to one another, James 5.16–**p. 1282**
to God, 1 John 1.5–2.2–**p. 1294**

CONFORMITY – to adopt the values and practices of
a group
to evildoers, Proverbs 4.10–19–**p. 652**
to the world, James 4.1–10,17–**p. 1279**

CONSCIENCE – awareness of one's actions as either
right or wrong (*see also* CONFESSION,
FORGIVENESS)
guilty, Psalm 38–**p. 577**
accuses us of sin, Romans 2.12–16–**p. 1166**
be sensitive to others', Romans 14–**p. 1178**;
1 Corinthians 8–**p. 1189**; 10.23–11.1–**p. 1191**
silencing of, *"Loss of Sensitivity"*–**p. 1221**
cleansed by Christ, Hebrews 10.19–22–**p. 1271**

Conversion – to turn away from sin and

to God through repentance and faith (*see also*
BORN AGAIN, PAUL, SALVATION)

result of God's love, Jeremiah 31.3–14–**p. 802**
of Samaritan woman, John 4.1–30,39–42–**p. 1095**
of an Ethiopian eunuch, Acts 8.26–40–**p. 1133**
of Paul, Acts 9.1–25–**p. 1134**; *"Recruiting from the
Opposition"*–**p. 1136**
of Lydia, Acts 16.11–15–**p. 1145**
of a jailer, Acts 16.22–34–**p. 1145**
become new through, 2 Corinthians 5.17–19–
p. 1203
by grace, Ephesians 2.1–10–**p. 1219**

CORINTH
church started, Acts 18.1–17–**p. 1147**
life in, *"The Last Place to Start a Church"*–**p. 1181**;
"Corinthian Slogans"–**p. 1188**
and Paul, *"A Book of Joy and Sadness"*–**p. 1197**; *"A
Mysterious Visit"*–**p. 1201**; *"Paul Has Had Enough"*–
p. 1206

CORNELIUS – first Gentile Christian, a Roman to
whom Paul preached
character profile, *"Least Likely Convert"*–**p. 1138**

COURAGE
the call to be courageous, Joshua 1–**p. 233**
David's, 1 Samuel 17.26–50–**p. 308**
shown by kings of Judah, *"The Great Reformers"*–**p. 461**
Esther's, *"A Profile of Courage"*–**p. 505**
Daniel's, *"Kidnapped"*–**p. 887**
Daniel's three friends, Daniel 3–**p. 892**
the apostles', Acts 4–**p. 1126**; 5.17–42–**p. 1128**

COVENANT – an agreement between two parties; a
solemn promise or vow, especially between God
and people
with Noah, Genesis 9.1–17–**p. 33**
with Abraham, Genesis 15–**p. 37**; 17.1–14–**p. 39**;
"Promises, Promises"–**p. 46**
with Israelites in Old Testament, *"Book of the Covenant"*–
p. 99; *"The Covenant"*–**p. 99**; Exodus 19.3–8,24–
p. 99; *"A Personal Plea"*–**p. 192**; Deuteronomy
29–**p. 223**
benefits of keeping, *"Healthier, Wealthier, and Wiser"*–
p. 205
illustrated by Joshua, *"Blessings and Curses"*–**p. 239**
with David, 2 Samuel 7.1–17–**p. 330**
punishment for breaking, *"Day of Reckoning"*–**p. 782**
new, *"A New Covenant"*–**p. 806**; 2 Corinthians 2.12–
3.18–**p. 1200**; Hebrews 8.7–13–**p. 1269**; 10.1–18–
p. 1271; *"More Perfect"*–**p. 1270**; *"A Vivid
Contrast"*–**p. 1274**
with Israelites in New Testament, *"A Crushing Blow to
Paul"*–**p. 1174**

COVETING – envious desire for something that
belongs to another (*see also* ENVY, GREED)
commandment on, Exodus 20.17–**p. 100**
Achan's, Joshua 7–**p. 237**
Ahab's, 1 Kings 21.1–14–**p. 381**
result of, James 4.1–10–**p. 1279**

CREATION
account of, Genesis 1–2–**p. 25**; *"God at Work"*–**p. 957**
God revealed through, Job 38–**p. 546**; Psalm 19.1–6–
p. 564; Romans 1.18–23–**p. 1165**
God's delight in, Psalm 104–**p. 618**
God's wisdom in, Proverbs 8.12–36–**p. 655**
Christ's work in, John 1.1–14–**p. 1091**; Colossians
1.15–17–**p. 1231**
renewal of, Romans 8.18–25–**p. 1172**

CRITICISM
by friends, *"The Attacks Get Personal"*—**p. 532**
of others, *"Unsettling Proverbs"*—**p. 1165**

CROSS — means by which Jesus died; also used as a metaphor for self-sacrifice
take up your, Mark 8.31—9.1—**p. 1037**
Jesus' crucifixion on, *"Death Without Dignity"*—**p. 1049**; Luke 23.26—49—**p. 1087**
center of preaching, 1 Corinthians 1.18—2.5—**p. 1184**
removed God's curse, Galatians 3.1—14—**p. 1212**
created peace and unity, Ephesians 2.11—18—**p. 1219**

CULTS — *see* FALSE TEACHERS

CULTURE
skills learned from Egypt, *"The Skills of Civilization"*—**p. 105**

CURSING — *see* PROFANITY

CYRUS — Persian king; allowed exiles to return to Jerusalem to rebuild the temple
character profile, *"Good Shepherd?"*—**p. 743**

D

DANCING
David before the ark, 2 Samuel 6.12—23—**p. 330**
in worship, Exodus 15—**p. 94**; Psalm 150—**p. 646**
in celebration, Luke 15.22—27—**p. 1076**
provocative, Matthew 14.1—12—**p. 1005**

DANIEL
character profile, see Introduction to Daniel—**p. 888**
interpreted dreams, Daniel 2—**p. 890**; 4—**p. 893**
in the lions' den, Daniel 6—**p. 896**
not Ezekiel's fellow exile, *"Different Daniel"*—**p. 865**
visions of, *"Long Delay"*—**p. 900**

DARKNESS
dispelled by God, Genesis 1.1—5—**p. 25**
picture of God's judgment, Joel 2.1—2—**p. 920**; Jude 8—13—**p. 1304**
Jesus came to dispel, John 1.1—9—**p. 1091**
symbol of evil, Romans 13.11—14—**p. 1178**; Ephesians 5.1—14—**p. 1222**; 1 Thessalonians 5.1—10—**p. 1238**
not in heaven, Revelation 22.1—5—**p. 1325**

DAVID — Israel's greatest king; associated with many of the psalms (*see also* JONATHAN, SAUL)
character profile, see Introduction to 2 Samuel—**p. 323**
chosen king, 1 Samuel 16—**p. 306**
and Goliath, 1 Samuel 17—**p. 307**
conflict with Saul, *"A Sense of God's Timing"*—**p. 315**
as a mercenary, *"Faking It"*—**p. 321**
as king, *"The Life of King David"*—**p. 322**; *"A Family Record"*—**p. 416**
and Joab, *"Easy on Joab"*—**p. 328**
God's promise to, 2 Samuel 7—**p. 330**; *"The Royal Line"*—**p. 420**; *"Conditional Promise"*—**p. 442**; *"The Imprint of the Master"*—**p. 966**
and Saul's family, *"Saul's Lame Grandson"*—**p. 332**
his love for God, *"What God Values"*—**p. 307**; *"Seeking Guidance"*—**p. 329**; *"David's Great Prayer"*—**p. 442**
and Bathsheba, 2 Samuel 11—12—**p. 333**; *"Adultery and Murder"*—**p. 336**;
results of his sin, *"Sin As a Cancer"*—**p. 342**
and Absalom, *"Absalom, Absalom!"*—**p. 344**
confession of sin, Psalm 51—**p. 585**; *"David's Finest Moment"*—**p. 335**; *"David Caught in the Act"*—**p. 586**
last words of, *"Final Words"*—**p. 350**
Jesus as son of, Matthew 1.1—18—**p. 989**; Luke 1.26—33—**p. 1053**
Jesus of Lord of, Matthew 21.41—45—**p. 1014**

DAY OF ATONEMENT (Yom Kippur)
described and reinterpreted, Leviticus 16—**p. 139**; *"Jewish Holy Days"*—**p. 110**

DAY OF THE LORD — a common Old Testament phrase for God's final victory over evil
as punishment for Israelites, Zephaniah 1.14—2.7—**p. 961**; *"The Day of the Lord"*—**p. 929**
as cleansing the world, Isaiah 24—**p. 720**; *"Beyond Darkness"*—**p. 958**

DEACON — an official in the early church who served the needs of people
established, Acts 6.1—4—**p. 1129**
requirements for, 1 Timothy 3.8—13—**p. 1247**

DEATH
physical:
result of sin, Genesis 3—**p. 27**; Romans 5.12—21—**p. 1170**
God cares about, *"Precious Death"*—**p. 628**
what happens at, *"Life after Death"*—**p. 562**; *"The Afterlife"*—**p. 870**
being unprepared for, Luke 12.13—21—**p. 1072**
victory over, 1 Corinthians 15—**p. 1195**
of Christians, *"The Sleep of Death"*—**p. 1239**
spiritual:
by nature true of everyone, Ephesians 2.1—10—**p. 1219**
to self, John 12.23—26—**p. 1108**
because of sin, *"A Matter of Life and Death"*—**p. 662**; *"Need for a Cure"*—**p. 1167**
to sin, Romans 6.1—23—**p. 1170**
of Lazarus, *"If Only . . ."*—**p. 1106**
of Jesus (*see* BLOOD OF CHRIST, CROSS)
of Stephen, Acts 7—**p. 1130**

DEBORAH — one of Israel's greatest judges and a prophetess
character profile, *"Multi-talented Woman"*—**p. 262**
delivers Israel, Judges 4—**p. 262**
song of, Judges 5—**p. 263**

DEBTS — (*see also* FORGIVENESS, LORD'S PRAYER)
compassion to debtors, Exodus 22.25—27—**p. 102**; *"Ruthless Bill Collectors"*—**p. 927**
warning against, *"Danger in Debt"*—**p. 654**
pay promptly, Romans 13.8—10—**p. 1178**

DEEDS — actions or accomplishments, often in the sense of attempts to please God through moral living (*see also* FAITH)
do not gain salvation, Ephesians 2.1—10—**p. 1219**
outgrowth of faith, *"Given, Not Earned"*—**p. 1219**; James 2.14—26—**p. 1278**; *"Words Are Not Enough"*—**p. 1275**

DELILAH — *see* SAMSON

DELIVERANCE
of Joseph, *"A Forgotten Man"*—**p. 68**
of Israelites, *"Free at Last"*—**p. 632**; *"Day of the Locusts"*—**p. 86**; *"Independence Day"*—**p. 90**
from any problem, *"Worst Case"*—**p. 623**

DEMONS — powerful evil spirits that can possess a person (*see also* EVIL)
driven out, Matthew 8.28—34—**p. 997**; Mark 5.1—10—**p. 1032**; Acts 16.16—19—**p. 1145**; *"Homeless"*—**p. 1065**
ignore teaching of, 1 Timothy 4.1—10—**p. 1247**

DESERT
of Sinai, *"Change of Scenery"*—**p. 96**

DEVIL — *see* SATAN

DISABILITIES
barriers to those with, *"Barriers to the Disabled"*—**p. 1028**

DISCIPLES
of John the Baptist, *"New Recruits"*—**p. 1034**

calling of, *"Gradual Disciples"*—**p. 1092**
training of, *"Training the 12 Disciples"*—**p. 1038**; *"Baffling Thoughts"*—**p. 1039**
doubting the Resurrection, *"Doubting Thomas"*—**p. 1120**
replacing Judas Iscariot, *"Inner Circle"*—**p. 1041**
transforming of, *"A Change of Heart and Mind"*—**p. 1119**; *"A Man Named 'The Rock' "*—**p. 1286**
make them of all nations, Matthew 28.6–20—**p. 1026**
called Christians, Acts 11.26—**p. 1139**

DISCIPLESHIP – the act of following and learning from a teacher, especially Jesus
not waiting, *"Burying His Father"*—**p. 1067**
cost of, Luke 14.25–34—**p. 1075**
evidence of, John 15.1–17—**p. 1112**
result of love, John 21.15–19—**p. 1122**

DISCIPLINE – training that molds, instructs, corrects
by parents, Proverbs 23.13–23—**p. 671**; *"How to Raise Children"*—**p. 670**
by God, *"Like Everybody Else"*—**p. 856**; Hebrews 12.1–13—**p. 1274**
by the church, 1 Corinthians 5—**p. 1187**
by God's word, 2 Timothy 3.14–17—**p. 1253**

DISCOURAGEMENT – (*see also* COMFORT)
overcoming, Joshua 1.1–9—**p. 233**; Psalm 42—**p. 580**; 77.1–15—**p. 601**; John 14.1–27—**p. 1111**; 2 Corinthians 4.7–12,16–18—**p. 1202**; *"For the Discouraged"*—**p. 1216**
of Job, *"Why Keep on Living?"*—**p. 519**
in life, *"Companion Book"*—**p. 686**

DISCRIMINATION – (*see also* RACISM)
against the Israelites, *"New Tyrant in Town"*—**p. 81**
on basis of wealth, *"Play No Favorites"*—**p. 1278**
eliminated in Christ, *"The Original Barbarians"*—**p. 1233**; Ephesians 2.11–18—**p. 1219**

DISEASE – (*see also* HEALING)
cleansing from, *"A Bird Set Free"*—**p. 136**
treatment of, *"Bad Medical Advice"*—**p. 457**

DISOBEDIENCE – (*see also* OBEDIENCE)
Israel's in entering Canaan, *"Imperfect Timing"*—**p. 171**
warnings against, *"Final Warnings"*—**p. 190**; *"A Scent of Doom"*—**p. 223**

DIVORCE
Mosaic law on, Deuteronomy 24.1–4—**p. 217**
God's view of, *"I Hate Divorce"*—**p. 980**
Jesus' teaching on, Matthew 19.1–12—**p. 1010**; Mark 10.2–12—**p. 1039**; *"Teaching on Divorce"*—**p. 1039**
a pardonable sin, John 4.4–42—**p. 1095**
Paul's teaching on, 1 Corinthians 7.10–16—**p. 1188**

Doubt (*see also* FAITH)

of Abraham, Genesis 12.10–20—**p. 36**
of Sarah, Genesis 18.1–15—**p. 40**
of Moses, Exodus 4.1–17—**p. 83**
of Gideon, Judges 6—**p. 264**
of Peter, Matthew 14.22–32—**p. 1006**
overcoming, Mark 9.14–29—**p. 1037**; 11.22–25—**p. 1042**; James 1.2–7—**p. 1277**
of John the Baptist, Luke 7.18–23—**p. 1063**
of Thomas, John 20.24–31—**p. 1119**

DREAMS – (*see also* VISIONS)
of Jacob, Genesis 28.10–22—**p. 53**
interpreted by Joseph, Genesis 37—**p. 64**; 41—**p. 68**
meaning of, *"A Nightmare"*—**p. 695**; *"A Nation of Dreamers"*—**p. 892**
false prophecy through, Jeremiah 23.25–32—**p. 794**; Ezekiel 13.1–9—**p. 848**
interpreted by Daniel, Daniel 2—**p. 890**; 4—**p. 893**
at the birth of Jesus, Matthew 2—**p. 990**

of Pilate's wife, Matthew 27.19—**p. 1022**
in the last days, Acts 2.14–21—**p. 1124**

Drinking Alcohol (*see also* WINE)

warnings about, Proverbs 20.1—**p. 667**; 23.29–35—**p. 671**; Isaiah 5.11–12—**p. 704**; *"The Dangers of Wine"*—**p. 672**; Ephesians 5.18—**p. 1222**
vow against, *"Teetotalers"*—**p. 809**
examples of overindulgence
of Noah, Genesis 9.20—**p. 33**
of Lot, Genesis 19.32–35—**p. 43**
of Ahasuerus, Esther 1.10—**p. 506**
at the Lord's Supper, 1 Corinthians 11.21—**p. 1192**

E

EARTH – (*see also* ECOLOGY)
created by God, Genesis 1.1–25—**p. 25**; *"Ecology Plus"*—**p. 618**
care for, Genesis 1.26–31—**p. 25**
exhibits God's love, Psalm 33.1–11—**p. 572**
not eternal, *"Outlasting the Universe"*—**p. 617**
ages of, *"Three Worlds"*—**p. 1291**
waits for redemption, Romans 8.18–25—**p. 1172**
destruction of, *"The Fate of the Earth"*—**p. 1292**
new, *"New Earth"*—**p. 764**; 2 Peter 3.3–13—**p. 1291**; Revelation 21.1–22.5—**p. 1324**; *"Eden Regained"*—**p. 1325**

ECOLOGY – keeping a proper balance in nature
God's concern for, *"Respect for Nature"*—**p. 215**
appreciation of, *"Ecology Plus"*—**p. 618**

EDOM – *see* Esau

EGYPT
Joseph taken there, Genesis 37—**p. 64**
Israelites moved there, Genesis 39–50—**p. 67**
exodus from, Exodus 1–13—**p. 81**
judgment of, Isaiah 19—**p. 716**; Jeremiah 42—**p. 814**; Ezekiel 29–30—**p. 866**
Jesus taken there, Matthew 2.13–20—**p. 990**

ELDER – a designated leader of the Jewish people and of the church
leaders of the Jewish council, Acts 5.17–42—**p. 1128**
leaders appointed in churches, Acts 14.21–25—**p. 1143**; Titus 1.5–9—**p. 1257**
Paul's farewell speech to, Acts 20.13–38—**p. 1152**
qualifications for, 1 Timothy 3.1–7—**p. 1246**

ELECTION – God's choosing a people for himself
of Abraham, Genesis 12.1–9—**p. 36**
of Israel, Exodus 19.1–6—**p. 99**; Deuteronomy 10.12–13—**p. 205**; Isaiah 41.8–16—**p. 738**
of Jesus' disciples, John 15.9–17—**p. 1112**
of Jacob, Romans 9.6–13—**p. 1173**
of the church, Ephesians 1.3–14—**p. 1218**; 1 Peter 2.1–10—**p. 1284**
make it sure, 2 Peter 1.3–10—**p. 1290**

ELI – a priest and judge of Israel
character profile, *"An End and a Beginning"*—**p. 293**
life of, 1 Samuel 1–4—**p. 289**

ELIJAH – Israelite prophet well known for his confrontation with the priests of Baal (*see also* BAAL, ELISHA)
character profile, *"Miracle Worker"*—**p. 376**
life of, 1 Kings 17–19—**p. 376**; 21—**p. 381**
and Baal, 1 Kings 18.16–46—**p. 378**; *"The Contest"*—**p. 377**
death of, 2 Kings 2—**p. 387**; *"An Obscure Compliment"*—**p. 388**

Eternal Life — life everlasting with God,
which begins at conversion (*see also* BORN
AGAIN, CONVERSION, SALVATION, HEAVEN)

F

Faith — trust in and reliance on God

shown by Ezra, *"Risk of Faith"*—**p. 487**

during suffering, *"When Bad Things Happened to a Good Person"*—p. 513; *"Seeing in the Dark"*—p. 551; *"Refiner's Fire"*—**p. 1284**

living by, *"Beyond Understanding"*—p. 689; *"Whom to Trust?"*—p. 787; Matthew 6.25–34—p. 995; *"Time to Decide"*—p. 1261

during crisis, *"A Time of Crisis"*—**p. 728**

lukewarm, *"When Faith Grows Weary"*—**p. 977**

necessary for salvation, Romans 3.21–5.11—p. 1167; Galatians 2–3—p. 1212; Ephesians 2.1–10—p. 1219

our part in, *"Working with God"*—**p. 1227**

heroes of, Hebrews 11—p. 1272; *"What Is True Faith?"*—p. 1272

shown by deeds, *"Bargain Hunting"*—p. 804; James 2.14–26—p. 1278; *"Words Are Not Enough"*—p. 1275

FAITHFULNESS
of God, Psalm 78—p. 601; Psalm 111—p. 626; Lamentations 3.22–32—**p. 834**

an aspect of the Spirit's fruit, Galatians 5.16–26—**p. 1215**

of Moses, Hebrews 3—**p. 1265**

expected of Christians, Revelation 2.8–11—**p. 1308**

FALSE PROPHETS
used by God, *"Whose Side Is Balaam On?"*—**p. 180**

tests for, *"Testing Prophets"*—**p. 209**

denounced, *"Doglike Prophets"*—**p. 755**

predicting good, *"Greedy Doctors"*—p. 776; *"Whitewash"*—p. 849; *"Plenty of Beer"*—**p. 944**

use of dreams, *"Questionable Dreams"*—**p. 795**

FALSE TEACHERS
avoiding, *"Unequal Yokes"*—**p. 1203**

recognizing, *"Battling the Cults"*—p. 1229; *"Foolish Questions"*—p. 1258; *"A Threat from Within"*—p. 1288; *"Who Were the Gnostics?"*—p. 1297; *"Undesirable Guests"*—p. 1298; *"Watch Out"*—**p. 870**

distorting the truth, *"Words That Get Polluted"*—**p. 1292**

Gnostics, *"Pesky Deceivers"*—**p. 1300**

emperor worship, *"Satan's Throne"*—**p. 1309**

FAME
transience of, Isaiah 14.9–20—**p. 711**

unreliability of, Ezekiel 33.30–32—**p. 872**

unimportant, 1 Corinthians 3.1–23—**p. 1185**

Family
established in Garden of Eden, Genesis 2.18–24—**p. 27**

obligations to, *"A Brother's Duty"*—**p. 66**

quarrels within, *"Family Battles"*—p. 65; *"Family Jealousy"*—**p. 168**

built by God, Psalm 127–128—**p. 636**

of God, *"For the Discouraged"*—p. 1216; Ephesians 2.19–22—**p. 1220**

family relations, Ephesians 5.21–6.4—p. 1222; Colossians 3.18–21—**p. 1233**

FAMINE
in Egypt and Palestine, *"An Unusual Famine"*—**p. 70**

in Israel, Ruth 1.1—p. 284; 1 Kings 17—p. 376; 2 Kings 6.25–8.2—**p. 393**

FASTING — abstinence from food or drink for a period of time, especially for spiritual reasons
at a time of national crisis, 2 Chronicles 20.1–13—p. 459; Esther 4—p. 509; Joel 2.15–17—**p. 921**

true, Isaiah 58—**p. 756**

proper time for, *"Repent for How Long?"*—**p. 971**

Jesus' teaching on, Matthew 6.16–18—**p. 995**

disciples', Acts 13.1–3—p. 1140; 14.23—**p. 1143**

FEAR — reverence and awe for God
commanded, Deuteronomy 6.10–25—p. 201; Ecclesiastes 12.8–14—**p. 689**

good, Psalm 33—**p. 572**

guide to living, *"The Fear of the Lord"*—**p. 656**

the beginning of wisdom, Proverbs 9.10–12—**p. 656**

FEAR — fright or alarm
combating, Psalm 23—p. 567; 56—p. 588; 91—p. 612; Jeremiah 1.4–19—p. 768; Luke 12.4–12—**p. 1072**

comfort in, John 14—**p. 1111**

FELLOWSHIP
expressed in sharing, Acts 2.42–47—p. 1125; 4.24–35—**p. 1127**

with the Holy Spirit, 2 Corinthians 13.14—**p. 1210**

in church, Ephesians 4.17–5.21—**p. 1221**

with God, 1 John 1—**p. 1294**

FESTIVALS — see JEWISH HOLY DAYS

FLATTERY
deceives, *"Flattering Advice"*—p. 342; *"Dangerous Flattery"*—**p. 677**

displeases God, Psalm 12—**p. 559**

FOOD
provided by God, *"No More Free Lunch"*—**p. 236**

provided by Christ, Matthew 14.13–21—p. 1006; John 6—**p. 1098**

glorify God through, 1 Corinthians 10.23–11.1—**p. 1191**

as god, Philippians 3.19—**p. 1228**

FOOL — (see also WISDOM)
in biblical terms, *"The Making of a Fool"*

FOREIGN NATIONS
opposing Judah and Israel, *"Troublesome Neighbors"*—**p. 401**

Israel's alliances with, *"Ahaz's Fateful Decisions"*—p. 403; *"The Siege Lifted"*—p. 810; *"False Hope"*—p. 836; *"The Runaways"*—p. 859; *"Unreliable Egypt"*—**p. 866**

praising God, *"Who are God's People?"*—p. 583; *"House of Prayer"*—**p. 755**

loved by God, *"God Reaches Out"*—**p. 593**

loss of power of, *"The Decline of Tyre"*—**p. 719**

Cyrus, *"Good Shepherd?"*—**p. 743**

cruelty of, *"Most Ruthless"*—**p. 867**

preaching gospel to, *"To All Nations"*—**p. 1044**

entering the church, *"Earthshaking Change"*—**p. 1139**

salvation of, *"Hope for the Gentiles"*—p. 783; *"The Wise Men"*—**p. 991**

judged by God, *"Just What They Deserved"*—**p. 862**

Forgiveness
human, Genesis 33—p. 60; 50.15–21—p. 80; Luke 15.17–24—p. 1076; Acts 7.60—**p. 1132**

God's, Exodus 34.4–7—p. 113; Psalm 103.8–12—p. 617; Micah 7.18–20—p. 949; *"Nobody Like God"*—**p. 948**

absolute, *"An End to Guilt"*—**p. 823**

for sins, Psalm 130—**p. 637**

how often, Matthew 18.21–35—**p.1010**

through Christ, Mark 2.1–11—p. 1028; Colossians 2.6–15—p. 1232; *"A Modern Peace Child"*—**p. 1168**

in the church, 2 Corinthians 2.5–11—**p. 1200**

FREE WILL
Pharaoh's, *"Pharaoh's Hard Heart"*—**p. 87**

Israel's, *"Free Choice"*—**p. 256**

David's, *"Satan or the Lord?"*—**p. 351**

FREEDOM
through obeying, *"Free At Last"*—**p. 632**

G

summarized, *"The Gospel in a Nutshell"*—**p. 1094**; *"What It's There For"*—**p. 1168**; Ephesians 2.1–10—**p. 1219**; Colossians 1.3–23—**p. 1231**

not ashamed of, Romans 1.16–17—**p. 1165**

only one, Galatians 1.6–9—**p. 1211**

GOSSIP

as a sin, Romans 1.29—**p. 1165**; 2 Corinthians 12.20—**p. 1208**

power of, *"Verbal Dynamite"*—**p. 664**

GOVERNMENT

confronting, Exodus 5–14—**p. 83**; 2 Samuel 12.1–14—**p. 335**; 1 Kings 21—**p. 381**

of Israel by judges, *"Freedom Fighters"*—**p. 256**

Israel's form of, *"Why Not a King?"*—**p. 297**

of Israel by theocracy, *"Church and State"*—**p. 439**

David's goals for, *"The Company You Keep"*—**p. 616**

qualities needed by, *"Good Government"*—**p. 673**

Judah lacking, *"Total Anarchy"*—**p. 702**

under tyrants, *"In the Hands of Tyrants"*—**p. 903**

disobedience toward, Acts 5.17–42—**p. 1128**

of Israel by Romans, *"Two Rulers"*—**p. 1157**

duty to, Romans 13.1–7—**p. 1177**; Titus 3.1–2—**p. 1258**; 1 Peter 2.13–17—**p. 1285**

GRACE — the undeserved love and salvation God gives

to Jacob, *"A Stairway to Heaven"*—**p. 54**

to Israel, *"Why the Israelites?"*—**p. 201**; *"The Turning Point"*—**p. 871**

parables of, *"Unfair Pay"*—**p. 1011**; Luke 15.11–31—**p. 1076**

through Christ, Romans 5—**p. 1169**

for salvation, Ephesians 2—**p. 1219**

GREED

defined, *"Never Enough"*—**p. 685**

futility of, Ecclesiastes 5.8–6.12—**p. 685**

as motive in preaching the gospel, *"Gospel Greed"*—**p. 1132**

evil of, Luke 12.13–34—**p. 1072**; 1 Timothy 6.3–10—**p. 1249**; James 5.1–6—**p. 1200**

GRIEF — see COMFORT, DISCOURAGEMENT, SORROW

GUIDANCE

of the Israelites, *"Unmistakable Guidance"*—**p. 165**

sought by Gideon, *"Putting Out a Fleece"*—**p. 266**

from God's word, Psalm 119—**p. 629**; 2 Timothy 3.14–17—**p. 1253**

practical, *"Uncommon Sense"*—**p. 647**

from Holy Spirit, John 16.5–16—**p. 1113**

Guilt (see also **CONFESSION, BACKSLIDING, FORGIVENESS**)

Old Testament guilt offering, Leviticus 5.14–6.7—**p. 126**

overwhelmed by, Psalm 38—**p. 577**

all guilty before God, Romans 3.10–23—**p. 1167**

acknowledging, Ezra 9—**p. 487**; Psalm 32—**p. 571**; 51—**p. 585**; 1 John 1.7–10—**p. 1294**

relief from, 1 John 1.5–2.2—**p. 1294**

H

HANNAH — mother of Samuel

character profile, *"Deepest Longing"*—**p. 291**

her life, 1 Samuel 1–2—**p. 289**

her prayer for a child, *"Sad, Not Drunk"*—**p. 290**

her life a picture of Israel, *"What Leadership Requires"*—**p. 287**

HARMAGEDON

in the valley of Megiddo, *"A Bloody Battlefield"*—**p. 476**

final role, *"The Battle of Harmagedon"*—**p. 1320**

HAPPINESS — see JOY

HEALING

prayers for, 2 Samuel 12.15–25—**p. 335**; 1 Kings 17.7–24—**p. 376**; 2 Kings 5—**p. 356**; 2 Corinthians 12.7–10—**p. 1208**

by Jesus' wounds, *"Healing Wounds"*—**p. 753**

by Jesus, Matthew 8.1–17—**p. 996**; Mark 5—**p. 1032**; Luke 4.38–41—**p. 1059**

by disciples, Acts 3.1–10—**p. 1125**; 5.12–16—**p. 1128**; 14.8–10—**p. 1142**; 28.7–10—**p. 1161**

encouraged, James 5.13–18—**p. 1282**

HEART — figuratively, the center of a person; that which gives direction to a person

obeying with your, *"Law of the Heart"*—**p. 219**

God knows, 1 Samuel 16.1–13—**p. 306**

cleansing of, Psalm 51—**p. 585**

undivided, *"Heart Surgery"*—**p. 608**

life flows from, Proverbs 4.23—**p. 653**

deceitful, Jeremiah 17.9–10—**p. 787**

leads to action, Matthew 12.33–37—**p. 1002**

Heaven — a place of perfect happiness and eternal communion with God

hints of in Old Testament, *"Life after Death"*—**p. 562**

God rules from, Psalm 99—**p. 615**; Isaiah 66.1–2—**p. 764**

new, Isaiah 65.17–25—**p. 764**; Revelation 21–22—**p. 1324**

treasures in, Matthew 6.19–24—**p. 995**

for righteous, Matthew 25.31–46—**p. 1019**

citizenship in, Philippians 3.12–4.1—**p. 1228**

inhabitants of, Hebrews 11—**p. 1272**

visions of, Revelation 4–5—**p. 1310**; 7—**p. 1312**

HELL — a place of eternal punishment and sorrow

hints of in Old Testament, Job 24.21–26—**p. 534**; Psalm 49.10–15—**p. 584**; Daniel 12—**p. 904**

to avoid, Matthew 5.21–30—**p. 993**; Romans 8.1–16—**p. 1172**

for evildoers, Matthew 13.24–30,36–43—**p. 1004**

punishment in, 2 Thessalonians 1.3–12—**p. 1241**; Jude 5–13—**p. 1304**; Revelation 20.11–14—**p. 1324**

keep others from, Jude 17–23—**p. 1304**

HERESIES — see FALSE TEACHERS

HEROD — name of a line of rulers of Palestine

character profile, the Herods: *"Lower Authority"*—**p. 1005**

the Great, Matthew 2—**p. 990**

Antipas, Matthew 14.1–12—**p. 1005**; *"Guards Without Allies"*—**p. 1140**

Agrippa I, Acts 12.1–23—**p. 1139**

HEZEKIAH — king of Judah for 29 years; reopened the temple his father had closed

character profile, *"Cleaning House"*—**p. 469**

life of, 2 Kings 18–20—**p. 406**; *"King of Contradictions"*—**p. 407**

restores worship, 2 Chronicles 29–31—**p. 468**

crisis with Isaiah, Isaiah 36–39—**p. 732**

HISTORY

God working in, *"God's Hand in History"*\MD/**p. 708**; *"Catastrophes Through God's Eyes"*—**p. 718**; *"Like a Wise Farmer"*—**p. 724**; *"A New Song"*—**p. 735**; *"Ransom for the Captives"*—**p. 741**; *"World at War"*—**p. 817**; *"Kidnapped"*—**p. 887**; *"In the Hands of Tyrants"*—**p. 903**; *"The Meaning of a Natural Disaster"*—**p. 917**; *"Light in a Dark Time"*—**p. 940**; *"A Look Behind the Scenes"*—**p. 1317**

as encouragement, *"Why the Cleanup?"*—**p. 420**

Holy Spirit — the third person of the Trinity; also known as the Counselor who is active in the lives of believers (*see also* FRUIT OF THE SPIRIT)

INFERTILITY
Sarah's, Genesis 18.1–15—**p. 40**
Hannah's prayer concerning, 1 Samuel 1.1–2.11—**p. 289**
Elizabeth's, Luke 1.7–25—**p. 1053**

INSPIRATION – the Bible as inspired by the Holy Spirit
(see BIBLE)

INTERCESSION – the prayer of one person for another
examples of, Genesis 18.23–32—**p. 41**; 1 Kings
8.33–51—**p. 364**; Ezra 9.5–15—**p. 487**; Daniel
9.3–19—**p. 900**
of Jesus for us, John 17—**p. 1114**; Romans 8.31–34—
p. 1173; Hebrews 7.24–25—**p. 1268**; 1 John 2.1—
p. 1294
of the Holy Spirit, Romans 8.26–27—**p. 1173**
commanded, 1 Timothy 2.1–2—**p. 1246**; James 5.16—
p. 1282

ISAAC – only son of Abraham by Sarah; born miraculously in their old age
character profile, "Ordinary People"—**p. 44**
birth predicted, Genesis 18.1–15—**p. 40**
as sacrifice, Genesis 22.1–19—**p. 45**
marries Rebekah, Genesis 24—**p. 47**
blesses sons, Genesis 27—**p. 52**; "Sense of Smell"—**p. 53**
death of, Genesis 35.16–29—**p. 62**
chosen by God, Romans 9.6–9—**p. 1173**; Galatians
4.21–31—**p. 1214**

ISAIAH
character profile, see Introduction to Isaiah—**p. 698**
as an author, "Prophet, Poet, and Politician"—**p. 697**
his call as prophet, Isaiah 6—**p. 705**
his reaction to his message, "A Prophet's Pain"—**p. 714**
his political involvement, "Foreign Policy"—**p. 715**; "A Time
of Crisis"—**p. 728**
as historian, "Isaiah the Historian"—**p. 731**

ISHMAEL – son of Abraham by Hagar
character profile, "Second Best"—**p. 39**

ISRAEL – name God gave to Jacob, the father of the Israelite nation (see also JACOB)
given name, Genesis 32.22–32—**p. 60**
twelve sons of, Genesis 49—**p. 76**

ISRAEL – nation of God's chosen people, composed of 12 tribes; its history makes up much of the Old Testament (see also JUDAH)
tribes of, "The Younger Brother"—**p. 76**; "Two for One"—
p. 155
and Egypt, "Final Escape"—**p. 93**
in the desert, "A Place for Everyone"—**p. 156**
census of, "How Many Israelites?"—**p. 157**; "Recount"—
p. 184; "Act of Pride"—**p. 436**
dividing Canaan, "Trouble Ahead"—**p. 189**; "Dividing Up
the Land"—**p. 245**
relationships between tribes, "Explosive Quarrel"—**p. 253**;
"A Soft Answer"—**p. 272**; "A State of Anarchy"—**p. 278**;
"Hanging by a Thread"—**p. 277**; "Unified Front"—**p. 454**;
"North Versus South"—**p. 346**; "Joseph's Heirs"—**p. 424**
size of the kingdom, "How Large Was Israel?"—**p. 360**
enemies of, "Troublesome Neighbors"—**p. 401**; "None
Escape"—**p. 822**
God's presence in, "Red-letter Day"—**p. 431**
relationship to God, "Experience Teaches"—**p. 199**; "A
Lesson from History"—**p. 762**; "God's Patience
Exhausted"—**p. 785**; "The Future of the Jews"—**p. 1176**
splitting into two nations, "The Nation Splits Apart"—
p. 371
governed by judges, "The Bad Old Days"—**p. 604**
promise of being reunited, "North and South Reunited"—
p. 877
images of restoration of, "New Hope"—**p. 917**
in prosperity, "Soft and Fat"—**p. 930**

ISRAEL – Northern Kingdom; the nation of the northern 10 tribes after rebelling against Rehoboam
ruled by Omri, "A Strong, Weak King"—**p. 375**
fall of, "The Great Wars of Israel"—**p. 384**
rulers of, "A Lineup of Rulers"—**p. 1349**
places of worship, "Northern Visitors"—**p. 456**
warnings to, "Tearing God's Heart"—**p. 905**; "Justice!"—
p. 923

J

JACOB – son of Isaac and Rebekah; younger brother of Esau (see also ISRAEL)
character profile, "Con Man in God's Family?"—**p. 52**
life of, Genesis 25–49—**p. 49**
steals birthright, Genesis 25.19–34—**p. 50**
steals blessing, Genesis 27—**p. 52**; "Con Man in God's
Family?"—**p. 52**; "Surface Reconciliation"—**p. 61**
dream of, Genesis 28.10–22—**p. 53**
his marriages, Genesis 29–30—**p. 55**
wrestles with God, Genesis 32—**p. 59**
symbolizing the nation Israel, "Jacob, a Man and a
Country"—**p. 915**

JAMES – son of Zebedee; an apostle and brother of apostle John
character profile, "Inner Circle"—**p. 1041**
call of, Matthew 4.18–22—**p. 992**
at transfiguration, Matthew 17.1–13—**p. 1008**
sought top place in kingdom, Mark 10.35–45—**p. 1040**
death of, Acts 12.1–2—**p. 1139**

JANNES AND JAMBRES
possible identification of, "Who Were Jannes and
Jambres?"—**p. 1253**

JEALOUSY
of God, Exodus 34.14—**p. 114**; Deuteronomy 32.15–22—
p. 226; "Idolatry"—**p. 790**
command against, Romans 13.13—**p. 1178**; 2 Corinthians
12.19–21—**p. 1208**
between people, 1 Corinthians 3.1–23—**p. 1185**

JEHOSHAPHAT – king of Judah
life of, 1 Kings 22—**p. 382**; 2 Chronicles 17–22—**p. 457**

JEPHTHAH – judge of Israel, known for his foolish vow
character of, "A Man Like David" **p. 271**

JEREMIAH
character profile, see Introduction to Jeremiah—
p. 766
as an author, "Jeremiah's Influence"—**p. 414**; "God's
Reluctant Messenger"—**p. 697**
reluctant, "Too Young?"—**p. 768**
warnings ignored, "Don't Worry, Be Happy"—**p. 774**
faithful, "No Social Life"—**p. 787**
motivation, "Fire in His Bones"—**p. 791**
protected by Babylonians, "Influential Prisoner"—**p. 812**
kidnapped, "Closed Minds"—**p. 814**
autobiography, "Autobiography of Pain"—**p. 833**
saved, "Life-saving Prophecy"—**p. 944**

JERICHO – city near the Dead Sea, destroyed by Joshua and later rebuilt
cursed by Joshua, "Cursed City"—**p. 237**; "A Curse from
Joshua"—**p. 376**
fall of, Joshua 5.13–6.27—**p. 236**
Jesus' healings there, Matthew 20.29–34—**p. 1012**

JEROBOAM I – first king of northern kingdom after split
character profile, "Blown Opportunity"—**p. 369**
life of, 1 Kings 11–14—**p. 367**

went to Egypt, Matthew 2–**p. 990**
went to Bethlehem, Luke 2–**p. 1055**

JOSHUA – successor to Moses who led the Israelites into Canaan
character profile, *"Filling Moses' Shoes"*–**p. 255**
spied out Canaan, Numbers 13–14–**p. 169**
commissioned, Numbers 27.12–23–**p. 184**
instructions from Moses, *"A Task for Joshua"*–**p. 220**
his leadership, *"The Difference 40 Years Can Make"*– **p. 230**
his life, *"Filling Moses' Shoes"*–**p. 254**
his farewell, *"Joshua's Farewell"*–**p. 254**

JOSIAH – son of Amon; King of Judah
character profile, *"Last Gasp"*–**p. 412**

Joy

in worshiping God, *"The Joy of the Lord"*–**p. 497**
in salvation, Isaiah 12–**p. 710**; 35–**p. 700**; 1 Peter 1.1–9–**p. 1283**
Jesus' teaching on, Matthew 5.1–12–**p. 992**
for repentance, Luke 15–**p. 1075**
through servanthood, John 13.1–17–**p. 1110**
an aspect of the Spirit's fruit, Galatians 5.16–26– **p. 1215**
always, Philippians 4.4–9–**p. 1228**
in all circumstances, *"Paul's Secret"*–**p. 1228**
in suffering, Colossians 1.24–**p. 1232**; James 1.2–18; 1 Peter 4.12–19; *"Like a Joy-filled Musical"*–**p. 1050**; *"Cheerful Sounds from a Jail Cell"*–**p. 1223**

JUDAH – Southern Kingdom; nation of the southern tribes of Benjamin and Judah that remained loyal to Rehoboam
loyalty of, *"The Nation Splits Apart"*–**p. 371**
invaded by Sennacherib, *"Invasion"*–**p. 473**
fall of, *"The Great Wars of Israel"*–**p. 384**; *"A Kingdom Disappears"*–**p. 415**; *"Total Destruction"*–**p. 828**
fighting with Israel, *"Ahaz's Fateful Decisions"*–**p. 403**
reform in, *"Too Little Too Late"*–**p. 413**
rulers of, *"A Lineup of Rulers"*–**p. 1349**; *"A Brighter Outlook"*–**p. 455**; *"The Great Reformers"*–**p. 461**
extent of its sin, *"Search for an Honest Person"*–**p. 774**; *"Light in a Dark Time"*–**p. 920**
complacency of, *"Practical Atheism"*–**p. 961**

JUDAS ISCARIOT – the disciple who betrayed Jesus
character profile, *"Devil Man"*–**p. 1100**
as betrayer, *"A Name Disgraced"*–**p. 1020**; Matthew 26.47–56–**p. 1020**
death of, Matthew 27.1–10–**p. 1021**; Acts 1.18–19– **p. 1123**
as treasurer, John 12.1–8–**p. 1108**

JUDGING OTHERS
unfairly, *"Unfair Accusation"*–**p. 524**
not to be done, Romans 14.1–13–**p. 1178**; James 4.9–12–**p. 1279**
Jesus' words on, Matthew 7.1–5–**p. 995**
with mercy, James 2.1–13–**p. 1278**

JUDGMENT
God as judge, Psalm 94–**p. 613**
Jesus as judge, Acts 10.34–43–**p. 1138**
God's standards for, *"A Higher Standard"*–**p. 406**
final, Matthew 24.36–25.46–**p. 1017**; 2 Thessalonians 1–2–**p. 1241**; Revelation 18–20–**p. 1321**

JUSTICE
through law, *"A National Law Library"*–**p. 143**
cry for, *"Self-Righteous?"*–**p. 569**; *"Rough Words"*–**p. 590**; *"What about Curses?"*–**p. 643**

God executes, Psalm 146–**p. 645**; *"Just What They Deserved"*–**p. 862**; *"God's Answer to Injustice"*–**p. 949**; *"God at Work"*–**p. 957**
for the oppressed, *"For the Voiceless"*–**p. 679**
through God's servant, *"The Solution"*–**p. 739**
as true worship, Isaiah 58–**p. 756**
injustice condemned, Amos 5–**p. 929**; Micah 6–**p. 947**
God's standards of, *"Justice!"*–**p. 923**; *"A Plumb Line"*– **p. 931**; *"Poetic Justice"*–**p. 933**

JUSTIFICATION – to be freed from guilt or blame
by faith, Romans 3.21–31–**p. 1167**; 4.1–5.11–**p. 1167**; Galatians 2.15–21–**p. 1212**

K

KINDNESS – a hospitable, friendly attitude toward others (*see* HOSPITALITY)
an aspect of the Spirit's fruit, Galatians 5.16–26–**p. 1215**

KING
God's requirements for, *"Prescription for a King"*–**p. 212**
Israel asks for, 1 Samuel 8–**p. 296**
Samuel's comments on, 1 Samuel 12–**p. 301**
as God's servant, *"The First King"*–**p. 299**
limits to power of, *"No King"*–**p. 268**; *"Limits on the King"*–**p. 299**
abuse of power of, *"A King of Excess"*–**p. 367**; *"A Stolen Vineyard"*–**p. 382**; *"Solomon's Forced Labor"*–**p. 446**; *"The Messianic Promise"*–**p. 794**
confusing names of, *"Two Kings, One Name"*–**p. 395**
rejected from tribe of Benjamin, *"Dynasty Rejected"*– **p. 425**
people's view of, *"A Wedding Fit for a King"*–**p. 582**
God as, Psalm 47–**p. 583**; 99–**p. 615**; 1 Timothy 1.15–17–**p. 1246**
Jesus as, *"The Killing of a King"*–**p. 1022**
Jesus on David's throne, Luke 1.26–38–**p. 1053**
Jesus now ruling at God's right hand, Ephesians 1.15–34–**p. 1219**; Hebrews 1.1–12–**p. 1263**

KINGDOM OF GOD (or KINGDOM OF HEAVEN) – wherever God is reigning; also, the people experiencing God's reign
parables of, Matthew 13.1–52–**p. 1002**; 18.10–14,21–35–**p. 1009**; 20.1–16–**p. 1011**; 21.28–46–**p. 1014**; 22.1–14–**p. 1014**; 25.1–46– **p. 1018**
has come in Jesus, Mark 1.14–15–**p. 1027**; Luke 7.18–22–**p. 1063**; 11.14–20–**p. 1070**
nature of, *"What Should a Leader Look Like?"*–**p. 1003**; *"Status-conscious Disciples"*–**p. 1084**
to be handed over to God, 1 Corinthians 15.20–28– **p. 1196**

L

LABAN – brother of Rebekah, father of Rachel and Leah
character profile, *"Cheater"*–**p. 56**

LAMB OF GOD – a title John the Baptist gave to Jesus
removes sin, John 1.29–42–**p. 1092**
receives praise, Revelation 5–**p. 1310**
worthy, *"A Startling Image of Jesus"*–**p. 1311**

LAUGHTER
of Sarah, Genesis 18.1–15–**p. 40**; 21.1–7–**p. 44**
God's, Psalm 2–**p. 554**
time for, Ecclesiastes 3.1–8–**p. 684**

LAW – a set of commandments given by God
concerning the firstborn, *"The Firstborn Principle"*–**p. 92**
given to Moses, Exodus 19.1–24.8–**p. 99**; *"Long-lasting Laws"*–**p. 100**; *"The Covenant"*–**p. 99**

Love

described, 1 Corinthians 13–p. 1194
an aspect of the Spirit's fruit, Galatians 5.13–26–
     p. 1215
of the world, 1 John 2.15–17–p. 1295
God is, 1 John 4.7–21–p. 1296

LUKE – author of the third Gospel; physician who
     traveled with Paul

sources, *"Luke the Historian"*–p. 1053; *"Jesus' Childhood"*–
     p. 1056
emphasis of, *"A Physician Looks at the Poor"*–p. 1060;
     "Severe and Gentle Stories"–p. 1075
travel companion of Paul, Acts 16.10–17–p. 1145; 20.5–
     21.18–p. 1151; 27.1–28.16–p. 1159

LUST – intense desire (*see* SEX)

LYING

by Abraham, *"Abraham's Half-Truth"*–p. 36
law against, Exodus 20.16–p. 100
penalty for, Leviticus 6.1–7–p. 126
by the Gibeonites, *"Tricked!"*–p. 240
by David, *"Disobeying the Law"*–p. 312; *"David's Double
     Game"*–p. 319
to David, *"The Traitor's' Story"*–p. 345
by Peter, Matthew 26.69–74–p. 1021
Satan the father of, John 8.44–p. 1103
by Ananias and Sapphira, *"Deadly Deceit"*–p. 1127
mark of old nature, Ephesians 4.17–5.21–p. 1221

M

MAGIC – *see* ASTROLOGY, WITCHCRAFT

MARK – author of the second Gospel and missionary
     helper to Paul and Barnabas
character profile, *"Slow Starter"*–p. 1144
as author, *"The Anonymous Author?"*–p. 1046

MARRIAGE (*see also* DIVORCE, HUSBAND, LOVE,
     WIFE)
God ordained, Genesis 2.18–25–p. 27; *"The First
     Marriage"*–p. 27
with unbelievers, *"Marrying Foreigners"*–p. 47;
     "Intermarriage"–p. 261; *"The First Sign of Trouble"*–
     p. 273; *"Inconsistent Ethics"*–p. 451; *"Corrupt Leaders"*–
     p. 489
for political reasons, *"Political Marriages"*–p. 396
importance of, *"Whom Should You Marry?"*–p. 669;
     Matthew 19.1–12–p. 1010
joys of, *"An Intoxicating Love"*–p. 680
Jewish customs about, *"More Than Engaged"*–p. 989
Jesus' teaching on, *"No-Fault Divorce?"*–p. 1011
relationship, Ephesians 5.22–33–p. 1222; Colossians
     3.18–19–p. 1233; 1 Peter 3.1–7–p. 1285
Paul's advice on, 1 Corinthians 7–p. 1188

MARTHA AND MARY – sisters of Lazarus; friends of
     Jesus
character profile, *"Doer and Seeker"*–p. 1070
Jesus at home of, Luke 10.38–42–p. 1069
at Lazarus's death, John 11–p. 1106
washed Jesus' feet, John 12.1–8–p. 1108

MARTYR – one who gives up life for the faith
Stephen as, Acts 7–p. 1130
Paul as, *"A Hint of Trials to Come"*–p. 1187; *"A Letter from
     Death Row"*–p. 1254
by Nero, *"Endangered Exiles"*–p. 1285
many examples of, Hebrews 11.35–40–p. 1274;
     Revelation 6.9–11–p. 1312

MARY – mother of Jesus; wife of Joseph
character profile, *"Saying Yes to God"*–p. 1055

Jesus born to, Matthew 1.18–2.23–p. 989; Luke
     1.26–56–p. 1053; 2–p. 1055
concerned for Jesus, Mark 3.20–35–p. 1029; Luke
     2.41–52–p. 1056
requests Jesus' first miracle, John 2.1–11–p. 1093
at crucifixion, John 19.16–27–p. 1117

MARY MAGDALENE – a close friend of Jesus
character profile, *"First to See"*–p. 1118
present at crucifixion, Mark 15.33–41–p. 1048
had been demon-possessed, Luke 8.1–3–p. 1064
first one at empty tomb, John 20.1–18–p. 1118

MATTHEW – author of the first Gospel; left his work
     to follow Jesus; also called Levi
transformed, *"Unpopular Profession"*–p. 997
hosted a dinner for Jesus, Mark 2.13–17–p. 1028

MEDIATOR – someone who helps bring harmony
     between two parties
Jesus as, 1 Timothy 2.1–6–p. 1246; Hebrews 9.11–28–
     p. 1270

MEDITATION – *see* QUIET TIME

MELCHIZEDEK – priest and king
character profile, *"The Twelfth Man"*–p. 625
blessed Abram, Genesis 14.17–20–p. 38
pointed to Christ, Psalm 110–p. 625; Hebrews 5.1–10–
     p. 1266; 7–p. 1267; *"Who is Melchizedek?"*–p. 1268
as example of leader, *"The Twelfth Man"*–p. 625

MEMORIALS
created for future generations, *"Monuments"*–p. 256

MEMORIES
giving hope, *"Fond Memories"*–p. 523; *"Remembering Our
     Past"*–p. 496; *"The Good Old Days"*–p. 709

Mercy

pleading for, Psalm 4–p. 555; Luke 18.9–14–
     p. 1078
of God, Psalm 108.8–12–p. 623; 123–p. 635; *"Too
     Merciful a God?"*–p. 940; Luke 1.46–79–
     p. 1054; Romans 9.15–18–p. 1174
for the merciful, *"A Key Characteristic"*–p. 579;
     James 2.12–13–p. 1278

MESSENGERS
in Persia, *"Pony Express"*–p. 509
of good news, *"Beautiful Feet"*–p. 751
Paul's, *"Mail Carriers"*–p. 1259

MESSIAH – a king and deliverer expected by the
     Jewish people; Christ
precedent for, *"Mystery Man"*–p. 38
promised by God, *"God's Great Promise"*–p. 331; *"Promise
     to David"*–p. 638
meaning of, *"The Messiah in the Psalms"*–p. 554
prophecies concerning, Psalm 2–p. 554; 110–p. 625;
     "The Song of the Cross"–p. 566; *"A Wedding Fit for a
     King"*–p. 582; *"The Suffering Servant"*–p. 752; Isaiah
     9.1–7–p. 707; 11.1–12–p. 709; 53.1–12–p. 751;
     61.1–3–p. 759; Daniel 7.13–14–p. 898; *"Jesus Asks a
     Question"*–p. 1082
as a leader, *"The Twelfth Man"*–p. 625
David's son as, *"A Bridge from Old to New"*–p. 981
Jesus as, Matthew 11.1–6–p. 999; *"The Killing of a King"*–
     p. 1022; *"Short-lived Acceptance"*–p. 1041; *"The Day of
     Execution"*–p. 1048; Luke 4.14–21–p. 1058

MICHAEL – the archangel appointed to guard the
     Jewish people
with Daniel, Daniel 10–p. 901; 12.1–13–p. 904
and war in heaven, Revelation 12–p. 1316

Money

N

"Colorful Language"—**p. 1279**; "Unnatural Botany"—
p. 1176
disasters in, "The Meaning of a Natural Disaster"—**p. 917**
power of, "Doomsday"—**p. 919**

NAZIRITE — Israelite consecrated to God for special
service
examples of, "Well-known Nazirites"—**p. 161**
described, Numbers 6.1–21—**p. 161**; "National
Reminders"—**p. 164**

NEBUCHADNEZZAR — ruler of Babylonian empire
who destroyed Jerusalem and took Jews into
captivity
character profile, "Power and Pride"—**p. 893**
takes Jerusalem, 2 Kings 25.1–26—**p. 414**; 2 Chronicles
36—**p. 477**; Jeremiah 39—**p. 812**
with Daniel, Daniel 1–4—**p. 889**

NEHEMIAH — a leader of the Jews who returned from
exile
character profile, see Introduction to Nehemiah—**p. 490**
life of, "A Man of Action"—**p. 489**
his character, "Politician Without Greed"—**p. 495**; "Never-
ending Task"—**p. 504**

NEIGHBOR
love as yourself, Leviticus 19.18—**p. 142**; Matthew
22.37–40—**p. 1015**; Romans 13.8–10—**p. 1178**
identification of, Luke 10.25–37—**p. 1069**

NICODEMUS — important Pharisee; attracted to Jesus
and his teachings
character profile, "A Reputation at Stake"—**p. 1094**
talks to Jesus, John 3.1–21—**p. 1093**; "A Reputation at
Stake"—**p. 1094**
argues for fair treatment of Jesus, John 7.50–52—
p. 1101
helps in Jesus' burial, John 19.38–42—**p. 1118**

NINEVEH — important city in Assyria
repentance of, Jonah 3–4—**p. 939**
and archaeology, "How Big a City?"—**p. 939**
its defense, "Battle Tactics"—**p. 952**
destruction predicted, Nahum 1–3—**p. 951**; Zephaniah
2.13–15—**p. 961**

NOAH
character profile, "Starting Over"—**p. 32**
ark and flood, Genesis 6–8—**p. 30**
covenant with, Genesis 9—**p. 33**

NUMBERS
as symbols, "Significant Numbers"—**p. 1312**
use of "7", "Dramatic Structure"—**p. 1313**

O

OATHS — see SWEARING

OBEDIENCE
reasons for, "Who Needs Laws?"—**p. 208**
understanding not necessary for, "God's Secrets"—**p. 224**
Israel's entering Canaan, "The Difference 40 Years Can
Make"—**p. 230**
Israel's, after exile, "A People of the Book"—**p. 498**; "The
Prophet Who Got Results"—**p. 963**
essential for Christians, Luke 6.46–49—**p. 1062**
Paul's, "Paul's Legal Battles"—**p. 1151**
to governing authorities, Romans 13.1–7—**p. 1177**
children's, Ephesians 6.1–4—**p. 1222**
in love, 1 John 3.11–24—**p. 1296**

OCCULT — (see also WITCHCRAFT)
avoid, Leviticus 19.26–31—**p. 142**

OFFERING
for the needy in Jerusalem, "No Cheating"—**p. 1152**; Acts
11.27–30—**p. 1139**; Romans 15.23–29—**p. 1179**;
1 Corinthians 16.1–4—**p. 1198**; 2 Corinthians 8–9—
p. 1204

OLD AGE
God's concern for those of, Psalm 71—**p. 597**
value in, Proverbs 16.31—**p. 665**; 20.29—**p. 668**

ONESIMUS — slave who ran away, became a
Christian, and returned to his master
Paul's love for, "Letter to a Slave Owner"—**p. 1259**
pun on name, "No Longer Useless"—**p. 1261**

OPPOSITION
to the returning exiles, "How to Stop God's Work"—**p. 482**
to Nehemiah, "Psychological Warfare"—**p. 495**

ORPHAN
care for, James 1.19–27—**p. 1278**

P

PAIN
reason for, "Pain as a Warning"—**p. 542**; "Pain with a
Purpose"—**p. 765**; "What Suffering Produces"—**p. 1204**
questioning, Job 1–42—**p. 516**; Jeremiah 15.15–21—
p. 786; Habakkuk 1–3—**p. 955**
not always punishment, "Pain as Punishment"—**p. 519**
God works in it for good, Romans 8.28–39—**p. 1173**
producing perseverance, "Productive Pain"—**p. 1277**;
Romans 5.1–5—**p. 1169**
wiped away, Revelation 21.1–4—**p. 1324**

PALESTINE — (see also CANAAN)
conquered by Israel, "Seven-Year Fight"—**p. 246**

PARABLE — a story told to illustrate an idea
use by Jesus foretold, "Speaking in Parables"—**p. 603**
of God's vineyard, "Grapevines"—**p. 605**; "What Can God
Do?"—**p. 703**
Jeremiah's, "Living Parables"—**p. 808**
purpose of, "Stories to Remember"—**p. 1002**; Matthew
13.10–17—**p. 1002**; "Handling Tough Questions"—
p. 1080
lack of in Mark, "Scarce Parables"—**p. 1031**
of the lost son, "Two Lost Brothers?"—**p. 1076**
list of, "Parables of Jesus"—**p. 1344**

PARENTS
honor, Exodus 20.12—**p. 100**
caring for, "Long-lost Relatives"—**p. 313**
lacking discipline, "Bad News for Eli"—**p. 292**; "Vicious
Children"—**p. 337**
as teachers, Proverbs 1.8–9—**p. 650**; 4—**p. 652**; "How to
Raise Children"—**p. 670**
influence on children, "Good Parenting"—**p. 670**; "Playing
Favorites"—**p. 56**
should be obeyed, Ephesians 6.1–4—**p. 1222**; Colossians
3.20–21—**p. 1233**

PASSOVER
reason for its menu, "Fast Food"—**p. 91**
instituted, Exodus 12.1–27—**p. 91**; "Independence Day"—
p. 90
celebrated by Hezekiah, "Delayed Passover"—**p. 470**
celebrated by Josiah, 2 Chronicles 35—**p. 475**
at time of Jesus' death, "Festival Time in Jerusalem"—
p. 1045

PASTOR — one who serves the church in the ministry
of preaching, teaching, and pastoral care
judged by message, "Style or Substance?"—**p. 1207**
gift of, Ephesians 4.1–16—**p. 1220**
lifestyle of, 1 Timothy 3–4—**p. 1246**

instructions for, 2 Timothy 1.8–4.8–**p. 1252**; Titus 1–3–
p. 1257

PATIENCE
of God, Exodus 34.6–**p. 114**; 2 Peter 3.1–9–**p. 1291**
of David, *"A Child with Its Mother"*–**p. 637**
an aspect of the Spirit's fruit, Galatians 5.16–26–**p. 1215**
commanded of Christians, Hebrews 12.1–13–**p. 1274**;
James 5.7–8–**p. 1280**

PAUL – apostle converted after Jesus' resurrection
who had a special mission of bringing the gospel
to the Gentiles; author of many New Testament
letters to new churches (*see also* SAUL)
character profile, *"Turnaround"*–**p. 1166**
teacher of, *"Questions, Anyone?"*–**p. 1174**
converted, Acts 9.1–31–**p. 1134**; *"Recruiting from the
Opposition"*–**p. 1136**; *"Three Versions"*–**p. 1154**
as preacher, *"Visiting Speaker"*–**p. 1141**
first missionary journey, Acts 13.1–14.28–**p. 1140**
second missionary journey, Acts 15.36–18.22–**p. 1144**;
"On the Road with the Apostle Paul"–**p. 1148**; *"A Tough
Audience"*–**p. 1147**; *"Paul at a Crossroads"*–**p. 1184**
third missionary journey, Acts 18.23–19.41–**p. 1148**
his family, *"Paul's Family"*–**p. 1155**
farewell, *"Emotional Farewell"*–**p. 1152**
on trial, *"Paul's Legal Battles"*–**p. 1151**; *"A Trumped-up
Charge"*–**p. 1153**; *"Paul Under Attack"*–**p. 1155**
theology of, *"A Most Demanding Audience"*–**p. 1162**;
"Nuggets of Theology"–**p. 1258**
in Rome, Acts 27.1–28.31–**p. 1159**; *"Rome at Last"*–
p. 1159; *"Second Imprisonment in Rome"*–**p. 1255**
relations with Corinth, *"The Last Place to Start a Church"*–
p. 1181; *"A Book of Joy and Sadness"*–**p. 1197**;
"A Mysterious Visit"–**p. 1201**
his friends, *"Paul's Friends"*–**p. 1180**
his opinions, *"Paul's Personal Opinions"*–**p. 1189**
his sufferings, *"On the Rebound"*–**p. 1199**; *"Paul's Many
Trials"*–**p. 1207**; *"The Thorn in Paul's Flesh"*–**p. 1208**
relations with Galatia; *"Paul's Anguish"*–**p. 1214**
response to critics, *"Paul Has Had Enough"*–**p. 1206**; *"Paul
Fights Back"*–**p. 1215**; *"Paul Defends His Actions"*–
p. 1237
imprisonment, *"Left in Chains"*–**p. 1156**; *"Letters from
Prison"*–**p. 1221**; *"Cheerful Sounds from a Jail Cell"*–
p. 1223; *"A Letter from Death Row"*–**p. 1254**
relations with Philippi, *"Paul's Partners"*–**p. 1225**
relations with Thessalonica, *"What Made Paul
Successful?"*–**p. 1234**
letters by, *"Time on His Hands"*–**p. 1161**; Romans–
p. 1163; 1 and 2 Corinthians–**p. 1182, 1198**;
Galatians–**p. 1210**; Ephesians–**p. 1217**; Philippians–
p. 1224; Colossians–**p. 1230**; *"Familiar Words"*–
p. 1233; 1 and 2 Thessalonians–**p. 1235, 1240**; 1 and
2 Timothy–**p. 1244, 1251**; Titus–**p.** ; Philemon–
p. 1260
letters hard to understand, *"Exactly What Will Happen?"*–
p. 1242
his prayers, *"Reading Between Lines"*–**p. 1220**
his successor, *"Passing the Torch"*–**p. 1250**

Peace

seeking, Psalm 34.11–14–p. 574; Colossians 3.15–
p. 1233; 1 Peter 3.8–12–p. 1285
in the kingdom of God, Isaiah 2.1–5–p. 701; Ezekiel
34.25–31–p. 874
Prince of, Isaiah 9.1–7–p. 707
formula for, *"Perfect Peace"*–p. 722
Jesus gives, John 14.25–27–p. 1112
with God, Romans 5.1–11–p. 1169
with others, Romans 12.18–21–p. 1177

an aspect of the Spirit's fruit, Galatians 5.16–26–
p. 1215
Jesus Christ is, Ephesians 2.14–18–p. 1219
coming from God, Philippians 4.4–9–p. 1228

PENTECOST – Jewish holiday, also called the festival
of weeks
instituted, Leviticus 23.15–21–**p. 147**
Holy Spirit given during, Acts 2–**p. 1123**

PERSECUTION
of prophets in Old Testament, Jeremiah 37–38–**p. 810**;
Matthew 23.29–39–**p. 1016**
rejoice in, Matthew 5.11–12–**p. 992**; Colossians 1.24–
p. 1232; James 1.1–18–**p. 1277**; 1 Peter 4.12–19–
p. 1287
of believers by Saul, *"Altered Mission"*–**p. 1135**
help in, Romans 8.28–39–**p. 1173**
patience in, James 5.7–11–**p. 1280**; 1 Peter 3.8–22–
p. 1285
helping to spread the church, *"The Danger in Being a
Christian"*–**p. 1133**
standing up under, *"Pep Talk"*–**p. 1274**; Hebrews
10.32–40–**p. 1272**
to be expected, *"A Word to the Suffering"*–**p. 1281**
during the ordeal, *"The Great Ordeal"*–**p. 1313**

PERSEVERANCE – standing firm in the faith (*see also*
BACKSLIDING)
commanded for believers, Hebrews 10.26–39–**p. 1272**;
James 1.1–12–**p. 1277**
warnings against backsliding, Hebrews 6.1–6–**p. 1267**;
Revelation 2–3–**p. 1308**
God's help available for, John 10.27–30–**p. 1106**;
Romans 8.31–39–**p. 1173**; Ephesians 6.10–20–
p. 1224; Philippians 1.1–11–**p. 1225**

PETER – originally named Simon; one of the disciples
closest to Jesus (and the one most frequently
mentioned in the Gospels); a strong leader in the
early church
character profile, *"A Man Named 'The Rock' "*–**p. 1286**
his call, Matthew 4.18–22–**p. 992**
his impulsiveness, *"Peter's Highs and Lows"*–**p. 1008**
disowned Christ, Matthew 26.31–75–**p. 1020**; *"Deserted
by His Friends"*–**p. 1085**
distinctive Galilean accent, *"Telltale Accent"*–**p. 1021**
his humility, *"Peter Learns Humility"*–**p. 1037**
Jesus' love for, *". . . and Peter"*–**p. 1049**; *"Do You Love
Me?"*–**p. 1120**
reinstated, John 21–**p. 1120**
in early church, Acts 2.1–5.42–**p. 1123**; *"A Shift from
Peter to Paul"*–**p. 1136**
vision of, Acts 10.1–11.18–**p. 1137**
as source for Gospel of Mark, *"Eyewitness Reports"*–
p. 1033
transformed, *"A Man Named 'The Rock' "*–**p. 1286**
opposing heresy, *"Approaching Death"*–**p. 1290**
and Paul, *"A Fellow Author"*–**p. 1292**

PHARAOH – title of ancient Egyptian rulers
with Joseph, Genesis 39–41–**p. 67**
with Moses, Exodus 1–15–**p. 81**
and God, *" 'Smart' Plagues"*–**p. 88**

PHARISEES – a strict Jewish sect; careful observers of
the law, known for their piety
offended, *"Pharisees Take Offense"*–**p. 1001**
Jesus confronting, Matthew 23–**p. 1016**; Mark 7.1–23–
p. 1035; Luke 11.37–54–**p. 1071**
opposing Jesus, *"Out to Get Jesus"*–**p. 1013**; *"A Double
Bind"*–**p. 1015**; Matthew 16.1–4–**p. 1008**; 22.15–45–
p. 1015
parable concerning, Luke 18.9–14–**p. 1078**
Paul's history with, Acts 23.6–11–**p. 1155**; Philippians
3.2–7–**p. 1227**

Power (*see also* MIRACLES)
of kings, *"Adultery and Murder"*—p. 336
of God, 1 Chronicles 29.10–13–p. 442; *"Chariots of Fire"*—p. 393; *"God Pulls Out the Stops"*—p. 547; *"God's Answer to Injustice"*—p. 949
temporary, *"Another Powerful City"*—p. 953
symbols of, *"Brute Power"*—p. 969
Jesus' perspective on, *"Taste of Power"*—p. 1069
in this world, *"Who Had Real Power?"*—p. 1074
of the gospel, Romans 1.16–17–p. 1165
not to be sought, Philippians 21–11–p. 1226

Q

R

REBELLION

against God, *"When God Was Obvious"*—**p. 104**; *"Forty Years of Misery"*—**p. 152**; *"The Worst Rebellion"*—**p. 169**; *"Children of the Desert"*—**p. 196**

at end of the present age, Matthew 24.4–25—**p. 1017**; 2 Thessalonians 2—**p. 1241**; Revelation 13–14—**p. 1318**

RECONCILIATION — to settle differences; to be in harmony again

of Jacob and Esau, *"Surface Reconciliation"*—**p. 61**

of Joseph and his brothers, *"Family Battles"*—**p. 65**

between people, Matthew 5.23–26—**p. 993**; Philippians 4.2–3—**p. 1228**

to God, *"Looking for an Arbitrator"*—**p. 523**; 2 Corinthians 5.11–6.2—**p. 1202**; Ephesians 2.11–22—**p. 1219**; Colossians 1.15–23—**p. 1231**

REDEEMER — one who frees or rescues another, especially from sin

Boaz as, *"Expensive Bride"*—**p. 287**

God as, Isaiah 54.1–8—**p. 753**; Luke 1.67–69—**p. 1054**

Christ as, Galatians 3.6–14—**p. 1212**; Colossians 1.13–14—**p. 1231**; Hebrews 9.11–14—**p. 1270**; *"A Modern Peace Child"*—**p. 1168**; 1 Peter 1.17–21—**p. 1284**

REHOBOAM — son of Solomon; first king of Judah

character profile, *"A Fool's Answer"*—**p. 453**

life of, 1 Kings 12—**p. 369**; 14—**p. 372**

RELIGION

true, *"Religion at Its Best"*—**p. 757**; *"What God Wants"*—**p. 947**; *"Which One Showed Love?"*—**p. 1069**

mixed, *"How to be Religious Without Pleasing God"*—**p. 912**; *"The New Golden Calf"*—**p. 914**

Paul on Greek religion, Acts 17.22–31—**p. 1147**

combating false, *"Battling the Cults"*—**p. 1229**

pure, James 1.26–27—**p. 1278**

Repentance — to feel sorry for and turn from sins; a common theme of Old Testament prophets

by Israel's kings, *"A Tardy Change of Mind"*—**p. 474**; *"Turnaround"*—**p. 1166**

"Unprecedented Response"—**p. 488**

of David, *"David Caught in the Act"*—**p. 586**

temporary, *"A Superficial Change"*—**p. 770**

call to, *"Before It's Too Late"*—**p. 928**

preached by Jesus, Matthew 4.12–17—**p. 992**; Luke 13.1–5—**p. 1073**

parable concerning, Luke 18.9–14—**p. 1078**

preached by Peter, Acts 2.38–41—**p. 1124**

preached by Paul, Acts 17.22–31—**p. 1147**

described by Paul, 2 Corinthians 7.9–10—**p. 1204**

RESPONSIBILITY

for sin, Ezekiel 18—**p. 853**

accepting, *"No Excuses"*—**p. 1165**

to love others, 1 John 3.11–24—**p. 1296**

REST

day of, Genesis 2.1–3—**p. 26**; Exodus 20.8—**p. 100**

for the land, *"Revenge of the Land"*—**p. 151**

year of, *"A Year of Freedom"*—**p. 501**

in God, Psalm 23—**p. 567**; 62—**p. 591**

for weary, Matthew 11.25–30—**p. 1001**

RESURRECTION

hinted in Old Testament, *"A Promise of Eternal Life"*—**p. 721**; *"Resurrection"*—**p. 905**; Job 19.23–27—**p. 530**; Ezekiel 37.1–14—**p. 876**; Daniel 12.1–2—**p. 904**

foretold, *"Resurrection!"*—**p. 561**; *"Stubbornly Unconvinced"*—**p. 1077**

of Jesus, Matthew 27.57–28.20—**p. 1023**; *"Final Glimpses of Jesus"*—**p. 1086**; *"More Than a Ghost"*—**p. 1125**

Jesus predicts his own, Mark 8.31—**p. 1037**; 9.31—**p. 1038**; 10.33–34—**p. 1040**

of the dead, 1 Corinthians 15—**p. 1195**; *"The Worst Danger of All"*—**p. 1195**; 1 Thessalonians 4.13–18—**p. 1238**

of the body, *"The Body as a Tent"*—**p. 1202**

as proof of God's power, *"Proven Power"*—**p. 1219**; Ephesians 1.15–23—**p. 1219**

spiritual in Christ, Romans 6.1–14—**p. 1170**; Colossians 2.9–15—**p. 1232**; 3.1–17—**p. 1233**

REVENGE — (see also CITIES OF REFUGE)

Joseph not taking, *"Weeping and Terror"*—**p. 73**

of David, *"Paying Back Joab"*—**p. 356**

belongs to God, *"God's Vengeance"*—**p. 227**

on enemies, *"Jehu's Slaughters"*—**p. 398**; do not take, Matthew 5.38–47—**p. 993**; Romans 12.17–21—**p. 1177**

REVERENCE — (see also FEAR)

for God, *"Living With Fire"*—**p. 121**; *"Touch and Die"*—**p. 159**; *"Is God Frightening?"*—**p. 574**

REVELATION — God's disclosure of himself and his truth

in nature, Psalm 19.1–6—**p. 564**; Acts 14.14–17—**p. 1142**; Romans 1.18–23—**p. 1165**

in Jesus Christ, John 1.1–18—**p. 1091**; Hebrews 1—**p. 1263**

in the Bible, 2 Timothy 3.14–17—**p. 1253**; 2 Peter 1.19–21—**p. 1291**

REWARD

everyone according to deeds, Leviticus 26—**p. 150**; Psalm 62.11–12—**p. 592**; Jeremiah 17.10—**p. 787**; 2 Corinthians 5.1–10—**p. 1202**

for evil, *"Short-Run Rewards"*—**p. 599**

for serving God, *"Why Serve God?"*—**p. 981**

in heaven, Matthew 5.3–12—**p. 992**; Mark 10.29–31—**p. 1040**; 1 Corinthians 3.10–15—**p. 1186**

RICHES — see MONEY, POOR, WEALTH

RIGHTEOUSNESS — the state of being perfect, without sin

attribute of God, Psalm 7—**p. 556**; Jeremiah 23.1–6—**p. 793**

rewarded by God, *"Never Abandoned"*—**p. 576**

from God, *"Luther's Gateway"*—**p. 1165**

by faith, *"What God Looks For"*—**p. 38**; *"The Benefits of Faith"*—**p. 572**; *"Righteous by Faith"*—**p. 956**; Romans 4.6–8—**p. 1169**; Galatians 2.15–21—**p. 1212**; Philippians 3.7–11—**p. 1228**

goal of Christian life, Matthew 6.25–34—**p. 995**; 1 Timothy 6.11–16—**p. 1249**; 1 Peter 2.24–25—**p. 1285**

ROCK

God as, Deuteronomy 32.1–4—**p. 226**; Psalm 18—**p. 561**; Isaiah 26—**p. 722**

Peter as, Matthew 16.16–20—**p. 1008**; John 1.35–42—**p. 1092**

Christ as, 1 Corinthians 10.1–4—**p. 1191**; 1 Peter 2.1–10—**p. 1284**

ROME — capital of the Roman empire; ruled Palestine during the time of Christ; a church was started here

Paul travels to, *"Rome at Last"*—**p. 1159**; Acts 27.1–28.31—**p. 1159**

letter (Romans) to church in, *"A Most Demanding Audience"*—**p. 1162**

treatment of Christians in, *"Christians and the Empire"*—**p. 1178**

RUTH— Moabite woman who married Boaz and became an ancestor of Jesus
character profile, *"Character Counts"*—**p. 286**
ethnic background, *"The Worst of Times"*—**p. 285**
friendship with her mother-in-law, *"A Rare Bond of Love"*—**p. 282**
in Jesus' genealogy, Matthew 1.5—**p. 989**

S

SABBATH— a day of worship and rest; traditionally Saturday for Jews
to be kept holy, Exodus 20.8–11—**p. 100**; Ezekiel 20.1–29—**p. 855**
laws concerning, Exodus 31.14–15—**p. 111**; Leviticus 23.1–3—**p. 145**
made for people, Mark 2.23–3.6—**p. 1029**
symbol of eternal rest, Hebrews 4.1–11—**p. 1266**

SACRIFICE— offering of something valuable to God
Cain's and Abel's, Genesis 4.1–5—**p. 29**
Noah's, Genesis 8.20–22—**p. 32**
Abraham's, Genesis 12.1–11—**p. 36**; 22.1–19—**p. 45**
prescribed, Leviticus 1–7—**p. 123**
offered as representative, *"The One for the Many"*—**p. 125**
types of, *"The Reason for Sacrifice"*—**p. 127**
choice of, *"The Very Best for God"*—**p. 145**
Christ as, Isaiah 53—**p. 751**; Hebrews 10—**p. 1271**
our lives as, Romans 12.1–2—**p. 1177**; *"A Better Sacrifice"*—**p. 579**
of praise, *"Sacrifice of Praise"*—**p. 1275**

SADDUCEES— a small but powerful Jewish sect in Christ's time; denied life after death
Jesus warns against, Matthew 16.1–12—**p. 1008**
Jesus confronts, Mark 12.18–23—**p. 1043**
opposed early church, Acts 4.1–22—**p. 1126**; 5.17–42—**p. 1128**
opposed Paul, Acts 23.1–11—**p. 1155**

Salvation— deliverance from danger or evil; especially deliverance from all that separates people from God (*see also* CONVERSION, JUSTIFICATION, REPENTANCE)
available to all, *"Who Can Be Saved?"*—**p. 754**; Romans 10.1–13—**p. 1175**
marked for, *"The Saving Mark"*—**p. 846**
Jesus' mission of, Luke 19.1–10—**p. 1079**
through faith, Acts 16.16–34—**p. 1145**
to be completed at end of time, Romans 5.6–11—**p. 1169**
by grace, Ephesians 2.1–10—**p. 1219**; Titus 3.3–8—**p. 1258**

SAMARITAN— an inhabitant of Samaria; a people held in contempt by the Jews
origin of, *"Scorched-Earth Policy"*—**p. 406**
conflict with returned exiles, Ezra 4–5—**p. 482**; Nehemiah 4–6—**p. 494**
parable of the good, Luke 10.25–37 —**p. 1069**
and the Jews, *"Bridging Differences"*—**p. 1095**
woman with Jesus, John 4.1–42—**p. 1095**

SAMSON— one of the last judges of Israel; a Nazirite known for his physical strength
character profile, *"Samson: A Weakness for Women"*—**p. 274**
life of, Judges 13–16—**p. 273**
and Delilah, Judges 16—**p. 275**; *"Samson: A Weakness for Women"*—**p. 274**
death of, *"Bring the House Down"*—**p. 276**

SAMUEL— last of the judges of Israel
character profile, *"Faithful Leadership"*—**p. 296**
his early years, 1 Samuel 1.1–3.21—**p. 289**
as a prophet, *"Still a Boy"*—**p. 293**
leads Israel, 1 Samuel 5.1–8.22—**p. 294**
with Saul, 1 Samuel 9.1–15.35—**p. 297**
anoints David, 1 Samuel 16.1–13—**p. 306**
his death, 1 Samuel 25.1—**p. 316**
man of faith, Hebrews 11.32—**p. 1273**

SANCTIFICATION— act of God by which a believer conforms more and more to the image of Christ (*see also* HOLY)
Jesus' prayer for, John 17.17–19—**p. 1115**
possible only in Christ, 1 Corinthians 1.1–2—**p. 1184**; 1 Thessalonians 5.16–24—**p. 1240**
by pressing on, Philippians 3.12–4.1—**p. 1228**
Christ's power in, 2 Peter 1.3–11—**p. 1290**

SANHEDRIN— highest Jewish court during Roman times
limits to power, *"Appeal for a Death Penalty"*—**p. 1047**
Jesus before, Matthew 26.57–68—**p. 1021**; John 18—**p. 1115**
apostles before, Acts 4.1–22—**p. 1126**; 5.17–42—**p. 1128**
Paul before, Acts 23.1–11—**p. 1155**

SARAH— wife of Abraham; gave birth to Isaac in her 90s
character profile, *"Who's Laughing?"*—**p. 41**
life of, Genesis 11.29–12.20—**p. 35**; 16.1–18.15—**p. 39**; 21.1–21—**p. 44**; *"The Women of Genesis"*—**p. 54**
death and burial of, Genesis 23.1–20—**p. 46**

SATAN— the enemy of God; also called the devil, Beelzebul
tempts Eve, Genesis 3—**p. 27**
restrained by God, *"The Extent of Satan's Power"*—**p. 516**
torments Job, Job 1–2—**p. 516**
metaphor for, *"Fall of the Day Star"*—**p. 713**
our accuser, Zechariah 3—**p. 969**
tempts Jesus, Matthew 4.1–11—**p. 991**
father of lies, John 8.42–47—**p. 1103**
resist, *"The Armor of God"*—**p. 1223**; 1 Peter 5.8–11—**p. 1287**
children of, 1 John 2.28–3.10—**p. 1295**
war against Christ and the church, Revelation 12—**p. 1316**
final victory over, Revelation 20—**p. 1324**

SAUL— the first king of Israel; became extremely jealous of David
character profile, *"Why Saul Was Rejected"*—**p. 305**
early days as king, 1 Samuel 9–15—**p. 297**
and David, 1 Samuel 16.1–30.31—**p. 306**
failures of, *"Big Ego"*—**p. 303**; *"Why Saul Was Rejected"*—**p. 304**
as a prophet, *"Out of Control"*—**p. 311**
death of, 1 Samuel 31.1–13—**p. 323**

SAUL— persecutor of Christians who later was converted and became Paul the missionary (*see also* PAUL)
persecution and conversion of, Acts 9.1–30—**p. 1134**
name changed to Paul, Acts 13.9—**p. 1141**

SAVIOR— one who rescues from danger or saves; used in connection with Christ (*see also* SALVATION)
prophecy concerning, Isaiah 59.15–21—**p. 758**
Jesus as, Acts 4.1–12—**p. 1126**; 13.13–52—**p. 1141**

SCAPEGOAT
taking the blame, *"Scapegoat"*—**p. 139**

SECOND COMING – the time when Christ will come again as King
Jesus' teaching on, Matthew 24–25–**p. 1017**; John 14.1–4–**p. 1111**; Acts 1.6–8–**p. 1123**
with resurrection, 1 Corinthians 15.12–28–**p. 1196**
unexpected, 1 Thessalonians 4.13–5.11–**p. 1238**
preceded by antichrist, 2 Thessalonians 2–**p. 1241**
reason for delay of, 2 Peter 3–**p. 1291**
preoccupation with, *"Preparing for the End"*–**p. 1238**; *"A Patient Who Didn't Follow Orders"*–**p. 1239**; *"A Book Full of Mysteries"*–**p. 1305**
vision of, Revelation 19–20–**p. 1322**

SECURITY
place of, *"The Hideout"*–**p. 591**
finding, *"Meek Will Inherit"*–**p. 962**; *"Safe Streets"*–**p. 971**
in God, Psalm 91–**p. 612**

SELF-CONTROL
necessary, *"Five Dangerous Responses"*–**p. 677**
an aspect of the Spirit's fruit, Galatians 5.16–26–**p. 1215**
achieving, *"Athlete in Training"*–**p. 1248**
importance of, *"The Need for Self-Control"*–**p. 1279**

SELFISHNESS – *see* AMBITION

SERMON ON THE MOUNT
words of, Matthew 5–7–**p. 992**

SERVANT
servant songs, Isaiah 49.1–6–**p. 747**; 50.4–9–**p. 749**; 52.13–53.12–**p. 751**
Jesus as, Mark 10.35–45–**p. 1040**; Philippians 2.6–11–**p. 1227**; 1 Peter 2.18–25–**p. 1285**
believers as, John 13.1–17–**p. 1110**; Galatians 5.13–26–**p. 1215**
Paul as, 1 Corinthians 9.19–23–**p. 1191**

Sex

God's laws concerning, *"Sex Rules"*–**p. 138**
in religion, *"Child Sacrifice and Sex"*–**p. 141**; *"Fertility Gods"*–**p. 260**; *"Real Prostitution"*–**p. 910**
joy in, Song of Solomon 1–8–**p. 1183**; *"An Intoxicating Love"*–**p. 680**
leading to trouble, *"Sexual Seduction"*–**p. 182**; *"Samson: A Weakness for Women"*–**p. 274**; *"Sin As a Cancer"*–**p. 342**
adulterous, Proverbs 5–**p. 653**; 6.20–7.27–**p. 654**
in marriage, Proverbs 5.15–20–**p. 653**; 1 Corinthians 7.1–7–**p. 1188**
and lust, Matthew 5.27–30–**p. 993**
avoid immoral, 1 Corinthians 6.9–20–**p. 1188**; Colossians 3.5–6–**p. 1233**
call to purity, 1 Thessalonians 4.1–8–**p. 1237**

SHADRACH, MESHACH, AND ABEDNEGO
and Daniel, Daniel 1–**p. 889**
faith of, *"Whether Rescued or Not"*–**p. 893**
in the fiery furnace, Daniel 3–**p. 892**

SHAME
consequence of sin, *"Sin and Shame"*–**p. 27**; Ezra 9.6–15–**p. 487**
Christians need not experience, Psalm 25–**p. 567**; Psalm 34.1–7–**p. 573**; Romans 1.16–17–**p. 1165**; 2 Timothy 1.8–14–**p. 1252**

SHEOL – *see* DEATH

SHEPHERD
comfort of, Psalm 23–**p. 567**
God as, Psalm 80.1–4–**p. 605**; Ezekiel 34–**p. 872**
bad, Jeremiah 23.1–4–**p. 793**
parable of, Matthew 18.12–14–**p. 1009**; Luke 15.3–7–**p. 1075**

at Jesus' birth, Luke 2.8–20–**p. 1055**
Jesus as good, John 10.1–21–**p. 1104**; Hebrews 13.20–21–**p. 1276**; *"A Modern Shepherd"*–**p. 1105**

SICKNESS – *see* DISEASE, HEALING, PRAYER

SILAS – prophet; co-worker with Paul on his second missionary journey
character profile, *"Singing in Prison"*–**p. 1146**

SIN – (*see also* CONFESSION, EVIL, FORGIVENESS, GUILT)
Adam's and Eve's, Genesis 3–**p. 27**
unintentional, *"Ignorance Isn't Bliss"*–**p. 125**
against another person, *"Double Jeopardy"*–**p. 128**
far-reaching results, *"Sin As a Cancer"*–**p. 342**
present in everyone, *"Who Seeks God?"*–**p. 560**
confession of, Psalm 32–**p. 571**; 51–**p. 585**
symbolized, *"Return to the Void"*–**p. 773**
sexual, *"Two Instances of Evil"*–**p. 913**
God's anger with, Romans 1.18–32–**p. 1165**; *"More Sin, More Forgiveness?"*–**p. 1170**
dead to, Romans 5.12–6.23–**p. 1170**
conflict with, Romans 7–**p. 1171**; *"Inner Struggles"*–**p. 1171**; *"Hidden Dangers"*–**p. 1172**
forgiveness of, 1 John 1.5–2.14–**p. 1294**

SINAI – name of the mountain where God talked with Moses; also called Mount Horeb
God appeared to Moses at, Exodus 3–**p. 82**
law given at, Exodus 19–**p. 99**
worshiping golden calf at, Exodus 32–**p. 111**
Elijah at, 1 Kings 19.8–18–**p. 380**

SINGING – (*see also* MUSIC, SONGS)
to the Lord, Ephesians 5.19–21–**p. 1222**; Colossians 3.16–**p. 1233**

SLAVERY
in Egypt, *"Oppressed by Egypt"*–**p. 84**
Israel's laws on, *"Slave Rights"*–**p. 101**
freedom from, Leviticus 25.35–55–**p. 149**; Jeremiah 34.8–22–**p. 807**
to sin, Romans 6.15–23–**p. 1170**; Galatians 4–**p. 1214**
Paul's advice to slaves, Ephesians 6.5–8–**p. 1223**; Colossians 3.22–25–**p. 1233**; 1 Timothy 6.1–2–**p. 1249**
Paul's advice to slave owner, Ephesians 6.19–**p. 1224**; Colossians 4.1–**p. 1234**; *"Letter to a Slave Owner"*–**p. 1259**
Peter's advice on, 1 Peter 2.18–25–**p. 1285**

SLEEP
peaceful, Psalm 3.5–**p. 555**
unable to, *"Sleepless Nights"*–**p. 601**; *"Lying in Bed"*–**p. 630**

SODOM AND GOMORRAH – cities that God destroyed because of wickedness
Lot saved in, Genesis 18.16–19.29–**p. 41**; *"A Catastrophe Sent from God"*–**p. 42**
sin of, Ezekiel 16.44–52–**p. 851**

SOLOMON – third and last king of united Israel; son of David and Bathsheba
character profile, see Introduction to 1 Kings–**p. 353**
becomes king, 1 Kings 1.1–4.34–**p. 355**; *"A Second Coronation"*–**p. 443**
builds temple, 1 Kings 5.1–9.9 –**p. 360**
wisdom of, 1 Kings 3.1–28–**p. 358**; 4.29–34–**p. 360**
his wealth, *"The Man Who Had Everything"*–**p. 352**; *"Prosperity under Solomon"*–**p. 362**
his personality, *"Wise Yet Ruthless"*–**p. 358**
God's anger with, 1 Kings 11.1–43–**p. 367**
and his wives, *"So Many Women"*–**p. 368**
his failures, *"Solomon's Peak"*–**p. 449**
and the Queen of Sheba, *"An Unfounded Rumor"*–**p. 452**

SON OF GOD
prophesied, *"The Son of God"*—**p. 626**
Christ as, Matthew 14.22–36—**p. 1006**
Peter's confession, Matthew 16.13–20–**p. 1008**

SON OF MAN
in Daniel's vision, *"A Son of Man"*—**p. 899**
Jesus as, *"Familiar Title"*—**p. 1308**

SONGS
of Moses, Exodus 15.1–18—**p. 94**; *"A Story for All Time"*—
p. 94
given to Moses, Deuteronomy 31.19–32.43–**p. 225**;
"Mixed Emotions"—**p. 226**
of David, *"David's Psalms"*—**p. 348**
addressed to God, *"Cries from the Heart"*—**p. 551**
at the passover, *"Psalms of the Last Supper"*—**p. 627**
in the New Testament church, Ephesians 5.18–20–
p. 1222; Colossians 3.15–17—**p. 1233**
in heaven, Revelation 5–6—**p. 1310**

SONS OF GOD
in the Old Testament, *"The Sons of God"*—**p. 31**; Psalm
82.6—**p. 606**; *"Among 'the Gods'"*—**p. 606**

SORROW — (*see also* COMFORT, DISCOURAGEMENT,
GRIEF)
God responds to, Exodus 3.1–9—**p. 82**
symbol of, *"Torn Hearts"*—**p. 921**
Jesus experiences, Matthew 26.36–46—**p. 1020**

SOUL — the nonphysical element in humans
(sometimes called "spirit")
in context of death, Ecclesiastes 12.7—**p. 689**; Revelation
6.9–10—**p. 1312**
distinguished from spirit, 1 Thessalonians 5.23—**p. 1240**;
Hebrews 4.12—**p. 1266**
activities of, Deuteronomy 6.1–5—**p. 200**; Psalm 42–
p. 580; 103—**p. 617**; 130—**p. 637**

SPEECH
power of, *"Who Owns Your Lips?"*—**p. 559**; *"Verbal
Dynamite"*—**p. 664**
control of, James 3.1–12—**p. 1279**

SPIRIT – *see* DEMONS, FRUIT OF THE SPIRIT, HOLY
SPIRIT

STARVATION
in Jerusalem, *"Starving to Death"*—**p. 835**

STEALING
command against, Exodus 20.15—**p. 100**; Ephesians
4.28–**p. 1222**
laws about, Exodus 22.1–15—**p. 102**; Leviticus
19.11–13—**p. 141**
robbing God, Malachi 3.8–10—**p. 988**

STEPHEN – the first Christian martyr
character profile, *"Dying to Live"*—**p. 1130**
chosen as deacon, Acts 6.1–7—**p. 1129**
tried and executed, Acts 6.8–8.3–**p. 1129**

STEWARDSHIP – management and accountability for
something that belongs to someone else;
especially human stewardship of God's gifts
parable concerning, Matthew 25.14–30–**p. 1018**
faithful, Luke 12.35–48—**p. 1073**; 16.10–12—**p. 1076**
of time, Ephesians 5.15–16—**p. 1222**

SUBMISSION
because of love for Christ, *"The Key to Submission"*—
p. 1222
of Christians to each other, Ephesians 5.21—**p. 1222**
to government, Romans 13.1–7—**p. 1177**; 1 Peter
2.13–17—**p. 1285**

Success

Lot's in Sodom, *"A Man of Substance"*—p. 42
basis for real, *"Secret of Success"*—p. 233
from God, Proverbs 3–p. 651
true, Matthew 5.1–12—p. 992; *"God and 'How-to-
Succeed' "*—p. 657
parable concerning, Luke 12.13–21—p. 1072
without love, 1 Corinthians 13–p. 1194
from God's perspective, *"Not Ashamed"*–p. 1273

SUFFERING – to endure physical or emotional loss
and pain (*see also* COMFORT,
DISCOURAGEMENT, PAIN)
the problem of, Job 1–42—**p. 516**; *"When Bad Things
Happened to a Good Person"*—**p. 513**; *"What Not to Say
to a Hurting Person"*—**p. 520**; *"When God Seems
Angry"*—**p. 528**; *"What Job Teaches about Suffering"*—
p. 545; *"A Silent Friend Decides to Speak Up"*—**p. 539**;
"Suffering and Sin"—**p. 1103**
God knows our, Psalm 69—**p. 595**
God's presence in, Psalm 73—**p. 598**; *"Pain in
Redemption"*—**p. 803**; *"Only Good Things?"*—**p. 1173**
without God, *"Total Devastation"*—**p. 920**
with Christ, Romans 8.12–17—**p. 1172**; 2 Corinthians
1.5—**p. 1199**; 1 Peter 4.12–19—**p. 1287**
compared to eternal glory, *"Worth the Struggle"*—**p. 1173**;
2 Corinthians 4.16–18 —**p. 1202**
for Christ, Colossians 1.24—**p. 1232**; Hebrews 10.32–39–
p. 1272; Revelation 1—**p. 1308**
benefits of, *"Waiting It Out"*—**p. 1281**; *"A Word to the
Suffering"*—**p. 1281**; *"Radical Shift"*—**p. 1287**
Christ's, 1 Peter 2.13–25—**p. 1285**; *"The Spirits in Prison"*—
p. 1287
for doing right, 1 Peter 3.8–22—**p. 1285**; 4.12–19–
p. 1287

SUICIDE – (*see also* JUDAS ISCARIOT, SAUL)
jailer saved from, Acts 16.22–36—**p. 1145**

SWEARING – taking an oath, making a solemn
promise (*see also* PROFANITY)
Jesus' teaching on, Matthew 5.33–37—**p. 993**
of God by himself, Hebrews 6.13–15—**p. 1267**
James's teaching on, James 5.12—**p. 1281**

SYMBOL
of peace, *"Peace Symbol"*—**p. 32**
of Christ, *"Bronze Snake"*—**p. 177**; *"Last-place Winner"*—
p. 629; *"Jesus as the Vine"*—**p. 1112**; *"Water, Blood, and
Spirit"*—**p. 1298**
of victory, *"Scalps"*—**p. 310**
of humiliation, *"Act of Humiliation"*—**p. 241**; *"Thumbs and
Big Toes"*—**p. 259**; *"David's Bad Conscience"*—**p. 316**
of importance, *"The Apple of Your Eye"*—**p. 655**
of evil, *"Gog and Magog"*—**p. 878**
of ineffectiveness, *"Kicking the Oxgoads"*—**p. 1158**
vine and kingdom of God, Psalm 80.8–18—**p. 605**;
Isaiah 5.1–7—**p. 703**; John 15.1–17—**p. 1112**
of believers, *"A Play on Words"*—**p. 1284**
in Revelation, *"Strange Creatures"*—**p. 1310**; *"Revelation's
Use of Symbols"*—**p. 1315**

T

TABERNACLE – place of worship for Israelites from
the time of the desert experience to the
completion of the temple when Solomon was
king
building instructions, Exodus 25–26—**p. 105**; *"Following
Orders"*—**p. 120**
where God dwells, *"A Portable Cathedral"*—**p. 115**
furnishings of, *"Sacred Furniture"*—**p. 117**

Temptation – something that tests a person's righteousness and strength of character

TRUST – *see* FAITH

TRUTH
worship in, John 4.19–26–**p. 1095**
God's word as, John 7.13–19–**p. 1100**
sets us free, John 8.31–38–**p. 1102**
Jesus is, John 14.5–14–**p. 1111**; *"No Lies"*–**p. 1257**
knowing and walking in, 2 Timothy 2.8–26–**p. 1253**;
    2 John–**p. 1299**; 3 John–**p. 1301**

U

UNBELIEF – (*see also* FAITH)
Abraham's, *"Laughing at God"*–**p. 40**
Israelites', *"Forty Years of Misery"*–**p. 152**

UNCLEANNESS
reason for rules of, *"Of Scallops and Rabbits"*–**p. 134**
law concerning, *"An Invisible Danger"*–**p. 133**; *"Types of Uncleanness"*–**p. 161**

Unity
Israel's need for, *"Hanging by a Thread"*–p. 277; *"The First King"*–p. 299; *"Accent on Unity"*–p. 429
goodness of, Psalm 133–p. 638
Jesus' prayer for, John 17–p. 1114
of early church, Acts 2.42–47–p. 1125; *"Paul the Fund-raiser"*–p. 1180; *"Personality Cults"*–p. 1186; *"Lessons from the Human Body"*–p. 1193; *"No Second-Class Christians"*–p. 1209
absent in Corinth, 1 Corinthians 1–4–p. 1184
symbolized in Lord's Supper, 1 Corinthians 10.16–17–p. 1191; 1 Corinthians 11.17–34–p. 1192
in Christ, Galatians 3.26–28–p. 1214; Ephesians 4.1–16–p. 1220

URIM AND THUMMIM
God's instruction concerning, Exodus 28.30–**p. 108**
given to Aaron and descendants, Leviticus 8.8–**p. 129**;
    Deuteronomy 33.8–11–**p. 228**
after the exile, *"The Need for Guidance"*–**p. 481**

V

VIRGIN BIRTH – the birth of Jesus Christ while his
    mother Mary was a virgin
predicted, Isaiah 7.1–14–**p. 705**
described, Matthew 1.18–25–**p. 989**; Luke 1.26–38–
    p. 1053

VISIONS – revelations; things seen through something
    other than ordinary sight
as guidance, *"Appealing to a Vision"*–**p. 518**
Isaiah's, Isaiah 6–**p. 705**
Ezekiel's, Ezekiel 1–3–**p. 840**; 37.1–14–**p. 876**; *"Dry
    Bones"*–**p. 876**
Daniel's, *"Kidnapped"*–**p. 887**; *"Symbols of Power"*–
    p. 898
in last days, Joel 2.28–32–**p. 922**
Peter's, Acts 10.1–11.18–**p. 1137**
Paul's, Acts 18.9–10–**p. 1147**; 2 Corinthians 12.1–10–
    p. 1208
John's, Revelation 1–22–**p. 1308**

W

WAR – (*see also* PEACE)
reasons for, *"Acts of War"*–**p. 188**; *"Reasons for Warfare"*–
    p. 203; *"Is a War Ever Holy?"*–**p. 243**; *"Old Enemies"*–
    p. 304; *"Comedy of Errors"*–**p. 435**

strategy in, *"War Strategy"*–**p. 238**; *"Battle Strategy"*–
    p. 319
methods of, *"Camel Power"*–**p. 264**; *"Military Setbacks"*–
    p. 259; *"Everyone Watched Goliath"*–**p. 307**; *"Not
    Ready for Chariots"*–**p. 332**
weapons of, *"Advanced Weaponry"*–**p. 244**; *"Deadly
    Rocks"*–**p. 308**
preparing for, *"A Military Hero"*–**p. 334**
hired soldiers in, *"Mercenaries"*–**p. 340**
necessary limits of, *"Limits of a Just War"*–**p. 467**
God's hand in, Psalm 79–**p. 604**; *"World at War"*–**p. 817**
will end, Isaiah 2.1–5–**p. 701**
images from, *"Victory Party"*–**p. 1200**
spiritual, Ephesians 6.10–20–**p. 1224**; Revelation 12–
    p. 1316

WARNINGS
to Judah, *"Prophet, Poet, and Politician"*–**p. 697**; *"Isaiah in
    His Prime"*–**p. 726**
to Christians, *"Like an Angry Letter from Home"*–**p. 1185**;
    "Watch Out"–**p. 870**

WATER
as symbol, *"An Astounding Trade"*–**p. 769**; *"River from the
    Temple"*–**p. 886**; John 4.10–14–**p. 1095**; 7.37–38–
    p. 1101; Revelation 22.1–2–**p. 1325**
importance of, *"Waters of Babylon"*–**p. 825**

WEALTH – (*see also* MONEY, POOR)
distribution of, *"Property Rights"*–**p. 149**
God's hand in, 1 Samuel 2.1–10–**p. 290**
Solomon's, *"The Man Who Had Everything"*–**p. 352**
of the wicked, *"Wicked People Prosper"*–**p. 531**; *"Money
    Can't Buy Life"*–**p. 584**
arrogance in, Amos 6.1–7–**p. 930**; 1 Timothy 6.3–19 –
    p. 1249
Jesus' teaching on, Matthew 19.16–30–**p. 1011**; *"The
    Wealth Barrier"*–**p. 1040**
no favoritism toward those with, James 2.1–13–**p. 1278**
because of obedience, *"Healthier, Wealthier, and Wiser"*–
    p. 205
reasons for, *"What Makes People Poor?"*–**p. 658**
doesn't bring happiness, *"When Life Seems Senseless"*–
    p. 680

WEAPONS – *see* WAR

WEEPING
of Joseph, *"Joseph in Tears"*–**p. 70**
of David, 2 Samuel 1–**p. 324**; 18.19–19.8–**p. 344**
doesn't last, *"One-night Guest"*–**p. 570**
of a woman with Jesus, Luke 7.36–50–**p. 1063**
of Jesus, Luke 19.41–44–**p. 1081**; John 11.1–43–
    p. 1106

WELFARE – (*see also* POOR)
God's programs of, *"A Form of Welfare"*–**p. 142**; *"Tithe to
    the Poor"*–**p. 210**; *"Don't Forget the Poor"*–**p. 1204**;
    "Caring for the Poor"–**p. 285**
in the early church, *"Welfare Mentality"*–**p. 1249**

WIDOW – a woman whose husband is dead; in
    ancient Israel a husband's death usually brought
    poverty and powerlessness
special to God, Exodus 22.22–24–**p. 102**; Deuteronomy
    24.17–22–**p. 218**; *"Poor and Helpless"*–**p. 664**
praised by Jesus, *"Exploiting Widows"*–**p. 1044**
in the church, 1 Corinthians 7.8–9–**p. 1188**; 1 Timothy
    5.3–16–**p. 1247**

WIFE – (*see also* HUSBAND, MARRIAGE)
virtuous, Proverbs 31.10–31–**p. 679**
relationship to husband, Ephesians 5.21–33–**p. 1222**;
    Colossians 3.18–19–**p. 1233**; 1 Peter 3.1–7–**p. 1285**

WILDERNESS – *see* DESERT

Will of God

in suffering, *"What Job Teaches about Suffering"*—p. 545; 1 Peter 4.12–19—p. 1287
submission to, *"The Potter and the Clay"*—p. 788; *"Counseling Surrender"*—p. 798; Matthew 26.36–46—p. 1020; James 4.13–15—p. 1280
Jesus came to do, John 4.34—p. 1095; 6.38—p. 1099; Philippians 2.5–11—p. 1226
discovering, Romans 12.1–8—p. 1177; 1 Thessalonians 4.1–8—p. 1237
everything done in accordance with, Ephesians 1.3–14—p. 1218

WINE (*see also* DRINKING ALCOHOL)

used in Persia, *"The Influence of Wine"*—p. 507
drunkenness from, Proverbs 23.29–35—p. 671
in the Lord's Supper, Matthew 26.17–30—p. 1020
water into, John 2.1–11—p. 1093
for health, 1 Timothy 5.23—p. 1249

WISDOM — practical insight; the skill of living successfully

Solomon's, *"Solomon's Wish"*—p. 359
comes from God, *"A Poem on Wisdom"*—p. 536
begins with fear of the Lord, Psalm 111—p. 626; Proverbs 1.1–7—p. 650
in understanding life, *"Uncommon Sense"*—p. 647
praise of, Proverbs 1.20–4.27—p. 650; 8.1–9.18—p. 655
love of, *"A Lifelong Quest"*—p. 652
in making choices, *"Be Careful"*—p. 662
through listening, *"The Supreme Gift of Wisdom"*—p. 661
spiritual, 1 Corinthians 2.6–16—p. 1184; James 1.5–8—p. 1277

WITCHCRAFT

displeases God, Leviticus 20.6–7—p. 142; Deuteronomy 18.10–12—p. 213; Isaiah 47.10–14—p. 746; Galatians 5.19–21—p. 1215
Saul's consulting of, 1 Samuel 28—p. 319
inadequacy of, Isaiah 8.19–22—p. 706
rejected by early church, Acts 8.9–24—p. 1132; Acts 13.6–12—p. 1141; 19.13–19—p. 1150

WITNESSING — (*see also* EYEWITNESSES)

to God's faithfulness, *"Courtroom Drama"*—p. 741
persistent, *"Group Faith"*—p. 1060
entrusted by God to believers, *"A Picture of Weakness"*—p. 1202; Acts 1.1–11—p. 1123; 10.34–43—p. 1138

WOMEN

creation of, Genesis 1.26–31—p. 25; 2.18–24—p. 27
with the patriarchs, *"The Women of Genesis"*—p. 54
offerings by, *"For Poor People"*—p. 134
rights of, *"Daughters' Rights"*—p. 248
as a judge, *"Deborah"*—p. 262
power of, *"Sexist Attitudes"*—p. 270
as political symbols, *"Women in Politics"*—p. 326; *"No Way Back"*—p. 341; *"After More than a Wife?"*—p. 357
as prophets, 2 Kings 22.14–20—p. 411; Acts 21.8–9—p. 1153; 1 Corinthians 11.2–16—p. 1192
value of, *"Whom Should You Marry?"*—p. 669
helping Jesus, *"Jesus' Support"*—p. 1064
involved in church work, Romans 16.1–2—p. 1180; Philippians 4.2–3—p. 1228
customs concerning, *"Women in Corinth"*—p. 1192
in Christ no male or female, Galatians 3.16–29—p. 1213

WORD OF GOD — (*see also* BIBLE)

as power of creation, Genesis 1—p. 25; Psalm 33.6–9—p. 572; Hebrews 11.1–3—p. 1272

not given for 400 years, *"Worst of All Famines"*—p. 932
our tool against Satan, Matthew 4.1–11—p. 991; Ephesians 6.10–17—p. 1224
Jesus as, John 1.1–18—p. 1091; *"Jesus the Word"*—p. 1092; Revelation 19.13–16—p. 1323
sharper than a sword, Hebrews 4.12–13—p. 1266
as power to regenerate, James 1.18—p. 1278; 1 Peter 1.22–25—p. 1284

Work (*see also* REST, SABBATH)

God's, Genesis 1.1–2.1—p. 25; *"God at Work"*—p. 957; Psalm 46—p. 583; Psalm 104.24–32—p. 619; John 5.16–30—p. 1097
Adam's, Genesis 2.15–20—p. 27; Genesis 3.17–19—p. 28
value of menial, *"Little People"*—p. 438
satisfaction in, Ecclesiastes 2.17–26—p. 683; Isaiah 28.23–29—p. 724
importance of, 2 Thessalonians 3.6–15—p. 1242

WORKS — *see* DEEDS

WORLD — values, ideas, practices, and relationships of the culture-at-large, especially those that are not God-directed

proclaiming gospel to, Matthew 28.16–20—p. 1026
Jesus came to save, John 3.1–21—p. 1093; 2 Corinthians 5.16–21—p. 1203
conforming to, Romans 12.1–8—p. 1177; 1 John 2.15–17—p. 1295
friendship with, James 4.1–12—p. 1279
overcoming, 1 John 5.1–5—p. 1297

WORRY — *see* ANXIETY

WORSHIP — giving reverence and honor to God (*see also* PRAISE, PRAYER)

only God, Exodus 20.4–5—p. 100; Matthew 4.10—p. 992
and the tabernacle, *"Tabernacle Layout"* p. 118
joyful, *"Seven Days of Rejoicing"*—p. 147; Psalm 100—p. 615
commanded, Deuteronomy 6.13–17—p. 201; Matthew 4.10—p. 992
costly, *"The Cost of True Worship"*—p. 352
dishes used in Israel's, *"Gold and Silver Dishes"*—p. 163
foundations of Israel's, *"Hope in a Time of Sorrow"*—p. 433; *"The Way They Worshiped"*—p. 595
David's preparation for, *"Major Enterprise"*—p. 440
through songs, *"Cries from the Heart"*—p. 551; *"Lyrics for the Living God"*—p. 573
true, Amos 5.18–27—p. 929
apathetic, *"When Faith Grows Weary"*—p. 977
in spirit and truth, John 4.20–24—p. 1095
instructions concerning, 1 Corinthians 11–14—p. 1192
in heaven, Revelation 5—p. 1310; 7—p. 1312

Y

YOUTH — (*see also* CHILDREN)

remember God in, Ecclesiastes 11.7–12.7—p. 689
will see visions, Joel 2.28–32—p. 922; Acts 2.13–36—p. 1124
not unqualified for leadership, *"Too Young for the Job?"*—p. 1247
set an example in, 1 Timothy 4.11–16—p. 1247

Z

ZACCHAEUS – a tax collector from Jericho
meets Jesus, Luke 19.1–10–**p. 1079**

ZECHARIAH – priest; father of John the Baptist
character profile, "End of an Era"–**p. 1053**

ZEDEKIAH – son of Josiah; puppet king of Judah for
Nebuchadnezzar
character profile, "The Bitter End"–**p. 415**

ZERUBBABEL – leader of first group of exiles to return
to Jerusalem
led Jews back, Ezra 2–**p. 480**

reinstituted worship of God, Ezra 3–**p. 481**
helped rebuild the temple, Ezra 4.1–5–**p. 482**; Ezra 5–
p. 483; Haggai 1.1–12–**p. 965**; Zechariah 4.1–9–
p. 970

ZION – one of the hills on which Jerusalem stood; also
used to refer to all Jerusalem, to the Jewish
people, or to heaven (see also HEAVEN,
JERUSALEM)
David captures, 2 Samuel 5.6–16–**p. 329**
as heaven, Psalm 9–**p. 557**; Hebrews 12.22–29–
p. 1275
the whole city of Jerusalem, Psalm 48–**p. 583**

The Student Bible, NRSV

Notes written and edited by *Philip Yancey and Tim Stafford*

Project management and editorial by *Anne McGuinness (1994), Michael Vander Klipp (1996)*

Interior design by *Sharon Wright, Belmont, MI*

Cover design by *Steve Allen, Snellville, GA*

Interior proofreading by *Peachtree Editorial and Proofreading Service, Peachtree City, GA*

Interior typesetting by *Auto-Graphics, Inc., Pomona, CA*

Printing and binding by *Quebecor Printing Hawkins, New Canton, TN*

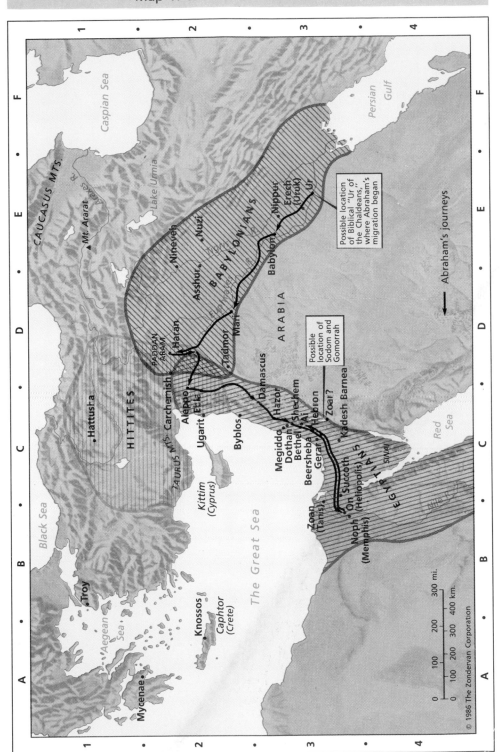

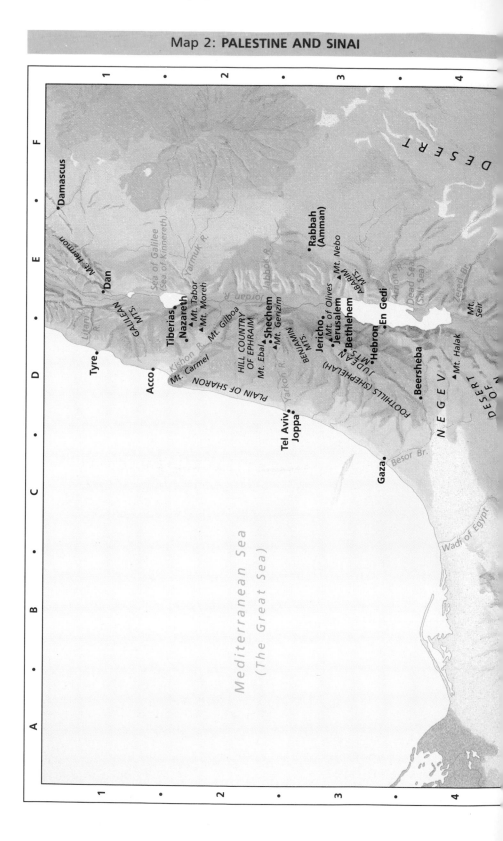

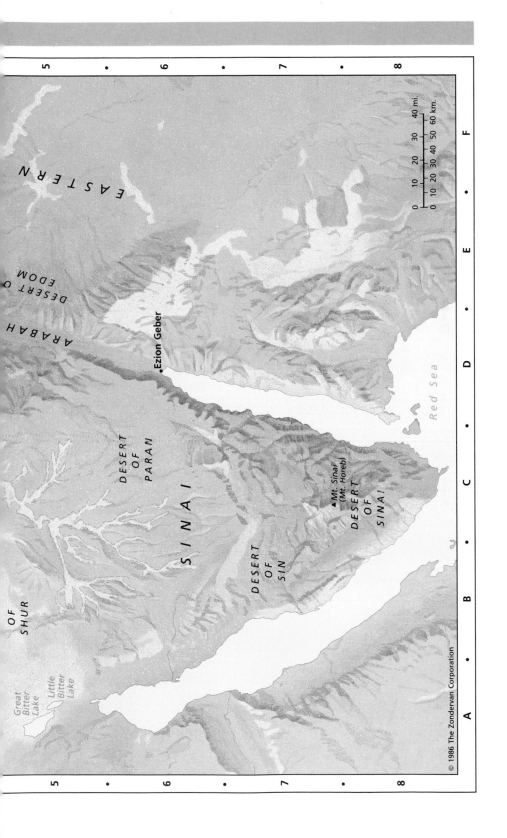

EASTERN

DESERT OF EDOM

ARABAH

•Ezion Geber

DESERT OF PARAN

S I N A I

DESERT OF SIN

▲Mt. Sinai (Mt. Horeb)

DESERT OF SINAI

Red Sea

OF SHUR

Great Bitter Lake

Little Bitter Lake

0   10   20   30   40 mi.
0 10 20 30 40 50 60 km.

© 1986 The Zondervan Corporation

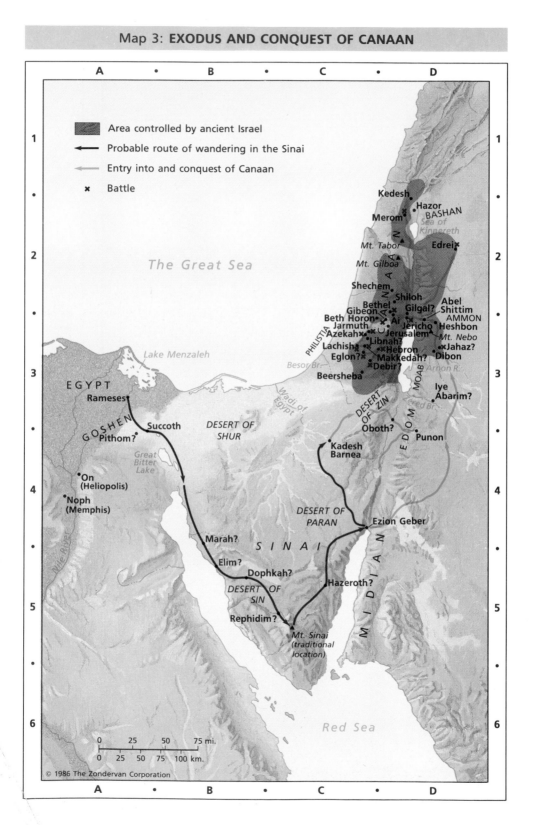

Map 3: EXODUS AND CONQUEST OF CANAAN

Area controlled by ancient Israel
Probable route of wandering in the Sinai
Entry into and conquest of Canaan
× Battle

The Great Sea

Kedesh
Hazor
Merom
BASHAN
Sea of Kinnereth
Mt. Tabor
Edrei
Mt. Gilboa
Shechem
Shiloh
Bethel
Abel
Gibeon
Gilgal?
Shittim
Beth Horon
Ai
AMMON
Jarmuth
Jericho
Heshbon
Azekah
Jerusalem
Mt. Nebo
Lachish
Libnah?
Jahaz?
Eglon?
Hebron
Dibon
Makkedah?
Debir?
Beersheba
MOAB
Arnon R.
DESERT OF ZIN
Iye
Abarim?
Sered Br.
Oboth?
Punon

Lake Menzaleh

Besor Br.

Wadi of Egypt

PHILISTIA

CANAAN

EGYPT
Rameses
GOSHEN
Pithom?
Succoth
DESERT OF SHUR
On (Heliopolis)
Great Bitter Lake
Noph (Memphis)
Nile River
DESERT OF PARAN
Ezion Geber
EDOM
Marah?
S I N A I
MIDIAN
Elim?
Dophkah?
Hazeroth?
DESERT OF SIN
Rephidim?
Mt. Sinai (traditional location)
Kadesh Barnea

Red Sea

0   25   50   75 mi.
0   25   50   75   100 km.

© 1986 The Zondervan Corporation

Map 4: LAND OF THE TWELVE TRIBES

Cities of refuge
• Other cities

Damascus

ARAM

Mt. Hermon

Litani R.

Pharpar R.

Ijon

Tyre

Dan

Kedesh

ASHER

NAPHTALI

Hazor

Acco

Cabul

Merom

EAST

The Great Sea

Rimmon

Sea of Kinnereth

Golan

Ashtaroth

ZEBULUN

Mt. Tabor

Yarmuk R.

MANASSEH

Dor

Mt. Moreh

Edrei

Megiddo

ISSACHAR

Taanach

Jezreel

Ramoth Gilead

Beth Shan

MANASSEH

Jabesh Gilead

Samaria

Tirzah

Mt. Ebal

Jabbok R.

Mahanaim?

Mt. Gerizim

Shechem

Succoth

Aphek

Shiloh

Jazer?

Joppa

EPHRAIM

GAD

Rabbah

DAN

Mizpah

Bethel

AMMON

Gezer

Gibeon

BENJAMIN

Gilgal

Ashdod

Kiriath Jearim

Jericho

Heshbon

Bezer

Ekron

Jerusalem

Mt. Nebo

Ashkelon

Gath

Beth Shemesh

Bethlehem

REUBEN

Lachish

Hebron

Gaza

Eglon?

En Gedi

Dibon

JUDAH

Salt Sea

Arnon

Aroer

Gerar

Ziklag

Beersheba

MOAB

Hormah

SIMEON

Zered Br.

EDOM

0   10   20   30 mi.
0 10 20 30 40 km.

© 1986 The Zondervan Corporation

Map 5: KINGDOM OF DAVID AND SOLOMON

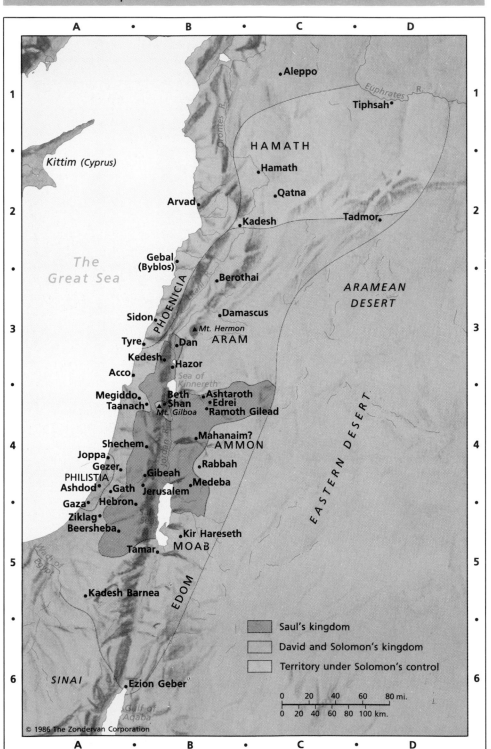

Aleppo

Tiphsah

Euphrates R.

Orontes R.

HAMATH

Hamath

Kittim (Cyprus)

Qatna

Arvad

Tadmor

Kadesh

The Great Sea

Gebal (Byblos)

Berothai

ARAMEAN DESERT

Sidon

PHOENICIA

Damascus

Mt. Hermon

Tyre

Dan

ARAM

Kedesh

Hazor

Acco

Sea of Kinnereth

Megiddo

Beth Shan

Ashtaroth

Taanach

Mt. Gilboa

Edrei

Ramoth Gilead

Mahanaim?

Shechem

AMMON

Joppa

Gezer

Rabbah

PHILISTIA

Gibeah

Jordan R.

EASTERN DESERT

Ashdod

Gath

Medeba

Jerusalem

Gaza

Hebron

Ziklag

Beersheba

Kir Hareseth

Tamar

MOAB

Wadi of Egypt

Kadesh Barnea

EDOM

Saul's kingdom

David and Solomon's kingdom

Territory under Solomon's control

SINAI

Ezion Geber

0   20   40   60   80 mi.

0 20 40 60 80 100 km.

Gulf of Aqaba

© 1986 The Zondervan Corporation

Map 6: PROPHETS IN ISRAEL AND JUDAH

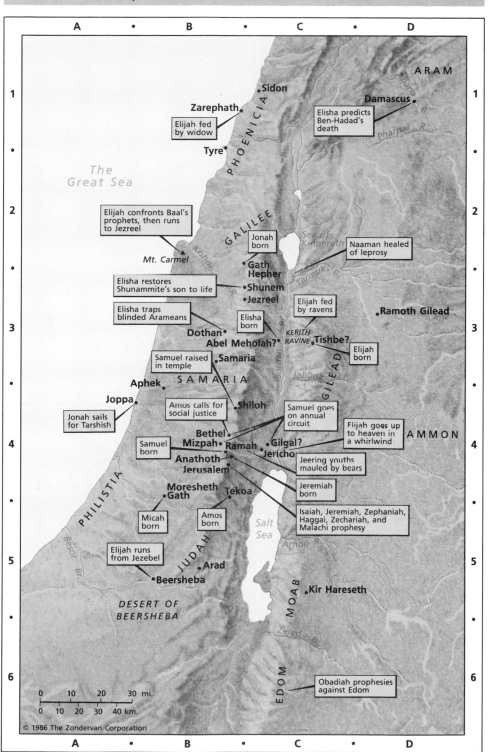

ARAM

Sidon

Damascus

Elisha predicts
Ben-Hadad's
death

Zarephath

Elijah fed
by widow

PHOENICIA

Tyre

The
Great Sea

Elijah confronts Baal's
prophets, then runs
to Jezreel

GALILEE

Jonah
born

Sea of
Kinnereth

Naaman healed
of leprosy

Mt. Carmel

Kishon R.

Gath
Hepher

Elisha restores
Shunammite's son to life

Shunem

Jezreel

Yarmuk R.

Elijah fed
by ravens

Ramoth Gilead

Elisha traps
blinded Arameans

Elisha
born

KERITH
RAVINE

Tishbe?

Elijah
born

Dothan

Abel Meholah?

Samaria

GILEAD

Jordan R.

Jabbok R.

Samuel raised
in temple

SAMARIA

Aphek

Joppa

Amos calls for
social justice

Shiloh

Samuel goes
on annual
circuit

Jonah sails
for Tarshish

Bethel
Mizpah

Ramah

Gilgal?

Jericho

Elijah goes up
to heaven in
a whirlwind

AMMON

Samuel
born

Anathoth
Jerusalem

Jeering youths
mauled by bears

Moresheth
Gath

Tekoa

Jeremiah
born

PHILISTIA

Micah
born

Amos
born

Salt
Sea

Arnon R.

Isaiah, Jeremiah, Zephaniah,
Haggai, Zechariah, and
Malachi prophesy

Besor Br.

Elijah runs
from Jezebel

JUDAH

Arad

Kir Hareseth

MOAB

Beersheba

DESERT OF
BEERSHEBA

Zered Br.

EDOM

Obadiah prophesies
against Edom

| 0 | 10 | 20 | 30 mi. |

| 0 | 10 | 20 | 30 | 40 km. |

© 1986 The Zondervan Corporation

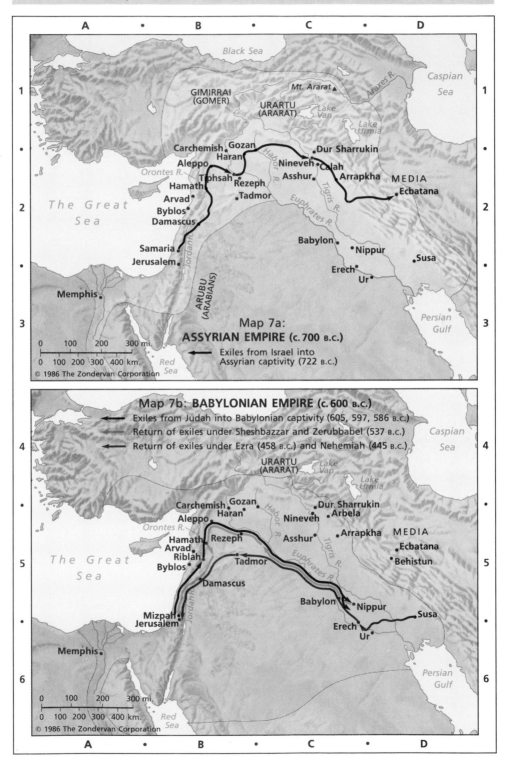

Map 7a: ASSYRIAN EMPIRE (c. 700 B.C.)

→ Exiles from Israel into Assyrian captivity (722 B.C.)

© 1986 The Zondervan Corporation

Map 7b: BABYLONIAN EMPIRE (c. 600 B.C.)

→ Exiles from Judah into Babylonian captivity (605, 597, 586 B.C.)
Return of exiles under Sheshbazzar and Zerubbabel (537 B.C.)
→ Return of exiles under Ezra (458 B.C.) and Nehemiah (445 B.C.)

© 1986 The Zondervan Corporation

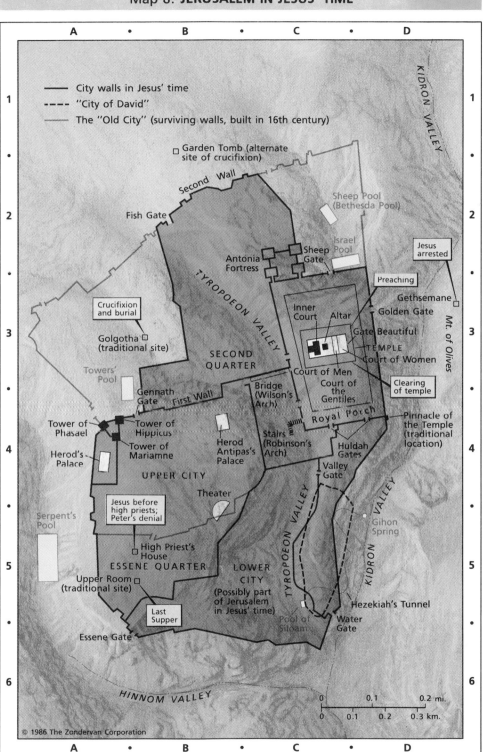

Map 8: JERUSALEM IN JESUS' TIME

City walls in Jesus' time
"City of David"
The "Old City" (surviving walls, built in 16th century)

KIDRON VALLEY

Garden Tomb (alternate site of crucifixion)

Second Wall

Sheep Pool (Bethesda Pool)

Fish Gate

Israel Pool

Jesus arrested

Antonia Fortress

Sheep Gate

Preaching

Gethsemane

Crucifixion and burial

Inner Court   Altar

Golden Gate

Gate Beautiful

Mt. of Olives

Golgotha (traditional site)

TEMPLE
Court of Women

TYROPOEON VALLEY

SECOND QUARTER

Court of Men

Towers' Pool

Bridge (Wilson's Arch)

Court of the Gentiles

Clearing of temple

Gennath Gate

First Wall

Royal Porch

Pinnacle of the Temple (traditional location)

Tower of Phasael

Tower of Hippicus

Stairs (Robinson's Arch)

Huldah Gates

Herod's Palace

Tower of Mariamne

Herod Antipas's Palace

Valley Gate

UPPER CITY

Theater

TYROPOEON VALLEY

KIDRON VALLEY

Jesus before high priests; Peter's denial

Serpent's Pool

Gihon Spring

High Priest's House

ESSENE QUARTER

LOWER CITY
(Possibly part of Jerusalem in Jesus' time)

Upper Room (traditional site)

Hezekiah's Tunnel

Last Supper

Pool of Siloam

Water Gate

Essene Gate

HINNOM VALLEY

0   0.1   0.2 mi.
0   0.1   0.2   0.3 km.

© 1986 The Zondervan Corporation

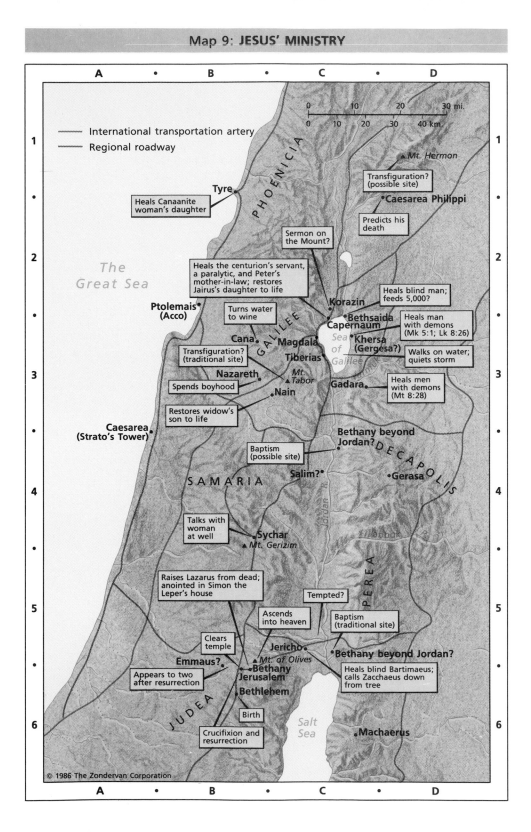

International transportation artery
Regional roadway

0   10   20   30 mi.
0   10   20   30   40 km.

Mt. Hermon

PHOENICIA

Transfiguration?
(possible site)

Caesarea Philippi

Tyre

Heals Canaanite
woman's daughter

Predicts his
death

Sermon on
the Mount?

Heals blind man;
feeds 5,000?

The
Great Sea

Heals the centurion's servant,
a paralytic, and Peter's
mother-in-law; restores
Jairus's daughter to life

Korazin

Ptolemais
(Acco)

Turns water
to wine

GALILEE

Bethsaida
Capernaum

Heals man
with demons
(Mk 5:1; Lk 8:26)

Cana

Magdala

Sea
of
Galilee

Khersa
(Gergesa?)

Transfiguration?
(traditional site)

Tiberias

Walks on water;
quiets storm

Nazareth

Mt.
Tabor

Gadara

Heals men
with demons
(Mt 8:28)

Spends boyhood

Nain

Restores widow's
son to life

Caesarea
(Strato's Tower)

Bethany beyond
Jordan?

DECAPOLIS

Baptism
(possible site)

SAMARIA

Salim?

Gerasa

Talks with
woman
at well

Sychar

Mt. Gerizim

PEREA

Raises Lazarus from dead;
anointed in Simon the
Leper's house

Tempted?

Ascends
into heaven

Baptism
(traditional site)

Clears
temple

Jericho

Emmaus?

Mt. of Olives

Bethany beyond Jordan?

Appears to two
after resurrection

Bethany
Jerusalem

Heals blind Bartimaeus;
calls Zacchaeus down
from tree

Bethlehem

JUDEA

Birth

Salt
Sea

Machaerus

Crucifixion and
resurrection

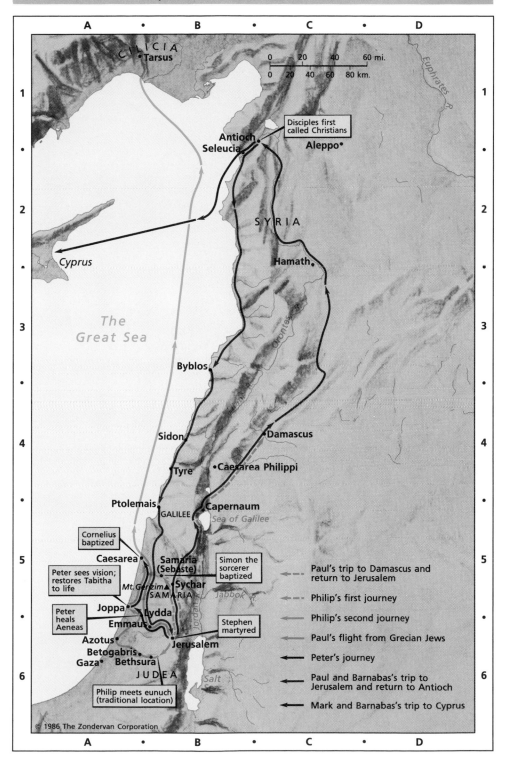

Map 10: APOSTLES' EARLY TRAVELS

CILICIA
Tarsus

0 20 40 60 mi.
0 20 40 60 80 km.

Disciples first
called Christians

Antioch
Seleucia

Aleppo

S Y R I A

Cyprus

Hamath

The
Great Sea

Byblos

Damascus

Sidon

Tyre

Caesarea Philippi

Ptolemais

Capernaum

GALILEE

Sea of Galilee

Cornelius
baptized

Caesarea

Samaria
(Sebaste)

Simon the
sorcerer
baptized

Peter sees vision;
restores Tabitha
to life

Mt. Gerizim

Sychar

SAMARIA

Jabbok r.

Peter
heals
Aeneas

Joppa

Lydda

Emmaus

Stephen
martyred

Azotus

Betogabris

Jerusalem

Gaza

Bethsura

J U D E A

Salt

Philip meets eunuch
(traditional location)

© 1986 The Zondervan Corporation

Euphrates R.

Orontes r.

Jordan r.

**Paul's trip to Damascus and
return to Jerusalem**

Philip's first journey

Philip's second journey

Paul's flight from Grecian Jews

Peter's journey

**Paul and Barnabas's trip to
Jerusalem and return to Antioch**

Mark and Barnabas's trip to Cyprus

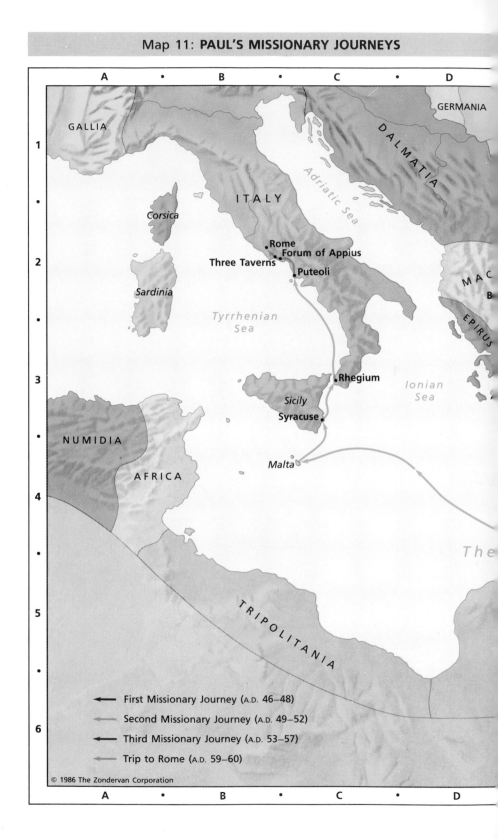

GERMANIA

GALLIA

DALMATIA

Adriatic Sea

ITALY

Corsica

Rome
Forum of Appius
Three Taverns
Puteoli

Sardinia

MAC
B

EPIRUS

Tyrrhenian
Sea

Rhegium

Ionian
Sea

Sicily
Syracuse

NUMIDIA

Malta

AFRICA

The

TRIPOLITANIA

◄——— First Missionary Journey (A.D. 46–48)
——— Second Missionary Journey (A.D. 49–52)
◄——— Third Missionary Journey (A.D. 53–57)
——— Trip to Rome (A.D. 59–60)

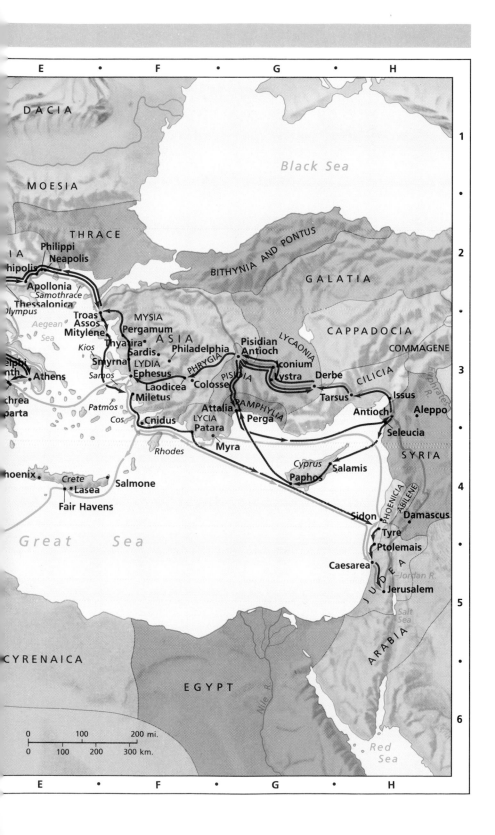

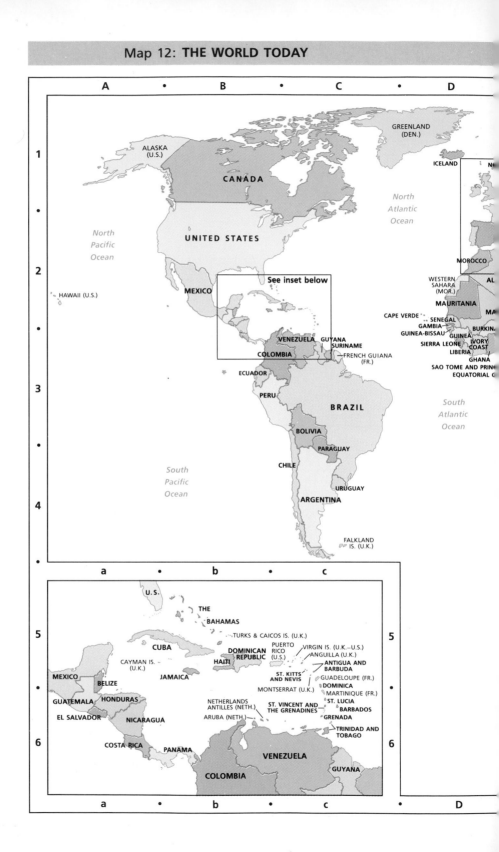

A • B • C • D

GREENLAND
(DEN.)

ICELAND

ALASKA
(U.S.)

CANADA

North
Atlantic
Ocean

North
Pacific
Ocean

UNITED STATES

MOROCCO

WESTERN
SAHARA
(MOR.)

MAURITANIA

HAWAII (U.S.)

MEXICO

See inset below

CAPE VERDE SENEGAL
GAMBIA
GUINEA-BISSAU GUINEA BURKIN.
SIERRA LEONE IVORY
COAST
LIBERIA
GHANA

VENEZUELA GUYANA
SURINAME

COLOMBIA FRENCH GUIANA
(FR.)

SAO TOME AND PRIN
EQUATORIAL G

ECUADOR

PERU

BRAZIL

South
Atlantic
Ocean

BOLIVIA

PARAGUAY

CHILE

South
Pacific
Ocean

URUGUAY

ARGENTINA

FALKLAND
IS. (U.K.)

a • b • c

U.S.

THE
BAHAMAS

TURKS & CAICOS IS. (U.K.)

PUERTO
RICO VIRGIN IS. (U.K.–U.S.)
ANGUILLA (U.K.)

CUBA DOMINICAN (U.S.)
REPUBLIC
HAITI ANTIGUA AND
BARBUDA

CAYMAN IS.
(U.K.) ST. KITTS GUADELOUPE (FR.)
AND NEVIS DOMINICA

MEXICO JAMAICA MARTINIQUE (FR.)
MONTSERRAT (U.K.) ST. LUCIA

BELIZE NETHERLANDS
ANTILLES (NETH.) ST. VINCENT AND BARBADOS
GUATEMALA HONDURAS THE GRENADINES

EL SALVADOR NICARAGUA ARUBA (NETH.) GRENADA

TRINIDAD AND
TOBAGO

COSTA RICA PANAMA

VENEZUELA

GUYANA

COLOMBIA

a • b • c • D

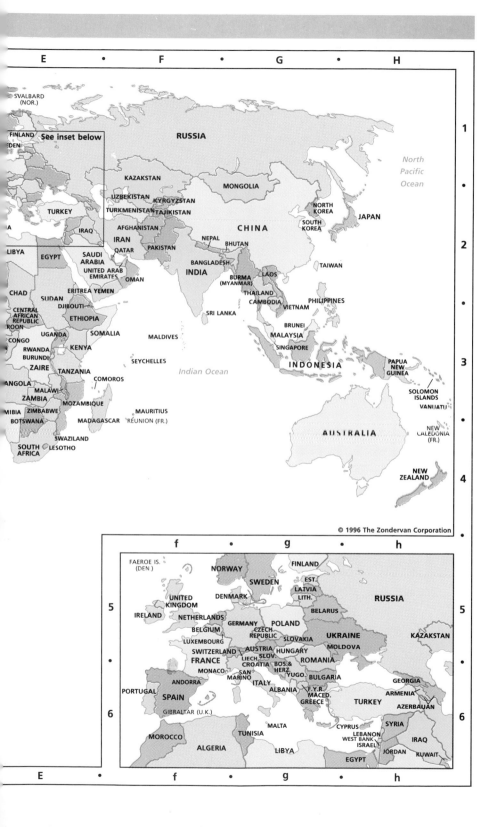

E · F · G · H

SVALBARD
(NOR.)

FINLAND
DEN
See inset below

RUSSIA

North
Pacific
Ocean

1

KAZAKSTAN

MONGOLIA

UZBEKISTAN KYRGYZSTAN
TURKMENISTAN TAJIKISTAN
TURKEY

IRAQ
AFGHANISTAN

NORTH
KOREA
SOUTH
KOREA
JAPAN

CHINA

IRAN
QATAR PAKISTAN
NEPAL
BHUTAN

2

LIBYA
EGYPT
SAUDI
ARABIA
UNITED ARAB
EMIRATES OMAN

BANGLADESH
INDIA
BURMA
(MYANMAR)
LAOS
TAIWAN

CHAD
SUDAN
CENTRAL
AFRICAN
REPUBLIC
ROON
ERITREA YEMEN
DJIBOUTI
ETHIOPIA
UGANDA SOMALIA
CONGO
RWANDA KENYA
BURUNDI
ZAIRE
TANZANIA
COMOROS
ANGOLA
MALAWI
ZAMBIA
MOZAMBIQUE
MIBIA ZIMBABWE
BOTSWANA MADAGASCAR
SWAZILAND
SOUTH LESOTHO
AFRICA

THAILAND
CAMBODIA
VIETNAM
PHILIPPINES
SRI LANKA

MALDIVES

SEYCHELLES

Indian Ocean

BRUNEI
MALAYSIA
SINGAPORE

INDONESIA

PAPUA
NEW
GUINEA

3

SOLOMON
ISLANDS
VANUATU

MAURITIUS
RÉUNION (FR.)

AUSTRALIA

NEW
CALEDONIA
(FR.)

NEW
ZEALAND

4

© 1996 The Zondervan Corporation

f · g · h

FAEROE IS.
(DEN)
NORWAY
FINLAND
SWEDEN
EST.
LATVIA
LITH.
RUSSIA

UNITED
KINGDOM
DENMARK
BELARUS

5

IRELAND
NETHERLANDS
GERMANY POLAND
BELGIUM
CZECH
REPUBLIC
SLOVAKIA
UKRAINE
KAZAKSTAN

LUXEMBOURG
SWITZERLAND
AUSTRIA HUNGARY
MOLDOVA
FRANCE
LIECH. SLOV.
CROATIA BOS. &
ROMANIA
MONACO
HERZ.
SAN
MARINO
YUGO. BULGARIA
GEORGIA
ANDORRA
ITALY
ALBANIA
F.Y.R.
MACED.
ARMENIA
PORTUGAL
SPAIN
GREECE
TURKEY
AZERBAIJAN

GIBRALTAR (U.K.)

MALTA
CYPRUS
SYRIA

MOROCCO
TUNISIA
LEBANON
WEST BANK
ISRAEL
IRAQ

ALGERIA
LIBYA
JORDAN KUWAIT
EGYPT

6

E · f · g · h

Map 13: **ROMAN EMPIRE**

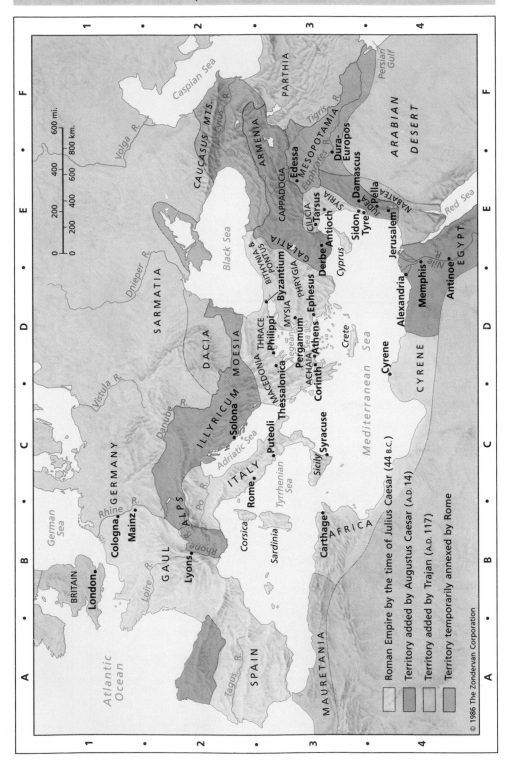

Roman Empire by the time of Julius Caesar (44 B.C.)

Territory added by Augustus Caesar (A.D. 14)

Territory added by Trajan (A.D. 117)

Territory temporarily annexed by Rome

© 1986 The Zondervan Corporation

600 mi.
800 km.
0   200   400   600
0   200   400

Atlantic Ocean

German Sea

BRITAIN
London

GAUL
Lyons
Cologna
Mainz
GERMANY

Rhine R.
Rhône R.
Po R.
Loire R.
Vistula R.
Danube R.
Dnieper R.
Volga R.

SPAIN
Tagus R.

Corsica
Sardinia

ITALY
ALPS
Rome
Puteoli

MAURETANIA
AFRICA
Carthage

Sicily
Syracuse
Tyrrhenian Sea

SARMATIA
DACIA
MOESIA
ILLYRICUM
Solona
Adriatic Sea

MACEDONIA
THRACE
Philippi
Thessalonica
Pergamum
MYSIA
Byzantium
BITHYNIA & PONTUS

Black Sea
Caspian Sea

PHRYGIA
GALATIA
Ephesus
Athens
ACHAIA
Corinth
Aegean Sea
Crete

CAPPADOCIA
CAUCASUS MTS.
ARMENIA
PARTHIA

Derbe
CILICIA
Tarsus
Antioch
SYRIA
Cyprus

Mediterranean Sea

Cyrene
CYRENE

Alexandria
Memphis
Antinoe
EGYPT
Nile R.

Sidon
Tyre
Damascus
Pella
JUDEA
Jerusalem
NABATEA

Edessa
MESOPOTAMIA
Dura-Europos
Tigris R.
Euphrates R.
Cyrus R.

ARABIAN DESERT
Persian Gulf
Red Sea